The Penguin Concise Encyclopedia

The Penguin

Concise Encyclopedia

Edited by David Crystal

PENGUIN BOOKS

PENGUIN BOOKS

Published by the Penguin Group
Penguin Books Ltd, 80 Strand, London, WC2R 0RL, England
Penguin Group (USA) Inc., 375 Hudson Street, New York, New York 10014, USA
Penguin Group (Canada), 10 Alcorn Avenue, Toronto, Ontario, Canada M4V 3B2
(a division of Pearson Penguin Canada Inc.)
Penguin Ireland, 25 St Stephen's Green, Dublin 2, Ireland (a division of Penguin Books Ltd)
Penguin Group (Australia), 250 Camberwell Road, Camberwell, Victoria 3124, Australia
(a division of Pearson Australia Group Pty Ltd)
Penguin Books India Pvt Ltd, 11 Community Centre, Panchsheel Park, New Delhi – 110 017, India
Penguin Group (NZ), cnr Airborne and Rosedale Roads, Albany, Auckland 1310, New Zealand
(a division of Pearson New Zealand Ltd)
Penguin Books (South Africa) (Pty) Ltd, 24 Sturdee Avenue, Rosebank 2196, South Africa

Penguin Books Ltd, Registered Offices: 80 Strand, London, WC2R 0RL, England

www.penguin.com

First published as *The Penguin Encyclopedia* 2002
Concise edition first published 2003
Second concise edition published 2005
This third concise edition published 2007

1

Copyright © Crystal Reference Systems Ltd, 2002, 2003, 2005, 2007
All rights reserved

The moral right of the author has been asserted

Set in TheAntiqua and TheSans
Typeset by Data Standards, Frome, Somerset
Printed in Finland by WS Bookwell

ISBN: 978-0-141-02621-3

Contents

Preface   vii

User Guide   viii

The Penguin Concise Encyclopedia   1

Acknowledgements

Crystal Reference

Editor
David Crystal

Associate Editor
Ann Rowlands

Editorial Assistance
Angie Beckett
Jan Thomas
Peter Preston
Todd Warden-Owen

Editorial Management
Hilary Crystal

Database Management
Tony McNicholl

Crystal Reference Administration
Ian Saunders
Rob Phillips

Penguin Books

Publishing Director
Adam Freudenheim

Designer
Richard Marston

Production
Andrew Henty

Typesetting
Data Standards

Preface

The Penguin Concise Encyclopedia provides a succinct, systematic and readable guide to the essential facts, events, issues, beliefs and achievements which make up the sum of human knowledge. Its aim is to act as a standard reference work for use in the home, school, library or office by both adult enquirers and young people of high-school age. In content it is an abridgement of *The New Penguin Encyclopedia* (third edition, 2006), but appropriately updated. The present book is the largest single-volume concise encyclopedia it has been my privilege to edit, comprising 1.6 million words and representing a much wider range of current topics, issues, locations and personalities than it has been possible to include in earlier books of this type.

The relevant statistics can be briefly summarized. The encyclopedia contains nearly 22,000 alphabetically organized entries, the majority of which are general topics, but there are also over 6,000 biographical entries, concentrating on persons of international distinction, and about 4,000 gazetteer entries. The entries have been written by a team of over 350 specialist contributors affiliated to universities, museums and other centres of excellence, and they are regularly revised to ensure a high level of up-to-dateness. The source database is actually updated day by day for current affairs, and this, along with a publishing procedure which allows new material to be added right up to just a couple of months before publication, ensures that the present edition, appearing in the second half of 2007, contains information from the first half of the year.

Internationalism is a major focus of *The Penguin Concise Encyclopedia*. There is of course systematic coverage of traditionally popular areas such as flora and fauna, history, art, music, literature, theatre, religion and mythology. But an encyclopedia for the 2000s has to reflect international issues, especially in politics, economics, technology and current affairs. In relation to entry treatment, probably the most noticeable characteristic of the book is its concern to present information in an accessible and interesting way. I have paid particular attention to the language of the entries to ensure that they are written in an intelligible style, without losing sight of the stylistic conventions identifying the subject area to which each entry belongs. A particular innovation is the systematic use of a specially condensed style for gazetteer, natural history and certain other types of entry, which provides information in a clear and direct manner, increases accessibility and saves a great deal of space. The principle of functional clarity has also been applied to the selection of illustrations, where I use a small set of clear, relevant line drawings. This is very much a text-based encyclopedia, focusing on description and explanation. People need to be able to talk about what they know, and it is text, rather than pictures, which is the only sure means of enabling them to do this. This is also why I give so much guidance on pronunciation and, where it is not obvious, I use a specially devised phonetic spelling.

The Penguin Concise Encyclopedia, accordingly, presents a knowledge base which is well suited to meeting the information needs of people in the new millennium. At the same time, it is important to recognize not only the strengths, but also the limitations of any general encyclopedia, and to strive to surmount them. Many readers will be more knowledgeable about certain topics than any encyclopedia team could ever be. I therefore very much welcome feedback from readers relating to any inadequacy in our coverage and treatment. The easiest way to do this is through the publishing address: Penguin Press Reference Editorial, Penguin Books, 80 Strand, London WC2R ORL. In this way, our knowledge base will grow with the times and reflect ever more closely the interests and concerns of those wishing to benefit from it.

David Crystal

Entry order

- The order of entries follows the English alphabet, ignoring capitals, accents, diacritics, or apostrophes.
- The ordering is letter by letter, ignoring all spaces and hyphens in compound headings, eg **seance** precedes **sea otter**, which precedes **sea pen**, which precedes **seaplane**. Exceptions include all **Mc** names, which are listed as if they were **Mac**, and all **St** names, which are listed as if they were **Saint**.
- When many people have the same name (eg **John**), we list monarchs before saints and popes, followed by others. Compound names (eg **John Paul I**) appear later than single-element names (eg **John, Otto**). Rulers with an identifying byname (eg **John of Austria**, **John the Baptist**) appear after single-element names following the letter-by- letter order of the constituent words (eg **John of Trevisa** precedes **John the Baptist**). The system groups all **John**s together, and occasionally provides an exception to the letter-by-letter convention (eg **John the Baptist** precedes **Johnson**).
- We list phrasal names under their most specific element, eg **Japan, Sea of**, and **Waterloo, Battle of**.
- In cases where headwords have the same spelling, the order is (1) places, (2) people, (3) general topics.
- We list identically spelled topic headwords according to the alphabetical order of their subject areas, eg **depression** (meteorology) precedes **depression** (psychiatry).
- We list rulers chronologically, ordering them by country if titles are the same, eg **Charles I** (of Austria-Hungary) is followed by **Charles I** (of England) then by **Charles II** (of England) and **Charles II** (of Spain). Names of non-English rulers, saints, etc. are anglicized, with a cross-reference used in cases where the foreign name is widely known, eg **Wilhelm** >> **William**.
- We list places with the same name on the basis of the alphabetical order of their countries, eg **Dover** (UK) precedes **Dover** (USA).
- Parts of a person's name that are not generally used are enclosed in parentheses, eg **Wells, H(erbert) G(eorge)** . Parenthesized elements are ignored in deciding alphabetical sequence, eg **Smith (Robert) Harvey** would precede **Smith, Henry**.

Entry conventions

- Where alternative spellings exist in headwords, we give British usage first, then American usage, eg **colour/ color television**. We give cross-references in all cases where spelling variation affects initial letters, eg **esophagus/oesophagus**.
- We transliterate names in non-Roman alphabets, and add a cross-reference in cases where confusion could arise because more than one transliteration system exists. Letter symbols from other languages which do not appear in the English alphabet are given their nearest English equivalents. Chinese names are given in pinyin (eg **Beijing** for **Peking**). In the case of Arabic names, we have not transliterated the alif and ain symbols. No accent is shown on French capital letters.
- A person's birthplace is usually cited with reference to the present-day town and country (eg Germany rather than Prussia), where this is known. Locations within the UK and USA are usually followed by the name of their country, state, etc., unless the two names are identical (as in the case of New York).
- People mentioned within entries usually have their dates of birth/death following their names; absence of these dates signifies that the person has his/her own entry elsewhere in the encyclopedia.

Other conventions

- Months in parenthesis are abbreviated to the first three letters (16 Sep 1941).
- Chemistry abbreviations are shown in the diagram located under Periodic table.
- A certain number of frequently used abbreviations maintain the succinctness of individual entries.

Abbreviations

AD	Anno Domini	E	east(ern)	Jap	Japanese	Port	Portuguese
BC	Before Christ	eg	for example	K	Kelvin	pt	pint(s)
c	century		(*exempli gratia*)	kg	kilogram(s)	r.	reigned
c.	circa (about)	Eng	English	km	kilometre(s)	R	River
C	Celsius	F	Fahrenheit	l	litre(s)	Russ	Russian
	(Centigrade)	Finn	Finnish	L	Lake	S	south(ern)
C	Central (in	fl.	flourished	Lat	Latin	s	second(s)
	locations)	Fr	French	lb	pound(s)	Span	Spanish
cc	cubic	ft	foot/feet	m	metre(s)	sq	square
	centimetre(s)	g	gram(s)	min	minute(s)	St	Saint
CFA	(for francs) *Com-*	Ger	German	mm	millimetre(s)	Sta	Santa
	munauté finan-	Gr	Greek	m/s	metres per	Ste	Sainte
	cière africaine	h	hour(s)		second	Swed	Swedish
Chin	Chinese	ha	hectare(s)	Mt	Mount(ain)	trans	translation
cm	centimetre(s)	Hung	Hungarian	Mts	Mountains	v.	versus
Co	County	I(s)	Island(s)	N	north(ern)	vol(s)	volume
cu	cubic	ie	that is (*id est*)	No/ no.	number	W	west(ern)
d.	died	in	inch(es)	oz	ounces	yd	yard(s)
e	estimate (for	Ir	Irish	p(p)	page(s)		
	populations)	Ital	Italian	pop	population		

Pronunciation guide

- We give a pronunciation whenever it is unpredictable from the spelling, or where there is a possibility that a reader might choose the wrong form. In foreign words/names we give an approximate foreign pronunciation, unless there is a well-known English version. In cases where both forms are used in English, we give both.
- Bold type is used to show stressed or strongly accented syllables, **Xerxes** [**zerk**seez]. We do not usually show the stress in languages (such as French, Chinese, Japanese) which have a very different rhythmical system to English, and where it would be misleading to identify one of the syllables as most prominent. We make exceptions in cases where there is a widely used or predictable English pronunciation.

Symbol	Sound	Symbol	Sound	Symbol	Sound	**Non-English sounds**	
a	h**a**t	i	s**i**t	r	**r**ed	ā	French *Nantes*
ah	f**a**ther	iy	l**ie**	s	**s**et	hl	Welsh *llan*
air	h**air**	j	**j**et	sh	**sh**ip	ī	French *Saint*
aw	s**aw**	k	**k**it	t	**t**in	ō	French *bon*
ay	s**ay**	l	**l**ip	th	**th**in	kh	Scots *loch*
b	**b**ig	m	**m**an	th	**th**is		German *ich*
ch	**ch**ip	n	**n**ip	u	p**u**t	oe	French *soeur*
d	**d**ig	ng	si**ng**	uh	c**u**p		German *möglich*
e	s**e**t	o	h**o**t	v	**v**an	õe	French *brun*
ee	s**ee**	oh	s**ou**l	w	**w**ill	ü	French *tu*
er	b**ir**d	oo	s**oo**n	y	**y**es		German *müde*
f	**f**ish	ow	c**ow**	z	**z**oo		
g	**g**o	oy	b**oy**	zh	lei**s**ure		

●No distinctive symbol is used for unstressed English vowels, in cases where the pronunciation can be intuitively deduced from the spelling, eg **echidna** [e**kid**na].

●The symbol [r] is used to mark cases where an r in the spelling may or may not be pronounced, depending on the accent, eg **Barbarossa** [bah(**r**)ba**ro**sa]. This symbol is not used when the transcription of a sound already contains an [r] symbol, as in [er].

a

Aachen [ahkhen], Fr **Aix-La-Chapelle** 50°47N 6°04E, pop (2000e) 252 000. Manufacturing city in Cologne district, Germany; N capital of Charlemagne's empire; annexed by France, 1801; given to Prussia, 1815; badly bombed in World War 2; railway; technical college; cathedral (14th-c) is a world heritage site.

Aalto, (Hugo Henrik) Alvar [awltoh] (1898–1976) Architect, born in Kuortane, Finland. He was a designer of modern public and industrial buildings in Finland, and also of contemporary furniture.

aardvark [ah(r)dvah(r)k] A southern African mammal (*Orycteropus afer*); length, 1–1·5 m/3¼–5 ft; long ears, pig-like snout, long sticky tongue, strong claws; digs burrows; eats ants and termites; mainly nocturnal; also known as **ant bear** or **earth pig**; the only member of the order Tubulidentata. (Family: Orycteropodidae.)

aardwolf [ah(r)dwulf] A rare southern African carnivore (*Proteles cristatus*) of the hyena family; slender, yellow with black stripes; lives in a den; nocturnal; also known as **maned jackal**.

Aarhus *Århus*

Aaron [airon] (15th–13th-c BC) Elder brother of Moses and the first high priest of the Israelites. He and his sons were ordained as priests after the construction of the Ark of the Covenant and the Tabernacle.

Aaron, Hank [airon], popular name of **Henry Louis Aaron**, nickname **Hammerin' Hank** (1934–) Baseball player, born in Mobile, AL. In 1974 he surpassed Babe Ruth's 39-year-old record of career home runs, and retired in 1976 with a total of 755 home runs, still a major league record.

abaca A fibre obtained from the leaf-stalks of a species of banana (*Musa textilis*) native to the Philippines; also called **Manila hemp**; used for cables, carpets, and ships' hawsers. (Family: Musaceae.)

abacus [abakuhs] A device for performing calculations by sliding bead counters along a set of rods or in grooves. It may have originated in Babylonia, and was used in ancient China, Greece, and Rome. It became widespread in Europe in the Middle Ages, as well as in China and Japan, where it is still in use, though increasingly being replaced by the calculator.

Abadan [abadahn] 30°20N 48°16E, pop (2000e) 418 000. Oil port in WC Iran at head of Persian Gulf; terminus of Iran's major oil pipelines; airport; severely damaged in the Iran–Iraq War.

abalone [abalohnee] A primitive marine snail characterized by a single row of holes extending back from the front margin of its ovoid shell; collected for decoration and for human consumption; also called **ormer**. (Class: Gastropoda. Order: Archaeogastropoda.)

Abba [aba] Swedish pop group, formed in 1973 by **Björn Ulvaeus** (1945– , guitar, vocals), married to **Agnetha Fältskog** (1950– , vocals), and **Benny Andersson** (1945– , keyboards, vocals), married to **Anni-Frid** (known as **Frida**) **Lyngstad** (1945– , vocals). The group's name derives from their first-name initials. Björn and Agnetha divorced in 1979, and Benny and Frida in 1981.

During the 1970s they were the most successful international group since the Beatles.

Abbas I [abas], known as **Abbas the Great** (1571–1629) Shah of Persia (1588–1629). His reign marked a peak of Persian artistic achievement, especially in painting, weaving, and manuscript illumination.

Abbas (c.566–c.652) Uncle of Mohammed, at first hostile to him, but ultimately the chief promoter of his religion. The **Abbasids** claimed descent from him, and thus a connection to the Prophet.

abbey A building or group of buildings used by a religious order for worship and living. It houses a community under the direction of an abbot or abbess as head, who is elected for a term of years or for life. Examples are La Grande Chartreuse (France), El Escorial (New Castile, Spain), and Fountains Abbey (near Ripon, North Yorkshire, UK).

Abbey Theatre A theatre situated in Dublin's Abbey Street, the centre of the Irish dramatic movement founded by Lady Gregory and W B Yeats. The present theatre was opened in 1966, after the earlier building had burnt down in 1951.

Abbott, Bud *Abbott and Costello*

Abbott and Costello Comedy film partners: **Bud Abbott**, originally **William A Abbott** (1896–1974), born in Asbury Park, NJ, and **Lou Costello**, originally **Louis Francis Cristillo** (1908–59), born in Paterson, NJ. They made a number of successful comedy films, beginning with *Buck Privates* (1941), Costello playing the clown and Abbott his straight man.

abdomen The lower part of the trunk, extending from within the pelvic floor to under the cover of the chest wall. It contains most of the alimentary canal (from stomach to rectum), the liver, pancreas, spleen, kidneys, and bladder, and the uterus in females.

Abdul-Jabbar, Kareem [abdul jaber], originally **Lewis Ferdinand Alcindor**, known as **Lew Alcindor** (1947–) Basketball player, born in New York City. A 7 ft 2 in/2 m 5 cm centre, he played most of his career with the Los Angeles Lakers. When he retired in 1989, he had played 1560 National Basketball League games, and had established an individual points record of 46 725.

Abel [aybel] Biblical character, the second son of Adam and Eve. He is described as a shepherd, whose offering God accepts; but he was then murdered by his brother, Cain (*Gen* 4.2–16).

Abelard, Peter [abelah(r)d] (1079–1142) Theologian, born near Nantes, France. While a lecturer at Notre-Dame, he married Héloïse, the 17-year-old niece of the canon Fulbert. Opposition to their marriage led Héloïse to enter a convent and Abelard to become a monk. He founded a monastic school, for many years defending his teaching against charges of heresy.

Aberconwy and Colwyn [aberkonwee, kolwin], Welsh **Aberconwy a Cholwyn** pop (2001e) 109 600; area 1130 km²/436 sq mi. County (unitary authority from 1996) in NC Wales, UK; renamed **Conwy**, 1998; drained by the R Conwy; administrative centre, Colwyn Bay; seaside resorts on north coast; part of Snowdonia National Park; castle at Conwy.

Aberdeen, ancient **Devana** 57°10N 2°04W, pop (2000e) 223 200. Seaport city council (Aberdeen City), and administrative centre of Aberdeenshire council, NE Scotland; on the North Sea; royal burgh since 1179; airport; helicopter port; ferries to Orkney and Shetland; railway; universities (1494, 1992); cathedral (1131); oil supply service, granite ('Granite City').

Aberdeen, George Hamilton Gordon, 4th Earl of (1784–1860) British statesman and prime minister (1852–5), born in Edinburgh. He became foreign secretary (1828–30, 1841–6), and in 1852 headed a coalition ministry. Vacillating policy and mismanagement during the Crimean War led to his resignation.

Aberdeen terrier Scottish terrier

Aberfan [abervan] 51°42N 3°21W. Village in coal-mining region, Merthyr Tydfil county, S Wales, UK; scene of major disaster in 1966, when a landslip of mining waste engulfed several houses and the school, killing 144, including 116 children.

Abernathy, Ralph D(avid) [abernathee] (1926–90) Baptist clergyman and civil rights activist, born in Linden, AL. Pastor of the West Hunter Street Baptist Church in Atlanta, GA, he became Martin Luther King's chosen successor as head of the Southern Christian Leadership Conference (1968–77).

aberrations 1 In optics, deviations from perfect images, as predicted by simple lens theory. They are consequences of the laws of refraction.
2 In astronomy, apparent changes in the observed position of a star, because of changes in relative velocity as the Earth orbits the Sun.

Aberystwyth [aberistwith] 52°25N 4°05W, pop (2000e) 12 700. Administrative centre of Cardiganshire county, W Wales, UK; university and resort town on Cardigan Bay; built around a castle of Edward I, 1227; railway; college of University of Wales (1872); National Library of Wales (1955).

Abidjan [abeejan] 5°19N 4°01W, pop (2000e) 3 049 000. Industrial seaport and former capital (1935–83) of Côte d'Ivoire, W Africa; airport; railway; university (1958); Ifan museum.

ABM antiballistic missile

Abney level clinometer

Åbo Turku

abolitionist movement A 19th-c movement to end slavery in the US South, which crystallized around the American Anti-Slavery Society, founded in 1833. It was distinguished from earlier anti-slavery movements by its uncompromising attitude.

A-bomb atomic bomb

Abomey [abomay] 7°14N 2°00E, pop (2000e) 90 900. Town in Zou province, S Benin, W Africa; capital of old Yoruba kingdom of Dahomey; Royal Palace of Djema, including the tomb of King Gbehanzin (still guarded by women), a world heritage site.

abominable snowman Bigfoot; Yeti

Aborigines [aborijineez] The indigenous inhabitants of Australia, the first of whom reached the continent c.60 000 years ago. By 1788, when European occupation began, there were c.600 territorially defined groups, subsisting on hunting and gathering, with a population of 300 000–1 million. Numbers then fell dramatically, partly through conflict with the Europeans, but mainly through European diseases, especially the smallpox epidemics of 1789 and 1829. By 1933 the population had fallen to c.66 000; it then steadily increased, and now numbers about 250 000. At first, Europeans portrayed Aboriginals as 'noble savages', but this image quickly gave way to contempt, and policies were designed to turn them into Christians with European lifestyles. Aborigines have not accepted their lot passively. In the 1950s they began moving into the cities of SE Australia and formed advancement groups; but it was not until the mid-1960s that activism became prominent. Their condition has since improved significantly, but they remain the most disadvantaged group in Australian society. A proposal to add a preamble to the constitution recognizing Aborigines

as 'the nation's first people' was heavily defeated in a 1999 referendum. In 2004, they formed Your Voice, thought to be the country's first national Aboriginal party.

abortion The spontaneous or induced termination of pregnancy before the fetus is viable. In the UK and for legal purposes, this is taken to be the 24th week, although some fetuses expelled before then may survive. In the USA and in some European countries, the time limit may be set some weeks earlier. Spontaneous abortion (miscarriage) occurs in about 15% of recognized pregnancies and may occur in up to 50% of all pregnancies. The moral issues surrounding abortion have received increasing publicity in the 1990s, with conflict between extremists from 'pro-life' (anti-abortion) and 'right-to-choose' (pro-abortion) groups leading to violent confrontation, especially in the USA. In the UK, a review of the 24-week limit was conducted in 2005 but doctors voted against calling for a reduction in the limit.

abortion pill contraception

Aboukir Bay, Battle of 1 (Aug 1798) A naval battle during the War of the Second Coalition, in which Nelson destroyed the French fleet under Brueys off the coast of Egypt; also known as the **Battle of the Nile**. **2** (Jul 1799) The last French victory of the Egyptian campaign, in which Napoleon's Army of Egypt captured Aboukir citadel, NE of Alexandria, defeating an Ottoman Turkish force under Mustafa Pasha; also known as the **Battle of Aboukir**.

Abraham, Abram, or **Ibrahiz** (after 2000 BC) Biblical character revered as the ancestor of Israel and of several other nations; also an important figure in Islam. At 100 years of age he is said to have had a son Isaac by his previously barren wife, Sarah (Gen 21). In Judaism, Isaac was seen as the fulfilment of the divine promises, although Abraham was ordered by God to sacrifice his heir at Moriah as a test of faith (Gen 22).

Abraham, Plains / Heights of The site of a battle (1759), Quebec City, Canada, in which British forces under Wolfe defeated French, Amerindian, and Canadian forces under Montcalm and Vaudreuil, and gained control over Quebec. Wolfe and Montcalm were both killed in the battle.

Abramovich, Roman Arkadyevich [abramovich] (1966–) Multi-billionaire businessman and entrepreneur, born in Saratov, Russia. While still a student at the Moscow Auto Transport Institute (1987), he set up a company producing plastic toys and its success enabled him to found an oil business in the Omsk region. He became head of the Sibneft company, completing a merger which made it the fourth biggest oil company in the world. Sibneft was sold in 2005. He became a familiar face in England after his acquisition of Chelsea Football Club in 2003.

abrasives Hard, rough, or sharp textured materials used to wear down, rub, or polish materials which are less hard, as in the traditional grindstone or whetstone. Naturally occurring abrasive substances include various forms of silica (sand, quartz, or flint), pumice, and emery (an aluminium oxide mineral). Artificial abrasives include silicon carbide, synthetic diamond, and boron carbide.

Abrikosov, Alexei A (1928–) Physicist, born in Moscow. He studied at Moscow State University (1948), and in 1991 joined the Materials Science Division at Argonne National Laboratory, Illinois. He is famous for the discovery of Type II superconductors and their magnetic properties (the **Abrikosov vortex lattice**). In 2003 he shared the Nobel Prize for Physics for pioneering contributions to the theory of superconductors and superfluids.

abscess A localized collection of pus in an organ or tissue, surrounded by an inflammatory reaction which forms a well-defined wall (an abscess cavity). It is commonly due to infection, but occasionally a foreign body is responsible.

Abse, Dannie [absee] (1923–) Writer and physician, born in Cardiff. His literary output includes poetry, novels, and plays, as well as the autobiographical volumes *A Poet in the Family* (1974) and *There was a Young Man from Cardiff* (1991). Later work includes *Twentieth Century Anglo-Welsh Poetry* (1997).

absolutism A theory of kingship elaborated and practised in early modern Europe, associated notably with Louis XIV of France. Absolute power was justified by the belief that monarchs were God's representatives on Earth.

absorbed dose *radioactivity units*

abstract art A form of art in which there is no attempt to represent objects or persons, but which relies instead on lines, colours, and shapes alone for its aesthetic appeal. It seems to have emerged c.1910, and was partly a reaction against 19th-c Realism and Impressionism. Early abstract artists include Kandinsky, Miró, Pevsner, and Brancusi. The term is often used imprecisely to cover a wide range of 20th-c art.

abstract expressionism *action painting*

absurdism The expression in art of the meaninglessness of human existence. Its potential for comedy and terror has been exploited especially in the theatre (**Theatre of the Absurd**), as in the plays of Ionesco, Beckett, and Pinter.

Abu-Bakr or **Abu-Bekr** [aboo baker] (c.573–634) Father of Mohammed's wife, Aïshah, born in Mecca. He became the prophet's most trusted follower, succeeded him as the first caliph (632), and began the compilation of the Qur'an. During his 2-year reign he put down a religious and political revolt, and initiated Arab conquests.

Abu Dhabi or **Abu Zabi** [aboo dabee] pop (2000e) 962 500; area c.67 600 km²/26 000 sq mi. Largest of the seven member states of the United Arab Emirates; capital Abu Dhabi, pop (2000e) 391 300; main oasis settlement, al-Ayn; vast areas of desert and salt flats; coastline 400 km/250 mi; a major oil region.

Abuja [abooja] 9°05N 7°30E, pop (2000e) 472 000. New capital (from 1991) of Nigeria, in Federal Capital Territory, C Nigeria, at the geographical centre of the country; government offices began moving from Lagos in the 1980s.

Abu Mena [aboo mena] A site in NW Egypt sacred to the 3rd-c AD martyr Abu Mena (St Menas). The ruins of the early 5th-c basilica erected here by the Emperor Arcadius are a world heritage site.

Abu Simbel [aboo simbel] 22°22N 31°38E. The site of two huge sandstone temples carved by Pharaoh Rameses II (c.1304–1273 BC) out of the Nile bank near Aswan; now a world heritage site. They were dismantled and relocated in the 1960s when the rising waters of the newly-constructed Aswan High Dam threatened their safety.

Abyssinia *Ethiopia*

Abyssinian cat A breed of domestic cat, popular in the USA (known as the **foreign short-haired**); reddish-brown, each hair with several dark bands; orange-red nose.

acacia *wattle*

Académie Française [akadaymee frōsez] French literary academy founded in 1634 by Cardinal Richelieu, and incorporated in 1635, for the purpose of maintaining standards of literary taste and to establish the literary language. Its membership is limited to 40 and has included many of the great names of French literature, such as Corneille, Voltaire, Racine, Hugo, Chateaubriand, and Bergson.

academy 1 A place of learning or association formed for scientific, literary, artistic, or musical purposes. From the Renaissance the term was applied in Europe to institutions of higher learning (eg the *Accademia della Crusca*, 1587) and advanced teaching (until the term 'university' became widespread in the 18th-c). **2** The American **Academy of Motion Picture Arts and Sciences**, widely known since 1927 for its annual awards for creative merit and craftsmanship in film production

Academy Award Categories

Best Picture
Best Actor (Leading Role)
Best Actor (Supporting Role)
Best Actress (Leading Role)
Best Actress (Supporting Role)
Best Foreign Language Film
Best Achievement in Animated Short Films
Best Achievement in Art Direction
Best Achievement in Cinematography
Best Achievement in Costume Design
Best Achievement in Directing
Best Achievement in Documentary Features
Best Achievement in Documentary Short Subjects
Best Achievement in Film Editing
Best Achievement in Live Action Short Films
Best Achievement in Makeup
Best Achievement in Music (Original Score)
Best Achievement in Music (Original Song)
Best Achievement in Sound
Best Achievement in Sound Effects Editing
Best Achievement in Visual Effects
Best Screenplay Written Directly for the Screen
Best Screenplay Based on Material Previously Produced or Published

(*see panel*). It has been influential in establishing technical standards.

Acadia [akaydia] Part of France's American empire; what is today Prince Edward Island, Nova Scotia, and New Brunswick, Canada. The first settlement was established at Port Royal in 1605 by Champlain. The Treaty of Utrecht (1713) handed most of Acadia to Britain.

acanthus [akanthuhs] A plant with thick, prickly leaves, representations of which are often used to decorate mouldings or carved parts of a building.

Acapulco [akapulkoh] or **Acapulco de Juárez** 6°51N 99°56W, pop (2000e) 713 000. Port and resort town in S Mexico, on the Pacific Ocean; airfield; tourism; badly damaged by hurricane Pauline in 1997.

Acari [akariy] *mite*

ACAS [aykas] Acronym for **Advisory, Conciliation and Arbitration Service**, a UK body set up in 1975. It provides facilities for conciliation, arbitration, and mediation in industrial disputes.

acceleration For linear motion, the rate of change of velocity with time; equals force divided by mass; symbol a, units m/s²; a vector quantity. For rotational motion, the rate of change of angular velocity with time; equals torque divided by moment of inertia; angular acceleration symbol α, units radians/s²; a vector quantity.

acceleration due to gravity The acceleration on an object close to the Earth, due to the Earth's gravitational field; symbol g. Its value is taken as 9·81 m/s², but it varies over the Earth's surface and decreases with height above sea level.

accent The features of pronunciation which mark a speaker's regional background or social class. Accent is to be distinguished from dialect, which involves the study of other linguistic features, such as grammar and vocabulary.

accentor A sparrow-like bird native to N Africa, Europe, and Asia; brownish-grey to chestnut above, often streaked; grey beneath. (Genus: *Prunella*, 12 species. Family: Prunellidae.)

accepting house A merchant bank which 'accepts', ie guarantees, three-month bills of exchange issued by companies. In the UK, the top accepting houses in London form the Accepting Houses Committee.

accordion A portable musical instrument of the reed organ type, fed with air from bellows activated by the player. In the most advanced models a treble keyboard is played with the right hand, while the left operates (usually) six rows of buttons, producing bass notes and chords. The earliest type was patented in Vienna in 1829.

accountancy The profession which deals with matters relating to money within an organization. It handles a wide range of activities, including financial planning, management accounting, taxation, and treasury management (managing money), as well as recording and presenting accounts for management, owners, and the tax authorities.

Accra [akrah] 5°33N 0°15W, pop (2000e) 1 253 000. Seaport capital of Ghana, on the Gulf of Guinea coast; founded as three forts and trading posts, 17th-c; capital of Gold Coast, 1877; capital of Ghana, 1957; airport; railway; university (1948) at Legon.

accumulator A device to store electricity, by accepting a charge and later releasing it; also called a **battery**. It is a lead–acid system, with plates of lead oxides and an electrolyte of sulphuric acid. Accumulators are widely used to start car engines, and also to propel electric vehicles such as milk floats. Other systems include nickel-iron (*Nife*) and nickel-cadmium (*Nicad*) plates, with alkaline electrolytes. Some are made in small sizes, to replace torch and other batteries with rechargeable versions.

acetaldehyde [asitaldihiyd] CH_3CHO, IUPAC **ethanal**, boiling point 21°C. The product of gentle oxidation of ethanol, intermediate in the formation of acetic acid; a colourless liquid with a sharp odour. A reducing agent, the compound is actually the one detected in the 'breathalyzer' test.

acetals [asitlz] Substances of the general structure $R_2C(OR)_2$, formed by the reaction of an alcohol with an aldehyde, water also being formed. Internal acetal formation gives most sugars ring structures.

acetic acid [aseetik] CH_3COOH, IUPAC **ethanoic acid**, boiling point 118°C. The product of oxidation of ethanol. The pure substance is a viscous liquid with a strong odour. Vinegar is essentially a 5% solution of acetic acid.

acetone [asitohn] CH_3COCH_3, IUPAC **propanone**, boiling point 56°C. A volatile liquid with an odour resembling ethers. It is a very widely used solvent, especially for plastics and lacquers.

acetyl [asitiyl] $CH_3CO–$, IUPAC **ethanoyl**. A functional group in chemistry, whose addition to a name usually indicates its substitution for hydrogen in a compound.

acetylcholine [asitiylkohleen] An acetyl ester of choline ($C_7H_{16}NO_2{}^+$) which functions as a neurotransmitter in most animals with nervous systems.

acetylene [asetileen] $HC≡CH$, IUPAC **ethyne**, boiling point −84°C. The simplest alkyne, a colourless gas formed by the action of water on calcium carbide. It is an important starting material in organic synthesis, and is used as a fuel, especially (mixed with oxygen) in the oxyacetylene torch.

Achaemenids [akiymenidz] The first royal house of Persia, founded by the early 7th-c BC ruler Achaemenes. Its capitals included Parsagadae and Persepolis.

Achebe, Chinua [achaybay], originally **Albert Chinualumogo** (1930–) Novelist, born in Ogidi, Nigeria. Four novels written between 1958 (*Things Fall Apart*) and 1966 (*A Man of the People*) describe tribal and racial tensions in pre-and post-colonial Nigerian society. After a period in politics and education, he wrote *Anthills of the Savannah* (1987). *Another Africa* appeared in 1998.

Achenbach, Andreas [akhenbakh] (1815–1910) Landscape and marine painter, born in Kassel, Germany. He was regarded as the father of 19th-c German landscape painting.

achene [akeen] A dry fruit, not splitting to release the single seed. It is usually small, often bearing hooks, spines, or other structures which aid in dispersal.

Achernar [akerna(r)] *Eridanus*

Acheron [akeron] In Greek mythology, the chasm or abyss of the Underworld, and the name of one of the rivers there. It is also the name of a river in Epirus, thought to be an entrance to Hades.

Acheson, Dean (Gooderham) [achesn] (1893–1971) US statesman and lawyer, born in Middletown, CT. Secretary of state (1949–53) in the Truman administration, he helped to establish the Marshall Plan (1947) and the North Atlantic Treaty Organization (1949).

Acheulian [ashoolian] In Europe, Africa, and Asia, a broad term for early prehistoric cultures using symmetrically-flaked stone handaxes, dating from c.1·5 million years ago. The name derives from finds made c.1850 at Saint-Acheul in the Somme Valley, N France.

Achilles [akileez] A legendary Greek hero, son of Peleus and Thetis, who dipped him in the R Styx so that he was invulnerable, except for the heel where she had held him. He was killed by Paris, who shot him in the heel with a poisoned arrow.

achondroplasia [aykondroplayzhuh] An inherited form of dwarfism, in which growth of the limb bones is disproportionately shortened. There is a characteristic bulging of the forehead, and a saddle nose.

acid Usually, a substance reacting with metals to liberate hydrogen gas, or dissolving in water with dissociation and the formation of hydrogen ions. Acids are classed as strong or weak depending on the extent to which this dissociation occurs. Strong acids are corrosive.

acidic oxides *oxides*

acid rain A term first used in the 19th-c to describe polluted rain in Manchester, England. Colloquially it is used for polluted rainfall associated with the burning of fossil fuels. Acid pollution can be wet (rain, snow, mist) or dry (gases, particles). A number of gases are involved, particularly sulphur dioxide (SO_2) and oxides of nitrogen (NO). Reactions in the atmosphere lead to the production of sulphuric acid (H_2SO_4) and nitric acid (HNO_3). Acid rain is implicated in damage to forests and the acidification of soils and lakes.

acne [aknee] A chronic inflammation of the sebaceous glands in the skin, notably affecting the face, upper chest, and back. It is particularly found in adolescents.

Aconcagua, Cerro [akonkagwa] 32°39S 70°01W. Mountain in the Andes, rising to 6960 m/22 834 ft in W Argentina; the highest peak in the W hemisphere.

aconite *monkshood; winter aconite*

acorn The fruit of the oak tree, actually a specialized nut borne in a cup-shaped structure, the cupule.

Acosta, Carlos (1973–) Ballet dancer and choreographer, born near Havana. At age nine his father enrolled him in the National Ballet School in Havana. He earned a student placement with the Turin Ballet in Italy (1990) and went on to win the prestigious Prix de Lausanne. He performed with the Houston Ballet and then joined the Royal Ballet (1998), where he became guest principal (from 2000). His choreographic debut, *Tocororo – A Cuban Tale*, was performed in 2003. He received a Laurence Olivier Award for outstanding achievement in dance in 2007.

acouchi [akooshee] A cavy-like rodent; inhabits Amazonian forests; resembles a small agouti, but with a longer tail (white, used for signalling). (Genus: *Myoprocta*, 2 species. Family: Dasyproctidae.)

acoustics The study of sound: the production, detection, and propagation of sound waves, and the absorption and reflection of sound. It includes the study of how electrical signals are converted into mechanical signals, as in loudspeakers, and the converse, as in microphones; also, how sound is produced in musical instruments, and perceived by audiences in concert halls; the protection of workers from damaging levels of sound;

and the use of detection techniques, such as sonar and ultra-sonic scanning.

ACP countries An acronym for a grouping of c.70 developing countries from **Africa, the Caribbean, and the Pacific**. It was established in the 1970s to facilitate the making of agreements with the European Union on economic assistance and trade.

Acre, Hebrew **Akko**, ancient **Ptolemais** 32°55N 35°04E, pop (2000e) 53 000. Ancient town in Northern district, NW Israel; resort centre on the Mediterranean Sea; capital of the Crusader kingdom after capture of Jerusalem in 1187; railway; ancient and modern harbour.

acridine [akrideen] $C_{13}H_9N$, melting point 111°C. A coal-tar base structurally related to anthracene. An important class of dye-stuffs is derived from it.

acromegaly [akrohmegalee] An adult disorder which arises from the over-secretion of growth hormone by the pituitary gland. There is coarsening and thickening of the subcutaneous tissues and the skin, and enlargement of the skull, jaw, hands, and feet.

Acropolis, The [akropolis] The citadel of ancient Athens, which contained the national treasury and many sacred sites and shrines, most of them (such as the Parthenon and the Erechtheum) associated with the worship of Athene. The pre-sent ruins date mainly from the second half of the 5th-c BC.

acrylic acid [akrilik] $CH_2=CH.COOH$, IUPAC **prop-2-enoic acid**. The simplest unsaturated carboxylic acid. Its nitrile is the monomer of a range of polymers used as fibres and paints. Its methyl ester and the related **methylmethacrylate** form other polymers used in paints, adhesives, and safety glass.

Actaeon [akteeon] A hunter in Greek mythology, who came upon Artemis, the goddess of chastity, while she was bathing. She changed him into a stag, which was then killed by his own hounds.

actinides [aktiniydz] Elements with an atomic number between 89 and 104 in which an inner electron shell is filling, the best known being uranium (92) and plutonium (94). Those heavier than uranium are known as the *transuranic elements*. All of their isotopes are radioactive, and most are artificially made.

action In mechanics, the difference between kinetic energy K and potential energy V ($K-V$), summed over time; symbol I or S, units J.s (joule.second).

action painting A form of abstract art which flourished in the USA from the late 1940s, its leading exponent being Jackson Pollock. The snappy term was introduced by the critic Harold Rosenberg in 1952 in preference to *abstract expressionism*. The physical act of applying paint to canvas is emphasized, rather than the picture as a finished artefact.

Actium, Battle of [aktium] (31 BC) The decisive victory of Octa-vian (later the Emperor Augustus) over the forces of Antony and Cleopatra off the coast of NW Greece.

Act of Congress A bill sanctioned by the US legislature, consist-ing of the two houses of Congress: the House of Representatives and the Senate. The bill must then be signed by the president to become law.

act of God In law, any natural phenomenon such as an earth-quake, hurricane or flood which, without human intervention, directly causes an accident. Heavy rain or fog to which drivers do not respond appropriately, with the result that their negli-gence leads to an accident, is not an act of God.

Act of Parliament A bill which has passed five stages (first read-ing, second reading, committee stage, report stage, third read-ing) in both houses of the UK parliament, and received the royal assent. The same kind of procedure applies in other par-liamentary systems.

Actors' Studio A workshop for professional actors founded in New York City by Elia Kazan, Cheryl Crawford, and Robert Lewis in 1947. Under Lee Strasberg, it was the major centre for US acting.

Acts of the Apostles A New Testament book, the second part of a narrative begun in Luke's Gospel, which traces the early pro-gress of Jesus's followers in spreading the Christian faith.

actuary A statistician specializing in life expectancy, sickness, retirement, and accident matters. Actuaries are employed by insurance companies, pension funds, and the government to calculate probability and risk.

actuator A mechanical or electrical device used to bring other equipment into operation; sometimes called a **servomotor**. It commonly refers to the equipment used for the automatic operation of brake valves in car or train brake systems.

acuity [akyooitee] Acuteness of perception, especially of vision or hearing; the smallest visual features (usually measured in terms of angular size in the retinal image) that can be seen, or auditory difference that can be heard.

acupressure A system of treatment said to be the forerunner of acupuncture. It involves the application of pressure using thumb and fingers, but sometimes also the palms, knees, elbows, and feet, to stimulate acupuncture points and meridians.

acupuncture A medical practice known in China for over 3000 years, which has come to attract attention in the West. It con-sists of the insertion into the skin and underlying tissues of a hot or cold needle, usually made of steel, several cm long. The site of insertion of the needle is chosen in relation to the site of the tissue or organ believed to be disordered, and several hun-dred specific points are identified on body maps or models. It is difficult to obtain a clear idea of which disorders benefit from acupuncture, but neuralgia, migraine, sprains, and asthma are claimed to respond, while infectious disease and tumours are unlikely to do so. It is also employed as an analgesic during surgery in the Far East. Its mechanism of action is unknown. Research has shown that brain tissue contains morphine-like substances called *endorphins*, and these may be released in increased amounts when deep sensory nerves are stimulated by injury near the body surfaces.

acyl [asiyl] IUPAC **alkanoyl**. In chemistry, the general name for an organic functional group R.CO–, where R represents H or an alkyl group.

ADA A computer programming language developed for the US Department of Defense which permits the development of very large computer systems. It was named after Augusta Ada King, Countess of Lovelace, daughter of Lord Byron, who worked with Charles Babbage.

Adair, Red [adair], popular name of **Paul Neal Adair** (1915–2004) Fire-fighting specialist, born in Houston, TX, called in as a troubleshooter to deal with major oil fires. In 1988 he and his team tackled the blaze aboard the Piper Alpha oil rig in the North Sea. He also helped to deal with the 700 fires in Kuwait following Operation Desert Storm (1991). In 1968 he was the subject of a film, *Hellfighters*, starring John Wayne.

Adam, Adolphe (Charles) [adã] (1803–56) Composer, born in Paris. He wrote several successful operas, but is chiefly remembered for the ballet *Giselle* (1841).

Adam, Robert (1728–92) Architect, born in Kirkcaldy, Fife. He and his brother **James Adam** (1730–94) succeeded in transforming the prevailing Palladian fashion in architecture by a series of romantically elegant variations on diverse classical originals. They also designed furniture and fittings to suit the houses they planned and decorated.

Adam and Eve Biblical characters described in the Book of Gen-esis as the first man and woman created by God. Traditions describe their life in the garden of Eden, their disobedience and banishment, and the birth of their sons Cain, Abel, and Seth.

Adamov, Arthur [adahmof] (1908–70) Playwright, born in Kislo-vodsk, Russia. His early absurdist plays, such as *L'Invasion* (1950, The Invasion) present the dislocations and cruelties of a meaningless world. Later plays show a transition to commitment.

Adams, Abigail, *née* **Smith** (1744–1818) Letter writer, born in Weymouth, MA. Her husband was the second president of the USA (1797–1801), and her correspondence became highly valued as a contemporary source of social history during the early days of the republic.

Adams, Ansel (Easton) (1902–84) Photographer, born in San Francisco, CA. Famous for his landscapes of the Western States, he was also an influential writer.

Adams, Douglas (Noel) (1952–2001) Writer, born in Cambridge, Cambridgeshire. He is known for his humorous science fiction novels, notably *The Hitch-hiker's Guide to the Galaxy* (1979, originally a radio series, 1978, 1980, later televised). Later works included *The Meaning of Liff* (1984, with John Lloyd) and *The Illustrated Hitch-hiker's Guide to the Galaxy* (1994). *The Salmon of Doubt*, a collection of unpublished pieces and fragments of an unfinished novel, was published posthumously in 2002.

Adams, Gerry, popular name of **Gerald Adams** (1948–) Northern Ireland politician, born in Belfast. In 1978 he became vice-president of Sinn Féin and later its president. In 1983–92 he was elected to the UK parliament as member for Belfast West, but declined to take up his seat at Westminster. He achieved national prominence as the chief spokesman for the IRA during the events relating to the IRA ceasefire (1994–6), and regained his seat in the 1997, 2001, and 2005 general elections. Elected to the newly formed Northern Ireland Assembly, 1998, he was a key actor in the implementation of the Good Friday Agreement which led to the transfer of power from London to Belfast in 1999. In July 2005 he formally announced the IRA's intention to end its armed campaign and to continue through exclusively peaceful means, and in the March Assembly elections he agreed to a historic power-sharing devolved government with Ian Paisley's UDP.

Adams, John (1735–1826) US statesman and second president (1797–1801), born in Braintree (now Quincy), MA. After eight years as vice-president under Washington (1789–97), he became the Federalist's choice for president. Defeated on seeking re-election in 1800, he retired to his home at Quincy.

Adams, John Couch (1819–92) Astronomer, born in Laneast, Cornwall. In 1845 he and Leverrier independently predicted the existence of Neptune by analyzing irregularities in the motion of Uranus.

Adams, John Quincy (1767–1848) US statesman and sixth president (1825–9), born in Quincy, MA, the son of John and Abigail Adams. As secretary of state under Monroe, he negotiated with Spain the treaty for the acquisition of Florida (1819), and was alleged to be the real author of the Monroe Doctrine (1823).

Adams, Richard (George) (1920–) Novelist, born in Newbury, Berkshire. He came to prominence with his first novel, *Watership Down* (1972). Later books include the novel *Shardik* (1974) and an autobiography, *The Day Gone By* (1990).

Adams, Samuel (1722–1803) American statesman, born in Boston, MA. He became governor (1794–7) of Massachusetts, helped to plan the Boston Tea Party, and was one of the signatories of the Declaration of Independence.

Adams, Tony (1966–) Footballer, born in Romford, Essex. He joined Arsenal as a centre back in 1983, eventually becoming team captain. He played 66 times for England, and was captain in 1994, 1995, and during the European Cup in 1996. He retired in 2000 and became manager of Wycombe Wanderers (2003–4). In 2006 he briefly joined Dutch club Feyenoord as coach of their under-21 squad.

Adamson, Joy (Friedericke Victoria), *née* **Gessner** (1910–80) Naturalist and writer, born in Austria. Living in Kenya with her third husband, British game warden **George Adamson** (1906–89), she made her name with books about the lioness Elsa, beginning with *Born Free* (1960). She was murdered in her home by tribesmen.

Adan *Aden*

adaptation (biology) The process of adjustment of an individual organism to environmental conditions. It may occur by natural selection, resulting in improved survival and reproductive success, or involve physiological or behavioural changes that are not genetic.

adaptive suspension A pneumatic or hydro-pneumatic suspension system fitted to a motor car or a commercial vehicle that damps out the variations in road surface, and maintains the vehicle at a constant level while in use. This levelling device can be controlled electronically.

adaptogen A substance which maintains or stimulates the body's mechanisms for adapting to change. Herbs such as *Eleutherococcus senticosus* are used as general adaptogens, but the term is also applied to more specific adaptors of self-regulation, such as immune stimulants.

ADD *attention*

Addams, Charles Samuel (1912–88) Cartoonist, born in Westfield, NJ. He is known for the ghoulish group which was immortalized on television in the 1960s as *The Addams Family*.

Addams, Jane (1860–1935) Social reformer, born in Cedarville, IL. She founded Hull House in Chicago, where she worked to secure social justice, female suffrage, and the cause of pacifism. In 1931 she shared the Nobel Peace Prize.

addax [adaks] A horse-like antelope (*Addax nasomaculatus*) native to N African deserts; resembles the oryx, but has thicker, spiralling horns; pale with clump of brown hair on the forehead; never drinks.

adder A venomous snake of family Viperidae; three species: *Vipera berus* (**European adder** or **common European viper**, the only venomous British snake) and the puff adders; also Australian **death adders** of the family Elapidae (2 species).

Addington, Henry *Sidmouth, 1st Viscount*

Addinsell, Richard [adinsel] (1904–77) Composer, born in Oxford, Oxfordshire. He composed much film music, including the popular *Warsaw Concerto* for the film *Dangerous Moonlight* (1941).

Addis Ababa or **Adis Abeba** [adis ababa] 9°02N 38°42E, pop (2000e) 2 157 000. Capital of Ethiopia; altitude 2400 m/7874 ft; founded by Menelik II, 1887; capital, 1889; occupied by Italy, 1936–41, declared capital of Italian East Africa; airport; railway to port of Djibouti; university (1950); cathedral.

Addison, Joseph (1672–1719) Essayist and poet, born in Milston, Wiltshire. He became a diplomat, under-secretary of state (1706–8), and an MP. Best known for his political writing, he contributed largely to the *Tatler* and the *Spectator* (which he co-founded with Steele in 1711).

Addison, Thomas (c.1793–1860) Physician, born in Longbenton, Northumberland. His chief researches were on pneumonia, tuberculosis, and the disease of the adrenal glands now known as **Addison's disease**.

Addison's disease A medical condition resulting from the destruction of the adrenal glands. A fall in the output of corticosteroids causes physical weakness, mental apathy, low blood pressure, and increased skin pigmentation. Taking synthetic steroids by mouth restores the patient to normal health.

additives Strictly, any chemical, even a vitamin, added to a food during its processing or preparation; more usually, chemicals which have been added in order to achieve a specific aim. They include (a) *preservatives*, which reduce spoilage by bacteria, (b) *anti-oxidants*, which prevent fats from becoming rancid, (c) *emulsifiers*, which permit a stable mixture of oil and water, (d) *colouring matter*, to vary colour to specifications, (e) *sweet-*

eners, and (f) *flavouring agents/enhancers*, to achieve a given flavour.

adduct *addition reaction*

Adela, Princess [adayla] (c.1062–1137) Fourth daughter of William the Conqueror. In 1080 she married Stephen-Henry, Count of Blois, by whom she had nine children. Her third son, Stephen, became King of England in her lifetime.

Adelaide 34°56S 138°36E, pop (2000e) 1 131 000. Port capital of South Australia, on the Torrens R; founded, 1837; the first Australian municipality to be incorporated, 1840; airfield; railway; two universities (1874, 1966); two cathedrals; major wine-growing area to the S and N.

Adélie Land [adaylee] or **Adélie Coast**, Fr **Terre Adélie** area c.432 000 km²/167 000 sq mi. Territory in Antarctica 66–67°S, 136–142°E; first seen by the French navy in 1840; French territory, 1938; research station at Base Dumont d'Urville.

Aden or **Adan** [aydn] 12°50N 45°00E, pop (2000e) 497 500. Port on the Gulf of Aden, at the entrance to the Red Sea; taken by British, 1839; capital of former Aden protectorate; British crown colony, 1937; scene of fighting between nationalist groups in 1960s; capital of former South Yemen, 1968–90; airport; oil refining, shipping.

Adenauer, Konrad [adenower] (1876–1967) German statesman, born in Cologne, who became the first chancellor of the Federal Republic of Germany (1949–63). He was president of the Prussian State Council 1920–33. As chancellor, he established closer post-war links with the Russians and the French.

adenine [adeneen] $C_4H_5N_5$. A base derived from purine; one of the five found in nucleic acids, where it is generally paired with thymine or uracil.

adenoids An accumulation of lymphoid tissue, arranged as a series of folds behind the opening of the auditory tube in the nasopharynx; also known as the **pharyngeal tonsils**. When enlarged in children they can fill the nasopharynx, giving an abnormal resonance to speech.

adenosine triphosphate (ATP) [adenoseen] A molecule formed by the condensation of adenine, ribose, and triphosphoric acid: HO–P(O)OH–O–P(O)OH–O–P(O)OH–OH. It is a key compound in the mediation of energy in both plants and animals.

adhesives Materials whose function is to bind one substance to another. Examples are (1) substances of biological origin, generally water soluble, known as *glues*, which are usually proteins or carbohydrates, and (2) synthetic materials, both thermoplastic and thermosetting resins and rubbers.

adiabatic process [adiabatik] In thermodynamics, a process in which no heat enters or leaves a system, such as in a well-insulated system, or in some process so rapid that there is not enough time for heat exchange. Sound waves in air involve adiabatic pressure changes.

Adie, Kate [aydee], popular name of **Kathryn Adie** (1945–) News reporter and correspondent, born in Sunderland, Tyne and Wear. As a reporter for BBC TV News (1979–81), correspondent (1982), and chief correspondent (1989–2003), she became a familiar figure presenting reports from the heart of war-torn countries around the world. Since 2003 she has presented a weekly BBC radio programme, *From Our Own Correspondent*.

Adi Granth [ahdee grahnt] (Hindi 'First Book') The principal Sikh scripture, originally called the *Granth Sahib* (Hindi 'Revered Book'). The text used today is an expanded version of Guru Arjan's original compilation, and is revered by all Sikhs.

adipic acid [adipik] HOOC–$(CH_2)_4$–COOH, IUPAC **hexanedioic acid**, melting point 153°C. It is one of the monomers for nylon, the other being 1,6-diaminohexane.

adipose tissue *fat 2*

Adirondack Mountains [adirondak] Mountain range largely in NE New York state, USA; rises to 1629 m/5344 ft at Mt Marcy; locations such as L Placid are noted winter resorts.

adjutant A stork native to tropical SE Asia. There are two species: the **greater adjutant stork** (*Leptoptilos dubius*), and the **lesser**, **haircrested**, or **Javan adjutant stork** (*Leptoptilos javanicus*); grey and white; head nearly naked.

Adler, Alfred (1870–1937) Pioneer psychiatrist, born in Vienna. A member of the psychoanalytical group that formed around Freud, his work led to one of the early schisms in psychoanalysis. His main contributions include the concept of the inferiority complex and his special treatment of neurosis as the exploitation of shock.

Admiral's Cup A yacht race for up to three boats per nation, first contested in 1957 and held biennially. Races take place in the English Channel, at Cowes, and around the Fastnet rock.

Admiralty Court An English court which is part of the Queen's Bench Division of the High Court. Its work deals with maritime claims in civil law, such as salvage and collisions at sea.

Admiralty Islands pop (2000e) 39 000; area 2000 km²/800 sq mi. Island group in N Papua New Guinea, c.40 islands, main island, Manus; chief town, Lorengau; German protectorate, 1884; under Australian mandate, 1920.

Adonis [adohnis] In Greek mythology, a beautiful young man who was loved by Aphrodite. He insisted on going hunting and was killed by a boar, but Persephone saved him on condition that he spent part of the year with her in the Underworld.

adoption A legal procedure in which a civil court makes an order giving parental rights and duties over a child to someone other than the natural parents. On adoption, the child becomes the legal child of his or her adoptive parents.

Adorno, Theodor (Wiesengrund) [adaw(r)noh], originally **Theodor Wiesengrund** (1903–69) Social philosopher and musicologist, born in Frankfurt, Germany. Director of the Frankfurt Institute for Social Research, his works include *Philosophy of Modern Music* (1949) and *Negative Dialectics* (1966).

Adrastea [adrasteea] A tiny natural satellite of Jupiter, discovered in 1979 by Voyager 2; distance from the planet 129 000 km/80 000 mi; diameter 24 km/15 mi.

adrenal glands [adreenl] Paired compound endocrine glands in mammals, each situated above each kidney; also known as the **suprarenal glands**. Each comprises an outer cortex, which produces specific hormones, and an inner medulla, which secretes a specific catecholamine (either adrenaline or noradrenaline).

adrenaline or **adrenalin** [adrenalin] A hormone released from the adrenal medulla in response to stress, and in some other circumstances; also known as **epinephrine** in the USA. It increases heart rate, raises blood pressure, and causes release of sugar into the blood from liver stores. It may also be a neurotransmitter in the brain.

Adrian IV, also **Hadrian**, originally **Nicholas Breakspear** (c.1100–59) The only Englishman to become pope (1154–9), born in Abbots Langley, Hertfordshire. In 1146 he was appointed Cardinal Bishop of Albano. As pope, he is said to have granted Ireland to Henry II.

Adrian, Edgar Douglas, 1st Baron Adrian (1889–1977) Neurophysiologist, born in London. A founder of modern neurophysiology, he shared the 1932 Nobel Prize for Physiology or Medicine for his work on the function of neurones.

Adriatic Sea [aydreeatik] Arm of the Mediterranean Sea, between the E coast of Italy and the Balkan Peninsula; length 800 km/500 mi; width 93–225 km/58–140 mi; maximum depth 1250 m/4100 ft; highly saline.

Advaita [adviyta] (Sanskrit, 'non-dual') An influential school of Vedanta Hinduism, revived in a modern form during the 20th-c. It holds that there is only one absolute reality, Brahman.

Advent In the Christian Church, a period of penitence and preparation for the celebration of the first coming of Christ at Christmas, and for his promised second coming to judge the world. It begins on **Advent Sunday**, the fourth Sunday before Christmas.

Adventists Those Christians whose most important belief is in the imminent and literal Second Coming of Christ. A separate movement began in the USA with William Miller (1781–1849), who predicted Christ's return (and the end of the world) in 1843–4, and whose followers eventually formed a denomination called Seventh Day Adventists. They believe that the Second Coming is delayed only by a failure to keep the Sabbath.

Advisory, Conciliation, and Arbitration Service *ACAS*

advocate A term generally applied to lawyers practising in the courts as professional representatives of those who bring or defend a case. In Scotland, the term is used as an equivalent to an English barrister, denoting exclusive right of audience before the superior courts; however, since 1993, a hybrid form of lawyer called a **solicitor advocate** has been created from existing solicitors who, on passing further examinations, is permitted to appear in the High Court or the Court of Session.

aechmea [akmaya] A member of a genus of plants (epiphytes) native to tropical America; rosettes of succulent leaves forming a water-filled cup in the centre; inflorescence on a stout, well-developed stalk. (Genus: *Aechmea*, 172 species. Family: Bromeliaceae.)

Aedes [ayeedeez] The yellow-fever mosquito, found in coastal and riverside habitats throughout the tropics and subtropics; eggs laid in stagnant water. (Order: Diptera. Family: Culicidae.)

Aegean Islands [eejeean] pop (2000e) 476 000; area 9122 km²/3521 sq mi. Island group and region of Greece; the name is generally applied to the islands of the Aegean Sea, including Lesbos, Chios, Samos, Limnos, and Thasos; a major tourist area.

Aegean Sea [eejeean] Arm of the Mediterranean Sea, bounded W and N by Greece, NE and E by Turkey, S by islands of Crete and Rhodes; dotted with islands on which the Aegean civilization of 3000–1000 BC flourished; length (N–S) 645 km/400 mi; width 320 km/200 mi; greatest depth, 2013 m/6604 ft.

Aegina [eejiyna], Gr **Aiyna** pop (2000e) 12 000; area 83 km²/32 sq mi. One of the largest of the Saronic Islands, Greece; chief town, Aiyna; a popular resort.

aegis [eejis] Originally a goatskin, and then, in Greek mythology, a fringed piece of armour or a shield. Zeus shakes his aegis, which may possibly be the thunder-cloud; Athene's is equipped with the Gorgon's head.

Aegisthus [eegisthuhs, eejisthuhs] In Greek legend, the son of Thyestes; while Agamemnon was absent at Troy he became the lover of Clytemnestra. Together they killed Agamemnon on his return to Argos. Aegisthus was later killed by Orestes.

Ælfric [alfrik, alfrich], also known as **Ælfric Grammaticus** ('The Grammarian') (c.955–c.1020) English writer, known for his use of the Anglo-Saxon vernacular. He taught at the monastery of Cerne Abbas, later becoming abbot of Eynsham.

Aelred of Rievaulx *Ailred of Rievaulx*

Aeneas [eeneeas] In Roman legend, the ancestor of the Romans. He was a Trojan hero, the son of Anchises and Venus, who escaped after the fall of Troy, bearing his father on his shoulders. His son founded Alba Longa, and a line of kings from whom Romulus was said to be descended.

aeolian harp [eeohlian] A wooden soundbox fitted with strings of various thicknesses, but tuned to a single pitch, which are made to vibrate freely by the surrounding air, producing an ethereal, 'disembodied' sound. It takes its name from Aeolus, god of the winds.

Aeolus [eeolus] In Greek mythology, the god of the winds. In the *Odyssey* Aeolus lived on an island, and gave Odysseus the winds tied in a bag so that his ship would not be blown off course. Odysseus' men opened the bag, thinking it contained treasure. As a result, the ship was blown far away.

Aepyornis [eepiaw(r)nis] *elephant bird*

aerial *antenna* (technology)

aerial photography Photography of the ground surface from an aerial viewpoint such as a balloon or aircraft. Applications include archaeology, ecology, geology, and wartime reconnaissance.

aerobe [airohb] An organism that requires the presence of oxygen for growth and reproduction. The great majority of all living organisms are aerobic, requiring oxygen for respiration. Some micro-organisms, typically bacteria, are anaerobic, able to grow only in the absence of oxygen; these are known as **anaerobes**.

aerobics [airohbiks] A system of physical training that exercises large muscle groups for long periods. Regular aerobic exercise improves the performance of the heart, lungs, and muscles, and these improvements can be measured on charts appropriate to different age groups. It includes exercises such as walking, running, swimming, and cycling. In the 1980s the term was particularly used for movement exercises in time to music, which became popular among keep-fit groups.

aerocapture A proposed technique for placing a spacecraft in orbit around a planet, without the expenditure of chemical propellants, by taking advantage of planetary atmosphere. The spacecraft would be equipped with an aerobrake and would be navigated into the planet's upper atmosphere, where friction would slow it down.

aerodynamics The study of the flow of air and the behaviour of objects moving relative to air; a subject which is applicable to other gases, and is part of the larger subject of fluid mechanics. Aerodynamic principles explain flight. The shape and orientation of an aircraft wing (curved upper surface, wing tilted down) mean that the air above the wing travels further than the air beneath. Air above the wing thus travels faster and so has lower pressure (Bernoulli's principle). The pressure difference provides lift to support the aircraft. The movement of an aircraft through the air produces a force which impedes motion, called *drag*, dependent on the aircraft size and shape. At velocities greater than the speed of sound (Mach 1, approximately 331·5 m/1088 ft per second) air can no longer be treated as incompressible and new rules apply, giving rise to **supersonic aerodynamics**. Passing from subsonic to supersonic speeds, aircraft cross the 'sound barrier', marked by a dramatic increase in drag. Aircraft flying at supersonic speeds produce sonic booms – shock waves in the air around the aircraft, produced because the aircraft's velocity is too great to allow the air pressure to adjust smoothly around it.

aeronautics The broad body of scientifically based knowledge describing aeroplanes as objects subject to the laws of physics. It covers such topics as the generation of lift to make the aeroplane fly, the production of thrust, the strength of the structure, and the way these elements are combined to produce a functioning vehicle.

aerophone Any musical instrument in which air is the main vibrating agent. Aerophones are subdivided into types according to (a) the main material they are made of, and (b) how the air is set in motion (via a mouthpiece, a reed, or neither).

aeroplane / airplane The general name given to a vehicle whose operational medium is air and which supports itself in the Earth's atmosphere by means of lift. Lift is produced through specially shaped fixed wings attached to the aeroplane's body or *fuselage*; these alter the airflow so that the pressure distribution of the air over the wing creates an upward force. The airflow is in turn produced by the aeroplane being 'pushed' or 'pulled' through the air by the propulsion device driven by a motor. By means of design, the lift produced by the wing can be made greater than the weight of the airframe and propulsive system, allowing a payload to be carried. George Cayley designed a glider in 1853, but the first truly powered flight was made by Orville Wright in December 1903, when he flew 260 m/852 ft. World War 2 saw the world's first operational jet fighter, the Me 262. In the period following the War, jet engines were applied to ever larger passenger aircraft, culminating in the introduction of the Boeing 747 Jumbo Jet in 1970. This period also saw the arrival of the supersonic Concorde in 1976. In 2005 the Airbus 380, the world's largest passenger plane to date, successfully completed its maiden flight. Later that year, its competitor, the new Boeing 777-200LR Worldliner jet broke the record for the longest non-stop commercial flight with a 12 500-mile trip from Hong Kong to London. Recent developments in civilian aircraft have been away from higher speed towards more economical and quieter operation, while military and large commercial aircraft are becoming increasingly reliant upon electronics to control and keep them stable in flight.

aerosol An airborne suspension of microscopic particles or liquid droplets, typically formed by forcing a liquid through a fine nozzle under pressure. Aerosol sprays are useful as a means of depositing fine even layers of material, such as in paint sprays.

aerospace medicine The study and prevention of the adverse affects of flight and space travel on the human body. The body is affected during high altitude flights by low oxygen levels, which lead to weakness and drowsiness; low pressure, which causes trapped air within the body to expand, producing pain; and high G-forces produced by rapid accelerations, which force blood away from the brain, leading to blackouts. Preventative measures include oxygen masks, pressurized cabins and suits.

Aeschines [eeskineez] (c.390 BC–?) Athenian orator, second only to Demosthenes. He was prominent in Athenian politics between 348 and 330 BC. Of his speeches, only three survive.

Aeschylus [eeskilus] (c.525–c.456 BC) Playwright, born in Eleusis, near Athens. Out of some 60 plays ascribed to him, only seven are extant, including the trilogy of the *Oresteia: Agamemnon, Choephori* (The Libation Bearers), and *Eumenides* (The Furies).

Aesculapius [eeskyulaypius] The Latin form of **Asclepius**, the Greek god of healing. His cult was transferred from Epidauros to Rome in 291 BC after a plague.

Aesop [eesop] (?6th-c BC) The traditional name of a Greek writer of fables. He is supposed to have been a native of Phrygia and a slave who, after being set free, travelled to Greece. The fables are anecdotes which use animals to make a moral point.

aesthetics / esthetics The philosophical investigation of art, understood to include the visual arts (painting, sculpture, photography, film), music, literature, drama, and dance. Aesthetics deals with such issues as what it is to perceive an object or a performance as a work of art; and whether there are objective standards for judging it.

aestivation hibernation

Æthel- (Anglo-Saxon name) *Athelstan; Ethelbert; Etheldreda; Ethelflaed; Ethelred I; Ethelred II*

aether *ether 2*

affenpinscher [afenpinsher] A breed of dog; small with long dark wiry coat; usually black; face like a monkey, with short muzzle and large black eyes; very old breed, originally from Germany, now rare.

affinity A relationship by marriage. Countries generally have rules prohibiting marriage between certain people where there is an affinity – for example between parents and their step-children. Prohibitions also apply where there is *consanguinity* (a blood relationship).

affirmative action Policies requiring institutions to act 'affirmatively' in employment or other recruitment practices to avoid discrimination on grounds of race, ethnic origin, or sex. They are usually found in the USA.

Affleck, Ben(jamin Geza) (1972–) Film actor, born in Berkeley, CA. He became internationally known following his appearance in *Good Will Hunting* (1997), for which he shared an Oscar for best original screenplay with fellow co-star Matt Damon. Later films include *Shakespeare in Love* (1998), *Pearl Harbor* (2001), *Hollywoodland* (2006), and *Smokin' Aces* (2007).

afforestation The planting of woodland areas. The aim may be to increase the extent of economically useful wood (eg conifer plantations in upland UK) or to protect against soil erosion and desertification by providing shelter belts and vegetation cover on bare ground.

Afghan hound A breed of dog; large, slender, with a bouncing step; hair very long, silky (short-haired forms also exist); long thin muzzle; originated in Middle East; was used for hunting in N Afghanistan; hunts by sight.

Afghanistan *pp.10–11*

Afghan Wars A series of wars (1838–42, 1878–80, 1919) between Britain and Afghanistan, prompted by the British desire to extend control in the region to prevent the advance of Russian influence towards India. The third Afghan War resulted in the country's independence (1922).

aflatoxin [aflatoksin] A toxin produced by the mould *Aspergillus flavus* (from *Aspergillus flavus toxin*) commonly found in peanuts, cottonseed, soybeans, wheat, barley, sorghum, and nuts such as pistachios, almonds, and cacao, where the climate favours its growth. Symptoms of poisoning include weight loss, loss of co-ordination, convulsions, and death.

AFL/CIO *American Federation of Labor – Congress of Industrial Organisations*

Africa area c.30·97 million km^2/11·6 million sq mi. Second largest continent, extending S from the Mediterranean Sea; bounded W by the Atlantic Ocean and E by the Indian Ocean and the Red Sea; bisected by the Equator; maximum length, 8000 km/5000 mi; maximum width, 7200 km/4500 mi; highest point, Mt Kilimanjaro (5895 m/19 340 ft); major rivers include the Congo, Niger, Nile, Zambezi. (*see map pp.12–13*)

African marigold A misleading name for *Tagetes erecta*, a popular garden annual, originating from Mexico, with deeply cut leaves and showy yellow, orange, or red flower-heads up to 10 cm/4 in diameter. **French marigold**, also from Mexico, is very similar but has smaller flower-heads. (Family: Compositae.)

African National Congress (ANC) The most important of the Black South African organizations opposed to the white regime. It began life in 1912. Banned by the South African government in 1961, it began a campaign of industrial and economic sabotage through its military wing, and in the 1980s it started attacking persons as well as property. It was unbanned, and suspended its armed struggle, in 1990. It dominated the first three sets of non-racial elections, taking 252 of the 400 seats in the Assembly in 1994, 266 seats in 1999, and 279 seats in 2004.

African Union An organization of African nations, founded in 1963 as the **Organization of African Unity** by representatives of 32 African governments meeting in Addis Ababa, which dedicated itself to the eradication of all forms of colonialism in Africa. Less active in recent years, it had 53 members in 2007. The decision to form a Pan-African Parliament was adopted in 2003 and it held its inaugural session in 2004. The body will eventually have 265 members. In May 2004 the AU officially launched a 15-member Peace and Security Council designed to intervene in African conflicts.

African violet A perennial with hairy leaves in a dense rosette (*Saintpaulia ionantha*); white, pink, blue, purple, or red flowers; native to tropical E Africa. Their wide colour range and long flowering period make them popular house plants. (Family: Gesneriaceae.)

Afrikaans South African or Cape Dutch, the language of Dutch

Afghanistan

☐ International Airport

official name **Islamic Emirate of Afghanistan**, Persian **Dowlat-e-Islami-ye-Afghanestan**

Local name Afghānestān

Timezone GMT + 4·5

Area 647 497 km²/249 934 sq mi

Population total (2002e) 27 756 000, plus an estimated 2·5 million nomadic tribesmen and c.5 million living in Pakistan and Iran as refugees.

Status Democratic republic

Date of independence 1919

Capital Kabul

Languages Pushtu, Dari

Ethnic groups Pathans (50%), Tajik (20%), Uzbek (9%), Hazara (9%), Chahar Aimak (3%), Turkmen (2%), Baluchi (1%)

Religions Muslim (Sunni 84%, Shi'ite 15%)

Physical features Mountainous, landlocked country centred on and divided E–W by the Hindu Kush mountain range which reaches heights of over 7 000 m/24 000 ft. Three distinctive regions: fertile valley of Herat in NW; arid uplands to the S; and 129 495 km²/50 000 sq mi of desert in the SW plateau (including the Rigestan Desert). Amu Darya (Oxus) R forms N border.

Climate Continental climate; summers warm everywhere except on highest peaks; rain mostly during spring and autumn; average annual rainfall 338 mm/13·25 in; winters generally cold, with much snow at higher altitudes (central highlands have a sub-polar climate); at lower levels desert or semi-arid climate.

Currency 1 Afghani (AFA) = 100 puls

Economy Traditionally based on agriculture, especially wheat, fruit, vegetables, maize, barley, cotton, sugar-beet, sugar cane, sheep, cattle, goats; natural-gas production in the N, largely for export; most sectors have been affected by civil war, especially sugar, carpets, textiles; natural resources also include oil, coal, copper, sulphur, lead, zinc, iron, salt, precious and semi-precious stones; many of these resources remain untapped owing to inaccessibility. Main trading partners: Eastern European and CIS countries, Japan, China.

GDP (2002e) $19 bn, per capita $700

History Nation first formed in 1747, under Ahmad Shah Durrani; seen as a bridge between India and the Middle East. Britain tried but failed to gain control during a series of Afghan Wars (the last in 1919); independence declared in 1919 after World War 1; feudal monarchy survived until after World War 2, when the constitution became more liberal under several Soviet-influenced five-year economic plans; king deposed in 1973, and a republic formed; new constitution, 1977; coup (1979) brought to power Hafzullah Amin, which led to invasion by USSR forces and establishment of Babrak Karmal as Head of State; new constitution in 1987 provided for an executive President, bicameral National Assembly, and council of ministers; Soviet withdrawal implemented 1988–9; new regime met with heavy guerrilla resistance from the Mujahideen (Islamic fghters); resignation of President Najibullah, 1992; Islamic State of Afghanistan declared, 1992; continuing unrest and disunity among Mujahideen groups, hindering implementation of UN-backed peace plans; new conflict, 1994–5, with the *taliban* (army of students), a Muslim force whose military organization emerged in late 1994; Taliban seize Kabul and drive out government forces, imposition of strict Islamic regime, and execution of Najibullah, 1996; government of Burhanuddin Rabbani continued to control part of the country in rebellion against the Taliban government under Mohammad Omar Akhondzada; called Ismalic Emirate of Afghanistan, 1997; following the attack on the World Trade Center in New York (11 Sep 2001), US-led coalition forces launch aerial

colonization, and a variety of West Germanic, but with many loan words from Bantu and other languages.

Afrika Korps A German expeditionary force of two divisions under the command of Rommel, sent to N Africa (Mar 1941) to reinforce Italian troops there. It proved highly effective in desert warfare between 1941 and 1944.

Afrikaners An early 18th-c term to describe those Europeans who had been born in the Dutch colony at the Cape (founded 1652) and were therefore 'Africans', also known as **Boers** (Dutch 'farmers'). After 1835, groups left Cape Colony and established independent republics in the interior. Following the Union of South Africa in 1910, the Afrikaners became the dominant force in White South African politics.

Afro-Asiatic languages The major language family in N Africa, the E horn of Africa, and SW Asia. It comprises more than 200 languages, spoken by 200 million people. The major subgroup

is the Semitic family. Amongst other subgroups are Cushitic, Berber, and Chadic.

Agadir [agadeer] 30°30N 9°40W, pop (2000e) 160 000. Seaport in W Morocco; on the Atlantic coast; named Santa Cruz by the Portuguese, 1505–41; taken by the French in 1913; extensive rebuilding after earthquake in 1960; airport.

Aga Khan [ahga kahn] Title of the hereditary head of the Ismailian sect of Muslims, notably **Aga Khan III** (1877–1957), in full **Aga Sultan Sir Mohammed Shah**, born at Karachi, who succeeded to the title in 1885. He owned several Derby winners. In the 20th-c, Aga Khan III served as president of the League of Nations, while Aga Khan IV became a noted philanthropist.

Agamemnon [agamemnon] King of Argos and commander of the Greek army in the Trojan War. On his return home he was murdered by his wife Clytemnestra and her lover Aegisthus.

agamid [agamid] A lizard native to Africa (except Madagascar), S bombardment of Taliban-controlled military installations linked to Osama bin Laden, Oct 2001; Afghan delegations agree to set up the interim administration under the auspices of the UN to end more that 20 years of war, Dec 2001; International Security Assistance Force (ISAF) established; US-led ongoing operations against remaining Taliban resistance, 2002; ISAF taken over by NATO, 2003; election victory for Hamid Karzai, 2004; fighting between Taliban and coalition forces renewed, 2006.

Democratic Republic of Afghanistan
Revolutionary Council – Head of State
1978–9 Nur Mohammad Taraki
1979 Hafizullah Amin
Soviet Invasion
1979–86 Babrak Karmal
1986–7 Haji Mohammad Chamkani *Acting*
1987 Ahmadzai Najibullah
Islamic Republic of Afghanistan
Head of State
1987–92 Mohammad Najibullah
1992 Seghbatullah Mujjaddedi
1992–6 Burhanuddin Rabbani
Head of Government
1929–46 Sardar Mohammad Hashim Khan
1946–53 Shah Mahmoud Khan Ghazi
1953–63 Mohammad Daoud
1963–5 Mohammad Yousef
1965–7 Mohammad Hashim Maiwandwal
1967–71 Nour Ahmad Etemadi
1972–3 Mohammad Mousa Shafiq
1973–9 *As President*
1979–81 Babrak Karmal
1981–8 Sultan Ali Keshtmand
Republic of Afghanistan
1988–9 Mohammad Hasan Sharq
1989–90 Sultan Ali Keshtmand
1990–2 Fazl Haq Khaleqiar
1992–3 Abdul Sabur Fareed
1993–4 Gulbardin Hekmatyar
1994–6 Arsala Rahmani *Acting*
1996 Gulbardin Hekmatyar
Interim Council
1996–2001 Mohammad Rabbani *Chairman*
Interim Government
2001–2 Hamid Karzai
Head of State
2002– Hamid Karzai

and SE Asia, and Australia; body usually broad, head large, scales with ridges and spines; tongue thick and fleshy; tail cannot be shed; some species able to change colour; also known as **chisel-tooth lizard**. (Family: Agamidae, 300 species.)

Agaña [agahnya] 13°28N 144°45E, pop (2000e) 1400. Port and capital town of Guam, Mariana Is, W Pacific Ocean; taken by Japan, 1941; destroyed during its recapture by the USA, 1944; US naval base; university (1952); cathedral (1669); frequent typhoons.

agar [aygah(r)] A jelly-like compound produced from seaweed. It is used, after sterilization and the addition of suitable nutrients, for culture of fungi or bacteria for medicinal or research purposes.

Agassi, Andre (Kirk) [agasee] (1970–) Tennis player, born in Las Vegas, NV. He turned professional in 1986, and went on to win Wimbledon (1992), the US Open (1994, 1999), the Australian

Open (1995, 2000, 2001, 2003), the French Open (1999), and other titles, leading the world rankings for much of 1995. At the beginning of 2006 he had a world ranking of number 7, and retired later that year.

agate [agayt] A form of chalcedony, a fine-grained variety of the mineral quartz. Colour variations result in semi-precious stones such as onyx (white/grey), carnelian (red), and chrysoprase (apple-green).

Agatha, St (?–251) Christian martyr from Catania, Sicily, who is said to have rejected the love of the Prefect Quintilianus, and suffered a cruel martyrdom in 251. She is the patron saint of Catania, and is invoked against fire and lightning. Feast day 5 February.

agave [agahvee] An evergreen perennial native to S USA, Central America, and N South America; stems very short, tough; leaves sword-shaped, often spiny on margins, thick, fleshy, and waxy, forming a rosette. The plant grows for many years, finally producing a huge branched inflorescence up to 7 m/23 ft high, with many flowers, after which it dies. Many species produce useful fibres, such as henequen, as well as alcoholic drinks such as pulque and mescal. (Genus: *Agave*, 300 species. Family: Agavaceae.)

Agee, James (Rufus) [ayjee] (1909–55) Writer, born in Knoxville, TN. He is best known for *Let Us Now Praise Famous Men* (1941), in collaboration with photographer Walker Evans. His novel, *A Death in the Family* (published 1957), was awarded a posthumous Pulitzer Prize.

ageing *senescence*

Agence France-Press (AFP) [azhãs frãs] An international news agency, with headquarters in Paris. The direct successor to Havas (established in 1832), AFP is the oldest surviving world agency, and one of the largest.

agenda setting The presumed power of interest groups, politicians, and the mass media to determine the public's perception of the salience and relative importance of issues. The agenda-setting hypothesis posits a cognitive correspondence on the part of the media, the public, and politicians (or other elites) on the way issues are seen, which is engineered in part by **spin doctors** and which serves the sectional interests of the powerful. Others argue that agenda setters more commonly respond to the public mood than create it.

Agent Orange (2,4,5-T or 2,4,5-trichlorophenoxy acetic acid) A herbicide used as a defoliant in jungle warfare, for example, by the British in Malaya and the USA in Vietnam. Its name derives from the orange rings painted around the containers used in Vietnam. It is toxic to humans and exposure is linked with serious health problems, notably genetic damage.

Aggeus [agayus] *Haggai, Book of*

aggiornamento [ajaw(r)namentoh] The process of making the life, doctrine, and worship of the Roman Catholic Church effective in the modern world. This was initiated by Pope John XXIII at the Second Vatican Council (1962–5).

Agincourt, Battle of [azhinkaw(r)t] (1415) A battle between France and England during the Hundred Years' War. Henry V of England was forced to fight near Hesdin (Pas-de-Calais) by the French. Though heavily outnumbered, the English won an overwhelming victory.

aging *senescence*

Agnew, Spiro T(heodore) [agnyoo] (1918–96) US Republican vice-president, born in Baltimore, MD, son of a Greek immigrant. As a compromise figure acceptable to most shades of Republican opinion, he was Nixon's running-mate in the 1968 election, and took office as vice-president in 1969. He resigned in 1973.

Agni [uhgni] The Hindu god of fire. He is welcome in every home as a principle of life and because he drives away demons.

Agnon, Shmuel Yosef, originally **Shmuel Josef Czaczkes** (1888–

1970) Novelist, born in Buczacz, Poland (now Buchach, W Ukraine), the first Israeli to win a Nobel Prize for Literature (1966). He wrote an epic trilogy of novels on Eastern European Jewry in the early 20th-c.

agnosia [agnohzia] A condition found in some brain-damaged individuals, whereby they are unable to recognize objects despite adequate basic visual and intellectual abilities; for example, a patient might be able to recognize by touch but not by sight.

agnosticism Strictly, the view that God's existence cannot be known (**theism**) nor denied (**atheism**). The term was derived from the 'unknown' God in *Acts* 17.23, and first used (by T H Huxley) in 1869: agnostics were contrasted with **gnostics**, or metaphysicians.

Agostini, Giacomo [agosteenee] (1944–) Motor-cyclist, born in Lóvere, Italy. He won a record 15 world titles between 1966 and 1975, including the 500 cc title a record eight times (1966–72, 1977).

agouti [agootee] A cavy-like rodent, native to Central and South America and Caribbean Is; length, 500 mm/20 in; rat-like with long legs and minute black tail. (Genus: *Dasyprocta*, 11 species. Family: Dasyproctidae.)

Agra [ahgra] 27°17N 77°58E, pop (2000e) 1 055 000. City in Uttar Pradesh, NE India; founded, 1566; Mughal capital until 1659; taken by the British, 1803; seat of the government of North-West Provinces, 1835–62; airfield; railway; university (1927); Taj Mahal (1632–54), Pearl Mosque of Shah Jahan (1662), Mirror Palace (Shish Mahal), a world heritage site.

Agre, Peter [ahg ray] (1949–) Biochemist, born in Northfield, MN. He became professor of biological chemistry at Johns Hopkins in 1993, and in 2003 shared the Nobel Prize for Chemistry for discoveries concerning channels in cell membranes.

agribusiness The combined businesses of: farmers, who produce commodities; input industries, which supply them with equipment, chemicals, and finance; and merchants, processors, and distributors, who convert commodities into foodstuffs, ready for sale to consumers.

Agricola, Georgius [agrikola], Latin name of **Georg Bauer** (1494–1555) Mineralogist, born in Glauchau, Germany. He made the first scientific classification of minerals in *De natura fossilium* (1546, On the Nature of Fossils).

Agricola, Gnaeus Julius [agrikola] (40–93) Rome's longest-serving and most successful governor in Britain (78–84). He subdued N England and Lowland Scotland, and actively encouraged the development of Roman-style towns in the S.

Agricola, Johann [agrikola], originally **Schneider** or **Schnitter**, also called **Magister Islebius** (1492–1566) Reformer, born in Eisleben, Germany, one of the most zealous founders of Protestantism. He was sent by Luther to Frankfurt (1525) to institute Protestant worship there.

Agricultural Revolution The name popularly given to a series of changes in farming practice occurring first in England and later throughout W Europe. The term usually covers the period 1700–1850. The main changes included: greater intensity of productive land use; the reduction of fallow land and waste lands; the introduction of crop rotation; the development of improved grasses; new crops, such as turnips and potatoes; the use of seed drills; and scientific animal breeding.

agriculture The cultivation of crops and the keeping of domesticated animals for food, fibre, or power. Agriculture enabled primitive people, who depended on hunting, fishing, and gathering, to settle down in communities, which could then grow as their agricultural productivity grew. This was aided by the development of such implements as ploughs, hoes, and sickles – and in drier countries by the construction of irrigation systems. Agricultural production is dominated by cereals: total world cereal production in 2006 was 2·02 thousand million tonnes.

agrimony [agrimonee] An erect perennial (*Agrimonia eupatoria*) growing to 60 cm/2 ft, native to Europe, W Asia, and N Africa; leaves hairy, with pairs of small leaflets alternating with large ones; flowers 5-petalled, yellow, in a long terminal spike. (Family: Rosaceae.)

Agrippa *Herod Agrippa I / II*

Agrippa, Marcus Vipsanius [agripa] (c.63–12 BC) Roman general and right-hand man of Octavian (later, the Emperor Augustus). He commanded the fleet at Actium (31 BC), and married Augustus's daughter, Julia.

Agrippina [agripeena], known as **Agrippina the Elder** (c.14 BC– AD 33) The granddaughter of the Roman Emperor Augustus, and mother of three potential imperial heirs. She became the focus of opposition to the Emperor Tiberius after the suspicious death of her husband, Germanicus (AD 19). Banished to the barren island of Pandateria (AD 29), she died there of starvation.

Agrippina [agripeena], known as **Agrippina the Younger** (15–59) The eldest daughter of Agrippina the Elder and Germanicus, and mother of the Emperor Nero. In 54 she ruthlessly engineered Nero's succession to the throne, poisoning Emperor Claudius, her husband at the time. Initially she ruled as virtual co-regent with Nero, but he tired of her influence and had her murdered.

agroforestry The cultivation of tree or bush crops (e.g. coffee, rubber), sometimes alternating with annual food crops, to give a sustainable and economically viable agricultural cropping system.

agronomy The theory and practice of field-crop production and soil management. The subject embraces several disciplines, including plant breeding, plant physiology, and soil conservation.

Agutter, Jenny [aguhter], popular name of **Jennifer (Ann) Agutter** (1952–) Film and stage actress, born in Taunton, Somerset. She became known following her role in *The Railway Children* (1970), and later film credits include *The Snow Goose* (1971, Emmy), *Equus* (1977, BAFTA), and *Blue Juice* (1995). Television work includes *A Respectable Trade* (1998), a new adaptation of *The Railway Children* (2000), and *The Alan Clark Diaries* (2004).

Ahab [ayhab] (9th-c BC) Son and successor of Omri as King of Israel (c.873–c.852 BC). His reign was marked by frequent battles against Syria, and a religious crisis when his wife Jezebel supported the worship of Baal in opposition to Yahweh.

Ahaggar Mountains [ahagah(r)] or **Hoggar Mountains** Mountain range in S Algeria, N Africa; rises to 2918 m/9573 ft at Mt Tahat, the highest point in Algeria.

Ahern, Bertie [ahern] (1951–) Irish politician and prime minister (1997–), born in Dublin. He became a member of the Dáil in 1977, and after holding posts as minister for labour (1987–91) and finance (1991–4), he became President of Fianna Fáil, and head of a coalition government after defeating John Bruton in 1997. He was elected for a second term in 2002.

Ahimsa [ahimsa] The principle of respect for all life and the practice of non-injury to living things. It is found in certain Hindu sects, Buddhism, and especially Jainism.

Ahmadabad or **Ahmedabad** [ahmadabad] 23°00N 72°40E, pop (2000e) 3 374 000. Commercial centre and industrial city in Gujarat, W India; founded, 1411; fell to the Mughals, 1572; British trading post, 1619; centre of Gandhi's activities during the 1920s and 1930s; airfield; railway; university (1949).

Ahura Mazda [ahura mazda] (Persian 'Wise Lord') The name for God used by Zoroaster and his followers. The world is the arena for the battle between Ahura Mazda and Ahriman, the spirit of evil – a battle in which Ahura Mazda will finally prevail and become fully omnipotent.

AI *artificial intelligence*

Aidan, St [aydn], known as the **Apostle of Northumbria** (?–651) Irish monk who was sent from Iona in 635 to found the Northumbrian Church in England. He established the monastery at Lindisfarne. Feast day 31 August.

AIDS Acronym for **acquired immuno-deficiency syndrome**, the result of infection with the human immuno-deficiency virus (HIV). The virus is transmitted sexually, or by inoculation with contaminated blood, and can also be passed from mother to baby at birth. In the West, the groups most at risk are homosexual or bisexual men, people with multiple sexual partners, intravenous drug abusers, and people who have had multiple transfusions of blood or blood products prior to 1986, such as haemophiliacs. The infection is endemic in parts of the developing world, such as sub-Saharan Africa and India. Its origin is unknown. It emerged in the 1960s, though the epidemic only became obvious in the 1980s, and one theory is that it spread to humans from African monkeys. The virus damages the immune system, notably T-helper cells, and slowly destroys the body's defence against other infections. Individuals with HIV may remain symptom-free for years; however, after a time illnesses develop, including infections due to micro-organisms that do not normally cause disease. There is also fatigue, weight loss, enlargement of lymph nodes, dementia, and a rare form of skin cancer (Kaposi's sarcoma). In developed countries, survival has been improved by treatment with combinations of powerful anti-retroviral therapies, including AZT. However, these drugs are expensive, and largely unavailable in poor countries. HIV was independently discovered by Luc Montagnier and Robert C Gallo (1983), and later shown by Françoise Barre-Sinoussi and Jean-Claude Chermann to be the virus responsible for AIDS.

Aiken, Conrad (Potter) [ayken] (1889–1973) Poet, novelist, and critic, born in Savannah, GA. Much influenced by T S Eliot, his *Selected Poems* won the 1930 Pulitzer Prize.

Aiken, Joan (Delano) [ayken] (1924–2004) Writer, the daughter of Conrad Aiken, born in Sussex. Her many books for children include *All You've Ever Wanted* (1953), *The Kingdom and the Cave* (1960), *Voices Hippo* (1988), *Dangerous Games* (1999), and *The Witches of Clatteringshaws* (2005, posthumously). Among her adult novels are *The Silence of Herondale* (1964), *Mansfield Revisited* (1985), and *Cold Shoulder Road* (1995).

aikido [iykeedoh] An ancient Japanese art of self-defence – a combination of karate and judo deriving from ancient jujitsu. There are two main systems, *tomiki* and *uyeshiba*.

Ailred of Rievaulx, St [aylred, reevoh], also **Aelred** or **Ethelred** (1109–66) Chronicler, born in Hexham, Northumberland. He became a Cistercian monk (later, abbot) at Rievaulx Abbey, Yorkshire. Feast days 12 January, 3 March.

Ainu [iynoo] The caucasoid aboriginals of Japan, now intermarried with other Japanese and culturally assimilated. Traditionally hunters and fishers, today many are factory workers and labourers.

air *atmosphere*

Airborne Warning and Control System (AWACS) [aywaks] An aircraft-mounted radar system able to detect and track hostile intruders at long range and direct friendly fighters to intercept them. The US, British and French Air Forces operate the Boeing E-3 Sentry AWACS.

air conditioning A system which improves the quality of air by purifying it (removing particles of dust, smoke, or pollen) and controlling its temperature and humidity (the amount of water in the air). In an air conditioner, a filter removes the larger particles of matter. Any tiny particles remaining are given a positive electric charge as the air passes over an electric grid. They are then attracted to a negatively charged grid and stick to it. Chemicals which cause smells are removed by passing the air through a charcoal filter. Air temperature is controlled by passing the air over pipes full of hot water to warm it or over pipes full of iced water to cool it. If the air is too dry, steam or water is sprayed into it. Air which is too humid or damp is cooled so that the moisture condenses out and drains away. It can also be passsed through chambers which contain moisture-absorbing chemicals such as silica gel.

aircraft Any vehicle designed to operate within the Earth's atmosphere, supporting itself by means of lift generated by wings or other methods.

aircraft carrier A naval vessel on which aircraft can take off and land, developed during World War 1. The first carrier, HMS *Furious* (1918), was a battle-cruiser with forward and after flight-decks. *Furious* was reconstructed in 1925 and fitted with an island bridge layout on the starboard side of a continuous flight-deck. This became the conventional carrier design. Later significant contributions were the steam catapult, the angled flight-deck, and the mirror landing-sight. The USS *Nimitz* (91487 tons displacement) has 260000 shaft horse-power, is 323 m/1092 ft long, has a crew of 5684, and carries over 90 aircraft. The first nuclear-powered carrier, the USS *Enterprise*, was completed in 1961.

air cushion vehicle (ACV) A revolutionary form of sea transport, in which the vehicle is supported on a cushion of air; also called a **ground effect machine**, or (following the principle proposed by Christopher Cockerell in 1950) a **hovercraft**. An ACV is propelled by an airscrew, and rides on a cushion of air trapped between the hull and the surface of the water by a flexible skirt, usually made of heavy-duty neoprene, which allows it to surmount obstacles. Because of delays in production, the first regular hovercraft service did not begin until 1962 (across the R Dee estuary in Britain). Hovercrafts are now in use worldwide in many varied forms.

Airedale terrier The largest breed of terrier; black and tan, thick wiry coat, stiff erect tail, small ears, short beard on chin; developed in Airedale valley (England) by crossing large hunting terriers (now extinct) and otterhounds.

air miles A consumer incentive scheme which offers the chance of free air travel in return for credits earned by frequent flyers who have joined the scheme. Credits may also be obtained through other means, such as authorized retail transactions, and flights of greater distance become possible as credits accumulate. An 'air mile' is a nautical mile as used by aircraft.

airplane *aeroplane*

airship A self-propelled steerable aircraft whose lift is generated by using lighter-than-air gases to provide buoyancy. The main body is cigar-shaped, with engines and gondolas (cabins) being suspended from it. The gas used to provide buoyancy was originally hydrogen, but its highly inflammable nature and poor safety record led to its replacement by helium.

Air Traffic Control (ATC) The guidance of an aircraft from one airport to another – a procedure which goes on day and night and in almost all weather conditions. From loading ramp to runway threshold, the pilot is directed by a ground controller. Take-off is directed by air traffic controllers in a control tower. They tell the pilot which runway to use and give them information on weather conditions. Each departing plane has a flight plan which has been agreed before the flight. This includes intended destination, expected flight time, and the altitude at which the plane will be flying. All this information is entered into the ATC computers. Each flight has a unique call sign which identifies it to the ATC officer. Once airborne and away from the airport, control of the aircraft is transferred to **Air Route Traffic Control (ARTC)**. Throughout the journey, the aircraft may be passed through several ARTCs. At all times it will be visible on radar, identified by its call sign, speed, and height. At the end of the journey, an aircraft may have to wait its turn to land. ATC at the destination airport directs the aircraft to circle a radio beacon about 50 km away from the air-

port. The aircraft forms part of a holding stack, keeping a vertical distance of 300 m/1000 ft between each plane. As an aircraft at the bottom of the stack is called to land, the others spiral down to the next level while they wait their turn. The ATC officer guides the aircraft on its approach to the runway, after which the pilot or the automatic control system locks on to a navigational beam called the **Instrument Landing System (ILS)**. The ILS beam guides the aircraft on to the correct glide slope and down the centre line of the runway.

Aïshah or **Ayeshah** [aeesha] (c.613–78) The favourite of the nine wives of Mohammed, but who bore him no children. On Mohammed's death, she resisted Ali, the Prophet's son-in-law, and secured the caliphate for her father, Abu-Bakr. Again opposing Ali, she was defeated in 656.

Aix-en-Provence [eks ã provãs] 43°31N 5°27E, pop (2000e) 130 000. Ancient city in Bouches-du-Rhône department, SE France; founded as Aquae Sextiae in 123 BC; important centre for Provençal literature since the 15th-c; airport; railway; university (1409); cathedral (11th–16th-c); archbishopric; home of Cézanne.

Ajaccio [azhakseeoh] 41°55N 8°40E, pop (2000e) 62700. Seaport and capital of the Island of Corsica, France; founded by the Genoese, 1492; made capital by Napoleon, 1811; Corsica's second largest port; airport; railway; car ferries to Marseille, Toulon, Nice; tourism; birthplace of Napoleon.

Ajanta Caves [ajanta] A group of 29 Buddhist cave-temples and monasteries cut into cliffs over R Wagurna (or Waghora), near Ajanta, Maharashtra, India; a world heritage site. The caves, built from the 2nd-c BC onwards, are particularly noted for their wall paintings.

Ajax [ayjaks] A legendary Greek hero during the Trojan War; the Latin form of Greek **Aias**; the son of Telamon, King of Salamis, therefore known as **Telamonian Ajax**. When the armour of the dead Achilles was not given to him, he went mad and killed himself.

Ajman [ajman] pop (2000e) 92 000; area c.250 km²/100 sq mi. Smallest of the seven member states of the United Arab Emirates; capital, Ajman; relatively undeveloped.

Akabusi, Kriss (Kezie Uche-Chukwu Duru) [akaboosee] (1958–) Athlete, born in London. One of the leading athletes of the 1990s, his achievements include gold medals in the 400 m hurdles at the 1990 European Championships (also breaking a 22-year world record) and the 4 x 400 m relay at the 1991 World Championships. His Olympic medals include silver in the 4 x 100 m relay (1984) and bronze for the same event in 1994. Since 1993 he has been a television presenter.

Akahito, Yamabe no [akaheetoh] (8th-c) Japanese poet, one of the 'twin stars' (with Hitomaro) of the great anthology of classical Japanese poetry known as the *Manyoshu* (Collection of a Myriad Leaves).

Akashi-Kaikyo Bridge [akashee kiykyoh] Suspension bridge across the Akashi Straits between Honshu and Shikoku, Japan, begun in 1988 and opened in 1998. With a main span of 1991 m/6532 ft (overall length 3911 m/12 831 ft) it is now the longest suspension bridge in the world.

Akbar the Great [akber], in full **Jalal ud-Din Muhammad Akbar** (1542–1605) Mughal Emperor of India, born in Umarkot, Sind, present day S Pakistan. He took over the administration from his regent in 1560. Within a few years, he had gained control of the whole of India N of the Vindhya Mts. A social and economic reformer, he pursued a policy of religious tolerance, and greatly encouraged the arts.

Akerlof, George A (1940–) Economist, born in New Haven, CT. A researcher at the University of California at Berkeley, he shared the Nobel Prize for Economics in 2001 for the analysis of markets with asymmetric information.

Akhenaton [akenaton], also **Akh(e)naten** or **Amenhotep (Ame-**

Albania

☐ International Airport   ∴ World heritage site

Albanian **Shqipni, Shqipri,** or **Shqipëri,** official name (1991) **Republic of Albania, Republica e Shqipërisë**

Local name Shqīpëri
Timezone GMT +1
Area 28 748 km²/11 097 sq mi
Population total (2002e) 3 108 000
Status Republic
Date of independence 1912
Capital Tiranë

Languages Albanian (official) (Gheg and Tosk, the main dialects), Greek

Ethnic groups Albanian (96%), Greek (2%), Macedonian, Vlach, Gypsy, Bulgarian

Religions Muslim (Sunni 70%), Roman Catholic (5%), Greek Orthodox (2%) (before April 1991, Albania was constitutionally atheist)

Physical features Mountainous country, relatively inaccessible and untravelled; geologically active – earthquakes severe and relatively frequent; N Albanian Alps rise to 2692 m/8832 ft; mountainous highlands (N, S, and E) account for c.70% of the land; coastal lowland in the W is agricultural; rivers include the Drin i zi, Shkumbin, Seman, Vijosë; 45% of land is forested; 25% is arable, mostly grain-producing; c.20% is permanent pasture land.

Climate Mediterranean climate, hot and dry on the plains in summer; average annual temperatures, 8–9°C (Jan), 24–5°C (Jul); thunderstorms frequent; mild, damp, cyclonic winters.

Currency 1 Lek (ALL) = 100 qintars

Economy Seventh fve-year plan (1981–5) focused on industrial expansion, especially in oil (new sources were located), mining, chemicals, natural gas; hydroelectric power plans for several rivers (eg the Koman hydroelectric complex on the Drin i zi R); agricultural product processing, textiles, oil products, cement; main crops are wheat, sugar-beet, maize, potatoes, fruit, grapes, oats; all industry is nationalized; progressive transformation of farm cooperatives into state farms; chromate, low-grade iron ore, and soft coal are exported; other natural resources: crude petroleum, asphalt, lignite (brown coal), phosphorus, bauxite, precious metals.

GDP (2002e) $15·69 bn, per capita $4400

Human Development Index (2002) 0·733

History Albanians descended from Illyrians, who occupied W Balkan peninsula c.1000 BC; King Argon and, after him, his wife Teuta conquered many territories, provoking the military might of Rome; despite Roman occupation and invasions by Visigoths, Slavs, and Huns, the Albanians were one of the few peoples to retain their Illyrian language and customs; Turkish invasions, 14th-c; independence after the end of Turkish rule, 1912; occupied by Italian forces, 1914-20; became a republic in 1925, and a monarchy in 1928, under King Zog I; occupied by Germany and Italy during World War 2; a new republic instigated in 1946, headed by Enver Hoxha (until 1985); dispute with the Soviet Union in 1961 led to withdrawal from Warsaw Pact in 1968, but close links with China maintained; People's Socialist Repub-

nophis) IV [amen**hoh**tep] (14th-c BC) Egyptian king of the 18th dynasty. He renounced the old gods and introduced a purified and universalized solar cult. One of his wives was Nefertiti.

Akhmatova, Anna [akh**mah**tofa], pseudonym of **Anna Andreeyevna Gorenko** (1889–1966) Poet, born near Odessa, Ukraine. Her works were condemned between 1922 and 1940, and again in 1946. Among her best-known works is *Requiem,* written in the late 1930s, an elegy for the prisoners of Stalin. She was 'rehabilitated' in the 1950s.

Akiba ben Joseph [a**kee**ba ben **johz**ef], also spelled **Akiva** (c.50–135) Rabbi and teacher in the formative period of rabbinic Judaism. He provided the basis for the Mishnah by his codification of the *halakhoth* (legal traditions). A supporter of bar Kokhba, he was put to death by the Romans.

Akihito [aki**hee**toh] (1933–) Emperor of Japan (1989–), the eldest son of Emperor Hirohito, born in Tokyo. Invested as Crown Prince in 1952, he became the first Crown Prince to marry a commoner, **Michiko Shoda** (1934–), in 1959. They have two

sons, **Crown Prince Naruhito** (1960–) and **Prince Akishino** (1963–). Their daughter, **Princess Sayako** (1969–), relinquished her royal status when she married a commoner in 2005. Prince Akishino and his wife, **Princess Kiko,** have three children: their son **Prince Hisahito** (b.2006), is third in line to the throne.

Akkadian [a**kay**dian] One of the oldest languages in the Semitic (Afro-Asiatic) family, with a substantial literature written in cuneiform script. It is now extinct.

Akmola *Astana*

Akrotiri [akro**teer**ee] 34°36N 32°57E. Bay on S coast of Cyprus; main port town, Limassol; British base on peninsula separating Akrotiri Bay (E) from Episkopi Bay (W).

Aksum 14°08N 38°43E. Ancient city in the highlands of N Ethiopia; a world heritage site. During the 1st–7th-c AD it was the capital of a powerful kingdom dominating trade between the Sudanese Nile Valley and the Roman Mediterranean.

Aktyubinsk [aktyoo**by**insk] 50°16N 57°13E, pop (2000e) 266 000.

lic instituted, 1976; renamed Republic of Albania, 1991; first free elections, 1991, giving a decisive majority to the communists; however general strike and demonstrations forced government to resign; Communist Party renamed itself the Socialist Party; Democratic Party elected in 1992 elections; collapse of fraudulent pyramid finance schemes, 1997, leading to rebellion in the S, arrival of UN protection force, and early elections, with unrest continuing in 1998; new constitution, 1998; People's Assembly (supreme legislative body) elects the President and Council of Ministers.

People's Socialist Republic of Albania
Head of State
1944–85 Enver Hoxha
1985–91 Ramiz Alia
1991–2 Fatos Nano *Provisional*
1992–7 Sali Berisha
1997–2002 Rexhep Mejdani
2002– Alfred Moisiu
Head of Government
1930–5 Pandeli Evangeli
1935–6 Mehdi Frashëri
1936–9 Koço Kota
1939–41 Shefqet Verlaci
1941–3 Mustafa Merlika-Kruja
1943 Eqrem Libohova
1943 Maliq Bushati
1943 Eqrem Libohova
1943 *Provisional Executive Committee* (Ibrahim Biçakçlu)
1943 *Council of Regents* (Mehdi Frashëri)
1943–4 Rexhep Mitrovica
1944 Fiori Dine
1944–54 Enver Hoxha
1954–81 Mehmed Shehu
1981–91 Adil Carcani
(Republic of Albania)
1991 Ylli Buf
1991–2 Vilson Ahmeti
1992–7 Alexander Meksi
1997 Baskim Fino
1997–8 Fatos Nano
1998–9 Pandeli Majko
1999–2002 Ilir Meta
2002 Pandeli Majko
2002–5 Fatos Nano
2005– Sali Berisha

Industrial city in NW Kazakhstan; established, 1869; airport; railway.

Alabama pop (2000e) 4 447 100; area 133 911 km²/51 705 sq mi. State in SE USA; the 'Heart of Dixie', the 'Camellia State', or 'Yellowhammer'; first permanent settlement by the French at Mobile, 1711; N Alabama became part of the USA in 1783, the remainder being acquired by the Louisiana Purchase in 1803; the 22nd state to be admitted to the Union, 1819; seceded, 1861; slavery abolished, 1865; re-admitted to the Union, 1868; highest point, Mt Cheaha (734 m/2 408 ft); mountainous NE, separated from the S coastal plain by the rolling plain of the Appalachian Piedmont; capital, Montgomery; diversified agriculture, after the boll weevil blight of 1915; iron and steel industry centred on Birmingham; many civil rights protests in the area in the 1950s and 1960s; areas devastated by Hurricane Katrina (notably Mobile) in 2005.

alabaster A fine-grained banded variety of the mineral gypsum;

pale and translucent. It is soft enough to be carved and polished by hand for ornamental use.

Alain-Fournier, Henri [alī foornyay], pseudonym of **Henri-Alban Fournier** (1886–1914) Writer, born in La Chapelle d'Angillon, Sologne, France. He was killed in the vicinity of Epargue, near Verdun, in World War 1, leaving a few short stories, and a novel, the nostalgic *Le Grand Meaulnes* (1913, trans The Lost Domain).

Alamo [alamoh] A battle fought during the 1836 Texan War of Independence against Mexico, when 180 Texans and US citizens held the old mission/fort of Alamo against a large number of Mexican troops. They held out for 13 days (23 Feb–6 Mar) until the last survivors were overwhelmed.

Alanbrooke (of Brookeborough), Alan Francis Brooke, 1st Viscount [alanbruk] (1883–1963) British field marshal, a leading strategist of World War 2, born in Bagnères-de-Bigorre, France. He commanded the 2nd corps of the British Expeditionary Force in France (1940), covering the evacuation from Dunkirk, and became Chief of the Imperial General Staff (1941–6). His war diaries presented a controversial view of Churchill and Eisenhower.

Alarcón (y Ariza), Pedro Antonio de [alah(r)hon] (1833–91) Writer, born in Guadix, Spain. He is best known for his *Sombrero de tres picos* (1874, The Three-Cornered Hat) on which Falla's ballet was based.

Alaric I [alarik] (c.370–410) King of the Visigoths from 395, and the first Germanic conqueror of Rome. The sack of Rome by his troops in 410 marks the beginning of the end of the Western Roman Empire.

Alaska pop (2000e) 626 900; area 1 518 748 km²/586 412 sq mi. US state in the extreme NW corner of the continent, 'The Last Frontier' or 'The Great Land', separated from the rest of the nation by Canada; first permanent settlement by Russians on Kodiak I, 1792; bought by the USA, 1867; gold discovered in 1889 and 1902; territorial status, 1912; Aleutian islands of Attu and Kiska occupied by the Japanese (Jun 1942–Aug 1943); granted statehood as the 49th state, 1959; large oil reserves discovered in 1968 (Alaska Pipeline from Prudhoe Bay to Valdez completed in 1977); the largest state, but the least populated; highest point Mt McKinley (6194 m/20 321 ft); capital, Juneau; major city, Anchorage; oil, natural gas, wide range of minerals; balance between industrial development and landscape preservation an ongoing controversy.

Alaska Highway An all-weather road which runs from Dawson Creek in British Columbia, Canada, to Fairbanks in Alaska. It was built in 1942 to supply military forces stationed in Alaska during World War 2.

Alaskan malamute [malamyoot] A breed of dog; a spitz bred by the Malamute Eskimos of Alaska as a sledge-dog (*husky*); largest sledge-dog breed; strong and active; thick grey and white coat.

Alawi (rulers) [alahwee] 1 Moroccan royal family, tracing their line to the grandson of the Prophet Mohammed, Hasan bin Ali, from which they derive their name. 2 Offshoot sect of Shiite Islam, found mainly in the NW mountains of Syria, as well as in Lebanon and Turkey. Persecuted over the centuries for their heterodox beliefs, the Alawis have observed the outward forms of Sunni Islam while observing their own rites in secret.

Alba, Duke of *Alva, duque de*

albacore [albakaw(r)] Large tuna fish (*Thunnus alalunga*) with long pectoral fins, widespread in open waters of tropical and warm temperate seas; length up to 1·3 m/4¼ ft, with an iridescent blue band on sides of body. (Family: Scombridae.)

Alba Iulia [alba yoolya], Ger **Karlsburg**, Lat **Apulum** 46°04N 23°33E, pop (2000e) 73 300. Capital of Alba county, WC Romania, on the R Mureş; founded by the Romans, 2nd-c AD; former seat of the princes of Transylvania; railway.

Alban, St [awlbn] (3rd-c) Roman soldier, who became the first British Christian martyr. Little is known about him, but he is said to have protected a Christian priest, and been converted by him. For this he was killed by the Romans in the 3rd-c or early 4th-c. Feast day 22 June.

Albania *pp.16–17*

Albany (Australia) 34°57S 117°54E, pop (2000e) 20 800. Resort and seaport in Western Australia; one of the oldest towns in Australia, founded in 1826; once used as a stopover point for vessels on their way to India; airfield; railway.

Albany (USA) 42°39N 73°45W, pop (2000e) 95 700. Capital of New York State USA; on the Hudson R; settled by the Dutch, 1614; state capital, 1797; railway; two universities (1844, 1848); State Capitol.

Albany Congress (1754) A US colonial gathering of delegates at which Benjamin Franklin proposed a 'plan of union' for the separate British colonies. Both the colonial governments and the British authorities rejected the idea.

albatross A large, slender-winged seabird, wingspan up to 3 m/ 10 ft; glides near water in air currents; lands only to breed. (Order: Procellariiformes (**tubenoses**). Family: Diomedeidae, 14 species.)

albedo [albeedoh] The ratio of the radiation reflected by a surface to the total incoming solar radiation, expressed as a decimal or percentage. The degree of reflectance varies according to the type of surface: snow-covered ice has an albedo of 0·8 (80%); a tropical rainforest 0·13 (13%).

Albee, Edward (Franklin) [awlbee, albee] (1928–) Playwright, born near Washington, DC. His major works are *The Zoo Story* (1958), *The American Dream* (1960), and *Who's Afraid of Virginia Woolf?* (1962, filmed 1966). *A Delicate Balance* (1966), *Seascape* (1975), and *Three Tall Women* (1991) won Pulitzer Prizes. Later plays include *Occupant* (2001) and *Peter & Jerry* (2004).

Albéniz, Isaac (Manuel Francisco) [albaynith] (1860–1909) Composer and pianist, born in Camprodón, Spain. He was especially known for his picturesque piano works based on Spanish folk music, notably *Iberia* (1906–9).

Albert, Lake, formerly also **Lake Mobuto Sésé Seko** area c.6400 km²/2500 sq mi. Lake in EC Africa; in the W Rift Valley on the frontier between the Democratic Republic of Congo and Uganda; length, c.160 km/100 mi; width, 40 km/25 mi; altitude, 619 m/2031 ft; receives the Victoria Nile (NE) and Semliki (SW) Rivers; Albert Nile flows N; European discovery by Samuel Baker, 1864; originally named after Queen Victoria's consort.

Albert II (1934–) King of Belgium (1993–), born in Brussels, the son of King Leopold III and the brother of King Baudouin. He was educated privately and in Geneva. Between 1962 and his succession to the throne, he held the post of honorary president of the administrative council of the Belgian Office of External Trade. In 1959 he married Donna Paola (1937–), daughter of Principe Don Fulco Ruffo di Calabria, Duca di Guardia Lombarda; they have three children. Since 1991 males and females have equal rights of succession. Prior to that date Belgium used Salic law.

Albert, Prince, in full **Francis Albert Augustus Charles Emmanuel, Prince of Saxe-Coburg-Gotha** (1819–61) Prince Consort of Queen Victoria of Great Britain, born at Schloss Rosenau, near Coburg, Germany. He married his cousin, an infatuated Queen Victoria, in 1840, and became her chief adviser, first as Consort (1842), then as Prince Consort (1857). He died of typhoid at Windsor Castle, Berkshire. The Albert Memorial in Kensington Gardens was erected to his memory in 1871.

Alberta pop (2000e) 2 851 000; area 661 190 km²/255 285 sq mi. Province in W Canada, bordered S by the USA; capital Edmonton; mainly a rolling plain, with edge of Rocky Mts in W; rivers, lakes, and forests in N, with much open prairie; treeless prairie in S; largest lakes, Athabasca, Claire, Lesser Slave; originally part of Rupert's Land, granted to Hudson's Bay Company, 1670; sovereignty acquired by the Dominion, 1870; status as province,

1905; governed by a lieutenant-governor and an elected Legislative Assembly; oil, natural gas, grain, cattle, timber products, coal, food processing, chemicals, fabricated metals, tourism.

Albert Hall *Royal Albert Hall*

Alberti, Leon Battista [albairtee] (1404–72) Architect, born in Genoa, Italy. One of the most brilliant figures of the Renaissance, his designs include the church of S Maria Novella in Florence.

Albertina An art gallery founded in 1768 by Duke Albert of Saxony-Tescha. Since 1795 it has been housed in the former Taroucca Palace in Vienna.

Albertus Magnus, St, Graf von (Count of) **Bollstädt,** known as **Doctor Universalis** ('Universal Doctor') (c.1200–80) Philosopher, bishop, and doctor of the church, born in Lauingen, Germany. He joined the Dominican order, becoming a teacher of theology, and did more than anyone to bring together theology and Aristotelianism. His most famous pupil was Thomas Aquinas. Feast day 15 November.

Albigenses [albijenseez] or **Albigensians** Followers of a form of Christianity which in the 11th-c and 12th-c especially had its main strength in the town of Albi, SW France; also known as **Cathari** or **Bogomils**. Condemned by the Roman Catholic Church, they were devastated in the early 13th-c crusade against them.

albinism A common inherited pigmentary disorder of vertebrates: affected individuals lack pigmentation of the skin, hair, eyes (iris), feathers, or scales. It is found in all human races: the absence of pigment (or *melanin*) results in white hair, pink skin, and pink irises.

Albinus *Alcuin*

Albright, Madeleine K(orbel) (1937–) US secretary of state (1997–2000), born in Prague. She studied at Columbia University, and took up a position on the National Security Council until appointed permanent US representative to the UN. In the second Clinton administration she became the first woman to head the State Department.

Albufeira [albufayra] 37°05N 8°15W, pop (2000e) 25 400. Fishing village and resort, S Portugal; Moorish-style architecture; Portugal's busiest seaside resort.

albumins [albyuminz] Part of a system of classification of simple proteins, usually referring to those proteins that are readily soluble in water and in dilute salt solutions. They are present in most animals and plants.

Albuquerque [albuhkerkee] 35°05N 106°39W, pop (2000e) 448 600. Largest city in C New Mexico, USA, on the Rio Grande; settled, 1706; city status, 1890; airport; railway; two universities (1889, 1940); base for many federal agencies; health resort; tourism.

Albuquerque, Affonso d' [albookerkay], known as **Affonso the Great** (1453–1515) Portuguese viceroy of the Indies, born near Lisbon. He landed on the Malabar coast of India in 1502, and conquered Goa, Ceylon, the Sundra Is, and Malacca.

Alcaeus [alseeus] (c.620–c.580 BC) Greek lyric poet, who was born and lived at Mytilene on the island of Lesbos. He was the inventor of Alcaic verse, which Horace transferred into Latin. Only fragments remain of his odes.

Alcestis [alsestis] In Greek mythology, the wife of Admetus; he was doomed to die, and she saved him by offering to die in his place. Heracles wrestled with the messenger of Death and brought her back to life. Her death and resurrection is the subject of Euripides' *Alcestis*.

alchemy The attempt from early times to find an elixir of immortal life. The first reference is by a Chinese Taoist in 140 BC, and the practice probably spread to Europe via Arab traders, where it was taken up by such scholars as Roger Bacon. Alchemists sought to convert base metals into gold – not to create wealth, but as a step towards discovering the recipe for eternity.

Because they needed accurate scales, clocks, and temperature control, their work facilitated important discoveries in chemistry, medicine, mineralogy, and pharmacology.

Alcibiades [alsibiyadeez] (c.450–404 BC) Athenian statesman and general from the aristocratic Alcmaeonid family. He was a leader against the Spartans in the Peloponnesian War, then sided with them against Athens. After further intrigues with the Athenians and Persians, he was assassinated.

Alcmaeonids [alkmiyonidz] An aristocratic Athenian family to which many prominent Athenian politicians belonged. It was particularly influential in the period 632–415 BC.

Alcock, Sir John William (1892–1919) Aviator, born in Manchester, Greater Manchester, who with Brown was the first to fly the Atlantic (14 Jun 1919). The trip, from Newfoundland to Ireland, was made in a Vickers-Vimy machine, and took 16 h 27 m.

Alcoholics Anonymous (AA) A self-help group for alcoholics trying to stop drinking. Founded in the USA in 1935, it consists of local groups where members (identified by first names only) meet to give each other support.

alcohols IUPAC **alkanols**. Generally organic compounds containing a hydroxyl (–OH) function bonded to a carbon atom which is not itself bonded to further atoms other than carbon or hydrogen. In everyday use, the word **alcohol** is often restricted to *ethanol* (**ethyl alcohol**), CH_3CH_2OH.

alcohol strength The measurement of the amount of ethanol (the active constituent) in alcoholic drinks, commonly expressed using either volumetric measures or proof strength. The volumetric measure declares the volume of ethanol present in a unit volume of the alcoholic beverage. *Proof spirit* is a mixture containing a standard amount of ethanol: in the UK it is 57·07% by volume, while in the USA it is 50%. Thus, a bottle of Scotch which claims to be 70° proof is in fact 70% of 57·07% (volume), or 40% ethanol by volume.

alcopops [alkohpops] Soft drinks with an alcoholic content, marketed in a wide range of brand names. Known since the 1970s, they became fashionable in the late 1990s, but raised considerable public concern about the wisdom of making alcohol more accessible to young people, and (through the use of terms such as 'alcoholic soft drink') reducing their awareness of its dangers.

Alcott, Louisa M(ay) (1832–88) Writer, born in Germantown, PA. Her *Little Women* (1868–9), *An Old-fashioned Girl* (1870), *Little Men* (1871), and *Jo's Boys* (1886), are firmly established among the classics.

Alcuin [alkwin], originally **Ealhwine**, Lat **Albinus** (c.737–804) Scholar, theologian, and adviser to the emperor Charlemagne, born in York, North Yorkshire. He was a major influence on the Carolingian revival of learning.

Alcyone *Halcyone*

Alda, Alan [awlda] (1936–) Actor, director, and writer, born in New York City. He is best known for the award-winning television series *M*À*S*H́ (1972–83). His acerbic sense of humour is evident in such films as *Canadian Bacon* (1995). Later films include *What Women Want* (2000) and *The Aviator* (2004), and in 2004 he joined the cast of the TV political drama series *The West Wing* (1999–2006), for which he won an Emmy for best supporting actor in 2006.

Aldabra Islands [aldabra] 9°25S 46°20E; area 154 km²/59 sq mi. Coral atoll nature reserve in SW Indian Ocean; outlying dependency of the Seychelles; habitat of the giant land tortoise; a world heritage site.

Aldebaran [aldebaran] *Taurus*

Aldeburgh [aldeberg] 52°09N 1°35E, pop (2000e) 2700. Coastal town in Suffolk, E England, UK; developed on the site of a mediaeval fishing centre; received royal charter, 1598; Moot Hall (16th-c), Martello Tower (19th-c); famous for its annual

music festival (Jun) founded in 1948; Maltings promenade concerts (Aug), poetry festival (Nov).

aldehydes [aldihiydz] IUPAC **alkanals**. Organic compounds containing a (–CHO) function. They are found in most sugars, notably glucose.

alder A small deciduous N temperate tree, often growing by water or in wet soils; leaves oval or rounded; male and female flowers on separate plants; male catkins long, pendulous; females short, erect, becoming woody and cone-like in fruit. (Genus: *Alnus*, 35 species. Family: Betulaceae.)

alderfly A slow, awkwardly flying insect with two pairs of large, translucent wings held over its body at rest; found around freshwater ponds and streams. (Order: Megaloptera. Family: Sialidae, c.50 species.)

Alderney [awldernee], Fr **Aurigny**, ancient **Riduna** pop (2000e) 2300; area 8 km²/3 sq mi. Third largest of the Channel Is, separated from France by the Race of Alderney; in the Bailiwick of Guernsey, with its own legislative assembly; chief town, Saint Anne; tourism, dairy farming.

Alderton, John (1940–) Actor, born in Gainsborough, Lincolnshire. A member of the York Repertory Company, he made his television debut (1961) in *Emergency Ward 10*, and became popularly known for series such as *Please Sir, My Wife Next Door*, and *Forever Green* (with actress wife Pauline Collins). His films include *It Shouldn't Happen to a Vet* (1976), *Clockwork Mice* (1995), and *Calendar Girls* (2003).

Aldington, Richard [awldingtn], originally **Edward Godfree** (1892–1962) Writer, editor, and biographer, born in Portsmouth, Hampshire. He edited *The Egoist*, the periodical of the Imagist school. His best-known novel is *Death of a Hero* (1929), and his biographies include *Wellington* (1946). He married Hilda Doolittle in 1913 (divorced, 1937).

Aldiss, Brian (Wilson) [awldis] (1925–) Writer and editor, best known for his science-fiction writing, born in East Dereham, Norfolk. His works include *Hothouse* (1962), *The Saliva Tree* (1966), histories of science fiction, and edited collections of short stories, and poetry. Later novels include *Dracula Unbound* (1991) and *Affairs at Hampden Ferrers* (2004). The short-story collection *Cultural Breaks* appeared in 2005.

aldosterone [aldosterohn] A type of hormone secreted from the adrenal cortex into the blood. Its primary role in humans is to stimulate sodium reabsorption and potassium excretion by the kidneys, in order to maintain electrolyte and water balance. Excessive secretion is known as **aldosteronism**.

Aldrin, Buzz [awldrin], popular name of **Edwin Eugene Aldrin** (1930–) Astronaut, born in Montclair, NJ. He was the second man to set foot on the Moon, after Neil Armstrong, in 1969.

Aldus Manutius [aldus manootius], Latin name of **Aldo Manucci** or **Manuzio** (c.1450–1515) Printer, born in Sermoneta, Latium, Italy. He was the first to print Greek books, and the first to use italics on a large scale.

ale An alcoholic beverage brewed from barley which has been malted (ie softened in water and allowed to germinate). It was a popular drink prior to the introduction of hops as a flavouring agent, thus creating beer. However, the term *ale* is still used to describe a hops-flavoured brew.

alecost *costmary*

Alentejo [alitezhu] Sparsely-populated agricultural area of SEC Portugal, SE of the R Tagus; low-lying plain with cork tree forests, heaths, maquis; prehistoric standing stones and chambered cairns; chief towns, Evora, Beja; noted for the Alter Real breed of horse.

Aleppo [alepoh], Arabic **Halab** 36°12N 37°10E, pop (2000e) 1 853 000. Chief commercial and industrial centre of N Syria; airport; road and rail junction; university (1960); old city, a world heritage site.

Aletsch [alech] area 117·6 km²/45·4 sq mi. Glacier in SC Switzerland, W and S of the Aletschhorn; length, 23·6 km/14·6 mi; the largest glacier in Europe.

Aleutian Islands [alooshn] or **Aleutians**, formerly **Catherine Archipelago** pop (2000e) 14500; area 18000 km²/7000 sq mi. Group of c.150 islands stretching c.1600 km/1000 mi from the Alaskan Peninsula, USA; many volcanic peaks over 1000 m/3000 ft; discovered by Russian explorers in 18th-c; purchased by USA, 1867; several military bases; wildlife refuge.

A level An abbreviation for **Advanced level**, the examination taken by British pupils, usually near the age of 18, which qualifies them for entrance to higher education and the professions. University matriculation requirements normally specify A levels in at least two subjects. One A level is deemed equivalent to two passes in the Advanced Supplementary (*A/S level*) examination.

alewife Deep-bodied herring-like fish (*Alosa pseudoharengus*), locally abundant along the American Atlantic seaboard; length up to 40 cm/16 in; migrates into rivers (Mar/Apr) to spawn in slow backwaters. (Family: Clupeidae.)

Alexander I (of Russia) (1777–1825) Tsar of Russia (1801–25), born in St Petersburg, the grandson of Catherine the Great. The early years of his reign were marked by the pursuit of a vigorous foreign policy. In 1805 Russia joined the coalition against Napoleon, but after a series of military defeats was forced to conclude the Treaty of Tilsit (1807) with France. When Napoleon broke the treaty by invading Russia in 1812, Alexander's armies forced the French army's retreat. His mysterious death at Taganrog caused a succession crisis.

Alexander VI, originally **Rodrigo Borgia** (1431–1503) Pope (1492–1503), born in Játiva, Spain. Father to Cesare, Lucretia, and two other illegitimate children, he endeavoured to break the power of the Italian princes, and to gain their possessions for his own family. Under his pontificate, he apportioned the New World between Spain and Portugal.

Alexander (Greek mythology) *Paris* (mythology)

Alexander of Hales, known as **Doctor Irrefragabilis** ('Irrefutable Doctor') (c.1170–1245) English theologian and philosopher, born in Hales, Gloucestershire. He became a professor of philosophy and theology in Paris, and later entered the Franciscan order.

Alexander (of Tunis), Sir Harold (Rupert Leofric George) Alexander, 1st Earl (1891–1969) British soldier, born in London. He served in Burma, and became commander-in-chief Middle East (1942–3), and supreme allied commander, Mediterranean theatre (1944). He later held posts as Governor-General of Canada (1946–52) and minister of defence (1952–4).

Alexander the Great (356–323 BC) King of Macedonia (336–323 BC), born at Pella, the son of Philip II and Olympias. He was tutored by Aristotle, and ascended the throne when less than 20 years old. After crushing all opposition at home, he set out to conquer Achaemenid Persia. By 330 BC, Darius III had fled, and the capitals of Babylon, Susa, Persepolis, and Ecbatana had been taken. In the next three years, the E half of the empire followed, and Alexander set out for India. He reached the Punjab, and had set his sights on the Ganges, when his troops mutinied and forced his return. He died shortly after at Babylon.

Alexander Nevski, St, also spelled **Nevsky** (c.1218–63) Russian hero and saint, born in Vladimir, Russia, who received his surname from his victory over the Swedes on the R Neva (1240). He was canonized by the Russian Orthodox Church in 1547. Feast day 30 August or 23 November.

Alexander technique A method of releasing unwanted physical and mental tension from the body by encouraging posture training and self-awareness, developed by the Australian actor **Frederick Matthias Alexander** (1869–1955). The technique is growing as a treatment for headache, backache, anx-

iety, and depression, and particularly benefits stage performers.

Alexandra, Queen (1844–1925) Eldest daughter of Christian IX of Denmark, who married the British Prince of Wales (later Edward VII) in 1863. In 1902 she founded Queen Alexandra's Imperial (now Royal) Army Nursing Corps.

Alexandra, Princess, the Hon Lady Ogilvy (1936–) Daughter of George, Duke of Kent, and Princess Marina of Greece. In 1963 she married Sir **Angus James Bruce Ogilvy** (1928–2004). They have a son, **James Robert Bruce** (1964–), and a daughter, **Marina Victoria Alexandra** (1966–). James married Julia Rawlinson and they have a daughter **Flora Alexandra** (1994–), and a son, **Alexander Charles** (1996–). Marina married Paul Mowatt (marriage dissolved) and they have a daughter, **Zenouska May Mowatt** (1990–), and a son, **Christian Alexander Mowatt** (1993–).

Alexandra Feodorovna [fyodorovna] (1872–1918) Empress of Russia upon her marriage with Nicholas II (1894), born in Darmstadt, Germany. She came under the influence of Rasputin, and meddled disastrously in politics. She was imprisoned and shot by Bolshevik revolutionaries, along with her husband and children, at Yekaterinburg.

Alexandria, Arabic **al-Iskandariya** 31°13N 29°55E, pop (2000e) 3958000. Second largest city of Egypt and the country's main port; founded in 332 BC by Alexander the Great; capital of the Ptolemies 304–30 BC; noted for its famous royal libraries; airport; railway; university (1942).

Alexandria, Library of A library founded by Ptolemy I and greatly extended by Ptolemy II. The greatest library in the Ancient World, it was destroyed in the civil wars of the 3rd-c AD. A new library, on the site of Cleopatra's former palace, opened in 2002.

Alexeyev, Vasiliy [aleksayef] (1942–) Weightlifter, born in Pokrovo-Shishkino, Russia. He set 80 world records (1970–7), more than any other athlete in any sport.

alexia **dyslexia**

Alexius I Comnenus [komneenus] (1048–1118) Byzantine Emperor (1081–1118), born in Constantinople, the founder of the Comnenian dynasty. His empire was invaded by the warriors of the First Crusade to Palestine (1096).

alfalfa **lucerne**

Al Fayed, Mohamed [al fayed] (1933–) Businessman, born in Egypt. Owner of the Ritz Hotel in Paris in 1979, and of Harrods in London in 1985, he is one of the world's wealthiest men. One of his children, **Dodi** (1955–97), received worldwide publicity in 1997 when the press discovered his relationship with Princess Diana. A graduate of Sandhurst Military Academy, Dodi briefly became a film producer, but was more renowned for his flamboyant lifestyle. He was killed along with Diana in a car accident in Paris while trying to escape the attentions of paparazzi. A British inquest into his death was opened in 2004 and was ongoing in 2007.

Alferov, Zhores Ivanovich [alferof] (1930–) Physicist, born in Vitebsk, NE Belarus. He joined the AF Ioffe Physico-Technical Institute in St Petersburg (1953) as an engineer and researcher, becoming director of the institute in 1987. He shared the 2000 Nobel Prize for Physics for his groundbreaking work in the development of semiconductor heterostructures.

Alföld [olfuld] Great Plain region of S Hungary, E of the R Danube, extending into adjoining countries. It is a flat area covering about half of Hungary, crossed by a system of canals which provide irrigation for grain and fruit.

Alfred, known as **Alfred the Great** (849–99) King of Wessex (from 871), born in Wantage, Oxfordshire, the fifth son of King Ethelwulf. He inflicted on the Danes their first major reverse at the Battle of Edington, Wiltshire (878), reorganized his forces into a standing army, built a navy, and established a network of *burhs* (fortified centres). These developments were complemented by his revival of religion and learning, and provided his successors with the means to reconquer the Danelaw and secure the unity of England. The famous story of his being scolded by a peasant woman for letting her cakes burn is first recorded in the 11th-c.

Alfvén, Hannes (Olof Gösta) [alfen] (1908–95) Theoretical physicist, born in Norrköping, Sweden. In 1942 he predicted the existence of waves in plasmas (*Alfvén waves*), which were later observed. He shared the Nobel Prize for Physics in 1970.

algae An informal grouping of primitive, mainly aquatic plants that have chlorophyll *a* as their primary photosynthetic pigment; body (*thallus*) not organized into root, stem, and leaf; range in form from simple unicellular plant plankton to massive seaweeds many metres in length.

Algarve [algah(r)v] area 5072 km²/1958 sq mi. Region and former province of S Portugal, bounded W and S by the Atlantic Ocean; Moorish kingdom, 1140; capital, Faro; the most popular tourist resort area in Portugal.

algebra A branch of mathematics in which unknown quantities are represented by letters or other symbols. It was developed and brought to Europe by the Moors, from whose word *al-jabr* the name of the subject is derived. In classical algebra (or **arithmetic algebra**), the operations in use are those of arithmetic; in **abstract algebra**, developed in the 19th–20th-c, different operations are defined.

Algeciras [aljeeseeras] 36°09N 5°28W, pop (2000e) 103 000. Seaport and resort in Cádiz province, Andalusia, SW Spain; founded by the Moors, 713; largely destroyed, 14th-c; rebuilt, 18th-c; railway; car ferries to Canary Is, Melilla, Tangier, Gibraltar.

Algeria *p.22*

Algiers [aljeerz], Fr **Alger** [alzhay] 36°50N 3°00E, pop (2000e) 3 545 000. Seaport capital of Algeria, N Africa; founded 10th-c by Berbers on the site of Roman Icosium; Turkish rule established by Barbarossa, 1518; taken by the French, 1830; Allied headquarters in World War 2; airport; railway; cathedral; University of Algeria (1879); university of sciences and technology (1974).

ALGOL [algol] An acronym of **ALGOrithmic Language**, a high-level programming computer language. It was developed in Europe in the late 1950s for mathematical and scientific use.

Algonkin [algongkin] or **Algonquin** Scattered small groups of American Indians speaking Algonkian languages, living in forest regions around the Ottawa R in Canada. Now only c.2000 survive.

Alhambra [alhambra] The palace-fortress of the Moorish kings built at Granada, Spain, in the 13th–14th-c; a world heritage site.

Alhazen [alhazen], Arabic **Abu al-Hassan ibn al Haytham** (c.965–1039) Mathematician and physicist, born in Basra (now in Iraq). The best known of his many books was the *Treasury of Optics* (first published in Latin in 1270).

Ali (?–661) The first convert to Islam and the fourth caliph (656–61), the cousin of Mohammed. He was the bravest follower of Mohammed, whose daughter Fatima he married. He encountered considerable opposition to his reign, and was assassinated in the mosque at Kufa. He is held by Shiah Muslims to be the only true successor to the prophet.

Ali, Muhammad, originally **Cassius (Marcellus) Clay, Jr** (1942–) Boxer, born in Louisville, KY. He won the world heavyweight title in 1964, defeating Sonny Liston in seven rounds. At that time he joined the Black Muslims and adopted the name Muhammad Ali. In 1971 he was beaten by Joe Frazier, but beat him in 1974, and went on to meet George Foreman later that year, knocking him out in eight rounds to regain his title. He was beaten by Leon Spinks (1953–) in a split decision (Feb 1978), but regained the title later that year – the first man to win

the world heavyweight title three times. His slogan 'I am the greatest' became a catch phrase. He retired in 1981. He was an almost universal choice as the 20th-century's most important sportsman.

Alicante [aleekantay], Lat **Lucentum** 38°23N 0°30W, pop (2000e) 264 000. Seaport in SE Spain; airport; railway; car ferries to Marseille, Oran, Ibiza, Palma de Mallorca; popular winter resort.

Alice Springs, formerly **Stuart** (to 1933) 23°42S 133°52E, pop (2000e) 22 600. Urban centre in Northern Territory, C Australia; administrative centre for the settlements of the Outback; established, 1890; airfield; railway terminus; Flying Doctor Service regional headquarters; tourist centre for the region.

Alien and Sedition Acts (1798–1800) US laws passed to crush political opposition, led by Thomas Jefferson, then vice-president. Two Alien Acts gave the president great power over foreigners. The Sedition Act authorized fining and imprisonment for public criticism of the government.

alienation Until the mid-20th-c, known mainly as a term referring either to the legal transfer of property or to progressive insanity. It then acquired currency as a key term in sociology, denoting the disorientation, depersonalization, and powerlessness of the individual in an increasingly bureaucratized industrial society.

alimentary canal A tube in which foodstuffs are ingested, digested, and absorbed, and waste products excreted; also known as the **gut**, or the **gastro-intestinal tract**. It may exist as a simple structure with only one opening to the exterior (as in coelenterates, platyhelminths), or as a more complex structure with two openings (as in vertebrates).

aliyah [ahleeah] (Heb 'ascend') The name given to the waves of Jewish migration to Palestine. The different waves were inspired by the push of persecution and the pull of Zionism, and drew Jews from Russia, C Europe, and the Middle East. The first two waves, spanning the years 1882–1914, brought an estimated 60–70 000 Jews to Palestine. The next three waves (1919–39) incurred opposition from Palestinian Arabs as 365 000 immigrants began to change the demographic balance. The sixth aliyah, coming mostly between 1945 and the establishment of the state of Israel, brought over 118 000 Jews, including many survivors of the Holocaust. Since statehood, numerous further waves of immigrants have reached Israel, such as emigrés from the former Soviet Union.

alkali [alkaliy] A strong base, especially sodium and potassium hydroxides. Solutions of alkalis have high values of pH, and are used as cleaning materials, as they dissolve fats. The **alkali metals** are Group I of the periodic table: lithium, sodium, potassium, rubidium, and caesium.

alkaline-earth Strictly, the elements calcium, strontium, barium, and radium, but often including beryllium and magnesium as well, hence Group II of the periodic table. These elements are largely responsible for the hardness of water.

alkaloids Organic, nitrogen-containing bases from plants which include complex ring structures. Many have been used as drugs, such as quinine, morphine, and cocaine. However, they may also be very toxic, as in the case of strychnine.

alkanamides *amides* 2

alkanes [alkaynz] Saturated hydrocarbons, having a general formula C_nH_{2n+2}, derived from methane by the addition of successive $-CH_2-$ groups. Also known as **paraffins**, they make up the major components of petroleum.

alkanet [alkanet] The name given to several plants of the borage family. True alkanet (*Alkanna tinctoria*) is a bristly perennial growing to 15 cm/6 in; leaves oblong; flowers with a red tube and blue lobes; native to S Europe. The roots yield a red dye of the same name. (Family: Boraginaceae.)

alkanoic acids *carboxylic acids*

alkanols *alcohols*

Algeria

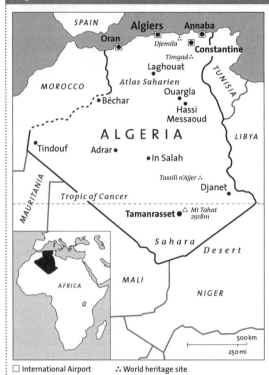

Fr **L'Algérie**, official name **The Democratic and Popular Republic of Algeria**, Arabic **al-Jumhuriya al-Jazairiya**
Local name(s) Al-Jazā'ir (Arabic), Algérie (French)
Timezone GMT +1
Area 2 460 500 km²/949 753 sq mi
Population total (2002e) 31 261 000
Status Democratic republic
Date of independence 1962
Capital Algiers (Alger)

Languages Arabic (official), Berber, French
Ethnic groups Arab (75%), Berber (25%)
Religions Muslim (Sunni 99%), Roman Catholic (0·5%)
Physical features Mountainous area in N Africa: mountains rise in a series of ridges and plateaux to the Atlas Saharien; Ahaggar Mts in the far S, rising to 2918 m/9573 ft at Mt Tahat; 85% of land is Saharan desert.
Climate Mediterranean in N, with cool, rainy winters and hot dry summers; average annual temperatures 12°C (Jan), 25°C (Jul); average annual rainfall 400–800 mm/15·8–31·5 in (mostly Nov–Mar); essentially rainless Saharan climate in S.
Currency 1 Algerian Dinar (DZD) = 100 centimes
Economy Petroleum products account for about 30% of national income; natural-gas liquification; jointly built with Italy first trans-Mediterranean gas pipeline; agriculture mainly on N coast: wheat, barley, oats, grapes, citrus fruits, vegetables; also food processing, textiles, clothing.
GDP (2002e) $173·8 bn, per capita $5400
Human Development Index (2002) 0·697
History Islamic Berber empires followed collapse of Numidian, Roman, Vandal, and Byzantine rule; Turkish invasion, 16th-c; French colonial campaign in 19th-c led to French control from 1902; guerrilla war (1954–62) with French forces by the National Liberation Front (FLN) led to independence, 1962; first President of the republic, Ahmed Ben Bella, replaced after coup, 1965; new constitution, 1976; military took control of government in 1992, and a state of emergency declared; continuing violence involving Islamic fundamentalists, including attacks on foreigners from 1993; legislative power shared by the President and National Assembly.

Head of State
1978–92 Chadli Benjedid
1992 Mohamed Boudiaf
1992–4 Ali Kaf
1994–9 Lamine Zeroual
1999– Abdelaziz Bouteflika
Head of Government
1994–5 Mokdad Sifi
1995–8 Ahmed Ouyahia
1998–9 Ismail Hamdani
1999–2000 Ahmed Benbitour
2000–3 Ali Benflis
2003–6 Ahmed Ouyahia
2006– Abdelaziz Belkhadem

---

alkanones *ketones*
alkenes [alkeenz] Hydrocarbons containing one or more double bonds; also called **olefins**. With one double bond, their general formula is C_nH_{2n}.
alkyl [alkiyl] A group $C_nH_{2n+1}–$, derived from an alkane, such as methyl ($CH_3–$), ethyl ($C_2H_5–$), and propyl ($C_3H_7–$).
alkynes [alkiynz] Hydrocarbons containing one or more triple bonds; also called **acetylenes**. With one triple bond, the general formula is C_nH_{2n-2}.
Allah [alah] The Islamic name for God. Prior to Mohammed, Allah was the supreme but not the sole deity in Arabia. It was Mohammed's mission to proclaim Allah as the sole God, the creator and sustainer of all things.
Allahabad [ahla-habahd] 25°25N 81°58E, pop (2000e) 947 000. City in Uttar Pradesh, NE India; founded, 1583; ceded to the British, 1801; airfield; railway; centre of Hindi literature.
All Blacks The New Zealand national rugby union football team. The term was first applied to the team that toured Britain in 1905.

Allcock, Tony, popular name of **Anthony Allcock** (1955–) British bowls player, born in Leicestershire. His achievements include world outdoor champion (1980, 1984, 1988), world outdoor singles champion (1992, 1996), world indoor singles champion (1986–7, 1998, 2002), and world indoor pairs champion with David Bryant (1986–7, 1989–92). The holder of a record 15 world bowls titles, he retired in 2003.
Allegheny Mountains [aluhgenee, aluhgaynee] Mountain range in E USA; W part of the Appalachian Mts; extends over 800 km/ 500 mi, highest point Spruce Knob, 1481 m/4859 ft; rich in timber, coal, iron, and limestone.
allegory A literary device by which another level of meaning is concealed within what is usually a story of some kind; also, the story itself. Myth and fable are both allegorical. Allegory has often been used for works with a religious or political bearing, such as Orwell's *Animal Farm* (1945). Two modern examples of allegorical drama have been Karel Čapek's *The Insect Play* (1921) and Edward Albee's *Tiny Alice* (1934).
allele [aleel, aleel] or **allelomorph** One of the alternative forms

of a gene which can occur at a given point on a chromosome. The term, introduced in 1902 to apply to Mendelian inheritance, is today increasingly applied to a short variant sequence of DNA, either within or adjacent to a functional gene.

allemande [alemahnd] A dance originating in the 16th-c, probably in Germany. It is in 4/4 time and moderate tempo, and usually begins with a short note before the first main beat.

Allen, Ethan (1738–89) American soldier, revolutionary leader, and writer, born in Litchfield, CT. He led the insurgent Green Mountain Boys (1770–5), and distinguished himself early in the revolutionary war by the capture of Fort Ticonderoga (1775). He later published the deist tract known as *Ethan Allen's Bible*.

Allen, Sir George Oswald Browning, known as **Gubby Allen** (1902–89) Cricketer, born in Sydney, New South Wales, Australia. He played for England in 25 Tests, and led the 1936–7 Ashes party to Australia.

Allen, Woody, originally **Allen Stewart Konigsberg** (1935–) Film actor, writer, and director, born in Brooklyn, NY. He is best known for a series of highly successful films which explore such themes as mortality, sexual inadequacy, show-business nostalgia, psychoanalysis, and urban living. They include *Annie Hall* (1977), *Hannah and Her Sisters* (1986, Oscar), *Bullets Over Broadway* (1994, Oscar), *Everyone Says I Love You* (1997), and *Match Point* (2005). *Husbands and Wives* (1992) coincided with the breakdown of his long-term relationship with actress **Mia Farrow**. In 1993 his private life received adverse publicity after losing a court battle for custody of three of their children, following the revelation of an affair with Farrow's adopted daughter, Soon-Yi (whom he married in 1997).

Allenby, Edmund Henry Hynman Allenby, 1st Viscount (1861–1936) British soldier, born in Brackenhurst, near Southwell, Nottinghamshire. He conducted a masterly campaign against the Turks in Palestine and Syria, capturing Jerusalem (1917), Damascus and Aleppo (1918), and securing an armistice.

Allende (Gossens), Salvador [ayenday] (1908–73) Chilean statesman and president (1970–3), born in Valparaíso. A medical doctor who helped found the Chilean Socialist Party (1933), he was elected in 1970 as leader of the left-wing Unidad Popular coalition. His government was overthrown by the armed forces in 1973, and he died in the presidential palace.

allergy An immune reaction to contact with certain foreign substances that are normally harmless and do not provoke a reponse in normal individuals. These substances are called **allergens**, and in sensitive individuals they react with antibodies produced within the body by cells of the immune system. Many substances found in nature (eg pollen) are actual or potential allergens, capable of inducing illnesses such as asthma and dermatitis.

All Fools' Day *April Fool*

Alliance *Liberal Party (UK); Social Democratic Party*

alligator A crocodile-like reptile of family Alligatoridae; short broad snout; fourth tooth from the front on each side of the lower jaw is hidden when the jaws are closed (unlike the crocodile); two species: **American alligator** (*Alligator mississippiensis*) from SE USA, and the rare **Chinese alligator** (*Alligator chinensis*).

allium A member of a large genus of perennials, all with a strong, distinctive onion smell, native to the N hemisphere; most form bulbs with a brown papery skin; leaves usually tubular; flowers have bell- or star-shaped segments in dense clusters. (Genus: *Allium*, 450 species. Family: Liliaceae.)

allophone *phoneme*

Allosaurus [alosawrus] A large flesh-eating dinosaur reaching 11 m/36 ft in length and two tonnes in weight; bipedal, powerful hindlimbs, and short forelimbs, both with three claws; muscular tail assisted in balancing; teeth with serrated edges; known

from the Upper Jurassic period of North America. (Order: Saurischia.)

alloy A blend of a metal with one or more other metals or with a non-metallic substance. Alloys known since ancient times include bronze (copper with tin), brass (copper with zinc), and pewter (lead with tin). Modern alloys include stainless steels (iron/chromium/nickel), and high temperature-resistant alloys for use in gas turbines (containing titanium).

All Saints' Day A Christian festival commemorating all the Church's saints collectively; held on 1 November in the Roman Catholic and Anglican Churches, and on the first Sunday after Pentecost in the Eastern Churches; formerly known as **All Hallows**.

All Souls' Day In the Roman Catholic Church, the day (2 Nov) set apart as a day of prayer for souls in purgatory; in the Eastern Orthodox Church celebrated about two months before Easter.

allspice An evergreen tree (*Pimenta dioica*) native to tropical America and the West Indies; leaves elliptical; flowers creamy; fruit small, round; also known as **pimento** or **Jamaican pepper**. Spice made from its dried, unripe fruits has a flavour like that of cinnamon, cloves, and nutmeg combined, hence the name. (Family: Myrtaceae.)

Allston, Washington [awlston] (1779–1843) Artist and writer, born at Allston plantation, Brook Green Domain on the Waccamaw R, SC. The earliest US Romantic painter, he graduated at Harvard, then studied at the Royal Academy in London before going on to Paris and Rome. He eventually settled at Cambridgeport, MA, in 1830. He painted large canvases, particularly of religious scenes, such as 'Belshazzar's Feast', 'The Flood', and 'Elijah in the Desert'.

Alma-Ata *Almaty*

Almagro, Diego de [almagroh] (c.1475–1538) Conquistador and collaborator with Pizarro, born in Spain. He briefly invaded Chile in 1536. Bitter rivalry then developed between Almagro and Pizarro, who defeated him in a desperate engagement near Cuzco. Soon after, Almagro was executed.

Almaty [almatee], formerly **Alma-Ata** (to 1995), **Vernyi** (to 1921) 43°15N 76°57E, pop (2000e) 1192000. Former capital city of Kazakhstan (to 1997, now Astana); established in 1854 as a military fortress and trading centre; destroyed by earthquake, 1887; airport; railway; university (1934); Academy of Sciences (1968); noted tourist and athletic centre.

Almohads [almuhhadz] *Berber*

almond A small deciduous, sometimes spiny tree (*Prunus dulcis*) growing to 8 m/26 ft, native to Asia; leaves narrowly oval, toothed; flowers pink fading to white; fruit greyish, velvety, 3.5–6 cm/1½–2½ in, oval; thin, leathery flesh surrounding pitted stone. The **sweet almond** (variety *dulcis*) is the source of edible almond nuts; **bitter almond** (variety *amara*) is inedible, but provides oil of bitter almonds used in industry. (Family: Rosaceae.)

Almoravids [almoravidz] *Berber*

aloe [aloh] A member of a large genus of shrub- or tree-like evergreens, native to Africa, especially S Africa, and Arabia; leaves sword-shaped, tough, fleshy, often waxy and toothed, in rosettes at tips of stems; flowers tubular, yellow to red; often planted for ornament. The drug **bitter aloes** is obtained from the sap. (Genus: *Aloe*, 275 species. Family: Liliaceae.)

Alonso, Fernando, in full **Fernando Alonso Díaz** (1981–) Motor racing driver, born in Oviedo, Asturias, Spain. He began karting as a child and won the world junior karting champion in 1996. He took up motor racing and joined Formula One in 2001, first driving for Minardi and then Renault. In the 2003 season he won the Hungarian Grand Prix and finished sixth in the world championship. He went on to take the title in 2005, repeating his success in 2006, making him the sport's youngest-ever double world champion. He left Renault to join McLaren for the 2007 season.

Alonso, Dámaso [alonsoh] (1898–1990) Poet and philologist, born in Madrid. *Hijos de la ira* (1944, Children of Wrath) is his best-known poetic work.

alopecia [alopeesha] Hair loss resulting from the failure of hair formation or the hair follicles. It may be inherited, or stem from an underlying general illness or toxin (eg a drug) which disturbs the follicular activity.

Aloysius, St *Gonzaga, Luigi*

alpaca [alpaka] A domesticated member of the camel family, from Peru and Bolivia (*Lama pacos*); resembles a long-haired llama, but with a shorter face, neck, and legs; kept mainly for wool.

Alpe Adria [alpay adria] A working association of 11 neighbouring regions in Austria, Germany, Italy, and Yugoslavia, linked by cultural and economic interests; established in 1978.

alphabet *see panel*

Alpha Centauri [alfa sentawree] *Centaurus*

alpha decay A naturally occurring radioactive decay process in which the atomic nucleus breaks up into a lighter nucleus and an alpha particle, which is ejected. It is governed by strong nuclear force.

alpha particle A particle emitted in alpha decay. It is composed of two neutrons plus two protons, the same as the helium nucleus, and was identified as such by British physicist Ernest Rutherford in 1906; charge +2.

Alpher, Ralph (Asher) (1921–) Physicist, born in Washington, DC. In 1948 with George Gamow he devised a theory of the processes emitting energy in the early life of the universe (the 'alpha, beta, gamma' theory – the name of physicist Hans Bethe being added in absentia to the authorship, to make the alphabetical joke work). This has become part of the 'big bang' model of the universe.

alphorn A musical instrument found in rural communities, particularly in the Swiss Alps. Most alphorns are about 1·8 m/6 ft long, made of wood, and can sound the first five or six harmonics; but examples up to twice that length are not uncommon.

Alps Principal mountain range of Europe, covering 259 000 km²/100 000 sq mi in Switzerland, France, Germany, Austria, Liechtenstein, Italy, and Montenegro; a series of parallel chains over 1000 km/600 mi SW–NE; originally formed by collision of African and European tectonic plates; source of many great European rivers, notably the Rhine, Po, and Rhône; Mont Blanc 4807 m/15 771 ft, highest peak in the range; notable passes include the St Bernard (Little and Greater), Simplon, St Gotthard, and Brenner; major tourist region for mountaineering and skiing.

al-Qaeda / al-Qa'ida (Arabic 'The Base') An Islamic network of fundamentalist organizations committed to the use of terrorism for the attainment of their goals. It was formed by Osama bin Laden (see separate entry) in the late 1980s to unite Sunni Arabs who had fought in Afghanistan against the USSR, and was based in Afghanistan until the removal of the Taliban regime in late 2001. Its political agenda is the replacement by Islamic governments based on the rule of Sharia (Islamic law)—a notion which includes several Arab regimes (especially Saudi Arabia) as well as the USA, whose influence throughout the Middle East it wishes to eliminate. Bin Laden has issued three fatwas (religious rulings) calling on Muslims to take up arms against the USA, and a 1998 statement asserted that it was the duty of all Muslims to kill US citizens and their allies.

The numbers of members in the organization is unknown, but probably totals several thousand. Since 1998 it has served as an umbrella organization called 'The Islamic World Front for the struggle against the Jews and the Crusaders' (Al-Jabhah al-

alphabet

The Development of the Early Alphabet

Old Phoenician	Hebrew	Early Greek	Classical Greek	Etruscan	Early Latin	Modern Roman
			A	A	ᐱ	Aa
		ᛒ	B		Ᏼ	Bb
		ᐱ	Γ	⟩	⟨	Cc
		ᐃ	Δ		D	Dd
		ᐃ	E	Ⴈ	ᐊ	Ee
			Φ		ᐅ	Ff
						Gg
		B	H	⊟	H	Hh
		I	I	I	I	Ii
						Jj
		ᛕ	K	ᛕ	K	Kk
		ᛐ	ᐱ	ᛃ	L	Ll
		ᛍ	M	ᛃ	M	Mm
		ᛃ	N	ᛃ	N	Nn
		ᐅ	O	ᐅ	O	Oo
		ᛐ	Π	ᛐ	Γ	Pp
		Φ	Q	ᛩ	Q	Qq
		ᐊ	P	ᛩ	ᐅ	Rr
		ᛋ	Σ	ᛋ	ᛋ	Ss
		T	T	T	T	Tt
		Y	Y	V	V	Uu
						Vv
						Ww
					X	Xx
						Yy
						Zz

The most economical and versatile form of writing system yet devised, because it breaks words down into their phonic components, assigning letters or combinations of letters to represent speech sounds. Thus, in English, the letter (or *grapheme*) *m* represents the sound (or *phoneme*) [m] in such words as *mat*; less obviously, the series *o...e* represents the long [ou] vowel sound in such words as *bone*. The symbols of an alphabetic writing system are not tied to the meanings of the words they represent, and the need for several thousand pictograms, for instance, is avoided. Most alphabets contain less than 30 symbols. However, they differ substantially in the regularity with which they correspond to the sound system: Spanish and Welsh, for instance, have a very regular system, whereas English and Irish Gaelic (particularly in its most traditional form) have many exceptional spelling patterns which can be learned only by special rules. Also, the alphabets of W European languages give vowels and consonants the same status, as full letters; but in the case of *consonantal* alphabets (eg the alphabets of India), the two types of sound are treated differently: the consonants are assigned the function of 'mapping out' the basic form of the word, and the vowels are added as diacritic marks. The Hebrew and Arabic alphabets take this system one step further, and allow the marking of the vowel diacritics to be optional. The model for all Western alphabets was the Etruscan (c.800 BC), itself based on the Greek alphabet, which had modified the Phoenician consonantal alphabet by adding vowel letters to it.

Islamiyyah al-'Alamiyyah li-Qital al-Yahud wal-Salibiyyin) which includes several Sunni Islamic extremist groups, such as the Egyptian al-Gama'a al-Islamiyya, the Islamic Movement of Uzbekistan, and the Harakat ul-Mujahidin.

Its most notorious terrorist act was the suicide attack by 19 of its members who hijacked and crashed four US commercial jets into US sites on 11 September 2001 – two into the World Trade Center in New York City, one into the Pentagon, Washington, and one into a field in Shanksville, Pennsylvania, killing nearly 3000. It was also responsible for the bombing of US embassies in Nairobi, Kenya and Dar es Salaam, Tanzania (1998), the attack on the USS *Cole* in the port of Aden (2000), other attacks on US military personnel in Kuwait and Yemen (2000–2), and the bombing of a hotel in Mombasa, Kenya (2002), and it may have been implicated in several other terrorist acts, such as the nightclub bombing in Bali, Indonesia (2002), the Madrid train bombings (2004), and the bombings in the London Underground (2005).

At the same time, the capture of al-Qaeda operatives has foiled several assassination and bombing plots, such as the arrest of Richard Colvin Reid, who attempted to ignite a shoe bomb on a transatlantic flight from Paris to Miami (2001) and the prevention of an attempt to shoot down an Israeli chartered plane with a surface-to-air missile at Mombasa airport (2002). However, the ongoing threat from the organization has led to unprecedented levels of security being put in place all over the world, especially at airports and public buildings in the USA and allied countries, and in areas where US influence is strong.

Alsace [alsas], Ger **Elsass**, Lat **Alsatia** pop (2000e) 1 699 000; area 8280 km²/3196 sq mi. Region of NE France; traditional scene of Franco-German conflict; formerly part of Lorraine before becoming part of German Empire; Treaty of Westphalia (1648) returned most of Alsace to France; ceded to Germany, 1871; returned to France, 1919; occupied by Germany in World War 2; chief towns, Strasbourg, Mulhouse, Colmar; fertile and industrially productive region.

alsatian *German shepherd*

Al Saud [sowd] Royal family and founders of the Kingdom of Saudi Arabia. **Abdul Aziz ibn Saud** (1880–1953), also known as **Ibn Saud**, came out of exile in Kuwait to consolidate his family's rule over a large part of the Arabian peninsula in the 1920s and, naming the country after his family, declared himself king of Saudi Arabia in 1932. **Faisal ibn Abd al-Aziz** (reigned 1964–75) led the kingdom to prominence by the strategic use of its oil power. The later rule of **Fahd ibn al-Aziz** (r.1982–2005), suffered from economic recession and regional insecurity, notably the two Gulf Wars. The current ruler is Fahd's half-brother, **Abdullah ibn Abd al-Aziz** (1924–).

alsike [alsiyk] A species of clover (*Trifolium hybridum*), probably native to Europe, grown as a fodder crop and now occurring in many temperate countries; a variable perennial growing to 60 cm/2 ft; leaves with three-toothed leaflets; pea-flowers white or pink. (Family: Leguminosae.)

Altaic [altayik] A hypothesized family of languages extending from the Balkan peninsula to the NE of Asia; not accepted as a genetic family by many linguists. About 40 languages fall into three groups: Turkic (of which Turkish is the main member), Mongolian, and Manchu-Tungus.

Altai Mountains [ahltiy], Chin **Altai Shan** Major mountain system of C Asia, extending from Russia SE along the border between NW China and Mongolia, into Mongolia itself; highest point, Mt Belukha (4506 m/14 783 ft); major mineral reserves.

Altair [altair] *Aquila*

Altamira [altameera] 43°18N 4°08E. A palaeolithic limestone cave of c.13 500 BC on the N Spanish coast near Santander, celebrated for its vivid ceiling paintings of game animals; a world heritage site.

altarpiece In a Christian church, a carved or painted screen placed above the altar facing the congregation; known as an *ancona* (Ital), *retable* (Fr), or *reredos* (Eng). The earliest examples appeared in the 10th–11th-c. An altarpiece consist-

ing of two panels is called a *diptych*; three panels make a *triptych*.

altazimuth [altazimuhht] A type of telescope mounting in which the telescope axis can be moved independently in altitude (swinging on a horizontal axis) and azimuth (swinging on a vertical axis).

Altdorfer, Albrecht [altdaw(r)fer] (c.1480–1538) Painter, engraver, and architect, born in Regensburg, Germany. A leading member of the Danube School of German painting, his major works are biblical and historical subjects set against atmospheric landscape backgrounds.

alternating current (AC) An electrical current whose direction of flow reverses periodically; the alternative is **direct current (DC)**, where the flow is in a single direction only. Household current is AC, with frequencies varying to some extent between countries, eg 50 Hz (UK), 60 Hz (USA).

alternative energy Sources of energy which do not rely on the burning of fossil fuels (eg coal, gas, oil) or nuclear power to provide energy. With the controversial nature of nuclear power, and the recognition that fossil fuels are a non-renewable resource and contribute significantly to pollution, there is considerable interest in alternative sources, such as solar, geothermal, hydroelectric, tidal, and wind power.

alternative fuel A fuel other than petrol for powering motor vehicles. These fuels include ethanol, methanol, and **biofuels** derived from organic material, such as biodiesel, obtained from various kinds of vegetable oil, and rape methyl esters (RME) from rape-oil. Such fuels are said to be environmentally friendly, but debate continues over whether they are as pollution-free as is claimed, and whether the land devoted to such crops might not be put to better use. The term often includes modifications which have been made to petrol to reduce harmful levels of lead emissions – the unleaded and superunleaded petrols (the latter giving better performance). Research continues into ways of modifying vehicle design to take advantage of such fuels (**alternative fuel vehicles**).

alternative medicine Approaches to the treatment of illness using procedures other than those recommended by orthodox medical science; also known as **complementary medicine**. There are many different approaches, and a recent publication on alternative medicine lists over 600 entries. Despite their current popularity, hardly any of the therapeutic methods used have been rigorously assessed, using the standard scientific techniques of critical assessment and refutation, or of comparison with the natural course of the ailment or with other remedies claimed to influence the ailment. At present, most of the claims for the success of alternative remedies remain anecdotal. However, there is a growing body of evidence to suggest that some alternative therapies may be effective.

Althusser, Louis [alt-hüser] (1918–90) Political philosopher, born in Algiers. He wrote influential works on the interpretation of Marxist theory, including *For Marx* (trans, 1965) and *Lenin and Philosophy* (trans, 1969).

Altichiero [altikyayroh] (c.1330–c.1395) Painter and possible founder of the Veronese School, born near Verona, Italy. He worked in Verona, then moved to Padua, where his frescoes are in the Basilica of San Antonio (painted 1372–9) and in the Oratory of San Giorgio (1377–84).

altimeter A device carried by an aircraft to measure its height above the ground. The usual type operates by sending out a radio signal, and measuring the time taken by the signal to return, since the speed at which the radio signal travels is known.

Altiplano [altiplahnoh] The arid plateau of W Bolivia and S Peru between the W and E cordilleras; elevation 3000–5000 m/9800–16 400 ft. The rivers and streams of the plateau drain into L Titicaca (Bolivia/Peru) and L Poopó (Bolivia).

altitude sickness Adverse effects experienced by individuals travelling to high altitudes, usually beginning at c.2500 m/ 8000 ft above sea level and getting worse with increasing elevation. The amount of oxygen in the air decreases with altitude, leading to shortness of breath and hyperventilation (rapid breathing). High altitudes also disturb the body's fluid balance and the blood is maintained at a more concentrated level, leading to the production of large amounts of urine and dehydration unless fluid input is maintained. The body is able to gradually adjust to high altitudes by producing more red blood cells to carry oxygen around the body. However, if ascent is too rapid there is insufficient time for the body to acclimatize, resulting in acute altitude sickness.

altocumulus clouds Middle-level clouds of the cumulus family at altitudes of c.2000–7000 m/6500–23 000 ft. They are white and/or grey in colour, and usually indicate fine weather. Cloud symbol: Ac.

altostratus clouds Middle-level clouds of the stratus family, similar to stratus clouds but less dense and occurring at higher elevations, typically c.2000–7000 m/6500–23 000 ft. They are greyish in colour with a sheet-like appearance, and give a warning of warm, rainy weather associated with the passage of a warm front. Cloud symbol: As.

alum Usually $KAl(SO_4)_2.12H_2O$. Hydrated potassium aluminium sulphate, **common alum**. Other alums have Al substituted by Fe (**iron alum**) or Cr (**chrome alum**).

alumina [aloomina] Al_2O_3. Aluminium (III) oxide, the principal ingredient of bauxite. It occurs in various forms, including emery or corundum (used as abrasives), and the coloured forms, rubies and sapphires.

aluminium [alyoominyuhm] or **aluminum** [aloominuhm] Al, element 13, melting point 660°C. A silvery metal, the third most abundant element in the Earth's crust, it forms a tough oxide coating and is then passive to further oxidation; with its relatively low density, 2·7 g/cm³, this makes it a valuable structural metal.

Alva or **Alba, Ferdinand Alvarez de Toledo, duque d'** (Duke of) (1507–82) Spanish general and statesman, born in Piedrahita, Spain. Sent to quell the Revolt of the Netherlands (1567), his Council of Blood promoted a ruthless campaign of repression. Later, Holland and Zeeland renewed their efforts against him, and his fleet was destroyed.

Alvarez Quintero [alvareth keentayroh] Playwrights and brothers: **Serafín Alvarez Quintero** (1871–1938) and **Joaquín Alvarez Quintero** (1873–1944), born in Utrera, Spain. They were the joint authors of well over 100 modern Spanish plays, all displaying a characteristic gaiety and sentiment.

alveoli *lungs*

alyssum [alisuhm] An annual to perennial, mat-forming or bushy but low-growing, native to Europe and Asia; leaves narrow; flowers cross-shaped, white, blue, or yellow. **Golden alyssum**, a grey-leaved, yellow-flowered perennial, is often grown in gardens. (Genus: *Alyssum*, 150 species. Family: Cruciferae.)

Alzheimer's disease [altshiymer] A common form of generalized cerebral atrophy which results in slowly progressive dementia affecting all aspects of brain function. The disease was first described in 1906 by a German neurologist, Alois Alzheimer (1864–1915).

Amado, Jorge [amahdoo] (1912–2001) Novelist, born in Ferradas, near Ilhéus, Brazil. Partly brought up on a cacao plantation in NE Brazil, his early writing focused on the poor social conditions of the plantation workers. Imprisoned for his political beliefs in 1935, he also spent several periods in exile. His novels include *Terras do sem-Fin* (1944, The Violent Land) and *Tenda dos milagres* (1969, Tent of Miracles).

Amal [amal] The first political organization of Lebanon's Shiite Muslims, the country's largest yet economically most disadvantaged community. Founded in the mid-1970s by the Imam Musa al-Sadr, the party has been led since al-Sadr's 1978 disappearance in Libya by the lawyer Nabih Berri (1938–).

amalgam An alloy of mercury with some other metal(s), known since classical times. Copper, zinc, and tin amalgams are used in dentistry.

Amalthea [amaltheea] The fifth natural satellite of Jupiter, discovered in 1892; distance from the planet 181 000 km/ 112 000 mi; diameter 270 km/168 mi.

Amanita *fly agaric*

amaranth [amaranth] An annual or perennial herb, native to tropical and temperate regions; flowers usually small and forming dense inflorescences; segments in whorls of three or five, often brightly coloured; also known as **pigweed**. Some Asian species yield a cereal substitute. (Genus: *Amaranthus*, 60 species. Family: Amaranthaceae.)

amaryllis [amarilis] A large bulb, native to tropical America (Genus: *Hippeastrum*, 75 species); flowers flaring, trumpet-shaped, up to 15 cm/6 in long, in a range of bright colours on a hollow stalk. (Family: Amaryllidaceae.)

Amaterasu [amaterasu] The principal deity in the Shinto religion of Japan. She is both the Sun-goddess who rules all the gods and the mother-goddess who ensures fertility.

Amazon, River *p.27*

Amazons [amaznz] In Greek mythology, a nation of women soldiers, located by Herodotos in Scythia (Russia). Strong and athletic, they were said to mutilate the right breast in order to use the bow.

ambassador An accredited diplomat sent by a state on a mission to a foreign country, or who is its highest-ranking permanent diplomat residing in a foreign country, officially representing his or her state in relations with foreign governments. Ambassadors are to be distinguished from **consuls**, whose chief functions are to protect citizens abroad, and to protect the commercial interests of these citizens.

Ambler, Eric (1909–98) Novelist, born in London. He specialized in the writing of spy thrillers, such as *Epitaph for a Spy* (1938), *The Mask of Dimitrios* (1939), and *The Intercom Conspiracy* (1970). Later books include *Here Lies: An Autobiography* (1985) and *The Story So Far* (1993).

Ambrose, St (c.339–97) Roman clergyman and doctor of the Church, born in Trier, Germany. He is especially remembered for his preaching, his literary works and hymns, and the Ambrosian ritual and chant. Feast day 7 December.

ameba *amoeba*

Amenhotep IV *Akhenaton*

amenorrhoea / amenorrhea [amenoreea] The absence of menstruation. It may be due to pre- or post-menopausal physiological reasons (eg pregnancy), or in the event of substantial weight loss, or to a variety of disorders including physical obstruction to the flow of menstrual blood and disturbances of the hormonal control of the uterus, ovaries, and pituitary gland.

American Ballet Theatre Renowned ballet company based at the Metropolitan Opera House in the Lincoln Center for the Performing Arts, New York. Originally named **Ballet Theatre**, it was launched in 1939 by Richard Pleasant under the direction (1945–80) of Lucia Chase and Oliver Smith. In 1992 the company's former principal dancer, Kevin McKenzie, was appointed artistic director.

American Civil Liberties Union A US pressure group concerned to promote civil rights. It is particularly concerned with freedom of speech and maintaining an open society.

American Civil War (1861–5) A conflict in the USA which resolved two great issues: the future of the Federal Union and the relative power of the states and the central government; and the existence of black slavery. The war began in the early months of

Amazon, River

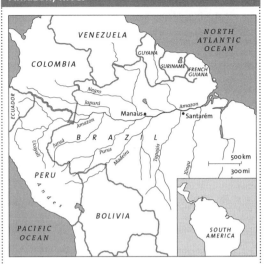

Port **Rio Amazonas** River in N South America, the largest in the world by volume, and the second longest; two major headstreams, the Marañón and the Ucayali, rising in the Andes of Peru (c.150 km/83 mi from the Pacific) and joining S of Iquitos; flows generally W–E across Brazil, entering the Atlantic in a wide delta; drains a basin c.7 000 000 km²/2 700 000 sq mi; more than 1100 tributaries; ocean steamers as far as Iquitos, 3680 km/2287 mi from the Atlantic; deepest point (37 m/121 ft) at the influx of the Trombetas R; large island, Ilha de Marajó, at the delta; length from L Lauricocha (at the headwaters of the Marañón) 6280 km/3902 mi; from L Vilafro following the Ucayali and Apurímac headwaters to the mouth of the Amazon via the Canal do Norte, 6449 km/4007 mi; river levels at Manaus fluctuate by over 15 m/50 ft; N channels of the delta made dangerous by a frequent tidal bore (*Pororoca*) moving up river at up to 65 kph/40 mph, with waves sometimes 5 m/16 ft high; cargo launches reach the interior, carrying fish, cedarwood, flour, rubber, and jute; discovered by Europeans, 1500; first descended 1541, ascended 1637; opened to world shipping, 1866; free navigation guaranteed by Colombia–Brazil treaty, 1929.

Lincoln's presidency. Although Lincoln was hostile to slavery, he did not believe that he could interfere where it existed. But to Southerners, he and the Republican Party were intolerable, and 11 Southern states withdrew from the Union, establishing the Confederate States of America. War broke out (12 Apr 1861) when Southern batteries opened fire on a Union emplacement in the harbour of Charleston, SC. At first Lincoln defined the issue as the preservation of the Union, without any reference to slavery. But he broadened the war aims (1 Jan 1863), proclaiming the emancipation without compensation of all slaves in areas then under arms against the government.

The winning strategy began in 1863, when Ulysses S Grant won control of the whole Mississippi Valley, isolating the W Confederate States from the rest. Meanwhile Robert E Lee was advancing into Pennsylvania, largely in the hope of winning foreign recognition for the Confederacy. His defeat at Gettysburg ended that possibility. By the autumn, the Chattanooga campaign put Northern troops in a position to bisect the Confederacy E to W, an act accomplished in late 1864 by General

Sherman's march through Georgia to the sea. Grant, now the overall Northern commander, adopted a strategy of relentless pressure on Lee's forces, regardless of his own losses. The end came in the spring of 1865, as Sherman marched N through the Carolinas while Grant continued his costly siege of Richmond. Lee finally abandoned the Confederate capital (2 Apr). His capitulation at Appomattox Court House left only scattered Southern forces in the field, and the last surrender took place on 26 May.

American eagle *bald eagle*

American Federation of Labor – Congress of Industrial Organizations (AFL/CIO) A US federation of trade unions, formed in 1955 from the merger of the AFL (mainly craft unions, founded in 1886) with the CIO (mainly industrial workers' unions, founded in 1935). It has c.13 million members.

American football *football, American*

American Indians The original inhabitants of the American continent, who arrived during the last glacial period (14–40 000 years ago) from Asia, crossing from Siberia over the Bering Strait, perhaps in three waves. They settled in North America, extending into Middle America (Mesoamerica) more than 10 000 years ago, and sometime after this into South America. From the 16th-c, with the coming of European settlers, the lives of most Indians were severely disrupted. Conflict over land resulted in numerous bloody clashes, and many died from diseases introduced by Europeans. In North America, the population was very much reduced, from an estimated 1·5 million at its height, and by the 1880s most Indians had been confined to reservations. In the past generation there has been increasing political activity on the part of Indians to reclaim land rights. In Middle America, the Indian population at its height was much larger than in North America – some suggest as many as 20 million. Today most Middle Americans live in small farming and trading village communities, are Roman Catholic and Spanish-speaking, and show a high rate of admixture with the descendants of the Spanish settlers. In South America, in the century before the Spanish invasion of the region, the Inca state brought together much of the Andean area in the New World's largest empire. Following the European conquest in the 16th-c, many groups became extinct, while others were absorbed into colonial society; but in a few remote parts, there are groups which have preserved their culture virtually intact.

American Legion In the USA, an association for former members of the armed forces (veterans), the largest in the world. Incorporated in 1919, its aims are to rehabilitate veterans, promote child welfare, ensure a strong national defence, and encourage patriotism.

American Muslim Mission *Black Muslims*

American ostrich *rhea* (ornithology)

American Revolution (1765–88) The movement that destroyed the first British Empire, establishing the United States and, indirectly, Canada; a much larger event than the War of Independence (1775–83). It can be divided into three main phases. In the first (1764–5), relations worsened between the colonies and Britain, primarily over the issue of Parliament's right to tax the colonies without reference to the colonial assemblies. Major events included the Stamp Act crisis (1765–6), resistance to the Townshend Acts (1767–70), the Boston Massacre (1770), the burning of the customs cruiser *Gaspée* (1772), and the Boston Tea Party (1773). This phase culminated in Parliament's passage of the Intolerable Acts (1774) to punish Massachusetts for the Tea Party, and the calling of the First Continental Congress (1774).

The second phase brought war and independence. Fighting began at Lexington and Concord, MA (Apr 1775), and lasted until the surrender of Lord Cornwallis to Washington at Yorktown,

VA, in 1781. Military conflict centred on Boston until the British withdrew (Mar 1776). From August 1776 until the beginning of 1780, the main theatre was the states of New York, New Jersey, and Pennsylvania. The American victory at Saratoga convinced the French to enter the war officially, bringing badly-needed material support, troops, monetary credit, and a fleet. After 1780, fighting shifted southward, when Sir Henry Clinton led an invasion of S Carolina. Cornwallis, his successor, led his army gradually N until Washington and the French Admiral de Grasse trapped him on the Yorktown peninsula. The defeat resulted in the fall of Lord North, the British prime minister who had prosecuted the war. Peace was signed at Paris two years later.

The third phase led to the creation of the modern United States. This process began with the writing of the first state constitutions, immediately after the Declaration of Independence (Jul 1776). At the same time, the Articles of Confederation were prepared by the Continental Congress as a basis for inter-state relations, but the document was not adopted until 1781. Its weaknesses, such as an inability to enforce Congressional decisions, soon became apparent. These, together with dissatisfaction about developments in the states, led to the Federalist movement. Initially, this sought merely to reform the Articles, but its great achievement, in 1787 and 1788, was to abolish that document completely, and establish the present US Constitution. At that point, the Revolution was effectively over.

American Samoa *see panel*

American Sign Language (ASL) A sign language widely used by the deaf in the USA; also known as **Ameslan**. The system contains over 4000 signs, and is used by over half a million deaf people.

American Society for the Prevention of Cruelty to Animals *RSPCA*

American whitewood *tulip tree*

America's Cup Yachting's most famous race, held approximately every four years. The trophy was originally called the One Hundred Guinea Cup, and was donated by the Royal Yacht Squadron for a race around the Isle of Wight in 1851. It was renamed when the US schooner *America* won the race six years later. Between 1870 and 1983 it remained in US ownership until the successful challenge of *Australia II*. The USA won it back in 1987, but lost it to New Zealand in 1995 and defeated an Italian challenge in 2000. Switzerland won in 2003.

Ameslan *American Sign Language*

amethyst A violet-to-purple form of quartz. It is prized as a precious stone.

Amhara A Semitic-speaking people of the Ethiopian C highlands who, with the Tigray, dominate the country. *Amharic* is the official language of Ethiopia. Population c.9 million.

amicable numbers Two numbers such that each is the sum of all the divisors of the other. Thus 284 and 220 are amicable, for the divisors of 284 are 1, 2, 4, 71, 142, whose sum is 220, and the divisors of 220 are 1, 2, 4, 5, 10, 11, 20, 22, 44, 55, 110, whose sum is 284. Note that 1 is counted as a divisor. Pythagoras is credited with the discovery of these numbers.

Amidah [ameeda] (Heb 'standing') The principal component of the daily prayers of Talmudic Judaism, recited while standing, and said silently except when in a congregational service. It consists of 19 benedictions.

amides [aymiydz, amidz] **1** Inorganic salts of ammonia, eg sodium amide ($NaNH_2$), strongly basic and hydrolysed by water to NH_3 and OH^-.

2 Organic compounds containing the function $-CO.NR_2$, also called **alkanamides**, derived from carboxylic acids. **Polyamides** include proteins and some artificial polymers, such as nylon.

Amiens [amyĩ], ancient **Samarobriva** 49°54N 2°16E, pop (2000e) 138 000. Agricultural market town in N France, on left bank of R

American Samoa

[samoha], formerly also **Loanda**, Portuguese **São Paulo de Loanda**

Local name Sao Paulo de Loanda (Portuguese)

Timezone GMT -11

Area 197 km²/76 sq mi

Population total (2002e) 62 000

Capital Fagatogo

Languages English (official), Samoan

Physical features Located in the CS Pacific Ocean, some 3500 km/2175 mi N of New Zealand; five principal volcanic islands (including Tutuila, Aunu'u, Ofu, Olosega, Ta'u, Rose, Swains I) and two coral atolls; main island, Tutuila, 109 km²/42 sq mi, rises to 653 m/2142 ft; islands mostly hilly, with large areas covered by thick bush and forest.

Climate Tropical maritime climate; average annual temperatures 28°C (Jan), 27°C (Jul) in Fagatogo; plentiful rainfall; rainy season (Nov–Apr); dry season (May–Oct); average annual rainfall 5000 mm/200 in; state of emergency declared after heavy rains caused severe flooding over much of the island, May 2003.

Currency 1 US Dollar (USD) = 100 cents

Economy Principal crops, taro, breadfruit, yams, bananas, coconuts; tuna fishing; local inshore fishing, handicrafts.

GDP (2000e) $500 mn, per capita $8000

History US acquired rights to American Samoa in 1899 and the islands were ceded by their chiefs, 1900–25; now an unincorporated territory of the USA, administered by the Department of the Interior; bicameral legislature established, 1948, comprising Senate and House of Representatives.

Somme; railway; university (1964); bishopric; war-time cemeteries at Arras to the E; Gothic cathedral (13th-c), a world heritage site.

Amies, Sir (Edwin) Hardy [aymeez] (1909–2003) Couturier, and dressmaker by appointment to Queen Elizabeth II, born in London. He became a managing designer in London in 1934, where he made his name especially with his tailored suits for women. He founded his own fashion house in 1946, and started designing for men in 1959.

Amin (Dada), Idi [ameen] (c.1925–2003) President of Uganda (1971–9), born in Koboko of a peasant family. He staged a coup deposing Obote in 1971, dissolved parliament, and was proclaimed president by the army. Throughout his presidency there were continual reports of widespread atrocities. Deposed by exiled Ugandans with the help of the Tanzanian army in 1979, he fled to Libya, eventually settling in Saudi Arabia.

amines [aymeenz, ameenz] Organic compounds derived from ammonia by the substitution of the hydrogen atoms by one, two, or three alkyl groups. Their solutions, when partially neutralized by strong acids, have pH values of about 9.

amino acids [ameenoh, amiynoh] Aminoalkanoic acids with the general formula $R–CH(NH_2)COOH$. About 24 are involved in protein synthesis; 10 of these cannot be made by the human body, and thus form an essential component of the diet (**essential amino acids**).

aminobenzene *aniline*

aminoethanoic acid *glycine*

Amis, Sir Kingsley (William) [aymis] (1922–95) Novelist and poet, born in London. He achieved a reputation by his first novel, *Lucky Jim* (1954), which added a new comic hero to English fiction. Later works on wider themes include *Jake's Thing* (1978), *The Old Devils* (1986, Booker), and *The Russian Girl* (1992). *The Letters of Kingsley Amis* (ed. Zachary Leader) were published in 2000. He was married (1965–83) to the novelist **Elizabeth Jane Howard** (1923–).

Amis, Martin (Louis) [aymis] (1949–) Novelist and journalist, born in Oxford, the son of Kingsley Amis. His works include the novels *The Rachel Papers* (1973), *Other People* (1981), *The Night Train* (1997), and *The Pregnant Widow* (2007), and the collection of short stories *'Heavy Water' and Other Stories* (1999). His memoirs, *Experience*, appeared in 2000, and he became a professor of creative writing at Manchester University in 2007.

Amman [aman] 31°57N 35°52E, pop (2000e) 1 996 000. Industrial and commercial capital city of Jordan; capital of the Ammonite kingdom in Biblical times; capital of Transjordan, 1923; many refugees after the Arab–Israeli Wars; airport; railway; university (1962); noted for its locally-quarried coloured marble.

ammonia NH_3, boiling point $-33°C$. A colourless gas with a pungent odour. It is a weak base; aqueous solutions partially neutralized with strong acid have a pH c.9·5. An important industrial chemical, it is mainly prepared by the Haber process.

ammonia–soda process *Solvay process*

ammonite An extinct, nautilus-like mollusc; found extensively as fossil shells from the Devonian to the Upper Cretaceous periods. (Class: Cephalopoda. Subclass: Ammonoidea.)

ammonium NH_4^+. A cation formed by the reaction of ammonia with acid. It is found in many salts, particularly the chloride (*sal ammoniac*) and the carbonate (*sal volatile*).

amnesia Memory disability, often associated with brain damage or a traumatic event. **Retrograde amnesia** is the inability to remember material learned before the precipitating events. **Anterograde amnesia** is difficulty in learning new material.

Amnesty International A human rights organization founded in London in 1961 largely by the efforts of Peter Benenson (1921–2005), a Catholic lawyer. Its fundamental concern is to seek the immediate and unconditional release of prisoners of conscience, as long as they have not advocated violence. It also campaigns against torture and the death penalty, and produces independent reports on abuses of human rights.

amniocentesis [amniohsenteesis] A diagnostic procedure performed at 14–18 weeks gestation which involves withdrawal of a small sample of amniotic fluid from within the uterus using a needle inserted through the abdominal wall under ultrasound guidance. Amniotic fluid is in close contact with the fetus, and contains cells that can be analysed to reveal many congenital fetal abnormalities. The procedure can also reveal the sex of the fetus.

amoeba / ameba [ameeba] A naked, single-celled protozoan which moves by protoplasmic flow, changing its shape by the formation of irregular lobes (*pseudopodia*); c.0·6 mm/ 0·025 in across; reproduces mainly by splitting in two (*binary fission*). (Phylum: Sarcomastigophora. Class: Rhizopoda.)

amoebiasis [ameebiyasis] A disease caused by infection with the protozoan parasite *entamoeba histolytica*, acquired by ingestion of food or water contaminated with faeces containing infected cysts. Inside the gut the cysts hatch to release the adult organisms, which irritate the gut lining resulting in severe bloody diarrhoea.

Amos (of Brondesbury), Valerie Ann Amos, Baroness [aymos] (1954–) British stateswoman, born in Guyana. After a career in local government (1981–9), in 2001 she became parliamentary under-secretary of state in the Foreign and Commonwealth Office, and took over as International Development Secretary after the resignation of Clare Short in mid-2003, becoming the first black woman to sit in the cabinet. Later that year she was appointed leader of the House of Lords. She was made a life peer in 1997.

Amos, Book of One of the twelve so-called 'minor' prophetic writings in the Hebrew Bible/Old Testament; attributed to

the prophet Amos, who was active in the N kingdom of Israel in the mid-8th-c BC.

Amoy (China) *Xiamen*

amp *ampere*

Ampère, André Marie [āpair] (1775–1836) Mathematician and physicist, born in Lyon, France. The first to devise techniques for measuring electricity, his name was given to the unit of electrical current.

ampere [ampair] The base SI unit of current; symbol A, often called **amp**. It is defined as the constant current which, if maintained in two straight parallel conductors of infinite length, of negligible cross-section, and placed 1 metre apart in vacuum, would produce a force equal to $2 \times 10^{-7} N/m$.

amphetamine A powerful stimulant of the central nervous system which causes wakefulness and alertness, elevates mood, increases self-confidence, loquaciousness, and the performance of simple mental tasks, and improves physical performance. Its effects are followed by mental depression and fatigue. Prolonged use may result in paranoia or clinical psychosis. As a drug of abuse it is called **speed**; it is illegally manufactured as a powder which can be sniffed ('snorted') or injected. Amphetamine sulphate was formerly available medically under the trade name **Benzedrine**. It is now available only as dexamphetamine sulphate, an isomer, under the proprietary name **Dexedrine**.

amphibian A vertebrate animal of class Amphibia (c.4000 species), exhibiting a wide range of characters and lifestyles; usually four legs and glandular skin, lacking scales or other outgrowths; adults breathe using lungs (and partly through the skin). There are three major groups: salamanders and newts (order: Urodela or Caudata), frogs and toads (order: Anura or Salientia), and the legless caecilians (order: Gymnophiona or Apoda).

amphiboles [amfibohlz] A group of hydrous silicate minerals of considerable chemical complexity, widely distributed in igneous and metamorphic rocks. Common varieties include hornblende, actinolite, and tremolite. Fibrous forms belong to the asbestos group of minerals.

amphioxus [amfioksuhs] A primitive chordate; body slender, length up to 70 mm/$2\frac{3}{4}$ in, tapered at both ends; notochord present, extending into head; possesses gill slits and segmented muscle blocks; 23 species found in shallow marine sediments; also known as **lancelet**. (Subphylum: Cephalochordata.)

amphisbaena [amfisbeena] A reptile native to South and Central America, Africa, SW Asia, and SW Europe; body worm-like with encircling rings; no legs or only front legs present; small eyes covered by skin; the only truly burrowing reptile; also known as **worm lizard** or **ringed lizard**. (Order: Squamata. Suborder: Amphisbaenia, 140 species.)

amphitheatre / amphitheater An open-air theatre where tiers of seats are situated round a central circular or oval performance space. The Romans developed this form of building for gladiatorial combats, naval exhibitions, and other events. The most famous example is the Colosseum in Rome (AD 72–80).

Amphitrite [amfitriytee] In Greek mythology, a goddess of the sea, married to Poseidon. She is the mother of Triton and other minor deities.

amphoteric [amfoterik] In chemistry, having two different properties, usually that of being an acid and a base. An example is aluminium hydroxide $(Al(OH)_3)$.

amplitude In a wave or oscillation, the maximum displacement from equilibrium or rest position; symbol A. It is always a positive number.

amplitude modulation (AM) In wave motion, the altering of wave amplitude in a systematic way, leaving frequency unchanged.

In AM radio, an electrical signal is used to modulate the amplitude of the broadcast carrier radio wave.

amputation The surgical removal of a part of the body because of disease or injury. The operation is carried out when the affected part has been irreparably damaged and is no longer functional, or when there is a risk of the disease (particularly infection) spreading to the rest of the body. It is sometimes possible to replace the removed part with a prosthesis, such as an artificial leg.

Amr ibn al-As [amribnalas] (?–664) Arab soldier, who joined the prophet Mohammed c.629 and took part in the conquest of Palestine. In 641 he took Alexandria after a 14 months' siege, and died governor of Egypt.

Amritsar [amritser] 31°35N 74°57E, pop (2000e) 833 000. City in Punjab, NW India; centre of the Sikh religion; founded in 1577 by Ram Das around a sacred tank, known as the pool of immortality; the Golden Temple contains the sacred book of the Sikhs, Adi Granth; centre of modern Sikh nationalism; massacre of Indian nationalists, 1919; battle between the Indian Army and Sikh militants inside the Golden Temple, 1984; airport; university (1969).

Amsterdam [amsterdam] 52°23N 4°54E, pop (2000e) 746 000. Major European port and capital city of The Netherlands; chartered, 1300; member of the Hanseatic League, 1369; capital, 1808; airport; railway; two universities (1632, 1880); harbour industry developed after World War 2; major transshipping point.

amu *atomic mass unit*

Amudarya, River [amudarya], ancient **Oxus** River forming part of the Turkmenia–Afghanistan border; flows W and NW to enter the Aral Sea in a wide delta; length 1415 km/879 mi; largest river of C Asia.

Amun [amun], also spelled **Amon, Ammon,** or **Amen** From the time of the Middle Kingdom, the supreme deity in Egyptian religion. Later he was given the qualities of the sun-god Re, hence the usual title **Amun-Re**. The name means 'the hidden one'.

Amundsen, Roald (Engelbregt Gravning) [amundsen] (1872–1928) Explorer, born in Borge, Norway. His Antarctic expedition of 1910 reached the Pole in December 1911, one month ahead of Scott.

Amur River [amoor], Chin **Heilong Jiang** River in NE China and Russia, part of the international border; flows generally E then NE to enter the Sea of Okhotsk; length, 4350 km/2700 mi.

amyl [aymiyl, amil] $CH_3CH_2CH_2CH_2CH_2$–, IUPAC **pentyl**. A group derived from pentane by removing one hydrogen atom. **Amyl alcohol** is a fraction of fusel oil, boiling point c.130°C. **Amylose** is a low molecular weight fraction of starch. **Amyloid** is a combination of protein and polysaccharides deposited as a fibrous substance in some animal organs affected by certain diseases (eg kuru).

amylases [amilayziz] A group of enzymes which speed up the breakdown of starch and glycogen into disaccharides and small polysaccharides. They occur widely in plants and animals.

amyl nitrite ($C_5H_{11}NO_2$) A drug in the form of a volatile liquid, administered by inhalation, which acts very rapidly and very briefly. It has some use in the treatment of angina but is also sold as a sex aid ('poppers').

Anabaptists The collective name given to groups of believers stemming from the more radical elements of the 16th-c Reformation; also known as **Rebaptizers**. They believed in the baptism of believing adults only, refusing to recognize infant baptism. They were associated with Thomas Müntzer and the Zwinglian prophets in Wittenberg (1521); the Swiss brethren in Zürich (1525); and Jan Mattys (d.1534) in Münster (1533–4). They were the forerunners of the Baptists, who are in many respects their spiritual heirs.

anatomy

The science concerned with the form, structure, and spatial relationships of a living organism, and the relation of structure to function. It originally referred to the cutting up of the body to determine the nature and organization of its parts, but nowadays it includes many other aspects of study. *Topographic* or *gross* anatomy deals with the relative positions of various body parts. *Systemic* anatomy is concerned with the study of groups of related structures (eg the respiratory system). *Applied* anatomy considers anatomical facts in relation to clinical medicine. *Functional* anatomy deals not only with the structural basis of function in the various systems (eg the musculo-skeletal system), but also with the relation of one system to another, and so merges with physiology. *Developmental* anatomy is concerned with the prenatal organization and structural changes within the embryo and fetus (*embryology*), and with postnatal growth and development. *Morbid* or *pathological* anatomy deals with the anatomy of diseased tissues. *Radiological* anatomy is the study of organs and tissues using radiographic techniques (X-rays, computer-assisted tomography, magnetic resonance imaging). *Neuroanatomy* is the study of the structure and function of nervous systems (central, peripheral, autonomic). *Comparative* anatomy describes and compares the form, structure, and function of different animals. *Veterinary* anatomy is the science dealing with the form and structure of the principal domesticated animals. Anatomical science also involves *histology*, the study of the architecture of tissues and organs, and *cell biology*, concerned with the basic elements of the cell.

anabolic steroids Drugs with structures similar to the male sex hormones (*androgens*) but with reduced androgenic activity and increased anabolic activity to promote weight and muscle development. They are used clinically to accelerate recovery from protein deficiency, in muscle-wasting disorders, and sometimes in breast cancer. They are used illegally to promote the performance of athletes and racing animals, and were first used by weightlifters and bodybuilders.

anabolism *metabolism*

anaconda A boa from South America (*Eunectes murinus*), the largest snake in the world; may be more than 11 m/36 ft long, weighing over 500 kg/1100 lb; dull colour with large irregular dark spots; inhabits slow-moving water; eats birds, mammals, caimans, turtles; also known as the **green anaconda**.

Anacreon [anakreeon] (c.570–c.475 BC) Greek lyric poet, born in Teos, modern Turkey. Of the five books of his poems, only a few genuine fragments have been preserved.

anaemia / anemia A reduction in the amount of oxygen-carrying pigment, haemoglobin, in the red cells circulating in the blood. There are many causes, including blood loss, excessively rapid destruction of red blood cells, and failure of their normal maturation in the bone marrow.

anaerobe *aerobe*

anaesthetics / anesthetics, general Drugs which produce a reversible state of unconciousness deep enough to permit surgery. They may be inhaled (eg halothane) or given intravenously (eg thiopentone); intravenous anaesthetics are used for short operations only. The first of these drugs, *nitrous oxide* ('laughing gas') was discovered by Joseph Priestley in 1776, and its use in surgical operations was suggested in 1799 by Humphry Davy. The medical speciality is known as **anaesthesiology**, and the presence of a specialist (an **anaesthetist**) is required during surgical operations.

anaesthetics / anesthetics, local Drugs which produce a revers-

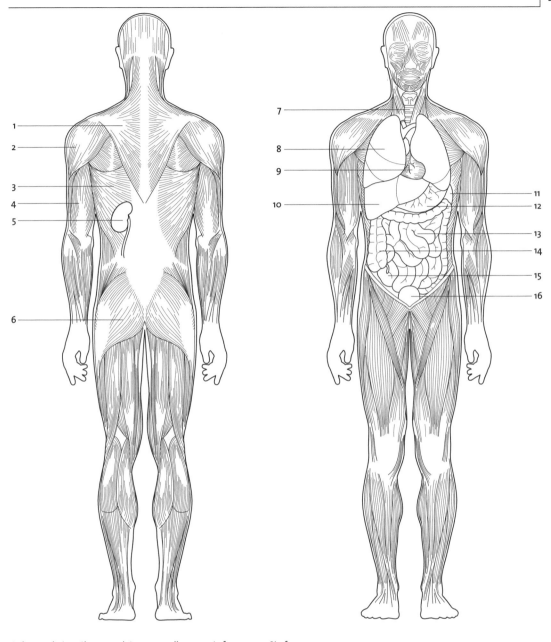

In human beings the musculature normally accounts for some 40% of
the total body weight. There are 639 named muscles in the human body.

1 trapezius muscle
2 deltoid muscle
3 latissimus dorsi muscle
4 triceps muscles (the biceps, at the front of
 the arm, cannot be seen from this view)
5 kidney
6 gluteus maximus muscle
 (largest muscle in the body)

7 trachea
8 lungs
9 heart
10 liver (only a small part of the
 liver can be seen in this illustration)
11 spleen

12 stomach
13 small intestine
14 colon
15 appendix
16 bladder

ible loss of sensation in a localized region of the body by blocking nerve impulses. It is achieved by topical application or by injection at the site of an operation (as in tooth extraction), near a main nerve trunk (eg to allow operations in limbs), or between spinal vertebrae (**epidural anaesthesia**). Examples include procaine, lignocaine (lidocaine), and benzocaine.

analgesics Drugs which relieve pain. **Narcotic analgesics** (eg codeine, morphine, heroin) act by mimicking the natural brain endorphins responsible for the subjective perception of pain. **Non-narcotic analgesics** (eg aspirin, paracetamol) act by blocking the synthesis of prostaglandins.

analog computer, also spelled **analogue** Computers which accept, as inputs, continuous electrical or mechanical variables (such as voltage or the rotation rate of a shaft) and respond immediately to calculate relevant output signals. Many of their former tasks are now done using the much more versatile digital computers.

analog-to-digital (A/D) conversion, also spelled **analogue** A process of converting analog signals, such as voltage, into a digital form which can be used in a digital computer. It is usually carried out by specialized electronic circuits or discrete integrated circuits called *analog-to-digital (A–D) converters*.

analytic / analytical geometry A method of attacking geometrical problems by referring to a point by its co-ordinates in a system; also known as **Cartesian** or **co-ordinate geometry**. For the plane, the commonest system is of two perpendicular axes, when all points can be identified by a number pair, (x,y). In three-dimensional geometry a number triple is needed (x,y,z).

Ananda [ananda] (5th–6th-c BC) The cousin and favourite pupil of the Buddha. He was instrumental in establishing an order for women disciples.

Ananke [anangkee] The 12th natural satellite of Jupiter, discovered in 1951; distance from the planet 21 200 000 km/ 13 174 000 mi; diameter 30 km/19 mi.

anaphylaxis [anafuhlaksis] A severe allergic reaction which occurs when an individual has been previously sensitized by contact with an allergen. Examples include asthma and hay fever.

anarchism A generic term for political ideas and movements that reject the state and other forms of authority and coercion in favour of a society based exclusively upon voluntary co-operation between individuals. Anarchists support civil disobedience action against the state, and on occasions political violence.

Anastasia [anastahzia], in full **Grand Duchess Anastasia Nikolaievna Romanova** (1901–?1918) Daughter of the Tsar Nicholas II of Russia, born near St Petersburg. Though she is thought to have died when the Romanov family were executed by the Bolsheviks in Yekaterinburg in 1918, several women later claimed to be Anastasia.

Anatolia [anatohlia], Turkish **Anadolu** Asiatic region of Turkey, usually synonymous with Asia Minor; a mountainous peninsula between the Black Sea (N), Aegean Sea (W), and the Mediterranean Sea (S).

Anatolian [anatohlian] A group of Indo-European languages, now extinct, spoken c.2000 BC in the area of present-day Turkey and Syria. The major language is Hittite, recorded on cuneiform tablets from the 17th-c BC: these are the oldest known Indo-European texts.

anatomy p.30

Anaxagoras [anaksagoras] (c.500–428 BC) Greek philosopher, born in Clazomenae. He taught in Athens, where he had many illustrious pupils, including Pericles.

Anaximander [anaximander] (c.611–547 BC) Greek philosopher, born in Miletus. He is credited with producing the first map, and with many scientific speculations, for example that the Earth is unsupported and at the centre of the universe. He was the successor and perhaps pupil of Thales.

Anaximenes [anakzimeneez] (?–c.500 BC) Greek philosopher, born in Miletus. He was the third of the great Milesian philosophers, succeeding Thales and Anaximander. He held air to be the first principle and the basis of matter from which other things were formed.

anchor A device which prevents a vessel from drifting. The flukes or arms of an anchor dig into the seabed, thus resisting a horizontal pull; it is made fast to the ship by a heavy cable, usually of studded chain.

Anchorage 61°13N 149°54W, pop (2000e) 260 300. City and seaport in SC Alaska, USA; largest city in the state; founded, 1914; severely damaged by earthquake, 1964; important transportation hub; a vital defence centre; airport; railway; university (1957).

anchovy [anchovee] Any of the small herring-like fishes of the family Engraulidae, widespread in surface coastal waters of tropical and temperate seas; support extensive commercial fisheries. (5 genera, including *Anchoa, Engraulis*.)

ancien régime [ãsyĩ rayzheem] The social and political system of France existing from the late 16th-c to the outbreak of the French Revolution (1789). The term implies a hierarchical, corporative society, bound closely to the dynastic state.

ancona altarpiece

Andalusia, Eng [andalooseea], Span **Andalucía** [andalootheea] pop (2000e) 6 950 000; area 87 268 km²/33 685 sq mi. Large and fertile autonomous region of S Spain; S coastal strip known for its tourist resorts on the Costa del Sol and the Costa de la Luz; chief cities, Málaga, Cádiz, Granada, Córdoba.

andalusite [andaloosiyt] A variety of mineral aluminium silicate (Al_2SiO_5), found in metamorphic rocks. Its importance lies as an indicator of the pressure and temperature of metamorphism in rocks.

Andaman and Nicobar Islands [andaman, nikohbah(r)] pop (2001e) 356 300; area 8300 km²/3200 sq mi. Union territory of India, comprising two island groups in the Bay of Bengal; over 300 islands, stretching 725 km/450 mi N to S; occupied by Japan in World War 2; part of India, 1950; British penal colony on Andaman Is, 1858–1945; Nicobar Is 120 km/75 mi S, a mountainous group of 19 islands; occupied by Denmark, 1756–1848; annexed by Britain, 1869; chief town, Nankauri; Andaman and Nicobar archipelago and most of S islands devasted by tsunami disaster, Dec 2004, with thousands of lives lost; over last 100 years Andaman aboriginal tribes have depleted from c.10 000 to c.900 by 2005.

Andean Community of Nations (CAN), also known as the **Andean Group**, Span **Comunidad Andina** An organization modelled on the European Union, with four member countries: Bolivia, Colombia, Ecuador, and Peru (Venezuela withdrew in 2006). It was previously known as the **Andean Pact** (1969–96).

Andersen, Hans Christian (1805–75) Writer, one of the world's great story-tellers, born in Odense, Denmark. The son of a poor shoemaker, he early displayed a talent for poetry. He is mainly remembered for such children's stories as 'The Tin Soldier' and 'The Ugly Duckling'.

Anderson, Carl (David) (1905–91) Physicist, born in New York City. He discovered the positron (1932), did notable work on gamma and cosmic rays, and confirmed the existence of intermediate-mass particles now called muons. He shared the Nobel Prize for Physics in 1936.

Anderson, Clive (Stuart) (1953–) Television presenter and barrister, born in London. He studied law at Cambridge, and was called to the bar in 1976. He joined BBC Radio 4 as chairman of the popular *Whose Line Is It Anyway?* (1988), was given his own Channel 4 television chat-show *Clive Anderson Talks Back* (1989–96), and presented BBC's *Clive Anderson All Talk* (1996–2000). *Unreliable Evidence*, in which he cross-examines some of the UK's most eminent legal figures, began on Radio 4 in 1998.

Anderson, Elizabeth Garrett, *née* **Garrett** (1836–1917) Physician, born in London, who pioneered the admission of women into medicine. She had difficulty qualifying as a doctor because of opposition to women, finally receiving an MD degree from the University of Paris (1870). She was elected Mayor of Aldeburgh in 1908 – the first woman mayor in England.

Anderson, Gerry (1929–) British creator of puppet-character programmes for television. He enjoyed great success with adventure series that combined a range of popular puppet characters with technologically advanced hardware and special effects, such as *Thunderbirds* (1964–6), *Captain Scarlett and the Mysterons* (1967), and *Terrahawks* (1983–4).

Anderson, Gillian (1968–) Actress, born in Chicago, IL. Brought up in London, her family returned to the USA, where she became involved in community theatre. Moving to Los Angeles, she was offered the part of Dana Scully in the TV series *The X-Files* (1993–2002), which has since become a cult classic. She also starred in the film *The X-Files: Fight the Future* (1998). Later work includes *Bleak House* for BBC TV (BAFTA, 2006).

Anderson, Lindsay (Gordon) (1923–94) British stage and film director, born in Bangalore, India. He began with short documentary films, such as *Thursday's Children* (1955, Oscar), and became a leading proponent of the Free Cinema critical movement. His feature films include *This Sporting Life* (1963), *O Lucky Man!* (1973), and *The Whales of August* (1987).

Anderson, Marian (1897–1993) Contralto concert and opera singer, born in Philadelphia, PA. In 1955 she became the first African-American singer at the New York Metropolitan Opera. President Eisenhower made her a delegate to the UN in 1958.

Andersson, Benny *Abba*

Andes [andeez] Major mountain range in South America, running parallel to the Pacific coast from Tierra del Fuego (S) to the Caribbean (N); extends over 6400 km/4000 mi; rises to 6960 m/22 834 ft in the Cerro Aconcagua (Argentina), the highest point in South America; several parallel ranges (*cordilleras*) and high plateaux; highest peaks on the Chile–Argentina border, with many lakes and tourist resorts; C Andes in Bolivia covers two-fifths of the country in an elevated plateau (*altiplano*) of 3000–3600 m/9800–11 800 ft; includes such active volcanoes as Chimborazo and Cotopaxi; connects via E Panama to the C American ranges.

Andhra Pradesh [andra pradaysh] pop (2001e) 75 727 500; area 276 814 km²/106 850 sq mi. State in S India, bounded E by the Bay of Bengal; capital, Hyderabad; made a separate state based on Telugu-speaking area of Chennai (Madras), 1953.

Andorra *p.34*

Andorra la Vella [andora la velya], Span **Andorra la Vieja**, Fr **Andorre la Vieille** 42°30N 1°30E, pop (2000e) 28 300. One of the seven parishes of the Principality of Andorra, with a capital town of the same name; altitude 1029 m/3376 ft; airports.

Andrássy, Gyula, Gróf (Count) [ondrahshee] (1823–90) Statesman and prime minister (1867–71), born in Kassa, Hungary (now Košice, Slovak Republic). A supporter of Kossuth, he was prominent in the struggle for independence (1848–9). When the Dual Monarchy was formed, he was made prime minister of Hungary (1871–9).

André, John [ondray] (1751–80) British soldier, born in London. He joined the army in Canada, and when in 1780 Benedict Arnold obtained the command of West Point, André was selected to make the arrangements for its betrayal. He was captured, tried as a spy, and hanged.

Andrea del Sarto *Sarto, Andrea del*

andrecium [andreesiuhm] *flower; stamen*

Andress, Ursula (1936–) Film actress, born in Bern, Switzerland. She made her international debut in *Dr No* (1963), her later films including *What's New, Pussycat?* (1965), *Casino Royale*

(1967), and *The Clash of the Titans* (1981). TV work includes *The Chinatown Murders* (1989).

Andrew, St (d.c.60) One of the 12 apostles, brother of Simon Peter. He is traditionally supposed to have preached the Gospel in Asia Minor and Scythia, and to have been crucified in Achaia by order of the Roman governor. He is the patron saint of Scotland and of Russia. Feast day 30 November.

Andrewes, Lancelot (1555–1626) Anglican clergyman, born in Barking, Essex. Considered one of the most learned theologians and preachers of his time, he became Bishop of Chichester (1605), Ely (1609), and Winchester (1618), and took part in the translation of the Bible.

Andrews, Eamon (1922–87) Broadcaster, born in Dublin. He was best known as television host of *What's My Line?* (1951–63, 1984–7) and *This is Your Life* (1955–87). He was also active as a chat-show host and children's programmes presenter.

Andrews, Dame Julie, originally **Julia Elizabeth Wells** (1935–) Singer and actress, born in Walton-on-Thames, Surrey. She became internationally known through her roles in the film musicals *Mary Poppins* (1964, Oscar) and *The Sound of Music* (1965). Later films include *Victor/Victoria* (1982), *A Fine Romance* (1992), and *The Princess Diaries* (2001). In 1998 an operation on her vocal cords left her singing voice badly damaged, but she recovered enough to undertake a short tour of the USA in 2002 with the Royal Philharmonic Orchestra. She was honoured with a lifetime achievement award from the Screen Actors Guild in 2006. Her husband is the film director Blake Edwards (1922–).

Androcles [androkleez] According to a Roman story, an escaped slave who met a lion, and extracted a thorn from its paw. When recaptured, he was made to confront a lion in the arena, and found it was the same animal, so that his life was spared.

androgens [androjenz] Chemical substances, usually steroid sex hormones, which induce masculine characteristics. In men the androgens *testosterone* and *dihydrotestosterone* are secreted in the testes. They are necessary for the development of male genitalia in the fetus. During puberty they promote the development of secondary sexual characteristics (growth of the penis and testes; the appearance of pubic, facial, and body hair; an increase in muscle strength; and deepening of the voice). In adults, they are required for the production of sperm and the maintenance of libido.

android *robotics* (cybernetics)

Andromache [andromakee] In Greek legend, the wife of Hector, the hero of Troy. After the fall of the city she became the slave of the Greek Neoptolemus.

Andromeda (astronomy) [andromida] A constellation in the N sky. Its brightest stars are Alpheratz and Mirach. It contains the **Andromeda galaxy**, the largest of the nearby galaxies, about 725 kiloparsec away.

Andromeda (mythology) [andromeda] In Greek mythology, the daughter of Cepheus and Cassiopeia. To appease Poseidon, she was fastened to a rock as an offering to a sea-monster. She was rescued by Perseus, who used the Gorgon's head to change the monster to stone.

Andropov, Yuri Vladimirovich [andropof] (1914–84) General secretary of the Soviet Communist Party (1982–4) and president of the USSR (1983–4), born in Nagutskoye, Russia. He was head of the KGB (1967–72), and became president following the death of Brezhnev, but died soon after.

Andros (Greece) area 380 km²/147 sq mi. Northernmost island of the Cyclades, Greece; length 40 km/25 mi; chief town, Andros; rises to 994 m/3261 ft.

anechoic chamber [anekohik] A room or chamber in which all walls and surfaces are lined with a sound-absorbing material to minimize reflected sound; also called a **dead room**. It is import-

Andorra

FRANCE
Arcalis
El Serrat
Coma Pedrosa 2942m
Canillo Valira Soldeu
Ordino
Pal A N D O R R A Pas de la Casa
Andorra- Encamp Grau-Roig
la-Vella
les Escaldes
Sant-Julià-de-Lòria
P Y R E N E E S SPAIN
10 km
5 mi

□ International Airport

[andora] or **the Valleys of Andorra, Catalan** Valls d'Andorra, **Fr** Vallée d'Andorre, **official name** Principality of Andorra, Principat d'Andorra

Local name Vallée d'Andorre (French), Valls d'Andorra (Spanish)

Timezone GMT +1

Area 453 km²/175 sq mi

Population total (2002e) 66 500

Status Independent State

Capital Andorra la Vella

Languages Catalan (official), French, Spanish

Ethnic groups Catalan (50%), Andorran (29%), French (8%), Portuguese (7%)

Religion Roman Catholic (94%)

Physical features Mountainous country, located on the S slopes of the C Pyrénées between France and Spain, peaks reaching 2946 m/9665 ft at Coma Pedrosa; two valleys (del Norte and del Orient) of the R Valira.

Climate Alpine climate: heavy snow in winter, warm summers; average annual temperature 2°C (Jan), 19°C (Jul); lowest average monthly rainfall, 34 mm/1·34 in (Jan).

Currency 1 euro (EUR) = 100 cents (previous to February 2002, 1 French Franc (FRF) = 100 centimes, 1 Peseta (ESA,ESB) = 100 céntimos)

Economy No restriction on currency exchange, and no direct value-added taxes, therefore a marketing centre for goods imported from Europe and Asia; commerce, agriculture; skiing at five mountain resorts; in recent years, textiles, publishing, leather, mineral water, tourism.

GDP (2000e) $1·3 bn, per capita $19 000

History One of the oldest states in Europe, under the joint protection of France and Spain since 1278; Co-Princes of Principality are the President of France and the Bishop of Urgel; General Council of the Valley appoints the head of the government; independent state since 1993.

Heads of State (Co-Princes): President of France and Bishop of Urgel, Spain

Head of Government (Chief Executive)

1989–94 Oscar Ribas Reig

1994– Marc Forné Molné

ant in acoustic experiments in which reflected sound would confuse results.

Aneirin or **Aneurin** [aniɣrin] (fl.6th–7th-c) British Celtic court poet. He was probably the author of the most famous Dark Age British poem, the *Gododdin*, which celebrates the British Celtic heroes killed by the Anglo-Saxons in the bloody Battle of Cattraeth (Catterick, North Yorkshire) sometime in the 6th-c.

anemometer A device for measuring the speed of a current of air. It is usually used to determine the speed of wind, or of a vehicle passing through air.

anemone [anemonee] A perennial found throughout N temperate and arctic regions, often forming large colonies; flowers with 5–9 segments ranging from white to yellow, pink, or blue, but hybrids exhibit an even greater colour range. (Genus: *Anemone*, 150 species. Family: Ranunculaceae.)

aneroid barometer *barometer*

anesthetics *anaesthetics*

Aneto, Pico de [peekoh thay anaytoh] 42°37N 0°40E. Highest peak of the Pyrenees Mts, rising to 3404 m/11 168 ft in Huesca province, NE Spain.

aneurysm [anyurizm] The abnormal enlargement of a segment of a blood vessel (usually an artery) due to the weakening or rupture of some of the layers of the wall of the vessel. Rupture of an aneurysm of the aorta or pulmonary trunk often proves fatal.

angel dust The street name of the drug **phencyclidine** (l-(l-phenylcyclohexyl) piperidine, or **PCP**) which is a hallucinogen. It was originally introduced in the 1950s as a general anaesthetic, but soon withdrawn.

Angeles, Victoria de los [anjeles], originally **Victoria Gómez Cima** (1923–2005) Soprano, born in Barcelona, Spain. She was noted particularly for her 19th-c Italian roles and for her performances of Spanish songs. She retired from the operatic stage in 1980 but continued to give recitals.

Angel Falls 5°57N 62°33W. Waterfall in SE Venezuela, on a tributary of the R Caroní; highest waterfall in the world, with a total drop of 980 m/3215 ft; named after the US aviator, Jimmy Angel, who crashed nearby in 1937.

angelfish Any of several small brightly coloured fish found in shallow waters of warm seas; deep, flattened body; small mouth, with gill cover bearing a spine; very popular in marine aquaria; also called **butterfly fish**. The name is also used for monkfish. (Family: Chaetodontidae.)

angelica [anjelika] A robust herb growing to 2 m/6 ft or more (*Angelica archangelica*), native from N and E Europe to C Asia; stem hollow; leaves divided into oval leaflets up to 15 cm/6 in; flowers small, greenish-white, in clusters. Aromatic oil, produced from the roots, is used in perfumes and herbal liqueurs. (Family: Umbelliferae.)

Angelico, Fra [anjelikoh], originally **Guido di Pietro**, monastic name **Giovanni da Fiesole** (c.1400–55) Early Renaissance painter, born in Vicchio, Italy. He entered the Dominican monastery at Fiesole in 1407. His most important frescoes are those in the Convent of St Mark (now a museum) in Florence, at Orvieto, and in the Nicholas Chapel of the Vatican. The ethereal beauty of his angelic figures gave him his new name.

Angelou, Maya [anjeloo], pseudonym of **Marguerite Ann John-**

son (1928–) Writer, singer, dancer, and African-American activist, born in St Louis, MO. She toured Europe and Africa in the musical *Porgy and Bess*, and in New York City joined the Harlem Writers Guild. In the 1960s she was involved in civil rights, then spent several years in Ghana as editor of *African Review*. Her multi-volume autobiography, commencing with *I Know Why the Caged Bird Sings* (1970), was a great success.

angelshark *monkfish*

Angevins [anjevinz] The ruling families of the mediaeval county (and later duchy) of Anjou in W France. Henry II, founder of the Angevin or Plantagenet dynasty in England, was a descendant of the earliest counts of Anjou.

angina [anjiyna] A sudden severe pain or sensation of constriction over the front of the chest which occurs when the oxygen demand of the heart muscle exceeds supply (**angina pectoris**). The pain is increased with exercise, and subsides with rest. It usually results from the narrowing or blockage of one or more of the arteries which supply the heart muscle with blood. It can be relieved by the use of drugs.

angiography [anjiografee] A radiological technique used to demonstrate the pathways and configuration of blood vessels in various parts of the body. A radio-opaque solution is injected into a main arterial trunk, which increases the X-ray contrast between the blood vessel and its surrounding tissues.

angioplasty *balloon angioplasty*

Angkor Thom [angkaw(r) tom] 13°26N 103°50E. The ancient capital of the Khmer Empire. The moated and walled city was built on a square plan, extending over 100 km^2/40 sq mi, and completed in the 12th-c. **Angkor Wat** is the largest of the temples surrounding the site.

anglerfish Any of about 13 families of bizarre shallow to deep-sea fishes which have a dorsal fin spine modified as a lure to attract prey; family Lophiidae includes large bottom-dwelling European species (length up to 1·5 m/5 ft) with broad flattened head, capacious mouth, and narrow tail; also called **goosefish**.

Angles A Germanic people thought to have originated from the S Danish peninsula and neighbouring Schleswig-Holstein. With the Saxons, they formed the bulk of the invaders who, in the two centuries following the Roman withdrawal from Britain (409), conquered and colonized most of what became England.

Anglesey [angglsee], Welsh **Sir Fôn** or **Ynys Môn** [uhnis mohn] pop (2001e) 66 800; area 715 km^2/276 sq mi. Island unitary authority (from 1996) in NW Wales, UK; separated from Gwynedd by Menai Strait, spanned by two bridges; chief towns, Holyhead, Llangefni; linked to Holy I by an embankment; ferry link from Holyhead to Dun Laoghaire and Dublin, Ireland.

Anglesey, Henry William Paget, 1st Marquess of [angglsee] (1768– 1854) British field marshal, born in London. He commanded the British cavalry at the Battle of Waterloo (1815), where he lost a leg.

Anglican chant *chant*

Anglican Communion A fellowship of some 26 independent provincial or national Churches, several extra-provincial dioceses, and Churches resulting from unions of Anglicans with other Churches, spread throughout the world. They share a close ecclesiastical and doctrinal relationship with the Church of England.

Anglicanism *Church of England*

Anglican–Roman Catholic International Commission *ARCIC*

angling The sport of catching fish, one of the world's most popular pastimes, performed in virtually every country, practised with a rod, line, and hook. Many forms of angling exist: freshwater fishing, fly fishing, game fishing, and deep sea fishing. The oldest fishing club still in existence is the Ellem Club in Scotland (founded 1829).

Anglo-Catholicism A movement within the Church of England, the term first appearing in 1838. It stresses the sacramental aspects of Christian faith, and continuity with the wider Church, especially with Roman Catholicism.

Anglo-Irish Agreement A joint agreement allowing the Irish Republic to contribute to policy in Northern Ireland for the first time since 1922, signed in 1985 by the British and Irish Prime Ministers, Margaret Thatcher and Garrett Fitzgerald. It established an intergovernmental conference to discuss political, security, and legal matters affecting Northern Ireland. Both governments pledged not to change the status of Northern Ireland without the consent of the majority. It was opposed by the Republic's Opposition party, Fianna Fáil, and Unionist leaders boycotted official bodies – a boycott which did not end until 1992. The Agreement was instrumental in leading to the 'Downing Street Declaration' of 1993, and also the talks which led to the Good Friday Agreement.

Anglo-Maori Wars A succession of conflicts (1843–7, 1860–70) in which Maori people attempted, unsuccessfully, to resist the occupation of New Zealand by British settlers. The main fighting finished in 1864 after the Kingite Maoris, who had led the resistance, retreated to the C North Island.

Anglo-Saxon *Old English*

Anglo-Saxons A term probably first used to distinguish the Saxons of England from those of the continent. It is now commonly employed for the entire Old English people from the incoming of Angles, Saxons, and Jutes in the 5th-c to the Norman Conquest.

Angola *p.36*

Angora cat [anggawra] A breed of domestic cat; white longhaired type originated in Turkey (*Angora* is an old name for Ankara); resembles the Persian cat, but with longer body and smaller head.

Angora goat [anggawra] A breed of domestic goat, originating in Turkey (*Angora* is an old name for Ankara); bred mainly in North America, S Africa, and Australasia for wool; silky hair (length up to 20 cm/8 in), called *mohair*.

angostura [anggostoora] A flavouring agent used in cocktails and some fruit juices, deriving from the bark of a S American tree (*Gallipea aspuria*). It was originally used in medicines.

Angra do Heroísmo [anggra duh eroeezhmu] 38°40N 27°14W, pop (2000e) 11 600. Fortified town and seaport in the Azores; a world heritage site, on S coast of Terceira I; founded, 1464; capital of the Azores until 1832; bishopric; airport.

Angry Brigade A left-wing group with anarchist sympathies, active in Britain in the 1960s and early 1970s. It took sporadic violent action against representatives of the establishment in the name of the working class.

Angry Young Men A term used to describe the authors of some novels and plays of the late 1950s and early 1960s in Britain, who felt a confident contempt for the (apparently) established order. They included Kingsley Amis, John Braine, John Osborne and Alan Sillitoe. The term was also applied to certain characters in their works, notably to Jimmy Porter, the hero of Osborne's *Look Back in Anger* (1956).

Ångström, Anders (Jonas) [angstruhm, ongstroem] (1814–74) Physicist, born in Lögdö, Sweden. He wrote on heat, magnetism, and especially spectroscopy. The unit used in crystallography and spectroscopy is named after him.

ångström or **angstrom** [angstruhm] Unit of length common in crystallography or any other subject which studies features of approximately atomic dimensions; symbol Å; equal to 10^{-10} m.

Anguilla *p.37*

angular acceleration *acceleration*

angular momentum A vector quantity in rotational motion, equal to the product of moment of inertia with angular velocity; also called the **moment of momentum**; symbol L, units kg.m^2/s. The rate of change of angular momentum is called *torque*.

Angola

☐ International Airport

[anggohla], official name **Republic of Angola**, Port **República de Angola**
Local name Angola
Timezone GMT +1
Area 1 246 700 km²/480 354 sq mi
Population total (2002e) 10 593 000 (excluding more than 400 000 refugees in D.R. of Congo and Zambia)
Status Republic
Date of independence 1975
Capital Luanda
Languages Portuguese (official), Bantu languages, including: Ovimbundu, Kimbundu, Bakongo, Chokwe
Ethnic groups Ovimbundu (37%), Mbundu (22%), Bakongo (13%), Lunda-Tchokwe (5%); also Nganguela, Nyaneka-Humbe, Herero, Ambo, Portuguese
Religions Traditional religions (12%), Roman Catholic (68%), Protestant (20%)

Physical features Located in SW Africa; narrow coastal plain; in S and E the planalto central (central plateau, continuation of great SW African plateau), covers c.60% of the country; in N, highland plateau, mean elevation 1200 m/4000 ft; highest point, Serro Môco 2619 m/8592 ft; coastal desert in W; in E, upland escarpments; c.40% of land forested.

Climate tropical plateau climate; at Huambo, on the plateau, average annual rainfall 1450 mm/57 in; rainfall varies greatly from SW to NE (negligible rainfall on SW coastal desert caused by Benguela current); average daily temperatures 24–9°C; temperature much reduced on the coast, which is semi-desert as far N as Luanda.

Currency 1 New Kwanza (AOK) = 100 iweis

Economy Reserves of several minerals; extraction and refining of oil (mainly off the coast of Cabinda Province) provides over 90% of current export earnings; diamond exporter; large producer of honey; principal livestock are cattle, goats, pigs, sheep; agriculture and fishing (mackerel and sardines) industries small; several airfields and railways.

GDP (2002e) $18·36 bn, per capita $1700

Human Development Index (2002) 0·403

History Became a Portuguese colony in 1482 after exploration; slave trade flourished, causing friction and war (in early 17th-c, c.10 000 slaves were exported from Luanda annually); boundaries formally defined during the Berlin West Africa Congress (1884-5); became an overseas province of Portugal, 1951; Portuguese finally withdrew in 1975, and the People's Republic of Angola achieved full independence; civil war followed independence, involving three internal factions – the Marxist MPLA (Popular Movement for the Liberation of Angola), UNITA (the National Union for the Total Independence of Angola), and the FNLA (National Front for the Liberation of Angola). Cuban combat troops arrived in 1976, at request of MPLA; at the end of 1988, Geneva agreement linked arrangements for independence of Namibia with withdrawal of Cuban troops, and the cessation of South African attacks and support for UNITA; peace agreement in 1991 established a one-party state, governed by a President, Council of Ministers, and National People's Assembly; adopted the name Republic of Angola; first multi-party legislative elections held in 1992. MPLA victory rejected by UNITA led to resumption of conflict in 1993; Lusaka peace protocol, October 1994; withdrawal of UN peace-keeping force (Jan 1999) as fighting resumed between government and UNITA forces; death of UNITA leader Jonas Savimbi, followed by peace agreement, 2002; lifting of UN economic sanctions against UNITA (Dec 2002).

Head of State
1975–9 Antonio Agostinho Neto
1979– José Eduardo dos Santos

Head of Government
1992– 6 Marcolino José Carlos Moco
1996–9 Fernando José França Van Dúnem
1999–2002 José Eduardo dos Santos
2002– Fernando da Piedade Dias dos Santos

---

angular velocity *velocity*
angwantibo [anggwantiboh] A West African primitive primate (prosimian); golden brown with pointed face; no tail; first finger reduced to a stump, and second short; also known as **golden potto**. (*Arctocebus calabarensis*. Family: Lorisidae.)
anhinga *darter*
anil [anil] A tropical American shrub (*Indigofera anil*), but culti-

vated in the Old and New World as a source of the blue dye indigo; also called **indigo plant**. (Family: Leguminosae.)
aniline [anileen] $C_6H_5NH_2$, **phenylamine**, or (IUPAC) **aminobenzene**, boiling point 184°C. A liquid with an unpleasant smell, it is the starting material for many dyestuffs, known as *aniline dyes*.
animal A living organism; one of the main kingdoms of bio-

Anguilla

□ International Airport

[angwila] (UK British Overseas Territory)

Timezone GMT -4

Area 155 km²/60 sq mi

Population total (2002e) 12 000

Capital The Valley

Physical features Most northerly of the Leeward Is, E Caribbean; also includes Sombrero I and several other offshore islets and cays; low-lying coral island, covered in low scrub and fringed with white coral-sand beaches.

Climate Tropical climate; average annual temperature ranges from 24–30°C; low and erratic annual rainfall, 550–1250 mm/ 22–50 in; hurricane season (Jul–Oct).

Currency 1 East Caribbean Dollar (XCD) = 100 cents

Economy Tourism, fishing, peas, corn, sweet potatoes, salt, boatbuilding.

GDP (2001e) $104 mn, per capita $8600

History Colonized by English settlers from St Kitts in 1650; ultimately incorporated in the colony of St Kitts-Nevis-Anguilla; separated, 1980; Governor appointed by the British sovereign; Legislative Assembly.

logical classification, **Animalia**, containing all vertebrates and invertebrates. The term 'animal' is sometimes used only for four-legged creatures (mammals, reptiles, and amphibians), but correctly fish and birds are also animals, as are insects, spiders, crabs, snails, worms, starfish, sponges, corals, jellyfish, and many other groups.

Animal Protection Society of America *RSPCA*

animism A belief in spiritual beings thought capable of influencing human events, based on the idea that animals, plants, and even inanimate objects have souls like humans. The 19th-c anthropologist Edward Tylor (1832–1917) regarded it as the earliest form of religion, a view not accepted by modern anthropologists.

anion [aniyon] A negatively charged atom or group of atoms, such as Cl⁻ (chloride) or SO_4^{2-} (sulphate). Anions are so called because they migrate towards the anode in an electrochemical cell.

Aniston, Jennifer (Joanne) [aniston] (1969–) Actress, born in Sherman Oaks, Los Angeles, CA. She worked in New York, then went to Hollywood, where she achieved success through her role as Rachel Green in the television series *Friends* (1994–2004). Roles in feature films include *She's the One* (1996), *The Object of My Affection* (1998), and *The Break-Up* (2006).

Anjou [āzhoo] Former province in the Paris Basin of NW France; former capital, Angers; lost provincial status in 1790.

Ankara [angkara], ancient **Ancyra**, European **Angora** 39°55N 32°50E, pop (2000e) 3 082 000. Capital city of Turkey; conquered by Alexander the Great, 4th-c BC; part of Roman and Byzantine Empires; under Turkish rule, 11th-c; government transferred here from Istanbul, 1923; airport; railway; three universities (1946, 1956, 1967).

ankh [ank] A cross with a loop for its upper vertical arm. In ancient Egypt it was an emblem of life.

ankle The region of the lower limb between the calf and the foot; specifically, the joint between the tibia and fibula and the talus (one of the tarsal bones). Movement at the joint is important during the stance phase of walking.

ankylosaur [angkilosaw(r)] A small four-legged dinosaur, heavily armoured with rectangular bony plates; head small, teeth reduced or absent; fed on vegetation; known from the Cretaceous period of North America. (Order: Ornithischia.)

ankylosing spondylitis [angkilohzing spondiliytis] A progressive inflammatory disease, mainly affecting young men, that attacks the joints of the spine leading to stiffness and pain in the back. Ocasionally other joints such as the hip and shoulder are affected. Its cause is unknown.

Annan, Kofi (Atta) (1938–) UN secretary-general (1997–2006), born in Kumasi, Ghana. He joined the UN in 1962, and became under-secretary-general for peace-keeping operations in 1993. He became the first secretary-general from sub-Saharan Africa. Jointly with the UN, he was awarded the 2001 Nobel Peace Prize.

Annapolis [anapolis] 38°59N 76°30W, pop (2000e) 35 800. Capital of state, Maryland, USA; port on the Severn R; named after Princess (later Queen) Anne, 1695; US capital, 1783–4; railway; business and shipping centre; US Naval Academy (1845).

Annapolis Convention (1786) In the American Revolution, a gathering at Annapolis, MD, of delegates from five states to discuss commercial problems. The main result was a call for a meeting the following year to consider changes in the Articles of Confederation.

Annapurna, Mount [anapoorna] Mountain massif in the C Himalayas, Nepal; length c.56 km/35 mi; includes Annapurna I (8091 m/26 545 ft), Annapurna II (7937 m/26 040 ft), Annapurna III (7556 m/24 790 ft), Annapurna IV (7525 m/24 688 ft), and several other peaks over 6000 m/20 000 ft.

Annas [anas] (1st-c) Israel's high priest, appointed in AD 6 and deposed by the Romans in 15, but still described later by this title in the New Testament. He apparently questioned Jesus after his arrest (*John* 18) and Peter after his detention (*Acts* 4).

Anne (1665–1714) Queen of Great Britain and Ireland (1702–14), born in London, the second daughter of James II. She was the last Stuart sovereign. In 1683 she married Prince George of Denmark (1653–1708), and Sarah Jennings (1660–1744), the wife of Lord Churchill (afterwards Duke of Marlborough), was appointed a lady of her bedchamber. For many years Lady Churchill had supreme influence over her, exerting this in favour of her husband. Anne bore 17 children, but only William, Duke of Gloucester (1689–1700), survived infancy.

Anne, St (fl.1st-c BC–1st-c AD) Wife of **St Joachim**, and mother of the Virgin Mary, first mentioned in the 2nd-c. She is the patron saint of carpenters. Feast day 26 July.

Anne (Elizabeth Alice Louise), Princess (1950–) Daughter of HM Elizabeth II and HRH Prince Philip, Duke of Edinburgh, born in London. She married **Mark Anthony Peter Phillips** (1948–) in 1973, but they were divorced in 1992. Their son is **Peter Mark Andrew** (1977–); their daughter **Zara Anne Elizabeth** (1981–). She married **Timothy Laurence** (1952–) in 1992. She was created Princess Royal in 1987. In recent years she has travelled widely on behalf of international charities and is a member of the International Olympic Committee (from 1988).

Anne Boleyn Boleyn, Anne

Anne of Austria (1601–66) Eldest daughter of Philip III of Spain and wife of Louis XIII of France, born in Valladolid, Spain. In 1643 she became Queen Regent for the baby Louis XIV.

Anne of Cleves (1515–57) German princess, the fourth Queen of Henry VIII. She was selected for purely political reasons after the death of Jane Seymour, and was married to Henry in 1540, who found her appearance disappointing. The marriage was annulled by parliament six months later.

Anne of Denmark (1574–1619) Wife (from 1589) of James VI of Scotland, later James I of England. She became a patron of the masque and other art forms.

annealing The relief of internal stresses in metals after heat treatment or working (hammering, forging, or drawing), or in glass after moulding or blowing. It is effected by maintaining the object at a moderate temperature to allow for molecular or crystalline re-arrangement.

Annecy [ansee] 45°55N 6°08E, pop (2000e) 53 500. Industrial town in E France, on N shore of Lac d'Annecy; railway; bishopric; popular tourist centre.

annelid [anelid] A ringed worm; a bilaterally symmetrical worm of phylum Annelida; body divided into cylindrical rings (segments) containing serially arranged organs; head typically well defined.

Annigoni, Pietro [anigohnee] (1910–88) Painter, born in Milan, Italy. He was one of the few 20th-c artists to put into practice the technical methods of the old masters. His most usual medium was tempera. His Renaissance manner is shown at its best in his portraits, such as those of Queen Elizabeth II (1955, 1970).

annual A plant which germinates, flowers, sets seed, and dies within one year. The definition is not strict: in mild weather some annuals may germinate late in the season, overwinter as seedlings or young plants, and complete their life-cycle in the next year.

annual ring One of the concentric rings visible when the stem or root of a woody plant is cut across. Usually one ring marks one year's growth, thus providing a means of calculating the age of trees.

annuity [anyooitee] A financial contract by which an insurance company agrees, in exchange for premiums which may be recurrent or lump-sum, to provide a regular income for life. An annuity enables the recipients to spend their capital as well as the income on it, without the risk of running out of funds before they die.

annulment A judicial declaration of nullity of marriage. A null marriage is one that was never valid, for example because it involved parties within the prohibited degrees of affinity or consanguinity. The term also refers to an incorrectly made bankruptcy order.

Annunciation The angel Gabriel's foretelling to Mary of the birth of Jesus and of the promise of his greatness (Luke 1.26–38). The feast day (25 Mar) is also known as **Lady Day**.

Annunzio, Gabriele d' d'Annunzio, Gabriele

anoa [anoha] A rare member of the cattle family, from Sulawesi; height, c.80 cm/30 in; straight backward-pointing horns; two species; also known as **dwarf buffalo**, **wood ox**, **sapi-utan**, or **sapi-outan**.

anode In electrolysis and gas discharge tubes, the positive electrode from which electrons leave the cell or tube. In a battery, the anode is the negative terminal by which electrons leave the battery.

anodizing A metal protection process, usually applied to aluminium or magnesium. The object is made the anode in an electrolytic bath which produces a thin but dense protective oxide layer.

anointing the sick The ritual application of oil performed in cases of (usually) serious illness or preparation for death. In the Roman Catholic and Orthodox Churches, it is recognized as a sacrament to be performed by a priest. It was formerly sometimes called **extreme unction**.

anole [anohlee] An iguana found from SE USA to N South America (including the West Indies); can change colour. (Genus: Anolis, several species.)

Anopheles [anofileez] The malaria mosquito, found in all major zoogeographical regions. The adult females transmit a malaria-causing agent when taking blood from vertebrates. (Order: Diptera. Family: Culicidae.)

anorexia nervosa [anoreksia nervohsa] A psychological illness which mainly affects young women, characterized by significant weight loss (usually deliberately induced), an unrealistic fear of being overweight, and a loss of normal menstrual functioning. Current views hold that there are both biological and psychological causes.

Anouilh, Jean (Marie Lucien Pierre) [onwee] (1910–87) Playwright, born in Bordeaux, France. He was influenced by the Neoclassical fashion inspired by Giraudoux. Among his many successful plays are Antigone (1944), Becket (1959), and La Culotte (1978, The Trousers).

Anoura Anura

Anschluss [anshlus] (Ger 'connection') The concept of union between Austria and Germany, prohibited by the Treaty of Versailles (1919). Hitler pursued the idea once in power, and in 1938 the Germans were 'invited' to occupy Austria.

Anselm, St (1033–1109) Theologian and philosopher, born of noble birth in Aosta, Italy. Appointed Archbishop of Canterbury (1093), he frequently came into conflict over Church rights, first with William Rufus, then with Henry I. He was the main figure in early scholastic philosophy, remembered especially for his ontological proof for the existence of God, and his theory of atonement. Feast day 21 April.

Anshan or **An-shan** 41°05N 122°58E, pop (2000e) 1 608 000. Town in Liaoning province, NE China; organized mining and smelting began here c.100 BC; railway; site of China's largest iron and steel complex.

ant A social insect, characterized by a waist of 1–2 narrow segments, forming perennial colonies in nests made in wood, soil, plant cavities, or other constructions. The nest contains one or more fertile queens, many wingless, sterile workers, and winged males that fertilize queens during mass nuptial flights. (Order: Hymenoptera. Family: Formicidae, c.14 000 species.)

Antananarivo [antananareevoh], formerly **Tananarive** or **Tananarivo** (to 1975) 18°52S 47°30E, pop (2000e) 1 076 000. Capital of Madagascar; altitude c.1350 m/4400 ft; airport; railway; university (1955); two cathedrals.

Antarctica p.39

Antarctic Circle Imaginary line on the surface of the Earth at 66°30S, marking the southernmost point at which the Sun can be seen during the summer solstice, and the northernmost point at which the midnight Sun can be seen in S polar regions.

Antarctic Ocean The S regions of the Atlantic, Indian, and Pacific Oceans surrounding Antarctica; narrowest point the Drake Pas-

Antarctica

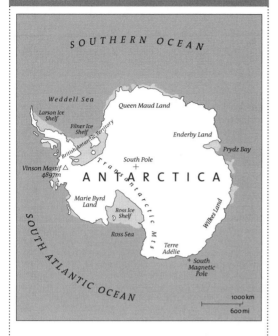

S Polar continent, area nearly 15.5 million km²/6 million-sq mi; surrounded by ice-filled ring of ocean waters containing scattered island groups; mainly S of 65°S, almost entirely within the Antarctic Circle; c.22 400 km/14 000 mi coastline, mainly of high ice cliffs; indented by Ross and Weddell Seas; divided into Greater and Lesser Antarctica, separated by the Transantarctic Mts, highest point 4897 m/16 066 ft at Vinson Massif; no permanent population; no flowering plants, grasses, large land mammals; species of algae, moss, lichen, and sea plankton provide food for fish, birds, whales, and seals; average depth of surface ice sheet 1500 m/5000 ft, overlying rock; inland ice moves slowly towards the periphery, pushing long tongues into the sea and creating shelf ice over large areas; drift ice develops along the whole coastline; many icebergs in adjacent waters, the largest of the tabular type (10–60 m/30–200 ft high); movement of pack ice varies widely in different longitudes; outward blowing winds prevail, often of hurricane force; blizzards common, especially in autumn and winter; lowest temperature on Earth (−88·3°C) recorded at Vostok Station; major scientific explorations since first winter base established in 1899 by Borchgevrink; during International Geophysical Year (1957–8) 12 countries maintained 65 bases in Antarctica; Antarctic Treaty signed by these nations in 1959, providing for international co-operation in scientific research, and prohibiting military operations, nuclear explosions, and disposal of radioactive waste; 50-year ban on mining and mineral extraction, 1991; territorial claims made by the UK (British Antarctic Territory), Norway (Dronning Maud Land), France (Terre Adélie), Australia (Enderby Land, Wilkes Land, George V Coast, part of Oates Coast), New Zealand (160°E to 150°W), Chile (90°W to 53°W), and Argentina (74°W to 25°W); South Pole first reached by Amundsen in 1911; major iceberg losses in Antarctic Peninsula, through global warming, 1987, 1995, 1998, 2000, 2002; annual ice loss c. 36 cu mi/150 cu km.

sage between South America and the Antarctic Peninsula (1110 km/690 mi).

Antares [antahreez] *Scorpius*

ant bear *aardvark*

anteater A mammal, native to Central and South America, which eats ants and termites; an edentate group, comprising four species; numbats are also known as *banded anteaters*, and pangolins as *scaly anteaters*. (Family: Myrmecophagidae.)

antelope A hoofed mammal, found mainly in Africa; classified as gazelles (tribe: Antilopini), four-horned antelopes (tribe: Boselaphini), spiral-horned antelopes (tribe: Strepsicerotini), dwarf (or pygmy) antelopes (tribe: Neotragini), grazing antelopes (subfamily: Hippotraginae, including horse-like antelopes of the tribe Hippotragini, and ox-antelopes of the tribe Alcelaphini), pronghorns (subfamily: Antilocaprinae), duikers (subfamily: Cephalophinae), and goat antelopes (subfamily: Caprinae, which includes goats and sheep). (Family: Bovidae, 116 species.)

antenna (biology) One of a pair of specialized sensory appendages on the head of an invertebrate animal; insects typically have one pair, crustaceans two pairs; varies in shape and size.

antenna (technology) The component of a radio or television system by which electromagnetic signals are transmitted or received; also known as the **aerial**. In high-frequency practice, additional elements termed *reflectors* and *directors* are included to increase directional efficiency.

Antheil, George [antiyl] (1900–59) Composer, born in Trenton, NJ. His works include the *Jazz Symphony* (1925), the *Ballet Mécanique* (1926), and the opera *Transatlantic* (1930).

anthelmintics [anthelmintiks] Drugs which paralyse or kill parasitic worms (*helminths*), such as ringworms, tapeworms, and schistosomes. They include mebendazole, piperazine, and niridazole.

anther *stamen*

Anthony, St *Antony, St; Antony of Padua*

Anthony, Susan B(rownell) (1820–1906) Women's suffrage leader, born in Adams, MA. From 1869 she was a leader of the National Woman Suffrage Association, becoming president of the US branch in 1892.

anthracene [anthraseen] $C_{14}H_{10}$, melting point 216°C. A colourless, cancer-causing, aromatic compound isolated from coal tar. Oxidized to **anthraquinone**, it is the raw material for the *alizarin* series of dyestuffs.

anthracite A hard and lustrous variety of coal, containing more than 90% carbon. It is the highest grade of coal, and burns with a very hot, virtually smokeless flame.

anthrax A disease resulting from infection with *Bacillus anthracis*. There are three types of anthrax, depending on where the infectious spore has arrived on the patient; cutaneous anthrax, the least serious of the three; intestinal anthrax caused by the consumption of contaminated meat; and respiratory anthrax, which happens when spores are breathed in by the patient and lodge in the lung. Blood poisoning, pneumonia, and death may occur, however, because the disease is not contagious, only those directly exposed to the spores have any chance of falling ill. In October 2001, powdered anthrax spores sent through the post were used in a terrorist attack against US government and media institutions, causing five deaths, the treatment of thousands of possible contacts and locations, much disruption of the postal service, and worldwide concern.

Anthropoidea [anthropoydia] A group of primates comprising monkeys and apes; face usually flat; ears small; fingers and toes with nails, not claws; live in complex social groups.

anthropology The scientific study of human beings, traditionally identified as a 'four-field' discipline, encompassing **archaeology**, **social** and **cultural anthropology**, **biological anthropology**, and often including **linguistics**. Cultural and social anthropologists study particular living societies, and attempt through comparison to establish the range of variation in human, social, and cultural institutions, and the reasons for these differences. Physical anthropologists study local biological adaptations and human evolutionary history.

anthropometry The comparative study of the dimensions of the human body and their change with time. The main dimensions examined include weight, height, skinfold thickness, mid-arm circumference, and waist-to-hip ratio. The study influences the design of many products, such as clothes, car seats, and space capsules.

anti-aircraft gun (AA-gun) A gun firing a shell at high velocity at a high angle designed to shoot down aircraft. On the modern battlefield, radar-guided 'Triple A' (standing for Anti-Aircraft Artillery) has an important role in providing low-level, close-in defence against hostile aircraft, helicopters, and missiles.

anti-anxiety drugs *benzodiazepines*

antiballistic missile (ABM) A missile capable of destroying hostile ballistic missiles or their payloads in flight at short, medium, or long ranges inside or outside the atmosphere.

Antibes [āteeb], ancient **Antipolis** 43°35N 7°07E, pop (2000e) 73 900. Fishing port and fashionable resort on the Riviera, SE France; best known for its luxurious villas and hotels sheltered by the pines of Cap d'Antibes; railway.

antibiotics Substances derived from one micro-organism which can selectively destroy other (infectious) organisms without harming the host. The development of penicillin (1941) was the start of the era of safe and effective antibiotics. Nearly 100 new antibiotics have since been discovered. Several are now synthesized.

antibodies Proteins which help protect against disease-causing micro-organisms (bacteria, viruses, parasites), present mainly in the gamma globulin fraction of serum; also known as **immunoglobulins**. The first exposure of the body to a foreign cell or molecule (an *antigen*) produces an immune response which is directed specifically against the antigen that triggered it. Antibodies are produced which eliminate the antigens by a number of mechanisms.

anticoagulants Drugs which slow down or prevent the normal process of blood clotting, such as heparin and warfarin. They are used in the treatment and prevention of diseases caused by thrombi (blood clots) which block blood vessels.

anticonvulsants Drugs used in the control of epilepsy. All sedatives are anticonvulsant at high doses, but useful drugs in current use include phenobarbitone, phenytoin, sodium valproate, and clonazepam.

Anti-Corn-Law League An association formed in Manchester (1838), largely under the patronage of businessmen and industrialists, to repeal the British Corn Laws, which imposed protective tariffs on the import of foreign corn. The Laws were repealed by Robert Peel in 1846.

anticyclone A meteorological term for a high pressure system. Anticyclones are areas of generally clear skies and stable weather conditions. In the N hemisphere, surface winds blow in a clockwise direction out of an anticyclone; in the S hemisphere the direction is anticlockwise.

antidepressants Drugs which cause elevation of mood in depressed patients. There are three major classes: *tricyclics* (eg imipramine, amitriptyline), *Monoamine oxidase inhibitors* (eg isocarboxazid, phenelzine) and *serotonin reuptake inhibitors* (SRIs) (eg Prozac).

Antietam, Battle of [anteetam] (1862) A battle of the American Civil War, fought in Maryland. In military terms the North won a technical victory. This helped dissuade Britain and France from giving diplomatic recognition to the Confederacy.

antifreeze A substance added to water in the cooling system of

an engine to prevent the system freezing during cold weather. Substances used as anti-freeze include ethanol and methanol; ethylene-glycol does not evaporate.

antigen *antibodies*

Antigone [antigonee] In Greek mythology, a daughter of Oedipus, King of Thebes. She is a symbol of the individual's right to defy the state over a matter of conscience.

Antigua or **Antigua Guatemala** [anteegwa] 14°33N 90°42W, pop (2000e) 40 700. City in S Guatemala; founded by the Spanish, 1543; capital, until largely destroyed by earthquake, 1773; old city now a world heritage site; cathedral (1534).

Antigua and Barbuda *p.41*

antihistamines Drugs used in the relief of allergic reactions, such as hay fever (but not asthma). They are so called because they act by blocking the action of the substance histamine, produced in the body during allergies.

antihydrogen *antiparticles*

antiknock A chemical substance added to a spark ignition engine's fuel to improve combustion and prevent knocking. An example is tetra-ethyl lead.

Antilles [antileez] The whole of the West Indies except the Bahamas; **Greater Antilles** include Cuba, Jamaica, Hispaniola (Haiti and the Dominican Republic), and Puerto Rico; **Lesser Antilles** include the Windward Is (S), Leeward Is (N), and the Netherlands Antilles.

antimatter *antiparticles*

antimony [antimonee] Sb (Lat *stibium*), element 51, melting point 631°C. A metalloid in the nitrogen family; expands on solidifying. It is used in alloys, and in semiconductors.

Antioch [anteeok], Turkish **Antakya**, ancient **Hatay** or **Antiochia** 36°12N 36°10E, pop (2000e) 138 000. Town in S Turkey; founded, 300 BC; centre of early Christianity; destroyed by earthquake, 526.

Antiochus I [antiohkus], known as **Antiochus Soter** (Gr 'Saviour') (324–261 BC) King of Syria (281–261 BC), the son and successor of Seleucus I. He received his nickname for his victory over the Gallic invaders of Asia Minor, but fell in battle with them.

Antiochus III [antiohkus], known as **Antiochus the Great** (c.242–187 BC) King of Syria (223–187 BC), the greatest of the Seleucid dynasty. He restored Seleucid prestige in the East (209–204 BC), and gained possession of Palestine and Coele Syria (198 BC). He was defeated by the Romans at Thermopylae (191 BC), and Magnesia (190 BC).

antioxidants Substances which slow down the oxidation of others, often by being oxidized themselves. The term is usually applied to additives in foods and plastics.

antiparticles Partners of subatomic particles having the same mass and spin but opposite charge, magnetic moment, and other quantum attributes. When antiparticles meet their particle partners the two annihilate, as predicted by British physicist Paul Dirac in 1928. The antiparticle is usually denoted by a bar over the symbol for the corresponding particle. **Antimatter** composed of antiparticles is possible, but highly unstable, and not observed naturally.

Antipater (of Idumaea) [antipater] (?–43 BC) A chieftain who dominated Jewish history from the 60s BC until his death. The father of Herod the Great, he laid the foundations of his family's ascendancy in Judaea during Roman times.

antiphon (chant) In the Roman Catholic and Greek Orthodox liturgies, a chant with a prose text which precedes or follows a psalm. A collection of antiphons is known as an **antiphoner**.

antipodes Any two places which are on the opposite sides of the Earth when connected by a straight line passing through the centre of the Earth. The term is also loosely used by Europeans to refer to Australasia.

antipope In the Roman Catholic Church, a claimant to the office

Antigua and Barbuda

☐ International Airport

[anteega, bah(r)**byoo**da]

Local name Antigua and Barbuda

Timezone GMT -4

Area 442 km²/171 sq mi; (Antigua: 280 km²/108 sq mi; Barbuda: 161 km²/62 sq mi; Redonda: 1 km²/0·4 sq mi)

Population total (2002e) 76 400

Status Independent republic within the Commonwealth

Date of independence 1981

Capital St John's (on Antigua)

Language English (official)

Ethnic groups African descent (92%), Portuguese, Lebanese, British (4%)

Religions Anglican (80%), Roman Catholic (10%)

Physical features Group of three islands in the Leeward group of the Lesser Antilles, E Caribbean; W part of Antigua rises to 470 m/1542 ft at Boggy Peak. Barbuda is a flat coral island reaching only 44 m/144 ft at its highest point, with a large lagoon on its W side; Redonda is an uninhabited, volcanic island, rising to 305 m/1000 ft at its highest point.

Climate Tropical; temperatures range from 24°C (Jan) to 27°C (Aug–Sep); mean annual rainfall 1000 mm/40 in.

Currency 1 East Caribbean Dollar (XCD) = 100 cents

Economy Tourism; sugar (40% of national income, marked decline in 1960s, now recovering); cotton.

GDP (2002e) $750 mn, per capita $11 000

Human Development Index (2002) 0·800

History Antigua claimed for Spain by Columbus, 1493; colonized by British, 1632; ceded to Britain, 1667; Barbuda colonized from Antigua, 1661; administered as part of the Leeward Is Federation, 1871–1956; associated state of the UK, 1967; independence achieved, 1981; legislative power is vested in a bicameral parliament; Governor-General appoints the Prime Minister and Cabinet.

Head of State
(British monarch represented by Governor-General)
1981–93 Sir Wilfred E Jacobs
1993– Sir James Carlisle

Head of Government
1981–94 Vere Cornwall Bird
1994–2004 Lester Bird
2004– Baldwin Spencer

---

of pope in opposition to one regularly and canonically appointed. Antipopes featured prominently in the period of Great Schism in the Western Church (1378–1417).

antiproton The antiparticle partner of the proton; symbol $\bar{p}$. Spin and mass are as for the proton, but the charge is −1. Discovered in 1955, antiprotons are created in particle accelerators by the collisions of protons with nuclei.

antirrhinum *snapdragon*

antiseptic A substance which kills or prevents the growth of micro-organisms (germs). Lister introduced the practice of antiseptic surgery (using phenol) in 1865. Commonly used antiseptics include alcohols, phenols, salts of heavy metals, and chlorine- and iodine-releasing compounds.

Antisthenes [antis**theneez**] (c.445–c.365 BC) Greek philosopher, considered to be the co-founder, with his pupil Diogenes, of the Cynic school. Only fragments of his many works survive.

antlers Bone outgrowths from the head of true deer; only on males, except in reindeer; *water deer* the only species without antlers; used in display, defence, and competition for mates; shed each year (unlike the 'horns' of other ruminants), and grow larger the following year; also known as **deer-horn**.

Antlia [**antleea**] (Lat 'air pump') A small S hemisphere constellation.

antlion The larva of a nocturnal, damselfly-like insect with a long abdomen and lightly patterned wings. (Order: Neuroptera. Family: Myrmeliontidae, c.600 species.)

Antofagasta [antofagasta] 23°38S 70°24W, pop (2000e) 249 100. Port city in N Chile; developed with 19th-c mineral and agricultural trade; airport; railway; two universities.

Antonine Wall [antoniyn] A defensive barrier built by the Roman Emperor, Antoninus Pius, in AD 142, at the N end of the British province. It ran from the Forth estuary to the Clyde.

Antonioni, Michelangelo [antoni**ohnee**] (1912–) Film director, born in Ferrara, Italy. He gained an international reputation with *L'avventura* (1959, The Adventure). Later films include *Blow-up* (1966) and *Zabriskie Point* (1969). He lost the power of speech after a stroke in 1985, but managed to make a further film, *Beyond the Clouds* (1995). He received an Academy lifetime achievement award in 1995.

Antonius, Marcus [antohnius] or **Mark Antony** (c.83–30 BC) Roman statesman and soldier. After Caesar's assassination, his speeches caused the flight of the conspirators from Rome, and left him with almost absolute power. He formed a triumvirate with Octavian and Lepidus to share the Roman world among themselves. While re-organizing the E provinces, Antony met and was captivated by Queen Cleopatra, whom he followed to Egypt (41 BC). On his return to Italy in 40 BC a new division of the Roman world was made at Brundisium, with Antony taking the East. His renewed liaison with Cleopatra provided Octavian with reasons to arouse the Roman people against him. Defeat at Actium (31 BC) followed, and Antony and Cleopatra both committed suicide.

Antony or **Anthony, St**, known as **Antony the Great**, also called **Antony of Egypt** (c.251–356) Religious hermit, one of the founders of Christian monasticism, born in Coma, Upper Egypt. Having sold his possessions for the poor, he spent 20 years in the desert, where he withstood a famous series of temptations, often represented in later art. In 305 he left his retreat and founded a monastery near Memphis and Arsinoë. In c.355, although over 100, he made a journey to Alexandria to dispute with the Arians, but retired soon after to his desert home. Feast day 17 January.

Antony or **Anthony of Padua, St** (1195–1231) Friar, born in Lisbon, who became one of the most active propagators of the Franciscan order. Canonized in 1232, he is the patron saint of Portugal, the lower animals, and lost property. Feast day 13 June.

antonym *synonym*

Antrim, Ir **Aontroim** pop (2000e) 714 100; area 2831 km²/ 1093 sq mi. County in NE Northern Ireland; rises N and E to the Antrim Mts; county town, Belfast; Giant's Causeway on N coast.

Antwerp, Flemish **Antwerpen**, French **Anvers** 51°13N 4°25E, pop (2000e) 476 400. City in N Belgium; on the right bank of the R Scheldt, 88 km/55 mi from the North Sea; chief port of Belgium and fourth largest port in the world; chartered, 1291; centre of the mediaeval cloth trade with England; airport; railway; colonial university (1920); cathedral (1352); major international centre of diamond trade; home of Rubens and van Dyck.

Anubis [anyoobis] An Egyptian god associated with death. He has the head of a jackal or wild dog of the desert.

Anura or **Anoura** [anoora] An order of amphibians comprising the frogs and toads (3500 species); adults with no tail; move by thrusting backwards with long hind legs; larvae called *tadpoles*; also known as **Salientia**.

Anuradhapura [anarahdapoora] 8°20N 80°25E, pop (2000e) 45 000. City in Sri Lanka; Sri Lanka's first capital; founded, 4th-c BC; Sri Mahabodhi Tree, all that remains of the Bo tree beneath which Buddha found Enlightenment, a world heritage site.

anus The terminal part of the gastro-intestinal tract, opening into the natal cleft between the buttocks; the lower limit of the anal canal. It is guarded by internal and external sphincters under autonomic and voluntary control respectively.

Anvers [ãvayr] *Antwerp*

ANZAC [anzak] An acronym of **Australia and New Zealand Army Corps**, a unit in which troops from both countries fought during World War 1 in the Middle East and on the Western Front. **Anzac Day** (25 Apr) commemorates the Gallipoli landing in 1915.

aorta [ayaw(r)ta] The largest blood vessel in the body, which conveys oxygenated blood from the left ventricle of the heart to the rest of the body. The thoracic branches supply the chest wall, and the abdominal branches supply the contents of the abdomen.

Aosta [ahosta], Fr **Aoste** 45°43N 7°19E, pop (2000e) 37 600. Town in NW Italy; largely French-speaking; railway; cathedral; old town surrounded by Roman walls.

aoudad [owdad] Wild sheep from the dry mountains of N Africa (introduced into SW USA); sandy colour, with long fringe along throat; curved horns up to 760 mm/30 in long; also known as **Barbary sheep**, **maned sheep**, **udad**, **arui**, or **fechstal**. (*Ammotragus lervia*.)

Aozou Strip [owzoo] A 100 km/60 mi-wide strip of mountainous desert in N Chad, NC Africa; area 114 000 km²/44 000 sq mi; disputed territory on the frontier with Libya, which occupied the area in 1973; returned to Chad by Libya, 1994; area rich in uranium and mineral deposits.

Apache [apahchee] American Indians who dominated much of the SW during the 19th-c. From 1861 they fought against Federal troops in the Apache and Navajo wars, eventually surrendering in 1886. Population c.57 000 (2000 census).

Apaloochy *Appaloosa*

apartheid (Afrikaans 'apartness') The former policy of separate racial development in the Republic of South Africa, supported traditionally by the Nationalist Party. Under the policy, different races were given different rights. In practice the system was one of white supremacy, blacks having no representation in the central state parliament. Many of the provisions of apartheid regarding labour, land segregation (*reserves, Homelands, Bantustans*), municipal segregation, social and educational separation, and a virtually exclusive white franchise were in place before the Nationalist victory of 1948, but after that date it was erected into a complete political, social, and economic system. The whole system was backed by extensive repression. Following widespread international condemnation, a commitment to dismantle apartheid was implemented by Frederik de Klerk in 1991. A new constitutional agreement was signed by de Klerk and Nelson Mandela in November 1993 and free elections were held in April 1994.

apatite [apatiyt] A common phosphate mineral widely distributed in many igneous and metamorphic rocks. Most varieties can be represented by the formula $Ca_5(PO_4)_3(OH,F,Cl)$.

Apatosaurus [apatosawrus] A giant, semi-aquatic dinosaur that probably ate vegetation around swamps and lakes; four-legged, limbs pillar-like, hindlimbs longer than forelimbs; tail whiplike; neck very long; known from the Upper Jurassic period of Colorado; formerly known as ***Brontosaurus***. (Order: Saurischia.)

ape An anthropoid primate; comprises the **lesser apes** (*gibbons*) and **great apes** (*orang-utan, gorilla, chimpanzee*); differs from most monkeys in having no tail and in using arms to swing through trees. (Family: Pongidae, 10 species.)

APEC Acronym for **Asia-Pacific Economic Co-operation**, a common market founded in 1989 to promote multi-lateral trade in the Asia-Pacific region; member nations comprise more than 2000 million people and account for half of the world's economic production.

Apennines [apeninyz], Ital **Appennino** Mountain range extending down the Italian peninsula into Sicily; length 1400 km/ 870 mi; width 30–150 km/20–90 mi; highest point Gran Sasso d'Italia (2914 m/9560 ft).

Apgar, Virginia (1909–74) Physician and anaesthesiologist, born in Westfield, NJ. Best known for pioneering work in anaesthesia relating to childbirth, in 1952 she developed the **Apgar Score** to evaluate newborns.

aphasia A disorder of language caused by brain damage; also (especially in the UK) known as **dysphasia**. **Broca's aphasia** is a disorder of production, characterized by word-finding difficulties and telegrammatic speech. **Wernicke's aphasia** is a disorder of comprehension, characterized by fluent but largely nonsensical speech.

aphelion *periapsis*

aphid A soft-bodied bug that feeds on plant sap. About 4000 species are known, mainly from the N hemisphere, including some that are serious pests, such as blackfly and greenfly. (Order: Homoptera. Family: Aphididae.)

aphrodisiacs Drugs, named after Aphrodite, the goddess of love, which induce sexual desire and/or improve sexual performance. Over 500 substances have been advocated throughout history, notably Spanish fly (responsible for many deaths), rhino horn, and mandrake root.

Aphrodite [afrodiytee] The Greek goddess of sexual love, said to have been born from the sea-foam at Paphos in Cyprus. This indication of an Eastern origin to her cult is borne out by resemblances to the worship of Ishtar.

Apia [apia] 13°48S 171°45W, pop (2000e) 47 700. Capital town of

Samoa (formerly Western Samoa), on N coast of Upolu I, SW Pacific Ocean.

apiculture The keeping of bees in hives for honey and wax production. Bees may be also used for pollinating orchards and crops, such as oilseed rape. As a hobby, collectors (**apiarists**) keep bees both for their honey and to study their habits.

Apis [aypis, ahpis] The Egyptian bull-god, representing or incarnating the Ptah of Memphis. An actual bull was selected from the herd, black with a triangular white patch on the forehead, and kept at Memphis; after death it was mummified and placed in a special necropolis, the Serapeum.

APL Abbreviation of **A Programming Language**, a scientific computer programming language, developed in the 1960s. It is of special interest to mathematicians.

apoapsis *periapsis*

apocalypse (Gr 'revelation of the future') A literary genre which can be traced to post-Biblical Jewish and early Christian eras; it especially comprises works in highly symbolic language which claim to express divine disclosures about the heavenly spheres, the course of history, or the end of the world. The most famous example is the Book of Revelation in the New Testament.

Apocalypse of John *Revelation, Book of*

Apocrypha, New Testament [apokrifa] Christian documents, largely from the early Christian centuries, which are similar in title, form, or content to many New Testament works, being called Gospels, Acts, Epistles, or Apocalypses. They are often attributed to New Testament characters, but not widely accepted as canonical.

Apocrypha, Old Testament [apokrifa] (Gr 'hidden things') Usually, a collection of Jewish writings found in the Greek version of the Hebrew Bible (the *Septuagint*), but not found in the Hebrew Bible itself. Most of these writings were also in the Latin version of the Christian Bible approved at the Council of Trent (the *Vulgate*), so Roman Catholics tend to consider them as authoritative, and designate them as *deuterocanonical*, while Protestants and most others attribute less authority to them, referring to them as **Apocrypha**. Modern studies prefer to limit the Apocrypha to 13 writings found in most Septuagint manuscripts, and to exclude additional works found only in the Vulgate, which are then assigned to a much larger body of writings called the Old Testament **Pseudepigrapha**. The Apocrypha would thus include: 1 Esdras, Tobit, Judith, Additions to the Book of Esther, Wisdom of Solomon, Ecclesiasticus (or Sirach), 1 Baruch, Letter of Jeremiah, Prayer of Azariah and Song of the Three Young Men, Susanna, Bel and the Dragon (the last three being Additions to the Book of Daniel), 1 and 2 Maccabees. Roman Catholics consider all of this list to be deuterocanonical except for 1 Esdras. Most of the Apocrypha were composed in the last two centuries BC.

apogee *periapsis*

Apollinaire, Guillaume [apolinair, giyom], pseudonym of **Wilhelm Apollinaris de Kostrowitzki** (1880–1918) Poet, born in Rome. He became a leader of the Parisian movement rejecting poetic traditions in outlook, rhythm, and language. His work is expressed chiefly in *Les Alcools* (1913) and *Calligrammes* (1918).

Apollo, (Phoebus) [apoloh] In Greek mythology, the god of poetic and musical inspiration; also a destructive force, sending disease with his arrows. In historic times he was the god who spoke through the Delphic oracle. Later poetry stresses his connection with the Sun.

Apollo asteroid An asteroid whose orbit crosses that of the Earth, but whose average distance from the Sun is greater than that of the Earth (ie more than one astronomical unit, 150 million km/93 million mi).

Apollonius of Perga [apolohnius], known as **the Great Geometer** (280–210 BC) Greek mathematician, born in Perga, Anatolia. He is the author of a major work on conic sections which laid the foundations of modern teaching on the subject.

Apollo programme The first crewed mission to the Moon, undertaken by NASA at the direction of President Kennedy in response to the space leadership position established by the USSR. The first landing (20 Jul 1969) was made by the Apollo XI crew of Neil Armstrong and Edwin Aldrin in the spacecraft *Eagle*. Over 300 kg/660 lb of soil, cores, and rocks were returned by all six landed missions. Long duration seismology and space physics experiments were deployed near the landers. The three-man crew in each mission was launched inside a Command Module which stayed in lunar orbit, while the Lunar Module with two crew members descended to the surface. Following the surface activities, part of the Lunar Module was launched to rendezvous with the Command Module in orbit. The crew were recovered from an ocean landing after re-entry and parachute descent. The last flight was undertaken (Dec 1972) by the Apollo 17 crew, who stayed 75 hours on the lunar surface and travelled 34 km/21 mi in the lunar rover.

Apollo–Soyuz project [soyoos] A landmark joint space mission conducted by the USA and USSR in 1975, following an agreement signed by President Nixon and Chairman Kosygin in 1972. It demonstrated the capability for joint operations between the major space powers and, as such, the potential for on-orbit emergency rescue missions. The rendezvous (17 Jul 1975) lasted 48 hours.

apologetics (Lat *apologia* 'defence') A branch of theology which justifies Christian faith in the light of specific criticisms or charges. An early example is Justin Martyr's *Apology* (2nd-c).

apostle In its broadest sense, a missionary, envoy, or agent; more narrowly used at times in the New Testament to refer to the 12 chosen followers of Jesus (less Judas Iscariot, replaced by Matthias according to *Acts* 1) who witnessed the resurrected Jesus and were commissioned to proclaim his gospel. At times the term also included Paul and other missionaries.

Apostles' Creed A statement of Christian faith widely used in Roman Catholic and Protestant Churches, and recognized by the Orthodox Churches. In its present form, it dates from the 8th-c, but its origins go back to the 3rd-c.

apothecary In most countries, an old term for a pharmacist at a time when drugs were crude and mostly derived from plants. In England, apothecaries were general medical practitioners; the Society of Apothecaries was founded by James I in 1617. As a licensing body, the examinations it sets are subject to approval by the General Medical Council.

Appalachian Mountains [apalayshuhn, apalaychian] Mountain system in E North America extending from the Gulf of St Lawrence SW to C Alabama (2570 km/1600 mi); a series of parallel ranges separated by wide valleys; highest peak Mt Mitchell (2037 m/6683 ft), North Carolina; rich in minerals, especially coal; major barrier to westward exploration in early US history; Appalachian Trail (world's longest continuous hiking trail, 3300 km/2050 mi).

Appaloosa A breed of horse; height, 14–15 hands/1·4–1·5 m/4·7–5 ft; short tail; dark with pale spots, or pale with dark spots; also called **Apaloochy** or **Palouse**.

appeal A legal procedure whereby a superior court considers an application by a party to a case concerning the decision reached in a lower court. In criminal cases, the appeal might concern the verdict or the sentence. In civil cases, it might concern the amount of damages awarded.

appendix A blind-ended tube, also known as the **vermiform appendix**, which arises from the beginning of the large bowel on the right side of the abdomen. In humans, it is variable in length (2–20 cm/³⁄₄–8 in) and its function is unknown. It tends to become blocked in later life, and if its single blood supply is cut off, it rapidly becomes infected and inflamed (**appendicitis**) and has to be removed as soon as possible.

Appian Way [apian] The first of Rome's major trunk roads, constructed in 312 BC by Appius Claudius Caecus. It ran initially from Rome SE to Capua, and later was extended to the Adriatic coast.

apple A small deciduous tree; flowers white or pinkish, in clusters, appearing with the oval leaves; fruit a swollen, fleshy receptacle (or *pome*), containing a core, which is the real fruit. There are over 1000 varieties of eating and cooking apples, which all derive from the cultivated apple of gardens and orchards (*Malus domestica*). (Genus: *Malus*, 35 species. Family: Rosaceae.)

applet A short program, written in a language such as JAVA, which can be called from a Web document while the document is being processed by a browser. When the applet is called, it is downloaded from the Web site and run in the user's machine. The JAVA language has been designed to allow applets to operate in user's machines without presenting a threat to user security.

Appleton layer A strongly ionized region of the upper part of the ionosphere, at heights of about 200–400 km/125–250 mi, which is responsible for the reflection of short radio waves back to Earth. Discovered in 1925 by Edward Appleton (1892–1965), it is also known as the **F layer**.

Appomatox Court House [apomatoks] The site in Virginia, USA, of the surrender of the Confederate army under Robert E Lee to Union forces under Ulysses S Grant. It marked the end of the American Civil War (9 Apr 1865).

apraxia [apraksia] Difficulty in controlling voluntary movements of the limbs or vocal organs; also called **dyspraxia**. In particular, there may be an inability to control sequences of sounds or gestures.

apricot A deciduous shrub or small tree (*Prunus armeniaca*) 3–10 m/10–30 ft, native to China and C Asia, and widely cultivated; flowers white or pale pink, appearing before the broadly oval, toothed leaves; fruits globose, velvety, 4–8 cm/1½–3 in, yellow or orange; flesh tart becoming sweet; stone ridged along one edge. (Family: Rosaceae.)

April Fool A person tricked or made a fool of on 1 April (All Fools' Day or April Fools' Day). In origin this may have been the final day of the festivities celebrating the spring equinox, which began on Old New Year's Day (25 Mar until 1564).

April Theses A programme of revolutionary action drawn up by Lenin in April 1917 shortly after the February Revolution. In it he advocated the transformation of the Russian 'bourgeois-democratic' revolution into a 'proletarian-socialist' revolution under the slogan of 'All power to the Soviets'.

Apuleius, Lucius [apulayus] (2nd-c) Roman satirist, born in Madaura, Numidia, N Africa. His romance, *Metamorphoses* or *The Golden Ass*, is a satire on the vices of the age, especially those of the priesthood and of quacks.

Apus [aypus] (Lat 'bird of paradise') A rather small and inconspicuous S hemisphere constellation.

Aqaba [akaba], ancient **Aelana** 29°31N 35°00E, pop (2000e) 77 000. Seaport in SW Jordan, on the border with Israel; Jordan's only outlet to the sea; airport; railway; popular winter seaside resort.

aquaculture *mariculture*

aquamarine A variety of the mineral beryl, used as a gemstone. It is transparent, usually sea-green or bluish-green.

aquaplaning A phenomenon which can take place when a tyre is operating on a wet road, and a layer of water becomes interposed between the tyre and the road. The tyre 'planes' (loses adhesion), and steering and braking can become ineffective.

aquarium A building suitably equipped for the display of aquatic plant and animal life. In recent times open-air **dolphinariums** have become popular for the displaying of dolphins, and underwater **oceanariums** can be found in popular tourist resorts, such as Disney World in Florida.

Aquarius [akwairius] (Lat 'water bearer') A constellation of the zodiac, lying between Pisces and Capricornus. It contains the Helix Nebula, the closest planetary nebula to us.

aquavit A colourless spirit, distilled from potatoes or cereals, and usually flavoured with caraway seeds. It is a popular drink in Scandinavia.

aqueduct An artificial channel for the conveyance of water. The Romans built thousands of miles of aqueducts to bring water to their towns. Many are in the form of arch bridges, such as the Pont du Gard at Nîmes, France.

aquifer Water-bearing rock strata, commonly sandstones or chalk with high porosity and permeability. They provide much of the world's water supply, which may be exploited directly by sinking wells or pumping into a reservoir.

Aquila [akwila] (Lat 'eagle') A constellation on the celestial equator. Its brightest star is Altair, distance 5·1 parsec.

aquilegia [akwileejuh] *columbine*

Aquinas, St Thomas [akwiynas], known as **Doctor Angelicus** ('angelic doctor') (1225–74) Scholastic theologian, born near Aquino, Italy. He was the first among 13th-c metaphysicians to stress the importance of sense perception and the experimental foundation of human knowledge. His *Summa theologiae*, the first attempt at a complete theological system, remains substantially the standard authority in the Roman Catholic Church. He was canonized in 1323. Feast day 7 March.

Aquino, Cory [akeenoh], popular name of **(Maria) Corazon Aquino**, *née* **Cojuangco** (1933–) Philippines politician and president (1986–92), born in Tarlac province. In 1956 she married opposition leader Benigno Aquino, and lived in exile with him in the USA until 1983, when he returned to the Philippines and was assassinated. She took up her husband's cause, leading a non-violent 'people's power' movement which brought the overthrow of President Marcos. She did not stand for re-election in 1992.

Aquitaine [akwitayn], Fr [akeeten], ancient **Aquitania** pop (2000e) 2 924 000; area 41 308 km²/15 945 sq mi. Region of SW France; chief town, Bordeaux; noted for wines; several spas and resort towns, notably Biarritz.

Ara (Lat 'altar') A small S hemisphere constellation.

arabesque [arabesk] Flowing linear ornament, based usually on plant forms. It occurs widely throughout history, but is especially favoured by Islamic artists.

Arabia area c.2 590 000 km²/1 000 000 sq mi. Peninsula of SW Asia, divided politically into the states of Saudi Arabia, Yemen, Oman, United Arab Emirates, Bahrain, Qatar, and Kuwait; an important world source of petroleum.

Arabian camel *dromedary*

Arabian Gulf *Persian Gulf*

Arabian hound *saluki*

Arabian Sea area 3 863 000 km²/1 492 000 sq mi. NW part of the Indian Ocean; principal arms include the Gulf of Oman (NW) and the Gulf of Aden (W); trade route between Indian subcontinent, Persian Gulf states, and Mediterranean.

Arabic A language of the S Semitic group within the Afro-Asiatic family, spoken by over 150 millions as a mother-tongue. **Colloquial Arabic** exists as the vernacular varieties of the major Arabic-speaking nation-states, which are not always mutually intelligible. **Classical Arabic**, the language of the Qur'an, in its modernized version (known as Standard or Literary Arabic) provides a basis for a common written form. The language is written from right to left.

Arab–Israeli Wars Five wars (1948, 1956, 1967, 1973, 1982) fought between Israel and the Arab states over the territorial and strategic consequences of the creation of the Jewish state. In 1948, the end of the British Mandate and the declaration of Israeli statehood on 14 May led to war. By the armistice of 1949, Israel had consolidated its hold over territorial Palestine except for the West Bank and Gaza Strip. These territories, along with the Golan Heights and Egyptian Sinai Peninsula, were occupied in the Six Day War of 1967. In all, some 800 000 Palestinians were made refugees in 1948 and another 300 000 in 1967. The wars of 1956 (the Suez Crisis) and 1973 (the Yom Kippur or Ramadan War) had no territorial consequences as Israel agreed to withdraw from captured land. In 1982, Israel invaded Lebanon in its only engagement primarily with Palestinian forces, and suffered domestic and international criticism for its conduct of the war.

Arab League A League of Arab States, founded in 1945, with the aim of encouraging inter-Arab co-operation. In 2007 it had 22 member states, including the Palestine National Authority. Its existence has been under pressure since Iraq's invasion of Kuwait (1990).

Arabs A diverse group of people, united by their use of Arabic as a first language, who live primarily in Iraq, Syria, the Arabian Peninsula, the Maghreb region of N Africa, Egypt, and Mauritania. A great unifying force is Islam, the religion of 95% of all Arabs. Population c.120 million.

Arachnida [arak**nid**a] A large, diverse class of mostly terrestrial arthropods, comprising c.70 000 species; body divided into *prosoma* (fused head and thorax) and *opisthosoma* (abdomen); head lacking antennae and compound eyes; four pairs of legs present, and a pair of fangs (*chelicerae*).

arachnodactyly [araknoh**dak**tilee] *Marfan's syndrome*

Arafat, Yasser [arafat], originally **Mohammed Abd al-Ra'uf Arafat** (1929–2004) Palestinian leader, born in Egypt. He helped to found the Palestine Liberation Movement, or Fatah, in Kuwait in 1959. In 1969, Fatah gained control over the Palestine Liberation Organization, and he became the chairman of its executive committee. With the 1988 declaration of Palestinian statehood in the West Bank and Gaza Strip, he was elected president by the PLO Central Committee. While his support for Saddam Hussein in the 1990 Gulf Crisis hurt Arafat's international standing, his reputation was largely restored after the Madrid peace talks of 1991. After the Palestinian National Authority was set up in Jericho and Gaza 1993, he was named chairman. He was elected president in 1996, and headed the Legislative Council, working to establish a Palestinian state. In October 2004, he was flown from his headquarters in Ramallah to a hospital near Paris to undergo tests, and died shortly afterwards. His body was taken to Cairo for a military funeral, before burial in Ramallah. He shared the Nobel Peace Prize in 1994.

Aragón [aragon] pop (2000e) 1 194 000; area 47 669 km²/ 18 400 sq mi. Autonomous region of NE Spain; featureless upland region largely occupying the basin of the R Ebro; Pyrenees in the N; sparsely populated; former kingdom, 11th–15th-c.

Aragon, Louis [aragõ] (1897–1982) Novelist, poet and journalist, born in Paris. He was one of the most brilliant of the Surrealist group, as shown by his first novel, *Le Paysan de Paris* (1926, trans The Night-Walker).

Aral Sea [ahral], Russian **Aral'skoye More** Inland sea, E of the Caspian Sea, mainly in Kazakhstan; world's eighth largest lake, originally c.65 000 km²/25 000 sq mi, but rapidly decreasing in size; shrunk by half since 1960 and twice as saline – caused chiefly by irrigation taking too much water from its feeder rivers; originally c.420 km/260 mi long, 280 km/175 mi wide, maximum depth 70 m/230 ft; heavily polluted; ambitious plan launched in 2003 to restore to health the N part of the Aral by building a massive dam to separate the two parts into which the sea has now split.

Aramaic [aramayik] A Semitic language still spoken by small communities in the Middle East. A dialect of Aramaic was the language used by Jesus and his disciples.

Araneae [aranee-ee] *spider*

Aran Islands Group of three islands (Inishmor, Inishmaan, Inisheer) off SW coast of Galway county, W Ireland; each has an airstrip; boat service from Rossaveel.

Ararat, (Great) Mount [ararat], Turkish **(Büyük) Ağri Daği** 39°44N 44°15E. Highest peak in Turkey; height 5165 m/ 16 945 ft; said to be the landing place of Noah's Ark; **Little Ararat** (Küçük Ağri Daği) lies to the SE, rising to 3907 m/12 818 ft.

Araucanians [arawkaynianz] South American Indian group of C Chile. They presently number c.200 000, living on reservations and in towns and cities in Chile and Argentina.

araucaria [arawkairia] An evergreen conifer, native to much of the S hemisphere except Africa; branches horizontal, in whorls; leaves usually scale-like, sometimes large; timber often sold as **parana pine**. (Genus: *Araucaria*, 18 species. Family: Araucariaceae.)

Arbor Day In the USA, New Zealand, and parts of Canada and Australia, a day (whose date varies from place to place) set apart each year for planting trees and increasing public awareness of the value of trees.

arboretum [ah(r)bo**ree**tum] A botanical garden, or a section of a botanical garden, used for the display and study of trees, shrubs, and vines.

arbor vitae [ah(r)baw(r) **vee**tiy] An evergreen coniferous tree or shrub native to North America, China, Japan, and Formosa; leaves scaly, overlapping, in opposite pairs, cones urn-shaped with thin scales. Individual species are called **cedars** or **thujas**, qualified by country of origin or timber colour. (Genus: *Thuja*, 6 species. Family: Cupressaceae.)

Arbuthnot, John [ah(r)**buht**hnot] (1667–1735) Physician and writer, born in Inverbervie, Aberdeenshire. A close friend of many literary celebrities of his day, he was a founder member of the satirical Scriblerus Club. His works include *The History of John Bull* (1712).

Arc, Joan of *Joan of Arc, St*

Arcadia (Ancient Greece) [ah(r)**kay**dia] The mountainous area in the centre of the Peloponnese. Its inhabitants claimed to be pre-Dorian, and the oldest settlers of Hellenic stock in Greece.

Arc de Triomphe [ah(r)k duh tree**õf**] A triumphal arch commemorating Napoleon's victories, designed by Jean Chalgrin (1739–1811) and erected (1806–35) in the Place Charles de Gaulle, Paris. It is 49 m/162 ft high and 45 m/147 ft wide.

Arcesilaus [ah(r)sesi**lay**us] (c.316–c.241 BC) Greek philosopher, born in Pitane in Aeolia. He became the sixth head of the Academy founded by Plato.

Arc-et-Senans [ah(r)k ay suhnõ] 47°02N 5°46E. A royal saltworks situated N of Arbois, France; architect, Claude-Nicolas Ledoux (1736–1806); a world heritage site. The works were abandoned by the end of the 19th-c.

arch *p.46*

Archaean or **Archean eon** [ah(r)**kee**an] The earlier of the two geological eons into which the Precambrian is divided; the period of time from the formation of the Earth (c.4600 million years ago) to 2500 million years ago.

Archaebacteria [ah(r)keebak**tee**ria] A recently established kingdom comprising the methane-producing bacteria (*Methanogens*). They possibly represent the oldest known life forms, existing more than 3 thousand million years ago.

archaeology / archeology The study of past peoples and societies through the systematic analysis of their material remains. The emphasis is on the study of human development over the period of more than 2 million years in which written records were non-existent (*prehistory*) or at best rudimentary (*protohistory*), and on the recovery of new data through excavation, field survey, laboratory study, and computer analysis. It now

arch

Part of a building, or a structure in its own right, made up of wedge-shaped stones or other pieces over an opening, which support both each other and any weight above. All classical and Norman arches are semicircular; other styles use a variety of shapes, including the elliptical, horseshoe, lancet, ogee, pointed, segmental, and Tudor. A **relieving** or **discharging** arch has no opening, being placed in a wall to direct weight away from an aperture further below.

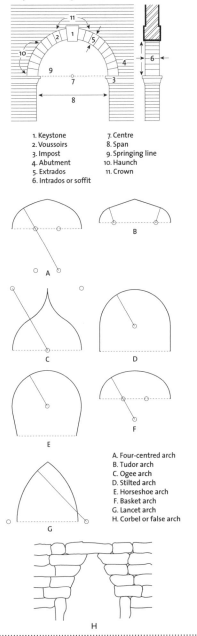

1. Keystone
2. Voussoirs
3. Impost
4. Abutment
5. Extrados
6. Intrados or soffit
7. Centre
8. Span
9. Springing line
10. Haunch
11. Crown

A. Four-centred arch
B. Tudor arch
C. Ogee arch
D. Stilted arch
E. Horseshoe arch
F. Basket arch
G. Lancet arch
H. Corbel or false arch

involves anthropology, ecology, and systematics alongside the more traditional preoccupations of history, art history, and taxonomy.

Archaeopteryx [ah(r)kiopteriks] The oldest fossil bird, known from the Jurassic period of Europe; characterized by feathers and a wishbone; long bony tail supported by vertebrae; three clawed fingers on wings; sharp teeth on both jaws. In 2004, computerized analysis of the archaeopteryx fossil in the Natural History Museum in London, UK revealed it to be a true bird capable of flight approx 147 m years ago.

Archangel, Russ **Arkhangelsk** 64°32N 40°40E, pop (2000e) 425 000. Port city in European Russia; harbour often icebound in winter; founded, 1584; airfield; railway.

archbishop A bishop appointed to have jurisdiction over other bishops; often, the head of a province. In Eastern Churches, a hierarchy of archbishops is recognized.

archdeacon A clergyman in the Anglican Church responsible for the administration of the whole or such part of a diocese as the bishop may authorize.

Archer (of Weston-Super-Mare), Jeffrey (Howard) Archer, Baron (1940–) Writer and former parliamentarian, born in Weston-Super-Mare, Somerset. He was a Conservative MP (1969–74), but resigned following bankruptcy. His books include *Not a Penny More, Not a Penny Less* (1975), *Kane and Abel* (1979), *First Among Equals* (1984), and *False Impression* (2006). He was created a life peer in 1992. In 1999 he stood as a Conservative candidate for the London mayoral election, but was forced to stand down following disclosures of malpractice relating to his successful libel action against *The Star* newspaper in 1987. He was sentenced to four years imprisonment after being found guilty of perjury and perverting the course of justice (2001), and was released on parole in 2003. Whilst still in jail he realeased *A Prison Diary* (2002), and a play based on the book premiered in 2004.

archerfish Any of the Asian marine and freshwater fishes renowned for their ability to dislodge or shoot down insect prey by spitting drops or jets of water over distances up to 3 m/10 ft; body length up to 25 cm/10 in. (Family: Toxotidae.)

archery The use of the bow and arrow, one of the first weapons used in battle. In the late 17th-c it gained popularity as a sport. The governing body, the *Fédération Internationale de Tir à l'Arc* was formed in 1931. In competition, a series of arrows is fired from 30, 50, 70, and 90 m (roughly 100–300 ft) for men, and 30, 50, 60, and 70 m (100–230 ft) for women. The circular target consists of 10 scoring zones.

Archimedes [ah(r)kimeedeez] (c.287–212 BC) Greek scientist, the most celebrated of ancient mathematicians, born in Syracuse. He proved that a body plunged in a fluid becomes lighter by an amount equal to the weight of the fluid it displaces (**Archimedes' principle**), and in popular tradition is remembered for his cry of *eureka* ('I have found it') at the moment of discovery.

Archimedes screw A device to raise water; named after the Greek mathematician Archimedes, who is said to have invented it. It consists of a broad threaded screw inside an inclined cylinder; as the screw is turned, the water is raised gradually between the threads and is run off at the top.

architecture The art or science of building. Architecture has traditionally been thought of as an aspect of higher culture, and its study has concentrated on the work of great artist-architects such as Wren and Schinkel. It now increasingly involves a variety of skills and disciplines, ranging from the technical considerations of structural engineering, environmental services, and energy conservation, to the functional considerations of room layout, interior design, and human comfort.

archives A place where historical records and other important documents are preserved; also, the materials themselves. Such institutions are also known as Public Record Offices. The first National Archives were established in France in 1789. In recent years, the term has also come to be used for the backup storage of computer data files.

ARCIC [ah(r)kik] An acronym for the **Anglican–Roman Catholic International Commission**, instituted in 1966 by Pope Paul VI and Archbishop Michael Ramsey. It produces statements on areas of substantial agreement between the two Churches.

Arctic *see panel*

Arctic Circle or **Polar Circle** An arbitrary boundary placed at 66°17N, but often defined as the area N of 70°N.

Arctic Council An organization formed in 1996 by seven countries bordering the Arctic Ocean: Canada, Denmark (for Greenland), Iceland, Norway, Sweden, Russia, and the USA, plus Finland. Based in Ottawa for the first two years, it would advise governments on issues to do with the protection and development of the Arctic's aboriginal peoples.

Arctic Ocean Body of water within the Arctic Circle; world's smallest ocean, 13 986 000 km²/5 400 000 sq mi; frozen all year except in marginal areas; hummocky icefields in winter, pack-ice during summer, carried S by surface currents; unexplored until Amundsen's flight, 1926; experiencing a period of warming; and in 2003 a 40 per cent thinning of the Ocean ice was confirmed.

Arctic tern A small tern found worldwide; migrates further than any other bird (approximately 36 000 km/22 000 mi per year); spends N summer in the Arctic, and N winter in the Antarctic. (*Sterna paradisaea*.)

Arcturus *Boötes*

Ardashir I [ah(r)dasheer] or **Artaxerxes** (c.211–41) King of Persia (224–41), destroyer of the Arsacid dynasty of Parthia, and founder of the new Persian dynasty of the Sassanids.

Arden, Elizabeth, originally **Florence Nightingale Graham** (?1878–1966) Beautician and businesswoman, born in Woodbridge, Ontario, Canada. A nurse by training, she went to New York City in 1907 and opened a beauty salon on Fifth Avenue in 1910. She produced cosmetics on a large scale, and developed a worldwide chain of salons.

Arden, John (1930–) Playwright, born in Barnsley, South Yorkshire. His plays include *The Workhouse Donkey* (1963), and *Serjeant Musgrave's Dance* (1959). He has collaborated with his wife, **Margaretta D'Arcy**, in several works, and written a number of novels, including *Jack Juggler and the Emperor's Whore* (1995).

Area of Outstanding Natural Beauty (AONB) An area in England and Wales which does not merit National Park status, but where special measures are needed to preserve its natural interest and beauty.

areca *betel-nut*

Arecibo Observatory [ariseeboh] A radio astronomy observatory in Puerto Rico, opened in 1963. A natural hollow has been lined with metal panels to create the world's largest single radio telescope, 305 m/1000 ft in diameter.

arena stage *theatre in the round*

Arendt, Hannah [arent] (1906–75) Philosopher and political theorist, born in Hanover, Germany. She moved to the USA in 1940 as a refugee from the Nazis. Her writings, which attracted a readership far beyond the academic world, include *Origins of Totalitarianism* (1951) and *The Life of the Mind* (1978).

Areopagus [arayopagus] In ancient Greece, the name for the hill in Athens which was the seat of the oldest council of state, and also for the council whose meetings took place there. The name means 'the hill of Ares' (the god of war).

Arequipa [araykeepa] 16°25S 71°32W, pop (2000e) 758 000. City in S Peru; altitude 2380 m/7808 ft; built on the site of an ancient Inca city; main commercial centre for S Peru; airfield; railway; two universities (1828, 1964); cathedral (1612, rebuilt 19th-c). The historic centre of the city is a world heritage site.

Arctic

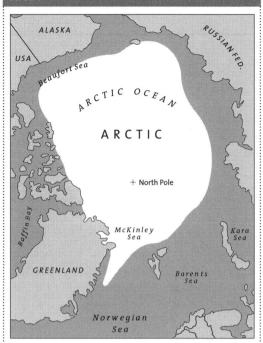

Area in the N hemisphere which lies N of the tree-line or, more loosely, to the N of the Arctic Circle; Arctic conditions of climate, vegetation, and life-forms obtain in Greenland, Svalbard, and the N parts of Canada, Russia, Alaska, and Iceland.

Ares [aireez] The Greek god of war, son of Zeus and Hera. He is often perceived as hostile, rather than as a national deity, as in other mythologies.

arête [aret] (Fr 'edge') A sharp, jagged mountain ridge separating cirques or valleys. It is formed by glacial erosion, and often further weathered by frost shattering.

Arezzo [aretsoh] 43°28N 11°53E, pop (2000e) 93 000. Town in NW Italy; on the site of an Etruscan settlement; birthplace of Petrarch; cathedral (begun 1277).

argali [ah(r)galee] A wild sheep from the margins of the Gobi Desert; the largest living sheep (1·2 m/4 ft tall at the shoulder); pale brown with white rump; large curling horns on either side of head; also known as **argalis**, **Siberian argali**, or **Marco Polo's sheep**. (*Ovis ammon*.)

Argentina *p.48*

argon Ar, element 18, boiling point −189°C. The commonest of the noble or rare gases, with no known compounds, it makes up about 1% of the Earth's atmosphere. It is used to provide inert atmospheres, especially inside incandescent light bulbs.

argonaut *paper nautilus*

Argonauts [ah(r)gonawts] In Greek mythology, the heroes who sailed in the ship *Argo* to find the Golden Fleece, under Jason's leadership.

Argos [ah(r)gohs, -gos] 37°38N 22°43E, pop (2000e) 22 500. Ancient town in Peloponnese region, S Greece, involved in wars with Sparta, 7th–4th-c BC; railway; commercial centre; many archaeological remains.

Argentina

☐ International Airport ∴ World heritage site

official name **The Argentine Republic**, Span **La República Argentina**

Local name Argentina

Timezone GMT -3

Area American continent: 2 780 092 km²/1 073 115 sq mi on Antarctic continent: 964 250 km²/372 200 sq mi

Population total (2002e) 36 446 000

Status Republic

Date of independence 1816

Capital Buenos Aires

Language Spanish (official)

Ethnic groups European origin (c.85%), mestizo European/Indian origin (15%)

Religions Roman Catholic (90%), Protestant and Jewish minorities

Physical features Divided into four regions: sub-tropical NE plains, the Pampa, Patagonia, and the Andes; the Andes stretch the entire length of Argentina (N–S), forming the boundary with Chile; highest peak, Aconcagua 6960 m/22 831 ft; uneven, semi-desert, arid steppes in the S (Patagonia); grassy, treeless Pampa to

E; N drained by the Paraguay, Paraná, and Uruguay rivers, which join in the R Plate estuary; island of Tierra del Fuego off the S tip.

Climate Moderately humid sub-tropical climate in the NE; average annual temperature 16°C; average annual rainfall 500–1000 mm/20–40 in; semi-arid in interior S lowlands; Pampa temperate, dry in W and humid in E, with temperatures ranging from tropical to moderately cool; S directly influenced by strong prevailing westerlies; serious flooding in NE (May 2003).

Currency 1 Argentinian Nuevo Peso (ARS) = 100 centavos (formerly the austral (ARA))

Economy Major contribution to economy from agricultural produce and meat processing; deposits of oil and natural gas, chiefly off the coast of Patagonia; important reserves of iron ore, coal, copper, lead, zinc, gold, silver, uranium, manganese.

GDP (2002e) $403·8 bn, per capita $10 500

Human Development Index (2002) 0·844

History Pre-colonially, nomadic Indian hunters lived in S and Inca farmers in NW; after a long battle settled in the 16th-c by the Spanish; declared independence as the federal Republic of Argentina in 1816, and United Provinces of the Río de la Plata established; dictatorship of Juan Manuel de Rosas during 1829–52; federal constitution in 1853; ranchers' oligarchy of 1916 ended by military coup in 1930; acquisition of the Gran Chaco after war with Paraguay, 1865–70; considerable European settlement since the opening up of the Pampas in the 19th-c; Juan Perón elected president (1946 and 1973); eventually succeeded by his wife Isabel (Martínez de Perón) who was deposed in 1976; attempt to control the Falkland Is (1982) failed following war with the UK; successive military governments, until federal constitution re-established in 1983; governed by a President and a bicameral National Congress, with a Chamber of Deputies and a Senate; four presidents resigned amid riots and lootings in protests over stringent economic sanctions (2001–Jan 2002).

Head of State/Government

1940–3 Ramón S Castillo
1943–4 Pedro P Ramírez
1944–6 Edelmiro J Farrell
1946–55 Juan Domingo Perón
1955–8 Eduardo Lonardi
1958–62 Arturo Frondizi
1962–3 José María Guido
1963–6 Arturo Illia
1966–70 Juan Carlos Onganía
1970–1 Roberto Marcelo Levingston
1971–3 Alejandro Agustín Lanusse
1973 Héctor J Cámpora
1973–4 Juan Domingo Perón
1974–6 María Estela (Isabelita) Martínez de Perón
1976–81 *Military junta* (Jorge Rafaél Videla)
1981 *Military junta* (Roberto Eduardo Viola)
1981–2 *Military junta* (Leopoldo Fortunato Galtieri)
1982–3 Reynaldo Bignone
1983–8 Raúl Alfonsín Foulkes
1988–99 Carlos Saúl Menem
1999–2001 Fernando de la Rua
2001 Ramon Puerta *Interim*
2001 Adolfo Rodriquez Saa *Interim*
2001 Eduardo Camano *Interim*
2002–3 Eduardo Duhalde
2003– Néstor Kirchner

Argus [ah(r)gus] In Greek mythology, **1** A watchman with a hundred eyes, appointed by Hera to watch over Io; after Argus was killed by Hermes, the eyes were placed in the tail of the peacock. **2** The name of Odysseus's dog.

Århus or **Aarhus** [aw(r)hoos] 56°08N 10°11E, pop (2000e) 271 300. Capital city in E Jutland, Denmark; cultural and educational centre; railway; university (1928); cathedral (1201).

aria A song with an Italian text, especially one which forms part of a larger work, such as an opera, oratorio, or cantata.

Ariadne [ariadnee] In Greek mythology, the daughter of the King of Crete (Minos). She enabled Theseus to escape from the labyrinth by giving him a ball of thread. She eventually became the wife of Dionysus.

Ariane launch vehicle [areean] A family of launch vehicles developed as a result of a 1973 agreement among member states of the European Space Agency (ESA). The first launch of Ariane 1 was in December 1979 from the Kourou launch site in French Guiana, and led to operational readiness in 1981. The latest version, Ariane 5, was qualified for operational use in October 1998 after an unsuccessful maiden flight in June 1996. An enhanced version of Ariane 5 veered off course on its inaugural flight (2002), and was blown up by remote control. Later flights were successful.

Arianism *Arius*

Arica [areeka] 18°28S 70°18W, pop (2000e) 219 400. Port city in Chile, on the Pacific coast; most northerly city in Chile; acquired from Peru, 1883; airport; railway; cathedral; major trading outlet for Bolivia.

Ariel [aireeuhl] The fourth-largest satellite of Uranus: distance from the planet 191 000 km/119 000 mi; diameter 1160 km/720 mi. It was discovered in 1851 by British amateur astronomer William Lassell (1799–1880).

Aries [aireez] (Lat 'ram') A constellation in the N sky; brightest star, Hamal. It is a spring sign of the zodiac, lying between Pisces and Taurus.

Ariosto, Ludovico [ariostoh] (1474–1533) Poet, born in Reggio nell'Emilia, Italy. His greatest work was *Orlando furioso* (1516), the Roland epic that forms a continuation of Boiardo's *Orlando innamorato*.

Aristarchus of Samos [aristah(r)kos], also spelled **Aristarchos** (c.310–230 BC) Alexandrian astronomer who proved by observation that the Sun is much further from the Earth than the Moon. He also maintained that the Sun is the centre of the planetary system.

Aristippus [aristipus] (4th-c BC) Greek philosopher, born in Cyrene, a pupil of Socrates. He was founder of the Cyrenaic school of hedonism, which argued that pleasure was the highest good.

Aristophanes [aristofaneez] (c.448–c.388 BC) Greek playwright. He is said to have written 54 plays, but only 11 are extant. His most sharply satirical works belong to his early period (up to c.425 BC): *The Acharnians*, *The Knights*, *The Clouds*, *The Wasps*, and *Peace*. In later years he wrote *The Birds*, *Lysistrata*, *Thesmophoriazusae*, *Frogs*, *The Ecclesiazusae*, and *The Plutus*.

Aristotle [aristotl] (384–322 BC) Greek philosopher, scientist, and physician, born in Stagira, Macedonia. At 18 he went to Athens, where he became associated with Plato's Academy for 20 years. He was for a while tutor to the young Alexander the Great. In 335 BC, he opened a school (the Lyceum). His followers were called 'Peripatetics', perhaps from his practice of walking up and down in the garden during his lectures. He wrote the first systematic treatises on logic; made major contributions to the study of natural change, psychology, and biology; and wrote some of the most influential philosophical works in the history of thought (*Metaphysics*, *Nicomachean Ethics*, *Politics*, *Rhetoric*, *Poetics*). In the Middle Ages, he was referred to simply as 'the Philosopher'.

arithmetic The practical skill of calculating with numbers, in contrast to number theory. The four operations of addition, subtraction, multiplication, and division are defined over the set of all real numbers, and used essentially for practical results.

arithmetic average / **mean** *mean*

arithmetic sequence A sequence in which the difference between any one term and the next is constant; sometimes called an **arithmetic progression**. The term **arithmetic series** is now usually reserved for the sum of the terms of the arithmetic sequence. Thus the terms 1,4,7,10 form an arithmetic sequence; 1+4+7+10 is an arithmetic series.

Arius [ahrius] (Gr *Areios*) (c.250–336) Founder of **Arianism**, born in Libya. He claimed (c.319) that, in the doctrine of the Trinity, the Son was not co-equal or co-eternal with the Father, but only the first and highest of all finite beings, created out of nothing by an act of God's free will. He was excommunicated in 321. The Council of Nicaea (Nice) in 325 defined the absolute unity of the divine essence, and the equality of the three persons of the Trinity.

Arizona pop (2000e) 5 130 600; area 295 249 km²/114 000 sq mi. State in SW USA; the 'Grand Canyon State'; Spanish exploration, 1539; part of New Spain, 1598–1821, then included in newly-independent Mexico; acquired by the USA in the Treaty of Guadalupe Hidalgo, 1848 and the Gadsden Purchase, 1853; a separate territory, 1863; joined the Union as the 48th state, 1912; bounded S by Mexico; highest point Humphreys Peak (3862 m/12 670 ft); to the S are desert basins interspersed with bare mountain peaks, then relatively low, desert plains; capital, Phoenix; cattle on irrigated land; produces two-thirds of the nation's copper supply; tourism the most important industry (Grand Canyon, Petrified Forest, meteor craters); largest Indian population in the USA.

Arjan Dev, known as **Guru Arjan Dev** (1581–1606) Sikh leader, the compiler of the Adi Granth in 1604, born in Goindwal, Punjab, India. The text used today is an expanded version of his original compilation and is revered by all Sikhs. He began the construction of the Harimandir, or Golden Temple, at Amritsar, and extended the social reforms and missionary work begun by earlier gurus. After the Mughal emperor Akbar died, his successor, Jahangir, began to oppress the Sikhs and ordered Guru Arjan to eliminate all sections of the Adi Granth that offended Hindus or Muslims. He refused and was tortured to death.

ark *Ark of the Covenant*; *Noah*

Arkansas [ah(r)kansaw] pop (2000e) 2 673 400; area 137 749 km²/53 187 sq mi. State in SC USA; the 'Land of Opportunity'; the first white settlement established by the French as part of French Louisiana, 1686; ceded to the US as part of the Louisiana Purchase, 1803; included in the Territory of Missouri, 1812; became a separate territory, 1819; joined the Union as the 25th state, 1836; seceded, 1861; re-admitted, 1868; highest point, Mt Magazine (860 m/2821 ft); the mountainous region is bisected by the Arkansas R valley; extensive plains in the S and E; over half the state covered by commercial forest; many lakes; capital, Little Rock; nation's leading producer of rice and a major tourist area; resistance to school desegregation made Little Rock a focus of world attention in 1957.

Ark of the Covenant A portable wooden chest overlaid with gold and having a cherub with extended wings mounted at each end of the golden lid. It had many successive functions – containing the two tablets of the Decalogue, serving as a symbol of the divine presence guiding Israel, and acting as a safeguard in war. It was constructed under Moses, and housed in the Temple under Solomon, but is now lost.

Arkwright, Sir Richard (1732–92) Inventor of mechanical cotton-spinning, born in Preston, Lancashire. In 1768 he set up his celebrated spinning-frame in Preston – the first machine that could produce cotton thread of sufficient strength to be used as warp.

Arles [ah(r)l] or **Arles-sur-Rhône** 43°41N 4°38E, pop (2000e) 55 000. Old town in SE France; capital of Gaul, 4th-c; formerly capital of Provence; railway; cathedral (11th-c); Roman remains, including a huge arena and theatre (a world heritage site).

Arlington pop (2000e) 189 500; area 68 km²/26 sq mi. County of Virginia, USA, a suburb of Washington, DC; site of the **Arlington National Cemetery** (1920); Pentagon Building; Washington National Airport.

Arlington, Henry Bennet, 1st Earl of (1618–85) English statesman, born in Arlington, Greater London. A member of the Cabal ministry under Charles II, and secretary of state (1662–74), he was created Earl of Arlington in 1672.

Arlott, (Leslie Thomas) John (1914–91) Writer, journalist, and broadcaster, born in Basingstoke, Hampshire. As a BBC cricket commentator on radio and television he became one of the country's most recognizable broadcasting voices.

arm A term commonly used to denote the whole of the upper limb; more precisely, in anatomy, the region between the shoulder and elbow joints, distinguished from the *forearm* (between the elbow and wrist joints), and the *hand* (beyond the wrist joint). The bones are the *humerus* in the arm, the *radius* (on the outside) and *ulna* (on the inside) in the forearm, the *carpals* in the wrist region, and the *Metacarpals* and *phalanges* in the hand.

armadillo [ah(r)madiloh] A nocturnal mammal (an edentate), found from South America to S USA; long snout and tubular ears; head and body covered with bony plates; large front claws for digging; eats ants, termites, and other small animals. (Family: Dasypodidae, 20 species.)

Armageddon [ah(r)magedn] A place mentioned in the New Testament (*Rev* 16.16) as the site of the final cosmic battle between the forces of good and evil in the last days.

Armagh (city) [ah(r)mah] 54°21N 6°39W, pop (2000e) 14 800. City in Armagh, SE Northern Ireland; seat of the kings of Ulster, 400 BC–AD 333; religious centre of Ireland in the 5th-c; Protestant and Catholic archbishoprics; city status, 1995; St Patrick's Cathedral, observatory (1791).

Armagh (county) [ah(r)mah], Ir **Ard Mhacha** pop (2000e) 132 300; area 1254 km²/484 sq mi. County in SE Northern Ireland; bounded S and SW by the Republic of Ireland; rises to 577 m/1893 ft at Slieve Gullion; county town, Armagh.

Armani, Giorgio [ah(r)mahnee] (1934–) Fashion designer, born in Piacenza, Italy. He became a designer for Nino Cerruti (1930–) in 1961, then set up his own company in 1975, designing first for men, and later for women. In 2003 he became the first fashion designer to be honoured with an exhibition at London's Royal Academy.

Armenia *p.51*

Armenia (Turkey) [ah(r)meenia], ancient **Minni** Ancient kingdom largely occupying the present-day Van region of E Turkey and parts of NW Iran and the republic of Armenia; ruled by the Ottoman Turks from 1514; E territory ceded to Persia, 1620; further districts lost to Russia, 1828–9; today Turkish Armenia comprises the NE provinces of Turkey; chief towns, Kars, Erzurum, Erzincan; Armenian nationalist movement developed in the 19th-c.

Armenians A people who came from Armenia, now in NE Turkey and the republic of Armenia. Of Indo-European origin, they speak a language of that family with some Caucasian features, and are Christians. Today 4·15 million live in the republics of the former USSR, including 2·7 million in Armenia; very few still live in Turkey.

Arminius, Jacobus [ah(r)minius], Lat name of **Jakob Hermandszoon** (1560–1609) Protestant theologian, born in Oudewater, The Netherlands. He was opposed to the Calvinistic doctrine of predestination, arguing that God bestows forgiveness on all who repent and believe in Christ. **Arminianism** influenced the development of religious thought all over Europe.

Armistice Day The anniversary of the day (11 Nov 1918) on which World War 1 ended, marked by a two-minute silence at 11 o'clock, the hour when the fighting stopped; replaced after World War 2 by **Remembrance Sunday**. The US equivalent is Veterans' Day.

Armory show An art exhibition, officially entitled The International Exhibition of Modern Art, held at the 69th Regiment Armory in New York, 1913. It introduced modern art to the USA.

armoured car Typically a four-wheel-drive, light-armoured fighting vehicle with protection against small-arms fire, armed with a machine gun or small calibre cannon in a rotating turret. The first mechanical armoured cars were developed just before 1914, with the roles of reconnaissance and rear area protection.

armoured fighting vehicle (AFV) A generic term for combat vehicles such as tanks, armoured cars, armoured personnel carriers, and infantry fighting vehicles which have armour protection against hostile fire.

arms, coats of *heraldry*

Armstrong, Lance (1971–) Racing cyclist, born in Plano, TX. He gained the World Championship title in 1993 and was ranked world number 1 in 1996 when he became ill with cancer. He later made a remarkable comeback, his achievements including a record-breaking seven times winner of the Tour de France (1999–2005), after which he retired. In 1996 he established the Lance Armstrong Foundation, a charity to aid the fight against cancer.

Armstrong, Louis, nicknames **Satchmo** and **Pops** (1898/1900–71) Jazz trumpeter and singer, born in New Orleans, LA. He moved to Chicago in 1922 to join Joe (King) Oliver's band. His melodic inventiveness established the central role of the improvising soloist in jazz, especially in a series of recordings known as the 'Hot Fives' and 'Hot Sevens' (1925–8). He was also a popular singer and entertainer, in such films as *Pennies from Heaven* (1936), and *High Society* (1956).

Armstrong, Neil (Alden) (1930–) Astronaut, born in Wapakoneta, OH. In 1966 he commanded Gemini 8, and as commander of Apollo 11 in 1969 became the first man to set foot on the Moon.

Armstrong-Jones, Antony *Snowdon, 1st Earl of*

Arnauld, Antoine [ah(r)noh], known as **the Great Arnauld** (1612–94) French philosopher, lawyer, mathematician, and priest, born in Paris. A controversialist, his activities as head of the Jansenists at Port-Royal, Paris, led to his expulsion from the Sorbonne, persecution, and ultimately refuge in Belgium. He collaborated with Pascal and Pierre Nicole (1625–95) on the *Port-Royal Logic* (1662).

Arne, Thomas (Augustine) (1710–78) Composer, born in London. He wrote over 50 operas and other works, notably 'Rule, Britannia' (from *The Masque of Alfred*).

Arnhem [ah(r)nem] 52°00N 5°53E, pop (2000e) 139 000. City in E Netherlands, on the right bank of the lower Rhine; seat of the law courts and the provincial government; charter, 1233; heavily damaged in World War 2; scene of unsuccessful airborne landing of British troops (Sep 1944); railway.

Arnhem Land [ah(r)nem] The peninsular plateau in N Australia, E of Darwin; named after the Dutch ship which arrived here in 1618; chief town, Nhulunbuy; Aborigine reserve; bauxite and uranium mining.

arni *water buffalo*

Arnold, Benedict (1741–1801) American general and turncoat, born in Norwich, CT. In the War of Independence he joined the colonial forces, and in 1778 was placed in command of Philadelphia. He later conspired with John André (1751–80) to betray West Point. When André was captured, Arnold fled to the British lines, and was given a command in the royal army.

Armenia

Date of independence 1991
Capital Yerevan
Language Armenian (official)
Ethnic groups (1991) Armenian (90%), Azer (3%), Kurd (2%), Russian (2%) (ethnic conflict since 1990 makes accurate statistical analysis impossible)
Religions Christian (Armenian Church), Russian Orthodox
Physical features Mountainous region in S Transcaucasia, rising to 4090 m/13 418 ft at Mt Aragats (W); rivers include Razdan and Vorotan; largest mountain lake is the Sevan, 1401 km²/541 sq mi – the main source of irrigation system and hydroelectric power.
Climate Varies with elevation; chiefly dry and continental with considerable regional variation.
Currency 1 Dram (AMD) = 100 ioumas
Economy Large mineral resources, chiefly copper; also molybdenum, gold, silver; electrical equipment and machinery, chemicals, textiles, cognac; agriculture based on fruits, wheat, wine grapes, cotton, tobacco.
GDP (2002e) $12·13 bn, per capita $3600
Human Development Index (2002) 0·754
History Proclaimed a Soviet Socialist Republic in 1920; constituent republic of the USSR from 1936; civil war over Nagorno-Karabakh began in 1989; declaration of independence, 1990; independence recognized and joined CIS, 1991; ongoing confict with Azerbaijan over disputed enclave of Nagorno-Karabakh.
Head of State
1991–8 Levon Ter-Petrosian
1998– Robert Kocharyan
Head of Government
1992–3 Khasrov Haroutunian
1993–6 Hrand Bagratian
1996–7 Armen Sarkisyan
1997–8 Robert Kocharyan
1998–9 Armen Darpinyan
1999 Vazgen Sarkisyan
1999–2000 Aram Sarkisyan
2000–7 Andranik Markaryan
2007– Serzh Sarkisyan

□ International Airport

(republic) [ah(r)meenia], official name **Republic of Armenia**, Armenian **Hayastani Hanrapetut'yun**
Local name Hayastan
Timezone GMT +3
Area 29 800 km²/11 500 sq mi
Population total (2002e) 3 800 000
Status Republic

Arnold, Sir Malcolm (Henry) (1921–2006) Composer and conductor, born in Northampton, Northamptonshire. His compositions include nine symphonies, 18 concertos, ballets, operas, and much film music, notably *Bridge over the River Kwai* (1957, Oscar). In 2004 he was the subject of a television documentary and a new biography.

Arnold, Matthew (1822–88) Poet and critic, born in Laleham, Surrey. Apart from his many poems, he wrote several works of criticism, such as *Culture and Anarchy* (1869), and books on religious themes such as *Last Essays on Church and Religion* (1877).

Arnold, Thomas (1795–1842) Teacher and scholar, born in East Cowes, I of Wight, the headmaster of Rugby School, and father of Matthew Arnold. He became headmaster of Rugby in 1828, reforming the school system and becoming both loved and feared (as recounted in Thomas Hughes's *Tom Brown's Schooldays*).

Arnold of Brescia [breshia] (c.1100–55) Clergyman and politician, born in Brescia, Italy. His preaching against the wealth and power of the Church led to his banishment from Italy (1139). He later became involved in an insurrection against the papal government, was condemned for heresy, and hanged.

aromatherapy A popular form of complementary medicine which uses concentrated essential oils extracted from plants. The application of oil to the skin is an effective way of getting active agents to be absorbed into the bloodstream, and aromatherapy treatment is often combined with massage. Cosmetic aromatherapy is offered by many beauty salons, sometimes in conjuction with facial massage, usually using proprietary brands of preblended oils.

Arp, Jean or **Hans**(1887–1966) Sculptor, painter, and poet, born in Strasbourg, France. He was one of the founders of the Dada movement in Zürich in 1916.

arquebus [ah(r)kwebuhs] A firearm dating from the 15th-c, a development of the hand cannon, in outline a forerunner of the musket. Fired in action by a flame held to the touch-hole, the weapon was supported by a forked rest holding up the barrel at the operator's chest height.

Arrabal, Fernando [arabal] (1932–) Playwright and novelist, born in Melilla, Spanish Morocco. Writing in the tradition of the Theatre of the Absurd, he coined the term *panic theatre*, intended to disorder the senses by shock.

Arran area 430 km²/166 sq mi. Island in North Ayrshire, W Scotland; separated from W coast mainland by the Firth of Clyde; rises to 874 m/2867 ft at Goat Fell; chief centres, Brodick, Lamlash, Lochranza; a major tourist area.

Arras [aras] 50°17N 2°46E, pop (2000e) 44 600. Old frontier town in N France; formerly famous for its tapestries; railway; bishopric; town hall (16th-c), cathedral (18th-c); birthplace of Robespierre; many war cemeteries nearby.

Arrau, Claudio [arow] (1903–91) Pianist, born in Chillán, Chile. He is noted for his interpretations of the 19th-c solo repertory.

array processor A particular type of digital computer which allows arrays of numbers to be processed simultaneously. In suitable applications, this can lead to marked increases in computing speeds.

arrest The stopping and detaining by lawful authority of a person suspected of a criminal offence; referred to as **apprehension** in Scotland. Arrests are carried out mainly by the police, but a **citizen's arrest** is possible in certain circumstances. A person wrongly arrested may bring civil proceedings for false imprisonment.

arrhythmia [arithmia] A disturbance of the normal regular rhythm of the heart. There are many types – some of them harmless, and a few that are a serious threat to life.

arrow-poison frog A slender frog, native to Central and South America; often brightly coloured; inhabits woodland; skin very poisonous; also known as **poison-arrow frog**. (Family: Dendrobatidae, 116 species.)

arrowroot A type of starch obtained from the tuberous roots of several plants. The most important is probably **West Indian arrowroot** (*Maranta arundinacea*), a perennial growing to 2 m/ 6½ ft; sepals and petals in threes; native to South America, and cultivated in New World tropics for edible starch.

Arrow War *Opium Wars*

arsenic As, element 33. A grey metalloid in the nitrogen family, used in some lead alloys and in semiconductors, especially gallium arsenide (GaAs). The name is commonly applied to arsenic (III) oxide (As_2O_3), the highly poisonous white arsenic of rodent control and detective novels.

arsine [ah(r)seen] AsH_3, boiling point $-55°C$. A gaseous hydride of arsenic, formed by reducing solutions of arsenic compounds.

art Originally, 'skill' (of any kind), a meaning the word still has in many everyday contexts. Modern usage referring especially to painting, drawing, or sculpture emerged by c.1700, but the modern sense of art as a uniquely significant form of creation and of the artist as a creative genius of a special kind arose somewhat later. The related concept of **fine arts**, considered as sharing common principles and distinct from science, religion, or the practical concerns of everyday life, also emerged in the 18th-c, together with a new subject, aesthetics, the philosophy of art. By the 19th-c, art was associated with the creative production of objects for abstract contemplation, with no useful function. The definition of art became controversial again in the 20th-c. New forms, such as film, television, street theatre, pop music, and happenings, were claimed by some to be art, by others not.

Artaud, Antonin [ah(r)toh] (1896–1948) Playwright, actor, theatre director, and theorist of the Surrealist movement, born in Marseilles, France. His chief work was *Le Théâtre et son double* (1938, The Theatre and its Double).

Art Brut [ah(r) broo] A term coined by French painter Jean Dubuffet (1901–85) for the art of untrained people, especially mental patients, prisoners, and socially dispossessed persons generally.

Art Deco [ah(r)t dekoh] A term abbreviated from the Paris *Exposition Internationale des Arts Décoratifs et Industriels Modernes* ('International Exhibition of Modern Industrial and Decorative Arts'), 1925. It has come to refer to decorative arts of the 1920s and 1930s generally, and the 'modernistic' style associated with them.

Artemis [ah(r)temis] In Greek mythology, the daughter of Zeus and Leto, twin sister of Apollo, and goddess of the Moon. Being connected with hunting, she is depicted with bow and arrows.

arteriole *artery*

arteriosclerosis [ah(r)teeriohsklerohsis] An umbrella term to describe hardening and thickening of arterial walls caused by a number of pathological processes. The most important is *atheroma*, in which fats and other substances are deposited in the inner wall of the artery.

artery A vessel of the body which usually conveys blood to body tissues. Large, medium, and small arteries (**arterioles**) can be distinguished. With increasing age, arteries tend to become blocked with deposits of cholesterol-based material (*atheroma*).

artesian basin A shallow basin-shaped aquifer with impermeable rock strata above and below it, thus confining the groundwater under pressure. Sinking a well into the aquifer allows the water to rise to the surface without pumping.

art gallery *Hermitage; Louvre; Metropolitan Museum of Art; National Gallery; National Gallery of Art; National Gallery of Australia; National Portrait Gallery; Pitti Palace; Prado; Rijksmuseum; Tate Gallery; Tretyakov Gallery; Uffizi*

arthritis An inflammation of one or more joints resulting in swelling, pain, redness, local heat, and limitation of movement.

arthropod [ah(r)thropod] A member of the largest and most diverse phylum of animals (Arthropoda), characterized by jointed limbs and an external chitinous skeleton. Arthropods have segmented bodies, most segments carrying a pair of limbs variously modified for locomotion, feeding, respiration, or reproduction. Size ranges from 80 μ to 3·6 m/11¾ ft. Arthropods include the insects, arachnids, crustaceans, trilobites, centipedes, millipedes, and several minor groups.

Arthur (?6th-c) A semi-legendary king of the Britons, who is represented as uniting the British tribes against the pagan invaders (5th–6th-c AD), and as the champion of Christianity. It is very doubtful if he is a historic figure. His story passed into literature and many legends became interwoven with it, including those of the Round Table and the Holy Grail (both from the 12th–13th-c).

artichoke *globe artichoke; Jerusalem artichoke*

Articles of Confederation The organizing document of the USA from 1781 to 1788. It established a single-house Congress, with one vote for each state and with no executive, courts, or independent revenue. It was replaced by the present Constitution in 1788.

artificial insemination (AI) The instrumental introduction of seminal fluid into the vagina in order to fertilize an ovum. The semen may be that of the husband (**AIH**) or of a donor (**AID**).

artificial intelligence (AI) A term applied to the study and use of computers that can simulate some of the characteristics normally ascribed to human intelligence, such as learning, deduction, intuition, and self-correction. The subject encompasses many branches of computer science, including cybernetics, knowledge-based systems, natural language processing, pattern recognition, and robotics.

artificial respiration A procedure to maintain the movement of air into and out of the lungs when natural breathing is inadequate or has ceased. A short-term emergency method is 'mouth-to-mouth' respiration. With the head of the patient bent backwards and the nose pinched, the resuscitator takes a deep breath and expels this into the open mouth and lungs of the victim, either directly or via a mouthpiece, repeating the manoeuvre 10–15 times a minute. When more prolonged assistance is required, a mechanical ventilator supplies a predetermined volume of oxygen at given intervals, usually via a tube inserted in the trachea.

artillery The heavy ordnance of an army; in particular, its longer-range weapons, as distinct from the small arms that each individual soldier carries. Modern artillery includes guns (known as 'tube' artillery) and missiles. Rocket artillery ranges from sim-

Aruba

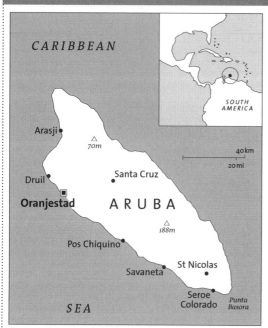

CARIBBEAN

SOUTH
AMERICA

Arasji
△
70m

40 km
20 mi

Druil
Santa Cruz

Oranjestad

A R U B A
△
188m

Pos Chiquino

St Nicolas
Savaneta

Seroe
Colorado   Punta
             Basora

SEA

□ International Airport

[arooba] Timezone GMT
Area 193 km²/74·5 sq mi
Population total (2002e) 100 000
Status Self-governing region of the Netherlands
Date of independence 1996
Capital Oranjestad

Languages Dutch (official) with Papiamento, English, and Spanish widely spoken

Ethnic groups Large majority of mixed European/Caribbean Indian descent

Religions Christian (Roman Catholic and Protestant), small Hindu, Muslim, Confucian, and Jewish minorities

Physical features Island in the Caribbean, the westernmost of the Lesser Antilles, N of Venezuela; flat, rocky terrain, dry, with little vegetation.

Climate Dry, tropical, with little seasonal temperature variation; average annual temperature 27°C; annual rainfall often falls to below 488 mm/19 in; lies just outside the Caribbean hurricane belt.

Currency 1 Aruban Guilder/Florin (AWG) = 100 cents

Economy Lack of natural resources limits agriculture and manufacturing; depends heavily on thriving tourist industry.

GDP (2002e) $1·94 bn, per capita $28 000

History Claimed by Dutch in 1634, but remained undeveloped; construction of an oil refinery brought employment and prosperity, 1929; acquired full internal self-government within kingdom of the Netherlands, 1954, as part of the Netherlands Antilles; growing resentment led to a campaign for Aruba's independence; closure of oil refinery, 1985; obtained separate status from the Netherlands Antilles with full internal autonomy in 1986; full independence in 1996; Sovereign of the Netherlands is Head of State, represented by a Governor-General, a Prime Minister, Council of Ministers and a unicameral legislature.

Head of State
(Dutch monarch represented by Governor-General)
1986–92 Felipe B Tromp
1992–2004 Olindo Koolman
2004– Fredis Refunjol

Head of Government
1986–89 Henry Eman
1989–94 Nelson Oduber
1994–2001 Henry Eman
2001– Nelson Oduber

ple, unguided bombardment missiles to medium-range, nuclear-armed battlefield missiles.

artiodactyl [ah(r)tiohdaktil] An ungulate mammal; foot with two or four toes (first always absent, second and fifth small or absent); weight carried on the third and fourth toe, which usually form a *cloven hoof*. (Order: Artiodactyla, 192 species.)

Art Nouveau [ah(r) noovoh] Literally 'new art' which flourished from c.1890 to c.1905, mainly in the decorative arts, characterized by naturalistic plant and flower motifs, and writhing patterns of sinuous, curling lines.

Arts and Crafts Movement A predominantly English movement in architecture, art ind the applied arts during the second half of the 19th-c, which advocated the renewed use of handicraft and simple decoration in reaction to industrial machinery and contemporary aesthetic eclecticism. The movement centred on William Morris.

art therapy The use of self-expression through drawing and painting as a form of treatment for emotional problems. It was introduced to England during the 1940s as a result of a collaboration between artist Adrian Hill and psychotherapist Irene Champernowne.

Aruba *see panel*

arum lily [aruhm, airuhm] A fleshy-stemmed perennial (*Zantedeschia aethiopica*) native to S Africa, and widely introduced elsewhere; leaves large, arrowhead-shaped, glossy; flower yellow and white; also called **calla lily**. (Family: Araceae.)

Arundel, Thomas [aruhndl] (1353–1414) English clergyman and statesman, who became Archbishop of York (1388) and of Canterbury (1396). He supported the nobles opposed to Richard II, who banished him (1397), but he returned to help seat Henry of Lancaster on the throne (1399).

Aryan [airian] A prehistoric people and their language, an extinct member of the Indo-European language family. Aryans reputedly colonized Iran and N India, and gave rise to the Indian subcontinent's Indo-Aryan languages.

Asante *Ashanti*

ASA rating *ISO speed rating*

asbestos The name applied to varieties of fibrous minerals of the serpentine and amphibole groups. Fibres can be separated and woven into cloths or felted into sheets. It is an excellent insulator of heat and electricity, does not burn, and is resistant to chemical attack. The varieties used in manufacture are principally *chrysotile* (white asbestos), a form of serpentine, and *crocidolite* (blue asbestos), an amphibole. Amosite (brown asbestos) has also had fairly widespread use. All forms of asbestos cause **asbestosis**, and crocidolite and amosite are carcinogenic; as a result, several countries have banned their use, either totally or partially.

Ascaris [askaris] A genus of parasitic roundworm found in vertebrate hosts, typically pigs and humans; usually present in low numbers in the small intestine. (Phylum: Nematoda.)

Ascension, Feast of In the Christian calendar, the fifth Thursday (being 40 days – *Acts* 1) after Easter. It commemorates Jesus's last appearance to his disciples, when he was 'lifted up' from them.

Ascension Island 7°56S 14°25W; pop (2000e) 1500; area 88 km²/ 34 sq mi. Small, arid, volcanic island in the S Atlantic; highest point, Green Mountain (859 m/2818 ft); discovered by the Portuguese on Ascension Day 1501; British territory, since 1815, administered under the Admiralty; made a dependency of St Helena in 1922; British and US air bases.

asceticism [asetisizm] A variety of austere practices involving the renunciation or denial of ordinary bodily and sensual gratifications. These may include fasting, meditation, a life of solitude, the renunciation of possessions, denial of sexual gratification, and, in the extreme, the mortification of the flesh.

Asch, Sholem or **Shalom** (1880–1957) Writer, born in Kutno, C Poland. He emigrated to America in 1914 and became a US citizen in 1920. His prolific output of novels and short stories, most of them originally in Yiddish, includes *The Mother* (1930), *The War Goes On* (1936), *The Nazarene* (1939), and *Moses* (1951).

Ascham, Roger [asham] (1515–68) Humanist, born in Kirby Wiske, North Yorkshire. He was tutor to Princess Elizabeth (1548–50), and later Latin secretary to Mary I. His main works were *Toxophilus* (1545), a treatise in defence of archery, and *The Scholemaster* (1570), a treatise on Classical education.

ASCII code [askee] A set of widely used binary codes, defined as the **American Standards Code for Information Interchange**. ASCII-96, an 8-bit code including a parity check bit, the most common code in use for storing text character strings in computers, allows 96 printing characters to be defined (letters, digits, arithmetic symbols, and punctuation characters) together with a number of control characters, such as printer carriage return.

Asclepios or **Asclepius** [askleepius] In Greek mythology, a hero who became a god of healing, the son of Apollo and Koronis. Because he restored Hippolytus to life, he was killed by the thunderbolt of Zeus.

Ascomycetes [askohmiyseeteez] A subdivision of the true fungi; includes cup fungi, yeasts, truffles, and many parasitic forms. (Division: Eumycota.)

ascorbic acid Vitamin C, largely found in citrus fruits, green vegetables, and potatoes. It functions in the body to maintain tissue integrity; a deficiency causes scurvy.

ASDIC [azdik] An acronym of **Allied Submarine Detection Investigation Committee** (1917), an early form of submarine detection device used on warships of the Royal Navy. Its operating principle was sonar.

asepsis [aysepsis] The absence of micro-organisms from body surfaces (eg the skin) or from wounds. In surgical operations, the procedures adopted include skin sterilization, the wearing of sterile gloves and gowns, sterilization of instruments, and the removal of contaminated air from the theatre.

asexual reproduction *reproduction*

Asgard [azgah(r)d] In Norse mythology, the home of the gods, created by Odin in the upper branches of the World-Tree, and therefore in the approximate centre of things.

ash A deciduous tree native to the N hemisphere; leaves pinnate; flowers borne in dense clusters appearing before leaves; seeds (*keys*) have a papery wing which aids in wind dispersal. (Genus: *Fraxinus*, 70 species. Family: Oleaceae.)

Ashanti or **Asante** [ashantee] A Kwa-speaking Akan people of S Ghana and adjacent areas. They form a confederacy of chiefdoms, founded in the late 17th-c. The independent Ashanti state became a major threat to British trade on the coast, until defeated (1873) by Sir Garnet Wolseley. The state was annexed by the British in 1902.

Ashbery, John (Lawrence) (1927–) Poet, born in New York City. He is recognized as the major postmodern poet of his generation,

and was given a lifetime achievement award by the Academy of American Poets in 2001. His works include *The Ice Storm* (1987), *Hotel Lautreamont* (1992), *Chinese Whispers* (2002), and *A Worldly Country: New Poems* (2007).

Ashcan School A derisive name given to a group of US Realist painters and illustrators, also called *The Eight*. Formed in 1907, they included John Sloan (1871–1951), and George Bellows (1882–1925). They painted everyday subjects in an attempt to bring art back into direct contact with ordinary life, especially street life in New York City.

Ashcroft, Dame Peggy, originally **Edith Margaret Emily Ashcroft** (1907–91) Actress, born in London. Her great roles include Juliet, in Gielgud's production (1935), Cleopatra (1935), and Hedda Gabler (1954). Her films include *A Passage to India* (1984), for which she won an Oscar as Best Supporting Actress.

Ashcroft, John (1942–) US attorney general, born in Chicago, IL. He became Missouri's state auditor (1973–4), assistant attorney general (1975–6), and attorney general (1976–84). Elected governor of Missouri for two terms (1984–92), he then entered the Senate (Republican, 1994–2000). His strongly conservative and religious background made him a controversial appointment as attorney general by George W Bush in 2001. During his office he drew up the Patriot Act which gave the FBI and other agencies increased powers relating to national security. He resigned following George W Bush's re-election in 2004.

Ashdod [ashdohd] 31°48N 34°38E, pop (2000e) 110 000. Seaport in W Israel; ancient Philistine city; modern city founded in 1956 as the major port of S Israel; railway.

Ashdown, Paddy, popular name of **Lord Jeremy John Durham Ashdown of Norton-sub-Hamdon** (1941–) British politician, born in New Delhi, India. Elected to parliament in 1983, he acted as a Liberal Party spokesman on trade and industry, and became leader (1988–99) of the newly constituted Social and Liberal Democratic Party. From 2002–6 he served as the international community's representative in Bosnia and Herzegovina with final responsibility for implementing the terms of the Dayton peace accord.

Asher, Jane (1946–) Actress and cake designer, born in London. From 1957 she performed regularly in the theatre and on television, and her films include *Alfie* (1966). Later stage work included roles in Alan Ayckbourn's plays *House* and *Garden* (2000), and for TV she appeared in the soap *Crossroads* (2003). Among her many books on baking are *Calendar of Cakes* (1989), *Jane Asher's Complete Book of Cake Decorating Ideas* (1993), and *Cakes for Fun* (2005). She is married to the cartoonist Gerald Scarfe.

Ashes, the A symbolic trophy contested by the cricket teams of England and Australia. It originated in 1882 after the *Sporting Times* printed an obituary to English cricket following the country's first defeat by Australia on home soil. An urn containing the ashes of a stump used in that match remains at Lord's cricket ground.

Ashkenazim [ashkenahzim] Jews of C and E European descent, as distinguished from Sephardim Jews, who are of Spanish or Portuguese descent. They have developed their own customs, traditions of interpretation of the Talmud, music, and language (Yiddish).

Ashkenazy, Vladimir [ashkenahzee] (1937–) Pianist and conductor, born in Nizhni Novgorod (formerly Gorky), Russia. After earning an international reputation as a concert pianist, he has turned increasingly to conducting, since 1987 directing the Royal Philharmonic Orchestra (1987–95), the Radio Symphony Orchestra, Berlin (1989–99), and the Czech Philharmonic Orchestra (1998–2003). In 2004 he was appointed music director of Tokyo's NHK Symphony Orchestra.

Ashley, Laura, *née* **Mountney** (1925–85) Fashion designer, born in Merthyr Tydfil, S Wales. In 1949, she started up a business designing and producing furnishing materials, later developing this into an international chain of boutiques selling clothes, furnishing fabrics, and wallpapers. Her work was characterized by a romantic style and the use of natural fabrics, especially cotton.

Ashmolean Museum A museum at Oxford University, England. Elias Ashmole (1617–92) donated the core of the collection to the University in 1675, and the museum was opened eight years later.

Ashmore and Cartier Islands Area c.3 km^2/1$\frac{1}{2}$ sq mi. Uninhabited Australian external territory in the Indian Ocean 320 km/ 200 mi off the NW coast of Australia; consists of the Ashmore Is (Middle, East and West) and Cartier I; formerly administered by the Northern Territory, it became a separate Commonwealth Territory in 1978.

ashram [ashram] An Indian religious community whose members lead lives of austere self-discipline and dedicated service. A well-known ashram was that of Mahatma Gandhi.

Ashton, Sir Frederick (William Mallandaine) (1906–88) British dancer and choreographer, born in Guayaquil, Ecuador. He became co-director of Sadler's Wells (later the Royal Ballet) (1952–63) and then director (1963–70).

Ashura [ashoora] A Muslim fast day observed on the 10th of Muharram, particularly among Shiite Muslims, in commemoration of the death of Husain, grandson of Mohammed.

Ashurbanipal *Assurbanipal*

Ash Wednesday The first day of Lent. The name derives from the ritual, observed in the ancient Church and continued in Roman Catholic and some Anglican Churches, of making a cross on the forehead of Christians with blessed ashes.

Asia area c.44.5 million km^2/17.2 million sq mi. The largest continent; maximum length, 8500 km/5300 mi; maximum width, 9600 km/6000 mi; chief mountain system, the Himalayas, rising to 8848 m/29 028 ft at Mt Everest; major rivers include the Yangtze (Chiangjiang), Yellow, Brahmaputra, Ayeyarwady (Irrawaddy), Indus, and Ganges. (*see map pp.56–57*)

Asia Minor *Anatolia*

Asian Games A multi-sport competition first held at New Delhi, India in 1951, and since 1954 held quadrennially. The Far Eastern Games, the predecessors of the Asian Games, were first held at Manila in 1913.

Asimov, Isaac [azimov] (1920–92) Biochemist and a master of science-fiction writing, born in Petrovichi, Russia. His family emigrated to the USA in 1923 and he was naturalized in 1928. His many novels and story collections included *I, Robot* (1950) and *The Foundation Trilogy* (1953). He was professor of biochemistry at the University of Boston, and after 1958 he worked mainly on textbooks and works of popular science.

Asmara or **Asmera** [asmera] 15°20N 38°58E, pop (2000e) 461 300. Capital of Eritrea region, Ethiopia; altitude 2350 m/7710 ft; occupied by Italians, 1889; regional capital, 1897; occupied by British, 1941; airport; university (1958); cathedral (1922), mosque (1937).

Asmoneans [azmoneeanz] *Maccabees*

Aśoka or **Ashoka** [ashohka] (3rd-c BC) King of India (c.264–238 BC), the last ruler of the Mauryan dynasty. He renounced armed conquest and became a convert to Buddhism, which subsequently spread throughout India. He advocated a policy called *dharma* (principles of right life), but after his death the Mauryan empire declined.

asp A venomous African snake (*Naja haje*) of family Elapidae; Cleopatra is said to have committed suicide by forcing this species to bite her; also known as the **Egyptian cobra**. The name is also used for venomous African **burrowing asps** (**atractaspid snakes** or **mole vipers**) of family Colubridae, and for the European *Vipera aspis* (**European asp, asp viper**, or **aspic viper**) of family Viperidae.

asparagus A perennial native to Europe and Asia; erect or spreading, some species climbers, all with feathery foliage; flowers tiny, white or yellow, bell- or star-shaped; berries green, red, or black. Young shoots of *Asparagus officinalis* are prized as a vegetable. (Genus: *Asparagus*, 300 species. Family: Liliaceae.)

Aspel, Michael (Terence) (1933–) Broadcaster and writer, born in London. He achieved public prominence as a television newsreader (1960–8), then became a freelance broadcaster, best known for his genial interviewing style in *Aspel and Company* (1984–93), and as presenter of *This is Your Life* (1988–2003) and *The Antiques Roadshow* (from 2000).

aspen A species of poplar (*Populus tremula*), also called **trembling aspen**, because the greyish-green, rounded-to-ovoid leaves have flattened stalks, allowing the blades to flutter in the slightest breeze. (Family: Salicaceae.)

Aspen Lodge *Camp David*

Aspergillus [aspenjilus] A genus of typically asexually reproducing fungus that can cause food spoilage and produce disease in humans. (Subdivision: Ascomycetes. Order: Eurotiales.)

asphalt A semi-solid bituminous residue of the evaporation of petroleum (formed by slow evaporation in nature or by distillation in industry). It is usually employed mixed with some solid mineral matter for roofing, road-making, etc.

asphodel [asfodel] The name applied to two related genera native to the Mediterranean region and Asia, with erect stems, narrow, grass-like leaves, and spikes of flowers each with six segments. *Asphodelus* (12 species) has leaves V-shaped in cross-section, flowers white or pink. *Asphodeline* (15 species) has leaves triangular in cross-section, flowers yellow. (Family: Liliaceae.)

aspidistra An evergreen perennial (*Aspidistra elatior*), native to E Asia; leaves long-stalked, elliptical, leathery, lasting several years; flowers bell-shaped, dull purple. It is much favoured as a pot-plant. (Family: Liliaceae.)

aspirin or **acetylsalicylic acid** A widely used drug effective against many types of minor pain (headache, menstruation, neuralgia), inflammation (it is frequently prescribed for rheumatoid diseases), and fever. It has more recently been discovered to prevent the formation of blood clots, and therefore to reduce the incidence of coronary and cerebral thrombosis.

Asquith, Herbert Henry Asquith, 1st Earl of Oxford (1852–1928) British Liberal statesman and prime minister (1908–16), born in Morley, West Yorkshire. He became an MP (1886), home secretary (1892–5), Chancellor of the Exchequer (1905–8), and premier. His regime was notable for the Parliament Act of 1911, suffragette troubles, the declaration of war (1914), and the Sinn Féin rebellion (1916).

ass A rare wild horse; small, long ears, short erect mane; pale grey or brown; domesticated thousands of years ago for carrying loads. The modern *donkey* (or *burro*) is a domesticated form of the African wild ass. (Genus: *Equus*. Subgenus: *Asinus*, 3 species.)

Assad, Hafez al- [asad] (1928–2000) Syrian general, statesman, and president (1971–2000), born in Qardaha, Syria. A member of the minority Alawi sect, he rose to high government office through the military and the Baath Party. He instigated a coup in 1970, became prime minister, and then president. Having long enjoyed Soviet support, he was left isolated by the end of the Cold War and the disappearance of Russian influence in the Middle East.

Assam [asam] pop (2001e) 26 638 400; area 78 523 km^2/ 30 310 sq mi. State in E India, almost completely separated from India by Bangladesh; important strategic role in World War 2; unicameral legislature; crossed by the R Brahmaputra; world's largest river island of Majuli is a pilgrimage centre; capital, Dispur; produces almost half of India's crude oil.

Assamese *Indo-Aryan languages*

assault An attack upon the person of another, causing them to fear actual injury (battery). Contact is not an essential ingredient of assault: threatening gestures can suffice.

assaying A chemical analysis which determines the amount of the principal or potent constituent of a mixture. The technique is mainly used for precious metals and for drugs.

assemblage Art objects formed by sticking together bits and pieces to make a three-dimensional whole. The term includes collages, readymades, and a variety of works made from crushed automobiles, old clothes, and other objects.

Assemblies of God A Christian pentecostalist denomination formed in the USA and Canada in the early 20th-c. It believes baptism by the Holy Spirit to be evidenced by speaking in tongues.

assembly language A set of convenient mnemonics corresponding to the machine-code instructions of a specific central processor unit or microprocessor, defined by the manufacturer. Assembly language is more convenient for the programmer than machine code, and is translated (**assembled**) into machine code by an **assembly program**, usually known as an **assembler**.

Assisi [aseezee] 43°04N 12°37E, pop (2001e) 25 500. Town in Umbria region, C Italy; famous religious and tourist centre; birthplace of Francis, Agnes, and Clare of Assisi; Basilica of St Francis (1228–53) has frescoes by Giotto and Cimabue that were damaged in earthquake of 1997; Basilica of St Clare (1257–65); Romanesque Cathedral of San Rufino (9th-c).

Assize Court A legal system in England and Wales, dating from the time of Henry II, which was abolished by the Courts Act, 1971. Assize Courts were presided over by High Court judges, who travelled on circuit to hear criminal and civil cases.

Associated Press (AP) An international news agency, with headquarters in New York City. Founded in 1848, it is the world's oldest and largest news-gathering co-operative.

associated state A former colony that has a free and voluntary arrangement with the UK as the former colonial power. The state enjoys the right of self-government, but recognizes the British sovereign as head. The concept was introduced for states (eg Antigua, Grenada) wishing to be independent, but economically unable to support themselves.

Association football *football, Association*

Association of Caribbean States An association created by 25 Caribbean basin countries in 1994, with the aim of promoting a common approach to regional economic and political issues. It included the members of the Caribbean Community and Common Market (CARICOM).

Association of South-East Asian Nations (ASEAN) An association formed in 1967 to promote economic co-operation between Indonesia, Malaysia, the Philippines, Singapore, and Thailand. Brunei joined in 1984 and Vietnam in 1995; Laos and Myanmar were formally admitted in 1997, Cambodia in 1999. In 2003 the 10 members signed a long-term plan, the Bali Concord II, to create a free-trade area by 2020.

associative operation In mathematics, the principle that the order in which successive additions are performed does not affect the result; for example $(2+3)+4 = 2+(3+4)$. Over the set of real numbers, addition and multiplication are associative; subtraction and division are not.

Assumption The claim concerning the Virgin Mary, mother of Jesus Christ, that on her death she was 'assumed' (taken up, body and soul) to heaven. This was defined by Pope Pius XII as an article of Roman Catholic faith in 1950.

assurance Chiefly in the UK, a general term for insurance related to a person's life. In exchange for recurrent or lump-sum premiums, the insurance company guarantees a fixed sum on the policy-holder's death, or at some agreed date if they survive. Such policies may be *without profits*, ie for a fixed sum, or *with* *profits*, in which case the amount received reflects the company's success in investing the premiums.

Assyria [asiria] The small area around the town of Assur on the Tigris in Upper Mesopotamia, then much later the vast empire that the rulers of Assur acquired through conquering their neighbours on all sides. At its height in the 9th-c and 8th-c BC, the empire was destroyed in 612 BC.

Astaire, Fred [astair], originally **Frederick Austerlitz** (1899–1987) Actor and dancer, born in Omaha, NE. He and his elder sister Adele (1897–1981) rose to stardom in the 1920s in *Lady be Good* and other stage shows. When Adele married, Fred continued with various partners, notably Ginger Rogers (1911–95). His many films include *Top Hat* (1935) and *Easter Parade* (1948). Later turning to straight acting, he received an Oscar nomination for *The Towering Inferno* (1974).

Astana, Kazakh 'capital', formerly **Akmola** (1995–7), **Tselinograd** (1961–95), **Akmolinsk** (to 1961) 51°10N 71°30E, pop (2000e) 300 000. Capital of Kazakhstan, on R Ishim; founded as a fortress, 1830; airport; railway junction.

Astarte [astah(r)tay] *Ishtar*

aster A member of a large group of mainly perennials from America, Eurasia, and Africa; flower-heads daisy-like, usually in clusters; outer ray florets blue, purple, pink, or white, often autumn or late-summer flowering. (Genus: *Aster*, 250 species. Family: Compositae.)

asteroids Rocky objects generally found in orbits lying between those of Mars and Jupiter, also called **minor planets**. This 'main belt' of asteroids has its inner edge c.100 million km/60 million mi outside Mars' orbit, and is c.165 million km/100 million mi wide. The orbits of c.10 000 of the larger asteroids are known. The first asteroid, Ceres (diameter 940 km/580 mi) was discovered in 1801, and has an orbital period of 4·6 years. Asteroids are believed to have originated in the formation of the Solar System, when planetesimals accreted from solar nebula. The first asteroid landing took place in February 2001, when the NEAR Shoemaker spacecraft landed on Eros (32 km/20 mi).

asthenosphere [astheenosfeer] The Earth's upper mantle. It extends from the base of the lithosphere at c.72 km/45 mi down to c.250 km/155 mi below the surface.

asthma A common condition in which there is narrowing and obstruction of the airways (bronchi and bronchioles). Narrowing results from the contraction of the bronchial muscles and inflammation of the bronchial walls. It may be an exaggerated response in hypersensitive individuals to various allergens. Common among these are pollen, house dust, and the detritus of house mites that inhabit mattresses, etc. Psychological factors and respiratory chest infection contribute in some cases. Attacks commonly consist of sudden episodes of breathlessness and wheezing which may last several hours or days. In most patients, treatment involves periodic inhalation of one or more of several available drugs which relax the airways or reduce any inflammation.

Asti 44°54N 8°13E, pop (2001e) 73 100.Town in Piedmont region, NW Italy; at the junction of Tanaro and Borbore rivers; centre of a fertile wine-producing area (Asti Spumante); bishopric; railway; Palio race (Sep).

astigmatism In vision, an actual asymmetry in the optical system of the eye, so that the eye's ability to focus horizontal and vertical lines is different. In optics, the term refers to aberrations of a lens image due to the position of an object off the lens axis.

Aston, Francis (William) (1877–1945) Physicist, born in Birmingham, West Midlands. He invented the mass spectrograph in 1919, for which he was awarded the Nobel Prize for Chemistry in 1922. The **Aston dark space** in electronic discharges is named after him.

Astor, John Jacob (1763–1848) Fur trader and financier, founder of the America Fur Company and the Astor family, born in Waldorf, Germany. In 1784 he moved to the USA, and rose to become one of the country's most powerful financiers.

Astor (of Hever), John Jacob Astor, Baron (1886–1971) Newspaper proprietor, born in New York City. He became an MP in 1922, and chairman of the Times Publishing Company after the death of Lord Northcliffe.

Astor, Nancy (Witcher) Astor, Viscountess, *née* **Langhorne** (1879–1964) British politician, born in Danville, VA. She succeeded her husband as MP for Plymouth in 1919, the first woman MP to sit in the House of Commons (1919–45), and became known for her interest in women's rights and social problems, especially temperance.

Astrakhan [astrakhahn], formerly **Khadzhi-Tarkhan** 46°22N 48°04E, pop (2000e) 508 000. City in SE European Russia; in the Volga delta, 22 m/72 ft below sea-level; protected from floods by dykes; founded, 13th-c; the most important port in the Volga–Caspian basin; airport; railway; university (1919); known for astrakhan fur.

astrobiology The multi-disciplinary study of the origin, distribution, and destiny of life in the universe. It addresses the questions of how does life begin and develop, does life exist elsewhere in the universe, and what is life's future on Earth and beyond. It is a major goal of NASA's science programmes.

astrolabe [astrolayb] An ancient instrument (c.200 BC) for showing the positions of the Sun and bright stars at any time and date. It was a forerunner of the sextant.

astrology A system of knowledge whereby human nature can be understood in terms of the heavens. It relies upon precise measurement and a body of symbolism which has come to be associated with each of the signs of the zodiac and the planets (including the Sun and Moon). It rests on the idea that the force which patterns the heavens likewise orders humanity. Today it thrives in several Eastern countries, and in the West is undergoing something of a rebirth, though the modern emphasis is on self-knowledge rather than on predicting events.

astrometry *astronomy*

astronaut The NASA term for a spacecraft crew member; originally applied to pilots, but now including scientists and payload specialists. Seventeen astronauts have lost their lives in accidents directly related to spaceflight.

Astronomer Royal An honorary title awarded to a distinguished British astronomer. Before 1972, the title was given to the director of the Royal Greenwich Observatory, England.

astronomical unit (AU) The mean distance of the Earth from the Sun, c.149·6 million km/93 million mi; a convenient measure of distance within the Solar System. There are 63 240 AU in one light year.

astronomy The study of all classes of celestial object, such as planets, stars, and galaxies, as well as interstellar and intergalactic space, and the universe as a whole. The branch of classical astronomy concerned with the precise measurement of the positions of celestial objects is known as **astrometry**. Modern astronomy began 450 years ago with Copernicus, who set the scene for the overthrow of the Hellenistic cosmology, asserting that the Sun, not the Earth, is at the centre of the Solar System. Newton described gravitational theory in the 17th-c, and thenceforth planetary astronomy became an exact science. In the 18th-c and 19th-c, techniques to build large telescopes were developed, culminating in the construction of observatories on mountain sites in the USA. Radio astronomy emerged rapidly after World War 2, and was the first of the invisible astronomies. The use of satellites above the blanket of the Earth's atmosphere enabled ultraviolet, X-ray, and infrared astronomies to be developed from the 1960s.

astrophysics The application of physical laws and theories to stars and galaxies, with the aim of deriving theoretical models to explain their behaviour. Its biggest triumph has been accounting for energy production inside stars, and there have been notable successes in explaining the properties of galaxies and quasars.

Asturias [astoorias] pop (2000e) 1 105 000; area 10 565 km²/ 4078 sq mi. Autonomous region and former principality of N Spain; largely occupied by the Cordillera Cantabrica, rising to 2646 m/8681 ft in the Picos de Europa; centre of Christian resistance to Muslim invasion, 8th–9th-c; part of Kingdom of Leon, 911; scene of unsuccessful left-wing revolution, 1934; provides nearly half of Spain's needs in coal.

Asturias, Miguel Angel [astoorias] (1899–1974) Novelist, born in Guatemala City. He is best known for his first novel, *El señor presidente* (1946, The President). Later novels include *Hombres de maíz* (1949, Men of Maize) and *Mulatta de tal* (1963, trans The Mulatta and Mr Fly). He received the Nobel Prize for Literature in 1967.

Asunción [asoonsyohn] 25°15S 57°40W, pop (2000e) 787 000. Federal capital of Paraguay; transport and commercial centre on the E bank of the R Paraguay; established, 1537; capital of La Plata region until 1580; airport; railway; two universities (1890, 1960).

Aswan [aswahn], ancient **Syene** 24°05N 32°56E, pop (2000e) 255 100. Town in S Egypt, on the E bank of the R Nile; Aswan Dam to the S (1898–1902); Aswan High Dam further S at head of L Nasser (1971); airfield; railway; winter tourism; Temple of Kalabsha (transported 55 km/34 mi from its original site and re-erected near Aswan High Dam).

Atacama Desert [atakahma], Span **Desierto de Atacama** Arid desert area in N Chile, claimed to be the world's driest area; a series of dry salt basins, extending 960 km/596 mi S from the Peru border; average altitude 600 m/2000 ft; almost no vegetation.

Atahualpa [atawalpa] (?–1533) Last Inca ruler of Peru. On his father's death (1525) he received the kingdom of Quito, and in 1532 seized Peru. He was captured by the Spaniards, and executed.

Atalanta [atalanta] In Greek mythology a heroine, nurtured by a she-bear, who grew up to be a strong huntress. She refused to marry any man who would not take part in a foot-race with her: those who lost were killed. Eventually Hippomenes (or Milanion) threw three golden apples of the Hesperides at her feet, so that her attention was diverted and she lost.

Atatürk [ataterk], originally **Mustafa Kemal** (1881–1938) Turkish army officer and president (1923–38), born in Salonika, Greece. Following a nationalist rebellion, he ruled as a dictator, and launched a social and political revolution introducing Western forms of dress, educational reform, and the replacement of Arabic script with the Latin alphabet. He transformed Turkey into a modern, secular state, abandoning the constitutional requirement that Islam be the state religion.

ataxia [ataksia] Inco-ordination of the arms or legs, arising from a failure of the central nervous system to control the movement of muscles in the limbs.

ATC (Automatic Train Control) *train protection systems*

Aten or **Aton** In Ancient Egypt, originally the name of the Sun's disc, and then that of the sun-god.

Athabascan or **Athapascan** [athabaskn] Various American Indian groups living in Alaska and NW Canada, W of Hudson Bay; also, the name of their language. Today most still live by hunting and fishing.

Athanasian Creed [athanayzhn] A statement of Christian faith, written in Latin probably in the 5th-c. It remains a historic statement of Trinitarian doctrine, still sometimes used liturgically.

Athanasius, St [athanayzius] (c.296–373) Christian leader, born in Alexandria. He led the opposition to the doctrines of Arianism, and his teaching was supported after his death at the Council of Constantinople (381). The *Athanasian Creed* (representing his beliefs) was little heard of until the 7th-c. Feast day 2 May.

atheism The denial of the existence of God or gods. It includes both the rejection of any specific belief in God or gods, and the view that the only rational approach to claims about divine existence is one of scepticism.

Athelstan or **Æthelstan** [athelstan] (c.895–939) Son of Edward the Elder, and the grandson of Alfred the Great. Acknowledged as King of Wessex and Mercia (924), he successfully invaded Northumbria, thus establishing himself as effectively the first King of all England (927).

Athene or **Athena** [atheena] The Greek goddess of wisdom. The patron of Athens, her emblem was the owl.

Athens, Gr **Athínai**, ancient **Athenae** 38°00N 23°44E, pop (2000e) Greater Athens 3 235 000. Capital city of Greece; ancient Greek city-state extending over Attica by the 7th-c BC; great economic and cultural prosperity under Pericles, 5th-c BC; taken by the Romans, 146 BC; part of the Ottoman Empire, 1456; capital of modern Greece, 1835; occupied by Germans in World War 2; two airports; railway; university (1837); port and industrial area at Piraeus; tourism; hill of the Acropolis (156 m/512 ft), with the Parthenon (5th-c BC), Propylaea (437–432 BC), Temple of Athena Niki (432–421 BC), Ionic Erechtheion (421–406 BC); location of the 2004 Summer Olympic Games.

atherosclerosis [atherohsklerohsis] The irregular deposition of fats (mainly cholesterol and triglycerides) and other substances in the inner wall of arteries; this causes narrowing of the affected blood vessel. Common sites are the aorta and blood vessels to the heart and brain, but any artery can be affected. Contributing causes include high fat (particularly saturated fat) dietary intake, high blood pressure, obesity, and lack of exercise.

Atherton, David (1944–) Conductor, born in Blackpool, Lancashire. He was founder and musical director of the London Sinfonietta (1967–73), later joining the Royal Liverpool Philharmonic Orchestra (1980–6), the BBC Symphony Orchestra (1985–9), and the Hong Kong Philharmonic Orchestra (1989–2000).

Atherton, Mike, popular name of **Michael Andrew Atherton** (1968–) Cricketer, born in Manchester, Greater Manchester. He made his debut for Lancashire in 1987, and his debut for England in 1989 against Australia. A leading batsman, he captained England in a record 51 Tests (1993–8). He retired from first-class cricket in 2001.

athlete's foot A common form of ringworm infection (*tinea pedis*) in which a fungus causes itching and fissuring of the skin of the soles of the feet and between the toes. It is usually acquired in swimming baths and from shower floors.

athletics Tests of running, jumping, throwing, and walking skills for trained athletes; also known, especially in the USA, as **track and field** events. The track events are divided into six categories: *sprint races* (100 m, 200 m, and 400 m); *Middle distance races* (800 m and 1500 m); *long distance races* (5000 m and 10 000 m); *hurdle races* (110 m – 100 m for women – and 400 m); *relay races* (4 × 100 m and 4 × 400 m); and the *steeplechase* (3000 m). In addition there is the endurance test of the *Marathon*. The field events involve jumping and throwing. *Jumping events* consist of the high jump, long jump, triple jump, and pole vault. The *throwing events* are the discus, shot put, javelin throw and hammer throw. *Walking races* take place on either the road or the track. In addition, two multi-event competitions exist in the form of the *decathlon* (10 events) for men and the *heptathlon* (7 events) for women. The governing body is the International Amateur Athletic Federation, founded in 1912.

Atkins, Robert Coleman (1930–2003) Cardiologist and business-man, born in Columbus, OH. He opened the Atkins Center for Complementary Medicine in New York City (closed Oct 2003), where he developed a dietary system based on the theory that people can lose weight by following a high-protein, high-fat diet with a significant restriction of dietary carbohydrate, published in *Dr. Atkins' Diet Revolution* (1972, revised 1992). Although the approach ran against most nutritional opinion of the time, the diet gained a huge following during the early 2000s but had faded in popularity by 2006.

Atkinson, Rowan (Sebastian) (1955–) Comic actor and writer, born in Newcastle upon Tyne, Tyne and Wear. He first appeared in Oxford University revues at the Edinburgh Festival Fringe, and in 1981 became the youngest performer to have had a one-man show in the West End. TV roles include *Not the Nine O'Clock News* (1979–82), *Blackadder* (1983–9), and *Mr Bean* (1990–4), and among his film credits are *Bean: the Ultimate Disaster Movie* (1997), *Johnny English* (2003), *Keeping Mum* (2005), and *Mr Bean's Holiday* (2007).

Atlanta 33°45N 84°23W, pop (2000e) 416 500. State capital in NW Georgia, USA; founded at the end of the railway in 1837 (named Terminus); renamed Atlanta, 1845; a Confederate supply depot in the Civil War; burned by General Sherman, 1864; capital, 1887; airport; railway; four universities (1835, 1836, 1865, 1913); professional teams, Braves (baseball), Hawks (basketball), Falcons (football).

Atlanta Campaign *Sherman, William Tecumseh*

Atlantic, Battle of the (1939–45) The conflict arising out of German attacks on shipping in the Atlantic during World War 2. The German strategy was to cut off Britain's supplies of food and munitions by submarine action. By 1943, Doenitz, commander of the Germany Navy, had 200 operational U-boats. British supplies were running out and many merchant vessels had been lost. The Allies countered with new technology, more merchant ships, increased air power, and improved intelligence, sinking 45 U-boats during April and May. Doenitz was forced to call off the battle (23 May 1943) to review tactics. As fighting continued, the Allies maintained the advantage thereby diminishing the German threat in the Atlantic for the remainder of the war. One of the longest campaigns in World War 2, between 75 000 and 85 000 Allied seamen were killed.

Atlantic Charter A declaration of common objectives by Roosevelt and Churchill after a secret meeting off Newfoundland (Aug 1941). It agreed principles which should govern post-war settlements. The Charter was endorsed by the USSR and 14 other states at war with the Axis Powers.

Atlantic City 39°21N 74°27W, pop (2000e) 40 500. Town in SE New Jersey, USA, on the Atlantic coast; railway; popular seaside resort with famed boardwalk (over 9 km/5½ mi long) and piers; many casinos; convention centre.

Atlantic Intracoastal Waterway *Intracoastal Waterway*

Atlantic Ocean Body of water extending from the Arctic to the Antarctic, separating North and South America (W) from Europe and Africa (E); area c.82 217 000 km²/31 700 000 sq mi; average depth 3700 m/12 000 ft; maximum depth, Puerto Rico Trench, 8648 m/28 372 ft; principal arms (W), Labrador Sea, Gulf of Mexico, Caribbean Sea; (E), North Sea, Baltic Sea, Mediterranean and Black Sea, Bay of Biscay, Gulf of Guinea; (S), Weddell Sea; continental shelf narrow off coast of Africa and Spain, broader in NW Europe and off Americas; 'S' shaped, submarine Mid-Atlantic Ridge between Iceland and the Antarctic Circle, centre of earthquake and volcanic activity; major surface circulation, clockwise in N, counter-clockwise in S; main currents include the Gulf Stream (N Atlantic Drift), and the N Equatorial, Canary, S Equatorial, Brazil, Benguela, and Equatorial Counter Currents.

Atlantic Wall An incomplete network of coastal fortifications, constructed in 1942–4 between the Pas-de-Calais and the Bay of Biscay as part of Hitler's plans for an impregnable 'Fortress Europe'. On D-Day its 'invincibility' was shown to be a myth.

Atlantis [atlantis] According to Plato, an island in the ocean W of Spain which disappeared into the sea. Its supposed existence has generated many speculative books and expeditions.

Atlas (astronomy) The 15th natural satellite of Saturn, discovered in 1980; distance from the planet 138 000 km/86 000 mi; diameter 40 km/25 mi.

Atlas (mythology) In Greek mythology, a Titan who was made to hold up the heavens as a punishment for taking part in the revolt against the Olympians. When books of maps came to be published, he was often portrayed as a frontispiece, hence the name 'atlas'.

Atlas Mountains A system of folded mountain chains in Morocco, Algeria, and Tunisia, NW Africa. Largest in the group is the **Haut Atlas** range, running SW–NE for 650 km/400 mi from Morocco's Atlantic coast, rising to Mt Toubkal (4165 m/13 665 ft).

atman [ahtman] (Sanskrit, 'soul' or 'self') In Hinduism, the human soul or essential self. It is seen as being one with the absolute, and identified with Brahman.

atmosphere *p.61*

atmospheric pressure The pressure exerted by the atmosphere on the Earth's surface. The average pressure at sea level is 1013·25 mb (millibars), 101 325 Pa (pascals), or 760 torr, and is taken as the standard *atmosphere*. Pressure is measured using a barometer.

atoll A roughly circular structure of coral reefs enclosing a lagoon. Atolls occur in warm, clear, tropical oceanic waters where corals and coralline algae can flourish. Darwin first theorized that they are the final stage in a progression of reef formations. In the first stage, a *fringing reef* grows adjacent to land with little or no lagoon separating it from the shore. The second stage, a *barrier reef*, lies offshore with a lagoon separating it from the land. An *atoll* is the third and most mature stage, where the original land is no longer present.

atom The smallest portion of a chemical element. Each atom comprises a positively charged nucleus surrounded by negatively charged electrons, whose number equals that of the protons contained within the nucleus. Electrons are attracted to the nucleus by electromagnetic force. They determine the chemistry of an atom, and are responsible for binding atoms together.

atomic bomb A nuclear explosive device (the **A-Bomb**) which achieves its destructive effects through energy released during the fission of heavy atoms (as in uranium-235 or plutonium-239). The first atomic bombs were used to destroy the Japanese cities of Hiroshima and Nagasaki (Aug 1945). Atomic weapons have been supplanted by thermonuclear weapons, but a fission weapon trigger is an essential component of these devices.

atomic clock *clock*

atomic mass unit (amu) Unit of mass; symbol *u*; defined as 1/12 of the mass of the carbon-12 atom; value $1u = 1.66 \times 10^{-27}$ kg; used to express relative atomic masses of atoms; sometimes called a **dalton**.

atomic number *proton number*

atomic spectra A set of specific frequencies of electromagnetic radiation, typically light, emitted or absorbed by atoms of a certain type. A given spectral line corresponds to the transition of an electron between two specific energy levels. The study of spectra is called **spectroscopy**, a major analytic technique in physics and chemistry.

atomic weight *relative atomic mass*

atom laser A device which creates a beam of atoms having properties akin to those of the light beam from a laser. In particular,

atmosphere

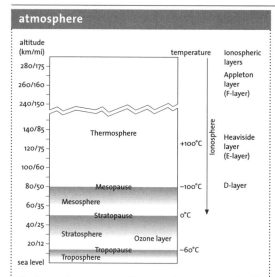

The layer of gas surrounding any planet or star. Earth's atmosphere is composed of air, which on average is made up of 78% nitrogen, 21% oxygen, and 1% argon, with traces of other rare gases, carbon dioxide, and hydrogen. Moist air may contain up to 31% water vapour. Earth's atmosphere is divided into several concentric shells, the lowest being the *troposphere*, followed by the *stratosphere*, *mesosphere*, and *thermosphere*. The outer shell of the atmosphere, at c.400 km/250 mi, from which light gases can escape, is termed the *exosphere*. The atmosphere contains the gases vital to life, and shields the Earth from harmful ionizing radiation.

the waves associated with the atoms are coherent, or in step, and the beam of an atom laser is much brighter than that of an ordinary (incoherent) atomic beam. An atom laser which created pulses of atoms was first demonstrated in 1997 by Wolfgang Ketterle's team at the Massachusetts Institute of Technology. Continuous atom laser beams were first produced by Theodor Hänsch and his team in Munich, Germany, in 1999.

atom optics The manipulation of beams of neutral atoms, in a way that parallels the manipulation of light in conventional optical systems, using atom optical equivalents of mirrors, lenses, beam splitters, and other elements. Atom optics can be used to fabricate microstructures directly via atom lithography, as an atom microscope, and as the basis for high-precision gyroscopic and gravitational measurements.

atonality The property of music which is not written in a key. The term is most commonly applied to music written in the post-tonal but pre-serial style of Schoenberg's *Ewartung* (1909) and other compositions of that period.

atonement [atohnmnt] In Christian theology, the process whereby sinners are made 'at one' with God, through the life, death, and resurrection of Jesus Christ.

Atonement, Day of *Yom Kippur*

ATP (Automatic Train Protection) *train protection systems*

atractaspid snake *asp*

atrium [aytrium] (plural **atria**) The entrance hall or open inner court of a Roman house; in mediaeval architecture, an open court in front of a church; generally, any cavity or entrance in a building. Atria became particularly fashionable in late-20th-c hotels and office blocks.

atropine [atropeen, atropin] A drug extracted from deadly night-

shade (*Atropa belladonna*), used as a poison during the Roman Empire and later. Safer derivatives are now used in a wide variety of disorders, commonly in motion-sickness preparations and in ophthalmology, to dilate the pupil during eye examinations.

Atropos [atropos] *Moerae*

attar A fragrant essential oil distilled from plants; also called **otto**. The best known is attar of roses, obtained from the petals of the damask rose (*Rosa damascena*), cultivated in the Balkans.

Attenborough, Sir David (Frederick) [atenbruh] (1926–) Naturalist and broadcaster, born in London, the brother of Richard Attenborough. He joined the BBC in 1952 as a trainee producer. The series *Zoo Quest* (1954–64) allowed him to undertake expeditions to remote parts of the globe to record wildlife in its natural habitat. He was the controller of BBC 2 (1965–8) and director of programmes (1969–72) before returning to documentary-making with such series as *Life on Earth* (1979), *The Private Life of Plants* (1995), *Life of Mammals* (2002), and *Planet Earth* (2006, 2 series).

Attenborough, Sir Richard (Samuel), Baron [atenbruh] (1923–) Film actor, producer, and director, born in Cambridge, Cambridgeshire, the brother of David Attenborough. His characterization of the vicious young hooligan in *Brighton Rock* (1947) led to many varied parts. He was actor/producer of several features in the 1960s, and became a director in 1969 with *O What a Lovely War!*, followed by such major epics as *Gandhi* (1982, eight Oscars), and *Cry Freedom* (1987). He later appeared in *In Love and War* (1996) and *Elizabeth* (1998). In 1999 he received a BAFTA Lifetime Achievement Award for his contribution to film.

attention A phenomenon where the processing capacity of the brain is directed towards a particular type of incoming, competing information. **Attention deficit (hyperactivity) disorder**, or **ADD**, includes a range of behaviour disorders, especially in children, with such symptoms as poor concentration, hyperactivity, and learning difficulties.

Attica [atika] The SE promontory of C Greece, and the most easterly part of the Greek mainland. In Classical Greece, it was the territory which made up the city-state of Athens.

Attila [atila], known as **the Scourge of God** (c.406–53) Hunnish King (434–53), whose dominion extended from the Rhine to the frontiers of China. He defeated the Emperor Theodosius, and in 451 invaded Gaul, but was defeated on the Catalaunian Plains by a joint army of Romans and Visigoths.

Attlee, Clem, popular name of **Clement Richard Attlee, 1st Earl Attlee** (1883–1967) British statesman and prime minister (1945–51), born in London. He was dominions secretary (1942–3) and deputy prime minister (1942–5) in Churchill's War Cabinet. As prime minister, he carried through a vigorous programme of nationalization, and introduced the National Health Service.

attorney A person who has power to act for another; **power of attorney** refers to the authority so given. The term is also used in some jurisdictions as a general label for lawyers.

attorney general The chief legal officer of a number of nations or states, who represents the government in its legal actions. In England and Wales, the attorney general is a member of the House of Commons and of the government. In the USA, the federal attorney general is an appointed member of the president's cabinet.

Attwell, Mabel Lucie (1879–1964) Artist and writer, born in London. From 1911 onwards she drew humorous postcards for Valentine's, usually featuring chubby children. Her 'cherubic' style was continued in children's books by her daughter, working under her mother's name.

aubergine [ohberzheen] A bushy perennial (*Solanum meleagrum*) with funnel-shaped, violet flowers and large, edible berries, native to New World tropics; also its fruit, variable in shape and colour, but typically egg-shaped and purple; also called **egg-plant**. (Family: Solanaceae.)

aubretia [awbreesha] A mat-forming perennial (*Aubretia deltoidea*); slightly greyish leaves; pink to purple or blue cross-shaped flowers; native to SE Europe. (Family: Cruciferae.)

Aubrey, John [awbree] (1626–97) Antiquary and folklorist, born in Easton Percy, Wiltshire. He left a large mass of materials, some of which were later published (notably in *Letters by Eminent Persons*, 1813, commonly called *Brief Lives*).

Aubusson, Pierre d' [ohbüsõ] (1423–1503) Grand Master of the Knights Hospitallers of St John of Jerusalem, born in Monteil-au-Vicomte, France. Mohammed II's career of conquest was halted by d'Aubusson and his small colony of Christian soldiers in Rhodes (1480).

Auchinleck, Sir Claude (John Eyre) [okhinlek] (1884–1981) British soldier, born in Aldershot, Hampshire. His regrouping of the 8th Army on El Alamein is now recognized as a successful defensive operation, but at the time he was made a scapegoat for the retreat, and replaced in 1942.

Auckland [awkland] 36°55S 174°43E, pop (2000e) 931 000 (urban area). Seaport city in North Island, New Zealand; principal port of New Zealand; founded, 1840; capital, 1840–65; airport; railway; university (1883); two cathedrals; Waitemata Harbour spanned by Auckland Harbour Bridge (1959).

auction bridge *bridge* (recreation)

Auden, W(ystan) H(ugh) [awden] (1907–73) Poet, born in York, North Yorkshire. His first volume of verse, *Poems* (1930), placed him in the forefront of a group of poets of left-wing sympathies, including Day-Lewis and Spender. He supported the Spanish Republic's cause, and (with Isherwood) reported on Japanese aggression in China in *Journey to a War* (1939). In 1939 he emigrated to New York, becoming a US citizen. His later conversion to Anglicanism left his writing more serious, and he developed a more reflective style, as in *City Without Walls* (1969).

Audenarde [ohdnah(r)d] *Oudenaarde*

audiology The study of the physiology of hearing, and of diseases that affect the ear and the associated nerve. It is specifically concerned with assessing the nature and degree of hearing loss and with the rehabilitation of people with hearing impairment. The scientific measurement of hearing is known as **audiometry**.

audiometry *audiology*

audio-visual aids Sources other than print which are used to help people teach and learn. These may include pieces of equipment such as still, overhead, and film projectors, tape recorders, and radio or television sets, as well as pictures, graphics, charts, films, videotapes, and audiotapes.

audit The process of checking that the accounts of an organization have been kept in accordance with good practice and with relevant laws, and that the accounts fairly reflect the activities of the organization and its state of affairs at a certain date. All limited companies must have accounts audited. Auditors are usually members of professional accountancy firms.

Audit Commission In the UK, an independent body set up by the government in 1982 to monitor local authority spending. It has also carried out reviews in the areas of education, health, and the police.

auditory tube A tube connecting the middle ear to the nasopharynx, also known as the **Eustachian tube**, after Italian physician Bartolommeo Eustachio (1520–74). It enables air to enter or leave the middle ear, so balancing the pressure on either side of the eardrum, thus allowing it to vibrate freely.

Audubon, John James [awduhbon] (1785–1851) Ornithologist, born in Les Cayes, Haiti. His *The Birds of America* (1827–38) contains coloured figures of 1065 birds, many natural size.

The National Audubon Society, dedicated to the conservation of birds in the USA, was founded in his honour in 1866.

Augsburg [owgsberg], Ger [owgsboork], ancient **Augusta Vindelicorum** 48°22N 10°54E, pop (2000e) 263 000. Industrial and commercial city in Germany; founded by the Romans, 15 BC; seat of the famous Diets of 1530 and 1555; railway; university (1970); birthplace of Brecht and Holbein; St Ulrich's Minster (1500).

Augsburg, League of [owgsberg] (1686) A defensive alliance formed by the Holy Roman Emperor, Bavaria, Spain, Sweden, and several German states to challenge Louis XIV's legalistic pursuit of territory. Continuing mutual provocation between France and the League resulted in the **War of the League of Augsburg** (1689–97), also known as the **War of the Grand Alliance**.

Augsburg Confession [owgsberg] A statement of faith composed by Luther, Melanchthon, and others for the Diet of Augsburg (1530). It became authoritative for the Lutheran Church.

augury [awgyuree] In ancient Rome, the principal means of divining the will of the gods. It involved observing natural phenomena such as lightning and the feeding habits of sacred chickens. The **augurs** themselves were distinguished public men who had undergone training and been admitted to the college of augurs – a select body of 16.

Augusta (Georgia) [awguhsta] 33°28N 81°58W, pop (2000e) 54 000. City in E Georgia, USA, on the Savannah R; founded as a river trading post; established in 1735; state capital, 1786–95; airfield; railway; popular resort with a notable golf club.

Augusta (Maine) [awguhsta] 44°17N 69°50W, pop (2000e) 18 600. State capital of Maine, USA; established as a trading post, 1628; city status, 1849; airfield.

Augustan age The age of the Emperor Augustus in Rome (27 BC–AD 14), graced by the poets Horace, Ovid, and Virgil; hence, the classical period of any national literature.

Augustine, St [awguhstin], also known as **Augustine of Canterbury** (?–604) Clergyman, the first Archbishop of Canterbury, born probably in Rome. He was prior of a Benedictine monastery at Rome, when in 596 Pope Gregory I sent him with 40 other monks to convert the Anglo-Saxons to Christianity. He was made Bishop of the English in 597. Feast day 26/27 May.

Augustine, St [awguhstin], originally **Aurelius Augustinus**, also known as **Augustine of Hippo** (354–430) The greatest of the Latin Fathers, born in Tagaste, Numidia (modern Algeria). His mother became St Monica. He was sent to Carthage to complete his studies, but yielded to the temptation of the city, and fathered a son before he was 18. An enthusiastic student of Plato, the Neoplatonists, and the Bible, he finally became a Christian in 387. Ordained priest in 391, he proved a formidable antagonist to the heretical schools in the Donatist and Pelagian controversies. His sacred autobiography, *Confessions*, was written in 397, and *De Civitate Dei*, a vindication of the Christian Church, in 413–26. Feast day 28 August.

Augustinians A religious order united in 1255 following the monastic teaching and 'rule' of St Augustine; also known as the **Augustinian** or **Austin Friars**; in full, the **Order of the Hermit Friars of St Augustine (OSA)**.

Augustus (Gaius Julius Caesar Octavianus) (63 BC–AD 14) Founder of the Roman Empire, the son of Gaius Octavius, and great-nephew, through his mother Atia, of Julius Caesar. On Caesar's assassination (44 BC), he raised an army, defeated Antony, and extorted a consulship from the Senate (43 BC). When Antony returned from Gaul in force later that year with Lepidus, Octavian made a deal with his former enemies, joining the so-called Second Triumvirate with them, and taking Africa, Sardinia, and Sicily as his province. A later redivision of power gave him the entire western half of the Roman world, and Antony the eastern. In 31 BC, the Battle of Actium made Octavian victorious as the sole ruler of the Roman world. The Romans awarded him the title *Pater Patriae* ('Father of his Country') in 2 BC, and on his death made him a god (*divus Augustus*).

Augustusburg The 18th-c Baroque residence of the former electors of Cologne at Brühl, NW Germany; a world heritage site. It was designed by Konrad Schlaun, and later Francois Cuvillié, for Elector Clemens August (1700–61).

auk A small, black-and-white, short-winged seabird; inhabits cool seas; excellent swimmer. (Family: Alcidae, 21 species.)

Aumann, Robert J (1930–) Mathematician, born in Frankfurt-am-Main, Germany. He went as a child with his family to the USA, where he studied, and in 1956 began working at the mathematics faculty of the Hebrew University of Jerusalem and later joined the Centre for Rationality there. He shared the 2005 Nobel Prize for Economics with Thomas Crombie Schelling for their work on game-theory analysis.

Aung San Suu Kyi, Daw [owng san soo kyee] (1945–) Political leader, born in Yangon, Myanmar (formerly Rangoon, Burma), the daughter of the assassinated General Aung San, who was hailed as the father of Burmese independence. She co-founded the National League for Democracy (NLD), and in 1989 was placed under house arrest by the military government. She was awarded the Nobel Peace Prize in 1991. She was released in July 1995, but continued to campaign for human rights in her country, and a further period of house arrest followed (Sep 2000–May 2002). In 2003, she was detained at Insein Prison near Rangoon despite worldwide criticism, and later placed under house arrest. By mid 2007 she had not been released.

Aurangzeb or **Aurungzib** [awrangzeb] ('ornament of the throne'), kingly title **Alamgir** (1618–1707) The last and most magnificent of the Mughal emperors of India (1658–1707), born at Dhod, Malwa. He was a fervent Muslim, which alienated the Hindus and led to war with the Marathas.

Aurelian [awreelian], in full **Lucius Domitius Aurelianus** (c.215–75) Roman emperor (270–5), a man of outstanding military talents. He took successful action against the Goths and Carpi on the Danube, Zenobia of Palmyra in the East, and the breakaway Gallic Empire in the West. He was awarded the title 'Restorer of the World'.

Aurelian Way *Roman roads*

Aurelius [awreelius], in full **Caesar Marcus Aurelius Antoninus Augustus**, originally **Marcus Annius Verus** (121–80) Roman emperor (161–80). The adopted son of Antoninus Pius, he ruled as his junior partner from 146. His reign saw constant warfare, and he personally directed operations on the Danube frontier.

Auric, Georges [ohrik] (1899–1983) Composer, born in Lodève, who became one of *Les Six*. His compositions ranged widely from full orchestral pieces to songs, and included many film scores.

auricular therapy [awrikyuler] A form of acupuncture which developed outside China, using points on the ear which relate to remote areas of the body. The entire body is said to be represented on the surface of the ear, and the application of needles, electronic stimulation, or laser to these points is said to cure disease in the related part. Ear acupuncture is now widely used to treat addictions and for pain relief during childbirth and dentistry.

Auriga [awriyga] (Lat 'charioteer') A prominent N hemisphere constellation in the Milky Way, containing many star clusters. Its brightest star is Capella, sixth-brightest in the sky, actually a close pair of giant yellow stars, distance 13 parsec.

Aurignacian [awrignayshn] In European prehistory, a division of Upper Palaeolithic culture. It is named after a cave site at Aurignac, Haute Garonne, SW France, excavated in 1852–60.

Auriol, Vincent [ohreeol] (1884–1966) French statesman, born in Revel, France. A socialist politician, he became president of the two constituent assemblies of 1946, and the first president of the Fourth Republic (1947–54).

aurochs [awroks] (plural, **aurochsen**) An extinct large wild ox (*Bos primigenius*), formerly widespread in Europe, Asia, and N Africa; the ancestor of domestic cattle; forward-pointing horns; last individual killed in Poland in 1627; also known as **urus**, or **wild ox**.

aurora (astronomy) [awrawra] A diffuse coloured light in the upper atmosphere (100 km/60 mi) over polar regions, visible at night. It is caused by charged particles from the Sun colliding with oxygen and nitrogen atoms in the atmosphere. In the N it is known as the *aurora borealis* or *northern lights*; in the S as the *aurora australis*.

Aurora (mythology) [awrawra] The Roman name of the goddess of the dawn, equivalent to the Greek Eos.

Aurungzeb(e) *Aurangzeb*

Auschwitz [owshvitz] The largest Nazi concentration and extermination camp, on the outskirts of Oświęcim, SW Poland. Estimates of the number of men, women, and children who died at Auschwitz vary greatly, but it is believed that about 1·6 million people were killed there, 1·3 million of whom were Jewish, the remainder consisting mainly of Poles, Soviet prisoners-of-war, and gypsies; a world heritage site.

Austen, Jane (1775–1817) Novelist, born in Steventon, near Basingstoke, Hampshire, where her father was rector. She later lived in Bath, Southampton, Chawton, and Winchester, where she died. Of her six great novels, four were published anonymously during her lifetime and two posthumously: *Sense and Sensibility* (1811), *Pride and Prejudice* (1813), *Mansfield Park* (1814), *Emma* (1816), *Persuasion* (1818), and *Northanger Abbey* (1818).

Auster, Paul [awster] (1947–) Novelist, born in Newark, NJ. His use of detective-story techniques to explore modern urban identity is evident in *The New York Trilogy* (1985–6). Later books include *The Music of Chance* (1990), *Timbuktu* (1999), *Oracle Night* (2003), and *Travels in the Scriptorium* (2007).

Austerlitz, Battle of [owsterlits] (1805) Napoleon's most decisive victory, also known as **the Battle of the Three Emperors**. It was fought in Moravia against a larger combined Austro-Russian army under Kutuzov.

Austin [awstin] 30°17N 97°45W, pop (2000e) 656 600. Capital of Texas, USA, on the Colorado R; settled, 1835; capital of the Republic of Texas, 1839; airfield; railway; two universities (1876, 1881); commercial centre for an extensive agricultural region.

Austin (of Longbridge), Herbert Austin, Baron (1866–1941) Car manufacturer, born in Little Missenden, Buckinghamshire. In 1895 he produced his first car, the Wolseley, and in 1905 opened his own works near Birmingham.

Austin, Stephen Fuller (1793–1836) Founder of the state of Texas, born in Austinville, VA. In 1822 he founded a colony on the Brazos R, and became leader of the movement for Texan independence.

Austin Friars *Augustinians*

Australasia A term used loosely to include Australia and the islands of Tasmania, New Zealand, New Guinea (including New Britain), New Caledonia, and Vanuatu; often described as equivalent to all of Oceania below the Equator and N of 47°S.

Australia *pp.64–65*

Australia, Order of An order according recognition to Australian citizens (and others). It was established by Queen Elizabeth II in 1975.

Australia Day A public holiday in Australia commemorating the founding of the colony of New South Wales on 26 January 1788.

Australian Alps Chain of mountains in SE Australia forming the S part of the Great Dividing Range; extends c.300 km/185 mi;

Australia

☐ International Airport　∴ World heritage site

official name **Commonwealth of Australia**

Local name Australia

Timezone GMT +8 (Western Australia); GMT +10 (New South Wales, Queensland, Tasmania, Victoria, Australian Capital Territory); GMT +9.5 (South Australia, Northern Territory)

Area 7 692 300 km²/2 969 228 sq mi

Population total (2002e) 19 702 000

Status Independent state within the Commonwealth

Date of independence 1901

Capital Canberra

Language English (official)

Ethnic groups European descent (95%), Asian and Pacific (2%), Aboriginal (1%)

Religions Christian (74%, including Roman Catholic 27%, Anglican 24%)

Physical features Variously viewed as the smallest continent or largest island; consists largely of plains and plateaux, most of which average 600 m/2000 ft above sea level; four main regions: Western Craton (or Western Shield), the Great Artesian Basin, the Great Dividing Range (or Eastern Uplands), and the Flinders-Mt Lofty ranges; W Australian Plateau occupies nearly half of the country; MacDonnell Ranges lie in the centre, highest point Mt Liebig, 1525 m/5000 ft; most of the plateau is dry, barren desert; Nullarbor Plain in the S is crossed by the Trans-Australian Railway; Great Dividing Range parallel to the Great Barrier Reef, rising to 2228 m/7310 ft at Mt Kosciuszko, Australia's highest point; Great Barrier Reef off NE coast stretches for over 1900 km/1200 mi; island of Tasmania rises to 1617 m/5305 ft at Mt Ossa; separated from the mainland by the Bass Strait; longest river is the Murray; chief tributaries, the Darling, Murrumbidgee, Lachlan; Lake Eyre occupies 8800 km²/3400 sq mi; c.18% of area forested; c.6% arable.

rises to 2228 m/7310 ft at Mt Kosciuszko; much used for winter sports.

Australian Antarctic Territory area 6 043 852 km²/2 332 927 sq mi of land, 84 798 km²/32 732 sq mi of ice shelf. Situated S of 60°S and lying between 142° and 136°E (excluding Terre Adélie);

claimed by Australia, 1936; scientific station at Mawson, 1954; Davis Base, 1957.

Australian Ballet Company The national ballet company of Australia. Founded in Melbourne in 1962, it grew out of the Borovansky Ballet Company and School founded by Edouard

Climate More than a third of Australia receives under 260 mm/ 10 in mean annual rainfall; less than a third receives over 500 mm/20 in; prolonged drought and frequent heatwaves in many areas; average daily temperature 26–34°C (Nov) and 19–31°C (Jul) in N; rainfall varies from 286 mm/15·2 in (Jan) to zero (Jul); fertile land with a temperate climate and reliable rainfall only in the lowlands and valleys near the E and SE coast, and a small part of the SW corner; Tasmania and Mt Kosciuszko have snowfields in winter; Mar 2006, NE coast hit by Cyclone Larry and NW by Cyclone Glenda.

Currency 1 Australian Dollar (AUD) = 100 cents

Economy Free-enterprise economy; world's largest wool producer, and a top exporter of veal and beef; most important crop is wheat; major mineral producer; petroleum reserves. Coal, bauxite, nickel, lead, zinc, copper, tin, uranium, iron ore, and other minerals in early 1960s; manufacturing industry expanded rapidly since 1945, especially engineering, shipbuilding, car manufacture, metals, textiles, clothing, chemicals, food processing, wine; self-sufficient in lumber; marine fishing (especially tuna) important, as are tourism and winter sports; Ghan railway linking Alice Springs to Darwin opened early 2004, completing the rail route from Adelaide.

GDP (2002e) $525·5 bn, per capita $26 900

Human Development Index (2002) 0·939

History Aboriginal people thought to have arrived in Australia from SE Asia c.40 000 years ago; first European visitors were the Dutch, who explored the Gulf of Carpentaria in 1606 and settled in 1616; became known as New Holland in 1644; Captain James Cook arrived in Botany Bay in 1770, and claimed the E coast for Britain; New South Wales established as a penal colony in 1788; gold discovered in New South Wales and Victoria in 1851, and in Western Australia in 1892; transportation of convicts to E Australia ended in 1840, but continued until 1853 in Tasmania and 1868 in Western Australia; during this period the colonies drafted their own constitutions and set up governments: New South Wales (1855), Tasmania and Victoria (1856), South Australia (1857), Queensland (1860), and Western Australia (1890); Commonwealth of Australia established in 1901, with Canberra subsequently chosen as capital, (1901); policy of preventing immigration by non-whites remained in force from the end of the 19th-c until 1974; the issue of Aboriginal civil rights has been a major issue since the 1960s. Northern Territory self-governing since 1978; divided into six states and two territories: each state has its own legislature, government, and constitution; legislature comprises a bicameral Federal Parliament with a Prime Minister and Cabinet; British monarch is Head of State, represented by a Governor-General; republican movement growing since the late 1980s; proposal on the issue rejected by referendum, late 1999.

Head of State
(British monarch represented by Governor-General)
1982–9 Sir Ninian Stephen
1989–96 Bill Hayden
1996–2001 Sir William Deane
2001–3 Peter Hollingworth
2003 Sir Guy Green *Acting*
2003– Michael Jeffery

Head of Government
1901–3 Edmund Barton *Prot*

1903–4 Alfred Deakin *Prot*
1904 John Christian Watson *Lab*
1904–5 George Houstoun Reid *Free/Prot**
1905–8 Alfred Deakin *Prot*
1908–9 Andrew Fisher *Lab*
1909–10 Alfred Deakin *Fusion*
1910–13 Andrew Fisher *Lab*
1913–14 Joseph Cook *Lib*
1914–15 Andrew Fisher *Lab*
1915–16 William Morris Hughes *Lab*
1916–17 William Morris Hughes *Nat Lab*
1917–23 William Morris Hughes *Nat*
1923–9 Stanley Melbourne Bruce, Viscount Bruce of Melbourne *Nat/Co**
1929–32 James Henry Scullin *Lab*
1932–8 Joseph Aloysius Lyons *UAP*
1938–9 Joseph Aloysius Lyons *UAP/Co**
1939 Earle Christmas Grafton Page *UAP/Co**
1939–40 Robert Gordon Menzies *UAP*
1940–1 Robert Gordon Menzies *UAP/Co**
1941 Arthur William Fadden *UAP/Co**
1941–5 John Joseph Curtin *Lab*
1945 Francis Michael Forde *Lab*
1945–9 Joseph Benedict Chifley *Lab*
1949–66 Robert Gordon Menzies *Lib/Co**
1966–7 Harold Edward Holt *Lib/Co**
1967–8 John McEwen *Lib/Co**
1968–71 John Grey Gorton *Lib/Co**
1971–2 William McMahon *Lib/Co**
1972–5 Gough Whitlam *Lab*
1975–83 John Malcolm Fraser *Lib/Co**
1983–91 Robert Hawke *Lab*
1991–6 Paul Keating *Lab*
1996– John Howard *Lib*
Co Country *Nat Lab* National Labor
Free Free Trade *Prot* Protectionist
Lab Labor *UAP* United Australia Party
Lib Liberal * Coalition
Nat Nationalist

Australian States *Name / Area (km² / sq mi) / State capital*
Australian Capital Territory / 2400 / 930 / Canberra
New South Wales / 801 400 / 309 400 / Sydney
Northern Territory / 1 346 200 / 519 800 / Darwin
Queensland / 1 727 200 / 666 900 / Brisbane
South Australia / 984 000 / 379 900 / Adelaide
Tasmania / 67 800 / 26 200 / Hobart
Victoria / 227 600 / 87 900 / Melbourne
Western Australia / 2 525 500 / 975 000 / Perth

External territories *Name / Area (km² / sq mi) / Population / Date under Australian administration*
The Ashmore and Cartier Islands / 3·0 / 2·0 / Uninhabited / 1931
Australian Antarctic Terr / 6 043 852·0 / 2 332 927·0 / Uninhabited / 1936
Christmas Island / 155·0 / 60·0 (2000e) / 2700 / 1958
Cocos (Keeling) Islands / 14·2 / 5·5 / (2000e) 780 / 1955
Coral Sea Island / 2·0* / 0·8* Uninhabited / 1969
Heard Island and McDonald Islands / 412·0 / 159·0 / Uninhabited / 1947
Norfolk Island / 35·0 / 13·0 / (2000e) 2200 / 1913

* Land figure only. Islands cover 1 000 000 km²/286 000 sq mi of ocean.

Borovansky in 1942, with British dance teacher, Peggy van Praagh, jointly becoming its artistic director with Robert Helpmann.

Australian Capital Territory pop (2000e) 309 300; area 2400 km²/925 sq mi. Territory in SE Australia, created in 1911 to provide a location for the national capital, Canberra; bordered on all sides by New South Wales; Jervis Bay on the E coast ceded (1915) for its use as a port; c.50% of the workforce employed by the government.

Australian Council of Trade Unions (ACTU) Australia's national trade union organization, formed in 1927. By 1992, there were 227 unions in the country, with a claimed total membership of 3·1 million.

Australian East Coast Temperate and Sub-Tropical Rainforest Parks A series of national parks and nature reserves along the length of the New South Wales coast; a world heritage area.

Australian Labor Party (ALP) Australia's oldest political party, founded in 1891 in New South Wales. It has always been a social democratic party, committed to evolutionary not revolutionary change.

Australian languages The aboriginal languages of Australia. About 50 survive, spoken by fewer than 50 000 people. There are now some bilingual school programmes, which will ensure the immediate survival of some languages.

Australian republicanism The desire to sever ties with Britain and install an Australian, non-hereditary head of state. An intermittent theme in Australian history since the 19th-c, republicanism has gained prominence since the late 1980s, and the Australian Republican Movement, supported by the Labor government of Paul Keating, aimed for a republic by 2001, the centenary of Australian federation. In 1998 the Constitutional Convention voted in favour of a republican system and a president; the proposals were placed before the electorate in late 1999, and closely defeated.

Australian Rules football *football, Australian Rules*

Australian Workers' Union (AWU) The largest Australian trade union from the early 1900s to 1970, and still one of the largest. It was formed in 1894, and has always been a conservative force in trade union and labour politics.

Australia Telescope An array of radio telescopes at three locations in New South Wales which use aperture synthesis to achieve very high resolving power.

Austral Islands [ostral] *Tubuai Islands*

Australopithecus [ostralohpithekus] Early hominids known from fossils found in Ethiopia, Kenya, Tanzania, and South Africa; dated c.5·5–1·0 mya (million years ago); although most finds are c.4·0–1·5 mya. They were truncally erect and bipedal, narrow-chested, and pot-bellied, with long powerful arms, and short legs. Face and jaws were strongly constructed and projecting; braincases were small. Features such as erect bipedalism, reduced canines, parabolic tooth rows, and rotary chewing reveal their close evolutionary links with humans. Several species are known. Bigger-brained hominids (*Homo*), probably evolved from *A. afarensis* or *A. africanus*; later species (*A. robustus* and *A. boisei*) persist well after earliest *Homo*, showing that they are not direct ancestors.

Austria *p.67*

Austria–Hungary, Dual Monarchy of, also known as the **Austro–Hungarian Empire** A constitutional arrangement created by the Ausgleich ('compromise') of 1867. In Austria–Hungary the Habsburg emperors Francis Joseph (until 1916), and Charles (1916–18), ruled over the twin kingdoms of Austria and Hungary. It was ultimately destroyed by defeat in World War 1.

Austrian Succession, War of the (1740–8) The first phase in the struggle between Prussia and Austria for mastery of the German states, developing after 1744 into a colonial conflict between Britain and the Franco-Spanish bloc. The fighting spread from C Europe to the Austrian Netherlands, the Mediterranean, and Italy, embroiling the New World and India before peace was concluded at the Treaty of Aix-la-Chapelle (1748).

Austro-Asiatic languages A group of over 100 languages spoken in SE Asia. The major group is the Mon–Khmer, which has three main languages: Mon (Tailang), Khmer, and Vietnamese.

Austronesian languages The most numerous and (after Indo-European) the most widely dispersed of the world's great language families. Extending from Taiwan to Madagascar and from Malaysia, the Philippines, and Indonesia E through the Pacific Islands, it contains over 700 separate languages.

Austro–Prussian War (1866) A war between Austria and Prussia occasioned by a dispute over the duchies of Schleswig and Holstein. It was declared on 14 June, decided by the Prussian victory at Königgrätz (sometimes known as Sadowa) on 3 July, and ended by the Treaty of Prague on 23 August.

Authorized Version of the Bible The English translation of the Bible commissioned by James I and accomplished by a panel of leading scholars of the day; widely called the **King James Bible**. It was published in 1611.

autism A condition characterized by abnormal functioning in social interaction together with repetitive behaviour and poor communication, almost always commencing before three years of age. One in 2000 children suffer from the disorder, which is four times more common in males. The cause is unknown.

auto-destructive art An artefact, typically a painting or piece of sculpture, deliberately constructed in a way guaranteed to self-destruct almost immediately. Examples include pictures executed with acid, and disintegrating kinetic machines.

autogiro A non-fixed-wing aircraft whose lift is provided (unlike a helicopter) by non-powered horizontal blades, which are brought into action by means of an engine providing horizontal thrust propelling the aircraft forward. This type of aeroplane was popular in the 1930s, but nowadays is mainly used for sport.

auto-immune diseases A group of apparently unrelated disorders which possess a common underlying immunological mechanism. The body is unable to distinguish accurately between 'self' and 'not-self' proteins, and mounts an immune response against its own cells. Antibodies are produced that damage the body's own tissues. Disorders include rheumatoid arthritis, diabetes mellitus, and Addison's disease.

automated teller machine (ATM) The formal name for the 'service tills' now common outside most banks and building societies, through which money can be withdrawn and other transactions carried out. The ATMs are linked to the banks' computers to enable on-line monitoring of customer's accounts to take place through the machines.

automatic pilot A device that automatically controls a vehicle (aircraft, ship, land vehicle) so that it will follow a preset course. It makes suitable adjustments to the vehicle's control systems to compensate for the offsetting effects of the environment or terrain.

automation The control of a technical process without using a human being to intervene to make decisions. The result of one operation is fed back to control the next. Central heating is a simple automatic system: the thermostat is a sensor, feeding information back to the heater, which then adjusts automatically, switching on and off as necessary. Computers are the most widespread example of automation.

automaton [awtomatn] A mechanical device that imitates the actions of a living creature, human or animal. Some are made as toys, but others are useful as research or control mechanisms, and in the remote handling of hazardous materials.

automobile *car; motor insurance*

autonomic nervous system (ANS) That part of the nervous system which supplies the glands (eg the salivary and sweat glands), heart muscle, and smooth muscle (eg the walls of blood vessels and the bladder). The *sympathetic* (S) system is distributed throughout the whole body, particularly to the blood vessels. The *parasympathetic* (P) system is distributed to the gastro-intestinal, respiratory, and urogenital systems, and to the eye. In general terms, the S system prepares the body for action, while the P is concerned with the conservation of energy.

autumnal equinox *equinox*

Austria

□ International Airport

Ger **Österreich**, official name **Republic of Austria**, Ger **Republik Österreich**

Local name Österreich

Timezone GMT +1

Area 83 854 km²/32 368 sq mi

Population total (2002e) 8 077 000

Status Republic

Date of independence 1955

Capital Vienna (Wien)

Languages German (official), Croatian, Slovene

Ethnic groups Austrian (99%), Croatian, Slovakian, Turkish, German

Religions Roman Catholic (85%), Protestant (12%), Muslim (1%), Jewish (1%)

Physical features One of the most mountainous countries in Europe; lies at E end of the Alps; highest point, Grossglockner, 3797 m/12 457 ft; largest lake, Neusiedler See; divided into three regions: Alpine; the highland Bohemian Massif; and the hilly lowland region, including the Vienna basin; R Danube drains whole country; most densely forested country in central Europe (40% of land is forested).

Climate Three climatic regions: the Alps (often sunny in winter, but cloudy in summer); the Danube valley and Vienna basin (driest region); and the SE, a region of often severe winters but warmer summers; average annual temperature: 2°C (Jan), 20°C (Jul) in Vienna; most rain in summer months; average annual rainfall 868 mm/34 in; winters cold, especially with winds from the E or NE; humid, continental climate in NE.

Currency 1 euro (EUR) = 100 cents (previous to 2002, 1 Schilling (ATS) = 100 groschen)

Economy Mixed free market; principal agricultural areas to the N of the Alps, and along both sides of the Danube; principal crops: cereals; dairy cattle and pigs; wine industry; wide range of metal and mineral resources; tourism (summer and winter); well-developed transportation networks; river ports at Linz and Vienna; airports at Vienna, Graz, Linz, Klagenfurt, Salzburg, Innsbruck; much power produced hydroelectrically.

GDP (2002e) $227·7 bn, per capita $27 900

Human Development Index (2002) 0·926

History Early Iron-Age settlement at Hallstatt; later Illyrian settlers driven out by the Celts; part of Roman Empire until 5th-c, then occupied by Germanic tribes, most signifcantly Bavarians; Charlemagne drove out the Slavic Avars who also settled in the region; area became a duchy and passed to the Habsburg family in 1282, who made it the foundation of their Empire; Hungarian nationalism and Habsburg defeats in 19th-c led to the dual monarchy of Austria-Hungary from 1867; nationalist protest resulted in assassination of Archduke Ferdinand in 1914 and World War 1, which ended the Austrian Empire; republic established, 1918; annexed by the German Reich in 1938 (the Anschluss) and named Ostmark; occupied by British, American, French, and Russian troops from 1945; obtained independence, 1955; neutrality declared, since when Austria has been a haven for many refugees; joined European Union, 1995; governed by a Federal Assembly; Federal President appoints a Federal Chancellor.

Head of State (Federal President)
1945–50 Karl Renner
1950–7 Theodor Körner
1957–65 Adolf Schärf
1965–74 Franz Jonas
1974–86 Rudolf Kirchsläger
1986–92 Kurt Waldheim
1992–2004 Thomas Klestil
2004– Heinz Fischer

Head of Government (Federal Chancellor)
1945 Karl Renner
1945–53 Leopold Figl
1953–61 Julius Raab
1961–4 Alfons Gorbach
1964–70 Josef Klaus
1970–83 Bruno Kreisky
1983–6 Fred Sinowatz
1986–97 Franz Vranitzky
1997–2000 Viktor Klima
2000– Wolfgang Schüssel

Auvergne [ohvairn] pop (2000e) 1 381 000; area 26 013 km²/10 041 sq mi. Region and former province of C France; Roman province, later a duchy and (10th-c) principality, united to France in 1527; capital, Clermont-Ferrand.

Auxerre [ohzair], Lat **Autissiodorum** 47°48N 3°32E, pop (2000e) 42 400. Market town in C France; on the R Yonne, surrounded by orchards and vineyards; railway; bishopric; Gothic cathedral (13th–16th-c).

auxiliary language A natural language adopted by people of different speech communities for the needs of trade, education, and communication, though it may not be the native language of any of them. English and French are used in this way in many parts of Africa.

auxiliary store *backing store*

avahi [avahhee] *indri*

Avalon [avalon] In Celtic mythology, the land of the dead, the place to which King Arthur was taken after his death. The name possibly means 'land of apples'.

avatar [avatah(r)] In Hinduism, the descent to Earth of deity in a visible form. The idea derives from the tradition associated with the deity Vishnu, who from time to time appears on Earth in order to save it from extraordinary peril.

Avebury [ayvbree] 51°27N 1°51W. Village in Wiltshire, S England; the largest megalithic monument in England, a world heritage site; in use c.2600–1600 BC; approached by a 2·4 km/1½ mi avenue of 100 paired stones; three stone circles within the enclosure, the largest of nearly 100 boulders; nearby Silbury Hill is the largest prehistoric construction in Europe.

Ave Maria [ahvay mareea] *Hail Mary*

avens [avinz] Either of two plants from the genus *Geum*, both native to temperate regions. **Wood avens** (*Geum urbanum*), also called **herb Bennet**, is an erect perennial growing to c.60 cm/2 ft; flowers 5-petalled, erect, yellow, petals spreading. **Water avens** (*Geum rivale*) is similar, but flowers are bowl-shaped, drooping, petals pinkish. (Family: Rosaceae.)

Averroës [averoheez], Latin form of **Ibn Rushd** (1126–98) The most famous of the Islamic philosophers, born in Córdoba, Spain. He wrote extensive commentaries on many of Aristotle's works.

aversion therapy A process in which an unpleasant experience is induced (eg by physical or electrical means) in association with an undesirable behaviour, in an attempt to inhibit or eliminate by this conditioning the undesirable behaviour. The technique has been used in a wide range of conditions, including smoking and alcohol dependence.

Avesta [avesta] The scriptures of Zoroastrianism, written in Avestan, a language of the E branch of the Indo-European family. Traditionally believed to have been revealed to Zoroaster, few portions of the original survive.

avian flu A highly infectious viral disease that affects poultry and other birds; often called **avian influenza** or popularly **bird flu**. It is spread by the movement of infected birds or contact with their secretions. There are about 100 strains of the disease. H5N1, the most deadly strain, which can be passed to humans, is a particular kind of H5 avian flu. Not all H5 viruses can infect human beings. H5N1 emerged in Hong Kong in 1997, killing or forcing the destruction of 1·5 million chickens, ducks and geese. It re-emerged in Korea in 2003, spread to other Asian countries and Russia, and in 2005 cases were confirmed in some European countries. By March 2006, 95 human deaths had been recorded in SE Asia from the H5N1 strain, and three deaths in Turkey were the first outside SE Asia. In April 2006, a swan found dead in Scotland tested positive for the H5N1 strain, the first reported case in the UK. At the start of 2007, the disease had claimed 157 lives. In February that year, the first UK outbreak of H5N1 in farmed poultry was confirmed at a large turkey farm in Suffolk, resulting in the cull of 159 000 turkeys.

Avicenna [avisena], Arabic **Ibn Sina** (980–1037) Islamic philosopher and physician, born near Bokhara, Kazakhstan. His medical system was long the standard in Europe and the Middle East.

Avignon [aveenyō], Lat **Avenio** 43°57N 4°50E, pop (2000e) 93 600. Walled town in SE France, on left bank of R Rhône; papal residence, 1309–76; railway; archbishopric; popular tourist centre; ruins of 12th-c Pont St Benezet, subject of the folk-song 'Sur le Pont d'Avignon'.

Ávila [aveela], also **Avila de los Caballeros**, ancient **Avela, Abula**, or **Abyla** 40°39N 4°43W, pop (2000e) 46 500. Ancient walled city in C Spain; altitude, 1126 m/3694 ft; bishopric; railway; birthplace of Queen Isabella and St Teresa; cathedral (11th-c); old town and churches are a world heritage site.

avocado [avohkahdoh] An evergreen tree growing to 18 m/60 ft (*Persea americana*), covered with aromatic oil glands, thought to be native to Central America; leaves oval, leathery; flowers greenish-white, 6-lobed; berry pear-shaped, leathery, growing to 15 cm/6 in long, green, yellow, or purplish, with thick yellowish-green edible flesh surrounding a single large stone. (Family: Lauraceae.)

avocet [avoset] A long-legged wading bird, found in fresh and saline waters worldwide; long, slender, up-curved bill. (Genus: *Recurvirostra*, 4 species. Family: Recurvirostridae.)

Avogadro, Amedeo [avohgadroh] (1776–1856) Scientist, born in Turin, Italy. In 1811 he formulated the hypothesis, known later as **Avogadro's law**, that equal volumes of gases contain equal numbers of molecules, when at the same temperature and pressure.

Avogadro's constant [avohgadroh] The physical quantity of molecules in a mole or of electronic charges in a faraday. Its approximate value is $6\cdot023 \times 10^{23}$.

Avon [ayvn] pop (2000e) 989 800; area 1347 km²/520 sq mi. Former county in SW England; created in 1974 from parts of Somerset and Gloucestershire; replaced in 1996 by the unitary authorities of Bath and NE Somerset, Bristol, South Gloucestershire, and NW Somerset.

Avon, River [ayvn] *England*

Avon, 1st Earl of *Eden, Sir Anthony*

AWACS [aywaks] *Airborne Warning and Control System*

AWS (Automatic Warning System) *train protection systems*

Axel, Richard (1946–) Biochemist, born in New York City. Professor of Pathology and Biochemistry at Columbia University in 1978, he joined the Howard Hughes Medical Institute there in 1984. In 2004 he shared the Nobel Prize for Physiology or Medicine with Linda B Buck for their discoveries of odorant receptors and the organization of the olfactory system.

Axelrod, Julius [akselrod] (1912–2004) Pharmacologist, born in New York City. As chief of the pharmacology section of the National Institute of Mental Health (1955–84), he discovered the substance which inhibits neural impulses, laying the basis for significant advances in neurophysiology. He shared the Nobel Prize for Physiology or Medicine in 1970.

axis deer *chital*

Axis Powers The name given to the co-operation of Nazi Germany and Fascist Italy (1936–45), first used by Mussolini. In September 1940, Germany, Italy, and Japan signed a tripartite agreement, after which all three were referred to as Axis Powers.

axolotl [aksolotl] A rare Mexican salamander (*Ambystoma mexicanum*) from high altitude in L Xochimilco; pale with three pairs of feathery gills; large fin around tail; family also known as **mole salamanders**. (Family: Ambystomatidae.)

axon *neurone*

axonometric and isometric projection A system for producing a three-dimensional drawing of an object without perspective and in which all lines are drawn to scale. Isometric projection is a particular case of axonometric projection, in which the three axes of height, width, and depth are drawn at 120° to each other, with width and depth axes at 30° to the horizontal. The method is widely used in engineering and architectural drawings.

ayatollah [iyatola] A Shiite Muslim religious title meaning 'sign of God', and referring to a clergyman who has reached the third level of Shiite higher education, is recognized as a mujtahid, and is over 40. The word is particularly associated today with the Islamic Republic of Iran.

Ayckbourn, Sir Alan [aykbaw(r)n] (1939–) Playwright, born in London. The first of many West End successes was *Relatively Speaking* (1967), establishing him as a master of farce. His plays include *Absurd Person Singular* (1973), *The Norman Conquests* (1974), *Invisible Friends* (1991), *Things We Do For Love* (1998), and *Improbable Fiction* (2005).

aye-aye [iyiy] A nocturnal primitive primate (prosimian) from Madagascar (*Daubentonia madagascariensis*); shaggy coat, long bushy tail, and large ears; fingers extremely long and slender; inhabits trees. (Family: Daubentoniidae.)

Ayer, Sir A(lfred) J(ules) [air] (1910–89) Philosopher, born in London. His antimetaphysical *Language, Truth, and Logic* (1936) was hailed as a lucid and concise rendering in English of the doctrines of the Vienna Circle of logical positivist philosophers.

Ayers Rock [airz], Aboriginal name **Uluru** 25°18S 131°18E. A huge red rock in SW Northern Territory, Australia, 450 km/280 mi SW of Alice Springs; rises from the desert to a height of 348 m/

Azerbaijan

☐ International Airport   ⌐⌐ Nagorno-Karabakh

[azerbiyjahn], Azerbaijani **Azärbayjan Respublikasi**, official name **Republic of Azerbaijan**

Local name Azerbaijan

Timezone GMT +3

Area 86 600 km²/33 428 sq mi

Population total (2002e) 8 176 000

Status Republic

Date of independence 1991

Capital Baku

Languages Azeri (official), Russian

Ethnic groups Azeri (83%), Russian (6%), Armenian (6%) (ethnic conflict since 1990 makes accurate statistical analysis impossible)

Religion Shi'ite Muslim

Physical features Mountainous country in E Transcaucasia: 10% of country is above 1494 m/4900 ft; 40% of land is lowland, 396–1494 m/1300–4900 ft; Bazar-Dyuzi rises to 4480 m/14 698 ft; rivers include the Kara and Araks.

Climate Central and eastern Azerbaijan dry and sub-tropical with mild winters and long, hot summers (often as hot as 43°C); SE is humid with annual rainfall of 1193–1396 mm/47–55 in.

Currency 1 Manat (AZM) = 100 gopik

Economy Once the former Soviet Union's most important oil-producing region, but now in decline; manufacturing industries include building materials, chemicals, textiles; mineral resources include natural gas, iron, copper, lead, zinc; exports include cotton, wheat, tobacco; Baku–Tblisi–Ceyhan oil pipeline (1760nbsp;km/1094 mi) connecting the oil-rich Caspian Sea to the Mediterranean formally opened, May 2005.

GDP (2002e) $28·61 bn, per capita $3700

Human Development Index (2002) 0·741

History Proclaimed a Soviet Socialist Republic, 1920; constituent republic of the USSR, 1936; declaration of independence, 1991; became a member of UN, 1992; ongoing conflict with Armenia over disputed enclave of Nagorno-Karabakh.

Head of State
1991–2 Ayaz Mutalibov
1992 Yagub Mamedov *Interim*
1992–3 Abulfaz Elchibey
1993–2003 Geidar Aliyev
2003– Ilham Aliyev

Head of Government
1991–2 Gasan Gasanov
1992–3 Feirus Mustafayev *Acting*
1993–4 Rakhim Guseinov
1994 Ali Masimov *Acting*
1994 Panakh Guseinov
1994–5 Surat Guseinov
1995–6 Fuad Guliyev
1996–2003 Artur Rasizade
2003 Ilham Aliyev
2003– Artur Rasizade

1142 ft; 3·6 km/2¼ mi long, 2·4 km/1½ mi wide, 8·8 km/5½ mi in circumference; the largest monolith in the world; named after South Australia premier, Sir Henry Ayers (1821–97).

Ayeshah *A'ishah*

Ayeyarwady, River, formerly **Irrawaddy** Major river dissecting Myanmar N–S, formed in N Myanmar; empties into Andaman Sea through a large delta; length c.1600 km/1000 mi; with the Nmai Hka headstream, c.2000 km/1300 mi; major rice-growing region.

Aykroyd, Dan (1952–) Actor, born in Ottawa, Canada. He wrote the screenplay for and starred in *The Blues Brothers* (1980), appeared in *Ghostbusters* (1984), and earned a Best Supporting Actor Oscar nomination for his first dramatic role in *Driving Miss Daisy* (1989). Later films include *Feeling Minnesota* (1996) and *Christmas with the Kranks* (2004).

Aylesbury [aylzbree] 51°50N 0°50W, pop (2000e) 61 400. County town of Buckinghamshire, SC England; railway.

Aylward, Gladys [aylwerd] (1902–70) Missionary in China, born in London. She arrived in China in 1930, and helped found an inn at Yangcheng. It was from here that in 1938 she made her famous trek across the mountains leading over 100 children to safety when the war with Japan brought fighting to the area.

Ayodhya [ayodya] Town in the N Indian state of Uttar Pradesh, and the location of the ancient Babri Masjid shrine. During the 1980s the shrine became the target of intense agitation by the Hindu followers of the Bharatiya Janata Paksh and related Hindu fundamentalist organizations. These asserted that the shrine lay over the birthplace of the god Rama, and that a temple should be built on the site. In 1992 a group of militant Hindus destroyed the shrine, and began to erect a temple. This sparked off intense communal violence in many parts of India.

Ayr [air] 55°28N 4°38W, pop (2000e) 49 800. Administrative centre of South Ayrshire, SW Scotland; on the Firth of Clyde, at mouth of R Ayr; railway.

Ayub Khan, Mohammad [ayub kahn] (1907–74) Pakistani soldier and president (1958–69), born in Hazara. He became president after a bloodless coup, and introduced a system of Basic Democracies. Following widespread civil disorder, he resigned in 1969, and martial law was re-established.

azalea [azaylia] A deciduous species of rhododendron. The name

Azores

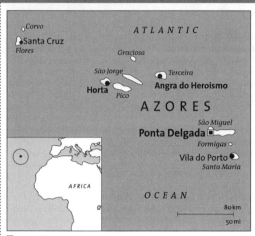

□ International Airport

[azaw(r)z], Port **(Arquipélago dos) Açôres**

Local name Ilhas dos Açôres, Port (Arquipélago dos) Açôres

Timezone GMT -1

Area 2300 km²/900 sq mi

Population total (2002e) 245 000

Status Semi-autonomous region of Portugal

Capital Ponta Delgada (on São Miguel Island)

Physical features Island archipelago of volcanic origin, 1400–1800 km/870–1100 mi W of mainland Portugal; three widely separated groups of nine islands; Flores and Corvo (NW), Terceira, Graciosa, São Jorge, Faial (Fayal), Pico (C), and Santa Maria with the Formigas Islands and São Miguel, the principal island (E); highest point, Pico, 2351 m/7713 ft; volcanic terrain.

Economy Agriculture; grain, fruit, tea, tobacco, wine.

History Settled by the Portuguese in 1439; under Spanish rule, 1580–1640; new constitution established in 1832, when islands were grouped into three administrative districts; given limited autonomous administration, 1895; has no central government, but a General Council.

is used in horticulture to distinguish it from the evergreen species. (Genus: *Rhododendron*. Family: Ericaceae).

Azerbaijan *p.69*

Azhar, al- [azhah(r)] Islamic mosque and university founded in Cairo, Egypt, in 970. It is said to be the oldest university in the world.

azidothymidine *AZT*

azimuth The direction of an object measured in degrees clockwise around the horizon from N point to a point on the horizon vertically beneath the object. The notion is used in astronomy, navigation, gunnery, and other contexts where it is important to determine a bearing as well as an altitude.

Aznar, (López) José Maria [aznah(r)] (1953–) Spanish statesman and prime minister (1996–2004), born in Madrid. He became a civil servant before his election to the Cortes (Spanish parliament) in 1982. He was prime minister of the autonomous region of Castilla y León, and has been president of the PP (Popular Party, formerly Popular Alliance) since 1990.

azo-dyes [azoh] An important class of dyes originally made (1861) by Peter Griess (1829–88), a German-born chemist who worked mainly as a brewery chemist at Burton-on-Trent, Staffordshire, UK. All have two nitrogen atoms joined: –N=N–.

azolla [azola] An aquatic, free-floating fern, native to tropical and subtropical regions; stem only a few cm long, branched with scale-like, overlapping fronds covered with non-wettable hairs, reddish in autumn. (Genus: *Azolla*, 6 species. Family: Azollaceae.)

Azores *see panel*

Azov, Sea of [azof], Russ **Azovskoye More** Gulf in NE of Black Sea; shallow water, tending to freeze (Nov–Mar); important source of freshwater fish for Russia.

AZT An abbreviation for **azidothymidine**, a drug which inhibits replication of viruses, including the AIDS virus, HIV. Developed as **zidovudine**, it was granted a licence unusually rapidly, in response to pressure from AIDS patients. Clinical trials have demonstrated the drug to be of limited use in therapy. It has inherent toxicity, and resistance develops rapidly.

Aztecs The most powerful people of Central America during the 15th–16th-c. Their main city, Tenochtitlan (present-day Mexico City), became the most densely populated city of the region. They built up a powerful despotic state, eventually ruling 400–500 small tribute-paying states. They developed a form of hieroglyphic writing, a complex calendar system, and built famous pyramids and temples. The Aztec empire was finally destroyed by the Spanish under Cortés in 1521.

b

Baader–Meinhof [bahder **miynhof**] The popular name for *Rote Armee Fraktion* (RAF), after leaders Andreas Baader (1943–77) and Ulrike Meinhof (1934–76); a left-wing German revolutionary terrorist group which carried out political bombings in Germany in the early 1970s.

Baal [bayl] (Heb 'lord') The Phoenician god of rain and fertility, his voice being the thunder; in the Bible, used for gods of various localities in Syria and Canaan.

Baalbek [bahlbek], ancient **Heliopolis** 34°00N 36°12E, pop (2000e) 17 000. Town in E Lebanon where the Phoenicians built a temple to the Sun-god, Baal; a world heritage site.

Baath or **Ba'ath** [bahth] (Arabic 'resurgence') The ideology of the Baath Arab Socialist Party, founded in 1940 by a Christian, Michel Aflaq, and a Muslim, Salah al-Din Bitar, synthesizing Marxism with a pan-Arab nationalism that aims to unite Arab nations. The party has been most prominent in Syria and Iraq.

Baba Malay *Malay* (language)

Babar or **Babur** (Arabic 'tiger'), originally **Zahir-ud-din Muhammad** (1483–1530) First Mughal Emperor of India, born in Ferghana, Uzbekistan. He was a distinguished soldier, as well as a poet and diarist of note.

Babbage, Charles (1791–1871) Mathematician and pioneer computer scientist, born in Walworth, London. He worked on the theory of logarithms, and built a 'difference machine', the forerunner of the computer, for which a system of programming was devised. His assistant was Byron's daughter, Augusta Ada, Lady Lovelace. In 1991, for the bicentenary of his birth, the Science Museum constructed a full-scale Difference Engine No 2 from original designs dating from 1847.

Babbitt, Bruce (Edward) (1938–) US statesman, born in Flagstaff, AZ. He trained as a lawyer, served as Arizona's attorney-general (1975–8), and became state governor (1978–87). An unsuccessful candidate for the Democratic presidential nomination in 1988, he was appointed secretary of the interior in 1993, and was reappointed in the 1997 administration.

babbler A songbird native to warmer regions of the Old World; soft, fluffy plumage and short wings. (Family: Timaliidae, over 280 species.)

Babel, Tower of Probably the site of an important temple shrine in the ancient city of Babylon. In the Bible (*Gen* 11.1–9) the legend is related of how its construction led to the confusion of languages, and the consequent dispersion of peoples, as a punishment by God for human pride.

Babi *Baha'i*

Babington, Antony (1561–86) Conspirator, born in Dethick, Derbyshire. In 1586, he was induced to lead a conspiracy to murder Queen Elizabeth and release Queen Mary of Scotland (the **Babington Plot**). The plot was discovered, and he was executed.

Babinski, Joseph (François Felix) [babinskee] (1857–1932) Neurologist, born in Paris. He is known for his description of an abnormal foot reflex which is symptomatic of upper motor neurone disease, and a reflex of the forearm believed to be due to a lesion in the spinal cord. Both reflexes are known as **Babinski's Sign**.

babirusa [babiroosa] A wild pig native to Sulawesi (*Babyrousa babyrussa*); pale, almost hairless body; long lower tusks; upper canines in the male grow from the top of the snout, and curl towards the eyes; inhabits riverbanks; swims well.

Babi Yar A huge ravine near Kiev in the Ukraine into which over 30 000 Jews were herded and massacred by Nazi German troops in 1941.

baboon A ground-dwelling African monkey; long dog-like muzzle with large teeth; males with swollen, naked buttocks. (Genera: *Papio*, 5 species; *Mandrillus*, 2 species; *Theropithecus*, 1 species.)

Babylon 32°33N 44°25E. From the 18th-c BC the capital of the Babylonian Empire, situated on the R Euphrates S of Baghdad, modern Iraq. Its massive city walls and 'hanging gardens' were one of the wonders of the ancient world.

Babylonia [babilohnia] The region in Lower Mesopotamia around the ancient city of Babylon, which formed the core twice in antiquity of extensive but short-lived empires. Under its greatest ruler Nebuchadnezzar (605–562 BC), it stretched as far W as the Mediterranean.

Babylonian exile The mass deportation of the Jews from Palestine to Babylonia in 587–6 BC, after the failure of their revolt against Nebuchadnezzar.

Bacall, Lauren [bakawl], originally **Betty Joan Perske** (1924–) Actress, born in New York City. She was given her first leading role in *To Have and Have Not* (1944), opposite Humphrey Bogart, whom she subsequently married. Later films include *The Big Sleep* (1946), *Key Largo* (1948), *The Shootist* (1976, BAFTA), *The Mirror Has Two Faces* (1996), *Dogville* (2004), and *Birth* (2004).

baccarat A casino card game, the most popular version being *baccarat banque*, in which the bank plays against the players. Another variant is *chemin de fer*, whereby all players take it in turn to hold the bank.

Bacchanalia [bakanaylia] The orgiastic rites of Bacchus (Dionysus), the god of nature, fertility, and wine. They were banned from Rome in 186 BC.

Bach, C(arl) P(hilipp) E(manuel), known as **the Berlin Bach** or **the Hamburg Bach** (1714–88) Composer, born in Weimar, Germany, the second surviving son of Johann Sebastian Bach. He wrote the first methodical treatment of clavier playing, and composed numerous concertos, keyboard sonatas, church music, and chamber music.

Bach, J(ohann) C(hristian), known as **the London Bach** or **the English Bach** (1735–82) Composer, born in Leipzig, Germany, the youngest son of Johann Sebastian Bach. In 1762 he settled in London, where he was employed at the King's Theatre and promoted an important series of subscription concerts.

Bach, Johann Sebastian (1685–1750) Composer, one of the world's greatest musicians, born in Eisenach, Germany. In 1707 he married a cousin, **Maria Barbara Bach** (1684–1720), and in 1711 became *Kapellmeister* to Prince Leopold of Anhalt-Cöthen, where he wrote mainly instrumental music, including the 'Brandenburg' Concertos (1721) and *The Well-tempered Clavier* (1722). Widowed in 1720, and left with four children, he married in 1721 **Anna Magdalena Wilcke** (1701–60), and had 13 children by her, of whom six survived. In 1723 he was appointed cantor of the Thomasschule in Leipzig, where his works included perhaps c.300 church cantatas, the *St Matthew Passion* (1727), and the *Mass in B Minor*. Almost totally blind, he died in Leipzig. His main achievement was the development of polyphony, but because of his success as an organist his genius as a composer was not fully recognized until the following century.

Bacher, Ali [bakher] (1942–) Cricketer and sports administrator, born in Roodepoort, South Africa. He captained Transvaal and South Africa with great success, but his Test career was cut short by international sports boycotts of South African teams. He was a leading figure in organizing the 'rebel' tours to South Africa in the 1980s, and in subsequent non-racial planning. In 1997 he became the first chairman of the International Cricket Council's development committee.

Bach flower remedies A system of flower remedies for illnesses, and especially for disharmonies of the personality and emotional state, devised by British medical microbiologist Edward Bach (1880–1936). Bach theorized that the dew condensing on a plant would, when exposed to sunlight, absorb the energy of the plant into the water molecules. From this premise he developed a system of herbal remedies prepared from 38 different species of flower.

bacillus [basiluhs] Any rod-shaped bacterium; also a large and diverse genus of rod-shaped bacteria, typically motile by means of flagella. Some are disease-causing, including the causative agent of anthrax. (Kingdom: Monera. Family: Bacillaceae.)

backgammon A board game for two players. Introduced to Britain by the Crusaders, it became known as backgammon from c.1750. Each player has 15 round flat pieces of a particular colour, which are moved around the board on the throw of two dice. The board is divided into two halves; the inner table and the outer table. The object is to move your own pieces around the board and home to your own inner table. You win by being the first to remove all your pieces from the board.

background radiation Naturally occurring radioactivity which can be detected at any place on Earth. It results from cosmic rays reaching the Earth from outer space, and from the radioactive decay of materials in the ground.

backing store A general term used in computing to describe the place where the computer stores the long term data needed to carry out its tasks; also known as **bulk store** or **secondary store**. It has a higher capacity but lower access time than the main memory of a computer, and is normally in the form of magnetic tape storage or magnetic disk storage.

Bacon, Francis, Viscount St Albans (1561–1626) Philosopher and statesman, born in London. He was in turn solicitor general (1607), attorney general (1613), privy counsellor (1616), Lord Keeper (1617), and Lord Chancellor (1618). His philosophy is best studied in *The Advancement of Learning* (1605) and *Novum Organum* (1620). His stress on inductive methods gave a strong impetus to subsequent scientific investigation.

Bacon, Francis (1909–92) Artist, born in Dublin. He began painting without any formal art education at the age of 19. He treated religious subjects in a highly individual manner, but made little impact until his 'Three Studies for Figures at the base of a Crucifixion' (1945). His style derives from Surrealism, often with a tendency towards the macabre.

Bacon, Kevin (1958–) Actor and musician, born in Philadelphia, PA. He studied acting at the Circle in the Square Theater in New York and gained his first feature film role in *National Lam-*

poon's Animal House (1981). Later films include *Apollo 13* (1995), *Hollow Man* (2000), *Mystic River* (2003), and *Saving Angelo* (2006). He also performs with The Bacon Brothers, a folk-rock group formed with his brother Michael.

Bacon, Nathaniel (1647–76) American colonial leader, born in Suffolk, England. He emigrated to Virginia in 1673, and made himself prominent by his raids against the Indians. His activities prompted the English governor to declare him a rebel in 1676, whereupon Bacon captured and burned Jamestown. For a time he controlled most of Virginia, but died suddenly, and the rebellion ended.

Bacon, Roger, known as **Doctor Mirabilis** ('Wonderful Doctor') (c.1220–92) Philosopher, probably born in Ilchester, Somerset. In 1247 he began to devote himself to experimental science, and in 1266–7 compiled, at the request of Pope Clement IV, his *Opus Majus* (Great Work). In 1277 his writings were condemned, and he was imprisoned until shortly before his death.

bacteria *p.73*

bacteriological warfare A form of warfare using organic agents such as micro-organisms and viruses which cause disease and death in humans. Many such agents have been investigated, including anthrax, plague, and botulinus toxin. Fears of bacteriological warfare surfaced in the aftermath of the terrorist attack on the United States of America on 11 Sep 2001 when a number of individuals were infected after coming into contact with anthrax-tainted letters and packages received through the postal service.

bacteriology The study of the biology of bacteria and of the diseases they cause. It involves identifying and classifying bacteria according to their characteristics, growing them in artificial media to determine the conditions under which they thrive, observing the disease processes they induce, and collecting and testing specimens to develop cures and vaccinations.

Bactria [baktria] The name given in antiquity to the area roughly corresponding to N Afghanistan and the adjacent parts of S Russia. It became an independent state in the second half of the 3rd-c BC.

Badajoz [badajoz], Span [bathahoth], ancient **Pax Augusta** 38°50N 6°59W, pop (2000e) 124 000. City in SW Spain, on R Guadiana; bishopric; former Moorish capital; scene of a battle in the Peninsular War, 1812; airport; railway; cathedral (13th-c).

Baden [bahdn], ancient **Thermae Pannonicae** 48°01N 16°14E, pop (2000e) 25 800. Town in NE Austria, on the R Schwechat; connected to Vienna by tram; principal Austrian spa, with sulphurous waters, known since Roman times; tourism.

Baden-Powell, Robert Stephenson Smyth Baden-Powell, Baron [baydn powel] (1857–1941) British general, born in London. He joined the army, served in India and Afghanistan, was on the staff in West Africa and Matabeleland, and won fame during the Boer War as the defender of Mafeking (1899–1900). In 1908 he founded the Boy Scout movement, and in 1910, with his sister **Agnes** (1858–1945), the Girl Guides.

Bader, Sir Douglas (Robert Stuart) [bahder] (1910–82) Wartime aviator, born in London. He lost both legs in a flying accident in 1931 and was invalided out of the RAF, but overcame his disability and returned to the service in 1939, commanding the first RAF Canadian Fighter Squadron. Captured in 1941, he set an example of fortitude and heroism that became a legend.

badger A nocturnal mammal, usually grey-brown with a black and white head; pointed face; length 0·5–1 m/1½–3¼ ft; lives in burrows. (Family: Mustelidae, 8 species.)

Badlands Arid region of SW South Dakota and NW Nebraska, USA; an area of barren, eroded landscapes and fossil deposits E of the Black Hills.

badminton An indoor court game played by two or four people

bacteria

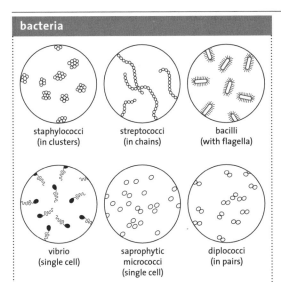

| staphylococci (in clusters) | streptococci (in chains) | bacilli (with flagella) |

| vibrio (single cell) | saprophytic micrococci (single cell) | diplococci (in pairs) |

(sing **bacterium**) A diverse division of microscopic organisms that all share a *procaryotic* cellular organization, ie each cell lacks a true nucleus bounded by a nuclear membrane. The genetic information is carried on a loop of deoxyribonucleic acid (DNA) in the cytoplasm. Most bacteria are single-celled. Basic bacterial shapes are spherical (*coccus*), rod-like (*bacillus*), and spiral (*spirillum*). These may occur singly, or in chains, pairs, clusters, or other groupings. Some (the actinomycetes) have a branching, filamentous structure, and may form a mycelium. Most have a rigid cell wall containing peptidoglycan, the exceptions being the mycoplasms and halobacteria. Cell division typically occurs by symmetrical binary fission; some form spores; mitosis never occurs. Bacteria range in size from less than $1\,\mu$ (*Chlamydia*) to about 0·5 mm (spirochaete), but most are between 1 and 10 μ; a bacterium *Thiomargarita namibiensis*, with a cell up to 0·75 mm, was reported in 1999. They differ greatly in their growth requirements. Some can grow only in the presence of oxygen (**aerobic bacteria**), while others grow only in the absence of oxygen (**anaerobic bacteria**). They occur in soil, water, and air, as well as in symbiotic associations with other organisms, and as parasites or disease-causing agents. They cause many human diseases, including anthrax, plague, pneumonia, syphilis, tetanus, and tuberculosis. The scientific study of bacteria is known as **bacteriology**.

using rackets and a shuttlecock. Its name derives from Badminton House, the seat of the Duke of Beaufort, where the Duke's family and guests played in the 19th-c. It developed from the children's game of *battledore and shuttlecock*.

Baedeker, Karl [baydeker] (1801–59) Publisher, born in Essen, Germany. He started his own publishing business at Koblenz in 1827, and is best known for the guidebooks which bear his name, published since 1872 at Leipzig.

Baez, Joan [biyez] (1941–) Folksinger, born in Staten I, New York City. Her crystalline soprano voice first attracted critical plaudits at the Newport Folk Festival of 1960, and her recordings in the decade that followed created a mass audience for folk music.

Baffin, William (c.1584–1622) Navigator, probably born in London. He was pilot in several expeditions in search of the Northwest Passage (1612–16). Baffin Bay is named after him.

Baffin Bay Ice-blocked Arctic gulf between Greenland (E) and

Baffin, Bylot, Devon, and Ellesmere Is (W); length c.1125 km/ 700 mi; width 110–650 km/70–400 mi; depth over 2400 m/ 8100 ft; navigation only in summer; first entered by John Davis, 1585; explored by William Baffin, 1615.

Baffin Island Largest island in the Canadian Arctic Archipelago, in the Arctic Ocean; became part of new Nunavut territory in 1999; area 318 186 km^2/122 820 sq mi; length c.1600 km/ 1000 mi; width 209–725 km/130–450 mi; irregular coastline, with several peninsulas and deep bays; first visited by Frobisher, 1576–8; Iqaluit is capital of Nunavut; population mainly Inuit.

BAFTA *British Academy of Film and Television Arts*

bagatelle [bagatel] A restricted form of billiards, played on a table with nine numbered cups instead of pockets. Popular in the UK, it is played in many different forms on a rectangular table.

Bagehot, Walter [bajuht] (1826–77) Economist, journalist, and political theorist, born in Langport, Somerset. His *English Constitution* (1867) is still considered a standard work.

Bagerat [bageraht] The former city of Khalifatabad, founded in the 15th-c by General Ulugh Khan Jahan in the S Ganges delta, present-day Bangladesh; a world heritage site.

Baghdad [bagdad] 33°20N 44°26E, pop (2000e) 6 247 000. Capital city of Iraq, on R Tigris; a commercial and transportation centre; founded, 762; enclosed on three sides by ancient walls; sacked by Mongols, 1258; later under Mongol, then Turkish rule; independent capital, 20th-c; airport; railway; university (1958); oil refining, distilling, tanning, tobacco, textiles, gum, brick, tiles, metal industry, cement; Abbasid palace, Mustansiriyah law college (13th-c); badly damaged through bombing during the Gulf War, 1991; taken by US-led coalition forces during the Iraq War, 2003; after the war, persistent street violence and bomb attacks between rival factions and against occupying forces, ongoing into 2007.

bagpipes A musical instrument of great antiquity consisting of a bag (usually of sheepskin) which the player fills with air through a blow-pipe or bellows, and squeezes with the arm so that the air then passes through several sounding pipes. The Highlands and Lowlands of Scotland have their different types of bagpipes, as also do Ireland, Northumberland, and several other parts of Europe.

Baguio [bagioh] 16°25N 120°37E, pop (2000e) 191 000. Summer capital of the Philippines, in NW Luzon I; mountain resort town and official summer residence of the president; two universities (1911, 1948); military academy.

Baha'i [bahiy] A religious faith arising out of a 19th-c anti-clerical movement in Iran, when Mirza Husayn-Ali (1817–92), known as Baha'u'llah ('Glory of God'), declared himself the prophet foretold by the founder of the Babi movement, Mirza Ali-Mohammed (1819–50). Baha'ism teaches the oneness of God, the unity of all faiths, the harmony of all people, universal education, and obedience to government. Its headquarters is in Haifa, Israel. There are around 7.5 million adherents in 2007.

Bahamas *p.74*

Bahia [baeea] pop (2000e) 13 536 000; area 561 026 km^2/ 216 556 sq mi. State in NE Brazil, bounded E by the Atlantic; capital, Salvador; site of first landing by Portuguese in 1500.

Bahía Blanca [baeea blangka] 38°45S 62°15W, pop (2000e) 302 500. City in E Argentina; includes naval base of Puerto Belgrano; founded in 1828; university (1956); airport; railway.

Bahrain *p.75*

Baikal or **Baykal, Lake** [biykal] area 31 500 km^2/12 160 sq mi. Crescent-shaped lake in S Siberia, Russia; largest freshwater lake in Eurasia, and deepest in the world; length (SW–NE) 636 km/ 395 mi; width 24–80 km/15–50 mi; maximum depth 1620 m/ 5315 ft; freezes over (Jan–Apr); measures to control serious pollution introduced since 1971.

Bahamas

□ International Airport

official name **Commonwealth of the Bahamas**
Local name Bahamas
Timezone GMT -5
Area 13 934 km²/5378 sq mi
Population total (2002e) 309 000

Status Independent state within the Commonwealth
Date of independence 1973
Capital Nassau
Language English (official)
Ethnic groups African (85%), European/N American descent (15%)
Religions Baptist (29%), Anglican (29%), Roman Catholic (23%)
Physical features Coral archipelago of 700 islands and 2400 uninhabited cays, forming a chain extending c.800 km/500 mi SE from the coast of Florida; population centres on the two oceanic banks of Little and Great Bahama; highest point, Mt Alvernia, 120 m/394 ft.
Climate Sub-tropical; average temperatures 21°C (Jan) and 27°C (Jul); mean annual rainfall 750–1500 mm/30–60 in; hurricanes frequent (Jun–Nov).
Currency 1 Bahamian Dollar (BSD) = 100 cents
Economy Market economy based on tourism; important financial centre (no income tax); oil refining, fishing, rum and liqueur distilling; cement; pharmaceuticals.
GDP (2002e) $4·59 bn, per capita $15 300
Human Development Index (2002) 0·826
History Visited by Columbus in 1492, but first permanent European settlement not until 1647 by British and Bermudan religious refugees; British Crown Colony from 1717; independence, 1973; governed by a bicameral Parliament.
Head of State
(British monarch represented by governor-general)
1988–92 Sir Henry Taylor
1992–5 Clifford Darling
1995–2001 Orville Turnquest
2001–5 Dame Ivy Dumont
2006– Arthur Dion Hanna
Head of Government
1973–92 Sir Lynden O Pindling
1992–2002 Hubert Alexander Ingraham
2002– Perry Christie

Baikonur or **Baykonyr Cosmodrome** [biykonoor] A Russian space centre constructed in 1955 in Karaganda oblast, Kazakhstan. It was from here that the first satellite to orbit the Earth, Sputnik 1, was launched in 1957. In 1961 Yuri Gagarin became the first man in space, and the first woman in space and the first person to walk in space also took off from Baikonur. In 1998 the first element of the International Space Station, the Russian-built Zarya control module, was launched. Baikonur celebrated its 50th anniversary in 2005.

bail The freeing from custody of a person charged with a crime and awaiting trial. There are often conditions imposed to secure the person's attendance at a court on a future date. Frequently the security involves a sum of money pledged by the person or a guarantor (a *surety*) with the police or a court. This money is liable to be forfeited in the event of the accused person's non-appearance. There are several differences in the operation of the bail procedure between legal systems. Breach of any bail condition is itself an offence.

Bailey, David (Royston) (1938–) Photographer, born in London. Originally a fashion photographer, he became known for his portraits expressing the spirit of the 1960s. He has been a director of televison commercials and documentaries since the 1970s.

Bailey bridge A prefabricated bridge used by combat engineers, which can be rapidly constructed on the battlefield. The system was devised by British engineer Sir Donald Bailey (1901–85) during World War 2.

bailiff An officer of the sheriff or the county court who is responsible for executing warrants, processes, and writs. He may also seize goods as a method of obtaining payment, such as for unpaid rent. The equivalent position in Scotland is that of the Sheriff officer.

Baillie, Dame Isobel [baylee] (1895–1983) Soprano, born in Hawick, Scottish Borders. She is regarded as one of the 20th-century's greatest oratorio singers.

Baily, Francis (1774–1844) Astronomer, born in Newbury, West Berkshire. He described the phenomenon now known as **Baily's beads** in 1836 – a broken ring of bright points around the edge of the Moon, formed in a total solar eclipse by the Sun's rays shining through the Moon's valleys at the moment of totality.

Bainbridge, Dame Beryl (Margaret) (1934–) Writer, born in Liverpool, Merseyside. She began writing in the 1960s, and became known for her terse, black comedies, such as *The Dressmaker* (1973, filmed 1979) and *Filthy Lucre* (1986). Several novels tackle historical subjects, such as *Young Adolf* (1978) and *The Birthday Boys* (1991). Later novels include *Master Georgie* (1998), *According to Queeney* (2001), and *The Girl in the Polka Dot Dress* (2007), and she has also published plays, stories, and collections of her journalistic essays.

Baird, John Logie (1888–1946) Television pioneer, born in Helensburgh, Argyll and Bute. In 1926 he gave the first demonstration of a television image. His 30-line mechanically scanned system was experimentally broadcast by the BBC in 1929; and during

Bahrain

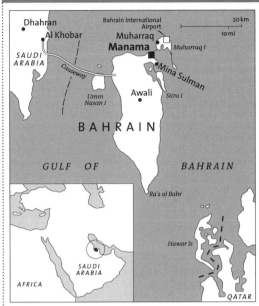

☐ International Airport

official name **State of Bahrain**
Local name al-Bahrayn
Timezone GMT +3
Area 678 km²/262 sq mi
Population total (2002e) 672 000
Status Independent state

Date of independence 1971
Capital Manama
Languages Arabic (official), Farsi, Urdu, and English
Ethnic groups Bahraini Arab (63%), Asian (13%), Arab (10%), Iranian (9%)
Religions Muslim (Shi'ite 65%), Sunni 35%)
Physical features Island of Bahrain c.48 km/30 mi long, 13–16 km/8–10 mi wide, area 562 km²/217 sq mi; highest point Jabal Dukhan, 135 m/443 ft; largely bare and infertile.
Climate Temperate (Dec–Mar); hot and humid (particularly Jun–Sep); cool N/NE winds with a little rain (Dec–Mar); average annual rainfall 35 mm/1·4 in; average annual temperature 19°C (Jan), 36°C (Jul).
Currency 1 Bahrain Dinar (BHD) = 1000 fils
Economy Major centre for oil trading, banking, commerce.
GDP (2002e) $9·91 bn, per capita $15 100
Human Development Index (2002) 0·831
History Flourishing centre of trade during 2000–1800 BC; treaty of protection with the UK, 1861; independence in 1971, with a constitutional monarchy governed by an Emir; National Assembly dissolved in 1975 and not yet revived; historic territorial dispute with Qatar over the Hawar Is began with the brief occupation of Fasht al-Dibal by Qatari troops, 1986; joined UN coalition during the Iraqi invasion of Kuwait, 1990; became monarchy, 2002.

Head of State (Emir; King, from 2002)
1869–1935 Isa I
1923–42 Hamad
1942–61 Salman II
1961–9 Shaikh Isa II bin Sulman al-Khalifa
1999– Shaikh Hamad II bin Isa al-Khalifa

Head of Government
1971– Shaikh Khalifa bin Sulman al-Khalifa

1936, transmissions of his improved 240-line system alternated with the rival Marconi-EMI 405-line electronic system, which was adopted in 1937.

Baja California [baha], Eng **Lower California** A long peninsula in NW Mexico; length 1220 km/760 mi; San Pedro Mártir Mts rise to 3095 m/10 154 ft; Colorado R flows into the N of the Gulf; geographical isolation much eased by highway completed in 1970s down the whole peninsula; chief towns, Mexicali, Ensenada, La Paz.

Bajazet *Bayezit I*

Baker, Sir Benjamin (1840–1907) Civil engineer, born in Keyford, Somerset. In 1861 he began a long association with engineer John Fowler, and together they constructed the London Metropolitan Railway, Victoria Station, and the Forth Rail Bridge (opened 1890).

Baker, James A(ddison), III (1930–) US secretary of state (1989–92), born in Houston, TX. He served President Reagan as White House chief-of-staff (1981–5) and secretary of the Treasury (1985–8) before resigning to manage George Bush's campaign for the presidency. After winning the election, Bush named him as secretary of state. In 1992 he returned to the White House as chief-of-staff, to run Bush's re-election campaign. He later served UN secretary-general Kofi Annan as his personal envoy for the Western Sahara (1997–2004).

Baker, Dame Janet (Abbott) (1933–) Mezzo-soprano, born in Hatfield, South Yorkshire. She had an extensive operatic career, especially in early Italian opera and the works of Benjamin Britten; she is also a noted interpreter of Mahler and Elgar. In 1994 she became a Companion of Honour.

Baker (of Dorking), Kenneth (Wilfred), Baron (1934–) British statesman. He became an MP in 1968, and in the Thatcher administration rose to become secretary of state for the environment (1985) and for education (1986). He was later appointed chairman of the Conservative Party (1989–90) and home secretary (1990–2).

Baker, Richard (Douglas James) (1925–) Broadcaster and writer, born in London. He joined the BBC as an announcer in 1950, and became known as a television newsreader (1954–82) and as a commentator on major state occasions. He also introduced the television productions of BBC Promenade Concerts (1960–95).

Bakewell, Joan (Dawson) (1933–) Broadcaster and writer, born in Stockport, Greater Manchester. She became known for her regular contributions and series on television, such as *Late Night Line Up* (1965–72), *Reports Action* (1976–8), and *The Heart of the Matter* (1988–2000). Her books include *The Complete Traveller* (1977), *Belief* (2005), and *The View from Here: Life at Seventy* (2006).

baking powder A mixture of sodium bicarbonate, tartaric acid, and potassium tartrate, used in baking. It is added to dough (a mixture of flour and water), and when heated, carbon dioxide is released, causing the dough to rise.

Bakst, Léon [bahkst], originally **Lev Samuilovich Rosenberg** (1866–1924) Painter and set designer, born in St Petersburg, Russia. He was associated with Diaghilev, designing the decor and costumes for numerous productions (1909–21).

Baku [bakoo] 40°22N 49°53E, pop (2000e) 1 174 000. Seaport capital of Azerbaijan; on the W coast of the Caspian Sea; airport;

railway; university (1919). The walled city is a world heritage site.

Balabanov, Aleksei (1959–) Film director, born in Yekaterinburg, Russia. In 1983, after studying languages in Gorky and working as a translator for the Soviet Army, he began working as a jobbing director at Sverdlovsk Film Studios. His directorial debut came in 1989 with *Yegor and Nastya*. Later films include *Brat* (1997, The Brother), the award-winning *Pro urodov I lyudej* (1998, Of Freaks and Men), and *Brat II* (2000, The Brother II).

Balaclava, Battle of (1854) A battle fought between British and Russian forces during the early stages of the Crimean War. The Russian attack on the British base at Balaclava was unsuccessful, but the British sustained the heavier losses.

Balakirev, Mili Alekseyevich [balakiryef] (1837–1910) Composer, born in Nizhni Novgorod, Russia. He became leader of the national Russian school of music. His compositions include two symphonies, many songs, and some highly individual piano music.

balalaika [balaliyka] A Russian musical instrument: a lute, with a triangular body, flat back, long neck, and three strings which are strummed by the player's fingers.

balance of payments The difference, for a country, between the income and expenditure arising out of its international trading activities. The *current account* includes the country's income from selling goods abroad (exporting), offset by its expenditure on goods imported. The difference between these two totals is the **trade balance**. Also included are 'invisible' services bought and sold abroad, such as banking, insurance, and tourism. The *capital account* deals with private and corporate investment abroad, borrowing and lending, and government financial transactions. A **balance of payments deficit** drains a nation's reserves of convertible currency and gold, and can lead to a devaluation of its currency.

balance sheet A statement of the assets and liabilities of a firm or organization at a moment in time, normally the end of a financial year. Assets include physical objects including land and buildings, plant and equipment, stocks of materials, work in progress and inventories of output not yet sold, and financial assets including cash and bank balances, securities held, and trade credit extended. Liabilities include long- and short-term debt, taxes due for payment, and trade credit. A solvent company's liabilities are less than these assets; to equate the two sides of the balance sheet the difference is treated as a debt to the shareholders of a company or members of an organization.

Balanchine, George [baluhncheen], originally **Georgi Melitonovich Balanchivadze** (1904–83) Ballet dancer and choreographer, born in St Petersburg, Russia. After a period in the Russian Ballet in Paris, he opened in 1934 the School of American Ballet in New York, and from then devoted most of his career to establishing a native American tradition of dance. In 1948 he became director of the New York City Ballet.

Balaton, Lake [boloton] area 598 km²/231 sq mi. Lake in WC Hungary; length 77 km/48 mi; width 8–14 km/5–9 mi; largest and shallowest lake in C Europe; Hungary's largest recreation area.

Balboa, Vasco Núñez de [balboha] (1475–1519) Explorer, born in Jerez de los Caballeros, Spain. He joined the expedition to Darién in 1511, and became the first European to see the Pacific Ocean (1513).

bald cypress *swamp cypress*

bald eagle A large eagle (length 80–100 cm/30–40 in), native to North America (*Haliaeetus leucocephalus*); the name refers to the white plumage on its head and neck. The national symbol of the USA, it is also known as the **American eagle**. (Family: Accipitridae).

Balder, Baldur, or **Baldr** [bawlder, balder] Norse god, the most handsome and gentle of the children of Odin and Frigga; the name means 'bright'. He taught human beings the use of herbs for healing.

baldness Commonly described as permanent loss of hair from the front and/or top of the head, usually in men, because of the degeneration and reduction in the size of hair follicles. Genetic factors, ageing, and androgens may be causative agents. There is no effective cure.

baldpate *wigeon*

Baldwin I (1172–c.1205) Count of Flanders (from 1194) and Hainault (from 1195), the youngest brother of Godfrey of Bouillon. He was a leader of the Fourth Crusade, and in 1204 was crowned as the first Latin Emperor of Constantinople.

Baldwin, James (Arthur) (1924–87) Writer, born in Harlem, New York City. He became an active member of the civil rights movement. His novels include *Go Tell it on the Mountain* (1954), *Tell Me How Long The Train's Been Gone* (1968), and *Just Above My Head* (1979).

Baldwin, Mark (Phillip) (1954–) Choreographer and dancer, born in Fiji. He became a dancer with the New Zealand Ballet and Australian Dance Theatre before joining the Rambert Dance Company in London (1982–92), also as choreographer (1992–4). He became resident choreographer with Sadlers Wells (1994–5) and with the Scottish Ballet (1996). In 1996 he received awards for his dance film video *Danse 8*. He was appointed artistic director of the Rambert Dance Company in 2002.

Baldwin (of Bewdley), Stanley Baldwin, 1st Earl (1867–1947) British Conservative statesman, who was three times prime minister (1923–4, 1924–9, 1935–7), born in Bewdley, Worcestershire. He was President of the Board of Trade (1921–2) and Chancellor of the Exchequer (1922–3), then unexpectedly succeeded Bonar Law as premier. His period of office included the General Strike (1926).

Balearic Islands *p.77*

baleen A fibrous material from the mouth of some species of whale; forms a sieve during feeding; formerly used in manufacturing, when strong, light, flexible material was needed; also known as **whalebone** (though it is not in fact bone).

Balenciaga, Cristóbal [balenthiahga] (1895–1972) Fashion designer, born in Guetaria, Spain. He left Spain for Paris as a result of the Spanish Civil War, producing clothes noted for dramatic simplicity and elegant design.

Balfour, Arthur James Balfour, 1st Earl [balfer] (1848–1930) British statesman and Conservative prime minister (1902–5), born in Whittingehame, East Lothian. He became chief secretary for Ireland (1887–91), where his policy of suppression earned him the name of 'Bloody Balfour'. As foreign secretary (1916–19) he was responsible for the **Balfour Declaration** (1917), which promised Zionists a national home in Palestine.

Bali [bahlee] pop (2000e) 3 265 000; area 5561 km²/2146 sq mi. Island province of Indonesia; mountainous, with peaks rising to 3142 m/10 308 ft at Gunung Agung (E); chiefly Hindu population; Dutch control by 1908; capital, Denpasar; major tourist area but badly affected following terrorist bomb attack which killed 202 in Kuta (Oct 2002); further bomb attacks (2003, 2004, 2005) with a number of deaths.

balkanization (*balkan*, Turkish 'mountain') The fragmentation of a region into smaller, often hostile, political units; specifically in the Balkans, where division is enhanced by their often mountainous geography. As the Ottoman empire weakened its hold on the Balkans in the 19th-c, ancient power struggles emerged. During the Ottoman period, most Albanians had converted to Islam, while most Serbs had adhered to a form of Christian orthodoxy. New political boundaries were drawn up after World Wars 1 and 2; a degree of autonomy and national independence was allowed to some groups, furthering ethnic separatism. This contributed to the polarization of ethnic groups into religious, cultural, geographic, and economic factions.

Balearic Islands

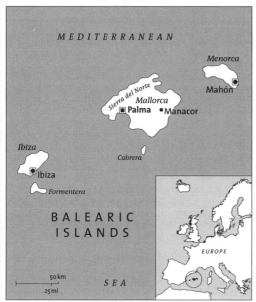

☐ International Airport

[baliarik], Span **Islas Baleares**

Local name Islas Baleares

Area 5014 km²/1935 sq mi

Population total (2000e) 712 000

Status Province of Spain

Capital Palma de Mallorca

Physical features Archipelago of five major islands and 11 islets in the Mediterranean, near the E coast of Spain; E group of islands consists of Mallorca (Majorca), Menorca, Cabrera; Ibiza and Formentera (W group); popular tourist resorts.

Climate Continental; average annual temperatures 11°C (Jan), 25°C (Jul); average annual rainfall 347 mm/14 in.

Currency 1 euro (EUR) = 100 cents (previous to February 2002, 1 Peseta (ESP) = 100 céntimos).

Economy Tourism; fruit, wine, grain, cattle, fishing, textiles, chemicals, cork; timber.

Balkan Wars (1912–13) A series of military campaigns fought in the Balkans. In 1912, Bulgaria, Serbia, Greece, and Montenegro attacked Turkey, securing swift victories. A preliminary peace was drawn up by the Great Powers in May 1913. Disputes between the Balkan allies over the spoils of war led to a second war (June–July 1913), in which Bulgaria attacked her former allies, and was defeated.

Balkhash, Lake [balkash] area 17 000–22 300 km²/6500–8500 sq mi. Crescent-shaped lake in SE Kazakhstan; length 605 km/376 mi; maximum width 74 km/46 mi; maximum depth 26 m/85 ft; no outlet; gradually shrinking.

Ball, Michael (Ashley) (1962–) Actor and singer, born in the West Midlands. His first starring role was in *The Pirates of Penzance* (1985, Manchester Opera House), and he made his West End debut in *Les Miserables* later that year. Other major productions include *Phantom of the Opera* (1987), *Aspects of Love* (1989, Broadway debut 1990), *Passion* (1996), and *The Woman in White* (2005). Television work includes his own series (1993, 1994) and he has made many recordings.

Ballantyne, R(obert) M(ichael) (1825–94) Writer of boys' books, born in Edinburgh. He joined the Hudson's Bay Company in 1841, and worked in the backwoods of N Canada until 1847. *The Coral Island* (1858) is his most famous work.

Ballarat or **Ballaarat** [balarat] 37°36S 143°58E, pop (2000e) 38 100. City in SWC Victoria, Australia; railway; centre of a wool-producing district; largest gold reserves in the country discovered here, 1851; scene of the Eureka Stockade, the gold-diggers' rebellion against state authority, 1854.

Ballard, J(ames) G(raham) (1930–) Writer, born in Shanghai, China. He specialized in the writing of science-fiction novels (eg his first, *The Drowned World*, 1962), later publishing an autobiographical novel *Empire of the Sun* (1984; filmed, 1987). Further novels include *Super-Cannes* (2000) and *Kingdom Come* (2006).

Ballesteros, Sevvy [ba-yestayros], popular name of **Severiano Ballesteros** (1957–) Golfer, born in Pedrena, Spain. His successes include the (British) Open (1979, 1984, 1988), the US Masters (1980, 1983), and the World Matchplay (1981–2, 1984–5, 1991).

ballet A theatrical form of dance typically combined with music, stage design, and costume in an integrated whole, based around a scenario. It can be divided roughly into historical periods; mid-19th-c Romantic ballets such as *La Sylphide*, *Giselle*, and the Russian classics (eg *Swan Lake*, *The Sleeping Beauty*); neoclassical works, such as Balanchine's *Apollo*; and modern ballets, such as Ashton's *Monotones* and MacMillan's *Gloria*. The ballet technique is based on turn out from the hip socket. There are five positions of the feet and a codified system of arm positions (*port de bras*). Intensive training is required from a young age, often in specialist schools.

Ballet Company *New York City Ballet*

Ballet Rambert *Rambert Dance Company*

Ballets Russes [balay roos] A ballet company created by Diaghilev and active in Europe 1909–29. It was famous for nurturing new talents and for collaborations between great painters (Bakst, Benois, Picasso), composers (Rimsky-Korsakov, Satie, Stravinsky), and choreographers (Fokine, Nijinsky, Massine, Nijinska, Balanchine).

Ballet Theatre *American Ballet Theatre*

ballistic missile A missile which acquires its energy during its launch phase, flying on a trajectory dictated by its initial velocity added to the factors of gravity and aerodynamic drag, until it reaches the target. A **cruise missile**, by contrast, flies with wings through the atmosphere under continuous power. A rifle bullet is in effect a ballistic missile, but more specifically the term applies to the big intercontinental and submarine-launched ballistic missiles which carry nuclear warheads.

ballistics The study of what takes place when a projectile is fired from a firearm. Ballistics has three aspects: (1) *internal*, concerning the way the object is thrown into the air; (2) *external*, investigating the way it moves in flight; (3) *terminal*, analyzing its impact on the target. **Forensic ballistics** helps in the investigation of gun crimes.

balloon A flexible envelope filled with a lighter-than-air gas which provides the buoyancy force to rise upwards. A popular children's toy, large balloons are also used for meteorological and scientific research as well as for pleasure. The envelope of a modern hot-air balloon is made from either nylon or Dacron, which is then coated with polyurethane applied under pressure to make the material more airtight.

balloon angioplasty [anjiohplastee] The insertion of a catheter into an artery that has narrowed pathologically. A balloon at the tip of the catheter is expanded at the site of the constriction, which causes the blood vessel to dilate. The procedure is successful in many cases of narrowing of the arteries to the limbs, kidney, and heart.

balm A name applied to various plants, but especially to **bee balm** or **lemon balm** (*Melissa officinalis*), a member of the mint family, Labiatae.

Balmoral Castle A castle and estate of 9700 ha/24 000 acres located on Upper Deeside, Aberdeenshire, Scotland. It has been in the possession of the British Royal family since 1852, and is used by them as a holiday home.

balsa A fast-growing tree (*Ochroma pyramidale*), reaching 25 m/80 ft or more, with very light, soft timber, native to lowland areas of tropical America; leaves broadly oval to circular, 30 cm/12 in or more in diameter; flowers 15 cm/6 in long, white. (Family: Bombacaceae.)

balsam An annual with a translucent stem; leaves alternate, opposite or in threes; flowers 2-lipped with funnel-shaped tube and curved spur, the capsule exploding to scatter seeds, especially when touched – hence the name **touch-me-not** (*Impatiens noli-tangere*) for the variety native to Europe and Asia. (Family: Balsaminaceae.)

Baltic Exchange An abbreviation for the **Baltic Mercantile and Shipping Exchange**, a major world market for cargo space on sea and air freight, which originated in the London coffee houses, and is still found in the City of London. The Exchange also handles the market in some commodities, such as grain.

Baltic Sea [bawltik], Ger **Ostsee**, ancient **Mare Suevicum** area 414 000 km²/160 000 sq mi. An arm of the Atlantic Ocean enclosed by Denmark, Sweden, Germany, Poland, Estonia, Latvia, Lithuania, Russia, and Finland; chief arms, the Gulfs of Bothnia, Finland, Riga; mean depth 55 m/180 ft; generally shallow, with large areas frozen in winter; navigation impossible for 3–5 months yearly.

Baltic Shield The geological name for the continental mass made up of Precambrian crystalline rocks exposed in parts of Norway, Sweden, and Finland, and forming the underlying basement of the continent. They are the oldest rocks in Europe.

Baltic states The countries of Estonia, Latvia, and Lithuania on the E shore of the Baltic Sea. Formed in 1918, the states remained independent until 1940, when they were annexed by the USSR. Their independence was reasserted in 1990, following the collapse of communism.

Baltimore [boltimaw(r)] 39°17N 76°37W, pop (2000e) 651 200. Port in N Maryland, USA, at the upper end of Chesapeake Bay; established, 1729; developed as a seaport and shipbuilding centre (Baltimore clippers); city status, 1797; rebuilt after 1904 fire; airport; railway; six universities; centre for culture and the arts; symphony orchestra; professional team, Orioles (baseball); first Roman Catholic cathedral in the USA (1806–21).

Baluchi [baloochee] Baluchi-speaking peoples of Baluchistan (Pakistan), Iran, Afghanistan, Punjab (India), and Bahrain. They are well known for their carpets and embroidery.

Baluchistan [baloochistahn] pop (2000e) 7 039 000; area 347 190 km²/134 015 sq mi. Province in W and SW Pakistan; treaties of 1879 and 1891 brought the N section under direct British control; incorporated into Pakistan in 1947–8; capital, Quetta; mountainous terrain, with large areas of desert.

Baluchitherium [baloochitheerium] *Indricotherium*

Balzac, Honoré de, originally **Honoré Balssa** (1799–1850) Novelist, born in Tours, France. His *La Comédie humaine* (1827–47, The Human Comedy), a series of novels and stories which present a complete picture of modern civilization, includes such works as *Le Père Goriot* (1834, Father Goriot). He produced 85 novels in 20 years.

Bamako [bamakoh] 12°40N 7°59E, pop (2000e) 910 000. Riverport capital of Mali, on the R Niger; mediaeval centre of Islamic learning; capital of French Sudan, 1905; airport; railway.

bamboo A giant woody grass, mostly tropical or subtropical, with a few temperate species; usually forming large clumps reaching heights of 36 m/120 ft; provides edible shoots and light timber, including garden canes. (Genera: *Bambusa* and others. Family: Gramineae.)

banana A giant perennial herb, superficially resembling a tree. The true stem lies underground, at intervals bearing buds which produce large, oar-shaped leaves. It is the closely sheathing bases of the leaves which form the soft, hollow, trunk-like 'stem' rising to a height of several metres above ground. Cultivated bananas are grown throughout the tropics as a staple food. Fruit for export is cut while still green, and ripened on the voyage. They are often sold as unblemished yellow fruits, but are not fully ripe until flecked with brown spots. (Genus: *Musa*, 35 species. Family: Musaceae.)

Banares *Benares*

Banda, Hastings (Kamuzu) (c.1906–97) Malawi statesman, prime minister (1963–6), and president (1966–94), born in Kasungu, Malawi. Leader of the Malawi African Congress, he was made life president in 1971. He was defeated in the 1994 elections.

Band Aid *Geldof, Bob*

Bandaranaike, S(olomon) W(est) R(idgeway) D(ias) [bandaraniy-kuh] (1899–1959) Sri Lankan statesman and prime minister (1956–9), born in Colombo. In 1951 he organized the Sri Lanka Freedom Party, which returned him to parliament as opposition leader and (1956) as prime minister on a policy of nationalization and neutralism. He was assassinated by a Buddhist monk, and succeeded by his wife **Sirimavo Ratwatte Dias Bandaranaike** (1916–2000), who became the world's first woman prime minister (1960–5, 1970–7).

Bandar Seri Begawan [bahndah seree begawan], formerly **Brunei Town** 4°56N 114°58E, pop (2000e) 90 600. Capital of Brunei, SE Asia; airport; town wharf used mainly for local vessels since opening of deep-water port at Muara in 1972.

bandicoot An Australasian marsupial (family: Peramelidae, 17 species); superficially rat-like, but larger with longer snout and ears; also includes the Australian **rabbit-eared bandicoots** (or **bilbies**) of family Thylacomyidae (2 species) from dry areas.

Bandung [bandung] 0°32N 103°16E, pop (2000e) 2 065 000. City in W Java, Indonesia; founded, 1810; former administrative centre of Dutch East Indies; **Bandung Conference** (1955), at which 29 non-aligned countries met to facilitate joint diplomatic action; airport; railway; two universities (1955, 1957); nuclear research centre (1964).

Bangalore [banggalaw(r)], officially **Bengalooru** (from 2006) 12°59N 77°40E, pop (2004e) 5 700 000. Capital of Karnataka, SC India; founded, 1537; airfield; railway; university (1964).

Banghazi *Benghazi*

Bangkok [bangkok] 13°44N 100°30E, pop (2000e) 6 746 000. Capital city of Thailand; on Chao Praya R; capital, 1782; old city noted for its many canals; since 1955, headquarters of the SE Asia Treaty Organization; airport; railway; subway (2004); eight universities.

Bangladesh *p.79*

Bangor [bangger] 53°13N 4°08W, pop (2000e) 48 700. City in Gwynedd, NW Wales, UK; railway; university (1884); cathedral (founded 6th-c).

Bangui [bahngwee] 4°23N 18°37E, pop (2000e) 767 800. Capital of Central African Republic; on the R Ubangi; founded, 1889; airport; university (1969); handles Chad trade.

Bani-Sadr, Abolhassan [banee sadr] (1935–) Iranian politician, who became the first president of the Islamic Republic of Iran. He was an important figure in the Iranian Revolution of 1978–9, and was elected president in 1980. Dismissed by Ayatollah Khomeini (mid-1981), he fled to France.

Banjalang One of the principal Aboriginal communities of NE

Bangladesh

☐ International Airport   ∴ World heritage site

[**banggladesh**], formerly **East Pakistan**, official name **People's Republic of Bangladesh**, **Gana Prajatantri Bangladesh**

Local name Bangladesh

Timezone GMT +6

Area 143 998 km²/55 583 sq mi

Population total (2002e) 133 377 000

Status Republic

Date of independence 1971

Capital Dhaka

Languages Bengali (official), also local dialects and English widely spoken

Ethnic groups Bengali (98%), Bihari (1%), tribal: Garo, Khasi, Santal (1%)

Religions Muslim (86%), Hindu (12%), Buddhist (1%), small Christian majority

Physical features Mainly a vast, low-lying alluvial plain, cut by a network of rivers, canals, swamps, marshes; main rivers the Ganges (Padma), Brahmaputra (Jamuna), Meghna; joining in the S to form the largest delta in the world, subject to frequent flooding (notably in 1998 and 2004); coast hit by tsunami disaster, Dec 2004; Chittagong Hill Tracts in the E rise to 1200 m/ 3900 ft.

Climate Tropical climate; monsoon season (Jun–Oct).

Currency 1 Taka (BDT) = 100 paisa

Economy Agriculture, especially rice (employs 86% of population); and supplies 80% of the world's jute; also paper, aluminium, textiles, glass, shipbuilding, fishing, natural gas.

GDP (2002e) $238·2 bn, per capita $1800

Human Development Index (2002) 0·478

History Part of the State of Bengal until Muslim East Bengal created in 1905, separate from Hindu West Bengal; reunited, 1911; partitioned again in 1947, with West Bengal remaining in India and East Bengal forming East Pakistan; rebellion in 1971 led to independence as the People's Republic of Bangladesh; political unrest led to suspension of constitution, and assassination of first President, Sheikh Mujib, 1975; further coups in 1975, 1977, and 1982; constitution restored, 1986; last military dictator, Hossain Mohammad Ershad, overthrown, 1990; constitutional amendments in 1991 restricted powers of President to ceremonial and restored full powers to unicameral legislature, *Jatiya Sangsad*; further amendment in 2004 reserved 45 seats for women in the 300-member legislature.

Head of State

1971–2 Sayed Nazrul Islam *Acting*
1972 Mujibur Rahman
1972–3 Abu Saeed Chowdhury
1974–5 Mohammadullah
1975 Mujibur Rahman
1975 Khondaker Mushtaq Ahmad
1975–7 Abu Saadat Mohammad Sayem
1977–81 Zia Ur-Rahman
1981–2 Abdus Sattar
1982–3 Abdul Fazal Mohammad Ahsanuddin Chowdhury
1983–90 Hossain Mohammad Ershad
1990–1 Shehabuddin Ahmed *Acting*
1991–6 Abdur Rahman Biswas
1996–2001 Shehabuddin Ahmed
2001–2 A.Q.M. Badruddoza Chowdhury
2002– Iajuddin Ahmed

Head of Government

1971–2 Tajuddin Ahmed
1972–5 Mujibur Rahman
1975 Mohammad Monsur Ali
1975–9 Martial Law
1979–82 Mohammad Azizur Rahman
1982–4 Martial Law
1984–5 Ataur Rahman Khan
1986–8 Mizanur Rahman Chowdhury
1988–9 Moudud Ahmed
1989–91 Kazi Zafar Ahmed
1991–6 Khaleda Zia
1996–2001 Hasina Wajed
2001 Latifur Rahman *Interim*
2001–6 Begum Khaleda Zia
2006–7 Iajuddin Ahmed *Interim*
2007– Fakhruddin Ahmed *Caretaker*

New South Wales, Australia. The Banjalang language is currently the object of a revival programme.

banjo A plucked string instrument developed in the 19th-c from earlier similar instruments used by W African slaves in the USA. It has a long neck and fingerboard, fretted like a guitar's, and five metal strings. These pass over a bridge which presses against a parchment (or plastic) membrane stretched over a circular frame.

Banjul [banjul], formerly **Bathurst** (to 1973) 13°28N 16°35W, pop (2000e) 68 700. Seaport capital of The Gambia, W

Africa; established in 1816 as a settlement for freed slaves; airport.

bank An organization which offers a wide range of services to do with the handling of money. Most banks are *commercial banks*, which keep money on behalf of their customers, lend it to them, and offer them various facilities. A *central bank* in a country (such as the Bank of England or the Banque de France) is the banker for the government, issuing money on its behalf and setting the chief interest rate for loans; it is much involved in the country's monetary policy. There are also several types of bank with restricted functions, such as merchant banks and international banks.

bank base rate A base lending rate for UK clearing banks, used as the primary measure for interest rates since 1981. It is decided by the Bank of England, on the advice of the Monetary Policy Committee.

Bankhead, Tallulah (1903–68) Actress, born in Huntsville, AL. She made her stage debut in 1918 and appeared in many plays and films. Her most outstanding film portrayal was in *Lifeboat* (1944).

Ban Ki-moon (1944–) UN secretary-general (2007–), born in Chungju, South Korea. He studied at Seoul University (1970) and Harvard (1985). He joined the South Korean Home Office in 1975 and held posts as national security adviser to the president (1996), ambassador to Austria (1998–2000), vice-foreign minister (2000–1), advisor on foreign affairs (2003–4), and foreign minister (2004–6). He succeeded Kofi Annan as UN secretary-general in January 2007.

Bank of England The central bank of Britain, founded in 1694. By the end of the 19th-c the Bank was acting as the government and bankers' bank only, and was not accessible to the public. In 1946 the Bank of England Act brought the Bank into public ownership. The monetary policy of the Bank of England used to be subject to control by the Treasury, but the Bank is now independent, advised by a nine-member Monetary Policy Committee. In 1997 the Treasury ceded its power to set interest rates to the Bank of England. Today the Bank's main functions are to act as a note-issuing authority, as the government and bankers' bank, as manager of the National Debt, and as custodian of the nation's gold reserves. It is popularly referred to as 'The Old Lady of Threadneedle Street'.

bank rate A former interest rate at which the Bank of England would lend to discount houses, and an important instrument of government economic policy. It was abandoned in 1973, and replaced by the minimum lending rate (MLR).

bankruptcy The state of being reduced to financial ruin. Legally, individuals and partnerships are in this state when a court in bankruptcy proceedings declares them to be bankrupt. These proceedings are started by a creditor (or sometimes the debtor) presenting a bankruptcy petition. The analogous concept of **liquidation** applies to companies.

Banks, Sir Joseph (1743–1820) Botanist, born in London. He accompanied Cook's expedition round the world (1768–71) and in 1772 visited the Hebrides and Iceland. As president of the Royal Society (1778–1820), he became an influential patron of science, sending explorers and botanists to many parts of the world. The colony of New South Wales owes its origin mainly to him: Linnaeus even proposed that it should be named Banksia.

Banks, Lynne (Reid) (1929–) Writer and actress, born in London. After a brief career as an actress (1949–54), she joined ITN as a reporter (1955–62), taught English in Israel (1963–71), and became a full-time lecturer from 1971. Her best-known novel is *The L-Shaped Room* (1960, filmed 1962). Her many books for children include *The Indian in the Cupboard* (1980, filmed 1995), *Angela and Diabola* (1997), and *Alice By Accident* (2000).

Banks, Tony, popular name of **Anthony Lewis Banks** (1943–

2006) British Labour statesman, born in Belfast. He was elected an MP in 1983. An avid association football fan, he became minister for sport in the 1997 Blair government. In 1999 he relinquished the post to lead the English bid for the 2006 association football World Cup competition.

banksia A low shrub or small tree, native to Australia; flowers commonly cream, also orange, red, or purplish. up to 1000 in spectacular globular or cylindrical heads; named after Sir Joseph Banks. (Genus: *Banksia*, 58 species. Family: Proteaceae.)

Banna, Hassan al- [bana] (1906–49) Islamic leader and reformer, born in Mahmudiya, near Cairo. In 1928 he founded in Egypt the Society of Muslim Brothers. Following the murder of the Egyptian prime minister by a Brotherhood member in 1948, Banna was himself assassinated.

Banner System A system of military organization in China used by the Manchu tribes. By the early 17th-c the Manchus were organized into companies of 300 troops under at first four and then eight banners. The system survived throughout the Qing dynasty.

Bannister, Sir Roger (Gilbert) (1929–) Athlete, born in Harrow, Greater London. He was the first man to run the mile in under 4 minutes (3 min 59.4 s), at Oxford (6 May 1954).

Bannockburn, Battle of (1314) A battle fought near Stirling between English forces under Edward II and the Scots under Robert Bruce. It resulted in a decisive victory for the Scots.

Banting, Sir Frederick Grant (1891–1941) Physiologist, born in Alliston, Ontario, Canada. With J J R Macleod he discovered insulin, for which they were jointly awarded the Nobel Prize for Physiology or Medicine in 1923.

Bantu-speaking peoples Ethnically diverse groups who speak one of 500 Bantu languages or dialects (which belong to the Benue–Congo sub-group of the Niger–Congo family). They comprise altogether about 60 million people living in the S part of Africa, occupying a third of the continent.

Bantustans *apartheid*

banyan A large evergreen species of fig (*Ficus benghalensis*), native to the Old World tropics. It is notable for its aerial roots, which grow from the horizontal branches to the ground, becoming trunk-like, so that an apparent group of trees may in fact be only one. (Family: Moraceae.)

baobab [bayohbab, bowbab] A deciduous tree (*Adansonia digitata*) native to arid parts of C Africa; its short but massive barrel- or bottle-shaped trunk 9–12 m/30–40 ft high and up to 9 m/ 30 ft in girth contains large stores of water. (Family: Bombacaceae.)

baptism A sacramental practice involving water. The Christian ritual is usually traced to the New Testament, where new converts were immersed in water, and where the rite is linked with the imparting of the Spirit and with repentance. Today, Church practices vary over infant and adult baptism, and over the use of immersion or sprinkling.

baptistery / baptistry A building or part of a building used to administer baptism, and containing the font. It is sometimes separate from the church.

Baptists A world-wide communion of Christians, who believe in the baptism only of believers prepared to make a personal confession of faith in Jesus Christ. They mainly derive from early 17th-c England and Wales, and late 19th-c USA. Strongly biblical, the emphasis in worship is on scripture and preaching. The Baptist World Alliance was formed in 1905. In 2007 there were 210 member denominations, representing over 47 million baptized members.

bar Unit of pressure; symbol bar; equal to 10^5 Pa (pascal, SI unit); 1 bar is approximately atmospheric pressure. The **millibar** (mb; 1 bar = 1000 mb) proves to be of greater use for practical measurements.

Barak, Ehud (1942–) Israeli statesman and Labour prime minister

Barbados

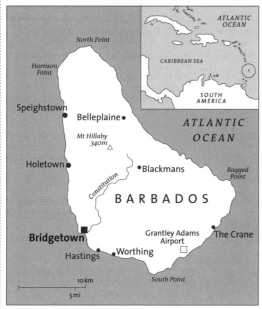

□ International Airport

[bah(r)**bay**dos]
Local name Barbados
Timezone GMT -4
Area 430 km²/166 sq mi
Population total (2002e) 270 000

Status Independent state within the Commonwealth
Date of independence 1966
Capital Bridgetown
Language English (official)
Ethnic groups African (80%), mixed race (16%)
Religions Anglican (40%), Protestant (15%), Roman Catholic (4%)
Physical features Small, triangular island in the Atlantic Ocean; length 32 km/20 mi (NW–SE); rising to 340 m/1115 ft at Mt Hillaby; ringed by a coral reef.
Climate Tropical climate, with average annual temperature 27°C; mean annual rainfall 1420 mm/56 in.
Currency 1 Barbados Dollar (BBD) = 100 cents
Economy Market economy based on tourism and sugar cane; cotton, bananas; natural gas; textiles.
GDP (2002e) $4·153 bn, per capita $15 000
Human Development Index (2002) 0·871

History Colonized by the British, 1627; self-government, 1961; independent within the Commonwealth, 1966; executive power rests with the Prime Minister, appointed by a Governor-General, the Senate, and the House of Assembly; plans to hold a referendum on change to a republican form of government announced, Feb 2005.

Head of State
(British monarch represented by Governor-General)
1984–90 Hugh Springer
1990–5 Dame Nita Barrow
1996– Sir Clifford Husbands
Head of Government
1966–76 Errol Walton Barrow
1976–85 J M G (Tom) Adams
1985–6 H Bernard St John
1986–7 Errol Walton Barrow
1987–94 L Erskine Sandiford
1994– Owen Seymour Arthur

(1999–2001), born in Kibbutz Mishmar Hasharon, Israel. He joined the Israeli army in 1959 and saw active service in both the Six-Day War and the Yom Kippur War. In 1991 he was appointed chief of the general staff and, following the signing of the Gaza–Jericho agreement, oversaw the Israeli Defence Force's redeployment in those areas. He was elected to the Knesset in 1996.

Barbados see panel
Barbary ape A monkey (macaque) native to N Africa (*Macaca sylvanus*), and maintained artificially on the Rock of Gibraltar; not an ape; stocky with no tail; also known as **magot** or **rock ape**.
Barbary Coast The coast of N Africa from Morocco to Tripolitania (Libya). It was famous for piracy between the 16th-c and 18th-c.
Barbary sheep *aoudad*
barbel Slender-bodied fish (*Barbus barbus*) of the carp family Cyprinidae, widespread in European rivers on clean gravel beds; body length up to 90 cm/3 ft; lips fleshy, bearing four long barbels.
Barber, Samuel (1910–81) Composer, born in West Chester, PA. His opera *Vanessa* (1958) and piano concerto (1962) were both awarded Pulitzer Prizes.
Barbera *Hanna-Barbera*
barberry A deciduous or evergreen shrub, native to N temperate regions and South America; long shoots with 3-pointed spines; leaves often spiny; flowers yellow, orange, or reddish; berries red, black, blue, yellow or purple, globose or cylindrical. The common barberry (*Berberis vulgaris*) is a necessary host in the

life-cycle of the cereal disease *black rust*. (Genus: *Berberis*, 450 species. Family: Berberidaceae.)
Barbie, Klaus, known as **the Butcher of Lyon** (1913–91) Nazi leader, born in Bad Godesberg, Germany. He worked for the Gestapo, and in Lyon sent thousands of people to Auschwitz. After the War he fled to South America, but was traced by Nazi hunters, and extradited in 1983. He was tried in France on 177 crimes against humanity, found guilty, and sentenced to life imprisonment.
Barbirolli, Sir John (Giovanni Battista) [bah(r)bi**rolee**] (1899–1970) Conductor, born in London of French and Italian parents. He was permanent conductor (1943–58) of the Hallé Orchestra, later becoming its principal conductor (1959–68). He married the oboist **Evelyn Rothwell** (1911–) in 1939.
barbiturates Drugs derived from barbituric acid, itself first prepared on St Barbara's Day, 1863. *Barbitone* (US *barbital*) was introduced into medicine in 1903; *phenobarbitone* (US *phenobarbital*) in 1912. Over 50 different barbiturates have been used at some time as sedatives, sleep inducers, and anti-epileptic drugs. They cause severe tolerance, ie increasingly higher doses are required to produce the same effect. The doses are progressively more dangerous, and poisoning becomes a major risk; they are also addictive.
Barbizon School [bah(r)**bizon**] A group of French landscape painters working c.1830–80 at Barbizon, a village in the Forest of Fontainebleau. Leading members included Théodore Rousseau and Charles François Daubigny.
Barbuda *Antigua and Barbuda*

barcarolle An instrumental or vocal piece in a lilting 6/8 metre, evoking the songs of the Venetian gondoliers. A well-known example is the Barcarolle in Offenbach's opera *Les Contes d'Hoffman* (Tales of Hoffman).

Barcelona [bah(r)selohna], Span [barthelohna], ancient **Barcino** or **Barcinona** 41°21N 2°10E, pop (2000e) 1 645 000. Major seaport in NE Spain; second largest city in Spain; airport; railway; two universities (1440, 1968); centre of Catalan art and literature, and of the separatist political movement; cathedral (13th-c); Casa Mila (1906–10), Casa Güell (1900–14), and Parque Güell (1900–14), architectural creations by Antonio Gaudí, now world heritage sites; Palau de la Música Catalana and Hospital de Sant Pau, world heritage sites; location of the 1992 Summer Olympic Games.

Barclay, Robert (1843–1913) British banker, under whom in 1896 the merger of 20 banks took place to form Barclay & Co Ltd. In 1917 the name was changed to Barclay's Bank Ltd.

barcode A pattern of black vertical lines, with information coded in the relative widths of the lines. This type of coding is very widely used in the retail market, such as on food packages. The bar-coded labels can be read by special bar-code scanners, and the output entered into a computer to link the product with such factors as price and stock level.

bard Among ancient Celtic peoples, a poet-minstrel who held a privileged place in society, singing the praises of chiefs and celebrating heroic deeds, historical events, and the passing of laws. In Wales, bardic standards declined after the Middle Ages; however, to this day, a contestant for the Chair at the National Eisteddfod must compose a poem in classical bardic verse-form.

Bardeen, John [bah(r)deen] (1908–91) Physicist, the first person to receive two Nobel Prizes for Physics, born in Madison, WI. He developed in 1947 with Brattain and Shockley the point contact transistor, for which they shared the Nobel Prize in 1956. His second prize (1972) was shared for his work on the first satisfactory theory of superconductivity (the Bardeen–Cooper–Schrieffer, or *BCS* theory).

Bardot, Brigitte [bah(r)doh], originally **Camille Javal** (1934–) Film actress, born in Paris. She was discovered by the director Roger Vadim, who subsequently married her, and from 1952 made her an international sex-symbol, with their greatest success in *Et Dieu créa la femme* (1956, And God Created Woman). They divorced in 1957. Her last major film was *Si Don Juan était une Femme* (1973, If Don Juan Were a Woman). In later years she has taken up the cause of endangered animal species. Her book *A Cry in the Silence* (2003) openly attacked the gay community, immigrants, and jobless people. In 2004, she was convicted of inciting racial hatred, her fourth such offence since 1997.

Barebone's Parliament The British 'Parliament of Saints' (4 Jul–12 Dec 1653), nominated by the Council of Officers of the Army to succeed the Rump Parliament; named after radical member Praise-God Barebone. It collapsed after disagreements over the abolition of tithes and lay patronage in the Church.

Barenboim, Daniel [barenboym] (1942–) Pianist and conductor, born in Buenos Aires, Argentina. A noted exponent of Mozart and Beethoven, he gained his reputation as pianist/conductor with the English Chamber Orchestra. He became musical director of the Chicago Symphony Orchestra (1991–2006) and general music director of the Deutsche Staatsoper, Berlin (1992–2002). He married the cellist Jacqueline du Pré in 1967.

Barents, Willem [baruhnts], also spelled **Barentz** (c.1550–97) Navigator, probably born in The Netherlands. Pilot to three Dutch expeditions (1594–6) in search of the Northeast Passage, he died off Novaya Zemlya. In 1871, Captain Carlsen found his winter quarters undisturbed after 274 years.

Barents Euro-Arctic Council An international organization established in 1993 to renew trade and economic co-operation in the Barents Sea region. Its members are Denmark, Finland, Iceland, Norway, Russia, and Sweden, with one Sami (Lapp) representative.

Barents Sea [barents], Russian **Barentsovo More**, Norwegian **Barents Havet** area 1 405 000 km^2/542 000 sq mi. Shallow arm of the Arctic Ocean, lying N of Norway and European Russia; warm North Cape Current disperses pack-ice in the S; Murmansk and Vardö ports are ice-free; fishing area.

Bari [baree] 41°07N 16°52E, pop (2000e) 357 000. Seaport in SE Italy; archbishopric; airport; car ferries; university (1924); cathedral (begun 1087); naval college; site of Italy's first atomic power station.

barite [bairiyt] The mineral form of barium sulphate (BaSO$_4$), the chief ore of barium. Found in hydrothermal vein deposits, it is used in paints, paper making, and drilling muds; earlier known as **barytes**.

barium [bairium] Ba, element 56, in Group II of the periodic table, melting point 725°C. It is a very reactive metal. Its soluble compounds are highly poisonous, but the very insoluble sulphate, BaSO$_4$, is used in the so-called **barium meal** to provide material opaque to X-rays.

bark In its everyday sense, the rough, protective outer layer of the woody parts of trees and shrubs; in botany, the term also embraces several inner tissues, including cork and phloem. Continued growth causes the bark to stretch, often cracking, flaking, or peeling in distinctive patterns.

Barker, Pat(ricia Margaret) (1943–) Novelist, born in Thornby-on-Tees, Cleveland. She is especially known for an acclaimed trilogy about World War 1: *Regeneration* (1991), *The Eye in the Door* (1993, Guardian Fiction Award), and *The Ghost Road* (1995, Booker). Later novels include *Double Vision* (2003).

Barker, Ronnie, popular name of **Ronald William George Barker** (1929–2005) Comic actor, born in Bedford, Bedfordshire. He made his professional debut in 1948. Adept at characterization, tongue-twisting comic lyrics, and saucy humour, his many radio and television appearances included *Porridge* (1974–7), *Open All Hours* (1976, 1981–5) and, in partnership with Ronnie Corbett, the long-running *The Two Ronnies* (1971–87). In 2004 he was honoured with a BAFTA tribute award for his contribution to comedy.

bar Kokhba, Simon [kokhba], also spelled **bar Kochba** (?–135) The leader of the Jews in their great but fruitless insurrection against the Emperor Hadrian (130–5). He was killed at Bethar. In 1960 some of his letters were found in caves near the Dead Sea.

bark painting A traditional product of Australian Aboriginal art: human and animal figures, sometimes geometrically stylized but occasionally naturalistic, painted on irregularly-shaped pieces of bark. They were created mainly for use in magical and initiation ceremonies.

barley A cereal of Middle Eastern origin (*Hordeum vulgare*), cultivated in temperate regions; dense head with long, slender bristles; grains in 2, 4, or 6 rows. It is more tolerant of drought, cold, and poor soil than wheat, and an important crop in such regions as N Europe. Germinated grains produce malt used in brewing beer and making whisky; its flour is used in cakes and porridge. It is also an important animal feed. (Family: Gramineae.)

Bar Mitzvah [bah(r) mitsva] (Heb 'son [*bar*]/daughter [*bat*] of the commandment') Jewish celebrations associated with reaching the age of maturity and of legal and religious responsibility, being 13 years plus one day for boys. The child reads a passage from the Torah or the Prophets in the synagogue on the Sabbath, and is then regarded as a full member of the congregation. Non-Orthodox synagogues have a **Bat Mitzvah** ceremony for girls at 12 years plus one day.

Barnabas [bah(r)nabas] (1st-c) Christian missionary, originally a Levite from Cyprus called Joseph. He was a companion and supporter of Paul during Paul's early ministry to the Gentiles. The so-called *Letter of Barnabas* is a spurious 2nd-c work.

barnacle A marine crustacean that lives attached by its base to hard substrates or to other organisms; body enclosed within a shell formed of calcareous plates; c.1000 species. (Subclass: Cirripedia.)

Barnard, Christiaan (Neethling) (1922–2001) Surgeon, born in Beaufort West, South Africa. At Groote Schuur Hospital he performed the first successful human heart transplant (Dec 1967). The patient, Louis Washkansky, died of double pneumonia 18 days later. Barnard's later transplants proved to be increasingly successful. He retired from medicine in 1983.

Barnardo, Thomas John [bah(r)nah(r)doh] (1845–1905) Founder of homes for destitute children, born in Dublin. He founded (1867) the East End Mission for destitute children, as well as a number of homes in Greater London, which came to be known as the *Dr Barnardo's Homes*.

Barnard's star One of the very few stars which is named after the astronomer who studied it, E E Barnard (1857–1923) of Yerkes Observatory, USA. The second-nearest star to the Sun, distance 1·82 parsec. It is a red dwarf, too faint to see with the naked eye.

Barnburners A faction within the US Democratic Party in New York State (1843–50), which arose through opposition to extending slavery into Western territory conquered during the Mexican War. Their name derived from the story of a Dutch farmer who burned down his barn (the Democratic Party) in order to drive out rats (slavery).

Barnes, William (1801–86) Pastoral poet, born in Sturminster Newton, Dorset. He was widely known for his idyllic poetry in the Dorset dialect.

barn owl An owl of worldwide distribution; legs feathered; eats small vertebrates, especially mammals and insects. (Genus: *Tyto*, 6 species. Family: Tytonidae.)

Barnum, P(hineas) T(aylor) (1810–91) Showman, born in Bethel, CT. He ran a museum in New York, introducing freak shows, at which he sponsored the famous dwarf 'General Tom Thumb' (1842). In 1881 he joined with his rival James Anthony Bailey (1847–1906) to found the Barnum and Bailey circus, 'the greatest show on earth'.

barograph *barometer*

Baroja (y Nessi), Pío [baroha] (1872–1956) Writer, born in San Sebastián, Spain. His first book of short stories, *Vidas sombrías* (1900, Sombre Lives), was the prelude to more than 70 volumes with a Basque setting.

barometer A meteorological instrument used to measure atmospheric pressure, invented in 1643 by Torricelli. It was based on the principle that the height of a column of mercury in a tube sealed at one end and inverted in a dish of mercury will change according to the atmospheric pressure exerted on the dish of mercury. The **aneroid barometer** is a metallic box containing a vacuum, with flexible sides which act as a bellows expanding and contracting with changing atmospheric pressure. Changes of pressure through time are recorded on a **barograph**.

baron / baroness In the UK, a title of nobility, ranking below viscount or count.

baronet (abbreviation **bart**) In the UK, a hereditary title, not part of the peerage and not a knighthood. The form, which was originally purchased by the holder, was created by James I in 1611 to raise money to pay the troops in Ireland.

Barons' Wars The wars in England during the reigns of John and Henry III. **1** (1215–17) Despite the granting of Magna Carta, many barons still defied John, and offered the crown to Prince Louis of France. After John's death, the French and baronial army was routed at Lincoln (1217). **2** (1264–7) After the Provisions of Oxford failed to achieve a settlement, barons led by Simon

de Montfort captured Henry III at Lewes (1264). Earl Simon was killed at Evesham (1265), and the king was restored to power.

Baroque (art and architecture) [barok, barohk] A style prevalent in the 17th-c and part of the 18th-c, characterized by curvilinear forms and ornate decoration arranged in dramatic compositions, often on a large scale and in a complicated fashion. Baroque art was especially associated with Louis XIV, but spread over most of W Europe until it was transformed into Rococo in the early 18th-c.

Baroque (music) [barok, barohk] A period in musical history extending from c.1580 to c.1730. Its features include a gradual replacement of modality by tonality, a love of melodic ornamentation, and the formation of the orchestra. Genres originating in the Baroque period include the opera, oratorio, cantata, sonata, and concerto.

barracuda [barakooda] Any of the voracious predatory fishes widespread in tropical and warm temperate seas; body slender, length up to 1·8 m/6 ft, jaws armed with many short teeth. (Genus: *Sphyraena*. Family: Sphyraenidae.)

Barranquilla [barankeelya] 11°00N 74°50W, pop (2000e) 1 053 000. Industrial city in N Colombia, Colombia's principal Caribbean port; founded, 1721; airport; three universities (1941, 1966, 1967).

Barras, Paul François Jean Nicolas, comte de (Count of) [bara] (1755–1829) French revolutionary, born in Fox-emphoux, France. An original member of the Jacobin Club, and a regicide, he played the chief part in the overthrow of Robespierre. He became one of the five members of the Directory (1795), and was overthrown by Bonaparte (1799).

barrel A measure of volume, its value depending on the substance contained. A barrel of alcohol is 189 litres; a barrel of petroleum is 159 litres.

barrel organ A mechanical musical instrument. By turning a handle at the side, the player both feeds a bellows and operates a rotating cylinder fitted with metal pins which allow air access to a set of pipes; the placing of the pins determines which pipes sound and when.

Barrie, Sir J(ames) M(atthew) (1860–1937) Novelist and playwright, born in Kirriemuir, Angus. His best-known plays are *The Admirable Crichton* (1902), *Dear Brutus* (1917), and *Peter Pan* (1904), for which he is chiefly remembered.

barrier reef *atoll*

barrigudo *woolly monkey*

Barringer Crater *Meteor Crater*

barrister A member of the legal profession in England and Wales whose work is mainly concerned with advocacy in the courts. Barristers have right of audience in the High Court as well as in all other courts. In addition to trials and preparation for trials, they also write advisory opinions.

Barry, Sir Charles (1795–1860) Architect, born in London. His designs include the new Palace of Westminster (Houses of Parliament, 1840–70), completed after his death by his son **Edward Middleton Barry** (1830–80).

Barrymore, Ethel, originally **Ethel Blythe** (1879–1959) Actress, born in Philadelphia, PA, the sister of John and Lionel Barrymore. She was a leading actress in many plays and films in the early decades of the century. **John** (1882–1942) made his name in Shakespearean roles, and appeared in many films such as *Grand Hotel* (1932). **Lionel** (1878–1954) was most widely known for his role as Dr Gillespie in the original *Dr Kildare* film series.

Barstow, Dame Josephine (Clare) (1940–) Soprano, born in Sheffield, South Yorkshire. Resident principal with Sadlers Wells (1967–8) and the Welsh National Opera (1968–70), she made her Covent Garden debut in 1969 and her US debut in 1977. She was made a dame in 1995.

Bart, Lionel (1930–99) Composer, born in London. His successful musicals include *Lock Up Your Daughters!* (1959) and *Oliver!* (1960).

Barth, Karl [bah(r)t] (1886–1968) Theologian, born in Basel, Switzerland. He played a leading role in the German Confessing Church. The major exponent of Reformed theology, his many works include the monumental *Church Dogmatics* (1932–67).

Barthes, Roland (Gérard) [bah(r)t] (1915–80) Teacher, critic, and writer on semiology and structuralism, born in Cherbourg, France. His works include *Mythologies* (1957), a semiological exploration of wrestling, children's toys, and other phenomena. From 1976 until his death he was the first professor of literary semiology at the Collège de France, Paris.

Bartholdi, (Frédéric) Auguste [bah(r)tholdee], Fr [bah(r)toldee] (1834–1904) Sculptor, born in Colmar, France. He specialized in enormous monuments, such as the bronze Statue of Liberty, New York harbour, unveiled in 1886.

Bartlett, John (1820–1905) Publisher and bookseller, born in Plymouth, MA. He is best known as the compiler of *Bartlett's Familiar Quotations* (1855).

Bartók, Béla [bah(r)tok] (1881–1945) Composer, born in Nagyszentmiklós, Hungary. His compositions were greatly influenced by Hungarian and Balkan folk music. Driven into exile by World War 2, he settled in the USA, where he composed several string quartets, concertos, and other orchestral works.

Bartoli, Cecilia [bah(r)tohlee] (1966–) Mezzo-soprano, born in Rome. She studied at the Conservatorio di Santa Cecilia in Rome and gave her debut performance in Zurich in 1988. She has won four Grammy Awards, and at the Classical Brits she has received the Outstanding Contribution to Music award (2003) and best female artist (2004). Her albums include *The Vivaldi Album* (1999), *The Salieri Album* (2003), and *Opera Proibita* (2005).

Bartolommeo, Fra [bah(r)tolomayoh], originally **Baccio della Porta** (1472–1517) Religious painter, born near Florence, Italy. He was a follower of Savonarola, at whose death he gave up painting and became a Dominican novice; but the visit of the young Raphael to Florence in 1504 led him to resume his art.

Baruch [barukh] (7th–6th-c BC) Biblical character, described as the companion and secretary of the prophet Jeremiah (*Jer* 36). His name became attached to several Jewish works of much later date.

barycentre For a group of objects, such as the Solar System or a cluster of stars, the point at which total mass may be considered to be concentrated ('the centre of gravity') for the purposes of calculating its gravitational effect on other objects.

baryon [barion] In particle physics, a collective term for heavy matter particles which experience strong interactions. The least massive baryon is the proton, into which other baryons decay.

barytes *barite*

baryton An obsolete musical instrument resembling a bass viol, with (usually) six strings which were bowed and a further 10–15 which were plucked. Between 1765 and 1778 Haydn wrote numerous pieces for the instrument.

basalt [basawlt] The most common extrusive igneous rock, characterized by low silica content, and composed essentially of plagioclase feldspar and pyroxene. It is commonly used as a building stone and road-stone aggregate.

base (chemistry) A substance liberating hydroxide ions in water, an acceptor of protons, or a donor of electron pairs: each of these definitions includes the previous one. The term is thus the opposite of an acid, whatever definition of acid is used.

base (mathematics) The number on which a system of counting is constructed (**number-base**). The numbers in common use are in base ten, ie numbers expressed in multiples of powers of ten; thus 'three hundred and forty two' is written 342, since it is $3 \times 10^2 + 4 \times 10 + 2$.

baseball *p.85*

Basel [bahzl], Eng **Basle** [bahl], Fr **Bâle** 47°35N 7°35E, pop (2000e) 179 000. City in N Switzerland, on the R Rhine; river port at the terminus of Rhine navigation; on the site of a Roman fort; mediaeval centre for silk, dyeing, and printing; joined the Swiss Confederacy, 1501; influential centre during the Reformation; scene of the first Zionist conference, 1897; airport (on French territory, shared with France); railway junction; oldest Swiss university (1460); Switzerland's leading centre for transshipment and international commerce; Gothic minster (11th-c, largely rebuilt 14th-c); town hall (1504–14), European World Trade and Convention Centre.

basenji [basenjee] A spitz breed of dog developed in C Africa for hunting; pale brown and white; short coat; cannot bark, but makes a yodelling noise.

Basho, Matsuo, pseudonym of **Matsuo Munefusa** (1644–94) Poet, born in Ueno (Iga), Japan. He was bred from a young age to poetry. Becoming master of the haiku, he started his own school, but later retired to a hermitage.

BASIC [baysik] Acronym of **Beginner's All-purpose Symbolic Instruction Code**, a high level computer programming language developed in the late 1950s at Dartmouth College in the USA. It has been widely adopted as a standard language by microcomputer manufacturers, but Microsoft has developed Visual Basic as a fourth generation language for programming client applications.

Basidiomycetes [basidiohmiyseeteez] A subdivision of the true fungi, characterized by a sexual reproduction process that forms a club-shaped structure (*basidium*) bearing four haploid spores (*basidiospores*); includes edible mushrooms, agarics, puffballs, and many parasitic forms. (Division: Eumycota.)

Basie, Count [baysee], popular name of **William Allen Basie** (1904–84) Bandleader and pianist, born in Red Bank, NJ. He joined Benny Moten's Kansas City Orchestra in 1929, became its leader in 1935, and took it to New York the next year. Its supple rhythmic drive propelled several brilliant soloists, elevating the band to top rank, known for such popular compositions as 'One O'Clock Jump' and 'Jumpin' at the Woodside'.

Basil, St, known as **Basil the Great** (c.329–79) One of the greatest of the Greek Fathers, born in Caesarea, Cappadocia. He was one of the leading defenders of Christian philosophy against Arianism. Feast day 1 Jan (E), 2 Jan (W).

basil A bushy aromatic annual or perennial (*Ocimum basilicum*), growing to 1 m/3¼ ft, but often less; stems square; leaves oval, pale, glossy, in opposite pairs; flowers 2-lipped, white or purplish, in whorls; probably native to SE Asia, but widely cultivated as a culinary herb and for use in perfumery. (Family: Labiatae.)

basilica [bazilika] Originally a royal palace or large oblong hall with double colonnades, for the administration of justice and commerce. It was later adopted by early Christians as a similarly arranged church with two or more aisles, timber roof, and apse.

Basiliensis, Regio [rejioh basilyensis] area 234 km²/90 sq mi. Transnational 'natural region' encompassing the frontier districts of France, Switzerland, and Germany; administrative centre, Basel; co-operation between local governments, industries, and universities promoted since 1963.

basilisk (mythology) A fabulous beast, a small dragon-like creature combining features of the snake and the cockerel. Its eye could freeze and kill, hence the expression 'If looks could kill'. It is equivalent to the **cockatrice**.

basilisk (zoology) An iguana native to South America; male with bony projections on head and prominent sail-like crests along back; tail long; may run upright on long hind legs. (Genus: *Basiliscus*, 5 species.)

baseball

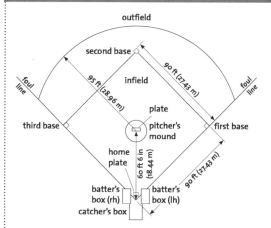

outfield

second base

infield

95 ft (28.96 m)

90 ft (27.43 m)

plate

third base

pitcher's mound

first base

home plate

60 ft 6 in (18.44 m)

90 ft (27.43 m)

batter's box (rh)

batter's box (lh)

catcher's box

foul line

foul line

Minimum distance along each foul line is 250 ft (72.2 m)
Distance to the farthest point in centre field is at least 400 ft (122 m)

A team game played on a wedge-shaped field, with a diamond-shaped infield (the *diamond*), by two sides of players with a bat and ball. One team, on offence or *at bat*, tries to score the most runs by having their players circle the bases before they are put *out* by the other team which is *in the field*. An out is made when the batter fails to hit a legally pitched ball on three successive occasions (a *strikeout*, see below), or when the fielding team catches a batted ball before it touches the ground, tags a member of the offensive team between the bases, or touches a base before an offensive player reaches that base. The defensive team is aided in stopping the offensive team by fielding batted balls with an oversized glove or *mitt*. Each game is made up of nine innings unless the score is tied, in which case the game is extended into *extra innings* until one team outscores the other in a particular inning. Each inning is divided into two parts – the *top* and *bottom*. The visiting team always bats first (the top) and the home team always bats last (the bottom). Each team at bat is allowed three outs in its half inning.

The major confrontation of the game centres on the *pitcher* and *batter*. The pitcher hurls the ball (at upwards of 145 kph/90 mph) towards the batter, who stands alongside the home plate poised to strike the ball. If the batter swings at the ball and fails to hit it, or if the pitcher throws the ball into a designated strike zone without the batter swinging at the ball, a *strike* is called. Three strikes causes a batter to be declared out. Conversely, if the pitcher fails to throw the ball into the strike zone and the batter does not swing, a *ball* is called. Four balls allow the batter to take first base. The home plate umpire, who stands behind the catcher, determines if the ball is within the strike zone (which comprises the area over home plate extending from the midway point between the top of the batter's shoulders to the top of his pants, down to the top of his knees). If the batter slices the ball outside the foul lines, the umpire call a 'ball'. If the batter strikes the ball beyond the playing area's limits (within the foul lines), or if he circles the bases before being put out, he has hit a *home run* (or *homer*).

Baseball is called the *national pastime* in the USA. Professional teams usually consist of 25 players. The *Major League* of North America is divided into the American League and National League, each consisting of an Eastern, Western, and (since 1994) Central division. In the National League 9 players can participate at one time for each team, while in the American League 10 take part because that league employs the designated hitter rule allowing a team to replace the pitcher in its batting order with a player who bats but does not play the field. The culmination of the season, which runs from April through October, is a best-of-seven game *World Series* between the champions of each league.

The origins of the game are unclear. The person most widely cited as the game's inventor is a West Point cadet, Abner Doubleday, who in 1839 laid out a diamond at Cooperstown, NY, where the modern day Baseball Hall of Fame stands. However, there is evidence that the game was played much earlier, and gradually evolved into its present form. The first formal set of baseball rules were drawn up by Alexander Cartwright in 1845. Baseball is becoming increasingly popular in Japan and Latin America, and in 1992 a Canadian team (the Toronto Blue Jays) won the World Series for the first time.

Basinger, Kim [bay**sinj**er] (1953–) Film actress, born in Athens, GA. She was a top model before making her feature film debut in *Hard Country* (1981). Other films include *The Real McCoy* (1993), *I Dreamed of Africa* (2000), *8 Mile* (2002), *Cellular* (2004), and *The Sentinel* (2006). She won an Oscar for Best Supporting Actress in *L.A. Confidential* (1997).

basketball A five-a-side team ball game, invented by James Naismith in 1891 in Springfield, MA. Played on a court, the object is to throw the ball through your opponent's basket, situated at the end of the court, and 10 ft (3·05 m) above the ground.

basking shark Extremely large, inoffensive shark (*Cetorhinus maximus*), second only to the whale shark as the largest living fish; length up to 10 m/33 ft, weight c.6000 kg/13 200 lb. (Family: Cetorhinidae.)

Basle *Basel*

Basque Provinces [bask], Span **País Vasco** or **Provincias Vascongadas**, Basque **Euskadi** pop (2000e) 2 121 000; area 7261 km²/2803 sq mi. Autonomous region of N Spain, comprising the provinces of Álava, Guipúzcoa, and Vizcaya; industries centred around Bilbao and San Sebastian.

Basques [basks] A people living in northern parts of Spain and neighbouring areas in France, and now thought to originate from local Mesolithic peoples; population c.805 000 in Spain, 130 000 in France, and 170 000 elsewhere, mainly South America and the United States of America. They are physically similar to their neighbours, and are Roman Catholics, but their language, Basque, spoken by c.500 000, does not relate to any other European language. Urbanized Basques retain strong ethnic identity, and their main city Bilbao is a centre of Basque nationalism. Since the death of Franco (1975), Basques have been granted some local autonomy (1978–9), but the more militant continue to agitate for a separate Basque state, engaging in terrorism for this end.

Basra [baz**r**a], Arabic **al-Basrah** 30°30N 47°50E, pop (2000e) 954 000. Port in SE Iraq, at head of the Shatt al-Arab; major centre of literature, theology, and scholarship in 8th–9th-c; badly affected in 1980s by Iran–Iraq war and again in 1991 during and after the Gulf War; attacked by US-led coalition forces (Mar 2003) during the Iraq War. modern administrative and commercial centre; airport; railway; university (1967).

bas-relief [bah ruh**leef**] Low relief sculpture, in which the design projects only very slightly from the background, as on a coin.

bass [bas] Marine and brackish-water fish (*Dicentrarchus labrax*) found in the surf zone around rocks and beaches of the NE Atlantic; body blue-grey with silver sides, length up to 1 m/3¼ ft. (Family: Serranidae.)

Bassae [ba**say**] A 5th-c BC temple dedicated to Apollo Epicurius on the slopes of Mt Lykaion, SW Arcadia, Greece; a world heritage site.

Bassano, Jacopo da [basahnoh], also known as **Giacomo da Ponte** (c.1510–92) Painter, founder of genre painting in Europe, born in Bassano, Italy. His best paintings are of peasant life and Biblical scenes with animals.

basse taille enamel [bas tiy] A technique of enamelling on silver, or occasionally gold, where the metal is carved and engraved, and translucent coloured enamel is applied on top with the image shining through.

Basse-Terre [bas tair] pop (2000e) 178 000; area 848 km²/327 sq mi. One of the two main islands of the French Overseas Department of Guadeloupe, E Caribbean; mountainous, with active volcano Grande Soufrière rising to 1484 m/4869 ft; capital, Basse-Terre, pop (2000e) 14 500; tourism.

Basseterre [bastair] 17°17N 62°43W, pop (2000e) 15 200. Capital and chief port of St Kitts-Nevis, E Caribbean, on SW coast of St Kitts I; airport; cathedral.

basset-horn An 18th-c musical instrument belonging to the clarinet family, with a lower compass than that of the normal clarinet. It fell into disuse in the 19th-c.

basset hound A breed of dog formerly used in France and Belgium for hunting; long, solid body, with very short legs; muzzle long and broad; ears long and pendulous; short-haired coat of white, black, and tan.

Bassey, Dame Shirley (Veronica) (1937–) Singer and entertainer, born in Tiger Bay, Cardiff. She left school at 15 and worked in a factory while performing at local working men's clubs at the weekends. She soon turned professional, and went on to international success spanning four decades. Her best-known songs include 'As Long as He Needs Me' (1960), 'What Now My Love' (1962), 'Goldfinger' (1964), and 'Diamonds are Forever' (1971). She was made a dame in 2000.

bassoon A musical instrument consisting of a jointed wooden pipe, about 2 m 54 cm/8 ft 4 in long, doubled back on itself, and fitted with metal keys and a curved crook with a double reed. The larger **double bassoon**, or **contrabassoon**, sounds one octave lower than the standard instrument.

Bass Strait [bas] A channel separating Tasmania from Victoria, Australia, maximum width 240 km/150 mi; named in 1798 after the British explorer George Bass (1771–1803).

basswood An American species of lime (*Tilia americana*), producing useful timber; stringy inner bark used for mats and ropes. (Family: Tileaceae.)

Bastia [basteea] 42°40N 9°30E, pop (2000e) 40 500. Port in NW Corsica, France; founded by the Genoese, 1380; capital of Corsica until 1811; chief town of the island; airport; railway.

Bastille [basteel] (Fr 'strongly fortified structure') A mediaeval fortress and prison in E Paris, the symbol of Bourbon despotism, stormed by a Parisian mob on 14 July 1789. The anniversary of the day is a French national holiday.

bat A nocturnal mammal, widespread in tropical and temperate regions; hibernates in winter in cold areas; usually hangs head-down at rest; the only mammal capable of sustained flight; probably evolved to exploit night-flying insects. Most members of the suborder Microchiroptera eat insects; some also eat fish, frogs, birds, or other bats. They use echolocation to detect prey and avoid obstacles, and have a nose and ears which are often complex in shape. In contrast, **fruit bats** (or *flying foxes*) of the Old World tropics (suborder: Megachiroptera, 170 species) eat fruit and flowers detected by smell. They include the largest bats, with large eyes and a dog-like head (small ears and a long muzzle). They have better vision than other bats, and few use echolocation. A quarter of living mammal species are bats. (Order: Chiroptera, 951 species.)

Batak Six closely-related ethnic groups of C Sumatra, Indonesia, speaking Austronesian languages. The most literate and Christianized group are the Toba Batak, well-known for trade and their key role in national government. They are one-third Muslim, one-third Christian, and the rest adhering to traditional religion.

Batalha, Monastery of [batalya] A Dominican abbey, in Batalha, W Portugal, one of the great examples of Christian Gothic architecture; a world heritage site. It was founded in 1388 by King João I in fulfilment of a vow made at the Battle of Aljubarrota, where Portuguese independence was established.

batch processing A defined series of tasks which are submitted to larger computers and executed only when time becomes available on the computer. This is in contrast to **interactive computing**, where the user accesses the computer in a conversational mode.

Bates, H(erbert) E(rnest) (1905–74) Writer, born in Rushden, Northamptonshire. He is one of the greatest exponents of the short-story form. His best-known novel is *Fair Stood the Wind for France* (1944). The Larkin family was introduced in *The Darling Buds of May* (1958).

Bates, H(enry) W(alter) (1825–92) Naturalist and traveller, born in Leicester, Leicestershire. In 1861 he described the phenomena of mimicry in animals (later known as **Batesian mimicry**), which contributed to the theory of natural selection.

Bateson, William (1861–1926) Biologist, born in Whitby, North Yorkshire. He laid the foundations of (and named) the science of genetics.

Bath, Lat **Aquae Calidae**, Old English **Akermanceaster** 51°23N 2°22W, pop (2000e) 84 400. Spa town, part of Bath and North East Somerset unitary authority (from 1996), SW England, on R Avon; noted since Roman times for its hot springs; chartered in 1189; railway; university (1966); Roman baths; City of Bath a world heritage site.

Bath, Most Honourable Order of the A British order of chivalry, formally created by George I in 1725, but traditionally founded by Henry IV in 1399 at the Tower of London, when he conferred the honour on the 46 esquires who had attended him at his bath the night before his coronation. The motto is *Tria juncta in uno* ('three joined in one').

Bathurst *Banjul*

bathymetry The measurement of the depths of sea-bottom features in large bodies of water. **Bathymetric charts** indicate the depths of water in feet, fathoms, or metres and are used to show the morphology of submarine topographic features.

bathyscaphe [bathiskayf] Any free-moving vessel designed for underwater exploration, consisting of a flotation compartment with an observation capsule underneath. Originally designed by Piccard in 1948, they have proved capable of reaching depths of over 10 000 m/32 000 ft.

batik [bateek] A form of dyeing in which parts of the fabric are left undyed because of wax printed or painted onto it. The fabric is then crushed to crack the wax, and dyed. Removal of the wax leaves undyed areas covered in fine lines. This method, a form of *resist dyeing*, originated in Indonesia.

Batista (y Zaldívar), Fulgencio [bateesta] (1901–73) Cuban dictator, born in Oriente province. In 1933, he organized a military coup (the 'sergeants' revolt'), and became president (1940–4). In 1952 he overthrew President Prio Socorras, and ruled as dictator until his overthrow by Fidel Castro (Jan 1959).

Bat Mitzvah *Bar Mitzvah*

Baton Rouge [baton roozh] 30°27N 91°11W, pop (2000e) 227 800. Capital of state in SE Louisiana, USA; a deep-water port on the Mississippi R; founded, 1719; ceded to the USA as part of the Louisiana Purchase, 1803; declared its independence under the name Feliciana, 1810; incorporated as a town within Louisiana, 1817; state capital, 1849–61 and since 1882; airfield; railway; university (1860).

Batten, Jean (1909–82) New Zealand pioneer aviator, born in

Rotorua, New Zealand. In 1934 she made the first England–Australia 'there and back' solo flight by a woman, breaking Amy Johnson's record, and in 1936 made a record-breaking flight from England to New Zealand.

battered baby / child syndrome *child abuse*

battery (electricity) A device that converts chemical energy into electrical energy. The first battery, made by Alessandro Volta in c.1800, was the basis of the *voltaic cell* – two chemicals immersed in an electrolyte, enabling electrons to travel from one to the other along a circuit. *Primary cells* only discharge electricity, whereas *secondary cells* (or *accumulators*) can also be recharged. The batteries commonly encountered in torches, toys, cameras, etc are 'dry' primary cells, in which the electrolyte has been treated so that it will not spill out of the battery. 'Wet' primary cells are used in telephone and railway signalling systems.

battery (law) The use of force against another person without that person's consent. It involves physical contact (unlike assault), but not necessarily physical damage. Consent may sometimes be implied, such as in the context of lawful sporting activity.

battery farming *factory farming*

battleship The most powerful warship capable of engaging an enemy. The largest battleship now in service is the USS *New Jersey* (58 000 tons), mounting nine 16-inch guns.

baud [bawd] A unit, named after the French inventor, J M E Baudot (1845–1903), which is used to measure the capacity of a communications channel to carry digital data. The baud rate of a communications channel is the number of signal changes per second with which the channel can cope. Using an analog link and current modem technology up to 16 bits can be coded into each signal change, hence a 2400 baud channel can carry 38 Kbps (kilobauds per second) of digital information.

Baudelaire, Charles (Pierre) [bohduhlair] (1821–67) French Symbolist poet, born in Paris. His masterpiece is a collection of poems, *Les Fleurs du mal* (1857), for which author, printer, and publisher were prosecuted for impropriety in 1864.

Baudot, Jean-Maurice-Emile [bawdoh] (1845–1903) Electrical engineer, born in Magneux, France. In 1874 he patented the Baudot code, used in telegraph systems, and in 1894 a system which allowed several messages to be sent along the same wire simultaneously (*multiplexing*).

Baudouin I [bohdwĩ] (1930–93) King of the Belgians (1951–93), born at Stuyvenberg Castle, near Brussels, the elder son of Leopold III and his first wife, Queen Astrid. He succeeded to the throne following the abdication of his father (Jul 1951), and in 1960 married the Spanish **Doña Fabiola de Mora y Aragón**.

Bauhaus [bowhows] An influential school of arts and crafts founded in the Weimar Republic by Walter Gropius in 1919. The aim was for artists and architects to work together to create a new unity in the arts. At first expressionist in style, the Bauhaus quickly championed the stark simplicity of functionalism. The school moved to Dessau in 1925, but was closed by Hitler in 1933, many members living thereafter in the USA. A new director was appointed in 1987, and the renamed Bauhaus Dessau Foundation now contains a collection, studio, academy, and workshop.

Baum, Vicki [bowm], originally **Vicki Hedvig** (1888–1960) Novelist, born in Vienna. Her works include *Grand Hotel* (1930), *Grand Opera* (1942), several short stories, and plays.

Bausch, Pina [bowsh], popular name of **Philippine Bausch** (1940–) Dancer, choreographer, and director, born in Solingen, Germany. She became ballet director of the Wuppertal Dance Theatre in 1973, later founding her own company. Her choreography and particularly her unusual stagings mark a turning point in contemporary dance, and have remained a powerful influence.

bauxite [bawksiyt] A natural mixture of hydrated aluminium oxide minerals produced by the weathering of rocks in hot, humid climates in which more soluble constituents are leached out. It is the chief ore of aluminium.

Bavaria, Ger **Bayern** pop (2000e) 11 677 000; area 70 553 km^2/ 27 233 sq mi. Largest province in former West Germany, and Europe's oldest existing political entity; capital, Munich; chief towns, Augsburg, Passau, Nuremberg, Würzburg, Regensburg; a third of the area is forested; many spas and climatic health resorts.

Bavarian Alps, Ger **Bayerische Alpen** Mountain range extending E and W from L Constance to Salzburg; highest peak, the Zugspitze (2962 m/9718 ft); called the **Tirol Alps** in Austria.

Bavarian Forest, Ger **Bayerische Wald** Mountain range bounded SW by the Danube valley; highest peak, the Einodriegel (1126 m/3694 ft); largest continuous forest in Europe.

Bax, Sir Arnold (Edward Trevor), pseudonym **Dermot O'Byrne** (1883–1953) Composer, born in London. His compositions include seven symphonies (1921–39), tone poems (such as *Tintagel*, 1917), choral works, chamber music, and piano concertos. In 1942 he was made Master of the King's (from 1952 Queen's) Musick.

Bayazid I *Bayezit I*

Bayeux Tapestry [biyuh, biyoe] An embroidered wall-hanging in coloured wool on linen, narrating events leading up to the invasion of England by William of Normandy, and the Battle of Hastings in 1066. Probably commissioned by William's half-brother Odo, Bishop of Bayeux in N France, and embroidered in S England c.1067–77, its length is 68 m/224 ft, and its height 46 cm–54 cm/18–21 in.

Bayezit I [bajazet], also spelled **Bajazet** or **Bayazid**, nickname **Yildrim** ('Thunderbolt') (c.1354–1403) Sultan in the Ottoman Empire (1389–1402). He conquered Bulgaria, parts of Serbia, Macedonia and Thessaly, and most of Asia Minor. In 1402 he was defeated near Ankara by Timur, in whose camp he died.

Baykonur Cosmodrome *Baikonur Cosmodrome*

Baylis, Lilian Mary (1874–1937) Theatrical manager, born in London. She founded the Old Vic Theatre in 1912, and in 1931 she re-opened Sadler's Wells Theatre, making it the home for the Vic Wells Ballet (later the Royal Ballet) and the English National Opera.

Baylis, Trevor (1937–) Engineer and inventor, born in London. In 1993 he began work on a clockwork ('wind-up') radio that dispensed with batteries and electric power, which could be used by isolated communities where energy resources were scarce or non-existent. By 1996 the radio was being commercially marketed, and has since been in demand globally. He later formed Trevor Baylis Brands, a company dedicated to helping inventors to develop, protect, and market their ideas.

Bay of Pigs The attempted invasion of Cuba (Apr 1961) by Cuban exiles supported by the USA. The invasion force of 1300 men landed at Bahía de Cochinos (Bay of Pigs) on the S coast, but was rapidly overwhelmed and defeated by Cuban troops commanded by Fidel Castro.

bayonet A steel blade, thought to have been invented in Bayonne, France, in the 17th-c, which turns an infantryman's firearm into a thrusting weapon. Originally plugging into the end of the musket, by the early 19th-c bayonets were designed to fit into a slot beneath the muzzle, allowing the weapon to be fired at will.

bayou [biyoo] A section of still or slow-moving marshy water cut off from a main river channel. It is often in the form of an oxbow lake. Bayous are typical of the Mississippi R delta in Louisiana, USA.

bay owl An owl native to Africa and SE Asia; inhabits wet tropical forest; eats insects and vertebrates. (Genus: *Phodilus*, 2 species. Family: Tytonidae.)

Bayreuth [biyroyt] 49°56N 11°35E, pop (2000e) 73 500. Industrial and marketing town in Germany, on a tributary of R Main; world famous as a festival city committed to the operas of Wagner; railway; university (1975).

bay tree *sweet bay*

Bazaar Malay *Malay* (language)

bazooka A US infantry weapon developed during World War 2 which fires a small rocket projectile from a simple launching tube. The projectile's warhead is effective against light tank armour.

bazouka *kazoo*

BBC Abbreviation of the **British Broadcasting Corporation**, the UK organization responsible for local, regional, national, and international television and radio services. It began radio broadcasts in 1922 as the British Broadcasting Company, and received a Royal Charter in 1927, thereafter maintaining a national radio service. It began its television service in 1936. Financed almost wholly by viewers' licence fees, it is formally independent of government, and committed to a public-service ethos.

BBC World Service A part of the British Broadcasting Corporation, providing radio services in English and 32 other languages. Based in London, it is funded by a grant from the Foreign and Commonwealth Office, but is editorially independent of the UK government.

BCG An abbreviation of *Bacille Calmette-Guérin*, a vaccine used to protect against tuberculosis named after French bacteriologists Albert Calmette (1863–1933) and Camille Guérin (1872–1961). It consists of attenuated living tubercle bacteria.

Beach Boys, The US singing/instrumental group, formed in California in 1961, consisting originally of brothers **Brian Wilson** (1942– , vocalist, bass guitar, keyboards, songwriter), **Carl Wilson** (1946–98, vocalist, guitar) and **Dennis Wilson** (1944–83, vocalist, drums), with cousin **Mike Love** (1941– , vocalist) and **Al(an) Jardine** (1942– , vocalist, bass guitar, guitar); later also **Bruce Johnston** (1944–) and others. They found fame in the 1960s with cheerful songs of teenage West Coast life, surfing, fast cars and motorcycles, and all-American girls, including 'I Get Around', 'California Girls', and 'Good Vibrations'. In 2004 Wilson performed his album *Smile* at London's Festival Hall. Although begun in the 1960s, the album was never completed and stayed unreleased.

Beachcomber *Morton, John Cameron*

beach flea *sand hopper*

Beaconsfield, Earl of *Disraeli, Benjamin*

beagle A breed of dog developed in Britain; a medium-sized hound with a sturdy body and short coat (coarse-haired forms exist); white, tan, and black; broad pendulous ears, deep muzzle; formerly used to track hares by scent.

Beaker culture A prehistoric culture defined archaeologically by finely-made, pottery drinking vessels for mead or beer, often burnished and geometrically decorated; found in graves of the 3rd millennium BC from Spain, Czech Republic, and Hungary to Italy and Britain.

Beale, Dorothea (1831–1906) Pioneer of women's education, born in London. From 1858 she was principal of Cheltenham Ladies' College, and in her later years became a suffragette. She sponsored St Hilda's Hall in Oxford for women teachers in 1894. In 2006 the college voted to admit men for the first time.

beam weapons *directed energy weapons*

bean A general name applied to the seeds of many plants, but particularly those belonging to the pea family, Leguminosae, many of which are edible.

bear A carnivorous mammal, widespread in the N hemisphere; head large with short, rounded ears and long muzzle; body bulky with thick (usually shaggy) coat and very short tail. (Family: Ursidae, 7 species.)

Beard, Dan(iel Carter), nickname **Uncle Dan** (1850–1941) Illustrator and youth leader, born in Cincinnati, OH. He wrote *What to Do and How to Do It: The American Boy's Handy Book* (1882), the first of 16 books on handicrafts. He organized the Sons of Daniel Boone (1905) and the Boy Pioneers of America (1909), was National Scout Commissioner (1910–41), and became 'Uncle Dan' to a generation of American boys.

bearded lizard An Australian agamid lizard; group of large spines behind each ear; body with numerous small spines; throat with deep pouch which can be enlarged as a threat display (hence 'beard'); also known as **bearded dragon**. (Genus: *Amphibolurus*, 3 species.)

bearded vulture *lammergeier*

Beardsley, Aubrey (Vincent) [beerdzlee] (1872–98) Illustrator, born in Brighton, East Sussex. He became well known through his posters and his black and white illustrations for *Morte d'Arthur* (1893) and other books. With Oscar Wilde he is regarded as leader of the 'Decadents' of the 1890s.

bearings Mechanical devices supporting rotating shafts with a minimal amount of frictional resistance. In the **ball bearing**, the rotating shaft is supported by a number of balls which are interposed in a cage between it and the fixed mounting.

bear market A stock market term which signifies that there are more sellers than buyers of stocks and shares. A **bear** is an individual who sells shares, hoping the price will then fall, so that they may be repurchased more cheaply.

beat generation A group of US writers of the 1950s who rejected conventional society and its values for a life and writing based on authentic individual experience, according to the poet Allen Ginsberg (*Howl*, 1957), 'of God, sex, drugs, and the absurd'. Besides Ginsberg, novelist Jack Kerouac (*On the Road*, 1957) and poets Gregory Corso (1930–2001) and Laurence Ferlinghetti (1919–) were principal beat writers.

beating the bounds In England, at Rogationtide, a traditional ceremonial walk round the boundaries of a parish, during which boundary stones are beaten with peeled willow wands, the better to fix their position in the memory.

Beatitudes The common name for the opening pronouncements of blessing upon the poor, the hungry, and others in Jesus's great Sermon on the Mount, reported in Matthew's gospel (nine listed in *Matt* 5.3–10) and the Sermon on the Plain in Luke's gospel (four listed in *Luke* 6.20–3).

Beatles, The (1960–70) British pop group, formed in Liverpool in 1960, consisting at that time of **John Lennon** (1940–80, rhythm guitar, keyboards, vocals), **Paul McCartney** (1942– , bass guitar, vocals), **George Harrison** (1943–2001, rhythm guitar, sitar, vocals), and **Pete Best** (1941– , drums). In 1962 Best was replaced by **Ringo Starr** (1940– , originally **Richard Starkey**), and the band signed a record contract. 'Love Me Do' became a hit in the UK, and their appearances at the Cavern Club in Liverpool and elsewhere in the UK overflowed with idolizing fans. 'Beatlemania' spread around the world in 1964, buoyed by international hits such as 'She Loves You' and by the overwhelming success of a concert tour in American stadiums. Their films included *A Hard Day's Night* (1964) and *Help* (1965). In 1966 the Beatles stopped performing in public. Their first studio production was *Sergeant Pepper's Lonely Hearts Club Band* (1967). The group dissolved acrimoniously in 1970, but the then three surviving members of the group sang together again in 1994.

Beaton, Sir Cecil (Walter Hardy) (1904–80) Photographer and designer, born in London. In the 1920s, as a staff photographer for *Vanity Fair* and *Vogue*, he became famous for his society portraits. After World War 2, he designed scenery and costumes for many productions, including *My Fair Lady* and *Gigi*.

Beaton or **Bethune, David** (1494–1546) Scottish statesman and Roman Catholic clergyman, born in Balfour, Fife. A persecutor of the Scottish Protestants, he had the reformer George Wishart burnt at St Andrews (1546), but was murdered in revenge three months later by a group of Protestant conspirators.

Beatrix, in full **Beatrix Wilhelmina Armgard** (1938–) Queen of the Netherlands (1980–), born in Soestdijk, who acceded to the throne on the abdication of her mother. In 1966 she married West German diplomat **Claus-Georg Wilhelm Otto Friedrich Gerd von Amsberg** (1926–2002). They have three sons.

Beatty, David Beatty, 1st Earl (1871–1936) Naval commander, born in Nantwich, Cheshire. He sank the *Blücher* (Jan 1915), and took part in the Battle of Jutland (May 1916). He became commander-in-chief of the Grand Fleet in 1916 and First Sea Lord in 1919.

Beatty, Warren [baytee], originally **Henry Warren Beaty** (1937–) Actor and film-maker, born in Richmond, VA, the younger brother of actress Shirley MacLaine (1934–). He produced *Bonnie and Clyde* (1967), co-wrote *Shampoo* (1975), and co-directed *Heaven Can Wait* (1978). He was the producer, co-writer, and star of *Reds* (1981), which won him an Oscar as best director, and later films include *Bulworth* (1998) and *Town and Country* (2001). In 2006 he received the Cecil B De Mille Award for lifetime achievement.

Beaufort, Henry [bohfert] (1377–1447) English cardinal, a major figure in English politics in the early 15th-c. He became a cardinal in 1426, and was Lord Chancellor on three occasions. During the 1430s he controlled the government of the young King Henry VI.

Beaufort Scale [byoofert, byoofaw(r)t] A scale of windspeed, ranging from 0 to 12, devised by Admiral Francis Beaufort (1774–1857) in the mid-19th-c, which uses descriptions of the way common outdoor features (eg smoke, trees) respond to different wind conditions. (*see panel p.90*)

Beauharnais, Alexandre, vicomte de (Viscount of) [bohah(r)nay] (1760–94) French army officer, born in Martinique. He eagerly embraced the French Revolution, and was made secretary of the National Assembly, but was guillotined (1794) for his failure to relieve Metz. In 1779 he married **Joséphine de la Pagerie**, afterwards wife of Napoleon.

Beaujolais [bohzholay] Sub-division of the old province of Lyonnais in EC France, now forming part of Rhône and Loire departments; major wine-growing region; N part known as Beaujolais Villages; centre, Villefranche.

Beaumarchais, Pierre Augustin Caron de [bohmah(r)shay], originally **Pierre Augustin Caron** (1732–99) Comic playwright, born in Paris. His most successful comedies were *Le Barbier de Séville* (1775, The Barber of Seville) and *Le Mariage de Figaro* (1784, The Marriage of Figaro).

Beaumont, Francis [bohmont] (c.1584–1616) Playwright, born in Gracedieu, Leicestershire. He formed a close association with John Fletcher, writing many plays. *The Woman Hater* (1607) is attributed solely to him, and he had the major share in *The Knight of the Burning Pestle* (1609).

Beauregard, P(ierre) G(ustave) T(outant) [bohregah(r)d] (1818–93) Confederate general, born near New Orleans, LA. He was appointed to the command at Charleston, where he commenced the war by the bombardment of Fort Sumter (1861).

beauty (physics) *bottom*

Beauvais [bohvay] 49°25N 2°08E, pop (2000e) 58 900. Market town in N France, on R Thérain; railway; bishopric; former tapestry-making centre; cathedral (13th–16th-c), with highest Gothic vault in existence (48 m/156 ft).

Beauvoir, Simone de *de Beauvoir, Simone*

Beaux-Arts, Ecole des [bohzah(r), aykol day] The main official art school in Paris. It dates from 1648 and was installed in its present quarters on the left bank of the Seine by 1830.

beaver A large squirrel-like rodent from North America, N Europe, and Asia; semi-aquatic; hind feet webbed; tail broad, flat, and scaly; builds a 'lodge' from logs and mud in woodland ponds; often dams streams to create ponds. (Family: Castoridae, 2 species.)

Beaverbrook (of Beaverbrook and of Cherkley), (William) Max(well) Aitken, Baron (1879–1964) Newspaper magnate and British politician, born in Maple, Ontario. In 1916 he took over the *Daily Express*, which he made into the most widely-read daily newspaper in the world. He became actively involved in World War 2, and was made minister of supply (1941–2), minister of production (1942), Lord Privy Seal (1943–5), and lend-lease administrator in the USA.

Beazley, Kim (Christian) (1948–) Politician, born in Perth, Western Australia. He was elected an MP in 1980, held a number of portfolios during the Australian Labor Party's 13 years in power, and became deputy Prime Minister (1995–6). He became leader of the Opposition in 1996, but resigned after the election defeat in 2001.

bebop A jazz style, also known as **bop**, characterized by fast tempos, extended chordal harmonies, and agitated rhythms. It was cultivated in the 1940s by small groups of musicians.

bèche de mer [besh duh mair] A French culinary term, referring to the food obtained from a marine animal found in the SW Pacific, also known as a **sea cucumber**.

Bechet, Sidney [beshay, beshay] (1897–1959) Jazz musician, born in New Orleans, LA. After starting on clarinet, he switched to soprano saxophone in order, he said, to dominate the brass in ensembles. Lionized in France on his first tour in 1919, he kept returning, and in 1949 became a permanent resident.

Bechstein, Karl [bekstiyn], Ger [bekhshtiyn] (1826–1900) Piano manufacturer, born in Gotha, Germany. He founded his famous factory in Berlin in 1856.

Beckenbauer, Franz [bekenbower], nickname **the Kaiser** (1945–) Footballer, born in Munich, Germany. He played in the West German side beaten by England in the 1966 World Cup, and led his country to World Cup success in 1974. He retired in 1983 and became manager of the German national team in 1986. He is currently president of FC Bayern Munich and in 1998 was appointed vice-president of the German Football Association.

Becker, Boris [beker] (1967–) Tennis player, born in Leiman, Germany. In 1985 he was the youngest winner of the men's singles at Wimbledon (17 years 227 days). He retained the title in 1986, lost it in the 1988 final to Stefan Edberg, but regained it in 1989. In 1988 he was the World Championship Tennis champion and the Masters champion, then won the US Open (1989), the Australian Open (1991, 1996), and the Association of Tennis Professionals World Title (1992). In 2003 he was inducted into the Tennis Hall of Fame.

Becket, St Thomas, also called **Thomas à Becket** (1118–70) Saint and martyr, born in London. In 1155, he became Chancellor, the first Englishman since the Conquest to hold high office. When created Archbishop of Canterbury (1162), he resigned the chancellorship, serving the Church as vigorously as he had the king, and coming into conflict with Henry II's aims to keep the clergy in subordination to the state. Henry's rashly-voiced wish to be rid of 'this turbulent priest' led to Becket's murder in Canterbury cathedral (29 Dec 1170) by four of the king's knights. He was canonized in 1173, and Henry did public penance at his tomb in 1174. Feast day 29 December.

Beckett, Margaret (Mary) (1943–) British stateswoman, born in Ashton-under-Lyne, Greater Manchester. Elected an MP in 1974, she became deputy leader of the Labour Party (1992–4, including a short term as leader in 1994). She served as president of the Board of Trade and secretary of state for trade and industry (1997), Leader of the House of Commons (1998–2001), secretary of state for environment, food and rural affairs (2001–6), and foreign secretary (2006–).

Beckett, Samuel (Barclay) (1906–89) Writer and playwright, born

Wind Force And Sea Disturbance

Beaufort number	Windspeed		Wind name	Observable wind characteristics	Sea disturbance number	Average wave height		Observable sea characteristics
	kph	mph				m	ft	
0	<1	<1	Calm	Smoke rises vertically	0	0	0	Sea like a mirror
1	1–5	1–3	Light air	Wind direction shown by smoke drift but not by wind vanes	0	0	0	Ripples like scales, without foam crests
2	6–11	4–7	Light breeze	Wind felt on face; leaves rustle; vanes moved by wind	1	0–3	0–1	More definite wavelets, but crests do not break
3	12–19	8–12	Gentle breeze	Leaves and small twigs in constant motion; wind extends light flag	2	0.3–0.6	1–2	Large wavelets; crests beginning to break; scattered white horses
4	20–28	13–18	Moderate	Raises dust, loose paper; small branches moved	3	0.6–1.2	2–4	Small waves becoming longer; fairly frequent white horses
5	29–38	19–24	Fresh	Small trees begin to sway; crested wavelets on inland waters	4	1.2–2.4	4–8	Moderate waves with longer form; many white horses; some foam spray
6	39–49	25–31	Strong	Large branches in motion; whistling heard in telegraph wires; difficult to use umbrellas	5	2.4–4	8–13	Large waves forming; more white foam crests; spray
7	50–61	32–38	Near gale	Whole trees in motion; difficult to walk against wind	6	4–6	13–20	Sea heaps up; streaks of white foam blown along
8	62–74	39–46	Gale	Breaks twigs off trees; impedes progress	6	4–6	13–20	Moderately high waves of greater length; well-marked streaks of foam
9	75–88	47–54	Strong gale	Slight structural damage occurs	6	4–6	13–20	High waves; dense streaks of foam; sea begins to roll; spray affects visibility
10	89–102	55–63	Storm	Trees uprooted; considerable damage occurs	7	6–9	20–30	Very high waves with overhanging crests; generally white appearance of surface; heavy rolling
11	103–17	64–72	Violent storm	Widespread damage	8	9–14	30–45	Exceptionally high waves; long white patches of foam; poor visibility; ships lost to view behind waves
12–17	≥118	≥73	Hurricane	Whole areas devastated	9	14	>45	Air filled with foam and spray; sea completely white; very poor visibility

Beaufort Scale

in Dublin. He settled in France in 1937. His early work was written in English, but he later wrote in French, notably the novels *Molloy* (1951) and *Malone Meurt* (1951, Malone Dies), and the play *En attendant Godot* (1954, Waiting for Godot), which later took London by storm. He was awarded the 1969 Nobel Prize for Literature.

Beckham, David (Robert Joseph) (1975–) Footballer, born in London. A midfield player, he joined Manchester United in 1993, and the England team in 1996, becoming England captain in the lead-up to the 2002 World Cup. He gained his 94th cap during the 2006 World Cup, and relinquished the captaincy following his country's quarter-final exit from the competition. His many honours with United include the treble of FA Cup, Premier League Championship, and European Cup in the 1998–9 season. He signed for Real Madrid in 2003, and in 2007 joined LA Galaxy. In 2005 he opened the David Beckham Academy soccer school in London, and a sister academy in Los Angeles, CA. He married Victoria Adams ('Posh Spice') in 1999.

Becquerel, (Antoine) Henri [bekerel] (1852–1908) Physicist, born in Paris. He shared the Nobel Prize with the Curies in 1903 for discovering the **Becquerel rays** emitted from uranium salts, which led to the isolation of radium.

becquerel [bekerel] The activity of a radioactive source as the number of disintegrations per second; SI unit; symbol *Bq*.

Bedchamber Crisis A British political crisis which occurred in May 1839, after Melbourne, Prime Minister in the Whig government, offered to resign, and advised the young Queen Victoria to appoint Peel and the Tories. The Queen refused to dismiss certain Ladies of the Bedchamber with Whig sympathies, whereupon Peel refused office and the Whig government continued.

Bede or **Baeda, St**, known as **the Venerable Bede** (c.673–735) Anglo-Saxon historian and theologian, born near Monkwearmouth, Durham. He wrote in the monastery at Jarrow, his most valuable work being the *Historia ecclesiastica gentis anglorum* (Ecclesiastical History of the English People). He was canonized in 1899. Feast day 25 May.

Bedford 52°08N 0°29W, pop (2001e) 147 900. County town of Bedfordshire, SC England; railway; John Bunyan was imprisoned here, during which time he wrote *The Pilgrim's Progress*.

Bedford Level *Fens, the*

Bedfordshire pop (2001e) 381 600; area 1235 km²/477 sq mi. County in SC England; drained W–E by the R Ouse; county town, Bedford; Luton a new unitary authority from 1997.

Bednorz, (Johannes) Georg [bednaw(r)ts] (1950–) Physicist, born in Germany. He worked with Swiss physicist K Alexander Müller (1927–) at the IBM Zürich Research Laboratory at Rüschlikon. Their work was chiefly directed to finding novel superconductors which would show superconductivity at higher temperatures than the near-absolute zero level previously observed. They shared the 1987 Nobel Prize for Physics.

Bedouin Arabic-speaking nomads of Arabia, Syria, Jordan, Iraq, and other desert areas in the Middle East. They mainly herd animals in the desert during winter months and cultivate land in summer. Many have been forced to settle in one locality, because of political or economic moves.

bedstraw An annual or perennial, found almost everywhere; weak, 4-angled stem, often with tiny hooks, narrow leaves in whorls; flowers tiny, white, yellow, or greenish, 4-petalled, in open clusters; fruits often burrs. (Genus: *Galium*, 400 species. Family: Rubiaceae.)

bee A winged insect that builds and provisions a nest for its young; the common name of several different types of hymenopteran, including solitary mining bees (Family: Andrenidae), carpenter bees (Family: Anthophoridae), bumblebees, orchid bees, stingless bees, and honeybees (all Family: Apidae). Social structure ranges from the solitary bees, in which each queen effectively raises her own brood, to honeybees, which form a complex society with a caste system and overlapping, co-operating generations. (Order: Hymenoptera.)

beech A deciduous, shallow-rooted tree native to the N hemisphere; leaves oval, margins wavy; flowers tiny, males in long-stalked clusters, females (and later, nuts) in pairs enclosed in 4-lobed, spiny case. (Genus: *Fagus*, 10 species. Family: Fagaceae.)

Beecham, Sir Thomas (1879–1961) Conductor, born in St Helens, Merseyside. He founded the Royal Philharmonic Orchestra in 1946. A noted champion of Delius's music, he published in 1958 a study of the composer's life and works. He was also known for his candid pronouncements on musical matters, his 'Lollipop' encores, and his after-concert speeches.

Beecher, Lyman (1775–1863) Presbyterian minister and revivalist, born in New Haven, CT, the father of Harriet Beecher Stowe. He preached in New York, Connecticut, and Massachusetts, his brand of Calvinism calling for constant church services and strong opposition to drinking. In 1832 he went to Cincinnati as head of the newly founded Lane Theological Seminary, and to serve as pastor of the Second Presbyterian Church.

Beecher Stowe, Harriet *Stowe, Harriet (Elizabeth) Beecher*

Beeching, Richard, Baron (1913–85) Engineer and administrator, born in Maidstone, Kent. As chairman of the British Railways Board (1963–5), he was responsible for the substantial contraction of the UK rail network (the **Beeching Plan**).

bee dancing The patterned movements of honey-bees used to signal the direction and distance of pollen and nectar to other members of the colony. The phenomenon was first documented by the Austrian biologist Karl von Frisch (1886–1982).

beefeater *Yeomen of the Guard*

bee-keeping *apiculture*

bee orchid The name for various species of the genus *Ophrys*, widespread throughout Europe, W Asia, and N Africa; remarkable for their flowers which mimic insects. The lower lip of the flower resembles a female insect in both colour and texture, and the flower emits a powerful pheromone-like scent to attract males of the same species. (Genus: *Ophrys*, 30 species. Family: Orchidaceae.)

beer An alcoholic beverage made from ale (malted barley) which has been flavoured with hops. It is currently an umbrella term covering a wide range of drinks, distinguished by the type of yeast used, such as *bitter* (a beer brewed with more hops and a lighter malt than *Mild*), *lager* (a light beer which matures over a long period of time at a low temperature), and *stout* or *porter* (types of dark ale produced from the brewing of roasted malt).

Beerbohm, Sir (Henry) Max(imilian) [beerbohm], nickname **the Incomparable Max** (1872–1956) Writer and caricaturist, born in London. He wrote many volumes of caricatures and parodying essays, but his best-known work was his novel on Oxford undergraduate life, *Zuleika Dobson* (1911).

Beerbohm Tree, Herbert *Tree, Sir Herbert (Draper) Beerbohm*

beeswax Wax secreted by bees of the family Apidae, including bumblebees, stingless bees, and honeybees. It is produced by glands beneath the abdominal body plates (*sterna* or *terga*), and used in nest construction.

beet An annual, biennial, or perennial native to Europe and Asia; leaves shiny, often tinged dark red. Cultivated beets, all derived from the wild beet (*Beta vulgaris*), are divisible into two groups: **leaf beets**, including spinach beets and chards, are grown as leaf vegetables; **root beets**, including beetroot and mangel-wurzel, are biennials grown for their edible, swollen roots. **Sugar-beet**, containing up to 20% sugar in the root, has largely replaced sugar-cane as the source of sugar in W Europe. (Genus: *Beta*, 6 species. Family: Chenopodiaceae.)

Beethoven, Ludwig van [baytohvn] (1770–1827) Composer, born in Bonn, Germany. He lived and worked in Vienna from 1792.

Though often in love with his noble pupils, he never married. His music is usually divided into three periods. In the first (1792–1802), which includes the first two symphonies, the first six quartets, and the 'Pathétique' and 'Moonlight' sonatas, his style gradually develops its own individuality. His second period (1803–12) begins with the 'Eroica' symphony (1803), and includes his next five symphonies, the difficult 'Kreutzer' sonata (1803), the Violin Concerto, the 'Archduke' trio (1811), and the 'Razumovsky' quartets. His third great period begins in 1813, and includes the Mass, the 'Choral' symphony (1823), and the last five quartets. His career was marred by deafness, which began in 1801 and was total by the early 1820s.

beetle A winged insect with forewings modified as rigid, horny cases covering membranous hindwings and abdomen beneath; hindwings used in flight, sometimes missing; biting mouthparts; range in size from less than 0·5 mm/0·2 in to c.170 mm/7 in; development includes distinct larval and pupal phases; c.350 000 species known, including many pests. (Order: Coleoptera.)

Beeton, Isabella Mary, *née* **Mayson**, known as **Mrs Beeton** (1836–65) Cookery writer, born in London. Her *Book of Household Management* (1859–60), covering cookery and other branches of domestic science, made her a household name.

beetroot *beet*

Begin, Menachem (Wolfovitch) [baygin] (1913–92) Israeli statesman and prime minister (1977–83), born in Brest-Litovsk, Belarus. In 1948 he founded the Herut Freedom Movement, becoming chairman of the Herut Party. In 1973 three parties combined to form the nationalist Likud Front with Begin as its leader, and in the 1977 elections he formed a coalition government. He attended peace conferences in Jerusalem (1977) and at Camp David at the invitation of President Carter (1978), and in 1978 he and President Sadat of Egypt were jointly awarded the Nobel Peace Prize.

begonia A perennial native to warm regions, especially America; leaves asymmetric, one side larger than the other, often spotted or marked with white or red; male flowers with two large and two small petals, females with 4–5 more petals; fruit a winged capsule. (Genus: *Begonia*, 900 species. Family: Begoniaceae.)

Behan, Brendan (Francis) [beean] (1923–64) Writer, born in Dublin. He was twice imprisoned for IRA activities, and had a period in hospital for alcoholism. His plays include *The Quare Fellow* (1956) and *The Hostage* (1958). His other writing includes an autobiographical novel, *Borstal Boy* (1958).

Behar *Bihar*

behaviourism / behaviorism The view that psychology is most effectively pursued by analyzing the overt behaviour of people and animals, in preference to subjective states, thoughts, or hypothetical internal dynamics. It has had an important influence on modern psychology, but is now rarely held in its extreme form.

behaviour / behavior therapy A type of psychological treatment formulated by psychotherapist Joseph Wolpe (1915–97) which emphasizes the alteration of thoughts and behaviour. It is often applied to neurotic illnesses (eg phobias) on the presumption that these are learned forms of behaviour which can be 'unlearned'. The term was coined by the British psychologist Hans Eysenck in the 1950s.

Beiderbecke, (Leon) Bix [biyderbek] (1903–31) Cornettist and composer, born in Davenport, IA. When expelled from a military academy, he began the short career that made him one of the most celebrated jazz performers of the 1920s. His later career was ravaged by alcoholism and he succumbed to pneumonia at the age of 28.

Beijing [bayzhing] or **Peking**, formerly **Beiping (Pei-p'ing)** 39°55N 116°25E; pop (2000e) 8 208 000, administrative region 12 062 000; municipality area 17 800 km²/6871 sq mi. Capital city and municipality of NE China; occupied by Japanese, 1937–45; capital of China, 1949; airport; railway; two universities (1898, 1950); Imperial Palace, formerly known as the 'Forbidden City'; Tiananmen (Gate of Heavenly Peace, built 1417, restored 1651), Niu Jie (oldest Muslim temple, 996).

Beira [bayra] 19°46S 34°52E, pop (2000e) 379 000. Seaport capital of Mozambique, SE Africa; occupied by the Portuguese, 1506; founded as the seat of the Mozambique Company, 1891; airport; railway.

Beirut [bayroot], Arabic **Bayrut**, Fr **Beyrouth**, ancient **Berytus** 33°52N 35°30E, pop (2000e) 1 690 000. Seaport capital of Lebanon; the 'Green Line' refers to the division of the city during the 1975–6 civil war into Muslim (W) and Christian (E) sectors; Israeli attack on Palestinian and Syrian forces in 1982 led to the evacuation of Palestinians to camps such as Sabra, Chatila, and Bourj Barajneh; severely damaged by continued fighting; reduction of tension and release of foreign hostages, 1991; S Beirut severely damaged during Israeli airstrikes in month-long war (2006) with Lebanese militant group Hezbollah; airport; railway; American University (1866), Lebanese University (1953), Arab University (1960); two cathedrals.

Békésy, Georg von [baykayshee] (1899–1972) Physiologist, born in Budapest. For his studies of how the human ear analyses sounds, he was awarded the Nobel Prize for Physiology or Medicine in 1961.

Bekka, the *Beqaa, el*

bel *decibel*

Bel and the Dragon An addition to the Book of Daniel, part of the Old Testament Apocrypha, or Chapter 14 of Daniel in Catholic versions of the Bible. It includes the tale of Daniel in the lion's den.

Belarus *p.93*

Belau *p.94*

Belém [belem], also called **Pará** 1°27S 48°29W, pop (2000e) 1 388 000. City in N Brazil; founded in 1616; airport; railway; university (1957); cathedral (1748).

Belfast, Ir **Beal Feirste** 54°35N 5°55W, pop (2000e) 285 800. Capital of Northern Ireland, NE Northern Ireland; at the mouth of the Lagan R, on Belfast Lough; original settlement and castle destroyed in 1177; settled in the 17th-c by English, Scots, and Huguenots, becoming a centre of Irish Protestantism; capital, 1920; well-defined Nationalist (Catholic) and Unionist (Protestant) areas; disrupted by civil unrest 1970s–90s; two airports; railway; university (1908); cathedral (begun 1898); Parliament House at Stormont.

Belgian Congo *Congo, Democratic Republic of*

Belgium *p.95*

Belgrade, Serbo-Croatian **Beograd**, ancient **Singidunum** 44°50N 20°30E, pop (2000e) 1 574 000. Capital city of Serbia (former federation of Yugoslavia), at the junction of the Danube and Sava Rivers; airport; railway; university (1863); arts university (1957); cathedral; damage from NATO bombing in Kosovo crisis (Apr–Jun 1999).

Belgrano, General [belgrahnoh] An Argentinian cruiser, sunk by HM submarine *Conqueror* during the Falklands conflict in 1982, with great loss of life. Her sinking proved to be one of the most controversial incidents of the war.

Belize *p.96*

Belize City 17°29N 88°10W, pop (2000e) 66 500. Seaport in Belize, Central America; capital until 1970; airport.

Bell, Alexander Graham (1847–1922) Educationist and inventor, born in Edinburgh, the son of Alexander Melville Bell. In 1871 he moved to the USA, where he invented the telephone (1872–6), and founded the Bell Telephone Company.

Bell, Alexander Melville (1819–1905) Educationalist, born in Edinburgh. He became a teacher of elocution, his numerous works including *Visible Speech* (1867).

Belarus

Capital Minsk (Mensk)

Languages Belorussian (official), Russian

Ethnic groups (1989) Belorussian (78%), Russian (13%), Polish (4%), Ukrainian (3%), Jewish (1%)

Religions Roman Catholic, Orthodox

Physical features Hilly lowlands with marshes, swamps; Dzyarz-hynskaya Mt rises to 346 m/1135 ft; largest lake, Narach; Belar-uskaya Hrada, largest glacial ridge, runs NW into Minsk Upland; rivers include the Pripyat and Dnepr; Pripyat marshes in E.

Climate Varies from maritime, near Baltic, to continental and humid; average annual temperatures, 18°C (Jul), -6°C (Jan); average annual rainfall 550–700 mm/22–8 in.

Currency Belorussian Rouble (BYR) = 100 kopec (in parallel with the Russian Rouble); currency coupons for food, alcohol, tobacco

Economy Main exports include textiles, timber, chemical products, fertilizers, electrical goods; valuable resource: peat marshes.

GDP (2002e) $90·19 bn, per capita $8700

Human Development Index (2002) 0·788

History Neolithic remains widespread; colonized by E Slavic tribes, 5th-c; Mongols conquered Slavs, 13th-c; Catherine the Great of Russia acquired E Belorussia (White Russia) in the first Polish partition in 1772; gained Minsk in 1793 and the remainder in 1795; W Belorussia ceded to Poland in 1921 as part of the Treaty of Riga which ended Soviet-Polish War; regained by Soviet Union as part of Nazi-Soviet Non-aggression Pact of 1939, and Belorussia became Belorussian Soviet Socialist Republic; admitted to UN, 1945; declared independence, 1991; co-founder of Commonwealth of Independent States (CIS), 1991.

Chairman of Supreme Council
1991–4 Stanislav Shushkevich
1994–6 Mechislav Grib
1996– Syamyon Sharetski

Head of State
1994– Alexander Lukashenko

Head of Government
1991–4 Vyacheslav Kebich
1994–6 Mikhail Chigir
1996–2000 Syargey Ling
2000–1 Uladzimir Yarmoshyn
2001–3 Henadz Navitski
2003– Sergey Sidorski

☐ International Airport

[belarus], official name **Republic of Belarus**, also spelled **Bye-larus**, formerly (to 1991) **Belorussian SSR** or **White Russia**, Russ **Belorusskaya**

Local name Belarus
Timezone GMT +3
Area 207 600 km²/80 134 sq mi
Population total (2002e) 9 933 000
Status Republic
Date of independence 1991

Bell, Martin (1938–) Television journalist and politician, born in Cambridge, Cambridgeshire. He joined the BBC in 1962, becoming one of their best known foreign correspondents. He fought an 'anti-sleaze' campaign in the 1997 general election, and was returned – much to his own surprise – as Independent MP for Tatton. He was unsuccessful in Brentwood and Ongar in the 2001 general election. In 2004 he was made an ambassador for the United Nations Children's Fund.

bell A hollow vessel of bronze or other material which, when struck, vibrates to produce a ringing sound. If the bell is tuned, the sound may be heard as a musical note of definite pitch. The *closed* (or *crotal*) variety is a hollowed sphere, with one or more slits in the surface, which is shaken to cause a loose pellet inside to strike against the inner surface. The *open* bell is cast in the shape of an upturned cup, usually sounded by means of a clapper suspended from the inside of the bell, but sometimes struck externally with a ramrod.

belladonna (Ital 'fair lady') A liquid extract of the deadly nightshade plant (*Atropa belladonna*), so called because Italian ladies used to apply it to their eyes to make the pupils dilate,

an effect deemed attractive. The main active constituent is atropine.

belladonna lily A large bulb (*Amaryllis bella-donna*), native to S Africa; leaves strap-shaped; flowers trumpet-shaped, 7–9 cm/ $2\frac{3}{4}$–$3\frac{1}{2}$ in long, white to pink, 6–12 on a solid stalk appearing in autumn after the leaves have died. (Family: Amaryllidaceae.)

Bellamy, David (James) (1933–) Botanist, writer, and broadcaster, born in London. A professor at Nottingham, and the writer of numerous conservation-oriented books, he is best known for his TV programmes designed to create a greater awareness of the natural environment, such as *Bellamy's Birds' Eye View* (1988), *Bellamy's Border Raids: The Peak District* (1994), and *A Welsh Herbal* (1998–9). He established the Conservation Foundation in 1988.

Bellarmine, St Robert [belermin], originally **Roberto Francesco Romolo Bellarmino** (1542–1621) Jesuit cardinal and theologian, the chief defender of the Church in the 16th-c, born in Montepulciano, Italy. He was canonized in 1930. Feast day 17 May.

bell-flower A member of a large variable genus of mostly annuals and herbaceous perennials, low and spreading to tall

Belau

□ International Airport

[below], also **Palau** or **Pelau**, official name **Republic of Belau**
Local names Belau, also Pelau, Palau
Timezone GMT +10
Area 494 km²/191 sq mi
Population total (2002e) 19 900
Status Republic
Date of independence 1994
Capital Koror
Languages Palauan, English
Ethnic groups Palauan (83%)
Religions Christianity (66%), traditional beliefs (25%)
Physical features A group of c.350 small islands and islets, c.960 km/600 mi E of the Philippines; most W group of the Caroline Is; largest island, Babeldoab ((367 km²/142 sq mi).
Climate Warm all year, with high humidity; average annual temperature 27°C; average annual rainfall, 3810 mm/150 in; typhoons common.
Currency 1 US Dollar (USD) = 100 cents
Economy Tourism, taro, pineapple, breadfruit, bananas, yams, citrus fruit, coconuts, pepper, fishing.
GDP (2001e) $174 mn, per capita $9000
History Smallest of the four political units to emerge out of the US Trust Territory of the Pacific Islands; organized into 16 states; held by Germany, 1899–1914; mandated to Japan by League of Nations, 1920; invaded by USA, 1944; compact of free association with the USA, signed in 1982, but not confirmed until 1993; independence, 1994; member of the UN, 1995; governed by a president and a National Congress consisting of a Senate and a House of Delegates.
Head of State
1993–2001 Kuniwo Nakamura
2001– Tommy Remengesau

and erect, native throughout N temperate regions; leaves very narrow to almost circular; flowers 5-lobed bells, usually large and showy, and almost always blue, sometimes pink or white. (Genus: *Campanula*, 300 species. Family: Campanulaceae.)

Bellingshausen, Fabian Gottlieb Benjamin von [belings-howzn] (1778–1852) Explorer, born in Ösel, Estonia. In 1819–21 he led an Antarctic expedition as far south as 70°, and gave his name to the Bellingshausen Sea.

Bellini [beleenee] A family of 15th-c Venetian painters. **Jacopo Bellini** (c.1400–70) studied under Gentile da Fabriano; only a few of his works remain. His son **Gentile Bellini** (c.1429–1507) worked in his father's studio, and is known for his portraits. His other son, **Giovanni Bellini** (c.1430–1516), was the greatest Venetian painter of his time. His innovations of light and colour became the hallmark of Venetian art, continued by his pupils Giorgione and Titian.

Belloc, (Joseph) Hilaire (Pierre René) [belok] (1870–1953) Writer, born in Saint-Cloud, near Paris. He became a British Liberal MP (1906–10), then continued as a writer, best known for his nonsensical verse for children, *The Bad Child's Book of Beasts* (1896) and the *Cautionary Tales* (1907). He was a leading Roman Catholic of his day.

Bellow, Saul, originally **Solomon Bellows** (1915–2005) Writer, born in Lachine, Quebec, Canada. His first novel was *Dangling Man* (1944), and others include *Herzog* (1964), *Humboldt's Gift* (1975, Pulitzer), *A Theft* (1989), and *The Actual* (1997). In 1976 he was awarded the Nobel Prize for Literature.

bell-ringing The art of ringing church bells, also known as **campanology**. Its two popular forms are **change ringing**, a hand-pulled method, and the **carillon** method, performed with the use of a keyboard connected to the clappers of the bells.

Bell's palsy Paralysis of the muscles of one side of the face innervated by the VIIth cranial nerve (the facial nerve). The condition is named after Scottish surgeon Charles Bell (1774–1842).

Belmopan [belmohpan] 17°18N 88°30W, pop (2000e) 6600. Capital of Belize, Central America; made capital in 1970, following major hurricane damage to Belize City in 1961.

Belo, Carlos (Felipe Ximenes) (1948–) Roman Catholic bishop, born in East Timor, Indonesia. Ordained bishop in 1983, he became an outspoken critic of the Indonesian regime's actions in East Timor, and shared the Nobel Prize for Peace in 1996.

Belo Horizonte [beloh oreezontay] 19°54S 43°54W, pop (2000e) 2786 000. Capital of Minas Gerais state, SE Brazil; altitude 800 m/2625 ft; Brazil's first planned modern city, founded, 1897; airport nearby; airfield; railway; three universities (1927, 1954, 1958); industrial area third largest in Brazil.

Belorussia *Belarus*

Belshazzar [belshazer], Gr **Balt(h)asar** (?–539 BC) Son of Nabonidus, King of Babylon (556–539 BC), and ruler under his father until his death at the capture of Babylon. In the Book of Daniel, mysterious writing appears on the wall of his palace, which Daniel interprets as predicting the fall of the Empire.

Beltane An ancient Celtic festival held at the beginning of May, and also in late June, when bonfires were lit on the hills. Beltane was formerly a quarter-day in Scotland.

Belton, Joshua Brewster (1954–) US Republican politician, born in Washington, DC. He studied at Princeton University and Stanford Law School (1975–80), and worked in private law prac-

Belgium

☐ International Airport

official name **Kingdom of Belgium**, Fr **Royaume de Belgique**, Flemish **Koninkrijk België**

Local names Belgique (French), België (Flemish)

Timezone GMT +1

Area 30 518 km²/11 780 sq mi

Population total (2002e) 10 280 000

Status Kingdom

Date of independence 1830

Capital Brussels

Languages Flemish/Dutch (56%), French (32%), German (1%); (Brussels officially bilingual Flemish/French)

Ethnic groups Flemish (Teutonic origin) (55%), Walloon (French Latin) (33%)

Religions Roman Catholic (75%), Muslim (1%), Protestant (0·4%)

Physical features Mostly low-lying, with some hills in the SE region (Ardennes), average elevation 300–500 m/1000–1600 ft; large areas of fertile soil, intensively cultivated for many centuries; main river systems linked by complex network of canals; low-lying, dune-fringed coastline.

Climate Cool and temperate with strong maritime infuences; average annual temperatures 2°C (Jan), 18°C (Jul) in Brussels; average annual rainfall 825 mm/35 in.

Currency 1 euro (EUR) = 100 cents (previous to 2002, 1 Belgian Franc (BEF) = 100 centimes)

Economy One of the earliest countries in Europe to industrialize, using rich coalfelds of the Ardennes; Flanders textile industry; long-standing centre for European trade; major iron and steel industry, with wide range of metallurgical and engineering products; agriculture mainly livestock; full economic union (Benelux Economic Union) between Belgium, Netherlands, and Luxembourg, 1948. Founder member of the European Union (formerly EC) 1958. Brussels is the headquarters of several major international organizations, including the Commission of the European Union.

GDP (2002e) $299·7 bn, per capita $29 200

Human Development Index (2002) 0·939

History Part of the Roman Empire until 2nd-c; then became part of the Frankish Empire following Celt and Germanic invasions; ruled by the Habsburgs from 1477 until the Peace of Utrecht in 1713, when sovereignty passed to Austria; conquered by the French, 1794; part of the French Republic and Empire until 1815, then united with the Netherlands; Belgian rebellion against Dutch rule in 1830, led to recognition as an independent kingdom under Leopold of Saxe-Coburg; occupied by Germany in both World Wars; became a constitutional monarchy with bicameral Parliament; political tension between Walloons in S and Flemings in N, 1980; federal constitution divided Belgium into the autonomous regions of Flanders, Wallonia, and Brussels, 1989; Constitutional Monarch has limited powers; a Chamber of Deputies and a Senate.

Head of State (Monarch)
1865–1909 Leopold II
1909–34 Albert I
1934–50 Leopold III
1950–93 Baudouin I
1993– Albert II

Head of Government
1950 Jean Pierre Duvieusart
1950–2 Joseph Pholien
1952–4 Jean van Houtte
1954–8 Achille van Acker
1958–61 Gaston Eyskens
1961–5 Théodore Lefèvre
1965–6 Pierre Harmel
1966–8 Paul Vanden Boeynants
1968–72 Gaston Eyskens
1973–4 Edmond Leburton
1974–8 Léo Tindemans
1978 Paul Vanden Boeynants
1979–81 Wilfried Martens
1981 Marc Eyskens
1981–92 Wilfried Martens
1992–9 Jean-Luc Dehaene
1999– Guy Verhofstadt

tice before entering politics. He became deputy assistant for legislative affairs to President George H W Bush (1990), then White House deputy chief-of-staff for policy (2001–3) and director of the office of management and budget (2005–) under President George W Bush. In 2006 President Bush appointed him chief-of-staff.

beluga (fish) [belooga] Very large sturgeon (*Huso huso*) found in the Caspian Sea, Black Sea, and adjacent rivers; body length up to 5 m/16 ft; weight over 1000 kg/2200 lb; fished commercially for caviar; one of the largest freshwater fish known. (Family: Acipenseridae.)

beluga (mammal) [belooga] A small toothed whale (*Delphinap-* *terus leucas*), native to shallow Arctic seas and rivers; white when adult; no dorsal fin; also known as the **white whale** or **sea canary**. (Family: Monodontidae.)

Benares or **Banares** [benahres], also **Varanasi**, ancient **Kasi** 25°22N 83°08E, pop (2000e) 1 087 000. City in N India, on N bank of R Ganges; one of the seven most sacred Hindu cities, reputed to be Shiva's capital while on Earth; also a holy city of Buddhists, Sikhs, and Jains; invaded by Afghans, 1033; ceded to Britain, 1775; airfield; railway; two universities (1916, 1958); over 1400 Hindu temples and shrines, including the Golden Temple (1777).

Benaud, Richie [benoh], popular name of **Richard Benaud**

Belize

MEXICO

Corozal

Orange
Walk

Ambergris Cay

B E L I Z E

Belize City

Turneffe Is

Lighthouse Reef

Belize

Belmopan

Dangriga

Gulf of
Honduras

Victoria Peak
1120m

Glovers Reef

MAYA MTS.

Independence

San Antonio

Punta Gorda

GUATEMALA

HONDURAS

CARIBBEAN
SEA

SOUTH
AMERICA

□ International Airport   ∴ World heritage site

[beleez], formerly **British Honduras** (to 1973)
Local name Belice (Spanish)
Timezone GMT -6
Area 22 963 km²/8864 sq mi
Population total (2002e) 251 000
Status Independent state within the Commonwealth
Date of independence 1981

Capital Belmopan
Languages English (official), Spanish, Garifuna, Maya
Ethnic groups Creole (40%), mestizo (33%), Mayan (9·5%), Carib (8%), Garifuna (8%)
Religions Roman Catholic (62%), Protestant (30%)
Physical features Located in Central America; extensive coastal plain; swampy in the N, fertile in the S; Maya Mts extend almost to the E coast, rising to 1120 m/3674 ft at Victoria Peak; Belize R fows W–E; inner coastal waters protected by world's second longest barrier reef.
Climate Generally sub-tropical, but tempered by trade winds; average annual temperature 24°C (Jan), 27°C (Jul); variable rainfall; average annual rainfall 1295 mm/51 in (N), 4445 mm/175 in (S); hurricanes frequent.
Currency 1 Belize Dollar (BZD) = 100 cents
Economy Developing free-market economy based on timber and forest products, more recently on agriculture; banana industry devastated by Hurricane Iris (Oct 2001).
GDP (2002e) $1·28 bn, per capita $4900
Human Development Index (2002) 0·784
History Evidence of early Mayan settlement; colonized in the 17th-c by shipwrecked British sailors and disbanded soldiers from Jamaica; created a British colony, 1862; administered from Jamaica until 1884; internal self-government, 1964; changed name from British Honduras to Belize, 1973; full independence, 1981; Guatemalan claims over Belize territory have led to a continuing British military presence; Guatemala accord, respecting Belize self-determination, 1991; bicameral National Assembly.
Head of State
(British Monarch represented by Governor-General)
1981–93 Dame Minita Elvira Gordon
1993– Colville Norbert Young
Head of Government
1981–4 George Cadle Price
1985–9 Manuel Esquivel
1989–93 George Cadle Price
1993–8 Manuel Esquivel
1998– Said Musa

(1930–) Cricketer and broadcaster, born in Penrith, New South Wales, Australia. He played in 63 Test matches for Australia (captain in 28), including three successful tours of England (1953, 1956, 1961). An all-rounder, he scored 2201 Test runs and took 248 wickets. Upon retirement he became a well-known cricket commentator. He made his last UK broadcast in 2005 on the final day of England's successful Ashes Test series.

Ben Bella, (Mohammed) Ahmed [ben bela] (1918–) Key figure in the Algerian War of Independence against France, and Algeria's first prime minister (1962–3) and president (1963–5), born in Maghnia, Algeria. Deposed in 1965, he was imprisoned until 1980, then went into voluntary exile, returning in 1990.

Benbow, John (1653–1702) English naval commander, born in Shrewsbury, Shropshire. His main engagements were in the War of the League of Augsburg (1690, 1693, 1694) and the War of the Spanish Succession.

Bendigo [bendigoh] 36°48S 144°21E, pop (2000e) 33 300. City in NC Victoria, Australia, NW of Melbourne; centre of a wine-producing area; gold mined here until the 1950s; railway.

Benedict of Nursia, St (c.480–c.547) The founder of Western monasticism, born in Nursia, Italy. At Subiaco he founded 12 small monastic communities which followed the rule he devised (c.515). He ultimately established a monastery on

Monte Cassino, which became one of the most famous in Italy. He was declared the patron saint of all Europe by Pope Paul VI in 1964. Feast day 11 July.

Benedict XVI, originally **Joseph Ratzinger** (1927–) Pope (2005–), born in Marktl am Inn, Bavaria, SE Germany. Raised in a traditional Bavarian farming family, he enrolled at the Traunstein Catholic seminary in 1939, but his studies were interrupted during World War 2 when he was conscripted into the Hitler Youth (1941) and drafted into the German army (1943). He was briefly held as a prisoner-of-war by the Allies in 1945. He was ordained in 1951 and taught at Münster University (1963–6). He was advisor to Cardinal Frings of Cologne during Vatican Council II and gained a reputation as a reformist. In 1966 he took a chair in dogmatic theology at the University of Tübingen, moving to Regensburg University in 1969. Made Archbishop of Munich in 1977, he was created cardinal by Pope Paul VI the same year. He became a close friend and confidante of Pope John Paul II, and served as head of the congregation of the Doctrine of the Faith in the Vatican for over 20 years. In 2002 he was named Dean of the College of Cardinals.

Benedictines A religious order following the 'rule' of St Benedict of Nursia; properly known as the **Order of St Benedict** (**OSB**). The order has a long tradition of scholarship and promotion of learning.

Benelux A customs union between Belgium, The Netherlands, and Luxembourg which came into existence in 1947. A treaty established a more ambitious economic union between the three in 1958.

Beneš, Edvard [benesh] (1884–1948) Czechoslovakian statesman and president (1935–8, 1939–45 in exile, 1946–8), born in Kožlany, Czech Republic. In 1935 he succeeded Masaryk as president, but resigned in 1938, setting up a government in exile, first in France, then in England. After returning in 1945, he was re-elected president, but resigned after the Communist coup of 1948.

Benesh, Rudolph (1916–75) and **Joan Benesh** (1920–) [benesh], *née* **Rothwell** Dance notators, husband and wife, born in London and Liverpool, Merseyside, respectively. Rudolph was a dancer and Joan a former member of the Sadler's Wells Ballet. Together they copyrighted (1955) a dance notation system, called Choreology, now used to document all important Royal Ballet productions.

Bengal, Bay of area 2 172 000 km²/839 000 sq mi. Arm of the Indian Ocean, on S coast of Asia; c.2000 km/1300 mi long, 1600 km/1000 mi wide; subject to heavy monsoon rains and cyclones.

Bengali *Indo-Aryan languages*

Bengalooru *Bangalore*

Benghazi or **Banghazi** [bengahzee] 32°07N 20°05E, pop (2000e) 610 000. Seaport in N Libya; first settled by Greeks; controlled by Turks, 16th-c–1911; Italian rule, 1911–42; military and naval supply base during World War 2; second largest city in Libya; airport; university (1955).

Ben-Gurion, David [ben gurion], originally **David Gruen** (1886–1973) Israeli statesman and prime minister (1948–53, 1955–63), born in Plonsk, Poland. In 1930 he became leader of the Mapai (Labour) Party, which was the ruling party in the state of Israel when the state was announced (May 1948).

Benidorm [benidaw(r)m] 38°33N 0°09W, pop (2000e) 42 600. Resort town in E Spain, on the Mediterranean Costa Blanca; a leading centre of low-cost package holidays.

Benigni, Roberto [beneenee] (1952–) Film director, actor, writer, and producer, born in Arezzo, Tuscany, Italy. At the age of 10 he became a member of a troubadour act in Tuscany, improvising songs and poetry. His film debut came with *Berlinger ti Volgio Bene* (1976, Have You Berliner). Other films include *The Son of the Pink Panther* (1993) and *Coffee and Cigarettes* (2003). His 1997 film, *La Vita e Bella* (Life is Beautiful), which he wrote, starred in, and directed, gained Oscars for Best Actor and Best Foreign Language Film.

Benin *p.98*

Ben Macdhui [muhkdooee], Gaelic **Ben Muich-Dhui** 57°04N 3°40W. Second highest mountain in the UK; in Cairngorm Mts, NC Scotland; height 1309 m/4295 ft.

Benn, Anthony (Neil) Wedgwood, known as **Tony Benn** (1925–) British statesman, son of Viscount Stansgate, born in London. He became a Labour MP (1950–60), but was debarred from the House of Commons on succeeding to his father's title. He renounced his title, and was re-elected in a by-election in 1963, since when he has held various government posts. He retired from the House of Commons in 2001.

Bennett, Alan (1934–) Playwright, actor, and director, born in Leeds, West Yorkshire. He came to prominence in the revue *Beyond the Fringe* in 1960. His stage plays include *Kafka's Dick* (1986), *Single Spies* (1988), *The Madness of George III* (1991, filmed 1995), and *The History Boys* (2004, 6 Tony Awards). He has also written much for television, such as *Talking Heads* (1987), and the autobiographical *The Lady in The Van* (1999). His sense for satire, both as writer and actor, relishes the foibles and eccentricities of the English. For his book *Untold Stories* (2006) he was named Author of the Year by the British Book Awards.

Bennett, (Enoch) Arnold (1867–1931) Novelist, born near Hanley, Staffordshire. Among his 30 novels are *Anna of the Five Towns* (1902), *The Old Wives' Tale* (1908), and the *Clayhanger* series, all of which reflect life in the Potteries.

Bennett, James Gordon (1795–1872) Newspaper editor, born in Keith, Moray. In 1819 he emigrated to America, where he founded the *New York Herald* (1835). His son, **James Gordon Bennett** (1841–1918), edited the paper from 1867, and financed several explorers, including Stanley's search for Livingstone (1870).

Bennett, Michael, originally **Michael Bennet Difiglia** (1943–87) Dancer, choreographer, director, and producer, born in Buffalo, NY. His first great success came on his fourth show, *Promises, Promises* (1968). His masterpiece, *A Chorus Line*, based on transcripts of workshop interviews with dancers (1975), was highly acclaimed, and he later developed *Ballroom* (1978) and *Dreamgirls* (1981) from similar workshops.

Bennett, Sir Richard Rodney (1936–) Composer, born in Broadstairs, Kent. Well known for his music for films, he has also composed operas, orchestral works, chamber music, experimental works, and pieces involving jazz. He was appointed Professor of Composition at the Royal Academy of Music in 1995.

Bennett, William J(ohn) (1943–) US Federal official, born in Brooklyn, NY. He became secretary of education (1985–8), and as President Bush's 'drug tzar' (1989–91) co-ordinated the campaign against drugs.

Ben Nevis 56°48N 5°00W. Highest mountain in the UK; in Grampian Mts, W Scotland; height 1344 m/4409 ft.

Benny, Jack, originally **Benjamin Kubelsky** (1894–1974) Comedian, born in Waukegan, IL. A child prodigy violinist, he made his film debut in 1928. *The Jack Benny Show* (1950–65) won him the warm affection of a mass audience. A gentle, bemused, self-effacing figure, he developed an act based on his ineptitude as a fiddler, his claiming of perennial youth, and an unfounded reputation as the world's cheapest man.

Bentham, Jeremy (1748–1832) Writer on jurisprudence and utilitarian ethics, born in London. He held that laws should be socially useful and not merely reflect the status quo, and that all actions are right when they promote 'the happiness of the greatest number'. He was a founder of University College London, where his skeleton, dressed in his clothes, is preserved.

Bentinck, William Henry Cavendish, 3rd Duke of Portland (1738–1809) British statesman and prime minister (1783, 1807–9), born in Bulstrode, Buckinghamshire. He is best remembered as home secretary under the Younger Pitt, with charge of Irish affairs (1794–1801).

Bentley, E(dmund) C(lerihew) (1875–1956) Journalist and novelist, born in Shepherd's Bush, London. He is chiefly remembered as the author of *Trent's Last Case* (1913). He also gave his name to the type of rhyming tag known as the *clerihew*.

Benton, Thomas Hart, known as **Old Bullion** (1782–1858) US statesman, born near Hillsborough, NC. He was a Missouri senator for over 30 years, and a leader of the Democratic Party. He received his byname from his opposition to paper currency.

Benton, Thomas Hart (1889–1975) Painter of large historical murals on American themes and realistic genre scenes, born in Neosho, MO. In the late 1920s he set about creating a populist American art based on ordinary Middle-Western experience – cowboys, gamblers, oil wells, and native Americans, as in 'Independence and the Opening of The West' (1959–62).

Bentsen, Lloyd Millard, Jr (1921–) US statesman, born in Mission, TX. A member of the US House of Representatives (1948–54), he became a senator for Texas in 1971, and was vice-presidential running-mate to Michael Dukakis in the Democrats' 1988 presidential challenge. In Bill Clinton's administration he served as secretary to the treasury (1993–4).

Benin

☐ International Airport

(republic) [beneen], formerly **Dahomey** (to 1975), official name **Republic of Benin**, Fr **République du Benin**, formerly (to 1990) **The People's Republic of Benin**

Local name Bénin

Timezone GMT +1

Area 112 622 km²/43 484 sq mi

Population total (2002e) 6 788 000

Status Republic

Date of independence 1960

Capital Porto Novo (nominal), Cotonou (political and economic)

Languages French (official), Fon (47%), Adja (12%), Bariba (10%), Yoruba (9%), Fulani (6%), Somba (5%), Aizo (5%)

Ethnic groups Fon (40%), Yoruba (10%), Bariba (20%), minority of Fulani nomads

Religions Traditional beliefs (c.70%), Christian (15%), Muslim (13%)

Physical features Located in N Africa; rises from a 100 km/62 mi-long, sandy coast with lagoons to low-lying plains; savannah plateau, c.400 m/1300 ft, in N; descend to forested lowlands in S fringing the Bight of Benin; Atakora Mts rise to over 500 m/1000 ft in NW; rivers include Ouémé, Alibori, Mekrou; Pendjari National Park in NW.

Climate Tropical climate divided into three zones: in the S, rain throughout the year, especially during the Guinea Monsoon (May–Oct); in C, two rainy seasons (peaks in May–Jun and Oct); in the N, one rainy season (Jul–Sep); dry season in N (Oct–Apr): hot, with low humidity, subject to the dry harmattan wind from the NE.

Currency 1 CFA Franc (XAF) = 100 centimes

Economy Agriculture, especially palm-oil products, cashew nuts, maize, cassava, rice, cotton, coffee; no known natural resources in commercial quantity; small offshore oilfield.

GDP (2002e) $7.38 bn, per capita $1100

Human Development Index (2002) 0.420

History Pre-colonially a collection of small, warring principalities, including the Fon Kingdom of Dahomey (founded 17th-c); Portuguese colonial activities centred on slave trade; subjugated by French, becoming the French Protectorate of Dahomey, 1892; territory within French West Africa from 1904; independent from 1960; Marxist-Leninist regime gained power, 1972; name changed from Dahomey to the People's Republic of Benin, 1975; Marxism-Leninism abandoned in 1989, and a new multi-party constitution approved, 1990; changed name to Republic of Benin, 1990; multi-party elections held, 1991; President elected for five-year term, and a National Assembly.

Head of State
1990–1 Mathieu Kerekou
1991–6 Nicéphore Soglo
1996–2006 Mathieu Kerekou
2006– Yayi Boni

Head of Government
1958–9 Sourou Migan Apithy
1959–60 Hubert Coutoucou Maga
1960–4 *As President*
1964–5 Justin Tométin Ahomadegbé
1965–7 *As President*
1967–8 Maurice Kouandete
1968–96 *As President*
1996–8 Adrien Houngbedji

Benue, River [baynway], Fr **Beboué** Major tributary of the R Niger in Nigeria; rises in Cameroon, and flows generally W across E and SC Nigeria; length 1295 km/805 mi.

Benue–Congo languages [baynway konggoh] *Niger–Congo languages*

Benz, Karl (Friedrich) (1844–1929) Engineer, born in Karlsruhe, Germany. In 1879 he constructed a two-stroke engine model and founded a factory for its manufacture. His first car – one of the earliest petrol-driven vehicles – was completed in 1885.

benzaldehyde [benzaldihiyd] C₆H₅CHO, IUPAC **phenylmethanal**, boiling point 179°C. A colourless liquid, with the odour of almonds, used as a flavouring. It is readily oxidized to benzoic acid.

Benzedrine *amphetamine*

benzene [benzeen] C₆H₆, melting point 5°C, boiling point 80°C. An aromatic liquid obtained from coal tar, the simplest of the large series of aromatic compounds. It is used in dyestuffs, plastics, insecticides, detergents, and several other products.

benzodiazepines [benzohdiyayzepeenz] A group of drugs each of which exerts, to varying degrees, anti-anxiety, anti-epileptic, hypnotic (sleep-inducing), muscle-relaxant, and sedative properties. The two tranquillizers *chlordiazepoxide* (Librium) and *diazepam* (Valium) were the first to be introduced, in 1960 and 1962 respectively. *Nitrazepam* (Mogadon) and *temazepam* (Normison) are commonly used as hypnotics, and *alprezalam* is widely prescribed to suppress anxiety. They are very safe drugs, with fatal overdose being very uncommon, and therefore they took over from the more dangerous barbiturates. Some concern is now being expressed at their very wide use, and evidence of addiction following long-term use is accumulating.

benzyl [benziyl, benzil] C₆H₅CH₂–, IUPAC **phenylmethyl**. A functional group containing a phenyl ring, whose addition to a name usually indicates its substitution for hydrogen in a compound.

Beqaa, al- [bekah], Eng **the Bekka** Governorate of E Lebanon, bounded NE and E by Syria; capital, Zahle; valley of strategic importance to both Israel and Syria, and a centre of Muslim Shiite activity.

Berber Afro-Asiatic-speaking peoples of Egypt, Algeria, Libya, Tunisia, and Morocco. They were originally settled in one area, but the Bedouin Arabs who invaded N Africa in the 12th-c turned many of them into nomads. The best-known groups include the Kabyle, Shluh, and Tuareg.

Berberian, Cathy *Berio, Luciano*

berberis *barberry*

Beresford, Bruce (1940–) Film director, born in Sydney, New South Wales, Australia. A key figure in the revival of the Australian film industry, he won the Australian Film Institute's Best Director award for *Don's Party* (1976) and *Breaker Morant* (1979). Later films include *Driving Miss Daisy* (1989, Oscar), *Evelyn* (2002), and *Orpheus* (2006, TV).

Berg, Alban (1885–1935) Composer, born in Vienna. He studied under Schoenberg, welding the 12-note system to a deeply traditional style. He is best known for his opera *Wozzeck* (1925).

Bergama [bergahma], ancient **Pergamon** or **Pergamum** 39°08N 27°10E, pop (2000e) 55 000. Town in W Turkey; former capital of Pergamum, and of the Roman province of Asia; parchment is supposed to have been invented here.

Bergamo [bairgamoh] 45°42N 9°40E, pop (2000e) 122 000. Town in N Italy; first seat of the Republican fascist government set up by Mussolini after his fall from power, 1943; airport; railway; 15th-c cathedral.

bergamot [bergamot] **1** An aromatic perennial, native to North America and Mexico; stem square; leaves oval, toothed, in opposite pairs; flowers 2-lipped, hooded, purple or red, in crowded whorls around stem; leaves provide medicinal Oswego tea. (Genus: *Monarda*, 12 species. Family: Labiatae.) **2** orange

Bergen (Belgium) [berkhen] *Mons*

Bergen (Norway) [bergn] 60°23N 5°20E, pop (2000e) 223 000. Seaport in SW Norway; second largest city in Norway; founded, 1070; capital, 12th–13th-c; occupied by Germans in World War 2; bishopric; airport; railway; university (1948); cathedral (13th-c); offshore oil services; tourist and cultural centre; birthplace of Grieg.

Berger, Samuel R, known as **Sandy Berger** (1945–) US public official and lawyer. Formerly the Deputy Assistant to the President for National Security Affairs (1993–6), he was appointed Assistant in Clinton's second administration. He is the author of *Dollar Harvest* (1971) on American rural politics.

Bergerac, Savinien Cyrano de *Cyrano de Bergerac, Savinien*

Bergman, (Ernst) Ingmar (1918–) Film director and writer, born in Uppsala, Sweden. His films became something of a cult for art-cinema audiences, such as *The Seventh Seal* (1956), *Wild Strawberries* (1957), *The Virgin Spring* (1960, Oscar), and *Through a Glass Darkly* (1961, Oscar), outstanding for their photographic artistry, haunting imagery, and subtle exploration of facial characteristics. Later films include *Fanny and Alexander* (1982, Oscar) and *Saraband* (2005).

Bergman, Ingrid (1915–82) Film actress, born in Stockholm, Sweden. Her early successes included *Casablanca* (1942), *For Whom the Bell Tolls* (1943), and *Gaslight* (1944), for which she won her first Oscar. The scandal of her relationship with the Italian director Rossellini, whom she subsequently married, led to her exclusion from Hollywood for a time. She won further Oscars for *Anastasia* (1956) and *Murder on the Orient Express* (1974).

Bergson, Henri (Louis) [bergsõ] (1859–1941) Philosopher and psychologist, born in Paris. He became known with his *Essai sur les données immédiates de la conscience* (1889, Time and

Free Will: an Essay on the Immediate Data of Consciousness). Later works include *L'Evolution créatrice* (1907, Creative Evolution). He was awarded the Nobel Prize for Literature in 1927.

Beria, Lavrenti Pavlovich [beria] (1899–1953) Soviet secret police chief, born in Mercheuli, Georgia. He became Soviet commissar for Internal Affairs in 1938, and during World War 2 was active in purging Stalin's opponents. After the death of Stalin (1953), he was shot after a brief 'treason' trial.

beri beri A nutritional disease due to an inadequate dietary intake of vitamin B_1. Peripheral nerves are affected (*polyneuritis*), and it also causes heart failure and oedema.

Bering, Vitus (Jonassen) [bayring], also spelled **Behring** (1681–1741) Navigator, born in Horsens, Denmark. In 1728 and again in 1741 he sailed towards the American continent, and finally sighted Alaska, but he was wrecked on the island of Avatcha (now Bering I), where he died. Bering Sea and Bering Strait are named after him.

Bering Sea [bayring] area 2 304 000 km²/890 000 sq mi. Part of the Pacific Ocean between Siberia (W) and Alaska (E); connected to the Arctic by the Bering Strait (90 km/56 mi wide at narrowest point); often ice-bound (Nov–May); contains boundary between Russia and USA.

Berio, Luciano [berioh] (1925–2003) Avant-garde composer and teacher of music, born in Oneglia, Italy. He married (1950–66) the American soprano **Cathy Berberian** (1925–83), for whom he wrote several works. His particular interest was in the combining of live and prerecorded sound, and the use of tapes and electronic music, as in the *Sequenza* series (1958–75).

Berkeley, Busby [berklee], originally **William Berkeley Enos** (1895–1976) Film director and choreographer, born in Los Angeles, CA. He was known for his extravagant stagings of dance numbers in Hollywood films, using the camera to move among the dancers.

Berkeley, George [bah(r)klee] (1685–1753) Anglican bishop and philosopher, born near Kilkenny, SE Ireland. His *Treatise Concerning the Principles of Human Knowledge* (1710) expounded his idealistic philosophy.

Berkeley, Sir Lennox (Randall Francis) [bah(r)klee] (1903–89) Composer, born in Boars Hill, Oxfordshire. He became professor of composition at the Royal Academy of Music, London (1946–68). His works include the operas *Nelson* (1953) and *Ruth* (1956), and several orchestral pieces.

Berkowitz, David [berkohvits] (c.1953–) Convicted US murderer, who dubbed himself 'Son of Sam' in a note to the New York Police Department. He terrorized the city for a year (1976–7), preying on courting couples and lone women. Finally arrested, he received a prison sentence of 365 years in 1977.

Berkshire [bah(r)ksheer], also known as **Royal Berkshire** pop (2000e) 781 700; area 1259 km²/486 sq mi. Former county of S England, UK; replaced in 1998 by the unitary authorities of Windsor and Maidenhead, Wokingham, Reading, Slough, West Berkshire, and Bracknell Forest; continues to receive widespread cultural recognition.

Berlin [berlin] 52°32N 13°25E, pop (2000e) 3 530 000; area 883 km²/341 sq mi. Capital of Germany; linked to the Oder and Elbe Rivers by canals; founded in the 13th-c; former residence of the Hohenzollerns and capital of Brandenburg; later capital of Prussia, becoming an industrial and commercial centre in the 18th-c; in 1949 West Berlin became a province of the Federal Republic of Germany and East Berlin a county of the German Democratic Republic; contact between the two halves of the city was restored in 1989, following government changes in East Germany; capital of a united Germany, 1990; two airports; railway; three universities (1809, 1948, 1946); German Academies of Sciences (1700); Kaiser Wilhelm Church, Brandenburg Gate, Unter den Linden, Pergamum museum; Holocaust memorial (opened 2005); host to the 2006 FIFA

World Cup final; former **East Berlin**, pop (1991) 1272600, area 403 km²/156 sq mi, capital of East Germany to 1990; former **West Berlin**, pop (1991) 2146300, area 480 km²/185 sq mi, enclave (city and province) lying entirely within East Germany.

Berlin, Irving [berlin], originally **Israel Baline** (1888–1989) Composer, born in Temun, Russia. He was a child when his family emigrated to New York City. 'Alexander's Ragtime Band' became an international hit in 1911, the first of many among more than 900 songs for which he wrote both the words and music, such as 'Always' (1925), 'Easter Parade' (1933), 'God Bless America' (1939), and 'White Christmas' (1942).

Berlin, Sir Isaiah (1909–97) Philosopher, born in Riga, Latvia. His family emigrated to England in 1920, and he spent most of his academic career at Oxford. His works on political philosophy included *Historical Inevitability* (1954) and *Two Concepts of Liberty* (1959). Later works included *The Magus of the North* (1993).

Berlin Airlift (1948–9) A massive airlift of essential supplies flown in to post-war Berlin – a city (pop 2 million) surrounded by Soviet-controlled East Germany – by British and US aircraft in round-the-clock missions. The airlift was carried out in response to the action of the Soviet military authorities in Berlin, who had attempted to isolate the city from the West by severing all overland communication routes (Jun 1948). A total of 277264 flights carried 2323738 tons of supplies. Stalin lifted the blockade in May 1949.

Berliner Ensemble [berliner] A theatre company in East Berlin which was formed by Brecht in 1949. In its early years it had an enormous influence on Western theatre.

Berlin Wall A concrete wall built by the East German government in 1961 to seal off East Berlin from the part of the city occupied by the three main Western powers. Built largely to prevent mass illegal emigration to the West, which was threatening the East German economy, the wall was the scene of the shooting of many East Germans who tried to escape from the Eastern sector. The wall, seen by many as a major symbol of the denial of human rights in E Europe, was unexpectedly opened on 9 November 1989, following increased pressure for political reform in East Germany. It has now been taken down.

Berlioz, (Louis-)Hector [berliohz] (1803–69) Composer, born in Côte-Saint-André, France. His works include the *Symphonie Fantastique* (1830), the symphony *Harold en Italie* (1834), the *Grande messe des morts* (1837), and the operas *Les Troyens* (1856–8) and *Béatrice et Bénédict* (1860–2).

Berlusconi, Silvio [berluskohnee] (1936–) Italian politician, prime minister (1994, 2001–6), and entrepreneur, born in Milan, Lombardy, N Italy. After building a thriving property business, he expanded his activities to include media, publishing, sport, and finance. In 1993 he entered politics, founding the right-wing party *Forza Italia*, which was successful at the 1994 elections. In 2003 he faced corruption allegations relating to his business affairs but the trial was halted when parliament approved a controversial law giving serving prime ministers immunity from prosecution while in office. In 2004 a constitutional court annulled this ruling and the trial resumed, ending wih his acquittal. He was defeated in the 2006 general election by Romano Prodi.

Bermuda *see panel*

Bermuda Triangle An area of the North Atlantic Ocean, roughly delimited by Bermuda, the Greater Antilles, and the US coast, which has become part of maritime mythology. Reports of vessels which have been abandoned or disappeared, vanishing aircraft, and other inexplicable events have been known for over a century, and have attracted diverse explanations. Although objective evidence, such as wreckage, is conspicuous by its absence, the Triangle continues to attract a great deal of imaginative writing.

Bern, Fr **Berne** 46°57N 7°28E, pop (2000e) 140 000. Federal cap-

---

Bermuda

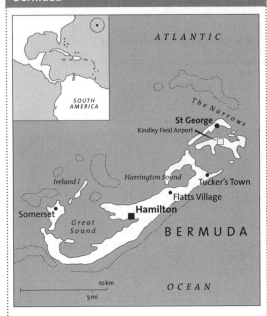

formerly **Somers Is** (UK British Overseas Territory)

Timezone GMT -4

Area 53 km²/20 sq mi

Population total (2002e) 82 000

Capital Hamilton

Physical features Archipelago in W Atlantic, c.900 km/560 mi E of Cape Hatteras, N Carolina; c.150 low-lying coral islands and islets, 20 inhabited, 7 linked by causeways and bridges; largest island, (Great) Bermuda; highest point, Gibb's Hill, 78 m/256 ft.

Climate Subtropical climate; generally humid; rain throughout year; warm summers, mild winters.

Currency 1 Bermuda Dollar (BMD) = 100 cents

Economy Mainly year-round tourism; increasingly an international company business centre; petroleum products, pharmaceuticals, aircraft supplies, boatbuilding, ship repair, vegetables, citrus fruits; fish-processing centre; hundreds of coastal properties destroyed by Hurricane Fabian, Sep 2003.

GDP (2002e) $2·25 bn, per capita $35 200

History Formerly called Somers Is, discovered by Spanish mariner, Juan Bermudez, in early 16th-c; colonized by English settlers, 1612; important naval station, and (to 1862) penal settlement; internal self-government, 1968; movement for independence caused tension in the 1970s, including assassination of the Governor-General; bicameral legislature.

---

ital of Switzerland; founded, 1191; joined the Swiss Confederation, 1353; capital, 1848; airport; railway junction; university (1834); Gothic cathedral (1421–1573); Zentrum Paul Klee (2005); old city is a world heritage site; headquarters of several international organizations.

Bernadette of Lourdes, St, originally **Marie Bernarde Soubirous** (1844–79) Visionary, born in Lourdes, France, the daughter of a miller. She claimed in 1858 to have received 18 apparitions of the Blessed Virgin at the Massabielle Rock, near Lourdes. She was beatified in 1925, and canonized in 1933. Feast day 18 February or 16 April.

Bernadotte, Folke, Greve (Count) [bernadot] (1895–1948)

Humanitarian and diplomat, born in Stockholm. Appointed by the UN to mediate in Palestine, he produced a partition plan, but was assassinated by Jewish terrorists in Jerusalem.

Bernadotte, Jean *Charles XIV* (of Sweden)

Bernard of Clairvaux, St [klairvoh], known as **the Mellifluous Doctor** (1090–1153) French theologian and reformer, born of a noble family at Fontaines, near Dijon. In 1113 he entered the Cistercian monastery of Cîteaux, and in 1115 became the first abbot of Clairvaux. He was canonized in 1174. The monks of his reformed branch of the Cistercians are often called **Bernardines**. Feast day 20 August.

Bernard of Menthon, St [mātō], known as **the Apostle of the Alps** (923–1008) Clergyman, born in Savoy, Italy. As Archdeacon of Aosta he founded the hospices in the Alpine passes that bear his name. In due course the hospices' dogs were also named after him. Feast day 28 May or 15 June.

Bernardines *Bernard of Clairvaux, St*

Berners-Lee, Sir Tim (1955–) Network designer, the inventor of the World Wide Web, born in London. In 1984 he took up a fellowship at CERN, Geneva, to work on distributed real-time systems for scientific data acquisition and system control. In 1989 he proposed a global hypertext project, initially with the international physics community in mind, which was implemented on the Internet in 1991. He joined the Massachusetts Institute of Technology in 1994, becoming the first holder of the 3 Com (Computer Communications Compatability) chair in 1999, and is also director of the World Wide Web Consortium.

Bernese Alps, Ger **Berner Alpen**, Fr **Alpes Bernoises** Mountain range in Switzerland, a N division of the Central Alps; highest peak, the Finsteraarhorn (4274 m/14 022 ft); also includes the Aletschhorn and Jungfrau; numerous tourist resorts.

Bernhard Leopold [bernhah(r)t], in full **Bernhard Leopold Frederik Everhard Julius Coert Karel Godfried Pieter** (1911–2004) Prince of The Netherlands, born in Jena. In 1937 he married future Queen Juliana, the only daughter of Wilhelmina, Queen of The Netherlands; they have four daughters. He helped establish the World Wildlife Fund in 1961, becoming its first president.

Bernhardt, Sarah [bernhah(r)t], originally **Henriette Rosine Bernard** (1844–1923) Actress and theatre producer, born in Paris. Her most famous roles included the title role in *Phèdre* (1877) and Marguerite (1884) in *La Dame aux camélias*. She founded the Théâtre Sarah Bernhardt in 1899.

Bernini, Gian Lorenzo [berneenee] (1598–1680) Baroque sculptor, architect and painter, born in Naples, Italy. In 1656 he decorated the apse of St Peter's with the so-called Cathedra Petri ('Chair of Peter'), designed the colonnade in front of the cathedral, and in 1663 the grand staircase to the Vatican.

Bernoulli, Daniel [bernoolee] (1700–82) Mathematician, born in Groningen, The Netherlands, the son of Swiss parents. He worked on trigonometrical functions, fractions, and the kinetic theory of gases, and solved an equation proposed by Jacopo Riccati, now known as 'Bernoulli's equation'. **Bernoulli's principle** (1738) states that as the speed of a moving fluid increases, its pressure decreases.

Bernoulli disk [bernoolee] A form of computer magnetic disk storage where the disk can be removed and replaced. It is named after Daniel Bernoulli.

Bernstein, Carl [bernstiyn] (1944–) Journalist and writer, born in Washington, DC. With Bob Woodward (1943–) he was responsible for unmasking the Watergate cover-up. They won for the *Washington Post* the 1973 Pulitzer Prize for public service, and wrote the best seller, *All the President's Men* (1974; filmed 1976).

Bernstein, Leonard [bernstiyn] (1918–90) Conductor, pianist, and composer, born in Lawrence, MA. His compositions include three symphonies, a television opera, a Mass, a ballet, and many choral works and songs. He is most widely known for his two musicals, *On the Town* (1944) and *West Side Story* (1957).

Berra, Yogi, popular name of **Lawrence Peter Berra** (1925–) Baseball player and coach, born in St Louis, MO. He played with the New York Yankees (1946–63), including 14 World Series (a record), and set the record for most home runs by a catcher in the American League (313). He went on to manage the Yankees, the New York Mets, and the Houston Astros.

Berry, Chuck, popular name of **Charles Edward Anderson Berry** (1926–) Rock singer, guitarist, and songwriter, born in St Louis, MO. Many of his songs belong to the standard repertoire of rock and roll, usually as hits for other singers: for example, 'Roll Over Beethoven' by The Beatles, and 'Sweet Little Sixteen' by The Beach Boys.

Berry, Halle [halee] (1966–) Actress, born in Cleveland, OH. She began modelling at age 16 and, after coming runner-up in the 1986 Miss USA pageant, decided on a career in acting. Her feature films include *The Flintstones* (1994), *Die Another Day* (2002), and *X-Men: The Last Stand* (2006). In 2002 she made Hollywood history as the first black woman to win an Academy Award for Best Actress for her role in *Monster's Ball*.

berserker [berserker] In Norse mythology, a warrior in a 'bearshirt' who fought in such a frenzy that he was impervious to wounds. The name is the origin of the phrase 'to go berserk'.

Bertolucci, Bernardo [bertohloochee] (1941–) Film director, born in Parma, Italy. He is best known for *Last Tango in Paris* (1972) and the epic *The Last Emperor* (1987, 9 Oscars). Later films include *Stealing Beauty* (1996), *Training Day* (2001), and *The Dreamers* (2003).

Bertrand, Henri Gratien, comte (Count) [bairtrã] (1773–1844) Military engineer and one of Napoleon's generals, born at Châteauroux, France. He shared the Emperor's banishment to St Helena, his shorthand diary giving a detailed account of Napoleon's life in exile.

Berwick-upon-Tweed [berik] 55°46N 2°00W, pop (2000e) 13 500. Town in Northumberland, NE England; disputed by England and Scotland, changed ownership 14 times, but part of England since 1482; railway.

beryl A beryllium, aluminium silicate mineral ($Be_3Al_2Si_6O_{18}$), occurring in granite pegmatites as greenish hexagonal prisms. Gemstone varieties are aquamarine and emerald. It is the commercial ore of beryllium.

beryllium [berilium] Be, element 4, melting point 1278°C. The metal forms an unreactive coat of BeO in air, making it inert to further oxidation. Its low density ($1·85 g/cm^3$) makes it a valuable component of alloys, but the poisonous nature of its compounds limits its use.

Berzelius, Jöns Jakob, Baron [berzaylius] (1779–1848) One of the founders of modern chemistry, born near Linköping, Sweden. His accurate determination of atomic weights established the laws of combination and the atomic theory. He also discovered the elements selenium, thorium, and cerium.

Besançon [bezãsõ], ancient **Vesontio** or **Besontium** 47°15N 6°00E, pop (2000e) 118 000. Industrial town in NE France, on R Doubs; former capital of Franche-Comté; railway; university (1485); archbishopric; cathedral (11th–13th-c); birthplace of Victor Hugo.

Besant, Annie [beznt], *née* **Wood** (1847–1933) Theosophist and social reformer, born in London. From secularism and Bradlaugh she passed in 1889 to Madame Blavatsky and theosophy, becoming its high priestess from 1891.

Beslan 43°12N 44°34E, pop (2002e) 33 600. Third largest town in the Republic of North Ossetia-Alania, Russia; founded 1847 as Tulatovo (after Beslan Tulatovo), renamed Iriston (1941), then Beslan (1950); became internationally known when 32 Islamic terrorists seized Middle School Number One (Sep 2004), holding over a thousand hostages in a siege lasting 52 hours, resulting in more than 340 deaths, over half being children.

Bessemer process [besemer] A process for converting pig iron (high carbon iron from the blast furnace) into steel (low carbon iron alloy). Air is blown through the molten iron; the oxygen of the air converts the carbon in the iron into carbon dioxide, which escapes. This reaction produces heat which keeps the iron molten. The process is named after British engineer Henry Bessemer (1813–98), who introduced it successfully into Britain in 1856.

Best, George (1946–2005) Footballer, born in Belfast. He made his debut for Manchester United at the age of 17 in 1963. A highly gifted player, he won 37 international caps for Northern Ireland, was the leading scorer for his club in the Football League First Division (1967–8), and in 1968 won a European Cup Medal and the titles of European Footballer of the Year and English Footballer of the Year. But his well-documented playboy lifestyle made him increasingly unable to cope with the pressure of top-class football and he left the club in 1974. Attempted come-backs with smaller clubs were short-lived, but he was recognized with a lifetime achievement award in 2000. He underwent a successful liver transplant operation in 2002 but was frequently beset by health problems. Belfast City airport was renamed in his honour in 2006.

best boy *gaffer*

bestiary A didactic literary form popular in classical and mediaeval times which presents human characteristics in the guise of animal behaviour: the Greek *Physiologus* is the model.

beta-blockers A group of drugs, introduced in the early 1960s, which lower heart rate and blood pressure. *Propranolol*, the first clinically useful beta-blocker, and *atenolol* are widely used in acute stress and panic, where they prevent symptoms such as racing of the heart, sweating, and tremor. There is current controversy over their use in some sports (eg snooker), where they may improve performance.

Betacam The trade name of a videotape cassette recorder and camera system of TV broadcast standard, introduced by Sony in 1981, initially for electronic news-gathering but widely adopted internationally for all forms of video production. **Betacam SP** is an improved version using metal-particle tape for higher bandwidth and better picture quality.

beta decay A naturally occurring radioactive decay process in which a neutron in an atomic nucleus spontaneously breaks up into a proton, which remains in the nucleus, and an electron (**beta particle**), which is emitted. The process is always accompanied by the emission of an antineutrino, and is governed by weak nuclear force.

Betamax The trade name for a videotape cassette recorder system developed by Sony in 1975 for the domestic market. Although economical, it never achieved the popularity of the competitive VHS system.

betatron [baytuhtron] A particle accelerator in which electrons are held in a circular orbit by a magnetic field, and accelerated by a varying electric field superimposed. It is used for research on high-energy electron behaviour or to produce high-energy X-rays.

Betelgeuse [beetlzherz, betljooz] A red supergiant star, prominent in Orion, over 500 times the diameter of the Sun. Distance: 131 parsec.

betel-nut A slender tree (*Areca catechu*) reaching 30 m/100 ft, native to SE Asia; leaves 8 m/26 ft, feathery; seeds 4–5 cm/1$\frac{1}{2}$–2 in, red or orange; also called the **areca palm**. The nuts are boiled with lime, then dried, and wrapped in betel leaf from the climbing species of pepper, *Piper betle*. The 'plug' is habitually chewed in the Indian subcontinent and SE Asia for its intoxicating effects, which are similar to alcohol. The juice stains teeth and saliva bright red. (Family: Palmae.)

Bethe, Hans (Albrecht) [baytuh] (1906–2005) Physicist, born in Strasbourg, France (formerly Germany). He held the chair of physics at Cornell (1937–75), and in 1939 proposed the first detailed theory for the generation of energy by stars through a series of nuclear reactions. He was awarded the 1967 Nobel Prize for Physics.

Bethlehem, Arabic **Beit Lahm** 31°42N 35°12E, pop (2000e) 25 000. Biblical town in Jerusalem governorate, Israeli-occupied West Bank, W Jordan; birthplace of Jesus and the home of David; trade centre; university (1973); Church of the Nativity, built by Constantine, 330 (scene of a 39-day siege by Israeli troops when a group of Palestinian men took refuge inside, 2002).

Betjeman, Sir John [bechuhman] (1906–84) Writer and poet, born in London. He is especially known for his light verse, much of which is to be found in his *Collected Poems* (1958) and in his verse autobiography, *Summoned by Bells* (1960). He was made poet laureate in 1972.

Bettany, Paul (1971–) Actor, born in London. Born into a show business family, his stage debut was in a West End production of *An Inspector Calls* (1992). His feature film roles include *A Beautiful Mind* (2001), *Master and Commander* (2003), *Wimbledon* (2004), and *The Da Vinci Code* (2006).

Better Business Bureau One of many local organizations, mainly in the USA and Canada, formed to protect communities against unfair or misleading advertising and selling practices. Established in the early years of the 20th-c by advertising men, it nowadays sets standards for business practice, and investigates complaints.

Beuys, Joseph [boys] (1921–86) Avant-garde artist, born in Krefeld, Germany. A professor at Düsseldorf Academy (1961–71), his sculpture consisted mainly of 'assemblages' of bits and pieces of rubbish; and he also staged multimedia 'happenings'. A prominent political activist, he was one of the founders of the Green Party in Germany.

Bevan, Aneurin, known as **Nye Bevan** (1897–1960) British statesman, born in Tredegar, Blaenau Gwent, SE Wales. He established a reputation as a brilliant, irreverent, and often tempestuous orator. As minister of health (1945–51), he introduced the National Health Service (1948). 'Bevanism' was a left-wing movement to make the Labour Party more socialist and less 'reformist'. He married **Jennie Lee** in 1934.

bevatron [bevatron] A thousand million electron volt proton accelerator, designed and built at Berkeley Radiation Laboratory, University of California, USA.

Beveridge, William Henry Beveridge, Baron (1879–1963) British economist, administrator, and social reformer, born in Rangpur, India. He is best known as the author of the *Report on Social Insurance and Allied Services* (**The Beveridge Report**, 1942), which became the foundation of the British Welfare State and the blueprint for much social legislation from 1944 to 1948.

Beverley 53°51N 0°26W, pop (2000e) 21100. Administrative centre of East Riding unitary authority, NE England; railway; market town; Beverley Minster (13th-c).

Beverly Hills 34°04N 118°25W, pop (2000e) 33 800. Residential city in Los Angeles County, SW California, USA; the home of many television and film celebrities.

Bevin, Ernest (1881–1951) British statesman, born in Winsford, Somerset. He built up the National Transport and General Workers' Union, and became its general secretary (1921–40). In 1940 he became a Labour MP, minister of labour and national service in Churchill's coalition government, and in the Labour government was foreign secretary (1945–51).

bézique [bezeek] A card game believed to have originated in Spain, and brought to England in 1861. Played with at least two players, each has a pack of cards but with the twos, threes, fours, fives, and sixes taken out. The object is to win tricks, and score points on the basis of the cards won.

Bhutan

☐ International Airport

[bootahn], Dzongkha **Druk-yul**, official name **Kingdom of Bhutan**

Local name Druk-yul

Timezone GMT +5·5

Area 46 600 km²/18 000 sq mi

Population total (2002e) 1 996 000

Status Kingdom

Capital Thimphu

Languages Dzongkha (official) (60%), Nepalese (25%), English

Ethnic groups Bhote (60%), Nepalese (25%), indigenous or migrant tribes (15%)

Religions Lamaistic Buddhist (75%), Hindu (20%), Muslim (5%)

Physical features High peaks of E Himalayas in the N, over 7 000m/23 000 ft; forested mountain ridges with fertile valleys

descend to low foothills in the S; rivers include Wong Chu, Manas; permanent snowfields in the mountains; sub-tropical forest in S.

Climate Affected by altitude; snowcapped in glaciated N; average monthly temperatures 4°C (Jan), 17°C (Jul); torrential rain common, average 1000 mm/40 in (C valleys) and 5000 mm/200 in (S).

Currency 1 Ngultrum (BTN) = 100 chetrum

Economy Largely based on agriculture, mainly rice, wheat, maize, mountain barley, potatoes, vegetables, fruit (especially oranges); also timber (large area of plantation forest); sales of tobacco products banned, 2004.

GDP (2002e) $2·7 bn, per capita $1300

Human Development Index (2002) 0·494

History British involvement since treaty of 1774 with the East India Company; S part of the country annexed, 1865; Anglo-Bhutanese Treaty signed, in which Britain agreed not to interfere in internal affairs of Bhutan, 1910; similar treaty (Indo-Bhutan Treaty of Friendship) signed with India, 1949, revised 2007; governed by a maharajah from 1907; now addressed as King of Bhutan; National Assembly (Tsogdu) established, 1953; constitutional monarchy with power shared between the King, the Council of Ministers, the National Assembly, and the monastic head of the kingdom's Buddhist priesthood; king devolved executive powers to the Council of Ministers, 1998; military offensive against separatist movements associated with Assam and Bodoland located in the S, 2004.

Head of State (Monarch)
1907–26 Uggyen Wangchuk
1926–52 Jigme Wangchuk
1952–72 Jigme Dorji Wangchuk
1972–2006 Jigme Singye Wangchuk
2006– Dasho Jigme Khesar Namgyel Wangchuk

Head of Government (Chairman of the Council of Ministers)
1998–9 Jigme Yoser Thinley
1999–2000 Sangay Ngedup
2000–1 Yeshey Zimba
2001–2 Khandu Wangchuk
2002–3 Kinzang Dorji
2003–4 Jigme Yoser Thinley
2004–5 Yeshey Zimba
2005–6 Sangay Ngedup

bezoar *goat*

Bhadgaon [badgown], also **Bhaktapur** 27°41N 85°26E, pop (2000e) 183 000. City and religious centre in C Nepal, in the Kathmandu Valley; altitude 1400 m/4600 ft.

Bhagavadgita or **Bhagavad Gita** [bahgavadgeeta] (Sanskrit 'The Song of the Lord') A poem forming part of the Hindu epic, the Mahabharata, consisting of an eve of battle dialogue between the warrior prince Arjuna and Lord Krishna (in the person of his charioteer). Most Hindus regard the poem, with its teaching that there are many valid ways to salvation, but that not all are universally appropriate, as the supreme expression of their religion.

bhangra [banggra] Originally traditional Punjabi dance music, developed by South Asian communities in the UK and elsewhere from the 1970s onwards into a hugely popular genre, at least within those communities. Prominent UK bhangra bands have included Alaap, Holle Holle, Heera, the Sahotas, and Pardesi.

Bharatiya Janata Paksh (BJP) [bahratya janata paksh] Hindu political party, formed in 1980 with the aim of transforming a secular and multicultural India into an organic Hindu nation.

From its base in the Hindi-speaking states of N India, it climbed to national prominence in the elections of 1989, capturing 12% of the popular vote. With the fundamentalist Vishwa Hindu Parishad, the Party made a disputed shrine at Ayodhya a major focus for agitation.

Bhopal [bohpahl] 23°20N 77°53E, pop (2000e) 1 248 000. Capital of Madhya Pradesh, C India; founded, 1723; scene of a major industrial disaster in December 1984, when poisonous isocyanate gas escaped from the Union Carbide factory, killing c.2500 people and leaving 100 000 homeless; airfield; railway; university (1970).

Bhutan *see panel*

Bhutto, Benazir [bootoh] (1953–) Pakistani stateswoman and prime minister (1988–91, 1993–6), born in Karachi, the daughter of Zulfikar Ali Bhutto. Placed under house arrest (1977–84) by General Zia ul-Haq, she moved to England (1984–6), becoming the joint leader in exile of the Opposition Pakistan People's Party. She returned to Pakistan amid massive popular acclaim, and in 1987 was elected prime minister. Her party was defeated in the 1991 election, and she later had to defend herself against charges of misconduct while in office. She continued to be a prominent focus of Opposition discontent, and won a further election in 1993, but was replaced in 1996. In 1999 she was convicted in absentia of corruption and sentenced (2002) to three years in prison. She continues to lead her party from abroad, being re-affirmed as PPP leader in 2002.

Bhutto, Zulfikar Ali [bootoh] (1928–79) Pakistani statesman, president (1971–3) and prime minister (1973–7), born in Larkana, Sind. He founded the Pakistan People's Party (PPP) in 1967, and after the secession of E Pakistan (now Bangladesh) in 1971, he became president. Opposition to his policies led to the army under General Zia ul-Haq seizing control after the 1977 elections. Tried for corruption and murder, he was sentenced to death in 1978. In spite of worldwide appeals for clemency, the sentence was carried out.

Biafra [biafra] The SE province of Nigeria, inhabited by the Igbo people. Under the leadership of Colonel Ojukwu, it attempted to break away from the federation, thus precipitating the civil war of 1967–70.

Białystok [byawistok] 53°09N 23°10E, pop (2000e) 267 000. Largest city in NE Poland; developed as a textile centre, 19th-c; devastated in World War 2; railway; medical academy.

Biarritz [beearits] 43°29N 1°33W, pop (2000e) 30 200. Fashionable resort town in SW France, on Bay of Biscay; noted for its mild climate and beaches.

biathlon A combined test of cross-country skiing and rifle shooting. Men's individual competitions are over 10 km and 20 km (6·2 and 12·4 mi), while women's are over 5 km and 10 km (3·1 and 6·2 mi). At designated points on the course, competitors have to fire either standing or prone at a fixed target.

Bible Either the Christian Scripture or the Jewish Scripture, those works recognized as sacred and authoritative writings by the respective faiths. The Christian Scriptures are divided between two *testaments*: the Old Testament (which corresponds roughly to the canon of Jewish Scriptures), and the New Testament. The Old Testament, or **Hebrew Bible**, is a collection of writings originally composed in Hebrew, except for parts of Daniel and Ezra that are in Aramaic. These writings depict Israelite religion from its beginnings to about the 2nd-c BC. The New Testament is so-called in Christian circles because it is believed to constitute a new 'testament' or 'covenant' in the history of God's dealings with his people, centring on the ministry of Jesus and the early development of the apostolic churches. The New Testament writings were in Greek.

bibliography 1 The study of the history, identification, and description of books, seen as physical objects, including the materials used and the methods of production (**critical** or **analytical bibliography**). **2** A book, or a list in a book, containing systematic details of an author's writings, or of publications on a given subject or period (**descriptive** or **enumerative bibliography**).

bicameral system A parliament of two chambers, which usually have different methods of election or selection. In some countries (such as the USA) the two chambers enjoy equal powers; but commonly one chamber enjoys supremacy over the legislative process, with the other enjoying powers of revision and delay (as in the UK).

bicarbonate HCO_3^-, IUPAC **hydrogen carbonate**. The anion corresponding to half-neutralized carbonic acid. **Sodium bicarbonate**, or baking soda, is used with weak acids as a source of carbon dioxide.

Bickerdyke, Mary Ann, *née* **Ball**, known as **Mother Bickerdyke** (1817–1901) Nurse and humanitarian, born in Knox Co, OH. When the Civil War broke out (1861) she volunteered to work as a nurse and caregiver both in battle and behind the lines, taking time out only to give speeches and gain support for the Sanitary Commission. She received a special pension from Congress in 1886.

bicycle A light-framed vehicle possessing two wheels fitted with pneumatic tyres, the rear wheel being propelled by the rider through a crank, chain, and gear mechanism. It is generally held that the modern pedal bicycle was invented by Kirkpatrick Macmillan of Dumfriesshire, Scotland, and first ridden by him in 1840. The pneumatic tyre was invented by Robert William Thomson in 1845 and first successfully applied to the bicycle in 1888 by John Boyd Dunlop.

Biennale [bee-enahlay] An international art exhibition held in Venice regularly since 1895, and imitated at Paris, Tokyo, and elsewhere. Since 1948 it has been a major showcase for the avant garde.

biennial A plant which flowers, sets seed, and dies in its second year. In the first year it produces only vegetative growth, usually a rosette of leaves which build up food reserves for the onset of flowering.

Bierce, Ambrose (Gwinett) [beers] (1842–?1914) Journalist and writer, born in Meigs Co, OH. He was the author of collections of sardonically humorous tales on the theme of death, such as *In the Midst of Life* (1898).

Biffen, Sir Rowland Harry (1874–1949) Botanist and plant breeder, born in Cheltenham, Gloucestershire. The first director of the Cambridge Plant Breeding Institute in 1912, he was largely responsible for the foundation of the modern science of plant breeding.

bigamy A criminal offence committed when someone who is already married enters into 'marriage' with another person. The offence is not committed where the first marriage has been ended by divorce or death, or where it has been declared void. In some jurisdictions, there is also a good defence if the accused has, for a period of time (7 years, in England and Wales), not known that his or her first marriage partner was alive.

'big bang' A hypothetical model of the universe which postulates that all matter and energy were once concentrated into an unimaginably dense state, or primaeval atom, from which it has been expanding since a creation event some 12 thousand million years ago. The main evidence favouring this model comes from cosmic background radiation and the redshifts of galaxies. Evidence of an expanding universe was announced by Edwin Hubble in 1929, and is now generally accepted.

Big Ben Originally the nickname of the bell in the clock tower of the Houses of Parliament, London, and now by association the clock and its tower. The bell, 2·7 m/9 ft in diameter and weighing 13 tonnes, was cast in 1858.

Big Dipper *Plough, the*

Bigfoot or **Sasquatch** In the mountaineering folklore of North America, a creature the equivalent of the abominable snowman or yeti, said to be 2–3 m/7–10 ft tall; its footprints are reported to be 43 cm/17 in long.

Biggs, Ronald (1929–) British convicted thief, a member of the gang who perpetrated the Great Train Robbery in 1963. Sentenced to 25 years for conspiracy and 30 years (to run concurrently) for armed robbery, he escaped from Wandsworth Prison in 1965, fled to Australia, and eventually settled in Brazil. Attempts at extradition failed, but he finally returned to Britain voluntarily in 2001 and was imprisoned.

bighorn A wild sheep, inhabiting mountains, especially cliffs; males with large curling horns; two species: **American bighorn sheep** (*Rocky Mountain sheep* or *Mountain sheep*) from North America (*Ovis canadensis*), and **Siberian bighorn** or **snow sheep** from NE Siberia (*Ovis nivicola*).

Bihar or **Behar** [beehah(r)] pop (2001e) 82 878 800; area 173 876 km²/67 116 sq mi. State in E India, bounded N by Nepal; crossed by the R Ganges; capital, Patna; major mineral deposits, including coal, copper, mica.

Bikini [bikeenee] Atoll in the Marshall Is, W Pacific, 3200 km/

2000 mi SW of Hawaii; site of 23 US nuclear tests, 1946–58; first H-bomb tested here (1952); inhabitants evacuated in 1946.

Biko, Stephen (Bantu) [beekoh], known as **Steve Biko** (1946–77) South African black activist, born in King William's Town. He was the founder and leader of the Black Consciousness Movement. In 1973 he was served with a banning order severely restricting his movements and freedom of speech and association. He died in police custody, allegedly as a result of beatings received. He was the subject of a successful film, *Cry Freedom* (1987), directed by Richard Attenborough.

bilateralism *multilateralism*

Bilbao [bilbow] 43°16N 2°56W, pop (2000e) 374 000. Major seaport in N Spain, founded, 1300; bishopric; airport; railway; university (1886); cathedral (14th-c); commercial centre of the Basque Provinces.

bilberry A small deciduous shrub (*Vaccinium myrtillus*), native to acid soils in Europe and N Asia, especially on high ground where it may form bilberry moors; leaves oval, toothed; 1–2 flowers in leaf axils, drooping, globose, greenish-white; berry black with bluish-white bloom, sweet, edible. Alternative names are **blaeberry**, **whortleberry**, and (in the USA) **huckleberry**. (Family: Ericaceae).

bilby *bandicoot*

bile A golden-yellow fluid produced by the liver. It is stored and concentrated in the gall bladder, until released into the duodenum in response to certain dietary substances (eg fats) in the duodenal cavity.

bilharziasis [bilhah(r)tsiyasis] *schistosomiasis*

Bilk, Acker, popular name of **Bernard Stanley Bilk** (1929–) Jazz musician, composer, and band leader, born in Pensford, Somerset. He joined Ken Colyer's Band as clarinettist, and forming the Bristol Paramount Jazz Band in 1951. His best-known hit single was 'Stranger on the Shore' (1961, first number 1 simultaneously in UK and USA).

billiards An indoor table game played in many different forms. The most popular is that played on a standard English billiard table measuring c.12 ft × 6 ft (3·66 m × 1·83 m). It is played with three balls; one red and two white. Scoring is achieved by *potting* balls, *going in-off* another ball, and *making cannons* (hitting your white ball so that it successively strikes the two others).

Billingsgate Market A fish-market in C London, dating from the 9th-c. Its name derived from a river-gate in the nearby city wall. The market was closed in 1982, and relocated further E, on the Isle of Dogs.

billion In earlier British usage, a million million (10^{12}); in US (and increasingly in technical international) usage, a thousand million (10^9). Because both senses are still encountered, however, many specialists avoid the term (and also *trillion* and other derivatives), preferring to state the numbers involved using superscripts, or in such a form as 'thousand million'. The latter usage is standard in this book.

bill of rights A list of citizens' rights set out in constitutional documents. Usually accompanying the document is an elaboration of the institutional means and powers by which such rights may be enforced. The best-known example is the first ten amendments to the US Constitution, adopted in 1791.

Billy the Kid *Bonney, William H, Jr*

Biloxi [biloksee] 30°24N 88°53W, pop (2000e) 50 600. Town in SE Mississippi, USA; named after an Indian tribe; settled, 1699; railway; Keesler Air Force Base; devastated by Hurricane Katrina, 2005.

bimetallic strip Two strips of different metals welded or riveted together face to face, which expand to different extents on heating because of their different coefficients of thermal expansion. This phenomenon can be used to actuate indicators or electric switches in response to changes in temperature.

binary code A code derived from the binary number system, using only two digits (0 and 1), in comparison with the decimal system, which has ten digits (0 to 9). The advantage of the binary system for use in digital computers is that only two electronic states, off and on, are required to represent all the possible binary digits.

binary number A number written in base two, ie in which every number is expressed as the sum of powers of 2; thus 'seven' (in base ten) is $4 + 2 + 1 = 1 \times 2^2 + 1 \times 2^1 + 1$; thus $7_{ten} = 111_{two}$.

binary star Two stars revolving around their common centre of mass. Perhaps half of all stars in our Galaxy are members of binaries.

binary weapon An expression describing how a munition used in chemical warfare can be configured. Two individually harmless chemicals are packed separately into, for example, an artillery shell; these are combined on detonation to form a deadly toxic agent.

Binchy, Maeve (1940–) Writer, born in Dublin. She has written plays for television and the stage, but is most widely known as a romantic novelist. Her books include *Light a Penny Candle* (1982), *The Glass Lake* (1994), *Scarlet Feather* (2000), and *Whitethorn Woods* (2006). Other work includes several volumes of short stories.

binding sites *receptors*

bindweed One of several related climbers with fleshy, rope-like roots, fast-growing twining stems, and large funnel-shaped flowers, all native to temperate regions; often pernicious weeds. *Convolvulus arvensis* is a coastal plant; leaves arrowhead-shaped; flowers pink, striped white above, maroon beneath. (Family: Convolvulaceae.)

Binet, Alfred [beenay] (1857–1911) Psychologist, born in Nice, France. He is principally remembered for the Binet–Simon scale (with colleague Théodore Simon) for measuring the intelligence of schoolchildren (1905) – the precursor of many of today's mental tests.

Binford, Lewis (Roberts) (1930–) US archaeologist, the acknowledged leader of the anthropologically-oriented school of archaeology which has powerfully influenced the discipline since the late 1960s. His works include *Bones* (1981) and *In Pursuit of the Past* (1983).

bingo A game played by any number of people, using cards normally containing 15 squares numbered between 1 and 90. The caller picks numbers at random, and if players have the corresponding number on their card they eliminate it, usually by crossing it through. The first person(s) to eliminate all numbers is the winner, and is usually identified by calling out 'bingo' or 'house'. Known as **lotto** or **housey-housey** for many years, it became popularized as bingo in the 1960s.

bin Laden *Osama bin Laden*

Binoche, Juliette [binosh] (1964–) Film actress, born in Paris. She attended acting school in the late 1970s and later took classes at the Paris Conservatoire. After various roles in French films and theatrical productions she received international success with the film version of Milan Kundera's novel, *The Unbearable Lightness of Being* (1988). Later films include *The English Patient* (1996, Oscar for Best Supporting Actress), *Chocolat* (2000), and *Breaking and Entering* (2006).

binoculars A magnifying optical instrument for use by both eyes simultaneously; also known as **field-glasses**. Two optical systems are mounted together, each consisting of two convex lenses (an eyepiece and an object lens) plus prisms to produce an upright image. Focusing is achieved by varying the distance between eyepiece and object lens.

binomial nomenclature The modern system of naming and classifying organisms, established by the Swedish naturalist Carl Linnaeus (1707–78) in the mid-18th-c. Every species has a unique scientific name (*binomen*) consisting of two words: a generic name and a specific name. For example, the scientific name of a lion is *Panthera leo* and that of the tiger *Panthera tigris*. They belong to the same genus, but are different species.

Bintley, David (Julian) (1957–) British choreographer and dancer. He joined Sadler's Wells Royal Ballet (1976–86), becoming resident choreographer and principal dancer. During 1986–93 he was resident choreographer and principal dancer with the Royal Ballet before joining the Birmingham Royal Ballet as artistic director (1995–).

binturong [bintoorong] A carnivorous mammal (*Arctictis binturong*), native to SE Asia; dense black fur, thickest on its grasping tail; tips of ears with prominent tufts; inhabits dense forests. (Family: Viverridae.)

Binyon, (Robert) Laurence (1869–1943) Poet and art critic, born in Lancaster, Lancashire. Extracts from his poem 'For the Fallen' (set to music by Elgar) adorn war memorials throughout the British Commonwealth.

bioassay [biyohasay] The measurement of amounts or activities of substances (such as the concentration of pollutants) using the responses of living organisms or cells; an abbreviation of **biological assay**.

biochemistry The branch of biology dealing with the chemistry of living organisms, especially with the structure and function of their chemical components.

biodegradable substance Any substance that can be decomposed by natural processes, particularly microbial decay, so that its constituents are rendered available for use within the ecosystem.

biodiversity A term used to cover the total variety of genetic strains, species, and ecosystems in the world, which change with evolution. A treaty to preserve biodiversity, including the sustainable development of biological resources, was signed at the Earth Summit in 1992.

bioengineering The design and production of mechanical and electronic medical devices that apply the latest technological developments to solving medical problems. Examples include machines for helping diagnosis; instruments to assist medical practice; and systems to enable more efficient delivery of drugs to disease sites.

biofeedback A technique by which an individual can learn to control autonomic responses (ie those not usually under conscious control) by using monitoring devices to give information about the results of current and past performance. For example, training in this way using an electroencephalogram can encourage the production of alpha brain waves which are associated with well-being and relaxation.

biogas A gas produced by the fermentation of organic waste. Decomposition of animal manure, crop residues, and food processing wastes in an airtight container produces a methane-rich gas which can be used as a source of energy.

biogeography The geographical study of the distribution of animals and plants at global, regional, and local scales. In particular it examines the factors responsible for their changing distribution in both time and space.

biography The narrative of a person's life. In classical and mediaeval times, biographical writing tended to be exemplary lives of kings, heroes, and saints, with little concern for the personal subject. But the Protestant and democratic spirit conferred greater value on the individual; Dr Johnson maintained that the narrative of any person's life would be worth reading.

Bioko [beeokoh], formerly **Fernando Po** or **Póo** (to 1973), **Macías Nguema Bijogo** (to 1979) pop (2000e) 93 400; area 2017 km² / 779 sq mi. Island off coast of Cameroon, W Africa; province of Equatorial Guinea; volcanic origin, rising to 3007 m/9865 ft at Pico de Basilé; chief town, and capital of Equatorial Guinea, Malabo; visited by Portuguese, 1471; originally named after Portuguese navigator; coffee, cocoa, copra.

biological assay *bioassay*

biological rhythm or **biorhythm** The rhythmical change in a biological function of a plant or animal. The frequency of rhythms varies from short (eg less than a second) to long (eg more than a year). Many rhythms arise from within organisms; others are entirely dependent upon external environmental factors (such as the alternation of light and dark). Examples of biological rhythms in humans are breathing, sleep, and waking.

biological sciences Specialized study areas which have developed to study living organisms and systems. All biological sciences are based on *taxonomy*, the description, naming, and classification of living organisms as a means of creating order out of the diversity of the natural world. The study of the distribution of organisms throughout the world is **biogeography**. The chemical processes that occur within living systems are studied as a whole (**biochemistry**) or at the level of interactions between large organic molecules (**molecular biology**). Functional aspects of living systems are the subject of disciplines such as **physiology** and **biophysics**. The study of the comparative behaviour of animals is known as **ethology**. **Genetics** encompasses heredity and variation. The study of the relationship between organisms and their environment is **ecology**. Each major group of organisms is the basis of its own special study area, such as bacteria (**bacteriology**), plants (**botany**), and animals (**zoology**).

biological shield A protective enclosure around the radioactive core of a nuclear reactor, to prevent the escape of radiation capable of damaging biological tissue. It usually consists mainly of massive concrete walls.

biological value In food science, the nutritional value of a protein, which depends upon the balance of amino acids it contains. Animal proteins such as egg have a high value, while vegetable proteins such as gluten have a low value.

biological warfare An expression that embraces *bacteriological warfare*, which uses naturally occurring micro-organisms as a weapon of war, and *toxins*, which are poisonous chemicals derived from natural sources. The manufacture and stockpiling of such agents is forbidden by a UN Convention of 1972, although research is allowed to continue.

biology The study of living organisms and systems. The beginnings of biology as a science are the natural history observations made by all who are in contact with the natural world. Its rapid development during the 20th-c has led to the increasing subdivision of biology into a variety of specialized disciplines.

bioluminescence The light produced by living organisms through a chemical reaction, and the process of emitting such biologically produced light. It can be found in some bacteria, fungi, algae, and animals such as deep-sea fishes, squid, fireflies, and glow-worms. It serves a variety of functions, such as signalling during courtship rituals and locating prey in the dark.

biome [biyohm] A major regional subdivision of the Earth's surface, broadly corresponding to the dominant ecological communities of the main climatic regions. Biomes are the largest recognized living communities classified on a geographical basis, such as tundra, desert, and tropical rainforest. Artificial biomes have also been created, as in the Eden Project in Cornwall, UK.

biomorphic art A type of abstract art based on shapes which vaguely resemble plants and animals. The most celebrated exponent was Hans Arp.

Biondi, Matt(hew) [byondee] (1965–) Swimmer, born in Morago, CA. At the 1986 world championships he won a record seven medals, including three golds, and at the 1988 Olympics won seven medals, including five golds.

bionics The construction of artificial mechanisms, models, circuits, or programs imitating the responses or behaviour of living systems. Its purpose is to adapt observed living functions to practical purposes in useful machines.

bionomics The study of organisms in relation to their environment. The term is used particularly with reference to ecological studies of single species.

biophysics The application of physics to the study of living organisms and systems. It includes the study of the mechanical properties of biological tissues and their functional significance.

biopsy [biyopsee] The removal by surgical operation or a needle of a small piece of tissue (eg from the skin, intestine, breast, or kidney) in order to assist the diagnosis of a suspected disease process.

biosphere That part of the Earth's surface and atmosphere in which living organisms are found, and with which they interact to form the global ecosystem.

biotechnology The application of biological and biochemical science to large-scale production. Examples include the large-scale production of penicillin in the 1940s, and research in genetic engineering.

bioterrorism *terrorism*

biotin One of the B vitamins, found in yeast and in the bacteria which inhabit the human gut. It acts as a co-factor in the synthesis of fatty acids and the conversion of amino acids to glucose.

biotite *micas*

birch A slender deciduous tree, occasionally a dwarf shrub, native to the N hemisphere; branches often pendulous, leaves ovoid, toothed; catkins pendulous, males long, females shorter, becoming cone-like in fruit; nutlets tiny with papery wings. (Genus: *Betula*, 60 species. Family: Betulaceae.)

Bird, Dickie, popular name of **Harold Dennis Bird** (1933–) Cricket umpire, born in Barnsley, South Yorkshire. He played county cricket for Yorkshire (1956–9) and Leicestershire (1960–4) before establishing himself as a popular and respected umpire. He umpired many major events, including 68 Test matches, retiring as a Test umpire in 1996. His autobiography in 1998 was the best-selling hardback book in British publishing.

bird A vertebrate animal assignable to the class Aves; any animal in which the adult bears feathers. The fore-limbs of birds are modified as wings; teeth are absent; and the projecting jaws are covered by horny sheaths to produce a bill or 'beak'. The female lays eggs with hard chalky shells. Flight has dominated the evolution of the birds, and their bodies are adapted accordingly. The bones of most birds are hollow, reducing weight; much of the wing and all of the tail is composed entirely of long feathers, these being strong but very light. The body is streamlined with a smooth covering of short overlapping feathers. Flight has also controlled size: no bird capable of horizontal flight in still air weighs more than 13 kg/30 lb. Larger birds, such as the modern ostrich (up to 150 kg/330 lb), are flightless. Birds evolved from reptiles approximately 150 million years ago. There are approximately 8600 living species of birds, and specialists indicate their relationships by grouping them into 29 orders and 181 families.

bird cherry *gean*

bird flu *avian flu*

bird of paradise A stout-billed, strong-footed bird native to SE Asian forests. The males use spectacular plumage to attract females. (Family: Paradisaeidae, 43 species.)

bird of prey Any bird that hunts large animals (especially mammals and birds) for food; also known as a **raptor**. They have a strong, curved bill and sharp claws.

Birdseye, Clarence (1886–1956) Businessman and inventor, born in New York City. He is best known for developing a process for freezing food in small packages suitable for retailing. He became president of Birdseye Frosted Foods (1930–4) and of the Birdseye Electric Company (1935–8). Some 300 patents are credited to him.

bird's-foot trefoil A perennial growing to 40 cm/15 in (*Lotus corniculatus*), native to Europe, Asia, and Africa; leaves with five oval leaflets; pea-flowers in stalked, rather flat-topped clusters of 2–8, yellow often tinged with red; pods up to 3 cm/1¼ in long, many-seeded; also called **eggs and bacon**. (Family: Leguminosae.)

birefringence A property exhibited by certain crystals, in which the speed of light is different in different directions because of the crystal structure; also called **double refraction**. Birefringent crystals such as calcite and quartz have two refractive indices, and can form double images.

bireme [biyreem] A galley, usually Greek or Roman, propelled by two banks of oars, rowed by slaves or criminals. It was also equipped with a square sail for use with a favourable wind.

Birgitta, St *Bridget, Brigit*, or *Birgitta (of Sweden), St*

Birkbeck, George (1776–1841) Educationist, born in Settle, North Yorkshire. He took a leading part in the formation of the London Mechanics' or Birkbeck Institute (1824), now Birkbeck College, part of London University.

Birmingham (UK) [bermingm] 52°30N 1°50W, pop (2001e) 977100. City in West Midlands, C England; Britain's second largest city; developed rapidly in the Industrial Revolution in an area with a large supply of iron ore and coal; heavily bombed in World War 2; railway; airport; three universities (Birmingham, 1900; Aston, 1966; Central England, 1992); National Exhibition Centre; cathedral (1839); football league teams, Aston Villa (Villa), Birmingham City (Blues), nearby West Bromwich Albion (Baggies), Walsall (Saddlers).

Birmingham (USA) [bermingham] 33°31N 86°48W, pop (2000e) 242800. City in NC Alabama, USA; settled, 1813; civil rights protests in the 1960s; airfield; railway; university (1842); leading iron and steel centre in the S.

Birmingham Six Six men convicted and sentenced to life imprisonment in 1975 for the bombing of two public houses in Birmingham, England, in which 21 people died. After a lengthy campaign by their supporters, they were freed by the Court of Appeal for England and Wales in 1991 and had their convictions quashed.

Biró, Lazlo [biro] (1899–1985) Hungarian inventor. Realizing the advantage of quick-drying ink he developed the ballpoint pen, to which eventually his name was applied – the **biro** [biyroh].

Birt (of Liverpool), John Birt, Baron (1944–) Broadcasting executive, born in Liverpool, Merseyside. He joined Granada Television (1968), and worked on the public affairs programme *World in Action* before moving to London Weekend Television (1971). Appointed BBC director-general (1993–2000), he initiated a radical and controversial programme of reforms ('Birtism'), including a market-driven approach to programme-making. He was knighted in 1998, and created a life peer in 2000. From 1999 to 2005 he was a strategy adviser to Labour prime minister Tony Blair.

birth control *contraception*

birthmark A skin blemish present at birth; also known as a **naevus/nevus**. There are two main causes: an accumulation of melanocytes (skin pigment cells) known as *moles*, which vary in colour from light brown to black; and a benign enlargement of blood and lymph vessels, the most common of which are 'strawberry marks' and 'port-wine stains'.

Birtwistle, Sir Harrison (1934–) Composer, born in Accrington, Lancashire. Among his later works are the operas *Punch and Judy* (1966–7) and *The Mask of Orpheus* (produced 1986), and *The Woman and the Hare* (1999) and *Theseus Game* (2002). In 1975 he became musical director of the National Theatre, and in

1993 composer in residence to the London Philharmonic Orchestra at the South Bank Centre.

Biscay, Bay of, Span **Golfe de Vizcaya**, Fr **Golfe de Gascogne** area 220 000 km²/85 000 sq mi. Arm of the Atlantic Ocean, known for strong currents and sudden storms; major fishing region.

Bishkek, formerly **Pishpek** (to 1926), **Frunze** (to 1991) 42°54N 74°46E, pop (2000e) 680 000. Capital city of Kyrgyzstan; altitude, 750–900 m/2500–3000 ft; founded, 1825; airport; railway; university (1951).

bishop An ecclesiastical office, probably equivalent to pastor or presbyter in the New Testament, and thereafter generally an ordained priest consecrated as the spiritual ruler of a diocese in Orthodox, Roman Catholic, and Episcopal Churches. The issue of whether women as well as men may be consecrated bishop aroused great controversy at the end of the 1980s, especially following the first such appointment (Rev Barbara Harris, as Bishop of Massachusetts) by the Episcopal Church of the United States in 1989.

Bishops' Wars (1639–40) Two brief conflicts between Charles I of England and the Scottish Covenanters, caused by his attempt to impose Anglicanism on the Scots and to take back former church lands from Scottish noblemen. They resulted in English defeats, and bankruptcy for Charles, who was forced to call the Short Parliament in 1640.

Bismarck (USA) 46°48N 100°47W, pop (2000e) 55 500. Capital of state in North Dakota, USA; established, 1873 (named after the German statesman); territorial capital, 1883; state capital, 1889; airfield; railway; trade and distribution centre for agricultural region.

Bismarck, Otto Eduard Leopold, Fürst von (Prince of) (1815–98) The first chancellor of the German Second Empire (1871–90), born in Schönhausen, Germany. Appointed prime minister in 1862, he became a guiding figure during the Schleswig-Holstein question and the war between Prussia and Austria. He was made a count in 1866, and created a prince and chancellor of the new German Empire. After the Peace of Frankfurt (1871), his policies aimed at consolidating and protecting the young Empire. In 1879, to counteract Russia and France, he formed the Austro-German Treaty of Alliance, which was later joined by Italy. Called the 'Iron Chancellor', he resigned the chancellorship in 1890, out of disapproval of Emperor William II's policy.

Bismarck Archipelago pop (2000e) 473 000; area 49 709 km²/19 188 sq mi. Island group, part of Papua New Guinea; main islands, New Britain, New Ireland, Admiralty Is, and Lavongai; mountainous, with several active volcanoes; annexed by Germany, 1884; mandated territory of Australia, 1920; occupied by Japan in World War 2; part of UN Trust Territory of New Guinea until 1975; chief town, Rabaul, on New Britain.

bismuth [bizmuhth] Bi, element 83. The heaviest element with stable isotopes, a metalloid which melts at 271°C, but forms alloys with much lower melting points.

bison A large mammal which inhabits forest and grassland; stocky; large hairy hump on shoulders; short upcurved horns; chin with beard; two species: the **American bison**, also called **boss** or (incorrectly) **buffalo** (*Bison bison*), and the **European bison** or **wisent** (*Bison bonasus*). The American bison has been crossbred with cattle to produce the hybrid *cattalo*. (Family: Bovidae.)

Bissau [beesow] 11°52N 15°39W, pop (2000e) 160 000. Seaport capital of Guinea-Bissau, W Africa; established as a fortified slave-trading centre, 1687; free port, 1869; capital moved here from Bolama, 1941; airport; cathedral.

Bissoondath, Neil (1955–) Novelist, born in Trinidad, West Indies, of Indian descent, the nephew of V S Naipaul. He emigrated to Canada in 1973. His acclaimed first novel, *A Casual Brutality* (1988) was short-listed for the Guardian Fiction Prize. Later books include short stories, *On the Eve of Uncertain Tomorrows*

(1990), and the novels *The Worlds Within Her* (2000) and *The Unyielding Clamour of the Night* (2005).

bit An abbreviation of **Binary digIT**. A bit may take only one of the two possible values in the binary number system, 0 or 1. All operations in digital computers take place using the binary number system.

Bitola or **Bitolj** [beetola], Turkish **Monastir** 41°01N 21°21E, pop (2000e) 164 000. Town in the Former Yugoslav Republic of Macedonia; under Turkish rule until 1912; second largest town in Macedonia; railway; carpets, textiles, tourism.

bitonality The property of music written in two keys simultaneously. The piquant dissonances that usually result were cherished particularly by *Les Six* in France during the first half of the 20th-c.

bittern A marsh-dwelling bird, widespread; heron-like but stouter, with shorter legs and neck; mottled brown plumage. (Family: Ardeidae, 12 species.)

bittersweet *woody nightshade*

bitumen 1 A mixture of tar-like hydrocarbons derived from petroleum either naturally or by distillation. It is black or brown and varies from viscous to solid, when it is also known as **asphalt**. It is used in road-making. **2** In art, a transparent, brown pigment made from tar, popular with painters in the 18th-c. Unfortunately, it never dries, but turns black and develops wide traction-cracks which are difficult to repair.

bivalve An aquatic mollusc with a body compressed sideways and enclosed within a shell consisting of two valves joined by a flexible ligament along a hinge line; typically feeds on small particles collected by large gills covered with tiny hairs (*cilia*); class contains over 20 000 species, many of great economic importance, such as oysters, clams, and mussels; also known as **lamellibranchs** and **pelecypods**. (Class: Pelecypoda.)

Bizerte or **Bizerta** [bizertuh], Lat **Hippo Diarrhytus** 37°18N 9°52E, pop (2000e) 170 000. City in N Tunisia on the Mediterranean coastline; occupied by Romans, Vandals, Arabs, Moors, Spanish, and French (1881); German base in World War 2, heavily bombed; French naval base until 1963; railway.

Bizet, Georges [beezay], originally **Alexandre César Léopold Bizet** (1838–75) Composer, born in Paris. His incidental music to Daudet's play *L'Arlésienne* (1872) was remarkably popular, and survived in the form of two orchestral suites. His masterpiece was the opera *Carmen* (1875).

Björling, Jussi [byerling], originally **Johan Jonaton Björling** (1911–60) Tenor, born in Stora Tuna, Sweden. He sang frequently at the Metropolitan Opera, New York, and made numerous recordings.

Black, Sir James (1924–) Pharmacologist, born in Uddingston, Scotland. He became professor of analytical pharmacology at King's College, London (1984–93). His work led to the discovery of beta-blockers (1964) and to advances in the treatment of stomach ulcers (1972), and he shared the Nobel Prize for Physiology or Medicine in 1988.

Black and Tans Additional members of the Royal Irish Constabulary, recruited by the British government to cope with Irish national unrest in the Irish War of Independence (1919–21), which reached a climax in 1920. The shortage of regulation uniforms led to the recruits being issued with khaki tunics and trousers and very dark green caps, hence their name.

black bear Either of two species of bear, usually black but sometimes brown in colour; the **American black bear** from North America (*Ursus americanus*), and the **Asiatic black bear, Himalayan bear**, or **moon bear** from S and E Asia, with a white chin and white 'V' on chest (*Selenarctos thibetanus*).

black beetle A dark beetle found in cellars and outhouses; larvae cylindrical; feeds on plant material. (Order: Coleoptera. Family: Tenebrionidae.)

blackberry A scrambling prickly shrub (*Rubus fruticosus*) with arching, biennial stems rooting at the tips; native to the Mediterranean region; flowers numerous, 5-petalled, white or pale pink; also known as **bramble**. The 'berry' is an aggregate of 1-seeded carpels, not separating from the core-like receptacle when ripe. (Family: Rosaceae.)

blackbird A thrush native to Europe, N Africa, and S and W Asia (*Turdus merula*); male black with yellow bill; female brown.

black box A complete unit in an electronics or computer system whose circuitry need not be fully understood by the user. The name is commonly used for the flight data recorder in an aircraft: this collects information about the aircraft's performance during a flight, which can be used to help determine the cause of a crash.

black bryony A perennial climber (*Tamus communis*) with a large, black tuber, related to the yam, native to Europe, W Asia, and N Africa; stems grow to 4 m/13 ft, twining; flowers tiny, 6-lobed, yellowish-green; berry red. (Family: Dioscoreaceae.)

blackbuck A gazelle native to India and Pakistan (*Antilope cervicapra*); inhabits plains and scrubland; adult males blackish-brown with white chin, white disc around eye, and white underparts; horns long, spiralling, ringed with ridges; females pale brown, hornless.

black consciousness An attitude, particularly in the USA, which asserts that African-Americans, by virtue of their ethnicity and history, possess a cultural tradition distinct from the wider population. Proponents aim to raise the awareness of blacks by espousing and publicizing these cultural traditions and values.

Black Consciousness Movement (South Africa) A movement formed by Steve Biko in 1969, when he founded the South African Students Organization. From this emerged the Black Peoples' Convention, which sought to create co-operation in social and cultural fields among all non-white peoples. Most of its leaders were imprisoned in 1977.

Black Country The industrial area of the English Midlands during and after the Industrial Revolution. It lies to the NW of Birmingham, in SW Staffordshire and N Worcestershire, England, UK.

blackcurrant An aromatic species of currant (*Ribes nigrum*) native to Europe and temperate Asia. It is widely cultivated, producing edible black berries on new wood. (Family: Grossulariaceae.)

Black Death The name given to the virulent bubonic and pneumonic plague which swept through W and C Europe from Asia (1347–51). Approximately 25 million people, about a third of the population, perished.

black economy In the UK, a term used for economic activities not reported to tax and other public authorities; also referred to as the **underground economy** or (in the USA) as 'off the books' activities. This allows one or both parties to avoid paying tax and/or social security contributions, and may conceal breaches of laws concerning such matters as job security, health and safety, and work permits.

Blackett, Patrick M(aynard) S(tuart) Blackett, Baron (1897–1974) Physicist, born in London. He was the first to photograph nuclear collisions involving transmutation (1925), and in 1932 independently discovered the positron. He pioneered research on cosmic radiation, for which he was awarded the Nobel Prize for Physics in 1948.

black-eyed Susan 1 A slender annual climber (*Thunbergia alata*) native to S Africa; stems twining to 2 m/6½ ft; leaves opposite, heart-shaped; flowers tubular with five spreading bright-yellow lobes, and a dark purplish or black central eye. (Family: Acanthaceae.)

2 In North America, members of the genus *Rudbeckia*.

blackfish *pilot whale*

blackfly A black-bodied aphid which feeds by sucking plant sap. (Order: Homoptera. Family: Aphididae.)

black fly A small biting fly found near running water; larvae aquatic; also known as **buffalo gnat**. The females of some species are blood-suckers, and serious cattle pests. (Order: Diptera. Family: Simuliidae.)

Blackfoot Three Algonkin Indian Groups (Blackfoot, Blood, Piegan) originally from the E who settled in Montana, USA and Alberta, Canada. Famous hunters and trappers. Population now c.32 000 (1990 census), chiefly on reservations.

Black Forest, Ger **Schwarzwald** Mountain range in Germany; extends 160 km/100 mi; highest peak, the Feldberg (1493 m/4898 ft).

Black Friars *Dominicans*

black grouse A grouse native to upland areas of N Europe and N Asia (*Tetrao tetrix*); the male (**blackcock**) black with a red comb above each eye; the female (**greyhen**) brown. (Family: Phasianidae.)

black gum *tupelo*

Black Hand A symbol and name for a number of secret societies which flourished in the 19th-c and early 20th-c. It was the name adopted by a secret organization formed in Serbia in 1911, led by army officers, whose objective was the achievement of Serbian independence from Austria and Ottoman Turkey. It planned the assassination of Archduke Francis Ferdinand of Austria in Sarajevo in June 1914.

black hole A region of spacetime from which matter and energy cannot escape; in origin, a star or galactic nucleus that has collapsed in on itself to the point where its escape velocity exceeds the speed of light. Its boundary is known as the *event horizon*: light generated inside the event horizon can never escape.

Black Hole of Calcutta A small, badly-ventilated room in which surviving British defenders were imprisoned overnight in an incident following Calcutta's capture (June 1756) by Siraj ud Daula, Nawab of Bengal. It was claimed that only 23 out of 146 prisoners survived. The incident became famous in the history of British imperialism, but its status is controversial, as the total number involved was probably much smaller.

blackjack A popular casino card game. The object is to accumulate a score of 21 with at least two cards (scoring 21 with a picture card and an ace is called a blackjack). There are several variations.

blackleg A debilitating disease of cattle and sheep, characterized by swollen legs; can be fatal; also known as **black legs** or **black quarter**.

black letter writing A style of writing, common in the mediaeval period, which formed the basis of early models of printers' type in Germany; sometimes called **Gothic**. It had relatively straight strokes in its letters.

blackmail The making of an unwarranted demand with menaces. The demand must be made with a view to either personal gain or loss to someone else. In the USA, many state penal codes subsume this offence under a general theft statute as theft by *extortion* (a term also used in Scotland).

black market An illegal trade in goods or currencies. The practice is well known in countries where there is rationing or restriction on the availability of food, petrol, clothing, and other essential commodities. These may be difficult or impossible to obtain using legal channels, but may be available (at a much higher price) 'on the black market'.

black Mass A blasphemous caricature of the Roman Catholic Mass, in which terms and symbols are distorted, and Satan is worshipped instead of God.

Blackmore, R(ichard) D(oddridge) (1825–1900) Novelist, born in Longworth, Oxfordshire. He wrote 15 novels, mostly with a

Devonshire background, of which *Lorna Doone* (1869) is his masterpiece.

Black Mountain College An experimental college in the USA founded in 1933 by John Andrew Rice, Theodore Dreier, and others. Originally located south of the village of Black Mountain, near Ashville, NC, the college sought to educate the 'whole' student through a combination of study, communal living, and manual work. An appreciation of the arts was central to its unorthodox curriculum. It relocated to its own campus at Lake Eden in 1941, where it remained until its closure in 1957.

Black Mountain poetry A school of poetry started in the 1950s by Charles Olson (1910–70), one-time rector of Black Mountain College in North Carolina, USA. It included such names as Robert Creeley (1926–2005) and Robert Duncan (1919–88).

Black Muslims A black separatist movement in the USA, founded in 1930 by W D Fard, Elijah Mohammed (1925–75); also known at different times as the **Nation of Islam**, the **American Muslim Mission**, and the **World Community of Islam in the West**. The movement holds that black Americans are descended from an ancient Muslim tribe. Members of the movement adopted Muslim names, and demanded a separate state for blacks. Malcolm X (*né* Little) was one of their foremost preachers, while Cassius Clay (Muhammad Ali) is undoubtedly the most famous member of the movement. They now repudiate their early separatism.

Black Pagoda *Sun Temple*

Black Panthers A militant, revolutionary African-American organization in the USA, founded in the late 1960s after the murder of Martin Luther King, Jr. The organization preached violence and acted as a protector of blacks. It rapidly went into decline with the arrest and exile of many of its leaders.

Blackpool 53°50N 3°03W, pop (2001e) 142 300. Town in NW Lancashire, NW England; unitary authority from 1998; the largest holiday resort in N England; railway; conference centre; Tower (based on Eiffel Tower); football league team, Blackpool (Tangerines); illuminations (autumn).

Black Prince *Edward the Black Prince*

Black Rod In the UK, since 1522, an official of the House of Lords. One of his chief ceremonial functions is to act as the official messenger from the Lords to the House of Commons. By tradition dating from 1643, to gain entrance to the Commons he must knock three times with his ebony staff of office (the black rod).

black rust *barberry*

Black Sea, ancient **Pontus Euxinus** (Euxine Sea), Bulgarian **Cherno More**, Romanian **Marea Neagra**, Russian **Chernoye More**, Turkish **Karadeniz** area 507 900 km²/196 000 sq mi. Inland sea between Europe and Asia, connected to the Mediterranean (SW) by the Bosporus, Sea of Marmara, and Dardanelles; 1210 km/752 mi long by 120–560 km/75–350 mi wide, maximum depth 2246 m/7369 ft; largest arm, Sea of Azov; opened by Treaty of Paris, 1856, to commerce of all nations, and closed to ships of war; now increasingly polluted; states bordering Black Sea met in Istanbul, 1992, to establish a new trading zone (Black Sea Economic Co-operation Project).

Blackshirts The colloquial name for members of Oswald Mosley's British Union of Fascists (BUF), formed in October 1932. It derived from the colour of the uniforms worn at mass rallies and demonstrations.

Blackstone, Sir William (1723–80) Jurist, born in London. In 1765–9 he published his influential *Commentaries on the Laws of England*, the first comprehensive description of the principles of English law.

blackthorn A deciduous spiny shrub (*Prunus spinosa*) growing to 6 m/20 ft; flowers white, appearing before ovoid, toothed leaves; fruits (**sloes**) globular, blue-black with waxy bloom, edible but very tart; native to Europe. (Family: Rosaceae.)

Black Watch The name of a famous Highland regiment of the British Army; first raised in 1725 as a group of six independent companies to police the Highlands, it became a regiment in 1739. Its name derives from its distinctive, very dark tartan. The two battalions known as the 42nd and 73rd Foot were amalgamated in 1881, and given the traditional title. Following service in Iraq in 2004, controversy surrounded its future as an independent regiment in the light of government plans to restructure the British Army in Scotland. From March 2006 the regiment became the 3rd Battalion The Royal Regiment of Scotland.

blackwater fever A complication of untreated or inadequately treated malaria, particularly due to *Plasmodium falciparum*. The name arises from the breakdown of red blood cells in the circulation, allowing the pigment haemoglobin to pass into the urine, darkening its colour.

Blackwell, Elizabeth (1821–1910) Physician and feminist, born in Bristol, SW England. She was responsible both for opening medical education to her sex and for establishing an infirmary for the poor of New York City. From 1869 she lived in England, founding the London School of Medicine for Women.

black widow A medium-sized, dark-coloured spider, found in warm regions worldwide. Its bite is venomous, causing severe pain, nausea, and breathing difficulties. It is occasionally fatal. (Order: Araneae. Family: Theridiidae.)

Blackwood, Algernon Henry (1869–1951) Writer, born in Shooter's Hill, Kent. His novels and stories reflect his taste for the occult, such as *Tales of the Uncanny and Supernatural* (1949).

Black Zionism The term applied to quasi-nationalist, messianic movements founded among African-Americans and West Indians. Africa is held in reverence, and there is a desire to return to the land of their forefathers.

bladder A rounded muscular organ situated behind the front of the pelvis (the *symphysis pubis*), but in children extending upwards into the abdominal cavity. The bladder receives urine from the kidneys via the ureters for temporary storage and eventual expulsion via the urethra (its capacity is c.600 ml/1·05 UK pt/1·3 US pt).

bladderwort A mostly aquatic carnivorous plant with finely divided leaves, the segments bearing tiny bladders; flowers 2-lipped, spurred, borne on a slender spike projecting above the water surface. The prey are insects or crustacea such as *Daphnia*; each bladder has a trap-door triggered when sensitive hairs are touched, sucking in the prey before the door closes again. (Genus: *Utricularia*, 120 species. Family: Utriculariaceae.)

blaeberry *bilberry*

Blaenau Gwent [bliyniy gwent] pop (2001e) 70 100; area 109 km²/42 sq mi. County (unitary authority from 1996) in SE Wales, UK; administrative centre, Ebbw Vale; former coal mining area.

Blaine, David [blayn] (1973–) Illusionist, born in Brooklyn, NY. He worked first as a street magician and, modelling himself on Harry Houdini, he began to perform seemingly impossible feats of endurance. In 1999 he was buried alive for one week beneath a glass tank filled with 4000 pounds of water. Further such feats followed, and in 2003 he apparently endured starvation in solitary confinement for 44 days in a perspex box suspended by a crane over the R Thames, the stunt gaining worldwide media coverage. In 2006 he was submerged in a water-filled sphere for seven days and, in a dramatic finale, failed to break the world record for holding breath under water, while simultaneously escaping heavy chains.

Blainey, Geoffrey Norman (1930–) Social historian, born in Melbourne, Victoria, Australia. *The Tyranny of Distance* (1966), *Triumph of the Nomads* (1975), and *A Land Half Won* (1980) formed a trilogy, *A Vision of Australian History*. Later works include *A Very Short History of the World* (2004). Through his books and a television programme, *The Blainey View*, he became well known in the 1980s.

Blair, Cherie *Blair, Tony*

Blair, Tony, popular name of **Anthony Charles Lynton Blair** (1953–) British politician and prime minister (1997–2007), born in Edinburgh. He became a barrister and was elected Labour MP for Sedgefield in 1983. He joined the shadow cabinet in 1988, becoming shadow secretary of state for energy (1988), employment (1989), and home affairs (1992). He became leader of the Labour Party in 1994, and led it to power in a landslide victory in 1997 and 2001. He encountered much public opposition over Britain's involvement in the invasion of Iraq (Mar 2003) by US-led coalition forces. In 2005 he made history as the only Labour leader to have won three successive general elections. His wife, **Cherie Blair** (1954–), is also a barrister.

Blake, Nicholas *Day-Lewis, Cecil*

Blake, Robert (1599–1657) English admiral, born in Bridgwater, Somerset. In 1649 he blockaded Lisbon, and in 1652–3 routed the Dutch in several battles. His greatest victory was at Santa Cruz, when he destroyed a Spanish treasure fleet off Tenerife; but he died on the return journey to England.

Blake, William (1757–1827) Poet, painter, engraver, and mystic, born in London. His first book of poems, the *Poetical Sketches* (1783), was followed by *Songs of Innocence* (1789) and *Songs of Experience* (1794), which express his ardent belief in the freedom of the imagination. These ideas found their fullest expression in his prophetic poems, especially *Jerusalem* (1804–20). His finest artistic work is to be found in the 21 *Illustrations to the Book of Job* (1826).

Blakey, Art [blaykee], popular name of **Arthur Blakey**, also known as **Abdulla Ibn Buhaina** (1919–90) Jazz drummmer and bandleader, born in Pittsburgh, PA. From the late 1940s he led groups under the name of the Jazz Messengers, playing 'hard bop', and introducing many future stars of jazz.

Blanc, Mont *Mont Blanc*

Blanc, Mel (1908–89) Entertainer, born in Los Angeles, CA. For over fifty years he provided the voices for some of the most famous cartoon characters including Bugs Bunny, Daffy Duck, Sylvester, and Tweety Pie. He took over the voice of the stammering Porky Pig ('Th-th-th-that's all, folks') in 1937, and in 1940 created the laugh for Woody Woodpecker. He was the voice of Barney Rubble in the television cartoon series *The Flintstones* (1960–66).

Blanchett, Cate (1969–) Actress, born in Melbourne, Victoria, Australia. She made her feature film debut in *Paradise Road* (1997). Further successes include *Elizabeth* (1998, Golden Globe, BAFTA, Oscar nomination), *The Talented Mr Ripley* (1999), *The Lord of the Rings* trilogy (2001–3), *The Aviator* (2004, BAFTA Best Supporting Actress; Oscar Best Supporting Actress), and *Babel* (2006, Best Supporting Actress Oscar nomination).

Blanda, (George) Frederick (1927–) Player of American football, born in Youngwood, PA. He played for the Chicago Bears (1949), the American Football League Houston Oilers (1960), and Oakland Raiders (1967). His 27 years as a active player with 340 matches played and 2002 points scored, are all-time NFL records.

blank verse Regular but unrhymed verse, in any metre but most usually the iambic pentameter of Shakespeare's plays, Milton's *Paradise Lost*, and Wordsworth's *Prelude*.

Blanqui, (Louis) Auguste [blãkee] (1805–81) Revolutionary socialist leader, born in Puget-Théniers, France. A passionate extremist, his opposition to the Bourbon regime led to repeated periods of imprisonment. He was arrested on the eve of the Paris Commune, of which he was nevertheless elected president (1871). His supporters were known as **Blanquists**.

Blantyre [blantiyr] 14°46N 35°00E, pop (2000e) 480 000. Town in S Malawi; altitude 1040 m/3412 ft; named after David Living-stone's birthplace in Scotland; Church of Scotland mission founded here, 1876; airport; railway; two cathedrals; Malawi's main commercial and industrial centre.

Blarney 51°56N 8°34W, pop (2000e) 2100. Small village in Cork county, S Ireland; visitors to Blarney Castle are supposed to gain the power of eloquent speech as they kiss the Blarney Stone; legend dates from the 16th-c, when Lord Blarney, by pure loquaciousness, avoided acknowledging to Queen Elizabeth's deputy that the lands of Blarney were held as a grant from the Queen and not as a chiefship.

Blasco Ibáñez, Vicente [blaskoh eevahnyeth] (1867–1928) Novelist, born in Valencia, Spain. *Los cuatro jinetes del Apocalipsis* (1916, The Four Horsemen of the Apocalypse) vividly portrays World War 1, and earned him world fame.

Blasis, Carlo [blasees] (1797–1878) Dancer, choreographer, and teacher, born in Naples, Italy. He was the author of several noted treatises on the codification of ballet technique.

blasphemy Any word, sign, or action which intentionally insults the goodness of or is offensive to God. Until the Enlightenment, it was punishable by death. In many Christian countries, it is technically a crime, and is extended to include the denial or ridicule of God, Christ, or the Bible; but the law is seldom if ever invoked. It is also a crime in certain non-Christian (eg Islamic) countries. The contemporary range of application of the law of blasphemy became an issue in the UK in 1989, following the publication of Salman Rushdie's book, *The Satanic Verses*.

blast furnace A furnace used for the primary reduction of iron ore to iron. Ore, coke, and limestone (which acts as a flux to remove silica) are loaded into the top of a tall furnace lined with mineral heat-resisting substances (such as fire-clay), in which the combustion of the coke is intensified by a pre-heated blast of air. At a certain temperature the iron ore is reduced to iron, which runs to the bottom of the furnace, where it is either tapped off and solidified as pig-iron, or conveyed while still molten to other plant for steel-making.

blastula [blastyula] An early embryonic stage in the development of multicellular animals. It typically consists of a hollow sphere of cells.

Blattaria *cockroach*

Blaue Reiter, der [blower riyter] (Ger 'blue rider') The name adopted by a group of avant-garde artists in Munich in 1911. It was apparently inspired by a coloured illustration of a horseman on the cover of a book. Members of the group included Wasily Kandinsky and Paul Klee.

Blavatsky, Helena Petrovna [blavatskee], *née* **Hahn**, known as **Madame Blavatsky** (1831–91) Theosophist, born in Yekaterinoslav (now Dnepropetrovsk), Ukraine. She helped to found the Theosophical Society in New York (1875), and later carried on her work in India.

blazar [blayzah(r)] A type of extremely luminous extragalactic object, similar to a quasar except that the optical spectrum is almost featureless.

blazonry The science of describing the pictorial devices used in heraldry. The basic colour (*tincture*) or background of the shield is known as the *field*, and this is overlaid with heraldic signs (*charges*). At their simplest, charges are broad bands, such as the vertical *pale*, or narrower stripes, such as the horizontal *fess*. The basic charges are called *ordinaries*. The *helm* or helmet appears above the shield, and denotes the rank of the bearer.

bleaching The removal of the colour of textiles or other materials, such as paper. **Bleaching powder** was used in immense quantities until its eventual replacement in the 1920s by cheap pure chlorine and sodium hypochlorite. So-called **optical bleaches** add a fluorescent emission to the basic colour of the textile.

bleaching powder A crude mixture of calcium hypochlorite

($Ca(ClO)_2$) and calcium chloride ($CaCl_2$). It is used as a bleach and as a disinfectant.

Bleasdale, Alan [bleezdayl] (1946–) Playwright, born in Liverpool, Merseyside. He became known through the popular TV series about a group of unemployed Liverpudlians, *The Boys from the Blackstuff* (1982). Later series were *GBH* (1991), *Melissa* (1997), and his adaptation of *Oliver Twist* (1999). His stage plays include *Are You Lonesome Tonight?* (1985) and *On the Ledge* (1992).

Blenheim, Battle of [blenim] (1704) The greatest military triumph of Marlborough and Prince Eugene in the War of the Spanish Succession. It marked the first significant defeat of Louis XIV's armies.

Blenheim Palace [blenim] A Baroque palace designed by Vanbrugh, and built (1705–24) at Woodstock, near Oxford, Oxfordshire; a world heritage site. The palace, with its estate of 809 ha/2000 acres, was a gift from the nation to the 1st Duke of Marlborough after the Battle of Blenheim.

blenny Any of the large family Blennidae (11 genera), of mostly small bottom-dwelling fishes of coastal waters; found worldwide in tropical to temperate seas, rarely in freshwater lakes; body stout, devoid of scales; jaws bearing many small teeth.

Blériot, Louis [blayryoh] (1872–1936) Airman, born in Cambrai, France. He made the first flight across the English Channel (25 Jul 1909) from Baraques to Dover in a small 24-hp monoplane.

blesbok *bontebok*

Blessed Virgin (Mary) *Mary* (mother of Jesus)

Blethyn, Brenda (1946–) Actress, born in Ramsgate, Kent. She has worked widely in British television in such programmes as *Chance In A Million* (1983–5), *Outside Edge* (1994–6), and *Belonging* (2004). She received international acclaim for her role in Mike Leigh's film *Secrets and Lies* (1996, Best Actress, Cannes). Later films include *Little Voice* (1998) and *Pride & Prejudice* (2005).

Bligh, William [bliy] (c.1754–c.1817) Naval officer, born in Plymouth, Devon. In 1787 he was sent as commander of HMS *Bounty* to Tahiti. On the return voyage, the men mutinied under his harsh treatment. In April 1789, Bligh and 18 men were cast adrift in an open boat without charts. In June, after great hardship, he arrived at Timor, near Java, having sailed his frail craft for 3618 miles. He was later appointed Governor of New South Wales (1805–11).

blight A general term applied to any of a variety of plant diseases, especially those caused by fungal infection.

blimp *airship*

blindness A substantial or total loss of vision in both eyes. It can be caused by degeneration of the retina of the eye (*macular degeneration*), cataract, glaucoma, or diabetes. In developing countries it can also be caused by infections.

blindworm *slowworm*

Bliss, Sir Arthur (Edward Drummond) (1891–1975) Composer, born in London. In 1953 he became Master of the Queen's Musick. His works include the ballet *Checkmate* (1937), the opera *The Olympians* (1949), chamber music, and piano and violin works.

blister beetle A brightly coloured beetle, usually from warm, dry regions. Adults produce a chemical (*cantharidin*) that causes skin blisters. (Order: Coleoptera. Family: Meloidae, c.3000 species.)

blister blight A serious airborne disease of tea (*Exobasidium vexans*), endemic in SE Asia. It can be controlled only by the application of expensive fungicidal sprays. (Order: Basidiomycetes.)

blitzkrieg [blitzkreek] (Ger 'lightning war') A term coined (Sep 1939) to describe the German armed forces' use of fast-moving tanks and deep-ranging aircraft, aiming the focus of effort at the enemy's rear areas rather than making frontal attacks.

Blix, Hans (1928–) Diplomat, born in Uppsala, Sweden. He qualified as a lawyer, then joined the Swedish Ministry for Foreign Affairs, becoming minister (1978), and served as director-general of the International Atomic Energy Agency (1981–97). He became widely known following his appointment in 2000 as head of the UN Monitoring, Verification and Inspection Commission, leading the investigation into the whereabouts of Iraq's weapons of mass destruction. In July 2003 he was appointed head of a Sweden-sponsored international commission on such weapons.

Blobel, Günter (1936–) Cell and molecular biologist, born in Waltersdorf, Germany. He joined Rockefeller University, New York City, in 1969, and received the 1999 Nobel Prize for Physiology or Medicine for the discovery that proteins have intrinsic signals that govern their transport and localization in the cell.

Bloch, Ernest [blokh] (1880–1959) Composer, born in Geneva, Switzerland. His works include the Hebrew *Sacred Service* (1930–3), and many chamber and orchestral works.

Bloch, Felix [blokh] (1905–83) Physicist, born in Zürich, Switzerland. He left Europe for the USA when Hitler came to power. He was appointed the first director-general of CERN (1954–5), and he shared the 1952 Nobel Prize for Physics for work on nuclear magnetic resonance. Several concepts and features dealing with superconductivity have been named after Bloch.

Bloc Québecois [kaybekwah] A separatist political organization in Quebec, Canada, formed in 1990 when Lucien Bouchard and other Conservative MPs from Quebec deserted the Mulroney government. In the 1993 federal election the *Bloc* won the second largest number of seats (all in Quebec) and became the official Opposition in Ottawa.

Bloemfontein [bloomfontayn] 29°07S 26°14E, pop (2000e) 350 000. Judicial capital of South Africa, and capital of Free State province; founded as a fort, 1846; taken by Lord Roberts in Boer War, 1900; airfield; railway; university (1855); cathedral.

Blondel or **Blondel de Nesle** [blodel] (12th-c) French minstrel, said to have accompanied Richard I of England to Palestine, and to have found him when imprisoned in the Austrian prison of Dürrenstein (1193) by means of a song they had jointly composed.

Blondin, Charles [blodĩ], originally **Jean François Gravelet** (1824–97) Acrobat and tightrope-walker, born in Saint-Omer, N France. In 1859 he crossed Niagara Falls on a tightrope, and later did the same with variations (eg blindfolded, with a wheelbarrow, with a man on his back, on stilts).

Blood, Thomas, known as **Colonel Blood** (c.1618–80) Irish adventurer, known for his activities during the English Civil War and Restoration. His most famous exploit was his attempt, disguised as a clergyman, to steal the crown jewels from the Tower of London (1671).

blood An animal tissue composed of cells, cell-like bodies, and fluid plasma that circulates around the body within vascular channels or spaces by the mechanical action of the channels or their specialized parts (primarily the heart). Present in many major classes of animals, it usually contains respiratory pigment, and transports oxygen, nutrients, waste-products, and many other substances around the body. In humans, the cells (red, *erythrocytes*, and white, *leucocytes*), cell-like bodies (*platelets*), and plasma constitute about 8% of total body weight; in an average-sized adult male, blood volume is c.5·5 l/9·7 UK pt/11·6 US pt; in an equivalent female, it is c.4·5 l/7·9 UK pt/9·5 US pt.

Blood, Council of A council established 1567–76 by the Duke of Alva, the Spanish Habsburg military commander in the Low Countries, on Philip II's orders, to suppress heresy and opposition during the Revolt of the Netherlands. It was also known as the **Council of Troubles**.

blood-bark *gum tree*

blood fluke A parasitic flatworm, found as an adult in the blood of some mammals, including humans; causes bilharzia. (Phylum: Platyhelminthes. Class: Trematoda. Genus *Schistosoma*.)

blood group systems A series of genetically determined systems of substances on the plasma membranes of red blood cells, which act as *agglutininogens* and which, when in contact with the complementary *agglutinin* in plasma cause the red cells to stick together. In humans, the most prominent system is the ABO. Everybody belongs to four main subdivisions of this system (A, B, AB, or O) determined by the presence or the absence of A and/or B substances on the red cell membrane. The absence of A or B antigen is usually associated with the presence of corresponding natural anti-A or anti-B antibodies in the plasma. Other well-known systems are the Rh (Rhesus) and MNSs.

bloodhound A breed of dog, known for its keen sense of smell; used for tracking; large powerful body with loose-fitting skin; short coat; tan or black and tan; long pendulous ears and jowls; long, deep muzzle.

blood poisoning *septicaemia*

blood pressure The hydrostatic pressure of the blood within the blood vessels. It usually refers to the pressure within arteries, the pressure within capillaries and veins being much lower. Arterial blood pressure depends on heart rate, the volume of blood ejected by the heart with each beat, and the *peripheral resistance* to the flow of blood through the arteries. It is measured, using a sphygmomanometer, as the height in millimetres of a column of mercury (mmHg). In health, the arterial blood pressure reaches a peak of around 120 mmHg with each heartbeat (*systolic pressure*) and falls to around 70 mmHg as the heart relaxes (*diastolic pressure*).

Blood River, Battle of *Great Trek*

blood sports The killing of animals for sport, such as foxhunting, hare-coursing, or bullfighting; often referred to as **field sports**. They have come under increasing attack in recent years from those concerned with animal welfare. In Britain, the Hunting Bill (2005), banned hunting with hounds in England and Wales. Deer-hunting and hare-coursing with dogs is also illegal.

bloodstone A type of chalcedony, a fine-grained variety of the mineral quartz. It is dark-green with red flecks.

blood transfusion The transfer of blood from one person to another. It was first carried out early in the 19th-c, but usually resulted in serious reactions. Clinically useful and safe blood transfusions were possible only after the discovery of blood groups.

blood vessels A closed system of tubes whereby blood permeates through all the tissues of the body, comprising the arteries, arterioles, capillaries, venules, and veins. In general, arteries and arterioles carry oxygenated blood from the heart, and venules and veins return deoxygenated blood back to it. However, the pulmonary arteries convey deoxygenated blood to the lungs from the heart, while the pulmonary veins return oxygenated blood to it from the lungs. Disorders of the circulatory system include aneurysm, embolism, haemorrhage, and thrombosis.

Bloody Assizes The name given to the western circuit assizes in England in the summer of 1685, presided over by Lord Chief Justice George Jeffreys after the defeat of the Duke of Monmouth at the Battle of Sedgemoor. About 150 of Monmouth's followers were executed, and 800 transported to the West Indies.

Bloody Mary *Mary I*

Bloom, Claire (1931–) Actress, born in London. A distinguished Shakespearean actress, her film roles also include *Limelight* (1952), *Look Back in Anger* (1959), *Sammy and Rosie Get Laid* (1987), *Wrestling with Alligators* (1999), and *Kalamazoo?* (2006).

Television work includes *Shadowlands* (1985, BAFTA) and *Imogen's Face* (1998).

Bloom, Orlando (1977–) Actor, born in Canterbury, Kent. He studied at the British American Drama Academy in London and the Guildhall School of Music and Drama, and went on to gain small parts on television and an appearance in the 1997 film *Wilde*. He became well known following his film role as the warrior elf Legolas Greenleaf in *The Lord of the Rings* trilogy (2001–3). Other films include *Pirates of the Caribbean* (2003, sequel 2006) and *Kingdom of Heaven* (2005).

Bloom, Ursula, pseudonym of **Mrs Gower Robinson** (1892–1984) Novelist and playwright, born in Chelmsford, Essex. Her novels, which include *The First Elizabeth* (1953), are mainly historical romances. Most of her plays were written for radio production.

Bloomer, Amelia, *née* **Jenks** (1818–94) Champion of women's rights and dress reform, born in Homer, NY. She founded and edited the feminist paper *The Lily* (1849–55). In her pursuit of dress equality she wore her own version of trousers for women, which came to be called **bloomers**.

Bloomsbury Group An informal association of intellectuals taking their name from the Bloomsbury area of London who were active around the time of World War 1: among them Virginia Woolf, Lytton Strachey, and E M Forster. In reaction against Victorian values, they had a significant influence on the Modernist movement in England.

Bloor, Ella (Reeve), known as **Mother Bloor** (1862–1951) Radical and feminist, born on Staten Island, New York City. Married at the age of 19, she became interested in women's rights, her political interests leading to her divorce in 1896. In 1919 she was one of the founders of the American Communist Party.

Blücher, Gebhard Leberecht von, Fürst von (Prince of) **Wahlstadt** [bloocher, blooker], nickname **Marshal Forward** (1742–1819) Prussian field marshal, born in Rostock, Germany. In 1813 he defeated Napoleon at Leipzig, and entered Paris (1814). In 1815 he saved Wellington from defeat at Waterloo by his timely appearance on the field.

blue In the UK, a sporting honour awarded at Oxford and Cambridge universities to students who represent their university against the other in the annual matches of certain sports. Ribbons of dark blue (Oxford) or light blue (Cambridge) were first awarded to competitors after the second Boat Race in 1836.

Bluebeard A wicked character in European folklore who gives his new wife charge of the house-keys, forbidding her to enter one room; she unlocks it out of curiosity, to discover the bodies of six previous wives. Her brothers arrive just in time to save her, and slay him.

bluebell A small herb with an annually renewed bulb (*Hyacinthoides non-scriptus*), native to W Europe; flowers bell-shaped, drooping, blue, sometimes pinkish or white. (Family: Liliaceae.)

blueberry A deciduous shrub, native to North America, and cultivated for fruit; flowers bell-shaped; berry blue-black, edible. (Genus: *Vaccinium*, c.20 American species. Family: Ericaceae.)

bluebird A thrush native to North and Central America; male with bright blue plumage on back; nests in holes in trees. (Genus: *Sialia*, 3 species.)

blue book A UK Government publication of official documents, presented to parliament, bound in a blue cover. Unlike other command papers, which put forward government proposals, blue books are more concerned with the provision of information.

bluebottle (botany) *cornflower*

bluebottle (entomology) A large fly with a metallic blue abdomen; lays eggs on decaying animal matter; legless larvae feed by liquefying food; adults feed by exuding digestive juices onto food and imbibing dissolved material. (Order: Diptera. Family: Calliphoridae.)

bluebuck / blue bull *nilgai*

bluegrass US 'hillbilly' country music. It features mandolins, banjos, fiddles, guitars, 'dobro' guitars (fitted with a metal resonator), and high ('high lonesome') singing in harmony, with its roots in black and European folk music. Originating from the Appalachian mountain regions, its virtuoso exponents include Bill Monroe (1911–96) and his Blue Grass Boys.

blue-green algae *blue-green bacteria*

blue-green bacteria Single-celled, colonial or filamentous organisms with an alga-like body and a bacterium-like (*prokaryotic*) cellular structure; photosynthetic pigment chlorophyll *a* found on a special membrane (*thylakoid*) not enclosed within chloroplasts as in true algae; very ancient organism, believed to have been responsible for enriching the Earth's atmosphere with oxygen as a by-product of its photosynthesis; over 1000 living species known, found mostly in aquatic habitats; formerly known as **blue-green algae**. (Division: Cyanophycota.)

blue moon 1 A phrase often used to refer to the second full moon in a calendar month in which two full moons occur – a rare event, only once every 2·7 years on average (though happening twice in one year in 1999 and 2018). However, research reported in 1999 suggested that this definition derives from an almanac misinterpretation of the 1940s, and that the phrase only makes sense in relation to a season of the year containing four (not the usual three) full moons. **2** Very rarely, the Moon's disc actually appears blue. If the atmosphere has particles 0·8–1·8 microns in diameter, for example from volcanoes or forest fires, red light gets scattered out of the line of sight, but the blue is allowed through.

Blue Mountains Mountain range in E New South Wales, Australia; part of the Great Dividing Range; rises to 1180 m/3871 ft at Bird Rock.

Blue Nile, Ethiopia **Abay Wenz**, Sudan **Bahr El Azraq** Upper reach of R Nile, NE Africa; length 1450 km/901 mi; issues from L Tana, Ethiopia; joins White Nile at Khartoum.

Blue Riband A notional honour awarded to the fastest passenger ship on the North Atlantic run. The final holder (1952) was the SS *United States* in a time of 3 days 11 hours 20 minutes at an average speed of 35·39 knots for the distance of 4745 km/2949 mi. The competition has ceased for economic reasons.

Blue Rider *Blaue Reiter, der*

Blue Ridge Mountains Mountain range, SE USA; E part of the Appalachian Mts; extends NE–SW for c.1050 km/650 mi; highest point Mt Mitchell (2037 m/6683 ft).

blues A style of US African-American music, related to slow jazz, originating c.1900. The singing of blues is essentially an improvisatory art, often reflecting a melancholy state of mind but also conveying the vitality of black working-class Americans. Blues songs may have a number of verses, but the standard pattern for each is one of three lines of 4 bars each, the second being a repetition of the first. The origins of the blues are associated particularly with the Mississippi region, and many of the most influential early singers, such as Bessie Smith, 'the Empress of Blues', were from the S States. Later departures were seen in the 'rhythm and blues' of the 1950s, and a great deal of rock 'n roll. Blues music is also now found in a wide range of instrumental manifestations, especially using the guitar.

blue shark Powerful slender-bodied shark (*Prionace glauca*) found worldwide in open tropical to temperate seas; length up to 3·8 m/12½ ft; pectoral fins elongate; deep blue dorsally, white underneath. (Family: Carcharhinidae.)

blueshift An astronomical effect observed when an object emitting electromagnetic radiation is moving towards an observer, increasing the observed frequency of its radiation. Spectral lines move to the blue end of the spectrum. Blueshifts are unusual, because almost all galaxies are moving away from us, and hence have redshifts.

bluetit A small typical tit common in gardens (*Parus caeruleus*); native to Europe, N Africa, and SW Asia; nests in hole in tree or wall; also known as **tomtit**. (Family: Paridae.)

blue whale A rare baleen whale (*Balaenoptera musculus*) of the rorqual family; the largest animal that has ever existed, length up to 30 m/100 ft; blue with pale spots; also known as the **sulphur-bottom whale**.

Blunden, Edmund (Charles) (1896–1974) Poet and critic, born in Yalding, Kent. He is essentially a nature poet, as is evident in *Pastorals* (1916), but his best-known work is his prose *Undertones of War* (1928).

blunderbuss A type of firearm, dating from the late 18th-c, with a large bore and a trumpet mouth. It is able to discharge 10 or 12 balls in one shot designed for very short-range use.

Blunkett, David (1947–) British statesman, born in Sheffield, South Yorkshire. His early education was in special schools for the blind. He became an MP in 1987, held several shadow ministerial posts, was chairman of the Labour Party (1993–4), and became secretary-of-state for education and employment in 1997 and home secretary in 2001. He resigned in 2004 following accusations that he fast-tracked a visa on behalf of an applicant with whom he had a personal connection. He was recalled to the cabinet in 2005 as work and pensions secretary, but resigned later that year after breaking the ministerial code of conduct over paid work he took while out of the cabinet.

Blunt, Anthony (Frederick) (1907–83) Art historian and Soviet spy, born in Bournemouth, Dorset. Influenced by Burgess, he acted as a 'talent-spotter' at Cambridge, supplying to him the names of likely recruits to the Russian Communist cause, and during his war service in British Intelligence was in a position to pass on information to the Russian government. In 1964, after the defection of Philby, a confession was obtained from Blunt in return for immunity from prosecution, and he continued as Surveyor of the Queen's Pictures until 1972. His full involvement in espionage was made public only in 1979, when his knighthood (1956) was annulled.

Blyth, Chay, popular name of **Charles Blyth** (1940–) Yachtsman, born in Hawick, Scotland, the first to sail single-handed 'the hard way' round the world (1970–1). In 1966 he rowed the Atlantic from W to E with John Ridgway (1938–), before making his epic voyage westward around the globe. With a crew of paratroopers he won the Whitbread Round the World Yacht Race (1973–4), travelling eastwards.

Blyton, Enid (Mary) (1897–1968) Children's writer, born in London. In the late 1930s she began writing her many children's stories featuring such characters as Noddy, the Famous Five, and the Secret Seven. The author of over 400 books, she is the third most translated British author, after Agatha Christie and Shakespeare.

B'nai B'rith [bniy brith] (Heb 'sons of the covenant') The oldest and largest Jewish service organization, founded in the USA in 1843. It pursues educational and community activities, and concerns itself with the rights of Jews throughout the world.

boa A snake native to the New World, N Africa, SW Asia, and Australasian islands; a constrictor; minute remnants of hind limbs; females give birth to live young (up to 80 at one time); includes the anaconda. (Family: Boidae, 39 species.)

Boadicea *Boudicca*

boar *pig*

Boas, Franz [bohas] (1858–1942) Anthropologist, born in Minden, Germany. Professor at Columbia University from 1899, he became the dominant figure in establishing modern anthropology in the USA. His approach is seen in a major collection of papers, *Race, Language and Culture* (1940).

Boat People Vietnamese who fled Vietnam by boat after the communist victory in 1975, travelling to Australia, Hong Kong, Japan, and several other parts of SE Asia (c.110 000 by the end of 1990). Many died on the long voyages, or were killed by pirates. Voluntary repatriation schemes gained momentum in 1989, and the first involuntary repatriation operation was carried out by the Hong Kong authorities that December. The term has since been applied to other groups who try to flee from a country using small craft.

Boat Race The annual rowing race between the crews of Oxford and Cambridge Universities. First held 10 June 1829 from Hambledon Lock to Henley Bridge, it is now raced over 6 km 780 m/ 4 mi 374 yd from Putney to Mortlake.

bobcat A nocturnal member of the cat family native to North America (*Felis rufus*); resembles a small lynx; length up to 1 m/ 3$\frac{1}{4}$ ft; brown with dark spots; tail very short.

bobolink An oriole native to North America (*Dolichonyx oryzivorus*); spends winter in South America; has the longest migration (8000 km/5000 mi) of any bird in its family.

bobsledding The art of propelling oneself along snow or ice on a sled (or sledge). The most popular forms of competitive bobsledding are **luge tobogganing** on a small sled, **bobsleighing** in a sophisticated streamlined sled, and the **skeleton**.

Boccaccio, Giovanni [bokahchioh] (1313–75) Writer, probably born in Italy. In 1353 he completed his great work, the *Decameron*, begun some 5 years before. He selected the plots of his stories from current popular fiction, and was a great influence on Chaucer, Shakespeare, and others.

Boccherini, Luigi (Rodolfo) [bokereenee] (1743–1805) Composer, born in Lucca, Italy. He was a cellist and prolific composer at the courts in Madrid and Prussia, best known for his chamber music, cello concertos, and sonatas.

Boccioni, Umberto [bochohnee] (1882–1916) Artist and sculptor, born in Reggio, Italy. The most original artist of the Futurist school and its principal theorist, he worked in Paris and Rome (1898–1914), and wrote a major survey of the movement.

Bocelli, Andrea [bochelee] (1958–) Tenor, born in Lajatico, Tuscany, Italy. Visually impaired from birth, he became blind at the age of 12 following a football injury. He recorded a demo tape of a duet, *Miserere*, that was heard by Pavarotti, who was persuaded to record the song with him. The duo scored a Europe-wide smash hit. International success followed with the single *Time To Say Goodbye* (1996), recorded with Sarah Brightman. His albums include *Romanza* (1997), *Cieli di Toscana* (2001), and *Amore* (2006).

Bochum [bokhum] 51°28N 7°12E, pop (2000e) 410 000. Industrial and commercial city in the Ruhr valley, Germany; originally developed around the coal and steel industries; railway; university (1965).

Bodensee *Constance, Lake*

Bode's law or **Titius–Bode law** A numerical relationship linking the distances of planets from the Sun, discovered in 1766 by German astronomer Johann Daniel Titius (1729–96), and published in 1772 by Johann Elert Bode (1747–1826), but now considered to be an interesting coincidence. The basis of this relationship is the series 0,3,6,12,...,384, in which successive numbers are obtained by doubling the previous one. If 4 is then added to create the new series 4,7,10,16,...,388, the resulting numbers correspond reasonably with the planetary distances on a scale, with the Earth's distance equal to ten units.

Bodh Gaya *Buddh Gaya*

Bodhidharma [bodhidah(r)ma] (6th-c) Monk and founder of the Ch'an (or Zen) sect of Buddhism, born near Chennai (Madras), India. He taught meditation as the means of return to Buddha's spiritual precepts.

bodhisattva [bodhisatwa] (Sanskrit, 'enlightened existence') In Mahayana Buddhism, one who has attained the enlightenment of a Buddha but chooses not to pass into Nirvana, voluntarily remaining in the world to help lesser beings attain enlightenment.

bodily harm A criminal offence against the person. **Grievous bodily harm** involves serious physical injury, such as wounding with a knife. **Actual bodily harm** involves a less serious attack, such as an assault causing unconsciousness. These terms are not used in all jurisdictions.

Bodleian Library [bodlian] The university library and national depository at Oxford; founded in 1595 by Sir Thomas Bodley (1545–1613).

Body art A type of modern art which exploits the artist's – or someone else's – physical presence as a work of art in its own right. Artists may stand in the gallery like a living statue, perhaps singing; photograph themselves performing some banal action, such as smiling; or may deliberately injure themselves. A typical fad of the 1960s, it emerged again in the 1990s, with people using paint, tattoo, rings, and a variety of attachments.

body colour *gouache*

body language *nonverbal communication*

body popping *street dance*

Boeing, William E(dward) [bohing] (1881–1956) Aircraft manufacturer, born in Detroit, MI. He formed the Pacific Aero Products Co in 1916, renamed as the Boeing Airplane Company in 1917. It eventually became the largest manufacturer of military and civilian aircraft in the world.

Boeotia [beeohsha] In antiquity, the area in C Greece bordering on Attica. Its chief city-state was Thebes, and its inhabitants were largely of Aeolian stock.

Boers *Afrikaners*

Boer Wars Two wars fought by the British and the Boers for the mastery of S Africa. The first Boer War (1880–1) ended with the defeat of the British at Majuba Hill, and the signing of the Pretoria and London Conventions of 1881 and 1884. The second Boer War (1899–1902) can be divided into three phases: (1) (Oct 1899–Jan 1900) a series of Boer successes, including the sieges of Ladysmith, Kimberley, and Mafeking, as well as victories at Stormberg, Modder River, Magersfontein, Colenso, and Moderspruit; (2) (Feb–Aug 1900) counter-offensives by Lord Roberts, including the raising of the sieges, the victory at Paardeberg, and the capture of Pretoria; (3) (Sep 1900–May 1902) a period of guerrilla warfare when Kitchener attempted to prevent Boer commandos raiding isolated British units and lines of communication. The Boers effectively won the peace. They maintained control of 'native affairs', and federated South Africa on their terms in 1910.

Boesak, Allan (Aubrey) [busak] (1945–) Clergyman, born in Kakamas, South Africa. A former president of the World Alliance of Reformed Churches (1982–97), he sees the Christian Gospel in terms of liberation of the oppressed. An outspoken opponent of apartheid, he became leader of the coloured (mixed-race) community in South Africa. In 1999, after a controversial trial, he was jailed for six years for embezzlement of funds sent to his organization. On appeal the sentence was reduced to three years.

Boethius, Anicius Manlius Severinus [boheethius] (c.AD 480–524) Roman statesman and philosopher, probably born in Rome. Made consul in 510, his uprightness of conduct brought him many enemies. He was accused of treason, imprisoned, and executed. During his imprisonment he wrote *De consolatione philosophiae* (The Consolation of Philosophy).

Bogarde, Sir Dirk [bohgah(r)d], originally **Derek Niven van den Bogaerde** (1921–99) Actor, born in London. He moved from the stage to films in 1946, playing mostly romantic or light comedy roles, such as *Doctor in the House* (1954) and its sequels. More challenging parts with varied characterization followed, as in *The Victim* (1961), *Death in Venice* (1971), and *Despair* (1981). He published several volumes of autobiography and some novels.

Bogart, Humphrey (DeForest) [bohgah(r)t] (1899–1957) Actor, born in New York City. Many of his performances have become classics, notably *The Maltese Falcon* (1941), *Casablanca* (1942), *The Big Sleep* (1946), and *The African Queen* (1951, Oscar). He married Lauren Bacall as his fourth wife in 1945.

bog burials Ancient human bodies recovered from N European peat bogs, their soft tissues and hair remarkably preserved by waterlogged, anaerobic conditions. Notable Iron Age examples are *Tollund Man* (c.200 BC) in Denmark, and the 25–30-year-old, 1·7 m/5 ft 7 in tall *Lindow Man*, buried naked c.300 BC in Lindow Moss, Cheshire, UK, and discovered in 1984.

Bognor Regis [bogner reejis] 50°47N 0°41W, pop (2000e) 60 500. Coastal resort town in West Sussex, S England; the title 'Regis' dates from 1929, when King George V came here to recuperate; railway.

Bogomils [bogohmilz] *Albigenses; Cathars*

Bogotá [bohgohta], official name **Santa Fe de Bogotá** 4°38N 74°05W, pop (2000e) 4 796 000. Federal capital of Colombia, on a plateau at 2650 m/8694 ft; founded by Spanish, 1538; former capital of Greater Colombia and of New Granada; airport; railway; several universities and colleges; cathedral.

Bohemia [bohheemia], Czech **Čechy**, Ger **Böhmen** Historic province of W Czech Republic, a plateau enclosed by mountains; major towns include Prague; highly industrialized area; coal, iron ore, uranium; part of Moravian Empire, 9th-c; at its peak in early Middle Ages, especially in 14th-c under Charles I; Hussite religious dissension; Habsburg rule from early 16th-c; became a province of Czechoslovakia, 1918; part of Czech Republic, 1993.

Bohemian Forest, Ger **Böhmerwald**, Czech **Český Les** Forested mountain range along the boundary between Germany and Czech Republic; highest German peak, Grosser Arber (1457 m/4780 ft).

Bohr, Niels (Henrik David) [baw(r)] (1885–1962) Physicist, born in Copenhagen. He greatly extended the theory of atomic structure when he explained the spectrum of hydrogen by means of an atomic model and quantum theory (1913). During World War 2 he assisted atom bomb research in the USA. He founded the Institute of Theoretical Physics Copenhagen, and was awarded the Nobel Prize for Physics in 1922.

Boiardo, Matteo Maria, conte di (Count of) **Scandiano** [boyah(r)doh] (c.1441–94) Poet, born in Scandiano, Italy. His fame rests on the *Orlando Innamorato* (1486), a long narrative poem about Roland, the greatest of Charlemagne's legendary heroes.

boil An abscess at the base of a hair follicle, which results in a raised, reddened, and often painful swelling in the skin. It usually results from infection with *Staphylococcus aureus*.

Boileau(-Despréaux), Nicolas [bwahloh] (1636–1711) Poet and critic, born in Paris. *L'Art poétique* (1674, The Art of Poetry), expressing the classical principles for the writing of poetry, was very influential in France and England.

boiling point The point at which heat added to a liquid is no longer used to increase temperature but instead to form gas from the liquid. Formally, the boiling point temperature is reached when a liquid's vapour pressure equals external pressure. Boiling points thus decrease with altitude.

boiling water reactor *nuclear reactor*

Bois de Boulogne [bwah duh booloyn] A park of 962 ha/2380 acres situated on the W outskirts of Paris. Originally a royal hunting forest, it became a popular recreation area for Parisians in the 17th-c.

Boise [boyzee] 43°37N 116°13W, pop (2000e) 185 800. State capital in SW Idaho, USA, founded after the 1862 gold rush; airfield; railway; trade and transportation centre.

Bolden, Buddy, popular name of **Charles Joseph Bolden** (1877–1931) Jazz cornetist, born in New Orleans, LA. He is a putative founder of jazz, a figure of mythic significance; no recorded evidence survives. In 1907, his uncontrollable fits of violence led to his incarceration for life, and he died in a fire at an asylum.

Boleyn, Anne [bolin], also spelled **Bullen** (c.1507–36) English queen, the second wife of Henry VIII (1533–6). Secretly married to Henry, she was soon declared his legal wife; but within three months his passion for her had cooled. It was not revived by the birth (1533) of a princess (later Elizabeth I), still less by that of a stillborn son (1536). She was charged with treason, and beheaded.

bolide [bohleed] An exceptionally brilliant meteor, or fireball, which explodes in our atmosphere. It makes a very loud bang, and in some cases scatters stony debris over a wide area.

Bolingbroke *Henry IV* (of England)

Bolívar, Simón [boleevah(r), bolivah(r)], known as **the Liberator** (1783–1830) The national hero of Venezuela, Colombia, Ecuador, Peru, and Bolivia, born in Caracas. He played the most prominent part in the wars of independence in N South America. In 1819, he was proclaimed and became president of the vast Republic of Colombia, which was finally liberated in 1822. He then took charge of the last campaigns for independence in Peru (1824).

Bolivia *p.117*

boll weevil A small weevil that prevents the normal development of cotton flowers by its feeding activities. It is an economically important pest of cotton. (Order: Coleoptera. Family: Curculionidae.)

Bologna [bolohnya] 44°30N 11°20E, pop (2000e) 411 000. Capital city in N Italy; ancient Etruscan city, enclosed by remains of 13th–14th-c walls; archbishopric; airport; rail junction; university (11th-c).

Bolsheviks (Russ 'majority-ites') Members of the hard-line faction of the Marxist Russian Social Democratic Labour Party, formed by Lenin at the party's second congress in 1903; the forerunner of the Communist Party of the Soviet Union (abolished in 1991). In October 1917 the Bolsheviks led the revolution in Petrograd which established the first Soviet government.

Bolshoi Ballet [bolshoy] (Russian 'Great Ballet') The leading ballet company of Russia and, formerly, of the Soviet Union. Based in Moscow, it traces its origins back to its foundation (1773) as the dancing school for the Moscow Orphanage. In 1825 the newly formed Bolshoi Theatre took over the ballet company of the Petrovsky Theatre and moved into its premises. By the mid-20th-c the Bolshoi was one of the world's foremost ballet companies. After the collapse of communism, its subsidies were drastically cut and it fell into decline. Under the current directorship of Alexei Ratmansky the theatre began a massive redevelopment in 2004.

Bolt, Robert (Oxton) (1924–95) Playwright, born in Sale, Greater Manchester. He worked as a teacher before achieving success with *A Man for All Seasons* (1960). He also wrote screenplays, including *Lawrence of Arabia* (1962), *Dr Zhivago* (1965), and *The Mission* (1986). He was an anti-nuclear activist in the 1960s, joining the 'Committee of 100', and was jailed for a month in 1961. He continued writing, despite being partly paralysed and left with speech difficulties, following a stroke in 1979.

Boltzmann, Ludwig (Eduard) [boltsman] (1844–1906) Physicist, born in Vienna. He worked on the kinetic theory of gases, and helped to develop the science of statistical mechanics. **Boltzmann's law**, the principle of the equipartition of energy, and the **Boltzmann constant**, used in the study of gases, are named after him.

bomb A device used to cause an explosion, usually consisting of a container, an explosive substance, and a fuse. Generally bombs are distinguished from other explosive devices by means of delivery: they normally use gravity (when dropped from aircraft) or are placed in position (as in the case of car bombs). Gravity and release speed determine an ordinary bomb's flightpath, although so-called **smart bombs** have a target-seeking guidance package in the nose which can pick up

Bolivia

□ International Airport

official name **Republic of Bolivia**, Span **República de Bolivia**

Local name Bolivia

Timezone GMT -4

Area 1 098 580 km²/424 052 sq mi

Population total (2005e) 8 857 000

Status Republic

Date of independence 1825

Capital La Paz (administrative), Sucre (legal)

Languages Spanish, Quechua, Aymará (all used offcially)

Ethnic groups Mestizo (30%), Quechua (30%), Aymará (25%), white (15%)

Religions Roman Catholic (95%), Baha'i (3%)

Physical features Landlocked country, bounded W by the Cordillera Occidental of the Andes, rising to 6542 m/21 463 ft at Sajama; separated from the Cordillera Real to the E by the flat, 400 km/ 250 mi-long Altiplano plateau, 3600 m/11 800 ft; major lakes, Titicaca and Poopó.

Climate Varies with altitude, ranging from consistently warm (26°C) and damp conditions (1800 mm/71 in of rainfall per year) in NE rainforests of Amazon Basin, to drought conditions in S; over 500 m/16 000 ft, conditions become sub-polar.

Currency 1 Boliviano (BOB) = 100 centavos

Economy Dependent on minerals for foreign exchange; silver largely exhausted, but replaced by tin (a fifth of world supply); oil and natural-gas pipelines to Argentina and Chile; illegally-produced cocaine.

GDP (2004e) $22·33 bn, per capita $2600

Human Development Index (2002) 0·653

History Part of Inca Empire, conquered by Spanish in 16th-c. Independence after war of liberation in 1825; much territory lost after wars with neighbouring countries; several changes of government and military coups during 1964–82; returned to civilian rule in 1982; resignation and exile of President Lozada (2003); governed by a bicameral Congress and an elected President and a Cabinet.

Head of State/Government

1979–80 Lydia Gueiler Tejada
1980–1 *Military junta* (Luis García Meza)
1981–2 *Military junta* (Celso Torrelio Villa)
1982 Guido Vildoso Calderón
1982–5 Hernán Siles Suazo
1985–9 Victor Paz Estenssoro
1989–93 Jaime Paz Zamora
1993–7 Gonzalo Sánchez de Lozada
1997–2001 Hugo Bánzer Suárez
2001–2 Jorge Quiroga Ramírez
2002–3 Gonzalo Sánchez de Lozada
2003–5 Carlos Mesa
2005 Eduardo Rodriguez *Acting*
2005– Evo Morales

signals from targets on the ground, and generate steering commands to guide the bomb onto a target.

Bombay *Mumbai*

Bombay duck Slender-bodied fish (*Harpadon nehereus*) with large jaws and barb-like teeth; common in the tropical Indian Ocean; length up to 40 cm/16 in; flesh soft and translucent; important food fish. (Family: Harpadontidae.)

Bonaire [bonair] pop (2000e) 11 500; area 288 km²/111 sq mi. Island of the S Netherlands Antilles; rises to 241 m/791 ft in the hilly NW; length 35 km/22 mi; capital, Kralendijk; airport.

Bonaparte, Jérôme [bohnapah(r)t] (1784–1860) Youngest brother of Napoleon, born in Ajaccio, Corsica. He served in the war against Prussia, was made king and ruled Westphalia (1807–14), and fought at Waterloo (1815).

Bonaparte, Joseph [bohnapah(r)t] (1768–1844) King of Naples and Spain, the eldest brother of Napoleon I, born in Corte, Corsica. He was made ruler of the Two Sicilies (1805) and King of Naples (1806). In 1808 he was transferred to the throne of Spain, but after the defeat of the French at Vittoria (1813) he abdicated. After Waterloo he escaped to the USA, but in 1832 returned to Europe.

Bonaparte, Napoleon [bohnapah(r)t] *Napoleon I / III*

Bonaventure or **Bonaventura, St** [bonavencher], known as **Doctor Seraphicus** ('Seraphic Doctor'), originally **Giovanni di Fidanza** (c.1221–74) Franciscan theologian and cardinal, born near Orvieto, Italy. He was canonized in 1482. Feast day 15 July.

Bond, Alan (1938–) Businessman, born in London. He emigrated to Fremantle, Western Australia, in 1951, where the Bond Corporation developed extensive interests in Australian newspapers and television, brewing, oil and gas, and gold mining. In 1996 he was sentenced to three years' imprisonment for failing to declare assets, and received an additional 4-year sentence for fraud in 1997.

Bond, Edward (1934–) Playwright and director, born in London. His early plays, such as *Saved* (1965), were notorious for their use of violence to portray contemporary society. Other plays include a reworking of Shakespeare's play *Lear* (1971), a trilogy *The War Plays* (1985), and *At the Inland Sea* (1996), sub-titled 'a play for young people'.

bond A loan to a company or a government. The loan carries interest payments and is repaid after several years. It can be bought and sold on the stock market, and is a relatively secure investment often held by insurance companies and pension funds.

Bondi [bondiy] A well-known resort beach in the Sydney suburb of Waverley, New South Wales, SE Australia.

Bondi, Sir Hermann (1919–2005) Mathematical physicist and astronomer, born in Vienna. He studied at Cambridge and was appointed professor of mathematics at King's College, London, in 1954. Further posts included director-general of the European Space Research Organisation (1967–71), chief scientific adviser, Ministry of Defence (1971–7), chief scientist, Department of Energy (1977–80), and Master of Churchill College, Cambridge (1983–90). He is best known as one of the originators of the steady-state theory of the universe.

bone The hard tissue component of the vertebrate skeleton. It is composed of an organic element (mainly collagen), 25% of the weight of the fully formed bone, and a mineral matrix (calcium, phosphate, and variable amounts of magnesium, sodium, carbonate, citrate, and fluoride), having a crystalline structure. It basically consists of many cylindrical units, each with a central canal, containing bone-forming cells (*osteoblasts*), blood vessels, and nerve filaments, surrounded by bony tissue. Long bones consist of a shaft (a hollow tube surrounded by compact bone) and the ends (a network of spongy bone). The growth in length occurs in the region between shaft and ends. When this region disappears (between puberty and 25 years) growth ceases, as the shaft has fused with the ends. Examples of bone disorders, diseases, and infections are dislocation, fracture, osteoarthritis, osteoporosis, Paget's disease, and rickets.

bone marrow An accumulation of cells and supporting tissues found within the central cavity of all bones. **Yellow marrow** consists of fat cells, blood vessels, and a minimal framework of reticular cells and fibres. **Red marrow** consists of numerous blood cells of all kinds. The functions of red marrow include the formation of red blood cells (*erythrocytes*), blood platelets, and granulocytes, and the destruction of old (c.120 days), worn-out erythrocytes.

Bonfire Night *Guy Fawkes Night*

bongos A pair of wooden conical or cylindrical drums with single heads of skin or plastic, played with the hands. Originating in Cuba c.1900, they are used throughout Latin America, and frequently elsewhere.

Bonham-Carter, Helena [bonam] (1966–) Actress, born in London. Her gift for playing quintessential English heroines brought her early fame; she made her cinematic debut as Lady Jane Grey in *Lady Jane* (1985). Later film credits include *Hamlet* (1990), *Twelfth Night* (1996), and *Charlie and the Chocolate Factory* (2005).

Bonhoeffer, Dietrich [bonhoefer] (1906–45) Lutheran pastor and theologian, born in Wrocław, Poland (formerly Breslau, Prussia). Deeply involved in the German resistance movement, he was arrested (1943), imprisoned, and hanged. His most influential works were *Ethik* (1949, Ethics) and *Widerstand und Ergebung* (1951, trans Letters and Papers from Prison).

Boniface, St [bonifas], originally **Wynfrith**, known as **the Apostle of Germany** (c.680–c.754) Benedictine missionary, born in Wessex, England. He became a monk in Exeter, and in 718 was commissioned to preach the Gospel to all the tribes of Germany. He was killed at Dokkum by heathens. Feast day 5 June.

Bonington, Sir Chris(tian John Storey) (1934–) Mountaineer, born in London. He was a member of the British team that took part in the first successful conquest of the N face of the Eiger (1962), a member of the expedition that climbed the S face of Annapurna (1970), and leader of the 1975 Everest expedition.

Bonin Islands, Jap **Ogasawara-shoto** area 104 km²/40 sq mi. Group of 27 volcanic islands in the W Pacific Ocean, c.965 km/600 mi S of Tokyo, Japan; first colonized by Europeans and Hawaiians, 1830; annexed by Japanese, 1876; taken by USA, 1953; returned to Japan, 1968.

Bonino, Emma [boneenoh] (1949–) Politician, born near Turin, Italy. She became known as a radical campaigner for law reform in such areas as abortion and divorce. First elected to European Parliament in 1979, she was re-elected in 1984 and 1999. Between 1995 and 1999 she served as European Commissioner with responsibility for the controversial Common Fisheries Policy. She was appointed minister for international trade in Romano Prodi's cabinet in 2006.

Bonn 50°43N 7°06E, pop (2000e) 300 000. Capital city of former West Germany, on R Rhine; early Roman fort on the Rhine; seat of Electors of Cologne (13th–16th-c); part of Prussia, 1815; badly bombed in World War 2; capital status since 1949; airport at Cologne; railway; university (1818); minster (11th–13th-c); birthplace of Beethoven.

Bonnard, Pierre [bonah(r)] (1867–1947) Painter and lithographer, born in Paris. A member of the *Intimist* group, he painted interiors and landscapes, subordinating everything to the subtlest rendering of light and colour effects.

Bonner, Neville Thomas (1922–99) Australian politician, born in Tweed Heads, New South Wales, Australia. President of the One People of Australia League (1967–73), he filled a casual Senate vacancy in 1971, becoming the first Aboriginal member of the Australian parliament. In 1972, standing for the Liberal Party, he was elected as a representative for Queensland.

Bonner, Yelena (1923–) Civil rights campaigner, born in Moscow. She married **Andrei Sakharov** in 1971, and for the next 14 years she and her husband led the Soviet dissident movement. Sakharov was banished to internal exile in Gorky (Nizhni Novgorod) in 1980, and Bonner suffered a similar fate in 1984. The couple were finally released in 1986, and remained prominent campaigners for greater democratization.

Bonney, William H, Jr, known as **Billy the Kid**, originally (?) **Henry McCarty** (1859–81) Bandit, born in New York City. He achieved notoriety for his robberies and murders in the SW states. He was finally tracked down and shot by Sheriff Patrick F Garrett.

Bonnie and Clyde Notorious robbery partners: **Clyde Barrow** (1909–34), born in Telico, TX, and **Bonnie Parker** (1911–34), born in Rowena, TX. The pair met in 1932. With their gang, which included Barrow's brother and wife, they robbed and murdered until they were shot dead at a police road-block in Louisiana.

Bonnie Prince Charlie *Stuart, Charles*

Bono *U2*

bonobo *chimpanzee*

bonsai The technique of growing dwarfed plants in small pots, in which all parts are in proportion. It was first practised in China and Japan.

bontebok [bontebok] An ox-antelope (*Damaliscus dorcas*) native to S Africa; long face; lyre-shaped horns ringed with ridges; dark brown with white face and underparts; two subspecies: **bontebok** (with white rump) and **blesbok** (with brown rump).

bonxie *skua*

bony fish Any of the very large group Osteichthyes, comprising all true bony fishes (18 000 species; 450 families); includes both the ray-finned fishes (Actinopterygii) and the fleshy-finned fishes (Sarcopterygii); endoskeleton made of bone; with air bladder or lungs.

booby A bird related to gannets, native to tropical and subtropical seas; streamlined, with a colourful pointed bill. It catches fish by diving vertically into the water. (Genus: *Sula*, 6 species. Family: Sulidae.)

Booker Prize, also called **Booker McConnell Prize** and (from 2002) the **Man Booker Prize** Britain's most prestigious literary prize, sponsored by the Man Group and Booker McConnell

Ltd, and administered by the National Book League in the UK. Established in 1969 and now worth £50 000, it is awarded annually to the best full-length novel written in English during the preceding 12 months by a citizen of the UK, the Commonwealth, Eire, Pakistan, or South Africa. The (Man) Booker International Prize was inaugurated in 2005. Awarded every two years, it recognizes a living writer of any nationality who has published fiction either originally in English, or generally available in translation in the English language. The winner receives £60 000 and can only win the award once. A further award to honour the work of translators was also introduced.

booklouse A small flattened insect which typically feeds on old books or dried organic material. It can cause extensive damage in libraries.

Book of Changes, Chin **Yijing** or **I-ching** One of Chinese literature's oldest and most treasured works, possibly dating in part from the 11th-c BC, with additions in the 7th-c and 1st-c BC. It comprises 64 hexagrams, each formed by combining two out of eight trigrams of three broken (*yin*) or unbroken (*yang*) lines. The *Yijing* could yield guidance on problems and imminent decisions, since each hexagram supposedly corresponded to typical human issues and life-change patterns, and the underpinning assumption was a unification of nature and humanity in the cosmos.

Book of Common Prayer The official directory of worship or service-book of the Church of England, widely followed in churches of the Anglican Communion. Largely composed by Archbishop Cranmer, it was first introduced in 1549, and revised in 1552, 1604, and finally 1662.

book of hours A prayer book, popular in the Middle Ages, and known in England as a **primer**. It typically contained the Little Office of Our Lady, psalms of penitence, and the Office of the Dead (usually in Latin).

bookworm The common name of various larval and adult insects that damage books by feeding on the paper and binding, and by burrowing activity. It is used particularly of the booklouse and silverfish.

Boole, George (1815–64) Mathematician and logician, born in Lincoln, Lincolnshire. He is primarily known for his *Mathematical Analysis of Logic* (1847) and *Laws of Thought* (1854), where he employed mathematical symbolism to express logical processes (**Boolean algebra**).

boomer *mountain beaver*

boomerang A throwing stick, so shaped as to fly great distances and strike a severe blow; mainly Australian but known elsewhere. Some are made to take a curved path and return, and are used mainly for play or training.

Boone, Daniel (c.1734–1820) Pioneer, born in Berks Co, PA. Twice captured by Indians, he repeatedly repelled (1775–8) Indian attacks on his stockade fort, now Boonesborough.

Boot, Sir Jesse, Baron Trent (1850–1931) Drug manufacturer, born in Nottingham, Nottinghamshire. In 1877 he opened his first chemist's shop in Nottingham, and by mass selling at reduced prices introduced the modern chain store.

Boötes [bohohteez] (Lat 'herdsman') A large N hemisphere constellation. It contains Arcturus, a red giant, the brightest star in the N sky, radius 28 times the Sun. Distance: 11 parsec.

Booth, John Wilkes (1839–65) Assassin, born near Bel Air, MD. In 1865 he entered into a conspiracy to avenge the defeat of the Confederates and shot President Lincoln at Ford's Theatre, Washington, DC (14 Apr). He fled to Virginia, but was tracked down and shot.

Booth, William (1829–1912) Founder and 'general' of the Salvation Army, born in Nottingham, Nottinghamshire. In 1865 he founded the Army (so named in 1878) on military lines with mission work in London's East End. His wife, **Catherine Booth**

(1829–90), also helped launch the movement, and his eldest son succeeded him as general.

Boothe, Clare *Luce, Clare Boothe*

Booths, Feast of *Sukkoth*

bootlegging The illegal manufacture or distribution of alcoholic drink or other highly taxed goods, such as cigarettes. The term is mainly used with reference to the smuggling of alcohol into the USA during the Prohibition era (1920–33).

bop *bebop*

Bophuthatswana [bopootatswahna], locally **Bop** Former independent black homeland in South Africa; comprised seven separate units of land in Cape, Free State, and Transvaal provinces; self-government, 1971; second homeland to receive independence from South Africa (not recognized internationally), 1977; incorporated into North West province in the South African constitution of 1994.

borage A robust annual (*Borago officinalis*), growing to 60 cm/ 24 in, covered in stiff, white bristles, native to C Europe and the Mediterranean region; leaves oval, rough; flowers bright blue, drooping, with five spreading petals and black anthers; cultivated as a herb. (Family: Boraginaceae.)

boranes [bohraynz] Compounds of boron and hydrogen, the simplest being diborane (B_2H_6). They are high-energy compounds, and have been used as rocket fuels.

borax [bohraks] $Na_2B_4O_7.10H_2O$; the hydrated salt of boric acid. It forms insoluble salts with Ca^{2+} and Mg^{2+} ions, and thus is useful as a water softener and cleanser. It is an important ingredient in borosilicate (Pyrex®) glasses.

Bordeaux [baw(r)doh], Lat **Burdigala** 44°50N 0°36W, pop (2000e) 222 000. Inland port in SW France, on R Garonne; cultural and commercial centre for SW; 100 km/60 mi from the Atlantic; held by the English, 1154–1453; temporary seat of government in 1870, 1914, and 1940; centre of wine-growing region; airport; railway; archbishopric; university (1441); cathedral.

Borden, Lizzie (Andrew) (1860–1927) Alleged murderess, born in Fall River, MA. In one of the most sensational murder trials in US history, she was accused of murdering her wealthy father and hated step-mother with an axe in 1892, but was acquitted. The case is immortalized in the rhyme *Lizzie Borden took an axe...*

Border, Allan (Robert) (1955–) Cricketer, born in Sydney, New South Wales, Australia. He made his Test debut against England in 1978–9, and was captain 1984–94. A left-hander, he was Australia's most prolific batsman since Don Bradman, and on his retirement in 1994 held Test records for the most Test appearances (156), and having captained Australia in more Tests than anyone (93). In 1993 he became the highest run-scorer in the history of Test cricket, with 10 123 runs, and he increased this record to a final 11 174 runs. He was Australian of the Year in 1990. His record was broken in 2006 by West Indian Brian Lara. Border was Australian of the Year in 1990.

Border terrier A breed of dog, developed in the Scottish/English border hills to hunt foxes; small and active; solid, flat-ended muzzle; small ears; thick, stiff, wiry coat; usually golden or reddish brown.

bore A nearly vertical wall of water that may be produced as a result of a tide, tsunami, or seiche. Bores usually occur in funnel-shaped estuaries with sloping bottoms. Bottom friction slows the advancing wave front, and water piles up behind to produce a nearly vertical bore face.

boreal forests The dense, coniferous forests of North America, Europe, and Asia. Characteristic tree species include fir, hemlock, spruce, and pine in more open areas.

borecole [baw(r)kohl] *kale*

Borg, Björn (Rune) (1956–) Tennis player, born in Södertälje, Sweden. He became Wimbledon singles champion five times (1976–80), a modern-day record, losing to McEnroe in the 1981 final. He also won the French singles title six times, and was the World Championship Tennis singles champion in 1976. At the 2006 BBC Sports Personality of the Year Awards he was honoured for lifetime achievement.

Borgå *Porvoo*

Borge, Victor [baw(r)guh], originally **Børge Rosenbaum** (1909–2000) Entertainer and pianist, born in Copenhagen. From 1940 he worked in the USA, and from 1956 performed with leading symphony orchestras on worldwide tours. He was best known for his comedy sketches combining music and narrative.

Borges, Jorge Luis [baw(r)khes] (1899–1986) Writer, born in Buenos Aires. From 1941 he wrote mainly short stories, including *Ficciones* (1945, Fictions) and *El Aleph* (1949, The Aleph). In 1980 he won the Cervantes Prize.

Borghese [baw(r)gayzay] A great 13th-c family of ambassadors and jurists of Siena, afterwards (16th-c) at Rome. The Borghese Palace and the Villa Borghese still contain one of the finest collections of paintings in Rome.

Borgia [baw(r)ja] Italian form of **Borja**, an ancient family in the Spanish province of Valencia. **Rodrigo Borgia** (1431–1503) became pope as Alexander VI (1492). Two of his children became especially notorious. **Cesare Borgia** (1476–1507) was a brilliant general and administrator, succeeding his brother (whom he may have murdered) as Captain-General of the Church. **Lucrezia Borgia** (1480–1519) was married three times by her father, for political reasons, finally becoming the wife of Alfonso d'Este, Duke of Ferrara. She has been represented as a person of wantonness, vices, and crimes; but she died enjoying the respect of her subjects, a patroness of learning and of the arts.

Borglum, (John) Gutzon (de la Mothe) [baw(r)gluhm] (1867–1941) Sculptor, born in St Charles, ID. He won renown for works of colossal proportions, such as the Mount Rushmore National Memorial.

Borlaug, Norman (Ernest) [baw(r)log] (1914–) Plant pathologist and geneticist, born in Cresco, IA. He developed 'dwarf' wheats which dramatically increased yields and made possible the 'green revolution', and was awarded the Nobel Peace Prize in 1970.

Bormann, Martin (1900–?45) Nazi politician, born in Halberstadt, Germany. One of Hitler's closest advisers, he became *Reichsminister* (1941) after Hess's flight to Scotland, and was with Hitler to the last. His own fate is uncertain.

Born, Max (1882–1970) Physicist, born in Wrocław, Poland (formerly Breslau, Prussia). He shared the 1954 Nobel Prize for Physics for work in the field of quantum physics.

Borneo [baw(r)neeoh] area 484 330 km²/186 951 sq mi. Island in SE Asia; comprises the Malaysian states of Sarawak and Sabah and the former British protectorate of Brunei (N); remainder comprises the four provinces of Kalimantan, part of Indonesia; formerly divided between the British and the Dutch; mountainous (N), rising to 4094 m/13 432 ft at Mt Kinabalu in Sabah; interior densely forested.

Bornholm [baw(r)nholm] pop (2000e) 46 700; area 588 km²/227 sq mi. Danish island in the Baltic Sea, 40 km/25 mi S of Sweden; length 37 km/23 mi; rises to 162 m/531 ft; taken by Sweden, 1645; returned to Denmark, 1660; administrative capital and chief port, Rønne.

Borobudur [borohbooder] A Buddhist sanctuary built between 750 and 850 in Java, Indonesia. The vast temple originally comprised 10 stepped terraces cut into the sides of a natural mound and culminating in a central shrine (*stupa*).

Borodin, Alexander Porfiryevich [borodeen] (1833–87) Composer and scientist, born in St Petersburg, Russia. His compositions include the unfinished opera *Prince Igor* (which contains the Polovtsian Dances) and three symphonies.

boron [bohron] B, element 5; melting point 2300°C. A hard, non-metallic solid, which as a pure element does not occur free in nature. It forms many compounds in which it is bound to oxygen.

borough In general terms, the second tier of local government in England and Wales, based on charters granted at different times by the monarchy. **Borough councils** were first elected in 1835, when their main function was law and order.

Borromeo, St Charles [boromayoh] (1538–84) Cardinal archbishop of Milan, born in Arona, Italy. He did much to bring the Council of Trent (1545–63) to a successful conclusion, and was renowned for his work for the poor. He was canonized in 1610. Feast day 4 November.

Borromini, Francesco [boromeenee], originally **Francesco Castello** (1599–1667) Baroque architect, born in Bissone, Italy. He spent all his working life in Rome, where his designs include San Carlo alle Quattro Fontane (1637–41).

Borrow, George (Henry) (1803–81) Writer and traveller, born in East Dereham, Norfolk. From 1825 to 1832 he wandered in England, sometimes in gypsy company, as described in *Lavengro* and *The Romany Rye*. As agent of the Bible Society he visited many European countries.

borstal *young offender institution*

borzoi [baw(r)zoy] A breed of dog, developed in Russia; an athletic breed, tall and slender; long thin muzzle; long tail; coat long, straight or curly; also known as **Russian wolfhound**.

Bosch, Hieronymus, originally **Jerome van Aken** (c.1450–1516) Painter, born in 's Hertogenbosch, The Netherlands. Noted for his allegorical pictures displaying macabre devils, freaks, and monsters, his best-known works include 'The Garden of Earthly Delights' (Prado) and 'The Temptation of St Anthony' (Lisbon).

Bosman, Jean-Marc (1964–) Footballer, born in Belgium. A youth international, his name entered football's vocabulary after he challenged the game's contract and transfer rules at the European Court of Justice after his club, FC Liège, refused to allow him a transfer to the French club Dunkerque. Bosman won a judgment in 1995 which made players free agents at the end of contracts and prevented limitations on the number of overseas players at clubs in the European Union.

Bosnia and Herzegovina *p.121*

boson [bohson] A subatomic particle having integer spin; named after Indian physicist **Satyendra Nath Bose** (1894–1974). Force-carrying particles, such as photons, gluons, and gravitons, are all bosons.

Bosporus or **Bosphorus** [bospuhruhs], Turkish **Karadeniz Boğazi** Narrow strait separating European from Asiatic Turkey, and connecting the Black Sea and the Sea of Marmara; length 32 km/20 mi; minimum width 640 m/2100 ft; an area of great strategic importance.

Bosporus Bridge [bosporus] A major steel suspension bridge across the Golden Horn at Istanbul, Turkey; completed in 1973; length of main span 1074 m/3524 ft.

Bosra Ancient Syrian city, S of Damascus; a world heritage site. Originally an Arab fortress, it flourished as capital of the province of Arabia.

boss (zoology) *bison*

Bossuet, Jacques Bénigne [bosway] (1627–1704) Catholic churchman and pulpit orator, born in Dijon, France. As Bishop of Meaux (1681) he took a leading part in the Gallican controversy, asserting the king's independence from the Roman Catholic Church in secular matters.

Boston 42°22N 71°04W, pop (2000e) 589 100. Capital of Massachusetts State, USA; largest city in New England; settled, 1630; capital of the Massachusetts Bay Colony, 1632; city status, 1822; a centre of opposition to British trade restrictions and scene of the Boston Tea Party, 1773; centre of the Unitarian Church movement; airport; railway; noted for its colleges and univer-

Bosnia and Herzegovina

☐ International Airport

[boznia, hertzegovina], Serbo-Croatian **Bosna-Hercegovina**, official name **Republic of Bosnia and Herzegovina**

Local name Bosna i Hercegovina

Timezone GMT +2

Area 51 129 km²/19 736 sq mi

Population total (2002e) 3 964 000

Status Republic

Date of independence 1992

Capital Sarajevo

Languages Bosnian (Bosniak), Serbian, Croatian

Ethnic groups (Pre-civil war) Slav (44%), Serbian (31%), Croatian (17%)

Religions Muslim (Sunni), Serbian Orthodox, Roman Catholic

Physical features Mountainous region in the Balkan peninsula, noted for its stone gorges, lakes, rivers, mineral springs; reaches heights of 1800 m/6000 ft above sea level; principal rivers are Bosna, Una, Drina, Neretva, Sava; in the SW lies the dry, limestone plateau (karst).

Climate Ranges from Mediterranean to mildly continental; sirocco wind brings rain from SW; strong NE wind (bora) affects coastal area in winter.

Currency 1 Convertible Mark (BAM) = 100 convertible pfennigs

Economy Highly industrialized, particularly iron and steel; large cellulose factory at Banja Luka; forestry strong in Bosnia; inflation rate high; war (1992–3) disrupted all economic activity.

GDP (2002e) $7·3 bn, per capita $1900

History Annexed by Austria in 1908; Serbian opposition to the annexation led to the murder of Archduke Francis Ferdinand and World War 1; ceded to Yugoslavia, 1918; declaration of sovereignty, 1991; Bosnian Serbs proclaimed three autonomous regions (Bosanska Krajina, Romanija, and Northern Bosnia), 1991; declaration of independence in 1992 led to ongoing military conflict between formerly integrated communities of Bosnians, Croats, and Serbs; UN peace-keeping forces deployed, and air-exclusion ('no-fly') zone imposed, 1992; conflict continued until ceasefire in Oct 1995; peace accord leaves Bosnia-Herzegovina a single state, comprising the Bosnian-Croat Federation (in the west) and the Bosnian Serb Republic (in the east), with Sarajevo a united city, centrally governed by a national parliament and president, and people allowed freedom of movement; NATO peace implementation force established; Bosnia-Herzegovina accused Serbia, as a nation, of genocide during the Yugoslavian Civil War, a claim rejected by the UN International Court of Justice in 2007.

Head of State
1992–8 Aliya Izetbegovic
Collective Presidency (Chairman)
1996–8 Alija Izetbegovic (Bosniak)
1998–9 Zivko Radisic (Serb)
1999–2000 Ante Jelavic (Croat)
2000 Alija Izetbegovic (Bosniak)
2000–1 Zivko Radisic (Serb)
2001–2 Jozo Krizanovic (Croat)
2001–2 Beriz Belkic (Bosniak)
2002–3 Mirko Sarovic (Serb)
2002– Sulejman Tihic (Bosniak)
2002–5 Dragan Covic (Croat)
2003– Borislav Paravac (Serb)
2005– Ivo Miro Jovic (Croat)

Head of Government
1992 Jure Pelivan
1992–3 Mile Akmadzic
1993–6 Haris Silajdzic
1996–7 Hasan Muratovic
1997–9 Boro Bosic (co-PM)
1997–2000 Haris Silajdzic (co-PM)
1999–2000 Svetozar Mihajlovic (co-PM)
2000 Spasoje Tusevljak
2000–1 Martin Raguz

sities (1869, 1898, 1906); large immigrant population; professional teams, Red Sox (baseball), Celtics (basketball), Bruins (ice hockey).

Boston Massacre (5 Mar 1770) The first bloodshed of the American Revolution. British guards at the Boston Customs House opened fire on a crowd, killing five.

Boston Strangler *Desalvo, Albert*

Boston Tea Party (1773) During the American Revolution, the climax of resistance to British attempts at direct taxation, resulting in the destruction in 1773 of 342 chests of dutied tea by working men disguised as Mohawks.

Boston terrier A breed of dog, developed in the USA by crossing existing terriers and bulldogs; small, deep-chested; large ears, spherical head, thick neck; coat short; white and brown or white and black.

Boswell, James (1740–95) Man of letters and biographer of Dr Johnson, born in Edinburgh. His *Journal of a Tour to the Hebrides* (1785) appeared after Johnson's death. He had, with Johnson's agreement, been storing up material for his great work, the *Life of Johnson*, since 1763, and he completed it in 1791.

Bosworth Field, Battle of (22 Aug 1485) The battle which put Henry Tudor on the English throne after victory over Richard III, who died in the conflict.

botanical garden A collection of living plants usually arranged by geographic or taxonomic principles, and maintained for the purposes of scientific research, education, and recreation. The first European botanical gardens were collections of medicinal plants used for study in monasteries.

botany The study of all aspects of plants, principally their structure, physiology, relationships, and biogeography. Important areas include genetics and plant breeding; vegetative reproduction and tissue culture; ecology and conservation, especially of endangered habitats; and the use of plants as indicators of pollution.

Botany Bay A shallow inlet 8 km/5 mi S of Sydney, New South Wales, Australia; now a residential part of Sydney; Captain Cook made his first landing here in 1770, naming the bay after the number of new plants discovered there.

bot fly A robust, hairy fly, whose larvae are parasites beneath the skin of mammals, feeding on fluids exuding from tissues. (Order: Diptera. Family: Oestridae.)

Botha, Louis [bohta] (1862–1919) South African statesman and soldier, the first prime minister of South Africa (1910–19), born in Greytown, Natal. He suppressed de Wet's rebellion (1914), and conquered German SW Africa (1914–15).

Botha, P(ieter) W(illem) [bohta] (1916–2006) South African statesman, prime minister (1978–84), and president (1984–9), born in Paul Roux, Orange Free State, South Africa. A defender of apartheid, he attempted to introduce constitutional reforms, involving limited power-sharing with non-whites. After suffering a stroke in 1989, he resigned as president later that year. In 1998 he was put on trial, and found guilty of contempt for refusing to appear before the country's Truth and Reconciliation Commission, but his conviction was overturned on appeal.

Botha, Roelof Frederik [bohta], known as **Pik Botha** (1932–) South African politician. He was foreign minister in the governments of P W Botha and F W de Klerk, and served as minister for minerals and energy (1994–6) in Nelson Mandela's first cabinet.

Botham, Ian (Terence) [bohtham] (1955–) Cricketer, born in Heswall, Merseyside. An all-rounder, he played for England in 102 Test matches, scored 5200 runs, took 383 wickets, and held 120 catches. His all-round figures are unsurpassed in Test cricket. He is well known for his walk from John o'Groats to Lands End, and for his aborted attempt to follow Hannibal's trek across the Alps, both ventures in aid of leukaemia research. He retired from first class-cricket in 1993.

Bothnia, Gulf of [bothneea] N arm of Baltic, between Sweden and Finland; length c.650 km/400 mi; width 80–240 km/50–150 mi; maximum depth c.100 m/330 ft; generally freezes over in winter.

Bothwell, James Hepburn, 4th Earl of (c.1535–78) Third husband of Mary, Queen of Scots. He was held responsible for the murder of Mary's second husband, Lord Darnley (1567). He was made Duke of Orkney, then married Mary, but fled to Denmark after Mary's surrender to rebel forces at Carberry Hill.

bo-tree *peepul*

Botswana *p.123*

Botticelli, Sandro [botichelee], originally **Alessandro Filipepi** (1445–1510) Painter of the early Renaissance, born in Florence, Italy. He produced many works on classical subjects – the finest his 'Birth of Venus' and 'Primavera' (Spring) in the Uffizi. He also painted frescoes for the Sistine Chapel at the Vatican.

bottlebrush An evergreen shrub native to Australia; flowers small, crowded in dense cylindrical spikes, stamens red or yellow, far exceeding length of petals. (*Callistemon*, 25 species. Family: Myrtaceae.)

bottle gourd *calabash*

bottom In particle physics, an internal additive quantum number conserved in strong and electromagnetic interactions, but not in weak interactions; symbol B. The notion was postulated in 1977 to explain the properties of upsilon mesons, discovered that year.

botulism [botyoolizm] A serious and often fatal illness resulting from the ingestion of a poisonous toxin produced by the *Clostridium botulinum* bacteria. It is one of the most severe forms of food poisoning, which affects the nervous system, and gives rise to rapidly developing paralysis and respiratory failure. The toxin is destroyed by cooking for 10 minutes at 80°C.

Bouchard, Lucien [booshahr(r)] (1938–) Canadian and Québecois statesman, and prime minister of Québec (1996–2001), born in Saint-Coeur-de-Marie, Lac-Saint-Jean, Québec, Canada. A lawyer, he entered parliament as a Conservative in 1988, then formed the Bloc Québecois. Following the 1993 elections, the Bloc became the official Opposition. An active campaigner for Québecois sovereignty, he became chairman of the Parti Québecois in 1996, resigning in 2001.

Boucher, François [booshay] (1703–70) Painter at the court of Louis XV, born in Paris. He is recognized as the purest exponent of the Rococo style in painting, known for his mythological and pastoral scenes, his female nudes, and his portraits of Madame de Pompadour.

Boudicca [boodika, boodika], also known as **Boadicea** (1st-c) British Celtic warrior-queen, wife of Prasutagus, king of the Iceni, a tribe inhabiting what is now Norfolk and Suffolk. Her army destroyed Camulodunum, Londinium, and Verulamium, putting to death as many as 70 000 Romans and Romano-Britons. Defeated in battle by Suetonius Paulinus, she took poison.

Boudin, (Louis) Eugène [boodĩ] (1824–98) Painter, born in Honfleur, France. A precursor of Impressionism, he is noted for his seascapes.

Bougainville [bohguhnvil] 6°12S 155°15E; pop (2000e) 160 000; area c.10 000 km²/4000 sq mi. Mountainous volcanic island in Papua New Guinea, SW Pacific; length, 190 km/118 mi; width, 50 km/31 mi; rises to 2743 m/9000 ft at Mt Balbi; chief port, Kieta; independence movement and guerrilla fighting from 1988, badly affecting economy; fragile ceasefire, 1998; peace agreement, 2001; autonomous region, 2005, providing for an eventual referendum on independence; copper mining, copra, cocoa, timber.

Bougainville, Louis Antoine, comte de (Count of) [booganveel] (1729–1811) Navigator, born in Paris. He led the first French circumnavigation of the world (1766–9). Several places, including the largest of the Solomon Is, are named after him, as well as the plant *bougainvillea*.

bougainvillea [booguhnvilia] A shrub, tree, or woody climber, native to South America; leaves oval; flowers tubular, in threes, surrounded by three lilac, purple, magenta, red, orange, pink, or white petal-like bracts. (Genus: *Bougainvillea*, 18 species. Family: Nyctaginaceae.)

Boulanger, Nadia [boolãzhay] (1887–1979) Composer, conductor, organist, and influential teacher of music, born in Paris. Several of her pupils became well-known composers.

boulder clay *till*

Boulder Dam *Hoover Dam*

boules [bool] A French ball game similar to bowls, played between two players or teams; also known as *pétanque*. The object is to place the ball nearer to a target ball, or jack, than the opposing player or team.

Boulez, Pierre [boolez] (1925–) Composer and conductor, born in Montbrison, France. Known especially as an interpreter of contemporary music, he became director of the Institut de Recherche et de Co-ordination Acoustique Musique (Ircam) at the Pompidou Centre in Paris (1977–91).

boulle *buhl*

Boulogne Eng [booloyn], Fr [boolon] or **Boulogne-sur-Mer** 50°43N 1°37E, pop (2000e) 46 300. Seaport in NW France; principal commercial harbour and fishing port of France; ferry and hovercraft links with Dover and Folkestone.

Boult, Sir Adrian (Cedric) [bohlt] (1889–1983) Conductor, born in

Botswana

ZAMBIA

AFRICA

ANGOLA

Cuando

Zambezi

Kavango

Kasane

Mabebe
Depression

ZIMBABWE

NAMIBIA

Tsau

Maun

Okavango
Delta

Makgadikgadi
Salt Pans

NGAMALAND

Francistown

Ghanzi

Selebi-Phikwe

B O T S W A N A

KALAHARI
Tropic of Capricorn

Khutse

Palapye

D E S E R T

Mochudi

Tshane

Gaborone ▣

Gemsbok
National
Park

Kanye

Lobatse

Limpopo

Tshabong

S O U T H   A F R I C A

200 km
100 mi

☐ International Airport

[botswahna], official name **Republic of Botswana**
Local name Botswana
Timezone GMT +2
Area 581 730 km²/224 711 sq mi
Population total (2002e) 1 679 000
Status Independent republic within the Commonwealth
Date of independence 1966

Capital Gaborone
Languages English (official), Tswana
Ethnic groups Tswana (75%), Shona (12%), San (Bushmen) (3%), Khoikhoin (Hottentot) (3%), Ndebele (1%)
Religions Mainly local beliefs; Christian (20%)
Physical features Landlocked S African republic; undulating, sand-filled plateau, part of the S African Plateau; mean elevation c.1000 m/3300 ft; N–S plateau divides country into two regions: hilly grasslands (velt) to E, and Okavango Swamps to W; most of the population lives in fertile, hilly E; SE terrain hilly, 1402 m/ 4600 ft; dry scrubland, savannah, and the Kalahari Desert in W; salt lakes in N.
Climate Largely sub-tropical; rainfall in N and E almost totally in summer (Oct–Apr); average annual temperature 26°C (Jan), 13°C (Jul) in Gaborone; average annual rainfall 450 mm/17·7 in.
Currency 1 Pula (BWP) = 100 thebes
Economy Mainly subsistence farming, especially livestock; continual problems of drought and disease; some crops, especially sorghum; main minerals, nickel, diamonds (jointly mined by the government and De Beers Consolidated Mines of South Africa), cobalt; tourism, especially wildlife observation; Central Kalahari Game Reserve (54 388 km²/21 000 sq mi) attracts tourists; principal trading partners, members of South African Customs Union.
GDP (2002e) $13·48 bn, per capita $8500
Human Development Index (2002) 0·572
History San (Bushmen) were the earliest inhabitants, followed by Sotho peoples who migrated to Botswana c.1600; explored by Europeans, 1801; visited by missionaries during 19th-c; London Missionary Society established a mission on the Kuruman R, 1813; Ndebele raided Botswana; Boers arrived, 1835; gold was discovered, 1867; under British protection from 1885; S became a Crown Colony, then part of Cape Colony, 1895; N became the Bechuanaland Protectorate; self-government from 1964; independence and change of name to Botswana, 1966; governed by a legislative National Assembly, President, and Cabinet; House of Chiefs considers chieftaincy matters but has no right of veto.
Head of State/Government
1966–80 Seretse Khama
1980–98 Quett K J Masire
1998– Festus Mogae

Chester, Cheshire. He became musical director of the BBC and conductor of the newly formed BBC Symphony Orchestra. He continued to conduct regularly until 1981.
Bounty Mutiny The most famous of English mutinies (28 Apr 1789). While HMS *Bounty* was returning to England from Tahiti, Fletcher Christian and several of the 44 crew seized control of the ship, and forced the commander, William Bligh, and 18 'loyalists' into a small boat. The 25 mutineers went back to Tahiti, 9 of whom (including Christian) travelled on to Pitcairn I. HMS *Endeavour* brought 14 surviving mutineers from Tahiti to England for trial, 3 of whom were eventually executed.
bourbon [berbn] A dark-coloured American whiskey, a distillate of at least 51% corn. It originated in Bourbon Co, Kentucky.
Bourbons [boorbõ] A French royal house descended from the Capetian St Louis IX (1215–70), associated with absolutist traditions at home and the extension of French influence abroad. Succeeding the last Valois, Henry IV (1589) established the dynasty. Under his son (Louis XIII) and grandson (Louis XIV), the long-standing rivalry between France and the Spanish Habsburgs came to a climax; it was concluded when a descendant, Philip of Anjou, ascended the Spanish throne (Phi-

lip V, reigned 1700–46), thereby founding the Spanish House of Bourbon.
Bourges [boorzh] 47°09N 2°25E, pop (2000e) 82 400. Ancient ducal town in C France; capital of Berry (12th-c); railway; bishopric; cathedral (13th-c).
Bourke-White, Margaret [berk], originally **Margaret White** (1906–71) Photo-journalist, born in New York City. She covered World War 2 for *Life*, and was the first woman photographer to be attached to the US armed forces, producing reports of the siege of Moscow (1941) and the opening of the concentration camps in 1944.
Bourne, Matthew (1960–) Choreographer and dancer, born in London. In 1987 he co-founded the dance company Adventures in Motion Pictures. He gained a reputation for his unconventional interpretations of classical ballets, and aroused controversy with his 1995 production of *Swan Lake* (Olivier Award, Tony) in which the 'swans' were replaced by dozens of bare-chested male dancers with wings. Later works include his staging of *Cinderella* (1997), *My Fair Lady* (2001), *Mary Poppins* (2004, Olivier Award), and *Edward Scissorhands* (2005).
Bournemouth [baw(r)nmuhth] 50°43N 1°54W, pop (2001e)

163 400. Unitary authority (from 1997) and resort town in S England, on Poole Bay; railway; university, 1992; conference centre; football league team, Bournemouth (Cherries).

Boutros-Ghali, Boutros [galee] (1922–) Egyptian diplomat, who took office as the sixth secretary-general of the United Nations (1992–7). The former deputy prime minister of Egypt, he was the first to hold the post from the continent of Africa. He became head of La Francophonie in 1997.

Bouts, Dierick [bowts], also spelled **Dirk**, or **Thierry** (c.1415–75) Painter, born in Haarlem, The Netherlands. He produced austere religious paintings, with rich and gem-like colour. His best-known work is 'The Last Supper' (Louvain).

bouzouki [buhzookee] A plucked string instrument of Greece, used especially in folk music. It has a very long neck, a fretted fingerboard, and three or four courses of metal strings.

Bovidae [bohvidee] A family of ruminant artiodactyl mammals (128 species), including cattle and antelopes; feed by grasping vegetation with their tongue, and cutting it with the lower incisor teeth; adult male (and usually female) with horns.

bovine mastitis The inflammation of mammary tissue in cattle, which results in serious loss of milk production. A wide variety of micro-organisms is involved.

bovine milk fever A metabolic disturbance due to a lack of circulating calcium following calving. There are muscle tremors and a general weakness leading to collapse and partial paralysis (*downer cow syndrome*) and the danger of heart changes. Most cases respond to prompt administration of calcium solutions.

bovine spongiform encephalopathy (BSE) [bohviyn spuhnji-faw(r)m ensefalopathi] A progressive, fatal disease of the central nervous system of cattle (*encephalopathy*: disease affecting the structure of the brain); usually referred to by its abbreviation, but also widely called **mad cow disease**. BSE appeared in the UK in 1985; clinical cases peaked in late 1992–early 1993 and have declined steadily since, following control measures. Affected cattle may show behavioural changes and lack of co-ordination. There is no known treatment or cure. BSE is probably caused by a type of protein organism (a *prion*) resistant to high temperatures and disinfectants. The BSE agent is unique amongst the transmissible spongiform encephalopathies in that it may have crossed the species barrier: it is believed that cattle may have become infected by eating feed containing tissue from scrapie-infected sheep. Fear that BSE may be transmitted to humans by eating the nervous tissue of affected cattle, possibly causing the comparable spongiform encephalopathy, Creutzfeldt-Jakob disease (CJD), has led to control measures being enforced. These have included the banning of certain meat and bone meals of ruminant origin, the destruction of specified bovine offals, and the selective slaughter of cattle. The indications are that the policies adopted will see the early elimination of BSE. By 2007, 25 countries had reported cases.

Bow, Clara [boh] (1905–65) Film actress, born in New York City. Having won a beauty contest, she went to Hollywood in 1921, and became a star of the silent screen, typifying the vivacious flapper of the Jazz Age. She starred in *It* (1927), and became popularly known as 'the It Girl'.

bow (weaponry) *crossbow*; *longbow*

Bowdler, Thomas [bowdler] (1754–1825) Man of letters, born in Ashley, Somerset. He is unhappily immortalized as the editor of *The Family Shakespeare* (1818), in which 'those words and expressions are omitted which cannot with propriety be read aloud in a family'.

bowerbird A bird native to New Guinea and Australia; related to birds of paradise. Males usually attract females by building ornate structures (*bowers*) on the ground. (Family: Ptilonorhynchidae, 18 species.)

Bowie, David [bowee], originally **David Robert Jones** (1947–)

Rock singer and actor, born in London. His career blossomed throughout the 1970s as he adopted a range of extreme stage images to suit a variety of musical styles. His albums include *Hunky Dory* (1971), *Heroes* (1977), *Hours* (1999), and *Reality* (2003). His film career includes roles in *The Man Who Fell to Earth* (1976), and *Basquiat* (1996). He received a Grammy Lifetime Achievement Award in 2006.

Bowie, Jim [booee, bohee], popular name of **James Bowie** (c.1796–1836) US pioneer, born in Logan County, KY. He is mainly remembered for his role in defending the Alamo (1836) during the Texas revolution. He was the inventor of the curved sheath knife named after him.

Bowles, Erskine [bowlz] (1945–) US public official, born in North Carolina. An investment banker (1975–93) and administrator of the US Small Business Administration (1993–4), he joined the White House as deputy chief-of-staff (1994–5), and after returning to his business career (1995–6) became chief-of-staff in Clinton's second administration (1997–2000).

bowling The act of delivering a ball at pins (as opposed to a target, as in bowls); a popular indoor sport and pastime, with an ancient history. The game of **ninepins** was taken to the USA by Dutch and German immigrants in the latter part of the 19th-c. When the sport was outlawed, a 10th pin was added as a way around the legislation. **Ten-pin bowling** is now the most popular form.

bowls An indoor and outdoor game played as singles, pairs, triples, or fours. Glasgow solicitor William Mitchell (1803–84) drew up the rules for modern bowls in 1848. There are two main variations: **lawn bowls** (also known as **flat green bowls**) is played on a flat, level rink, whereas **crown green bowls** is played on an uneven green raised at the centre. In both varieties the object is to deliver your bowl nearer to the *jack* (a smaller target ball) than your opponent(s). Bowls have a bias which causes them to curve, imparted by flattening one side of the bowl.

box An evergreen shrub or small tree (*Buxus sempervirens*) growing to 10 m/30 ft, often less, native to Europe and N Africa; flowers green, lacking petals; fruit a woody capsule. (Family: Buxaceae.)

box camera The simplest form of camera for amateur photography: a rectangular box containing holders for paper-backed roll film advanced by an external winder, a fixed-focus lens, and a shutter for instantaneous exposure. Early examples are the original Kodak camera of 1888 and the Box Brownie of 1900 which popularized snapshot photography.

boxer A breed of dog; large muscular body; rounded compact head; ears soft, pendulous; muzzle short and broad, with pronounced jowls and prominent lower jaw; developed from the bulldog in Germany (late 19th-c).

Boxer Rising An anti-foreign movement in China (1898–1900). Its name derives from the secret society to which the rebels belonged, the 'Righteous and Harmonious Fists', whose members adopted boxing and other rituals, convinced by their mixture of magical beliefs that foreign weapons could not harm them. It originated in N China, as a reaction to economic distress and Western territorial seizures. Many foreigners were killed, and the foreign legations in Tianjin and Beijing were besieged. The rising was eventually suppressed, and The Boxer Protocol (1901) imposed massive indemnities on China.

boxing Fighting with fists, a sport recorded from the earliest times. The first rules were drawn up by John Broughton in 1743. Boxing was with bare knuckles, and each round lasted until one fighter was knocked down. The *Queensberry Rules*, as drawn up in 1867 by the 8th Marquess of Queensberry, laid the foundation of the modern sport. Professional championship bouts comprise twelve 3-min rounds. Amateur contests are over three rounds, and all fighters must wear a vest. All fights last until one fighter is knocked out or retires, the referee halts the fight, a fighter is disqualified, or the designated number of rounds is reached. If the fight goes the distance, judges then mark the fighters according to winning punches, etc. It is possible to have a draw. Four bodies recognize world champions; the *World Boxing Council (WBC)*, founded in 1963; the *World Boxing Association (WBA)*, founded in 1927 as the National Boxing Association; the *International Boxing Federation (IBF)*, founded in 1983; and the *World Boxing Organization (WBO)*, founded in 1988. In 2004 there were 17 different weight divisions, ranging from straw-weight to heavyweight. (*see panel*)

Boxing Day In the UK and the Commonwealth, the day after Christmas Day. It is so called because traditionally on that day gifts from boxes placed in church were distributed to the poor, and apprentices took a box round their masters' customers in the hope of getting presents of money from them.

boyars Members of the highest stratum of the Russian feudal aristocracy from the 10th-c to the early 18th-c. The *Boyarskaya Duma* ('Boyars' Council') was a major legislative and deliberative assembly under the mediaeval tsars.

Boycott, Charles Cunningham (1832–97) British soldier, born in Burgh St Peter, Norfolk. A land agent in Co Mayo, Ireland, when he ruthlessly evicted tenants in 1880, Parnell suggested they avoid any form of contact or communication with him. His name thus became the source of the verb *to boycott*.

Boycott, Geoffrey (1940–) Cricketer and broadcaster, born in Fitzwilliam, Yorkshire. In 1981 he overtook Gary Sobers's world record of 8032 Test runs, and in 108 Tests for England scored 8114 runs (average 47·72). Captain of Yorkshire 1971–8, he was a brilliant but often controversial batsman. Since retiring from first-class cricket in 1986, he has become known as a cricket commentator.

Boyd, Michael (1955–) Stage director, born in Belfast. Founding artistic director of the Tron Theatre, Glasgow (1985–9), he became an associate director of the Royal Shakespeare Company (RSC) in 1996, and won an Olivier Award for best director for the *Henry VI* trilogy (2000). In 2003 he succeeded Adrian Noble as artistic director of the RSC.

Boyer, Charles [boyay] (1899–1978) Actor, born in Figeac, France. A star of the French stage and cinema, he settled in Hollywood in 1934, and was known as the screen's 'greatest lover' from such romantic roles as *Mayerling* (1936) and *Algiers* (1938). His later appearances included *Barefoot in the Park* (1967) and *Stavisky* (1974).

Boyer, Paul D (1918–) Chemist, born in Provo, UT. He graduated from the University of Wisconsin in 1943, and taught at the University of California, Los Angeles. He shared the 1997 Nobel Prize for Chemistry for his contribution towards the elucidation of the enzymatic mechanism underlying the synthesis of adenosine triphosphate.

Boyer, Sir Richard (James Fildes) [boyer] (1891–1961) Broadcasting administrator, born in Taree, New South Wales, Australia. He became chairman of the Australian Broadcasting Company in 1945. The ABC Lectures were renamed the **Boyer Lectures** in his honour after his death.

Boy George, popular name of **George O'Dowd** (1961–) Pop singer and songwriter, born in Eltham, Kent. In 1981 he formed his own band, Culture Club, and had a string of hit records including a number 1 single, 'Karma Chameleon' (1983). A flamboyant cross-dresser and admitted drug user, controversy dogged his career. He underwent successful treatment for drug dependence, re-emerging as a solo artist with the hit single 'Everything I Own' (1987). During the 1990s he forged a new career as a DJ on the club scene. In 2002, his musical *Taboo*, charting his own life-story in the world of pop music, opened in London.

Boylan, Clare (1948–2006) Writer, born in Dublin. She won the Dublin Journalist of the Year Award in 1983. Her first novel, *Holy Pictures*, appeared that year, as did a book of short stories, *A Nail in the Head*. Later books include *Black Baby* (1998), *Beloved Stranger* (1999), and *Emma Brown* (2003). Non-fiction works include *The Agony and the Ego* (1993) and *The Literary Companion to Cats* (1994).

Boyle, Danny, popular name of **Daniel Boyle** (1956–) Director, born in Bury, Greater Manchester. He was artistic director of London's Royal Court Theatre Upstairs (1982–7), an experimental venue for new writing, then moved into television directing, where he made his name with *Mr Wroe's Virgins*, a period drama. His directorial film debut was *Shallow Grave* (1994), which won a BAFTA award for Best British Film, and he achieved critical and box-office success in 1996 with *Trainspotting*. Later films include *A Life Less Ordinary* (1997) and *The Beach* (2000).

Boyle, Robert (1627–91) Physicist and chemist, born at Lismore Castle, Co Waterford. In 1661 he published his *Sceptical Chymist*, in which he criticized the current theories of matter, and in 1662 arrived at **Boyle's law**, which states that the pressure and volume of gas are inversely proportional.

Boyle, T(homas) C(oraghessan) (1948–) Novelist and storyteller, born in Peekshill, NY. He joined the Iowa Writers' Workshop in 1972, and published in 1979 his first collection of short stories, *Descent of Man* (St Lawrence Award for Short Fiction). Later books include *World's End* (1988, PEN/Faulkner Award), *The Road to Wellville* (1993), and *Friend of the Earth* (2000).

Boyne, Battle of the (1690) A battle fought near the River Boyne, Drogheda, Ireland, between Protestant forces under William of Orange, and smaller Catholic forces led by the exiled James II. William's decisive victory marked a critical stage in the English reconquest of Ireland.

Boy Scouts *scouting*

Brabham, Jack [brabuhm], popular name of **Sir John Arthur Brabham** (1926–) Motor-racing driver and constructor, born in Sydney, New South Wales, Australia. Australia's first world champion, he won in 1959 and 1960 in a Cooper, and in 1966 took both the driver and constructor titles in a Brabham. He won the constructor's title again in 1967.

Brachiopoda [brakiopoda] *lamp shell*

bracken A perennial fern (*Pteridium aquilinum*) with far-creeping rhizomes; fronds solitary, up to 2–4 m/6½–13 ft; tri-pinnate; common on acid soils, especially in woods and heaths. It is poisonous, and not grazed by animals such as sheep and rabbits. (Family: Polypodiaceae.)

bract A modified leaf immediately below a flower or inflorescence. It is usually green, but may be brightly coloured and petal-like.

Bracton, Henry de (?–1268) English jurist. His *De legibus et consuetudinibus Angliae* (On the Laws and Customs of England) is the earliest attempt at a systematic treatment of English law.

Bradbury, Sir Malcolm (Stanley) (1932–2000) Writer and critic, born in Sheffield, South Yorkshire. The travels and travails of an academic have provided material for several of his novels, such as *The History Man* (1975), *The Atlas of Literature* (1996), and *To The Hermitage* (2000).

Bradbury, Ray(mond Douglas) (1920–) Science-fiction writer, born in Waukegan, IL. His collections of short stories include *The Martian Chronicles* (1950) and *The Golden Apples of the Sun* (1953). He is best known for film adaptations of two of his novels, *The Illustrated Man* (1951) and *Fahrenheit 451* (1953). Later novels include *Ahmed and the Oblivion Machines* (1998) and *Let's All Kill Constance* (2002).

Bradford 53°48N 1°45W, urban area pop (2001e) 467 700. Town in West Yorkshire, N England; 19th-c development was based on the wool textile industry; railway; university (1966); cathedral (15th-c); football league team, Bradford City (Bantams); scene of major disaster (1985) when wooden stand of Bradford City Football Club caught fire, killing 56.

Bradford, Barbara Taylor (1933–) Journalist and novelist, born in Leeds. She worked for several newspapers and magazines, both in the UK and USA, before gaining success with her first novel, *A Woman of Substance* (1980). Later books include *The Women in his Life* (1990), *Her Own Rules* (1996), *Where You Belong* (2000), and *The Ravenscar Dynasty* (2006).

Bradford, William (1590–1657) Colonist and religious leader, born in Austerfield, South Yorkshire. One of the moving spirits in the Pilgrim Fathers' expedition, he sailed on the *Mayflower*, and in 1621 became governor of Plymouth Colony.

Bradlaugh, Charles [bradlaw] (1833–91) Free-thinking social reformer, born in London. In 1880 he became an MP, and claimed the right as an unbeliever to make an affirmation of allegiance instead of taking the parliamentary oath, but the House refused to allow this. He was re-elected on three occasions, and was finally admitted (1886).

Bradlee, Benjamin (Crowninshield) (1921–) Journalist and writer, born in Boston, MA. In 1965 he became managing editor of the *Washington Post*, and encouraged the investigative journalism which reached its high point in the Watergate scandal.

Bradley, Omar N(elson) (1893–1981) US general, born in Clark, MO. In World War 2, he played a prominent part in Tunisia and Sicily, and in 1944 led the US invading armies through France and Germany.

Bradman, Sir Don(ald George) (1908–2001) Cricketer, born in Cootamundra, New South Wales, Australia. He played for Australia 1928–48, and was captain from 1936. He set up many batting records, including a highest score (452 not out in 1930) which he held until 1994, and his Test batting average was 99·94 runs per innings. He later became chairman of the Australian Cricket Board (1960–3, 1969–72).

Bradstreet, Anne, *née* **Dudley** (1612–72) Poet, born in Northampton, Northamptonshire. She emigrated with her husband to Massachusetts in 1630, and is acknowledged as the first poet of note in British America.

Brady, Ian (1938–) Convicted murderer, born in Glasgow. In a case which horrified the public, it was revealed that Brady, with his lover **Myra Hindley** (1942–2002), lured young children into their home in Manchester and subjected them to torture before killing them. The lovers were described as the 'Moors Murderers' because they buried most of their victims on Saddleworth Moor in the Pennines.

Brady Bill A gun control measure in the USA mandating a five-day waiting period and background checks before a handgun can be purchased, enacted in 1993. The law is named after James Brady, Ronald Reagan's press secretary, who was severely wounded in the assassination attempt on the president in 1981.

Braemar [braymah(r)] 57°01N 3°24W. Village in Aberdeenshire council, Scotland, 10 km/6 mi W of Balmoral Castle; Highland games (Aug).

Braga [brahga], ancient **Bracara Augusta** 41°32N 8°26W, pop (2000e) 90 000. Fourth largest city in Portugal, former capital of the old region of Entre Minho and Douro; seat of the Primate of Portugal; university; cathedral (11th-c).

Braganza [braganza], Port **Bragança** [bragansa], ancient **Juliobriga** 41°47N 6°46W, pop (2000e) 16 400. City in NE Portugal; original seat of the House of Braganza, rulers of Portugal, 1640–1910; castle (1187); bishopric; cathedral.

Bragg, Billy, popular name of **Steven William Bragg** (1957–) Rock singer, musician, and songwriter, born in Barking, Essex. A committed left-wing political performer, he began performing in the 1970s with the punk group Riff Raff, then briefly joined the British army. Starting a solo career, he became known as the leading figure of the anti-folk movement of the 1980s. His albums include *Brewing Up With Billy Bragg* (1984), *Mermaid Avenue* (1998, 2000), and *Must I Paint You a Picture? The Essential Billy Bragg* (2003).

Bragg (of Wigton), Melvyn Bragg, Baron (1939–) Novelist and broadcaster, born in Wigton, Cumbria. His novels include *Love and Glory* (1983), *A Time to Dance* (1990), *A Son of War* (2001), and *Crossing the Lines* (2003). He has been presenter and editor of ITV's *The South Bank Show* since 1978, was presenter of BBC Radio 4's *Start the Week* (1988–98), and currently presents *In Our Time*. He became chairman of Border Television in 1990, and was reappointed as controller of arts and features at London Weekend Television in 2000.

Brahe, Tycho [brahhoe, tiykoh] (1546–1601) Astronomer, born in Knudstrup, Sweden (then under the Danish crown). In 1573 he discovered serious errors in the astronomical tables, and commenced work to rectify this by observing the stars and planets with unprecedented positional accuracy.

Brahma [brahma] The personified creator god of Hinduism. The deities Vishnu, Shiva, and Brahma form the *Trimurti* of classical Indian thought. As Vishnu and Shiva represent opposite forces, Brahma represents the balance between them.

Brahman cattle *zebu*

Brahmanism [brahmanizm] An early religion of India (though not the earliest), to which, historically, Indians have looked as the source of their religious traditions. It came to dominance during the Vedic Period (c.1200–500 BC) and was a religion of ritual and sacrifice.

Brahmaputra, River [bramapootra], Chin **Yalu Zangbu**, Bangla **Jamuna** River in SW China and India, rising in the Chinese Himalayas; flows E then S into Assam, then S into Bangladesh, joining the R Ganges before entering the Bay of Bengal through a vast delta; length c.2900 km/1800 mi.

Brahmins [brahminz] The highest of the four Hindu social classes. A priestly class, the Brahmins dominated Indian society for many centuries. Many of their descendants have now taken up secular occupations.

Brahms, Johannes (1833–97) Composer, born in Hamburg, Germany. He earned his living as a pianist until 1853, when he was able to concentrate on composition, settling in Vienna. His main works include four symphonies, two piano concertos, a violin concerto, a large amount of chamber and piano music, and many songs. His greatest choral work is the *German Requiem* (first performed complete in 1869).

braille [brayl] A communication system designed to enable blind people to have access to written language; devised in 1829 by French teacher Louis Braille (1809–52). It consists of a sequence of cells, each of which contains a 3 × 2 matrix of embossed dots, whose patterns can be sensed through the fingers. Computer-assisted systems are now available which can turn written text into braille.

brain *see panel*

brain death The cessation of brain activity, in particular in the parts of the brain stem concerned with respiration and other vital functions. It must be certified by two doctors who can demonstrate the absence of electrical impulses from the brain surface (a flat EEG) and the failure of brainstem reflexes, including the reaction of pupils to light and oscillation (*nystagmus*) in response to the introduction of warm and cold water into the external ear canal. The diagnosis is usually made on an individual in a coma whose respiration is being artificially sustained and whose heart has not ceased to beat.

Braine, John (Gerard) (1922–86) Writer, born in Bradford, West Yorkshire. The success of his first book, *Room at the Top* (1957), enabled him to embark on a career as a novelist, identified with the 'Angry Young Men' of the 1950s. His novels deal mostly with the north of England and northerners, and include *The Vodi* (1959), *Life at the Top* (1962), and *One and Last Love* (1981).

brain stem That part of the nervous system between the spinal cord and the forebrain, consisting of a thick bundle of transversely running fibres called the *pons*, with the *midbrain* above it and the *medulla oblongata* below. The cardiac, respiratory, vasomotor, and other 'vital' physiological centres are located in the medulla.

brake A device used to apply a force to an object to retard its motion. The most common method is to bring the moving surface into contact with a fixed surface, thereby generating friction which opposes the direction of movement. The two types of brake most commonly used on motor cars are **drum brakes** and **disc brakes**.

Bramah, Joseph [brama] (1748–1814) Inventor, born in Stainborough, South Yorkshire. His inventions include a hydraulic press, a machine for numbering banknotes, and a safety lock which remained pickproof for over 60 years.

Bramante, Donato [bramantay], originally **Donato di Pascuccio d'Antonio** (c.1444–1514) Architect and painter, born near Urbino, Italy. He drew up plans for the renovation of the Vatican and St Peter's (1505–6), and much influenced the development of Renaissance architecture in Italy.

bramble *blackberry*

brambling A finch native to the N Old World (*Fringilla montifringilla*); migrates to the Mediterranean and N Africa for winter. (Family: Fringillidae.)

bran The protective coat surrounding a cereal seed which, because of its high fibre content, is becoming increasingly common as a component of human foods. It comprises about 12% of the seed.

Branagh, Kenneth (Charles) [brana] (1960–) Actor and director, born in Belfast. He joined the Royal Shakespeare Company in 1984, co-founded the Renaissance Theatre Company (1987), and in 1998 co-founded the Shakespeare Film Company. He has directed and appeared in several films, such as *Henry V* (1989), *Much Ado About Nothing* (1993), *Hamlet* (1997), *Love's*

brain

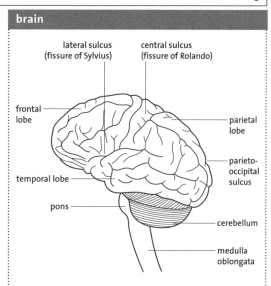

lateral sulcus (fissure of Sylvius)

central sulcus (fissure of Rolando)

frontal lobe

parietal lobe

parieto-occipital sulcus

temporal lobe

pons

cerebellum

medulla oblongata

The part of the central nervous system of bilaterally symmetrical animals which co-ordinates and controls many bodily activities to an extent that depends upon the species. In humans, in addition to the control of movement, sensory input, and a wide range of physiological processes, it acts as the organ of thought, with several areas being specialized for specific intellectual functions (eg language, calculation). It occupies the cranial cavity, and can be divided into the **forebrain** (the *cerebral hemispheres* and *diencephalon*), **midbrain**, and **hindbrain** (the *cerebellum*, *pons*, and *medulla oblongata*). It is continuous with the spinal cord at the medulla oblongata (part of the **brain stem**). The cerebral hemispheres and brain stem contain cavities (the *ventricles*) which are continuous with the central canal of the spinal cord, and within which cerebrospinal fluid is produced. The brain also gives rise to the 12 pairs of cranial nerves. Examples of brain disorders, diseases, and infections are cerebral palsy, dementia, encephalitis, epilepsy, hydrocephalus, and meningitis.

Labour's Lost (2000), and *The Magic Flute* (2006). He was married to actress Emma Thompson (1989–96).

Branchiopoda [brangkiopoda] A diverse class of aquatic crustaceans found mostly in inland waters; characterized by leaf-like trunk limbs that act as food-gathering apparatus and as gills; contains c.820 living species.

Brancusi, Constantin [brankoozee] (1876–1957) Sculptor, born in Pestisani, Romania. His 'Sleeping Muse' (1910, Muzeul de Artă, Bucharest) shows Rodin's influence, and is the first of many characteristic, highly polished, egg-shaped carvings.

Brandeis, Louis (Dembitz) [brandiys] (1856–1941) Jurist, born in Louisville, KY. His opinions on issues of governmental power and legal procedure rank him as a major legal theoretician, and he became the first Jewish member of the Supreme Court. Brandeis University in Waltham, MA, was named after him.

Brandenburg or **Brandenburg an der Havel** [brandnberg] 52°25N 12°34E, pop (2000e) 99 200. Industrial city in EC Germany, former centre of the Prussian province of Brandenburg; much rebuilding after severe damage in World War 2; railway.

Brandenburg Gate An arch designed by Carl Langhans (1733–1808) and erected in Berlin in 1788–91. The monument, which was badly damaged during World War 2, was restored in 1958.

Brando, Marlon (1924–2004) Film and stage actor, born in Omaha, NE. He was a product of the New York Actors' Studio, with its emphasis on 'method' acting. His films include *The Godfather* (1972), *Apocalypse Now* (1977), *Don Juan de Marco* (1995), and *The Score* (2001). His most outstanding role was in *On the Waterfront* (1954), for which he won his first Oscar, but he refused to accept a second, for *The Godfather*, in protest against the persecution of the Indians.

Brandt, Bill [brant], popular name of **William Brandt** (1904–83) Photographer, born in Hamburg. He portrayed life in London during the Blitz, and later made a striking series on the nude, in which his essays in pure form, as published in *Perspective of Nudes* (1961) and *Shadows of Light* (1966), approached the surreal.

Brandt, Willy [brant], originally **Karl Herbert Frahm** (1913–92) West German statesman and Chancellor (1969–74), born in Lübeck, Germany. In 1966 he led the Social Democratic Party into a coalition government with the Christian Democrats, and in 1969 was elected Chancellor in a coalition government with the Free Democrats. He was awarded the 1971 Nobel Peace Prize. He later chaired a commission on the world economy (the **Brandt Commission Report**, 1980).

brandy A spirit distilled from fruit fermentation, usually grapes, but also from stone fruits such as cherries. Cognac is produced in the Charente basin, France, from white grapes aged for a minimum of 2 years in barrels of Limousin oak. Armagnac is produced to the S of this area, and matured in 'black' oak. Calvados is made from cider in Normandy.

Brandywine, Battle of the (11 Sep 1777) A battle fought during the War of Independence, taking its name from the Brandywine Creek near Philadelphia. British forces under Howe defeated Washington's troops.

Branson, Sir Richard (Charles Nicholas) (1950–) Businessman, born in Sharnley Green, Surrey. He opened his first shop in London in 1971, under the name Virgin. This was followed by a series of highly successful business enterprises, including a recording company, various retailing operations, the travel company Voyager Group (1980), the airline Virgin Atlantic (1984), Virgin Radio (1993), Virgin Direct (1995), V2 Music (1996), and Virgin Trains (1996). He is also known for his sporting achievements, notably the record-breaking Atlantic crossing in *Virgin Atlantic Challenger II* in 1986, and the first crossing by hot-air balloon of the Atlantic (1987) and Pacific (1991).

Braque, Georges [brak] (1882–1963) Painter, born in Argenteuil, France. He was one of the founders of classical Cubism, and worked with Picasso from 1908 to 1914. After World War 1 he developed a personal nongeometric, semi-abstract style.

Brasília [brazilia] 15°45S 47°57W, pop (2000e) 2 080 000. Capital of Brazil in WC Brazil; construction began in 1956; capital moved from Rio de Janeiro in 1960; principal architect Oscar Niemeyer (1907–); laid out in the shape of a bent bow and arrow; airport; university (1961); cathedral; light industry; famous for its modern sculpture; designated a world heritage site.

Braşov [brashov], formerly **Kronstadt** (to 1918), **Stalin** (1950–60) 45°39N 25°35E, pop (2000e) 319 000. City in C Romania; founded, 13th-c; ceded by Hungary after World War 1; railway junction; university (1971); summer resort and winter sports centre.

brass An alloy composed of copper and zinc; yellowish, malleable, and ductile. Its properties and applications may be altered by varying the proportions of copper and zinc. It is the most widely used non-ferrous alloy.

brassica A member of a genus of plants containing numerous economically important vegetables, including turnip and mustard, but often in a gardening sense referring more specifically to cabbages, cauliflower, broccoli, and Brussels sprouts, all derived from the wild cabbage, *Brassica oleracea*. (Genus: *Brassica*, 30 species. Family: Cruciferae.)

brass instrument A musical instrument made of brass or other metal, in which air is made to vibrate by means of the player's lips and breath, usually through a narrow mouthpiece. In simple instruments, such as the bugle, the notes available are restricted to the lower end of a single harmonic series; in others, valves or slides enable the fundamental note to be altered, and consequently a greater number of pitches to be obtained.

Bratby, John (1928–92) Artist and writer, born in London. One of the leading representatives of the English Realist School, in the mid-1950s, he was associated with the 'kitchen sink' school, as typified in 'Baby in Pram' (Liverpool).

Bratislava [bratislahva], Ger **Pressburg**, Hung **Pozsony**, ancient **Posonium** 48°10N 17°08E, pop (2000e) 450 000. River port and capital of the Slovak Republic; on R Danube; stronghold of Great Moravian Empire, 9th-c; capital of Hungary, 1541–1784; centre of emergent Slovak national revival; incorporated into Czechoslovakia in 1918; airport; railway; university (1919); technical university (1938); cathedral (13th-c).

Brattain, Walter H(ouser) (1902–87) US physicist, born in Amoy, China. In 1929 he joined Bell Telephone Laboratories, where he worked on the surface properties of semiconductors, and also helped to devise the point contact transistor, for which he shared the Nobel Prize for Physics in 1956.

Braun, Eva [brown] (1910–45) The mistress of Adolf Hitler, born in Munich. She met Hitler in the early 1930s, and is said to have married him before they committed suicide together during the fall of Berlin.

Braun, Wernher von [brown] (1912–77) Rocket pioneer, born in Wyrzysk, Poland (formerly Wirsitz, Germany). In 1936 he directed a rocket research station at Peenemünde, where he perfected and launched the V-2 rockets against Britain (Sep 1944). After the war, he became a naturalized American, and was chiefly responsible for the launching of the first American artificial Earth satellite (1958).

Brautigan, Richard (Gary) [brawtigan] (1933–84) Writer, born in Tacoma, WA. He became a cult figure as one of the San Francisco poets and an embodiment of the 1960s counterculture, writing surrealistically random novels and poems about alienation. His books include the novel, *Trout Fishing in America* (1967), and the collected poems, *The Pill Versus the Springhill Mine Disaster* (1968). Disheartened by public indifference to his later works, he committed suicide.

Brazil *p.129*

Brazil nut An evergreen tree (*Bertholletia excelsa*) growing to 30 m/100 ft, native to the jungles of Brazil; flowers white; fruit a woody or rounded capsule containing 3-sided seeds familiarly called by the same name. (Family: Lecythidaceae.)

brazing The joining of two pieces of metal (the same or different) by heating, then filling in the junction with a metal of lower melting point than those being joined. A flux is generally necessary.

Brazzaville [brazavil] 4°14S 15°14E, pop (2000e) 1 098 000. River-port capital of the Congo, W Africa, on right bank of R Congo; founded, 1880; capital of French Equatorial Africa, 1910; headquarters of Free French forces in World War 2; capital of Congo, 1960; airport; railway terminus from coast; university (1972); cathedral.

bread A widely used staple food made by baking a mixture of flour and water; the flour used is most commonly wheat, which may be mixed with flour from oatmeal, rye, or barley. The mix

Brazil

☐ International Airport   ∴ World heritage site

Port **Brasil**, official name **The Federative Republic of Brazil**, Port **República Federativa do Brasil**

Local name Brasil

Timezone GMT -2 (Atlantic Islands); GMT -3 (E); GMT -4 (mid-W); GMT -5 (extreme W)

Area 8 511 965 km²/3 285 618 sq mi

Population total (2002e) 174 619 000

Status Republic

Date of independence 1822

Capital Brasília

Language Portuguese (official)

Ethnic groups White (53%), mixed (34%), black (6%)

Religions Roman Catholic (89%), Protestant, Spiritualist

Physical features Located in E and C South America; low-lying Amazon basin in the N; where forest canopy cleared, soils susceptible to erosion; Brazilian plateau in the C and S, average height 600–900 m/2000–3000 ft; Guiana Highlands (S) contain Brazil's highest peak, Pico da Neblina, 3014 m/9888 ft; eight river systems, notably Amazon (N), Sao Francisco (C), Paraguay, Paraná, and Uruguay (S); 30% of population concentrated on a thin coastal strip on the Atlantic, c.100 km/325 mi wide.

Climate Almost entirely tropical, equator passing through the N region, and Tropic of Capricorn through the SE; Amazon basin,

annual rainfall 1500–2000 mm/60–80 in; no dry season; average midday temperatures 27–32°C; dry region in the NE, susceptible to long droughts; hot, tropical climate on narrow coastal strip, with rainfall varying greatly N–S; S states have a seasonal temperate climate.

Currency 1 Cruzeiro Real (BRL) = 100 centavos

Economy One of the world's largest farming countries, agriculture employing 35% of population; world's largest exporter of coffee, second largest exporter of cocoa and soya beans. Iron-ore reserves (possibly world's largest). Timber reserves, the third largest in the world; but continuing destruction of the Amazon rainforest is causing much concern; road network being extended through the Amazon rainforest.

GDP (2002e) $1·376 tn, per capita $7600

Human Development Index (2002) 0·757

History Claimed for the Portuguese by Pedro Alvares Cabral, 1500, first settlement at Salvador da Bahia; King of Portugal moved seat of government to Brazil, 1808; his son, Dom Pedro, declared himself emperor, 1818; independence established, 1822; Dom Pedro forced to abdicate in 1831 and succeeded by his 14-year-old son, Dom Pedro II, 1840; abolition of slavery in 1888, persuaded former slave-owners in declining sugar-plantation areas to join Republican opposition to the king, who was overthrown in the coup of 1889; ruled by dictator, Getúlio Vargas, 1930–45; Vargas deposed by military, and liberal republic restored, 1946; returned to office, 1950, but committed suicide, 1954; capital moved from Rio de Janeiro to Brasília, 1960; another coup in 1964 led to a military-backed presidential regime; President da Costa e Silva resigned and military junta took control, 1969; new elections, 1985; new constitution approved, transferring power from the President to the Congress, 1988; bicameral National Congress.

Head of State/Government

1945–51 Eurico Gaspar Dutra
1951–4 Getúlio Dornelles Vargas
1954–5 João Café Filho
1955 Carlos Coimbra da Luz
1955–6 Nereu de Oliveira Ramos
1956–61 Juscelino Kubitschek de Oliveira
1961 Janio da Silva Quadros
1961–3 João Belchior Marques Goulart
1963 Pascoal Ranieri Mazilli
1963–4 João Belchior Marques Goulart
1964 Pascoal Ranieri Mazilli
1964–7 Humberto de Alencar Castelo Branco
1967–9 Artur da Costa e Silva
1969–74 Emílio Garrastazu Médici
1974–9 Ernesto Geisel
1979–85 João Baptista de Oliveira Figueiredo
1985–90 José Sarney
1990–2 Fernando Collor de Mello
1992–5 Itamar Franco
1995–2002 Fernando Henrique Cardoso
2002– Luiz Inacio Lula da Silva

results in a dough which may be kneaded, a process that stretches and aligns the protein molecules of the wheat. The product is then either immediately baked to give **unleavened bread**, or allowed to rise, through the production of carbon dioxide, to give **leavened bread**. The carbon dioxide can be produced either chemically or by using yeast.

breadfruit An evergreen tree (*Artocarpus altilis*) growing to 12–18 m/40–60 ft, probably native to Malaysia; rounded, multiple fruits, 10–20 cm/4–8 in diameter, and green to brownish when ripe, filled with a white, fibrous pulp. (Family: Moraceae.)

break dancing *street dance*

breaking stress *tensile strength*

Breakspear, Nicholas *Adrian IV*

Bream, Julian (Alexander) [breem] (1933–) Guitarist and lutenist, born in London. Several composers, including Britten and Walton, have written works for him. He formed the Julian Bream Consort in 1961, specializing in early ensemble music.

bream Deep-bodied freshwater fish (*Abramis brama*) found in quiet lowland rivers and lakes of N Europe; length up to c.60 cm/2 ft. (Family: Cyprinidae.)

breast The milk-producing organ of the female reproductive system; also known as the **mammary gland**. It is composed of glandular tissue supported by fibrous tissue covered by skin and a thick layer of fat. The two breasts in humans are found on the front of the chest: they are small in children, but at puberty the female breasts increase rapidly in size, whereas in males they remain rudimentary. During pregnancy the breasts enlarge, being largest during milk secretion (*lactation*). At the apex of the breast is the *nipple*, surrounded by the darker *areola*.

breastbone *sternum*

breast cancer One of the commonest malignant tumours in women, first appearing as a lump within breast tissue, it spreads locally to the skin, which may ulcerate, and to the lymph nodes. Treatment includes surgical removal of the tumour or breast (*mastectomy*) and a combination of hormonal and anti-cancer drugs.

breathalyzer / breathalyser A device used with a driver suspected of having drunk an excessive amount of alcohol. Formerly, the driver blew into a tube; crystals in the device changed colour if there was alcohol present; and the extent of the change indicated that the driver had exceeded the alcohol limit, which in the UK is 80 mg per 100 ml of blood. Modern devices are battery-operated, the suspect blows through a tube, and lights indicate the alcohol level. The initial test is given by a uniformed police officer; if positive, the driver may be arrested, and given a further blood or urine test at a police station with a doctor present.

breathing *respiration*

Brecht, (Eugene) Bertolt (Friedrich) [brekht] (1898–1956) Poet, playwright and theatre director, born in Augsburg, Germany. Popularity came with *Die Dreigroschenoper* (1928, The Threepenny Opera). Hitler's rise to power forced him to leave Germany, and he lived in exile for 15 years. During this period, he wrote some of his greatest plays, including *Mutter Courage und ihre Kinder* (1938, Mother Courage and her Children) and *Der Kaukasische Kreidekreis* (1945, The Caucasian Chalk Circle). After his return to East Berlin in 1948, his work with the Berliner Ensemble firmly established his influence as a major figure in 20th-c theatre.

Breckland, The A sandy region of heathland on the border of Norfolk and Suffolk, UK. It was an important area of Neolithic flint mining.

Brecon Beacons [brekn] National park in S Wales; area 1434 km²/ 553 sq mi; established in 1957; three main peaks of 'the Beacons', Pen-y-Fan, Corn Du, and Cribyn, rise to c.900 m/2950 ft.

Breda [brayda] 51°35N 4°45E, pop (2000e) 132 000. Industrial city in S Netherlands; bishopric; important cultural centre; charter, 13th-c; known for the **Compromise of Breda**, a protest against Spanish tyranny (1566); railway; cathedral (1510).

Breeches Bible A name sometimes applied to the **Geneva Bible**, because of the rendering of *Gen* 3.7, which refers to Adam and Eve having sewn fig leaves together 'and made themselves breeches'. This translation, though, is not unique to the Geneva Bible.

breeder reactor *nuclear reactor*

Bremen [braymen] 53°05N 8°48E, pop (2000e) 569 000. Commercial city and seaport in Germany; on the R Weser; railway; university (1970); cathedral (11th-c).

Bremerhaven [braymerhahvn] 53°34N 8°35E, pop (2000e) 134 000. Seaport in Germany; on the Weser estuary; city status, 1851; united with Wesermunde, 1938; railway; Europe's largest fishing port for many years, declining in 1990s.

Bremner, Rory (Keith Ogilvy) (1961–) Satirical impressionist, writer, and performer, born in Edinburgh. He began performing in tours and one-man shows in 1985. He made several series for BBC television (1986–92) and *Rory Bremner – Who Else?* for

Channel 4 (from 1992), as well as a number of videos. Awards include the Top Male Comedy Performer BAFTA (1994, 1995, 1996).

Brendan, St, known as **the Navigator** (?–c.577) Abbot, born in Tralee, Ireland. The Latin *Navigation of St Brendan* (7th–8th-c) recounts his legendary voyage to a land of saints far to the W and N, possibly the Northern Isles, Iceland, or even N America. He founded the monastery of Clonfert in Co Galway (561). Feast day 16 May.

Bren gun A light machine-gun, the standard section weapon of the British Army during World War 2. The name derives from Brno in Czechoslovakia, where the gun was designed, and Enfield in Britain, where it was manufactured.

Brenner, Sydney (1927–) Molecular biologist, born in Germiston, NE South Africa. He joined the MRC Molecular Biology Laboratory in Cambridge (1957), becoming its director in 1980. He did notable work on the information code of DNA, and in the 1970s moved to basic studies designed to relate, in detail, an animal's nervous system to its genetic make-up. He shared the Nobel Prize for Physiology or Medicine in 2002.

Brenner Pass [brenuh], Ger **Brenner Sattel**, Ital **Passo del Brennero** 47°02N 11°32E. Mountain pass in the C Tirol Alps between Italy and Austria; altitude 1371 m/4498 ft; open all seasons of the year.

Brentano, Clemens von [brentahnoh] (1778–1842) Writer, born in Ehrenbreitstein, Germany. He was a founder of the Heidelberg Romantic school. With Achim von Arnim (1781–1831) he edited *Des Knaben Wunderhorn* (1805–8), a collection of folk songs.

Brescia [braysha] 45°33N 10°13E, pop (2000e) 209 000. Industrial town in N Italy; rail junction; Roman remains; cathedrals (11th-c, 17th-c).

Brest (Belarus), formerly **Brest-Litovsk**, Pol **Brześć nad Bugiem** 52°08N 23°40E, pop (2000e) 279 600. River port in Belarus; on the Polish border; founded by Slavs, 1017; railway; major transportation centre.

Brest (France) 48°23N 4°30W, pop (2000e) 154 000. Fortified port and naval station in NW France, used as a German submarine base in World War 2; rebuilt after heavy bombing; railway; extensive dockyards, naval stores, arsenals.

Brest-Litovsk, Treaty of (1918) A bilateral treaty signed at Brest between Soviet Russia and the Central Powers. Under its terms, Russia withdrew from World War 1, and the new Soviet state ceded nearly half of its European territory to Germany.

Breton, André [bruhtõ] (1896–1966) Poet, essayist and critic, born in Tinchebray, France. In 1919 he joined the Dadaist group, and became a founder of the Surrealist movement. His major novel, *Nadja*, was published in 1928, and his collected poems in 1948.

Breton The Celtic language of Brittany, introduced by migration from Cornish-speaking S England in the 5th-c AD. There are no official figures for Breton speakers, but it is thought they are now less than 250 000. There is a substantial body of literature from the mediaeval period onwards.

Bretton Woods Conference An international conference held at Bretton Woods, NH, USA, in 1944, to consider the stabilization of world currencies and the establishment of credit for international trade in the post-war years. It led to the establishment of the International Monetary System, including the International Monetary Fund (IMF) and the World Bank.

Breughel *Brueghel*

breviary A book of liturgical material (psalms, hymns, lessons, prayers) used in the Daily Office, and required to be recited by all priests and clerics in major orders of the Roman Catholic Church.

brewing The art and technique of producing an alcoholic beverage (most often a variety of beer) from cereals. Grain is steeped in water, and allowed to germinate. The germination is halted by heating (*malting*), and after *milling*, to crush the grain and expose the contents, the malt is *mashed* (leached with hot water) to give a solution of fermentable carbohydrates (the *wort*). Sugar may be added. The wort is boiled in a *copper* with hops (to give aroma and flavour). When cool, a brewer's yeast is added.

Brezhnev, Leonid Ilich [brezhnyef] (1906–82) Russian statesman, general secretary of the Soviet Communist Party (1964–82), and president of the Supreme Soviet (1977–82), born in Kamenskoye, Ukraine. He succeeded Khrushchev (1964), and was the first to hold simultaneously the positions of general secretary and president.

Brezhnev Doctrine [brezhnef] The term applied to the policies of Leonid Brezhnev, which combined strict political control internally with détente abroad. It also justified intervention in the internal affairs of other socialist states, as in Czechoslovakia (1968).

Brian [breean], known as **Brian Boroimhe** or **Boru** ('Brian of the Tribute') (c.926–1014) King of Ireland (1002–14). He became King of Leinster (984), and his rule was later acknowledged over the whole of Ireland.

Briand, Aristide [breeã] (1862–1932) French socialist statesman and prime minister, born in Nantes, France, who was 11 times French premier (1909–11, 1913, 1915–17, 1921–2, 1925–6, 1929). He shared the 1926 Nobel Peace Prize.

briar The woody root of two species of heath, *Erica scoparia* and *Erica arborescens*, used to make tobacco pipes. (Family: Ericaceae.)

Brickhill, Paul (Chester Jerome) (1916–91) Writer, born in Sydney, New South Wales, Australia. He served with the Royal Australian Air Force during World War 2, was shot down in North Africa, and for two years was a prisoner-of-war in Stalag Luft III, Germany. He described his escape from the camp in *The Great Escape* (1951); other books include *The Dam Busters* (1951) and *Reach for the Sky* (1954).

bricks Blocks, usually of clay or a clay mixture, baked by the Sun or by fire. Most are now made by machine, and fired in kilns. The fixing of bricks in place to provide a strong wall is called **bricklaying**. Bricks are laid in mortar, a mixture of cement or lime with sand and water.

Bride, St *Bridget, Brigid*, or *Bride, St*

bridge (engineering) A structure carrying a road, path, or railway over an obstacle. The principal types are **arch bridges**, **girder bridges**, and **suspension** bridges. The greatest spans are achieved by suspension bridges, the longest at present being the Akashi-Kaikyo, Japan (1991 m/6532 ft). The greatest single span arch bridge is the New River Gorge, W Virginia, USA (518 m/1700 ft).

bridge (recreation) A popular card game developed from whist, using the full set of 52 playing cards, and played by two pairs of players. In **auction bridge**, trumps are decided by a preliminary bid or auction that is intended to be low, because the declarer is given credit for all tricks, whether contracted or not. In the more aggressive **contract bridge**, the side winning the contract, and so naming trumps, scores towards game only the number of tricks contracted for in the bidding. Auction bridge was displaced by contract bridge in the 1920s, and is now rarely played.

Bridgend [brijend] pop (2001e) 128 600; area 246 km²/95 sq mi. County (unitary authority from 1996) in S Wales, UK; administrative centre, Bridgend; castle (12th-c).

Bridge of Sighs An enclosed 16th-c bridge in Venice, through which condemned prisoners would pass from the Doge's Palace to the Prigioni prison.

Bridges, Robert (Seymour) (1844–1930) Poet, born in Walmer, Kent. He published three volumes of graceful lyrics (1873, 1879, 1880), and several plays, and a great deal of literary criticism. He became poet laureate in 1913. In 1929, on his 85th birthday, he issued his most ambitious poem, *The Testament of Beauty*.

Bridget, Brigid, or **Bride, St** (453–523) Patron saint of Leinster, Ireland. She founded four monasteries, the chief at Kildare. Feast day 1 February.

Bridget, Brigit, or **Birgitta (of Sweden), St** (c.1302–73) Patron saint of Sweden, born in Finstad, the founder of a monastic order which flourished in Sweden until the Reformation (the **Bridgettine Order**). She was canonized in 1391. Feast day 23 July or 8 October.

Bridgetown 13°06N 59°36W, pop (2000e) 6100. Port capital of Barbados, West Indies; University of the West Indies (1963); cathedral.

Bridgewater Canal An inland waterway in England commissioned by Francis Egerton, 3rd Duke of Bridgewater (1736–1893), and constructed (1762–72) by James Brindley. The canal links Worsley to Manchester, and continues to Liverpool. It is 64 km/40 mi long.

brig Any two-masted, square-rigged sailing vessel. Brigs became common in the mid-18th-c, and are still used as sail-training vessels.

Briggs (of Lewes), Asa Briggs, Baron (1921–) Educationalist and historian, born in Keighley, West Yorkshire. Professor of modern history at Leeds University (1955–61), he became professor of history, then Vice Chancellor (1967), of the University of Sussex, and provost of Worcester College, Oxford, in 1976. A pioneer in distance learning, he was instrumental in establishing Britain's Open University (1969), and became its Chancellor in 1978. His books include *A Social History of England* (1983, 1994) and *Modern Europe 1789–1989* (1997).

Bright, John (1811–89) Radical British statesman and orator, born in Rochdale, Greater Manchester. He became a leading member of the Anti-Corn-Law League (1839), and was closely associated with the Reform Act of 1867.

brightness *luminous intensity*

Brighton 50°50N 0°10W, pop (2000e) 144 400. Resort city in Brighton and Hove unitary authority, SE England, on the English Channel; city status, 2000; railway; two universities (1961, 1992); conference centre; marina; Royal Pavilion (1811), designed by John Nash; pier (built 1866) badly damaged by fire in 2003; Palace Pier (1891); football league team, Brighton and Hove Albion (Seagulls); London–Brighton veteran car run (Nov).

Brigid, St *Bridget, Brigid*, or *Bride, St*

Brigit, St *Bridget, Brigit*, or *Birgitta (of Sweden), St*

brill Large flatfish (*Scophthalmus rhombus*) found mainly in shallow waters of NE Atlantic and Mediterranean; body length up to c.60 cm/2 ft; both eyes on left side, mouth large and curved; sandy brown with dark and light flecks. (Family: Scophthalmidae.)

brimstone (chemistry) *sulphur*

brimstone (entomology) A wide-winged butterfly; wings lemon-yellow in male, greenish-white in female, each with an orange spot. (Order: Lepidoptera. Family: Pieridae.)

Brindisi [breendisee], ancient **Brundisium** 40°37N 17°57E, pop (2000e) 90 000. Seaport in S Italy, on the Adriatic; used by Crusaders as a naval base; archbishopric; airport; railway; cathedral (11th-c, rebuilt 18th-c).

Brindley, James (1716–72) Engineer, born in Thornsett, Derbyshire. His inventions recommended him to the Duke of Bridgewater, who employed him (1759) to build the canal between Worsley and Manchester.

Brinell hardness test [brinel] A test for the hardness of metal, named after Swedish engineer, Johann August Brinell (1849–1925). A hard steel ball is pressed into the test piece with a known and reproducible force, producing a depression. The dimensions of the depression provide a measure of hardness.

Brink, André (Philippus) (1935–) Writer, critic, and translator, born in Vrede, South Africa. An Afrikaner dissident, he emerged as a writer in the 1950s, but it was not until his seventh novel – which he later translated into English as *Looking on Darkness* (1974) – that he began to attract international attention. Later books include *Rumours of Rain* (1978), *Imaginings of Sand* (1996), *The Other Side of Silence* (2003), and *Praying Mantis* (2005).

Brisbane [brizbn] 27°30S 153°00E, pop (2000e) 1 506 000. State capital of Queensland, Australia, on the Brisbane R; founded as a penal colony, 1824; state capital, 1859; third largest city in Australia; airport; railway; two universities (1909, 1975).

brisling Small Norwegian fish, *Sprattus sprattus*, usually canned in oil.

Brissot (de Warville), Jacques Pierre [breesoh] (1754–93) French revolutionary politician, born near Chartres. He established *Le Patriote français* ('The French Patriot'), the organ of the earliest Republicans, and became leader of the Girondins (or **Brisso-tins**). In the Convention his moderation made him suspect to Robespierre, and he was guillotined.

bristletail A primitive wingless insect with long tail filaments; the group includes the silverfish. **Two-pronged bristletails** (Order: Diplura, 660 species) are blind and found in the soil, feeding on decaying organic matter. **Three-pronged bristle-tails** (Order: Thysanura, 600 species) are mostly found in the soil and forest leaf litter.

bristleworm An aquatic annelid worm; body segments typically with paired lateral lobes bearing various bristles and scales; body length from 1 mm–3 m/0·04 in–10 ft; c.8000 species. (Class: Polychaeta.)

Bristol, Anglo-Saxon **Bricgstow** 51°27N 2°35W, pop (2001e) 380 600. Unitary authority in SW England; former (to 1996) administrative centre of Avon county; county status 1373; major port in 17th–18th-c, much involved in the slave trade; two airports; railway; universities (1909, 1992); 12th-century cathedral, Roman Catholic cathedral (1973), Theatre Royal (1766), Clifton suspension bridge (1864); football league teams, Bristol City (Robins), Bristol Rovers (Pirates).

Bristol Channel An inlet of the Atlantic Ocean and an extension of the R Severn estuary, between Wales and England; extends 128 km/79 mi E–W, with a varying width of 5–80 km/3–50 mi at its mouth; the greatest tidal range in England.

Bristow, Eric, nickname **the Crafty Cockney** (1957–) Darts player, born in London. He was world professional champion a record five times (1980–81, 1984–6), and won several other champion-ships during the 1980s.

Britain *United Kingdom*

Britain, Battle of The name given to the air war campaign of late summer 1940 in which the German Luftwaffe attempted to destroy the Royal Air Force (RAF) as a prelude to the invasion of Great Britain. British resistance proved stubborn, with the Spitfires and Hurricanes of RAF Fighter Command being dir-ected by radar onto the incoming bomber streams. Between 1 July and 31 October the Luftwaffe lost 2848 aircraft to the RAF's 1446.

Brit Awards British popular music awards established in 1977 by the British Music Industry to mark the Queen's silver jubilee. Since 1982 the awards have been presented annually. Nominees in various categories are voted for by an academy of over 1000 members from business and the media. Some winners are voted for by the public, while the Outstanding Contribution to British Music Award is gifted by the British Record Industry. In 2000 the spin-off Classical Brit Awards were established.

British *Celtic languages*

British Academy of Film and Television Arts (BAFTA) A media academy which began in 1947 as the British Film Academy, becoming the Society of Film and Television Arts in 1959, and changing its name to its present title in 1975. The BAFTA award, a bronze theatrical mask, was originally nicknamed a 'Stella'. Over the years the categories have varied and widened and currently include awards for best film, director, actor/actress, screenplay, cinematography, music, and production design.

British Antarctic Territory British colonial territory 20–80°W and S of 60°S; includes South Orkney Is, South Shetland Is, Antarc-tic Graham Land Peninsula, and the land mass extending to the South Pole; area 5·7 million km²/2·2 million sq mi; population solely of scientists of the British Antarctic Survey.

British Association for the Advancement of Science An organiza-tion whose aims are to promote interest and progress in science. It was founded in 1831 by a group of scientists disillu-sioned with the elitist and conservative attitude of the Royal Society.

British Athletic Federation (BAF) The former governing body for athletics in England and Wales. It was formed in 1991 as a result of a merger between the Amateur Athletic Association, founded in 1880, and the Women's Amateur Athletic Associ-ation, founded in 1922. Bankruptcy led to its reconstitution in 1998 as UK Athletics.

British Broadcasting Corporation *BBC*

British Columbia pop (2000e) 3 675 000; area 947 800 km²/365 945 sq mi. Mountainous province in SW Canada, bordered S by USA and W by the Pacific; Rocky Mts in the E, Coast Mts in the W; largest islands, Queen Charlotte, Vancouver; ranges cut by fertile valleys of Fraser, Thompson, and Columbia Rivers; many lakes; capital, Victoria; Captain Cook landed at Vancouver I, 1778; sea otter fur trade flourished; border with USA settled by Oregon Treaty, 1846; gold rush to Fraser R, 1858; entered feder-ation of Canada, 1871; Canadian Pacific Railway completed, 1885; governed by a lieutenant-governor and a Legislative Assembly.

British Commonwealth *Commonwealth* (British)

British Council An organization founded in 1934 to spread the influence of British culture, ideas, and education. Its headquar-ters is in London, with (in 2007) offices based in 109 countries throughout the world.

British currency The basic units of the present British currency are the pound (£) and the (new) **penny**. 100p = £1. Coins are issued for 1p, 2p, 5p, 10p, 20p, 50p, £1, and £2 (with £5 struck for special occasions). The British currency was decimalized in 1971. The basic unit, the pound or pound sterling, survived, the sym-bol £ deriving from the Latin *libra* (originally a pound weight of silver). The pre-decimal currency units include the penny, abbreviated to *d* from the Latin *denarius*, with 240 pence equal to £1 and 12 pence equal to one shilling. The Norman design for the penny showed a crossed indentation on one side, allowing the coin to be broken in half to serve as a **half-penny**, and into quarters to become a **farthing**. The first round farthing and halfpenny coins were struck in 1279. The shilling (abbreviated to *s*), was introduced under Henry VII, 20 shillings equalling £1. This combination of entities is the source of the term *Lsd* for money. The farthing was withdrawn from circu-lation in 1960. Other old units were the halfpenny coin (two halfpence equalling 1 penny, 480 halfpence equalling £1); the threepence ('threepenny bit') and the sixpence coins, both introduced under Edward III; the florin or two-shilling piece (equalling 24 pence, with ten florins equalling £1); the **half-crown**, equalling 30 pence, with eight half-crowns equalling £1; the **crown**, with one crown equalling five shillings and four crowns equalling £1, and the **guinea**, whose value was fixed at 21 shillings in 1717 and which was last coined in 1813. This guinea is still used as a unit of account, for example, in art auctions. Archaic terms include the **groat**, with one groat equal-ling 4 pence, coined in 1351–2 and remaining in circulation until 1662.

British Indian Ocean Territory

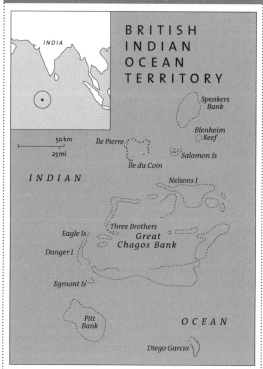

B R I T I S H
I N D I A N
O C E A N
T E R R I T O R Y

INDIA

Speakers Bank

Blenheim Reef

50 km
25 mi

Île Pierre

Île du Coin

Salomon Is

I N D I A N

Nelsons I

Eagle Is.

Three Brothers
Great
Chagos Bank

Danger I

Egmont Is

Pitt Bank

O C E A N

Diego Garcia

pop (2006e) 4000 (no permanent inhabitants); land area 60 km²/23 sq mi. British territory in the Indian Ocean, 1900 km/1180 mi NE of Mauritius, comprising the Chagos Archipelago; the islands cover c.54 400 km²/21 000 sq mi of ocean, in six main island groups; acquired by France, 18th-c; annexed by Britain, 1814; dependency of Mauritius until 1965; strategic UK–US air and naval base on Diego Garcia, the largest island; copra plantations.

British Empire, Most Excellent Order of the In the UK, an order of chivalry, instituted in 1917 by George V. It has five classes: Knights and Dames Grand Cross (GBE), Knights and Dames Commanders (KBE/DBE), Commanders (CBE), Officers (OBE), and Members (MBE).

British Expeditionary Force (BEF) An army, first established in 1906, sent to France (Aug 1914 and Sep 1939) to support the left wing of the French armies against German attack. In World War 2 its total strength was 394 000, of whom 224 000 were safely evacuated, mainly from Dunkirk, in May–June 1940.

British Indian Ocean Territory *see panel*

British Isles Group of islands off the NW coast of Europe. It consists of two main islands (Great Britain and Ireland) and many smaller islands, notably the Isle of Man, Isle of Wight, Channel Is, Western Is, Orkney, and Shetland.

British Legion *Royal British Legion*

British Library The national depository created by the British Library Act of 1972 through the amalgamation of the British Museum Library with two other libraries. Its reference division is based in London; its lending division in West Yorkshire. A new site for the library, in Euston Road, London, opened in 1997 after many delays.

British Lions The name used by representative touring rugby teams: British Isles in Rugby Union, Great Britain in Rugby League. British RU teams first went to New Zealand and Australia in 1888, although they were only fully representative from 1910. The 'Lions' nickname has been used by 18 teams since its adoption on the 1924 tour of South Africa. They enjoyed only limited playing success until the 1970s, when the 1971 team beat New Zealand, and the 1974 team won in South Africa. Further wins came in Australia (1989) and in South Africa (1997). The first British RL team went to Australia and New Zealand in 1910, but the name was not adopted until players formed the British Rugby League Lions Association in 1945. They won in Australia in 1946, 1958, 1962, and 1970, and in New Zealand in 1954, 1966, 1970, 1974, 1979, and 1990.

British Museum The national museum of archaeology and ethnography in Bloomsbury, London. It dates from 1753, when the collection of Sir Hans Sloane was acquired for the nation. Since 1881 the natural history collection has been housed separately, and the library moved to the Euston Road site in 1997. In 2003 the museum celebrated its 250th anniversary.

British South Africa Company A company, formed by Cecil Rhodes, which secured a Royal Charter from the British government in 1889. In 1923–4, its territories were divided into Northern Rhodesia (Zambia after 1964) and Southern Rhodesia (Zimbabwe after 1980).

British Sports Association for the Disabled An organization, founded in 1961, which aims to provide sports and recreation opportunities for people with disabilities throughout the UK. Its membership of c.50 000 is represented in over 500 clubs, schools, and associations, participating in over 20 different sports.

British Standards Institution (BSI) The recognized UK body for the preparation of nationally accepted standards for engineering and industrial materials, consumer products, and codes of practice. There are similar bodies in over 130 other countries.

British Summer Time *Daylight Saving Time*

British thermal unit In thermodynamics, an old unit of heat; symbol Btu; $1 Btu = 1055 J$ (joule, SI unit); defined as the heat needed to raise the temperature of a pound of water from 63°F to 64°F; a *therm* is 10^5 Btu.

British Virgin Islands *Virgin Islands, British*

Brittain, Vera (Mary) [britn] (1893–1970) Writer, born in Newcastle-under-Lyme, Staffordshire. She served as a nurse in World War 1, recording her experiences in *Testament of Youth* (1933). Her daughter is the politician, Shirley Williams.

Brittan (of Pennithorne), Leon Brittan, Baron (1939–) British Conservative statesman, born in London, who became Home Secretary (1983–5) and secretary for trade and industry (1985–6). Following a conflict with Michael Heseltine over the takeover of Westland helicopters, he resigned from the Cabinet. He became a vice-president of the European Commission in 1989. He resigned in 1999 following the publication of a report severely critical of European administration.

Brittany, Fr **Bretagne** pop (2000e) 2 923 000; area 27 208 km²/10 502 sq mi. Region and former province of NW France; rugged and striking coastline; rises to 391 m/1283 ft at Monts d'Arrée; arrival of Celts from Britain 5th–6th-c AD, from which came a distinctive culture and language (Breton); chief towns, Nantes, Rennes, Lorient, Quimper, Brest; high concentration of megaliths; major tourist area.

Britten (of Aldeburgh), (Edward) Benjamin Britten, Baron (1913–76) Composer, born in Lowestoft, Suffolk. His works were largely vocal and choral – exceptions include the famous *Variations and Fugue on a Theme of Purcell* (also known as *The Young Person's Guide to the Orchestra*). His operas include *Peter Grimes* (1945), *Billy Budd* (1951), and *Death in Venice*

(1973). He was also an accomplished pianist, often accompanying Peter Pears, and helped to found (1948) the annual Aldeburgh Festival.

brittle bone syndrome A hereditary disease of the skeleton, characterized by the deficient formation of bone and connective tissue, resulting in excessive skeleton fragility; also known as **osteogenesis imperfecta**. Seriously afflicted babies suffer multiple fractures and die in infancy.

brittle star A starfish-like marine invertebrate (echinoderm) which typically has five slender arms sharply demarcated from the central disc; arms sometimes branched; c.2000 species. (Class: Ophiuroidea.)

Brittonic *Celtic languages*

Brno [bernoh], Ger **Brünn** 49°11N 16°39E, pop (2000e) 390 000. Third largest city in Czech Republic; founded in 10th-c; part of Bohemia, 1229; free city, 1243; airport; railway; university (1919); technical university (1899); Špilberk fortress, 15th-c cathedral.

broad bean An annual growing to 80 cm/30 in (*Vicia faba*); peaflowers in small clusters, white with purplish-black wings; pods up to 20 cm/83 in long, hairy, black; containing few large seeds each 2–3 cm/^{3}/$_4$–1^1/$_4$ in across; also called **horse bean**. (Family: Leguminosae.)

broadcasting The provision of television and radio programmes and commercials for the general public; also, the technical transmission of television and radio signals. Starting in the 1920s, broadcasting, whether of the commercial or 'public-service' variety, quickly established itself at regional, national, and international levels as a popular source of entertainment, information, and education. In recent years **narrowcasting** has been introduced for services geared to special interest groups.

Broadmoor A hospital for the criminally insane, established in 1863 near Crowthorne, Berkshire, S England. It is the prototype special hospital, and has lent its name to the generic description **Broadmoor institutions**.

Broads, The, also known as **The Norfolk Broads** An area (c.2000 ha/5000 acres) of low-lying and shallow lakes in East Anglia, UK. The lakes are flooded peat pits, excavated during the 11th-c and 12th-c. It is a popular holiday area.

Broadway The name of a street in New York City (25 km/15·5 mi long) which since the 1890s has become famous as a symbol of commercial theatre in the USA. In the 1950s the label **Off-Broadway** emerged to distinguish those theatrical enterprises in New York which operated outside the crippling economics of Broadway. By the mid-sixties the rising economic pressures of Off-Broadway in their turn spawned an Off-Off-Broadway movement.

broccoli A type of cultivated cabbage (*Brassica oleracea*) grown for the immature flowers, which are edible. **Winter broccoli** has large, white heads similar to cauliflower; **sprouting broccoli** (**calabrese**) produces numerous small, purplish, green or white spears. (Family: Crucifereae.)

Brockhouse, Bertram N (1918–2003) Physicist, born in Lethbridge, Alberta, Canada. He joined Chalk River Nuclear Laboratories in Ontario (1950–9), later moving to McMaster University (1962–84). He shared the Nobel Prize for Physics in 1994 for his work in developing the field of neutron spectroscopy.

Broderick, Matthew (1962–) Actor, born in New York City. He made his film debut in *War Games* (1983), and earned Tony awards for his Broadway appearances in *Brighton Beach Memoirs* (1982–3) and *How to Succeed in Business Without Really Trying* (1995). Later films include *Election* (1999), *The Stepford Wives* (2004), and *Deck the Halls* (2006).

Brodkey, Harold (Roy), originally **Aaron Roy Weintraub** (1930–96) Novelist and short-story writer, born in Staunton, IL. The short stories he wrote for the magazine *New Yorker* were collected in *First Love and Other Sorrows* (1957). His autobiograph-

ical novel, *The Runaway Soul* (1991), was compared to Marcel Proust's *Remembrance of Things Past*.

Broglie, Louis (Victor Pierre Raymond), 7^e duc de (7th Duke of) [broy, brolee] (1892–1987) Physicist, born in Dieppe, France. In 1929 he was awarded the Nobel Prize for Physics for his pioneer work on the wave nature of the electron (**de Broglie waves**).

Broken Hill 31°57S 141°30E, pop (2000e) 26 200. Mining town in New South Wales, Australia; centre of silver, lead, and zinc mining; Royal Flying Doctor Service based here (1938).

bromeliad Any member of the pineapple family; typically fleshy, spiny-leaved epiphytes, especially common in the canopy of tropical forests, and notable for the reservoir of water which collects in the cup-shaped centre of the leaf rosette. (Family: Bromeliaceae.)

bromine [brohmeen] Br, element 35, freezing point −7°C, boiling point 58·8°C. A corrosive brown liquid with an unpleasant and irritating odour. Its main uses are in 1,2-dibromoethane, a petrol adduct, and silver bromide, used in photographic emulsions.

Bron, Eleanor (1938–) Actress and writer, born in Stanmore, Greater London. From the early 1960s she made regular stage appearances, and on television became known in *Not So Much a Programme, More a Way of Life* (1964). Her films include *Alfie* (1966), *Black Beauty* (1994), and *Wimbledon* (2004). Her books include a novel, *Double Take* (1996).

bronchi [brongkee] A series of branching tubes which gradually decrease in size, conveying air from the trachea to the lungs. The larger bronchi contain cartilage rings to keep the tubes open. The smaller tubes, known as respiratory *bronchioles*, have sac-like dilatations (*alveoli*) where gaseous exchange occurs.

bronchitis [brongkiytis] Inflammation of the airways (bronchi). **Acute bronchitis** is a serious disease in infants, usually caused by viruses such as influenza which produce intense inflammation of the respiratory tract that may lead to asphyxia. **Chronic bronchitis** affects adults who smoke cigarettes.

bronchopneumonia *pneumonia*

Brontë, Anne [brontee], pseudonym **Acton Bell** (1820–49) Poet and novelist, born in Thornton, West Yorkshire. She wrote two novels: *Agnes Grey* (1847) and *The Tenant of Wildfell Hall* (1848).

Brontë, Charlotte [brontee], pseudonym **Currer Bell** (1816–55) Novelist and poet, born in Thornton, West Yorkshire. Her first novel, *The Professor*, was not published until after her death (1857). Her masterpiece, *Jane Eyre*, appeared in 1847, and this was followed by *Shirley* (1849). *Emma* remained unfinished at her death.

Brontë, Emily (Jane) [brontee], pseudonym **Ellis Bell** (1818–48) Novelist and poet, born in Thornton, West Yorkshire. Her single novel, *Wuthering Heights* (1847), remains one of the major works of English prose fiction.

Brontosaurus *Apatosaurus*

Bronx or the **Bronx** 40°50N 73°52W, pop (2000e) 1 332 600, area 109 km²/42 sq mi. A mainland borough of N New York City and County of New York State, USA; named after Jonas Bronck, an early Dutch settler.

bronze One of the earliest known alloys; two parts copper and one part tin. Hard and resistant to corrosion, it is traditionally used in bell casting, and is the most widely used material for metal sculpture.

Bronze Age *Three Age System*

Bronzino, Il [bronzeenoh], originally **Agnolo di Cosimo di Mariano** (1503–72) Florentine Mannerist painter, born in Monticelli, Italy. His portraits include most of the Medici family, as well as Dante, Boccaccio, and Petrarch.

Brook, Peter (Stephen Paul) (1925–) Theatre and film director, born in London. He worked with the Royal Shakespeare Company in the 1960s, his successes including *King Lear* (1962),

Marat/Sade (1964), and *A Midsummer Night's Dream* (1970). Among his films are *Lord of the Flies* (1962), *The Mahabharata* (1989), and *The Tempest* (1990).

Brooke, Rupert (Chawner) (1887–1915) Poet, born in Rugby, Warwickshire. His *Poems* appeared in 1911, and *1914 and Other Poems* after his death. He was a favourite poet among young people in the interwar period.

Brooklyn 40°40N 73°58W, pop (2000e) 2 465 300. Borough of New York City, USA; area 182 km²/70 sq mi; a major port, at the SW corner of Long Island.

Brooklyn Bridge A suspension bridge built (1869–83) across East R from Brooklyn to Manhattan I, New York City; length of main span 486 m/1595 ft.

Brookner, Anita (1928–) Writer and art historian, born in London. An authority on 18th-c painting, she joined the Courtauld Institute of Art in 1977. Her novels include *Hôtel du Lac* (1984, Booker), *Altered States* (1996), and *Leaving Home* (2005).

Brooks, Mel, originally **Melvin Kaminsky** (1926–) Film actor and director, born in New York City. He is known for zany comedies satirizing established movie styles, among them *Blazing Saddles* (1974), *Robin Hood: Men in Tights* (1993), and *Svitati* (1999). He usually writes the script, and acts in his productions, as well as directing them. In 2001 he adapted his 1967 film, *The Producers*, into a musical comedy for the New York stage, taking the show to London in 2004. He married actress **Anne Bancroft** (1931–2005) in 1964.

broom A shrub (*Cytisus scoparius*) native to Europe, growing to 2·5 m/8 ft; branches numerous, green, straight, and stiff; pea-flowers golden yellow, up to 2 cm/³⁄₄ in long, pods up to 4 cm/1¹⁄₂ in long, black. (Family: Leguminosae.)

Broome, David (1940–) Show jumper, born in Cardiff. He won the World Championship on *Beethoven* in 1970, and was the individual bronze medallist at the 1960 and 1968 Olympics. He returned to the British Olympic team in 1988.

broomrape An annual or perennial, parasitic and lacking chlorophyll; leaves reduced to scales; flowers 2-lipped, in subdued colours, mainly browns; mainly native to Old World warm temperate regions. (Genus: *Orobanche*, 140 species. Family: Orobanchaceae.)

Brosnan, Pierce [broznan] (1953–) Actor, born in Navan, Co Meath, Ireland. After several stage roles in London, he moved to Los Angeles, becoming known when he took on the role of James Bond in *Goldeneye* (1995), followed by *Tomorrow Never Dies* (1997), *The World is Not Enough* (1999), and *Die Another Day* (2002). Other films include *The Long Good Friday* (1980), *The Thomas Crown Affair* (1999), and *The Matador* (2005).

Brouwer or **Brauer, Adriaen** [brower] (c.1605–38) Painter, born in Oudenaarde, Belgium. His favourite subjects were scenes from tavern life, country merrymakings, and all kinds of roisterers.

Brown, Sir Arthur Whitten (1886–1948) Aviator, born in Glasgow. He trained as an engineer, and was the companion of Alcock on the first transatlantic flight (1919).

Brown, Capability Brown, Lancelot

Brown, Charles Brockden (1771–1810) Novelist, born in Philadelphia, PA. He was the first professional American writer, and is often called 'the father of the American novel'. *Wieland* (1798), *Ormund* (1799), and *Jane Talbot* (1804) are among his Gothic Romances.

Brown, Ford Madox (1821–93) British historical painter, born in Calais, France. Among his major works are 'Manfred on the Jungfrau' (1841) and 'Chaucer reciting his poetry' (1851). He later produced designs for furniture and stained glass.

Brown, George (Alfred) George-Brown, Baron

Brown, George Mackay (1921–96) Poet, novelist, and short-story writer, born in Stromness, Orkney. He published his first collection of poems, *The Storm* (1954), while at Edinburgh University. He lived most of his life on Orkney. His stories include

A Calendar of Love (1967) and *A Time to Keep* (1969, Katherine Mansfield Memorial Prize). In 1988 he was awarded the James Tait Black Memorial Prize, and a novel *Beside the Ocean of Time* was nominated for the 1994 Booker Prize. *Selected Poems* was published in 1991, and *Travellers* posthumously in 2001.

Brown, (James) Gordon (1951–) British statesman and prime minister (2007–), born in Glasgow. He became Opposition chief secretary to the Treasury (1987–9), Opposition trade and industry secretary (1989–92), and shadow chancellor (1992–97) under John Smith, then Tony Blair, and Chancellor of the Exchequer (1997–2007) in the Labour government.

Brown, John (1800–59) Militant abolitionist, born in Torrington, CT. In 1859 he led a raid on the US Armory at Harper's Ferry in Virginia, trying to launch a slave insurrection. The raid failed, and he was hanged. The song 'John Brown's Body' commemorates the raid.

Brown, John (1826–83) Manservant, born in Crathie, Deeside, Scotland. Raised on a farm, he was employed at Balmoral Castle at the time of its purchase (1852) by Queen Victoria and Prince Albert. He was ghillie to Albert and favourite servant to Victoria, and after Albert's premature death (1861) he became a great support to the grieving queen. She came to depend on him but the unlikely relationship fuelled gossip and he became resented by the royal family, gaining many enemies.

Brown, Lancelot, known as **Capability Brown** (1715–83) Landscape gardener, born in Kirkharle, Northumberland. His gardens, such as those at Blenheim Palace and Kew are characterized by an imitation of nature. His nickname arose from his habit of saying that a place had 'capabilities'.

Brown, Robert (1773–1858) Botanist, born in Montrose, Angus. In 1831 he was the first to recognize the nucleus as the basis of a cell. He also discovered the effect later known as **Brownian motion**.

brown algae A large group of predominantly marine seaweeds, characterized by their photosynthetic pigments; over 1500 species known; body form ranges from filament-like to large blades. (Class: Phaeophyceae.)

brown bear A bear widespread in the N hemisphere (*Ursus arctos*); thick brown coat and pronounced hump on shoulders; includes the **big brown bear** and **grizzly bear** from the Rocky Mts, and the **Kenai bear** and **Kodiak bear** (both from S Alaska); Kodiak bear is the largest living carnivore (length 2·7 m/9 ft; weight up to 780 kg/1720 lb).

brown dwarf A hypothetical very large planet, which is just below the critical mass needed to ignite a stellar nuclear reaction in its interior. There is evidence for brown dwarfs as companions to a handful of stars.

Browne, Charles Farrar, pseudonym **Artemus Ward** (1834–67) Humorist, born in Waterford, ME. He wrote a description of an imaginary travelling menagerie, followed by a series of comic letters marked by puns, grotesque spelling, and satire.

Browne, Hablot Knight, pseudonym **Phiz** (1815–82) Artist, born in London. He is best known for his Dickens illustrations, beginning with *The Pickwick Papers* (1836).

Browne, Sir Thomas (1605–82) Writer, born in London. His greatest work is his earliest, the *Religio medici* (c.1635), revealing a deep insight into the spiritual life.

Brownian movement or **motion** The ceaseless erratic motion of fine particles in suspension, first observed by British botanist Robert Brown in 1827 using pollen grains in water. The effect was explained by Einstein in 1905 as the result of the irregular bombardment of the suspended matter by molecules of solution.

Browning, Elizabeth Barrett, née **Barrett** (1806–61) Poet, born in Durham, Co Durham. About 1821 she seriously injured her spine, and was long an invalid. In 1845 she met Robert Browning, with whom she eloped in 1846. Her best-known work is *Sonnets from the Portuguese* (1850, 'Portuguese' being Browning's pet name for her).

Browning, Robert (1812–89) Poet, born in London. *Bells and Pomegranates* (1841–6) included several of his best-known dramatic lyrics, such as 'How they Brought the Good News from Ghent to Aix'. In 1846 he married Elizabeth Barrett, and with her settled at Florence. After the death of his wife (1861) he settled in London, where he wrote his masterpiece, *The Ring and the Book* (1869).

Browning automatic rifle A gas-operated light machine-gun designed by US gunsmith John Moses Browning (1855–1926) in 1917, and produced until 1950. The weapon had a 20-round magazine and an effective range of 600 m/2000 ft.

Brown judgment *civil rights*

Brownshirts Members of an early Nazi paramilitary organization, officially the *Sturmabteilungen*, or *SA* ('assault division'). Formed in 1920, it had expanded to over 2 million members by 1933. After Hitler's accession to power (1933), they challenged the autonomy of the German army. They were crushed in the 'Night of the Long Knives' (29–30 Jun 1934).

Brown University *Ivy League*

browser A type of computer program which uses the Internet to locate and transfer documents held on Web sites, and presents the documents to the user of the program in a way which makes them easy to read and understand. The two most common browsers in use are Netscape Communicator and Microsoft Internet Explorer.

Brubeck, Dave, popular name of **David Warren Brubeck** (1920–) Jazz pianist, bandleader, and composer, born in Concord, CA. In 1951 the Dave Brubeck Quartet was formed featuring saxophonist **Paul Desmond** (1924–77). His best-known pieces are 'Take Five', 'Unsquare Dance', and 'Blue Rondo à la Turk'.

Bruce, James, nickname **the Abyssinian** (1730–94) Explorer, born in Larbert, Falkirk, Scotland. In 1770 he reached the source of the Blue Nile.

Bruce, Lenny, originally **Leonard Alfred Schneider** (1925–66) Satirical comedian, born in New York City. The satire and 'black' humour of his largely improvised act often transgressed the conventions of respectability. In 1961 he was imprisoned for obscenity.

Bruce, Robert (1274–1329) King of Scots (1306–29), as Robert I. He joined the Scottish revolt under Wallace, was crowned king at Scone (1306), and defeated the English at Bannockburn (1314). The Treaty of Northampton (1328) recognized the independence of Scotland and his right to the throne.

brucellosis [brooselohsis] A disease of animals, especially cattle, caused by micro-organisms of genus *Brucella*; can be caught by humans, when it is called **undulant fever** or **Malta fever**; named after British bacteriologist Sir David Bruce (1855–1931); also known as **contagious abortion**.

Bruch, Max [brukh] (1838–1920) Composer, born in Cologne, Germany. He is best known for his Violin Concerto in G minor and the *Scottish Fantasy*.

Brücke, die [brüker] (Ger 'bridge') The name adopted by a group of avant-garde artists active in Dresden, 1905–13, including Ernst Ludwig Kirchner and Emil Nolde. Their most striking works are prints, especially bold and expressive woodcuts.

Bruckheimer, Jerry [brukhiymer], popular name of **Jerome Bruckheimer** (c.1944–) Film producer, born in Detroit, MI. In 1983 he teamed up with Don Simpson (1943–96) to head a company that produced such successful films as *Beverly Hills Cop* (1984) and *Dangerous Minds* (1995). His later productions include *Armageddon* (1998), *Pearl Harbor* (2001), *Pirates of the Caribbean* (2003, sequel 2006), and *Déjà Vu* (2006).

Bruckner, Anton [brukner] (1824–96) Composer and organist, born in Ansfelden, Austria. His fame chiefly rests on his nine

symphonies (the last unfinished), but he also wrote four impressive masses and many choral works.

Brueghel, Pieter [broygl], also spelled **Bruegel** or **Breughel**, known as **the Elder** (c.1520–69) Flemish painter, probably born in the village of Brueghel, near Breda. The most original of all 16th-c Flemish painters, he settled in Brussels, where he painted his genre pictures of peasant life. His eldest son, **Pieter Brueghel**, byname **the Younger** (c.1564–1637) is known as 'Hell' Brueghel, because of his paintings of devils, hags, and robbers. His younger son, **Jan Brueghel** (1568–1625), known as 'Velvet' Brueghel, painted still-life, flowers, landscapes, and religious subjects on a small scale.

Bruges [broozh], Flemish **Brugge** 51°13N 3°14E, pop (2000e) 119 600. Port in NW Belgium; chief market town of the Hanseatic League and a major centre of the woollen and cloth trade; railway; one of the best-preserved mediaeval European cities; a world heritage site.

Brugge [brooguh] *Bruges*

Bruijn, Inge de [brown] (1973–) Swimmer, born in Barendrecht, W Netherlands. She won two gold medals and set a European record in the 100 m butterfly event at the European championships in 1999. In 2000 she set world records in the 50 m and 100 m freestyle and the 50 m and 100 m butterfly. She then won gold medals in the 50 m and the 100 m freestyle and the 100 m butterfly at the Sydney Olympics (2000) and set new world records in each of these events.

Brummell, George Bryan, known as **Beau Brummell** (1778–1840) Dandy, a leader of early 19th-c fashion, born in London. For 20 years he had the prince regent (later George IV) as friend and admirer. They quarrelled in 1813, and gambling debts forced Brummell to flee to France (1816), where he died in a lunatic asylum.

Bruna, Dick [broona] (1927–) Artist and writer, born in Utrecht, The Netherlands. The creator of a highly successful series of picture books for young children, his books include such characters as Miffy the rabbit, and the small dog Snuffy.

Brundage, Avery (1887–1975) International athletics administrator, born in Detroit, MI. He was president of the US Olympic Association (1929–53) and of the International Olympic Committee (1952–72).

Brundtland, Gro Harlem [bruntland], *née* Harlem (1939–) Norwegian stateswoman and first woman prime minister of Norway (1981, 1986–9, 1990–6), born in Bærum, Norway. She was appointed environment minister (1974–9) and, as leader of the Labour Party group, became prime minister for the first time. In 1987 she chaired the World Commission on Environment and Development which produced the report *Our Common Future*. She served as director-general of the World Health Organization (1998–2003).

Brundtland Commission *World Commission on Environment and Development*

Brunei *p.137*

Brunel, Isambard Kingdom [broonel] (1806–59) Engineer, born in Portsmouth, Hampshire. He designed the *Great Western* (1837), the first steamship built to cross the Atlantic, the *Great Britain* (1843), the first ocean screw-steamer, and the *Great Eastern* (1853–8), then the largest vessel ever built.

Brunelleschi, Filippo [brooneleskee] (1377–1446) Architect, born in Florence, Italy. He designed the dome for the Cathedral (1417–34) in Florence. The first great Renaissance architect, he had a profound influence upon his successors.

Bruno, Giordano, originally **Filippo Bruno**, nickname **Il Nolano** (1548–1600) Philosopher, born in Nola, Italy. At first a Dominican, his unorthodox views caused him to leave the order. His pantheistic views and support of Copernicus caused his arrest by the Inquisition in 1593, and after a 7-year trial he was burned in Rome.

Brunei

☐ International Airport

Status Independent state
Date of independence 1984
Capital Bandar Seri Begawan
Languages Malay (official), English
Ethnic groups Malay (65%), Chinese (20%)
Religions Muslim (Sunni 65%), Buddhist (12%), Christian (9%)
Physical features Swampy coastal plain; equatorial rainforest covers 75% of land area; rivers include Belait, Tutong Brunei; mountainous tract on Sarawak border, average height 500 m/ 1640 ft.
Climate Tropical; high temperatures and humidity and no marked seasons; average daily temperature 24–30°C; average annual rainfall 2540 mm/100 in on coast, doubling in the interior.
Currency 1 Brunei Dollar (BND) = 100 cents
Economy Largely dependent on oil (discovered 1929) and gas resources.
GDP (2002e) $6·5 bn, per capita $18 600
Human Development Index (2002) 0·856
History Formerly a powerful Muslim sultanate, with dominion over all of Borneo, its neighbouring islands, and parts of the Philippines by early 16th-c; under British protection from 1888; occupied by Japanese, 1941; liberated and reverted to former status as a British residency, 1945; internal self-government in 1971 and full independence, 1984; a constitutional monarchy with the Sultan as Head of State, who presides over a Council of Cabinet Ministers, a Religious Council, and a Privy Council.
Head of State/Government (Sultan)
1885–1906 Hashim Jalil-ul-Alam Akam-ud-Din
1906–24 Muhammad Jamal-ul-Alam II
1924–50 Ahmad Taj-ud-Din
1950–67 Umar Ali Sa if-ud-Din III
1967– Muda Hassan al Bolkiah Mu'izz-Din-Waddaulah

[brooniy], official name **State of Brunei Darussalam** (Islamic Sultanate of Brunei)
Local name Negara Brunei Darussalam
Timezone GMT +8
Area 5765 km²/2225 sq mi
Population total (2002e) 351 000

Bruno of Cologne, St (c.1030–1101) Monastic founder, born in Cologne, Germany. In 1084 he withdrew to the wild mountains of Chartreuse, near Grenoble, where he founded the austere Carthusians. Feast day 6 October.
Brunswick [brownshviyk], Ger **Braunschweig** 52°17N 10°28E, pop (2000e) 268 000. Manufacturing and commercial city in Germany; capital of former duchy of Braunschweig; railway; technical university (1745); cathedral (12th-c), castle (12th-c).
Brussels, Flemish **Brussel**, Fr **Bruxelles**, ancient **Broucsella** 50°50N 4°21E, pop (2000e) 1 069 000 (including suburbs). Capital of Belgium lying at the geographical mid-point of the country; inner city surrounded by 18 suburbs with independent administrations; major mediaeval wool centre; capital of Spanish and Austrian Netherlands; headquarters of many international organizations, such as the European Union and NATO; linguistic frontier between Flemings and Walloons runs just S of the city; officially Brussels is bilingual, but French predominates in the centre, Flemish in the suburbs; archbishopric; airport; railway; underground system; Free University of Brussels (1834); cathedral (13th–15th-c); industry largely outside the city, leaving the centre to the service sector.
Brussels, Treaty of 1 (1948) A treaty of economic, social, and cultural collaboration and collective self-defence signed by Belgium, France, Luxembourg, the Netherlands, and the UK. **2** (1973) A treaty which enabled Britain, Denmark, and Ireland to join the European Economic Community.
Brussels sprout A type of cultivated cabbage (*Brassica oleracea*) producing shoots or sprouts in all the axils of the leaves on the

main stem. These sprouts resemble miniature cabbages, and can be harvested over a long period, especially in winter. (Family: Crucifereae).
Brutalism or **New Brutalism** An architectural concept of the 1950s, in which the buildings often have large distinct blocks of exposed concrete. It is typified by the work of Le Corbusier at Chandigarh, India.
Bruton, John (1947–) Irish statesman and prime minister (1994–7), born in Dublin. Elected to the Dáil Éireann in 1969, he was minister of finance under FitzGerald (1981–2, 1986–7), and became leader of Fine Gael (1990–2001). In 1994, he formed a coalition with the Labour and Democratic Left parties. He maintained the momentum of the Northern Ireland peace process, producing with British prime minister John Major a joint framework document on the decommissioning of terrorist arms (1995).
Brutus, Marcus Junius [brootus] (c.85–42 BC) Roman politician. When the civil war broke out, he submitted to Caesar, and was appointed Governor of Cisalpine Gaul. Cassius persuaded him to join the conspiracy against Caesar (44 BC), but he killed himself after the defeat at Philippi.
Bruxelles [brüksel] *Brussels*
Bryggen [brüggen] A world heritage site in Bergen, SW Norway. Probably founded in the 11th-c, it is the best surviving example of the traditional wooden towns of N Europe.
bryophyte A spore-bearing, non-vascular plant belonging to the division Bryophyta, which includes some 25 000 species of moss, liverwort, and hornwort. Bryophytes have conducting

cells but lack true vascular tissue; they have rhizoids, thread-like outgrowths which anchor the plant and conduct water, but no true roots. They are mainly terrestrial plants, mostly restricted to damp and humid habitats. They are increasingly regarded as important indicator plants (eg in pollution studies).

Bryozoa [briyozoha] A phylum of small, aquatic animals that typically form colonies comprising a few to a million individuals; c.4 000 living species, mostly marine, and attached to hard substrates or seaweeds; also known as **moss animals**.

Bryson, Bill (1951–) Writer, born in Des Moines, IA. In 1977 he moved to England and settled in North Yorkshire. His travel books include *The Lost Continent* and *Neither Here Nor There* (1991). *Notes From A Small Island* (1995) recounts his final trip around Britain before returning to America, when he produced *Notes From a Big Country* (1998). Later books include *A Short History of Nearly Everything* (2003) and *The Life and Times of the Thunderbolt Kid* (2007). He settled in England again in 2003.

Brythonic *Celtic languages*

Brzezinski, Zbigniew [bzhuhzinskee] (1928–) Educator and statesman, born in Poland. He served as National Security Adviser under President Carter (1977–80).

BSE *bovine spongiform encephalopathy*

BSE crisis A European Commission (EC) ban on the sale of British beef as a result of the discovery of bovine spongiform encephalopathy (BSE) in British cattle in the 1980s. In an attempt to stop the spread of the diseasse, a ban on feed derived from protein was introduced in 1988, and a decision to slaughter all BSE-affected cattle was made the same year. In 1989, the EC banned the export of cattle born before July 1988, and in 1990 restricted exports to cows under six months old. Following a British government announcement of a suspected link between BSE and CJD (Creutzfeldt-Jakob disease) in March 1996, a worldwide export ban on British beef was introduced. The British government then applied for a phased lifting of the ban, and this was agreed, with various preconditions. The ban was first removed on certified herds in Northern Ireland in March 1998, and the following November was lifted for the whole of the UK, with a residual ban on sales of beef-on-the-bone lifted a year later.

BSI *British Standards Institution*

BTU *British thermal unit*

bubble chamber A device for detecting the paths of sub-atomic particles, devised in 1952 by Donald Glaser. The chamber contains a liquid prevented from boiling by pressure. The pressure is briefly released. Before general boiling can take place, the passage of a particle produces a local instability which initiates boiling, forming visible bubbles of gas along its path.

bubble memory A type of computer memory first produced as a storage medium in the mid-1970s. These devices operate as read/write memories by circulating very small polarized magnetic bubbles which represent single bits. They have the advantage of being extremely sturdy, but they are relatively slow and expensive.

Buber, Martin [boober] (1878–1965) Jewish theologian and philosopher, born in Vienna. He was professor of comparative religion at Frankfurt (1923–33), then directed the Central Office for Jewish Adult Education until 1938, when he fled to Palestine. His most influential work as a figure of religious existentialism was the early *Ich und Du* (1923, I and Thou).

bubonic plague *plague*

Bucaramanga [bookaramangga] 7°08N 73°10W, pop (2000e) 401 900. City in NC Colombia; altitude, 1018 m/3340 ft; 'the garden city of Colombia'; founded, 1622; university (1947).

buccaneers Pirates and adventurers who preyed upon Spanish and other shipping in the West Indies and along the Spanish Main in the 17th-c; mainly Dutch, English, and French. Referred to by the Spanish as *corsarios* ('corsairs'), by the Dutch as *vrij-buiter* ('freebooters'), and by the English as *privateers*, they flourished between 1630 and 1689.

Bucer or **Butzer, Martin** [butser] (1491–1551) Protestant reformer, born in Sélestat, France (formerly Schlettstadt, Germany). He joined the Dominicans, but in 1521 left the order. He adopted a middle course in the disputes about the Eucharist between Luther and Zwingli.

Buchan, John, Baron Tweedsmuir [buhkn] (1875–1940) Writer and statesman, born in Perth, Perth and Kinross. He was MP for the Scottish Universities (1927–35), and became Governor-General of Canada until 1940. Despite his busy public life, Buchan wrote over 50 books, especially fast-moving adventure stories, such as *Prester John* (1910) and *The Thirty-nine Steps* (1915).

Buchanan, James [byookanan] (1791–1868) US statesman and 15th president (1857–61), born near Mercersburg, PA. A Democratic senator from 1834, he became secretary of state in 1845. He supported the establishment of Kansas as a slave state, but his compromise failed to avert the Civil War.

Bucharest [bukarest], Romanian **Bucureşti**, ancient **Cetatea Dambovitei** 44°25N 26°07E, pop (2000e) 2 066 000. Capital of Romania; founded, 14th-c; capital of Wallachia, 1698; capital of Romania, 1861; badly damaged by German bombing in World War 2; airport; railway; university (1864); technical university (1819).

Buchman, Frank (Nathan Daniel) [buhkman] (1878–1961) Evangelist, born in Pennsburg, PA. In 1921, believing that there was an imminent danger of the collapse of civilization, he founded at Oxford, UK, the 'Group Movement'. It was labelled the 'Oxford Group' until 1938, when it rallied under the slogan 'Moral Rearmament'.

Buck, Linda B (1947–) Neurobiologist, born in Seattle, WA. After a series of academic posts, in 2002 she joined the Fred Hutchinson Cancer Research Center, Seattle. In 2004 she shared the Nobel Prize for Physiology or Medicine with Richard Axel for their discoveries of odorant receptors and the organization of the olfactory system.

Buck, Pearl (Comfort) S(ydenstricker), pseudonym **John Sedges** (1892–1973) Novelist, born in Hillsboro, WV. *The Good Earth* (1931) earned her the Pulitzer Prize, and in 1938 she was awarded the Nobel Prize for Literature. Five novels were written under her pseudonym.

buckhound *deerhound*

Buckingham Palace The 600-room residence of the British sovereign in London, built for George IV on the site of his parents' home, Buckingham House. The architect was John Nash. The palace remained unused until Queen Victoria's accession in 1837. Some rooms were opened to the public for the first time in 1993.

Buckinghamshire pop (2001e) 479 000; area 1883 km²/727 sq mi. County in SC England; crossed in the S by the Chiltern Hills; extensive woodland; county town, Aylesbury; Milton Keynes a unitary authority from 1997.

Buckley, William F(rank), Jr (1925–) Political writer and editor, born in New York City. He founded the political journal *National Review* in 1955, making it the primary voice of the intellectual US right. In the 1970s he turned to writing spy novels.

buckminsterfullerene [buhkminsterfulereen] C_{60}. An almost spherical molecule, thought to be an ingredient of soots; also called **soccerene**.

buckthorn A thorny, spreading, deciduous shrub or small tree (*Rhamnus catharticus*) 4–10 m/13–30 ft, native to Europe and the Mediterranean region; flowers tiny, green, parts in fours; berry black, mildly poisonous, and purgative. (Family: Rhamnaceae.)

buckwheat An erect annual (*Fagopyrum esculentum*) with spear-shaped leaves and a terminal cluster of tiny pink or white flowers; fruit a triangular nut c.6 mm/¼ in long; native to C Asia and cultivated as a substitute for cereals. (Family: Polygonaceae.)

Budaeus, Guglielmus [budayus], Latin name of **Guillaume Budé** (1467–1540) Scholar, born in Paris. At his suggestion Francis I founded the Collège de France. As royal librarian he founded the collection which later became the Bibliothèque Nationale.

Budapest [boodapest] 47°29N 19°05E, pop (2000e) 1 966 000. Capital of Hungary, on R Danube; old-world Buda on W bank hills, modern Pest on E bank, unified in 1873; scene of popular uprising, crushed by Soviet troops, 1956; airport; railway; underground; Eötvös Loránd University (1635); universities of medicine (1769), economic science (1948), horticulture (1853); Hungarian Academy of Sciences; Buda castle and banks of the Danube are a world heritage site; location for World Fair (Expo) in 1996.

Budd, Zola, married name **Pieterse** (1966–) Athlete, born in Bloemfontein, South Africa. She caused a controversy by obtaining British citizenship in 1984 and then being selected for the British Olympic squad. There was further controversy at the Los Angeles Games when she was involved in an incident which led to Mary Decker (USA) being tripped during the 3000 m. She set the 5000 m world record in 1984 and 1985, and was world cross-country champion in 1985 and 1986. A hip injury and public attitudes caused her to retire in 1988.

Buddha ('the enlightened one') (c.563–c.483 BC) The founder of Buddhism, born the son of the rajah of the Sakya tribe ruling at Kapilavastu, N of Benares. His personal name was **Siddhartha**, but he was also known by his family name of **Gautama**. When about 30, he left the luxuries of the court, his beautiful wife, and all earthly ambitions for the life of an ascetic; after several years of severe austerities he saw in meditation and contemplation the way to enlightenment. For some 40 years he taught, gaining many disciples and followers, and died at Kusinagara in Oudh.

Buddh Gaya or **Bodh Gaya** [bud gahya] A sacred Buddhist site in Bihar, India. Since the 3rd-c BC, shrines have marked the spot where Gautama Buddha attained enlightenment.

Buddhism A tradition of thought and practice originating in India c.2500 years ago, and now a world religion (over 370 million Buddhists estimated in 2007), deriving from the teaching of Buddha (Siddhartha Gautama), who is regarded as one of a continuing series of enlightened beings. The teaching of Buddha is summarized in the *Four Noble Truths*, the last of which affirms the existence of a path leading to deliverance from the universal human experience of suffering. A central tenet is the law of *karma*, by which good and evil deeds result in appropriate reward or punishment in this life or in a succession of rebirths. Through a proper understanding of this condition, and by obedience to the right path, human beings can break the chain of karma. The Buddha's path to deliverance is through morality (*sila*), meditation (*samadhi*), and wisdom (*panna*), as set out in the *Eightfold Path*. The goal is *Nirvana*, which means 'the blowing out' of the fires of all desires, and the absorption of the self into the infinite.

There are two main traditions within Buddhism, dating from its earliest history. **Theravada Buddhism** adheres to the strict and narrow teachings of the early Buddhist writings: salvation is possible for only the few who accept the severe discipline and effort necessary to achieve it. **Mahayana Buddhism** is more liberal, and makes concessions to popular piety: it teaches that salvation is possible for everyone, and introduces the doctrine of the *bodhisattva* (or personal saviour). As Buddhism spread, other schools grew up, among which are Ch'an or Zen, Lamaism, Tendai, Nichiren, and Soka Gakkai. The only complete canon of Buddhist scripture is called the Pali canon, after the language in which it is written.

buddleia or **buddleja** [buhdlia] A deciduous shrub or small tree, native to warm regions; flowers small, various colours, often scented, crowded in dense spikes or globular clusters. It is very attractive to insects, especially butterflies, hence the name **butterfly bush** given to *Buddleia davidii*, the most commonly cultivated species. (Genus: *Buddleia*, 100 species. Family: Loganiaceae.)

Budé, Guillaume *Budaeus, Guglielmus*

budgerigar A small parrot native to C Australia, and introduced in Florida (*Melopsittacus undulatus*). It is a popular cage-bird, with many colour variations, but is usually green in the wild. (Family: Psittacidae.)

Buenaventura [bwenaventoora] 3°51N 77°06W, pop (2000e) 189 400. Pacific seaport in SW Colombia; founded, 1540.

Buenos Aires [bwaynos iyrees] 34°40S 58°30W, pop (2000e) 3 333 000. Federal capital of Argentina; on S bank of R Plate; founded in 1536 as the city of the 'Puerto de Santa Maria del Buen Aire'; destroyed by Indians, and refounded, 1580; formerly capital of the Spanish viceroyalty of La Plata; airport; railway; metro; nine universities; cathedral.

Buerk, Michael (Duncan) [berk] (1946–) Television journalist and presenter, born in Solihull, West Midlands. He joined the BBC in 1970, becoming a special correspondent (1981–2) and Africa correspondent (1983–7). He has presented Radio 4's *The Moral Maze* (from 1990), and for television the new format *Ten O'Clock News* (2000–2) and *The Hand of God* (2003). An autobiography, *The Road Taken*, appeared in 2004.

Buffalo 42°53N 78°53W, pop (2000e) 292 600. Port on the Niagara R at the NE end of L Erie; second largest city in New York State, USA; railway; two universities (1846, 1867); professional teams, Bills (football), Sabres (ice hockey).

buffalo *African buffalo; bison; water buffalo*

Buffalo Bill *Cody, William F*

buffalo-weaver *weaverbird*

buffer (computing) In computing, a temporary storage area in memory for data. Buffers are often used when transmitting data between two devices with different working speeds, such as between a keyboard and the central processor.

buffer state A small state lying between two or more larger and potentially belligerent states, as a means of reducing border friction between them. For example, after World War 1, attempts were made to create a buffer state between Germany and France.

Buffon, Georges-Louis Leclerc, comte de (Count of) [bufõ] (1707–88) Naturalist, born in Montbard, Burgundy. In 1739 he was made director of the Jardin du Roi, with its museum, and formed the design of his *Histoire naturelle* (1749–67, Natural History). His wide-ranging ideas foreshadowed the theory of evolution.

bug (computing) An error in a computer program or a fault in computer hardware. The process of detecting and correcting errors is known as **debugging**.

bug (entomology) An insect with forewings leathery at base, membranous near the tip, and folded over membranous hindwings at rest; diverse in form and feeding habits; mouthparts modified into a snout for piercing and sucking; includes many crop pests and disease carriers. (Order: Heteroptera.)

Bugatti, Ettore (Arco Isidoro) [boogatee] (1881–1947) Car manufacturer, born in Milan, Italy. He began designing cars in 1899 and set up his works in Strasbourg in 1907. His racing cars won international fame in the 1930s.

Buginese or **Bugi** A major ethnic group of Celebes (Sulawesi), Indonesia. They live as rice cultivators, traders, and seafarers.

bugle (music) A musical instrument made of brass or copper, curved elliptically and ending in a large bell. It normally has no valves and can therefore produce only those notes forming the first half-dozen harmonics above the fundamental (usually B♭). It has been used above all for sounding military calls.

bugloss [byooglos] A bristly annual or biennial (*Anchusa arvensis*) growing to 50 cm/20 in, native to Europe and Asia; leaves narrowly oblong with wavy margins; inflorescence coiled; flowers 5 mm/¼ in diameter with curved white tube, spreading bright-blue lobes, and white eye. (Family: Boraginaceae.)

buhl or **boulle [bool]** A technique of furniture decoration involving very elaborate inlays of brass, tortoiseshell, mother-of-pearl, and coloured wood. Introduced into France in the 16th-c from Italy, it was perfected by André Charles Boulle (1642–1732) and his sons.

building biology The study of the interaction between a building and its environment, especially with respect to the effects upon the health of the occupants. It deals with the location and geometry of the building, its colour scheme, lighting, and furnishings, and the selection of non-toxic and ecologically 'friendly' building materials.

building society An institution which lends money to enable people to buy property (via a mortgage loan). Their funds are derived from investors who obtain interest on the sum deposited. Interest paid to the society by the borrower is higher than the rate paid out. In the UK there are some 150 societies, but their numbers have been falling through amalgamations. The US equivalent is the **savings and loan association**.

Bujumbura [bujumboora], formerly **Usumbura** 3°22S 29°21E, pop (2000e) 400 000. Port capital of Burundi, C Africa, at NE end of L Tanganyika; altitude 805 m/2641 ft; founded in 1899 by German colonists; airport; university (1960).

Bukharin, Nikolay Ivanovich [bookharin] (1888–1938) Russian Marxist revolutionary and political theorist, born in Moscow. He played a leading role in the organization of the October Revolution in Moscow. In 1937 he was arrested in Stalin's Great Purge, tried on trumped-up charges, and shot.

Bulawayo [boolawayoh] 20°10S 28°43E, pop (2000e) 612 100. Second largest city in Zimbabwe; founded, 1893; airport; railway junction; commercial, industrial, and tourist centre.

bulb A highly modified shoot forming an underground storage organ. It is composed of overlapping leaves or leaf bases, swollen with food reserves which nourish early growth. The bulbs usually persist from year to year, the reserves being replenished before the plant dies back.

bulbil A small organ resembling a bulb, but produced above ground, either in a leaf axil or in the inflorescence in place of some flowers. It produces a new plant after falling from the parent.

bulbul A bird native to tropical Africa, Madagascar, and S Asia; short wings, long tail; stiff bristles at base of pointed bill. (Family: Pycnonotidae, 120 species.)

Bulfinch, Charles (1763–1844) Architect, born in Boston, MA. America's first native-born architect, he succeeded Latrobe as architect of the US Capitol (1817–30). His domed capitol buildings influenced the design of state capitals across the country throughout the 19th-c.

Bulganin, Nikolay Alexandrovich [bulgahnin] (1895–1975) Soviet statesman and prime minister (1955–8), born in Nizhni Novgorod, Russia. He was made premier after Malenkov resigned (1955), with Khrushchev wielding real power. 'B and K' travelled extensively abroad, conducting propaganda through lengthy letters to Western statesmen.

Bulgaria *p.141*

Bulgarian *Slavic languages*

Bulge, Battle of the (1944) The last desperate German armoured counter-offensive through the Ardennes in World War 2 (beginning 16 Dec). It achieved early success, but the Germans were then forced to retreat by the Allies by the end of January 1945.

bulimia nervosa [byoolimia nervohsa] A condition typified by repeated episodes of binge eating and frequent vomiting and purging, associated with a preoccupation with control of body weight and a feeling of lack of control over eating behaviour. The vast majority of patients are female.

bulk store *backing store*

Bull, Deborah (Clare) (1963–) Ballerina, born in Derby, Derbyshire. In 1981 she joined the Royal Ballet (principal dancer from 1992), and retired in 2001. She was then appointed artistic director of the Linbury Studio Theatre and Clore Studio Upstairs at the Royal Opera House.

Bull, John (c.1562–1628) Musician, born in Somerset. A virtuoso player, he was one of the founders of contrapuntal keyboard music. He has been credited with composing the air 'God save the King'.

bull (religion) An important, formal communication or edict from a pope, originally sealed with his signet-ring (Lat *bulla*, 'seal') and identified by the opening Latin words.

bull (zoology) A male mammal belonging to one of several species; female usually called *cow*; young called *calf*; used especially for uncastrated male cattle (male castrated when young called a *bullock*, *ox*, or *steer*; if castrated when fully grown, called a *stag*).

bullace [boolis] A type of small, wild plum (*Prunus domestica*), usually a thorny shrub with spherical black fruit with waxy bloom; native to Europe. (Subspecies *institia*. Family: Rosaceae.)

bulldog A breed of dog, used in mediaeval Britain for the sport of bull-baiting; heavy body with short, bowed legs and short tail; large round head with flat upturned muzzle; ears and eyes small; short brown or brown and white coat.

bulletin board A form of electronic notice board which occurs frequently in data communications networks, particularly those linking academic institutions; also called a **bulletin board system (BBS)**. The bulletin board hosts notices of meetings, technical papers, or even computer programs. Its readership is worldwide.

bullfighting The national sport in Spain, also popular in some regions of S France, and in Latin-American countries. Known as the *corrida de toros* ('running of the bulls') it is regarded as an art in Spain. Leading bullfighters (*matadors*) are treated as national heroes. Picadors are sent into the bull ring to weaken the bull before the matador enters the arena to make the final killing.

bullfinch A bird native to Europe, Scandinavia, and Asia E to Japan and the Philippines; causes serious damage in orchards. (Genus: *Pyrrhula*, 6 species. Family Fringillidae.)

bullhead Small bottom-dwelling fish found in clear streams and lakes of N Europe; body stout, length up to 10 cm/4 in, with broad flattened head; also called **sculpin** or **miller's thumb**. (Genus: *Cottus*. Family: Cottidae.)

bull market A stock market term which signifies that the prices of stocks and shares are on a rising trend, due to buying demand. A **bull** buys shares hoping that the price will rise, so that they can be sold later at a profit.

bull-mastiff A breed of dog, developed in Britain by crossing bulldogs and mastiffs; thick-set body; brown short-haired coat; soft ears and powerful muzzle.

Bull Run, Battles of Major victories by Confederate forces in the American Civil War; also known as the **Battles of Manassas**.

bull terrier A breed of dog, developed for bullbaiting in Britain by crossing bulldogs and terriers; powerful body; long tail; ears pointed, erect; head broad with small eyes; coat short, usually white. The **American pit bull terrier** attracted widespread publicity during the 1980s, following several attacks on people; it became subject to controls and registration in the UK in 1991, along with the *tosa fila Braziliera* and *dogo Argentino*.

bulrush An aquatic, rush-like perennial (*Scirpus lacustris*), found almost everywhere; stems to 3 m/10 ft; leaves in tufts; flowers

Bulgaria

200 km
100 mi

EUROPE

R O M A N I A

SERBIA

Danube

Ruse

Iskur

Pleven

Balkan Mountains

Varna

B U L G A R I A

Sofia

Kazanluk

Rila

Burgas

Stara Zagora

BLACK
SEA

Maritsa

Plovdiv

Rhodope Mountains

Pirin
Mts

MACEDONIA

GREECE

TURKEY

☐ International Airport

[buhl**gai**reea], official name **Republic of Bulgaria**, Bulgarian **Republika Bulgariya**, formerly **People's Republic of Bulgaria** (1941–90)
Local name Bǎlgarija
Timezone GMT +2

Area 110 912 km^2/42 812 sq mi
Population total (2002e) 7 890 000
Status Republic
Date of independence 1908
Capital Sofia
Languages Bulgarian (official), Turkish
Ethnic groups Bulgarian (85%), Turkish (9%)
Religions Bulgarian Orthodox (85%), Muslim (13%)
Physical features Traversed W–E by the Balkan Mts, averaging 2000 m/6500 ft; in the SW, Rhodope Mts, rising to 3000 m/ 9600 ft; rivers include Maritsa, Iskur, Danube.
Climate Continental climate, with hot summers, cold winters; average annual temperatures -2°C (Jan), 21°C (Jul); average annual rainfall 635 mm/25 in.
Currency 1 Lev (BGL) = 100 stotinki
Economy Mainly agricultural produce; coal, iron ore; offshore oil (Black Sea), natural gas; tourism; tobacco, wine exports.
GDP (2002e) $49·23 bn, per capita $6500
Human Development Index (2002) 0·779
History Bulgars crossed the Danube in the 7th-c; their empire continually at war with Byzantines until destroyed by Turks, 14th-c; remained under Turkish rule, 1396-1878; full independence, 1908; became a kingdom, 1908–46; aligned with Germany in both World Wars; occupied by USSR, 1944; Socialist People's Republic founded, 1946; unicameral National Assembly established, 1971; proclaimed Republic of Bulgaria in 1990; new constitution, 1991; joined EU 2007; governed by an elected President, and a 250-member National Assembly.

Head of State
1991–6 Zhelyu Zhelev
1996–2001 Petar Stoyanov
2001– Georgi Parvanov

Head of Government
1995–6 Zhan Videnov
1997 Stefan Sofianski *Interim*
1997–2001 Ivan Kostov
2001–5 Simeon Borisov Sakskoburggotski
2005– Sergei Stanishev

tiny, perianth reduced to six rough bristles, in oval, brown spikelets. (Family: Cyperaceae.)

bulrush millet *millet*

Bultmann, Rudolf (Karl) (1884–1976) Lutheran theologian and New Testament scholar, born in Wiefelstede, Germany. He is best known for his highly influential programme (1941) to 'demythologize' the New Testament and interpret it existentially, employing the categories of the earlier work of Heidegger.

Bulwer-Lytton, Edward George Earle *Lytton, Edward George Earle Bulwer-Lytton*

bumblebee A large bee found mainly in the temperate N hemisphere. The adults transport pollen on the modified outer surface of the hindleg. (Genus: *Bombus*. Family: Apidae.)

Bunche, Ralph (Johnson) [buhnch] (1904–71) US diplomat, born in Detroit, MI. He directed the United Nations Trusteeship department (1947–54), and became UN mediator in Palestine, where he arranged for a ceasefire. He was awarded the Nobel Peace Prize in 1950.

Bundy, McGeorge (1919–96) US statesman and educator, born in Boston, MA. As National Security Adviser to presidents Kennedy and Johnson he was one of the architects of the Vietnam War.

bungee jumping The activity of jumping from a high point to which the jumper is attached by a strong rubber cable fastened to the ankles. The length and tension of the cable is calculated to ensure that the jumper bounces up before reaching the ground. The activity became popular in the early 1990s, and is now practised as a sport in several countries.

Bunin, Ivan Alexeyevich [boonin] (1870–1953) Writer, born in Voronezh, Russia. His best-known work is *Gospodin iz San-Francisco* (1922, The Gentleman from San Francisco). He was the first Russian to receive the Nobel Prize for Literature (1933).

bunion A painful, inflamed hardening and thickening of the skin of the sole of the foot at the base of the great toe. It is often induced by ill-fitting footwear.

Bunker Hill, Battle of (1775) The first pitched battle of the US War of Independence, fought during the siege of Boston. It was technically an American defeat, but very high British casualties forbade attempts on other American emplacements.

bunraku [bunrakoo] The classical Japanese puppet theatre. Puppets are two-thirds life size, hand-held by a puppet master, generally with two 'invisible' assistants in black. The movements are accompanied by a singer-narrator and musicians.

Bunsen burner A gas burner, used mainly in chemistry laboratories. Gas enters through a jet at the lower end of a tube, and is drawn through a side tube whose aperture can be controlled. The controllable gas–air mixture makes possible a flame of quality, ranging from luminous to hot non-luminous. The idea is attributed to German scientist Robert Wilhelm Bunsen (1811–99).

bunting A small seed-eating bird, usually dull in colour with a short stout bill. It belongs to a widespread family, thought to have evolved in the Americas, spread across the Bering Straits to Asia, then colonized Europe and Africa. (Family: Emberizidae, c.290 species.)

Buñuel, Luis [buhnwel] (1900–83) Film director, born in Calanda, Spain. He directed such major films as *Viridiana* (1961), *The Discreet Charm of the Bourgeoisie* (1972), and *That Obscure Object of Desire* (1977). His work is characterized by a poetic, often erotic, use of imagery, a black humour, and a hatred of Catholicism.

Bunyan, John (1628–88) Writer, born in Elstow, Bedfordshire. In 1653 he joined a Christian fellowship, preaching around Bedford. While imprisoned in the town gaol, he wrote the first part of the allegorical work *The Pilgrim's Progress* (1678). The second part was published in 1684.

Bunyan, Paul In American folklore, a lumberjack of superhuman size and strength. He could refashion geography, creating lakes, rivers, and even the Grand Canyon.

bunyip In the mythology of the Australian aborigines, the source of evil. The Rainbow Serpent, the mother of life, confined bunyip to a waterhole: he haunts dark and gloomy places.

Buonaparte *Napoleon*

buoy A fixed, floating object attached by a cable or chain to the seabed to mark safe channels, approaches to harbours, and dangers to navigation. Buoys are generally made of steel or fibre-glass reinforced plastic; they may be fitted with bells or whistles, usually operated by the motion of the waves. There are also mooring buoys, used for the anchoring of ships. In addition to a battery-powered light which allows recognition at night, a buoy may be fitted with a fog signal and a *racon* (a radar beacon that can be identified and located by its response to a radar signal).

buoyancy The upward thrust on an object immersed in liquid or gas, equal to the weight of the displaced fluid. The human body is more buoyant in salt water than in fresh water, as the former is 3% denser.

Burbage, Richard [berbij] (c.1569–1619) Actor, born in London. He was the leading performer with Shakespeare's company from 1594 until his death.

Burbank, Luther (1849–1926) Horticulturalist, born in Lancaster, MA. He developed the *Burbank potato* on a farm near Lunenberg, MA, and in 1875 moved to Santa Rosa, CA, where he bred over 800 new strains of fruits and flowers.

burbot Elongate slender-bodied fish (*Lota lota*) widespread in rivers and lakes of N Eurasia and North America; the only freshwater species in the cod family Gadidae; length up to 1 m/3¼ ft; single barbel beneath mouth; also called **eelpout**.

Burford, Eleanor *Hibbert, Eleanor*

Burgess, Anthony, pseudonym of **John Anthony Burgess Wilson** (1917–93) Writer and critic, born in Manchester, Greater Manchester. His many novels include *A Clockwork Orange* (1962), *Earthly Powers* (1980), and *Any Old Iron* (1989). He wrote several critical studies and film scripts, including *Jesus of Nazareth* (1977), and his musical compositions include symphonies, a ballet, and an opera. In his later years, he lived in Monaco. In 2004, his widow Liana Burgess opened the International Anthony Burgess Foundation in Manchester as a focal point for his life and work.

Burgess, Guy (Francis de Moncy) (1910–63) British traitor, born in Devonport, Devon. He studied at Cambridge, where he became a communist, and was recruited as a Soviet agent in the 1930s. Recalled from Washington in 1951 for 'serious misconduct', he and Maclean disappeared, re-emerging in the Soviet Union in 1956.

Burgh, Hubert de [ber] (?–1243) Justiciar of England under King John and Henry III (1215–32). He is chiefly remembered as the gaoler of Prince Arthur.

burgh *borough*

Burghley or **Burghleigh, Lord** *Cecil, William*

burglary A crime which involves entering a building as a trespasser, either with the intent to commit theft, grievous bodily harm, rape or criminal damage; or, having entered, stealing or attempting to steal anything, or committing or attempting to commit grievous bodily harm. The term is not used in all jurisdictions.

Burgos [boorgos] 42°21N 3°41W, pop (2000e) 163 000. City in N Spain; former capital of Old Castile; archbishopric; railway; cathedral (13th–16th-c), castle; a world heritage site; home and burial site of El Cid.

Burgoyne, John, nickname **Gentleman Johnnie** (1722–92) British general and playwright, born in Sutton, Bedfordshire. In 1777 he was sent to America, where he led an expedition from Canada, taking Ticonderoga, but was forced to surrender at Saratoga. His best-known work was his comedy, *The Heiress* (1786).

Burgundy, Fr **Bourgogne** pop (2000e) 1 683 000; area 31 582 km²/12 191 sq mi. Region and former province of EC France; former kingdom of Burgundia (5th–10th-c); famous wine-producing area (eg Beaujolais, Beaune, Chablis); chief town, Dijon; industry centred on Le Creusot.

burials *bog burials; Hochdorf; Kofun; Maes Howe; Mount Li; New Grange; Pazyryk; shaft graves; Ship of Cheops; Sutton Hoo ship burial*

Burke, Edmund (1729–97) British statesman and political philosopher, born in Dublin. His early writing includes his *Philosophical Inquiry into the Origin of Our Ideas of the Sublime and Beautiful* (1756). His *Reflections on the French Revolution* (1790) was read all over Europe.

Burke, William (1792–1829) Murderer, born in Orrery, Waterford, Ireland. With his partner, **William Hare** (c.1790–c.1860), born in Londonderry, he carried out a series of infamous murders in Edinburgh in the 1820s, with the aim of supplying dissection subjects to an anatomist. Hare turned king's evidence, and died a beggar in London; Burke was hanged, to the general satisfaction of the crowd.

Burke's Peerage A reference guide to the aristocratic and titled families of Great Britain, first published by John Burke (1787–1848) in 1826 under the title *Genealogical and Heraldic Dictionary of the Peerage and Baronetage of the United Kingdom*.

Burkina Faso *p.143*

Burma *Myanmar*

burn A wound in which tissues are damaged or destroyed by heat or electricity. Burns are classified into *partial* or *full* thickness. In a partial thickness burn, enough of the surface layer is preserved to allow spontaneous regeneration; full thickness burns usually require skin grafts.

Burne-Jones, Sir Edward Coley (1833–98) Painter and designer, born in Birmingham, West Midlands. His later oils, inspired by the early Italian Renaissance, are characterized by a Romantic and contrived Mannerism. He also designed stained glass and tapestries, and illustrated several books.

burnet An erect, tuft-forming perennial, native to Europe, W Asia, or N Africa; flowers in a globular head, four sepals, petals absent. The **salad burnet** (*Sanguisorba minor*) grows to 40 cm/15 in, flowers green or purple-tinged; crushed foliage smelling of cucumber. (Family: Rosaceae.)

Burnet, Alastair [bernet], popular name of **Sir James William Alexander Burnet** (1928–) British journalist and television news presenter. He was editor of *The Economist* (1965–74) and *The Daily Express* (1974–6), and became a nationally known personality when he joined ITN as a news presenter

Burkina Faso

□ International Airport

[berkeena fasoh], formerly **Upper Volta** (to 1984), then (Fr) **République de Haute-Volta**

Local name Burkina Faso
Timezone GMT
Area 274 200 km²/105 870 sq mi
Population total (2002e) 12 603 000

Status Republic
Date of independence 1960
Capital Ouagadougou
Languages French (official), with Moré, Mossi, Mande, Fulani, Lobi, and Bobo also spoken
Ethnic groups Mossi (48%), over 50 other groups
Religions Traditional beliefs (45%), Muslim (43%), Christian (12%)
Physical features Landlocked republic in W Africa; low-lying plateau, falling away to the S; tributaries of the Volta and Niger unnavigable in dry season; wooded savannahs in S; semi-desert in N.
Climate Tropical; average annual rainfall 894 mm/35 in; dry season (Dec–May), rainy season (Jun–Oct); average annual temperature 24°C (Jan), 28°C (Jul) in Ouagadougou; violent storms (Aug); subject to drought conditions.
Currency 1 CFA Franc (XAF) = 100 centimes
Economy Based on agriculture, largely at subsistence level; millet, corn, rice, livestock, peanuts, sugar cane, cotton.
GDP (2002e) $14·51 bn, per capita $1100
Human Development Index (2002) 0·325
History Mossi empire in 18th–19th-c; Upper Volta created by French, 1919; abolished in 1932, with most land joined to Ivory Coast; original borders reconstituted, 1947; autonomy within French community, 1958; independence, 1960, with several military coups since; changed name from Upper Volta to Burkina Faso ('land of upright men'), 1984; end of military rule, 1991; governed by a president and an appointed Council of Ministers; new constitution, 1991, which promulgated an Assembly of People's Deputies (from 1997, with 111 members).

Head of State
1984–7 Thomas Sankara (Chairman)
1987– Blaise Compaoré

Head of Government
1992–4 Youssouf Ouedraogo
1994–6 Roch Christian Kabore
1996–2000 Kadre Desire Ouedraogo
2000– Paramanga Ernest Yonli

(1976–91), later becoming associate editor for *News at Ten* (1982–91). He was knighted in 1984.

Burnet, Sir (Frank) Macfarlane [bernet] (1899–1985) Medical scientist, born in Traralgon, Victoria, Australia. A world authority on viral diseases, he shared the 1960 Nobel Prize for Physiology or Medicine for research into immunological intolerance in relation to skin and organ grafting.

Burnett, Frances (Eliza) Hodgson (1849–1924) Writer, born in Manchester, Greater Manchester. She wrote several plays and over 40 novels, notably *Little Lord Fauntleroy* (1886) and *The Secret Garden* (1911).

Burnett, Ivy Compton Compton-Burnett, Ivy

Burney, Fanny, popular name of **Frances Burney**, married name **Madame d'Arblay** (1752–1840) Writer and diarist, born in King's Lynn, Norfolk. Her first and best novel, *Evelina*, was published anonymously in 1778, and influenced Jane Austen. Her *Letters and Diaries* (1846) show her skill in reporting events of her time.

burning bush dittany; summer cypress

Burns, George, originally **Nathan Birnbaum** (1896–1996) Comedian and actor, born in New York City. He made his debut at the age of 13, and in 1923 teamed up with **Gracie Allen** (1905–64). They became a husband-and-wife comedy duo popular for over three decades in vaudeville, radio, films, and television. Well known for his omnipresent cigar, dry wit, and comic timing, he received an Oscar for his role in *The Sunshine Boys* (1975).

Burns, Robert (1759–96) Scotland's national poet, born in Alloway, South Ayrshire. On his father's death (1784) he was left in charge of the farm. At the same time his entanglement with Jean Armour (1767–1834) began, and as the farm went to ruin, his poverty, passion, and despair produced in 1785 an extraordinary output of poetry, including 'The Jolly Beggars'. Looking for money to emigrate to Jamaica, he published the famous Kilmarnock edition of his poems (1786), which brought such acclaim that he was persuaded to stay in Scotland. Going to Edinburgh, where he was feted, he began the epistolary flirtations with 'Clarinda' (Agnes Maclehose, 1759–1841). In 1788 he married Jean Armour and leased a farm near Dumfries. By 1790, when he wrote 'Tam o' Shanter', the farm was failing. He left for Dumfries, where he died.

Burnside, Ambrose Everett (1824–81) US general, born in Liberty, IN. In the Civil War he was repulsed at Fredericksburg (1862), but held Knoxville (1863), and led a corps under Grant through the battles of the Wilderness and Cold Harbor (1864). He lent his name to a style of side whiskers, later known as 'sideburns'.

Burns Night The evening of 25 January, anniversary of the birth of Robert Burns. It is celebrated with a special meal (**Burns Supper**) including haggis, potatoes, and swedes, followed by a set formula of toasts and performances of Burns's works.

Burra, Edward (1905–76) Artist, born in London. Well known as a colourist, his Surrealist paintings of figures against exotic (often Spanish) backgrounds are invariably in watercolour.

Burroughs, Edgar Rice [buhrohz] (1875–1950) Writer, born in Chicago, IL. He had many unsuccessful jobs, before making his name with the 'Tarzan' stories, beginning with *Tarzan of the Apes* (1914).

Burroughs, William S(eward) [buhrohz] (1914–97) Writer, born in St Louis, MO. His novels *Naked Lunch* (1959) and *The Soft Machine* (1961) established him as a spokesman of the 'beat' movement of the late 1950s. His later work includes *The Wild Boys* (1971), and *The Western Lands* (1987).

Bursa [boorsah], ancient **Brusa** or **Prusa** 40°12N 29°04E, pop (2000e) 1 005 000. City in NW Turkey; founded, 3rd-c BC; airfield; railway; noted for its silk textiles.

Burt, Sir Cyril (Lodowic) (1883–1971) Psychologist, born in London. He was largely responsible for the theory and practice of intelligence and aptitude tests, ranging from the psychology of education to the problems of juvenile delinquency. In the 1980s, the validity of some of his techniques was called into question.

Burton, Richard, originally **Richard Walter Jenkins** (1925–84) Stage and film actor, born in Pontrhydfen, South Wales. His early Hollywood films include *The Robe* (1953), for which he received one of his six Oscar nominations. His romance with Elizabeth Taylor during the making of *Cleopatra* (1962) and their eventual marriage (1964–74) projected them both into the 'superstar' category. Among his later films were *Becket* (1964), *Equus* (1977), and *1984* (released after his death). In his later years, interest in his social life grew, especially after his remarriage to Elizabeth Taylor (1975–6).

Burton, Sir Richard (Francis) (1821–90) Explorer and language expert, born in Torquay, Devon. In 1856 he set out on the journey which led to the discovery (1858) of L Tanganyika. He translated several Eastern works, notably, *The Arabian Nights* (1885–8).

Burton, Robert (1577–1640) Writer, born in Lindley, Leicestershire. His great work was the *Anatomy of Melancholy* (1621), a satire on the inefficacy of human learning and satire.

Burundi *p.145*

bus (computing) A form of wiring within or between computers in which any electronic message to be transferred is sent down the wire and is taken off the wire only by the particular device to which the message is being sent. Inside a computer there are usually an **address bus**, a **data bus**, and an **input–output bus**.

Busan *Pusan*

Busby, Sir Matt(hew) (1909–94) Footballer and football manager, born in Bellshill, North Lanarkshire. He became manager of Manchester United in 1945, winning the FA Cup in 1948 and the League shortly afterwards. His side was largely wiped out in an air crash at Munich airport. He himself was severely injured, but he reconstructed the team, achieving European Cup success in 1968.

Bush, George (Herbert Walker) (1924–) US statesman and 41st president, born in Milton, MA. He entered politics in 1964, and became US permanent representative to the United Nations. Under President Ford he headed the US Mission to Beijing (Peking), then became director of the CIA. In 1980 he campaigned for the Republican nomination, but lost to Reagan, later becoming his vice-president. In 1988 he won the Republican nomination for the presidency, and defeated Governor Michael Dukakis of Massachusetts in the general election, but lost to Bill Clinton in the 1992 election.

Bush, George W(alker), also known as **George Bush Jr** (1946–) US statesman and 43rd president (2001–), born in New Haven, CT, the eldest child of president George Bush. He graduated from Yale University and Harvard Business School and entered the oil business in West Texas in the 1970s. In 1994 he became the

46th governor of Texas, and easily won re-election in 1998 as an exponent of 'compassionate conservatism'. In 2000 he was declared president following five weeks of complex legal argument over the voting procedure in the presidential election. Following a terrorist attack on the World Trade Center in New York City (11 Sep 2002), he created the Department of Homeland Security responsible for coordinating a national strategy against terrorism. Key defence initiatives included Project BioShield, the Terrorist Threat Integration Center, and disarming Saddam Hussein. Iraq's apparent failure to comply with UN resolution 1441 to eliminate its weapons of mass destruction led to the Iraq War (Mar–Apr 2003) and the removal and eventual capture of Saddam Hussein. In November 2004 he won a second term in office after a closely fought contest with Senator John Kerry, receiving more popular votes than any other candidate in US history, and winning a majority of that vote, the first president to do so since his father won in 1988.

Bush, Laura Welch (1946–) US First Lady (2001–), born in Midland, TX. She studied library science at the University of Texas, Austin (1973), and worked as a librarian in public schools in Texas until 1977, when she married future president George W Bush. In her role as First Lady, she promotes the importance of libraries and reading for children, and is a member of many education advisory boards. She also supports the Texas Health Department, the American Cancer Society, and other health organizations.

bushbaby A primitive primate (*prosimian*), whose cry sounds like a human baby; large eyes and ears; thick coat, very long tail; long hind legs; agile; also known as **galago**. (Family: Lorisidae, 7 species.)

bushbuck A spiral-horned antelope (*Tragelaphus scriptus*) native to Africa S of the Sahara; reddish-brown with white spots or thin white lines; females without horns; lives in pairs; nocturnal.

bush cat *genet*

bushmaster A rare pit viper (*Lachesis muta*), native to Central and South America; largest venomous snake in the New World; length, up to 3.5 m/11½ ft; the only New World viper to lay eggs; nocturnal.

Bushmen *Khoisan*

bushrangers Australian rural outlaws who operated from 1790 to 1900. Some attained folk hero status, such as Ben Hall (killed 1865), and Ned Kelly (hanged 1880).

business cycle The tendency for the aggregate level of real activity in a country to fluctuate over time rather than growing steadily; also called a **trade cycle**. Such fluctuations have been observed as far back as economic records reach. They are believed to be due to a variety of causes, including irregular timing of changes in techniques and geographical discoveries, natural catastrophes such as earthquakes, political upsets such as wars and revolutions, and changes in the policies followed by governments or central banks.

Busoni, Ferruccio (Benvenuto) [busohnee] (1866–1924) Composer and pianist, born in Empoli, Italy. An infant prodigy, in 1889 he became professor of pianoforte at Helsinki. The influence of Liszt is apparent in his great piano concerto.

Bussell, Darcey (Andrea) [buhsel] (1969–) Ballerina, born in London. She joined the Royal Ballet as soloist in 1988, and went on to become the company's youngest principal dancer. She has made guest appearances internationally for various companies, and danced leading roles in works by MacMillan and Ashton. In 2005 she retired as principal dancer with the Royal Ballet, but remains as guest dancer.

bussing A government policy adopted in the 1960s (particularly in the USA) to promote social integration among school children in ethnically divided urban communities. Children (especially black and Asian) were taken by bus from disadvantaged

Burundi

☐ International Airport

[burundee], official name **Republic of Burundi**

Local name Burundi

Timezone GMT +2

Area 27 834 km²/10 747 sq mi

Population total (2002e) 6 373 000

Status Republic

Date of independence 1962

Capital Bujumbura

Languages French and Kirundi (official), Swahili

Ethnic groups Hutu (82%), Tutsi (14%), Twa Pygmy (1%)

Religions Roman Catholic (62%), traditional beliefs (32%)

Physical features Located in C Africa; lies across Nile-Congo watershed; interior plateau, c.1500 m/5000 ft; highest point, Mt Karonje 2685 m/8809 ft; R Ruzizi forms part of NW frontier with Zaïre and links Lake Kiki in Rwanda, with Lake Tanganyika in S and E; river Malagarasi valley in E.

Climate Equatorial; moderately wet; dry season (Jun–Sep); average annual temperature 23°C; average annual rainfall at Bujumbura, 850 mm/33·5 in.

Currency 1 Burundi Franc (BIF) = 100 centimes

Economy Mainly agriculture; cash crops include coffee, cotton, tea; light consumer goods, shoes, blankets; reserves of rare-earth metals.

GDP (2002e) $3·146 bn, per capita $500

Human Development Index (2002) 0·313

History Ruled by the Tutsi kingdom, 16th-c; occupied by Germany in 1890, and included in German East Africa, 1890; League of Nations mandated territory, administered by Belgians, 1919; joined with Rwanda to become the UN Trust Territory of Ruanda-Urundi, 1946. Independent, 1962; full republic following the overthrow of the monarchy, 1966; civil war, 1972; military coup, 1976; new constitution provided a National Assembly, 1981; Assembly dissolved and constitution suspended after 1987 coup; Military Council for National Salvation disbanded, 1990; new constitution, 1992; political instability following assassination of president, 1993; inter-ethnic (Hutu/Tutsi) conflict, 1993– ; transitional government agreed, 1994–8; ongoing conflict led to a further period of transitional governance, 2001; ceasefire signed (Dec 2002) by President Buyoya and main Hutu rebel group CNDD-FDD; talks on power sharing, early 2003; Domitien Ndayizeye, a Hutu, took over for 18-month term as agreed, Apr 2003; government signed peace agreement with FDD, Nov 2003; peace talks with Hutu rebel group NFL began Jan 2004; new interim constitution, Nov 2004; Pierre Nkurunziza, a Hutu former rebel leader, elected democratically (Aug 2005).

Head of State

1993 Melchior Ndadye
1994 Cyprien Ntaryamina
1994–6 Sylvestre Ntibantunganya
1996–2003 Pierre Buyoya *Military coup*
2003–5 Domitien Ndayizeye
2005– Pierre Nkurunziza

Head of Government

1993–4 Sylvie Kinigi
1994–5 Anatole Kanyenkiko
1995–6 Antoine Nduwayo
1996–8 Pascal-Firmin Ndimira

---

urban contexts to schools elsewhere. In the USA, bussing became controversial, and the policy was abandoned in 1972.

bustard A large, long-legged, ground-living bird native to Africa, S Europe, Asia, and Australia; walks rather than flies (but flies well). Permission for the reintroduction of the bird to Britain (on to Salisbury Plain, Wiltshire), was granted in 2003. (Family: Otididae, 24 species.)

busy Lizzie *impatiens*

butadiene [byootadiyeen] $CH_2=CH–CH=CH_2$, **buta-1,3-diene**, boiling point $-4°C$. A gas, an important monomer of synthetic rubbers.

butane [byootayn] $CH_3CH_2CH_2CH_3$, boiling point $0°C$. An easily liquefied alkane gas, obtained as a petroleum fraction. It is supplied as a liquid under pressure for use as a fuel, as in Calor(r) gas.

butanedioic acid *succinic acid*

butcherbird *shrike*

Buthelezi, Mangosuthu Gatsha [bootuhlayzee], known as **Chief Buthelezi** (1928–) South African Zulu leader and politician, born in KwaZulu Natal, South Africa. He is leader of the Zulu-based movement, Inkatha, which in the early 1990s was involved in a violent struggle for political leadership among black South Africans. In 1994 he was appointed minister for home affairs in Nelson Mandela's first cabinet, a position he retained (1999–2004) under President Thabo Mbeki.

Butler, Joseph (1692–1752) Moral philosopher and theologian, born in Wantage, Oxfordshire. His major work, *The Analogy of Religion* (1736), argued that objections against revealed religion may also be levelled against the whole constitution of nature.

Butler, Reg(inald Cotterell) (1913–81) Sculptor, born in Bunting-ford, Hertfordshire. He was one of the leading exponents of 'linear' constructions in wrought iron.

Butler, R(ichard) A(usten), Baron Butler, known as **Rab Butler** (1902–82) British Conservative stateman, born in Attock Serai, India. He became minister of education (1941–5), introducing the Education Act of 1944. Later posts included Chancellor of the Exchequer (1951), home secretary (1957), deputy prime minister (1962), and foreign secretary (1963–4). He was then appointed Master of Trinity College, Cambridge (1965–78).

Butler, Samuel (1612–80) Poet and satirist, baptized at Stren-sham, Worcestershire. His great 3-part poetic work, *Hudibras* (1663, 1664, 1678), is a burlesque satire on Puritanism.

Butler, Samuel (1835–1902) Writer, painter, and musician, born at Langar Rectory, Nottinghamshire. In his Utopian satire, *Ere-whon* (1872) – the word is an inversion of 'nowhere' – many conventional practices and customs are reversed. He is best known for his autobiographical novel *The Way of All Flesh* (1903).

Butlin, Billy, popular name of **Sir William (Edmund) Butlin** (1899–1980) Holiday camp promoter, born in South Africa. He opened his first camp at Skegness, UK, in 1936. In World War 2 he served as director-general of hostels to the ministry of supply.

Butskellism A compound of the names of UK Conservative politician R A Butler and the Labour leader Hugh Gaitskell, used in the 1950s and early 1960s to imply a high degree of similarity between the policies of the two main parties.

butte [byoot] Isolated, flat-topped, steep-sided residual hills formed by erosion of a mesa, when a remnant of hard rock protects the softer rock underneath.

butter A pale yellow foodstuff derived from the churning of cream, typically used in baking, cooking, or for spreading on bread. It comprises c.82% fat and c.16% water.

buttercup A member of a large and diverse genus of annuals or perennials, some aquatic, especially found in the N hemisphere; flowers cup-shaped, 5-petalled, glossy yellow, sometimes white or red. (Genus: *Ranunculus*, 400 species. Family: Ranunculaceae.)

butterfish *gunnel*

butterfly An insect belonging to the order Lepidoptera, which comprises the butterflies and moths. Butterflies are usually distinguished from moths by being active during the daytime, by folding their wings upright over their bodies when at rest, and by having small knobs at the tips of their antennae; but there are exceptions.

butterfly bush *buddleia*

butterflyfish *angelfish*

butterwort A small carnivorous perennial native to the N hemisphere and the mountains of South America; flowers solitary on leafless stems, 2-lipped, spurred; white, lilac, or violet. (Genus: *Pinguicula*, 46 species. Family: Lentibulariaceae.)

buttress A mass of masonry built against a wall, usually on the outside of a building to oppose the lateral thrust of an arch, roof, or vault. Varied in form, the most notable type is the **flying buttress**, which consists of a segment of an arch, stretching from a higher wall (sometimes, from a detached pier) to an external buttress.

Buttrose, Ita (Clare) (1942–) Journalist, publisher, and broadcaster, born in Sydney, New South Wales, Australia. In 1981 she joined News Limited as editor-in-chief of the *Sunday Telegraph*, becoming the first woman in Australia to edit either a daily or a Sunday paper. In 1988 she was editor of that paper's opposition, *The Sun Herald*, and by 1989 had started her own magazine, called *Ita*.

butyl [byootiyl, byootil] $CH_3CH_2CH_2CH_2-$. A four-carbon aliphatic group.

Buxtehude, Diderik or **Dietrich** [bukstehooduh] (1637–1707) Composer and organist, born in Oldesloe or Helsingborg, Sweden (formerly in Denmark). In 1668 he was appointed organist at the Marienkirche, Lübeck, where he began the famous *Abend-musiken* – Advent evening concerts of his own sacred music and organ works.

Buys Ballot, Christoph H(endrick) D(iederick) [biyz balot] (1817–90) Meteorologist, born in Kloetinge, The Netherlands. The law relating wind direction to areas of high and low pressure (**Buys Ballot's law,** 1857) arose from his work.

buzzard A large hawk found worldwide (except Australasia and Malaysia); brown, grey, and white; soaring flight, but spends much time perching; kills prey on ground. (Genus: *Buteo*, 25 species.)

buzz-bomb *V-1*

Byatt, Dame A(ntonia) S(usan), *née* **Drabble** (1936–) British novelist and critic, born in Sheffield, South Yorkshire, the sister of Margaret Drabble. Her novels include *Virgin in the Garden* (1978) and *Still-Life* (1985), the first two parts of a projected sequence tracing English life from the mid-1950s to the present day, *Possession* (1990, Booker), *Babel Tower* (1996), *The Biographer's Tale* (2000), and *A Whistling Woman* (2002). Her short story collections include *Little Black Book of Stories* (2003).

Byblos [biblos] 34°07N 35°39E. An ancient trading city on the Lebanese coast N of Beirut; a world heritage site. It was the chief supplier of papyrus to the Greeks, which they accordingly nicknamed 'byblos' – hence the word 'bible' (literally, 'the papyrus book').

Byelarus; Byelorussia *Belarus*

Byng, George, 1st Viscount Torrington (1663–1733) English sailor, born in Wrotham, Kent. In 1708 he defeated the French fleet of James Stuart, the Pretender, and in 1718 destroyed the Spanish fleet off Messina.

Byng (of Vimy), Julian Hedworth George Byng, 1st Viscount (1862–1935) British general, born in Wrotham Park, Middlesex. He commanded the 9th Army Corps in Gallipoli (1915), the Canadian Army Corps (1916–17), and the 3rd Army (1917–18). After World War 1 he became Governor-General of Canada (1921–6).

Byrd, Richard E(velyn) (1888–1957) Rear admiral, explorer, and aviator, born in Winchester, VA. He made the first aeroplane flight over the North Pole (1926), then flew over the South Pole (1929).

Byrd, William (1543–1623) Composer, probably born in Lincoln, Lincolnshire. He was organist of Lincoln Cathedral until 1572, when he was made joint organist with Tallis of the Chapel Royal. He wrote music for both the Catholic and the Anglican services, as well as madrigals, songs, keyboard pieces, and music for strings.

Byron (of Rochdale), George (Gordon) Byron, 6th Baron, known as **Lord Byron** (1788–1824) Poet, born in London. After a grand tour of Europe, he published the popular *Childe Harold's Pilgrimage* (1812), becoming the favourite of London society, and giving to Europe the concept of the 'Byronic hero'. Later works include *Don Juan* (1819–24). He gave active help to the Italian revolutionaries, and in 1823 joined the Greek insurgents who had risen against the Ottoman Turks. He died of malaria at Missolonghi.

byte A fixed number of bits (binary digits), usually defined as a set of 8 bits. An 8-bit byte can therefore take 256 different values corresponding to the binary numbers 00000000, 00000001, 00000010, through to 11111111. A **kilobyte** is one thousand bytes (actually 1024); a **megabyte** is one million bytes (1024 × 1024); a **gigabyte** is one thousand million bytes (1024 × 1024 × 1024).

Byzantine Empire [bizantiyn] The E half of the Roman Empire, with its capital at Constantinople, formerly Byzantium. Founded in AD 330, Byzantium survived the collapse of the W Empire by nearly a thousand years, falling to the Ottoman Turks in 1453.

C

C A computer programming language, developed by AT&T in the USA to be used with the Unix operating system. It has since been adopted much more widely, and is now available on personal computers. A further development was C++.

Cabal [kabal] An acronym taken from the initials of the five leading advisers of Charles II of England between 1667 and 1673: Clifford, Arlington, Buckingham, Ashley Cooper (Shaftesbury), and Lauderdale. The name is misleading, since these five were by no means Charles's only advisers, nor did they agree on a common policy, but the overtones of intrigue found in the general use of the word *cabal* made the acronym attractive.

cabbage A vegetable (*Brassica oleracea*) grown for its dense leafy head, which is harvested before the flowers develop and the head elongates. There are numerous cultivars, all derived from wild cabbage, native to W Europe and the Mediterranean. (Family: Cruciferae.)

cabbage white butterfly A large butterfly, found in Europe, N Africa, and North America; wings mainly white with black markings, and yellow on undersides of hindwings. The caterpillars are pests of cabbage family crops. (Order: Lepidoptera. Family: Pieridae.)

Cabbala *Kabbalah*

Cabell, James Branch [kabl] (1879–1958) Novelist and critic, born in Richmond, VA. He made his name with his novel *Jurgen* (1919), the best known of a sequence of 18 novels, collectively called *Biography of Manuel*, set in the imaginary mediaeval kingdom of Poictesme.

caber tossing The art of tossing a tree trunk (**caber**), practised in Scotland. The competitor has the caber, about 3–4 m/12–18 ft in length, placed vertically into the palms of his hands. He then runs with it and tosses it; the caber should revolve longitudinally, its base landing away from him. The tradition is popular at Highland Games gatherings.

Cabinda [kabeenda] area 7270 km²/2800 sq mi. Province of Angola on the SW coast of Africa; surrounded by the Congo; attached to Angola in 1886 by agreement with Belgium; seaport and chief town, Cabinda.

cabinet In a parliamentary system, a group of senior ministers usually drawn from the majority party. In Britain (where cabinet government originated), the cabinet has no constitutional status other than the conventions by which it operates. It forms the link between the executive and legislative branches of government, as its members must be drawn from the legislature. Cabinet members are bound by the doctrine of collective responsibility: ministers must publicly support decisions taken by the cabinet, or its committees, or else resign. A cabinet may also be found in a non-parliamentary system, such as that of the USA, where it provides the president with an additional consultative body.

cable television The distribution of video programmes to subscribers by co-axial cable or fibre-optic links, rather than by broadcast transmission. It provides a wide range of choice to individual homes within a specific area.

Cabot, John [kabot], Ital **Giovanni Caboto** (1425–c.1500) Navigator, born possibly in Genoa, who discovered the mainland of North America. He set sail in 1497 with two ships, sighting Cape Breton I and Nova Scotia on 24 June.

Cabot, Sebastian [kabot] (1474–1557) Explorer and navigator, born in Venice or Bristol, the son of John Cabot. In 1512 he entered the service of Ferdinand V of Spain as a cartographer, and in 1526 explored the coast of South America for Charles V.

Cabral or **Cabrera, Pedro Alvarez** [kabral] (c.1467–c.1520) Explorer, born in Belmonte, Portugal. In 1500 he sailed from Lisbon bound for the East Indies, but was carried to the unknown coast of Brazil, which he claimed on behalf of Portugal.

Cabrini, St Frances Xavier [kabreenee] (1850–1917) Nun, born near Lodi, Italy. She founded the Missionary Sisters of the Sacred Heart (1880), emigrating to the USA in 1887. Canonized in 1946, she was the first American saint. Feast day 13 November.

cacao An evergreen tree native to Central America (*Theobroma cacao*), widely cultivated elsewhere; leaves oblong; flowers pink, borne in clusters directly on trunks and older branches; fruit an ovoid yellow pod, leathery and grooved, enclosing up to 100 beans. The beans are dried, roasted, and ground to produce cocoa powder, used in drinks and chocolate. (Family: Sterculiaceae.)

Cáceres [katheres], Arabic **Qazris** 39°26N 6°23W, pop (2000e) 72 400. Walled town in W Spain; railway; a world heritage site; Roman settlement, 1st-c BC.

cachalot [kashalot] *sperm whale*

cache memory [kash] A very high-speed buffer memory which operates between the computer processor and main memory in high performance computer systems.

cacomistle [kakomisl] A mammal native to S USA and Central America; pale brown with lighter underparts; long bushy tail with black bands; also known as **cacomixl** or **ringtail**. (Genus: *Bassariscus*, 2 species. Family: Procyonidae.)

cactus A member of a large family of plants typical of arid zones but found in a number of habitats; almost all are confined to the New World. In the Old World they are paralleled by various members of the spurge family (Euphorbiaceae). Cacti exhibit a wide variety of size, form, and adaptations to dry conditions, some very sophisticated. All species are succulents and store water, sometimes in the roots but usually in swollen, often barrel-like, stems. The plants are leathery with a thick waxy cuticle. The spines can be very intricate, ranging from simple prongs to parasols and long, soft hairs; they shade or insulate the cactus, protect it from animals, reflect light, and collect and absorb droplets of dew – an important source of water. There is a wide range of flowers, often large and conspicuous. (Family: Cactaceae, c.2000 species.)

cactus moth A small, dull moth with narrow forewings and broad hindwings (*Cactoblastis cactorum*); introduced successfully into Australia in 1925 as a measure to control the spread of prickly pear cactus. (Order: Lepidoptera. Family: Pyralidae.)

Cadbury, George (1839–1922) Businessman, born in Birmingham,

West Midlands. In partnership with his brother **Richard Cadbury** (1835–99), he expanded his father's cocoa and chocolate business, and established for the workers the model village of Bournville (1879), a prototype for modern methods of housing and town planning.

caddis fly A dull-coloured, moth-like insect; forewings hairy, held at oblique vertical angle at rest. (Order: Trichoptera.)

Cade, Jack [kayd] (?–1450) Irish leader of the insurrection of 1450 against Henry VI. Assuming the title of Captain of Kent, he marched on London with a great number of followers, and entered the city. A promise of pardon sowed dissension among the insurgents, and he was killed.

cadenza An improvised (or improvisatory) passage, usually of a virtuoso and rhythmically free character, which the soloist in a concerto plays as a kind of adjunct to the main body of the piece. The orchestra is usually silent.

Cader Idris [kader idris] (Welsh 'chair of Idris') 52°42N 3°54W. Mountain ridge in NW Wales, UK; SW of Dolgellau; rises to 892 m/2928 ft at Pen-y-Gader.

Cádiz [kadiz], Span [kadeeth], ancient **Gadier** or **Gades** 36°30N 6°20W, pop (2000e) 156 000. Seaport in SW Spain; Francis Drake burned the ships of Philip II at anchor here, 1587; bishopric; airport; railway; university; naval harbour of La Carraca; cathedral (18th-c).

cadmium Cd, element 48, density 8·7 g/cm³, melting point 321°C, colour bluish-white. A metal, normally occurring with other metals as the sulphide, CdS. The metal is recovered for use in low-melting alloys and as an absorber for neutrons in atomic reactors. Cadmium compounds (which are very toxic) are used as phosphors in colour television tubes.

caecilian [seesilian] An amphibian of the worldwide tropical order Gymnophiona (163 species); length, up to 1·5 m/5 ft; body worm-like with encircling rings and no legs.

Caedmon [kadmon] (?–c.680) The first English poet of known name, to whom the *Song of Caedmon* is attributed. Bede reports that, unlearned till mature in years, Caedmon became aware in a semi-miraculous way that he was called to exercise the gift of religious poetry. He became a monk at Whitby, N Yorkshire.

Caelum [kiyluhm] (Lat 'chisel') An inconspicuous S hemisphere constellation.

Caen [kã] 49°10N 0°22W, pop (2000e) 118 000. Port in NW France; airport; railway; university (1432, refounded 1809); badly damaged in World War 2; tomb of William the Conqueror.

Caernarfon [kiyrnarvon], Eng **Caernarvon** [kuhnah(r)vn] 53°08N 4°16W, pop (2000e) 9800. County town of Gwynedd, NW Wales, UK; on Menai Strait; yachting centre; Galeri arts centre (2005); castle (1284), birthplace of Edward II is a world heritage site; investiture of Prince Charles as Prince of Wales, 1969.

Caernarfonshire *Gwynedd*

Caerphilly [kiy(r)filee], Welsh **Caerffili** pop (2001e) 169 500; area 279 km²/108 sq mi. County (unitary authority from 1996) in SE Wales, UK; administrative centre, Hengoed; original home of Caerphilly cheese; Caerphilly Castle (13th-c), the largest in Wales.

Caesar, in full **Gaius Julius Caesar** (c.101–44 BC) Roman politician of patrician origins but slender means, whose military genius enabled Rome to extend her empire to the Atlantic seaboard, but whose ruthless ambition led to the breakdown of the Republican system of government at home. In 60 BC he joined with Pompey and Crassus (the so-called First Triumvirate) to protect his interests in the state. For nine years (58–50 BC) he conducted campaigns (the Gallic Wars) which extended Roman power in the West. In 55 BC he invaded Britain, and on a second invasion in 54 BC crossed the R Thames and enforced at least the nominal submission of the SE of the island. In 49 BC, to avoid being humbled by his enemies at Rome, he led his army across the R Rubicon into Italy and plunged the state into civil war. Victory over the Pompeian forces at Pharsalus (48 BC), Zela (47 BC), Thapsus (46 BC), and Munda (45 BC) left him in sole control at Rome, taking the title 'Dictator for Life' in 44 BC. His person was declared sacred, his statue placed in temples, his portrait struck on coins, and the month Quintilis renamed July in his honour. He was murdered by Republican-minded Romans under the leadership of Brutus and Cassius.

caesarian / cesarian section [seezairian] The surgical removal of the fetus from the uterus. It is undertaken when normal labour and vaginal delivery is causing or is likely to cause significant harm to the mother or fetus.

caffeine C₈H₁₀N₄O₂. An alkaloid, also called **theine**, a weak stimulant of the central nervous system. It is found in both coffee and tea.

Cage, John (Milton) (1912–92) Composer, born in Los Angeles, CA. His works use such resources as electronics and the 'prepared piano' (distorting the sound of the instrument with objects placed inside). He also experimented with silence as an art form, and with musical chance, in which (for example) a dice would be thrown to determine the elements of a composition.

Cage, Nicolas, originally **Nicholas Coppola** (1964–) Film actor, born in Long Beach, CA. He became well known after his appearances in *The Cotton Club* (1984) and won critical acclaim for *Leaving Las Vegas* (1995, Oscar). Later films include *Captain Corelli's Mandolin* (2001), *Adaptation* (2002), and *World Trade Center* (2006).

Cagliari [kalyahree], ancient **Carales** 39°13N 9°08E, pop (2000e) 236 000. Seaport in S Sardinia, Italy; archbishopric; airport; railway; university (1956); cathedral (1312), Roman amphitheatre.

Cagliostro, Alessandro, conte di (Count of) [kalyohstroh], originally **Giuseppe Balsamo** (1743–95) Adventurer and charlatan, born in Palermo, Italy. Successful alike as physician, philosopher, alchemist, and necromancer, he carried on a lively business in his 'elixir of immortal youth'.

Cagney, James (1899–1986) Film actor, born in New York City. His film performance as the gangster in *The Public Enemy* (1931) brought him stardom. Later films include *Angels with Dirty Faces* (1938) and *Yankee Doodle Dandy* (1942, Oscar).

Cahokia [kahohkia] A prehistoric city of Middle Mississippi Indians in E St Louis, IL, USA. It was founded c.600 and, at 13 km²/5 sq mi, is the largest such settlement in North America; a world heritage site.

Caiaphas [kiyafas] (1st-c) Son-in-law of Annas, eventually appointed by the Romans to be his successor as high priest of Israel (c.18–36). In the New Testament he interrogated Jesus after his arrest.

Caicos Islands [kaykos] Island group in the W Atlantic, SE of the Bahamas, forming a British overseas territory with the Turks Is. It was settled by Loyalist planters from the S States of America after the War of Independence.

caiman or **cayman** [kayman] A member of the alligator family (5 species), native to Central and South America; length, up to 2 m/6½ ft; inhabits rivers and swamps.

Cain [kayn] Biblical character, the eldest son of Adam and Eve, the brother of Abel and Seth. He is portrayed as a farmer whose offering to God was rejected, in contrast to that of his herdsman brother Abel. This led to his murder of Abel, and Cain's punishment of being banished to a nomadic life.

Caine, Sir Michael [kayn], properly **Sir Maurice Micklewhite** (1933–) Film actor, born in London. He became known with roles such as down-at-heel spy Harry Palmer in *The Ipcress File* (1965) and its two sequels, and as the Cockney Romeo in *Alfie* (1966). Later films include, *California Suite* (1978), *Educating Rita* (1983), *Hannah and Her Sisters* (1986, Oscar), *The Cider House Rules* (1999, Oscar for Best Supporting Actor), *The*

Quiet American (2002, Oscar nomination), and *Children of Men* (2006).

Cainozoic era *Cenozoic era*

Cairngorms or **Cairngorm Mountains** Mountain range in NEC Scotland, part of Grampian Mts; rises to 1309 m/4295 ft in Ben Macdhui; winter sports region, centre at Aviemore.

Cairns [kairnz] 16°51S 145°43E, pop (2000e) 54 500. Resort and seaport on the NE coast of Queensland, Australia; starting point for tours to the Great Barrier Reef and the Cape York Peninsula; railway; airfield.

Cairns Group An informal association of agricultural exporting countries, established in Cairns, Australia, in 1986. Its aims are to introduce reforms in international agricultural trade, such as the reduction of export subsidies and internal support measures. It had 17 members in 2007.

Cairo [kiyroh], Arabic **al-Qahira** 30°03N 31°15E, pop (2000e) 7 630 000 (Greater Cairo). Capital of Egypt, at head of R Nile delta; largest African city; originally founded as El Fustat in AD 642; occupied by British, 1882–1946; airport; railway; four universities (1908, 1919, 1950, and Muslim university in Mosque of al-Azhar, 1972); Islamic Cairo a world heritage site; major archaeological sites nearby, including pyramids at El Giza.

caisson [kaysn] A permanent structure for keeping water or soft ground from flowing into the site when building foundations. There are several types: **open caissons** open at the top and bottom; **box caissons** open at the top and closed at the bottom; and **pneumatic caissons**, containing a working chamber in which compressed air excludes the water.

caisson disease [kaysn] *decompression sickness*

calabash A trailing or climbing vine (*Lagenaria siceraria*), native to warm Old World regions, with white flowers and woody, bottle-shaped fruits; also called **bottle gourd**. (Family: Cucurbitaceae.)

calabash tree An evergreen tree (*Crescentia cujete*) growing to 12 m/40 ft, native to tropical America; flowers bell-shaped; fruit a woody berry up to 30 cm/12 in long or more, flask-shaped and used as a container. (Family: Bignoniaceae.)

calabrese [kalabrayzee] *broccoli*

Calabria [kalaybria], Ital [kalabria] pop (2000e) 2 008 000; area 15 079 km²/5820 sq mi. Region of S Italy, occupying the 'toe' of the country, capital, Catanzaro; underdeveloped area with mixed Mediterranean agriculture; subject to earthquakes, floods, and erosion.

Calais [kalay] 50°57N 1°52E, pop (2000e) 79 300. Seaport in NW France; on the Straits of Dover, at the shortest crossing to England, 34 km/21 mi SE of Dover; captured by England, 1346; retaken by France, 1558; British base in World War 1; centre of heavy fighting in World War 2; airport; railway; ferry services.

calamine [kalamiyn] A mixture of zinc carbonate and ferric oxide, used as an ointment for many skin conditions.

Calamity Jane, popular name of **Martha Jane Burke**, *née* **Cannary** (c.1852–1903) Legendary frontier figure, born in Princeton, MO. Raised in Virginia City, MT (1864), she became an expert markswoman and rider and (dressed as a man) held her own in rough, mining-town society. Allegedly a pony-express rider and then a scout for General George Custer in Wyoming (1870s), she was companion to **'Wild Bill' Hickok** (1837–76). She is said to have threatened 'calamity' for any man who tried to court her, but in 1891 she married **Clinton Burk(e)** in El Paso, TX, who soon left her. She died in poverty, and is buried beside Hickok in Deadwood.

calceolaria [kalsiohlairia] A member of a large genus of annuals, perennials, or shrubs native to Central and South America; characteristic 2-lipped flowers with lower lip inflated and pouch-like; commonly grown ornamentals are mainly hybrids with yellow, orange, or red spotted flowers. (Genus: *Calceolaria*, 300–400 species. Family: Scrophulariaceae.)

calcite [kalsiyt] A mineral form of calcium carbonate ($CaCO_3$), and the main constituent of limestone and marble. It can form stalactites and stalagmites, and the structure of coral reefs. Good crystals formed in vein deposits are transparent, and termed *Iceland spar*.

calcium Ca, element 20, melting point 839°C. A very reactive, silvery metal only found combined in nature; the metal is obtained by electrolysis. It is the fifth most common element in the Earth's crust, occurring mainly in fluorite (CaF_2), gypsum ($CaSO_4.2H_2O$), and limestone ($CaCO_3$). Ca^{2+} ions are largely responsible for hardness in water. Calcium is used in the structural tissue of both plants and animals; its compounds are common components of agricultural fertilizers, and are ingredients of both glass and cement.

calculi [kalkyooliy] In medicine, small stone-like concretions which form within certain organs and ducts. The most common sites include the salivary glands, urinary tract, and biliary tract.

calculus *differential calculus; integral calculus*

Calcutta [kalkuhta], official name **Kolkata** (Jan 2001) 22°36N 88°24E, pop (2000e) 12 750 000. Port capital of West Bengal, E India; third largest city in India; founded by the British East India Company, 1690; capital of British India, 1773–1912; airport; railway; three universities; Queen Victoria Memorial Museum; cathedral (1787), Nakhoda Mosque (1926), Jain temples (1867), Hindu Bengali Temple of Kali (1809).

Caldecott, Randolph [kawldikot] (1846–86) Artist and illustrator, born in Chester, Cheshire. He illustrated Washington Irving's *Old Christmas* (1876) and numerous children's books, such as Aesop's Fables (1883). The **Caldecott Medal** has been awarded annually since 1938 to the best US artist-illustrator of children's books.

Calder, Alexander [kawlder], known as **Sandy Calder** (1898–1976) Artist, born in Philadelphia, PA. His best-known works are the abstract, hanging wire mobiles, which he began to make in 1934.

caldera [kaldaira] A large volcanic crater formed when the remains of a volcano subside into a magma chamber, emptied after a violent eruption. The caldera may subsequently fill with water, and become a crater lake.

Calderón de la Barca, Pedro [kolduhron duh la bah(r)ka] (1600–81) Playwright, born in Madrid. He was appointed to the court of Philip IV, where he wrote over 100 plays, masques, and operas for the court, the church, and the public theatres.

Caldwell, Erskine (Preston) [kawldwel] (1903–87) Writer, born in White Oak, GA. His best-known novels are *Tobacco Road* (1932) and *God's Little Acre* (1933). Much of his work addresses issues of social injustice in the US South.

Caledonian Canal A line of inland navigation following the Great Glen (Glen More) in Highland council, Scotland; extends from Inverness (NE) to Loch Eil near Fort William (SW), thus linking North Sea and Irish Sea; total length 96 km/60 mi; built by Telford.

calendar *French Republican / Gregorian / Julian calendar; month / year equivalents (see panel p.150)*

Calgary 51°05N 114°05W, pop (2000e) 795 500. Town in S Alberta, Canada, centre of rich grain and livestock area; growth following arrival of Canadian Pacific Railway, 1883; oil found to the S, 1914; airport; university (1945); ice hockey team, Calgary Flames; Calgary Tower (1967, 190 m/623 ft).

Cali [kalee] 3°24N 76°30W, pop (2000e) 1 561 000. City in W Colombia, at centre of rich sugar-producing region; founded, 1536; airport; two universities (1945, 1958); cathedral.

calico bush *mountain laurel*

Calicut *Kozhikode*

California pop (2000e) 33 871 600; area 411 033 km²/158 706 sq mi. State in SW USA; the 'Golden State'; discovered by the

Calendar Year Equivalents

Jewish[1] (AM)	Islamic[2] (H)	Hindu[3] (SE)
5766 (4 Oct 2005–22 Sep 2006)	1426 (10 Feb 2005–30 Jan 2006)	1927 (22 Mar 2005–21 Mar 2006)
5767 (23 Sep 2006–12 Sep 2007)	1427 (31 Jan 2006–19 Jan 2007)	1928 (22 Mar 2006–21 Mar 2007)
5768 (13 Sep 2007–29 Sep 2008)	1428 (20 Jan 2007–9 Jan 2008)	1929 (22 Mar 2007–21 Mar 2008)
5769 (30 Sep 2008–18 Sep 2009)	1429 (10 Jan 2008–28 Dec 2009)	1930 (22 Mar 2008–21 Mar 2009)
5770 (19 Sep 2009–8 Sep 2010)	1430 (29 Dec 2009–17 Dec 2010)	1931 (22 Mar 2009–22 Mar 2010)

Gregorian equivalents are given in parentheses and are AD (= Anno Domini).
[1] Calculated from 3761 BC, said to be the year of the creation of the world, AM = Anno Mundi.
[2] Calculated from AD 622, the year in which the Prophet went from Mecca to Medina, H = Hijra.
[3] Calculated from AD 78, the beginning of the Saka era (SE), used alongside Gregorian dates in Government of India publications since 22 Mar 1957. Other important Hindu eras include: Vikrama era (58 BC), Kalacuri era (AD 248), Gupta era (AD 320), and Harsa era (AD 606).

Calendar Month Equivalents

Gregorian equivalents to other calendars are given in parentheses; the figures refer to the number of solar days in each month.

Gregorian (Basis: Sun)	Jewish (Basis: Moon)	Islamic (Basis:Moon)	Hindu (Basis:Moon)
January (31)	Tishri (Sep–Oct) (30)	Muharram (Sep–Oct) (30)	Caitra (Mar–Apr) (29 or 30)
February (28 or 29)	Heshvan (Oct–Nov) (29 or 30)	Safar (Oct–Nov) (29)	Vaisakha (Apr–May) (29 or 30)
March (31)	Kislev (Nov–Dec) (29 or 30)	Rabi I (Nov–Dec) (30)	Jyaistha (May–Jun) (29 or 30)
April (30)	Tevet (Dec–Jan) (29)	Rabi II (Dec–Jan) (29)	Asadha (Jun–Jul) (29 or 30)
May (31)	Shevat (Jan–Feb) (30)	Jamada I (Jan–Feb) (30)	Dvitiya Asadha *certain leap years*
June (30)	Adar (Feb–Mar) (29 or 30)	Jumada II (Feb–Mar) (29)	Svrana (Jul–Aug) (29 or 30)
July (31)	Adar Sheni *leap years only*	Rajab (Mar–Apr) (30)	Dvitiya Sravana *certain leap years*
August (31)	Nisan (Mar–Apr) (30)	Shaban (Apr–May) (29)	Bhadrapada (Aug–Sep) (29 or 30)
September (30)	Iyar (Apr–May) (29)	Ramadan (May–Jun) (30)	Asvina (Sep–Oct) (29 or 30)
October (31)	Sivan (May–Jun) (30)	Shawwal (Jun–Jul) (29)	Karttika (Oct–Nov) (29 or 30)
November (30)	Tammuz (Jun–Jul) (29)	Dhu al-Qadah (Jul–Aug) (30)	Margasirsa (Nov–Dec) (29 or 30)
December (31)	Av (Jul–Aug) (30)	Dhu al-Hijjah (Aug–Sep) (29 or 30)	Pausa (Dec–Jan) (29 or 30)
	Elul (Aug–Sep) (29)		Magha (Jan–Feb) (29 or 30)
			Phalguna (Feb–Mar) (29 or 30)

Spanish, 1542; colonized mid-18th-c; developed after gold discovered in the Mother Lode, 1848; ceded to the USA by the treaty of Guadalupe Hidalgo, 1848; joined the Union as the 31st state, 1850; now the most populous US state; mountainous in the N, W and E, with dry, arid depressions in the S; Coast Ranges in the W run parallel to the Pacific; Sierra Nevada in the E, rising to 4418 m/14 495 ft at Mt Whitney (state's highest point); Central Valley a major fruit-producing area; a zone of faults (the San Andreas Fault) extends S from N California along the coast; earth tremors commonplace; major earthquakes in San Francisco 1906, 1989, and in Los Angeles, 1993; devastating wildfires in the south, 2003; record heatwave caused 136 deaths (Jul 2006); deal agreed to cut carbon dioxide emissions (2006); capital, Sacramento; major towns, San Francisco, Los Angeles, Oakland, and San Diego; centre of the US microelectronics industry in Silicon Valley; vineyards in over 40 Californian counties; increasing Hispanic and Asian populations; a major tourist state, with several national monuments and parks (Yosemite, Kings Canyon, Sequoia, Redwood), the film industry, and Disneyland.

California, Gulf of Arm of the Pacific Ocean between Mexican mainland (E) and Baja California (W); Colorado R delta (N); maximum depth 2595 m/8514 ft; 1130 km/700 mi long by 80–130 km/50–80 mi wide.

California redwood *mammoth tree*

California sorrel *palomino*

Caligula [kaligyula], nickname of **Gaius Julius Caesar Germanicus** (12–41) Roman emperor (37–41), the youngest son of Germanicus and Agrippina, born in Antium. Brought up in an army camp, he was nicknamed Caligula from his little soldier's boots (*caligae*). Extravagant, autocratic, vicious, and mentally unstable, he wreaked havoc with the finances of the state, and terrorized those around him, until he was assassinated.

calimanco cat *tortoiseshell cat*

calisthenics The art and practice of bodily exercises designed to produce beauty and grace rather than muscular development. They are often performed with the aid of hand-held apparatus, such as rings and clubs.

Callaghan (of Cardiff), (Leonard) James Callaghan, Baron [kalahan], known as **Jim Callaghan** (1912–2005) British Labour statesman and prime minister (1976–9), born in Portsmouth, Hampshire. He was Chancellor of the Exchequer (1964–7), home secretary (1967–70) and foreign secretary (1974–6), and became prime minister on Wilson's resignation. He resigned as Leader of the Opposition in 1980, and became a life peer in 1987.

Callaghan, Morley (Edward) [kalahan] (1903–90) Novelist, short-story writer, and memoirist, born in Toronto, Ontario, Canada.

His novels include *Strange Fugitive* (1928), *The Loved and the Lost* (1951), and *A Time for Judas* (1983).

calla lily *arum lily*

Callao [kalyahoh] 12°05S 77°08W, pop (2000e) 688 000. Port in W Peru; handles 75% of Peru's imports and c.25% of its exports; occupied by Chile, 1879–84; airport.

Callas, Maria (Meneghini) [kalas], originally **Maria Kalogeropoulos** (1923–77) Operatic soprano, born in New York City. She sang with great authority in all the most exacting soprano roles, excelling in the intricate *bel canto* style of pre-Verdian Italian opera.

calligraphy The art of penmanship, or writing at its most formal. It is a major art form in many countries of E Asia and in Arabic-speaking countries, and there has been a revival of interest in Europe and America since the 19th-c.

Callimachus [kalimakus] (5th-c BC) Greek sculptor working in Athens in the late 5th-c BC. Vitruvius says he invented the Corinthian capital.

Callimachus [kalimakus] (299–210 BC) Greek poet, grammarian, and critic, born in Cyrene, Libya. He became head of the Alexandrian Library, for which he prepared a catalogue in 120 volumes.

calliope [kaliyopee] A steam organ patented by J C Stoddard of Worcester, MA, in 1855. Most calliopes had about 15–30 whistles, operated by a keyboard, and were fitted to the top decks of river showboats.

Calliope [kaliyopee] In Greek mythology, the Muse of epic poetry. She is sometimes said to be the mother of Orpheus.

Callisto (astronomy) [kalistoh] The fourth natural satellite of Jupiter, discovered in 1610 by Galileo; distance from the planet 1 883 000 km/1 170 000 mi; diameter 4800 km/3000 mi; orbital period 16·689 days. Its dark surface is a mixture of ice and rocky material, and is heavily cratered.

Callisto (mythology) [kalistoh] In Greek mythology, an Arcadian nymph attendant upon Artemis. Loved by Zeus, she became pregnant, and was sent away from the virgin band. She was later changed into a she-bear, and eventually into the constellation Ursa Major.

Calmar *Kalmar*

Calmette, (Léon Charles) Albert [kalmet] (1863–1933) Microbiologist, born in Nice, France. He is best known for the vaccine BCG (Bacille Calmette–Guérin), which provides protection against tuberculosis, jointly developed with Dr Camille Guérin (1872–1961).

caloric *thermodynamics*

calorie In thermodynamics, an old unit of heat, symbol *cal*; 1 cal = 4·184 J (joule, SI unit); defined as the quantity of heat required to raise the temperature of a gram of water from 14·5°C to 15·5°C. The calorie is an extremely small unit of energy, the average person requiring 2·5 million calories per day. To overcome the obvious problem in counting such small units, the preferred term in scientific literature is the *kilocalorie*, symbol *kcal* or *Cal*, where 1 Cal = 1000 cal, and this is the term commonly used in describing the energy content of foodstuffs. However, the public have continued to use the familiar word; so, in popular usage, 1 kilocalorie is often thought of as 1 Calorie.

calorimetry The measurement of energy transferred in some physical or chemical process, such as the energy evolved by burning some substance. In nutrition, **calorimeters** are used to measure the number of calories in a given substance, or to measure the heat output of humans, equivalent to caloric expenditure.

Calvary [kalvaree] (Lat *calvaria*, 'skull', translating Semitic *Golgotha*) The site where Jesus was crucified, presumed to be a place of execution just outside Jerusalem. The term appears in the Authorized Version (*Luke* 23.33).

Calvin, John (1509–64) Protestant reformer, born in Noyon, France. At Basel he issued his influential *Christianae religionis institutio* (1536, Institutes of the Christian Religion), and at Geneva was persuaded to help with the reformation. The father figure of Reformed theology, he left a double legacy to Protestantism by systematizing its doctrine and organizing its ecclesiastical discipline.

Calvinism [kalvinizm] A term with at least three applications. **1** The theology of the 16th-c Protestant reformer, John Calvin. **2** The principal doctrines of 17th-c Calvinist scholars, including the 'five points of Calvinism' affirmed by the Synod of Dort (1618–19). **3** More broadly, the beliefs of those Churches in the Reformed tradition which arose under the influence of Calvin. Historically, Calvinism has emphasized the sovereignty of God, the Bible as the sole rule of faith, the doctrine of predestination, and justification by faith alone. There has been a Neo-Calvinist renewal in the 20th-c under the influence of the theologian Karl Barth.

Calypso (astronomy) The 14th natural satellite of Saturn, discovered in 1980; distance from the planet 295 000 km/183 000 mi; diameter 30 km/19 mi.

calypso (music) A song tradition from Trinidad, with roots in West African music. It regularly features satirical, social, political, or other topical comment sung to the accompaniment of guitar and maracas, or steel drums, with a syncopated beat. The music has been one of several influences on the development of reggae and its variants, and has itself developed (some would say degenerated) into soca.

calyx *flower; sepal*

Calzaghe, Joe [kalzagee], popular name of **Joseph Calzaghe** (1972–) Boxer, born in London. The son of an Italian father and Welsh mother, he settled with his family in Newbridge, South Wales when a young boy. He joined the Newbridge Boxing Club and went on to win three consecutive British ABA titles (1991–3) in welter, light-middle, and middleweight divisions. He turned professional in 1993, and in 1997 defeated Chris Eubank for the vacant WBO super-middleweight crown. In 2006 he became the undisputed world super-middleweight champion after a convincing win over IBF super-middleweight champion Jeff Lacy. He rounded off a successful year by winning the Wales Sports Personality of the Year award.

Camargue [kamah(r)g] area 750 km²/290 sq mi. District in R Rhône delta, SE France; alluvial island, mainly saltmarsh and lagoon; nature reserve for migratory birds; centre for breeding bulls and horses; chief locality, Saintes-Maries-de-la-Mer; tourism.

Camberwell beauty A colourful butterfly; wings velvet brown with yellow margin and line of blue spots. (Order: Lepidoptera. Family: Nymphalidae.)

Cambodia *p.152*

Cambodian *Austro-Asiatic languages; Khmer*

Cambrian period The earliest geological period of the Palaeozoic era, lasting from c.590 to 505 million years ago. Characterized by widespread seas, its rocks contain a large variety of marine invertebrate fossils.

Cambridge (UK), Lat **Cantabrigia** 52°12N 0°07E, pop (2000e) 121 200. County town of Cambridgeshire, EC England; on the R Cam (Granta); Roman settlement, AD 70; airfield; railway; one of the world's great universities, established 13th-c; football team, Cambridge United ('U's).

Cambridge (USA), formerly **New Towne** (to 1638) 42°22N 71°06W, pop (2000e) 101 400. City in E Massachusetts, USA; on the Charles R; founded, 1630; city status, 1846; railway; Harvard University (1636) is the oldest US college; Massachusetts Institute of Technology (1859) moved from Boston in 1915.

Cambridge Platonists A group of 17th-c philosophers, centred on Cambridge University, who took Plato (more than his doc-

Cambodia

☐ International Airport ∴ World heritage site

[kambohdia], formerly **Kampuchea** (1975–89) and **Khmer Republic** (1970–5), official name (from 1993) **Kingdom of Cambodia**, Khmer **Preah Reach Ana Pak Kampuchea**
Local name Cambodia
Timezone GMT +7
Area 181 035 km²/69 879 sq mi
Population total (2002e) 13 414 000
Status Kingdom
Date of independence 1953
Capital Phnom Penh
Languages Khmer (official), French
Ethnic groups Khmer (93%), Chinese (3%), Cham (2%)

Religions Theravada Buddhist (88%), Muslim (2%)
Physical features Kingdom in SE Asia. Crossed E by floodplain of Mekong R; Cardamom mountain range 160 km/100 mi across Thailand border, rising to 1813 m/5948 ft at Phnom Aural; Tonlé Sap (Greek Lake) in NW.
Climate Tropical monsoon climate, with a wet season (May–Sep). High temperatures in lowland region throughout the year; average annual temperature 21°C (Jan), 29°C (Jul); average annual rainfall 5000 mm/71 in (SW), 1300 mm/51 in (interior lowlands).
Currency 1 Riel (KHR) = 100 sen
Economy Most of population employed in subsistence agriculture, rice and corn; industrial development disrupted by the civil war.
GDP (2002e) $20·42 bn, per capita $1600
Human Development Index (2002) 0·543
History Originally part of Funan Kingdom, then part of the Khmer Empire, 6th-c; in dispute with Vietnamese and Thais from 15th-c; French Protectorate, 1863; formed French Indo-Chinese Union with Laos and Vietnam; 1887; independence, 1953; Prince Sihanouk deposed and Khmer Republic formed in 1970; fighting throughout the country involved troops from N and S Vietnam and the USA; surrender of Phnom Penh to the Khmer Rouge, and country renamed Kampuchea, 1975; attempt to reform economy on cooperative lines by Pol Pot (1975–8) caused the deaths of an estimated 3 million people; further fighting 1977–8; Phnom Penh captured by the Vietnamese, causing Khmer Rouge to flee, 1979; 1981 constitution established a Council of State and a Council of Ministers; name of Cambodia restored, 1989; Vietnamese troops completed withdrawal, 1989; UN peace plan agreed, with ceasefire and return of Sihanouk as Head of State, 1991; Sihanouk crowned King, 1993; further conflict following Khmer Rouge refusal to take part in 1993 elections; following eleven months of political deadlock, the two main parties agreed to form a coalition government, 2004; abdication of King Sihanouk, Oct 2004, Prince Norodom Sihamoni appointed successor.

Head of State (Monarch)
1993–2004 Norodom Sihanouk II (*restored*)
2004 Norodom Ranariddh *Interim*
2004– Norodom Sihamoni
Head of Government
1993–7 Norodom Ranariddh (*joint*)
1993–8 Hun Sen (*joint*)
1997–8 Ing Huot (*joint*)
1998– Hun Sen

trines) as their model. The movement was noted for its emphasis on reason in religion and ethics and its opposition to dogmatism.
Cambridgeshire pop (2001e) 552 700; area 3409 km²/1316 sq mi. County of EC England; flat fenland to the N; county town, Cambridge; Peterborough a unitary authority in 1998.
Cambridge University The second oldest university in England, after Oxford. The first college, Peterhouse, was founded in 1284. Prestigious institutions include the Fitzwilliam Museum, the Cavendish Laboratory of experimental physics, the Cambridge University Press (founded 1534), and the University library. (*see panel p.153*)
camcorder A small, portable video camera with an integral narrow-gauge videotape recorder, also known as the **camera cassette recorder** (CCR). It offers immediate play-back through a domestic television receiver.
Camden (UK) 51°33N 0°09W, pop (2001e) 198 000. Borough of N Greater London, UK; includes suburbs of Hampstead, St Pancras, and Holborn; named after an 18th-c Lord Chancellor.

Camden (USA) 39°56N 75°07W, pop (2000e) 79 900. City in W New Jersey, USA; port on E bank of Delaware R; city status, 1828; railway; university (1934); home of Walt Whitman (1873–92).
Camden, William (1551–1623) Scholar, antiquary, and historian, born in London. His *Britannia* (1586) was the first comprehensive topographical survey of the British Isles. The *Camden Society* (founded 1838), which promoted historical publications, was named after him.
Camden, Battle of (1780) A battle of the US War of Independence, fought in S Carolina. Americans under Horatio Gates were defeated by British troops under Lord Cornwallis.
Camden Town Group A group of artists who flourished 1905–13 in London. Sickert was the leading member. They shared an enthusiasm for recent French painting.
Camdessus, Michel (Jean) [kādesy] (1933–) Managing director and chairman of the International Monetary Fund (1987–2000), born in Bayonne, SW France. Deputy-director of the Bank of France from 1982, he became its director in 1984, a post he held until he was appointed to the IMF.

camel A mammal of the family Camelidae (2 species): the **Bactrian** (or **two-humped**) **camel** (*Camelus bactrianus*) from cold deserts in C Asia, and domesticated elsewhere, and the **dromedary**; eats any vegetation; humps are stores of energy-rich fats.

Camelidae [kamelidee] The camel family of mammals (6 species), found from N Africa to Mongolia (*camels*), or in the Andes (*llama, alpaca, guanaco, vicuña*); artiodactyls; unusual walk (move both right legs, then both left).

camellia [kameelia] An evergreen shrub or tree, native to China, Japan, and SE Asia; flowers usually large and showy, often scented, usually 4–7 petals, but often numerous in cultivars; white, pink, or crimson. (Genus: *Camellia*, 82 species. Family: Theaceae.)

camel(e)opard [kameluhpah(r)d] *giraffe*

Camelopardalis [kamelopah(r)dalis] (Lat 'giraffe') A large constellation in the N hemisphere, also known as **Camelopardus**. It lacks any bright stars.

Camelot [kamelot] The legendary capital of King Arthur's Britain. It is variously located at Cadbury in the West Country, Colchester (Camulodunum), and Winchester.

cameo A method of carving a relief image into a shell or semiprecious stone with different coloured layers. It was popular in the Roman Empire, and has been used ever since in W European art, often copied in glass and ceramic.

camera An apparatus which produces an image of an external scene. In the early **camera obscura** (literally 'darkened room'), light passing through a small hole or lens formed a picture on the opposite wall. Portable versions in boxes served as artist's guides in landscape drawing, and early 19th-c attempts to record the image led to the first photographic camera: a light-tight box containing a glass or metal plate with a light-sensitive surface on which the image was formed by a lens. In the 1880s photographic film in continuous strips revolutionized camera design. The first miniature camera to use perforated film 35 mm wide was the Leica in 1925, and this compact cassette-loaded form was widely adopted for other sizes. Camera operation has become increasingly simplified with automatic focus setting and exposure; built-in synchronized electronic flash and motor drive for film advance and repeated operation are also now available. Digital cameras became widely available in the 1990s, and have now largely replaced traditional models.

camera obscura *camera*

Cameron, David (William Donald) (1966–) British statesman, born in Oxfordshire. He studied at Eton and Brasenose College, Oxford, and began his political career in the Conservative Party research department (1988), before becoming special adviser to chancellor Norman Lamont (1992) and to home secretary Michael Howard (1993). Elected MP for Witney in Oxfordshire (2001), he became deputy chairman of the Conservative Party (2003) and shadow education secretary (2004). In December 2005 he was voted party leader, taking over from Michael Howard.

Cameron, James (1954–) Film director, screenwriter, and producer, born in Kapuskasing, Ontario, Canada. His credits as writer/director include *The Terminator* and its sequels (1984, 1991), *Aliens* (1986), *The Abyss* (1989), *True Lies* (1994), and *Titanic* (1997, 11 Oscars, including Best Film and Best Director). He directed and produced *Aliens of the Deep* in 2005.

Cameroon *p.154*

Camoens or **Camões, Luís Vaz de** [kamohenz] (1524–80) Poet, born in Lisbon. He went to India (1553) and was shipwrecked while returning to Goa (1558), losing everything except his major poem, *Os Luciados* (The Lusiads, or Lusitanians). The work has since come to be regarded as the Portuguese national epic.

camomile *chamomile*

Cambridge University

College	Founded
Peterhouse	1284
Clare	1326
Pembroke	1347
Gonville (refounded as Gonville and Caius 1558)	1348
Trinity Hall	1350
Corpus Christi	1352
King's	1441
Queens'	1448
St Catharine's	1473
Jesus	1496
Christ's	1505
St John's	1511
Magdalene	1542
Trinity	1546
Emmanuel	1584
Sidney Sussex	1596
Homerton[*]	1768
Downing	1800
Girton	1869
Newnham[1]	1871
Selwyn	1882
Hughes Hall[3]	1885
St Edmund's[3]	1896
New Hall[1]	1954
Churchill	1960
Lucy Cavendish[1]	1964
Darwin[2]	1964
Wolfson	1965
Clare Hall[2]	1966
Fitzwilliam	1966
Robinson	1977

[1] Women's colleges
[2] Graduate colleges
[3] Graduate and affiliated graduate colleges
[*] Only offers education courses leading to BEd or PGCE

Campaign for Nuclear Disarmament *CND*

campanile [kampaneelay] The Italian name for a bell tower, usually tall and detached from the main building. The most famous example is the circular Leaning Tower of Pisa, with eight arcaded storeys.

campanology *bell-ringing*

campanula *bell-flower; Canterbury bell*

Campbell, Sir Colin, Baron Clyde (1792–1863) British field marshal, born in Glasgow, W Scotland. In the Crimean War (1854–6) he commanded the Highland Brigade in a campaign which included the renowned repulse of the Russians by the 'thin red line' at Balaclava. During the Indian Mutiny he effected the final relief of Lucknow.

Campbell, John W(ood), Jr, pseudonym **Don A Stuart** (1910–71) Science-fiction writer, born in Newark, NJ. He developed in his stories the new idea that machines could dominate humans, notably in *Twilight* (1934). His works were highly influential, and he has come to be regarded as the father of modern science-fiction.

Campbell, Kim (Avril Phaedra Douglas) (1947–) Canadian stateswoman, and Canada's first woman prime minister (1993), born in Port Alberni, British Columbia, Canada. She was elected for British Columbia in 1988 as a federal conservative, and served in Brian Mulroney's cabinet. She became leader of her party in

Cameroon

NIGER

Lake Chad

AFRICA

100 km
50 mi

Mokolo
Maroua
Chari
Mandara Mts
Benue
CHAD
Garoua

N I G E R I A

Ngaoundéré

Foumban
Tibati
Bétaré Oya
CENTRAL
AFRICAN
REPUBLIC

C A M E R O O N
• Nkongsamba
Mt Cameroon
4070m
Batouri •
Sanaga
Limbe △
■ Yaoundé
Douala
Yokadouma
∴ Dja Reserve
Sangha
Bioko
Kribi
Dja

EQUAT.
GUINEA
GABON
CONGO

☐ International Airport   ∴ World heritage site

[kameroon], official name **Republic of Cameroon**, Fr **Républi-que du Cameroun**
Local name Cameroun
Timezone GMT +1
Area 475 442 km²/183 569 sq mi

Population total (2002e) 16 185 000
Status Republic
Date of independence 1960
Capital Yaoundé
Languages French and English (official); 24 major African languages including Fang, Bamileke, Luanda, Fulani, Tika, Maka
Ethnic groups Highlanders (31%), Equatorial Bantu (19%), Kirdi (11%), Fulani (10%)
Religions Christian (40%), traditional beliefs (39%), Muslim (21%)
Physical features Located in W Africa. Equatorial forest, with low coastal plain. C plateau 1300 m/4200 ft. W forested and mountainous; Mt Cameroon, 4070 m/13 353 ft (active volcano and the highest peak in W Africa). Low savannah, semi-desert towards L Chad; rivers include Sanaga and Dja.
Climate Rain all year in equatorial S; daily temperature in Yaoundé 27–30°C; average annual rainfall 4030 mm/159 in.
Currency 1 CFA Franc (XAF) = 100 centimes
Economy Agriculture (employs c.80% of workforce); world's fifth largest producer of cocoa; tourism, especially to national parks.
GDP (2002e) $26·84 bn, per capita $1700
Human Development Index (2002) 0·512
History First explored by Portuguese navigator Fernando Po; later by traders from Spain, Netherlands, Britain. German protectorate of Kamerun from 1884. Divided into French and British Cameroon in 1919; confirmed by League of Nations mandate in 1922; UN trusteeships, 1946. French Cameroon independent as Republic of Cameroon in 1960: N sector of British Cameroon voted to become part of Nigeria, S sector part of Cameroon; became Federal Republic of Cameroon, with separate parliaments, 1961. Federal system abolished in 1972, and name changed to United Republic of Cameroon. Changed name to the Republic of Cameroon in 1984; multiparty legislative and presidential elections, 1992; governed by a President, an executive Prime Minister, Cabinet, and national assembly.
Head of State
1960–82 Ahmadou Ahidjo
1982– Paul Biya
Head of Government
1991–2 Sadou Hayatou
1992–6 Simon Achidi Achu
1996–2004 Peter Mafany Musonge
2004– Ephraim Inoni

spring 1993, but disastrously lost the general election some months later.

Campbell, Sir Malcolm (1885–1948) Racing motorist, born in Chislehurst, Kent. He was the first to exceed 300 mph (483 kph) (at Bonneville Salt Flats, Utah, 1935). His son, **Donald Campbell** (1921–67), set a water speed record 444·7 kph/276·33 mph on Lake Dumbleyung, Australia, in 1964. He also set a land vehicle record in 1964 at Lake Eyre, Australia of 652·37 kph/405·45 mph. Donald died in an accident on Coniston Water, Cumbria while trying to break his own water speed record (achieving 528 kph/328 mph).

Campbell, Sir Menzies, known as **Ming Campbell** (1941–) British politician, born in Glasgow. He studied law at Glasgow University (1962–5) and at Stanford University, CA (1966–7), and also excelled in athletics. He was called to the Scottish Bar in 1968 and was made QC in 1982. Entering politics, he was elected MP for North East Fife in 1987, and for the Liberal Democrat Party has served as shadow foreign secretary (1997–2003), deputy party leader (2003–6), and shadow secretary-of-state for for-

eign and Commonwealth affairs (2003–). In 2006 he succeeded Charles Kennedy as party leader. He was knighted in 2004.

Campbell, Mrs Patrick, *née* **Beatrice Stella Tanner** (1865–1940) Actress, born in London. She went on the stage in 1888, achieving fame with *The Second Mrs Tanqueray* (1893). She played Eliza in Shaw's *Pygmalion* (1914) and formed a long friendship with the author.

Campbell-Bannerman, Sir Henry (1836–1908) British statesman and Liberal prime minister (1905–8), born in Glasgow, W Scotland. He was chief secretary for Ireland (1884), war secretary (1886, 1892–5), Liberal leader (1899), and prime minister. His popularity united the Liberal Party.

Camp David The US presidential retreat established in 1942 by President Roosevelt in Catoctin Mountain Park, Maryland. It has been used for a number of historic meetings between heads of state.

Camp David Accords The framework for 'a just, comprehensive, and durable settlement of the Middle East conflict', reached by Egyptian President Sadat, Israeli Prime Minister Begin, and US

President Jimmy Carter at Camp David, MD, in September 1978. Based on the principle of exchanging land for peace embodied in UN Security Council Resolution 242, the accords laid the foundation for the March 1979 peace treaty between Egypt and Israel. A settlement of the Palestinian–Israeli dispute was still being negotiated at the beginning of the 2000s.

Campese, David (Ian) [kampeezee], nickname **Campo** (1962–) Rugby union player, born near Queanbeyan, New South Wales, Australia. A flamboyant player, he set a world record 64 tries as an international, and an Australian record for the most matches played, 101. He was the star of Australia's 1991 World Cup victory. After retiring in 1998, he was appointed national coach to the Singapore Rugby Union.

camphor $C_{10}H_{16}O$, melting point 179°C. A colourless, waxy material (a terpene), occurring especially in the tree *Cinnamonium camphora*, and also synthesized from α-pinene. It is used in many lotions, mainly for its characteristic odour. **Camphorated oil** is a 20% solution of camphor in olive oil.

Campi, Giulio [kampee] (c.1502–72) Architect and painter, born in Cremona, Italy. He founded the Cremonese school of painting, to which his brothers **Vincenzo Campi** (1539–91) and **Antonio Campi** (1536–c.91) also belonged.

Campin, Robert [kāmpīn] (c.1378–1444) Artist born in Tournai, Belgium. He was called **the Master of Flémalle** from his paintings in the Abbey of that name near Liège.

Campinas [kampeenas] 22°54S 47°60W, pop (2000e) 1 108 000. Town in SE Brazil; NW of São Paulo; airport; railway; two universities (1941, 1962); agricultural institute; cathedral.

campion An annual or perennial herb, native to the temperate N hemisphere; calyx tubular, 5 petals, red or white depending on species. (Genus: *Silene*. Family: Caryophyllaceae.)

Campion, Edmund, St (1540–81) The first of the English Jesuit martyrs, born in London. After circulating his *Decem rationes* (Ten Reasons) against Anglicanism in 1581, he was tortured, tried on a charge of conspiracy, and hanged at Tyburn, London. He was beatified in 1886, and canonized in 1970. Feast day 1 December.

Campion, Jane (1954–) Film director, born in Waikanae, New Zealand. Her films include *Peel* (1984), which won the 1986 Cannes Palme d'Or for best short film, *Sweetie* (1989), and *An Angel at My Table* (1990). *The Piano* (1993), which she wrote and directed, shared the Palme d'Or at the 1993 Cannes Film Festival. Later films include *The Portrait of a Lady* (1996) and *In the Cut* (2003).

Campoli, Alfredo [kampohlee] (1906–91) Violinist, born in Rome. During the 1930s he became known for his salon orchestra, disbanded at the beginning of the war. He later emerged as one of the outstanding violinists of the time.

camshaft A rotating shaft upon which **cams** are fixed. A cam is a flat plate which rotates about an axis perpendicular to the plane of the plate. The shape of the cams and their relative orientation actuate and time the lifting of valves as part of an engine's operating cycle.

Camulodunum [kamulodoonum] The name for ancient Colchester, the capital first of the Belgic kingdom of Cunobelinus and for a time of the Roman province of Britain.

Camus, Albert [kahmü] (1913–60) French existentialist writer, born in Mondovi, Algeria. He earned an international reputation with his nihilistic novel, *L'Etranger* (1942, The Outsider). Later novels include *La Peste* (1947, The Plague) and *La Chute* (1956, The Fall). He received the Nobel Prize for Literature in 1957.

Canaan [kaynan, kanayan] The land of the ancient Semitic-speaking peoples, living in the coastal areas of modern Israel and Syria. It was divided into various city-states during the early 2nd millennium BC, but mostly fell under the control of Israelites and other powers from the late 13th-c BC.

Canada *pp.156–57*

Canada Day A public holiday in Canada (observed 1 Jul), the anniversary of the union of the provinces in 1867; formerly known as **Dominion Day**.

Canada First Movement A political movement in Canada, founded in Ontario in 1868. Its objectives were to ensure that the newly-confederated Dominion of Canada would not collapse over regional disputes.

Canadian National Tower C N Tower

Canadian Pacific Railway (CPR) A transcontinental railway, constructed 1881–5, linking the Dominion of Canada with British Columbia. It produced a chain of western railway towns terminating in Vancouver on the Pacific coast.

Canadian Rocky Mountain Parks A group of five national parks (Banff, Jasper, Waterton Lakes, Kootenay, Yoho) in Alberta and British Columbia, Canada. Together with the Burgess Shale region, these constitute a world heritage site.

Canadian Shield or **Laurentian Shield** Vast area of ancient pre-Cambrian rocks, forming a low plateau covering over half of Canada, extending into parts of N USA; many lakes and swamps, remnants of Pleistocene glaciation; generally infertile, but a rich source of minerals, forest products, and hydroelectricity.

canal An artificial watercourse for inland navigation. The first modern canal in the UK was the Sankey Brook from the Mersey to St Helens, built by Henry Berry between 1755 and 1772. Thousands of miles of canal were built, and they were the major method of transporting goods until the mid-19th-c, when the railways superseded them. After a long period of decline, more recently many canals have been restored, and nowadays are principally used for leisure activities.

Canaletto [kanaletoh], originally **Giovanni Antonio Canal** (1697–1768) Painter, born in Venice, Italy. He painted a renowned series of views in Venice, and his views of London and elsewhere proved extremely popular. His nephew and pupil, **Bernardo Bellotto** (1720–80), known as **Canaletto the Younger**, was also born in Venice, where he worked as a painter and engraver.

canary A small finch, native to the Old World; prized as a songbird; also known as **serin**. All domestic varieties of the cage canary were developed from one species, *Serinus canaria*, from the Canary Is. (Genus: *Serinus*, 32 species. Family: Fringillidae.)

Canary Islands *p.157*

Canary whitewood *tulip tree*

canasta A card game similar to rummy. It derives from the Spanish word *canasta* ('basket'), probably referring to the tray into which cards were discarded. Its most popular form is played with two standard packs of playing cards, together with four jokers. The object is to collect as many cards of the same denomination as possible.

Canaveral, Cape [kanaveral], formerly **Cape Kennedy** 28°28N 80°28W. Cape in E Florida, USA; US crewed space flights launched from here since 1961.

Canberra [kanbera] 35°18S 149°08E, pop (2000e) 308 300. National and regional capital in Australian Capital Territory, SE Australia, on the Molonglo R; building started in 1913; Commonwealth Parliament moved from Melbourne, 1927; airport; railway; two universities (1946, 1989); Parliament House (1927, new building opened in 1988 by the Queen); devastating bush fires in suburbs (Jan 2003).

Cancer (Lat 'crab') An inconspicuous N constellation of the zodiac, lying between Gemini and Leo. It contains an open star cluster, Praesepe, just visible by eye.

cancer A general term to denote all forms of malignant tumour. Tumours occur when the cells of a tissue or organ multiply in an uncontrolled fashion unrelated to the biological requirements of the body and not to meet the needs of repair or of

□ International Airport

formerly **British North America** (to 1867)
Local name Canada
Timezone GMT W -9, to E -3
Area 9 971 500 km²/3 848 900 sq mi
Population total (2002e) 31 244 000
Status Independent nation within the Commonwealth
Date of independence 1867 (Dominion of Canada)
Capital Ottawa
Languages English and French (official)
Ethnic groups British origin (45%), French origin (29%), other European, Indian, and Inuit (23%)
Religions Roman Catholic (49%), United Church (18%), Anglican (12%)
Physical features Dominated in the NE by the Canadian Shield; flat prairie country S and W of the Shield, stretching to the Western Cordillera, which includes the Rocky, Cassiar, and Mackenzie Mts; coast Mts flank a rugged, heavily indented coastline; Mt Logan in the Yukon, 5950 m/19 521 ft, the highest peak in Canada; major rivers; the Mackenzie (W), and St Lawrence (E); Great Bear, 31 330 km²/11 030 sq mi, and Great Slave, 28 570 km²/11 030 sq mi, are lakes in NW Territories.

Climate N coast permanently ice-bound or obstructed by ice floes, but for Hudson Bay (frozen c.9 months each year); mild winters and warm summers on Pacific coast and around Vancouver Island; rainfall ranges from near-desert conditions of less than 300 mm/12 in per year in the far N to very wet conditions of more than 2400 mm/90 in in parts of the W coast.

Currency 1 Canadian Dollar (CAD) = 100 cents

Economy Traditionally based on natural resources and agriculture: world's second largest exporter of wheat; world's largest producer of asbestos, zinc, silver, nickel; second largest producer of potash, gypsum, molybdenum, sulphur; hydroelectricity, oil (especially Alberta), natural gas; major industrial development in recent decades.

GDP (2002e) $934.1 bn, per capita $29 300

Human Development Index (2002) 0.940

History Evidence of Viking settlement c.1000; Newfoundland claimed for England, 1583; Champlain founded Quebec, 1608; Hudson's Bay Company founded, 1670; conflict between British and French in late 17th-c; Britain gained large areas from Treaty of Utrecht, 1713, after Seven Years' War, during which British General James Wolfe captured Quebec from Louis Montcalm's forces in 1759; Treaty of Paris gave Britain almost all France's possessions in North America; Province of Quebec created, 1774; migration of loyalists from USA (1783) after War of Independence led to division of Quebec into Upper and Lower Canada; reunited as Canada, 1841; Dominion of Canada created (1867) by confederation of Quebec, Ontario, Nova Scotia, and New Brunswick; Rupert's Land and Northwest Territories bought from Hudson's Bay Company, 1869–70; joined by Manitoba (1870), British Columbia (1871), Prince Edward I (1873), Alberta and Saskatchewan (1905), and Newfoundland (1949); recurring political tension in recent decades arising from French-Canadian separatist movement in Quebec; separatist referendum rejected in 1980, and again in 1995, but only by a 1% margin; Inuit territory of Nunavut created, 1999; Canada Act, 1982, gave Canada full responsibility for constitution; bicameral Federal Parliament includes Senate and a House of Commons; British monarch is Head of State, represented by a Governor-General.

Head of State
(British monarch represented by Governor-General)
1999–2005 Adrienne Clarkson
2005– Michaëlle Jean

Head of Government
1867–73 John Alexander MacDonald *Con*
1873–8 Alexander Mackenzie *Lib*
1878–91 John Alexander MacDonald *Con*
1891–2 John J C Abbot *Con*
1892–4 John Sparrow David Thompson *Con*
1894–6 Mackenzie Bowell *Con*
1896 Charles Tupper *Con*
1896–1911 Wilfrid Laurier *Lib*
1911–20 Robert Laird Borden *Con*
1920–1 Arthur Meighen *Con*
1921–6 William Lyon Mackenzie King *Lib*
1926 Arthur Meighen *Con*
1926–30 William Lyon Mackenzie King *Lib*
1930–5 Richard Bedford Bennett, 1st Viscount Bennett *Con*
1935–48 William Lyon Mackenzie King *Lib*
1948–57 Louis Stephen St Laurent *Lib*
1957–63 John George Diefenbaker *Con*
1963–8 Lester Bowles Pearson *Lib*
1968–79 Pierre Elliott Trudeau *Lib*
1979–80 Charles Joseph Clark *Con*
1980–4 Pierre Elliott Trudeau *Lib*
1984 John Napier Turner *Lib*
1984–93 (Martin) Brian Mulroney *Con*
1993 Kim Campbell *Con*
1993–2003 Jean Chrétien *Lib*
2003–6 Paul Martin *Lib*
2006– Stephen Harper *Con*
Con Conservative *Lib* Liberal

Canadian provinces and territories
Name / Area (km² / sq mi) / Capital
Alberta / 661 190 / 255 285 / Edmonton
British Columbia / 947 800 / 365 945 / Victoria
Manitoba / 649 950 / 250 945 / Winnipeg
New Brunswick / 73 440 / 28 355 / Fredericton
Newfoundland / 405 720 / 156 648 / St John's
Northwest Territories / 1 346 106 / 519 597 / Yellowknife
Nova Scotia / 55 490 / 21 424 / Halifax
Nunavut / 2 093 190 / 807 971 / Iqaluit
Ontario / 1 068 580 / 412 578 / Toronto
Prince Edward Island / 5 660 / 2 185 / Charlottetown
Quebec / 1 540 680 / 594 856 / Quebec City
Saskatchewan / 652 380 / 251 883 / Regina

Canary Islands

□ International Airport

Span **Islas Canarias**
Local name Islas Canarias
Area 7273 km²/2807 sq mi
Population total (2000e) 1 475 000
Status Forms two provinces of Spain
Chief town Las Palmas
Physical features Island archipelago, located in the Atlantic, 100 km/60 mi off the NW coast of Africa; includes the islands of Tenerife, La Palma, Gomera, Hierro, Grand Canary (Gran Canaria), Fuerteventura, Lanzarote, and several uninhabited islands; major ports, Las Palmas, Santa Cruz; volcanic and mountainous, the Pico de Teide rises to 3718 m/12 198 ft on Tenerife; tourist resorts on main islands.
Climate Continental; average annual temperature 18°C (Jan); 24°C (Jul); average annual rainfall 196 mm/8 in.
Currency 1 euro (EUR) = 100 cents (previous to February 2002, 1 Peseta (ESP) = 100 céntimos).
Economy Tourism; agriculture, fishing, canning, textiles, leatherwork, footwear, cork, timber, chemical and metal products.

normal replacement. In contrast to *benign* tumours, which enlarge in a specific place, and cause damage by pressure on adjacent tissues, *malignant* tumours invade, destroy, and spread to other tissues. The cells of a malignant tumour may also be carried in the blood stream and lymphatics, and lodge in distant organs where they continue to spread and enlarge (*metastases*). Cancer kills by destroying vital tissues, by interfering with the performance of their functions through ulceration, bleeding, and infection, and by affecting bodily nutrition. The cause of cancer is unknown, but appears to depend upon an interplay between factors in the environment and the genetic component of body cells. Only a small number of cancers are determined solely by inherited factors. The great majority are related to exposure to one or more environmental factors which predisposes to the cancer. These factors are known as **carcinogenic** agents.

candela [kandayla] Base SI unit of luminous intensity; symbol *cd*; defined as the luminous intensity, in a given direction, of a source that emits monochromatic radiation of frequency 540×10^{12} Hz, and has a radiant intensity in that direction of 1/683 watt per steradian; obsolete name **candle**.

Candida [kandida] A genus of fungi known from its yeast-like vegetative state; parasitic in animals. (Family: Cryptococcaceae.)

candidiasis [kandidiyasis] A disease caused by *Candida albicans*, a yeast which normally inhabits the gut and vagina. The organism may invade the surface of the skin and the mucous membranes of the vagina and gastro-intestinal tract, including the mouth, where white patches can be seen. This is known as **thrush**.

candle A light source typically consisting of a wax cylinder (stearic acid, paraffin wax, etc) with a central fibrous wick, known from ancient times (at least 3000 BC). Light is generated by burning liquid wax melted by the flame and drawn up the wick by capillary action.

Candlemas A Christian festival (2 Feb) commemorating the purification of the Virgin Mary after the birth of Jesus, and the presentation of Jesus in the Jerusalem temple (*Luke* 2). The name is derived from the lighted candles carried in procession on that day.

candytuft An annual, biennial, or evergreen perennial, native to Europe and Asia; leaves narrow; flowers white or mauve, in flattened heads, cross-shaped with outer two petals of outermost flowers enlarged. (Genus: *Iberis*, 30 species. Family: Cruciferae.)

cane *bamboo; sugar cane*

Canea *Chania*

cane sugar *sugar cane*

Canes Venatici [kaneez venatisiy] (Lat 'hunting dogs') An inconspicuous constellation in the N hemisphere which includes the famous Whirlpool Galaxy.

Canetti, Elias [kanetee] (1905–94) Writer born in Rustschuk, Bulgaria. His interest in crowd psychology produced two important works: the novel *Die Blendung* (1936, trans as both Auto da Fé and The Tower of Babel) and the study *Masse und Macht* (1960, Crowds and Power). He was awarded the Nobel Prize for Literature in 1981.

Canidae [kanidee] The dog family of carnivores (36 species), usually with slender legs, lean muzzles, large erect ears, and bushy tails; four toes on hind feet, usually five on front; blunt claws not retractable; colour usually without stripes or spots.

canine parvovirus A serious viral infection of dogs and other canids, which emerged in the late 1970s. Its most characteristic feature is very severe persistent diarrhoea with blood, and there may be vomiting and a high fever. The disease is now well controlled by effective vaccines.

Canis Major [kanis] (Lat 'great dog') A constellation in the S hemisphere, partly in the Milky Way. It includes Sirius, the brightest star in our sky.

Canis Minor [kanis] (Lat 'little dog') A small N hemisphere constellation. Its brightest star is Procyon, just 3·5 parsec away, and the eighth brightest star in the sky.

canker (botany) A general term for a localized disease of woody plants, in which bark formation is prevented; typically caused by bacteria or fungi.

canker (zoology) A disease of animals, characterized by open sores or ulcers. The name is used for several conditions.

canna A tuberous perennial, native to Central and tropical North America; flowers in a spike, three sepals, three petals, 4–6 stamens, petal-like and brightly coloured; fruit a warty capsule; often grown for the showy flowers. (Genus: *Canna*, 55 species. Family: Cannaceae.)

cannabinoids *cannabis*

cannabis A preparation of the plant *Cannabis sativa*, widely used as a recreational drug for its euphoric, relaxing properties: its extracts are found as **hashish** and **marihuana**. The plant, also called **ganja** or **hemp**, is an annual growing to 2·5 m/8 ft; its leaves have 5–7 narrow, toothed, spreading, finger-like lobes; there are tiny green flowers in terminal clusters, with males and females on separate plants. It is native to Asia, but widely cultivated elsewhere. It is a source of rope fibre and birdseed, but is best known as a narcotic resin. (Family: Cannabidaceae.)

Cannes [kan] 43°33N 7°00E, pop (2000e) 72600. Fashionable resort town on the French Riviera; airport; railway; major tourist centre, with many beaches and yachting harbours; International Film Festival (May).

Cannes Film Festival Awards One of the world's leading film festivals, established in 1939. Now held annually in May, over the years the categories have varied and widened and awards are currently given for best film, which receives the Palme d'Or (inaugurated 1955), director, actor and actress.

Canning, George (1770–1827) British statesman, born in London. He became treasurer of the Navy (1804–6), and minister for foreign affairs (1807). His disapproval of the Walcheren expedition led to a misunderstanding with Castlereagh, which resulted in a duel. As foreign secretary (1822), he was the first to recognize the free states of Spanish America, and promoted the cause of Greece (1827). In 1827 he formed an administration with the aid of the Whigs, but died the same year.

canning A food preservation process relying on the sterilization of foods by heating in a container sealed before or immediately after the heat treatment. The idea was first applied in 1810 by Nicolas Appert (c.1750–1841) to foods sealed in bottles and heated, but since 1839 in cans. The processes are now highly automated.

Cannon, Annie Jump (1863–1941) Astronomer, born in Dover, DE. She reorganized the classification of stars in terms of surface temperature, and developed great skill in cataloguing them. Her classification of over 225000 stars brighter than 9th or 10th magnitude was a major contribution.

Cano, Juan Sebastian del [kahnoh] (?–1526) Navigator, born in Guetaria, Spain, the first to journey around the world. In 1519 he sailed with Magellan, after whose death he safely navigated the *Victoria* home to Spain.

canoe A small, double-ended open craft propelled with paddles. There are two main types: a vessel carrying three or four people, made from a light wooden framework, traditionally covered with birch bark; and the Pacific dugout canoe, often fitted with an outrigger, which could be made capable of ocean voyages.

canoeing A water sport practised in canoes, developed by British barrister John Macgregor (1825–92) in 1865. The Canoe Club was formed the following year. Two types of canoe are used in competition: the *kayak*, which has a keel and the canoeist sits in the boat, and the *Canadian canoe*, which has no keel and the canoeist kneels.

canon (music) A strictly ordered texture in which polyphony is derived from a single line by imitation of itself at fixed intervals of time and pitch. In other words, all the canonic parts are the same, but they overlap each other.

canon (religion) The ecclesiastical title of clergy attached to cathedrals or certain endowed churches; either *secular* or, if living under semi-monastic rule, *regular* (eg Augustinian). In the Church of England, *residentiary* canons are the salaried staff of a cathedral, responsible for the upkeep of the building; *non-residentiary* canons are unsalaried, but have certain privileges.

canonization The culmination of a lengthy process in the Roman Catholic Church whereby, after a long process of enquiry, a deceased individual is declared a saint, or entitled to public veneration. In the Orthodox Church, there is a similar but less formal procedure.

canon law In the Roman Catholic Church, a body of rules or laws to be observed in matters of faith, morals, and discipline. It developed out of the decisions of the Councils of the Church, and the decrees of popes and influential bishops.

Canopus [kanohpus] *Carina*

Canova, Antonio [kanohva] (1757–1822) Sculptor, born in Possagno, Italy. He is regarded as the founder of a new Neoclassicist school. In 1802 he was appointed by Pius VII as curator of works of art.

Cantabria [kantabria] pop (2000e) 531 000; area 5289 km²/ 2041 sq mi. Autonomous region of N Spain, co-extensive with the modern province of Santander; capital, Santander.

cantata Music which is 'sung'. The Italian solo cantata of the 17th–18th-c was a setting of secular (usually amatory) verses, alternating recitative and aria. The Lutheran cantatas (eg those of Bach) were church compositions for soloists, choir, and instruments. More recent cantatas are usually choral and orchestral pieces.

Canterbury, Lat **Durovernum**, Anglo-Saxon **Cantwaraburh** 51°17N 1°05E, pop (2001e) 135 300. Market town in Kent, SE England; St Augustine began the conversion of England to Christianity here, 597; Thomas Becket murdered in Canterbury Cathedral, 1170; seat of the Primate of the Anglican Church; railway; University of Kent (1965); cathedral (11th–15th-c).

Canterbury bell A robust hairy biennial (*Campanula medium*), native to Italy; flowers 4–5 cm/1½–2 in, bell-shaped, dark blue, in long spikes; garden forms in many colours. (Family: Campanulaceae.)

Canterbury Tales A series of linked narrative poems (and prose pieces) by Geoffrey Chaucer: the most important English work of literature from mediaeval times. Modelled on Boccaccio's *Decameron*, the tales are told by a group of 29 pilgrims on the road to Canterbury. Their 24 tales (the plan is incomplete) are told in a variety of poetic styles.

Canticles *Song of Solomon*

cantilever A horizontal building element where the part hidden within the building bears a downward force, and the other part projects outside without external bracing, and so appears to be self-supporting.

canton A territorial division of land. In Switzerland, cantons have their own separate governments; in France, cantons are subdivisions of *arrondissements*, which are themselves sub-divisions of the regional *départements*.

Cantona, Eric [kantona] (1966–) Footballer, born in Paris. Brought up in Marseille, he made his professional debut in 1983, and won his first French cap in 1987, moving to Leeds United in 1991 and to Manchester United in 1993. An aggressive and tempestuous player, his career was interrupted by a series of suspensions. He announced his retirement in 1997, and began a career in films. In 2003 he received the Overseas Player of the Decade award, presented by the FA Premier League.

Cantonese *Chinese*

Cantor, Georg (Ferdinand Ludwig Philipp) (1845–1918) Mathematician, born in St Petersburg, Russia. He worked out a highly original arithmetic of the infinite which resulted in a theory of sets of irrational numbers.

Canute or **Cnut**, sometimes known as **the Great** (c.995–1035) King of England (from 1016), Denmark (from 1019), and Norway (from 1028), the younger son of Sweyn Forkbeard. He defeated Edmund Ironside in 1016 at the Battle of Assandun, secured Mercia and Northumbria, and became king of all England after Edmund's death. A story is told by the 12th-c historian, Henry of Huntingdon, that Canute rebuked his flatterers by showing that even he, as king, could not stop the incoming tide, nor by implication, the might of God.

canyon A deep valley with almost vertical sides which have been cut by a river, often in arid or semi-arid regions.

Canyon de Chelly [shay] National monument in NE Arizona, USA; established in 1931 to protect notable Indian cliff dwellings, dating from c.350 AD; area 339 km²/131 sq mi.

capacitance The measure of a system's ability to store electric charge; symbol *C*, units F (*farad*). For an electrical circuit, elements are usually quoted as μF (*Microfarad*, 10^{-6} F) or pF (*picofarad*, 10^{-12} F).

Cape Breton Island pop (2000e) 200 500; area 10 295 km²/ 3974 sq mi. Island in Nova Scotia province, E Canada; almost bisected by Bras d'Or Lake (arm of the sea); chief towns, Sydney, Glace Bay, Louisburg; many people of Scottish descent, with Gaelic still spoken; originally French (Ile Royale), taken by British, 1758; joined to Nova Scotia, 1820.

Cape Cod A sandy peninsula of SE Massachusetts, USA; length 105 km/65 mi; width up to 32 km/20 mi; crossed by the 13 km/ 8 mi Cape Cod Canal; pilgrims from the *Mayflower* landed near Provincetown in November 1620; airfield at Provincetown; popular resort area.

Cape Coloured or **Coloured** A term used by the South African government to refer to a group of people of mixed descent, arising from the unions of Europeans with slaves or Khoikoi (Hottentots). They number about 3·2 million people (c.8·5% of the total population), mainly living in the towns and rural areas of the Western Cape province. In South Africa's racial hierarchy, they were ranked between Europeans and Black Africans.

Čapek, Karel [chapek] (1890–1938) Writer, born in Schwadonitz, Czech Republic. His best-known work is his play *R. U. R.* (Rossum's Universal Robots), produced in 1921, showing mechanization rampant, and the comic fantasy *Ze Života hmyzu* (1921, The Insect Play), written with his brother **Josef Čapek**.

Capella [kapela] *Auriga*

Cape Provinces, Afrikaans **Kaapprovinsie** Former province in South Africa; founded, 1652; formally ceded to Britain (Cape Colony), 1814; separate parliament, 1850; joined Union of South Africa, 1910; since the 1994 constitution, divided into three provinces: Northern, Western, and Eastern.

caper A sprawling, deciduous, spiny shrub (*Capparis spinosa*), native to S Europe; flowers 5–7 cm/2–2¾ in in diameter, 4-petalled, white with numerous long purple stamens. Its pickled flower buds are eaten. (Family: Capparidaceae.)

capercaillie [kaperkaylee] A large grouse native to Europe and N Asia; usually solitary. (Genus: *Tetrao*, 2 species. Family: Tetraonidae.)

Capet, Hugo or **Hugh** [kapet] (c.938–96) King of France, founder of the third Frankish royal dynasty (the Capetians), which ruled France until 1328. His 40 years in power were marked by constant political intrigue and struggle.

Capetians A French ruling dynasty for over 300 years (987–1328), founded by Hugh Capet in succession to the Carolingians. Two dynamic royal descendants were Philip II Augustus (reigned 1180–1223) and Louis IX (reigned 1226–1270). The Capetians laid the foundations of the French nation-state.

Cape Town, Afrikaans **Kaapstad** 33°56S 18°28E, pop (2000e) Greater Cape Town 1 285 000. Seaport capital of Western Cape province, South Africa; on Table Bay at the foot of Table Mt; legislative capital of South Africa; founded by the Dutch East India Company, 1652; occupied by the British, 1795; airport; railway; university (1829); cathedral; Union Houses of Parliament.

Cape Verde *p.160*

capillarity A surface tension effect in which liquids rise up narrow tubes or spread through porous solids; caused by the difference in attraction between liquid and air molecules for the material of the solid; also called **capillary action**. An example is ink soaking into blotting paper.

capillary [kapilaree] A minute, thin-walled blood vessel situated between arterioles and venules. It is the site of the exchange of

Cape Verde

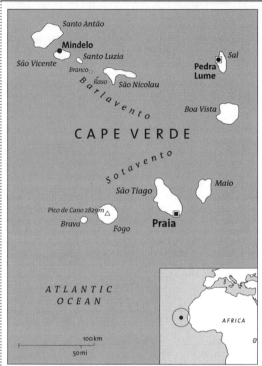

☐ International Airport

[kayp **vaird**], official name **Republic of Cape Verde**, Port **República de Cabo Verde**
Local name Cabo Verde
Timezone GMT -1
Area 4033 km²/1557 sq mi
Population total (2002e) 453 000

Status Island group
Date of independence 1975
Capital Praia (on Sao Tiago Island)
Languages Portuguese (official), Crioulo (Portuguese-based creole)
Ethnic groups Creole (mulatto) (60%), African (28%), European (2%)
Religion Roman Catholic (80%), others (20%)
Physical features Island group in the Atlantic Ocean off W Coast of Africa, c.500 km/310 mi W of Dakar, Senegal; Barlavento (windward) group in N, Sotavento (leeward) group in S; mostly mountainous islands of volcanic origin; highest peak, Pico do Cano, 2829 m/9281 ft; active volcano on Fogo I; fine sandy beaches on most islands.
Climate Arid climate; located at N limit of tropical rain belt; low and unreliable rainfall (Aug–Sep); small temperature range throughout year; average annual temperature 23°C; average annual rainfall 250 mm/10 in.
Currency 1 Escudo (CVE) = 100 centavos
Economy Suffering because of drought; substantial emigration in early 1970s; c.70% of workforce are farmers occupying irrigated inland valleys; increase in fishing since 1975.
GDP (2002e) $600 mn, per capita $1400
Human Development Index (2002) 0·715
History Colonized by Portuguese in 15th-c, also used as a penal colony; administered with Portuguese Guinea until 1879; overseas province of Portugal, 1951; independence, 1975; governed by a President, Council of Ministers, and People's National Assembly; multi-party elections held, 1991.
Head of State
1975–91 Aristides Pereira
1991–2001 Antonio Mascarenhas Monteiro
2001– Pedro Verona Rodrigues Pires
Head of Government
1975–91 Pedro Pires
1991–2000 Carlos Viega
2000–1 António Gualberto do Rosário
2001– José Maria Pereira Neves

materials (oxygen, nutrients, carbon dioxide) between capillary blood and surrounding tissues.

capital (accountancy) Business sources of finance to buy assets, such as buildings, machinery, stocks, or investment in other firms. **Equity capital** is supplied by shareholders, either by buying shares or by ploughing back profits into the business. **Loan capital** or **debt** is borrowed from a financial institution or individual, and interest is paid.

capital (architecture) The top part of a column, pilaster, or pier, identifiable in classical architecture as one of the five main orders. Romanesque and Gothic types include basket, bell, crocket, cushion, protomai (with animal figures), scalloped, and water-leaf.

capital gains tax (CGT) A tax on the increase in the value of assets. This is usually payable only when an asset is realized by sale or bequest. CGT is levied in various countries – in the UK since 1965. In the USA it is a federal income tax.

capitalism A set of economic arrangements which developed in the 19th-c in Western societies following the Industrial Revolution. The concept derives from the writings of Marx and rests upon the private ownership of the means of production by the capitalist class, or *bourgeoisie*. It has been the most productive economic system to date, though it has brought with it massive environmental (eg pollution) and social (eg unemployment) problems.

capital punishment Sentence of death passed by a judicial body following trial. Capital punishment for murder has been abolished in the UK, though proposals for its reinstatement are regularly debated by parliament, and it remains the penalty for high treason. It is still available in several states of the USA, and in many other countries. Countries employ a variety of procedures in carrying out executions, including lethal injection, electrocution, hanging, gassing, and shooting.

Capitol The Assembly of the US Congress on Capitol Hill, Washington, DC. The building was designed in 1792 by William Thornton (1759–1828), but a succession of architects supervised its construction.

Capitoline Hill The highest of the seven hills upon which Rome was built. Once the political and religious centre of Ancient Rome, it is now the site of the Piazza del Campidoglio.

Capone, Al(phonse) [kapohn] (1899–1947) Gangster, born in Brooklyn, NY. He achieved worldwide notoriety as a racketeer during the prohibition era in Chicago. In 1931 he was sentenced to 11 years' imprisonment for tax evasion.

Capote, Truman [kapohtee], pseudonym of **Truman Streckfus Persons** (1924–84) Writer, born in New Orleans, LA. His novels include *Breakfast at Tiffany's* (1958), which was highly successful as a film, and *In Cold Blood* (1966), described as a 'non-fiction novel' because of the way he tells of actual events in novelistic form. In 2004 the manuscript of his first novel, *Summer Crossing*, was discovered; written in the 1940s, he had claimed to have destroyed it. The novel was published in 2005.

Capp, Al, originally **Alfred Gerald Caplin** (1909–79) Strip cartoonist, born in New Haven, CT. His chief comic-strip creation, the hill-billy character *L'il Abner* (1934), inspired two films, a stage musical, and an animated series.

Cappadocia [kapadohshia], Turkish **Kapadokya** Ancient name for the mountainous region of C Turkey, between the Black Sea and the Taurus Mts; a province of the Roman Empire from AD 17; largest town, Nevşehir.

Capri [kapree], Ital [kapree], ancient **Capreae** area 10·5 km²/ 4 sq mi. Italian island in the Tyrrhenian Sea; length 6 km/ 4 mi; maximum width 2·5 km/1·5 mi; rugged limestone crags rise to 589 m/1932 ft; capital, Capri; major tourist centre; home of Emperor Tiberius.

Capriati, Jennifer (Marie) [kapriahtee] (1976–) Tennis player, born in New York City. She turned professional in 1990 and went on to win a gold medal at the Barcelona Olympics in 1992. In 1994 personal problems resulted in an extended break from tennis, but in 2001 she made a successful comeback, winning the French Open and Australian Open singles titles that year. She retained the Australian title in 2002. In 2005 she had a world ranking of number 10 but a shoulder injury has since kept her out of the game.

capriccio (music) [kaprichioh] A short musical composition, usually of a light or fanciful kind and often (though not necessarily) for piano.

Capricornus (Lat 'goat') A S constellation of the zodiac, lying between Sagittarius and Aquarius.

capsid A small to medium-sized bug that typically feeds on plants; c.10 000 species, distributed worldwide. (Order: Heteroptera. Family: Miridae.)

capuchin [kapuchin] A New World monkey, the most numerous captive monkey in the USA and Europe; tail partly adapted for grasping; acrobatic and intelligent; also known as **ring-tailed monkey** or **organ-grinder's monkey**. (Genus: *Cebus*, 4 species.)

Capuchins [kapyoochinz] (Ital *capuche*, a kind of cowl) A monastic order stemming from the Franciscans; in full, the **Order of Friars Minor of St Francis Capuccinorum**; abbreviated as **OM Cap** or **OSFC**. It was formed in 1528 by Matteo di Bassi (c.1495–1552), and observes a very strict rule, stressing poverty and austerity.

capybara [kapibahra] A cavy-like rodent (*Hydrochoerus hydrochaeris*), native to Central and South America; largest living rodent (length, over 1 m/3¼ ft); dog-like with deep square snout; no tail; lives in or near water; part-webbed toes; eats vegetation. (Family: Hydrochoeridae.)

car, also **motor car** (UK), **automobile** (USA) The general name for a passenger-carrying, self-propelled vehicle designed for normal domestic use on roads. The motive power system includes the engine (of whatever type), and its fuel supply, and the lubrication, exhaust, and cooling systems. The power developed by the engine is transmitted to the wheels by the transmission system, which includes gears, clutches, shafts, axles, and brakes. The engine and transmission are housed in the carriage unit, which also provides the compartment for the driver and passengers to sit, and in which the steering, engine controls, suspension, and electrical components can be mounted. The motor car became a reality with the invention in 1884 of the medium-speed internal combustion engine by Daimler in Germany. However, it was not until the early 1900s, and the application in the USA of mass production techniques

to the motor car by Henry Ford, that mass motoring started to become a reality.

carabao [karabow] *water buffalo*

caracal [karakal] A member of the cat family, native to Africa and S Asia (*Felis caracal*); reddish-brown; slender with long legs, short tail, long tufted ears.

Caracas [karakas] 10°30N 66°55W, pop (2000e) 2 208 000. Federal capital of Venezuela; altitude, 960 m/3150 ft; founded in 1567; often damaged by earthquakes; airport; airfield; railway; metro; three universities (1725, 1953, 1970); cathedral; birthplace of Bolívar; Ciudad Universitaria de Caracas is a world heritage site.

Caractacus [karaktakus], **Caratacus**, or **Caradoc** (1st-c) A chief of the Catuvellauni, the son of Cunobelinus, who fought unsuccessfully against the Romans in the years following the Claudian conquest (43). He was taken to Rome (51), where he was exhibited in triumph.

caracul *karakul*

carat or (US) **karat 1** A measure of the purity of gold in some alloy. A gold carat is a 24th part of the whole, and the purity of a gold alloy is stated by the number of such parts it contains. Pure gold is 24-carat gold. A 12-carat ring is one in which half the metal is gold.

2 A unit of weight for precious stones, equal to 200 mg.

Caratacus *Caractacus*

Caravaggio [karavajioh], originally **Michelangelo Merisi** (1573–1610) Baroque painter, born in Caravaggio, Italy, whence his nickname. His works include several altarpieces and religious paintings, using dramatic contrasts of light and shade, notably 'Christ at Emmaus' (c.1602–3).

caravel [karavel] A sailing vessel with up to four masts developed by the Portuguese in the 15th-c. The illustration shows the typical lateen rig sails with the long curved spars.

caraway A much-branched annual (*Carum carvi*), growing to 1 m/3¼ ft, native to Europe; flowers small, petals whitish, deeply notched; fruit (the 'seeds') strong-smelling when crushed, used as a spice and for flavouring bread, cakes, and cheese. (Family: Umbelliferae.)

carbamide *urea*

carbide Any compound of carbon, especially those in which carbon is ionic. It is often used specifically for **calcium carbide**, CaC_2, a salt of acetylene.

carbohydrate A non-nitrogen-containing compound based on carbon, hydrogen, and oxygen, generally with two hydrogen atoms per atom of oxygen. The molecules may be small (glucose) or large (cellulose, starch). Most carbohydrates comprise one or more 6-carbon units, of which glucose is by far the most abundant.

carbolic acid *phenol*

carbon C, element 6. It has two main forms: **graphite** (the stable form, very soft and black with a density of c.2 g/cm³) and **diamond** (the hardest substance known, density 3·5 g/cm³). Both of these melt above 3500°C. Coal is mainly graphite. Carbon also occurs naturally in compounds, particularly as **carbonates**, and in the atmosphere as carbon dioxide. In virtually all its compounds, it is covalently bonded, and shows a valency of 4. Carbon compounds are the basis of all living matter, and form the subject matter of organic chemistry. There are two simple oxides, **carbon monoxide** (CO), a very poisonous gas, boiling point −191°C, formed from the incomplete combustion of carbon and hydrocarbons, and **carbon dioxide** O=C=O, the product of complete combustion. Carbon dioxide is in turn the raw material for photosynthesis, regenerating combustibles. Solid carbon dioxide, or *dry ice*, sublimes at −78°C without passing through a liquid phase. It accounts for less than 0·03% of the gases of the atmosphere.

Carbonari [kah(r)bonahree] (Ital 'charcoal burners') Neapolitan secret societies, linked with freemasonry and probably founded under Napoleonic occupation. They played a major role in the Neapolitan revolution of 1820 and in the early stages of the Risorgimento.

carbonates Salts of carbonic acid, containing the ion CO_3^{2-}. Important natural carbonates include the almost insoluble **calcium carbonate** ($CaCO_3$), or limestone; **magnesium carbonate** ($MgCO_3$); and **dolomite** ($CaMg(CO_3)_2$). **Sodium carbonate**, known as 'washing soda' in its hydrated form ($Na_2CO_3.10H_2O$), is a cleansing agent and water softener.

carbon cycle The cycle through which carbon is transferred between the biological and non-biological parts of the global ecosystem. It involves the fixation of gaseous carbon dioxide during photosynthesis to form complex organic molecules, as well as the process through which it returns to the atmosphere by respiration and decomposition.

carbon dating *radiocarbon dating*

carbon dioxide *carbon*

carbon fibre A high-strength material made by the controlled heat treatment of acrylic fibre. Woven as a fabric, it has the property of absorbing poisonous gas, and is used for protective underwear for military personnel, and for firehoods. The fibres are several times stronger than steel, and are extensively used where laminates of great strength and low weight are needed, as in components for rockets and aeroplanes.

carbonic acid H_2CO_3; the hydrated form of carbon dioxide (CO_2). It is a weak acid, dissociating in two stages to give hydrogen carbonate (HCO_3^-) and carbonate (CO_3^{2-}) ions. Rain water containing pure carbonic acid has a pH of about 5.

Carboniferous period A geological period of the Palaeozoic era, extending from 360 to 286 million years ago, and characterized by extensive swampy forests with conifers and ferns which now form most of the present-day coal deposits. It was also marked by the first appearance of reptiles and seed-bearing plants. In the USA, the period is termed the **Mississippian** (earlier) and the **Pennsylvanian** (later).

carborundum The trade name for silicon carbide (SiC), a highly refractory material formed by fusing together sand and coke. It is almost as hard as diamond, and is used in grinding wheels and cutting tools.

carboxylic acids [kah(r)boksilik] Organic compounds containing the group –COOH; formed by the oxidation of alcohols or aldehydes; also called **alkanoic acids**. Many are found in nature, particularly as part of fats (*fatty acids*).

carbuncle An infection in sweat glands and under the skin. It forms multiple confluent abscesses that discharge pus onto the surface through two or more tracts.

carburettor / carburetor A device fitted to a spark ignition engine that mixes its fuel of air and petrol in suitable proportions for combustion. As the engine draws in its air/petrol mixture, the carburettor ensures that small droplets of petrol are carried along with the airstream. These droplets then vaporize on their way to the engine to form the highly inflammable mixture used in the engine's power stroke.

Carcassonne [kah(r)kason], ancient **Carcaso** 43°13N 2°20E, pop (2000e) 47100. Ancient city in S France, in foothills of Pyrenees; railway; bishopric; the Cité (altitude 200 m/650 ft) is the best preserved example of a French mediaeval fortified town (world heritage site); basilica (5th-c, rebuilt 11th–13th-c), cathedral (late 13th-c, restored 1840).

Carchemish [kah(r)kemish] An ancient trading city in N Syria. It was ruled by the Hittites in the second millennium BC, and remained an important centre of Hittite culture until its conquest by Assyria in 716 BC.

carcinogen [kah(r)sinojn] An agent which is capable of inducing cancer in tissues exposed to it. Several carcinogens have been identified by studies of the frequency of specific tumours in relation to different occupations, lifestyles, exposure to injurious chemical agents, drugs, ionizing radiations, ultraviolet light, and certain tumour-inducing (*oncogenic*) viruses. Exposure to such agents does not cause cancer immediately, but only after a period which may be months or years.

carcinoma *sarcoma*

Card, Andrew H, Jr (1947–) US Republican politician, born in Brockton, MA. He served four terms in the Massachusetts House of Representatives (Republican, 1975–83), then under Ronald Reagan as a special assistant for intergovernmental affairs (1983–7), and under George Bush as deputy chief-of-staff (1989–92) and as secretary of transportation (1992–3). He was appointed White House chief-of-staff by George W Bush (2001–6).

cardamom [kah(r)damom] A perennial native to India (*Elettaria cardamomum*); stem to 3·5 m/11½ ft; flowers small, white with blue and yellow markings, in clusters 60 cm/2 ft long; fruit a capsule 2 cm/0·8 in long. The dried ripe fruits are used as spice. (Family: Zingiberaceae.)

card games *playing cards*

cardiac resuscitation Emergency treatment following cardiac arrest (the sudden complete cessation of heart function); also known as **external cardiac massage**. It must be started within three minutes if the brain is not to suffer irreversible damage. It involves administering regular, firm compressions to the chest over the sternum, at a rate of about 70 per minute, in order to force blood round the body artificially. The procedure is usually combined with mouth-to-mouth ventilation, and five compressions are given for each breath. Resuscitation needs to be continued until either the heart starts beating spontaneously, or until facilities are available to attempt to restart it using an electric shock applied to the chest (*defibrillation*).

Cardiff, Welsh **Caerdydd** 51°30N 3°13W, pop (2001e) 305 300. Capital of Wales, in Cardiff county, S Wales, UK; at the mouth of the Taff, Rhymney, and Ely Rivers, on the Bristol Channel; Roman fort, 1st-c AD; Norman castle, c.1090; city charter, 1147; capital status, 1955; airport; railway; university college (1893); registry for University of Wales; Llandaff Cathedral, Welsh National Folk Museum (St Fagans), Cardiff Castle, Millennium Stadium (1999), Wales Millennium Centre for performing arts in Cardiff Bay (2004), Welsh Assembly building (2006); football league team, Cardiff City (Bluebirds).

Cardiff Arms Park Welsh rugby and cricket ground, the home ground of Cardiff Rugby Club from 1876. It became the venue for the Welsh national team in 1884 and for Glamorgan County Cricket Club in 1888. Redeveloped in the 1960s into the National Stadium, it was still popularly known as the Arms Park. The National Stadium was demolished in 1997, to be replaced by the Millennium Stadium (on the same site) for the 1999 Rugby World Cup.

Cardiff Singer of the World International singing competition founded by BBC Wales in 1983 to celebrate the opening of St David's Hall in Cardiff, S Wales, UK, and held every two years. Generally regarded as the world's leading vocal contest, it is a showcase for singers of opera and Lieder who are on the threshold of professional careers. The overall winner receives £10 000 and a specially commissioned trophy.

Cardigan, James Thomas Brudenell, 7th Earl of (1797–1868) British general, born in Hambleden, Buckinghamshire. He led the Charge of the Light Brigade against the Russians at Balaclava (1854). The woollen jacket known as a *cardigan* is named after him.

Cardiganshire, Welsh **Sir Aberteifi** pop (2001e) 75 400; area 1797 km²/694 sq mi. County (unitary authority from 1996) in W Wales, UK; administrative centre, Aberystwyth; Aberystwyth university and National Library of Wales.

Cardin, Pierre [kah(r)dĩ] (1922–) French fashion designer, born in Venice, Italy. He went to Paris in 1944, opened his own house in 1953, and has since been prominent in fashion for both women and men.

cardinal (ornithology) Either of two species of bird of genus *Cardinalis*, native to the Americas: the **red** or **northern cardinal** (*Cardinalis cardinalis*), or the **vermilion cardinal** (*Cardinalis phoeniceus*); males bright red. (Family: Emberizidae.)

cardinal (religion) A name originally given to one of the parish priests, bishops, or district deacons of Rome, then applied to a senior dignitary of the Roman Catholic Church, being a priest or bishop nominated by a pope to act as counsellor. The office carries special insignia, such as the distinctive red cap.

Cardinals, College of An institution consisting of all the cardinals of the Roman Catholic Church. It is responsible for the government of the Church during a vacancy in the papacy, and since 1179 has been responsible for the election of a pope.

care proceedings The procedure adopted by a court or tribunal in relation to children, taken with a view to ensuring their protection and, if necessary, their reception into care. Care proceedings encompass children who are or may be the victims of abuse or neglect, those who are beyond the control of their parents, and those who are failing to receive a proper education. Many jurisdictions also include children and young persons who are committing offences in this category, though there has been an increasing tendency in some countries to separate child offenders from other children in need of care, protection, or control.

Carew, Thomas [karoo] (1595–1639) Poet, born in West Wickham, Kent. He wrote polished lyrics in the Cavalier tradition, and a masque *Coelum britannicum* (1634) which was performed at court.

Carey, George (Leonard) [kairee] (1935–) Anglican churchman, born in London. He became bishop of Bath and Wells in 1987, and Archbishop of Canterbury (1991–2002).

Carey, Peter [kairee] (1943–) Writer, born in Bacchus Marsh, Victoria, Australia. His first book, *The Fat Man in History* (1974), was a collection of short stories. Later books include the novels *Illywhacker* (1985), *Oscar and Lucinda* (1988, Booker), *The True History of the Kelly Gang* (2001, Booker), *My Life as a Fake* (2003), and *Theft: A Love Story* (2006).

cargo cult The Melanesian variety of a widely occurring type of social movement (millenarianism) in which people look to some supernatural event to bring them prosperity. It is so-called because, in Melanesia, people performed rituals in an effort to obtain European material goods (referred to as 'cargo'). The movement first appeared in the late 19th-c.

Carib American Indian groups of the Lesser Antilles and neighbouring South America (the Guianas and Venezuela); also the name of the largest family of South American Indian languages.

Caribbean Community (CARICOM) An association chiefly of former British colonies in the Caribbean Sea. In 1968 many of the islands agreed to the establishment of the **Caribbean Free Trade Area (CARIFTA)**. In 2007 it had 15 member states.

Caribbean Sea area 2 515 900 km²/971 100 sq mi. Arm of the Atlantic Ocean between the West Indies and Central and South America; linked to the Pacific by the Panama Canal; deepest point, Cayman Trench, 6950 m/22 802 ft; main island groups, Greater and Lesser Antilles.

caribou *reindeer*

CARICOM *Caribbean Community*

caries (dentistry) [kaireez] A non-specific bacterial disease in which infecting organisms penetrate the enamel coating of a tooth. A high consumption of sugar predisposes to the development of caries, while an adequate amount of fluoride in drinking water (one part in a million) increases the resistance of the enamel to bacteria.

CARIFTA *Caribbean Community*

carillon A set of bells, usually with a compass of two octaves or more, installed in a tower or other high construction, and operated mechanically or by hand to play melodies or more complex polyphonic music. Many carillons are incorporated into elaborate public clocks.

Carina [kariyna] (Lat 'keel') A S hemisphere constellation, formerly part of Argo Navis. It contains Canopus, the second-brightest star in our sky, a supergiant. Distance: 96 parsec.

Carling, Will, popular name of **William David Charles Carling** (1965–) Player of rugby union football, born in Bradford-on-Avon, Wiltshire. He made his England debut in 1988, was appointed captain (1988–96), and played a major role in the Grand Slam victories of 1991, 1992, and 1995. He received national publicity in 1995 when the media focused on rumours of a possible relationship with Princess Diana.

Carlisle [kah(r)liyl], Lat **Luguvallum** 54°54N 2°55W, pop (2001e) 100 700. County town in Cumbria, NW England; at the W end of Hadrian's Wall; important fortress in Scots–English border wars; airfield; railway junction; cathedral (11th–12th-c), castle (11th-c); football league team, Carlisle United.

Carlow (county) **[kah(r)loh]**, Ir **Cheatharlach** pop (2000e) 41 000; area 896 km²/346 sq mi. County in SE Ireland; capital, Carlow, pop (2000e) 14 400; castle (12th-c), cathedral (19th-c).

Carlsson, Arvid (1923–) Pharmacologist, born in Uppsala, Sweden. Professor of pharmacology at the University of Göteborg, Sweden (1959, emeritus 1989), he shared the 2000 Nobel Prize for Physiology and Medicine for discoveries concerning signal transduction in the nervous system.

Carluccio, Antonio (Mario Gaetano) [kah(r)loochioh] (1937–) Restaurateur, born in Vietri Sul Mare, Italy. He joined the Neal Street Restaurant in London as restaurateur (1981), became proprietor (1989), and joint proprietor of Carluccio's food retailers (1992). His television appearances include the series *Antonio Carluccio's Italian Feasts* (1996) with accompanying book. Later books include *Antonio Carluccio's Italia* (2007).

Carlyle, Robert (1961–) Actor, born in Glasgow, W Scotland. He became known for his role in the television series *Hamish Macbeth* (1995–7), and his film credits include *Trainspotting* (1996), *The Full Monty* (1996), *Angela's Ashes* (1999), and *The Mighty Celt* (2005).

Carlyle, Thomas (1795–1881) Man of letters, born in Ecclefechan, Dumfriesshire. In 1826 he married **Jane Baillie Welsh** (1801–66). His best-known works are *Sartor Resartus* (1833–4), and studies on the French Revolution (3 vols, 1837) and Frederick the Great (6 vols, 1858–65). In 1866 his wife died, leaving letters and a journal showing her to have been one of the most accomplished women of her time.

Carmarthen [ka(r)mahthen] 51°52N 4°19W, pop (2000e) 15 800. County town of Carmarthenshire, SW Wales, UK; on R Towy; chartered, 1227; railway.

Carmarthenshire, Welsh **Sir Caerfyrddin** pop (2001e) 173 600; area 2398 km²/926 sq mi. County (unitary authority from 1996) in SW Wales, UK; drained by R Teifi and R Tywi; administrative centre, Carmarthen; Laugharne (home of Dylan Thomas); Carreg Cennen and Kidwelly castles.

Carme [kah(r)mee] The 11th natural satellite of Jupiter, discovered in 1938; distance from the planet 22 600 000 km/14 044 000 mi; diameter 40 km/25 mi.

Carmelites A Roman Catholic monastic order originating in the 12th-c from the Hermits of Mount Carmel (Israel); properly known as the **Order of the Brothers of the Blessed Virgin Mary of Mt Carmel**, or **White Friars**; abbreviated **OCarm**. Carmelite nuns were officially recognized in 1452, reformed by Teresa of Ávila in Spain (1562) as strictly cloistered **Discalced Carmelites** (**ODC**). (The term 'discalced' derives from the practice of wearing sandals.) The male order was similarly reformed by St John of the Cross, and in 1593 was recognized as a separate order.

Carmichael, Hoagy, popular name of **Hoagland Howard Carmichael** (1899–1981) Songwriter, singer, pianist, bandleader, and actor, born in Bloomington, IN. His much-loved compositions (often written with others) included 'Stardust', 'Georgia on my Mind', and '(Up a) Lazy River'.

Carmichael, Stokely, after 1969, also known as **Kwame Ture** (1941–98) Radical activist, born in Port-of-Spain, Trinidad. He popularized the phrase 'black power', and as a Black Panther came to symbolize black violence to many whites. He later favoured forging alliances with radical whites, which led to his resignation from the Panthers in 1968. He and his wife, **Miriam Makeba**, moved to Guinea in 1969, where he supported Pan-Africanism.

Carnac A peninsula on the S coast of Brittany, N France, renowned for its megalithic alignments, stone circles, and chambered tombs of Neolithic date. About 3000 stones survive, extending over some 5 km/3 mi.

Carnap, Rudolf (1891–1970) Philosopher, born in Wuppertal, Germany. He was one of the leaders of the 'Vienna Circle' of logical positivists. His writings include *Der logische Aufbau der Welt* (1928, The Logical Construction of the World), and *Meaning and Necessity* (1947).

carnation A perennial species of pink (*Dianthus caryophyllaceus*), native to the Mediterranean; leaves tufted; flowers with spreading, slightly frilly petals. Ornamental hybrids and garden cultivars are various colours and may have multiple petals. (Family: Caryophyllaceae.)

Carneades [kah(r)neeadeez] (c.214–129 BC) Greek philosopher, born in Cyrene. He became head of the Academy, which under his very different, sceptical direction became known as the 'New Academy'.

Carnegie, Andrew [kah(r)naygee, or **karnegee**] (1835–1919) Industrialist and philanthropist, born in Dunfermline, Fife. His family emigrated to Pittsburgh, PA, in 1848. He gave millions of dollars to libraries and other public institutions in the UK and USA, and several buildings are named after him.

Carnegie Hall International concert venue located in New York City, USA. Named after industrial tycoon Andrew Carnegie, the building was inaugurated in 1891 with a five-day music festival at which Tchaikovsky conducted several of his works. It was designated a national historic landmark in 1964.

carnitine A chemical substance (an *amine*) derived from the essential amino acid, lysine. Although once considered a vitamin, it is probably not an essential component of the diet.

Carnival A traditional festive period prior to Lent, celebrated in the Catholic countries of S Europe and their former colonies, and characterized by feasting, sexual licence, dancing, processions, masking, satire, and social levelling. Well known examples are those of Rome, Venice, New Orleans, and Rio de Janeiro. The term is also applied to similar festivals, such as the Notting Hill Carnival in London.

carnivore [kah(r)nivaw(r)] A primarily meat-eating mammal, preying on other vertebrates; lower jaw moves only up and down; canine teeth long; some cheek teeth (*carnassials*) specialized for cutting flesh; 4–5 clawed toes on each foot. (Order: Carnivora, 7 families, 238 species.)

carnivorous plant A plant which traps animals, usually insects and small invertebrates, and secretes digestive enzymes which break down the resulting products to be absorbed; also known as an **insectivorous plant**.

Carnot, Lazare (Nicolas Marguerite) [kah(r)noh] (1753–1823) French statesman, born in Nolay, France, known as 'the organizer of victory' during the Revolutionary Wars. He was one of the Directors (1795), became minister of war (1800), helped to organize

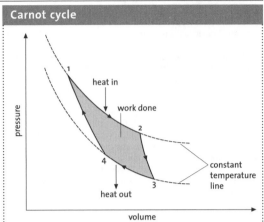

Carnot cycle

heat in

work done

pressure

volume

constant temperature line

heat out

[kah(r)noh] The fundamental thermodynamic cycle proposed by French engineer Sadi Carnot in 1824, in an attempt to explain the working of the steam engine. It comprises four stages: isothermal then adiabatic expansions, followed by isothermal and adiabatic compressions. A **Carnot engine** is the most efficient heat engine possible (**Carnot's law**). For intake temperature T_i and exhaust temperature T_o, thermal efficiency e is $e = (T_i - T_o)/T_i$. Because of physical and metallurgical problems, the Carnot cycle is not practical, and other cycles have been developed that meet the needs of real engines. Such cycles reflect more closely the way heat is actually added to and taken from the gases of a real engine.

the Italian and Rhenish campaigns, and during the Hundred Days was minister of the interior.

Carnot, (Nicholas Léonard) Sadi [kah(r)noh] (1796–1832) Scientist, born in Paris. He spent much of his life investigating the design of steam engines, and his findings were the foundation of the science of thermodynamics.

Carnot cycle *see panel*

Carnot's law *Carnot cycle*

carob An evergreen tree or shrub (*Ceratonia siliqua*), growing to 10 m/30 ft, native to the Mediterranean region; flowers lacking petals; pods to 20 cm/8 in long, pendent, violet-brown when ripe; also called **locust tree**. (Family: Leguminosae.)

Caroline, Radio The best-known UK pirate radio station of the 1960s. Operating illegally from a ship off the Essex coast, and financed by advertising, Radio Caroline broke the BBC's monopoly of domestic radio broadcasting and 'created' a youth audience through non-stop pop music, thus prompting the creation of BBC Radio 1.

Carolingians A Frankish ruling dynasty which rose to power as mayors of the palace, and ultimately replaced the Merovingians when Pepin II became King of the Franks in 751. The Carolingian Empire created by Charlemagne embraced most of the former territory of the Roman Empire in the West.

carp Deep-bodied freshwater fish (*Cyprinus carpio*) native to Black Sea coasts but now introduced worldwide; length up to 1 m/3$\frac{1}{4}$ ft; two pairs of barbels on upper jaw; important food fish; broadly, any member of the large family Cyprinidae.

Carpaccio, Vittore [kah(r)pachioh] (c.1460–c.1525) Painter, born in Venice. His most characteristic work is seen in the nine subjects from the life of St Ursula (1490–5).

carpal tunnel syndrome A weakness of the thumb and hand, with numbness or tingling in the thumb and adjacent two or three fingers. It is caused by pressure on the nerve that supplies the muscles and skin in this area (the *median nerve*) as it passes through a band of tissue that encircles the wrist (the *carpal tunnel*). The carpal tunnel is inflexible, and so the median nerve becomes compressed if there is swelling of other tissues within it. Symptoms can often be relieved by rest and splinting of the wrist, but surgery may be required to release the pressure on the nerve.

Carpathian Mountains Mountain system of EC Europe; extends 1400 km/870 mi in a semi-circle from Czech Republic to Romania; highest point, Mt Gerlach (2655 m/8711 ft).

carpel Part of the innermost whorl of a flower, collectively forming the *gynecium*: it typically consists of an ovary, style, and stigma, which together are sometimes called the **pistil**.

Carpentaria, Gulf of [kah(r)pentayria] Major inlet on N coast of Australia between Cape Arnhem and Cape York; 595 km/370 mi long by 491 km/305 mi wide; named by Tasman in honour of the Governor-General of Dutch East Indies, 1642.

carpet A floor covering made from wool, silk, jute, mohair, or other fibres, traditionally woven but currently produced by other methods such as bonding or machine-stitching the pile to a base. The technique is thought to have originated in Persia in ancient times; in the 18th-c, it became widespread in Britain, France, and other West European countries.

Carpetbaggers A derogatory term for US Northerners who went to the defeated South after the Civil War to aid freed blacks and take part in rebuilding. Supposedly they carried all their belongings in bags made of carpet.

Carr, Philippa *Hibbert, Eleanor*

Carracci [karahchee] A family of Italian painters, born in Bologna. The most famous was **Annibale Carracci** (1560–1609), who with his brother, **Agostino Carracci** (1557–1602), painted the gallery of the Farnese Palace, Rome. With their cousin, **Ludovico Carracci** (1555–1619), they founded an influential academy of painting in Bologna (1582).

carrack [karak] A 15th-c development of the Portuguese caravel, distinguished by having square sails in addition to lateen sails.

Carrantuohill [karantoouhl] Mountain in SW Ireland in the Macgillycuddy's Reeks range, rising to 1041 m/3415 ft; highest peak in Ireland.

Carreras, José Maria [karairas] (1946–) Lyric tenor, born in Barcelona, Spain. He made his debut at Covent Garden and at the Metropolitan Opera in 1974. After severe illness in the mid-1980s, he returned to the stage.

Carrey, Jim, popular name of **James Eugene Carrey** (1962–) Actor and entertainer, born in Newmarket, Ontario. He moved to Los Angeles in 1981, where he worked in nightclubs as a stand-up comedian and impressionist. His films include *Earth Girls Are Easy* (1989), *The Mask* (1994), *Batman Forever* (1995), *The Truman Show* (1998), and *Fun with Dick and Jane* (2005).

Carrington, Peter (Alexander Rupert) Carrington, 6th Baron (1919–) British Conservative statesman, born in London. He served as secretary of state for defence (1970–4) and foreign secretary (1979–82), but resigned over the Argentinian invasion of the Falkland Is. He later became Secretary-General of NATO (1984–8) and Chancellor of the University of Reading.

Carroll, Lewis, pseudonym of **Charles Lutwidge Dodgson** (1832–98) Writer, mathematician, and photographer, born in Daresbury, Cheshire. He took orders in 1861, and was a lecturer in mathematics (1855–81). His nursery tale, *Alice's Adventures in Wonderland* (1865), and its sequel, *Through the Looking-Glass* (1872), quickly became classics. 'Alice', to whom the story was originally related during boating excursions, was the second daughter (who died in 1934) of Henry George Liddell, the head of his Oxford college. He wrote a great deal of humorous and nonsense verse, such as *The Hunting of the Snark* (1876), and was also a respected portrait photographer.

carrot A biennial herb (*Daucus carota*) growing to 1 m/3.3 ft,

native to Europe, temperate Asia, and N Africa; flowers white or pink, the central flower usually dark purple; fruits spiny. The cultivated carrot (subspecies *sativus*), with a large fleshy orange or whitish tap root, is an important human dietary food. (Family: Umbelliferae.)

Carrott, Jasper, originally **Bob Davies** (1945–) Comedy entertainer, born in Acocks Green, Birmingham. He had a hit record with 'Funky Moped' (1975), and in 1978 starred in his own television show *An Audience with Jasper Carrott*. Later series include *Carrott Confidential* (1987–9), *Canned Carrott* (1990–1), and *The Detectives* (1989, 1993–7). In 2002 he took on a more serious acting role in the TV sitcom *All About Me*.

Carson, Johnny, popular name of **John William Carson** (1925–2005) Television personality and businessman, born in Corning, IA. He starred in *The Johnny Carson Show* (1955–6), and was engaged as an occasional host of *The Tonight Show*, a position that was made permanent in 1962. Consistently top of the ratings, his breezy, relaxed manner, comic monologue, and selection of guests made him an American institution. He retired from the show in 1992.

Carson, Kit, popular name of **Christopher Carson** (1809–68) Frontiersman, born in Madison Co, KY. He was Indian agent in New Mexico (1853), and fought for the Union in the Civil War. Several places are named after him.

Carson, Rachel (Louise) (1907–64) Naturalist and publicist, born in Springdale, PA. In 1962 her *Silent Spring* directed public attention to the problems caused by agricultural pesticides, and she became a pioneer in the conservationist movement of the 1960s.

Carson City 39°10N 119°46W, pop (2000e) 52 500. State capital in W Nevada, USA; founded, 1858; trade centre for a mining and agricultural area; tourism; gambling centre.

Cartagena (de los Indes) (Colombia) [kartakhayna] 10°24N 75°33W, pop (2000e) 590 200. Port in NW Colombia; founded, 1533; sacked by Drake, 1586; airfield; university (1824); old colonial quarter is a world heritage site.

Cartagena (Spain) [kah(r)tajeena], Span [kartakhayna], Lat **Carthago Nova** 37°38N 0°59W, pop (2000e) 169 000. Fortified seaport and naval base in SE Spain; founded by the Carthaginians, 221 BC; two airports; railway.

Carte, Richard D'Oyly *D'Oyly Carte, Richard*

cartel [kah(r)tel] An agreement by a number of companies in the same industry to fix prices and/or quantities, thus avoiding cut-price competition or overproduction. It is often seen as not being in the public interest, since it does not allow market forces to operate freely.

Carter, Angela (1940–92) Writer, born in Eastbourne, East Sussex. Her novels and short stories are characterized by feminist themes and fantasy narratives; they include *The Magic Toyshop* (1967), *Nights at the Circus* (1984), and *Wise Children* (1991).

Carter, Betty, originally **Lillie Mae Jones** (1930–98) Jazz singer and arranger, born in Flint, MI. She was perhaps the major jazz singer of the 1980s and 1990s. In her younger days she sang with Charlie Parker and Dizzy Gillespie, and became known as 'Betty Bebop'. Later she worked with Ray Charles and other blues artists, and continued performing into her sixties.

Carter, Howard (1874–1939) Archaeologist, born in Swaffham, Norfolk. His discoveries included the tombs of Hatshepsut (1907), Thutmose IV and, most notably, Tutankhamen (1922), a find on which he worked for the remainder of his life.

Carter, Jimmy, popular name of **James (Earl) Carter** (1924–) US statesman and 39th president (1977–81), born in Plains, GA. In 1976 he won the Democratic presidential nomination, and went on to win a narrow victory over Gerald Ford. He arranged the peace treaty between Egypt and Israel (1979), and was much concerned with human rights at home and abroad. His administration ended in difficulties over the taking of US hostages in

Iran, and the Soviet invasion of Afghanistan, and he was defeated by Ronald Reagan in the 1980 election. He has been much involved in international diplomacy, notably in relation to the crisis in Haiti in 1994. He was awarded the Nobel Prize for Peace in 2002.

Cartesian geometry *analytic geometry*

Carthage 36°54N 10°16E. Ancient town in Tunisia, N Africa, now a suburb of Tunis; a world heritage site; reputedly founded by the Phoenicians in 814 BC; destroyed by Rome following the Punic Wars, 146 BC; refounded by Caesar and Octavian, 29 BC; restored as capital by the Vandals, AD 439–533, but destroyed again by the Arabs, 698.

Carthusians A Roman Catholic monastic order founded in 1084 by Bruno of Cologne in Chartreuse, near Grenoble, France; properly known as the **Order of Carthusians**; abbreviated **OCart**. At the mother-house, 'La Grande Chartreuse', a famous liqueur is distilled, the profits being distributed to local charities.

Cartier, Jacques [ka(r)tyay] (1491–1557) Navigator, born in St-Malo, France. Between 1534 and 1542 he made three voyages of exploration to North America, surveying the coast of Canada and the St Lawrence R.

Cartier-Bresson, Henri [ka(r)tyay bresõ] (1908–2004) Photographer, born in Paris. His first exhibitions were in 1933 in Madrid and New York. He returned to Europe at the outbreak of the Spanish Civil War, recording events on both still and film cameras, resulting in the film *Victoire de la Vie* (1937). In the later 1930s he was an assistant to the film director Jean Renoir, working on *Partie de Campagne* (1936) and *La Régle du Jeu* (1939). He photographed the liberation of Paris in 1944 and made the documentary film *Le Retour* (1945). He worked only in black-and-white (except for some early commercial work), concerned exclusively with the capturing of visual moments illustrating contemporary life. In the mid-1970s he gave up photography, and returned to his earlier interests of painting and drawing.

cartilage Tissue supplementary to bone in the skeleton, found for example in the nose, ear, and larynx; sometimes called **gristle**. It is composed of living cells surrounded by an intercellular substance containing collagen. It is not hard or strong (so can be easily cut or damaged by high pressure), and is relatively nonvascular, being nourished by tissue fluids (particularly at joint surfaces).

cartilaginous fish [kah(r)tilajinuhs] Any fish of the class Chondrichthyes (800 species), having a cartilaginous endoskeleton that may be calcified but not ossified (true bone), and lacking air bladder or lungs; comprises the sharks and rays (Elasmobranchii) and ratfishes (Holocephalii).

Cartland, Dame (Mary) Barbara (Hamilton) (1901–2000) Popular romantic novelist, born in Edgbaston, West Midlands. After her first novel, *Jigsaw* (1923), she wrote over 700 books, mostly romantic novels but also biographies of 'romantic' figures, and books on food, health, and beauty. She was active in charitable causes, and well known for her views on health and fitness in old age.

cartography The method of construction of maps and charts. Through the use of symbols, lettering, and shading techniques, data concerning an area (eg its relief, population density) are portrayed on a map in such a way that it can be interpreted by the user to find out information about a place. Data come from many sources, such as fieldwork, surveying, and remote sensing.

cartridge tape drive *magnetic tape* 2

Cartwright, Edmund (1743–1823) Inventor of the power loom (1785–90), born in Marnham, Nottinghamshire. Attempts to use the loom met with fierce opposition, and it was not until the 19th-c that it came into practical use.

Caruso, Enrico [karoozoh] (1873–1921) Operatic tenor, born in Naples, where he made his debut in 1894. The extraordinary power of his voice, combined with his acting ability, won him worldwide recognition.

Carver, George Washington (1861–1943) Scientist, born near Diamond Grove, MO. He was born into an African-American slave family, and received little formal education in his early years. He became renowned for his research into agricultural problems and synthetic products, and was an influential teacher and humanitarian.

Cary, John [kairee] (c.1754–1835) English cartographer, who began as an engraver in London. His *New and Correct English Atlas* appeared in 1787, followed by county atlases, and the *New Universal Atlas* of 1808.

Cary, (Arthur) Joyce (Lunel) [kairee] (1888–1957) Writer, born in Londonderry, Northern Ireland. His best-known work is his trilogy, *Herself Surprised* (1941), *To be a Pilgrim* (1942), and *The Horse's Mouth* (1944).

caryatid [kareeatid, kariatid] A sculptured female figure, used as a column or support for an entablature or other building element. The name derives from the ancient Greek women of Caryae sold into slavery.

Casablanca [kasablangka], Arabic **Dar el Beida** 33°20N 71°25W, pop (2000e) 3 141 000. Seaport in W Morocco; founded by the Portuguese as Casa Branca, 1515; seriously damaged by an earthquake in 1755 and rebuilt; French occupation, 1907; meeting place of Churchill and Roosevelt, 1943; airport; railway; university; handles over 75% of Morocco's trade; world's second largest mosque (King Hassan II Mosque) opened, 1993; target of terrorist suicide bomb attacks, May 2003.

Casablanca Conference A meeting in N Africa between Roosevelt and Churchill during World War 2 (Jan 1943), at which it was decided to insist on the eventual unconditional surrender of the Axis states.

Casals, Pablo [kasals], Catalan **Pau** (1876–1973) Cellist, conductor, and composer, born in Vendrell, Spain. He began to appear as a soloist in 1899, and in 1919 founded the Barcelona Orchestra, which he conducted until he left Spain at the outbreak of the Civil War (1936). During his later years, he conducted many master classes.

Casanova (de Seingalt), Giacomo Girolamo [kasanohva] (1725–98) Adventurer and author, born in Venice, Italy. By 1750 he had worked as a clergyman, secretary, soldier, and violinist in various countries. Alchemist, cabalist, and spy, he visited many parts of Europe, was everywhere introduced to the best society, and had always to 'vanish' after a brief period of felicity. His main work is his autobiography, first published in 1960, in which he emerges as one of the world's great lovers. His seductions are the first things many think of in connection with his name.

Cascade Range Mountain range in W North America; extends over 1120 km/700 mi from N California to British Columbia; named after the cascades of the Columbia R where it passes through the range in a canyon c.1200 m/4000 ft deep; highest point, Mt Rainier (4392 m/14 409 ft), Washington; Crater Lake National Park in the S.

case-control study A scientific method used in medicine to determine the cause of a disease. Two groups of people, one with the disease under investigation and the other without, are analysed to see whether the diseased group has had a statistically greater exposure to the suspected risk factor.

casein [kayseen] The main protein in milk and cheese, rich in associated calcium and phosphorus. Casein is heat-stable, but is precipitated at a pH of about 4.2 (mildly acid). This is exploited in cheese-making, where the initial step is the precipitation of the curd (casein and fat) from the whey.

Casement, Roger (David) [kaysment] (1864–1916) British consular official, born in Dun Laoghaire (formerly Kingstown), Co Dublin, Ireland. In 1916 he was arrested on landing in Ireland from a German submarine to head the Sinn Féin rebellion, and hanged for high treason in London. His controversial 'Black Diaries' were long suppressed by the government, but ultimately published in 1959.

Cash, Johnny (1932–2003) Musician and actor, born in Kingsland, AR. A singer, guitarist, and songwriter, he became one of the greatest stars of country music. He recorded his first hits for Sun Records, 'I Walk the Line' and 'Folsom Prison Blues' in 1956. He appeared regularly on the 'Grand Ole Opry' radio broadcasts in the early 1960s, and performed the first of many free jailhouse shows in San Quentin Prison. In 1968 he married country singer **June Carter** (1929–2003), and the next year began hosting his own television programme, 'The Johnny Cash Show'. He also appeared in film and television roles. A biopic of his life, *Walk the Line*, appeared in 2005.

cashew A small evergreen tree (*Anacardium occidentale*), native to South America; flowers in terminal clusters, petals red, narrow, and reflexed; the receptacle thick, fleshy, pear-shaped in fruit, and bearing the curved nut. (Family: Anacardiaceae.)

cashmere The highly-prized fine warm undercoat fibres from the Kashmir goat; mainly produced in China and Iran. It is used principally in knitwear.

casino An establishment where gambling takes place. The first legal casino opened in Baden-Baden in 1765, and rules governing their operation are very strict in most countries.

Casper 42°51N 106°19W, pop (2000e) 49 600. City in EC Wyoming, USA; largest city in the state; airfield; railway; trade centre of a farming, ranching, and mineral-rich area.

Caspian Sea [kaspian], ancient **Mare Caspium** or **Mare Hyrcanium** area 371 000 km²/143 200 sq mi. Largest inland body of water on Earth, surrounded on three sides by republics of the former USSR, and in the S by Iran; c.28 m/90 ft below sea-level, but much variation in level; maximum depth, 980 m/3215 ft in S; shallow N area; low salinity; frozen in N for several months in severe winters; no outlet and no tides; pollution an increasing problem; Caspian Sea pact (agreed Nov 2003) aims to reduce amount of sewage and industrial waste pumped into sea.

Cassandra [kasandra] In Greek legend, the daughter of Priam, King of Troy. She was favoured by Apollo, who gave her the gift of prophecy. Because she did not return his love, he decreed that she would never be believed. After the fall of Troy she was murdered on her arrival in Argos.

Cassatt, Mary [kasat] (1844–1926) Impressionist painter, born in Allegheny, PA. A pupil and close follower of Degas, she was renowned for her etching and drypoint studies of domestic scenes.

cassava A food plant (*Manihot esculenta*), also called **manioc**, important throughout the tropics. It ranges from low herbs to shrubs or slender trees, with fleshy, tuberous roots and fan-shaped, 5–9-lobed leaves. The raw roots are poisonous without treatment. It can then be made into a wide range of products, including cassava flour, bread, and tapioca. (Family: Euphorbiaceae.)

Cassegrain telescope [kasuhgran] A telescope designed by French scientist Laurent Cassegrain (c.1629–93) in 1672, and now the commonest optical system for a telescope. It has a paraboloid primary mirror with a central hole, a hyperboloid secondary mounted inside the focus of the primary, and the eyepiece behind the primary. A variant of it, the Schmidt-Cassegrain, has a thin correcting lens as well, and is popular for amateur astronomy.

Cassidy, Butch, originally **Robert LeRoy Parker** (1866–?1909) Outlaw, born in Beaver, UT. He joined the infamous Wild Bunch and was partner with the Sundance Kid, robbing banks, trains, and mine stations with the law in constant pursuit. From 1901 they lived mainly in South America, where (according to one theory) they were trapped and killed.

Cassini, Giovanni Domenico [kaseenee], also known as **Jean Dominique Cassini** (1625–1712) Astronomer, born in Perinaldo, Italy. In 1669 he became the first director of the observatory at Paris. **Cassini's division** (the gap between two of Saturn's rings) is named after him. **Cassini's laws**, describing the rotation of the Moon, were formulated in 1693.

Cassini–Huygens mission A spacecraft mission to Saturn and Titan undertaken as an international project by NASA, the European Space Agency (ESA), the Italian Space Agency (ASI), and several European academic and industrial partners. Launched in October 1997 on a Titan IVB-Centaur, the spacecraft requires several gravity assists (Venus–Earth–Jupiter) to reach Saturn. In May 2004, Cassini transmitted the first detailed pictures of the moon Phoebe, and in July 2004 successfully entered into orbit around Saturn, returning the first close-up pictures of the planet's rings. It revealed the existence of two previously unknown moons in August 2004, bringing the total of natural satellites to 33. In December 2004 the spacecraft released Huygens towards Titan, Saturn's largest moon, and in January 2005 the probe landed successfully on the surface, the furthest from Earth a spacecraft has ever landed. The first ever images of the surface were received soon after.

Cassiopeia (astronomy) [kasiohpeea] A large N constellation that includes rich star fields in the Milky Way. It contains **Cassiopeia A**, the strongest radio source in the sky after the Sun.

Cassiopeia (mythology) [kasiohpaya] In Greek mythology, the beautiful daughter of Arabus who gave his name to the country called Arabia. She is said to have been the wife of King Cepheus of Ethiopia by whom she bore Andromeda. Cassiopeia was turned into a constellation.

Cassirer, Ernst [kaseerer] (1874–1945) Neo-Kantian philosopher, born in Wrocław, Poland (formerly Breslau, Prussia). His best-known work, *Die Philosophie der symbolischen Formen* (1923–9, The Philosophy of Symbolic Forms), analyses the symbolic functions underlying all human thought, language, and culture.

Cassius [kasius], in full **Gaius Cassius Longinus** (?–42 BC) Roman soldier and politician. Despite gaining political advancement through Caesar, he later turned against him and played a leading part in the conspiracy to murder him (44 BC). Defeated by Caesar's avengers at Philippi (42 BC), he committed suicide.

Casson, Sir Hugh (Maxwell) [kasn] (1910–99) Architect, born in London. He directed the architecture of the Festival of Britain (1951), and was professor of interior design at the Royal College of Art (1953–75).

cassowary [kasohwairee] A large flightless bird native to S Australasia; naked head has a bony outgrowth (*casque*), used as a shovel to uncover food; feet with long claws; its kick may be fatal. (Genus: *Casuarius*, 3 species. Family: Casuariidae.)

castanets Pairs of wooden (usually chestnut) discs, slightly concave, worn on the thumbs and clicked together rhythmically to accompany dancing, especially in Spain.

caste A system of inequality, most prevalent in Hindu Indian society, in which status is determined by the membership of a particular lineage and associated occupational group into which a person is born. Contact between castes is held to be polluting, and must be avoided.

Castiglione, Baldassare, conte di (Count of) **Novilara** [kasteelyohnay] (1478–1529) Writer and diplomat, born near Mantua, Italy. His chief work, *Il cortegiano* (1528, The Courtier), is a manual for courtiers.

casting The pouring of molten metal into a mould, where it solidifies into an ingot of manageable size for further processing, or into a desired final shape. Some metals can be **continuously cast**, solidified metal being removed at one end of a continuous length as more molten metal is added at the beginning. Some alloys (often containing zinc) can be **die-cast**, ie cast under pressure into a complex re-usable mould to give intricate shapes.

cast iron The primary product of the blast furnace: iron with about 4% carbon (**pig iron**). It has a low melting point and solidifies well into the shape of the mould. It is therefore valuable for casting, but has to be purified or modified before being used for manufacture.

Castle (of Blackburn), Barbara (Anne) Castle, Baroness, *née* **Betts** (1911–2002) British stateswoman, born in Bradford, West Yorkshire. She was a controversial minister of transport (1965–8), introducing a 70 mph speed limit and the 'breathalyser' test. She became secretary of state for employment and productivity (1968–70) and for social services (1974–6), and a member of the European Parliament, where she was vice-chair of the Socialist group (1979–86). She became a life peer in 1990.

castle One of the products of feudal society as it spread across Europe and into the Crusader kingdoms. Found in France from the mid-10th-c, they reached England as a result of the Norman Conquest, where they were built in large numbers by the new Norman elite. The earliest English castles were normally earthen mounds surrounded by ditches and topped by wooden towers. In 12th-c England, castle-builders increasingly used stone for towers and walls, and in the 13th-c Edward I built a fine series of castles in Wales (eg Caernarfon, Conwy, Harlech). Castles served as residences, seats of justice, administrative centres, and symbols of lordly authority. Later, especially in England, increasing emphasis was placed on their non-military roles, with greater concessions to domestic comfort and ornamental display.

Castlebar [kaslbah(r)], Ir **Caisleán an Bharraigh** 53°52N 9°17W, pop (2000e) 7800. Capital of Mayo county, W Ireland; residential and agricultural market town; Irish Land League founded here in 1879; airfield; railway.

Castlereagh, Robert Stewart, Viscount [kaslray] (1769–1822) British statesman, born in Dublin. His major achievements date from 1812, when, as foreign secretary under Lord Liverpool, he was at the heart of the coalition against Napoleon (1813–14). He represented Britain at Chaumont and Vienna (1814–15), Paris (1815), and Aix-la-Chapelle (1818), advocating 'Congress diplomacy' to avoid further warfare.

Castor and Pollux, Gr **Kastor** and **Polydeuces** Two heroes of classical mythology, known as the **Dioscuri**, usually pictured as twin brothers on horseback. They were children of Leda, at least one being fathered by Zeus. After death they became divine beings, and were turned into the constellation Gemini.

castor-oil plant An evergreen plant (*Ricinus communis*), in its native tropics forming a tall shrub or tree, in temperate regions only a stout herb; flowers tiny, green, in dense clusters; processed seeds yield castor oil. (Family: Euphorbiaceae.)

castration The surgical removal of the sex glands (testes or ovaries). When carried out in children, secondary sexual characteristics do not develop. In adults physical changes are less marked, but the individuals are sterile. In contrast with surgical castration, medical castration consists of giving drugs that block the normal effects of male or female sex hormones. It is used in the treatment of some forms of cancer.

castrato A male singer who underwent castration before puberty in order to preserve his treble voice. The practice probably originated at the Vatican in the 16th-c to compensate for the absence of women's voices from the choirs. Castrati took many of the leading roles in Italian opera during the 17th-c and 18th-c.

Castries [kastrees] 14°01N 60°59W, pop (2000e) 56 500. Port capital of St Lucia; founded, 1650; rebuilt after a fire in 1948; airport.

Castro (Ruz), Fidel (1927–) Cuban revolutionary, prime minister (1959–), and president (1976–), born near Birán, S Cuba. He led a successful rising against Batista in 1958, proclaimed a 'Marxist–Leninist programme', and set about far-reaching reforms. His overthrow of US economic dominance, and the routing of the US-connived emigré invasion at the Bay of Pigs (1961) was balanced by his dependence on Russian aid. In August 2006 he temporarily handed power to his brother, **Raul (Ruz) Castro** (1931–), after undergoing surgery in hospital.

cat A carnivorous mammal of the family Felidae; name popularly used for the domestic cat, *Felis catus*, other species having individual names (lion, tiger, etc); domestic cats known in Egypt 4000 years ago and may have evolved there from the **wild cat** (or **caffre cat**); numerous modern breeds; male called a *tom*, female a *queen*, young are *kittens*.

catabolism *metabolism*

catacombs Subterranean Jewish or early Christian cemeteries found in certain parts of the Roman world – notably Rome itself. The practice is believed to have been derived from ancient Jewish cave burials.

Catalan *Romance languages*

Catalaunian Plains, Battle of the [katalawnian] (451) The decisive defeat in E France suffered by Attila the Hun at the hands of the Romans and Visigoths.

catalepsy The adoption of a body posture which would normally be unsustainable; also referred to as **waxy flexibility**. It occurs in serious psychotic illness or as a hysterical reaction.

Çatal Hüyük [chatahl hooyuk] A prehistoric riverside settlement of c.6500–5500 BC in S Turkey, the largest Neolithic site known in the Near East. The *tell* (mound) is 20 m/65 ft high, and covers 13 ha/32 acres.

Catalonia [katalohnia], Span **Cataluña**, Catalan **Catalunya** pop (2000e) 6 038 000; area 31 932 km²/12 320 sq mi. Autonomous region of NE Spain, with a distinctive culture and Romance language; united with Aragon, 1137; part of Spain following union of Castilian and Aragonese crowns, 1469–79; strong separatist movement since the 17th-c; Catalan republic established, 1932; abolished by Franco during the Civil War, 1936–9; new government established, 1979; industry centred on Barcelona; major tourist resorts on the Costa Brava.

catalysis [katalisis] The acceleration or slowing of a chemical reaction by the action of a material (**catalyst**) which is recovered unchanged at the end of the reaction. Catalysts include iron in the Haber process for ammonia, and chlorophyll in photosynthesis.

catalytic converter An antipollution device often fitted to a car exhaust system. It contains a platinum catalyst for chemically converting unburned hydrocarbons and nitrogen oxides to compounds harmless to the environment.

catamaran [katamaran, katamaran] A twin-hulled vessel of Tamil origin, offering advantages in speed and stability. Propelled nowadays either by sail or power, it has become very popular as a yacht design in the past 25 years, and the advantages of the design have also proved attractive to firms introducing a new generation of car/passenger ferries.

catamount *cougar*

Catania [katahnia] 37°31N 15°06E, pop (2000e) 364 000. Port in Sicily, S Italy; at foot of Mt Etna, on E coast; archbishopric; airport; railway; university (1444).

cataract Opacities in the lens of the eye which cause slowly progressive loss of vision. Senile cataract is the most common type, but cataracts may also follow excessive exposure to ultraviolet light or injury to the eye, as well as being a complication of diabetes and other conditions. When severe, the lens can be removed and the vision corrected with the aid of spectacles and an artificial lens implantation.

catastrophe theory The mathematical study of sudden change, in contrast to continuous change. For example, in Necker's cube, the location of a dot appears first either in the centre of one face or in a corner of another face, then suddenly changes. It is not possible to say in which face any one viewer will first see it, but it always changes suddenly. Catastrophe theory was created in the late 1950s by French mathematician René Thom (1923–2002) and developed in particular by Stephen Smale, Vladimir Arnold, Christopher Zeeman, and others.

catatonia A psychiatric state in which there is stupor associated with catalepsy, or overactivity associated with stereotyped behaviour. This condition was first described by the German physician Karl Ludwig Kahlbaum (1828–99) in 1874, and is seen particularly in manic-depressive illnesses and schizophrenia.

Catch-22 The title of a novel by Joseph Heller, published in 1961. US airmen seeking to be excused bombing missions in World War 2 on grounds of mental derangement are judged ineligible to apply, since such a request proves their sanity. Hence 'Catch-22' signifies any logical trap or double bind.

catchfly An annual or perennial herb, part of the same genus as campions, but with hairy, sticky stem; native to the temperate N hemisphere; five petals, white, pink, or yellow. (Genus: *Silene*. Family: Caryophyllaceae.)

catechism A manual of Christian doctrine, usually in question-and-answer form. It derived from the early Church period of instruction for new converts, and was later applied to the instruction of adults baptized in infancy. Some have avoided the question-and-answer format, such as the Roman Catholic 'New Catechism' of 1966 and the 'Universal Catechism' of 1992.

catecholamine [katekohlameen] The chemical classification of a group of biologically important components widely distributed among animals and plants. Those occurring in mammalian tissues are dopamine, noradrenaline, and adrenaline. They are crucial in the control of blood pressure, and in the 'flight or fight' response.

caterpillar The larval stage of butterflies and moths (Order: Lepidoptera), usually feeding on plants; occasionally also used for the larvae of sawflies. (Order: Hymenoptera.)

caterpillar bird *cuckoo shrike*

Catesby, Robert [kaytsbee] (1573–1605) Chief conspirator in the Gunpowder Plot (1605), born in Lapworth, Warwickshire. A Catholic of wealth and lineage, he had suffered much as a recusant both by fines and imprisonment. He was shot dead while resisting arrest after the plot's failure.

catfish Any of about 28 families of typically elongate bottom-living fishes; flattened head, smooth skin, long barbels around mouth; includes freshwater Siluridae, Bagridae, Clariidae, Ictaluridae, and marine Ariidae, Plotosidae.

cat flu A highly infectious viral disease of the upper respiratory tract of cats. Ulceration of the tongue and palate as well as obstruction of the nasal passages leads to lack of appetite and further debility. Recovered cats can remain as carriers, and may start to shed the virus when stressed. Cats may be protected by the use of vaccines, and most cat-boarding establishments require evidence of up-to-date vaccination before accepting an animal.

catgut A tough cord prepared from the intestines of sheep (sometimes horse or ass, but never a cat). It has been used for musical instrument strings and surgical sutures. *Cat* seems to be derived from *kit* 'fiddle'.

Cathars [kathah(r)z] (Gr *kathari* 'pure ones') Originally, 3rd-c separatists from the Church, puritan and ascetic, following the teaching of the 3rd-c Roman bishop Novatian. In the Middle Ages, as a sect, they were known in Bulgaria as **Bogomils** and in France as **Albigenses**. They survived until the 14th-c.

cathartid vulture *vulture*

cathedral (Lat *cathedra*, 'chair') The chief church of a bishop of a diocese; originally, the church which contained the throne of the bishop, then the mother church of the diocese. The most famous are the W European Gothic cathedrals built in the Middle Ages, such as those at Reims and Chartres, France (both 13th-c).

Catherine II, known as **Catherine the Great**, originally **Princess Sophie Friederike Auguste von Anhalt-Zerbst** (1729–96) Empress of Russia (1762–96), born in Stettin. She carried out an energetic foreign policy and extended the Russian Empire S to the Black Sea as a result of the Russo–Turkish Wars (1774, 1792), while in the W she brought about the three partitions of Poland (1772, 1793, 1795). In 1774 she suppressed the popular rebellion led by Pugachev. Her private life was dominated by a long series of lovers, most notably Potemkin.

Catherine de' Medici [maydeechee] (1519–89) Queen of France, wife of Henry II, and Regent (1560–74), born in Florence, the daughter of Lorenzo de' Medici. During the minority of her sons, Francis II (1559–60) and Charles IX (1560–3), she assumed political influence, which she retained as Queen Mother until 1588. She was drawn into political and religious intrigues, conniving in the infamous Massacre of St Bartholomew (1572).

Catherine of Aragon [aragon] (1485–1536) Queen of England, the first wife of Henry VIII (1509–33), and fourth daughter of Ferdinand and Isabella of Spain, born in Alcalá de Henares, Spain. She was first married in 1501 to Arthur (1486–1502), elder son of Henry VII, and following his early death was betrothed to her brother-in-law Henry, then a boy of 11. She bore him five children, but only the Princess Mary survived. Henry divorced her in 1533, and she retired to an austere religious life.

Catherine of Braganza [braganza] (1638–1705) Wife of Charles II of England, the daughter of King John IV of Portugal, born in Vila Viçosa, Portugal. She was married to Charles in 1662 as part of an alliance between England and Portugal, but failed to produce an heir.

Catherine of Siena, St [syayna], originally **Caterina Benincasa** (1347–80) Dominican nun and mystic, born in Siena, Italy. She prevailed on Pope Gregory XI to return the papacy from Avignon to Rome. Christ's stigmata were said to be imprinted on her body. She was canonized in 1461, and is the patron saint of Italy. Feast day 29 April.

catheter [katheter] A fine tube made of rubber or synthetic material for insertion into parts of the body cavities, such as the bladder and blood vessels. It is used either to introduce drugs and fluids, to withdraw blood and body fluids for analysis, or to measure pressure or rates of flow.

cathode The positive terminal in a battery. In cathode-ray tubes (eg television tubes) and thermionic valves, a heated cathode is a source of electrons. In electrolysis, cations (positive ions) move towards the cathode. For a battery in a completed circuit, positive current flows from the cathode through the circuit to the **anode**.

cathode rays *electron*

cathode-ray tube (CRT) An electronic device in which an image is formed on a phosphor screen in a vacuum tube by a beam of electrons deflected in electric or magnetic fields. It is used in oscilloscopes, display screens, and television receivers.

Catholic Church (Gr *katholikos*, 'general', 'universal') **1** As in the Apostles' Creed, the universal Church which confesses Jesus Christ as Lord.
2 Christian Churches with episcopal order and confessing ancient creeds.
3 Specifically, the Roman Catholic Church and other Churches recognizing the primacy of the Pope.

Catholic Emancipation Act A reluctant religious concession to Roman Catholics in the British Isles, granted by the British Tory government in 1829, following mounting agitation led by Daniel O'Connell and the Catholic Association. Roman Catholics were permitted to become MPs; and certain offices of state were opened to Catholics. However, Roman Catholics remain excluded from the British throne.

Catiline [katiliyn], in full **Lucius Sergius Catilina** (c.108–62 BC) An impoverished Roman politician who tried to exploit the economic unrest of Rome in the 60s BC for his own political ends. His conspiracy against the state was foiled by Cicero in 63 BC.

cation [katiyon] An ion bearing a positive charge, so called because it will migrate towards the cathode in an electrochemical cell.

catmint A square-stemmed perennial (*Nepeta cataria*), growing to 1 m/40 in, native to Europe and Asia; flowers 2-lipped, white spotted with purple, in whorls forming spikes; also called **catnip**. A relative of true mints, its strong scent is attractive to cats. (Family: Labiatae.)

catnip *catmint*

Cato, Marcus Porcius [kaytoh], known as **Cato the Elder** or **Cato the Censor** (234–149 BC) Roman statesman, orator, and man of letters. Sent on a mission to Carthage (c.157 BC), he was so impressed by the power of the Carthaginians that afterwards he ended every speech in the Senate with the words: 'Carthage must be destroyed'.

Cato, Marcus Porcius [kaytoh], known as **Cato the Younger** or **Cato Uticensis** (95–46 BC) Roman statesman, the great-grandson of Cato the Censor. His career was marked by an unswerving opposition to Caesar. A supporter of Pompey in the Civil War, after Pharsalus (48 BC) he escaped to Africa.

Cato Street conspiracy [kaytoh] A plot in February 1820, formulated by Arthur Thistlewood (1770–1820) and fellow radical conspirators, to blow up the British Tory cabinet as it attended a dinner at the house of the Earl of Harrowby. The plot was infiltrated by a government agent, and the leaders were arrested and hanged.

CAT scanning *computerized tomography*

cat's eyes Rubber road studs fitted with a pair of light reflectors, designed to mark road lanes at night by reflecting a vehicle's headlights; devised by UK inventor Percy Shaw in 1934. The device can be compressed by the vehicle's wheels without doing damage to itself or the wheel.

Catskill Mountains Mountain group in SE New York State, USA; part of the Appalachian system; rises to 1282 m/4206 ft at Slide Mt.

cat's tail *reedmace*

cattalo *bison*

cattle Domesticated mammals, developed from wild aurochs (*Bos taurus*); now worldwide with numerous breeds; kept for milk and/or meat or for hauling loads; also known as **oxen**. (Family: Bovidae.)

cattle plague *rinderpest*

cattleya [katlia] An orchid (mainly an epiphyte) native to the forests of Central and South America. Most kinds have swollen, bulb-like stems (*pseudobulbs*) bearing 1–3 leaves, and spikes of up to 47 large, showy flowers. They are one of the most widely used orchids of floristry. (Genus: *Cattleya*, 30 species. Family: Orchidaceae.)

Catullus, Gaius Valerius [katuhlus] (c.84–c.54 BC) Lyric poet, born in Verona, Italy. He settled in Rome (c.62 BC), where he met 'Lesbia' whom he addressed in his verses. His extant works comprise 116 pieces, many of them extremely brief.

Caucasus Mountains [kawkasus], Russ **Kavkaz** Major mountain system in SW Europe and Asia; comprises the **Greater Caucasus** and the **Lesser Caucasus**; extends c.1120 km/700 mi SE; in the W is Mt Elbrus (5642 m/18 510 ft).

caucus A meeting, public or private, restricted to persons sharing a common characteristic, usually membership of a political party, held to formulate decisions or nominate candidates in forthcoming elections. It is most often applied to the USA, where the caucus–convention system is significant in selecting presidential and vice-presidential candidates, and where caucuses are the authoritative voice of the parties in Congress.

cauliflower A type of cultivated cabbage (*Brassica oleracea*) grown for the immature inflorescence which forms the edible white head. (Family: Cruciferae.)

Causley, Charles (Stanley) [kawzlee] (1917–2003) Poet, born in Launceston, Cornwall. He became known as a poet of the sea, and also as a children's poet. His *Collected Poems 1951–1997* were published in 1997.

caustic In chemistry, descriptive of substances (normally strongly alkaline) which are destructive, particularly to biological tissue. **Caustic soda** is sodium hydroxide; **caustic potash** is potassium hydroxide.

Cavalcanti, Guido [kavalkantee] (c.1230–1300) Poet, born in Florence, Italy. He was a friend of Dante, and wrote about 50 poems in the 'new style' of the period.

Cavalier poets Poets of the mid-17th-c who supported Charles I in the Civil War. Their (mostly love) poems are characterized by urbanity, elegance, and wit.

Cavaliers Those who fought for Charles I in the English Civil War. The name was used derogatorily in 1642 by supporters of Parliament to describe swaggering courtiers with long hair and swords, who reportedly welcomed the prospect of war. Similarly, the Parliamentarians were labelled 'Roundheads' by Cavaliers, dating from the riotous assemblies in Westminster during Strafford's trial in 1641, when short-haired apprentices mobbed Charles I's supporters outside the House of Lords.

Cavan (county) [kavn] pop (2000e) 53 000; area 1891 km²/ 730 sq mi. County in NC Ireland; capital, Cavan; pop (2000e) 5300.

cave A natural cavity in the Earth's surface, generally hollowed out by the action of water, and most spectacularly developed in limestones (soluble in mildly acid rainwater), in which huge vaults and interconnected river systems may form. Caves are also made by the action of sea water against cliffs.

cave art *Palaeolithic art*

cavefish Small blind North American fish confined to limestone caves of SE states; body lacking pigment (Genera: *Amblyopsis*, *Typhlichthys*, four species); also two species (Genus: *Chologaster*) with small eyes and pigmented skin from coastal swamps. (Family: Amblyopsidae.)

Cavell, Edith [kavel] (1865–1915) Nurse, born in Swardeston, Norfolk. Matron of the Berkendael Institute, Brussels, she tended friend and foe alike, yet was executed by the Germans for helping Belgian and Allied fugitives to escape capture.

Cavendish, Henry (1731–1810) Physicist and chemist, born in Nice, France. In 1760 he studied the 'inflammable air', now known as hydrogen gas; and later ascertained that water resulted from the union of two gases. The 'Cavendish Experiment' was an ingenious means of estimating the density of the Earth.

Cavendish, Spencer Compton, 8th Duke of Devonshire, known (1858–91) as the **Marquess of Hartington** (1833–1908) British statesman, born in Lower Holker, Lancashire. In 1875 he became Leader of the Liberal Opposition during Gladstone's temporary abdication, and led the breakaway from the Liberal Party, becoming head of the Liberal Unionists from 1886. His younger brother, **Lord Frederick Cavendish** (1836–82), was also a Liberal MP (1865–82). He was appointed chief secretary for Ireland, but immediately after his arrival in Dublin was murdered by 'Irish Invincibles' in Phoenix Park.

caviar The prepared roe (eggs) of the female sturgeon, beluga, sevruga, and starlet. These fish are caught in the winter months in the rivers flowing into the Baltic Sea and the Danube.

Cavour, Camillo Benso, conte di (Count of) [kavoor] (1810–61) Piedmontese statesman who brought about the unification of Italy (1861), born in Turin. As premier (1852–9), he brought the Italian question before the Congress of Paris, and in 1860 secretly encouraged the expedition of Garibaldi.

cavy A rodent native to South America; includes **guinea pigs** (Genus: *Cavia*), and a wide range of cavy-like rodents. (Family: Caviidae, 15 species.)

Caxton, William (c.1422–c.1491) The first English printer, born possibly in the Weald of Kent. In Cologne (1471–2) he probably learned the art of printing, and soon after printed the first book in English, *The Recuyell of the Historyes of Troye* (1475). A year later he set up his wooden press at Westminster. Of about 100 books printed by him, over a third survive only in unique copies or fragments.

Cayenne [kayen] 4°55N 52°18W, pop (2000e) 60 000. Port capital of French Guiana, NE South America; founded, 1643; used as penal settlement, 1854–1938; airport; source of Cayenne pepper.

cayenne *pepper* 1

Cayley, Sir George [kaylee] (1773–1857) Pioneer of aviation, born in Scarborough, North Yorkshire. In 1808 he constructed and flew a glider, probably the first heavier-than-air machine, and in 1853 made the first successful man-carrying glider.

cayman *caiman*

Cayman Islands *see panel*

Cazaly, Roy [kazaylee] (1893–1963) Legendary Australian Rules footballer, born in Melbourne, Victoria, Australia. Leaping master of the high mark (jumping above other players to catch the ball), the call 'Up there Cazaly' was chanted by South Melbourne crowds and became a rallying cry for Australian troops in World War 2.

CBE *British Empire, Order of the*

CBI *Confederation of British Industry*

CD *compact disc*

CDC *Commonwealth Development Corporation*

CD-ROM [seedeerom] An acronym of **Compact Disk Read Only Memory**, a computer storage medium based on the use of the standard 5 in (25 mm) compact disk, licensed by Sony and Philips, and usually used for digital audio. One CD-ROM disk can store more than 600 megabytes of computer information. A read-only device, the main applications have been in providing access to large volumes of information such as encyclopedias. A **CD-writer** is a device which can be used to write data to writable CD-ROMS, thus allowing the CD-ROM to be used in a way similar to a floppy disk.

CD-writer *CD-ROM*

Ceanannus Mór, formerly **Kells** 53°44N 6°53W, pop (2000e) 3600. Urban district in Meath county, E Ireland; noted for its monastery (founded by St Columba); **Book of Kells** (now in Trinity College, Dublin) produced there c.800.

Ceauşescu, Nicolae [chowsheskoo] (1918–89) Romanian statesman and president, born in Scorniceşti, Romania. He became general secretary of the Romanian Communist Party in 1969, and under his leadership, Romania became increasingly independent of the USSR. As the first president of the Republic in 1974, he established a strong personality cult. In 1989 he was deposed when the army joined a popular revolt against his repressive government. Following a trial by military tribunal, he and his wife, Elena, were shot on Christmas Day 1989.

Cech, Thomas R [chek] (1947–) Biochemist, born in Chicago, IL. He showed that RNA could have an independent catalytic function aiding a chemical reaction without being consumed or changed. This had major implications for genetic engineering, as well as for understanding how life arose, and he shared the 1989 Nobel Prize for Chemistry.

Cecil, Robert (Arthur Talbot Gascoyne), 3rd Marquess of Salisbury [sesil] (1830–1903) British Conservative statesman and prime minister (1885–6, 1886–92, 1895–1902), born in Hatfield, Hertfordshire. Much of the time as prime minister he served as his

Cayman Islands

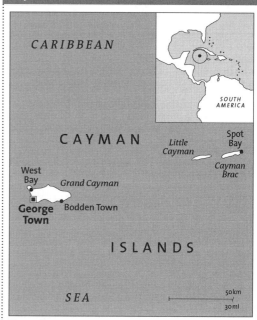

□ International Airport

[kayman] (UK British Overseas Territory)

Timezone GMT -5

Area 260 km²/100 sq mi

Population total (2002e) 40 000

Capital George Town

Physical features Located in W Caribbean, comprising the islands of Grand Cayman, Cayman Brac, and Little Cayman, c.240 km/150 mi S of Cuba; low-lying, rising to 42 m/138 ft on Cayman Brac plateau; ringed by coral reefs.

Climate Tropical climate; average temperatures 24–32°C (May–Oct), 16–24°C (Nov–Apr); average annual rainfall 1420 mm/56 in; hurricane season (Jul–Nov).

Currency 1 Cayman Island Dollar (KYD) = 100 cents

Economy Tourism; international finance, property development; over 450 banks and trust companies established on the islands; oil transshipment; crafts, jewellery, vegetables, tropical fish.

GDP (2002e) $1·27 bn, per capita $35 000

History Visited by Colombus, 1503; ceded to Britain, 1670; colonized by British settlers from Jamaica; British Crown Colony, 1962; a Governor represents the British sovereign, and presides over a Legislative Assembly.

own foreign secretary. He was head of government during the Boer War (1899–1902).

Cecil, William, 1st Baron Burghley or **Burghleigh** [sesil] (1520–98) English statesman, born in Bourn, Lincolnshire. In 1558 Elizabeth appointed him chief secretary of state, and for the next 40 years he was the chief architect of Elizabethan greatness, influencing her pro-Protestant foreign policy, securing the execution of Mary, Queen of Scots, and preparing for the Spanish Armada. He used an army of spies to ensure security at home.

Cecilia, St (2nd-c or 3rd-c) Patroness of music, especially church music. She was a convert to Christianity, and is said to have suffered martyrdom at Rome. Feast day 22 November.

cedar An evergreen conifer with a massive trunk and flat, wide-spreading crown, native to the mountains of N Africa, the Himalayas, and the E Mediterranean; needles sometimes bluish, in tufts; timber fragrant and oily. (Genus: *Cedrus*, 4 species. Family: Pinaceae.)

Ceefax [seefaks] A UK alphanumeric teletext system operated by the BBC since 1974. The name derives from 'see facts'.

Celebes *Sulawesi*

celeriac A variety of celery (*Apium graveolens* variety *rapaceum*), also called **turnip-rooted celery**, with a tuberous base to the stems, cooked as a vegetable or used in salads. (Family: Umbelliferae.)

celery A strong-smelling biennial herb (*Apium graveolens*), growing to 1 m/3$\frac{1}{4}$ ft, native to Europe, SW Asia, and N Africa; stems deeply grooved; flowers minute, greenish-white. (Family: Umbelliferae.)

celesta A musical instrument resembling a small upright piano, but with metal plates instead of strings and a shorter (five-octave) compass. It was invented in 1886 by French instrument maker Auguste Mustel (1842–1919).

celestial equator The great circle in which the plane of the Earth's equator cuts the celestial sphere. This is the primary circle for the co-ordinates' right ascension and declination.

celestial mechanics The study of the motions of celestial objects in gravitational fields. Founded by Isaac Newton, it deals with satellite and planetary motion within the Solar System, using Newtonian gravitational theory.

celestial sphere An imaginary sphere surrounding the Earth, used as a reference frame to specify the positions of celestial objects on the sky. Its N and S poles lie over those of Earth, and its equator is the projection of the terrestrial Equator.

celiac disease *coeliac disease*

Céline, Louis-Ferdinand [sayleen], pseudonym of **Louis-Ferdinand Destouches** (1894–1961) Writer, born in Paris. His reputation is based on the two autobiographical novels he wrote during the 1930s: *Voyage au bout de la nuit* (1932, Journey to the End of the Night) and *Mort à crédit* (1936, trans Death by Instalments).

cell (biology) The basic unit of plant and animal bodies; it comprises, at least, a nucleus or nuclear material and cytoplasm enclosed within a cell membrane. Many cells contain other specialized structures (*organelles*), such as mitochondria, chloroplasts, Golgi bodies, and flagella. Many simple organisms comprise a single cell, and may lack a membrane separating nuclear material from cytoplasm. Advanced organisms consist of a variety of co-operating cells, often specialized to perform particular functions and organized into tissues and organs. Plant cells are typically surrounded by an outer cell wall containing cellulose. Cell division may occur by splitting into two parts (*fission*), by mitosis, and (in the case of reproductive cells) by meiosis. All nucleated cells contain within their nuclei the entire inherited genetic information of that individual, but in specialized cells, such as a liver or brain cell, only a minute fraction of their genetic database is operational.

Cellini, Benvenuto [cheleenee] (1500–71) Goldsmith, sculptor, engraver, and author, born in Florence, Italy. He is particularly known for his autobiography (1558–62). At the siege of Rome (1527), he killed the Constable de Bourbon. His best work includes the gold saltcellar made for Francis I of France, and his bronze 'Perseus'.

cello or **violoncello** [cheloh] The bass instrument of the violin family, with four strings tuned one octave below the viola's. The modern instrument is fitted with an adjustable endpin which rests on the floor.

cellophane *cellulose*

cellular radio *mobile communications*

cellulite According to certain beauty experts, the dimpled fat around the thighs and buttocks, which is said to resist dieting. However, available scientific evidence shows that when an individual diets, fat is lost from all fat deposits in the body.

cellulitis [selyooliytis] Inflammation of the connective tissue that supports organs and structures in the body, usually caused by a bacterial infection. It is potentially dangerous, as the infection may enter the bloodstream or affect adjacent organs, and is best treated by an appropriate antibiotic.

celluloid The earliest commercial plastic (c.1865–9), consisting of cellulose nitrate plasticized with camphor. It had the great virtue of dimensional stability, which kept it in vogue for photographic film in spite of its dangerous inflammability. It was eventually superseded as a film base by dimensionally stable forms of cellulose acetate.

cellulose ($C_6H_{10}O_5)_n$. A structural polysaccharide found mainly in the cell walls of woody and fibrous plant material, such as cotton. It is the main raw material for paper. Important derivatives include rayon (**cellulose acetate**) and guncotton (**cellulose nitrate** or **nitrocellulose**).

celostat *coelostat*

Celsius (temperature) A temperature scale that takes the triple point of water to be 0·01°C, which corresponds roughly to taking the freezing point of water as 0°C and the boiling point as 100°C; named after Swedish astronomer Anders Celsius (1701–44); still often called by the old name *degrees Centigrade*.

Celtiberia [keltibeeria] The territory in NC Spain inhabited by the Celtiberians, a warlike people of mixed Celtic and Iberian ancestry. Staunch opponents of the Romans, they were pacified in 133 BC.

Celtic languages [keltik] The languages of the Celts. The dialects spoken on the continent are known as **Continental Celtic**; traces remain in several inscriptions and place-names in *Gaulish* and *Celtiberian*. **Insular Celtic** is the name given to the Celtic languages of the British Is and Brittany. There are two branches: *Goidelic* comprises the Gaelic spoken in Ireland (Irish or Erse), which spread to the Isle of Man (Manx) and Scotland (Gaelic); Welsh, Cornish, and Breton comprise the *Brythonic* (also called the *Brittonic* or *British*) branch.

Celtic Sea [keltik] Part of the Atlantic Ocean S of Ireland; separated from the Irish Sea by St George's Channel; main inlet, Bristol Channel; average depths of 100–200 m/330–650 ft.

Celts Different groups of peoples who probably originated in present-day France, S Germany, and adjacent territories during the Bronze Age, and developed in the later first millennium BC. Celtic-speaking societies expanded through armed raids into the Iberian Peninsula, British Is, C Europe, Italy, Greece, Anatolia, Egypt, Bulgaria, Romania, Thrace, and Macedonia. They were finally repulsed by the Romans and Germanic tribes. They were famous for their burial sites and hill forts, and their bronze and iron art and jewellery. Their modern descendents are found chiefly in Ireland, Scotland, and Wales.

cement In general, any substance used to adhere to each of two materials which cannot themselves adhere. More usually, it refers to **Portland cement**, an artificial mineral substance used in building and engineering, made from heating clay and limestone. The addition of water produces a soft manageable substance which sets hard. It is commonly mixed with other mineral substances (sand, stone) to form various grades of concrete, or used as a mortar for joining brickwork.

Cenozoic era [seenozohik], or **Cainozoic** [kaynozohik] The most recent of the four eras of geological time, beginning c. 65 million years ago and extending to the present day; subdivided into the *Tertiary* and *Quaternary* periods. It was characterized by widespread changes in the fauna, with the dominance of mammals and flowering plants.

censors In Republican Rome (5th-c–1st-c BC), two officials (usually ex-consuls) elected every five years to compile a register of citizens and their property for military, legislative, electoral, and fiscal purposes.

census A count of the population resident in an area at a given time, together with the collection of social and economic data, made at regular intervals, often every ten years. The USA conducted its first national census in 1790, and France and the UK began to collect census data in 1801. The first Chinese census was AD 2, when the population was recorded at 59 594 978.

centaur [sentaw(r)] In Greek mythology, a creature combining the upper half of a man and the rear legs of a horse; later and more popularly imagined as having the entire body of a horse. Centaurs came from Thessaly, and most were beastly and wild.

Centaurus [sentawrus] (Lat 'centaur') A large and rich S constellation. Its brightest star, **Alpha Centauri**, is actually three stars, the faintest of which, **Proxima Centauri**, is the closest star to the Sun, 1·29 parsec away from Earth.

centaury An annual, sometimes perennial, found almost everywhere; flowers pink, tubular with 4–5 spreading lobes, borne in dense heads. (Genus: *Centaurium*, c.50 species. Family: Gentianaceae.)

centigrade *Celsius* (temperature)

centimetre *metre* (physics)

centipede A carnivorous, terrestrial arthropod, commonly found in soil, leaf litter, and rotting wood; body up to 30 cm/12 in long, divided into head (bearing feelers and mouthparts) and many-segmented trunk; each trunk segment has one pair of legs; c.2500 species, some venomous. (Class: Chilopoda.)

Central (Scotland) pop (2000e) 274 700; area 2631 km²/1016 sq mi. Former 1975 region in C Scotland; replaced in 1996 by Stirling, Clackmannanshire, and Falkirk councils.

Central African Republic *p.174*

Central America A geographical region that encompasses the independent states to the S of Mexico and to the N of South America; includes Guatemala, El Salvador, Belize, Honduras, Nicaragua, Costa Rica, and Panama.

Central American Common Market (CACM) An economic association initiated in 1960 between Guatemala, Honduras, El Salvador, Nicaragua, and (from 1963) Costa Rica. Its early apparent success was offset by growing political crisis in the late 1970s.

Central Committee Under Soviet party rules, the highest decision-making authority in the former USSR, apart from Congress, which elected it. It exercised little influence, partly because of its unwieldy size and partly because of the concentration of power in the Politburo.

Central Criminal Court *Old Bailey*

Central Intelligence Agency (CIA) The official US intelligence analysis organization responsible for external security, established under the National Security Act (1947). It suffered a loss of credibility following the investigation into the Watergate affair in the mid-1970s.

central nervous system (CNS) A collection of nerve cells connected in an intricate and complex manner, involved in the control of movement and the analysis of sensation, and in humans also subserving the higher-order functions of thought, language, and emotion. In vertebrates it consists of the brain and spinal cord.

Central Powers Initially, the members of the Triple Alliance (Germany, Austria–Hungary, Italy) created by Bismarck in 1882. As Italy remained neutral in 1914, the term was later used to describe Germany, Austria–Hungary, their ally Turkey, and later Bulgaria in World War 1.

central processing unit (CPU) *digital computer*

Central Valley or **Great Central Valley** Valley in California, USA, between the Sierra Nevada (E) and the Coast Range (W). The Central Valley Project is a series of dams and reservoirs for flood-control, irrigation, and hydroelectricity.

Centre Beaubourg [sätruh bohboorg] The popular name for the Centre National d'Art et de Culture, or **Pompidou Centre**, situated on the Plateau Beaubourg in Paris. Designed by Renzo Piano and Richard Rogers, and opened in 1977, the six-storey building houses a modern art gallery and a centre for industrial design. Display space has been maximized by placing all services on the outside of the transparent exterior walls.

centrifuge A device for separating the components of a mixture (solid-in-liquid or liquid-in-liquid) by applying rapid rotation and consequent centrifugal force. It may be equipped for the technical separation of materials (eg cream) or for scientific observation (eg the **ultracentrifuge**, which separates particles of macromolecular size).

centrography In geography, the study of descriptive statistics for the determination and mapping of measures of central tendency. For example, the mean centre of population distribution can be mapped to show the main focus of a country's population distribution.

century The smallest unit in a Roman legion. Probably consisting originally of 100, under the Empire there were 80 soldiers in a century.

century plant A species of agave (*Agave americana*), so-called from the length of time once thought to pass between germination and flowering – up to 100 years. In Mexico its sap is one of the sources of the national drink, pulque, as well as a spirit, mescal. (Family: Agavaceae.)

cephalic index A skull's breadth as a percentage of its length. Skulls of different relative breadths are termed *brachycephalic* (broad), *mesocephalic* (intermediate), and *dolichocephalic* (long).

Cephalonia [kefalohnia], Gr **Kefallinía** pop (2000e) 33 700; area 781 km²/301 sq mi. Largest of the Ionian Is, Greece; length 48 km/30 mi; hilly island, rising to 1628 m/5341 ft; capital, Argostolion.

Cephalopoda [sefalopoda] A class of carnivorous, marine molluscs characterized by the specialization of the head-foot into a ring of tentacles, typically armed with hooks or suckers, and by their method of swimming using jets of water squirted out of a funnel; mouth typically with a powerful beak; eyes usually well developed.

Cephas [seefas] *Peter, St*

Cepheid variable [seefeeid] A class of variable star with a period of 1–50 days, characterized by precise regularity. The observed period of a Cepheid indicates its distance from Earth, and is consequently of great importance in determining the distance scale of the universe.

Cepheus (astronomy) [seefyoos] A N constellation which includes the famous star **delta Cephei**, the prototype of regular variables used for calibrating the distance scale of the universe.

Cepheus (mythology) [seefyoos] In Greek mythology, the son of Belus. He became the husband of Cassiopeia and was the father of Andromeda. He ruled over the Cephenes who were said to live partly on the banks of the Euphrates and partly in Ethiopia. At his death he was succeeded by his grandson, Perses.

ceramics The products of the baking of clay, giving hard, strong, non-conducting, brittle, heat-resistant substances. They are useful for technical purposes (eg abrasives, cutting tools, refractory linings) and for decoration. Clays of many kinds are used, from the coarse clay used for bricks to the fine white clay used for porcelain. Ceramics may be made in stages, such as the many ways of producing a *glaze*, a coating of a second clay or glass-like substance, which confers impermeability (as in making pipes) or decorative colours.

Ceratopsia [seratopsia] The horned dinosaurs; typified by enormous bony frill extending back over neck from posterior part

Central African Republic

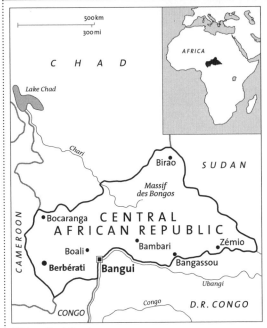

□ International Airport

Fr **République Centrafricaine**
Local name République Centrafricaine
Timezone GMT +1
Area 622 984 km²/240 535 sq mi
Population total (2002e) 3 643 000
Status Republic
Date of independence 1960
Capital Bangui
Languages French (official), Sangho
Ethnic groups Baya (34%), Banda (28%), Sara (10%), over 80 other groups
Religions Christian (50%), (Protestant 25%, Roman Catholic 25%), also Muslim and traditional beliefs

Physical features Located in C Africa; plateau forming a watershed between Chad and Congo river basins; Massif des Bongos rises 1400 m/4593 ft in NW; granite ranges of Mont Karre, 1220 m/4003 ft in W.

Climate Tropical; single rainy season in N (May–Sep); average annual rainfall 875–1000 mm/34–9 in; more equatorial climate in S; rainfall 1500–2000 mm/60–80 in.

Currency 1 CFA Franc (XAF) = 100 centimes

Economy Agriculture employs c.85% of working population; also sawmilling, brewing, diamond splitting, leather and tobacco processing.

GDP (2002e) $4·296 bn, per capita $1200

Human Development Index (2002) 0·375

History Part of French Equatorial Africa (Ubangi Shari); autonomous republic within the French community, 1958; independence, 1960; coup deposed country's first President, David Dacko, 1965; Jean-Bédel Bokassa declared himself emperor for life, and country's name changed to the Central African Empire, 1976; Bokassa deposed and country reverted to a republic, 1979; military coup established Committee for National Recovery, 1981–5; Committee dissolved and National Assembly established, 1987; movement toward multi-party democracy, 1991; multiparty legislative and presidential elections, 1993, elected Ange-Félix Patasse; President Patasse overthrown in coup, 2003, by Gen. Bozize; governed by a president, prime minister, and 85-member National Assembly.

Head of State
1981–93 André Kolingba
1993–2003 Ange-Félix Patasse
2003 *Military Coup*
2003– François Bozize

Head of Government
1991–2 Edouard Frank
1992–3 Thimothée Malendoma
1993 Enoch Derant Lakoue
1993–5 Jean-Luc Mandaba
1995–6 Gabriel Koyambounou
1996–7 Jean-Paul Ngoupandé
1997–8 Michel Gbezera-Bria
1999–2001 Anicet Georges Dologuélé
2001–3 Martin Ziguele
2003 Abel Goumba
2003–5 Célestin Gaombalet
2005– Elie Dote

of skull; usually with median horns in nasal region and paired horns behind eyes; evolved during the Upper Cretaceous period. (Order: Ornithischia.)

Cerberus [serberus] In Greek mythology, the dog which guards the entrance to the Underworld, originally 50-headed, later with three heads. Heracles carried him off as one of his labours.

cereals Grain-bearing grasses which provide staple foods for most of the world's population. The grains are much larger than those of other grass species, and are rich in protein and carbohydrates. There are eight major cereals: rice, wheat, oats, barley, rye, sorghums, millets, and maize. All derive from wild species, and their domestication in early times (c.8000 BC in the case of wheat and barley) marks a turning-point in human history. The replacement of *ramassage* (the gathering of wild grains) by a more dependable crop allowed the development of a more settled lifestyle. The development of modern cereals is very sophisticated, with strains tailored for specific purposes and conditions. (Family: Gramineae.)

cerebellum [serebelum] A mass of neural tissue that occupies the lower back part of the cranial cavity within the skull. Its principal function is the control of posture, repetitive movements, and the geometric accuracy of voluntary movements; it also appears to have an important role in learning.

cerebral haemorrhage / hemorrhage An episode of acute bleeding within the substance of the brain. It tends to occur when the blood pressure is high, or when the wall of the cerebral blood vessel is weakened by degenerative change (eg atherosclerosis) or is the site of a localized distension (*aneurysm*). The neurological disability that follows depends on the severity and site of the haemorrhage.

cerebral palsy A disorder resulting from damage to the brain during fetal development or in infancy, characterized by weakness, paralysis, rigidity, and lack of co-ordination of movement; the muscular spasms involved have led to the use of the term **spastic** for these children. A high proportion of children also suffer from epilepsy, and some are retarded mentally. Several types of brain injury are responsible, but the cause is unknown in many cases.

cerebrospinal fluid (CSF) A clear, colourless, protein-free fluid circulating through the cerebral ventricles of the brain, the central canal of the spinal cord, and the subarachnoid space in vertebrates, which provides the brain with mechanical support and nutrients. In humans, CSF is sometimes collected (by *lumbar puncture*) and analysed for diagnostic purposes.

cerebrum [serebruhm] A large mass of neural and supporting tissue which occupies most of the cranial cavity within the skull. It is separated into right and left halves (the right and left **cerebral hemispheres**), connected by a body of nerve fibres known as the *corpus callosum*. Each hemisphere can be divided into four *lobes* which are named according to the skull bone that they are most closely related to (ie *frontal, parietal, temporal,* and *occipital*). The surface of each hemisphere is formed by a layer of *grey matter* known as the *cerebral cortex*, containing the cell bodies of the neurones responsible for the functions of the cerebrum. Within the cortex the hemispheres are formed by a large mass of *white matter* consisting largely of the axons of the neurones in the cerebral cortex.

The surface of the cerebrum is thrown into a series of folds (*gyri*) separated by troughs (*sulci*): for example, the *central sulcus* separates the frontal and parietal lobes. Immediately in front of the central sulcus is the *motor cortex*, in which the opposite half of the body is represented upside down: the face lies lowest, then the hand (a very large area), then the arm, trunk, and leg. Stimulation here results in contraction of the appropriate voluntary muscles on the opposite side of the body. Below the area of the brain representing the face, on the left side, lies the speech area (*Broca's area*). Immediately behind the central sulcus is the *sensory cortex*, which receives sensory information from the opposite side of the body via the brain stem and thalamus.

The occipital lobe is involved with vision. The parietal lobe is in general responsible for sensory functions such as the perception of touch, pressure, and body position, as well as three-dimensional perception, the analysis of visual images, language, and calculations. The frontal lobe subserves motor functions, and also governs the expression of the intellect and personality. The upper part of the temporal lobe is involved in the perception of sound, with the remainder being concerned with memory and various emotional functions.

Ceres (astronomy) [seereez] The first asteroid to be found, discovered on the first night of the 19th-c. Much the largest known asteroid, its diameter is 940 km/580 mi (over one-quarter of the Moon's). It was upgraded to dwarf planet (or pluton) status in 2006. Dwarf planets take more than 200 years to orbit the Sun.

Ceres (mythology) [seereez] The ancient Italian corn-goddess, an early cult at Rome. She was given characteristics and stories associated with Demeter.

CERN *European Laboratory for Particle Physics*

Cerne Abbas [sern abas] 50°49N 2°29W, pop (2000e) 800. Village in Dorset, S England, UK; 10 km/6 mi N of Dorchester; ruins of 10th-c abbey where Ælfric was abbot; tithe barn (14th-c), church (15th-c); famous tourist attraction is the Cerne Giant, a 45 m/150 ft high figure cut into the chalk downs overlooking the village.

Cervantes (Saavedra), Miguel de [servanteez], Span [thairvantes] (1547–1616) Writer of *Don Quixote*, born in Alcalá de Henares, Spain. Tradition maintains that he wrote *Don Quixote* in prison at Argamasilla in La Mancha. When the book came out (1605), it was hugely popular. He wrote the second part in 1615, after several years writing plays and short novels.

cervical cancer [serviykl] A malignant tumour arising from the lining of the cervical canal. It is one of the leading causes of cancer death among women. Its occurrence is related to fre-

quent sexual intercourse with several partners, and most cases arise in association with genital infection by the human papilloma virus. Early stages of the cancer can be detected by the cervical smear test and effectively treated.

cervix [serviks] The lower tapering third of the uterus (womb). Its lower, blunt part projects into the vagina; its upper part communicates with the body of the uterus.

cesarian section *caesarian section*

Cestoda [sestoda] *tapeworm*

Cetacea [seetayshia] *whale*

cetane number An index defining the ignition quality of fuel for diesel internal combustion engines. The number is the cetane percentage in a mixture of cetane and alpha-methyl naphthalene, adjusted to match the characteristics of the fuel under test.

Cetewayo or **Cetshwayo** [ketewayoh] (c.1826–84) Ruler of Zululand from 1873, born near Eshowe, South Africa. In 1879 he defeated the British at Isandhlwana, but was himself defeated at Ulundi.

Cetus [seetus] (Lat 'whale') The fourth largest constellation, lying on the celestial Equator, but inconspicuous because it has few bright stars.

Ceuta [thayoota] 35°52N 5°18W, pop (2000e) 69 000. Freeport and military station, at E end of the Strait of Gibraltar, on the N African coast of Morocco; became Spanish in 1580; cathedral (15th-c).

Cévennes [sayven], ancient **Cebenna** Chief mountain range in the S of France, on the SE edge of the Massif Central; highest peak, Mt Mézenc (1754 m/5754 ft).

Cézanne, Paul [sayzan] (1839–1906) Postimpressionist painter, born in Aix-en-Provence, France. He abandoned his early sombre expressionism for the study of nature, and began to use his characteristic glowing colours. In his later period (after 1886), he constructed his pictures from a rhythmic series of coloured planes, thus becoming the forerunner of Cubism. Among his best-known paintings are 'The Card Players' (1890–2, Musée d'Orsay, Paris) and 'The Gardener' (1906, Tate). Picasso called him 'the father of us all'.

CFCs The acronym for **chlorofluorocarbons**, also called **Freons**; derivatives of methane and ethane containing both chlorine and fluorine. They are inert, volatile compounds, used as refrigerants and aerosol sprays. Their decomposition in the atmosphere damages the Earth's ozone layer. International agreements propose replacing them with less harmful substances.

Chabrier, (Alexis) Emmanuel [shabreeyay] (1841–94) Composer, born in Ambert, France. His best-known pieces were inspired by the folk music of Spain, notably his orchestral rhapsody *España* (1883).

Chabrol, Claude [shabrol] (1930–) Film critic and director, born in Paris. Identified with the French *Nouvelle Vague*, his most widely known films are dramas of abnormality in the provincial bourgeoisie, such as *Le Boucher* (1970, The Butcher), and *L'Enfer* (1993, Torment). Later films include *Rien ne va plus* (1997) and *L'Ivresse du pouvoir* (2006, Comedy of Power).

Chaco Canyon A remote desert canyon in New Mexico, 160 km/100 mi NW of Albuquerque, the hub in AD c.950–1300 of the Anasazi Indian culture of the American SW; now a world heritage site. A National Monument since 1907, its road network links c.125 D-shaped pueblos.

chaconne A dance of Latin-American origin. The harmonies and basses traditionally associated with it were widely used as material for arias and instrument variations in the 17th–18th-c.

Chaco War (1932) A territorial struggle between Bolivia and Paraguay in the disputed Northern Chaco area. Owing to the brilliant tactics of Col José Félix Estigarribia (1888–1940), Paraguay won most of the area.

Chad

□ International Airport

Fr **Tchad**, official name **Republic of Chad**, Fr **République du Tchad**

Local name Tchad

Timezone GMT +1

Area 1 284 640 km²/495 871 sq mi

Population total (2002e) 8 997 000

Status Republic

Date of independence 1960

Capital N'djamena

Languages Arabic and French (official), many local languages spoken

Ethnic groups Sara, Bagirmi, and Kreish (30%); Sudanic Arab (26%), Teda (17%), Masalit, Maba, Mimi (6%), over 200 groups

Religions Muslim (50%), Christian (Roman Catholic 21%, Protestant 12%), and local religions

Physical features Landlocked in C Africa; mostly arid, semi-desert plateau at edge of Sahara Desert; average altitude of 200–500 m/650–1650 ft; Tibesti Mts (N) rise to 3415 m/11 204 ft at Emi Koussi; rivers in S (Chari and Logne) flow NW to Lake Chad.

Climate Tropical, moderately wet in S (May–Oct); hot, arid N, almost rainless; C plain hot, dry, with brief rainy season (Jun–Sep).

Currency 1 CFA Franc (XAF) = 100 centimes

Economy Severely damaged in recent years by drought, locusts, and civil war; export of cotton, kaolin, animal products; salt mined around L Chad; country's first oil pipeline (length 1000 km/621 mi) from Doba in S to Cameroon's offshore Kribi oil terminal opened, 2003.

GDP (2002e) $9·297 bn, per capita $1000

Human Development Index (2002) 0·365

History Part of French Equatorial Africa, 1908; colonial status, 1920; independence, 1960; Libyan troops occupied the Aozou Strip in extreme N, 1973; fighting between Libyan-supported rebels and French-supported government until ceasefire agreed, 1987; continuing civil war with some further periods of ceasefire during the 1990s; new constitution adopted, 1991; transitional charter, 1993; Aouzou strip returned to Chad by Libya, 1994; peace agreement with northern rebel movement, 2002; draft peace agreement signed with the National Resistance Army (ANR), 2003; governed by a president, prime minister, Council of Ministers, and a 57-member Higher Transitional Council; constitution amended to lift limit on number of presidential terms, May 2004.

Head of State
1982–90 Hissne Habré
1990– Idriss Déby

Head of Government
1992–3 Joseph Yodemane
1993 Fidèle Moungar
1994–5 Delwa Kassire Koumakoye
1995–7 Koibla Djimasta
1997–9 Nassour Ouaidou Guelendouksia
1999–2002 Negoum Yamassoum
2002–3 Haroun Kabadi
2003–5 Moussa Faki Mahamat
2005–7 Pascal Yoadimnadji
2007– Nouradine Delwa Kassiré Koumakoye

Chad see panel

Chadic [chadik] A group of 100 languages, spoken by over 25 million people in parts of Ghana and the Central African Republic. It is assigned to the Afro-Asiatic family, though its position there is unclear.

Chadwick, Sir James (1891–1974) Physicist, born in Manchester, Greater Manchester. He discovered the neutron (1932), for which he received the Nobel Prize for Physics in 1935, and led the UK's work on the atomic bomb in World War 2.

Chadwick, John *Ventris, Michael*

Chadwick, Lynn (Russell) (1914–2003) Sculptor, born in London. He studied architecture, but after war service he began making mobiles (c.1946), then rough-finished solid metal sculptures.

chafer A large, nocturnal beetle; adults feed on leaves; larvae fleshy, C-shaped, burrow in soil eating roots, often taking 3–4 years to develop. (Order: Coleoptera. Family: Scarabaeidae.)

chaffinch Either of two species of bird of genus *Fringilla*. *Frin-*

gilla coelebs is native to Europe, N Africa, the Azores, and SW Asia; inhabits forest and human habitations; colour varies over range; N populations move S for winter. The **blue chaffinch** (*Fringilla teydea*) is from the Canary Is. (Family: Fringillidae.)

Chagall, Marc [shagal] (1887–1985) Artist, born in Vitebsk, Belarus. He moved to Paris and the USA, and became best known for his fanciful painting of animals, objects, and people from his life, dreams, and Russian folklore. The word 'Surrealist' is said to have been coined by Apollinaire to describe the work of Chagall.

Chaikin, Joseph [chiykin] (1935–) Actor and theatre director, born in New York City. He acted with the Living Theater, and in 1963 founded The Open Theater, which for a decade produced some of the most original work in the US theatre.

Chain, Sir Ernst Boris [chayn] (1906–79) Biochemist, born in Berlin. He shared the Nobel Prize for Physiology or Medicine in

1945 for the development of penicillin, and also worked on snake venoms and insulin.

chain reaction In nuclear physics, a reaction in which nuclear fission induced by a neutron releases further neutrons that in turn may cause further fission through some material. Nuclear power and atomic bombs rely on chain reactions in uranium or plutonium.

chakras The seven centres of energy in the yogic system. Roughly equivalent to the autonomic nervous system and endocrine glands of Western medicine, they are important for channelling vital energy and consciousness. An imbalance of energy may lead to physical, mental, emotional, or spiritual disharmony.

Chalcedon, Council of [kalseedn] (451) A Council of the Church which agreed that Jesus Christ is truly God and truly man, two natures in one person (the *Chalcedonian definition*).

chalcedony [kalsedonee] A group name for the compact varieties of mineral silica (SiO_2) composed of very fine-grained crystals of quartz. Banded varieties are agate and onyx, and coloured varieties include carnelian, jasper, bloodstone, and chrysoprase.

Chalcis [kalsis], Gr **Khalkis** 38°27N 23°42E, pop (2000e) 48 600. Capital of Euboea, Greece; railway; local ferries; Aristotle died here.

Chalcolithic *Three Age System*

chalcopyrite [kalkopiyriyt] A copper iron sulphide mineral ($CuFeS_2$) found in veins associated with igneous rocks; brass-coloured and metallic. It is the main ore of copper.

Chaldaeans [kaldeeanz] **1** Originally the name of a Semitic people (*Kaldu*) from Arabia who settled in the region of Ur in Lower Mesopotamia. **2** In the 7th-c and 6th-c BC, a generic term for Babylonians.

chalk A fine-grained limestone rock, mainly of calcite, formed from the shells of minute marine organisms. Often pure white in colour, it is characteristically seen in rocks of the Upper Cretaceous period of W Europe, its most famous exposures being on either side of the English Channel. Blackboard chalk is calcium sulphate.

Challoner, Richard [chaloner] (1691–1781) Roman Catholic clergyman and writer, born in Lewes, East Sussex. His best-known works are the prayer book, *The Garden of the Soul* (1740), and his revision of the Douai version of the Bible (5 vols, 1750).

Chalmers, Thomas (1780–1847) Theologian and reformer, born in Anstruther, Fife. In the Disruption of 1843 he led 470 ministers out of the Established Church of Scotland to found the Free Church of Scotland.

Chamaeleon [kameelion] A faint S constellation.

chambered tomb In European prehistory, megalithic monuments usually constructed of uprights (*orthostats*) and capstones beneath a cairn or mound of earth, the burial chamber sometimes being provided with a corbelled vault; also known as a **dolmen**.

Chamberlain, Sir (Joseph) Austen (1863–1937) British Conservative statesman, born in Birmingham, West Midlands, eldest son of Joseph Chamberlain. He was Chancellor of the Exchequer (1903–6, 1919–21), secretary for India (1915–17), Unionist leader (1921–2), foreign secretary (1924–9), and First Lord of the Admiralty (1931). He received the 1925 Nobel Peace Prize for negotiating the Locarno Pact.

Chamberlain, Joseph (1836–1914) British statesman, born in London. From 1889 he was leader of the Liberal Unionists, and in the Coalition Government of 1895 was secretary for the Colonies.

Chamberlain, Lindy, *née* **Alice Lynne Murchison** (1948–) Mother of the 'dingo baby', born in Whakatane, New Zealand. The disappearance of her nine-week-old daughter, Azaria, at Uluru (Ayers Rock) in 1980 made her the subject of national obsession in Australia. Married to pastor **Michael Chamberlain** (tried with her, since divorced), she claimed the baby was taken by a dingo. She was found guilty of murder, and gaoled, but released in 1986 when a baby's jacket was found at the base of the rock. Following a judicial inquiry, all convictions against the couple were quashed, and they received A$1 million in compensation.

Chamberlain, (Arthur) Neville (1869–1940) British statesman and Conservative prime minister (1937–40), born in Birmingham, West Midlands, the son of Joseph Chamberlain. He advocated 'appeasement' of Italy and Germany, returning from Munich with his claim to have found 'peace for our time' (1938). Criticism of his war leadership and initial military reverses led to his resignation (1940).

Chamberlain, Wilt(on) Norman, nickname **Wilt the Stilt** (1936–99) Basketball player, born in Philadelphia, PA, height 1·85 m/ 7 ft 1 in. He was seven times the National Basketball Association leading scorer (1960–6). During his career (1960–73) he scored 31 419 points at an average of 30·1 per game.

Chamberlain, Lord In the UK, the chief official of the royal household, overseeing all aspects of its management. The office should be distinguished from the **Lord Great Chamberlain**, whose duties are largely ceremonial; in particular, at coronations, he presents the sovereign to the people.

chamber music Music for two or more players intended for performance in a room rather than a concert hall, with only one player to a part. The string quartet has been looked upon as the chamber ensemble *par excellence*, but any wind, string, or keyboard instrument might participate in chamber music.

chamber of commerce An association of business enterprises in a district, whose aims are to promote the area and its members' businesses. The International Chamber of Commerce (ICC), based in Paris, was set up in 1920, and has the affiliation of over 40 national institutions.

Chambers, Ephraim (c.1680–1740) Encyclopedist, born in Kendal, Cumbria. While apprentice to a globemaker in London, he conceived the idea of a cyclopaedia (2 folio vols, 1728). A French translation gave rise to the great French *Encyclopédie*.

Chambers, William (1800–83) Publisher and writer, born in Peebles, Scottish Borders. In 1832 he started *Chambers's Edinburgh Journal*, and soon after united with his brother **Robert** (1802–71) in founding the printing and publishing firm of W & R Chambers.

Chambord [shãbaw(r)] 47°37N 1°31E, pop (2000e) 220. A village 18 km/11 mi E of Blois, France, noted for its chateau and estate; a world heritage site. Once a hunting lodge of the counts of Blois, the chateau was reconstructed (1519–33) as a royal residence.

chameleon [kameelion] A lizard native to Africa, the Middle East, S Spain, India, and Sri Lanka; body flattened from side to side; can change colour rapidly; tail clasping, cannot be shed; eyes move independently of one another; tongue longer than head and body, with sticky tip that shoots out to hit insect prey. (Family: Chamaeleontidae, 85 species.)

chamois [shamwah] A goat-antelope from S Europe (*Rupicapra rupicapra*) (introduced in New Zealand); brown with pale patches on face or neck; horns short, vertical, with backward-hooked tips; inhabits rugged mountains; skin formerly used to make 'shammy leather'.

chamomile or **camomile** [kamomiyl] A perennial growing to 30 cm/12 in (*Chamaemelum nobile*), native to W Europe and N Africa; flower-heads up to 2·5 cm/1 in across, solitary; outer ray florets spreading, white; inner disc florets yellow. It is widely used to make chamomile tea, and is a popular additive to shampoos, hair washes, etc. (Family: Compositae.)

champagne A sparkling wine produced in the Champagne region of NE France, using either a mixture of black and white grapes, or white grapes only. The effervescent nature of champagne is due to the fact that some of the fermentation takes place in the bottle. The amount of sugar determines the style of the champagne, ranging from very sweet to very dry: *doux, demi-sec, sec, extra-sec, brut,* and *extra brut.* Bottle sizes increase from the basic bottle to a *magnum* (2 bottles), *jeroboam* (4), *rehoboam* (6), *methuselah* (8), *salmanazar* (12), *balthazar* (16), and *nebuchadnezzar* (20).

Champagne-Ardenne [shāpanyah(r)den] pop (2000e) 1 410 000; area 25 606 km²/9884 sq mi. Region of NE France comprising the departments of Ardennes, Aube, Marne, and Haute-Marne; a long-standing scene of conflict between France and Germany; noted for the production of champagne wine.

Champlain, Samuel de [shāplī] (1567–1635) Governor of Canada, born in Brouage, France. In a series of voyages he travelled to Canada (1603), exploring the E coast (1604–7), and founding Quebec (1608). L Champlain is named after him.

champlevé [shomluhvay] A technique of enamelling on metal, which involves engraving the image out of the metal surface, and filling it with vitreous pastes of different colours, which are then fired.

Champollion, Jean François [shāpolyō] (1790–1832) Founder of Egyptology, born in Figeac, France. He is best known for his use of the Rosetta Stone to decipher Egyptian hieroglyphics (1822–4).

chancel The E end of a church, containing the altar, choir, and clergy; more generally, the body of the church to the E of the nave.

Chancellor, Lord (High) *Lord Chancellor*

Chancellor of the Exchequer The senior minister in charge of the UK Treasury, and a senior minister in the cabinet. The Chancellor takes responsibility for the preparation of the budget, and (in contrast to most other countries) is economic as well as finance minister.

Chancery Division A division of the High Court of England and Wales created by the Judicature Acts (1873–5). It is mainly concerned with real property, trusts and probate matters, also company law, patents and intellectual property, presided over by the Lord Chancellor. In Scotland, the Court of Chancery is part of the Sheriff Court, and deals with the issue of land titles for heirs of deceased persons.

chancroid A sexually transmitted disease common in Africa and South Asia, resulting from infection with *Haemophilus Ducreyi.* It causes ulceration of the genital organs.

Chandigarh [chandigah(r)] pop (2001e) 901 000; area 114 km²/44 sq mi. City and union territory (1966) in NW India; serves as the joint state capital of the Punjab and Haryana; airfield; railway; university (1947); city designed by Le Corbusier.

Chandler, Raymond (Thornton) (1888–1959) Writer, born in Chicago, IL. His 'private-eye' novels include *The Big Sleep* (1939) and *Farewell, My Lovely* (1940). He is the creator of the cynical but honest detective anti-hero, Philip Marlowe.

Chandrasekhar, Subrahmanyan [chandrasayker] (1910–95) Astrophysicist, born in Lahore, Pakistan (formerly India). Working in the USA, he studied the final stages of stellar evolution, showing that the final fate of a star depends on its mass. Massive stars will be unable to evolve into white dwarfs, and this limiting stellar mass (about 1·4 solar masses) is called the **Chandrasekhar limit**. He was awarded the Nobel Prize for Physics in 1983.

Chanel, Coco [shanel], popular name of **Gabrielle Chanel** (?1883–1971) Fashion designer, born in Saumur, France. She revolutionized women's fashions during the 1920s, her designs including the 'chemise' dress and the collarless cardigan jacket. She retired in 1938, but made a surprisingly successful come-back in 1954.

Chaney, Lon [chaynee], originally **Alonso Chaney** (1883–1930) Film actor, born in Colorado Springs, CO. He was famous for spine-chilling deformed villains and other horrific parts, as in *The Hunchback of Notre Dame* (1923) and *The Phantom of the Opera* (1925). His son, **Lon Chaney, Jr** (1907–73), also acted in horror films.

Changchun or **Ch'ang-ch'un** [changchun] 43°50N 125°20E, pop (2000e) 2 444 000. Capital of Jilin province, NE China; developed during Japanese military occupation, 1933–45, as capital of Manchukuo; airfield; railway; university (1958).

change ringing A British form of bell-ringing devised by 17th-c Cambridge printer Fabian Stedman. A set of differently tuned bells, usually those in a church tower, are rung in various permutations so that no sequence (**change**) is sounded more than once. A full diatonic scale of eight bells allows 40 320 changes.

Changsha or **Ch'ang-sha** [changshah] 28°10N 113°00E, pop (2000e) 1 536 000. River port and capital of Hunan province, SE China; founded before 1000 BC; early craft, industrial, and educational centre; foreign trade port, 1904; airfield; railway; university (1959).

Chania [khanya] or **Cania** 35°31N 24°01E, pop (2000e) 139 000. Town on N shore of Crete I; founded, 13th-c; capital of Crete until 1971; airport.

Channel Islands *p.179*

channel swimming Swimming the English Channel, first achieved on 24–25 August 1875 by Captain Matthew Webb (1848–83), who covered the 34 km/21 mi from Dover to Calais Sands in 21 h 45 min. The record is now 7 h 40 min.

Channel Tunnel A tunnel linking France and Britain, first proposed in 1802. In 1985 Eurotunnel, an Anglo-French consortium, was set up to finance the tunnel and operate it once it opened. Built by the Anglo-French Transmanche Link, it consists of twin rail tunnels between Cheriton near Folkestone and Fréthun near Calais. Opened in 1994, it is 50 km/31 mi long (38 km/23 mi under the sea). In November 1996 a fire in a freight train caused serious damage and temporary closure.

chansons de geste [shāsō duh zhest] (Fr 'poems of action') French poems from the 12th–13th-c, celebrating historical figures and events on an epic scale. Different cycles centre on Charlemagne (including the *Chanson de Roland*) and the Crusades.

chant A monotone or a melody, usually restricted in range, mainly stepwise in interval and free in rhythm, to which a text (especially a liturgical one) is declaimed. **Plainchant**, originally sung in unison and without accompaniment, was used for the services of the mediaeval Roman Catholic Church and later incorporated into polyphonic music. **Anglican chant** is a type of harmonized melody to which the psalms and canticles are sung in Church of England services.

chanterelle [shanterel] The bright yellow, edible fruiting body of the fungus *Cantharellus cibarius;* funnel-shaped, diameter up to 10 cm/4 in; gill-like ridges present on lower surface; common in Europe and North America. (Order: Agaricales.)

Chanukah *Hanukkah*

chaos [kayos] A state of disorder and irregularity whose evolution in time, though governed by simple exact laws, is highly sensitive to starting conditions: a small variation in these conditions will produce wildly different results. Chaos is an intermediate stage between highly ordered motion and fully random motion. It is present in most real systems, such as in weather patterns and the motion of planets about the Sun. The modern theory of chaos is based on the work of US meteorologist Edward Lorenz (1917–) in 1963, arising from the study of convection in the atmosphere.

chaparral [shaparal] (Span *chaparro* 'scrub oak') The evergreen scrub vegetation of semi-arid areas with a Mediterranean-type climate in SW USA and NW Mexico. It is a plant community adapted to frequent fires. Typical species includes evergreen scrub oak, laurel sumac, and ceanothus.

chapati [chapahtee] A thin, flat, unleavened bread, made from a

Channel Islands

☐ International Airport

Fr **Iles Anglo-Normandes** (UK, British Islands) Timezone GMT

Area 194 km²/75 sq mi

Population total (2002e) 145 000

Status Crown dependency of the United Kingdom

Capital St Helier (on Jersey), St Peter Port (on Guernsey)

Languages English and Norman-French

Physical features Island group of the British Isles in the English Channel, W of Normandy; comprises the islands of Guernsey, Jersey, Alderney, Sark, Herm, Jethou, Brechou, and Lihou.

Economy Tourism, fruit, vegetables, flowers, dairy produce, Jersey and Guernsey cattle; used as a tax haven; not part of the European Community.

History Granted to the Dukes of Normandy, 10th-c; only British possession to have been occupied by Germany during World War 2; a dependent territory of the British Crown, with individual legislative assemblies and legal system; divided into the Bailiwick of Guernsey and the Bailiwick of Jersey; Bailiff presides over the Royal Court and the Representative Assembly (the States).

mixture of water and wheat flour containing c.95% of the original wheat. It is a traditional accompaniment to many Asian dishes.

chapel Originally, a place to house sacred relics; now generally a church. In England and Wales, the term is used of Nonconformist places of worship; in N Ireland and Scotland, of Roman Catholic churches. It may also be a place of worship belonging to a college or institution, the chancel of a church or cathedral, or part of a cathedral containing a separate altar.

Chaplin, Charlie, popular name of **Sir Charles Spencer Chaplin** (1889–1977) Film actor and director, born in London. In his early silent comedies he adopted the bowler hat, out-turned feet, moustache and walking-cane which became his hallmark, as in *The Gold Rush* (1925), and many others. His first sound film

was *The Great Dictator* (1940). In *Limelight* (1952) he acted, directed, and composed the music and dances. He was awarded an Oscar in 1972.

Chapman, George (c.1559–1634) Poet and playwright, born near Hitchin, Hertfordshire. He is best known for his translations of Homer's *Iliad* (1598–1611) and *Odyssey* (1616). He collaborated in the composition of *Eastward Ho* (1605), and in 1607 appeared *Bussy d'Ambois*, which had a sequel in 1613.

Chappaquiddick [chapakwidik] (Algonquian 'separated-island-at') Island to the E of Martha's Vineyard I, USA; in the Nantucket Sound, off the SE coast of Massachusetts; briefly achieved worldwide fame in 1969, as the site of a car accident involving US senator Edward Kennedy.

Chappell, Greg(ory Stephen) (1948–) Cricketer, born in Unley, South Australia, the brother of Ian Chappell. He played 88 times for his country (1970–84), 48 as captain, and scored 24 Test centuries. In 2005 he took over as coach of India's national team, resigning in 2007.

Chappell, Ian (Michael) (1943–) Cricketer, born in Unley, South Australia, the brother of Greg Chappell. He played 75 times for Australia (1976–80), scoring over 5000 runs and 14 Test centuries. He is now a sports commentator.

characin [karasin] Any of a large family of colourful carp-like freshwater fishes common in South and Central America and Africa; mostly carnivorous; 40 genera, including piranhas, tigerfish, headstanders, tetras, and penguinfish. (Family: Characidae.)

character recognition The technology associated with the ability of computer-based systems to recognize specific patterns; sometimes referred to as **pattern recognition**. In particular, the ability to read printed characters is known as **optical character recognition (OCR)**. Another common type is **magnetic ink character recognition (MICR)**, used worldwide to read automatically such things as account numbers on cheques.

Charadriiformes [karadriuhfaw(r)meez] An order of essentially water-loving birds (18 families).

charcoal An impure form of carbon made by heating animal or vegetable substances in the absence of air to drive off the volatile constituents. It burns without flame or smoke. Animal charcoal is known as *bone-black*.

chard A type of cultivated beet (*Beta vulgaris* variety *cicla*) lacking a swollen root but with swollen midribs and leaf-stalks; also called **Swiss chard**. (Family: Chenopodiaceae.)

Chardin, Pierre Teilhard de *Teilhard de Chardin, Pierre*

Chargaff, Erwin [chah(r)gaf] (1905–2002) Biochemist, born in Czernowitz, Czech Republic. His work on the ratio of bases present in DNA (the **Chargaff rules**) provided a fundamental contribution to the double helix structure for DNA advanced in 1953.

charge A quantity of electricity (**electrical charge**), the source of an electric field; symbol Q, units C (*coulombs*). The elementary unit of charge $e = 1.602 \times 10^{-19}$ C, equal in size but opposite in sign to the electron's charge, a fundamental constant. Two types of charge are possible: **positive** and **negative**. Like-sign charges repel, opposite-sign charges attract; the force between charges is expressed by Coulomb's law. Moving charges constitute a *current*. The study of stationary charges and the forces between them is called **electrostatics**.

charge card *credit card*

charge-coupled device (generally abbreviated **CCD**) An image sensor which in a video camera comprises a mosaic of minute photo-conductive diodes corresponding to the pixels and lines of a television system. Charges produced in each element by incident light are stored until read off in the required scanning sequence.

Charge of the Light Brigade An incident during the Battle of Balaclava (25 Oct 1854), when the Light Brigade, under the command of Lord Cardigan, charged the main Russian artillery, with massive loss of life. It resulted from the misunderstanding of an order given by the commanding officer, Lord Raglan, to stop guns captured by the Russians being carried away during their retreat.

Charing Cross An area in C London, UK, traditionally viewed as the city centre. It takes its name from a cross erected to mark the site of the resting-place of the body of Queen Eleanor, who died in 1290.

charismatic movement [karizmatik] A movement of spiritual renewal, which takes a variety of forms in Roman Catholic, Protestant, and Eastern Orthodox Churches. It emphasizes the present reality and work of the Holy Spirit in the life of the Church and the individual.

Charlemagne or **Charles the Great** [shah(r)luhmayn] (742–814) King of the Franks (sole ruler, 771–814) and Emperor of the West (800–14). He defeated the Saxons and Lombards and took control of most of Christian W Europe. In his later years he consolidated his vast empire, promoting Christianity, education and learning, agriculture, the arts, manufacture, and commerce, so much so that the period has become known as the **Carolingian Renaissance**.

Charleroi [shah(r)lrwah] 50°25N 4°27E, pop (2000e) 210 000. Town in SW Belgium; location of World War 1 German attack against the French (Aug 1914); centre of coal-mining area.

Charles I (of England) (1600–49) King of Britain and Ireland (1625–49), born in Dunfermline, Fife. His marriage to the French princess, Henrietta Maria (1609–69), disturbed the nation, for the marriage articles permitted her the free exercise of the Catholic religion. He warred with France (1627–9), and in 1630 made peace with Spain, but his continuing need for money led to unpopular economic policies. His attempt to anglicize the Scottish Church brought active resistance (1639). In 1642, having alienated much of the realm, Charles entered into the Civil War, which saw the annihilation of his cause at Naseby (14 Jun 1645), and he surrendered to the Scots at Newark (1646). After a second Civil War (1646–8), he came to trial at Westminster, where his dignified refusal to plead was interpreted as a confession of guilt. He was beheaded at Whitehall.

Charles II (of England) (1630–85) King of Britain and Ireland (1660–85), born in London, the son of Charles I. On his father's execution (1649), he assumed the title of king, and was crowned at Scone (1651). Leading poorly organized forces into England, he met defeat at Worcester (1651). He then lived in exile until an impoverished England summoned him back as king (1660). In 1662 he married the Portuguese Princess Catherine of Braganza. His war with Holland (1665–7) was unpopular, and led to the dismissal of his adviser, Lord Clarendon (1667), who was replaced by a group of ministers (the Cabal). For the last four years of his life, he ruled without parliament.

Charles V (Emperor) (1500–58) Holy Roman Emperor (1519–56), born in Ghent, Belgium. His rivalry with Francis I of France dominated W European affairs, and there was almost constant warfare between them, including the formation of the Holy League against Charles by Pope Clement VII, Henry VIII, Francis, and the Venetians. At the Diet of Augsburg (1530) he confirmed the 1521 Edict of Worms, which had condemned Luther, and in 1538 the pope, Francis, and Charles agreed to a truce. Charles's league with the pope drove the Protestants to rebellion, resulting in his defeat by Maurice of Saxony in 1552, and the granting of legal recognition to Protestantism.

Charles XIV (of Sweden), originally **Jean Baptiste Jules Bernadotte** (1763–1844) King of Sweden (1818–44), born a lawyer's son at Pau, France. He became marshal in the French army in 1804, fought in several Napoleonic campaigns (1805–9), then in 1810 was elected heir to the throne of Sweden. He refused to comply with Napoleon's demands, and in 1814 was rewarded with the Kingdom of Norway.

Charles (Philip Arthur George), Prince of Wales (1948–) Eldest son of Queen Elizabeth II and Prince Philip, Duke of Edinburgh, and heir apparent to the throne of Great Britain, born in London (at Buckingham Palace). Duke of Cornwall as the eldest son of the monarch, he was given the title of Prince of Wales in 1958, and invested at Caernarfon (1969). He served in the RAF and the Royal Navy (1971–6), and in 1981 married **Lady Diana Frances Spencer** (1961–97), younger daughter of the 8th Earl Spencer. They had two sons: **Prince William Arthur Philip Louis** (1982–) and **Prince Henry Charles Albert David** (1984–). The couple separated in 1992, and divorced in 1996. During this period he was, along with Princess Diana, the focus of continual media interest, attracting unprecedented attention from biographers. Diana was killed in a car crash in 1997. The announcement of his marriage to divorcée Camilla Parker Bowles, in April 2005, was accompanied by legal controversy. The civil service took place in Windsor Guildhall followed by a service of dedication in Windsor Castle.

Charles, Jacques Alexandre César [shah(r)l] (1746–1823) Physicist, born in Beaugency, France. He made the first ascent by hydrogen balloon, reaching 3000 m/9800 ft in 1783.

Charles, (William) John, nickname **the Gentle Giant** (1931–2004) Footballer, born in Swansea, S Wales. He joined Leeds United Football Club in 1949 and gained his first cap for Wales the next year. In 1957 he made history as the first British player to sign for a foreign club when he transferred to Italy's Juventus for a then British record £65 000. With Juventus his honours included three Serie A championships (1958, 1960–1) and the Italian Cup (1959, 1960). He returned briefly to Leeds (1962), had a season with Roma (1962–3), and ended his playing career at Cardiff City (1963–6). He gained a total of 38 caps and was never booked or sent off.

Charles, Ray, originally **Ray Charles Robinson** (1930–2004) Singer, pianist, and composer, born in Albany, GA. Blind from the age of six, he attended a special school and studied music. Influenced by jazz and blues, he became a versatile performer, developing an original blend of music identified as 'soul'. He had many hit records, 'What'd I say' (1959) being his first million-seller. He received eight Grammy Awards, and co-wrote an autobiography *Brother Ray: Ray Charles' Own Story* (1978). He gave his 10 000th concert in 2003, and his final album, *Genius Loves Company* (2004), was released a few months after his death. In 2005 he received eight posthumous Grammy Awards.

Charles Edward Stuart *Stuart, Charles Edward*

Charles Martel [mah(r)tel] (Old French, 'the hammer') (c.688–741) Mayor of the palace for the last Merovingian kings of the Franks, and the undisputed head of the Carolingian family by 723. He conducted many campaigns against the Frisians and Saxons, and halted Muslim expansion in W Europe at the Battle of Poitiers (732).

Charles's law A law discovered by and named after French physicist Jacques Charles (1746–1823): at constant pressure, the volume of a given mass of an ideal gas is directly proportional to a constant plus its temperature measured on any scale. The value of this constant fixes the zero of the absolute scale of temperature; in other words if temperature is given in K then at constant pressure volume is directly proportional to temperature.

Charleston (South Carolina) 32°46N 79°56W, pop (2000e) 96 600. Port in SE South Carolina, USA; founded in 1670; captured and held by the British, 1780–2; Confederate attack on nearby Fort Sumter (12–13 Apr 1861) began the Civil War; evacuated by Confederate forces in 1865 after a 2-year siege; devastated by an earthquake in 1886; badly damaged by hurricane Hugo in 1989; airfield; railway; US naval and air force base.

Charleston (West Virginia) 38°21N 81°38W, pop (2000e) 53 400. Capital of state in West Virginia, USA; developed around Fort Lee in the 1780s; city status, 1870; capital, 1870–5 and from 1885; airfield; railway; an important transportation and trading centre.

Charleston (dance) A jazz dance of black origin popularized in the 1920s, and first seen at Charleston, SC, USA in 1903. It can be danced either solo, with a partner, or in a group. Music is in 4/4 time and with syncopated rhythms.

Charleston, Battles of (1780) During the US War of Independence, the victorious British siege of Charleston, SC. It marked the beginning of the Southern phase of British strategy.

Charlestown 17°08N 62°37W, pop (2000e) 1790. Capital and port of Nevis I, St Kitts-Nevis; formerly famous for its thermal springs.

charlock A roughly hairy annual (*Sinapis arvensis*), 30–80 cm/12–30 in, found in most temperate regions; flowers yellow, cross-shaped, capsule cylindrical, long-beaked. Once grown as a leaf vegetable, it is now a pernicious weed of arable land. (Family: Cruciferae.)

Charlotte 35°13N 80°51W, pop (2000e) 540 800. City in S North Carolina, USA; settled c.1750; incorporated, 1768; Mecklenburg Declaration of Independence was signed here, 1775; largest city in the state; airfield; railway; two universities (1867, 1946); birthplace of President Polk; professional team, Hornets (basketball).

Charlotte Amalie [shah(r)lot amalyuh], formerly **St Thomas** (1921–36) 18°22N 64°56W, pop (2000e) 13 300. Port capital of the US Virgin Is; founded by the Danes, 1672; important cruise ship port.

Charlottenburg Palace A palace in Berlin built (1695–1796) by Elector Frederick for his wife, Sophie Charlotte. The building houses a museum.

Charlottesville 38°02N 78°30W, pop (2000e) 45 000. City in C Virginia, USA, settled in the 1730s; named after the wife of King George III; railway; university (1819); Ash Lawn (home of James Monroe); Monticello (home of Thomas Jefferson) and University of Virginia are world heritage sites.

Charlottetown 46°14N 63°09W, pop (2000e) 17 200. Principal capital of Prince Edward Island, NE Canada; founded by the French in the 1720s; capital since 1765; scene of Charlottetown Conference, 1864, which promoted plans for the union of Canada (achieved 1867); university (1969).

Charlottetown Accord A Canadian constitutional package for a new federal structure, put together by the prime minister (Brian Mulroney), provincial and territorial leaders, and First Nations representatives in 1992. It recognized aboriginal demands as legitimate, and promised to integrate First Nations' leadership in future constitutional discussions. It was rejected in a national referendum.

Charlton, Bobby, popular name of **Sir Robert Charlton** (1937–) Footballer, born in Ashington, Northumberland, the brother of Jack Charlton. He spent most of his playing career with Manchester United, surviving the Munich air disaster (1958). A member of the successful England World Cup winning team in 1966, he played for England 105 times, and scored a record 49 goals.

Charlton, Jack(ie), popular name of **John Charlton** (1935–) Footballer, born in Ashington, Northumberland, the brother of Bobby Charlton. He played for Leeds United, and also for England, later becoming manager of Middlesborough (1973), Sheffield Wednesday (1977), and Newcastle United (1984). In 1986 he was appointed manager of the Ireland team, retiring in 1996.

charm In particle physics, an internal additive quantum number conserved in strong and electromagnetic interactions, but not in weak interactions; symbol *C*. It was postulated in 1964.

Charon (astronomy) [kairon] Pluto's only known satellite, dis-

covered photographically in 1978; distance from the planet 19 600 km/12 200 mi; diameter 1200 km/745 mi. It has a surface of mainly water ice. Charon was upgraded to dwarf planet (or pluton) status in 2006. Dwarf planets take more than 200 years to orbit the Sun.

Charon (mythology) [kairon] The ferryman of the Underworld, who carried the shades or souls of the dead across the R Acheron. The Greeks placed a small coin in the mouth of a corpse as Charon's fee.

charr Freshwater or anadromous (ascending rivers to breed) fish in lakes and rivers of N hemisphere; length up to 1 m/3¼ ft; includes the **Arctic charr** (*Salvelinus alpinus*) and **brook charr** or **brook trout** (*Salvelinus fontinalis*). (Family: Salmonidae.)

Charteris, Leslie [chah(r)teris], originally **Leslie Charles Bowyer Yin** (1907–93) Crime-story writer, born in Singapore. He settled in the USA (1932), becoming known as the creator of Simon Templar, 'the Saint'.

Chartism A largely working-class radical movement which achieved substantial but intermittent support in Britain between the late 1830s and the early 1850s. Its objective was democratic rights for all men, and it took its name from 'The People's Charter', first published in 1838. Its six points were: universal male suffrage; the abolition of property qualifications for MPs; parliamentary constituencies of equal size; a secret ballot; payment for MPs; and annual general elections by ballot.

Chartres [shah(r)truh], ancient **Autricum**, **Civitas Carnutum** 48°29N 1°30E, pop (2000e) 43 700. City in NC France; railway; bishopric; agricultural centre and wheat market; Gothic cathedral (1195–1220), a world heritage site.

Chartreuse, La Grande [la gräd chah(r)troez] The principal monastery of the Carthusian order, founded in 1084 by St Bruno in the Dauphin Alps of SE France. The present structure (which is now a museum) dates from the 17th-c. Chartreuse liqueur was first distilled here in 1607.

Charybdis [karibdis] In Greek mythology, a whirlpool which swallowed ships whole, encountered by Odysseus on his wanderings.

Chase, James Hadley, pseudonym of **René Raymond** (1906–85) Novelist, born in London. He started the vogue for tough realism in gangster stories with his *No Orchids for Miss Blandish* (1939).

Chase, Salmon P(ortland) (1808–73) Jurist and statesman, born in Cornish, NH. He became secretary of the Treasury (1861–4), and in 1864 was appointed Chief Justice of the USA.

chat The name given to numerous birds: 51 species of thrush (Family: Turdidae), 5 species of New World warblers (Family: Parulidae), and 5 species of Australian chats (Family: Ephthianuridae).

chateau Originally, a mediaeval fortified residence in France, acting as the focus of the feudal community. By the 15th-c chateaux had become private seignoral residences, while the 16th-c saw the emergence of less fortified buildings.

Chateaubriand, François Auguste René, vicomte de (Viscount of) [shatohbreeä] (1768–1848) Writer and French politician, born in St Malo, France. *Le Génie du christianisme* (1802, The Genius of Christianity) made him prominent among men of letters. In his later years, he wrote his celebrated autobiography, *Mémoires d'outre-tombe* (Memoirs from Beyond the Tomb), not published as a whole until 1902.

Chatham, 1st Earl of ▸ *Pitt, William, 1st Earl of Chatham*

Chatham Islands [chatm] pop (2000e) 800; area 963 km²/372 sq mi. Islands of New Zealand in the SW Pacific Ocean; 850 km/528 mi E of South Island; visited in 1791 by the British brig *Chatham*; chief settlement, Waitangi.

Chatsworth One of the great English country houses, built (1687–1707) for the 1st Duke of Devonshire near Edensor village, Derbyshire, UK. The original design by William Talman (1650–1719) was altered and extended by successive architects. In 1950 the 11th Duke of Devonshire opened the house and gardens to a fee-paying public. It is now visited by more than 650 000 each year.

Chattanooga Campaign (1863) A series of battles in Tennessee, during the American Civil War, leading to Southern victory at Chickamauga, and Northern victories at Lookout Mountain and Missionary Ridge. It placed Northern troops in a position to bisect the Confederacy on an E–W axis.

chattels *property*

Chatterton, Thomas (1752–70) Poet, born in Bristol, SW England. In 1768 he hoaxed the whole city with a description, 'from an old manuscript', of the opening of Bristol Bridge in 1248. His poems, purporting to be by Thomas Rowley, a 15th-c monk, were denounced as forgeries, and the debate over their authenticity raged for 80 years. His death was considered suicide until modern research suggested that he had overdosed on arsenic as a cure for a sexually transmitted disease.

Chaucer, Geoffrey (c.1343–1400) Poet, probably born in London. Travelling extensively abroad on the king's service, he also held royal posts at home, including that of Comptroller of the Petty Customs (1382). In 1386 he was elected a knight of the shire for Kent. During this time he wrote *Troilus and Criseyde*, and several other major works. His early writings followed French trends, but were greatly influenced by Italian authors, notably Boccaccio and Petrarch. His later period includes his most famous work, the unfinished *Canterbury Tales*. Chaucer was the first great poet of the English nation; and in the Middle Ages he stands supreme.

Chautauqua movement [shuhtawkwuh] A late 19th-c and early 20th-c US adult education movement, organized under Methodist auspices by Lewis Miller (1829–99) and Bishop John H Vincent (1832–1920). The original centre at L Chautauqua, New York, continues its activities.

Chauvin, Yves (1930–) Chemist, born in France. He joined the French Petroleum Institute (IFP) in 1960 as a research engineer in thermodynamics and applied kinetics, becoming research director (1991–5). He shared the 2005 Nobel Prize for Chemistry with Richard Schrock and Robert Grubbs for his work in the early 1970s on the development of the metathesis method in organic synthesis.

Chavez, Cesar (Estrada) [chavez, chahvez] (1927–93) Labour leader, born in Yuma, AZ. In 1962 he started the National Farm Workers Association. He became widely known for organizing a series of national grape boycotts that helped the union to gain improved wages and working conditions for its members.

Chechnya [chechnya] Republic in the C Caucasus, bordered S by the main Caucasus range and Georgia; capital, Grozny (named Dzhoxhar Ghala, 1997); economy based on oil, with major refining centre at Grozny; population mainly Chechen (c.60%, Muslim); history of resistance to Russian rule, especially in 19th-c; became an administrative region (*oblast*) within the Soviet Union; amalgamated with Ingushetiya (**Checheno-Ingushetiya**) as an autonomous republic (ASSR) in 1934, dissolved by Stalin in 1944, with its population deported, but re-established in 1957; area 19 3000 km²/7400 sq mi; pop (2002e) 1 080 000, but uncertain numbers of deaths and refugees in ongoing war; Chechnya declared independence from Russia, 1991; Chechnya and Ingushetiya separated, 1992; civil war between forces loyal to Chechen president Dzhokar Dudayev and former leader of the opposition Ruslan Khasbulatov; invasion of Russian troops with aim of restoring Moscow control, 1994; Dudayev killed, peace accord signed between Yeltsin and new Chechen leadership, but hostilities renewed, 1996; Russian troops finally withdrawn by end of 1996, with fresh elections in early 1997; renewed Russian invasion against Chechen rebels, following a series of terrorist bombings in Russian cities and incursions into Dagestan, 1999; major assault on the capital by Rusian troops, with displacement of most of the population and widespread destruction; tentative peace negotiations, 2001, but conflict still ongoing into 2004; President Akhmad Kadyrov assassinated in Grozny bomb attack, May 2004; President Alu Alkhanov sworn in (Oct 2004) amid tight security; power struggle developed with Prime Minister Ramzan Kadyrov, son of Akhmad Kadyrov; President Putin of Russia dismissed Alkhanov (Feb 2007), naming Ramzan Kadyrov as successor.

check *cheque*

checkers *draughts*

Cheddar 5°17N 2°46W, pop (2000e) 4400. Market town in Somerset, SW England; famous for the limestone features of the Cheddar Gorge and for the Cheddar cheese originally made here.

cheese A dairy foodstuff made from milk. Milk proteins are soluble in water at a neutral pH, but when the pH falls to a critically low level of about 4·6, the proteins precipitate out to form the curd of sour milk, which is the basis of cheese manufacture. The wide variety of cheeses is achieved by allowing particular strains of bacteria to cause the fall in pH by fermenting lactose. The curd is then processed into cheese by a variety of methods, some of which require quite lengthy maturation in the presence of moulds. Others are matured in a smoky atmosphere, and others mixed with cream to form very creamy cheeses. Many regions of Europe have produced cheeses for which they are famous. France alone has more than 400 varieties, including Brie, Camembert, and Roquefort. Other well-known cheeses include Swiss Gruyère and Emmenthal; English Cheddar, Cheshire, and Stilton; Italian Parmesan and Gorgonzola; and Dutch Gouda and Edam. Versions of these cheeses are now made in many other countries.

cheetah A member of the cat family (*Acinonyx jubatus*), native to Africa and SW Asia; fastest land animal (can reach 110 kph/ 70 mph); only cat unable to retract its claws completely; pale with solid dark spots; lean with long legs and tail.

Cheka An acronym from the Russian letters **che** + **ka**, for the All-Russian Extraordinary Commission for Combating Counter-Revolution and Sabotage, established in 1917. During the Civil War it was responsible for executing thousands of political opponents in what came to be called the 'Red Terror'.

Chekhov, Anton (Pavlovitch) [chekof] (1860–1904) Playwright and master of the short story, born in Taganrog, Russia. His first book of stories appeared in 1886. His early full-length plays were failures, but when *Chayka* (1896, The Seagull) was revived in 1898 it was a great success. He then wrote his masterpieces: *Dyadya Vanya* (1900, Uncle Vanya), *Tri sestry* (1901, The Three Sisters), and *Vishnyovy sad* (1904, The Cherry Orchard).

chelation therapy [keelayshn] A treatment for heavy metal poisoning in which biochemical substances are given to a patient intravenously to bind the poisonous metal so that it is inactivated and can be removed from the body. The substances administered are known as **chelating agents** and vary according to the toxic substance to be inactivated.

Chelmsford 51°44N 0°28E, pop (2001e) 157 100. County town of Essex, SE England; railway; university (1992); cathedral (15th-c).

Chelonia [kelohnia] An order of reptiles (244 species); body encased in a domed shell of bones covered by large horny scales; no teeth; jaws form a hard beak; most withdraw head and legs into the shell for protection.

Chelsea *Kensington and Chelsea*

Chelsea pensioners Occupants of the hospital for old and disabled soldiers in Chelsea, London. Founded by Charles II in 1682, the Royal Hospital takes in about 420 men, usually aged over 65. Chelsea pensioners wear distinctive uniforms, navy blue in winter and scarlet in summer.

Cheltenham [cheltnm] 51°54N 2°04W, pop (2001e) 110 000. Residential town in Gloucestershire, SWC England; famous spa in 18th-c; railway; schools (Cheltenham College, Cheltenham Ladies' College); Cheltenham Gold Cup horse-race (Mar).

Chelyabinsk [chilyabinsk], also **Tchelyabinsk** 55°12N 61°25E, pop (2000e) 1 142 000. Industrial city in W Siberian Russia; founded in 1736 as a frontier outpost; airport; road and rail junction.

chemical bond The electric forces linking atoms in molecules and non-molecular solid phases. The energy required to break a chemical bond (eg to convert a chlorine molecule to two chlorine atoms) is called the **bond energy**.

chemical elements The simplest substances into which matter can be broken without nuclear reactions. Each element is characterized by the number of protons in the nuclei of its atoms, the atomic number of the element, and is identified by a one- or two-letter symbol. There are about 90 elements which have been found in nature. Several more have been artificially made, with those greater than atomic number 112 being referred to as superheavy elements.

chemical engineering The theory and practice of designing, setting up, and operating apparatus for the large-scale manufacture of the products of chemical reactions. University departments, professional training, and professional institutions devoted to chemical engineering have developed in all industrialized countries since 1900.

chemical laser A laser in which a chemical reaction provides the energy for laser action. For example, in a laser containing carbon dioxide with hydrogen and fluorine, the laser action would take place in the carbon dioxide, powered by the reaction of hydrogen and fluorine to give hydrogen fluoride.

chemical reaction A process in which one or more compounds are converted into others, usually with the gain or loss of energy by the system, by the breaking and forming of chemical bonds.

chemical warfare The use of deadly or disabling gases in warfare. It was forbidden by a declaration of the Hague Conference in 1899, but one of the signatories, Germany, was the first to use such weapons, the first attack being made against British troops at Ypres in April 1915. Chemical weapons are not forbidden by treaty, and large quantities were stockpiled by the USA and the former Soviet Union. Other agents of chemical warfare include non-lethal harassing and incapacitating agents, hallucinogenic substances, and herbicides.

chemiluminescence *bioluminescence*

chemin de fer [shuhmī duh **fair**] A casino card game, often referred to as 'chemmy'. A variant of *baccarat banque*, it is played by up to 12 players. The object is to obtain a total as near as possible to 9 with two or three cards.

chemistry The study of the composition of substances and the changes that they undergo. Antoine Lavoisier is usually considered the father of modern chemistry, with his distinction between *elements* and *compounds* formed from elements, and his insistence that chemical reactions are quantitative in nature. With the development of the atomic theory of John Dalton, chemistry evolved rapidly in the 19th-c. **Organic chemistry** originated from the isolation of medicinal compounds from animals and plants, and **inorganic chemistry** from the study of minerals. **Physical chemistry** (studying the relationship of physical properties to chemical composition, structure, and reactivity) and **analytical chemistry** (studying the composition of material) also developed in parallel, particularly with 20th-c developments in spectroscopic and electrochemical methods. Modern chemistry has also been advanced by the elucidation of the nature of chemical bonding. Chemistry today is the basis of a worldwide industry concerned with almost every aspect of life, including food, fuel, clothing, building materials, and medicines.

chemoreception The perception of chemical stimuli by living organisms; usually performed by specialized receptor cells or organs. Chemoreception includes both olfaction (the perception of smells) and gustation (the perception of taste).

chemotherapy The drug treatment of infectious diseases (using antibiotics), parasitic diseases, and cancer. Cancer chemotherapy usually involves the administration of a cocktail of cytotoxic drugs (ie which kill or damage cells). These also attack normal cells (especially bone marrow) causing reduced resistance to infection, loss of hair, and sterility, though supportive therapy can now help with these problems.

Chenab, River [chaynab] River in Kashmir and Pakistan; one of the five rivers of the Punjab; rises in the Himalayas and flows into Pakistan, finally joining the R Indus; length 1087 km/675 mi.

Cheney, Dick [chaynee], popular name of **Richard B(ruce) Cheney** (1941–) US Republican politician, born in Lincoln, NE. He went to Washington as a congressional intern, and became special assistant to Donald Rumsfeld in the Nixon administration (1969–70) and Gerald Ford's chief-of-staff (1975–6). He then worked in the private sector until elected to the House of Representatives in 1978, becoming minority whip in 1988. Secretary of defence under George Bush (1989–93), he formed the coalition to execute Operation Desert Storm. In the Democrat years he was chief executive officer of Halliburton Co, but returned to politics as George W Bush's running-mate in 2000, and became vice-president in 2001.

Chengchow; Cheng-chou *Zhengzhou*

Chengdu or **Cheng-tu** [chengdoo] 30°37N 104°06E, pop (2000e) 3 295 000. Capital of Sichuan province, SWC China; founded 200 BC as Zhou dynastic capital; regional industrial base since 1949; airfield; railway; university (1931); home of Sichuan opera.

Cheng-hsien *Zhengzhou*

Cheops, Ship of *Ship of Cheops*

cheque (UK) or **check** (US) An order in writing to a bank to pay the person or institution named the sum of money specified. Cheques are commonly printed by banks for the use of their customers, but may be written on anything.

cheque card A flexible plastic card (c.54 × 85 mm/2⅛ × 3⅜ in) issued by banks to customers who have a cheque book. It shows the customer's name and account number, and guarantees that the bank will honour a cheque (up to a specified sum) where the name and number correspond.

Chequers [chekerz] The official country residence of British prime ministers, located in the Chiltern Hills, Buckinghamshire. It is mentioned in the Domesday Book.

Cher, in full **Cherilyn La Piere Sarkisian** (1946–) Singer and actress, born in El Centro, CA. She was originally paired in a singing act with her husband **Salvatore 'Sonny' Bono** (1935–98) as Sonny and Cher, best known for the rock anthem 'I Got You Babe' (1965). Cher found greater success on her own, both as a singer and as a stage and film actress, notably in *Moonstruck* (1987, Oscar). Later films include *Tea With Mussolini* (1999).

Cherbourg [sherboorg], Fr [shairboor], ancient **Carusbur** 49°38N 1°37W, pop (2000e) 30 000. Fortified seaport in NW France; harbour protected by a long breakwater, 1853; France's third largest naval base; shipbuilding and dockyards; ferry services to Southampton, Weymouth, Rosslare.

Cherenkov *Čerenkov*

Chernenko, Konstantin Ustinovich [chernyengko] (1911–85) Soviet statesman and president (1984–5), born in Bolshaya Tes, Russia. Regarded as a conservative, Chernenko was a rival of Andropov in the Party leadership contest of 1982, and became Party general secretary and head of state after Andropov's death in 1984. He suffered from ill health, and died soon after, to be succeeded by Gorbachev.

Chernobyl [chernobil] 51°16N 30°15E. City in Ukraine; near the junction of the Pripyat and Ushk Rivers, N of Kiev; scene of the world's largest known nuclear disaster (26 Apr 1986); nuclear reactor complex shut down in 2000.

chernozem [chernozem] A dark, rich and fertile soil found in cool, low-humidity regions. It is typical of the Russian steppes.

Cherokee [cherokee] North American Indian people, originally from the Great Lakes, who migrated to the SE after their defeat by the Iroquois and Delaware, and were later resettled in Oklahoma. They are now the largest Native American group in the USA, numbering c.730 000 (2000 census).

cherry A deciduous, mostly N temperate tree; often with distinctive, shiny, reddish-brown, banded bark; clusters of white flowers and bright red or purplish fruits which are sour or sweet, depending on the species or variety. (Genus: *Prunus*. Subgenus: *Cerasus*. Family: Rosaceae.)

chert A very fine-grained form of silica (SiO_2), in which the quartz crystals are too small to be observed by optical microscopy. It is characteristically formed on the ocean bed by the accumulation and subsequent recrystallization of the silica shells of diatoms and radiolaria.

cherubim [cheruhbim], singular **cherub** In the Hebrew Bible/Old Testament, winged celestial creatures or beasts of various descriptions. Their roles include guarding the tree of life in the Garden of Eden (*Gen* 3.24), and accompanying the throne chariot of God (*Ezek* 1, 10).

Cherubini, (Maria) Luigi (Carlo Zenobio Salvatore) [kerubeenee] (1760–1842) Composer, born in Florence, Italy. He wrote a succession of operas, notably *Les Deux Journées* (1880, trans The Water-Carrier). His later work was mainly ecclesiastical.

chervil A hollow-stemmed annual (*Anthriscus cerefolium*), growing to 70 cm/27 in, native to Europe and Asia; flowers small, white; fruits oblong, smooth. It is often grown for its aromatic leaves, used as a flavouring. (Family: Umbelliferae.)

Cherwell, Frederick Alexander Lindemann, 1st Viscount [chah(r)-wel] (1886–1957) Scientist, born in Baden-Baden, Germany. In 1914 he became director of the Experimental Physics Station at Farnborough, where he evolved the mathematical theory of aircraft spin, and later became director of the Clarendon laboratory. A close friend of Winston Churchill, he became his scientific adviser in 1940.

Chesapeake Bay [chesapeek] 38°40N 76°25W. An inlet of the Atlantic Ocean in Virginia (S) and Maryland (N) states, USA; over 300 km/185 mi long; part of the Intracoastal Waterway; an early area of US settlement (explored 1607).

Cheshire pop (2001e) 673 800; area 2328 km²/899 sq mi. County of NWC England; county town, Chester; Warrington and Halton new unitary authorities from 1998.

Cheshire (of Woodhall), (Geoffrey) Leonard Cheshire, Baron (1917–92) British bomber pilot and philanthropist, several times decorated (including the VC, 1944) for his bombing missions. He was one of the official British observers of the destruction caused by the atomic bomb over Nagasaki (1945). This experience, together with his new-found faith, Catholicism, made him devote the rest of his life to tending the incurably sick, by founding 'Cheshire Homes' (220, in 45 countries). In 1959 he married **Sue Ryder, Baroness Ryder** (1923–2000), who in 1953 founded the Sue Ryder Foundation for the sick and disabled. In several countries, projects now function under the auspices of the Ryder–Cheshire Foundation.

chess A game for two players played on a board containing 64 squares alternately black and white. Each player has 16 pieces, either black or white, consisting of eight *pawns*, two *rooks* (also known as *castles*), two *knights*, two *bishops*, a *queen*, and a *king*. The game is one of strategy, the object being to capture the opponent's king. The earliest reference to chess is from AD c.600; the current pieces have existed in standard form for more than 500 years. The international body which supervises the game is the World Chess Federation (*Fédération Internationale des Echecs*, or FIDE). It traditionally organizes the world chess championships and other international competitions, though in 1987 a disagreement between Russian grandmaster Gary Kasparov and FIDE over levels of prize funding and FIDE's alleged autocratic methods led Kasparov to promote a breakaway body (the *Professional Chess Association*). Following the collapse of the PCA, and the subsequent collapse of the *World Chess Council* set up to replace it, the 2000 world championship was contested under the aegis of Braingames Network, an Internet company. An agreement was signed in Prague (May 2002) to unify the various competing federations under FIDE, and a reunification match eventually took place in late 2006, in which Vladimir Kramnik beat FIDE champion Veselin Topalov.

Chessman, Caryl (Whittier), nickname **The Red Light Bandit** (1921–60) Convict and writer, born in St Joseph, MI. He was sentenced to death in 1948 on 17 charges of kidnapping, robbery and sexual assault, but was granted eight stays of execution, amounting to a record period of 12 years under sentence of death without a reprieve. During this period he conducted a brilliant legal battle from prison, and wrote best-selling books against capital punishment, including *Cell 2455 Death Row* (1956).

chest *thorax*

Chester, Lat Deva, Devana Castra, Welsh **Caerleon**, Anglo-Saxon **Legaceaster** 53°12N 2°54W, pop (2001e) 118 200. County town of Cheshire, NWC England; on the R Dee; important Roman port and military centre; railway; aircraft construction (Broughton); cathedral (13th–15th-c); commercial centre; city walls; football league team, Chester City; Chester Zoo.

Chesterton, G(ilbert) K(eith) (1874–1936) Critic, novelist and poet, born in London. The amiable detective-priest who brought him popularity with a wider public first appeared in *The Innocence of Father Brown* (1911). He became a Catholic in 1922, and thereafter wrote mainly on religious topics.

Chetniks (Serbo-Croatian *četnici*) Yugoslav, mainly Serbian, guerrillas during World War 2. Under the leadership of Drazha Mihailovic, they fought Tito's communist Partisans rather than the Axis occupiers. Abandoned by the Allies in 1944, they were defeated by the Partisans, and Mihailovic was tried and executed in 1945. Since 1990 the name has been adopted by Serb irregular forces in the former state of Yugoslavia.

Chevalier, Maurice [shevalyay] (1888–1972) Film and vaudeville actor, born in Paris. His first Hollywood film was *The Innocents of Paris* (1929), and 30 years later his individual, straw-hatted, *bon-viveur* personality, with his distinctive French accent, was still much acclaimed, as in the musical *Gigi*. He received a special Academy Award in 1958.

Cheviot Hills [cheeviuht] Hill range on the border between Scotland and England; extends 56 km/35 mi SW; rises to 816 m/2677 ft at The Cheviot; gives its name to a famous breed of sheep.

chevrotain [shevrotin] A ruminant artiodactyl mammal, native to tropical forest in Africa, India, Sri Lanka and SE Asia; small with stocky bodies and short slender legs; no horns or antlers; male with long protruding canine teeth; also known as **mouse deer** or **deerlet**. (Family: Tragulidae, 4 species.)

chewing gum A sugared and flavoured product made from the concentrated juice of latex of the sapodilla tree, especially popular in the USA. It is chewed for its flavour, but not swallowed.

Cheyenne (Wyoming) [shiyan] 41°08N 104°49W, pop (2000e) 53 000. State capital in SE Wyoming, USA; founded at a railway junction, 1867; territorial capital, 1869; railway; livestock market and shipping centre.

Cheyenne (Indians) [shiyan] North American Plains Indians, divided since the 1830s into N and S groups. They live mainly in Montana and Oklahoma, numbering c.18 200 (2000 census).

Chiang Ch'ing *Jiang Qing*

Chiang Kai-shek *Jiang Jieshi*

Chiang Mai [jee-eng miy] 18°48N 98°59E, pop (2000e) 191 000. City in NW Thailand; N Thailand's principal city since 1296, when it was founded as the capital of Lan Na Thai kingdom; airfield; railway; university.

chiaroscuro [keearoskooroh] (Ital 'light-dark')In painting, the use of strong light and shadow to define forms in space. The technique was developed in Italy by Leonardo da Vinci and Caravaggio, and perfected by Rembrandt in 17th-c Holland.

Chicago [shikahgoh] 41°53N 87°38W, pop (2000e) 2 896 000. Third largest city in the USA, in NE Illinois, on L Michigan; built on the site of Fort Dearborn; settled in the 1830s; city status, 1837; much of the city destroyed by fire, 1871; notorious gangster activity in the Prohibition years, 1920s; now the major industrial, commercial, financial and cultural centre for the US interior; a quarter of the nation's steel produced in and around the city; transport centre of the USA, with one of the busiest airports in the world; major rail network and inland port; seven universities; Sears Tower (1974), the world's second tallest building in 1999 (443 m/1454 ft); professional teams, Cubs, White Sox (baseball), Bulls (basketball), Bears (football), Black Hawks (ice hockey).

Chicago School (architecture) The name given to a group of Chicago architects and office buildings in the late 19th-c. The buildings were the forerunners of 20th-c skyscrapers, and are characterized by the pioneering use of steel frame construction, clothed in masonry and with large expanses of windows, often to a great height.

Chicago School (economics) A group of economists at Chicago University, led by Milton Friedman from 1948 to 1979. They hold the monetarist view that competition and market forces should be allowed to act freely, and with minimal government interference, for the best results.

Chichén Itzá [cheechen eetza] Toltec/Maya capital of the Yucatan peninsula, Mexico, AD c.1000–1200. Its monumental centre (area 3 km/1¾ mi by 2 km/1¼ mi) contains temple pyramids and the largest known Meso-American ballcourt.

Chichester [chichester] 50°50N 0°48W, pop (2001e) 106 400. County town of West Sussex, S England; founded by the Romans; railway; cathedral (11th–12th-c); bishop's palace (12th-c); Chichester Festival Theatre.

Chichester, Sir Francis (Charles) [chichester] (1901–72) Yachtsman, born in Barnstaple, Devon. In 1953 he took up yacht racing, winning the first solo transatlantic yacht race (1960) in *Gipsy Moth III*, sailing from Plymouth to New York in 40 days. He made a successful solo circumnavigation of the world (1966–7) in *Gipsy Moth IV*, sailing from Plymouth to Sydney in 107 days and from there back to Plymouth, via Cape Horn, in 119 days.

chickadee A name used in the USA for certain small birds of the tit family. (Family: Paridae, 7 species.)

chickaree *red squirrel*

chicken *domestic fowl*

chickenpox A highly infectious and usually benign disease of childhood, caused by *herpes zoster*, the same virus that is responsible for shingles. It causes characteristic blister-like eruptions on the skin.

chick-pea A branching annual (*Cicer arietinum*), probably native to Asia, growing to 50 cm/20 in or more; pea-flowers white or bluish, solitary on long stalks; pods inflated, usually 2-seeded; also called **garbanzos**. It has been cultivated since ancient times as a fodder plant and for its edible seeds. (Family: Leguminosae.)

chickweed A slender, spreading, often pale-green annual (*Stellaria media*); a very common weed, often flowering throughout the year; flowers tiny, white, five petals, deeply cleft into two parts. (Family: Caryophyllaceae.)

chicle An evergreen tree (*Achras zapota*) growing to 18 m/60 ft, native to Central America; flowers tiny, greenish-white, 6-petalled; fruit 5–10 cm/2–4 in, greyish to reddish-brown with yellow flesh. The copious white latex provides the elastic base for chewing gum; the edible fruit is called **sapodilla plum**. (Family: Sapotaceae.)

chicory A perennial growing to 120 cm/5 ft (*Cichorium intybus*), with a long stout tap root, native to Europe, W Asia, and N Africa; flower-heads nearly stalkless, bright blue, rarely pink or white. Dried and ground roots are used as a coffee substitute. (Family: Compositae.)

Chief Justice The presiding justice of the United States Supreme Court, nominated by the US president and confirmed by a majority of the Senate. The Chief Justice serves for life, presides in both public session and at private court conferences, assigns the task of writing majority opinions, and administers the oath of office to the US president.

chiffchaff A bird belonging to a group of Old World warblers (*Phylloscopus collybita*); native to Europe, N Africa, and Asia. (Family: Silviidae.)

chigger *harvest-mite*

Chihuahua [chiwahwa] 28°40N 106°06W, pop (2000e) 639 000. City in N Mexico; altitude 1428 m/4685 ft; centre of Pancho Villa's revolutionary activities; railway; university (1954); cathedral (18th-c).

chihuahua [chiwahwa] The smallest domestic breed of dog, developed in Mexico; tiny body; head disproportionately large with bulbous forehead, large widely spaced eyes, and large ears.

chilblains Bluish and slightly swollen areas of the skin of fingers and toes, caused by exposure to excessive cold. The lesions become red and itchy on warming.

child abuse The treatment of a child by an adult in a way unacceptable in a given culture at a given time; also referred to technically as **non-accidental injury of childhood** and popularly as **battered baby/child syndrome**. Abuse may be physical (soft and bony tissue injury, burns and scalds, poisoning and suffocation), sexual, emotional, or through neglect. Most abuse is perpetrated by parents, particularly non-related cohabitants. Such activities may result in both criminal proceedings being taken against the adult concerned, and care proceedings in respect of the victim.

Childers, (Robert) Erskine [childerz] (1870–1922) Irish nationalist and writer, born in London. He wrote a popular spy story, *The Riddle of the Sands* (1903), and several works of non-fiction. He later joined the Irish Republican Army, and was active in the Civil War, but was captured and executed at Dublin. His son, **Erskine Childers** (1905–74) was President of Ireland in 1973–4.

Children's Crusade A movement in 1212 of thousands of children from Germany and France, aiming to reach the Holy Land and recapture Jerusalem from the Turks. Some reached Genoa, Italy, but did not embark; some reached Marseille, France, whence they were shipped to N Africa and sold into slavery.

Child Support Agency (CSA) In the UK, a government agency responsible for assessing and collecting obligatory child maintenance payments from non-resident parents. Introduced in 1993, it took over its role from the courts, and became part of the Department of Social Security. Although its aim of alleviating single-parent poverty was welcomed, widespread complaints in the mid-1990s about its practices made its work controversial, and led to several procedural reforms.

Chile *p.186*

Chile pine *monkey-puzzle*

chili *pepper 1*

Chilopoda [keelopoda] *centipede*

Chile

☐ International Airport

[chilee], official name **Republic of Chile**, Span **República de Chile**

Local name Chile

Timezone GMT -4

Area 756 626 km²/292 058 sq mi (excluding territory claimed in Antarctica)

Population total (2002e) 15 082 000

Status Republic

Date of independence 1818

Capital Santiago

Language Spanish (official)

Ethnic groups Mestizo (92%), Indian (6%), European (2%)

Religions Roman Catholic (89%), Protestant (10%), small Jewish and Muslim minority

Physical features Coastal Cordillera, Pampa Central, and the Chilean Andes are parallel regions running almost the entire length of the country; narrow coastal belt, backed by Andean mountain ridges rising in the NW to 6910 m/22 660 ft at Ojos del Salado; Atacama Desert in far NW, rich in minerals; arable land and forest in the S; S Andes still experiences volcanic activity; main river, the Bío-Bío; Punta Arenas located on southern tip of Chile's mainland; Chilean possessions include a rock measuring 424 m/1390 ft on Horn Island in the Wollaston group, and 1 250 000 km²/500 000 sq mi of Antarctic territory.

Climate Varied climate (spans 37° of latitude, with altitudes from Andean peaks to coastal plain); extreme aridity in N Atacama Desert, temperatures averaging 20°C; cold, wet, and windy in far S; Mediterranean climate in C Chile, with warm wet winters and dry summers; average temperature at Santiago 19°C (Jan), 8°C (Jul); average annual rainfall 375 mm/14·8 in.

Currency 1 Chilean Peso (CLP) = 100 centavos

Economy Based on agriculture and mining; wheat, corn, potatoes, sugar beet, fruit, livestock; fishing in N, timber in S; copper, iron ore, nitrates, silver, gold, coal, molybdenum; oil and gas discovered in far S (1945); steel, wood pulp, cellulose, mineral processing.

GDP (2002e) $156·1 bn, per capita $10 100

Human Development Index (2002) 0·831

History Originally occupied by South American Indians; arrival of Spanish in 16th-c; part of Viceroyalty of Peru; independence from Spain declared in 1810, with a provisional government set up in Santiago; Spain reasserted its authority, 1814; patriot leader, Bernardo O'Higgins, escaped and returned, with military help of José de San Martín, to defeat the Spanish at Chacabuco, 1817; O'Higgins became first president and independence was declared, 1818; border disputes with Bolivia, Peru, and Argentina brought Chilean victory in War of the Pacific, 1879–84; economic unrest in late 1920s led to military dictatorship under Carlos Ibáñez until 1931; Marxist coalition government of Salvador Allende Gossens ousted in 1973, and replaced by military junta under Augusto Pinochet Ugarte, which banned all political activity; constitution providing for eventual return to democracy came into effect, 1981; plebiscite held in 1988 resulted in a defeat for Pinochet's candidacy as president beyond 1990, and limited political reforms; National Congress restored, comprising a Senate and a Chamber of Deputies in 1990; 6-year term for president agreed in 1994; Michelle Bachelet voted Chile's first woman president, 2006.

Head of State/Government

1910–15 Ramón Barros Luco
1915–20 Juan Luis Sanfuentes
1920–4 Arturo Alessandri
1924–5 *Military juntas*
1925 Arturo Alessandri
1925 Luis Barros Borgoño *Vice President*
1925–27 Emiliano Figueroa
1927–31 Carlos Ibáñez
1931 Pedro Opaso Letelier *Vice President*
1931 Juan Esteban Montero *Vice President*
1931 Manuel Trucco Franzani *Vice President*
1931–2 Juan Estaban Montero
1932 *Military juntas*
1932 Carlos G Dávila *Provisional President*
1932 Bartolomé Blanche *Provisional President*
1932 Abraham Oyanedel *Vice President*
1932–8 Arturo Alessandri Palma
1938–41 Pedro Aguirre Cerda
1941–2 Jerónimo Méndez Arancibia *Vice President*
1942–6 Juan Antonio Ríos Morales
1946–52 Gabriel González Videla
1952–8 Carlos Ibáñez del Campo
1958–64 Jorge Alessandri Rodríguez
1964–70 Eduardo Frei Montalva
1970–3 Salvador Allende (Gossens)
1973–90 Augusto Pinochet Ugarte
1990–4 Patricio Aylwin Azócar
1994–9 Eduardo Frei Ruíz-Tagle
1999–2006 Ricardo Lagos Escobar
2006– Michelle Bachelet

Chiltern Hills Low chalk hill range in SE England; extends 88 km/ 55 mi NE between S Oxfordshire and Bedfordshire; rises to 260 m/853 ft at Coombe Hill.

Chiltern Hundreds In the UK, a legally fictitious office of profit under the Crown: Steward or Bailiff of Her Majesty's Chiltern Hundreds of Stoke, Desborough, and Burnham. To accept this office disqualifies an MP from the House of Commons. As an MP cannot resign, application to be appointed to the Chiltern Hundreds is the conventional manner of leaving the Commons.

Chi-lung *Jilong*

Chimaera *Chimera*

chimaera (zoology) [kimeera] Cartilaginous fish (*Chimaera monstrosa*) with robust body, large pelvic fins, and long tapering tail; common in deeper waters of N Atlantic and Mediterranean; length up to 1·5 m/5 ft; cream with brown patches and metallic sheen; also called **ratfish** or **rabbitfish**. (Family: Chimaeridae.)

Chimborazo [cheemborasoh] 1°28S 78°48W. Inactive Andean volcano in C Ecuador; height 6310 m/20 702 ft.

Chimbote [cheembohtay] 8°59S 78°38W, pop (2000e) 356 000. Port in N Peru; one of the few natural harbours on the W coast; a new port has been built to serve the national steel industry.

Chimera [kiymeera, kimeera], also **Chimaera** In Greek mythology, a fabulous monster with the head of a lion, the body of a goat and the tail of a serpent, which breathed fire.

chimpanzee An ape native to equatorial Africa, believed to be the closest living relative to humans; height, 1–1·7 m/3¼–5½ ft; black coat; hair on head parted or directed backwards; face and ears naked; skin pale or dark; spends most time on the ground; eats fruit and some insects, but may kill small vertebrates; uses twigs, etc as tools to obtain food; two species: **chimpanzee** (*Pan troglodytes*) and the smaller, black-faced **pygmy chimpanzee** or **bonobo** (*Pan paniscus*).

Chimu [cheemoo] A South American Indian people of Peru, the most important political and cultural group before the Incas in the 14th-c, with a highly stratified social system. They were conquered by the Incas (1465–70), who absorbed many aspects of their culture.

China *pp.188–89*

china clay *kaolin*

Chi-nan *Jinan*

chinch bug A small, short-winged bug that feeds by sucking juices from grasses; an important corn and grain pest in America. (Order: Heteroptera. Family: Lygaeidae.)

chinchilla A South American cavy-like rodent; small (length, 35 cm/14 in); thick soft grey coat, bushy tail, large round ears. It is widely farmed for its fur, which is the most expensive in the world. (Genus: *Chinchilla*, 2 species. Family: Chinchillidae.)

chinchilla cat A breed of domestic cat, of the long-haired type; round head with short face; very dense white coat; each hair tipped with black (the *blue chinchilla* has the hairs tipped with blue-grey); also known as **silver Persian** or **silver**.

chinchilla rabbit A breed of domestic rabbit with thick soft grey fur resembling that of a chinchilla.

Chindits Members of the 3rd Indian Division, raised in 1942 by Brigadier Orde Wingate for long-range guerrilla operations in Japanese-occupied Burma. High casualties were sustained in 1943 and 1944, and their military value has been questioned.

Chinese The Sinitic branch of the Sino-Tibetan group of languages, comprising eight major varieties, commonly called 'dialects'. This classification is an artifact of the writing system of Chinese, which is used by all varieties. Although the orthography transfers from one variety to another, the varieties themselves are, in some cases, not mutually intelligible. The two best-known varieties are *Cantonese*, spoken in the S, and *Mandarin*, spoken in the N, C, and W, the Beijing form being the

basis of the modern standard language. There have been numerous attempts to romanize the Chinese writing system, and in 1958 the *pinyin* 'phonetic spelling' system was officially adopted, with the further aim of popularizing the grammar, vocabulary, and pronunciation of the codified standard Mandarin, now known as *putonghua* ('common language'). Chinese has the largest number of mother-tongue speakers of all the world's languages, at over 1000 million.

Chinese block *wood block*

Chinese gooseberry *kiwi fruit*

Ching-tao *Qingdao*

chinoiserie [sheenwazeree] Silks, porcelain, and lacquer from China, which were very much admired in Europe from the time they were first imported in the late Middle Ages, and consequently much imitated. From the 17th-c a separate Western style evolved, using Chinese and Japanese motifs in an original manner. It reached its height in the 18th-c, being used throughout the decorative arts, as well as in such fields as book illustration, furniture, and gardening.

Chinook A North American Indian people of Washington and Oregon, one of the NW Indian groups with an artistic tradition. White contact, dating back to 1805, eventually eroded their culture.

chinook wind *Föhn wind*

Chios [keeos], Gr **Khíos**, Ital **Scio** pop (2000e) 55 000; area 842 km²/325 sq mi; length 48 km/30 mi. Greek island in the Aegean Sea, off the W coast of Turkey; crossed N–S by hills rising to 1298 m/4258 ft; chief town, Chios, pop (2000e) 32 400; noted for its wine and figs.

chip A commonly used name for an integrated circuit. Strictly, the term refers to the small 'chip' of silicon on which the electronic circuits reside, rather than the encapsulated package.

chipmunk A type of squirrel, all species native to North America except *Eutamias sibiricus* from W Asia; back with alternating pale and dark longitudinal stripes; cheeks with internal pouches for carrying seeds. (Genera: *Tamias*, 1 species; *Eutamias*, 22 species.)

Chipp, Don(ald) Leslie (1925–) Australian politician, born in Melbourne, Victoria, Australia. He founded the Australian Democrats in 1977, a centrist group, and served as their parliamentary leader from 1978 until 1986, when he retired.

Chippendale, Thomas (1718–79) Furniture-maker and designer, baptised at Otley, West Yorkshire. He made his name following publication of *The Gentleman and Cabinet-maker's Director* (1754), a comprehensive range of furniture designs in the Rococo, chinoiserie, and Gothic Revival styles.

Chippewa *Ojibwa*

Chirac, Jacques (René) [shirak] (1932–) French prime minister (1974–6, 1986–8) and president (1995–2007). He resigned over differences with Giscard d'Estaing and broke away to lead the Gaullist Party. Mayor of Paris since 1977, he was an unsuccessful candidate in the 1981 and 1988 presidential elections, but won in 1995. He won a landslide victory in the second round of the 2002 presidential election after voters surged to the polls to keep out the far-right candidate, Jean-Marie Le Pen. His government supported the proposed European constitution but it was rejected by French voters in a referendum in May 2005.

Chirico, Giorgio de [kireekoh] (1888–1978) Artist, born in Volos, Greece. A major influence on the Surrealists, his whole style after 1915 is often called 'metaphysical painting', including semi-abstract geometric figures and stylized horses. In the 1930s he reverted to an academic style.

chirography [kiyrografee] The various forms and styles of handwriting. Early Western styles included *majuscule*, as seen in the chiselled capital letters of early Greek and Roman inscriptions from c.300 BC; *minuscule*, the use of small letters found in

China

□ International Airport ∴ World heritage site

official name **People's Republic of China**, Chin **Zhonghua Renmin Gonghe Guo** or **Zhongguo**

Local name Zhongguo

Timezone GMT +8

Area 9 597 000 km²/3 705 000 sq mi (also claims island of Taiwan)

Population total (2002e) 1 284 211 000

Status People's republic

Capital Beijing (Peking)

Languages Standard Chinese (Putonghua) or Mandarin, also Yue (Cantonese), Wu, Minbei, Minnan, Xiang, Gan and Hakka

Ethnic groups Han Chinese (92%), over 50 minorities, including Chuang, Manchu, Hui, Miao, Uighur, Hani, Kazakh, Tai and Yao

Religions Officially atheist; widespread Confucianism and Taoism (20%), Buddhism (6%)

Physical features Over two-thirds of country are upland hills, mountains, and plateaux; highest mountains in the W, where the Tibetan plateau rises to average altitude of 4000 m/13 000 ft; Mt Everest rises to 8848 m/29 028 ft on the Nepal-Tibet border; land descends to desert/semi-desert of Xinjiang and Inner Mongolia (NE); broad and fertile plains of Manchuria (NE); further E and S, Sichuan basin, drained by Yangtze R (5980 km/3720 mi in length); Huang He (Yellow) R runs for 4840 km/3010 mi; heavily populated S plains and E coast, with rich, fertile soils.

Climate Varied, with seven zones; (1) NE China: cold winters, with strong N winds, warm and humid summers, unreliable rainfall;

Greek from the 8th-c AD; *uncial* writing, large rounded letters found in Latin and Greek manuscripts from the 4th-c AD; *cursive*, used from c.4th-c BC, in which the letters are joined together in rounded strokes to promote speed; and *italic*, developed in Italy in the 16th-c, a forerunner of italic letters in printing.

Chiron [kiyron] In Greek mythology, a good and wise centaur who kept a school for princes in Thessaly. He educated Asclepius in the art of medicine and music, Jason the Argonaut, and Achilles.

chiropody [chiropodee] The study of the structure and function of the foot in health, and of its disorders and deformities. It is also known as **podiatry**.

chiropractic [kiyrohpraktik] The study of the alignment of the bones of the skeleton and of the anatomical relations of the nerves and muscles of the body to them. The discipline was founded in 1895 by US physician Daniel David Palmer (1845–1913). It is mainly concerned with the bones of the spine. Chiropractors treat disorders by manipulation without the use of drugs or surgery.

(2) C China: warm and humid summers, sometimes typhoons or tropical cyclones on coast; (3) S China: partly within tropics; wettest area in summer, frequent typhoons; (4) SW China: summer temperatures moderated by altitude, winters mild with little rain; (5) Xizang autonomous region: high plateau surrounded by mountains; winters severe with frequent light snow and hard frost; (6) Xinjiang and W interior: arid desert climate, cold winters; rainfall well distributed throughout year; (7) Inner Mongolia: extreme continental climate; cold winters, warm summers.

Currency 1 Renminbi Yuan (CNY) = 10 jiao = 100 fen

Economy Since 1949, economy largely based on heavy industry; more recently, light industries; special economic zones set up to attract foreign investment; rich mineral deposits; largest oil-producing country in Far East; major subsistence crops include rice, grain, beans, potatoes, tea, sugar, cotton; economy hit by SARS epidemic (2003).

GDP (2002e) $5·989 tn, per capita $4700

Human Development Index (2002) 0·726

History Chinese civilization believed to date from the Xia dynasty (2200–1799 BC); Qin dynasty (221–207 BC) unified warring states and provided system of centralized control; expansion W during Western and Eastern Han dynasties (206 BC– AD 220), and Buddhism introduced from India; split into Three Kingdoms (Wei, Shu, Wu, 220–65); period of Six dynasties (221–581); from 4th-c, series of N dynasties set up by invaders, with several dynasties in S; gradually reunited during the Sui (590–618) and Tang (618–906) dynasties; partition into the Five Dynasties (907–60); Song (Sung) dynasty (960–1279), remembered for literature, philosophy, inventions; Kublai Khan established Mongol Yuan dynasty which ruled China 1279–1368; visits by Europeans, such as Marco Polo, 13th-14th-c; Ming dynasty (1368–1644) increased contacts with West; overthrown by Manchus, who ruled China during 1644–1911 under the Qing dynasty, and enlarged empire to include Manchuria, Mongolia, Tibet, Taiwan; opposition to foreign imports led to Opium Wars 1839–42, 1858–60; Sino-Japanese War, 1895; Hundred Days of Reform movement, 1898; Boxer Rising, 1900; Qing dynasty overthrown, 1911; Republic of China founded by Sun Yatsen, 1912; May Fourth Movement, 1919; unification under Jiang Jieshi (Chiang Kai-shek), who made Nanjing capital in 1928; conflict between Nationalists and Communists led to the Long March, 1934–5, with Communists moving to NW China under Mao Zedong (Mao Tse-tung); Nationalist defeat by Mao and withdrawal to Taiwan in 1950; People's Republic of China proclaimed, 1949, with capital at Beijing; first Five-Year Plan (1953–7) period of nationalization and collectivization; Great Leap Forward, 1958–9, emphasized local authority and establishment of rural communes; Cultural Revolution initiated by Mao Zedong, 1966; many policies reversed after Mao's death in 1976, and drive towards rapid industrialization and wider trade relations with West; after 1980, Deng Xiaoping became the dominant figure within the ruling Chinese Communist Party; he retired from his last official post in 1990, but remained influential until his death in 1997; Hong Kong returned to China, 1997; Hu Jintao elected Communist Party chief, 2002; China's first manned space mission launched 2003; Qinghai–Tibet railway linking E China to Lhasa, opened 2006; Nathu La Pass historic trade route between China and India (closed 1962) reopened 2006; international concern following China's destruction of weather satellite during ground-based ballistic missile test (Jan 2007); governed by elected National People's Congress who elect a State Council.

President of the Executive Council
1928–30 Tan Yankai
1930 Song Ziwen (T V Soong) *Acting*
1930 Wang Jingwei (Wang Ching-wei)
1930–1 Jiang Jieshi (Chiang K'ai-shek)
1931–2 Sun Fo
1932–5 Wang Jingwei
1935–7 Jiang Jieshi (Chiang K'ai-shek)
1937–8 Wang Chonghui (Wang Ch'ung-hui) *Acting*
1938–9 Kong Xiangxi (K'ung Hsiang-hsi)
1939–44 Jiang Jieshi (Chiang K'ai-shek)
1944–7 Song Ziwen (T V Soong)
1945–9 *Civil war*
1948 Wang Wenhao (Wong Wen-hao)
1948–9 Sun Fo
1949 He Yingqin (Ho Ying-ch'in)
1949 Yan Xishan (Yen Hsi-shan)

People's Republic of China
Head of State
1949–59 Mao Zedong (Mao Tse-tung)
1959–68 Liu Shaoqi
1968–75 Dong Biwu
1975–6 Zhu De
1976–8 Song Qingling
1978–83 Ye Jianying
1983–8 Li Xiannian (Li Hsien-nien)
1988–93 Yang Shangkun
1993–2003 Jiang Zemin
2003– Hu Jintao

Head of Government
1949–76 Zhou Enlai (Chou En-lai)
1976–80 Hua Guofeng
1980–7 Zhao Ziyang (Chao Tzu-yang)
1987–98 Li Peng
1998–2003 Zhu Rongji
2003– Wen Jiabao

Communist Party Chairman
1935–76 Mao Zedong
1976–81 Hua Guofeng
1981–2 Hu Yaobang (Hu Yao-pang)

General Secretary
1982–7 Hu Yaobang
1987–9 Zhao Ziyang
1989–2002 Jiang Zemin (Chiang Tse-min)
2002– Hu Jintao

Chiroptera [kiyroptera] *bat*

Chirripó Grande [chiripoh granday] 9°50N 83°25W. Highest peak of Costa Rica and S Central America; in the Cordillera de Talamanca; height 3819 m/12 529 ft.

chiru [chiroo] A goat-antelope (*Pantholops hodgsoni*) native to the high plateau of Tibet and China; pale-pinkish brown; nose swollen at tip; male with black face and long slender vertical horns growing apart towards tips; female without horns; also known as **Tibetan antelope**.

chisel-tooth lizard *agamid*

Chisholm Trail A cattle trail in the USA, from Texas across Oklahoma to the railhead at Abilene, KS. It is named after Jesse Chisholm, who pioneered the route in 1866.

chital [cheetl] A true deer (*Axis axis*), native to India and Sri Lanka; pale brown with white spots; antlers long, lyre-shaped; also known as **axis deer** or **spotted deer**.

chitarrone [kitarohnay] A long-necked lute or theorbo, used in the 16th–17th-c to accompany singing. There were usually six pairs of gut or metal strings running over a fretted keyboard, and eight longer bass strings which were not stopped (ie each produced one note only). The instrument might be as long as 1 m 90 cm/6 ft 3 in.

chitin [kiytin] A long chain-like molecule (a linear homopolysaccharide of N-acetyl-D-glucosamine) found as a major constituent of the horny covering (cuticle) of insects and cell walls of fungi. When cross-linked, these chains produce a lightweight but strong material.

chiton [kiytn] A marine mollusc characterized by a dorsal shell consisting of eight overlapping calcareous plates; muscular foot used for attachment to a substrate; also known as **coat-of-mail shell**. (Class: Polyplacophora.)

Chittagong [chitagong] 22°20N 91°48E, pop (2000e) 2 386 000. Principal port of Bangladesh; conquered by Nawab of Bengal, 1666; ceded to British East India Company, 1760; damaged during 1971 Indo-Pakistani War; many Hindu and Buddhist temples; university (1966).

Chittagong Hill Tracts area 8680 km²/3350 sq mi. Region in SE Bangladesh, reaches heights of 500–1000 m/1500–3000 ft in the SE; divided into four fertile valleys, covered with thick planted forest.

Chitwin or **Royal Chitwin** area 932 km²/360 sq mi. National park in SC Nepal; established in 1973; a world heritage site.

chive A perennial growing to 40 cm/15 in (*Allium schoenoprasum*); tufts of narrow, tubular leaves; pink or purple flowers; native to the N hemisphere. Its leaves are used as flavouring. (Family: Liliaceae.)

Chlamydia [klamidia] A genus of spherical, non-motile bacteria that multiply only within the cytoplasm of true nucleated (*eukaryotic*) cells. Virulent strains can cause eye, mouth, genital, and other diseases of humans and other animals. (Kingdom: Monera. Family: Chlamydiaceae.)

chloracne [klawraknee] Acne-like lesions on the skin with pimple-like (*papular*) formations which may become infected (*pustular*). Its occurrence is linked to industrial exposure to chlorinated hydrocarbons.

chloral CCl_3CHO, IUPAC **2,2,2-trichloroethanal**, boiling point 97°C. **Chloral hydrate** is a sedative.

chlorates Salts of an oxyacid of chlorine, usually a chlorate(V), containing the ion ClO_3^-, including the weedkiller **sodium chlorate** ($NaClO_3$). Chlorate(I) or **hypochlorite** is ClO^-; chlorate(VII) or **perchlorate** is ClO_4^-.

chlordiazepoxide *benzodiazepines*

Chlorella [klorela] A genus of non-motile, single-celled green algae containing a cup-shaped chloroplast; very common in a variety of freshwater habitats.

chlorides Compounds containing chlorine, especially those containing the ion Cl^-. Common salt is **sodium chloride** (Na^+Cl^-).

chlorine [klawreen] Cl, element 17, boiling point −35°C. A greenish-yellow gas, containing diatomic molecules (Cl_2). It does not occur free in nature, but is recovered from deposits of NaCl or KCl by electrolysis. It may also be recovered from sea water. The gas has an intense odour and is very poisonous. Chlorine is mainly used in propellants, cleaning fluids, rubber production, and as a disinfectant, such as in swimming pools.

chlorofluorocarbons *CFCs*

chloroform $CHCl_3$, IUPAC **trichloromethane**, boiling point 62°C. A dense liquid, used as a solvent and as an anaesthetic.

Chlorophyceae [klorohfiysee-ee] *green algae*

chlorophyll [klorohfil] The green pigment (a magnesium-porphyrin derivative) found in plants, which absorbs radiant energy from sunlight, mainly in blue (wavelength 435–438 nm) and red (wavelength 670–680 nm) regions of the spectrum.

Chlorophyta [klorofita] The green algae that form zoospores or gametes having cup-shaped grass-green chloroplasts and at least two anterior flagella; classified as a phylum of the kingdom Protoctista.

chloroplast [klorohplast] A specialized structure found within plant cells. It contains some genetic material (DNA), and partly controls the synthesis of its own proteins.

chlorpromazine *phenothiazines*

Chobham armour *reactive armour*

chocolate and **cocoa** A foodstuff derived from the cacao bean, cultivated mainly in W Africa. **Cocoa butter** is rich in fat, and **cocoa powder** contains a mixture of protein (25%), fat (30%), and carbohydrate (45%). **Milk chocolate** is produced by mixing finely ground cocoa powder with some cocoa butter, sugar, and dried milk.

choir The part of a church for the singers; usually part of the chancel, and separated from the nave by a screen or a rail.

Choiseul(-Amboise), Etienne François, duc de (Duke of) [shwazoel] (1719–85) French statesman, minister of Louis XV, born in Lorraine, NE France. He arranged in 1756 the alliance between France and Austria against Frederick the Great, and obtained good terms for France at the end of the Seven Years' War (1763).

cholecystitis [kohlesistiytis] Acute inflammation of the gall bladder, often induced by a blockage or partial blockage of the flow of bile by gallstones. It presents with severe upper right-sided abdominal pain accompanied by vomiting and fever.

cholera [kolera] An acute infection of the gastro-intestinal tract by *Vibrio cholerae*, acquired by drinking contaminated water. The bacteria cause profuse watery diarrhoea, which so depletes the body of water and electrolytes as to induce shock and death within 24–48 hours. Adequate treatment involving the replacement of body fluids can prevent death and allow a full recovery.

cholesterol [kolesterol] The most abundant steroid in animals. It is ingested in the diet as a constituent of egg-yolk, meats (particularly offal), and some shellfish; transported in the blood; and synthesized in the liver, gastro-intestinal tract, and other tissues. It is implicated as a cause of atherosclerosis.

choline [kohleen] The most common form of the variable part of phospholipids, which play a key role in the structure of biological membranes. It is an essential component of the diet of some species, but not humans. Phospholipids containing choline are also known as *lecithin*, commonly sold in health-food shops to reduce cholesterol absorption, a feat which it does not achieve.

Chomsky, (Avram) Noam (1928–) Linguist and political activist, born in Philadelphia, PA. He became professor of linguistics at the Massachusetts Institute of Technology, where he wrote *Syntactic Structures* (1957), introducing a new theory of language called transformational generative grammar. Later works include *Aspects of the Theory of Syntax* (1965), *Language and Mind* (1968), *Knowledge of Language* (1986), and *On Nature and Language* (2002). His opposition to the Vietnam War involved him in the radical movement, which led to such works as *American Power and the New Mandarins* (1969). Later works include *Imperial Ambitions* (2005) on the Iraq War.

Chongqing or **Chungking** [chungching], also **Pahsien** 31°08N 104°23E, pop (2000e) 3 486 000. City in SWC China; founded 12th-c; treaty port, 1891; capital of China, 1937–46; most important industrial city in SW; airfield; railway; river transport.

Chopin, Frédéric (François) [shohpĩ] (1810–49) Composer and pianist, born in Zelazowa Wola, Poland. His works for the piano include 50 mazurkas, 27 études, 25 préludes, 19 nocturnes, 14 waltzes, and 12 polonaises. He lived with the novelist George Sand from 1838 until 1847, when they became estranged.

Chopin, Kate [shohpin], *née* **Katherine O'Flaherty** (1851–1904) Novelist, short-story writer, and poet, born in St Louis, MO. She married **Oscar Chopin**, a Creole cotton trader from Louisiana, by whom she had six children. Her realistic novel of sexual passion, *The Awakening* (1899), was harshly condemned by the public, but she has since been praised for her concerns about the freedom of women.

chorale 1 A hymn of the Lutheran church. The qualities most associated with its music – harmonic strength and a firm, regular metre – are those of Bach's harmonizations.

2 The term *chorale* is also used for a choir, especially in the USA.

chord In music, two or more notes sounded simultaneously. In tonal music of the period c.1600–1920, a chord functions as a unit in a harmonic progression related to (or diverging from) a particular key centre. In post-tonal music, chords have been formed on serial or other principles, without reference to a key centre.

Chordata [kaw(r)dahta] or **chordates** A phylum of animals having bilateral symmetry, a stiffening rod (*notochord*) running along the back, a hollow dorsal nerve cord, a tail extending backwards beyond the anus, and gill slits. There are three subphyla: Cephalochordata (*lancelets*), Tunicata (*sea squirts* and *salps*), and Vertebrata (*vertebrates*). Vertebrates are chordates in which the dorsal nerve cord is surrounded by *vertebrae* made from cartilage or bone.

chordophone Any musical instrument in which the sound is produced by the vibrations of one or more strings. Chordophones are divided into (i) those without resonators, or with resonators that can be detached while leaving the strings in place (*simple chordophones*: piano, zither, etc), and (ii) those in which an integral resonator serves to keep the strings in place (*composite chordophones*: violin, lute, etc). Each type may be further subdivided (eg according to whether the strings are bowed, plucked, or struck); but in the perception of most people the main divisions are between those with keyboards, those with bows, and those with neither.

chorea [koreea] Involuntary jerky movements caused by damage to the part of the brain that controls muscular co-ordination. It may occur due to genetic disease (Huntington's chorea), stroke, or in children as a complication of rheumatic fever due to streptococcal infection (Sydenham's chorea).

choreography Originally, the writing of dances in notation; in its current general use, the making of dances by the selection of movements for a particular dance purpose, linked together to form a whole. The choreographic structure is often derived from music but can also be independent of it, based directly on the rhythm of movement.

chorionic villus sampling [korionik viluhs] A technique for obtaining samples of placental tissue, ideally at 8–12 weeks gestation. A needle is introduced through the mother's abdominal and uterine walls under ultrasound guidance. It is advanced to the edge of the placenta, a small piece of which is removed. Analysis of the tissue can identify the presence of several genetically determined disorders.

chorus The collective or impersonal voice in a drama (as distinct from the individual characters), which serves to introduce and comment on the action. It was an essential feature in classical drama, but less common later.

Chou En-lai *Zhou Enlai*

chough [chuhf] A crow-like bird, especially the **red-billed** or **Cornish chough** (*Pyrrhocorax pyrrhocorax*), native to Europe and Asia. (Family: Corvidae, 3 species.)

chow chow or **chow** A breed of dog, developed in China before 1000 BC; heavy body with thick coat and lion-like mane; blue tongue; tail curled over back; kept in temples, and bred with stern expressions to frighten away evil spirits; introduced to Europe in the 18th-c.

Chrétien, (Joseph Jacques) Jean [kraytyen] (1934–) Canadian statesman and prime minister (1993–2003), born in Shawinigan, Quebec, Canada. He served under Lester Pearson and Pierre Trudeau, and in 1990 became leader of the Liberal Party. He was returned to power for a second term in 1997, and again in 2000, and retired in 2003.

Chrétien de Troyes [kraytyī duh trwah] (?–c.1183) Mediaeval poet, born in Troyes, France. His best-known works are the metrical Arthurian romances, such as *Lancelot* and *Perceval*, which employ all the traditional ingredients of Celtic legend, and introduce into European literature the theme of the mystical Holy Grail.

Christ *Jesus Christ*

Christadelphians [kristadelfianz] A Christian sect, founded by John Thomas (1805–71) in the USA, which teaches a return to primitive Christianity, and that Christ will soon come again to establish a theocracy lasting for a millennium. The name means 'Brothers of Christ'.

Christchurch 43°33S 172°40E, pop (2000e) 334 000 (urban area) 315 700. City on the E coast of South Island, New Zealand; founded, 1850; airport; railway; university (1873); corn and sheep trade from the Canterbury Plains; scene of 1974 Commonwealth Games.

Christian X (1870–1947) King of Denmark (1912–47), born in Charlottenlund, E Denmark. During the German occupation (1940–5), he attracted great acclaim by remaining in Denmark.

Christian, Fletcher (18th-c) Seaman, born in Cockermouth, Cumbria. He was the ringleader in the mutiny on the *Bounty*, which sailed to Tahiti 1787–8. In 1808 his descendants were found on Pitcairn I.

Christian Aid A large UK-based charity supported by most Churches in Britain. It pays for development projects in the poorest countries of the world, particularly in agriculture, water supply, and health, using its own experts as advisors.

Christian Democratic Union *Christian Democrats*

Christian Democrats Members of Christian Democratic political parties, most of which were formed in W Europe after 1945, and which have since become a major political force. The Christian Democratic philosophy is based upon strong links with the Catholic Church and its notions of social and economic justice. It emphasizes the traditional conservative values of the family and church, but also more progressive, liberal values such as state intervention in the economy and significant social welfare provision.

Christianity (Gr *christos* 'anointed') A world religion (with over 2000 million adherents in 2007) centred on the life and work of Jesus of Nazareth in Israel, and developing out of Judaism. The earliest followers were Jews who, after the death and resurrection of Jesus, believed him to be the Messiah or Christ, promised by the prophets in the Old Testament, and in unique relation to God, whose Son or 'Word' (*Logos*) he was declared to be. During his life he chose 12 men as *disciples*, who formed the nucleus of the Church as a society or communion of believers. The Gospel ('Good News') of Jesus by the end of the 1st-c was reduced to writing and accepted as authoritative scriptures of the New Testament, understood as the fulfilment of the Jewish scriptures, or Old Testament. Through the witness of the 12 earliest leaders (*Apostles*) and their successors, the Christian faith spread through the Greek and Roman world, and in 315 was declared by Emperor Constantine to be the official religion of the Roman Empire, and formed the basis of civilization in the Middle Ages in Europe.

Major divisions, separated as a result of differences in doctrine and practice, are the *Eastern* or *Orthodox Churches*, the *Roman Catholic Church*, acknowledging the Bishop of Rome as head (the *Pope*), and the *Protestant Churches* stemming from the split with the Roman Church in the 16th-c Reformation. All Christians recognize the authority of the Bible, read at public worship, which takes place at least every Sunday, the first day of the week, to celebrate the resurrection of Jesus Christ. Most Churches recognize at least two sacraments (Baptism, and the Eucharist, Mass, or Lord's Supper) as essential. The impetus to spread Christianity to the non-Christian world in missionary movements, especially in the 19th-c and 20th-c, resulted in the creation of numerically very strong Churches in the developing countries of Asia, Africa, and South America. A powerful ecumenical movement in the 20th-c, promoted by, among others, the World Council of Churches, sought to recover unity among divided Christians.

Christian Science A movement, founded by Mary Baker Eddy, which seeks to reinstate the original Christian message of salvation from all evil, including sickness and disease as well as sin. The first Church of Christ, Scientist, was established in 1879 in Boston, MA, USA. Eddy's *Science and Health with Key to the Scriptures* (1875) and the Bible are the principal texts of the movement.

Christian Social Union *Christian Democrats*

Christie, Dame Agatha (Mary Clarissa), *née* **Miller** (1890–1976) Writer, born in Torquay, Devon. She wrote more than 70 detective novels featuring the Belgian detective, Hercule Poirot, or the inquiring village lady, Miss Marple. Her play *The Mousetrap* opened in 1952 at the Ambassador Theatre, and holds the record for the longest unbroken run in a London theatre. Several of her stories have become popular films, such as *Murder on the Orient Express* (1974) and *Death on the Nile* (1978).

Christie, John Reginald Halliday (1898–1953) Murderer, born in Yorkshire. He was hanged at London for the murder of his wife, and confessed to the murder of six other women, including the wife of **Timothy John Evans**, who lived in the same house. Evans had been convicted and hanged for the murder of his infant daughter in 1950, and was also charged with his wife's murder. After a special inquiry, Evans was granted a free pardon in 1966.

Christie, Julie (1940–) Actress, born in Chukua, Assam. She became known through her role in *Billy Liar* (1963), and in 1965 won an Oscar for *Darling*. Later films include *Dr Zhivago* (1965), *The Go-Between* (1971), *Heat and Dust* (1982), *Hamlet* (1996), *Afterglow* (1997), and *Troy* (2004).

Christie, Linford (1960–) Sprinter, born in Jamaica, now living in Britain. In 1993 he held the World, Olympic, Commonwealth, and European Cup titles for the 100 m, achieving 9·87 seconds at the world championships in Stuttgart, Germany (a European record).

Christmas The Christian festival commemorating the birth of Jesus, observed by most branches of the Church on 25 December but by some denominations in January. The practice of celebrating Christmas on 25 December began in the Western Church early in the 4th-c; it was a Christian substitute for the pagan festival held on that date to celebrate the birth of the unconquered Sun. The name is often abbreviated to **Xmas**, *X* being the first letter (*chi*) of the Greek word **Christos**.

Christmas disease *haemophilia*

Christmas Island (Kiribati) *Kiritimati*

Christmas Island (Indian Ocean) 10°25S 105°39E, pop (2000e) 2700; area 135 km²/52 sq mi. Island in the Indian Ocean; administered by Australia as an external territory; annexed by the UK, 1888; sovereignty passed to Australia, 1958; airport.

Christmas tree *Norway spruce*

Christology The orderly study of the significance of Jesus Christ for Christian faith. Traditionally, the term was restricted to the study of the person of Christ, and in particular to the way in which he is both human and divine. Latterly, an emphasis on the inseparability of Christ's person and work has meant that Christology often encompasses enquiry into his saving significance (*soteriology*) as well.

Christophe, Henry [kristof] (1767–1829) Haitian revolutionary, born a slave on the island of Grenada. He joined the black insurgents on Haiti against the French (1790), was appointed president in 1807, and proclaimed king in the N part of the island as Henry I in 1811.

Christopher, St (3rd-c) Syrian saint, said to have been 12 ft/3·6 m tall, and to have suffered martyrdom under the Emperor Decius (249–51). His name is from the Greek, 'Christ-bearer', from the legend of his carrying the Christ child across a river. He is the patron saint of wayfarers, and now motorists. Feast day 25 July.

Christopher, Warren M(inor) (1925–) Lawyer and government official, born in Scranton, ND. Deputy attorney general (1967–9) and deputy secretary of state (1977–81), he remained a respected voice in the Democratic Party, and was appointed secretary of state in 1993. He resigned after the 1996 election.

Christ's Hospital An independent co-educational boarding school, founded in London (1552), but since 1902 at Horsham, Sussex. It is known as the **Blue Coat School**, because of the blue cloak which was part of the pupils' uniform.

chromakey An image-combination process in video production where an area of strong colour in one scene is replaced ('keyed') by the picture from another source; also termed **colour separation overlay (CSO)**.

chromaticism An attribute of music which uses notes, intervals, and chords outside the prevailing key; a note which does not belong to the diatonic scale is called a **chromatic note**.

chromatin [krohmatin] The network of substance in a cell nucleus that takes up stain, and which can thus be made visible under the microscope during the process of cell division. It is organized into distinct bodies (the chromosomes).

chromatography The separation of components of a mixture (the *mobile phase*) by passing it through another phase (the *stationary phase*), making use of the different extents to which the various components are adsorbed by the stationary phase. Many systems have been developed. One is **paper chromatography**, illustrated by the separation of the constituent dyes of an ink when it is spilled on a paper tissue. Another is **gas–liquid chromatography (GLC)**, used to separate mixtures of gases.

chromatophore [krohmatofaw(r)] A pigment-bearing cell, or structure within a cell. In many animals chromatophores are cells containing pigment granules. By dispersing or contracting these granules, the animal is able to change colour.

chrominance The component of a video signal which determines the hue and saturation of a reproduced colour. The term is sometimes abbreviated to 'chroma'.

chromium Cr, element 24, density 7·2 g/cm³, melting point 1857°C. A hard, lustrous metal, found combined with oxygen, and generally prepared as a metal by reduction of the ore with aluminium. Its principal uses are in plating and as a component of steels, to which it gives corrosion resistance.

chromosome *p.193*

chromosphere Part of the outer gaseous layers of the Sun (and other stars), a few thousand km deep. It is visible as a thin crescent of pinkish light during a total eclipse of the Sun.

chronic fatigue syndrome *ME syndrome*

chronicle plays Plays (from any period) based upon historical events, often using the written record as both source and structure. Marlowe and Shakespeare used Holinshed's chronicles for their plays from English history. Epic theatre (after Brecht) has revived this mode of drama.

Chronicles or **Paralipomenon, Books of** Two books of the Hebrew Bible/Old Testament, originally a single work, part of a history of Judah from its beginnings to its restoration under Ezra and Nehemiah.

chronogram The practice of hiding a date within a series of words, by using the letters for Roman numerals (C = 100, V = 5, etc). It is often used on tombstones and foundation stones to mark the date of the event being commemorated.

chrysalis *pupa*

chromosome

The threads within the nucleus of a cell which become visible during cell division. The chromosomes were postulated to be the carriers of inherited information in 1903, after a study of the close correspondence between their behaviour and Mendelian factors. They occur in pairs – one member of maternal and one of paternal origin. They are the major carriers of genetic material, consisting of chromatin (DNA and various types of proteins, mostly his-

tones). The position of a particular gene on a chromosome is called its *locus*. The number of chromosomes differs from species to species. A normal human cell has 46 chromosomes: 22 pairs of autosomes together with (in females) one matching pair of X chromosomes and (in males) one non-matching pair, the X and Y chromosomes. By the end of 2003, the genetic map of four human chromosomes (14, 20, 21, 22) had been published.

chrysanthemum A name applied in a broad sense to various members of the family Compositae. The large-flowered 'chrysanthemums' of gardens (Genus: *Dendranthema*) have a long history of cultivation, especially in China and Japan, and modern plants are derived from complex hybrids whose exact parentage is uncertain.

Chrysippus [kriysipus] (c.280–c.206 BC) Stoic philosopher, born in Soli, Cilicia. The third and greatest head of the Stoa, he wrote over 700 works (only fragments remain) elaborating the Stoic system in what became its definitive and orthodox form.

chrysoprase [krisoprayz] The apple-green form of chalcedony.

Chrysostom, St John [krisostom] (c.347–407) Church Father, born in Antioch. In 398 he was made Archbishop of Constantinople, but his reproof of vices moved the Empress Eudoxia to have him deposed and banished (403). His name comes from the Greek, 'golden mouthed', on account of his eloquence. Feast day 13 September.

chrysotile [krisotiyl] The fibrous form of serpentine. It is a member of the asbestos group of minerals.

Chu, Steven (1948–) Physicist, born in St Louis, MO. He held posts at Bell Laboratories and Stanford University, and shared the 1997 Nobel Prize for Physics for his contribution to the

development of methods to cool and trap atoms with laser light.

chub Fish mainly found in European streams and rivers (*Leuciscus cephalus*); body elongate, rather cylindrical, length up to 60 cm/2 ft; greenish-grey above, sides silver, underside white. (Family: Cyprinidae.)

Chubb Crater A meteorite crater c.410 m/1350 ft deep in Quebec, Canada; occupied by Crater Lake, 260 m/850 ft deep; discovered in 1949 by a prospector, F W Chubb; also known as **Ungava–Quebec Crater**.

chuckwalla An iguana (*Sauromalus obesus*) from North America, found in rocky deserts; dark body with thick blunt yellow tail; no crest along back; eats plants.

Chukchi or **Chuckchee** A people of NE Siberia. They are divided into **maritime Chukchi**, who are hunters and fishers of the Arctic and Bering Sea, and the previously nomadic **reindeer Chukchi**, who live inland and herd reindeer.

Chukchi Peninsula [chukchee], Russ **Chukotskiy Poluostrov** NE extremity of Asia, in Russia; bounded N by the Chukchi Sea, E by the Bering Strait; rises to heights above 1000 m/3300 ft.

Chu-kiang *Zhu Jiang*

Chungking *Chongqing*

church

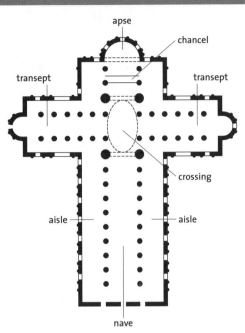

In architecture, a building used for public religious worship, especially Christian. First adapted by the early Christians from the Roman basilicas and martyrs' shrines, it was later developed in the Romanesque architecture of the 11th-c and 12th-c into the now more usual Latin cross plan, typically consisting of nave with side aisles, transepts, chancel, and apse, such as Pisa Cathedral (mainly 1063–1118) and the Panthéon (Sainte Geneviève), Paris (1757–90), architect J G Soufflot. The centrally-planned circular or Greek cross plan was briefly favoured in Renaissance Italy, such as Santa Maria della Consolazione, Todi (1508–1604). In the 20th-c, church design has become increasingly eclectic, most famously the Chapel of Notre Dame, Ronchamp, France (1950–5), architect Le Corbusier; the Roman Catholic Cathedral, Liverpool, UK (1960–7), architect Frederick Gibberd; and also in numerous smaller, usually urban churches.

church *see panel*

Church, Charlotte (1986–) Soprano, born in Cardiff. At age 11 she performed 'Pie Jesu' on a television talent show, and was immediately signed to a recording contract. With her debut album, *Voice of an Angel* (1998), she became the youngest ever artist to make number 1 in the UK classical charts. Later albums include *Dream A Dream* (2001) and *Prelude* (2002). In 2005 she released her first pop album, *Tissues and Issues*. She began hosting *The Charlotte Church Show* for Channel 4 television in 2006.

Church Army An Anglican organization of volunteer lay workers, founded in 1882. Its aims are evangelical, but it concentrates on social welfare and rehabilitation work, mainly in cities.

Churcher, Betty, popular name of **Elizabeth Ann Churcher** (1931–) Arts administrator, born in Brisbane, Queensland, Australia. The author of the award-winning book *Understanding Art* (1974), she became director of the Australian National Gallery (1990–7).

Churchill, Lord Randolph (Henry Spencer) (1849–95) British Con-

servative statesman, born in Blenheim Palace, Oxfordshire, the father of Winston Churchill. He was secretary for India (1885–6), and for a short while Chancellor of the Exchequer and Leader of the House of Commons.

Churchill, Sir Winston (Leonard Spencer) (1874–1965) British statesman, prime minister (1940–5, 1951–5), and author, born in Blenheim Palace, Oxfordshire. Initially a Conservative MP (1900), he joined the Liberals in 1904, and was colonial under-secretary (1905), President of the Board of Trade (1908), home secretary (1910), and First Lord of the Admiralty (1911). After World War 1 he was secretary of state for war and air (1919–21), and Chancellor of the Exchequer (1924–9). In 1929 he returned to the Conservative fold, but remained out of step with the leadership until World War 2, when he returned to the Admiralty. On Chamberlain's defeat (May 1940) he formed a coalition government, and, holding both the premiership and the defence portfolio, led Britain through the war against Germany, Italy, and Japan with great oratory and steely resolution. Defeated in the July 1945 election, he became a pugnacious Leader of the Opposition. In 1951 he was prime minister again, and after 1955 remained a venerated backbencher. He was awarded the Nobel Prize for Literature in 1953. His widow, **Clementine Ogilvy Hozier**, whom he had married in 1908, was made a life peer in 1965 for her indefatigable charitable work (**Baroness Spencer-Churchill of Chartwell**).

Church of England The official state Church of England, a national Church having both Protestant and Catholic features, based on episcopal authority, and with the monarch of England formally as its head. It originated when Henry VIII broke ties with the Roman Catholic Church (c.1532–4), its doctrine and liturgy developing in the Book of Common Prayer (1549, 1552), and the 39 Articles. The Church today consists of 44 dioceses in the two provinces of Canterbury and York, with over 16 000 churches and other places of worship. Local parishes are arranged into rural deaneries and dioceses, with each diocese led by a bishop. In 1970 the General Synod was established for the purpose of reaching decisions and expressing views on issues of interest to the Church. It meets three times a year, and has over 500 members, divided between the three houses: the Houses of Clergy, of Bishops, and of Laity. In 1992 it voted in favour of the ordination of women priests – an event which took place for the first time in 1994, and in 2005 the Synod voted to begin the legal process to ordain women as bishops. In 2006 the appointment of Bishop Katharine Jefferts Schori as head of the US Episcopal Church, the first woman to hold this authority, was highly controversial. In 2003, the first consecration of an openly gay minister, as Bishop of New Hampshire, USA, took place amid much controversy. There were over 82 million Anglicans in 2007.

Church of Scotland The national Church in Scotland, founded at the Reformation of 1560 under the leadership of John Knox. Presbyterian in its governing organization and discipline, laymen or *elders* (ordained) play a leading part with ministers in church courts at local, congregational level (in *Kirk Session*), district level (*presbyteries*, overseeing congregations in a given area), provincial synods, and the *General Assembly*. Ministers (women and men), who are ordained by presbytery, are alone authorized to administer the sacraments of baptism (of infants as well as adults) and the Lord's Supper (*communion*).

Church Slavonic *Slavic languages*

Chu-teh *Zhu De*

CIA *Central Intelligence Agency*

Cibber, Colley [siber] (1671–1757) Actor and playwright, born in London. He spent most of his career at the Theatre Royal in Drury Lane. From 1730 he was poet laureate.

cicada [sikahda] A large, typically tropical insect that spends most of its long life-cycle as a nymph burrowing underground, feeding on sap from roots; adults live in trees; males typically have well-developed sound-producing organs. (Order: Homoptera. Family: Cicadidae.)

Cicero, Marcus Tullius [siseroh], also known in English as **Tully** (106–43 BC) Roman orator, statesman, and philosopher, born in Arpinum, Latium. Though he foiled Catiline's revolutionary plot, he broke the law by executing Roman citizens without a trial, and fled to Thessalonica (58 BC) in exile. In 57 BC he was recalled by the people, but lost the esteem of both Caesar's and Pompey's factions by vacillating between the two. Living in retirement (46–44 BC), he wrote most of his chief works on rhetoric and philosophy. In 43 BC he delivered his famous speeches against Antony, the so-called 'Philippics', and was murdered by Antony's soldiers as he tried to escape.

cichlid [siklid] Any of a large family of freshwater fishes found in South and Central America, Africa, and India; body usually perch-like; feeding and breeding habits extremely diverse. (20 genera, including *Haplochromis*, *Tilapia*. Family: Cichlidae.)

CID An abbreviation of **Criminal Investigation Department**, formed in 1878 as a branch of the London Metropolitan Police, and responsible for the investigation and prevention of crime and the gathering of criminal intelligence. Most provincial forces in Scotland, England, and Wales now have their own CIDs.

Cid, El [sid], Span [theed], popular name of **Rodrigo** or **Ruy Díaz de Vivar** (c.1043–99) Spanish hero, born in Burgos. He became known as the *Cid* (from the Moorish *Sidi*, 'lord'); his great achievement was the capture of Valencia (1094).

cider An alcoholic drink produced from the fermentation of apples, traditionally made in SW England and Normandy, France. Its alcoholic content varies widely, from 3% to 9% ethanol. In the USA, ciders are either 'sweet' (non-alcoholic) or 'hard' (containing alcohol).

Ciechanover, Aaron (1947–) Biologist born in Haifa, Israel. Professor at the Unit of Biochemistry and director of the Rappaport Family Institute for Research in Medical Sciences at the Technion in Haifa, Israel (1992–), in 2004 he shared the Nobel Prize for Chemistry for the discovery of ubiquitin-mediated protein degradation.

Cienfuegos [syenfwaygohs] 22°10N 80°27W, pop (2000e) 132 600. Port on S coast of Cuba; founded, 1819; important industrial centre; naval base.

cigar *cigarette*

cigarette A thin roll of finely-cut tobacco, wrapped in paper, used for smoking. The origins of the cigarette lie in Central and South America, where native Indians wrapped crushed tobacco leaves in a reed or vegetable casing. Spanish explorers then introduced the practice to Europe in the form of the *cigar*. By the 16th-c, *cigarillos* ('little cigars') had emerged, re-using the tobacco found in discarded cigar butts by wrapping it in paper. *Cigarettes* (the term is French) spread throughout Europe in the following century.

ciliate [siliuht] A microscopic, single-celled organism typically possessing short hair-like appendages (**cilia**) on its surface; commonly also with a specialized mouth region (*cytostome*); found free-living in all kinds of aquatic and terrestrial habitats, and as parasites. (Phylum: Ciliophora.)

Cilicia [siylisia, silisha] The ancient name for the S coastal part of Turkey around the Taurus Mts. It was famous for its timber and its pirates.

Cimabue [cheemabooay], originally **Cenni di Peppi** (c.1240–c.1302) Painter, born in Florence, Italy. He at first adopted traditional Byzantine forms, but soon turned to nature, and led the way to the naturalism of his great pupil, Giotto. He executed several important frescoes in the Church of St Francis at Assisi; these were badly damaged in an earthquake in 1997.

cimbalom [simbalom] A kind of dulcimer, native to Hungary but found also in other E European countries. The concert cimbalom has been used as an orchestral instrument by Liszt, Kodály, Bartók, and others.

Cimbri [kimbree] A Germanic people from N Europe who migrated S towards the end of the 2nd-c BC in search of new lands. They were defeated and destroyed by the Romans (101 BC) in the Po valley.

cimetidine *H2 blockers*

Cincinnati [sinsinatee] 39°06N 84°01W, pop (2000e) 331 300. City in SW Ohio, USA, on Ohio R; Fort Washington built here, 1789; city status, 1819; large numbers of German immigrants in the 1840s; airport; railway; two universities (1819, 1831); several centres for culture, music, and the arts; professional teams, Reds (baseball), Bengals (football); birthplace of William Howard Taft.

Cincinnatus, Lucius Quinctius [sinsinahtus] (5th-c BC) Roman statesman, farmer and folk hero. Called from the plough and given absolute power to rescue the Roman army of the consul Minucius, which had been trapped by the Aequi (458 BC), he voluntarily gave up this power and returned to his farm, as soon as the crisis was over.

CinemaScope A system of wide-screen cinematography, based on Henri Chrétien's invention of 1927 and adopted by 20th Century Fox in 1953. A squeeze factor of 2:1 horizontally is used, resulting in a screened picture of aspect ratio (width:-height) 2·35:1.

cinematography The presentation of moving pictures as a series of photographic images recorded and reproduced in rapid succession, the eye's persistence of vision giving the impression of continuous movement. Film in continuous strips provided the material for Edison's pioneer Kinetoscope camera of 1891, but projecting the image on a screen for a large audience originated with the Lumière brothers in 1895, establishing the film production and cinema industries. Pictures were exposed in the camera at a rate of 16 per second, the film being held stationary for each exposure and then advanced one frame at a time while a shutter obscured the lens. After developing this film as a negative, a positive print was made for projection, again with an intermittent mechanism and shutter. In the late 1920s synchronized sound was added to the picture presentation, after 1927 from a sound track on the film itself, the frame rate being increased to 24 pictures per second.

cinéma vérité (Fr 'truth cinema') A style of film production stressing realistic documentary treatment even for fictional drama. The approach prefers non-professional actors and minimal script and rehearsal, using the mobile viewpoint of a handheld camera and natural sound.

Cinerama One of the first systems of wide-screen cinema presentation in 1952, using three synchronized projectors to cover a very large curved screen in three blended panels. Its cost and complexity limited its use to showing travelogues in specially adapted theatres, and it ceased after 1962.

cineraria A dwarf shrub growing to 60 cm/2 ft or more, native to Africa and Madagascar; flower-heads numerous, daisy-like, in dense flat-topped clusters, red to deep blue-violet. (Genus: *Cineraria*, c.50 species. Family: Compositae.)

Cinna, Lucius Cornelius [sina] (?–84 BC) Prominent Roman politician of the turbulent 80s BC. Driven from Rome while consul in 87 BC, he recaptured the city with the help of Marius amid much bloodshed, and was all-powerful there until his murder.

cinnabar (entomology) [sinabah(r)] A medium-sized, nocturnal tiger moth; forewings dark grey with carmine patches, hindwings carmine with black margins; also called **cinnabar moth**. (Order: Lepidoptera. Family: Arctiidae.)

cinnabar (metallurgy) [sinabah(r)] A mineral of mercury sulphide (HgS), the chief ore of mercury. It consists of small, red, soft crystals, and is used in the mineral pigment vermilion.

cinnamon A small evergreen tree (*Cinnamomum zeylanicum*) growing to 6 m/20 ft, native to SE Asia; flowers greenish; berries black. The spice is obtained from the bark of young trees. (Family: Lauraceae).

cinquefoil [singkfoyl] The name of various species of *Potentilla*, with 5-petalled, white, yellow, or purple flowers. (Genus: *Potentilla*. Family: Rosaceae.)

Cinque Ports [singk] Originally, the five S English coast ports of Dover, Hastings, Hythe, Romney, and Sandwich, associated by royal authority (under Edward the Confessor) to provide ships for naval defence; Rye and Winchelsea were added later. They received royal privileges, and were governed by a Lord Warden. Their role declined with the growth of the navy, and the status was abolished in 1835.

cipher A secret way of writing; also, anything written in such a manner. The letters comprising a message in ciphers are normally either replaced by others (*substitution*) or re-ordered (*transposition*) according to a frequently changing scheme. In either case the appropriate key is needed to decipher and understand the message.

circadian rhythm [serkaydian] (Lat *circa* 'about' + *dies* 'day') A biological rhythm that has a periodicity of about one day. This periodicity can be seen, for example, in the sleep cycle in animals and the growth cycles of plants.

Circassians A people from the Caucasus, divided into Adyghians and Kabardians; they are Sunni Muslims. Most live in Russia as farmers and pastoralists.

Circe [sersee] In the *Odyssey*, an enchantress who detained Odysseus and his followers on the island of Aeaea. She transformed Odysseus's men into swine with a magic drink, but he was able to defeat her charms through the protection of the herb *Moly*.

Circinus [sersinus] (Lat 'compasses') A small obscure S constellation.

circle The locus of a point that is a constant distance from a fixed point. The constant distance is called the *radius*, and the fixed point the *centre*. From this definition are obtained all the properties of the circle. The area of a circle radius r is πr^2; the circumference is $2\pi r$.

circotherm oven An oven with a fan to circulate internal hot air. It is designed to achieve uniformity of heating and to economize in heating or cooking time.

circuit An administrative division of the judicial system of England and Wales. Each circuit has a circuit administrator and two presiding judges, one senior, one junior. In the USA, federal and state judicial systems have similar administrative divisions, also known as circuits.

circuit riders Early itinerant Methodist preachers on horseback who covered a circuit of churches and carried messages to new settlements. They were instrumental in the rapid expansion of early Methodism.

circulation In physiology, the vertebrate system in which blood is pumped intermittently from the heart and flows continuously around the body (**systemic circulation**) or to the lungs (**pulmonary circulation**) and back to the heart by a network of blood vessels. By means of the systemic circulation, tissues are provided with oxygen, nutrients, hormones, and enzymes. The pulmonary circulation is concerned with the exchange of oxygen and carbon dioxide with the environment. In mammals and birds, the circulatory system also functions in body temperature regulation.

circumcision The widespread practice of removing all or part of the foreskin of the penis. The age of circumcision varies; male Jewish babies, for example, are circumcised eight days after birth, while other groups circumcise just before or at puberty as part of an initiation ceremony. In female circumcision, some or all external genitalia are removed. Circumcision may also be carried out for health reasons.

Circumcision, Feast of the A Christian festival (1 Jan) in honour of the circumcision of Jesus eight days after his birth (*Luke* 2).

circumpolar star A star which never sets when viewed from a particular location. In Europe and North America the stars of Ursa Minor and Ursa Major are always visible. In Australia, Crux is a circumpolar constellation.

circus Historically, games in ancient Rome involving horse and chariot races, gladiatorial combat, and wild animals; in modern times, a travelling show featuring animals and feats of human endurance and skill. The modern-day circus was initiated in 1768 by trick horseback rider Philip Astley (1742–1814), who built his own 'arena' in which to display his skills. The most famous 19th-c circuses were Barnum and Bailey's, Astley's and Spengler's. In recent times the shows of Bertram Mills, Billy Smart, and David Chipperfield have been popular, though have suffered a decline in recent years. At the beginning of the 21st century, European and Asian circuses, such as those of Moscow and China, continue to provide spectacular shows, and tour regularly, as does Canada's Cirque du Soleil.

Cirencester [siyrensester, sisister], ancient **Corinium Dobunorum** 51°44N 1°59W, pop (2000e) 15700. Market town in Gloucestershire, SWC England; second largest town in Roman Britain during 2nd-c AD; Royal Agricultural College.

cire perdue [seer perdoo] or **'lost wax' process** A technique for casting metals, mainly for sculpture. The desired shape is formed (eg in clay), and a mould is made, the inside of which is then coated in wax. The inside of the wax is coated with further heat-resisting material, giving a gap filled with wax. The wax is then melted out, leaving a hollow into which molten metal can be poured.

cirque [serk] A bowl-shaped, steep-sided hollow formed at the head of a mountain valley by the erosion of ice in glaciated regions; termed **corrie** or **cwm** in Scotland and Wales respectively. Two cirques cutting back into a ridge forms an *arete*, while three or more result in pyramidal peaks such as the Matterhorn in the Alps.

cirrhosis [sirohsis] A chronic diffuse disorder of the liver, in which liver cells are destroyed and progressively replaced by scar tissue (*fibrosis*). The most common cause is long-continued excessive consumption of alcohol.

Cirripedia [siripeedia] *barnacle*

cirrocumulus clouds [sirohkyoomyuluhs] High-level clouds above c.5000 m/16 000 ft, composed of ice crystals. They are white in thin sheets or layers, but have the rounded appearance of cumulus clouds. Cloud symbol: Cc.

cirrostratus clouds [sirohstratuhs] High-level stratus or layered clouds, in which there is a transition from supercooled water droplets to ice crystals. Found at altitudes above c.5000 m/16 000 ft, they are sheet-like and white/grey in colour. Their arrival precedes the warm front of a depression. Cloud symbol: Cs.

cirrus clouds [siruhs] High-level clouds above c.5000 m/16 000 ft, composed of ice crystals. They are white and wispy in appearance, elongated by strong winds in the upper atmosphere. They are an indication of the leading edge of a warm front at altitude. Cloud symbol: Ci.

CIS *Commonwealth of Independent States*

Cisalpine Gaul [sizalpiyn gawl] *Gaul*

Cisalpine Republic [sizalpiyn] N Italian state created by Napoleon I at the Peace of Campoformio (1797). By the Treaty of Lunéville (1802), it became the Italian Republic, with Bonaparte as president.

***cis*-butenedioic acid** *maleic acid*

Ciscaucasia The N Caucasus territory of Kuban, Stavropol, Terek, and the Black Sea, formed in 1924. It existed until 1934.

Ciskei [siskiy] Former independent black homeland in NE Cape province, South Africa, established in 1981; military coup, 1990;

incorporated into Eastern Cape province in the South African Constitution of 1994.

Cistercians [sistershnz] A religious order formed by Benedictine monks by St Robert of Molesme in Citeaux, France, in 1098, under a strict rule, with an emphasis on solitude, poverty, and simplicity. In the 17th-c it was divided into communities of **Common Observance** (now abbreviated **SOCist**) and of **Strict Observance** (in full, the **Order of the Reformed Cistercians of the Strict Observance**, abbreviated **OCSO**). The latter were revived in France after the Revolution by *Trappists* (former members of the monastery of La Trappe).

cithara *kithara*

Citizen's Advice Bureaux (CAB) In the UK, a national network of information offices, set up in 1939 to inform the public about the emergency wartime regulations. It has remained in operation to provide free and confidential information, particularly concerning the social services, housing, legal aid, consumer services, and family matters. Its 462 offices (in 2007) are staffed by trained counsellors, 90% of whom are volunteers, and each office is funded by the local authority.

citizens' band (CB) radio A short-range two-way radio communication system for use by members of the public, typically consisting of a transceiver (a combined transmitter-receiver) and aerial. CB originated in the USA in the 1940s, and is particularly associated with long-distance truck drivers, who evolved special codes and jargon to keep their messages from being understood by the police and public. In the UK, the use of CB was illegal until 1981, when a special channel was authorized. The technology has now been largely replaced by cellular phones.

Citlaltépetl [seetlaltaypetl] or **Pico de Orizaba** 19°02N 97°02W. Highest peak in Mexico, rising to 5699 m/18 697 ft; a dormant volcano, inactive since 1687.

citric acid cycle *Krebs cycle*

citron A citrus fruit (*Citrus medica*), 10–25 cm/4–10 in in diameter; ovoid, with thick, rough, yellowish-orange rind, and green or yellow flesh. (Family: Rutaceae.)

citrus A member of a group of plants bearing distinctive juicy, acid-tasting fruits of great economic importance. The majority belong to the genus *Citrus*, but a few come from close relatives. All species are spiny evergreen shrubs or trees. The fruit is a type of berry, in which the carpels are enclosed in a thick, leathery rind. Both the foliage and rind of the fruit have numerous glands containing aromatic essential oils. The species include the orange, lemon, lime, and grapefruit, as well as more local fruits, such as the shaddock. They are now grown in the tropics and warm temperate regions throughout the world, mainly the Mediterranean, S USA, S Africa, and Australia, and have become a major export crop for several countries. (Genus: *Citrus*, 12 species. Family: Rutaceae.)

cittern A plucked string instrument of great antiquity, particularly popular in the 16th–17th-c. It resembled a lute, but with a smaller, pear-shaped body, a flat (or slightly convex) back, and usually four, five, or six courses of strings played with a plectrum.

city A settlement larger than a town or village, the definition of which varies according to national conventions. In Britain the term is used of cathedral towns (eg Ely) and certain other towns upon which the title has been conferred by royal authority (eg Birmingham); in the USA it is used of urban centres which have a particular local government structure.

City, the A square mile of C London, UK, housing some of the world's major financial institutions, including the Stock Exchange, money markets, commercial and merchant banks, the insurance institutions, and commodity exchanges. The term is also used as a collective noun to denote the major British financial institutions and their interests.

city-state *polis*

city technology college (CTC) A type of secondary school, established by the 1988 Education Act, which specializes in science and technology. It is independent of the local education authority and receives its annual grant direct from the government.

Ciudad Guayana [syoodad gwayana] 8°22N 62°37W, pop (2000e) 656 400. New city in E Venezuela, founded in 1961; population of 1 million is planned; airfield; railway; commercial port at San Félix.

civet A carnivorous mammal, found in 17 species (mostly Asian); also known as **civet cat** or **bush dog**, but the name *civet* is often used for any member of this family. (Family: Viverridae.)

Civic Trust A charitable organization in the UK which exists to promote conservation and improvement of the environment in town and country. It encourages high standards in architecture and planning, and the preservation of buildings of historic and architectural interest.

civil defence (CD) The organization of civilian defences, able to limit damage and keep communications and production moving. It became a vital part of a nation's defences during the bombing campaigns of World War 2. Countries which maintain active organizations include Switzerland, Sweden, and the USA, where Civil Defense copes with natural disasters.

civil disobedience A political strategy adopted by M K Gandhi and his followers in India in 1930, in opposition to Britain's imperial rule: a non-violent, mass, illegal protest, intended to discredit the authority of the state. The strategy was later used by Martin Luther King Jr to good effect, and was a path sometimes advocated by opponents of nuclear weapons.

civil engineering A branch of engineering which deals with the design and construction of public works: buildings, bridges, tunnels, waterways, canals, streets, sewerage systems, railways, and airports. The subject includes structural, sanitary, and hydraulic engineering.

civil law 1 A branch of law regulating relationships between private citizens. An aggrieved person must generally initiate proceedings personally in order to obtain a remedy. In a narrower sense, it refers to domestic law, seen in contrast with international law. **2** The term also refers to civil law systems such as those of continental Europe and Japan, where law is codified. The *Code Napoléon* is an influential example. The contrast is with **common law** systems, where the emphasis is on the development of law through individual cases under a system of precedent.

civil liberties Individual freedoms that are thought to be essential to the operation of liberal democratic societies. These include freedom of speech, association, religion, conscience and movement, freedom before the law, and the right to a fair trial.

civil list In the UK, since 1760, a payment made from public funds for the maintenance of the royal household and family (except the Prince of Wales). It covers the salaries of the household staff, travel, entertaining, and public engagements at home and abroad. For 1991–2000 the civil list was fixed at £10 420 000, of which £7 900 000 was intended for the Queen. In 1992 it was decided that only the Queen, the Queen Mother and the Duke of Edinburgh would receive payments from the civil list.

civil list pension In the UK, pensions originally paid from the sovereign's civil list, but now granted separately. They are awarded by the monarch on advice from the prime minister to persons who have given service to the Crown or public.

civil rights The rights guaranteed by the state to its citizens. It incorporates the belief that governments should not arbitrarily act to infringe these rights, and that individuals and groups, through political action, have a legitimate role in determining and influencing what constitutes them. In common usage, the term is taken to mean the rights of groups, as opposed to the rights of the individual, although there is a clear element of overlap. Women's rights, gay rights, ethnic and racial minority rights, and others are all commonly cited in this connection, but the term has come to be especially associated with movements in the USA, especially 1954–68, which aimed to secure the legal enforcement of the guarantees of racial equality contained in the 13th, 14th, and 15th Amendments to the US Constitution. Beginning as an attack on specific forms of racial segregation in the Southern states, it broadened into a massive challenge to all forms of racial subordination, and achieved considerable success, especially at the level of legal and juridical reform.

civil service Civilian personnel or officials employed on behalf of the state to administer central governmental policies, as distinct from the wider generality of public officials employed in such areas as local government, public corporations, and education, or as civilian staff of the armed forces. Most civil servants are permanent, remaining in post upon a change in government. Civil services are hierarchically organized, operate according to established rules of procedure, and are accountable through ministers to the Crown or the state.

civil union *homosexuality*

CJD *Creutzfeldt-Jakob disease*

cladistics A method of classifying organisms employing evolutionary hypotheses as the basis for classification. It uses recency of common ancestry as the criterion for grouping species together, rather than data on apparent similarity between species.

Cladocera [kladosera] *water flea*

Clairvaux [klairvoh] A Cistercian abbey founded in 1115 by St Bernard near Ville-sous-la-Ferté, Champagne, France. The site is now occupied by a prison.

clairvoyance The gaining of information about an object or a contemporaneous external physical event by alleged paranormal means. The term **precognitive clairvoyance** is used to refer to the supposed paranormal gaining of information about an external physical source which will come into existence at some time in the future.

clam The common name for a variety of bivalve molluscs; includes the giant clams, soft-shelled clams, and venus clams. (Class: Pelecypoda.)

clapper board In motion-picture production, a board or 'slate' with subject details, photographed at the beginning of each scene for identification. A hinged arm is 'clapped' to mark a synchronization point in the separate picture and sound records.

Clapton, Eric (1945–) Rock guitarist and singer, born in Ripley, Surrey. In the 1960s he was in British rhythm-and-blues bands The Yardbirds and John Mayall's Bluesbreakers, then in Cream and Blind Faith. 'Layla' (1970) is considered a rock classic by many, as are 'I Shot the Sheriff', 'Lay Down Sally', and 'Wonderful Tonight'. His 2005 album, *Back Home*, followed an historic Cream reunion in London's Royal Albert Hall. One of his guitars became the most expensive to sell at auction, fetching £527 000 in 2004.

Clare, Ir **An Chláir** pop (2000e) 92 000, area 3188 km²/1231 sq mi. County in W Ireland; capital, Ennis.

Clare of Assisi, St (1194–1253) Abbess, born of a noble family in Assisi, Italy. In 1215 she founded with St Francis the order of Franciscan nuns known as the Poor Clares. Canonized in 1255, she is the patron saint of television. Feast day 11 August.

Clare, Anthony (Ward) (1942–) British psychiatrist and broadcaster. He became professor at St Bartholomew's Hospital, London (1982–8), and at Trinity College, Dublin (1985–95), and

widely known through his BBC television series, *In the Psychiatrist's Chair* (from 1982). Among his books are *Depression and How to Survive It* (1993, with Spike Milligan), *In the Psychiatrist's Chair II* (1995), and *On Men* (2000).

Clare, John (1793–1864) Poet, born in Helpston, Cambridgeshire. His works include *Poems Descriptive of Rural Life* (1820). He spent the last 23 years of his life in an asylum at Northampton, where he wrote some of his best poetry.

Clarendon, Edward Hyde, 1st Earl of (1609–74) English statesman and historian, born near Salisbury, Wiltshire. He headed the Royalist opposition in the Commons until 1642, and became High Chancellor in 1658. Unpopular as a statesman, in 1667 he fell victim to a court cabal. Impeached for high treason, he left the country for France. His major work is the *History of the Rebellion in England* (3 vols, 1704–7).

Clarendon Code A series of British Acts passed between 1661 and 1665 which re-asserted the supremacy of the Church of England after the collapse of the 'Puritan Revolution' in 1660. Nonconformity was recognized as lawful, but many restrictions were placed on the activities of Nonconformists.

Clarendon, Constitutions of (1164) A written declaration of rights claimed by Henry II of England in ecclesiastical affairs, with the purpose of restoring royal control over the English Church. Promulgated at Clarendon, near Salisbury, the Constitutions brought the Archbishop of Canterbury Thomas Becket and Henry II into open conflict.

claret *wine*

clarinet A woodwind instrument, with a cylindrical bore and a single reed. It has been in regular use as a solo and orchestral instrument since the late 18th-c. It is a transposing instrument, the most common models being pitched in A or B♭. The larger **bass clarinet** (in B♭) sounds one octave lower than the standard instrument.

Clark, Alan (Kenneth McKenzie) (1928–99) British politician, military historian, and diarist. A barrister, he was elected a Conservative MP in 1974, and brought into government by Mrs Thatcher where he held posts at employment (1983–6), trade (1986–9), and defence (1989–92). He left parliament before the 1992 general election but returned in 1997. Three volumes of his diaries have been published (1994, 2000, 2002).

Clark, Helen (Elizabeth) (1950–) New Zealand politician and prime minister (1999–), born in Hamilton, New Zealand. A former lecturer in political studies at Auckland University, she became an MP in 1981, and served in Labour administrations in the 1980s. She became deputy prime minister (1989), leader of the party (1993), and New Zealand's first elected woman prime minister (1999), winning a second term in 2002. She secured a narrow win in the 2005 general election and formed a Labour-led coalition deal with minor parties.

Clark, Jim, popular name of **James Clark** (1936–68) Motor-racing driver, born in Kilmany, Fife. After joining the Lotus Team in 1960, he went on to become World Champion Racing Driver (1963, 1965). He won 25 Grands Prix, and was killed during a Formula Two race at Hockenheim, Germany.

Clark, Kenneth (Mackenzie) Clark, Baron (1903–83) Art historian, born in London. In addition to his acclaimed scholarly work on Leonardo da Vinci, he wrote many popular books on his subject, and became widely known through his television series *Civilisation* (1969).

Clark, Michael (1962–) Dancer and choreographer, born in Aberdeen, Scotland. He studied at the Royal Ballet School and formed his own company in the mid-1980s. Best known for his outlandish costumes, stage props and innovative dance technique.

Clark, William (1770–1838) Explorer, born in Caroline Co, VA. He became joint leader with Meriwether Lewis of the successful transcontinental expedition to the Pacific coast and back (1804–6).

Clarke, Sir Arthur C(harles) (1917–) Writer of science fiction, born in Minehead, Somerset. He became especially known for *2001: a Space Odyssey* (1968) which, under the direction of Stanley Kubrick, became a highly successful film. Later works include the sequels to *2001, 2010: Space Odyssey II* (1982, film 1984), *2062: Odyssey III* (1988), and *3001: the Final Odyssey* (1997). He emigrated to Sri Lanka in the 1950s.

Clarke, Jeremiah (c.1674–1707) Composer, probably born in London. The real composer of the Trumpet Voluntary long attributed to Purcell, Clarke wrote theatre music, religious and secular choral works, and music for the harpsichord.

Clarke, Kenneth (1940–) British statesman, born in Nottingham, Nottinghamshire. He became a Conservative MP in 1970, and was appointed secretary of state for health (1988), home secretary under John Major (1992), and Chancellor of the Exchequer (1993–7). He failed in his bids for leadership of the party, in 1997 against William Hague and in 2001 against Ian Duncan Smith. In 2005 he launched his third bid, to succeed Michael Howard, but was eliminated in the first round.

clarkia An annual native to western North America and Chile; flowers in spikes, 4-petalled, white, pink, or violet; cultivated as ornamentals. (Genus: *Clarkia*, 36 species. Family: Onagraceae.)

Clarkson, Jeremy (Charles Robert) (1960–) Journalist and television presenter, born in Doncaster, South Yorkshire. He joined the BBC as presenter on *Top Gear* (1989–1998) and *Jeremy Clarkson's Motorworld* (1995–). He is a regular columnist for leading newspapers and for *Top Gear* magazine, which he founded in 1993, and in 2002 returned as presenter of a new-look *Top Gear*. His publications include *The World According to Clarkson* (2004) and its sequel, *And Another Thing ...* (2006).

class A set or group of people sharing the same socio-economic position. A **class society** is a system of social inequality based on the unequal distribution of income and wealth between different classes.

classical music Music which is part of a long written tradition, which lends itself to sophisticated study and analysis in conservatories and universities, and which is heard in concert halls, opera houses, and churches (rather than in dance halls, public houses, and discotheques). These days, the distinction between classical music on the one hand and folk music, light music, jazz, pop, etc on the other is felt to be largely unnecessary, and even injurious.

classicism An adherence, in any period, to the standards of Greek and Roman art, traditionally understood in terms of 'correct' proportions of the figure, dignified poses and gestures (as in Raphael, Poussin), but also powerful expression of feeling (as in Donatello, David). In Western art the pendulum seems to swing between classical and non-classical (eg Gothic, Mannerist, Baroque, Romantic), although in certain periods a tension between the two is maintained. In literature, classicism is associated especially with Latin poets such as Horace and Virgil. It implies the skilful imitation and adaptation of permanent forms and themes, rather than new departures and 'originality'.

Claude Lorrain [klohd], originally **Claude Gellée** (1600–82) Landscape painter, born in Lorraine, France. He painted about 400 landscapes, including several with biblical or Classical themes, such as 'The Sermon on the Mount' (1656, New York). He also produced many drawings and etchings.

Claudianus, Claudius [klawdius] (340–410) The last of the great Latin poets, born in Alexandria, Egypt. Several of his works have survived, notably his epic poem *De raptu Proserpinae* (The Rape of Proserpine), the work for which he was famed in the Middle Ages.

Claudius [klawdius], in full **Tiberius Claudius Caesar Augustus Germanicus** (10 BC–AD 54) Roman emperor (41–54), the grandson of the Empress Livia, brother of Germanicus, and nephew of the Emperor Tiberius. Kept in the background because of his physical disabilities, he devoted himself to historical studies, and thus survived the vicious in-fighting of the imperial house. Through his lavish public works and administrative reforms, he made a lasting contribution to the government of Rome and the empire, and through the annexation of Britain, Mauretania, and Thrace, a significant extension of its size.

Clause Four *New Labour*

Clausewitz, Karl (Philip Gottlieb) von [klowzevits] (1780–1831) General, born in Burg, Germany. His posthumously published *Vom Kriege* (1833, On War), advocating a policy of total war, revolutionized military theory.

Clausius, Rudolf (Julius Emanuel) [klowzius] (1822–88) Physicist, born in Koszalin, NW Poland (formerly Köslin, Germany). He formulated the second law of thermodynamics, and was influential in establishing thermodynamics as a science.

clavichord A keyboard instrument used from the 15th-c to the late 18th-c and revived in recent times, mainly for performing early music. The keys, when depressed, cause metal tangents to strike the strings, which run at right angles to the keys and are tuned in pairs.

clavicle The curved bone, also known as the **collar bone**, lying almost horizontally at the base of the neck between the breastbone (*sternum*) and the shoulder blade (*scapula*); part of the pectoral girdle.

Clay, Cassius *Ali, Muhammad*

Clay, Henry (1777–1852) US statesman and orator, born in Hanover Co, VA. He was active in bringing on the war of 1812–15 with Britain. He made several attempts to hold the Union together in the face of the issue of slavery, for which he earned the title of 'the great pacificator'.

clay A fine-grained sedimentary deposit composed mainly of clay minerals with some quartz, feldspar, and gypsum. Wet clay can be shaped into bricks, pottery, or sculpture, and when fired forms a durable solid. Clay-rich soils are characteristically sticky, with poor drainage when wet, or cracked and hard when dry.

clay minerals Hydrous sheet silicates which form fine, flaky crystals, and which can absorb water, giving clay its characteristic plasticity when wet. They are formed as the product of the weathering of rocks, and are often deposited by rivers. They are used as fillers for paper, rubber, and paint.

claymore (Gael 'great sword') A large, double-edged sword used by Scottish Highlanders in the 17th-c. It had a broad, flat blade, and was wielded with both hands. An 18th-c development was a single-edged broadsword with a basket hilt.

clay-pigeon shooting A pastime and sport in which clay targets are released into the air using an automatic machine, and are fired at with shotguns. It is also known as **trap shooting**.

clay tokens Small clay artifacts of several distinctive shapes, used in the Middle East since at least the 9th millennium BC as a system of accounting. Some of the symbols used on the earliest known writing tablets from the same area (c.3500 BC) show a striking resemblance in shape to those of the clay tokens.

Clayton, Adam *U2*

Clayton, Lisa (1959–) Yachtswoman, born in Birmingham, West Midlands. In 1995 she became the first British woman to circumnavigate the globe, in a single, unaided, continuous journey. Her voyage, in a 39 ft sloop, *Spirit of Birmingham*, took 285 days.

Cleanthes [kleeantheez] (c.331–232 BC) Greek Stoic philosopher, born in Assos, Troas. He studied under Zeno of Citium, and succeeded him as head of the Stoa in 262. His own contributions to Stoicism were especially in the areas of theology and cosmology.

clearing house In economics, any institution whose function is to co-ordinate and settle the debts owed by its various members; in particular, a place where cheques from different banks are sorted, and the amounts owed by and to each bank are calculated. Since 1984, the process has been mainly automated in the UK through the Clearing House Associated Payments System (CHAPS). In the USA, the equivalent organization is the Clearing House Interbank Payments System (CHIPS).

cleavage The process by which a fertilized egg cell (*zygote*) divides to give rise to all the cells of an organism. The *deuterostomes*, which include vertebrates and echinoderms, display radial cleavage. The *protostomes*, which include molluscs and arthropods, display spiral cleavage.

cleavers *goosegrass*

Cledwyn (of Penrhos), Cledwyn Hughes, Baron [kledwin] (1916–2001) British statesman, born in Holyhead, Anglesey. A solicitor, he was elected Labour MP for Anglesey (1951–79), becoming minister of state for the Commonwealth (1964–6), secretary of state for Wales (1966–8), and minister of agriculture, fisheries and food (1968–70). He later served as leader of the Opposition in the Lords (1982–92). He was made a life peer in 1979.

Cleese, John (Marwood) [kleez] (1939–) Comic actor and writer, born in Weston-super-Mare, Somerset. He became well known through his performances in TV's *Monty Python's Flying Circus* (1969–74), and enjoyed great success as the co-writer and star of the series *Fawlty Towers* (1975, 1979). His feature films include *A Fish Called Wanda* (1988), *Fierce Creatures* (1997), *The World is Not Enough* (1999), and *Around the World in 80 Days* (2004). He also founded Video Arts Ltd, producing industrial training films.

cleft lip and palate A congenital abnormality of development of the lips and palate, occurring in about 1 in 1000 live births. It consists of a fissure or cleft on one or both sides of the upper lip, occurring either alone or associated with a cleft in the palate.

Cleisthenes [kliystheneez] (6th-c BC) Prominent Athenian politician of the Alcmaeonid family, and through his constitutional reforms (c.508 BC) the founder of Athenian democracy.

Cleland, John [klayland] (1709–89) Novelist, born in London. He published in 1750 *Fanny Hill, or the Memoirs of a Woman of Pleasure*. A best-seller in its time, it achieved a second *succès de scandale* on its revival and prosecution under the Obscene Publications Act in 1963.

clematis [klemaytis] A member of a genus of woody climbers native throughout temperate regions; stalk sensitive on the lower side, acting as a tendril and bending around supports on contact; flowers with four petaloid segments, styles long and feathery. (Genus: *Clematis*, 250 species. Family: Ranunculaceae.)

Clemenceau, Georges [klemãsoh] (1841–1929) French statesman and prime minister (1906–9, 1917–20), born in Mouilleron-en-Pareds, France. He was a leader of the extreme left in the Chamber of Deputies. Known as 'the tiger', he presided at the Versailles Peace Conference in 1919, showing an intransigent hatred of Germany.

Clemens, Samuel Langhorne *Twain, Mark*

Clement I, St, known as **Clemens Romanus** or **Clement of Rome** (late 1st-c) One of the apostolic Fathers, reckoned variously as the second or third successor of St Peter at Rome, possibly 88–97 or 92–101. The first of two epistles attributed to him is generally accepted as his (written c.96). Feast day 23 November.

Clement VII, originally **Giulio de' Medici** (1478–1534) Pope (1523–34), born in Florence, Italy. He allied himself with Francis I of France against the Holy Roman Emperor Charles V. His refusal to sanction Henry VIII's divorce from Catherine of Aragon hastened the Reformation.

Clement of Alexandria, St, Lat **Clemens Alexandrinus** (c.150–c.215) Theologian and Father of the early Church, probably born in Athens. He became head of the celebrated Catechetical school at Alexandria, where he related Greek philosophical thought to Christian belief. Feast day 5 December.

Clementi, Muzio [klementee] (1752–1832) Composer and pianist, born in Rome. In 1817–26 he wrote the *Gradus ad Parnassum*, on which subsequent piano methods have been based.

Cleon [kleeon] (?–422 BC) The first Athenian of rich, bourgeois stock to play a prominent role in 5th-c BC politics. His capture of the Spartans on the island of Sphacteria (425 BC) gave Athens her trump card in the peace negotiations of the late 420s BC.

Cleopatra VII (69–30 BC) Queen of Egypt (51–48 BC, 47–30 BC), the daughter of Ptolemy Auletes. A woman of great intelligence, she made the most of her physical charms to strengthen her own position within Egypt, and to save the country from annexation by Rome. Thus, Julius Caesar, to whom she bore a son Caesarion, supported her claim to the throne against her brother (47 BC), while Antony, by whom she had three children, restored to her several portions of the old Ptolemaic Empire, and even gave to their joint offspring substantial areas of the Roman East (34 BC). Defeated along with Antony at Actium (31 BC), she committed suicide.

clergy *abbey; archbishop; archdeacon; bishop; canon* **3**; *cardinal* (religion); *curate; deacon; dean; priest; rector; vicar*

Clerk Maxwell, James *Maxwell, James*

Clermont-Ferrand [klairmõ ferã] 45°46N 3°04E, pop (2000e) 142 000. City in C France; capital of Auvergne, 16th-c; Clermont merged with Montferrand, 1630; geographical and economic centre of the Massif Central; railway; bishopric; university (1896); cathedral (begun 1248); birthplace of Pascal.

Cleveland (UK) [kleevland] pop (2000e) 567 600; area 583 km²/225 sq mi. Former county of NE England; created in 1974 from parts of Yorkshire and Durham; replaced in 1996 by Hartlepool, Redcar and Cleveland, Middlesbrough, and Stockton-on-Tees unitary authorities.

Cleveland (USA) [kleevland] 41°30N 81°42W, pop (2000e) 478 400. Port on L Erie, NE Ohio, USA; city status, 1836; largest city in Ohio; airfield; railway; three universities (1826, 1886, 1923); medical research centre; professional teams, Indians (baseball), Cavaliers (basketball), Browns (football).

Cleveland, (Stephen) Grover (1837–1908) US statesman and the 22nd and 24th president (1885–9, 1893–7), born in Caldwell, NJ. In 1895 he caused worldwide excitement by applying the Monroe Doctrine to Britain's dispute with Venezuela.

Cleveland bay One of the oldest English breeds of horse; height, 15–16 hands/1·5–1·6 m/5 ft–5 ft 4 in; reddish-brown with long body, shortish legs, muscular hindquarters; also known as the **Chapman horse**.

Cleveland Way Long-distance footpath in North Yorkshire, England; length c.150 km/90 mi; stretches from Helmsley to near Filey.

Clewlow, Warren (Alexander Morten) (1936–) Businessman, born in KwaZulu Natal, South Africa. He became executive chairman of the Barlow Rand Group of Companies (now Barloworld), South Africa's largest industrial corporation. He is also chairman of the State President's Economic Advisory Council, and president of the South Africa Foundation.

click beetle An elongate, usually dark-coloured beetle; an adult lying on its back can right itself with a jack-knifing movement that produces a loud click; can be serious crop pests, known as **wireworms**. (Order: Coleoptera. Family: Elateridae.)

cliff dwellings Houses of the Pueblo Indians in SW USA from the Pueblo III cultural period (AD c.1100–1300). Made with stone blocks and adobe mortar, some were several storeys high, and built in arched recesses of cliff walls.

Clijsters, Kim [kliysterz] (1983–) Tennis player, born in Bilzen, Belgium. At age 15, she became the youngest national A champion. A professional from 1998, by the end of 2003 she had won 19 titles, including the Australian Open and French Open (2000). Further achievements include the Paris Open (2004) and US Open (2005), and she began 2007 ranked world number 5.

climacteric *menopause*

climate The long-term prevailing weather conditions in a region or place. The climate of a place is influenced by several factors. Latitude determines the amount of solar radiation received, with the greatest in equatorial regions. Elevation affects both temperature and precipitation; mountainous areas are generally cooler and wetter. Location close to the sea or large bodies of water moderates temperature. Aspect is of local importance; in the N hemisphere, S- and W-facing slopes are warmer than N- and E-facing slopes. The scientific study of climate, describing and attempting to explain climatic differences from place to place, is known as **climatology**.

climbing plant A plant which reaches towards the light by clinging to neighbouring plants, walls, or other supports, sometimes referred to by the general term **vine**. Various means are used, including twining stems and leaf-stalks, tendrils, and aerial roots. **Ramblers** merely grow against and lean on their supports, but often have thorny hooks to help grip. **Lianes** have long, woody stems which reach high into the forest canopy, and are found especially in the tropics.

clinical psychology The application of psychological knowledge to the assessment, prevention, and treatment of a variety of psychological disorders, involving behavioural, emotional, or cognitive disturbances.

clinometer A hand-held surveying instrument, also known as an **Abney level**. It is used to measure the angles of a slope by bringing a level-bubble on a graduated circle into coincidence with a wire in a sighting tube.

Clinton, Bill, popular name of **William Jefferson Clinton**, born **William Jefferson Blythe** (1946–) US statesman and 42nd president (1993–2000), born in Hope, AR. He trained as a lawyer, becoming attorney general (1977–9), then governor of AR (1979–81, 1983–93). Overcoming serious charges concerning extramarital affairs and questions about his draft deferment during the Vietnam War, he became the first Democratic Party candidate to win a presidential election since 1976, defeating George Bush. He was elected for a second term in 1996, defeating Bob Dole.

In 1997, media attention was taken up by a civil suit against Clinton by Paula Jones, a former Arkansas state employee, who alleged sexual harassment by him in 1991. During the enquiries, a fresh series of allegations emerged concerning Monica Lewinsky, a White House intern with whom Clinton was alleged to have had a sexual relationship. Allegations that he had committed perjury by denying the affair, and had attempted to suborn a witness, raised the issue of his resignation or impeachment. Whitewater investigator Kenneth Starr was authorized to extend his investigations, which lasted throughout 1998. However, strong support from Hillary Clinton, suggestions of a right-wing conspiracy to discredit the president, criticism of the motives and tactics of Starr (a Republican), and growing feeling among the US public that the president's private and public lives were separate, led to his continuing to receive strong popular support. Despite a campaign of personal public apology, the release of the Starr report led to the establishment of a House of Representatives judiciary committee, which voted for impeachment. A Senate trial took place in 1999, but Clinton was acquitted.

Despite the controversy surrounding his personal life, Clinton governed from the centre of US politics. His economic policies helped produce a balanced budget, he joined Republicans in reforming the welfare system, and saw a reduction in the crime rate during his presidency. Sustained prosperity helped maintain his job ratings at a high level during his second term. His presidency was marked by a notable international profile, including intervention in Haiti, the Middle East, and Northern Ireland. He maintained the existing policy towards Iraq, and oversaw the expansion of the North Atlantic Treaty Organization (NATO) into Eastern Europe. His historical reputation will depend on how his personal life is viewed in the perspective of his political career. An autobiography, *My Life*, appeared in 2004.

In 2002 he set up the charitable Clinton Foundation to work on issues including AIDS, poverty, women's empowerment, and religious and racial reconciliation. He was appointed the United Nations' special envoy for tsunami relief in Asia in 2005.

Clinton, Hillary (Rodham) (1947–) Lawyer and US first lady (1993–2000), born in Park Ridge, IL. She married fellow law graduate Bill Clinton in 1975, and emerged as a dynamic and valued partner of her husband amid the allegations of extramarital affairs which surfaced during his 1992 presidential nomination campaign. She performed an active political role following his election, heading a task force on national health reform in 1993. Her defence of her husband during the Lewinsky affair was widely admired, and her personal political presence was greatly enhanced following her effective role supporting Democratic candidates during the mid-term elections in November 1998. In 2000 she won a senate seat representing New York state, and in 2007 she announced her bid to run for Democratic candidate in the 2008 presidential elections. A volume of memoirs, *Living History*, appeared in 2003.

Clio [kliyoh] In Greek mythology, the Muse of history, and of lyre-playing.

clipper ship A mid-19th-c revolutionary US design of sailing ship. Its principal features were finer bow and stern lines, greater rake to the masts, and greater beam than in traditional vessels, resulting in faster ships with improved windward performance.

clitoris [klitoris] Part of the female external genitalia, composed of erectile tissue partly surrounded by muscle. It is the equivalent of the male penis (though it does not convey the urethra), and enlarges upon tactile stimulation.

Clive (of Plassey), Robert Clive, Baron (1725–74) Soldier and adminstrator in India, born in Styche, Shropshire. In January 1757 he recaptured Calcutta from the Nawab, and at Plassey on the 23 June defeated a large Indian–French force. For three years he was sole ruler in all but name of Bengal. In Calcutta he effectively reformed the civil service, and re-established military discipline.

cloaca [klohayka] The terminal region of the gut into which the alimentary canal, urinary system, and reproductive system all open and discharge their products via a single common aperture.

clock A mechanism for measuring and indicating the passage of time, and for recording the duration of intervals. Its essential elements are a source of energy to drive the mechanism, and a device to maintain a regular (usually stepwise) rate of motion. The first clockwork escapement was Chinese, AD 724, and water-powered clocks are noted in China from the 760s. In mediaeval and many later clocks, the drive was a falling weight; from the 16th-c, it was the coiled mainspring; and from the late 19th-c, it was electric current from batteries or mains. From c.1670 a balance wheel was used for small clocks and watches. In modern times, clocks are powered by electric synchronous motors maintained by the mains frequency, by a maintained tuning fork, or by the oscillation of a quartz crystal.

Clodion [klodyō], pseudonym of **Claude Michel** (1738–1814) Sculptor, born in Nancy, France. One of the most brilliant Rococo sculptors, he specialized in small terracottas and low reliefs of erotic dancing nymphs and satyrs.

cloisonné [klwazonay] A method of enamelling on metal, and occasionally ceramic, in which the different fields of colour are separated by metal wires soldered to the surface to be decorated. Principally an oriental technique, it was much used in Byzantine and Mediaeval art.

cloisters Covered walkways around an open space or court, with a colonnade or arcaded inner side and a solid outer wall. Cloisters are used in a monastery or convent to connect the church to other parts of the building.

cloning (genetics) The process of asexual reproduction observed, for example, in bacteria and other unicellular micro-organisms which divide by simple fission, so that the daughter cells are genetically identical to each other and to the parent (except when mutation occurs). In higher organisms, genetically identical individuals may be produced by cloning. A body (*somatic*) cell is taken from an embryo in an early stage of development or from an adult, the nucleus transferred to an unfertilized ovum from which the nucleus has been removed, and the product grown in culture; daughter cells from the earliest divisions are removed, and grown in culture or implanted into host mothers to give genetically identical offspring. The successful cloning of a sheep (named Dolly, 1996–2003) was reported by scientists from the Roslin Institute, Edinburgh, UK, in February 1997. There is considerable potential application in animal rearing, but its application to humans is extremely unlikely (except in some rare instances of *in vitro* fertilization). The term *molecular cloning* is used in recombinant DNA technology, where a section of foreign DNA is inserted into an artificial bacterial chromosome (plasmid) and divides with it, thus 'cloning' the DNA. In 1998, a Council of Europe protocol banning the cloning of human beings was signed in Paris by 19 states – the first international treaty on the issue. However, in 1999, predictions were being made about the application of the technique in other areas, such as bone-marrow grafting in leukaemia, and transplant medicine in general, and the controversy surrounding the ethics of human cloning continued to exercise professional and public opinion. In 2004, Newcastle University received Britain's first licence to clone human embryos.

Clonmel [klonmel], Ir **Cluain Meala** 52°21N 7°42W, pop (2000e) 15 700. Capital of Tipperary county, S Ireland; centre of Irish greyhound racing and salmon fishing; railway.

Clooney, George (1961–) Actor and director, born in Lexington, KY. He became well-known for his role as Dr Doug Ross in the TV series *ER* (1994–9), and his film credits include *Batman and Robin* (1997), *O Brother, Where Art Thou?* (2000, Best Comedy Actor Golden Globe), *Ocean's Twelve* (2004), and *Syriana* (2005, Best Supporting Actor Oscar and Golden Globe). He directed and appeared in *Confessions of a Dangerous Mind* (2003) and *Good Night, and Good Luck* (2005, Oscar nomination).

closed circuit television (CCTV) Any system of image presentation in which a video camera and its display screen are directly linked, even at a considerable distance, rather than by broadcast transmission or intermediate recording. Applications include surveillance, surgical and scientific demonstration, and industrial remote examination.

closed shop A company or works where some grades of worker are required to belong to a recognized trade union; the opposite situation is known as an **open shop**. Unions prefer the closed shop, as it gives them more members, and gives their members a better chance of getting any available jobs. Employers accept the closed shop for the sake of industrial peace, though they know it weakens their bargaining position in the event of an industrial dispute. Closed shops are banned in many US states.

Clostridium A genus of rod-shaped bacteria that are typically motile by means of flagella, and produce spores (*endospores*). They are widespread in the soil and in the intestinal tract of humans and other animals. The genus includes the causative

agents of botulism, gas gangrene, and tetanus. (Kingdom: Monera. Family: Bacillaceae.)

Clotho *Moerae*

cloud A visible collection of particles of ice and water held in suspension above the ground. Clouds form when air becomes saturated and water vapour condenses around nuclei of dust, smoke particles, and salt. Four main categories of clouds are recognized: **nimbus clouds**, which produce rain; **stratus clouds**, which resemble layers; **cumulus clouds**, which resemble heaps; and **cirrus clouds**, which resemble strands or filaments of hair. These names are further modified by an indication of cloud height: *strato* – low level clouds; *alto* – middle level clouds; *cirro* – high level clouds. Fog can be considered as cloud close to ground level.

cloud chamber A device for detecting subatomic particles; invented by Charles Wilson in 1912. It comprises a chamber containing vapour prone to condensing to liquid. The passage of particles forms ions, which act as centres for condensation, and the particle paths become visible as trails of mist. The device has been superseded by other particle detectors.

clouded tiger *tortoiseshell cat*

Clough, Arthur Hugh [kluhf] (1819–61) Poet, born in Liverpool, Merseyside. His works include *The Bothie* (1848) and *Amours de Voyage* (1849). His best-known poem, beginning 'Say not the struggle nought availeth', was published posthumously in 1862.

clover A low-growing annual or perennial, occurring in both temperate and subtropical regions, but mainly in the N hemisphere; leaves with three toothed leaflets; small pea-flowers, white, pink, or red, clustered into often dense, rounded heads. Several species are extensively grown as fodder for cattle, and they are also valuable pasture plants. Yellow-flowered species are generally called **trefoils**. (Genus: *Trifolium*, 250 species. Family: Leguminosae.)

clove tree An evergreen tree growing to 12 m/40 ft, native to Indonesia; flowers yellow, 4-petalled, in terminal clusters. The flower buds are dried to form the spice cloves. (*Syzygium aromaticum*. Family: Myrtaceae.)

Clovis [klohvis] The earliest identifiable Indian culture of North America; hunter-gatherers exploiting the mammoth herds of the plains towards the end of the last glaciation, c.10 000–9000 BC. It is characterized archaeologically by bifacially-flaked spear points found across the USA, notably near Clovis, NM, in 1963.

club foot A congenital deformity of one or both feet, in which the child cannot stand on the sole of the affected foot. The sole of the foot is turned inwards. Improvement may be achieved by the application of a series of graded splints, or in severe cases by surgical operation.

clubmoss A spore-bearing plant related to ferns and horsetails; stem long, regularly branched, clothed with numerous small leaves. It is found almost everywhere, many in heathland or similar habitats. (Genus: *Lycopodium*, 450 species. Family: Lycopodiaceae.)

clubroot A disease of cabbage-family plants (the Brassicaceae) that causes gall-like swellings of roots and discoloration of leaves; caused by the parasitic slime mould *Plasmodiophora brassicae*.

Cluj-Napoca or **Cluj** [kloozh napoka], Ger **Klausenburg** 46°47N 23°37E, pop (2000e) 323 000. City in NEC Romania, on the R Someş; a former capital of Transylvania; ceded from Hungary, 1920; airfield; railway; university (1872), technical university (1948).

Clune, Frank [kloon], popular name of **Francis Patrick Clune** (1893–1971) Writer of biography, history, and travel, born in Sydney, New South Wales, Australia. He wrote over 60 books, often in collaboration with P R ('Inky') Stephensen, such as *Ben Hall the Bushranger* (1947), and *Wild Colonial Boys* (1948).

Cluny Abbey [klúnee] A Benedictine abbey founded in 910 at Cluny, EC France, known for the monastic reforms it introduced, promoting a stricter observance of the Benedictine rule. The abbey was forced to close in 1790, during the French Revolution.

clustered wax flower *stephanotis; wax plant*

Cluster project A space project undertaken by the European Space Agency (ESA) for launch in 2000 following the destruction of the original Cluster spacecraft on the first Ariane 5 launch in June 1996. Four identical satellites are designed to study the interaction of the solar wind and the Earth's magnetic field.

clutch A mechanical device that allows an engine to be connected and disconnected from its load while the engine is running. The most common application is in the motor car, where normally a plate covered with high friction material is sandwiched and held in place between a disc attached to the engine's flywheel and a disc fixed to the gear-box.

Clutha, River [klootha] Longest river of South Island, New Zealand; length c.320 km/200 mi.

cluttering A disorder of speech fluency, in which the main symptom is excessive rapidity while speaking. The cause is unknown, though a physical explanation in terms of the brain's motor control of speech has been suggested.

Clwyd [klooid] pop (2000e) 422 200; area 2426 km²/937 sq mi. Former county in NE Wales, UK; created in 1974, and replaced in 1996 by the counties of Denbighshire, Flintshire, and Wrexham.

Clyde, Lord *Campbell, Sir Colin*

Clyde, River River in S Scotland; passes through Scotland's most important industrial area, including Glasgow, then expands into the Firth of Clyde estuary leading to the Atlantic Ocean; length 170 km/100 mi; Clyde Arc Bridge in Glasgow opened, 2006.

Clydesdale A breed of horse, produced in Scotland by crossing local mares with large Flemish stallions; a heavy horse, developed in the 18th-c for hauling coal; height c.16·1 hands/1·7 m/5 ft 5 in; reddish-brown with white face and legs.

Clydeside pop (2000e) 1 624 100. Urban area in WC Scotland, focused on the R Clyde; airport; railway; major industrial area of Scotland.

Clytemnestra [kliytemnestra] or **Clytemestra** In Greek legend, the twin sister of Helen and the wife of Agamemnon. She murdered him on his return from Troy, assisted by her lover, Aegisthus. She was killed in revenge by her son, Orestes.

CND An acronym of the **Campaign for Nuclear Disarmament**, a mass organization founded in the UK in 1958 to mobilize public opinion against the nuclear-weapons programme and for unilateral disarmament. It organized peaceful mass marches between London and Aldermaston, where the Atomic Weapons Research Establishment was based, and was successful in securing acceptance of a resolution at the 1960 Labour Party Conference for Britain's unilateral disarmament. During the 1980s it underwent a revival, as concern over the proliferation of nuclear weapons grew. However, following disarmament agreements between the USA and USSR, the organization became less prominent.

Cnidaria [nidaria] *coelenterate*

CNS *central nervous system*

C N Tower or **Canadian National Tower** The world's tallest self-supporting tower, erected in Toronto, Ontario, Canada (1973–5); 555·3 m/1822 ft high.

Cnut *Canute*

coal A black or brown sedimentary rock found in beds or seams, and formed by heat and pressure over millions of years on vegetation accumulated in shallow swamps. Successive stages in the formation of coal involve an increase in carbon content or 'rank': **peat** is the first stage, followed by **lignite** or **brown coal** (60–70% carbon), **bituminous coal** (more than 80% carbon), and **anthracite** (more than 90% carbon).

coalfish *saithe*

coalition An inter-party arrangement established to pursue a common goal, most obviously government. Coalition governments are relatively common in electoral systems using proportional representation and/or in multiparty systems. The nature of the coalition is defined by those parties with seats in the cabinet.

coal mining Extracting coal from beneath the ground. In **opencast mining**, the coal is near the surface: the overburden is stripped away, the coal removed, and the overburden restored for environmental conservation. In **drift mining**, the coal lies within a slope: a horizontal tunnel is driven into the side of the slope, and the coal removed on level railways or conveyors. **Deep mining** relies on vertical shafts with horizontal approaches to the seams. Coal is dug (mainly now by mechanical means) and removed by conveyors to the shaft bottom for haulage to the surface. Reserves are estimated at around 1 million million tonnes. World production in 2005 was c.4970 million tonnes.

Coalsack The finest visual example of an obscuring cloud of dust in space, 180 parsec away. It is in the constellation Crux, where it causes a gaping hole in the Milky Way.

coal tar A volatile by-product of heating coal in the absence of air to form coke; a black viscous liquid consisting of a complex mixture of organic compounds. Further distillation of coal tar produces a large number of chemicals which form the basis of explosives, dyes, and drugs.

Coastal Command A separate functional Command within the British Royal Air Force (1936–69). During World War 2, it played a decisive role in winning the Battle of the Atlantic.

coastguard An institution whose duty is to keep watch on the coastline and organize rescue and lifeboat services to help those in trouble. The nature of these services varies widely; some nations use their naval forces, whereas others operate through voluntary organizations. The largest service is the US Coastguard, responsible for search and rescue, lighthouses and lightships, pilotage, fishery protection, security at ports, enforcement of maritime legislation, and oceanography.

Coast Range Mountain belt in W North America, extending along the coast of the Pacific Ocean from Alaska to Mexico Mts; highest point, Mt Logan (5950 m/19 521 ft).

coast redwood A massive evergreen conifer (*Sequoia sempervirens*), the tallest tree in the world at over 100 m/325 ft high and 8 m/26 ft thick; bark almost 1 m/3¼ ft thick, reddish, fibrous, spongy. It is now confined to the misty bottomlands of coastal California and SW Oregon. (Family: Taxodiaceae.)

Coates, Eric (1886–1957) Composer, born in Hucknall, Nottinghamshire. Among his best-known compositions are 'London Suite' (1933) and 'The Three Elizabeths' (1944), and a number of popular waltzes, marches, and other melodies, such as 'By the Sleepy Lagoon' (1930) (which became the signature tune for the BBC radio programme 'Desert Island Discs' for over fifty years), and 'The Dambusters March' (1954).

coati [kohahtee] A raccoon-like mammal, found from S USA to South America; reddish-brown; long banded tail; long narrow muzzle with overhanging tip; solitary males called *coatimundis* (or *koatimundis*). (Genus: *Nasua*, 2 species. Family: Procyonidae.)

coat of arms *heraldry*

coat-of-mail shell *chiton*

coaxial cable A form of electrical wiring with relatively low loss which is used in the home as a connector from a television aerial to the television set. In computer systems it is the standard form of inter-connection wiring for local area networks, and in many computer networks by unshielded twisted pair (UTP) cabling.

cob A type of horse, often produced when crossing a heavy carthorse with a racehorse; height, 14·2–15·2 hands/1·5–1·6 m/4 ft 10 in–5 ft 2 in; short deep body; calm natured; also known as **rouncy** or **roncey**.

cobalt Co, element 27, density 9 g/cm³, melting point 1495°C. A hard metal, which occurs in ores as its sulphide (CoS), along with copper and nickel. It is used mainly as a metal in steel alloys, especially for permanent magnets.

Cobb, Ty(rus Raymond), nickname **the Georgia Peach** (1886–1961) Baseball player, born in Narrows, GA. An outstanding base runner and batter, in a 23-year career with Detroit and Philadelphia he hit over 4000 base hits, a record which survived 57 years until broken in 1985.

Cobbett, William (1763–1835) Journalist and social reformer, born in Farnham, Surrey. He started his famous *Weekly Political Register* in 1802, changing in 1804 from its original Toryism to an uncompromising Radicalism. His works include a *History of the Protestant Reformation* (1824–7) and *Rural Rides* (1830).

Cobden, Richard (1804–65) Economist and politician, 'the apostle of free trade', born in Heyshott, West Sussex. In 1838 he helped to found the Anti-Corn-Law League, becoming its most prominent member. His speeches focused opinion on the Corn Laws, which were repealed in 1846.

Coblenz *Koblenz*

COBOL [kohbol] An acronym of **COmmon Business Orientated Language**, a high-level computer language widely used in the business community. It uses statements written in English which are relatively easy to understand.

cobra A venomous snake, native to S Asia and Africa; neck has loose folds of skin which can be spread as a 'hood' when alarmed; fangs short; venom attacks the nervous system; usually inhabits forests, but also open country. (Family: Elapidae, many species, most in genus *Naja*.)

cocaine C₁₇H₂₁NO₄, melting point 98°C. A white alkaloid extracted from the leaves of the South American shrub *Erythroxylon coca*, and used for its stimulant properties, similar to those of amphetamine. It is widely abused; the powder is sniffed and the purified form can be smoked (*freebasing*). It causes addiction, particularly when freebased. Street names include 'Charlie', and 'charge'.

coccus Any spherical bacterium. It varies in size, and may occur in chains, clusters, or other groupings. Examples are *Staphylococcus* and *Streptococcus*.

coccyx [koksiks] The lowest part of the vertebral column, forming the tail in many animals. In humans it is small and triangular, comprising three to five rudimentary vertebrae.

Cochabamba [kochabamba] 17°26S 66°10W, pop (2000e) 517 000. City in C Bolivia; altitude 2500 m/8200 ft; country's third largest city; founded, 1542; airfield; railway; university (1832); important agricultural centre.

Cochin [kochin] 9°55N 76°22E, pop (2000e) 663 000. Naval base and seaport in Kerala, SW India; Portuguese trading station, 1502; Fort Cochin, first European settlement in India; tomb of Vasco da Gama.

cochineal [kochineel] A dye (**carminic acid**) obtained from the dried bodies of a female bug, *Dactylopus coccus*. The bug feeds on cacti, and is native to Peru and Mexico. (Order: Homoptera. Family: Coccidae.)

cockatiel [kokateel] An Australian parrot of the cockatoo family (*Nymphicus hollandicus*); long tapering crest on head; male with colourful facial markings. (Family: Cacatuidae.)

cockatoo An Australasian parrot, separated from other parrots

mainly by features of its skull, and in having an erectile crest of feathers on the head. (Family: Cacatuidae, 18 species.)

cockatrice *basilisk* (mythology)

cockchafer A large, dark-coloured chafer; adults nocturnal, feeding on leaves; fleshy, C-shaped larvae burrow in ground for 3–4 years, feeding on roots before emerging as flying adults, typically in May, hence alternative name of **maybug**. (Order: Coleoptera. Family: Scarabaeidae.)

Cockcroft, Sir John Douglas (1897–1967) Nuclear physicist, born in Todmorden, West Yorkshire. With E T S Walton (1903–95) he succeeded in disintegrating lithium by proton bombardment in 1932, pioneering the use of particle accelerators, and shared the Nobel Prize for Physics (1951). He became the first director of Britain's Atomic Energy Establishment at Harwell in 1946.

Cockerell, Sir Christopher (Sydney) (1910–99) Engineer, born in Cambridge. He first worked on radio and radar, before turning to hydrodynamics, and in the early 1950s invented the amphibious hovercraft.

cocker spaniel or **American cocker spaniel** A breed of dog, developed in the USA from the **English cocker spaniel**; recognized as a separate breed in 1941; smaller than ancestral stock; longer coat; black or golden brown; popular as pets.

cockfighting A blood sport in which *gamecocks* aged 1–2 years, wearing steel spurs on their legs, were set against each other. It was a popular sport in England until 1849, when it was banned.

cockle A marine bivalve mollusc whose shell comprises two more or less equal valves closed by two adductor muscles; an active burrower in inter-tidal sediments; fished extensively for human consumption. (Class: Pelecypoda. Order: Veneroida.)

cockroach An active, typically nocturnal insect; body depressed; legs long and adapted for running; forewings hard and leathery; hindwings membranous, sometimes lost; will eat almost any organic matter. (Order: Blattaria, c.3700 species.)

cocoa *chocolate*

coco de mer [kohkoh duh **mair**] A species of palm endemic to the Seychelles (*Lodoicea maldavica*). The fruit is one of the largest known, up to 20 kg/45 lb, taking 10 years to ripen; buoyant and often washed ashore, it was well known before the tree itself was discovered. (Family: Palmae.)

coconut palm A tree with a characteristic curved trunk (*Cocos nucifera*), growing to 30 m/100 ft, with feathery leaves up to 6 m/20 ft long; the large, single-seeded fruits (coconuts) have a fibrous outer husk and a hard inner shell enclosing a layer of white flesh and a central cavity filled with milky fluid. Coconut leaves are woven into mats and baskets and are used for thatching; the outer husk of the nuts makes coir, a tough fibre used for matting. Coconut milk is a refreshing drink, and the white flesh is eaten raw or cooked, sold as desiccated coconut, or dried to form copra, the world's principal source of vegetable fat. (Family: Palmae.)

cocoon *pupa*

Cocos Islands [kohkohs] or **Keeling Islands** 12°05S 96°53E, pop (2000e) 780, total land area 14·2 km²/5½ sq mi. Two separate groups of atolls in the Indian Ocean, 3685 km/2290 mi W of Darwin, Australia; an Australian external territory comprising 27 small, flat, palm-covered coral islands; visited in 1609 by William Keeling; first settled 1826, and developed by the Clunies-Ross family; annexed to the British Crown, 1857; granted by Queen Victoria to George Clunies-Ross, 1886; placed under Australian administration as the Territory of Cocos (Keeling) Islands, 1955; Australia purchased Clunies-Ross interests in the islands, 1978; inhabitants voted to be part of Northern Territory, 1984.

Cocteau, Jean [koktoh] (1889–1963) Poet, playwright, and film director, born in Maisons-Lafitte, near Paris. His best-known works include his novel *Les Enfants terribles* (1929, trans Children of the Game), his play *Orphée* (1926, Orpheus), and his film *La Belle et la bête* (1946, Beauty and the Beast).

cod Any of the family Gadidae (15 genera; 100 species) of marine fishes, found mainly in cool temperate shelf waters of N hemisphere; body with 2–3 dorsal and 1–2 anal fins; length up to 120 cm/4 ft; greenish to reddish, freckled, with a pale lateral line; supports very important trawl and net (seine) fisheries.

code A system of rules for matching signs, linguistic or otherwise, which makes communication possible. It may be governed by informal, unwritten conventions (eg body language) or by officially agreed rules (eg some types of sign language), and may be culturally specific or universal in its use. Computer programmers may apply an alphanumeric code, while linguists often view language as a code or set of rules pairing sounds with meaning.

codec Acronym for **coder/decoder**, a device for converting the analogue signals used by audio and video equipment to digital form so that the signals can be sent over digital telecommunications networks. Pulse Code Modulation is used for the conversion.

codeine A painkiller related to morphine that is used for treating mild types of pain (eg headache); it is rarely addictive. It is also used in some cough mixtures, since it inactivates the cough reflex.

Code Napoléon The French Civil Code, introduced (though not devised) by Napoleon Bonaparte as First Consul in 1804, to fill the void left by the abolition of the legal and social customs of pre-revolutionary France. It established the principles of equality between people, liberty of person and contract, and the inviolability of private property. From 1804 to 1810 the Code was introduced into those areas of Europe under direct French control, and is still substantially extant in France, Belgium, Luxembourg, and Monaco today.

cod-liver oil An oil obtained from the fresh liver of the cod and refined. It provides a rich source of vitamins A and D. It is now believed to be protective in heart disease because of its high content of unsaturated fatty acids.

codon [kohdon] The sequence of three nucleotides in DNA or RNA which determine (or 'code for') the particular amino acid to be inserted into a polypeptide chain.

Cody, William F(rederick) [kohdee], known as **Buffalo Bill** (1846–1917) Showman, born in Scott Co, IA. He was known as 'Buffalo Bill' after killing nearly 5000 buffalo in eight months for a contract to supply workers on the Kansas Pacific Railway with meat. He served as a scout in the Sioux wars, but from 1883 toured with his Wild West Show.

Coe (of Ranmore), Sebastian (Newbold) Coe, Lord [koh] (1956–) Athlete, born in London. The world's outstanding middle-distance runner of the 1980s, he broke eight world records altogether, including the mile three times. At the 1980 Olympics he won the gold medal in the 1500 m and the silver in the 800 m, repeating the achievement 4 years later. He retired from running in 1990 and became a Conservative MP in 1992, but lost his seat in the 1997 general election. In 2004 he was appointed the new leader of London's successful campaign to host the 2012 Olympics.

coelacanth *Crossopterygii*

coelenterate [seelenteruht] A simple, multicellular animal with a body plan comprising two primary layers separated by a layer of gelatinous material (*Mesoglea*); most are marine, and all are carnivorous; most exhibit radial symmetry, and possess stinging cells (*nematocysts*) for prey capture and defence. (Phylum: Cnidaria.)

coeliac / celiac disease [seeliak] A disorder of the small intestine, which develops in childhood, caused by a hypersensitivity reaction to gluten, a protein found in wheat and cereals. This damages the lining of the intestine, preventing absorption of nutrients, particularly fats, and leading to retarded growth, anaemia, and the passage of pale bulky stools. A gluten-free diet, maintained for life, will reverse these adverse features.

coelostat / celostat [seeluhstat] A flat mirror driven by a clock mechanism in such a way as to project the same part of the heavens into a fixed telescope. This is particularly used for solar telescopes, as a means of controlling costs.

Coelurus [seeloorus] A lightly built, flesh-eating dinosaur; slender neck and long tail; skull long, with large orbits; two-legged; forelimbs short with three digits, one facing the other two; known from the Upper Jurassic period of Wyoming; formerly known as *Ornitholestes*. (Order: Saurischia.)

Coetzee, J(ohn) M(axwell) [kootzee] (1940–) Novelist and critic, born in Cape Town, South Africa. His novels include *Dusklands* (1974), *In the Heart of the Country* (1977), *Life and Times of Michael K* (1983, Booker), *The Master of Petersburg* (1994), *Disgrace* (1999, Booker), and *Slow Man* (2005). He received the 2003 Nobel Prize for Literature.

coffee An evergreen shrub; flowers white, fragrant, 5-petalled; cherry-like fruits, red, fleshy, containing two seeds (the coffee beans) rich in caffeine. **Arabian coffee** (*Coffea arabica*) is native to Ethiopia, and was introduced first to Arabia, later the E Indies, W Indies, South America, and Africa. The major world producer is now Brazil, where in 2004 scientists mapped the plant's genome anticipating the production of higher quality coffee beans. (Genus: *Coffea*, 40 species. Family: Rubiaceae.)

cofferdam A temporary structure designed to keep water or soft ground from flowing into a site when building foundations. A cofferdam usually consists of a dam or sheet piling.

cognitive science The formal study of mind, in which models and theories originating in artificial intelligence (AI) and in the human sciences (particularly cognitive psychology, linguistics, and philosophy) are subject to interdisciplinary development. The dominant partner in this enterprise is often the AI scientist, since the major criterion for success is usually whether a program can be written and successfully implemented on a computer.

Cohen, William S (1940–) US statesman and writer, born in Bangor, ME. He became Republican senator for Maine in 1973, serving three terms before retiring in 1996. He was appointed secretary of defense (1997–2001), following Clinton's election promise to appoint a Republican to his cabinet.

Cohen-Tannoudji, Claude [kohī tanoojee] (1933–) Physicist, born in Constantine, Algeria. He graduated in 1962 from the Ecole Normale Supérieure, Paris, where he went on to work. In 1997 he shared the Nobel Prize for Physics for his contribution to the development of methods to cool and trap atoms with laser light.

cohort study A scientific method used in medicine to determine the cause of a disease. A group of people exposed to a suspected risk factor is followed up over time and compared to a group not exposed, to determine whether there is a statistically significant difference in the proportion of each group that develop the disease under investigation.

Coimbatore [kohimbataw(r)] 11°00N 76°57E, pop (2000e) 1 002 000. City in Tamil Nadu, S India; stronghold of successive Tamil kingdoms, 9th–17th-c; ceded to Britain, 1799; airfield; railway; university (1971); agricultural centre.

Coimbra [kweembra], ancient **Conimbriga** 40°12N 8°25W, pop (2000e) 95 000. City in C Portugal; former capital of Portugal, 12th–13th-c; oldest university in Portugal (founded at Lisbon in 1290, transferred here in 1537); bishopric; two cathedrals.

Coke, Sir Edward [kook], commonly called **Lord Coke of Cooke** (1552–1634) Jurist, born in Mileham, Norfolk. He brutally prosecuted Essex, Raleigh, and the Gunpowder conspirators, but after 1606 stood forth as a vindicator of national liberties against the royal prerogative. The Petition of Right (1628) was largely his doing.

Coke, Thomas William *Leicester of Holkham, Thomas William Coke*

coke A form of charcoal made by heating coal to over 1000°C in the absence of air to remove the volatile constituents. It is a brittle, porous substance consisting mainly of carbon, and used mainly in steelmaking for fuelling blast furnaces.

cola *kola*

Colbert, Claudette [kolbair], originally **Lily Claudette Chauchoin** (1903–96) Film actress, born in Paris. She started in films with spirited comedy roles, becoming a star with *It Happened One Night* (1934, Oscar). On the stage her career continued into the 1980s.

Colbert, Jean Baptiste [kolbair] (1619–83) French statesman, born in Reims, France. In 1651 he entered the service of Mazarin, and in 1661 became the chief financial minister of Louis XIV. He introduced a series of successful reforms, reorganized the colonies, improved the civil code, and introduced a marine code. However, his successes were undone by wars and court extravagance.

Colchester, Lat **Camulodunum**, Anglo-Saxon **Colneceaster** 51°54N 0°54E, pop (2001e) 155 800. Town in Essex, SE England; railway; university (1961); claimed to be the oldest town in England, founded by Cunobelinus AD c.10; castle (12th-c); football league team, Colchester United ('U's).

colchicine [kolchiseen] A drug, effective against gout, extracted from the corm and seeds of the meadow saffron, *Colchicum autumnale* ('autumn crocus'), so called because it is native to Colchis on the Black Sea.

cold An infection of the upper respiratory tract caused by several different viruses, usually a rhinovirus; also known as the **common cold** or **coryza** [koriyza]. It is characterized by a sore throat, and profuse nasal secretions.

cold-bloodedness *poikilotherm*

cold front A meteorological term for the leading edge of a parcel of cold or polar air. In a depression, the passage of a cold front is often preceded by heavy rainfall, and as it passes there is a sharp fall in temperature.

cold fusion Nuclear fusion occurring at room temperature. In March 1989, US chemist Stanley Pons and British chemist Martin Fleischmann claimed to have observed nuclear fusion in an electrolytic cell comprising platinum and titanium electrodes in heavy water. Their claims are now known to be false. The way in which Pons and Fleischmann announced their results to the media so soon, the lack of independent checking by other experimental groups, and the claims and counter-claims that followed their announcement created a scientific incident without parallel in recent times.

Cold Harbor, Battles of (1864) Battles of the American Civil War, fought in Virginia as part of General Grant's strategy of unrelenting pressure on the South. Grant lost 12 000 men in one day's fighting.

cold sore (*Herpes labialis*) A localized blister-like rash affecting the lips and adjoining skin around the mouth, the lining of the mouth, and the tongue. The lesions are due to a virus which usually lies dormant but is activated by intermittent illness or debility.

cold storage Storage for perishable foodstuffs at a temperature just above freezing point. This process minimizes deterioration from chemical or biological action, but does not subject the food to damage by ice crystal formation on freezing. It is carried on in large buildings with cold air or brine circulated from a central refrigeration plant.

Cold War A state of tension or hostility between states that is expressed in economic and political terms, and stops short of a 'hot' or shooting war. The term is often used to describe the relationship between the USSR and the major Western non-communist powers – especially the USA – between 1945 and the mid- to late 1960s when the nuclear 'arms race' intensified.

Cole, George (1925–) Actor, born in London. His many films include the *St Trinian's* series and other comedies, but he is probably best known in the UK as Arthur Daly from the television series, *Minder*, also *My Good Friend* (1995–6), and *Dad* (1997–9).

Cole, Nat King, originally **Nathaniel Adams Cole**, family name formerly **Coles** (1919–65) Singer, jazz pianist, composer, and actor, born in Montgomery, AL. During the 1930s he became popular as a jazz pianist, forming his own instrumental trio of piano, guitar, and double bass in 1937. As a singer of romantic ballads, his many hit records including 'Route 66', 'Walking My Baby Back Home', and 'Unforgettable'.

Coleoptera [kolioptera] *beetle*

Coleridge, Samuel Taylor (1772–1834) Poet and man of letters, born in Ottery St Mary, Devon. As a result of his friendship with William and Dorothy Wordsworth, a new English Romantic poetry emerged, in reaction against Neoclassic artificiality. The publication of *Lyrical Ballads* (1798), which opens with his magical 'Rime of the Ancient Mariner', achieved a revolution in literary taste and sensibility. In 1800 he moved to the Lake District, but his career prospects were blighted by his moral collapse, partly due to opium. In 1816 he published 'Christabel' and the fragment, 'Kubla Khan', both written in his earlier period of inspiration.

Colet, John [kolet] (c.1467–1519) Theologian and Tudor humanist, born in London. In 1505 he became Dean of St Paul's, where he delivered controversial lectures on the interpretation of Scripture, and founded St Paul's School (1509–12).

Colette, Sidonie Gabrielle [kolet] (1873–1954) Novelist, born in Saint-Sauveur-en-Puisaye, France. Her novels include the *Claudine* series (1900–3), *Chéri* (1920), and *Gigi* (1944). She won many awards for her work, and died a legendary figure in Paris.

coleus A perennial native to Java (*Coleus blumei*); small flowers pale blue or white, in whorls forming slender spikes; a very popular pot-plant. (Family: Labiatae.)

coley *saithe*

colic [kolik] Excessive contraction and spasm of smooth (involuntary) muscle, tending to occur in waves, and giving rise to severe short-lived but recurring bouts of pain. It particularly affects the smooth muscle of the gut (**intestinal colic**), the common bile duct (**biliary colic**), and the renal pelvis and ureters (**renal colic**). Calculi in the ducts are the common causes of colic. Babies are prone to develop intestinal colic as a result of feeding difficulty.

Coligny, Gaspard II de, seigneur de (Lord of) **Châtillon** [koleenyee] (1519–72) Huguenot leader, born in Châtillon-sur-Loing, France. In 1557 he became a Protestant, and commanded the Huguenots during the second and third Wars of Religion. He was one of the first victims in the St Bartholomew's Day massacre.

colitis [koliytis] Inflammation of the large bowel (*colon*) leading to diarrhoea, abdominal pain, and bleeding. It may be due to infection with micro-organisms, auto-immune processes (ulcerative colitis and Crohn's disease), or inadequate blood supply (ischaemic colitis).

collage [kolahzh] A technique of picture-making introduced by the Cubists c.1912 in which pieces of paper, fabrics, or other materials are glued to the surface of the canvas. It was much used by the Surrealists in the 1920s.

collagens [kolajenz] A family of fibrous proteins found in all multicellular animals, constituting 25% of the total protein in mammals, and playing an essential role in providing tissue strength. A particularly important type is found in skin, tendon, bone, ligaments, the cornea, and internal organs.

collar bone *clavicle*

collateral [kolateral] A valuable item used as security for a loan –

often land, shares, or an insurance policy. If the borrower fails to repay the debt, the collateral can be sold and the debt (along with any costs) deducted from the proceeds.

collective bargaining Trade union negotiations on behalf of a group of workers in relation to pay and conditions of employment. If the negotiations break down, the dispute may result in industrial action, or the matter may be referred to arbitration by another body.

collective farm A large co-operative farm, commonly found in socialist countries, where many small peasant holdings have been pooled to create a single unit capable of exploiting the economies of scale associated with mechanized agriculture. They were first introduced on a large scale in the USSR during Stalin's campaign for the enforced collectivization of the Russian peasantry (1928–33).

collectivism A set of doctrines asserting the interests of the community over the individual, and the preference for central planning over market systems. It advocates that economic and political systems should be based upon co-operation, state intervention to deal with social injustice, and central administration to ensure uniformity of treatment.

college *university*

College of Arms *heraldry*

college of education A college specializing in the initial and in-service training of teachers. In the UK, such colleges were formerly called **training colleges**, and since the 1970s many have diversified into different fields, or merged with other colleges (as **colleges of higher education**), universities, or polytechnics.

collie A medium-sized domestic dog; several breeds developed in Scotland as sheepdogs; **collie**, usually brown and white, with a long pointed muzzle; black and white **Border collie**, similar; **bearded collie** (or **Highland collie**), with a long shaggy coat.

collimator [kolimayter] **1** An optical device for changing a divergent beam of light (from a point source) into a parallel beam, which is required for control of the optical behaviour of the beam (as in a spectroscope).

2 A small telescope fixed to a large one, to help in preliminary alignment.

Collingwood, Cuthbert, Baron (1748–1810) British admiral, born in Newcastle upon Tyne. He fought at Brest (1794), Cape St Vincent (1797), and Trafalgar (1805), where he succeeded Nelson as commander.

Collins, Joan (Henrietta) (1933–) Actress, born in London. She made her film debut in *Lady Godiva Rides Again* (1951), and used her sultry appeal and headline-catching private life to build a career as an international celebrity. She is best known for her role in the television soap opera *Dynasty* (1981–9). Her sister is the best-selling novelist **Jackie Collins** (1942–).

Collins, Michael (astronaut) (1930–) US astronaut, born in Rome. He was one of the members of the Gemini 10 project, and remained in the command module during the successful Apollo 11 Moon-landing expedition.

Collins, Michael (politician) (1890–1922) Irish politician and Sinn Féin leader, born near Clonakilty, Co Cork. He became an MP (1918–22), and with Arthur Griffith was largely responsible for the negotiation of the treaty with Great Britain in 1921. He was killed in an ambush by his former compatriots, who had come to regard him as a traitor.

Collins, Pauline (1940–) Actress, born in Exmouth, Devon. She became known in the popular television series *Upstairs, Downstairs* (1971–5). Later series include *Forever Green* (1989–91), with actor husband John Alderton (married 1969), *The Ambassador* (1998), and *Bleak House* (2005). Her film credits include *Shirley Valentine* (1989, Best Actress Oscar nomination) and *Paradise Road* (1997).

Collins, (William) Wilkie (1824–89) Novelist, born in London. A master of the mystery story, his best-known works are *The Woman in White* (1860) and *The Moonstone* (1868).

colloid [koloyd] A state midway between a suspension and a true solution. It is classified in various ways, particularly into **sols** (eg milk), in which liquid properties predominate, and **gels** (eg gelatine), which are more like solids.

colobus [kolobuhs] An Old World monkey, native to tropical Africa; slender with long tail; thumbs absent; also known as **guereza**. (Genus: *Colobus*, c.6 species.)

Cologne [kolohn], Ger **Köln** 50°56N 6°58E, pop (2000e) 986 000. Manufacturing and commercial river port in Germany, on W bank of R Rhine; capital of N Roman Empire (3rd-c); badly bombed in World War 2; noted for its trade fairs; archbishopric; railway; university (1388); cathedral (begun 1248).

Colombia *p.208*

Colombo [kolomboh], originally **Kalan-Totta** 6°55N 79°52E, pop (2000e) 689 000. Chief city and seaport of Sri Lanka; on the W coast; outer suburb, Sri-Jayawardenapura, the official capital since 1983; settled by the Portuguese in 1517 and by the Dutch in 1656; under British control, 1796; British defence base, 1942–5; road and rail centre; university (1972).

Colombo Plan A plan drawn up by British Commonwealth foreign ministers in Colombo, Sri Lanka (Jan 1950), whose purpose was the co-operative development of the countries of S and SE Asia.

Colón [kolon], formerly **Aspinwall** 9°21N 79°54W, pop (2000e) 157 000. Port city in N Panama, at the Caribbean end of the Panama Canal; second largest free port in World (after Hong Kong); founded, 1850; railway.

colon *intestine*

Colonial and Imperial Conferences A series of conferences at which representatives of the British colonies and dominions discussed matters of common imperial concern; usually held in London. The first Colonial Conference was held in 1887, and the first Imperial Conference in 1911. After World War 2 they were replaced by the Conferences of Commonwealth Prime Ministers.

colonnade A series of columns in or outside a building, usually supporting an entablature, roof, or arches. The most famous example is the 284-column colonnade that forms the Piazza of St Peter's, Rome (1655–67).

Colonsay [kolonsay] or **St Columba's Isle** Island in Argyll and Bute council, W Scotland; separated from Oronsay by a low channel which is dry at low water; rises to 142 m/468 ft at Carn Eoim; Augustinian priory.

colony An area of land or a country held and governed by another country, usually for the purpose of economic or other forms of exploitation. The present Commonwealth comprises the former colonies and the **Crown Colonies** (those still directly administered by Britain), which made up the British Empire.

colophony *rosin*

color (entries) *colour / color*

Colorado pop (2000e) 4 301 000; area 269 585 km²/104 091 sq mi. State in WC USA; the 'Centennial State'; E part included in the Louisiana Purchase, 1803; W part gained from Mexico by the Treaty of Guadalupe Hidalgo, 1848; settlement expanded after the gold strike of 1858; became a territory, 1861; joined the Union as the 38th state, 1876; contains the Ute Indian reservation (SW); Rocky Mts run N–S through the centre, divided into several ranges; highest point, Mt Elbert (4399 m/14 432 ft); forms part of the High Plains in the E, the centre of cattle and sheep ranching; capital, Denver; several notable national parks and monuments; world's largest deposits of molybdenum; growing tourist industry.

Colorado beetle A small, leaf beetle; yellow back with 10 longitudinal black stripes on wing cases; females lay eggs on potato

Colombia

CARIBBEAN SEA

NETHS. ANTILLES

Santa Marta
Barranquilla
Cartagena
Pico Cristobal Colón 5800m
Gulf of Venezuela
Panama Canal
Lake Maracaibo

VENEZUELA

PANAMA
Medellin
Bucaramanga
PACIFIC OCEAN
Puerto Carreño
Orinoco
Buenaventura
Cauca
Magdalena
■ Bogotá
COLOMBIA
Cali
△ *Nevado de Huila 5750m*
Guaviare

Tumaco
Pasto
Vaupés
Equator
Mitu

ECUADOR
Caquetá

Putumayo

SOUTH AMERICA
PERU
Leticia
Amazon

BRAZIL

250 km
150 mi

□ International Airport

[kolombia], official name **Republic of Colombia**, Span **República de Colombia**
Local name Colombia

Timezone GMT -5
Area 1 140 105 km²/440 080 sq mi
Population total (2002e) 41 008 000
Status Republic
Date of independence 1819
Capital Bogotá
Language Spanish (official)
Ethnic groups Mestizo (58%), European descent (20%), mulatto (14%)
Religion Roman Catholic (95%), other (5%)
Physical features Located in NW South America, includes several island possessions (Providencia, San Andrés and Mapelo); Andes run N–S, dividing narrow coastal plains from forested lowlands of Amazon basin; Cordillera Central rises 5000 m/16 000 ft to the high peak of Huila, 5750 m/18 865 ft; rivers include Vaupés, Magdalena, Cauca, and Guaviare.
Climate Hot, humid coastal plains (NW and W); annual rainfall over 2500 mm/100 in; drier period on Caribbean coast (Dec–Apr); hot, humid tropical lowlands in E.
Currency 1 Colombian Peso (COP) = 100 centavos
Economy Virtually self-sufficient in food; major crops include coffee, bananas, cotton; leather; gold, silver, emeralds, coal, oil; widespread illegal cocaine trafficking.
GDP (2002e) $251·6 bn, per capita $6100
Human Development Index (2002) 0·772
History Spanish occupation from early 16th-c, displacing Amerindian peoples; governed by Spain within Viceroyalty of Peru, later Viceroyalty of New Granada; independence in 1819, after the campaigns of Simón Bolívar; Union with Ecuador, Venezuela, and Panama as Gran Colombia, 1821–30. Civil war in 1950s; left-wing rebel groups FARC (Revolutionary Armed Forces of Colombia) and ELN (National Liberation Army) formed in 1960s; continuing political unrest led to rise of right-wing militias (1980s); new constitution, 1991; FARC-controlled zone established in S (1998) as part of peace negotiations (collapsed 2002); conflict ongoing (2007) with significant US military presence; governed by a President, bicameral Congress and Cabinet.
Head of State/Government
1994–8 Ernesto Samper Pizano
1998–2002 Andrés Pastrana Arango
2002– Alvaro Uribe Velez

plants; larvae fat, reddish-yellow with black side spots; causes great damage to potato crops. (Order: Coleoptera. Family: Chrysomelidae.)
Colorado Desert Depressed arid region in SE California and N Baja California, USA; area 5000–8000 km²/2000–3000 sq mi.
Colorado River River in SW USA; rises in the Continental Divide, N Colorado; empties into the Golfo de California; length c.2350 km/1450 mi; used extensively for irrigation, flood-control, and hydroelectric power.
Colorado Springs 38°50N 104°49W, pop (2000e) 360 900. City in C Colorado, USA; established, 1872; city status, 1886; railway; university; nearby mineral springs make it a popular health resort.
coloratura Florid ornamentation, or 'colouring', of a melody, especially in vocal music. A **coloratura soprano** is one with a high voice who specializes in such music.
colorization The addition of colour by electronic means to the videotape transfer of a motion picture originally photographed in black-and-white. Sometimes the former picture quality is sacrificed, and the technique has therefore proved to be controversial.

Colossians, Letter to the [koloshnz] New Testament writing attributed to Paul while he was in prison. It bears many similarities to the *Letter to the Ephesians*, but there is much current debate about whether the work is genuinely from Paul.
Colossus of Rhodes A huge, bronze statue of the Sun-god, Apollo, which bestrode the harbour entrance of the seaport of Rhodes. It was built c.280 BC.
colour / color *complementary colour; light; primary colour; quark; spectrum*
colour / color blindness *colour / color vision*
colour / color cinematography Early attempts to show motion-pictures in colour included projecting successive frames through red and blue-green filters (Kinemacolor, 1906), or optically superimposing three separate colour images on projection (Francita, Opticolor, 1930–7, Dufay mosaic, 1931–40), but none was very successful. In 1932 Technicolor introduced a three-colour camera exposing three black-and-white separation colour negatives, with prints in three-colour dye-transfer which became the dominant medium for professional colour cinematography until Kodak produced their masked Eastman-color negative. By 1955 the three-strip camera was obsolete, but

dye-transfer printing continued into the 1970s. Eastmancolor negative/positive films opened the way to a vast expansion of colour cinematography, and similar materials are now manufactured worldwide.

Coloured *Cape Coloured*

colour / color filter A transparent material which transmits light from only a selected portion of the visible spectrum, partially or completely absorbing the remainder. Colour filters are used to provide light of a required spectral composition, or to give an overall colour balance to a colour photograph.

colouring / coloring agents Dyes used for colouring food which are either natural, nature identical, or synthetic. Tartrazine is an example of a synthetic colouring agent, while carotene is a natural colourant.

colourization *colorization*

colour / color photography The photographic reproduction of colour from negatives recording separately the red, green, and blue light components of a scene. A positive picture is formed by the superimposition of three corresponding images, either projected in the light of the same hues (*additive*) or printed in the complementary colours, cyan, magenta, and yellow (*subtractive*). A major advance was the integral *tripack*, recording in three separate photographic layers on a common base and developed with colour couplers. The first was Kodachrome, in 1935.

colour / color separation overlay *chromakey*

colour / color television A broadcasting medium, introduced in the 1950s. The image formed by the lens of a camera is divided into its components of red, green, and blue (RGB) light which are combined in the proportions of 30% R, 59% G, and 11% B to form the *luminance* signal, Y, representing the picture in neutral tones from white to black. The colour information, *chrominance*, is handled as two colour-difference signals, B−Y and R−Y, which are coded in phase relationship and added to the luminance signal for transmission, in what is termed the *composite mode*. In the late 1980s, the alternative *component mode* was developed, in which the chrominance signals are kept separate from the luminance, but compressed in time to occupy the same period. This provides improved picture quality, and is widely used in the latest generation of videotape recorders. In a colour receiver, chrominance and luminance are decoded to give separate RGB signals controlling the three electron guns of a shadow-mask tube. As these beams are scanned across the screen they stimulate groups of minute phosphor dots which glow in the corresponding colour, red, green and blue, to form the elements of the complete picture by additive colour mixture.

colour / color therapy The use of psychological and physical effects of coloured light for healing purposes. Since both infrared and ultraviolet radiation are used in orthodox medicine for healing purposes, colour therapists claim that the intervening wavelengths of visible light may also have healing properties, since the body is thought to absorb electromagnetic radiation as well as to emit it. An unhealthy body emits an unbalanced vibration pattern, and colour therapy is designed to restore balance using such methods as exposure to coloured light, wearing particular colours of clothing, or eating coloured foods. Therapists may also be asked to advise on the selection of colours in buildings.

colour / color vision The ability to detect differences between light of various wavelengths reaching the retina by converting them into colours. It is dependent on the presence of light-sensitive pigments in the cones (*retinal photoreceptors*), each being sensitive to light of a specific wavelength. In humans, the cones contain pigments most sensitive to red, green, or blue light. Absence of one or more of these pigments results in **colour blindness**: red-blindness (*protanopia*) affects the ability

to distinguish red and green; blue-blindness (*deuteranopia*) affects blue and yellow; and green-blindness (*tritanopia*) affects the green range of the spectrum. Colour blindness is a sex-linked characteristic, about 20 times more common in males.

Colt, Samuel (1814–62) Inventor, born in Hartford, CT. In 1835 he took out his first patent for a revolver, which after the Mexican war was adopted by the US army, founding the fortunes of his company.

Coltrane, John (William) (1926–67) Jazz tenor and soprano saxophonist, born in Hamlet, NC. He was little known in 1955 when Miles Davis chose him for his quintet. On forming his own quartet in 1960, Coltrane quickly became the most influential jazz musician of the day, with such recordings as *Giant Steps* (1959), *Africa/Brass* (1961), and *A Love Supreme* (1964).

coltsfoot A perennial with long whitish rhizomes (*Tussilago farfara*), native to Europe, W and N Asia, and N Africa; flower-heads bright yellow, solitary on stems to 15 cm/6 in, appearing before the leaves. It is an old herbal medicine for chest complaints. (Family: Compositae.)

colugo [koloogoh] A nocturnal mammal, native to SE Asia; face lemur-like; large gliding membrane along each side of body, extending to tips of fingers, toes, and long tail; lives in trees; only member of the order Dermoptera; also known as **flying lemur**. (Family: Cynocephalidae, 2 species.)

Colum, Padraic (1881–1972) Poet and playwright, born in Co Longford, Ireland, a leader of the Irish literary revival. He wrote several plays for the Abbey Theatre, and helped to found the *Irish Review* (1911).

Columba, St, also **Columcille** or **Colm** (521–97) Missionary and abbot, born in Gartan, Donegal. He founded monasteries at Derry (546) and Durrow (553), and then at Iona, in the Inner Hebrides (c.563), from where he and his followers brought Christianity to Scotland. Feast day 9 June.

Columba (Lat 'dove') A small S constellation.

Columbae *Columbiformes*

Columban or **Columbanus, St** (c.543–615) Missionary and abbot, 'the younger Columba', born in Leinster, Ireland. About 585 he went to Gaul and founded the monasteries of Anegray, Luxeuil, and Fontaine in the Vosges. Feast day 23 November.

Columbia 34°00N 81°03W, pop (2000e) 116 300. State capital in C South Carolina, USA; settled, early 1700s; state capital, 1786; city status, 1854; burned by General Sherman, 1865; airfield; railway; two universities (1801, 1870); commercial and trading centre in a rich farming area.

Columbia River River in NW USA and SW Canada; rises in the Rocky Mts in E British Columbia, enters the Pacific at Cape Disappointment, SW of Vancouver, Washington; length 1953 km/1214 mi; source of irrigation and hydroelectric power.

Columbia University *Ivy League*

Columbiformes [koluhmbifaw(r)meez] An order of birds encompassing the pigeons, sandgrouse, the extinct dodo, and dodo-like solitaires; also known as **Columbae**.

columbine A perennial (*Aquilegia vulgaris*) native to Europe, N Africa, and Asia; flowers blue, rarely white, each of the five petals with a curved backward-pointing spur containing nectar. Garden forms are often called **aquilegias**. (Family: Ranunculaceae.)

Columbus 39°58N 83°00W, pop (2000e) 711 500. Capital of state in C Ohio, USA; founded, 1812; state capital, 1824; city status, 1834; railway; three universities (1850, 1870, 1902); air force base; centre for research in science and information technology.

Columbus, Christopher, Ital **Cristoforo Colombo**, Span **Cristóbal Colón** (1451–1506) European discoverer of the New World, born in Genoa, Italy. His plans to reach India by sailing W were supported by Ferdinand and Isabella of Spain. He set sail from Saltes (3 Aug 1492) in the *Santa Maria*, reaching the Bahamas

(12 Oct), Cuba, and Hispaniola (Haiti). His second voyage (1493–6) led to the discovery of several Caribbean islands. On his third voyage (1498–1500) he discovered the S American mainland. His last great voyage (1502–4) was along the S side of the Gulf of Mexico.

Columbus Day A national holiday in the USA, held in most states on the second Monday in October in commemoration of Christopher Columbus's discovery of America (12 Oct 1492). It is also celebrated in several countries of Central and South America.

column A vertical support in a building, usually made up of a base, circular shaft, and spreading capital, and designed to carry an entablature or arch. It is also used as an aesthetic device to add ornament or to divide a space.

Colwyn *Aberconwy and Colwyn*

coly [kohlee] A bird native to Africa S of the Sahara, also known as **mousebird**; small, greyish; head crest, short curved bill, long tail; outer toe reversible. It is placed in a separate order (Coliiformes). (Genus: *Colius*, 6 species. Family: Coliidae.)

coma (medicine) A state of unconsciousness from which individuals cannot be roused. Brain functions are progressively depressed, but the vital activities of respiration and constriction of the heart continue. The causes include trauma to the brain, meningitis, alcohol and drug overdosage, and metabolic disorders.

coma (physics) *aberrations* 1

Coma Berenices [kohma bereniyseez] (Lat 'Berenice's hair') A faint N constellation established in 1551 by Gerardus Mercator. It includes the huge Coma cluster of galaxies, located 100 megaparsec away.

Comanche [komanchee] Shoshonean-speaking North American Plains Indians who migrated S from Wyoming and became a powerful fighting group. They were settled on reservations in the 19th-c.

Comaneci, Nadia [komaneech] (1961–) Gymnast, born in Onesti, Moldova. She was the star of the 1976 Olympic Games when, at the age of 14, she won gold medals in the beam, vault, and floor disciplines. In 1989 she defected to the USA via Hungary, amid much publicity.

combassou *whydah*

Combination Acts British legislation passed in 1799 and 1800 which prohibited the coming together (*combination*) of workers in trade unions. The Acts were repealed in 1824–5, and trade unions legalized.

Combined Operations Command A British force established in 1940 to co-ordinate British commando raids against German-occupied Europe. Combined Operations techniques were to play a crucial role in the Allied invasion of France.

combine harvester A machine which cuts, threshes, and cleans all types of cereals, oilseeds, and legumes. Most combines are now self-propelled, and are equipped for handling grain and seed in bulk.

combing In spinning, a post-carding process which removes unwanted short fibres, termed *noil*, and straightens and aligns the remaining fibres (*sliver*). The sliver may then be spun into fine smooth yarns.

comb jelly *ctenophore*

combustion A burning, usually in a supply of oxygen to form oxides. The complete combustion of a hydrocarbon yields carbon dioxide and water. The energy associated with the combustion of a mole of a substance is called its **heat of combustion**.

COMECON *Council for Mutual Economic Assistance*

Comédie-Française, La [komaydee frãsez], official name *Le Théâtre Français* The oldest surviving theatre company in France, dating officially from 1680. It is organized as a co-operative society, with its longest serving actor as the Doyen or head of the company. All full members of the society, as shareholders, are eligible for a pension on retirement.

comet A small Solar System body made of ice and dust. Comets are asteroidal in appearance at distances of many astronomical units from the Sun (when they consist of a bare, inactive nucleus), and are often spectacularly active when nearer to the Sun. The characteristic bright head (*coma*) and streaming tails (both dust and ions) are created by solar heating, with emission of light from gas molecules and scattered light from the dust. The comet nucleus is a few km in size, irregularly shaped and very dark; dust in the coma contains carbon and silica; there is evidence of polymerized organic molecules; the gases of the coma include water, carbon monoxide, carbon dioxide, ammonia, methane, and hydrocarbons. The source of comets of long orbital periods is believed to be a spherical halo cloud about the Sun called the *Oort Cloud*. Observable comets are occasionally scattered into the inner Solar System by the gravitational fields of nearby stars and giant molecular clouds. Some (eg Halley's comet) are captured into relatively short period orbits as a result of gravitational interactions with giant planets. A small 'armada' of spacecraft (Sakigake and Suisei, VEGA 1 and 2, Giotto) encountered Halley's comet in 1986. In 2004, the Stardust probe captured particles from Comet Wild 2 and returned to Earth in January 2006. In 2005, NASA's Deep Impact Spacecraft released an 'impactor' directly into the path of Comet Tempel 1. The projectile successfully shattered on impact throwing up a huge plume of icy debris. The data collected will be studied by scientists who hope to gain new information on the Solar System's original composition.

comfrey A bristly perennial, native to Europe and the Mediterranean region; flowers drooping, tubular, or funnel-shaped, white, yellow, or pink in bud, and opening blue. (Genus: *Symphytum*, 25 species. Family: Boraginaceae.)

comic opera A light, amusing opera, particularly one which (like those of Gilbert and Sullivan) alternates songs and ensembles with spoken dialogue. The modern equivalent is the **musical**.

Cominform An abbreviation for the former USSR's **Communist Information Bureau**, and a successor to the Comintern. It was established upon Stalin's orders at a meeting in Poland (Sep 1947), its purpose being the co-ordination of the 'voice' and activities of European communist parties. It was dissolved in 1956.

Comino [komeenoh] 36°00N 14°20E; area 2·7 km²/1·04 sq mi. Smallest of the three main islands of the Maltese group, midway between Malta and Gozo; highest point, 247 m/810 ft; no cars allowed.

Comintern An abbreviation for the **Communist International**, founded in Moscow (Mar 1919) at the behest of the Russian Communist Party, its purpose being the rallying of left-wing socialists and communists. It was disbanded in 1943.

command economy *market economy*

commedia dell'arte [komaydia delah(r)tay] (Ital 'comedy of the profession') A distinctive form of theatre which originated in Italy about the middle of the 16th-c. Its performance was the prerogative of professional troupes, and performance skills were passed on from player to player. The comedy relied on stock characters, many represented by masks. The tradition survives in puppetry, the harlequinade, mime, and pantomime.

Commission for Racial Equality A body of between 8 and 15 individuals set up in England and Wales under the Race Relations Act (1976) to work towards the elimination of discrimination because of colour, race, nationality, or ethnic origin. The Commission, which is appointed by the home secretary under the 1976 Act, also works to promote equality of opportunity and good relations between racial groups. The Protection from Harassment Act (1997) also imposes penalties for racial harassment.

commodity market A market where buyers and sellers of commodities – mainly agricultural crops and metals – trade (**commodity trading**). Often prices are fixed on a bargain-by-bargain basis. The dealers who negotiate on behalf of clients are known as **commodity brokers**.

Common Agricultural Policy (CAP) The most important of the common policies of the European Community, absorbing c.65% of the total Community budget. The basic principles behind the CAP are free trade for agricultural commodities within the Community, Community preference for domestic production, control of imports from the rest of the world, and common financing. The use of high price-support measures has generated surpluses in most major commodities (eg the 'butter mountain' and 'wine lake').

common law A source of English law, the first source common to the entire kingdom, replacing over a period of centuries local courts and customs. It emphasizes the development of law through individual cases rather than prescriptive codes.

Common Market *European Economic Community*

Commons, House of The lower, and effectively the ruling, chamber of the bicameral legislature of the UK. It contains 659 members, elected by universal adult suffrage, each representing a single constituency. The Commons is elected for a maximum period of five years, though the prime minister may call an election at any time within that period, and the government is drawn from the party that wins the majority of seats.

Commonwealth (British) A free association of independent nations formerly subject to British imperial government, and maintaining friendly and practical links with the UK. In 1931 the Statute of Westminster established the British Commonwealth of Nations; the adjective 'British' was deleted after World War 2. Most of the states granted independence, beginning with India in 1947, chose to be members of the Commonwealth. Ireland resigned from the association in 1948, South Africa in 1961, Pakistan in 1972, and Fiji in 1987; Pakistan re-entered in 1989, South Africa in 1994, and Fiji in 1997; Nigeria was suspended 1995–99; Pakistan was suspended in 1999, and re-admitted 2004. Zimbabwe was suspended for a year in March 2002, and withdrew after the 2003 conference reaffirmed its suspension. There were 53 members at the start of 2007.

Commonwealth (English history) English republican regime, established in 1649, and lasting until the Instrument of Government created a Protectorate in 1653. It failed to achieve political settlement at home, but its armies pacified Scotland and Ireland.

Commonwealth Conference An annual meeting of prime ministers of the independent nations that now comprise the Commonwealth. It acts as a forum for maintaining political and economic links between the member countries.

Commonwealth Day The second Monday in March, celebrated with receptions, educational events, etc throughout the Commonwealth; originally instituted as **Empire Day** (by which name it was known until 1960).

Commonwealth Games A multi-sport gathering every 4 years by representatives of the nations of the Commonwealth. The first Games were at Hamilton, Canada in 1930. The 2002 games held in Manchester was the first major multi-sport event to include Elite Athletes with a Disability (EAD).

Commonwealth Institute An organization founded in 1959 to replace the Imperial Institute, itself founded in 1886 to promote commerce and industry between the countries of the British Empire. Its main activity is the promotion of the heritage and culture of its member nations.

Commonwealth of Independent States *p.212*

Commune of Paris An uprising by Parisian Republicans (18 Mar–28 May 1871) following France's humiliating defeat in the Franco-Prussian War. The insurgents rose against the Versailles government, but were defeated, leaving an unprecedented legacy of bitterness.

communicable disease A disease caused by a micro-organism which can be transmitted to humans from infected animals, other people, or the environment. The infection may be by direct contact (eg venereal diseases), via the air (eg influenza), by ingestion (eg dysentery), or by insect transmission (eg malaria).

communication 1 The sharing of meaning by individuals, groups, or organizations through the conveying of facts, ideas, feelings, values, etc from one party to another. The codes used may be linguistic (as in speech, writing, or signing) or those of non-verbal communication (eg gestures or clothes), but they require to be common to both parties for the most complete sharing of meaning or the fullest communication to take place. The act of communicating may be direct and face-to-face (**interpersonal** communication) or indirect and at a distance, using technical means such as television, radio, cinema, books, newspapers, or magazines (**mass** communication). Though usually considered as a deliberate process, communication can also take place unintentionally; sweating, for instance, may be a sign of embarrassment, fear, or simply being over-heated. As with every sign, its interpretation will depend to a degree on the context in which it is produced and received. **2** The technical means by which links are established between individuals, organizations, countries, etc for the purpose of the transfer of messages. These involve an *initiator*, who formulates a message and sends it as a signal (by means of a particular *channel*) to a *receiver*, who decodes and interprets the meaning. **3** A system of routes (road, rail, sea, air) for transporting people and goods from one place to another. Historically used for the movement of troops and supplies, the notion is now more often associated with commercial transactions.

communication theory The application of information theory to human communication in general. Communication is seen to involve an information source encoding a message which is transmitted via a channel to a receiver, where it is decoded and has an effect. Efficient, error-free transmission is assumed to be the primary goal, especially in engineering contexts.

Communion, Holy *Eucharist*

communism A political ideology which has as its central principle the communal ownership of all property, and thereby the abolition of private property. Modern communism is specifically associated with the theories of Karl Marx, who saw the emergence of a communist society as being the final stage in a historical process that was rooted in human material needs, preceded by feudalism, capitalism, and (a transitional stage) socialism. Communism, according to Marx, would abolish class distinctions and end the exploitation of the masses inherent in the capitalist system. The working class, or proletariat, would be the instrument of a revolution that would overthrow the capitalist system and liberate human potential. The Communist Party of the Soviet Union (CPSU), first of all under Lenin's leadership and followed by Stalin, re-interpreted Marxist ideology as Marxism–Leninism–Stalinism, the major feature of which is democratic centralism. The CPSU provided the ideological lead for European communist parties. During the latter part of the 20th-c, however, its compulsory leadership was questioned. In 1989, the establishment of a non-communist Government in Poland, popular uprisings in Eastern Europe, and the decision by the Soviet Union not to intervene saw the dominant position of the Communist Party overturned and an immediate reduction in the status and influence of other communist parties. This change was symbolized best

Commonwealth of Independent States (CIS)

☐ International Airport

Russ **Sodruzhestvo Nezavisimykh Gosudarstv** Organization formed to replace Gorbachev's Union of Sovereign States, which was thwarted by the abortive political coup of 19–22 August 1991; administrative centre, Minsk. The agreement on the creation of the CIS declares that 'the USSR no longer exists as a subject of international law and geopolitic reality'. The initiative was taken by Belarus, the Russian Federation, and the Ukraine at a meeting in Minsk, and signed by the three parties on 8 December 1991. The Alma-Ata Declaration (21 Dec 1991) saw the original three members joined by the independent republics of Armenia, Azerbaijan, Kazakhstan, Kyrgyzstan, Moldova, Tajikistan, Turkmenistan, and Uzbekistan. Georgia joined in 1993. The aims of the CIS include: to cement historical ties; to build democracy on the rule of law; to recognize the sovereignty and territorial integrity of individual states within their existing borders; to promote mutually beneficial co-operation in the spheres of economy, transport, and communications; and to recognize the rights of the individual. There was to be an agreement on the joint command of strategic forces and the central control of nuclear weapons.

by the demolition of the Berlin Wall, a structure which had stood for the division of Europe into two ideologically opposed camps. There remain a number of countries in which communist parties continue to rule, notably the People's Republic of China, North Korea, Vietnam, Laos, and Cuba. However, even in these the system is showing signs of strain, and in China the aging rulers (adherents to the variant of communism known as Maoism) had to resort to force to crush demands for reform in the Tiananmen Square Massacre in 1989. Only in North Korea and Cuba does a fully-blown totalitarian democratic-centralist regime continue in power.

Communism Peak, since 1998 known as **Ismoil Somoni Peak** (also spelled **Ismail Samani**), formerly **Mt Garmo** (to 1933), **Mt Stalin** (1933–62) 39°00N 72°02E. Highest peak in the former USSR, in the Pamir range, N Tajikistan; height, 7495 m/ 24 590 ft; first climbed in 1933.

Communist Party of the Soviet Union (CPSU) The party which controlled political, economic, and social life in the former USSR. Many posts were confined to party members, who comprised only c.10% of the population. The party was ruled illegal by Boris Yeltsin following the failed 1991 coup, but Russia's constitution court reinstated some of their activities.

community charge A flat-rate charge on every adult resident in a particular area to contribute towards the provision of local government services. As the **poll tax**, it was first levied on each adult or 'head' (Middle English, *polle*) in 1377, and periodically reimposed (eg in 1513, 1641, and during the reign of Charles II). Most tax systems have abandoned the poll tax, but in the UK it was revived as a way of overcoming weaknesses in the domestic rating system, applying to all adults who use the services in a district, not just to those who own property. The charge came into operation in Scotland in 1989, and was introduced in England and Wales from 1990. The intention was to induce voters to impose greater financial responsibility on local authorities. In practice, the level had to be 'capped' (ie limited by central government) in some cases. The system proved to be extremely unpopular and difficult to enforce, with claims that it was unjust in its impact on the poorer members of society. Following a campaign of non-payment and increasing dissatisfaction, the tax was replaced in 1993 by a **council tax**, which reverts to the system of basing local taxation on property values.

community medicine A branch of medicine which assesses and meets the health needs of populations rather than individuals; also known as **social medicine** and **public health**.

community school / college A school or college which is open to the whole community. It may therefore be open seven days a week, during evenings as well as through the day, and in some cases children and adults may study together.

community service order A sentence of the criminal courts

Comoros

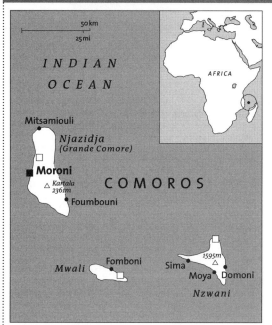

INDIAN
OCEAN

AFRICA

Mitsamiouli

Njazidja
(Grande Comore)

■ **Moroni**
△ *Kartala*
2361m

COMOROS

Foumbouni

Mwali Fomboni Sima *1595m* △
Moya Domoni

Nzwani

☐ International Airport

[komoros], official name **Federal and Islamic Republic of the Comoros**, République Fédérale Islamique des Comores

Local name Comores
Timezone GMT +3
Area 1 862 km²/719 sq mi
Population total (2002e) 583 000
Status Federal republic

Date of independence 1975
Capital Moroni (on Njazidja Island)
Languages Arabic, French (official), Kiswahili
Ethnic groups Comorian (97%), Makua (2%)
Religions Sunni Muslim (86%), Roman Catholic (14%)
Physical features Located in the Mozambique Channel between mainland Africa and Madagascar; a group of three volcanic islands: Njazidja (Grande Comore), Nzwani (Anjouan), and Mwali (Mohéli); largest island, Njazidja, with an active volcano, Mt Kartala, 2361 m/7746 ft.
Climate Tropical; dry season (May–Oct), hot, humid season (Nov–Apr); average temperatures, 20°C (Jul), 28°C (Nov).
Currency 1 Comorian Franc (KMF) = 100 centimes
Economy Largely agricultural economy: vanilla, copra, cacao, sisal, coffee, cloves, vegetable oils; perfume.
GDP (2002e) $441 mn, per capita $700
Human Development Index (2002) 0.511
History Under French control, 1843–1912; French overseas territory, 1947; internal political autonomy, 1961; unilateral independence declared, 1975; Mayotte, island in the archipelago, has remained under French rule; established as a Federal Islamic Republic, 1978; a one-party state, governed by a President, Council of Ministers, and unicameral Federal Assembly; new constitution, 2001, provided for the creation of a new federation, the Comoros Union, with greater autonomy for each of the three islands; presidency of the union rotates between the three islands; president is elected for a 4-year term, heads a central government, and 33-member legislature.

Head of State/Government
1999–2002 Azali Assoumani
2002 Hamada Madi *Interim*
2002–6 Azali Assoumani
2006– Ahmed Abdallah Mohamed Sambi

Prime Minister
1999–2000 Tarmidi Bianrifi
2000–2 Hamada Madi

whereby a convicted defendant can be required to undertake constructive unpaid work in the community, rather than being detained or paying a fine.

Como 45°49N 9°06E, pop (2000e) 96 000. City in NW Italy, at SW end of L Como; cathedral (1396).

Como, Lake (Ital **Lago di**) or **Lario**, ancient **Larius Lacus** area 146 km²/56 sq mi. Narrow lake in N Italy, length 50 km/31 mi; maximum depth 412 m/1353 ft.

Comodoro Rivadavia [kohmohdohroh reevadavia] 45°50S 67°30W, pop (2000e) 135 300. Seaport in Patagonia, S Argentina; university (1961); railway; airfield; natural gas pipeline to Buenos Aires.

Comoros *see panel*

compact disk (CD) A plastic disk of 120 mm/4·7 in diameter, holding on a single side up to an hour of digitally encoded sound recording, stored as a succession of pits and plateaux in tracks 1·6 μm wide. The disk is coated in a reflective material (usually aluminium), which either scatters or reflects back into a photoelectric detector a laser beam used to read (play) the encoded sound when the disk is rotated at high constant linear speed. Launched in 1982–3 by Philips and Sony jointly, digital compact disks are free of stylus wear, are essentially immune to surface blemishes, and thus appear near to perfection in sound recording.

Companions of Honour, Order of the (CH) In the UK, an award instituted in 1917, made to members of either sex for outstanding service to the nation. It consists of the sovereign and a maximum of 65 members.

company An association existing for a commercial or business purpose, considered to be a legal entity independent of its members. It may be formed by Act of Parliament, by Royal Charter, or by registration under company law (referred to as a **limited liability** or **joint-stock company**). *Ltd* after the company's name signifies *limited*, and *PLC* (**public limited company**) indicates that its shares are widely held. In the USA, companies are registered in a particular state – Delaware being especially favoured – and become *Incorporated* (*Inc*).

comparative linguistics The comparison of the features of different languages or dialects, or the different historical states of a language. In the 19th-c, the concern was exclusively historical, the field being known as **comparative philology**.

comparative philology *comparative linguistics*

compass A device for determining a horizontal geographical direction or bearing. The **magnetic compass** depends on a magnet, free to rotate in a horizontal plane, locating itself in line with the Earth's magnetic field.

compensation order In British law, an order, made by a court to someone convicted of an offence which has caused personal injury, loss, or damage, to pay a specified amount of compensation to the victim, in addition to any other sentence imposed by the court (typically a fine). Many other jurisdictions have introduced similar arrangements, some of which are restricted to financial compensation while others involve an element of service either to the victim or to the community in general.

competence In linguistics, an idealized conception of language, representing the system of grammatical rules which any speaker of a language subconsciously knows. It is contrasted with **performance**, the way in which sentences actually appear, containing 'imperfections' such as hesitations, and grammatical errors.

compiler A computer program which translates (**compiles**) the source code of a high-level computer language program, such as BASIC, into a set of machine-code instructions which can be understood by the central processing unit. Compilers are very large programs, and contain error-checking and other facilities.

complementary medicine *alternative medicine*

Complicite [komplisitay] *Theatre de Complicite*

Composite order The most decorative of the five main orders of classical architecture, combining the Ionic volute with the acanthus leaves of the Corinthian order.

compost *manure*

compound In chemistry, an entity with a definite composition, containing atoms of two or more elements.

comprehensive school A school catering for the whole of the ability range; opposed to a **selective school**, which takes only a section of the population. In countries such as Sweden and the USA, these schools were commonplace for most of the 20th-c. In other places, such as the UK, the non-selective school did not become widespread until the 1960s.

Compton, Arthur (Holly) (1892–1962) Physicist, born in Wooster, OH. The **Compton effect**, explaining the change in the wavelength of X-rays when they collide with electrons, is named after him. He shared the Nobel Prize for Physics in 1927.

Compton, Denis (Charles Scott) (1918–97) Cricketer, born in London. He played cricket for England 78 times, and scored 5807 runs. During his career (1936–57) he made 38 942 runs and took 622 wickets. A winger at soccer, he won an England cap during the war years. His later career was as a journalist and broadcaster.

Compton-Burnett, Dame Ivy [bernet] (1884–1969) Novelist, born in Pinner, Middlesex. Her novels, set in upper-class Victorian or Edwardian society, include *Pastors and Masters* (1925) and *Mother and Son* (1955, James Tait Black).

computer A device which can be programmed to store and process numerical and alphabetical data. The first mechanical adding device was developed in 1642 by Pascal. In 1835, Charles Babbage formulated his concept of an 'analytical machine' which combined arithmetic processes with decisions based on the results of the computations. This was really the forerunner of the modern digital computer, in that it combined the principles of sequential control, branching, looping, and storage units. J Presper Eckert and John W Mauchly produced the first all-electronic digital computer, ENIAC (Electronic Numerical Integrator and Calculator), at the University of Pennsylvania in 1946. Very significant contributions were made around this time by Johann von Neumann, who converted the ENIAC principles to give the EDVAC computer (Electronic Discrete Variable Automatic Computer) which could modify its own programs in much the same way as suggested by Babbage. Advances were accelerated from the mid-1960s by the successful development of miniaturization techniques in the electronics industry. The first microprocessor, which might be regarded as a computer on a chip, appeared in 1971, and nowadays the power of even the most modest personal computer can equal or outstrip the early electronic computers of the 1940s. The key elements in computing today are miniaturization and communications. Hand-held computers, with input via a stylus, can be linked to central systems through a mobile telephone.

computer game A small personal computer supplied with a computer program which allows one or more users to play some game. The game could be chess, in which case a single user plays against the computer, or it could be driving a car, in which case two users could compete against each other in a race. Many games are concerned with a series of trials (eg fighting a dragon) in which the player has to win the trial before being allowed to proceed. Increasingly, computer games require the user to wear a visor (so that the player sees only the computer display) and gloves (so that the computer can record arm and hand movements) – a technique known as *virtual reality*.

computer generations Different eras of technical development of digital computers, defined as different 'generations'. **First-generation** computers were the early devices in the 1940s and 1950s, built using thermionic valves. **Second-generation** computers replaced these valves by discrete transistors. **Third-generation** computers replaced transistors by integrated circuits. **Fourth-generation** computers were built with very large scale integrated circuits (VLSI). **Fifth-generation** computers are those showing artificial intelligence with which we can communicate in natural language.

computer graphics The use of computers to display information in graphical or pictorial form, usually on a visual display unit (VDU), a printer, or a plotter. Applications include the manipulation of highly detailed engineering drawings, computer games, high definition views in aircraft simulators, and the automatic production of animated film.

computerized tomography (CT), also **computerized axial tomography (CAT)** A medical X-ray scanning technique which makes a series of pictures that are then reconstructed by computer programs to represent a 'slice' through the patient. The X-ray tube rotates round the patient and produces images in sequence on a number of detectors. These machines are especially used in setting up radiotherapy treatment for precise action on small target areas in the patient.

computer language *programming language*

computer memory A part of a computer which stores, either permanently or temporarily, programs and data. There are two basic types of internal memory used in digital computers: **Random Access Memory** (RAM) and **Read-Only Memory** (ROM) or variants thereof.

computer network A group of computers, linked together by telecommunications lines, for the purpose of working together. During the preparation of this encyclopedia, for example, several computer terminals in one building were linked through a network to a computer containing the encyclopedia database, thus enabling different editorial tasks to be carried out simultaneously.

computer package A computer program, or group of computer programs, sold as a 'package' for the performance of a specific function. An example is an accounting package, which contains all the routines and calculations necessary for the analysis and presentation of accounts.

computer peripheral Any device which can be connected to a computer. It may be an input device or an output device. Examples include printers, magnetic disks, scanners, visual display units, and plotters.

computer printer A computer output device which produces characters or graphics on paper. Many different types exist, and the optimum choice for any given situation depends on the acceptable cost, printing speed, print quality, and operating noise.

computer program A complete structured sequence of statements in a programming language which directs a computer to carry out a specific task. The task of writing computer programs is known as **programming**.

computer science The whole area of knowledge associated with the use and study of computers and computer-based processes. It encompasses computer design and programming, and inter-computer communication.

computer terminal Any device which can be attached to a computer, possibly over a telecommunications line, to allow a user to interact with the computer. Examples are visual display units and some kinds of personal computers using appropriate software while linked to another computer.

computer virus A term applied to computer programs which can spread from computer to computer, usually via shared software, and damage other programs stored on the computers. The 'virus' program is often attached, by the human perpetrator, to a genuine program and is not readily detectable.

Comte, Auguste [kõt] (1798–1857) Philosopher and sociologist, the founder of positivism, born in Montpellier, France. In his philosophy, all sciences are regarded as having passed through a theological and then a metaphysical stage into a positive or experiential stage. In positive religion, the object of reverence is humanity, and the aim the well-being and progress of the race.

Conakry [konakree] 9°30N 13°43W, pop (2000e) 966 000. Seaport capital of Guinea, W Africa; on Tumbo island; linked to the mainland by a causeway; established in 1889; airport; railway terminus; technical college (1963).

Conan Doyle *Doyle, Arthur Conan*

concentration camp Originally, a compound where non-combatants were detained, first instituted by Lord Kitchener during the Second Boer War (1900–2). During the Nazi regime in Germany (1933–45), the term was applied to places of internment for unwanted people, specifically Jews, but also for religious dissidents, communists, gypsies, and the handicapped. At least 22 camps (*Konzentrazionslager* or *KZ*) were operated by the Nazis; some, such as Auschwitz, were set up for the extermination and incineration of men, women, and children. Among Jews alone, an estimated 6 million died in the camps and ghettos, or were shot by mobile killing squads (the Holocaust). In the Soviet Union an estimated 15 million prisoners were sent to the forced-labour camps (*Gulags*) in Siberia during Stalin's purges. Concentration camps were also widely used in China under Mao. More recent examples of civilian incarceration include the notorious Serb and Croat camps set up during the Yugoslav civil war, where 'ethnic cleansing' of the Muslim population was carried out.

Concepción [konsepsyohn] 36°49S 73°03W, pop (2000e) 351 900. Industrial city in C Chile; founded, 1550; often damaged by earthquakes; airfield; railway; university (1919).

concertina A portable reed organ similar in principle to the accordion, but hexagonal in vertical cross-section, smaller, and without a keyboard. The English type, fully chromatic, was patented in 1844: it was largely superseded by the fully developed piano accordion.

concertino [konsherteenoh] **1** A musical work for soloist(s) and orchestra, shorter than a concerto and usually with a lighter accompaniment.

2 The solo group in a concerto grosso.

concerto A musical work for one or more solo instruments and orchestra. The early concerto with a single soloist is associated above all with Vivaldi, whose three-movement form (fast–slow–fast) was adopted by J S Bach, and remained standard in the concertos of Mozart, Beethoven, and most later composers.

concerto grosso A musical work in which a small group of instruments (*concertino*: typically two violins and cello) is contrasted with the full string orchestra (*ripieno*). The Baroque concerto grosso, in four or more movements, was cultivated with particular distinction by Corelli and Handel.

conch A large marine snail found in shallow seas around coral reefs; the queen conch, *Strombus gigas*, is abundant in the Caribbean, and is gathered for food and the curio trade. (Class: Gastropoda. Order: Mesogastropoda.)

conclave (Lat *cum clave*, 'with a key') A meeting of cardinals of the Roman Catholic Church. Its original purpose was to elect a pope; by a tradition dating from 1271, the cardinals are locked into an apartment to hasten election.

Concord (Massachusetts) 42°28N 71°21W, pop (2000e) 17 000. Town in E Massachusetts, USA; 8 km/5 mi NW of Boston; in April 1775 British soldiers attempted to seize military stores in Concord but were resisted by minutemen; battles at Concord (19 Apr) and Lexington marked the start of the American War of Independence; railway.

Concord (New Hampshire) 43°12N 71°32W, pop (2000e) 40 700. Capital of New Hampshire State, USA; established, 1727; city status, 1853; state capital, 1808; railway; home of Mary Baker Eddy.

Concorde The world's first supersonic airliner, built jointly by the British Aircraft Corporation and the French company, Aérospatiale. It entered full-time operational service in January 1976. Its maximum speed was 2·2 times the speed of sound, though normal cruising speed was reduced to twice the speed of sound, ie c.2000 kph/1300 mph. The maximum range was c.6400 km/4000 mi, and the time taken to cross the Atlantic was 3½ hours. It was temporarily withdrawn from service in July 2000 after an Air France Concorde crashed shortly after take-off in Paris killing 113 people. After undergoing a complete overhaul it became operational once more in 2001 but British Airways later decided to retire the aircraft as it was no longer profitable. Concorde was finally withdrawn from service on 24 October 2003.

concrete art An art form defined by the Dutch artist Theo van Doesburg (1883–1931) in 1930 as a totally abstract art 'constructed entirely from purely plastic elements, that is to say planes and colours'.

concrete music *musique concrète*

concrete poetry Poetry which emphasizes the visual presentation of the poem on the page. Classical inscriptions provide a model, and 17th-c emblem poems are simple examples. The French poets Mallarmé and Apollinaire considerably extended visual techniques. Later experiments include the use of different typefaces, colour, collage, and computer graphics.

concussion A state of reversible unconsciousness which may immediately follow a severe blow to the head, but which outlasts the trauma. On regaining consciousness there is impaired memory of the accident or of immediately preceding events.

Condé [kõday] The junior branch of the French royal line, the House of Bourbon, which played a prominent role in French dynastic politics, particularly in the 16th–17th-c. Ten generations bore the title of **Prince de Condé**, the most eminent being Louis XIV's general, Louis II de Bourbon (1621–86), better known as the **Great Condé**.

condensation (physics) The process by which water changes from a gaseous state (*water vapour*) to a liquid state. It can result from uplift of air, radiation cooling on a calm cloudless night, or when warm moist air comes into contact with a cooler surface. In such situations, vapour condenses around condensation nuclei, such as salt, dust, and smoke particles in the air. When condensation occurs at altitude, clouds form; close to the ground, it results in fog or dew.

condensed matter physics *solid-state physics*

Condillac, Etienne Bonnot de [kõdeeyak] (1715–80) Philosopher, born in Grenoble, France. He based all knowledge on the senses, his works including *Essai sur l'origine des connaissances humaines* (1746, Essay on the Origin of Human Knowledge) and *Traité des sensations* (1754, Treatise on Sensations).

condition In law, a relatively important term in a contract. In

English law, breach of condition gives the innocent party the right to treat the contract as terminated. Contracts may also contain **warranties**, which may (eg in Scotland), in the event of a breach, justify repudiating the contract. Breach of a warranty in England is considered less important, and does not give the innocent party the right to end the contract, though a claim for damages may be possible.

conditionality The practice of lenders, in particular the International Monetary Fund (IMF), to impose conditions on the recipients of loans. These conditions include measures such as reducing budget deficits, currency devaluation, or liberalization of trade controls.

conditioning An elementary associative learning process. In **Pavlovian**, **classical**, or **respondent conditioning**, a stimulus which reliably precedes another stimulus of biological significance (eg food, pain, a potential mate) comes to evoke a new pattern of reaction (a **conditioned response**) similar to that evoked by the biologically significant (**unconditioned**) stimulus. For example, salivation, normally evoked by the taste of food, comes to be evoked by the sight of food or the sound of a dinner gong.

condominium 1 In government, the joint rule, tenancy, or co-ownership of a territory by two or more countries, often suggested as appropriate where ownership of a territory is disputed. For example, the former New Hebrides (now the republic of Vanuatu) was, until 1980, jointly administered by Britain and France. **2** A type of co-operative ownership of a domestic dwelling. A person owns a unit (an apartment, or flat) in the building, and typically enters into an arrangement with other unit-owners to share the responsibility for the services to the building and the general upkeep of the site. The concept is particularly associated with property dealing in the USA, where the term is used both for the building as a whole and for the units within it.

condor Either of two species of New World vulture; the **Californian condor** (*Gymnogyps californianus*) and the **Andean condor** (*Vultur gryphus*). The Andean condor, which inhabits the mountains, has the largest wingspan of any living bird (up to 3 m/10 ft). The Californian condor is in danger of extinction. (Family: Cathartidae.)

Condorcet, Marie Jean Antoine Nicolas de Caritat, marquis de (Marquess of) [kŏdaw(r)say] (1743–94) French statesman, philosopher, and mathematician, born in Ribemont. At the Revolution he became president of the Legislative Assembly (1791), siding usually with the Girondists. Condemned by the extreme party, he was found dead in prison. In his philosophy, he proclaimed the ideal of progress, and the indefinite perfectibility of the human race.

conductance *resistance*

conducting The task of directing an orchestra, choir, or other musical group in the performance of a musical work. The conductor establishes a musical rhythm and interpretation, signalling this in a performance by conventional hand and arm movements, as well as by movements of the body and facial expression. A thin stick, or baton, held in the right hand, became widely used only in the mid-19th-c to give a clearly visual emphasis to the basic rhythm; but many modern conductors have dispensed with it, using only their hands. The special role of the conductor emerged only in the 19th-c; previously, the task of keeping the musicians together was performed by one of the leading players. The prestige now associated with the role developed with the emergence of composers (such as Berlioz) who also conducted, and with the serious intellectual and aesthetic demands of major works (such as those by Wagner) in which as much effort had to be devoted to the context of the work and the interpretation of the score as to the accuracy of the playing.

conduction *electrical conduction; thermal conduction*

conductivity *resistivity*

cone In gymnosperms, a spike-like structure formed of woody, overlapping scales bearing seeds. Clubmosses and horsetails have similar structures bearing spores. The term is also used for the cone-like fruits of some flowering plants.

coneflower *rudbeckia*

cones *rods and cones*

coney *pika; rabbit*

Coney Island [kohnee] (Dutch 'rabbit') 40°35N 73°59W. Resort on the S coast of Long Island in New York State, USA; developed as a pleasure resort since the 1840s.

Confederacy *Confederate States of America*

Confederate States of America The official name of the states that seceded in 1860–1, precipitating the American Civil War: Virginia, N Carolina, S Carolina, Georgia, Florida, Tennessee, Alabama, Mississippi, Louisiana, Texas, and Arkansas. Its only president was Jefferson Davis of Mississippi. It never won foreign recognition, and collapsed in 1865.

Confederation (Canada) A movement in the 1860s devoted to the unification of the British North American colonies within a federal framework. New Brunswick, Nova Scotia, Quebec, and Ontario were so joined in 1867. Confederation marked the birth of modern Canada, and it is celebrated annually on 1 July.

Confederation, Articles of *Articles of Confederation*

Confederation of British Industry (CBI) A federation of UK employers, founded in 1965, with a membership of over 250 000 companies. Its role is to ensure that the needs, intentions, and problems of business organizations are generally understood.

Conference on Security and Co-operation in Europe *Organization for Security and Co-operation in Europe*

Confessing Church A Church formed in Germany by Evangelical Christians opposed to Nazism. Its Synod of Barmen published the Barmen Declaration (1934), which became influential in Germany and beyond as a basis for resistance to oppressive civil authorities.

confession 1 A declaration or profession of faith, originally by an individual martyr, later by a group or church. Such a document became common after the Reformation. **2** An acknowledgment of sin, made either corporately in the course of public worship or privately and individually 'into the ear' of a priest.

confessional poetry Poetry which takes as its subject the intimate details of the poet's own life. Generally considered a recent phenomenon, it has been encouraged by US poets such as Robert Lowell and Sylvia Plath.

confirmation The Christian sacrament of initiation. Performed only by the laying on of hands (or by anointing with oil, or both) by a bishop. Children are not usually confirmed before reaching seven years of age, and many Churches prefer them to reach adolescence.

Confucius [konfyooshuhs], Lat name of **Kongfuzi** or **K'ung Fu-tse** (Chin 'Venerated Master Kong') (551–479 BC) Philosopher, born in the state of Lu (modern Shantung), China. Largely self-educated, in 531 BC he began his career as a teacher, aiming to resurrect traditional values and reinforce the structure of social obligations and behaviours which manifested them. Fundamental was benevolence, humanity or goodness, which embraced duty, loyality, and sincerity – fundamental for the maintenance at all levels of society. His precepts are preserved in the Analects (*lunyu*), probably written by some of his 22 disciples. No writings can definitely be attributed to him. His teachings later inspired a cult of veneration. Confucianism became the state religion of China, but he was denounced as a class-exploiter during the Cultural Revolution (1966–76). There are now thought to be over 6 million Confucians.

Congo

200 km
100 mi

AFRICA

CENTRAL AFRICAN
REPUBLIC

Sangha

CAMEROON

Souanké
Impfondo
Ouesso

Sangha

Oubangui

Equator

GABON

Owando

CONGO

Congo

Gamboma

Djambala

Mont de la Lékéti 1040m △

Mbé

Kasaï

Sibiti

Loubomo
Brazzaville

Pointe-Noire

Kinshasa

Cabinda (Ang.)

Congo

D. R. CONGO

ANGOLA

□ International Airport

[konggoh], official name **Republic of the Congo** (1991), formerly **People's Republic of the Congo** (from 1968), Fr **République du Congo**
Local name Congo

Timezone GMT +1
Area 341 945 km²/132 047 sq mi
Population total (2002e) 2 899 000
Status Republic
Date of independence 1960
Capital Brazzaville
Language French (official), with local languages, including Kongo and Téké
Ethnic groups Kongo (45%), Sangha (15%), Téké (20%)
Religions Roman Catholic (40·5%), Protestant (9·5%), local traditional beliefs
Physical features Niari valley rises to 1040 m/3412 ft at Mont de la Lékéti; mainly covered by dense grassland, mangrove, and tropical rainforest; rivers include Sangha and Alima in N.
Climate Hot, humid equatorial climate; annual rainfall 1250–1750 mm/50–70 in, annual daily temperature 28–33°C in Brazzaville; dry season (Jun–Sep).
Currency 1 CFA Franc (XAF) = 100 centimes
Economy Mainly agriculture and forestry; sugar cane, coffee, cocoa, palm oil, tobacco; oil, timber, diamonds; sugar-refining.
GDP (2002e) $2·5 bn, per capita $900
Human Development Index (2002) 0·512
History Visited by Portuguese, 14th-c; part of French Equatorial Africa, known as 'Middle Congo', 1908–58; independence as Republic of Congo, 1960; military coup created first Marxist state in Africa, renamed People's Republic of the Congo, 1968; Congolese Labour Party (PCT), the single ruling party in Congo, renounced Marxism, 1990; transitional government formed, 1991, and country renamed the Republic of Congo; new constitution, 1992, recognized a multi-party system; violence following disputes over the election process, 1993; new constitution, 2001; executive authority vested in the President, elected for a 7-year term, and a bicameral legislature.
Head of State
1992–7 Pascal Lissouba
1997– Denis Sassou-Nguesso
Head of Government
1992–3 Claude Antoine Dacosta
1993–6 Jacques-Joachim Yhombi-Opango
1996–7 Charles David Ganao
1997–2002 Bernard Kolelas

conga An Afro-Cuban dance usually performed (often with singing) in a long line, using simple and repetitive steps. It was popular in Western ballrooms in the mid-20th-c.
congenital abnormality An anatomical or physiological abnormality found at birth or within a few weeks of birth. Some are caused by chromosome abnormalities or genetic defects. Others are caused by environmental factors, such as infections (eg rubella) and drugs given to the mother (eg thalidomide). Some have no obvious cause, such as failure of the testicles to descend, malformations of the heart, and cleft lip and palate.
conger eel Predatory marine fish (*Conger conger*) found in shallow coastal waters of N Europe and Mediterranean, usually within cover of rocks, jetties, or wrecks; body cylindrical, length up to 2·7 m/8¾ ft; jaws powerful, teeth conical and close-set; may be dangerous to divers. (Family: Congridae.)
conglomerate (mineralogy) Sedimentary rock composed of rounded pebbles of pre-existing rocks and embedded in a fine matrix of sand and silt. It is commonly formed along beaches or on river beds.
Congo see panel

Congo, Democratic Republic of *p.218*
Congonhas do Campo [kongohnyas] 23°38S 46°38W, pop (2000e) 30 100. A town in the Brazilian highlands, noted for its 18th-c Sanctuary of Bom ('good') Jesus, an imposing church with chapels and gardens; a world heritage site and pilgrimage centre.
Congo, River [zaheer] (1971–97, known as **River Zaire**) River in C and W Africa; length c.4670 km/2900 mi, second longest in Africa; rises in SE Zaire; enters the Atlantic Ocean.
Congregationalism A movement which sees the Christian Church as essentially a gathered community of believers, covenanting with God, keeping God's law, and living under the Lordship of Christ. It derived from the Separatists of the 16th-c Reformation in England, of whom Robert Browne (c.1550–1633) was an early leader. Persecution drove the Congregationalists to Holland and the USA (the Pilgrim Fathers, 1620). Church affairs, including calling a minister and appointing deacons to assist, are regulated by members at a 'Church Meeting'.
Congress The national, or federal, legislature of the USA, consisting of two elected chambers: the Senate and the House of

Congo, Democratic Republic of

☐ International Airport   ∴ World heritage site
1 Lake Albert   2 Lake Edward   3 Lake Kivu   4 Lake Tanganyika

formerly **Congo Free State** (1885–1908), **Belgian Congo** (1908–60), **Democratic Republic of the Congo** (1960–71), **Republic of Zaire** [zaheer] (1971–97)

Local name République Démocratique du Congo

Timezone GMT +1 (W) to +2 (E)

Area 2 234 585 km²/905 365 sq mi

Population total (2002e) 52 557 000

Status Republic

Date of independence 1960

Capital Kinshasa

Languages French (official), English, with various Bantu dialects (including Swahili, Lingala, Ishiluba, and Kikongo) spoken

Ethnic groups Bantu, with Sudaneseic, Nilotes, Pygmies, Hamite and Angolan minorities

Religions Christian (70%) (Roman Catholic 50%, Protestant 20%), Kimbanguist (10%), Muslim (10%), traditional beliefs (10%)

Physical features Located in C Africa, land rises E from a low-lying basin to a densely forested plateau; Ruwenzori Mts (NE) rise to 5110 m/16 765 ft in the Mt Stanley massif; Mitumba Mts further S; Rift Valley chain of lakes, Albert, Edward, Kivu, and Tanganyika; Congo R.

Climate Equatorial, hot and humid; average annual temperature, 26°C (Jan), 23°C (Jul) in Kinshasa; average annual rainfall 1125 mm/44 in; dry coastal region; dry season (May–Sep) S of the Equator, (Dec–Feb) N of the Equator.

Currency 1 Congolese Franc (CDF) = 100 centimes

Economy Subsistence farming employs c.80% of population; palm oil, rubber, quinine, fruit, vegetables, tea, cocoa; extensive mineral reserves; world's biggest producer of cobalt; industrial diamonds, copper; coffee, petroleum, cotton, tobacco processing, chemicals, cement.

GDP (2002e) $34 bn, per capita $600

Human Development Index (2002) 0.431

History Visited by the Portuguese, 1482; expeditions of Henry Morton Stanley, 1874–7; claimed by King Leopold of Belgium, recognized, 1885; Congo Free State ceded to the state, 1907, and renamed Belgian Congo; independence as the Democratic Republic of the Congo, 1960; shortly after, mineral-rich Katanga (later, Shaba) province claimed independence, leading to civil war; UN peace-keeping force present until 1964; renamed the Republic of Zaïre, 1971; further conflict, 1977–8, as Katangese rebels invaded Shaba province from Angola; President Mobutu announced proposals for the introduction of a new constitution in 1990, including the adoption of a three-party system; dissatisfaction with proposals resulted in boycotting of elections scheduled for 1992; conflict between president and opposition party over appointment of prime minister, 1993; new constitutional act, and period of transition established, 1994; further conflict, 1996; Alliance of Democratic Forces for the Liberation of Congo-Zaire, led by Laurent Kabila, take control; formation of new transitional government, May 1997, with president assuming full executive, legislative, and military powers; further fighting with rebel movements, 1998, with troops from Uganda and Rwanda supporting rebels, and troops from Zimbabwe, Angola, and Namibia supporting government; assassination of Laurent Kabila, 2001; peace negotiations disrupted by ongoing fighting, 2002; peace agreement signed with Rwanda and Uganda, 2002; power-sharing agreement signed between government and key rebel groups (Dec 2002); agreement signed with Uganda providing for withdrawal of Ugandan forces from the NE (Feb 2003); emergency UN peacekeeping force deployed in Bunia (Ituri province) after heavy fighting broke out (May 2003); President Joseph Kabila named an interim government (Jun 2003), leaders of main rebel groups sworn in as vice-presidents (Jul 2003); new constitution adopted, 2006.

Head of State
1960–5 Joseph Kasavubu
1965–97 Mobutu Sese Seko (formerly Joseph Mobutu)

Democratic Republic of Congo
1997–2001 Laurent Kabila
2001– Joseph Kabila

Head of Government
1960 Patrice Emergy Lumumba
1960 Joseph Ileo
1960–1 *College of Commissioners*
1961 Joseph Ileo
1961–4 Cyrille Adoula
1964–5 Moïse Tshombe
1965 Evariste Kimba
1965–6 Mulamba Nyungu wa Kadima
1966–77 *As President*
1977–80 Mpinga Kasenga
1980 Bo-Boliko Lokonga Monse Mihambu
1980–1 Nguza Karl I Bond
1981–3 Nsinga Udjuu
1983–6 Kengo wa Dondo
1986–8 *No Prime Minister*
1988 Sambwa Pida Nbagui
1988–9 Kengo wa Dondo
1989–91 Lunda Bululu
1991 Mulumba Lukeji
1991 Etienne Tshisekedi
1991 Bernardin Mungul Diaka
1991–2 Jean Nguza Karl-I-Bond
1992–3 Etienne Tshisekedi
1993–4 Fouistin Birindwa *Acting*
1994–7 Kengo Wa Dondo
1997 Etienne Tshisekedi
1997 Likulia Bolongo
1997–2003 *As President*
2003– Yerodia Abdoulaye Ndombasi (*Vice President*)

Representatives. Unusually powerful for a modern legislature, Congress can initiate legislation, and significantly amend or reject presidential legislative proposals. For a bill to become law it must be passed in identical form by both chambers and signed by the president. A presidential veto may be overturned by a two-thirds majority in both chambers. Legislation receives detailed consideration in the powerful Congressional committees. The majority party leader of the House occupies the influential position of Speaker.

Congress of Racial Equality A prominent US civil rights organization which campaigns for the rights of African-Americans, and which was particularly involved in the attack on racism in the 1960s. It is regarded as one of the more militant black rights organizations.

Congreve, William [konggreev] (1670–1729) Playwright and poet, born in Bardsey, West Yorkshire. His comedies include *The Old Bachelor*, *The Double Dealer* (1693), and *The Way of the World* (1700).

conic sections *see panel*

conifer A cone-bearing tree; strictly, any member of the gymnosperm order Coniferales.

Coniston Water [konistn] Lake in the Lake District of Cumbria, NW England; length 9 km/6 mi; scene of world water speed record by Malcolm Campbell in 1939; Donald Campbell killed here in 1967 trying to break this record.

conjoined twins *Siamese twins*

conjunction (astronomy) The alignment of two celestial bodies seen from Earth, for example a planet with the Sun. The exact moment of conjunction occurs when the two bodies have the same celestial longitude.

conjunctivitis Inflammation of the membrane covering the inner surface of the eyelids and the front surface of the eye (the **conjunctiva**). It results in feeling of grittiness in the eyes, and is associated with stickiness of the eyelids and a discharge. The whites of the eyes are red and bloodshot.

Connacht or **Connaught** [konawt] pop (2000e) 428 000; area 17 121 km²/6609 sq mi. Province in W Ireland, comprising counties of Sligo, Leitrim, Mayo, Roscommon, Galway.

Connaught *Connacht*

Connecticut [kuhnetikuht] pop (2000e) 3 405 000; area 12 996 km²/5018 sq mi. A state in NE USA, the 'Constitution State', 'Nutmeg State' or 'The Insurance State'; densely populated; explored by Adriaen Block, 1614; one of the original states of the Union, fifth to ratify the Federal Constitution, 1788; highest point, Mt Frissell (725 m/2379 ft); coast largely urbanized, with many industries; interior mainly woodland and forest; capital, Hartford.

connectionism A form of computer modelling in which information processing is carried out by a network of inter-connected units. It is sometimes called **parallel distributed processing**, because information is processed in many parts of the network simultaneously.

Connelly, Jennifer (Lynn) (1970–) Actress, born in Catskill Mountains, NY. She began a modelling career and her acting debut came in an episode of the British TV series *Tales of the Unexpected* (1979). Her first film role was in *Once Upon a Time in America* (1984), and later films include *Mulholland Falls* (1996), *A Beautiful Mind* (2001, Best Actress Golden Globe, BAFTA, Oscar nomination), and *Blood Diamond* (2006).

Connemara [konemahra] Mountainous region in W Galway county, Ireland; rocky coastline with mountains rising to 765 m/2510 ft at Croagh Patrick; peat bogs; numerous lakes.

Connery, Sir Sean, originally **Thomas Connery** (1930–) Film actor, born in Edinburgh. In 1963 he appeared in the highly successful *Dr No* as Ian Fleming's secret agent James Bond, a part he played in seven other films. Other films include *The Untouchables* (1987, Oscar), *The Russia House* (1991), *Entrap-*

conic sections

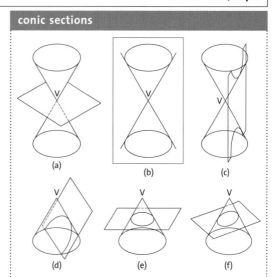

(a)   (b)   (c)

(d)   (e)   (f)

The figure in which a plane cuts a right circular double cone. Several cases arise: (1) If the plane passes through the vertex *V* of the cone, it may cut the cone in a single point *V* (*a*), or in two straight lines (*b*) through *V*, generators of the cone. (2) If the plane is at right angles perpendicular to the axis of the cone, and not through *V*, it cuts the cone in a circle (*e*). (3) If the plane is parallel to a generator of the cone, it cuts the cone in a parabola (*d*); otherwise it cuts the cone in an ellipse (*f*) or a hyperbola (*c*).

ment (1999), and *The League of Extraordinary Gentlemen* (2004). In 1998 he received a BAFTA Fellowship award.

Connolly, Billy (1942–) Comedian, actor, and television presenter, born in Glasgow, Scotland. After leaving school, he worked as an apprentice welder in Glasgow, then entered show business, becoming well known during the 1980s for his one-man theatre comedy performances and television appearances. His film credits include *Mrs Brown* (1997), *Still Crazy* (1998), and *The Man Who Sued God* (2003), and his TV work includes the documentary series *World Tour of New Zealand* (2004).

Connolly, Maureen (Catherine), nickname **Little Mo** (1934–69) Tennis player, born in San Diego, CA. The first woman to win all four major titles in one year (1953), she won the Wimbledon singles in 1952–4, the US title in 1951–3, the French Open in 1953–4, and the Australian title in 1953.

Connors, Jimmy, popular name of **James Scott Connors**, nickname **Jimbo** (1952–) Tennis player, born in Belleville, IL. He became Wimbledon champion in 1974 (against Ken Rosewall) and 1982 (against John McEnroe). He won the US Open in 1974, 1976, 1978, and 1982–3. In 1998 he was elected to the International Tennis Hall of Fame.

conquistador [konkeestadaw(r)] (Span 'conqueror') The standard term for the leaders of the Spanish expeditions of the early 16th-c that undertook the invasion and conquest of America.

Conrad, Joseph, originally **Józef Teodor Konrad Nalecz Korzeniowski** (1857–1924) Novelist, born in Berdichev, Ukraine. His best-known works are *The Nigger of the Narcissus* (1897), *Lord Jim* (1900), *Nostromo* (1904), *The Secret Agent* (1907), *Under Western Eyes* (1911), and *Chance* (1914). He also wrote many short stories.

Conran, Jasper (1959–) Fashion designer, born in London. In 1978

Constellations: northern sky

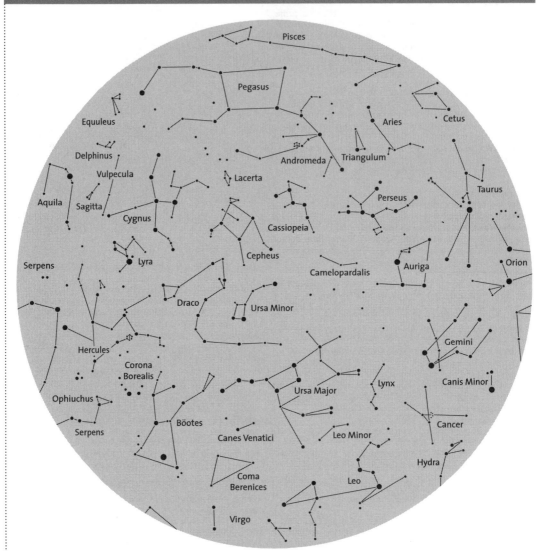

From ancient times, a group of stars that form a recognizable shape or picture. The stars in most constellations are not genuinely related, but lie at greatly different distances from the Solar System. Different cultures have their own ways of delineating the constellations. The system in use by astronomers today has its origins in ancient Mesopotamia, and still includes many names from Greek mythology. Until the 20th-c, the traditional mythological figures were still used to illustrate star atlases.

The boundaries of the constellations were at first drawn using arbitrary curves. This led to great confusion until half of them were agreed along lines of right ascension and declination in

he founded his own company, producing his first collection of easy-to-wear, quality clothes.

Conran, Sir Terence (Orby) (1931–) Designer and businessman, born in Esher, Surrey. He founded and ran the Habitat Company, based on his own success as a furniture designer and the virtues of good design and marketing. His many books include

Terence Conran on Design (1996) and *The Ultimate House Book* (2003).

conscription The practice, dating from the Napoleonic era, of compelling young men (and women, in some countries) of eligible age and fitness to serve by statute in the armed forces of a nation. Conscription was introduced in Great Britain in

Constellations: southern sky

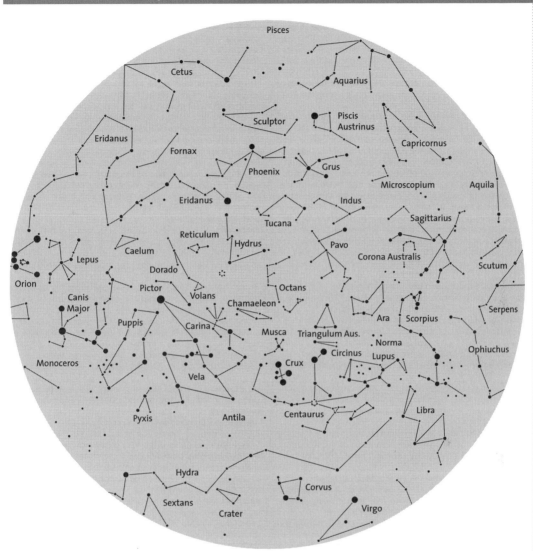

1875, with the remainder being adopted by the International Astronomical Union in 1930. The whole patchwork quilt now includes 88 constellations, which vary enormously in size and shape: the largest, Hydra, is 20 times bigger in area than the smallest, Crux. The Egyptian astronomer Claudius Ptolemy listed 48 constellations in *Almagest* AD c.140; the modern ones were mostly invented in the 16th–18th-c. The brightest stars are named after the constellation in which they are found, using the Greek alphabet and the Latin genitive or possessive form for the constellation: *alpha Ursae Majoris* is thus the brightest star in Ursa Major. Modern astronomers use numerical co-ordinates that computers can readily interpret, to map the sky.

early 1916 and then in the USA (1917). It was again enforced in Britain from 1939–45, continuing in peacetime as **National Service**, which was finally abolished in 1962. In popular US usage, conscription is often referred to as **the draft**, last time invoked during the Vietnam war.

conservation (earth sciences) The protection and preservation of the Earth's resources (eg plants, animals, land, energy, minerals) or of historical artefacts (eg books, paintings, monuments) for the future. The World Conservation Strategy (1980) concluded that conservation of living resources was needed to preserve genetic diversity, to maintain essential ecological processes, and to ensure the sustainable use of species and ecosystems.

conservation laws Sets of rules describing quantities which are the same before and after some physical process. The identification of these laws is central to physics; all physical laws express conservation principles. A conservation law is related to a symmetry of the system. The most important such law is the **conservation of energy**, which is related to the symmetry of physical systems under translation in time. **Conservation of momentum** results from symmetry under translation in space.

conservatism A set of political ideas, attitudes, and beliefs which stress adherence to what is known and established in the political and social orders, as opposed to the innovative and untested. Generally associated with right-wing political parties, conservatives view humanity as inherently imperfect, emphasizing the need for law and order and the value of tradition.

Conservative Party, nickname **Tories** One of the two main political parties in the UK, its full name being the **Conservative and Unionist Party**, due to its adherence to union of the countries making up the UK. It has been the most successful party electorally this century. In common with other Conservative parties, it is on the right of the political spectrum, though in the 1980s it fused conservative with radical neo-liberal ideas. It developed out of the Tory Party in the 1830s, and spent long periods power 1886–1905 and 1922–45. Later periods in office are 1951–64 (under Churchill, Eden, Macmillan and Home), 1970–4 (under Heath) and 1979–97 (under Thatcher and Major), when it was defeated by the Labour Party.

consols [konsolz] Loan-stock issued by the British government, first introduced in 1751; its name derives from *consolidated fund*. It is a form of gilt-edged stock, but 'undated' – no redemption date is given for the return of the capital.

Constable, John (1776–1837) Landscape painter, born in East Bergholt, Suffolk. Among his best-received works were 'Haywain' (1821, National Gallery, London) and 'White Horse' (1825, New York). His work was especially popular in France. He is today considered, along with Turner, as the leading painter of the English countryside.

Constance, Ger **Konstanz**, ancient **Constantia** 47°39N 9°10E, pop (2000e) 77 400. Lake port in Germany, on L Constance; former episcopal see and imperial city; railway; university (1966); cathedral (15th-c).

Constance, Lake, Ger **Bodensee**, ancient **Lacus Brigantinus** area 541 km²/209 sq mi. Lake on the N side of the Swiss Alps, forming a meeting point of Switzerland, Austria, and Germany; length, 64 km/40 mi; part of the course of the R Rhine.

Constance, Council of, Ger **Konzil von Konstanz** (1414–18) The first large Church assembly of the Middle Ages, convened in Constance, SW Germany, to settle the question of papal succession. It also dealt with the question of reform and condemned as heretical the doctrines of John Wycliffe and Jan Huss. The election of Pope Martin V ended the schism between the popes of Rome and Avignon.

Constant (de Rebeque), (Henri) Benjamin [kōstã duh rebek] (1767–1830) Novelist and politician, born in Lausanne, Switzerland. He supported the Revolution, but was banished in 1802 for his opposition to Napoleon. His best-known work is the novel *Adolphe* (1816), based on his relationship with Madame de Staël.

Constanţa [konstantsa], Eng **Constantza**, ancient **Tomis** or **Constantinia** 44°10N 28°40E, pop (2000e) 307 000. Major port in SE Romania, on the W shores of the Black Sea; established as a Greek colony, 7th-c BC; under Roman rule from 72 BC; named after Constantine I (4th-c AD); ceded to Romania, 1878; airport; railway.

Constantine [konstanteen], ancient **Ciria**, **Qacentina** 36°22N 6°40E, pop (2000e) 549 200. Town in NE Algeria; oldest city in Algeria, important since the 3rd–4th-c BC; Roman provincial capital of Numidia; destroyed in AD 311 during a civil war, rebuilt by Constantine I; seat of successive Muslim dynasties in Middle Ages; French occupation in 1837; airport; railway; university (1969).

Constantine I (Emperor), known as **the Great**, originally **Flavius Valerius Constantinus** (c.274–337) Roman emperor, born in Naissus, Moesia. He became emperor of the West after his defeat of Maxentius at the Milvian Bridge in Rome (312), and emperor of the East after his victory over Licinius (324). Believing that his victory in 312 was the work of the Christian God, he became the first emperor to promote Christianity, whence his title 'Great'. His edict of Milan (313), issued jointly with Licinius, brought toleration to Christians throughout the empire.

Constantine II (of Greece) (1940–) King of Greece (1964–73), born near Athens, who succeeded his father, Paul I. In 1964 he married **Princess Anne-Marie of Denmark** (1946–) and has two sons and a daughter. He fled to Rome (Dec 1967) after an abortive coup against the military government which had seized power, and was deposed in 1973.

constellations *pp.220–21*

constituency A territorial division that in many countries serves as a unit in the election of one or more political representatives to national assemblies. Population usually serves as the main criterion in determining the size of each constituency. For example, in the USA 435 people are elected to the House of Representatives from constituencies with roughly equivalent populations, while two senators are elected from each state, regardless of population size. The UK contains 659 single-member constituencies, most with electorates of c.65 000.

constitution Usually a written document which contains the rules determining the way that a country may be governed in terms of the sources, purpose, use, and limits upon the exercise of political power. The UK is one of a few exceptions in having an unwritten constitution, although in all countries the identification of constitutional principles include reference to statute law, judicial interpretation, tradition, and other constitutional practices.

Constitutional Convention (1787) A gathering at Philadelphia during the American Revolution that produced the present US Constitution; 12 of the original 13 states were represented.

Constitution of the United States A constitution founded upon the principles of the Declaration of Independence, and based on the concepts of limited and responsible government, and federalism. The constitutional document comprises a short preamble followed by seven articles which include: the organization, powers and procedures of the legislative branch (Congress); the powers of the president and executive; the powers of the judiciary, including the Supreme Court; the rights of the states; and procedures for amending the constitution. The articles are then followed by 26 amendments, the first 10 of which are known as the *bill of rights*.

Constitutions of Clarendon *Clarendon, Constitutions of*

constrictor A snake which wraps its body tightly around its prey and, by squeezing, induces suffocation; teeth carry no venom.

Constructivism An imprecise term usually applied to a form of abstract art that began in Russia in 1917, using machine-age materials such as steel, glass, and plastic. Leading practitioners included Antoine Pevsner and Naum Gabo. Their ideas exerted a deep influence on abstract artists in the West (**International Constructivism**).

consubstantiation A theory attributed to Luther, describing the presence of Christ in the Eucharist 'under or with the elements of bread and wine'. It is to be contrasted with the Roman Catholic doctrine of transubstantiation.

consul 1 In Republican Rome (5th-c–1st-c BC), a chief executive officer of state, with military and judicial functions. Two con-

Continents

Name	Area		% of	Lowest point below sea level			Highest elevation		
	km²	sq mi	total		m	ft		m	ft
Africa	30 293 000	11 696 000	20.2	Lake Assal, Djibouti	156	512	Kilimanjaro, Tanzania	5 895	19 340
Antarctica	13 975 000	5 396 000	9.3	Bently subglacial trench	2 538	8 327	Vinson Massif	5 140	16 864
Asia	44 493 000	17 179 000	29.6	Dead Sea, Israel/Jordan	400	1 312	Mt Everest, China/ Nepal	8 848	29 028
Oceania	8 945 000	3 454 000	6.0	Lake Eyre, S Australia	15	49	Puncak Jaya (Ngga Pulu), Indonesia	5 030	16 500
Europe	10 245 000	3 956 000	6.8	Caspian Sea, Russia	29	94	Elbrus, Russia	5 642	18 510
North America	24 454 000	9 442 000	16.3	Death Valley, California	86	282	Mt McKinley, Alaska	6 194	20 320
South America	17 838 000	6 887 000	11.9	Peninsular Valdez, Argentina	40	131	Aconcagua, Argentina	6 959	22 831

suls were elected annually. The consulship was the highest rank in the hierarchy of offices (the *cursus honorum*) and could not be held before the age of 36.

2 *ambassador*

consumerism The promotion of policies aimed at regulating the standards of manufacturers and sellers in the interests of buyers. The stimulus may come from a government, through legislation, from an industry itself, through setting up codes of practice, or from consumer pressure groups.

consumption (economics) The part of national income used to satisfy immediate human needs. This includes both consumer spending by individuals or families, and government consumption. Consumption is contrasted with investment, or spending to create the means of future production. Consumer goods are divided between consumer non-durables, such as food, clothing, heating, or travel, and consumer durables such as furnishings or cars. For most countries consumption is the largest component of national expenditure.

contact In England and Wales, under the Children Act (1989), a concept which replaced the former concepts of access and custody of a child by a parent or guardian during or after divorce, judicial separation, or the annulment of a marriage. Court orders made under the Act are known as *Section 8 orders*, and include *residence orders*, which formalize arrangements about where a child is to live, and *contact orders*, which permit a parent or anyone with whom the child has lived for the last three years to communicate with or stay with the child regularly.

contact lens A disc of plastic which fits over the front of the eye, usually to correct vision problems, in the same way as spectacles. Coloured contact lenses can change the apparent colour of the eye, generally for theatrical or cosmetic reasons. Contact lenses first became available in the 1930s. Early devices, called *scleral* or *haptic* lenses, covered the complete front of the eyeball. Modern lenses are the much smaller *corneal* lenses, and fit over the coloured part of the eye (the iris). Contact lenses can be *hard* or *soft*, offering different possibilities with respect to such features as visual improvement, maintenance, length of wear, comfort, convenience, and side-effects. Hard lenses are made from perspex (polymethylmethacrylate, or PMMA). Those which allow oxygen to pass through are called *rigid gas permeable* (RGP) and are made from cellulose acetate butyrate (CAB). Soft lenses are made from hydroxyethylmethacrylate – a plastic which contains water and is like a gel.

Contadora, Isla [eeslya kontadohra] 8°40N 79°02W. Island of Panama, in the Pearl Is, Gulf of Panama; meeting place of the foreign ministers of Colombia, Mexico, Panama, and Venezuela

(the Contadora Group) in 1983 to discuss the problems of Central America; their proposed solutions became known as the **Contadora process**.

contagious abortion *brucellosis*

container ship A cellular ship, designed to carry 6 m/20 ft or 12 m/40 ft boxes in predetermined positions, thus largely dispensing with the lashing or stowage problems associated with traditional cargo. The first purpose-built ships were commissioned in 1966 by a British company; by the early 1990s there were 26 million gross tonnes of container ships in the world.

containment building A steel or concrete structure enclosing a nuclear reactor, designed to withstand high pressure and high temperature and, in an emergency, to contain the escape of radiation. Such a building must also withstand external hazards, such as high winds and heavy snow.

conté crayon [kõtay] A type of synthetic chalk named after its French inventor, Nicolas Jacques Conté (1755–1805). It is used by artists, and is available in black, white, red, and brown.

contempt of court A wide-ranging term which includes failure to comply with an order of the court, and conduct which obstructs the process of the courts (eg by intimidating witnesses or causing a disturbance in court). A person in contempt may be committed to prison or fined.

Conti, Tom [kontee], popular name of **Thomas A Conti** (1942–) Actor and director, born in Paisley, W Scotland. He made his acting debut in 1960, and has since performed and directed regularly in London theatres, receiving a Tony Award for Best Actor in 1979. Among his films are *Merry Christmas, Mr Lawrence* (1982), *Shirley Valentine* (1989), and *Don't Go Breaking My Heart* (1998). TV appearances include *The Norman Conquests* and *Glittering Prizes*, and the later *Donovan* (2004).

continent A term applied to the seven large land masses on the Earth's surface: Asia, Africa, North America, South America, Antarctica, Europe, and Australia, in decreasing order of size. The continents (including the submerged continental shelves) make up about 35% of the Earth's crust, the rest being made up of the oceanic plates. (*see panel*)

Continental Congress (1774–88) The gathering that declared and led the struggle for American independence. Each of the 13 colonies (states after 1776) had one vote. The First Congress met for six weeks in 1774. The Second (convened Apr 1775) did not formally dissolve until replaced by the government under the present Constitution, adopted in 1788.

Continental Divide or **Great Divide** A line of mountain peaks in North America extending SE from NW Canada down the W USA into Mexico, Central America, and South America where it meets the N end of the Andes; a major watershed, with rivers running to the Atlantic and the Pacific; includes the Rocky Mts in Canada and the USA.

continental drift A theory which proposes that the present positions of the continents and oceans results from the breaking up of a single large land mass or 'supercontinent', termed *Pangaea*, c.200 million years ago. The idea is generally ascribed to Alfred Wegener (1910) but gained little support until the 1960s, when the theory of plate tectonics was established.

Continental System The process of economic warfare introduced by Napoleon to destroy British commercial power, after Trafalgar put paid to his invasion plans. The Decrees of Berlin (1806) and Milan (1807) established a blockade of European and neutral trade with Britain and her colonies.

continuo The practice, common to most Baroque music, of filling out the harmonic texture by reference to a specially notated bass line (a *figured bass*). The continuo is usually supplied by a harmony instrument (harpsichord, organ, lute, etc) reinforced by a melodic bass instrument (cello, double bass, bassoon, etc).

continuous assessment The appraisal of students' work on a regular basis rather than exclusively by final examination. Essays, practical work, projects, and assignments done during the course might form all or part of the final assessment, which can be based on marks, grades, or a profile.

contrabassoon *bassoon*

contraception The prevention of pregnancy following sexual intercourse; also known as **birth control** or **family planning**. For centuries its practice was opposed by the Church and the medical profession, but it has come to be widely advocated in order to control populations, protect against venereal disease, and regulate the size of families. Many methods are in use. The use of a 'safe period' – the **rhythm method** – is based on the fact that both spermatozoa and ova survive for only a day or two after release. Attractive to the Roman Catholic Church, it is fallible because of the difficulty in timing ovulation and the variability of the duration of the menstrual cycle. The condom, made of siliconed latex with an expanded part or teat on the end, is widely advocated because its mechanical protection guards not only against pregnancy but also against AIDS. Other **mechanical devices** include shields, diaphragms, or caps inserted into the vagina over the cervix. Their effectiveness can be improved by the use of spermicidal agents. **Intrauterine devices** (IUD) are coils or hooks made out of plastic or metal that are inserted by a trained person into the uterus. They act by preventing the products of conception becoming embedded in the wall of the uterus. The **contraceptive pill** contains synthetic steroids similar to the female sex hormones oestrogen and progesterone, either together or progesterone alone. They inhibit ovulation and induce changes in the lining and secretions of the cervix, uterus, and uterine tubes that makes them hostile to sperm. **Post-coital contraceptives** (the 'morning-after pill') contain the synthetic oestrogen stilboestrol, which prevents implantation of any fertilized egg. It is insufficiently safe to be used as an ordinary contraceptive device, and is reserved for emergencies (eg if a condom splits, or in the event of unplanned unprotected intercourse). Substance RU-486 (mifepristone, often referred to as the 'abortion pill') was launched in 1988, surrounded by considerable controversy; designed for use in the early stages of pregnancy, it causes the womb lining to shed as in normal menstruation.

contract A legally enforceable agreement. A contract has certain essential features – for example, the parties must have *legal capacity* (ie be legally able to enter into the agreement – such as by being old enough). There is no general rule that a contract must be in writing – buying something in a shop is a contractual agreement.

contract bridge *bridge* (recreation)

Contras *Nicaragua*

control *seance*

control engineering The branch of engineering concerned with the control and adjustment of systems. A human operator need not be involved. Control is achieved by using closed loop systems: when an error is detected, the information is returned to the input and used to correct the error – a system known as *feedback*.

contrology *Pilates*

convection The flow of heat by the actual movement of a gas or liquid. For example, air warmed by a fire expands, becomes less dense, and so rises, creating a **convection current** as fresh cool air is drawn in to replace the warmed air.

conversation piece A type of small group portrait which flourished in 18th-c England, representing a family and/or friends grouped informally either indoors or in a landscape or garden setting.

conveyance A legal document which, when signed, sealed, and delivered, transfers ownership of real property (eg in England and Wales) or heritable property (eg in Scotland) such as houses or land (specified in the document) from one party to another. In the USA, the document is usually a deed (a seal is no longer required in most US jurisdictions). In the UK, the Administration of Justice Act (1985) permits licensed conveyancing to be carried on for payment by a class of persons who are not solicitors. These **licensed conveyancers** are subject to the professional controls of the Council for Licensed Conveyancers. In the USA, private parties may convey land.

Convocation A gathering of Church of England clergy to regulate affairs of the Church. The **Upper House** consists of the archbishop and bishops; the **Lower House** of representatives of the lower clergy. The two convocations form the Church Assembly, which meets two or three times a year.

convolvulus *bindweed*

convulsion An involuntary contraction of all the muscles in the body, with widespread muscle spasms, rolling eyeballs, laboured breathing, and tightly clenched teeth. It may be due to epilepsy or metabolic disturbances, and can occur as a reaction to fever in children (*febrile convulsion*).

Conwy, Eng **Conway** 53°17N 3°50W, pop (2000e) 13 900. Historic market town and resort in Aberconwy and Colwyn county, NC Wales, UK; at head of R Conwy (Conway); 13th-c castle (a world heritage site); road tunnel beneath river.

cony *hyrax; pika; rabbit*

Cook, Mount 43°37S 170°08E. Mountain in W South Island, New Zealand, in the Southern Alps; height, 3764 m/12 349 ft; highest peak in New Zealand; in Mount Cook National Park, a world heritage site; landslide in 1991 lowered its summit by 11 m to 3753 m/12 313 ft.

Cook, James (1728–79) Navigator, born in Marton, North Yorkshire. He surveyed the area around the St Lawrence R, Quebec, then in the *Endeavour* carried the Royal Society expedition to Tahiti to observe the transit of Venus across the Sun (1768–71), circumnavigated New Zealand, and charted parts of Australia. In his second voyage he sailed round Antarctica (1772–5), and visited several Pacific island groups. His third voyage (1776–9) aimed to find a passage round the N coast of America from the Pacific; but he was forced to turn back, and on his return voyage was killed by natives on Hawaii.

Cook, Peter (Edward) (1937–95) Comedian and actor, born in Torquay, Devon. He became known as one of the writers and performers of *Beyond the Fringe* (1959–64), and for his collaboration with Dudley Moore in the irreverent television programme, *Not Only... But Also* (1965–70).

Cook, Robin, popular name of **Robert Finlayson Cook** (1946–2005) British statesman, born in Bellshill, North Lanarkshire, Scotland. He became an MP in 1974, held various posts in the shadow cabinet, and was chairman of the Labour Party (1996–

8). He became foreign secretary in the Labour government (1997) and Leader of the Commons (2001), but resigned in 2003 over his opposition to war in Iraq.

Cook, Sue, popular name of **Susan Lorraine Cook** (1949–) Broadcaster, born in Ruislip, Greater London. She joined Capital Radio as a producer and presenter (1974–6), then moved to the BBC. She became well known for her television work, including *Breakfast Time*, *Holiday*, and *Crimewatch UK*, while also working with several charities. In 2005 she began presenting *Making History* for BBC Radio 4.

Cook, Thomas (1808–92) British railway excursion and tourist pioneer, born in Melbourne, Derbyshire. In the 1860s he became an agent for the sale of travel tickets and built up the business of Thomas Cook & Son, now a worldwide organisation.

Cooke, (Alfred) Alistair (1908–2004) Journalist and broadcaster, born in Manchester, Greater Manchester. A sympathetic and urbane commentator on current affairs and popular culture in the USA, where he lived from 1937, his 'Letter from America', broadcast by the BBC from 1946 to 2004, was the longest-running solo radio feature programme. His BBC TV series *America* (1972–3) also produced a best-selling book. He received an honorary knighthood in 1973, and in 2003 was inducted into the newly established Radio Hall of Fame. He retired from broadcasting at the beginning of March 2004, because of illness, and died within the month.

Cook Islands pop (2000e) 20 400; area 238 km²/92 sq mi. Widely scattered group of 15 volcanic and coral islands, c.3200 km/2000 mi NE of New Zealand, S Pacific Ocean; self-governing country in free association with New Zealand; capital, Avarua (on Rarotonga); timezone GMT −10; mainly Polynesian population; main religion, Christianity; official language, English, with local languages widely spoken; unit of currency, New Zealand dollar; highest island, Rarotonga, rises to 650 m/2132 ft; climate damp and tropical; placed under British protection, 1888–1901; New Zealand dependency, 1901; internally self-governing, 1965; Legislative Assembly, with a premier as head of state; economy mainly agriculture and fishing.

Cookson, Dame Catherine (Ann) (1906–98) Novelist, born in East Jarrow, Tyne and Wear. Most of her novels are set in the NE of England, several of them belonging to a series tracing the fortunes of a single character or family, such as *Tilly Trotter* (1981). Other novels include *Rooney* (1957), *The Round Tower* (1968), *The Thursday Friend* (1998), and *Kate Hannigan's Girl* (2000, posthumously). In 1988 a third of all fiction borrowed from public libraries in the UK was by this author.

Cook Strait Channel of the Pacific Ocean separating North Island from South Island, New Zealand; 23–130 km/14–80 mi wide; visited by Captain Cook in 1770.

Coolidge, (John) Calvin (1872–1933) US statesman and 30th president (1923–9), born in Plymouth, VT. A strong supporter of US business interests, he was triumphantly re-elected by the Republicans in 1924, but refused renomination in 1928. His economic policies were later questioned because of the depression that followed his administration.

Coombs, Herbert Cole, nickname **Nugget Coombs** (1906–97) Australian public servant, born in Perth, Western Australia. He joined the [Australian] Commonwealth Bank, becoming its governor in 1949, and in 1959 was inaugural governor of the Reserve Bank of Australia. Pro-Chancellor of the Australian National University in 1959, he became Chancellor in 1968. He was personal adviser to seven Australian prime ministers.

Cooper, Gary (Frank) (1901–61) US film actor, born in Helena, MT. He was the archetypal hero of many Westerns, notably in *High Noon* (1952) and in the Hemingway epics *A Farewell to Arms* (1932) and *For Whom the Bell Tolls* (1943). In addition to two

Oscars for Best Actor he received a Special Academy Award in 1960.

Cooper, Sir Henry (1934–) Boxer, born in Bellingham, Kent. The only man to win the Lonsdale Belt outright on three occasions, he beat Brian London to win his first British heavyweight title in 1959, but lost the title in a disputed contest against Joe Bugner in 1971. After flooring Cassius Clay at Wembley in 1963, he had his only world title fight in 1966, when a bad cut against Muhammad Ali (formerly, Cassius Clay) forced his early retirement from the contest. He does much work for charity, and is a popular television personality.

Cooper, James Fenimore (1789–1851) Novelist, born in Burlington, NJ. He is best known for his frontier adventures such as *The Last of the Mohicans* (1826) and *The Pathfinder* (1840). He also wrote novels and historical studies about the sea.

Cooper, Jilly, *née* **Sallitt** (1937–) Writer and journalist, born in London. Her books include several general interest works, such as *Jolly Marsupial* (1982) and *Angels Rush In* (1990), and the novels *Polo* (1991), *Score!* (1999), and *Wicked!* (2006).

Cooper, Leon Neil (1930–) Physicist, born in New York City. His theory of the behaviour of electron pairs (**Cooper pairs**) in certain materials at low temperatures was a major contribution to the theory of superconductivity. He shared the Nobel Prize for Physics in 1972.

Cooper, Dame Whina (1895–1994) Maori leader, born in Hokianga, New Zealand. From the 1930s she became nationally known for her efforts to help her people recover from the problems caused by European settlement. In 1951 she became the founding president of the Maori Women's Welfare League, and in 1975 led a historic march to publicize Maori land claims.

Cooper, William, pseudonym **H(arry) S(ummerfield) Hoff** (1910–2002) Novelist, born in Crewe, Cheshire. In the 1930s he published four novels under his own name, but it was *Scenes from Provincial Life* (1950) that established his reputation and influenced the 'Angry Young Men' of the 1950s. Later works included *Scenes from Married Life* (1961), *Scenes from Metropolitan Life* (1982), and *Scenes from Later Life* (1983).

co-operative *collective farm; farmer co-operative*

co-operative society A business venture owned by its members, who may be customers (in the case of a retail co-operative) or the employees (in a manufacturing company). The profits are distributed among members only. The first society was set up in 1844 in Rochdale, and soon each town had a 'co-op' store. In 1862, the retail co-operative societies set up the **Co-operative Wholesale Society (CWS)**, which manufactures and distributes goods to its members, its profits being ploughed back or distributed to member societies.

co-ordinate geometry *analytic geometry*

coot A bird of the rail family, inhabiting fresh water; widespread; front of head with horny shield; sides of toes lobed, to assist swimming; pelvis and legs modified for diving. (Genus: *Fulica*, 9 species.)

Copán [kopahn] 14°52N 89°10W. An ancient Mayan city in the Motagua Basin of W Honduras, noted for its three-dimensional stone carving; flourished in the 8th-c AD; area 39 km²/15 sq mi; now a world heritage site; town of Copán (or Santa Rosa de Copán) nearby.

Cope, Wendy (Mary) (1945–) Poet, writer, and journalist, born in Kent. Her first collection of poems, *Making Cocoa for Kingsley Amis*, was published in 1986. She won the Cholmondeley Award for poetry in 1987, and the Michael Braude Award for Light Verse in 1995. She has also written many books for children.

Copenhagen [kohpnhaygn], Danish **København**, Lat **Hafnia** 55°43N 12°34E, pop (2000e) 478 400. Capital city of Denmark; developed around 12th-c fortifications; charter, 1254; capital, 1443; airport; railway; university (1479); technical university of Denmark (1829); shipping and commercial centre; old citadel of Frederikshavn; Tivoli amusement park (May–Sep); Amalienborg Palace (residence of Danish monarch since 1794); Christiansborg Palace; cathedral; Little Mermaid sculpture (1913).

copepod [kohpepod] A small aquatic arthropod; free-living forms extremely abundant in most marine and freshwater habitats, forming a vital link in the food chain by feeding on minute plant plankton; the subclass contains c.9000 species. (Subphylum: Crustacea. Subclass: Copepoda.)

Copernican system A model of the Solar System in which the Sun is at the centre, with the Earth and other planets moving in combinations of circular movements around it (a *heliocentric* system). Prior to the publication of this theory in 1543, it was held by European astronomers that the Earth lay at the centre of the universe.

Copernicus, Nicolas [kopernikus], Polish **Mikolaj Kopernik** (1473–1543) The founder of modern astronomy, born in Toruń, Poland. His 400-page treatise, *De revolutionibus orbium coelestium* (completed 1530, On the Revolutions of the Celestial Spheres) had a hostile reception when it was published (1543).

Copland, Aaron [kohpland] (1900–90) Composer, born in New York City. Among his compositions are those tapping a deep vein of US tradition and folk music, as in the ballets *Billy the Kid* (1938) and *Appalachian Spring* (1944). He also composed film scores, two operas, and three symphonies.

Copleston, Frederick (Charles) [kohplston] (1907–94) Jesuit philosopher, born near Taunton, Somerset. He wrote several books on individual philosophers and movements, as well as an eight-volume *History of Philosophy* (1946–66).

copper Cu, element 29, density 9 g/cm³, melting point 1080°C. The only brown metal, known from ancient times; its name derives from Cyprus, the main source in Roman times. It corrodes slowly, conducts electricity well, and is used mainly in electrical apparatus.

Copper Age *Three Age System*

Copperbelt pop (2000e) 2 119 400; area 31 328 km²/12 093 sq mi. Province in C Zambia; economic centre of the country because of its vast copper and cobalt reserves, the world's largest known deposits; capital, Ndola.

Copperhead A term for members of the US Democratic Party who opposed the Civil War. It is derived from the name of a poisonous snake.

copperhead A pit viper (*Agkistrodon contortrix*) native to SE USA; top of head reddish-brown; bites more people in North America than any other venomous snake, but venom is weak and deaths are rare.

Coppola, Francis Ford [kopohla] (1939–) Film director and screenwriter, born in Detroit, MI. Among his outstanding productions are *The Godfather* (1972; *Part II*, 1974; *Part III*, 1990) and his controversial study of the Vietnam War, *Apocalypse Now* (1979). Later films include *Peggy Sue Got Married* (1987) and *The Rainmaker* (1997).

Coppola, Sofia (1971–) Director and actress, born in New York City. The daughter of film director Francis Ford Coppola, she gained attention with her performance as Mary Corleone in her father's final part of *The Godfather* trilogy. As a director her work includes *The Virgin Suicides* (1999), *Lost in Translation* (2003, Oscar for best original screenplay), and *Marie-Antoinette* (2006), for which she also wrote the screenplay.

copra The dried kernel of the coconut. In the 1860s, to supplement supplies of animal fats, manufacturers of soap, margarine, and lubricants turned to tropical vegetable oils, especially coconut oil. Plantations were set up to produce copra, from which the oil is extracted by crushing.

co-processor A second computer processor, an optional extra processor on most personal computers, which allows the computer to carry out specific tasks more quickly. Examples are mathematics and graphics co-processors.

Coptic Church (Gr *aigyptos* 'Egyptian') The Christian Church in Egypt of ancient origin, claiming St Mark as founder. After the Council of Chalcedon (451), the Copts split from the rest of the Church, preserving the **Coptic language**, and observing the liturgy and sacraments of the ancient Alexandrian rite. It maintains a monastic tradition and structure, its head (called a *pope*) being elected by a religious tribunal and confirmed by the Egyptian government.

copyright Ownership of and right of control over all possible ways of reproducing a 'work', ie the product of an original creative act by one or more people, in a form which makes it possible to be copied. In particular, copyright protection is given to literary, dramatic, and artistic works (paintings, drawings, photographs, etc), sound recordings, films, television and sound broadcasts, and various productions of new technology. At some time or other the work falls into public ownership and can be copied without permission: in the UK, since 1996, the period is 70 years after the creator's death (previously, 50); in the USA, since 1978, the period is 50 years for most works (previously 28, once renewable).

coracle A small circular craft first constructed from reeds in basket form by ancient Britons. It was light enough to be carried on a man's back. The tradition mainly survives in Wales, where coracles are still used by salmon fishermen.

coral A typically massive hydroid, found in colonies in warm shallow seas; many produce a calcareous external skeleton forming coral reefs. (Phylum: Cnidaria. Class: Hydrozoa.)

Coral Sea or **Solomon Sea** area 4 791 000 km²/1 850 200 sq mi. Arm of the Pacific Ocean, bounded W by NE Australia, N by Papua New Guinea and the Solomon Is, many coral islands; scene of US victory over Japanese, 1942.

Coral Sea Islands, Territory of the Uninhabited territory in the Coral Sea off the NE coast of Australia, administered by the Australian government since 1969; comprises scattered reefs and islands (including the Great Barrier Reef) over a sea area of about 1 million km².

cor anglais [kawr ongglay] (Fr 'English horn') A woodwind instrument with a slightly conical bore, a double reed, and a distinctive bulb-shaped bell. Neither English nor a horn, it is in effect a tenor oboe.

corbelling A prehistoric method of constructing a vault, using courses of dry stone stepped successively inwards until they come close enough together to span with a single slab or capstone. The chambered tombs of Maes Howe and New Grange afford notable early examples in N Europe.

Corbett, Ronnie, popular name of **Ronald Balfour Corbett** (1930–) Comedian, born in Edinburgh. His television series include *Sorry!* (1981–8), *Small Talk* (1994–6), and a fruitful partnership with Ronnie Barker led to the long-running *The Two Ronnies* (1971–87). Film appearances comprised *Casino Royale* (1967) and *No Sex Please, We're British* (1972).

Corday (d'Armont), (Marie) Charlotte [kaw(r)day] (1768–93) Noblewoman, born in St Saturnin, France. A sympathizer with the aims of the Revolution, she came to be horrified by the acts of the Jacobins. She managed to obtain an audience with Marat, while he was in his bath, and stabbed him. She was guillotined four days later.

Cordeliers, Club of the [kaw(r)delyay] An extreme revolutionary club founded in Paris (1790) by Danton and Marat; also called the **Society of the Friends of the Rights of Man and Citizen**.

Córdoba (Argentina) [kaw(r)dohba], Span [korthoba] 31°25S 64°11W, pop (2000e) 1 327 000. City in C Argentina; founded, 1573; renowned as a Jesuit mission centre; airport; railway; three universities (including Argentina's first, 1613); cathedral (1758). The Jesuit Block in Córdoba is a world heritage site.

Córdoba (Spain) [**kaw(r)**dohba], Span [**kort**hoba] 37°50N 4°50W, pop (2000e) 305 000. City in Andalusia, S Spain; capital of

Moorish Spain, 8th-c; bishopric; airport; railway; cathedral; Great Mosque (completed 990) is a world heritage site.

Córdoba Cathedral Originally a mosque built (785–6) by Abd-er-Rahman I (731–88) in Córdoba, Spain. It has been used as a Christian cathedral since 1238, and is now a world heritage site.

Corelli, Arcangelo [korelee] (1653–1713) Composer, born in Fusignano, Italy. His concerti grossi, and his solo and trio sonatas for violin, mark an epoch in chamber music, and influenced a whole generation of composers.

Corelli, Marie [korelee], pseudonym of **Mary Mackay** (1855–1924) Novelist, born in London. Her romantic melodramas, such as *Barabbas* (1893) and *The Sorrows of Satan* (1895), were extremely popular.

Corfu [kawfoo], Gr **Kérkira** pop (2000e) 110 000; area 592 km²/228 sq mi. Northernmost and second largest of the Ionian Is, Greece, off NW coast of Greece; length 64 km/40 mi; semi-mountainous terrain (highest point 907 m/2976 ft), dense vegetation; chief town, Corfu, pop (2000e) 36 500; airport.

corgi The only British spitz breed of dog; small with short legs, pointed muzzle, large erect ears; two varieties: short-tailed **Pembroke** and long-tailed **Cardigan**; also known as **Welsh corgi**.

coriander An annual (*Coriandrum sativum*), growing to 50 cm/20 in, native to N Africa and W Asia; flowers white or pink, petals unequal; fruit globular. The leaves are used in Chinese, Indian, and Mexican cooking; the fruits are used as a spice in sausages, curries, confectionery, and liqueurs. (Family: Umbelliferae.)

Corinth, Gr **Kórinthos** 37°56N 22°55E, pop (2000e) 30 200. City in Greece, on an isthmus separating the Adriatic Sea from the Aegean; founded before 3000 BC; influential Greek city-state of Dorian origins; destroyed by Romans 146 BC; ancient Kórinthos, 7 km/4 mi SW; transferred to new site in 1858, after a severe earthquake; railway; extensive remains, including Archaic Temple of Apollo.

Corinthian order One of the five main orders of classical architecture, characterized by a fluted shaft and a decorative acanthus capital. It was first invented in Athens in the 5th-c BC.

Corinthians, Letters to the Two New Testament writings, widely accepted as genuinely from the apostle Paul to the church that he founded in Corinth.

Coriolanus, Gaius or **Gnaeus Marcius** [koriolaynus] (5th-c BC) Roman folk hero, so named from his capture of the Volscian town of Corioli. Banished by the Romans for tyrannical behaviour (491 BC), he took refuge with the Volscians, and proceeded to lead them against his native city. After entreaties from his mother and wife, he spared Rome, and was executed by the Volscians.

Coriolis force [koriohlis] An apparent force acting on objects moving across the Earth's surface; named after French mathematician Gustave Gaspard Coriolis (1792–1843). A result of the Earth's rotation, it is responsible for wind and ocean current patterns, and is applicable to rotating systems generally.

Cork (county), Ir **Chorcaigh** pop (2000e) 415 000; area 7459 km²/2880 sq mi. County in Munster, S Ireland; capital, Cork, pop (2000e) 176 000; third largest city in Ireland; airport; railway; university (1845); two cathedrals.

cork A spongy, protective layer just beneath the outer bark in trees, made up of thin-walled cells impregnated with a waxy substance (*suberin*). The cork layer may be built up over several years, becoming very thick.

corm A short underground shoot containing food reserves. Early growth of foliage and flowers totally depletes the reserves, and a new corm is formed on top of the old one at the end of each year before the plant dies back.

cormorant A large gregarious seabird, found worldwide; dark plumage, often with bright naked facial skin; flies fast, usu-

ally close to water surface. (Family: Phalacrocoracidae, 31 species.)

corn A generic term usually referring to the most widely cultivated cereal crop in a country or region. In North America, corn normally refers to maize, in Britain to wheat, and in Scandinavia to barley.

corn belt The major agricultural region of the US Midwest. It is centred on the states of Iowa and Illinois, and includes parts of S Dakota, Minnesota, Nebraska, Kansas, Missouri, Ohio, and Indiana. Its main products are corn (maize) and other feed-grain.

corncrake A bird of the rail family (*Crex crex*), native to Europe and W Asia, also known as the **landrail**; migrates to tropical Africa in winter.

cornea [kaw(r)nia] The transparent front part of the outer protective fibrous coat of the eyeball. It is largely responsible for the fraction of light entering the eye, focusing it approximately on the retina, so that the lens can make the final fine adjustment. A large inequality in its vertical and horizontal curvatures is known as *astigmatism*.

Corneille, Pierre [kaw(r)nay] (1606–84) Playwright, born in Rouen, France. Among his major tragedies are *Le Cid* (1636), *Horace* (1639), *Cinna* (1639), and *Polyeucte* (1640). *Le Menteur* (1642, The Liar) entitles him to be called the father of French comedy as well as of French tragedy.

Cornell, Eric A (1961–) Physicist, born in Palo Alto, CA. A researcher at the National Institute of Standards and Technology at the University of Colorado, he shared the 2001 Nobel Prize for Physics for the achievement of Bose–Einstein condensation in dilute gases of alkali atoms, and for early fundamental studies of the properties of the condensates.

cornet A musical instrument made of brass. The modern cornet, resembling a small trumpet with three valves, is used above all in brass bands.

cornetfish Colourful tropical marine fish found around reefs and sea-grass beds; head and body very slender, length up to 1·8 m/6 ft; scaleless, tail bearing a whip-like process; also called **flutemouth**. (Family: Fistulariidae.)

cornett A musical instrument in use from the 15th-c to the mid-18th-c, made from two pieces of hollowed wood, glued together and covered with leather to form a tube, usually curved, with a conical bore. This was provided with finger-holes and a cup-shaped mouthpiece like that of a brass instrument.

cornflour The flour of the maize seed, favoured by cooks as a thickening agent in sauces and soups.

cornflower A branched annual (*Centaurea cyanus*) growing to 80 cm/30 in, native to SE Europe; flower-heads solitary, long-stalked; outer florets bright blue, spreading, larger than the inner red-purple florets; also called **bluebottle**. (Family: Compositae.)

cornice [kaw(r)nis] In classical or Renaissance architecture, the crowning, projecting part of an entablature. In a general sense, it may refer to any crowning ornamental projection along the top of a building or wall.

Cornish The Celtic language once spoken to the W of the R Tamar in Cornwall. The last speakers died in c.1800, and there is some interest in a modern revival of the language.

Corn Laws British legislation regulating the trade in corn. The most famous Corn Law was introduced in 1815, which imposed prohibitively high duties on the import of foreign corn. Following widespread criticism, the Corn Laws were amended in 1828, and repealed by Peel in 1846.

corn poppy An erect annual (*Papaver rhoeas*), growing to 60 cm/2 ft, producing white latex, native to Europe and Asia, and introduced elsewhere; flowers round, four petals, bright scarlet; capsule pepper-pot shaped with a ring of pores around the rim. It is a poignant symbol of World War 1, when fields bloomed with poppies after being churned by battle. (Family: Papaveraceae.)

cornucopia [kaw(r)nyukohpia] A classical motif of a ram's horn overflowing with fruit and flowers, symbolizing abundance and plenty. It was much used in Renaissance and later decorative schemes to do with eating and drinking.

Cornwall, Celtic **Kernow** pop (2001e) 499 100; area 3564 km²/ 1376 sq mi. County in SW England; county town, Truro; Cornish nationalist movement revived the Stannary (Tinners' Parliament) in 1974, and there is renewed interest in the Cornish language; heavy rains in N Cornwall caused severe flooding (Aug 2004), notably in the village of Boscastle.

Cornwall, Duchess of, formerly **Camilla (Rosemary) Parker Bowles**, née **Shand** (1947–) Consort of Charles, Prince of Wales, the eldest son of Elizabeth II of the United Kingdom. She grew up in Sussex and was educated at the Queen's Gate School in London before attending finishing school in Switzerland and France. She first met Prince Charles in 1970 and they became close friends. In 1973 she married cavalry officer Andrew Parker Bowles (divorced 1995); they have two children. Following Charles's divorce from Princess Diana (1996), Camilla became Charles's constant companion. The couple were married in April 2005 at a civil ceremony in Windsor Guildhall, followed by a service of dedication in St George's Chapel at Windsor Castle.

Cornwallis, Charles Cornwallis, 1st Marquess [kaw(r)nwolis] (1738– 1805) British general and statesman, born in London. He defeated Gates at Camden (1780), but was forced to surrender at Yorktown (1781). In 1786 he became Governor-General of India, where he defeated Tippoo Sahib, and introduced the series of reforms known as the **Cornwallis Code**.

Cornwell, Patricia (Daniels) (1957–) Novelist, born in Miami, FL. In the 1990s she became one of the world's best-selling women novelists, producing a book each year, and known especially for the character of medical examiner Dr Kay Scarpetta introduced in her first novel *Postmortem* (1990). Later books include *Cause of Death* (1996), *Blow Fly* (2003), *Trace* (2004), and *At Risk* (2006).

corolla *flower; petal*

Coromandel Coast [korohmandl] The E coast of India, extending more than 650 km/400 mi from Point Calimere in the S to the mouth of the Krishna R in the N.

corona (astronomy) [korohna] The outermost layers of the Sun's atmosphere, visible as a pearly halo of light during a total eclipse, temperature c.1–2 million K. It is a source of strong X-rays.

corona (botany) [korohna] An extension of the corolla (petals) of a flower, such as the central trumpet of a daffodil.

Corona Australis [korohna awstralis] (Lat 'southern crown') A small but prominent S constellation on the fringes of the Milky Way.

Corona Borealis [korohna borialis] (Lat 'northern crown') A small N constellation, the stars forming a striking semicircle.

coronary heart disease Atherosclerosis of the coronary arteries, the most important cause of death over 40 in the West, and the commonest cause of angina pectoris and myocardial infarction; also known as **ischaemic/ischemic heart disease**. There are large differences in the prevalence of coronary artery disease between countries and communities. Risk factors include family history, smoking, diabetes, high blood pressure, high levels of cholesterol in the blood, and stress. In developed countries, people from deprived areas have higher rates of disease.

coroner A public officer who investigates the cause of a death, especially one where there is reason to suspect that it was due to violent or unnatural causes, in some cases holding an official inquiry, or *inquest*. Coroners are appointed by the Crown, and must be qualified as a medical doctor or a lawyer.

Corot, (Jean Baptiste) Camille [koroh] (1796–1875) Landscape painter, born in Paris. Several of his masterpieces, such as 'La Danse des nymphes' (1850) are in the Louvre.

corporation tax A tax levied on company profits by the UK government, created in 1966; its predecessor was the **profits tax**. The tax rate payable has been changed over the years, and small firms pay the tax at a lower rate. In the USA there are federal, state, and local taxes on corporations.

Corpus Christi, Feast of [kaw(r)pus kristee] A festival of the Roman Catholic Church in honour of the Eucharist, instituted by Pope Urban IV in 1264 and observed on the Thursday after Trinity Sunday.

Correggio [korejioh], originally **Antonio Allegri** (c.1494–1534) Renaissance painter, born in Correggio, Italy. In 1518 he began his great series of mythological frescoes for the convent of San Paolo at Parma. The decoration of the cathedral of Parma was commissioned in 1522.

corrie *cirque*

corrosion Destructive oxidation, usually by air in the presence of water; most marked for metals, especially iron. It is an electro-chemical process, occurring most rapidly when two different metals are in contact with one another and with air and water.

corsairs Dutch, English, and French privateers licensed by governments to prey upon enemy shipping in the Channel and Atlantic during the Wars of the League of Augsburg (1689–97) and the Spanish Succession (1702–13).

Corsica [kawsikuh], Fr **Corse** pop (2000e) 261 000; area 8680 km²/3350 sq mi. Mountainous island and region of France in the Mediterranean Sea; length 183 km/114 mi; width up to 84 km/52 mi; part of France since 1768; France's largest island; mountainous interior, rising to 2710 m/8891 ft at Mont Cinto; capital, Ajaccio; airport; major scenic area, with a wide range of tourist activities.

Cort, Henry (1740–1800) Ironmaster, born in Lancaster, Lancashire. In 1784 he invented the 'puddling' process for converting pig iron to wrought iron, as well as a system of grooved rollers for the production of iron bars.

Cortés, Hernán [kaw(r)tez], Span [kawrtays], also spelled **Cortéz** (1485–1547) The conqueror of Mexico, born in Medellín, Spain. In 1519 he commanded an expedition against Mexico, marching on the Aztec capital, and capturing the king, Montezuma; but the Mexicans rose, and Cortés was forced to flee. He then launched a successful siege of the capital, which fell in 1521.

cortex An outer layer of an organism or biological system. In the brain of vertebrates, the cerebral cortex is a layer of grey matter lying above each cerebral hemisphere.

corticosteroids Steroid hormones produced and secreted by the adrenal glands, including **hydrocortisone**, **corticosterone**, and **aldosterone**. They have numerous effects in the body, influencing metabolism, salt and water balance, and the function of many organs.

cortisol [kaw(r)tisol] A steroid hormone found in the adrenal cortex of vertebrates; also known as **hydrocortisone**. It promotes the conversion of protein and fat into glucose, and has an important role in the body's resistance to physical and psychological stress, especially after trauma.

Cortona, Pietro (Berrettini) da [kaw(r)tohna] (1596–1669) Painter and architect, born in Cortona, Italy. One of the founders of the Roman High Baroque style in painting, he specialized in highly illusionistic ceiling painting, seen notably in his 'Allegory of Divine Providence' and 'Barberini Power' (1633–9) at the Palazzo Barberini in Rome.

corundum [korundum] A mineral formed from aluminium oxide (Al₂O₃); extremely hard and used as an abrasive. Gemstone varieties are ruby and sapphire.

Corunna [koruhna], Span **La Coruña**, Galician **A Coruña**, ancient **Caronium** 43°20N 8°25W, pop (2000e) 248 000. Seaport in NW Spain; base of the Spanish Armada, 1588; city sacked by Drake,

1589; scene of British victory during the Peninsular War (1809), and the death of Sir John Moore, 1809; airport; railway.

corvette [kaw(r)vet] A small single-screw warship designed for convoy escort duties in World War 2. In former times, it was a single gun-decked, three-masted, square-rigged sailing vessel.

Corvus [kaw(r)vus] (Lat 'crow') A small S constellation, named in ancient times.

coryphaena [korifeena] *dolphinfish*

coryza [kuhriyza] *cold*

Cos, Gr **Kós**, Ital **Coo** area 290 km^2/112 sq mi. Island of the Dodecanese, E Greece, in the Aegean Sea, off the SW coast of Turkey; length 43 km/27 mi; width 2–11 km/1$\frac{1}{4}$–7 mi; rises to 846 m/2776 ft at Mt Dikaios; severely damaged by earthquakes in 1933; capital, Cos, pop (2000e) 15 300; famous in antiquity for the cult of Asclepius and its doctors, notably Hippocrates.

Cosby, Bill [kozbee], popular name of **William Henry Cosby** (1937–) Comedian, born in Philadelphia, PA. His television series *The Cosby Show* (1984–92, 1996) consistently topped the ratings. His films include *Uptown Saturday Night* (1974), *California Suite* (1978), and *Leonard: Part VI* (1987).

Cosgrave, William Thomas [kozgrayv] (1880–1965) Irish statesman and first president of the Irish Free State (1922–32), born in Dublin. His son, **Liam Cosgrave** (1920–) was prime minister (1973–7).

Cosmas and **Damian, Saints** (3rd-c) Arabian twin brothers, said to have been physicians at Aegaea, Cilicia, who were beheaded by Diocletian. They are the patron saints of physicians. Feast day 26 September (W), 1 July/1 November (E).

Cosmic Background Explorer (COBE) A NASA satellite launched in November 1989 to study the cosmic background radiation from the universe. COBE precisely measured the temperature of this radiation as 2·73 K. In 1992 it also discovered minuscule temperature variations in the radiation, attributed to slight fluctuations in the density of the early universe.

cosmic background radiation A weak radio signal that comes from the entire universe; also called **microwave background radiation**. It has a spectrum identical to a perfect black body a mere 2·73 degrees above absolute zero. It is a relic of an early very hot phase in the universe, a fossil of the 'big bang' itself. In 1992, satellite observations showed slight 'ripples' in the strength of this radiation, believed to be due to differences in density in the early universe which gave rise to the formation of galaxies.

cosmic dust Microscopic grains of dust of extraterrestrial origin; also called **Brownlee particles**, after the original collector. It enters Earth's atmosphere at high velocity, and is slowed down by friction in the uppermost atmosphere. The particles are a few microns in size, often with porous structure. Some are believed to be dust from comets.

cosmic rays High energy electrons and ions moving through space, thought to be produced by exploding stars. When the particles strike the Earth's atmosphere, secondary rays comprising mostly pions and muons are produced. Cosmic rays are a useful source of high-energy particles for experiments.

cosmic string Hypothetical massive filaments of matter (10^{19} kg/cm) predicted in supersymmetry theory as an important component of the very early universe.

cosmogony [kozmoguhnee] *cosmology*

cosmological argument An argument for the existence of God as the first cause of all things, championed especially by Aquinas. The argument appeals to the intuitions that the existence of the universe cannot be explained by things *in* the universe, and that there should be only one first cause.

cosmology The study of the universe on the largest scales of length and time, particularly the propounding of theories concerning the origin, nature, structure, and evolution of the universe. The study of the origin and mode of formation of various celestial objects is known as **cosmogony**.

cosmonaut The Russian term for a spacecraft crew member. Over 70 crewed flights, including three women (one British), were carried out by the Soviet (later, Russian) space programme to the beginning of 1992.

Cossacks Originally, members of semi-independent communities of fugitive peasants and military adventurers inhabiting the steppelands of S Russia and the Ukraine. In the 18th–19th-c they were formed into military organizations (*hosts*), and earned a reputation for ferocious fighting and skilled horsemanship.

Cossington-Smith, Grace (1892–1984) Painter, born in Sydney, New South Wales, Australia. She was instrumental in introducing Postimpressionism to her country. Her 1915 painting, 'The Sock Knitter', is seen as a key work in the Australian Modernist movement.

Costa Azul [azul] Atlantic coastline of W Portugal between the Ponta da Arrifana and the mouth of the R Sado; the name means 'blue coast'.

Costa Blanca [blangka] The coastal resort regions of Murcia, Alicante, and part of Almería provinces, E Spain; on the Mediterranean coast; the name means 'white coast'.

Costa Book Awards British book prizes, established in 1973 and known as the Whitbread Book Awards until 2006. The awards were initially given in four categories (novel, first novel, poetry, and biography) to works by writers who must have been resident in Great Britain or Ireland for at least six months per year for the preceding three years. Category winners are also eligible to become the Costa Book of the Year, which is announced two weeks later. The Costa Children's Book of the Year is announced as a separate award. The total prize fund is £50 000: each of the category award winners receives £5000, and the overall winner receives a further £25 000.

Costa Brava [brahva] The Mediterranean coastal resort region of Catalonia, E Spain, between Barcelona and the French border; the name means 'wild coast'.

Costa de la Luz [loos] Resort region on the Atlantic coastline of Huelva and Cádiz provinces, S Spain; the name means 'coast of light'.

Costa del Azahar [asakhahr, athakhahr] Mediterranean coastal resort region of Castellón de la Plana and Valencia provinces, E Spain; the name means 'orange-blossom coast'.

Costa del Sol [sol] Mediterranean coastal resort region in Andalusia, S Spain; the name means 'coast of the sun'.

Costa Dorada [dorahda] Mediterranean coastal resort region S of the Costa Brava, Barcelona, and Tarragona provinces, E Spain; the name means 'golden coast'.

Costa Dourada [dorada] Atlantic coastline of W Portugal between the Ponta da Arrifana and the mouth of the R Sado; the name means 'golden coast'.

Costa Rica *p.230*

Costello, Elvis, originally **Declan Patrick MacManus** (1955–) Singer and songwriter, born in London. His debut album *My Aim Is True* established his reputation. For his second album, *This Year's Model* (1978), he was joined by a three-piece group, The Attractions, and they worked together on most of his recordings over the next eight years. He had a hit single with 'She' from the *Notting Hill* film soundtrack (1999). Later albums include *North* (2003) and *River in Reverse* (2006).

Costello, Lou *Abbott and Costello*

costmary A sweetly aromatic perennial (*Balsamita major*) growing to 90 cm/3 ft, native to W Asia; flower-heads numerous, in flat-topped clusters; spreading outer florets white, inner disc florets yellow; also called **alecost**. Its strong-smelling foliage was formerly used for flavouring ales. (Family: Compositae.)

Costner, Kevin (1955–) Film actor and director, born in Compton,

Costa Rica

□ International Airport

[kosta reeka], official name **Republic of Costa Rica**, Span **República de Costa Rica**

Local name Costa Rica

Timezone GMT -6

Area 51 022 km²/19 694 sq mi

Population total (2002e) 3 960 000

Status Republic

Date of independence 1821

Capital San José

Language Spanish (official)

Ethnic groups European (87%), mestizo (7%), black/mulatto (3%), E Asian (mostly Chinese) (2%), Amerindian (1%)

Religions Roman Catholic (85%), Protestant (15%)

Physical features Second smallest republic in Central America; formed by series of volcanic ridges: Cordillera de Guanacaste (NW), Cordillera Central, and Cordillera de Talamanca; highest peak, Chirripó Grande, 3819 m/12 529 ft. C plateau; swampy land near coast, rising to tropical forest.

Climate Tropical; small temperature range; abundant rainfall; dry season (Dec–May); average annual temperature 26–8°C.

Currency 1 Costa Rican Colón (CRC) = 100 céntimos

Economy Primarily agriculture, mainly coffee (especially in Meseta Central), bananas, sugar, cattle; silver, bauxite; exploration for oil in collaboration with Mexico.

GDP (2002e) $32 bn, per capita $8300

Human Development Index (2002) 0·820

History Visited by Columbus, 1502; named Costa Rica ('rich coast') in the belief that vast gold treasures existed; independence from Spain, 1821; member of Federation of Central America, 1824–39; new constitution, 1949, established Costa Rica as a democratic state; governed by an executive President, legislative assembly, and Cabinet.

Head of State/Government

1962–6 Francisco José Orlich Bolmarcich
1966–70 José Joaquín Trejos Fernández
1970–4 José Figueres Ferrer
1974–8 Daniel Oduber Quirós
1978–82 Rodrigo Carazo Odio
1982–6 Luis Alberto Monge Alvarez
1986–90 Oscar Arias Sánchez
1990–4 Rafael Angel Calderón Fournier
1994–8 José María Figueres
1998–2002 Miguel Angel Rodríguez Echeverría
2002–6 Abel Pacheco
2006– Oscar Arias

CA. He established a reputation with *Bull Durham* (1988) and *Field of Dreams* (1989), then directed and starred in *Dances With Wolves* (1990, 7 Oscars). Later starring roles include *Robin Hood: Prince of Thieves* (1991), *JFK* (1991), *The Postman* (1998), and *The Guardian* (2006).

cost of living (index) *retail price index*

Cosway, Richard (1742–1821) Miniaturist, born in Tiverton, Devon. He was a fashionable painter of portraits; the use of watercolour on ivory is a notable feature of his work. In 1781 he married the artist **Maria Hadfield** (1759–1838), also a miniaturist.

cot death *sudden infant death syndrome*

Côte d'Ivoire p.231

cotinga [kotingga] A bird native to the New World tropics; inhabits woodland. Most species eat fruit; some catch insects in flight. (Family: Cotingidae, 65 species.)

Cotman, John Sell (1782–1842) Watercolourist, born in Norwich, Norfolk. A leading member of the Norwich School, his best work shows a masterly arrangement of masses of light and shade, as in 'Greta Bridge' (c.1805, Norwich).

cotoneaster [kotohniaster] A deciduous or evergreen shrub or small tree, native to N temperate regions; variable in size and shape, branches arching, spreading or erect; leaves oval to rounded, often with bright autumn colours; flowers usually in clusters, 5-petalled, white or pink; berries yellow, red, or black. (Genus: *Cotoneaster*, 50 species. Family: Rosaceae.)

Cotonou [kohtonoo] 6°24N 2°31E, pop (2000e) 831 800. Port in S Benin, W Africa; largest city in Benin, and its political and eco-

nomic centre, though not the official capital; airport; railway; university (1970).

Cotopaxi [kohtopaksee] 0°40S 78°26W. Active Andean volcano in NC Ecuador; height 5896 m/19 344 ft; national park, area 340 km²/131 sq mi established in 1975.

Cotswold Hills or **Cotswolds** [kotzwohld] Hill range mainly in Gloucestershire, SE England; extends 80 km/50 mi NE from Bath to Chipping Camden; rises to 333 m/1092 ft at Cleeve Cloud.

Cottee, Kay (1954–) Yachting record holder, born in Sydney, New South Wales, Australia. In 1988 she was the first woman to complete a solo, nonstop, unassisted circumnavigation of the world, in her sloop *First Lady*. Her time of 189 days was a women's record. She was named Australian of the Year in 1989.

Cotten, Joseph (1905–94) Film actor, born in Los Angeles, CA. A member of Orson Welles Mercury Theater radio ensemble from 1937, he starred in *Citizen Kane* (1941), *The Magnificent Ambersons* (1942), and *Journey into Fear* (1942). His many later films include *The Third Man* (1949) and *Heaven's Gate* (1980).

cotton The name of both a plant and the fibre it produces. Plants are annuals or perennials, many shrubby and growing up to 6 m/20 ft high; funnel-shaped flowers, up to 5 cm/2 in diameter, with creamy-white, yellow, or reddish petals. Ovoid seed pods (*bolls*) burst when ripe to reveal tightly packed seeds covered with creamy-white fibres which contain 87–90% cellulose. Cotton is graded according to the length (*staple*) and appearance of the fibres. The bolls are picked when ripe, either

Côte d'Ivoire

300 km
150 mi

M A L I

AFRICA

GUINEA

Odienné   Ferkessédougou   BURKINA FASO
           Korhogo
                        ∴ Comoé
                          Nat. Park   Black
                                           Volta

C Ô T E   D ' I V O I R E

△ Mt Nimba   ● Bouaké
  1752 m ●
    Man   Yamoussoukro
         ●
         Daloa   GHANA
                      Bandama   Comoé
         ● Gagnoa
LIBERIA   Abidjan
     ∴ Taï Nat.   ▫
       Park   Sassandra   Grand
           Sassandra   Bassam

ATLANTIC OCEAN

☐ International Airport   ∴ World heritage site

[koht deevwah(r)], official name **Republic of Côte d'Ivoire** (Eng **Ivory Coast**), Fr **République de Côte d'Ivoire**

Local name Côte d'Ivoire
Timezone GMT
Area 322 462 km²/124 503 sq mi
Population total (2002e) 16 805 000
Status Republic

Date of independence 1960
Capital Yamoussoukro (formerly Abidjan)
Languages French (official), Akan, Kru
Ethnic groups Akan (41%), Kru (17%), Voltaic (16%), Malinke (15%), Southern Mande (10%)
Religions Traditional beliefs (63%), Muslim (25%), Christian (12%)
Physical features Sandy beaches and lagoons backed by broad forest-covered coastal plain; Mt Nimba massif in NW, 1752 m/ 5748 ft; rivers include Comoé, Sassandra, Bandama.
Climate Tropical, varying with distance from coast; average annual rainfall at Yamoussoukro 2100 mm/83 in; average annual temperatures 25–7°C.
Currency 1 CFA Franc (XAF) = 100 centimes
Economy Largely based on agriculture (employs c.82% of the population): palm oil, rice, maize, ground nuts, bananas; world's largest cocoa producer, third largest coffee producer.
GDP (2002e) $24·03 bn, per capita $1400
Human Development Index (2002) 0·428
History Explored by Portuguese, 15th-c; declared a French protectorate, 1889; colony, 1893; territory within French West Africa, 1904; independence, 1960; constitution provides for a multiparty system, however, opposition parties only allowed to function since 1990; post of Prime Minister created, 1990; governed by a National Assembly, executive President, and Council of Ministers; during 2002 fighting escalated between emerging rebel groups in W of country; ceasefire agreed (Oct 2000) but breached, leading to intervention by French troops, 2002; UN mission to facilitate peace plan, 2003; ceasefire announced (Nov 2003), but renewed fighting and French intervention (Nov 2004); peace process initiated by Pretoria Agreement (Apr 2005).

Head of State
1960–93 Félix Houphouët-Boigny
1993–9 Henri Konan Bédié
1999–2000 Robert Guéi
2000– Laurent Gbagbo

Head of Government
1990–3 Alassane D Ouattara
1993–9 Daniel Kablan Duncan
2000 Seydou Diarra
2000–3 Affi N'Guessan
2003–5 Seydou Diarra
2005– Charles Konan Banny

by hand or by machine. Four processes then follow: removal of the seeds (*ginning*), cleaning and separating (*carding*), stretching (*drawing*), and finally *spinning* into yarn. Major producing countries include the USA, Russia, China, India, Egypt, and Turkey. (Genus: *Gossypium*, c.20 species. Family: Malvaceae.)

cotton gin A machine, invented in 1793 by Eli Whitney in the USA, which separated the seeds from the cotton boll quickly and efficiently. It greatly increased productivity.

cottonmouth A pit viper (*Agkistrodon piscivorus*) native to SE USA; inside of mouth white; lives near water; mainly nocturnal; one of the few snakes to eat carrion; venom very dangerous; also known as **water moccasin**.

cottontail A type of rabbit, native to the New World; inhabits open country or woodland clearings. (Genus: *Sylvilagus*, 13 species.)

cotton tree *kapok tree*

cottonwood *poplar*

cotyledons [kotileednz] Embryo leaves present in a seed. They are either fleshy and remain underground as a food store, or are

thin and raised above ground to act as the first leaves of the seedling.

Coubertin, Pierre de [koobairtī] (1863–1937) Educator, born in Paris. He toured the USA and Europe to study educational methods, and visited Greece, where excavators were uncovering the ancient Olympic site. The visit inspired his proposal to revive the Olympic Games, and he became the first president (1896–1925) of the International Olympic Committee.

couch grass [kooch, kowch] A dull-green perennial grass (*Elymus repens*) with numerous creeping rhizomes, native to temperate regions; spikelets set edge-on to stem in a stiff, erect spike; a tenacious weed; also called **twitch grass**. (Family: Gramineae.)

Coué, Emile [kooay] (1857–1926) Pharmacist, hypnotist, and pioneer of 'auto-suggestion', born in Troyes, France. His system became world-famous as *Couéism*, expressed in the famous formula 'Every day, in every way, I am becoming better and better'.

cougar A member of the cat family (*Felis concolor*), found from Canada to South America; grey or; reddish-brown; solitary; territorial; also known as **puma, mountain lion, catamount, panther, painter**.

coulomb [koolom] SI unit of electric charge; symbol *C*; named after French physicist Charles Coulomb (1736–1806); defined as the quantity of electricity transported by a current of 1 ampere in 1 second.

Council for Mutual Economic Assistance (COMECON) A body founded in 1949 by Stalin, and dominated by the Soviet Union; its purpose was ostensibly the economic integration of the Eastern bloc as a means of counteracting the economic power of the EEC and EFTA. It was disbanded in 1991, and replaced by the **Organization for National Economic Co-operation**.

Council for the Protection of Rural England A pressure group founded in 1926 as the Council for the Preservation of Rural England. It aims to promote the protection and improvement of the countryside and rural amenities. The Council for the Protection of Rural Wales is a similar organization.

Council of Baltic States A grouping of Baltic countries established at a meeting in Copenhagen in 1992, with the aim of regional economic co-operation. Its members are Denmark, Estonia, Finland, Germany, Iceland, Latvia, Lithuania, Norway, Poland, Russia, and Sweden.

Council of Constance *Constance, Council of*

Council of Europe A loose association now including most of the states of Europe, established in 1949. Membership was originally limited to Western Europe (including Scandinavia), but since the collapse of communism it has been extended to Central and Eastern Europe, including Russia. It has a Committee of Ministers and a representative at the parliamentary assembly, whose role is essentially advisory. Its most important achievement has been the signature of the European Convention on Human Rights. It had 46 members in 2007. Several other nations have observer status.

Council of Ministers The body (established 1958) within which legislative decisions are jointly made by the national government of the European Union, the minister involved depending on the subject under consideration. Agriculture and foreign affairs have the most frequent meetings.

Council of the Church In the Orthodox and Roman Catholic Churches, a meeting of bishops of the whole Church to regulate doctrine and discipline. The Roman Catholic Church recognizes a Council if called by a pope, and its decisions, if approved by the pope, as infallible, and binding on the whole Church.

council tax *community charge*

count (textiles) In spinning, a numerical system indicating the fineness of yarn. The *tex* unit (from *textile*), is the weight mass in grams of one kilometre of yarn, and is gradually replacing older systems such as 'cotton count' and 'denier'.

count and **countess** The English translation of various foreign titles, such as Fr *comte/comtesse*. It is not part of the UK peerage. However, the title is used for the wife of an earl, and for female holders of earldoms.

counterfeiting Imitating some object (chiefly, currency notes and coin) in order to pass off the imitation as genuine. It is a criminal offence to counterfeit coins currently in circulation. Alterations to coins are also covered by statute.

counter-intelligence *military intelligence*

counterpoint In music, the simultaneous combination of two or more melodic strands; distinct from 'harmony', which implies (in general terms) a chordal texture accompanying one or more melodic lines.

Counter-Reformation A general movement of reform and missionary activity in the Roman Catholic Church from the mid 16th-c, stimulated in part by the Protestant Reformation. It included the revival of the monastic movement; doctrinal formulations by the Council of Trent; and liturgical and moral reforms. In a secular sense, the term also refers to the success of Roman Catholic powers in Europe in the late 16th-c and early 17th-c.

countertenor The falsetto voice of the adult male, trained and developed to sing alto parts, especially in sacred polyphony. The revival of interest in the countertenor as a solo voice has been largely due to the artistry of Alfred Deller.

country and western A type of popular US music stemming from the hillbilly tradition of the years between the two World Wars. The country music of that time was played at barn dances, fairs, and similar gatherings, typically on a violin, banjo, and guitar. 'Country and western', a post-war fusion of the hillbilly tradition with the more jazz-orientated country music of the SW, has been popularized by such performers as Merle Haggard (1937–), Johnny Cash (1932–2003), and Charley Pride (1938–). The recognized centre of country and western music is Nashville, TN.

country dance Historic social dances based on John Playford's *The English Dancing Master* (1651). The emphasis was on spatial design, with couples in long or circular sets, using simple walking steps.

Country Party (Australia) *National Party* (Australia)

Countryside Commission, formerly (to 1991) **Countryside Commission for England and Wales** A UK government amenity agency set up in 1968 to replace the National Parks Commission. It advises the government on matters of countryside interest, and formulates policy for National Parks. The Commission now covers England only; there is a separate Countryside Commission for Wales.

county council The body elected to carry out such responsibilities as may be statutorily determined, within a defined geographical boundary. In areas of England and Wales without all-purpose local authorities, it is the higher in a two-tier local government system whose powers are delegated by parliament.

County Court A court system of England and Wales, concerned with civil disputes, established in 1846. It deals with certain cases of contract and tort, landlord and tenant disputes, matrimonial cases (including divorce), and the relatively informal small-claims procedure.

Couperin, François [kooperǐ] (1668–1733) Composer, born in Paris. Known mainly as a harpsichord composer (whose influence on Bach was profound), he also composed chamber concertos and church music.

courante [koorahnt] A Baroque dance in triple metre; it became a standard movement of the instrumental suite.

Courbet, Gustave [koorbay] (1819–77) Painter, born in Ornans, France. The founder of Realism, in 1844 he began exhibiting pictures in which everyday scenes were portrayed with complete sincerity and absence of idealism, such as 'Studio of the Painter: an Allegory of Realism' (1855, Musée d'Orsay, Paris).

courgette [koorzhet] (UK) or **zucchini** (US) A variety of marrow with small, green or yellow fruits (*Cucurbita pepo*). (Family: Cucurbitaceae.)

Courrèges, André [koorezh] (1923–) Fashion designer, born in Pau, France. He opened his own house in 1961, and is famous for his stark, futuristic, 'Space Age' designs.

courser A long-legged, short-winged, running bird, native to Africa and SW Asia; inhabits deserts; dull-coloured plumage; long curved bill; three forward-pointing toes only on each foot; seldom flies; nests on ground. (Family: Glareolidae. Subfamily: Cursoriinae, 7 species.)

coursing A blood sport involving greyhounds, which seek out their prey by sight and not scent. The dogs pursue in pairs, as opposed to being in packs, and the performance of one dog against another is judged.

Court, Margaret (Jean) [kaw(r)t], *née* **Smith** (1942–) Lawn tennis player, born in Albury, New South Wales, Australia. She was the winner of more Grand Slam events than any other player: 10 Wimbledon titles (including the singles in 1963, 1965, 1970), 22 US titles, 13 French, and 21 Australian.

court martial A court which tries offences against naval, military (ie army), and air force law. The court is composed of three to five serving officers advised on the law by a judge advocate, a barrister.

Court of Appeal An English court, with civil and criminal divisions, which hears appeals from the High Court, and most county court decisions. The civil division hears appeals from the High Court and the county court; its head is the Master of the Rolls. The criminal division hears appeals from the Crown Court; its head is the Lord Chief Justice.

Court of Auditors The body within the institutions of the European Union which is responsible for overseeing the implementation of the budget. Its role is to counter fraud and inefficiency.

Court of Justice of the European Communities The European Court which sits at Luxembourg, an institution of the European Union (EU), with its judges being appointed by the member states. Its functions involve the interpretation of EU treaties and legislation, and ruling on relevant points of law referred to it by domestic courts of member states.

court of law A forum for settling legal disputes. There are two broad categories of courts as traditionally distinguished: **civil courts**, dealing with disputes between private persons; and **criminal courts**, dealing with offences against society generally.

Court of Session A Scottish court, sitting in Edinburgh, which deals with civil matters. It has an Outer House and a more senior Inner House, analogous to the High Court and Court of Appeal respectively.

Cousins, Frank [kuhzinz] (1904–86) Trade union leader, born in Nottingham. In 1955 he became general secretary of the Transport and General Worker's Union. He was also minister of technology (1964–6) until he resigned over the prices and incomes policy.

Cousins, Robin (1957–) Ice skater, born in Bristol, SW England. In 1980 he became only the second British male to win an Olympic figure-skating gold medal, and he was world freeskating champion for three successive years (1978–80). He turned professional in 1980, and became artistic director of the Ice Castle International Training Center in California in 1989. He later returned to England and in 1997 co-founded the company, Adventure! on Ice, creating and producing programmes for television. In 2000 he announced his retirement from professional ice skating.

Cousteau, Jacques (Yves) [koostoh] (1910–97) Naval officer and underwater explorer, born in Saint-André, France. He invented the Aqualung diving apparatus (1943) and a process of underwater television. He wrote widely on his subject, and his films included the Oscar-winning *The Golden Fish* (1960).

covalent *chemical bond*

covenant 1 A term used in certain legal systems for a written document under seal; also known as a **deed**. It contains a promise to act in a certain way, which is signed, sealed, and takes effect on delivery. The term is often used in the UK for members of charities to covenant their membership subscriptions. The charity claims back from the tax authorities a sum equal to the tax paid by the member.
2 In the Hebrew Scriptures, the agreement between God and his chosen people which was the basis of Jewish religion; especially identified with the giving of the law to Moses on Mt Sinai, but preceded by a covenant with Abraham.

Covenanters Originally, signatories (and their successors) of the **National Covenant** (1638) in Scotland, who resisted the theory of the 'Divine Right of Kings' and the imposition of an episcopal

system on the Presbyterian Church of Scotland. Until Presbyterianism was established in 1690, they were savagely persecuted.

Covent Garden [kovnt] A square in C London, known for the fruit and vegetable market that operated there for nearly three centuries; it also gives its name to the Royal Opera House close by. Once the garden of a convent in Westminster, the site was developed in the 17th-c. The market was relocated in 1974, and the buildings restored.

Coventry [kovntree], Middle Eng **Couentrey** 52°25N 1°30W, pop (2001e) 300 800. Industrial city in West Midlands, C England; Benedictine priory founded in 1043, around which the town grew; important centre of clothing manufacture from 17th-c; railway; University of Warwick (1965), Coventry University (1992); old cathedral (1433) destroyed during World War 2; new cathedral designed by Sir Basil Spence (consecrated 1962); football league team, Coventry City (Sky Blues).

Coverdale, Miles (1488–1568) Bible scholar, born in York, North Yorkshire. His translation of the Bible (**Coverdale's Bible**, the first complete one in English) appeared in 1535, and he then superintended the work which led to the *Great Bible* (1539). He also edited the work known as *Cranmer's Bible* (1540).

covered wagon *prairie schooner*

cow *bull* (zoology)

Coward, Sir Noel (Pierce) (1899–1973) Actor, playwright, and composer, born in London. Among his many successes were *The Vortex* (1924), *Hay Fever* (1925), *Private Lives* (1930), and *Blithe Spirit* (1941), all showing his strong satirical humour, and a gift for witty dialogue. He wrote the music as well as the lyrics for most of his works, including the musical *Bitter Sweet* (1929), the play *Cavalcade* (1931), and the revue *Words and Music* (1932), with its 'Mad Dogs and Englishmen'. He was also an accomplished singer, produced several films based on his own scripts, and became known as an actor following his role in *The Italian Job*. He published two volumes of autobiography, *Present Indicative* (1937) and *Future Indefinite* (1954), and was knighted in 1970.

Cowell, Simon (1959–) Record producer and manager, born in Brighton, East Sussex. In 2001 he was a judge on the first series of UK's *Pop Idol* show, and again for *American Idol* (2002–), and with his production company, Syco, he created, and was a judge on, a British TV talent show, *The X Factor* (2004–). Known for his acerbic humour, he published *I Don't Mean to be Rude, But...* in 2004.

Cowes [kowz] 50°45N 1°18W, pop (2000e) 17 500. Town in the Isle of Wight, S England; a notable yachting centre; Cowes Castle (1543); Osborne House; Cowes Week (Aug).

Cowley, Abraham (1618–67) Poet, born in London. His main works were the influential *Pindarique Odes* (1656) and his unfinished epic on King David, *Davideis* (1656).

cow parsley A biennial or perennial (*Anthriscus sylvestris*), growing to 1·5 m/5 ft, native to Europe, temperate Asia, and N Africa; stems hollow, grooved; flowers small, white; fruit smooth; also called **Queen Anne's lace** and **keck**. (Family: Umbelliferae.)

cow parsnip *hogweed*

Cowpens, Battle of (1781) During the US War of Independence, an engagement in S Carolina in which a small American army under Daniel Morgan (1736–1802) defeated a British force under Banastre Tarleton (1754–1833).

Cowper, William [kooper] (1731–1800) Poet, born in Berkhamsted, Hertfordshire. His ballad of John Gilpin (1783) was highly successful, as was his long poem about rural ease, *The Task* (1785).

cow pox A virus disease of cattle characterized by small blisters (*pocks*) on the teats; also known as **kine pox**. The contents of these blisters were used by Edward Jenner in 1798 to vaccinate humans against the related *smallpox*.

cowrie A marine snail with a glossy, smooth, and often highly patterned shell, largely covered by lobes of mantle; used as decorations and even as currency on Pacific Islands. (Class: Gastropoda. Order: Mesogastropoda.)

cowslip A perennial (*Primula veris*) with a rosette of oblong, slightly crinkled leaves, native to Europe and Asia; flowers 1–30 at the tip of a common stalk, drooping, petals yellow with orange spots at base. (Family: Primulaceae.)

Cox (Arquette), Courteney (1964–) Actress, born in Birmingham, AL. She became well known through her role as Monica Geller in the acclaimed television series *Friends* (1994–2004). Her feature film roles include *Scream* and its sequel (1996, 1998), *Commandments* (1997), and *Zoom* (2006). She married actor David Arquette in 1999.

coyote [koyohtee] A member of the dog family (*Canis latrans*), native to North and Central America; inhabits grassland and open woodland; also known as **prairie wolf, barking wolf, little wolf**, or (in fur trade) **cased wolf**. Coyotes have been subject to bounties, and are still often hunted by ranchers and farmers.

coypu [koypoo] A cavy-like rodent (*Myocastor coypus*), native to South America (introduced elsewhere); large (length over 1 m/3¼ ft); rat-like with broad blunt muzzle; farmed for soft underfur; also known as **nutria**. (Family: Myocastoridae.)

CPU *digital computer*

crab A typically marine crustacean with a front pair of legs specialized as pincers (*chelipeds*) and used for food capture, signalling, and fighting; usually walks sideways, using four pairs of walking legs; also capable of swimming; body broad, flattened, with a hard outer covering (*carapace*); abdomen permanently tucked up beneath body; eyes usually movable on stalks; many species exploited commercially for food. (Class: Malacostraca. Order: Decapoda.)

Crabbe, George (1754–1832) Poet, born in Aldeburgh, Suffolk. His best-known early work is *The Village* (1783). His later narrative poems include *The Parish Register* (1807) and *The Borough* (1810).

crabeater seal A true seal (*Lobodon carcinophagus*), native to the Antarctic and sub-Antarctic; teeth with deeply notched margins, forming a sieve when mouth is shut; eats krill (despite its name); fastest true seal on land (up to 25 kph/15 mph); one of the world's most numerous large mammals.

Crab nebula The remnant of a star seen by Chinese astronomers to explode spectacularly on 4 July 1054. Photographs show a tangled web of filaments threading a luminous nebula. The explosion which triggered the nebula was a supernova, which left a dense neutron star at the centre, now observed as a pulsar rotating 30 times a second.

crab-plover *plover*

Crabtree, Joseph [krabtree, ?krabtray] (1754–1854) Poet and polymath, born in Bristol, SW England, UK. According to the records of the Crabtree Foundation, he was a precocious child, who spent some time at Oxford University (1773) before travelling in Europe, where he developed a great friendship with Wordsworth, inspiring several of his poems. A latter-day Renaissance man, Crabtree made contributions to science, engineering, and mathematics, as well as achieving recognition as a traveller, translator, and lawyer. He is thought to have met virtually all the leading figures of his time, often suggesting ideas and inventions later attributed to them. Little was known of him until the 20th-c, when the Crabtree Foundation was founded in 1954 at University College London, dedicated to the exposition of his life and work. It continues to organize annual orations in his memory.

crack A blend of cocaine, baking powder, and water. The cocaine hardens to white cinder chunks which can be smoked in a small pipe. The effect is immediate. This form of cocaine is held to be extremely addictive.

Cracow *Kraków*

Cradock, Fanny, *née* **Phyllis Primrose-Pechey** (1909–94) British writer and television cook. From 1955 she became known for the television programmes presented with her husband, Johnny. She wrote cookery books, children's books, novels, and press columns which were notorious for their social pretension and outspoken opinions.

Craig, Daniel (Wroughton) (1968–) Actor, born in Chester, Cheshire. While at school he successfully auditioned for the National Youth Theatre (1984) and later joined the London Guildhall School of Music and Drama (1988–91). His film debut was in *The Power of One* (1992), and later films include *Lara Croft: Tomb Raider* (2001), *Road to Perdition* (2002), *Layer Cake* (2004), and *The Invasion* (2007). Controversially cast in *Casino Royale* (2006) as the first blonde James Bond, the film proved a box-office success, winning the Evening Standard Best Actor Award.

Craig, Edward (Henry) Gordon (1872–1966) Stage designer, actor, director, and theorist, born in Stevenage, Hertfordshire. He published the theatre journal, *The Mask* (1908–29), which together with his scene designs and his books, *On the Art of the Theatre* (1911) and *The Theatre Advancing* (1921), had a profound influence on modern theatre practice.

crake The name often given to any smallish rail with a short, chicken-like bill (45 species).

Cram, Steve, popular name of **Stephen Cram** (1960–) Athlete, born in Gateshead, Tyne and Wear. He won the World Championship gold medal at 1500 m in 1983, and the Commonwealth Games gold medals at 1500 m (1982, 1986) and 800 m (1986). In 1985 he set three world records in 20 days at 1500 m, 1 mi, and 2000 m.

Cranach, Lucas [krahnakh], known as **Lucas Cranach the Elder** (1472–1553) Painter, so named from Kronach, near Bamberg, Germany, where he was born. He was closely associated with the German Reformers, many of whom (including Luther) he painted. A 'Crucifixion' in the Stadtkirche, Weimar, is his masterpiece. Of three sons, all painters, the second, **Lucas Cranach the Younger** (1515–86), painted so like his father that their works are difficult to distinguish.

cranberry A dwarf, creeping, evergreen shrub (*Vaccinium oxycoccos*), native to N temperate regions; flowers on long, slender stalks, pink, four petals, curling backwards; berry round or pear-shaped, red- or brown-spotted, edible. (Family: Ericaceae.)

Crane, (Harold) Hart (1899–1932) Poet, born in Garrettsville, OH. His most important work is contained in *White Buildings* (1926), a collection on New York life, and *The Bridge* (1930), an epic using Brooklyn Bridge as its focal point.

Crane, Stephen (Townley) (1871–1900) Writer and war correspondent, born in Newark, NJ. He became known as a novelist through *Maggie: a Girl of the Streets* (1893) and *The Red Badge of Courage* (1895), a vivid story of the Civil War.

crane (engineering) A machine which can lift and position loads. It essentially consists of an arm (or *jib*) carrying a pulley, attached to a post round which it can rotate, and with a rope which can be wound round a barrel. Cranes are much used in docks (with special designs used for container traffic), in construction (**tower cranes**), and in engineering (often as **gantry cranes**).

crane (ornithology) A long-legged, long-necked bird, height 0·6–1·5 m/2–5 ft; worldwide except South America, New Zealand, and the Pacific; adult usually with head partly naked; inhabits flat wetlands and wet plains. (Family: Gruidae, 15 species.)

cranefly A long-legged, true fly; adult body slender, legs fragile, readily discarded if trapped; larvae known as **leatherjackets**; adults also known as **daddy longlegs**; c.13 500 species. (Order: Diptera. Family: Tipulidae.)

cranesbill An annual or perennial of the genus *Geranium*, native to temperate regions; flowers usually white to purple or blue, 5-

petalled; fruit with long beak resembling a bird's bill, exploding when ripe. (Genus: *Geranium*, 400 species. Family: Geraniaceae.)

Cranko, John [krangkoh] (1927–73) Dancer, choreographer, and director, born in Rustenburg, South Africa. He choreographed for both Sadler's Wells and the Royal Ballet companies, and in 1961 became ballet director of the Stuttgart Ballet.

Cranmer, Thomas (1489–1556) Archbishop of Canterbury, born in Aslockton, Nottinghamshire. He annulled Henry VIII's marriages to Catherine of Aragon and to Anne Boleyn (1536), and divorced him from Anne of Cleves (1540). He was largely responsible for the Book of Common Prayer (1549, 1552). On Henry's death, he agreed to the plan to divert the succession from Mary to Lady Jane Grey (1553), for which he was arraigned for treason and burned alive.

craps A casino dice game of American origin, adapted from the game *hazard* by Bernard de Mandeville in New Orleans in 1813. Using two dice, a player loses throwing 2, 3, and 12, but wins with 7 or 11. If the player's first throw makes 4, 5, 6, 8, 9, or 10, this number is called the *point*; the player then continues to throw until the same number is rolled again (*making the point*), thus giving a win, or throws a 7 and thus loses (*craps out*).

craquelure [krakuhlür] The distinctive pattern of fine cracks on the surface of a painting or glazed pottery. Normally the result of aging, craquelure can be faked.

Crashaw, Richard [krayshaw] (c.1613–49) Religious poet, born in London. He is best known for his volume of Latin poems, *Epigrammatum sacrorum liber* (1634, A Book of Sacred Epigrams) and *Steps to the Temple* (1646).

Crassus, Marcus Licinius, nickname **Dives** (Lat 'wealthy') (c.115–53 BC) Roman politician. A friend of Caesar, he formed the First Triumvirate with him and Pompey (60 BC). In 53 BC, as Governor of Syria, he attacked the Parthians, but was killed at the Battle of Carrhae.

Crater (Lat 'cup') A small, faint constellation in the S sky.

crater A circular depression on the surface of a planetary body. Those on Mercury, the Moon, and most of the natural satellites of planets have been formed by impacts with meteorites and comets in the remote past. The Moon, Mars, Venus, and Io (one of Jupiter's satellites) also have volcanic craters. Craters on Earth have been caused by meteorites (eg Meteor Crater, Arizona) and by volcanic explosions (eg Crater Lake, Oregon).

Crater Lake (Canada) *Chubb Crater*

Crater Lake (USA) Circular crater lake in SW Oregon, USA, in the Cascade Range; 9.5 km/6 mi across; area 52 km²/20 sq mi; 604 m/1982 ft deep; altitude 1879 m/6165 ft; in a large pit formed by the destruction of the summit of a prehistoric volcano.

Crawford, Joan, originally **Lucille Fay Le Sueur** (1904–77) Film actress, born in San Antonio, TX. She became an established star in the 1930s and 1940s, winning an Oscar for *Mildred Pierce* (1945); her last great role was in *Whatever Happened to Baby Jane?* (1962). A very critical biography, *Mommie Dearest*, by her adopted daughter Christine, was filmed in 1981.

Crawford, Michael (1942–) Actor and singer, born in Salisbury, Wiltshire. In the 1970s the television series *Some Mothers Do 'Ave 'Em* made him a household name in Britain, and he went on to star in musicals, such as *Billy* (1974), *Barnum* (1981), *The Phantom of the Opera* (1986, Tony), and *The Woman in White* (2004). His films include *Hello Dolly* (1968), *Condorman* (1980), and *Once Upon a Forest* (1993). In 1999 he published his autobiography, *Parcel Arrived Safely: Tied With String*.

crayfish A typically freshwater, lobster-like crustacean with a well-developed abdomen and front pair of legs modified as powerful pincers (chelipeds); many species exploited commercially for food. (Class: Malacostraca. Order: Decapoda.)

Crazy Horse, Sioux name **Tashunka Witco** (c.1842–77) Oglala Sioux Chief, born in South Dakota. Regarded as the foremost Sioux military leader, he defeated General Custer at the Battle of the Little Bighorn (1876). He is regarded as a symbol of Sioux resistance and as their greatest leader.

cream of tartar *tartaric acid*

creationism Originally, the belief that God creates a soul for each human individual at conception or birth. It is now commonly applied to the belief that the Genesis account of creation in the Bible accurately describes the origins of the world and humanity. It is opposed to the theory of evolution.

Crécy, Battle of [kraysee] (1364) A battle between France and England in the Hundred Years' War. Edward III routed Philip VI of France and his larger army, mainly cavalry, near Abbeville (Somme).

credit card A plastic card which is used instead of cash or cheque to pay for goods or services. The best-known companies are *Visa*, *Mastercard*, and *American Express*. Credit cards differ from **charge cards**, in that there is a specified credit limit. Charge cards have no limit, but full repayment is to be made each month.

credit rating A system used to assess the ability of a company (or individual) to pay for goods and services, or the ability to borrow and repay. Popular rating systems in the USA are *Moody* and *Standard and Poor*. All companies are assigned a rating code: the highest is AAA, next is AA, and so on.

credits The recognition given to someone who has successfully completed a part of a modular course. American education is firmly based on the notion of accumulated credits. A particular advantage is that students know from the beginning how many credits they must acquire in order to obtain the qualification they seek.

credit union A co-operative venture where members save together and lend to each other, mainly short-term consumer loans. The system is popular in North America, where there are some 50 000 credit unions.

Cree A North American Algonkin Indian group from the Canadian Subarctic region, originally hunters and fishermen.

Creek A North American Indian people, originally from Georgia and Alabama, c.71 000 (2000 census). They were forcibly moved to Oklahoma in 1837, where they became one of the Five Civilized Tribes.

cremation Burning the remains of a dead person. The practice was recorded in ancient Greece for soldiers killed in battle. Discouraged in the past by Christians because of its pagan associations, it is the regular form of disposal by Hindus. Today cremation is becoming more common because of lack of space in cemeteries.

creodont An extinct flesh-eating mammal; known from the early Tertiary period around the world except Australia and South America; distinguished from true carnivores by shorter limbs, unfused wrist bones, cleft claw bone, and shearing teeth (*carnassials*) formed from molars. (Order: Creodonta.)

creole A pidgin language which has become the mother-tongue of a speech community, as has happened with Jamaican creole. A creole develops a wider range of words, grammatical structures, and styles than is found in a pidgin.

Creon or **Kreon** [kreeon] A name (meaning 'ruler') given to several legendary Greek kings, but especially to the brother of Jocasta, regent of Thebes, who awarded the throne to Oedipus.

creosote [kreeosoht] A fraction of coal tar, boiling point c.250°C, containing a variety of toxic aromatic compounds giving it strong antiseptic and preservative properties.

cress The name given to several different members of the cabbage family, often small weeds, some cultivated as salad plants. (Family: Cruciferae.)

Cressida [kresida] In mediaeval accounts of the Trojan War, the daughter of Calchas, a Trojan priest. Beloved by Troilus, a Trojan prince, she deserted him for Diomedes when transferred to the Greek camp.

Cretaceous period [kretayshuhs] The last geological period of the Mesozoic era, lasting from 144 to 65 million years ago, characterized by the emergence of flowering plants and the dominance and extinction of dinosaurs.

Crete, Gr **Kríti**, Ital **Candia**, ancient **Creta** pop (2000e) 561 000; area 8336 km²/3218 sq mi. Island region of Greece, in the Mediterranean Sea, S of the Cyclades island group; length 256 km/159 mi; width 14–60 km/9–37 mi; largest of the Greek islands; highest point, Psiloritis (2456 m/8058 ft); evidence of settlement from c.6000 BC; important Minoan civilization, c.2000 BC; ruled at various times by Greeks, Romans, Turks, and Arabs; passed to Greece in 1913; German occupation in World War 2, after airborne invasion, 1941; capital, Heraklion; ancient sites at Knossos, Gortys, Lato, Phaistos.

cretinism A condition affecting children who suffer from inadequate production of thyroid hormones (*thyroxine*). There is a failure of normal growth and development, with short stature, puffiness of the skin, notably of the face, enlarged tongue, hairloss, and mental deficiency.

Creutzfeldt-Jakob Disease [kroytsvelt yakob] A prion disease involving degeneration of the nervous system; named after German neuropathologists Heinz Creutzfeldt and Andreas Jakob. Hereditary and sporadic cases have been documented since the 1920s, characterized by an onset between 45 and 60 years of age, and neurological symptoms including dementia, problems with speech and balance, abnormal movements, and paralysis. There are typical electroencephalographic changes and pathological changes in the brain identifiable at post-mortem. The disease progresses steadily, with death occurring within 12 months. More recently, a new form of the disease has been described, variant Creutzfeldt-Jakob disease (vCJD), thought to be due to an infectious agent. It affects younger people, and has a more aggressive course. It is possible that infection may occur following inoculation with infected tissue, eg during medical procedures. There is also concern that transmission may occur from animals by the consumption of infected meat, particularly beef products.

cribbage A card game popular in public houses in the UK, played by two, three, or four people with a standard pack of 52 cards and a holed board known as the **cribbage board** or *peg board*. Points are scored according to cards dropped (ie for playing a card that makes a pair, a run of three or more, etc). All scores are marked on the peg board.

Crick, Francis (Harry Compton) (1916–2004) Biophysicist, born in Northampton, Northamptonshire. With J D Watson in 1953 he constructed a molecular model of the complex genetic material DNA; and in 1958 proposed that DNA determines the sequence of amino acids in a polypeptide. He shared the Nobel Prize for Physiology or Medicine in 1962.

cricket (entomology) A large, grasshopper-like insect; forewings box-like and bent down round sides of body; many species have a well-developed sound-producing mechanism for auditory communication; c.2000 species. (Order: Orthoptera. Family: Gryllidae.)

cricket (sport) *p.237*

Crimea [kriymeea], Russ **Krym** area 25 900 km²/10 000 sq mi. Peninsula in S Ukraine; bounded S and W by the Black Sea, and E by the Sea of Azov; length, 320 km/200 mi; Greek colonization, 7th-c BC; autonomous Soviet republic, 1921; an oblast of the Russian SFSR, 1946; transferred to the Ukraine, 1954; tourism on coast.

Crimean War (1854–6) A war fought in the Crimean peninsula by Britain, France, Turkey, Piedmont, and Austria against Russia. Major battles were fought in 1854 at the R Alma (20 Sep), Balaclava (25 Oct), and Inkerman (5 Nov). The fall of the Russian fortress at Sebastopol (Sep 1855) led to peace negotiations, finally agreed at the Treaty of Paris (Mar 1856).

Crime Writers' Association A British literary association open to all published writers who write about crime – fiction or non-fiction – with the aim of promoting the prestige and appreciation of crime writing. The first meeting was convened by John Creasey in 1953. Annual awards include the Gold Dagger for the best novel published in the English language that year, and the Debut Dagger for the best new writer previously unpublished.

Criminal Injuries Compensation Scheme A British scheme established in 1964, whereby the state pays compensation to certain victims who have suffered personal injury attributable to a crime of violence. Certain classes of victims, offences, and injuries are excluded, and any payment made is reduced by the amount of damages or compensation awarded by a civil or criminal court. The first such scheme was established in New Zealand in 1963.

Criminal Investigation Department *CID*

criminal law A branch of law which deals with offences against society generally. Investigation of breaches of the criminal law is generally the responsibility of the police. The responsibility for prosecution varies between jurisdictions: for example, in England and Wales, it belongs to the Director of Public Prosecutions and the Crown Prosecution Service; in most US jurisdictions, to a local district attorney or county prosecutor; and in federal jurisdictions, to a US attorney.

crimp The waviness which occurs naturally in wool fibres, imparting a soft bulkiness to yarns. Crimping of synthetic fibres extends their range of uses into knitting and carpet yarns, and the manufacture of softer woven fabrics.

crinoid [kriynoyd] A primitive marine invertebrate (echinoderm), typically attached to the seabed by a long stalk; mouth and arms on upper surface; long fossil record; c.650 living species; also known as **sea lilies** and **feather stars**. (Phylum: Echinodermata. Class: Crinoidea.)

Crippen, Hawley Harvey, known as **Dr Crippen** (1862–1910) Physician and murderer, born in Michigan. He settled in London in 1900. After poisoning his wife, he and his mistress attempted to escape to Canada on board the SS *Montrose*. The suspicious captain contacted Scotland Yard by radiotelegraphy (the first use of radio for a murder case). They were arrested, and Crippen was hanged in London.

Cripps, Sir (Richard) Stafford (1889–1952) British Labour statesman, born in London. During the 1930s he was associated with several extreme left-wing movements, and was expelled from the Labour Party in 1939 for his 'popular front' opposing Chamberlain's policy of appeasement. In the 1945 Labour government, he was readmitted to the Party and appointed President of the Board of Trade. In 1947 he became minister of economic affairs and then Chancellor of the Exchequer, introducing a successful austerity policy.

Cristofori, Bartolomeo [kristoforee] (1655–1731) Harpsichord maker, born in Padua, Italy. He is usually credited with the invention of the pianoforte in c.1710.

critical mass The smallest mass of material of a given type and formed into a given shape able to sustain a nuclear-fission chain reaction. For a mass of material greater than the critical mass, large amounts of energy are released via the fission-chain reaction in a small fraction of a second.

Crittenden Compromise (1860) In the months preceding the American Civil War, an attempt by Senator John J Crittenden of Kentucky to resolve the crisis between North and South by formally recognizing slavery in territories S of 36°30. This proved unacceptable to Abraham Lincoln.

croaker *drumfish*

Croatia *p.238*

cricket

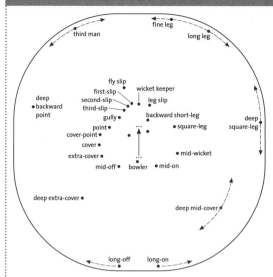

third man • • fine leg

long leg

fly slip
first-slip • wicket keeper
deep second-slip • leg slip
• backward third-slip •
point gully • backward short-leg
point • deep
cover-point • • square-leg square-leg
cover •
extra-cover • • mid-wicket
mid-off • bowler • mid-on

deep extra-cover •

deep mid-cover •

long-off long-on

(sport) A bat-and-ball team game of 11-a-side. A wicket consisting of three stumps surmounted by a pair of bails is placed at each end of a grassy pitch 22 yd (20·1 m) in length. Each team takes it in turn to bat and bowl. The aim of the batting team is to defend the two wickets while trying to score as many runs as possible before being dismissed. Each member of the team must bat, and two batsmen (or, in a female team, batswomen) are on the field at any one time, one in front of each wicket (unless one is injured, and a 'runner' is needed). After the captains of the two sides have tossed a coin to decide who bats first, the fielding team assembles on the field. At any one time it will consist of a bowler, a wicket-keeper (who stands behind the wicket that the bowler is attacking), and nine fielders, who are placed at strategic positions around the field. A bowler delivers an 'over' of (usually) six balls to one wicket, before a different bowler attacks the other wicket.

If the batsman hits a ball (and in certain other circumstances,

such as the bowler bowling too wide or the wicket-keeper missing the ball), he may decide it is safe to run between the two wickets, exchanging places with the other batsman, in which case he scores a 'run'. Several runs may be scored following a single hit, but if the ball reaches the boundary of the field, four runs are scored automatically, and six if it has not bounced on the way. A batsman is out if he is 'bowled' (the ball from the bowler knocks his wicket down), 'caught' (the batsman hits the ball so that it is caught by a fielder without bouncing), 'stumped' (the wicket-keeper knocks the wicket down with the ball while the defending batsman is standing outside his 'safe ground' or 'crease'), 'run out' (the wicket towards which one of the batsmen is running is knocked down before the batsman reaches the safe ground, and 'leg before wicket', or 'lbw' (the batsman's body obstructs the ball's path to the wicket without the bat having first made contact). He may also be out if he hits his own wicket while playing a shot, hits the ball twice, prevents a fielder taking a catch ('obstructing the field'), uses a hand to prevent the ball hitting the wicket ('handled the ball') or takes more than three minutes to replace the previous batsman once the wicket has fallen ('timed out'). Once 10 batsmen have been dismissed, the innings comes to a close, but a team can stop its innings ('declare') at any time before that, if it thinks it has made enough runs. In first-class cricket, the pre-eminent form of the game, each team has two innings, and the one with the greater number of runs at the end of the match is the winner, provided the other side has completed – or declared – both its innings. It is possible, however, to forfeit innings in order to obtain a definite result.

The game has been traced back to 1300, but the first known county match was in 1719. The earliest known laws of cricket were drawn up in 1744, and the Marylebone Cricket Club (MCC) was founded in 1787. The first Test match was played in Melbourne in March 1877. Principal domestic competitions in the UK consist of the County Championship, Cheltenham and Gloucester Trophy, NPower Twenty20 Cup, and the NatWest Pro40 National League. In 1998 the counties voted to introduce two championship divisions from 2000. The Pura Milk Cup (previously the Sheffield Shield) is the principal competition in Australia. Test matches are staged over five days, county championship matches over four days. Limited-over competitions are normally concluded in one day, and last for a specific number of overs per side. For practical reasons, the World Cup (1975 to date) is strictly limited-overs.

Croce, Benedetto [krohchay] (1866–1952) Italian statesman, philosopher, historian, and critic, born in Pescasseroli, Italy. He founded the review *La Critica* in 1903, and made major contributions to idealistic aesthetics in his *Estetica* (1902, Aesthetic) and *La Poesia* (1936, Poetry). He was opposed to totalitarianism, and with the fall of Mussolini (1943) helped to resurrect Liberal institutions in Italy.

Crockett, Davy, popular name of **David Crockett** (1786–1836) Backwoodsman, born in Green Co, TN. He died fighting for Texas at the battle of the Alamo. Highly embellished stories of his exploits have assumed mythological proportions.

crocodile A reptile native to tropical rivers and estuaries worldwide; length, up to 7·5 m/25 ft; fourth tooth from the front on each side of the lower jaw is visible when the jaws are closed (unlike the alligator); eats a range of vertebrate prey; eggs have hard shells. Crocodilians (crocodiles, alligators, and the gharial) are the descendants of an ancient reptile group, the *archosaurs* (which included the extinct dinosaurs and pterodactyls). (Order: Crocodilia. Family: Crocodilidae, 14 species.)

crocus A perennial producing corms, native to Europe and Asia; leaves grass-like with distinctive silvery stripe down centre;

stalkless flowers, goblet-shaped with long, slender tube, mainly white, yellow, or purple, closing up at night. (Genus: *Crocus*, 75 species. Family: Iridaceae.)

Croesus [kreesuhs] (?–c.546 BC) The last king of Lydia (c.560–546 BC), who succeeded his father, Alyattes. His conquests and mines made his wealth proverbial. Cyrus II defeated and imprisoned him (546 BC), but his death is a mystery.

crofting A form of small-scale subsistence farming once characteristic of the Highlands and Islands of Scotland. A croft usually comprised a house, a few hectares of arable land, and grazing rights on the hill.

Crohn's disease [krohn] A persisting but fluctuating disorder affecting any part of the alimentary canal. The lining of the mouth, stomach, and especially the small intestine becomes inflamed and ulcerated. It is named after US physician Burrill Crohn (1884–1983).

Cro-Magnon Man [krohmanyon] The earliest fully modern humans (*Homo sapiens sapiens*) from late Pleistocene Europe (40 000–10 000 BC), named after the 1868 discovery of fossil skeletons at Cro-Magnon in SW France. Cromagnons were specialist hunters (mammoth, reindeer) occupying rock shelters in

Croatia

☐ International Airport

[krohaysha], official name **Republic of Croatia**, Serbo-Croatian **Republika Hrvatska**

Local name Hrvatska

Timezone GMT +1

Area 56 538 km²/21 824 sq mi

Population total (2002e) 4 405 000

Status Republic

Date of independence 1991

Capital Zagreb

Language Croatian

Ethnic groups (1990) Croat (75%), Serb (12%), Slovenes (1%)

Religions Roman Catholic, Eastern Orthodox

Physical features Fertile Pannonian Plain in C and E; mountainous, barren coastal region near Dinaric Alps; Adriatic coast to W; one third of country is forested; main rivers: Drava, Danube, Sava. Coastal Velebit and Velika Kapela ranges reach heights of 2200 m/7200 ft; islands include Korčula, Lsinj, Dugi Otok, Cres, Krk.

Climate Continental in Pannonian Basin: average temperatures 19°C (Jul), -1°C (Jan); average annual rainfall 750 mm/30 in; Mediterranean climate on Adriatic coast: average temperatures 24°C (Jul), 6°C (Jan).

Currency 1 Kuna (HRK) = 100 lipa

Economy Agriculture; corn, oats, sugar-beet, potatoes, meat and dairy products; tourism on Adriatic coast. Electrical engineering; metal-working; machinery manufacture; lumber; aluminium, textiles, petroleum refining, chemicals, rubber; natural resources include bauxite, coal, copper, iron; all economic activity adversely affected by war of independence.

GDP (2002e) $43.12 bn, per capita $9800

Human Development Index (2002) 0.809

History Slavic Croat tribes (Chrobati, Hrvati) migrated to White Russia (now Ukraine) during 6th-c; converted to Christianity between 7th and 9th-c and adopted Roman alphabet; Frankish and Byzantine invaders repelled, and Croat kingdom reached its peak during 11th-c; Lázló I of Hungary claimed Croatian throne, 1091; Turkish defeat of Hungary in 1526 placed Pannonian Croatia under Ottoman rule; rest of Croatia elected Ferdinand of Austria as king and fought Turkey; Croatia and Slovenia became part of Hungary until collapse of Austria-Hungary in 1918; formed the Kingdom of Serbs, Croats and Slovenes with Montenegro and Serbia, 1918; Yugoslavia, 1929; proclaimed an independent state during occupation by the Axis Powers, 1941–5; became a republic of Yugoslavia again in 1945; nationalist upsurges during 1950s against Communist rule, culminating in a bloody war with Serbian-dominated Yugoslav army, 1991; declaration of independence, 1991; autonomy claimed by Serb-dominated Krajina area; UN peacekeeping forces deployed, 1992; continued fighting between Croatian forces and Bosnian Serbs in the civil war in Bosnia-Herzegovina; 1995 offensive restored territorial balance in Bosnia; ceasefire followed by peace treaty (Nov) recognized Bosnian-Croat Federation in W Bosnia; governed by an Assembly consisting of a Chamber of Deputies and a Chamber of Districts.

Head of State

1991–9 Franjo Tudjman
1999 Vlatko Pavletic *Acting*
2000– Stjepan Mesic

Head of Government

1991–2 Franjo Greguric
1992–3 Hrvoje Sarinic
1993–5 Nikica Valentic
1995–2000 Zlatko Matesa
2000–3 Ivaca Racan
2003– Ivo Sanader

W Europe and hut campments on the steppe and tundra of C Europe and Russia.

Crome, John, known as **Old Crome** (1768–1821) Landscape painter, the chief of the Norwich School, born in Norwich, Norfolk. His subjects derived from the scenery of Norfolk, such as 'Poringland Oak' and 'Mousehold Heath' (Tate, London).

cromlech *megalith*

cromoglycate or **sodium cromoglycate** [krohmohgliysayt] An anti-allergy drug used especially in the prevention of asthma, also known as **cromolyn**. It is administered using a special inhaler which dispenses very fine powder into the inspired air.

Crompton, Richmal, pseudonym of **Richmal Samuel Lamburn** (1890–1969) Writer of children's books, born in Bury, Lancashire. She wrote the first of the 'William' books (*Just William*) in 1922, and had written 40 of them before her death.

Crompton, Samuel (1753–1827) British inventor of the *spinning-mule*, born in Firwood, Greater Manchester. In 1779 he devised a machine which produced yarn of astonishing fineness, and although he was forced to sell his idea to a Bolton manufacturer he was later awarded a national grant of £5000.

Cromwell, Oliver (1599–1658) English soldier and statesman, born in Huntingdon, Cambridgeshire. A convinced Puritan, when war broke out (1642) he fought for the parliament at Edgehill. He formed his unconquerable Ironsides, and it was his cavalry that secured the victory at Marston Moor (1644), while under Fairfax he led the New Model Army to decisive success at Naseby (1645). He brought Charles I to trial, and was one of the signatories of his death warrant (1649). Having established the Commonwealth, Cromwell suppressed the Levellers, Ireland (1649–50), and the Scots (under Charles II). He dissolved the Rump of the Long Parliament and established a Protectorate (1653). He was succeeded by his son **Richard Cromwell** (1626–1712), who was forced into French exile in 1659.

Cromwell, Thomas, Earl of Essex (c.1485–1540) English statesman, born in London. He arranged Henry VIII's divorce from Catherine of Aragon, and put into effect the Act of Supremacy (1534) and the dissolution of the monasteries (1536–9). He held several offices, proving himself a highly efficient adviser to the king; but Henry's aversion to Anne of Cleves, consort of Cromwell's choosing, led to his ruin. He was sent to the Tower and beheaded.

Cronenberg, David (1943–) Film director and screenplay writer, born in Toronto, Ontario, Canada. His plots typically concern the aftermath of some disastrous biological mishap, as in the highly successful *The Dead Zone* (1983) and *The Fly* (1986), which gave him cult status. Later films include the controversial *Crash* (1996), *Spider* (2002), and *A History of Violence* (2005).

Cronin, A(rchibald) J(oseph) [krohnin] (1896–1981) Novelist, born in Cardross, Argyll and Bute. His books include *The Citadel* (1937) and *The Keys of the Kingdom* (1942). Several were filmed, and the television series *Dr Finlay's Casebook* was based on his stories.

Cronkite, Walter (Leland), Jr [krongkiyt] (1916–) Journalist and broadcaster, born in St Joseph, MO. He joined the United Press (1939–48), and provided vivid eye-witness accounts of the war in Europe. At CBS from 1950, he became a national institution as the anchorman of the *CBS Evening News* (1962–81).

Cronus [kronus] or **Kronos** In Greek mythology, the second ruler of the Universe, a Titan, the youngest son of Uranus, who rebelled against his father. Probably a pre-Greek deity, he is often confused with *chronos* 'time'.

croquet [krohkay] A ball-and-mallet game for two to four players, played on a lawn about 32 m/35 yd long and 25 m/28 yd wide, on which have been arranged six hoops and a central peg. The object is to strike your own ball through the hoops in a prescribed order before finally hitting the central peg.

Crosby, Bing, popular name of **Harry Lillis Crosby** (1904–77) Singer and film star, born in Tacoma, WA. He began to make films, specializing in light comedy roles, and his distinctive style of crooning made him one of the best-known names in the entertainment world. His recordings of 'White Christmas' and 'Silent Night' were the hits of the 20th-c. He starred in many films, notably the *Road* films with Bob Hope and Dorothy Lamour. A keen golfer, he continued to perform and give concerts until his death on a golf course in Spain.

Crosland, Tony, popular name of **(Charles) Anthony Raven Crosland** (1918–77) British Labour statesman, born in St Leonards, East Sussex. His posts include secretary for education and science (1965–7), environment secretary (1974–6), and foreign secretary (1976–7). A key member of the revisionist wing of the Labour Party, he wrote one of its seminal texts, *The Future of Socialism* (1956).

cross The main symbol of Christianity, signifying the execution of Jesus by crucifixion, but a widespread religious symbol even in pre-Christian times. Many popular variations of the cross-symbol have appeared in Christian worship and art.

cross-bencher The name given to a member of the House of Lords who sits as an independent peer rather than accepting a party whip. The name comes from the position in the Lords chamber of the benches upon which this group of peers sit.

crossbill A finch native to the N hemisphere, especially N regions. The tips of its bill cross over, an adaptation for extracting seeds from pine cones. (Genus: *Loxia*, 4 species. Family: Fringillidae.)

crossbow A form of bow mounted in a stock, with a crank to wind

back and tension the bow itself, and a trigger to discharge the arrow, or 'bolt'. It was much used in the Crusades. China had crossbows before the 4th-c BC.

cross-country running An athletic running event using a pre-determined course over natural terrain. The length of race varies, but world championships are over 12 km/7·5 mi for men and 5 km/3·1 mi for women.

Cross Fell Highest peak of the Pennine Chain in Cumbria, NW England; rises to 893 m/2930 ft.

Crossman, Richard (Howard Stafford) (1907–74) British Labour statesman, born in Cropredy, Oxfordshire. He became minister of housing and local government (1964–6), then secretary of state for social services and head of the Department of Health (1968–70). His best-known work is his series of political diaries, begun in 1952, keeping a detailed record of the day-to-day workings of government. They were published in four volumes (1975–81), despite attempts to suppress them.

Crossopterygii [krosopterijeeiy] A subclass of bony fishes comprising the tassel-finned (or lobe-finned) fishes, having an extensive fossil record from the Devonian to Cretaceous periods. The only living representative is the coelacanth, *Latimeria*.

cross sums *kakuro*

croup [kroop] A hollow crowing noise during respiration and on coughing. It occurs in children due to swelling and narrowing of the vocal cords due to infection with one of several viruses.

Crow North American Sioux-speaking Plains Indians. In 1868 they were settled on reservations in Montana, where most Crow still live.

crow A bird of the worldwide family Corvidae. It can be a common name for the whole family, or just for the 40 species of the genus *Corvus*, or just for some species of *Corvus*.

crowberry A spreading, evergreen, heather-like shrub (*Empetrum nigrum*), native to arctic and N temperate moors; three sepals, three petals; berry black. (Family: Empetraceae.)

Crowe, Russell (1964–) Actor, born in Wellington, New Zealand. He made his acting debut on the Australian television soap *Neighbours* in 1985. His films include *The Insider* (1999, Oscar nomination), *Gladiator* (2000, Best Actor Oscar), *A Beautiful Mind* (2001, Best Actor Golden Globe; BAFTA), *Master and Commander* (2003), and *Cinderella Man* (2005).

Crowley, Aleister, originally **Edward Alexander Crowley** (1875–1947) British writer and 'magician'. He became interested in the occult, and founded the order known as the Silver Star (1906). He liked to be known as 'the great beast' and 'the wickedest man alive'.

Crown Agents (for Overseas Governments and Administrations) A UK agency which provides professional, financial, and commercial services to governments and other public authorities in developing countries and to international agencies. It also acts on behalf of the World Bank.

Crown Colony *colony*

Crown Court A court in England and Wales, established by the Courts Act (1971), which abolished the Assizes and Quarter Sessions. Crown Courts have unlimited power to deal with indictable offences, and also hear most appeals from magistrates' courts.

Crown Estate Property belonging by heredity to the British sovereign, comprising over 120 000 ha/300 000 acres in England, Scotland, and Wales. Over half of Britain's foreshore is included, together with the sea bed within territorial waters.

crown jewels Regalia and jewellery belonging to a sovereign. The British crown jewels have been displayed at various sites in the Tower of London for 300 years, since 1967 in the Jewel House. Most of the crown jewels date from the Restoration (1660). They include St Edward's Crown, used in most coronations since that of Charles II; the Imperial State Crown; and Queen

The Main Crusades To The East

	Background	Leader(s)	Outcome
First Crusade (1096–9)	Proclaimed by Urban II to aid the Greeks against the Seljuk Turks in Asia Minor, liberate Jerusalem and the Holy Land from Seljuk domination, and safeguard pilgrim routes to the Holy Sepulchre.	Bohemond I Godfrey of Bouillon Raymond, Count of Flanders Robert Curthose, Duke of Normandy Stephen, Count of Blois	Capture of Nicaea in Anatolia (Jun 1097); Turks vanquished at Battle of Dorylaeum (Jul 1097); capture of Antioch in Syria (Jun 1098), Jerusalem (Jul 1099). Godfrey of Bouillon became ruler of the new Latin Kingdom of Jerusalem, and defeated the Fatimids of Egypt near Ascalon in Palestine (Aug 1099). Three other crusader states were founded: Antioch, Edessa, Tripoli.
Second Crusade (1147–8)	Proclaimed by Eugenius III to aid the crusader states after the Muslim reconquest of Edessa (1144).	Conrad III of Germany Louis VII of France	German army heavily defeated by Turks near Dorylaeum (Oct 1147), and the French at Laodicea (Jan 1148); Damascus in Syria invested, but siege abandoned after four days (Jul 1148). The crusaders' military reputation was destroyed, and the Syrian Muslims united against the Latins.
Third Crusade (1189–92)	Proclaimed by Gregory VIII after Saladin's defeat of the Latins at the Battle of Hattin (Jul 1187) and his conquest of Jerusalem (Oct 1187). (By 1189 all that remained of the Kingdom of Jerusalem was the port of Tyre).	Frederick Barbarossa Philip II Augustus of France Richard I of England	Cyprus conquered from Greeks (May 1191), and established as new crusader kingdom (survived until 1489); capture of Acre in Palestine (Jul 1191); Saladin defeated near Arsuf (Sept 1191); three-year truce guaranteeing safe-conduct of Christian pilgrims to Jerusalem. Most cities and castles of the Holy Land remained in Muslim hands.
Fourth Crusade (1202–4)	Proclaimed by Innocent III to recover the Holy Places.	Boniface of Montferrat	Despite papal objections, crusade diverted from Egypt or Palestine (1) to Zara, a Christian town in Dalmatia, conquered for Venetians (Nov 1202); (2) to Byzantium, where embroilment in dynastic struggles led to sack of Constantinople (Apr 1204) and foundation of Latin Empire of Constantinople (survived until 1261). The crusading movement was discredited; the Latins in Palestine and Syria were hardly helped at all; the Byzantine empire never fully recovered; and the opportunity was lost of a united front between the Latins and Greeks against the Muslims.

Elizabeth the Queen Mother's crown, which is set with the Koh-i-Noor ('mountain of light') diamond.

Crown Prosecution Service In England and Wales, a body of lawyers responsible for assessing the evidence collected by the police, and for deciding whether to prosecute an individual or a corporate body and what the particular charge should be. Established in 1985, it is independent of the police, and is headed by the Director of Public Prosecutions.

crucifixion A common form of capital punishment in the Roman world, in which a person was nailed or bound to a wooden cross by the wrists and feet, and left to die. The method was inflicted only upon slaves and people of low social status (*humiliores*). It was regularly preceded by flagellation.

Cruden, Alexander [krooden] (1701–70) Scholar and bookseller, born in Aberdeen, NE Scotland. In 1737 appeared his *Concordance of the Holy Scriptures*.

	Background	Leader(s)	Outcome
Fifth Crusade (1217–21)	Proclaimed by Innocent III when a six-year truce between the Kingdom of Jerusalem and Egypt expired.	Andrew II of Hungary John of Brienne, King of Jerusalem Leopold, Duke of Austria	Three indecisive expeditions against Muslims in Palestine (1217); capture of Damietta in Egypt after protracted siege (May 1218–Nov 1219); further conquests attempted, but crusaders forced to relinquish Damietta (Aug 1221) and withdraw.
Sixth Crusade (1228–9)	Emperor Frederick II, who first took the Cross in 1215, married the heiress to the Kingdom of Jerusalem in 1225. Excommunicated by Gregory IX for delaying his departure, he finally arrived at Acre in Sept 1228.	Frederick II	Negotiations with Egyptians secured Jerusalem and other places, including Bethlehem and Nazareth (Feb 1229); Frederick crowned King of Jerusalem in church of Holy Sepulchre (Mar 1229). Jerusalem was held until recaptured by the Khorezmian Turks in 1244.
Seventh Crusade (1248–54)	Proclaimed by Innocent IV after the fall of Jerusalem and defeat of the Latin army near Gaza by the Egyptians and Khorezmians (1244).	Louis IX of France	Capture of Damietta (June 1249); defeat at Mansurah (Feb 1250); surrender of crusaders during attempted withdrawal; Damietta relinquished and large ransoms paid (May 1250). Louis spent four years in Palestine, refortifying Acre, Caesarea, Joppa and Sidon, and fruitlessly attempting to regain Jerusalem by alliances with the Mameluks and Mongols.
Eighth Crusade (1270–2)	Proclaimed after the Mameluk conquest of Arsuf, Caesarea, Haifa (1265), Antioch and Joppa (1268).	Charles of Anjou, King of Naples-Sicily Edward of England (later Edward I) Louis IX of France	Attacked Tunisia in N Africa (Jul 1270); Louis died in Aug; Charles concluded treaty with Tunis and withdrew; Edward negotiated 11-years truce with Mameluks in Palestine. By 1291 the Latins had been driven from the Holy Land.

Cruelty, Theatre of A notion developed during 1931–6 by French poet, actor, and theorist Antoine Artaud to describe his vision of a metaphysical theatre in which both actors and audience could experience, without any avoidance or illusion, existential realities. Using gesture, movement, sound, and rhythm, rather than words, he aimed to release the audience's inhibitions.

Cruft, Charles (1852–1939) British showman, who organized the first dog show in London in 1886. The annual shows have since become world-famous, and have helped to improve standards of dog breeding.

Cruikshank, George [krookshangk] (1792–1878) Caricaturist and illustrator, born in London. His best-known work includes Grimm's *German Popular Stories* (1824–6) and Dickens's *Oliver Twist*.

Cruise, Tom [krooz] (1962–) Film actor, born in Syracuse, NY. His films include *Top Gun* (1985), *Rain Man* (1988), *Born on the*

Fourth of July (1989), and *Mission: Impossible* (1996, sequels 2000, 2006). In 1999 he co-starred with second wife Nicole Kidman (divorced, 2001) in *Eyes Wide Shut*. Among later films are *Vanilla Sky* (2001), *The Last Samurai* (2003), and *War of the Worlds* (2005). He married actress **Katie Holmes** (1978–) in 2006.

cruise missile A type of missile which flies continuously on wings, and is propelled continuously by an engine using air from the atmosphere as its oxidant to mix with the fuel it carries. The German V-1 of 1944 was a cruise missile. It now provides a comparatively cheap means of delivering a nuclear or conventional warhead over a long distance, using onboard computer power to provide pinpoint accuracy.

cruiser A medium-sized warship designed to protect trade routes and to act as a scout for a battle fleet.

crumhorn A musical instrument made from wood with a small cylindrical bore, and curved at the end like a hockey stick. It was widely used in Europe in the 16th–17th-c, and revived in the 20th-c for performing early music.

Crusades Holy Wars authorized by the Pope in defence of Christendom and the Church. They were fought against the Muslims in the East, Germany, and Spain, against heretics and schismatics who threatened Catholic unity, and against Christian lay powers who opposed the papacy. (*see panel pp. 240–41*)

crustacean [kruhstayshn] A typically aquatic arthropod possessing a pair of jaws (*mandibles*) and two pairs of antennae situated in front of the mouth in adults; group contains c.40 000 species. (Subphylum: Crustacea.)

Crutzen, Paul (1933–) Chemist, born in Amsterdam. In 1970 he was among the first to draw attention to the vulnerability of the ozone layer, and demonstrated that the presence of nitrogen oxides increase the rate of ozone's decomposition. He shared the 1995 Nobel Prize for Chemistry.

Crux (Lat 'cross') The smallest constellation in the sky, and one of the most distinctive, better known as **the Southern Cross**, it features on the national flags of Australia and New Zealand.

Cruyff, Johan(nes Hendrikus) [kriyf] (1947–) Footballer, born in Amsterdam. He won 11 Dutch League and Cup medals with Ajax, and helped them to three consecutive (1971–3) European Cup successes. In 1973 he joined Barcelona, and in 1974 captained Holland in the World Cup final (beaten by West Germany). He returned to Barcelona as manager (1988–96), guiding the Spanish champions to the European Cup for the first time in 1992. His son, Jordi (1974–), joined Manchester United Football Club (1996–2000).

Cruz, Penélope (1974–) Actress, born in Madrid. Her work for the Spanish cinema includes *Belle Epoque* (1993) and *All About My Mother* (1999), both of which won Best Foreign Film Oscars. In the USA her films include *The Hi-Lo Country* (1998), *Captain Corelli's Mandolin* (2001), and and *Volver* (2006, Best Actress Oscar nomination).

crwth [krooth] A Celtic (especially Welsh) lyre, played with a bow or plucked. The earliest types, known from the 12th-c onwards, had three strings, but by the 18th-c it had acquired a further three.

cryogenics The study of physical systems at temperatures less than c.90 K ($-183°$C). Some processes can be observed only at low temperatures, either because of masking by thermal effects or because the phenomena (eg superconductivity) exist only at low temperature.

cryolite [kriyoliyt] A mineral composed of sodium, aluminium, and fluorine (Na_3AlF_6), used in the smelting of aluminium ores. It occurs in important quantities in Russia and Greenland.

crypt Part of a building below the main floor and usually underground. In particular, it refers to the part of a church containing graves and relics.

cryptanalysis The deciphering or codebreaking of messages intended for others. This involves firstly intercepting a message, then analyzing it to reveal its contents. Since languages can be distinguished by the different frequencies with which the letters of the alphabet occur, the prime task is to search for such enciphered patterns.

cryptography The alteration of the form of a message by codes and ciphers to conceal its meaning. Codewords, normally from a code book, stand for one or more words of the *plaintext* (the original message). With ciphers, the letters of the plaintext are individually substituted or transposed (re-ordered), according to a secret key.

Crystal, Billy (1947–) Film actor, born in Long Beach, NY. Well known for his role in the American comedy series, *Soap*, his feature films include *Throw Momma From the Train* (1987), *When Harry Met Sally* (1989), *City Slickers* and its sequel (1991, 1994), *Forget Paris* (1995), which he also directed, *Analyze This* (1999), and *Analyze That* (2002).

crystal defects Irregularities in otherwise perfectly regular crystals. Some, such as cracks and dislocations, strongly influence crystal mechanical properties, typically causing weakness. Others, such as impurities, affect electrical properties (eg the semiconductor crystals used in electronics) or give colour to crystals (eg chromium in red ruby).

Crystal Palace An iron-framed, prefabricated, glass building designed by Sir Joseph Paxton to house the Great Exhibition of 1851. The structure was erected in London's Hyde Park, re-erected in S London, but destroyed by fire in 1936.

crystals True solids, made up of regularly repeating groups of atoms, ions, or molecules. In contrast with liquids and other amorphous materials, the properties of crystals vary with the direction in which they are measured. A complete crystal structure is defined by giving both a lattice of points, of which only 14 types are possible, and the group of atoms associated with each lattice point. The study of crystals is called **crystallography**.

crystal therapy In alternative medicine, a technique which uses precious and semi-precious stones, credited with particular astrological, esoteric, and physical properties. Each stone has a particular vibration pattern which some believe can act upon the body's energy field to increase the available energy and also to correct any imbalance or blockages.

CS gas US military designation for a chlorinated compound, 1-*o*-chlorophenyl-2,2-dicyanoethylene, $Cl-C_6H_4-CH=C(C\equiv N)_2$. It causes irritation and watering of the eyes, and is widely used in riot control.

ctenophore [tenofaw(r)] A marine animal with a transparent, jelly-like (gelatinous) body, which swims using eight comb-like rows of plates (**ctenes**); carnivorous, using paired tentacles armed with stinging cells to catch prey; c.80 species; known as **comb jellies** or **sea gooseberries**. (Phylum: Ctenophora.)

CT scanning *computerized tomography*

Cuba *p.243*

Cuban Missile Crisis A period of acute international tension between the USA and USSR in October 1962, following the USA's discovery of Soviet nuclear missile sites in Cuba. The crisis pushed the world to the brink of a nuclear war. President Kennedy demanded the dismantling of the base and the return of the missiles, and threw a naval blockade around the island. The crisis ended when Soviet leader Khrushchev agreed to Kennedy's demands.

Cubism A modern art movement out of which grew most of the early forms of abstraction. About 1907 Picasso and Braque rejected Renaissance perspective and Impressionist attention to light and atmosphere. Objects, painted in sombre shades of brown and grey, were analysed into geometrical planes with several views depicted simultaneously (**analytic cubism**). After c.1912 a flatter, more colourful and decorative hard-edged style

Cuba

☐ International Airport

official name **Republic of Cuba**, Span **República de Cuba**

Local name Cuba

Timezone GMT -5

Area 110 860 km²/42 792 sq mi

Population total (2002e) 11 267 000

Status Republic

Date of independence 1902

Capital Havana

Language Spanish (official)

Ethnic groups Mulatto (50%), Spanish (37%), African origin (11%)

Religions Roman Catholic (40%), Protestant (3%), Afro-Cuban syncretist (2%), non-religious (55%): Castro regime discourages religious practice

Physical features Archipelago in the Caribbean Sea, comprising the island of Cuba, Isla de la Juventud, and c.1600 islets and cays; main island of Cuba, 1250 km/777 mi; three mountainous regions range E–W, the Oriental, including Cuba's highest

peak, Pico Turquino, 2005 m/6578 ft, Central, and Occidental ranges; longest river is Rio Cauto in E.

Climate Subtropical climate, warm and humid; average annual temperature 25°C; dry season (Nov–Apr); mean annual rainfall, 1375 mm/54 in; hurricanes (Jun–Nov).

Currency 1 Cuban Peso (CUP) = 100 centavos

Economy World's second largest sugar producer (accounting for 75% of export earnings); world's fifth largest producer of nickel; fish, coffee, tobacco, citrus fruits, rice.

GDP (2002e) $30·69 bn, per capita $2700

Human Development Index (2002) 0·795

History Visited by Columbus, 1492; Spanish colony until 1898, following revolution under José Martí with support of USA; independence, 1902; struggle against dictatorship of General Batista led by Fidel Castro Ruz finally successful in 1959, and a Communist state was established; invasion of Cuban exiles with US support defeated at Bay of Pigs, 1961; US naval blockade, after Soviet installation of missile bases discovered in Cuba (Cuban Missile Crisis), 1962. Communist Party of Cuba established as the sole legal party, 1965; President of the State Council is Head of State; State Council, appointed by National Assembly of People's Power.

Head of State/Government

1902–6 Tomas Estrada Palma
1906–9 *US rule*
1909–13 José Miguel Gómez
1913–21 Mario García Menocal
1921–5 Alfredo Zayas y Alfonso
1925–33 Gerardo Machado y Morales
1933 Carlos Manuel de Céspedes
1933–4 Ramón Grau San Martín
1934–5 Carlos Mendieta
1935–6 José A Barnet y Vinagres
1936 Miguel Mariano Gómez y Arias
1936–40 Federico Laredo Bru
1940–4 Fulgencio Batista
1944–8 Ramón Grau San Martín
1948–52 Carlos Prío Socarrás
1952–9 Fulgencio Batista
1959 Manuel Urrutia
1956–76 Osvaldo Dorticós Torrado
1976 Fidel Castro Ruz *Prime Minister and First Secretary*
1976– Fidel Castro Ruz *President*

emerged (**synthetic cubism**), using collage and painted relief constructs.

Cubitt, Thomas (1788–1855) Builder, born in Buxton, Norfolk. With his brother **Lewis Cubitt** (1799–1883) he worked on the development of Belgravia, London; later, Thomas's buildings included Osborne House and the E front of Buckingham Palace; Lewis's best-known building is Kings Cross Station.

Cuchulain [kuhoolin] Ir **Cu Chulainn** The hero of many Irish legends, the chief warrior of Ulster. He obtained his name (meaning 'the hound of Culaan') after killing a huge dog.

cuckoo A bird of the worldwide family Culculidae (130 species), mostly inhabiting woodland. About 50 species do not build nests, but lay eggs in the nests of other birds, with the young reared by 'foster' parents.

cuckoo-pint *lords-and-ladies*

cuckoo-roller *roller*

cuckoo shrike A bird native to the Old World, especially the tropics; also known as the **caterpillar bird**; dull, greyish plumage. It is neither a true cuckoo nor a shrike. (Family: Campephagidae, 70 species.)

cuckoo-spit insect *froghopper*

cucumber A vine (*Cucumis sativa*), trailing or climbing by means of tendrils, cultivated from early times as a salad vegetable; flowers yellow, funnel-shaped; fruit up to 45 cm/18 in or more, green, fleshy, cylindrical or oval. (Family: Cucurbitaceae.)

Cúcuta [kookoota] 7°55N 72°31W, pop (2000e) 441 300. City in NE Colombia; founded, 1734; destroyed by earthquake, 1875, then rebuilt; a focal point in Colombia's fight for independence; airfield; university (1962).

Cudworth, Ralph (1617–88) Philosopher and theologian, born in Aller, Somerset. The leader of the 'Cambridge Platonists', his best-known work is *The True Intellectual System of the Universe* (1678).

Cuenca [kwenka] 2°54S 79°00W, pop (2000e) 234 400. City in SC Ecuador; founded by Spanish, 1557; airfield; railway; two universities (1868, 1970); old and new cathedrals.

Cukor, George D(ewey) [kooker] (1899–1983) Film director, born in New York City. He was particularly successful with the great actresses of the star system – Garbo, Crawford, Hepburn – but his range was wide, including *Gaslight* (1944), *A Star is Born* (1954), and *My Fair Lady* (1964, Oscar).

cu lan *loris*

Culicidae [kyoolisidee] A family containing c.3000 species of true flies, including mosquitoes and gnats. Many species are of primary medical and veterinary importance as carriers of diseases. (Order: Diptera.)

Cullinan diamond [kuhlinan] The largest gem diamond ever found, weight 3255 carats (650 grams/22·9 avoirdupois ounces). It was found in Premier Diamond Mine, Transvaal in 1905 and named after Sir Thomas Cullinan, who had discovered the mine.

Culloden Moor, Battle of [kuhlodn] (1746) A battle fought near Inverness, marking the end of the Jacobite rebellion of 1745 led by Charles Edward Stuart. His force, mainly of Scottish highlanders, was crushed by a superior force of English and lowland Scots under the Duke of Cumberland.

Culpeper, Nicholas (1616–54) Astrologer and physician, born in London. In 1649 he published an English translation of the College of Physicians' Pharmacopoeia, *A Physical Directory*, and in 1653 appeared *The English Physician Enlarged, or the Herbal*.

cult Any set of beliefs and practices associated with a particular god or group of gods, forming a distinctive part of a larger religious body. The focus of devotion may be an animal (eg the whale cult in Eskimo religions), a particular deity (eg the Hindu cult devoted to Shiva), or even a deified human being (eg the emperor cult in ancient Rome).

cultivar A contraction of **cultivated variety**; in names further abbreviated to **cv**. It refers to any distinct type of plant produced in cultivation but not growing in the wild.

cultivator An agricultural implement carrying rows of prongs (*tines*); some versions carry blades. It is used for breaking up soil and creating a seed-bed before planting, and is also used in the control of weeds.

cultural anthropology *anthropology*

Cultural Revolution An abbreviation for the Great Proletarian Cultural Revolution, a radical Maoist mass movement initiated as a rectification campaign in 1966, which ended only with the death of Mao Zedong and the arrest of the Gang of Four in the autumn of 1976. Mao appealed directly to the masses, in particular to young students, the Red Guards, who with the support of the People's Liberation Army overthrew not only party leaders but all so-called 'bourgeois reactionaries' in authority in schools, universities, factories, and the administration. The '10 lost years' of social and political turmoil saw the closure of schools and universities, factories at a standstill, tens of thousands of deaths, and millions of people sent to undertake manual labour in the countryside as re-education.

culture (microbiology) An artificially maintained population of micro-organisms, or of dissociated cells of a tissue, grown in a nutrient medium and reproducing by asexual division. The process is used in experimental microbiological research and also in medical applications, chiefly as part of the task of diagnosis.

Cumae [kyoomee] The oldest Greek colony in Italy, founded c.750 BC near present-day Naples. It was famous in Roman times as the home of the oracular prophetess, the Sibyl.

Cumberland A former county of NW England; part of Cumbria since 1974.

Cumberland, William Augustus, Duke of (1721–65) British general, the second son of George II, born in London. He crushed the Young Pretender's rebellion at Culloden (1746), and by his harsh policies afterwards earned the lasting title of 'Butcher'.

Cumbria pop (2001e) 487 600; area 6810 km²/2629 sq mi. County in NW England, 40% of the county within the Lake District and Yorkshire Dales national parks; created in 1974 from the former counties of Westmorland and Cumberland; county town, Carlisle; atomic energy at Sellafield and Calder Hall (operational 1956–2003).

cumin A slender annual (*Cuminum cyminum*) growing to 50 cm/20 in, native to N Africa and SW Asia; flowers white or pink; fruit oblong with slender ridges. It is cultivated for the aromatic fruits, used for spice, and is an ingredient of curry powder. (Family: Umbelliferae.)

Cummings, E(dward) E(stlin) (1894–1962) Writer and painter, born in Cambridge, MA. His several successful collections of poetry, starting with *Tulips and Chimneys* (1923), are striking for their unorthodox typography and linguistic style. *Complete Poems* appeared in 1968.

cumquat *kumquat*

cumulonimbus clouds [kyoomyulohnimbuhs] Clouds of the cumulus family which rise to great heights (up to 10 km/6 mi). They are often dark and threatening when seen from below, and are associated with thunderstorms and the arrival of a cold front during the passage of a depression. Cloud symbol: Cb.

cumulus clouds [kyoomyuluhs] A family of clouds with a predominantly vertical extent but relatively horizontal base. They range from small, white fluffy clouds typical of summer afternoons, to black and threatening storm or cumulonimbus clouds. Cloud symbol: Cu.

Cunard, Sir Samuel [kyoonah(r)d] (1787–1865) Ship-owner, born in Halifax, Nova Scotia, Canada. He emigrated to Britain in 1838, and helped to found the British and North American Royal Mail Steam Packet Company, later known as the **Cunard Line**. The modern Cunard Line runs luxury cruises and officially launched *Queen Mary 2*, the world's largest ocean liner, in January 2004.

cuneiform A form of writing used throughout the Middle East for over 3000 years until about the 1st-c BC. Originally derived from pictograms, the symbols were later used to represent words, syllables, and phonetic elements. At first, the symbols took the form of impressions made on soft clay with a stylus, but subsequently a harder writing surface was used.

Cunningham, Jack, popular name of **John Cunningham** (1939–) British statesman, born in Felling, Durham. He was a university lecturer and full-time trade union official before becoming a Labour MP (1970). He was minister for energy (1976–9) in the Callaghan government, and under Blair he became minister of agriculture (1997–8), then minister for the cabinet office and chancellor of the Duchy of Lancaster (1998–9).

Cunningham, Merce (1919–) Dancer, choreographer, teacher, and director, born in Centralia, WA. He started his own company in 1952, and is one of the major figures in the development of a concern with form and abstraction in modern dance.

Cunobelinus *Cymbeline*

Cuomo, Mario [kwohmoh] (1932–) US politician, born in New York City. He became Governor of New York State (1983–94), and was mentioned as a possible Democratic presidential candidate in 1988 and 1992.

Cupid The Roman god of Love, son of Venus, depicted as a naked winged boy with bow and arrows. Apuleius tells the story of *Cupid and Psyche*. He is equivalent to Greek Eros.

cupola [kyoopohla] A small dome over a circular, square, or polygonal part of a building, usually above a roof or turret; more loosely, a dome of any size. Good examples are found at the Royal Pavilion, Brighton (1815–23).

cuprite [kyoopriyt] A red copper oxide (Cu_2O) mineral, which is widely distributed. It is an important source of copper.

cupronickel [kyooprohnikl] An alloy of copper and nickel, silver in colour. It is used extensively for coinage.

Curaçao [koorasahoh] pop (2000e) 150 000; area 444 km²/171 sq mi. Largest and most populous island of the Netherlands Antilles, E Caribbean; rises to 373 m/1224 ft in the NW; length 58 km/36 mi; width 13 km/8 mi; visited by Europeans, 1499; Dutch colony, 1634; capital, Willemstad; airport; known for its liqueur.

curare [kyoorahree] An extract of the South American plants *Chondrodendron tomentosum* or *Strychnos toxifera*, used as an arrow poison for hunting by South American Indians. The active principle, tubocurarine, is widely used to induce muscle paralysis during surgery.

curassow [kyoorasoh] A large, tree-dwelling, turkey-like bird, native to C and N South America; head with a conspicuous crest of curved feathers; legs long, strong. (Family: Cracidae, 13 species.)

curate Strictly, a Christian clergyman admitted to the 'cure of souls' and having the 'cure' or charge of a parish. Popularly, the term is used of an assistant or unbeneficed clergyman, helping or temporarily replacing the priest, rector, vicar, or other incumbent of the parish.

curia In ancient Rome, the Senate house. It stood on the NW side of the forum, adjacent to the site of the legislative assembly.

Curia Romana *Roman Curia*

Curie, Marie [kyooree], *née* **Manya Sklodowska** (1867–1934) Physicist, born in Warsaw, who worked in Paris with her French husband **Pierre Curie** (1859–1906) on magnetism and radioactivity. Together they discovered and isolated polonium and radium (1898), and shared the 1903 Nobel Prize for Physics with Becquerel for the discovery of radioactivity. Madame Curie published her treatise on radioactivity in 1910 and was awarded the Nobel Prize for Chemistry in 1911. She died of leukaemia, probably caused by long exposure to radiation.

curie [kyooree] In radioactivity, defined as 3.7×10^{10} disintegrations per second; symbol Ci; 1 Ci $= 3.7 \times 10^{10}$ Bq (becquerel, SI unit); original definition related to the activity of radioactive radon; named after French physicists Pierre and Marie Curie.

Curie point *Curie temperature*

Curie's law A law for paramagnetic materials which states that the magnetization is proportional to B/T, where B is magnetic flux density and T is temperature in kelvins; stated by French physicist Pierre Curie in 1895.

Curie temperature In ferromagnetism, the material-dependent temperature above which a ferromagnetic material becomes merely paramagnetic; symbol T_c, units K; introduced by French physicist Pierre Curie in 1895; also called **Curie point**. For iron, $T_c = 1043$ K.

Curitiba [kooreecheeba] 25°24S 49°16W, pop (2000e) 1 604 000. Industrial city in S Brazil; altitude 900 m/2950 ft; railway; airfield; two universities (1912, 1959); cathedral (1894); commercial centre.

Curl, Robert, Jr (1933–) Chemist, born in Alice, TX. He shared the Nobel Prize for Chemistry in 1996 for his contribution to the discovery of fullerenes).

curlew A long-legged sandpiper; breeds in the N hemisphere, but flies S (some as far as Australia) in N winter; long, down-curved bill; probes for food in sediments. (Genus: *Numenius*, 8 species.)

curling A game played usually by teams of four on an ice-rink, using special stones fitted with handles. The object is similar to that of bowls, to deliver the stones nearest to a target object, known as the *tee*. The ice is swept with brooms in front of the running stone to help it to travel further. It is particularly popular in Canada, Scotland, the Nordic countries, and the USA.

currant A deciduous shrub, native to N temperate regions and the Andes; flowers borne in clusters on short lateral shoots, 4–5 sepals and petals; berries juicy. The currants used for 'fruit' cakes are dried grapes. (Genus: *Ribes*, 150 species. Family: Grossulariaceae.)

currency A country's money. A currency is *convertible* if it can be exchanged into other currencies without restriction. A currency *depreciates* if it becomes cheaper relative to other currencies.

current (electricity) The flow of electric charge, symbol i or I, units A (amp). A current of one amp means that a charge of one coulomb flows every second. Current flows positive to negative by convention. **Current density**, symbol j or J, is the total current divided by the cross-sectional area of the conductor.

current (oceanography) *p.246*

curry A spiced dish of fish, meat, poultry, or vegetables, originating in the East. Among the spices used in curries are coriander, cumin, chilli, cinnamon, cardamom, cloves, fenugreek, ginger, and turmeric.

Curtin, John (Joseph) (1885–1945) Australian statesman and Labor prime minister (1941–5), born in Creswick, Victoria. As premier, he organized national mobilization during the Japanese war.

Curtis, Tony, originally **Bernard Schwarz** (1925–) Actor, born in New York City. After many small film parts early in his career, he proved he could play light comedy roles as in *Some Like It Hot* (1959) while also displaying his dramatic ability in *The Boston Strangler* (1968). Other films include *The Vikings* (1958), *Spartacus* (1960), *The Great Impostor* (1961), *The Mirror Crack'd* (1980), and *The Continued Adventures of Reptile Man* (1996).

Curtiss, Glenn (Hammond) (1878–1930) Engineer and aeronaut, born in Hammondsport, NY. In 1908 he won the *Scientific American* trophy for the first public flight of 1 km in the USA, and in 1911 he demonstrated the practicality of the seaplane.

Curwen, John (1816–80) Music educationist, born in Heckmondwike, West Yorkshire. He devoted himself to promoting the tonic sol-fa musical system, and established a publishing house for music.

Curzon, Sir Clifford (1907–82) Pianist, born in London. He taught for some years at the Royal Academy of Music, later devoting himself to concert work.

Curzon (of Kedleston), George Nathaniel Curzon, Marquess (1859–1925) British statesman, born in Kedleston Hall, Derbyshire. In 1898 he was made Viceroy of India, where he introduced many social and political reforms, established the NW Frontier Province, and partitioned Bengal. He was also foreign secretary (1919–24).

Curzon Line A line of territorial demarcation between Russia and Poland proposed in 1920 by the British foreign secretary, Lord Curzon. It was recognized in 1945 as the frontier between Poland and the USSR.

cuscus [kuskus] *phalanger*

Cush *Kush*

Cushing, Peter (1913–94) Actor, born in Kenley, Greater London. He is chiefly known for his long association with the Gothic horror films produced by Hammer, such as *The Curse of Frankenstein* (1956) and *Dracula* (1958). His numerous other films include *Dr Who and the Daleks* (1965) and *Star Wars* (1977).

Cushing's syndrome A disorder caused by excessive levels of glucocorticoid hormones. It produces a range of characteristic clinical features, including a round red face, thin easily bruised skin, obesity, muscle wasting, osteoporosis, amenorrhoea, and hypertension.

cusp In Gothic architecture, a projecting point formed by the intersection of two or more curves in the tracery; hence, usually carved in stone.

custard apple A deciduous tree (*Annona squamosa*) growing to 6 m/20 ft, native to tropical America; flowers with six greenish-yellow petals; fruit 10 cm/4 in, roughly heart-shaped, greenish, containing numerous seeds buried in a sweet pulp; also called **sweet sop**. (Family: Annonaceae.)

Custer, George Armstrong (1839–76) US soldier, born in New Rumley, OH. He served in the campaigns against the Indian tribes of the Great Plains. His defeat by a combined Sioux–Cheyenne force at the Little Bighorn, Montana (25 Jun 1876), shocked the nation, but did no lasting good to the Indians'

currents

→ cold ocean currents		1 California Current	4 South Equatorial Current	7 Brazil Current	10 Agulhas Current	13 Kuro Shio
→ warm ocean currents		2 North Equatorial Current	5 Peru Current	8 Benguela Current	11 West Wind Drift	14 Oya Shio
----→ seasonal drift during Northern winter		3 Equatorial Counter Current	6 Gulf Stream	9 North Atlantic Drift	12 Southwest Monsoon Current	

Flowing water in the ocean. The surface currents depicted on atlases of the seas are long-term averages of the direction of water motion at the sea surface, driven primarily by the winds. Because most do not extend deeper than 300–500 m/1000–1600 ft, they can be conveniently separated from the circulation of intermediate and deep waters, driven by varying densities of sea water caused by differences in temperature and salinity. (The situation is more complex, in fact, because the Antarctic Circumpolar Current and even parts of the Gulf Stream system do extend all the way to the sea floor.)

The surface circulation has certain similarities in each of the major ocean basins. The strong, persistent *trade winds*, blowing out of the NE in the N hemisphere and out of the SE in the S hemisphere, produce major W-flowing **equatorial currents**. These currents flow along bands of latitude until, deflected by continents, they form **boundary currents** flowing N or S. In the Atlantic and Pacific Oceans these equatorial and boundary currents are parts of semi-enclosed circulation cells called *gyres*. The gyres are oval-shaped, elongated E–W, and centred in the subtropics (30°N and S). Their centres are displaced towards the W side of ocean basins because of the rotation of the Earth, which results in an intensifying of boundary currents on the W side and a weakening of E boundary currents.

In general, a subtropical gyre has four components. (1) An equatorial current travelling W in response to the Trade Winds. (2) A W boundary current flowing towards the Poles; these currents are important in transporting heat from lower to higher latitudes; they are narrow, swift, and deep. (3) An E-flowing current pushed along by the bands of W winds at temperate latitudes. (4) An E boundary current flowing towards the Equator; these currents transport cool water from higher to lower latitudes, and are broad, shallow, and weak. Smaller subpolar gyres, turning in the opposite direction to the subtropical gyres, are present especially in the N hemisphere where continents deflect current flow.

The W-flowing N and S equatorial currents of the N and S subtropical gyres are separated by an E-flowing equatorial counter-current. **Counter-currents** are developed at the inter-tropical convergence (ITC), the area of weak and variable winds known as *the Doldrums*. The ITC is not found at the geographic equator, but is shifted to c.5°N in the Atlantic and Pacific and to c.7°S in the Indian Ocean. The shift of this 'climatic equator' away from the geographic equator is the result of the unequal distribution of land and sea between the N and S hemispheres.

cause. Although a lieutenant-colonel in the cavalry, he is often referred to by his Civil War rank of general.

custody Formerly, the assigning of a child by a court to the care of one or other of the parents or guardian following a divorce, a separation, or the nullification of a marriage. In England and Wales, since the Children Act (1989) custody and access orders are no longer available, having been replaced by the concept of *parental responsibility*. Both parents have responsibility for the child if they are married to each other; and if not, the parental responsibility is conferred on the mother. In Scotland, the terms *custody* and *access* have been superseded by the terms *residence* and *contact*.

customs and excise The UK government department charged with collecting taxes due on specified goods and services, and controlling imports into a country where there are tariffs or quota restrictions, or where the imports are illegal. It is most visible at airports and ports checking goods imported, and charging tax (*duty*) as appropriate. The department also handles value-added tax.

customs union A group of countries with a common external tariff and free trade between its members. Examples include Benelux, set up in 1948, and the European Economic Community (now the European Union), set up in 1958.

Cuthbert, St (c.635–87) Missionary, born in Ireland or Northumbria. He became prior of Melrose (661) and of Lindisfarne (664), and in 684 became bishop of Hexham, then of Lindisfarne. Feast day 20 March.

Cutner, Solomon *Solomon* (music)

cutter A single-masted, fore-and-aft-rigged sailing vessel with more than one headsail, usually requiring a bowsprit. The term is still in use, especially in compounds (eg **revenue cutter**). In the USA it applies to vessels which would elsewhere be called **sloops**.

cutting A portion of a plant, usually a side shoot but also a leaf or root which, when removed from the parent, will grow to form a new individual. It is commonly used by gardeners as a means of propagation.

cuttlefish A squid-like marine mollusc with eight arms and two tentacles, used to capture prey; internal calcareous shell (**cuttlebone**) may be straight or curved; capable of rapid colour changes. (Class: Cephalopoda.)

Cuvier, Georges (Léopold Chrétien Frédéric Dagobert), Baron [küvyay] (1769–1832) Anatomist, born in Montbéliard, France. Professor of natural history at the Collège de France, he originated the natural system of animal classification, and through his studies of animal and fish fossils he established the sciences of palaeontology and comparative anatomy.

Cuyp or Cuijp, Albert [kiyp] (1620–91) Painter, born in Dordrecht, The Netherlands. He excelled in the painting of landscapes, often suffused with golden sunlight, and containing cattle and other figures.

Cuzco [kooskoh] 13°32S 71°57W, pop (2000e) 327 000. City in S Peru; altitude 3500 m/11 500 ft; ancient capital of the Inca empire; oldest continuously occupied city in the Americas; airfield; railway; a world heritage site; university (1969); cathedral (17th-c); trade centre of an agricultural region; extensive Inca ruins.

cwm *cirque*

cyanide A compound containing the group –C–N in a molecule, or salts of hydrocyanic acid containing the ion CN⁻. It is a very rapidly acting poison, which can kill within minutes. Cyanide gas has been used in gas chambers. Amyl nitrite (by inhalation) can treat cyanide poisoning if administered in time.

cyanocobalamin [siyanohkohbalamin] The chemical name for vitamin B_{12}, involved in cell division and in the manufacture of the sheath surrounding nerve cells. It is found predominantly in animal-derived food, so that a true deficiency rarely occurs except among vegans, who eat no animal food.

Cyanophycota [siyanohfiykuhta] *blue-green bacteria*

Cybele [siybeelee] In Greek mythology, a mother-goddess, especially of wild nature, whose cult originated in Phrygia, and was taken over by the Greeks. She was depicted with a turreted mural crown, and was attended by lions.

cyberintelligence The (usually covert) gathering of information via computer networks and databases, and the subsequent analysis and evaluation of this information in a useable form. With organizations now increasingly dependent on computer systems for the conduct and recording of business, cyberintelligence is undertaken by third parties in order to gain access to these systems. Those involved are mainly national and international intelligence agencies, including criminal agencies, which apply information-warfare techniques to obtain their aim. Private-sector firms also seek cyberintelligence about clients and competitors, forcing the latter to install more powerful critical infrastructure protection. Target systems are accessed by hacking, with their contents typically copied rather than altered or destroyed. **Intelligent agents** are computer programs associated with browsers which search the Web for specific information on behalf of the user and then analyse it.

cybernetics The study of control systems that exhibit characteristics similar to those of animal and human behaviour. The term was coined by Norbert Wiener in the 1940s, based on a Greek word meaning 'steersman'. It is a broad-based discipline which includes information, message, and noise theories.

cyberspace *Internet*

cycad [siykad] A tropical or subtropical gymnosperm, palm-like in appearance, trunk usually unbranched, with a crown of tough, feathery leaves; flowers borne in separate male and female cones, the female very large. Cycads are considered to be the most primitive living seed-plants, appearing in the late Palaeozoic era. (Family: Cycadaceae, 100 species.)

Cyclades [sikladeez], Gr **Kikládhes** pop (2000e) 99 300; area 2572 km²/993 sq mi. Island group in the Aegean Sea, Greece; capital, Siros; several now popular holiday resorts.

cyclamate [siklamayt] A derivative of cyclohexylsulphamic acid. It has c.30 times the sweetening power of sucrose, and was previously used widely in sweetening 'diet foods'. It is less used now because of possible health risks.

cyclamen [siklamen] A perennial with leaves growing direct from a fleshy corm, native to Europe and Asia; flowers nodding, white, pink, or purple. (Genus: *Cyclamen*, 15 species. Family: Primulaceae.)

cycling The riding of a bicycle for fitness, pleasure, or as a sport. There are several popular forms of cycling as a sport. In *time trials* cyclists race against the clock. *Cyclo-cross* is a mixture of cycling and cross-country running, with the bike on the shoulder. *Track racing* takes place on purpose-built concrete or wooden velodromes. *Criteriums* are races around town or city centres. *Road races* are normally in excess of 150 km/100 mi in length, and take place either from one point to another, or involve several circuits around a predetermined road course. *Stage races* involve many days' racing, each consisting of 150 km/100 mi or more. The most famous cycle race is the *Tour de France*.

cyclone *depression* (meteorology); *hurricane*

cyclophosphamide [siyklohfosfamiyd] An important drug in the treatment of cancers. It belongs to a class of drug called the *nitrogen mustards*, developed from mustard gas which was used in the first world war. Nitrogen mustards are so-called *alkylating* agents, which work by binding to the DNA of cells, thus stopping them from dividing. Cyclophosphamide is usually given in a cocktail of different classes of anti-cancer drug to optimize therapy and minimize side effects.

Cyclops [siyklops], plural **Cyclopes** In Greek mythology, a race of one-eyed giants who worked as smiths and were associated with volcanic activity. In the *Odyssey*, the Cyclops Polyphemus is outwitted and blinded by Odysseus.

cyclostome [siyklohstohm] Any of a group of jawless fishes with a large sucking mouth.

cyclotron A machine for accelerating charged particles, typically protons; developed by US physicist Ernest Lawrence and others in 1931, and now largely superseded in particle physics by the synchrotron. Acceleration is provided by an oscillating electric field.

Cygnus [signus] (Lat 'swan') A large N constellation, associated by the ancient Greeks with the swan into which Zeus changed to

Cyprus

☐ International Airport

[siypruhs], Gr **Kypros**, Turkish **Kibris**; official name **Republic of Cyprus**, Gr **Kypriaki Dimokratia**, Turkish **Kibris Cumhuriyeti**

Local names Kipros (Greek), Kibris (Turkish)

Timezone GMT +2

Area 9251 km²/3571 sq mi

Population total (2002e) 802 000

Status Republic

Date of independence 1960

Capital Nicosia (Lefkosia to Greek Cypriots, Lefkosa to Turkish Cypriots)

Languages Greek and Turkish (official), English

Ethnic groups Greek (78%), Turkish (18%), other (4%)

Religions Greek Orthodox (78%), Sunni Muslim (18%), other Christian (4%)

Physical features Third largest island in Mediterranean; Kyrenia Mts extend 150 km/90 mi along N coast, Mt Kyparissovouno, 1024 m/3360 ft; forest-covered Troödos Mts in SW, rising to 1951 m/6401 ft at Mt Olympus; fertile alluvial Mesaoria plain extends across island centre; SE plateau region slopes towards indented coastline, with several long, sandy beaches; major rivers include the Pedios, Karyota, Kouris.

Climate Mediterranean, with hot, dry summers and warm, wet winters; average annual rainfall ranges from 300–400 mm/12–

16 in on the Mesaoria Plain to 1200 mm/47 in in the Troödos Mts; mean daily temperatures in Nicosia 10°C (Jan), 28°C (Jul); temperatures range from 22°C on Troödos Mts, to 29°C on Central plain (Jul–Aug); snow on higher land in winter.

Currency Greek Cyprus: 1 Cyprus Pound (CYP) = 100 cents; Turkish Cyprus: 1 Turkish Lira (TRL) = 100 kurus

Economy Main exports include cement, clothing, footwear, citrus, potatoes, grapes, wine; tourism; financial services; Famagusta (chief port prior to 1974 Turkish invasion) now under Turkish occupation, and declared closed by Cyprus government; Turkish Cypriot economy heavily dependent on agriculture.

GDP (2001e) Greek $9·4 bn, per capita $15 000
Turkish $787 mi, per capita $6000

Human Development Index (2001) 0·891

History Recorded history of 4000 years; rulers included Greeks, Ptolemies, Persians, Romans, Byzantines, Arabs, Franks, Venetians, Turks (1571–1878), and British; British Crown Colony from 1925; Greek Cypriot demands for union with Greece (enosis) led to guerrilla warfare, under Grivas and Makarios, and four-year state of emergency, 1955–9; independence, 1960, with Britain retaining sovereignty over bases at Akrotiri and Dhekelia; Greek-Turkish fighting throughout 1960s, with UN peacekeeping force sent in 1964; Greek junta engineered coup d'état, 1974; Turkish invasion in 1974 led to occupation of over a third of the island; island divided into two parts by the Attila Line, cutting through Nicosia where it is called the Green Line; almost all Turks now live in N sector (37% of island); governed by a president (head of state), elected for a 5-year term by the Greek community, and a House of Representatives of 80 elected members (including 24 seats nominally reserved for Turkish Cypriots); Turkish members ceased to attend in 1983, when the Turkish community declared itself independent (as 'Turkish Republic of Northern Cyprus', or TRNC, with Raul Denktas as president, recognized only by Turkey); UN peace proposals rejected, 1984; summit meeting between Kyprianou (Greek president of Cyprus) and Denktas failed, 1985; president Georgios Vassiliou renewed talks with Denktas, 1988, but soon abandoned; UN-sponsored peace negotiations, 1997; representatives of both sides in a new series of talks, 2002; Green Line border opened for daytime crossings (Apr 2003); restrictions eased further with lifting of travel ban on Greek Cypriots to Turkey (May 2003); accession of Greek Cyprus as EU member (from 1 May 2004) ratified, July 2003; Greek Cypriots reject UN plan to reunite the island, April 2004; inter-island trade between TRNC and Greek Cyprus resumed, Aug 2004.

Head of State/Government

1960–77 Archbishop Makarios III
1977–88 Spyros Kyprianou
1988–93 Georgios Vassiliou
1993–2003 Glafkos Clirides
2003– Tassos Papadopoulos

---

seduce Queen Leda of Sparta. Its brightest star is Deneb, a supergiant, distance 990 parsec.

cymbals Musical instruments of great antiquity. Modern orchestral cymbals are made in pairs, from an alloy of copper and tin, with a diameter of about 40–50 cm/16–20 in. They are clashed together, or suspended from a stand and played with a drumstick. An array of free-standing cymbals is also an important part of the jazz drummer's kit.

Cymbeline [simbeleen], also known as **Cunobelinus** (?–c.43) Pro-Roman king of the Catuvellauni, who from his capital at Camulodunum (Colchester) ruled most of SE Britain. Shakespeare's

character was based on Holinshed's half-historical Cunobelinus.

cymbidium [simbidium] A member of a genus of orchids (epiphytes) native to tropical forests from Asia to Australia. They are widely cultivated for the spikes of large, showy flowers much used in floristry and the cut-flower trade. (Genus: *Cymbidium*, 40 species. Family: Orchidaceae.)

cyme [siym], **cymose** *inflorescence*

Cynewulf [kinewulf] (8th-c) Anglo-Saxon poet, identified by some with Cynewulf, bishop of Lindisfarne (737–80). Four of his poems have his name worked into the text in runes.

Czech Republic

☐ International Airport

[chek], Czech **Česká Republika**
Local name Česká republika
Timezone GMT +1
Area 78 864 km²/30 441 sq mi
Population total (2002e) 10 210 000
Status Republic
Date of independence 1993
Capital Prague
Languages Czech (official), with several minorities
Ethnic groups Czech (94%), Slovak (4%), Hungarian, Polish, German, and Ukrainian minorities

Religions Roman Catholic (39%), Protestant (2%)
Physical features Landlocked in C Europe; Bohemian Massif, average height, 900 m/2953 ft, surrounds the Bohemian basin in W; Elbe-Moldau river system flows N into Germany; fertile plains of the Morava R divide Czech from Slovak Republic; c.40% land is arable.
Climate Continental, with warm, humid summers and cold, dry winters; average annual temperatures 2°C (Jan), 19°C (Jul) in Prague; average annual rainfall, 483 mm/19 in.
Currency 1 Koruna (CZK) = 100 haléř
Economy Steel production around Ostrava coalfields; machinery, iron, glass, chemicals, motor vehicles, cement; wheat, sugar beet, potatoes, rye, corn, barley.
GDP (2002e) $157·1 bn, per capita $15 300
Human Development Index (2002) 0·849
History From 880 ruled by the Premyslid dynasty; rise of Bohemian royal power, 14th-c; ruled by Austrian Habsburgs, early 17th-c; Czech lands united with Slovakia to form separate state of Czechoslovakia, 1918; occupied by Germany, 1938; government in exile in London during World War 2; Czechoslovakian independence, with loss of some territory to USSR, 1946; communist rule imposed by Russia following 1948 coup; attempt at liberalization by Dubček terminated by intervention of Warsaw Pact troops, 1968; fall from power of the Communist Party, 1989; 1992 agreement to divide Czechoslovakia into its constituent republics, Czech and Slovak, by Jan 1993; Czech Republic now comprises former provinces of Bohemia, Silesia, Moravia; governed by a Chamber of Deputies and (1996) 81-member Senate; member of European Union, 2004.

Head of State
1993–2003 Václav Havel
2003– Václav Klaus

Head of Government
1993–7 Václav Klaus
1997–8 Josef Tosovsky
1998–2002 Miloš Zeman
2002–4 Vladimir Spidla
2004–5 Stanislav Gross
2005–6 Jiri Paroubek
2006– Mirek Topolanek

Cynics (Gr 'dogs') A discontinuous group of philosophers, early members of which included Antisthenes and Diogenes of Sinope, influential in Greece and Rome 4th-c BC–6th-c AD. They taught by their example an ascetic life in conformity with nature.

cypress An evergreen conifer, native to the temperate N hemisphere; leaves small, scale-like; cones like the head of a mace, with 4–12 woody scales joined at their margins. (Genus: *Cupressus*, 15–20 species. Family: Cupressaceae.)

Cyprian, St [siprian], originally **Thascius Caecilius Cyprianus** (c.200–58) One of the great Fathers of the Church, probably born in Carthage. He suffered martyrdom under Valerian (reigned 253–60). At a synod in Carthage in 256 he argued for a notion of Church unity as expressed through the consensus of bishops. Feast day 16 September.

Cyprus p.248

Cyrano de Bergerac, Savinien [siranoh duh berzherak] (1619–55) Satirist and playwright, born in Paris. In his youth he fought more than a thousand duels, mostly on account of his extremely large nose. His life was the subject of the play by Edmond Rostand (1897).

Cyrenaics [sirenayiks] A school of 4th-c and 3rd-c BC Greek phil-

osophers, whose founder was Aristippus of Cyrene. They believed that the immediate sensation of pleasure is the only good, that all such sensations are equal in worth, and that past and future pleasures have no present value.

Cyrene [siyreenee] 32°49N 21°52E. A prosperous Greek city-state in N Africa, famous in antiquity for the export of silphium, a plant used in ancient medicine. It is now a world heritage site, and the location of the village of Shahhat, E Libya.

Cyril, St (c.827–69) Christian missionary and saint, born in Thessaloniki, Greece, who with his brother **St Methodius** (c.825–85), also born in Thessaloniki, became missionaries to the Slavs. Together they went to Moravia, where they prepared a Slavonic translation of the Scriptures and the chief liturgical books, and introduced a new, Greek-based alphabet (the *Cyrillic alphabet*). Feast day 14 February (W), 11 May (E).

Cyril of Alexandria, St (376–444) Theologian, one of the Fathers of the Church, born in Alexandria. He expelled the Jews from the city (415), and relentlessly persecuted Nestorius, whose doctrine was condemned at the Council of Ephesus (431). Feast day 9 June (E) or 27 June (W).

Cyril of Jerusalem, St (c.315–86) Theologian and Bishop of Jerusalem, who took a leading part in the doctrinal controversies concerning Arianism. He spoke for the Orthodox churchmen at the Council of Constantinople (381). Feast day 18 March.

Cyrillic alphabet [sirilik] An alphabet attributed to St Cyril, and used for Slavonic languages, such as Russian and Bulgarian. It is used for many non-Slavonic languages in the republics of the former USSR.

Cyrus II [siyrus], known as **the Great** (?–529 BC) The founder of the Achaemenid Persian Empire, the son of Cambyses I. His empire eventually ran from the Mediterranean to the Hindu Kush. He had a policy of religious conciliation: the nations which had been carried into captivity in Babylon along with the Jews were restored to their native countries.

cyst (biology) [sist] Any relatively thick-walled resting cell formed by an organism as a means of dispersal or as a way of surviving a period of adverse conditions. Eggs and spores are often protected in cysts, but whole organisms may also encyst, to re-emerge when favourable conditions return.

cyst (medicine) [sist] A benign (non-malignant) swelling within a tissue, very often containing fluid. It is sometimes caused by the blockage of a duct (eg a sweat-gland cyst in the skin), by abnormal embryological development, or by infection.

cystic fibrosis [sistik fiybrohsis] A genetically determined disorder that causes the mucous secretions in many parts of the body to become thickened and viscid. The thick mucus particularly affects the respiratory and digestive symptoms. It accumulates in the airways, which dilate and are prone to recurrent infection. It also blocks ducts in the pancreas, preventing pancreatic secretions, which are essential for digestion, from reaching the intestines.

cystitis [sistiytis] Inflammation of the wall of the urinary bladder, usually due to an infection. It induces frequency of urination, with a burning sensation on passing urine.

cytokines [siytokiynz] Messenger molecules within the immune system which are involved in modulating the immune response. Some (eg interferon) have been genetically engineered, and tested (though not with particular success) in diseases such as cancer.

cytology [siytolojee] The study of the structure and function of cells. Microscopic studies of cells, using a variety of staining techniques to identify cell types, are important in the diagnosis of some diseases, especially cancer.

cytoplasm [siytoplazm] That part of an animal or plant cell enclosed by the cell membrane (*plasma membrane*) but excluding the nucleus. The cytoplasm contains a range of organelles, each with a specialized function.

cytosine [siytoseen] $C_4H_5N_3O$. A base derived from pyrimidine, one of the four found in nucleic acids, where it is generally paired with guanine.

cytotoxic drugs *chemotherapy*

czar *tsar*

Czechoslovakia [chekoslovahkia], Czech **Československo**, official name **Czech and Slovak Federative Republic** pop (1992e) 15 605 000; area 127 899 km^2/49 369 sq mi. Former federal state consisting of the Czech Republic (W) and the Slovak Republic (E); capital, Prague; official languages, Czech and Slovak; population, 65% Czech, 30% Slovak, with several minorities; unit of currency, the koruna or crown of 100 haler; formerly ruled by Austrian Habsburgs; Czech lands united with Slovakia to form separate state, 1918; Mazaryk elected first president of parliamentary democracy; communist rule followed 1948 coup; attempt at liberalization by Dubček terminated by intervention of Warsaw Pact troops, 1968; strong dissident protest movement led to fall of communism in 1989, amd election of President Havel; each republic was governed by a National Council; with overall power vested in the Federal Assembly, which elected the president, and comprised the Chamber of Nations (75 Czech and 75 Slovak delegates) and Chamber of the People (200 elected deputies); agreement to divide into the two constituent republics made in 1992, effective 1 January 1993.

Czech Republic *p.249*

dab European flatfish (*Limanda limanda*) abundant on sandy bottoms in inshore waters; both eyes on right side of head; scales rough; body length up to 40 cm/16 in; valuable food fish. (Family: Pleuronectidae.)

dabchick The common name for some smaller birds of the grebe family.

Dacca *Dhaka*

dace Freshwater fish (*Leuciscus leuciscus*) widespread in rivers of Europe and Russia; length up to 30 cm/1 ft, body slim; olive-green above, underside silvery white. (Family: Cyprinidae.)

dachshund A breed of dog, developed from small terriers in Germany; small, with long back, short legs; long muzzle, pendulous ears; used for hunting (sent into burrows); also known as **sausage dog**.

dactylology [daktilolojee] A means of communication in which the fingers are used to sign the different letters of the alphabet; also known as **finger-spelling**. Both two-handed and one-handed manual alphabets have been devised.

dactyloscopy *fingerprint*

Dada (Fr 'rocking horse') or **Dadaism** A modern art movement founded in Zürich in 1916, which attacked traditional artistic values. The name was chosen at random from a dictionary. Important contributors included Arp, Duchamp, Ernst, Picabia, and Ray. Their deliberate shock-tactics were revived by some artists in the 1960s.

daddy longlegs *cranefly; harvestman*

Daedalus [deedalus] A legendary Athenian inventor, who worked for King Minos in Crete and constructed the labyrinth. Any archaic work of skill was ascribed to him, and he was a patron saint of craftsmen in Ancient Greece.

daffodil A species of narcissus (*Narcissus pseudonarcissus*), yellow, with a central trumpet up to 2·5 cm/1 in long, and darker than the six surrounding segments; native to Europe. (Family: Amaryllidaceae.)

Dafoe, Willem [dafoh] (1955–) Film actor, born in Appleton, WI. He made his film debut with a small part in *Heaven's Gate* (1980), and went on to the Oscar-nominated role of Sergeant Elias in *Platoon* (1986) and the controversial title role in *The Last Temptation of Christ* (1988). Later films include *The English Patient* (1996) and *Inside Man* (2006).

Dafydd ap Gwilym [davith ap gwilim] (c.1320–c.1380) Poet, born probably in Brogynin, Cardiganshire. He wrote love songs, satirical poems, and nature poems in the complex *cywydd* metre which he perfected, much extending the range of such poetry.

daguerreotype [dageruhtiyp] An early system of photography established by Louis Daguerre (1789–1851) in France in 1839. A silver-plated sheet was sensitized by iodine vapour, and after a long exposure in the camera the image was developed over heated mercury and fixed in a solution of common salt. It became obsolete in the 1850s.

Dahl, Roald (1916–90) Writer, born in Llandaff, Cardiff, of Norwegian parents. He specialized in writing short stories of unexpected horror and macabre surprise, such as in *Someone Like You* (1953). His children's books, such as *James and the Giant Peach* (1961) and *Charlie and the Chocolate Factory* (1964), display a similar taste for the grotesque.

dahlia [daylia] A tuberous perennial up to 8 m/26 ft high, native to mountains from Mexico to Colombia. Several species with large, showy flower-heads were introduced into cultivation, originally for the tubers, which were eaten as a vegetable; but they are now commonly grown as garden ornamentals. (Genus: *Dahlia*, 28 species. Family: Compositae.)

Dahomey [dahohmee] W African kingdom based on its capital at Abomey, which in the late 17th-c extended its authority from the coast to the interior. The state was annexed by the French in 1883, and regained its independence (later renaming itself Benin) in 1960.

Dáil Éireann [doyl airan] (Gaelic 'Assembly of Ireland') The lower house of the parliament of the Republic of Ireland. Unlike the upper house, the Senate (*Seanad Éireann*), which is appointed, the Dáil is elected by proportional representation for a period of 5 years.

Daimler, Gottlieb (Wilhelm) [daymler], originally [diymler] (1834–1900) Engineer, born in Schorndorf, Germany. He worked from 1872 on improving the gas engine, and in 1885 designed one of the earliest roadworthy motor cars.

dairy farming A farming system specializing in the production of milk – usually from cows, but in some regions from sheep, goats, yaks, buffalo, or reindeer. Specialist dairy-cow breeds include Friesians, Ayrshires, and Jerseys. Farmers sell their milk to dairy manufacturers, who make butter, cheese, cream, yogurt, and skimmed milk. These foods are **dairy products**.

daisy A perennial native to Europe and W Asia (*Bellis perennis*), with a basal rosette of oval or spoon-shaped leaves; leafless flowering stems up to 20 cm/8 in, each bearing a solitary flower-head; outer ray florets white often tinged red, inner disc florets yellow. (Family: Compositae.)

daisy-wheel printer A type of impact printer, used in computer systems and in typewriters, in which the individual print characters are carried on separate 'petals' of a segmented disk called the **daisy-wheel**. The daisy-wheel is rotated to bring the relevant character in front of a striking hammer. Daisy-wheel printers are relatively slow, but are capable of producing high quality typescript.

Dakar [dakah(r)] 14°38N 17°27W, pop (2000e) 2 183 000. Seaport capital of Senegal; founded, 1857; capital of French West Africa, 1902; part of Dakar and Dependencies, 1924–46; held by Vichy forces during World War 2; capital of Senegal, 1958; airport; railway terminus; university (1957); cathedral (consecrated, 1936).

Daladier, Edouard [daladyay] (1884–1970) French statesman and prime minister (1933, 1934, 1938–40), born in Carpentras, France. As premier (1938) he supported appeasement policies and signed the Munich Pact. In 1940 he resigned, became successively War and Foreign Minister, and on the fall of France was arrested and interned until 1945.

Dalai Lama [daliy lahma] (Mongolian, 'ocean-like guru') Spiritual and temporal head of Tibet, regarded as a manifestation of the Bodhisattva Avalokiteshavara. Tenzin Gyatso (1935–), held to be the 14th incarnation, ruled in Tibet from 1940 to 1959. Following the Chinese invasion of the country, he escaped to India. He received the Nobel Peace Prize in 1989.

Daldry, Stephen [doldree] (1960–) Film and theatre director, born in Dorset. He began his career with the Crucible Theatre, Sheffield (1986–8), later moving to London where he became artistic director of the Gate Theatre (1990–2) and the English Stage Company (1992–9), and associate director of the Royal Court (1999). He received Best Director Oscar nominations for the films *Billy Elliot* (2000) and *The Hours* (2002), and directed the stage musical version of *Billy Elliot* (2005) in London's West End.

Dalglish, Kenny [dalgleesh], popular name of **Kenneth Mathieson Dalglish** (1951–) Footballer and manager, born in Glasgow. He joined Glasgow Celtic in 1967, transferring to Liverpool in 1977, and won 102 caps for Scotland. Unexpectedly invited to manage Liverpool while still a player, in his first season Liverpool won both Cup and League. He joined Newcastle United as manager (1997–8), returning to Celtic as director of football in 1999.

Dalhousie, James Andrew Broun Ramsay, 1st Marquess of [dalhowzee] (1812–60) British Governor-General of India (1847–56), born at Dalhousie Castle, Midlothian. He annexed Satara (1847) and Punjab (1849), but the annexation of Oudh (1856) caused resentment which fuelled the 1857 Rebellion.

Dali, Salvador (Felipe Jacinto) [dahlee], Span **Dalí** (1904–89) Artist, born in Figueras, Spain. One of the principal figures of the Surrealist movement, his study of abnormal psychology and dream symbolism led him to represent 'paranoiac' objects in landscapes remembered from his Spanish boyhood. One of his best-known paintings is 'The Persistence of Memory' (known as 'The Limp Watches', 1931, New York). A major retrospective of his work marking the centenary of his birth was held at the Palazzo Grassi in Venice (2004–5).

Dalian [dalyan], also **Lüda**, **Lü-ta**, **Dairen**, **Ta-lien** 38°53N 121°37E, pop (2000e) 2 770 000. Port city in NE China; port built by Japanese, 1899–1930; Soviet occupation, 1945–54; resort beaches nearby; airfield; railway; centre of fruit-growing area.

Dallas 32°47N 96°49W, pop (2000e) 1 188 600. City in NE Texas, USA; commercial and financial centre of the SW; largest city in the USA; founded, 1841; city status, 1871; President Kennedy assassinated here (22 Nov 1963); airport (Dallas–Fort Worth); railway; two universities (1910, 1956); scene of the television series *Dallas*; professional teams, Mavericks (basketball), Cowboys (football).

Dalmatia [dalmaysha] A name applied since early times to the strip of territory bordering the Adriatic Sea in W Yugoslavia; largely mountainous and barren; formerly part of the Greek province of Illyria; occupied by Slavs, 7th-c AD.

dalmatian A breed of dog, officially from the Balkans W coastal region, but probably developed in India many centuries ago; large, lightly built, with long legs, tail, and muzzle; ears short, pendulous; coat short, white with black or brown spots.

Dalton, John [dawltn] (1766–1844) Chemist, born in Eaglesfield, Cumbria. His chief physical researches were on mixed gases, the force of steam, the elasticity of vapours, and the expansion of gases by heat. His development of the atomic theory of matter (c.1810) elevated chemistry to a quantitative science.

dalton *atomic mass unit*

dam A barrier constructed to control the flow of water, thus forming a reservoir. Dams are built to allow storage of water, giving a controlled supply for domestic or industrial consumption, for irrigation, to generate hydro-electric power, or to prevent flooding. They are built either as **gravity dams**, where the strength is due entirely to the great weight of material; as **arch**

dams, where abutments at either side support the structure; or as **arch gravity dams**, a combination of the two. The earliest known dams were in China, 6th-c BC. Modern examples are Aswan High Dam (Egypt), Grand Coulee Dam (NE Washington, USA), and Hoover Dam (Arizona, USA).

daman *hyrax*

Daman and Diu [damahn, deeoo] pop (2001e) 158 100; area 456 km²/176 sq mi. Union territory in W India; chief town, Daman; island of Diu taken by Portugal, 1534; Daman area N of Mumbai ceded to Portugal, 1539; occupied by India, 1961; part of Union Territory of Goa, Daman and Diu until 1987.

Damascus [damaskus], Arabic **Dimashq** 33°30N 36°19E, pop (2000e) 1 860 000. Capital city of Syria; claimed to be the world's oldest continuously inhabited city; a world heritage site; satellite city Dimashq ad-Jadideh; airport; railway; university (1923); famous for its crystallized fruits, brass and copper ware, silks, woodwork; Great Mosque (8th-c, burned 1893, then restored).

Damien, Father Joseph [damyï], originally **Joseph de Veuster** (1840–89) Missionary, born in Tremelo, Belgium. He was renowned for his great work among the lepers of the Hawaiian island of Molokai, where he lived from 1873 until his death from the disease. He became internationally known after Robert Louis Stevenson published a passionate defence of his character and work.

Damocles [damokleez] (4th-c BC) Legendary courtier of the elder Dionysius, tyrant of Syracuse (405–367 BC), who was shown the precarious nature of fortune in a singular manner. While seated at a richly-spread table, Damocles looked up to see a keen-edged sword suspended over his head by a single horsehair.

Damon, Matt (1970–) Film actor, born in Cambridge, MA. He gained a starring role in the film *Good Will Hunting* (1997), for which he shared an Oscar for Best Original Screenplay with co-star Ben Affleck. Later films include *Saving Private Ryan* (1998), *The Talented Mr Ripley* (1999), *The Bourne Identity* (2002, sequel 2004), *The Departed* (2006), and *Ocean's Thirteen* (2007).

Damon and Pythias [daymon, pithias], also found as **Phintias** (4th-c BC) Two Pythagoreans of Syracuse, remembered as the models of faithful friendship. Condemned to death by the elder Dionysius, Pythias begged to be allowed to go home to arrange his affairs, and Damon pledged his own life for his friend's. Pythias returned just in time to save Damon from death. Struck by so noble an example, Dionysius pardoned Pythias.

Dampier, William [dampeer] (1652–1715) Navigator and buccaneer, born near Yeovil, Somerset. In 1683 he sailed across the Pacific, visiting the Philippines, China, and Australia. He then led a voyage of discovery to the South Seas (1699), exploring the NW coast of Australia, and giving his name to the *Dampier Archipelago* and *Strait*.

damping Reduction of the size of oscillations by the removal of energy. For example, the indicator needles of gauges are often immersed in oil to give frictional damping; and resistive circuit components reduce electrical oscillations.

damselfish Any of the family Pomacentridae; small brightly coloured marine fishes widespread in tropical and temperate seas around reefs and rocky shores; body length 10–25 cm/4–10 in. (7 genera, including *Chromis* and *Pomacentrus*.)

damselfly A large, long-bodied insect with two pairs of slender wings typically held together over the abdomen at rest. Damselflies are powerful predators, both as aquatic larvae and as flying adults. (Order: Odonata. Suborder: Zygoptera, c.3000 species.)

damson A type of plum (*Prunus domestica*, subspecies *institia*) in which the small, ovoid fruit is purplish with a waxy bloom; thought to be a cultivated form of bullace. (Family: Rosaceae.)

Danae [danayee] In Greek mythology, the daughter of King Acrisius of Argos. When an oracle prophesied that her son would kill his grandfather, Acrisius imprisoned her in a bronze tower, where Zeus visited her in the form of a golden shower. She gave birth to a son, Perseus, who accidentally killed Acrisius with a discus.

Danakil Depression [danakil] Desert area in NE Ethiopia and Eritrea; mountainous in parts, rising to 1000 m/3000 ft; land also dips to 116 m/381 ft below sea-level; extremely hot area, temperatures close to 60°C; major salt reserves; crossed by Djibouti–Addis Ababa railway.

Da Nang [dah nang], formerly **Tourane** 16°04N 108°13E, pop (2000e) 445 100. Seaport in C Vietnam; site of an important US military base during the Vietnam War.

Dance, George, known as **George Dance the Elder** (1695–1768) Architect, born in London. He designed the Mansion House (1739) and many other London buildings. His son, **George Dance, the Younger** (1741–1825), was also an architect. An exponent of Neoclassicism, his best-known building was Newgate Prison (1770–83).

dance notation The recording of dance movement through symbols. More than 100 systems have been created, using letter abbreviations (15th-c), track drawings (18th-c), stick figure and music note systems (19th-c), and abstract symbol systems. Three are in current use; Benesh, Eshkol, and Labanotation.

dance of death A common theme in late mediaeval art: the allegorical representation of a dance or procession in which the living and the dead take part. Holbein the Younger designed a famous set of woodcuts on this theme (published 1538).

dance therapy A form of group psychotherapy, with or without music, which encourages spontaneous movements rather than teaching formal dance sequences. It is particularly used as a way of enabling people who have difficulty in talking about their feelings to express their emotions through body movements.

D and C *dilatation and curettage*

dandelion A perennial, native to Europe and W Asia; flowerheads solitary, borne on leafless hollow stems, florets yellow; fruits with a parachute of white hairs attached by a long stalk, the whole fruiting head forming the familiar 'clock'. The best-known species, *Taraxacum officinale*, is a cosmopolitan weed, its flower-heads sometimes used for wine-making, and its young leaves for salad. (Genus: *Taraxacum*, c.60 species. Family: Compositae.)

Dandie Dinmont A breed of dog, developed in Britain in the 19th-c from wire-haired hunting terriers; small terrier with long body and short legs; long soft hair, especially on the head; ears pendulous; tail long.

Dandolo, Enrico [dandoloh] (c.1110–1205) Italian statesman, born in Venice, Italy. He became Doge of Venice (1192), and in 1202 marched at the head of the Fourth Crusade.

dandruff Fine dry scales which fall from an eruption of the skin of the scalp, usually noticed when the scales fall on to clothing around the shoulders. It possibly results from infection with the fungus *Pityrosporum*.

Dane, Clemence, pseudonym of **Winifred Ashton** (1888–1965) Novelist and playwright, born in Greenwich, London. Her novels include *Regiment of Women* (1917), and *The Flower Girls* (1954). Many of her plays achieved long runs, notably *A Bill of Divorcement* (1921).

Danelaw That part of E England where Danish conquest and colonization in the late 9th-c left an imprint not only on legal and administrative practices, but on place-names, language, and culture.

Danes, Claire (Catherine) (1979–) Actress, born in New York City. She became known through her role in the US television series *My So-Called Life* (1994–5), and went on to star as Juliet in Baz Luhrmann's film *William Shakespeare's Romeo + Juliet* (1996). Later films include *The Rainmaker* (1997), *Igby Goes Down* (2002), and *Stage Beauty* (2004).

Daniel, Glyn (Edmund) (1914–86) Archaeologist, born in Barry, Vale of Glamorgan. He stimulated popular interest in archaeology through writing, editing, and broadcasting, and achieved particular popularity on British television in the 1950s as the genial chairman of the archaeological panel game, *Animal, Vegetable, Mineral*.

Daniel, Book of A book of the Hebrew Bible/Old Testament named after Daniel, its main character. Although some date the work in the 6th-c BC, many prefer a later date of the 3rd–2nd-c BC, with several stages of compilation.

danio [daynioh] Colourful freshwater fish (*Danio malabaricus*) from India and Sri Lanka, extremely popular among aquarists; body with blue and golden side stripes, length up to c.13 cm/5 in. (Family: Cyprinidae.)

Danish *Danish literature*; *Germanic languages*; *Scandinavian languages*

Dannay, Frederic, originally **Daniel Nathan** (1905–82) Novelist, born in New York City. First cousin to **Manfred B Lee** (originally Manford Lepofsky (1905–71)), also born in New York City. They wrote many popular books, using 'Ellery Queen' both as their pseudonym and as the name of their detective. They also used the pseudonym **Barnaby Ross** as the author of their other detective, Drury Lane.

d'Annunzio, Gabriele [danuntseeoh] (1863–1938) Writer, born in Pescara, Italy. During the 1890s he wrote several novels, influenced by the philosophy of Nietzsche, notably *Il trionfo della morte* (1894, The Triumph of Death). His major plays include the tragedy *La gioconda* (1899), which he wrote for the actress Eleonora Duse. Their tempestuous relationship was exposed in his erotic novel, *Il fuoco* (1900, trans The Flame of Life). He became a national hero following his active service in World War 1, though he later supported fascism.

Dante (Alighieri) (1265–1321) Poet, born in Florence, Italy. In 1274, when he was nine, a meeting with **Beatrice** (c.1265–90), possibly the daughter of the Florentine aristocrat Folco Portinari, influenced the rest of his life. The lyric poems, *Vita nuova*, which tells of his boyish passion for Beatrice, are probably his earliest work. By far the most celebrated is the *Divina commedia* (Divine Comedy), a vision of hell, purgatory, and heaven which gives an encyclopedic view of the highest culture and knowledge of his age. He also wrote several shorter poems, as well as treatises on government and language.

Danton, Georges (Jacques) [dãtõ] (1759–94) French revolutionary politician, born in Arcis-sur-Aube, France. He voted for the death of the king (1793), and was one of the original members of the Committee of Public Safety. He tried to abate the pitiless severity of his own Revolutionary Tribunal, but lost the leadership to Robespierre, and was guillotined.

Danu In Celtic religion, a mother-goddess who is associated with hills and the earth.

Danube, River, Ger **Donau**, Bulgarian **Dunav**, Russian **Dunai**, Romanian **Dunarea** River in C and SE Europe, rising in the Black Forest, SW Germany; flows generally E and S to enter the Black Sea through a wide, swampy delta; second longest river in Europe (2850 km/1770 mi); flows through Vienna, Budapest, and Belgrade.

Danube School Pioneers of imaginative landscape painting who worked in the Danube region in the early 16th-c. Their members included Altdorfer and Cranach.

Danzig *Gdańsk*

Daoism *Taoism*

Daphne In Greek mythology, the daughter of a river-god, Ladon (or, in another story, Peneios). Pursued by the god Apollo, she was saved by being turned into a laurel, which became Apollo's sacred tree.

Daphnia [daf nia] A genus of water flea, commonly found in freshwater bodies. (Class: Branchiopoda. Order: Cladocera.)

Daphnis In Greek mythology, a Sicilian shepherd, half-brother of Pan, who was loved by a nymph. He did not return her love, so she blinded him. He became the inventor of pastoral poetry.

Dardanelles or **Hellespont** [dah(r)danelz], Turkish **Çanakkale Boğazi**, ancient **Hellespontus** Narrow strait in NW Turkey, connecting the Aegean Sea (W) and the Sea of Marmara (E); length 65 km/40 mi; width varies from 1·6–6·4 km/1–4 mi; scene of an unsuccessful Allied campaign in World War 1.

Dar es Salaam [dahr es salahm] 6°51S 39°18E, pop (2000e) 1 800 000. Seaport in E Tanzania; founded, 1882; occupied by German East Africa Company, 1887; capital of German East Africa, 1891; occupied by the British in World War 1; capital of Tanganyika, 1916–64; capital of Tanzania until 1974; industrial, commercial, and financial centre; airport; university (1970).

Darién [daryen] pop (2000e) 51 000; area 16 803 km²/6486 sq mi. Province of E Panama; capital, La Palma; attempted settlement by the Scots in the 1690s (the **Darién Scheme**).

Darío, Rubén [dareeoh], pseudonym of **Félix Rubén García Sarmiento** (1867–1916) Poet, born in Metapa, Nicaragua. His *Azul* (1888, Blue) and *Prosas profanas* (1896, Profane Hymns) gave new vitality to Spanish poetic modernism.

Darius I [dariyus, dahrius], known as **the Great** (548–486 BC) King of Persia (521–486 BC), one of the greatest of the Achaemenids. He is noteworthy for his administrative reforms, military conquests, and religious toleration. His conquests, especially in the East and Europe (Thrace and Macedonia) consolidated the frontiers of the empire, but he was defeated at Marathon (490 BC).

Darjeeling or **Darjiling** [dah(r)jeeling] 27°02N 88°20E, pop (2000e) 80 000. Hill station in West Bengal, NE India; centre of a tea-growing region.

Dark Ages A term once used to describe the period of Western European history from c.500 to c.1000, but misleading because of its negative implications. Historians usually describe the whole period c.500–c.1500 as the **Middle Ages**.

dark matter Material in space which does not emit light, and which therefore cannot be seen with conventional astronomical instruments; also known as the **missing mass**. Over 95% of the universe is thought to be composed of dark matter. According to one view, most of this matter consists of *machos* (*massive compact halo objects*) – large structures which do not emit light (such as black holes and brown dwarfs). An opposing view conceives of dark matter as consisting of new kinds of subatomic particle which have so far not been detected, known as *wimps* (*weakly interacting massive particles*).

Darling, Grace (1815–42) Heroine, born in Bamburgh, Northumberland. She lived with her father **William** (1795–1860), the lighthouse keeper on one of the Farne Islands. In 1838 she braved raging seas in an open rowing boat to rescue the survivors of the *Forfarshire* steamboat, which was stranded on one of the other islands in the group.

Darling Range Mountain range in Western Australia, near Perth; extends 320 km/200 mi S along the SW coast, and rises to 582 m/1909 ft at Mt Cooke.

Darling River Longest tributary of the Murray R; flows generally SW to join the Murray R; length 3070 km/1908 mi; used for irrigation in New South Wales.

Darnley, Henry Stewart, Lord (1545–67) Nobleman, the second husband of Mary, Queen of Scots and father of James I of England, born at Temple Newsom, Yorkshire. His part in the murder (1566) of the Queen's secretary, David Rizzio, caused his downfall. He became estranged from the Queen, and during an illness was killed at Edinburgh.

Darrow, Clarence (Seward) (1857–1938) Lawyer, born in Kinsman, OH. Known for his defences of trade union leaders, he was also involved in several notable cases, including the trial of John T Scopes (1925) for the teaching of Darwinian evolution in school.

Dart, Raymond (Arthur) (1893–1988) Palaeoanthropologist, born in Brisbane, Queensland, Australia. His discovery (1924) of *Australopithecus africanus* substantiated Darwin's view of Africa as the cradle of the human species.

Dart, Thurston (1921–71) Keyboard player, conductor, and musical scholar, born in London. A specialist in early music, he edited several editions of 16th-c and 17th-c English works.

darter A slender bird native to warm regions worldwide; spears fish underwater with long pointed bill; swims with only head and long neck out of water; called **anhinga** in the New World, **darter** in the Old World; also known as **snake bird** and **water turkey**. (Genus: *Anhinga*, 1 or 2 species; experts disagree. Family: Anhingidae.)

Dartmoor National park in Devon, S England; area 913 km²/352 sq mi; established in 1951; noted for its granite tors and hanging oak woods; highest point, High Willhays, 621 m/2039 ft; prison (1806–13).

Dartmoor pony A small pony, developed on Dartmoor, England; tough and sure-footed; calm-natured; height, up to 12·2 hands/1·3 m/4 ft 2 in; usually brown or black; slim legs, long bushy tail and mane, short erect ears.

Dartmouth College *Ivy League*

darts An indoor game played by throwing three darts (or 'arrows') at a circular board of 20 numbered segments. The throwing distance is normally 8 ft (2·4 m), and the height from the floor to the centre of the board (known as the *bull*) is 5 ft 8 in (1·7 m). The modern game is credited to a Lancashire carpenter Brian Gamlin (1852–1903) who devised the present-day board and scoring system.

Darwin (Australia), formerly **Palmerston** (to 1911), **Port Darwin** 12°23S 130°44E, pop (2000e) 86 300. Seaport capital of Northern Territory, Australia; first European settlement (1869) destroyed by hurricane in 1879; bombed by the Japanese, 1942; destroyed by cyclone Tracy, 1974; airport; railway; university college; cathedral (1902).

Darwin (Falkland Is) 51°48S 58°59W. Settlement on East Falkland, Falkland Is; c.70 km/43 mi from Stanley.

Darwin, Charles (Robert) (1809–82) Naturalist, the discoverer of natural selection, born in Shrewsbury, Shropshire. In 1831 he became the naturalist on HMS *Beagle*, surveying South American waters, and returned in 1836, having travelled extensively throughout the S Pacific. From 1842 he spent his time at Downe, Kent, working in his garden and breeding pigeons and fowls, and here he devoted himself to his major work, *On the Origin of Species by Means of Natural Selection* (1859). An epoch-making work, it was given a mixed reaction throughout Europe, but in the end received widespread recognition.

Darwinism The theory of evolution proposed jointly by Charles Darwin and Alfred Russel Wallace, and later expanded upon by Darwin in *On the Origin of Species by Means of Natural Selection*. Individuals of a species show variation. On average, more offspring are produced than are needed to replace the parents, but population size remains more or less stable in nature. There must therefore be competition for survival; and it is the best adapted (the fittest) variants which survive and reproduce. Evolution occurs by means of natural selection acting on individual variation, resulting in the survival of the fittest. The discovery of the genetic mechanism causing variation has resulted in a modified version of the theory, known as **neo-Darwinism**.

Darwin's finches A closely related group of birds, native to the Galapagos Is (off Ecuador); also known as **Galapagos finches**. The classification of the group is currently uncertain; they may be put in the family Fringillidae (finches) or the family Emberizidae (buntings and their allies). Charles Darwin's observations on this group were important to his ideas about natural selection.

dasheen *taro*

Dassanowsky, Elfriede von [dasanofskee] (1924–) Operatic singer, pianist, and music educator, born in Vienna. She promoted the rebuilding of democratic cultural institutions in post-war Austria and Germany, and was instrumental in the revival of German-language cinema. She moved to the USA in 1955, and has since come to be recognized as a leading figure of post-war European culture.

dassie *hyrax*

dasyure [dasyoor] A marsupial native to Australia and New Guinea; includes quolls, dunnarts, and the Tasmanian devil. (Family: Dasyuridae, 51 species.)

data In computing, the stored facts and figures on which computers operate in order to perform their assigned task. For example, in a payroll operation the data would be the employee details, the details of the hours worked, absences, etc, and the national insurance, pension, and taxation rules to be applied. The task of taking facts (eg names, addresses) and figures from a form and entering them into a computer system is known as **data entry**. Nowadays, this is normally done by teams of clerks keying the data directly into the computer using visual display units, though some data entry is done using automatic character recognition.

database A file of computer data structured in such a way that it can be of general use and is independent of any specific application. This information can be managed by a **database management system (DBMS)**, a software system or program which allows data to be modified, deleted, added to, and retrieved from one or more databases.

data processing (DP) A general term used to describe various uses of computers in business. These include clerical functions (eg scheduling and stock control), financial functions (eg salaries and budget management), and many other aspects of business management and planning.

data protection The techniques of maintaining the privacy and the integrity of computer-based information. The UK Data Protection Act (1987) requires formal registration of all computer users who store information on individuals, and gives certain rights to people who wish to obtain access to this information. There is similar legislation in several other countries.

data warehousing The use of special techniques and database software to interrogate selected company data, with the aim of identifying business trends and patterns. Because databases are being used for decision-support, they are optimized for queries rather than transactions. Typically, data are exported from a company's main database to a more accessible secondary database which has been specially designed to handle user queries from company managers.

Date Line *see panel*

date palm A tree reaching 30 m/100 ft (*Phoenix dactylifera*); thick trunk covered with old, spiny leaf bases; leaves feathery; native to Near East, and widely cultivated since 6000 BC. A single tree produces up to 250 kg/550 lb of deep orange, sugary dates each year for up to 100 years or more. (Family: Palmae.)

date plum *persimmon*

Datong or **Ta-t'ung** [dahtoong] 40°12N 113°12E, pop (2000e) 1 424 000. City in Shanxi province, NEC China; founded in the 4th-c as capital of N Wei dynasty; railway.

Daubigny, Charles François [dohbeenyee] (1817–78) Artist, born in Paris. He was a member of the Barbizon School, painting landscapes, especially moonlight and river scenes, such as 'The Banks of the Oise' (1872, Reims).

Daudet, Alphonse [dohday] (1840–97) Writer, born in Nîmes, France. He wrote several theatrical pieces, including *L'Arlésienne* (1872), for which Bizet composed incidental music. His sketches of Provençal subjects appeared as *Lettres de mon moulin* (1866, Letters from My Mill).

Date Line

An imaginary line, based by international agreement on the meridian of 180° (with deviations to keep certain islands in the same zone as their respective mainlands); the date is altered to compensate for the gain or loss of time (1 hour per 15°) which occurs when circumnavigating the globe.

Daughters of the American Revolution A patriotic society organized in the USA in 1890; members must be directly descended from soldiers or patriots of the Revolutionary period.

Daumier, Honoré (Victorin) [dohmyay] (1808–79) Painter and caricaturist, born in Marseille, France. He won contemporary fame for satirical cartoons about government corruption, and was imprisoned for caricaturing the king.

Dauphin [dohfi] The title of the eldest son of the reigning French monarch in the period 1350–1830, acquired in 1349 when the future King Charles V purchased the lands known as Dauphiné.

daurian jackdaw *jackdaw*

Davao or **Davao City** [davow] 7°05N 125°38E, pop (2000e) 1 043 000. Seaport in S Mindanao, Philippines; founded, 1849; formerly held by the Japanese; airfield; university (1965); commercial centre.

Davenant or **d'Avenant, Sir William** [davenant] (1606–68) Poet and playwright, born in Oxford, Oxfordshire. His father kept the Crown, at which Shakespeare used to stop between London and Stratford – hence the rumour that he was Shakespeare's illegitimate son. His most successful work was *The Wits* (1636), a comedy. He became poet laureate in 1638.

Davenport, Lindsay (1976–) Tennis player, born in Palos Verde, CA. In 1996 she won the Olympic gold medal, in 1997 four titles, and in 1998 three, including the US Open. She took the Wimbledon title in 1999, beating Steffi Graf, and the Australian Open title in 2000. She began 2005 and 2006 as the world number 1, but her ranking had fallen to 25 by 2007.

David (?–c.962 BC) Second King of Israel. According to Jewish tradition the author of several of the Psalms, and according to some Christian traditions the ancestor of Jesus. He was a warrior under King Saul, but his successes against the Philistines (including the killing of Goliath) caused the king's jealousy, and he was forced to become an outlaw. After Saul's death, he was chosen king of all Israel. He made Jerusalem the centre of his kingdom, building a palace for himself on its highest hill, Zion (the 'city of David'). He was succeeded by Solomon, his son by Bathsheba.

David or **Dewi, St** (?–601) Patron saint of Wales, born near St Bride's Bay, Pembrokeshire. He was Bishop of Moni Judeorum, or Menevia (afterwards St David's), presided over two Welsh synods, at Brefi and Caerleon, and founded many churches in the S of Wales. Feast day 1 March.

David, Hal (1921–) Lyricist, born in Brooklyn, NY. He teamed up with composer Burt Bacharach in 1957 and among their many successful songs are '24 Hours From Tulsa' (1964), 'Walk On By' (1964), and 'What's New Pussycat?' (1965). He received an Academy Award for 'Raindrops Keep Falling On My Head' (1969), and in 1999 was the first non-Briton to receive the Ivor Novello Award.

David, Jacques Louis [dahveed] (1748–1825) Painter, born in Paris. He became known for his paintings of classical themes and historical events, such as 'The Oath of the Horatii' (1784, Louvre) and 'The Rape of the Sabines' (1799, Louvre), and in 1804 was appointed court painter by Napoleon.

Davies, Paul (Charles William) (1946–) Physicist and popularizer of science, born in London. Professor of mathematical physics at Adelaide, Australia, his numerous popular books on science, such as *The Mind of God* (1992) and *About Time* (1995), reflect his research interests in cosmology, the origin of the universe, and quantum gravity as well as in the links between science and religion. He received the Templeton Prize for Progress in Religion in 1995.

Davies, Sir Peter Maxwell (1934–) Composer, born in Manchester, Greater Manchester. He founded and co-directed the Pierrot Players (1967–70) and was founder/artistic director of The Fires of London (1971–87). His works include *Taverner* (1972) and three other operas, *Eight Songs for a Mad King* (1969), symphonies, and concertos. He was made composer laureate in 1994 and Master of the Queen's Musick in 2004.

Davies, W(illiam) H(enry) (1871–1940) Poet, born in Newport, Wales. He lived a wandering life to raise enough money to have his poems printed (1905). Once known, he wrote several books of poetry, essays, and a prose work, *The Autobiography of a Super-tramp* (1908).

da Vinci, Leonardo *Leonardo da Vinci*

Davis, Sir Andrew (Frank) (1944–) Conductor, born at Ashridge House, Hertfordshire. He became musical director of the Toronto Symphony Orchestra (1975–88), then music director of the Glyndebourne Festival Opera, and (from 1989) chief conductor of the BBC Symphony Orchestra. In 2000 he was appointed director of the Chicago Lyric Opera.

Davis, Bette, popular name of **Ruth Elizabeth Davis** (1908–89) Film actress, born in Lowell, MA. Her leading roles included *Of Human Bondage* (1934), *Dangerous* (1935, Oscar), *Jezebel* (1938, Oscar), *Whatever Happened to Baby Jane?* (1962), and *Death on the Nile* (1979).

Davis, Carl (1936–) Composer and conductor, born in New York City. Among his works for ballet are *Liaison Amoureuses* (1988), *The Savoy Suite* (1993), and *Alice in Wonderland* (1995). His music for television includes *The World at War* (1972, Emmy) and *Pride and Prejudice* (1995), and for film *The French Lieutenant's Woman* (1981, BAFTA) and *Waterloo* (1995). In 2003 he received a BAFTA special award for his contribution to film, television, and theatre.

Davis, Sir Colin (Rex) (1927–) Conductor, born in Weybridge, Surrey. He was chief conductor of the BBC Symphony Orchestra (1967–71), musical director at Covent Garden (1971–86), and chief conductor of the Bavarian Radio Symphony Orchestra (1983–92). He was principal conductor of the London Symphony Orchestra (1995–2006), and became its president in 2007.

Davis, Geena (1957–) Film actress, born in Wareham, MA. She won an Oscar for Best Supporting Actress for *The Accidental Tourist* (1988), and critical acclaim for her role as Thelma in the controversial film *Thelma and Louise* (1991). Later films include *The Long Kiss Goodnight* (1996) and *Stuart Little* (1999, sequels 2002, 2005). Television work includes the drama series *Commander and Chief* (2005, Golden Globe).

Davis, Jefferson (1808–89) US statesman, and president of the Confederate States during the Civil War (1861–5), born in Christian Co, KY. In the Senate he led the extreme States' Rights Party, and supported slavery. At the close of the War he was imprisoned for two years, then released on bail, and included in the amnesty of 1868.

Davis, Joe, popular name of **Joseph Davis** (1901–78) Billiards and snooker champion, born in Whitwell, Derbyshire. Responsible for inaugurating the World Championship in 1927, he won every title between then and 1946, when he retired from world championship play. His brother, **Fred Davis** (1913–98), followed the same career, winning the first of his 10 world titles in 1948.

Davis, John (c.1550–1605) Navigator, born in Sandridge, Devon. In 1585–7 he undertook three Arctic voyages in search of a Northwest Passage, in the last of which he reached 73°N, and discovered the Strait later named after him.

Davis, Miles (Dewey) (1926–91) Trumpeter, composer, and bandleader, born in Alton, IL. He became the most admired instrumentalist of the post-war era, from 1948 leading a nonet that introduced the style known as 'cool jazz'.

Davis, Raymond (1914–2006) Physicist, born in Washington, DC. A researcher at the University of Pennsylvania, he shared the 2002 Nobel Prize for Physics for his pioneering contributions to astrophysics, in particular for the detection of cosmic neutrinos.

Davis, Sammy, Jr (1925–90) Singer, actor, and dancer, born in New York City. He starred on Broadway in *Mr Wonderful* (1956) and in *Golden Boy* (1964), and his films include *Porgy and Bess* (1959), *Robin and the Seven Hoods* (1964), and *Taps* (1980).

Davis, Steve (1957–) Snooker player, born in London. He dominated snooker in the 1980s, winning the world championship six times: 1981, 1983–4, and 1987–9. In 1982, during the Lada Classic, he became the first man to compile a televised maximum 147 break. In 1997 he won the Benson & Hedges Masters tournament. At the age of 48 he reached the final of the 2005 UK Championship, but lost to 18 year-old Ding Junhui of China.

Davis Cup An annual lawn tennis competition for international male teams, first held in 1900, named after the US public official, Dwight Filley Davis (1879–1945), who donated the trophy.

Davis Strait Sea passage between Greenland and Baffin I, connecting Atlantic and Arctic Oceans; c.650 km/400 mi long by 290 km/180 mi wide at its narrowest point; visited by British navigator John Davis in 1587.

Davos [davohs], Romansch **Tavau** 46°54N 9°52E, pop (2000e) 11 100. Fashionable resort town in E Switzerland; altitude, 1560 m/5118 ft; railway; noted health resort and winter sports centre.

Davy, Sir Humphry (1778–1829) Chemist, born in Penzance, Cornwall. His fame chiefly rests on his discovery that chemical compounds could be decomposed into their elements using electricity. In this way he discovered potassium, sodium, barium, strontium, calcium, and magnesium. In 1815 he invented the miner's safety lamp. In 1820 he became president of the Royal Society.

Dawes, Charles G(ates) (1865–1951) US statesman and financier, who became Republican vice-president under Coolidge (1925–9), born in Marietta, OH. He was head of the Commission which drew up the **Dawes Plan** (1924) for German reparation payments to Europe after World War 1, for which he shared the Nobel Peace Prize in 1925.

Dawkins, (Clinton) Richard (1941–) British zoologist, born in Nairobi, Kenya. One of the most successful popularizers of his subject, he became Charles Simonyi professor of public understanding of science at Oxford in 1995. His work on animal behaviour and genetics emphasizes that apparently selfish behaviour is designed to ensure survival of the gene, apparently above that of the carrier (*The Selfish Gene*, 1976), and this and wider views on behaviour and evolution have been developed in *The Blind Watchmaker* (1986), *Climbing Mount Improbable* (1996), and *The Ancestor's Tale* (2004). *The God Delusion* appeared in 2006. He remains a controversial media figure, known as much for his aggressive atheism as for his scientific views on evolution.

Dayak or **Dyak** The Malayo-Polynesian-speaking indigenous inhabitants of Borneo and Sarawak. They mostly live along rivers in small village communities.

Dayan, Moshe [diyan] (1915–81) Israeli general and statesman, born in Deganya. Fighting with the Allies in World War 2, he lost his left eye, thereafter wearing his distinctive black eye patch. He formed the Rafi Party with Ben-Gurion in 1966, served as defence minister when Israel defeated Egypt, Jordan, and Syria in the Six Day War (1967), and was foreign minister when Egypt and Israel signed their historic peace treaty (1977).

Day-Lewis, C(ecil) (1904–72) Poet, born in Ballintubber, Ireland. During the 1930s, he became known as a leading left-wing writer, but in 1939 broke away from communism. Under the pseudonym of **Nicholas Blake** he wrote detective stories. His *Collected Poems* appeared in 1954, and he became poet laureate in 1968.

Day-Lewis, Daniel (1957–) Film actor, born in London. He became well known for *My Beautiful Launderette* (1985) and *Room With A View* (1985), and won several awards for his portrayal of handicapped Irish writer Christy Brown in *My Left Foot* (1989, Oscar). Later films include *The Last of the Mohicans* (1992), *The Crucible* (1996), *Gangs of New York* (2002, BAFTA; Oscar nomination), and *The Ballad of Jack and Rose* (2005).

Daylight Saving Time A means of making fuller use of the hours of daylight over the summer months, usually by putting clocks forward one hour so that daylight continues longer into the evening. Adopted during World War 1 by Germany in 1917, it was retained after the war by the UK, where it is known as (British) **Summer Time**. In the USA it was enacted in a federal regulation of 1966, but states were given the choice of whether to ignore it (and some have done so).

dBase IV® A widely used computer package for personal computers which allows users to design and implement their own database. Most of the features of a relational database management system are available.

D-Day The term used for a secret date on which a military operation is to begin. The most famous D-day is 6 June 1944, when the Allies launched the greatest amphibious operation in history (code-named 'Overlord'), and invaded German-occupied Europe. By the end of D-Day, 130 000 troops had been landed on five beach-heads along an 80 km/50 mi stretch of the coast of Normandy, at a cost of 10 000 Allied casualties.

DDT A chemical mixture, largely consisting of dichlorodiphenyltrichloroethane. One of the earliest successful insecticides, it has now been largely abandoned both because new strains of insects have developed immunity to it and because its decomposition products are harmful.

deacon (Gr *diakonos*, 'servant') An official of the Christian Church appointed to assist the minister or priest in administrative, pastoral, and financial affairs. In the late 20th-c, ecumenical factors revived interest in an order of deacons (the **diaconate**).

deadly nightshade A stout, large-leaved perennial (*Atropa belladonna*) up to 1·5 m/5 ft high, native to limestone and chalk areas of Europe, W Asia, and N Africa; dull flowers, solitary, tubular, brownish-violet; berry shiny black. All parts of the plant are narcotic and highly poisonous. (Family: Solanaceae.)

dead-nettle An annual or perennial, found almost everywhere, except in the tropics; flowers 2-lipped, the upper hooded, in whorls at the nodes. When not in flower, some species, especially white dead-nettle, resemble true nettles but lack stinging hairs; hence the name. (Genus: *Lamium*, c. 50 species. Family: Labiatae.)

dead room anechoic chamber

Dead Sea, ancient **Lacus Asphaltites**, Hebrew **Bahrat Lut** (Sea of Lot), Old Testament **Salt Sea, Sea of the Plain, East Sea** Inland lake in the Great Rift Valley on the Jordan–Israel border; lowest point on Earth, 400 m/1312 ft below sea-level; 80 km/50 mi long; up to 18 km/11 mi wide; area 900 sq km/350 sq mi; fed by Jordan R (N), but no outlet; one of the most saline lakes in the world.

Dead Sea Scrolls Parchment scrolls in Hebrew and Aramaic, many representing books of the Old Testament, 1000 years older than previously known copies, found accidentally in 1947 and 1952–5 concealed in pottery jars in 11 caves near Qumran on the Dead Sea. They are thought to represent the library of an ascetic Jewish sect, the Essenes, concealed when their settlement was overrun by the Roman army in AD 68.

deafness Inability or reduced capacity to hear external sounds. **Conductive deafness** is caused by blockage of the entry of sound to the external canal of the ear (eg through wax in ear), or by abnormalities of the eardrum (tympanic membrane) or bones (ossicles) in the middle ear (eg through middle-ear infection). All sounds irrespective of their pitch are heard with difficulty. **Sensorineural deafness** results from a disturbance of the cochlea, auditory nerve, or neuronal pathways in the brain. Loss of hearing tends to be patchy, affecting only certain frequencies, and amplified or loud sounds are distorted.

Deák, Francis [dayak] (1803–76) Statesman, born in Zala (formerly Söjtör), Hungary. He practised as an advocate, and in the restored Diet of 1861, emerged as leader of moderate liberalism and negotiated the *Ausgleich* of 1867, establishing the Dual Monarchy of Austria–Hungary.

Deakin, Alfred (1856–1919) Australian Liberal statesman and prime minister (1903–4, 1905–8, 1909–10), born in Melbourne, Victoria, Australia. He helped to draft Australia's constitution, and as prime minister helped to form many of the new country's policies, notably the White Australia policy.

Dean, Christopher *Torvill and Dean*

Dean, Dixie, popular name of **William Ralph Dean** (1907–80) Footballer and record goal-scorer, born in Birkenhead, Merseyside. He joined Everton in 1925, and scored 349 goals in 399 games. He still holds the scoring record of 60 League goals in one season.

Dean, Howard (1948–) US politician and physician, born in New York City. He studied at Yale University (1971) and Albert Einstein College of Medicine (1978), then set up in private practice. Entering politics as a Democrat, he served in the Vermont House of Representatives (1982–6), becoming lieutenant governor (1986–91) and governor (1991–2002). Late in 2003 he emerged as a front-runner in the race to secure the Democrat nomination in the 2004 US presidential election, but after failing to win a number of key primaries he dropped out of the race early in 2004. He was elected Democratic Party chairman in 2005.

Dean, James (Byron) (1931–55) Film star, born in Marion, IN. He gained overnight success in the film *East of Eden* (1955), and made only two more films, *Rebel Without a Cause* (1955) and *Giant* (released 1956), before he was killed in a car crash at Paso Robles, CA. He became a cult figure, for many years after his death remaining a symbol of youthful rebellion and self-assertion.

dean (ultimately from Lat *decem*, 'ten') Originally, in a monastery, a monk in charge of 10 novices. Later, the term denoted a senior clergyman (after the bishop) in a cathedral chapter or diocese. In lay terms, it is used for a head of a university or college faculty.

Deane, Sir William (Patrick) (1931–) Governor-general of Australia (1996–2001), born in Melbourne, Victoria, Australia. He was made a judge in the Supreme Court of New South Wales (1977) and the Australian High Court (1982). As governor-general, he was outspoken on the question of reconciliation with Australia's indigenous population, and other issues.

death The exact definition of death is controversial, and varies among legal systems, although it can be regarded as the cessation of all vital cellular activity. It is no longer enough to rely solely on criteria such as the absence of heartbeat or respiration, since medical science can sometimes revive people who have temporarily lost these functions. This matter is of particular importance when faced with uncertainty over the state of a person who has been on a life-support system for a long time without showing any change. The decision is made in some countries by applying the criteria for brain death.

death cap A deadly poisonous, mushroom-like fungus; cap pale greenish or white, with white gills on underside; common on the ground in broad-leaved woodland in late summer and autumn. (Order: Agaricales. Family: Amanitaceae.)

'death of God' theology A style of theology popular especially in the USA in the 1960s. It sought to assert the rationality of the Christian faith and belief in the uniqueness of Christ, without belief in a transcendent God.

death's-head moth A large, nocturnal hawk-moth; wingspan up to 12 cm/$4\frac{3}{4}$ in; forewings dark with yellow markings; hindwings ochre-yellow with black bands; black thorax with yellow skull-like marking. (Order: Lepidoptera. Family: Sphingidae.)

Death Valley SE California, USA; ancient rift valley lake bed beside the Nevada border; one of the hottest places in the world; contains the lowest point in North America (the Bad-water River, altitude −86 m/−282 ft); 225 km/140 mi long; 6–26 km/$3\frac{3}{4}$–16 mi wide; highest point Telescope Peak (3367 m/11 046 ft); less than 50 mm/2 in rainfall per year; named in 1849 by a party of gold prospectors, some of whom died while trying to cross it.

deathwatch beetle A small, brownish beetle, 5–9 mm/$\frac{1}{8}$–$\frac{1}{3}$ in long; now found mostly in house timbers; larvae bore into wood; adults tap on wood at mating time (Apr–May). Larvae leave large holes in timber when they emerge. (Order: Coleoptera. Family: Anobiidae.)

Deayton, (Gordon) Angus [deeton] (1956–) Writer and broadcaster, born in Caterham, Surrey. He became well known for his role in BBC TV's *One Foot in the Grave* (from 1989), went on to host *Have I Got News for You* (1990–2002), and was writer/presenter of *In Search of Happiness* (1995). He later starred in the black comedy series *Nighty Night* (2005) and hosted the TV series *Help Your Self* (2006).

de Beauvoir, Simone [duh bohvwah(r)] (1908–86) Existentialist writer and novelist, born in Paris. Closely associated with Sartre's literary activities after World War 2, she remained his companion until his death (1980). Her own works provide existentialism with an essentially feminine sensibility, notably *The Second Sex* (1949) on women's rights, which became a classic of feminist literature, and *Les Mandarins* (1954, Prix Goncourt).

debenture [debencher] A loan raised by a company, usually with a fixed interest rate and possibly a definite redemption date. Debenture holders have no control over the company as long as their interest is paid, but if it is not they can take over control.

de Bernières, Louis (1954–) Writer, born in London. He trained as a teacher and taught English in Colombia, an experience which greatly influenced his early work. His fourth novel, *Captain Corelli's Mandolin* (1994), set on the Greek island of Cephalonia during World War 2, became a best-selling book and successful film (2001). The later *Birds Without Wings* (2004) was shortlisted for the Whitbread novel prize. Other work includes a short-story collection, *Red Dog* (2001), and he contributes regularly to newspapers and magazines.

de Bono, Edward (Francis Charles Publius) [duh bohnoh] (1933–) Psychologist and writer, born in Malta. He became known for his promotion of the skills of thinking which break out of the trammels of the traditional (*lateral thinking*). He has been secretary-general of the Supranational Independent Thinking Organization since 1983.

Debrecen [debretsen] 47°33N 21°42E, pop (2000e) 207 000. City in E Hungary; second largest city in Hungary; railway; three universities (1868, 1912, 1951); commercial centre for agricultural region.

Debrett's Peerage A reference guide to the titled aristocracy of Great Britain, named after John Debrett (c.1752–1822). It also offers information on forms of address, precedence, the wearing of decorations, and etiquette.

de Broglie *Broglie, duc de*

Debs, Eugene V(ictor) (1855–1926) US politician, born in Terre Haute, IN. He helped to establish the Socialist Party of America, was imprisoned for labour agitation, and between 1900 and 1920 stood five times as socialist candidate for president.

debt Borrowing by individuals, companies, or governments. Interest is normally payable. Companies with high debts are 'highly geared', or 'highly leveraged', and face financial difficulties if their profits fall or interest rates rise. Individuals in debt through consumer credit or via mortgages on their house also face difficulties if interest rates rise, or if their incomes fall through unemployment.

debugging *bug* (computing)

Debussy, Claude (Achille) [debüsee] (1862–1918) Composer, born in St Germain-en-Laye, France. His early successes were the *Prélude à l'après-midi d'un faune* (1894), and his piano pieces,

Images and *Préludes*, producing the pictures in sound which led to his work being described as 'musical Impressionism'.

Decalogue *Ten Commandments*

Decapoda [dekapoda] A large order of mostly marine crustaceans characterized by three pairs of thoracic legs modified as pincers for feeding, and five pairs of walking legs; horny covering fused along back to form gill chamber above leg bases; contains c.10 000 living species. (Class: Malacostraca.)

decathlon A multi-event track-and-field discipline consisting of 10 events, held over two days. The events, in order, are: 100 m, long jump, shot, high jump, 400 m, 110 m hurdles, discus, pole vault, javelin, and 1500 m. Points are awarded in each event based on individual performance.

Decatur, Stephen [deekayter] (1779–1820) US naval commander, born in Sinepuxent, MD. He gained great distinction in the war with Tripoli (1801–5). In the war with England in 1812 he captured the frigate *Macedonian*, but in 1815 surrendered to the British.

decay rate *mean life*

Deccan [dekan], Sanskrit **Dakshin** Eastward sloping plateau occupying most of CS India; average altitude 600 m/2000 ft; noted for cotton.

Decembrists A group of progressive-minded Russian army officers who attempted a coup against the autocratic government of Nicholas I (12 Dec 1825). They were later regarded as martyrs and founders of the 19th-c Russian revolutionary movement.

decibel Unit of sound level intensity; symbol db; named after US inventor Alexander Graham Bell; defined as $10\log_{10}(I/I_o)$, where I is the sound level intensity in question and I_o is defined as 10^{-12}W/m^2; a tenth of a **bel**.

deciduous plants Plants which shed their leaves before the onset of harsh seasons, during which they remain dormant. Leaf fall prevents excessive water loss during drought, or when water is locked up as ice, and minimizes frost damage.

decision theory A set of principles designed to enable an agent to make rational choices of self-interest in situations of uncertainty where there are various options, each of whose probable consequences must be assessed. It is used most often in economics and management studies.

Declaration of Independence Following the American Revolution, the document adopted by the Continental Congress to proclaim the separation of the 13 colonies from Britain. It was written mainly by Thomas Jefferson.

Declaration of Rights An English statute which ended the brief interregnum after James II quit the throne in December 1688, establishing William III and Mary II as joint monarchs. One of the fundamental instruments of constitutional law, the Bill effectively ensured that monarchs must operate with the consent of parliament.

Declaration of the Rights of Man and Citizen A fundamental document of French constitutional history, embodied in the French constitution of 1791. The declaration made by the French National Assembly (27 Aug 1789), proclaiming liberty of conscience, of property, and of the press, and freedom from arbitrary imprisonment.

decompression sickness An occupational disease which occurs when individuals who have been working under higher than atmospheric pressure, such as in underwater exploration, return to normal atmospheric pressure too quickly. Nitrogen comes out of solution in the blood and tissues and forms tiny bubbles which cause damage to the tissues, especially if they lodge in small blood vessels and cut off the blood supply. Permanent brain damage or death can occur. Less severe cases result in dizziness and pain in the muscles and joints (the *bends*).

Decorated Style The form of English Gothic architecture prevalent in the late 13th-c and 14th-c, characterized by a maximum of surface decoration, usually in the form of stylized leaves and the double S-shaped curve known as an *ogee*.

Decoration Day *Memorial Day*

decorative arts The design and ornamentation of objects, usually with some practical use and outside the field of 'fine art' (painting, sculpture, and architecture); nowadays more exactly called the **applied arts**. Metalwork, ceramics, glass, textiles, and woodwork have all been wrought and decorated to a degree which transcends their functional purpose.

Decroux, Etienne-Marcel [duhkroo] (1898–1991) French actor and mime. A pupil and collaborator of Charles Dullin (1885–1949), he was the first to develop a systematic language of physical expression, which led to the 20th-c revival of mime.

Dedication, Feast of *Hanukkah*

Dee, River, Welsh **Afon Dyfrdwy** River in N Wales and adjoining parts of Cheshire, England; rises in the Snowdonia region, and flows past Chester to an estuary lying W of the Wirral peninsula; length 110 km/70 mi.

Dee, Jack (1962–) Comedian and actor, born in Petts Wood, Orpington, London. He began his stage career in 1986 as a stand-up comedian at London's Comedy Store, becoming known for his deadpan humour, and since 1990 has toured extensively with his one-man show. Television credits include five series of his own show for Channel 4 and two series of *Jack Dee's Happy Hour* (BBC 2000–1). In 2006 he starred in the comedy series *Lead Balloon* for BBC4.

Dee, John (1527–1608) Alchemist, geographer, and mathematician, born in London. He travelled widely in Europe, brought back many astronomical instruments, and earned the reputation of a sorcerer. He was astrologer to the court of Elizabeth I.

deed *covenant 1*

deep-freezing Freezing to −20°C or below in either a chest freezer or cabinet freezer. The level of ability of a freezer cabinet to maintain a sufficiently low temperature for prolonged food preservation is shown on the cabinet by a series of stars; deep-freezers will allow 3 months storage, a level which is symbolized by four stars.

Deeping, (George) Warwick (1877–1950) Novelist, born in Southend, Essex. His early novels were mainly historical, and it was not until after World War 1 that he gained recognition with his bestseller, *Sorrell and Son* (1925).

Deep Space Network (DSN) A NASA tracking and telecommunications system used to operate interplanetary spacecraft. Stations are located at three widely spaced locations around the world (Goldstone, CA, USA; Canberra, Australia; Madrid, Spain) to provide a continuous communications capability in all parts of the Solar System.

deer A type of hoofed mammal of families Cervidae (**true deer**, 36 species), Moschidae (**musk deer**), and Tragulidae (**mouse deer**); an artiodactyl; only true deer have antlers; true deer found worldwide except Africa and Australasia; usually found in or near woodland; male called a *stag* or *buck*, female a *hind* or *doe*, young a *fawn* or *kid* (names depend on species).

deerhound A breed of dog, developed in Scotland from Mediterranean ancestors; tall, slim; very long legs, long tail; shaggy grey coat; head small with short soft ears; also known as the **Scottish deerhound**, **staghound**, or **buckhound**.

deerlet *chevrotain*

defamation The publication or communication of a false statement which tends to injure reputation or lower a person in the view of the community. In England, Wales, and the USA, the form can be either permanent (libel) or non-permanent (slander); Scottish law does not distinguish between the two terms, recognizing only defamation. Both are actionable at civil law, and in certain jurisdictions libel can exist as a criminal offence.

Defence of the Realm Act A British Act introduced in 1914 at the beginning of World War 1 to give the government greater controls over the activities of its citizens. The most important control related to restrictions on press reporting and other forms of censorship.

defendant In law, the person who is called on to answer proceedings brought against him or her by some other person, called the **plaintiff**. In criminal cases the defendant is the accused; in civil cases, the person who is sued. The term **defender** is used in Scotland.

Defender of the Faith (Lat *fidei defensor*) A title conferred on Henry VIII of England by Pope Leo X as a reward for the king's written opposition to the teachings of Martin Luther. It is still used by British sovereigns.

defibrillation *cardiac resuscitation*

deficiency diseases A wide range of medical disorders caused by insufficient dietary intake of essential substances, either carbohydrates and proteins, or vitamins and minerals.

deflation A government economic policy designed to reduce inflationary pressures. Steps taken include higher interest and tax rates, and a tighter money supply.

Defoe, Daniel [defoh] (1660–1731) Writer, born in London. In 1702 his satire *The Shortest Way with the Dissenters* raised Queen Anne's anger, and he was imprisoned at Newgate, where he continued his pamphleteering. He achieved lasting fame with *Robinson Crusoe* (1719–20). His other major works include *A Journal of the Plague Year, Moll Flanders* (both 1722), and *Roxana* (1724).

De Forest, Lee [di forist] (1873–1961) Inventor, born in Council Bluffs, IA. He became a pioneer of radio, introducing the grid into the thermionic valve, and inventing the Audion and the four-electrode valve. He was widely honoured as 'the father of radio' and 'the grandfather of television'.

Degas, (Hilaire Germain) Edgar [popularly **daygah**, Fr **duhgahs**] (1834–1917) Artist, born in Paris. He associated with the Impressionists and took part in most of their exhibitions from 1874 to 1886. Among his best-known works are 'Dancer Lacing her Shoe' (c.1878, Paris) and 'Jockeys in the Rain' (1879, Glasgow).

de Gaulle, Charles (André Joseph Marie) [duh gohl] (1890–1970) French general and first president of the Fifth Republic (1958–69), born in Lille, France. With the fall of France (Jun 1940), he fled to England to raise the standard of the 'Free French', and entered Paris in the vanguard of one of the earliest liberation forces (Aug 1944). In late 1958 he became president, and practised a high-handed yet extremely successful foreign policy, repeatedly surviving political crises by the lavish use of the referendum. He developed an independent French nuclear deterrent and withdrew French suppport for NATO, signed a historic reconciliation treaty with West Germany, and blocked Britain's entry into the European Economic Community. He resigned in 1969 after the defeat of his referendum proposals for senate and regional reforms.

degaussing [deegows*ing*] The neutralizing of an object's magnetic field using current-carrying coils to produce an opposing magnetic field of equal strength. The process is applied to ships, to protect them from magnetically activated mines.

de Havilland, Sir Geoffrey [duh haviland] (1882–1965) Aircraft designer, born in Haslemere, Surrey. He built his first plane in 1908 and became director of the firm bearing his name, producing many types of aircraft, including the Tiger Moth, the Mosquito, and the Vampire jet.

De Havilland, Olivia (Mary) (1916–) Actress, born in Tokyo. Brought up in the USA, she joined Warner Brothers (1935–42). She received Best Supporting Actress nominations for her roles in *Gone With the Wind* (1939) and *Hold Back The Dawn* (1941), and won Oscars for *To Each His Own* (1946) and *The Heiress* (1949).

dehydration Literally, 'loss of water'; but in medicine, the process of salt depletion as well as water loss. Loss of salt-containing fluids occurs after severe vomiting, diarrhoea, excessive sweating, burns, or excessive urination. It particularly affects the circulation, with a rise in pulse rate and falling blood pressure.

Deighton, Len [daytn], popular name of **Leonard Cyril Deighton** (1929–) Thriller writer, born in London. A leading author of spy novels, notable titles are *The Ipcress File* (1962), *Funeral in Berlin* (1964), and the trilogy *Berlin Game* (1984), *Mexico Set* (1985), and *London Match* (1986). Later books include *Charity* (1997).

Deimos [diymos] One of the two natural satellites of Mars, discovered in 1877; distance from the planet 23 460 km/14 580 mi; diameter c.15 km/9 mi; orbital period 30 h 17 min. Like Phobos, it has a dark, cratered surface.

deism [dayizm] Belief in the existence of a supreme being who is the ground and source of reality but who does not intervene or take an active interest in the natural and historical order. It also designates a largely British 17th-c and 18th-c movement of religious thought emphasizing natural religion as opposed to revealed religion, and seeking to establish reasonable grounds for belief in the existence of God.

Dekker, Thomas (c.1570–c.1641) Playwright, born in London. His best-known works are the comedy *The Shoemaker's Holiday* (1600) and *The Honest Whore* (1604; part II, 1630). He wrote several plays in collaboration with other Elizabethan playwrights.

de Klerk, F(rederick) W(illem) [duh klairk] (1936–) South African statesman and president (1989–94), born in Johannesburg, South Africa. He served in National Party cabinets under P W Botha, becoming president when Botha resigned. He then set about the dismantling of apartheid, releasing Nelson Mandela and lifting the state of emergency. The culmination of the process was the signing of a new constitutional agreement with Mandela in late 1993. In the same year, he and Mandela were jointly awarded the Nobel Peace Prize. He served as vice-president (1994–6) in the Mandela administration, and announced his retirement from politics in August 1997.

Delacroix, (Ferdinand Victor) Eugène [duhlakrwah] (1798–1863) Painter and a leader of the Romantic movement, born in Charenton, France. In his later work he moved away from traditional treatment in his canvases of historical and dramatic scenes, often violent or macabre in subject, such as 'Liberty Guiding the People' (1831, Louvre).

de la Mare, Walter (John) [mair] (1873–1956) Writer, born in Charlton, Kent. He wrote several volumes of poetry, novels, and short stories, including the prose romance *Henry Brocken* (1904), the poetic collection *The Listeners* (1912), and his fantastic novel *Memoirs of a Midget* (1921).

Delaney, Shelagh [delaynee] (1939–) Playwright, born in Salford, Greater Manchester. She left school at 16 and began writing her first and best known play, *A Taste of Honey* (1958) a year later. Later works failed to achieve equal acclaim, though she produced some notable screenplays.

de la Renta, Oscar (1932–) Fashion designer, born in Santo Domingo, Dominican Republic. He started his own company in 1965. He has a reputation for opulent, ornately trimmed clothes, particularly evening dresses, but he also designs day wear and accessories.

de la Roche, Mazo [rosh] (1885–1961) Novelist, born in Newmarket, Ontario, Canada. In 1927 she wrote *Jalna*, the first of a series of novels about the Whiteoak family. *Whiteoaks* (1929) was dramatized with considerable success.

Delaroche, (Hippolyte) Paul [duhlarosh] (1797–1856) Painter, born in Paris. A master of large historical painting, his major work was the series of murals for the Ecole des Beaux-Arts, where he became professor of painting in 1833.

de la Tour, Georges *La Tour, Georges de*

de la Tour, Maurice Quentin *La Tour, Maurice Quentin de*

Delaunay, Robert [duhlohnay] (1885–1941) Painter, born in Paris.

He was associated with the *Blaue Reiter* (1911–2), but is principally known as the founder of Orphism. His research into colour orchestration as applied to abstract art was influential.

Delaware pop (2000e) 783 600; area 5296 km²/2045 sq mi. State in E USA; the 'First State', 'Diamond State', or 'Blue Hen State'; part of Pennsylvania until 1776; one of the original states and first to ratify the Federal Constitution, 1787; highest point, Ebright Road (135 m/443 ft); capital, Dover; the second smallest state; mainly an industrial state; several large corporations based in Wilmington, taking advantage of the state's taxation laws.

Delaware River River in E USA; rises in the Catskill Mts, New York, and empties into Delaware Bay; length 450 km/280 mi; navigable to Trenton.

Delbrück, Max [delbrük] (1906–81) Biophysicist, born in Berlin. He did much to create bacterial genetics, and to inspire early work in biophysics and molecular biology. He shared the Nobel Prize for Physiology or Medicine in 1969.

Delft 52°01N 4°22E, pop (2000e) 94 000. Ancient city in W Netherlands, famous for linen-weaving (14th-c), pottery, and porcelain (16th-c); William the Silent assassinated here, 1584; railway; technical university (1863); birthplace of Vermeer.

Delftware The Dutch and English version of faience, named after the town of Delft where it was made in large quantities in the 17th-c. Usually blue and white, its decoration is generally copied from Chinese and Japanese porcelain.

Delhi [delee], Hindi **Dilli**, formerly **Shahjahanabad** 28°38N 77°17E, pop (2001e) 13 783 000. Capital of India; second largest city in India; **Old Delhi**, enclosed within the walls built by Shah Jahan in 1638, on R Yamuna; Mughal architecture and thronged bazaars contrast with formal architecture and wide boulevards of **New Delhi** to the S, largely designed by Lutyens; New Delhi the administrative centre of India since 1912; airport; railway junction; metro system (first phase completed in 2006); university (1922).

Delian League [deelian] The association of Greek city-states formed after the Persian Wars (478–477 BC) for the continuing defence of the Aegean area against the Persians. It was so called because the treasury of the League was initially on the island of Delos.

Delibes, (Clément Philibert) Léo [duhleeb] (1836–91) Composer, born in St Germain du Val, France. He wrote light operas, of which *Lakmé* had the greatest success, but is chiefly remembered for the ballet *Coppélia* (1870).

Delilah [deliyla] Biblical character, who at the instigation of the Philistines enticed Samson to reveal the secret of his great strength – his uncut hair, according to his Nazirite vow. She contrived to cut his hair to weaken him (*Judges* 16).

DeLillo, Don [deleeloh] (1936–) Writer, born in New York City. His novels, recognized as leading examples of American postmodernism, include *Americana* (1971), *End Zone* (1972), *White Noise* (1984), *Underworld* (1997), *Cosmopolis* (2003), and *Falling Man* (2007). A play, *Love-Lies-Bleeding*, premiered in 2006.

delirium tremens A form of delirium which occurs following withdrawal of alcohol from alcoholics. Hallucinations often take the form of a sensation of insects crawling on the skin or visions of Lilliputian individuals or objects. It is usually associated with tremor of the hands and arms.

Delius, Frederick [deelius] (1862–1934) Composer, born in Bradford, West Yorkshire. He wrote six operas, including *A Village Romeo and Juliet* (1901), and a variety of choral and orchestral works, such as *On Hearing the First Cuckoo in Spring* (1912). In 1924 he became paralysed and blind, but with the assistance of Eric Fenby (1906–97), his amanuensis from 1928, he continued to compose.

Deller, Alfred (George) (1912–79) Countertenor, born in Margate, Kent. He made many recordings of early English songs, and in 1950 formed the Deller Consort, devoted to the authentic performance of early music.

Del Mar, Norman (René) (1919–94) Conductor and horn player, born in London. He became principal conductor of the English Opera Group (1948–56), and conductor of the BBC Scottish Symphony Orchestra (1960–5). His son, **Jonathan Del Mar** (1951–), also became a conductor.

Delon, Alain [delõ] (1935–) Film actor, born in Paris. He became known following his success in *Purple Moon* (1960). Later films include *The Leopard* (1962), *Swann in Love* (1984), *The Day and the Night* (1997), and *Le Lion* (2003, TV).

de Lorris, Guillaume [duh lorris] *Guillaume de Lorris*

Delors, Jacques [duhlaw(r)] (1925–) French and European statesman, born in Paris. He joined the French Socialist Party in 1973, and served as minister of economy and finance under President Mitterrand (1981–4). He became President of the European Commission in 1985, and was elected to a second 4-year term in 1988, extended until 1995. He was president of the International Commission on Education for the Twenty-first Century (1993–6) established by UNESCO.

de los Angeles, Victoria *Angeles, Victoria de los*

Delphi [delfiy], Gr **Dhelfoí**, formerly **Pytho** 38°29N 22°30E. Village and ancient site in Greece, on the slopes of Mt Parnassos; altitude 520–620 m/1706–2034 ft; renowned throughout the ancient Greek world as the sanctuary of Apollo and the seat of his oracle.

delphinium A tall perennial, native to the N hemisphere; flowers blue, rarely pink or white, each with a conical spur and borne in long showy spikes. It contains poisonous alkaloids including delphinin. (Genus: *Delphinium*, 250 species. Family: Ranunculaceae.)

Delphinus [delfiynus] (Lat 'dolphin') A small N constellation.

delta A fan-shaped body of alluvium enclosed within the bifurcating channels at the mouth of a river. It is formed when a river deposits sediment as its speed decreases, and the coastal processes of erosion are not sufficiently strong to carry the material away. Deltas may form large, fertile plains, but are subject to frequent flooding.

Deluge *Flood, the*

dementia A decline in intellectual capacity as a result of an alteration of brain functioning which leads to impaired social or occupational abilities. It is commonly due to cerebrovascular disease and the ageing process, in which brain cells are destroyed and brain size is markedly reduced. Features include loss of memory, alteration of personality, impaired judgment, poor impulse control, and a failure to recognize friends and relatives.

Demeter [deemeeter] The Greek goddess of agriculture, especially corn, so that a basket or an ear of corn is her symbol. She is the mother of Persephone.

de Meung, Jean *Jean de Meung*

De Mille, Agnes [duh mil] (1905–93) Dancer, choreographer, and writer, born in New York City. She became best known in America for the choreography of the musicals *Oklahoma!* (1943) and *Carousel* (1945).

De Mille, Cecil B(lount) [duh mil] (1881–1959) Film producer and director, born in Ashfield, MA. He made a reputation for box-office spectacles with such films as *The Ten Commandments* (1923, re-made in CinemaScope, 1956), and *The Greatest Show on Earth* (1952).

Demme, Jonathan (1944–) Film director, born in Long Island, NY. He directed pop videos, documentaries, and television episodes, making his cinema directorial debut with *Caged Heat* (1974). He won a Best Director Oscar for the psychological thriller *Silence of the Lambs* (1991). Later films include *Philadelphia* (1993), *Beloved* (1998), and *The Manchurian Candidate* (2004).

democracy From Greek *demos* ('people') and *kratia* ('authority'), hence 'rule by the people'; contrasted with rule by the few (**oligarchy**) or by one (**monarchy** or **tyranny**); also known as a **liberal democracy**. Since the Greeks first introduced *demokratia* in many city states in the 5th-c BC, there has been disagreement about what constitutes the essential elements of democracy. One debate concerns who should compose 'the people', and only in the 20th-c did this notion come to be viewed as covering the total adult citizenship. Another relates to how the people should rule, particularly in relation to the increasing size of states, which has resulted in a shift from direct democracy to systems of representation. Elections, including the right to choose among different groups of representatives offering different doctrines and party programmes, have therefore become seen as essential to democracy.

Democratic Labor Party (DLP) An Australian political party, formed in 1957 from anti-communist groups which had formerly been part of the Australian Labor Party (ALP). At its height, in the late 1950s and through the 1960s, its importance lay in its ability to prevent the ALP from winning national government.

Democratic Party One of the two major parties in contemporary US politics. It was originally composed in the late 18th-c of those opposed to the adoption of the US Constitution. Its first successful presidential candidate was Thomas Jefferson. The party was split over slavery and secession during the Civil War (1861–5), after which it became conservative. It held a majority position in 1932, when Roosevelt introduced his 'New Deal', and added large urban areas and ethnic, racial, and religious support to its conservative Southern base. It retains the preference of the majority of Americans, but has won the Presidency on only three occasions since 1968. The party made gains in the 1998 elections, regained a working majority and assumed control of the House of Representatives in 2001, but lost it to the Republicans in the mid-term elections in 2002. In the 2006 mid-term elections, the Democrats won control of the House of Representatives and of the Senate.

Democritus [demokritus] (c.460–370 BC) Greek philosopher, born in Abdera in Thrace. He travelled in the East, and was by far the most learned thinker of his time. He wrote many physical, mathematical, ethical, and musical works, but only fragments survive.

demography A branch of sociology which studies the population patterns of the past, present, and future. Demography has been very important in estimating future trends in population growth in order to calculate the pressures on global resources.

demoiselle [demwazel] A crane (*Anthropoides virgo*), native to S Europe, Asia, and N Africa (migrates further S in winter); mainly white with dark chest and throat; ornamental feathers on head. (Family: Gruidae.)

demonology An outmoded branch of theology relating to the Devil and demons, elaborated from the later Middle Ages particularly in association with belief in witches and their power to do harm. Its most influential work was the *Malleus maleficarum* (Hammer of the Witches) by the Dominicans Kramer and Sprenger, published at Cologne in 1484.

Demosthenes [demostheneez] (c.383–322 BC) The greatest of the Greek orators. He came to prominence in 351 BC, when he delivered the first of a long series of passionate speeches (the 'First Philippic') advocating all-out resistance to Philip of Macedon. Swayed by his oratory, the Athenians did eventually go to war (340 BC), only to be defeated at Chaeronea (338 BC). Put on trial by the peace party of Aeschines, he fully vindicated himself in his oratorical masterpiece, 'On the Crown'.

Denbighshire [denbeesheer], Welsh **Sir Ddinbych** pop (2001e) 93 100; area 844 km²/326 sq mi. County (unitary authority from 1996) in NC Wales, UK; drained by R Clwyd; administra-

tive centre, Ruthin; St Asaph cathedral (founded 573); international eisteddfod at Llangollen (Jul).

Dench, Dame Judi, popular name of **Dame Judith Olivia Dench** (1934–) Actress, born in York, North Yorkshire. She studied at the Central School of Dramatic Art in London, and joined the Old Vic Company (1957–61), becoming one of Britain's most distinguished classical actresses. Her television credits include the popular sitcom *A Fine Romance* (1981–4), with actor husband **Michael Williams** (1935–2001). Her many films include *Iris* (2002, BAFTA Best Actress) and *Notes on a Scandal* (2006, Best Actress Oscar nomination; Best Actress Evening Standard Award), and she played the role of *M* in the later James Bond films.

dendrite *neurone*

dendrochronology The construction of archaeological chronologies from annual tree-ring sequences. Rings vary in width and structure from year to year, depending on the prevailing climatic conditions; overlapping patterns observed in preserved timbers can therefore be matched and linked to form an accurate and absolute chronology extending back thousands of years from the present day.

Deneb *Cygnus*

Deneuve, Cathérine [duhnoev], originally **Cathérine Dorléac** (1943–) Actress, born in Paris. She became well known through the unexpected popularity of the musical *Les Parapluies de Cherbourg* (1964, The Umbrellas of Cherbourg). Other films include *Belle de Jour* (1967), *Le Dernier Métro* (1980), *Dancer in the Dark* (2000), and *Les Temps qui changent* (2004).

dengue [denggee] A serious disease caused by a virus, transmitted by mosquitoes. Classic dengue with fever, headache, joint pain, weakness, and skin rashes usually resolves in a few weeks. Haemorrhagic dengue is characterized by vomiting, abdominal pain, circulatory collapse, and a high mortality. Gastric dengue attacks the vital organs, and can kill within hours.

Deng Xiaoping [duhng syowping] or **Teng Hsiao-p'ing** (1904–97) Leader of the Chinese Communist Party, born in Sichuan province, China. In 1954 he became secretary-general of the Chinese Communist Party, but reacted strongly against the excesses of the Great Leap Forward (1958–9). When Mao Zedong launched the Cultural Revolution (1966), Deng was criticized and purged, but was restored to power in 1974. From 1978 he took China through a rapid course of pragmatic reforms.

denier [denier] A unit of weight in textiles, measuring the fineness of yarn in such materials as silk, rayon, or nylon. It is equal to the weight in grams of 9000 m of the yarn. Materials of 15 denier would be finer than the material of 20 denier. It is now being replaced by the *tex*.

denim A popular clothing fabric made originally by filling indigo-dyed warp yarns with undyed cotton weft to give a twill structure. The indigo slowly leaches out of the fabric, causing a characteristic lightening of the blue colour. The fabric is hard-wearing, and was used for working clothes, but from the 1950s acquired a fashionable cult status.

De Niro, Robert [duh neeroh] (1943–) Actor and director, born in New York City. His many films include *The Godfather, Part II* (1974), *The Deer Hunter* (1978), *Raging Bull* (1980, Oscar), *Heat* (1995), and *Meet the Fockers* (2004). In 2006 he directed and starred in *The Good Shepherd*.

Denis or **Denys, St** [denis], Fr [duhnee] (3rd-c) Traditional apostle of France and first Bishop of Paris, who was sent from Rome about 250 to preach the Gospel to the Gauls. He was martyred at Paris under the Roman Emperor Valerian (reigned 253–60). Feast day 9 October.

Denis, Maurice [duhnee] (1870–1943) Artist and art theorist, born in Grandville, France. One of the original group of Symbolist painters, *Les Nabis*, he helped to found the Studios of Sacred Art (1919), devoted to the revival of religious painting.

Denmark

□ International Airport

Dan **Danmark**, official name **Kingdom of Denmark**, Dan **Kongeriget Danmark**

Local name Danmark

Timezone GMT +1

Area 43 076 km²/16 627 sq mi (excluding Greenland and Faroe Islands)

Population total (2002e) 5 364 000

Status Kingdom

Capital Copenhagen

Language Danish (official)

Ethnic groups Danish (97%), Turkish (0·5%), other Scandinavian (0·4%)

Religions Evangelical Lutheran (97%), Roman Catholic (0·5%), Jewish (0·1%)

Physical features Consists of most of the Jutland peninsula, several islands in the Baltic Sea, and some of the N Frisian Is in the North Sea; coastline 3400 km/2100 mi; uniformly low-lying; no large rivers and few lakes; shoreline indented by many lagoons and fjords, largest is Lim Fjord.

Climate Modified by Gulf Stream; cold and cloudy winters, warm and sunny summers; average annual temperatures range from 0·5°C (Jan) to 17°C (Jul); average annual rainfall 800 mm/32 in.

Currency 1 Danish Krone (DKK) = 100 øre

Economy Lack of raw materials has resulted in development of processing industries; intensive agriculture; wide range of food processing; machinery, textiles, furniture, electronics; dairy products.

GDP (2002e) $155·3 bn, per capita $28 900

Human Development Index (2002) 0·926

History Part of Viking kingdoms, 8th–10th-c; Danish Empire under Canute, 11th-c; joined with Sweden and Norway under Queen Margrethe of Denmark, 1389; Sweden separated from union in 16th-c, followed by Norway; 1814; Schleswig-Holstein lost to Germany, 1864; N Schleswig returned after plebiscite, 1920; occupied by Germany during World War 2; Iceland independent 1944; Greenland and Faroe Is remain dependencies; constitutional monarchy since 1849; unicameral system adopted, 1953; legislative power lies with the Monarch and the Diet jointly; member of European Union, 1973.

Head of State (Monarch)
1863–1906 Christian IX
1906–12 Frederik VIII
1912–47 Christian X
1947–72 Frederik IX
1972– Margrethe II

Head of Government
1975–82 Anker Jorgensen
1982–93 Poul Schlüter
1993–2001 Poul Nyrup Rasmussen
2001– Anders Fogh Rasmussen

Denmark *see panel*

Denning (of Whitchurch), Alfred Thompson Denning, Baron (1899–1999) British judge, born in Whitchurch, Hampshire. As Master of the Rolls (1962–82) he was responsible for many, often controversial, decisions. Among his books are *The Road to Justice* (1955) and *What Next in the Law* (1982).

density (physics) The mass of a substance divided by its volume; symbol ρ, units kg/m³. The density of water is 1000 kg/m³. Density is measured using a hydrometer.

dentistry The treatment and prevention of diseases of the mouth and teeth. Dentistry was studied at the Chinese Imperial Medical College from 620, and toothbrushes and toothpaste were known by Song times (10th–13th-c). In the West, it was first practised by barber surgeons, surgeon dentists forming a separate guild in France in the reign of Louis XIV. The trend in dental practice has moved from the repair of individual teeth, or their wholesale removal for the relief of pain, to that of conservation and the prevention of disease (**conservative dentistry**). Several special branches of the subject have developed. **Periodontics** is concerned with the prevention, diagnosis, and treatment of disorders of tissues that surround and support the teeth. **Orthodontics** is concerned with correcting the malposition of teeth, usually arising from faults in dental development.

The provision of artificial **prosthesis** attempts to restore oral function after the loss of teeth or of tissue (**prosthodontics**). **Oral surgery** is concerned with the repair of injury to the jaws by disease or by trauma. In some countries, **dental hygienists** provide services such as X-rays, scaling of teeth, and dental health education.

Denver 39°44N 104°59W, pop (2000e) 554 600. State capital in NC Colorado, USA; largest city in the state and a port on the S Platte R; founded, 1860; airport; railway; university (1864); processing, shipping, and distributing centre for a large agricultural area; professional teams, Nuggets (basketball), Broncos (football), Colorado Rockies (baseball).

Deodoro da Fonseca, Manuel [dayodooroo da fonsayka] (1827–92) Brazilian general and president (1889–91), born in Alagoas province, Brazil. He headed the revolt that overthrew Emperor Pedro II, and instituted the republic.

deoxyribonucleic acid *DNA*

deoxyribose [deeoksiriybohs] $C_5H_{10}O_4$. A 5-carbon sugar, particularly important for its role in the genetic material DNA.

De Palma, Brian (1940–) Film director, born in Newark, NJ. He made his feature-length debut with *The Wedding Party* (1966), and had commercial success with *Carrie* (1976) and *The Untouchables* (1987). Later films include *Bonfire of the Vanities*

(1990), *Mission: Impossible* (1996), *Mission to Mars* (2000), and *The Black Dahlia* (2006).

Dépardieu, Gérard [daypah(r)dyoe] (1948–) Actor and director, born in Châteauroux, France. His films include *Le Dernier Métro* (1980), *Danton* (1982), *Jean de Florette* (1986), *Cyrano de Bergerac* (1990), *The Man in the Iron Mask* (1998), and *Last Holiday* (2006). He played the lead role in the television serial *Le Comte de Monte Cristo* (1998).

depilatory [depilatree] A chemical used to remove unwanted hair on the skin, including alkalis, metallic sulphides, and mercaptans. They act by disrupting the chemical structure of the hair protein.

Depp, Johnny, popular name of **John Christopher Depp II** (1963–) Actor, born in Owensboro, KY. He dropped out of high school and played with several rock bands before turning to acting. He made his feature film debut in *A Nightmare on Elm Street* (1984) and later films include *Edward Scissorhands* (1990) and *Donnie Brasco* (1997). He received Best Actor Oscar nominations for *Pirates of the Caribbean* (2003, sequel 2006) and *Finding Neverland* (2004).

depression (economics) An economic situation where demand is slack, order-books are low, firms dispense with staff, and profits are poor or absent. A less severe form is a *recession*.

depression (meteorology) A meteorological term for a low pressure system at high and mid-latitudes; also known as a **cyclone** at low latitudes. A depression is initiated when a wave develops on a *front* (a boundary between cold and warm air masses). Pressure falls at the crest of the wave. A *warm front* is the leading edge of the depression, followed by the *cold front*, with a warm sector between the two fronts. As the cold front travels faster than the warm front, it catches up, to produce an *occluded front*. When this happens, pressure rises and the depression loses velocity. Depressions are typically 1000–2000 km/600–1250 mi across, but are temporary features with an average lifespan of 4–7 days.

depression (psychiatry) A mental condition in which there are feelings of low mood, despondence, self-criticism, and low esteem. It may be associated with a change (up or down) in appetite for sleep, food, or sex. There is a wide variety of treatments that can be used for this condition, including psychotherapy, drugs, and electroconvulsive therapy.

Depression, the, the *Great Depression*

depth charge A munition used by surface warships as a means of destroying submarines, typically an explosive-packed container dropped from a warship, armed by a fuse primed to detonate when it senses the water-pressure at a predetermined depth. Nuclear depth charges with explosive radii greater than one kilometre are now in service with nuclear-equipped navies.

de Quincey, Thomas [duh kwinsee] (1785–1859) Writer and critic, born in Manchester, Greater Manchester. On a visit to Bath, he met Coleridge, and through him Southey and Wordsworth; and in 1809 went to live near them in Grasmere. His *Confessions of an English Opium Eater* appeared as a serial in 1821, and brought him instant fame.

Derain, André [duhrî] (1880–1954) Artist, born in Chatou, France. Best known for his Fauvist landscape pictures (1904–8), he also designed for the theatre (notably the Diaghilev ballet).

Derby [dah(r)bee] 52°55N 1°30W, pop (2001e) 221700. City and unitary authority (from 1997) in Derbyshire, C England; chartered in 1637; railway; cathedral (1525); first silk mill (1719); porcelain centre in 18th-c (Derby ware); football league team, Derby County (Rams).

Derby, Edward Geoffrey Smith Stanley, 14th Earl of [dah(r)bee] (1799–1869) British statesman and prime minister (1852, 1858–9, 1866–8), born at Knowsley Hall, Lancashire. He entered parliament as a Whig in 1828, and as colonial secretary (1833) carried the Act for the emancipation of West Indian slaves.

In 1834 he joined the Conservatives, and became party leader, 1846–68. His third administration passed the Reform Bill (1867).

Derbyshire [dah(r)bisheer] pop (2001e) 734600; area 2631 km²/1016 sq mi. County of C England; rises to The Peak at 636 m/2086 ft; county town, Matlock; Derby a new unitary authority from 1997.

Dere Street *Roman roads*

derivatives Securities whose value depends on the prices of other securities. For example, a financial institution may borrow, promising repayment proportional to some index of security prices, such as the FT–SE share price index, or may sell an option giving the other party the right but not the obligation to buy or sell a given share or currency at a fixed price on some future date. New forms of derivatives are continually being invented.

Dermaptera [dermaptera] *earwig*

dermatitis [dermatiytis] The commonest skin disorder; involving an allergic reaction in the skin; also known as **eczema**. It may be provoked by chemical and physical irritants (eg detergents, watch straps), or ingested food and drugs. There is a hereditary element, in that affected individuals often have a family history of dermatitis and other allergic disorders.

dermatology The scientific study of the structure and function of the skin and of its diseases. It is a specialized branch of medical practice.

Derrida, Jacques [derida] (1930–2004) French philosopher-linguist, born in Algeria. His critique of the referentiality of language and the objectivity of structures founded the school of criticism called *deconstruction*. The award of an honorary degree by Cambridge University in 1992 was publicly contested, prompting attacks on and defences of his work.

Derry (city), official name **Londonderry** (but **Derry City Council** since 1984) 55°00N 7°19W, pop (2000e) 77600. City in Derry, NW Northern Ireland; monastery founded by St Columba, c.546; James I proclaimed the city to be part of the Corporation of London, 1613; renamed London-Derry, and settled by a Protestant colony; resisted a siege by James II for 105 days, 1689; railway; cathedral (1628–33).

Derry (county), official name **Londonderry**, Ir **Doire** pop (2000e) 227300; area 2067 km²/798 sq mi. County in N Northern Ireland, bounded NW by the Republic of Ireland; hilly, with part of the Sperrin Mts rising in the S; county town, Derry.

dervish A member of an Islamic ascetic or mystical fraternity. Since the founding of the Qadiriya order in the 12th-c, numerous orders with lodges situated across the Muslim world have been established. One of the most famous is the Mevlevi, or **whirling dervishes**.

DES An abbreviation of **diethylstilboestrol/diethylstilbestrol** – a synthetic oestrogen for the treatment of menopausal symptoms and prostate cancer. It is also used as the 'morning-after' pill.

Desai, Morarji (Ranchhodji) [daysiy] (1896–1995) Indian statesman and prime minister (1977–9), born in Gujarat, India. He became deputy prime minister in 1969 to lead the Opposition Congress Party. Detained during the state of emergency (1975–7), he was then appointed leader of the newly-formed Janata Party.

desalination The removal of salt from sea-water or brine to produce potable or industrially usable water, or water for ships' boilers. Distillation is the oldest process, still widely used. Membrane processes, electrodialysis, and the freezing out of ice are also used. About half of the world's desalinated water is produced in the Middle East.

Desalvo, Albert [desalvoh] (?–1973) Convicted US sex offender. After his arrest in late 1964 for sex attacks on women in their homes, he confessed that he was the Boston Strangler who had murdered 13 women between 1962 and 1964 in Boston, MA. He was found stabbed to death in his cell in Walpole Prison, MA.

descant A melody sung or played above another well-known one, such as a hymn tune. The term (often as **discant**) is also used for a type of mediaeval polyphony, and to distinguish the highest-pitched member of a family of instruments (eg the descant recorder).

Descartes, René [daykah(r)t], Lat **Renatius Cartesius** (1596–1650) Rationalist philosopher and mathematician, 'the father of modern philosophy', born in La Haye, near Tours. His aim, to refound human knowledge on a basis secure from scepticism, is expounded in his most famous work, the *Meditationes de prima philosophia* (1641, Meditations on First Philosophy). This work introduced his famous principle that one cannot doubt one's own existence as a thinking being – *cogito ergo sum* ('I think, therefore I am') – and presented the argument that mind and body are distinct substances. He virtually founded co-ordinate or analytic geometry, and made major contributions to optics.

desensitization An experimental treatment designed to prevent allergic reactions in sensitive individuals. It involves small repeated subcutaneous injections of the allergen believed to be responsible for the reaction. The antibody produced in response to the injections coats tissue cells, and blocks the access of a later dose of the offending allergen to which the individual was sensitive.

desert An arid and empty region of the Earth, characterized by little or no vegetation, and meagre and intermittent rainfall, high evaporation rates, and low humidity and cloud cover. Low-latitude deserts such as the Sahara are hot and dry, caused by high pressure air masses which prevent precipitation. Mid-latitude deserts such as the Gobi are cold and dry, and are related to mountain barriers which seal off moist maritime winds. Polar deserts of the Arctic and Antarctic are permanently covered by snow and ice. Approximately one third of the Earth's land surface is desert. (*see panel*)

desert fox *fennec fox*

desert rat *jerboa*

Desert Rats Members of the 7th British Armoured Division, which in 1940 took as its badge the jerboa or desert rat, noted for remarkable leaps. The media applied the name generally to all British servicemen in the North Africa campaign.

Desert Shield / Storm *Gulf War* (Jan–Feb 1991)

de Sica, Vittorio [seeka] (1901–74) Actor and film director, born in Sora, Italy. He achieved international success in the neo-realist style with *Sciuscià* (1946, Shoeshine), *Ladri di biciclette* (1948, Bicycle Thieves), and *Miracolo a Milano* (1951, Miracle in Milan).

Desiderio da Settignano [dezideryoh da setinyahnoh] (c.1428–61) Sculptor, born in Settignano, Italy. He worked in the early Renaissance style, producing many notable portrait busts of women and children.

design, argument from An argument, especially popular in the 18th-c and 19th-c, that the existence of complex organisms can be explained only by the existence of a supremely wise, powerful, beneficent God. The argument lost its appeal with the development of evolutionary theory.

designer drugs Synthetic drugs, usually similar to amphetamines, which are not controlled by law in the USA; they are so called because they are specifically designed by chemists to be slightly different structurally to drugs that are controlled by law (which are 'named', and thus illegal), yet still chemically so close to them that they have similar biological effects.

desk-top publishing The preparation of typeset output using a microcomputer with appropriate software for the composition of text, the creation of illustrations, the editing of structured pages, and typography. 'Publishing' in this now familiar turn of phrase is a misnomer: 'typesetting' or 'text composition' would be more appropriate.

desman An insectivore of the mole family (2 species), native to the Pyrenees and W Asia; red-brown; long mobile snout; webbed hind feet; long tail flattened from side to side; lives in streams and pools.

Des Moines [dimoyn] 41°35N 93°37W, pop (2000e) 198 700. Capital of state in C Iowa, USA; developed around a fort established in 1843; city status, 1857; state capital in 1881; airport; railway; university (1881); important commercial and transportation centre in the heart of Iowa's Corn Belt.

Desmoulins, (Lucie Simplice) Camille (Benoist) [daymoolî] (1760–94) French revolutionary and journalist, born in Guise, France. An effective crowd orator, he played a dramatic part in the storming of the Bastille. He was elected to the National Convention, and voted for the death of the king. He actively attacked the Girondists, then argued for moderation, and was guillotined.

Desprez, Josquin *Josquin Desprez*

Dessalines, Jean Jacques [desaleen] (c.1758–1806) Emperor of Haiti (1804–06), born a slave, probably at Grande Rivière du Nord, Haiti (formerly St Domingue). In the slave insurrection of 1791 he was second only to Toussaint L'Ouverture. His despotic behaviour as emperor led to his assassination.

De Stijl [duh shteel] A group of Dutch artists and architects formed in 1917, strongly influenced by Cubism, Dutch Calvinism, and theosophy. The group advocated a new, wholly

Largest Deserts

Name/location	Area*	
	km²	sq mi
Sahara, N Africa	8 600 000	3 320 000
Arabian, SW Asia	2 330 000	900 000
Gobi, Mongolia/NE China	1 166 000	450 000
Patagonian, Argentina	673 000	260 000
Great Basin, SW USA	492 000	190 000
Chihuahuan, Mexico	450 000	175 000
Great Sandy, NW Australia	450 000	175 000
Great Victoria, SW Australia	325 000	125 000
Sonoran, SW USA	310 000	120 000
Kyzyl-Kum, Kazakhstan/ Uzbekistan	300 000	115 000
Takla Makan, N China	270 000	105 000
Kalahari, SW Africa	260 000	100 000
Kara-Kum, Turkmenistan	260 000	100 000
Kavir, Iran	260 000	100 000
Syrian, Saudi Arabia/Jordan/ Syria/Iraq	260 000	100 000
Nubian, Sudan	260 000	100 000
Thar, India/Pakistan	200 000	77 000
Ust'-Urt, Kazakhstan/Uzbekistan	160 000	62 000
Bet-Pak-Dala, Kazakhstan	155 000	60 000
Simpson, C Australia	145 000	56 000
Dzungaria, China	142 000	55 000
Atacama, Chile	140 000	54 000
Namib, SE Africa	134 000	52 000
Sturt, SE Australia	130 000	50 000
Bolson de Mapimi, Mexico	130 000	50 000
Ordos, China	130 000	50 000
Alashan, China	116 000	45 000

*Desert areas are very approximate, because clear physical boundaries may not occur.

abstract aesthetic style composed solely of straight lines, primary colours, and black and white, typified by the paintings of Mondrian. The group formally ended in 1931.

destroyer A small fast warship designed in the late 19th-c to destroy enemy torpedo boats. It has since adopted many other roles: submarine hunting, evacuation, invasion, assault support, and convoy escort. Modern destroyers are usually guided-missile carriers.

detached retina *retina*

detente [daytawnt] An attempt to lower the tension between states as a means of reducing the possibility of war and of achieving peaceful coexistence between different social and political systems. A prominent feature of relations between the USA and USSR in the 1970s, it led to several agreements over arms (SALT) and security and co-operation (Helsinki); the concept was overtaken by events, following the break-up of the Soviet Union in 1990.

detention centre *young offender institution*

detergent A material which lowers the surface tension of water, and makes it mix better with oils and fats. Most detergents contain molecules or ions with a combination of polar (water-seeking) and non-polar (oil-seeking) parts, which serve to bind oil and water together.

deterrence A concept that has developed in strategic military thinking since the 1930s, following the emergence of long-range weapons of mass destruction. It is based on the threat of effective military or economic counter-action as a means of discouraging acts of aggression. There is considerable debate over the effectiveness of deterrence in different circumstances.

detonator A sensitive explosive (eg mercuric fulminate, lead azide) used in a small quantity to initiate the function of larger quantities of principal explosive. By extension, the term is used for any device containing a detonating explosive actuated by heat, percussion, friction, or electricity.

Detroit [deetroyt] 42°20N 83°03W, pop (2000e) 951 300. Port in SE Michigan, USA; tenth largest city in the USA; founded by the French as a fur-trading outpost, 1701; surrendered to the British during the Seven Years War, 1760; handed over to the USA, 1796; much of the city rebuilt after a fire in 1805; capital of state, 1837–47; airport; railway; two universities (1877, 1933); the nation's leading manufacturer of cars and trucks; professional teams, Tigers (baseball), Pistons (basketball), Red Wings (ice hockey), Lions (football).

Dettori, Frankie [detoree], popular name of **Lanfranco Dettori** (1970–) British jockey, born in Milan, Italy. A champion apprentice in 1990, his major wins of the decade include The Oaks (1994, 1995, 2002), St Leger (1995, 1996, 2005, 2006), Two Thousand Guineas (1996, 1999), and One Thousand Guineas (1998). He was champion jockey for two successive seasons (1994, 1995), and again in 2004, and in 1996 was winner of all seven races on one card at Ascot. In 2003 he won the Hong Kong Cup and the title of top jockey in the World Racing Series.

Deucalion [dyookaylion] In Greek mythology, a son of Prometheus. When Zeus flooded the world, Deucalion and his wife Pyrrha built an 'ark' which grounded on the top of Parnassus. They restored the human race by throwing stones over their shoulders, which turned into human beings.

deus ex machina [dayus eks makina] (Lat 'god from the machine') A device used mainly by classical dramatists to resolve by supernatural intervention (the god descending from above the stage) all the problems which have arisen during the course of a play.

deuterium A heavy isotope of hydrogen, in which the nucleus comprises a proton and a neutron rather than a proton alone (as for common hydrogen); symbol D or ^2H. It forms 0·015% of naturally occurring hydrogen. Water made with deuterium is called *heavy water*, and is used in some nuclear reactors.

Deuteronomy, Book of [dyooteronomee] The fifth and last book of the Pentateuch, in the Hebrew Bible/Old Testament. It was traditionally attributed to Moses, but many date it much later, c.7th-c BC. It surveys Israel's wilderness experiences, and presents an extensive code of religious laws and duties.

Deutsch, David [doych] (1953–) British theoretical physicist, born in Haifa, Israel. Educated at Cambridge and Oxford universities, in 1978 he took up a position at the University of Texas at Austin, and in 1985 returned to Oxford. He pioneered the theory of quantum computation.

de Valera, Eamon [devalayra] (1882–1975) Irish statesman, prime minister (1932–48, 1951–4, 1957–9), and president (1959–73), born in New York City. A commandant in the 1916 rising, he was arrested and narrowly escaped the firing squad. In 1926 he became leader of Fianna Fáil, his newly-formed Republican opposition party, which won the 1932 elections. In spite of his colourful early career, his leadership was moderate, and he opposed extremism and religious intolerance.

devaluation A fall in the amount of foreign currency which can be obtained per unit of a country's own currency. For example, if the £ has been selling for $1·60 and falls to $1·40, it is devalued. Devaluation makes a country's exports cheaper abroad and its imports dearer at home, as long as domestic prices do not change. This tends to improve the balance of payments. Rises in import costs tend to create domestic inflation, however, so that the initial competitive advantage obtained does not last.

Devanagari [devanagahree] A range of alphabets used for Indian languages, consisting of a set of consonantal letter-symbols. Vowels are represented by a system of diacritics.

development In photography, the process by which the latent image formed by exposure to light is made visible. It generally involves reducing the exposed silver compounds in the sensitive material to black metallic silver. In colour photography, couplers may be used to form a coloured dye image at the same time.

developmental psychology A branch of psychology which examines the biological, social, and intellectual development of people from before birth throughout the life-course. Most attention has been paid to young children, in whom shifts in understanding appear more obvious.

Devi, Phoolan [devee], known as **Dasyu Sundari** ('Beautiful Bandit') (1957–2001) Bandit and folk hero, born in India. After a childhood of abuse, she was kidnapped by bandits, then joined the gang, to become one of India's most notorious criminals while attracting a national reputation among oppressed people. She surrendered in 1983 in a much publicized ceremony. Released from prison in 1994, she became a Buddhist convert, and in 1995 launched a new political party in support of the lower castes. In 1996 she won a seat in the federal Parliament. Mala Sen's story of her life, *India's Bandit Queen* (1991) was the basis of the film *Bandit Queen* (1995). She was assassinated at her Delhi home.

Devil A supernatural evil agent thought to influence human behaviour, in many religious beliefs; when referring to a specific character in the Judaeo-Christian tradition, the chief of the evil spirits or fallen angels; also known as **Satan**. In religious literature the Devil appears in many different guises, human or animal, and with many different names (eg *Beelzebul, Belial, ahuras, jinn*). Exorcism of individuals possessed by demons is long attested in the Judaeo-Christian tradition, but cults of devil-worship (or Satanism) involving witchcraft, black magic, and the occult have persisted despite opposition throughout most of Christian history.

devil ray Any of the giant rays widespread in surface waters of tropical and warm temperate seas; pectoral fins forming large triangular wings; body width up to 6 m/20 ft; sides of head

The Dewey Decimal System

000 Generalities	320 Political science	650 Business and related enterprises
010 Bibliographies and catalogues	330 Economics	660 Chemical technology, etc
020 Library science	340 Law	670 Manufactures
030 General encyclopedic works	350 Public administration	680 Assembled and final products
040 (Unassigned)	360 Welfare and association	690 Buildings
050 General periodicals	370 Education	700 The arts
060 General organizations	380 Commerce	710 Civic and landscape art
070 Newspapers and journalism	390 Customs and folklore	720 Architecture
080 General collections	400 Language	730 Sculpture and the plastic arts
090 Manuscripts and book rarities	410 Linguistics and non-verbal language	740 Drawing and decorative arts
100 Philosophy and related	420 English and Anglo-Saxon	750 Painting and paintings
110 Ontology and methodology	430 Germanic languages	760 Graphic arts
120 Knowledge, cause, purpose, man	440 French, Provençal, Catalan	770 Photography and photographs
130 Pseudo- and parapsychology	450 Italian, Romanian, etc	780 Music
140 Specific philosophic viewpoints	460 Spanish and Portuguese	790 Recreation (recreational arts)
150 Psychology	470 Italic languages	800 Literature and rhetoric
160 Logic	480 Classical and Greek	810 American literature in English
170 Ethics (moral philosophy)	490 Other languages	820 English and Anglo-Saxon literature
190 Modern Western philosophy	500 Pure sciences	830 Germanic languages literature
200 Religion	510 Mathematics	840 French, Provençal, Catalan literature
210 Natural religion	520 Astronomy and allied sciences	850 Italian and Romanian literature
220 Bible	530 Physics	860 Spanish and Portuguese literature
230 Christian doctrinal theology	540 Chemistry and allied sciences	870 Italic languages literature
240 Christian moral and devotional theology	550 Earth sciences	880 Classical and Greek literature
250 Christian pastoral, parochial etc	560 Paleontology	890 Literature of other languages
260 Christian social and ecclesiastical theology	570 Anthropological and biological sciences	900 General geography and history, etc
270 History and geography of Christian Church	580 Botanical sciences	910 General geography
	590 Zoological sciences	920 General biography and genealogy
280 Christian denominations and sects	600 Technology (applied science)	930 General history of ancient world
290 Other religions and comparative religion	610 Medical sciences	940 General history of modern Europe
	620 Engineering and allied operations	950 General history of modern Asia
300 The social sciences	630 Agriculture and agricultural industries	960 General history of modern Africa
		970 General history of North America
		980 General history of South America
310 Statistical method and statistics	640 Domestic arts and sciences	990 General history of rest of world

prolonged as fleshy 'horns'; tail whip-like. (Genera: *Mobula*, *Manta*. Family: Mobulidae.)

Devil's Island *Salut, Iles du*

Devil's Tower 44°31N 104°57W. The first US national monument, in NE Wyoming, USA; a natural tower of volcanic rock with a flat top, 263 m/863 ft high; used as the setting for the film *Close Encounters of the Third Kind* (1977).

devise *property*

devolution The delegation of authority from a country's legislature or government to a subordinate elected institution on a more limited geographical basis. Devolution is distinguished from **federalism**, where the powers of the central government and the federal bodies are set out in the constitution. Under devolution, the subordinate body receives its power from the government, which retains some right of oversight.

Devolution, War of A conflict prompted by Louis XIV of France in pursuit of his wife's legal claims to the Spanish Netherlands. Louis's armies overran Flanders, prompting the Dutch, England, and Sweden to negotiate the Triple Alliance (1668). The war ended with a secret treaty of compromise between Louis and the Emperor Leopold (1668).

Devon pop (2001e) 704 500; area 6711 km²/2590 sq mi. County of SW England; rises to Dartmoor in SW and Exmoor in NE; county town, Exeter; Plymouth and Torbay new unitary authorities from 1998; naval base at Plymouth.

Devonian period A geological period of the Palaeozoic era extending from 408 to 360 million years ago. It contains the oldest widespread continental deposits in Europe (Old Red

Sandstone) as well as extensive marine sediments containing fossils of armoured fish, corals, ammonites, and molluscs.

Dewar, Donald (Campbell) (1937–2000) British statesman, born in Glasgow, W Scotland. A lawyer, he became a Labour MP in 1966, becoming Labour chief whip (1995–7). He was secretary of state for Scotland (1997–9), and became Scotland's inaugural first minister in the new Scottish Parliament (1999–2000).

Dewar flask An insulated vessel with double walls, the inner space being made into a vacuum and silvered; heat losses by convection and radiation are thus reduced to a minimum. It was devised in 1892 by British chemist James Dewar (1842–1923) to hold gases liquefied at very low temperatures, and later developed industrial and domestic uses for maintaining liquids at constant high or low temperatures. Everyday names include **vacuum flask** and the trade name **Thermos flask**.

de Wet, Christiaan (Rudolf) [wet] (1854–1922) Afrikaner statesman and general, born in Smithfield district, Orange Free State, South Africa. He became conspicuous in the Transvaal war of 1880–1; and in the war of 1899–1902 was the most audacious of all the Boer commanders.

Dewey, John (1859–1952) Philosopher and educator, born in Burlington, VT. A leading exponent of pragmatism, he developed a philosophy of education which stressed development of the person, understanding of the environment, and learning through experience.

Dewey decimal system A library classification system in widespread international use, devised in 1873 by US librarian Melvil

Dewey (1851–1931). It recognizes 10 main classes of subject-matter, each class containing 100 numbers, with decimal subdivisions for unlimited supplementary classes. (*see panel p.267*)

dew point temperature The temperature at which a parcel of air would become saturated with water vapour if it were cooled without a change in pressure or moisture content. When moist air is cooled to below this temperature, condensation in the form of dew or hoar frost occurs.

dextrin A complex sugar, a mixture of glucose polymers obtained from starch. Its main use is to improve the palatability of starchy foods, and to reduce the osmotic load on the stomach in convalescent drinks.

dextrose *glucose*

Dhaka [daka], former spelling **Dacca** 23°42N 90°22E, pop (2000e) 7 137 000. Capital city of Bangladesh; capital of Mughal province of East Bengal, 1608–1704; capital of British province of East Bengal and Assam, 1905–12; major expansion since becoming capital of East Pakistan, 1947; centre of the world's greatest jute-growing region; airport; railway; two universities (1921, 1961); known as 'the city of mosques' (over 1000); Bashundhara City shopping/leisure complex opened, 2004.

dharma [dah(r)ma] In Hinduism, the universal law that applies to the universe, human society, and the individual. It is both a general code of ethics applicable to all, and a moral law specific to an individual's station in life.

dhole [dohl] A member of the dog family (*Cuon alpinus*), native to S and SE Asia; red-brown, with white underneath; black tip to tail; hunts large mammals in packs; also known as **Asiatic wild dog** or **Indian wild dog**.

diabetes mellitus [diyabeeteez melitus] A common metabolic disorder in which the pancreas fails to produce insulin in the amounts needed to control sugar metabolism. The blood sugar level rises above normal values (*hyperglycemia*) and spills over into the urine, causing large volumes to be produced (*polyuria*). Diabetes is a leading cause of death and disability in developed countries, as a result of the complications that develop over a long period. These can be minimized by careful management of blood sugar, often requiring insulin injections under the skin several times a day.

diablotin [diyablotin] *oilbird*

Diaghilev, Sergei Pavlovich [deeagilef] (1872–1929) Ballet impresario, born in Novgorod, Russia. His company was founded in 1909, and remained perilously in existence for 20 years, triumphantly touring Europe. Many of the great dancers, composers, and painters of his period contributed to the success of his Ballets Russes. He also encouraged several major choreographers.

diagnosis In medicine, the determination by a medical practitioner of the nature of a disease in a patient by first taking a history of the patient's current symptoms, previous complaints, illnesses in the family, and social circumstances; then by conducting a physical examination to look for signs of disease; and finally by using additional investigations such as blood tests and X-rays.

dialect *dialectology*

dialectic The study of the logic involved in conversational argument. As used by Hegel and Marx, dialectic is an analogous process that occurs in nature.

dialectical materialism A central doctrine of Marxism. Its claims are that quantitative changes in matter yield qualitative changes (for example, the emergence of mind); that nature is a unity of contradictory opposites; and that the result of one opposite (thesis) clashing with another (antithesis) is a synthesis that preserves and transcends the opposites.

dialectology The study of varieties of a language (**dialects**) which are regionally or socially distinctive. They are marked by having distinctive words, grammatical structures, and pronunci-

ations. Dialects are studied by wide-ranging questionnaires which gather information about the way linguistic features are used in a geographical area. A **dialect atlas** shows dialect areas and boundaries.

dialysis [diyalisis] A process of separating dissolved substances (solutes) of different molecular weights by using the differences in their rates of diffusion across thin layers of certain materials (eg cellulose). Artificial kidney machines (**dialysers**) perform **haemodialysis**, whereby waste products (such as urea or excess salts) are removed from the patient's blood, while blood cells and protein are retained.

Diamond, Neil (Leslie) (1941–) Singer and songwriter, born in New York City. He wrote the hit 'I'm A Believer' (1966) for the Monkees, and had his first number 1 hit with 'Cracklin' Rosie' (1970). His albums include *Jonathon Livingston Seagull* (1974), *Headed for the Future* (1986), *Tennessee Moon* (1996), and *12 Songs* (2005).

diamond A naturally occurring form of crystalline carbon formed at high pressures and temperatures deep in the Earth's crust; the hardest natural substance known. It is the most precious of gemstones. Major mines near Kimberley, South Africa (1871–2005). **Black diamonds**, generally of poorer quality, are used for industrial purposes.

diamondback North American rattlesnake with bold diamond-shaped markings along back; also known as **diamondback rattlesnake**; the **Eastern diamondback rattlesnake** (*Crotalus adamanteus*) is the most venomous snake in North America.

diamondbird A small woodland bird native to Australia, also known as **pardalote**; short tail and bill; nests in holes. (Genus: *Pardalotus*, 5 or 8 species; experts disagree. Family: Dicaeidae.)

diamorphine *heroin*

Diana [diyana] Roman goddess, associated with the Moon, virginity, and hunting. She was considered to be equivalent to the Greek Artemis.

Diana, Princess of Wales, formerly **Lady Diana (Frances) Spencer** (1961–97) Former wife of Charles, Prince of Wales, and youngest daughter of the 8th Earl Spencer, born at Sandringham, Norfolk. She became Lady Diana Spencer when her father succeeded to the earldom in 1975, and worked as a kindergarten teacher in Pimlico before marrying the Prince of Wales to great popular acclaim in 1981. They had two sons, **Prince William (Arthur Philip Louis)** (1982–) and **Prince Henry (Charles Albert David)** (1984–), known as **Prince Harry**. Seriously interested in social concerns, she became a popular public figure in her own right, and was president of Relate and many other charities. The royal couple were legally separated in 1992, and divorced in 1996. She continued to travel and work with a range of good causes, both in Britain and abroad, while receiving unprecedented worldwide media attention, with newspapers competing to report on her family situation and on her (real or imaginary) personal relationships; and it was while trying to escape the pursuit of paparazzi in Paris that she died in a car accident in August 1997. A British inquest into her death was opened in 2004 and was ongoing in 2007.

diaphragm (anatomy) A sheet of muscle and tendons separating the thoracic and abdominal cavities. It is the principle muscle of respiration, and is also an important muscle used in expulsive acts: coughing, vomiting, micturition, defecation, and childbirth.

diaphragm (photography) An opening, usually circular, and generally adjustable in diameter or area, which controls the amount of light passing through a lens into an optical system, such as a camera.

diarrhoea / diarrhea [diyareea] The frequent passage of semi-formed or liquid motions. Acute diarrhoea usually results from inflammation of the bowel, chemical irritants in food, or infection by micro-organisms (eg dysentery). Important consequences are loss of body water and salts, which may lead to dehydration.

Diaspora [diyaspora] (Gr 'scattering', Heb *golah* or *galut* 'exile') The Jews scattered in the world outside Palestine, from either voluntary or compulsory resettlements; also known as the **Dispersion**.

diastole [diyastolee] The interval between successive contractions of the heart. During this period, the heart chambers fill with blood flowing from the veins into the atria, and continuing into the ventricles.

diastrophism [diyastrofizm] The deformation of large masses of the Earth's crust to form mountain ranges, ocean basins, and continents.

diathermy [diyathermee] The application of heat to muscles or joints for the relief of pain. The heat is produced by means of high-frequency electric current, high-frequency electromagnetic short-wave radiation, or ultrasound.

diatom [diyatm] A microscopic, single-celled green alga common in marine and freshwater habitats; possesses an often ornate, external shell (*frustule*) containing silica, and consisting of two separate valves. (Class: Bacillarophyceae.)

Diaz or **Dias, Bartolomeu** [deeas], Span also [deeath], Port [deeazh] (c.1450–1500) Navigator and explorer, probably born in Portugal. The first man to sail round the Cape of Good Hope (1487), he also travelled with Vasco da Gama in 1497, and with Cabral in 1500.

Diaz, Cameron [deeas] (1972–) Film actress, born in San Diego, CA. Her big break into cinema came in 1994 when she auditioned for a small part in *The Mask* and was offered the lead. From 1997 onwards she was propelled into international stardom with *My Best Friend's Wedding* (1997) and *There's Something About Mary* (1998). Later films include *Gangs of New York* (2002) and *The Holiday* (2006).

Díaz, (José de la Cruz) Porfirio [deeas] (1830–1915) President of Mexico (1876–80, 1884–1911), born in Oaxaca, S Mexico. Defeated in the presidential election of 1875, he seized power, and served as president for 30 years, until forced into exile.

diazepam *benzodiazepines*

diazo process *photocopying*

Dibdin, Michael (John) (1947–2007) Novelist, born in Wolverhampton, West Midlands. In 1988 he won the Crime Writer's Award, the Gold Dagger, for *Ratking*. Later books include *Dirty Tricks* (1991), *Cosi Fan Tutti* (1996), *And Then You Die* (2001), *Back to Bologna* (2005), and *End Games* (2007), the 11th of his novels featuring Inspector Aurelio Zen.

DiCaprio, Leonardo (1974–) Film actor, born in Los Angeles. He began his acting career in television at the age of 14, moved into films, and became known after his Oscar-nominated role for Best Supporting Actor in *What's Eating Gilbert Grape?* (1993). Later films include *Romeo + Juliet* (1996), *Titanic* (1997), *The Beach* (2000), *Gangs of New York* (2002), *The Aviator* (2004, Golden Globe Best Actor; Oscar nomination), and *Blood Diamond* (2006, Best Actor Oscar nomination).

Dickens, Charles (John Huffam) (1812–70) Novelist, born in Landport, Hampshire. He took up journalism, at 22 joining a London newspaper. In 1836 his *Sketches by Boz* and *Pickwick Papers* were published; and that year he married Catherine Hogarth. They had 10 children, but were separated in 1858. Dickens worked relentlessly, producing several successful novels, which first appeared in monthly instalments, notably *Oliver Twist* (1837–9), *Nicholas Nickleby* (1838–9) and *The Old Curiosity Shop* (1840–1). His later novels include *David Copperfield* (1849–50), *Bleak House* (1852–3), *A Tale of Two Cities* (1859), *Great Expectations* (1860–1), and the unfinished *The Mystery of Edwin Drood* (1870). His novels included vigorous campaigns against some of the social abuses of the time, and influenced several reforms. They

have provided the basis for many successful theatre, cinema, radio, and television adaptations.

Dickinson, Emily (Elizabeth) (1830–86) Poet, born in Amherst, MA. At the age of 23 she withdrew from all social contacts, and lived a secluded life at Amherst, writing in secret over 1000 poems. Hardly any of her work was published before her death.

dicotyledons [diykotileednz] One of the two major divisions of the flowering plants, often referred to simply as **dicots**; contrasted with **monocotyledons**. The seed embryo has two cotyledons, and the primary root of the seedling persists, forming a taproot. About 250 different families of dicots are currently recognized. (Subclass: Dicotyledonae.)

dictator In strict terms, a single ruler who is often not elected but enjoys authority by virtue of some personal characteristic, ie an **autocrat**. In practice, a dictatorship often refers to rule by several people, unelected and authoritarian, such as a military dictatorship.

dictionary A work of reference, traditionally in the form of a book, and now often available as a computational database, giving linguistic information about the words of a language, arranged in alphabetical order under headwords. Some dictionaries (especially those falling within the US and European – particularly French and German – traditions) add encyclopedic data, or provide special features, such as notes on usage or closely related words. The process of compiling dictionaries, and the study of the issues involved, is known as **lexicography**.

Dicynodon [diysiynodon] A plant-eating fossil reptile known from the late Permian period; jaws with horny plates for cutting and crushing vegetation; upper canine tusks prominent. (Order: Therapsida.)

Diderot, Denis [deederoh] (1713–84) Writer and philosopher, born in Langres, France. He was the chief editor of the *Encyclopédie* (1751–65), a major work of the age of the Enlightenment. A prolific and versatile writer, he published novels, plays, satires, essays, and letters.

didgeridoo, also spelled **didjeridoo** or **didjeridu** A primitive trumpet of the Australian aborigines, made from a hollow eucalyptus branch about 120–150 cm/4–5 ft long. It is used to accompany singing and dancing.

Dido [diydoh] In the *Aeneid*, the daughter of the King of Tyre, who founded Carthage. Aeneas was diverted to Africa by storms, and told her his story. They fell in love, and when Aeneas deserted her she committed suicide.

Didrikson, Babe, nickname of **Mildred Ella Zaharias**, *née* **Didrikson** (1914–56) Sportswoman, born in Port Arthur, TX. After an outstanding career in athletics, she became a leading golfer, and was also renowned at diving, billiards, and lacrosse. As a professional she won the US Women's Open in 1948, 1950, and 1954.

Diefenbaker, John G(eorge) [deefenbayker] (1895–1979) Canadian Conservative statesman and prime minister (1957–63), born in Neustadt, Ontario. His government introduced important agricultural reforms, and extended the federal franchise to Canada's native peoples.

dielectric A non-conducting material whose molecules align or polarize under the influence of applied electric fields. Dielectrics are an essential constituent of capacitors.

dielectric constant *permittivity*

Diemen, Antony Van *Tasman, Abel Janszoon*

diencephalon [diyensefalon] The part of the forebrain which lies deep within the cerebral hemispheres. The *thalamus* is the largest part, whose diverse functions include various motor, sensory, and emotional responses.

Dieppe [dyep] 49°55N 1°05E, pop (2000e) 38 300. Seaport in NW France; scene of heavy fighting in World War 2; ferry links with Newhaven.

Dieri [diree] Aboriginal community of the L Eyre region of South Australia. After 1860, they were drawn into European-controlled cattle stations and missions, and many now live in the cities of Adelaide and Port Augusta.

Diesel, Rudolf (Christian Carl) [deezl] (1858–1913) Engineer, born in Paris. Subsidized by the Krupp company, he constructed a 'rational heat motor', demonstrating the first compression-ignition engine in 1897.

diesel engine An internal combustion engine, working upon the diesel cycle, which ignites its fuel/air mixture by heating it to combustion point through compression. Because of this, the diesel engine is classed as a compression-ignition engine.

diet The combination of foods which provide the necessary nutrients for the body. Often the term is used to imply a restriction of calories for slimming: strictly speaking this is a 'low-calorie' diet, just as there are low-fat diets, low-salt diets, or high-fibre diets.

Diet, Imperial The assembly of the Holy Roman Empire, mediaeval in origin, representing the separate estates of electors, princes, and free cities, and summoned at the will of the Emperor. It became increasingly little more than a permanent congress of ambassadors during the last century and a half of its existence (1663–1806).

dietary fibre The part of the diet made up of plant material that is indigestible by humans; also known as **roughage**. Fibre is an important component of the diet, it absorbs water and helps to bulk out the gut contents, thereby increasing the rate of passage through the intestines.

dietetics The clinical management of a patient through dietary intervention, as practised professionally by **dietitians**. The two problems most commonly treated by dietitians are obesity and diabetes.

diethylstilboestrol DES

Diet of Worms Worms, Diet of

Dietrich, Marlene [deetrikh], originally **Maria Magdalene von Losch** (1901–92) Film actress, born in Berlin. She became famous in a German film Der blaue Engel (1930, The Blue Angel), and developed a glamorous and sensual film personality in such Hollywood films as Morocco (1930).

differential calculus A system of mathematical rules which considers small increments of a variable x, and the corresponding changes in $f(x)$, to find the rate at which $f(x)$ is changing. The early development of calculus was associated with Isaac Newton, and independently with Gottfried Leibniz.

Differential GPS Global Positioning System

diffraction An interference effect, a property of waves, responsible for the spreading of waves issuing from a small aperture (eg sound waves from a public address loudspeaker). Diffraction causes the waves to 'bend round' objects, which in light produces shadows surrounded by tiny light and dark bands (**diffraction fringes**).

diffusion (science) In physics and chemistry, the movement of atoms or particles through bulk material via their random collisions. For example, atoms of a gas introduced into a volume of still air will become evenly distributed through it by diffusion.

Digby, Sir Kenelm (1603–65) Diplomat, scientist, and writer, born in Gayhurst, Buckinghamshire. During the Civil War he was imprisoned by the parliament (1642–3), and had his estate confiscated. After the Restoration, he was chancellor to Queen Henrietta Maria until 1664.

digestion A physiological process of animals in which complex foodstuffs are broken down by enzymes into simpler components (monosaccharides, amino acids, fatty acids, and other substances) which can be used by body cells. In certain animals (eg protozoa, porifera), digestion is entirely intracellular. Many animals (eg vertebrates, arthropods) depend entirely on extracel-

lular digestion, in which enzyme-rich fluids are secreted into the cavity of the alimentary canal.

Diggers A radical group in England formed during the Commonwealth, led by Gerrard Winstanley (1609–72), preaching and practising agrarian communism on common and waste land. The movement was suppressed and its communities dispersed by local landowners.

digital Descriptive of any method of representing information (numbers, strings of characters, sounds, pictures) by a sequence of electronic pulses of fixed duration. The existence of a voltage denotes a '1' and the absence denotes a '0'. This allows all numbers to be represented by their binary equivalents. Other forms of information are first represented as a set of numbers and then those numbers are coded in digital electronic form. Digital representation is preferred because it is less vulnerable to noise, easy to compress, and easy to encrypt, preventing unauthorized capture of the information.

digital computer A programmable machine which operates using binary digital data. The basic operations carried out are simple arithmetic or logical operations, but in combination and at high speed these provide a very powerful facility. Digital computers contain (i) a central processing unit which controls and co-ordinates all the functions of the computer, and performs the arithmetic and logical operations; (ii) a memory, which holds data and program instructions; and (iii) input/output devices, which allow communication to and from the outside world.

digitalis [dijitahlis] An extract of Digitalis purpurea (the foxglove) which has been used for the treatment of heart failure and oedema ('dropsy') for at least 800 years. The extract contains cardiac glycosides as active ingredients.

digital media The use of digital recording to store media on computers and allow them to be processed by computer software. Different standards have been developed for the compression and storage of images, audio recordings, and video recordings: **GIF (Graphics Interchange Format)** is a standard for the storage of still images; **JPEG (Joint Photographic Experts Group)** is a standard for the compression and storage of continuous tone still images; **MIDI (Musical Instrument Digital Interface)** is a format for representing the output from musical instruments which can be processed by a MIDI synthesizer, whether a computer or a sound reproduction system; **MPEG (Motion Picture Experts Group)** is a standard for compressing video (including audio) sequences; **MPEG-1** is used for the storage of movies on CD-ROM; **MPEG-2** is for long-distance video transmission over digital communication lines; **WAV (Windows Waveform)** is a format for recording sound digitally. **MIME (Multipurpose Internet Mail Extension)** is a protocol for sending image, audio, and video sequences across the Internet; it can handle images in GIF and JPEG formats, and video in MPEG format.

digital recording A technique of sound recording, developed in the 1970s, in which a series of coded pulses replaces the waveform analogues of earlier methods. The advantages are that tape noise, pitch fluctuations, and distortion are virtually eliminated, as happens in the case of the compact disk and digital audiotape. Developments in the 1990s include digital audio broadcasting, a high-quality transmission system for radio; the digital compact cassette, a format for tape cassettes; and the digital video disk (DVD; originally, digital versatile disk), a disk similar to a compact disk, but double-sided and multi-layered, thus vastly increasing storage capacity.

dihydroxybutanedioic acid tartaric acid

Dijon [deezhõ], ancient **Dibio** 47°20N 5°00E, pop (2000e) 153 000. Industrial and commercial city in E France; railway; bishopric; university (1722); cathedral; historic capital of Burgundy; famous for its restaurants and its mustard; centre of wine trade.

dik-dik A dwarf antelope, native to Africa; small (height, up to 40 cm/16 in); large ears, elongate nose; male with short straight horns and pronounced secretory gland in front of eye. (Genus: *Madoqua*, 3 species.)

dikkop [dikop] *thick-knee*

dilatation and curettage (D and C) [dilatayshn, kyooretij] A gynaecological operation to investigate the cause of menstrual disorders and possible carcinoma of the uterus. A special type of scoop (*curette*) is passed through the dilated cervix into the uterine cavity. Tissue lining the cavity is removed and examined microscopically.

dill An aromatic annual (*Anethum graveolens*), growing to 60 cm/2 ft, native to India and SW Asia; leaves feathery; flowers yellow; fruit ellipsoid, strongly compressed, dark brown with a paler wing. It is cultivated as a culinary herb. (Family: Umbelliferae.)

Dillane, Stephen, originally **Stephen Delaney** (1958–) Actor, born in London. In 1999 he won the Evening Standard Theatre Award for Best Actor in *The Real Thing*, and after its transfer to Broadway the Tony Award for Best Actor (2000). His feature films include *Welcome to Sarajevo* (1997), *The Hours* (2002), and *King Arthur* (2004).

Dillinger, John (Herbert) [dilinjer] (1903–34) Gangster, born in Indianapolis, IN. He specialized in armed bank robberies, terrorizing Indiana and neighbouring states (1933–4). He was shot dead by FBI agents in Chicago.

Dillon, Matt (1964–) Film actor, born in Larchmont, NY. His first major film role was in Francis Ford Coppola's *The Outsiders* (1983). Later films include *Beautiful Girls* (1996), *City of Ghosts* (2002), *Crash* (2005, Best Supporting Actor Oscar nomination), and *You, Me and Dupree* (2006).

DiMaggio, Joe [dimajioh], popular name of **Joseph (Paul) DiMaggio**, nicknames **Joltin' Joe** and **the Yankee Clipper** (1914–99) Baseball player, born in Martinez, CA. He spent his entire career with the New York Yankees (1936–51), holding the record for hitting safely in 56 consecutive games (1941). His second wife was the film star, Marilyn Monroe.

Dimbleby, David (1938–) Broadcaster, born in London, the son of Richard Dimbleby. Since the 1970s he has become a leading presenter and interviewer on BBC television current-affairs programmes, such as *Panorama* and *Election and Results*, and is also chairman of the BBC's *Question Time* (from 1994). In 2005 he presented the series *A Picture of Britain* and wrote the accompanying book.

Dimbleby, Jonathan (1944–) Broadcaster, writer, and journalist, born in London, the son of Richard Dimbleby. Well known as a presenter of television current-affairs documentaries (1972–88), he regularly fronts programmes on major national events. His controversial 'official' biography of the Prince of Wales appeared in 1994.

Dimbleby, Richard (Frederick) (1913–65) Broadcaster, born in Richmond on Thames, Greater London. He became the BBC's first foreign correspondent and its first war correspondent. In the post-war era, he established himself as a magisterial TV anchorman on *Panorama*, and a commentator on major events.

dimer [diymer] A compound formed when two units (**monomers**), react together either by addition or by condensation.

dimethylpropane *pentane*

diminished responsibility A limited defence to a charge of murder which reduces the crime to one of manslaughter (England and Wales) or culpable homicide (Scotland), thereby avoiding the mandatory sentence of life imprisonment. It relates to a state of mind which substantially impairs a person's mental responsibility and which, while not amounting to insanity, borders on it.

diminishing returns, law of A prediction in economics that, as more capital and labour is put into a factory, the resulting increases in output will eventually start to get smaller. Ultimately the average output per unit of labour or capital will also fall.

Dinaric Alps [dinarik], Serbo-Croatian **Dinara Planina**, Ital **Alpi Dinariche** Mountain range following the Adriatic coast of Croatia and NW Albania; rises to 2522 m/8274 ft at Durmitor.

d'Indy, (Paul Marie Théodore) Vincent [dãdee] (1851–1931) Composer, born in Paris. His works include several operas and orchestral pieces, notably *Symphonie sur un chant montagnard français* (1886, Symphony on a French Mountaineering Song).

dingo An Australian subspecies of domestic dog (*Canis familiaris dingo*), descended from dogs introduced thousands of years ago with aboriginal settlers; tawny yellow; cannot bark; eats kangaroos (and now rabbits and sheep); viewed as a pest.

Dinka E Sudanic-speaking transhumant cattle herders of the Upper Nile in the Sudan Republic.

dinoflagellate [diynohflajeluht] A microscopic, single-celled organism classified either as an alga (Class: Dinophyceae) or as a flagellate protozoan (Phylum: Mastigophora); characterized by two whip-like organelles (*flagella*); most species enclosed in a rigid shell (*test*) encrusted with silica.

dinosaur A member of a group of reptiles (Subclass: Archosauria) that dominated life on land for 140 million years from the late Triassic period until their extinction at the end of the Cretaceous period, 64 million years ago. There are over 800 species of dinosaurs, all sharing the specialized kind of hip joint that allowed upright posture. They fall into two contrasting groups: the **reptile-hipped dinosaurs** (Order: Saurischia), and the **bird-hipped dinosaurs** (Order: Ornithischia). Many attained great size. *Diplodocus* reached a length of 28 m/90 ft but weighed only 10 tonnes, whereas *Apatosaurus* was shorter at 25 m/80 ft, but weighed 30 tonnes. These giants were slow-moving (3–4 kph/2–2½ mph), probably lived in herds and were warm-blooded. Dinosaurs laid eggs, often on a nest mound of mud, and there is evidence that some protected their young. The reason for their extinction is unknown, but a combination of climatic changes and competition from mammals in the changing conditions seems most probable. A widely promulgated theory is that the climatic changes came about as the result of a meteoritic impact.

Dinosaur Provincial Park A provincial park in Alberta, SW Canada; a world heritage site. In the early 20th-c the fossil remains of some 60 different species of dinosaur were discovered here.

Dio Cassius [diyoh kasius], also found as **Dion Cassius** and **Cassius Dio Cocceianus** (c.150–c.235) Roman senator and prominent man of affairs, from Bithynia in Asia Minor, who wrote a comprehensive history of Rome in Greek, extending from the foundation of the city down to his own day (229).

Diocletian [diyokleeshn], in full **Gaius Aurelius Valerius Diocletianus** (245–316) Roman emperor (284–305), a Dalmatian of humble birth, born in Diocles, who became the greatest of the soldier emperors of the 3rd-c. In 286 the Empire was split in two, with Diocletian retaining the East, and Maximian taking the West. Later, he divided the Empire into four.

diode An electronic valve having two electrodes (an anode and a cathode); invented in 1904 by British physicist John Ambrose Fleming. It permits current flow in only one direction, and is thus widely used as a rectifier, changing alternating current (AC) into direct current (DC).

Diogenes of Sinope [diyojeneez] (c.410–c.320 BC) Cynic philosopher, born in Sinope, Pontus. His unconventional behaviour, which became legendary in antiquity (eg looking with a lantern in daylight for an honest man), was intended to portray the ideal of a life lived according to nature.

Diomedes [diyohmeedeez] or **Diomede** A Greek hero who fought in the Trojan War, even taking on the gods in battle; also a wise counsellor, the partner of Odysseus in various schemes.

Dione [diyohnee] The fourth natural satellite of Saturn, discovered in 1684; distance from the planet 377 000 km/234 000 mi; diameter 1120 km/700 mi; orbital period 2·737 days; heavily cratered.

Dionne, Cécile, Yvonne, Annette, Emilie, and **Marie** [deeon] (1934–) Quintuplets successfully delivered to their French-Canadian parents, Oliva and Elzire Dionne in N Ontario, Canada. As the first documented quintuplets to survive, they soon became international celebrities. Emilie died in 1954, Marie in 1970, and Yvonne in 2001.

Dionysius of Halicarnassus [diyoniysius] (1st-c BC) Influential Greek critic, historian and rhetorician, from Halicarnassus in Asia Minor, who lived in Rome at the time of Augustus. Much of his writing survives, including about half of his masterpiece, the *Early Roman History*.

Dionysius the Areopagite [diyoniysius, ariopagiyt] (1st-c) Greek Church leader, one of the few Athenians converted by the apostle Paul (*Acts* 17.34). Tradition makes him the first Bishop of Athens and a martyr.

Dionysius the Elder [diyoniysius] (c.431–367 BC) Tyrant of Syracuse (405–367 BC) and ruler of half of Sicily. His reign was dominated by warfare with the Carthaginians. A patron of the arts, he invited Plato to his court.

Dionysius the Younger [diyoniysius] (c.397–? BC) Tyrant of Syracuse (367–357/6 BC, 347/6–344 BC), the son and successor of Dionysius the Elder. Groomed by Plato as a potential philosopher-king, he turned out to be a rake and an oppressor.

Dionysus or **Dionysos** [diyoniysus] In Greek mythology, the god of wild and uncontrolled ecstasy; later, more specifically, the god of wine, associated with music and dramatic festivals. He is the son of Zeus and Semele.

Diophantus [diyofantus] (c.200–c.284) Greek mathematician, who flourished in Alexandria c.250. Of his three known works, only six books of *Arithmetica*, the earliest extant treatise on algebra, have survived.

dioptre / diopter [diyopter] In optics, the power of a lens; symbol *dpt*; defined as 1 divided by focal length in metres; used mostly in optometry.

Dior, Christian [deeaw(r)] (1905–57) Fashion designer, born in Granville, Normandy. He founded his own Paris house in 1945, and in 1947 achieved worldwide fame with his long-skirted 'New Look'. His later designs included the 'H' line and the 'A' line.

dioxin (**tetrachlorodibenzo-*p*-dioxin**, or **TCDD**) A highly toxic contaminant of the chlorophenoxy group of herbicides whose level is currently regulated at 0·1 parts per million or less. It causes a severe form of skin eruption (*chloracne*), and in laboratory animals causes cancer and damages the fetuses of mothers exposed to it.

diphtheria A disease caused by *Corynebacterium diphtheriae*. The bacterium infects the nose and throat, and occasionally wounds on the skin. The illness is severe and potentially lethal. In the West, better standards of living and the use of a vaccine have led to a dramatic fall in incidence.

diphthong A vowel in which there is a change in auditory quality during a single syllable, as in *my*, *how*. The term is also used for a sequence of two written vowels within the same syllable, eg *fear*, *weight*.

Diplodocus [diplodokus] A semi-aquatic, long necked dinosaur; body length up to 28 m/92 ft, including an extremely long, whip-like tail; plant-eating; four-legged, hindlimbs longer than forelimbs; known from the Upper Jurassic period of North America and Europe. (Order: Saurischia.)

diplomatic service The body of public servants who are official representatives of their country in another country, or who provide support to them.

diplopia *double vision*

Diplopoda [diplopoda] *millipede*

Dipnoi [dipnoy] A subclass of bony fishes, comprising the lungfishes.

dipper A starling-like bird, native to mountains of Eurasia and the W New World; inhabits fast-flowing streams; swims underwater using wings. (Genus: *Cinclus*, 4 species. Family: Cinclidae.)

Diprotodon [diyprohtodon] A heavily built, fossil marsupial known from the Pleistocene epoch of Australia; large, up to 2 m/6½ ft tall at the shoulder; front legs short; plant-eating. (Order: Diprotodonta.)

Diptera [diptera] *fly*

diptych [diptik] A picture consisting of two panels, hinged like the pages of a book. Small portable devotional pictures and altarpieces sometimes took this form in the late Middle Ages.

Dirac, Paul A(drien) M(aurice) [dirak] (1902–84) Physicist, born in Bristol, SW England. His main research was in the field of quantum mechanics, especially the incorporation of special relativity and development of the theory of electron spin. He received the Nobel Prize for Physics in 1933.

direct current *alternating current*

directed energy weapons A technology under investigation for military purposes, using energy sources such as laser beams, particle beams, plasma beams, and microwave beams, all of which travel at the speed of light. Such weapons are regarded as a vital component of the US Strategic Defense Initiative.

Directoire Style A French style of furniture, and women's clothes, strictly belonging to the years 1795–9, but generally used to describe the furniture fashionable between the outbreak of the French Revolution and the introduction of the Empire Style. It was a restrained Neoclassical style strongly influenced by antique Greek art.

Director of Public Prosecutions *Crown Prosecution Service*

Directory The government of the First Republic of France (1795–9), established in the Thermidorian reaction to the Reign of Terror, with two legislative houses and a Council of five executive Directors. It was overthrown by the coup of 18 Brumaire (9–10 Nov 1799), bringing Napoleon to power.

dirigible A cigar-shaped, steerable, rigid-framed, fabric-covered airship. It is fitted with horizontal engines driving propellers which provide the forward thrust.

disaccharide [diysakariyd] A carbohydrate consisting of two simple sugars joined together, condensed with the elimination of water. The most abundant in nature are *sucrose* (table sugar) which combines one glucose and one fructose molecule, and *lactose*, the sugar of milk, which is a combination of glucose and galactose. Fructose, glucose, and galactose are single-unit sugars, classed as **monosaccharides**.

disarmament Arms control which seeks to promote international security by a reduction in armed forces and/or weapons. General (ie applies to all countries) and comprehensive (ie applies to all categories of forces and weapons) disarmament was first attempted in the 1920s by the League of Nations, and by the United Nations in the 1950s, but such moves have not been successful. Disarmament is therefore limited to agreements between two or a few countries, and restricted to particular classes of weapons and troop levels. Problems arise in determining equivalences between different types of weapons held by different countries, and in verifying arms reduction treaties, especially in respect of nuclear weapons.

discant *descant*

discount house 1 In the UK, financial institutions which buy short-dated government stock (Treasury Bills) with money borrowed from commercial banks for very short periods. The difference between the borrowing rate and the lending rate provides the discount house with its profit.

2 In the USA, a retail store which sells goods at a lower (**discounted**) price than is standard practice. When the use of the house is available only to members of a particular group (eg a trade union), it is a **closed-door discount house**. Such stores have also developed in other consumer countries, though not always with this label.

Discovery programme A NASA programme of Solar System exploration missions of relatively low cost and payload mass similar in nature to the astrophysics Explorers. **Discovery 1** Mars Pathfinder, launched Dec 1996, landed Jul 1997. **Discovery 2** NEAR (Near Earth Asteroid Rendevous mission), renamed NEAR-Shoemaker, launched Feb 1996, encountered 433 Eros Feb 2000. **Discovery 3** Lunar Prospector, launched Jan 1998, low polar orbits of Moon then controlled impact, Jul 1999. **Discovery 4** Stardust, launched Feb 1999 with encounter in Jan 2004; capsule containing particles and dust samples from Comet Wild-2 [pronounced: vilt] returned to earth, Jan 2006. **Discovery 5** Genesis, launched Aug 2001, solar wind samples returned to Earth Sep 2004, capsule damaged on re-entry but contents not lost. **Discovery 6** Contour, tour of three comet nuclei launched Jul 2002, but lost soon after. **Discovery 7** Deep Impact, made rendezvous with comet P/Tempel 1, Jan 2004–Aug 2005. **Discovery 8** Messenger, to orbit Mercury, scheduled 2004–8;. **Discovery 9** Dawn, to visit the two oldest and most massive asteroids in the Solar System, 4 Vesta and 1 Ceres, 2006–2010 (for Vesta) and 2014 (for Ceres). **Discovery 10** Kepler survey, to look for planets around stars, launch scheduled for 2008.

discus throw An athletics field event using a circular disc of wood with metal plates, weighing 2 kg/4·4 lb for men and 1 kg/2·2 lb for women. The competitor throws the discus with one hand from within the confines of a circle 2·5 m/8·2 ft in diameter, with the aim of achieving a greater distance than anyone else. The current world record for men is 74·08 m/243 ft, achieved by Jürgen Schult (Germany) in 1986; for women it is 76·80 m/251 ft, achieved by Gabriele Reinsch (Germany) in 1988.

diseconomies *externalities*

disequilibrium A situation in which the plans made by various individuals and firms are mutually inconsistent. Firms may, for example, be planning to sell more carpets than customers are planning to buy. Inconsistent plans cannot all be carried out, and as a result some will be changed. An accumulation of unsold carpets will cause firms either to cut production or reduce prices. Disequilibrium is usually widespread in the world economy. *Comparative statics* is the part of economics which considers what would constitute a new equilibrium after any change. *Dynamics* is the part of economics which considers the process of change, and examines whether this will lead to an equilibrium.

dish In telecommunications using microwaves, an antenna having a concave reflecting surface which acts as a secondary radiator to concentrate the signal on the main pick-up element. In television broadcasting by satellite, the main transmission dish is 2–3 m/6–10 ft in diameter, but for domestic reception 30 cm/12 in may be sufficient.

disinfectant A material toxic to bacteria. Phenol (carbolic acid) was one of the earliest used, but is also toxic and corrosive to humans. Phenol derivatives are, however, used in chemical toilets.

disintermediation The practice of companies borrowing directly from the public rather than from financial intermediaries such as banks. This has the advantage of saving the administrative costs and profit margins of financial intermediaries. Disintermediation is used mainly by large firms, with good reputations and names which are household words.

disk *magnetic disk*

disk operating system *DOS*

dislocation (medicine) The displacement of a bone from its joint with another bone by force. Ligaments within or around the affected joint (*capsule*) binding adjacent bones together are torn or otherwise damaged. Most dislocations can be restored manually.

dislocation (physics) *crystal defects*

Disney, Walt(er Elias) (1901–66) Artist, motion-picture animator, and film producer, born in Chicago, IL. After World War 1, he set up a small studio with the artist U B Iwerks (1901–71) in which he produced animated cartoons, his most famous character being Mickey Mouse (1928), for whom he provided the original voice. His first full-length coloured cartoon film was *Snow White and the Seven Dwarfs* (1937). This was followed by *Pinocchio* (1940), *Dumbo* (1941), and *Fantasia* (1940). In 1948 he began his series of coloured nature films, including *The Living Desert* (1953). He also directed several films for young people, such as *Treasure Island* (1950), and family films such as *Mary Poppins* (1964). In 1929 the **Walt Disney Company** was founded, a US corporation that became the best-known distributor of child and adult entertainment in the 20th-c. The company opened **Disneyland**, the first of several family amusement parks, in California in 1955, and others followed in Florida (1971), and Paris (1992). His studios are still highly active, making feature films for cinema and television. The studio made cinematographic history in 1995 with *Toy Story*, the first full-length computer-animated cartoon film. In 2003, worldwide celebrations marking the 75th birthday of cartoon legend Mickey Mouse were led by the Disney Company.

Dispersion *Diaspora*

Disraeli, Benjamin, 1st Earl of Beaconsfield [dizraylee, bekuhnsfeeld] (1804–81) British statesman and twice prime minister (1868, 1874–80), born in London, the eldest son of an anglicized Jew, and baptized in 1817. He made his early reputation as a novelist, and is especially known for his two political novels, *Coningsby* (1844) and *Sybil* (1846). He came to prominence as a critic of Peel's free trade policies, and was Chancellor of the Exchequer in Derby's minority governments of 1852, 1858–9, and 1866–8, when he piloted the 1867 Reform Bill through the Commons. He became prime minister on Derby's resignation in 1868, but was defeated in the general election. During his second administration, Britain became half-owner of the Suez Canal (1875), and the queen assumed the title Empress of India (1876).

Dissenters Christians who separate themselves from the established Church or general religious belief of a country. In a wider sense, it is applied to those who dissent from the very principle of an established or national Church.

dissidents People who oppose the particular regime under which they live, often through peaceful means, and who as a result suffer discrimination and harassment from the authorities. They tend to take a moral rather than an overtly political stance in their opposition.

distalgesic [distaljeezik] The trade name of co-proximol, a compound of dextropropoxyphene hydrochloride and paracetamol, which is used to treat pain. Dextropropoxyphene is a morphine-like drug, but is less potent.

distance education Teaching people, usually at home or in their place of work, by means of correspondence units, radio, cassettes, telephone, television, or microcomputer, rather than through face-to-face contact. Often a tutor may be involved to give advice or mark written work, either at a distance or through occasional meetings.

distemper A viral disease of the dog (**canine distemper**) and ferret families, which may also spread to the seal family. It is a life-threatening disease, characterized by attacks of catarrh and severe neurological signs, such as fits. Vaccination is very effective.

Distinguished Flying Cross (DFC) In the UK, a decoration instituted in 1918, awarded to officers and warrant-officers in the RAF for acts of gallantry performed on active service. The ribbon is violet and white (equal diagonal stripes).

Distinguished Service Cross (DSC) In the UK, a decoration awarded to warrant officers and officers below the rank of captain in the Royal Navy for acts of gallantry or devotion to duty. The ribbon has equal stripes: black, white, black.

Distinguished Service Order (DSO) A military award in the UK, founded in 1886, to recognize special service by officers of the army, navy, merchant navy, and airforce. The ribbon is red edged with blue.

distortion (lens) *aberrations* **1**

district attorney In the USA, the state or county prosecutor, who acts on information supplied by the police or a member of the public, and decides whether to initiate a prosecution; also called a **public prosecutor**, when employed by local government; an **attorney general**, when employed by the state; and a **US attorney**, when working federally.

District of Columbia pop (2000e) 572 100; area 174 km²/67 sq mi. Federal district in E USA, co-extensive with the city of Washington; established 1790–1 from land taken from Maryland and Virginia.

dittany An aromatic herb (*Dictamnus albus*), native to Europe; flowers 4-petalled, purple or white. It gives off a highly inflammable volatile oil, which in hot conditions can ignite and burn without harming the plant; hence its alternative name, **burning bush**. (Family: Rutaceae.)

diuretics [diyuretiks] Drugs which increase the production of urine, used in the treatment of fluid retention, heart failure, and high blood pressure. Certain other substances also have a diuretic effect, such as coffee.

diver A large diving bird native to N waters of the N hemisphere; plumage with fine contrasting patterns, usually black and white; also known in the USA as the **loon**. (Genus: *Gavia*, 5 species. Family: Gaviidae.)

diverticulosis A disorder of the large bowel that affects older people. Small pouches form in the lining of the bowel that penetrate the muscle coat of the gut at points of weakness.

divertimento A light musical composition. Mozart and his contemporaries wrote divertimentos in five or more movements for an ensemble of soloists.

dividend An allocation of the profits of an enterprise to its shareholders. Companies may pay out all profits as dividends, retain a proportion, or pay out nothing. There is no legal obligation to pay; the distribution depends on the level of profits and the company's financial needs. Dividends are also sometimes paid, out of reserves accumulated from past profits, when there have been no profits, but management is confident about the future, and wishes to retain the confidence of the public and shareholders.

divination A term applied to several traditional methods of attempting to acquire information by alleged paranormal means. The information to be interpreted is conveyed by some physical source, such as dowsing or palm reading.

Divine Right of Kings The concept of the divinely-ordained authority of monarchs, widely held in the mediaeval and early modern periods. It is often associated with the absolutism of Louis XIV of France and the assertions of the Stuarts.

diving Any method of descending under water. The most common form at competitive level is by jumping from an elevated board into a swimming pool. Springboard events take place from a board 3 m (9 ft 10 in) above the water; platform diving is from a rigid board 10 m (30 ft 5 in) above the water.

Divisional Court A court in England and Wales presided over by at least two judges from a division of the High Court. One of its functions is to hear certain appeals.

Divisionism In painting, a technique (sometimes called **Pointillism**) whereby small patches or spots of pure colour are placed close together so that they mix in the eye of the beholder. It was developed by some of the French Postimpressionists, notably Seurat, and designated **Neoimpressionism** by the French critic Félix Fénéon (1861–1944).

divorce The termination by court order of a valid marriage, the criteria for which vary greatly between countries and jurisdictions. English courts now recognize only one ground for divorce: the irretrievable breakdown of marriage. In England and Wales, the Family Law Act (1996) which reformed the law on divorce, is being implemented gradually; its aim is to remove the acrimony of divorce proceedings by banishing the idea of fault. No divorce will be made until the welfare of the children and financial arrangements have been settled. After a *Statement of Marital Breakdown* is filed a period of 9 to 15 months follows with the emphasis on reconciliation; if this fails a *Divorce Order* is applied for replacing the old decrees nisi and absolute. Most US jurisdictions recognize no-fault divorce based on incompatibility, irreconcilable differences, living separate and apart for a fixed time (usually 1–3 years), or mutual consent to divorce; however, the grounds for divorce vary considerably.

Diwali [deewahlee] The Hindu festival of lights, held in October or November (Asvina K 15) in honour of Rama, an incarnation of the god Vishnu, and Lakshmi, goddess of wealth and luck; lamps are lit and gifts exchanged. Diwali is also a Sikh and a Jain religious festival.

Dix, Dorothea (Lynde) (1802–87) Humanitarian, born in Hampden, ME. She was largely responsible for the emergence of the concept of mental illness in the USA, and for the establishment of mental hospitals there. In 1861 she became superintendent of women nurses for the federal government, overseeing some 2000 women who cared for the Union war-wounded.

Dixieland A style of jazz associated with the 'classic' New Orleans school, and especially with white musicians who based their music on that of the Original Dixieland Jazz Band in the early 1920s.

Djakarta *Jakarta*

Djem, el- [el jem] The world's most intact example of a Roman amphitheatre, situated in the present-day village of el-Djem in W Tunisia; a world heritage monument. It had a capacity for 35 000 people.

Djemila [jemila] The former Roman garrison of Cuicul in N Algeria; a world heritage site. Founded in the late 1st-c AD, the ruins include temples, forums, thermal baths, and Christian basilicas.

Djibouti (city) [jibootee] 11°36N 43°08E, pop (2000e) 380 600. Free-port capital of Djibouti, NE Africa; built 1886–1900 in Arab style; official port of Ethiopia, 1897; airport.

Djibouti (country) *p.275*

DNA or **deoxyribonucleic acid** *p.276*

DNA profiling A biochemical process used both to determine paternity and to identify criminals from human material (eg blood, hair, skin) left at the scene of a crime; developed in 1986 by Alec Jeffreys of Leicester University, UK. The process involves isolating DNA patterns using enzymes to break up the sample before passing an electric current through the material and exposing it to X-ray film, eventually producing an *autorad*, or DNA profile. This profile is thought to be as distinctive as fingerprints.

Dnepr, River [dneeper], Eng **Dnieper**, ancient **Borysthenes** River in W Russia, rising in the S Valdayskaya Vozvyshennost range; enters the Black Sea at Kherson; length, c.2200 km/1400 mi; third longest river in Europe.

Djibouti

Status Republic

Date of independence 1977

Capital Djibouti

Language Arabic (official)

Ethnic groups Somali (47%), Afar (20%), Arab (mostly Yemeni) (6%), European (4%), other refugees (10%)

Religions Muslim (94%), Christian (Roman Catholic 4%, Protestant 1%, Orthodox 1%)

Physical features Located in NE Africa; series of plateaux dropping down from mountains to flat, low-lying, rocky desert; fertile coastal strip around the Gulf of Tadjoura; highest point, Moussa Ali, rising to 2020 m/6627 ft in the N.

Climate Semi-arid climate, with hot season (May–Sep); very high temperatures on coastal plain all year round; average temperatures 26°C (Jan), 36°C (Jul); slightly lower humidity and temperatures in interior highlands; low rainfall; average annual rainfall 130 mm/5 in.

Currency 1 Djibouti Franc (DJF) = 100 centimes

Economy Crop-based agriculture possible only with irrigation; livestock-raising among nomadic population; some fishing on coast; port of Djibouti provides an important transit point for Red Sea trade, particularly for Ethiopia; small industrial sector.

GDP (2002e) $619 mn, per capita $1300

Human Development Index (2002) 0.445

History French colonial interest in mid-19th-c; annexed by France as French Somaliland, 1896; French Overseas Territory, following World War 2; French Territory of the Afars and the Issas, 1967; independence, 1977. Political parties combined in 1979 to form People's Progress Assembly (RPP) as single ruling party; overwhelming majority voted in favour of a multi-party constitution, 1992; governed by a President, a Legislative Chamber, an executive Prime Minister, and a Council.

Head of State
1977–99 Hassan Gouled Aptidon
1999– Ismael Omar Guelleh

Head of Government
1977–8 Abdallah Mohammed Kamil
1978–2001 Barkat Gourad Hamadou
2001– Dileita Mohamed Dileita

□ International Airport

(country) [jibootee], official name **Republic of Djibouti**, Arabic **Jumhouriya Djibouti**

Local name Jumhouriyya Djibouti

Timezone GMT +3

Area 23 200 km²/8958 sq mi

Population total (2002e) 473 000

Dnepropetrovsk [duhnyepropyetrofsk], formerly **Ekaterinoslav** (to 1926) 48°29N 35°00E, pop (2000e) 1 168 000. Port in Ukraine, on R Dnepr; founded in 1783 on the site of a Cossack village; airport; railway; university (1918); cathedral (1830–5); iron and steel centre.

Dnestr, River *Dniester, River*

Dniester, River [dneester], also **Dnestr**, Pol **Dniestr** River in Ukraine and Moldova, rising in the Carpathian Mts; enters the Black Sea, SW of Odessa; length, 1400 km/870 mi.

Doberman(n) pinscher [dohberman pinsher] A breed of dog, developed c.1900 by a German dog-catcher, Herr Dobermann, who crossbred stray dogs, intending to produce the most vicious dog possible; subsequently crossbred with greyhounds and terriers, and now less vicious; large, lean; short brown or black and tan coat; long neck and muzzle.

dobsonfly A large, soft-bodied insect; adult wingspan up to 16 cm/6¼ in, but flight clumsy and fluttering; found near streams. (Order: Megaloptera. Family: Corydalidae, c.200 species.)

Docetism [dositizm] The belief, arising in early Christianity, that the natural body of Jesus Christ was only apparent (Gr *dokeo*, 'appear, seem') and not real, thereby stressing the divinity of Christ and denying any real physical suffering on his part.

dock (botany) A perennial N temperate herb with strong roots; leaves large; flowers tiny; fruit a 3-sided nut enclosed in papery, often reddish valves. (Genus: *Rumex*, c.200 species. Family: Polygonaceae.)

Docklands An area of E London along the R Thames, formerly of great poverty, which attracted new housing and office developments in the 1980s. It includes the Canary Wharf tower, the tallest building in Europe. There is a new Docklands airport, and a railway connecting the area with the City.

Doctors Without Borders *Médecins Sans Frontières*

Doctor Who A science-fiction series first broadcast on BBC television in 1963. Eleven actors have portrayed the character of the Doctor: in the television series these were William Hartnell (1963–6), Patrick Troughton (1966–9), Jon Pertwee (1970–4), Tom Baker (1974–81), Peter Davison (1982–4), Colin Baker (1984–6), and Sylvester McCoy (1987–9). In addition, Peter Cushing appeared as the Doctor in two films for television (1965, 1966), Richard Hurndall appeared in a special production (1983), and Paul McGann starred in a 1996 feature film. A new TV series starring Christopher Eccleston aired in 2005, followed by a second series starring David Tennant (2006–). The series has generated a worldwide cult following, its fans being known as **Whovians**.

DNA (deoxyribonucleic acid)

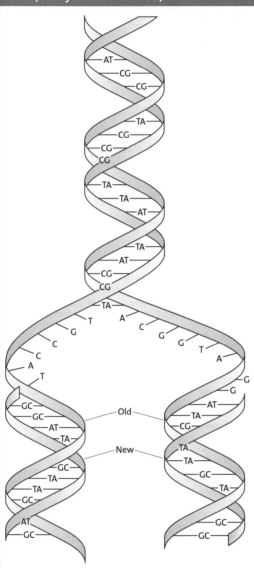

The nucleic acid which occurs in combination with protein in the chromosomes, and which contains the genetic instructions. It consists of four nitrogenous bases (adenine, guanine, thymine, cytosine), a sugar (2-deoxy-D-ribose), and phosphoric acid, arranged in a regular structure. The skeleton of the DNA consists of two chains of alternate sugar and phosphate groups twisted round each other in the form of a double helix; to each sugar is attached a base; and the two chains are held together by hydrogen bonding between the bases. The sequence of bases provides in code the genetic information, which is transcribed, edited, and translated by the RNA. Each diploid human cell nucleus contains approximately 6×10^9 base pairs of DNA, totalling in length about $2\,m/6{\cdot}6\,ft$, but coiled upon itself again and again, so that it fits inside the cell nucleus of less than $10\,\mu m$ in diameter. DNA replicates itself accurately during cell growth and duplication, and its structure is stable, so that heritable changes (mutations) are infrequent. The structure of DNA was discovered by geneticists James Watson and Francis Crick in 1953.

document description language A methodology which enables documents to be handled in a consistent way when being electronically processed, through the use of special codes (*tags*). The first widely used system, **HTML (HyperText Mark-up Language)**, made use of tags indicating which kind of document element (eg main heading, sub-heading, figure caption) a particular section of text happens to be. A browser uses the tags in order to be able to decide how to present the document to the user. **HTTP (HyperText Transfer Protocol)** is a protocol for locating documents stored on the World Wide Web and transferring the documents over the Internet from the Web site to the browser. **XML (Extensible Mark-up Language)** is a development of HTML which allows much more varied elements (eg video sequences) to be built into Web documents for transfer over the Internet.

dodder A parasitic annual reduced to a reddish, thread-like stem bearing clusters of tiny white or pink flowers; native to temperate and tropical regions. The germinating seed produces a short-lived root and a twining stem which moves in search of a host. A wide variety of host plants are attacked, including crop plants. (Genus: *Cuscuta*, 170 species. Family: Convolvulaceae.)

Dodecanese [dohdekaneez], Gr **Sporádhes** area 2000 km²/ 1000 sq mi. Group of 12 main islands and several islets in the SE Aegean Sea, Greece, off SW coast of Turkey; part of Greece since 1947; chief islands include Cos, Patmos, and Rhodes; several major tourist centres.

Dodgson, Charles Lutwidge *Carroll, Lewis*
dodo An extinct bird related to pigeons; native to high forests in Mascarene I, E of Madagascar; turkey-like with large bill and rudimentary wings. Probable dates of extinction were during the 17th–18th-c. (Family: Raphidae, 3 species.)
Dodoma [dohdohma] 6°10S 35°40E, pop (2000e) 270 000. Capital of Tanzania, E Africa; altitude 1120 m/3674 ft; replaced Dar es Salaam as capital in 1974.
Doenitz or **Dönitz, Karl** [doenits] (1891–1980) German naval commander, born in Grünau, Germany. He planned Hitler's U-boat fleet, was made its commander in 1936, and in 1943 became commander-in-chief of the German Navy. Becoming führer on the death of Hitler, he was responsible for the final surrender to the Allies.
dog A carnivorous mammal (*Canis familiaris*), probably evolved from the wolf; first animal to be domesticated; c.400 modern domestic breeds, sometimes classed as *working*, *sporting*, *hound*, *terrier*, *non-sporting*, and *toy*. The name is also used for some mammals of other families (eg the *prairie dog*). The male of several mammal species is called a *dog*, the female a *bitch*, and the young a *pup*. (Family: Canidae.)
dog daisy *ox-eye daisy*
Doge's Palace [dohzh] The residence of the former Doges of Venice. Parts of the structure date from the 12th-c, but the loggias and marble facade are Renaissance additions.
dogfish Small bottom-living shark found from Norway to the Mediterranean; length to 75 cm/30 in, skin very rough; sold in shops as **rock eel**, **rock salmon**, or **huss**.
Dogger Bank A large sandbank forming the shallowest part of the North Sea, c.17–37 m/55–120 ft deep, 250 km/155 mi N of the Norfolk coast, England.
Dogme [dogmuh] A set of rules for the making of feature films. Formulated in the mid-1990s by four Danish film directors, **Lars von Trier** (1956–), **Thomas Vinterberg** (1969–), **Christian Herrring**, and **Soren Kragh-Jacobsen** (1947–) in a document entitled *Dogma 95*, it set out a 'vow of chastity', made up of 10 sections which prescribe strict methods of film-making that run counter to modern cinematic practices. Methods include filming only in real time, always on location, using a hand-held camera and natural light, doing without all superficial action, using the 35 mm format, doing without a musical score, creating the sound at the same time as the images, shooting the film where the story takes place, using no flashbacks, props, or make-up, and not crediting the director on screen.
Dog Star *Sirius*
dogwood A deciduous shrub or small tree (*Cornus sanguinea*), growing to 6 m/20 ft, native to Europe, SW Asia, and North America; leaves turning purple in autumn, veins prominent; flowers small, numerous, in flat-topped clusters; petal-like bracts, white, pink, red; berries black. (Family: Cornaceae.)
Doha [dohha], Arabic **ad-Dawhah** 25°25N 51°32E, pop (2000e) 281000. Seaport capital of Qatar; reclamation of West Bay has created New Doha; airport; university.
Doherty, Peter (Charles) [dokertee] (1940–) Immunologist, born in Brisbane, Queensland, Australia. He shared the Nobel Prize for Physiology or Medicine in 1996 for his contribution to the discovery of how the immune system recognizes virus-infected cells – research which was first reported in 1974.
Dohnányi, Ernst von [dohnanyee], Hung **Ernő** (1877–1960) Composer and pianist, born in Pozsony, Hungary (now Bratislava, Czech Republic). He is best known for his piano compositions, especially *Variations on a Nursery Song*, for piano and orchestra.
Dolby system The first effective and still the most widely used noise reduction system, devised originally for professional tape recording (**Dolby A**) by Dr Ray Dolby (1933–) in the mid-1960s. He adapted the circuitry to a simpler form (**Dolby B**) widely

incorporated in cassette tape players. **Dolby C** followed in the 1980s, giving noise reduction of up to 20 dB and over a wider frequency range.
Dolci, Danilo [dohlchee] (1924–97) Social worker, born in Trieste, Italy. He qualified as an architect, but decided to fight poverty in Sicily, building schools and community centres in the poorest areas. Although not a communist, he was awarded the Lenin Peace Prize in 1956.
Doldrums Traditionally a zone of cloudy, calm conditions, with light, westerly winds associated with low atmospheric pressure. Formerly, sailing ships would often get becalmed in the Doldrums. The word has since passed into general usage to express listless despondency.
Dole, Bob, popular name of **Robert Joseph Dole** (1923–) US Republican politician, born in Russell, KS. A senator for Kansas, and for several years the minority leader in the Senate, he sought the Republican nomination for the presidency in 1980 and 1988. He resigned in 1996 to campaign for the presidency but was defeated by Bill Clinton. His wife, Elizabeth Dole, is also a politician.
Dole, Elizabeth, *née* **Hanford**, popularly known as **Liddy Dole** (1936–) US Republican politician, born in Salisbury, NC. Secretary of Transportation in the Reagan administration (1983–7), and Secretary of Labor under George Bush (1989–90), she became president of the American Red Cross in 1990, but resigned in early 1999 to campaign for the Republican presidential nomination for 2000 (withdrawing in October). She won a Senate seat in the mid-term elections in 2002. She is married to Senator Robert Dole.
dolerite [doleriyt] A medium-grained basic igneous rock, dark-green in colour and composed mainly of plagioclase feldspar and pyroxene crystals. It is the common rock of dykes and sills throughout the world.
dollar ($) A unit of currency in the USA, Canada, Australia, New Zealand, and certain other countries. The US dollar is the world's most important currency. Much international trade is conducted in it, and prices of goods and commodities are often quoted in it. Also, over half the official reserves of countries are held in US dollars.
Dollfuss, Engelbert [dolfoos] (1892–1934) Austrian statesman and chancellor (1932–4), born in Texing, Austria. In 1934 he suspended parliamentary government, drove the socialists into revolt and militarily crushed them. An attempted Nazi putsch in Vienna culminated in his assassination.
dolmen *chambered tomb*
Dolomites [dolomiyts], Ital **Alpi Dolomitiche** Alpine mountain range in NE Italy; limestone formation of jagged outlines and isolated peaks, rising to 3342 m/10 964 ft at Marmolada.
dolphin A small, toothed whale. The name is usually used for species with a long slender snout and streamlined body. Species with less streamlined bodies and blunt snouts are usually called **porpoises** (especially in genera *Phocoena*, *Phocoenoides*, and *Neophocoena*); worldwide. (Family: Delphinidae, c.28 species.)
dolphinarium *aquarium*
dolphinfish Large, predatory, marine fish widespread in tropical and temperate seas; length up to 1·5 m/5 ft, greenish-blue above, underside silver. (Genus: *Coryphaena*. Family: Coryphaenidae.)
Domagk, Gerhard (Johannes Paul) [dohmak] (1895–1964) Biochemist, born in Lagow, Germany. He discovered the chemotherapeutic properties of sulphanilamide, and thus ushered in a new age in chemotherapy. In 1939, on instruction from the German government, he refused the Nobel Prize for Physiology or Medicine.
domain name system The system which enables recognizable names (such as *bbc.co.uk*) to be associated with Internet loca-

Dominica

☐ International Airport

[domineeka], Fr **Dominique**, official name **Commonwealth of Dominica**

Local name Dominica
Timezone GMT -4
Area 751 km²/290 sq mi
Population total (2002e) 71 700
Status Independent republic within the Commonwealth

Date of independence 1978
Capital Roseau
Languages English (official), with French widely spoken
Ethnic groups African or mixed African-European descent (97%), Amerindian (2%)
Religions Christian (Roman Catholic 77%, Protestant 16%)
Physical features Island in the Windward group of the West Indies; c.50 km/30 mi long and 26 km/16 mi wide; rises to 1447 m/4747 ft at Morne Diablotin; volcanic origin; central ridge, with several rivers; 67% of land area forested.
Climate Warm and humid tropical climate; temperatures ranging 25·6–32·2°C; rainy season (Jun–Oct); heavy rainfall, varies from 1750 mm/70 in average on the coast, to 6250 mm/246 in inland.
Currency 1 East Caribbean Dollar (XCD) = 100 cents
Economy Agriculture; tourism; coconut-based products, cigars, citrus fruits (notably limes), bananas, coconuts, bay oil.
GDP (2002e) $380 mn, per capita $5400
Human Development Index (2002) 0·779
History Visited by Columbus, 1493; colonization attempts by French and British in 18th-c; British Crown Colony from 1805; part of Federation of the West Indies, 1958–62; independent republic within the Commonwealth, 1978; governed by a House of Assembly, President, Prime Minister, and Cabinet.

Head of State
1993–8 Crispin Sorhaindo
1998–2003 Vernon Shaw
2003– Dr Nicholas Liverpool

Head of Government
1995–2000 Edison James
2000 Rosie Douglas
2000–4 Pierre Charles
2004– Roosevelt Skerrit

tions (Internet Protocol numbers) that serve as routing addresses on the Internet. It is a directory organized in a hierarchy of levels, with each level separated by a dot. The **top-level domain** is the name which occurs at the top of the Internet domain-name hierarchy – the rightmost element of a domain name. Examples include country codes (eg *uk* in *bbc.co.uk*) or non-geographical generic codes (eg *org* in *www.icann.org*). Most US addresses, for historical reasons, do not end in a country code. Within countries, regional administrators control what **second-level domains** are recognized. These relate to different types of activity, such as *co* for commercial enterprises and *ac* for academic establishments.

Domenichino [domenikeenoh], originally **Domenico Zampieri** (1581–1641) Painter, born in Bologna, Italy. His masterpiece is 'The Last Communion of St Jerome' (1614) in the Vatican.

Dome of the Rock A masterpiece of Islamic architecture completed in AD 691 on Mt Moriah, Jerusalem. The shrine, which is built on an octagonal plan and surmounted by a gilded wooden cupola, encloses the holy rock where, according to tradition, Mohammed ascended to heaven and Abraham prepared to sacrifice Isaac.

Domesday Book [doomzday] The great survey of England S of the Ribble and Tees rivers (London and Winchester excepted), compiled in 1086 on the orders of William the Conqueror; sometimes spelled **Doomsday Book** (though the *dome* refers to houses, not to doom). Information is arranged by county and, within each county, according to tenure by major land-

holders; each manor is described according to value and resources.

domestic fowl A bird kept worldwide for its meat or eggs, also known as the **chicken** or **hen**; domesticated over 5000 years ago. Modern breeds are grouped as **Mediterranean** or **Asian**.

Domingo, Plácido [dominggoh] (1941–) Tenor, born in Madrid. He moved to Mexico with his family, and took his first tenor role in 1960. His vocal technique and acting ability have made him one of the world's leading lyric–dramatic tenors, notably in works by Puccini and Verdi. He received an honorary knighthood in 2002.

Dominic, St (c.1170–1221) Founder of the Order of Friars Preachers, born in Calaruega, Old Castile. His preaching order was approved by Pope Honorius III in 1216. He was canonized in 1234. Feast day 8 August.

Dominica *see panel*

Dominican Republic *p.279*

Dominicans A religious order, officially *Ordo Praedicatorum* (Lat 'Order of Preachers'), abbreviated **OP**; also known as the **Friars Preachers**, **Black Friars**, or **Jacobins**. It was founded by St Dominic in 1215 in Italy to provide defenders of the Roman Catholic Faith, and is devoted mainly to preaching and teaching.

Dominion Day *Canada Day*

Domino, Fats, originally **Antoine Domino** (1928–) Singer, pianist, and composer, born in New Orleans, LA. His cheerful boogie-woogie piano style helped popularize rock-and-roll in the

Dominican Republic

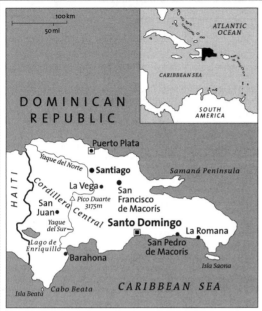

□ International Airport

Span **República Dominicana**
Local name República Dominicana
Timezone GMT -4
Area 48 442 km²/18 699 sq mi
Population total (2002e) 8 833 000
Status Republic

Date of independence 1844
Capital Santo Domingo
Language Spanish (official)
Ethnic groups Spanish, or mixed Spanish and African descent
Religions Roman Catholic (92%), other (mostly Evangelical Protestant and followers of voodoo) (8%)
Physical features Crossed NW–SE by Cordillera Central, with many peaks over 3000 m/10 000 ft; Pico Duarte, 3175 m/10 416 ft is highest peak in the Caribbean; wide coastal plain in E; main rivers include Yaque del Sur, Yaque del Norte, Yuna (E).
Climate Tropical maritime climate with rainy season (May–Nov); Santo Domingo, average temperature 23·9°C (Jan), 27·2°C (Jul); annual rainfall 1400 mm/55 in; hurricanes (Jul–Nov).
Currency 1 Dominican Peso (DOP) = 100 centavos
Economy Mainly agriculture, especially sugar, cocoa; tourism expanding with new resort complexes on N coast.
GDP (2002e) $53·78 bn, per capita $6300
Human Development Index (2002) 0·727
History Visited by Columbus, 1492; Spanish colony, 16th–17th-c; E province of Santo Domingo remained Spanish after partition of Hispaniola, 1697; taken over by Haiti on several occasions; independence from Haiti, 1844, as Dominican Republic; occupied by USA, 1916–24, 1965; comprises 26 provinces and a National District which contains the capital; governed by a President and National Congress (Senate and Chamber of Deputies).

Head of State/Government
1965–6 Héctor García Godoy Cáceres
1966–78 Joaquín Videla Balaguer
1978–82 Antonio Guzmán Fernández
1982–6 Salvador Jorge Blanco
1986–96 Joaquín Videla Balaguer Ricardo
1996–2000 Leonel Fernandez Reyna
2000–4 Hipólito Mejía
2004– Leonel Fernandez

1950s. His songs include 'Blueberry Hill', 'Ain't That a Shame', and 'I'm Walkin''.
dominoes An indoor game which involves the matching of a series of rectangular blocks, with the face of each block divided into two halves, each half containing a number of spots. No two dominoes have the same markings on them. In a double-six set of dominoes, every combination between 6–6 and 0–0 is marked on the 28 dominoes. The object of the basic game is to lay out a sequence (or 'line') of dominoes, each player in turn having to put down a domino of the same value as the one left at either end of the line by a previous player.
Domitian [domishn], in full **Titus Flavius Domitianus** (51–96) Roman emperor (81–96), the younger son of Vespasian, and the last of the Flavian emperors. After the armed revolt of Saturninus (89), he unleashed a reign of terror in Rome which lasted until his own assassination.
Don, River River in SW European Russia, rising SE of Tula; enters the Sea of Azov; length, 1958 km/1217 mi.
Donat, Robert [dohnat] (1905–58) Actor, born in Manchester, Greater Manchester. His many films include *The Thirty-nine Steps* (1935), *Good-bye, Mr Chips* (1939, Oscar), and *The Winslow Boy* (1948).
Donatello [donateloh], originally **Donato di Betto Bardi** (c.1386–1466) The greatest of the early Tuscan sculptors, born in Florence, Italy. He may be regarded as the founder of modern sculpture, as the first producer since classical times of statues complete and independent in themselves. Among his works

are the marble statues of saints Mark and George for the exterior of Or San Michele, Florence.
Donatists [donatists] African Christian schismatics named after Donatus (4th-c), elected as rival to the Bishop of Carthage. The movement was rigorist and puritan, supported rebaptism, and declared invalid the sacraments celebrated by priests suspected of collaboration in times of persecution. Despite condemnation by the Catholic Church (411), it continued until the 7th–8th-c.
Donatus, Aelius [donaytus] (c.300–c.399) Latin grammarian and rhetorician, who taught at Rome AD c.360. His treatises on Latin grammar were in the Middle Ages the only textbooks used in schools, so that 'Donat' in W Europe came to mean a grammar book.
Donau, River Danube, River
Doncaster, ancient **Danum** 53°32N 1°07W, urban area pop (2001e) 286 900. Town in South Yorkshire, N England; founded as a fort 1st-c AD, later an important Roman station on road from Lincoln to York; railway; railway engineering; St Leger Stakes, the oldest horse-race in England (Sep); football league team, Doncaster Rovers; nearby Robin Hood Airport opened 2005.
Donegal [donigawl, donigol], Ir **Dún na nGall** pop (2000e) 130 000; area 4830 km²/1865 sq mi. Scenic county in N Ireland; Slieve Snaght (N) rising to 752 m/2467 ft at Errigal; capital, Lifford; tweed manufacture, agriculture, livestock.
Donegan, Lonnie, originally **Anthony Donegan** (1931–2002)

Singer and guitarist, born in Glasgow, W Scotland. During the 1950s he had success both in Britain and the USA with such songs as 'Rock Island Line' (which launched a skiffle craze), 'Gamblin' Man', and 'Cumberland Gap', and was a widely acknowledged influence on later British guitar-based rock and pop music.

Donetsk [donyetsk], formerly **Stalino** (to 1961), **Yuzovka** (to 1924) 48°00N 37°50E, pop (2000e) 1101000. Industrial city in Ukraine; in the Donbas coal basin; founded, 1870; airport; railway; university (1965).

Dönitz, Karl *Doenitz, Karl*

Donizetti, (Domenico) Gaetano (Maria) [donizetee] (1797–1848) Composer, born in Bergamo, Italy. The work which carried his fame beyond Italy was *Anna Bolena* (1830), and he had several other successes, notably *Lucia di Lammermoor* (1835).

Don Juan [hwan] A legendary figure probably derived from Spanish literature sources. He is a philanderer who has no heart, and whose career is terminated by divine intervention. This comes in the shape of a stone statue, who insists on being Juan's guest and who carries him off to Hell. Mozart's opera uses the Italian name, *Don Giovanni*.

donkey *ass; mule* (zoology)

Donleavy, J(ames) P(atrick) (1926–) Writer, born in New York City. His first novel, *The Ginger Man* (1955), was hailed as a comic masterpiece. Among his other works are *A Singular Man* (1963), *The Onion Eaters* (1971), and *The Wrong Information is Being Given Out at Princeton* (1997). He has been an Irish citizen since 1967.

Donne, John [duhn] (?1572–1631) Poet and priest, born in London. Originally a Roman Catholic, he joined the established Church, becoming Dean of St Paul's, where his sermons were extremely popular. His creative years fall into three periods. The first (1590–1601) was a time of passion and cynicism, as seen in his *Elegies* and *Songs and Sonnets*; the second is represented by his *Anniversaries* and funeral poems; and his third includes a wide range of sonnets and hymns.

Doohan, Mick [dooan], popular name of **Michael Doohan** (1965–) Motor-cyclist, born in Brisbane, Queensland, Australia. He first raced in 1984, and won 54 Grand Prix before retiring from riding after a serious accident in 1999. He won five successive 500 cc world championships (1994–8), and set a new record for the number of wins in a season (12) in 1997.

Doolittle, Hilda, pseudonym **H D** (1886–1961) Poet, born in Bethlehem, PA. She lived in London from 1911, and became an exponent of Imagism. Her books of poetry include *Sea Garden* (1916) and *Hymen* (1921).

Doomsday Book *Domesday Book*

dopamine [dopameen] A chemical compound (*catecholamine*) widely distributed in the brain and peripheral nervous system. The degeneration of certain dopamine-containing brain cells results in Parkinsonism, and is probably also implicated in schizophrenia.

doping In chemistry, adding a controlled amount of an impurity, which can radically change the properties of a substance. For example, the addition of minute quantities of aluminium or phosphorus to silicon will increase its semiconducting properties greatly.

Doppler effect or **shift** The change in wavelength observed when the separation between a wave source and an observer is changing; named after Austrian physicist Christian Doppler (1803–53). The wavelength increases as the source and observer move apart, and decreases as they come closer. The changing tone of passing motor vehicles represents the Doppler shift in sound waves.

Dorado [dorahdoh] (Span 'gilded') A S constellation which includes the Large Magellanic Cloud; also known as 'swordfish' or 'goldfish'.

dorcas gazelle A gazelle (*Gazella dorcas*), native to N Africa and S Asia; light brown with white underparts; dark smudge along flank and along side of face; short backward-curving horns ringed with ridges; also known as **jebeer**.

Dorchester, ancient **Durnovaria** 50°43N 2°26W, pop (2000e) 15800. County town of Dorset, S England; on the R Frome; model for Casterbridge in Hardy's novels; railway; brewing.

Dordogne Eng [daw(r)doyn], Fr [dawrdon], ancient **Durenius** area 9224 km²/3597 sq mi; Department of SW France in the Aquitaine region; capital, Périgueux; popular tourist area.

Dordogne, River Eng [daw(r)doyn], Fr [dawrdon], ancient **Duranius** River in SW France, rising in the Auvergne hills; meets R Garonne to form the Gironde estuary; length 472 km/293 mi.

Dordrecht [daw(r)drekht], also **Dordt** or **Dort** 51°48N 4°39E, pop (2000e) 117000. River port and industrial city in W Netherlands; founded, 1008; Synod of Dort, 1618–19; railway.

Dorians [dawrianz] A sub-group of Hellenic peoples, thought to have migrated into Greece around 1100 BC. Dorian settlements there included Argos, Corinth, and Sparta.

Doric order The earliest of the five main orders of classical architecture, characterized by a fluted shaft and plain capital. It is sub-divided into **Greek Doric** and **Roman Doric**, the former having no base.

dormouse A mouse-like rodent of family Gliridae (10 species); native to Africa, Europe, and C Asia; intermediate between squirrels and true mice; most resemble mice, with long bushy tails.

Dornier, Claude [daw(r)nyer] (1884–1969) Aircraft engineer, born in Kempten, Germany. In 1911 he designed the first all-metal plane. He later made seaplanes and flying-boats, and a twin-engined bomber used in World War 2.

Dors, Diana, originally **Diana Fluck** (1931–84) Actress, born in Swindon, Wiltshire. She made her film debut in *The Shop at Sly Corner* (1946), and became a popular sex symbol in various low-budget comedies. Later films cast her in several good character parts, as in *The Amazing Mr. Blunden* (1972).

Dorset pop (2000e) 682800; area 2654 km²/1024 sq mi. County of S England; bounded S by the English Channel; extensive heathlands and chalk down; county town, Dorchester; Bournemouth and Poole new unitary authorities from 1997; setting for many of Hardy's novels.

Dorsey, Tommy [daw(r)see], popular name of **Thomas Dorsey** (1905–56) Trombonist and bandleader, born in Shenandoah, PA. His big bands were sometimes co-led by his brother **Jimmy Dorsey** (1904–57, alto saxophone, clarinet). The Dorsey Brothers Orchestra existed from 1932 to 1935, reforming again in 1953 until Tommy's death.

Dortmund [daw(r)tmund] 51°32N 7°28E, pop (2000e) 619000. Industrial, mining, and commercial city in Germany; river port in the Ruhr valley, connected to the North Sea by the Dortmund–Ems Canal (272 km/169 mi); railway; university (1966).

DOS [dos] An acronym of **Disk Operating System**, referring to the computer program – part of the operating system – which oversees the communication of data between the computer processor and its magnetic disks, as well as the management of files and programs on the disks.

dose equivalent *radioactivity units*

Dos Passos, John (Roderigo) (1896–1970) Novelist and war correspondent, born in Chicago, IL. His best-known work is the trilogy on US life, *U.S.A.* (1930–6).

Dostoevsky or **Dostoyevsky, Fyodor (Mikhailovich)** [dostoyefskee] (1821–81) Novelist, born in Moscow, the son of a surgeon. Joining revolutionary circles in St Petersburg, he was condemned to death (1849), reprieved at the last moment, and sent to hard labour in Siberia. In 1859 he returned to St Petersburg, where he wrote his masterpiece, *Prestupleniye i nakazaniye* (1866, Crime and Punishment). Other important books are *Idiot* (1868–9, The Idiot) and *Bratya Karamazovy* (1879–80, The Brothers Karamazov).

dot-matrix printer A type of impact printer, where characters are formed by the selection of sets of dots from a rectangular matrix. It is widely used with microcomputer systems, being relatively fast and inexpensive, but it can be noisy. Today the dot-matrix printer has been largely replaced by the ink-jet printer.

Dou or **Douw, Gerard** [dow] (1613–75) Painter, born in Leyden, The Netherlands. His 200 works include his own portrait, 'The Poulterer's Shop' (National Gallery, London) and his celebrated 'Dropsical Woman' (Louvre).

Douai [dooay] 50°22N 3°04E, pop (2001e) 42 600. Town in Nord department, N France; on the R Scarpe; probably a 4th-c Roman fortress; belonged to the counts of Flanders in the Middle Ages, received charter, 1228; passed to the dukes of Burgundy (1384), then to the Spanish Habsburgs (1477); seized by Louis XIV (1667), restored to France by the Peace of Utrecht (1713); Roman Catholic college for English priests founded here (1568) by William Allen for the translation of the Reims–Douai Bible.

Douai Bible [dooay] An early English translation of the Bible by Roman Catholic scholars. The New Testament was first published at Reims in 1582; the Old Testament in 1609. It is sometimes called the **Reims–Douai translation** (the English college at Douai having moved to Reims in 1578).

Douala or **Duala** [dooala] 4°04N 9°43E, pop (2000e) 1 878 000. Seaport in Cameroon, W Africa; capital of German Cameroon, as Kamerunstadt, 1885–1901; present name, 1907; capital of French Cameroon, 1940–6; airport; railway; many import-export companies; centre for petroleum exploration.

double bass The largest and lowest in pitch of the orchestral string instruments. There are two basic types: the first, belonging to the viol family, has sloping shoulders and a flat back; the other, belonging to the violin family, has squarer shoulders and a slightly rounded (sometimes also flat) back. Both types have four strings, tuned in fourths. The strings are often plucked, almost invariably so in jazz and dance music.

double coconut *coco de mer*

double jeopardy The legal doctrine that no person can be convicted twice for the same crime, or for different crimes arising from the same set of facts unless the crimes involve substantially different wrongs. Also, no person having been acquitted of an offence can be subjected to a second trial for the same offence.

double refraction *birefringence*

Doublespeak Awards Mock awards made annually by the National Council of Teachers of English in the USA to those public figures who have used language that is distorted, unfactual, deceptive, evasive, or euphemistic. An example is 'collateral damage', referring to civilians killed in war.

double star A pair of stars that appear close together in our sky when viewed through a telescope. Some pairs are stars at very different distances that merely coincide from our vantage point. If the stars are close enough to be linked through their gravitational attractions, they constitute a binary star.

double vision A weakness or paralysis of one or more of the muscles which move one or other of the eyes, resulting in a failure of the eyes to move together in parallel; also known as **diplopia**. As a result, light from a single object does not fall on comparable parts of the two retinae, and the object appears as two images.

Douglas 54°09N 4°29W, pop (2000e) 23 700. Seaport capital of the Isle of Man; railway; House of Keys, Manx National Museum.

Douglas, Gawain or **Gavin** (c.1474–1522) Poet and bishop, born in Tantallon Castle, East Lothian. His works include *The Palace of Honour* (c.1501) and a translation of the *Aeneid* (finished c.1513), the first to be published in English.

Douglas, Kirk, originally **Issur Danielovitch Demsky** (1916–) Film actor, born in Amsterdam, NY. He began his screen career in 1946, his films including *Champion* (1949), *Lust for Life* (1956), and *Spartacus* (1960), and from the 1970s he also worked as a director.

Douglas, Michael (Kirk) (1944–) US film actor and producer, born in New Brunswick, NJ, the son of Kirk Douglas. He co-produced *One Flew Over the Cuckoo's Nest* (1975), which won five Academy Awards, and won a Best Actor Oscar for his performance in *Wall Street* (1987). Other acting roles include *Fatal Attraction* (1987) and *A Perfect Murder* (1998). Later films include *Traffic* (2000), in which he co-starred with wife Catherine Zeta-Jones (married 2000), and *The Sentinel* (2006). In 2004 he received a Golden Globe Lifetime Achievement Award.

Douglas-Home, Sir Alec *Home of the Hirsel*

Doulton An English firm which began making chimney-pots and large architectural ornaments in London in the first half of the 19th-c. They later became leading art potters renowned for tiles, figures, and decorative panels in faience.

Dounreay [doonray] Former nuclear research station, Caithness, Highland, N Scotland; site of world's first experimental fast-breeder nuclear reactor; decommissioning likely to take until 2033.

Douro, River [dawru], Eng [dooroh], Span **Río Duero** [dwero], ancient **Durius** River of Spain and Portugal; rises in NC Spain, and crosses N Portugal, emptying into the Atlantic near Oporto; used extensively for irrigation and hydroelectric power; length 895 km/556 mi.

douroucouli [doorookoolee] A nocturnal New World monkey (*Aotus trivirgatus*); long tail, large eyes, spherical head; cannot see in colour; moves silently; the only nocturnal monkey; also known as **night monkey**, **night ape**, or **owl monkey**.

dove (ornithology) A bird of the pigeon family. Usually the large-bodied species with rounded tails are called *pigeons*; the smaller-bodied ones with longer slender tails are called *doves*.

Dover (UK), Fr **Douvres**, ancient **Dubris Portus** 51°08N 1°19E, pop (2001e) 104 500. Seaport in Kent, SE England; principal cross-Channel port, the shortest link with France (35 km/21³⁄₄ mi); railway; Dover Castle (13th–14th-c).

Dover (USA) 39°10N 75°32W, pop (2000e) 32 100. Capital of state in C Delaware, USA; founded, 1683; state capital, 1777; city status, 1929; railway; university.

Dowding, Hugh (Caswell Tremenheere) Dowding, Baron (1882–1970) British air chief marshal of World War 2, born in Moffat, Dumfries and Galloway. As commander-in-chief of Fighter Command (1936–40), he organized the air defence of Britain, which resulted in the victorious Battle of Britain (1940).

Dow Jones Index [dow] A statistic showing the state of the New York Stock Exchange, computed on working days by Dow Jones and Co. It enables a measurement to be made of changes in the price of shares of 30 leading US corporations, and is the primary indicator of share price movements in the USA.

Dowland, John (1563–1626) Composer, lutenist, and songwriter, born possibly in Westminster, London. He produced several collections of music, including *Lachrimae* (1605, Tears), which contains some of the finest instrumental consort music of the period.

Down, Ir **An Dun** pop (2000e) 404 000; area 2448 km²/945 sq mi. County in SE Northern Ireland; coastline indented (N–S) by Strangford Lough, Dundrum Bay, and Carlingford Lough; Mourne Mts in the S; rises to 852 m/2795 ft at Slieve Donard; county town, Downpatrick.

Downing Street A street off Whitehall in C London. Of the original terraced houses only numbers 10 (since 1735 the prime minister's official residence), 11 (used by the Chancellor of the Exchequer), and 12 (used by the party whip) remain.

Downing Street declaration A joint agreement between the British and Irish governments, made in 1993, intended to provide the basis of a peace initiative in Northern Ireland. The declaration was made by British and Irish prime ministers John Major and Albert Reynolds, and recommended closer co-operation over Northern Ireland affairs, taking further the initiatives of the 1985 Anglo-Irish agreement.

Downpatrick, Ir **Dun Padraig** 54°20N 5°43W, pop (2000e) 11 000. County town in Down, SE Northern Ireland. St Patrick is said to have landed here in 432; reputed burial place of Saints Patrick, Columbus, and Bridget of Kildare; cathedral (1798–1812).

Downs Low-lying chalk hill ranges rising in Dorset and Hampshire and extending into Surrey, Kent, and East and West Sussex, S England; North Downs rise to 294 m/964 ft at Leith Hill, South Downs to 264 m/866 ft at Butser Hill.

downsizing A term, used by organizations employing computers extensively, which describes the process of changing from the use of very large computers centrally to the use of networks of computer workstations. These workstations are distributed around the organization, possibly as personal computers in individual offices.

Down's syndrome A common congenital abnormality especially liable to affect babies born to mothers over 40 years. Affected individuals have high cheek-bones, a flattened nose, and slanted eyes with a prominent fold over the inner part of either eye. The hands are short and broad with a single palmar crease. There are varying degrees of mental handicap and there may be associated malformations of the heart. The defect stems from a failure of one chromosome of a reproductive germ cell to split in the normal way to form a healthy ovum with 23 chromosomes. The condition is named after English physician J L H Down (1828–96), and is sometimes referred to as **mongolism**.

dowsing A technique in which a held rod, pendulum, or other indicator moves when it is brought near to a certain substance. This technique has been used to search for a wide variety of substances, including water, oil, and mineral deposits. The medical applications date from the 1920s when a French priest, the Abbé Mermet, used a pendulum for diagnosis and to select suitable herbal remedies. Many people believe that detecting the object of dowsing is a supersensory phenomenon, and that the use of an indicator is entirely incidental.

Doyle, Sir Arthur Conan (1859–1930) Writer, the creator of Sherlock Holmes, born in Edinburgh. His first book, *A Study in Scarlet* (1887), introduced the super-observant, deductive Holmes, his good-natured question-raising friend, Dr Watson, and the whole apparatus of detection mythology associated with Baker Street, Holmes's fictional home. After *The Adventures of Sherlock Holmes* was serialized in the *Strand Magazine* (1891–3), the author tired of his popular creation, and tried to kill off his hero, but was compelled in 1903 to revive him.

Doyle, Roddy (1958–) Novelist, born in Dublin. His first success came with *The Commitments* (1987), the first of the internationally acclaimed Barrytown trilogy, which he completed with *The Snapper* (1990) and *The Van* (1991). Later novels include *Paddy Clarke Ha Ha Ha* (1993, Booker), *A Star Called Henry* (1999), *Oh, Play That Thing* (2004), and *Paula Spencer* (2006).

D'Oyly Carte, Richard [doylee kah(r)t] (1844–1901) Impresario and manager, born in London. He built the Savoy Theatre (1881) and the Royal Opera House (1887), and is best known as the first producer of the Gilbert and Sullivan operas.

DRA (Driver Reminder Appliance) *train protection systems*

Drabble, Margaret (1939–) Novelist, born in Sheffield, South Yorkshire. Her novels include *The Radiant Way* (1987), *The Gates of Ivory* (1991), *The Peppered Moth* (2001), and *The Sea*

Lady (2006). She was the editor of the 5th edition of the *Oxford Companion to English Literature* (1985).

Draco (astronomy) [draykoh] (Lat 'dragon') The eighth-largest constellation, a sinuous zone of the N sky.

Draco (law-giver) [draykoh] (7th-c BC) Athenian legislator. His harsh codification of the law in 621 BC has given us the word 'draconian'. With death the penalty of almost every offence, the code was so unpopular that it was largely abolished by Solon (594 BC).

draft *conscription*

dragonet Any of a small family of fishes, widespread in coastal waters of tropical to warm temperate seas; includes European *Callionymus lyra* found from Norway to the Mediterranean; length up to 30 cm/1 ft, body rather flattened, pelvic fins broad, dorsal fin striped blue and yellow in male; gill openings small on top of head, eyes prominent. (Family: Callionymidae.)

dragon-fish Deep-water fish with slender snake-like body; length up to 40 cm/16 in; short head and very long mouth, bearing fang-like jaw teeth; light organs present in rows along underside of body, behind eye, and on long chin barbel that serves as lure to attract prey. (Family: Stomiatidae.)

dragonfly A large, long-bodied insect with two pairs of slender wings held horizontally at rest; large compound eyes enable adults to catch insects in flight. (Order: Odonata. Suborder: Anisoptera.)

dragon-tree An evergreen tree (*Dracaena draco*), native to the Canary Is and Madeira; short, thick branches, bearing clusters of greyish or bluish sword-shaped leaves at the tips; flowers small, greenish-white; berries orange. Red resin exuded by the trunk is known as **dragon's blood**, used in varnish. (Family: Agavaceae.)

drag racing A specialized form of motor racing which is a test of acceleration. Large-engined 'vehicles' with big rear wheels and small front ones race normally two at a time on a 400 m/440 yd straight track, from a standing start. Parachutes are fitted to the machines to help with braking.

Drake, Sir Francis (c.1540–96) Elizabethan seaman, born near Tavistock, Devon. In 1577 he set out with five ships for the Pacific, through the Straits of Magellan, but after his fleet was battered by storm and fire, he alone continued in the *Golden Hind*. He then struck out across the Pacific, reached the Pelew Is, and returned to England via the Cape of Good Hope in 1580. In 1585 he sailed with 25 ships against the Spanish Indies, bringing home tobacco, potatoes, and the dispirited Virginian colonists. In the battle against the Spanish Armada (1588), which raged for a week in the Channel, his seamanship and courage brought him further distinction.

Drakensberg Mountains [draknzberg], Zulu **Kwathlamba** or **Quathlamba** Mountain range in South Africa, highest peak, Thabana Ntlenyana (3482 m/11 424 ft).

dramatherapy The use of drama as a creative medium to help in clarifying and alleviating personal and social problems. As a practice it fuses both artistic and therapeutic skills.

draughts A popular board game played on a standard chessboard containing 64 squares of alternate colours (normally black and white); known as **checkers** in the USA. It is played by two players; each has 12 small, flat, round counters (*pieces*), one set normally being black, the other white. The pieces are lined on alternate squares on the first three rows at either side of the board. The object is to remove your opponent's pieces from the board by jumping over them onto a vacant diagonal square.

Dravidian languages [dravidian] A group of more than 20 languages, spoken mainly in S India. The principal ones are Telugu, Tamil, Kannada, and Malayalam, which together have over 150 million speakers within the S states.

Drayton, Michael (1563–1631) Poet, born in Hartshill, Warwickshire. His best-known works are *England's Heroical Epistles* (1597) and *Poly-Olbion* (1612–22), an ambitious description of the English countryside.

Dr Barnardo's Homes *Barnardo, Thomas John*

dreaming Sensory perceptions experienced during sleep; specifically during the period of sleep associated with rapid movement of the eyes (*REM sleep*). Perceptions are usually visual, but sound, smell, taste, and touch can also be experienced.

Dreamtime or **The Dreaming** In the mythology of the Australian Aborigines, one of the names for the time of the Ancestors, who created the world and are still alive in the sacred places. This time continues to exist, and it may be possible to find it through dreams.

dredger A vessel designed to remove spoil from the seabed in order to maintain or increase the depth in a harbour or approaches. Dredgers are also used to obtain sand and gravel from the seabed for constructional purposes.

Dred Scott decision A ruling by the US Supreme Court in 1857 which made slavery legal in all US territories. Dred Scott was a slave who had been taken by his master from Missouri (a slave state) to Illinois and Wisconsin (both free areas). After returning to Missouri, Scott sued for his freedom on the grounds that by living in a free state he had altered his status. The Missouri Supreme Court overruled a decision by a lower court which had considered Scott to be free, and was eventually supported in its view by the Supreme Court. The decision was an important element in the polarization of opinions which led to the American Civil War.

Dreiser, Theodore (Herman Albert) [dreiyzer] (1871–1945) Writer, born in Terre Haute, IN. His first novel *Sister Carrie* (1900), starkly realistic, was criticized for obscenity. Later works include *Jennie Gerhardt* (1911) and *An American Tragedy* (1925).

Dresden [drezdn] 51°02N 13°45E, pop (2000e) 512 000. City in Germany; close to the Czech frontier; former capital of Saxony; almost totally destroyed by bombing in 1945, now rebuilt; airport; railway; technical university (1828); Dresden china now manufactured in Meissen.

dressage [dresahzh] An equestrian discipline which is a test of the horse's obedience skills, consisting of a series of movements at the walk, trot, and canter. Dressage can have its own competition or form part of a *three-day event*.

Dreyer, John (Louis Emil) [drayer] (1852–1926) Astronomer, born in Copenhagen. He produced the standard catalogue on star clusters, nebulas, and galaxies, the *New General Catalogue* (NGC), which is still in use today.

Dreyfus, Alfred [drayfuhs] (1859–1935) French Jewish army officer, born in Mulhouse, France. Falsely charged with delivering defence secrets to the Germans, he was court-martialled and transported to Devil's I, French Guiana. The efforts of his wife and friends to prove him innocent provoked a vigorous response from militarists and anti-Semites. After the case was tried again (1899), he was found guilty but pardoned, and in 1906 the verdict was reversed. Proof of his innocence came when German military documents were uncovered in 1930.

Dreyfuss, Richard [drayfus] (1947–) Actor, born in New York City. He became well known following his performances in *Jaws* (1975), *Close Encounters of the Third Kind* (1977), and *The Goodbye Girl* (1977, Oscar). Later films include *Postcards from the Edge* (1990), *The American President* (1995), *Silver City* (2004), and *Poseidon* (2006).

drill A baboon (*Mandrillus leucophaeus*), native to W African forests; resembles the mandrill, but smaller, with a black face. Drills live to the N of the Sanaga R in Cameroun; mandrills live to the S.

Drogheda [drouhduh], Ir **Droichead Átha** 53°43N 6°21W, pop (2000e) 25 000. Industrial seaport in E Ireland; Irish parlia-

ments met here until 1494; railway; Battle of the Boyne field (1690) 6 km/3¾ mi SW.

Drogheda, Statutes of *Poynings' Law*

dromedary A camel formerly wild in Arabia (*Camelus dromedarius*), now known only in domestication; comprises 90% of the world's camels; found in hot deserts from N Africa to SW Asia (introduced elsewhere); also known as the **Arabian camel** or **one-humped camel**.

Dromgoole, Dominic (1964–) Theatre director, born in Bristol, SW England. He studied at Cambridge University, and began work as a part-time assistant director at London's Bush Theatre, rising to become artistic director (1990–7). He followed this with a spell at the Old Vic where he directed new plays for Peter Hall's company, and then took over at the Oxford Stage Company (1998–2005). In 2006 he succeeded Mark Rylance as artistic director of Shakespeare's Globe.

drone The male of colonial ants, bees, and wasps, whose only function is to mate with fertile females. It plays no part in brood maintenance. (Order: Hymenoptera.)

drongo A bird native to the Old World tropics; plumage usually glossy black; long forked tail; inhabits woodland. (Family: Dicruridae, 20 species.)

Dronning Maud Land *Queen Maud Land*

dropwort An erect perennial (*Filipendula vulgaris*), growing to 80 cm/30 in, native to Europe, W Asia, and N Africa; roots tuberous; flowers 6-petalled, cream tinged with purple, forming an irregular terminal mass. (Family: Rosaceae.)

Drosophila [drosofila] A genus of brownish-yellow fruit flies with typically red eyes. They lay eggs near fermenting fruit, on which the larvae feed. There are c.2600 species, some of which are economically important pests of fruit. (Order: Diptera. Family: Drosophilidae.)

Droste-Hülshoff, Annette Elisabeth, Freiin (Baroness) **von** [drostuh hülshohf] (1797–1848) Poet, born near Münster, Germany, commonly regarded as Germany's greatest woman writer. Her poetry is mainly on religious themes and on the Westphalian countryside.

drug addiction or **drug dependence** A state whereby an addict habitually takes a drug, the compulsion being fuelled by a continuous need to experience the psychic effect of the particular drug or to avoid the discomfort of its absence. Frequently, addicts need to increase the dose of the drug they are taking to feel the same effect (*drug tolerance*). Addictive drugs include narcotics (eg heroin, cocaine), many types of sedative and tranquillizer, and nicotine.

drug resistance A state in which a patient does not respond to a therapeutic drug. Bacteria may acquire resistance through gene mutation to a particular antibiotic by its overuse or misuse. Cancer cells may also acquire resistance to drugs which had previously been effective, requiring a change in the course of treatment. Similarly, insects and other pests acquire resistance to agents which previously controlled them.

Druids A religious sect among the ancient Celts of pre-Christian Britain and Gaul. They acted as priests, teachers, and judges, taught the immortality of the soul and a doctrine of reincarnation, and it is also thought they offered human sacrifice. They studied ancient verse and natural philosophy, and were expert in astronomy. They were suppressed in Gaul by the Romans, and probably a little later in Britain.

drum A musical instrument consisting of a membrane of skin or plastic (rarely of other materials) stretched over a hollow resonator or frame, usually of wood or metal. Drums are normally played by striking the membrane with a stick or with the hands, and may be classified according to their shape (eg conical, cylindrical, 'hourglass', kettledrums) and whether they have a single membrane or are double-headed.

drumfish Any of a large family of marine and estuarine fishes that have the ability to produce sounds by resonating the swimbladder; also known as **croakers**. (Family: Sciaenidae.)

drumlins Small, streamlined, ice-moulded hills made of till, produced by the pressure of moving ice over glacial deposits. They often occur in groups producing a 'basket of eggs' topography. The shape indicates ice flow direction.

Drummond (of Hawthornden), William (1585–1649) Poet, born at Hawthornden, near Edinburgh. He was the first Scottish poet to write in a form of English not from Scotland. His chief collection, *Poems*, appeared in 1616.

drupe A fleshy fruit in which each of one or more seeds is enclosed by a stony layer.

Druze [drooz] A religious faith which originated during the closing years of the Fatimid caliph al-Hakim (996–1021), whom some extremist Ismailis regarded as a manifestation of the Divinity. The Druze, who survive in parts of Jordan, Lebanon, and Syria, deviate considerably in belief and practice from the main Muslim body. They number c.500 000.

dryad [driyad] In Greek mythology, a being originally connected with oak-trees, but more usually referring to a wood-nymph, living in or among the trees. Dryads were usually friendly, but could frighten travellers.

dry cleaning The cleaning of textiles using organic solvents rather than water. Oil and grease is dissolved by the solvent, so that solid dirt falls away easily.

Dryden, John (1631–1700) Poet, dramatist, and critic, born in Aldwinkle, Northamptonshire. In 1658 he wrote *Heroic Stanzas* in homage to Oliver Cromwell. On the restoration of Charles II, he published *Astraea Redux* (1660) in praise of the new monarch. In 1668 he became poet laureate and in 1670 historiographer royal. Called to defend the king's party, he wrote a series of satires, notably *Absalom and Achitophel* (1681), which did much to turn the tide against the Whigs. To this era also belong the didactic poem *Religio laici* (1682), which argues the case for Anglicanism, and *The Hind and the Panther* (1687), marking his conversion to Catholicism. On the accession of William III (1688), a Protestant, Dryden forfeited his laureateship for refusing to take the oath of allegiance to the king.

dry ice *carbon; sublimation* (chemistry)

Dryopithecus [driyopithekus] A fossil ape abundant in Africa and the Mediterranean region during the Miocene epoch; about the size of a rhesus monkey; walked on all fours; brain gibbon-like; jaw projecting moderately; canine teeth prominent; includes *Proconsul*. (Superfamily: Hominoidea. Family: Pongidae.)

drypoint A method of intaglio printing whereby the metal plate is incised by direct pressure using a steel point. The greatest master was Rembrandt, who often combined drypoint with straightforward etching.

dry rot A serious type of timber decay caused by the fungus *Serpula lacrymans*; infected wood shows a surface growth of white filaments; common on structural timbers of buildings in damp, poorly ventilated conditions. (Subdivision: Basidiomycetes.)

Drysdale, Russell (1912–81) Painter, born in Bognor Regis, West Sussex. His powerful scenes of the outback were a major contribution to modern art in Australia.

DTP *desk-top publishing*

Duala *Douala*

dualism In philosophy, any theory which asserts the existence of two different kinds of thing. The most familiar dualism, held by Plato, Descartes, and many others, is between mind and matter.

Dubai or **Dubayy** [doobiy] pop (2000e) 601 700; area 3900 km²/1505 sq mi. Second largest of the United Arab Emirates; capital, Dubai, pop (1995e) 392 000; oil discovered in 1966.

du Barry, Marie Jeanne Gomard de Vaubernier, comtesse (Countess), *née* Bécu (c.1743–93) The favourite mistress of Louis XV, born in Vaucouleurs, France. Her influence reigned supreme

until the death of Louis in 1774. She was tried before the Revolutionary Tribunal, and guillotined.

dubbing The combination of several separate sound recordings into the final composite sound track for a motion-picture or video production; sometimes known as **mixing**. The term also refers to the operation of replacing spoken dialogue of a completed sound track by its equivalent in another language, producing a **dubbed** version.

Dubček, Alexander [dubchek] (1921–92) Czechoslovakian statesman, born in Uhrovek, Slovakia. He rose to become first secretary in the Communist Party (1968), then introduced a series of far-reaching economic and political reforms. His liberalization policy led to the occupation of Czechoslovakia by Warsaw Pact forces (Aug 1968), and in 1969 he was replaced by Husak. In 1989, following a popular uprising, he was elected chairman of the Czechoslovak Federal Assembly.

Dublin (city), Ir **Baile Átha Cliath**, ancient **Eblana** 53°20N 6°15W, pop (2000e) 485 000. Capital of the Irish Republic; at mouth of R Liffey; on site of Viking settlement; first Sinn Féin parliament met here, 1919; airport; railway; ferries to Liverpool and Holyhead; two universities (1591, 1908); two cathedrals; Dublin Castle, Abbey Theatre.

Dublin (county), Ir **Baile Átha Cliath** pop (2000e) 1 038 000; area 922 km²/356 sq mi. County in E Ireland; Wicklow Mts to the S; capital, Dublin.

Du Bois, W(illiam) E(dward) B(urghardt) [doo boyz] (1868–1963) Historian, sociologist, and equal rights campaigner, born into a small black community at Great Barrington, MA. His writings explored the history and lives of African-Americans, and he helped found the National Association for the Advancement of Colored People.

Dubrovnik [doobrovnik], Ital **Ragusa** 42°40N 18°07E, pop (2000e) 69 500. Port on the Dalmatia coast of Croatia; capital of Dalmatia; earthquake damage, 1979; badly damaged during siege by the Federal Army in the civil war, 1991; airport; car ferries to Italy and Greece; mediaeval town walls surrounding the old town, a world heritage site; cathedral.

Dubuffet, Jean [dübüfay] (1901–85) Artist, born in Le Havre, France. He invented the concept of Art Brut, and is regarded as a forerunner of the Pop Art and Dada-like fashions of the 1960s.

Duccio di Buoninsegna [doochioh dee bwoninsenya] (c.1260–c.1320) Painter, founder of the Sienese School, born in Siena, Italy. His masterpiece is the 'Maestà' for the altar of Siena cathedral (1311).

Duchamp, Marcel [düshã] (1887–1968) Painter, born in Blainville, France. He was associated with several modern movements, including Cubism and Futurism, and was one of the pioneers of Dadaism. He laboured eight years on his best-known work, 'The Bride Stripped Bare by Her Bachelors, Even' (1915–23, Philadelphia).

Duchovny, David (1960–) Actor, born in New York City. He achieved star success when he was given the role of Fox Mulder in the cult TV series *The X-Files* (1993–2002), for which he received a Golden Globe Best Actor award in 1997. His feature films include *Working Girl* (1988), *Beethoven* (1992), *The X-Files: Fight the Future* (1998), and *Full Frontal* (2003).

Duchy of Cornwall The oldest of English duchies, instituted by Edward III in 1337 to provide support for his eldest son, Edward, the Black Prince. Since 1503 the eldest son of the sovereign has inherited the dukedom; it consists of lands (totalling c.52 000 ha/130 000 acres) in Cornwall, Devon, Somerset, and S London, including the Oval cricket ground.

Duchy of Lancaster A duchy created in 1267 by Henry III of England for his son Edmund. It was attached to the Crown in 1399 when the last Duke of Lancaster became Henry IV. The duchy lands consist of some 21 000 ha/52 000 acres of farmland and moorland, mostly in Yorkshire. It is controlled by the Chancellor of the Duchy of Lancaster, a political appointment generally held by a member of the cabinet.

duck A smallish bird (the larger species are called **geese** or **swans**), primarily aquatic, with full webbing between the three front toes; relatively long neck; blunt flattened bill; male has penis (rare in birds). (Family: Anatidae.)

duck-billed platypus A mammal native to E Australia (*Ornithorhynchus anatinus*); length, up to 75 cm/30 in; thick brown fur, soft duck-like bill, short legs with webbed feet, short flattened tail; pouch inside each cheek; male with venomous 'spur' on hind leg; also known as **platypus** or **duck-bill**. (Family: Ornithorhynchidae.)

duck hawk *peregrine falcon*

duckweed A tiny floating or submerged herb found in freshwater everywhere. It consists of a flat or convex green plant-body a few millimetres across, with a groove concealing the flowers on the margin, and roots on the underside. (Genus: *Lemna*, 15 species. Family: Lemnaceae.)

ductless glands *endocrine glands*

Dufay, Guillaume [düfiy] (c.1400–74) Composer, probably born in Cambrai, France. He wrote many motets, such as *Nuper rosarum flores* (1436), Masses, and a large number of secular songs.

Dufourspitze [doofoorshpitsuh], Ital **Punta Dufour** 45°57N 7°53E. Mountain peak in Switzerland; second highest Alpine peak; height 4634 m/15 203 ft.

Dufy, Raoul [düfee] (1877–1953) Artist and designer, born in Le Havre, France. He produced many fabric designs and engraved book illustrations, and (from 1919) a series of calligraphic sketches of seascapes, regattas, and racecourse scenes.

dugong [doogong] A marine mammal (*Dugong dugon*), native to tropical coasts of the Old World; streamlined, with a short broad head; male with short tusks hidden beneath fleshy cheeks; front legs are flippers; hind legs absent; tail with pointed horizontal blades. (Family: Dugongidae. Order: Sirenia.)

Duhamel, Georges [dooamel] (1884–1966) Novelist, poet, and man of letters, born in Paris. His best-known works are his novel cycles *Salavin* (1920–32) and *Chronique des Pasquier* (1933–44, The Pasquier Chronicles).

duiker [diyker] A small African antelope; both sexes with arched back and short horns separated by a tuft of long hairs; two types: the **common** (**grey**, **savanna**, or **bush**) **duiker** (*Sylvicapra grimmia*), and the **forest duiker** (Genus: *Cephalophus*, 16 species).

Duisburg [düsboork] 51°27N 6°42E, pop (2000e) 552 000. Industrial and commercial city in Germany; port on R Ruhr; largest inland port in Europe; badly bombed in World War 2; railway; university (1972); home of Gerhard Mercator.

Duisenberg, Willem (Frederik) [dowsenberkh] (1935–2005) Banker and politician, born in Heerenveen, The Netherlands. He was director of The Netherlandsche Bank, professor of macro-economics at the University of Amsterdam, finance minister in the Den Uyl cabinet (1973–7), and vice-chairman of the Radobank Nederland BV. During 1998–2003 he served as the first president of the European Central Bank.

Dukas, Paul (Abraham) [dükah] (1865–1935) Composer, born in Paris. His best-known work is the symphonic poem *L'Apprenti sorcier* (1897, The Sorcerer's Apprentice). He also wrote several orchestral and piano pieces.

duke In the UK, a nobleman of the highest order. A royal duke is a son of the sovereign who has been given a dukedom, such as Queen Elizabeth's son Andrew, Duke of York.

Dukeries, the Area of NW Nottinghamshire, C England; includes Sherwood Forest and the parks of former ducal seats at Clumber, Thoresby, Welbeck, and Worksop.

dulcimer A type of zither, consisting of a wooden soundbox strung with a variable number of metal strings which pass over (or through) one or more bridges held in place by the pressure of the strings themselves. It is played with hammers of various types.

Dulles, John Foster [duhlez] (1888–1959) US Republican secretary of state (1953–9), born in Washington, DC. In 1945 he advised at the Charter Conference of the UN, thereafter becoming US delegate to the General Assembly. As secretary of state, he opened a vigorous diplomacy of personal conferences with statesmen in other countries.

Duluth [duhlooth] 46°47N 92°07W, pop (2000e) 86 900. Port in NE Minnesota, USA, at the W end of L Superior; established in the 1850s; airfield; railway; major lake port handling grain and iron ore.

duma A political assembly in pre-revolutionary Russia. Municipal dumas (town councils) were introduced as part of local government reforms in 1870. After the 1905 revolution the State Duma, a quasi-parliamentary body, was established with limited constitutional powers. The Duma is also the name given to the lower house of the Russian legislature.

Dumas, Alexandre [dümah], known as **Dumas *père*** ('father') (1802–70) Novelist and playwright, born in Villers-Cotterêts, France. He gained enduring success as a storyteller, his purpose being to put the history of France into novels. Among his best-known works are *Le Comte de Monte Cristo* (1844–5, The Count of Monte Cristo) and *Les Trois Mousquetaires* (1845, The Three Musketeers). In 2005 a further novel, *Le Chevalier de Sainte-Hermine*, discovered in the National Library of France, was published. His son, **Alexandre Dumas** (1824–95), often known as **Dumas *fils***, was also a writer, whose best-known work was *La Dame aux camélias* (1848).

du Maurier, Dame Daphne [dü mohryay] (1907–89) Novelist, born in London, the granddaughter of George du Maurier. She wrote several successful period romances and adventure stories, including *Jamaica Inn* (1936), *Rebecca* (1938), and *The Flight of the Falcon* (1965).

du Maurier, George (Louis Palmella Busson) [dü mohryay] (1834–96) Artist and illustrator, born in Paris. He gained a reputation as a designer and book illustrator, then joined the staff of *Punch* and became widely known as a gentle, graceful satirist of fashionable life.

Dumfries [duhmfrees] 55°04N 3°37W, pop (2000e) 31 000. Market town and administrative centre of Dumfries and Galloway, SW Scotland; railway; Burns's House, Mausoleum.

Dumfries and Galloway pop (2000e) 149 500; area 6370 km²/2459 sq mi. Local government council in SW Scotland; capital, Dumfries; Stranraer linked by ferry to Larne in N Ireland.

Du Mont, Allen B(alcom) [doomont] (1901–65) Electronics engineer, born in New York City. In 1931 he developed cathode-ray tubes for use in oscilloscopes and television. He also invented the radio set's 'magic eye' tuning indicator.

Dunant, (Jean) Henri [dünã] (1828–1910) Philanthropist, born in Geneva. He inspired the foundation of the International Red Cross, brought about the conference at Geneva (1863) from which came the Geneva Convention (1864), and in 1901 shared the first Nobel Peace Prize.

Dunaway, Faye (1941–) Film actress, born in Bascom, FL. Her first starring role was in *Bonnie and Clyde* (1967). Later films include *Chinatown* (1974, Oscar nomination), *Network* (1976, Oscar), *The Thomas Crown Affair* (1999), and *Jennifer's Shadow* (2004).

Dunbar, William [duhnbah(r)] (c.1460–c.1520) Poet, probably born in East Lothian, Scotland. He was a courtier of James IV, who gave him a pension in 1500. His poems include *Lament for the Makaris* and several satires, such as *The Dance of the Sevin Deadly Synnis*.

Dunblane [duhnblayn] Town near Stirling, Perthshire, Scotland, the scene in March 1996 when 16 children and their teacher were killed by gunman Thomas Hamilton, who then killed himself. One of the consequences was a major national movement directed towards the stricter control of firearms, as well as various measures aimed at improving school security.

Duncan I *Macbeth*

Duncan, Isadora, originally **Angela Duncan** (1877–1927) Dancer and choreographer, born in San Francisco, CA. She was one of the pioneers of modern dance, basing her work on Greek-derived notions of beauty and harmony, but using everyday movements such as running, skipping, and walking. Her unconventional views on marriage and women's liberation gave rise to scandal.

Duncan Smith, Iain (1954–) British politician, born in Edinburgh. A former member of the Scots Guards, he joined the Conservative Party in 1981 and was elected MP in 1992, rising to be shadow secretary of state for social security (1997–99) and defence (1999–2001). A die-hard Eurosceptic, he defeated Kenneth Clarke in the contest for leadership of the Conservative Party in 2001, the first such leader to be elected by ordinary party members. In October 2003 he lost a vote of confidence in his leadership following a ballot of Conservative MPs, and was replaced by Michael Howard.

Dundalk [duhndolk], Ir **Dun Dealgan** 54°01N 6°25W, pop (2000e) 30 000. Capital of Louth county, NE Ireland; railway.

Dundee 56°28N 3°00W, pop (2000e) 170 700. Port and (since 1996) local council (Dundee City), E Scotland; royal burgh since 12th-c; airfield; railway; university (1881); Claypotts Castle (1569–88).

Dundee, John Graham of Claverhouse, 1st Viscount, known as **Bloody Claverse** or **Bonnie Dundee** (c.1649–89) Scottish soldier, born of a noble family. Joined by the Jacobite clans, he raised the standard for James against William and Mary, but died from a musket wound after his successful battle against Mackay at the Pass of Killiecrankie.

Dunedin [duhneedin] 45°52S 170°30E, pop (2000e) 119 000. City in Otago, SE South Island, New Zealand; founded by Scottish settlers, 1848; airfield; railway; university (1869).

Dunfermline [dunfermlin] 56°04N 3°29W, pop (2000e) 51 900. City in Fife, E Scotland; royal burgh since 1588; ancient residence of Scottish kings and the burial place of several, including Robert the Bruce; birthplace of Charles I; railway; Dunfermline Abbey and Palace (11th-c foundation).

Dungeness Head [duhnjnes] 50°55N 0°58E. Point on the S coast of Kent, S England, UK, projecting into the English Channel SE of Lydd; nearby is Dungeness nuclear power station. **Dungeness A**, with gas-cooled, graphite-moderated reactors (operational 1965–2006). **Dungeness B**, an advanced gas-cooled reactor, opened in 1983.

Dunkirk [duhnkerk], Fr **Dunkerque**, Flemish **Duinekerke** 51°02N 2°23E, pop (2000e) 74 300. Seaport in NW France; ferry connections to Dover and Harwich; during World War 2, the retreating British Expeditionary Force was rescued from the beaches near the town; railway.

Dun Laoghaire [doonlaee], Eng **Dunleary** [duhnleeree], formerly **Kingstown** 53°17N 6°08W, pop (2000e) 56 000. Port town in Dublin county, E Ireland; dormitory town for Dublin; named Kingstown when George IV landed here in 1821; railway; ferries to Holyhead.

dunlin A small wading bird (*Calidris alpina*), native to the N hemisphere; mottled brown plumage with pale underside; slender probing bill. (Family: Scolopacidae.)

Dunlop, (Ernest) Edward, nickname **Weary** (1907–93) Army surgeon, born in Wangaratta, Victoria, SE Australia. He enlisted in the Australian Army Medical Corps in 1939, and in 1942, as a prisoner-of-war, was forced by the Japanese to work on the Burma–Siam Railway. He ministered to the sick under appalling conditions, and was hailed as the 'Christ of the Burma Road'. After the war he continued his work as a surgeon, and fostered Australian–Asian relations. Named Australian of the Year in 1977, by the time he died he was a national hero.

Dunlop, Joey, popular name of **(William) Joseph Dunlop** (1952–2000) Motor-cyclist, an outstanding rider at Isle of Man TT races, born in Ballymoney, Northern Ireland. He won the Formula One TT for the sixth successive season in 1988, and was Formula One world champion 1982–6. He was killed in a road race in Estonia.

Dunlop, John Boyd (1840–1921) Inventor, born in Dreghorn, North Ayrshire. In 1888 he obtained patents on the pneumatic tyre (invented 1845) for bicycles. His company, formed in 1889, became known as the Dunlop Rubber Company in 1900.

Dunmore, Helen (1952–) Poet and novelist, born in Leeds, West Yorkshire. Her work includes the poetry collections *The Apple Fall* (1983) and *Secrets* (1994), and the children's books *Going to Egypt* (1992), *Fatal Error* (1996), and *The Lilac Tree* (2004). In 1996 she won the inaugural Orange Prize for women fiction writers for her novel *A Spell of Winter*, and later novels include *Mourning Ruby* (2003) and *House of Orphans* (2006).

Dunmow flitch A side of bacon offered as a prize to any married couple, if the husband could in honesty swear that for a year and a day he had not quarrelled with his wife, nor wished himself unmarried. Instituted at Little Dunmow, Essex, in the 13th-c or earlier, the custom has been revived in modern times.

Dunne, Finley Peter (1867–1936) Journalist and humorist, born in Chicago, IL. As 'Mr Dooley', he became widely known from 1900 as the exponent of American-Irish humorous satire on current personages and events.

dunnock A small, grey-brown, ground-feeding bird with short slender bill (*Prunella modularis*); native to Europe and W Asia (N Africa in winter); also known as **(European) hedge sparrow** or **hedge accentor**. (Family: Prunellidae.)

Dunois, Jean d'Orléans, comte (Count) [dünwah], known as **the Bastard of Orléans** (1403–68) French general in the Hundred Years' War, born in Paris, the natural son of Louis, Duke of Orléans. He defended Orléans with a small force until its relief by Joan of Arc (1429), then inflicted several defeats on the English, forcing them out of Paris, Normandy, and Guyenne.

Duns Scotus, Johannes [duhnz skohtus], known as **Doctor Subtilis** (Lat 'the Subtle Doctor') (c.1265–1308) Mediaeval philosopher and Franciscan theologian, probably born in Maxton, Scottish Borders. A critic of preceding scholasticism, his dialectical skill gained him his nickname; but his defence of the papacy led to his ideas being ridiculed at the Reformation (hence the word 'dunce').

Dunstable [duhnstabl] 51°53N 0°32W, pop (2000e) 50 300. Town in Bedfordshire, SC England; at the junction of the Roman Watling Street and the earlier Icknield Way; Whipsnade Zoo nearby.

Dunstable, John [duhnstabl] (?–1453) The most important English composer of the 15th-c. He wrote motets, Masses, and secular songs including the three-part *O rosa bella*.

Dunstan, St (c.909–88) Abbot, born near Glastonbury, Somerset. He became abbot of Glastonbury in 945. An adviser to King Edmund, he later became Bishop of Worcester (957) and of London (959), then (under King Edgar) Archbishop of Canterbury (960). Feast day 19 May.

Dunwoody, Richard (Thomas), nickname **the Prince** (1964–) Jockey, born in Belfast. Champion jockey in 1993–5, he was Grand National winning rider in 1986 and 1994. He rode at least 100 winners in Britain every season from 1989–90. In 1999, he rode home his 1679th winner, setting a National Hunt record, and retired at the end of that year.

duodenal ulcer [dyoo-ohdeenl] A peptic ulcer occurring on the first part of the duodenum.

duodenum [dyoo-ohdeenm] A region of the alimentary canal in vertebrates, important in digestion. In humans it is the C-shaped first part of the small intestine, providing a large area for the absorption of digestive products.

Du Pont [doo pont] Franco-American industrial family; in full, **du Pont de Nemours**. Their firm has a long history of manufacturing gunpowder, fibres, plastics, and chemicals, and played an important economic role in 19th-c Delaware.

du Pré, Jacqueline [doo pray] (1945–87) Cellist, born in Oxford, Oxfordshire. In 1967 she married the pianist Daniel Barenboim, with whom she gave many recitals. Her career as a player ended in 1973, when she developed multiple sclerosis.

Duralumin [dyuralyumin] The trade name for an alloy of aluminium (over 90%) with copper (about 4%) and minor amounts of magnesium and manganese. It is used in the aircraft industry.

Duras, Marguerite [düra], pseudonym of **Marguerite Donnadieu** (1914–96) Novelist, born in Gia Dinh, Vietnam. Her reputation was made by the novels she wrote in the 1950s, such as *Le Marin de Gibraltar* (1952, The Sailor from Gibraltar). She achieved a wider celebrity with the screenplay for Alain Resnais' film *Hiroshima Mon Amour* (1959, Hiroshima, My Love). Her autobiographical novel *L'Amant* (1984, The Lover, Prix Goncourt) was made into a successful film (1992).

Durban or **Port Natal** 29°53S 31°00E, pop (2000e) 860 000. Seaport in KwaZulu Natal province, South Africa; situated on Indian Ocean coast; South Africa's third largest city; mission settlement founded here, 1834; airport; railway; university (1960).

Dürer, Albrecht [dyoorer], Ger [dürer] (1471–1528) Painter and engraver, born in Nuremberg, Germany. In 1497 he set up his own studio, producing many paintings, then in 1498 published his first great series of designs on wood, the illustrations of the Apocalypse.

Durga Puja *Navaratri*

Durham (city) [duhruhm] 54°47N 1°34W, pop (2001e) 87 700. City and administrative centre of County Durham, NE England; on the R Wear; founded in the 10th-c by monks who had fled from Lindisfarne; railway; university (1832); cathedral (1093) and castle (11th-c) designated a world heritage site.

Durham (county) [duhruhm] pop (2001e) 493 500; area 2436 km²/941 sq mi. County in NE England; county town, Durham; Darlington a new unitary authority from 1997; coal-mining.

Durkheim, Emile [derkhiym] (1858–1917) Sociologist, born in Epinal, France, generally regarded as one of the founders of sociology. He is perhaps best known for his concept of 'collective representations', the social power of ideas stemming from their development through the interaction of many minds.

Durmitor [doormitaw(r)] 43°08N 19°01E. Highest mountain in Montenegro; in the Dinaric Alps, rising to 2522 m/8274 ft; in a national park, which is a world heritage site.

Durrell, Gerald (Malcolm) [duhrel] (1925–95) British zoologist, traveller, writer, and broadcaster, born in Jamshedpur, India, the brother of Lawrence Durrell. His popular animal stories and reminiscences include *My Family and Other Animals* (1956) and *Birds, Beasts and Relatives* (1969). He founded a zoo and wildlife centre in Jersey.

Durrell, Lawrence (George) [duhrel] (1912–90) British novelist and poet, born in Darjeeling, India. He is best known for the *Alexandria Quartet* (1957–60): *Justine*, *Balthazar*, *Mountolive* and *Clea*. A series of five novels commenced in 1974 with *Monsieur*, followed by *Livia* (1978), *Constance* (1982), *Sebastian* (1983), and *Quinx* (1985).

Dürrenmatt or **Duerrenmatt, Friedrich** [dürenmat] (1921–90) Writer, born in Konolfingen, Switzerland. His plays include *Die Ehe des Herrn Mississippi* (1952, The Marriage of Mr Mississippi), which established his international reputation, and *Die Physiker* (1962, The Physicists).

Durrës [dooruhs], formerly **Durazzo**, Turkish **Draj** 41°18N 19°28E, pop (2000e) 97 500. Seaport in W Albania, on the Adriatic Sea; founded as Epidamnos, 627 BC, and renamed Dyrrhachium, 229 BC; occupied by Italians and Austrians in World War 1, when capital of Albania, 1912–21; railway; a seaside health resort.

durum A wheat (*Triticum durum*) with a high protein content, whose flour is used to make pasta. The flour is harder than that produced by other varieties of wheat, used in bread-making.

Duse, Eleonora [doozay] (1859–1924) Actress, born near Venice, Italy. She became the mistress of Gabriele d'Annunzio, who wrote *La Gioconda* for her. Her histrionic genius ranks 'The Duse' as one of the world's greatest actresses.

Dushanbe [dyooshambe], formerly **Kishlak** (to 1925), **Diushambe** (to 1929), **Stalinabad** (1929–61) 38°38N 68°51E, pop (2000e) 743 000. Capital city of Tajikistan, on the R Dushanbe; airfield; railway; university (1948).

Düsseldorf [düseldaw(r)f] 51°13N 6°47E, pop (2000e) 594 000. Industrial city in Germany; on the lower Rhine; city status, 1288; railway; university (1965); administrative centre of North Rhine–Westphalia province's heavy industry; birthplace of Heinrich Heine.

Dust Bowl The semi-arid area of the US prairie states from Kansas to Texas, which suffers from dust storms. In the 1930s, after several years of overcultivation, strong winds and dry weather resulted in major dust storms and soil erosion.

Dutch A member of the W Germanic family of languages, spoken by c.20 million in The Netherlands, Belgium, Suriname, and the Antilles. It is the official language of The Netherlands, and is also spoken in Belgium, where it is called **Flemish**; both dialects are officially referred to as **Nederlands**.

Dutch elm disease A disease affecting all species of elm (genus: *Ulmus*) caused by the fungus *Ceratocystis ulmi*; symptoms include wilting, yellowing of foliage, and eventually death; transmitted from tree to tree by elm-bark beetle. (Order: Eurotiales.)

Dutch New Guinea *Irian Jaya*

Dutch Reformed Church The largest Protestant Church in Holland, stemming from the Calvinist Reformation in the 16th-c. The Dutch Reformed Church in South Africa (totally separated from the Church in Holland) was the official Church of dominant White Afrikaans-speaking nationals.

Dutch Wars Three wars between England and the Dutch Republic (1652–4, 1664–7, 1672–4) concerned with issues of world trade and the colonies. The wars brought on the decline of Dutch power, and signalled the growing predominance of the English.

Dutch West India Company The organization of Dutch merchants responsible for the settlement of New Netherland, now New York. The Company was established in 1621, and was dissolved in 1674.

Duval, Claude [düval] (1643–70) Highwayman, born in Domfront, France. He moved to England at the Restoration (1660), and pursued a successful career, gaining a popular reputation. He was hanged at Tyburn, London.

Duvalier, François [doovalyay], known as **Papa Doc** (1907–71) Haitian politician and president (1957–71), born in Port-au-Prince, Haiti. His regime saw the creation of the civilian militia known as the Tonton Macoute. He became president for life in 1964, and was succeeded in this post by his son, **Jean-Claude Duvalier** (1951–), known as **Baby Doc**, whose regime lasted until 1986.

Duvall, Robert [dooval] (1931–) Actor, born in San Diego, CA. He earned Oscar nominations for *The Godfather* (1972), *Apocalypse Now* (1979), and *The Great Santini* (1980), before winning the award for *Tender Mercies* (1983). Later films include *The Apostle* (1997) and *Thankyou for Smoking* (2005).

Dvořák, Antonín (Leopold) [dvaw(r)zhak] (1841–1904) Composer, born near Prague. His work, basically classical in structure, but with colourful Slavonic motifs, won increasing recognition, culminating in European acclaim for his *Stabat mater* (1880). In the USA he wrote his ninth symphony, the ever-popular 'From the New World'.

dwarf buffalo *African buffalo; anoa*

dwarfism A disorder of slowed growth in children. It may be due to a variety of factors, including genetic effects (eg achondroplasia) and hormone imbalances, especially deficiencies of thyroid and growth hormones, but also increased secretion of testosterone, which causes premature closure of the growing ends of bone, arresting their linear growth. It may also be due to nutritional deficiencies such as malnutrition or rickets, or generalized chronic illness.

dwarf planet *planet*

dwarf star Strictly, any star in which the source of energy is the nuclear burning of hydrogen in its core to helium, and therefore lying on the main sequence of stellar evolution. Our Sun, 109 times the diameter of Earth, is a dwarf star.

Dyak *Dayak*

dyeing The process of permanently changing the colour of a material. This ancient art has developed into a high-technology industry for the coloration of textiles, leather, and other goods. Dyes are usually applied by soaking the material in a solution, which is fixed onto the material by heating.

dyer's rocket *weld*

dyestuff Strongly coloured substances, generally complex organic molecules, which are absorbed by textile materials. Indigo and cochineal are two of the best-known natural dyes. The synthetic *vat* dyes produce strong, bright colours of the highest fastness, and are often used on cotton furnishing fabrics.

Dyfed [duhvid] pop (2000e) 357 500; area 5768 km²/2227 sq mi. Former county in SW Wales, UK; created in 1974, and replaced in 1996 by Cardiganshire, Carmarthenshire, and Pembrokeshire counties.

Dyke, Greg(ory) (1947–) Broadcasting executive, born in London. He was editor-in-chief at TVam (1983–4) then director of programmes at TVS (1984–7) and LWT (1987–91), becoming managing director and group chief executive of LWT in 1990. He was chairman and chief executive at Pearson Television (1995–9) before taking over from John Birt at the BBC (2000). He resigned in 2004 after the Hutton Report severely criticised the BBC.

dyke (geography) A ditch or natural watercourse. The term is also used to describe a long ridge or embankment constructed to prevent flooding, such as those in the Netherlands made to hold back the sea.

Dylan, Bob [dilan], pseudonym of **Robert Zimmerman** (1941–)

Singer, musician, and songwriter, born in Duluth, MN. Opposition to war, the nuclear bomb, and racial and social injustice were the themes of his most famous songs, such as 'Blowin' in the Wind' and 'The Times They are a-Changin''. Later albums include *Bringing It All Back Home* (1965), *Blood on the Tracks* (1974), *Street Legal* (1978), *Love and Theft* (2001), and *Modern Times* (2006). *Chronicles*, the first volume of his memoirs, appeared in 2004.

dynamics (economics) *disequilibrium*

dynamics (mechanics) In mechanics, the study of the properties of the motion of objects, and the relation of this motion to the forces causing it.

dynamite Once a specific name, now a general term for industrial high explosives consisting of nitroglycerine absorbed on some porous or granular non-explosive substance to minimize its vulnerability to shock.

dysentery [disentree] Intestinal infection leading to profuse diarrhoea with the passage of blood and mucus in the stool. **Bacillary dysentery** is caused by *Shigella*; the disease is usually mild and short-lived. **Amoebic/amebic dysentery** is caused by a protozoan, *Entamoeba histolytica*, and is more serious.

dyslexia Reading disability, in people with apparently adequate intellectual and perceptual abilities and adequate educational opportunities; sometimes called **alexia**. **Developmental dyslexia** is the term applied to people who have never learned to read. **Acquired dyslexia** describes those who could once read, but who have lost this ability as a result of brain damage. There is no single theory which explains dyslexia, and the nature of the problem has been a source of some dispute; nevertheless it is common for several members of a family to exhibit similar difficulties with reading and writing.

dysmenorrhoea / dysmenorrhea [dismenoreea] Discomfort or pain in the lower abdomen associated with menstruation. It is a common, usually mild (but sometimes very painful) complaint, which lasts 12–24 hours from the start of bleeding.

dyspepsia *indigestion*

dysphasia *aphasia*

dysplasia A malformation of bone or other body tissue. Cells divide more quickly than normal and do not mature properly, thereby affecting their function. It is a normal finding in damaged tissue while it is repairing. In some parts of the body (eg the cervix) the dysplastic cells are a precursor of malignancy.

dyspraxia *apraxia*

Dzaoudzi [dzoodzee] 12°47S 45°12E; pop (2000e) 12 000; area 6·7 km²/2·6 sq mi. Capital of Mayotte, on La Petite Terre I; airport.

dzo *yak*

e

eagle A large-bodied bird of prey that kills its own food (smaller birds of prey – buzzards, falcons, hawks, harriers, or kites). (Family: Accipitridae, 30 species.)

Ealing Studios, popular name of **Associated Talking Pictures, Ltd** An English motion-picture studio based at Ealing, Greater London, UK. Founded in 1929 by the film producers Basil Dean and Reginald Baker with the financial support of the Courtauld family, the company produced several vaudeville-style musical comedies as well as serious feature films during the 1930s. In World War 2 it created propaganda films for the British Ministry of Information. The studio became internationally renowned for a series of satirical 'Ealing Comedies' such as *Kind Hearts and Coronets* (1949), *The Lavender Hill Mob* (1951), and *The Lady-killers* (1955). It ceased production in 1955 when it was sold to the British Broadcasting Corporation.

ear *p.290*

Earhart, Amelia [ay(r)hah(r)t] (1897–1937) Aviator, born in Atchison, KS. She was the first woman to fly the Atlantic, as a passenger, and followed this by a solo flight in 1932. In 1937 she set out to fly round the world, but her plane was lost over the Pacific.

earl In the UK, a member of the third most senior order of noblemen, and the most ancient title, dating from before the Norman Conquest (Danish *jarl*). The wife of an earl is a *countess*.

Earl Marshal In the UK, the hereditary post held by the Howard Dukes of Norfolk. One of the great officers of state, the Earl Marshal is head of the College of Arms and is also responsible for organizing state ceremonies.

Early English Style The form of English Gothic architecture prevalent during the 13th-c, characterized by pointed arches, rib vaults, and a greater stress on the horizontals than is found in French Gothic architecture.

EAROM [eeayrom] An acronym of **Electrically Alterable Read-Only Memory**, a type of integrated circuit read-only memory, where the data can be altered electronically while the EAROM remains in circuit.

Earp, Wyatt (Berry Stapp) [erp] (1848–1929) Gambler, gunfighter, and lawman, born in Monmouth, IL. During his stay in Tombstone, AZ, he befriended Doc Holliday, who joined with the Earp brothers against the Clanton gang in the famous gunfight at the OK Corral (1881). Earp collaborated in the writing of his biography *Wyatt Earp, Frontier Marshal* (1931), published after his death, which portrayed him as a heroic frontiersman of the Wild West.

Earth The third major planet from the Sun, having the following characteristics: mass 5.97×10^{24}kg; orbital period 365.26 days; radius (equatorial) 6378 km/3963 mi; obliquity 23°27'; mean density $5.52\,g/cm^3$; orbital eccentricity 0.017; equatorial gravity 978 cm/s^2; mean distance from the Sun 149.6×10^6 km/ 93×10^6 mi; rotational period 23 h 56 min 4 s. It has one large natural satellite, the Moon. There is an oxygen/nitrogen-rich atmosphere, liquid water oceans filling lowland regions between continents, and permanent water ice caps at each pole. It is unique in the Solar System in being able to support life, for which there is fossil evidence in rocks dating from 3.5 thousand million years ago; human population over 6500 million (2006). The interior of the planet is differentiated into zones: an iron/nickel-rich molten *core* (radius c.3500 km/2175 mi) an iron–magnesium silicate *Mantle* (c.85% by volume of the Earth); and a *crust* of lighter metal silicates (relatively thin, c.6 km/3$\frac{1}{2}$ mi thick under the oceans to c.50 km/30 mi under the continents).

earth pig *aardvark*

earthquake *p.291*

earth sciences A general term for the study of the Earth and its atmosphere, encompassing geology and its subdisciplines as well as oceanography, glaciology, meteorology, and the origin of the Earth and the Solar System.

earthstar A ground-living fungus with a globular fruiting body; when ripe, outer layer splits into rays, and peels back into a star-shaped structure. (Order: Lycoperdales. Genus: *Geastrum*.)

Earth Summit The name given to the **United Nations Conference on Environment and Development (UNCED)** held in Rio de Janeiro in June 1992, at which 178 governments were represented. The aim was to find ways of minimizing the damage done to the environment by the processes associated with economic development. The *Framework Convention on Climate Change* introduced measures designed to reduce the threat of global warming. The *Convention on Biological Diversity* put forward proposals to preserve the Earth's biological diversity. *Agenda 21* was an action plan aimed at introducing sustainable development, The *Rio Declaration* included 27 principles to guide action on development and the environment. The *Forest Principles* emphasized the right of states to exploit their own forest resources while advocating general principles of sustainable forest management. Follow up conferences were held in New York in 1997 (Rio + 5), attended by 185 countries, and in Johannesburg in 2002 (**UN World Summit on Sustainable Development**, Rio + 10).

earthworm A terrestrial segmented worm found in soil, feeding mainly on decomposing organic matter; head simple, without sensory appendages; body cylindrical, length up to 4 m/13 ft. (Phylum: Annelida. Class: Oligochaeta.)

earwig A slender insect with large pincers at rear end of body, used for courtship, defence, grooming, or predation; forewings small and hard; hindwings membranous; c.1500 species, most abundant in tropics. (Order: Dermaptera.)

East Bank Region in Jordan, E of the R Jordan; corresponds roughly to the former Amirate of Transjordan.

East End An area of London situated N of the R Thames and E of Shoreditch and Tower Bridge. The Dockland Development scheme has recently sought to bring industry and finance into the area.

Easter The chief festival of the Christian Church, commemorating the resurrection of Christ after his crucifixion. Observed in the Western Churches on a Sunday between 22 March and 25

ear

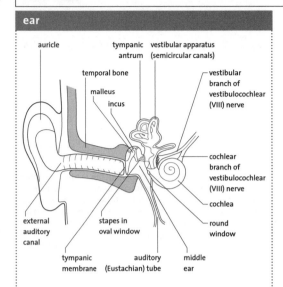

auricle — tympanic — vestibular apparatus
antrum (semicircular canals)

temporal bone — vestibular branch of vestibulocochlear (VIII) nerve

malleus

incus

cochlear branch of vestibulocochlear (VIII) nerve

cochlea

external auditory canal — stapes in oval window — round window

tympanic membrane — auditory (Eustachian) tube — middle ear

A compound organ concerned with hearing and balance, situated on the side or (in some animals) the top of the head. The **external ear** consists of the *pinna* (commonly referred to as 'the ear') and the *external acoustic meatus* (or *auditory canal*), a tube leading to the eardrum (*tympanic membrane*). In many animals (eg dogs, horses), the pinna can be moved to scan the environment to locate sounds. The **middle ear** (*tympanic cavity*) is an air-filled space, separated from the external ear by the tympanic membrane, and from the internal ear by the oval and round windows. It is continuous with the nasopharynx via the auditory (Eustachian) tube, and contains the auditory *ossicles* (the *malleus*, *incus*, and *stapes*) and two small muscles which act to damp down their vibrations. The **internal ear** consists of a number of parts, but can be divided into that concerned with hearing (the *cochlea*) and that concerned with assessing head position and its movements (the *vestibular apparatus*). The round window is filled with a fibrous membrane which allows movement of the fluid (*perilymph*) within the cochlea, when compressed by the stapes. Sound waves directed down the external auditory canal cause the tympanic membrane to vibrate; movements of the malleus are conveyed to the oval window (via the incus and stapes), where the vibrations are transmitted to the basilar membrane of the cochlea. The *vestibulocochlear nerve* (the VIIIth cranial nerve) conveys information from both parts of the internal ear to the brain. Blockage of the auditory tube leads to the loss of pressure in the middle ear (due to the absorption of air), increased concavity of the tympanic membrane, and progressive deafness. When the blockage is associated with infection of the middle ear, the accumulation of fluid causes the tympanic membrane to bulge towards the external auditory canal, again leading to increasing deafness.

April inclusive, depending on the date of the first full moon after the spring equinox; the Orthodox Church has a different method of calculating the date.

Easter Island [paskwa], Span **Isla de Pascua** 27°05S 109°20W; pop (2000e) 2800; area 166 km²/64 sq mi; maximum length 24 km/15 mi; maximum width 12 km/7 mi. Chilean island 3790 km/2355 mi W of Chile; rises to 652 m/2139 ft at Terevaka; first European discovery by Dutch admiral Jacob Rog-

geveen on Easter Sunday 1722; islanders largely of Polynesian origin; capital, Hanga Roa; airport; famous for its *Moai* stone statues depicting the human head and trunk of local ancestors.

Eastern Cape One of the nine new provinces established by the South African constitution of 1994, in SE South Africa, incorporating the former Transkei and Ciskei homelands, and formerly part of Cape Provinces; capital, Bisho; pop (2000e) 6 170 000; area 170 616 km²/65 858 sq mi; chief languages, Xhosa (85%), Afrikaans, English; second poorest province; automotive industry at Port Elizabeth; agriculture, forestry, tourism (coastal amenities and nature reserves).

Eastern Orthodox Church *Orthodox Church*

Easter Rising, also **Easter Rebellion** A rebellion in Dublin of Irish nationalists, organized by two revolutionary groups, the Irish Republican Brotherhood led by Patrick Pearse, and the socialist 'citizen armies' organized by James Connolly (1868–1916). The rising was put down and several leaders were executed.

East Germany *Germany*

East India Company, British A British trading monopoly, established in India in 1600, which later became involved in politics, eventually wielding supreme power through a Board of Control responsible to the British parliament. During the 18th-c it received competition from other European countries, in particular France and Holland. Its monopoly was broken in 1813, and it ceased to exist as a legal entity in 1873.

Eastman, George (1854–1932) Inventor and philanthropist, born in Waterville, NY. In 1889 he manufactured the transparent celluloid film used by Edison and others in experiments which made possible the moving-picture industry.

East Sea, also known as **Sea of Japan** area 978 000 km²/ 378 000 sq mi. Arm of the Pacific Ocean, bounded by S and N Korea (SW), Russia (N and W), and the islands of Japan (E and S).

East Sussex *Sussex, East*

East Timor *p.292*

Eastwood, Clint (1930–) Film actor and director, born in San Francisco, CA. He began acting in television Westerns, notably the *Rawhide* series (1959–65), and became an international star with three Italian-made 'spaghetti Westerns', beginning with *A Fistful of Dollars* (1964). Later films include *Unforgiven* (1992, two Oscars), *Bridges of Madison County* (1995), and *Million Dollar Baby* (2004, Golden Globe Best Director; Oscar Best Director and Best Film). Further work as a director includes *Mystic River* (2003, Best Director Oscar nomination), *Flags of Our Fathers* (2006), and *Letters From Iwo Jima* (2006, Golden Globe Best Foreign Language Film; Best Director Oscar nomination).

eau de Cologne mint *mint*

Ebadi, Shirin [ebahdee] (1947–) Lawyer and human rights activist, born in Hamadan, Iran. She studied at Tehran University and became the first female judge in Iran, serving as president of the Tehran City Court from 1975. Forced to resign in 1979 with the advent of the Islamic republic, she went on to set up her own law practice. Her campaigns for greater rights for Iranian women and children and for the reform of family laws have made her a key figure in the reformist movement. In 2003 she was awarded the Nobel Peace Prize for her efforts for democracy and human rights.

EBCDIC code [ebseedik] An acronym of **Extended Binary Coded Decimal Interchange Code**, a binary code used by IBM for information exchange: 256 different characters are defined using an 8-bit code.

Ebola A virus, first isolated in 1976 in Africa, belonging to the *Filoviridae* family, which causes severe and often fatal haemorrhagic fevers in humans and non-human primates. It is classified as a biosafety level 4 agent because of its extreme pathogenicity and the lack of a protective vaccine or anti-

earthquake

Key:
▲ Volcano
— Transform fault
Plate boundaries:
— Constructive
- - - Destructive
······ Uncertain

A series of shock waves generated at a point (*focus*) within the Earth, and caused by the movement of rocks on a fault plane releasing stored strain energy. The point on the surface of the Earth above the focus is the *epicentre*. Major earthquakes are associated with the edges of plates that make up the Earth's crust, and along mid-oceanic ridges where new crust is forming. The greatest concentration of earthquakes is in a belt around the Pacific Ocean (the 'ring of fire'), and along a zone from the Mediterranean E to the Himalayas and China. The magnitude of an earthquake is measured on the Richter scale. Major earthquakes, such as in San Francisco in 1906 and Japan in 1923, can cause much damage to property and loss of life. Further dangers arise from associated effects, especially tsunamis.

viral drug. Little is known of its natural history and its host is still unidentified.

ebonite *vulcanite*

ebony An evergreen or deciduous tree, native to tropical and subtropical regions; flowers solitary or in small clusters, urn-shaped with 3–5 spreading lobes, white, yellow, or reddish; fruit a berry; cultivated especially for its hard, black heartwood, and for the edible fruits. (Genus: *Diospyros*, 500 species. Family: Ebenaceae.)

Ebro, River [ebroh], ancient **Iberius** Longest river flowing entirely in Spain; rises in the Cordillera Cantabrica and flows SE to enter the Mediterranean; length, 910 km/565 mi.

Eccles, Sir John (Carew) (1903–97) Physiologist, born in Melbourne, Victoria, Australia. A specialist in neurophysiology, he shared the 1963 Nobel Prize for Physiology or Medicine for his work on the functioning of nervous impulses.

Ecclesiastes, Book of [ekleeziasteez] A Biblical work, specifically attributed to 'The Preacher, the son of David, King of Jerusalem', who has traditionally been identified as Solomon, although the work is more usually now dated in the post-exilic period of Israel's history.

Ecclesiasticus, Book of [ekleeziastikus] (Lat 'the Church (Book)') Part of the Old Testament Apocrypha or Catholic deuterocano-

nical writings, originally attributed to a Jewish scribe c.180 BC, but later translated into Greek by his grandson; also called **The Wisdom of Jesus, the Son of Sirach**, or just **Sirach** or **Ben Sira**.

ecclesiology [ekleeziolojee] The theological study of the nature of the Christian Church. The term can also signify the science of church construction and decoration.

ECG *electrocardiography*

echidna [ekidna] An Australasian mammal; coat with spines; minute tail; long claws used for digging; long narrow snout and sticky tongue; eats ants and termites, or larger insects and earthworms; young develop in pouch. (Family: Tachyglossidae, 2 species.)

Echidna [ekidna] In Greek mythology, a fabulous creature, half-woman and half-snake, who was the mother of various monsters.

echinoderm [ekiynoderm] A spiny-skinned marine invertebrate characterized by its typically 5-radial symmetry; body enclosed by a variety of calcareous plates, ossicles, and spines; water vascular system operates numerous tubular feet used in feeding, locomotion, and respiration. (Phylum: Echinodermata.)

Echinoidea [ekinoydia] *sea urchin*

Echiura [ekiyoora] *spoonworm*

Echo In Greek mythology, a nymph of whom several stories are

East Timor, Democratic Republic of

Local name Port **Timor Leste**, Tetum **Timor Loro Sae** (*see map p.460*)

Timezone GMT + 8

Area 14 874 km²/5743 sq mi

Population total (2002e) 738 000

Status Republic

Date of independence 2002

Capital Dili

Languages Tetum and Portuguese (official), Indonesian and English widely spoken

Ethnic groups Tetum

Religion Roman Catholic (91·4 %), traditional animist beliefs

Physical features Occupies E half of the mountainous island of Timor and the enclave of Ocussi (Ambeno) in West Timor, SE Asia, in the Sunda Group, NW of Australia; W half of the island belongs to Indonesia (part of East Nusa Tengarra province); highest peak, Tata Mailau (2950 m/9679 ft); many rivers flowing from the mountains through the coastal plains.

Climate Hot with monsoon rains falling between December and March; average daily temperatures 32°C (Oct–Dec), 21°C (Jan–Sep)

Currency 1 US Dollar (USD) = 100 cents

Economy 90% of the population live off the land, with one in three households living below the poverty line; coffee is the main export crop, also coconuts, cloves, cacao, and marble; potential for gas and oil exports.

GDP (2001e) $440 mn, per capita $500

History Former Portuguese colony of East Timor declared itself independent as the Democratic Republic of East Timor, 1975; invaded by Indonesian forces and annexed, the claim not recognized by the UN; administered by Indonesia as the province of Timor Timur; considerable local unrest (1989–90), and mounting international concern over civilian deaths; independence movement (Fretilin) largely suppressed by 1993; UN-sponsored talks, 1993; ongoing conflict, mid-1990s; President Habibie grants referendum, 1999, resulting in 78·5% vote in favour of independence, immediately followed by widespread violence and destruction of property by pro-Jakarta militia groups, and major refugee movements; growing threat to the UN presence in Dili led to arrival of UN-sponsored, Australian-led intervention force; administered by the UN since 1999, with a transitional administration, 2000; elections for an 88-member Constituent Assembly, 2001; Council of Ministers of the Second Transitional Government, 2001; presidential elections (Apr), followed by full independence, May 2002; UN Mission of Support in East Timor (Unmiset) remained in place until 2004; parliamentary system of government with a largely ceremonial president; army and police split by internal disputes and gang violence, President Xanana Gusmao assumes emergency powers to control looting and unrest (May 2006); José Ramos-Horta appointed prime minister (Jul 2006) then president (2007); unrest ongoing in 2007.

Head of State
2002–7 Xanana Gusmao
2007– José Ramos-Horta

Head of Government
2007– Estanislau Aleixo da Silva (*Interim*)

---

sound waves, typically high-frequency sounds. The process is used by some animals, such as bats and whales, for orientation and prey location.

echo-sounding Bouncing sound waves off the sea-floor to determine the depth of water in the oceans. A device known as a *precision depth recorder* (PDR) is used to print a visual trace of the water depth and provide a picture of the sea-floor topography.

Eckhart, Johannes [ekhah(r)t], also spelled **Eckart** or **Eckehart**, known as **Meister Eckhart** ('Master Eckhart') (c.1260–c.1327) Dominican theologian and mystic, born in Hochheim, Germany. In 1325 he was arraigned for heresy, and two years after his death his writings were condemned by Pope John XXII.

eclipse 1 The passage of a planet or satellite through the shadow cast by another body. In the case of our Sun, a **solar eclipse** can occur only at new Moon, when the Moon is directly between the Earth and the Sun. A **total eclipse**, when the whole disc is obscured, lasts a maximum of 7·5 min. A **partial eclipse** of much longer duration occurs before, after, and to each side of the path of totality. Sometimes the apparent size of the lunar disc is just too small for a total eclipse, and an **annular eclipse** results, in which a bright ring of sunlight surrounds the Moon. A **lunar eclipse** occurs when the Moon passes into the shadow of the Earth, which can happen only at full moon. **2** The total or partial disappearance from view of an astronomical object when it passes directly behind another object. In binary star systems it is also possible for one star to eclipse another (an *eclipsing binary star*).

ecliptic That great circle which is the projection of the Earth's orbit onto the celestial sphere, and therefore is the apparent path of the Sun across our sky.

eclogue [eklog] A short dramatic poem, originally with a pastoral setting and theme. Of classical derivation (notably in Theocritus and Virgil), the form was popular in the 16th–17th-c (as Spenser's *Shepheardes Calendar*, 1579).

Eco, Umberto [aykoh] (1932–) Semiotician, novelist, and critic, born in Allesandra, Italy. His novel *Il nome della rosa* (1981, The Name of the Rose), an intellectual detective story, achieved instant fame, and attracted much critical attention; it was filmed in 1986. Later novels are *Foucault's Pendulum* (trans, 1988) and *The Mysterious Flame of Queen Loana* (2005). A critical work, *On Literature*, appeared in 2004.

ecology The study of the interaction of living organisms with their physical, biological, and chemical environment. The ecological movement of the 1960s onwards has argued that people must live within the limitations of the Earth's finite supply of resources, and that humanity is very much dependent on its environment.

e-commerce The trend, by business and administration, to use data communications to link their computer systems directly to those of their suppliers and customers, also called **electronic commerce**. This allows many transactions to take place without any human involvement, particularly the ordering of materials from suppliers on a just-in-time basis. The term is increasingly used for the marketing of goods and services directly to customers through the Internet. Data communications need to be highly secure, using sophisticated techniques for encryption and authentication.

Economic Community of West African States (ECOWAS) An economic organization formed in 1975 by 15 W African signatories to the Treaty of Lagos: Benin, Gambia, Ghana, Guinea, Guinea-Bissau, Côte d'Ivoire (Ivory Coast), Liberia, Mali, Niger, Nigeria, Senegal, Sierra Leone, Togo, and Upper Volta (now Burkina Faso); Cape Verde joined in 1977; Mauritania left in 2002.

economics The study of the allocation of scarce resources among competing ends, the creation and distribution of wealth, and

---

told. Either she was beloved by Pan, and was torn to pieces, only her voice surviving; or she was punished by Hera so that she could only repeat the last words of another speaker. She loved Narcissus, who rejected her, so that she wasted away to a voice.

echolocation The perception of objects by means of reflected national income. The first major economist was Adam Smith, and the economic theory of the classical school (*equilibrium*) dominated thinking until the 1930s. The main change in thinking at that time was the result of work by J M Keynes, whose economic theories attempted to solve the problems of depression and economic stagnation. **Microeconomics** is the study of the economic problems of firms and individuals, and the way individual elements in an economy behave. **Macroeconomics** is the study of the country as a whole, including such matters as trade, monetary policy, prices, national income, output, exchange rates, growth, and forecasting (**econometrics**).

ecosocialism A branch of socialism of relatively recent origin which wishes to see socialist practice linked with concern for environmental and ecological matters.

ecosystem An ecological concept which helps to explain the relationships and interactions between one or more living organisms and their physical, biological, and chemical environment (eg a pond and its associated plants, fish, insects, birds, and mammals). The study of ecosystems is commonly based on transfers of energy along a food chain. In most natural ecosystems, several food chains interact to form complex food or energy webs.

ecotourism *tourist industry*

ecstasy A designer drug which is supposedly mildly hallucinogenic; also called **MDMA** (methylenedioxymethamphetamine), 'E' or 'Adam'. It is reported to heighten the tactile senses of touch and skin sensations, and thereby act as an aphrodisiac.

ectoplasm A substance said to exude from the body of a medium during a seance, from which materializations sometimes supposedly form. It is the subject of much controversy, as some mediums were discovered to simulate such effects fraudulently.

ECU *European Monetary System*

Ecuador *p.294*

ecumenism [ekyoomenizm] (Gr *oikoumene*, 'the inhabited world') A movement seeking visible unity of divided churches and denominations within Christianity. The 4th-c and 5th-c 'Ecumenical Councils' had claimed to represent the Church in the whole world. The movement encourages dialogue between churches of different denominations, joint acts of worship, and joint service in the community.

eczema *dermatitis*

edaphology [eedafolojee] The study of soil as a medium for growth of living organisms. The word is from Greek *edaphos* 'ground, soil'.

Edda (Old Norse 'great-grandmother') The name of two separate collections of Old Norse literature. The **Elder Edda**, dating from the 9th-c to the 12th-c, consists of heroic and mythological poems; the **Younger** or **Prose Edda** was written (mainly in prose) in the early 13th-c by the Icelandic poet Snorri Sturluson.

Eddington, Sir Arthur S(tanley) (1882–1944) Astronomer, born in Kendal, Cumbria. In 1919 his observations of star positions during a total solar eclipse gave the first direct confirmation of Einstein's general theory of relativity. He became a renowned popularizer of science, notably in *The Expanding Universe* (1933).

Eddy, Mary Baker, married name **Glover** (1821–1910) Founder of the Christian Scientists (1876), born in Bow, NH. In 1866 she received severe injuries after a fall, but read about the palsied man in Matthew's Gospel, and claimed to have risen from her bed similarly healed. Thereafter she devoted herself to developing her spiritual discovery, and in 1879 organized at Boston the Church of Christ, Scientist.

Edelman, Gerald (Maurice) [aydlman] (1929–) Biochemist, born in New York City. His research into the antibodies which form a major part of a vertebrate animal's defence against infection led to his sharing the Nobel Prize for Physiology or Medicine in 1972.

edelweiss [aydlviys] A perennial (*Leontopodium alpinum*) growing to 20 cm/8 in, native to the mountains of SE Europe; flowerheads yellowish-white, arranged in a flat-topped cluster surrounded by pointed, spreading, star-like, woolly bracts. (Family: Compositae.)

edema *oedema*

Eden, Sir (Robert) Anthony, 1st Earl of Avon [eedn] (1897–1977) British statesman and Conservative prime minister (1955–7), born in Windlestone, Durham. He became foreign secretary (1935), resigning in 1938 over differences with Chamberlain. Again foreign secretary (1940–5, 1951–5), he succeeded Churchill as prime minister. In 1956 he ordered British forces into the Suez Canal Zone – an action which led to his resignation.

Eden, Garden of Biblical place associated with **Paradise**, where Adam and Eve lived prior to their sin and expulsion (*Gen* 2, 3).

Eden Project A sustainable garden development created as a tourist attraction near St Austell, Cornwall, opened in 2001. Sited in the crater of a disused clay pit are two bubble shaped geodesic domes known as *biomes*. One biome is designed to recreate a tropical rainforest climate, while the other controls a warm temperate climate. They house a spectacular and diverse collection of plants from around the world as well as locally-grown specimens. Future developments include a dry-tropics biome.

Edentata [eedntahta] (Lat 'with no teeth') An order of mammals characterized by having extra contacts between some of the bones in the spine, and by having no front teeth.

Ederle, Gertrude (Caroline) [ayderlee] (1905–2003) The first woman to swim the English channel, born in New York City. She won a gold medal at the 1924 Olympic Games as a member of the US 400 m relay team. On 6 August 1926 she swam the Channel from Cap Gris Nez to Kingsdown in 14 h 31 min, very nearly two hours faster than the existing men's record.

Edgar or **Eadgar** (943–75) King of Mercia and Northumbria (957) and (from 959) King of all England, the younger son of Edmund I. In c.973 he introduced a uniform currency based on new silver pennies.

Edgar the Ætheling ('Prince') [athuhling] (c.1050–1125) Anglo-Saxon prince, the grandson of Edmund Ironside. Though chosen as king after the Battle of Hastings, he was never crowned. He submitted to William the Conqueror, then rebelled and fled to Scotland (1068). He was finally reconciled with King William in 1074.

Edgar Awards Annual awards given by the Mystery Writers of America for the best in mystery fiction and non-fiction published the previous year. The awards began in 1954 and are named in honour of Edgar Allan Poe. Categories include Best Novel, Best Fact Crime, Best Juvenile, and the Grand Master Award.

Edgeworth, Maria (1767–1849) Writer, born in Blackbourton, Oxfordshire. She is best known for her children's stories, and her novels of Irish life, such as *Castle Rackrent* (1800) and *The Absentee* (1812).

Edinburgh [edinbruh] 55°57N 3°13W, pop (2000e) 445 400. Capital of Scotland; port facilities at Leith; castle built by Malcolm Canmore (11th-c); charter granted by Robert Bruce, 1392; capital of Scotland, 1482; in the 1760s, New Town area designed by James Craig (1744–95), but the business centre remained in the Old Town; Nor' Loch separating old and new towns was drained and laid out as gardens (Princes Street Gardens); new local council status in 1996 (as City of Edinburgh); airport; railway; three universities (1583, 1966, 1992); cathedral (15th-c); commercial, business, legal, and cultural centre; Edinburgh Castle (oldest part, St Margaret's Chapel, 12th-c); Royal Mile from castle to Palace of Holyroodhouse; Holyrood Park, con-

Ecuador

□ International Airport

[ekwadaw(r)], official name **Republic of Ecuador**, Span **República del Ecuador**

Local name Ecuador

Timezone GMT -5

Area 270 699 km²/104 490 sq mi (including the Galápagos Islands, 7812 km²/3015 sq mi)

Population total (2005e) 13 363 000

Status Republic

Date of independence 1830

Capital Quito

Languages Spanish (official), with Quechua also spoken

Ethnic groups Quechua (50%), Mestizo (40%), white (8·5%), other Amerindian (5%)

Religions Roman Catholic (94%), other (6%)

Physical features Located in NW South America; includes the Galápagos Is, Ecuadorian island group on the equator 970 km/600 mi W of South American mainland; coastal plain in the W, descending from rolling hills (N) to broad lowland basin; Andean uplands in C rising to snow-capped peaks which include Cotopaxi, 5896 m/19 343 ft; forested alluvial plains in the E, dissected by rivers flowing from the Andes towards the Amazon (source of the Amazon located in Peru).

Climate Hot and humid, wet equatorial climate on coast; rain throughout year (especially Dec–Apr); average annual rainfall 1115 mm/44 in; average annual temperatures in Quito, 15°C (Jan), 14°C (Jul).

Currency 1 US Dollar (USD) = 100 cents (before 2000, the Sucre (ECS))

Economy Agriculture (employs c.35% of population); beans, cereals, livestock; bananas, coffee, fishing (especially shrimps); petrochemicals, steel, cement, pharmaceuticals; oil piped from the Oriente basin in E to refineries at Esmeraldas.

GDP (2004e) $49·51 bn, per capita $3700

Human Development Index (2002) 0·732

History Formerly part of Inca Empire; taken by Spanish, 1534; within Viceroyalty of New Granada; independent, 1822; joined with Panama, Colombia, and Venezuela to form Gran Colombia; left union, to become independent republic, 1830; highly unstable political history; constitution, 1978; comprises 21 provinces, including the Galápagos Is, each administered by a governor; governed by a President and a unicameral National Congress.

Head of State/Government

1966 Clemente Yerovi Indaburu
1966–8 Otto Arosemena Gómez
1968–72 José María Velasco Ibarra
1972–6 Guillermo Rodríguez Lara
1976–9 *Military junta*
1979–81 Jaime Roldós Aguilera
1981–4 Oswaldo Hurtado Larrea
1984–8 León Febres Cordero Rivadeneira
1988–92 Rodrigo Borja Cevallos
1992–6 Sixto Durán Ballén
1996–7 Abdala Bucaram
1997 Rosalia Arteaga *Acting*
1997–8 Fabián Alarcón Rivera
1998–2000 Jamil Mahuad Witt
2000–2 Gustavo Noboa Bejarano
2002–5 Lucio Gutiérrez
2005–6 Alfredo Palacio
2006– Rafael Correa

taining Arthur's Seat, extinct volcano; Scott Monument (1844), 61 m/200 ft high; Military Tattoo (Aug); International, Fringe, Jazz, Book, and Film Festivals, and Highland Games (Aug–Sep); named the world's first City of Literature by UNESCO in 2004.

Edinburgh, Prince Philip, Duke of [edinbruh] (1921–) The husband of Queen Elizabeth II of the United Kingdom, the son of Prince Andrew of Greece and Princess Alice of Battenberg, born in Corfu. He became a naturalized British subject in 1947, when he was married to the Princess Elizabeth (20 Nov). In 1956 he began the **Duke of Edinburgh Award Scheme** to foster the leisure activities of young people.

Edison, Thomas (Alva) (1847–1931) Inventor, born in Milan, OH. He was the author of over 1000 inventions, including the printing telegraph (1871), the phonograph (1877), the electric light bulb (1879), and motion picture equipment.

Edmonton 53°34N 113°25W, pop (2000e) 691000. Capital of Alberta province, W Canada; Fort Edmonton built by Hudson's

Bay Company, 1795; destroyed by Indians, 1807, and rebuilt on new site, 1819; chosen as capital, 1905; rapid growth after discovery of oil nearby, 1947; airport; airfield; University of Alberta (1906) and Athabasca University (1972); ice hockey team, Edmonton Oilers.

Edmund I (921–46) King of the English (from 939), the half-brother of Athelstan. He re-established control over the S Danelaw (942) and Northumbria (944), and for the remainder of his life ruled a reunited England.

Edmund II, known as **Edmund Ironside** (c.980–1016) King of the English, the son of Ethelred the Unready. Chosen king by the Londoners on his father's death (Apr 1016), he defeated Canute, but was routed at Ashingdon (Oct 1016), and died soon after.

Edmund, St, originally **Edmund Rich** (1170–1240) Clergyman and Archbishop of Canterbury, born in Abingdon, Oxfordshire. He became the spokesman of the national party against Henry III, defending Church rights. Feast day 16 November.

Edomites [eedomiyts] According to the Bible (*Gen* 36), the descendants of Esau who settled in the mountainous area S of the Dead Sea to the Gulf of Aqabah; in Greek, **Idumeans**. Enemies of Israel, they became a kingdom in the 8th-c BC.

educational drama The use of drama within an educational system, both as a means of learning and as a subject in its own right. Often more emphasis is placed on improvisation and exploration than on performance skills – on drama as process rather than on theatre as product.

educational psychology A branch of psychology which applies the findings of psychology to the understanding of learning. The traditional role of the educational psychologist was often limited to one of testing children and placing 'backward' ones into special education. Today, more attention is paid to the task of assisting teachers in programmes designed to help individual children, and in advising schools about their function as organizations.

Edward, Lake, Democratic Republic of Congo **Lake Rutanzige** area 4 000 km²/1 500 sq mi. Lake in EC Africa, on the frontier between the Democratic Republic of Congo and Uganda; length, c.80 km/50 mi; width, 50 km/30 mi; altitude, 912 m/2992 ft; European discovery by Stanley in 1889; named after the Prince of Wales (later Edward VII).

Edward I (1239–1307) King of England (1272–1307), born in London, the elder son of Henry III and Eleanor of Provence. In the Barons' War (1264–7), he defeated Simon de Montfort at Evesham (1265), then won renown as a crusader to the Holy Land in the Eighth Crusade (1270–2). In two campaigns (1276–7, 1282–3), he annexed N and W Wales, building magnificent castles, and reasserted English claims to the overlordship of Scotland thus beginning the Scottish Wars of Independence.

Edward II (1284–1327) King of England (1307–27), born in Caernarfon, Wales, the fourth son of Edward I and Eleanor of Castile. In 1301 he was created Prince of Wales, the first English heir apparent to bear the title. He was humiliated by reverses in Scotland, where he was decisively defeated at Bannockburn (1314). Throughout his reign, he mismanaged the barons, who sought to rid the country of royal favourites. He was deposed by his wife Isabella, and her lover Roger Mortimer Earl of March, and was murdered in Berkeley Castle.

Edward III, known as **Edward of Windsor** (1312–77) King of England (1327–77), born in Windsor, the elder son of Edward II and Isabella of France. By banishing Queen Isabella from court, he assumed full control of the government (1330), and began to restore the monarchy's authority and prestige. He defeated the Scots at Halidon Hill (1333), and in 1337 revived his hereditary claim to the French crown, thus beginning the Hundred Years' War. He destroyed the French navy at the Battle of Sluys (1340), and won another major victory at Crécy (1346).

Edward IV (1442–83) King of England (1461–70, 1471–83), born in Rouen, France, the eldest son of Richard, Duke of York. He entered London in 1461, was recognized as king on Henry VI's deposition, and defeated the Lancastrians at Towton. Forced into exile by the Earl of Warwick (1470), he recovered the throne after victories at Barnet and Tewkesbury.

Edward V (1470–83) King of England (Apr–Jun 1483), born in London, the son of Edward IV and Elizabeth Woodville. He and his younger brother Richard, Duke of York, were imprisoned in the Tower by their uncle Richard, Duke of Gloucester, who usurped the throne as Richard III. The two princes were never heard of again, and were most probably murdered (Aug 1483) on their uncle's orders.

Edward VI (1537–53) King of England (1547–53), born in London, the son of Henry VIII by his third queen, Jane Seymour. During his reign, power was first in the hands of his uncle, the Duke of Somerset, then of John Dudley, Duke of Northumberland. Under the Protectors the English Reformation flourished.

Edward VII (1841–1910) King of the United Kingdom (1901–10), born in London, the eldest son of Queen Victoria. In 1863 he married Alexandra of Denmark, by whom he had six children. As Prince of Wales, his behaviour led him into several social scandals, and the queen excluded him from affairs of state.

Edward VIII (1894–1972) King of the United Kingdom (Jan–Dec 1936), born in Richmond, Greater London, the eldest son of George V. He abdicated in the face of opposition to his proposed marriage to Wallis Simpson, an American who had been twice divorced. He was then given the title of Duke of Windsor, and the marriage took place in France in 1937. His wife, the **Duchess of Windsor** (1896–1986), lived in seclusion in Paris, after her husband's death.

Edward (Antony Richard Louis), Prince (1964–) Prince of the United Kingdom, the third son of Queen Elizabeth II. After studying history at Cambridge, he joined the Royal Marines in 1986, but left the following year and began a career in the theatre, beginning as a production assistant with Andrew Lloyd Webber's Really Useful Theatre Company. In 1993 he formed his own company, Ardent Productions. He was made Earl of Wessex on his marriage to Sophie Rhys-Jones (1965–) in 1999. Their daughter, Lady Louise Windsor, was born in 2003.

Edward the Black Prince (1330–76) Eldest son of Edward III, born in Woodstock, Oxfordshire. In 1346, though still a boy, he fought at Crécy, and is said to have won his popular title from his black armour. He won several victories in the Hundred Years' War, including Poitiers (1356).

Edward the Confessor, St (c.1003–66) King of England (1042–66), the elder son of Ethelred the Unready. Although in 1051 he probably recognized Duke William of Normandy (later William I) as his heir, on his deathbed he nominated Harold Godwinson (Harold II) to succeed, the Norman Conquest following soon after. Edward's reputation for holiness began in his lifetime, and he was canonized in 1161. Feast day 13 October.

Edward the Elder (c.870–924) King of Wessex (899–924), the elder son of Alfred the Great. He built on his father's successes and established himself as the strongest ruler in Britain, conquering the S Danelaw (910–18), and assuming control of Mercia (918).

Edward the Martyr, St (c.963–78) King of England (975–8), son of Edgar. He was murdered at Corfe, Dorset, by supporters of his stepmother, Elfrida, and canonized in 1001. Feast day 18 March.

Edwardes, Sir Michael (Owen) (1930–) British business executive, born in South Africa. After moving to Britain in 1966, he developed a reputation for rescuing ailing companies, and in 1977 was challenged to rescue British Leyland from commercial collapse, which he succeeded in doing over the next five years.

Edwards, Blake, originally **William Blake McEdwards** (1922–) Director and writer born in Tulsa, OK. A former actor and radio scriptwriter, he made his film directorial debut in 1955 with *Bring Your Smile Along*. He is best known for *Breakfast at Tiffanys* (1961), and his series of *Pink Panther* films (1964–78) starring Peter Sellers. Other films include *Operation Petticoat* (1959), *S.O.B.* (1981), and *Son of the Pink Panther* (1993).

Edwards, Huw (1961–) Television journalist and presenter, born in Llangennech, nr Llanelli. He joined the television newsroom in BBC Wales (1985), becoming their parliamentary correspondent (1986) and chief political correspondent for BBC News 24 (1988). He has presented the Six O Clock News (1999–2002) and the Ten O Clock News (2003–), and also several general-interest programmes, notably *The Story of Welsh* (2003) and *The Welsh in London* (2006).

Edwards, Jonathan (1703–58) Calvinist theologian and metaphysician, born in East Windsor, CT. His works, which include *Freedom of the Will* (1754), led to the religious revival known as the 'Great Awakening'.

Edwards, Jonathan (1966–) Triple jump athlete, born in London.

His sporting achievements include Commonwealth Games gold (2002), Olympic gold (2000), European Championship title (1998), and two World Championship gold medals (1995, 2001). He holds the world record of 18·29 m, set at the 1995 Championships in Gothenburg, Sweden. He retired in 2003.

Edwin, St (584–633) King of Northumbria (616–33), brought up in North Wales. Under him, Northumbria became united, and he obtained the overlordship of all England, save Kent. He was converted to Christianity, and baptized with his nobles in 627. Feast day 12 October.

EEC *European Economic Community*

EEG *electroencephalography*

eel Any of numerous marine and freshwater fishes with an elongate cylindrical body form; median fins continuous, pelvics absent, and pectorals present or absent; adults live in fresh water, returning to sea to spawn; common European eel (*Anguilla anguilla*. Family: Anguillidae) an important food fish.

eelpout Slender-bodied fish (*Zoarces viviparous*) with broad head, long dorsal and anal fins, well-developed pectorals, abundant in European coastal waters; length up to 50 cm/20 in. (Family: Zoarcidae.)

eelworm *nematode*

Efate [efatee], Fr **Vaté**, Eng **Sandwich Island** 17°40S 168°23E; pop (2000e) 39 200; area 985 km²/380 sq mi. Volcanic island, Vanuatu, SW Pacific; length, 42 km/26 mi; width, 23 km/14 mi; capital, Vila.

EFTA *European Free Trade Association*

egalitarianism A political philosophy which places a high value on equality among members of society, and advocates the removal of barriers to it. Egalitarianism was one of the tenets of the French Revolution, and is associated with radical and socialist politics.

Egbert, in Anglo-Saxon **Ecgberht** or **Ecgbryht** (?–839) King of Wessex (from 802). His successes gave him mastery over S England from Kent to Land's End, and established Wessex as the strongest Anglo-Saxon kingdom.

egg The mature female reproductive cell (*ovum*) in animals and plants; also the fertilized ovum in egg-laying animals, such as birds and insects, after it has been laid. This type of egg is covered by egg membranes, including the hard shell, which prevent it from drying out or being damaged. The eggs produced by domestic poultry (especially hens) are widely used as food. The yolk is rich in cholesterol, which has led some people for health reasons to restrict their egg intake. In 1987 an increase in food-poisoning cases due to *Salmonella* bacteria led to advice that eggs should be thoroughly cooked before being eaten.

egg-plant *aubergine*

eggs and bacon *bird's-foot trefoil*

eglantine A species of rose (*Rosa eglanteria*) with aromatic, sweet-smelling foliage; also called **sweet briar**. (Family: Rosaceae.)

Egmont, Mount, Maori **Taranaki** 39°18S 174°05E. Symmetrical volcanic peak, W North Island, New Zealand, S of New Plymouth; height, 2518 m/8261 ft.

egret The name used for a number of heron species. It is not applied consistently; some species are called *egret* by some observers, and *heron* by others.

Egypt *p.297*

Egypt, Ancient Dynasties *see panel*

Egyptian An extinct Afro-Asiatic language, which survives in inscriptions and papyrus manuscripts. In the 2nd-c AD, it evolved into **Coptic**, which is still used as a language of devotion by the Monophysite Christians in Egypt.

Egyptian cobra *asp*

Egyptian mongoose *ichneumon* (mammal)

Ehrenburg, Ilya Grigoryevich [airenberg] (1891–1967) Writer, born in Kiev. His novels include *Padeniye Parizha* (1941, The Fall of

Paris) and *Burya* (1948, The Storm), both of which won Stalin Prizes.

Ehrlich, Paul [airleekh] (1854–1915) Bacteriologist, born in Strzelin, Poland. He was a pioneer in haematology, immunology, and chemotherapy, discovering a cure for syphilis. He shared the Nobel Prize for Physiology or Medicine in 1908.

Eichmann, (Karl) Adolf [iykhman] (1906–62) Nazi war criminal, born in Solingen, Germany. He became a member of the SS in 1932, and organizer of anti-Semitic activities. Captured by US forces in 1945, he escaped from prison and in 1950 reached Argentina. He was traced and kidnapped by Israeli agents, taken to Israel in 1960, tried, convicted of crimes against humanity, and executed.

Eid-al-Adha; Eid-al-Fitr *Id al-Adha; Id al-Fitr*

eider [iyder] Any of four species of sea duck native to the northern N hemisphere; also known as **eider duck**. The female lines her nest with the soft downy feathers from her breast; these are collected commercially as **eiderdown**. (Subfamily: Anatinae. Tribe: Somateriini.)

eidophor [iydofaw(r)] A large-screen projection television system in which a scanning electron beam modulated by the video signal distorts the surface of an oil layer in a vacuum tube to refract the beam of light from a xenon lamp. Colour requires a triple-tube unit with the light divided by filters and recombined in projection.

Eiffel, (Alexandre) Gustave [efel] (1832–1923) Engineer, born in Dijon, France. Apart from his most famous project, the *Eiffel Tower*, he also designed the steel framework of the Statue of Liberty, NY.

Dynasties of Rulers: Ancient Egypt

dynasty	period	date BC
I	early dynastic period	c.3100–2890
II		c.2890–2686
III	old kingdom	c.2686–2613
IV		c.2613–2494
V		c.2494–2345
VI		c.2345–2181
VII	first intermediate period	c.2181–2173
VIII		c.2173–2160
IX		c.2160–2130
X		c.2130–2040
XI		c.2133–1991
XII	middle kingdom	1991–1786
XIII		1786–1633
XIV	second intermediate period	1786–c.1603
XV		1674–1567
XVI		c.1684–1567
XVII		c.1660–1567
XVIII	new kingdom	1567–1320
XIX		1320–1200
XX		1200–1085
XXI	third intermediate period	1085–945
XXII		945–730
XXIII		8172–730
XXIV		720–715
XXV		751–668
XXVI	late period	664–525
XXVII		525–404
XXVIII		404–399
XXIX		399–380
XXX		380–343
XXXI		343–332

Egypt

400 km
200 mi

TURKEY

AFRICA

MEDITERRANEAN
SEA

JORDAN

Alexandria
Matrûh
El Alamein
Siwa
Qattara
Depression
−133m

Port
Said
∴ Abu Mena
Suez
Canal
Cairo
Giza
Giza Pyramids
& Sphinx

ISRAEL

Suez

Sinai

SAUDI
ARABIA

El Minya

Hurghada

LIBYA

E G Y P T

RED
SEA

Thebes
Valley of the Kings ∴ ∴
El Kharga

Luxor

The Great
Oasis

Aswan

Tropic of Cancer

Dam
∴ Philae

Lake Nasser

S A H A R A

Abu Simbel ∴.

D E S E R T   SUDAN

☐ International Airport   ∴ World heritage site   — — Border in dispute

official name **Arab Republic of Egypt**, Arabic **Jumhuriyah Misr Al-Arabiya**
Local name Misr
Timezone GMT +2
Area 1 001 449 km²/386 559 sq mi
Population total (2002e) 66 341 000
Status Republic
Date of independence 1922
Capital Cairo
Language Arabic (official)
Ethnic group Population mainly of E Hamitic origin (90%)
Religions Sunni Muslim (c.90%), minority largely Coptic Christian (c.10%)
Physical features R Nile flows N from Sudan, dammed S of Aswan, creating L Nasser; huge delta N of Cairo, 250 km/150 mi across and 160 km/100 mi N–S; narrow Eastern Desert, sparsely

inhabited, between Nile and Red Sea; broad Western Desert, covering over two-thirds of the country; Sinai Peninsula (S), desert region with mountains rising to 2637 m/8651 ft at Gebel Katherina, Egypt's highest point; 90% of population lives on Nile floodplain (c.3% of country's area).

Climate Mainly desert climate, except for 80 km/50 mi wide Mediterranean coastal fringe; very hot on coast where dust-laden khamsin wind blows N from Sahara (Mar–Jun); Alexandria, average maximum daily temperatures 18–30°C; elsewhere rainfall less than 50 mm/2 in.

Currency 1 Egyptian Pound (EGP) = 100 piastres

Economy Agriculture on floodplain of R Nile accounts for about a third of national income; building of Aswan High Dam extended irrigated cultivation; a major tourist area.

GDP (2002e) $289·8 bn, per capita $4000

Human Development Index (2002) 0·642

History Neolithic cultures on R Nile from c.6000 BC; Pharaoh dynasties from c.3100 BC; Egyptian power greatest during the New Empire period, 1576–1085 BC; became Persian province, 6th-c BC; conquered by Alexander the Great, 4th-c BC; Ptolemaic Pharaohs ruled Egypt until 30 BC; conquered by Arabs, AD 672; Suez Canal constructed in 1869; revolt in 1879 put down by British in 1882; British protectorate from 1914; declared independence, 1922; King Farouk deposed by Nasser, 1952; Egypt declared a republic, 1953; attack on Israel followed by Israeli invasion, 1967; Suez Canal remained blocked, 1967–75; changed name to Arab Republic of Egypt, 1971; Yom Kippur War against Israel, 1973; Camp David peace conference with Israel, 1978; Israel returned disputed Taba Strip, 1989; participated in Gulf War with US-led coalition, 1991; governed by a People's National Assembly, President, Prime Minister, and Council of Ministers; constitution amended (May 2005) to allow contested presidential elections.

Monarch
1922–36 Fouad I
1936–7 Farouk *Trusteeship*
1937–52 Farouk I
Head of State
1952–4 Mohammed Najib
1954–70 Gamal Abdel Nasser
1970–81 Mohammed Anwar el-Sadat
1981– Mohammed Hosni Mubarak
Head of Government
1980–1 Mohammed Anwar el-Sadat
1981–2 Mohammed Hosni Mubarak
1982–4 Fouad Monyi ed-Din
1984 Kamal Hassan Ali
1985–6 Ali Lotfi
1986–96 Atef Sidqi
1996–9 Kamal Ahmed Ganzouri
1999–2004 Atef Ebeid
2004– Ahmed Nazif

Eiffel Tower [iyfl] A famous city landmark in Paris, designed by Gustave Eiffel and erected (1887–9) in the Champs-de-Mars for the Paris Exhibition of 1889. At 300 m/984 ft high, it was the tallest building in the world until 1930.

Eiger [iyger] 46°34N 8°01E. Mountain peak with three ridges in the Bernese Alps, Switzerland; height, 3970 m/13 025 ft; first ascent by Charles Barrington in 1858; N face first climbed in 1938.

Eigg [eg] Island in Highland, W Scotland; S of Skye, 11 km/7 mi from mainland (E); area 67 km²/26 sq mi; rises to 397 m/1302 ft.

Eight, the *Ashcan School*

Eightfold Path The fourth of Buddha's Four Noble Truths, prescribing the way to enlightenment. The Path involves right understanding, right aspiration, right speech, right conduct, right means of livelihood, right endeavour, right mindfulness, and right contemplation.

Eijkman, Christiaan [iykman] (1858–1930) Physician, born in Nijkerk, The Netherlands, the first to propose the concept of essential food factors, later called vitamins. He shared the Nobel Prize for Physiology or Medicine in 1929.

Eilat or **Elat** [aylat] 29°33N 34°57E, pop (2000e) 34 000. Seaport in S Israel, founded in 1949; airfield; terminus of oil pipeline from Ashkelon.

Eindhoven [iynthohvn] 51°26N 5°30E, pop (2000e) 203 000. Modern industrial city in S Netherlands; airport; railway; technical university (1956); Centre of Micro-Electronics.

Einstein, Albert (1879–1955) Mathematical physicist, born in Ulm, Germany. He became world famous by his special (1905) and general (1916) theories of relativity, and was awarded the Nobel Prize for Physics in 1921. After Hitler's rise to power, he left Germany, became a US citizen. He spent the later part of his life attempting by means of his unified field theory (1950) to establish a merger between quantum theory and his general theory of relativity. He was also a champion of pacifism and liberalism.

Einthoven, Willem [aynthohfn] (1860–1927) Dutch physiologist, born in Semarang, Indonesia. He invented the string galvanometer for measuring the elecrical rhythms of the heart (1903), introduced the term 'electrocardiogram', and was awarded the Nobel Prize for Physiology or Medicine in 1924.

Eisenhower, Dwight D(avid) [iyznhower], nickname **Ike** (1890–1969) US general and 34th president (1953–61), born in Denison, TX. In 1942 he commanded Allied forces for the amphibious descent on French N Africa. His talent for smooth co-ordination of the Allied staff led to his selection as Supreme Commander for the 1944 cross-channel invasion of the continental mainland. In 1952 the popularity which he had gained in Europe swept him to victory in the presidential elections, standing as a Republican, and he was re-elected in 1956. During his presidency the US government was preoccupied with foreign policy, and pursued a campaign against Communism, but was also actively involved in the civil rights movement.

Eisenstein, Sergey (Mikhaylovich) [iyznstiyn] (1898–1948) Film director and artist, born in Riga, Latvia, a major influence on the development of the cinema. His films include *Potemkin* (1925), *Alexander Nevski* (1938), and *Ivan the Terrible* (1944–6).

eisteddfod [iystethvod] A Welsh gathering of 12th-c origin for competitions in music and literature. The annual National Eisteddfod is held in August (entirely in Welsh) alternately in N and S Wales.

Ekaterinburg *Yekaterinburg*

Ekwensi, Cyprian (Odiatu Duaka) [ekwensee] (1923–) Writer, born in Minna, C Nigeria. His most successful novel is *Jagua Nana* (1961), about a group of vibrant characters who forsake their rural origins for the attractions of city life. His experiences of civil war are chronicled in *Survive the Peace* (1976) and *Divided We Stand* (1980). He was awarded the Dag Hammarskjöld International Prize in Literature in 1968.

El Alamein, Battle of (23 Oct–4 Nov 1942) A World War 2 battle, named after a village on Egypt's Mediterranean coast. It ended in the victory of the British Eighth Army commanded by Montgomery over Rommel's Afrika Korps.

Elam [eelam] The name given in antiquity to what is now SW Iran. Its main city was Susa, and at its zenith in the 13th-c BC it ruled an empire stretching from Babylonia in the W to Persepolis in the E.

eland [eeland] An African spiral-horned antelope; cattle-like, with narrow face and straight horns; the largest antelope (shoulder height, up to 1·8 m/6 ft); easily tamed; two species: the **common** (or **Cape**) **eland** (*Taurotragus oryx*) and the **giant** (or **derby**) **eland** (*Taurotragus derbianus*).

Elara [eelara] The seventh natural satellite of Jupiter, discovered in 1905; distance from the planet 11 740 000 km/7 295 000 mi; diameter 80 km/50 mi.

elasticity (physics) In solids, the property that a stressed material will return to its original size and shape when the stress is removed. It usually corresponds to a direct proportionality between stress and strain.

elastic rebound theory *isostasy*

elastomers [eelastomerz] Materials, usually synthetic, having elastic properties (ie capable of recovery from severe deformation). Examples include natural rubber and polyisoprene.

Elat *Eilat*

E layer *Heaviside layer*

Elba, Gr **Aithalia**, Lat **Ilva** pop (2000e) 11 000; area 223 km²/86 sq mi. Italian island in the Ligurian Sea, between the N Italian coast and Corsica; length 27 km/17 mi; width 18·5 km/11½ mi; chief town, Portoferraio; Napoleon lived here after his abdication (1814–15).

ElBaredei, Mohamed (1942–) Director-general of the International Atomic Energy Agency (IAEA), born in Cairo, Egypt. He studied law at the University of Cairo (1962) and at the New York University School of Law (1974). In 1964 he joined the Egyptian Diplomatic Service and served in the Permanent Missions of Egypt to the UN. A senior member of the IAEA secretariat since 1984, he became director-general in 1997. He shared the 2005 Nobel Peace Prize with the IAEA.

Elbe, River [elbuh], Czech **Labe**, ancient **Albis** River in the Czech Republic and Germany, flowing N to enter the North Sea at Cuxhaven, Germany; length 1158 km/720 mi; navigable to beyond the Czech border.

Elbert, Mount 39°05N 106°27W. Mountain in C Colorado, USA; the highest peak in the Rocky Mts (4399 m/14 432 ft).

elbow The region of the upper limb between the arm and forearm; specifically, the joint between the humerus and the radius/ulna. Banging the medial side of the elbow (the 'funny bone') against a solid object may cause pain and a tingling sensation over the hand; when this happens, the ulnar nerve has been compressed between the object and the humerus.

Elbrus, Mount [elbruhs] 43°21N 42°29E. Highest peak of the Caucasus range, S European Russia; height 5642 m/18 510 ft; highest peak in Europe.

El Cid *Cid, El*

elder (botany) A deciduous shrub (*Sambucus nigra*), growing to 10 m/30 ft, very widespread; bark furrowed, corky; flowers creamy, in large, flat-topped clusters; berries purplish-black. The flowers and berries are used in wines and preserves, but all other parts of the plant are poisonous. (Family: Caprifoliaceae.)

elder (religion) One who by reason of age or distinction is entrusted with shared authority and leadership in a community. **1** In the ancient Biblical world, the elders of Israel exercised both religious and civil influence from the tribal period onwards; and city elders were active at a local level. In the New Testament, elders were church officials with a collective authority for general oversight of a congregation. **2** In Reformed Churches, an officer ordained to 'rule' along with the minister (a 'teaching' elder). Elders exercise discipline, and oversee the life of a congregation and its individual members.

El Dorado [el dorahdoh] Literally, 'the gilded one'; a powerful early colonial Spanish-American legend of a ruler coated in gold, believed to exist in New Granada (now Colombia); by extension, a land of fabulous wealth.

Eleanor of Aquitaine (c.1122–1204) Queen consort of Louis VII of France (1137–52) and of the future Henry II of England (1154–89). She was imprisoned (1174–89) for supporting the rebellion of her sons, two of whom became kings as Richard I (in 1189) and John (in 1199).

Eleanor of Castile [kasteel] (1246–90) Queen consort of Edward I of England (1254–90). She accompanied Edward to the Crusades, and is said to have saved his life by sucking the poison from a wound. The 'Eleanor Crosses' at Northampton, Geddington, and Waltham Cross are survivors of the 12 erected by Edward at the halting places of her cortège.

Eleatics [eliatiks] A group of presocratic Greek philosophers in the 5th-c BC – Parmenides, Melissus, and Zeno – from Elea, Italy, who argued that reality is unbegotten, imperishable, atemporal, indivisible, motionless, and utterly changeless. The arguments profoundly influenced subsequent Greek philosophy.

elections *franchise* (politics)

electoral college A body made up of people who are responsible for electing a person to some office. These people can hold a particular office themselves (as in the case of the College of Cardinals who elect the Pope) or be elected from a wider electorate. The most famous college is the one that elects the president of the USA.

Electra [elektra] In Greek tragedies, but not in Homer, the daughter of Agamemnon and Clytemnestra, who assisted her brother Orestes when he arrived in Argos to avenge his father, and who later married his friend Pylades.

electrical conduction The transport of electrical charge through some substance. Only metals conduct electricity well; conduction is by means of the free electrons in the electron gas characteristic of metal structure. Ionic and covalently bound solids are insulators; but ionic solids such as salt (sodium chloride) conduct when dissolved in water, as the electrically charged ions become free to move.

electrical engineering A branch of engineering which studies the practical applications of electricity and electronics. It deals with the production, distribution, control, and use of electricity in all its forms, as in radio, radar, lighting, motors, power generators, and transmission systems. **Electronic engineering** developed as a subdivision of electrical engineering, and is now primarily concerned with automation, missile control systems, satellites, spacecraft, and communication systems.

electrical power The rate of transfer of energy in electrical circuits; symbol P, units W (watt). An electric light of power 60 W running for 1 hour consumes as much energy as a 30 W light running for 2 hours.

electric-arc furnace An electric furnace used particularly in steel making, where a very high temperature is generated in the 'arc' or discharge between two electrodes, the current passing through material evaporated from the electrodes. The original process was devised in 1870 by Siemens.

electric car A motor car designed to be propelled by an electric motor. Although electric traction has been used extensively in delivery vehicles such as milk floats (UK) and in golf carts (USA), it has not been possible for the electric car to compete with the internal-combustion-engined car because of the size and weight of batteries needed.

electric charge *charge*

electric conductance *electrical conduction; resistance*

electric dipole moment Symbol p, units C.m (coulomb.metre), a vector quantity; for charges $+q$ and $-q$ separated by distance l (a *dipole*), the electric dipole moment is $p = ql$.

electric eel Large freshwater fish (*Electrophorus electricus*) found in shallow streams of the Orinoco and Amazon basins; body cylindrical at front, length up to 2·4 m/8 ft; long anal fin; produces powerful electric shocks. (Family: Electrophoridae.)

electric field The region of electric influence surrounding positive or negative electric charges; symbol E, units V/m (volts per metre); a vector quantity.

electric grid In the UK, the system of distributing electricity, across the country and internationally, using a network of cables to provide supplies matching peak and lesser demands with maximum economy. The largest pylons carry the primary supplies at 400 000 or 275 000 volts; smaller ones carry secondary supplies at 132 000 and 66 000 volts.

electricity Phenomena associated with electrical charges and currents, and the study of such phenomena. Between collections of positive and negative charges there exists a potential difference. If a conducting path exists between the two charge groups, charges will flow from one to the other, constituting an electric current. Electric charge which builds up on an insulator and is thus unable to flow is termed **static electricity**.

electric ray Any of a family of sluggish bottom-living marine rays, widespread in tropical to temperate seas; body disc rounded, skin smooth, tail robust; well-developed electric organs produce strong shocks to stun prey; also called **torpedo rays**. (Family: Torpedinidae.)

electric resistance *resistance*

electrocardiography The investigation of the electrical activity of the heart. The electric voltages accompanying heartbeats can be recorded from the surface of the skin in the form of an electrocardiogram (**ECG**). Electrodes are attached to the skin of the limbs and chest, and the voltages between various pairs of electrodes are recorded.

electrochemistry The study of chemical change in a solution, resulting from the uptake of electrons from an external circuit or their supply to a circuit. Storage batteries (*accumulators*) illustrate this process, as they charge and discharge respectively.

electroconvulsive therapy (ECT) A highly successful treatment for patients with severe psychiatric disorders, in which an electric current is passed through the brain of an anaesthetized patient. The technique is often used in depression and schizophrenia.

electrocution Death or severe injury from contact with electric current. High-voltage electric shock induces spasm of the skeletal muscles and rapid irregular contractions of the heart, which stops pumping. Electrocution is used as a method of capital punishment in some countries (eg in some US states).

electrodynamics The study of the motion of electric charges caused by electric and magnetic fields.

electroencephalography [electrohensefalografee] The investigation of the electrical activity of the brain, using electrodes applied to the scalp, and usually recorded as a tracing on paper (an electroencephalogram, or **EEG**). The EEG changes with the mental activity of the subject, and characteristic patterns of electrical activity (eg for sleep, coma, epileptic seizure) can be recognized. The *alpha rhythm* (c.10 Hz) appears with relaxation and eye closure. The *delta rhythm* (1–4 Hz) appears in deep sleep.

electrolysis The splitting of a compound into simpler forms by the input of electrical energy.

electrolyte A system, usually a solution, in which electrochemical reactions occur. It must be sufficiently conducting to allow current to pass.

electromagnet *magnet*

electromagnetic radiation Oscillating electric and magnetic fields which propagate together through empty space as a radiated wave; velocity c, the velocity of light. They include radio waves, light, and X-rays.

electromagnetism *p.300*

electromotive force The work done by some source in separating electrical charges to produce a potential difference capable of driving current round a circuit; often abbreviated **emf**. The unit of emf is the volt.

electron A fundamental particle, denoted e^-, where the minus sign indicates that the charge is negative; charge of $-1·602 \times 10^{-19}$C; mass $9·110 \times 10^{-31}$ kg or $0·511$ MeV, approximately 1/1836 that of the proton; spin $\frac{1}{2}$ fermion; stable against decay; no known size, assumed point-like; no known substructure; a carrier of negative charge in matter, including electrical currents in conductors. Electrons together with the positively charged nucleus form atoms. They were discovered by British physicist J J Thomson in 1897.

electromagnetism

The electromagnetic spectrum

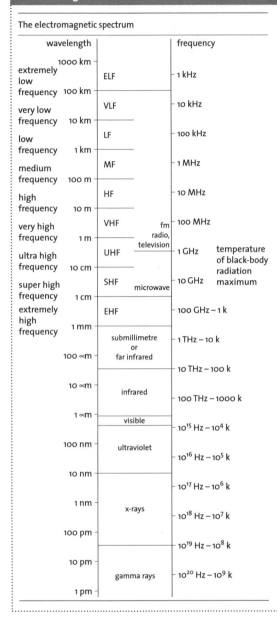

Phenomena involving both electric and magnetic fields, and the study of such phenomena. The first indication of a link between electricity and magnetism was shown by Hans Christian Ørsted, who demonstrated that an electrical current caused the deflection of a compass needle (1819). This established that magnetic effects are produced by a moving electrical charge. Ørsted's observation was interpreted by Michael Faraday in terms of lines of magnetic influence circulating around the wire. Ampère deduced an expression for the magnetic force between two current-carrying wires to give the original form of what is now called Ampère's law (1827). Faraday demonstrated that switching off a current in a circuit produced a momentary current in a nearby circuit, and that moving a magnet close to a circuit also produced momentary currents (1831). This established that electrical charge can be made to flow by changing magnetic fields, the basis of electromagnetic induction (expressed as Faraday's law). Similar work was performed by Joseph Henry (1829). The first generator was built by Faraday in 1831.

The unification of electricity and magnetism into a single theory of electromagnetism is due to James Clerk Maxwell, who first expressed the laws of Faraday and Ampère in their modern form as two of the four Maxwell's equations. Using his equations of electromagnetism, Maxwell postulated that light is electromagnetic disturbance with velocity

$$c = \frac{1}{\sqrt{\varepsilon_0 \mu_0}},$$

where ε_0 and μ_0 are the permittivity and permeability of empty space, respectively (1864). Heinrich Hertz used oscillating electrical circuits to produce radio waves which travelled at the velocity of light (1887), thereby providing experimental support for Maxwell's work. The expression of the velocity of light in terms of fundamental constants suggested to Einstein that it should always be the same for all observers. This conclusion is central to his theory of special relativity (1905), which in turn explains more fully the relationship between electric and magnetic effects. While an observer stationary with respect to an electric charge will see it as a source of electric field only, a second observer moving relative to the first will see the same charge as a source of both electric and magnetic fields in a way dictated by special relativity.

---

electron gun A device for producing electron beams. A heated cathode produces electrons by thermionic emission. It is an essential component of television tubes, electron microscopes, and cathode ray tubes.

electronic cash *smart card*

electronic commerce *e-commerce*

electronic data interchange (EDI) A set of standards which have been established between different computer users to enable data created by one to be sent to another in an understandable form. For example, department stores use EDI to transmit orders to suppliers.

electronic games Games programmed and controlled by a small microprocessor. Most electronic games are connected to a visual display unit and are known as **video games**. Multi-coloured visual effects and varying sounds are incorporated. The first video game appeared in the USA in the early 1970s; it was called *Pong*, and was a simple form of table tennis.

electronic mail or **e-mail** The use of computer systems to transfer messages between users. Messages are usually stored centrally until acknowledged by the recipient.

electronic music Music in which the sound is generated by electronic instruments (especially synthesizers), processed by means of tape recorders heard through loudspeakers.

electronic photography Exposure of a single picture in a special video camera (a *still video camera*, or *SVC*), which records the image in either an analogue or digital way on a rotating 50 mm floppy magnetic disk or a solid state memory card. This has the capacity for up to 25 individual shots, which are available for immediate display on a video screen or as a paper printout within 90 seconds.

electronic publishing The issuing to identified users of selected, edited, textual and illustrative material taken from an electronic database. The data may be communicated on-line to the customer's computer, or transferred to a portable medium such as magnetic tape or disk or CD-ROM disk. The term is used generally to cover all publishing except print on paper.

electronics The scientific study and application of the movement of electrons. Transistors facilitated the miniaturization of electronic components, as did the silicon chip and the integrated circuit. The social impact of electronics is far-reaching, including the development of television, computerized office systems, video games, personal computers, pacemakers, and spacecraft.

electron microscope A microscope using a beam of electrons instead of light, and magnetic or electrostatic fields as lenses. In the **transmission electron microscope** the direct passage of the beam through the specimen produces an image on a fluorescent screen. The specimen must be very thin, but the resolution is high: c.0·2–0·5 nm. In the **scanning electron microscope**, the specimen is scanned by the beam, which produces secondary electron emission, imaged on a cathode ray screen. The specimen can be thicker, and an image of some depth produced, but resolution is limited to c.10–20 nm.

electron volt A unit of energy common in atomic, nuclear, and particle physics; symbol eV; equals the change in energy of an electron moving through a potential difference of 1 volt; $1 \text{ eV} = 1·602 \times 10^{-19}$ J (joule, SI unit); commonly used as keV (10^3 eV), MeV (10^6 eV), and GeV (10^9 eV).

electrophone Any musical instrument in which the sound is generated by mechanical or electronic oscillators (eg a synthesizer) or in which acoustically generated vibrations require electrical amplification before they can be heard (eg the electric guitar).

electroplating The depositing of a metal on another metal by electrolysis. The object to be plated is made the cathode; the metal to be deposited is derived from the anode. The plating may be intended for decoration, or to provide resistance to corrosion.

electro-pollution High and low frequency electromagnetic emissions (EMF) produced by such equipment as microwave ovens, computer terminals, and high voltage cables. Exposure to the EMF field may have adverse long-term effects on health and lead to such problems as headaches, impaired concentration, and stress-induced disorders.

electroscope A device for detecting the presence of an electric charge and estimating its amount. The simplest form consists of two thin gold leaves which repel each other when charged, the degree of divergence indicating the amount of the charge.

electrosleep *shock therapy*

electrostatic generator A device for producing a large electric charge, usually by the repetition of an induction process and the successive accumulation of the charge produced. Modern, very high voltage machines are versions of the Van de Graaff belt-operated generator (1929).

electrostatics The study of fields and potentials due to stationary electric charges. Electrostatic forces bind electrons to the nucleus in atoms.

elegy In classical times, any poem in elegiac metre (a couplet consisting of one hexameter and one pentameter), such as those written (in Greek) by Archilochus (7th-c BC), and (in Latin) by Propertius. In modern literatures, it is a poem of mourning or lament, as in Gray's *Elegy Written in a Country Churchyard* (1751).

elementary particle physics *particle physics*

elements (chemistry) *chemical elements*

elephant A large mammal of family Elephantidae; the only living members of order Proboscidea (many extinct forms); almost naked grey skin; massive forehead; small eyes; upper incisor teeth form 'tusks'; snout elongated as a muscular grasping 'trunk'; ears large and movable (used to radiate heat). There are two living species. The **African elephant** is the largest living land animal (height up to 3·8 m/12½ ft), with three subspecies (*Loxodonta africana*). The smaller **Asian elephant** has four subspecies (*Elephas maximus*).

Elephanta Caves A group of Hindu cave-temples located on Elephanta I off the W coast of Maharashtra, India; a world heritage site.

elephant bird An enormous bird, known from the Pleistocene and Holocene epochs; fossil remains found on Madagascar; flightless, stood up to 3 m/10 ft tall, and laid eggs more than 30 cm/1 ft long. (Family: Aepyornithidae.)

elephantiasis [elifantiyasis] A gross swelling of one or both legs, scrotum, and occasionally arms as a result of blockage of the lymphatic channels by filariasis. The condition is found only in the tropics.

elephant seal A huge true seal; adult male up to 6 m/20 ft long, weight 3700 kg/8150 lb; swollen pendulous snout. (Family: Phocidae, 2 species.)

elephant's-ear *begonia*

Eleusinian Mysteries [elyoosinian] The secret initiation ceremonies connected with the worship of the corn-goddess Demeter and her daughter Persephone, held annually at Eleusis near Athens in ancient times.

elevator (chiefly American English) or **lift** (chiefly British English) A device which carries people or objects from one level to another in a building with several floors. The elevator car is moved by a system of cables and pulleys, which link the car to a counterweight, the power usually being generated by electricity (earlier lifting systems had used a variety of methods, such as animal, steam, and water power). The invention of the elevator fostered the development of the skyscraper in modern cities. Following the invention of a safety device by Otis in 1852, the first (steam-powered) passenger elevator was introduced in New York City in 1857.

eleven-plus examination In the UK, a test taken by pupils towards the end of their primary education, in areas where there are selective secondary schools, to determine which school they shall attend. It declined, though did not disappear, with the spread of comprehensive schools in the 1960s and 1970s.

Elgar, Sir Edward (1857–1934) Composer, born in Broad Heath, Worcestershire. The *Enigma Variations* (1899) and the oratorio *The Dream of Gerontius* (1900) made him the leading figure of his day in English music. From 1924 he was Master of the King's Musick.

Elgin Marbles [elgin] Marble sculptures of the mid-5th-c BC from the Parthenon of Athens. Acquired in 1801–3 by Thomas Bruce, 7th Earl of Elgin (1766–1841), in circumstances of doubtful legality while Greece was under Turkish rule, they were shipped to England, and in 1816 purchased by the government for the British Museum, where they remain on display. In the 1980s in particular, the question of their return to Greece became a heated political issue there, and the matter continues to be raised, given a focus by the ongoing restoration of the Parthenon. A request to borrow the Marbles for the 2004 Olympic Games was turned down.

El Greco *Greco, El*

Elijah [eliyja] (9th-c BC) Hebrew prophet, whose activities are portrayed in four Bible stories (1 *Kings* 17–19, 21; 2 *Kings* 1–2). By virtue of his loyalty to God he was depicted as ascending directly into heaven.

elint The practice of 'electronic *int*elligence' gathering, in which one finds out the performance factors of hostile weapons systems by interpreting their electronic emissions.

Elion, Gertrude (Belle) (1918–99) Chemist, born in New York City. In 1951, working with George Hitchings (1905–98), she made and tested 6-mercaptopurine (6MP) which proved useful in cancer treatment, especially childhood leukaemia, then worked on a wide range of other drugs. She shared the Nobel Prize for Physiology or Medicine in 1988.

Eliot, George, pseudonym of **Mary Ann Evans** or **Marian Evans** (1819–80) Novelist, born at Arbury Farm, Astley, Warwickshire. She became the centre of a literary circle, one of whose members was G H Lewes (1817–78), with whom she lived until his death. Her major novels were *Adam Bede* (1859), *The Mill on the Floss* (1860), *Silas Marner* (1861), *Middlemarch* (1871–2), and *Daniel Deronda* (1876).

Eliot, T(homas) S(tearns) (1888–1965) Poet, critic, and playwright, born in St Louis, MO. The enthusiastic support of Ezra Pound led to his first book of poetry, *Prufrock and Other Observations* (1917). He then published *The Waste Land* (1922) and *The Hollow Men* (1925), and edited the quarterly review, *The Criterion*, from its beginning to its demise (1922–39). Later works include his major poetic achievement, *Four Quartets* (1944), and a series of verse dramas, notably *Murder in the Cathedral* (1935). In 1948 he was awarded the Nobel Prize for Literature.

Elisabethville *Lubumbashi*

Elisha [eliysha] (second half of 9th-c BC) Hebrew prophet in succession to Elijah; his activities are portrayed in 1 *Kings* 19 and 2 *Kings* 2–9,13. He was active in Israel under several kings from Ahab to Jehoash.

Elizabeth I, known as **the Virgin Queen** and later **Good Queen Bess** (1533–1603) Queen of England and Ireland (1558–1603), the daughter of Henry VIII by his second wife, Anne Boleyn, born in Greenwich, London. She saw her role in Europe as a Protestant sovereign, and it is from this time that the Anglican Church was formally established. Mary, Queen of Scots, was thrown into her power (1568) and imprisoned, causing endless conspiracies among English Catholics. After the most sinister plot was discovered (1586), Elizabeth was reluctantly persuaded to execute Mary (1587), and subsequently persecuted Catholics. Philip of Spain then attacked England with his 'invincible armada' (1588), but England managed to repel the attack. A strong, cruel, and capricious woman, the 'Virgin Queen' was nevertheless popular with her subjects, as indicated by her other byname, 'Good Queen Bess'; and her reign is seen as the period when England assumed the position of a world power.

Elizabeth II (1926–) Queen of the United Kingdom (1952–) and head of the Commonwealth, born in London, the daughter of George VI. Formerly **Princess Elizabeth Alexandra Mary**, she was proclaimed queen on 6 February 1952, and crowned on 2 June 1953. Her husband was created Duke of Edinburgh on the eve of their wedding (20 Nov 1947), and styled Prince Philip in 1957. They have three sons, **Charles Philip Arthur George** (1948), **Andrew Albert Christian Edward** (1960), and **Edward Anthony Richard Louis** (1964), and a daughter, **Anne Elizabeth Alice Louise** (1950). In 2006 she celebrated her 80th birthday and attended various public events to mark the occasion.

Elizabeth (Queen Mother), originally **Lady Elizabeth Bowes-Lyon** (1900–2002) Queen-consort of Great Britain, born in St Paul's Walden Bury, Hertfordshire. Her father became 14th Earl of Strathmore in 1904. Much of her childhood was spent at Glamis Castle in Scotland, where she helped the nursing staff in World War 1. In 1923 she married the **Duke of York**, second son of George V; **Princess Elizabeth** (later Queen Elizabeth II) was born in 1926 and **Princess Margaret** in 1930. She was a strong support to her husband, during the period of Edward VIII's abdication in 1936, and after her husband came to the throne as King George VI, she scored striking personal success in royal visits to Paris (1938) and to Canada and the USA (1939). She was with the king when Buckingham Palace was bombed in 1940, travelling with him to visit heavily damaged towns throughout the war. After George VI's death (1952), she continued to undertake public duties and became a widely loved figure. In 1978 she became Lord Warden of the Cinque Ports, the first woman to hold the office. Even after her 100th birthday, which prompted a nation-wide celebration, she continued to attend public events. Her death generated a wave of popular emotion, with thousands queuing many hours to walk past her coffin in Westminster Hall. A million people lined the route of her funeral, and the nation marked her death with a level of ceremony not seen in the UK for half a century.

Elizabethan Style A form of early English Renaissance architecture of the period 1558–1603, characterized by symmetrical facades combined with Netherland decoration and over-sized windows. The name derives from Queen Elizabeth I of that period. A good example is Longleat, Wiltshire (c.1568 onwards).

Elizabeth Petrovna [petrovna] (1709–62) Empress (tsaritsa) of Russia (1741–62), the daughter of Peter the Great and Catherine I, born near Moscow. A war with Sweden was brought to a successful conclusion, and she took part in the War of the Austrian Succession and in the Seven Years' War.

elk The largest of the true deer (*Alces alces*) (shoulder height, 2·4 m/8 ft); widespread in temperate N hemisphere; usually solitary; long snout; throat with loose flap of skin; antlers broad; also known in North America as **moose**.

elkhound A spitz breed of dog, used in Scandinavia (especially Norway) to hunt elk; medium-sized, broad, solid body with thick grey coat; also known as **Norwegian elkhound** or **elk**.

Ellesmere Island [elezmeer] Arctic island in Northwest Territories, Canada; area 196 236 km^2/75 747 sq mi; barren and mountainous; several small settlements.

Ellice Islands *Tuvalu*

Ellington, Duke, popular name of **Edward Kennedy Ellington** (1899–1974) Composer, arranger, bandleader, and pianist, born in Washington, DC. He developed a unique sound for his musicians by blending instruments ingeniously into startling harmonies, as in 'Creole Love Call' (1927) and 'Mood Indigo' (1930). His creative peak is generally said to be 1939–42, with such recordings as 'Cotton Tail' and 'Take the A Train'. Later works included suites such as 'Such Sweet Thunder' (1957) and 'Gutelas Suite' (1971), film scores, ballets, and a series of 'sacred concerts' (1968–74) performed in cathedrals around the world. He led his band until a couple of months before his death from cancer, when it was taken over by his son, **Mercer Ellington** (1919–96).

Elliott, Herb, popular name of **Herbert James Elliott** (1938–) Athlete, born in Perth, Western Australia. Winner of the gold medal in the 1500 m at the 1960 Olympics in Rome, his time of 3 min 35·6 s for that event was unbeaten for seven years. He was noted for the rigour and severity of his training schedule.

ellipse In mathematics, the locus of a point which moves so that the sum of its distances from two fixed points (or *foci*) is constant. The Cartesian equation of an ellipse can be put in the form $x^2/a^2 + y^2/b^2 = 1$. The planets move around the Sun in ellipses, and the shape is much used in art and architecture.

elliptic geometry *geometries, non-Euclidean*

Ellis, Alice Thomas, originally **Anna Margaret Haycraft**, *née* **Lindholm** (1932–2005) Novelist, born in Liverpool, Merseyside. A writer of cookery books under her original name, it was *The Sin Eater* (1977), which established her reputation as a novelist. *The 27th Kingdom* (1982) is often considered her most successful novel. Other books include *Valentine's Day* (2000), *Fish, Flesh and Good Red Herring, A Gallimaufry* (2004), and an autobiography, *A Welsh Childhood* (1990).

Ellis, (Henry) Havelock (1859–1939) Physician and writer on sex, born in Croydon, Greater London. The seven-volume *Studies in the Psychology of Sex* (1897–1928), the first detached treatment of the subject, was highly controversial at the time.

Ellis Island A small island (27·5 acres) in New York Bay, USA; named after New Jersey merchant Samuel Ellis, who owned it in the 18th-c. It served as the main immigration centre to the USA from 1892 to 1943, with c.2000 immigrants a day arriving there in the peak years of the early 20th-c. It became part of the Statue of Liberty National Monument in 1965. Sovereignty of the island changed from New York to New Jersey, following a US Supreme Court decision in 1998.

Ellison, Ralph (Waldo) (1914–94) Writer, born in Oklahoma City, OK. His major work was the novel, *Invisible Man* (1952), a semi-autobiographical account of a young black intellectual's search for identity. His short story *Flying Home*, was published posthumously in 1996.

elm A deciduous N temperate tree; leaves ovoid, doubly toothed, asymmetric at base; flowers tiny, appearing before leaves; seed oval, with broad papery wing. In recent years the European and N American elm populations have been largely destroyed by Dutch elm disease, first identified in Holland in 1967. (Genus: *Ulmus*, 45 species. Family: Ulmaceae.)

El Niño [neenyoh] An anomalous seasonal ocean current along the coast of Peru. Under normal conditions, upwelling along the coast brings up nutrient-enriched deeper waters which result in high biological productivity. During El Niño, wind patterns along the Peruvian coast change, the upwelling is interrupted, and there is massive mortality of marine organisms. The phenomenon usually occurs around Christmas, hence the name, which is Spanish for 'the Child'. Once thought to be produced by changes in local wind conditions affecting the ocean, it is now known to be part of a much larger phenomenon related to changes in atmospheric pressure in the S Pacific, called the *southern oscillation*. The phenomenon may recur every 2–10 years, and has been blamed for such wide-ranging effects as severe storm damage along the W coast of the Americas, more frequent tropical cyclones, and severe winters in Europe and North America. Its effects were especially noticeable during 1997, with some locations experiencing dramatic climatic change (eg a major increase of rainfall on Christmas I). There is a complementary effect, known as **La Niña**, a cooling of the Pacific water, in intervening years.

elocution The study and practice of excellence in the manner and style of vocal delivery, dating from classical Greek and Roman times. Grammar, choice of vocabulary, and style are all taken into account to achieve the greatest effect in using the voice.

Elohim [elohheem] (Heb 'gods') A divine name for the God of Israel, the plural form here being purged of its polytheistic meaning, and used as a plural of majesty.

El Paso [el pasoh] 31°45N 106°29W, pop (2000e) 563 600. City in W Texas, USA; port on the Rio Grande; founded, 1827; part transferred to Mexico in 1963; airfield; railway; university (1913).

El Salvador *p.304*

Elsinore [elsinaw(r)], Danish **Helsingør** 56°03N 12°38E, pop (2000e) 58 200. Seaport on The Sound, NE Zealand, Denmark, opposite Helsingborg, Sweden; railway; site of Kronborg Castle,

a world heritage site, famous as the scene of Shakespeare's *Hamlet*.

Eluard, Paul [elwah(r)], pseudonym of **Eugène Grindel** (1895–1952) Poet, born in Saint-Denis, France. He was one of the founders of the Surrealist movement in literature. His first collection of poetry was *Capitale de la douleur* (1926, Capital of Sorrow).

Elvström, Paul [elvstroem] (1928–) Yachtsman, born in Gentofte, Copenhagen. He is the only yachtsman to win four individual Olympic gold medals: in the Firefly class in 1948 and the Finn class in 1952, 1956, and 1960.

Elway, John (1960–) Player of American football, born in Port Angeles, Washington, DC. He spent his entire career with Denver Broncos, leading them to the NFL quarterback record 148 victories and throwing for 51 475 yds, the second highest total in NFL history. He won the NFL Most Valuable Player award in 1997 before retiring. In 2004 he was inducted into the Professional Football Hall of Fame.

Ely [eelee] 52°24N 0°16E, pop (2000e) 10 500. Small city in E Cambridgeshire, EC England; on R Ouse; railway; 12th-c cathedral; Isle of Ely (higher ground surrounded by fens) the location of Hereward the Wake's defence against the Normans.

Elyot, Sir Thomas, also spelled **Eliot** (c.1490–1546) Writer and diplomat, born in Wiltshire. His chief work, *The Boke Named the Gouernour* (1531), is the earliest English treatise on moral philosophy.

Elysée, Palais de l' [pale duh layleezay], Eng **Elysée Palace** Since 1873 the official residence of the French president, situated on the Rue du Faubourg Sainte-Honoré in Paris. It was built in 1718 for the Compte d'Evreux.

Elysium [elizium] or **Elysian fields** In Greek and Roman mythology, the happy fields, often located on the borders of the Underworld, where the good remain after death in perfect happiness.

ema *rhea* (ornithology)

e-mail *electronic mail*

Emancipation Proclamation A document issued (1863) by President Lincoln during the American Civil War, declaring the freedom of all slaves in areas then in arms against the US government.

Ember Days In the Christian Church, the Wednesday, Friday and Saturday of the weeks (Ember Weeks) following the first Sunday in Lent, Whitsunday, Holy Cross Day (14 Sep) and St Lucia's Day (13 Dec); formerly observed as special times of fasting and abstinence.

embezzlement The dishonest taking of money or other property entrusted to an employee on behalf of his or her employer. Many penal codes subsume this offence under theft. However, in Scots law it is distinguished from both theft and fraud.

embolism [embolizm] An obstruction of a blood vessel by the accumulation and adhesion of any undissolved material (such as a blood clot) carried to the site in the bloodstream. It is usually identified according to the vessel involved (cerebral, coronary, pulmonary) or the undissolved material (air, fat).

embroidery The ornamentation of fabrics with decorative stitching – an art which dates from very early times (as shown in Egyptian tomb paintings), when the designs were sewn onto a base fabric by hand. It was highly developed in the Middle and Far East, and in India. In Europe, church vestments provided consistently sumptuous examples. While hand-embroidery survives as a craft, many of today's goods are embroidered using computer-controlled sewing machines, capable of reproducing complex multi-coloured patterns.

embryo [embrioh] In flowering plants, the young plant developed from an ovum and contained within the seed; in animals, the developing young, contained either within the egg membranes or inside the maternal body.

El Salvador

☐ International Airport

Religions Roman Catholic (93%), other (mostly Evangelical Protestant) (7%)

Physical features Smallest of Central America republics; two volcanic ranges run E–W; narrow coastal belt in S, rises to mountains in N; highest point, Santa Ana, 2381 m/7812 ft; many volcanic lakes; earthquakes common.

Climate Varies greatly with altitude; hot tropical on coastal lowlands; single rainy season (May–Oct); temperate uplands; average annual temperature at San Salvador 23°C (Jul), 22°C (Jan); average annual rainfall 1775 mm/70 in.

Currency 1 US Dollar (USD) = 100 cents (before 2001, the Colón (SVC))

Economy Largely based on agriculture; main crops coffee and cotton; sugar, maize, balsam (world's main source); chemicals, rubber, rubber goods, oil products.

GDP (2002e) $29·41 bn, per capita $4600

Human Development Index (2002) 0·706

History Originally part of the Aztec kingdom; conquest by Spanish, 1526; independence from Spain, 1821; member of the Central American Federation until its dissolution in 1839; independent republic, 1841; war with Honduras, 1965, 1969; considerable political unrest in 1970s and 80s, with guerrilla activity directed against the US-supported government; civil war, 1979–91; peace plan agreed, 1991; governed by a President, and Council of Ministers; unicameral Legislative Assembly.

Head of State/Government
1962–7 Julio Adalberto Rivera
1967–72 Fidel Sánchez Hernández
1972–7 Arturo Armando Molina
1977–9 Carlos Humberto Romero
1979–82 Military juntas
1982–4 *Government of National Unanimity* (Alvaro Magaña)
1984–9 José Napoleón Duarte
1989–94 Alfredo Cristiani Burkard
1994–9 Armando Calderón Sol
1999–2004 Francisco Flores
2004– Tony Saca

official name **Republic of El Salvador**, Span **República de El Salvador**

Local name El Salvador

Timezone GMT -6

Area 21 476 km²/8290 sq mi

Population total (2002e) 6 354 000

Status Republic

Date of independence 1841

Capital San Salvador

Language Spanish (official)

Ethnic groups Spanish-Indian (89%), Indian (mostly Pipil) (5%)

embryology The study of the development of animals from the first division of the fertilized egg (*zygote*), through the differentiation and formation of the organ systems, to the ultimate hatching or birth of the young animal.

emerald A gem variety of beryl, coloured green by minor amounts of chromium oxide. The finest crystals are from Colombia.

Emerson, Ralph Waldo (1803–82) Poet and essayist, born in Boston, MA. His works include his prose rhapsody, *Nature* (1836), and many poems and essays, notably *The Conduct of Life* (1860). He was a transcendentalist in philosophy, a rationalist in religion, and a bold advocate of spiritual individualism.

emery A natural mixture of crystalline corundum with iron oxides, occurring as dark granules. Very hard, it is used as an abrasive.

emigration *migration* 1

Emin, Tracey (1963–) Multimedia artist, born in London. She gained attention with her controversial entry for the 1999 Turner Prize, 'My Bed'. In 2001 her solo exhibition, 'You Forgot to Kiss My Soul', opened at the White Cube Gallery in London. It included sculptures, embroidered blankets, drawings, photographs, a video, and some work in neon. Her first piece of public art, a sculpture entitled 'The Roman Standard', was unveiled in Liverpool in 2005.

Emmy In America, a series of annual awards presented by the National Academy of Television Arts and Sciences since 1957; it is the television equivalent of the Oscar. It recognizes excellence in television with the Emmy Award for news, sports, daytime, public service and technology. The Academy of Television Arts and Sciences rewards excellence in prime time programming. The International Academy of Television Arts and Sciences was founded in 1969.

Empedocles [empedokleez] (c.490–c.430 BC) Greek philosopher and poet, born in Acragas, Sicily. In *On Nature* he introduced the doctrine of four everlasting elements, Earth, Water, Air, and Fire, which became central to Western thought for 2000 years through its adoption by Aristotle.

emperor moth A large, broad-winged moth; wings grey or grey-brown with conspicuous eye-spots on forewings and hindwings. (Order: Lepidoptera. Family: Saturniidae.)

emperor penguin The largest of penguins (*Aptenodytes forsteri*), 1·2 m/4 ft tall; inhabits seas around Antarctica; single egg incubated on the male's feet for 64 days during bitter polar blizzards.

emphysema [emfiseema] A disorder of the lungs in which there is destruction of the elastic fibres that normally cause lung tissue to recoil during expiration. The condition is common in heavy cigarette-smokers in whom inhaled cigarette products activate enzymes that digest the elastic tissue.

Empire Day *Commonwealth Day*

Empire State Building An office block in Manhattan, New York City, built 1930–1. At 449 m/1472 ft high (including a 68 m/222 ft high television mast added in 1951) it was the tallest building in the world until 1970.

Empire Style The style of decoration associated with Napoleon I's court after he became Emperor in 1804. It is massive, and heavily ornamented with classicizing motifs, particularly Egyptian sphinxes, winged lions, and caryatids. The equivalent style in Britain was **Regency**.

empiricism A philosophical tradition which maintains that all or most significant knowledge is based on sense experience; it is usually contrasted with rationalism. Mathematical knowledge and language competence provide difficult cases for empiricism.

employers' association or **trade association** A society of companies in the same line of business, whose purpose is to discuss matters of common interest, make representations to government on industrial matters, and negotiate with trade unions.

Empson, Sir William (1906–84) Poet and critic, born in Howden, Hull. He wrote several major critical works, notably *Seven Types of Ambiguity* (1930), his *Collected Poems* were published in 1955, and *The Complete Poems of William Empson* (ed. John Haffenden) appeared in 2000.

empyema [empiyeema] A collection of pus between the two layers of membranes which cover the lung (the *pleura*). It is most commonly due to the spread of infection from pneumonia in the lungs.

Ems, River, Dutch **Eems**, ancient **Amisia** German river, rises N of Paderborn; enters the North Sea in a 32 km/20 mi-long estuary; length 328 km/204 mi.

Ems telegram A despatch (13 Jul 1870) from the Prussian king William I to his chancellor, Bismarck, describing the refusal of the king to accept French conditions over the disputed candidature to the Spanish throne. Altered and published by Bismarck, it helped achieve his aim of provoking Napoleon III of France into declaring war on Prussia.

emu A flightless bird native to Australia (*Dromaius novaehollandiae*); the second largest living bird (after the ostrich), 1·9 m/$6\frac{1}{4}$ ft tall; runs at nearly 50 kph/30 mph; swims well; related to the cassowary. (Family: Dromaiidae.)

emulsifiers Chemical substances which help liquids to mix with each other, forming an emulsion. For example, oil and water, which do not normally mix, can be combined into a single phase using an emulsifier, as in margarine and mayonnaise. Emulsifying agents include algin, agar, and lecithin.

emulsion A suspension of one liquid in another, particularly of an oil in water. All emulsions eventually separate, 'stable' emulsions merely separating more slowly than 'unstable' ones.

emu wren A small, brightly coloured bird native to Australia, also known as the **Australian wren** or **wren-warbler**. (Genus: *Stipiturus*, 3 species. Family: Maluridae.)

enamelling The use of brightly coloured substances similar to glass which are fired on to metalwork or ceramics as decoration. The techniques used on metalwork are champlevé, cloisonné, basse taille, and painting. Enamel decoration on ceramics is applied during a second or subsequent firing at a lower temperature on top of the main body and glaze.

Enceladus [enseladus] The second natural satellite of Saturn, discovered in 1789; distance from the planet 238 000 km/148 000 mi; diameter 500 km/310 mi; orbital period 1·370 days.

encephalitis [ensefaliytis] Inflammation of the brain, usually caused by a viral infection. The clinical features are fever, headache, drowsiness, and confusion, as well as hallucinations, paralysis, and abnormal movements.

encopresis *enuresis*

encounter group A form of group therapy in which the leader facilitates the acquisition of insight and sensitivity to others, using such techniques as bodily contact and the sharing of emotional experiences. Also known as *T*- ('training') *groups*,

sessions vary greatly in length and type, and can have both positive and negative effects on members.

encyclical, papal [ensiklikl] Originally, a letter sent to all the churches in a particular area. The term is now restricted to official letters of instruction, usually doctrinal or pastoral in nature, issued by a pope to the whole Roman Catholic Church.

Encyclopaedists / Encyclopedists A collective term for the distinguished editors (Diderot and d'Alembert) and contributors to the *Encyclopédie*, a major work of social and political reference published in France (1751–76), associated with the French Enlightenment.

endangered species Plant and animal species which are in danger of becoming extinct. Their classification as endangered species is made by the International Union for the Conservation of Nature and Natural Resources. The danger of extinction generally comes from habitat loss and disturbance caused by human activity, overexploitation, and in many cases pollution.

Ender, Kornelia (1958–) Swimmer, born in Bitterfeld, Germany. In 1976 she became the first woman to win four gold medals (for East Germany) at one Olympic Games: the 100 m and 200 m freestyle, the 100 m butterfly, and the 4 × 100 m medley relay.

endive An annual or biennial (*Cichorium endivia*) growing to 120 cm/4 ft, native to S Europe; flower-heads blue, in clusters of 2–5. It is widely grown as a salad plant. (Family: Compositae.)

endocarditis Infection and inflammation of the lining of the heart, particularly of the heart valves. Bacteria circulating in the blood colonize and multiply on the heart valves and initiate an inflammatory process; the inflamed valves become thickened and misshapen and are unable to open and close properly; normal control of blood flow through the heart is lost. Clinical features include fever, fatigue, and shortness of breath. Auscultation of the heart may reveal abnormal sounds (murmurs) due to altered blood flow through the valves. Severe infections result in heart failure. Treatment with antibiotics is required to eradicate the infection, and replacement of the valves may be necessary if they have been permanently damaged.

endocrine glands [endokriyn] Ductless glands, present in some invertebrates (certain molluscs, arthropods) and all vertebrates, which synthesize and secrete chemical messengers (hormones) into the blood stream, or lymph for transport to target cells. In vertebrates they collectively form a major communication system (the **endocrine system**) which with the nervous system regulates and co-ordinates body functions. Disorders of the endocrine glands are numerous, and may result in disturbances of growth and development, metabolism, and reproduction. The study of the structure, function, and disorders of the endocrine glands is **endocrinology**.

endogamy and **exogamy** The broad social rules that define who are to be regarded as legitimate marriage partners in society. **Endogamy** allows marriage between members of one's own group or lineage; **exogamy** allows marriage only between members of different groups.

endogenous opioids *opioid peptides*

endometriosis A common disorder in which the cells that normally line the uterine cavity (*endometrium*) grow in other sites of the body, such as the ovaries, rectum, and bladder. The cause is unknown, but it is possible that endometrial cells migrate up through the uterine tubes and implant in the pelvis (*retrograde-menstruation*). Endometrial cells outside the uterus respond to the same hormonal signals as those within it: they proliferate and swell every month, then slough off during the next menstrual period. This provokes an inflammatory reaction on other pelvic organs, which can lead to scarring and damage, and on the uterus can lead to the formation of blood-filled cysts (*chocolate cysts*).

endorphins [endaw(r)finz] Natural substances present through-

England

☐ International Airport

Lat **Anglia** (UK)
Area 130 357 km²/50 318 sq mi
Population total (2001e) 49 138 800
Status Constituent part of the United Kingdom
Capital London
Languages English, with c.300 minority languages
Ethnic groups & Religions (*see* **United Kingdom**)
Physical features Largest area within the United Kingdom, forming the S part of the island of Great Britain; since 1974 divided into 46 counties; includes the Isles of Scilly, Lundy, and the Isle of Wight; largely undulating lowland, rising (S) to the Mendips, Cotswolds, Chilterns, and North Downs, (N) to the N–S ridge of the Pennines, and (NW) to the Cumbria Mts; drained E by the Tyne, Tees, Humber, Ouse, and Thames Rivers, and W by the Eden, Ribble, Mersey, and Severn Rivers; Lake District (NW) includes Derwent Water, Ullswater, Windermere and Bassenthwaite; linked to Europe by ferry and hovercraft, and (from 1994) by the Channel Tunnel.
Economy North Sea oil and gas, coal, tin, china clay, salt, potash, lead ore, iron ore; vehicles, heavy engineering, petrochemicals, pharmaceuticals, textiles, food processing, electronics, telecommunications, publishing, brewing, fishing, livestock, agriculture, horticulture, pottery and tourism.
History (*see* **United Kingdom**)

Counties of England

County / Area (km² / sq mi) / Population total (2000e) / Admin Centre

Avon / 1345 / 520 / 989 800 / Bristol
Bedfordshire / 1235 / 477 / 555 500 / Bedford
Berkshire / 1259 / 486 / 781 700 / Reading
Buckinghamshire / 1883 / 727 / 671 700 / Aylesbury
Cambridgeshire / 3409 / 1316 / 711 000 / Cambridge
Cheshire / 2328 / 899 / 979 700 / Chester
Cleveland / 583 / 225 / 567 600 / Middlesbrough
Cornwall / 3564 / 1376 / 484 800 / Truro
Cumbria / 6810 / 2629 / 497 900 / Carlisle
Derbyshire / 2631 / 1016 / 968 600 / Matlock
Devon / 6711 / 2591 / 1 074 600 / Exeter
Dorset / 2654 / 1025 / 682 800 / Dorchester
Durham / 2436 / 941 / 617 100 / Durham
Essex / 3672 / 1418 / 1 600 000 / Chelmsford
Gloucestershire / 2643 / 1020 / 553 500 / Gloucester
Greater London / 1579 / 610 / 7 077 000 / no central authority
Greater Manchester 1287 / 497 / 2 607 000 / no central authority
Hampshire / 3777 / 1458 / 1 623 000 / Winchester
Herefordshire / 2181 / 842 / 162 000 / Hereford
Hertfordshire / 1634 / 631 / 1 022 000 / Hertford
Humberside / 3512 / 1356 / 904 000 / Beverley
Isle of Wight / 381 / 147 / 124 200 / Newport
Kent / 3731 / 1441 / 1 558 000 / Maidstone
Lancashire / 3063 / 1183 / 1 440 000 / Preston
Leicestershire / 2553 / 986 / 926 300 / Leicester
Lincolnshire / 5915 / 2284 / 621 200 / Lincoln
Merseyside° / 652 / 252 / 1 447 000 / Liverpool
Norfolk / 5368 / 2073 / 781 700 / Norwich
Northamptonshire / 2367 / 914 / 607 000 / Northampton
Northumberland / 5032 / 1943 / 312 100 / Morpeth
Nottinghamshire / 2164 / 836 / 1 051 000 / Nottingham
Oxfordshire / 2608 / 1007 / 613 100 / Oxford
Shropshire / 3490 / 1347 / 421 200 / Shrewsbury
Somerset / 3451 / 1332 / 489 900 / Taunton
Staffordshire / 2716 / 1049 / 1 069 000 / Stafford
Suffolk / 3797 / 1466 / 637 300 / Ipswich
Surrey / 1679 / 648 / 1 057 000 / Kingston/Thames
Sussex, East / 1795 / 693 / 743 100 / Lewes
Sussex, West / 1989 / 768 / 721 100 / Chichester
Tyne and Wear° / 540 / 208 / 1 160 000 / Newcastle/Tyne
Warwickshire / 1981 / 765 / 506 000 / Warwick
West Midlands° / 899 / 347 / 2 657 000 / Birmingham
Wiltshire / 3481 / 1344 / 608 000 / Trowbridge
Worcestershire / 1813 / 700 / 550 000 / Worcester
Yorkshire, North / 8309 / 3208 / 738 300 / Northallerton
Yorkshire, South / 1560 / 602 / 1 325 000 / Barnsley
Yorkshire, West° / 2039 / 787 / 2 141 000 / Wakefield
 New counties in 1974 were formed as follows:
Avon: parts of Somerset and Gloucestershire
Cleveland: parts of Durham and Yorkshire
Cumbria: Cumberland, Westmoreland, parts of Lancashire and Yorkshire
Greater London: London and most of Middlesex
Greater Manchester: parts of Lancashire, Cheshire, and Yorkshire
Hereford and Worcester: Hereford, most of Worcestershire (Reverted to separate counties in 1998)
Humberside: parts of Yorkshire and Lincolnshire
Merseyside: parts of Lancashire and Cheshire
West Midlands: parts of Staffordshire, Warwickshire, and Worcestershire
Tyne and Wear: parts of Northumberland and Durham
° The councils of these metropolitan councils were abolished in 1986.

a Stoke-on-Trent
b Gillingham &
   Rochester upon Medway
c Southampton
d Thamesdown
e S Gloucestershire
f Bath & NE Somerset
g NW Somerset
h Newbury
i Reading
j Wokingham
k Bracknell Forest
l Windsor & Maidenhead
m Slough
n Portsmouth

▲ St Helens
  Wigan
  Bolton
  Bury
  Rochdale
  Salford
  Trafford
  Manchester
  Oldham
  Tameside
  Stockport

△ Leeds
  Bradford
  Kirklees
  Wakefield

† Barnsley
  Sheffield
  Rotherham
  Doncaster

+ Wolverhampton
  Walsall
  Dudley
  Sandwell
  Birmingham
  Solihull
  Coventry

◆ Sefton
  Knowsley
  Liverpool
  Wirral

Newcastle upon Tyne
North Tyneside
Gateshead
South Tyneside
Sunderland

Hartlepool
Middlesbrough
Redcar & Cleveland

Darlington

York

East Riding of Yorkshire
Kingston upon Hull

NE Lincolnshire

Blackpool
Blackburn

Halton

Warrington

Derby
Nottingham

Rutland

The Wrekin

Leics.

Peterborough

Herefordshire

Bristol

Luton

Thurrock
Southend

LONDON

Poole

Bournemouth

Isle of Wight

Brighton & Hove

Torbay

Plymouth

200 km
100 mi

Two-tier authority areas

1 NORTHUMBERLAND	19 ESSEX
2 DURHAM	20 HERTFORDSHIRE
3 CUMBRIA	21 BEDFORDSHIRE
4 LANCASHIRE	22 BUCKINGHAMSHIRE
5 NORTH YORKSHIRE	23 OXFORDSHIRE
6 CHESHIRE	24 BERKSHIRE
7 DERBYSHIRE	25 HAMPSHIRE
8 NOTTINGHAMSHIRE	26 SURREY
9 LINCOLNSHIRE	27 WEST SUSSEX
10 STAFFORDSHIRE	28 EAST SUSSEX
11 SHROPSHIRE	29 KENT
12 LEICESTERSHIRE	30 GLOUCESTERSHIRE
13 WORCESTERSHIRE	31 WILTSHIRE
14 WARWICKSHIRE	32 DORSET
15 NORTHAMPTONSHIRE	33 SOMERSET
16 CAMBRIDGESHIRE	34 DEVON
17 NORFOLK	35 CORNWALL &
18 SUFFOLK	ISLES OF SCILLY

*Unitary authorities of London

City of London	Hammersmith	Lambeth
Barking &	& Fulham	Lewisham
Dagenham	Haringey	Merton
Barnet	Harrow	Newham
Bexley	Havering	Redbridge
Brent	Hillingdon	upon Thames
Bromley	Hounslow	Southwark
Camden	Islington	Sutton
Croydon	Kensington	Tower Hamlets
Ealing	& Chelsea	Waltham Forest
Enfield	Kingston-	Wandsworth
Greenwich	upon-Thames	Westminster
Hackney		

Unitary authority areas

County boundary

out the body which have similar (but more controlled) effects to morphine and other narcotics. Isolated in 1975, the substances are believed to act as neurotransmitters.

endoscopy [endoskopee] The introduction of an instrument into a body aperture or duct for direct visual inspection and biopsy. It is carried out with a flexible glass fibre **endoscope**.

endothelium *epithelium*

Endymion [endimion] In Greek mythology, a handsome shepherd of Mt Latmos, who was loved by the Moon-goddess Selene. He was also said, as King of Elis, to have founded the Olympic Games.

energy An abstract calculable quantity associated with all physical processes and objects, whose total value is found always to be conserved; symbol *E*, units J (joule); one of the most important concepts in physics. It is an additive, scalar quantity, which may be transferred but never destroyed, and so provides a useful book-keeping device for the analysis of processes. It is sometimes called the capacity for doing work. The main sources of electric energy are fossil fuels (petroleum, coal, and natural gas), water power, and nuclear power. Solar power, wind power, and coal provide c.75% of world energy needs; natural gas c.20%; water power (hydroelectricity) c.2%; and nuclear energy c.1%. The search for new sources of energy is a continuing one, since that provided by the fossil fuels will eventually run out.

Enfield, Harry (1961–) British comedian, actor, and writer, known for his character-based comedy shows. *Sir Norbert Smith – a Life?* (1989) won the Silver Rose at Montreux, as did *The End of an Era* (1994). He achieved national recognition after his own BBC television series in 1991–2, following this with *Harry Enfield and Chums* (1994, 1996) and the later *Ruddy Hell! It's Harry and Paul* (2007).

Engels, Friedrich (1820–95) Socialist philosopher, founder of 'scientific socialism', born in Barmen, Germany. He collaborated with Marx on the *Communist Manifesto* (1848).

engine A mechanical device that transforms some of the energy of its fuel into a convenient and controllable form for use by other devices. The majority convert the motion of an oscillating piston in a cylinder to rotary motion by means of a crank linkage mechanism. The piston is made to oscillate by means of gases expanding and contracting. These gases may be created internally within the cylinder (as in **spark ignition** and **diesel engines**) or externally (as in **steam engines**). Other types of engine use the hot gases to create rotary motion direct (**gas turbine** and **Wankel engines**), while others eject their gases direct to the environment to create thrust (**jet engines**).

engineering The branch of technology which makes power and materials work for people. Engineers study ways of harnessing power sources, such as the use of gasoline and other fuels to power vehicles, and the conversion of water power into hydroelectricity. They also analyse and use many types of material, depending on the problem to be solved. The field as a whole was traditionally subdivided into five main branches: **civil**, **mechanical**, **mining and metallurgical**, **chemical**, and **electrical engineering**. New fields have now developed, such as aeronautical, aerospace, computer, control, marine, nuclear, and systems engineering.

England *pp.306–7*

Engle, Robert F (1942–) Economist, born in Syracuse, NY. Professor of management of financial services at New York University, in 2003 he shared the Nobel Prize for Economics with Clive W J Granger for work on using statistics to predict the future.

English (language) A language belonging to the Germanic branch of the Indo-European family. Its unbroken literary heritage goes back to the inflecting language, Anglo-Saxon, notably in the 8th-c epic poem *Beowulf*. Standard English prose evolved from the Chancery (law-court) English of the 14th-c. Over 400 million people now speak English as a mother-tongue, and another 600 million or so use it as a second language; at least a further 600 million use it with some competence as a foreign language. English is used by over 60 countries as an official or semi-official language. It is the main world language of book and newspaper publication, of science and technology, of advertising and pop music, of cinema, and of computer information storage. It is also . the medium for auxiliary (restricted) languages, such as those used by international airline pilots and seafarers for intercommunication.

English Channel, Fr **La Manche**, Lat **Mare Britannicum** Arm of the Atlantic Ocean, bounded N by England and S by France; connected to North Sea by Straits of Dover (E), 34 km/21 mi wide; 565 km/350 mi long by 240 km/150 mi wide at its widest point (Lyme Bay–Golfe de St-Malo); crossings by ferry and hovercraft, one of the world's busiest shipping lanes; tunnel opened, 1994; first aeroplane crossing by Bleriot, 1909; first swum by Matthew Webb, 1875; main islands, I of Wight, Channel Is.

English Civil War (1642–8) The country's greatest internal conflict, between supporters of Parliament and supporters of Charles I, caused by Parliamentary opposition to royal policies. The first major engagement took place at Edgehill in October 1642. It was a draw, but Royalist forces then threatened London, the key Parliamentary stronghold. The crucial event of 1643 was Parliament's alliance with the Scots in the Solemn League and Covenant, which led to the major Royalist defeat at Marston Moor (1644). Royalist successes in the W at Lostwithiel and Newbury (both 1643) were overtaken by major Parliamentary victories at Naseby and Langport (both 1645). The next year brought to an end the first civil war, Charles surrendering to the Scots at Newark. From June 1646 to April 1648 there was an uneasy peace and attempts at compromise. The climax came (Aug 1647) when the army presented the king with the Heads of Proposals, calling for religious toleration, and Parliamentary control of the armed forces. Charles made a secret alliance with the Scots, promising to establish Presbyterianism in England; they invaded England (Apr 1648), and were repulsed only after the Battle of Preston (Aug). Bitterly fought, the second war earned Charles the epithet 'that man of blood' and, ultimately, his execution (30 Jan 1649).

English Heritage In the UK, a body directly responsible for protecting and preserving England's collection of 12 500 designated monuments and over 300 000 'listed' buildings. The Historic Buildings and Monuments Board for Scotland, and Cadw (Welsh 'heritage'), have similar functions.

English National Ballet A classical ballet company which tours nationally and internationally from its studio base in Westminster, London. Founded in 1950 by the Polish-born impresario Julian Braunsweg as the London Festival Ballet, the company changed its name to the English National Ballet in 1988.

English National Opera Opera company founded in 1931 by Lilian Baylis as the Vic-Wells Opera, named after the Old Vic and Sadler's Wells theatres that she also managed. The company moved to its present location at the London Coliseum in 1968 and was renamed English National Opera in 1974.

English Nature A British governmental agency, set up by the Environmental Protection Act (1990), and responsible for the conservation of England's wildlife and natural features. It continues the work of its predecessor, the Nature Conservancy Council, and works closely with the Scottish Natural Heritage and Countryside Council for Wales.

English-Speaking Union A charity founded by Sir Evelyn Wrench (1882–1966) in 1918 with the purpose of 'improving understanding about people, international issues, and culture through the bond the English language provides'. Based in

London, in 2006 the Union had branches in over 50 countries, two-thirds in the UK and the USA.

engraving A process of printmaking by the intaglio method; also the resulting print. The term is often used less precisely to mean any process whereby a design is printed on paper.

enhanced radiation weapon *neutron bomb*

enkephalins *opioid peptides*

Enlightenment or **Age of Reason** (Ger *Aufklärung*) A European literary and philosophical movement of the 18th-c, rooted in the 17th-c Scientific Revolution and the ideas of Kant, Locke, and Newton. Its basic belief was the superiority of reason as a guide to all knowledge and human concerns; from this flowed the idea of progress and a challenging of traditional Christianity.

Enlil The Mesopotamian god of the wind, son of Anu the sky-god, king of the gods before the creation of Marduk.

Enniskillen [iniskilin], also **Inniskilling**, Ir **Inis Ceithleann** 54°21N 7°38W, pop (2000e) 11 500. Town in Fermanagh, SW Northern Ireland; scene of a victory of William III over James II, 1689; became an important Protestant stronghold; scene of an IRA bombing at the Remembrance Day service in 1987, killing 11 people; airfield; castle ruins (15th–16th-c); cathedral (17th–18th-c).

Ennius, Quintus [enius] (c.239–169 BC) Latin epic poet and dramatist, born in Rudiae, Calabria, Italy. He introduced the hexameter into Latin; but only fragments of his many writings survive.

Enoch [eenok] Biblical character, son of Jared, father of Methuselah. In the Graeco-Roman era his name became attached to Jewish apocalyptic writings allegedly describing his visions (1, 2, and 3 *Enoch*).

enosis [enohsis] A political movement in Cyprus for union with Greece, reflecting the demands of Cypriots opposed to foreign rule, and closely associated with the leadership of the Greek Orthodox Church. Now independent, Cyprus has never achieved this union because of Turkish opposition.

Enright, D(ennis) J(oseph) (1920–2002) Writer, born in Leamington, Warwickshire. He wrote five novels and much criticism, but is best known for his poetry. Work spanning five decades is represented in *Collected Poems 1948-1998* (1998).

Ensor, James (Sydney) Ensor, Baron (1860–1949) Painter, born in Ostend, Belgium. He became known for his bizarre and fantastic images, using masks, skeletons, and other ghostly effects as symbols of the evils of society.

entablature [entablachoor] The horizontal element supported by the orders of classical architecture. It consists of an architrave, frieze, and cornice.

Entebbe [entebay] 0°05N 32°29E, pop (2000e) 32 000. Town in S Uganda, E Africa; on N shore of L Victoria, founded, 1893; former capital of Uganda, 1894–1962; airport; railway; scene in 1976 of a dramatic rescue by Israeli forces of Israelis whose plane had been hijacked by a group of Palestinian terrorists.

entellus [entelus] A langur native to S Asia (*Presbytis entellus*), and traditionally sacred in India; sandy brown, with a black face; long tail; also known as **entellus langur** or **hanuman monkey**.

enteric fever *typhoid fever*

enterprise zones Parts of a country designated by the government as areas where business start-up schemes will get favourable financial help. They are usually located in inner-city areas with high unemployment levels. Schemes of this kind are in operation in many countries.

enthalpy [enthalpee] An energy quantity appearing frequently in thermodynamics; symbol H, units J (joule); defined as $H = U + pV$, where U is internal energy, p is pressure, and V is volume. There is no absolute zero of enthalpy, so only changes in enthalpy can be measured.

entomology The branch of biology dealing with the study of insects, the most diverse group of organisms on Earth. The development of insecticides and alternative techniques for controlling pest insects forms the basis of **applied economic entomology**. **Medical entomology** is a specialized field dealing with the study of insect carriers of numerous diseases and with the methods of controlling them.

entresol *mezzanine*

entropy [entropee] A thermodynamic quantity which always increases for irreversible processes, giving a direction in time for processes which might otherwise appear reversible from energy considerations alone; symbol S, units J/K (joules per kelvin). Entropy may be understood as a measure of disorder at a microscopic level, caused by the addition of heat to collections of atoms. The second law of thermodynamics states that for all processes entropy either is constant or increases.

E-number A code number on food labels, used by food manufacturers in member states of the European Union, which identifies all materials added to the food ($E = European$). Among food additives, four categories (preservatives, colourants, anti-oxidants, and emulsifiers) each have code numbers. For example, E102 is the colourant tartrazine.

enuresis [enyureesis] A condition typified by involuntary voiding of urine. The involuntary passage of faeces is known as **encopresis**.

Enver Pasha (1881–1922) Turkish soldier and politician, born in Istanbul. A leader in the revolution of Young Turks in 1908, he later became minister of war (1914). He fled to Russia in 1918 after the Turkish surrender, and was killed in an insurrection in Turkestan.

environment The conditions and influences of the place in which an organism lives. The **physical environment** describes the characteristics of a landscape (eg climate, geology) which have not been changed markedly by human impact, whereas the **geographical environment** includes the physical environment together with any human modifications (eg industrialization, urbanization). The relationship between living organisms and their environment forms part of the subject of *ecology*. Concern that large parts of the physical environment are suffering from misuse and overexploitation is central to conservation.

Environment Agency The body established by the Environment Act (1995) of England and Wales to enforce and regulate pollution controls. The Agency carries out the functions of the former National Rivers Authority, Her Majesty's Inspectorate of Pollution, and the waste regulation authorities. It is also responsible for certain other functions connected with the environment, such as controlling effluent and sewage sludge in agriculture, land drainage, and coastal defence.

Environmentally Sensitive Areas (ESAs) A European Community scheme introduced in 1985 to protect areas of ecological and landscape importance from drainage and loss caused by agricultural change. Examples include the Broads and the Breckland in East Anglia, UK.

Environmental Protection Agency A US government agency established in 1970. Its job is to determine, regulate, and enforce environmental pollution controls, such as legislation governing the use of pesticides.

environmental studies Those aspects of biology, ecology, and geography which are related to an understanding of the environment: its physical and human components. It is sometimes used synonymously with *ecology*, though environmental studies are more wide-ranging.

enzyme A specialized protein molecule produced by a living cell, which acts as a biological catalyst for biochemical reactions. The names of enzymes typically end in *-ase*, and they are derived from the substrates on which they act; for example, lipase is an enzyme that breaks down lipid (fat).

Eocene epoch [eeohseen] The second of the five geological epochs of the Tertiary period, lasting from 55 to 38 million years ago. It was characterized by a warmer climate and the appearance of modern flora and fauna.

Eohippus [eeohhipus] *Hyracotherium*

EOKA [ayohka] The acronym for **Ethniki Organosis Kipriakou Agonos** ('National Organization of Cypriot Struggle'), a Greek Cypriot underground movement seeking to end British rule and achieve the union of Cyprus with Greece. Founded in 1955 by Colonel George Grivas, with the support of Archbishop Makarios III, it pursued a campaign of anti-British violence. EOKA was disbanded following Makarios's acceptance of Cypriot independence (1958). In 1971–4 it was unsuccessfully resurrected as EOKA B.

Eos [eeohs] In Greek mythology, the goddess of the dawn, daughter of Helios, mother of Memnon.

Epaminondas [epaminondas] (c.418–362 BC) Theban general and statesman, whose victory at Leuctra (371 BC) broke the military power of Sparta and made Thebes the most powerful state in Greece.

ephedrine [efedrin, efedreen] A drug with similar actions to adrenaline, used as a nasal decongestant. Earlier, it was also used in the treatment of asthma and low blood pressure.

ephemeral An annual plant with a very short life-cycle, usually producing several generations in a single season. Many weed species are ephemeral, as are desert plants which experience very short favourable seasons.

Ephemeroptera [efemeroptera] *mayfly*

Ephesians, Letter to the [efeezhnz] New Testament writing attributed to Paul, but of disputed authorship. It sets out God's purposes in establishing the Church and uniting both Jews and Gentiles in it.

Ephesus [efesus], Turkish **Efes** 37°5N 27°19E. Ancient city of Lydia and important Greek city-state on the W coast of Asia Minor; centre of worship of Artemis/Diana, whose temple was one of the Seven Wonders of the Ancient World; in Roman times, principal city of the province of Asia visited by St Paul.

epic A heroic poem; a long narrative of wars and adventures where larger-than-life characters perform deeds of great significance. The earlier epic poems, in the oral tradition, reach back into myth and legend, where men and gods moved on the same scene; among these are the Sumerian epic *Gilgamesh* (c.3000 BC), the Homeric epics *Iliad* and *Odyssey* (c.1000 BC), and the Indian *Mahabharata* (c.500 BC): also the N European epics such as the Old English *Beowulf* (8th-c) and the 13th-c German *Niebelungenlied*. The term **secondary epic** refers to works such as Virgil's *Aeneid* (30–19 BC) and Milton's *Paradise Lost* (1667), written in conscious imitation of these primary epic models. The poetic and mythological aspects are generally missing when modern works are described as 'epic'.

epicalyx An additional whorl of flower parts attached outside the sepals or calyx, which they resemble in both form and function. It is characteristic of some plants, such as members of the Rosaceae.

epicentre *earthquake*

Epictetus [epikteetus] (c.50–c.130) Stoic philosopher, born in Hierapolis. At first a Roman slave, on being freed he devoted himself to philosophy. His *Enchiridion* is a collection of maxims dictated to a disciple.

Epicurus [epikyoorus] (c.341–270 BC) Greek philosopher, founder of Epicureanism, born in Samos. He held that pleasure is the chief good, by which he meant freedom from pain and anxiety, not (as the term **epicurean** has since come to mean) one who indulges sensual pleasures without stint.

Epidauros Small town located 32 km/20 mi from Nafplion, on the Saronic Gulf in the N Peloponnese. In ancient Greece it was an important commercial centre, but is today famed for its 4th-c BC temple of Asclepius, the god of healing, and for the amphitheatre (350 BC) carved out of a hillside where the annual summer Epidauros Festival is held.

Epidaurus [epidawrus] A Greek city-state situated in the E Peloponnese. It was famous in antiquity for its sanctuary to Asclepius, the god of healing, and for its magnificent open theatre, which is still used today.

epidemiology The study of the distribution and causes of disease in populations. It developed in the 19th-c, when the study of the occurrence of outbreaks in relation to the social conditions prevailing at the time led to effective measures for their control.

epidermis [epidermis] The outermost layer of a plant or animal. In plants and many invertebrates, the epidermis is a single cell thick. In vertebrates, it is many cells thick, and in terrestrial vertebrates it is formed from dead, hardened cells.

epididymis [epididimis] *testis*

epidural anaesthesia [epidyooral] The injection of a local anaesthetic into the epidural space located within the vertebral canal outside the dura (a membrane covering the spinal cord). It is often used in surgical procedures on the lower half of the body, and in normal or abnormal childbirth.

epiglottis A pear-shaped sheet of elastic fibrocartilage, broad above (where it lies immediately behind the tongue) and narrow below. It moves on swallowing, and partly covers the opening into the larynx.

Epigoni [epigonee] In Greek mythology, the 'next generation' of heroes. After the failure of the Seven Champions to take Thebes, their sons made another expedition and succeeded.

epigram Originally, an inscription on a statue; hence, any short, pithy poem. Coleridge's definition is also an example: 'What is an epigram? A dwarfish whole,/Its body brevity, and wit its soul'.

epigraphy [epigrafee] The study of ancient inscriptions, variously inscribed on memorial stones, clay pots and tablets, marble, wood, wax, and other hard surfaces, and using a wide variety of techniques (eg carving, embossing, painting).

epilepsy [epilepsee] A transient seizure or fit usually associated with a short-lived disturbance of consciousness. It stems from a synchronous high-voltage electrical discharge from groups of neurones in the brain. The disorder takes several forms, which include loss of consciousness with generalized convulsions (**grand mal**), short periods of loss of consciousness in which patients simply stop what they are doing and look blank ('absence' or 'drop attacks', or **petit mal**), seizures with involuntary movements of only part of the body, such as a limb (**Jacksonian epilepsy**), and short-lived sensations of smell and smacking of the lips (**temporal lobe epilepsy**). The majority of cases do not have an obvious cause.

Epimetheus [epimeethius] The 11th natural satellite of Saturn, discovered in 1980; distance from the planet 151 000 km/94 000 mi; diameter 140 km/90 mi.

epinephrine [epinefrin] *adrenaline*

Epiphany A Christian festival (6 Jan) which commemorates the showing of the infant Jesus to the Magi (*Matt* 2), the manifestation of Jesus's divinity at his baptism (*Matt* 3), and his first miracle at Cana (*John* 2). Its eve is Twelfth Night.

epiphyte A plant not rooted in the soil, but growing above ground level, usually on other plants. It uses such hosts for support only, and should not be confused with **parasites**, which also obtain food from their hosts. Epiphytes are especially common in tropical rainforests, where the adoption of this lifestyle allows them to grow in the light, which is otherwise shut out by the dense canopy.

episcopacy [episkopasee] (Gr *episkopos*, 'bishop', 'superintendent') A hierarchical (as opposed to consistorial) system of Church government, with bishops occupying the dominant role and authority. In the Roman Catholic, Orthodox, and Anglican communions, those consecrated bishops are the chief ecclesiastical officers of a diocese, and have the power to ordain priests and confirm baptized members of the Church.

Episcopal Church, Protestant The Anglican Church in the USA, formally established in 1784 after the War of Independence. Traditionally, it has allowed more lay participation in the government of the Church than has the Church of England.

epistemology The branch of philosophy dealing with the theory of knowledge – its sources, limits, kinds, and reliability. These central issues divide such major schools as empiricists, rationalists, and sceptics.

epithelium [epitheelium] A layer of cells lining all internal surfaces (organs, tubes, ducts) and covering the external surface of the body; the internal lining is also known as **endothelium**. Its function varies in different regions of the body (eg protection, secretion, absorption).

epoch In geology, an arbitrary unit of time used as a subdivision of a *period*.

epoxy resin [ipoksee rezin] A polymer formed by the condensation of epichlorohydrin and bisphenol-A. The resulting hard material is useful as an adhesive, a coating, and an embedding material for electrical components.

EPROM [eeprom] An acronym for **electrically programmable read-only memory**, a type of integrated circuit read-only memory which can be reused by removing the chip from the computer, erasing its contents, electrically writing new data into it, and replacing it in the computer.

Epsom salts *magnesium*

Epstein, Sir Jacob [epstiyn] (1880–1959) Sculptor, born in New York City. Several of his symbolic sculptures, such as 'Ecce homo' (1934), resulted in accusations of indecency and blasphemy. In the 1950s, his last two large works, 'Christ in Majesty' (in aluminium; Llandaff Cathedral) and 'St Michael and the Devil' (in bronze; Coventry Cathedral), won more immediate acclaim.

Equal Opportunities Commission A body set up in England and Wales under the Sex Discrimination Act (1975) to work towards the elimination of discrimination on the grounds of sex or marital status and to promote equality of opportunity between men and women generally. The Commission also reviews the working of the Sex Discrimination Acts and Equal Pay Act (1970).

equations The statement that one mathematical expression is equal to another. Those containing only one unknown quantity are classified by the *degree* of that unknown. Equations of degree one, called **linear equations**, are of the form $ax = b$, and have the solution $x = b/a$, given $a \neq 0$. Equations of degree two, **quadratic equations**, are of the form $ax^2 + bx + c = 0$, and $a \neq 0$ have solutions $x = [-b \pm \sqrt{(b^2 - 4ac)}]/2a$. Equations of degree three are called **cubic equations**. A **polynomial** equation contains the sum of multiples of powers of a variable, say $a_0 x^n + a_1 x^{n-1} + a_2 x^{n-2} \dots = 0$, where $a_0 \neq 0$; n, the highest power of the unknown, is called the degree of the polynomial.

Equator The great circle on the Earth's surface, halfway between the Poles, dividing the Earth into the N and S hemispheres; known as the **terrestrial equator**. Its own latitude is $0°$, and from here latitude is measured in degrees N and degrees S. The **celestial equator** is the great circle in the sky in the same plane as the terrestrial equator.

Equatorial Guinea *p.312*

equestrianism The skill of horsemanship. As a sport it can fall into one of four categories; **show jumping**, **dressage**, **three-day eventing** (also known as **horse trials**), and **carriage driv-**

ing. The governing body is the International Equestrian Federation.

equinox 1 Either of the two points on the celestial sphere where the ecliptic intersects the celestial equator. Physically these are the points at which the Sun, in its annual motion, appears to cross the celestial equator – the **vernal equinox** as it crosses from S to N, and the **autumnal equinox** as it crosses from N to S. **2** Either of the two instants of time at which the Sun crosses the celestial equator, being about 21 March (vernal) and 23 September (autumnal).

equisetum *horsetail*

equity (economics) The capital of a company, belonging to the shareholders. It consists of issued share capital (the money received from the sale of shares); the profits retained (traditionally known as *reserves*); share premiums (excess receipts from the sale of shares over their nominal value); and the revaluation reserve (sums resulting from the increase in the value of assets since their purchase). The shares themselves are called **equities**.

equity (law) A source of English and Scottish law, originally developed by the Lord Chancellor and later by the Court of Chancery. It arose from the right of litigants to petition the monarch. Trust law and equitable remedies (such as the injunction) are examples.

Equuleus [ekwoolius] (Lat 'little horse') An insignificant N constellation, the second-smallest in the N sky.

era The second largest of the time divisions used in geology, each being divided into a number of periods.

Erasistratus (of Ceos) [erasistratus] (c.250 BC) Greek founder of a school of medicine, born in Ceos. He studied the nature of the nervous system, and came near to discovering the circulation of the blood.

Erasmus, Desiderius [erazmus], originally **Gerrit Gerritszoon** (1466–1536) Humanist, born in Rotterdam, The Netherlands. He moved to England in 1498, becoming professor of divinity and of Greek at Cambridge. In 1519 appeared his masterpiece, *Colloquia*, an audacious handling of Church abuses. He also made the first translation of the Greek New Testament into English (1516), and edited the works of St Jerome (1519).

Erastianism [erastianizm] An understanding of the Christian Church which gives the state the right to intervene in and control Church affairs. It is associated with Thomas Erastus (1524–83), who, in 16th-c Heidelberg, had argued against Calvinists for the rights of the state in Church affairs.

Erato [eratoh] In Greek mythology, the Muse responsible for lyric poetry and hymns.

Eratosthenes [eratostheneez] (c.276–c.194 BC) Greek astronomer and scholar, born in Cyrene. He is remembered for the first scientific calculation of the Earth's circumference.

Erechtheum [erekhtheeum] The latest building on the Athenian Acropolis, named after the legendary king Erechtheus of Athens. It is a symmetrical, two-part Ionic marble temple, built during the Peloponnesian War (c.420–407 BC).

ergonomics The study of work, including the design of the work situation, the analysis and training of work skills, the effects of physical and psychological environments, work-stress, errors, and accidents; also called **human engineering**. The systematic study of work developed from the early 20th-c introduction of mass production, and the use of time and motion study for job analysis and improvement. The subject has applications in such areas as factory design and the design of vehicle instruments.

ergot [ergot] A fungal disease of grasses caused by *Claviceps purpurea*; forms hard black fruiting bodies (*sclerotia*) in flower-heads of infected grasses, including cereal crops. (Class: Pyrenomycetes.)

ergotism [ergotizm] A condition which results from eating bread

Equatorial Guinea

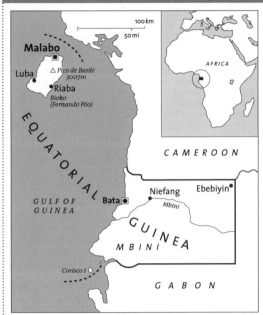

☐ International Airport

[ginee], official name **Republic of Equatorial Guinea**, Span **República de Guinea Ecuatorial**

Local name Guinea Ecuatorial

Timezone GMT +1

Area 26 016 km²/10 042 sq mi (mainland area)
28 051 km²/10 828 sq mi (total area)

Population total (2002e) 498 000

Status Republic
Date of independence 1968
Capital Malabo
Language Spanish (official)
Ethnic groups Mainland population, mainly Fang (83%), Bubi (10%), Ndowe (4%), Annobonés (2%), Bujeba (1%)
Religions Roman Catholic (80%), traditional beliefs (5%)
Physical features Located in WC Africa; comprises the mainland area (Río Muni) and several islands in the Gulf of Guinea; mainland rises sharply from a narrow coast of mangrove swamps towards the heavily forested African plateau; Bioko, fertile volcanic island in NW, contains Guinea's highest point, Pico de Basilé, 3007 m/9865 ft.
Climate Hot and humid equatorial climate; average maximum daily temperature, 29–32°C; average annual rainfall c.2000 mm/80 in.
Currency 1 CFA Franc (XAF) = 100 centimes
Economy Largely based on agriculture; cocoa, coffee, timber, bananas, cassava, palm oil, sweet potatoes.
GDP (2002e) $1·27 bn, per capita $2700
Human Development Index (2002) 0·679
History First visited by Europeans in 15th-c; island of Fernando Póo claimed by Portugal, 1494–1788; occupied by Britain, 1781–1843; rights to the area acquired by Spain, 1844; independence, 1968; military coup, 1975; governed by Supreme Military Council headed by a President; new constitution, 1991; first multi-party elections held, 1993.

Head of State
1968–79 Francisco Macias Nguema
1979– Teodoro Obiang Nguema Mbasogo

Head of Government
1993–6 Silvestre Siale Bileka
1996–2001 Angel Serafin Seriche Dougan
2001–4 Candido Muatetema Rivas
2004–6 Miguel Abia Biteo Borico
2006– Ricardo Mangue Obama Nfube

made from rye infected with ergot. Victims develop burning sensations in the limbs, gangrene, and convulsions. Outbreaks were referred to as *St Anthony's fire*, in the belief that a visit to the tomb of this saint would bring a cure.

erica *heath*

Eridanus [eridanus] (name of a river) A long and rambling S constellation, sixth-largest in the sky. Its brightest star is Achernar. Distance: 44 parsec.

Eridu [ayridoo] The oldest of the Sumerian city-states, lying SW of Ur. Excavations of the site have revealed a continuous series of temples starting in the sixth millennium BC and ending in the third with the great ziggurat.

Erie, Lake [eeree] Fourth largest of the Great Lakes, North America, on frontier between Canada and USA; 388 km/241 mi long, 48–92 km/30–57 mi wide; area 25 667 km²/9907 sq mi; Welland Ship Canal bypasses Niagara Falls; generally closed by ice during winter months (Dec–Mar); major (US) ports include Buffalo, Cleveland, Detroit; British defeated at Battle of Lake Erie, 1813.

Erie Canal [eeree] An artificial waterway extending 580 km/360 mi between Albany and Buffalo, New York State. Constructed 1817–25, it provided a water route from the Hudson R to L Erie.

Erigena, John Scotus [erijena], also known as **John the Scot** (c.810–c.877) Philosopher and theologian, born in Scotia (now Ireland). His major work, *De divisione naturae* (c.865, On the Division of Nature), tried to fuse Christian and Neoplatonic doctrines and to reconcile faith and reason, but was later condemned for its pantheistic tendencies.

Eriksson, Sven Goran (1948–) Footballer and football manager, born in Torsby, W Sweden. A knee injury in 1975 brought his career as a player to an end. He joined IFK Gothenburg in 1980 and with them won the Swedish championship and the 1982 UEFA Cup. He went next to Portuguese side Benfica (1982–84, 1989–91), and Italian teams AS Roma (1984–86), Fiorentina (1987–98), Sampdoria (1991–96), and Lazio (1997–2001). He was manager of the England football team (2001–6).

Erik the Red, originally **Erik Thorvaldsson** (10th-c) Norwegian sailor who explored the Greenland coast, and founded the Norse colonies there (985). His son Leif Eriksson landed in 'Vinland', often identified as America (1000).

Erinyes [ereenyeez] In Greek mythology, spirits of vengeance, depicted as carrying torches and covered with snakes. Their names are Alecto 'never-ceasing', Megaira 'grudger', and Tisiphone 'avenger of blood'.

Eris [eris] In Greek mythology, the daughter of Night and the sister of Ares. She was present at the wedding of Peleus and Thetis and threw a golden apple 'for the fairest'; this brought Hera, Athene, and Aphrodite into contention, and was the first cause of the Trojan War.

Eris The largest object discovered in our Solar System since Neptune in 1846, and designated a dwarf planet (or pluton) in 2006. First detected in the Kuiper Belt in 2003 (and given the tem-

Eritrea

S U D A N
Mersa
Tek'lay
Algena •
RED
AFRICA
Kerkebet   Enghershatu   Nak'fa
2576m △
E R I T R E A   Massawa
Ak'ordat   Asmara
Teseney
Dek'emaré
Barentu   Adi Ugri •   • Adi K'eyah
• Sen'afe
SEA
Tekeze
E T H I O P I A   Aseb
Ramlu
2131m
200 km
100 mi

☐ International Airport

[eritraya], Amharic **Ertra**
Local name Ertra
Timezone GMT+3
Area 93 700 km²/36 200 sq ml
Population total (2002e) 3 981 000
Status Republic
Date of independence 1993
Capital Asmara
Language Tigrinya, Tigray, Amharic

Ethnic groups Tigray, Amhara
Religions Islam (50%), Coptic Christianity (50%)
Physical features Ethiopian plateau drops to low plains; E plain includes the Danakil Depression, descending to 116 m/381 ft below sea level.
Climate Tropical climate, varied by altitude; annual temperature at Asmara, 16°C, at Mitsiwa (on coast) 30°C; hot, semi-arid NE and SE lowlands receive less than 500 mm/20 in rainfall annually; severe droughts have caused widespread famine.
Currency 1 Nafka (ERN) = 100 cents (before 1997, the Ethiopian Birr (ETB))
Economy Largely devoted to agriculture, but badly affected by drought, and heavily dependent on irrigation and foreign aid; textiles, leather, salt, food production.
GDP (2002e) $3·3 bn, per capita $700
Human Development Index (2002) 0·421
History Federated as part of Ethiopia, 1952; province of Ethiopia, 1962, which led to political unrest; civil war in the 1970s, with separatists making major gains; Soviet- and Cuban-backed government forces regained most areas after 1978 offensive; fall of President Mengistu (1991) led to new status as an autonomous region, with a provisional government established by the Eritrean People's Liberation Front; referendum followed by the declaration of independence, 1993; transitional government for 4 years, consisting of a National Assembly, which elects the president, and State Council; escalating conflict with Ethiopia over disputed border territory, 1999–2000; Permanent Court of Arbitration at The Hague issued a border ruling, 2002; Ethiopian government announced acceptance 'in principle' of ruling, Nov 2004, but regional tension continues.
Head of State
1993– Issais Afewerki

---

porary name of Xena (2003 UB313)), it was confirmed in 2005. It is made of rock and ice and measures c.2398 km/1490 mi across, making it slightly larger than Pluto. It is estimated to be three times as far away as Pluto, in an orbit at an angle to the orbits of the main planets.
Eritrea *see panel*
ERM *European Monetary System (EMS)*
ermine *stoat*
Ermine Street *Roman roads*
Ernst, Max(imillian) (1891–1976) Painter, born in Brühl, nr Cologne, Germany. A founder in 1919 of the German Dada group, he later participated in the Surrealist movement in Paris.
Eros (astronomy) [eeros] Asteroid 433, discovered in 1898. It passed within 23 million km/14 million mi of Earth in 1975. The Near Earth Asteroid Rendevous (NEAR) spacecraft encountered and photographed it in 1998.
Eros (mythology) [erohs], commonly [eeros] In Greek mythology, the son of Aphrodite and Ares. He is first depicted on vases as a handsome athlete, then as a boy with wings and arrows, and finally, in the Hellenistic period, as a chubby baby.
erosion In geology, the alteration of landforms through the removal and transport of material by water, wind, glacial movement, gravity, or living organisms. Rivers are the most effective agents of erosion, forming the pattern of hills and valleys, while wave action forms the coastlines.
Erse *Irish*
Ershad, Hussain Muhammad [airshad] (1929–) Bangladeshi soldier, chief martial law administrator, and president (1983–90).

Appointed army chief-of-staff in 1978, he led a bloodless military coup in 1982. He resigned in 1990, and was imprisoned (1991–7).
Erté [ertay], originally **Romain de Tirtoff** (1892–1990) Fashion designer, born in St Petersburg, Russia. He went to Paris, where he became a dress and theatrical-costume designer. He worked for the *Folies-Bergère* (1919–30), and designed the costumes for the American musical revues *The Ziegfeld Follies* and *George White's Scandals*. In the 1960s he produced lithographs and sheet-metal sculptures. His autobiography, *Things I Remember*, was published in 1976.
erysipelas [erisipelas] An infectious skin disease caused by haemolytic strains of *Streptococcus*. The skin becomes reddened and swollen, resembling the texture of an orange, and the infected area spreads rapidly. Usually associated with a high fever, it is treated with penicillin.
erythrocytes [erithrosiyts] Haemoglobin-containing blood cells, also known as **red blood cells**, present in most vertebrates. Their primary function is the transport of oxygen and carbon dioxide in the blood. They are manufactured in bone marrow.
ESA *European Space Agency*
Esarhaddon [eesah(r)hadn] (?–669 BC) King of Assyria (680–669 BC), son of Sennacherib and father of Assurbanipal. He is best known for his conquest of Egypt (671 BC).
Esau [eesaw] Biblical character, the elder son of Isaac. He was depicted as his father's favourite son, but was deprived of Isaac's blessing and his birthright by his cunning brother Jacob (*Gen* 27).
Esbjerg [aysbyer] 55°28N 8°28E, pop (2000e) 85 000. Seaport in

SW Jutland, Denmark; railway; ferry link with UK and Faroe Is; base for North Sea oil and gas exploration.

escape velocity Spacecraft velocity at which the energy of a craft is sufficient to overcome the gravitational attraction of the parent body, and will thus not return to that body. Earth escape velocity is c.11 km/s (7 mi/s) (root 2 × circular orbit velocity).

Escaut, River *Schelde, River*

eschatology [eskatolojee] The Christian doctrine concerning 'the last things' – the final consummation of God's purposes in creation, and the final destiny of individual souls or spirits and of humanity in general. The notion is sometimes represented as a present spiritual condition rather than as a future cosmic event. Some continue to adhere to the early belief in the literal 'second-coming' of Christ.

Escherichia [esherikia] A genus of rod-shaped bacteria that occur in the intestinal tract of animals, including humans, and are common in soil and aquatic habitats. They can cause bacterial dysentery. The only species, *Escherichia coli*, has been intensively studied by microbiologists. (Kingdom: Monera. Family: Enterobacteriaceae.)

Escorial, El [eskorial] A palace-monastery built (1563–84) for Philip II in New Castile, Spain; a world heritage site. It was built by Juan Bautista de Toledo and his successor Juan de Herrara.

Esdras, Books of [ezdras] **1** The **First Book of Esdras**, known also as **3 Esdras** (in the Vulgate), part of the Old Testament Apocrypha; an appendix to the Catholic Bible.
2 The **Second Book of Esdras**, known also as **4 Esdras** (in the Vulgate) or **4 Ezra**, sometimes considered part of the Old Testament Apocrypha; also an appendix to the Catholic Bible. Dated probably late 1st-c; chapters 1–2 and 15–16 may be two later Christian additions, today sometimes called 5 Ezra and 6 Ezra, respectively.

Esfahan [esfahahn], ancient **Isfahan**, **Aspadana** 32°40N 51°38E, pop (2000e) 1 383 000. Third largest city in Iran; airport; railway; university (1950).

esker [esker] A long, narrow hill of gravel and sand which may wind for long distances along a valley floor, probably formed by water flowing in tunnels underneath glaciers.

Eskimo or (in Canada) **Inuit** Eskimo–Aleut-speaking peoples of North America, Russia, and Greenland, living along the N edge of the continent, from Alaskan and E Asian shores in the W to Greenland and Labrador in the E, mostly S of the Arctic Circle. They are closely related to the Aleut. An economy based on nomadic hunting and fishing has now largely given way to village settlement and seasonal employment in the wage economies of the countries where they live, mainly as labourers in the mining and oil industries. The combined populations of Eskimos and Aleuts in Russia is c.1300, with 33 000 in Alaska, 24 000 in Canada, and 43 000 in Greenland.

eskimo dog *husky*

esophagus *oesophagus*

ESP *extrasensory perception*

esparto A tufted perennial grass (*Stipa tenacissima*), native to N Africa, and naturalized elsewhere, consisting of spikelets with long, feathery bristles in narrow panicles. The leaves are used to make paper. (Family: Gramineae.)

Esperanto The best known of the world's artificial languages, invented by Ludwig Lazarus Zamenhof in 1887, designed to overcome problems of international communication. Newspapers and journals are published in Esperanto, together with the Bible and the Qur'an. It is used for broadcasting, and is taught as a school subject in many countries.

ESPRIT [espree] An abbreviation for the **European Strategic Programme for Research and Development in Information Technology**, a programme of research funded by the European Commission. It aims to develop the European computer industry by supporting joint pre-competitive research projects

across institutions in the member countries of the European Union.

Essen 51°28N 6°59E, pop (2000e) 647 000. Industrial city in Germany; badly bombed in World War 2; bishopric; railway; headquarters of many large corporations; important centre of retail trade; Minster (9th–14th-c).

Essenes [eseenz] A Jewish sect renowned in antiquity for its asceticism, communistic lifestyle, and skill in predicting the future.

essential amino acids *amino acids*

essential fatty acids *carboxylic acids*

essential oil A natural volatile oil produced by plants, giving a distinctive aromatic scent to the foliage. Mostly terpenoids, the oils are common in plants from hot dry habitats.

Essequibo, River [esekeeboh] Largest river in Guyana, South America; flows c.970 km/600 mi N to meet the Atlantic at a 32 km/20 mi-wide delta, W of Georgetown.

Essex pop (2001e) 1 310 900; area 3672 km²/1418 sq mi. County of SE England; county town, Chelmsford; Southend and Thurrock new unitary authorities from 1998.

Essex, Robert Devereux, 2nd Earl of (1566–1601) English soldier and courtier to Elizabeth I, born in Netherwood, Herefordshire. At court, he quickly rose in the favour of Elizabeth, despite his clandestine marriage in 1590 with Sir Philip Sidney's widow. He became a privy councillor (1593) and earl marshal (1597), but alienated the Queen's advisers, and there were constant quarrels with Elizabeth. His six months' lord-lieutenancy of Ireland (1599) proved a failure, and he was imprisoned. He attempted to raise the City of London, was found guilty of high treason, and beheaded.

estate duty A tax formerly levied in the UK on the estate of a deceased person, based on the total value of the estate; small estates were exempt, and the levels of tax were varied from time to time. It has now been replaced by the **inheritance tax**. The USA has a federal **estate tax** and a related **gift tax**.

ester A compound obtained by the condensation of an alcohol with an acid. Esters are named as if they were salts, the first part being derived from the alcohol, and the second part from the acid (eg ethyl acetate from ethanol and acetic acid).

Esther, Book of A book of the Hebrew Bible/Old Testament, telling the popular story of how Esther became the wife of the Persian king Ahasuerus (Xerxes I) and prevented the extermination of Jews. The **Additions to the Book of Esther** are several enhancements found in the Septuagint but not in the Hebrew Bible. They are part of the Old Testament Apocrypha, and appear as *Esther* 11–16 in the Catholic Bible.

Estonia *p.315*

Estremadura [ishtremadoora], Lat **Extrema Durii** ('farthest land on the Douro') area 3249 km²/1254 sq mi. Region and former province of WC Portugal; chief town, Lisbon; popular tourist region.

estrildid finch *finch*

estrogens *oestrogens*

Esztergom [estergom], Ger **Gran**, ancient **Strigonium** 47°47N 18°44E, pop (2000e) 29 100. River-port town in N Hungary; on R Danube; fortress in Roman times; capital, 10th-c; seat of primate, 1198; railway; school of forestry; birthplace of St Stephen, Hungary's first king.

ETA (Basque, *Euzkadi Ta Azkatasuna* 'Homeland and Liberty') Basque separatist organization whose goal is Basque self-determination. Founded in 1959, it split off from its parent Partido Nacionalista Vasco (PNV), fragmenting further in 1966 to produce a more violent Marxist-Leninist wing. The Franco government responded with a brutal policy of assaults and torture, but the post-Franco government granted partial Basque autonomy and pardoned ETA members. In 1978 a political wing, *Herri Batasuna*, was founded. In the 1990s it continued terrorist

Estonia

International Airport

[estohnia], official name **Republic of Estonia**, Estonian **Eesti Vabariik**, Russ **Estonskaya**

Local name Eesti

Timezone GMT +2

Area 45 100 km²/17 409 sq mi

Population total (2002e) 1 359 000

Status Republic

Date of independence 1991

Capital Tallinn

Languages Estonian (official), also Russian

Ethnic groups Estonian (65%), Russian (28%), Ukrainian (3%), Belorussian (2%)

Religions Evangelical Lutheran, with Orthodox minority

Physical features Consists of mainland area and c.800 islands (including the Baltic island of Saaremaa); S covered with morainal hills, C with elongated glacial hills usually arrayed in the direction of glacial movement; most lakes and rivers drain either E into Lake Peipus, N into the Gulf of Finland; a few W into Gulf of Riga.

Climate Mild climate. Average annual temperatures −6°C (Jan) and 17°C (Jul); average annual rainfall 650 mm/26 in.

Currency 1 Kroon (EEK) = 100 cents

Economy Major industries: agricultural machinery, electric motors; agricultural produce of grain, vegetables; livestock.

GDP (2002e) $15·52 bn, per capita $11 000

Human Development Index (2002) 0·826

History Ceded to Russia, 1721; independence, 1918; proclaimed a Soviet Socialist Republic, 1940; occupied by Germany in World War 2; resurgence of nationalist movement in the 1980s; declared independence, 1991; 105-member Parliament; 495-member Congress of Estonia; joined European Union, 2004.

Head of State
1991–2 Arnold Rüütel
1992–2001 Lennart Meri
2001–6 Arnold Rüütel
2006– Toomas Hendrik Ilves

Head of Government
1997–9 Mart Siimann
1999–2002 Mart Laar
2002–3 Siim Kallas
2003–5 Juhan Parts
2005– Andrus Ansip

---

activities despite declaring a ceasefire in 1994. In 1998 the murder of a hostage taken by ETA, a town councillor, caused widespread outrage. ETA announced a truce, followed by a resumption of direct talks with the Spanish government (1999). ETA offered new terms for negotiation, including the key demand for a referendum in the Basque region, but these were turned down, and further bombings have since taken place. The Basque separatist party Batasuna was outlawed in March 2003. ETA announced a permanent ceasefire in March 2006 but in December that year Spain's prime minister suspended talks with the organization after a car bomb attack at a Madrid airport.

etching A form of intaglio printing invented in the early 16th-c, whereby the design on a copper plate is bitten with acid, rather than cut directly with the engraving tool (*burin*). The greatest master of the technique was Rembrandt.

Eteocles [etiokleez] In Greek legend, the elder of Oedipus's two sons, both of whom he cursed. King of Thebes after his father's death, he refused to share power with his brother Polynices. Seven Champions attacked the city, and Eteocles was killed by Polynices.

ethanal *acetaldehyde*

ethane [eethayn, ethayn] C_2H_6, boiling point −89°C. The second member of the alkane series; an odourless gas, used for refrigeration, which forms explosive mixtures with air.

ethanedioic acid *oxalic acid*

ethanoic acid [ethanohik] *acetic acid*

ethanol CH_3CH_2OH, boiling point 78°C, also called **ethyl alcohol**, **grain alcohol**, and simply **alcohol**. It is a colourless liquid with a characteristic odour, mainly prepared by the fermentation of sugars. An important solvent, disinfectant, and preservative, it is mainly known for its intoxicating properties in beverages.

ethanoyl *acetyl*

Ethelbert or **Æthelbert** [ethelbert] (c.552–616) King of Kent (560–616). In his reign Kent achieved (c.590) control over England S of the Humber, and Christianity was introduced by St Augustine (597). To him we owe the first written English laws.

Etheldreda or **Æthelthryth, St** [etheldreeda], also known as **St Audrey** (c.630–679) Daughter of the King of East Anglia. She founded a double monastery on the Isle of Ely in 673. Feast day 23 June.

Ethelred I [ethelred], also spelled **Æthelred** (c.830–71) King of Wessex (865–71), the elder brother of Alfred the Great. During his reign the Danes launched their main invasion of England and established their kingdom (866). He died soon after his victory over the invaders at Ashdown, in the former county of Berkshire.

Ethelred II [ethelred], known as **Ethelred the Unready**, also spelled **Æthelred** (c.968–1016) King of England (from 978), the son of Edgar. In 1013 Sweyn Forkbeard secured mastery over England, forcing Ethelred into exile in Normandy. After Sweyn's death (1014), he returned to oppose Canute, but the unity of English resistance was broken when his son, Edmund Ironside, rebelled. 'Unready' is a mistranslation of *Unraed*, which means 'ill advised'.

Ethelred, St *Ailred of Rievaulx, St*

Ethelwulf, also spelled **Æthelwulf** (d.858) Anglo-Saxon king of England (839–56), the son of the West Saxon king, Egbert. In 851 he fought a victorious battle against the Danish army at Aclea in Surrey. In 856 he was deposed by rivals on his return from Rome, but continued to rule Kent until his death. Four of his sons became kings of Wessex, including Alfred the Great.

ethene *ethylene*

ether [eether] **1** An organic compound containing an oxygen atom bonded to two alkyl groups. The best known is **ethyl ether** (CH_3CH_2–O–CH_2CH_3), a volatile liquid, boiling point 35°C, used as an anaesthetic.
2 A substance once believed to pervade all space, thought necessary as the medium of the propagation of light; also spelled **aether**. The notion is no longer required by the modern theory of light.

Etherege, Sir George [etherij] (1635–92) Restoration playwright, probably born in Maidenhead, England. His plays, such as *The Comical Revenge; or, Love in a Tub* (1664), were highly popular in their day, and introduced the comedy of manners to English theatre.

Ethernet A model of a local area network in which the workstations of the network are linked by coaxial cable. If any network station wishes to communicate with another, it sends an addressed message along the cable; this is then recognized and picked up only by the workstation to which it is addressed. A **'thin' ethernet** uses telephone wires but transmits data more slowly than in the standard **'thick' ethernet**. More recently, versions of Ethernet, using unshielded twisted pair (UTP) cables linked to a central hub and operating at 100 Mbps (Megabauds per second), have been developed.

ethics The branch of philosophy dealing with the concepts and principles of morality, and including such theoretical questions as the source and foundation of morality, the status and justification of moral rules, the relationship between moral and other human objectives, and the nature of responsibility. Ethics has various subfields of application, such as medical ethics and business ethics, and its meaning shades into the more everyday, descriptive sense of 'a set of standards'.

Ethiopia *p.317*

ethnic cleansing The systematic removal of a racial, political, religious, or cultural group from a geographical area. Ethnic cleansing differs from **genocide** in that the objective is not to exterminate all members of the group; however, mass murder, either organized or on an ad hoc basis, has often been part of the process of ethnic cleansing. The term became widely applied to the activities of various governments in the Balkans during the break-up of former Yugoslavia.

ethnicity A term which may be confused with 'race', but which refers to a shared cultural identity that has a range of distinctive behavioural and possibly linguistic features, passed on through socialization from one generation to another. Ethnic differences have been a source of political unrest, often associated with religious or clan differences.

ethnography A detailed description of the culture of a particular society, based on fieldwork by ethnographers or anthropologists, using the method of participant observation. In Europe, the subject is often referred to as **ethnology**.

ethnolinguistics The study of the relationship between language and culture. It is concerned with all aspects of language, including its structure and usage, which have any connection with culture and society.

ethnomethodology The sociological theory developed out of the work of the US sociologist Harold Garfinkel (1917–) and others in the 1960s. It studies the methods people use to accomplish successful social interaction.

ethnomusicology The scientific study of folk and national music, especially that of non-Western countries, in its anthropological, cultural, and social contexts. It was not until sound recording became easily available that the discipline could establish itself on a scientific basis.

ethnoscience A branch of social/cultural anthropology which investigates folk beliefs or ideologies that correspond to such fields of Western science as medicine, astronomy, and zoology.

ethology [eetholojee] The study of animal behaviour from the viewpoint of zoology and ecology. It considers the fine details of individual species behaviour in relation to properties of the natural environment to which the species has adapted (its *ecological niche*). The data are derived from direct observation and monitoring (eg by radio-tracking) of animals under natural or quasi-natural conditions.

ethyl [eethiyl, ethil] C_2H_5–. A functional group derived from ethane. Adding it to a name usually indicates its substitution for hydrogen in that compound.

ethyl alcohol *ethanol*

ethylene [ethileen] CH_2=CH_2, IUPAC **ethene**, boiling point −104°C. A colourless gas, the first member of the alkene series. It is a very important industrial chemical, which polymerizes to **polyethylene**.

ethyne [eethiyn] *acetylene*

Etna, Mount [etna], in Sicily **Mongibello** 37°45N 15°00E. Isolated volcanic mountain in E Sicily, Italy; height 3390 m/11 122 ft; Europe's largest active volcano; recent major eruptions, 1949, 1971, 1986, 1992, 2001, 2002–3; fertile lower slopes, growing oranges, lemons, olives, vines.

Eton *Windsor* (UK)

Etruria [etrooria] The heartland of the Etruscan people, roughly corresponding to modern Tuscany.

Etruscans [etruhsknz] A people of obscure origin who sprang to prominence in WC Italy in the 8th-c BC. Although they succumbed to the Romans politically in the 3rd-c BC, culturally their influence remained strong. Their lavishly equipped tombs show that they were particularly skilled in metal work.

etymology The study of the origins of the form and meaning of words and their history; a branch of historical linguistics. The **etymological fallacy** maintains that the 'real' meaning of a word is an earlier one, for example that *villain* really means 'farm labourer', because it once had this meaning.

Euboea [yoobeea], Gr **Évvoia**, Ital **Negropon** pop (2000e) 218 000; area 3655 km²/1411 sq mi. Second largest Greek island, in the Aegean Sea; length 144 km/89 mi; rises to 1744 m/5722 ft; capital, Chalcis.

eucalyptus *gum tree*

eucaryote or **eukaryote** [yookarioht] An organism in which cells have an organized nucleus, surrounded by a nuclear envelope, with paired chromosomes containing DNA that are recognizable during mitosis and meiosis. It includes all animals, plants, fungi, and many micro-organisms.

Eucharist (Gr *eucharistia*, 'thanksgiving') For most Christian denominations, a sacrament and the central act of worship, sometimes called the **Mass** (Roman Catholic), **Holy Communion**, or **Lord's Supper** (Protestant). It is based on the example of Jesus at the Last Supper, when he identified bread and wine with his body and blood, and generally consists of the consecration of bread and wine by the priest or minister and distribution among the worshippers (*communion*). Theological interpretations vary from the literal transformation of the

Ethiopia

250 km
150 mi

SUDAN

Gulf of Aden

ERITREA

AFRICA

Aksum • Danakil
Ras Dashen
△ 4620 m
Lake Tana • Gondar
Lalibela
DJIBOUTI
Rift Valley
E T H I O P I A
Blue Nile • Dire Dawa
■ • Awash • Harar
Addis Ababa
Jimma •
Omo Wenz
Yirga 'Alem
Wabe Shebele Wenz
Lake Turkana
S O M A L I A
K E N Y A

☐ International Airport

[eethiohpia], official name **Federal Democratic Republic of Ethiopia**, formerly **Abyssinia**, Amharic **Hebretesebawit Ityopia**

Local name Ityopiya

Timezone GMT +3

Area 1 251 282 km²/483 123 sq mi

Population total (2002e) 67 673 000

Status Republic

Capital Addis Ababa

Language Amharic (official)

Ethnic groups Oromo (40%), Amhara and Tigray (32%)

Religions Muslim (45%), Ethiopian Orthodox (37%), traditional beliefs (11%)

Physical features Located in NE Africa; dominated by mountainous C plateau, mean elevation 1800–2400 m/6–8000 ft; split diagonally by the Great Rift Valley; highest point, Ras Dashan Mt, 4620 m/15 157 ft; crossed E–W by Blue Nile; Danakil Depression (NE) dips to 116 m/381 ft below sea level.

Climate Tropical climate, moderated by higher altitudes; distinct wet season (Apr–Sep); hot, semi-arid NE and SE lowlands receive less than 500 mm/20 in of rainfall annually; severe droughts in 1980s caused widespread famine, deaths, and resettlement; major famine, 2003.

Currency 1 Ethiopian Birr (ETB) = 100 cents

Economy One of the world's poorest countries; over 80% of population employed in agriculture, especially subsistence farming; production severely affected by drought; distribution of foreign aid hindered by internal civil war and poor local organization.

GDP (2002e) $48·53 bn, per capita $700

Human Development Index (2002) 0·327

History Oldest independent country in sub-Saharan Africa; first Christian country in Africa; Italian presence in north from 1885; defeat of Italians at Adowa (1896), but northern region (Eritrea) ceded to them in peace treaty; independence of Abyssinia (former name of Ethiopia) recognized by League of Nations, 1923; Haile Selassie became Emperor in 1930, and began programme of modernization and reform; Italian invasion, 1935; annexation as Italian East Africa, 1936–41; Italians forced from Ethiopia by the Allies, and Haile Selassie returned to power in 1941; military coup, 1974; ongoing conflict with Somalia over Ogaden region; internal conflict with regional separatist Eritrean and Tigrean forces; transfer of power to People's Democratic Republic, 1987; government overthrown by separatist forces, 1991; Council of Representatives formed; multi-party elections, 1994; new constitution, 1994, recognizing a federal government of nine states, and providing for regional autonomy (allowing the right of secession); new Council of People's Representatives formed, 1995; escalating conflict with Eritrea over disputed border territory, 1999–2000; Permanent Court of Arbitration at The Hague issued a border ruling, 2002, but tension in the region continues.

Monarch
1889–1911 Menelik II
1911–16 Lej Iyasu (Joshua)
1916–28 Zawditu
1928–74 Haile Selassie (Emperor from 1930)

Provisional Military Administrative Council Chairman
1974–7 Teferi Benti
1977–87 Mengistu Haile Mariam

People's Democratic Republic Head of State
1987–91 Mengistu Haile Mariam
1991–5 Meles Zenawi
1995–2001 Negaso Gidada
2001– Woldegiorgis Girma

Head of Government
1991–5 Tamirat Layne
1995– Meles Zenawi

elements into the body and blood of Christ, to symbolism representing the real presence of Christ and a simple memorial meal.

Euclid [yooklid], Gr **Eucleides** (4th–3rd-c BC) Greek mathematician who taught in Alexandria c.300 BC. His chief extant work is the 13-volume *Elements*. The approach which obeys his axioms became known as **Euclidean geometry**.

Eudoxos of Cnidus [yoodoksus, niyduhs] (c.408 BC–c.353 BC) Greek geometer and astronomer, born in Cnidus, Asia Minor. He established principles that laid the foundation for Euclid, then applied the subject to the study of the Moon and planets.

Eugene of Savoy, Prince, in full **François Eugène de Savoie Carignan** (1663–1736) Austrian general, born in Paris. He defeated the Turks on several occasions, fought against France, and while in command of the imperial army helped Marlborough at Blenheim (1704), Oudenaarde (1708), and Malplaquet (1709).

eugenics [yoojeniks] The science that deals with the effects on the individual of biological and social factors. The term was coined in 1883 by Francis Galton as 'the science which deals with all influences that improve the inborn qualities'. The responsible study of eugenics was made difficult in the earlier years of the 20th-c by the propagation (eg in Germany and the USA) of political doctrines, in the name of eugenics, which were nonscientific and brutal.

Eugenics Society [yoojeniks] A society founded in London in 1907 as the Eugenics Education Society, adopting its present name in

1926. Its American counterpart changed its name in 1971 to the Society for the Study of Social Biology. It promotes research into the biological, genetic, social, and cultural factors relating to human reproduction, development, and health.

Eugénie, Empress *Napoleon III*

Euglena [yoogleena] A genus of freshwater, single-celled micro-organisms with a whip-like flagellum at their front end used for swimming; usually contains chlorophyll in chloroplasts, and classified as a green alga (Class: Chlorophyceae); sometimes lacks chlorophyll, and classified as a protozoan flagellate (Phylum: Mastigophora).

eukaryote *eucaryote*

Eulenspiegel, Till [oylenshpeegl] A legendary 14th-c peasant prankster of Brunswick, Germany. He is celebrated in an epic poem by Gerhard Hauptmann (1928) and musically in a tone poem by Richard Strauss (1894).

Euler, Leonhard [oyler] (1707–83) Mathematician, born in Basel, Switzerland. A highly prolific scholar, his many works dealt with number theory, geometry, calculus, and applications in astronomy and technology. Several important notions in mathematics are named after him. He had a prodigious memory, which enabled him to continue mathematical work and to compute complex calculations in his head, even after becoming totally blind in his 60s.

Eumenides [yoomenideez] A euphemistic name given to the Erinyes after being domesticated at Athens in Aeschylus's play of the same name. The name means 'the kindly ones'.

Eumycota [yoomiysuhta] *Ascomycetes; Basidiomycetes; fungus*

Eupen [uhpen] 50°38N 6°02E, pop (2000e) 17500. Principal town in German-speaking Belgium; popular health resort and holiday centre; railway.

euphonium A musical instrument of the tuba family, much used in brass bands and occasionally in orchestral music.

euphorbia *spurge*

Euphrates, River [yoofrayteez], Arabic **Al-Furat**, Turkish **Firat** Longest river in W Asia; length 2735 km/1700 mi; formed in EC Turkey, flows into Iraq, uniting with the Tigris to form the Shatt al-Arab, which enters the Persian Gulf; remains of several ancient cities along banks.

EURATOM [yooratm] Acronym for **European Atomic Energy Community**. It was established as an independent body in 1957, but brought into the EEC in 1962. Its objectives are the promotion of peaceful uses of atomic energy, particularly nuclear power for electricity.

Eureka Stockade [yureeka] In Australian history, an armed clash between goldminers and a combined police and military force at the Eureka Stockade, Ballarat, Victoria (1854). The miners had objected to the expensive mining licence imposed by the government. Public opinion swung behind the miners, and the government was forced to back down.

eurhythmics [yurithmiks] A system of musical training devised by Jaques-Dalcroze, designed to develop a quick response to changing rhythms by fitting bodily movements to pieces of music.

Euripides [yuripideez] (c.480–406 BC) Greek tragic playwright, born in Athens. He wrote about 80 dramas, of which 19 survive, such as *Alcestis*, *Medea*, *Orestes*, and *Electra*.

Euro [yooroh], symbol € The common currency unit used in 12 countries of the European Union (from 1 Jan 1999 in Belgium, Germany, Spain, France, Ireland, Italy, Luxembourg, Netherlands, Austria, Portugal, Finland, and from 1 Jan 2001 in Greece), and also from 1999 in Andorra, Monaco, San Marino, and the Vatican. Euro notes and coins entered general circulation on 1 Jan 2002, at which point each country had a period of time to phase out its old currency, replacing it with Euro currency to be used throughout the Euro area ('Eurozone'). Notes are in units of 5, 10, 20, 50, 100, 200, and 500. In the business world, all

payment and accounting systems began to use the Euro on 1 January 1999, each national currency unit being irrevocably fixed in relation to it; for example, the exchange rate with the Deutschmark was set at 1·95583, and in the UK 1 Euro was worth approximately 70p. The 2002 launch was celebrated with ceremonies and special events throughout the Eurozone.

Eurocurrency *Euromoney*

Eurodollar US dollars held in banks in Europe. Considerable sums are involved, resulting from such major concerns as the oil industry, where trade is conducted in dollars.

Eurofighter The name given to the standardized air-to-air and ground-attack aircraft with which it is planned to equip several European air forces. A major multi-national collaborative development programme involved Germany, Italy, Spain, and the UK. Revised planning and production schedules delayed the plane's availability until 2003. It was named *Euro-fighter Typhoon* in 1998. The four partner nations had (in 2006) ordered 638 of the aircraft.

Euromoney or **Eurocurrency** Convertible currencies such as pounds sterling, French and Swiss francs, Deutschmarks, and US dollars held in banks outside the country of origin. They can be borrowed by commercial undertakings for trade.

Europa (astronomy) [yurohpa] The second natural satellite of Jupiter, discovered by Galileo in 1610; distance from the planet 671 000 km/417 000 mi; diameter 3140 km/1950 mi; orbital period 3·551 days.

Europa (mythology) [yurohpa] or **Europe** [yoorohpee] In Greek mythology, the daughter of Agenor, king of Tyre, who was abducted by Zeus in the shape of a bull. Her children were Minos and Rhadamanthus.

Europa Nostra [yurohpa nostra] (Lat 'our Europe') An international federation established in 1963 for the preservation of historic sites, buildings, and monuments. It represents more than 200 organizations from 20 countries.

Europe Second smallest continent, forming an extensive peninsula of the Eurasian land-mass, occupying c.7% of the Earth's surface; bounded E by Asia beyond the Ural Mts; supports over 25% of the world's population. (*see map pp.320–21*)

European Atomic Energy Community *EURATOM*

European Bank for Reconstruction and Development A bank founded in 1990 to assist the economic reconstruction of C and E Europe. It has 59 members.

European Central Bank (ECB) A bank established in Frankfurt (am Main) on 1 June 1998 to oversee the introduction and development of the Euro, and to set interest rates (3 per cent, at the outset). The Bank reports to the European Parliament on a yearly basis. The ECB and the national central banks together form the **European System of Central Banks** (ESCB), which govern the conduct of the single monetary policy, and whose primary objective is to maintain price stability.

European Coal and Steel Community (ECSC) The first European economic institution, set up in 1952. It worked to remove customs duties and quota restrictions in coal, iron ore, and scrap, and aimed to ensure that competition in these commodities was fair.

European Commission The administrative and executive bureaucracy of the European Union. Its functions are to uphold the European ideal, propose new policy initiatives, and ensure that existing policies are implemented. It comprises 20 commissioners directly nominated by the member states; they serve a 5-year term, are each responsible for a specific area of work, and are supported by a bureaucracy employing c.15 000 people. The Commission decides by majority vote, and is collectively responsible to the European Parliament. In 1999 a strict code of conduct for commissioners was adopted.

European Community (EC), formerly **European Communities** The name generally used in 1967–93 to refer to the organization which then became the European Union. A community of Western European states initially created to achieve economic integration, but with the longer-term goal of political integration also in mind. It grew out of the European Coal and Steel Community which was established in 1952 under the Treaty of Paris by Belgium, France, Italy, Luxembourg, The Netherlands, and West Germany. In 1957, under the two Treaties of Rome, the same six states established the European Economic Community (essentially a customs union), and also the European Atomic Community (EURATOM). In 1967 the executive bodies of the three communities were merged to form the 'European Community'. A further nine members later joined the Community. They were Denmark, Ireland, and the UK (1973), Greece (1981), Portugal and Spain (1986), and Austria, Finland, and Sweden (1995). Several other countries are seeking to become members. In 1993, the area covered by the EC became a single market, which was extended to incorporate the seven countries of the European Free Trade Association in 1994 (as the European Economic Area). Also in 1993, the EC member states concluded the process of ratifying the Maastricht Treaty on European Union, designed to strengthen the degree of co-operation within the Community and to enhance political integration. The Community (now the European Union) is governed by a series of supra-national and international institutions: the European Council, the Council of Ministers, the European Commission, the European Parliament, the European Court of Justice, and the Court of Auditors.

European Convention on Human Rights A convention which sets out the main rights and fundamental freedoms to be protected, contained in the Universal Declaration of Human Rights: the right to life, to a fair trial, and to freedom of thought, conscience, religion, and education. Originally formulated by the Council of Europe in 1950, it came into force in 1953, and may only investigate a complaint if all possible remedies in the national courts have been tried. It attempts to reach a friendly settlement of any breach of the Convention, but failing this the breach may be referred to the European Court of Human Rights, whose judgments have acquired the force of law in most Western European countries. The Court has become the final court of appeal on human rights issues for the European Court of Justice. The Human Rights Act (1989) gave effect in the United Kingdon to rights and freedoms guaranteed by the European Convention on Human Rights.

European Council The body which brings together the heads of state and/or government of the member states of the European Union. Formally constituted in 1974 it takes the main decisions in the European Union, for instance on such issues as institutional reform and the admission of new members. The European Council became an official part of the European Community's structure in 1987.

European Court of Human Rights (ECHR) A judicial court established by the European Convention on Human Rights, based in Strasbourg, France. It was founded in 1950 to safeguard the rights of free expression and to protect against discrimination. In countries that recognize the Convention within their own legal systems, verdicts in domestic courts concerning discrimination are not binding, and cases can be referred to the ECHR by reference to the Convention. The Convention was incorporated into English law in 2000 by the Human Rights Act (1998).

European Court of Justice *Court of Justice of the European Communities*

European Currency Unit (ECU) *European Monetary System*

European Defence Community A supranational community which was to ensure the security of its members against aggression, and produce a more coherent grouping than the North Atlantic Treaty Organization. A treaty was signed in May 1952 by the six members of the European Coal and Steel Community, but was never ratified by the French parliament, and the project was abandoned.

European Economic Area (EEA) A trading bloc linking the European Union and the European Free Trade Association, introduced in January 1994. Its 372 million members make it the world's biggest free-trade area.

European Economic Community (EEC) A grouping of European states established in 1958 after the Treaties of Rome (1957), referred to as the **Common Market**. It was essentially a customs union, providing a common external tariff and a common market with the removal of internal trade barriers. A common agricultural policy was established in 1963, and common policies were introduced for fisheries, regional development, industrial intervention, and economic and social affairs. The four principle institutions of the EEC were the European Commission, the Council of Ministers, the Court of Justice and the European Assembly (later to become the European Parliament). At the level of the European Commission, the EEC merged in 1967 with the European Atomic Energy Community (EURATOM) and the European Coal and Steel Community (ECSC), and was thereafter unofficially known as the European Community (EC), though this title was not adopted until 1993.

European Environment Agency *Environment Agency*

European Free Trade Association (EFTA) An association originally of seven W European states who were not members of the European Economic Community (EEC), intended as a counter to the EEC; it was established in 1959 under the Stockholm Convention. The members (Austria, Denmark, Norway, Portugal, Sweden, Switzerland, and the UK) agreed to eliminate over a period of time trade restrictions between them. Both the UK (1973) and Portugal (1986) left to join the EEC, but there has been a free trade agreement between the remaining EFTA countries and the European Community. Finland joined in 1985. The two groupings united as the European Economic Area in 1994.

European Laboratory for Particle Physics (CERN) The principal European centre for experimental research in particle physics, located in Geneva. Supported by most European countries, CERN was founded in 1954 by the Conseil Européene pour la Recherche Nucléaire for fundamental research into the structure of matter and the interactions governing it. CERN houses particle accelerators that are among the largest scientific instruments in the world.

European Monetary Institute An institution established in Frankfurt in January 1994, as a precursor to a European central bank – the second stage towards economic and monetary union. Its aims were to strengthen central bank co-operation and monetary policy co-ordination, and to prepare for the establishment of the European System of Central Banks for the conduct of a single monetary policy and the creation of a single currency. The Institute was liquidated following the establishment of the European Central Bank in 1998.

European Monetary System (EMS) A financial system set up in 1979 by member states of the European Economic Community with the immediate aim of stabilizing exchange rates and the ultimate aim of achieving Economic and Monetary Union (EMU), with a single European currency. A **European Currency Unit (ECU)** was created, but only as a unit of account; later named the **Euro**. Central banks were to consult on exchange rates, and to assist each other in stabilizing them both bilaterally and through a European Monetary Cooperation Fund. Members could join an **Exchange Rate Mechanism (ERM)**, which limited fluctuations in the exchange rates between its members. The first stage of formal EMU was established in 1990, when the Committee of Governors of the Central Banks of the EEC member states was given additional responsibilities to engage in the required preparatory work. The sec-

Novaya
Zemlya

Kara
Sea

Arctic Circle

R U S S I A N

F E D E R A T I O N

Kazakhstan

Volga

Caspian Sea

E

Sea of
Azov

Caucasus

c k   S e a   Georgia

Azerbaijan

ond stage was the replacement of this body by the European Monetary Institute (1 Jan 1994), whose activities included the introduction of a new Exchange Rate Mechanism (ERM II), adopted in mid-1997. The third stage, the adoption of the Euro by those member states which satisfied the entry conditions laid down by the EU Council, began on 1 January 1999. A new European Central Bank was set up (1 Jun 1998) to control monetary policy in the third stage.

European Parliament The representative assembly of the European Union. Despite its name, it has few legislative powers, but it does have the right to be consulted by the Council of Ministers, to dismiss the Commission, and to reject or amend the European Union's budget. It has been directly and democratically elected since 1979. European-wide elections for the 732 seats (626 before 1 May 2004) are held every five years. Seats are distributed among the EU members on their respective populations, and members do not sit in national blocs. Until the Maastricht Treaty (1991), its legislative powers were largely advisory. The bulk of the Parliament's administration is located in Luxembourg; its plenary sessions are normally held in Strasbourg, and most of its committees meet in Brussels, where the European Union is based and the Councils meet.

European Recovery Program *Marshall Plan*

European Space Agency (ESA) A consortium space agency of 13 European countries (Belgium, Denmark, Germany, France, Ireland, Italy, the Netherlands, Spain, Sweden, Switzerland, UK (founding nations) together with Austria and Norway, and associate member Finland) to promote space research, technology, and applications for exclusively peaceful purposes. It was created in 1975 and its headquarters is in Paris. Launches use the Ariane family of vehicles from a launch centre in Kourou, French Guiana.

European Steel and Coal Community *European Community*
European System of Central Banks *European Central Bank*
European Union (EU), formerly known as the **European Community (EC)** An organization of European nations committed to increasing economic integration and political, judicial and social co-operation among its member states. Its founder members of 1958 – Belgium, France, West Germany, Italy, Luxembourg, and The Netherlands – were joined by the UK, Denmark, and the Republic of Ireland (1973), Greece (1981), and Spain and Portugal (1986). East Germany was incorporated on German reunification in 1990, and Austria, Finland and Sweden joined in 1995. In 1993 the 12 European Community members, in accordance with the Maastricht Treaty on European Union (1991), agreed to extend their co-operation in matters of justice, home affairs, and a common foreign and security policy. The UK government was unwilling to agree to all the proposals adopted by the other countries (notably over the single European currency and a common social policy), and a compromise providing opt-out clauses for the UK was devised; of these, only the opt-out concerning the single currency remains. The designation *European Union* in place of *European Community* was formally introduced in 1993. Cyprus, Czech Republic, Estonia, Hungary, Latvia, Lithuania, Malta, Poland, Slovakia, and Slovenia joined in 2004 and plans for expansion of membership continued in 2007 with Bulgaria and Romania, and with Turkey a longer-term prospect. A European constitution was finalized in 2004 after long negotiations among EU governments. Member states can ratify the constitution through a referendum or by parliamentary vote. By mid-2005 nine countries had ratified the constitution, but in May/June that year it was rejected by French and Dutch voters. The EU's first military operation took place in March 2003, when it took over NATO's role in Macedonia.

Europoort *Rotterdam*
Eurostar International high-speed passenger train service

between London (St Pancras, formerly Waterloo) and Continental Europe via the Channel Tunnel. Direct services include Paris (and Disneyland), Brussels, Calais, and Lille, as well as Bourg St-Maurice and Moutier in the French Alps. Operated jointly by Eurostar (UK) Ltd, the French Railways (SNCF) and Belgium Railways (SNCB), it commenced operations in 1994. There are 27 trains in the fleet, 392 m/1286 ft in length, each containing 766 passenger seats, and capable of speeds of 300 kph/186 mph. On 30 July 2003, a Eurostar train broke the UK rail speed record, reaching 335 kph/208 mph on the 70 km/43·5 mi first section of the new high-speed track from the Channel Tunnel to London's St Pancras Station (open in Nov 2007).

Eurovision Song Contest An annual contest organized by television companies throughout Europe (and Israel) to choose a winning pop song from among those entered by the participating countries. The first was held at Lugano, Switzerland, in 1956.

Eurozone Those 12 countries within the European Union that have adopted the € as their common currency. In 2002 Euro notes and coins entered general circulation in Belgium, Germany, Spain, France, Ireland, Italy, Luxembourg, Netherlands, Austria, Portugal, Finland, and Greece.

Eurydice [yooridisee] In Greek mythology, a dryad, the wife of Orpheus. After her death, Orpheus went down to the Underworld and persuaded Hades to let her go by the power of his music. The condition was that she should follow him, and that he should not look at her until they reached the light. Not hearing her footsteps, he looked back, and she disappeared.

eurypterid [yooripterid] An extinct, aquatic, water scorpion; large, up to 3 m/10 ft in length; known from the Ordovician period to the end of the Palaeozoic era. (Phylum: Arthropoda. Class: Eurypterida.)

Eusebio [yoosaybioo], in full **Eusebio Ferreira da Silva**, nickname **the Black Pearl** (1942–) Footballer, born in Lourenço Marques, Mozambique. He made his international debut in 1961, and played for his country 77 times. At club level he played for Benfica. He retired in 1978, and was later appointed coach to Benfica.

Eusebius of Caesarea [yooseebius] (c.264–340) Historian of the early Church, probably born in Palestine. His great work, the *Ecclesiastical History*, is a record of the chief events in the Christian Church until 324.

Euskadi Ta Askatasuma *Basques*

Eustachian tube [yustayshn] *auditory tube*

eustasy [yoostasee] Worldwide changes in sea level caused by the advance or recession of the polar ice caps. This caused a gradual rise in the sea-level during the 20th-c.

Euston Road School A group of English painters working 1937–9 in London, including William Coldstream (1908–87), Victor Pasmore (1908–98), Graham Bell (1910–43), and Claude Rogers (1909–79). They rejected abstraction and surrealism, and practised a quiet naturalism concentrating on domestic subjects.

Euterpe [yooterpee] In Greek mythology, one of the Muses, usually associated with flute-playing.

euthanasia The painless ending of life, usually as an act of mercy to relieve chronic pain or suffering. It has been advocated by pressure groups such as *Exit*, as a dignified death for the elderly who have lost the will to live. Since the 1980s, several cases of *doctor-assisted suicide* (the death of a terminally ill patient, through taking lethal drugs provided by a doctor), and associated notions such as *medicide* (*medically assisted suicide*), have been given publicity, and fuelled the medical ethical debate. During the 1990s, several US states made these practices illegal. In 1996 Australia's Northern Territory legalized euthanasia, but the law was repealed after nine months. The Netherlands made doctor-assisted death legal in 2002, followed by Belgium, the first countries to sanction the practice.

Evangelical Alliance A religious movement, founded in 1846 – the formal expression of an international evangelical community embracing a variety of conservative evangelical churches and independent agencies. In the USA it has been succeeded by the National Council of Churches of Christ in the United States of America.

evangelicalism Since the Reformation, a term which has been applied to the Protestant Churches because of their principles of justification through faith alone and the supreme authority accorded to scripture. It has been applied more narrowly to Protestant Churches emphasizing intense personal conversion ('born-again Christianity') and commitment in their experience of justification and biblical authority.

Evangelical United Brethren Church A Christian denomination established in the USA in 1946 through the merger of the Church of the United Brethren in Christ and the Evangelical Church. In 1968 it merged with the Methodist Church to form the United Methodist Church.

evangelist (Gr *evangel*, 'good news') One who preaches the gospel of Jesus Christ. Although evangelizing is now understood to be the task of the whole Church, the term has been more recently applied to popular preachers at missionary rallies.

Evans, Sir Arthur (John) (1851–1941) Archaeologist, born in Nash Mills, Hertfordshire. Between 1899 and 1935 he excavated the city of Knossos, discovering the remains of the civilization which in 1904 he named 'Minoan', after Minos, the Cretan king of Greek legend.

Evans, Chris (1966–) Disc jockey and television presenter, born in Warrington, Cheshire. For television's Channel 4 he launched *The Big Breakfast* and hosted *Don't Forget Your Toothbrush* and *TFI Friday*. He presented breakfast shows for Radio 1 and later Virgin, and in 1998 he received a Sony gold award for his contribution to the radio industry, but in 2001 was dismissed by Virgin Radio for breach of contract. He joined BBC Radio 2 in 2005, and also began hosting *OFI Sunday* for ITV1. He was married to singer and actress Billie Piper (2001–6).

Evans, David *U2*

Evans, Dame Edith (Mary) (1888–1976) Actress, born in London. She earned a great reputation for her versatility, with many notable appearances in the plays of Shakespeare and Shaw. She continued to be active on both stage and screen into her eighties.

Evans, Sir Geraint (Llewellyn) (1922–92) Baritone, born in Pontypridd, S Wales. He made his operatic debut at Covent Garden in 1948, and became particularly known for his comic roles. He retired from the operatic stage in 1984.

Evans, Timothy John *Christie, John*

Evans, Walker (1903–75) Photographer, born in St Louis, MO. His work with the writer James Agee to document the lives of the share-croppers of the Deep South, eventually published as *Let Us Now Praise Famous Men* (1941), is considered to be one of the best writer–photographer collaborations.

evaporation The passing from a liquid phase to a gas phase; in particular, the process by which water is lost from the Earth's surface to the atmosphere as water vapour. Rates of evaporation depend on such factors as solar radiation, the temperature difference between the evaporating surface and the overlying air, humidity, and wind.

Eve *Adam and Eve*

Eve, Trevor (1951–) Actor and producer, born in Birmingham, West Midlands. In 1980 he became well known for his lead in the television series *Shoestring*, and later TV appearances include *The Politician's Wife* (1995), *David Copperfield* (1999), the series *Waking the Dead* (2001–), and *The Family Man* (2006).

Evelyn, John [evelin, eevlin] (1620–1706) Writer, born in Wotton,

Surrey. His main literary work is his *Diary*, a detailed source-book on the social, political, and religious life of 17th-c England.

evening primrose The name given to several very similar species of erect, robust biennials, native to North America; flowers large, broadly funnel-shaped with four narrow sepals and four overlapping yellow (sometimes red or white) petals, usually fragrant and opening at night. The oil from *Oenothera biennis* and *Oenothera lamarkiana* is claimed to be beneficial in several disorders. (Genus: *Oenothera*, 80 species. Family: Onagraceae.)

Evenki [evengkee] *Altaic*

event horizon *black hole*

Everest, Mount [evuhrest], Nepali **Sagarmatha**, Chin **Qomolangma Feng** 27°59N 95°26W. Mountain peak in the Himalayas of C Asia; height (1999 calculation) 8850 m/29 035 ft; highest mountain in the world; named after Sir George Everest (1790–1866), surveyor-general of India; summit first reached via the Southeast Ridge on 29 May 1953 by Sir Edmund Hillary and Sherpa Tenzing Norgay of Nepal in a British expedition under Col John Hunt.

Everglades S Florida, USA; swampy, subtropical region, length c.160 km/100 mi, width 80–120 km/50–75 mi, area c.12 950 km²/5000 sq mi; covers most of the Florida peninsula S of L Okeechobee; Everglades National Park in the S, a world heritage site.

evergreen plants Plants which retain their leaves throughout the year. They either grow in climates which have no adverse seasons or have leaves adapted to withstand cold and drought. The leaves are shed and replaced gradually, so that the plant always bears foliage.

Everly Brothers, The [eve(r)lee] American duo **Don Everly** (1937– , guitar, vocals), and **Phil Everly** (1939– , guitar, vocals). They had their first major hit with 'Bye Bye Love' (1957), and the style – close harmonies over acoustic guitars and a rock 'n' roll beat – became their trademark. They split up in 1973, but reformed in 1983 with a sell-out concert in London.

Evert (Lloyd), Chris(tine Marie) [evert] (1954–) Tennis player, born in Fort Lauderdale, FL. She won her first Wimbledon title in 1974 at age 19, and later won in 1976 and 1981; she also won the US singles title in 1975–80 and 1982, and several other titles. She married British tennis player John Lloyd (marriage dissolved 1987), and in 1988 US skier Andy Mill. She retired from professional tennis in 1989 and was elected to the International Tennis Hall of Fame in 1995.

Evesham [eevshm] 52°06N 1°56W, pop (2000e) 17 300. Town in Worcestershire, WC England; in the Vale of Evesham in a fruit- and vegetable-growing area; railway.

evidence-based medicine The use by physicians of the current best scientific evidence in making decisions about the medical care of patients. Increasingly, systems are being developed, including powerful electronic databases, to enable physicians to identify up-to-date information on the causes, diagnosis, and treatment of diseases.

Evita *Perón, Eva*

evolution Any gradual directional change; now most commonly used to refer to the cumulative changes in the characteristics of populations of organisms from generation to generation. Evolution occurs by the fixation of changes (*mutations*) in the structure of the genetic material, and the passing on of these changes from ancestor to descendant. It is well demonstrated over geological time by the sequence of organisms preserved in the fossil record.

Evora [evura], ancient **Ebora** or **Liberalitas Julia** 38°33N 7°57W, pop (2000e) 38 600. Ancient walled market town in S Portugal; a world heritage site; airfield; railway; cathedral (1186), Roman Temple of Diana, old university (1551).

Evreux [ayvroe] 49°00N 1°08E, pop (2000e) 53 800. City in NW France; railway; cathedral (begun 11th-c).

Ewe [evay, ayway] A cluster of Kwa-speaking agricultural peoples of Togo, Ghana, and Benin. The coastal peoples also fish.

ewe *sheep*

Excalibur [ekskaliber] In Arthurian legend, the name of King Arthur's sword, which was given to him by the Lady of the Lake. As he lay dying he instructed Sir Bedivere to throw it back into the lake, where a hand drew it under.

exchange rates The price at which a currency may be bought in terms of a unit of another currency. Until the 1970s, rates were fixed from time to time; today, most are *floating* (ie the rate is determined by the ongoing supply and demand for the currency).

excise tax A tax levied on many goods and services by governments as a way of raising revenues; often called **duty**. Best known are the duties on tobacco, alcoholic drinks, and fuel, Value Added Tax in the UK, and Sales Tax in the USA.

executor(s) The individual(s) named in the will by a deceased person as being responsible for ensuring that his or her wishes are carried out. These duties include paying any debts from the estate, and ensuring that any balance is distributed amongst the beneficiaries according to the instructions in the will.

Exeter, ancient **Isca Dumnoniorum** 50°43N 3°31W, pop (2001e) 111 100. County town of Devon, SW England; on the R Exe; founded by the Romans 1st-c AD; railway; airfield; university (1955); cathedral (12th-c), Guildhall (12th-c); football league team, Exeter City (Grecians).

existentialism A philosophical movement, closely associated with Kierkegaard, Camus, Sartre, and Heidegger. Its most salient theses are that there is no ultimate purpose to the world; that persons find themselves in a world which is vaguely hostile; that persons choose and cannot avoid choosing their characters, goals, and perspectives; and that truths about the world and our situation are revealed most clearly in moments of unfocused psychological anxiety or dread. These themes have influenced literature, psychoanalysis, and theology.

Exmoor National park in Somerset and Devon, England; area 686 km²/265 sq mi; established in 1954; highest point, Dunkery Beacon, 520 m/1707 ft; known for its ponies; major tourist area.

Exmoor pony The oldest British breed of horse; a small pony developed on Exmoor, Devon; height, 11·2–12·3 hands/1·2–1·3 m/3 ft 10 in–4 ft 3 in; very hardy; broad chest, deep body, stiff springy coat; brown with cream muzzle.

Exmouth [eksmuhth] 50°37N 3°25W, pop (2000e) 34 200. Resort town in Devon, SW England; on the R Exe; centre for recreational sailing; railway.

exobiology The study of extraterrestrial life. Techniques include the monitoring of radio waves emitted by other star systems, and the use of space-probe experiments designed to detect life forms, or the presence of the molecules required for life to develop.

Exodus, Book of The second book of the Pentateuch in the Hebrew Bible/Old Testament. It narrates stories about the deliverance of the Jews from slavery in Egypt, and the giving of the Law to Israel through a revelation to Moses on Mt Sinai.

exogamy *marriage*

exon *intron*

exoplanet A planet orbiting a star outside the Solar System; short for **extrasolar planet**. The first such planet, orbiting 51 Pegasi, was discovered by Michael Mayor and Didier Queloz of Geneva in 1995. Others were announced in 1996 in 70 Virginis, 47 Utsaa Rajoris, and 55 Cancri, and several more have since been discovered.

exosphere The outer shell in the atmosphere (at c.400 km/250 mi) from which light gases can escape.

expanding universe *'big bang'*

expert system A computer system which can perform at least some of the functions of the relevant human expert. Expert

eye

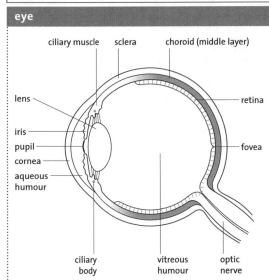

ciliary muscle sclera choroid (middle layer)

lens
iris
pupil
cornea
aqueous humour
retina
fovea

ciliary body — vitreous humour — optic nerve

retina — lens of eye
back of eye — front of eye

Normal eye
The image is in focus on the retina without a correcting lens in front

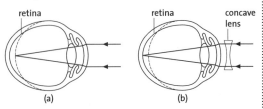

retina retina concave lens

(a) (b)

Short-sighted eye
(a) The eye is too long and the image is not in focus on the retina
(b) The use of a concave lens brings the image into focus

retina retina convex lens

(a) (b)

Long-sighted eye
(a) The eye is too short and the image is not in focus on the retina
(b) The use of a convex lens brings the image into focus

A specialized receptor organ responding to light stimuli. Various forms exist, such as the stigmata of certain protozoa, the ocelli of annelids, and the compound eye of insects. In land-based vertebrates, such as humans, the eyeball is composed of two parts: the transparent *corneal* part at the front, and the opaque *scleral* part at the back. Three concentric coats form the wall of the eyeball: an outer *fibrous* coat, consisting of the cornea and sclera; a middle *vascular* coat, consisting of the choroid, ciliary body, and iris; and an inner *nervous* coat (the *retina*). The coats surround and partly divide the contents of the eyeball. The *vitreous body* (a jelly-like substance containing a meshwork of fine fibres) lies between the lens and the retina. The space between the lens and the cornea contains a watery fluid (the *aqueous humour*), and is further partly divided by the iris into front and rear chambers. The *lens* is transparent and biconvex, lying between the iris and the vitreous body; changes in its convexity alter its focal length (the greater the convexity, the shorter the focal length), and are brought about by the action of the ciliary muscles. The lens is soft and elastic in the fetus, but becomes hardened and flatter with increasing age, making focusing on close objects more difficult (*presbyopia*); it may also become opaque in the elderly (*cataract*). Light entering the eye is refracted by the cornea, and passes through the lens, which focuses it to form an inverted image on the retina. This image is coded by the retina and sent to the visual areas of the cerebral cortex for interpretation, thus enabling the original pattern of light stimuli to be 'seen'. The amount of light entering the eye is determined by the size of the pupil, which in turn is determined by the degree of contraction of the iris. If the image from distant objects is focused in front of the retina, the condition is known as *myopia*, with vision being better for near objects ('short-sightedness'). If the image is focused beyond the retina, the condition is known as *hypermetropia*, with vision being better for distant objects ('long-sightedness'). Glasses using concave lenses are used to correct short sight; a convex lens is used for long sight.

systems have been developed for use in areas, such as medical diagnosis, which require a large amount of organized knowledge plus deductive skills.

Explorer 1 The first US space satellite (launched 31 Jan 1958). The simple 14-kg/31-lb spacecraft was launched on a Redstone (Jupiter C) rocket vehicle from Cape Canaveral. 'Explorer' later became the generic name of a series of relatively simple Earth orbital space physics and astronomy missions carried out by NASA.

explosives Substances capable of undergoing a rapid chemical change to produce hot gases which occupy a much greater volume, and therefore exert a sudden very high pressure. Most military and industrial explosives consist largely of nitrated carbon compounds. (The chief exception is the oldest explosive, gunpowder.) They are distinguished as **propellants** and **high explosives**. Propellants burn rapidly but smoothly, so as to exert a great but steady pressure on a projectile in the barrel of a gun. High explosives change so fast as to produce a violent and disruptive shock in adjacent material.

exposure (photography) The controlled presentation of a photosensitive surface to light in order to record an image. Exposure level is determined by the intensity of the light and the time of exposure, and must be correctly set to ensure satisfactory reproduction of tone and colour. In still cameras this is done by a suitable combination of lens aperture and shutter speed, but in motion-picture and video cameras the exposure time is normally fixed, and level is set by the lens aperture. An **exposure meter** is an instrument for measuring light, giving a scale reading from which lens aperture and shutter setting may be determined.

exposure (physics) A measure of exposure to ionizing radiation, based on the amount of ionization produced in dry air by X-rays or gamma rays; symbol *X*, units R (röntgen). The modern notions of *absorbed dose* and *dose equivalent* are generally more useful.

Expressionism A movement in art, architecture, and literature which aims to communicate the internal emotional realities of a situation, rather than its external 'realistic' aspect; the term was first used in Germany in 1911, but the roots of the movement can be traced to van Gogh and Gauguin in the 1880s. Traditional ideas of beauty and proportion are disregarded, so that artists can express their feelings more strongly by means of distortion, jarring colours, and exaggerated linear rhythms. The movement was also influential in literature, especially in German theatre after World War 1.

Extensible Mark-up Language *document description language*

externalities The effects of economic processes on people other than those conducting them. External *diseconomies* are effects harmful to others, such as traffic congestion or environmental pollution. External *economies* are effects beneficial to others, such as the sight of pleasant private buildings or gardens visible to the public. Externalities may arise from both productive and consumer activities.

extinction The disappearance of a species from a particular habitat (*local* extinction), or the total elimination of a species worldwide. Animal species are categorized as extinct if they have not been definitely located in the wild for the past 50 years.

extracellular fluid (ECF) The fluid which surrounds the cells of the body. In humans the adult volume is c.14 l/25 UK pt/30 US pt, and consists of blood plasma, the interstitial fluid of tissues, and transcellular fluids.

extradition The removal of a person by a state in which that person is currently located to the territory of another state where the person has been convicted of a crime, or is said to have committed a crime. Extradition treaties are normally restricted to more important crimes, but exclude political crimes.

Extranet *Intranet*

extrasensory perception (ESP) The apparent gaining of information about an object or event (mental or physical; past, present, or future) by means other than those currently understood by the physical sciences. Clairvoyance, telepathy, and precognition are specific types of extrasensory perception.

extraversion *introversion / extraversion*

Extremadura [ekstraymadoora] or **Estremadura** [aystraymadoora] pop (2000e) 1 064 000; area 41 602 km²/16 058 sq mi. Autonomous region of W Spain on the Portuguese frontier; considerable industrial development since the 1970s.

extreme unction *anointing the sick*

extrusive rock Igneous rocks which have formed from molten magma, or volcanic fragments ejected onto the Earth's surface; also termed **volcanic rock**. They are most commonly basalt or pyroclasts.

Eyck, Jan van [iyk] (c.1389–1441) Flemish painter, born (possibly) in Maaseik or Maastricht. The first master of the new realistic approach to painting in the 15th-c Netherlands, his skill is well-attested by the highly-finished 'Arnolfini Wedding Portrait' (1434, National Gallery, London).

eye *p.324*

eyespot A splash-borne disease of wheat and barley (*Pseudocercosporella herpotrichoides* = *Tapesia yallundae*), causing decay at the bases of growing stems. The disease is carried between seasons on crop residues, so that infection is more severe when successive susceptible crops are grown on the same field. It may be controlled by fungicidal spray or by crop rotation. (Order: Ascomycetes.)

Eyre, Sir Richard (Charles Hastings) [air] (1943–) Theatre, film, and television director, born in Barnstaple, Devon. Associate director of the National Theatre, London (1981–8), he became artistic director (1988–97). Films for television include *Tumbledown* (1988, BAFTA for best single drama), *The Absence of War* (1995), and *King Lear* (1998). Among his feature films are *Iris* (2000), *Stage Beauty* (2004), and *Notes on a Scandal* (2006).

Eyre Lakes [ayr] Dry salt lakes in NE South Australia; includes L Eyre North (145 km/90 mi long, 65 km/40 mi wide, area 7692 km²/2969 sq mi) and L Eyre South (61 km/38 mi long, 26 km/16 mi wide, area 1191 km²/460 sq mi); L Eyre North is the largest lake in Australia, normally a shallow pan of glistening white salt; 15 m/50 ft below mean sea-level; site of Donald Campbell's world land speed record (1964).

Eysenck, Hans (Jurgen) [iysingk] (1916–97) Psychologist, born in Berlin. Much of his work was psychometric research into the normal variations of human personality and intelligence. He often held controversial views, particularly with his study of racial differences in intelligence.

Ezekiel or **Ezechiel, Book of** [eezeekiel] A major prophetic work in the Hebrew Bible/Old Testament, attributed to Ezekiel, a 6th-c BC priest among the Jews exiled in Babylonian territories. The prophecies may have been the work of a later editor.

Ezra the Scribe [ezra] (5th–4th-c BC) Religious leader who lived in Babylon during the reign of King Artaxerxes (I or II), who reorganized the Jewish community in Jerusalem. An Old Testament book bears his name, as well as the apocryphal works of 1 and 2 Esdras (the Greek equivalent of 'Ezra').

Fabergé, Peter Carl [faberzhay], originally **Karl Gustavovich Fabergé** (1846–1920) Goldsmith and jeweller, born in St Petersburg, Russia. He moved from the design of conventional jewellery to the creation of more elaborate and fantastic objects, notably the imperial Easter eggs commissioned by Alexander III for his tsarina in 1884.

Fabian Society A socialist group established in 1884 which took its name from the Roman general Fabius Cunctator, noted for his cautious military tactics. It adopts a gradualist approach to social reform. In 2007 it had 6000 members, including over 250 MPs.

Fabius Maximus, Quintus [faybius maksimus], known as **Fabius Cunctator** (Lat 'the delayer') (c.260–203 BC) Roman general, statesman, and hero of the Second Punic War, whose refusal to engage Hannibal in set battle earned him his nickname. Originally a term of abuse, it became an honorific title after 216 BC, when Rome's defeat at the Battle of Cannae proved that his cautious tactics had been right.

fabliau [fablioh] A short narrative poem popular in 12th–14th-c France, and also appearing in English (eg Chaucer's *Miller's Tale*). The subjects were usually bawdy, misogynist, and anticlerical.

Fabriano, Gentile da [fabriahnoh] (c.1370–c.1427) Painter, born in Fabriano, Italy. He painted religious subjects, notably 'The Adoration of the Magi' (1423, Florence), but few of his paintings have survived.

Fabricius, Hieronymus [fabreetsius], also known as **Girolamo Fabrici** (1537–1619) Anatomist, born in Acquapendente, Italy. He made the first detailed description of the valves of the veins, the placenta, and the larynx.

fabrics *batik; coated fabrics; denim; felt; non-woven fabrics; tweed; twill*

Fabritius, Carel [fabreetsius] (c.1624–54) Painter, born in Beemster, The Netherlands. Vermeer was much influenced by his sensitive experiments in composition and the painting of light, as in the tiny 'View of Delft' (1652, National Gallery, London).

facilities management The process of efficient planning, integration, and operation of the different elements which make up a work environment. This environment may be anything from a small office to a major institution, and the facilities may include everything from day-to-day activities of catering, cleaning, and security to long-term planning considerations of office lay-out, refurbishment, and ergonomics.

facsimile machine *fax*

factor VIII One of a series of enzymes present in the blood which controls the clotting process. Sufferers from classical haemophilia lack this factor, and are treated by intravenous administration of factor VIII that has been separated from fresh blood. This process carries the risk of transferring infections such as AIDS from the blood donor; in future, haemophiliacs may be cured by gene therapy, which would enable them to make factor VIII themselves.

factoring The purchase of goods for resale without further processing. **Debt factoring** is the purchase of debts due from a company's customers with the view to collecting them. When payment is problematical the debt will be bought at a discount.

Factory Acts Legislation passed in Britain from 1802 onwards to regulate employment in factories. The early Acts were generally concerned to limit the hours of work of women and children.

factory farming An intensive form of livestock production, usually carried out indoors with strict control over the environment and feeding regimes; also known as **battery farming**. Currently the predominant production technique for eggs, poultry meat, and pig meat, it is opposed by many environmentalists.

faeces / feces [feeseez] Material discharged from the alimentary canal, consisting mainly of the undigested remains of ingested matter, bacteria, and water. The odour is the result of the formation of certain amines by intestinal bacteria.

Faeroe or **Faroe Islands** [fairoh], Danish **Faerøerne** 62°00N 7°00W; pop (2002e) 47 000; area 1400 km²/540 sq mi. Group of 22 sparsely vegetated volcanic islands in the N Atlantic between Iceland and the Shetland Is; 17 inhabited; settled by Norse, 8th-c; passed to Denmark, 1380; self-governing region of Denmark since 1948; capital, Tórshavn; largest islands, Strømø, Østerø; inhabitants speak Faroese.

Fahrenheit, Gabriel (Daniel) [farenhiyt] (1686–1736) Physicist, born in Gdańsk, Poland (formerly Danzig, Germany). He invented the alcohol thermometer in 1709, following this with a mercury thermometer in 1714.

Fahrenheit temperature [farenhiyt] A scale which takes the freezing point of water as 32°F and the boiling point as 212°F; symbol °F; introduced by German physicist Gabriel Fahrenheit.

faience [fiyahns] Earthenware decorated with an opaque glaze containing oxide of tin; the name derives from the Italian town of Faenza. English and Dutch Delftware and Italian maiolica employ exactly the same technique.

fainting A brief episode of loss of consciousness, usually sudden in onset; also known as **syncope**. It is caused either by the reduction of blood supply to the brain or by changes in its electrical activity. Less commonly, low blood sugar may be responsible.

Fairbanks 64°50N 147°50W, pop (2000e) 30 200. City in C Alaska; terminus of the Alaska railway and highway; founded in 1902 after the discovery of gold; university (1922).

Fairbanks, Douglas, (Elton), Snr, originally **Douglas Elton Ulman** (1883–1939) Film actor, born in Denver, CO. He made a speciality of swashbuckling hero parts, as in *The Three Musketeers* (1921) and *Robin Hood* (1922). His son **Douglas Fairbanks Jr** (1909–2000), followed in his footsteps, starring in such films as *The Prisoner of Zenda* (1937).

Fairfax (of Cameron), Thomas Fairfax, 3rd Baron (1612–71) English Parliamentary general, born in Denton, North Yorkshire. In the

Civil War, he distinguished himself at Marston Moor (1644), and in 1645 was given command of the New Model Army, defeating Charles I at Naseby.

fairy tales Traditional stories mainly for children, deriving from folk tales, and usually involving magic and fairies or other supernatural creatures. One of the oldest collections is *The Arabian Nights' Entertainments* or *A Thousand and One Nights*, compiled c.1450. The first published collections of European tales were by Perrault (1697) and the Brothers Grimm (1812). These included such favourites as 'Cinderella', 'The Sleeping Beauty', and 'The Goose Girl'.

Faisalabad [fïysalabad], formerly **Lyallpur** (to 1979) 31°25N 73°09E, pop (2000e) 1 776 000. City in Punjab province, Pakistan; in an important cotton and wheat-growing region; railway.

faith healing The alleviation of physical and mental ailments by the prayer of a healer relying on a higher source (usually, the power of God) working in response to faith. Known in several religions, the practice is now a major feature of Christian pentecostal and charismatic movements. Critics assert that it is difficult to ascribe healing to the action of the higher source, because so little is currently understood about the effects of psychological attitudes upon the body's biochemistry.

Fajans, Kasimir [fahyans] (1887–1975) Physical chemist, born in Warsaw. He is best known for **Fajans's rules**, dealing with the types of bond between atoms in compounds.

falabella The smallest breed of horse in the world; height, 7 hands/0·7 m/2 ft 4 in; developed by the Falabella family in Argentina; descended from a small thoroughbred and Shetland ponies.

Falange [falanj], Span **[falankhay]** A Spanish fascist movement, founded in 1933 by José Antonio Primo de Rivera (1903–36). It was fused by Franco in 1937 with other rightist forces to form the single party of Nationalist Spain.

falcon Any bird of prey of the family Falconidae (c.60 species); worldwide; includes the carrion-feeding **caracara**, the **forest falcon** (large eyes, acute hearing, hunts in near-darkness), and the **true falcon** (a fast-flying predator which usually kills its prey in flight).

Falcone, Giovanni [falkohnay] (1939–92) Judge, born in Palermo, Sicily. In 1978 he was appointed to Palermo where he began a campaign against the Mafia, leading to the successful prosecution of 338 top members in 1987. He was killed when a bomb exploded under his car.

Faldo, Nick [faldoh], popular name of **Nicholas Alexander Faldo** (1957–) Golfer, born in Welwyn Garden City, Hertfordshire. His successes include the Professional Golf Association championships (1978, 1980, 1981), the Open Championship (1987, 1990, 1992), and the US Masters (1989, 1990, 1996). In 2006 he was chosen to captain the European Ryder Cup team in 2008.

Falkenlust *Augustusburg*

Falkland Islands *see panel*

Falklands War A war between Britain and Argentina, precipitated by the Argentine invasion of the Falkland Is, known to Argentinians as the **Malvinas**. Britain had ruled the islands continuously since 1833, but Argentina claimed them by inheritance from the Spanish Empire and through their proximity to her shores. When talks broke down, the Argentinian government of General Galtieri issued a warning to the British, and on 19 March merchants landed on South Georgia, ostensibly to demolish a whaling station, but they also raised the Argentine flag. On the night of 1–2 April the full-scale invasion of the Falklands began. The British immediately began to fit out a task force of almost 70 ships to retake the islands, under the command of Rear Admiral John Woodward. A 200-mile maritime exclusion zone was declared around the Falklands, and on 2 May the Argentine cruiser *General Belgrano* was sunk by the nuclear submarine *Conqueror*. South Georgia was retaken on 25

Falkland Islands

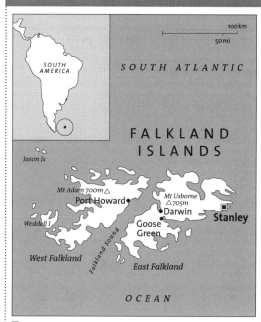

☐ International Airport

Span **Islas Malvinas** (UK British Overseas Territory)

Timezone GMT -4

Area c.12 200 km²/4700 sq mi

Population total (2002e) 3000

Capital Stanley (on East Falkland)

Physical features Located in the S Atlantic, c.650 km/400 mi NE of the Magellan Strait; consists of East Falkland and West Falkland, separated by the Falkland Sound, with over 200 small islands; hilly terrain, rising to 705 m/2313 ft at Mt Usborne (East Falkland) and 700 m/2297 ft at Mt Adam (West Falkland).

Climate Cold, strong westerly winds; low rainfall; narrow temperature range 19°C (Jan), 2°C (Jul); average annual rainfall 635 mm/25 in.

Currency 1 Falkland Pound (FKP) = 100 pence

Economy Agriculture; oats, sheep; service industries to the continuing military presence in the islands.

History Seen by several early navigators, including Capt John Strong in 1689–90, who named the islands; French settlement, 1764; British base established, 1765; French yielded their settlement to the Spanish, 1767; occupied in the name of the Republic of Buenos Aires, 1820; Britain asserted possession, became a British Crown Colony, 1833; formal annexation, 1908 and 1917; the whole island claimed since independence by Argentina; Falklands War, precipitated by the Argentine invasion of the islands in April 1982, led to the dispatch of the British Task Force and the return of the islands to British rule in June 1982; external affairs and defence are the responsibility of the British government, which appoints civil and military commissioners; internal affairs are governed by executive and legislative councils.

April and 5000 British troops were landed at Port San Carlos on 21 May. The British forces, under the command of Major General Jeremy Moore, took Darwin and Goose Green on 28 May, and after the recapture of the capital, Port Stanley, the Argentinians surrendered on 14 June.

Falla, Manuel de [falya] (1876–1946) Composer, born in Cadiz, Spain, whose works became known for their colourful national Spanish idiom. He is best known for his ballet, *The Three-Cornered Hat* (1919).

Fallopian tubes *uterine tubes*

fallout *radioactive fallout*

fallow deer A true deer (*Dama dama*) native to Mediterranean countries (introduced elsewhere); in summer, pale brown with white spots; in winter, grey without spots; antlers long, usually flattened with marginal projections.

Fältskog, Agnetha *Abba*

Falun Gong (Chin 'law of the wheel') A spiritual sect established in China by Li Hongzhi (1951–) now claiming 100 million adherents worldwide. It offers a mixture of Buddhist meditation, physical exercise, Taoist philosophy, martial arts, and pantheistic mysticism. The sect's beliefs are laid down in its core text, *Zhuan Falun*, written by Li. It first came to public notice in 1992 when a centre was opened in Beijing. In 1999, the Chinese government banned Falun Gong's activities and publications.

Falwell, Jerry L [fawlwel] (1933–) Religious leader, born in Lynchburg, VA. In 1956, he founded Thomas Road Baptist Church, Lynchburg, VA, which became the basis of an extensive evangelical campaign. He was also responsible for founding The Moral Majority, Inc, and Liberty University.

Famagusta [famagoosta], Gr **Ammokhostos**, Turkish **Magusa** 35°07N 33°57E, pop (2000e) 21 300. Port in E Cyprus; occupies site of ancient Arsinoë, 3rd-c BC; strongly fortified by Venetians, 15th–16th-c; now under Turkish occupation; cathedral (14th-c).

family of languages A set of 'daughter' languages which derive from the same 'parent' language, and which are thus genetically related. They can be represented by a *family tree*, as with the Indo-European languages, in which Celtic, Germanic, and Romance languages are all interrelated.

family planning *contraception*

family therapy A type of psychiatric treatment in which the family is the therapeutic unit, and an attempt is made to change the structure and functioning of the unit as well as to improve relationships within it. The main development of this technique took place in the 1960s as a form of psychotherapy.

famine A period of food scarcity which may lead to malnutrition and death through starvation. The causes of famines are complex; they may result from natural causes, such as failure of a harvest following lack of rainfall and drought, or from combinations of political and economic circumstances such as war. Famine may also occur in a region where food is not completely scarce, but is unavailable to a sector of the population.

fandango A Spanish dance in triple time, usually accompanied by guitars and castanets. It was known from c.1700 as a popular dance at roadside inns, and later became fashionable in aristocratic ballrooms.

Fanfani, Amintore [fanfahnee] (1908–99) Italian statesman and prime minister, born in Pieve Santo Stefano, Italy. A former professor of political economics, he was prime minister on five occasions – in 1954, 1958–9, 1960–3 (twice), and 1982–3. He was a member of the Christian Democratic Party.

Fangio, Juan Manuel [fanjioh] (1911–95) Racing motorist, born in Balcarce, Argentina. He first took part in European Grand Prix racing in 1949, and by 1957 had won the World Championship a record five times (1951, 1954–7). After his retirement (1958) he joined Mercedes-Benz in Argentina.

fantail The name used for a group of birds of uncertain affinity, native to SE Asian forests. (Genus: *Rhipidura* contains most of the c.42 species.)

fantasia An instrumental piece in which the composer's imagination is allowed free rein in one direction or another. An element of improvisation is often suggested, but some fantasias (such as Purcell's for strings) are carefully structured.

Fantin-Latour, (Ignace) Henri (Jean Théodore) [fãtĩ latoor] (1836–1904) Painter, pastellist, and lithographer, born in Grenoble, France. He is best known for his flower studies and portrait groups, such as 'Hommage à Manet' (1870, Louvre).

fanworm A sedentary marine worm that lives within a tube which it constructs; possesses a crown of tentacles or gills (*branchiae*) around its mouth, used for catching suspended food particles and for respiration; c.800 species. (Class: Polychaeta. Order: Sabellida.)

farad SI unit of capacitance; symbol F; defined as the capacitance of a capacitor comprising two parallel plates between which is a potential difference of one volt when the capacitor is charged with one coulomb of electricity; commonly used as μF (**microfarad**, 10^{-6} F) and pF (**picofarad**, 10^{-12} F).

Faraday, Michael (1791–1867) Chemist, experimental physicist, and natural philosopher, born in Newington Butts, Surrey. His research contributed to an extremely broad area of physical science: he discovered benzene and the laws of electrolysis, invented an electric motor, dynamo and transformer, and was the creator of classical field theory. His major work is the series of *Experimental Researches on Electricity* (1839–55), in which he reports a wide range of discoveries and the relationship between electricity and magnetism.

faraday The electrical charge on a mole (6.02×10^{23}) of electrons, 9.65×10^4 coulombs.

Faraday cage *screening*

farandole [farandol] A folk dance originating in Provence performed to music in a slow tempo; usually played on a flute and a drum.

farce A comic dramatic genre which focuses on both the limitations and liberties of the human body. Throughout a varied history (from Greek and Roman mimes to the Marx Brothers) it has never surrendered its anarchic purpose. Ruthless in pursuit of laughter, farce demands precision plotting and playing, bold stereotyping and mimicry, an aggressive sense of the incongruous, and a forthright recognition of the physical. Its themes never wander far from basic bodily functions.

Farm Credit Administration (FCA) A system set up in the USA in the 1920s and 1930s to revive agriculture by providing adequate finance, especially mortgages. It was made independent in 1953, and is still in existence.

farming *arable / dairy / dryland / extensive / factory / intensive / livestock / organic farming*

Farnaby, Giles [fah(r)nabee] (c.1560–1640) Composer, probably born in Truro, Cornwall. His works include madrigals and settings of the psalms, but he is best remembered for his keyboard music.

Farne Islands or **The Staples** A group of basaltic islets in the North Sea, 3 km/1¾ mi NE off Northumberland, NE England; St Cuthbert lived and died here; scene of heroic rescue in 1838 by Grace Darling and her father, William Darling (1795–1860), the lighthouse keeper, of survivors of the *Forfarshire*.

Faro [faru] 37°01N 7°56W, pop (2000e) 31 600. Industrial seaport in S Portugal; airport; railway; focal point of Algarve tourism; cathedral.

Faroe Islands *Faeroe Islands*

Faroese *Germanic languages; Scandinavian languages*

Farouk [farook] (1920–65) King of Egypt (1936–52), born in Cairo. The defeat of Egypt by Israel (1948) and continuing British occupation led to increasing unrest, and the Free Officers' coup (1952) forced his abdication and exile.

Farquhar, George [fah(r)ker] (c.1678–1707) Playwright, born in Londonderry, Northern Ireland. His first comedy, *Love and a Bottle* (1699), proved a success, as were several other plays, notably *The Beaux' Stratagem* (1707).

Farragut, David (Glasgow) [faraguht] (1801–70) US naval commander, born near Knoxville, TN. In the Civil War he led the Union forces that captured New Orleans (1862), and took part in the siege and capture of Vicksburg (1863) and Mobile Bay (1864).

Farr-Jones, Nick, popular name of **Nicholas Campbell Farr-Jones** (1962–) Rugby union player, born in Sydney, New South Wales, Australia. He won 63 caps for Australia (1984–93), captaining them 36 times including their victory in the 1991 World Cup.

Farrow, Mia (1945–) Film actress, born in Los Angeles, CA. Her film roles include *Rosemary's Baby* (1968), *The Great Gatsby* (1973), and several Woody Allen films, notably *The Purple Rose of Cairo* (1985), *Hannah and Her Sisters* (1986), and *Husbands and Wives* (1992). Earlier married to Frank Sinatra (1966–8), her relationship with Woody Allen broke up in acrimony in 1992, following her discovery of Allen's affair with their adopted teenage daughter.

Farsi *Iranian languages*

farthing Formerly the coin of the lowest value in British currency, a quarter of an old (pre-decimalization) penny, its value therefore being 1/960th of £1. It was withdrawn from circulation in 1960.

Fasching [fashing] or **Fastnacht** The period of merrymaking in S Germany and Austria, between Epiphany (6 Jan) and Lent.

fasciation The abnormal, flattened growth of a single shoot, which resembles several stems fused together and often bears several inflorescences. It is common in such plants as dandelions and plantains.

Fasciola [fasiyola] *liver fluke*

fascism A term applied to a variety of vehemently nationalistic and authoritarian movements that reached the peak of their influence in 1930–45. The original fascist movement was founded by Mussolini in Italy (1921), and during the 1930s several such movements grew up in Europe, the most important being the German Nazi Party. The central ideas of fascism are a belief in the supremacy of the chosen national group over other races, and the need to subordinate society to the leadership of a dictator who can pursue national aggrandisement without taking account of different interests.

Fashoda [fashohda] A settlement (now called Kodok) on the upper White Nile, which was the scene of a major Anglo-French crisis in 1898. French forces withdrew following a British ultimatum.

Fasil Ghebbi [fasil gebee] The royal complex of Emperor Fassilides (1632–67) in Gondar, NW Ethiopia; a world heritage site.

Fassbinder, Rainer Werner [fasbinder] (1946–82) Film director, writer, and actor, born in Bad Wörishofen, Germany. He completed over 40 full-length films, largely politically committed criticisms of contemporary Germany, as in *Die Ehe der Maria Braun* (1979, The Marriage of Maria Braun). The most prolific writer-director-actor of the New German Cinema of the 1970s, he died at 36 as a result of alcohol and drug abuse.

Fassett, Kaffe [kayf] (1937–) Fashion designer, born in San Francisco, CA. He migrated to England in 1964, where he formed a design company producing knitting kits, needlepoint, and fabrics. His television broadcasts and books have made his colourful designs popular in Europe and the USA.

Fastnacht *Fasching*

Fastnet Challenge Race A biennial yacht race from Cowes in the Isle of Wight to Plymouth in the SW of England via the Fastnet rock in the Atlantic Ocean, 6·5 km/4 mi off Cape Clear, Co Cork, SW Ireland. Arguably the toughest race in the British sailing calendar, it was first contested in 1925. Between 1957 and 1999 it formed the final race of the Admiral's Cup competition before it was redesigned as a stand-alone event.

fast reactor *nuclear reactor*

fat 1 A complex mixture of many different triglycerides, each formed when three molecules of fatty acids combine with one of glycerol. It is the major storage fuel of plants and animals. **2** A white or yellowish animal tissue (*adipose tissue*) in which individual cells are swollen with the accumulation of fat forming a single globule within the cytoplasm. The stored triglycerides are an energy source for the organism. Fat acts as a packing and insulating material in many animals, but it can also act as a shock-absorber (eg under the heel). Human excess accumulation of body fat (*obesity*) arises when energy intake (diet) exceeds energy output (physical activity).

Fatah [fata] *PLO*

Fateh Singh, Sant [fate sing] (1911–72) Sikh religious leader and campaigner for Sikh rights, born in the Punjab. During the 1950s he agitated for a Punjabi-speaking autonomous state, which was achieved with the creation of the Indian state of Punjab in 1966.

Fates *Moerae; Parcae*

Father Christmas *Santa Claus*

Father of the House (of Commons) The honorary and affectionate title given to the longest serving MP in the British parliament. In 2004, this was Tam Dalyell, MP for Linlithgow, Scotland. He stepped down after the 2005 general election and was succeeded by Alan Williams, MP for Swansea West.

Father's Day In some countries, a day on which fathers are honoured. In the USA and the UK, it is held on the third Sunday in June; in Australia, the first Sunday in September.

Fathers of the Church A title usually applied to the leaders of the early Christian Church, recognized as teachers of truths of the faith. The study of their writings and thought is known as *patristics*.

Fatima (Portugal) [fatima], also **Fátima** 39°37N 8°38W, pop (2000e) 7700. Pilgrimage town in C Portugal, where three peasant children claimed to have seen 'the Virgin of the Rosary' in 1917; Basilica (begun 1928, consecrated 1953).

Fatima (religion) (c.605–33) The youngest daughter of Mohammed, and wife of the fourth Muslim caliph, Ali. From them the Fatimids, the dynasty of Shiite caliphs, who ruled over Egypt and N Africa (909–1171), and later over Syria and Palestine, traced their descent.

fatty acids *carboxylic acids*

Faulkner (of Downpatrick), (Arthur) Brian (Deane) Faulkner, Baron [fawkner] (1921–77) Politician, born at Helen's Bay, Co Down, Northern Ireland. The last Unionist leader to be prime minister of Northern Ireland, he was minister of home affairs (1959–63) at Stormont, and was elected leader of the Parliamentary Unionists in 1971. In 1973 he entered into Anglo-Irish talks, agreeing to share power with Irish Republicans at an Assembly in Stormont and to take part in a Council of Ireland (the Sunningdale agreement). Unable to maintain Unionist unity, he resigned as leader in 1974, and was created a baron in 1976.

Faulkner, William (Cuthbert) [fawkner], originally **Falkner** (1897–1962) Writer, born in New Albany, MS. With *The Sound and the Fury* (1929) he began to experiment in literary form and style. *Sartoris* (1929) was the first in a series dealing with the social and racial problems of an imaginary Southern county, Yoknapatawpha. Other major novels include *As I Lay Dying* (1930), *Absalom, Absalom!* (1936), and *The Reivers* (1962). He was awarded the Nobel Prize for Literature in 1949.

fault In geology, a fracture in rock along which displacement has occurred due to stresses in the Earth. **Tear faults** release compressional stress by sideways displacement, the best known example being the San Andreas Fault in California. Major faults can create significant features of landscape, such as block mountains and rift valleys.

Fauré, Gabriel (Urbain) [fohray] (1845–1924) Composer, born in Pamiers, France. Though chiefly remembered for his songs, including the evergreen 'Après un rêve' (c.1865), he also wrote operas and orchestral pieces, and a much-performed *Requiem* (1887–90).

Faust [fowst] or **Faustus** [fowstus, fawstus] A legendary German scholar of the early 16th-c (derived from a historical magician of that name), who sold his soul to the devil in exchange for knowledge, magical power, and prolonged youth. His story has inspired several literary and musical works.

Fauvism [fohvizm] (Fr *les fauves* 'the wild beasts') A name given by a hostile critic to a group of modern painters (1898–1908) who were experimenting with vivid colours; they included Matisse, Derain, and Vlaminck. Their work was inspired by van Gogh, Gauguin, and Cézanne.

Favre, Brett (Lorenzo) [fahvr] (1969–) Player of American football, born in Pass Christian, MS. He joined the Atlanta Falcons in 1991, then the Green Bay Packers as quarterback. He became only the second player to win the NFL's Most Valuable Player Award in consecutive years (1995–6). He shared the award again in 1997 becoming the only three-times winner of the award for the NFL. In 2005 he notched up 50 000 passing yards, only the third player ever to do so.

Fawcett, Dame Millicent, *née* **Garrett** (1847–1929) Women's rights campaigner, born in Aldeburgh, Suffolk. She was president of the National Union of Women's Suffrage Societies (1897–1919).

Fawkes, Guy (1570–1606) Catholic conspirator, born in York, North Yorkshire. He served in the Spanish army in The Netherlands (1593–1604). He crossed to England at Catesby's invitation, and became a member of the Gunpowder Plot. Discovered and arrested on the night of 4–5 November, he was, together with his fellow-conspirators hanged, drawn, and quartered.

fax The facsimile transmission of documents, diagrams, and photographs over a telephone network, widely available for international communication since 1986. The original is scanned by laser beam and digitally coded for transmission to the receiver, where it is printed out line by line on either thermo-sensitive paper or plain paper.

FBI *Federal Bureau of Investigation*

feather A structure formed from the skin of birds. It may be less than 0.5 cm/$\frac{1}{4}$ in long, or more than 1.5 m/5 ft. Birds evolved from reptiles, and feathers are modified scales. The central shaft bears many side branches (*barbs*), each barb having small side branches (*barbules*). The barbules of adjacent barbs interlock, creating the familiar flattened structure (*vane*). 'Down' feathers have flexible and sometimes branched barbs, and the barbules hold the barbs in a three-dimensional shape. Down feathers provide insulation; vaned feathers provide smooth aerodynamic surfaces. In many species feathers are important in display, and may be modified in shape and colour.

February Revolution (France) The revolution in France (22–24 Feb 1848) which resulted in the abdication of King Louis Philippe, the proclamation of a republic, and the establishment of a provisional government.

February Revolution (Russia) Popular demonstrations, strikes, and military mutinies in Petrograd, Russia (Feb–Mar 1917), which led to the abdication of Nicholas II and the collapse of the tsarist government.

feces *faeces*

Fechner, Gustav (Theodor) [fekhner] (1801–87) Physicist and psychologist, born in Gross Särchen, Germany. His interest in mind-body relationships led to his book *Elemente der Psychophysik* (1860, Elements of Psychophysics), in which he developed the ideas of Ernst Heinrich Weber on the measurement of sensory thresholds, and laid the foundations for psychophysics.

Fedayeen [fedayeen] A label commonly used to describe commandos who operated under the umbrella of the Palestine Liberation Organization. The name is from the Arabic *fidai*, 'one who sacrifices oneself' (for a cause or country).

Federal Bureau of Investigation (FBI) The US organization primarily concerned with internal security or counter-intelligence operations. It is a branch of the Department of Justice.

Federal Constitutional Convention *Constitutional Convention*

federalism A form of territorial political organization which aims to maintain national unity while allowing for regional diversity. This is achieved by distributing different constitutional powers to national and regional governments. The key features of federalism usually are: (at least) two tiers of government enjoying their own right of existence under the constitution; separate legislative and executive powers; separate sources of revenue; an umpire (normally the supreme court) to decide upon disputes between the different levels; and a bicameral parliament which provides for representation in regional or state government. Beyond that, federalism takes a variety of forms: examples include the USA, Canada, Australia, and Germany.

Federalist Party One of the two political parties that took shape in the USA in the 1790s. Washington (in office 1789–97) and John Adams (in office 1797–1801) were Federalist presidents, but after the 1800 election the Federalists never held the presidency, and the party slowly faded.

Federal Reserve System (FRS) The USA Central Bank, known as 'The Fed', set up in 1913. It divides the USA into 12 districts, each with its own Federal Reserve Bank, carries out the normal duties of a central bank, and also manages cheque clearance on behalf of member banks.

Federal Theater Project A US project inaugurated in 1935 by an Act of Congress as part of the Works Projects Administration. It sought to provide employment to theatre professionals during the Depression, and 'free, adult, uncensored theatre' throughout the country. This experiment in federal sponsorship was terminated by Congress in June 1939.

Federer, Roger [federer] (1981–) Tennis player, born in Basel, Switzerland. In 2003 he became the first Swiss man to win a Grand Slam title when he became Wimbledon singles champion. During 2004 he won the Australian Open, the US Open, the ATP Masters, and retained the Wimbledon title. He was ranked number 1 at the start of 2005 and that year won Wimbledon and the US Open. He retained the number 1 spot at the start of 2006, winning the Australian Open, his fourth successive Wimbledon singles title, and the US Open. Number 1 again in 2007, he won his third Australian Open, and also became the longest reigning number 1, completing 161 consecutive weeks at the top.

feedback The process by which information is conveyed to the source of the original output; also, the information itself. The term comes from cybernetics, and is applied both to machines and to animal and human communication, whereby it enables the sender of a message to monitor its reception and make any necessary modification.

Feininger, Lyonel (Charles Adrian) [fiyninger] (1871–1956) Painter, born in New York City. After World War 1 he taught at the Bauhaus in Weimar and Dessau, and adopted a style reminiscent of Cubism. He later helped to found the New Bauhaus in Chicago.

feldspar or **felspar** An important group of minerals constituting about half of the rocks of the Earth's crust. All are aluminosilicates containing various proportions of potassium, sodium, and calcium (and, rarely, barium). Important minerals of the group are *orthoclase* and *Microcline* (both $KAlSi_3O_8$), *albite* ($NaAlSi_3O_8$) and *anorthite* ($CaAl_2Si_2O_8$). Na,Ca feldspars are termed *plagioclase*.

Felidae [felidee] The cat family (37 species); a family of muscular carnivores with camouflaged coloration; round head with powerful jaws, long canine teeth; sharp claws (usually retractable); cannot chew food; eats meat almost exclusively.

feline immunodeficiency virus (FIV) A viral disease related to but quite separate from human immunodeficiency virus (HIV). It does not affect humans. A wide variety of clinical signs is seen in cats, as other organisms overcome the immune system.

feline infectious enteritis (FIE) A serious, often fatal disease of cats and other Felidae; also known as **panleucopenia (FPL)**, and occasionally by the blanket term **cat flu**. It is caused by a virus of the parvovirus group. Young cats are very vulnerable, but protection by the use of a vaccine is effective.

Fellini, Federico [feleenee] (1920–93) Film director, born in Rimini, Italy. His highly individual films, always from his own scripts, include *La strada* (1954, The Road; foreign film Oscar winner, 1957), *Fellini's Roma* (1972) and, his most famous and controversial work, *La dolce vita* (1960, The Sweet Life; Cannes Festival prizewinner). He was presented with an Honorary Academy Award in 1993.

felony Originally, at common law, every crime which occasioned the forfeiture of land and goods, usually punishable by death. In modern times, in the USA, a felony is a crime which carries a potential punishment in a state prison of not less than one year. It corresponds roughly to an **indictable offence** in the UK, and is distinguished from a **misdemeanour**.

felspar *feldspar*

felt A non-woven cloth consisting of loose 'webs' of natural or synthetic fibre, or formed in fabrics by the action of moisture, heat, and repeated pressure. Felts are important industrial and domestic materials.

feminism A socio-political movement whose objective is equality of rights, status, and power for men and women. It has its roots in early 20th-c struggles for women's political emancipation (the suffragettes), but has been broadened in its political scope by the influence of radical left-wing beliefs, especially Marxism, which has led feminists to challenge both sexism and the capitalist system which is said to encourage patriarchy.

femur [feemer] The long bone of the thigh, having a rounded head, neck, and shaft, and an expanded lower end. It is the largest and longest bone in the body.

fencing The art of fighting with a sword, one of the oldest sports, which can be traced back to the ancient Egyptians c.1300 BC. Modern weapons consist of the *sabre, foil,* and *épée*. In competitive fencing, different target areas exist for each weapon, and contestants wear electronically wired clothing to indicate successful hits.

Fénelon, François de Salignac de la Mothe [faynelō] (1651–1715) Roman Catholic theologian, born in Fénelon, France. His chief work, *Les Aventures de Télémaque* (1699, The Adventures of Telemachus), received the censure of Louis XIV for its political undertones. Also controversial was his *Explication des maximes des saints sur la vie intérieure* (1697, Explanation of the Sayings of the Saints on the Interior Life), which was condemned by the Pope.

Fenians [feenianz] (Gaelic *Fianna* 'warriors') The short title of the Irish Republican Brotherhood, a nationalist organization founded as the Fenian Brotherhood in New York in 1857 and as the Irish Republican Brotherhood in Ireland in 1858. The movement quickly espoused violent rebellion as a means of achieving its objectives. In England, they attempted to seize Chester Castle; they rescued two of their members in Manchester (1867); and in an unsuccessful bid to rescue Irish prisoners in London the same year, killed 12 people. Several Fenians were executed and hundreds more imprisoned.

Fenn, John B (1917–) Chemist, born in New York City. A researcher at Virginia Commonwealth University, he shared the 2002 Nobel Prize for Chemistry for the development of soft desorption ionization methods for mass spectrometric analyses of biological macromolecules.

fennec fox A small nocturnal fox (*Vulpes zerda*) native to deserts in N Africa and Kuwait; smallest member of the dog family; thick pale coat, enormous ears; also known as **desert fox**.

fennel A strong-smelling, bluish-green biennial or perennial (*Foeniculum vulgare*), growing to 2·5 m/8 ft, native to the Mediterranean region; flowers yellow; fruit ovoid, ribbed. The leaves are used as a flavouring. Certain forms are eaten raw in salads or cooked as a vegetable. (Family: Umbelliferae.)

Fens, the or **the Fen Country** Flat marshy land surrounding the Wash, in Lincolnshire, Norfolk, Suffolk, and Cambridgeshire, E England; extends 112 km/70 mi N–S and 6 km/4 mi E–W; remnant of a silted-up North Sea bay; major reclamation in 17th-c under 5th Earl of Bedford; market gardening, fruit, vegetables, grazing.

Fenton, James (Martin) (1949–) Poet and essayist, born in Lincoln, Lincolnshire. His first collections of poems, *Terminal Moraine* (1972), won the Eric Gregory Award. Later works of poetry include *The Memory of War* (1982) and *Out of Danger* (1993). He was professor of poetry at Oxford (1994–9).

fenugreek An annual (*Trigonella foenum-graecum*) growing to 50 cm/20 in, a native of SW Asia; pea-flowers yellowish-white, solitary or in pairs; pod up to 10 cm/4 in long. Grown for fodder, its seeds are edible (used in curries), and it is also employed medicinally. (Family: Leguminosae.)

fer-de-lance [fair duh lahns] (Fr 'spearhead') A New World pit viper; powerful venom; two species: *Bothrops atrox* (**Southern fer-de-lance**) and *Bothrops asper* (**Central American fer-de-lance**); also known as **lancehead viper**.

Ferdinand (of Castile), known as **the Catholic** (1452–1516) King of Castile, as Ferdinand V (from 1474), of Aragon and Sicily, as Ferdinand II (from 1479), and of Naples, as Ferdinand III (from 1503), born in Sos, Aragon (Spain). In 1469 he married Isabella, sister of Henry IV of Castile, and ruled jointly with her until her death. He introduced the Inquisition (1478–80), and in 1492, after the defeat of the Moors, expelled the Jews. Under him, Spain gained supremacy following the discovery of America, and by 1512 he had become monarch of all Spain.

Ferdinand, Rio (Gavin) (1978–) Footballer, born in London. He made his debut for West Ham in 1996, joining Leeds in 2000 for a record fee of £18 million. He made his England debut in 1997, was a member of the England squad for the FIFA World Cup in 1998, 2002, and 2006, bringing his caps to 52. He became the world's most expensive defender when he was bought by Manchester United in 2002 for £30 million. In September 2003 he failed to attend for a routine drugs test, and was charged with misconduct by the Football Association, resulting in a fine and an 8-month suspension (Jan–Sep 2004).

Ferdusi *Firdausi*

Ferghana [fergana] A strategic point on the ancient Silk Road from China, lying E of Samarkand. The area, now in Uzbekistan, is famous for its horses.

Ferguson, Sir Alex(ander Chapman) (1941–) Football player and manager, born in Glasgow. A former Queens Park Rangers player, he became a manager, and had success with Aberdeen (1978–86) before taking over at Manchester United, where his achievements include the FA Cup (1990), the European Cup Winners' Cup (1991), the League and Cup double (1994, 1996, 1999), and the European Cup (1999). In 2003 he received the Manager of the Decade award, presented by the FA Premier League. He celebrated 20 years as manager of Manchester United in November 2006.

Ferguson, Sarah *Andrew, Duke of York*

Fermanagh [fermana], Ir **Fear Manach** pop (2000e) 54 100; area 1876 km²/715 sq mi. District and county in SW Northern Ireland;

Fermat's principle

A principle in physics: light rays travel between two points in such a way that the time taken is a minimum; stated by Pierre de Fermat in 1657. It is a special case of the least-action principle.

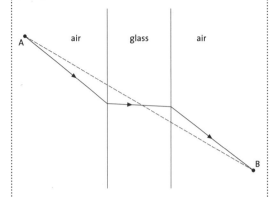

The dotted line shows the shortest path between A and B. A light beam follows the solid line, consistent with the laws of refraction, because the velocity of light in the glass is less than in air. The solid line is the path of least time.

rises to 667 m/2188 ft at Cuilcagh; Upper and Lower Lough Erne run SE–NW; county town, Enniskillen.

Fermat, Pierre de [fermah] (1601–65) Mathematician, born in Beaumont-de-Lomagne, France. He became a lawyer, and then turned to mathematics, making many discoveries in the properties of numbers, probabilities, and geometry.

Fermat's last theorem A mathematical theorem proposed by Pierre de Fermat, which states that there are no positive integers x, y, z, and n (where n is greater than 2), such that $x^n + y^n = z^n$. The theorem was proved by British mathematician Andrew Wiles in 1994.

Fermat's principle see panel

fermentation A chemical reaction in which an organic compound is broken down through the action of an enzyme. This process is typically carried out using bacteria or yeast to metabolize carbohydrates in the absence of oxygen. The two most common end-products are lactic acid and ethanol.

Fermi, Enrico [fermee] (1901–54) Nuclear physicist, born in Rome. In 1934 he and his colleagues in Rome split a number of nuclei by bombardment with neutrons, for which he was awarded the 1938 Nobel Prize for Physics. In the USA, he played a prominent part in developing atomic energy, and constructed the first nuclear reactor at Chicago (1942).

fermion Subatomic particle having half integer spin; the particle of matter; named after Italian physicist Enrico Fermi. Electrons, protons, and quarks are all fermions.

fern A member of a large group of spore-bearing, vascular plants related to clubmosses and horsetails. The visible plant typically has one or more large, often much-divided fronds which are characteristically coiled in a crozier shape when young, unfurling as they grow. Ferns embrace a large number of forms. A few are annuals, but most are perennials with tough rhizomes. Although more or less cosmopolitan, the majority of species are concentrated in the tropics and in the warmer, more humid parts of the world. (Class: Filicopsida or Filicinae, c.10 000 species.)

Fernandel [fernãdel], stage name of **Fernand Joseph Désiré Con-**tandin (1903–71) Film comedian, born in Marseilles, France. From 1930 he appeared in over 100 films, establishing himself internationally as the country priest of *Le Petit Monde de Don Camillo* (1953, The Little World of Don Camillo). He was renowned for his wide grin and his remarkable facial mobility.

Fernando Póo *Bioko*

Ferrar, Nicholas (1592–1637) Anglican clergyman and spiritual mystic, born in London. At Little Gidding in Huntingdonshire he founded a small religious community, which was broken up by the Puritans in 1647.

Ferrara [fayrahra] 44°50N 11°38E, pop (2000e) 148 000. Ancient town in N Italy; seat of the Council of Ferrara, 1438, and of the 15th-c Renaissance court; archbishopric; railway; university (1391); cathedral (12th–14th-c).

Ferrari, Enzo [ferahree] (1898–1988) Racing-car designer, born in Modena, Italy. He became a racing driver in 1920, and in 1929 founded the company which bears his name, remaining president until 1977.

Ferraro, Geraldine A(nne) [ferahroh], married name **Zacarro** (1935–) US politician, born in Newburgh, NY. She was elected as a Democrat to the US House of Representatives in 1981, and was selected in 1984 by Walter Mondale to be the first female vice-presidential candidate of a major party. In 1992 and 1998 she ran in the New York senatorial primary, but lost the nomination despite much popular support.

ferrate A compound containing iron as part of an anion.

ferret A domesticated form of the European polecat (*Mustela putorius*); yellowish-white with pink eyes; sent down burrows to chase out rabbits; bred white so it is not mistaken for a rabbit.

Ferrier, Kathleen (1912–53) Contralto singer, born in Higher Walton, Lancashire. One of her greatest successes was in Mahler's *Das Lied von der Erde* (The Song of the Earth) at the first Edinburgh Festival (1947).

ferrimagnetism The magnetic property of materials (eg ferrites) for which neighbouring atomic magnetic moments are of different strengths and are aligned antiparallel. It is related to ferromagnetism, but exhibiting much weaker gross magnetic properties.

ferrites A class of ceramic materials composed of oxides of iron and some other metal such as copper, nickel, or manganese. Of low electrical conductivity, they are used as core material in high-frequency electrical coils, loudspeaker magnets, and video/audio tape-recorder heads.

ferro-alloys Combinations of elements added to molten steel to impart various properties, such as greater corrosion resistance or strength.

ferrocene [feroseen] $Fe(C_5H_5)_2$, orange solid, melting point 173°C, first prepared in 1951, in which an iron atom is symmetrically bonded to two cyclopentadienyl rings. It was the first of a series of transition metal organometallic compounds called **metallocenes**.

ferromagnetism A property of ferromagnetic substances (eg iron, nickel, cobalt, gadolinium, dysprosium, and many alloys) arising from large-scale alignment between atomic magnetic moments. An applied magnetic field intensity, supplied by a surrounding electric coil, causes a disproportionately large magnetic flux density to appear in the bulk material. A field may remain in the material even when the external field has been removed, resulting in permanent magnets.

fertility drugs Drugs which treat infertility in women – usually successfully if it is due to a failure to ovulate. Early fertility drugs caused multiple pregnancies, but newer drugs such as clomiphene are not so extreme, though the incidence of twins is 10% of all successful pregnancies.

fertilization The union of two gametes to form a zygote, as occurs during sexual reproduction. The gametes are typically male (a sperm) and female (an egg), and both are haploid (possess a single chromosome set). Fertilization involves the fusion of the two haploid nuclei to form a diploid zygote that develops into a new individual.

fertilizer A substance which provides plant nutrients when added to soil. The term normally refers to inorganic chemicals containing one or more of the basic plant nutrients: nitrogen, phosphorus, or potash. It may also refer to compounds containing trace elements such as boron, cobalt, copper, iron, manganese, molybdenum, and zinc; to lime, which is used to correct acidity; or to a concentrated organic substance such as dried blood and bonemeal.

Fès *Fez*

fescue A tufted grass with inrolled, bristle-like leaves, found almost everywhere; important as pasture grass. (Genus: *Festuca*, c.80 species. Family: Gramineae.)

Festival of Britain An event organized in 1951 to mark the centenary of the Great Exhibition held in London in 1851. The Royal Festival Hall was built for the occasion.

fetch *wave* (oceanography)

fetus / foetus The embryo of a mammal, especially a human, at a stage of development when all the main features of the adult form are recognizable. In humans, this stage is from 8 weeks to birth.

feudalism In a narrow sense, the mediaeval military and political order based on reciprocal ties between lords and vassals, in which the main elements were the giving of homage and the tenure of fiefs. Polemicists apply the term to whatever appears backward or reactionary in the modern world.

Feuerbach, Ludwig (Andreas) [foyerbakh] (1804–72) Philosopher, born in Landshut, Germany. His most famous work was *Das Wesen des Christentums* (1841, The Essence of Christianity). His naturalistic materialism was a strong influence on Marx and Engels.

Feuillants, Club of the [foeyā] An association of moderate deputies and former members of the Jacobin Club, who aimed at establishing a constitutional monarchy in France during the first stage of the Revolution (1791).

fever A clinical condition when the temperature of the body rises above the upper limit of normal; also known as **pyrexia**. Normal temperature is between 36·6 and 37·7°C, measured with a rectal thermometer. Fever is most often a result of infection.

feverfew An aromatic perennial (*Tanacetum parthenium*) growing to 60 cm/2 ft, probably native to SE Europe; flower-heads long-stalked in loose, flat-topped clusters; spreading outer florets white, inner disc florets yellow. As a medicinal herb, it is reputed to provide relief from migraines, but it has toxic side-effects. (Family: Compositae.)

Feynman, Richard (Phillips) [fiynman] (1918–88) Physicist, born in Far Rockaway, NY. He shared the Nobel Prize for Physics in 1965 for his work on quantum electrodynamics, and is also known for his graphical representation of the behaviour of interacting particles, known as **Feynman diagrams**.

Fez or **Fès** [fez] 34°05N 5°00W, pop (2000e) 653 000. City in NC Morocco; Old Fez, a world heritage site, founded in 808; New Fez founded in 1276; modern Fez (Ville Nouvelle) S of the railway; name given to a type of red felt hat worn by many Islamic followers; railway; Karaouine mosque (first built, 9th-c) became famous as a Muslim university.

Fianna Fáil [fiana foyl] (Ir 'Militia of Ireland') An Irish political party founded in 1926 by those opposed to the 1921 Anglo-Irish Treaty. It first came to power under de Valera in 1932, and has been the governing party for most of the period since. It has consistently supported the unification of Ireland.

fiber *fibre*

Fibonacci, Leonardo [fibonahchee], also known as **Leonardo**

Pisano (c.1170–c.1250) Mathematician, born in Pisa, Italy, arguably the most outstanding mathematician of the Middle Ages. He popularized the modern decimal system of numerals, and made an advanced contribution to number theory. He also discovered the **Fibonacci sequence** of integers in which each number is equal to the sum of the preceding two (0,1,1,2,3,5,8...).

fibre / fiber That part of plant carbohydrates which cannot be digested by the normal carbohydrate-digesting enzymes in the small intestine. Fibre is largely contained in the structural part of plants, ie the roots, stem, seed coat, or husk. The most abundant fibre in nature, cellulose, is made up of repeating glucose units in long single strands, making it ideal for conversion into the fabric cotton.

fibre-glass / fiber-glass A composite material for the construction of light, generally complex-curved structures, made of glass fibres embedded in a polyester or epoxy resin which can be moulded before setting; more fully described as **glass fibre reinforced plastic**. It is much used for hulls of boats, tanks for liquids, and occasionally for car bodies. In the USA, *Fibreglas* is a registered trade mark for this material.

fibre optics *optical fibres*

fibres / fibers The fundamental units from which textiles are made. Natural fibres include wool, cotton, linen, jute, cashmere, and silk. Synthetic fibres are made from polymers using oil as the raw material; examples include nylons, polyesters and acrylics.

fibroid A benign tumour that develops within or is attached to the uterine wall; also known as a **leiomyoma**. It results from an abnormal overgrowth of the muscle and connective tissue of the uterus. The cause is unknown, but is probably related to oestrogen stimulation, since fibroids tend to enlarge with oestrogen therapy (such as oral contraceptives) and during pregnancy. They continue to grow during a woman's reproductive lifetime, and regress after the menopause.

fibrositis [fiybruhsiytis] An imprecise lay term referring to aching in the muscles, which may be locally tender. It is usually felt in the neck, shoulders, or back. The underlying nature of the disorder is unknown in the majority of cases.

fibula [fibyoola] A long slender bone in the calf, which articulates with the foot (via the ankle joint) and the tibia. It is thought to have no weight-bearing function, but gives attachment to many of the muscles of the calf.

Fichte, Johann Gottlieb [fikhtuh] (1762–1814) Philosopher, born in Rammenau, Germany. An ardent disciple of Kant, he modified the Kantian system by substituting for the 'thing-in-itself' as the absolute reality, the more subjective *Ego*, the primitive act of consciousness. In *Reden an die deutsche Nation* (1807–8, Addresses to the German Nation) he invoked a metaphysical German nationalism to resistance against Napoleon.

Fichtelgebirge [fikhtelgebeerguh], Czech **Smrčiny** Horseshoe-shaped mountain range in Bavaria, Germany; highest peak Schneeberg (1051 m/3448 ft).

Ficino, Marsilio [ficheenoh] (1433–99) Philosopher, born in Figline, Italy. He was a major influence in the Renaissance revival of Platonism, which he attempted to reconcile with Christianity.

fiddler crab A marine crab commonly found on inter-tidal mud flats in tropical and subtropical regions; males have a large claw used for signalling during courtship. (Class: Malacostraca. Order: Decapoda.)

FIDE [feeday] *chess*

Fidei Defensor *Defender of the Faith*

Field, John (1782–1837) Composer and pianist, born in Dublin. An infant prodigy, he wrote mainly for the piano (including seven concertos), and is credited with originating the nocturne. His music influenced Chopin.

field emission The emission of electrons from a metal surface caused by the application of an intense electric field. Field emission microscopes guide electrons emitted from a sharp metal point to a screen, forming a highly magnified image of the metal's structure.

fieldfare A thrush native to Europe and Asia (*Turdus pilaris*); found in S Greenland since 1937; brown back, mottled breast, grey head.

Fielding, Helen (1958–) Novelist, born in Morley, West Yorkshire. She worked in newspaper and television journalism, which led to her first work of fiction, *Cause Celeb* (1994). However, it was her comic novel *Bridget Jones's Diary* (1996, filmed 2001) – originally a weekly newspaper column about the fictional life of a single woman – that brought her enormous success. A sequel *Bridget Jones: The Edge of Reason* appeared in 2000 (filmed 2004). In 2005 she revived her *Bridget Jones's Diary* weekly column for *The Independent* newspaper.

Fielding, Henry (1707–54) Playwright and novelist, born at Sharpham Park, Glastonbury, Somerset. On Richardson's publication of *Pamela* (1740), he wrote his famous parody, *Joseph Andrews* (1742). Several other works followed, notably *The History of Tom Jones, A Foundling* (1749), which established his reputation as a founder of the English novel.

fieldmouse A mouse of genus *Apodemus* (**Old World field mice** or **wood mice**, 13 species) or of genus *Akodon* (**South American field mice** or **grass mice**, 41 species). Old World fieldmice often jump; South American fieldmice have short legs, and are less athletic.

Field of the Cloth of Gold, the A meeting between Henry VIII and Francis I near Calais in 1520, in which France hoped to gain English support against the Emperor Charles V; named for the lavish pavilions of golden cloth erected by the French.

Fields, Dame Gracie, originally **Grace Stansfield** (1898–1979) Singer and variety star, born in Rochdale, Greater Manchester. With her sentimental songs and broad Lancashire humour, she won a unique place in the affections of British audiences. Her theme tune, 'Sally', she first sang in 1931.

Fields, W C, originally **William Claude Dukenfield** (1879–1946) Actor, born in Philadelphia, PA. He established his comic persona in silent films such as *Sally of the Sawdust* (1925), but his characteristic gravelly voice found its full scope with the coming of sound in the cinema during the 1930s.

Fields Medal An award established by the 1924 International Congress of Mathematicians to honour outstanding mathematical achievement. Professor J D Fields donated funds to establish the award, which is available to mathematicians up to the age of forty. Equivalent to the Nobel Prize, since 1936 the medals have been presented every four years; since 1966 up to four medals may be awarded.

Fiennes, Joseph (Alberic) [fiynz] (1970–) Actor, born in Salisbury, Wiltshire, the brother of Ralph Fiennes. His first feature film appearance was in *Stealing Beauty* (1996), and he became known after his role in *Elizabeth* (1998). Later films include *Shakespeare in Love* (1998), *Enemy at the Gates* (2000), and *The Darwin Awards* (2006).

Fiennes, Ralph (Nathaniel) [rayf fiynz] (1962–) Actor, born in Suffolk. A theatre actor in the late 1980s, his film debut was in *Emily Bronte's Wuthering Heights* (1991). Later films include *Schindler's List* (1993, Golden Globe, Oscar nomination), *The English Patient* (1996, Oscar nomination), *The End of the Affair* (1999), *Harry Potter and the Goblet of Fire* (2005), and *The Constant Gardener* (2005).

Fiennes, Sir Ranulph (Twisleton-Wykeham-) [fiynz] (1944–) Explorer and expedition leader, born in Windsor, England. He was leader of several expeditions, including the Transglobe (1979–82), tracing the Greenwich Meridian across both Poles. With Michael Stroud he completed the first unsupported crossing on foot of the Antarctic in 1993, covering 2300 km/1350 mi

in 95 days. In 2000 he was forced to abandon his 520-mile solo trek to the North Pole because of frostbite. In 2003 he successfully completed the challenge to run seven marathons in seven continents in seven days, taking him to Santiago in Chile, the Falkland Is, Sydney, Singapore, London, Cairo, and New York.

FIFA [feefa] The abbreviation of **Fédération Internationale de Football Association**, the world governing body of association football, founded in Paris in 1904. FIFA stages its World Cup tournament every four years.

Fife, also sometimes called **Kingdom of Fife** pop (2000e) 354 500; area 1307 km²/505 sq mi. Local council in E Scotland, bounded by the Firth of Tay (N), North Sea (E), and the Firth of Forth (S); Lomond Hills in the W; capital, Glenrothes.

fife A small, high-pitched, transverse flute, with six finger-holes and (in modern and some older instruments) metal keys. Fifes have been mainly military instruments, used (like the bugle) for calls and signals, and also, in 'drum and fife' bands, for marching.

Fifteen Rebellion The name given to the first of the Jacobite rebellions against Hanoverian monarchy to restore the Catholic Stuart Kings to the British throne. The rising was begun at Braemar (Sep 1715) by the Earl of Mar, proclaiming James Edward Stuart ('the Old Pretender') as king. Jacobite forces were defeated at Preston in November, and the rebellion collapsed early in 1716.

fifth column A popular expression from the early days of World War 2 to describe enemy sympathizers who might provide active help to an invader. The name originally described the rebel sympathizers in Madrid in 1936 during the Spanish Civil War, when four rebel columns were advancing on the city.

fifth force A new force postulated by US physicist Ephraim Fischbach (1942–) and others in 1986, in addition to the four recognized fundamental forces. It is weaker than gravity, and of intermediate range. However, experimental results were ambiguous, and the theory is no longer taken seriously.

fifth-generation computers *computer generations*

fifty-four forty or fight A slogan used in the 1840s to advocate US seizure of British Columbia, whose N boundary is at 54°40N. The issue was resolved in 1846 by a treaty establishing the present US–Canadian border, at 49°N.

fig A member of a large genus of trees, shrubs, and climbers, mostly native to the tropics; tiny flowers borne on the inner surface of a hollow, fleshy receptacle which forms the fruit after fertilization. Many species are large evergreen trees, such as the indiarubber tree and the banyan. (Genus: *Ficus*, 800 species. Family: Moraceae.)

figurative art Any form of visual art in which recognizable aspects of the world, especially the human figure, are represented, in however simplified, stylized, or distorted a form, in contrast to abstract or **non-figurative art**.

figurative language Language used in such a way that 'simple' meaning is elaborated and complicated by various rhetorical means. Language has been described as 'a graveyard of dead metaphors', and all forms of emphasis and parallelism, as well as imagery, may be considered 'figurative'.

figwort A perennial (*Scrophularia nodosa*), native to Europe and Asia; flowers with greenish, almost globose tube and five small lobes, the upper two forming a reddish-brown lip. (Family: Scrophulariaceae.)

Fiji *p.335*

filariasis [filariyasis] A disease common in tropical areas caused by nematode worms. Larvae are transmitted to uninfected human beings by mosquitoes. Lymph nodes enlarge and interfere with the flow of lymph, causing gross oedema of the limbs.

filbert A species of hazel (*Corylus maxima*), native to the Balkans, and cultivated elsewhere for its edible nuts, which are com-

Fiji

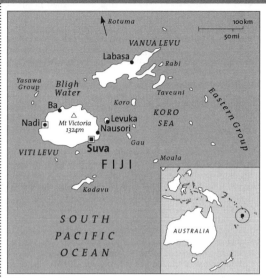

International Airport

[feejee], official name **Sovereign Democratic Republic of Fiji**

Local name Viti

Timezone GMT +12

Area 18 333 km²/7076 sq mi

Population total (2002e) 824 000

Status Republic

Date of independence 1970

Capital Suva (on Viti Levu Island)

Language English (official)

Ethnic groups Indigenous Fijians (44%), Indian (51%)

Religions Native Fijians, mainly Christian (Methodist c.85%, Roman Catholic 12%); Indo-Fijians, mainly Hindu (c.70%) and Muslim (25%)

Physical features Melanesian group of 844 islands and islets in the SW Pacific Ocean; highest peak, Tomaniivi (Mt Victoria) on

Viti Levu, 1324 m/4344 ft; most smaller islands consist of limestone, little vegetation; Great Sea Reef stretches 500 km/300 mi along W fringe; dense tropical forest on wet, windward side (SE); mainly treeless on dry, leeward side.

Climate Tropical oceanic climate, high humidity; average annual temperature 27°C, ranging from 35°C (Dec–Apr) to 16°C (Jun–Sep); heavy rainfall; occasional hurricanes.

Currency 1 Fijian Dollar (FJD) = 100 cents

Economy Agriculture; sugar cane (accounts for over two-thirds of export earnings); bananas, ginger; gold, silver, limestone, timber; major tourist area.

GDP (2002e) $4·822 bn, per capita $5600

Human Development Index (2002) 0·758

History Visited by Tasman, 1643, and by Cook, 1774; British colony from 1874; independence within the Commonwealth, 1970; 1987 election brought to power an Indian-dominated coalition, which led to military coups (May and Sep), and proclamation of a republic outside the Commonwealth; civilian government restored, Dec 1987; constitution, 1990 and 1997; readmitted to Commonwealth, 1997; coup, with prime minister and others held hostage, May–Jul 2000; suspended from Commonwealth, Jun 2000 (readmitted, 2001); parliamentary elections, 2001; military coup, Dec 2006; bicameral Parliament of a nominated Senate and an elected House of Representatives.

Republic

Chairman

1987 Sitiveni Rabuka

Head of State

1987–93 Penaia Ganilau
1993–2000 Kamisese Mara
2000–6 Ratu Josefa Iloilo
2006–7 Frank Bainimarama *Military coup*
2007– Ratu Josefa Iloilo *Reinstated*

Head of Government

1987–92 Kamisese Mara
1992–9 Sitiveni Rabuka
1999–2000 Mahendra Chaudhry
2000 *Military Administration*
2000–1 Laisenia Qarase *Interim*
2001–6 Laisenia Qarase
2006 *Military coup*
2007– Frank Bainimarama *Interim*

pletely enclosed in a leafy cup, constricted above the nut to form a neck. (Family: Corylaceae.)

filefish Deep-bodied fish common in shallow tropical and warm temperate waters; body strongly compressed, length up to 25 cm/10 in; dorsal fin spiny; scales finely toothed and rough to touch; also called **porky**. (Genus: *Stephanolepis*. Family: Balistidae.)

filibuster To hold up the passage of a bill in the US Senate, by organizing a continuous succession of long speeches in opposition. The term is also more generally applied to any attempt to delay a decision or vote by exercising the right to talk on an issue.

Filioque [filiohkway] (Lat 'and from the Son') A dogmatic formula expressing the belief that the Holy Spirit 'proceeds' from the Son as well as from the Father. The term does not appear in the original Nicene–Constantinopolitan Creed, but was inserted by the Western Church, and insistence on its retention was a major source of tension and eventual breach between the Western (Roman Catholic) and Eastern (Orthodox) Churches in 1054.

Fillmore, Millard (1800–74) US statesman and 13th President (1850–3), born in Summerhill, NY. He was vice-president to

Zachary Taylor in 1848, becoming president on his death. On the slavery question he was a supporter of 'compromise'.

film A light-sensitive photographic emulsion on a thin flexible transparent support, originally celluloid (cellulose nitrate), but later the less inflammable cellulose triacetate. Film for still cameras is supplied in cut sheets and film packs, but more generally as short rolls in various standard widths. Motion-picture film is used in long rolls, up to 300 m, in widths 16, 35, and 70 mm.

Filofax The trade name of a 'personal organizer', or portable information and filing system. Paperback-size, loose-leaf, with a flexible binder, filofaxes typically contain a diary, address book, notebook, and information sections (hence 'file of facts').

filter 1 A device for removing fine solid particles from a mixture. It usually consists of some woven or felted material (eg paper, textile), and is thus distinct from a **sieve**, which removes coarse particles with a wire mesh or perforated metal. By analogy, the term is also used for any device which separates the components of a wave system (eg sound, light, radio-frequency currents). **2** In photography, a transparent material which modifies the light passing in a specified manner. It is used in front of light sources to alter colour temperature, reduce intensity, or scatter light by diffusion.

fin The external membranous process of an aquatic animal, such as a fish or cetacean, used for locomotion and manoeuvring; may be variously modified as suckers and claspers. The **median fins** are called *dorsal, anal,* and *caudal* (tail); the paired **lateral fins** are *pectorals* and *pelvics*.

finch Any bird of the family Fringillidae; commonly kept as songbirds; bill internally modified to crush seeds.

fine A financial penalty paid to the state, following conviction by a court for a criminal offence. Limits are normally set on the levels of fines inferior courts are permitted to levy, and the offender's means are generally taken into account. Failure to pay a fine without good cause can lead to imprisonment for default.

Fine Gael [feenuh gayl] (Ir 'United Ireland') An Irish political party created out of the pro-Anglo-Irish Treaty (1921) wing of Sinn Féin. The first government of the Irish Free State, it has largely been in opposition since the 1930s. It supports an Irish confederation.

finfoot A water-bird, native to Central America, S Africa, and S Asia; slender, with long pointed bill; toes with side lobes; inhabits fresh or brackish water margins; angle of wing bears a claw; also called **sungrebe**. (Family: Heliornithidae, 3 species.)

Fingal's Cave A cave situated on the coast of Staffa in the Inner Hebrides, Scotland. The cavern, which is renowned for its natural beauty, is celebrated in Mendelssohn's *Hebrides Overture.* It is 69 m/227 ft deep and of volcanic origin, being formed from huge hexagonal pillars of basalt. The name derives from the legendary Irish figure, Finn MacCool.

Finger Lakes A group of long, narrow, finger-like lakes in W New York State, USA; includes (W–E) Canandaigua, Keuka, Seneca, Cayuga, Owasco, and Skaneateles lakes.

fingerprint An impression made on a surface by the pattern of ridges at the ends of fingers and thumbs. No two people have the same fingerprints, and the technique of fingerprinting has thus long been used by law enforcement agencies as a means of identification, based on the general shape of the ridge pattern, its size and position on the finger, the number of ridges in loops and whorls, and other such indicators. The formal process of fingerprinting is called **dactyloscopy**.

finger-spelling *dactylology*

Finisterre, Cape [finistair] (Span **Cabo**) 42°50N 9°16W. Cape at La Coruña, NW Spain; the most W point on the Spanish mainland; scene of a British naval victory against the French in 1747.

Finland *p.337*

Finland, Gulf of Arm of the Baltic Sea (E), bounded N by Finland, S and E by Russia; c.4600 km/2900 mi long, 16–120 km/10–75 mi wide; ice cover (Dec–Mar).

Finlay, Carlos Juan (1833–1915) Physician, born in Camagüey, Cuba. He first suggested the mosquito as the carrier of yellow fever in 1881, and specified the correct species, now known as *Aëdes aegypti* the following year. Later experiments validated his theory.

Finney, Albert (1936–) Actor, born in Salford, Greater Manchester. His definitive portrayal of the working-class rebel in *Saturday Night and Sunday Morning* (1960) established him as a star. He received Oscar nominations for *Tom Jones* (1963), *Murder on the Orient Express* (1974), *The Dresser* (1983), and *Under the Volcano* (1984). Later films include *Amazing Grace* (2006). Television work includes *My Uncle Silas* (2001) and *The Gathering Storm* (2002, Emmy; Golden Globe).

Finn MacCool A legendary Irish hero, the son of Cumhall, and father of Ossian (Oisin). He became leader of the Fenians, and was famous for his generosity.

fiord *fjord*

Fiordland [fyaw(r)dland] area 10 232 km²/3949 sq mi. National park, SW South Island, New Zealand; established in 1904; a world heritage site.

fir *silver fir*

Firdausi or **Ferd(a)usi** [firdowsee], pseudonym of **Abú al-Qásim Mansúr** (940–c.1020) The greatest of Persian poets, born near Tús, Khorassan. His major work was the epic poem, *Shah Náma* (1010, The Book of Kings).

Fire, Andrew Zachary (1959–) Geneticist, born in Palo Alto, CA. He studied at the University of California, Berkeley (1978) and the Massachusetts Institute of Technology (1983), then became a postdoctoral fellow at Cambridge. He went on to work at the Carnegie Institution of Washington's Department of Embryology in Baltimore, where his initial work on double-stranded RNA as a trigger of gene silencing was published. In 2003 he joined the Stanford University School of Medicine. He shared the 2006 Nobel Prize for Physiology or Medicine with Craig Mello for 'their discovery of RNA interference – gene silencing by double-stranded RNA'.

fireclay Clay with high alumina content that can withstand high temperatures without excessive deformation. It is used for making firebricks and other refractory materials.

firecrest A small bird (*Regulus ignicapillus*) native to Europe, N Africa, and Madeira; head with orange stripe and white 'eyebrows'; Europe's smallest breeding bird. (Family: Regulidae, sometimes placed in Silviidae.)

firedamp Methane found in coal mines. A mixture of methane and air is inflammable or explosive in certain proportions, and has been the cause of many pit disasters. One of the best methods of firedamp detection remains the Davy safety lamp.

firefly A small, mostly nocturnal beetle; males with soft wing cases, females larva-like, often wingless; jaws hollow, used to inject digestive juices into prey; luminous organs near tip of abdomen used to produce mating signals; also known as **glow-worms** and **lightning bugs**. (Order: Coleoptera. Family: Lampyridae, c.2000 species.)

Fire of London A devastating fire which started in a baker's shop in Pudding Lane (2 Sep 1666) and lasted several days, engulfing c.160 ha/400 acres – four-fifths of the city. Casualties were low (no more than 20 died).

firethorn A thorny, evergreen shrub (*Pyracantha coccinea*) growing to c.1·5 m/5 ft, occasionally a small tree, native to S Europe; flowers numerous, 5-petalled, white, in small clusters; berries bright red. (Family: Rosaceae.)

firewall A technology which is used by organizations that have linked their enterprise computer systems into the Internet. The firewall prevents users from outside the organization doing anything which would corrupt the system inside. One standard approach uses the firewall to filter out suspicious messages and discard them. Another approach offers a caller a copy of a system so that, if the caller does anything that is malicious, this can be seen before the real system is damaged.

fireworks Artificial devices, normally used for display purposes, which when ignited produce an array of coloured lights, sparks, and explosions. They contain flammable and explosive materials (eg charcoal, sulphur) which react with oxygen-yielding substances (eg nitre, chlorate of potash). The making of fireworks is called *pyrotechny*.

firmware A concept intermediate between software and hardware, used to describe devices which combine elements of each. A computer program stored in an unalterable form in an integrated circuit such as a read-only memory could be described as firmware.

First, Ruth (1925–82) Radical opponent of apartheid, as activist, journalist, writer, and academic, born in Johannesburg, South Africa. In 1949 she married Joe Slovo; both were arrested and

Finland

☐ International Airport

Finn **Suomi**, official name **Republic of Finland**, Finn **Suomen Tasavalta**, Swed **Republiken Finland**

Local name Suomi (Finnish)
Timezone GMT +2
Area 338 145 km²/130 524 sq mi
Population total (2002e) 5 201 000
Status Republic
Date of independence 1917
Capital Helsinki
Languages Finnish and Swedish (official), also Saame (Lappish)
Ethnic groups Finnish (94%), Swedish, Lappish, Russian minorities

Religions Lutheran (90%), Finnish/Greek Orthodox
Physical features Low-lying, glaciated plateau, average height 150 m/500 ft; highest peak Haltiatunturi, 1328 m/4357 ft, on NW border; over 60 000 shallow lakes in SE, providing a system of inland navigation; over a third of the country located N of the Arctic Circle; Archipelago of Saaristomeri (SW), with over 17 000 islands; including Åland Is (Ahvenanmaa) (SW); forest covers 65% of the country, water covers 10%.

Climate Extreme, N of the Arctic Circle: average annual temperatures -30°C (Jan), 27°C (Jul); half annual precipitation falls as snow; sun does not go down beyond the horizon for over 70 days during summer; average temperatures -6°C (Jan), 17°C (Jul) at Helsinki; average annual rainfall 618 mm/24 in.

Currency 1 euro (EUR) = 100 cents (previous to 2002, 1 Markka (FIM) = 100 penni)

Economy Traditional focus on forestry, farming; rapid economic growth since 1950s; metals, clothing, chemicals; copper, iron-ore mining; wide use of hydroelectric power.

GDP (2002e) $133·8 bn, per capita $25 800

Human Development Index (2002) 0·930

History Ruled by Sweden from 1157 until ceded to Russia in 1809; Grand Duchy of the Russian Czar, 19th-c; independent republic, 1917; parliamentary system created, 1928; invaded by Soviets, 1939–40 (Winter War); lost territory to USSR, including Petsamo and Porkkala peninsula, 1944; signed a friendship treaty with Soviet Union in 1948 (renewed 1955, 1970, 1983), undertaking to resist any attack made on the Soviet Union launched through Finnish territory; Harri Holkeri became Finland's first post-war conservative Prime Minister, 1987; governed by a single-chamber House of Representatives and President assisted by a Council of State; joined the European Union, 1995.

Head of State
1946–56 Juho Kusti Paasikivi
1956–81 Urho Kaleva Kekkonen
1982–94 Mauno Koivisto
1994–2000 Martti Ahtisaarsi
2000– Tarja Halonen

Head of Government
1979–82 Mauno Koivisto
1982–87 Taisto Kalevi Sorsa
1987–91 Harri Holkeri
1991–5 Esko Aho
1995–2003 Paavo Lipponen
2003 Anneli Jaatteenmaki
2003– Matti Vanhanen

charged with treason in 1956. In 1982 she was assassinated by a parcel bomb in her office at Maputo, Mozambique.

First Amendment Legislation enacted in 1789 amending the Constitution of the United States to guarantee freedom of worship, of speech, of the press, of assembly, and of petition to the government for redress of grievances. The Supreme Court has held that freedom of speech does not include the right to refuse to testify before a Congressional investigating committee.

first cause *cosmological argument*

first fleet In Australian history, the name given to the 11 ships which left Portsmouth, England (1787), carrying the first European settlers to E Australia. The fleet carried officials, 212 marines and their families, and 579 convicts plus provisions. The fleet's captain, Arthur Phillip, decided that Botany Bay was

unsuitable and proceeded north to Sydney Cove, Port Jackson, where he hoisted the British flag (26 Jan 1788).

first-footing *Hogmanay*

first-generation computers *computer generations*

First Ladies A title applied to the wives of the Presidents of the United States of America. The term seems to have originated during the last quarter of the 19th-c, but came into general use around 1911 after a play written by Charles Nirdlinger, *The First Lady of The Land*, became popular. During the 20th-c, the wives of presidents became more active in pursuing social causes, following the example of Eleanor Roosevelt (1933–45). As a result of the professional activities of Hillary Rodham Clinton (1993–2000), federal courts have described the work undertaken by the First Lady as making her in legal terms an employee of the federal government.

First Nations A term used in Canada to describe Canadian aboriginal peoples. It was introduced in the 1980s as a response to French- and English-Canadian claims to be the 'two founding nations'.

First World Three Worlds theory

First World War World War 1

Firth, Colin (1960–) Actor, born in Grayshott, Hampshire. He received a BAFTA nomination for his role in the television production of *Tumbledown* (1989), and another for *Pride and Prejudice* (1995), where his brooding performance as the handsome Mr Darcy attracted unprecedented public interest. His films include *The English Patient* (1996), *Bridget Jones's Diary* (2001, sequel 2004), *Love Actually* (2003), and *The Last Legion* (2007).

fiscal policy The use by government of tax and its own rate of spending to influence demand in the economy. When a government decides to lower taxes or raise public expenditure, the effect is to stimulate economic activity by increasing the demand for goods and services. In contrast, a tightening of fiscal policy is where taxes are raised or public expenditure is reduced, in order to reduce aggregate demand.

Fischer, Bobby, popular name of **Robert (James) Fischer** (1943–) Chess player, born in Chicago, IL. He was world champion in 1972–5, taking the title from Boris Spassky (USSR) in a much-publicized match. He resigned his title shortly before a defence against Anatoly Karpov in 1975, and did not then compete at a major international level until 1992, when he defeated Spassky in a match which generated unprecedented levels of publicity for a chess match. In 1992, he disappeared after breaking international sanctions by going to Yugoslavia to play Boris Spassky. He lived undetected in Europe and Japan until 2004, when he was arrested in Tokyo for passport irregularities and the US requested his extradition. In 2005 he left for Iceland having been granted an Icelandic passport and citizenship.

Fischer-Dieskau, Dietrich [fisher deeskow] (1925–) Baritone, born in Berlin. He is one of the foremost interpreters of German *Lieder*, particularly the song cycles of Schubert.

Fischer von Erlach, Johann Bernard [fisher fon airlakh] (1656–1723) Architect, born in Graz, Austria. A leading exponent of the Baroque style, he designed many churches and palaces, notably the Karlskirche at Vienna, and the University Church at Salzburg.

fish Any cold-blooded aquatic vertebrate without legs, but typically possessing paired lateral fins as well as median fins. There is a 2-chambered heart, a series of respiratory gills present throughout life in the sides of the pharynx, and a body usually bearing scales and terminating in a caudal (tail) fin. As a subgroup of the Vertebrata, the fishes are sometimes referred to collectively as *Pisces*. The *Chondrichthyes* (800 living species), containing the sharks, rays, and ratfishes, are characterized by a cartilaginous skeleton, and are commonly referred to as the **cartilaginous fishes**. By far the largest extant group are the **bony fishes** (*Osteichthyes*; 20 000 living species), exhibiting a rich diversity and found in all aquatic habitats. Although many fish have the familiar elongate shape, body form shows great variety. Body length ranges from as small as a few centimetres to over 18 m/60 ft in the massive whale shark. Many species have bright coloration, others well-developed camouflage patterns. Light organs are common in those forms living in the darkness of deep oceanic waters.

Fishbourne Roman palace near Chichester, West Sussex, discovered in 1960. Probably erected in the AD 60s for the British client-king Cogidubnus, it continued in use into the 4th-c.

Fishburne, Larry, popular name of **Laurence John Fishburne III** (1961–) Actor, born in Augusta, Georgia, USA. He won a Tony Award for his performance in the Broadway play *Two Trains Running*, later starring in the films *School Daze* (1988) and *Boyz*

N the Hood (1991). Later films include *The Matrix* (1999) and its sequels *The Matrix Reloaded* and *Matrix Revolutions* (both 2003), and *Bobby* (2006).

fish eagle osprey; sea eagle

Fisher, John, St (1469–1535) Clergyman and humanist, born in Beverley, East Riding of Yorkshire. In 1527 he pronounced against the divorce of Henry VIII, and was sent with More to the Tower. In 1535 he was made a cardinal, and soon after was tried and beheaded on Tower Hill. He was canonized in 1935. Feast day 22 June.

Fisher (of Lambeth), Geoffrey Fisher, Baron (1887–1972) Archbishop of Canterbury (1945–61), born in Higham-on-the-Hill, Leicestershire. In 1939 he became Bishop of London, and as Archbishop crowned Queen Elizabeth II in Westminster Abbey (1953).

fisher A mammal, related to the marten, native to North America; length, up to 1 m/3$\frac{1}{4}$ ft; thick brown-black coat; inhabits dense forest; also known as **pekan**. (*Martes pennanti*. Family: Mustelidae.)

fishing angling

fission A method of asexual reproduction by splitting into two (**binary fission**) or more (**multiple fission**) parts, each of which develops into an independent organism. The process is common among single-celled micro-organisms.

fitchet polecat

Fitt, Gerry, popular name of **Gerard, Baron Fitt (of Bell's Hill)** (1926–2005) Northern Ireland politician, born in Belfast. He founded and led the Social Democratic and Labour Party (1970–9), until he resigned the leadership to sit as an Independent Socialist. He served as Labour MP for West Belfast (1966–83), and received a peerage in 1983.

Fitzgerald, Ella (1918–96) Singer, born in Newport News, VA. Discovered in 1934 singing in an amateur contest in Harlem, she joined Chick Webb's band and recorded several hits, notably 'A-tisket A-tasket' (1938). Her series of recordings for Verve (1955–9) in multi-volume 'songbooks' are among the treasures of American popular song.

Fitzgerald, F(rancis) Scott (Key) (1896–1940) Novelist, born in St Paul, MN. He captured the spirit of the 1920s – 'the Jazz Age' – in *The Great Gatsby* (1925), his best-known book. His other novels include *The Beautiful and the Damned* (1922) and *Tender is the Night* (1934).

Fitzgerald, Garrett (Michael) (1926–) Irish statesman and prime minister (1981–2, 1982–7), born in Dublin. In 1969 he was elected Fine Gael member of the Irish parliament for Dublin SE, and became minister for foreign affairs (1973–7), and leader of the Fine Gael Party (1977–87).

Fitzgerald, George Francis (1851–1901) Physicist, born in Dublin. Independently of Lorentz, he concluded that, to a stationary observer, a moving body appears shorter, the degree of forshortening being larger at higher velocities (the **Lorentz–Fitzgerald contraction**), a notion embraced by Einstein as part of his theory of special relativity.

Fitzsimmons, Bob, popular name of **Robert Prometheus Fitzsimmons** (1863–1917) Boxer, born in Helston, Cornwall. He moved to the USA in 1890, where he won the world middleweight (1891), heavyweight (1897), and light heavyweight championships (1903).

Fiume Rijeka

Five, the A group of 19th-c Russian composers, also known as **the Mighty Handful**, who came together to promote nationalist ideals and styles in music. The group, led by Balakirev, also contained Borodin, Moussorgsky, Rimsky-Korsakov, and César Cui (1835–1918).

Five Civilized Tribes The Muskogean-speaking nations of Indians (Chickasaws, Creeks, Choctaws, Cherokees, Seminoles) who originally inhabited the present SE USA. The Cherokees, in particular, adopted white ways, acquiring literacy in their own language and English.

fives A handball game played by two or four players, derived from the French game *jeu de paume* ('palm [of hand] game'). The first recorded game was at Eton School in 1825.

fjord A long, narrow, steep-sided coastal inlet extending far inland and often reaching very great depths. The best-known fjords are in Norway and E Greenland.

flag (botany) A species of iris (*Iris pseudacorus*) with yellow flowers 7·5–10 cm/3–4 in diameter, found in wet, swampy ground in Europe, W Asia, and N Africa. (Family: Iridaceae.)

flagellate [flajiluht] A microscopic, single-celled organism that possesses 1, 2, 4, or more thread-like organelles (**flagella**), typically used for swimming. (Phylum: Mastigophora.)

flagellum [flajelum] A thread-like structure found on some bacteria and on or in many eucaryotic organisms. Flagella usually function in locomotion, bacterial flagella rotating and eucaryotic flagella undulating as they beat.

flageolet [flajiohlet] A simple, high-pitched, end-blown flute, made of wood, with six fingerholes; later, often fitted with metal keys and an ivory mouthpiece. It was popular during the 16th–18th-c, and did not become obsolete until about the mid-19th-c.

Flagstad, Kirsten (1895–1962) Soprano, born in Hamar, Germany. She excelled in Wagnerian roles. In 1958 she was made director of the Norwegian State Opera.

Flamboyant The style of French late Gothic architecture prevalent in the 15th-c, characterized by wavy flame-like tracery. It was especially common in Normandy.

flamenco A traditional song and dance of the Rom (gypsies) of Andalusia in southern Spain. It evolved over centuries of fusion between Rom, Moorish, Andalusian and other traditions. It involves intricate toe- and heel-clicking steps and graceful body- and hand-movements.

flamingo A large wading bird, native to South America, Africa, S Europe, and W Asia; plumage white or pink; inhabits shallow soda or brine lakes; stout, downwardly angled bill; swims well; forms immense flocks. (Family: Phoenicopteridae, 5 species.)

Flaminian Way The second of Rome's major trunk roads, constructed in 220 BC. It ran NE from Rome across the Apennines to Rimini on the Adriatic coast.

Flaminius, Gaius [flaminius] (?–217 BC) Roman general and statesman at the time of the Second Punic War, whose name lived on in his two most popular projects: the **Flaminian Way** and the chariot-racing arena, the **Circus Flaminius**.

Flamsteed, John (1646–1719) The first Astronomer Royal of England (1675–1719), born in Denby, Derbyshire. In 1676 he instituted reliable observations at Greenwich, near London, providing data from which Newton was later able to verify the gravitational theory.

Flanders, Flemish **Vlaanderen**, Fr **Flandre** Historical region of NW Belgium and NE France; autonomous in early Middle Ages; densely populated industrial area; chief towns include Bruges, Ghent; traditional textile industry; intensive farming; scene of heavy fighting in both World Wars.

flatfish Any of the bottom-dwelling mainly shallow-water fishes in which the adult body is strongly compressed laterally and asymmetrical, with both eyes on the same side of the head; nine families; important food fish.

flat foot A condition affecting the normal arches of the foot. Loss of the arches strains the ligaments and muscles of the foot, and can lead to discomfort on standing.

Flathead A Salish-speaking Indian group living on L Flathead, Montana, the most easterly-based of Plateau Indian groups.

flathead Bottom-living fish of the Indo-Pacific and tropical Atlantic oceans; body slender, length up to 1 m/3¼ ft, flattened

anteriorly with prominent spinose fins. (Genera: *Platycephalus*, *Thysanophrys*. Family: Platycephalidae.)

Flatley, Michael (1958–) Dancer and choreographer, born in Chicago, IL. At age 11 he began dance lessons and in 1975 became the first American to win the All World Championships in Irish dancing. He shot to fame after the success of his stage routine *Riverdance* at the Eurovision Song Contest in Dublin in 1994, and went on to create, choreograph and star in the show *The Lord of the Dance* (1996). He announced his retirement from the stage in 2001. A new show, *Celtic Tiger*, premiered in the US in 2005.

flat racing *horse racing*

flatworm A flattened, worm-like animal with a definite head but without a true body cavity (*coelom*); parasitic forms include tapeworms and flukes. (Phylum: Platyhelminthes.)

Flaubert, Gustave [flohbair] (1821–80) Novelist, born in Rouen, France. His masterpiece was *Madame Bovary* (1857), which was condemned as immoral and its author (unsuccessfully) prosecuted. *Trois contes* (1877, Three Tales) reveals his mastery of the short story.

flavouring agent Any compound when added to a food to alter its taste, the most widely used being salt and sugar. Monosodium glutamate is an example of a flavour enhancer, bringing out a 'meaty flavour'.

flax A slender erect annual (*Linum usitatissimum*), growing to 60 cm/2 ft; flowers numerous, blue, with five spreading petals; fruit a capsule with numerous seeds. It is cultivated throughout temperate and subtropical regions for flax fibre obtained from the stems, and for linseed oil from the seeds. (Family: Linaceae.)

Flaxman, John (1755–1826) Sculptor and illustrator, born in York, North Yorkshire. He furnished the Wedgwood house with renowned pottery designs, and illustrated the *Iliad* and *Odyssey* (1793), and other works.

F layer *Appleton layer*

flea A small, wingless insect that as an adult is a blood-feeding external parasite of warm-blooded animals (mostly mammals, but including some birds); body flattened from side to side, usually hairy; mouthparts specialized for piercing and sucking; hindlegs adapted for jumping; c.1750 species, many carriers of disease. (Order: Siphonaptera.)

fleabane A leafy perennial (*Pulicaria dysenterica*) growing to 60 cm/2 ft, native to marshes in Europe, N Africa, and Asia Minor; flower-heads golden yellow, daisy-like; fruit with a parachute of hairs. Its dried leaves were formerly burned to repel insects. (Family: Compositae.)

fleawort The name applied to certain species of the genus *Senecio*. **Field fleawort** (*Senecio integrifolius*) is a variable perennial growing to 70 cm/27 in; smaller clusters of flower-heads with c.13 bright yellow outer ray florets; native to much of Europe. (Family: Compositae.)

Flecker, (Herman) James Elroy (1884–1915) Poet, born in London. His best-known works are the drama *Hassan* (1922) and *The Golden Journey to Samarkand* (1913).

Flémalle, Master of *Campin, Robert*

Fleming, Sir Alexander (1881–1955) Bacteriologist, born near Darvel, East Ayrshire. He was the first to use antityphoid vaccines on human beings, pioneered the use of Salvarsan against syphilis, and discovered the antiseptic powers of lysozyme. In 1928 he discovered penicillin, for which he shared the Nobel Prize for Physiology or Medicine in 1945.

Fleming, Ian (Lancaster) (1908–64) Writer and journalist, born in London. He achieved worldwide fame and fortune as the creator of 12 sophisticated spy novels, starting with *Casino Royale* (1953), built round the exploits of his amoral hero James Bond.

Fleming, Sir John Ambrose (1849–1945) Physicist, born in Lancaster, Lancashire. He invented the thermionic valve, and was a pioneer in the application of electricity to lighting and heating on a large scale.

Fleming and Walloon The two main linguistic and cultural groups of present-day Belgium. Flemings are based in the N and W, and speak Flemish (Vlaams). The French-speaking Walloons live in the S and E. Linguistic disputes between the two groups are a major feature of Belgian politics.

Flemish *Dutch*

Flemming, Walther (1843–1905) Biologist, born in Sachsenberg, Germany. In 1882 he gave the first modern account of cytology, including the process of cell division, which he named *mitosis*.

Fletcher, John (1579–1625) Playwright, born in Rye, East Sussex. He is best known for his collaboration with Beaumont in such works as *The Maid's Tragedy* (1611). Collaboration with Shakespeare probably resulted in *Two Noble Kinsmen* and *Henry VIII*.

Fleury, André-Hercule de [floeree] (1653–1743) French prelate and statesman, born in Lodève, France. He became chief minister in 1726, and also a cardinal, and effectively controlled the government of Louis XV until 1743. His moderation gave France the tranquility her tangled finances demanded, and he carried out legal and economic reforms which stimulated trade.

Flinders, Matthew (1774–1814) Explorer, born in Donington, Lincolnshire. In 1795 he sailed to Australia, where he explored the SE coast, and later (1801–3) circumnavigated the country. The Flinders R in Queensland, and the Flinders range in South Australia are named after him.

Flinders Ranges *Lofty–Flinders Ranges, Mount*

flint A type of chert, occurring as grey, rounded nodules in chalk or other limestone. It breaks into sharp-edged flakes and hence was used as a Stone Age tool.

flint glass Heavy crystal glass, containing lead, highly suitable for cutting and engraving. It was first introduced c.1675, and so called because early examples were made with powdered flint instead of the more usual sand.

Flintoff, Andrew, nickname **Freddie** (1977–) Cricketer, born in Preston, Lancashire. A fast bowler and batsman, he joined Lancashire County Cricket Club at age 17, debuted for England against South Africa in 1998, and made his one-day international debut against Pakistan in 1999. In his first Ashes series, in England in 2005, he contributed to his country's victory with a tally of 24 wickets and 402 runs, winning England's Man of the Series Award. He took over as England captain during the team's Test series against India in March 2006. He was then out of the game for some months with an ankle injury but was named captain for England's unsuccessful defence of the Ashes in Australia at the end of the year. He was named Leading Cricketer of the World for 2005 by Wisden Cricketers' Almanack.

Flintshire, Welsh **Sir y Fflint** pop (2001e) 148 600; area 437 km²/ 169 sq mi. County (unitary authority from 1996) in NE Wales, UK; administrative centre, Mold; castles at Flint, Hawarden; St Winifred's Well at Holywell; Theatre Clwyd.

FLN The acronym for the **Front de Libération Nationale**, an organization founded in the early 1950s, which fought for Algerian independence from France under the leadership of Mohammed Ben Bella. France's inability to defeat the FLN led to the Evian conference in 1962, and complete Algerian independence. The FLN became the governing party of independent Algeria, and until 1991 was the only legal party in the country.

floating rate *exchange rates*

Flodden, Battle of (9 Sep 1513) A victory of the English over the Scots, fought in the Scottish Borders. James IV, allied with France, invaded England in August, but was defeated by English forces under Thomas Howard, Earl of Surrey. The Scots lost perhaps as many as 10 000 dead, including James IV himself. The battle ended the Scottish threat for a generation.

Flood, the In the Bible, the story that in Noah's time God caused a widespread deluge to destroy all people because of their sin (except Noah and his family), this purge providing a new start for mankind (*Gen* 6–8) and the animal world. Similar legends are found also in other ancient near-eastern sources.

floppy disk or **floppy** A flexible plastic disk coated with magnetic material, used as a storage medium for microcomputers. The disks generally have a diameter of 5·25 in (13·3 cm). In use, the disks are rotated at some 300 revolutions per minute and are written to, or read from, by movable magnetic heads. 5·25 in disks can store up to 1 megabyte or more of information, the exact amount depending on the particular system. The term has also come to be used by analogy for the rigid 3·5-in/7·9-cm disk.

Flora An ancient Roman goddess of flowers and flowering plants, who appears with the Spring. She was given a temple in 238 BC, and her games were celebrated on 28 April.

Florence, Ital **Firenze** 43°47N 11°15E, pop (2000e) 408 000. Ancient city in Tuscany, Italy, on R Arno; ancient Etruscan town; cultural and intellectual centre of Italy from the Middle Ages; badly damaged by floods, 1966; archbishopric; airport; railway; university (1321); city centre a world heritage site; famed for its many religious buildings and palaces, such as the Baptistery of San Giovanni (c.1000), the Duomo (1296); Palazzo degli Uffizi (1560–74), Palazzo Pitti (15th-c and later), Ponte Vecchio (rebuilt 1345); birthplace of Dante and Macchiavelli.

floret A very small or reduced flower, usually one of many aggregated together in a head which may itself resemble a single flower, as in members of the daisy family.

Florida pop (2000e) 15 982 400; area 151 934 km²/58 664 sq mi. State in SE USA; the 'Sunshine State' or 'Peninsular State'; discovered and settled by the Spanish in the 16th-c; ceded to Britain in 1763, and divided into East and West Florida; given back to Spain after the War of Independence, 1783; West Florida gained by the US in the Louisiana Purchase, 1803; East Florida purchased by the US, 1819; admitted as the 27th state of the Union, 1845; seceded, 1861; slavery abolished, 1865; re-admitted to the Union, 1868; a long peninsula bounded W by the Gulf of Mexico and E by the Atlantic Ocean; C state has many lakes, notably L Okeechobee; highest point in Walton County (105 m/345 ft); S almost entirely covered by the Everglades; SE coast protected from the Atlantic by sandbars and islands, creating shallow lagoons and sandy beaches; warm sunny climate; capital, Tallahassee; many famous resorts (Palm Beach, Miami Beach); Everglades National Park, Walt Disney World entertainment park, John F Kennedy Space Center at Cape Canaveral; the nation's greatest producer of citrus fruits; the second largest producer of vegetables; large Hispanic population (especially from Cuba).

Florida Keys A series of small islands curving approx 240 km/ 150 mi SW around the tip of the Florida peninsula, USA; Overseas Highway (1938) runs from the mainland to Key West, 198 km/123 mi long.

florin A type of coin first made in the Italian city of Florence in 1252. In 1849, Britain issued its first silver florin, the two-shilling piece, which became the 'old' 10p piece after the coinage was decimalized in 1971. This 10p piece was replaced in 1993.

Flotow, Friedrich, Freiherr von (Baron) [flohtoh] (1812–83) Composer, born in Teutendorf, Germany. He made his reputation with several operas, including *Martha* (1847).

flotsam, jetsam, and **lagan** [laygn] Terms used in describing goods or wreckage found in the sea. **Flotsam** refers to anything found floating. **Jetsam** includes anything deliberately jettisoned from a ship. **Lagan** refers to goods on the bottom of the sea.

flounder Common European flatfish (*Platichthys flesus*) found in shallow inshore waters; upper body surface grey-brown with dark patches and orange spots, underside white; length up to 50 cm/20 in. (Family: Pleuronectidae.)

flour The finely ground product of a cereal seed, especially wheat, primarily used to make bread. A wheat seed consists of an outer coat (husk), with the germ (embryo), and a starchy centre (endosperm). When the seed is ground, it forms a wholemeal flour suitable for baking; if the flour is refined to increase the proportion of endosperm, white flour is produced. Wholemeal flour is richer in fibre, and an important constituent of high-fibre diets.

flower The reproductive organ of a flowering plant (*angiosperm*) derived from a leafy shoot of limited growth in which the leaves are modified for specific roles. It typically consists of four distinct *whorls* of parts attached to a receptacle: the sepals (*calyx*), the petals (*corolla*), the stamens (*andrecium*), and the carpels or ovary (*gynecium*). Structurally, flowers can be divided into two types: **actinomorphic** or radially symmetrical, and **zygomorphic** or bilaterally symmetrical.

flowering plants One of the two divisions of seed plants, sometimes referred to as the **angiosperms**, the other division being the **gymnosperms**. They are characterized by having the seed enclosed in an ovary which has a specialized extension (the *stigma*) for receiving pollen. The group includes all plants in which the reproductive organ is a flower, hence the commonly used name. The flowering plants are divided into **monocotyledons** and **dicotyledons** on the basis of cotyledon number. They are the most common in terms of both numbers and distribution, with an estimated 250 000 species occurring in all parts of the globe. (Class: Angiospermae.)

flowering quince *japonica*

flows *stocks*

flugelhorn [flooglhaw(r)n] A musical instrument made of brass, somewhat like a cornet and with a similar compass, but with a slightly larger bell. It is a standard instrument in British brass bands, and is used in jazz, but is rarely found in orchestras.

fluid A substance which flows and is able to fill its container: a liquid, gas, or plasma. The mechanical properties of fluids are governed by the laws of fluid mechanics.

fluidics The study of control and detection systems based on fluid movement. Available devices include fluid amplifiers (in which a small flow modifies a large flow), logic circuits, and switches.

fluid mechanics The study of the mechanics of fluids. **Fluid statics** is concerned with the properties of fluids at rest. **Fluid dynamics** considers the properties peculiar to moving fluids. **Hydrostatics** and **hydrodynamics** are the study of stationary and moving incompressible fluids (usually liquids), respectively. **Aerodynamics** is concerned with the flow of gases, especially air. The properties of fluids include *density*, the mass per unit volume, and *compressibility*, which is high for gases but essentially zero for liquids. A fluid also exerts a *pressure* on an object immersed in it, which is the same in all directions. Objects immersed in fluid experience an upward *buoyancy* force. *Viscosity* measures a fluid's reluctance to flow, more properly its internal friction. *Flow rate* is the mass of fluid passing some point every second.

fluke Either of two groups of parasitic flatworms; **digenetic flukes**, typically parasites of vertebrates as adults, with complex life-cycles involving at least two hosts; **monogenetic flukes**, usually external parasites of fishes with single host life-cycles. (Phylum: Platyhelminthes. Class: Trematoda.)

fluorescence Light produced by an object excited by means other than heating, where light emission ceases as soon as the energy source is removed. It is a type of luminescence, exploited in dyes and in the coating of fluorescent light tubes.

fluorescent lamp A lamp consisting of a tube, coated inside with fluorescent material (phosphor), filled with mercury vapour, and with an electrode at each end. Light is generated by passing a current between the electrodes through the vapour, producing ultraviolet light that is converted to visible light by phosphor fluorescence.

fluoridation of water The production of water containing small amounts of fluorine (1 part per million), whose regular consumption greatly reduces the incidence of caries of the teeth. Water supplies in many regions contain fluorine naturally in sufficient concentrations to increase the resistance of teeth to attack. This has led the authorities to recommend the addition of fluorine to reservoirs deficient in the element. While this is done in many instances, a vociferous minority of the population who object to adding 'chemicals' to water have succeeded in preventing it from becoming universal.

fluoride A compound containing fluorine, especially one containing F^- ions. **Sodium fluoride** (NaF) is commonly added in small amounts to drinking water or dentifrice to supply fluoride ions necessary for strong dental enamel.

fluorine Element 9, composed of molecules F_2, boiling point $-187°C$. A yellow gas, the first of the halogens, the most electronegative element, oxidation state -1 in nearly all its compounds. It is very corrosive and toxic, and occurs mainly in the mineral *fluorite* (CaF_2).

fluorite or **fluorspar** A common mineral of calcium fluoride (CaF_2), typically blue or purple in colour, and the main source of fluorine. It is used as a flux in steel production.

fluorocarbons Compounds of carbon and fluorine, the simplest being CF_4, tetrafluoromethane. The C–F bond is very stable, and saturated fluorocarbons are very unreactive.

fluoroscope A medical instrument that projects radiation through the body to form an image of the internal organs on a fluorescent screen, used by physicians to assist in diagnosis. Conventional radiographic images are capable of demonstrating greater detail, but fluoroscopy is preferable when a live moving image is required.

fluorosis [floo-orohsis] Chronic poisoning by drinking water which contains an excessive amount of fluoride. It results in discoloration of the teeth and a disabling arthritis which chiefly affects the spine. The concentration necessary to produce fluorosis is many times that added to drinking water in reservoirs to prevent dental caries.

fluorspar *fluorite*

Flushing, Dutch **Vlissingen**, Fr **Flessingue** 51°27N 3°35E, pop (2000e) 46 000. Seaport in W Netherlands, at the mouth of the Schelde river estuary; scene of Allied landing, 1944; railway; site of a nuclear power station; 14th-c Grote Kerk.

flute Broadly speaking, a musical instrument in which a column of air is activated by the player blowing across a mouth-hole or (as in the recorder) against a sharp edge towards which the breath may be directed through a duct. The unqualified term 'flute' generally refers to the transverse concert type. This is made of wood or (more often now) of metal in three jointed sections, with 13 tone-holes, and an elaborate system of keys.

flutemouth *cornetfish*

flux (technology) Any substance used in metallurgical processes to promote the flow of molten metal and waste (*slag*) and to segregate unwanted impurities. Limestone fulfils this purpose in iron smelting. In soldering, rosin is often used.

fly The common name of many small flying insects. True flies have a single pair of membranous flying wings only; hindwings modified as club-shaped, balancing organs (*halteres*); mouthparts form a *proboscis* adapted for sucking, occasionally for piercing; larvae maggot-like, lacking true legs; c.150 000 species, many carriers of disease. (Order: Diptera.)

fly agaric [agarik] A toadstool (*Amanita muscaria*) that forms a bright red fruiting body, typically with white patches on cap;

common on ground under trees such as birch and pine during autumn; produces hallucinogenic poisons that can be fatal to humans if eaten. (Order: Agaricales.)

flycatcher A name applied to birds of three distinct groups: **New World** or **tyrant flycatchers** (Family: Tyrannidae, 375 species); **Old World flycatchers** (Family: Muscicapidae, 150 species); and **silky flycatchers** (Family: Ptilogonatidae, 4 species). All usually eat insects caught in flight.

flying doctor service The provision of medical services to isolated communities spread over wide areas, based on the use of Air Ambulances. It is particularly well-known in the Australian interior.

Flying Dutchman A ghost ship of disastrous portent, haunting the seas around the Cape of Good Hope; its captain had sworn a blasphemous oath when he failed to round the Cape in a storm, and was condemned to sail those waters forever. The story inspired Wagner's opera *Der Fliegende Holländer* (1843).

flying fish Small surface-living fish with greatly enlarged pelvic and pectoral fins, and the ability to jump and glide above the water surface; *Exocoetus volitans* (length up to 30 cm/1 ft), is widespread in tropical and warm temperate seas. (Family: Exocoetidae.)

flying fox *bat*

flying snake A snake from SE Asia; glides between trees; launches itself into the air, then flattens the body and forms several S-shaped curves. (Genus: *Chrysopelea*, 2 species. Family: Colubridae.)

flying squirrel A squirrel with a large flap of skin between its front and hind legs; glides between trees (up to 450 m/1475 ft in one leap); 33 species in Asia and 2 species in North America.

Flynn, Errol (Leslie Thomson) (1909–59) Film star, born in Hobart, Tasmania. His first American film, *Captain Blood* (1935), established him as a hero of historical adventure films, and his good looks and athleticism confirmed him as the greatest Hollywood swashbuckler, in such films as *The Adventures of Robin Hood* (1938) and *The Sea Hawk* (1940). During the 1940s his off-screen reputation for drinking, drug-taking, and womanizing became legendary.

flywheel A wheel attached to the shaft of an engine, whose distribution of weight enables it to act as a smoothing device for the engine's power output.

f-number A numerical system of indicating the size of the aperture stop in a camera lens, which determines how much light is transmitted to the film and hence the control of exposure in conjunction with shutter speed. The f-number is calculated by dividing the focal length of the lens by the diameter of the clear aperture of the lens as given by the iris diaphragm.

Fo, Dario [foh] (1926–) Playwright, designer, and actor, born in San Giano, Italy. His populist plays use the comic traditions of farce and slapstick, as well as surreal effects, notably in *Morte accidentale di un anarchico* (1970, Accidental Death of an Anarchist). He was awarded the Nobel Prize for Literature in 1997.

Foale, Michael [fohl] (1957–) Astronaut, born in Louth, Lincolnshire. In October 2003 he was chosen to command the International Space Station (ISS), spending 200 days performing routine maintenance and conducting scientific experiments, and thereby clocking up more hours in space than any other US astronaut.

Foch, Ferdinand [fosh] (1851–1929) French marshal, born in Tarbes. He proved himself a great strategist at the Marne (1914), Ypres, and other World War 1 battles, and commanded the Allied armies in 1918.

foetus *fetus*

fog A cloud which occurs at ground level, resulting in low visibility. It forms when two air masses with differing temperatures and moisture contents mix together. **Radiation fog**

develops on cold, clear nights when terrestrial radiation cools the ground surface, and lowers the temperature of the air close to the ground, causing condensation. **Advective fog** forms when warm, moist air blows over a cold ground surface, is cooled, and condensation results.

Föhn / Foehn wind [foen] A warm, dry wind descending on the leeward side of a mountain. As moist air rises on the windward side, it cools and loses moisture before descending and warming. It is found in the European Alps and other mountainous areas.

Fokine, Michel [fokeen], originally **Mikhail Mikhaylovich Fokine** (1880–1942) Dancer and choreographer, born in St Petersburg, Russia. He is credited with the creation of modern ballet from the artificial, stylized mode prevalent at the beginning of the 20th-c.

Fokker, Anthony Herman Gerard (1890–1939) Aircraft engineer, born in Kediri, Java. He built his first plane in 1911, and in 1913 founded the factory at Schwerin, Germany, which made warplanes for the German air force in World War 1.

folic acid A B vitamin found in liver and most green vegetables, required for the synthesis and functioning of red cells. A deficiency, which is rare in developed countries, leads to anaemia.

Folies-Bergère [folee bairzhair] A music hall in Paris, opened in 1869. By the end of the 19th-c its stage was dominated by circus acts and semi-nude female performers. It remains famous for its lavish displays.

folklore The traditional songs, tales, proverbs, legends, and beliefs of a people, embracing material culture (utensils, arts and crafts) and non-material culture (festivals, dances and rituals). A scientific study of folklore was first undertaken by Jacob Grimm.

folk music Music which is transmitted orally, usually with modifications from generation to generation and from place to place, so that its original form and composer are forgotten. Sound recording greatly facilitated the collecting and transcribing of folk music in the 20th-c.

folk tales Traditional stories told orally and found all over the world, known – as far as one can tell – from earliest times. They fall into various categories, such as animal tales, tales involving magic, tales recounting tests, tricks, or reversals of fortune, and tales explaining the origin of customs, topographical features, or the entire cosmos.

Fomalhaut [fomalhoht] A bright S hemisphere star in Piscis Austrinus. Distance: 7·7 parsec.

Fonda, Henry (Jaynes) (1905–82) Actor, born in Grand Island, NE. His early performances, such as in *The Grapes of Wrath* (1940), established him in the role of the American folk hero, and he played many such parts over the next 30 years. His last major appearance was in *On Golden Pond* (1981, Oscar).

Fonda, Jane (1937–) Actress and human-rights activist, born in New York City, the daughter of Henry Fonda. She married director Roger Vadim (1965–73), with whom she made *La Ronde* (1964) and *Barbarella* (1968). Further roles widened her dramatic scope, such as in *Klute* (1971, Oscar), *Coming Home* (1978, Oscar), *On Golden Pond* (1981), *Old Gringo* (1989), and the later *Monster-in-Law* (2005). She is politically active in anti-nuclear and feminist peace movements, and in the 1980s became involved with women's health and fitness activities.

Fontainebleau [fõtenbloh] A magnificent 16th-c chateau built by Italian craftsmen for Francis I on the site of an earlier royal chateau-fortress at Fontainebleau in France; a world heritage site.

Fontana, Domenico [fontahna] (1543–1607) Architect, born in Melide, Switzerland (formerly Italy). He was papal architect in Rome, employed on the Lateran Palace, the Vatican Library, and St Peter's dome.

Fontenay Abbey [fŏtnay] A Cistercian abbey, founded in 1119 by Bernard of Clairvaux at Fontenay in NE France; a world heritage monument.

Fonteyn, Margot [fontayn], in full **Dame Margot Fonteyn de Arias**, originally **Margaret Hookham** (1919–91) Ballerina, born in Reigate, Surrey. She joined the Sadler's Wells Ballet (later the Royal Ballet) in 1934, and became one of the greatest ballerinas of the 20th-c. A new partnership with Nureyev in the 1960s extended her performing career.

Foochow *Fuzhou*

food allergy A true allergic reaction in which there is accompanying evidence of abnormal immunological response to the food items. A reaction is set up in the body involving immunoglobulins (IgE, IgG, or IgM), which results in the release of substances (*kinins*) causing inflammation and tissue damage.

Food and Agriculture Organization (FAO) A specialized agency of the United Nations dealing with agriculture and nutrition. The FAO was set up in 1945 and has its headquarters in Rome. It conducts research and surveys, and publishes statistics, in the areas of agriculture, forestry, and fisheries, and the distribution of their products. It also provides technical assistance to improve agricultural productivity, with the aim of preventing famines and improving standards of living in rural areas.

food chain The sequence of organisms on successive feeding (*trophic*) levels within an ecological community, through which energy is transferred by feeding. Energy enters the food chain mainly during photosynthesis by green plants (*primary producers*), passes to the herbivores (*primary consumers*) when they eat plants, and then to the carnivores (*secondary and tertiary consumers*) when they prey on herbivores.

food fortification Food to which a nutrient has been added. Many breakfast cereals are fortified with iron by the choice of the manufacturer. Margarine manufacturers are obliged to add vitamins A and D to their product.

food labelling The provision of identifying labels on packaged food, which must not only declare the product and manufacturer but also provide data on the product weight, the additives which have been incorporated, and nowadays a brief outline of key nutritional data.

food poisoning An illness that arises from eating food or liquid contaminated with infectious micro-organisms or chemicals that affect the gastro-intestinal tract, causing vomiting and diarrhoea. Infectious causes include *salmonella* and botulism. Non-bacterial food poisoning may be due to eating poisonous mushrooms and shellfish.

food preservation The treatment of food to maintain its quality and prevent deterioration. Drying removes the water necessary for the growth of spoilage organisms, while bacterial growth can be prevented by acidifying (pickling), salting, heating, canning, freezing, and now by irradiation.

food sensitivity A state of intolerance to a food item, in which there may or may not be evidence of an abnormal immunological reaction. The reactions may be allergic, psychological or pharmacological (eg to additives), a direct irritant effect of food on the gut lining (eg wheat), and some enzyme deficiencies in which the body is unable to process the constituents. Most food sensitivities are temporary, and can be reintroduced into the diet after a period of avoidance.

fool's gold *pyrite*

Foot, Michael (Mackintosh) (1913–) British statesman, born in Plymouth, Devon. He joined the staff of the *Tribune* in 1937, becoming editor (1948–52, 1955–60). He became a Labour MP in 1945, and was secretary of state for employment (1974–6), and deputy leader (1976–80) then leader (1980–3) of the Labour Party. He retired from the Commons in 1992. A pacifist, he has long been a supporter of the Campaign for Nuclear Disarmament.

foot The terminal part of the lower limb which makes contact with the ground; an instrument of support when standing, and of propulsion and restraint when walking or running. In humans there are seven tarsal bones, five metatarsals, two phalanges in the big toe, and three in the other toes.

foot-and-mouth disease A contagious feverish disease of artiodactyls characterized by blistering inside the mouth and in the cleft of the hooves; also known as **hoof-and-mouth disease**. It can be caught by humans. In domestic stock, diagnosis (at least in Western countries) would lead to the immediate destruction of the affected herd, as happened with the British outbreak in 2001.

football, American *p.344*

football, Association *p.344*

football, Australian Rules *p.345*

football, Rugby League A team game played with an oval ball on a rectangular playing area. Rugby League originated when the North of England clubs seceded from the Rugby Football Union in 1895 over its refusal to permit 'broken time' payments for time off work to play rugby. They formed the Northern Rugby Football Union, which became the Rugby Football League in 1922. The Rugby League became openly professional in 1898 and gradually developed into a distinctive game through rule changes such as the reduction of teams from 15 to 13 players and the abolition of the line-out for returning the ball to play. The means of scoring are the same as in Rugby Union, but with different scoring values: try 4, conversion 2, penalty goal 2, drop goal 1.

football, Rugby Union *p.346*

Football League The oldest association football league in the world, formed after a formal meeting at the Royal Hotel, Manchester on 17 April 1888. Twelve clubs became founder members.

foraminiferan [foraminiferan] An amoeba-like protozoan that secretes an external shell (*test*), typically calcareous and chambered; feeds and moves by means of protoplasmic processes (*pseudopodia*) extruded through shell openings; largely marine; includes many fossils. (Order: Foraminifera.)

Forbidden City The Imperial Palace in Beijing, the residence of the imperial rulers of China from its construction in 1420 until the fall of the Qing dynasty in 1911. The walled and moated palace complex covers 74 ha/183 acres.

force An influence applied to an unrestrained object which results in a change in its motion, causing it to accelerate in some way; symbol *F*, units N (newton); a vector quantity. Force equals mass of object multiplied by acceleration (Newton's second law).

forces of nature In physics, taken to mean gravitation, electromagnetism, strong nuclear force, and weak nuclear forces. (*see panel p.346*)

Ford, Anna (1943–) Broadcaster, born in Tewkesbury, Gloucestershire. She worked with Granada TV and the BBC before becoming an ITN newscaster (1978–80) and helping to present *TV am* (1980–2). She then worked as a freelance broadcaster and writer, and (from 1989) with BBC news and current affairs, retiring in 2006.

Ford, Elbur *Hibbert, Eleanor*

Ford, Ford Madox, originally **Ford Hermann Hueffer** (1873–1939) Writer and literary critic, born in Merton, Surrey. He is best known for his novel *The Good Soldier* (1915) and for founding the *English Review* (1908). Later works include a series of war novels, and the tetralogy *Parade's End* (1920s).

Ford, Gerald R(udolph) (1913–2006) US statesman and 38th president (1974–6), born in Omaha, NE. A Republican member of the House of Representatives (1949–73), on the resignation of Spiro Agnew in 1973 he was appointed vice-president, and became president when Nixon resigned because of the Water-

football, American

goal

160 ft (48.8 m)

18 ft (5.64 m)

5
10
15
20
25
30
35
40
45
50
45
40
35
30
25
20
15
10
5

120 yd (109.8 m)

100 yd (91.4 m)

side zone

5 yd (4.57 m)

70 ft 9 in (21.5 m)

goal line

end zone

end line

American football

The national fall (autumn) and winter sport in the USA, played between September and January. It resembles rugby, but forward passing of the ball is permitted. It is played on a rectangular field 360 ft (110 m) by 160 ft (49 m), divided into 5-yd (4·6-m) segments which give the field a gridiron effect. The object is to score *touchdowns* - the moving of the ball across the goal line in a running or passing play. This is similar to the *try* in rugby, but progress has to be made upfield by a series of *plays*, and a team must make 10 yd (9·1 m) of ground within four plays, otherwise it loses possession of the ball. Six points are awarded for a touchdown and one point for a *conversion* (kicking the ball between the posts and over the crossbar), as in rugby. A goal kicked from anywhere on the field (a *field goal*) is worth 3 points. Teams consist of more than 40 squad members, but only 11 are allowed on the field for each team at any one time. Special units come on for specific roles. When a team is attacking, the 11 players will be different from those on the field when they are on the defence. The game was first played in US colleges in the mid-19th-c, and the first rules were drawn up at Princeton College in 1867. The professional game in the USA comes under the auspices of the National Football League, which is divided into the American Football Conference (AFC) and National Football Conference (NFC). The leading teams of the two conferences meet in a series of play-off games each January for the Super Bowl (instituted 1966–7).

football, Association

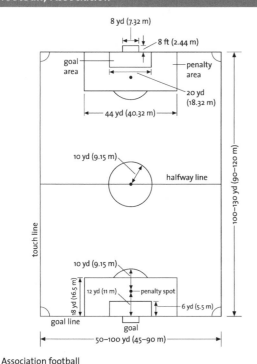

8 yd (7.32 m)

8 ft (2.44 m)

goal area

penalty area

20 yd (18.32 m)

44 yd (40.32 m)

10 yd (9.15 m)

halfway line

100–130 yd (90–120 m)

touch line

10 yd (9.15 m)

18 yd (16.5 m)

12 yd (11 m)

penalty spot

6 yd (5.5 m)

goal line

goal

50–100 yd (45–90 m)

Association football

An 11-a-side team game played on a grass or synthetic pitch (or field) measuring 90–120 m/100–130 yd in length, and 45–90 m/50–100 yd wide. At each end of the field is a goal net measuring 8 yd (7·3 m) wide by 8 ft (2·4 m) high. The object is to move the ball around the field, with the feet or head, until a player is in a position to put the ball into the net and score a goal. The goalkeeper defends the goal, and he is the only person allowed to touch the ball with his hands while it is in play, provided he touches it within his specifically defined area. The ancient Greeks, Chinese, Egyptians, and Romans all played a form of football. In the early 19th-c it became an organized game in Britain, and was played in most universities and public schools. Standard rules were drawn up at Cambridge University in 1848, and in 1863 the Football Association was formed. The first FA Cup final was played in 1872. Professionalism increased amongst northern clubs, and the game was legalized in 1885. The Football League was formed in 1888. The world governing body, the Fédération Internationale de Football Association (FIFA), was formed in Paris in 1904. The first World Cup was organized in Uruguay in 1930. The European governing body, the Union of European Football Associations (UEFA), was formed in 1954, and it controls the major European club competitions.

football, Australian Rules

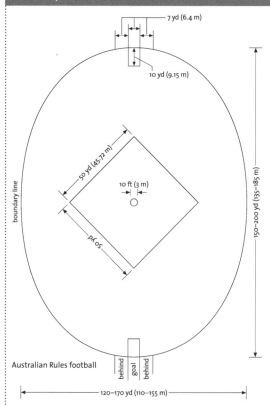

7 yd (6.4 m)

10 yd (9.15 m)

50 yd (45.72 m)

10 ft (3 m)

50 yd

boundary line

150–200 yd (135–185 m)

Australian Rules football

behind | goal | behind

120–170 yd (110–155 m)

A handling and kicking game which is a cross between association football and rugby. Surprisingly, it has few rules. It is played with 18 players per side on an oval field measuring c.165 m/180 yd long by c.137 m/150 yd wide. The object is to score goals by kicking the ball between the opponent's goal posts for six points. Smaller posts are positioned either side of the main goal, and if the ball is kicked through that area then 1 point is scored. The first recorded game was played between Scotch College and Melbourne Grammar School in 1858.

gate scandal. The full pardon he granted to Nixon made him unpopular, and he was defeated in the 1976 presidential election by Jimmy Carter.

Ford, Harrison (1942–) Actor, born in Chicago, IL. He achieved stardom in *Star Wars* (1977) and its two sequels, and also found great popularity as the archaeologist adventurer 'Indiana Jones' in a series of films beginning with *Raiders of the Lost Ark* (1981). Later films include *Witness* (1985, Oscar nomination), *The Fugitive* (1993), *What Lies Beneath* (2000), and *Firewall* (2005).

Ford, Henry (1863–1947) Automobile engineer and manufacturer, born in Dearborn, MI. He produced his first petrol-driven motor car in 1893, and in 1899 founded a company in Detroit, designing his own cars. In 1903 he started the Ford Motor Company, pioneering the modern 'assembly line' mass-production techniques for his famous Model T (1908–9). In 1919 he was succeeded by his son **Edsel Ford** (1893–1943), and in 1945 by his grandson **Henry Ford** (1917–87).

Ford, John (c.1586–c.1640) Playwright, born in Ilsington, Devon. His plays include *The Lover's Melancholy* (1629) and *'Tis Pity She's a Whore* (1633).

Ford, John, originally **Sean Aloysius O'Fearna** (1895–1973) Film director, born in Cape Elizabeth, ME. His skilful portrayal of US pioneering history reached a peak with *Stagecoach* (1939), *The Informer* (1935, Oscar), and *The Grapes of Wrath* (1940, Oscar). Later films include *How Green Was My Valley* (1941, Oscar) and *The Quiet Man* (1952, Oscar).

Ford Foundation A philanthropic foundation set up in 1936 by Henry Ford and his son, Edsel, as an international charity mainly concerned with food shortages and population control in developing nations.

Foreign Legion The elite formation of the French Army, recruited from non-French nationals. *La Légion Etrangère* was first raised in 1831, and retains its reputation for toughness.

forensic medicine The discipline which relates the practice of medicine to the law. It includes such areas as abortion, the provision of medicines, and the supply of human tissues for surgical transplantation. *Forensic pathology* includes the study of wounds self-inflicted or caused by others, and of death in which other factors than natural causes might have played a part.

Forester, C(ecil) S(cott) (1899–1966) Writer, born in Cairo. Chiefly a novelist, he also wrote biographical and travel books. He is known especially for his creation of Captain Horatio Hornblower. Several of his works have been filmed, notably *The African Queen* (1935).

forestry The business of growing, harvesting, and marketing trees and managing the associated wildlife and recreational resources. Over 31% of the world's land area is covered by forest and woodland. Total world production of forest products reached 3.9 thousand million cubic m/5.1 thousand million cubic yd in 1990.

forgery The act of falsely making, reproducing, altering, or signing a document or instrument with the intention of defrauding others. It is essential to the criminal offence of forgery that the false document is to be used as if it were genuine, as in the cases of wills and bank-notes.

football, Rugby Union

Rugby Union football

A team ball game played with an oval ball on a rectangular playing area. Rugby developed from the kicking game of football, taking its name from the public school at Rugby, Warwickshire, C England, which had its own distinct form of football, although there was no formal separation from football until a dispute over rules led in 1871 to clubs seceding from the Football Association to form the Rugby Football Union. The first international, England v. Scotland, was also played in 1871. Rugby itself split in 1895 when the leading North of England clubs formed the Northern Union (subsequently Rugby League). Rugby is most popular in Britain and the former White Commonwealth (Australia, New Zealand, and South Africa) with only France so far offering a serious challenge to British and former colonial dominance. The first World Cup was played in 1987 and the game accepted professionalism in 1995. There are 15 players (reduced from 20 in 1876). The aim of the game is to score either through tries - grounding the ball behind the opposing goal line - or goals, kicking the ball through the opposition posts, above the uprights. Current scoring values are: try 5 points, conversion 2, penalty goal or drop goal 3. (*see also* **football, Rugby League**)

---

forget-me-not An annual or perennial, native to temperate regions; flowers tubular with five spreading lobes, often pink in bud, opening blue. (Genus: *Myosotis*, 50 species. Family: Boraginaceae.)

formaldehyde [faw(r)maldehiyd] HCHO, IUPAC **methanal**, boiling point $-21°C$. The simplest aldehyde, a gas with a characteristic odour, which polymerizes readily and reversibly to **paraformaldehyde** $(CH_2O)_n$. An aqueous solution, called *formalin*, is used as a disinfectant and preservative.

Formalists A school of critics in early 20th-c Russia who believed that formal properties were of primary importance in a work of art. Roman Jakobson (1896–1982) later exported their ideas, which had considerable influence on later criticism.

Forman, Miloš (1932–) Film director, born in Caslav, Czech Republic. His tragi-comedy of insanity, *One Flew Over the Cuckoo's Nest* (1975), won five Oscars, and was followed by

Hair (1979), *Amadeus* (1983, Oscar), *The People vs. Larry Flynt* (1996), and *Man on the Moon* (1999).

Formentera [formentayra] $38°43N$ $1°26E$; pop (2000e) 4390; area $100 km^2/39$ sq mi. Island in the Balearic Is, Spain; capital, San Francisco.

formic acid HCOOH, IUPAC **methanoic acid**, boiling point $101°C$. A liquid with a pungent odour, the simplest carboxylic acid. It is a moderately strong acid; partially neutralized solutions have a pH of about 4. Formic acid is secreted by some insects, especially red ants, in the sting. It is used in textile and leather manufacture, and as an industrial solvent.

Fornax (Lat 'furnace') A faint S constellation.

Forster, E(dward) M(organ) (1879–1970) Writer, born in London. His works include *Where Angels Fear to Tread* (1905), *The Longest Journey* (1907), *A Room with a View* (1908), *Howard's End* (1910), and his masterpiece, *A Passage to India* (1924).

Forces Of Nature

	gravity	electro-magnetism	weak nuclear force	strong nuclear force
Range m	infinite	infinite	10^{-18} (subatomic)	10^{-15} (subatomic)
Relative strength	6×10^{-39}	1/137	10^{-5}	1
Examples of application	orbit of Earth around Sun	force between electrical charges	radioactive β-decay	binds atomic nuclei together

Forsyth, Bruce [faw(r)siyth], popular name of **Bruce Joseph Forsyth-Johnson** (1928–) Entertainer, born in Edmonton, Greater London. He trained as a dancer, but is best known as the compère or host on many UK television shows, such as *Sunday Night at the London Palladium* (1958–60), *The Generation Game* (1971–8, 1992–4), and *Play Your Cards Right* (three series). He has co-hosted BBC's *Strictly Come Dancing* since 2003.

Forsyth, Frederick [faw(r)siyth] (1938–) Writer of suspense thrillers, born in Ashford, Kent. His reputation rests on three taut thrillers, *The Day of the Jackal* (1971), *The Odessa File* (1972), and *The Dogs of War* (1974). Later novels include *The Fourth Protocol* (1984), *Avenger* (2003), and *The Afghan* (2006).

forsythia A deciduous shrub, suckering and rooting from the tips of arching branches, native to SE Europe and E Asia; flowers yellow, with four spreading petals, in clusters appearing before leaves on last season's wood. (Genus: *Forsythia*, 7 species. Family: Oleaceae.)

Fortaleza [faw(r)talayza] 3°45S 38°35W, pop (2000e) 2 069 000. Port in NE Brazil; airfield; railway; commercial and industrial centre, especially for agriculture; two universities (1955, 1973); cathedral.

Fort-de-France [faw(r) duh frãs], formerly **Fort Royal** 14°36N 61°05W, pop (2000e) 114 000. Capital town of Martinique, Lesser Antilles, E Caribbean; airport; naval base; cathedral (1895).

Forth, River River in SEC Scotland; formed at Aberfoyle by the confluence of headstreams rising on Ben Lomond; flows generally E, widening into the Firth of Forth estuary; length 186 km/116 mi.

Fort Knox A US army post established in Kentucky in 1917, and noted as the site, since 1937, of the US Bullion Depository. Built in 18 months at a cost of $560 000, the door alone of its steel and concrete vault weighs more than 20 tons.

FORTRAN [faw(r)tran] An acronym of **FORmula TRANslation**, a widely used high-level computer programming language developed in the USA during the 1960s for mathematical, engineering, and scientific use.

Fortuna [faw(r)toona] The ancient Roman goddess of Fortune. In the Middle Ages she was highly revered as a divine and moral figure, redressing human pride. Her wheel is frequently referred to, with figures seen climbing and falling off.

Fort William 56°49N 5°07W, pop (2000e) 110 000. Town in Highland, W Scotland; on E side of Loch Linnhe; airfield; railway; Inverlochy castle; Ben Nevis (SE).

Fort Worth 32°45N 97°18W, pop (2000e) 534 700. City in NE Texas, USA, on the Trinity R; established as an army post, 1847; important livestock market centre; airport at Dallas–Fort Worth; airfield; railway; university (1873).

Forty-five Rebellion The Jacobite rebellion of 1745–6 to restore the Catholic Stuart kings to the British throne. It began in July 1745 when Charles Edward Stuart ('the Young Pretender') arrived in Scotland and proclaimed his father ('the Old Pretender') King James III. The Jacobite forces reached as far south as Derby, but the rebellion was crushingly defeated at Culloden in 1746.

forty-niners Adventurers who swarmed to California in 1849, after the discovery of gold there the previous year. Their number may have been as high as 100 000.

forum The Roman equivalent of the Greek *agora*; originally the market-place of a town, later its civic centre. Besides shops and stalls, it contained the principal municipal buildings, such as the Council chamber and law courts.

Fosse Way *Roman roads*

fossil The remains of a once-living organism, usually restricted to organisms that lived prior to the last Ice Age. Fossils typically comprise the bodies or part of the organisms themselves, but also include a variety of trace fossils such as tracks and faeces.

fossil fuel Fuels derived from the fossilized remains of plants and animals, such as peat, coal, and crude oil.

Foster, Jodie, originally **Alicia Christian Foster** (1962–) Film actress, born in Los Angeles, CA. Known for her child roles in such films as *Bugsy Malone* (1976), as an adult actress she received Oscars for her roles in *The Accused* (1988) and *The Silence of the Lambs* (1991), and made her directorial debut with *Little Man Tate* (1991). Later films include *Contact* (1997), *Anna and the King* (1999), *Panic Room* (2002), and *Inside Man* (2006).

Foster, Stephen (Collins) (1826–64) Songwriter, born in Pittsburgh, PA. Songs such as 'Oh! Susanna' (1848), 'The Old Folks at Home' (1851), and 'Beautiful Dreamer' (1864) sold thousands of song-sheets, and became seminal works of the American songwriting tradition.

Foucault, (Jean Bernard) Léon [fookoh] (1819–68) Physicist, born in Paris. He determined the velocity of light, invented the gyroscope (1852), and improved the mirrors of reflecting telescopes (1858).

Foucault, Michel [fookoh] (1926–84) Philosopher, born in Poitiers, France. He sought consistently to test cultural assumptions in given historical contexts. His most important writings include *Histoire de la folie* (1961, trans Madness and Civilization) and *Les mots et les choses* (1966, trans The Order of Things).

Foucault pendulum [fookoh] A pendulum that is free to swing in any direction, such that the plane of swing gradually rotates as the Earth turns under it; devised by French physicist Léon Foucault in 1851. It was used as proof that the Earth spins.

Fouché, Joseph, duc d'Otrante (Duke of Otranto) [fooshay] (1759–1820) French statesman, born in Nantes, France. He was elected to the National Convention in 1792 as a Jacobin, and in 1799 became Minister of Police, a post which he held successfully until 1815.

foul marten *polecat*

foumart [foomah(r)t] *polecat*

founding Casting molten metal in a mould made to a high degree of precision. Mould materials are compounded of sand and clay, packed over a pattern to which the eventual casting is to conform.

Fountains Abbey A Cistercian monastery founded in 1132 near Ripon, North Yorkshire, UK; a world heritage site. The abbey ruins stand in the magnificent water gardens of Studley Royal.

Fouqué, Friedrich Heinrich Karl, Baron de la Motte [fookay] (1777–1843) Romantic author, born in Brandenburg, Germany. He published a long series of romances based on Norse legend and old French poetry, his masterpiece being *Undine* (1811).

Fouquet, Jean [fookay] (c.1420–c.1480) Painter, born in Tours, France. His most notable illuminations are found in the *Antiquities of the Jews* of Josephus and the *Hours of Etienne Chevalier* at Chantilly.

Fouquet, Nicolas, vicomte de (Viscount of) **Melun et de Vaux, Marquis de Belle-Isle** [fookay] (1615–80) French statesman, born in Paris. Mazarin made him *procureur-général* to the parliament of Paris (1650) and Superintendent of Finance (1653). He became extremely rich, and was ambitious to succeed Mazarin, but was arrested for embezzlement (1661), and imprisoned.

Four Freedoms Four basic human rights proclaimed in an annual message to Congress by President Roosevelt. They included freedom of speech and worship, and freedom from want and fear.

Four Horsemen of the Apocalypse Symbolic Biblical characters described in *Rev* 6 (also *Zech* 6.1–7). Each comes on a steed of different colour, symbolizing devastations associated with the world's end (black = famine; red = bloodshed, war; pale = pestilence, death), except for the white horse, which has a 'crown' and is sent 'to conquer'.

France

200 km
100 mi

NORTH SEA

UNITED KINGDOM

EUROPE

BEL.
LUX.
GERMANY

Calais
Boulogne
Cherbourg   Dieppe   Lille
Amiens
Le Havre   Nancy
Seine   Strasbourg
Paris
BRITTANY   Chartres   Fontainebleau
Nantes   Dijon
Tours   SWITZ.
F R A N C E
Limoges   Lyon   A L P S
Bay of Biscay   △ Mont Blanc 4807m
Bordeaux   Grenoble   ITALY
MASSIF CENTRAL
Bayonne   Marseille   Nice   MONACO
SPAIN   PYRÉNÉES   Côte d'Azur   Corsica
MEDITERRANEAN SEA

□ International Airport

ancient **Gallia**, official name **Republic of France**, Fr **République Française**

Local name France

Timezone GMT +1

Area 551 000 km²/212 686 sq mi

Population total (2002e) 59 440 000

Status Republic

Capital Paris

Languages French (official), Breton, Occitan and Alsatian are also spoken

Ethnic groups Celtic and Latin origin (91%), Breton, Catalan, and large immigrant population (including Portuguese, Algerian, Moroccan, and Arab minorities)

Religions Roman Catholic (90%), Protestant (4%), Muslim (3%), Jewish (1%)

Physical features Bounded S and E by large mountain ranges,

notably (interior) the Massif Central, Jura, and Alps (E), rising to 4807 m/15 771 ft at Mont Blanc, and the Pyrénées (S); chief rivers include Loire (longest at 1020 km/633 mi), Rhône, Seine, Garonne; 60% of land arable.

Climate Mediterranean climate in S, with warm, moist winters and hot, dry summers; average temperatures, 3°C (Jan), 18°C (Jul); continental climate in E; average annual rainfall 786 mm/31 in; heatwave in August 2003 caused deaths of many elderly people.

Currency 1 euro (EUR) = 100 cents (previous to February 2002, 1 French Franc (FRF) = 100 centimes).

Economy Main industries include wine, fruit, cheese; perfume, textiles, clothing; steel, chemicals, machinery, cars, aircraft; natural resources of coal, iron ore, bauxite, timber; tourism important.

GDP (2002e) $1·558 tn, per capita $26 000

Human Development Index (2002) 0·928

History Celtic-speaking Gauls dominant by 5th-c BC; part of Roman Empire, 125 BC to 5th-c AD; feudal monarchy founded by Hugh Capet, 987; Plantagenets of England acquired several territories, 12th-c; lands gradually recovered in Hundred Years' War, 1337–1453, apart from Calais (regained in 1558); Capetian dynasty followed by the Valois, from 1328, and the Bourbons, from 1589; Wars of Religion, 1562–95; monarchy overthrown by the French Revolution, 1789; First Republic declared, 1792; French Revolutionary Wars 1793–99; First Empire, ruled by Napoleon, 1804–14; monarchy restored, 1814–48; Second Republic, 1848–52, and Second Empire, 1852–70, ruled by Louis Napoleon; Third Republic, 1870–1940; great political instability between World Wars, with several governments holding office for short periods; occupied by Germany 1940–4, with pro-German government at Vichy, and Free French in London under de Gaulle; Fourth Republic, 1946; war with Indo-China, 1946–54; conflict in Algeria, 1954–62; Fifth Republic, 1958; founder member of European Union (formerly EC), 1958; referendum on European constitution rejected, May 2005; governed by a President, an appointed Prime Minster, a Council of Ministers, bicameral National Assembly, and Senate.

Head of State
1969–74 Georges Pompidou
1974–81 Valéry Giscard d'Estaing
1981–95 François Mitterrand
1995–2007 Jacques René Chirac
2007– Nicolas Sarkozy

Head of Government
1959–62 Michel Debré
1962–8 Georges Pompidou
1968–9 Maurice Couve de Murville
1969–72 Jacques Chaban Delmas
1972–4 Pierre Messmer
1974–6 Jacques Chirac
1976–81 Raymond Barre
1981–4 Pierre Mauroy
1984–6 Laurent Fabius
1986–8 Jacques Chirac

Fourier, (Jean Baptiste) Joseph, Baron [fooryay] (1768–1830) Mathematician, born in Auxerre, France. While working on the flow of heat he discovered the theorem which now bears his name, that any function of a variable can be expanded in a series of sines of multiples of the variable (the **Fourier series**).

Four Noble Truths The summary of the central teachings of Buddha. **1** All life involves suffering, and is inevitably sorrowful. **2** The cause of suffering and sorrow is craving or desire arising

from ignorance. **3** There is escape from suffering, because craving and desire can end. **4** There is an Eightfold Path leading to the end of suffering and sorrow.

four-stroke engine An engine that works on a practical cycle with one in every four strokes of the piston being the power stroke. This is the type of engine normally used to drive motor cars.

Fourteen Points A peace programme outlined by US President Wilson to Congress in 1918. The Germans subsequently asked

☐ International Airport

1988–91 Michel Rocard
1991–2 Edith Cresson
1992–3 Pierre Bérégovoy
1993–5 Edouard Balladur
1995–7 Alain Juppé
1997–2002 Lionel Jospin
2002–5 Jean-Pierre Raffarin
2005–7 Dominique de Villepin
2007– François Fillon

Internal Collective Territory
Island of Corsica in the Mediterranean Sea: area 8680 km^2/ 3350 sq mi; capital, Ajaccio; GMT +1

Overseas departments
Name / Area (km^2/sq mi) / Capital / GMT
Guadeloupe / 1779 / 687 / Basse-Terre / -4
Guiana / 90 909 / 35 091 / Cayenne / -3
Martinique / 1079 / 416 / Fort-de-France / -4
Mayotte / 374 / 144 / Dzaoudzi / +3
Réunion / 2512 / 970 / St Denis / +4
St-Pierre-et-Miquelon / 240 / 93 / St Pierre / -3

Overseas territories
Name / Area (km^2/sq mi) / Capital (chief centre) / GMT
French Polynesia / 3941 / 1521 / Papeete / -6
New Caledonia / 18 575 / 7170 / Nouméa / +11
Southern and Antarctic Territories / 10 100 / 3900 / Port-aux-Français
Wallis and Futuna / 274 / 106 / Matu Utu / +12

Wilson for an armistice agreement based on their acceptance of these points, which, with two reservations, were accepted by the Allied powers as the basis for a peace settlement.
Fourth of July, July Fourth, or **Independence Day** A public holiday in the USA, commemorating the adoption of the Declaration of Independence (4 Jul 1776).
Fou Ts'ong [foo tsong] (1934–) Concert pianist, born in Shanghai, China. Acclaimed as an interpreter of Mozart and Chopin, in

1958 he made his base in London, and performed extensively on the international circuit.
Fowler, H(enry) W(atson) (1858–1933) Lexicographer, born in Tonbridge, Kent. With his brother, **F(rank) G(eorge) Fowler** (1871–1918), they began a literary partnership which led to *The King's English* (1906) and the *Concise Oxford Dictionary* (1911). Henry later wrote the *Dictionary of Modern English Usage* (1926).
Fowler, William A(lfred) (1911–95) Astrophysicist, born in Pittsburgh, PA. He worked on the application of nuclear physics to all aspects of astronomy, and is considered the founder of the theory of nucleosynthesis, he was awarded the Nobel Prize for Physics in 1983.
Fowles, John (Robert) (1926–2005) Writer, born in London. His major works include *The Magus* (1966), *The French Lieutenant's Woman* (1969, filmed 1981) and *Tessera* (1993). Other work includes the autobiographical *Daniel Martin* (1977), a book of essays entitled *Wormholes* (1998), and *The Journals: Volume 1* (2003).
fowl pest The name applied to two diseases of birds, **fowl plague** and **Newcastle disease**; several strains, caused by viruses; attacks nervous, digestive, and respiratory systems; often fatal.
Fox A North American Algonkin Indian group originally from N Wisconsin. They settled permanently in Iowa in 1842, retaining many traditional organizational features.
Fox, Charles James (1749–1806) British statesman and foreign secretary (1782, 1783, 1806), born in London. He became secretary of state after Lord North's downfall, and in 1783 formed a coalition with him, which held office for a short period.
Fox, George (1624–91) Founder of the Quakers, born in Fenny Drayton, Leicestershire. He became a travelling preacher and a missionary, and was imprisoned on several occasions. As a writer he is remembered by his *Journal* (posthumously published), which records the birth of the Quaker movement.
fox A small member of the dog family (21 species), worldwide except SE Asia; usually thin muzzle, large pointed ears, long bushy tail; hunts alone; renowned for its cunning; often nocturnal; lives in a den.
foxglove A softly hairy biennial (*Digitalis purpurea*) growing to 150 cm/5 ft, native to Europe; tall flower-spike produced in second year; flowers all on one side of the stem, bell-shaped with five very short lobes, drooping, usually pink to purple. It is the original source of the heart drug digitalin. (Family: Scrophulariaceae.)
fox-grape *grapevine*
foxhound A domestic dog bred for hunting foxes; large with brown, black, and white coat; soft ears; two breeds: the **English foxhound**, and its larger descendant, the **American foxhound**.
foxhunting A blood sport, which developed in the UK in the late 17th-c, and which since the early 19th-c has been regarded as the pastime of the aristocracy and the wealthy. The foxhunting season lasts from November to April. Each hunt is controlled by a *master of hounds*, and the hounds are controlled by the *huntsman*. In recent years, animal rights saboteurs have attempted to thwart hunts, and there is a movement to try to get the sport banned in the UK. In November 2004 the Parliament Act was invoked to force through a bill banning hunting with hounds in England and Wales. The Hunting Bill, in force from February 2005, over-rode the objections from the House of Lords, which fought the legislation for seven years.
foxtail millet *millet*
fox terrier An active British terrier with a deep chest, pointed muzzle, and soft, folded ears held high; tail usually docked short when young; usually white with black and brown markings; two forms: **wire-haired** and **smooth-haired**.
Foxx, Jamie, originally **Eric Morlon Bishop** (1967–) Actor and singer, born in Terrell, TX. His success as a stand-up comedian/impersonator led him to Los Angeles, where he gained parts in

the TV comedy sketch show *In Living Color* (1990), and later had his own series *The Jamie Foxx Show* (1996). His feature films include *Any Given Sunday* (1999), *Ali* (2001), *Collateral* (2004, Golden Globe, Oscar nomination), *Ray* (2004, Golden Globe, Oscar), and *Dreamgirls* (2006).

Foyle, Lough Inlet of the Atlantic, on the N coast of Ireland; mouth 1·5 km/0·9 mi wide; length, 24 km/15 mi; width, 16 km/10 mi.

fractals Geometrical entities characterized by basic patterns that are repeated at ever decreasing sizes. For example, trees describe an approximate fractal pattern, as the trunk divides into branches which further subdivide into smaller branches which ultimately subdivide into twigs; at each stage of division the pattern is a smaller version of the original. They were devised in 1967 by French mathematician Benoit Mandelbrot.

fractions *numbers*

fracture (medicine) A physical break in the continuity of a bone, most commonly the result of external force. The break takes a number of forms, from a hairline transverse fracture with no displacement (a **greenstick fracture**) to a severe fracture in which the bone is shattered into a number of small pieces (**comminuted fracture**). Well-aligned fragments may unite while being kept in place by a simple splint. Displaced fractures may need manipulation and the insertion of metal pins to hold the pieces together while they heal.

frame relay A technology developed by telephone companies in North America to transfer digitally coded messages over the telephone network at very high speed using fibre-optic cabling. SONET (Sychronous Optical NETwork) is the name given to a fibre-based mesh network employing frame relay to deliver various levels of service, on demand, to a customer. OC-1 offers 51·84 Mbps (megabauds per second) while OC-12 offers 622·08 Mbps (12 × OC-1).

Framework programme A programme of research, funded by the European Commission, designed to improve the level of technical expertise and application within the European Union. It includes the ESPRIT and RACE programmes.

Frampton, Sir George James (1860–1928) Sculptor, born in London. Among his works are 'Peter Pan' in Kensington Gardens, London, and the lions at the British Museum.

franc The former currency unit of many countries, notably France, Belgium, and Switzerland, now replaced by the Euro in EU countries. The name derives from the words on a 14th-c gold coin, *Francorum rex* ('King of the Franks').

France *pp.348–49*

France, Anatole [frãs], pseudonym of **Jacques Anatole François Thibault** (1844–1924) Writer, born in Paris. He wrote several lively novels, which contrast with his later, satirical works, notably *L'Île des pingouins* (1908, Penguin Island). The Dreyfus case (1896) stirred him into politics as a champion of internationalism. He was awarded the Nobel Prize for Literature in 1921.

Francis I (1494–1547) King of France (1515–47), born in Cognac. The dominant feature of his reign was his rivalry with the Emperor Charles V, which led to a series of wars (1521–6, 1528–9, 1536–8, 1542–4). After establishing his military reputation against the Swiss at Marignano (1515), he later suffered a number of reverses, including his capture at Pavia (1525).

Francis II (Emperor) (1768–1835) Last Holy Roman Emperor (1792–1806), the first Emperor of Austria (1804–35), and King of Hungary (1792–30) and Bohemia (1792–1835), born in Florence, Italy. Defeated on several occasions by Napoleon, he made a short-lived alliance with him, but later joined with Russia and Prussia to win the Battle of Leipzig (1813).

Francis of Assisi, St [aseezee], originally **Giovanni Bernardone** (?1181–1226) Founder of the Franciscan Order, born in Assisi, Italy. In 1205 he left his worldly life, and by 1210 had formed a brotherhood for which he drew up a rule which became the Franciscan way of life. He was canonized in 1228. He is often represented in art among animals and birds, which he called his sisters and brothers. Feast day 4 October.

Francis of Sales, St [saylz], Fr [sahl] (1567–1622) Roman Catholic bishop and writer, born in Sales, France. A distinguished preacher, he became Bishop of Nicopolis (1599) and Bishop of Geneva (1602), where he helped to found a congregation of nuns of the Visitation. He was canonized in 1665. Feast day 24 January.

Franciscans Religious orders founded by St Francis of Assisi in the early 13th-c. The first order, of **Friars Minor**, is now divided into three groups: the **Observants** (**OFM**), the **Conventuals** (**OFM-Conv**), and the **Capuchins** (**OFMCap**). The second order is made up of nuns, known as the **Poor Clares** (**PC**). The third order is a lay fraternity.

Francis Joseph I, Ger **Franz Josef I** (1830–1916) Emperor of Austria (1848–1916) and king of Hungary (1867–1916), born near Vienna. He was defeated by the Prussians in 1866, and established the Dual Monarchy of Austria–Hungary in 1867. His attack on Serbia in 1914 precipitated World War 1.

Francistown 21°11S 27°32E, pop (2000e) 67 300. Independent township in Botswana, S Africa; altitude 990 m/3248 ft; area 79 km²/49 sq mi; industrial and commercial centre of Botswana; airfield; railway.

Francis Xavier, St [zayvier], Span **San Francisco Javier**, known as **the Apostle of the Indies** (1506–52) Roman Catholic missionary who brought Christianity to India and the Far East, born in Navarre, Spain. He became one of the first seven members of the Jesuit order (1534), and began his missionary work in Goa, India (1542). He was canonized in 1622. Feast day 3 December.

Franck, César (Auguste) [frãk, sayzah(r)] (1822–90) Composer, born in Liège, Belgium. His reputation rests on a few masterpieces all written after the age of 50, the best known being a violin sonata, a string quartet, a symphony, and the *Variations symphoniques* (1885) for piano and orchestra.

Franco (Bahamonde), Francisco [frangkoh], popular name **el Caudillo** ('the leader') (1892–1975) Spanish general and dictator (1936–75), born in El Ferrol, Galicia. He led the repression of the Asturias miners' revolt (1934), and during 1935 served as chief-of-staff. In 1936 he joined the conspiracy against the Popular Front government, becoming *generalísimo* of the rebel forces. Between 1936 and 1939 he led the Nationalists to victory, and presided over the construction of an authoritarian regime that endured until his death. During World War 2, he opted for non-belligerency rather than neutrality, having offered in 1940 to fight on the side of Hitler. During the 1950s, his anti-communism made possible a rapprochement with the Western powers. In 1969 he announced that upon his death the monarchy would return in the person of Juan Carlos, grandson of Spain's last ruling king.

Franco-German Treaty of Co-operation A treaty signed (Jan 1963) by President de Gaulle and Chancellor Adenauer. It made provisions for regular summit meetings, and co-operation and consultation in foreign, economic, and cultural affairs.

francolin A partridge native to Africa and S Asia; large bird with patches of bare skin on head and neck. (Genus: *Francolinus*, 40 species.)

Francome, John [frangkuhm] (1952–) Jockey and trainer, born in Swindon, Wiltshire. In 1970–85 he rode a record 1138 winners over fences. He was seven times National Hunt champion jockey (1976, 1979, 1981–5).

Franco-Prussian War (1870–1) A conflict occasioned by the Hohenzollern candidature for the Spanish throne and the Ems telegram, and caused by the changing balance of power in Europe. It resulted in crushing defeats for France at Sedan and Metz, the siege of Paris, and the humiliating Treaty of Frankfurt.

frangipani [franjipahnee] A shrub or small tree (*Plumeria rubra*) growing to c.6 m/20 ft, native to tropical America; leaves oval; flowers in large clusters, very fragrant, five petals, white, yellow, or pink. The scented flowers are often placed in Buddhist temples. (Family: Apocynaceae.)

Frank, Anne (1929–45) Jewish diarist and concentration camp victim, born in Frankfurt, Germany. Her family fled from the Nazis to The Netherlands in 1933, and after the Nazi occupation hid with her family in a sealed-off office flat in Amsterdam from 1942 until they were betrayed in 1944. She died in Belsen concentration camp. The lively, moving diary she kept during her concealment was published in 1947. The flat where the family hid, at 263 Prinsengracht, is now the Anne Frankmuseum. In 2007, previously undisclosed records of her family's attempts to emigrate to the USA in 1941 were found in a Jewish archive in New York.

Frankenstein A soulless creature made from parts of corpses and animated by supposed scientific means. In Mary Shelley's novel (1818), Frankenstein was the name of the monster's creator, but it has since become transferred to the monster itself. The story was made into a film in 1931 by James Whale, with Boris Karloff as the monster, and has since given rise to a whole genre of cinema films.

Frankfort [frangkfert] 38°12N 84°52W, pop (2000e) 27 700. Capital of state in NC Kentucky, USA; founded by Daniel Boone, 1770; state capital, 1792; railway; university; trade and shipping centre for tobacco, livestock, and limestone.

Frankfurt (am Main) [frangkfoort, miyn] 50°07N 8°40E, pop (2000e) 661 000. Manufacturing and commercial city in Germany; port on R Main; most of the German emperors crowned here; international junction for rail, road, and air traffic; university (1914); headquarters of the leading German stock exchange; birthplace of Goethe; cathedral (13th–15th-c), many trade fairs.

Frankfurt (an der Oder) [frangkfoort, ohder] 52°50N 14°31E, pop (2000e) 91 900. City in Germany on R Oder; badly bombed in World War 2; railway.

frankincense An evergreen tree or shrub (*Boswellia carteri*) growing to 6 m/20 ft, native to Somaliland; flowers white, 5-petalled. Aromatic resin is obtained from cuts in the bark. (Family: Burseraceae.)

Franklin, Benjamin (1706–90) US statesman, writer, and scientist, born in Boston, MA. He set up a printing house in Philadelphia, and built a reputation as a journalist. In 1746 he began his research into electricity, proving that lightning and electricity are identical, and suggesting that buildings be protected by lightning conductors. In 1776 he was actively involved in framing the Declaration of Independence. He was US minister in Paris until 1785, then three times president of the State of Pennsylvania. After taking part in the Federal Constitutional Convention (1787), he retired from public life, and wrote an acclaimed autobiography.

Franklin, Sir John (1786–1847) Arctic explorer, born in Spilsby, Lincolnshire. He commanded an expedition to discover the Northwest Passage, but his ships were beleaguered by thick ice in the Victoria Strait, and he and his crew died. Their remains, and a record of the expedition, were found several years later.

Franklin, (Stella Maria Sarah) Miles, pseudonym **Brent of Bin Bin** (1879–1954) Novelist, born in Talbingo, New South Wales, Australia. Her best-known novel, *My Brilliant Career* (1901), has been described as the first Australian novel. The annual *Miles Franklin Awards* are now among Australia's most prestigious literary prizes.

Franks Germanic peoples, originally from the lower Rhine region. Charlemagne, their greatest ruler, attempted to revive the Roman Empire in the West. They gave their name to Francia, which by the 13th-c stood for what is now France.

Franks, Tommy, popular name of **Thomas Ray Franks** (1945–) US general, born in Wynnewood, OK. He graduated from military school at Fort Still, OK (1967), served in West Germany (1980s) and Korea, and was commander of the Third US Army, Fort McPherson, GA. Promoted to general (2000), he was appointed commander-in-chief of the US Central Command (2000–3). He had responsibility for the campaign in Afghanistan to destroy the Taliban regime (2001) and commanded the US-led invasion of Iraq (Mar–Apr 2003). He retired in 2003.

Franz Josef Land, Russ **Zemlya Frantsa-Iosifa** area 20 700 km²/8 000 sq mi. Archipelago in the Arctic Ocean, NW Russia; over 160 islands of volcanic origin; declared Soviet territory in 1926; uninhabited save for a meteorological station.

Fraser, Lady Antonia, *née* **Pakenham** (1932–) British writer. She is best known for her books about important historical figures, such as *Mary Queen of Scots* (1969, James Tait Black), *Kings and Queens of England* (1975, 1988), *The Six Wives of Henry VIII* (1992), *Marie Antoinette: The Journey* (2001), and *Love and Louis XIV: The Women in the Life of the Sun King* (2006). She married Harold Pinter in 1980.

Fraser, Dawn (1937–) Swimmer, born in Sydney, New South Wales, Australia. She is the only swimmer to take the same individual title at three consecutive Olympics, winning the 100 m freestyle in 1956, 1960, and 1964. She also won a gold medal in the 4 × 100 m freestyle relay in 1956. In 1964 she was banned by the Australian association for 10 years (later reduced to four) when she and some colleagues tried to take a souvenir flag from the emperor's palace in Tokyo after winning her third Olympic title. She was elected an Independent member of the New South Wales Legislative Assembly in 1988–91.

Fraser, (John) Malcolm (1930–) Australian statesman and Liberal prime minister (1975–83), born in Melbourne, Victoria, Australia. He was minister for the army (1966–8), defence (1969–71), and education and science (1968–9, 1971–2), and became prime minister in a Liberal–National Country coalition.

Fraser, Simon (1776–1862) Fur trader, born in Bennington, VT. He moved to Canada in 1784, worked as a clerk in the North-West Co, and was sent in 1805 to establish the first trading posts in the Rocky Mountains. In 1808 he followed the Fraser R, named after him, to its mouth. Simon Fraser University, in British Columbia, is also named after him.

Fraser River River in SW Canada, rises in the Rocky Mts, and enters the Pacific Ocean 16 km/10 mi S of Vancouver; length 1368 km/850 mi.

fraternity and sorority In the USA, associations at universities, for men and women respectively, named usually with two or three letters of the Greek alphabet (eg *Kappa Lamda*, *Sigma Chi*). They are formed mainly for social purposes; membership is by invitation, and is in some cases discriminatory. They are banned in some universities.

fraud A false statement made knowingly, recklessly, or without belief in its truth; the fact that there may have been no intention to cheat anyone is irrelevant. Any person injured by fraud may bring an action to recover damages in the tort (or delict) of deceit. Any contract induced by fraud can be rescinded or sometimes reformed at the instance of the innocent party.

Fraunhofer, Joseph von [frownhohfer] (1787–1826) Physicist, born in Straubing, Germany. In 1807 he founded an optical institute at Munich, where he improved prisms and telescopes, enabling him to discover the dark lines in the Sun's spectrum, since named after him.

Fray Bentos [friy bentohs] 33°10S 58°20W, pop (2000e) 22 100. River port in W Uruguay, on R Uruguay; airfield; railway; ferry; former centre of meat packing and canning industry (especially corned beef), plant now closed and made into an industrial museum.

Frazer, Sir James George (1854–1941) Social anthropologist, classicist, and folklorist, born in Glasgow, W Scotland. His major work was *The Golden Bough* (1890; rewritten in 12 vols, 1911–15).

Frears, Stephen Arthur (1941–) Director, born in Leicester, Leicestershire. He studied law at Cambridge University and gained his first experience of film production with Karel Reisz (1926–2002) and Lindsay Anderson in the 1960s. He won international acclaim with his cult classic, *My Beautiful Launderette* (1985). Other films include *Dangerous Liaisons* (1988), *Mrs Henderson Presents* (2005), and *The Queen* (2006, Best Director Oscar nomination; Evening Standard Alexander Walker Special Award; BAFTA Best Film).

Frederick I (Emperor), known as **Frederick Barbarossa** ('Redbeard') (c.1123–90) Holy Roman Emperor, born of the Hohenstaufen family, who succeeded his uncle Conrad III in 1152. His reign was a continuous struggle against unruly vassals at home, the city republics of Lombardy, and the papacy. He went on several campaigns in Italy, but was severely defeated at Legnano (1176). He also led the Third Crusade against Saladin (1189).

Frederick I (of Prussia) (1657–1713) Elector of Brandenburg from 1688 (as Frederick III) and the first King of Prussia from 1701, born in Königsberg. He maintained a large court, established a standing army, and was a great patron of the arts and learning.

Frederick II (Emperor) (1194–1250) Holy Roman Emperor (from 1220), born in Jesi, near Ancona, the grandson of Frederick I, the last of the Hohenstaufen line. He was also King of Sicily (1198) and of Germany (1212). He devoted himself to organizing his Italian territories, but his plans were frustrated by the Lombard cities and by the popes. Embarking on the Sixth Crusade in 1228, he took possession of Jerusalem, and crowned himself king there (1229).

Frederick II (of Prussia), known as **the Great** (1712–86) King of Prussia from 1740, born in Berlin, the son of Frederick William I. He seized Silesia, and defeated the Austrians at Mollwitz (1741) and Chotusitz (1742). The second Silesian War (1744–5) left him with further territories which he retained after fighting the Seven Years' War (1756–63). In 1772 he shared in the first partition of Poland. Under him, Prussia became a leading European power.

Fredericksburg, Battle of (1862) In the American Civil War, a fruitless attempt by the Northern army of 113 000 to capture the town of Fredericksburg, VA, defended by a Southern army of 75 000.

Frederick William (of Brandenburg), known as **the Great Elector** (1620–88) Elector of Brandenburg (1640–88), born near Berlin. He regulated the finances of the state, and reorganized the army and administrative system. He gained East Pomerania by the Treaty of Westphalia (1648), retrieving the sovereignty of Prussia from Poland (1657). His reforms laid the foundation of future Prussian greatness.

Frederick William III (of Prussia) (1770–1840) King of Prussia (1797–1840), the son of Frederick William II, born in Potsdam. He was severely defeated by Napoleon at Jena and Auerstadt, but after major military reforms shared in the decisive victory of Leipzig (1813). By the Treaty of Vienna (1815) he recovered his possessions.

Fredericton 45°57N 66°40W, pop (2000e) 52 000. Capital of New Brunswick, Canada, on the St John R; originally settled by Acadians, 1731, as St Anne's Point; renamed 1785 for Prince Frederick, second son of George III; capital, 1787; airfield; railway; university (1783); cathedral (1853).

Freedom Building *World Trade Center*

freedom of the press *press freedom*

freefalling *skydiving*

Free French French men and women who answered General de Gaulle's appeal, broadcast from London (18 Jun 1940) to reject the impending armistice between France and Germany, and join him in fighting on. He became leader of the Free French forces.

freehold Land or property held for use by the owner for an indefinite period of time. This is in contrast to **leasehold**, where the leaseholder has possession only for some finite period (eg 99 years), subject to payment of ground rent, reversion of the property to the ground landlord at the end of the lease, and possibly restrictions on the uses to which the property can be put.

Freeman, Morgan (1937–) Actor, born in Memphis, TN. He made his Broadway debut in 1967 in an all-black production of *Hello, Dolly*. His film credits include *Street Smart* (1987, Oscar nomination), *Driving Miss Daisy* (1989), *Seven* (1995), *Million Dollar Baby* (2004, Oscar Best Supporting Actor), and *Paradise Now* (2006).

freemasonry A movement whose members (**masons**) are joined together in an association based on brotherly love, faith, and charity; the one essential qualification for membership is a belief in a supreme being. It is known for its rituals and signs of recognition that date back to ancient religions and to the practices of the mediaeval craft guild of the stonemasons (in England). During the 17th-c the masons' clubs, or *lodges*, began to be attended by gentlemen who had no connection with the trade, and the Grand Lodge of England was founded in 1717. The organization regularly comes under attack for the secrecy with which it carries out its activities. In 2007 freemasons numbered five million worldwide, with 300 000 in England and Wales.

free port An area near a port or airport where business enterprises may import materials and components free of tax or import duties, as long as the resulting finished articles are exported. The world's largest ports in this category are Hong Kong and Singapore. The UK set up six free ports in 1984, including Liverpool and Southampton.

free radicals Oxygen molecules with one, two, or three additional electrons produced by oxidative process within the body, and thought to be responsible for tissue damage and disease. Antioxidant vitamins C and E and other micro-nutrients such as ß carotene and selenium are thought to prevent this process and may be protective against a range of disorders.

freesia A perennial (*Freesia refracta*) growing to 75 cm/30 in, producing corms, native to S Africa; flowers up to 5 cm/2 in long, goblet-shaped, creamy white, fragrant, in one-sided sprays; cultivars with orange-to-crimson or blue-to-mauve flowers. (Family: Iridaceae.)

Free State, formerly (1910–94) **Orange Free State** pop (2000e) 2 534 000; area 129 437 km²/49 963 sq mi. One of the nine new provinces established by the South African constitution of 1994, in EC South Africa; capital, Bloemfontein (also, the judicial capital of South Africa); chief languages, Sesotho (56%), Afrikaans, Xhosa; claimed by British as the Orange River Sovereignty, 1848; independence, 1854; joined Union of South Africa as Orange Free State, 1910; a largely rural province ('the breadbasket of South Africa'); rich gold deposits.

Freetown 8°30N 13°17W, pop (2000e) 722 000. Seaport capital of Sierra Leone; visited by the Portuguese, 15th-c; founded in the 1790s as a foundation for freed slaves; capital of British West Africa, 1808–74; capital of Sierra Leone, 1961; airport; university (1827).

free trade An economic doctrine that trade between countries should not be controlled in any way; there should be no tariffs or other barriers. Since the 19th-c, tariff barriers have become very common, but groups of countries may agree to lower or remove them, forming a **free-trade area**, as in the case of the EU.

free verse Verse which, while being rhythmical, observes no strict or recurrent metrical pattern. Much if not most 20th-c verse was written in free verse. Many poets (such as T S Eliot) have maintained it is more difficult to write well than formal verse.

freeze drying *lyophilization*

freezing *deep-freezing*

Frege, (Friedrich Ludwig) Gottlob [frayguh] (1848–1925) Mathematician and logician, born in Wismar, Germany. His *Begriffsschrift* (1879, 'Concept-script') outlined the first complete system of symbolic logic, and this was followed by his *Grundlagen der Arithmetik* (1884, The Foundations of Arithmetic), which influenced Bertrand Russell.

Frei (Montalva), Eduardo [fray] (1911–82) Chilean statesman and president (1964–70), born in Santiago. He became one of the leaders of the Social-Christian Falange Party in the late 1930s, and of the new Christian Democratic Party after 1957.

Freire, Paulo (Reglus Neves) [frairay] (1921–97) Philosopher and educator, born in Recife, Brazil. A lawyer, he turned to teaching and became the first director of the Department of Cultural Extension at Recife University (1961–4). Regarded as a socialist pedagogue, following the military coup of 1964 he was briefly jailed and then exiled. In Geneva he was appointed special educational adviser for the World Congress of Churches, and on his return to Brazil (1979) was made secretary of education for São Paulo. He was awarded UNESCO's Peace Prize in 1987.

Fremantle [freemantl] 32°07S 115°44E, pop (2000e) 26 300. Seaport city in Western Australia, at the mouth of the Swan R; founded as a penal colony, 1829; railway terminus; the Round House (1830), a former jail; a notable sailing club.

French *Romance languages*

French, Dawn (1957–) Comedy writer and actress, born in Holyhead, Anglesey. She met Jennifer Saunders at drama school and formed a comedy partnership, becoming widely known with the television series *French and Saunders* (from 1987). Her own series include *Murder Most Horrid* and *The Vicar of Dibley* (1994–2005; Emmy, 1998). In 2006 she appeared in the series *Jam and Jerusalem*, written by Saunders. She is married to comedy performer Lenny Henry.

French, John (Denton Pinkstone), Earl of Ypres (1852–1925) British field marshal (1913), born in Ripple, Kent. Chief of the Imperial General Staff (1911–14), he held supreme command of the British Expeditionary Force in France (1914–15), but was criticized for indecision, and resigned.

French, Marilyn (1929–) Writer, born in New York City. She is best known for her first novel, *The Woman's Room* (1977), hailed as a pioneering feminist text for its angry study of the continuing subjection of women. Later books include *Her Mother's Daughter* (1992), *Our Father* (1994), and *In the Name of Friendship* (2006).

French bean *haricot bean*

French Guiana [geeahna], Fr **La Guyane Française** pop (2000e) 173 200; area 90 909 km²/35 091 sq mi. Overseas department of France in South America, bordering the Atlantic; capital, Cayenne; timezone GMT −3; mixed Creole, European, and Amerindian population; chief religion, Roman Catholicism; official language, French; unit of currency, the euro; low-lying near the coast; rises to 635 m/2083 ft at Mont Saint Marcel; many rocky islets along the coast, notably Devil's Island; hot and humid tropical climate; area settled by Europeans, 17th-c; territory of France, 1817; used as penal colony, 1798–1935; overseas department of France, 1946; elects two members to the French National Assembly; timber the main export, from forests covering c.80 000 km²/30 000 sq mi; only 0·1% of land under cultivation.

French horn *horn*

French Polynesia [polineezhuh], formerly **French Settlements in Oceania** (to 1958), official name **Territory of French Polynesia**, Fr **Territoire de la Polynésie Française** pop (2000e) 246 000;

area 3941 km²/1521 sq mi. Island territory comprising five scattered archipelagoes in the SE Pacific Ocean, between the Cook Is (W) and the Pitcairn Is (E); capital, Papeete; timezone GMT −6; chief ethnic group, Polynesian; chief religion, Christianity (87%); official language, French and Tahitian, with local languages widely spoken; mainly volcanic, mountainous, and ringed with coral reefs; hot and humid climate (Nov–Apr); French missionary activity, 19th-c; French protectorates introduced from 1843; 'French Oceania' became an Overseas Territory, 1958; administered by a high commissioner and Council of Ministers, elected by a Territorial Assembly; economy based on agricultural smallholdings (vegetables, fruit) and plantations (coconut oil, copra); French nuclear test base.

French Republican calendar A calendar introduced during the French Revolution to herald the beginning of a new epoch, Year 1 dating from the declaration of the Republic (22 Sep 1792). Twelve 30-day months were introduced and divided into three 10-day weeks, eliminating Sundays. The system was abolished under Napoleon (1805).

French Revolution A complex upheaval, considered a significant turning point in French history. The first major event was the summoning of the States General (spring 1789). Subsequently the National Assembly responded to public pressure, such as the storming of the Bastille (14 Jul 1789), with wide-sweeping political, social, and economic measures (1789–91), including the abolition of feudal, aristocratic, and clerical privileges, and a Declaration of the Rights of Man. Meanwhile the royal family had been removed from Versailles to Paris (Oct 1789), but after their flight to Varennes (Jun 1791) their fate was sealed. A Legislative Assembly was elected, and France was declared a republic (1792). Louis XVI and his queen, Marie Antoinette, were executed (1793). The Revolution then entered more dramatic phases, marked by political extremism and bitter rivalry between Girondins and Jacobins (the latter led by Robespierre). Though the Jacobins seized control of the Committee of Public Safety (Jul 1793) and instituted the dictatorship of the Terror, Robespierre's short-lived triumph ended with his execution (1794). The Convention suppressed the *sans-culottes* with military force before establishing the government of the Directory (1795), which was in turn overthrown by Napoleon Bonaparte in the Brumaire coup (1799). (*see panel p.354*)

French Revolutionary Wars (1792–9) A series of campaigns between France and neighbouring European states hostile to the Revolution and to French hegemony, merging ultimately into the Napoleonic Wars (1799–1815). In the War of the First Coalition (1792–7), French forces attacked the Rhine, the Netherlands, and Savoy, and later Britain, Holland, and Spain. After successfully invading the Netherlands (1794), the French broke the Coalition (1795–6), isolating Britain (1797). A Second Coalition (1798) expelled French forces from Italy and the Rhinelands, before suffering defeat by Napoleon (1799–1800).

French Southern and Antarctic Territories, Fr **Terres Australes et Antarctiques Françaises** French overseas territory, comprising Adélie Land in Antarctica and certain islands in the S Indian Ocean; established, 1955.

French West Indies A geographical label for two French overseas departments, the islands of Martinique and Guadeloupe, and their dependencies, notably the sub-prefectures of St Martin and St Barthélémy (St Barth). The islands have been departments of France since 1946.

Freneau, Philip (Morin) [frenoh] (1752–1832) Sailor and poet, born in New York City. He commanded a privateer in the American War of Independence, was captured by the British, and wrote *The British Prison Ship* (1781) and other patriotic poems. He founded and edited the *National Gazette* (1791–3).

Freon *CFCs*

frequency The number of complete cycles per second for a

Events Of The French Revolution 1789–1799

1789

Mar–May	Election of deputies to the Estates General.
5 May	Opening of the Estates General.
17 Jun	Title of National Assembly adopted by the Third Estate.
Jul	The 'Great Fear'.
14 Jul	Seizing of the Bastille in Paris.
4 Aug	Abolition of the feudal regime.
26 Aug	Declaration of the Rights of Man and Citizen.
Oct	Foundation of the Club des Jacobins.
5–6 Oct	Louis XVI brought to Paris from Versailles.
19 Oct	National Assembly installed in Paris.

1790

19–23 Jun	Abolition of hereditary nobility and titles.
Jul	Foundation of the Club des Cordeliers.

1791

20–21 Jun	Flight of the King to Varennes.
16 Jul	Foundation of the Club des Feuillants.
13 Sep	Acceptance of the Constitution by the King.
Oct	Formation of the Legislative Assembly.

1792

9–10 Aug	Attack on the Tuileries, Functions of the King suspended.
12 Aug	King and royal family imprisoned in the Temple.
2–6 Sep	Massacre of nobles and clergy in prisons.
21 Sep	Abolition of the monarchy.
22 Sep	Proclamation of the Republic.

1793

17 Jan	National Convention votes for the death of the King.
21 Jan	Execution of the King.
1 Feb	Declaration of war against England and Holland.
Mar	Tribunal created in Paris (later called the Revolutionary Tribunal).
6 Apr	Creation of the Committee of Public Safety.
27 Jul	Robespierre elected to the Committee of Public Safety.
5 Sep–27 Jul 1794	Reign of Terror.
11 Sep	Creation of the Revolutionary Army of Paris.
16 Oct	Trial and execution of Marie Antoinette.
24–31 Oct	Trial and execution of the Girondins.

1794

5 Apr	Execution of the Cordeliers, including Danton.
24 Mar	Execution of the Hebertists.
8 Jun	Inaugural Feast of the Supreme Being and of Nature.
27 Jul (9 Thermidor)	Fall of Robespierre.
19 Nov	Closure of the Club des Jacobins.

1795

21 Feb	Separation of Church and State.
31 May	Suppression of the Revolutionary Tribunal.
8 Jun	Death of Louis XVII in the Temple.
5 Oct (13 Vendémiaire)	Royalists crushed by Bonaparte.
27 Oct–4 Nov 1799	Institution of the Directory.
9 Nov (18 Brumaire)	Abolition of the Directory.

vibrating system or other repetitive motion; symbol f or v; units Hz (hertz). For wave motion, it corresponds to the number of complete waves per second.

frequency modulation (FM) In wave motion, the altering of frequency in a systematic way, leaving amplitude unchanged. In FM radio, an electrical signal modulates the frequency of a broadcast carrier radio wave by an amount proportional to the signal amplitude. Demodulation takes place in the radio receiver to give a copy of the original signal.

fresco An ancient technique for painting on walls, perfected in the 14th–16th-c in Italy. The wall is prepared with layers of plaster, sometimes as many as four, the penultimate being marked out with the artist's design (underdrawing or *sinopia*). The final layer of lime-plaster is then laid and, while it is still wet (*fresco* means 'fresh' in Italian), the artist works on this with a water-based paint.

Fresno [freznoh] 36°44N 119°47W, pop (2000e) 427 700. City in C California, USA; founded, 1872; city status, 1885; airfield; railway; university; centre of a wine-producing region; often called the world's raisin centre.

Freud, Anna [froyd] (1895–1982) Psychoanalyst, born in Vienna, the daughter of Sigmund Freud. She emigrated with her father to London in 1938, where she became a founder of child psychoanalysis.

Freud, Sigmund [froyd] (1856–1939) Founder of psychoanalysis, born in Freiburg, Moravia (now Príbor, Czech Republic). He studied medicine at Vienna, then specialized in neurology, and later in psychopathology. His method of 'free association' allowed the patient to express thoughts in a state of relaxed consciousness, and included the data of childhood and dream recollections. In 1900 he published his major work, *Die Traumdeutung* (The Interpretation of Dreams), arguing that dreams are disguised manifestations of repressed sexual wishes. In 1902, he was appointed to a professorship in Vienna, out of which grew the Vienna Psychoanalytical Society (1908) and the International Psychoanalytic Association (1910). In 1933 Hitler banned psychoanalysis, and after Austria had been overrun, Freud and his family were allowed to emigrate. He settled in London, where he died.

Frey *Freya*

Freya or **Freyja** [fraya] In Northern mythology, the goddess of love and beauty. She and her brother **Frey**, the male fertility god, were the children of Niord and Skadi.

friar A member of one of the mendicant ('begging') Christian religious orders founded in the Middle Ages. Unlike monks, they are not confined to a single monastery or abbey.

friarbird A bird of the honeyeater family, native to N Australia and the adjacent islands of SE Asia, also known as the **leatherhead**; songbird with head partly or totally naked. (Genus: *Philemon*, 17 species. Family: Meliphagidae.)

friar's balsam A resin from the stem of *Styrax benzoin* and *Styrax paralleloneurus* containing aromatic acids (benzoic and cinnamic acids), prepared in an alcoholic solution. It is used as an inhalation in the treatment of chronic bronchitis.

Fribourg [freeboorg], Ger **Freiburg** [friyboork] 46°49N 7°09E, pop (2000e) 36000. Mediaeval town in W Switzerland; founded, 1178; bishopric; railway junction; university (1889); cathedral (13th–15th-c).

Frick, Henry (Clay) (1849–1919) Industrialist, born in West Overton, PA. He became chairman of the Carnegie Steel Co in 1889, reorganizing it to become the largest steel manufacturing company in the world, and in 1901 became director of United States Steel. Among his various endowments is the Frick Collection of fine art, bequeathed to New York City.

Fricker, Peter (Racine) (1920–90) Composer, born in London. He wrote several symphonies, the oratorio *The Vision of Judgment* (1957–8), and other chamber, choral, and keyboard works.

friction A force acting against the direction of motion for two objects in contact sliding across one another. Friction may be sufficient to prevent actual relative motion. It is caused by surface roughness, and by the attraction of the atoms of one surface for those of the other.

Friedan, Betty (Naomi) [freedan], *née* **Goldstein** (1921–2006) Feminist leader and writer, born in Peoria, IL. She is best known for her book *The Feminine Mystique* (1963). She was the founder and first president of the National Association for Women in 1966 and became one of the most influential feminist leaders of the late 20th-c.

Friedman, Milton [freedman] (1912–2006) Economist, born in Brooklyn, New York City. Professor of economics at Chicago (1948–83), and a leading monetarist, his work included the permanent income theory of consumption, and the role of money in determining events. He was awarded the Nobel Prize for Economics in 1976.

friendly society A voluntary mutual-aid organization in the UK which provides financial assistance to members in times of sickness, unemployment, or retirement. Their operations are governed by the Friendly Society Acts (1974–1984).

Friends, Society of A Christian sect founded by George Fox and others in mid-17th-c England, and formally organized in 1667; members are popularly known as **Quakers**, possibly because of Fox's injunction 'to quake at the word of the Lord'. Belief in the 'inner light', a living contact with the divine Spirit, is the basis of its meetings for worship, where Friends gather in silence until moved by the Spirit to speak. They emphasize simplicity in all things, and are active reformers promoting tolerance, justice, and peace.

Friends of the Earth An international federation of environmental pressure groups with autonomous organizations in member countries. It conducts campaigns on topics such as safe energy, tropical rainforest destruction, and the preservation of endangered species.

frieze The middle part of an entablature on a classical building, usually decorated. It may also be the decorative band running along the upper part of an internal wall and below the cornice.

frigate A small warship in World War 2, superior in speed and armament to a corvette, but less powerful and smaller than a destroyer. Its present role is mainly anti-submarine and general-purpose.

frigate bird A large bird, native to tropical seas; male with coloured inflatable pouch on throat. (Genus: *Fregata*, 5 species. Family: Fregatidae.)

Frigg or **Frigga** In Norse mythology, the wife of Odin, and goddess of married love (often confused with Freya).

frilled lizard An agamid lizard (*Chlamydosaurus kingi*) native to New Guinea and N Australia; slim body; neck with large cape-like frill of brightly coloured skin; frill usually folded, but can be expanded in courtship and to deter predators.

Friml, (Charles) Rudolf [friml] (1879–1972) Composer, born in Prague. In 1906 he settled in the USA, where he made a name as a composer of light operas, including *Rose Marie* (1924) and *The Vagabond King* (1925).

Fringe, the Cultural events, particularly theatrical performances, presented around a Festival but not central to it. The term has thus come to be applied to theatre groups working on the margins of the establishment, or to any style of theatre not part of orthodoxy.

Fringillidae [frinjilidee] A family of small seed-eating birds (c.125 species); native to the Americas, Eurasia, and Africa, and introduced in Australasia; also known as **finches**.

Frisch, Karl von (1886–1982) Ethologist, born in Vienna. A key figure in the development of ethology, he is best known for his 40-year study of the honey bee, which showed that forager bees communicate information in part by the use of coded dances. In 1973 he shared the Nobel Prize for Physiology or Medicine.

Frisch, Max (Rudolf) (1911–91) Playwright and novelist, born in Zürich, Switzerland. His novels include *Stiller* (1954), a satire on the Swiss way of life, and *Bluebeard* (1983). His plays, modern morality pieces, include *Andorra* (1962) and *Triptych* (1981).

Frisch, Otto Robert (1904–79) Physicist, born in Vienna. He and Meitner first described 'nuclear fission' in 1939, and in 1945 he became head of the nuclear physics division at Harwell. During World War 2 he was involved in atomic research at Los Alamos, CA.

Frisch, Ragnar (Anton Kittil) (1895–1973) Economist, born in Oslo, a pioneer of econometrics. In 1969 he shared the first Nobel Prize for Economics.

Frisian *Germanic languages*

Frisian Islands [frizeeuhn] Island chain in the North Sea, extending along the coasts of The Netherlands, Germany, and Denmark, and politically divided between these countries; includes the **North Frisian Is** (Ger **Nordfriesische Inseln**), the German **East Frisian Is** (Ger **Ostfriesische Inseln**), and the Dutch **West Frisian Is** (Dutch **Friese Eilanden**); several areas of reclaimed land.

fritillary (botany) [fritilaree] A perennial with a small scaly bulb (*Fritillaria meleagris*), native to Europe; stem growing to 50 cm/ 20 in; leaves grass-like, bluish; flower a broad bell 3–5 cm/1$\frac{1}{2}$– 2 in, drooping, dull purple rarely white, with a distinctive chequered pattern. (Family: Liliaceae.)

fritillary (entomology) [fritilaree] A colourful, day-flying butterfly; wings typically yellow-brown with black markings; forelegs reduced, non-functional. (Order: Lepidoptera. Family: Nymphalidae.)

Frobisher, Sir Martin [frohbisher] (c.1535–94) Navigator, born in Altofts, West Yorkshire. He made several attempts to find a Northwest Passage to Cathay (1576–8), reaching Labrador and Hudson Bay.

Froebel, Friedrich (Wilhelm August) [froebl] (1782–1852) Educationist, born in Oberweissbach, Germany. In 1816 he put into practice his educational system whose aim, to help the child's mind grow naturally and spontaneously, he expounded in *Die Menschenerziehung* (1826, The Education of Man). In 1836 he opened his first kindergarten school at Blankenburg.

frog An amphibian of order Anura (3500 species), found worldwide except in the Arctic and Antarctic; short body with fewer than 10 vertebrae in the spine. The smooth wet-skinned species are called **frogs**; the rough dry-skinned species (adapted to drier habitats) are called **toads**.

froghopper A small, hopping insect that feeds by sucking the sap of plants; also known as **cuckoo-spit insect** and **spittlebug**. The eggs are laid on the plants, and hatch into sedentary larvae which surround themselves with mucus-like 'cuckoo spit' that protects them against drying out and predation. (Order: Homoptera. Family: Cercopidae, c.2500 species.)

frogmouth A large, nocturnal, nightjar-like bird native to Australasia (except New Zealand) and SE Asia; short but very broad bill (hence the name). (Family: Podargidae, 12 species.)

Froissart, Jean [frwasah(r)] (c.1333–c.1404) Historian and poet, born in Valenciennes, France. His *Chronicles*, covering European history from 1325 to 1400, were heavily influenced by his devotion to chivalric principles.

Frome [froom] 51°14N 2°20W, pop (2000e) 22 000. Town in Somerset, SW England; Anglo-Saxon origin; railway; Longleat House (1568) nearby.

Fromm, Erich (1900–80) Psychoanalyst, born in Frankfurt, Germany. Professor of psychiatry at New York from 1962, he was a neo-Freudian, known for his investigations into motivation. His works include *Escape from Freedom* (1941) and *The Sane Society* (1955).

Frondes, the [frōd] A series of civil revolts in France during the Regency of Anne of Austria, caused by economic grievances and the excessive opportunism of central government, directed by Cardinal Mazarin. The disturbances developed into two phases: the Parlementary Fronde (1648–9), and that of the Princes (1650–3). They were crushed by royal forces under Turenne.

front A meteorological term for the sharp boundary between two parcels of air of different origin and characteristics, along which a steep horizontal temperature gradient exists. A **warm front** is the leading boundary of tropical or warm air, and a **cold front** is the leading boundary of polar or cold air. In a depression, the meeting of the cold front with the warm front results in an **occluded front**.

Front de Libération Nationale *FLN*

Frontenac, Louis de Buade, comte de (Count of) [frōtenak] (1620–98) French-Canadian statesman, born in St Germain-en-Laye, France. He extended the boundaries of New France down the Mississippi, repulsed the British siege of Quebec, and broke the power of the Iroquois.

front-line states An informal grouping of seven states bordering South Africa, defined by their position with respect to the apartheid system: Angola, Botswana, Mozambique, Namibia, Tanzania, Zambia, Zimbabwe.

Frost, Sir David (Paradine) (1939–) Broadcaster and businessman, born in Tenterden, Kent. He presented *That Was the Week That Was* (BBC, 1962–3), has hosted many programmes in Britain and America, such as *The Frost Report* (1966–7) and *Breakfast with Frost* (1992–2005), and interviewed world leaders in such programmes as *The Nixon Interviews* (1976–7). In 2006 he joined Arab-language Qatar-based TV station al-Jazeera as presenter on its new English-language channel. He was a co-founder of London Weekend Television, and also of Britain's TV–AM. In 2005 he was honoured with a BAFTA Fellowship.

Frost, Robert (Lee) (1874–1963) Poet, born in San Francisco, CA. *A Boy's World* (1913) and *North of Boston* (1914) gave him an international reputation. *New Hampshire* (1923) won the Pulitzer Prize, as did his first *Collected Poems* (1930), *A Further Range* (1936), and *A Witness Tree* (1942).

Frost, Sadie, originally **Sadie Liza Vaughn** (1967–) Actress, born in London. She became known for her role as a vampire in *Bram Stoker's Dracula* (1992), and later films include *Splitting Heirs* (1993), *Captain Jack* (1998), and *Uprising* (2001). She married actor Jude Law in 1997 (divorced 2003).

frost A meteorological condition which occurs when the air temperature is at or below the freezing point of water, causing condensation. It may cause considerable damage to plants, especially if ground frost is accompanied by air frost.

frostbite The damage of exposed parts of the body by the direct effect of extreme cold. The fingers, nose, and feet are especially vulnerable, and the part may die and become gangrenous.

frottage [frotahzh] A technique used by some modern artists, notably Max Ernst, whereby paper is placed over a textured surface, such as a plank of wood, and rubbed with a pencil or crayon producing an impression.

Froude, James Anthony [frood] (1818–94) Writer and historian, born in Dartington, Devon. A member of the Oxford Movement, his early novels were controversial, notably *The Nemesis of Faith* (1848). He then worked as an essayist and editor, and wrote his *History of England* (12 vols, 1856–69).

fructose $C_6H_{12}O_6$. A simple sugar (a *monosaccharide*) found mainly in fruits in combination with glucose to produce the *disaccharide* sucrose (table sugar). Fructose is twice as sweet as glucose, and has been used as a sweetening agent.

fruit Strictly, the ripened ovary and seeds of a plant, but more generally used to include any structures closely associated with these, such as a swollen receptacle. Fruits can be divided into two main groups: **dry** and **fleshy**. In the latter, the middle layer of the ovary wall becomes succulent. Further classification is based mainly on carpel or seed number, **dehiscence** (ie whether the fruit splits to release the seeds), and to a lesser extent on derivation of tissues.

fruit fly A common name for flies of the families Drosophilidae and Tephritidae; mostly tropical. The latter contains c.4000 species of colourful flies, feeding on sap and fruit. (Order: Diptera.)

Frunze [frunzye] *Bishkek*

Fry, Christopher, pseudonym of **Christopher Harris** (1907–2005) Playwright, born in Bristol, SW England. He wrote a series of major plays in free verse, often with undertones of religion and mysticism, including *A Phoenix Too Frequent* (1946) and *The Lady's Not For Burning* (1949). His later works included *Curtmantle* (1962) and *A Yard of Sun* (1970).

Fry, Elizabeth (1780–1845) Quaker prison reformer, born in Norwich, Norfolk. After seeing the terrible conditions for women in Newgate prison, she devoted her life to prison reform at home and abroad.

Fry, Roger (Eliot) (1866–1934) Art critic, aesthetic philosopher, and painter, born in London. He is mainly remembered for his support of the Postimpressionist movement in England. He propounded an extreme formal theory of aesthetics.

Fry, Stephen (John) (1957–) Writer, actor, and comedian, born in London. He studied at Queens' College, Cambridge (1979–82), and joined the Footlights Revue where he met Hugh Laurie. They formed a comedy writing partnership, notably for the television series *A Bit of Fry and Laurie* (1986–95). He appeared in *Blackadder* (1986), *Jeeves and Wooster* (1990–3), and *Kingdom* (2007), and his films include *Wilde* (1997), *Gosford Park* (2001), and *A Cock and Bull Story* (2005). His literary output also includes humorous books, novels, and an autobiography, *Moab is My Washpot* (2003). He appears regularly on radio and television panel shows.

FT–SE Index (Financial Times–Stock Exchange Index), nickname **Footsie** A UK share index which records changes in the prices of shares of 100 leading British companies. It has been in operation since 1982, when it started with a notional value of 1000.

FT30 Index (Financial Times Index) A UK share index which records changes in the prices of shares of 30 leading British companies. It started in 1935 with a notional value of 100.

Fu-chou *Fuzhou*

Fuchs, Klaus (Emil Julius) [fooks] (1912–88) Physicist and atom spy, born in Rüsselsheim, Germany. From 1943 he worked in the USA on the atom bomb, and in 1946 became head of the theoretical physics division at Harwell, UK. In 1950 he was imprisoned for disclosing nuclear secrets to the Russians, and later worked at East Germany's Central Institute for Nuclear Research.

Fuchs, Sir Vivian Ernest [fookhs] (1908–99) Antarctic explorer and scientist, born in Freshwater, Isle of Wight. As leader of the British Commonwealth Trans-Antarctic Expedition (1956–8), he made an overland crossing from Shackleton Base via the S Pole to Scott Base (3500 km/2200 mi). He was director of the British Antarctic Survey (1958–73).

fuchsia [fyooshuh] An evergreen or deciduous shrub, native to Central and South America and New Zealand; flowers pendulous with a long, red 4-lobed tube surrounding a purple bell with projecting stamens and style; cultivars show a wide range of flower colours. (Genus: *Fuchsia*, 100 species. Family: Onagraceae.)

fuel A substance capable of releasing thermal energy in chemical, electrochemical, or nuclear processes. The oldest are combustible natural fuels (such as wood and cow dung). The chief solid **fossil fuels** are fossil vegetable matter in various degrees of carbonization, such as coal, lignite, and peat. **Liquid fuels** include some vegetable oils, but are mainly petroleum products. **Gaseous fuels** mainly comprise manufactured and natural gas. Some use is made of gaseous products arising from the degradation of biological waste. **Fuel cells** operate on an electrochemical reaction which takes place between hydrogen and oxygen. **Nuclear fuels** consist of radioactive isotopes, emitting energy spontaneously by nuclear change. **Rocket fuels** operate by reaction against high speed gases emitted on combustion.

fuel injection 1 In a diesel engine, the system that injects the fuel at high pressure directly into the combustion chamber. **2** In a petrol engine, a system that uses a special fuel/mixture control unit, as an alternative to a carburettor, to produce improved running and transient performance. The petrol is usually injected into the port immediately preceding the inlet valve rather than directly into the cylinder.

Fuentes, Carlos [fwentes] (1928–) Novelist and playwright, born in Mexico City. His novel *La muerte de Artemio Cruz* (1962, The Death of Artemio Cruz) established him as a major international writer. He became professor of Latin American Studies at Harvard in 1987. A collection of essays, *An A–Z of a Writer's Life*, appeared in 2004.

Fugard, Athol (Harold Lanigan) [foogah(r)d] (1932–) Playwright and theatre director, born in Middleburg, Cape Province, South Africa. His plays, set in contemporary South Africa, met with official opposition, notably *The Blood Knot* (1960) and *Boesman and Lena* (1969). Later works include *The Captain's Tiger* (1998), and *Sorrows and Rejoicings* (2002). He has also written film scripts and a novel, *Tsotsi* (1980, filmed 2005).

fugu [fugoo] A Japanese globe fish or puffer fish, eaten at special restaurants, cooked in small slices, raw. Parts are poisonous and cause instant death. Only restaurant staff who have passed the official examination and have a special licence are allowed to prepare it.

fugue A musical composition (or part of one) in which a single theme announced by each 'voice' in turn serves to generate the whole. It usually reappears in different keys and sometimes in different guises.

Fujairah, al- [al fujiyra] pop (2000e) 77 600; area 1150 km²/444 sq mi. Member state of the United Arab Emirates; partly mountainous, with a fertile coastal plain and no desert; capital, al-Fujairah; people live mostly in scattered villages, depending on agriculture.

Fuji, Mount [fujee], or **Fujiyama**, also known as **Fuji-san** 35°23N 138°42E. Highest peak in Japan, in C Honshu; 88 km/55 mi SW of Tokyo; dormant volcano rising to 3776 m/12 388 ft; crater diameter c.600 m/2000 ft; last eruption, 1707; snow-capped (Oct–May); sacred since ancient times.

Fujiwara Style [fujiwahra] A style of art which flourished in Japan during the late Heian period (9th–12th-c). The aristocratic Fujiwara clan built temples and pagodas, decorated in a delicate, refined manner.

Fukuoka [fukwoka], formerly **Najime** 33°39N 130°21E, pop (2000e) 1 277 000. Port in NE Kyushu, Japan; airport; railway; university (1911); institute of technology (1909).

Fulani [fulahnee], also called **Fulbe** or **Peul** Fula-speaking peoples dispersed across the Sahel zone of W Africa from Senegal to Cameroon. Originally pastoralists, they are today socially very diverse, and in many places are assimilated into the local culture.

Fulbright, J(ames) William (1905–95) US Democratic politician, lawyer, and writer, born in Sumner, MO. As chairman of the Senate Committee on Foreign Relations, he became a major critic of the Vietnam War. He was also known for introducing the international exchange programme for scholars (*Fulbright scholarships*).

Fuller, (Sarah) Margaret (1810–50) Writer, feminist, and revolutionary, born in Cambridgeport, MA. Her *Woman in the Nineteenth Century* (1845) is the earliest major piece of US feminist writing.

Fuller, R(ichard) Buckminster, known as **Bucky** (1895–1983) Inventor, designer, poet, and philosopher, born in Milton, MA. He developed the Dymaxion ('dynamic and maximum efficiency') House in 1927, and the Dymaxion streamlined, omnidirectional car in 1932. He also developed the geodesic dome.

Fuller, Roy (Broadbent) (1912–91) Poet and novelist, born in Oldham, Lancashire. His first collection, *Poems*, appeared in 1939, and his war-time experiences prompted *The Middle of a War* (1942) and *A Lost Season* (1944). His novels include *Second Curtain* (1953) and *Image of a Society* (1956). *New and Collected Poems, 1934–84* was published in 1985.

fullerenes A series of molecular allotropes of carbon, of which the best characterized are C_{60} and C_{70}; named after the designer Buckminster Fuller. First made and its structure proposed in 1985 by the astrophysicists D R Huffman (USA) and W Krätschmer (Germany), their properties are being actively investigated, such as for superconductivity.

Fuller's earth Fine earthy material containing montmorillonite clay; formerly used for cleansing oil and grease from wool (*fulling*), and now used for clarifying vegetable oils by absorbing impurities.

fulmar A marine tubenosed bird, native to N oceans (*Fulmarus glacialis*) or S oceans (2 species); comes to land only to breed. (Family: Procellariidae.)

fulminate A salt containing the ion CNO^-, also called **isocyanate**. It is an explosive; $Hg(CNO)_2$ is used as a detonator.

Fulton, Robert (1765–1815) Engineer, born in Lancaster Co, PA. His inventions included a dredging machine and the torpedo, but he is best known for his development of the steamboat, which he made a commercial success in the USA.

fumaric acid [fyoomarik] $C_2H_2(COOH)_2$, IUPAC **trans-butene-dioic acid**, melting point 300°C (in a sealed tube). An unsaturated dicarboxylic acid, used in the manufacture of polyester resins.

fumitory A brittle-stemmed annual, sometimes scrambling or climbing, native to the N hemisphere and S Africa; flowers strongly zygomorphic, 2-lipped, with rounded spur. (Genus: *Fumaria*, c.50 species. Family: Fumariaceae.)

Funafuti [foonafootee] 8°30S 179°12E, pop (2000e) 3500. Port capital of Tuvalu, SW Pacific; airfield; US military base.

Funchal [funshal] 32°40N 16°55W, pop (2000e) 109 000. Capital of Madeira, on S coast of Ilha da Madeira; third largest Portuguese city; bishopric; important port and tourist resort; cathedral (1485).

functional group A part of a molecule with characteristic reactions. Important examples include the hydroxyl group, –OH, characteristic of alcohols, and the amino group, $-NH_2$, characteristic of amines.

functionalism (art and architecture) The theory, rooted in Greek philosophy, that beauty should be identified with functional efficiency. It became fashionable in the 1920s especially under Bauhaus influence. In architecture, the form of a building was to be determined by the function it was meant to fulfil – as in the famous definition of a house as a machine for living in.

functionalism (sociology) A theory widely accepted in social anthropology and sociology in the mid-20th-c, according to which particular social institutions, customs, and beliefs all have a part to play in maintaining a social system. The central notion is that a community or society has an enduring structure, its parts fitting together to form a single integrated system.

fundamental constants A set of numerical quantities having the same fixed value for all observers. Values of these constants control all physical processes. Examples include the velocity of light, the gravitational constant, and the electron charge.

fundamental forces *forces of nature*

fundamentalism A theological tendency seeking to preserve what are thought to be the essential doctrines ('fundamentals') of a religion. The term was originally used of the conservative US Protestant movement in the 1920s, characterized by a literal interpretation of the Bible. Generally, it is any theological position opposed to liberalism, with important manifestations (often violent) found today in all major religions, notably Islam.

fundamental particles Those subatomic particles that are thought to be indivisible into smaller particles. They are the **matter particles** (quarks, neutrinos, electrons, muons, and taus) and the **force particles** (gluons, photons, W and Z bosons, and gravitons).

Fundy, Bay of A bay separating the provinces of New Brunswick and Nova Scotia, E Canada. The world's greatest tidal height (16·2 m/53 ft) is used to generate electricity.

Fünen *Fyn*

fungal infection Infection with fungi that cause disease. Examples include *Candida albicans*, the cause of thrush; *Aspergillus*, responsible for respiratory disorders; and *Actinomyces*, which produces fungal swellings in the body (*mycetomas*).

fungicide Any chemical (eg sulphur compounds) used to control fungi that are harmful to plants, animals, or foodstuffs. It is particularly important in controlling rusts in cereals, blight in potatoes, and mildew in fruit.

fungus A primitive plant that obtains its nourishment either *saprophytically*, by secreting enzymes to dissolve insoluble organic food externally before absorption, or *parasitically*, by absorbing food from a host. True fungi belong to the division Eumycota of the kingdom Plantae, containing all fungi except the slime moulds and their allies. Fungi are sometimes classified as a separate kingdom characterized by their lack of flagella at all stages of the life-cycle; those with flagellae are transferred to the kingdom Protoctista. Many are pests of crops or are human pathogens; some are edible or produce useful by-products.

funk A term used for various genres of (mainly black) popular music. From the 1950s it described 'hard bop' jazz with a 'soul' feeling, as performed by Julian 'Cannonball' Adderley and others. Later in the 1960s it was used more generally for soul and rhythm-and-blues music, epitomized by James Brown and by George Clinton's Parliament/Funkadelic bands; and from the 1970s on for a variety of black dance and disco music and its white derivatives.

funnel-web spider A predatory spider that constructs a funnel-shaped web to trap its prey. Some species are venomous. (Class: Arachnida. Order: Araneae.)

Furchgott, Robert F (1916–) Pharmacologist, born in Charleston, SC. He worked at the State University of New York Health Science Center, and shared the 1998 Nobel Prize for Physiology or Medicine for his contribution to the discovery of nitric oxide as a signalling molecule in the cardiovascular system.

Furies *Erinyes*

furniture beetle A small, brown beetle; larvae, known as **woodworm**, are C-shaped, white and fleshy with tiny legs, which bore into dead wood as they feed; adults emerge leaving typical woodworm holes. (Order: Coleoptera. Family: Anobiidae.)

Fürstenbund [fürstenbunt] ('League of Princes') A league of German Princes founded in 1785 at Frederick the Great's instigation in the last phase of his conflict with the Austrian Habsburgs.

further education A level of educational provision offered in many countries, often distinguished from **higher education**. Further education is post-school education leading, usually, to qualifications at sub-degree level, though it may not lead to any award at all but simply be taken for its own sake. Higher education takes place in institutions where most or all of the work is at degree level or above.

Furtwängler, (Gustav Heinrich Ernst Martin) Wilhelm [foortvengler] (1886–1954) Conductor, born in Berlin. He became conductor of the Gewandhaus concerts in Leipzig and of the Berlin Philharmonic, his highly subjective interpretations of the German masters arousing controversy.

furze *gorse*

Fuseli, Henry [fyoozelee], originally **Johann Heinrich Füssli** (1741–1825) Painter and art critic, born in Zürich, Switzerland. His 200 paintings include 'The Nightmare' (1781) and two series to illustrate Shakespeare's and Milton's works, by which he is chiefly known.

fusel oil [fyoozl] Organic material obtained along with ethanol in fermentation, mostly alcohols of higher molecular weight. The presence of a very small proportion of the alcohols contributes to the characteristic flavour of fermented beverages.

fusion A development of jazz that started in the late 1960s, when jazz artists sought to revitalize the music by drawing on elements from other musical traditions, and particularly rock, soul, and dance music. Miles Davis's albums *In A Silent Way* and *Bitches Brew* (both 1969) were major influences on the genre. At the same time, rock groups like Soft Machine and King Crimson were looking to jazz for fresh inspiration. The term is also used for other blendings of music genres, such as rock and folk, or jazz and classics.

futhark [fuhthah(r)k] *runes*

futon [futon] A Japanese quilt, equivalent to Western eiderdowns or duvets. Most Japanese sleep on a thick futon on the tatami matting. All bedding is kept in a cupboard during the day, leaving the room free for use.

futures In economics, a market where commodities are bought and sold for delivery at some future date. Speculators may buy futures in the hope that the price will rise, and thus be able to make a profit by selling on to others.

Futurism A modern art movement founded by the poet Marinetti in Milan in 1909. Futurism glorified machinery, war, speed, and the modern world generally; artists worked in a style derived from Cubism. It had petered out by c.1918.

Fuzhou, Fu-chou, or **Foochow** [foojoh] 26°09N 119°17E, pop (2000e) 1 564 000. City in SE China; on N bank of Min Jiang R, founded 202 BC; capital of autonomous state, 10th-c; treaty port, 1842; airfield; railway; many important pagodas and temples.

Fyn [fün], or **Funen**, Ger **Fünen** pop (2000e) 476 300; area 3486 km²/1346 sq mi. Danish island between S Jutland and Zealand; capital, Odense; second largest island in Denmark; agriculture ('the garden of Denmark').

g

gabbro A coarse-grained basic (low in silica) igneous rock composed of calcic plagioclase feldspar, pyroxene, and sometimes olivine.

Gable, (William) Clark (1901–60) Film actor, born in Cadiz, OH. His first leading film role was in *The Painted Desert* (1931). Growing popularity in tough but sympathetic parts soon labelled him 'the King of Hollywood', reaching its peak with his portrayal of Rhett Butler in *Gone With the Wind* (1939).

gable The section of wall which conceals the triangular end of a pitched roof. The term is generally used of Gothic architecture. A gable is steeper than its Classical equivalent – the pediment – and is often elaborately decorated.

Gabo, Naum [gahboh], originally **Naum Neemia Pevsner** (1890–1977) Sculptor, born in Bryansk, Russia. In 1920 he helped to form the group of Russian Constructivists, who had considerable influence on 20th-c architecture and design. He moved to the USA in 1946.

Gabon *p.360*

Gabor, Dennis [gabaw(r)] (1900–79) Physicist, born in Budapest. Leaving Germany in 1933, he became professor of applied electron physics at Imperial College, London (1958–67). In 1971 he received the Nobel Prize for Physics for his invention of holography.

Gaborone [gabuhrohnay] 24°45S 25°55E, pop (2000e) 165 900. Independent township and capital of Botswana, S Africa; altitude 1000 m/3300 ft; area 97 km²/37 sq mi; capital moved there from Mafeking, 1965; airport; university.

Gabriel An angel named in both the Old and New Testaments. He is said to have helped Daniel interpret visions (*Dan* 8, 9), and is also recorded as foretelling the births of John the Baptist and of Jesus (*Luke* 1).

Gabriel, Peter (1950–) Singer and songwriter, born in Surrey. He co-founded the rock group Genesis, but left to pursue a solo career in 1975. A collection of his video hits was released as *CV* (1988), topping the UK music video chart. Later credits include the score for the controversial film *The Last Temptation of Christ* (1988) and music for the inaugural Greenwich Millennium Dome celebration. He also founded the 'World of Music, Arts and Dance' (WOMAD) festival (1982). Other albums include *Us* (1992) and *Up* (2002).

Gabrieli, Andrea [gabrielee] (c.1533–86) Composer, born in Venice, Italy. He became organist of St Mark's Church, writing madrigals, Masses, and other choral works. Several of his organ pieces foreshadow the fugue.

Gaddafi or **Qaddafi, Colonel Muammar** [gadafee] (1942–) Libyan political and military leader, born into a nomadic family. He formed the Free Unionist Officers Movement which overthrew King Idris in 1969, and became Chairman of the Revolutionary Command Council. He set about eradicating colonialism by expelling foreigners and closing down British and US bases. A somewhat unpredictable figure, Gaddafi has openly supported violent revolutionaries in other parts of the world, has waged a war in Chad, and in 1986 the US bombed Libya

in an attempt to eliminate him. In 1999 he released for trial the alleged perpetrators of the bombing of the PanAm flight which crashed on Lockerbie, Scotland in 1988, and in 2003 agreed to pay compensation to the victims' families, following which UN sanctions were lifted.

Gaddi, Taddeo [gadee] (c.1300–66) Painter, born in Florence, Italy, the godson and best pupil of Giotto. His finest work is seen in the frescoes of 'The Life of the Virgin' in the Baroncelli chapel of San Croce.

Gaddis, William (1922–98) Novelist, born in New York City. He worked as a freelance speech and scriptwriter before making his mark with the novel *The Recognitions* (1955). A radical satirist, he was one of America's most prominent contemporary novelists; his other works include *JR* (1976), *Carpenter's Gothic* (1985), and *A Frolic of His Own* (1993).

gad fly A robust, biting fly; eyes usually large, often iridescent; females suck blood of cattle and horses. (Order: Diptera. Family: Tabanidae, c.2000 species.)

Gadidae [gadiday] The cod family of fishes, a large group comprising about 15 genera and 100 species of marine fish found primarily in continental shelf waters of the cool temperate N hemisphere; includes cod, burbot, haddock, ling, pollack, saithe, torsk, and whiting.

Gadsden Purchase (1853) An area in S Arizona and New Mexico bought from Mexico for $10 000 000 as a route for a transcontinental railroad. The purchase, named after US minister to Mexico James Gadsden (1788–1858), defined the present-day US/Mexican border.

gadwall A duck (*Anas strepera*) native to the N hemisphere S of 60°; male grey with black rear end; female brown; feeds at surface; eats weeds and small animals. (Family: Anatidae.)

Gaea, Gaia, or **Ge** [geea, giya, gee] In Greek mythology, 'the Earth' personified, and then the goddess of the whole Earth (not a particular piece of land). Her Roman equivalent was **Tellus**.

Gaelic *Irish; Scottish Gaelic*

gaffer The chief electrician in a film or television production crew, working closely with the lighting director. The chargehand electrician working directly under the gaffer is known as the **best boy**.

Gagarin, Yuri (Alekseyevich) [gagahrin] (1934–68) Russian cosmonaut, born in Gzhatsk, Russia. He joined the Soviet Air Force in 1957, and in 1961 became the first man to travel in space, completing a circuit of the Earth in the *Vostok* spaceship satellite. After his death, Gzhatsk was renamed Gagarin.

Gage, Thomas (1721–87) British general, born in Firle, Sussex. In 1763 he became commander-in-chief of the British forces in America. In 1775 (18 Apr) he sent a force to seize a quantity of arms at Concord; and next day the skirmish of Lexington took place which began the Revolution.

Gaia hypothesis [giya] A hypothesis, first proposed by James Lovelock in 1972, which considers the Earth as an intimately linked system of physical, chemical, and biological processes,

Gabon

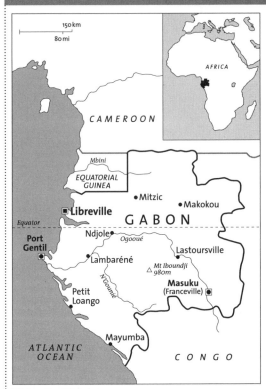

☐ International Airport

[gabohn], official name **Gabonese Republic**, Fr **République Gabonaise**
Local name Gabon
Timezone GMT +1
Area 267 667 km²/103 349 sq mi
Population total (2002e) 1 300 000

Status Republic
Date of independence 1960
Capital Libreville
Languages French (official), Fang, Myene, Bateke, and other Bantu dialects spoken
Ethnic groups c.40 Bantu tribes (Fang 30%, Eshira 25%, Bateke and Bapounou 10%) and c.10% expatriate Africans and Europeans
Religions Christian (96%) (Roman Catholic 65%, Protestant 19%, other 12%), traditional beliefs
Physical features Located in W Africa; lies on the equator for 880 km/550 mi W–E; land rises towards the African central plateau, cut by several rivers, notably the Ogooué and N'Gounié; highest point, Mont Ibounoji, 980 m/3215 ft.
Climate Typical equatorial climate: hot, wet, and humid; mean annual temperature 27°C; annual average rainfall 1250–2000 mm/50–80 in inland.
Currency 1 CFA Franc (XAF) = 100 centimes
Economy Small area of land under cultivation, but employing 65% of population; coffee, cocoa, palm oil, rubber; timber extraction; rapid economic growth since independence, largely because of offshore oil, natural gas, and minerals; manganese, uranium, iron ore.
GDP (2002e) $8·354 bn, per capita $6500
Human Development Index (2002) 0·637
History Visited by Portuguese, 15th-c; under French control from mid-19th-c; slave ship captured by the French in 1849, the liberated slaves forming the settlement of Libreville; occupied by France, 1885; one of four territories of French Equatorial Africa, 1910; independence, 1960; multi-party elections held, 1990; new constitution, 1991; governed by a President, an appointed Council of Ministers, and a legislative National Assembly.
Head of State
1960–7 Léon M'ba
1967– Omar (Albert-Bernard, to 1973) Bongo
Head of Government
1960–75 *As President*
1975–90 Léon Mébiame (Mébiane)
1990–4 Casimir Oyé M'ba
1994–9 Paulin Obame-Nguema
1999–6 Jean-François Ntoutoume-Emane
2006– Jean Eyeghe Ndong

interacting in a self-regulating way to maintain the conditions necessary for life. Although named after the Greek Earth goddess, it has a scientific rather than a mystical basis.

gaillardia [gaylah(r)dia] An annual or perennial, mostly native to North America; two species are the parents of many garden hybrids: *Gaillardia pulchella*, an annual growing to 30–60 cm/1–2 ft, yellow outer ray florets coloured crimson at the base; and *Gaillardia aristata*, a perennial growing to 70 cm/27 in with yellow and red ray florets. (Family: Compositae.)

Gainsborough, Thomas [gaynzbruh] (1727–88) Landscape and portrait painter, born in Sudbury, Suffolk. He moved to Bath in 1759, where he established himself with his portrait of Earl Nugent (1760). His best-known paintings include 'The Blue Boy' (c. 1770, San Marino), 'The Harvest Wagon' (1767, Birmingham), and 'The Watering Place' (1777, Tate, London).

Gaiseric or **Genseric** [giyserik] (c.390–477) King of the Vandals and Alans (428–77), who led the Vandals in their invasion of Gaul. He captured Hippo (430) and Carthage (439), and in 455 sacked Rome.

Gaitskell, Hugh (Todd Naylor) (1906–63) British Labour politician, born in London. An MP in 1945, he was minister of fuel and power (1947) and of economic affairs (1950), and Chancellor of the Exchequer (1950–1). In 1955 he was elected Leader of the Opposition.

galactose A simple sugar (monosaccharide), found in the sugar of milk along with glucose; otherwise, it is rare in nature.

galago *bushbaby*

Galahad, Sir One of King Arthur's knights, son of Lancelot and Elaine. Distinguished for his purity, he alone was able to succeed in the adventures of the Siege Perilous and the Holy Grail.

Galápagos finches *Darwin's finches*

Galápagos giant tortoise The largest known tortoise (*Geochelone elephantopus*); length of shell up to 1·2 m/4 ft; native to the Galápagos Is; each island has its own subspecies, differing in shell shape. (Family: Testudinidae.)

Galápagos Islands [galapagohs], Span **Archipiélago de Colón** pop (2000e) 12 100; area 7812 km²/3015 sq mi. Ecuadorian island group on the Equator, 970 km/600 mi W of South American mainland; highest peak, Volcán Wolf (1707 m/5600 ft) on Isabela I; visited by Spanish, 1535, but no colony established; Ecuador took possession, 1832; became well known after visit of Charles Darwin, 1835; volcanic origin with some active cones; diverse vegetation and landforms, from lava deserts to tropical forests; many unique species of flora and fauna evolved independent of mainland; marine iguanas on Isla Fernandina; giant tortoises, mostly on Isabela; Galápagos National Park established in 1934; a world heritage site.

Galatians, Letter of Paul to the [galayshnz] New Testament writing, widely accepted as genuinely from the apostle Paul to the churches in some part of Galatia in C Asia Minor.

galaxy A huge family of stars held together by their mutual gravitational attractions. Galaxies exist in a great variety of forms, ellipticals predominating, but spirals feature prominently in popular books on account of their notable shapes. Masses range from a few million suns to 10 million million times as many. The nearest galaxies to the Milky Way are the Magellanic Clouds, some 55 000 parsec away.

Galaxy The huge star family to which our Sun belongs, seen as the Milky Way. In shape it is basically a bulging flat disc, diameter 35 kiloparsec, thickness 3000 parsec at the centre, and 300 parsec elsewhere. The Sun is 8000 parsec from the nucleus. A pair of spiral arms merges from the nucleus and is superimposed on the general distribution of stars. The Galaxy as a whole rotates, faster at the centre than further out. There are over 100 000 000 000 stars in all, and the Galaxy is 10–15 thousand million years old.

Galbraith, John Kenneth [golbrayth] (1908–2006) Economist and diplomat, born in Iona Station, Ontario, Canada. He became professor of economics at Harvard (1948–75), and for two years (1961–3) was US ambassador to India. He was a key adviser to presidents Kennedy and Johnson, and one of the major intellectual forces in American liberalism.

Galdós, Benito Pérez *Pérez Galdós, Benito*

Galen [gaylen], in full **Claudius Galenus** (c.130–201) Greek physician, born in Pergamum, Mysia. He wrote at length on medical and philosophical subjects, becoming the authority used by subsequent Greek and Roman medical writers.

galena [galeena] A lead sulphide (PbS) mineral, with very dense, dark-grey crystals. It is an important source of lead.

Galicia [galeesha] pop (2000e) 2 745 000; area 29 434 km²/11 361 sq mi. Autonomous region of Spain in the NW corner of the Iberian peninsula extending S to the Portuguese border; a mediaeval kingdom within Castile, 11th-c; ports include Corunna and Vigo; there is a separatist political movement.

Galilean moons The four principal natural satellites of Jupiter, discovered by Galileo in 1610: Io (the innermost), Europa, Ganymede, and Callisto. They are in the same size range as the Moon, lack sensible atmospheres, and lie in near circular orbits in Jupiter's equatorial plane.

Galilee [galilee], Hebrew **Galil** N region of former Palestine and now of Israel, chiefly associated in Biblical times with the ministry of Jesus; scene of fierce fighting during the Arab invasion of Israel, 1948.

Galilee, Sea of *Tiberias, Lake*

Galileo [galilayoh], in full **Galileo Galilei** (1564–1642) Astronomer and mathematician, born in Pisa, Italy. He became professor of mathematics at Padua (1592–1610), where he improved the refracting telescope (1610), and was the first to use it for astronomy, discovering the four largest satellites of Jupiter. His realization that the ancient Aristotelian teachings about the structure of the universe were unacceptable brought severe ecclesiastical censure, and he was forced to retract before the Inquisition. By 1637 he had become totally blind. The validity of his scientific work was formally recognized by the Roman Catholic Church in 1993.

Galileo Project A NASA spacecraft mission to Jupiter, launched in October 1989, and designed to study the planet's atmosphere, satellites, and surrounding magnetosphere for two years starting in December 1995. Launched by the space shuttle, it was the first mission to encounter an asteroid (Gaspra) and to photograph an asteroid' moon (that of Ida). Having operated for five years longer than originally planned, the spacecraft burned up in Jupiter's atmosphere (Sep 2003).

Gall, Franz Joseph [gal] (1758–1828) Anatomist, born in Tiefenbrunn, Germany. As a physician in Vienna (1785), he evolved a theory in which a person's talents and qualities were traced to particular areas of the brain.

gall An abnormal outgrowth of tissue which can appear on any part of a plant, caused by insects, bacteria, fungi, nematodes, or mites. Common examples are oak-apples and the pincushion galls of roses.

Galla *Oromo*

Gallaudet College [galuhdet] A college of higher education for the deaf, in Washington, DC. It was founded by Edward Miner Gallaudet (1837–1917) in 1857, and is financed both privately and publicly.

gall bladder A small muscular sac found near or in the liver of many vertebrates, which acts as a reservoir for the storage and concentration of bile. During digestion the gall bladder expels bile into the intestine via the biliary duct system.

Galle, Johann Gottfried [gahluh] (1812–1910) Astronomer, born in Pabsthaus, Germany. In 1846, at Berlin Observatory, he discovered the planet Neptune.

galleon An elaborate, four-masted, heavily armed 16th-c warship, with a pronounced beak reminiscent of the ram on a galley, hence 'galleon'.

Galliano, Sir John (Charles) [galiahnoh] (1960–) Fashion designer, born in Gibraltar. He set up a studio in London, receiving the British Fashion Council Designer of the Year Award in 1987. After moving to Paris in 1994, he again won the British Designer Award (1994, 1995), and after a period with Givenchy became designer-in-chief at Christian Dior in 1996. He received a knighthood in 2001.

galliard *pavane*

Gallic Wars The name traditionally given to Julius Caesar's brutal campaigns (58–51 BC) against the Celtic tribes of Gaul (ancient France). They were also the occasion of his two unsuccessful invasions of Britain.

Galliformes [galifaw(r)meez] A worldwide order of medium-sized, mainly ground-feeding birds; also known as **gallinaceous birds**.

gallinaceous birds *Galliformes*

gallinule [galinyool] A water-bird of the rail family (c.12 species); native to the Old World and much of South America and Australia; toes often very long for walking on floating vegetation.

Gallipoli [galipolee], Turkish **Gelibolu** Narrow peninsula in NW Turkey; between the Dardanelles (SE) and the Aegean Sea (W); length c.100 km/60 mi.

Gallipoli campaign [galipolee] A major campaign of World War 1 (1915–16). With stalemate on the Western Front, the British War Council advocated operations against the Turks to secure the Dardanelles and aid Russia. The land campaign began with amphibious assaults on the Gallipoli peninsula (Apr 1915). Australian and New Zealand forces were heavily involved. It was abandoned as a costly failure.

gallium Ga, element 31. A metal with a remarkable liquid range (melting point 28°C, boiling point 2400°C), relatively rare and found chiefly as an impurity in ores of other elements. It is important mainly as gallium arsenide (GaAs), a compound converting electrical energy into visible light, used in light-emitting diodes.

gall midge A minute, delicate fly; eggs and hatching larvae often cause gall-like swellings on host plants. (Order: Diptera. Family: Cecidomyiidae, c.4000 species.)

Gambia, The

☐ International Airport

official name **Republic of the Gambia**
Local name Gambia
Timezone GMT
Area 11 295 km²/4361 sq mi
Population total (2002e) 1 418 000
Status Independent republic within the Commonwealth
Date of independence 1965

Capital Banjul
Languages English (official), also Madinka, Wolof and Fula
Ethnic groups Madinka (40%), Fula (19%), Wolof (15%), Dyola (10%), Sonike (8%)
Religions Muslim (85%), Christian (14%), traditional local beliefs (1%)
Physical features Located in W Africa; surrounded, except for coastline, by Senegal; strip of land 322 km/200 mi E–W along R Gambia; flat country, not rising above 90 m/295 ft; c.25% of land arable.
Climate Tropical climate; average temperatures 23°C (Jan), 27°C (Jul), rising upland to over 40°C; rainy season (Jun–Sep) with high humidity and high night temperatures; rainfall decreasing inland.
Currency 1 Dalasi (GMD) = 100 butut
Economy Agriculture, especially groundnuts; cotton, rice, millet, sorghum, fruit, vegetables, livestock; groundnut processing, brewing, soft drinks, agricultural machinery assembly, metal working, clothing, tourism.
GDP (2002e) $2·582 bn, per capita $1800
Human Development Index (2002) 0·405
History Visited by Portuguese, 1455; settled by English in 17th-c; independent British Crown Colony from 1843; independent member of Commonwealth, 1965; republic, 1970; joined Confederation of Senegambia, 1982–9; signed treaty of friendship with Senegal, 1991; military coup, 1994; governed by a House of Representatives, President and Cabinet.
Head of State/Government
1965–94 Dawda Kairaba Jawara
1994– 6 *Military administration* Yayeh Jameh *Chairman*
1996– Yayeh Jameh

Galloway *Dumfries and Galloway*

gallstones Small stones in the gall bladder and its associated ducts. They are found in about 20% of individuals, but give rise to symptoms in only a small proportion of these. Most stones are composed of cholesterol with a little admixture of calcium. When they cause significant discomfort or jaundice, they are usually removed surgically. In some cases small stones may be dissolved by giving a derivative of bile salts by mouth.

Gallup, George (Horace) (1901–84) Public opinion expert, born in Jefferson, IA. A professor of journalism, in 1935 he founded the American Institute of Public Opinion, and evolved the **Gallup polls** for testing the state of public opinion via representative samples.

gall wasp A very small wasp, each species causing a characteristic gall on its host plant, typically the oak. (Order: Hymenoptera. Family: Cynipidae, c.2000 species.)

Galsworthy, John [golzwerthee] (1867–1933) Novelist and playwright, born in Kingston Hill, Surrey. His great sequence, *The Forsyte Saga* (1906–28), recording the life of the affluent British middle class before 1914, began a new vogue in novel writing. His plays, such as *Strife* (1909), illustrate his interest in social and ethical problems. He was awarded the Nobel Prize for Literature in 1932.

Galton, Sir Francis [gawltn] (1822–1911) Scientist and explorer, born in Birmingham, West Midlands. He is best known for his studies of heredity and intelligence, such as *Hereditary Genius* (1869), which led to the field he called *eugenics*.

Galuppi, Baldassare [galoopee] (1706–85) Light operatic composer, born near Venice, Italy. His comic operas were extremely popular, and he also composed sacred and instrumental music.

He is the subject of a well-known poem by Browning, 'A Toccata of Galuppi's'.

Galvani, Luigi [galvahnee] (1737–98) Physiologist, born in Bologna, Italy, known for his studies of the role of electrical impulses in animal tissue. The galvanometer, an instrument for measuring small electrical currents, is named after him.

galvanizing The application of a zinc coating to iron or steel to protect against atmospheric corrosion. Although the term 'galvanizing' derives from Galvani, the process was not devised by him, but by Henry William Crawford in 1837.

Galway [gawlway], Ir **Na Gaillimhe** pop (2000e) 183 000; area 5939 km²/2293 sq mi. County in Connacht province, W Ireland; largest Gaelic-speaking population in Ireland; capital, Galway, pop (2000e) 52 000; port at head of Galway Bay; airfield; railway; university (1849); technical college.

Galway, Sir James [gawlway] (1939–) Flautist, born in Belfast. He has followed a highly successful solo career, playing on a solid gold flute of great tonal range. He was honoured at the 2005 Classical Brit Awards for his outstanding contribution to music over 30 years.

Gama, Vasco da [gahma] (c.1469–1525) Navigator, born in Sines, Portugal. He led the expedition which discovered the route to India round the Cape of Good Hope (1497–9).

Gambetta, Leon (Michel) [gãbeta] (1838–82) French Republican statesman, born in Cahors, France. After the surrender of Napoleon III he helped to proclaim the Republic (1870), became minister of the interior, made a spectacular escape from the siege of Paris in a balloon, and for five months was dictator of France. He was briefly prime minister (1881–2).

Gambia, The *see panel*

gambling The wagering of either money or material goods of value on the outcome of a chance happening, such as roulette or dice-throwing, or where an element of skill can be used to judge the likelihood of an outcome, such as in horse racing or football. Gambling takes place in some form in every country of the world, but is legal only in certain locations. In America, it is legal only in some cities and states; Las Vegas and Reno were granted the first licences in 1931. In Britain, legislation in the early 1960s allowed the opening of bookmaker's shops where 'off-course' bets could be legally laid. All licensed gambling provides revenue for the city, state, or country, and there are firm rules and conditions to ensure fairness to individuals placing the bet. In addition, many places also run lotteries, where purchasing either a pre-set series of random numbers or choosing a set personally can bring the winner a considerable fortune, while providing funds for charitable works. Britain's National Lottery was established in 1994 (renamed Lotto, 2002).

Gambon, Sir Michael (John) (1940–) Actor, born in Dublin. He joined the National Theatre in 1963, also working widely in repertory and with the Royal Shakespeare Company (1982–3). His television appearances include *The Singing Detective* (1986, BAFTA), *Longitude* (2000, BAFTA), and *Perfect Strangers* (2001, BAFTA). His films include *A Dry White Season* (1990) and *Gosford Park* (2001), and he played Dumbledore in *Harry Potter and the Prisoner of Azkaban* (2004) and *Harry Potter and the Goblet of Fire* (2005).

gamelan [gamelan] An ensemble used for traditional and ceremonial music, especially in Bali and Java. It consists mainly of tuned gongs, chimes, and other percussion instruments.

gamete [gameet] A specialized reproductive cell which fuses with another gamete of the opposite sex or mating type, during fertilization, to form a zygote. Gametes are typically *haploid* (possessing a single chromosome set), and the zygote is *diploid* (possessing a double set, one derived from each gamete). Gametes are usually differentiated into male and female.

gamete intrafallopian transfer (GIFT) A procedure undertaken to remedy infertility. Ova are collected from the surface of the ovaries after stimulation with drugs, then introduced into the uterus together with spermatozoa, permitting natural fertilization to occur.

game theory The branch of mathematics that analyzes a range of problems involving decision-making, with important applications to military strategy, economics, and other applied sciences. Game theory was developed principally by French mathematician Emile Borel (1871–1956) and US mathematician John Von Neumann (1903–57).

gametophyte The sexual (ie gamete-producing or *haploid*) generation in the life of a plant. It is the dominant part of the life-cycle in algae and bryophytes; it is the free-living but minor generation in ferns; while in flowering plants it is represented only by the pollen tube and embryo sac.

gamma globulins The most abundant fraction of the antibodies in blood serum, produced by the plasma cells of B lymphocytes (derived from bone marrow); also known as **immunoglobulin G (IgG)**. Gamma globulins combine with antigens such as viruses and parasites to kill them.

gamma rays Electromagnetic radiation of very short wavelength, less than 3×10^{-11} m; particle-like properties; no electric charge; highly penetrating. Emitted in natural radioactivity, it is the result of transitions from high-energy excited states to lower-energy states in atomic nuclei.

Gamow, George [gamov], originally **Georgy Antonovich Gamov** (1904–68) Physicist, born in Odessa, Ukraine. In 1948 he helped to develop the 'big bang' theory of the origin of the universe, and contributed to the analysis of the double helix model of DNA (1953). He was also a highly successful popular science writer.

Gand [gã] *Ghent*

Gandhi, (Mohandas Karamchand) [gandee], known as **the Mahatma** (Hindi 'of great soul') (1869–1948) Indian nationalist leader, born in Poorbandar, Kathiawar. He studied law in London, but in 1893 went to South Africa, where he spent 20 years opposing discriminatory legislation against Indians. In 1914 he returned to India, where he became leader of the Indian National Congress, advocating a policy of non-violent non-co-operation to achieve independence. Following his civil disobedience campaign (1919–22), he was jailed for conspiracy (1922–4). In 1930 he led a 320 km/200 mi march to the sea to collect salt in symbolic defiance of the government monopoly. In 1946 he negotiated with the Cabinet Mission which recommended the new constitutional structure. After independence (1947), he tried to stop the Hindu–Muslim conflict in Bengal, a policy which led to his assassination in Delhi by Nathuram Godse, a Hindu fanatic.

Gandhi, Indira (Priyadarshini) [gandee] (1917–84) Indian stateswoman and prime minister (1966–77, 1980–4), born in Allahabad, the daughter of Jawaharlal Nehru. She became president of the Indian Congress Party (1959–60), minister of information (1964), and prime minister after the death of Shastri. She achieved a considerable reputation through her work as a leader of the developing nations, but was unable to stem sectarian violence at home. She was assassinated in New Delhi by Sikh extremists, and succeeded by her elder son, **Rajiv Gandhi**; her other son, **Sanjay Gandhi** (1946–80), was killed in an air crash.

Gandhi, Rajiv [gandee] (1944–91) Indian statesman and prime minister (1984–9), born in Mumbai (Bombay), India, the eldest son of Indira Gandhi. Following the death of his brother **Sanjay Gandhi** in an air crash in 1980, he was elected to his brother's parliamentary seat. After the assassination of Indira Gandhi (1984), he became prime minister, securing a record majority. He resigned after his party was defeated in the 1989 election, and was assassinated 18 months later while campaigning for the Congress Party. His Italian-born widow, **Sonia**, was elected Congress president in 1998, and was elected to parliament in 1999, becoming leader of the Opposition.

Gandolfini, James [gandolfeenee] (1961–) Actor, born in Westwood, NJ. He made his film debut in *A Stranger Among Us* (1992), and later films include *Get Shorty* (1995) and *The Mexican* (2001). He became well known for his role as Tony Soprano in the television series *The Sopranos* (1999–), for which he received Best Actor Golden Globe (1999) and Emmy (2000, 2001, 2003) awards.

Ganges, River [ganjeez], Hindi **Ganga** River in N India, formed in the E Himalayas; flows W onto the Ganges Plain, then through Bihar and West Bengal; joined by the R Brahmaputra, it continues through Bangladesh as the river Padma, to form the vast Ganges–Brahmaputra delta in the Bay of Bengal; length 2510 km/1560 mi; the most sacred Hindu river.

ganglion 1 In anatomy, an aggregation of grey (non-myelinated) nervous tissue within the nervous system, constituting the bulk of many invertebrate central nervous systems. They are often the site of communication between nerve cells. **2** In clinical medicine, a cyst which forms in relation to a tendon sheath, producing a painless, harmless swelling.

Gang of Four 1 A description given by Mao Zedong to the Shanghai-based hard-core radicals of the Cultural Revolution: Zhang Chunqiao (1917–2005), Yao Wenyuan (d.2005), Wang Hongwen (d.1992), and Jiang Qing. All were members of the politburo when they were arrested and disgraced in 1976. **2** In British politics, the name given to the four politicians who broke away from the Labour Party to found the Social Democratic Party in 1981: Roy Jenkins, William Rodgers, David Owen, and Shirley Williams.

gangrene Death of body tissue which occurs in parts of the body deprived of their blood supply, such as a toe or foot, or internal organ. Without infection, the affected part blackens and shrivels (**dry gangrene**). If it is infected, the affected part becomes swollen and ulcerated and the area of dead tissue spreads, requiring urgent surgery.

ganja *cannabis*

gannet A large marine bird closely related to the booby; native to the N Atlantic, S Africa, Australia, and New Zealand; long blue bill with no external nostrils; bare patches of blackish skin on face. (Family: Sulidae, 3 species.)

Ganymede (astronomy) [**ganimeed**] The third natural satellite of Jupiter, discovered by Galileo in 1610; distance from the planet 1 070 000 km/665 000 mi; diameter 5260 km/3270 mi; orbital period 7·155 days. The brightest of the Galilean satellites, it seems to have a large rocky core surrounded by a mantle of water and a thick crust of ice.

Ganymede (mythology) [**ganimeed**] In Greek mythology, a beautiful boy, the son of Tros, a Trojan prince. He was carried up to Olympus, where he became the cup-bearer.

Gao, Xingjian [gow, shingjian] (1940–) Novelist, playwright, and painter, born in Ganzhou, E China. During the Cultural Revolution (1966–76) he was sent to a re-education camp. His book of collected plays, *The Other Shore* (1986), was banned in China, and the next year he settled in Paris as a political refugee, later taking French citizenship. In 2000 he became the first Chinese writer to receive the Nobel Prize for Literature.

Gaoxiong [gowshyung] or **Kao-hsiung** 22°36N 120°17E, pop (2000e) 1 509 000. Special municipality and seaport in SW Taiwan; largest seaport and industrial city in Taiwan; world's largest shipbreaking centre, occupied by the Japanese, 1895–1945; airport; railway.

gar Primitive slender-bodied fish confined to fresh and brackish rivers and lakes of North America; length up to 3 m/10 ft, scales rhomboidal, jaws prolonged to form a narrow snout; also called **garpikes**. (Genus: *Lepisosteus*. Family: Lepisosteidae.)

Garamba National park established in 1938 in N Democratic Republic of Congo, area 4480 km²/1730 sq mi; noted for its unique population of white rhinoceroses; a world heritage site.

garbanzos *chick-pea*

Garbo, Greta, originally **Greta Lovisa Gustafsson** (1905–90) Film actress, born in Stockholm. She moved to the USA in 1925, where she starred in such successes as *Anna Karenina* (1935) and *Ninotchka* (1939). She retired from films in 1941, and became a US citizen in 1951, living in seclusion in New York City.

García Lorca, Federico *Lorca, Federico García*

García Márquez, Gabriel *Márquez, Gabriel García*

Gard, Pont du [pō dü gah(r)] An aqueduct built by the Romans early in the 1st-c AD to carry the water supply of the city of Nîmes in S France. It is c.275 m/900 ft long and towers 55 m/180 ft above the R Gard; a world heritage site.

Gard, Roger Martin du *Martin du Gard, Roger*

Garda, Lake, ancient **Lacus Benacus** area 370 km²/143 sq mi. Largest Italian lake, between Lombardy and Venetia; length 52 km/32 mi; width 5–16·5 km/3–10 mi; maximum depth 346 m/1135 ft.

garden bunting *ortolan*

garden city In the UK, a planned settlement designed to provide a spacious, high-quality, living and working environment. The concept is based on 19th-c ideas of Utopian communities, and was developed by Ebenezer Howard in 1898. The first was built at Letchworth, Hertfordshire, in 1903, followed by Welwyn in 1919. The ideas were developed further in the British 'new towns' of the 1950s, and were also influential in Europe and the USA.

garden cress A slender annual (*Lepidium sativum*), single stem 20–40 cm/8–15 in; flowers small, white, cross-shaped; possibly native to W Asia. Long cultivated as a salad plant, it is the cress of mustard and cress. (Family: Cruciferae.)

gardenia An evergreen shrub or small tree, native mostly to the Old World tropics, China, and Japan; flowers white, fragrant, petals forming a tube with spreading lobes. (Genus: *Gardenia*, 250 species. Family: Rubiaceae.)

Gardiner, Stephen (c.1483–1555) Clergyman, born in Bury St Edmunds, Suffolk. He supported the royal supremacy, but opposed doctrinal reformation, and for this was imprisoned on Edward VI's accession. Released and restored by Mary in 1553, he became an arch-persecutor of Protestants.

Gardner, Ava (Lavinnia), originally **Lucy Johnson** (1922–90) Film actress, born in Smithfield, NC. A green-eyed brunette, once voted the world's most beautiful woman, she remained a leading lady for two decades. Her films include *Mogambo* (1953), *The Barefoot Contessa* (1954), and *Night of the Iguana* (1964). She was married to Mickey Rooney, Artie Shaw, and Frank Sinatra.

Gardner, Erle Stanley (1889–1970) Crime novelist, born in Malden, MA. He is best known as the writer of the 'Perry Mason' books, later the basis of a long-running television series.

Garfield, James A(bram) (1831–81) The 20th president of the USA (Mar–Sep 1881), born in Orange, OH. He identified himself with the cause of civil service reform, thereby irritating many in his own party. He was shot at Washington, DC by a disappointed office-seeker, Charles Guiteau.

garfish *needlefish*

Garfunkel, Art (1941–) Singer and actor, born in Forest Hills, NY. He teamed up with Paul Simon as a teenager, achieving major hits with 'The Sound of Silence' (1965) and the soundtrack for *The Graduate*. The duo split up following his decision to go into acting. His films include *Catch 22* (1970), *Carnal Knowledge* (1971), and *Boxing Helena* (1993). He continued to record as a soloist, achieving a UK No 1 with 'Bright Eyes' in 1979. In 2004 they reunited for their successful Old Friends tour, performing across America and Europe. He released his 12th solo album, *Some Enchanted Evening*, in 2007.

garganey [gah(r)ganee] A small, slender duck (*Anas querquedula*), native to S Eurasia, W and NE Africa, and Indonesia; male brown with white stripe from eye to back of neck; migrates to tropics for winter. (Family: Anatidae.)

gargoyle In Gothic architecture, a stone rainwater spout carved in the form of a grotesque animal or human face, with its mouth open as if spewing the water. It is usually built so as to project well out from the parapet, thus sending the water away from the building.

Garibaldi, Giuseppe [garibawldee] (1807–82) Italian patriot, born in Nice, France. At the outbreak of Italy's war of liberation he sailed from Genoa (May 1860) with his 'thousand' volunteers, and assisted Mazzinian rebels to free Sicily from Neapolitan control. He swiftly overran much of S Italy, and drove King Francis of Naples from his capital (Sep 1860). Thereafter he allowed the conquest of S Italy to be completed by the Sardinians under Victor Emmanuel II.

Garland, Judy, originally **Frances Gumm** (1922–69) Actress and singer, born in Grand Rapids, MN. She became a juvenile film star in *Broadway Melody of 1938*, followed by *The Wizard of Oz* (1939) and *Meet Me in St Louis* (1944), directed by Vincente Minelli, whom she later married. Concerts and occasional films continued with public success, but her private life was full of overwhelming difficulties, and she died in London, apparently from an overdose of sleeping pills.

garlic A perennial bulb (*Allium sativum*) up to 60 cm/2 ft; greenish-to-purple star-shaped flowers mixed with bulbils. Native to Asia, it has been cultivated in the Mediterranean region since ancient times for the strongly flavoured bulbs. (Family: Liliaceae.)

Garner, Jay (1938–) US general, born in Arcadia, FL. He joined the US Army in 1960, served in Vietnam, and during the 1991 Gulf War supervised the deployment of Patriot missile batteries. After the war he commanded Operation Provide Comfort for the resettlement of Kurdish refugees in N Iraq. In 1994 he became commander of the US Space and Strategic Defense Command, and was assistant chief-of-staff until his retirement in 1997. Following the Iraq War (Mar–Apr 2003), he was briefly appointed director of the Office of Reconstruction and Humanitarian Assistance for Iraq.

garnet A group of silicate minerals occurring mainly in metamorphic rocks. It displays a wide range of composition and colour. Some varieties are important as gemstones.

Garonne, River [garon], ancient **Garumna** Chief river of SW France, rising in the Pyrenees; meets the R Dordogne to form the Gironde estuary; length 575 km/357 mi.

garpike *gar*

Garrett, Lesley (1955–) Soprano, born in Doncaster, South Yorkshire. In 1984 she joined the English National Opera as principal soprano. Her television work includes two series of *Lesley Garrett Tonight* (BBC 1998, 2000), and among her albums are *Soprano in Red* (1995), *I Will Wait for You* (2000), and *So Deep is the Night* (2003). In 2006 she appeared in Andrew Lloyd Webber's revival of *The Sound of Music* at the London Palladium.

Garrett, Peter (Robert) (1953–) Popular singer and political activist, born in Sydney, New South Wales, Australia. Trained as a lawyer, during 1997–2002 he was lead singer with the band Midnight Oil, known for its songs dealing with issues such as Aboriginal land rights, conservation, and prison reform. He became widely known in 1984, when he stood for parliament. He was president (1989–93, 1998–2004) of the Australian Conservation Foundation, and was awarded the Order of Australia in 2003.

Garrick, David (1717–79) Actor, theatre manager, and playwright, born in Hereford, Herefordshire. For 30 years he dominated the English stage, in a wide range of parts. As joint manager of Drury Lane (1747–76) he encouraged innovations in scenery and lighting design.

garrigue [gareeg] Evergreen scrubland vegetation found in areas with thin soils and a Mediterranean-type climate; also known as **garigue** or **garriga**. Low, thorny shrubs and stunted oak are characteristic.

Garrison, William Lloyd (1805–79) Abolitionist, born in Newburyport, MA. He emerged in 1830 as the foremost anti-slavery voice in the USA, founding the American Anti-Slavery Society.

Garter, the Most Noble Order of the (KG) The most ancient order of chivalry in Europe, founded by Edward III of England between 1344 and 1351. The emblem of the order is a gold-edged blue garter, inscribed in gold with *Honi soit qui mal y pense* (Fr 'Shamed be he who thinks evil of it'), traditionally the words spoken by Edward after he picked up the Countess of Salisbury's dropped garter.

gas 1 A state of matter in which atoms are disordered and highly mobile, moving in a random way with little interaction. Gases are characterized by low densities (typically 1/1000 of a solid), an ability to flow and to fill a container, and high compressibility.
2 A fuel which includes both **manufactured gas**, derived from solid or liquid fossil fuels, and **natural gas**, drawn from existing gaseous subterranean accumulations. Manufactured gas (or **town gas**) was made from the early 19th-c by the distillation of coal; more recently by the chemical conversion of surplus naphtha from the petroleum industry or natural solid fuels other than coal. Natural gas occurs on its own or in association with oil deposits. The main constituent of town gas is hydrogen; that of natural gas is methane. The calorific value of natural gas is about double that of town gas.

Gascoigne, Paul [gaskoyn], nickname **Gazza** (1967–) Footballer, born in Gateshead, Tyne and Wear. After Tottenham Hotspur signed him in 1988, he established himself as an outstanding player and a flamboyant personality, becoming a member of the England team. During the 1991 FA Cup Final, he sustained a serious knee injury that delayed his transfer to Italian club, Lazio, where he was again dogged by injury. He joined Rangers (1995) and then Middlesbrough (1998–2000), played briefly for a succession of clubs and had a short-lived spell as manager at Kettering Town (2005).

Gascony [gaskonee], Fr **Gascogne**, Lat **Vasconia** Former province in SW France; part of the Roman Empire; conquered by the Visigoths, later by the Franks, who made it a duchy; joined to Guienne, 1052; in English hands, 1154–1453.

gas-cooled reactor *nuclear reactor*

gas engine A specially adapted or designed internal combustion engine which uses gas as its fuel. The gas (usually methane) is stored in pressurized tanks as a liquid.

gas gangrene An infection of muscle and soft tissue by *Clostridium perfringens*. The bacteria infect wounds and secrete a toxin that digests tissues, producing gas bubbles from fermentation.

Gaskell, Elizabeth (Cleghorn), *née* **Stevenson**, known as **Mrs Gaskell** (1810–65) Writer, born in London. She did not begin to write until middle age, when she published *Mary Barton* (1848). Her other works include *Cranford* (1853) and *Wives and Daughters* (1865, televised 2000).

gas laws Boyle's and Charles's Laws together, interrelating pressure, volume, and temperature for a given mass of an ideal gas. These laws may be summarized in a single equation: $pV = nRT$, where p is the pressure exerted by n moles of a gas contained in a volume V at an absolute temperature T.

gasohol A mixture of gasoline with 5/15 % ethanol (ethyl alcohol which must be water-free), useful as a high-octane rating fuel in internal combustion engines.

gas oil A liquid fuel, the heavier fraction of petroleum distillation. It is used as a heating fuel and in diesel engines.

gasoline *petrol*

gastric juice A mixture of substances secreted by cells and glands within the stomach, consisting of hydrochloric acid, pepsinogen, mucus, and intrinsic factor. Excessive secretion of acid and pepsinogen may lead to the formation of **gastric ulcers**.

gastritis [gastriytis] Inflammation of the stomach lining as a result of irritants, such as alcohol, cigarettes, spicy food, or strongly acid substances such as aspirin. These cause patches of inflammation which sometimes bleed. This leads to upper abdominal pain, nausea, and vomiting, sometimes with blood. Persistent irritation leads to chronic gastritis, with thinning of the lining of the stomach and sometimes ulcers.

gastro-enteritis [gastrohenteriytis] Irritation and inflammation of any part of the gastro-intestinal tract, usually by an infectious micro-organism, characterized by abdominal pain, vomiting, diarrhoea, and severe prostration in some cases.

gastro-intestinal tract *alimentary canal*

gastropod [gastropod] The snails, slugs, and snail-like molluscs; body consists of a head, muscular foot, and visceral mass largely covered by a calcareous shell, usually spirally coiled; includes land and freshwater snails and slugs, as well as a great diversity of marine snails. (Phylum: Mollusca. Class: Gastropoda.)

gastrotrich [gastrotrik] A minute, worm-like animal found in or on bottom sediments and in association with other aquatic organisms in various habitats; body covered in a horny layer (cuticle), and may have bristles. (Phylum: Gastrotricha, c.150 species.)

gastrula [gastrula] The stage following the blastula in the embryonic development of animals. During this phase (**gastrulation**), cells of the embryo move into their correct position for development into the various organ systems of the adult.

gas turbine An engine that passes the products of the combustion of its fuel/air mixture over the blades of a turbine. The turbine drives an air compressor, which in turn provides the air for the combustion process. The energy of the combustion products not taken up by the compressor can be used to provide a jet of exhaust gases, or drive another turbine.

gas warfare *chemical warfare*

Gates, Bill, popular name of **William Henry Gates** (1955–) Computer engineer and entrepreneur, born in Seattle, WA. In 1977, he co-founded Microsoft to develop and produce DOS, his basic operating system for computers. When in 1981 International Business Machines (IBM) adopted DOS for its line of personal computers, his company took a giant step forward, and by age 35 he had become one of the wealthiest men in America. In 1998 the government sued Microsoft for alleged anti-trust violations (*see* **Microsoft** entry). Well known for his donations to charity, the Bill and Melinda Gates Foundation was established in 2000.

Gates, Horatio (1728–1806) US general, born in Maldon, Essex. He joined the British army, served in America in the Seven Years' War (1756–63), and then settled there. In the War of Independence he sided with his adoptive country, and in 1777 compelled the surrender of the British at Saratoga. In 1780 he commanded the army of the South, but was routed by Cornwallis near Camden.

Gates, Robert (Michael) (1943–) Public official and intelligence officer, born in Wichita, KS. He studied at William and Mary College and Indiana University, gaining a PhD in international relations. He entered the Central Intelligence Agency (CIA), where he rose to become director (1991–3). He played a key role in US policy in the first Gulf War, in the Iran hostage crisis, and the Soviet invasion of Afghanistan. In 2006 he was named secretary of defense by President George W Bush following the resignation of Donald Rumsfeld.

Gatling, Richard Jordan (1818–1903) Inventor, born in Maney's Neck, NC. He is remembered for his invention of the **Gatling gun** (1861–2), a revolving battery gun, with 10 parallel barrels, firing 1200 shots a minute. His weapon came to public notice again in 1991 when it was used as the principal weapon platform on US A10 aircraft during the Gulf War.

GATT *General Agreement on Tariffs and Trade*

gaucho [gowchoh] A nomadic, fiercely independent mestizo horseman of the Argentine pampa, first appearing in the 17th-c. Gaucho skills live on among the rural population of Argentina and Uruguay.

Gaudí (I Cornet), Antonio [gowdee] (1852–1926) Architect, born in Reus, Spain. He was the most famous exponent of Catalan *Modernisme*, one of the branches of the Art Nouveau movement, and is best known for the ornate Church of the Holy Family in Barcelona, which occupied him from 1884 until his death, and which is still unfinished.

Gaudier-Brzeska, Henri [gohdyay breska] (1891–1915) Sculptor, born in St Jean de Braye, France. A pioneering modernist who drew upon African tribal art, he rapidly developed a highly personal abstract style exemplified in both carvings and drawings.

Gaudron, Mary [godron] (1943–) Judge, born in Moree, New South Wales, Australia. Seen as a progressive, in 1987 she became the first woman to be appointed to the High Court of Australia.

Gauguin, (Eugène Henri) Paul [gohgĩ] (1848–1903) Postimpressionist painter, born in Paris. He visited Martinique (1887), and became the leader of a group of painters at Pont Aven, Brittany (1888). From 1891 he lived mainly in Tahiti and the Marquesas Is, using local people as his subjects, and evolving his own style, *synthétisme*, reflecting his hatred of civilization and the inspiration he found in primitive peoples.

Gaul (Lat *Gallia*) In ancient geography normally used for **Transalpine Gaul**, bounded by the Alps, the Rhine, and the Pyrenees. Julius Caesar completed the Roman conquest in 58–51 BC. With the gradual Roman withdrawal in the 5th-c, Germanic colonies became independent kingdoms. Unity was superficially achieved under Clovis and Charlemagne, and Gaul later developed into the mediaeval kingdom of France. **Cisalpine Gaul** lay S of the Alps and N of the Apennines. Conquered by the Romans in 201–191 BC, it was incorporated into Italy in 42 BC.

Gaulish *Celtic languages*

Gaullists Members of the French political party, the *Rassemblement pour la République* (RPR) whose programmes are based on the doctrine developed by President de Gaulle in 1958–69. Nationalistic in character, Gaullists emphasize the need for strong government, especially in relations with the European Union and foreign powers such as the USA.

Gaultier, Jean-Paul [gohtyay] (1952–) Fashion designer, born in Paris. He joined the houses of Jacques Esterel and Jean Patou before producing his own independent collection in 1976. He reached a new audience as co-host of the magazine show *Eurotrash* on British television.

Gaumont, Léon Ernest [gohmõ], Eng [gohmont] (1864–1946) Cinema inventor, manufacturer, and producer, born in Paris. He was responsible for the first talking pictures, demonstrated at Paris in 1910. He also introduced an early form of coloured cinematography in 1912.

Gaunt, John of *John of Gaunt*

Gauss, (Johann) Carl Friedrich [gows] (1777–1855) Mathematician, born in Brunswick, Germany. A mental prodigy, he pioneered the application of mathematics to such areas as gravitation, magnetism, and electricity.

Gauss's law [gows] In electrostatics, the total electric flux through some closed surface is proportional to the total charge enclosed by that surface. The constant of proportionality is $1/\varepsilon$, where ε is permittivity.

Gauteng [khowteng] (Sesotho 'place of gold') One of the nine new provinces established by the South African constitution of 1994, in NC South Africa, occupying the area formerly known as the PWV (Pretoria–Witwatersrand–Vereeniging) triangle; capital, Johannesburg; pop (2000e) 8 118 000; area 18 760 km^2/ 7241 sq mi; chief languages, Afrikaans, Zulu, English; Pretoria is the administrative capital of South Africa; smallest province, most densely populated; commercial, financial, and industrial heartland of South Africa, containing c.70% of the labour force, and producing c.37% of GDP.

Gautier, Théophile [gohtyay] (1811–72) Writer and critic, born in Tarbes, France. In 1835 his celebrated novel, *Mademoiselle de Maupin*, appeared. His most important collection was *Emaux et camées* (1852, Enamels and Cameos).

gavial *gharial*

gavotte [gavot] A French folk dance, popular also as a court dance during the 17th–18th-c, and often included in instrumental and orchestral suites of the period. It was in a moderately quick duple or quadruple metre.

Gawain or **Gawayne** [gawayn] One of King Arthur's knights, the son of King Lot of Orkney, whose character varies in different accounts. In the mediaeval *Sir Gawayn and the Grene Knight*, he is a noble hero undergoing a test of faith.

Gay, John (1685–1732) Poet and playwright, born in Barnstaple, Devon. He wrote poems, pamphlets, and popular satirical *Fables*, and is best known for *The Beggar's Opera* (1728).

Gay-Lussac, Joseph Louis [gay luhsak] (1778–1850) Chemist and physicist, born in St Léonard, France. He made balloon ascents to study the laws of terrestrial magnetism, and to collect samples of air for analysis, which led to his major discovery, the law of volumes named after him (1808).

Gazankulu [gazangkooloo] Former national state or non-independent black homeland in Transvaal province, NE South Africa; achieved self-governing status in 1973; incorporated into Northern Province in the new constitution of 1994.

Gaza Strip pop (2000e) 1 163 000, including c.8500 Jewish settlers; area 202 km²/78 sq mi. A narrow strip of land bounded NW by the Mediterranean Sea; length, 50 km/30 mi; chief town, Gaza; formerly part of Egyptian Sinai, after Arab–Israeli War of 1948–9; Israeli-occupied district under military administration containing many Palestinian refugee camps, 1967–94; considerable tension in the area after the beginning of the uprising (*intifada*) in 1988; peace agreement (1993) with PLO assigned it to Palestine; evacuation of Jewish settlers by Israeli army (Aug–Sep 2005) in line with Prime Minister Sharon's disengagement plan.

gazelle An elegant athletic antelope, native to Africa and S Asia; usually pale brown above with white underparts; when alarmed, moves by 'pronking' (or 'stotting') – a vertical leap using all four legs simultaneously. (Tribe: Antilopini, 18 species.)

gazelle hound *saluki*

GCSE Abbreviation of **General Certificate of Secondary Education**, introduced in England and Wales for the first time in 1988. It merged what had previously been two separate examinations for pupils aged about 16 or older – the *General Certificate of Education* (GCE), originally aimed at about the top 20% of the ability range, and the *Certificate of Secondary Education* (CSE), which was meant for the next 40%.

Gdańsk [gdansk], formerly Ger **Danzig** 54°22N 18°38E, pop (2000e) 469 000. Industrial port in N Poland; held by Prussia, 1793–1919; free city within the Polish tariff area, 1919; Lenin shipyard the scene of much labour unrest in 1980s, in support of Solidarity; part of the *Tri-city* with Sopot and Gdynia; airport; railway; two universities (1945, 1970); maritime research institutes; largest shipyard in Poland.

GDP *gross domestic product*

gean [geen] A species of cherry (*Prunus avium*) native to Europe and Asia, forming a tall tree with white flowers and dark, purplish-red, sweet or sour fruit; also called **wild** or **bird cherry**. (Family: Rosaceae.)

gear A device used to transform one rotary motion into another, in terms of speed and direction. The fundamental type of gear is the toothed gear wheel, which can be used in a wide variety of ways to produce the desired ratio of output rotation to input rotation.

Gebrselassie, Haile [gabruhselasee, hiylee] (1973–) Athlete, born in Arssi, Ethiopia. The dominant long-distance runner of the 1990s, he was four times world champion (1993, 1995, 1997, 1999) and twice Olympic champion (1996, 2000) at 10 000 m. He broke his first world record in 1994, and had set a total of 15 world records by 2000. He was International Athletics Federation Athlete of the Year in 1998.

gecko A lizard native to warm regions worldwide; body usually flattened top to bottom; skin soft; eyes large, without movable eyelids; tongue short, often used to lick eyes; most individuals nocturnal; males are the only lizards with loud calls. (Family: Gekkonidae, 800 species.)

Geelong [jeelong] 38°10S 144°26E, pop (2000e) 161 000. Port in S Victoria, Australia; railway; university (1974); customs house the oldest wooden building in Victoria.

gegenschein [gaygenshiyn] *zodiacal light*

Gehrig, (Henry) Lou(is) [gerig], nickname **the Iron Horse** (1903–41) Baseball player, born in New York City. He played 2130 consecutive games for the New York Yankees between 1925 and 1939. An outstanding first-baseman, he scored 493 home runs. His final illness (amyotrophic lateral sclerosis) is widely known as 'Lou Gehrig's disease' in the USA.

Geiger counter [giyger] A device for counting atomic particles,

named after German physicist Hans Geiger (1882–1945). Gas between electrodes is ionized by the passage of a particle, and so transmits a pulse to a counter.

Geisel, Ernesto [giyzl] (1908–96) Brazilian general and president (1974–9), born in Rio Grande do Sul. His military presidency was notable for its policy of 'decompression', which led to the restoration of democracy in 1985.

gel [jel] A colloidal suspension of a solid in a liquid, in which the properties of the solid predominate. An example is gelatine.

gelatin(e) [jelatin] A protein formed when collagen (a fibrous protein found in animal bones, skin, and hair) is boiled in water. It is used in foods, adhesives, and photographic emulsions.

Geldof, Bob [geldof], popular name of **Robert Frederick Xenon Geldof** (1954–) Rock musician and philanthropist, born in Dublin. He formed the successful rock group **the Boomtown Rats** (1975–86). Moved by television pictures of widespread suffering in famine-stricken Ethiopia, he established the pop charity 'Band Aid' trust in 1984, which raised £8 million for African famine relief through the release of the record 'Do they know it's Christmas?'. Other successful 'Live Aid' charity concerts followed, and he was awarded an honorary knighthood in 1986. In 2004 he was appointed a member of the newly-launched Commission for Africa initiative. The same year a new 'Band Aid' recorded a successful second version of 'Do they know it's Christmas?' to raise funds for Darfur in W Sudan. In support of the Make Poverty History campaign, in 2005 he organized the 'Live 8' charity pop concerts timed to coincide with the G8 summit on world poverty.

gelignite A group of industrial explosives consisting of a gelatinized mixture of nitroglycerine and nitrocellulose. Inert non-explosive material promotes safety in handling.

Gellhorn, Martha (Ellis) (1908–98) Journalist and writer, born in St Louis, MO. In 1936 she met Ernest Hemingway (whom she married in 1940 and divorced in 1946) and the following year became war correspondent for *Collier's Weekly*. Later she reported from wars in Vietnam (1966), the Middle East (1967), and Central America (1983–5). She is best known for her books of collected journalism and memoirs, notably *Travels with Myself and Others* (1978).

Gell-Mann, Murray [gelman] (1929–) Theoretical physicist, born in New York City. He introduced the concept of *strangeness* into the theory of elementary particles, and helped to devise the idea of quarks as constituents of all nuclei, and the idea of weak currents for understanding a type of nuclear interaction. He was awarded the Nobel Prize for Physics in 1969.

Gemara [gemahra] (Aramaic 'completion') A commentary on the Jewish Mishnah, which together with the Mishnah constitutes the Talmud.

Gemayel [zhemiyel] One of the leading political families of Lebanon's Maronite Christian community. **Sheikh Pierre** (1905–84) founded the Kataeb or Phalangist Party in 1936. Originally a youth group modelled along fascist lines, its members were first elected to the Lebanese parliament in 1960. His younger son **Bashir** (1947–82), a Lebanese army officer, rose through the party and its militia during the 1975–6 civil war, and was elected President of Lebanon in 1982. Upon his assassination 20 days later he was succeeded by his elder brother **Amin** (1942–). Politically more moderate than Bashir, in his six years as president he proved unable to resolve the communal conflict stemming from the civil war.

Gemini [jeminiy] (Lat 'twins') A conspicuous N constellation of the zodiac, with a bright pair of stars **Castor** and **Pollux**, lying between Taurus and Cancer. Castor is a double star, easily divided through a small telescope; orbital period 470 years; distance: 15·8 parsec. Pollux is a bright orange star, the nearest giant star to Earth; distance: 10·3 parsec.

Gemini North and South Telescopes Large 8·1 m/320 in optical telescope sited on Mauna Kea, Hawaii Island, which became operational in 1999. It is able to achieve very high resolution by the use of adaptive optics, a technique that continually flexes the main mirrors to counteract the defocusing effects of Earth's turbulent atmosphere. A twin telescope, Gemini South, on the top of Cerro Pachon in the Chilean Andes, was officially opened in January 2002.

Gemini programme [jeminiy] The second-generation US-crewed spacecraft programme, following Mercury and preceding Apollo, using a two-member crew. It was used to demonstrate the new capabilities of extravehicular activity, and extended astronaut endurance to a degree needed to accomplish lunar landing missions. There were 10 successful missions between March 1965 and November 1966.

gemsbok *oryx*

gemstones A general term for precious or semi-precious stones or minerals valued for their rarity, beauty, and durability; usually cut and polished as jewels. The most highly valued are hard and transparent crystals such as diamond, ruby, emerald, and sapphire.

gender (sociology) The social expression of the basic physiological differences between men and women – social behaviour which is deemed to be appropriate to 'masculine' or 'feminine' roles and which is learned through primary and secondary socialization.

gene A unit of heredity; a segment of the DNA which contains the instructions for the development of a particular inherited characteristic. A gene in the nuclear DNA codes or carries the information for a particular protein (or part of a protein).

genealogy The study of family history. Since the 16th-c, records of family descent have been strictly kept in many countries. A chart showing genealogical descent is a *pedigree*. In countries where wealth and position were commonly inherited, such as the UK, genealogy has been very important; but even in countries where the legal and social reasons for interest in genealogy are fewer, such as the USA and Australia, many individuals attempt to trace their 'family tree'.

General Agreement on Tariffs and Trade (GATT) An agency of the United Nations, founded in 1948 to promote international trade. GATT was based in Geneva, and had 125 members in December 1994. It successfully concluded several rounds of negotiations which greatly reduced world tariffs. It was not, however, able to stem the spread of non-tariff barriers to trade, such as voluntary export restraints. GATT was succeeded by the World Trade Organization (WTO) in 1995.

General Agreement on Trade in Services (GATS) An international agreement to begin to liberalize trade in services. GATS was set up as part of the Uruguay Round of trade negotiations which led to the creation of the World Trade Organization in 1995. It was intended to start the process of extending to international trade in services the liberalization of trade in goods which had been achieved under the General Agreement on Tariffs and Trade (GATT) since 1948. Initial results have not been great; countries stipulate which sectors are subject to liberalization, and can specify exempt parts of these. Several rounds of negotiation are likely to be needed to achieve major liberalization of trade in services.

General Assembly (politics) *United Nations*

General Assembly (religion) The highest court, in Churches of Presbyterian order. It normally meets annually and comprises equal numbers of ministers and elders, elected by presbyteries in proportion to their size. It is presided over by a *Moderator*, elected annually.

General Medical Council (GMC) The statutory body in the UK which controls the professional standing and conduct of members of the medical profession. It is responsible for maintaining the Medical Register of those entitled to practise medicine.

general relativity A theory of gravity deriving almost entirely from Einstein (1916). It supersedes Newton's theory of gravitation, and replaces the Newtonian notion of instantaneous action at a distance via the gravitational field with a distortion of space–time due to the presence of mass. For example, as the Earth moves round the Sun there is distortion of space–time by the Sun's greater mass. An analogy represents space–time as a rubber sheet distorted by a heavy ball representing the Sun; a smaller ball rolling by, representing a planet, will tend to fall into this depression, apparently attracted. General relativity is supported by experiments which measure the bending of starlight due to the presence of the Sun's mass, and also the precession of Mercury's orbit.

General Strike (4–12 May 1926) A national strike in Britain, organized by the Trades Union Congress (TUC) in support of the miners' campaign to resist wage cuts. The government organized special constables and volunteers to counter its most serious effects. The TUC called off the strike after nine days, though the miners' strike continued fruitlessly for three more months.

generation, computer *computer generations*

generative grammar A type of grammar, devised by US linguist Noam Chomsky in the 1950s, which explicitly defines the set of grammatical sentences in a language. Each is assigned a unique structural description, representing the grammatical knowledge (or *competence*) which a native speaker uses. In **transformational grammar**, one set of rules assigns a structure to a basal set of sentences, and another 'transforms' those structures into the forms in which they will actually occur in a language.

Genesis, Book of The first book of the Hebrew Bible/Old Testament and of the Pentateuch; traditionally attributed to Moses, but considered by many modern scholars to be composed of several distinct traditions. It presents stories of the creation (Chapters 1–11), then focuses on God's dealings with the people destined to become Israel.

Genet, Jean [zhuhnay] (1910–86) Writer, born in Paris. His first novel, *Notre-Dame des fleurs* (1944, Our Lady of the Flowers) created a sensation for its portrayal of the criminal world. He later turned from novels to plays, such as *Les Bonnes* (1947, The Maids) and *Les Paravents* (1961, The Screens). Sartre's book *Saint Genet* (1952) widened his fame among the French intelligentsia.

genet or **genette** [jenit] An African or European carnivore of the family Viverridae; pale with rows of dark spots and banded tail; also known as **bush cat**. (Genus: *Genetta*, 10 species.)

gene therapy *somatic gene therapy*

genetically modified organisms (GMOs) Organisms whose genetic make-up has been altered using genetic engineering technology that does not involve natural methods of reproduction; they can be plants, animals, or other organisms. Animals can be modified to produce pharmacologically active compounds in their milk, to change the texture of the parts that are eaten, or to add genes to make body parts suitable for transplant into humans (*xenotransplantation*). Bacteria, yeast, and mammalian cultured cells can have genes added to allow them to produce large amounts of specific proteins such as insulin, growth hormone, and blood-clotting factors. Agricultural food crops can be genetically modified by the addition of gene-coding for enzymes that change the metabolic pathways and allow them to be sprayed with otherwise toxic herbicides, or for the production of proteins poisonous to specific pests. Genetically-modified food crops have caused considerable controversy because the imprecise integration of the transgene into its host genome may cause effects other than those desired, and for which they have not been fully tested. There are also concerns that the GM crop will cross with weedy relatives, making them resistant to herbicides, or that large monoculture crops will cause insects to mutate to become resistant to pesticide transgenes faster than is usual.

genetic code The code in which genetic instructions are written, using an alphabet based on the four bases in DNA and RNA: *adenine, cytosine, guanine*, and *thymine* (for DNA) or *uracil* (for RNA). Each triplet of bases indicates that a particular kind of amino acid is to be synthesized. The code is non-overlapping; the triplets are read end-to-end in sequence (eg UUU = phenylalanine, UUA = leucine, CCU = proline); and there are three triplets not translated into amino acid, indicating chain termination. The code is universal and applies to all species.

genetic counselling / counseling Advice given to prospective parents concerned at the risk of their future child suffering from a genetic disease. The procedure consists of confirmation of the diagnosis in the affected individual; calculation of the risk of occurrence of the disease from the family history and relevant clinical investigations; advice on the risk; discussion of the implications if the child should be affected; and advice on procedures by which the birth of an affected child can be avoided.

genetic engineering The formation of artificial combinations of heritable genetic material which does not involve the use of natural methods of sexual or asexual reproduction. Nucleic acid molecules, produced chemically or biologically outside the cell (eg by recombinant DNA technology), are inserted into a host organism in which they do not naturally occur, but in which they are capable of continued propagation. Biological compounds can be produced industrially (eg human insulin, vaccines). New synthetic capabilities can be incorporated into plants (eg for nitrogen fixation). Ultimately it may be possible to repair genes responsible for hereditary disease or insert a normal copy of a gene sequence ('gene therapy'). The implications of genetic engineering have led to public debate, and in most countries there is government control over recombinant DNA work. There is also some public fear that the presence of foreign genetic elements may adversely affect the normal functions of cells. To counter this, safety measures are used to minimize the risk of spread of engineered organisms. Physical containment makes use of microbiological techniques and equipment designed to prevent escape. Biological containment minimizes the chance of a host organism surviving outside the laboratory, usually by using host cells carrying deleterious mutations which permit their growth only under restricted artificial laboratory conditions. However, a great deal of concern has been expressed over the release into the agricultural environment of viable genetically engineered organisms that are capable of reproducing and spreading.

genetics The science of heredity. It originated with the discovery by Gregor Mendel that observable hereditary characteristics are determined by factors transmitted without change and in predictable fashion from one generation to the next. The term was coined by British biologist William Bateson in 1907. Genetics occupies a unique position, for its principles and mechanisms extend throughout almost all biology, tying together all branches that deal with individual and population variation, and giving a unifying core at all levels – the molecular structure of cells and tissues, the development of individuals, and the evolution of populations.

genette *genet*

Geneva [jeneeva], Fr **Genève**, Ger **Genf**, Ital **Ginevra** 46°13N 6°09E, pop (2000e) 175 000. City in SW Switzerland, W end of L Geneva; built on the site of a Roman town; independent republic until becoming a Swiss canton in 1814; centre of the Reformation under Calvin; former seat of the League of Nations, 1920–46; capital of French-speaking Switzerland; airport; railway; university (1559); world capital of high-class

watchmaking and jewellery; headquarters of over 200 international organizations; renowned for its numerous quays and its fountain, Jet d'Eau; cathedral (12th-c).

Geneva, Lake, Fr **Lac Léman**, Ger **Genfersee**, Lat **Lacus Lemanus** area 581 km²/224 sq mi. Lake in SW Switzerland and SE France; largest of the Alpine lakes; height, 371 m/1217 ft; maximum depth, 310 m/1017 ft; maximum width, 14 km/9 mi.

Geneva Accord A peace plan for the Middle East devised by Israeli and Palestinian moderates, launched in Switzerland in December 2003. The Israeli army would withdraw from the Gaza Strip and most of the West Bank, and an independent Palestinian state would be established. The West Bank's borders would be defined by the 1967 Green Line, but areas of land would be exchanged between Palestine and Israel. East Jerusalem would be the capital of the Palestinian state and West Jerusalem the capital of Israel. Palestine would have sovereignty over most of the Old City. The Palestinians would forego the 'right of return' for Palestinian refugees who fled from what became Israel in 1948. The Palestinians would recognize Israel's existence and right to live in peace, and Israel would recognize the Palestinian state in the same way. The Accord did not have the backing of the Israeli or Palestinian governments, and its key compromises (over the division of Jerusalem and the right of return) attracted the opposition of radical groups on both sides. In its emphasis on an immediate political settlement, it differed from the 'road-map' proposed earlier in 2003, which had as its primary phase the establishing of secure conditions under which a settlement would eventually take place. In August 2005 the army evacuated Jewish settlers from the Gaza Strip in line with Israeli Prime Minister Sharon's disengagement plan.

Geneva Bible An English translation of the Bible, prepared and published in Geneva by Protestant exiles from England. It first appeared complete in 1560.

Geneva Convention An international agreement on the conduct of warfare first framed in 1864 and ratified in 1906. It is chiefly concerned with the protection of wounded and the sanctity of the Red Cross, while prohibiting methods of war that might cause unnecessary suffering.

Genghis Khan [jengis kahn], also spelled **Jingis** or **Chingis Khan** ('Very Mighty Ruler'), originally **Temujin** (1162/7–1227) Mongol conqueror, born in Temujin, Mongolia. From 1211, in several campaigns, he overran the empire of N China, the Kara-Chitai empire, the empire of Kharezm, and other territories, so that by his death the Mongol empire stretched from the Black Sea to the Pacific.

genie *jinni*

genital warts Cauliflower-like lesions on the penis, vulva, and around the anus due to overgrowth of the epidermis. They are caused by infection with a papilloma virus similar to that which causes warts on other parts of the body. They are spread by sexual contact.

Genoa [jenoha], Ital **Genova** 44°24N 8°56E, pop (2000e) 700 000. Largest seaport in Italy; founded as a Roman trading centre; leading Mediterranean port by 13th-c; rebuilt after World War 2; archbishopric; airport; railway; ferries; university (1471); birthplace of Columbus; Doge's Palace (13th-c), cathedral (12th–14th-c).

genocide The crime under international law of the deliberate and systematic destruction of a race of people or an ethnic group by mass murder. The word was coined after events in Europe in 1933–45 and the mass destruction of Jews and Rom by Germany. In 1948 the UN General Assembly adopted a Convention on the Prevention and Punishment of the Crime of Genocide; this confirmed the policy that genocide was a crime under international law as much in peacetime as in war, and was not a matter of private concern for an individual state. Perpetrators

Geological Time Scale

Eon	Era	Period	Epoch	Million years ago	Geological events	Sea life	Land life
Phanerozoic	Cenozoic	Quaternary	Holocene		Glaciers recede. Sea level rises. Climate becomes more equable.	As now.	Forests flourish again. Humans acquire agriculture and technology.
				0·01			
			Pleistocene		Widespread glaciers melt periodically, causing seas to rise and fall.	As now.	Many plant forms perish. Small mammals abundant. Primitive humans established.
				2·0			
		Tertiary	Pliocene		Continents and oceans adopting their present form. Present climatic distribution established. Ice caps develop.	Giant sharks extinct. Many fish varieties.	Some plants and mammals die out. Primates flourish.
				5·1			
			Miocene		Seas recede further. European and Asian land masses join. Heavy rain causes massive erosion. Red Sea opens.	Bony fish common. Giant sharks.	Grasses widespread. Grazing mammals become common.
				24·6			
			Oligocene		Seas recede. Extensive movements of Earth's crust produce new mountains (eg Alpine-Himalayan chain).	Crabs, mussels, and snails evolve.	Forests diminish. Grasses appear. Pachyderms, canines, and felines develop.
				38·0			
			Eocene		Mountain formation continues. Glaciers common in high mountain ranges. Greenland separates. Australia separates.	Whales adapt to sea.	Large tropical jungles. Primitive forms of modern mammals established.
				54·9			
			Palaeocene		Widespread subsidence of land. Seas advance again. Considerable volcanic activity. Europe emerges.	Many reptiles become extinct.	Flowering plants widespread. First primates. Giant reptiles extinct.
				65			
	Mesozoic	Cretaceous	Late		Swamps widespread. Massive alluvial deposition. Continuing limestone formation. S America separates from Africa. India, Africa and Antarctica separate.	Turtles, rays, and now-common fish appear.	Flowering plants established. Dinosaurs become extinct.
			Early	97·5			
				144			
		Jurassic	Malm	163	Seas advance. Much river formation. High mountains eroded. Limestone formation. N America separates from Africa. Central Atlantic begins to open.	Reptiles dominant.	Early flowers. Dinosaurs dominant. Mammals still primitive. First birds.
			Dogger	188			
			Lias	213			
				213			
		Triassic	Late		Desert conditions widespread. Hot climate slowly becomes warm and wet. Break up of Pangea into supercontinents Gondwana (S) and Laurasia (N).	Ichthyosaurs, flying fish, and crustaceans appear.	Ferns and conifers thrive. First mammals, dinosaurs, and flies.
			Middle	231			
			Early	243			
				248			
	Palaeozoic	Permian	Late		Some sea areas cut off to form lakes. Earth movements form mountains. Glaciation in southern hemisphere.	Some shelled fish become extinct.	Deciduous plants. Reptiles dominant. Many insect varieties.
			Early	258			
				286			
		Carboniferous			Sea-beds rise to form new land areas. Enormous swamps. Partly-rotted vegetation forms coal.	Amphibians and sharks abundant.	Extensive evergreen forests. Reptiles breed on land. Some insects develop wings.
			Pennsylvanian	320			
			Mississippian				
				360			

Eon	Era	Period	Epoch	Million years ago	Geological events	Sea life	Land life
Phanerozoic	Palaeozoic	Devonian	Late Middle Early	374 387	Collision of continents causing mountain formation (Appalachians, Caledonides, and Urals). Sea deeper but narrower. Climatic zones forming, Iapetus ocean closed.	Fish abundant. Primitive sharks. First amphibians.	Leafy plants. Some invertebrates adapt to land. First insects.
		Silurian	Pridoli Ludlow Wenlock Llandovery	408 414 421 428	New mountain ranges form. Sea level varies periodically. Extensive shallow sea over the Sahara.	Large vertebrates.	First leafless land plants.
		Ordovician	Ashgill Caradoc Llandeilo Llanvirn Arenig Tremadoc	438 448 458 468 478 488	Shore lines still quite variable. Increasing sedimentation. Europe and N America moving together.	First vertebrates. Coral reefs develop.	None.
		Cambrian	Merioneth St David's Caerfai	505 525 540	Much volcanic activity, and long periods of marine sedimentation.	Shelled invertebrates, Trilobites.	None.
Proterozoic	Precambrian	Vendian		590	Shallow seas advance and retreat over land areas. Atmosphere uniformly warm.	Seaweed. Algae and invertebrates.	None.
		Riphean	Late Middle Early	650 900 1 300	Intense deformation and metamorphism.	Earliest marine life and fossils.	None.
		Early Proterozoic		1 600	Shallow shelf seas. Formation of carbonate sediments and 'red beds'.	First appearance of stromatolites.	None.
Archaen		Archaean (Azoic)		2 500 4 600	Banded iron formations. Formation of the Earth's crust and oceans.	None.	None.

may be tried whether they are rulers, public officials, or private individuals, and may be tried by the state in which the act was committed or by an international tribunal or court whose jurisdiction is accepted by the contracting parties to the Convention.

genome [jeenohm] The complete genetic information about an organism. In most organisms this is contained in the DNA sequences within chromosomes, while in RNA-based viruses it is the total RNA sequence. Genome sizes have a 100 000 fold range from a few thousand base pairs in simple viruses to 10^{11} base pairs in some plants.

genotype The genes carried by an individual member of an organism. The interaction of gene products (RNA, protein) with each other and with the environment in which the organism develops gives rise to the **phenotype** – the characteristics that are observed.

genre painting Realistic scenes from everyday life, typically on a small scale, as produced by Dutch 17th-c masters such as Steen and Vermeer. The term may be applied, however, to any period.

Genscher, Hans-Dietrich [gensher] (1927–) German statesman, born in Reideburg, Germany. In 1974 he became vice-chancellor, foreign minister, and (until 1985) Chairman of the Free Democratic Party. In 1989–90 he worked vigorously for Ger-

man reunification and became the first foreign minister of the unified Germany.

Genseric *Gaiseric*

Gent *Ghent*

gentian Any of several species, mostly perennials, found almost everywhere, except for Africa; many are low-growing alpines; flowers usually several cm long, funnel- or bell-shaped, with often long tubes and five spreading lobes, usually deep blue, but also white, yellow, or red. (Genus: *Gentiana*, 400 species. Family: Gentianaceae.)

Gentile da Fabriano *Fabriano, Gentile da*

Gentlemen at Arms, Honourable Corps of In the UK, non-combatant troops in attendance upon the sovereign. They provide an escort at coronations, state openings of parliament, receptions, royal garden parties, and during state visits.

genus [jeenuhs] A category in biological classification consisting of one or more closely related and morphologically similar species. The name of the genus (eg *Panthera*) and the species (eg *leo*) together form the scientific name of an organism (eg the lion, *Panthera leo*).

geochemistry A branch of geology concerned with the abundances of elements and their isotopes in the Earth, and the processes that affect their distribution. It also subsumes the study of chemical processes in the evolution of the Earth and the Solar System.

geochronology The science of dating rocks or geological events in absolute terms (ie in years), usually by radiometric dating. For more recent rocks, varve counting may be applicable to Pleistocene sediments, or tree-ring dating can measure ages back to about 7000 years before the present.

geodesic dome A structurally stable dome constructed of a grid of straight members connected to each other to form a continuous surface of small triangles. It was invented by Buckminster Fuller in the 1950s.

geodesy [jeeodesee] A branch of science concerned with the size and shape of the Earth, its gravitational field, and the location of fixed points. Geodesic surveying, unlike plane surveying, takes into account the Earth's curvature.

Geoffrey of Monmouth (Gaufridus Monemutensis) (c.1100–54) Welsh chronicler, consecrated Bishop of St Asaph in 1152. His *Historia regum Britanniae* (History of the Kings of Britain), composed before 1147, introduced the stories of King Lear and Cymbeline, the prophecies of Merlin, and the legend of Arthur in the form we know.

geography The study of the nature of the physical and human environments. It is often divided broadly into **physical geography**, which concerns the Earth's physical environment, and **human geography**, the study of people and their activities. It can be divided into a number of specialist disciplines: for example, **geomorphology**, the scientific study of the origin and development of landforms; **population geography**, concerned with the composition, distribution, growth, and migration of populations; and **resource geography**, the study of the location and exploitation of natural resources.

geological time scale Divisions and subdivisions of geological time, based on the relative ages of rocks determined using the methods of stratigraphy. Correlations between rocks of the same age are made from a study of the sedimentary sequences and the characteristic fossils they contain. The major divisions are termed *eons* (or *aeons*) which are further subdivided into *eras, periods*, and *epochs*. (*see panel pp.370–71*)

geology The science of the Earth as a whole: its origin, structure, composition, processes, and history. Geology is applied to the exploration for mineral and oil deposits in the Earth.

geomagnetic field The magnetic field of the Earth which arises from the metallic core, and which may be regarded as produced by a magnetic dipole pointing towards the geomagnetic N and S Poles. Local anomalies in the magnetic field are due to variations in the nature and structure of the rocks in the crust.

geomancy [geeohmansee] The study of 'earth mysteries', originally a means of divination by scattering earth on a surface and analyzing the resulting patterns. The notion now extends to studying how the Earth's own energy affects daily life.

geometric sequence A sequence in which the ratio of any one term to the next is constant; sometimes called a **geometric progression**. The terms 1,2,4,8 form a geometric sequence; $1+2+4+8$ is a **geometric series**.

geometrid moth A moth, small to medium-sized, often with large and cryptically coloured wings; c.20 000 species, including many serious pests. (Order: Lepidoptera. Family: Geometridae.)

geometries, non-Euclidean Geometries developed by varying Euclid's fifth axiom, as stated by the British mathematician John Playfair (1748–1819), 'Through any one point there can be drawn one and only one straight line parallel to a given straight line'. Variations on this took either the form 'Through any one point can be drawn more than one straight line parallel to a given straight line' or 'Through any one point can be drawn no straight line parallel to a given straight line'. The first form was called **hyperbolic geometry**, the second **elliptic geometry**. There are other non-Euclidean geometries.

geometry The branch of mathematics which studies the properties of shapes and space, originally (as its name suggests) of the Earth. The Greeks from c.300 BC developed geometry on a logical basis, many of the early results being collected in Euclid's *Elements*. In the past 200 years, abstract geometries have been developed, notably by Gauss and Lobachevsky.

geomorphology A branch of geology (or geography) which studies and interprets landforms and the processes of erosion and deposition which form the surface of the Earth and other planets.

geopathic stress [geeohpathik] A term which covers all forms of naturally occurring environmental stress, but most often applied to the adverse effects which result from electromagnetic fields and other forms of radiation, including radon gas. Environmental factors contributing to geopathic stress may include ley lines, artificial structures such as power lines, and sun spots which disturb the Earth's magnetic field.

geophagy [jeeofajee] *pica*

geophysics A broad branch of geology which deals with the physical properties of Earth materials and the physical processes that determine the structure of the Earth as a whole. Major subjects include seismology, geomagnetism, and meteorology, as well as the study of large-scale processes of heat and mass transfer in the Earth and variations in the Earth's gravitational field.

George I (of Great Britain) (1660–1727) King of Great Britain and Ireland (1714–27), born in Osnabrück, Germany, the great-grandson of James I of England. Elector of Hanover from 1698, he took relatively little part in the government of Britain, living in Hanover as much as possible.

George II (of Great Britain) (1683–1760) King of Great Britain and Ireland (1727–60), and Elector of Hanover, born at Herrenhausen, Hanover, the son of George I. In 1705 he married Caroline of Ansbach (1683–1737). In the War of the Austrian Succession, he was present at the Battle of Dettingen (1743), the last occasion on which a British sovereign commanded an army in the field.

George III (1738–1820) King of Great Britain and Ireland (1760–1820), Elector (1760–1815) and King (from 1815) of Hanover, born in London, who succeeded his grandfather, George II. Eager to govern as well as reign, he caused considerable friction. With Lord North he shared in the blame for the loss of the American colonies. In 1810 he suffered a recurrence of a mental derangement, and the Prince of Wales was made regent. DNA research in 2004 on a sample of his hair concluded that his condition was probably made more acute due to the application of arsenic powder as a skin cosmetic and wig dressing.

George IV (1762–1830) King of Great Britain and Hanover (1820–30), born in London, the eldest son of George III. Rebelling against a strict upbringing, he went through a marriage ceremony with a Roman Catholic, which was not recognized in English law. The marriage was later declared invalid, and in 1795 he married Princess Caroline of Brunswick, whom he tried to divorce when he was king. Her death in 1821 ended a scandal in which the people sympathized with the queen.

George V (1865–1936) King of the United Kingdom (1910–36), born in London, the second son of Edward VII. His reign saw the Union of South Africa (1910), World War 1, the Irish Free State settlement (1922), and the General Strike (1926). His consort, **Mary** (1867–1953), originally **Princess Victoria Mary Augusta Louise Olga Pauline Claudine Agnes of Teck**, was born in London, and married Prince George in 1893. She organized women's war work (1914–18), and continued with many public and philanthropic activities after the death of her husband. They had five sons and one daughter.

George VI (1895–1952) King of the United Kingdom (1936–52), born at Sandringham, Norfolk, the second son of George V. He studied at Dartmouth Naval College and Trinity College, Cambridge, and served in the Grand Fleet at the Battle of Jutland (1916). In 1920 he was created Duke of York, and married Lady Elizabeth Bowes-Lyon in 1923. They had two children: Princess Elizabeth (later Queen Elizabeth II) and Princess Margaret. An outstanding tennis player, he played at Wimbledon in the All-England championships in 1926. He ascended the throne in 1936 on the abdication of his elder brother, Edward VIII. During World War 2 he set a personal example coping with wartime restrictions, continued to reside in bomb-damaged Buckingham Palace, visited all theatres of war and delivered many broadcasts, for which he overcame a speech impediment. His last great public occasion was the opening of the Festival of Britain in 1951.

George, St (fl. 3rd-c) Patron of chivalry, and guardian saint of England and Portugal. His name was early obscured by fable, such as the story of his fight with a dragon to rescue a maiden. Feast day 23 April.

George, David Lloyd *Lloyd George, David*

George-Brown, Baron, originally **George (Alfred) Brown** (1914–85) British Labour politician, born in London. As secretary of state for economic affairs (1964–6), he instigated a prices and incomes policy, and later became foreign secretary (1966–8).

George Cross (GC) In the UK, a decoration bestowed on civilians for acts of great heroism or conspicuous bravery, or on members of the armed forces for actions in which purely military honours are not normally granted. It was instituted in 1940 and named after George VI.

George Medal (GM) In the UK, the second highest award which may be bestowed on civilians for acts of bravery; instituted in 1940 by George VI. The ribbon is scarlet with five narrow blue stripes.

George Town (Cayman I) 19°20N 81°23W, pop (2000e) 19 400. Capital of the Cayman Is, W Caribbean, on Grand Cayman I; airport nearby.

George Town (Malaysia) *Pinang* (city)

Georgetown 6°46N 58°10W, pop (2000e) 148 000. Port capital of Guyana; founded, 1781; airport; airfield; railway; university (1963); cathedral (1887).

Georgia (republic) *p.374*

Georgia (USA) pop (2000e) 8 186 500; area 152 571 km²/58 910 sq mi. State in SE USA; the 'Empire State of the South' or the 'Peach State'; discovered by the Spanish; settled as a British colony, 1733; named after George II; the fourth of the original 13 states (first Southern state) to ratify the Constitution, 1788; seceded from the Union, 1861; suffered much damage in the Civil War (especially during General Sherman's March to the Sea, 1864); slavery abolished 1865; last state to be re-admitted, 1870; highest point, Mt Brasstown Bald (1457 m/4780 ft); low coastal plain in the S, heavily forested; fertile Piedmont plateau, Appalachian plateau, and Blue Ridge Mts in the N; capital, Atlanta; many local paper mills in the S; leads the nation in production of pulp; major cotton textile producer; grows nearly half US crop of peanuts.

Georgian Style English architecture of the period 1714–1830. The name is derived from the kings George I, II, III, and IV of that period. The style is characterized by a restrained use of classical elements in low relief on the exterior, and more elaborately decorated interiors.

geosynchronous Earth orbit A spacecraft orbit about the Earth's Equator, where the period of the orbit matches the Earth's day and causes the spacecraft to appear stationary at the longitude in question; orbit altitude is 36 000 km/22 500 mi. The orbit is ideally suited for communications satellites.

geothermal energy Energy extracted in the form of heat from the Earth's crust, arising from a combination of the slow cooling of the Earth since its formation, and heat released from natural radioactive decay. Geologically active regions such as

plate margins have higher heat flow values and result in hot springs and geysers.

geranium The name used for two related plant genera: the **cranesbills** (Genus: *Geranium*) and the geraniums of horticulture, the **pelargoniums** (Genus: *Pelargonium*).

Gérard, François (Pascal Simon), Baron [zhayrah(r)] (1770–1837) Painter, born in Rome. His portrait of Isabey the miniaturist (1796) and his 'Cupid and Psyche' (1798), both in the Louvre, established his reputation. He later painted several historical subjects, such as the 'Battle of Austerlitz' (1808, Versailles).

gerbil A type of mouse, native to Africa, Middle East, and C Asia; long hind legs and long furry tail; inhabits dry open country; digs burrows; one species, the **Mongolian gerbil** (*Meriones unguiculatus*) is a popular pet; also known as **jird**. (Subfamily: Gerbilinae, 81 species.)

Gere, Richard [geer] (1949–) Actor, born in Philadelphia, PA. After some years in theatre, he made his screen debut in 1975, and went on to star in such films as *Yanks* (1979), *American Gigolo* (1980), and *Pretty Woman* (1990). Later films include *Runaway Bride* (1999), *Chicago* (2002), and *The Hoax* (2006).

gerenuk [gerenuk] An E African gazelle (*Litocranius walleri*); pale brown; slender, with long neck and small head; male with thick horns (usually curling forward at tips); also known as **giraffe antelope**.

geriatrics The study of the health needs of the aged and their provision. The numbers of elderly persons have increased in recent years in most Western societies, making increasing demands on specialized health and social services, such as district nurses, home helps, meals on wheels, and health visitors. The branch of medicine which investigates the process and problems of aging is known as **gerontology**.

Géricault, (Jean Louis André) Théodore [zhayreekoh] (1791–1824) Painter, born in Rouen, France. He painted many unorthodox and realistic scenes, notably 'The Raft of the Medusa' (1819, Louvre), as well as racing scenes and landscapes.

German, Sir Edward, originally **Edward German Jones** (1862–1936) Composer, born in Whitchurch, Shropshire. In 1901 he emerged as a light opera composer, completing Sullivan's *The Emerald Isle* after the composer's death, and writing *Merrie England* (1902). He also wrote two symphonies, orchestral suites, chamber music, and songs.

German *Germanic languages; German literature*

germander An annual or perennial, sometimes shrubby, found almost everywhere; flowers greenish, pink, or purple with spreading 5-lobed lower lip, upper lip absent. (Genus: *Teucrium*, 300 species. Family: Labiatae.)

Germanic languages A branch of Indo-European comprising the **North Germanic** Scandinavian languages in N Europe, and the **West Germanic** languages English, Frisian, German, and Dutch (with its colonial variant Afrikaans in South Africa) in the W. Scandinavian inscriptions in the runic alphabet date from the 3rd-c AD. Old English and Old High German, precursors of modern English and German, are evidenced from the 8th-c, and the Scandinavian languages from the 12th-c. **East Germanic** languages are extinct, though there are manuscript remains of Gothic.

Germanicus [jermanikus], in full **Gaius Germanicus Caesar** (15 BC–AD 19) The son, father, and brother of Roman emperors (Tiberius, Caligula, and Claudius respectively), and heir apparent himself from AD 14. His sudden and suspicious death in Antioch marked a turning point in Tiberius's reign.

germanium [jermaynium] Ge, element 32, melting point 937°C. A metalloid found in composite ores, especially with silver and zinc. It is extracted from other metals as GeCl$_4$, which boils at c.80°C. Its main use is in transistor manufacture.

German measles *rubella*

German shepherd A breed of large dog developed in Germany in

Georgia

200 km
100 mi

RUSSIAN FEDERATION

INDIA

AFRICA

C a u c a s u s

Gagra
ABKHAZIA
Sukhumi

M o u n t a i n s

OSSETIA

Kazbek 5047m

BLACK
SEA
Kutaisi

GEORGIA

Poti
Rioni

Batumi
Borzhomi
Kura
Telavi
Rustavi

Tbilisi

TURKEY
ARMENIA
AZERBAIJAN

☐ International Airport

(republic), official name **Republic of Georgia**, Georgian **Sakartvelos Respublika**

Local name Georgia

Timezone GMT +4

Area 69 700 km²/26 900 sq mi

Population total (2002e) 4 961 000

Status Republic

Date of independence 1991

Capital Tbilisi

Languages Georgian (official), also Russian

Ethnic groups Georgian (69%), Armenian (9%), Russian (7%), Azerbaijani (5%), Ossetian (3%), Abkhazian (2%)

Religion Georgian Church, independent of the Russian Orthodox Church since 1917

Physical features Mountainous country in C and W Transcaucasia; contains the Greater Caucasus (N) and Lesser Caucasus (S); highest point in the republic, Mt Shkhara, 5203 m/17 070 ft; chief rivers, Kura and Rioni; c.39% of land forested.

Climate Greater Caucasus in N borders temperate and subtropical climatic zones; average temperatures 1–3°C (Jan), 25°C (Jul) in E Transcaucasia; humid, subtropical climate with mild winters in W Mediterranean climate with humid winters, dry summers in N Black Sea region.

Currency 1 Lari (GEL) = 100 tetri

Economy Kakhetia region famed for its orchards and wines; holiday resorts, spas on the Black Sea; manganese, coal, iron and steel, oil refining; tea, fruits, tung oil, tobacco, vines, silk, textiles, food processing.

GDP (2002e) $16·05 bn, per capita $3200

Human Development Index (2002) 0·748

History Proclaimed a Soviet Socialist Republic, 1921; linked with Armenia and Azerbaijan as Transcaucasian Republic, 1922–36; made a constituent republic within the Soviet Union, 1936; declaration of independence, 1991; quest for regional autonomy led to declaration of secession by S Ossetia, 1991, and declaration of independence by Abkhazia, 1992; did not join Commonwealth of Independent States (CIS), 1991; President Gamsakhurdia overthrown in civil war, 1992, bringing military council to power; Parliament dismissed and powers transferred to a State Council headed by Shevardnadze, 1992; joined Commonwealth of Independent states, 1993; Head of State holds executive power, advised by Cabinet of Ministers; new constitution, 1995; Shevardnadze forced to resign following a people's revolution, replaced by leader of the opposition Mikhail Saakashvili in January 2004; post of prime minister reintroduced, 2004.

Head of State

1991–2 Zviad Gamsakhurdia
1992 *Military Council*
1992–2003 Eduard Shevardnadze
2003–4 Nino Burjanadze *Acting*
2004– Mikhail Saakashvili

Head of Government

1992–3 Tengiz Sigua
1993–5 Otar Patatsia
2004–5 Zurab Zhvania
2005– Zurab Noghaideli

Minister of State

1992–3 Tengiz Sigua
1993–5 Otar Patatsia
1995–8 Nikoloz Lekishvili
1998–2000 Vazha Lortkipanidze
2000–3 Gia Arsenishvili
2003–4 Zurab Zhvania

the late 19th-c by crossing spitz breeds with local sheepdogs; thick coat; long pointed muzzle and ears; trains well; also known as **alsatian**.

Germany *pp.376–77*

germ-line therapy or **transfer** An attempt to insert a gene with 'therapeutic' intention into sex cells. Germ-line genetic manipulation does not have any therapeutic effect for the individual possessing an inherited disease; therefore, many argue that gene-line gene 'transfer' is a more appropriate term. In contrast to somatic cell gene therapy, success in this task alters the inheritance of genetically derived disorders in offspring. The concept has caused a great deal of controversy, because of its potential to be used for character 'enhancement' or alteration, rather than for gene correction purposes, giving rise to fears of a new wave of eugenics. As in the case of gene therapy, the procedure remains experimental.

Geronimo [jeronimoh], Indian name **Goyathlay** (1829–1909)

Chiricahua Apache Indian, born along the Gila River in present-day Arizona. The best known of all Apaches, he forcibly resisted the internment of his people on a reservation, escaping from white control on several occasions.

gerontology *geriatrics*

Gershwin, George, originally **Jacob Gershvin** (1898–1937) Composer, born in New York City. In 1924 he began collaborating with his brother **Ira** (1896–1983) as lyricist, producing numerous classic songs, such as 'Lady Be Good' (1924) and 'I Got Rhythm' (1930). He also composed extended concert works including *Rhapsody in Blue* (1924), *An American in Paris* (1928), and the opera *Porgy and Bess* (1935).

Gervais, Ricky [zhairvayz] (1962–) Actor, writer, and director, born in Reading, Berkshire. He shot to fame with his role as branch manager David Brent in the BBC television cult show *The Office* (2001–2), a series he co-wrote with Stephen Merchant. In 2002 the show won double BAFTA awards for Gervais for Best Sitcom and Best Comedy Performance, and he repeated this success in 2003 and 2004. At the 2003 Golden Globe awards he won Best TV Comedy Actor and *The Office* won best comedy show. He teamed up with Merchant again for the comedy series *Extras* (2005–).

Gestapo [geshtahpoh] An abbreviation of *Geheime Staatspolizei*, the secret police of the German Third Reich, founded in 1933 by Goering. From 1936 it came under the control of Himmler, as head of the SS (*Schutsstaffel*).

Gethsemane [gethsemanee] A place outside Jerusalem near the Mt of Olives where Jesus and his disciples went to pray immediately before his betrayal and arrest (*Mark* 14.32ff); described as a 'garden' in *John* 18.1.

Getty, J(ean) Paul (1892–1976) Oil executive, multi-millionaire, and art collector, born in Minneapolis, MN. He entered the oil business and went on to control more than 100 companies, becoming one of the richest men in the world. He founded the J Paul Getty Museum at Malibu, CA, in 1953.

Gettysburg, Battle of (Jun–Jul 1863) A major series of engagements in the American Civil War between the army of N Virginia (Confederate) and the army of the Potomac (Union). Union victory ended any prospect of foreign recognition for the Confederacy.

Gettysburg Address (19 Nov 1863) During the American Civil War, a speech given by President Lincoln at the dedication of a war cemetery in Pennsylvania on the site of the Battle of Gettysburg.

geyser [geezer, giyzer] A natural spring which erupts intermittently, throwing up fountains of superheated water and steam from a crack deep in the Earth's crust. Geysers occur in volcanically active areas in New Zealand, Iceland, and the USA.

Ggantija Temples [jgantiya] A Copper Age temple complex on Gozo, NW Malta; a world heritage site. The two temples, built 3600–3300 BC, were excavated in 1827.

Ghana *p.378*

gharial [gairial] or **gavial** A rare S Asian crocodile-like reptile (*Gavialis gangeticus*) of family Gavialidae; length up to 6·6 m/21½ ft; very narrow snout; nostrils of male swollen as a bulbous 'pot'.

Ghats [gahts] Two mountain ranges in India; **Eastern Ghats** runs parallel to the Bay of Bengal, forming the E edge of the Deccan Plateau; **Western Ghats** runs parallel to the Arabian Sea, forming the W boundary of the Deccan plateau; length c.1600 km/ 1000 mi; highest point, Anai Mudi Peak (2695 m/8842 ft) in the Cardamon Hills.

ghee [gee] An edible fat derived from butter by removing all or most of the water. It is popular in hot climates, where the absence of water improves the keeping quality of the butter-fat.

Ghent [gent], Flemish **Gent**, Fr **Gand** 51°02N 3°42E, pop (2000e) 234 200. River port in NW Belgium, at the confluence of the Scheldt and Leie Rivers; third largest urban region in Belgium; focus of Flemish nationality; railway; university (1816); cathedral (begun 10th-c).

gherkin A variety of cucumber (*Cucumis sativa*) or its very small fruits. (Family: Cucurbitaceae.)

Ghibellines [gibeleenz] The pro-imperial party in Italian cities of the 13th–14th-c, favouring the involvement of the Holy Roman Emperor in Italian politics.

Ghiberti, Lorenzo [geebairtee] (1378–1455) Goldsmith, bronze-caster, and sculptor, born in Florence, Italy. In 1401 he won the competition to make a pair of bronze gates for the Baptistry of Florence Cathedral.

Ghirlandaio, Domenico [geerlandahyoh], originally **Domenico di Tommaso Bigordi** (1449–94) Painter, born in Florence, Italy. His main works were frescoes, notably a series illustrating the lives of the Virgin and the Baptist in the choir of Santa Maria Novella, Florence (1490).

Ghose, Zulfikar (1935–) Writer, born in Sialkot, NE Pakistan (formerly, India). He and his family moved to England in 1952, but in 1969 he moved to the USA. His first novel, *The Contradictions* (1966), was followed by a trilogy, *The Incredible Brazilian* (1972–8). Other works include the novel *The Triple Mirror of the Self* (1992) and *Selected Poems* (1991). Non-fiction works include *The Art of Creating Fiction* (1991) and an autobiography, *Confessions of a Native-Alien* (1965).

Giacconi, Riccardo (1931–) Astrophysicist, born in Genoa, Italy. He became director of the Space Telescope Science Institute in Baltimore (1981), specializing in X-ray astronomy. He shared the 2002 Nobel Prize for Physics for pioneering contributions to astrophysics, which have led to the discovery of cosmic X-ray sources.

Giacometti, Alberto [jiakometee] (1901–66) Sculptor and painter, born in Stampa, Switzerland. He joined the Surrealists in 1930, producing many abstract constructions of a symbolic kind, arriving finally at the characteristic 'thin man' bronzes, such as 'Pointing Man' (1947, Tate, London).

Giant's Causeway 55°14N 6°30W. Volcanic basalt formation on the N coast of Co Antrim, Northern Ireland; a world heritage site; according to legend, the causeway was built for giants to travel across to Scotland.

giardiasis [jeeah(r)diyasis] The infestation of the intestinal tract of vertebrates with the parasite *Giardia lamblia*, which can cause severe diarrhoea. It is one of the few infections which can be transmitted from people to animals. It is named after the French biologist Alfred Giard (1846–1908).

Gibbon, Edward (1737–94) Historian, born in Putney, Surrey. After a visit to Rome in 1764 he began his major work, *The History of the Decline and Fall of the Roman Empire* (5 vols, 1776–88).

Gibbon, Lewis Grassic, pseudonym of **James Leslie Mitchell** (1901–35) Writer, born in Auchterless, Aberdeenshire. He published the historical novels *Three Go Back* (1932) and *Spartacus* (1933) under his own name, but the trilogy *A Scots Quair* (1946) appeared under his pseudonym.

gibbon An ape native to rainforests of SE Asia; acrobatic; slender with small head; thumb small; fingers long; arms as long as body and legs together; also known as **lesser ape**. (Genus: *Hylobates*, 6 species.)

Gibbons, Grinling (1648–1721) Sculptor and woodcarver, born in Rotterdam, The Netherlands. At Chatsworth, Burghley, and other mansions he executed an immense quantity of carved fruit and flowers, cherubs' heads, and other typical Baroque embellishment.

Gibbons, Orlando (1583–1625) Composer, born in Oxford, Oxfordshire. His compositions include services, anthems, and madrigals (notably 'The Silver Swan'), and also hymns, fantasies for viols, and music for virginals.

Gibbons, Stella (Dorothea) (1902–89) Writer, born in London. Her *Cold Comfort Farm* (1932), a light-hearted satire on melodramatic rural novels, has established itself as a classic of parody.

Gibbs, J(osiah) Willard (1839–1903) Mathematician and physicist, born in New Haven, CT. The field of chemical thermodynamics developed largely from his work, and he was a founder of physical chemistry.

Gibraltar [jibrawlter], Span [kheevraltahr], Arabic **Jebel Tariq** 36°09N 5°21W; pop (2002e) 27 000; area 6·5 km²/2·5 sq mi. British Crown Colony; a narrow rocky peninsula rising steeply from the low-lying coast of SW Spain at the E end of the Strait of Gibraltar; length, c.5 km/3 mi; width 1·2 km/¾ mi, narrowing to the S; 8 km/5 mi from Algeciras; timezone GMT +1; official language, English, with Spanish widely spoken; units of currency, the Pound Sterling (GBP) and the Gibraltar Pound (GIP); limestone massif, 'The Rock', height 426 m/1398 ft, connected to the Spanish mainland by a sandy plain; home of the Barbary apes,

Germany

☐ International Airport

Ger **Deutschland**, official name **Federal Republic of Germany**, Ger **Bundesrepublik Deutschland**

Local name Bundesrepublik Deutschland

Timezone GMT +1

Area 357 868 km²/138 136 sq mi

Population total (2002e) 82 506 000

Status Federal republic

Capital Berlin

Languages German (official)

Ethnic groups German (93%), Turkish (2%), Yugoslav (1%), Italian (1%), other European Community (3%)

Religions Lutheran (55%), Roman Catholic (38%), Muslim (3%)

Physical features Lowland plains rise SW through C uplands and Alpine foothills to the Bavarian Alps; highest peak, the Zugspitze, 2962 m/9718 ft; C uplands include the Rhenish Slate Mts, Black Forest, and Harz Mts; Rhine crosses the country S–N; complex canal system links chief rivers, Elbe, Weser, Danube, Rhine, Main.

Climate Oceanic climatic influences strongest in NW, where winters are mild, stormy; elsewhere continental climate; lower winter temperatures in E and S, with considerable snowfall; average annual temperatures -0.5°C (Jan) to 19°C (Jul); average annual rainfall 600–700 mm/23–7 in.

Currency 1 euro (EUR) = 100 cents (previous to February 2002, 1 Deutsche Mark (DEM) = 100 pfennige).

Economy Economically powerful member of EC (accounts for 30% of European Community output): substantial heavy industry in NW, wine in Rhine and Moselle valleys; increasing tourism, especially in the S; leading manufacturer of vehicles, electrical and electronic goods; much less development in the E, after the period of socialist economy; following unification, a major socio-economic division emerged between W and E, leading to demonstrations in the E provinces, 1991.

GDP (2002e) $2·16 tn, per capita $26 200

Human Development Index (2002) 0·925

History Ancient Germanic tribes united in 8th-c within the Frankish Empire of Charlemagne; elective monarchy after 918 under Otto I, with Holy Roman Empire divided into several hundred states; after Congress of Vienna, 1814–15, a confederation of 39 states under Austria; under Bismarck, Prussia succeeded Austria as the leading German power; union of Germany and foundation of Second Reich, 1871, with King of Prussia as hereditary German Emperor; aggressive foreign policy, eventually leading to World War 1; after German defeat, Second Reich replaced by democratic Weimar Republic; world economic crisis led to collapse of Weimar Republic and rise of National Socialist movement, 1929; Adolph Hitler became dictator of the totalitarian Third Reich, 1933; acts of aggression led to World War 2 and a second defeat for Germany, with collapse of the German political regime; partition of Germany in 1945, with occupation zones given to UK, USA, France, and USSR, who formed a Control Council; USSR withdrew from the Control Council in 1948, dividing Germany into W and E: W Germany controlled by the three remaining powers, UK, USA and France; E administered by USSR.

West Germany (former Federal Republic of Germany) Area 249 535 km²/96 320 sq mi; population total (1990) 62 679 035; including West Berlin; established, 1949; gained full sovereignty, 1954; entered NATO, 1955; founder member of the European Union (formerly EC), 1958; federal system of government, built around 10 provinces (Länder) with considerable powers;

the only native monkeys in Europe; settled by Moors, 711; taken by Spain, 1462; captured by Anglo-Dutch force, 1704; ceded to Britain by Spain, 1713; Crown Colony, 1830; played a key role in Allied naval operations during both World Wars; proposal to end British rule defeated by referendum, 1967; Spanish closure of frontier, 1969–85; Spain continues to claim sovereignty; British–Spanish talks ongoing, 2002; referendum (Nov 2002) resulted in 99 percent rejection of joint sovereignty by Gibraltarians; collapse of talks, 2003; celebrations marking 300 years of British rule strongly criticized by Spain, 2004; new consti-

tution (Jan 2007) allows devolution of additional powers from UK; British monarch represented by a governor and House of Assembly; military base; important strategic point of control for the W Mediterranean; economy largely dependent on the presence of British forces; airport; car ferries to Tangier.

Gibraltar, Strait of, Arabic **Bab al Zakak**, Lat **Fretum Herculeum** Channel connecting the Mediterranean Sea to the Atlantic Ocean; length, 60 km/37 mi; width between the Rock of Gibraltar and Cape Ceuta (the Pillars of Hercules), 24 km/15 mi; widest point, 40 km/25 mi; narrowest point, 15 km/9 mi.

☐ International Airport

People's Chamber, a single-chamber parliament (Volkskammer) which elected a Council of State, a Council of Ministers, and a National Defence Council; movement for democratic reform culminated in Nov 1989 in the opening and removal of the Wall and other border crossings to the West, and a more open government policy; first free all-German elections since 1932 held in Mar 1990, paving the way for a currency union with West Germany, Jul 1990, and full political unification, Oct 1990.

United Germany The 10 provinces of West Germany joined by the 5 former East German provinces abolished after World War 2 (Brandenburg, Mecklenburg-West, Pomerania, Saxony, Saxony-Anhalt, Thuringia), along with unified Berlin; West German electoral system adopted in East Germany; first national elections, Dec 1990.

German Democratic Republic (East Germany)

Head of State
1949–60 Wilhelm Pieck

Chairman of the Council of State
1960–73 Walter Ulbricht
1973–6 Willi Stoph
1976–89 Erich Honecker
1989 Egon Krenz
1989–90 Gregor Gysi *General Secretary as Chairman*

Head of Government
1949–64 Otto Grotewohl
1964–73 Willi Stoph
1973–6 Horst Sindermann
1976–89 Willi Stoph
1989–90 Hans Modrow
1990 Lothar de Maizière

German Federal Republic (until 1990 West Germany)

Head of State
1949–59 Theodor Heuss
1959–69 Heinrich Lübke
1969–74 Gustav Heinemann
1974–9 Walter Scheel
1979–84 Karl Carstens
1984–94 Richard von Weizsäcker
1994–9 Roman Herzog
1999–2004 Johannes Rau
2004– Horst Koehler

Head of Government (Federal Chancellor)
1949–63 Konrad Adenauer
1963–6 Ludwig Erhard
1966–9 Kurt Georg Kiesinger
1969–74 Willy Brandt
1974–82 Helmut Schmidt
1982–98 Helmut Kohl
1998–2005 Gerhard Schröder
2005– Angela Merkel

two-chamber legislature, consisting of Federal Diet (Bundestag) and Federal Council (Bundesrat).

East Germany (former German Democratic Republic) Area 108 333 km²/41 816 sq mi; population total (1990) 16 433 796; administered by USSR after 1945 partition, and Soviet model of government established, 1949; anti-Soviet demonstrations put down, 1953; recognized by USSR as an independent republic, 1954; flow of refugees to West Germany continued until 1961, largely stopped by the Berlin Wall built along zonal boundary, dividing western sectors of Berlin from eastern; governed by the

Gibson, Guy (Penrose) (1918–44) British airman, born in Simla, NE India. As a wing-commander in the RAF he led the famous 'dambusters' raid on the Möhne and Eder dams in 1943, an exploit for which he received the VC. He was killed during a later operation.

Gibson, Mel, originally **Columcille Gerard Gibson** (1956–) Film actor, born in Peekskill, NY. He made his film debut in Australia in 1977, and became known following his role in the action-packed *Mad Max* films (1979, 1981, 1985). Other films include *Lethal Weapon* (1987) and its sequels (1989, 1992, 1998), *Hamlet*

(1990), *Braveheart*, which he also directed (1995, Oscar Best Film), and *Payback* (1999). Later work as a director includes the controversial *The Passion of the Christ* (2004), and *Apocalypto* (2006).

Gibson Desert Central belt of the Western Australian Desert; area c.220 000 km²/85 000 sq mi.

Gide, André (Paul Guillaume) [zheed] (1869–1951) Writer, born in Paris. Among his best-known works are *Les Nourritures terrestres* (1897, Fruits of the Earth) and *Les Faux Monnayeurs* (1926,

Ghana

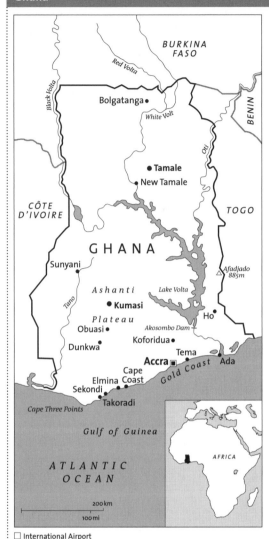

☐ International Airport

[gahna], official name **Republic of Ghana**

Local name Ghana

Timezone GMT

Area 238 537 km²/92 100 sq mi

Population total (2002e) 20 244 000

Status Republic

Date of independence 1960

Capital Accra

Languages English (official), Akan, Ewe, Ga, several minority languages

Ethnic groups c.75 tribal groups, including Akan (44%), Mole-Dagbani (16%), Ewe (13%), and Ga (8%)

Religions Christian (43%), traditional local beliefs (38%), Muslim (12%)

Physical features Located in W Africa; low-lying plains inland, leading to the Ashanti plateau (W) and R Volta basin (E), dammed to form L Volta; mountains (E) rise to 885 m/2903 ft at Mt Afadjado; Ashanti plateau in W and Akwapin Toto Mts in E.

Climate Tropical climate, including a warm dry coastal belt (SE); a hot, humid SW corner; and a hot, dry savannah (N); average temperatures 27°C (Jan), 25°C (Jul) in Accra.

Currency 1 Cedi (GHC) = 100 pesewas

Economy Agriculture; cocoa (world's leading producer) provides two-thirds of export revenue; tourism; commercial reserves of oil, diamonds, gold, manganese, bauxite, timber.

GDP (2002e) $41·25 bn, per capita $2000

Human Development Index (2002) 0·548

History Visited by Europeans in 15th-c; centre of slave trade, 18th-c; modern state created by union of two former British territories, British Gold Coast (Crown Colony, 1874) and British Togoland, merging to form Ghana and declaring independence, 1957; independent republic within the Commonwealth, 1960; constitution provides for a Parliament, executive President, Cabinet, and Council of State; series of military coups (1966, 1972, 1979, 1982) led to the creation of a Provisional National Defence Council, which rules by decree; new multi-party constitution, 1992, allowing for a directly elected executive President and legislature.

Head of State/Government
(Chairman of the Provisional National Defence Council)
1981–92 Jerry John Rawlings

President
1992–2001 Jerry John Rawlings
2001– John Kufuor

The Counterfeiters), as well as his *Journal*. He received the Nobel Prize for Literature in 1947.

Gideons International An international organization, which began in Wisconsin in 1898, with the aim of spreading the Christian faith by the free distribution of copies of the Bible to public places. It is named after the Biblical judge, Gideon, who led Israel against the Midianites.

Gielgud, Sir (Arthur) John [geelgud] (1904–2000) Actor and director, born in London. He established a reputation as Hamlet (1929), and became a leading Shakespearean actor. His film appearances include *Arthur* (1970, Oscar), *Prospero's Books* (1991), and *Elizabeth* (1998). The London *Globe* theatre was renamed after him in 1994.

GIF [gif] *digital media*

Gigantes [jiyganteez, giganteez] In Greek mythology, the sons of Earth and Tartaros, with snake-like legs; their name means 'the giants'. They made war on the Olympian gods, were defeated, and are buried under various volcanic islands.

Giggs, Ryan (1973–) Footballer, born in Cardiff. He made his league debut for Manchester United in 1991, and first played for Wales later that year, becoming the youngest-ever Welsh cap. He has twice been named the Professional Football Association's Young Player of the Year (1991–2). His honours with United include the FA Cup, Premier League Championship, and European Cup in the 1998–9 season, and a third consecutive league championship (2000–1). By the end of 2006 he had gained 59 caps for Wales.

Gigli, Beniamino [jeelyee] (1890–1957) Tenor, born in Recanati, Italy. He won a worldwide reputation as a lyric-dramatic tenor of great vitality, at his best in the works of Verdi and Puccini.

gigue [zheeg] A lively dance, probably of British origin, popular during the 17th–18th-c. It became a standard movement in instrumental suites of the period.

gila monster [heela] An American lizard of family Helodermatidae; the only venomous lizard; length up to 600 mm/24 in; dark with yellow mottling; bead-like scales; blunt head; fat tail; two species.

Gilbert, Cass (1859–1934) Architect, born in Zanesville, OH. He designed the first tower skyscraper, the 60-storey Woolworth Building in New York City (1912), at that time the tallest building in the world.

Gilbert, William, also **Gylberde, William** (1544–1603) Physician and physicist, born in Colchester, Essex. He established the magnetic nature of the Earth, and was the first to use the terms 'electricity', 'electric force' and 'electric attraction'. The *gilbert*, unit of magnetomotive power, is named after him.

Gilbert, Sir W(illiam) S(chwenck) (1836–1911) Parodist, and librettist of the 'Gilbert and Sullivan' light operas, born in London. He wrote much humorous verse under his boyhood nickname 'Bab', collected in 1869 as the *Bab Ballads*. He is remembered for his partnership with Sir Arthur Sullivan, begun in 1871, with whom he wrote 14 popular operas, from *Trial by Jury* (1875) to *The Gondoliers* (1889).

Gilbert and George Avant-garde artists: **Gilbert Proesch** (1943–) and **George Passmore** (1944–). They made their name in the late 1960s as performance artists (the 'singing sculptures'), with faces and hands painted gold, holding their poses for hours at a time. Tate Modern held a retrospective exhibition of their work in 2007.

Gilbert of Sempringham, St (c.1083–1189) Priest, born in Sempringham, Lincolnshire. In 1131 he founded the Order of Gilbertines for monks and nuns, the only mediaeval order to originate in England. He was canonized in 1202. Feast day 4 February.

Gilbert Islands pop (2000e) 82 000; area 264 km²/102 sq mi. Island group of Kiribati, C Pacific Ocean; chain of 17 coral atolls spread over c.680 km/420 mi; part of the British colony of Gilbert and Ellice Is until 1977; capital, Tarawa.

Gilchrist, Ellen [gilkrist] (1935–) Writer, born in Vicksburg, MI. She has written poetry, short stories, and novels, and is known especially for her satirical treatment of the upper-class world of the southern states of the USA. Her novels include *The Annunciation* (1983) and *Net of Jewels* (1993). Short-story collections include *Victory Over Japan* (1984) and *The Cabal and Other Stories* (2000).

gilding The ancient craft of sticking gold (or other metallic) leaf on to a surface, usually wood. Gilding flourished in the Middle Ages in manuscript illumination and panel painting, and later for picture-frames and furniture.

Giles, Bill, popular name of **William George Giles** (1939–) Weatherman, born in Dittisham, Devon. He joined the Meteorological Office in 1959 and became a radio broadcaster in 1972. He moved to television in 1975 and was head of the Weather Centre at the BBC (1983–2000). His books include *The Story of Weather* (1990).

Giles, Carl [jiylz] (1916–95) Cartoonist, born in London. From 1937 he produced his distinctive and popular drawings, first for *Reynolds News*, then (from 1943) for the *Express* newspapers.

Gilgamesh [gilgamesh] A Babylonian epic poem, named after its hero, the Sumerian King Gilgamesh (3rd millennium BC). It includes a story of the Flood that has striking parallels with the Biblical account.

Gill, (Arthur) Eric (Rowton) [gil] (1882–1940) Carver, engraver, and typographer, born in Brighton, East Sussex. Among his main works is 'Prospero and Ariel' (1931) at Broadcasting House, London.

Gillespie, Dizzy [gilespee], popular name of **John Birks Gillespie** (1917–93) Jazz trumpeter and composer, born in Cheraw, SC. He worked in prominent swing bands (1937–44), and as a leader, often with Charlie Parker on saxophone, he developed the music called *bebop*, with dissonant harmonies and poly-rhythms, a reaction to swing.

Gillette, King C(amp) [jilet] (1855–1932) Inventor of the safety razor, born in Fond du Lac, WI. He founded his razor blade company in 1903.

Gilliam, Terry [gilyam] (1940–) Artist and film director, born in Minneapolis, MI. Originally known for his fantasy animations in TV's 'Monty Python's Flying Circus' (1969–74), he went on to work in film, directing such imaginative adventures as *The Time Bandits* (1980), *The Adventures of Baron Munchausen* (1988), *Fear and Loathing in Las Vegas* (1998), and *The Brothers Grimm* (2005).

gilliflower *stock*

Gillray, James [gilray] (1757–1815) Caricaturist, born in London. He issued about 1500 caricatures of political and social subjects, notably of Napoleon, George III, and leading politicians.

Gilman, Charlotte Anna Perkins, *née* **Perkins**, earlier married name **Stetson** (1860–1935) Feminist and writer, born in Hartford, CT. Her most notable books are *Women and Economics* (1898), *The Home* (1903), and *Man-Made World* (1911).

gilt-edged securities The name given to UK government loan stock, considered to be a safe investment. The name derives from the book in which transactions were originally recorded, which was edged in gold.

gin A spirit distilled from grain or malt, and flavoured with juniper berries. **Dutch gin** is drunk neat with beer, while **London** or **dry gin** is usually mixed with tonic.

Ginckell or **Ginkel, Godert de** [gingkel] (1630–1703) Dutch general, born in Utrecht. He accompanied William III to England in 1688, and fought at the Battle of the Boyne (1690).

ginger A perennial native to SE Asia (*Zingiber officinale*); stem to 1 m/3¼ ft; yellow and purple flowers. The aromatic underground stem contains the essential oil *zingiberene*, used in perfumes as well as food and drink (such as ginger ale). (Family: Zingiberaceae.)

gingivitis [jinjiviytis] Inflammation of the gums caused by excessive deposits on the teeth of plaque, consisting of food debris, mucus, and bacteria, leaving them prone to infection. The infection can spread to the tissues and bone that support the teeth, ultimately resulting in their loss.

Gingrich, Newt(on Leroy) [ginggrich] (1943–) US politician, born in Hummelstown, PA. He was elected as Republican representative for Georgia in 1979, and became Speaker of the House in 1995 with the promise of enacting a new conservative agenda. He resigned in November 1998 following the poor performance of his party in the mid-term elections.

ginkgo A deciduous gymnosperm (*Ginkgo biloba*) originally from SW China, but probably no longer existing in the wild; seed with a fleshy outgrowth covering the edible kernel; also called **maidenhair tree**. (Family: Ginkgoaceae.)

Ginola, David [zhinola] (1967–) Footballer, born in Gassin, France. He played for Paris St Germain, moving to the UK to join Newcastle United (1995), Tottenham Hotspur (1997), Aston Villa (2000), and Everton (2002–3), where he finished his playing career. He won 17 caps for France, and in 1994 was voted French Footballer of the Year, but he lost his place in the national team after France failed to qualify for the 1994 World Cup. In 1998 he highlighted the international campaign against land mines by visiting an Angolan minefield. After retiring from football, he began a career in acting.

gin rummy *rummy*

Ginsberg, Allen (1926–97) Poet, born in Newark, NJ. His first book, *Howl* (1957), presented the prototype poetry of the 'beat' school. His *Collected Poems* were published in 1987.

ginseng Either of two species of thick-rooted perennial (*Panax pseudoginseng*, *Panax quinquefolium*), native to North America and Asia; 5-petalled, yellowish-green flowers; round, red fruits. The powdered roots are said to have aphrodisiac as well as medicinal and rejuvenative properties. It is popular as a tonic and dietary supplement. (Family: Araliaceae.)

Ginzburg, Vitaly L (1916–) Physicist, born in Moscow. In 1940 he joined the P N Lebedev Physical Institute of the Russian Academy of Sciences in Moscow. In 2003 he shared the Nobel Prize for Physics for pioneering contributions to the theory of superconductors and superfluids.

Giorgione [jiaw(r)jiohnay], also called **Giorgio da Castelfranco**, originally **Giorgio Barbarelli** (c.1478–1510) Painter, born in Castelfranco, Italy. A great innovator, he created the small, intimate easel picture and a new treatment of figures in landscape, 'the landscape of mood'. One of his best-known works is 'The Tempest' (c.1505, Venice).

Giotto (di Bondone) [jiotoh] (c.1266–1337) Painter and architect, born near Vespignano, Italy, the founder of the Florentine School of painting. His major work was the fresco cycle, 'The Lives of Christ and the Virgin', in the Arena Chapel, Padua (1305–8). In 1334 he was appointed Master of Works in Florence, designing the Campanile. The fresco cycle on the life of St Francis in the Basilica of St Francis in Assisi is also attributed to him; it was severely damaged in an earthquake in 1997.

Giotto project [jiotoh] The first European interplanetary spacecraft launched in 1985 from Kourou, French Guiana, to intercept Halley's Comet. It encountered the comet successfully (13 Mar 1986) at a distance of 500 km/300 mi from the active nucleus, protected by a dust shield, and obtained TV images of the nucleus, and measurements of gases and dust.

Gipsy *Rom*

giraffe An African ruminant mammal (*Giraffa camelopardalis*), the tallest land animal (height, 5·5 m/18 ft); extremely long legs and neck; an artiodactyl; head with 2–5 blunt 'horns'; usually pale with large angular brown blotches; also known as **camel(e)opard**. (Family: Giraffidae.)

giraffe antelope *gerenuk*

Giralda [heeralda] A bell tower adjacent to Seville Cathedral, in Spain. Built (1163–84) as an Islamic minaret, the tower is 93 m/305 ft high, and takes its name from the *giraldillo* or weathervane which surmounts it.

Giraldus Cambrensis [jiraldus kambrensis], also known as **Gerald of Wales** or **Gerald de Barri** (c.1147–1223) Historian and clergyman, born in Manorbier Castle, S Wales. He wrote an account of Ireland's natural history and inhabitants, and in 1188 travelled through Wales to recruit soldiers for the Third Crusade, writing up his observations in the *Itinerarium Cambriae* (1191, Itinerary of Wales) and *Cambriae descriptio* (1194, Description of Wales).

Giraudoux, (Hippolyte) Jean [zheerohdoo] (1882–1944) Writer and diplomat, born in Bellac, France. He is chiefly remembered for his plays, mainly fantasies based on Greek myths and biblical lore, such as *Ondine* (1939), and *La Folle de Chaillot* (1945, The Mad Woman of Chaillot).

girl guide / scout *scouting*

giro [jiyroh] A state-operated low-cost banking system which commenced in the UK in 1968. Now called **Girobank PLC**, it is operated by the Post Office Corporation through its 20 000 post offices, carrying out the normal range of banking services.

Girondins [jirondinz], Fr [zhirõdĩ] A group of deputies in the Legislative Assembly (1791–2) and French Convention (1792–5). Sympathetic to the provinces rather than to Paris (their name derived from the Gironde region of SW France), many were executed during the Reign of Terror (1793).

Girtin, Thomas [gertin] (1775–1802) Landscape painter, born in London. His works were among the first to exploit watercolour as a true medium, as distinct from a tint for colouring drawings.

Gisborne [gizbaw(r)n] 38°41S 178°02E, pop (2000e) 34 000. Port and resort town in North Island, New Zealand; site of Captain Cook's first landing, 1769; airfield; railway.

Giscard d'Estaing, Valéry [zheeskah(r) daystī] (1926–) French statesman and president (1974–81), born in Koblenz, Germany. He became finance minister (1962–6), and launched his own Party (National Federation of Independent Republicans). He returned to the finance ministry in 1969, defeated Mitterrand to become president in 1974, and was then beaten by Mitterrand in 1981.

Gish, Lillian, originally **Lillian de Guiche** (1893–1993) Actress, born in Springfield, OH. She started in silent films as an extra under D W Griffith in 1912, and became the girl heroine in all his classics from *The Birth of a Nation* (1915) to *Orphans of the Storm* (1922). Her character roles continued into the 1970s.

Gissing, George (Robert) (1857–1903) Novelist, born in Wakefield, West Yorkshire. *Workers in the Dawn* (1880) was the first of over 20 novels largely presenting realistic portraits of poverty and misery. His best-known novel is *New Grub Street* (1891).

gittern A mediaeval musical instrument resembling a lute, but with a shorter neck. It usually had three or four courses of strings played with a plectrum.

Giuffre, Jimmy [joofree], popular name of **James Peter Giuffre** (1921–) Jazz musician and composer, born in Dallas, TX. He played clarinet and saxophones with various bands during the 1940s, then specialized in the clarinet, developing a distinctive breathy tone. His compositions include several chamber and ballet pieces, and he was also active in music education.

Giuliani, Rudolph W(illiam) [jooliahni] (1944–) US lawyer, politician, and mayor of New York City, born in New York City. He spent several years in private law practice, then ran for Mayor of New York City as a Republican in 1993, being re-elected in 1997. He decided to run for the US senate in 2000, but withdrew on health grounds. His popularity soared in the aftermath of the terrorist attack on New York on 11 Sep 2001, and his adept handling of the situation in the city led to calls for his term of office to be extended, but he stood down. In 2007 he announced his bid to run for Republican candidate in the 2008 presidential elections. He was awarded an honorary knighthood by the UK in 2002.

Giulio Romano [joolioh romahnoh], originally **Giulio Pippi de' Giannuzzi** (c.1499–1546) Painter and architect, born in Rome. He assisted Raphael in several of his later works, and in 1524 went to Mantua, where he protected the city from floods.

Giza [geeza], al-Giza, Gizeh, or **al-Jizah** 30°03N 32°15E, pop (2000e) 2 667 000. Town in N Egypt; on W bank of R Nile, 5 km/3 mi SW of Cairo; railway; Sphinx, and pyramids of Khufu (Cheops), Khafra, and Mankara nearby.

glaciation The coverage of the surface of the Earth by glaciers, as well as the erosive action produced by the movement of ice over the land surface. The most extensive period of recent glaciation was in the Pleistocene epoch, when polar ice caps repeatedly advanced and retreated, covering up to 30% of the Earth's surface.

glacier A body of ice originating from recrystallized snow in cirques in mountain areas and flowing slowly downslope by creep under its own weight (**alpine glaciers**). Huge glaciers on continental plateaux are termed **ice sheets**.

glaciology The scientific study of ice in all its forms, including its crystal structure and physical properties, as well as glaciers and ice sheets.

gladiators In ancient Rome, heavily armed fighting men who fought duels, often to the death, in public. They were usually slaves, prisoners of war, or condemned criminals.

gladiolus A perennial with a large fibrous corm, native to Europe, Asia, and Africa; flower with a short tube and six spreading or hooded segments in a variety of colours, in one-sided spikes. (Genus: *Gladiolus*, 300 species. Family: Iridaceae.)

Gladstone, W(illiam) E(wart) (1809–98) British Liberal statesman and prime minister (1868–74, 1880–5, 1886, 1892–4), born in Liverpool, Merseyside. He was twice Chancellor of the Exchequer (1852–5, 1859–66), and in 1867 became leader of the Liberal Party. Frequently in office until 1894, he succeeded in carrying out a scheme of parliamentary reform which went a long way towards universal male suffrage. In his last two ministries he introduced bills for Irish Home Rule, but both were defeated.

Glamorgan *Mid Glamorgan; South Glamorgan; Vale of Glamorgan; West Glamorgan*

gland A single cell or group of cells secreting specific substances (eg hormones) for use elsewhere in the body. In mammals, most glands are **exocrine**: their secretions are discharged via duct systems into the cavity of a hollow organ (eg the salivary glands), or open directly onto an outer epidermal surface (eg the sweat glands of mammals). Vertebrates and some invertebrates also possess **endocrine glands** (eg the pituitary glands in vertebrates), whose secretions are released directly into the blood stream.

glanders or **the glanders** A malignant disease of horses, characterized by a swelling of the glands (especially beneath the jaw) and a mucous discharge from the nostrils; fatal and contagious; may be caught by humans.

glandular fever A generalized and sometimes prolonged infectious disease due to Epstein–Barr virus (EBV), which tends to affect young people. The blood contains a large number of mononuclear cells, and the condition is technically known as **infectious mononucleosis**. There is no specific antiviral remedy.

glare *Polaroid 1*

Glaser, Donald A(rthur) [glayzer] (1926–) Physicist, born in Cleveland, OH. He developed the 'bubble chamber' for observing the paths of atomic particles, for which he received the Nobel Prize for Physics in 1960.

Glasgow 55°53N 4°15W, pop (2000e) 678 700. City and local council (as City of Glasgow), W Scotland; on R Clyde; largest city in Scotland; airport; railway; underground; University of Glasgow (1451); Strathclyde University (1964); Glasgow Caledonian University (1992, formerly Glasgow Polytechnic); shipyards, engineering, commerce, whisky blending and bottling, chemicals, textiles, carpets; cathedral (12th-c), Cathcart castle (15th-c), Crookston castle (15th-c), Haggs castle (1585); European City of Culture, 1990.

glasnost (Russ 'speaking aloud') A term describing the changes in attitude on the part of leaders of the Soviet Union since 1985 under Gorbachev, which brought about a greater degree of openness both within Soviet society and in its relations with foreign powers.

Glass, Philip (1937–) Composer, born in Baltimore, MD. A proponent of minimalism in music, he attracted public notice with the first of his 12 operas, *Einstein on the Beach* (1976). Later works include *The Hydrogen Jukebox* (1990), the multimedia opera *Monsters of Grace* (1998), and the film scores *Kundun* (1998), *The Hours* (2002, BAFTA), and *Notes on a Scandal* (2006). His opera, *Waiting for the Barbarians*, premiered in Germany in 2005.

glass 1 Any non-crystalline solid; one in which there is no orderly pattern, or arrangement of atoms. It is usually formed by the rapid cooling of a viscous liquid, such that the atoms have insufficient time to align into a crystal structure.

2 The transparent or translucent product of the fusion of lime (calcium oxide), soda (sodium carbonate), and silica (silicon(IV) dioxide). There may be other constituents, yielding a great variety of properties. Having no sharp melting point, glass can be

formed by many techniques while hot, most being variants on blowing or moulding. The best flat glass is today made by the 'float' process: molten glass flows continuously over a bed of molten tin.

glass harmonica *musical glasses*

glass snake A lizard native to North America, Europe, and Asia; snake-like, with no limbs; length, up to 1·3 m/4¼ ft; tail can be shed to confuse predators, and may break into several pieces; also known as **glass lizard**. (Genus: *Ophisaurus*, several species. Family: Anguidae.)

glasswort An annual herb growing along coasts and in salt marshes more or less everywhere; fleshy, leafless jointed stems, with flowers sunk into stems; also called **marsh samphire**. It was burnt to provide soda for early glass-making. (Genus: *Salicornia*, 35 species. Family: Chenopodiaceae.)

Glauber, Roy (Jay) (1925–) Physicist, born in New York City, NY. He graduated from the Bronx High School of Science and went on to earn a doctorate from Harvard University, later working on the Manhattan Project. He was appointed professor of physics at Harvard and adjunct professor of optical sciences at the University of Arizona. In 2005 he was awarded one half of the Nobel Prize for Physics for his contribution to the quantum theory of optical coherence.

Glauber's salt Hydrated sodium sulphate, $Na_2SO_4.10H_2O$. It is named after the German chemist Johann Rudolph Glauber (1604–70), a follower of Paracelsus. It is a mild laxative, an ingredient of many mineral waters, and was once credited with remarkable medicinal properties.

glaucoma [glawkohma] A rise in the pressure of the aqueous fluid within the eye. Acute glaucoma arises when drainage of this fluid is blocked because of infection or cataract surgery. There is sudden pain in the affected eye and variable interference with vision, which may develop rapidly into blindness.

glaze In oil painting, a transparent layer of paint sometimes mixed with varnish laid over dry underpainting. In pottery it is a thin vitreous coating fused to the surface of a pot by firing.

Glazunov, Alexander (Konstantinovich) [glazunof] (1865–1936) Composer, born in St Petersburg, Russia. Among his compositions are eight symphonies, and works in every branch of music except opera.

Glendower, Owen [glendower], Welsh **Owain Glyndwr** or **Owain ap Gruffudd** (c.1354–c.1416) Welsh chief, born in Powys, E Wales. In 1400 he rebelled against Henry IV, proclaimed himself Prince of Wales, and joined the coalition with Harry Percy Hotspur, who was defeated at the Battle of Shrewsbury (1403).

Glenn, John H(erschel) (1921–) Astronaut, the first American to orbit the Earth, born in Cambridge, OH. He became an astronaut in 1959, and in 1962 made a three-orbit flight in the Friendship 7 space capsule. He was a senator from Ohio (1975–98), and sought the Democratic nomination for the presidency in 1984 and 1988. He became the oldest astronaut to travel in space when he joined the 9-day space-shuttle mission in November 1998.

Glennie, Dame Evelyn (Elizabeth Ann) (1965–) Percussionist and composer, born in Ellon, Aberdeenshire. Although profoundly deaf, she studied at the Royal Academy of Music, London, winning several prizes, and made her debut recital at the Wigmore Hall in 1986. She has since received international recognition as a percussionist, playing with orchestras all over the world. She was made a dame in 2007.

Glenrothes [glenrothis] 56°12N 3°11W, pop (2000e) 36 200. Administrative centre of Fife, E Scotland, designated a new town in 1948; airfield; centre for electronic research.

gliadin [gliyadin] A simple protein occurring mainly in wheat. An adverse reaction to this protein is a feature of coeliac disease.

glider An aircraft that flies without the aid of mechanical propulsion. The wings may be fixed or flexible, and if the latter, the machine is known as a **hang glider**. The first piloted glider was designed in 1853 by aviator and inventor Sir George Cayley (1773–1857).

Glinka, Mikhail (Ivanovich) [glingka] (1804–57) Composer, born in Novospasskoye, Russia. His opera *Russlan and Ludmilla* (1842) pioneered the style of the Russian national school of composers.

global economy The view of the whole world as a single market. Globalization means that goods and services, capital, and labour are traded on a worldwide basis, and information and the results of research flow readily between countries. The rise of cheap sea transport and the telegram in the 19th-c, and of cheap air travel, the telephone, and the computer in the 20th-c, together with the rising importance of multinational companies and the general relaxation of controls on trade and international investment, mean that the world has moved some way towards a global economy. It is possible that the rise of the Internet and the start which has been made on liberalizing international trade in services will take this movement further in the 21st-c. The world has, however, a very long way to go before its economy is fully global. In particular, international mobility of labour is tightly restricted, and poor transport and communications in most developing countries mean that only the economies of the richer and more advanced countries are really at all global.

Global Positioning System (GPS) A means of determining an exact position on the Earth using a GPS receiver and a system of satellites. Twenty-four satellites make up the American NAVSTAR system, orbiting about 20 000 km above the Earth. Each satellite makes a complete orbit of the Earth every 12 hours. Their positions are carefully calculated so that, from any point on the Earth, four or more of the satellites will be in direct line of sight to the GPS receiver. The GPS receiver picks up signals which are being transmitted continuously from the satellites. Each satellite carries four atomic clocks, so that the transmission time of the signals is known precisely. Using the time difference between the signals being transmitted and received, the GPS calculates the distance to that satellite. It has to lock on to at least three different satellite signals in order to locate itself in three-dimensional space. The **Standard Positioning Service (SPS)** is accurate to about 100 m (325 ft) and the **Precise Positioning Service (PPS)** is accurate to 20 m (65 ft). The **Differential GPS (DGPS)** also uses additional fixed stations on Earth and gives horizontal position accuracy to about 3 m (10 ft). NAVSTAR was begun in the 1970s and all 24 satellites were in operation by 1994.

global warming *greenhouse effect*

globe artichoke A robust perennial (*Cynara scolymus*) growing to 2 m/6½ ft; leaves up to 80 cm/30 in, deeply divided; flowerheads blue, very large, surrounded by distinctive leathery, oval bracts. The soft receptacle of the young flower-heads and the fleshy bases to the bracts are eaten as a vegetable. (Family: Compositae.)

Globe Theatre A theatre completed in 1599 on Bankside in London. Nearly all of Shakespeare's greatest works were performed here. A project to build a working replica of the theatre on the original site was initiated in 1970 under the direction of US actor and film producer Sam Wanamaker (1919–93), and opened in 1996. In 1989, part of the foundations of the Globe was discovered and designated a scheduled area. An exhibition area opened beneath the theatre in 2000.

globigerina [globijeriyna] A type of amoeba-like microscopic organism commonly found in marine plankton.

globular cluster A swarm of old stars arranged characteristically as a compact sphere. It contains tens of thousands to millions of stars, formed at the same time.

globulin [globyulin] A simple protein folded into a globular 3-dimensional shape. It is insoluble or only sparingly soluble in water, but soluble in dilute salt solutions.

glockenspiel [glokenshpeel] A musical instrument consisting of tuned metal bars arranged in two rows like a piano keyboard, and played with small hammers held in each hand.

glomerulonephritis [glomerulohnefriytis] An inflammation of the glomeruli (part of the kidneys responsible for the initial blood-filtering process) caused by foreign antigens invading the body, and stimulating the production of antibodies; the antigens combine with the antibodies to form protein complexes which circulate in the blood stream and settle in tissues. Damage to the glomeruli impairs the filter, and leads to proteins and blood cells escaping into the urine. The illness leads to oedema and elevation of blood pressure. In young people it usually resolves in two to three weeks, but in adults may lead to persisting kidney failure.

Glorious Revolution or **Bloodless Revolution** The name given to the events (Dec 1688–Feb 1689) during which James II fled from England, and William III and Mary II were established by parliament as joint monarchs. The title celebrates the bloodlessness of the event, and the assertion of the constitutional importance of parliament.

glossolalia The practice of 'speaking in tongues' – uttering sounds whose meaning is unknown to the speaker, who is undergoing a religious experience. It is found in several Christian groups, such as Pentecostalists or charismatic Catholics, and interpreted among its practitioners as a supernatural sign of religious sincerity or conversion.

glottis The narrow part of the larynx at the level of the vocal cords (or vocal folds), which is most directly concerned with the production of sound.

Gloucester [gloster], Lat **Glevum**, Celtic **Caer Glou** 51°53N 2°14W, district pop (2001e) 109 900. County town of Gloucestershire, SWC England; founded by Romans 1st-c AD; railway; airfield; cathedral (13th-c).

Gloucester, Richard (Alexander Walter George), Duke of [gloster] (1944–) British prince, the younger son of Henry, Duke of Gloucester (the third son of George V). In 1972 he married **Birgitte van Deurs** (1946–); they have one son, **Alexander, Earl of Ulster** (1974–) and two daughters, **Lady Davina Windsor** (1977–) and **Lady Rose Windsor** (1980–).

Gloucestershire [glostersheer] pop (2001e) 564 600; area 2643 km²/1020 sq mi. County in SWC England; features include the Cotswold Hills, Forest of Dean; drained by the R Severn; county town, Gloucester; South Gloucestershire became a unitary authority in 1996.

glowworm *firefly*

gloxinia A member of a Brazilian genus of plants with large, showy, funnel-shaped flowers in a variety of colours; related to the African violet. (Genus: *Siningia*, 20 species. Family: Gesneriaceae.)

Glubb, Sir John Bagot, known as **Glubb Pasha** (1897–1986) British soldier, born in Preston, Lancashire. In Transjordan he organized the Arab Legion's Desert Patrol, and became Legion Commandant (1939), gaining immense prestige among the Bedouin.

glucagon [glookagon] A hormone (a polypeptide) found in vertebrates, synthesized in the pancreas. Its main action is to raise blood glucose levels by promoting the conversion of liver glycogen into glucose.

Gluck, Christoph (Willibald) [glook] (1714–87) Composer, born in Erasbach, Bavaria. In the late 1770s, Paris was divided into those who supported Gluck's French opera style and those supporting the Italian style of Niccolo Piccinni (1728–1800) – the *Gluckists* and *Piccinnists*. Gluck finally conquered with his *Iphigénie en Tauride* (1779), and retired from Paris full of honour.

glucocorticoids [glookohkaw(r)tikoydz] Steroid hormones synthesized and released from the adrenal cortex of vertebrates, important in carbohydrate metabolism and the resistance of the body to stress. In humans they include *cortisol* (*hydrocortisone*), *corticosterone*, and *cortisone*.

glucose $C_6H_{12}O_6$, also called **dextrose**. By far the most common of the six-carbon sugars, the primary product of plant photosynthesis. Starch and cellulose are both condensation polymers of glucose.

glue *adhesives*

gluon A fundamental particle that carries the strong force between quarks, and binds them together into other subatomic particles; symbol *g*; mass 0, charge 0, spin 1.

gluten The main protein of wheat, subdivided into two other proteins, **gliadin** and **glutenin**. When mixed with water and kneaded, these proteins become aligned along one plane, imparting an elastic property to the dough. The small intestine in some people is abnormally sensitive to gliadin, a condition known as *coeliac disease*.

glutton *wolverine*

glycerides [gliseriydz] Esters of glycerol. Glycerol forms three series of ester: mono-, di- and triglycerides. Fats are examples of triglycerides.

glycerine *glycerol*

glycerol [gliserol] OHCH₂–CH(OH)–CH₂OH, IUPAC **1,2,3-trihydroxypropane**, also known as **glycerine**, boiling point 290°C. A colourless, viscous, and sweet-tasting liquid, obtained from all vegetable and animal fats and oils by hydrolysis, and thus a by-product of soap manufacture.

glycine [gliyseen] NH₂–CH₂–COOH, IUPAC **aminoethanoic acid**, melting point 260°C. A colourless solid, freely soluble in water. It is the simplest of the amino acids, found in almost all proteins, and obtainable from them by acid hydrolysis.

glycogen [gliykojen] ($C_6H_{10}O_5$)$_n$. A polysaccharide found in both plant and animal tissue as an energy store. It is essentially a condensation polymer of glucose, and very similar to starch.

GMDSS *Global Maritime Distress and Safety System*

GM food *genetically modified organisms*

gnat 1 An alternative name for mosquitoes.
2 A swarming gnat; a type of small, delicate fly. The males fly in dancing swarms low over water or in woodland clearings. (Order: Diptera. Family: Epididae.)

Gneisenau, August (Wilhelm Anton), Graf (Count) **Neithardt von** [gniyzuhnow] (1760–1831) Prussian general, born in Schildau, Germany. He helped to reorganize the army after its defeat by Napoleon (1807), and in the war of liberation gave distinguished service at Leipzig (1813) and Waterloo (1815).

gneiss [niys] A coarse, high-grade metamorphic rock with a banded appearance due to the segregation of light- and dark-coloured minerals.

Gnosticism [nostisizm] (Gr *gnosis*, 'knowledge') A system of belief which became prominent within 2nd-c Christianity. It emphasized salvation through acquiring secret revealed knowledge about cosmic origins and the true destiny of the spirit within people. Gnosticism was considered a heresy by the early Church Fathers.

GNP (gross national product) *gross domestic product*

gnu [noo] *wildebeest*

go The national game of Japan, first played in China c.1500 BC. It is a tactical game, played on a board divided into 324 squares (18 × 18). Each player has a supply of black or white counters. They take it in turn to fill up the board with the intention of surrounding the opponent's pieces and capturing them.

Goa [goha] pop (2001e) 1 344 000; area 3496 km²/1363 sq mi. State in W India; capital, Panaji; taken by Portugal, 1510; occupied by India, 1961; part of Union territory of Goa, Daman and Diu until 1987; churches and convents are world heritage monuments; burial place of St Francis Xavier.

goat A mammal of family Bovidae; may be classified as an ante-lope; tail with naked undersurface; both sexes with horns; males with beard; male called a *billy*, female a *nanny*, young a *kid*; six species in genus *Capra*, including the **bezoar** and **ibex**.

goatfish *red mullet*

Gobbi, Tito (1915–84) Baritone, born in Bassano del Grappa, Italy. He appeared regularly with the Rome Opera from 1938, and soon made an international reputation, especially in Verdian roles such as Falstaff and Don Carlos.

Gobelins, Manufacture nationale des [gohbuhlî] A factory on the Left Bank of the R Seine in Paris. It was established in 1440 by Jean Gobelin as a dye works, and in the 17th-c a number of tapestry workshops were brought together here.

Gobi Desert [gohbee] Desert in C Asia; area c.1 295 000 km²/500 000 sq mi, extends c.1600 km/1000 mi E–W across SE Mongolia and N China; on a plateau, altitude 900–1500 m/3000–5000 ft; completely sandy in W.

goby [gohbee] Any of a large family of mostly small, elongate fishes with stout head, fleshy lips, and large eyes, abundant in coastal waters of tropical to temperate seas; length up to 25 cm/10 in, many less than 5 cm/2 in; pelvic fins joined to form single sucker-like fin. (Family: Gobiidae.)

God Supernatural being or power, the object of worship. In some world religions (eg Christianity, Judaism, Islam) there is one God only (*monotheism*), who is transcendent, all-powerful, and related to the cosmos as creator. In other religions (eg Hinduism, Classical Greek and Roman religions, and primitive religions) many gods may be recognized (*polytheism*), with individual gods having particular properties and powers. In the Judaeo-Christian tradition, God is believed to have revealed himself in history through the life and response of the people of Israel, and, in the Christian tradition, in the life, death, and resurrection of Jesus of Nazareth, the Christ. The conviction that Jesus stood in a unique relation to God led to the development in Christian thought of the Trinitarian understanding, whereby the one God is confessed as three persons (Father, Son, and Holy Spirit) of one substance. In the mainstream Western tradition, influenced by Classical Greek philosophy as well as Christianity, God is conceived as 'being itself' or 'pure actuality' (St Thomas Aquinas), in whom there is no unactualized potentiality or becoming; as absolute, infinite, eternal, immutable, incomprehensible (ie unable to be comprehended by human thought), all-powerful (omnipotent), all-wise (omniscient), all-good (omnibenevolent), and everywhere present (omnipresent). From the time of the ancient Greeks, philosophers have tried to prove the existence of God by reason alone (ie not by divine revelation). While the philosophical consensus seems now to be that none of these arguments is coercive, discussion in the 20th-c of the matter continued unabated. Attempts to disprove the existence of God or to show concepts of God to be incoherent have been likewise generally unpersuasive.

Godard, Jean-Luc [gohdah(r)] (1930–) Film director, born in Paris. His first major film *A bout de souffle* (1960, Breathless) established him as one of the leaders of *Nouvelle Vague* cinema. His prolific output includes *Weekend* (1968), *Je vous salue, Marie* (1985, trans Hail Mary), *For Ever Mozart* (1997), and *Notre musique* (2004, trans Our Music).

Goddard, Robert H(utchings) (1882–1945) Physicist and rocketry pioneer, born in Worcester, MA. He elaborated the theory of rocketry, developing the first successful liquid-fuelled rocket, launched in 1926.

Gödel or **Goedel, Kurt** [goedl] (1906–78) Logician, born in Brno, Czech republic. He showed in 1931 that any formal logical system adequate for number theory must contain propositions not provable in that system (**Gödel's proof**).

Godfrey of Bouillon [booeeyõ] (c.1061–1100) Duke of Lower Lorraine (1089–95), born in Baisy, Belgium. He was elected one of the principal commanders of the First Crusade, and later became its chief leader. After the capture of Jerusalem (1099) he was proclaimed king, but he refused the crown, accepting only the title Defender of the Holy Sepulchre.

Godiva, Lady [godiyva] (11th-c) An English lady and religious benefactress, who, according to tradition, rode naked through the market-place at Coventry, in order to obtain the remission of a heavy tax imposed by her husband, Leofric, upon the townsfolk (1040).

Godolphin, Sidney Godolphin, 1st Earl of [godolfin] (1645–1712) English statesman, born near Helston, Cornwall. He held various treasury positions under William III and Queen Anne, and his able management of the finances helped Marlborough in the War of the Spanish Succession (1701–13).

Godoy, Manuel de [gothoy] (1767–1851) Spanish court favourite and chief minister (1792–1808) under Charles IV. He achieved dictatorial power at the age of 25 through the favour of the Queen, Maria Luisa, and in 1795 assumed the title 'Prince of the Peace'. In 1796 he allied with France against England – a move which contributed to Spain losing her American Empire.

godparents In Christianity, those who act as sponsors for a child at its baptism or christening and who thereafter assume some sort of moral guardianship over the child. They are usually one or two persons of the same sex and one of the opposite. This duty is now often a simple formality; however, in S Europe and Latin America the institution is still used to create important social ties among adults.

Godthåb or **Godthaab** [gothop] Eskimo **Nûk** or **Nuuk** 64°11N 51°44W, pop (2000e) 12 900. Capital and largest town of Greenland; founded, 1721; ruins of 10th-c Norse settlement nearby.

Godunov, Boris (Fyodorovich) [goduhnof], Russ [goduhnof] (c.1552–1605) Tsar of Russia (1598–1605), previously Regent (from 1584) for Fyodor, the imbecile elder son of Ivan IV (the Terrible).

Godwin, also spelled **Godwine** (?–1053) Earl of Wessex, probably son of the South Saxon Wulfnoth. He became powerful under King Canute, and in 1042 helped to raise Edward the Confessor to the throne. His son Harold was for a few months Edward's successor.

Godwin, Mary Wollstonecraft *Wollstonecraft*

Godwin, William (1756–1836) Political writer and novelist, born in Wisbech, Cambridgeshire. His major work of social philosophy was *An Enquiry Concerning Political Justice* (1793). His masterpiece was the novel, *The Adventures of Caleb Williams* (1794). He married Mary Wollstonecraft in 1797.

Godwin-Austen, Mount *K2*

godwit A large sandpiper, native to the N hemisphere but may winter in the S; bill long, very slightly upcurved. (Genus: *Limosa*, 4 species.)

Goebbels or **Göbels, (Paul) Joseph** [goeblz] (1897–1945) Nazi politician, born in Rheydt, Germany. A bitter anti-Semite, his gift of mob oratory made him a powerful exponent of the more radical aspects of Nazi philosophy. He retained Hitler's confidence to the last, and in the Berlin bunker he and his wife committed suicide, after taking the lives of their six children.

Goeppert-Mayer, Maria [goepert mayer], *née* **Goepert** (1906–72) Physicist, born in Katowice, Poland. In 1948 she discovered the 'magic numbers' of subnuclear particles, and from 1950 devised a complete shell theory of nuclear structure. She shared the Nobel Prize for Physics in 1963.

Goering or **Göring, Hermann (Wilhelm)** [goering] (1893–1946) Nazi politico-military leader, born in Rosenheim, Germany. He founded the Gestapo, and set up the concentration camps for political, racial, and religious suspects. In 1940 he became economic dictator of Germany, and was made Marshal of the Reich, the first and only holder of the rank. In 1946 he was sentenced to death at the Nuremberg War Crimes Trial, but hours before his execution he committed suicide.

Goethe, Johann Wolfgang von [goetuh] (1749–1832) Poet, dramatist, novelist, and scientist, born in Frankfurt, Germany. He captured the spirit of German nationalism with his drama, *Götz von Berlichingen* (1773), following this with his novel *Die Leiden des jungen Werther* (1774, The Sorrows of Young Werther). He wrote much lyric poetry at this time, inspired by his relationships with a series of women, culminating in a profound attachment to Charlotte von Stein. Visits to Italy (1786–8, 1790) contributed to a greater preoccupation with poetical form, seen in such plays as *Iphigenie auf Tauris* (1789). In his later years he wrote the novel *Wilhelm Meisters Lehrjahre* (1796, Wilhelm Meister's Apprentice Years), continued as *Wilhelm Meisters Wanderjahre* (1821–9, Wilhelm Meister's Journeyman Years). His masterpiece is his version of *Faust*, on which he worked for most of his life, published in two parts (1808, 1832).

Gog and Magog [gog, maygog] Biblical names, applied in different ways to depict future foes of the people of God. *Rev* 20.8 and rabbinic literature treat Gog and Magog as paired figures representing Satan in the final conflict against God's people. In British folklore, the names are given to the survivors of a race of giants annihilated by Brutus, the founder of Britain.

Gogol, Nikolai (Vasilievich) [gohgl] (1809–52) Novelist and playwright, born in Sorochintsi, Ukraine. He became famous through two masterpieces: *Revizor* (1836, The Inspector General), a satire exposing the corruption and vanity of provincial officials, and a novel, *Myortvye dushi* (1842, Dead Souls).

Goiânia [gohyania] 16°43S 49°18W, pop (2000e) 1 227 000. City in WC Brazil; founded, 1933; railway; two universities (1959, 1960).

Goidelic [goydelik] *Celtic languages*

goitre / goiter [goyter] A swelling in the neck resulting from enlargement of the thyroid gland. It is often caused by iodine deficiency.

Golan or **Golan Heights** [gohlan], Arabic **al-Jawlan** pop (2000e) 32 000; area 1176 km²/454 sq mi. Israeli-occupied area of Syria administered as part of N Israel; of great strategic importance; occupied by Israel in 1967, and annexed in 1981; rises to 1204 m/ 3950 ft at Mt Avital.

Gold, Thomas (1920–2004) Astronomer, born in Vienna. He worked with Hermann Bondi and Fred Hoyle on the steady-state theory of the origin of the universe (1948). In 1968 he suggested that pulsars are rapidly rotating neutron stars, as was later confirmed.

gold Au, element 79, melting point 1064°C. A soft yellow metal of high density (19 g/cm³), known from ancient times. It is rare and found uncombined in nature. Much of its value is due to its lack of reactivity, its main uses being for decoration and for monetary reserves.

Goldberg, Whoopi, originally **Caryn Elaine Johnson** (1955–) Film actress, born in New York City. She achieved instant fame with her role in *The Color Purple* (1985), for which she received a Golden Globe Award. Later films include *Ghost* (1990, Oscar for Best Supporting Actress) and *Get Bruce* (1999).

Goldblum, Jeff (1952–) Film actor, born in Pittsburgh, PA. His film debut was in 1974, and he has since become well known especially for his roles in science-fiction films, including *The Fly* (1986), *Earth Girls Are Easy* (1989), *Jurassic Park* and its sequel (1993, 1997), and *Independence Day* (1996). Among later films are *Igby Goes Down* (2003) and *Man of the Year* (2006).

Gold Coast (Africa) *Ghana*

goldcrest A small woodland bird (*Regulus regulus*), native to Europe and Asia; head with orange or yellow stripe; also known as the **golden-crested wren**. (Family: Regulidae, sometimes placed in family Silviidae.)

Golden Bull Any document whose importance was stressed by authentication with a golden seal (Lat *bulla*). Specifically, the term is used for the edict promulgated by Emperor Charles IV in 1356 to define the German constitution.

golden calf An idolatrous image of worship, fashioned by Aaron and the Israelites at Sinai (*Ex* 32), and destroyed by Moses.

Golden Fleece In Greek mythology, the object of the voyage of the *Argo*. Hermes saved Phrixus from sacrifice by placing him upon a golden ram, which bore him through the air to Colchis, where a dragon guarded the Fleece in a sacred grove. Jason obtained the fleece with Medea's help.

Golden Gate Bridge A major steel suspension bridge across the Golden Gate, a channel in California, USA, connecting San Francisco Bay with the Pacific; completed in 1937; length of main span 1280 m/4200 ft.

Golden Globe awards Annual awards given by the Hollywood Foreign Press Association (HFPA) to honour achievements in film and television during the preceding year. Founded in 1943, the first awards took place in 1944. Winners receive a trophy representing a golden globe encircled with a strip of motion-picture film and mounted on a pedestal. For motion pictures, awards are currently presented in the categories of best picture, actor/actress, supporting actor/actress, director, screenplay, original score, original song, foreign film, and lifetime achievement. Similar awards are given for television productions.

Golden Pavilion *Kinkakuji*

golden-rain tree *laburnum; pride of India*

golden ratio In mathematics, a proportion obtained if a point P divides a straight line AB in such manner that $AP : PB = AB : AP$; also known as the **golden section**. It was applied to architecture by Vitruvius, and much discussed during the Renaissance.

golden retriever A breed of dog, developed in Britain in the late 19th-c; large with long golden or cream coat; solid body, strong legs, long muzzle; calm temperament; popular choice as a guide-dog for blind people.

goldenrod The name applied to several species of *Solidago*. The plant commonly grown in gardens is **Canadian golden rod** (*Solidago canadensis*), a late-flowering perennial growing to 1·5 m/5 ft, native to North America; flower-heads numerous, tiny, golden-yellow, arranged in a dense pyramidal panicle. (Genus: *Solidago*. Family: Compositae.)

Golden Rule The name given today to the saying of Jesus about one's duty to others: 'Whatever things you wish that people would do to you, do also yourselves similarly to them' (*Matt* 7.12; *Luke* 6.31).

Golden Temple *Harimandir*

goldfinch A bird native to the N hemisphere; one species in the Old World, *Carduelis carduelis*, three in the Americas; closely related to the siskin. (Genus: *Carduelis*, 4 species. Family: Fringillidae.)

goldfish Colourful carp-like freshwater fish, native to weedy rivers and lakes of Eurasia, but now very widely distributed as popular ornamental fish; body length up to 30 cm/1 ft; mouth lacking barbels. (*Carassius auratus*. Family: Cyprinidae.)

Golding, Sir William (Gerald) (1911–93) Novelist, born near Newquay, Cornwall. His first novel was *Lord of the Flies* (1954), and this was followed by *The Inheritors* (1955), *Pincher Martin* (1956), *Free Fall* (1959), and *The Spire* (1964). Later novels include *Rites of Passage* (1980, Booker) and *The Paper Men* (1984). He was awarded the Nobel Prize for Literature in 1983.

Goldoni, Carlo [goldohnee] (1707–93) Playwright, born in Venice, Italy. He wrote over 200 plays, including 150 comedies. Among his best-known works are *Il servitore di due padroni* (1746, the Servant of Two Masters), *Il teatro comico* (1750, The Comic Theatre), and *Il ventaglio* (1766, The Fan).

Goldsmith, Oliver (1728–74) Playwright, novelist, and poet, born in Kildare, Ireland. *The Vicar of Wakefield* (1766) secured his reputation as a novelist, *The Deserted Village* (1770) as a poet, and *She Stoops to Conquer* (1773) as a dramatist.

Goldstone, Richard (1938–) Judge and human rights campaigner, born in Boksburg, NE South Africa. He was appointed to the Supreme Court of South Africa in 1980, and became Chairman of the South African Commission of Inquiry into the Prevention of Public Violence and Intimidation (1990–4), then a Justice of the South African Constitutional Court. He also served as Chief Prosecutor at the International War Crimes Tribunal at The Hague (1994–6).

Goldsworthy, Andy (1956–) Artist and sculptor, born in Cheshire. He works closely with nature, producing ephemeral works assembled from natural materials, such as stone, wood, foliage and water, which are then photographed. His Sheepfolds project in Cumbria, to rebuild c.100 traditional drystone sheep corrals, was completed in 2000 and is open to the public.

Goldwater, Barry M(orris) (1909–98) US politician and writer, born in Phoenix, AZ. In 1964 he became Republican nominee for the presidency, but was defeated by Lyndon Johnson. He was one of the architects of the conservative revival within the Republican Party.

Goldwyn, Samuel, originally **Samuel Goldfish** (1882–1974) Film producer, born in Warsaw, Poland. He emigrated to the USA and in 1917 founded the Goldwyn Pictures Corporation, and in 1925 the Metro-Goldwyn-Mayer Company, allying himself with the United Artists from 1926. A colourful personality, many of his off-the-cuff remarks (*Goldwynisms*) have become catch phrases, such as 'include me out'.

golf A popular pastime and competitive sport, played on a course usually consisting of 18 holes. A *hole* consists of three areas: the flat starting point where the player hits the ball (the *tee*), a long stretch of mown grass (the *fairway*), and a putting *green* of smooth grass where the hole itself (10·8 cm/$4\frac{1}{4}$ in) is situated. Obstacles, such as areas of sand (*bunkers*) and trees, are placed at various points. The object is to hit a small, rubber-cored ball from a starting point into the hole, which is generally 90–450 m/100–500 yd away. The winner is the player who completes a round with the lowest number of strokes. The expected number of strokes a good player would be expected to play for any given hole is referred to as the *par* for that hole. If the player holes the ball in one stroke below par, this is called a *birdie*; two strokes below is an *eagle*, one shot over par is a *bogey*; an occasional possibility is a *hole in one*. Players may carry up to 14 clubs in their golf bag, each designed for a specific purpose and shot. The ruling body of the game in Britain is the Royal and Ancient Club at St Andrews, Scotland. Major tournaments include the Open Golf Championship, the US Open, the US Professional Golfers' Association (PGA), and the US Masters.

golf-ball printer A high quality impact printer with a spherical print head used mainly in typewriters. The printhead is removable, allowing different typesets to be used.

Golgotha *Calvary*

goliards Wandering scholars and clerks of the 12th–13th-c, who wrote reckless celebrations of women and wine, and satirical verses against the Church.

Goliath [goliyath] Biblical character described (1 *Sam* 17) as a giant from Gath in the Philistine army who entered into single combat with the young David and was slain by a stone from David's sling, resulting in Israel's victory.

Gollancz, Sir Victor [golangks, golants] (1893–1967) Publisher, author, and philanthropist, born in London. He founded his own firm in 1928, and after World War 2 founded the Jewish Society for Human Service, and War on Want (1951).

Gompers, Samuel [gomperz] (1850–1924) Labour leader, born in London. He migrated to New York City in 1863, founded the American Federation of Labor in 1886, and except for one year was its president until his death.

Gomułka, Władysław [gomoolka] (1905–82) Polish communist leader, born in Krosno, Poland. He was vice-president of the first post-war Polish government (1945–8), but his criticism of

240 million years ago
The single supercontinent *Pangaea* is formed, with a single superocean, *Panthea-lassa*

120 million years ago
Tethys, a broad gulf, divides Pangaea into two huge land-masses: *Laurasia* in the north: *Gondwana* in the south

60 million years ago
Laurasia and Gondwana have split to begin to form the continents as we know them today

[gond**wah**naland] The name given to the postulated S 'supercontinent' which began to break away from the single land mass Pangaea about 200 million years ago. It included Australia, Africa, Antarctica, India, and South America; the N supercontinent was Laurasia.

the Soviet Union led to his arrest (1951–4). He later returned to power as party first secretary (1956–71).

gomuti palm *sugar palm*

gonad The organ responsible for the production of reproductive cells (*germ cells* or *gametes*): in males the gonads (*testes*) produce spermatozoa, in females the gonads (*ovaries*) produce ova. In vertebrates the gonads also synthesize and secrete sex hormones.

Goncourt brothers [gōkoor] **Edmond de Goncourt** (1822–96) and **Jules de Goncourt** (1830–70) Novelists, born respectively at Nancy and Paris. They are especially remembered for their *Journal*, begun in 1851, a detailed record of French social and literary life which Edmond continued for 40 years. Edmond

also founded in his will the Académie Goncourt to foster fiction.

Gondar *Fasil Ghebbi*

Gondwanaland *see panel*

gong A percussion instrument: a circular bronze plaque, commonly suspended from a frame or bar and struck with a soft beater. The orchestral gong (or **tam-tam**) is of indefinite pitch; other, usually smaller, gongs are tuned to precise pitches.

Góngora y Argote, Luis de [gongora ee ah(r)**goh**tay] (1561–1627) Lyric poet, born in Córdoba. His reputation largely rests on his later, longer poems, such as *Solidades* and *Polifemo* (both 1613), executed in an elaborate style which came to be called **gongorism**.

gonorrhoea / gonorrhea [gonuh**ree**a] An acute infection of the genital tract caused by *Neisseria gonorrhoeae*, acquired by sexual intercourse with an infected partner. Males suffer from a discharge from the penis, with pain on urination. Females may suffer a vaginal discharge, but may have no symptoms.

Gonzaga, Luigi, St [gon**zah**ga], known as **St Aloysius** (1568–91) Jesuit, born near Brescia, Italy. In a plague at Rome he devoted himself to the care of the sick, but was himself infected and died. He was canonized in 1726, and is the Italian patron saint of youth. Feast day 21 June.

Gonzales, Alberto R (1955–) US attorney general, born in San Antonio, TX. After military service, he studied at Rice University and Harvard Law School (1982), then joined a private law firm (1982–95). He was named secretary of state for Texas (1997–9), where his duties included senior advisor to then Governor George W Bush, chief elections officer, and head liaison officer on Mexico and border issues. In 1999 he was appointed justice to the Texas Supreme Court, and from 2001 served as Counsel to the President. He was appointed attorney general in 2004, the first Hispanic to hold the office.

González, Felipe [gon**thah**leth] (1942–) Spanish statesman and prime minister (1982–96), born in Seville. He became secretary-general of the Spanish Socialist Workers' Party in 1974, and led it to victory in the 1982 elections, forming the first left-wing administration since 1936.

Gooch, Graham (Alan) (1953–) Cricketer, born in Leytonstone, Greater London. He began his career playing for Essex. As England captain (1988–93) he led a notable victory over the West Indies in Jamaica (1989). The leading England Test run-scorer, and most-capped player, he announced his retirement in January 1995, with 8900 runs scored in 118 Tests, at an average of 42·58.

Good Friday In the Christian Church, the Friday before Easter, commemorating the crucifixion of Jesus Christ; in many Christian denominations, a day of mourning and penance.

Good Friday Agreement Talks between the British government and the representatives of Northern Ireland, concluded in April 1998. Under the agreement, Sinn Féin accepted that Northern Ireland would remain part of the United Kingdom as long as a majority of the population was in favour. Power would be devolved from Westminster to a new 108-member Assembly, elected by proportional representation, and a 12-member Northern Ireland executive, structured to ensure cross-community participation. There would be 'North–South' bodies linking northern and southern Ireland and a Council of the Isles linking these regions with Britain, and including members from Scottish and Welsh assemblies. The deal was approved in referenda staged in Northern Ireland and the Irish Republic, and took effect in December 1999.

Goodman, Benny, popular name of **Benjamin David Goodman**, nickname **the King of Swing** (1909–86) Clarinettist and bandleader, born in Chicago, IL. He reigned as the 'King of Swing' in the big-band era. Among his band's hit recordings were 'Let's Dance', 'Stompin' at the Savoy', and 'One O'Clock Jump'. He also featured trios and quartets with Lionel Hampton and other African-American jazz musicians.

Goodman, John (1952–) Film actor, born in St Louis, MO. He became well known for his role as the husband Dan in the television comedy series *Roseanne* (1988–97). His films include *King Ralph* (1991), *Barton Fink* (1991), *The Flintstones* (1994), *Bringing Out the Dead* (1999), and *Beyond the Sea* (2004).

Goodricke, John (1764–86) English astronomer, born in Groningen, N Netherlands. In 1782 he noticed that the brightness of the star known as Algol varied, and was the first to establish the periodic nature of this variation. He also suggested that the variability of Algol was due to its being eclipsed by a darker companion body, a theory eventually confirmed and which forms the basis of the class of stars known as eclipsing variables.

Goodyear, Charles (1800–60) Inventor, born in New Haven, CT. His work led to the invention (1844) of vulcanized rubber.

Google A multilingual Internet search engine that indexes and caches pages on the World Wide Web; derived from *googol* (1 followed by 100 zeroes). It was founded in 1998 by Stanford graduates Sergey Brin (1973–) and Larry Page (1972–), following their success in 1996 with the prototype *BackRub*. By the end of 1999 Google employed 39 people and was answering 3 million search queries per day. In 2006 it had over 5000 employees, covered more than 8 billion items, and the number of daily searches was over 200 million. The company was floated on the stock-market in August 2004.

Goons, The Four comedians who came together after World War 2 to create the Goon Show, which revolutionized British radio comedy: **Spike Milligan**, **Peter Sellers**, **Harry Secombe**, and **Michael Bentine** (1922–96). They first performed on radio together in 1951: the show, called *Crazy People*, soon became *The Goon Show*, running for nine years and winning a worldwide band of devotees. The Goons prefigured much of British comedy since the fifties, especially in their imaginative use of sound effects, their mixture of surrealism and slapstick, and their anarchic humour.

goosander A sea-duck (*Mergus merganser*) native to N areas of the N hemisphere, also known in the USA as the **common merganser**; dark head and long red bill; male with dark back. (Family: Anatidae.)

goose A term not applied precisely, but used for large birds with more terrestrial habits than the 'swans' or 'ducks' comprising the rest of the family. (Family: Anatidae.)

gooseberry A deciduous shrub (*Ribes uva-crispa*) growing to c.1 m/3¼ ft, native to Europe and N Africa; stems and branches spiny; flowers greenish, tinged purple; edible berry oval, up to 4 cm/1½ in long, green or reddish, bristly or smooth. (Family: Grossulariaceae.)

goosefish *anglerfish*

goosegrass An annual, sometimes overwintering; a common weed (*Galium aparine*) native to Europe and Asia; fruit a burr with two more or less equal globular halves covered in whitish bristles, dispersed by clinging or cleaving to animals; hence the alternative name **cleavers**. (Family: Rubiaceae.)

Goose Green 51°52S 59°00W, pop (2000e) 100. Settlement on East Falkland, Falkland Is.

Goossens, Sir Eugène (1893–1962) Composer and conductor, born in London. As conductor of the Sydney Symphony Orchestra and director of the New South Wales Conservatory (1947–56), he became a major influence on Australian music.

Goossens, Léon (1897–1988) Oboist, born in Liverpool, Merseyside. He was the brother of the conductor Eugène Goossens; his sisters **Marie Goossens** (1894–1991) and **Sidonie Goossens** (1899–2004) became well-known harpists.

gopher A name used in North America for many animals which burrow.

goral A small goat-antelope (*Nemorhaedus goral*), native to the high mountains of E Asia; thick yellow-grey coat, pale throat; both sexes with short horns; also known as the **Himalayan chamois**.

Gorbachev, Mikhail Sergeyevich [go(r)bachof] (1931–) Soviet statesman, born in Privolnoye, Russia. He became Central Committee secretary for agriculture (1979–85); candidate member (1979–80) and full member (1980–91) of the Politburo of the Central Committee (1979–80); and, on the death of Konstantin Chernenko, general secretary of the Central Committee (1985–91). In 1988 he also became chairman of the Presidium of the Supreme Soviet (ie head of state) and in 1990 the first executive president of the USSR, with increased powers. He launched a radical programme of reform and restructuring (*perestroika*) of the Soviet economic and political system. A greater degree of civil liberty was allowed under the policy of *glasnost* ('openness' of information). In foreign and defence affairs he pursued a policy of detente and nuclear disarmament with the West. He survived an attempted coup in August 1991, but following the break-up of the USSR resigned all his offices in December of that year.

Gorbals, The A district of Glasgow, Scotland, which by the end of the 19th-c had become infamous as an area of overcrowding and deprivation. Redevelopment started in the late 1950s, and most of the old buildings were demolished in the next 20 years.

Gordian knot In Phrygia, a complicated knot with which the legendary King Gordius had tied up his wagon. An oracle said that whoever succeeded in untying it would rule Asia. Alexander the Great cut it with his sword.

Gordimer, Nadine (1923–) Writer, born in Springs, South Africa. In novels such as *The Conservationist* (1974) and *A Sport of Nature* (1987), she adopts a liberal approach to problems of race and repression. Later books include *The House Gun* (1998), *The Pickup* (2001), and *Get a Life* (2005). She was awarded the 1991 Nobel Prize for Literature.

Gordon, Charles George (1833–85) British general, born in Woolwich, Greater London. In 1860 he crushed the Taiping Rebellion, for which he became known as **Chinese Gordon**. In 1877 he was appointed Governor of the Sudan. He was besieged at Khartoum for 10 months by the Mahdi's troops, and was killed there two days before a relief force arrived.

Gordon Riots Anti-Catholic riots in London in early June 1780. They occurred after Lord George Gordon (1751–93), leader of the Protestant Association, had failed in his attempt to have clauses in the 1778 Catholic Relief Act (removing restrictions on the activities of priests) lifted.

Gore, Al(bert Arnold, Jr) (1948–) US vice-president (1993–2000), born in Washington, DC. He studied at Harvard and Vanderbilt Universities, worked as a journalist, then became a Democratic congressman (1977–85) and senator (1985–92). He was elected vice-president to Bill Clinton in 1992. In 1999 he was the leading candidate for the Democratic presidential nomination. He conceded defeat to George W Bush after five weeks of complex legal argument over the voting procedure in the presidential election in 2000.

Górecki, Henryk Mikolaj [goreskee] (1933–) Composer, born in Czernica, near Rybnik, Poland. His work, usually based on tragic themes and in very slow tempi, was virtually unknown in the West until 1993, when his *Symphony No. 3: Symphony of Sorrowful Songs* (1973) sold over half a million copies worldwide. Later works include *Miserere* (1981) and *Kleines Requiem* (1993).

Gorée Island [goray] A small island off the Cape Verde peninsula, Senegal, formerly a major centre of slave storage before shipping to the Americas. It is now a world heritage site.

Göreme [goereme] Valley in Cappadocia, C Turkey; noted for its cave dwellings; a world heritage site.

Gorgon A terrible monster of Greek mythology. There were three

Gorgons, who had snakes in their hair, ugly faces, and huge wings; their staring eyes could turn people to stone. Perseus killed Medusa (the only mortal one), and cut off her head.

gorilla An ape (*Gorilla gorilla*) native to the rainforests of WC Africa; the largest primate (height, up to 1·8 m/6 ft); massive muscular body; usually walks on all fours; adult male with marked crest; black, except in old males (*silverbacks*), which have a silvery grey torso.

Göring, Hermann *Goering, Hermann*

Gorky *Nizhni Novgorod*

Gorky, Arshile, originally **Vosdanig Manoog Adoian** (1905–48) Painter, born in Khorkom Vari, Turkish Armenia. He emigrated in 1920, and played a key role in the emergence of the New York school of Action painters in the 1940s.

Gorky, Maxim, pseudonym of **Alexey Maksimovich Peshkov** (1868–1936) Novelist, born in Nizhni Novgorod, Russia. He produced several Romantic short stories, then social novels and plays, notably the drama *Na dne* (1902, The Lower Depths). An autobiographical trilogy (1915–23) contains his best writing. He was the first president of the Soviet Writers Union. His birthplace was renamed Gorky in his honour (1929–91).

Gormley, Antony (Mark David) (1950–) Sculptor, born in London. He won the Turner Prize in 1994 and his later projects include the giant steel statue 'The Angel of the North' (1998) near Gateshead in Tyneside, and a 29 m/95 ft high metal structure named 'Quantum Leap' (2000) sited outside the Millennium Dome in London. His exhibition 'Domain Field' (2003), a series of life-size metal skeletons, was held at Tyneside's Baltic Centre. Among further works is 'Another Place' (2005), 100 life-size iron figures sited on Crosby Beach, Merseyside.

gorse A spiny shrub (*Ulex europaeus*) growing to 2 m/6½ ft, from Europe and NW Africa; leaves reduced to rigid needle-like spines, or small scales in mature plants; pea-flowers yellow, fragrant; also called **furze**. (Family: Leguminosae.)

Gorsedd [gaw(r)seth] A society of Welsh bards, founded in 1792 by Iolo Morganwg. It takes a major part in the organization of the National Eisteddfod, in particular the bardic ceremony.

Gorton, Sir John Grey (1911–2002) Australian statesman and prime minister (1968–71), born in Melbourne, Victoria, Australia. He served in the governments of Sir Robert Menzies and Harold Holt before becoming prime minister. In 1971 he resigned in favour of William McMahon, becoming deputy leader of the Liberal Party (until 1975).

goshawk [gos-hawk] A smallish hawk with short rounded wings and a long tail (20 species). The **northern goshawk** (*Accipiter gentilis*) is found in much of the N hemisphere; other species are native to Africa, S and SE Asia, and Australia. (Family: Accipitridae.)

Gospel (music) Music developed in black churches of the US South from a secular musical style in the early decades of the 20th-c. It was practised both by soloists and choirs, often with instrumental accompaniment, and became known for its infectious rhythms, close harmonies, and lively presentation. Noted solo performers include Sister Rosetta Tharpe and Mahalia Jackson. The style later had a major influence on other musical styles, especially soul music. The term is also associated with the revivalist movement of the late 19th-c, and the *Gospel Hymns* (1875–94) of US evangelists Philip Paul Bliss (1838–76) and Ira David Sankey (1840–1908).

Gospels, canonical Four books of the New Testament, known as the Gospels according to Matthew, Mark, Luke, and John; called 'gospels' by the 2nd-c Church (Gr *euangelion*, 'good news'). Each portrays a perspective on the ministry and teaching of Jesus of Nazareth, concluding with an account of his arrest, crucifixion, and resurrection.

Gothenburg [gothenberg], Swed **Göteborg** 57°45N 12°00E, pop (2000e) 450 000. Seaport in SW Sweden; second largest city in Sweden; founded, 1619; free port, 1921; railway; ferry services to UK, Denmark, Germany; university (1891), technical university (1829); cathedral (1633).

Gothic *black letter writing; Germanic languages*

Gothic architecture A form of architecture, usually religious, prevalent in W Europe from the 12th-c to the late 15th-c. It is characterized by a structural system comprising the pointed arch, rib vault, flying buttress, and a propensity for lofty interiors and maximum window area.

Gothic novel A type of fiction, written in reaction to 18th-c rationalism, which reclaims mystery and licenses extreme emotions. Some (eg Lewis's *The Monk*, 1797) make confident forays into the unconscious, exploring sexual fears and impulses. The Gothic horror stories of the 20th-c represented a fresh development for the genre, providing the input for a new medium of expression, the horror film.

Gothic Revival The movement to revive Gothic architecture, prevalent during the late 18th-c and 19th-c, popular in England, France, Germany, and North America. The style was applied to a multitude of buildings including churches, railway stations, hotels, town halls, and the parliament buildings at London and Ottawa.

Goths Germanic peoples who moved S, possibly from the Baltic area (Gotland), dividing into two confederations, Ostrogoths and Visigoths. Displaced by the Huns, they created two kingdoms in the 5th-c out of the ruins of the Roman Empire in the W.

Gotland, Gottland, or **Gothland** pop (2000e) 60 000; land area 3140 km²/1212 sq mi. Island county of Sweden, in the Baltic Sea off the SE coast; colonized by Germans, 12th-c; taken by Sweden in 1280, by Denmark in 1361, and again by Sweden in 1645; capital, Visby.

gouache [gooahsh] A type of opaque watercolour paint, also known as 'body colour', or 'poster paint' – familiar to most people from school art lessons. It was used in ancient Egypt, and widely in the Middle Ages, especially in illuminated manuscripts.

Goujon, Jean [goozhõ] (c.1510–c.68) The foremost French sculptor of the 16th-c, probably born in Normandy. His finest work is a set of reliefs for the Fountain of the Innocents (1547–9, Louvre).

Gould, Shane (Elizabeth) (1956–) Swimmer, born in Brisbane, Queensland, Australia. She created Olympic history by being the first and only woman to win three individual gold swimming medals in world record time. She retired in 1973, at the age of 17.

Gounod, Charles (François) [goonoh] (1818–93) Composer, born in Paris. His major works include the comic opera, *Le Médecin malgré lui* (1858, trans The Mock Doctor), and his masterpiece, *Faust* (1859).

gourd Any of several members of the cucumber family, with hard, woody-rinded fruits of various shapes and colours. All are trailing or climbing vines with tendrils, funnel-shaped flowers, and round pear- or bottle-shaped fruits. (Family: Cucurbitaceae.)

gout A disorder arising from a raised concentration of uric acid in the blood, which is deposited in the joints and soft tissues. It predominantly affects overweight males.

Gower, David (Ivon) (1957–) Cricketer, born in Tunbridge Wells, Kent. He was captain of England (1984–6, 1989), and for a while was the leading Test run-scorer, with 8231 runs in Test cricket over 117 matches. He retired in 1993, to follow a career in the media.

Gower, John (c.1325–1408) Mediaeval poet, born in Kent, a friend of Chaucer. His best-known work is the long English poem, *Confessio amantis* (c.1383), comprising over 100 stories on the theme of Christian and courtly love.

Gowers, Sir Ernest (Arthur) (1880–1966) British civil servant, and author of an influential work on English usage. He wrote *Plain Words* (1948) in an attempt to maintain standards of clear English, especially in official prose.

Goya (y Lucientes), Francisco (José) de [gohya] (1746–1828) Artist, born in Fuendetodos, Spain. He became famous especially for his portraits, and in 1799 was made court painter to Charles IV, which led to 'The Family of Charles IV' (1800, Prado) and other works.

Goyen, Jan van [goyen] *van Goyen, Jan*

Gozo [gohzoh], Maltese **Ghaudex**, ancient **Gaulus** 36°00N 14°13E; pop (2000e) 28 000 (with Comino); area 67 km²/ 26 sq mi Island in the Maltese group, often called 'the Isle of Calypso'; 6 km/4 mi NW of the main island of Malta; coastline, 43 km/27 mi; chief town, Victoria (Rabat).

Gozzi, Carlo, conte (Count) [gotzee] (1720–1806) Playwright, born in Venice, Italy. His best-known works include the comedy, *Fiaba dell' amore delle tre melarance* (1761, The Love of the Three Oranges) and *Re Turandot* (1762).

graben [grahbn] A rift valley, usually of great size, formed when a narrow block of the Earth's crust drops down between two normal faults.

Grable, Betty, originally **Ruth Elizabeth Grable** (1916–73) Actress, born in St Louis, MO. She worked as a chorus girl from the age of 13 and made her film debut in the musical *Whoopee!* (1930). She had her first major film role in *Hold 'em Jail* (1932), and became more established with *Pigskin Parade* (1936), and *Million Dollar Legs* (1939). She was adopted by American GI's during World War 2 as a pin-up girl. She went on to appear on Broadway in *Hello, Dolly* (1965).

Gracchi, (the brothers) [grakee], in full **Tiberius Sempronius Gracchus** (c.168–133 BC) and **Gaius Sempronius Gracchus** (c.159–121 BC) Roman politicians who attempted to solve the major social and economic problems of their day by forcing through sweeping reforms while they were tribunes of the plebs (133 BC, 123–122 BC). The ruthlessness of their methods provoked a backlash which led to Tiberius being killed, and Gaius committing suicide.

Grace, W(illiam) G(ilbert) (1848–1915) Cricketer, born in Downend, Bristol, SW England. He twice captained the English team. His career in first-class cricket (1865–1908) as batsman and bowler brought 126 centuries, 54 896 runs, and 2876 wickets.

Graces, the (Gr *Charites*) In Greek mythology, three daughters of Zeus and Hera, embodying beauty and social accomplishments. They are sometimes called **Aglaia**, **Euphrosyne**, and **Thalia**.

grackle A bird of the New World, any of 11 species of the family Icteridae (American blackbirds and orioles). The name is also used for several starlings from SE Asia and Indonesia (family: Sturnidae).

Grade (of Elstree), Lew Grade, Baron, originally **Louis Winogradsky** (1906–98) Theatrical impresario, born near Odessa, Ukraine, the eldest of three brothers who were to dominate British showbusiness for over 40 years. He arrived in Britain in 1912, along with his younger brother Boris (1909–94), who became **Baron Bernard Delfont of Stepney**. Bernard entered theatrical management in 1941, and from 1958 to 1978 presented the annual Royal Variety Performance. Lew became managing director of ATV in 1962, and headed several large film entertainment and communications companies. His nephew, *Michael Grade* (1943–), became chairman of the BBC (2004–6) and executive chairman of ITV (from 2006).

Graf, Steffi [grahf], popular name of **Stefanie Maria Graf** (1969–) Tennis player, born in Brühl, nr Heidelberg, Germany. She won the French Open in 1987, and took all four major titles in 1988, as well as the Olympic crown. She won the Wimbledon title again in 1989, 1991, 1992, 1993, 1995, 1996, and the French Open

in 1999, retiring later that year. In 2001 she married tennis player Andre Agassi.

graffito *sgraffito*

graft (botany) The portion of a woody plant inserted into a slot cut in the stem or rootstock of another plant, so that the vascular tissues combine and growth continues. It is successful only between closely related species.

graft (medicine) A tissue or organ that can be used for transplantation. An **allograft** (**homograft**) is taken from a member of the same species but one that is genetically dissimilar. An **autograft** is taken from the animal's or the patient's own body or a genetically identical individual (eg an identical twin). A **xenograft** (**heterograft**) is taken from a species different to that of the host.

Graham, Billy, popular name of **William Franklin Graham, Jr** (1918–) Evangelist, born in Charlotte, NC. He was ordained a Southern Baptist minister in 1939, and quickly gained a reputation as a preacher. Since the 1950s he has conducted a series of highly organized revivalist campaigns in the USA, UK, and elsewhere. He received the Templeton Prize in 1982.

Graham, Martha (1894–1991) Dancer, teacher, and choreographer, born in Pittsburgh, PA. She started the Martha Graham School of Contemporary Dance in 1927, and became the most famous exponent of Expressionist modern dance in the USA. The company appeared at the Edinburgh Festival in 1996, performing reconstructions of her early works.

Grahame, Kenneth (1859–1932) Writer, born in Edinburgh. He wrote several stories for children, the best known being *The Wind in the Willows* (1908).

Graham Land Mountainous Antarctic peninsula; rises to c.3600 m/11 800 ft at Mt Jackson.

Grail, Holy or **Sangreal** In the Arthurian legends, the dish or chalice used by Christ at the Last Supper. Joseph of Arimathea brought it to Glastonbury. It appeared at Pentecost at King Arthur's table, and the knights set out to find it.

Grainger, Percy (Aldridge), originally **George Percy Grainger** (1882–1961) Composer and pianist, born in Melbourne, Victoria, Australia. He championed the revival of folk music, in such works as 'Molly on the Shore' and 'Shepherd's Hey' (1911), which make skilful use of traditional dance themes.

gram *kilogram*

grammar The study of the structure of words (also known as *morphology*), phrases, clauses, and sentences (also known as *syntax*). A **prescriptive grammar** lays down conventions of usage regarded by some sections of society as being 'correct', such as 'Never end a sentence with a preposition'. By contrast, a **descriptive grammar** describes actual usage patterns, without making value judgments about their social standing. A **comparative grammar** compares the grammatical features of languages that are genetically related, and a **universal grammar** investigates those grammatical features shared by the structure of all languages.

grammar school In the UK, a selective school choosing usually the most able 15–25% of 11-year-olds on the basis of the eleven-plus examination. The oldest schools date back to mediaeval times, and were originally established to teach Latin.

Grammer, Kelsey (1955–) Actor, born on St Thomas, US Virgin Islands. He is best known for his role as Dr Frasier Crane, originally seen in *Cheers* (1982–93) and *Wings*, and then in *Frasier* (from 1993–2004, 32 Emmys). His feature films include *Down Periscope* (1996), *The Real Howard Spitz* (1998), and *X-Men: The Last Stand* (2006).

Grammy An annual popular music award given by the US National Academy of Recording Arts and Sciences for special achievements in the record industry. It was established in 1958. (*see panel p.390*)

gramophone An acoustic device for reproducing sounds, stored

Grammy Award Categories

The 31 Grammy domains listed below are subdivided into 108 categories (as of 2006).

General Field	World Music
Pop	Polka
Dance	Children's
Traditional Pop	Spoken Word
Rock	Musical Show
Alternative Music	Film/TV/Visual Media
R&B	Composing/Arranging
Rap	Package
Country	Album Notes
New Age	Historical
Jazz	Non-Classical Production
Gospel	Surround Sound
Latin	Classical Production
Blues	Classical
Folk	Music Video
Reggae	

as acoustically generated, laterally cut grooves in the flat surface of a disc rotated on a turntable beneath a stylus. It was first demonstrated in 1888 by US inventor Emile Berliner (1851–1929).

Grampian pop (2000e) 548 400; area 8704 km²/3360 sq mi. Former region in NE Scotland; created in 1975, and replaced in 1996 by Moray and Aberdeenshire councils.

Grampians (Australia) Mountain range in SWC Victoria, Australia; rises to 1167 m/3829 ft at Mt William.

Grampians (Scotland) or **Grampian Mountains** Mountain system extending SW–NE across Scotland; rises to 1344 m/4409 ft at Ben Nevis.

grampus A toothed whale; correctly the **grey grampus** or **Risso's dolphin** (*Grampus griseus*), a widespread temperate and tropical deep-water species of short-nosed dolphin. (Family: Delphinidae.)

Gramsci, Antonio [gramshee] (1891–1937) Political leader and theoretician, born in Ales, Sardinia, Italy. He helped to establish the separate Italian Communist Party in 1921, and in 1924 became leader of the party in parliament. In prison from 1926, his *Lettere del carcere* (1947, Letters from Prison) is now regarded as one of the most important political texts of the 20th-c.

Granada 37°10N 3°35W, pop (2000e) 257 000. City in Andalusia, S Spain; founded by the Moors, 8th-c; capital of the Kingdom of Granada, 1238; last Moorish stronghold in Spain, captured in 1492; archbishopric; airport; railway; university (1531); cathedral (16th-c), with tombs of Ferdinand and Isabella; Generalife Palace and the Alhambra, a world heritage site.

granadilla Any of several species of passion flower which produce edible fruits. **Purple granadilla** (*Passiflora edulis*) has purple fruits, 5–7.5 cm/2–3 in long. (Family: Passifloraceae.)

Granby, John Manners, Marquess of (1721–70) British army officer, the eldest son of the Duke of Rutland. His reputation was made in the Seven Years' War (1756–63), when he led the British cavalry in a major victory over the French at Warburg (1760).

Gran Canaria [gran kanaria], Eng **Grand Canary** 28°00N 15°35W; area 1532 km²/591 sq mi. Volcanic Atlantic island in the Canary Is; highest point, Pozo de las Nieves (1980 m/6496 ft); chief town, Las Palmas de Gran Canaria; airport; tourism.

Gran Chaco [gran chakoh] Lowland plain covering part of N Argentina, W Paraguay, and S Bolivia; scrub forest and grassland, with a tropical savannah climate and sparse population; cattle raising.

Grand Army of the Republic (GAR) An organization of veterans of the Union side in the American Civil War. Established in 1866, the GAR became an important force in post-war politics.

Grand Banks A major fishing ground in the N Atlantic Ocean, off the coast of Newfoundland, Canada, formed by an extensive submarine plateau on the continental shelf.

Grand Canal, Chin **Da Yunhe** Canal in E China, length 1794 km/1115 mi, average width, 30 m/100 ft; longest artificial waterway in the world; from Beijing municipality to Hangzhou in Zhejiang province; opened in AD 610.

Grand Canyon Enormous gorge in NW Arizona, USA; 349 km/217 mi long; 8–25 km/5–15 mi wide from rim to rim; maximum depth c.1900 m/6250 ft; the result of large-scale erosion by the Colorado R.

Grand Coulee [koolee] Valley in Douglas County, NE Washington, USA; the **Grand Coulee Dam** is a major gravity dam on the Columbia R, impounding L Franklin D Roosevelt; built 1933–42; height 168 m/550 ft; length 1272 m/4173 ft.

Grand Guignol [grã geenyol] Short sensational shows, in vogue in Paris in the late 19th-c, which depict violent crimes in a style designed to shock and titillate. Guignol was originally a puppet in the French marionette theatre.

grand mal [grã mal] *epilepsy*

Grand National The most famous steeplechase in the world, first held at Maghull near Liverpool in 1836. The race moved to its present course at Aintree in 1839. Raced over 4 mi/855 yd (7.2 km) the competitors have to negotiate 31 difficult fences.

Grand Remonstrance The statement of Charles I of England's abuses, and of reforms made by the Long Parliament in 1640–1.

Granger, Clive W J (1934–) Economist, born in Swansea, S Wales. He joined the University of California at San Diego, USA, and in 2003 shared the Nobel Prize for Economics for work on using statistics to predict the future.

Granger, Stewart, originally **James Lablanche Stewart** (1913–93) Film actor, born in London. He assumed his professional name in the 1930s, to avoid confusion with actor James Stewart, and developed into a leading romantic star, his films including *The Man in Grey* (1943), *King Solomon's Mines* (1950), and *The Wild Geese* (1977).

granite A coarse-grained, acid (high in silica) igneous rock containing orthoclase feldspar, quartz, and mica (and/or hornblende); pale pink or grey in colour, its durability makes it an important building stone.

Grant, Cary, originally **Archibald Leach** (1904–86) Actor, born in Bristol, SW England. From the late 1930s he developed in leading comedy roles, and also provided several performances for Hitchcock, such as in *Suspicion* (1941) and *North by North-West* (1959).

Grant, Duncan (James Corrow) (1885–1978) Painter, born in Rothiemurchus, Inverness, Highland. Associated with the London Group, his works were mainly landscapes, portraits, and still life.

Grant, Hugh (John Mungo) (1960–) Actor, born in London. He became internationally known following his role in *Four Weddings and a Funeral* (1994, Best Actor Golden Globe). Later films include *Notting Hill* (1999), *Bridget Jones's Diary* (2001, sequel 2004), *Love Actually* (2003), and *American Dreamz* (2006).

Grant, Richard E(sterhuysen) (1957–) Actor, born in Mbabane, Swaziland. He became known following his role as the down-and-out thespian in *Withnail and I* (1987), and later films include *The Player* (1992), *The Portrait of a Lady* (1996), *Gosford Park* (2001), and *Penelope* (2006). He made his directorial debut with *Wah-Wah* (2005). He provided the voice for Doctor Who in an animated TV series *Doctor Who: Scream of the Shalka* (2003).

Grant, Ulysses S(impson) (1822–85) US general and 18th president (1869–77), born in Point Pleasant, OH. He led Union forces to victory in the Civil War (1861), first in the Mississippi Valley, then in the final campaigns in Virginia, and accepted the Confederate surrender at Appomattox Court House (1865). Elected president in 1868 and 1872, he presided over the reconstruction of the South. His memoirs have been much acclaimed.

Granth Sahib *Adi Granth*

grant-maintained school A school, established by the 1988 Education Act, which is independent of the local education authority and receives its annual grant directly from the government. In order to 'opt out' of local authority control a majority of parents must vote in favour by secret ballot.

granulation (astronomy) *photosphere*

Granville-Barker, Harley (1877–1946) Actor, playwright, and director, born in London. His writing includes a famous series of prefaces to Shakespeare's plays (1927–45).

Granz, Norman (1918–2001) Concert impresario and record producer, born in Los Angeles, CA. He was chiefly known for his staging of the national and international tours called Jazz at the Philharmonic, and was widely recognized as a leading disseminator of jazz music around the world.

grape *grapevine*

grapefruit A citrus fruit (*Citrus paradisi*) 10–15 cm/4–6 in diameter, globose with thick, pale, yellow rind; some varieties may be slightly pear-shaped or have thin or pinkish rind. (Family: Rutaceae.)

grapevine A deciduous woody climber (*Vitis vinifera*); flowers numerous, tiny, green; ripe fruits sweet, yellowish or purple, often with a waxy, white bloom. Probably native to E Asia, many varieties are now cultivated in most temperate regions, especially those with a Mediterranean climate. It is of considerable economic importance as the source of wine. Dried grapes are sold as currants, raisins, and sultanas. (Family: Vitaceae.)

graph A diagram illustrating the relationship between two sets of numbers, such as the relationship between the height of a plant in centimetres and the time in days since germination. The sets of numbers can be purely algebraic; for example, described by the equation $y = x − 1$.

graphic design A set of skills and techniques employed in the design of all printed matter. The major skills include typography, photography, illustration, and printmaking.

graphics tablet A device by which the movements of a pen over a special surface can be translated into digital input for a computer. This provides a means of converting two-dimensional information, such as maps and drawings, into computer-readable form.

graphic user interface (GUI) The screen interface with a computer's operating software, where graphical components such as icons are used to represent computer files and programs. Users simply click on the icons to activate the program or file.

graphite A mineral form of carbon, found in metamorphic rocks; black, soft, and greasy to the touch. It is a very good electrical conductor and dry lubricant. Mixed with clay, it is used in pencil 'leads'.

graphology 1 The analysis of handwriting as a guide to the character and personality of the writer. It was introduced during the late 19th-c by the French abbot, Jean Hippolyte Michon (1806–81).
2 In linguistics, the study of the writing system of a language; also the writing system itself.

Grappelli, Stéphane [grapelee] (1908–97) Jazz violinist, born in Paris. He and Django Reinhardt were the principal soloists in the Quintet of the Hot Club of France (1934–9), the first European jazz band to exert an influence in the USA.

Grasmere 54°28N 3°02W, pop (2000e) 1220. Scenic resort village in Cumbria, NW England; by L Grasmere; home (Dove Cottage) and burial place of Wordsworth.

Grass, Günter (Wilhelm) (1927–) Writer and political activist, born in Gdańsk, Poland (formerly Danzig, Germany). He achieved a European reputation with his first novel, *Die Blechtrommel* (1959, The Tin Drum). Other political novels include *Hundejahre* (1963, Dog Years) and *Die Ratten* (1987, The Rats). Later novels include *Crabwalk* (2003). He was awarded the 1999 Nobel Prize for Literature. An autobiography, *Beim Häuten der Zwiebel* (While Skinning the Onion) appeared in 2006, causing controversy through its revelation that he had been a member of the Waffen-SS.

grass A member of one of the largest flowering-plant families, with over 9000 species distributed worldwide. They are monocotyledons, ranging from tiny annuals to perennials over 30 m/100 ft high. A typical grass has fibrous roots and hollow, cylindrical stems which branch at the base to form a tuft. Long, narrow leaves grow singly from the nodes of the stem and have an upper part (the *blade*), and a lower part (the *sheath*), which fits around the stem like a sleeve. The junction of blade and sheath often bears a flap or ring of hairs (the *ligule*), which is diagnostically important. Grasses occur in every type of habitat, terrestrial and aquatic, including the sea, and especially in the vast, open prairies, savannah, and steppe. They are the most important economic plant group. As well as providing forage for animals in the form of grazing, hay, and silage, they include grain-bearing species (the *cereals*), which are staple foods for most of the world's population. They also provide sugar, materials for thatching, paper, mats, and even light timber. They have an important role as soil stabilizers, and are used for lawns and verges. A few are ornamentals but a number are tenacious weeds. (Family: Gramineae.)

grasshopper A medium to large, terrestrial insect with hindlimbs adapted for jumping; forewings leathery; hindwings forming membranous fan, or reduced; many produce sound by rubbing together forewings or hindlimbs. (Order: Orthoptera.)

grass snake A harmless snake native to the Old World from Europe to SE Asia, and to North America; lives near water; often called **water snake** in the USA. (Genus: *Natrix*, many species. Family: Colubridae.)

Grattan, Henry (1746–1820) Irish statesman, born in Dublin. He secured Irish free trade in 1779, and legislative independence in 1782.

Gravenhage, 's- [skhrahvenhahguh] *Hague, The*

Graves, Robert (Ranke) (1895–1985) Poet and novelist, born in London. His best-known novels are *I, Claudius* and its sequel, *Claudius the God* (both 1934), which were adapted for television in 1976. His *Collected Poems* (1975) draws on more than 20 volumes and confirms his status as a major poet of the 20th-c.

Graves' disease *hyperthyroidism*

Gravesend 51°27N 0°24E, pop (2001e) 51 200. Seaport in Kent, SE England; on S bank of the R Thames facing Tilbury; pilot station for the Port of London; Pocahontas is buried in St George's churchyard.

Gravettian [gravetian] A European archaeological culture of the Upper Palaeolithic Age, c.26 000–18 000 BC (sometimes referred to as the **Later Aurignacian/Later Perigordian**). It is named after the cave at La Gravette, Dordogne, SW France.

gravitation The mutually attractive force between two objects due to their masses; expressed by Newton's law of gravitation $F = Gm_1m_2/r^2$, where F is the force between objects of mass m_1 and m_2 separated by distance r, and G is the gravitational constant. The direction of force is along a line joining the two bodies. It is the weakest of all forces, important only on a large scale. **Gravity** refers to the intensity of gravitation at the surface of the Earth or some other celestial body.

gravitational collapse A phenomenon which occurs when the supply of nuclear energy in the core of a star runs out, and the star cools and contracts; a prediction of general relativity.

Once the star radius is less than a critical value (Schwarzschild radius, $R = 2MG/c^2$, value 3 km/2 mi for the Sun), the collapse cannot be reversed by any force now known to physics. Implosion to a black hole seems inevitable.

gravitational constant A fundamental constant, symbol G, value $6.673 \times 10^{-11} \text{Nm}^2/\text{kg}^2$, which measures the strength of gravitation.

gravity *gravitation*

gravity assist The additional increment of velocity acquired by a spacecraft on passing a planet. Through accurate targeting, it can be used to speed up a spacecraft to achieve a trajectory not possible using present launch capabilities.

gravure A form of printing, known as **intaglio**, in which the image to be communicated is engraved or etched into the surface of a metal cylinder; after inking, surplus ink is removed from the surface of the cylinder, and the ink retained in the engraved cells is transferred to paper when that is brought into contact with the cylinder.

Gray, Asa (1810–88) Botanist, born in Sauquoit, NY. His main works were the *Flora of North America* (1838–42), which he compiled with John Torrey, and the *Manual of the Botany of the Northern United States* (1848), often known simply as 'Gray's Manual'.

Gray, Thomas (1716–71) Poet, born in London. His masterpiece is 'Elegy Written in a Country Churchyard' (1751), set at Stoke Poges, Buckinghamshire.

gray In radioactivity, the unit of absorbed dose, ie the energy deposited in an object by radiation, divided by the mass of the object; SI unit; symbol Gy; 1 Gy defined as 1 J/kg.

grayling Freshwater fish (*Thymallus thymallus*) widespread in clean swift rivers of N Europe; length up to 50 cm/20 in; body silvery with longitudinal violet stripes; good food fish. (Family: Thymallidae; sometimes placed in Salmonidae.)

Gray's Inn *Inns of Court*

Graz [grahts] 47°05N 15°22E, pop (2000e) 242 200. City in SE Austria; second largest city in Austria; railway; two universities (1585, 1811); cathedral (15th-c); 28 m/92 ft-high clock tower (1561); Piber Stud Farm, where Lippizaner horses bred for the Spanish Riding School in Vienna, 3.5 km/2 mi NE.

Great Australian Bight Area of the Southern Ocean off the S coast of Australia (1450 km/900 mi).

Great Awakening A widespread 18th-c Christian revival movement in the USA, which reached its high point in the 1740s in New England. Jonathan Edwards and George Whitefield were among its leaders.

Great Barrier Reef Coral reef in the Coral Sea off the NE coast of Australia, 50–150 km/30–90 mi offshore and 2000 km/1200 mi long; the largest accumulation of coral known, yielding trepang, pearl-shell, and sponges.

Great Basin area 500 000 km²/193 000 sq mi. Vast interior region in W USA, between (W) the Sierra Nevada and the Cascade Range and (E) the Wasatch Range and Colorado Plateau; rugged N–S mountain ranges; semi-arid climate; several deserts; some minerals and grazing land.

Great Bear Lake Lake in Northwest Territories, NW Canada, on the Arctic Circle; 320 km/200 mi long; 40–177 km/25–110 mi wide; maximum depth 413 m/1356 ft; area 31 153 km²/12 025 sq mi.

Great Bitter Lake, Arabic **Buheiret Murrat al-Kubra** Lake on Suez Canal between Ismailiya (N) and Suez (S); Little Bitter Lake lies SE.

Great Britain *United Kingdom*

great circle A circle described on the surface of a sphere with its plane passing through the centre of the sphere. The shortest distance between any two points on a sphere lies along a great circle.

Great Dane One of the largest breeds of dog (height, 0.75 m/

2½ ft), perfected in Germany from a mastiff-like ancestor; long powerful legs; square head with deep muzzle and pendulous ears; coat short, pale brown with dark flecks.

Great Depression The worldwide slump in output and prices, and the greatly increased levels of unemployment, which developed between 1929 and 1934. It was precipitated by the collapse of the US stock market (the 'Wall Street crash') in October 1929.

Great Divide *Continental Divide*

Great Dividing Range Mountain range in Queensland, New South Wales, and Victoria, Australia; extends 3600 km/2200 mi; rises to 2228 m/7310 ft at Mt Kosciuszko.

Greater Manchester *Manchester, Greater*

Great Exhibition An international exhibition held in Hyde Park, London (May–Oct 1851), celebrating 'the Works of Industry of all Nations'. Prince Albert helped to organize the Exhibition, for which the Crystal Palace was constructed.

Great Indian Desert *Thar Desert*

Great Lakes The largest group of freshwater lakes in the world, in C North America, on the Canada–USA border; drained by the St Lawrence R; consists of Lakes Superior, Michigan (the only one entirely in the USA), Huron, Erie, Ontario; sometimes L St Clair is included; water surface c.245 300 km²/94 700 sq mi, c.87 270 km²/33 700 sq mi in Canada; connected by navigable straits and canals; pollution a recent problem.

Great Leap Forward A movement in China, initiated in 1958, which aimed at accelerating both industrial and agricultural progress. It planned the creation of 'communes' in a true collective system, but failed miserably.

Great Malvern *Malvern*

Great Northern War (1700–21) A war between Russia and Sweden for the mastery of the Baltic coastal region. Charles XII of Sweden defeated Peter I of Russia's army at Narva in 1700, but Peter later defeated Sweden at Poltava (1709). The war was concluded by the Treaty of Nystadt.

Great Plains Region of C North America; a sloping plateau, generally 650 km/400 mi wide, bordering the E base of the Rocky Mts from Alberta (Canada) to New Mexico and Texas; limited rainfall, short grass; used chiefly for stock grazing and grain growing; dry farming on unsuitable land and overpasturing led to the **Dust Bowl**, semi-arid regions where wind storms carry off large quantities of topsoil.

Great Red Spot The largest, best-known, and probably longest-lived 'storm' feature of Jupiter's atmosphere; a reddish oval feature in the S hemisphere, about 30 000 km/19 000 mi across. It is a region high in atmosphere exhibiting a counter-clockwise rotation lasting about six days. Its red colour is ascribed to chemicals (eg sulphur, phosphorus) in the atmosphere.

Great Rift Valley *Rift Valley*

Great Salt Lake Large inland salt lake in NW Utah, USA; length 120 km/75 mi; width 80 km/50 mi; average depth 4 m/13 ft; has no outlet and fluctuates greatly in size; water is 20–7% saline; commercial salt extraction.

Great Sandy Desert N belt of the Western Australian Desert; area c.450 000 km²/175 000 sq mi.

Great Slave Lake Lake in W Northwest Territories, C Canada; 480 km/300 mi long; 50–225 km/30–140 mi wide; maximum depth over 600 m/2000 ft; area 28 570 km²/11 030 sq mi.

Great Smoky Mountains Mountain range, part of the Appalachians, USA; rises to 2025 m/6644 ft at Clingmans Dome.

Great Train Robbery *Biggs, Ronald*

Great Trek The movement of parties of Boers (*Voortrekkers*) which made them the masters of large tracts of the interior of S Africa. They began to leave Cape Colony in 1836 in separate trekking groups, settling in the Transvaal and Natal, and often encountering considerable native opposition.

Great Victoria Desert or **Victoria Desert** S belt of the Western Australian Desert, area c.325 000 km²/125 000 sq mi.

Great Wall of China (Chin *chang cheng*, 'long wall') The defensive and symbolic frontier stretching 4100 km/2550 mi across N China from the Yellow Sea to the C Asian desert; a world heritage site. The earliest connected wall was built from 221 BC to repel attacks from nomads to the N, and was improved during later dynasties. The wall is c.7·6 m/25 ft high and 3·7 m/12 ft broad, made of earth and stone with a facing of bricks. A four-year study to determine its exact route, length, and condition began in May 2007.

Great Zimbabwe Stone ruins covering an area of 25 ha/62 acres in SE Zimbabwe; a world heritage site. The site was probably occupied from the 4th-c, and the ruins date from the 8th-c onwards. The term *zimbabwe* is Bantu for 'stone houses'.

grebe An aquatic bird, native to temperate regions or high tropical lakes worldwide; swims underwater using feet; toes lobed and slightly webbed. (Family: Podicipedidae, 22 species.)

Greco, El [grekoh] ('El' Span 'the', 'Greco' Ital 'Greek'), nickname of **Domenikos Theotokopoulos** (1541–1614) Painter, born in Candia, Crete, Greece. He became a portrait painter whose reputation fluctuated because of the suspicion which greeted his characteristic distortions, such as his elongated, flamelike figures. His most famous painting is probably the 'Burial of Count Orgaz' (1586) in the church of San Tomé, Toledo. His work *The Baptism of Christ* (1567–70) was discovered in 2004.

Greece *p.394*

Greek–Persian Wars *Persian Wars*

Greek Orthodox Church The self-governing (*autocephalous*) Orthodox Church of Greece. After the schism of 1054, the Orthodox Church in Greece remained under the patriarch of Constantinople, but was declared independent in 1833.

Greek religion *p.395*

Greeley, Horace (1811–72) Editor and politician, born in Amherst, NH. He was editor of the weekly *New Yorker* in 1834, and in 1841 founded the daily New York *Tribune*. He was its leading editor until his death, and exerted a supreme influence on US opinion.

Green (politics) *Greens*

green algae A large and diverse group of alga-like plants characterized by the photosynthetic pigments, chlorophylls *a* and *b*, which give them their green colour; found predominantly in fresh water. (Class: Chlorophyceae.)

Greenaway, Kate, popular name of **Catherine Greenaway** (1846–1901) Artist and book illustrator, born in London. She became well known in the 1880s for her coloured portrayals of child life, in such works as *The Birthday Book* (1880). The **Greenaway Medal** is awarded annually for the best British children's book artist.

Greenaway, Peter (1942–) Film-maker and painter, born in Newport, S Wales. In 1982, *The Draughtsman's Contract* won him critical acclaim, and he went on to direct a series of films preoccupied with sex, death, decay, and gamesmanship. His films include *Prospero's Books* (1991), *The Pillow-Book* (1996), and *8 ½ Women* (1999).

green belt A planning measure in which areas are designated free from development to prevent urban sprawl encroaching into the countryside, and the merging of neighbouring towns. It provides open land for recreation, and protects agricultural land.

Greene, Maurice (1974–) Athlete, born in Kansas City, KS. Among his achievements are World Championship gold medals for the 100 m in 1997 and 1999 (world record), and for the 200 m in 1999.

Greene, (Henry) Graham (1904–91) Writer, born in Berkhamsted, Hertfordshire. In his major novels, central religious issues and moral dilemmas emerge, especially concerning Catholicism, such as in *Brighton Rock* (1938), *The Power and the Glory* (1940), *The End of the Affair* (1951), and *A Burnt-Out Case* (1961). He also wrote plays, film scripts (notably, *The Third Man*, 1949), short stories, and essays, as well as three volumes of autobiography.

Greene, Nathanael (1742–86) US general, born in Warwick, RI. In the American Revolution, he took command of the Southern army in 1780, and though Cornwallis defeated him at Guilford Courthouse, the victory was so costly that Greene was able to recover S Carolina and Georgia, paving the way to American victory in the South.

Greene, Robert (1558–92) Playwright, born in Norwich, Norfolk. His most popular work was the comedy *Friar Bacon and Friar Bungay* (c.1589), and his *Pandosto* (1588) was a source for Shakespeare's *The Winter's Tale*.

greenfinch A bird of the finch genus, *Carduelis* (4 species), native to S Europe and S Asia. (Family: Fringillidae.)

greenfly A soft-bodied aphid that feeds by sucking plant sap; wingless female has plump, greenish body, winged male darker; a complex life-cycle, with up to 10 generations each year produced asexually.

Greengard, Paul (1925–) Biochemist, born in New York City. He became head of the Laboratory of Molecular and Cellular Neuroscience, The Rockefeller University, in 1983. In 2000 he shared the Nobel Prize for Physiology or Medicine for discoveries concerning signal transduction in the nervous system.

Greenham Common The site of a US military base in West Berkshire, England. It was subjected to continuous picketing during most of the 1980s by the Women's Peace movement, who were opposed in particular to the siting of Cruise missiles in Britain, and in general to nuclear weaponry. The base closed down in 1992.

greenhouse effect A planetary atmosphere warming phenomenon, resulting from the absorption of infrared radiation by atmospheric constituents. Radiant energy arrives at the planetary surface mainly as visible light from the Sun, which is then re-emitted by the surface at infrared wavelengths as heat. Carbon dioxide and water vapour in the atmosphere absorb this infrared radiation and behave as a blanket, with the net effect that atmospheric temperatures rise. On Earth, the burning of fossil fuels and large-scale deforestation enhance the effect. In 2007 the Intergovernmental Panel on Climate Change predicted that, by 2100, temperatures may rise by up to 6·4°C and sea levels by up to 43 cm, with Arctic sea ice disappearing. (The term 'greenhouse' is misleading, since the mechanism by which glasshouses provide warming is mainly due to the inhibition of convection.)

Greenland *p.396*

Greenland Sea area 1 205 000 km²/465 000 sq mi. Gulf connecting the Atlantic and Arctic Oceans; cold surface current from the Arctic brings icebergs and fog.

Green Line 1 The dividing line between Muslim W Beirut and Christian E Beirut, Lebanon, during the 1975–6 civil war. **2** The dividing line between N (Turkish) and S (Greek) sectors of Nicosia.

green monkey *vervet monkey*

Green Mountain Boys A movement in the American Revolution that created the state of Vermont, from territory disputed between New York and New Hampshire. They helped capture the British fort at Ticonderoga (1775).

green paper In the UK, a document published by the government for discussion by interested parties, usually prior to formulating or changing policy. The practice first began in the late 1960s in response to calls for more consultation.

Greenpeace An international environmental pressure group which began in Canada and the USA in 1971. It campaigns by direct action (non-violent, passive resistance) against commer-

Greece

☐ International Airport

ancient **Hellas**, Gr **Ellás**, official name **The Hellenic Republic**, Gr **Elliniki Dimokratia**

Local name Ellás

Timezone GMT +2

Area 131 957 km²/50 935 sq mi

Population total (2002e) 10 994 000

Status Republic

Date of independence 1830

Capital Athens (Athínai)

Languages Greek (official), English and French widely spoken

Ethnic groups Greek (98%), Albanian, Slav, Turkish minorities, and others (2%)

Religions Christian (98%) (Greek Orthodox 97·5%, Roman Catholic 0·4%, Protestant 0·1%), Muslim, Judaism, and others (2%)

Physical features Located in SE Europe, occupying the S part of the Balkan peninsula and numerous islands in the Aegean and Ionian seas; mainland includes the Peloponnese (S), connected via the narrow Isthmus of Corinth; over 1400 islands (only 169 inhabited), including Crete, the largest, 8336 km²/3218 sq mi, Rhodes, Milos, Corfu, Lesbos, Kos; nearly 80% of Greece mountainous or hilly; Pindus Mts run N to S; highest point, Mt Olympus, 2917 m/9570 ft; principal rivers include the Néstos, Strimón, Arakhthos; c.30% of land arable or under permanent cultivation; c.20% forested.

Climate Mediterranean climate for coast and islands, with mild, rainy winters and hot, dry summers; rainfall almost entirely in winter; island of Corfu receives maximum rainfall 1320 mm/52 in; severe winters in mountains; average annual temperatures 9°C (Jan), 28°C (Jul) in Athens.

Currency 1 euro (EUR) = 100 cents (previous to February 2002, 1 Drachma (GRD) = 100 lepta)

Economy Strong service sector accounts for c.60% of national income; agriculture based on cereals, cotton, tobacco, fruit, figs, raisins, wine, olive oil, vegetables; major tourist area, especially on islands; world's largest shipping fleet (under own and other flags); member of the European Union (formerly EC) from 1981.

GDP (2002e) $203·3 bn, per capita $19 100

Human Development Index (2002) 0·885

History Prehistoric civilization culminated in the Minoan-Mycenean culture of Crete; Dorians invaded from the N, 12th-c BC; Greek colonies established along N and S Mediterranean and on the Black Sea; many city-states on mainland, notably Sparta and Athens; Persian invasions, 5th-c BC, repelled at Marathon, Salamis, Plataea, Mycale; Greek literature and art flourished, 5th-c BC; conflict between Sparta and Athens (Peloponnesian War) weakened both, and hegemony passed to Thebes, and then Macedon under Philip II, 4th-c BC; his son, Alexander the Great, conquered the Persian Empire; Macedonian power broken by the Romans, 197 BC; part of the Eastern Roman and Byzantine empires; ruled by the Ottoman Turks from 15th-c until 19th-c; national reawakening led to independence as kingdom, 1830; territorial gains after Balkan War and World War 1; absorbed over 1 00 000 refugees after defeat in Asia Minor, 1922; republic established, 1924–35; German occupation, 1941–4; civil war, 1944–9; military coup, 1967; abolition of monarchy, 1969; democracy restored, 1974; governed by a Prime Minister; Cabinet, unicameral Parliament, and President.

Monarch

1935 Georgios Kondylis *Regent*
1935–47 Georgios (George) II
1947–64 Pavlos (Paul) I
1964–7 Konstantinos (Constantine) II
1967–73 *Military junta*
1973 Georgios Papadopoulos *Regent*

Head of State

1973 Georgios Papadopoulos
1973–4 Phaedon Gizikis
1974–5 Michael Stasinopoulos
1975–80 Konstantinos Tsatsos
1980–5 Konstantinos Karamanlis
1985–90 Christos Sartzetaki
1990–5 Konstantinos Karamanlis
1995–2005 Konstantinos Stephanopoulos
2005– Karolos Papoulias

Head of Government

1973 Spyridon Markezinis
1973–4 Adamantios Androutsopoulos
1974–80 Konstantinos Karamanlis
1980–1 Georgios Rallis
1981–9 Andreas Georgios Papandreou
1989 Tzannis Tzannetakis
1989–90 Xenofon Zolotas
1990–3 Konstantinos Mitsotakis
1993–6 Andreas Papandreou
1996–2004 Kostas Simitis
2004– Kostas Karamanlis

Greek religion

Principal Greek Gods

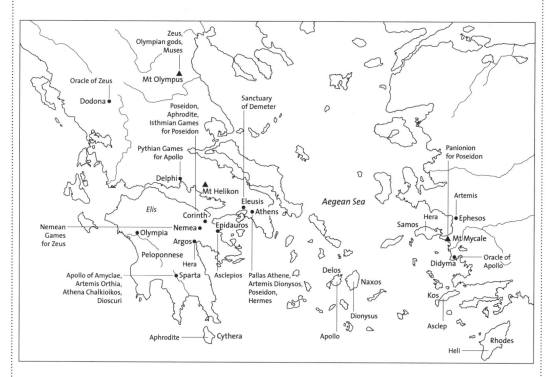

The religion of the Ancient Greeks was polytheistic, as were earlier systems of belief in the Near East. The gods each had a sphere of influence (eg Poseidon over the sea) or an attachment to a locality (eg Athena at Athens); often both. Though mythologists try to systematize the relationships between the gods, it is unwise to take their tidying up too seriously. It is doubtful whether the average Greek knew more than is contained in Homer. Besides the 12 major Olympian gods, there were later introductions of 'Oriental' deities, especially female, such as Cybele and Isis, who acquired great influence. The Homeric gods are very human in their passions and spiteful jealousies; the main difference is that they do not eat human food, and they do not die. They shade into a lower group of demi-gods and heroes, special people whose cults centred on their tombs. In the cults, ritual and sacrifice were important duties, in return for which the suppliant expected benefits. The system had to be seen to work, as in the case of the oracle at Delphi. In the 5th-c the whole basis of religion was challenged by the Sophists, and the weakening of supernatural belief reinforced Greek humanism. Yet, at the same time, the Eleusinian and Orphic mystery cults began to grow; though highly secret, they were concerned with personal survival after death. Finally, after Alexander the Great had himself proclaimed as a god, the way was open to the ruler-cults of the Roman Empire.

Greenland

Dan **Grønland**, Eskimo **Kalâtdlit-Nunât**

Local names Kalaalit Nunaat (Greenlandic), Grønland (Danish), Kalâtdlit-Nunât (Inuit)

Timezone GMT 0, -1, -4;

Area 2 175 600 km²/839 800 sq mi

Population total (2002e) 57 000

Status Self-governing province of Denmark

Capital Nuuk (Godthåb)

Languages Danish (official), Inuit

Ethnic groups Largely Inuit (Eskimo), with Danish admixtures

Religions Lutheran, Shamanist

Physical features Located in N Atlantic and Arctic Oceans; largely covered by an ice-cap (up to 4300 m/14 000 ft thick); coastal mountains rise to 3702 m/12 145 ft at Gunnbjørn Fjeld (SE); less than 5% of island is habitable.

Climate Arctic to subarctic.

Currency 1 Danish Krone (DKK) = 100 óre

Economy Largely dependent on fishing from ice-free SW ports; hunting for seal and fox furs in N and E; reserves of lead, zinc, molybdenum, uranium, coal, cryolite.

GDP (2001e) $1·1 bn, per capita $20 000

History Settled by seal-hunting Eskimos from North America c.2500 BC; Norse settlers in SW, 12th–15th-c AD; explored by Frobisher and Davis, 16th-c; Danish colony from 1721; self-governing province of Denmark, 1979; elected Provincial Council sends two members to the Danish Parliament.

Head of State (Monarch)
1972– Margrethe II

Head of Government
1987–2002 Jonathan Motzfeldt
2002– Hans Enoksen

□ International Airport

---

cial whaling and seal culling, the dumping of toxic and radio-active waste at sea, and the testing of nuclear weapons.

green pound The special agricultural exchange rates in the EU, which ensure that currency movements are not reflected in national farm prices. The aim is that the price of each agricultural product should be the same throughout the EU.

Greens A label applied to members of political parties and social movements which espouse ideologies having as a central tenet a concern over the damaging effect human activity is having on the environment. The first green party (the Values Party) was formed in New Zealand in 1972, to be followed in 1974 by People in the UK. The most successful in parliamentary terms has been the German Green Party, which has had members of the Bundestag since 1983 and of the European Parliament since 1984. There is also a much larger green movement made up of environmental pressure groups and individuals.

greenshank A wading bird (*Tringa nebularia*), native to N Europe and N Asia; long pale green legs; long bill slightly upturned. (Family: Scolopacidae.)

green tourism *tourist industry*

Greenwich [grenich], Anglo-Saxon **Grenawic** 51°28N 0°00, pop (2001e) 214 500. Borough of EC Greater London, UK; site of the original Royal Greenwich Observatory; birthplace of Henry VIII, Elizabeth I, and Mary I; railway; Greenwich Hospital (1694), Royal Naval College, National Maritime Museum; clip-per *Cutty Sark* and Francis Chichester's *Gypsy Moth IV* at Greenwich Pier; maritime Greenwich made a world heritage site in 1997; Millennium Dome.

Greenwich Mean Time (GMT) [grenich] The basis for world time zones, set by the local time at Greenwich, near London. This is located on the Greenwich Meridian, longitude 0°, from which other time zones are calculated. It is now known as **co-ordinated universal time.**

Greenwich Village [grenich] A district of Manhattan, New York City, which became famous during the 20th-c as the quarter of writers, intellectuals, and bohemians. It has recently developed into a more fashionable residential area.

Greer, Germaine (1939–) Feminist, writer, and lecturer, born in Melbourne, Victoria, Australia. Her best-known book, *The Female Eunuch* (1970), portrayed marriage as a legalized form of slavery for women, and attacked the misrepresentation of female sexuality by male-dominated society. Later books include *The Whole Woman* (1999) and *Whitefella Jump Up* (2004).

Gregorian calendar A calendar instituted in 1582 by Pope Gregory XIII, and now used in most of the world. Its distinguishing feature is that a century year is a leap year if, and only if, divisible by 400. This gives a year of 365·2425 days when averaged over 400 years. When introduced, a discrepancy of 10 days had built up, which was eliminated by jumping straight from 4 to 15

October in Catholic countries. Britain and its colonies (including America) switched in 1752, and also moved New Year's Day from 25 March back to 1 January.

Gregorian chant The monophonic and (in its purest form) unaccompanied chant of the Roman Catholic liturgy. The compilation of the repertory has been credited to Pope Gregory the Great.

Gregory I, St, known as **the Great** (c.540–604) Pope (590–604), a Father of the Church, born in Rome. There he saw some Anglo-Saxon youths in the slave market, and was seized with a longing to convert their country to Christianity. As pope, he was a great administrator, reforming all public services and ritual, and systematizing the sacred chants. He was canonized on his death. Feast day 12 March.

Gregory VII, St, originally **Hildebrand** (c.1020–85) Pope (1073–85), the great representative of the temporal claims of the mediaeval papacy, born near Soana, Italy. As pope, he worked to change the secularized condition of the Church, which led to repeated conflict with the German Emperor Henry IV. Gregory was canonized in 1606. Feast day 25 May.

Gregory of Tours, St [toor], originally **Georgius Florentinus** (c.538–c.594) Frankish historian, born in Arverna (now Clermont). His *Historia Francorum* is the chief authority for the history of Gaul in the 6th-c. Feast day 17 November.

Grenada *p.398*

grenade A munition, typically an explosive-packed container with a simple ring-pull fuse, designed for use in close-quarters fighting. It may be either thrown by hand or projected from a launcher.

Grenadines, The [grenadeenz] Group of 600 small islands and islets in the Windward Is, E Caribbean; administered by St Vincent (**N Grenadines**) and Grenada (**S Grenadines**); five airfields.

Grenoble [gruhnobl], ancient **Cularo**, **Gratianopolis** 45°12N 5°42E, pop (2000e) 157 000. Ancient fortified city in E France; Mont Blanc to the NE; railway; bishopric; university (1339); cathedral 12th–13th-c; important sports and tourist centre; scene of 1964 Olympic skating championships and 1968 Winter Olympics.

Grenville, Sir Richard (c.1542–91) English naval commander, a cousin of Sir Walter Raleigh. In 1585 he commanded the seven ships carrying Raleigh's first colony to Virginia. In 1591, as commander of the *Revenge*, he fought alone against a large Spanish fleet off the Azores, dying of wounds on board a Spanish ship.

Grenville, William Wyndham Grenville, 1st Baron (1759–1834) British statesman, born in Wotton House, Buckinghamshire. The son of prime minister George Grenville (1712–1770), he became paymaster-general (1783), home secretary (1790), and foreign secretary (1791), and in 1806–7 formed the coalition 'Government of All the Talents', which abolished the slave trade.

Greville, Sir Fulke, 1st Baron Brooke (1554–1628) Poet, born in Beauchamp Court, Warwickshire. He wrote several didactic poems, over 100 sonnets, and two tragedies. He was Chancellor of the Exchequer (1614–22).

Grey, Charles Grey, 2nd Earl (1764–1845) British statesman and prime minister (1830–4), born in Fallodon, Northumberland. A leading supporter of parliamentary reform, he secured the passage of the 1832 Reform Bill, and carried the Act for the abolition of slavery in the colonies.

Grey, Lady Jane (1537–54) Queen of England for nine days in 1553, born in Broadgate, Leicestershire, great-granddaughter of Henry VII. The Duke of Northumberland aimed to secure the succession by marrying Jane (against her wish) to his son. Three days after the death of Edward VI, she was named as his successor, but was forced to abdicate in favour of Mary, and beheaded.

Grey, Zane, pseudonym of **Pearl Grey** (1872–1939) Novelist, born in Zanesville, OH. Best known of his many popular books was *Riders of the Purple Sage* (1912).

greyhound A breed of dog, now raced for sport; thin with short coat; long legs, tail, and muzzle; the **Italian greyhound** is a miniature breed developed in Italy. Greyhound racing takes place on an enclosed circular or oval track, round which dogs are lured to run by a mechanical hare. The first regular track was at Emeryville, CA, in 1919.

grey mullet Any of a large family of fish, widespread in tropical and warm temperate seas; body elongate, robust; dorsal profile rather flat; blue-grey above, sides silvery; valuable food fish in some areas. (*Chelon labrosus*. Family: Mugilidae, 4 genera.)

Grey-Thompson, Dame Tanni (1969–) Paralympian, born in Cardiff. Born with spina bifida and paralyzed from the waist down, she took up wheelchair racing and made her debut for Wales at the Junior National Championships aged 15. Her first Olympic success was at Seoul in 1988 when she won the 400 m race, and went on to achieve a remarkable medal haul at successive games. At Barcelona in 1992 she won four gold medals (100 m, 200 m, 400 m, 800 m) and one silver (4 x 100 m relay); at Atlanta in 1996 she won gold in the 800 m, and three silver (100 m, 200 m, 400 m); at Sydney in 2000 she won four gold medals (100 m, 200 m, 400 m, 800 m); at Athens in 2004 she won gold in the 100 m and 400 m. She was honoured with a damehood in 2005.

Gribbin, John Richard (1946–) Astronomer, writer, and broadcaster, born in Maidstone, Kent. His first book, *The Jupiter Effect* (1974) was followed by over 50 others, including *In Search of Schrödinger's Cat* (1984), *The Universe* (2007), and biographies of Stephen Hawking and Albert Einstein. In 1993 he became a visiting fellow in astronomy at the University of Sussex.

gribble A small wood-boring crustacean that burrows into boat hulls and other submerged timber, causing extensive damage. (Class: Malacostraca. Order: Isopoda.)

grid reference A unique set of numbers locating any place on a map onto which a grid of numbered squares has been imposed. References in the UK are based on the National Grid. The distance eastwards (*easting*) is always given before the distance northwards (*northing*) when giving a National Grid reference.

Grieg, Edvard (Hagerup) [greeg] (1843–1907) Composer, born in Bergen, Norway. A strongly nationalist writer, his major works include the incidental music for Ibsen's *Peer Gynt* (1876), and the A minor piano concerto.

Grierson, John [greerson] (1898–1972) Producer of documentary films, born in Kilmadock, Stirling. He made his name with *Drifters* (1929), and is regarded as the founder of the British documentary movement.

griffin or **gryphon** A fabulous beast, originating in Greek tales of the Arimaspians, who hunted the creature for its gold. It had a lion's body, and an eagle's head, wings, and claws.

Griffith, Arthur (1872–1922) Irish nationalist politician, born in Dublin. In 1905 he founded Sinn Féin, editing it until 1915, became an MP (1918–22), signed the peace treaty with Great Britain, and was a moderate president of the Dáil Eireann (1922).

Griffith, D(avid) W(ark) (1875–1948) Pioneer film director, born in La Grange, KY. He experimented with new techniques in photography and production, and brought out two masterpieces, *The Birth of a Nation* (1915) and *Intolerance* (1916).

Griffith, Melanie (1957–) Actress, born in New York City. She appeared in a number of films as a teenager, then after a gap of four years her adult career commenced with *Body Double* (1984). Later films include *Bonfire of the Vanities* (1990), *Lolita* (1997), and *Tempo* (2003).

griffon (ornithology) An Old World vulture, native to S Europe, Africa, and S Asia; head and neck lack long feathers. (Genus: *Gyps*, 7 species.)

Grignard, (François Auguste) Victor [greenyah(r)] (1871–1935)

Grenada

□ International Airport

[grenayda]

Local name Grenada
Timezone GMT -4
Area 344 km²/133 sq mi
Population total (2002e) 101 900
Status Independent state within the Commonwealth
Date of independence 1974
Capital St George's
Languages English (official), French patois

Ethnic groups African descent (84%), mixed (12%), E Indian (3%) European (1%)

Religions Roman Catholic (64%), Protestant (21%)

Physical features Most southerly of the Windward Is, E Caribbean; comprises the main island of Grenada, 34 km/21 mi long, 19 km/12 mi wide; and the S Grenadines; Grenada volcanic in origin, with a ridge of mountains along its entire length, the highest point, Mt St Catherine, rising to 843 m/2766 ft; many rivers and lakes, including Grand Étang.

Climate Sub-tropical climate; average annual temperature 23°C; wet season (Jun–Dec); annual rainfall varies from 1270 mm/150 in (coast) to 5000 mm/200 in (interior); lies within Caribbean hurricane zone.

Currency 1 East Caribbean Dollar (XCD) = 100 cents

Economy Economy based on agriculture, notably fruit, vegetables, cocoa, nutmegs, bananas, mace; processing of agricultural products and their derivatives; cocoa and nutmeg crops destroyed by Hurricane Ivan, Sep 2004.

GDP (2002e) $440 mn, per capita $5000

Human Development Index (2002) 0·747

History Visited by Columbus and named Concepción, 1498; settled by French, mid-17th-c; ceded to Britain, 1763; retaken by France, 1779; ceded again to Britain, 1783; British Crown Colony, 1877; independence, 1974; popular people's revolution, 1979; Prime Minister Maurice Bishop killed during further uprising, 1983; a group of Caribbean countries requested US involvement, and troops invaded the island in Oct 1983, to restore stable government; governed by a Senate, House of Representatives, Prime Minister, and Cabinet.

Head of State
(British monarch represented by Governor-General)
1996– Daniel Charles Williams

Head of Government
1974–9 Eric Matthew Gairy
1979–83 Maurice Bishop
1983–4 Nicholas Brathwaite *Chairman of Interim Council*
1984–9 Herbert Augustus Blaize
1989–90 Ben Jones *Acting*
1990–5 Nicholas Brathwaite
1995 George Brizan
1995– Keith Mitchell

Organic chemist, born in Cherbourg, France. He introduced the use of organo-magnesium compounds (**Grignard reagents**), which form the basis of the most valuable class of organic synthetic reactions, for which he shared the Nobel Prize for Chemistry in 1912.

Grigson, Sophie, popular name of **Hester Sophia Frances Grigson** (1959–) Cookery writer and broadcaster, born in Swindon, Wiltshire. A newspaper cookery correspondent from 1986, she became widely known through her television programmes for Channel 4, such as *Sophie's Meat Course* (1995). Among her books are *Sophie Grigson's Feasts for a Fiver* (1999), *Country Kitchen* (2004), and *Vegetables* (2006).

Grimaldi, Joseph [grimaldee] (1779–1837) Comic actor, singer, and acrobat, born in London. From 1800 until 1828, he dominated the stage of Sadler's Wells as the figure of 'Clown' in the English harlequinade.

Grimes Graves Prehistoric flint mines on the Norfolk Breckland, E England, in use c.3000–2500 BC.

Grimké sisters [grimkay] Abolitionists and feminists: **Sarah Moore Grimké** (1792–1873) and **Angelina Emily Grimké** (1805–79), born to a major slaveholding family in Charleston, SC. The sisters rejected their family's way of life, and joined the Quakers, who were officially anti-slavery. They became public figures, committed to social change.

Grimm brothers Folklorists and philologists: **Jacob Ludwig Carl Grimm** (1785–1863) and **Wilhelm Carl Grimm** (1786–1859), both born in Hanau, Germany. Between 1812 and 1822 they published the three volumes known as *Grimm's Fairy Tales* (Ger *Kinder und Hausmärchen*). Jacob's *Deutsche Grammatik* (1819, Germanic Grammar, revised 1822–40) is perhaps the greatest philological work of the age; he also formulated **Grimm's Law** of sound changes.

Grimmelshausen, Hans Jakob Christoffel von [grimels-howzen] (c.1622–76) Writer, born in Gelnhausen, WC Germany. In later life he wrote a series of novels, the best of them on the model of the Spanish picaresque romances, such as the *Simplicissimus* series (1669–72).

Grimond (of Firth), Jo(seph) Grimond, Baron [grimuhnd] (1913–93) British politician, born in St Andrews, Fife. Elected leader of the Liberal Party (1956–67), he was largely responsible for the modernizing of both the Party and Liberalism, and called for a 'realignment of the left' of British politics. He was also Chancellor of the University of Kent (1970–90).

Grimsby, formerly **Great Grimsby** 53°35N 0°05W, pop (2000e)

90 900. Port town in North East Lincolnshire, NE England; railway; largest fishing port in England; football league team, Grimsby Town (Mariners).

grip The member of a camera crew in film or TV production who moves equipment and mountings. A **key grip** may also take part in associated set construction.

Griqualand [greekwaland] Region of Eastern Cape province, South Africa; **East Griqualand** joined to Cape Colony in 1879; **West Griqualand**, including the former diamond fields of Kimberley, joined in 1880.

grisaille [greeziy] A painting executed entirely in shades of grey. This may be done for its own sake, or to look like sculpture as part of a decorative scheme. Many Renaissance painters began their pictures with a grisaille underpainting.

Grisham, John (1955–) Novelist, born in Jonesboro, AR. His first novel, the crime thriller *A Time To Kill* (1989), was followed by a string of best-sellers, many of which have been made into successful films, and include *The Rainmaker* (1995), *The Brethren* (2000), and *The Broker* (2005). His first work of non-fiction, *The Innocent Man: Murder and Injustice in a Small Town*, appeared in 2006.

Grivas, Georgeios (Theodoros) [greevas] (1898–1974) Leader of EOKA, born in Trikomo, Cyprus. In 1955 he became head of the underground campaign against British rule in Cyprus, calling himself 'Dighenis' after a legendary Greek hero. In 1971 he returned secretly to Cyprus and, as leader of EOKA-B, directed a terrorist campaign for union with Greece until his death.

grivet monkey *vervet monkey*

grizzly bear *brown bear*

Groening, Matt [grayning] (1954–) Cartoonist, born in Portland, OR. He studied at The Evergreen State College in Olympia, WA, then moved to Los Angeles (1977). He is known as creator of the popular cartoon family *The Simpsons* which debuted as a series in 1990, and won an Emmy for Best Animated Series. It celebrated its 350th episode in 2005. In 1999 he created the animated series *Futurama*.

Gromyko, Andrei Andreevich [gromeekoh] (1909–89) Soviet statesman and president (1985–8), born near Minsk, Belarus. As longest-serving foreign minister (1957–85), he was responsible for conducting Soviet relations with the West during the Cold War.

Groningen [khroningn] 53°13N 6°35E, pop (2000e) 177 000. City in N Netherlands; bishopric; connected to its outer port, Delfzijl, by the Eems Canal; airport; railway; university (1614); large market, dealing in cattle, vegetables, fruit, and flowers.

Gropius, Walter (Adolph) [grohpius] (1883–1969) Architect, born in Berlin. He was appointed director of the Grand Ducal group of schools of art in Weimar, which he reorganized to form the Bauhaus, aiming at a new functional interpretation of the applied arts. When Hitler came to power, he moved to London (1934–7), and then to the USA, where he was professor of architecture at Harvard (1937–52).

grosbeak [grohsbeek] A name applied to birds of several unrelated groups, all with a large, stout bill: the finch family Fringillidae (12–32 species); the weaver family Ploceidae (1 species); and the **cardinal grosbeaks** of the family Emberizidae (14 species).

Gros Morne [groh maw(r)n] National park on the W coast of Newfoundland, Canada, established in 1970; area 2000 km²/775 sq mi; noted for its landscape and wildlife; a world heritage site.

Gross, David J(onathan) (1941–) Theoretical physicist, born in Washington, DC. Director of the Institute of Physics at Santa Barbara, California (1997–), in 2004 he shared the Nobel Prize for Physics for work contributing to the discovery and exploration of the force that binds particles inside an atomic nucleus.

Gross, Michael [grohs], nickname **the Albatross** (1964–) Swimmer, born in Frankfurt, Germany. In 1981–7 he won a record 13 gold medals at the European Championships, and won three Olympic gold medals: the 100 m butterfly and 200 m freestyle in 1984, and the 200 m butterfly in 1988.

gross domestic product (GDP) A measure of national income, calculated in any of three ways. The *output method* is the total of selling prices less the cost of bought-in materials. The *income method* is the total of wages, rents, dividends, interest, and profits. The *expenditure method* is the national expenditure on goods and services (known as 'GDP at factor cost'). The **gross national product (GNP)** is similarly calculated, but includes residents' income from economic activity overseas and excludes UK incomes accruing to foreign residents.

Grosseteste, Robert [grohstest] (c.1175–1253) Scholar, bishop, and Church reformer, born in Stradbroke, Suffolk. He undertook the reformation of abuses in the Church, which brought him into conflict both locally and with the papacy.

Grossglockner [grohsglokner] 47°05N 12°44E. Mountain in the Hohe Tauern range, SC Austria; height 3797 m/12 457 ft; highest peak in Austria.

Grossmith, George [grohsmith] (1847–1912) Comedian and entertainer, born in London. With his brother, **Weedon Grossmith** (1853–1919), he wrote *Diary of a Nobody* in *Punch* (1892). His son **George Grossmith** (1874–1935) was a well-known musical-comedy actor, songwriter, and manager of the Gaiety Theatre, London.

Grosz, George [grohs] (1893–1959) Artist, born in Berlin. While in Germany he produced a series of bitter, ironical drawings attacking German militarism and the middle classes. He fled to the USA in 1932, where he produced many oil paintings of a symbolic nature.

Grotius, Hugo [grohshius], also found as **Huig de Groot** (1583–1645) Jurist and theologian, born in Delft, The Netherlands. In 1625 he published his great work on international law, *De jure belli ac pacis* (On the Law of War and Peace).

ground beetle An active, terrestrial beetle; adults mostly predatory, found in litter or vegetation. (Order: Coleoptera. Family: Carabidae, c.30 000 species.)

ground elder A perennial (*Aegopodium podagraria*) native to Europe and temperate Asia; long creeping underground stems give rise to numerous leafy shoots and stems to 1 m/3¼ ft; flowers white. It is a persistent weed of gardens. Family: Umbelliferae.)

groundhog *woodchuck*

Groundhog Day A day (2 Feb) recognized in US popular tradition when the groundhog (or woodchuck), an American marmot, is supposed to appear from hibernation; it is said that if the groundhog sees its shadow, it goes back into hibernation for six more weeks, thereby indicating six weeks of winter weather to come.

ground ivy A creeping perennial (*Glechoma hederacea*), native to Europe and Asia; leaves rounded, bluntly toothed, in opposite pairs; flowers in pairs, 2-lipped, with long tube, violet-blue. (Family: Labiatae.)

groundnut *peanut*

groundsel A very variable annual (*Senecio vulgaris*) growing to 45 cm/18 in, native to Europe, Asia, and N Africa; flower-heads numerous, cylindrical, surrounded by narrow black-tipped bracts; florets yellow; fruit with a parachute of hairs. It is a common and often problematic weed. (Family: Compositae.)

Ground Zero The name given to the site of the former World Trade Center in lower Manhattan, New York City, USA, where rescue teams worked to clear the wreckage and debris left after the terrorist attack on 11 September 2001. The term was originally used with reference to the part of the ground situated immediately under an exploding bomb (especially an atomic bomb).

grouper Large heavy-bodied fish with mottled cryptic coloration; prized as a sport fish and food fish; **Indo-Pacific grouper**, *Epinephelus lanceolatus*, may reach 3·7 m/12 ft, weight 270 kg/600 lb. (Family: Serranidae.)

group therapy The interaction of several individuals on a cognitive and emotional level, as part of a therapeutic programme. It incorporates the sharing of personal experiences and feelings, with the purpose of increasing self-understanding and the treatment of psychological problems.

groupware Computer programs which are developed especially for the purpose of enabling groups of people either in the same or different locations to work together on a common task. A special case of groupware is the computer conference.

grouse A plump, ground-dwelling bird of the family Tetraonidae (19 species); inhabits high latitudes of the N hemisphere; camouflaged coloration; short curved bill; nostrils covered by feathers; legs feathered; eats vegetation and insects.

Grove, Sir George (1820–1900) Musicologist, born in London. His major work was as editor of the *Dictionary of Music and Musicians* (1878–89).

growth hormone (GH) A hormone (a polypeptide), secreted by the front lobe of the pituitary gland in vertebrates with jaws, which stimulates body growth; also known as **somatotrophin** or **somatotrophic hormone**. Its abnormal secretion may result in dwarfism or gigantism.

growth ring *annual ring*

Grozny [groznee] 43°21N 45°42E, pop (2003e) 80–160 000 (estimates affected by refugee and militia movements). Capital city of Chechnya, SE European Russia; founded as a fortress, 1818; airfield; railway; university (1972); major damage and disruption during war with Russia, 1995; virtually totally destroyed in renewed fighting, 1999–2000.

Grubbs, Robert (1942–) Organic chemist, born in Calvert City, KY. He studied at the University of Florida (1963–5), Columbia University (1968), and Stanford University (1968–9). In 1978 he joined the California Institute of Technology, Pasadena, and has been the Victor and Elizabeth Atkins Professor of Chemistry since 1990. He shared the 2005 Nobel Prize for Chemistry with Richard Schrock and Yves Chauvin for his work on the development of the metathesis method in organic synthesis.

Grünewald, Matthias [grünevalt], originally **Mathis Gothardt** (?1470–1528) Artist, architect, and engineer, probably born in Würzburg, Germany. In 1516 he completed the great Isenheim altarpiece (Colmar Museum).

grunion Slender-bodied fish (*Leuresthes tenuis*) confined to inshore waters of the Californian coast; length up to 18 cm/7 in; body with silvery side-stripe. (Family: Atherinidae.)

grunt Any of the family Haemulidae (formerly Pomadasyidae, 5 genera) of mainly tropical fishes common in shallow coastal waters and around coral reefs. They are so called because they produce audible sounds by grinding their pharyngeal teeth.

Grus [groos] (Lat 'crane') A S constellation.

gryphon *griffin*

G-7 (Group of Seven) An economic grouping formed between states in 1975 with the aim of co-ordinating efforts to promote growth and stability in the world economy and to bring the world's key exchange rates into line. It consists of the seven leading industrialized countries: Canada (from 1976), France, Germany, Italy, Japan, UK, and USA. Its annual meetings are attended by the president or prime minister of each member country. The European Union is also now represented, and Russia became a full member in 1998, to make the group G-8. Other groupings include G-10 (comprising 11 countries, the G-7 members plus Belgium, Netherlands, Switzerland, and Sweden) and G-24 (whose membership comes from developing countries).

guacharo *oilbird*

Guadalajara [gwadalakhahra] 20°30N 103°20W, pop (2000e) 1 960 000. City in WC Mexico; altitude 1567 m/5141 ft; founded, 1530; second largest city in Mexico; airport; railway; two universities (1792, 1935); cathedral (1561–1618), Hospicio Cabañas (a world heritage site); scene of a major industrial accident (gasline explosion) in 1992.

Guadalcanal [gwadalkanal] pop (2000e) 76 000; area 5302 km²/2047 sq mi. Largest of the Solomon Is, SW Pacific; rises to 2477 m/8126 ft at Mt Makarakomburu; capital, Honiara; airport; scene of the first World War 2 Allied Pacific invasion northward (1942).

Guadalquivir, River [gwadalkiveer] (Span **Río**), ancient **Baetis**, Arabic **Wad-el-kebir** River rising in the Sierra de Cazorla, Andalusia, S Spain; enters the Atlantic at Sanlúcar de Barrameda; length, 657 km/408 mi.

Guadalupe Hidalgo, Treaty of [gwadaloop hidalgoh] (1848) The agreement that settled the Mexican War, with Mexico yielding all of Texas, Arizona, Nevada, California, and Utah, and parts of New Mexico, Colorado, and Wyoming.

Guadeloupe [gwadeloop] pop (2000e) 425 000; area 1779 km²/687 sq mi. Overseas department of France, a group of seven islands in the C Lesser Antilles, E Caribbean; capital, Basse-Terre; largest town, Pointe-à-Pitre; timezone GMT −4; 90% black or mulatto population, with several minorities; chief religion, Roman Catholicism; official language, French; unit of currency, the French franc; main islands of Grand-Terre and Basse-Terre accommodate over 90% of the population; warm and humid climate; average annual temperature, 28°C; visited by Columbus, 1493; occupied by France, 1635; later held by Britain and Sweden; returned to France, 1816; departmental status, 1946; administrative region, 1973; Commissioner advised by a General Council and a Regional Council; economy mainly agricultural processing, especially sugar refining and rum distilling.

Guam *p.401*

guanaco [gwanahkoh] A wild member of the camel family (*Lama guanicoe*), native to the Andean foothills and surrounding plains; brown with white underparts and grey head; possibly ancestor of llama and alpaca.

Guangzhou [kwangjoh], **Canton**, also **Kwang-chow** or **Kuang-chou** 23°08N 113°20E, pop (2000e) 4 387 000. City in S China, on Pearl R delta; founded in 200 BC; opened to foreign trade following Opium War of 1839–42; occupied by Japan, 1938–45; airport; railway; university (1958); medical college (1953); industrial and foreign trade centre in S China.

guanine [gwaneen] $C_5H_5N_5O$. One of the purine bases in DNA, normally paired with cytosine.

guano [gwahnoh] An accumulation of animal droppings, typically of birds but also of mammals such as bats. Guano deposits are a rich source of phosphates and nitrates, and are often used as a fertilizer.

guarana [gwarahna] A woody liana (*Paullinia cupana*) with coiled tendrils, fern-like leaves and clusters of small, 5-petalled flowers; native to tropical America, cultivated in Brazil. The seeds are rich in caffeine, and it is used like cacao to produce a drink called guarana. (Family: Sapindaceae.)

Guaraní [gwaranee] A Tupian-speaking South American Indian group, who lived in Brazil, Paraguay, and Argentina, practising slash-and-burn agriculture, hunting, and fishing. About a million now speak Guaraní.

Guardi, Francesco [gwah(r)dee] (1712–93) Painter, born in Venice, Italy. He was noted for his views of Venice, full of sparkling colour, with an impressionist's eye for effects of light.

guardian A person who by right or appointment acts on behalf of another, taking care of that person's interests in full (or some cases to a limited or specified degree) as a result of the other's inability, either due to youth or (in some jurisdictions) mental

Guam

[gwahm] (USA Formal Dependencies)

Local name Guam (*see map p.582*)

Timezone GMT +10

Area 541 km²/209 sq mi

Population total (2002e) 630 000

Status Unincorporated territory of the United States of America

Capital Agaña

Languages Chamorro and English (official), Japanese is also spoken

Ethnic groups Chamorro (47%), Filipino (29%), Caucasian (18%), Micronesian (13%)

Religion Roman Catholic

Physical features Largest and southernmost of the Mariana Islands, covering c.48 km/30 mi in the Pacific Ocean; volcanic island fringed by a coral reef; relatively flat limestone plateau, with narrow coastal plains in N, low rising hills in C and mountains in S; highest point, 406 m/1332 ft at Mt Lamlam.

Climate Tropical maritime climate; average annual temperature 24-30°C; average annual rainfall 2125 mm/84 in; wet season (Jul-Dec); hit by Typhoon Pongsona (Dec 2002).

Currency 1 US Dollar (USD) = 100 cents

Economy Economy highly dependent on government activities; military installations cover 35% of the island; diversifying industrial and commercial projects; oil refining, dairy products, furniture, watches, copra, processed fish; rapidly growing tourist industry.

History Originally settled by Malay-Filipino peoples; Ferdinand Magellan landed on the island, 1521; claimed for Spain, 1565; rebellion against Spanish missionaries, 1670–95; US consulate established, 1855; ceded to US by Spain after defeat in Spanish-American War, 1898; occupied by Japan, 1941–4; unincorporated territory of the US, Organic Act, 1950; elected Governor and a unicameral legislature.

incapacity. In the case of a child, the parents are normally the guardians, having full parental rights and duties, but they may arrange for the appointment of another person as guardian, in the event of their death.

Guareschi, Giovanni [gwareskee] (1908–68) Writer and journalist, born in Parma, Italy. He achieved fame with his stories of the village priest, beginning with *The Little World of Don Camillo* (1950).

Guarini, (Giovanni) Battista [gwareenee] (1538–1612) Poet, born in Ferrara, Italy. His chief work was the pastoral play, *Il pastor fido* (1585, The Faithful Shepherd), which helped to establish the genre of pastoral drama.

Guarini, Guarino [gwareenee], originally **Camillo Guarini** (1642–83) Architect, philosopher, and mathematician, born in Modena, Italy. His influential *Architettura civile* (published posthumously in 1737), concerned the relationship of geometry and architecture, and he was responsible for the spread of Baroque architecture beyond Italy.

Guarnieri [gwah(r)nyayree], also found as **Giuseppe Guarneri**, known as **Giuseppe del Gesù** (1687–1745) A celebrated Italian family of violin-makers of Cremona, including **Andrea Guarnieri** (c.1626–98), his sons **Giuseppe Guarnieri** (1666–c.1740) and **Pietro Guarnieri** (1655–1720), and (most notably) Giuseppe's son **Giuseppe Guarnieri** (1698–1744).

Guatemala *p.402*

Guatemala City or **Guatemala** [gwatuhmahla] 14°38N 90°22W, pop (2000e) 1 389 000. Capital city of Guatemala; founded to serve as capital, 1776; almost totally destroyed by earthquakes

in 1917–18, and since rebuilt; altitude 1500 m/4920 ft; airport; railway; University of San Carlos (1680) and four other universities; cathedral (1782–1815).

Guayaquil [gwiyakeel] 2°13S 79°54W, pop (2000e) 1 861 000. Seaport in W Ecuador; founded 1537; airport; railway; four universities (1867, 1958, 1962, 1966); banana trade (world's chief exporter).

Gucci, Guccio [goochee] (1881–1953) Fashion designer, born in Florence, Italy. He opened his first shop in Florence in 1920, becoming known for his leather craftsmanship and accessories. His four sons joined the firm, and in 1953 (the year he died) the first overseas shop opened in New York City. His grandson, **Maurizio** (1949–95) oversaw the resurrection of the firm in the 1980s. Following a series of legal and family disputes, the company was sold to Investcorp in 1993.

gudgeon Small bottom-dwelling freshwater fish (*Gobio gobio*) widespread in Europe; body elongate, cylindrical, length up to 20 cm/8 in; head large, mouth with pair of barbels; greenish-brown with darker patches on back, sides yellowish, underside silver. (Family: Cyprinidae.)

guelder rose [gelder] A deciduous shrub or small spreading tree (*Viburnum opulus*), growing to 4 m/13 ft, native to Europe and W Asia; flowers 5-petalled, white, in a cluster, outer flowers much larger than the inner; fruits berry-like, red, often persisting after the leaves have fallen. It is much grown as an ornamental under the name **snowball tree**. (Family: Caprifoliaceae.)

Guelph [gwelf] 43°34N 80°16W, pop (2000e) 98 600. Town in SE Ontario, Canada; founded, 1827; railway; university (1964); agricultural centre.

Guelphs The pro-papal, anti-imperial party in Italian cities in the 13th–14th-c, opposed to the power of the Holy Roman Emperors. Allied with the papacy, the Guelphs resisted the claims of potential successors, and dominated Florentine politics.

guenon [guhnon] An Old World monkey native to Africa S of the Sahara; round head with beard, and 'whiskers' at side of face; slender, with long hind legs and tail. (Genus: *Cercopithecus*, c.17 species.)

Guercino, Il [eel gwercheenoh], nickname of **Giovanni Francesco Barbieri** (1591–1666) Painter of the Bolognese School, born in Cento, Italy. His major work is the ceiling fresco 'Aurora' at the Villa Ludovisi in Rome for Pope Gregory XV.

guereza *colobus*

Guericke, Otto von [gayrikuh] (1602–86) Physicist, born in Magdeburg, Germany. He improved a water pump so that it would exhaust air from a container (1650), and was able with this air pump to give dramatic demonstrations of pressure reduction (the **Magdeburg hemisphere**).

Guernica [gairneeka] 43°19N 2°40W, pop (2000e) 16 300. Basque town in N Spain; German planes bombed the town in 1937, during the Spanish Civil War, an event recalled in a famous painting by Picasso (now in Madrid).

Guernsey [gernzee] pop (2000e) 66 200; area 63 km²/24 sq mi. Second largest of the Channel Is; rises to c.90 m/300 ft; airport; ferries to the UK and France; forms the Bailiwick of Guernsey with Alderney, Sark, and some smaller islands; chief town, St Peter Port.

Guevara, Che [gayvahra], popular name of **Ernesto Guevara (de la Serna)** (1928–67) Revolutionary leader, born in Rosario, Argentina. He trained as a doctor (1953), then played an important part in the Cuban revolution (1956–9), after which he held government posts under Castro. He left Cuba in 1965 to become a guerrilla leader in South America, and was captured and executed in Bolivia.

Guggenheim, Solomon R(obert) [gugenhiym] (1861–1949) Businessman and art collector, born in Philadelphia, PA. With the assistance of Hilla Rebay, he collected important Modernist

Guatemala

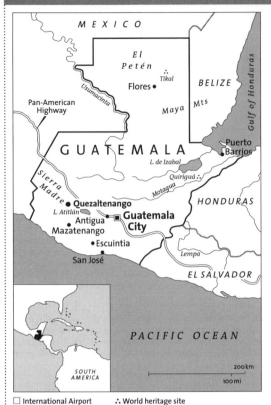

☐ International Airport   ∴ World heritage site

[gwatemahla], official name **Republic of Guatemala**, Span **República de Guatemala**
Local name Guatemala
Timezone GMT -6

Area 108 889 km²/42 031 sq mi
Population total (2002e) 11 987 000
Status Republic
Date of independence 1838
Capital Guatemala City
Languages Spanish (official), c.40% speak Indian dialects, including Quiche, Cakchiquel, Kekchi
Ethnic groups Indian (41%) and Mestizo
Religions Roman Catholic (75%), Protestant (25%)
Physical features Northernmost of the Central American republics; over two-thirds mountainous, with large forested areas; narrow Pacific coastal plain, rising steeply to highlands of 2500–3000 m/8000–10 000 ft; many volcanoes on S edge of highlands; low undulating tableland of El Petén to the N.
Climate Humid tropical climate on lowlands and coast; average annual temperatures 17°C (Jan), 21°C (Jul) in Guatemala City; rainy season (May–Oct); average annual rainfall 1316 mm/51·8 in; area subject to hurricanes and earthquakes; village of Panabaj in S buried by mudslide with 1500+ deaths (Oct 2005).
Currency 1 Quetzal (GTQ) = 100 centavos; also 1 US Dollar (USD) = 100 cents
Economy Agricultural products account for c.65% of exports, chiefly coffee, bananas, cotton, sugar; on higher ground, wheat, maize, beans; on the Pacific coastal plain, cotton, sugar cane, rice, beans.
GDP (2002e) $53·2 bn, per capita $3900
Human Development Index (2002) 0·631
History Mayan and Aztec civilizations before Spanish conquest, 1523–4; independence as part of the Federation of Central America, 1821; independence as the Republic of Guatemala, 1838; 1985 constitution provides for the election of a President (who appoints a Cabinet), and a National Assembly; long-standing claim over Belize resolved in 1991.

Head of State/Government
1986–91 Marco Vinicio Cerezo Arévalo
1991–3 Jorge Serrano Elias
1993–6 Ramiro de Léon Carpio
1996–9 Alvaro Arzú Irigoyen
1999–2003 Alfonso Portillo Cabrera
2003– Oscar Berger

paintings and established the Solomon R Guggenheim Foundation (1937). This was the source of funds for the Solomon R Guggenheim Museum, designed by Frank Lloyd Wright in 1959.
GUI *graphic user interface*
guided missile A weapon system which has the ability to fly towards its target under its own power. Its progress is directed either by an external source of command or by an internal computer which sends electronic guidance instructions to the missile's control surfaces.
guide dog A dog trained to assist the blind in finding their way, notably in urban traffic and crowded areas. The dogs are selectively bred, and include labradors, often crossed with golden retrievers, and German shepherd dogs.
Guido d'Arezzo [gweedoh daretzoh], also known as **Guido Aretino** (c.990–c.1050) Benedictine monk and musical theorist, probably born in Arezzo, Italy. The invention of the musical staff is ascribed to him, and he introduced the system of naming the notes of a scale with syllables.
Guildford [gilferd] 51°14N 0°35W, pop (2001e) 129 700. Town in Surrey, SE England; railway; University of Surrey (1966); cathedral (completed in 1964).
Guildford Four [gilferd] Three men and a woman who were con-

victed and sentenced to life imprisonment in England in 1975 for the bombing of two Guildford public houses in which seven people died, as well as for a bombing in Woolwich. The four were freed in 1989 after the Court of Appeal quashed their convictions.
guilds Religious and trade organizations, mediaeval in origin, but lasting into early-modern times. Trading and craft guilds controlled economic life in mediaeval towns; religious guilds flourished in cities and villages.
Guilin, Kuei-lin, or **Kweilin** [gwaylin] 25°21N 110°11E, pop (2000e) 626 000. Town in S China; contains majority of China's Muslim population; badly damaged while US air base in World War 2; airfield; railway.
Guillain Barre syndrome [geean baray] A rare disorder that affects the peripheral nerves and leads to a loss of function of the body that is variable in severity but usually completely reversible. It tends to follow viral infections, particularly of the respiratory tract, and is due to an auto-immune response induced by the infection that attacks nerve cells and destroys the coating around them (*myelin*) that is essential to the transmission of nerve impulses. The most obvious clinical feature is a progressive symmetrical paralysis, but loss of sensation and loss of

Guinea

SENEGAL
MALI
GUINEA-BISSAU
Fouta Djallon
Mt Tangue 1537m
Niger
Labé
Siguiri
Boké
Konkouré
Sénégal
GUINEA
Fria
Kouroussa
Kindia
Kankan
Conakry
SIERRA LEONE
CÔTE D'IVOIRE
Nzérékoré
St Paul
AFRICA
LIBERIA
ATLANTIC OCEAN
200 km
100 mi

□ International Airport

[ginee], Fr **Guinée**, formerly **French Guinea**, official name **Republic of Guinea**, Fr **République de Guinée**
Local name Guinée
Timezone GMT
Area 245 857 km²/94 926 sq mi
Population total (2002e) 7 775 000
Status Republic
Date of independence 1958
Capital Conakry
Languages French (official), Fulani, Malinké, Susu, Kissi, Kpelle
Ethnic groups Fulani (40%), Malinké (25%), Susu (11%), Kissi (6%), Kpelle (5%)
Religions Muslim (75%), traditional beliefs (24%)

Physical features Located in W Africa; coast characterized by mangrove forests, rising to a forested and widely cultivated narrow coastal plain; Fouta Djallon massif beyond, c.900 m/3000 ft; higher peaks near Senegal frontier include Mt Tangue, 1537 m/5043 ft; savannah plains in E; forested Guinea Highlands in S.

Climate Tropical climate; wet season (May–Oct); annual rainfall 4923 mm/194 in at Conakry; average temperature 32°C (dry season) on coast, 23°C (wet season).

Currency 1 Guinean Franc (GNF) = 100 cauris

Economy Agriculture (employs 75% of population); rich in minerals, with a third of the world's bauxite reserves; gold, diamonds; independence brought a fall in production as a result of withdrawal of French expertise and investment.

GDP (2002e) $18·69 bn, per capita $2100

Human Development Index (2002) 0·414

History Part of Mali empire, 16th-c; French protectorate, 1849; governed with Senegal as Rivières du Sud; separate colony, 1893; constituent territory within French West Africa, 1904; overseas territory, 1946; independent republic, 1958; death of Sékou Touré, Guinea's first President (1961–84); coup in 1984 established a Military Committee for National Recovery (CMRN); CMRN replaced by a mixed military and civilian Transitional Committee of National Recovery (CTRN), 1991; ethnic tension fuelled by acute economic problems and uncertainty over successor to ailing President Conté; state of siege declared (Feb 2007), Lansana Kouyate appointed prime minister after weeks of civil disturbance and martial law; governed by a President and Council of Ministers; new constitution, 1990.

Head of State
1961–84 Ahmed Sékou Touré
1984– Lansana Conté

Head of Government
1958–72 Ahmed Sékou Touré
1972–84 Louis Lansana Beavogui
1984–5 Diarra Traore
1985–96 *No Prime Minister*
1996–9 Sidia Toure
1999–2004 Lamine Sidime
2004 Francois Fall
2004–6 Cellou Dalein Diallo
2006–7 *No Prime Minister*
2007– Lansana Kouyate

---

involuntary regulation of blood pressure and bowel and bladder control also occur. Most patients survive and begin to recover in a few weeks.

Guillaume de Lorris [geeyohm duh loris] (c.1200–?) Poet, born in Lorris-en-Gatinais, France. He wrote the first 4000 lines of the *Roman de la Rose* (c.1235, Romance of the Rose) an allegory which was widely influential throughout mediaeval Europe.

Guillaume de Machaut [geeyohm duh mashoh] (c.1300–77) Poet and musician, born possibly in Reims, France. One of the creators of the harmonic art, he wrote a Mass, motets, songs, and ballads. His poetry greatly influenced Chaucer.

Guillem, Sylvie [gee-em] (1965–) Ballet dancer and choreographer, born in Paris. She trained at the Paris Opéra Ballet School (1977–80) and at age 16 joined the company's corps de ballet. She made her first solo appearance in 1981 and gained the status of *étoile* in 1984. In 1988 she partnered Rudolf Nureyev in a production of *Giselle* performed with the Royal Ballet in London, and from 1989 became principal guest artist with the company.

guillemot [gilimot] An auk with a long pointed bill, also known as **tystie** or (in USA) **murre**. (Genera: *Uria*, 2 species, or *Cepphus*, 4 species. Family: Alcidae.)

Guillotin, Joseph Ignace [geeyohtĩ] (1738–1814) Physician and revolutionary, born in Saintes, France. He proposed to the Constituent Assembly, of which he was a deputy, the use of a decapitating instrument as a means of execution. This was adopted in 1791 and named after him.

guillotine In the UK, a parliamentary device whereby debate on particularly contentious items of government business can be limited so that those opposing the business cannot instigate tactics designed to filibuster. It is used by all governments, usually on major pieces of legislation.

Guimarães [geemarĩysh] 41°26N 8°19W, pop (2000e) 47 800. Fortified city in N Portugal; first capital of Portugal; birthplace of Alfonso I; castle (10th-c).

Guinea *see panel*

Guinea, Gulf of area 1 533 000 km²/592 000 sq mi. Arm of the Atlantic Ocean, lying in the great bend of the W African coast; the Equator lies to the S.

Guinea-Bissau

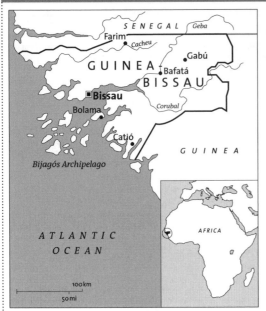

☐ International Airport

[ginee bisow], offical name **Republic of Guinea-Bissau**, Port **Republica da Guiné-Bissau**, formerly **Portuguese Guinea** (to 1974)

Local name Guiné-Bissau

Timezone GMT

Area 36 125 km²/13 948 sq mi

Population total (2002e) 1 345 000

Status Republic

Date of independence 1973

Capital Bissau

Languages Portuguese (official), Criolo, Balante

Ethnic groups Balanta (32%), Fula (22%), Mandyako (14%), Mandingo (13%), Pepel (10%)

Religions Traditional beliefs (54%), Muslim (38%), Christian (5%)

Physical features Located in W Africa; indented coast backed by forested coastal plains; main rivers, Geba and Cacheu; low-lying, with savannah-covered plateaux (S, E), rising to 310 m/1017 ft on the Guinea border; includes the heavily-forested Bijagos archipelago located in the Atlantic Ocean off the shores of the mainland.

Climate Tropical climate, hot and humid; wet season (Jun-Oct); average annual rainfall at Bissau, 1950 mm/76·8 in; average annual temperature 24°C (Jan), 27°C (Jul) in Bissau.

Currency 1 CFA Franc (XAF) = 100 centimes

Economy Based on agriculture, especially rice, maize, beans, peanuts, coconuts, palm oil, groundnuts, shrimps, fish, timber; reserves of petroleum, bauxite, phosphate.

GDP (2002e) $901·4 mn, per capita $700

Human Development Index (2002) 0·349

History Visited by the Portuguese in 1446; Portuguese colony, 1879; overseas territory of Portugal, 1952; independence, 1973; military coup, 1980; new constitution, 1984; National Assembly elects Council of State; President of the Council of State also the Head of Government; introduction of a multi-party system, 1991; governed by a president, prime minister, and a 100-seat National People's Assembly; President Yalla deposed in military coup after repeatedly cancelling elections, 2003; transitional government formed; fresh elections, Jun 2005.

Head of State
1974–80 Luis de Almeida Cabral
1980–4 Joao Bernardo Vieira (President of the Military Council)
1984–99 Joao Bernardo Vieira
1999–2000 Malam Bacai Sanhá
2000–3 Kumba Yalla
2003 Verissimo Correira Seabre *Military junta*
2003–5 Henrique Rosa *Interim*
2005– Joao Bernardo Vieira

Head of Government
1992–4 Carlos Correia
1994–7 Manuel Saturnino da Costa
1997–8 Carlos Correia
1998–2000 Francisco Fadul
2000–1 Caetano N'Tchama
2001 Faustino Imbali
2001–2 Alamara Ntchia Nhasse
2002–3 Mario Pires
2003–4 Antonio Artur Sanha *Interim*
2004– Carlos Gomes Junior

Guinea Bissau *see panel*

guinea corn *sorghum*

guinea flower *fritillary* (botany)

guinea fowl A sturdy, ground-dwelling bird native to Africa; plumage speckled grey; head and neck virtually naked; top of head may bear crest of feathers or horny projection (*casque*). (Family: Numididae, 7 species.)

guinea pig *cavy*

guineaworm A thread-like parasitic worm, a serious human parasite in Africa and India; larvae swallowed in untreated drinking water; adult worm develops in musculature of lower limbs. (Phylum: Nematoda.)

Guinevere [gwiniveer] King Arthur's queen; originally **Guanhamara** in Geoffrey of Monmouth's *History*, and there are other spellings. In later romances, much is made of her affair with Sir Lancelot (an example of courtly love).

Guinness, Sir Alec (1914–2000) Actor, born in London. His famous stage performances include Hamlet (1938) and Macbeth (1966). In 1958 he received an Academy Award for his part in the film

The Bridge on the River Kwai. Later roles include Ben Kenobi in the *Star Wars* series, and Smiley in the television versions of John Le Carré's novels (1979, 1982). He was knighted in 1959 and made a Companion of Honour in 1994. He wrote three volumes of autobiography: *Blessings in Disguise* (1985), *My Name Escapes Me: Diary of a Retiring Actor* (1997), and *A Positively Final Appearance* (1999).

Guise [geez] French ducal house of Lorraine, named after the town of Guise, whose members were prominent as staunch leaders of the Catholic Party during the 16th-c civil wars. The first duke was Claude de Lorraine (1496–1550). The line became extinct in the 17th-c.

guitar In its modern form, a musical instrument with a wooden, 'waisted' body, flat back, fretted neck, and six strings which are plucked (usually by fingers or fingernails) or strummed. Since its earliest days the guitar has been associated with folk and popular music, especially Spanish flamenco. Its elevation to the status of a recital and concerto instrument owes much to the example and influence of Segovia. The **electric guitar**, the sound of which is amplified and fed through a loudspeaker, exists in two types: the semi-acoustic, with a hollow body, and the more common type with a solid body acting not as a resonator but as an anchor for the strings, and a panel to which the electronic pickups and tone and volume controls are attached. The standard instrument has six strings, played with plectrum or fingers; the **bass guitar** has four strings, tuned one octave below the four lowest strings of the standard instrument.

guitar fish Bottom-dwelling, ray-like fish of families Rhinobatidae or Rhynchobatidae, in which the flattened head, broad pectoral fins, and slender body resemble the shape of a guitar or violin.

Guiyang or **Kuei-yang** [kwayyahng] 26°35N 106°40E, pop (2000e) 1 856 000. Capital of Guizhou province, S China; airfield; railway; steel, machinery, aluminium.

Guizot, François (Pierre Guillaume) [geezoh] (1787–1874) Historian and statesman, born in Nîmes, France. As the king's chief adviser (1840), he promoted reactionary methods of government, and was forced to escape to London with Louis Philippe in 1848.

Gujarat [goojaraht] pop (2001e) 50 597 000; area 195 984 km²/ 75 650 sq mi. State in W India; independent sultanate, 1401; part of Mongol Empire, 1572; part of Bombay state, 1947; created in 1960 from the N and W Gujarati-speaking areas of Bombay state; capital, Gandhinagar; airfield; six universities; highly industrialized; scene of flood disaster in 1983, after bursting of the Fodana Dam; major earthquake in 2001, with 100 000 deaths recorded.

Gujarati [gujarahtee] *Indo-Aryan languages*

Gujranwala [gujrahnvala] 32°06N 74°11E, pop (2000e) 1 069 000. City in NE Punjab province, Pakistan; Sikh ruler Ranjit Singh born there, 1780; former Sikh capital; railway.

gulag [goolag] Acronym for **Glavnoye Upravleniye Ispravitelno-Trudovykh Lagerey** (Main Administration of Corrective Labour Camps), the Soviet Union's secret police department which administered the system of forced labour for those found guilty of crimes against the state.

Gulbenkian, Calouste (Sarkis) [gulbengkian] (1869–1955) Financier, industrialist, and diplomat, born in Scutari, Turkey. A major figure in international oil negotiations for over 50 years, he left $70 million and vast art collections to finance an international Gulbenkian Foundation.

Gulf, The *Persian Gulf*

Gulf Co-operation Council (GCC) An organization which encourages co-operation among the Arab states in the Persian Gulf area. It was established in 1981 by Bahrain, Kuwait, Oman, Qatar, Saudi Arabia, and the United Arab Emirates. The relationship with Yemen is under consideration.

Gulf Intracoastal Waterway *Intracoastal Waterway*

Gulf Stream Ocean current named after the Gulf of Mexico; flows along the E coast of the USA and across the Atlantic Ocean (the N Atlantic Drift); its warm water has an important moderating effect on the climate of NW Europe.

Gulf War (1980–8) *Iran–Iraq War*

Gulf War (Jan–Feb 1991) A war caused by the invasion of Kuwait by Iraq (Aug 1990). Iraq failed to comply with a UN resolution calling on it to withdraw, which resulted in the formation of a 29-member coalition, led by the USA, launching an air attack against Iraq (Operation Desert Storm) on 16 January 1991, followed by a ground war (Operation Desert Sabre) on 24 February. Kuwait was liberated two days later, and hostilities were suspended on 28 February (a total of 43 days fighting). Iraq then accepted the UN resolutions. Among notable events of the conflict were the Scud missile attacks on Israel; Iraq's pumping of Kuwaiti oil into the Gulf; and the burning of Kuwaiti oil wells (all capped by Nov 1991).

gull A medium or large bird, found worldwide, usually near water; feet webbed; plumage white, grey, and black; wings long and slender; bill long, stout. (Family: Laridae, 44 species.)

gullet *oesophagus*

gum arabic A resin which exudes from the branches of several species of *Acacia*, particularly *Acacia senegal*, a shrub or small tree native to dry areas of Africa, from Senegal to Nigeria. The gum is used as an adhesive, and in ink and confectionery manufacture. (Family: Leguminosae.)

gumbo *okra*

gums Dense fibrous connective tissue surrounding the base of the teeth, firmly attached to the underlying bone (the alveolar bone of the jaws). They are covered by a smooth vascular mucous membrane continuous with the lining of the lips and cheeks.

gum tree A member of a genus of evergreen trees, native to and typical of Australia. Groups of species can be recognized by their characteristic bark: smooth gum trees, scaly bloodwoods, fibrous stringy-barks, and hard iron-barks. They are fast-growing (the tallest reaching 97 m/318 ft), and provide useful timber and oils, including eucalyptus oil. (Genus: *Eucalyptus*, 500 species. Family: Myrtaceae.)

gun-cotton *nitrocellulose*

gundog *sporting dog*

gun-metal A form of bronze once favoured for the making of weapons. Modern gun-metal, with a composition of c.88% copper, 10% tin, and some zinc, has good anti-corrosion properties.

Gunn, Thom(son William) (1929–2004) Poet, born in Gravesend, Kent. He settled in California (1954), where he taught English at Stanford and Berkeley. His often erotic poems are written in an intriguing variety of regular and free forms. Volumes include *Fighting Terms* (1954), *The Passages of Joy* (1982), *The Man With Night Sweats* (1992), and *Boss Cupid* (2000).

gunnel Small slender-bodied fish found in inshore and intertidal habitats of the N Atlantic and Pacific Oceans; length up to 30 cm/1 ft; pelvic fins reduced or absent. (Family: Pholidae.)

Gunnell, Sally (Janet) (1966–) Athlete, born in Chigwell, Essex. She gained international recognition with a gold medal for the 100 m hurdles in the 1986 Commonwealth Games. She won the 400 m hurdles in the 1992 Olympics, and in 1993–4 became European Cup, Commonwealth, and World Cup champion in the hurdles. She published a book about her career, *Running Tall* (1994).

gunpowder The oldest known explosive, a mixture of sulphur, charcoal and saltpetre (nitre, potassium nitrate). It was the principal military explosive until late in the 19th-c, and is still valuable in primers, fuses, and pyrotechnics.

Gunpowder Plot A conspiracy by Catholic gentry, led by Robert Catesby, to blow up the English Houses of Parliament. It failed when Guy Fawkes, who placed the explosives, was arrested (5 Nov 1605). The scheme reflected Catholic desperation after the failure of previous plots to remove James I in 1603; peace with Spain in 1604, which ended the prospect of foreign support; and new sanctions imposed against recusant Catholics, resulting in 5000 convictions in the spring of 1605 alone.

Gunwinggu An Australian Aboriginal people of W Arnhem Land. Many still live in small 'outstations' on Aboriginal land, gaining most of their subsistence by hunting and gathering, and selling bark paintings.

Guomindang or **Kuomintang (KMT)** [gwohmindang] The Chinese National People's Party (or Nationalists), founded by Sun Yat-sen in 1912 and later led by Jiang Jieshi. It ruled China from Nanjing, 1927–37 and 1945–9, and from Chonqing during the war with Japan, 1937–45. It retreated to Taiwan in 1949.

guppy Small freshwater fish (*Poecilia reticulata*) native to South and Central America but now widespread through the aquarium trade; length up to 3 cm/1¼ in; males with metallic blue-green coloration. (Family: Poecilidae.)

Gupta Empire [gupta] (320–540) A decentralized state system covering most of N India. It was materially prosperous, and is known as India's 'Classical' or 'Golden' Age, when norms of Indian literature, art, architecture, and philosophy were established.

Gur Amir or **Gur Emir** [goor ameer] The mausoleum of Timur, Ulugh Beg, and others of the house of Timur, built in Samarkand (in present-day Uzbekistan) in the 15th-c. It was restored in 1967.

gurdwara [goordwara] (Sanskrit, 'guru's door') A Sikh temple, or any place where the scripture is installed.

Gurkhas [gerkuhz] **1** The name of the Nepalese ruling dynasty since 1768.

2 An elite infantry unit of the British army recruited from the hill tribes of Nepal. Their characteristic weapon, the *kukri* fighting knife with its curved blade, has contributed to their fame. As many as 100 000 fought in World War 1, 132 000 in World War 2, and in 2007 there were 3400 serving. Thirteen Gurkhas have been awarded the Victoria Cross.

gurnard [gernah(r)d] Any of the bottom-living marine fishes of the family Triglidae, widespread in inshore waters of tropical to temperate seas; also called **sea robins**; length up to 75 cm/ 30 in; head armoured with bony plates; pectoral fin rays used as feelers or as stilts.

guru [gooroo] In Hinduism, a spiritual teacher or guide who gives instruction to a disciple or pupil, who in return is required to render reverence and obedience. In Sikhism, it is identified with the inner voice of God, of which the 10 Gurus were the human vehicles. The term has developed a more general sense in recent years, referring to anyone who comes to be recognized as leader or originator of a cult or idea, not necessarily to do with religion.

Gush Emmunim [gush emuneem] (Heb 'Group of those who keep the faith') A militant Israeli movement set up after the 1973 elections, dedicated to an active settlement policy in territories such as the West Bank, occupied by the Israelis after the 1967 war.

Gustav I, originally **Gustav Eriksson Vasa** (1496–1560) King of Sweden (1523–60), founder of the Vasa dynasty. He led a peasant rising against the occupying Danes, capturing Stockholm (1523) and driving the enemy from Sweden.

Gustav II Adolf or **Gustavus Adolphus** (1594–1632) King of Sweden (1611–32), born in Stockholm. He recovered his Baltic provinces from Denmark, ended wars with Russia (1617) and Poland (1629), and carried out major military and economic reforms at home. In 1630 he entered the Thirty Years' War, and won several victories, notably at Breitenfeld (1631).

gut *alimentary canal*

Gutenberg, Johannes (Gensfleisch) [gootnberg] (1400–68) Printer, regarded as the inventor of printing from movable type, born in Mainz, Germany. His best-known work is the 42-line Bible, often called the Gutenberg Bible (c.1455).

Guterson, David (1956–) Writer, born in Seattle, WA. His works include a collection of short stories, *The Country Ahead of Us, The Country Behind* (1996), a best-selling novel, *Snow Falling On Cedars* (1995, PEN/Faulkner Award), *East of the Mountains* (2000), and *Our Lady of the Forest* (2003).

Guthrie, Sir (William) Tyrone (1900–71) Theatrical director, born in Tunbridge Wells, Kent. He was responsible for many fine productions of Shakespeare at the Old Vic during the 1930s, and became administrator of the Old Vic and Sadler's Wells (1939–45).

Guthrie, Woody, popular name of **Woodrow Wilson Guthrie** (1912–67) Folksinger and songwriter, born in Okemah, OK. He took to the road during the Great Depression, and wrote hundreds of songs, notably 'So Long, It's Been Good to Know You' and 'This Land Is Your Land'.

gutta percha A grey-black substance similar to rubber, but non-elastic, obtained from the latex of *Palaquium*, a genus of tropical trees related to chicle. It has been widely used in dental fillings, electrical insulation, and (especially) golf balls. (Family: Sapotaceae.)

Guy, Thomas [giy] (c.1644–1724) Philanthropist, born in London. In 1721 he founded the hospital in Southwark, London, which bears his name.

Guyana *p.407*

Guy Fawkes Night or **Bonfire Night** The evening of 5 November, the anniversary in the UK of the Gunpowder Plot, celebrated with fireworks and bonfires, on which are often burned effigies of Guy Fawkes known as *guys*.

Gwalior [gwaliaw(r)] 26°12N 78°09E, pop (2000e) 814 000. City and former princely state in Madhya Pradesh, C India; founded, 8th-c; famous cultural centre, 15th-c; Mughal city, 15th–16th-c; taken by the British, 1780; railway; commercial centre.

Gwent pop (2000e) 456 500; area 1376 km²/531 sq mi. Former county in SE Wales, UK; created in 1974, and replaced in 1996 by Monmouthshire, Blaenau Gwent, Torfaen, and Newport counties.

Gwyn or **Gwynne, Nell**, popular name of **Eleanor Gwyn** (c.1650–87) Mistress of Charles II of England, possibly born in London. She lived precariously as an orange girl before going on the boards at Drury Lane, where she established herself as a comedienne.

Gwynedd [gwineth] pop (2001e) 116 800; area 3869 km²/1494 sq mi. County in NW Wales, UK; created in 1996; formerly (1974–96) a wider area, including Anglesey, now consists only of Caernarfonshire and Merionethshire; rises to 1085 m/3560 ft at Snowdon in Snowdonia National Park; bilingual language policy; administrative centre, Caernarfon; castles at Caernarfon, Conwy, Criccieth, Harlech.

Gyllenhaal, Jake, popular name of **Jacob Benjamin Gyllenhaal** (1980–) Actor, born in Los Angeles, CA. Born into a show business family, he made his film debut at age 10 in *City Slickers* (1991). He gained recognition for his role in *Donnie Darko* (2001), and later films include *The Day After Tomorrow* (2004), *Brokeback Mountain* (2005, Best Supporting Actor BAFTA and Oscar nomination), and *Jarhead* (2005).

gymkhana A mixed sports meeting in a public place, especially one involving a range of horse-riding skills for young riders. They originated in India in 1860. In the USA, the term is often used for an obstacle competition for automobiles.

gymnastics A series of physical exercises now used primarily for sporting contests. Men compete on the parallel bars, pommel horse, horizontal bar, rings, horse vault, and floor exercise. Women compete on the asymmetrical bars, beam, horse vault, and floor exercise.

gymnosperms The commonly used name for one of the two divisions of seed plants, the other being the *flowering plants* (**angiosperms**). They are characterized by having naked seeds (ie not enclosed in an ovary). They contain both living (eg conifers) and entirely fossil groups. Early gymnosperms became the dominant vegetation during the Jurassic and Cretaceous periods. (Class: Gymnospermae.)

gymnure [jimnyoor] *moonrat*

gynaecology / gynecology [giynikolojee] The study of the functions and disorders of the female organs of reproduction. Disorders of menstruation and of fertility constitute a major part of the discipline. Liberalization of the laws relating to abortion has increased the need for specialized gynaecological care.

gynecium / gynoecium *carpel; flower*

Györ [dyür], Ger **Raab**, Lat **Arrabona** 47°41N 17°40E, pop (2000e) 126 000. Industrial city in NW Hungary; railway; bishopric; noted for its modern ballet company; cathedral (12th-c, rebuilt 18th-c).

Guyana

☐ International Airport

[giyahna], official name **Co-operative Republic of Guyana**, formerly (to 1966) **British Guiana**
Local name Guyana

Timezone GMT -3
Area 214 969 km²/82 978 sq mi
Population total (2002e) 775 000
Status Co-operative republic
Date of independence 1966
Capital Georgetown
Languages English (official), Hindi, Urdu, Amerindian dialects
Ethnic groups E Indian (51%), black (30·5%), Amerindian (5%) (Carib 4%, Arawak 1%)
Religions Christian (42%), Hindu (37%), Muslim (9%)
Physical features Located on N coast of South America; inland forest covers c.83% of land area; highest peak Mt Roraima, rising to 2875 m/9432 ft in the Pakaraima Mts (W); main rivers, Essequibo, Rupununi, and Corantijn, with many rapids and waterfalls in upper courses.
Climate Equatorial climate in the lowlands; hot, wet, with constant high humidity; average annual temperature 26°C (Jan), 27°C (Jul) in Georgetown; two seasons of high rainfall (May–Jul, Nov–Jan); average annual rainfall 2175 mm/87 in.
Currency 1 Guyana Dollar (GYD) = 100 cents
Economy High unemployment, influenced by labour unrest, low productivity, and high foreign debt; economy largely based on sugar, rice, bauxite, shrimps, livestock, cotton, molasses, timber.
GDP (2002e) $2·628 bn, per capita $3800
Human Development Index (2002) 0·708
History Sighted by Columbus, 1498; settled by the Dutch, late 16th-c; several areas ceded to Britain, 1814; consolidated as British Guiana, 1831; independence, 1966; cooperative republic within the Commonwealth, 1970; governed by a President who holds executive power and appoints a Prime Minister and National Assembly, elected every five years.

Head of State/Government
1997–9 Janet Jagan
1999– Bharrat Jagdeo
Prime Minister and First Vice-President
1985–92 Hamilton Green
1992–7 Samuel Hinds
1997 Janet Jagan
1997– Samuel Hinds

gypsum A mineral of calcium sulphate ($CaSO_4.2H_2O$) found in evaporite deposits as crystals (*selenite*) or fine-grained masses (*alabaster*). When partly dehydrated, it forms *plaster of Paris*, a fine, quick-setting, white powder.
Gypsy *Rom*
gypsy moth A medium-sized tussock moth; rare in Britain but a pest of fruit trees in North America; wings whitish with dark zigzag markings. (Order: Lepidoptera. Family: Lymantridae.)
gyrfalcon [jerfawlkn] The largest of all falcons (*Falco rusticolus*) (length 50–60 cm/20–24 in); native to Arctic regions; plumage white, grey, or dark.
gyrocompass A form of gyroscope which is set to maintain a N-

seeking orientation as an aid to navigation.
gyromagnetic ratio For spinning particles, the ratio of magnetic moment to particle spin; symbol γ, units $T^{-1}s^{-1}$ (per tesla per second). For protons, $\gamma = 2.675 \times 10^8 T^{-1}s^{-1}$.
gyroscope An instrument consisting of a rapidly spinning wheel so mounted as to utilize the tendency of such a wheel to maintain a fixed position in space, and to resist any force which tries to change it. A free vertically spinning gyroscope remains vertical as the carrying vehicle tilts, so providing an artificial horizon. A horizontal gyroscope will maintain a certain bearing, and therefore indicate a vessel's heading as it turns.

h

Haakon VII [hawkon] (1872–1957) King of Norway (1905–57), born in Charlottenlund, Denmark. During World War 2, he remained active in Norwegian resistance to Nazi occupation from England.

Haarlem *Harlem* (The Netherlands)

Habakkuk or **Habacuc, Book of** [habakuk] One of the 12 so-called 'minor' prophetic books of the Hebrew Bible/Old Testament, attributed to the otherwise unknown prophet Habakkuk, possibly of the late 7th-c BC.

habeas corpus [haybias kaw(r)pus] (Lat 'you must have the body') An ancient and fundamental common-law right that requires a person who detains another to appear in court and justify that detention. If there is no good reason for the detention, release is ordered.

Haber, Fritz [hahber] (1868–1934) Chemist, born in Wrocław, W Poland (formerly Breslau, Prussia). He invented the process for making ammonia from the nitrogen in the air, and was awarded the Nobel Prize for Chemistry in 1918.

Habsburgs One of the principal dynasties of modern Europe, pre-eminent in C Europe from the mediaeval period as sovereign rulers of Austria, from which the family extended its influence to secure the title of Holy Roman Emperor (1452–1806). The zenith of Habsburg power was reached under Charles V (1500–58). His inheritance was divided between his son and brother, thus creating the **Spanish Habsburg** line, rulers of Spain until 1700, and the **Austrian Habsburgs**, whose descendants ruled in C Europe until 1918.

hacker A computer user who communicates with other remote computers, usually via the telephone network or Internet. In recent years, the term has acquired a pejorative sense, referring to those who access remote computers without permission. Computer systems are vulnerable to the infiltration of viruses or 'bugs' which give control of the computers to hackers with malicious intent.

Hackman, Gene (1931–) Film actor, born in San Bernardino, CA. He earned a Best Supporting Actor Oscar nomination for his performance in *Bonnie and Clyde* (1967), an Oscar for his role in *The French Connection* (1971), and further nominations for *Mississippi Burning* (1989), and *Unforgiven* (1992). Later films include *Wyatt Earp* (1994), *Get Shorty* (1995), *The Royal Tenenbaums* (2001, Golden Globe), and *Superman II* (2006).

hackney horse An English breed of horse; height, 14·3–16 hands/1·5–1·6 m/4 ft 11 in–5 ft 4 in; graceful and spirited, with an emphasized strutting step; black or brown with tail held high.

haddock Bottom-living fish (*Melanogrammus aeglefinus*) widespread in cold N waters of the Atlantic; length up to c.80 cm/32 in; body dark greenish-brown on back, sides silvery grey with dark patch above pectoral fins, underside white, lateral line black; important food fish, exploited commercially throughout the N Atlantic. (Family: Gadidae.)

Hades [haydeez] In Greek mythology, the king of the Underworld, terrible but just; he was responsible for the seizure of Persephone. To the Greeks, Hades was always a person, never a place, but by transference the Underworld became known by that name.

Hadith [hadeeth] Sayings attributed to the Prophet Mohammed, prefaced by a chain of authorities through whom the tradition is said to have been transmitted. One of the chief sources of Islamic law, it is second in authority only to the Qur'an.

Hadlee, Sir Richard (John) (1951–) Cricketer, born in Christchurch, New Zealand. He has scored 3124 Test runs since making his debut in 1973, in 1988 he surpassed Ian Botham's record of 383 Test wickets, and went on to a total of 431 before retiring in 1990, when he was knighted.

Hadrian [haydrian], in full **Publius Aelius Hadrianus** (76–138) Roman emperor (117–38), successor of Trajan. He spent little of his reign at Rome, but tirelessly toured the empire, consolidating the frontiers, visiting the provinces, and promoting urban life.

Hadrian IV (Pope) *Adrian IV*

Hadrian's Wall The principal N frontier of the Roman province of Britain. Built AD 122–8 on the orders of the Emperor Hadrian, it runs 117 km/73 mi from the Solway Firth to the R Tyne, the wall itself 4·5 m/15 ft high (probably with a 2 m/6 ft timber parapet), its forward defensive ditch c.8·5 m/28 ft wide and 3 m/10 ft deep. Overrun by N tribes in AD 139 and again in 367, the wall was finally abandoned c.400–410. It is now a world heritage site.

hadron In particle physics, a collective term for all composite particles which experience strong interactions. All baryons and mesons are hadrons (eg protons and pions).

hadrosaur [hadrosaw(r)] A duck-billed dinosaur; front of snout flattened and expanded to form duck-like bill; dentition specialized, with several rows of teeth; widely distributed during the Cretaceous period. (Order: Ornithischia.)

Haeckel, Ernst (Heinrich Philipp August) [haykl] (1834–1919) Naturalist, born in Potsdam, Germany. One of the first to sketch the genealogical tree of animals, he strongly supported Darwin's theories of evolution.

haemangioma [heemanjiohma] A benign tumour of vascular tissues, most commonly affecting the skin and liver; often found on the skin at birth as a result of a local overgrowth of capillaries during fetal development, where they appear as well demarcated red patches (*portwine stains*). Sometimes the capillaries form larger blood-filled sinuses, causing the discoloured area to be swollen and raised from the skin surface (a *strawberry naevus*).

haematite / hematite A mineral iron oxide (Fe_2O_3), the most important ore of iron. Powdered haematite is used as a pigment (red ochre).

haematology / hematology [heematolojee] The study of the formation and function of the cells which circulate in the bloodstream and reside in the bone marrow and lymph nodes, and of the abnormalities that cause diseases.

haemodialysis *dialysis; kidney dialysis*

haemoglobin / hemoglobin [heemoglohbin] A widely occurring red-coloured protein, found for example in some protozoa, many invertebrates, vertebrates, certain yeasts, and plants of the family Leguminosae. In vertebrates it is the oxygen-carrying pigment present in red blood cells (*erythrocytes*).

haemophilia / hemophilia [heemofilia] An inherited disorder of blood coagulation, resulting from a deficiency in one of the proteins responsible for normal blood clotting. This is the antihaemophilic factor (AHF, or *factor VIII*), which is normally produced by the liver and circulates in the blood. The gene responsible is X-linked, so the condition is transmitted by the mother and reveals itself in the sons. It causes recurrent bleeding after minor trauma, mainly into joints. Bleeding can be ameliorated by giving fresh plasma which contains factor VIII, or by giving a concentrate of the factor prepared from freshly donated blood.

haemorrhage / hemorrhage [hemerij] Loss of blood externally or internally from any size of blood vessel. It is caused by injury to a blood vessel, or by a defect in normal blood clotting, as in haemophilia.

haemorrhoids / hemorrhoids [hemeroydz] A cluster of distended veins at the junction of the rectum and the anal canal, 2–3 cm/^{3}/$_4$–1^1/$_8$ in above the opening of the anus; also known as **piles**. Usually there is no detectable cause. Haemorrhoids are very common, and can be removed surgically when large and giving discomfort; otherwise they may be treated by injections of a sclerosing solution.

Haerbin / Haerhpin *Harbin*

Háfiz or **Háfez**, pseudonym of **Shams-ed-Din Mohammad** (c.1326–c.1390) Lyrical poet, born in Shiraz, Iran. A member of the mystical sect of Sufi philosophers, his short poems (*ghazals*), all on sensuous subjects, contain an esoteric signification to the initiated.

Haganah [hagahna] The Jewish underground militia in Palestine, founded during the period of the British Mandate in the 1920s. After the declaration of the State of Israel in 1948, the Haganah became the official Israeli army.

Hagen [hahgn] 51°22N 7°27E, pop (2000e) 222 000. Industrial city in Germany; at junction of important traffic routes; railway.

hagfish Primitive marine fish lacking true jaws, vertebrae, paired fins, and scales; body eel-like, covered in copious slime, length up to 60 cm/2 ft; mouth slit-like surrounded by stout barbels. (Family: Myxinidae, 3 genera.)

Haggai, Book of [hagiy] One of the 12 'minor' prophetic books of the Hebrew Bible/Old Testament, attributed to the prophet Haggai, a contemporary of Zechariah, both of whom supported the rebuilding of the Temple in Jerusalem in c.520 BC after the return from exile.

Haggard, Sir H(enry) Rider (1856–1925) Novelist and social historian, born at Bradenham Hall, Norfolk. His novel *King Solomon's Mines* (1885) immediately acquired the status of a children's classic, and was followed by *She* (1887) and several other stories.

haggis A traditional Scottish dish comprising the minced heart, liver, and lungs of a sheep, as well as suet, oatmeal, and various seasonings. The ingredients are cooked in a bag made from the *rumen* or forestomach of a sheep.

Hagia Sophia [hahgia sohfeea], or **Santa Sophia** A masterpiece of Byzantine architecture built (532–7) at Constantinople (now Istanbul). The lavishly-decorated, domed basilica was commissioned by Emperor Justinian I and designed by Anthemius of Tralles and Isidore of Miletus.

Hague, The [hayg], Dutch **Den Haag** or **'s-Gravenhage** 52°05N 4°16E, pop (2000e) 466 000. City in W Netherlands, and seat of the Dutch government; third largest city in The Netherlands; meeting-place of the States-General, 1527; centre of European diplomacy from 17th-c; Hague Convention (1907) formulated much of the law governing international warfare; headquarters of several international organizations, including the International Court of Justice; railway; noted for its furniture, pottery, and silverware.

Hague, William (Jefferson) [hayg] (1961–) British politician, born in Rotherham, South Yorkshire. Elected an MP in 1989, he acted as parliamentary private secretary to Chancellor of the Exchequer Norman Lamont (1990–3), then became under-secretary (1993–4) and minister of state for social security (1994–5), and minister for Wales (1995–7). He won the leadership of the Conservative Party following John Major's resignation in 1997. He resigned as leader after the general election defeat of 2001, but returned in 2005 as shadow foreign secretary.

Hague Agreement A convention of 1899 for the Pacific Settlement of International Disputes. It established a Permanent Court of Arbitration – the forerunner of the World Court.

Hahn, Otto (1879–1968) Physical chemist, born in Frankfurt, Germany. In 1938 he bombarded uranium with neutrons to find the first chemical evidence of nuclear fission products. He was awarded the Nobel Prize for Chemistry in 1944.

Hahnemann, (Christian Friedrich) Samuel [hahnuhman] (1755–1843) Physician and founder of homeopathy, born in Meissen, Germany. He experimented on the curative power of bark, but his methods caused him to be prosecuted wherever he tried to settle.

Haida [hiyda] A Pacific Northwest Coast American Indian group in Queen Charlotte I, British Columbia, famous for their wood carvings, totem poles, and canoes.

Haidar Ali [hiyder alee], also spelled **Hyder Ali** (1722–82) Muslim ruler of Mysore, born in Budikote, Mysore, India. He waged two wars against the British, in the first of which (1767–9) he won several gains; but in 1781–2 he was defeated.

Haider, Jörg [hiyder] (1950–) Austrian politician, born in Upper Austria. A lawyer, he entered parliament for the ultra-right wing Freedom Party (FPÖ) in Carinthia, and in 1983 was elected chairman of the Carinthian branch. From 1986 to 2000 he was leader of the national FPÖ, campaigning against further immigration, and expressing sympathy for the Nazi cause. The FPÖ was returned as Austria's second largest party in the 1999 elections, and in 2000 he joined in coalition with the conservative People's Party. Protests erupted in Austria against the Freedom Party's presence in the national government, and European Union sanctions were introduced by member states. He then resigned as leader of the Freedom Party and returned to his base as governor of Carinthia.

Haifa or **Hefa** [hiyfa] 32°49N 34°59E, pop (2000e) 322 000. Industrial centre and seaport in NW Israel; third largest city in Israel; airfield; railway; university (1963); Bahai Shrine.

Haig, Alexander (Meigs) [hayg] (1924–) US army officer and statesman, born in Philadelphia, PA. A full general by 1973, he retired from the army to become White House chief-of-staff during the last days of the Nixon presidency. He served President Reagan as secretary of state in 1981–2, and sought the Republican nomination for the presidency in 1988.

Haig (of Bemersyde), Douglas Haig, 1st Earl [hayg] (1861–1928) British field marshal, born in Edinburgh. In 1914 he led the 1st Army Corps in France, and in 1915 became commander of the British Expeditionary Force. He waged a costly and exhausting war of attrition, for which he was much criticized, but led the final successful offensive (Aug 1918).

haiku [hiykoo] A Japanese poetic miniature, consisting of three lines of 5, 7, and 5 syllables. This highly concentrated form has proved very popular outside Japan.

hail A form of precipitation comprising small balls or pieces of ice, which may reach up to 50 mm/2 in in diameter. It is generally associated with rapidly rising convection currents in low latitudes, or the passage of a cold front in temperate latitudes.

Haile Selassie I [hiylee selasee], originally **Prince Ras Tafari**

Makonnen (1892–1975) Emperor of Ethiopia (1930–6, 1941–74), born near Harer, Ethiopia. He led the revolution in 1916 against Lij Yasu, and became regent and heir to the throne, westernizing the institutions of his country. The disastrous famine of 1973 led to mutiny among the armed forces, and he was deposed (1974). Accusations of corruption levelled at him have not destroyed the reverence in which he is held by certain groups, notably the Rastafarians.

Hailey, Arthur (1920–2004) Popular novelist, born in Luton, Bedfordshire. He became a naturalized Canadian in 1947. He wrote many best-selling blockbusters about disasters, several of which became successful films, such as *Airport* (1968) and *Wheels* (1971). Later novels include *The Evening News* (1990) and *Detective* (1997).

Hail Mary (Lat *Ave Maria*) A prayer to the Virgin Mary, also known as the **Angelic Salutation**, used devotionally since the 11th-c in the Roman Catholic Church. The first two parts are quotations from scripture (*Luke* 1.28, 42), the third part being added later.

Hailsham, Quintin (McGarel) Hogg, 2nd Viscount [hay**l**sham] (1907–2001) British Conservative statesman, born in London. His many posts included minister for science and technology (1959–64), and secretary of state for education and science (1964). In 1970 he was created a life peer (**Baron Hailsham of Saint Marylebone**) and became Lord Chancellor (1970–4, 1979–87).

Hain, Peter (Gerald) [hayn] (1950–) British politician, born in Nairobi, Kenya. He was a trade union research officer (1976–91) before becoming Labour MP for Neath (1991–), having left the Liberal Party in the early 1980s. He became under-secretary at the Welsh Office in 1997. Following the Welsh Assembly election (1998) he was moved to the Foreign Office, then had a brief spell as energy minister before returning to the Foreign Office as minister for Europe after the 2001 general election. He became secretary of state for Wales in 2002, combining this with the post of Northern Ireland secretary from 2005, and served as Leader of the Commons (2003–5).

Hainan Island [hiynan] area 34 000 km²/13 000 sq mi. Island off S coast of China; rises to 1879 m/6165 ft at Wuzhi Shan; airport; opened to tourism and foreign trade in 1982; principal cities, Haikou, Dongfang.

Haiphong [hiyfong] 20°50N 106°41E, pop (2000e) 1 730 300. Seaport in N Vietnam; founded, 1874; badly bombed in Vietnam War; third largest city in Vietnam; rail link to Kunming, China.

hair A thread-like structure consisting of dead keratinized cells produced by the epidermis in mammalian skin. The covering of hair in mammals helps to maintain constant body temperature by insulating the body.

hairstreak An inconspicuous butterfly; wings typically blackish-brown, often with coloured patches; wingspan up to 40 mm/1½ in. The name is applied to several different species of the family Lycaenidae. (Order: Lepidoptera.)

Haiti *p.411*

Haitink, Bernard [hiytingk] (1929–) Conductor, born in Amsterdam. He conducted the Amsterdam Concertgebouw Orchestra (from 1961) and the London Philharmonic (1967–79), and was appointed musical director at Glyndebourne (1978–88) and at Covent Garden (1988–2002). He was music director at the Royal Opera House (1987–98) and then of Dresden Staatskapelle (2002–4), and became principal conductor of the Chicago Symphony Orchestra in 2006. He was granted an honorary knighthood in 1977 and was made an honorary Companion of Honour in 2002.

Hajj [haj] A formal pilgrimage to the holy city of Mecca during the Islamic month of Dhu-ul-Hijja. It is one of the Five Pillars of Islam.

hake Commercially important, edible, cod-like fish widely distributed in offshore continental shelf waters of temperate seas; length up to c.1 m/3¼ ft, head and jaws large, teeth strong; blue-grey on back, underside silvery white. (Genus: *Merluccius*. Family: Merlucciidae.)

Hakluyt, Richard [hakloot] (c.1552–1616) Geographer, born in Hertfordshire. He wrote widely on exploration and navigation, notably his *Principal Navigations, Voyages, and Discoveries of the English Nation* (1589). The *Hakluyt Society* was instituted in 1846.

Halakhah [halakah] The subject matter contained in the Talmudic and Rabbinic literature of Judaism dealing with the laws governing religious or civil practice in the community. It is distinguished from the **Haggadah**, which is not concerned with religious law, and includes such material as parables, fables, and prayers.

Halcyone or **Alcyone** [halsiyonee] In Greek mythology, **1** A daughter of Aeolus, who married Ceyx, son of the Morning Star. Both were changed into sea-birds – halcyons, or kingfishers – who are fabled to calm the sea.
2 One of the Pleiades.

Hale, George Ellery (1868–1938) Astronomer, born in Chicago, IL, who discovered magnetic fields within sunspots. He initiated the construction of some of the world's largest telescopes, including the 5 m Palomar telescope.

Haleakala Crater [halayakala] or **Kolekole** 20°42N 156°16W. Dormant volcano in E Maui I, Hawaii, USA; rises to 3055 m/10 023 ft; contains the largest inactive crater in the world.

Hale–Bopp The name given to a comet discovered independently by amateur astronomers Alan Hale and Thomas Bopp in 1995, passing closest to the Sun in April 1997. Some 40 km/25 mi in diameter, it proved to be the biggest and brightest comet in recent times.

Halévy, (Jacques François) Fromental (Elié) [alayvee] (1799–1862) Composer, born in Paris. He is best known for his opera, *La Juive* (1835).

Haley, Bill, popular name of **William Haley** (1927–1981) Popular singer and musician, born in Highland Park, MI. With his group 'The Comets' he popularized rock-and-roll in the 1950s. His most famous song, 'Rock Around the Clock', was used in the film *Blackboard Jungle* (1955).

half-life In radioactivity, the time taken for a group of atoms to decay to half their original number; symbol $T_{\frac{1}{2}}$, units s (second), also minutes and years. The half-life of plutonium-239 is 24 000 years; for helium-6 it is 0·8 seconds. The term also applies to the decay of excited atoms by the emission of light.

half-marathon *marathon*

halibut Largest of the Atlantic flatfishes (*Hippoglossus hippoglossus*), found on sandy and stony bottoms in cold N waters; length up to 2·5 m/8 ft; eyes on right side, mouth and teeth large; brown to greenish-brown with white underside; edible, commercially important, and prized by sea anglers. (*Hippoglossus hippoglossus*. Family: Pleuronectidae.)

Halicarnassus [halikah(r)nasus] A Greek city-state founded by the Dorians on the coast of SW Asia Minor; modern Bodrum, Turkey. It was the birth-place of Herodotos, and the site of the Tomb of Mausolus.

Halifax 44°38N 63°35W, pop (2000e) 127 700. Seaport, provincial capital of Nova Scotia, Canada; major transatlantic port and rail terminus; founded in 1749 as a British military and naval base; scene of harbour disasters, 1917, 1945; airport; four universities (1789, 1802, 1818, 1925); Citadel Hill (height 82 m/269 ft).

Halifax, Charles Montagu, 1st Earl of (1661–1715) English Whig statesman, born in Horton, Northamptonshire. He established the Bank of England (1694), and as Chancellor of the Exchequer (1694–5), introduced a new coinage. On Queen Anne's death he was made a member of the Council of Regency, and on George I's arrival (1714) became prime minister.

Haiti

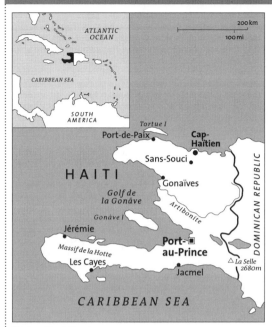

☐ International Airport

[haytee], locally [hiytee], also written **Haïti**, official name **Republic of Haiti**, Fr **République d'Haiti**

Local name Haïti

Timezone GMT -5

Area 27 750 km²/10 712 sq mi

Population total (2002e) 7 064 000

Status Republic

Date of independence 1804

Capital Port-au-Prince

Languages French (official), with Creole French widely spoken

Ethnic groups African descent (95%), European (mulatto) (5%)

Religions Roman Catholic (80%), voodoo

Physical features Consists of two mountainous peninsulas, Massif du Nord (N) and Massif de la Hotte (S), separated by a deep structural depression, the Plaine du Cul-de-Sac; highest peak, La Selle, 2680 m/8793 ft; includes islands of Gonâve (W) and Tortue (N).

Climate Tropical climate; average annual temperatures 25°C (Jan) 29°C (Jul) in Port-au-Prince; wet season (May–Sep); average annual rainfall for N coast and mountains 1475–1950 mm/58–

77 in, but only 500 mm/20 in on W side; hurricanes common; severe flooding and 2000+ deaths from Hurricane Jeanne (Sep 2004).

Currency 1 Gourde (HTG) = 100 centimes

Economy Based on agriculture; large plantations grow coffee, sugar, sisal, rice, bananas, corn, sorghum, cocoa; sugar refining, textiles, flour milling; cement, bauxite; tourism; light assembly industries.

GDP (2002e) $10·6 bn, per capita $1400

Human Development Index (2002) 0·471

History Visited by Columbus, 1492; created when W third of island ceded to France as Saint-Domingue, 1697; slave rebellion followed by independence as Haiti, 1804; united with Santo Domingo (Dominican Republic), 1822–44; under US occupation, 1915–34; Duvalier family had absolute power, 1957–86; after 1986 coup, new constitution provided for a bicameral National Congress consisting of a Senate and National Assembly; military coup in 1992 forced Jean-Bertrand Aristide to flee the country, and a provisional government created; Marc Bazin resigned as head of an army-backed coalition government, 1993; talks between deposed President Aristide and coup leader Cédras reached deadlock, June 1993; peaceful invasion by US forces to restore democratic government, September 1994; Aristide re-elected in 2000 amid claims of fraudulent procedure; conflict escalated early 2004 when international delegation failed to persuade Aristide's political opposition to agree to a US-backed power-sharing plan; rebel uprising forced Aristide into exile, March 2004; René Préval declared president (Feb 2006) after claims of ballot irregularities by his supporters is upheld.

Head of State

1990 Ertha Pascal-Trouillot *Interim*
1990–1 Jean-Bertrand Aristide
1991 Raoul Cédras *Military Junta*
1991–2 Joseph Nerette *Interim*
1992–4 Marc Bazin
1994–6 Jean Bertrand Aristide
1996–2000 René Préval
2001–4 Jean Bertrand Aristide
2004–6 Boniface Alexandre
2006– René Préval

Head of Government

1992–3 Marc Bazin
1993–4 Robert Malval
1994–5 Smarck Michel
1995–6 Claudette Werleigh
1996–7 Rosny Smarth
1997–9 *No prime minister*
1999–2001 Jacques-Edouard Aléxis
2001–2 Jean-Marie Chéréstal
2002–4 Yvon Neptune
2004–6 Gerard Latortue *Interim*
2006– Jacques-Edouard Aléxis

halite [haliyt] The mineral form of sodium chloride (NaCl); also known as **rock salt**.

Hall, Ben(jamin) (1837–65) Bushranger, born in New South Wales, Australia. From 1862 he was increasingly involved in robbery, and became known for a series of audacious exploits. He was killed in a police ambush at the age of 28.

Hall, John (1934–) Physicist, born in Denver, CO. He studied at the Carnegie Institute of Technology (1956–8) and Carnegie-Mellon University (1961), after which he joined the National Institute of Standards and Technology, Boulder, CO, becoming senior fellow in 1988. Since 1964 he has also been fellow of the JILA research institute at the University of Colorado. He

shared one half of the 2005 Nobel Prize for Physics with Theodor Hänsch for their contributions to the development of laser-based precision spectroscopy, including the optical frequency comb technique. The other half was awarded to Roy Glauber.

Hall, Sir Peter (Reginald Frederick) (1930–) Theatre, opera, and film director, born in Bury St Edmunds, Suffolk. He became director of the Royal Shakespeare Company (1960–8), director of the Covent Garden Opera (1969–71), and successor to Olivier as director of the National Theatre (1973–88). He launched the Peter Hall Company in 1988, and became artistic director of the Rose Theatre in Kingston-upon-Thames in 2003.

Halle or **Halle an der Saale** [haluh] 51°29N 12°00E, pop (2000e) 310 000. City in EC Germany; railway; university (1694); Academy of Agricultural Science; birthplace of Handel.

Hallé, Sir Charles [halay] (1819–95) Pianist and conductor, born in Hagen, Germany. The 1848 revolution drove him to England, and he ultimately settled in Manchester, where in 1858 he founded his famous orchestra. He was knighted in 1888.

Halley, Edmond [halee, hawlee] (1656–1742) Astronomer and mathematician, born in London. From 1676 he investigated orbits in the Solar System, discovering that some comets pursue elliptical orbits. From this he successfully predicted the return of the comet named after him.

Halley's comet [halee] The most famous of all comets, first recorded by Chinese astronomers in 467 BC, a spectacular periodic comet orbiting the Sun in a retrograde direction with a period of 76 years. During its 1986 apparition, it was the subject of an intense study by an 'armada' of spacecraft. The images revealed a nucleus of irregular shape, about 16 × 8 km/10 × 5 mi. The very dark surface of the nucleus, and the presence of carbon in the comet dust, indicate that there are significant quantities of organic molecules in the nucleus.

hallmarks The official marks struck on all modern and much old English, Scottish, and Irish silver and gold, and since 1975 on platinum. The metal is tested (*assayed*) for standard or quality. Hallmarks date from 1300, and each assay office had its own mark.

Hallowe'en The evening of 31 October, when spirits of the dead are supposed to return to their former homes, and witches and demons are thought to be abroad at night. This was the last day of the Celtic and Anglo-Saxon year, and many Hallowe'en customs have their origin in pagan ceremonies. In the USA, children go around demanding 'trick or treat' – if no 'treat' or present is forthcoming a 'trick' or practical joke will be played on the householder.

Hallstatt [halshtat] 47°34N 13°39E, pop (2000e) 1200. Small market town in N Austria; known for the **Hallstatt period**, the first phase of the European Iron Age (8th–4th-c BC), characterized by goods from burial tombs nearby.

hallucination A sensory perception occurring without any stimulation of the sense organ. In its true form the individual is fully awake and the perception is located out of the body. Hallucinations indicate a loss of contact with reality, but they can be a normal phenomenon, such as during grief.

hallucinogens or **psychotomimetic drugs** Drugs that produce hallucinations, angel dust, LSD, magic mushrooms, and mescaline; also called **psychedelic drugs**. Many naturally occurring hallucinogens have been used in ancient medicine and in religious ceremonies. Some are widely used (illegally) for recreational purposes.

Halmahera [halmahera], formerly **Djailolo** area 17 936 km²/6923 sq mi, pop (2000e) 129 000. Largest island in the Moluccas, Indonesia; forested mountain chains, including active volcanoes; taken by the Dutch in 1683; independence, 1949.

halogens [halojnz] The group of the periodic table with seven valence electrons. It comprises fluorine, chlorine, bromine, iodine, and the artificial element astatine.

Hals, Frans [hals] (c.1580–1666) Portrait and genre painter, probably born in Antwerp. Among his best-known works are 'The Laughing Cavalier' (1624, Wallace Collection, London) and 'Gypsy Girl' (c.1628–30, Louvre).

Hal Saflieni [hal saflyenee] A vast prehistoric rock-cut catacomb (*hypogeum*) for multiple burial in Paola, SE Malta; a world heritage site. The excavation, which was in use throughout the Copper Age, was discovered in 1902.

Hälsingborg *Helsingborg*

hamadryad (mythology) [hamadriyad] In Greek mythology, a tree-nymph. The hamadryad was offended or died when the tree containing her was harmed.

hamadryad (zoology) [hamadriyad] *king cobra*

hamadryas baboon [hamadriyas] A baboon (*Papio hamadrya*) native to NE Africa and SW Arabia; silver-brown fur; naked face; long tail; sacred to ancient Egyptians; also known as **sacred baboon**.

HAMAS (acronym for *Harakat al-Muqawama al-Islamiyya* 'movement of Islamic resistance') An Islamic resistance movement founded in Gaza in 1987 from a faction of the Muslim Brotherhood. Its aims are to carry on a jihad (struggle) against the Israeli 'occupation' of Palestine, largely through suicide bombings and attacks. It refused to recognize peace with Israel and did not join the government of the Palestine National Authority (PNA). Both the PNA and Israel have vowed to curb its activities. Its leader Sheikh Ahmad Yassin was arrested by the Israelis but released in 1997 to Gaza. He was assassinated in an Israeli air attack in March 2004 and Khaled Meshaal became head of the movement. The leader in Gaza, Abdel Aziz al-Rantissi, was assassinated in April 2004. In January 2006, HAMAS won a surprise victory over the ruling Fatah party in the Palestine elections, and **Ismail Haniya** was appointed prime minister. A resurgence of factional violence later that year led to the formation of a national unity cabinet (Mar 2007), with independents holding key ministerial posts.

Hamburg [hamberg] 53°33N 10°00E, pop (2000e) 1 703 000; area 755 km²/291 sq mi (including islands of Neuwerk and Scharhörn). Industrial port city in Germany; on the R Elbe, 109 km/68 mi from its mouth; largest German port; second largest city of Germany; founded by Charlemagne in the 9th-c; badly bombed in World War 2; railway; university (1919); birthplace of Brahms and Mendelssohn.

Hamer, Robert (1911–63) Film director, producer, and scriptwriter, born in Kidderminster, Worcestershire. At Ealing Studios he directed many successful films, including *Kind Hearts and Coronets* (1949), *Father Brown* (1954), and *School for Scoundrels* (1960).

Hamersley Range Mountain range in NW Western Australia, extends for 257 km/160 mi; rises to 1244 m/4081 ft at Mt Meharry; the great iron-bearing area of Western Australia.

Hamilcar [hamilkah(r)], known as **Hamilcar Barca** ('Lightning') (c.270–228 BC) Carthaginian statesman and general at the time of the First Punic War, the father of Hannibal. He founded a new Carthaginian Empire in Spain, conquering most of the S and E of the peninsula.

Hamilton (Bermuda) 32°18N 64°48W, pop (2000e) 1180. Port, resort, and capital of Bermuda, on Great Bermuda; modern berthing and container facilities; founded 1612; capital since 1815; cathedral.

Hamilton (Canada) 43°15N 79°50W, pop (2000e) 356 600. City in SE Ontario, Canada, at head (W) of L Ontario; founded, 1813; site of Battle of Stoney Creek (1813); railway; McMaster University (1887); football team, Hamilton Tiger-Cats.

Hamilton (New Zealand) 37°46S 175°18E, pop (2000e) 162 000. City in North Island, New Zealand; airfield; railway; university (1964); noted for horse breeding and agricultural research.

Hamilton, Alexander (1757–1804) US statesman, born in the West Indian island of Nevis. He fought in the American Revolution, becoming Washington's aide-de-camp (1777–81), and was instrumental in the movement to establish the USA in its present political form, becoming secretary of the Treasury (1789–95). He was leader of the Federalist Party until his death. His successful effort to thwart the ambition of his rival, Aaron Burr, led to a duel in which Hamilton was killed.

Hamilton, Emma, Lady, *née* **Emily Lyon** (c.1765–1815) Lord Nelson's mistress, probably born in Ness, Cheshire. In 1791 she married Sir William Hamilton (1730–1803). She first met Nelson in 1793, and bore him a daughter, Horatia (1801–81). After the death of her husband and Nelson, she became bankrupt, and fled to Calais, where she died.

hamiltonian The total energy of a mechanical system; symbol *H*, units J (joule); after Irish mathematician William Hamilton (1805–65). It is equal to the sum of kinetic energy *K* and potential energy *V*.

Hammarskjöld, Dag (Hjalmar Agne Carl) [hamershohld] (1905–61) Swedish statesman, who became secretary-general of the United Nations (1953–61), born in Jönköping. At the UN, he helped to set up the Emergency Force in Sinai and Gaza (1956), and worked for conciliation in the Middle East (1957–8). He was awarded the 1961 Nobel Peace Prize.

hammerhead shark Large active shark of inshore tropical and temperate waters, characterized by a flattened head with broad lateral lobes; eyes and nostrils widely spaced; length up to 6 m/20 ft. (Genus: *Sphyrna*. Family: Sphyrnidae.)

Hammerstein, Oscar, II [hamerstiyn] (1895–1960) Librettist, born in New York City. He wrote the book and lyrics for many operettas and musical comedies. With composer Jerome Kern, he wrote *Show Boat* (1927), and with Richard Rodgers (1902–79), *Oklahoma!* (1943), *South Pacific* (1949), *The King and I* (1951), and *The Sound of Music* (1959). **Oscar Hammerstein I** was his impresario grandfather.

hammer throw An athletics field event in which the contestant throws with both hands a hammer (in fact, a metal ball with a wire handle) weighing 16 lb (7·6 kg), from within the confines of a 7 ft (2·13m) circle. The current world record is 86·74 m/284 ft 7 in, achieved by Yuriy Sedykh of Russia in 1986 at Stuttgart, Germany; for women it is 77·80 m/255 ft 2·7 in, achieved by Tatyana Lysenko of Russia, in 2006 at Tallinn, Estonia.

Hammett, (Samuel) Dashiell (1894–1961) Writer, born in St Mary's Co, MD. He became the first US author of authentic 'private eye' crime stories. His best-known books are *The Maltese Falcon* (1930) and *The Thin Man* (1934).

Hammond, Dame Joan (1912–96) Soprano, born in Christchurch, New Zealand. She made her operatic debut in 1929, and became noted particularly for her Puccini roles.

Hammurabi [hamurahbee] (18th-c BC) Amorite king of Babylon (c.1792–1750 BC), best known for his Code of Laws, and for his military conquests that made Babylon the greatest power in Mesopotamia.

Hampden, John (1594–1643) English parliamentarian and patriot, born in London. In 1634 he became famous for refusing to pay Charles I's imposed levy for outfitting the navy ('ship money'). He was one of the five members whose attempted seizure by Charles (1642) precipitated the Civil War.

Hampi The site of the former Hindu capital of Vijayanagar, near the SW Indian village of Hampi. The city was founded in the 14th-c, and is a world heritage site.

Hampshire pop (2001e) 1 240 000; area 3777 km²/1458 sq mi. County of S England; crossed by the North Downs in the NW and W; county town, Winchester; major ports at Portsmouth, Southampton (new unitary authorities from 1997); naval bases at Portsmouth and Gosport.

Hampshire, Susan (1938–) Actress, born in London. She won Emmys for Best Actress in the television series *The Forsyte Saga* (1970), *The First Churchills* (1971), and *Vanity Fair* (1973). Later series include *The Grand* (1997–8) and *Monarch of the Glen* (2000–5). She has written about her problems with dyslexia in *Susan's Story* (1981).

Hampton Court The royal residence situated by the R Thames near London, built by Cardinal Wolsey, who occupied it until 1529. Queen Victoria declared it open to the public in 1851, and its gardens and maze are a major tourist attraction.

Hampton Institute A privately funded, co-educational college established in 1869 by Samuel Chapman (1839–93) in Hampton,

VA, to provide vocational training for slaves freed after the American Civil War. It is an important centre for studies in black American history.

hamster A small rodent of the subfamily Cricetinae (24 species); short tail, large ears; food can be stored in internal cheek pouches. One species, the **golden hamster** (*Mesocricetus auratus*), is a popular pet.

Hamsun, Knut [hamsoon], pseudonym of **Knud Pedersen** (1859–1952) Writer, born in Lom, Norway. His best-known books are *Sult* (1888, Hunger) and *Markens grøde* (1917, The Growth of the Soil). He received the Nobel Prize for Literature in 1920.

Han Term used in China to differentiate the 93% of native Chinese population from the 7% made up of 50 ethnic minorities, including Hakka, Mongols, and Tibetans.

Hancock, Lang(ley) George (1909–92) Australian mining industrialist, born in Perth, Western Australia. After discovering iron ore in several locations, he initiated the growth of Australian extractive industries. He held controversial right-wing views on politics and Aboriginal affairs, and in 1974 formed a secessionist movement in Western Australia.

Hancock, Tony, popular name of **Anthony John Hancock** (1924–68) Comedian, born in Birmingham, West Midlands. He achieved national popularity with the radio (later TV) series *Hancock's Half Hour* (1954–61). He committed suicide in Australia while attempting a television comeback.

hand The terminal part of the upper limb, used to manipulate (motor function) or assess (sensory function) the environment. It is richly endowed with sensory nerve endings and consists of a number of bony elements whose size and arrangement differs between species. In humans the bony elements are the eight carpals, the five metacarpals, the three phalanges in each finger, and the two phalanges in the thumb.

handball An indoor and outdoor game first played in Germany c.1890, resembling association football, but played with the hands. The indoor game is played with seven on each side. The outdoor game (known as **field handball**) is played on a field with 11 on each side.

Handel, George Frideric (1685–1759) Composer, born in Halle, Germany. In Italy (1706–10) he established a great reputation as a keyboard virtuoso and had considerable success as an operatic composer. While in London (from 1720), he developed a new form, the English oratorio, which proved to be highly popular. His most memorable work includes *Saul* (1739), *Israel in Egypt* (1739), and *Messiah* (1742). His vast output included over 40 operas, about 20 oratorios, cantatas, sacred music, and orchestral, instrumental, and vocal works.

Handley, Tommy, popular name of **Thomas Reginald Handley** (1892–1949) Comedian, born in Liverpool, Merseyside. In 1939 he achieved nationwide fame through his weekly programme *ITMA* (It's That Man Again), whose wit and satire helped to boost wartime morale.

handwriting *chirography*

Handy, W(illiam) C(hristopher) (1873–1958) Composer, born in Florence, AL. He was the first to introduce the 'blues' style to printed music, his most famous work being the 'St Louis Blues' (1914).

Han dynasty Major Chinese dynasty (206 BC–AD 220), commonly divided into Early or Western Han (206 BC–AD 8), which had its capital at Changan (modern Xian), and Later or Eastern Han (25–220), with its capital at Luoyang. The Han period saw the conquest of what is now N Korea, N Vietnam, Kyrgyzstan, Uzbekistan, and Xinjiang, as well as major developments in education, science, technology, astronomy, and public health. Buddhism was introduced to China, and trade links developed with Europe via the Middle East.

Hangchow *Hangzhou*

hang glider A person-carrying glider using a delta-shaped flexible wing, developed for NASA in the late 1950s as a gliding parachute. The pilot is suspended by a harness from the light frame holding the wing, and controls the movement of the craft by body movement. Later, engines were fitted, and the type developed into a form of ultra-light aircraft called a **microlight**. Although popularized in the mid-1970s, hang gliding was pioneered in the 1890s by Otto Lilienthal in Germany.

hangul *red deer*

Hangzhou or **Hangchow** [hahngjoh], also **Kinsai** 30°18N 120°07E, pop (2000e) 1 645 000. City in E China; founded, 2200 BC; capital of several kingdoms and dynasties, 8th–12th-c; airfield; railway; technical university (1927); university (1959).

Hani, Chris [hanee], popular name of **Martin Thembisile Hani** (1942–93) South African political leader, born in Cofimvaba, South Africa. In 1991, he joined the ANC's National Executive Committee, and was also elected secretary-general of the South African Communist Party. He was shot dead by a white right-winger, and his murder triggered massive protests.

Hanks, Tom, popular name of **Thomas J Hanks** (1956–) Film actor, born in Concorde, CA. His major films include *Sleepless in Seattle* (1993), *Apollo 13* (1995), *Saving Private Ryan* (1998), and *The Green Mile* (1999), and he received universal acclaim for his character performances in *Philadelphia Story* (1993, Oscar; Golden Globe) and *Forrest Gump* (1994, Oscar). He made his directorial debut in 1996 with *That Thing You Do!*, and in 2001 collaborated with Steven Spielberg on the TV mini-series *Band of Brothers* (Golden Globe; Emmy). Later films include *Catch Me If You Can* (2002) and *The Da Vinci Code* (2006). In 2004 he received the BAFTA Stanley Kubrick Award for Excellence in Film.

Hanna–Barbera [hana bah(r)bera] Animated cartoonists, in partnership for nearly 50 years. **William (Denby) Hanna** (1910–2001), born in Melrose, NM, became one of the first directors at the new MGM animation studio in 1937. He then teamed up with **Joseph (Roland) Barbera** (1911–2006), born in New York City, who had joined MGM as an artist. Together they created the first *Tom and Jerry* cartoons, winning seven Oscars between 1943 and 1952. They later created numerous television cartoon series using computer animation, including *The Flintstones*, *Yogi Bear*, and *Huckleberry Hound*.

Hannibal [hanibl] (247–182 BC) Carthaginian general and statesman, the son of Hamilcar Barca. In the Second Punic War, he left New Carthage on his famous journey (218 BC), defeated the Gauls, and crossed the Alps in fifteen days. He marched on Rome, and defeated the Romans at L Trasimene (217 BC) and at Cannae (216 BC), but was defeated by Scipio at Zama (202 BC). After several years in exile, he committed suicide to avoid Roman capture.

Hannover *Hanover*

Hanoi [hanoy] 21°01N 105°52E, pop (2000e) 2 398 900. Capital of Vietnam, on Red R; former capital of Vietnamese Empire, 11th–17th-c; capital of French Indo-China, 1887–1946; occupied by the Japanese in World War 2; severely damaged by bombing in Vietnam War; university (1956).

Hanover, Ger **Hannover** 52°23N 9°44E, pop (2000e) 530 000. Commercial and industrial city in Germany; chartered, 1241; Elector George Louis became George I of Great Britain, 1714; badly bombed in World War 2; railway; three universities (1831, 1913, 1961).

Hanover, House of A dynasty of British monarchs, encompassing George I (1714–27), George II (1727–60), George III (1760–1820), George IV (1820–30), William IV (1830–7), and Victoria (1837–1901), though only the Georges and William are usually referred to as 'Hanoverians'.

Hansard, Luke (1752–1828) British printer. He entered the office of Hughes, printer to the House of Commons, in 1798 succeeding as sole proprietor of the business. He and his descendants

printed regular parliamentary reports from 1774 to 1889, and the name is still used for these reports.

Hänsch, Theodor W(olfgang) [hensh] (1941–) Physicist, born in Heidelberg, Germany. He went to the USA to teach and carry out research at Stanford University (1970), and later returned to Germany where he was appointed professor of physics at Ludwig Maximilians University in Munich, later joining the Max Planck Institute for Quantum Optics. In 2005 he shared one half of the Nobel Prize for Physics with John Hall for their contributions to the development of laser-based precision spectroscopy, including the optical frequency comb technique. The other half was awarded to Roy Glauber.

Hanseatic League A late mediaeval association of 150 N German towns, including Bremen, Hamburg, and Lübeck. It dominated trade from the Atlantic to the Baltic, and fought successful wars against neighbours between 1350 and 1450.

Hansen's disease An ancient chronic infectious disease due to *Mycobacterium leprae* that still affects 20 million people, mainly in the tropics, but is also endemic in the Middle East and S Europe; named after Norwegian bacteriologist Armauer Hansen (1841–1912), who discovered the bacillus in 1879. For centuries the disease was known as **leprosy** – a name applied to a variety of skin disorders, and still retaining (along with *leper*) strong negative emotional connations from the era when the basis of this disease was not understood; the trend in modern medical usage is to avoid this stigmatized term. The organisms show a predilection for the skin, peripheral nerves, and upper respiratory tract.

Hanson, Pauline (1954–) Politician, born in Brisbane, Queensland, Australia. She stood as a Liberal candidate for Oxley in the Queensland parliament in 1966, but backing was withdrawn when she made derogatory remarks about Aborigines. She won the seat as an Independent, and went on to form her own party, One Nation. A highly controversial figure, in the 1998 general election her party failed to win a seat. She resigned as leader of One Nation in 2002. In 2003 she was found guilty of electoral fraud and sentenced to three years in jail but the conviction was quashed on appeal.

Hanukkah or **Chanukah** [hanuka] An annual Jewish festival held in December (begins 25 Kislev), commemorating the rededication of the Temple at Jerusalem after the victory of Judas Maccabaeus over the Syrians in 165 BC; also known as the **Feast of Dedication** or **Feast of Lights**.

Hanuman [hanuman] The monkey-god of the Ramayana epic, who is the courageous and loyal supporter of Rama. A popular Hindu deity, he is represented as half-human and half-monkey.

hanuman monkey *entellus*

Harald III Sigurdsson, nickname **Harald Hardrada** ('the Ruthless') (1015–66) King of Norway (1045–66). He waged war against Denmark until 1064. In 1066 he landed in England to aid Tostig against the English King Harold II, but fell at Stamford Bridge.

Harappa [harapa] A prehistoric city in the Pakistani Punjab, occupied c.2300–1750 BC. Its ancient population numbered c.25 000.

Harare [harahray], formerly **Salisbury** (to 1982) 17°43S 31°05E, pop (2000e) 980 700. Capital and largest city of Zimbabwe; altitude, 1473 m/4833 ft; founded in 1890, and named after Lord Salisbury; airport; railway; university (1970); two cathedrals.

Harbin, also spelled **Haerhpin** or **Haerbin** 45°54N 126°41E, pop (2000e) 3 334 000. City in NE China; founded, 12th-c; developed as major rail junction; airfield.

Harburg, Edgar 'Yip', originally **Isidore Hochberg** (1898–1981) Songwriter, born in New York City. Almost alone among his colleagues, he was politically active in civil rights groups. In his music, his convictions were realized in a quiet idealism that a better world was in the offing, as in 'April in Paris' (1932, with

Hardness Scale

Friedrich Mohs (1773–1839) introduced a simple definition of hardness, according to which one mineral is said to be harder than another if the former scratches the latter. The Mohs scale is based on a series of common minerals, arranged in order of increasing hardness.

Mineral	Composition	Simple hardness test	Hardness
Talc	$Mg_3Si_4O_{10}(OH)_2$	Crushed by finger nail	1
Gypsum	$CaSO_4 \cdot 2H_2O$	Scratched by finger nail	2
Calcite	$CaCo_3$	Scratched by copper coin	3
Fluorite	CaF_2	Scratched by glass	4
Apatite	$Ca_5(PO_4)_3F$	Scratched by penknife	5
Orthoclase (feldspar)	$KAlSi_3O_8$	Scratched by quartz	6
Quartz	SiO_2	Scratched by steel file	7
Topaz	$Al_2SiO_4F_2$	Scratched by corundum	8
Corundum	Al_2O_3	Scratched by diamond	9
Diamond	C		10

Vernon Duke) and his masterwork 'Somewhere Over the Rainbow' (1939, with Harold Arlen). He also wrote the clown songs for *The Wizard of Oz* (1939), and collaborated on *Finian's Rainbow*.

hard disk A rigid magnetic storage disk for computer data. It is generally capable of storing much more data than a similar-sized floppy disk.

Hardicanute [hah(r)dikanoot], also spelled **Harthacnut** (c.1018–42) King of Denmark (1035–42), and the last Danish King of England (1040–2), the only son of Canute and Emma of Normandy. His death without children led to the restoration of the Old English royal line in the person of Edward the Confessor.

Hardie, (James) Keir (1856–1915) British politician, born near Holytown, North Lanarkshire. He became a journalist and the first Labour candidate, entering parliament in 1892, and later served as chairman of the Labour Party (1906–8).

Harding, Warren G(amaliel) (1865–1923) US statesman and 29th president (1921–3), born in Corsica, OH. Emerging as a power in the Republican Party, he won the presidency in 1920, campaigning against US membership of the League of Nations. His presidency was wracked with corruption.

hardness A measure of a material's resistance to denting, scratching, and abrasion, related to the yield stress and tensile strength of the material. It is determined using indentation tests, which measure the size of a hole formed by a hard indenter driven into the material, as in the Vickers and Brinell tests. It is sometimes classified using the Mohs test of mineral hardness (devised by German mineralogist Friedrich Mohs in 1812), which rates talc as hardness 1 and diamond as hardness 10. (*see panel*)

hardware In computing, a term used, in contrast to **software**, to include all the physical units which make up an electronic or computer system, such as keyboards, magnetic disks, circuits, and visual display units.

Hardy, Oliver *Laurel and Hardy*

Hardy, Thomas (1840–1928) Novelist and poet, born in Upper Bockhampton, Dorset. Unable to publish his poetry, he turned to the novel, and found success with *Far from the Madding Crowd* (1874). Later novels include *The Return of the Native* (1878), *The Mayor of Casterbridge* (1886), *Tess of the D'Urbervilles* (1891), and *Jude the Obscure* (1896). His main works were all tragedies, increasingly pessimistic in tone, and after *Tess* he was dubbed an atheist. He then took up poetry again, writing several volumes of sardonic lyrics, and the epic drama, *The Dynasts* (1903–8).

Hare, Sir David (1947–) Playwright and director, born in St Leonard's-on-Sea, East Sussex. His politically engaged plays include *Slag* (1970) and *Plenty* (1978); *The Secret Rapture* (1988) won two awards for best play of the year. He has also written several films and television plays. Later works include *Amy's View* (1997), *The Judas Kiss* (1998), and *The Vertical Hour* (2006).

Hare, William *Burke, William*

hare A mammal of the genus *Lepus* (11 species); also known as **jackrabbit**. There are several differences from the closely related rabbit: hares give birth to young (*leverets*) with fur, are larger, have black tips to the ears, are more solitary, and do not burrow. (Family: Leporidae. Order: Lagomorpha.)

harebell A slender perennial (*Campanula rotundifolia*), native to N temperate regions; stems growing to 40 cm/15 in; flowers 5-lobed bells, blue, rarely white, drooping on slender stalks; the bluebell of Scotland. (Family: Campanulaceae.)

Hare Krishna movement [haree krishnah] A religious movement founded in the USA in 1965 by His Divine Grace A C Bhaktivedanta, Swami Prabhupada, as the International Society for Krishna Consciousness. It is one of the best known of the new religious movements coming from the East, largely as a result of saffron-robed young people gathered in town centres chanting the Maha mantra. Devotees practise vegetarianism, do not use intoxicants, do not gamble, and are celibate apart from procreation within marriage.

hare lip *cleft lip and palate*

Harewood, George Henry Hubert Lascelles, 7th Earl of [hah(r)wud] (1923–) Elder son of Princess Mary, and cousin of Queen Elizabeth II, born in Harewood, West Yorkshire. Since the 1950s he has been much involved in the direction of operatic and arts institutions, such as at Covent Garden, Edinburgh, and Leeds.

Hargreaves, James (c.1720–78) Inventor, probably born in Blackburn, Lancashire. He invented the *spinning jenny* (named after his daughter) in c.1764; and erected a spinning mill in Nottingham.

Hargreaves, Roger (1935–88) Children's writer, born in Cleckheaton, West Yorkshire. He began writing after creating the storybook character 'Mr Tickle' for his son **Adam** in 1971. A hugely popular series of Mr Men books followed, which he also illustrated, and in 1981 he began the series of Little Miss books. In 2003 Adam wrote and illustrated a further set of books, crediting his father as author.

haricot bean An annual (*Phaseolus vulgaris*) growing to 3 m/10 ft, sometimes climbing, a native of South America; pea-flowers white, yellow, or bluish, in small shortly stalked clusters; pods up to 20 cm/8 in long, containing edible ellipsoid or kidney-shaped seeds; numerous varieties are cultivated as a vegetable; also called **kidney bean** and **French bean**. (Family: Leguminosae.)

Harimandir [harimandeer] or **Golden Temple** The centre of the Sikh religion at Amritsar, Punjab, India. The temple dates from 1766, and houses the Granth Sahib, the holy book of the Sikhs.

Harlem (The Netherlands), Dutch **Haarlem** 52°23N 4°38E, pop (2000e) 157 000. City in W Netherlands; founded, 10th-c; charter, 1245; sacked by the Spaniards (1573); railway; centre for tulip, hyacinth, and crocus bulbs.

Harlem (USA) District in New York City, largely in N Manhattan Island, centred on 125th St; named (1658) after Haarlem, The Netherlands; a chiefly black residential area, known for its poverty and racial tension; area to the E contains a large Puerto Rican community (**Spanish Harlem**), and several other minority groups also live in the district; centre of a literary movement in the 1920s (the **Harlem Renaissance**).

Harlem Globetrotters An American professional touring basketball team, usually all-black, formed in 1927 under the name Saperstein's Globetrotters. They developed a comedy routine to add to their skills, and now tour worldwide giving exhibitions. The team was inducted into the Basketball Hall of Fame in 2002.

Harlequin Columbine's young lover in the English harlequinade, with a costume of multi-coloured diamond-shaped patches, whose cunning and ingenuity has had a long and varied theatrical history.

harlequinade An English theatrical entertainment developed in the 18th-c by the actor John Rich, who specialized in the acrobatic and pantomimic portrayal of Harlequin. Scenes of this character's comic courtship of Columbine interspersed the performance of a serious play, which they served to satirize. They were the immediate precursors of the English pantomime.

Harley, Robert, 1st Earl of Oxford (1661–1724) British statesman, born in London. In 1710 he was made Chancellor of the Exchequer, head of the government, and (1711) Lord High Treasurer. The principal act of his administration was the Treaty of Utrecht (1713).

Harlow, Jean, originally **Harlean Carpentier**, nickname **the Blonde Bombshell** (1911–37) Film star, born in Kansas City, MO. From film performances such as *Platinum Blonde* (1931) and *Bombshell* (1933), and the scandals of her private life, she earned her nickname.

Harman, Harriet (1950–) British stateswoman, born in London. She studied at York University, became a solicitor, and was legal officer for the National Council of Civil Liberties (1978–82). She became a Labour MP in 1982, and held a number of shadow ministerial posts before becoming secretary of state for social security and minister for women (1997–8). She was appointed solicitor general after the 2001 election, and in 2005 became a minister in the Department for Constitutional Affairs.

Harmattan [hah(r)matan] A hot, dry wind which blows from the Sahara desert in W Africa. Dust carried by the Harmattan may be blown across to the Caribbean.

harmonic A pitch sounded by a string or column of air vibrating at a half, a third, a quarter, etc of its length. The timbre of a voice or instrument depends on the prominence or otherwise of these harmonics (or *upper partials*) when the fundamental note is sounded.

harmonica A musical instrument, popularly known as the **mouth organ**, in which metal 'reeds' arranged in a row are made to vibrate by the inhalation and exhalation of the player's breath. Virtuosi such as Larry Adler (1914–2001) and Tommy Reilly (1919–2000) have inspired many serious composers to write for it.

harmonium A type of reed organ patented in 1842 by French instrument maker A F Debain (1809–77). The name has been widely used for reed organs in general.

harmony The combining of musical notes into chords, and then into sequences of chords, with emphasis on the 'vertical' component of the music rather than on the 'horizontal' fitting together of melodic strands (counterpoint). Harmony is thus generally thought of as accompanying, or 'clothing', one or more lines of melody.

Harmsworth, Alfred (Charles William), 1st Viscount Northcliffe (1865–1922) Journalist and newspaper magnate, born near Dublin. In 1896 he revolutionized Fleet Street with his *Daily Mail*, introducing popular journalism to the UK. In 1908, he became proprietor of *The Times*.

Harmsworth, Harold (Sydney), 1st Viscount Rothermere (1868–1940) Newspaper magnate, born in London. He founded the Glasgow *Daily Record* and in 1915 the *Sunday Pictorial*, and after his brother's death acquired control of the *Daily Mail* and *Sunday Dispatch*.

harness racing A horse race in which the rider is seated in a small two-wheeled cart, known as a *sulky*. The horses either trot or *pace*, and must not gallop. Races are run on an oval dirt track measuring 400–1500 m/$\frac{1}{2}$–1 mi in circumference.

Harold I, nickname **Harold Harefoot** (c.1016–40) King of England (1037–40), the younger son of Canute and Ælfgifu of Northampton. Canute had intended that Hardicanute should succeed him in both Denmark and England, but in view of Hardicanute's absence in Denmark, Harold was accepted in England.

Harold II (c.1022–66) Last Anglo-Saxon king of England (1066), the second son of Earl Godwin. He defeated his brother Tostig and Harold Hardrada, King of Norway, at Stamford Bridge (Sep 1066), but Duke William of Normandy then invaded England, and defeated him near Hastings (14 Oct 1066), where he died, shot through the eye with an arrow.

Harold III *Harald III Sigurdsson*

harp A musical instrument of great antiquity existing in a wide variety of forms and sizes, its distinguishing characteristic being that its strings run in a plane perpendicular to the resonator. The modern concert harp, designed in 1810 by French pianoforte maker Sébastien Erard (1752–1831), has a single row of 46 or 47 strings tuned to the major scale of C♭, and seven pedals by means of which any pitch may be raised by a semitone or a tone.

Harpers Ferry Raid (1859) An attack on the Federal arsenal in Virginia, led by abolitionist John Brown, intending to launch a slave insurrection. The raiders were captured, and Brown was executed amidst great publicity.

Harpies [hah(r)peez] In Greek mythology, fabulous monsters with women's features and bird's wings and claws. They were originally rapacious ghosts or the storm-winds.

Harpocrates *Horus*

harpsichord A keyboard instrument in use from the 15th-c to the early 19th-c and revived in recent times, mainly for performing early music. The keys, when depressed, cause wooden *jacks*, fitted with plectrums to pluck the strings, which extend away from the keyboard and are dampened when the jacks fall into place again.

Harrelson, Woody (1961–) Actor, born in Midland, TX. He became well known for his role as the bartender in the popular TV series *Cheers* (1983–93). His feature films include *Indecent Proposal* (1993), *The People vs. Larry Flynt* (1996, Oscar nomination), *The Hi-Lo Country* (1999), and *A Scanner Darkly* (2006).

harrier (ornithology) A medium-sized hawk of the worldwide genus *Circus* (10 species); wings and tail long; most nest on ground. (Family: Accipitridae.)

harrier (zoology) A hound used for hunting hares; slightly smaller than a foxhound, with a keen sense of smell.

Harriman, W(illiam) Averell (1891–1986) US statesman and diplomat, born in New York City. He became ambassador to the USSR (1943) and to Britain (1946), Governor of New York (1955–8), and US representative at the Vietnam peace talks in Paris

(1968). He negotiated the partial nuclear test-ban treaty between the USA and USSR in 1963.

Harris S part of the Lewis with Harris island district, Western Isles, NW Scotland; area c.500 km²/200 sq mi; tweed manufacture.

Harris, Sir Arthur Travers, nickname **Bomber Harris** (1892–1984) British airman, born in Cheltenham, Gloucestershire. As commander-in-chief of Bomber Command in World War 2 (1942–5) he organized mass bomber raids on industrial Germany.

Harris, Joel Chandler (1848–1908) Writer, born in Eatonton, GA. He became known for his stories of *Uncle Remus* (1880), and several other children's books, noted for their distinctive use of Southern African-American folklore and dialect.

Harris, Joanne (Michèle Sylvie) (1964–) Novelist, born in Barnsley, South Yorkshire. Her first successful novel, *Chocolat* (1999; filmed 2000), was shortlisted for the Whitbread Book Award. Further books include *Blackberry Wine* (2000), *Holy Fools* (2003), and *Gentlemen and Players* (2005).

Harris, Rolf (1930–) Entertainer and artist, born in Bassendean, Perth, Western Australia. He studied art in London, and on his return to Australia became presenter of a children's television programme and also had commercial success with his recordings. Settling in Britain, he has since appeared widely on stage and television, and fronted BBC's popular long-running series *Animal Hospital* (1994–2003). He was commissioned to paint a portrait of Queen Elizabeth II to mark her 80th birthday in 2006.

Harris, Roy, popular name of **LeRoy Ellsworth Harris** (1898–1979) Composer, born in Lincoln Co, OK. His works are ruggedly American in character and include 16 symphonies, as well as much instrumental, choral, and chamber music.

Harrisburg 40°16N 76°53W, pop (2000e) 48 900. Capital of state (since 1812) in S Pennsylvania, USA, on the Susquehanna R; scene of the Harrisburg Convention, 1788; scene of nuclear power station accident on Three Mile Island, 1979; railway; former steel industry giving way to a more diversified economy.

Harrison, Benjamin (1833–1901) US Republican statesman and 23rd president (1889–93), born in North Bend, OH, grandson of William Henry Harrison. In 1888 he defeated Cleveland on the issue of the protective tariff, but failed to gain re-election in 1892.

Harrison, George (1943–2001) Singer, guitarist, and songwriter, born in Liverpool, Merseyside. He played lead guitar and sang with the Beatles, and developed an interest in Indian music and Eastern religion. His solo albums include *All Things Must Pass* (1970), *Dark Horse* (1974), and *Somewhere in England* (1981). His company HandMade Films produced feature films, including *Withnail and I* (1987). He was wounded following a knife attack by an intruder at his Henley home at the end of 1999, and died in 2001 from cancer.

Harrison, Sir Rex, originally **Reginald Carey Harrison** (1908–90) Actor, born in Huyton-with-Roby, Lancashire. His charming, somewhat blasé style attracted many star comedy parts, such as in *Blithe Spirit* (1945), *The Constant Husband* (1958), and *My Fair Lady* (1964, Oscar).

Harrison, Tony (1937–) Poet, born in Leeds, West Yorkshire. He became known with *The Loiners* (1970) and the translation *Palladas Poems* (1975). Poems on social conflict ('V'. 1985, televised 1987) and the Gulf War ('A Cold Coming', 1991) underline his commitment to public issues, confirmed in *The Gaze of the Gorgon* (1992). Later works include *The Prince's Play* (1996) and *Under the Clock* (2005).

Harrison, William Henry (1773–1841) US soldier, statesman, and ninth president (1841), born in Charles City Co, VA. In the war of 1812–14 he defeated the British in the Battle of the Thames (1813). He was elected president in 1841, but died a month after his inauguration.

Harrow 51°35N 0°20W, pop (2001e) 207 400. Borough of NW Greater London; it is thought that there was once a temple on top of Harrow on the Hill; railway; Harrow School (1572); church of St Mary (1087) on Harrow Hill.

Harsanyi, John C(harles) (1920–2000) Economist, born in Budapest. He moved to the USA in 1956, joining the Haas School of Business at the University of California, Berkeley, in 1964. He shared the Nobel Prize for Economics in 1994 for his contribution to the analysis of equilibria in the theory of non-co-operative games.

Harte, Bret, pseudonym of **Francis Brett Hart** (1836–1902) Writer, born in Albany, NY. In 1868 he founded and edited the *Overland Monthly*, to which he contributed several short stories, notably those later collected in *The Luck of Roaring Camp* (1870).

hartebeest [hah(r)tibeest] An ox-antelope closely related to the topi; pale brown; two species: the **hartebeest** or **kongoni** (*Alcelaphus buselaphus*, 12 subspecies), and **Lichtenstein's hartebeest** (*Alcelaphus lichtensteini*).

Hartford 41°46N 72°41W, pop (2000e) 121 600. Capital of Connecticut, USA; founded by Dutch settlers, 1633; city status, 1784; railway; university; world's largest concentration of insurance companies; professional team, Whalers (ice hockey).

Hartington, Lord *Cavendish, Spencer Compton*

Hartley, L(eslie) P(oles) (1895–1972) Writer, born near Peterborough, Cambridgeshire. His early short stories, such as *Night Fears* (1924), established his reputation as a master of the macabre. Later novels include *The Boat* (1950) and *The Go-Between* (1953).

Hartnell, Sir Norman (1901–78) Fashion designer and court dressmaker, born in London. His work included costumes for leading actresses, wartime 'utility' dresses, and Princess Elizabeth's wedding and coronation gowns.

Hartwell, Leland H, known as **Lee Hartwell** (1939–) Geneticist, born in Los Angeles, CA. He became professor of genome sciences at the University of Washington in 1968, and director of the Fred Hutchinson Cancer Research Center, Seattle, in 1997. He shared the 2001 Nobel Prize for Physiology or Medicine for his pioneering work in yeast genetics, which contributed to understanding the key regulators of the cell cycle.

haruspices [haruspikayz] In ancient Rome, the practitioners of the Etruscan system of divination, of which inspection of the entrails of sacrificial animals was the main part. Their art survived well into the Christian era.

Harvard University *Ivy League*

harvestman An extremely long-legged arthropod; body compact, carried on four pairs of long legs; female with long egg-laying tube; also called **daddy longlegs**. (Class: Arachnida. Order: Opiliones, c.4500 species.)

harvest-mite A small, predatory mite; tiny, red-coloured, 6-legged larvae often occur in large numbers in damp fields in autumn; feed by sucking blood of small mammals and humans; larvae known as **chiggers**. (Order: Acari. Family: Thrombidiidae.)

harvest mouse A mouse of genus *Reithrodontomys* (**American harvest mouse**, 19 species) from Central and North America; also, **Old World harvest mouse** (*Micromys minutus*) from Europe and Asia, the smallest living rodent (may weigh as little as 5 g/0·2 oz).

Harvey, Caroline *Trollope, Joanna*

Harvey, William (1578–1657) Physician, born in Folkestone, Kent, the first European to discover the circulation of the blood. His celebrated treatise, *De motu cordis et sanguinis in animalibus* (On the Motion of the Heart and Blood in Animals) was published in 1628.

Harwich [harich] 51°57N 1°17E, pop (2000e) 20 000. Port in Essex,

SE England; railway; container freight terminal; ferries to Denmark, Germany, Holland.

Hasdrubal [hazdrubl] The name of several Carthaginian leaders, notably **1** Hamilcar Barca's son-in-law and successor in Spain (died 221 BC), and **2** Hannibal's younger brother, who died in battle with the Romans at the R Metaurus (207 BC).

Hašek, Jaroslav [hashek] (1883–1923) Novelist and short-story writer, born in Prague. He is best known for his novel *The Good Soldier Švejk* (1921–3), a satire on military life and bureaucracy.

Haselrig, Sir Arthur [hayzlrig], also spelled **Hesilrige** (?–1661) English parliamentarian, one of the five members whose attempted seizure by Charles I in 1642 precipitated the Civil War. After the Restoration, he died a prisoner in the Tower.

Hashemites Arab princely family of sharifs, or descendants of the Prophet, who ruled parts of Arabia and the Fertile Crescent in the 20th-c. They include the current royal family of Jordan.

hashish *cannabis*

Hasmoneans *Maccabees*

Hastert, J(ohn) Dennis [hastert], known as **Denny Hastert** (1942–) US politician, born in Aurora, IL. He was elected to the state legislature in 1980, and ran successfully for the US House of Representatives in 1986. He became Speaker in 1999 with a small working majority of Republicans amid promises of bipartisan co-operation.

Hastings, Warren (1732–1818) British colonial administrator in India, born in Churchill, Oxfordshire. He joined the East India Company in 1750, and by 1774 was Governor-General of Bengal, making the Company's power paramount in many parts of India. On his return to England in 1784 he was charged with corruption, and after a seven-year trial, acquitted.

Hastings, Battle of (1066) The most decisive battle fought on English soil. Norman cavalry overcame the resolute defence of the Anglo-Saxon army fighting on foot, and Harold II's death in battle cleared the way for Duke William of Normandy's coronation.

Hatfield 51°46N 0°13W, pop (2000e) 33 900. Town in Hertfordshire, SE England; 30 km/19 mi N of London; designated a 'new town' in 1948; railway; University of Hertfordshire (1992, formerly Hatfield Polytechnic).

Hathaway, Anne *Shakespeare, William*

Hathor [hahthaw(r)] The ancient Egyptian goddess of love, together with joyful music and dancing. She was identified by the Greeks with Aphrodite.

Hatra [hatra] An ancient Parthian fortress city located between the Tigris and Euphrates rivers in N Iraq; a world heritage site. Founded in the 1st-c BC, it flourished as a trading and religious centre for four centuries.

Hatshepsut [hatshepsoot] (c.1540–c.1481 BC) A queen of Egypt of the XVIIIth dynasty, the daughter of Thutmose I. She acted as Regent for Thutmose III, then had herself crowned as Pharaoh. She was represented with the regular pharaonic attributes, including a beard.

Hattersley, Roy (Sydney George), Baron (1932–) British statesman, born in Sheffield, South Yorkshire. He was secretary of state for prices and consumer protection (1976–9), and has since been Opposition spokesman on the environment and on home affairs, shadow Chancellor, and deputy leader of the Labour Party (1983–92). He was created a life peer in 1997.

Hattusas [hatusas] or **Hattusha** The ancient capital of the Hittites, now Bogazkoy in C Turkey, taken by the Hittites in the 17th-c BC, and destroyed in 1200 BC by the Sea Peoples. The ruins are a world heritage site.

Haughey, Charles (James) [hokhee] (1925–2006) Irish statesman and prime minister (1979–81, 1982, 1987–92), born in Castlebar, Co Mayo. He became a Fianna Fáil MP in 1957, and held posts in justice, agriculture, and finance. After two years as minister of health and social welfare, he became premier in 1979, and defeated Garrett Fitzgerald in the 1987 elections. He was forced to resign in 1992 following allegations of his involvement in a phone-tapping scandal.

Hausa [howsa] A Chadic-speaking, predominantly Muslim people of Nigeria and Niger; the largest ethnic group in the area. They are intensive farmers, and Hausa traders are found throughout W Africa; they are also famed for their crafts. The Hausa language which has c.25 million mother-tongue speakers, is used as a lingua franca throughout N Nigeria and adjacent territories.

Haussmann, Georges Eugène, Baron [howsman] (1809–91) Financier and town planner, born in Paris. He became prefect of the Seine (1853), improving Paris by widening streets, laying out boulevards and parks, and building bridges.

haustorium A sucker-like organ inserted by a parasite into the cells of the host, through which food is withdrawn. It is found in fungi and parasitic flowering plants, such as dodder.

Havana [havana], Span **La Habana** 23°07N 82°25W, pop (2000e) 2 263 000. Capital city of Cuba; founded on this site, 1519; airport; railway; country's chief port on fine natural harbour; university (1721); cathedral (1704); trade in sugar, cotton, tobacco; old city centre a world heritage site.

Havel, Václav [havl, **vahts**laf] (1936–) Playwright, president of Czechoslovakia (1989–92), and president of the Czech Republic (1993–2003), born in Prague. In 1977 he became co-founder of the Charter 77 human rights initiative, was under-house arrest in 1978–9, was imprisoned for four years, and again in 1989, but later that year was released and elected president by popular vote, following the collapse of communism. He resigned in 1992 in protest at the dissolution of Czechoslovakia, but was elected the first president of the new Czech Republic in January 1993, and retired at the end of his second term.

Hawaii (state) [hawahee] pop (2000e) 1 211 500; area 16 759 km²/6471 sq mi. Pacific state of the US, a group of eight major islands (Hawaii, Kahoolawe, Kauai, Lanai, Maui, Molokai, Niihau, Oahu) and numerous islets in the C Pacific Ocean; the 'Aloha State'; reached by the Polynesians over 1000 years ago; discovered by Captain Cook in 1778, and named the Sandwich Is; monarchy overthrown, 1893; ceded itself to the USA, 1898; surprise attack by Japanese planes on the US naval base at Pearl Harbor, Oahu (7 Dec 1941) brought the USA into World War 2; admitted to the Union as the 50th state, 1959; highest point Mauna Kea, a dormant volcano on Hawaii I (4201 m/13 783 ft) a major astronomical site; Mauna Loa (4169 m/13 678 ft) an active volcano; capital, Honolulu; defence installations at Pearl Harbor; major tourist area.

Hawaii (island) [hawahee] pop (2000e) 132 000; area 10 488 km²/4048 sq mi. Largest island of the US state of Hawaii; the 'orchid isle'; chief town, Hilo.

Hawaiian guitar A guitar with a straight body placed across the player's knees. It has metal strings which are stopped with a steel bar, instead of the fingers of the left hand, to produce the characteristic scooping (glissando) sound. Electric Hawaiian (or 'steel') guitars, sometimes free-standing, have been manufactured since the 1930s.

hawfinch A stout finch (*Coccothraustes coccothraustes*) native to Europe, Asia, and N Africa; golden-brown with black face; bill huge, strong, used for cracking tree fruits. (Family: Fringillidae.)

Haw-Haw, Lord *Joyce, William*

hawk (ornithology) A bird of prey of the family Accipitridae, the name being used especially for smaller members of the family. In the USA, the name is also used for some falcons (Family: Falconidae.)

Hawke, Bob, popular name of **Robert (James Lee) Hawke** (1929–) Australian statesman and Labor prime minister (1983–91), born in Bordertown, South Australia. He was a skilled negotiator who won praise for his handling and settling of industrial disputes. In 1987 he became the first Labor prime minister to win a third term in office, and won a fourth term in 1990, but was defeated in a leadership contest by Paul Keating the following year.

Hawke (of Towton), Edward Hawke, Baron (1705–81) British admiral, born in London. His major victory was against the French at Quiberon Bay (1759), which caused the collapse of their invasion plans.

Hawking, Stephen (William) (1942–) Theoretical physicist, born in Oxford, Oxfordshire. His work has been concerned with cosmology, dealing with black holes, singularities, and the 'big bang' theory of the origin of the universe. His popular writing includes *A Brief History of Time* (1988), *The Universe in a Nutshell* (2002), and *A Briefer History of Time* (2005). Since the 1960s he has suffered from a neuromotor disease, amyotrophic lateral sclerosis, causing extreme physical disability.

Hawkins, Sir John *Hawkyns, Sir John*

hawk-moth A medium to large moth, typically with long, triangular wings and an elongate body, most abundant in tropics. (Order: Lepidoptera. Family: Sphingidae, c.1000 species.)

Hawks, Howard (Winchester) (1896–1977) Film director, born in Goshen, IN. He had many successes over some 40 years, in such varied genres as airforce dramas (*The Dawn Patrol*, 1930), detection and crime (*The Big Sleep*, 1946), Westerns (*Rio Lobo*, 1970), and comedy (*Man's Favorite Sport?*, 1962).

Hawksmoor, Nicholas (1661–1736) Architect, born in East Drayton, Nottinghamshire. His works include the London churches, St Mary Woolnoth, St George's (Bloomsbury), and Christ Church (Spitalfields).

hawkweed A widely distributed perennial, mostly in the N hemisphere; flower-heads solitary or in loose clusters, florets usually yellow. (Genus: *Hieracium*, c.250 species. Family: Compositae.)

Hawkyns or **Hawkins, Sir John** (1532–95) British sailor, born in Plymouth, Devon. He became navy treasurer (1573), and was knighted for his services against the Armada in 1588. In 1595, with his kinsman Drake, he commanded an expedition to the Spanish Main.

Hawn, Goldie (Jeanne) [hawn] (1945–) Actress, born in Washington, DC. She became known through her comedy roles in Rowan and Martin's *Laugh In* (1968–70), then won a Best Supporting Actress award for her first film role in *Cactus Flower* (1969). Later films include *Private Benjamin* (1980), *First Wives Club* (1996), *The Out-of-Towners* (1999), and *The Banger Sisters* (2002).

hawthorn A spiny, deciduous shrub or tree (*Crataegus monogyna*), growing to 18 m/60 ft, native to Europe; leaves deeply 3–7-lobed; flowers white, in clusters; berries (*haws*) red to maroon, flesh thin over a large stone; forms dense stock-proof hedges and attractive park or street trees; also called **quickthorn** and **may**. (Family: Rosaceae.)

Hawthorne, Nathaniel (1804–64) Novelist and short-story writer, born in Salem, MA. His first success was a collection of short stories, *Twice-Told Tales* (1837), but his best-known works are his novels, notably *The Scarlet Letter* (1850) and *The House of the Seven Gables* (1851).

Hawthorne, Sir Nigel (Barnard) (1929–2001) Actor, born in Coventry, West Midlands. He theatrical work included *Privates On Parade* (1978, SWET and Clarence Derwent awards), *Shadowlands* (1989, Tony) and *The Madness of George III* (1991, Olivier). He achieved television fame for his acclaimed role as Sir Humphrey Appleby in the series *Yes Minister* (1980) and its sequel. His films include *The Madness of King George* (1994, Oscar nomination), and in 1997 he was awarded a BAFTA Best Actor award for *The Fragile Heart*. He was knighted in 1999.

Hay, Will (1888–1949) Comedian and actor, born in Stockton-on-Tees, England. He joined Fred Karno's comedy troupe (1914–18), going on to star in several films, such as *Good Morning Boys* (1937), *Oh Mr Porter* (1938), and *My Learned Friend* (1944).

Hayden, Bill, popular name of **William George Hayden** (1933–) Australian statesman, born in Brisbane, Queensland, Australia. He replaced Gough Whitlam as Labor Party leader (1977–83), then served as foreign minister in Bob Hawke's government (1983–8). He was Governor-General of Australia (1989–96).

Haydn, Franz Joseph [hiydn] (1732–1809) Composer, born in Rohrau, Austria. He entered the service of the Esterházy family as musical director in 1761, staying with them until 1790. Among his innovations were the four-movement string quartet and the 'classical' symphony. His works include 104 symphonies, about 50 concertos, 84 string quartets, 24 stage works, 12 Masses, orchestral divertimenti, keyboard sonatas, and diverse chamber, choral, instrumental, and vocal pieces.

Hayes, Helen, originally **Helen Hayes Brown** (1900–93) Actress, born in Washington, DC. Her adult stage productions brought her national popularity, and include *The Glass Menagerie* (1956) and *Long Day's Journey into Night* (1971). She also appeared in several films, notably *The Sin of Madelon Claudet* (1931, Oscar), and *Airport* (1970, Oscar). The Helen Hayes Theater in New York City was named after her.

Hayes, Rutherford B(irchard) (1822–93) US Republican statesman and 19th president (1877–81), born in Delaware, OH. Under his presidency, the country recovered commercial prosperity. His policy included reform of the civil service and the conciliation of the Southern states.

hay fever An allergic reaction affecting the eyes and nasal passages, resulting in watering of the eyes, nasal congestion, and sneezing. It is usually provoked by exposure to the pollen of grasses in the air, but the reaction is not confined to any season or to a single stimulus. Symptoms can be reduced by antihistamine drugs.

haymaker *pika*

Haywood, William D(udley), nickname **Big Bill Haywood** (1869–1928) US labour leader, born in Salt Lake City, UT. In 1905 he helped to found the Industrial Workers of the World, which was committed to revolutionary labour politics. He was convicted of sedition in 1917, and fled from the USA in 1921, taking refuge in Russia.

Hayworth, Rita, originally **Margarita Carmen Cansino** (1918–87) Film actress, born in New York City. She partnered both Fred Astaire and Gene Kelly in musicals of the 1940s, and found her best-known lead in *Gilda* (1946). A scandal involving her romance with Aly Khan (1949–51), whom she later married, effectively closed her Hollywood career.

hazardous substances Generally human-made substances, potentially damaging to health, which when incorrectly disposed of result in contamination and pollution of the environment. They include toxic substances, heavy metal pollutants (eg lead, mercury), and radioactive waste produced in the generation of nuclear power.

hazel A deciduous shrub or small tree (*Corylus avellana*), native to Europe and Asia Minor; leaves broadly oval, toothed; male catkins long, pendulous; females short, bud-like with prominent red stigmas; edible nut partially enclosed in a ragged green leafy cup. (Family: Corylaceae.)

Hazlitt, William (1778–1830) Essayist, born in Maidstone, Kent. His best-known essay collections are *Table Talk* (1821) and *The Spirit of the Age* (1825).

H-bomb *hydrogen bomb*

HDI *Human Development Index*

headache An aching sensation over the vault of the skull, temples, or back of the head, usually diffuse and poorly localized. The brain itself is insensitive to touch, and headaches arise from the stretching or distortion of its covering membranes, from tension arising from the muscles overlying the skull, or from vascular dilatation with increased blood supply, as occurs in generalized fevers or over-indulgence in alcohol.

Head Start A project begun in the USA in the early 1960s to help pre-school children from a disadvantaged background prepare for schooling. The main emphasis was on language and social development, but attention was also paid to health care and parent education.

Healey (of Riddlesden), Denis (Winston) Healey, Baron (1917–) British statesman, born in Eltham, Kent. He was secretary of state for defence (1964–70), Chancellor of the Exchequer (1974–9), deputy leader (1980–3), and in 1983 was appointed shadow foreign minister, retiring in 1992.

healing Any method by which an illness or injury is cured; specifically, the use of a technique which is not recognized within orthodox medicine and involves no form of physical therapy or manipulation. Techniques such as the 'laying on of hands' are seen as involving the transmission of energy from, or channelling through, a healer and into the sick person. Sometimes prayer, visualization, meditation, or other methods are used by the patient, healer, or both to help focus beneficial thoughts and energy onto the illness.

health foods An umbrella term for so-called 'whole food', additive-free food, and diet supplements such as minerals, vitamins, trace elements, essential fatty acids, and other nutrients. Many are sold simply as a supplement to diet, but some make therapeutic claims. Most health-food shops are now actively promoting alternative medicine.

Health Maintenance Organizations (US) Private health insurance groups that in the last quarter of the 20th-c dominated the way in which Americans under the age of 65 received medical coverage, popularly known as **HMOs**. Begun in the 1960s, HMOs offered an attractive programme of 'managed care' that emphasized cost-cutting, careful review of patient claims and diagnoses, and an emphasis on preventative methods and a healthy lifestyle. In the 1990s they captured an ever-growing share of the health-care market, but encountered serious problems in providing affordable care to a burgeoning population of needy patients.

Heaney, Seamus (Justin) [heenee, shaymus] (1939–) Poet, born on a farm near Castledawson in Co Londonderry, Northern Ireland. His works include *Death of a Naturalist* (1966), *Field Work* (1979), and *Station Island* (1984). He became professor of rhetoric and oratory at Harvard in 1985, and professor of poetry at Oxford in 1989. Volumes of selected poems appeared in 1980, 1990, and 1998. Later work includes *The Spirit Level* (1996, Whitbread), his reworking of the Anglo-Saxon epic poem *Beowulf* (1999, Whitbread), *Finders Keepers: Selected prose 1971-2001* (2002), and *District and Circle* (2006, T S Eliot Prize). He was awarded the Nobel Prize for Literature in 1995.

Heard and McDonald Islands area 412 km²/159 sq mi. Island group in S Indian Ocean, about 4000 km/2500 mi SW of Fremantle, Australia; an Australian external territory since 1947; made a world heritage site in 1997.

hearing *auditory perception; cochlea; ear*

hearing aid A device for amplifying sound, used by persons with defective hearing. Modern aids are electronic, consisting of a microphone, amplifier, and earphone, usually compressed into a very small container to fit directly on to the ear.

Hearne, Samuel [hern] (1745–92) Explorer of N Canada, born in London. He joined the Hudson's Bay Company, and became the first European to travel overland by canoe and sled to the Arctic Ocean.

Hearns, Thomas [hernz], nicknames **Hit Man** and **Motor City Cobra** (1958–) Boxer, born in Memphis, TN. In 1991 he became the first man to win world titles at six different weights.

hearsay A complex rule of evidence in common-law countries which prohibits an out-of-court oral or written statement from being used in court to prove the truth of an issue. The rule is still widely followed in the USA, but has been virtually abolished in civil cases Scotland, and in England and Wales. It has many exceptions, generally situations in which the speaker is likely to be truthful, such as dying declarations.

Hearst, William Randolph (1863–1951) Newspaper owner, born in San Francisco, CA. He revolutionized journalism by the introduction of banner headlines, lavish illustrations, and other sensational methods. His career inspired the film *Citizen Kane* (1941).

heart *p.421*

heartburn A burning sensation usually felt intermittently within the chest over the lower part of the breastbone. It results from regurgitation of the contents of the stomach into the lower part of the oesophagus, inducing a spasm.

heart disease Disease of the heart and the associated blood vessels. The heart is essentially a pump. Interference with its function whatever the cause gives rise to the cardinal symptoms of shortness of breath, fluid retention (*oedema*), palpitations, chest pain, and fainting.

heart–lung machine An apparatus which takes over the pumping action of the heart, together with the breathing action of the lungs, so that the heart can be stopped and operated upon. The blood is filtered and kept at a suitable temperature during its passage through the machine – if necessary, for several hours.

heartsease A species of violet (*Viola tricolor*), also called **wild pansy**, native to Europe. The flowers are blue, yellow, white, or a combination of these colours. (Family: Violaceae.)

heat The transfer of energy from one object to another, due solely to their difference in temperatures; symbol Q, units J (joule). The quantity of heat sometimes ascribed to an object or process is the total amount of energy transferred in this way.

heat capacity The quantity of heat needed to produce a temperature rise of one kelvin (or 1°C) in some material. **Specific heat capacity** c (also called **specific heat**), units J/(kg.K), is the heat capacity per kilogram of material. For water, $c = 4180$ J/(kg.K).

heat engine The name given to a device that transforms disordered heat energy into ordered, useful, mechanical work. This is achieved by taking a working fluid at high temperature and high heat energy, and subjecting it to a thermodynamic cycle involving compression and expansion, during which time heat is expelled at a lower temperature. The differences in heat energy of the working fluid between input and output appear as work.

Heath, Sir Edward (Richard George), known as **Ted Heath** (1916–2005) British statesman and prime minister (1970–4), born in Broadstairs, Kent. He was minister of labour (1959–60), then Lord Privy Seal (1960–3) and the chief negotiator for Britain's entry into the European Economic Community. Elected Leader of the Conservative Party in 1965, he was Leader of the Opposition until his 1970 victory. Replaced as leader by Mrs Thatcher in 1975, he continued to play an active part in politics, and was Father of the House from 1997 to his retirement in 2001. He was known for his interests in yachting and music.

heath A low evergreen shrub or small tree, native to Europe, Asia, N Africa, and especially S Africa; flowers often numerous, bell- or urn-shaped, pink, purple, or white. They are also called **ericas**, and are widely known as **heathers**, which is a source of possible confusion with true heather. (Genus: *Erica*, c.500 species. Family: Ericaceae.)

heather 1 A small, bushy, evergreen shrub (*Calluna vulgaris*), native to Europe, especially N and W; flowers tiny, in loose spikes, four sepals, four petals, all purple; also called **ling**. (Family: Ericaceae.)

2 *heath*

heat storage Any means by which heat can be stored for release

heart

Labels (left, top to bottom): right pulmonary artery — innominate artery — arch of aorta — left common cartoid — left subclavian artery — ascending aorta — superior vena cava — pulmonary trunk — right pulmonary veins — pulmonary semilunar valve — right atrium — valve of interior vena cava — tricuspid valve — chordae tendineae — inferior vena cava — right ventricle — papillary muscle

Labels (right): remains of ductus arteriosus — left pulmonary artery — left pulmonary veins — left atrium — aortic semilunar valve — bicuspid valve — left ventricle — left ventricular septum — descending thoracic aorta

A hollow muscular organ, divided into chambers (right and left *atria*, right and left *ventricles*) and enclosed within a fibrous sac (the *pericardium*) found within the thorax. It lies directly under the sternum, being protected by it and the adjacent ribs. It is the first organ to develop in the embryo (in humans by three weeks). In mammals it is separated into right and left halves concerned with pulmonary and systemic circulation respectively. It consists mainly of cardiac muscle (the *myocardium*) enclosed between two sheets of fibrous and elastic tissue, the *epicardium* and the *endocardium*. The myocardium forms a network of sheets and strands which have a characteristic arrangement in different parts of the heart. The heart also possesses a fibrous skeleton which surrounds and strengthens many of its openings. In humans, the ventricles have a capacity of between 90 and 120 ml. The right atrium receives deoxygenated blood from the body (via the superior and inferior *venae cavae*) and from the heart itself (via the *coronary sinus*) during diastole, and conveys it to the right ventricle via the right atrioventricular opening (guarded by the *tricuspid valve*). The right ventricle expels blood into the *pulmonary trunk* (guarded by the *pulmonary valve*) and thence to the lungs. The left atrium receives oxygenated blood from the lungs and conveys it to the left ventricle via the left atrioventricular opening (guarded by the *mitral valve*). The left ventricle forcibly expels blood into the *aorta* (guarded by the *aortic valve*) and thence to the rest of the body. In the fetus, blood bypasses the non-functioning lungs in two ways. Freshly oxygenated blood returning from the placenta enters the right atrium and passes directly into the left atrium through the *foramen ovale*, an opening in the inter-atrial septum, to be distributed to body tissues via the left ventricle. Deoxygenated blood returning to the right atrium passes into the right ventricle and pulmonary trunk and then into the descending aorta by a communicating channel (the *ductus arteriosus*). After birth, the foramen ovale closes (failure to do so leads to a 'hole in the heart', with the mixing of pulmonary and systemic blood), and the ductus arteriosus becomes obliterated. The conducting system of the mammalian heart consists of a 'pacemaker' (the *sinuatrial node*), a 'relay station' (the *atrioventricular node*), and the *atrioventricular bundle* within the *interventricular septum*. Both nodes are situated in the right atrium. The contractile impulse begins at the sinuatrial node, reaches the atrioventricular node via atrial muscle fibres, and reaches the ventricles via the atrioventricular bundle. Damage to the atrioventricular bundle (by disease or experimentally) causes the ventricles to contract independently and at a slower rate than the atria (known as 'heart block'). The sinuatrial node has the highest degree of inherent rhythmicity, and determines the rate of the heart beat. It is influenced by the autonomic nervous system. The walls of the heart are supplied by the coronary arteries, and drained by the cardiac veins and by *venae cordae minimae* (small veins draining the deeper layers of myocardium). A **heart attack** (*myocardial infarction*) occurs when part of the coronary arterial supply becomes blocked by a blood clot (*thrombus*), leading to the cessation of blood flow and death of the myocardium.

later. Domestic electric storage heaters usually contain large, heat-absorbing bricks. They also contain electric coils which are wound through thousands of tiny holes in the bricks. During the night, the electric current switches on the coils in the storage heater and they heat up. In the morning the current switches off, and the bricks slowly give off their heat during the day. Other heat storage systems use the principle that a substance will give off heat as it changes from one state to another (*a phase change*). An example is Glauber's salt, which melts at about 31°C. It is liquefied during the night when electricity is cheap, and gives off its stored heat during the day as it changes back into a solid.

heat stroke A raised body temperature (often above 41°C) which occurs when heat production exceeds heat loss, for example during heavy exercise, feverish illness, or when the environmental temperature is excessive. Treatment is by urgent cooling of the body, and rehydration. The condition is also known as **sunstroke**, though it may occur with or without exposure to direct sunlight.

heaven Generally, the dwelling-place of God and the angels, and in traditional Christianity the ultimate eternal destiny of the redeemed, there to reign with Christ in glory. In modern theology, the emphasis is more on the fully-revealed presence of God, and the perfection of the divine–human relationship, than on a place.

Heavenly Twins *Gemini*

Heaviside layer A region of the ionosphere between c.90–120 km/55–75 mi responsible for the reflection of radio waves back to Earth; also known as the **E layer**. It was discovered in 1902 independently by Oliver Heaviside (1850–1925) in England and Arthur E Kennelly (1861–1939) in the USA (where it is also known as the **Kennelly layer**).

heavy metal music A form of rock music developed from electrified blues music, with heavily amplified guitars, bass guitars, and drums, and often strident vocals. Early pioneers were Jimi Hendrix and the band Cream with Eric Clapton; classic exponents of the genre included US bands Grand Funk (Railroad), Vanilla Fudge, and Mountain, and the British Led Zeppelin, Deep Purple, and Black Sabbath.

heavy water *deuterium*

Hebe [heebee] In Greek mythology, the goddess of youth and youthful beauty, daughter of Zeus and Hera. She became cup-bearer to the Olympians, and was married to Heracles after he was deified.

Hébert, Jacques René [aybair] (1757–94) French revolutionary extremist, born in Alençon, France. He played a major part in the September Massacres and the overthrow of the monarchy. After denouncing the Committee of Public Safety for its failure to help the poor, he tried to incite a popular uprising, but he and 17 of his followers (**Hébertists**) were guillotined.

Hebrew A Semitic language which dates from around the 2nd millennium BC. Classical Hebrew is the written language of Judaism, and its modern variety is the official language of the state of Israel. It is spoken by c.4 million people around the world.

Hebrews, Letter to the New Testament writing of unknown authorship and recipients. It is sometimes attributed to Paul, but this attribution was widely doubted even from early times.

Hebrides [hebrideez] Over 500 islands off the W coast of Scotland; divided into the **Inner Hebrides** (notably Skye, Rhum, Eigg, Coll, Mull, Iona, Staffa, Islay, Jura) and **Outer Hebrides** (notably Lewis with Harris, the Uists, Barra), separated by the Minch.

Hebron, Arabic **al-Khalil**, Hebrew **Hevro** 31°32N 35°06E, pop (2000e) 135 000. City in Israeli-occupied West Bank, W Jordan; one of the oldest cities in the world, built 1730 BC; a religious centre of Islam; the home of Abraham.

Hecate [hekatee, hekat] In Greek mythology, the goddess associated with witchcraft, spooks, and magic. She is worshipped with offerings at places where three roads cross, and so given three bodies in sculpture.

Heckman, James J (1944–) Economist, born in Chicago, IL. He joined the faculty at the University of Chicago (1973), where he became professor of economics. In 2000 he shared the Nobel Prize for Economics for work in the field of microeconometrics.

Hector [hektaw] According to Greek legend, the bravest Trojan, who led out their army to battle; the son of Priam, and married to Andromache. Achilles killed him and dragged his body behind his chariot.

Hecuba [hekyooba] or **Hecabe** [hekabee] In Greek legend, the wife of Priam, King of Troy, and mother of 18 children, including Hector and Cassandra. After the Greeks took Troy, she saw her sons and her husband killed, and was sent into slavery.

hedgehog A mammal (an insectivore) native to Europe, Africa, and Asia; body covered with spines; tail short; many species dig burrows. When frightened, it can roll its body into a ball. (Family: Erinaceidae, 12 species.)

hedging *futures*

hedonism 1 An ethical doctrine, held by Cyrenaics, Epicureans, and most utilitarians, which maintains that the only intrinsic good is pleasure; the only intrinsic evil is pain.
2 A psychological thesis which claims that people are always motivated to seek pleasure and avoid pain.

Heeger, Alan J (1936–) Physical chemist, born in Sioux City, IA. He became professor of physics at the University of California, Santa Barbara (1982). In 2000 he shared the Nobel Prize for Chemistry for the discovery and development of conductive polymers.

Hegel, Georg Wilhelm Friedrich [haygl] (1770–1831) Philosopher, born in Stuttgart, Germany. His major works include *Phänomenologie des Geistes* (1807, The Phenomenology of the Mind), *Wissenschaft der Logik* (1812–16, Science of Logic), and *Enzyklopädie der philosophischen Wissenschaften* (1817, trans Encyclopedia of the Philosophical Sciences), in which he set out his tripartite system of logic, philosophy of nature, and mind. His approach rejects the reality of finite and separate objects and minds in space and time, and establishes an underlying, all-embracing unity, the Absolute. The quest for greater unity and truth is achieved by the famous dialectic, positing something (*thesis*), denying it (*antithesis*), and combining the two half-truths in a *synthesis* which contains a greater portion of truth in its complexity.

Heidegger, Martin [hiydeger] (1889–1976) Philosopher, born in Messkirch, Germany. In his uncompleted main work *Sein und Zeit* (1927, Being and Time), he presents an exhaustive ontological classification of 'Being', through the synthesis of the modes of human existence. He was a key influence in Sartre's Existentialism.

Heidelberg [hiydlberg] 49°23N 8°41E, pop (2000e) 141 000. Industrial city in Germany; centre of German Calvinism during the 16th-c; railway; oldest university in Germany (1386); castle (1583–1610).

Heifetz, Jascha [hiyfets] (1901–87) Violinist, born in Vilnius, Lithuania. After the Revolution he settled in the USA, becoming a US citizen in 1925.

Heilong Jiang *Amur River*

Heine, (Christian Johann) Heinrich [hiynuh] (1797–1856) Poet and essayist, born in Düsseldorf, Germany, of Jewish parentage. He established his reputation with his four-volume *Reisebilder* (1826–7, 1830–1, Pictures of Travel) and *Das Buch der Lieder* (1827, The Book of Songs). He later became leader of the cosmopolitan democratic movement, writing widely on French and German culture.

Heinz, H(enry) J(ohn) [hiynts] (1844–1919) Food manufacturer and packer, born in Pittsburgh, PA. His company was founded in 1876, introducing the famous slogan '57 varieties' 20 years later.

Heisenberg, Werner (Karl) [hiyznberg] (1901–76) Theoretical physicist, born in Würzburg. He helped to develop quantum mechanics, and formulated the revolutionary principle of indeterminacy in nuclear physics (1927). He received the Nobel Prize for Physics in 1932.

Hel or **Hela** In Norse mythology, the youngest child of Loki. She was assigned by Odin to rule **Helheim** (the Underworld).

Helen In Greek legend, the wife of Menelaus of Sparta, famous for her beauty; her abduction by Paris the Trojan caused the Trojan War. She was the daughter of Zeus and Leda, in mythical accounts.

Helena, St (c.255–c.330) Mother of the Roman Emperor Constantine (the Great), born in Bithynia, Asia Minor. She early became a Christian, and in 326, according to tradition, visited Jerusalem, where she founded the basilicas on the Mount of Olives and at Bethlehem. Feast day 18 August (W), 21 May (E).

Helfgott, David [helfgot] (1947–) Pianist, born in Melbourne, Victoria, Australia. After a nervous breakdown, he developed a mood disorder which left him with a distinctive mode of playing often accompanied by vocalization. His life-story was dramatized in the film *Shine* (1995). A world tour in 1997 received a cool reception from music critics, but sell-out support and enthusiasm from the public.

helical scan A system of magnetic tape recording in which the tape is wrapped in a partial helix around a drum carrying two or more rotating heads which trace a series of tracks diagonally across its width. It enables very high frequencies to be recorded economically.

Helicon [helikon] The largest mountain in Boeotia. In Greek mythology, it was the sacred hill of the Muses, whose temple was to be found there.

helicopter A vertical take-off and landing aircraft whose lift is provided by means of a horizontal, large-diameter set of powered blades which force the air downwards and by reaction create a lifting force upwards. Forward flight is achieved by tilting the plane of the blades in the direction of flight, varying their angle to the horizontal as they rotate.

Heligoland, Ger **Helgoland** 54°09N 7°52E, pop (2000e) 3640. Rocky North Sea island of the North Frisian Is, Germany; area 2·1 km²/0·8 sq mi; captured from Denmark by the UK, 1807;

ceded to Germany in exchange for Zanzibar, 1890; German naval base in both World Wars.

heliocentric system Any theory of our planetary system that has the Sun at the centre. It was proposed by Aristarchus in the 3rd-c BC, and revived with great success by Copernicus in 1543.

Helios [heelios] In Greek mythology, the Sun-god, represented as a charioteer with four horses. In the late classical period, there was an Imperial cult of the sun, *Sol Invictus*.

heliotrope A small evergreen shrub (*Heliotropium peruvianum*) 0·5–2 m/1½–6½ ft, a native of Peru; flowers small, tubular, with spreading lobes, white to lilac or violet, in terminal clusters. (Family: Boraginaceae.)

helium He, element 2, the most inert of the chemical elements, forming no stable compounds; the lightest of the *noble* or *inert* gases. It condenses to a liquid only at −269°C (4 K). Because of its inertness and low density (less than 15% of the density of air), it is used to fill balloons. Liquid helium is used as the ultimate coolant, and was important in the discovery of super-conductivity.

hell In traditional Christian thought, the eternal abode and place of torment of the damned. Much contemporary Christian thought rejects the idea of vindictive punishment as incompatible with belief in a loving God. The emphasis acccordingly shifts from hell as a place of retribution to a state of being without God.

hellebore [helibaw(r)] A perennial with glossy divided leaves and large flowers, native to Europe and W Asia; flowers with five green, white, or pinkish-purple petaloid sepals, and up to 20 prominent 2-lipped nectar-secreting glands; highly poisonous. (Genus: *Helleborus*, 20 species. Family: Ranunculaceae.)

helleborine [heliborin] Either of two closely related genera of orchids. *Epipactis* (24 species), from N temperate regions and parts of the tropics, has stalked flowers in which the lower lip forms a nectar-containing cup with a tongue-like extension. *Cephalanthera* (12 species), from N temperate regions, has stalkless flowers which never open fully. (Family: Orchidaceae.)

Hellenistic Age The period from the death of Alexander the Great (323 BC) to the beginning of the Roman Empire (31 BC), during which a number of Greek or Hellenized dynasties ruled the entire area from Greece to the N of India.

Heller, Joseph (1923–99) Novelist, born in New York City. His wartime experience formed the background for his first novel, *Catch-22* (1961), which was an immediate success; a sequel, *Closing Time*, appeared in 1994. Other books include *Something Happened* (1974), *Picture This* (1988), and the autobiographical *Now and Then* (1998).

Hellespont *Dardanelles*

Hell's Canyon or **Grand Canyon of the Snake** Gorge on the Snake R, USA; with a depth of c.2450 m/8030 ft, it is one of the deepest gorges in the world; length 65 km/40 mi.

Helmholtz, Hermann von (1821–94) Physiologist and physicist, born in Potsdam, Germany. The key figure in the development of science in Germany in the later 19th-c, his works are principally connected with the eye, the ear, and the nervous system. He is best known for his statement of the law of the conservation of energy.

helminthology The study of parasitic worms (**helminths**), including roundworms, flatworms, and their larval stages.

Helmont, Jan Baptista van (1579–1644) Chemist, born in Brussels. He invented the term *gas*, and was the first to take the melting point of ice and the boiling point of water as standards for temperature.

Héloïse *Abelard, Peter*

Helpmann, Sir Robert (Murray) (1909–86) Dancer, actor, and choreographer, born in Mount Gambier, South Australia, Australia. He was first dancer of the newly founded Sadler's Wells Ballet (1933–50), and also appeared in many films.

Helsingborg, Swed **Hälsingborg** 56°03N 12°43E, pop (2000e) 115 000. Seaport and commercial town in SW Sweden; opposite Helsingør, Denmark; railway; ferry services to Denmark.

Helsingfors [helsingfaw(r)z] *Helsinki*

Helsingør *Elsinore*

Helsinki [helsingkee], Swed **Helsingfors** 60°08N 25°00E, pop (2000e) 507 000. Seaport capital of Finland; founded by Gustavus Vasa in 1550; capital, 1812; heavily bombed in World War 2; airport; railway; university (transferred from Turku, 1828); technical university (1908); cathedral (completed 1852).

Helvellyn [helvelin] 54°32N 3°02W. Mountain in the Lake District of Cumbria, NW England; rises to 950 m/3117 ft; Striding Edge descends to the E.

Helvetii [helwaytiee] Celtic people forced S by Germanic tribesmen in the 2nd-c BC into modern Switzerland. The official names for Switzerland derive from this source: *Helvetia* and *Confederatio Helvetica*.

hem- *haem-*

hemichordate A bottom-living, marine invertebrate with gill slits in its pharynx similar to those of primitive vertebrates; includes the acornworms and graptolites. (Phylum: Hemichordata.)

Hemingway, Ernest (Miller) (1899–1961) Writer, born in Oak Park, IL. His major novels include *A Farewell to Arms* (1929), *For Whom the Bell Tolls* (1940), and *The Old Man and the Sea* (1952, Pulitzer). In 1954 he was awarded the Nobel Prize for Literature.

hemione *ass*

hemiplegia *paralysis*

Hemiptera [hemiptera] A group of insects comprising two orders, the Homoptera and the Heteroptera.

hemispheric specialization *laterality*

hemlock 1 An evergreen conifer native to North America and E Asia; branches drooping. It yields timber, Canada pitch, and tanning bark. (Genus: *Tsuga*, 15 species. Family: Pinaceae.) **2** A biennial growing to 2·5 m/8 ft, native to Europe and temperate Asia; stem hollow, furrowed, spotted with purple; flowers white; fruit ovoid; a fetid smell; all parts very poisonous; used as a poison since classical times. (*Conium maculatum*. Family: Umbelliferae.)

hemo- *haemo-*

hemp *abaca; cannabis*

Hempleman-Adams, David (1956–) British explorer and expedition leader, born in Swindon, Wiltshire. In 1998, he completed the explorer's 'Grand Slam', having reached the North and South Geographic and Magnetic Poles (in 1996) and climbed the highest mountain on each continent, including Mount Everest in 1993. He is the first person to fly a balloon over the Andes (1998) and the North Pole (2000), and the first person to cross the Atlantic solo in an open wicker basket (2003). In March 2004 he claimed a new altitude record of 12 800 m (42 000 ft) for an ascent in a Roziere balloon with wicker basket near Denver, USA.

hen *domestic fowl*

henbane An annual or biennial (*Hyoscyamus niger*), sticky-haired and fetid, native to Europe, W Asia, and N Africa; petals 5-lobed, lurid yellow and purple; poisonous. Its extracts are still used in modern medicine, mainly as sedatives. (Family: Solanaceae.)

Henderson, Fletcher (1897–1952) Pianist, arranger, and jazz bandleader, born in Cuthbert, GA. In 1924 he put together a big band, attracting the finest instrumentalists and arrangers of the time. His orchestrations helped set the standard for the swing era.

Hendrix, Jimi, popular name of **James Marshall Hendrix** (1942–70) Rock guitarist, singer, and songwriter, born in Seattle, WA. He explored electronic tricks on his guitar at ear-splitting amplitude, to which he added stage gimmicks, playing behind his back or with his teeth. His raucous blues style influenced heavy metal bands.

Hendry, Stephen (Gordon) (1969–) Snooker player, born in Edinburgh. He became a professional in 1985, and dominated the game in the 1990s. His wins include seven Embassy world championships (1990, 1992–6, 1999). In 1997–8 he won his 29th ranking event, but lost his number 1 world record ranking position to John Higgins. In 2003 he added the British Open title to his achievements. In 2007 he compiled his 700th century, a record in professional competition.

Hengist and **Horsa** Brothers, leaders of the first Anglo-Saxon settlers in Britain, said by Bede to have been invited over by Vortigern, the British king, to fight the Picts in about AD 450.

Henie, Sonja [henee] (1912–69) Figure skater, born in Oslo. The winner of three Olympic gold medals (1928, 1932, 1936), she also won a record 10 individual world titles (1927–36).

Henin-Hardenne, Justine [aynī ah(r)den], *née* **Justine Henin** (1982–) Tennis player, born in Liège, Belgium. She won her first WTA Tour event as a professional at Antwerp in 1999. In 2003 she won her first two Grand Slam events, the French Open and the US Open. At the beginning of 2004 she was ranked world number 1 and her further achievements include the Australian Open (2004) and French Open (2005, 2006). She was world number 1 again at the start of 2007.

Henley Royal Regatta Rowing races which take place annually on the R Thames at Henley-on-Thames, Oxfordshire, UK, inaugurated in 1839. It is as much an elegant social occasion for the public as a sporting one.

Henman, Tim(othy) (1974–) Tennis player, born in Oxford, Oxfordshire. He turned professional in 1993, his achievements including the British National Championships (singles and men's doubles, 1995–6, singles 1996). He had become Britain's number 1 player by early 1997, and although he lost this position to Greg Rusedski later that year, he regained it during 1998. He reached the semi-finals at Wimbledon in 1998, 1999, 2001, and 2002, and rose to fourth in the world rankings in 2002. He won the Paris Masters in 2003. At the beginning of 2005 he had a world ranking of 7, but this had fallen to 39 in 2007.

henna An evergreen shrub (*Lawsonia inermis*) growing to 3 m/10 ft, native to the Old World tropics; flowers 4-petalled, white, pink, or red; fruit a 3-chambered capsule. The powdered leaves produce a red dye, used as a cosmetic for skin and hair since ancient times. (Family: Lythraceae.)

Henrietta Maria (1609–69) Queen of Charles I of England, born in Paris, the youngest child of Henry IV of France. She married Charles in 1625, but her French attendants and Roman Catholic beliefs made her unpopular. In 1642, under the threat of impeachment, she fled to Holland and raised funds for the Royalist cause.

Henry I (of England) (1068–1135) King of England (1100–35) and Duke of Normandy (1106–35), the youngest son of William the Conqueror. Under Henry, the Norman Empire attained the height of its power. He nominated his daughter Empress Matilda as his heir for both England and Normandy, but after Henry's death the crown was seized by Stephen, son of his sister, Adela.

Henry II (of England) (1133–89) King of England (1154–89), born in Le Mans, France, the son of Empress Matilda, Henry I's daughter and acknowledged heir, by her second husband Geoffrey of Anjou. He founded the Angevin or Plantagenet dynasty of English kings, and ruled England as part of a wider Angevin Empire. His efforts to restrict clerical independence caused conflict with his former Chancellor Thomas Becket, Archbishop of Canterbury, which was ended only with Becket's murder (1170). He led a major expedition to Ireland (1171), which resulted in its annexation.

Henry II (of France) (1519–59) King of France (1547–59), born near Paris, the second son of Francis I, who became heir to the throne in 1536. He formed an alliance with Scotland, and declared war against England, which ended in 1558 with the taking of Calais. He also continued the long-standing war against the Emperor Charles V.

Henry III (of England) (1207–72) King of England (1216–72), the elder son and successor, at the age of nine, of John. His arbitrary assertion of royal rights conflicted with the principles of Magna Carta, and antagonized many nobles. Simon de Montfort and the barons rebelled, and captured the king at Lewes (1264), but were defeated at Evesham (1265).

Henry III (of France) (1551–89) King of France (1574–89), born in Fontainebleau, the third son of Henry II. His reign was a period of almost incessant civil war between Huguenots and Catholics. In 1588 he engineered the assassination of the Duke of Guise, enraging the Catholic League. He joined forces with the Huguenot Henry of Navarre, and while marching on Paris was assassinated.

Henry IV (of England), originally **Henry Bolingbroke** (1366–1413) King of England (1399–1413), the first king of the House of Lancaster, the son of John of Gaunt, who was the fourth son of Edward III. He was surnamed **Bolingbroke**, from his birthplace in Lincolnshire. In 1397 he supported Richard II against the Duke of Gloucester, but was banished in 1398. On returning to England, he induced Richard to abdicate in his favour. Henry's attack on Scotland in 1400 ended in his defeat. Henry Percy (Hotspur) and his house joined with the Scots and the Welsh against him, but they were defeated at Shrewsbury (1403).

Henry IV (of France), originally **Henry of Navarre** (1553–1610) The first Bourbon king of France (1589–1610), born in Pau, France. He became leader of the Protestant Party, and after the massacre of St Bartholomew's Day (1572) was spared by professing himself a Catholic. In 1576 he revoked his conversion, and resumed command of the army in opposition to the Catholic League. On his accession, he became a Catholic again, thereby unifying the country, and granted Protestants liberty of conscience.

Henry V (of England) (1387–1422) King of England (1413–22), born in Monmouth, Monmouthshire, the eldest son of Henry IV. The main effort of his reign was his claim to the French crown. In 1415 he invaded France, and won the Battle of Agincourt against great odds. He was recognized as heir to the French throne and Regent of France, and married Charles VI's daughter, Catherine of Valois.

Henry VI (of England) (1421–71) King of England (1422–61, 1470–1), born in Windsor, S England, the only child of Henry V and Catherine of Valois. Although crowned King of France in Paris in 1431, he gradually lost England's French conquests. Richard, Duke of York, seized power as Lord Protector in 1454, and defeated the king's army at St Albans (1455), the first battle of the Wars of the Roses. York's heir was proclaimed king as Edward IV after Henry's deposition (1461). In 1464 Henry returned from exile in Scotland to lead the Lancastrian cause, but was captured and imprisoned (1465–70). Richard Neville, Earl of Warwick, restored him to the throne (Oct 1470), his nominal rule ending when Edward IV returned to London (Apr 1471). After the Yorkist victory at Tewkesbury (May 1471), where his only son was killed, Henry was murdered in the Tower.

Henry VII (of England) (1457–1509) King of England (1485–1509), born at Pembroke Castle, Pembrokeshire. His claim to the throne was traced back through his father, Edmund Tudor, the younger son of Catherine of France and the Welshman Owen Tudor. Through his mother, Margaret Beaufort, Henry claimed descent from Edward III's son, John of Gaunt, and Katherine Swynford. He founded the Tudor dynasty by defeating Richard III at Bosworth in 1485. As king, his policy was to restore peace and prosperity to the country, and this was helped by his marriage of reconciliation with Elizabeth of York. Peace was concluded with France, and the marriage of his heir to Catherine of Aragon cemented an alliance with Spain.

Henry VIII (of England) (1491–1547) King (1509–47), born in Greenwich, Greater London, the second son of Henry VII. Soon after his accession he married Catherine of Aragon. From 1527 he determined to divorce Catherine, whose children, except for Mary, had died in infancy, and in defiance of the Roman Catholic Church was privately married to Anne Boleyn (1533). In 1534 it was enacted that his marriage to Catherine was invalid, and that the king was the Supreme Head of the English Church. In 1536 Catherine died, and Anne Boleyn was executed for infidelity. Henry then married Jane Seymour (c.1509–37), who died leaving a son, afterwards Edward VI. In 1540 Anne of Cleves became his fourth wife, in the hope of attaching the Protestant interest of Germany; but dislike of her appearance caused him to divorce her speedily. He then married Catherine Howard (1540), who two years later was executed on grounds of infidelity (1542). In 1543 his last marriage was to Catherine Parr, who survived him. His later years saw ineffectual and expensive wars with France and Scotland, but a powerful English navy was created.

Henry the Navigator (1394–1460) Portuguese prince, the third son of John I, King of Portugal, and Philippa, daughter of John of Gaunt, Duke of Lancaster. He sponsored many exploratory expeditions along the W African coast.

Henry, Joseph (1797–1878) Physicist, born in Albany, NY. He discovered electrical induction independently of Faraday, and constructed the first electromagnetic motor (1829). The unit of inductance is named after him.

Henry, Lenny, popular name of **Lenworth George Henry** (1958–) Comedian and actor, born in Dudley, West Midlands. He joined the children's television show *Tiswas* in the 1970s, and went on to star in his own BBC television series the *Lenny Henry Show* (1984–95) and *Chef* (from 1992). He also hosts the annual BBC *Comic Relief* telethon. He is married to Dawn French.

Henry, O, pseudonym of **William Sydney Porter** (1862–1910) Writer, master of the short story, born in Greensboro, NC. His stories provide a romantic and humorous treatment of everyday life, and are noted for their use of coincidence and trick endings.

Henry, Patrick (1736–99) American revolutionary and statesman, born in Studley, VA. He was outspoken in his opposition to British policy towards the colonies, and he made the first speech in the Continental Congress (1774).

Henry, Thierry (Daniel) [onree] (1977–) Footballer, born in Les Ulis, Paris. He was admitted to France's football academy, Clairefontaine, at the age of 13, and within four years was playing for the French first division side AS Monaco (1994–9). He signed for Arsenal in 1999. His honours include the Professional Football Association Player of the Year (2003, 2004), a record three-times Football Writers' Association Player of the Year (2003, 2004, 2006), and twice runner-up FIFA World Player of the Year (2003, 2004). In 2005 his 186th goal for Arsenal made him the club's leading goal scorer, breaking the record previously held by Ian Wright. He gained his 85th cap as member of France's 2006 World Cup squad, his team losing the final to Italy.

henry SI unit of inductance; symbol *H*; named after Joseph Henry; defined as the inductance of a closed circuit in which a current changing at the rate of 1 ampere per second produces an electromotive force (emf) of 1 volt.

Henry's law In chemistry, a law formulated by British chemist William Henry (1774–1836): the solubility of a gas in a liquid at any given temperature is proportional to the pressure of the gas on the liquid.

Henryson, Robert [henrison] (c.1425–1508) Scottish mediaeval poet. His works include *The Testament of Cresseid*, and a metrical version of 13 *Morall Fabels of Esope*, often viewed as his masterpiece.

Henslowe, Philip (c.1550–1616) Theatre manager, born in Lindfield, West Sussex. In 1587 he built the Rose Theatre on the Bankside, London. His business diary (1593–1609) contains invaluable information about the stage of Shakespeare's day.

Henson, Jim, popular name of **James Maury Henson** (1936–90) Puppeteer, born in Greenville, MS. His 'Muppets' (Marionettes/puppets) achieved nationwide popularity on the children's television workshop, *Sesame Street*, from 1969, and *The Muppet Show* (1976–81), appearing also in a string of films and on a Grammy-winning album (1979). Later series included *Fraggle Rock* (from 1983) and *The Storyteller* (from 1987).

Henze, Hans Werner [hentsuh] (1926–) Composer, born in Gütersloh, Germany. He was influenced by Schoenberg, exploring beyond the more conventional uses of the 12-tone system. His works include operas, ballets, symphonies, and chamber music.

heparin [heparin] A chemical substance (a polysaccharide) found in the mast cells of the liver, lungs, and intestinal mucosa. It prevents blood clotting.

hepatitis *infectious hepatitis*

Hepburn, Audrey, originally **Eda van Heemstra** (1929–93) Actress and film star, born in Brussels, Belgium. She was given the lead in the Broadway production of *Gigi* (1951), and went on to win international acclaim for *Roman Holiday* (1953, Oscar). Other popular film roles included *The Nun's Story* (1959) and *Breakfast at Tiffany's* (1961).

Hepburn, Katharine (Houghton) (1907–2003) Actress, born in Hartford, CT. From 1932 she attained international fame as a film actress, notably in *Morning Glory* (1933), *Guess Who's Coming to Dinner* (1967), *The Lion in Winter* (1968), and *On Golden Pond* (1981), all of which gained her Oscars, and *The African Queen* (1952).

Hephaestus [hefeestus] In Greek mythology, a god of fire, associated with volcanic sites; then of the smithy and metalwork. He was the son of Hera, who was annoyed at his lameness and threw him out of heaven.

heptane C_7H_{16}. An alkane hydrocarbon with seven carbon atoms. There are nine structural isomers, most of which occur in the gasoline fraction of petroleum.

heptathlon A multi-event track-and-field competition, discipline for women. It consists of seven events: 100 m hurdles, shot put, high jump, 200 m, long jump, javelin, and 800 m. The world record of 7291 points was set by Jacqueline Joyner-Kersee (1962–) of the USA, at Seoul, South Korea, in 1988.

Hepworth, Dame (Jocelyn) Barbara (1903–75) Sculptor, born in Wakefield, West Yorkshire. She was one of the foremost non-figurative sculptors of her time, as seen in her 'Contrapuntal Forms' (1951).

Hera [heera] In Greek mythology, the daughter of Cronus and wife of Zeus. She was associated with Argos and hostile to Troy.

Heracles [herakleez], Lat **Hercules** Greek hero, who undertook Twelve Labours for Eurystheus of Argos: (1) to kill the Nemean Lion, (2) to kill the Hydra of Lerna, (3) to capture the Hind of Ceryneia, (4) to capture the Boar of Erymanthus, (5) to clean the Stables of Augeas, (6) to shoot the Birds of Stymphalus, (7) to capture the Cretan Bull, (8) to capture the Horses of Diomedes, (9) to steal the Girdle of the Amazon, (10) to capture the oxen of the giant Geryon, (11) to fetch the Apples of the Hesperides, (12) to capture Cerberus, the guardian of Hades.

Heraclitus or **Heracleitos** [herakliytus] (?–460 BC) Greek philosopher, born in Ephesus. He thought that all things are composed of opposites, constantly at strife with one another, and thus in perpetual change. Only fragments of his writings survive.

Heraklion [heraklion], Gr **Iráklion**, Ital **Candia** 35°20N 25°08E, pop (2000e) 275 000. Administrative centre and capital town of Crete region (since 1971), S Greece; on N coast of Crete I; airfield; cathedral (19th-c); old city within Venetian walls (begun 1538).

heraldry The granting and designing of pictorial devices (*arms*) originally used on the shields of knights in armour to identify them in battle. The science of describing such devices is *blazonry*. Arms are regarded as insignia of honour, and their unauthorized display is subject to legal sanction in most European countries.

herb A plant with a distinctive smell or taste, used to enhance the flavour and aroma of food. Herbs are usually grown in temperate climates (whereas spices are usually tropical). Some are often used for their medicinal properties, hence the speciality of the **herbalist**.

herbaceous plant Any non-woody plant which dies at the end of the growing season; often referred to simply as **herb**. Herbaceous perennials die back to ground level, but survive as underground organs such as bulbs or tubers, sending up new growth in the spring.

herbalism The use of herbs to prevent and cure illness; also called **herbal medicine** or **phytotherapy**. The treatment is based upon a holistic assessment of the patient, and uses whole plants, or parts of plants, rather than separating and purifying the active constituents. A computerized data bank is now available, and a pharmacopoeia has been produced by the British Herbal Medical Association.

Herbert (of Cherbury), Edward Herbert, Baron (1583–1648) English soldier, statesman, and philosopher, born in Eyton, Shropshire, brother of George Herbert. He is regarded as the founder of English deism. His main works are *De veritate* (1624, On Truth), and *De religione Gentilium* (published 1663, On the Religion of the Gentiles).

Herbert, George (1593–1633) Clergyman and poet, born at Montgomery Castle, Powys, E Wales. His verse is collected in *The Temple* (1633), and his chief prose work, *A Priest to the Temple*, was published in *Remains* (1652).

herbicide A chemical compound which kills weeds. **Nonselective** herbicides may be used to kill all vegetation before cultivation and planting begin. Once the crop has emerged, **selective herbicides** target the troublesome weeds only.

herbivore [herbivaw(r)] An animal that feeds on vegetation – a label used especially of the large plant-eating mammals, such as the ungulates. Its teeth are typically adapted for grinding plants, and its gut is adapted for digesting cellulose.

Herculaneum [herkyulaynium] In Roman times, a prosperous town situated near Mt Vesuvius in SW Italy. It was destroyed in the volcanic eruption of AD 79 (now a world heritage site). A 10-year restoration project began in 2004.

Hercules (astronomy) [herkyuleez] A constellation in the N sky, the fifth-largest of all, but hard to recognize because its stars are faint.

Hercules (mythology) [herkyuleez] *Heracles*

Herder, Johann Gottfried von (1744–1803) Critic and poet, born in Mohrungen, Germany. He wrote on folksongs, poetry, and mythology, developing a historical method best seen in his masterpiece, *Ideen zur Geschichte der Menschheit* (1784–91, Outlines of a Philosophy on the History of Man). He was a major influence on Goethe and German Romanticism.

heredity *genetics*

Hereford [hereferd] 52°04N 2°43W, pop (2000e) 51 500. Administrative centre of Herefordshire (unitary authority from 1998), WC England; on the R Wye at the centre of a rich farming region; railway; cathedral (11th-c) contains the *Mappa Mundi*, a mediaeval map of the world; football league team, Hereford United.

Hereford and Worcester [hereferd, wuster] Former county (1974–98) of WC England, UK, created by the amalgamation of Herefordshire and Worcestershire; following local opposition, the separate status of the counties was restord in 1998.

Herefordshire [hereferdsheer] pop (2004e) 177 800; area 2180 km²/841 sq mi. County in WC England, UK (formerly Hereford and Worcester, 1974–98); bounded W by Monmouthshire and Powys in Wales; drained by Wye and Lugg Rivers; Malvern Hills to E; county town Hereford.

heresy False doctrine, or the formal denial of doctrine defined as part of a particular faith. If consciously adhered to, heresy entails excommunication. Total heresy or the rejection of all faith is termed **apostasy**.

Hereward, known as **Hereward the Wake** (?–c.1080) Anglo-Saxon thegn who led the last organized Anglo-Saxon resistance against the Norman invaders. He held the Isle of Ely against William the Conqueror for nearly a year (1070–1).

Hergé [herzhay], Fr [airzhay], pseudonym of **Georges Rémi** (1907–83) Strip cartoonist, the creator of 'Tintin' the boy detective, born in Etterbeek, C Belgium. He drew his first strip, *Totor*, for a boy scouts' weekly in 1926. He created the *Tintin* strip for the children's supplement of the newspaper *Le Vingtième Siècle*, using the pseudonym Hergé, a phonetic version of his initials, RG. In 2007 the Pompidou Centre in Paris staged an exhibition of original drawings and colour plates to mark the 100th anniversary of his birth.

herm *term*

Herman, Woody, popular name of **Woodrow Charles Herman** (1913–87) Jazz musician, bandleader, singer, and composer, born in Milwaukee, WI. Playing clarinet and alto saxophone, he formed the white swing band called **the Woodchoppers** in 1936, following this with the first **Herman's Herd** in 1944.

Hermandszoon, Jakob *Arminius, Jacobus*

hermaphrodite An animal or plant having both male and female reproductive organs. Species in which both sets of organs mature simultaneously often have mechanisms that prevent self-fertilization.

Hermaphroditus [hermafrodiytus] In Greek mythology, the son of Hermes and Aphrodite. The nymph Salmacis, unloved by him, prayed to be united with him; this was granted by combining them in one body.

hermeneutics [hermenyootiks] The theory of the interpretation and understanding of texts. Though its origins lie in ancient Greek philosophy, hermeneutics received fresh impetus in 18th-c discussions of the problems of biblical interpretation. It now includes many fields, including literary theory, the social sciences, and aesthetics.

Hermes (astronomy) [hermeez] An asteroid which came within 760 000 km/475 000 mi of Earth in 1937, at that time a record. It was only a few km in diameter.

Hermes (mythology) [hermeez] In Greek mythology, the ambassador of the gods, the son of Zeus and Maia; depicted with herald's staff and winged sandals. He is variously associated with stones, commerce, roads, cookery, and thieving; also arts such as gymnastics.

Hermitage A major art gallery in St Petersburg, Russia, built in the 18th–19th-c to house the art collection of the tsars, and opened to the public in 1852. After the deposition of the tsar, this became the headquarters of Kerensky's provisional government, but was stormed by the Bolsheviks (Nov 1917). It now contains over 3 million works of art, and almost 400 rooms.

hermit crab A crab-like crustacean which uses an empty snail shell as a portable refuge covering its soft abdomen; it changes shells as it grows. (Class: Malacostraca. Order: Decapoda.)

hernia The protrusion of tissue from its natural site through an adjacent orifice or tissue space. Examples are *inguinal, femoral,* and *umbilical* herniae, in which abdominal contents such as intestines push through weak sites in the abdominal wall; the herniae emerge as externally protruding masses in the groin, over the upper thigh, and at the navel, respectively.

Hero of Alexandria (1st-c) Greek mathematician and inventor. He devised many machines, among them the 'aeolipile', the earliest known steam engine. He also devised the formula for expressing the area of a triangle in terms of its sides.

Hero and Leander [heeroh, leeander] A Greek legend first found in the Roman poet, Ovid. Two lovers lived on opposite sides of the Hellespont; Hero was the priestess of Aphrodite at Sestos, and Leander, who lived at Abydos, swam across each night guided by her light. When this was extinguished in a storm, he was drowned, and Hero committed suicide by throwing herself into the sea.

Herod [herod], known as **the Great** (c.73–4 BC) King of Judea, the younger son of the Idumaean chieftain, Antipater. He owed his initial appointment as Governor of Galilee (47 BC) to Julius Caesar, and his elevation to the kingship of Judea (40 BC) to Marcus Antonius. An able administrator, he did much to develop the economic potential of his kingdom. His cruelty is reflected in the Gospel account of the Massacre of the Innocents.

Herod Agrippa I [herod agripa] (10 BC–AD 44) King of Judaea (41–4), the grandson of Herod the Great, reared at the court of the Emperor Augustus. Caligula gave him two thirds of the former kingdom of Herod the Great, while Claudius added the remaining third (41). He executed St James and imprisoned St Peter.

Herod Agrippa II [herod agripa] (c.27–c.93) King of Chalcis (49/50–53), ruler of the Ituraean principality (53–c.93), the son of Herod Agrippa I. A supporter of Rome in the Jewish War (66–70), he was rewarded for it afterwards with grants of land in Judaea. It was before him that St Paul made his defence and was found innocent.

Herod Antipas [herod antipas] (?–AD 39) The son of Herod the Great and ruler (tetrarch) of Galilee and Peraea (4–39) after Herod's death. In the Christian tradition, he looms large as the capricious murderer of John the Baptist.

Herodotos or **Herodotus** [herodotus] (c.485–425 BC) Greek historian, born in Halicarnassus, Asia Minor. He travelled widely in the Middle East, collecting material for his great narrative history, which gave a record of the wars between the Greeks and the Persians.

heroin or **diamorphine** A derivative of morphine developed in 1896, and soon found to be extremely addictive. It is used to ease the severe pain that can accompany terminal illness, but even this medical use is banned in the USA. It is widely abused.

heron A wading bird related to the bittern; worldwide (mainly tropical); flies with neck retracted, not extended. (Family: Ardeidae, 64 species.)

Herophilus [herofilus] (c.335–c.280 BC) Greek anatomist, born in Chalcedon. He was the first to dissect the human body, and to compare it with that of other animals.

herpes labialis *cold sore*

herpes simplex [herpeez simpleks] A viral infection which affects the lips, the mouth, or the genital region. Recurrent attacks are common, between which the virus lies dormant.

herpes zoster *shingles*

Herrick, Robert (1591–1674) Poet, born in London. His writing is mainly collected in *Hesperides* (1648), and includes such well-known lyrics as 'Cherry ripe'.

herring Surface-living marine fish (*Clupea harengus*) abundant in the N Atlantic and Arctic; body length up to 40 cm/16 in; colour deep blue on back, underside silvery white; supports important commercial fisheries, being sold fresh, smoked as kippers or bloaters, or preserved in salt or vinegar; first-year herring sold as whitebait; during the 1990s, there was increasing international concern over reduced stocks, and controversy over fishing quotas. (Family: Clupeidae.)

Herriot, James, pseudonym of **James Alfred Wight** (1916–95) Veterinary surgeon and writer, born in Glasgow, W Scotland. Beginning in the 1970s, he brought the vet's world to the notice of the public with a number of best-selling books, such as *It Shouldn't Happen to a Vet*. Feature films and television series made his work known all over the world, especially the television series *All Creatures Great and Small* (1977–80). The stories prompted a thriving tourist industry based on 'Herriot country', and transformed the public image of his profession, making veterinary medicine one of the most competitive university subjects. In 1992 he was the first recipient of the Chiron Award, created by the British Veterinary Association for exceptional service to the profession.

Herschel, Sir (Frederick) William [hershl], originally **Friedrich Wilhelm Herschel** (1738–1822) Astronomer, born in Hanover, Germany. He built the largest reflecting telescopes made at the time, discovered Uranus in 1781, extensively observed double stars, and produced a notable star catalogue.

Hershko, Avram (1937–) Biologist born in Karcag, Hungary. Professor at the Unit of Biochemistry, the Rappaport Family Institute for Research in Medical Sciences at the Technion in Haifa (1980–), in 2004 he shared the Nobel Prize for Chemistry for the discovery of ubiquitin-mediated protein degradation.

Hertford [hah(r)tferd] 51°48N 0°05W, pop (2000e) 23 500. County town in Hertfordshire, SE England; railway; castle (12th-c).

Hertfordshire [hah(r)tferdsheer] pop (2001e) 1 034 000; area 1634 km²/631 sq mi. County of SE England; county town, Hertford.

Hertz, Heinrich (Rudolf) (1857–1894) Physicist, born in Hamburg, Germany. His main work was on electromagnetic waves (1887), and he discovered radio waves. The unit of frequency is named after him.

hertz SI unit of frequency; symbol *Hz*; named after Heinrich Hertz; defined as the number of complete cycles per second.

Hertzog, J(ames) B(arry) M(unnik) [hertzokh] (1866–1942) South African statesman and prime minister (1924–39), born in Wellington, Cape Colony, South Africa. In 1914 he founded the Nationalist Party, advocating complete South African independence. As premier, he pursued a legislative programme which destroyed the African franchise, and tightened land segregation.

Hertzsprung–Russell diagram [hertshprung]

Hertzsprung-Russell diagram *p.428*

Herzl, Theodor [hertsl] (1860–1904) Zionist leader, born in Budapest. He was converted to Zionism, and in the pamphlet *Judenstaat* (1896, The Jewish State) called for a world council to discuss the question of a homeland for the Jews. He became the first president of the World Zionist Organization.

Herzog, Werner [hertzog], originally **Werner Stipetic** (1942–) Film director, screenwriter, and producer, born in Sachrang, Germany. He became recognized as a leading member of the New Cinema in Germany with his feature *Aguirre, der Zorn Gottes* (1973, Aguirre, Wrath of God). His general themes are metaphysical in character, often with remoteness in time or location, as in *Where the Green Ants Dream* (1984). Later films include *The White Diamond* (2004) and *Rescue Dawn* (2006).

Heselrig, Sir Arthur *Haselrig, Arthur*

Heseltine, Michael (Ray Dibdin), Lord [heseltiyn] (1933–) British Conservative statesman, born in Swansea, S Wales. He was appointed secretary of state for the environment (1979–83), and then defence secretary (1983–6). He resigned from the government in dramatic fashion by walking out of a cabinet meeting over the issue of the takeover of Westland helicopters. He

Hertzsprung–Russell diagram

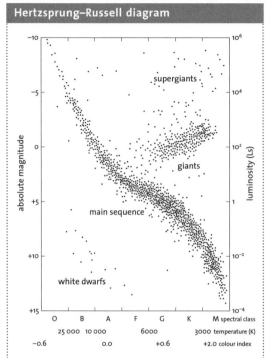

[hertshprung] The graphical representation of the correlation between the spectrum and luminosity for a sample of stars, discovered independently by Danish astronomer Ejnar Hertzsprung (1873–1967) and US astronomer Henry Norris Russell (1877–1957). The diagram achieves its astrophysical significance when the plotted points are restricted to a particular sample (such as all the members of a star cluster) or a particular type (such as one class of variable star). It then effectively graphs surface temperature against luminosity. In the diagram, normal stars that are burning hydrogen form a broad band known as the *main sequence*. Evolved stars clump together as red giants. Almost defunct stars are grouped as white dwarfs. The theory of stellar evolution explains the main features of the diagram.

stood unsuccessfully as a candidate in the leadership contest following Mrs Thatcher's resignation (1990), and under John Major became environment secretary (1990–2), President of the Board of Trade (1992–5), and deputy prime minister (1995–7). He was made a Companion of Honour in 1997.

Hesiod [heesiod] (fl.8th-cBC) Greek poet, born in Ascra. His *Works and Days* deals with the farmer's life; *Theogony* teaches the origin of the universe and the history of the gods.

Hesperides [hesperideez] In Greek mythology, the daughters of the evening star (**Hesper**), who guard the Golden Apples together with the dragon, Ladon.

Hess, Dame Myra (1890–1965) Pianist, born in London. An immediate success on her first public appearance in 1907, during World War 2 she organized the lunchtime concerts in the National Gallery.

Hess, (Walter Richard) Rudolf (1894–1987) German politician, Hitler's deputy as Nazi Party leader, born in Alexandria, Egypt. In 1941, he flew alone to Scotland to plead the cause of a negotiated Anglo-German peace. He was held in Britain until the Nuremberg Trials (1946) when he was sentenced to life imprisonment. He remained in Spandau prison, Berlin (after 1966, as the only prisoner) until his death.

Hesse [hesuh], Ger **Hessen** pop (2000e) 5 891 000; area 21 114 km²/8151 sq mi. A state formed in 1945 from the former Prussian province of Hesse-Nassau; wine produced along Rhine valley; capital, Wiesbaden.

Hesse, Hermann [hesuh] (1877–1962) Novelist and poet, born in Calw, Germany. His works include *Rosshalde* (1914), *Siddhartha* (1922), *Steppenwolf* (1927), and *Das Glasperlenspiel* (1945, The Glass Bead Game). He was awarded the Nobel Prize for Literature in 1946. His psychological and mystical concerns made him something of a cult figure after his death.

Hestia [hestia] Greek goddess of the hearth, the daughter of Cronus and Rhea.

Heston, Charlton, originally **John Charles Carter** (1924–) Actor, born in Evanston, IL. De Mille's *The Greatest Show on Earth* (1951) and *The Ten Commandments* (1956) brought him great success, and he won an Oscar for *Ben Hur* (1959). He continued in heroic roles, his later films including *The Awakening* (1980), *True Lies* (1994), and *Any Given Sunday* (1999). He has played a prominent role in US arts, theatre, and cinema organizations. He received the inaugural Charlton Heston Prize in 2003, awarded by the American Film Institute.

Heteroptera [heteroptera] A large order of insects comprising the true bugs; body typically depressed, forewings usually leathery at base and membranous at tip; mouthparts modified for piercing and sucking; c.35 000 species, including many crop pests and disease carriers.

Hewish, Antony (1924–) Radio astronomer, born in Fowey, Cornwall. With his student Susan Jocelyn (Burnell) Bell (1943–), he discovered the first pulsars. He shared the Nobel Prize for Physics in 1974 with his former teacher, Sir Martin Ryle.

Hewitt, Lleyton (1981–) Tennis player, born in Adelaide, South Australia. His wins include the Queen's Club Championship three years in succession (2000–2), the US Open singles title (2001), the ATP Tour World Championships (2001, 2002), and the 2002 Wimbledon singles title. At the start of 2007 he had a world ranking of 20.

Hewitt, Patricia (Hope) (1948–) British stateswoman, born in Canberra, Australia. She was general secretary of the National Council for Civil Liberties (1974–83), and deputy director of the Institute for Public Policy Research (1989–94). Elected a Labour MP in 1997, she served as minister for trade and industry (1997–8), economic secretary to the Treasury (1998–9), information technology minister (1999–2001), trade and industry secretary and minister for women (2001–5), and minister for health from 2005.

Hewson, John (1946–) Australian politician and economist, born in Sydney, New South Wales, Australia. He became shadow minister for finance (1988–9) and shadow treasurer (1989–90), and was elected leader of the Liberal Party (1990–4).

Hewson, Paul ⟩ **U2**

hexachlorophene [heksaklorofeen] $C_{13}H_6Cl_6O_2$. A white powder with antiseptic properties, widely used in toilet preparations.

hexadecanoic acid *palmitic acid*

hexadecimal coding A number notation using the number base 16. The 16 individual characters are 0–9, and A–F inclusive, representing decimal 10 to decimal 15 respectively. The notation provides a convenient means of writing binary numbers.

hexane C_6H_{14}. An alkane hydrocarbon with six carbon atoms. There are five structural isomers. The straight-chain compound, n-hexane, $CH_3CH_2CH_2CH_2CH_2CH_3$, has boiling point 69°C.

hexanedioic acid *adipic acid*

Heyer, Georgette [hayer] (1902–74) Writer, born in London. Her early work includes historical novels, and fictional studies of real figures in crisis, such as William I. An outstanding authority on the Regency period, she had success with *Regency Buck* (1935) and later novels.

Heyerdahl, Thor [hiyerdahl] (1914–2002) Anthropologist, born in Larvik, Norway. In 1947 he proved, by sailing a balsa raft (the *Kon-Tiki*) from Peru to Tuamotu I in the S Pacific, that the Peruvian Indians could have settled in Polynesia. In 1970 he sailed from Morocco to the West Indies in a papyrus boat, *Ra II*, and made the journey from Iraq to Djibouti in a reed boat, the *Tigris*, in 1977–8.

Heyhoe Flint, Rachel [hayhoh flint] (1939–) British cricketer. A member of the Women's England Cricket Team (1960–83, captain 1966–77), she captained England to victory in the first women's World Cup in 1973. She also played for the England women's hockey team as goalkeeper in 1964. She later became a journalist and public relations consultant.

Heysel stadium [hayzl] A football stadium in Brussels, Belgium; scene of a tragedy during the European Champions' Cup Final between Liverpool and Juventus (Turin) in 1985, when a wall and safety fence collapsed during a riot, killing 39 and injuring over 200. After that event, English football clubs were not allowed to play matches in Europe for several years – a ban which began to be lifted in 1990.

Heywood, Thomas (c.1574–1641) Playwright and poet, born in Lincolnshire, England. He shared in the composition of over 200 plays, and wrote 24 of his own, notably his domestic tragedy, *A Woman Killed with Kindness* (1607).

Hezbollah or **Hizbullah, Hizbollah** [hizbulah] (Arabic 'party of God') The largest of the Shiite Islamic fundamentalist parties in Lebanon. Under Iranian sponsorship, Hezbollah has called for the creation of an Islamic republic in Lebanon. The group was associated in particular with the kidnapping of Westerners to advance its political aims, some hostages were executed, though most were released. Hezbollah has been in conflict with Israeli forces in the south of Lebanon since the 1982 invasion by Israel. Lebanon became the scene of renewed fighting in 2006 when Israel launched a major military offensive against Hezbollah, sparked by the movement's capture of two Israeli soldiers. After a month-long war, in which Hezbollah displayed unanticipated resilience, the United Nations brokered a fragile ceasefire.

hiatus hernia [hiyaytus] A protrusion of the upper part of the stomach into the chest through the hole in the diaphragm that allows the oesophagus to pass into the abdomen. It is a common condition, and most individuals affected are untroubled. However, it predisposes to a reflux of acid from the stomach into the oesophagus, which lacks a protective lining and becomes inflamed, producing heartburn.

Hiawatha [hiyawotha], Indian name **Heowenta** (16th-c) The name of a real American Indian, used by Longfellow for his hero in *The Song of Hiawatha*. The poem retells Indian legends in the manner and metre of the Finnish *Kalevala*.

Hibbert, Eleanor (Alice Burford) (1906–93) Novelist, born in London. She was a prolific writer of romantic novels, writing under several pseudonyms. She began with **Eleanor Burford** (*Daughter of Anna*, 1941), and under the name of **Jean Plaidy** wrote over 40 historical novels, beginning with *Together They Ride* (1945). Her other pseudonyms were **Elbur Ford**, beginning with *The Flesh and the Devil* (1950), **Kathleen Kellow** (*Danse Macabre*, 1952), **Ellalice Tate** (*Queen of Diamonds*, 1958), **Victoria Holt** (*Mistress of Mellyn*, 1961), and **Philippa Carr** (*The Miracle at St Bruno's*, 1972).

hibernation A strategy for passing the cold winter period in a torpid or resting state, found in mammals and some other animals. The animal enters a deep sleep, surviving on food reserves stored in its body during a favourable summer period. The similar strategy for surviving a hot, dry summer is known as **aestivation**.

hibiscus An annual, perennial, or shrub native to warm regions; flowers often very large and showy, 5-petalled, the stamens united into a central column. (Genus: *Hibiscus*, 300 species. Family: Malvaceae.)

hiccup / hiccough An involuntary contraction of the diaphragm causing an intake of air which is halted by spasm (closure) of the glottis, thereby producing a sharp, characteristic, inspiratory sound. Its cause is unknown, but there are many folk-remedies, such as drinking from the 'wrong side of the glass'.

Hickock, Wild Bill *Calamity Jane*

hickory A tall deciduous tree, sometimes with shaggy bark, native to E Asia and E North America; flowers small, green, lacking petals; nut 4-valved, edible. (Genus: *Carya*, 25 species. Family: Juglandaceae.)

hidden curriculum The unwritten, informal code of conduct to which children are expected to conform in the classroom. Children are said to be rewarded not only for learning their subject curriculum but appearing to do so with enthusiasm, alertness, and deference to and respect for authority.

hieroglyphics *see panel*

hi-fi *high fidelity sound system*

Higgins, Alex(ander Gordon), nickname **Hurricane Higgins** (1949–) Snooker player, born in Belfast. He has had a tempestuous career since becoming the youngest world champion in 1972, at age 23. He won the title for a second time in 1982.

Higgins, John (1975–) Snooker player, born in Wishaw, Lanarkshire. He turned professional in 1992, his wins including the German Open (1995, 1997), the British Open (1995, 1998, 2004),

hieroglyphics

Egyptian Hieroglyphic

swallow		go	
beetle		find	
eat		fresh	
sun, sun god, daytime		moon, month	
star, hour, time to pray		mountain	
city, town		see	
pray, adore, praise		weep, grief	

The study of the symbols of ancient Egyptian writing; also, the symbols themselves. The characters were originally pictograms, and were named **hieroglyphs** (from the Greek 'sacred carving') because of their frequent use in religious contexts, such as temple and tomb inscriptions. The symbols are usually written from right to left, and were developed to represent three kinds of information: some are ideograms, representing objects or concepts in the real world; others stand for a consonant or consonant sequence; and a third type has no phonetic value, but serves to disambiguate a hieroglyph with more than one meaning.

the European Open (1997), and the LG Cup (2005). His win in the Embassy World Championship (1998) gave him the number 1 ranking position which he retained in 1999. He won the Masters title in 2006. When competing in the British Open tournament in 2003, he made history as the first player to compile maximum 147 breaks in successive matches.

Higgs particle In particle physics, a yet to be discovered particle implicated in the process of mass generation; named after British physicist Peter Higgs (1929–). It is assumed to be very heavy, and to have charge 0. Spontaneous symmetry breaking arises when the symmetry of the lowest energy state of a system is less than that of the interaction governing the system. The Higgs mechanism is the manifestation of symmetry breaking in quantum field theory, and shows how the breakdown of symmetry leads to massive particles where field theory alone predicts massless particles. Finding the Higgs particle, or **Higgs boson**, remains one of the great challenges of particle physics. However, in 2001 a CERN study concluded that it might not exist.

High Commissioner A person carrying out the same duties and possessing the same rank as an ambassador, representing one Commonwealth country in another Commonwealth country.

High Court (of Justice) A court established for England and Wales by the Judicature Acts (1873–5), principally a trial court for civil cases. It hears appeals on points of law from magistrates' courts in both civil and criminal cases, and also undertakes judicial review. In Scotland, the **High Court of Justiciary** is the supreme criminal court.

high-definition television (HDTV) Any television system using substantially more scanning lines than the 500–600 of established broadcast standards, with improved picture quality in a wide-screen format. For example, the Japanese NHK system, Hi-Vision, uses 1125 lines at 60 fields per second (60 Hz).

high energy physics *particle physics*

higher education *further education*

high fidelity sound system An assembly of sound reproduction components capable of regenerating an original musical performance to the highest attainable quality across the whole range of audible frequencies (20–20 000 Hz) and amplitudes; also known as **hi-fi**. It was a concept which emerged after World War 2, made possible by new record material (vinylite), stereophonic recording, and transistors. Digital recording, noise reduction, FM radio, and the compact disk were later embellishments.

high jump An athletics field event in which competitors attempt to clear a bar without any aids. The height of the bar is gradually increased, and competitors are allowed three attempts to clear each new height; they are eliminated if they fail. The current world record for men is 2·45 m/8 ft$\frac{1}{2}$ in, achieved by Javier Sotomayor (Cuba) in 1993 at Salamanca, Spain; for women, it is 2·09 m/6 ft 10$\frac{1}{4}$ in, achieved by Stefka Kostadinova (Bulgaria) in 1987 at Rome.

Highland pop (2000e) 213 100; area 25 391 km^2/9804 sq mi. Council in N Scotland, includes Inner Hebrides; sparsely inhabited region of great scenic beauty; Grampian, Monadhliath, and Cairngorm Mts; rises to 1344 m/4409 ft in Ben Nevis (SW); capital, Inverness.

Highland Games Athletic meetings held in Scotland; the first Games were organized in 1819. A range of events takes place, in addition to specifically Scottish events such as tossing the caber. The most famous meeting is the Braemar Gathering.

high-level language A computer language in which every instruction or statement is equivalent to several machine-code instructions. High-level languages, such as BASIC and PASCAL, are written using notations which are relatively easy for the user to understand.

high school The common form of secondary school in the USA

for 15–19-year-olds, following the **junior high school** phase for 11–15-year-olds. The schools are non-selective.

Highsmith, Patricia (1921–95) Writer, born in Fort Worth, TX. Her first novel was *Strangers on a Train* (1949, filmed 1957), but her best novels describe the criminal adventures of her psychotic hero Tom Ripley, beginning with *The Talented Mr Ripley* (1956, filmed 1999).

high-speed anti-radiation missile (HARM) A guided missile developed initially by the US Navy after Vietnam. HARMs are equipped with a 'homing head' designed to lock onto enemy ground-based radar transmitters.

high-speed photography The photographic recording of transient phenomena with very short periods of exposure. Electronic flash can be as brief as one-millionth of a second, and non-mechanical shutters (such as the polarizing Kerr cell) can operate 200 times faster. In cinematography the limit for mechanical intermittent film movement is about 600 pictures per second.

Hijra [hijra], formerly also spelled **Hegira** The migration of the Prophet Mohammed from Mecca to Medina in 622. The departure marks the beginning of the Muslim era.

Hilary (of Poitiers), St (c.315–c.368) Clergyman and Doctor of the Church, born in Limonum (Poitiers), France. A leading opponent of Arianism, his principal work is on the Trinity. His feast day marks the beginning of a term at Oxford and Durham universities, and English law sittings. Feast day 13 January.

Hildesheim [hildes-hiym] 52°09N 9°55E, pop (2000e) 108 000. Port in Germany; founded, 1300; railway; St Michael's Church (11th-c) and cathedral (1054–79), world heritage sites.

Hill, Benny, popular name of **Alfred Hawthorne Hill** (1925–92) Comedian, born in Southampton, Hampshire. Named TV personality of the year in 1954, he gained national popularity with the saucy *The Benny Hill Show* (1957–66), and spent over two decades writing and performing in top-rated television specials.

Hill, Damon (Graham Devereux) (1960–) Motor-racing driver, born in London, the son of Graham Hill. He drove for Brabham in his first Grand Prix at Silverstone in 1992, and went on to win over 20 grands prix in the next four years, succeeding Nigel Mansell on the Williams team. He took third place in the world championship in 1993, was runner-up in 1994, and won in 1996. The next season he joined the TWR Arrows Yamaha team, and in 1998 drove for the Benson & Hedges Jordan Mugen Honda team. He retired from Formula One in 1999.

Hill, Geoffrey (William) (1932–) Poet, born in Bromsgrove, Worcestershire. His works include *For the Unfallen* (1959), *The Mystery of the Charity of Charles Péguy* (1983), *The Triumph of Love* (1998), and *Selected Poems* (2006).

Hill, (Norman) Graham (1929–75) Motor-racing driver, born in London. He was world champion in 1962 (in a BRM) and in 1968 (Lotus), and won the Monaco Grand Prix five times (1963–5, 1968–9). His son, Damon, also went into motor-racing.

Hill, Octavia (1838–1912) Housing reformer and founder of the National Trust, born in Wisbech, Cambridgeshire. She worked among the London poor, and in 1864 commenced an influential project to improve the homes of working men in the slums.

Hill, Sir Rowland (1795–1879) Originator of penny postage, born in Kidderminster, Worcestershire. In his *Post-office Reform: its Importance and Practicability* (1837), he advocated a low and uniform rate of postage, to be prepaid by adhesive stamps, and in 1840 a uniform penny rate was introduced.

Hillary, Sir Edmund (Percival) (1919–) Mountaineer and explorer, born in Auckland, New Zealand. As a member of Hunt's Everest expedition he reached, with Tenzing Norgay, the summit of Mt Everest in 1953. With a New Zealand party he reached the South Pole in 1958. In 2003 he was granted honorary citizenship of

Nepal to mark the 50th anniversary of the first ascent of Mt Everest.

Hillel [hilel], known as **Hillel Hazaken** (the Elder), or **Hillel Haba-bli** ('the Babylonian') (1st-c BC–1st-c AD) One of the most respected Jewish teachers of his time, probably born in Babylonia. Noted for his use of seven rules in expounding Scripture, his views were influential for later rabbinic Judaism.

Hillery, Patrick (John) (1923–) Irish politician and president of the Irish Republic (1976–90), born in Co Clare. He was previously foreign minister (1969–72) and European Commissioner for social affairs (1973–6).

Hilliard, Nicholas (1547–1619) Court goldsmith and miniaturist, born in Exeter, Devon. He founded the English school of miniature painting.

Hillsborough Football stadium in Sheffield, England. It was the scene of the worst disaster in British sporting history, when 95 Liverpool fans died and 400 people were injured at the FA Cup semi-final match between Liverpool and Nottingham Forest (15 Apr 1989).

Hilton, Conrad (Nicholson) (1887–1979) Hotelier, born in San Antonio, NM. He formed the Hilton Hotels Corporation in 1946, diversifying the company in the 1950s to include car-rental and credit-card operations.

Hilton, James (1900–54) Novelist, born in Leigh, Lancashire. His books include *Lost Horizon* (1933, Hawthornden Prize), and *Goodbye Mr Chips* (1934).

Hilversum 52°14N 5°10E, pop (2000e) 89 000. City in W Netherlands; famous for its radio and television stations; fashionable residential district of Amsterdam; railway.

Himalayas [himahlyaz, himalayaz] Gigantic wall of mountains in C Asia; length over 2400 km/1500 mi; three main ranges, the Outer, Middle, and Inner Himalayas, which become five ranges in Kashmir; Mt Everest rises to 8848 m/29 028 ft on the Nepal–Tibet border; other major peaks include K2 in the Karakorams (8611 m/28 251 ft), Kangchenjunga (8586 m/28 169 ft); in Hindu mythology the mountains are highly revered.

Himalia [himahlia] The sixth natural satellite of Jupiter, discovered in 1904; distance from the planet 11 480 000 km/7 134 000 mi; diameter c.186 km/116 mi.

Himmler, Heinrich (1900–45) Nazi leader and chief of police, born in Munich, Germany. In 1929 he was made head of the SS (*Schutzstaffel*, 'protective force'), which he developed into a powerful party weapon, and also directed the secret police (*Gestapo*). He was captured by the Allies (1945), and committed suicide at Lüneburg.

Hindemith, Paul [hinduhmit] (1895–1963) Composer, born in Hanau, Germany. His works include operas, concertos, and a wide range of instrumental pieces. The modernity of his music caused it to be banned by the Nazis in 1934.

Hindenburg, Paul (Ludwig Hans Anton von Beneckendorff und) von [hindenberg] (1847–1934) German general and president (1925–34), born in Poznan, Poland (formerly Posen, Prussia). Recalled from retirement at the outbreak of World War 1, he won victories over the Russians (1914–15), but was forced to direct the German retreat on the Western Front (to the **Hindenburg line**). In 1933 he appointed Hitler as chancellor.

Hindenburg [hindnberg] A famous airship, of rigid-frame construction, built by the German government in 1936, capable of carrying 72 passengers in a style matching the ocean liners of the day. After 63 successful flights, it caught fire in May 1937 while coming in to moor in New Jersey.

Hindi *Indo-Aryan languages*

Hindley, Myra *Brady, Ian*

Hinduism [hinduizm] The Western term for a religious tradition developed during the first millennium and intertwined with the history and social system of India. It emphasizes the right way of living (*dharma*) rather than a set of doctrines, and thus embraces diverse religious beliefs and practices. Common to most forms is the idea of reincarnation or transmigration. *Samsara* refers to the process of birth and rebirth continuing for life after life. The particular form and condition (pleasant or unpleasant) of rebirth are the result of *karma*, the law by which the consequences of actions within one life are carried over into the next. The ultimate spiritual goal of Hindus is *mohsha*, or release from the cycle of *samsara*. No specific text is regarded as uniquely authoritative. The earliest extant writings come from the Vedic period (c.1200–500 BC), and are known collectively as the Veda. Later (c.500 BC–AD 500) came the religious law books which codified the classes of society (*varna*) and the four stages of life (*ashrama*). To these were added the great epics, the Ramayana and the Mahabharata. The latter includes one of the most influential Hindu scriptures, the Bhagavadgita. Brahma, Vishnu, and Shiva are the chief gods of Hinduism, and together form a triad (the *Trimurti*). There are numerous lesser deities, including the goddesses Maya and Lakshmi. There is a great emphasis upon the performance of complex and demanding rituals under the supervision of Brahman priests and teachers. There were over 840 million Hindus in 2007.

Hindu Kush [hindoo kush], ancient **Paropamisus** Mountain range in C Asia, an extension of the Himalayan system, covering c.800 km/500 mi; world's second highest range; rising to 7690 m/25 229 ft in Tirich Mir.

Hines, Earl (Kenneth) [hiynz], nickname **Fatha** ('Father') **Hines** (1903–83) Jazz pianist and bandleader, born in Duquesne, PA. He revolutionized jazz piano, improvising single-note lines in the treble clef and punctuating them with internal rhythms in the bass, in a style that became known as 'trumpet piano'.

Hingis, Martina [hingis] (1981–) Tennis player, born in Kosice, Slovak Republic. She was brought up in Switzerland and, playing for that country, in 1997 became the youngest-ever world number 1 when she replaced the injured Steffi Graf. Winner of the 1996 and 1998 Wimbledon doubles title, she won the singles title in 1997 at the age of 16, and that same year won the US and Australian titles, retaining the latter in 1998 and 1999. Injury forced her retirement in 2003, but she returned to competitive tennis at the start of 2006 and began 2007 ranked world number 7.

hinny **mule** (zoology)

hip The outer rounded region at the side of the upper thigh. It is the joint between the head of the femur and the pelvis, possessing great strength and stability.

hip-hop A US black popular music culture first developed in New York in the 1970s. The music may be created by disco DJs 'scratching' – manipulating dance-music records on the turntable to produce new sounds and rhythms – or, more recently, by 'sampling' – selecting and mixing digital samples from recordings by other artists. It relies on hard and heavy percussion, often from electronic drum machines, and this can provide a backing for improvised rap lyrics. Hip-hop culture also encompasses break-dancing and 'body-popping', street graffiti, and baggy-clothes fashion.

Hipparchos / Hipparchus [hipah(r)kus] (2nd-c BC) Astronomer, born in Nicaea, Rhodes. He is noted for his catalogue of the positions of 850 stars. He also found the length of the solar year (correct to 7 min).

Hipparcos [hipah(r)kos] A satellite launched in 1989 by the European Space Agency to measure positions, brightness, distances, and motions of the stars far more accurately than possible through telescopes on Earth, where the unsteadiness of the atmosphere interferes with observations. The Hipparcos catalogue, containing data for over 100 000 stars, was published in 1997.

hippeastrum [hipeeastruhm] *amaryllis*

Hippocrates [hipokrateez] (c.460–c.377 BC) Physician, born on the Greek island of Cos. He is traditionally regarded as 'the father of medicine'.

Hippocratic oath An ethical code attributed to Hippocrates. Parts of it are still used in medical schools throughout the world to encourage young graduates to aspire to conduct that befits those who care for sick people.

Hippolytus [hipolitus] A Greek hero, son of Theseus and Hippolyta. Theseus's new wife, Phaedra, made advances to Hippolytus, which were refused; so she falsely accused Hippolytus of rape. Theseus invoked a curse, Poseidon sent a frightening sea-monster, and Hippolytus was thrown from his chariot and killed.

hippopotamus (Gr 'river horse') A mammal of family Hippopotamidae; an artiodactyl, found in two species: **hippopotamus** (*Hippopotamus amphibius*) of tropical African rivers; body large, barrel-shaped; spends day in water, emerges at night; large oblong head; four webbed toes on each foot; **pygmy hippopotamus** (*Choeropsis liberiensis*) from W Africa; inhabits swamps and forests; shoulder height, 750 mm/30 in; also known as **hippo**.

hippotigris *zebra*

hire purchase (UK) / **installment credit** (US) A legal agreement to buy an article by means of small regular payments, meanwhile having use of the article. Payment may include an element of interest as well as part of the cost of the article.

Hirohito [hirohheetoh] *Showa Tenno*

Hiroshige, Ando [hirohsheegay] (1797–1858) Painter, born in Edo (modern Tokyo). He is celebrated for his impressive landscape colour prints.

Hiroshima [hirosheema, hiroshima] 34°23N 132°27E, pop (2000e) 1 094 000. City in S Honshu I, Japan; founded as a castle, 1594; atomic bomb dropped here (6 Aug 1945), c.150 000 killed or wounded, 75% of the buildings destroyed or severely damaged; town rapidly rebuilt; airport; railway; university (1949); Peace Memorial Park.

Hirst, Damien (1965–) Avant-garde artist, born in Bristol, SW England. He became known for works which made use of dead animals, preserved in formalin, such as 'Mother and Child Divided' – four tanks contained the severed halves of a cow and calf. At the centre of debate over the nature and role of art, he became an established figure after being awarded the Turner Prize in 1995. Later work includes the exhibition *Romance in the Age of Uncertainty* (2003), and the bronze statue entitled 'Exquisite Pain' (2006), depicting the Christian martyr St Bartholomew flayed alive.

Hislop, Ian (1960–) Writer, editor, and broadcaster, born in Mumbles, near Swansea, SC Wales. He became a television scriptwriter for *Spitting Image* (1984–9) and editor of the satirical magazine *Private Eye* (from 1986). He is also a team captain of the BBC's popular *Have I Got News For You* (1991–), and wrote the TV comedy sitcom series, *My Dad's The Prime Minister* (2003).

Hispanic American Any person resident in the USA who comes from, or whose parents came from, Spanish-speaking countries in Central and South America, including the Caribbean. They are now thought to number c.35 million, but the figures are highly inaccurate because there are many illegal immigrants. The main groups are Mexican Americans, Puerto Ricans, and Cubans.

Hispaniola [hispanyohla], formerly **Santo Domingo** Second largest island of the Greater Antilles, E Caribbean; W third occupied by Haiti, remainder by the Dominican Republic; highest peak in the West Indies rises to 3175 m/10 416 ft at Pico Duarte.

Hiss, Alger [aljer] (1904–96) US State Department official, born in Baltimore, MD. He reached high office as a State Department official, then stood trial twice (1949, 1950) on a charge of perjury, having denied before a Congressional Un-American Activities Committee that he had passed secret state documents to a communist spy ring. The case roused great controversy, but he was sentenced to five years' imprisonment. Revelations from American intelligence intercepts point to his guilt.

histamine [histameen] A local hormone derived from the amino acid *histidine*, found in virtually all mammalian tissues, and particularly abundant in the skin, lungs, and gut. It is released by antigen–antibody reactions, and after skin damage by heat, venom, or toxins. Its actions include the dilation of blood vessels, and the stimulation of gastric acid secretion.

histochemistry The chemistry of living biological tissue. It is particularly significant in the study of immune response, such as in organ transplant surgery.

histology The microscopic study of the tissues of living organisms. Particular use is made of staining techniques to differentiate between cell types and between parts of cells.

histopathology The microscopic examination of diseased tissues to determine the nature of the condition. Small pieces of tissue taken at autopsy or by biopsy are stained with chemicals that colour the cell membrane, cytoplasm, and nucleus, rendering them more easily visible.

Hitchcock, Sir Alfred (Joseph) (1899–1980) Film producer, born in London. He directed his first film in 1925, and rose to become an unexcelled master of suspense, internationally recognized for his intricate plots and novel camera techniques. His British films included *The Thirty-Nine Steps* (1935) and *The Lady Vanishes* (1938). His first US film, *Rebecca* (1940), won an Oscar. Later films included *Psycho* (1960), *The Birds* (1963), and *Frenzy* (1972).

Hitchings, George (Herbert) (1905–98) Chemist, born in Hoquiam, WA. From 1942 he worked at the Burroughs Wellcome Research Laboratories in Tuckahoe, New York, being joined by Gertrude Elion in a major programme of drug development. In 1988 they shared, with James Black, the Nobel Prize for Physiology or Medicine.

Hitler, Adolf, popular name **der Führer** ('the Leader') (1889–1945) German dictator, born in Braunau, Upper Austria, the son of a minor customs official, originally called **Schicklgruber**. In 1919 he joined a small political party which in 1920 he renamed as the National Socialist German Workers' Party. In 1923, he attempted to overthrow the Bavarian government, but was imprisoned for nine months in Landsberg jail, during which time he produced his political testament, *Mein Kampf* (1925, My Struggle). Made chancellor in 1933, he suspended the constitution, silenced all opposition, and brought the Nazi Party to power. He created 'Greater Germany' by the Anschluss with Austria (1938), and absorbed the German-populated Sudeten region of Czechoslovakia. He then demanded from Poland the return of Danzig and free access to East Prussia, which, when Poland refused, precipitated World War 2 (3 Sep 1939). His domestic policy was one of total Nazification, enforced by the Secret State Police (*Gestapo*). He established concentration camps for political opponents and Jews, over 6 million of whom were murdered in the course of World War 2. With his early war successes, he increasingly ignored the advice of military experts, and the tide turned in 1942 after the defeats at El Alamein, Stalingrad, and Kursk. When Germany was invaded, he retired to his *Bunker*, an air-raid shelter under the Chancellory building in Berlin, where he went through a marriage ceremony with his mistress, Eva Braun. All available evidence suggests that he and his wife committed suicide and had their bodies cremated (30 Apr 1945). Hitler used tremendous forcefulness, charisma, oratory, and his ability to appeal to people's baser instincts to manipulate them. He rose at a time of defeat and disillusionment. His 'Thousand-Year Reich' lasted 12 years and three months.

Hittites A people of uncertain origin who became prominent in

C Asia Minor in the first part of the second millennium BC. At their zenith (1450–1200 BC), their Empire covered most of Anatolia and parts of N Syria.

HIV Abbreviation of **human immunodeficiency virus**; a retrovirus that can cause the breakdown of the human immune system known as *acquired immunodeficiency syndrome* (AIDS).

hives *urticaria*

Hizbollah *Hezbollah*

Hizbullah *Hezbollah*

Hoad, Lew(is Alan) [hohd] (1934–94) Tennis player, born in Sydney, New South Wales, Australia. With his doubles partner, Ken Rosewall (1934–), he had a meteoric rise to fame, winning the Wimbledon doubles title and a Davis Cup challenge match against the USA before he was 20 years old. He defeated Rosewall in the Wimbledon final of 1956, and won again the following year, but then turned professional.

hoarhound *horehound*

hoatzin [hohatsin] An unusual South American bird (*Opisthocomus hoazin*), found on wooded banks of the Amazon and Orinoco; large wings and tail; small head with untidy crest. (Family: Opisthocomidae.)

Hobart [hohbah(r)t] 42°54S 147°18E, pop (2000e) 200 600. Seaport and state capital in SE Tasmania, Australia; on the Derwent R; fine natural harbour; founded as a penal colony, 1804; state capital, 1812; city status, 1842; airport; railway; University of Tasmania (1890).

Hobbema, Meindert [hobema], originally **Meyndert Lubbertsz(oon)** (1638–1709) Landscape painter, probably born in Amsterdam. His masterpiece, 'The Avenue, Middelharnis' (1689, National Gallery, London) greatly influenced modern landscape artists.

Hobbes, Thomas (1588–1679) Political philosopher, born in Malmesbury, Wiltshire. After being introduced to Euclidean geometry, he thought to extend its method into a comprehensive science of man and society. He wrote several works on government, notably *Leviathan* (1651).

hobbits The name for the reluctant heroes, living in holes in the ground, found in the works of Tolkien. Among their number are Bilbo and Frodo Baggins. In the 1960s a cult developed, with peace-loving people sporting badges saying 'Frodo lives'. Frodo lived again in the new millennium, when the film trilogy *The Lord of the Rings* (2001–3) was released to international acclaim.

Hobbs, Jack, popular name of **Sir John Berry Hobbs** (1882–1963) Cricketer, born in Cambridge, Cambridgeshire. He played in county cricket for Surrey (1905–34) and for England (1908–30). He made 3636 runs, including 12 centuries, in test matches against Australia, and a record number of 197 centuries and 61 237 runs in first-class cricket.

hobby A small falcon native to the Old World. (Genus: *Falco*, 4 species. Family: Falconidae.)

hobby-horse A horse made of wood, wicker, and cloth, sometimes with a real horse's head or skull, and donned by a man in traditional rituals and dances in many parts of Europe. Hobby-horse customs are associated with fertility and general well-being, and the mock animals are probably group emblems or totems.

Hobday, Peter (1937–) British journalist and broadcaster. He joined the BBC, working in both radio and television, becoming known for his contributions to such programmes as BBC2's *The Money Programme* (1979–81) and *Newsnight* (1980–2), and Radio 4's *Today* (from 1981).

Hobsbawm, Eric (John Ernest) (1917–) Historian, born in Alexandria, N Egypt. He became a lecturer at Birkbeck College, University of London (1947), and professor of Economic and Social History there (1970–82, emeritus 1982). His many works include *The Age of Revolution* (1962), *The Age of Capital* (1975), and *Age of Extremes: the Short Twentieth Century* (1994).

Hochhuth, Rolf [hokhhoot] (1931–) Playwright, born in Eschwege, Germany. His play *Der Stellvertreter* (1963, The Representative), focusing on the role of the Pope in World War 2, excited controversy and introduced the fashion for 'documentary drama'.

Ho Chi-Minh [hoh chee min], originally **Nguyen That Thanh** (1892–1969) Statesman, prime minister (1954–5) and president (1954–69) of North Vietnam, born in Central Vietnam. He directed the successful military operations against the French (1946–54), and was a leading force in the war between North and South Vietnam during the 1960s.

Ho Chi Minh City [hoh chee min], formerly **Saigon** (to 1976) 10°46N 106°43E, pop (2000e) 4 568 900. Largest city in Vietnam; on R Saigon; former capital of French Indochina, 1887–1902; former capital of South Vietnam; occupied by the USA in Vietnam War; airport; chief industrial centre of Vietnam.

hockey *see panel*

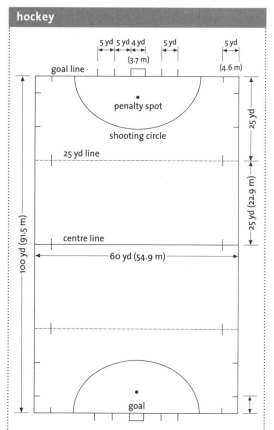

hockey

A stick-and-ball game played by two teams, each of 11 players; also known as **field hockey**, especially in the USA. The object is to move the ball around the field with the stick until a player is in a position to strike the ball into the opposing side's goal. The playing area is 100 yd (91 m) long and 60 yd (54 m) wide. A game lasts 70 minutes, split into two 35-minute halves. A similar game to hockey was played by the ancient Greeks c.2500 BC. Modern hockey dates from 1875, when the English Hockey Association was formed in London. Indoor hockey is increasingly popular during the winter months.

Hockney, David (1937–) Artist, born in Bradford, West Yorkshire. Associated with the Pop Art movement from his earliest work, he has also worked in printmaking and photography, and designed sets and costumes. He became well-known for his 'swimming pool' paintings, prompted by his fascination with the representation of water.

Hoddinott, Alun (1929–) Composer, born in Bargoed, Caerphilly, S Wales. He is a prolific composer of operas, symphonies, concertos, and a large corpus of choral and chamber works.

Hoddle, Glenn (1957–) Football manager and player, born in Hayes, Greater London. He began his career with Tottenham Hotspur (1975–86), and after spells with other clubs became manager of England in 1996. Following a controversial newspaper interview in 1999 that offended the disabled community, the Football Association relieved him of his duties. He later managed Southampton (2000), Tottenham (2001–3), and Wolverhampton Wanderers (2004–6).

Hodgkin, Dorothy Mary, *née* **Crowfoot** (1910–94) Chemist, born in Cairo. A crystallographer, she was awarded the Nobel Prize for Chemistry in 1964 for her discoveries, by the use of X-ray techniques, of the structure of certain molecules, including penicillin, vitamin B^{12}, and insulin.

Hodgkin, Thomas (1798–1866) Pathologist, born in Tottenham, Greater London. He held various posts at Guy's Hospital, London, and described the glandular disease *lymphadenoma*, named after him (**Hodgkin's disease**).

Hoffman, Dustin (1937–) Actor, born in Los Angeles, CA. His first leading film role was *The Graduate* (1967), and this was followed by a number of similar 'anti-hero' roles, such as in *Midnight Cowboy* (1969) and *Marathon Man* (1976). He found wider scope in *All The President's Men* (1976), *Kramer v Kramer* (1979, Oscar), and *Rain Man* (1988, Oscar). His later films include *Outbreak* (1995), *Runaway Jury* (2003), and *Perfume* (2006).

Hoffman, Philip Seymour Film and stage actor, born in Fairport, NY. He studied drama at the Tisch School of the Arts, New York University (1989). His breakthrough into feature films came with *Boogie Nights* (1997), and he quickly established his reputation in such films as *Happiness* (1998), *Flawless* (1999), *State and Main* (2000), and *Capote* (2005, Oscar).

Hoffnung, Gerard (1925–59) Cartoonist and musician, born in Berlin, but raised in England. He was staff cartoonist on the London *Evening News* (1947), and later freelanced for *Punch* and other magazines. His interest in music led to his creation of the Hoffnung Music Festivals at the Royal Festival Hall.

Hofmannsthal, Hugo von [hofmanztahl] (1874–1929) Poet and playwright, born in Vienna. His plays include *Electra* (1903) and the morality play *Jedermann* (1912, Everyman). He also collaborated with Richard Strauss, for whom he wrote the libretti for *Der Rosenkavalier* (1911) and other works.

hog *pig*

Hogan, Ben(jamin William), nickname **The Hawk** (1912–97) Golfer, born in Dublin, TX. In 1948 he became the first man in 26 years to win all three US major titles. He won the US Open four times before retiring in 1970.

Hogan, Paul (1939–) Comedian and actor, born in Lightning Ridge, New South Wales, Australia. He is best known for the successful films *Crocodile Dundee* (1986, Golden Globe) and *Crocodile Dundee II* (1988). His series of television advertisements for the Australian Tourist Board did much to promote his country, and he has become something of a national folk hero. Later films include *Crocodile Dundee in Los Angeles* (2001).

Hogarth, William [hohgah(r)th] (1697–1764) Painter and engraver, born in London. His 'modern moral subjects' include 'A Rake's Progress' (1733–5, Sir John Soanes Museum, London), and his masterpiece, the 'Marriage à la Mode' (1743–5, Tate, London). His crowded canvases are full of revealing details and pointed subplots.

hogfish Deep-bodied bottom-living fish, *Lachnolaimus maximus*, belonging to the wrasse family, Labridae, found in the warmer waters of the W North Atlantic; length up to 90 cm/3 ft; excellent food fish, but now scarce in some areas.

Hogg, James, known as the **Ettrick Shepherd** (1770–1835) Writer, born near Ettrick, Scottish Borders. He tended sheep in his youth, and became a writer of ballads which achieved some success, thanks to the patronage of Walter Scott.

Hogg, Quintin *Hailsham, Viscount*

Hoggar Mountains *Ahaggar Mountains*

Hogmanay [hogmanay, hogmanay] The name in Scotland for New Year's Eve, the last day of the year. One custom associated with Hogmanay is *first-footing*, the first-foot being the first person to enter a house on New Year's Day. Traditionally the first-foot should be tall, dark-haired, and male, and should carry gifts of food, drink, and fuel.

hogweed A very variable robust biennial (*Heracleum sphondylium*), growing to 3 m/10 ft, native to N temperate regions; leaves up to 30 cm/12 in; flowers white or pinkish; also called **keck** or **cow parsnip**. The closely related **giant hogweed** (*Heracleum mantegazzianum*) is distinguished by its greater size, growing to 5 m/16 ft tall; native to SW Asia. It can cause painful skin irritations if touched in bright sunlight. (Family: Umbelliferae.)

Hohenstaufen [hohenshtowfn] A German dynasty named after the castle of Staufen in Swabia. They ruled as German kings or king-emperors (1138–1254), and as kings of Sicily (1194–1266).

Hohenzollerns [hohentzolernz] A German ruling dynasty of Brandenburg–Prussia (1415–1918) and Imperial Germany (1871–1918).

Hohokam [hohhokam] The prehistoric inhabitants of the S Arizona desert c.300 BC–AD 1400, ancestors of the modern Pima and Papago Indians.

Hokan languages [hohkn] A group of about 30 North American Indian languages, forming a bridge between the indigenous languages of North and South America.

Hokkaido [hokaeedoh], formerly **Yezo** or **Ezo** pop (2000e) 5 811 000; area 83 513 km^2/32 236 sq mi. Northernmost and second largest island of the Japanese archipelago; 418 km/260 mi N–S, 450 km/280 mi E–W; largely mountainous, with active and inactive volcanic cones (C); rises to 2290m/7513 ft at Mt Asahidake; originally populated by the Ainu; capital, Sapporo.

Hokusai, Katsushika [hokusiy] (1760–1849) Artist and wood engraver, born in Edo (modern Tokyo). He early abandoned traditional styles of engraving for the coloured woodcut designs of the *ukiyo-e* school. He is best known for his 'Hundred Views of Mount Fuji' (1835), many of which grace Western homes in reproduction today.

Holbein, Hans [holbiyn], known as **the Younger** (1497–1543) Painter, born in Augsburg, Germany, the son of **Hans Holbein the Elder** (c.1460–1524), also a painter of merit. In 1536 he became court painter to Henry VIII, his works including several portraits of eminent English people of the time, notably of Henry and his wives.

Hölderlin, (Johann Christian) Friedrich [hoelderlin] (1770–1843) Poet, born in Lauffen, Germany. He began to publish, with the help of Schiller, notably the philosophical novel, *Hyperion* (1797–9).

holding company A company which effectively controls another by owning at least half of the nominal value of its ordinary share capital or controlling the composition of its board of directors. The owned company is thereby a *subsidiary* of the holding company.

Holi [hohlee] A Hindu festival in honour of Krishna, occurring in February or March (Phalguna S 15), characterized by boisterous revelry, including the throwing of coloured water over people.

Holiday, Billie, originally **Eleanora Fagan**, nickname **Lady Day** (1915–59) Singer, born in Baltimore, MD. Her troubled life made sensational reading in her 1956 'autobiography' (actually written by William Dufty), *Lady Sings the Blues*.

Holinshed, Raphael [holinshed] (?–c.1580) English chronicler, born apparently of a Cheshire family. His compilation of *The Chronicles of England, Scotland, and Ireland* (1577), was a major source for many of Shakespeare's plays.

holism A thesis which maintains that some wholes cannot be fully understood in terms of their parts; the wholes could be biological organisms, societies, art works, or networks of scientific theories.

holistic medicine An approach to medical treatment based on the theory that living creatures and the non-living environment function together as a single integrated whole (*holism*). The approach insists on the study not only of individual disease but also of the response of people to their disease, physically, psychologically, and socially.

Holland *Netherlands, The*

Holloway, Stanley (1890–1982) Entertainer, born in London. He was an original member of The Co-Optimists revue group (1921–30). Popular on radio and in pantomime, he became widely known for his monologue readings about the adventures of Albert and the Ramsbottom family (created by his fellow Co-Optimist, Marriott Edgar), Sam Small, and others. He was also a genial comedy actor in such Ealing film classics as *Passport to Pimlico* (1948) and *The Lavender Hill Mob* (1951). He is perhaps best known for his role of Alfred Dolittle in *My Fair Lady* on Broadway (1956–8) and later on film (1964). He published an autobiography, *Wiv a Little Bit of Luck* (1969).

Hollows, Fred(erick) Cossom (1929–93) Ophthalmologist, born in Dunedin, New Zealand. Chairman of ophthalmology at Prince of Wales Hospital, Sydney, he was famed for his work on blinding eye infections among Australian Aborigines, Eritreans, and Vietnamese. In 1991 he was named Australian of the Year.

Holly, Buddy, popular name of **Charles Hardin Holley** (1936–59) Rock singer, songwriter, and guitarist, born in Lubbock, TX. His band, The Crickets, was among the first to use the now standard rock-and-roll line-up of two guitars, bass, and drums. Following his death in a plane crash, he became an important cult figure. His most popular records include 'That'll Be The Day', 'Peggy Sue', and 'Oh Boy'.

holly An evergreen tree or shrub (*Ilex aquifolium*) growing to 10 m/30 ft, native to Europe; bark silvery-grey; leaves leathery, glossy above with wavy, spiny margins, prickly to the touch; flowers 4-petalled, white, followed by red berries; much-used at Christmas for decoration. (Family: Aquifoliaceae.)

hollyhock A biennial or perennial (*Althaea rosea*), native to China; stem growing to 3 m/10 ft in second year; flowers in a wide range of colours, forming a long spike. (Family: Malvaceae.)

Hollywood A suburb of Los Angeles, CA, which after 1912 developed into the centre of film production in the USA. Its studios dominated the world motion-picture market from the 1920s.

Holmes, Dame Kelly (1970–) Athlete, born in Pembury, Kent. She won English Schools' 1500 m titles at junior and senior level, and later joined the army as a physical training instructor. Her first major international title was the 1500 m gold in the 1994 Commonwealth Games. Further achievements include an Olympic 800 m bronze at the Sydney Games (2000), 1500 m gold at the 2002 Commonwealth Games, and Olympic gold in the 800 m and 1500 m events at the 2004 games in Athens. She received the International Association of Athletics Federations Award for the best women's performance in the world during 2004, and later that year was voted BBC TV Sports Personality of the Year. She was made a dame in 2005, and retired from athletics at the end of that year.

Holmes, Larry, nickname **the Easton Assassin** (1949–) Boxer, born in Cuthbert, GA. He beat Ken Norton for the World Boxing Council heavyweight title in 1978, and held it until 1985, when he lost to Michael Spinks.

Holmes, Oliver Wendell, Jr, nickname **the Great Dissenter** (1841–1935) Judge, born in Boston, MA, son of the writer, **Oliver Wendell Holmes** (1809–94). He was associate justice of the US Supreme Court (1902–32).

HOLMES Abbreviation for **Home Office Large Major Enquiry System**, a computer system introduced in the 1980s for crime detection in the UK.

Holmes a Court, (Michael) Robert Hamilton [hohmz uh kaw(r)t] (1937–90) Entrepreneur, born in South Africa. He established the Bell Group, which in 1984 stunned the business world by bidding for BHP, Australia's largest company. His company recovered well after the 1987 stock-market crash, and he continued as one of the wealthiest people in Australia. After his death, his widow **Janet Holmes a Court** (1943–) became chair of the family company.

Holocaust The attempt by Nazi Germany to systematically destroy European Jews. Jews were driven from their homes and transported to concentration camps, slave-labour camps, and extermination camps. There they were herded into gas chambers and their bodies burned in crematoria. By the end of the war in 1945, more than 6 million had been murdered. Other minorities were also subject to Nazi atrocities. The major consequence was the acceleration of the establishment of the state of Israel.

Holocene epoch [holoseen] The most recent of the two geological epochs of the Quaternary period, from 10 000 years ago to the present time.

holography A method of lensless photography which gives true three-dimensional images; invented by Dennis Gabor in 1948. Modern holograms are made using laser light. The light beam is divided into two parts: one falls directly onto photographic film; the other is reflected onto the film via the object. An interference pattern forms, which is recorded on the film; and the processed film is the hologram. The image is generally viewed by illuminating the hologram using laser light.

holoplankton *plankton*

Holothuroidea [holothuhroydia] *sea cucumber*

Holst, Gustav (Theodore) (1874–1934) Composer, born in Cheltenham, Gloucestershire. He emerged as a major composer with the seven-movement suite *The Planets* (1914–16). Among his other major works are *The Hymn of Jesus* (1917), and his orchestral tone poem, *Egdon Heath* (1927).

Holt, Harold (Edward) (1908–67) Australian politician and prime minister (1966–7), born in Sydney, New South Wales, Australia. He joined the United Australia Party (later, the Liberal Party of Australia), becoming deputy leader in 1956, and leader and prime minister when Robert Menzies retired in 1966. He died in office.

Holt, Victoria *Hibbert, Eleanor*

Holyfield, Evander [holeefeeld] (1962–) Boxer, born in Atlanta, GA. He became the World Boxing Association (WBA) heavyweight champion in 1996 and the International Boxing Federation (IBF) heavyweight champion in 1998. He was undisputed heavyweight champion of the world in 1990–2. He lost the WBA crown to John Ruiz in 2001.

Holy Ghost *Holy Spirit*

Holyhead [holeehed], Welsh **Caergybi** 53°19N 4°38W, pop (2000e) 12 900. Port on Holy I, Anglesey, NW Wales, UK; railway; ferry to Dun Laoghaire and Dublin, Ireland; Holyhead Mountain 216 m/710 ft; breakwater (1845–73), 2·4 km/1½ mi long; St Cybi's Church (founded 6th-c) within 3rd-c Roman walls; Ucheldre Centre; Maritime Museum.

Holy Innocents' Day A Christian festival (28 Dec) which commemorates the killing of the male children around Bethlehem by Herod (*Matt* 2).

Holy Island *Holyhead; Lindisfarne*

Holy League The name given to a number of European alliances formed during the 15th-c, 16th-c, and 17th-c. The Holy League of 1495 was forged between the Hapsburg Emperor Maximilian I, Pope Alexander VI, Spain, Venice, Milan, and England to protect Italy from French ascendancy. The League of 1511–13, organized by Pope Julius II, included England, Spain, Venice, the Hapsburg Empire, and Switzerland. The Holy League of 1526 was formed against Spain by France, the Papacy, England, Venice, and Milan. In 1571 an alliance was formed between Venice, Spain, and the Papacy to counter Turkish supremacy in the E Mediterranean, before disagreements divided the Allies. The French Holy League of 1576, led by the Guise faction during the French Wars of Religion, was dissolved in 1577, but revived in 1584 to play a major part in the War of the Three Henrys (1585–9). The Holy League of 1609 was an alliance of the German Catholic princes, formed at the start of the Jülich Succession (1606–14). In 1683 a Holy League was formed against Ottoman Turkey following the Imperial repossession of Vienna, consisting of Poland, the Hapsburg Empire, Venice, and the Papacy. Pope Innocent XI planned further crusades in Hungary, Greece, and Moldavia; the latter failed (1686), but after several years' fighting (1683–99) most of Hungary was recovered for the Hapsburgs.

Holy of Holies The innermost and most sacred part of the Jewish tabernacle, and later of the Jerusalem Temple, cubic in shape, which contained the Ark of the Covenant.

Holy Orders *Orders, Holy*

Holy Roman Empire The revived mediaeval title of the Roman Empire, dating from the 9th-c, when the papacy granted the title to Charlemagne, King of the Franks. It was later bestowed upon German princely families, including the Hohenstaufens, Luxemburgs, and Habsburgs, lasting until 1806.

Holyroodhouse, Palace of [holeeroodhows] The official residence in Scotland of the reigning monarch. Built in the 16th-c at Edinburgh, the palace was reconstructed in the 1670s by the architect Sir William Bruce (d.1710).

Holy Shroud or **Shroud of Turin** A relic, alleged to be the burial-sheet of Jesus Christ, known since the 14th-c, and preserved in the Cathedral at Turin since 1578. It portrays an image (clearer when shown using a photographic negative) of the front and back of a man's body, with markings that seem to correspond to the stigmata of Jesus. Controversy over its authenticity resulted in the use of independent radiocarbon-dating tests by three research centres in 1988, using a tiny piece of the fabric. The results indicated a late provenance for the shroud, but controversy continued over the methods used. The question of how the body image was produced remains open. In 2004, a second image was discovered during a restoration project, and in early 2005 previous results were contradicted when a thermochemical test report indicated that the shroud was between 1300 and 3000 years old.

Holy Spirit A term used to denote the presence or power of God, often imbued with personal or quasi-personal characteristics; in Christian thought considered the third person of the Trinity, alongside the Father and the Son. In the New Testament, the Church is described as receiving the Spirit at Pentecost, from which time it continued to direct the Church's missionary activities.

Holy Week In the Christian Church, the week before Easter, beginning on Palm Sunday. It includes Maundy Thursday and Good Friday.

Holywell [holeewel], Welsh **Treffynnon** 53°17N 3°13W, pop (2000e) 12 400. Town in Flintshire, NE Wales, UK; 'the Welsh Lourdes', place of pilgrimage since the 7th-c, where St Winefride (Gwenfrewi) was beheaded.

Home of the Hirsel, Baron [hyoom], formerly **Sir Alec Douglas-Home**, originally **Alexander Frederick Douglas-Home, 14th Earl of Home** (1903–95) British Conservative statesman and prime minister (1963–4), born in London. He became Commonwealth Relations secretary (1955–60) and foreign secretary (1960–3). After Macmillan's resignation, he astonished everyone by emerging as premier, renouncing his peerage and fighting a by-election. He was foreign secretary again in Edward Heath's 1970–4 government.

home counties Those counties which border London, and into which the city has expanded. These are Essex, Kent, Surrey, Buckinghamshire, Hertfordshire, and the former counties of Middlesex and Berkshire.

Home Guard A home defence militia, raised during the summer of 1940, when the German armies seemed poised to complete the conquest of W Europe by invading the UK. At first called the Local Defence Volunteers, the force was finally stood down in 1945.

Homelands *apartheid; South Africa*

homeopathy A practice of medicine devised by German physician Samuel Hahnemann in the early 19th-c with the principles of (1) like cures like; and (2) drug activity is enhanced by dilution.

homeostasis / homoeostasis [hohmiohstaysis] A term initially used to describe the stability of the extracellular fluid apparent in healthy individuals. Nowadays it is often used to describe the ways in which this stability is achieved, in both humans and other animals. For example, body temperature in warm-blooded mammals is maintained by active metabolic mechanisms such as shivering, if it falls too low, or panting, if it rises too high.

Homer, Greek **Homēros** (c.8th-c BC) Greek poet to whom are attributed the great epics, the *Iliad*, the story of the siege of Troy, and the *Odyssey*, the tale of Odysseus's wanderings. Arguments have long raged over whether his works are in fact by the same hand, or have their origins in the lays of Homer and his followers (*Homeridae*). Of the true Homer, nothing is positively known.

Homer, Winslow (1836–1910) Marine and genre painter, born in Boston, MA. He painted rural and domestic scenes, but was at his best in his seascapes.

home rule The handing down of certain legislative powers and administrative functions, previously exercised by a higher authority, to an elected body within a geographically defined area. Since the early 1970s in the UK, for political movements such as the Scottish National Party and Irish republicans, home rule has tended to become synonymous with separatism.

Homestead Act (1862) A US law allowing a grant of 160 acres of public land to settlers, conditional on their staying five years, the making of improvements to the property, and the payment of fees.

homicide The unlawful killing of one human being by another. The term varies in its application among different jurisdictions. In England and Wales, for example, unlawful homicide includes the crimes of murder, manslaughter, and infanticide. In certain circumstances homicide may be lawful, such as in self-defence, but the action taken has to be reasonable in the circumstances. In both Scotland and the USA, homicide involves causing the death of another either by an act or by an intentional or negligent omission when there is a legal duty to act. Criminal homicide usually includes murder (first and second degree), manslaughter, and negligent homicide.

homing overlay device Part of a US experiment to achieve a practical ballistic missile defence using space-based systems.

A 'layer' of defences would be established outside the atmosphere to intercept incoming nuclear warheads.

hominid A member of the primate family Hominidae, containing humans, their immediate ancestors, and close extinct relatives. Two genera are usually recognized: *Australopithecus* and *Homo*. Anatomical and molecular evidence indicate that the hominid and African ape lineages separated c.6–8 million years ago. The earliest definite hominid fossils are c.5·5 million years old, although most finds are <4 million years.

Homo [homoh] (Lat 'man') A genus of the family Hominidae, order Primates. *Homo* features include a medium-large brain (500–2000 cm^3), a high brain:body ratio, bipedal gait, upright posture, and adaptable hands with a precision grip based on thumb–index finger opposition. The genus probably evolved in Africa c.2 million years ago (mya) from *Australopithecus*. Environmental change (increased seasonality, grassland expansion, forest contraction) may have promoted the evolution of *Homo* species by favouring co-operative behaviour in food-gathering and sharing, the making and use of tools involving hand–eye co-ordination, improved communication, and a progressively extended period of infant care and childhood learning. There are five named species of *Homo*, four extinct.

Homo habilis known from Olduvai Gorge in Tanzania, L Turkana (Rudolf) in Kenya, Sterkfontein in South Africa, and possibly elsewhere, is dated c.2–1·5 mya. It had a lightly built braincase (capacity 500–700 cm^3), projecting face and jaws, relatively large front teeth, but small narrow cheek teeth. Body size was 25–40 kg/55–88 lb with long, powerfully-muscled arms and hands suggesting climbing ability, and short hindlimbs.

Homo rudolfensis, known only from sites around L Turkana dated 1·9–1·7 mya, was probably bigger-bodied than *H. habilis*, with more modern limb proportions. It was bigger-brained (750–900 cm^3), with a broader, flatter face and larger cheek teeth.

Homo erectus, also known from sites around L Turkana dated at 1·8–1·6 mya, had strongly built but otherwise largely modern bodily proportions. The skull was also strongly built, with a retreating frontal, flat, thick-walled vault (800–1200 cm^3 capacity), big face and jaws, but only moderate-sized teeth.

Homo floresiensis specimens were discovered on the Indonesian island of Flores in 2004 and dated 18 000–12 000 years ago. It probably evolved from a *Homo erectus* group cut off on the isolated island about 800 000 years ago. The skull is similar to *Homo erectus*, though with slighter brow ridge and smaller brain (380 cm^3) capacity. It had a smaller skeleton (height 1 m/3 ft), a very wide pelvis, a bipedal stance, and was capable of tool-making.

The evolutionary relationships of *H. habilis*, *H. rudolfensis*, and *H. erectus* are unclear, but since they overlap in time and space they do not form a single evolutionary sequence. On balance, *H. rudolfensis* and *H. erectus* appear more closely related to each other than either is to *H. habilis*, which may be an advanced 'human-like' *Australopithecus* rather than true *Homo*. More evidence is needed to clarify these and other issues. Crude pebble tools and modified bones are known for the same sites as the early *Homo* species, but it is not clear which were tool-making – perhaps all three were. *H. habilis* and *H. rudolfensis* disappear around 1·7–1·5 mya, but *H. erectus* persists for c.1·5 my down to c.300 000 years ago. There are increasing fossil finds in Africa c.1·5–0·6 mya, together with better-made tools (hand axes) and larger sites with more animal bones, suggesting skilled hunting. By 700 000 years ago *H. erectus* had expanded beyond Africa, with finds in Java and China, where evidence of fire indicates ability to exploit a range of habitats and climates. *Homo sapiens*, our own species, evolved from *H. erectus* through archaic, big-faced forms such as Neanderthal Man (Europe, Middle East) and equivalents in Africa and Asia, to fully modern man.

H. sapiens sapiens, which is first known from Africa c.100–120 000 years ago, and shortly afterwards in the Middle East. This subspecies has a relatively light build, a large rounded braincase (12 000–2000 cm^3 – average 1400 cm^3), a high forehead, flat and lightly-built face and jaws, slight or no brow ridges, small crowded teeth, and a definite chin. The earliest fossils (Africa, Middle East) have tools no different from those of archaic *H. sapiens* but later specimens (40 000 years ago) are found with more complex, specialized tool kits which include bone, ivory, and antler as well as stone artefacts, and fine engraving, carving, and cave art. These innovations reflect more complex behaviour patterns that enabled *H. sapiens sapiens* to colonize all continents save Antarctica by the final Pleistocene (10 000 years ago). Subsequent developments include agriculture, domestication, and civilization, and more recently industrialization and explosive population growth.

Homo floresiensis The name assigned to the remains of a partial human skeleton discovered on Flores Island, Indonesia in 2004, a new member of the family Hominidae, genus *Homo*. Archaeologists unearthed the bones while digging at Liang Bua, one of many limestone caves on Flores. The 18 000-year-old specimen, known as Liang Bua 1 or LB1, is a significant find. Measuring only 1 m/3 ft in height, with a child-size skull, the skeleton is that of an adult female who walked upright. *H. floresiensis* probably evolved from the species *Homo erectus*, whose remains have been found on the Indonesian island of Java. Skeleton parts belonging to six other similar individuals have since been found, ranging in date from 95 000 years ago to 12 000 years ago. The tiny human resembles the diminutive people of local folklore, known as Ebu Gogo, suggesting they might have survived into recent times.

Following publication of the discovery, controversy ensued as some researchers expressed doubts over the study's findings. In 2006 the American National Academy of Sciences reported that further research and a new analysis of the skeleton indicated that it probably belonged to an early human suffering from microcephaly, a condition that causes an abnormally small head and other deformities. The report concluded that 'The skeletal remains do not represent a new species, but some of the ancestors of modern human pygmies who live on the island today'.

homoiothermy [homoyohthermee] The regulation of internal body temperature at a relatively constant level. Higher vertebrates, such as mammals and birds, are warm-blooded (**homoiothermic**), and typically have insulated body coverings to aid temperature regulation.

homology The relationship between equivalent structures and traits in living organisms, derived from the same part of the embryo but existing in different states in related organisms. The forelimb of a horse, the wing of a bird, and the human arm are all homologous structures.

Homoptera [homoptera] A large order of insects comprising c.45 000 species, including the cicadas, plant hoppers, froghoppers, leaf hoppers, psyllids, whiteflies, aphids, scale insects, and mealybugs; hindlegs often adapted for jumping; feeding on plants, with modified mouthparts for piercing and sucking.

homosexuality A form of sexuality in which the sexual attraction is between members of the same sex. There are both clinical (eg Freudian psycho-medical) and sociological theories to account for homosexuality. Most sociological theories see any form of sexuality as a social construction rather than as displaying any specific, pre-given biological process. Homosexuality has been a subject of considerable political controversy in the West, especially since the formation of the Gay Liberation Movement and the onset of the AIDS virus. The Netherlands became the first country to offer full civil marriage rights to gay couples in 2001. Same-sex unions (or *civil unions* or *partnerships*) are now legalized in several European countries, and became official in Britain in December 2005, with the event receiving high-profile coverage following the union of singer Elton John and David Furnish. In the USA, Congress has so far failed to rule on the matter, but individual states are able to make their own decisions regarding homosexual unions. Civil unions give gay and lesbian couples the same rights as heterosexual couples, especially in relation to such areas as next-of-kin status, inheritance tax, and pension rights.

Homs or **Hims**, ancient **Emesa** 4°44N 36°43E, pop (2000e) 665 000. Industrial city in WC Syria; road and rail junction; commercial centre in well-irrigated area.

Honduras *see panel*

Honecker, Erich [honeker] (1912–94) East German statesman, born in Neunkirchen, Germany. He was elected party chief in 1971, becoming head of state from 1976 to 1989, when he was dismissed as a consequence of the anti-communist revolution. Although charges were brought against him in the new united Germany, he was allowed to leave for Chile in 1993 on grounds of illness.

Honegger, Arthur [oneger] (1892–1955) Composer, born in Le Havre, France. He became one of the group of Parisian composers known as *Les Six*. His dramatic oratorio *King David* established his reputation in 1921. His other works include five symphonies.

honey A substance prepared by bees from nectar found in blossoms. Because of its palatability and its relative rarity, honey has always been a highly prized food. Its colour and flavour varies with the flora on which bees feed.

honey badger *ratel*

honeybee The European honeybee (*Apis mellifera*) and three other species of the genus *Apis* (Order: Hymenoptera. Family: Apidae). It is a bee that forms true perennial societies, typically consisting of one queen, several hundred drones, and 50 000 to 80 000 workers.

honeyeater An Australasian bird specialized to eat nectar; tongue long with brush-like tip; shows great variation in bill shape and lifestyle. (Family: Meliphagidae, 167 species.)

honeyguide A small brownish bird native to Africa and S or SE Asia; inhabits evergreen forest; eats insects (especially bees) and beeswax; some said to lead animals to bees' nests. (Family: Indicatoridae, c.13 species.)

honeysuckle A member of a large genus mainly comprising shrubs, with a few well-known species of woody climbers with twining stems, deciduous or evergreen; native to the N hemisphere; flowers tubular, 2-lipped, often fragrant; berries red, blue, or black. The **common honeysuckle** or **woodbine** produces sweet scent at night. (Genus: *Lonicera*, 200 species. Family: Caprifoliaceae.)

Hong Kong *p.439*

Honiara [hohniahra] 9°28S 159°57E, pop (2000e) 46 000. Port

Honduras

☐ International Airport   ∴ World heritage site

[hondyooras], official name **Republic of Honduras**, Span **República de Honduras**

Local name Honduras

Timezone GMT -6

Area 112 088 km²/43 266 sq mi

Population total (2002e) 6 561 000

Status Republic

Date of independence 1821

Capital Tegucigalpa

Languages Spanish (official), a number of Indian dialects also spoken by aboriginal population

Ethnic groups Spanish-Indian origin (90%), Indian (7%), black (2%)

Religions Roman Catholic (85%), Protestant (mainly Fundamentalist, Moravian, and Methodist) (10%)

Physical features Coastal lands (S) separated from Caribbean coastlands by mountains running NW–SE; S plateau rises to 2849 m/9347 ft at Cerro de las Minas; includes Bay Is in the Caribbean Sea and nearly 300 islands in the Gulf of Fonseca.

Climate Tropical climate in coastal areas, temperate in C and W; average annual temperatures 19°C (Jan), 23°C (Jul) in Tegucigalpa; two wet seasons in upland areas (May–Jul, Sep–Oct); country devastated by Hurricane Mitch in 1998.

Currency 1 Lempira (HNL) = 100 centavos

Economy Agriculture (provides a third of national income), forestry, mining, cattle raising; bananas, coffee, beef, cotton, tobacco, sugar; exports of silver, lead and zinc; offshore oil exploration in the Caribbean.

GDP (2002e) $16·29 bn, per capita $2500

Human Development Index (2002) 0·638

History Centre of Mayan culture, 4th–9th-c; settled by the Spanish in early 16th-c, and became province of Guatemala; independence from Spain, 1821; joined Federation of Central America; independence, 1838; several military coups in 1970s; since 1980, a democratic constitutional republic, governed by a President and National Assembly.

Head of State/Government

1982–6 Roberto Suazo Córdova
1986–90 José Azcona Hoyo
1990–4 Rafael Callejas
1994–7 Carlos Roberto Reina
1997–2001 Carlos Roberto Flores Facussé
2001–5 Ricardo Maduro
2005– Manuel Zelaya

Hong Kong

20 km
10 mi

CHINA

C H I N A

Deep Bay

Shek Wu Hui

Yueng • Long   Tai Po

Tuen Mun   *NEW TERRITORIES*
Tsuen Wan   • Sha Tin

Chek Lap Kok   Tsing Yi

Hong Kong   Kowloon

Lantau Is   Hong Kong I

Stanley

H O N G   K O N G

SOUTH CHINA SEA

□ International Airport

Chin **Hsiang Kang** (Special administrative region of China)
Timezone GMT +8
Area 1066 km²/412 sq mi
Population total (2002e) 7 049 000
Capital Hong Kong

Languages English and Cantonese (official), with Mandarin widely spoken

Ethnic groups Chinese (98%), including many illegal immigrants from China and refugees from Vietnam; 59% of population born in Hong Kong, 37% in China

Religions Buddhist, Taoist and Confucianist majorities, Christian, Muslim, Hindu, Sikh, and Jewish minorities

Physical features Located off the coast of SE China, on the South China Sea; divided into Hong Kong Island, Kowloon, and New Territories (includes most of the colony's 235 islands); highest point, Tai Mo Shan, 957 m/3140 ft; hilly terrain, sharply indented coastline; natural harbour between Kowloon and Hong Kong Island; built-up areas on artificially levelled or reclaimed land.

Climate Subtropical climate, with hot, humid summers and cool, dry winters; average annual temperatures 16°C (Jan), 29°C (Jul); average annual rainfall 2225 mm/88 in.

Currency 1 Hong Kong Dollar (HKD) = 100 cents

Economy Based on banking, import-export trade, tourism, shipbuilding, and a diverse range of light industry; an important freeport acting as a gateway to China for the West; economy hit by SARS epidemic (2003).

GDP (2002e) $198·5 bn, per capita $27 200

Human Development Index (2002) 0·888

History Ceded to Britain, 1842; New Territories leased to Britain, 1898; occupied by the Japanese in World War 2; British Crown Colony, Governor represented the British Crown, advised by an Executive Council; in 1997, Britain's 99-year lease of the New Territories expired, whereupon Hong Kong was restored to China; China has designated Hong Kong a special administrative region from 1997; it will remain a freeport, foreign markets will be retained, and the Hong Kong dollar will remain as official currency; new Chief Executive appointed (first incumbent, Tung Chee-hwa), with new membership of advisory councils; however, anxiety over the colony's political future remains.

Chief Executive
1997–2005 Tung Chee-hwa
2005– Donald Tsang

capital of the Solomon Is, SW Pacific; airport; developed around the site of US military headquarters.

Honolulu [honolooloo] 21°19N 157°52W, pop (2000e) 371 700. State capital in Hawaii, USA; noted tourist resort, with the famous beach at Waikiki; harbour entered by William Brown, an English captain, 1794; capital of the Kingdom of Hawaii, 1845; US naval base at Pearl Harbor, attacked by the Japanese (7 Dec 1941); airport; three universities; headquarters of US Pacific Fleet.

Honorius, Flavius [onawrius] (384–423) Roman Emperor of the West (393–423). A feeble ruler, he abandoned Britain to the barbarians, and stayed in Ravenna while the Goths besieged and sacked Rome (408–10).

honours list In the UK, the military and civil awards suggested by the prime minister and approved by the sovereign at New Year and on the sovereign's official birthday.

Honshu [honshoo] pop (2000e) 102 151 000; area 231 119 km²/89 212 sq mi. Largest of the four main islands of Japan; c.1290 km/800 mi long, 48–240 km/30–150 mi wide; highest peak, Mt Fuji (3776 m/12 388 ft); coastal lowlands include most of the population, and several major cities; earthquakes common; wide range of industries.

Honthorst, Gerrit van [honthaw(r)st] (1590–1656) Painter, born in Utrecht, The Netherlands. He is known for his portraits and also for his candle-lit interiors.

Hooch or **Hoogh, Pieter de** [hohkh] (c.1629–c.1684) Genre painter,

born in Rotterdam, The Netherlands. His 'Courtyard of a House in Delft' (1658, National Gallery, London) is one of the best-known examples of the Dutch School of the 17th-c.

Hood (of Whitley), Samuel Hood, 1st Viscount (1724–1816) British admiral, born in Thorncombe, Dorset. He fought during the American Revolution, when he defeated the French in the West Indies (1782). In 1793, he directed the occupation of Toulon and the operations in the Gulf of Lyon.

Hood, Thomas (1799–1845) Poet and humorist, born in London. In his *Whims and Oddities* (1826) he showed his graphic talent in 'picture-puns', of which he seems to have been the inventor.

hoof-and-mouth disease *foot-and-mouth disease*

Hooke, Robert (1635–1703) Chemist and physicist, born in Freshwater, Isle of Wight. He formulated the law governing elasticity (**Hooke's law**), invented the balance spring for watches, and helped develop the telescope and microscope.

Hooker, Richard (1554–1600) Theologian, born near Exeter, Devon. His major work, on the basis of Church government, is the eight-volume *Of the Laws of Ecclesiastical Polity* (1594, 1597, 1648, 1662). It is mainly to this work that Anglican theology owes its tone and direction.

Hook of Holland, Dutch **Hoek van Holland** Cape in SW Netherlands; also the name of a port 27 km/17 mi W of Rotterdam; ferry links with Harwich, UK.

hookworm infestation An important cause of anaemia and ill health in tropical countries, caused by nematode worms that become hooked on to the lining of the small intestine and suck blood.

Hoon, Geoffrey (1953–) British statesman, born in Derby, Derbyshire. He studied at Nottingham and Cambridge universities and worked as a lecturer before becoming a barrister. He joined the Labour Party in 1977, became an MEP (1984–94), and was elected MP for Ashfield in 1992. Following posts within the Lord Chancellor's Department (1998) and the Foreign Office (1999), he was appointed defence secretary (1999–2005), Leader of the Commons (2005–6), and minister for Europe (2006–).

hoopoe A ground-dwelling bird (*Upupa epops*) native to Africa and S Eurasia; pink body; black and white wings and tail; large crest; long curved bill. (Family: Upupidae.)

Hoover, Herbert (Clark) (1874–1964) US Republican statesman and 31st president (1929–33), born in West Branch, IA. His opposition to direct governmental assistance for the unemployed after the world slump of 1929 made him unpopular, and he was beaten by Roosevelt in 1932.

Hoover, J(ohn) Edgar (1895–1972) US public servant, born in Washington, DC. He became FBI director in 1924, and remained in charge until his death, campaigning against city gangster rackets in the inter-war years, and against Communist sympathizers in the post-war period. He was later criticized for abusing his position by engaging in vendettas against liberal activists.

Hoover Dam, formerly **Boulder Dam** (1936–47) 36°01N 114°45W. One of the world's major dams, on the Colorado R, Arizona, USA, impounding L Mead; built 1931–6; height 221 m/726 ft; length 379 m/1244 ft; can generate 1345 megawatts of hydroelectricity; named after President Hoover.

hop A perennial climber (*Humulus lupulus*) native to Europe and W Asia; stems 3–6 m/10–20 ft, twining clockwise with small hooks to aid support. Only the fruiting heads are used to flavour and preserve beer. (Family: Cannabidaceae.)

Hope, A(lec) D(erwent) (1907–2000) Poet and critic, born in Cooma, New South Wales, Australia. His *Collected Poems* (1972) is one of the major books of Australian verse.

Hope, Anthony, pseudonym of **Sir Anthony Hope Hawkins** (1863–1933) Writer, born in London. He is best known for his 'Ruritanian' romance, *The Prisoner of Zenda* (1894).

Hope, Bob, originally **Leslie Townes Hope** (1903–2003) Comedian, born near London, whose parents emigrated to the USA in 1907. In partnership with Bing Crosby and Dorothy Lamour he appeared in the highly successful *Road to...* comedies (1940–52), and in many others until the early 1970s. He was given a special Academy Award on five occasions, and he received an honorary knighthood in 1998. His 100th birthday was marked with various celebrations across America.

Hope, Christopher (1944–) Writer, born in Johannesburg, South Africa. His novels include *Kruger's Alp* (1984, Whitbread), *Serenity House* (1992, shortlisted for the Booker Prize), *Signs of the Heart* (1999), and *My Mother's Lovers* (2006). Among his nonfiction works are *White Boy Running* (1988) and *Brothers Under the Skin: Travels in Tyranny* (2003).

Hopewell The native American culture of C USA c.100 BC–AD 400. It is notable for its geometric ceremonial earthworks and richly furnished burial mounds.

Hopi [hohpee] A Shoshonean-speaking Pueblo Indian group living in Arizona, c.15 000 (2000 census). They farmed corn and other crops and became famous for their basketry and pottery.

Hopkins, Sir (Philip) Anthony (1937–) Actor, born in Port Talbot, S Wales. A member of the National Theatre, London, he made his film debut in 1967. His films include *The Silence of the Lambs* (1991, Oscar), *The Remains of the Day* (1994), *Amistad* (1997), *The Human Stain* (2003), and *All the King's Men* (2006). He received a Golden Globe for lifetime achievement in 2006.

Hopkins, Gerard Manley (1844–89) Poet, born in Stratford, London. He became a Catholic in 1866, joined the Jesuit order and was ordained in 1877. None of his poems was published in his lifetime. Robert Bridges published an edition in 1918, which was given a very mixed reception, notably to Hopkins' skilful experiments with 'sprung rhythm'; but a new edition in 1930 established him as a major poet in the English language. His best-known poems include 'The Wreck of the *Deutschland*' and 'The Windhover'.

Hopkins, Harry L(loyd) (1890–1946) US administrator, born in Sioux City, IA. Under Franklin D Roosevelt he headed the 'New Deal' projects (1935–8), became secretary of commerce (1938–40), supervised the lend-lease programme (1941), and undertook several important missions to Europe during World War 2.

Horace, in full **Quintus Horatius Flaccus** (65–8 BC) Latin poet and satirist, born near Venusia, Italy. His earliest works were chiefly satires and lampoons, and through the influence of Virgil he came under the patronage of Maecenas. The unrivalled lyric poet of his time, he produced his greatest work, the three books of *Odes*, in 19 BC.

Horatii and Curiatii [horahtiee, kyooriahtiee] An early Roman legend used to justify appeals. Under Tullus Hostilius there was war between Rome and Alba. Two groups of three brothers were selected from Rome (the Horatii) and Alba (the Curiatii) to fight, the winners to decide the battle. All were killed except one Horatius. When his sister, who was betrothed to a Curiatius, abused him, he murdered her, but was acquitted after appealing to the Roman people.

Hordern, Sir Michael (Murray) (1911–95) Actor, born in Berkhamsted, Hertfordshire. He made his professional debut in 1937. His major classical roles included King Lear (1960) and Prospero (1978), as well as several modern roles, such as in Tom Stoppard's *Jumpers* (1972) and Howard Barker's *Stripwell* (1975).

Horeb, Mount *Sinai, Mount*

horehound or **hoarhound** A perennial occurring in two species, native to Europe, Asia, and N Africa, both related to mint; leaves wrinkled; flowers 2-lipped, in whorls. **White horehound** (*Marrubium vulgare*) is used as a medicinal herb for cough remedies. (Family: Labiatae.)

hormone replacement therapy (HRT) The use of synthetic oestrogen and progesterone, taken orally in combination, to replace natural female hormones when the body has stopped producing them, usually after the menopause. It is commonly taken to relieve symptoms of the menopause such as hot flushes, night sweats, poor sleep, and vaginal dryness; it also has the beneficial effect of reducing osteoporosis. Potential side effects include thrombosis, vaginal bleeding, and an increased risk of breast cancer.

hormones Chemical messengers synthesized and secreted in small amounts by the endocrine glands of vertebrates and some invertebrates (eg certain molluscs and arthropods), which affect the functioning of the body's cells and organs. They are usually classified chemically into *amines* (eg noradrenaline, thyroxine), *peptides* (eg oxytocin), *proteins* (eg insulin), and *steroids* (eg aldosterone, testosterone).

Hormuz, Strait of [haw(r)mooz] Passage linking the Persian Gulf to the Arabian Sea; 50–80 km/30–50 mi wide; a strategic route controlling ocean traffic to the oil terminals of the Gulf.

horn A musical instrument made from metal (usually brass) tubing, with a conical bore, coiled and twisted several times and ending in a wide bell. It was traditionally associated with hunting. The tubing of the orchestral horn (or **French horn**) is about 3·6 m/12 ft in length; it has four valves and is a transposing instrument pitched in F.

hornbeam A deciduous tree (*Carpinus betulus*) growing to 30 m/100 ft, native to Europe and Asia Minor; flowers tiny in pendulous catkins; nutlets each with a 3-lobed wing-like bract; often called **ironwood** in the USA. (Family: Corylaceae.)

hornbill A large bird native to tropical Africa, S Asia, and Australasian islands; bill large, often brightly coloured, topped with large ornamental outgrowth; plumage black, brown, and white. (Family: Bucerotidae, 45 species.)

hornblende A common variety of the amphibole group of ferromagnesian silicate minerals; a hydrated calcium magnesium iron aluminosilicate that is dark green or black in colour.

Horne, Donald (Richmond) (1921–2005) Writer, academic, and arts administrator, born in New South Wales, Australia. His best-known book is *The Lucky Country* (1964), the title of which has become a common Australian expression. A leading member of the Australian Republican Movement, he wrote *The Coming Republic* (1992) and *The Public Culture* (1994), which analyse societies and nation-states.

hornet The largest social wasp; a fierce predator, up to 35 mm/$1\frac{1}{2}$ in long; yellow and black coloration. (Order: Hymenoptera. Family: Vespidae.)

Horne-Tooke, John *Tooke, John Horne*

Horney, Karen, *née* **Danielsen** (1885–1952) Psychoanalyst, born near Hamburg, Germany. During the 1920s she took issue with orthodox Freudianism, particularly in relation to women's psychosexuality, and in the 1930s developed theories about the importance of sociocultural factors in human development. In 1934 she moved to New York City, where in 1941 she helped found the Association for the Advancement of Psychoanalysis.

hornpipe A dance of British origin, popular in the 16th–19th-c. Although the best-known example is the 'Sailors' Hornpipe', the dance was not associated particularly with the navy.

hornwort A submerged aquatic perennial without roots; stems growing to 1 m/$3\frac{1}{4}$ ft; one flower at each node, tiny, lacking petals; fruits warty and sometimes spiny. (Genus: *Ceratophyllum*, 10 species. Family: Ceratophyllaceae.)

Horologium [horolohjium] (Lat 'clock') A faint S constellation contrived in the 1750s by French astronomer Nicolas Lacaille.

Horowitz, Vladimir [horovits] (1904–89) Pianist, born in Kiev. He settled in the USA and became a US citizen, but in 1986 he played again in Russia.

Horrocks, Sir Brian (Gwynne) (1895–1985) British general, born in Ranikhet, India. In 1942 he commanded the 9th Armoured Division and then the 13th and 10th Corps in N Africa, and headed the 30th Corps during the Allied invasion (1944).

Horsa *Hengist and Horsa*

horse A hoofed mammal with many domestic breeds. Modern breeds are thought to have developed from three wild ancestral types: the heavy **forest** type, and the lighter **steppe** and **plateau** types. Technically any horse up to 14·2 hands/1·5 m/58 in high at the shoulder is termed a *pony*; taller than this it is a *horse*. An *entire* (ie not castrated) male horse aged 1–4 years is called a *colt*; older than 4 years it is a *stallion*; a castrated male is a *gelding*. A female of 1–4 years is a *filly*; older than 4 years it is a *mare*. A horse less than one year old is a *foal* (*colt foal* or *filly foal*). The domestication of the horse was crucial in world history, both for agrarian and military purposes; for example, superior cavalry enabled the rapid expansion of the Huns. Fundamental, also, was the Chinese invention of the breast strap, collar harnesses (5th–6th-c AD), and stirrup (before 300). (*Equus caballus*. Order: Perissodactyla. Family: Equidae.)

horse chestnut A large, spreading, deciduous tree (*Aesculus hippocastanum*) growing to 25 m/80 ft, native to the Balkans; leaves with 5–7 leaflets, widest above the middle; flowers 4-petalled, white with yellow and pink spots, in pyramidal spikes; nuts (*conkers*) brown, shiny, two in a leathery, prickly capsule. (Family: Hippocastanaceae.)

horse fly A biting fly with large, often iridescent eyes; mouthparts form a piercing proboscis in females, inflicting painful bites. (Order: Diptera. Family: Tabanidae, c.2000 species.)

Horse Guards An elite regiment of the British Army, first raised in 1661, known as the Royal Horse Guards, whose nickname was 'the Blues'. Amalgamated in 1969 with the Royal Dragoon Guards, 'the Blues and Royals' form, with the Life Guards, the British Sovereign's *Household Cavalry*.

Horsehead nebula A famous dark nebula in the constellation Orion, resembling the silhouette of a horse's head.

Horse Latitudes Two belts of ocean calm at 30° N and S of the Equator, where conditions of high atmospheric pressure exist almost permanently.

horsepower Unit of power; symbol *hp*; equal to 745·7 W (watt, SI unit); almost obsolete, but still used in engineering to describe the power of machinery; equal to 1·0139 metric horsepower.

horse racing The racing of horses against one another, each ridden by a jockey. Popularized in England in the 12th-c, most monarchs have supported the sport, which has thereby become known as 'the sport of kings'. **Flat racing** is a straightforward race on a flat surface (grass or dirt) over a predetermined distance which can be anything between 5 furlongs (1 km) and $2\frac{1}{2}$ mi (4 km). **National hunt racing** involves the horses negotiating fences which can be either movable *hurdles* or fixed fences. These races (eg the Grand National) are longer than flat races, and can be anything up to $4\frac{1}{2}$ mi (6·5 km) in length. Bets are usually placed on the horses likely to come first (a *win*), second (a *place*), or third (a *show*), with professional bookmaking emerging in the 19th-c (along with a host of illegal or semi-legal activities), and the Totalizator concept in the 1920s.

horse-radish A perennial (*Armoracia rusticana*), probably native to S Europe, but long cultivated for the pungent seasoning prepared from the fleshy, cylindrical roots. (Family: Cruciferae.)

horsetail A primitive, spore-bearing perennial related to ferns and clubmosses; the only living genus of a formerly widespread group, the Sphenopsida, dominant during the Carboniferous period. All extant species are herbaceous. (Genus: *Equisetum*, 23 species. Family: Equisetaceae.)

horst An uplifted block of the Earth's crust, usually of great size, bounded by two normal faults. It is often elongated in shape, and may form block mountains.

Horthy (de Nagybánya), Miklós [haw(r)tee] (1868–1957) Hungarian statesman and regent (1920–44), born in Kenderes, Hungary. Minister of war in the counter-revolutionary 'White government' (1919), he opposed Bela Kun's communist regime, which he suppressed (1920). In World War 2 he supported the Axis Powers until Hungary was overrun by the Germans in 1944.

horticulture The business of growing, harvesting, and marketing fruit, vegetables, flowers, and shrubs; also practised widely as a hobby and an art form. It is usually associated with the intensive production of high-value crops, and often involves the use of irrigation in drier areas, and glass or polythene protection in cooler areas.

Horus [hawrus] An ancient Egyptian sky-god in the shape of a man with a hawk's head; also depicted as the child of Isis, when he is often called **Harpocrates**.

Horvitz, H Robert (1947–) Microbiologist, born in Chicago, IL. A researcher at the Massachusetts Institute of Technology, he shared the 2002 Nobel Prize for Physiology or Medicine for discoveries concerning the genetic regulation of organ development and programmed cell death.

Hosea, Book of, also spelled **Osee** [hohzeea] The first of the 12 so-called 'minor' prophetic writings of the Hebrew Bible/Old Testament; attributed to the prophet Hosea, who was active in the N kingdom of Israel c.750–725 BC.

Hoskins, Bob, popular name of **Robert William Hoskins** (1942–)

Actor, born in Bury St Edmunds, Suffolk. He became known with the TV series *Pennies From Heaven* (1978) and as the menacing hoodlum in the film *The Long Good Friday* (1980). He gained international stardom with his award-winning performance in *Who Framed Roger Rabbit* (1988), and later films include *Hook* (1991), *Last Orders* (2001), and *Mrs Henderson Presents* (2005).

hospice A type of hospital normally reserved for the treatment of the terminally ill, usually catering for specific age groups, typically children or the elderly. The term was originally used for a refuge attached to a monastery.

hospital An institution in which certain kinds of illness are investigated and treated. In most developed countries today, hospitals are run as either private charities or public (state) institutions, with 'teaching hospitals' closely related to universities. Most hospitals not only cater for emergencies of all types and for those whose illnesses develop acutely and unexpectedly (the *acute hospital*), but they contain specialized departments for non-emergency work and for numerous branches of medicine. Other hospitals have become exclusively specialized, and cater for the needs of single categories of ill health, such as psychiatric, orthopaedic, maternity, paediatric, and geriatric hospitals. An additional important role is the provision of out-patient departments providing consultative services for the patients of general practitioners who are under care in their own home. In the 1990s, in the UK, hospitals were allowed to opt out of local health authority control, forming themselves into *hospital trusts* (or *NHS trusts*), the others remaining as *directly-managed units* (*DMUs*).

Hospitallers Members (priests or brother knights subject to monastic vows) of the Order of the Hospital of St John of Jerusalem, originally a purely charitable organization to care for sick pilgrims to the Holy Land. From the 12th-c they played a prominent role in the Crusades as an international religious-military order. After the loss of Acre in 1291, they transferred their headquarters to Cyprus (1292), Rhodes (1309), then Malta (1530), which they held until 1798. The Sovereign Order is now based in Rome.

hot-air balloon *balloon*

hot spring A spring of hot or warm groundwater which emerges at the Earth's surface and which often contains dissolved minerals and sulphurous gases. Very hot springs emerge as geysers, and may be used as sources of geothermal energy.

Hotspur, Harry *Percy*

Hottentots *Khoisan*

Houdini, Harry [hoodeenee], originally **Erich Weiss** (1874–1926) Magician, born in Budapest. He gained an international reputation as an escape artist, freeing himself from handcuffs, and other devices, often while imprisoned in a box under water or in mid-air.

Houdon, Jean Antoine [oodõ] (1741–1828) Classical sculptor, born in Versailles, France. His works as a portrait sculptor include busts of Diderot, Voltaire, and Napoleon.

hound A category of domestic dog; name applied to breeds developed for hunting, especially those which track by scent.

housefly A small, darkish fly; females lay masses of 100–150 eggs on decaying organic matter or dung; white, worm-like maggots mature in a few days. (Order: Diptera. Family: Muscidae.)

Household Cavalry *Horse Guards*

housemaid's knee A painful inflammation of the liquid-filled pouch (*bursa*) in front of the knee joint, provoked by trauma or excessive kneeling. It is so called because of its former frequent occurrence as an occupational hazard.

house music Popular dance music that spread from south Chicago, USA, in the early 1980s. Its instrumentation is often no more than a synthesizer and drum machine; the music is loud and repetitive, with a heavy beat and baseline, insistent riffs,

and 'sampled' extracts from more imaginative recordings. A well-known example is 'Pump Up The Jam' from Technotronic.

House of Commons *Commons, House of*

House of Lords *Lords, House of*

House of Representatives In the USA, one of the two chambers of the bicameral legislature, in which, under the constitution, all legislative power is vested. There are 435 members, and each state has at least one representative.

Houses of Parliament The Palace of Westminster in London. The first palace on the site was built by King Canute in the 11th-c. By 1860 the two new, purpose-built Houses of Parliament, to accommodate the Lords and the Commons, and St Stephen's clock tower (Big Ben) had been completed.

house sparrow A small, brown and grey, ground-feeding bird (*Passer domesticus*), native to Europe, Asia, and N Africa, and introduced worldwide; also known as the **English sparrow**. (Family: Ploceidae.)

Housman, A(lfred) E(dward) (1859–1936) Scholar and poet, born near Bromsgrove, Worcestershire. He is best known for *A Shropshire Lad* (1896), a cycle of short, lyrical and often melancholy poems with a country setting, and *Last Poems* (1922). He saw himself chiefly as a Latinist, and devoted much of his life to an annotated edition (1903–30) of Manilius.

Houston [hyoostn] 29°46N 95°22W, pop (2000e) 1 953 600. Port in SE Texas, USA; on the Houston Ship Channel (1914); fourth largest city and third busiest port in the USA; settled, 1836; capital of the Republic of Texas, 1837–9, 1842–5; two airports; railway; five universities; major oil centre with huge refineries and the largest petrochemical complex in the world; corporate headquarters of numerous energy companies; base for several space and science research firms; professional teams, Astros (baseball), Rockets (basketball), Oilers (football).

Houston, Sam(uel) [hyoostn] (1793–1863) US soldier and statesman, born in Lexington, VA. As commander-in-chief in the Texan War, he defeated the Mexicans on the San Jacinto in 1836, and achieved Texan independence. He was then elected president of the republic, and after annexation (1845) became a member of the US Senate. Houston, TX, is named after him.

Houston, Whitney (1963–) Singer and actress, born in Newark, NJ. The album *Whitney Houston* (1985) won a Grammy award and included her first US number 1 hit single 'Saving All My Love For You'. Later albums include *My Love is Your Love* (1999) and *One Wish – The Holiday Album* (2003). In 1988 she broke a US chart record with seven consecutive number 1 hits. Her films include *The Bodyguard* (1992) and *The Preacher's Wife* (1996).

hovercraft *air cushion vehicle*

hoverfly A medium to large-sized fly often found hovering over flowers; adults resemble wasps. (Order: Diptera. Family: Syrphidae, over 5000 species.)

Howard, Catherine (?–1542) Fifth wife of Henry VIII, a granddaughter of the 2nd Duke of Norfolk. She became queen in 1540. After Henry learned of her alleged premarital affairs (1541), she was accused of treason and beheaded in the Tower.

Howard, Charles, 1st Earl of Nottingham (1536–1624) English lord high admiral, a cousin of Queen Elizabeth I, who commanded the English fleet against the Spanish Armada (1588). In 1601 he quelled Essex's rising.

Howard, Sir Ebenezer (1850–1928) Founder of the garden-city movement, born in London. His *Tomorrow* (1898) led to the laying out of Letchworth (1903) and Welwyn Garden City (1919) in Hertfordshire.

Howard, Elizabeth Jane (1923–) Novelist, born in London. Her first novel, *The Beautiful Visit* (1950), won the John Llewellyn Rhys Memorial Prize. The *Cazalet Chronicles* comprises *The Light Years* (1990), *Marking Time* (1991), *Confusion* (1993), and *Casting Off* (1995). Later novels include *Falling* (1999), dramatized for television in 2005.

Howard, John (1726–90) British prison reformer, born in London. As high sheriff for Bedfordshire, he investigated the condition of prisons and prisoners. As a result, two acts were passed in 1774, one providing for fixed salaries to jailers, and the other enforcing cleanliness.

Howard, John (Winston) (1939–) Australian prime minister (1996–), born in Sydney, New South Wales, Australia. He became an MP in 1974, and went on to be deputy-leader (1983–5) then leader of the Liberal Party in Opposition (1985–9, 1995–6). He became prime minister following his party's general election victory in 1996. He won a third term in 2001.

Howard, Leslie, originally **Leslie Howard Stainer** (1893–1943) Actor, born in London. During the 1930s he had many leading film roles, such as in *Gone with the Wind* (1939), and *The Scarlet Pimpernel* (1935). He was killed when a special mission flight from Lisbon to London was shot down.

Howard, Michael (1941–) British statesman, born in Gorseinon, near Swansea. He studied at Cambridge and was called to the bar in 1964. He was elected an MP in 1983, and after several junior posts became minister for local government (1987–8), minister for water and planning (1988–90), secretary of state for employment (1990–2) and the environment (1992–3), and home secretary (1993–7). He served as shadow foreign secretary (1997–9) and shadow chancellor (2001–3), and in 2003 was elected unopposed as party leader. Defeated in the 2005 general election, he stepped down in December that year.

Howard, Ron(ald William) (1954–) Actor, director, and producer, born in Duncan, OK. Born into a show business family, he appeared on stage, television, and in films from an early age. Among his best-known TV series are *The Andy Griffith Show* (1960–8) and *Happy Days* (1973–80). He made his directorial debut with *Grand Theft Auto* (1977), and later films include *Apollo 13* (1995), *A Beautiful Mind* (2002, Oscar Best Director; Golden Globe Best Film), and *The Da Vinci Code* (2006).

Howard, Trevor (Wallace) (1916–88) Actor, born in Cliftonville, Kent. He sprang to stardom with *Brief Encounter* (1945), followed by *The Third Man* (1949) and *Outcast of the Islands* (1951). His versatile and often eccentric characterizations were regularly in demand for both film and television.

Howard League for Penal Reform A charity dedicated to the cause of penal reform, named after John Howard; formed by the amalgamation of the Howard Association with the Prison Reform League in 1921.

Howe, Elias (1819–67) Inventor, born in Spencer, MA. He is best known for his invention (1846) of the sewing machine.

Howe (of Aberavon), (Richard Edward) Geoffrey Howe, Baron (1926–) British Conservative statesman, born in Port Talbot, S Wales. He was Chancellor of the Exchequer (1979–1983) and foreign secretary (1983–9), and in 1989 deputy prime minister, Lord President of the Council, and Leader of the House of Commons. He resigned from the government in 1990 in opposition to Mrs Thatcher's hostility towards European monetary union.

Howe, Richard Howe, 1st Earl (1726–99) British admiral, born in London. In the French Revolutionary Wars he defeated the French at 'the Glorious First of June' (1794).

Howe, William Howe, 5th Viscount (1729–1814) British soldier who commanded the army in North America during the American Revolution. In the American War of Independence his victories included Bunker Hill (1775), the Brandywine (1777), and the capture of New York City (1776).

Howerd, Frankie, originally **Francis Alex Howard** (1922–92) Comedian and actor, born in London. He appeared regularly on television and in films, his most famous role being that of a Roman slave in *Up Pompeii* (1970–1). In the 1980s he presented several successful television series, including *Frankie Howerd on Campus* (1990).

howitzer An artillery piece in which the shell is projected at a high angle of trajectory, typically at low muzzle velocity, to fall on to its target as plunging fire.

Hoxha, Enver, also spelled **Hodja [hoja]** (1908–85) Albanian statesman, born in Gjirokastër, Albania. He founded and led the Albanian Communist Party (1941) in the fight for national independence, and became head of state, first as prime minister (1946–54), then as first secretary of the party (1954–85).

Hoyle, Sir Fred(erick) (1915–2001) Astronomer, mathematician, astrophysicist, and science fiction writer, born in Bingley, West Yorkshire. He was known for his work on the origin of chemical elements, and was a leading proponent of steady state cosmology, of the notion that viruses come from outer space, and a believer in an extraterrestrial origin for life on Earth.

Hradčany Castle [radchanee] Since 1918, the official residence of the Czech president in Prague. The Přemysl dynasty founded a stronghold and royal residence on the site in the late 9th-c. This was destroyed by fire in 1303, and the present citadel, which incorporates both Gothic and Renaissance architecture, was built from 1344 onwards. The complex includes St Vitus's Cathedral and the royal palace.

HRT *hormone replacement therapy*

HTLV An abbreviation of **Human T-cell Leukaemia/lymphoma Virus**, a virus that causes aggressive forms of leukaemia and lymphoma and a disease called *tropical spastic paraparesis*, a severe progressive disorder of the nerves that produces paralysis. The infection is spread by sexual intercourse or by inoculation with contaminated needles.

HTML *document description language*

HTTP *document description language*

H2 blockers, also called **H2 (histamine-2)** A family of drugs which act as receptor antagonists. H2 blockers revolutionized the treatment of gastric ulcers because they can heal an ulcer in around six weeks and obviate the need for surgery. They work by stopping the local hormone histamine from stimulating acid secretion into the stomach. The first H2 blocker to be used clinically was cimetidine, also known as Tagamet in the UK.

Hua Guofeng [hwah gwohfeng], also spelled **Hua Kuo-feng** (1920–) Chinese statesman and prime minister (1976–80), born in Jiaocheng, Shanxi province. Under him China adopted a more pragmatic domestic and foreign policy, with emphasis on industrial and educational expansion, and closer relations with Western and Third World countries.

Huang He; Huang Ho *Yellow River*

Huascarán [waskaran] area 3400 km^2/1312 sq mi. National park in W Peru; a world heritage site; part of the Andean Cordillera Occidental; it rises to 6768 m/22 204 ft.

Hubbard, L(afayette) Ron(ald) (1911–86) Writer, founder of Dianetics® healing technology and of the Scientology® applied religious philosophy, born in Tilden, NE. During the 1930s he became a prolific writer of novels and short stories in several different genres. His most famous work, *Dianetics: the Modern Science of Mental Health* (1950), became an instant best seller, and the basic text of the Scientology movement. Later books include the science-fiction novel *Battlefield Earth* (1982) and the 10-volume *Mission Earth* series (from 1985).

Hubble, Edwin (Powell) (1889–1953) Astronomer, born in Marshfield, MO. His work led to the discovery of the expanding universe, by attributing the redshifts of galaxies to velocities of recession. The **Hubble constant** is a measure of the rate at which the expansion of the universe varies with distance.

Hubble constant The figure that specifies the rate at which the universe is expanding, from which the time elapsed since the 'big bang' can be estimated. To derive the Hubble constant, both the speed of recession of galaxies and their distances must be known. Improved distance measurements, aided by the Hubble Space Telescope, give the constant a value of around 60 km/sec per million parsecs. At this rate of expansion, the universe would have taken about 16 billion years to reach its present size. In practice, the expansion was probably faster in the past, and a revision announced in 1999 suggested that the true age of the universe is closer to 12 billion years.

Hubble Space Telescope An orbiting observatory, a joint project of the European Space Agency and NASA, launched in 1990 with a 2·4m (94in) aperture telescope; named after Edwin Hubble. It was expected to image objects more sharply than telescopes on Earth, and detect fainter sources. However, following the launch, a defect was discovered in the main mirror, which limited its performance. A space shuttle mission added optics to correct the defect and carried out other repairs in 1993. Further new equipment was installed by astronauts on servicing missions in 1997 and 2002, but in 2004 NASA announced it was halting its maintenance programme. This decision was reversed in 2006, with a shuttle mission to service and upgrade the telescope planned for 2008.

huckleberry An evergreen or deciduous shrub which varies from mat-forming to erect, native to the New World; flowers urn- or bell-shaped; berries black, edible. (Genus: *Gaylussacia*, 49 species. Family: Ericaceae.)

Huddersfield 53°39N 1°47W, urban area pop (2000e) 220 200. Town in West Yorkshire, N England; on the R Colne; railway; university, 1992; woollen and worsted textiles; football league team, Huddersfield Town (Terriers).

Huddleston, (Ernest Urban) Trevor (1913–98) Anglican missionary, ordained in 1937. He became Bishop of Masasi, Tanzania (1960–8), Bishop Suffragan of Stepney until 1978, then Bishop of Mauritius and Archbishop of the Indian Ocean. After his retirement, he became president of the Anti-Apartheid Movement (1981–94).

Hudson, Henry (?–1611) English navigator, who explored the NE coast of North America. He sailed in search of a passage across the Pole (1607), reached Novaya Zemlya (1608), entered the river which was named after him (1609), and (1610) travelled through the strait and bay which now bear his name.

Hudson Bay area c.1 232 250 km²/476 000 sq mi. Inland sea in Northwest Territories, Canada; maximum length c.1600 km/ 1000 mi, including James Bay (S); maximum width c.1000 km/650 mi; generally ice-clogged (but open to navigation mid-July–Oct).

Hudson River River rising in the Adirondack Mts, New York State, USA; flows 560 km/350 mi S to the Atlantic Ocean.

Hudson River School A group of 19th-c US landscape painters, including Thomas Cole (1801–48) and Thomas Doughty (1793–1856). The Hudson R valley and Catskill Mts provided favourite subjects.

Hudson's Bay Company A London-based corporation which was granted a Royal Charter to trade (principally in furs) in most of N and W Canada (Rupert's Land) in 1670. It annexed its main competitor, the Northwest Company, in 1821.

Hué [hway] 16°28N 107°35E, pop (2000e) 310 300. Town in C Vietnam; former capital of Annam and of the Vietnamese Empire; many historical sites destroyed in Vietnam War; railway; university (1957).

Hueffer, Ford Hermann *Ford, Ford Madox*

Huelva [welva], Lat **Onuba** 37°18N 6°57W, pop (2000e) 143 000. Port in Andalusia, SW Spain; bishopric; railway.

Hugh Capet *Capet, Hugh*

Hughes, Howard (Robard) (1905–76) Millionaire businessman, film producer and director, and aviator, born in Houston, TX. He inherited his father's oil-drilling equipment company at 18, and in 1926 began to involve himself in Hollywood, producing several films. In 1932 he began to design, build, and fly aircraft. He broke most of the world's air speed records (1935–8), then

abruptly returned to film making, including *The Outlaw* (1943). He eventually became a recluse.

Hughes, Owain Arwel (1942–) Conductor, born in Cardiff, S Wales. His posts include associate conductor of the BBC Welsh Symphony Orchestra (1980–6), the Philharmonia Orchestra, London (1985–90), and principal conductor of the Aalborg Symphony Orchestra, Denmark (1994–9). In 2003 he was appointed principal associate conductor of the Royal Philharmonic and conductor/music director of the National Youth Orchestra of Wales.

Hughes, Richard (Arthur Warren) (1900–76) Writer, born in Weybridge, Surrey. *The Fox in the Attic* (1961) was the first of a projected series of novels about the rise of fascism in Germany, but only one other book was completed. He also wrote several children's stories.

Hughes, Ted, popular name of **Edward (James) Hughes** (1930–98) Poet, born in Mytholmroyd, West Yorkshire. Best known for his distinctive animal poems, his first collections were *The Hawk in the Rain* (1957) and *Lupercal* (1960). He married US poet Sylvia Plath in 1956, but the marriage deteriorated, and he left her in 1962. After her suicide, he destroyed the final volume of her journal, to avoid her children seeing it – an action which brought criticism as Plath's reputation grew, and he became increasingly reclusive. He was nonetheless responsible for bringing her work before a wider public, editing her collected poems in 1981. He became poet laureate in 1984. Later works include *Rain Charm for the Duchy* (1992) and *Tales from Ovid* (1997, Whitbread). *Birthday Letters*, a series of poems about his relationship with Plath, written over 25 years, appeared unexpectedly in 1998, and won several literary prizes.

Hughes, Thomas (1822–96) Novelist, born in Uffington, Berkshire. He is primarily remembered as the author of the public school classic, *Tom Brown's Schooldays* (1857), based on his school experiences at Rugby under the headmastership of Arnold.

Hughes, William Morris, known as **Billy** (1862–1952) Australian statesman and prime minister (1915–23), born in London. He was the major proponent of conscription in World War 1, and represented Australia at the Versailles conference. He founded the United Australian Party in the early 1930s.

HUGO [hyoogoh] Acronym for **Human Genome Organization**, set up in 1989 as the first international group co-ordinating activities within the human genome project. Its legal headquarters is in Geneva, while its administrative headquarters is currently in London.

Hugo, Victor (Marie) (1802–85) Writer, born in Besançon, France. The most prolific French writer of the 19th-c, his early works include *Odes et Ballades* (1822, 1826), *Hernani* (1830), the first of the 'five-act lyrics' which compose his drama, and the novel *Notre Dame de Paris* (1831, trans The Hunchback of Notre Dame). He joined the democratic republicans; but in 1851, after the coup, he fled into exile, where he wrote several major works, notably his panoramic novel of social history, *Les Misérables* (1862). He returned to Paris in 1870, and upon his death was given a national funeral.

Huguenots [hyoogenohz] French Calvinist Protestants whose political rivalry with Catholics (eg the House of Guise) led to the French Wars of Religion (1562–98). Their leader, Henry of Navarre, succeeded to the throne (1589), granting them important concessions on his conversion to Catholicism (Edict of Nantes, 1598); these were later revoked by Louis XIV (1685), resulting in persecution and emigration.

Hu Jintao (1942–) Chinese president (2003–). He became party secretary in Guizhou (1984) and Xizang (Tibet) (1988), where he pursued a hardline policy, crushing anti-Chinese demonstrations at Lhasa in 1989. A member of the Politburo standing committee in 1992, he was appointed vice-president in 1998, and succeeded Jiang Zemin as president in 2002 and as head of the Central Military Commission (2004–).

Hull (Canada) 45°26N 75°45W, pop (2000e) 67 900. City in SW Quebec, Canada, on the Ottawa R; founded in 1801 by settlers from the USA; railway; timber.

Hull (UK), properly **Kingston-upon-Hull** 53°45N 0°20W, pop (2001e) 243 500. Seaport and unitary authority (from 1996), NE England; city status granted, 1897; a major UK container port; railway; ferry service to Rotterdam, Zeebrugge; two universities (1954, 1992); football league team, Hull City (Tigers); The Deep aquarium centre.

Hull, Clark L(eonard) (1884–1952) Psychologist, born in Akron, NY. He developed a rigorous mathematical theory of the learning process that attempted to reduce learned behaviour to a few simple axiomatic principles. Much of his work was based on reinforcement theory, as seen in *Principles of Behavior* (1943).

Hull, Cordell (1871–1955) US statesman, born in Overton, TN. He became secretary of state under Roosevelt in 1933, and attended most of the great wartime conferences. He helped to organize the United Nations, for which he received the Nobel Peace Prize in 1945.

Hull House A settlement house founded (1889) in Chicago by the social reformer Jane Addams and her associates. Set up primarily as a welfare agency for needy families, it also assisted immigrants to learn English and become American citizens. Originally housed in a single building, the settlement later expanded to become one of the largest institutions of its kind in the USA.

Hulme, Keri (Ann Ruhi) [hyoom] (1947–) Writer, born in Otautahi, Christchurch, New Zealand. She acquired international renown when her novel, *The Bone People* (1984), was awarded the Booker Prize. Maori themes figure prominently in her work. Among her short-story collections is *Stonefish* (2004).

Human Development Index (HDI) The United Nations (UN) Human Development Index was developed in 1990 by the Pakistani economist Mahbub ul Haq, and has been used since 1993 by the UN Development Programme in its annual report. The index measures poverty, literacy, education, life expectancy, and other factors, and is a standard means of measuring human progress in a country.

human engineering ergonomics

human genome project An ambitious plan launched in 1985 to determine the exact sequence of all 3×10^9 base pairs in the human genome. The project is loosely co-ordinated by a number of national and international organizations, including HUGO. The project was over 90% complete by 2002.

human immuno-deficiency virus AIDS

humanism Historically, a movement that arose with the Italian Renaissance, in the writings of Ficino, Pico, and later Erasmus and More. The humanists drew on classical literature and emphasized the centrality of human achievements and potential, in opposition to many of the claims of dogmatic theology and science.

human rights A concept deriving from the doctrine of natural rights, which holds that individuals, by virtue of their humanity, possess fundamental rights beyond those prescribed in law. First formally incorporated into the US Declaration of Independence (1776), most written constitutions contain a bill of rights. The UN's General Assembly adopted a Universal Declaration of Human Rights in 1948, followed in 1953 by the European Convention on Human Rights. The European Court of Human Rights was established within this framework.

Human T-cell Leukaemia/lymphoma Virus HTLV

Humber, River River estuary in NE England; runs 64 km/40 mi E and SE; entrance dominated by Spurn Head; Humber Bridge, 1981.

Humber Bridge Single-span suspension bridge, built (1973–81)

across the R Humber, E England; length of main span 1410 m/4626 ft; total length 2220 m/7283 ft; second-longest suspension bridge (after Akashi-Kaikyo) in the world.

Humberside pop (2000e) 904 000; area 3512 km²/1356 sq mi. Former county of NE England; created in 1974 from parts of Lincolnshire and Yorkshire; replaced in 1996 by unitary authorities of East Riding of Yorkshire, Hull, North Lincolnshire, and North East Lincolnshire.

Humboldt, (Friedrich Wilhelm Heinrich) Alexander, Freiherr (Baron) von [humbohlt] (1769–1859) Naturalist and geographer, born in Berlin. His major work, *Kosmos* (1845–62), endeavours to provide a comprehensive physical picture of the universe. The ocean current off the W coast of South America is named after him.

Humboldt, (Karl) Wilhelm von [humbohlt] (1767–1835) German statesman and philologist, born in Potsdam, Germany. He was the first to study Basque scientifically, and also worked on the languages of the East and of the South Sea Is.

Hume, (George) Basil, Cardinal [hyoom] (1923–99) Roman Catholic Benedictine monk and cardinal. Ordained in 1950, he became Abbot of Ampleforth in 1963, where he remained until created Archbishop of Westminster and a cardinal in 1976.

Hume, David [hyoom] (1711–76) Philosopher and historian, born in Edinburgh. His major works include *A Treatise of Human Nature* (1739–40), consolidating and extending the empiricist legacy of Locke and Berkeley, the six-volume *History of England* (1746–62), and *Essays Moral and Political* (1741–2). He wrote the posthumously published *Dialogues concerning Natural Religion* in the 1750s.

Hume, John (1937–) Northern Ireland politician, born in Londonderry. Leader of the Social Democratic Labour Party, in 1993 he and Sinn Féin leader Gerry Adams began a series of talks, the Hume–Adams peace initiative, intended to bring about an end to violence in Northern Ireland. He shared the 1998 Nobel Peace Prize with David Trimble for his efforts to find a peaceful solution to the conflict. He stepped down as leader of the SDLP in 2001 and as an MEP in 2004.

humidity The amount of water vapour in a sample of air, usually expressed as relative or absolute humidity. **Absolute humidity** is the total mass of water in a given volume of air, expressed in grams per cubic centimetre. Warmer air is able to hold more water vapour than cold air.

hummingbird A small bird restricted to the New World; often brightly coloured; feeds on nectar from plants; fast wing-beat and modification of wing structure allows hovering. (Family: Trochilidae, 320 species.)

humpback whale A baleen whale of the rorqual family (*Megaptera novaeangliae*), found worldwide; dark back and pale undersurface; wide tail and very long slender flippers; jaws and flippers with many rough knobs; have complex 'songs' unique to each population.

humped cattle zebu

Humperdinck, Engelbert (1854–1921) Composer, born in Siegburg, Germany. He composed several operas, one of which, *Hänsel und Gretel* (1893), was highly successful.

Humperdinck, Engelbert, popular name of **Arnold George Dorsey** (1936–) Singer, born to British parents in Chennai (Madras), SE India, and brought up in Leicester, UK. In 1965 he changed his name and had his first hit single 'Release Me' (1967). He had further hits with 'There Goes My Everything' (1967) and 'The Last Waltz' (1967). After the 1970s his career as a cabaret artist blossomed in America.

Humphrey, Doris (1895–1958) Dancer, choreographer, and teacher, born in Oak Park, IL. She wrote the key text on dance composition in modern dance, *The Art of Making Dances* (1959).

Humphrey, Hubert H(oratio) (1911–78) US Democratic statesman, born in Wallace, SD. He built up a strong reputation as a liberal, but, as vice-president from 1964 under Johnson, alienated many of his supporters by defending the policy of continuing the war in Vietnam. He narrowly lost the 1968 election to Nixon.

Humphries, (John) Barry (1934–) Comic performer and satirical writer, born in Melbourne, Victoria, Australia. He created the Barry McKenzie comic strip in *Private Eye* (1964–73), and wrote and appeared in *The Adventures of Barry McKenzie* (1972). He is best known for his characters **Sir Les Patterson** and 'housewife megastar' **Dame Edna Everage**, who have frequently appeared on television and in film.

Humphrys, John (Desmond) (1943–) Television journalist and presenter, born in Cardiff, S Wales. In 1966 he joined the BBC, and became a foreign and diplomatic correspondent, then presenter on the Nine O'Clock News (1981–6). He joined the *Today* programme on Radio 4 (1987), and began to present *On the Record* for BBC 1 (1993). In 2003 he became host of the revived classic TV quiz show *Mastermind*. He received the 2001 Media Society Award and the 2003 Sony Radio Award.

humus Decomposed organic matter, usually present in the topsoil layers. It improves soil structure, making cultivation easier, and gives the soil a characteristic dark colour.

hundred An old subdivision of a shire, sometimes containing about 100 hides (c.12 000 acres), which had its own court, and formed a unit of local administration in the government of England from at least the 10th-c to the 19th-c.

Hundred Days (Mar–Jun 1815) The period between Napoleon I's escape from Elba and his defeat at the Battle of Waterloo, during which he returned to Paris and tried to reconstitute the Empire.

Hundred Years' War A series of wars between England and France dated by convention 1337–1453. When Edward III claimed the French throne, from 1340 styling himself 'king of England and France', traditional rivalries exploded into a dynastic struggle. In 1417 the English turned from raiding to territorial conquest, a task ultimately beyond their resources. Eviction from Guyenne (1453) reduced England's French territories to Calais (lost 1558) and the Channel Is.

Hungarian uprising (Oct–Nov 1956) National insurgency in Budapest following the denunciation of Stalin at the 20th Soviet Communist Party Congress. When the new prime minister, Imre Nagy, announced plans for Hungary's withdrawal from the Warsaw Pact, Soviet and Hungarian troops and tanks crushed the uprising, and Nagy was executed.

Hungary p.447

Hunniford, Gloria (1940–) British broadcaster, born in Portadown, Co Armagh. She became widely known with her daily radio programme for BBC's Radio 2 (1982–95), while participating in several shows, including London Weekend Television's *Sunday Sunday* (1982–91) and BBC's *Gloria Live* (1990–3). She has written an autobiography, *Gloria* (1994), and *Next to You* (2005), a best-selling biography of her daughter, **Caron Keating** (1962–2004).

Huns An Asiatic people who in 375 overran the Gothic tribes of S Russia, and precipitated the great Germanic migration into the Roman Empire. United under Attila, they laid waste parts of Gaul, the Balkans, and Italy (451–2), but were then forced to retreat.

Hunt, (R) Tim(othy) (1943–) Biochemist, born in London. In 1990 he joined the Cell Cycle Control Laboratory at the Imperial Cancer Research Fund in London. He shared the 2001 Nobel Prize for Physiology or Medicine for his contributions to understanding the key regulators of the cell cycle.

Hunt, Henry, known as **Orator Hunt** (1773–1835) Radical agitator, born in Upavon, Wiltshire. He was a well-to-do farmer who in

1800 became a staunch radical, and spent his life advocating the repeal of the Corn Laws and parliamentary reform.

Hunt, (William) Holman (1827–1910) Painter, born in London. He helped to inaugurate the Pre-Raphaelite Brotherhood. His works in this vein included, notably, 'The Light of the World' (1854, Oxford).

Hunt (of Llanfair Waterdine), (Henry Cecil) John Hunt, Baron (1910–98) Mountaineer, born in Marlborough, Wiltshire. In 1953 he led the first successful expedition to Mt Everest, and in 1958 led the British party in the British–Soviet Caucasian mountaineering expedition.

Hunt, (James Henry) Leigh (1784–1859) Poet and essayist, born in Southgate, Greater London. From 1808 he edited with his brother *The Examiner*, which became a focus of Liberal opinion. His *Autobiography* (1850) is a valuable picture of the times.

hunter–gatherers Populations living entirely, or almost so, by hunting animals and gathering food. In 10 000 BC the entire world population consisted of hunters and gatherers; today they are fewer than 0·001%, including the Pygmies in Africa and Australian Aborigines.

Huntingdon 52°20N 01°12W, pop (2000e) 21 300, with Godmanchester. Town in Cambridgeshire, EC England; on Great Ouse R; railway; birthplace of Oliver Cromwell.

Huntingdon, Selina Hastings, Countess of, *née* **Shirley** (1707–91) Methodist leader, born in Staunton Harold, Leicestershire. Joining the Methodists in 1739, she made Whitefield her chaplain, and assumed a leadership among his followers, who became known as 'the Countess of Huntingdon's Connexion'.

Huntingdonshire Former county of EC England; part of Cambridgeshire since 1974.

Huntington's chorea [koreea] An inherited degenerative disorder of the brain, in which slowly developing dementia is associated with uncontrolled jerking or slow writhing movements. It is named after US physician George Sumner Huntington (1850–1916).

Huntsville 34°44N 86°35W, pop (2000e) 158 200. Town in N Alabama, USA; railway; university; major US space research centre.

Hunyady, János [hoonyodi] (c.1387–1456) Hungarian statesman and warrior. His life was one unbroken crusade against the Turks, whom he defeated in several campaigns, notably in the storming of Belgrade (1456).

Hurd (of Westwell), Douglas (Richard), Baron [herd] (1930–) British statesman, born in Marlborough, Wiltshire. A Conservative MP from 1974, he became Northern Ireland secretary (1984), home secretary (1985), and foreign secretary (1989–95). He stood unsuccessfully as a candidate in the leadership contest following Mrs Thatcher's resignation (Nov 1990), remaining foreign secretary under John Major. He was made a Companion of Honour in 1996, and received a life peerage in 1997. His writing includes memoirs and political novels.

hurdling 1 An athletics event which involves foot racing while clearing obstacles (**hurdles**) en route. Race distances are 100 m and 400 m for women, 110 m and 400 m for men. The height of a hurdle varies according to the type of race: $2\frac{3}{4}$ ft (84 cm) for the 100 m; 3 ft (91·4 cm) for the 400 m; and $3\frac{1}{2}$ ft (106·7 cm) for the 110 m. Hurdles are also included in the steeplechase. **2** A form of horse race in which the horses have to clear hurdles. It is not as testing as the steeplechase.

hurdy-gurdy A mechanically bowed string instrument known since mediaeval times. The player turns a handle which causes a wooden wheel to rotate and to sound a number of accompanimental drone strings. Melodies are played on a simple keyboard, operated by the other hand.

hurling or **hurley** An Irish 15-a-side team field game played with curved sticks and a ball. The object is to hit the ball with the stick into your opponents' goal: under the crossbar scores 3

Hungary

□ International Airport

Hung **Magyarország**, official name **Republic of Hungary**, Hung **Magyar Köztársaság**

Local name Magyarország

Timezone GMT +1

Area 93 033 km²/35 912 sq mi

Population total (2002e) 10 162 000

Status Republic

Date of independence 1918

Capital Budapest

Language Hungarian (Magyar) (official)

Ethnic groups Magyar (92%), German (2%), Slovak (1%), Romanian and Yugoslav minorities

Religions Roman Catholic (67%), Calvinist (20%), Lutheran (5%)

Physical features Drained by the R Danube (flows N–S) and its tributaries; crossed (W) by a low spur of the Alps; highest peak, Kékestetö, 1014 m/3327 ft; frequent flooding, especially in the Great Plains (E); 54% of land arable; 18% forested.

Climate Fairly extreme continental climate, due to landlocked position; average annual temperature 0°C (Jan), 21°C (Jul) in Budapest; wettest in spring and early summer; average annual rainfall 600 mm/23·6 in; cold winters; R Danube sometimes frozen over for long periods; frequent fogs.

Currency 1 Forint (HUF) = 100 fillér

Economy Large-scale nationalization as part of centralized planning strategy of the new republic, 1946–9; greater independence to individual factories and farms, from 1968; grain, potatoes, sugar beet, fruit, wine; coal, bauxite, lignite; metallurgy, engineering, chemicals, textiles, food processing.

GDP (2002e) $134 bn, per capita $13 300

Human Development Index (2002) 0·835

History Kingdom formed under St Stephen I, 11th-c; conquered by Turks, 1526; part of Habsburg Empire, 17th-c; Austria and Hungary reconstituted as a dual monarchy, 1867; republic, 1918; communist revolt led by Béla Kun, 1919; monarchical constitution restored, 1920; new republic with communist government, 1949; uprising crushed by Soviet forces, 1956; during 1989, pressure for political change towards a multi-party system; multi-party elections in 1990 saw an end to communist rule; governed by a National Assembly which elects a Presidential Council and Council of Ministers; joined European Union, 2004.

Head of State
1987–8 Károly Németh
1988–9 Brunó Ferenc Straub
1989–90 Mátyás Szűrös
1990–2000 Arpád Göncz
2000–5 Ferenc Madl
2005– László Sólyom

Head of Government
1987–8 Károly Grosz
1988–90 Miklós Németh
1990–3 József Antall
1993–4 Peter Boross
1994–8 Gyula Horn
1998–2002 Viktor Orban
2002–4 Peter Medgyessy
2004– Ferenc Gyurcsany

---

points; above the crossbar but between the posts scores 1 point. It has been played since 1800 BC.

Huron [hyooron] Iroquoian-speaking North American Indians, who settled in large towns and farming villages in Quebec and Ontario in the 16th-c. Defeated by the Iroquois in 1648–50, they were finally driven by whites to Oklahoma.

Huron, Lake [hyooron] Second largest of the Great Lakes, North America, on the US–Canadian frontier; 330 km/205 mi long; 294 km/183 mi wide; area 59 570 km²/22 994 sq mi, 60% in Canada; empties into L Erie (E) via the St Clair R, L St Clair, and the Detroit R; generally ice-bound in winter months (Dec–Apr).

hurricane An intense, often devastating, tropical storm which occurs as a vortex spiralling around a low pressure system. Wind speeds are very high (above 34 m/s/75 mph), but the centre (*eye*) of the storm is characterized by calm weather. Hurricanes usually develop between July and October, and move in a W or NW direction (SW in the S hemisphere), losing energy as they reach land. They are also known as **typhoons** in

the western N Pacific and **cyclones** in the Bay of Bengal. Each year they are named in alphabetical sequence as they occur (excluding rare letters, such as Q and X), to avoid confusion when more than one storm is being followed at the same time. Different sets of names are used in the central Pacific, eastern Pacific, and the Atlantic Basin. In the Atlantic, for example, the names are English, Spanish, and French, and occur in a six-year cycle. Originally female names were used, but male names were introduced for the first time in 1978. Names are sometimes retired, if their storms are exceptionally damaging (such as David in 1979 and Bob in 1991).

Hurt, John (1940–) Actor, born in Chesterfield, Derbyshire. He won BAFTA awards for *Midnight Express* (1978) and *The Elephant Man* (1980); other films include *Alien* (1979), *Rob Roy* (1995), and *Outlander* (2007). Theatre work includes Samuel Beckett's solo play *Krapp's Last Tape* (2000), and for TV he starred in *Bait* (2002) and *The Alan Clark Diaries* (2004).

Hurt, William (1950–) Actor, born in Washington, DC. He won a Best Actor Oscar for *Kiss of The Spiderwoman* (1985), and Oscar nominations for *Children Of A Lesser God* (1986) and *Broadcast News* (1987). Later films include *A History of Violence* (2005, Best Supporting Actor nomination) and *The Good Shepherd* (2006).

husky A domestic dog, one of several spitz breeds traditionally used in the Arctic as a beast of burden (especially to pull sledges); also known as **eskimo dog**.

Huss or **Hus, John** (c.1369–1415) Bohemian religious reformer, born in Husinec, Czech Republic. After writing his main work, *De ecclesia* (1413, On the Church), he was called before a General Council at Constance, and burned after refusing to recant. The anger of his followers in Bohemia led to the Hussite Wars.

Hussain, Nasser [husayn] (1968–) Cricketer, born in Madras, India. A batsman, he joined Essex in 1987 and made his England debut in 1990. He achieved a career-best 207 runs against Australia at Edgbaston in 1997, and during 1998–9 he was England's most successful batsman in the Ashes series defeat in Australia. Appointed England captain in 1999, he led his country to its first series victory over the West Indies on home soil since 1969. Following a captaincy of mixed fortunes, he announced his retirement as one-day captain in 2003, and later stepped down as Test captain. He retired from first class cricket in 2004.

hussars Light cavalry, regiments of which were formed in many national armies from the late 18th-c onwards. They were modelled on an idealized 'Hungarian' style of horseman-warrior, with an exotic uniform and an elaborate fur helmet.

Hussein (ibn Talal) [husayn] (1935–99) King of Jordan (1952–99), born in Amman. He steered a middle course in the face of the political upheavals inside and outside his country, favouring the Western powers, while supporting Arab nationalism. After increasingly frequent raids by the PLO into Israel from Jordan, he ordered the Jordanian army to move against them, and after a short civil war (1970), the PLO leadership fled abroad. His decision to cut links with the West Bank (1988) prompted the PLO to establish a government in exile. In 1994 he signed an official peace with Israel. He was married four times; his second wife, Toni Gardiner, was an Englishwoman, by whom he had an heir, Abdullah, in 1962.

Hussein, Saddam [husayn], also spelled **Sadam Husain** (1937–2006) President of Iraq (1979–2003), born in Awja, Takrit, Iraq. He played a prominent part in the 1968 revolution and on the retirement of al-Bakr, became sole president. His disastrous attack on Iran in 1980, led to a war of attrition which ended in 1988. He invaded Kuwait in 1990, but was forced to withdraw when he was defeated by a coalition of Arab and Western forces in Operation Desert Storm (1991). Iraq then suffered international isolation and economic sanctions. His breaching of the peace terms led to further military strikes during the next decade, but he continued to resist UN and US pressure for a programme of weapons inspection within Iraq. World opinion was divided in 2002 following President Bush's threat of war as part of a renewed campaign to remove him from office. UN weapons experts resumed inspections, 2002–3, but Iraq's apparent failure to comply with UN resolutions to eliminate its weapons of mass destruction led to a US-led military invasion in March 2003. He was deposed the following month, but his whereabouts in the immediate aftermath of the war were unknown. In December 2003 he was captured by US forces on a farm in the town of Al-Dawr, near Takrit, and held as a prisoner-of-war. His trial for war crimes began in Baghdad in 2005 and was frequently beset by interruptions and delays. In November 2006 he was found guilty of crimes against humanity and executed the following month.

Husserl, Edmund (Gustav Albrecht) [huserl] (1859–1938) Philosopher, founder of the school of phenomenology, born in Prossnitz, Czech Republic. His chief work was the two-volume

Logische Untersuchungen (1900–1, Logical Investigations) defending the view of philosophy as an *a priori* discipline.

Hussites Followers of John Huss, who in the early 15th-c constituted a movement for the reform of the Church in Bohemia (Czech Republic). They anticipated many aspects of the 16th-c Reformation.

Huston, John (Marcellus) [hyoostn] (1906–87) Film director, born in Nevada, MO. His films include *The Maltese Falcon* (1941), *The African Queen* (1951), *Moby Dick* (1956), and the musical, *Annie* (1982).

Hutton, James (1726–97) Geologist, born in Edinburgh. His book *A Theory of the Earth* (1795) forms the basis of modern geology.

Hutton, Len, popular name of **Sir Leonard Hutton** (1916–90) Cricketer, born in Fulneck, West Yorkshire. He was the inspiration of England after World War 2, and skipper of the team which regained the Ashes in 1953. Playing for England against Australia at the Oval in 1938, he scored a world record 364 runs. During his first-class career (1934–60) he scored 40 140 runs (average 55·51), including 129 centuries.

Hutton, Sir James Brian Edward, Lord (1931–) Judge, born in Belfast. He studied at Oxford (1953) and Queen's University, Belfast, and was called to the Northern Ireland Bar (1954) and the English Bar (1972). He was appointed Judge of the High Court of Justice (NI) 1979–88, Lord Chief Justice of Northern Ireland (1988–97), and Lord of Appeal in Ordinary (1997–2004), and was knighted in 1988. He was appointed to chair the enquiry (2003–4) into the circumstances surrounding the death of Dr David Kelly, the Ministry of Defence's chief scientific officer and weapons inspector, who was a key figure in the row between the government and the BBC over claims that Downing Street 'sexed up' a dossier on Iraq's weapons capability. Having been identified by the press, Kelly became the centre of media attention and committed suicide soon after. In his report (Jan 2004), Lord Hutton criticised the BBC for its editorial procedures and attached no blame to the government for the naming of Kelly. The apparently 'black-and-white' nature of the conclusions led to the report being controversially received.

Hutu and Tutsi Bantu-speaking peoples of the republics of Burundi and Rwanda, EC Africa, speaking the same language and having a common culture. The Hutu, mostly peasant farmers, comprise more than 80% of the total population in both countries. They were subjugated by the Tutsi, warrior–pastoralists of Nilo-Hamitic stock, who migrated S in the 14th–15th-c. The Tutsi dominated Rwanda until 1961, when Belgian colonial rulers helped the Hutu to seize power and form the first independent government, and 10 000 Tutsi were killed. In Burundi, the Hutu led an unsuccessful revolt against the Tutsi in 1971, in which over 100 000 Hutu were massacred by the army, and 120 000 fled to Tanzania. In 1994, following the shooting down of an aircraft carrying President Habyarimana, Hutu militias sought revenge on the Tutsi minority. About a million people were killed in subsequent months. Following successes by the Tutsi-led Rwanda Patriotic Front, over the next year some 2 million refugees (mainly Hutu) fled to neighbouring countries. Conflict continued in 2002, against a backdrop of international concern, but a ceasefire was announced in December.

Huxley, Aldous (Leonard) (1894–1963) Novelist and essayist, born in Godalming, Surrey. His reputation was made with his satirical novels *Crome Yellow* (1921) and *Antic Hay* (1923). Later novels include *Point Counter Point* (1928) and his best-known work, *Brave New World* (1932).

Huxley, Sir Andrew Fielding (1917–) Physiologist, born in London. He helped to provide a physico-chemical explanation for nerve transmission, and outlined a theory of muscular contraction. He shared the Nobel Prize for Physiology or Medicine in 1963.

Huxley, Elspeth (Josceline) (1907–97) Novelist and essayist, born in London. Her best-known novel, *The Flame Trees of Thika* (1959), was about her childhood in Kenya, as was *The Mottled Lizard* (1962) and *Love Among the Daughters* (1968). She also wrote detective novels, such as *Death of an Aryan* (1939, also known as *The African Poison Murders*).

Huxley, Sir Julian (Sorell) (1887–1975) Biologist, born in London. He applied his scientific knowledge to political and social problems, formulating a pragmatic ethical theory based on the principle of natural selection. He was the first director-general of UNESCO (1946–8), the grandson of T H Huxley.

Huxley, T(homas) H(enry) (1825–95) Biologist, born in Ealing, Greater London. He became the foremost expounder of Darwinism, to which he added an anthropological perspective in *Man's Place in Nature* (1863). He also wrote essays on theology and philosophy from the viewpoint of an 'agnostic', a term he introduced.

Huygens, Christiaan [hoygenz] (1629–95) Physicist and astronomer, born in The Hague, The Netherlands. In 1655 he discovered the ring and fourth satellite of Saturn, and in 1657 made the first pendulum clock. In optics he propounded the wave theory of light, and discovered polarization.

Huysmans, Joris Karl [hoysmahnz] (1848–1907) Novelist of Dutch origin, born in Paris. His best-known works are *À rebours* (1884, Against the Grain), a study of aesthetic decadence, and the controversial *Là-bas* (1891, Down There), which dealt with devil-worship.

hyacinth A bulb native to the Mediterranean region and Africa; flowers bell-shaped, held horizontally or drooping in spikes. (Genus: *Hyacinthus*, 30 species. Family: Liliaceae.)

Hyades [hiyadeez] A bright open cluster of stars 46 parsec distant. It makes a V-shaped group for the bull's face in the zodiacal constellation Taurus.

hyaena *hyena*

hybrid An individual animal or plant resulting from cross-breeding between genetically dissimilar parents. It is typically used for the offspring of mating between parents of different species or subspecies, such as the mule (produced by cross-breeding an ass and a horse).

Hyde, Douglas, Ir *Dubhighlas de Hide* (1860–1949) Writer, philologist, and first president of Ireland (1937–45), born in Frenchpark, Co Roscommon. He was founder and first president (1893–1915) of the Gaelic League, and professor of Irish in the National University (1909–32).

Hyde Park A royal park covering 255 ha/630 acres in C London. It was first opened to the public during the reign of James I. The Albert Memorial, Speaker's Corner, and Marble Arch are situated in the park. The Diana, Princess of Wales Memorial Fountain was opened in 2004.

Hyderabad (India) [hiydrabad] 17°22N 78°26E, pop (2000e) 3 529 000. Capital of Andhra Pradesh, S India; founded in 1589 as capital of the Kingdom of Golconda; joined with India, 1948; Muslim stronghold in S India; airfield; railway; four universities (1918, 1964, 1972, 1974); commercial centre.

Hyderabad (Pakistan) [hiydrabad], also **Haidarabad** 25°23N 68°24E, pop (2000e) 1 300 000. City in Sind province, SE Pakistan; on the R Indus; provincial capital from 1768 until captured by the British in 1843; airfield; railway; university (1947).

Hyder Ali *Haidar Ali*

Hydra (Greece) [hiydra], Gr **Ídhra** pop (2000e) 3960; area 50 km²/20 sq mi. Island in the Aegean Sea, Greece, off the E coast of the Peloponnese; chief town, Hydra; tourism.

Hydra (astronomy) [hiydra] (Lat 'sea serpent') The largest and longest constellation in the sky, extending from the celestial equator into the S hemisphere, but with no particularly bright stars.

Hydra (mythology) [hiydra] In Greek mythology, a many-headed monster, the child of Typhon and Echnida, whose heads regrew when struck off. It was killed by Heracles.

Hydra (zoology) [hiydra] A genus of solitary, freshwater coelenterates; stalk-like body attached at the base; apical mouth surrounded by tentacles; typical green colour derived from green algal cells contained in body. (Phylum: Cnidaria. Class: Hydrozoa.)

hydrangea [hiydraynja] An evergreen or deciduous shrub, or a climber with aerial roots, native to Asia, and North/South America; **lacecaps** have heads with large, sterile flowers surrounding the fertile ones; **hortensias** or **mop-heads** have heads composed entirely of large, sterile flowers. Both forms produce blue flowers on acid soils, pink on alkaline soils. (Genus: *Hydrangea*, 80 species. Family: Hydrangaceae.)

hydrate A compound containing water, usually one in which the water is present as 'water of crystallization', such as in gypsum ($CaSO_4.2H_2O$), a hydrate of calcium sulphate.

hydraulics The study of systems using liquids, whether stationary or moving, for the transmission of force; often, water or oil is the transmitting fluid. Any machine which uses, controls, or conserves a liquid makes use of the principles of hydraulics. The applications include such fields as irrigation, domestic water supply, hydroelectric power, and the design of dams, canals, and pipes. Most motor vehicles have hydraulic braking systems.

hydrobiology The branch of biology dealing with the study of life in aquatic habitats, especially those in freshwater. Its core is formed by the study of planktonic plants and animals.

hydrocarbons Compounds containing only carbon and hydrogen. Many hundreds of such compounds are known, and most occur in coal, petroleum, or natural gas. There are two main subdivisions: **aliphatic hydrocarbons**, of which methane (CH_4) is the simplest, and **aromatic hydrocarbons**, based on benzene.

hydrocephalus [hiydrohsefaluhs] The abnormal accumulation of cerebrospinal fluid within the ventricular system inside the brain. It causes distension of the brain and, in infants, enlargement of the skull.

hydrochloric acid An aqueous solution of hydrogen chloride (HCl), a strong acid, fully dissociated into H^+ and Cl^-. Gastric juice in the human stomach is 2% hydrochloric acid.

hydrocortisone *corticosteroids; cortisol*

hydrocyanic acid [hiydrohsiyanik] Hydrogen cyanide (HCN), or its aqueous solution; also known as **prussic acid**. Pure hydrogen cyanide is an exceedingly poisonous liquid, boiling at 26°C, and having an odour of almonds.

hydrodynamics *fluid mechanics*

hydroelectric power (HEP) Electricity generated using the potential energy of water. It is a renewable energy source with considerable potential worldwide, although it accounts for only a small proportion of the world's energy needs. The world's largest HEP scheme is at Itaipú on the Parana R.

hydrofluoric acid Hydrogen fluoride (HF), or its aqueous solution. Although extremely corrosive, it is only a moderately strong acid, partially neutralized solutions having a pH of about 3.

hydrofoil A vessel able to raise itself clear of the water on attaining a certain speed. Foils are fitted at a depth greater than the draft of the hull. Successful trials were first held in Italy in 1906, but 50 years elapsed before the Italians put it to commercial use. Speeds of around 40 knots are common in commercial service.

hydrogen H, element 1, the lightest of the chemical elements, the commonest isotope having only one proton and one electron in an atom. Its stable form is a gas with diatomic molecules (H_2). Although it makes up more than 90% of the atoms in the universe, it is much less common on Earth, and mainly occurs combined with oxygen in water and with carbon in hydrocarbons.

hydrogenation The addition of hydrogen to a compound, also often called **reduction**. It occurs, for example, in the conversion of ethylene to ethane, important in the saturation of fats and in petroleum refining.

hydrogen bomb The popular name (often shortened to **H-bomb**) for thermonuclear weapons which achieve their destructive effects through the intense release of heat and blast produced when the nuclei of hydrogen isotope materials used in the construction of the weapon are fused together in a nuclear reaction. The reaction is triggered by the detonation of an atomic bomb used as the weapon's core. The hydrogen bomb was first developed in the USA at Los Alamos laboratories. The first successful test was made at Enewetak Atoll in November 1952.

hydrography The science of charting the water-covered areas of the Earth, including the determination of water area, coastline, and depth, as well as the flow characteristics of rivers, lakes, and seas.

hydrology The science concerned with the occurrence and distribution of water on or near the Earth's surface, in oceans and in the atmosphere, particularly in relation to the interaction of water with the environment and fresh water as a resource. **Applied hydrology** covers topics such as irrigation schemes, dam design, drainage, flood control, and hydroelectric power.

hydrolysis [hydrolisis] The splitting of a molecule by the action of water. The technique is applied, for example, in the conversion of an ester into an alcohol and an acid (eg fats into fatty acids and glycerol).

hydrophobia *rabies*

hydroponics The growing of plants in nutrient solutions, without soil. The method is especially used in the production of high-quality tomatoes and cucumbers, under glass.

hydrostatics *fluid mechanics*

hydrotherapy *hyperthermia*

hydroxide The ion OH^- or a compound containing it. The only metal hydroxides soluble in water are those of the alkali metals and, to a lesser extent, calcium, strontium, and barium.

hydroxybenzene *phenol*

hydroxybutanedioic acid *malic acid*

hydroxypropanoic acid *lactic acid*

Hydrozoa [hiydrozoha] A class of mainly marine coelenterates in which the life-cycle involves alternation between attached polyp and planktonic medusa phases. (Phylum: Cnidaria.)

Hydrus [hiydrus] (Lat 'water snake') An inconspicuous constellation of the S hemisphere.

hyena or **hyaena** [hiyeena] A nocturnal carnivorous mammal; stocky, dog-like, with short back legs; large head with strong jaws; inhabits plains in SW Asia and Africa. (Family: Hyaenidae, 3 species.)

Hygeia [hiygeea] In Greek mythology, a minor deity, the daughter of Asclepius; the name is a personification of the word for 'health'.

hygrometer [hiygrometer] A meteorological instrument used for measuring the relative humidity of the air. A **hygrograph** gives a continuous record of relative humidity.

Hyksos [hiksos] The so-called 'shepherd kings' of ancient Egypt, who founded the XVth dynasty there c.1670 BC. They were originally desert nomads from Palestine.

Hymen [hiymen] In ancient Greece and Rome, the god of marriage. He is depicted as a youth with a torch.

Hymenoptera [hiymenoptera] A diverse order of insects containing about 130 000 species, including the sawflies, horntails, wasps, bees, and ants; adults typically with two pairs of membranous wings; mouthparts adapted for chewing, or sucking nectar; social organization exhibited by many species.

hymn A song of praise to God, usually with a non-Biblical text in verses. It is sung congregationally with accompaniment on the organ or other instruments.

Hypatia [hiypateea] (c.375–415) Greek philosopher, daughter of Theon, an astronomer and mathematician of Alexandria. Associated by many Christians with paganism, she was murdered by a fanatical mob.

hyperactivity The combination of overactive, poorly controlled behaviour with inattention and lack of concentration for a particular task. This condition is most frequently seen in children.

hyperbola In mathematics, the locus of a point which moves so that the difference of its distances from two fixed points (*foci*) is constant. Some of the comets move in hyperbolae, and the curve is much used in architecture.

hyperbole Exaggeration, used often for comic or rhetorical effect, as throughout the writings of Rabelais, or in the mouth of Shakespeare's Falstaff. Charles Dickens used it skilfully. It is the staple of the tabloid press, and also of ordinary conversation ('I'm dying for a drink').

Hyperboreans In Greek mythology, an unvisited people of fabled virtue and prosperity, living in the land 'beyond the North Wind'.

hypercube (computing) An arrangement of computers in the form of a cube. Communications links between the computers enable them to carry out tasks in parallel.

hyperglycemia / hyperglycaemia [hiypergliyseemia] A level of blood sugar above the upper limit of the normal range (>160 mg/100 ml).

Hyperion (astronomy) [hiypeerion] The seventh natural satellite of Saturn, discovered in 1848; distance from the planet 1 481 000 km/920 000 mi; diameter 400 km/250 mi; orbital period 21·277 days.

Hyperion (mythology) [hiypeerion] In Greek mythology, a Titan, son of Uranus and Gaia, and father of Eos (the Dawn), Helios (the Sun), and Selene (the Moon); later identified with the Sun.

hypermedia A form of document which can be held on a computer, consisting of elements of text, audio and video sequences, and computer programs, linked together in such a way that users can move from one element to another and back again. When these operations are carried out within a database consisting solely of texts, the domain is known as **hypertext**.

hypermetropia *eye*

Hyperrealism *Photorealism*

hypersensitivity *allergy*

hypertension A condition in which both systolic and diastolic blood pressure (BP) rise above normal levels. All levels of BP above normal damage blood vessels; the greater the increase, the greater the damage. In the majority of cases the cause of high BP is unknown.

hypertext *document description language; hypermedia*

HyperText Mark-up Language / Transfer Protocol *document description language*

hyperthermia The use of artificial fever for the treatment of disease. The fever can be induced by heat, hydrotherapy (water-treatment, in the form of steam or hot bath immersion), diathermy, and the injection of foreign protein. Since fever is one of the body's natural reactions to the presence of infection or other disease, it is reasoned that a high body temperature may have beneficial effects.

hyperthyroidism Oversecretion of thyroid hormones, leading to an increase in the body's metabolic rate; also known as **Graves disease** after Irish physician Robert James Graves (1796–1853). Symptoms include a warm skin with tremor of the hands, weight loss, a rapid heart rate with palpitations, and protrusion of the eyes.

hypnosis A temporary trance-like state induced by suggestion, in which a variety of phenomena (eg increased suggestibility and alterations in memory) can be induced in response to verbal or other stimuli. A hypnotic trance is not in any way related to sleep, but there is a constriction of responses by the hypnotized subject. The technique was first used by Mesmer in France, and the term *hypnosis* was coined by the British surgeon James Braid (1795–1860).

hypnotics Drugs that promote drowsiness and sleep. They include benzodiazepines and barbiturates.

hypo Popular name for sodium thiosulphate, incorrectly known as 'hyposulphite'. It is used as a fixing solution in photographic processing.

hypochondria A preoccupation with physical health and excessive anxiety about illness. The hypochondriac interprets common physical symptoms as being due to a serious disease, for example headache is believed to be due to a brain tumour. The fear of disease can interfere with daily life, often leading to medical examinations, but persists despite medical reassurance.

hypoglycemia / hypoglycaemia [hiypohgliyseemia] A blood sugar level below the lower limit of normal. It is rare except in diabetics who have mistakenly administered themselves with too much insulin. It initially produces weakness, sweating, and confusion, which may be followed by fainting and coma. Blood sugar can be restored by giving sugar by mouth or by intravenous injection.

hypophysis [hiypofisis] *pituitary gland*

hypothalamus [hiypohthalamus] A region of the vertebrate brain, situated below the thalamus, which has an important regulatory role regarding the internal environment (eg water balance, body temperature in mammals). It is also involved in the control of emotions by the limbic system.

hypothermia [hiypohthermia] A deep body temperature of 35°C or less, measured clinically by a rectal thermometer. It occurs after immersion in cold water, exposure to low environmental temperatures, and following prolonged unconsciousness or immobilization. Treatment is by gradual rewarming.

hypothyroidism [hiypohthiyroydizm] Reduced function of the thyroid gland, with a fall in the secretion of thyroid hormones. Body metabolism falls, and patients develop an increased dislike of cold weather; physical and mental activity slows down.

Hyracotherium [hiyrakotheerium] The first fossil horse, known from the early Eocene epoch of North America, Europe, and Asia; four hoofed toes on forelimbs, three on hind limbs; formerly known as *Eohippus*. (Family: Equidae.)

hyrax [hiyraks] A mammal, native to Africa and Arabia; superficially resembles a large guinea pig, with pointed muzzle and round ears; the only members of the order Hyracoidea; also known as **daman**, **dassie**, **rock rabbit**, or (in Bible) **cony**. (Family: Procaviidae, 11 species.)

Hyrcanus I, John [heerkaynus] (2nd-c BC) High priest of Israel and perhaps also a king subject to Syrian control (c.134–104 BC); the son of the high priest Simon, and in the line of Hasmonean priestly rulers.

hyssop [hisop] A small, shrubby perennial (*Hyssopus officinalis*) growing up to 60 cm/2 ft, native to S Europe and W Asia; flowers 2-lipped, violet-blue, in whorls forming long, loose 1-sided spikes; originally cultivated as a medicinal herb. (Family: Labiatae.)

hysterectomy [histerektomee] The surgical removal of the uterus. This operation is indicated in cases of malignant tumours of the uterus, in benign growths (*fibroids*) when these have become large, and in the event of excessive, uncontrollable vaginal bleeding.

hysteria In its most general sense, a colloquial and derogatory term, used especially for histrionic behaviour. More specifically, it is used in psychiatry to describe a personality profile or a neurotic illness. It may also describe a symptom in which there is a physical manifestation without an organic cause.

i

iamb [iyam] A metrical foot consisting of one unstressed and one stressed syllable, as in the word 'release'. It is the most common measure in English verse.

Iapetus (astronomy) [iyapitus] The eighth natural satellite of Saturn, discovered in 1671; distance from the planet 3 560 000 km/ 2 212 000 mi; diameter 1460 km/910 mi; orbital period 79·33 days.

Iapetus (mythology) [iyapitus] In Greek mythology, one of the Titans, the father of Prometheus, Epimetheus, Atlas, and Menoetius.

IAU *International Astronomical Union*

Ibadan [ibadan] 7°23N 3°56E, pop (2000e) 1 578 000. City in Nigeria; founded in the 1830s; British control, 1896; airfield; railway; regarded as the intellectual centre of the country; university (1948).

Ibáñez, Vicente Blasco Blasco Ibáñez, Vicente

Ibárruri (Gómez), Dolores [eebaruree], known as **la Pasionaria** ('The Passionflower') (1895–1989) Spanish politician and orator, born in Gallarta, Spain. With the outbreak of the Civil War (1936), she became the Republic's most emotional and effective propagandist. After the war, until 1977, she took refuge in the USSR, becoming president of the Spanish Communist Party in exile.

Iberian Peninsula [iybeerian] area c.593 000 km²/229 000 sq mi. The region of Europe SW of the Pyrenees, including Portugal and Spain; Iberia is an ancient name for Spain.

Iberians A group of iron-age peoples inhabiting the S and E periphery of present-day Spain, and extending N into present-day France as far as the Rhône valley.

ibex A wild goat with high sweeping curved horns; horns round in cross-section and ringed with ridges; two species: **ibex** (*Capra ibex*) from the mountains of Europe, N Africa, and S Asia; **Spanish ibex** (*Capra pyrenaica*) from the Pyrenees.

Ibibio [ibibeeoh] A cluster of Kwa-speaking peoples of SE Nigeria. Agriculturalists, they are also renowned for their woodcarvings.

ibis A wading bird native to tropical and warm temperate regions; long curved bill; face naked. (Family: Threskiornithidae, c.23 species.)

Ibiza [ibeetha] or **Iviza** [eeveetha], ancient **Ebusus** pop (2000e) 71 000; area 572 km²/221 sq mi. Third largest island in the Balearic Is; a major tourist island; capital, Ibiza, pop (2000e) 30 000, founded by the Carthaginians, 645 BC.

IBM *International Business Machines*

Ibo *Igbo*

Ibsen, Henrik (Johan) (1828–1906) Playwright and poet, born in Skien, Norway. His international reputation began with *Brand* and *Peer Gynt* (1866–7). He regarded his historical drama, *Kejser og Galilaeer* (1873, Emperor and Galilean) as his masterpiece, but his fame rests more on the social plays which followed, notably *Et Dukkehjem* (1879, A Doll's House) and *Gengangere* (1881, Ghosts). In his last phase he turned more to

Symbolism, as in *Vildanden* (1884, The Wild Duck), *Rosmersholm* (1886), and *Bygmester Solness* (1892, trans The Master-Builder). The realism of *Hedda Gabler* (1890) was a solitary escape from Symbolism.

Icaria [ikaria], Gr **Ikaría** area 255 km²/98 sq mi. Greek island in the Aegean Sea; named after the legendary Icarus; Ayios Kyrikos is a popular resort.

Icarus (astronomy) [ikarus] Asteroid no.1566, discovered in 1949, diameter 1·5 km/0·9 mi. It has an orbital period of 1·12 years and occasionally passes close to the Earth.

Icarus (mythology) [ikarus] In Greek mythology, the son of Daedalus. His father made him wings to escape from Crete, but he flew too near the Sun; the wax holding the wings melted; and he fell into the Aegean at a point now known as the Icarian Sea.

ICBM *intercontinental ballistic missile*

ice The common solid form of water, stable below 0°C. Unlike most solids, it is less dense than its liquid, because the strong hydrogen bonds formed hold the molecules in a relatively open network.

Ice Age A period of time in the Earth's history when ice sheets and glaciers advanced from polar regions to cover areas previously of temperate climate. Several ice ages are known, the most recent ('the Ice Age') being from c.1 million years ago and lasting until c.10 000 years ago.

iceberg A floating mass of ice, detached from ice sheets or glaciers, drifting on ocean currents for up to several years and for many hundreds of kilometres before melting. With only a fraction of their mass above water level they are a danger to shipping, particularly in the N Atlantic.

icebreaker A vessel designed to clear waterways of ice by propelling itself onto the surface of the ice, breaking it with the weight of the fore part of its hull, which is specially shaped and strengthened for this purpose. Icebreakers are commonly employed in Russia, the Baltic, and Canada.

ice hockey *p.453*

Iceland *p.454*

Icelandic *Germanic / Scandinavian languages; Icelandic literature*

Iceland spar *calcite*

Iceni [ikaynee] An ancient British tribe occupying what is now Norfolk and NW Suffolk. They rebelled in AD 47 and again in 60, when their queen, Boudicca, led them and other tribes in a major revolt against Rome.

ice skating 1 Figure skating, artistic dancing on ice. Competitions are held for individual, pairs, and ice dancing. **2 Speed skating**, in which one competitor races against another on an oval ice track over distances of 500–10 000 m (550–11 000 yds).

I-ching [ee ching] *Book of Changes*

ichneumon (entomology) [iknyoomn] A slender, parasitic wasp; females often have elongate egg-laying tube; larvae feed on other insects as parasites. (Order: Hymenoptera. Family: Ichneumonidae.)

ichneumon (mammal) [iknyoomn] The largest living mongoose

ice hockey

A sport played on ice between two teams of six players all wearing ice skates and protective clothing. It is a fast, aggressive game, played with sticks and a small, circular, rubber puck, on a rink 56–61 m/184–200 ft long and 26–30 m/85–98 ft wide. The aim is to hit the puck into the opponent's goal. Players (apart from the goalie) are often substituted during the game, and may enter and leave while the game is in play. Ice hockey is thought to have been first played in Canada in the 1850s. The National Hockey League (NHL) was established in 1917, and consists of US and Canadian professional teams. The sport's chief prize is the Stanley Cup, first awarded in 1893 in Canada, and later presented by the NHL. The governing body is the International Ice Hockey Federation, founded in 1908.

(*Herpestes ichneumon*) (length, 1 m/3¼ ft), native to Africa and the Middle East; also known as **Egyptian mongoose** or **Pharaoh's rat**.

ichthyosaur [ikthiosaw(r)] An aquatic reptile with streamlined body for fast swimming; tail typically large, paddle-like; known mainly from the Jurassic period. (Subclass: Ichthyopterygia.)

Icknield Way [ikneeld] A Neolithic track linking Salisbury Plain in SE England to the E coast. The Romans gravelled it and used it as a secondary road.

Ickx, Jacky [iks] (1945–) Motor-racing driver, born in Brussels. He was world champion in 1982–3 (both Porsche), and won the Le Mans 24-hour race a record six times.

icon (art and religion) (Gr *eikon*, 'image') A representation of Christ, the Virgin Mary, angels, saints, or even events of sacred history, used since the 5th-c for veneration and an aid to devotion, particularly in the Greek and Russian Orthodox Churches. They are typically in Byzantine style, flat, and painted in oils on wood, often with an elaborately decorated gold or silver cover.

icon (computing) In computing, a small image or symbol used in graphic displays to represent an item such as a program or disk drive. Commands can be given to the computer using a mouse to point at an icon, thereby selecting the task related to the icon that needs to be performed.

iconoclasm [iykonoklazm] (Gr 'image breaking') The extreme rejection of the veneration of images. The practice was supported by the pope and the Roman emperor in the 8th-c, and again by certain Reformers in the 16th-c.

iconography The branch of art history which, faced with a picture, or any kind of image, takes as its central question: who or what is represented? Originally concerned with the identification of portraits, it now covers the whole science of subject-matter and symbolism.

Ictinos or **Ictinus** [iktiynus] (5th-c BC) Greek architect, who shares with Callicrates the glory of designing the Parthenon at Athens (447–438 BC).

Idaho [iyda-hoh] pop (2000e) 1 294 000; area 216 422 km²/ 83 564 sq mi. State in NW USA; the 'Gem State'; first European exploration by Lewis and Clark, 1805; held jointly by Britain and the USA until 1846; Territory of Idaho established, 1863; admitted to the Union as the 43rd state, 1890; bounded N by Canada (British Columbia); highest point Borah Peak (3860 m/ 12 664 ft); largely rugged, mountainous country, with nearly half the state (mostly N) under national forest; Snake R Plain is one of the largest irrigated areas in the USA; capital, Boise; mainly an agricultural state; contains one of the deepest gorges in the world (Hell's Canyon).

Id al-Adha [eed al adha] The Muslim 'Feast of Sacrifice', celebrating the faith of Abraham, who was willing to sacrifice his son at Allah's request.

Id al-Fitr [eed al feeter] A Muslim festival, the 'Feast of Breaking Fast', occurring on the first day after Ramadan.

ide *orfe*

idealism In philosophy, the theory that the material world is in some sense created by the mind and does not exist independently of it; the only things which really exist are minds and their contents. Physical objects are collections of ideas that exist only in so far as they are perceived by finite, human minds or by the infinite mind, God.

ideography [idiografee] The study of writing systems which use symbols called **ideographs** or **ideograms** – a development from primitive picture writing, found in early systems of the Far and Middle East. An ideograph represents an abstract concept to which its shape bears no clear relationship; for example, a hand might represent friendship. Most of the symbols come to represent words, and are thus more precisely referred to as *logographs*.

idiolect [idiohlekt] The total linguistic system of an individual, in a given language, at any specific time. Different preferences in usage, grammar, vocabulary, and pronunciation serve to keep idiolects apart.

idiophone Any musical instrument whose sound proceeds from

Iceland

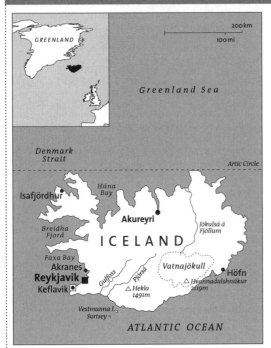

☐ International Airport

Icelandic **Ísland**, official name **Republic of Iceland**, Icelandic **Lýdhveldidh Ísland**

Local name Ísland
Timezone GMT
Area 103 000 km²/40 000 sq mi
Population total (2002e) 288 000
Status Republic
Date of independence 1944
Capital Reykjavík

Language Icelandic (official)

Ethnic groups Homogeneous (96%), with European minorities

Religions Protestant (95%) (Evangelical Lutheran 93%, other Lutheran 2%), Roman Catholic (1%), non-religious (1%)

Physical features Several active volcanoes, including Hekla, 1491 m/4920 ft; Helgafell, 215 m/706 ft; and Surtsey, 174 m/570 ft; famous for its geysers; many towns heated by subterranean hot water; heavily indented coastline with many long fjords; high ridges rise to 2119 m/6952 ft at Hvannadalshnjúkur (SE); several large snowfields and glaciers.

Climate Changeable; summers cool and cloudy, mild winters; average annual temperature 1°C (Jan), 11°C (Jul); Reykjavík generally ice-free throughout year; average monthly rainfall reaches 94 mm/3·7 in (Oct)

Currency 1 Króna (ISK) = 100 aurar

Economy Based on inshore and deep-water fishing (75% of national income); stock and dairy farming, potatoes, greenhouse vegetables; aluminium, diatomite; tourism.

GDP (2002e) $8·444 bn, per capita $30 200

Human Development Index (2002) 0·936

History Settled by the Norse, 9th-c; world's oldest Parliament (Althing), 10th-c; union with Norway, 1262; union with Denmark, 1380; independent kingdom in personal union with Denmark, 1918; independent republic, 1944; extension of the fishing limit around Iceland in 1958 and 1975 precipitated the 'Cod War' disputes with the UK; ceased whaling in 1992 but resumed in 2003; governed by a bicameral Parliament (Althing), President, Prime Minister, and Cabinet.

Head of State
1944–52 Sveinn Björnsson
1952–68 Asgeir Asgeirsson
1968–80 Kristján Eldjárn
1980–96 Vigdís Finnbogadóttir
1996– Olafur Ragnar Grimsson

Head of Government
1980–3 Gunnar Thoroddsen
1983–7 Steingrímur Hermannsson
1987–8 Thorsteinn Pálsson
1988–91 Steingrímur Hermannsson
1991–2004 Davíd Oddsson
2004–6 Halldor Asgrimsson
2006– Geir Haarde

the body of the instrument itself, without the action of vibrating strings, membranes, loudspeakers, or columns of air.

Idomeneus [iydomenyus] The leader of the Cretans who assisted the Greeks at Troy. Being caught in a storm at sea, he vowed to sacrifice the first thing he met on his safe return. This was his own son; and after carrying out the sacrifice he was driven into exile.

Idumeans *Edomites*

Ife [eefay] A ceremonial and trading centre in SW Nigeria, occupied from the 11th-c AD, from which the Yoruba dispersed to found their kingdoms. The related Benin tradition may also derive from Ife.

Igbo or **Ibo** [eeboh] An agricultural people of E Nigeria; their language is a member of the Kwa branch of the Niger–Congo family. They established the short-lived state of Biafra (1960–70).

Ignarro, Louis J (1941–) Pharmacologist, born in New York City. He worked at the University of California, Los Angeles (from 1985), and shared the 1998 Nobel Prize for Physiology or Medicine for his contribution to the discovery of nitric oxide as a signalling molecule in the cardiovascular system.

Ignatius (of Antioch), St [ignayshus] (c.35–c.107) One of the apostolic Fathers, reputedly a disciple of St John, the second Bishop of Antioch. According to Eusebius, he died a martyr in Rome. Feast day 17 October.

Ignatius de Loyola, St *Loyola, Ignatius of, St*

igneous rock Rocks that have formed by crystallization of magma originating within or below the Earth's crust. *Plutonic* rocks form deep in the Earth and are coarse-grained (eg granite); *volcanic* rocks form on the Earth's surface and are fine-grained (eg basalt); and *hypabyssal* rocks form at relatively shallow depths (eg dolerite).

ignis fatuus [ignis fatyoouhs] Flickering lights sometimes seen at night in marshy areas, and thought to be due to the spontaneous combustion of marsh gas (methane) generated by decaying vegetation. It is commonly termed **will-o'-the-wisp** or **Jack-o'-lantern**.

Iguaçu [igwasoo], Brazil **Iguaçu**, Argentina & Paraguay **Iguazú** National park close to the borders of Argentina, Brazil and Paraguay; area 1950 km²/750 sq mi; 82 m/269 ft-high Iguaçu Falls; a world heritage site.

iguana [igwahna] A lizard, native to the New World, Madagascar,

Fiji, and Tonga; often has crest of tooth-like projections along back; tongue thick and fleshy. (Family: Iguanidae, 650 species.)

Iguanodon [igwahnodon] A heavily built two-legged dinosaur; up to 8 m/26 ft in length; plant-eating; known mainly from the Lower Cretaceous period of Europe. (Order: Ornithischia.)

Ijsselmeer or **Ysselmeer** [eselmair] area 1240 km²/480 sq mi. Shallow lake in NW Netherlands, formed from the S part of the Zuider Zee inlet by the construction of the Afsluitdijk Sea Dam (1932).

Ikaría *Icaria*

ikebana [eekaybahna] The formal Japanese style of flower arrangement, which selects a few blooms or leaves and places them in a very careful relationship to one another.

Illinois [ilinoy] pop (2000e) 12 419 300; area 145 928 km²/56 345 sq mi. State in NC USA; the 'Prairie State'; 21st state admitted to the Union, 1818; explored by Jolliet and Marquette in 1673 and settled by the French; included in French Louisiana, it was ceded to the British in 1763 and by the British to the USA in 1783; capital, Springfield; mostly flat prairie producing maize, soybeans, wheat; chief cities include Chicago; highest point, Charles Mound (376 m/1234 ft); diverse manufacturing centred on the Chicago area.

illiteracy *literacy*

illuminance In photometry, the incident luminous flux per unit area, ie the amount of visible light available to provide illumination per square metre; symbol E, units lx (lux); also called **illumination**.

Illyria [iliria] In antiquity, the E seaboard of the Adriatic and its mountainous hinterland. It was roughly the equivalent of the W half of former Yugoslavia and NW Albania.

ilmenite [ilmeniyt] A black oxide mineral, iron titanate (FeTiO₃), found in basic igneous rocks and beach sand deposits. It is the major ore of titanium.

ILO *International Labour Organization*

Ilyushin, Sergey Vladimirovich [ilyooshin] (1894–1977) Aircraft designer, born in Dilialevo, Russia. His designs include the Il-4 long-range bomber, which was important in World War 2. Afterwards his passenger aeroplanes became the basic Soviet carriers.

imagery Figurative language; the illustration and emphasis of an idea by analogies and parallels of different kinds, to make it more concrete and objective. Images may be explicit in the form of a simile ('As cold as any stone') or implicit in the form of a metaphor ('You blocks, you stones, you worse than senseless things'). Imagery is often thought of as mainly visual, but images often invoke the other senses and may operate even on an abstract level.

imaginary number *numbers*

Imagism An early Anglo-American 20th-c poetic movement which sought to return (and confine) poetry to its essential ingredient, the image, which 'presents an intellectual and emotional complex in an instant of time' (Ezra Pound). It has been widely influential.

imam [imahm] **1** A religious leader and teacher of a Sunni Muslim community, who leads worship in the mosque.
2 A title given to the founders or great leaders of Muslim communities or schools.
3 A charismatic leader among Shiite Muslims, who believe that in every generation there is an imam who is an infallible source of spiritual and secular guidance. The line of imams ended in the 9th-c, and since then the ayatollahs serve as the collective caretakers of the office until the return of the expected imam.

IMAX [iymaks] A large-screen cinematograph system, developed in Canada in 1968. Film is projected on a screen typically 18–23 m/60–75 ft wide and 14–18 m/45–60 ft high, and viewed by an audience seated comparatively close so that the picture fills their field of vision. OMNIMAX was a further development in

1972, using wide-angle lenses for projection on a domed screen c.23 m/75 ft in diameter.

Imhotep [imhohtep] (fl.27th-c BC) Egyptian physician and adviser to King Zoser (3rd dynasty). He was later worshipped as the life-giving son of Ptah, god of Memphis. The Greeks identified him with Asclepius.

Immaculate Conception The belief that the Virgin Mary from the moment of her conception was free from sin. It was promulgated as a dogma of the Roman Catholic Church by Pope Pius IX in 1854.

immigration *migration* 1

immortelle The name applied to various species of the daisy family (Compositae), cultivated for the papery flower-heads which retain their colour and are often used dried in flower arrangements.

immunity (law) A state of freedom from certain legal rules and their consequences. Diplomatic immunity is a provision of the Vienna Convention on Diplomatic Relations (1961), an international treaty, which states that diplomatic agents will have immunity from all criminal jurisdiction of the receiving state and immunity from certain civil jurisdiction. The ambassador may waive immunity.

immunity (medicine) The reaction of the body to material that it perceives to be 'not-self'. The term was originally used to describe the body's ability to resist the development of disease in the event of exposure to a disease-causing micro-organism. It now also includes the body's response to other foreign proteins such as transplants and allergens. Naturally occurring or **innate immunity** protects individuals from infections with which they have not had previous contact; it is a non-specific response to any material perceived as 'not-self'. **Acquired** or **adaptive immunity** is a specific response mediated by lymphocytes and antibodies.

immunization The artificial introduction into the body of immunity against infectious micro-organisms. *Passive immunization* involves administering antibodies against the infectious agent, derived from the blood of another individual who has recovered from the disease. *Active immunization (vaccination)* involves administering proteins (*antigens*) belonging to the infectious agent itself.

immunoglobulin *antibodies*

immunology Originally the study of the biological responses of a living organism to its invasion by bacteria, viruses, or parasites, and its defence against these. It now also includes the study of the body's reaction to other foreign substances, particularly proteins, such as those in transplanted organs.

immunosuppression The suppression of the immune response of the body to the presence of foreign protein. It may occur in a number of special clinical conditions, such as organ transplantation, and in the treatment of certain malignant tumours and auto-immune diseases. Immunosuppression renders patients vulnerable to infections in general, and also to micro-organisms which are not commonly the cause of disease in normal individuals.

impact printer A printer which relies on the character being pressed onto the paper via an inked ribbon. Examples include dot matrix, daisy-wheel, golfball, and line printers.

impala [impahla] An African grazing antelope (*Aepyceros melampus*); golden brown, paler on underside; dark stripe each side of tail; male with lyre-shaped horns ringed with ridges.

impatiens [impayshienz] A member of a large genus of annuals and perennials, native to Europe, Asia, most of Africa, and North America; translucent, watery stems; flowers hanging horizontally from a slender stalk, showy; fruit a capsule exploding audibly and scattering seeds. Hybrids between *Impatiens holstii* and *Impatiens sultanii*, with mostly red, pink, or white flowers, are popular ornamentals known as

busy Lizzie. (Genus: *Impatiens*, 500–600 species. Family: Balsaminaceae.)

impeachment A legal process for removing undesirable persons from public office. Originating in mediaeval England, it was revived in the 17th-c during the conflict between the monarch and parliament. Impeachment is a cumbersome method because of the problem of defining unacceptable behaviour and crimes. The move to impeach US President Nixon did, however, force his resignation, whereas the attempt to impeach President Clinton in 1999 failed.

impedance In alternating current circuits, a measure of the restriction of current flow (in much the same way as resistance is used for direct current circuits); defined as voltage divided by current; symbol Z, units Ω (ohm).

Imperial Conferences *Colonial and Imperial Conferences*

imperialism The extension of the power of the state through the acquisition, normally by force, of other territories, which are then subject to rule by the **imperial power**. The main era of imperialism was the 1880s to 1914, when many European powers sought to gain territories in Africa and Asia. The term is now often applied to any attempts by developed countries to interfere in underdeveloped countries. There is also increasing interest in the idea of *neocolonialism*, where certain countries are subjugated by the economic power of developed countries, rather than through direct rule.

Imperial War Museum The Museum of British and Commonwealth military operations since 1914, founded in London as a memorial to those who died in World War 1. A new branch, the Imperial War Museum North, opened in Manchester in 2002.

impetigo [impetiygoh] A superficial infection of the skin common in children, usually due to *Staphylococcus aureus*. Infection affects the face, hands, and knees.

impotence Inability in males to engage in sexual intercourse because of failure to achieve an erection. A minority of cases of impotence are from organic diseases, and physiological problems (such as insufficient bloodflow or the side-effects of medication) may also be factors. More commonly a number of psychological causes are responsible, such as the strength of the sexual drive, and marital, family, and social relationships.

Impressionism (art) A modern art movement which started in France in the 1860s; the name, coined by a hostile critic, was taken from Claude Monet's picture, 'Impression: sunrise' (1872). The Impressionists rejected the dark tones of 19th-c studio painting, set up their easels out-of-doors, and tried to capture the brilliant effects of sunlight on water, trees and fields, and pretty girls.

imprinting (behaviour) The process whereby animals rapidly learn the appearance, sound, or smell of significant individual members of their own species (eg parent) or important sub-categories (eg suitable mates) through being exposed to them, often during a restricted period of life.

imprinting (genetics) The specific silencing of some DNA regions from a parent during meiosis and the formation of sperm or egg. In the resulting offspring the genes in these areas will not be able to be active. Disease can occur where a DNA deletion from the non-imprinted parent is matched by imprinting on the corresponding chromosome from the other parent (as with Angelman and Prader-Willi syndromes).

improvisation The performance of music without following a predetermined score; an important constituent of music for many centuries. In the classical concerto, for example, the cadenza provided a major formal context for brilliant soloistic improvisation. The art of improvising on a given theme has survived mainly in organ lofts and in jazz, where both individual and ensemble improvisations have always played an important role.

Imran Khan, in full **Ahmad Khan Niazi Imran** (1952–) Cricketer, born in Lahore, Pakistan. A fast bowler, adaptable batsman, and astute captain, he inspired Pakistan's rise to prominence in world cricket. After leading Pakistan to the 1992 World Cup, he retired with a total of 3807 runs and 362 wickets in Test matches. His highly publicized nine-year marriage to Jemima Goldsmith ended in 2004. In addition to following a career in politics, forming his own party, Pakistan Tehrik-i-Insaaf (Pakistan Justice Movement), he is a cricket commentator.

incandescent lamp A lamp which produces visible light from a heated source or filament. Examples include arc lamps, gas lights, and filament electric light bulbs.

Incarnation (Lat 'the putting on of flesh') In Christianity, the union between the divine and human natures in the one Jesus Christ; the 'Word' of God becoming 'flesh' (*John* 1.14). The term is also appropriate to other religions (eg Hinduism) in which a life-spirit is given a material form.

Incas or **Inka** Originally a small group of Quechua-speaking Indians living in the C Andean highlands; during the 15th-c, one of the world's major civilizations, and the largest Precolumbian state in the New World, with an estimated population of 5–10 million. In the 11th-c, they established their capital at Cuzco, the Sacred City of the Sun, where they built huge stone temples and fortresses, and covered their buildings in sheets of gold. During the 15th-c, they brought together much of the Andean area, stretching along the entire W length of South America. In 1523, Spanish invaders under Pizarro captured the emperor Atahualpa, whom they later murdered, and by the 1570s Indian power was totally destroyed.

Ince, Paul (1967–) Footballer, born in Ilford, Greater London. A midfielder, he played for West Ham, Manchester United, and Inter Milan, signing for Liverpool (1997), Middlesbrough (1999), Wolverhampton Wanderers (2002–6), and Swindon Town (2006). In 2006 he became player-manager at Macclesfield Town. A member of the Euro 2000 team, he won 53 caps playing for England.

incendiary bomb A bomb which causes its destructive effects by burning fiercely and igniting the structures on which it lands. It was used with great effect by both sides during World War 2.

incense A mixture of gums and spices which gives off a fragrant odour when burnt. It is widely used in many religious rites, and its smoke is often regarded as symbolic of prayer.

incest Sexual relations with close kin. In Western society, it refers to sex in the nuclear family other than between man and wife, but the precise specification of when a relationship is too close to allow sexual relations varies between cultures.

Inch'n [inchon], also **Jinsen** or **Chemulpo** 37°30N 126°38E, pop (2000e) 1 996 000. City in W Korea; on the coast of the Yellow Sea; scene of battle between Japanese and Russian navies, 1904; UN forces landed there during Korean War, 1950; major port for Seoul, to which it is linked by subway; university (1954).

incomes policy *prices and incomes policy*

income tax A major source of government revenue, levied on personal incomes. Income below some lower limit is usually exempt, and the tax rate levied on further slices of income varies, at rates fixed from time to time in the budget. There may also be a range of special tax allowances, such as for charitable covenants.

incontinence The involuntary loss of urine or faeces, which tends to occur when intra-abdominal pressure is increased, such as during coughing. Common in children, it can also affect the elderly due to a loss of tone in the muscular rings (*sphincters*) that control the passage of urine and faeces from the bladder and bowel; these muscles may also be damaged by childbirth.

incubator (neonatal) A chamber, used for small, premature, or unwell newborn babies, designed to provide a sterile environment with a constant temperature. It may be used in conjuction with other instruments and machines, such as a ventilator as in the case of respiratory distress syndrome.

incubus [ingkyubus] A malevolent male spirit supposed in mediaeval superstition to have intercourse with women in their sleep. Witches and demons were the offspring of such unions. The equivalent female spirit was a **succubus**.

Independence Day *Fourth of July*

Independence Hall A building in Independence National Historical Park, Philadelphia, PA, where the Declaration of Independence was proclaimed (1776); a world heritage site. The Liberty Bell, rung at the proclamation, is kept here.

Independent Labour Party (ILP) A British political party, socialist in aim, formed in 1893 with the objective of sending working men to parliament. Many of its leaders played a major part in founding the Labour Party in 1906, to which it was affiliated until 1932. In 1975, the ILP returned to the Labour Party as a publishing body and pressure group.

independent schools Schools in the UK which are not dependent on either the government or local authorities for their income, but derive it principally from the fees paid by parents.

index (bibliography) *indexing*

index (mathematics) A notation which simplifies the writing of products, eg $2 \times 2 \times 2 \times 2$ is written 2^4, where 4 is the index (or *exponent*); it can be extended to give meaning to fractional, negative, and other indices.

indexation A system under which contracts provide for regular revision of prices, wages, pensions, or rents in line with some chosen index of prices. The argument for indexation is that it offers stability of real incomes in times of inflation to workers or pensioners, and avoids the need for repeated ad hoc renegotiation of wages, etc. The disadvantage of widespread indexation is that if the various revisions are staggered over time, as seems inevitable, this gives rise to a wage–price spiral, making inflation extremely difficult to stop once it has started. Many countries have adopted some degree of indexation.

index fund An investment fund where shares are bought in all the companies listed in the main stock exchange index, then held. In this way the portfolio of shares will always equal movements in the stock market.

indexing The compiling of systematic guides to the location of words, names, and concepts in books and other publications. An index consists of a list of entries, each of which comprises a heading, together with any qualifying phrase and/or subheading(s), and at least one page reference or cross-reference ('see...'). Several procedures are available, such as 'letter-by-letter' indexing (in which *seabird* would appear before *sea horse*) and 'word-by-word' indexing (in which *sea horse* would appear before *seabird*).

Index Librorum Prohibitorum [indeks librawrum prohhibitawrum] (Lat 'index of forbidden books') A list of books which members of the Roman Catholic Church were forbidden to read. It originated with the Gelasian Decree (496), and was frequently revised, but in 1966 it was decided to publish no further editions.

India pp.458–59

Indiana [indiana] pop (2000e) 6 081 000; area 93 716 km²/ 36 185 sq mi. State in E USA, S of L Michigan; the 'Hoosier State'; 19th state to join the Union, 1816; visited by La Salle in 1679 and 1681; occupied by the French, who ceded the state to the British in 1763; scene of many Indian battles; hilly in the S, fertile plains in the C, and flat glaciated land in the N; capital, Indianapolis; grain, soybeans, pigs, cattle; bituminous coal, limestone, steel and iron, chemicals, motor vehicles, electrical goods.

Indianapolis [indianapolis] 39°46N 86°09W, pop (2000e) 782 000. Capital of state in C Indiana, USA, on the White R; founded, 1820; state capital, 1825; airport; railway; university

(1855); professional teams, Indiana Pacers (basketball), Colts (football); Motor Speedway (where the world-famous 'Indianapolis 500' motor race is held).

Indian dance An ancient dance tradition based on Hindu thought, but showing Arab and Mughal influences. Classical dance forms are of religious or court origin, while folk forms are social and based in village life. Religious or mythical themes rely on the poetic language of codified hand gestures and facial expressions. They are accompanied by traditional instruments such as the tabla and sitar, and by voices, often in rhythmic counterpoint to the dance.

Indian languages *Devanagari; Dravidian languages; Indo-Aryan*

Indian Mutiny (1857–9) A serious uprising against British rule, triggered off by the belief among Indian troops in British service that new cartridges had been greased with animal fat – something which would have been abhorrent to both Hindus and Muslims. The mutiny at Meerut (10 May 1857) spread throughout N India; Delhi quickly fell; and Kanpur and Lucknow garrisons were beseiged. The British finally regained full control in mid-1858.

Indian National Congress A broad-based political organization, founded in 1885, which spearheaded the nationalist movement for independence. It has been the dominant political party in India since 1947.

Indian Ocean, ancient **Erythræan Sea** area 73 426 000 km²/ 28 350 000 sq mi. Third largest ocean in the world; width c.6400 km/4000 mi at the Equator; maximum depth of 7125 m/23 375 ft in the Java Trench; linked to the Mediterranean by the Suez Canal.

Indian Territory Land set aside in the USA as a 'permanent' home for native Americans removed from the area E of the Mississippi R between 1825 and 1840. Originally it included most of Oklahoma and parts of Kansas and Arkansas, but by the end of the 19th-c most of it had been opened to whites.

indiarubber tree An evergreen tree (*Ficus elastica*) with elliptical, leathery, very glossy leaves, native to India and SE Asia. A source of rubber, young specimens are sold as house-plants under the name **rubber plants**. (Family: Moraceae.)

indictment [indiytment] A document specifying the particulars of an offence of which a person is accused. **Indictable offences** in England and Wales are those triable before a judge (or Sheriff in Scotland) and jury, such as murder. However, in some jurisdictions some less serious indictable offences, such as theft, may be tried on a summary basis in a lower court or without a jury. The Fifth Amendment to the US constitution guarantees the right to indictment by a Grand Jury for 'capital or infamous crimes'.

indigestion Upper abdominal pain or discomfort related to eating; also known as **dyspepsia**. It is an extremely common complaint that may be precipitated by overeating, or by particular foods such as spices, fried foods, or alcohol. The condition is usually relieved by taking antacids.

indigo A dye obtained from a species of *Indigofera*, particularly anil (*Indigofera anil*), a tropical American shrub, and *Indigo tinctoria*, a shrubby perennial growing to 2·5 m/8 ft; peaflowers red, in short clusters. It is now mainly used to dye the warp yarns of denim. (Family: Leguminosae.)

indigo bird / finch *whydah*

indirect rule A form of colonial rule especially characteristic of British rule in Africa during the interwar years, involving the use of existing political structures, leaders and local organs of authority. It was adopted on grounds of its cheapness and to allow for independent cultural development, but was increasingly criticized for its failure to introduce a modernizing role into colonial administration, and was gradually given up after 1945.

Indo-Aryan languages The easternmost branch of the Indo-Euro-

India

□ International Airport **- - -** Disputed boundary J&K Jammu & Kashmir
- - - India/Pakistan line of control

Hindi **Bharat**, official name **Republic of India**

Local name Bhārat (Hindi)

Timezone GMT +5·5

Area 3 166 829 km²/1 222 396 sq mi

Population total (2002e) 1 047 671 000

Status Republic

Date of independence 1947

Capital New Delhi

Languages Hindi and English (official); others include Urdu, Panjabi, Gujarati, Marathi, Bengali, Oriya, Kashmiri, Assamese, Kannada, Malayalam, Sindhi, Tamil and Telugu

Ethnic groups Indo-Aryan (72%), Dravidian (25%), with Mongoloid and other minorities

Religions Hindu (83%), Muslim (11%), Christian (2%), Sikh (2%), Buddhist (1%)

Physical features Seventh largest country in the world, located in S Asia; includes Andaman and Nicobar Is in the Bay of Bengal, and Laccadive Is in the Indian Ocean; folded mountain ridges and valleys in N, highest peaks over 7000 m/23 000 ft; C river plains of the Ganges, Yamuna, Ghaghari, and Brahmaputra to the S – control measures needed to prevent flooding; Thar Desert in NW bordered by semi-desert areas; Deccan Plateau in the S peninsula, with hills and wide valleys, bounded by the Western and Eastern Ghats; the coastal plains are important areas of rice cultivation.

Climate Dominated by the Asiatic monsoon; rains come from the SW (Jun–Oct); rainfall decreases E–W on the N plains, with desert conditions in extreme W; tropical in S even in cool season; average annual temperature 14°C (Jan), 31°C (Jul) in New Delhi; average annual rainfall 640 mm/25·2 in; cyclones and storms on SE coast (especially Oct–Dec).

Currency 1 Indian Rupee (INR) = 100 paisa

Economy Agriculture employs over two-thirds of the labour force; tea, rice, wheat, coffee, sugar cane, cotton, jute, oil seed, maize, pulses, milk; floods and drought cause major problems; considerable increase in industrial production since independence; iron, steel, oil products, chemicals, fertilizers, chromite, barytes, oil, natural gas; tourism.

GDP (2002e) $2·664 tn, per capita $2600

Human Development Index (2002) 0·577

History Indus civilization emerged c.2500 BC, destroyed in 1500 BC by the Aryans, who developed the Brahmanic caste system; Mauryan Emperor Asoka unified most of India, and established Buddhism as the state religion, 3rd-c BC; spread of Hinduism, 2nd-c BC; Muslim influences during 7th-8th-c AD, with sultanate established at Delhi; Mughal Empire established by Babur in 1526 and extended by Akbar and Aurangzeb; Portuguese, French, Dutch, and British footholds in India, 18th-c; conflict between France and Britain, 1746–63; development of British interests represented by the East India Company; British power established after the Indian Mutiny crushed, 1857; movement for independence from the late 19th-c; Government of India Act of 1919 allowed election of Indian ministers to share power with appointed British governors; a further Act in 1935 allowed election of independent provincial governments; passive-resistance campaigns of Mohandas Gandhi from 1920s; independence granted in 1947, on condition that a Muslim state be established (Pakistan); Indian states later reorganized on a linguistic basis;

pean languages, comprising some 500 languages spoken in N and C India. Its subgroupings are exemplified by Panjabi (or Punjabi, c.73 million) in the NW; Gujarati (c.43 million) and Marathi (c.65 million) in the W and SW; Hindi and Urdu (together, 240 million) in the mid-N; and Bengali and Assamese (together, c.93 million) in the E. (Figures are for first-language speakers.)

Indo-European languages The family of languages which developed in Europe and S Asia, and which gave the modern languages of W Europe (eg the Germanic, Romance, and Celtic languages) as well as many in the Baltic states, Russia and N India. The parent language of the family has been labelled **Proto-Indo-European** (PIE); there is no documentary evidence for it, but it is thought to have been spoken before 3000 BC.

Indo-Iranian languages The E branch of the Indo-European family of languages. It comprises the Iranian and Indo-Aryan subgroups.

Indonesia p.460

Indo-Pacific languages A hypothesized group of languages, centred on Papua New Guinea. There seem to be about 3·5 million speakers, but little is known of the languages, and many tribes have not been contacted. The grouping is highly speculative, linking the Papuan languages (themselves genetically diverse) with Andamanese and the extinct languages of Tasmania.

Indra In Hinduism, the Vedic king of the gods, to whom many of the prayers of the Rig Veda are addressed.

indri or **indris** A leaping lemur (*Indri indri*), the largest living primitive primate (body length, 70 cm/27½ in); very short tail; dark with white legs and hindquarters; fluffy round ears; has a very loud, far-reaching cry.

Indricotherium [indrikotheerium] The largest land mammal that ever lived; known from the Oligocene epoch of C Asia; a gigan-

Pakistan-India war over disputed territory in Kashmir and Jammu, 1948; federal democratic republic within the Commonwealth, 1950; Hindu-Muslim hostility, notably in 1978, and further India-Pakistan conflict in 1965 and 1971; separatist movements continue, especially relating to Sikh interests in the Punjab; suppression of militant Sikh movement in 1984 led to assassination of Indira Gandhi; Rajiv Gandhi assassinated, 1991; ongoing tension with Pakistan over Kashmir, with some fighting, 2001, escalating into a major crisis, mid-2002; ceasefire announced (Nov 2003) and diplomatic ties resumed; SE coast, especially Tamil Nadu, devasted by tsunami, 2004; each of the 27 states administered by a governor appointed by the President; each state has an Assembly; the President, advised by a Council of Ministers, appoints a Prime Minister; Parliament comprises the President, an Upper House, and a House of the People.

Head of State
1950–62 Rajendra Prasad
1962–7 Sarvepalli Radhakrishnan
1967–9 Zakir Husain
1969 Varahagiri Venkatagiri *Acting*
1969 Mohammed Hidayatullah *Acting*
1969–74 Varahagiri Venkatagiri
1974–7 Fakhruddin Ali Ahmed
1977 B D Jatti *Acting*
1977–82 Neelam Sanjiva Reddy
1982–7 Giani Zail Singh
1987–92 Ramaswami Venkataraman
1992–7 Shankar Dayal Sharma
1997–2002 K(ocheril) R(aman) Narayanan
2002– Avul Pakir Jaunilabdeen Abdul Kalam

Head of Government
1947–64 Jawaharlal Nehru
1964 Gulzari Lal Nanda *Acting*
1964–6 Lal Bahadur Shastri
1966 Gulzari Lal Nanda *Acting*
1966–77 Indira Gandhi
1977–9 Morarji Ranchhodji Desai
1979–80 Charan Singh
1980–4 Indira Gandhi
1984–9 Rajiv Gandhi
1989–90 Vishwanath Pratap Singh
1990–1 Chandra Shekhar
1991–6 P V Narasimha Rao
1996 Atal Bihari Vajpayee
1996–7 Deve Gowda
1997–8 Inder Kumar Gujral
1998–2004 Atal Bihari Vajpayee
2004– Manmohan Singh

tic, hornless rhinoceros standing 5·5 m/18 ft at the shoulder. (Order: Perissodactyla.)

inductance A measure of a coil's ability to produce a voltage in another coil (**mutual inductance**, *M*) or in itself (**self inductance**, *L*) via changing magnetic fields; units H (henry). It is equal to the ratio of electromotive force produced to rate of change of current.

induction (logic) An inference from particular, observed instances to a general law or conclusion. The premisses of a sound induction may give good reason for believing the conclusion ('The Sun has always risen in the past, therefore it will rise tomorrow') but do not logically entail the conclusion.

induction (obstetrics) The initiation of childbirth by artificial means. A common technique is the injection of the hormone oxytocin, which causes contractions of the uterus.

indulgences In Roman Catholicism, grants of remission of sin to the living, following repentance and forgiveness; also, to the dead in purgatory. Abuses in the Middle Ages, leading to the 'buying and selling' of places in heaven, finally occasioned Martin Luther's '95 Theses', which launched the Reformation. Little reference is made to them today.

Indurain, Miguel [induhran] (1964–) Racing cyclist, born in Villava, Spain. In 1991 he won the first of five successive Tours de France races (1991–5) becoming the first to achieve this distinction, and in 1996 won an Olympic Gold in the time trial. He retired in 1997.

Indus (astronomy) (Lat 'Indian') An inconspicuous constellation of the S hemisphere.

Indus, River, Sanskrit **Sindhu** River of Asia, the longest of the Himalayan rivers (3000 km/1900 mi); rises in Xizang region (Tibet); flows into Pakistan; enters the Arabian Sea in a level, muddy delta.

indusium *sorus*

industrial action The activities of trade unions, or groups of workers or employers, to bring pressure on the others when negotiations and/or arbitration have failed to settle industrial disputes. Action by workers can include go-slows or 'working to rule', overtime bans, or strike action; action by employers may involve lockouts.

industrial disease *occupational diseases*

industrial espionage The illicit acquisition of information about a company's activities. Such information may concern formulae, designs, personnel, or business plans. Methods include theft of documents, telephone tapping, and computer hacking.

industrial relations The dealings and relationships between the management and the workforce of a business, particularly one where trade unions are present and collective bargaining is normal; also known as **labour** or **employee relations**. The main topics covered include pay, hours and conditions of work, holidays, security of employment, and disciplinary and grievance procedures.

Industrial Revolution A term usually associated with the accelerated pace of economic change, the associated technical and mechanical innovations, and the emergence of mass markets for manufactured goods. It began in Britain in the last quarter of the 18th-c with the mechanization of the cotton and woollen industries of Lancashire, C Scotland, and the West Riding of Yorkshire. The mechanization of heavier industries (iron and steel) was slower, but sustained the Industrial Revolution in its second phase from c.1830.

industrial textiles Textiles used for industrial purposes, as found in the manufacture of conveyor belts, filter cloths, geotextiles, and ropes. Some 30% of all textile products are categorized as industrial.

industry A group of business enterprises which produce or supply goods or services. **Primary industries** are those based on the use of the earth for cultivation (eg agriculture, forestry, fishing) or the extraction of raw materials (eg mining, quarrying). **Secondary industries** (or **manufacturing industries**) are those which process raw materials into consumer products and components; they are often divided into **heavy industries**, involving the large-scale use of plant, machinery, personnel, and output (eg iron and steel, machinery) and **light industries**, involving production on a much smaller scale (eg electronics, food processing). **Tertiary industries** (or **service industries**) are those which do not produce goods, but provide support for other areas of the economy (eg banking, law) or are concerned with quality of life (eg tourism, entertainment).

Indus Valley Civilization The earliest known S Asian civilization, flourishing c.2300–1750 BC around the R Indus in Pakistan. Over 100 sites have been identified with important urban centres at Mohenjo-daro and Harappa (Pakistan), and Kalibangan and Lothal (W India).

Indonesia

□ International Airport

[indohneezha], official name **Republic of Indonesia**, Bahasa Indonesia **Republik Indonesia**, formerly **Netherlands Indies, Dutch East Indies, Netherlands East Indies, United States of Indonesia**

Local name Indonesia

Timezone GMT +7 to +9

Area 1 906 200 km²/735 800 sq mi

Population total (2002e) 211 023 000

Status Republic

Date of independence 1945

Capital Jakarta

Languages Bahasa Indonesia (official), English, Dutch, and Javanese widely spoken

Ethnic groups Madurese (40%), Javanese (33%), Sudanese (15%), Bahasa Indonesian (12%)

Religions Muslim (88%), Christian (9%) (Roman Catholic 6%, Protestant 2%), Hindu (2%), Buddhist (1%)

Physical features World's largest island group of 13 677 islands and islets, of which c.6000 are inhabited; five main islands: Sumatra, Java, Kalimantan (two-thirds of Borneo I), Sulawesi, Irian Jaya (W half of New Guinea I); characterized by mountainous volcanic landscape and equatorial rainforest; many volcanic peaks – over 100 on Java, 15 active.

Climate Hot and humid equatorial climate; dry season (Jun–Sep), rainy season (Dec–Mar); average annual temperature 26°C (Jan), 27°C (Jul) in Jakarta; average annual rainfall 1775 mm/69 in.

Currency 1 Indonesian Rupiah (IDR) = 100 sen

Economy Mainly agrarian, notably rice; oil, natural gas, and petroleum products from Borneo and Sumatra account for nearly 60% of national income; small manufacturing industry.

GDP (2002e) $714·2 bn, per capita $3100

Human Development Index (2002) 0·684

History Settled in early times by Hindus and Buddhists, whose power lasted until the 14th-c; Islam introduced, 14th–15th-c; Portuguese settlers, early 16th-c; Dutch East India Company established, 1602; Japanese occupation in World War 2; independence proclaimed with Sukarno as President, 1945; changed name from Netherlands East Indies to the Republic of the United States of Indonesia, 1949; federal system replaced by unified control, 1950, and the unitary Republic of Indonesia proclaimed (W New Guinea remained under Dutch control until 1963 and is now called Irian Jaya); military coup, 1966; governed by a President elected by a 700-member People's Consultative Assembly, and advised by a Cabinet and several advisory agencies; separatist movements in Irian Jaya, East Timor, and Aceh; referendum in East Timor in favour of independence (Sep 1999), with subsequent violence by anti-independence militias, and arrival of a UN-sponsored force; independence achieved, May 2002; terrorist bomb in Kuta, Bali, killed 202 people (Oct 2002); military offensive launched in Aceh after failed peace talks with rebel Free Aceh Movement (GAM), May 2003; truce signed (Aug 2005) between GAM (to disarm) and government (to withdraw troops); earthquake off NW coast of Sumatra caused devastating tsunami, 2004; earthquake hit Java with over 6000 deaths, 2006.

Republic of Indonesia
Head of State/Government
1949–66 (Achmed) Sukarno
1966–98 (T N J) Suharto
1998–9 Bacharuddin Jusuf Habibie
1999–2001 Abdurrahman Wahid
2001–4 Megawati Sukarnoputri
2004– Susilo Bambang Yudhoyono

inertia The reluctance of a massive object to change its motion. Inherent to mass, it is present in the absence of gravity. Newton's first law is sometimes called the **law of inertia**.

inertial guidance An automatic navigation system used in guided missiles, aeroplanes, and submarines, which depends on the tendency of an object to continue in a straight line (*inertia*). Any changes in the direction and magnitude of motion of the vehicle are sensed and corrected automatically.

infallibility In the Roman Catholic Church, the claim that state-

ments on matters of faith or morals, made by a pope speaking *ex cathedra* (Lat 'from the throne'), or by a General Council if confirmed by the pope, are guaranteed the assistance of the Holy Spirit (ie free from error). The claim is rejected by Protestants.

Infante / Infanta [infantay, infanta] In Spain and Portugal, the title given to the sons and daughters of the sovereign.

infanticide The putting to death of the newborn with the consent of the parent, family, or community. In England and Wales, the term is also used where a mother wilfully causes the death of her child. The child must be under 1 year old, and the mother must have been disturbed in her mind as a result of the stress of the birth. In the USA, the offence is usually subsumed under the general homicide statute, and in Scotland it is usually tried as culpable homicide.

infantile paralysis *poliomyelitis*

infant school A UK school taking children from the age of 5 up to 7 or 8. In areas with middle schools, such schools are sometimes known as **first schools**.

infection The invasion of the body by micro-organisms that are capable of multiplying there and producing illness. An infection begins by the entry of an organism at a specific site, such as the skin, urinary, and respiratory tracts. This is followed by a short interval in which the person feels well (the *incubation period*), during which the micro-organisms multiply. They may cause disease locally or disperse throughout the body causing disease in other tissues and organs, such as in cystitis (the bladder) or pneumonia (the lungs).

infectious hepatitis [hepatiytis] Inflammation of the liver, which may be caused by several different viruses. The best known are hepatitis A, B, and C. **Hepatitis A** infection may be debilitating for several months, and possibly fatal in older people, but causes no long-term effects. **Hepatitis B** and **C** infections can cause an acute illness similar to hepatitis A, but can also cause long-term liver damage, resulting in cirrhosis and liver cancer.

inference In logic, a sequence of steps leading from a set of premises to a conclusion. Rules of inference are rules for the construction of good and valid arguments.

inferiority complex A fundamental sense of inadequacy and insecurity out of proportion to real circumstances. An example may be short individuals who have a driven need to assert themselves in social situations to overcome their sensitivity about their height.

infertility The inability of a couple to conceive, affecting about 10% of couples, with a wide range of causes affecting both partners. In the female, factors include failure of ovulation, obstruction of the uterine (Fallopian) tubes, or abnormalities in the uterus. In the male, factors include the absence or inadequate production of sperm.

infinity In mathematics, a number greater than any other number. The symbol ∞ was first used for infinity by the English mathematician John Wallis (1616–1703).

inflammation The body's reaction to injury, whether caused by a physical or chemical insult, an infectious agent, or an autoimmune process. Certain types of white blood cells are attracted to the site, and these engulf and digest damaged tissue and infected micro-organisms. The reaction is accompanied by pain, heat, swelling and redness.

inflation An economic situation of widespread and persistent increases in prices and wages. Common measures of inflation are the Retail Price Index, which covers a wide range of consumer goods, and the gross domestic product deflator, an index of all goods prices. Economists differ over the cause of inflation: the main models blame excess demands and excessive pay rises in the money supply. Cost inflation, in which each price or wage rate rises because others have risen, or are expected to rise, does not explain how inflation starts, but does explain why it is so persistent once it has started. Governments have often tried to cure inflation, frequently incurring unemployment in the process, without much success.

inflorescence The arrangement of more than one flower on the stem, together with any associated structures. The type of inflorescence is often significant in recognizing plant families. In **cymose inflorescences** the *meristem* of the main axis differentiates into a flower with new growth coming from a lateral branch (*monochasia*) or branches (*dichasia*) which in turn are

terminated by a flower. In **racemose** [rasimohz] **inflorescences**, the main axis continues to grow, flowers being formed below the tip.

influenza or **flu** A disease caused by the influenza virus. It causes an acute respiratory illness with cough and congested airways, as well as headache, fever, and muscle pain. Vaccination is difficult, because the virus develops different strains with varying antigenic properties. The name is derived from *influentia coeli*, a mediaeval name for the disease, thought to be due to the influence of the sky.

information superhighway *Internet*

information technology A term commonly used to cover the range of technologies relevant to the transfer of information, in particular to computers, digital electronics, and telecommunications. Developments during the 1970s and 1980s, such as satellite and optical-based communication methods, have been responsible for enormous scientific and commercial growth in this area.

information theory The mathematical theory of information, deriving from the work of the US mathematicians Claude E Shannon and Warren Weaver, in particular *The Mathematical Theory of Communication* (1949), and from the theory of probability. It is concerned with defining and measuring the amount of information in a message, with the encoding and decoding of information, and with the transmission capacity of a channel of communication.

infrared astronomy The study of celestial objects by their radiation in the wavelength range 1000 nm–1 mm. Many objects emit most of their radiation in the infrared waveband. This type of astronomy has increased in importance with the availability of two-dimensional detector arrays.

infrared photography Photography which uses wavelengths beyond visible red light. Black-and-white film has medical and forensic application. Multilayer colour film including an infrared sensitive emulsion gives a false colour rendering in which natural vegetation appears red or magenta; this is used in aerial surveying.

infrared radiation Electromagnetic radiation of a wavelength a little longer than light, between 10^{-3} m and 7.8×10^{-7} m; discovered by William Herschel in 1800. Emitted by oscillating and rotating molecules and atoms, and invisible to the naked eye, it is perceived by us as 'radiant heat'. Infrared detectors are used in night and smoke vision systems (for fire fighting), intruder alarms, weather forecasting, and missile guidance systems.

infrasound Sound having a frequency of less than 20 Hz. Such waves cannot be heard by humans, but may be felt. Infrasonic waves are produced by explosions and by an unsteady airflow past an object.

infrastructure The network of factors which enables a country's economy or an industrial operation to function effectively. They include such matters as transport, power, communication systems, housing, and education.

Inge, William Ralph [ing], known as **the Gloomy Dean** (1860–1954) Clergyman, born in Crayke, North Yorkshire. He was Dean of St Paul's (1911–34), earning his byname from the pessimism displayed in his sermons and newspaper articles.

Ingham, Sir Bernard [ingam] (1932–) Journalist, born in Hebden Bridge, West Yorkshire. A government press adviser (1976) and under-secretary in the Department of Energy (1978–9), he became nationally known after his appointment as chief press secretary to prime minister Margaret Thatcher (1979–90).

Ingrams, Richard (Reid) (1937–) Writer and journalist, born in Westcliffe-on-Sea, Essex. In 1962 he co-founded the satirical magazine *Private Eye*, whose editor he remained until 1986. In 1992 he founded *The Oldie*, a lively magazine for older readers. Other writings include the satirical *Dear Bill: the Collected*

Letters of Denis Thatcher (1980) and a biography of Malcolm Muggeridge (1995).

Ingres, Jean Auguste Dominique [ĩgruh] (1780–1867) Painter, born in Montauban, France. He was the leading exponent of the Classical tradition in France, and is especially known for his nudes, including 'Baigneuse' (1808, Louvre) and 'La Source' (completed 1856, Musée d'Orsay).

inheritance tax A UK tax started in 1986 which replaced capital transfer tax. It is levied on the value of a deceased person's 'estate', and includes property, land, investments, and other valuable assets. In the USA, such taxes are collected by the individual states.

Initial Teaching Alphabet *i.t.a.*

injection The administration by a syringe of a drug or other pharmacological preparation in solution or suspension through a needle inserted into the skin (*intradermal*), underneath the skin (*subcutaneous*), into the muscle tissue (*intramuscular*), or into a vein (*intravenous*).

injection engine *fuel injection*

injection moulding A process used in the manufacture of plastics. Raw plastic, usually in granular form, is heated until soft enough to squeeze through a nozzle into a mould of the shape of the desired article. This type of manufacture is highly automated.

injunction A court order in equity instructing a defendant to refrain from committing some act or, less commonly (but found for example in the USA), to carry out some act; the term **interdict** forbidding a particular act is used in Scots law. It is a remedy; for example, a prohibitory injunction might be granted to stop a continuing nuisance.

ink A substance, usually coloured, used for writing, drawing, or printing; known in China before 1100 BC. At its simplest, it is a solution of a pigment or dye in a liquid (eg soot in water).

Inka *Incas*

Inkatha [inkahta] A Zulu-based political organization, founded in South Africa in 1928, and now led by Chief Buthelezi; in full, **Inkatha yeNkululeku yeSizwe**. *Inkatha* refers to the woven heading worn by the Zulu to support loads; *yeNkululeku yeSizwe* means 'freedom for the nation'. Its disagreement with the politics of the African National Congress and its fear that the ANC was being privileged in constitutional talks in the mid-1990s led to violent conflict between members of the two organizations, despite efforts for reconciliation between Buthelezi and Mandela.

ink-jet printer A type of fast and relatively quiet printer which produces characters or graphics by squirting very fine jets of rapid-drying ink onto paper.

INLA *Irish National Liberation Army*

inlaying A method of decorating furniture and other wooden objects by cutting away part of the surface of the solid material, and replacing it with a thin sheet of wood in another contrasting colour.

Inner Mongolia, Chin **Nei Mongol** pop (2000e) 23 921 000; area 450 000 km²/173 700 sq mi. Autonomous region in N China; two-thirds grasslands, remainder desert; capital, Hohhot.

Inner Temple *Inns of Court*

Innis, (Emile Alfredo) Roy (1934–) Civil rights activist, born in St Croix, US Virgin Isles. He joined the Congress of Racial Equality (CORE) in 1963, advocating black separatism and community school boards, and became CORE national president in 1968.

Innocent III, originally **Lotario de' Conti di Segni** (1160–1216) Pope (1198–1216), born in Anagni, Italy. His pontificate is regarded as the high point of the temporal and spiritual supremacy of the Roman see. He proclaimed the Fourth Crusade (1202–4) to recover the Holy Places. He excommunicated King John for refusing to recognize Stephen Langton as Archbishop of Canterbury.

Innocents' Day *Holy Innocents' Day*

Innsbruck [inzbruk] 47°17N 11°25E, pop (2000e) 119 600. City in W Austria; in the valley of the R Inn, surrounded by mountains; a mediaeval old town, with narrow and irregular streets and tall houses in late Gothic style; popular winter skiing centre; 1964 and 1976 Winter Olympic Games held here; university (1914–23); cathedral (1717–22).

Inns of Court Voluntary unincorporated societies having the exclusive right to confer the rank of barrister in England, Wales, and Northern Ireland. For England and Wales, four Inns have existed in London since the 14th-c: the Inner Temple, the Middle Temple, Lincoln's Inn, and Gray's Inn.

inoculation *immunization*

Inönü, Ismet [inoenü], originally **Mustafa Ismet** (1884–1973) Turkish soldier, prime minister (1923–37, 1961–5), and president (1938–50), born in Izmir, Turkey. As the first premier of the new republic, he introduced many political reforms, and was elected president in 1938 on Atatürk's death.

inorganic chemistry That branch of chemistry which deals with the structures, properties, and reactions of the elements and compounds of elements other than carbon.

inositol A component of phytic acid in cereal and other vegetable foods. Some species (eg mice) require inositol for growth; humans do not, though large amounts are present in the body, especially in the brain.

input–output analysis In economics, an analysis showing flows of goods and services between industries. It assists economists in understanding how different sectors of the economy are interrelated.

Inquisition A tribunal for the prosecution of heresy, originally of the mediaeval Christian Church, introduced by Pope Gregory IX (13th-c). The activities of the inquisitors were later characterized by extremes of torture and punishment, notoriously in the case of the **Spanish Inquisition**.

INRI The first letters of the Latin wording of the inscription placed on Jesus's cross at Pilate's command (*John* 19.19–20): *Iesus Nazarenus, Rex Iudaeorum* ('Jesus of Nazareth, the king of the Jews').

insect An arthropod belonging to the largest and most diverse class of living organisms, the Insecta; c.1 million recognized species, grouped into 28 orders; head typically bears a pair of feelers (*antennae*) and a pair of compound eyes; each of three thoracic segments bears a pair of legs, the last two also typically bear a pair of wings each.

insecticide A substance which kills insects. Most commonly these are synthetic organic compounds, applied as sprays by farmers. There is current concern about these substances entering the food chain and having a detrimental impact on wildlife, and perhaps on humans.

insectivore The most primitive of placental mammals, native to Africa, Europe, Asia, and North America; small with narrow pointed snout; eats insects and other invertebrates. (Order: Insectivora, 345 species.)

insectivorous plant *carnivorous plant*

insider dealing (UK) or **insider trading** (US) A business situation where an individual takes advantage of information about a company before it is made public, in order to make a profit (or avoid a loss) by dealing in the company's stocks or shares. It is illegal in most countries.

insolation The amount of solar radiation (both diffuse and direct) which reaches the Earth. Insolation varies with latitude and season: it is consistently high at the Equator, and high at the Poles during the polar summer, but zero in winter.

insomnia Unsatisfactory sleep, whether in quantity or in quality.

It may be a component of a variety of physical or mental disorders. There may be difficulty in either initiating or maintaining sleep, a preoccupation about sleep, and interference with social and occupational functioning.

installment credit *hire purchase*

instinct An unlearned tendency to behave in a particular way. Instinctive behaviours are those actions or reactions to specific stimuli, shown in similar form by all normally developed members of a species (or sex or age-group thereof), no specific life experience being necessary for their emergence.

insulation *thermal insulation*

insulator A material or covering which prevents or reduces the transmission of electricity, heat, or sound. All electrical devices are insulated for protection from the passage of electricity. Thermal insulators keep things hot, cold, or maintain an even temperature. Sound insulators act as mufflers.

insulin [insyulin] A protein of vertebrates, secreted by B-cells of the islets of Langerhans (in the pancreas) in response to increases in blood glucose concentration (eg after a meal). Its main action is to lower blood glucose concentration by accelerating its uptake by most tissues (except the brain), and promoting its conversion into glycogen and fat.

insurance A system of guarding an individual or institution against the possibility of an event occurring which will cause some harm – usually financial. The insured pays a fee (the *premium*) to an insurance company. The size of the premium (calculated by actuaries) depends on the size of the risk at stake, the number of premiums to be received, and the risk (or chance) of the event occurring. There are four main classes of insurance: marine, fire, life, and accident.

intaglio [intahlioh] 1 A technique of printmaking. The design is incised into a metal plate, ink is forced into the cut lines and wiped off the rest of the surface; damp paper is laid on top; and both plate and paper are rolled through a press.
2 A type of engraved gem in which the design is cut into the stone, instead of standing up in relief as in a *cameo*.

integers *numbers*

integrated circuit A single chip of semiconductor, such as silicon, in which a large number of individual electronic components are assembled. Integrated circuits are smaller, lighter, and faster than conventional circuits. They use less power, are cheaper, and last longer. The circuit is usually made from pure silicon, doped with impurities – the type of impurity determining the job of that part of the chip: transistors, diodes, or resistors.

integrated optics The study of minute optical devices linked by light guides into single units containing several components, and known as a **photonic integrated circuit** (**pic**). The first commercially successful pic was launched by Infera in 2004, as part of a network system for long-distance fibre-optic telecommunications.

Integrated Services Digital Network (ISDN) A service provided by the Posts, Telegraph and Telephones Authorities, which allows voice and data communications to be effected on the same line. This enables voice messaging to be carried out in the same way as data transmission. Facilities are available also for transmitting television pictures of medium quality.

intelligence The ability to respond adaptively to novel situations. Psychologists attempt to measure this ability by constructing tests which appear related to intelligence, and extensively using these tests on a target population, so enabling them to assess the mental age of any individual. **IQ** (**intelligence quotient**) equals mental age divided by actual (chronological) age.

intelligence service A state agency which gathers information regarded as important to state security concerning foreign threats. In democratic countries it is usually kept separate from internal security agencies, whereas in such countries as the former USSR the KGB was responsible both for external espionage and internal counter-intelligence. In the USA and UK, the CIA and MI6 respectively are examples of the former, while the FBI and MI5 are examples of the latter. The extent to which the UK government has been concerned to suppress all information relating to MI5 operations was apparent in the lengthy court battle in Australia and the UK to prevent publication, or reporting in the media, of the book *Spycatcher*. This was written by Peter Wright, a former intelligence officer, who alleged misconduct and 'misuse' of the law by MI5, in particular as it related to a 'plot' to destabilize the Wilson government of the 1970s. In 1991 the first woman to head MI5 was appointed (Stella Rimington, 1935–). This was also the first time that the name of the head of the service was made public. Following the end of the Cold War the emphasis has changed to economic intelligence and the fight against domestic terrorism.

intelligent agent *cyberintelligence*

intelligent building / home A building in which all areas of the building have been linked by cable capable of providing voice, video, and data communications. These communications could be used, for example, to provide continuous monitoring of the building, to ensure that the temperature, lighting, and environment always obey preset parameters. An **intelligent home** is one in which domestic appliances, meters, and alarms are linked to a central computer for the purposes of remote monitoring and control.

intensive care The continuous monitoring of several vital bodily functions in very seriously ill patients or in premature infants. The variables most commonly assessed (depending on the nature of the illness) are pulse rate, systemic arterial blood pressure, pulmonary artery blood pressure, heart output, central venous pressure, respiratory rate, body temperature, levels of oxygen, carbon dioxide, sugar, and acidity in the blood, and the electrical activity of the heart.

intensive farming Farming with relatively high input levels, especially of fertilizers, sprays, and pharmaceuticals. It produces higher yields per hectare, which may compensate for limited farm size and allow the small farmer to make an acceptable income.

interactive video A closed-circuit recorded video system in which the display responds to the instructions of the viewer. Applications range from simple press-button or touch-screen question-and-answer interactions to complex branched learning programmes.

intercellular fluid *interstitial fluid*

intercontinental ballistic missile (ICBM) A very large, long-range nuclear-armed missile developed by the USA and the former Soviet Union from the late 1950s onwards. ICBMs are based in silos spread out over a wide land mass.

interest The amount of money charged by a person or institution that lends a sum to a borrower. The sum lent, on which interest is calculated, is known as the *principal*. The **interest rate** is the percentage payable; for example, an 8% interest rate on £100 gives the lender £8 interest at the end of a year. In **simple interest**, the interest gained in a given year is paid to the lender, so that the principal available does not change from year to year. In **compound interest**, the interest gained in a given year is not paid to the lender, but is added to the principal, which thereby increases year by year.

interest group *pressure group*

interference In physics, the result of two or more waves of similar frequency passing through the same point simultaneously. An interference pattern is determined by the relative phases of the constituent waves. Interference is a property of all types of waves, including light. It is exploited in interferometers, including certain telescopes, compact disc players, phased-array radar, and holography.

interferometer A device which relies on monitoring the interference pattern formed by combining two wave beams, usually light, derived from a single source. The technique is used in the study of gas flow, in wind tunnels, and in plasma physics.

interferons A class of protein molecules produced by body cells that are part of the body's defences against infection, notably by viruses. They appear to inhibit the multiplication of viruses within cells, and to stimulate the immune system to combat infection. Their use in medical practice remains uncertain.

Intergovernmental Panel on Climate Change (IPCC) A panel established by the World Meteorological Organization and the UN Environment Programme in 1988 to assess the scientific information relating to climatic change, such as emissions of greenhouse gases and ensuing alterations to the Earth's climate. Comprised of more than 400 scientists from 25 countries, the panel first reported in 1990. In 2007 the panel announced that, by 2100, temperatures may rise up to 6.4°C and sea levels by up to 43 cm, with Arctic sea ice disappearing. More heatwaves and stronger tropical storms are also predicted.

intermezzo An instrumental piece, especially for piano, in a lyrical style and in no prescribed form. Earlier it was used for short, comic interludes performed on stage between the acts of a serious opera.

internal combustion engine An engine (such as a diesel or petrol engine) which burns its fuel/air mixture within the engine as part of its operating cycle. This cycle may be *two stroke* (one power stroke for every two strokes of the piston) or *four stroke* (one power stroke for every four strokes of the piston).

internal energy In thermodynamics, the difference between the heat supplied to a system and the work done by that system on its surroundings; symbol U, units J (joule).

International An abbreviation of **International Working Men's Association**, the name given to attempts to establish international co-operative organizations of socialist, communist, and revolutionary groups. The **First International** was created in 1864 with Marx playing a significant role in its development. The **Second International** was formed in Paris in 1889, and still survives as a forum for reformist socialist parties. The **Third International** (Comintern) was founded by Lenin, and represented communist parties until abolished in 1943. There was a brief attempt in the 1930s by Trotsky to launch a **Fourth International**.

International Amateur Athletic Federation (IAAF) The supreme governing body which controls athletics worldwide. Founded in Stockholm in 1912, it is responsible for ratifying world records. By 2007 there were 212 member federations.

International Astronomical Union (IAU) The organization responsible for co-ordinating international co-operation and standardization in astronomy, founded in 1919, with its secretariat in Paris. There were 87 participating countries and 9783 individual members in late 2006. The IAU is the sole internationally recognized authority for naming celestial bodies and their surface features.

International Atomic Energy Agency (IAEA) An international agency which promotes research and development into the peaceful uses of nuclear energy, and oversees a system of safeguards and controls governing the misuse of nuclear materials for military purposes. Founded in 1957, and based in Vienna, by March 2007 it had 144 member countries. In 2005 the Agency shared the Nobel Peace Prize with its director general, Mohamed ElBaredei.

International Baccalaureate An award taken by 18-year-old school leavers, and accepted in most countries as a qualification for entry to higher education. It is particularly popular in international schools or with students whose parents have to work abroad.

International Bank for Reconstruction and Development (IBRD) A bank, generally known as the **World Bank**, founded in 1945, to help raise standards of living in the developing countries. It is affiliated to the United Nations, and based in Washington, DC.

International Bill of Rights *Universal Declaration of Human Rights*

International Brigades In the Spanish Civil War (1936–9), foreign volunteer forces recruited by the Comintern and by individual communist parties to assist the Spanish Republic. They played a particularly important role in the defence of Madrid (1936–7).

International Bureau for American Republics *Pan-American Union*

International Business Machines Inc (IBM) A US computer manufacturing and sales company, for many years the most successful in the world. Although initially concerned with mainframe computers, it launched the IBM personal computer in 1983. Their machines, now including other personal computers of the same design (**IBM compatible** computers), occupy c.85% of the personal computer market.

International Campaign to Ban Landmines (ICBL) A campaign, launched in 1991, with the aim of banning antipersonnel landmines. There are thought to be over 100 million such mines scattered over large areas on several continents. Around 20 000 people annually, many of them children, are killed or disfigured by mines. The campaign is coordinated by an advisory board of 21 members, and brings together over 1200 non-governmental organizations in over 60 countries. The campaign and its coordinator, Jody Williams, shared the Nobel Peace Prize in 1997. A treaty signed by 133 countries, and ratified by 58, to ban the use, production, stockpiling, and transfer of landmines, became international law in March 1999.

International Confederation of Free Trade Unions (ICFTU) An association of some 241 trade union federations from 156 countries and territories (in 2007) on all five continents, with a membership of 155 million, located in Brussels, and founded in 1949. Its aim is collaboration between free and democratic trade unions throughout the world.

International Court of Justice A court established by the United Nations Organization for the purpose of hearing international law disputes; known widely as the 'World Court'. The court sits at The Hague, The Netherlands.

international date line *Date Line*

International Development Association (IDA) An organization affiliated to, but distinct from, the International Bank for Reconstruction and Development, based in Washington, DC. It was set up in 1960 to provide help to the world's 50 poorest countries by giving them aid on very easy terms.

International Finance Corporation (IFC) An institution for lending to the private sector in developing countries, based in Washington, and affiliated to the World Bank. The IFC was founded in 1956 to supplement other banks which lent only to the state sector or with state guarantees.

International Gothic A style of art which flourished in W Europe c.1375–c.1425, characterized by jewel-like colour, graceful shapes, and realistically-observed details.

International Labour Organization (ILO) An autonomous agency associated with the League of Nations, founded in 1919, which became a specialized agency of the United Nations in 1946; it had 180 members in 2007. It is concerned with industrial relations and the pay, employment, and working conditions of workers.

international law The law that governs relationships between nation states. It is based principally on custom; there is no worldwide international legislature, and thus the enforcement of international law may pose problems. Although there is an International Court, it may only adjudicate with the consent of the parties.

International Monetary Fund (IMF) A financial agency affiliated to the United Nations, and located in Washington, DC. Formed in 1945, its functions include promoting international monetary co-operation and assisting states in need. It had 184 members in 2007.

international monetary system A financial system which enables international trade to function effectively. Until 1914, the pound sterling was the currency in which most world trade was conducted. By 1945, the US dollar had taken over the role. The EU nations have moved towards a linked currency system, with most adopting the Euro. Some countries have convertible currencies, in that they can be bought and sold freely and exchanged for one another.

International Olympic Committee (IOC) The multi-sport organizational body responsible for the summer and winter Olympics, formed in 1894. Member countries of the IOC are allowed two delegates on the organization's ruling body.

International Organization for Standardization A non-governmental organization established in 1947 for the preparation of international standards for materials, products, and codes of practice; its headquarters are in Geneva, Switzerland. It coordinates the activities of over 130 regional standardization organizations.

International Packet Switching Service (IPSS) A service provided by the Posts, Telegraph and Telephones Authorities which allows a computer to send a packet of data to another computer anywhere in the world, without a dedicated physical wire communication being established between the two. The sender is charged only for the number of packets and their destination, and not for the length of time that the sender and receiver are linked together.

International Space Station (ISS) A multinational space station planned to orbit Earth at an altitude of 400 km/250 mi with an inclination of 51·6°. Begun as a NASA project in the 1980s, the ISS has evolved into an international programme led by the USA and involving Russia, Canada, Japan, Brazil, and the 11 nations of the European Space Agency. About 160 US and Russian spacewalks are required over five years to construct and maintain the ISS. The six laboratories of the ISS will be used for research in space medicine, gravitational biology, and microgravity sciences such as crystal growth, materials science, and combustion science. In April 2001 the station welcomed its first 'space tourist', retired American businessman, Dennis Tito.

International Standard Book Numbering (ISBN) A system of 10-digit numbers allocated to books on publication. Internationally adopted in 1971, each book has its own number printed on the reverse of the title page and on the back cover. From January 2007 the length of ISBNs was changed to 13 digits.

International Style 1 A term sometimes used by art historians to refer to the more or less homogeneous Gothic style which flourished throughout Europe c.1400.
2 A term first used in the USA to describe a new style of architecture developed in the 1920s, principally in Europe; also known as the **Modern Movement**. It is characterized by geometric shapes, an absence of decoration, white rendered walls, flat roofs, large expanses of glass, and asymmetrical compositions.

International Telecommunication Union (ITU) An agency of the United Nations, which since 1947 has promoted worldwide co-operation in all aspects of telecommunications, such as the regulation global telecom networks and radio frequencies.

International UN Agencies *United Nations*

International Union of Pure and Applied Chemistry *IUPAC*

International Working Men's Association *International*

International Youth Hostel Association An organization found in over 50 countries which provides simple, low-cost accommodation for those wishing to travel. In many youth hostels the guests cook their own meals and help with the cleaning. The first hostel was created by Richard Schirrmann at Altena Castle, NW Germany in 1912.

Internet An association of computer networks with common standards which enable messages to be sent from any host on one network to any host on any other. It developed in the 1970s in the USA as an experimental network designed to support military research, and steadily grew to include federal, regional, campus, and other users. It is now the world's largest computer network, with around 400 million hosts connected in 2006, providing an increasing range of services and enabling unprecedented numbers of people to be in touch with each other through electronic mail, discussion groups, and the provision of digital 'pages' on every conceivable topic. The **World Wide Web** is an Internet facility designed for multimedia use, in which individuals or organizations make available 'pages' of information to other users anywhere in the world, generally at no cost, but in the case of certain commercial operations (such as an encyclopedia) through subscription. Some commentators have likened the Internet to an amalgam of television, telephone, and conventional publishing, and the term **cyberspace** has been coined to capture the notion of a world of information present or possible in digital form (the **information superhighway**). During the 1990s, alongside claims that the Internet provides fresh opportunities for self-publishing, creativity, and freedom of speech, there was increasing concern about the safeguarding of rights of privacy and intellectual property, the application of existing laws to the Internet (in such domains as pornography and libel), the extent to which the content of some of the new 'virtual communities' can or should be regulated, and the impact that the growing numbers of Internet communities ('cyburbia') will have on individuals and on society as a whole. The potential of the Internet is also currently limited by relatively slow data-transmission speeds, and by the problems of information management and retrieval posed by the existence of such a vast amount of information.

Internet Service Provider (ISP) An organization which offers access to the Internet to individuals who do not belong to an organization (such as a large company) which is connected directly. A home PC can be linked to the ISP via a modem and the public telephone network; the ISP then provides the additional connection to the Internet. Most ISPs also offer many value-added services, such as mailboxes and Web pages.

interplanetary matter Material in the Solar System other than the planets and their satellites. It includes streams of charged particles from the solar wind, dust, meteorites, and comets.

Interpol [interpol] Originally the telegraphic address, adopted in 1946, of the **International Criminal Police Organization** (earlier, **Commission**), initiated by Prince Albert I of Monaco in 1914. The address became widely used as a name, and was formally incorporated into the organization's title in 1956 as **ICPO–Interpol**. It is an international organization which exists to promote international co-operation in law enforcement. Member states are linked by a secure messaging system, and have direct access to specially designed international law enforcement databases. Interpol manages and stores information on behalf of its members, and provides criminal analysis services. A key factor in international co-operation is understanding the different legal frameworks within which national police forces work; Interpol works to promote harmonization in this area, and offers model legislation on such topics as extradition. Based in Lyon, France, it had 186 members in 2007.

intersection (mathematics) *set*

interstitial fluid [interstishl] That part of the extracellular fluid which lies outside the vascular system and surrounds the tissue cells of animals; also known as **tissue fluid** and **intercellular fluid**.

intestacy The situation where a person dies without a valid will. In the case of a **partial intestacy**, the will does not provide for the disposal of the entire estate.

intestine A tube of muscular membrane extending from the pyloric opening of the stomach to the anus, generally divided into the **small intestine** (*duodenum, jejunum,* and *ileum*), the **large intestine** (*caecum, appendix,* and the *ascending, transverse, descending,* and *sigmoid colon*), and the **rectum**. The length of the small intestine is c.6 m/20 ft and of the large intestine c.1 m/5 ft, but there is considerable variation. Medical problems affecting the intestine include coeliac disease, colic, colitis, diverticulosis, dysentery, hernia, and irritable bowel syndrome.

Intifada [intifahda] A Palestinian uprising which erupted in 1987 in the Gaza Strip and quickly spread to the West Bank. The uprising reflected frustrations with two decades of Israeli military occupation, the expansion of Israeli settlement in the Occupied Territories, and the failure of the PLO and the Arab states to change the status quo. The armed response from Israeli forces claimed nearly 1000 Palestinian lives. However, the Intifada is credited with breaking the political deadlock. The term is now used to mean any mass uprising against oppressive rule.

Intolerable Acts (1774) The American name for laws passed by parliament to punish Massachusetts for the Boston Tea Party (1773).

intonaco *fresco*

intonation The melody of an utterance, brought about by the distinctive use of pitch patterns in sentences. It has several functions, notably the marking of grammatical structure (eg statements with a falling pitch, and questions with a rising pitch), and the expression of speaker attitudes.

intoxilyzer *breathalyzer*

intracellular fluid The fluid contained within cells. In humans the total adult volume is about 28 l/49 UK pt/59 US pt. Its principal components (apart from water) are potassium ions, organic phosphates, and proteins.

Intracoastal Waterway A shipping route extending 5000 km/3100 mi along the E coast of the USA from Massachusetts to Florida (the **Atlantic Intracoastal Waterway**) and from Florida to Texas (the **Gulf Intracoastal Waterway**). It consists of natural water routes, such as bays and rivers, linked by canals.

Intranet The use of Internet technology to provide an organization with an internal communications network. A development of the mid-1990s, such networks can either be linked to the global Internet, or be completely isolated from it. An Intranet system which permits links to selected outside organizations is an *Extranet*.

intra-ocular lens implantation A perspex lens introduced into the front chamber of the eye following surgical removal of a cataract.

intra-uterine device *contraception*

Intrepid *Stephenson, William*

introversion / extraversion Psychological terms formerly used as two categories of personality (**introvert** or **extravert**). The distinction is now considered to be a dimension with high levels of extraversion and introversion at the extremes. Strongly extraverted individuals are sociable, excitement-seeking, and care-free. They are often aggressive, may lose their temper quickly, and be unreliable. Strongly introverted individuals are quiet, reserved, and have few friends. They dislike excitement, are reliable, serious-minded, and like a well-ordered life.

intrusive rock Igneous rock formed by the emplacement and crystallization of magma formed at depth into higher levels of the Earth's crust. Igneous intrusions form a variety of rock masses.

Inuit *Eskimo*

Invalides, Hôtel des [ohtel dayzávaleed] A hospital for the care of old and disabled soldiers, founded in Paris by Louis XIV and built in 1671–6. The main building, which is now mainly given over to a museum, was designed by Libéral Bruant (c.1635–97). The courtyard is the location of Napoleon's tomb.

Invar (trademark) [invah(r)] An alloy containing 65% iron with 35% nickel. It has very low thermal expansion, and hence is used in surveying rods and pendulum bars.

Inverness 57°27N 4°15W, pop (2000e) 43 500. Capital of Highland, NE Scotland; at mouth of R Ness; city status, 2000; airfield; railway; NE terminus of the Caledonian Canal.

inversion temperature *Joule–Thompson effect*

invertebrate A multicellular animal that lacks a vertebral column. It includes the vast majority (over 97%) of all animal species.

invert sugar *sucrose*

investment A term used in economics in two different, though related, senses: the acquisition of financial assets with a view to income or capital gains; and the creation of productive assets, which may be 'fixed investment' (ie buildings and equipment) or stocks and work in progress. In ordinary speech the term is even more widely used: people 'invest' in works of art and antiques, and even in football pools.

investment bank A US bank handling new share issues, often in a syndicate with others. It is similar in function to the British merchant bank.

investment company or **investment trust** A company which holds a portfolio of shares in a range of other companies, aimed at obtaining a reasonable dividend yield, growth, and with less risk (ie a *balanced portfolio*).

invisibles The export and import of services; opposed to goods, which are known as **visibles**. Invisible exports include tourism, shipping, air freight, banking, insurance, and other financial services.

in vitro fertilization *test-tube baby*

Io (astronomy) [iyoh] The first natural satellite of Jupiter, discovered by Galileo in 1610; distance from the planet 422 000 km/262 000 mi; diameter 3630 km/2260 mi; orbital period 1·769 days.

Io (mythology) [iyoh] In Greek mythology, the daughter of Inachos of Argos. She was beloved by Zeus, who turned her into a heifer to save her from Hera's jealousy.

iodine I, element 53, melting point 114°C. A violet solid with a sharp odour; a halogen, not found free in nature, but as an impurity in sodium nitrate deposits, and concentrated in kelp and other seaweeds. An essential element in biological systems, lack of it causes goitre in humans. It is used in medicine as an antiseptic.

iodoform [iyohdofaw(r)m] CHI_3, triiodomethane, melting point 119°C. A yellow solid with a peculiar odour, used as a mild antiseptic.

ion An atom which has lost one or more electrons (a *positive* ion) or which has gained one or more electrons (a *negative* ion). Atoms with a net positive charge are called **cations**; those with a net negative charge, **anions**. The type and magnitude of a charge is indicated by a superscript sign; for example, the positively charged sodium ion is identified as Na^+, and the negatively charged chloride ion as Cl^-. The formation of ions is called **ionization**. Ions are present in all animal and plant cells, where they are involved in many important and diverse roles, including the activation of enzymes, osmotic balance, and nerve impulse conduction.

Iona [iyohna] A remote island off Mull, W Scotland, the site of a monastery established in AD 563 by the Irish missionary St Columba to convert the inhabitants of N Britain to Christianity. In c.1200 a Benedictine abbey was founded on the site.

Ionesco, Eugène [yoneskoh] (1912–94) Playwright, born in Slatina, Romania. He became a prolific writer of one-act plays which came to be seen as typical examples of the Theatre of the Absurd, such as *Rhinoceros* (1959). After 1970, his writing was mainly non-theatrical, including essays, children's stories, and a novel.

Ionia [iyohnia] In antiquity, the C part of the W coast of Asia Minor. It was the birthplace of Greek philosophy and science.

Ionian Islands [iyohnian], Gr **Ioníai Nísoi** or **Eptánisos** pop (2000e) 200 000; area 2307 km²/890 sq mi. Region and island group of W Greece; a chain of about 40 islands, including Corfu; under British control, 1815–64.

Ionian Sea [iyohnian] Part of the Mediterranean Sea, lying W of the Greek islands and S of Italy.

ionic *chemical bond*

Ionic order [iyonik] One of the five main orders of classical architecture, displaying slim, usually fluted shafts, and spiral scrolls known as *volutes* on the capitals. It originated in Ionia in the 6th-c BC.

ionization *ion*

ionizer [iyoniyzer] An electrical apparatus which generates a negative electrical charge that is taken up by airborne particles, including smoke and dust; these are then attracted to earth, thus clearing the air. The electrical activity from appliances such as heaters, computers, and televisions tends to destroy negative charges, leaving the atmosphere with a relative positive charge which is thought to contribute to respiratory problems, headaches, allergies, and depression.

ionosphere The region of the Earth's upper atmosphere from c.50–500 km/30–300 mi in height where short-wave radiation from the Sun is absorbed and partly ionizes the gas molecules or atoms, removing their outer electrons and leaving them positively charged. The ionized layers reflect short-wavelength radio waves, and so make long-distance radio communication possible.

ion plating Coating a metal surface by exposing it to ions of a metal, generated by discharge or thermionically. The ions are directed to the metal by making it the cathode in a low pressure discharge circuit. The process is able to coat intricate surfaces uniformly and firmly.

Ios [eeos] 36°43N 25°17E; area 108 km²/42 sq mi. Island of the Cyclades, Greece, in the Aegean Sea. Homer is said to have died here.

Iowa [iyohwa] pop (2000e) 2 926 300; area 145 747 km²/56 275 sq mi. State in NC USA; the 'Hawkeye State'; 29th state admitted to the Union, 1846; became part of USA with the Louisiana Purchase, 1803; became a state, 1846; capital moved from Iowa City to Des Moines, 1857; highest point is Ocheyedan Mound (511 m/1677 ft); almost entirely prairie-land (95%) with rich soil; chief crops corn and soybeans; leads the nation in corn and pig production; industry dominated by food processing and machinery manufacture.

IPCC *Intergovernmental Panel on Climate Change*

ipecacuanha [ipikakyooahna] A perennial (*Cephaelis ipeca-cuanha*) with roots thickened to resemble a string of beads, native to Brazil; flowers small, white, in heads. The roots provide a drug used to induce vomiting and to treat dysentery. (Family: Rubiaceae.)

Iphigeneia [iyfijeniya] According to Greek legend, the daughter of Agamemnon and Clytemnestra. She was about to be sacrificed at Aulis as the fleet could not sail to Troy, because the winds were against it. At the last moment she was saved by Artemis.

Ipswich, Anglo-Saxon **Gipeswic** 52°04N 1°10E, pop (2001e) 117 100. Port and county town in Suffolk, E England; at the head of the R Orwell estuary; a major wool port in the 16th-c; railway; home of Thomas Gainsborough; football league team, Ipswich Town.

IQ *intelligence*

Iqbal, Sir Mohammed [ikbal] (1876–1938) Poet and philosopher, born in Sialkot, Pakistan (formerly, India). He achieved fame through his mystical and nationalistic poetry. His efforts to establish a separate Muslim state contributed to the formation of Pakistan.

Iquique [eekeekay] 20°13S 70°09W, pop (2000e) 171 700. Free port in N Chile; founded in 16th-c; partly destroyed by earthquake, 1877; airfield; railway.

Iquitos [eekeetohs] 3°51S 73°13W, pop (2000e) 314 000. City in NE Peru; on W bank of the Amazon, 3700 km/2300 mi from its mouth; limit of navigation for ocean vessels; access only by air and river; chief town of Peru's jungle region; university (1962).

IRA Abbreviation of **Irish Republican Army**, an anti-British paramilitary force established in 1919 by Irish nationalists to combat British and Protestant Irish forces in Ireland. It was suppressed by the Irish government in the 1922 rising, and remained largely inactive until the late 1960s. In 1969, a major split in its ranks led to the formation of the **Provisional IRA** alongside the **Official IRA**, and a serious schism between the two sides in the early 1970s. The Official IRA generally supported political action to achieve Irish unity. The Provisionals became the dominant republican force, responsible for shootings and bombings in the N of Ireland, Britain, and W Europe.

The organization announced a ceasefire (Sep 1994), but this was withdrawn (Feb 1996) following dissatisfaction with political progress, and a new campaign began, with bombs causing severe damage in Docklands, London, and Manchester, UK. The ceasefire was resumed (July 1997), and Sinn Féin, the political wing of the IRA, entered into talks with the new Blair government. These led to the Good Friday Agreement, 1998, when the IRA accepted that Northern Ireland would remain part of the UK in return for a Northern Ireland Assembly and executive, structured to ensure cross-community participation. The Unionists dropped their demand that decommissioning of arms must precede Sinn Féin's participation in government, and the new Northern Ireland Assembly came into effect in December 1999. Within the framework of the Assembly, former IRA activists assumed power-sharing roles, among them the former IRA commander Martin McGuinness.

A perceived lack of progress on the decommissioning issue led to the reimposition of UK rule in February 2000. In 2001 the IRA announced that it would begin the process of arms decommissioning. Negotiations aimed at restoring devolved government began (Sep 2004) and by December a power-sharing agreement had been reached, though its implementation remained in doubt following the IRA's refusal to produce photographic evidence of decommissioning. Talks collapsed in early 2005 when the IRA withdrew its offer to decommission weaponry. In July that year the IRA formally announced its intention to end its armed campaign and to continue through exclusively peaceful means. NI secretary Peter Hain set out a 2-year plan on demilitarization. In September, the IRA formally declared that its process of arms decommissioning had been completed.

Iran *p.468*

Iran–Contra scandal or **Irangate** The popular nickname for a political scandal in 1986 that grew out of the Reagan administration's efforts to obtain the release of US captives held in the Middle East by the covert supply of arms to the government of Iran. In an additional complication, officials (notably, Colonel Oliver North) tried to use the proceeds of arms sales to Iran as a means of financing support for the anti-government *Contra* rebels in Nicaragua, without the knowledge of the president.

Irangate *Iran–Contra scandal*

Iranian languages A branch of the E Indo-European language family, spoken in the region of present-day Iran and Afghanistan. Modern Iranian languages, of which Persian (Farsi) is one of the major examples, are spoken by over 60 million people.

Iran

□ International Airport   ∴ World heritage site

[iran], formerly **Persia** (to 1935), official name **Islamic Republic of Iran**, Farsi **Jumhuri-e-Eslami-e-Iran**

Local name Īrān

Timezone GMT + 3·5

Area 1 648 000 km²/636 128 sq mi

Population total (2002e) 65 457 000

Status Islamic Republic

Date of independence 1925

Capital Tehran

Languages Farsi (Persian) (official), several minority languages including Kurdish, Baluchi, Luri, and Turkic (including Afshari, Shahsavani, and Turkish)

Ethnic groups Persian (63%), Turkic (18%), other Iranian (13%), Kurdish (3%), Arab, and other Semitic (3%)

Religions Muslim (Shi'ite 93%, Sunni 5%), Zoroastrian (2%), Jewish, Baha'i, and Christian (1%)

Physical features Largely composed of a vast arid C plateau, average elevation 1200 m/4000 ft; bounded N by the Elburz Mts, rising to 5670 m/18 602 ft at Mt Damavand; Zagros Mts in W and S.

Climate Mainly a desert climate, hot and humid on Persian Gulf; average annual temperatures 2·2°C (Jan), 29·4°C (Jul) in Tehran; average annual rainfall 246 mm/9·7 in; frequent earthquakes; preserved medieval city of Bam in SE destroyed in earthquake, 2003.

Currency 1 Iranian Rial (IRR) = 100 dinars

Economy World's fourth largest oil producer, but production severely disrupted by 1978 revolution, and Gulf War, 1991; agriculture and forestry (employs a third of population); natural gas, iron ore, copper, coal, salt; textiles, sugar refining, petrochemicals; traditional handicrafts (especially carpets).

GDP (2002e) $458·3 bn, per capita $6800

Human Development Index (2002) 0·721

History Early centre of civilization, dynasties including the Achaemenids and Sassanids; ruled by Arabs, Turks, and Mongols until the Sasavid dynasty in the 16th–18th-c, and the Qajar dynasty in the 19th–20th-c; military coup, 1921, with independence under Reza Shah Pahlavi, 1925; changed name from Persia to Iran, 1935; protests against Shah's regime in 1970s led to revolution, 1978; exile of Shah, and proclamation of Islamic Republic under Ayatollah Khomeini, 1979; Islamic Cultural Revolution under Khomeini saw a return to strict observance of Muslim principles and traditions; occupation of US Embassy in Tehran, 1979–81; Gulf War following invasion of Iraq, 1980–8; overall authority exercised by appointed spiritual leader: post of Prime Minister abolished, 1989; governed by a President and a Consultative Assembly (Majlis).

Shah

1896–1907 Muzaffar-ud-Din
1907–9 Mohammed Ali
1909–25 Ahmad Mirza
1925–41 Reza Khan
1941–79 Mohammed Reza Pahlavi

Republic
Leader of the Islamic Revolution

1979–89 Ayatollah Khomeini
1989– Ayatollah Sayed Ali Khamenei

Head of State/Government

1980–1 Abolhassan Bani-Sadr
1981 Mohammed Ali Rajai
1981–9 Seyed Ali Khamenei
1989–97 Ali Akbar Hashemi Rafsanjani
1997–2005 Sayed Mohammad Khatami
2005– Mahmoud Ahmadinejad

Iranian Revolution A revolution in Iran (1978–9), the consequence of widespread discontent at rapid socio-economic change and the authoritarian rule of the shah. It took the exiled religious scholar Ayatollah Khomeini as its figurehead, and ended with the exile of the shah and the establishment of the Islamic Republic.

Iran–Iraq War A war between Iran and Iraq, which began as an Iraqi attempt under the aggressive leadership of Saddam Hussein to overthrow the Islamic republic of Iran under Ayatollah Khomeini. The secular regime in Baghdad claimed it feared Iranian attempts to export its revolution. The Iraqi invasion was soon halted, and after a series of futile and costly battles both sides reluctantly accepted a UN ceasefire in 1988. There

was no victor, but one million casualties, great economic hardship, and widespread destruction.

Iraq *p.469*

Iraq War (2003) A war (Mar–Apr 2003) between Iraq and US-led coalition forces, brought about by Iraq's apparent continued failure to comply with UN Security Council Resolution 1441 to disarm itself of weapons of mass destruction. US President George W Bush, supported by UK Prime Minister Tony Blair, set a deadline for Iraqi cooperation. No positive response was received from Iraqi leader, Saddam Hussein, and the conflict began with air missile strikes on the capital, Baghdad (20 Mar), launched from warships in The Gulf in a 'shock and awe' campaign. The strategically important port of Umm Qasr was sur-

Iraq

□ International Airport   ∴ World heritage site

[irak], official name **Republic of Iraq**, Arabic **al-Jumhuriya al-Iraquia**

Local name Al-ʿĪrāq

Timezone GMT +3

Area 434 925 km²/167 881 sq mi

Population total (2002e) 24 002 000

Status Republic

Date of independence 1932

Capital Baghdad

Languages Arabic (official), also English, Kurdish, Persian, Turkish, and Assyrian spoken

Ethnic groups Arab (79%), Kurd (largely in NE) (16%), Persian (3%), Turkish (2%)

Religions Muslim (95%) (Shi'ite 63%, Sunni 32%), Christian (3%)

Physical features Comprises the vast alluvial tract of the Tigris-Euphrates lowland (ancient Mesopotamia); Tharthar and Euphrates rivers, divided by al-Jazirah plain, flow over dense swampland and join to form the navigable Shatt al-Arab; mountains (NE) rise to over 3000 m/9800 ft; desert in other areas.

Climate Mainly arid climate; summers very hot and dry; winters often cold; average annual temperature 10°C (Jan), 35°C (Jul) in Baghdad; average annual rainfall 140 mm/5.5 in.

Currency 1 New Iraqi Dinar (NID) = 1000 fils

Economy World's second largest producer of oil, but production severely disrupted during both Gulf Wars (several oil installations destroyed); natural gas, oil refining, petrochemicals, cement, textiles; dates, cotton, winter wheat, rice, sheep, cattle.

GDP (2002e) $58 bn, per capita $2400

Human Development Index (1998) 0.583

History Part of the Ottoman Empire from 16th-c until World War I; captured by British forces, 1916; British-mandated territory, 1921; independence under Hashemite dynasty, 1932; monarchy replaced by military rule, and Iraq declared a republic, 1958; since 1960s, Kurdish nationalists in NE fighting to establish a separate state; invasion of Iran in 1980, led to the Iran-Iraq War, lasting until a ceasefire in 1988; invasion and annexation of Kuwait in Aug 1990 led to the 1991 Gulf War (Jan–Feb); UN imposed a no-fly zone over S Iraq to protect the Shi'ites, and a security zone in N Iraq to protect Kurdish refugees, 1992; ongoing confrontation with UN (1997–8) over access of weapons inspectors to sensitive sites, leading to US/UK air-strikes (Operation Desert Fox) from 1998; UN weapons experts resumed inspections, 2002–3, but with increasing dissatisfaction from US-led coalition over Iraq's apparent failure to comply with UN resolution to eliminate its weapons of mass destruction; build-up of US-led military forces in the Gulf leading to invasion by coalition forces (Mar 2003) begins Iraq War; Saddam Hussein's regime toppled, Apr 2003; capture of Saddam (Dec 2003); attacks on occupying forces in Iraq ongoing; Iraqi Governing Council established to oversee task of drawing up new Iraqi constitution and set date for elections; interim constitution signed (Mar 2004); handover of power to an interim Iraqi government (Jun 2004); US and Iraqi forces launch assault against insurgents in cities of Fallujah and Mosul (Nov 2004); elections held Jan 2005, Shia United Iraqi Alliance (UIA) form coalition government; voting in referendum on Iraq's constitution to make country an Islamic federal democracy (Oct 2005), high turn out amid heavy security; constitution approved; Iraqis go to the polls to elect first full-term government since the invasion, Dec 2005; UIA gain victory (Jan 2006) but fail to get absolute majority.

Monarch
1921–33 Faisal I
1933–9 Ghazi I
1939–58 Faisal II (Abdul Illah Regent 1939–53)

Republic
Commander of the National Forces
1958–63 Abdul Karim Qassem

Head of Council of State
1958–63 Mohammed Najib ar-Rubai

Head of State/Government
1963–6 Abdus Salaam Mohammed Arif
1966–8 Abdur Rahman Mohammed Arif
1968–79 Said Ahmad Hassan al Bakr
1979–2003 Sadam Hussein at-Takriti
2003–5 Coalition Provisional Authority (CPA) *Interim administration*

President
2004–5 Sheikh Ghazi al-Yawer *Interim*
2005– Jalal Talabani

Prime Minister
2004–5 Iyad Allawi *Interim*
2005–6 Ibrahim Jaafari *Interim*
2006– Jawad al-Maliki

---

rounded and US troops marched towards Baghdad where they took control of the international airport, and entered the city. British troops advanced towards Basra and surrounded the city.

On entering they met limited resistance, but widescale looting by Iraqi civilians became a major problem. A large US force advanced through Kurdish N Iraq to secure the oilfields around

Ireland

ATLANTIC OCEAN

EUROPE

North Channel

Aran I ∪ ULSTER Northern
Donegal
Donegal Bay   Lough Neagh   Belfast
Sligo   Ireland
Achill I   □ Knock   ULSTER   Dundalk
CONNACHT   ●Drogheda
Croagh Patrick 765m
IRELAND
Galway   Dublin ■ Dun
Liffey   Laoghaire
LEINSTER
Shannon □   IRISH SEA
Limerick   Kilkenny
●Tralee MUNSTER   Slaney
Killarney   Waterford ● ●Rosslare
△ Carrauntoohil 1041m   □ Cork ●
Macgillycuddy's Reeks
Bantry Bay   CELTIC SEA

□ International Airport

(republic), Ir **Eire** [ayruh], official name also **Republic of Ireland**

Local name Éire (Gaelic)

Timezone GMT

Area 70 282 km²/27 129 sq mi

Population total (2002e) 3 926 000

Status Republic (occupying S, C, and NW Ireland; bounded NE by Northern Ireland, part of the UK)

Capital Dublin

Languages Irish Gaelic and English (official)

Ethnic groups Celtic (94%), small English minority

Religions Roman Catholic (95%), Anglican (Church of Ireland) (3%), Presbyterian (1%)

Physical features Mountainous landscapes in W, part of Caledonian system of Scandinavia and Scotland with quartzite peaks weathered into conical mountains such as Croagh Patrick, 765 m/2510 ft; landscape of ridges and valleys in SW, rising towards Macgillycuddy's Reek Mts; lowlands in E drained by slow-moving rivers such as the Shannon (S), Liffey (E), and Slaney (SE).

Climate Mild and equable climate. Average annual temperature 5°C (Jan), 15°C (Jul); rainfall heaviest in W, often over 3000 mm/20 in.

Currency 1 euro (EUR) = 100 cents (previous to February 2002, 1 Irish Pound/Punt (IEP) = 100 new pence)

Economy Primarily agriculture (two-thirds of country covered by improved agricultural land); forestry developed since 1950s; fishing; food, drink, tobacco, textiles; recent growth in light engineering; synthetic fibres, electronics, pharmaceuticals; several peat-fired power stations; Kinsale natural-gas field near Cork; major tourist area; member of the European Union (formerly EC), 1973.

GDP (2002e) $113·7 bn, per capita $29 300

Human Development Index (2002) 0·925

History Occupied by Goidelic-speaking Celts during the Iron Age; conversion to Christianity by St Patrick, 5th-c; SE attacked by Vikings, c.800; Henry II of England declared himself lord of Ireland, 1171, but English influence restricted to area round Dublin (the Pale); Henry VIII took the title 'King of Ireland', 1542; Catholic rebellion during English Civil War suppressed by Oliver Cromwell, 1649–50; supporters of deposed Catholic King James II defeated by William III at Battle of the Boyne, 1690; struggle for Irish freedom developed in 18th-19th-c, including such revolutionary movements as Wolfe Tone's United Irishmen, 1796–8, and later Young Ireland, 1848, and the Fenians, 1866–7; Act of Union, 1801; Catholic Relief Act enabling Catholics to sit in Parliament, 1829; population reduced by half during famine, 1846; Land Acts, 1870–1903, attacking Irish poverty; Home Rule Bills introduced by Gladstone, 1886, 1893; third Home Rule Bill passed in 1914, but never came into effect because of World War I; armed rebellion, 1916; republic proclaimed by

---

Kirkuk and Mosul. The campaign was notable for its live global television coverage, which included the historic moment (9 Apr) when Saddam Hussein's giant statue in Baghdad was toppled by a US tank. The search then began for Saddam and his senior officials, some of whom were later captured. US diplomat Paul Bremer was appointed to the task of restoring civil order and forming an interim administration in Iraq, supported by retired US general Jay Garner. In December 2003, Saddam was captured by US forces on a farm in the town of Al-Dawr, near Tikrit, and held as a prisoner-of-war. Fighting has since continued between local militias and occupying forces. Official handover of power to an interim Iraqi government took place on 28 June 2004. Following Saddam's removal, the mainly Sunni Muslim city of Fallujah became the headquarters of rebel resistance, led by Jordanian-born terrorist Abu Musab al-Zarqawi. In November 2004, interim Iraqi Prime Minister Iyad Allawi endorsed a major ground assault on Fallujah by US

and Iraqi soldiers, as part of the aim to stabilize the country for elections in January 2005. The Shia United Iraqi Alliance (UIA) party polled nearly half the vote and began the process of forming a coalition government. Abu Musab al-Zarqawi was killed in a US air raid 2006. Saddam was found guilty of crimes against humanity and executed in December 2006.

Ireland (island), Lat **Hibernia** Island on W fringe of Europe, separated from Great Britain by the Irish Sea; maximum length 486 km/302 mi, maximum width 275 km/171 mi; since 1921, divided politically into the independent 26 counties of the **Republic of Ireland** (area 70 282 km²/27 129 sq mi; pop (1995e) 3 499 000), and **Northern Ireland**, part of the UK, containing six of the nine counties of the ancient province of Ulster (area 14 120 km²/5450 sq mi; pop (1995e) 1 631 000); known poetically as **Erin**, the name is also in widespread use for the Republic of Ireland.

Ireland (republic) *see panel*

Sinn Féin, 1919; partition proposed by Britain, 1920; treaty signed, giving dominion status, 1921; right of Northern Ireland to opt out was exercised, and frontier agreed, 1925; renamed Éire, 1937; left Commonwealth, 1949; Anglo-Irish Agreement signed, 1985; a President (Uachtarán na h'Éireann) elected for seven years; a Prime Minister (Taoiseach); the National Parliament (Oireachtas) includes a House of Representatives (Dail Éireann) and a Senate (Seanad Éireann).

Head of State
1976–90 Patrick J Hillery
1990–7 Mary Robinson
1997– Mary McAleese

Head of Government
1987–92 Charles Haughey
1992–4 Albert Reynolds
1994–7 John Bruton
1997– (Patrick) Bertie Ahern

Counties of Ireland
County / Area (km² / sq mi) / Population total (2000e) / Admin centre
Carlow / 896 / 346 / 41 000 / Carlow
Cavan / 1891 / 730 / 53 000 / Cavan
Clare / 3188 / 1231 / 92 000 / Ennis
Cork / 7459 / 2880 / 415 000 / Cork
Donegal / 4830 / 1865 / 130 000 / Lifford
Dublin / 922 / 356 / 1 038 000 / Dublin
Galway / 5939 / 2293 / 183 000 / Galway
Kerry / 4701 / 1815 / 123 000 / Tralee
Kildare / 1694 / 654 / 124 000 / Naas
Kilkenny / 2062 / 796 / 75 000 / Kilkenny
Laoighis (Leix) / 1720 / 664 / 53 000 / Portlaoise
Leitrim / 1526 / 589 / 24 000 / Carrick
Limerick / 2686 / 1037 / 164 000 / Limerick
Longford / 1044 / 403 / 31 000 / Longford
Louth / 821 / 317 / 92 000 / Dundalk
Mayo / 5398 / 2084 / 112 000 / Castlebar
Meath / 2339 / 903 / 107 000 / Trim
Monaghan / 1290 / 498 / 52 000 / Monaghan
Offaly / 1997 / 771 / 59 000 / Tullamore
Roscommon / 2463 / 951 / 53 000 / Roscommon
Sligo / 1795 / 693 / 55 000 / Sligo
Tipperary / 4254 / 1642 / 134 500 / Clonmel
Waterford / 1869 / 710 / 92 000 / Waterford
Westmeath / 1764 / 681 / 63 000 / Mullingar
Wexford / 2352 / 908 / 103 000 / Wexford
Wicklow / 2025 / 782 / 98 000 / Wicklow

Ireland, John (Nicholson) (1879–1962) Composer, born in Bowdon, Greater Manchester. He established his reputation with his Second Violin Sonata (1917), and between the wars was a prominent member of the English musical renaissance.

Irenaeus, St [irenayus] (c.130–c.200) One of the Christian Fathers of the Greek Church, probably born near Smyrna. He is chiefly known for his opposition to Gnosticism, and for his attempts to prevent a rupture between Eastern and Western Churches over the computing of Easter. Feast day 28 June (W), 23 August (E).

Irene (mythology) [iyreenee] In Greek mythology, a personification of 'peace'; one of the Horae, or 'seasons'.

Ireton, Henry [iy(r)tn] (1611–51) English soldier, born in Attenborough, Nottinghamshire. Cromwell's son-in-law from 1646, he was one of the most implacable enemies of the king, and signed the warrant for his execution.

Irgun (Zvai Leumi) [irgun zviy loomee] (Heb 'National Military Organization') A Jewish resistance group in Palestine, founded in 1937, whose aim was the establishment of the State of Israel by any means. Led by Menachem Begin, it was the nucleus for the Herut Party in Israel.

Irian Jaya [irian jiyah], officially **Papua** (from 2002), formerly **West Papua, West Irian**, earlier **Dutch New Guinea** pop (2000e) 1 928 000; area 421 981 km²/162 885 sq mi. Autonomous province of Indonesia, comprising the W half of New Guinea and adjacent islands; rises to 5029 m/16 499 ft at Jaya Peak; part of Indonesia, 1963; bicameral council introduced, 2002; ongoing separatist Free Papua Movement (OPM); capital, Jayapura.

iridology [iridolojee] The detailed study of the visible parts of the eye, especially the iris, which is used as a diagnostic aid in conjunction with other forms of therapy. Iridologists claim that, since the nervous system comes to the body surface in the eyes, so the condition of all parts of the body is reflected in the eye's appearance.

iridosmine *osmiridium*

iris (anatomy) The coloured part of the vertebrate eye, an opaque diaphragm extending in front of the lens and having a circular opening (the *pupil*). The contraction of these muscle fibres alters pupil size and so regulates the amount of light entering the eye. Bright light decreases and dim light increases pupil size.

iris (botany) A perennial, sometimes evergreen, native to N temperate regions; flowers large, showy, the parts in threes and structurally complex, often in a combination of colours; fruit a capsule, sometimes with brightly coloured seeds. (Genus: *Iris*, 300 species. Family: Iridaceae.)

Iris (mythology) In Greek mythology, the goddess of the rainbow, which seems to reach from Earth to heaven. She therefore became the messenger of the gods.

Irish The Celtic language spoken in Ireland; also known as **Erse**. Designated the first official language of the Republic of Ireland, there are over a million users, and an active literary tradition. Most speakers of Irish as a mother-tongue come from the W fringes of the country, which have been designated as an area of protection for the language, the *Gaeltacht*.

Irish Famine, also known as the **Great Hunger** The widespread starvation of Irish peasantry which followed the effects of potato blight in 1845–7, due to the destruction of the crop by a fungus, *Phytophthora infestans*. Because of starvation, disease, and emigration, the population of Ireland fell by almost 25 per cent between 1845 and 1851.

Irish National Liberation Army (INLA) The military wing of the Irish Republican Socialist Party, a small paramilitary group which committed few terrorist attacks, but was noted for the ruthless nature of those it does carry out. It was responsible for the killing of the Conservative MP Airey Neave (1979). It announced a ceasefire in August 1998.

Irish Republican Army *IRA*

Irish Republican Socialist Party A political party formed in 1974 largely as a breakaway group from the official Sinn Féin. It was involved in a feud with the Official IRA in the 1970s, and subsequently moved closer to the Provisional Sinn Féin.

Irish Sea area 103 600 km²/39 990 sq mi. Arm of the Atlantic Ocean between Ireland and Great Britain; 210 km/130 mi long by 225 km/140 mi at its widest point.

Irish setter A breed of dog, developed in Ireland, with a glossy red-brown coat; hair forming fringes on tail, underside, and backs of legs; also known as **red setter**.

Irish terrier An active medium-sized terrier with a coarse reddish-tan coat; ears soft, held high; tip of muzzle with a surrounding brush of longer hair; tail docked, but left longer than in most terriers.

Irish wolfhound The tallest domestic breed of dog (shoulder height, 80 cm/30½ in); very old breed, used for hunting by the Celts; long (usually grey) coat; soft ears.

Irkutsk [irkutsk] 52°18N 104°15E, pop (2000e) 635 000. Capital city in S Siberian Russia; founded as a fortress, 1661; airport; on the Trans-Siberian Railway; university (1918); one of the largest economic centres of E Siberia.

iron Fe (from Lat *ferrum*), element 26, a metal with density of 7·8 g/cm^3, melting point 1535°C. It is the fourth most common element in the Earth's crust, not found uncombined except in some meteorites. Learning to recover (*smelt*) it from its ores (mainly the oxide Fe$_2$O$_3$) was a major step in human civilization. Most iron is used as metal, usually alloyed with some quantities of other elements, especially carbon and silicon. Steel is iron alloyed with other metals, mainly vanadium, chromium, manganese, and nickel. It is an essential element in biology, particularly as part of haemoglobin.

Iron Age *Three Age System*

Ironbridge A historic industrial town in the Severn R gorge, Shropshire, the birthplace of England's Industrial Revolution. In 1778–9 Europe's first iron bridge was cast and erected here; 196 ft (59·8 m) long, its centre span 100 ft (30·5 m). Ironbridge Gorge is a world heritage site.

ironclad A 19th-c term for warships which were either protected by iron plates or built entirely of iron, and more recently of steel. The first ironclad was the French frigate *La Gloire* of 1859.

Iron Cross A military decoration (an iron cross edged with silver) instituted in Prussia in 1813, reinstated in 1870 for the Franco-Prussian War and as a German medal in 1914 and 1939 for the two World Wars. The ribbon is black, white, and gold.

iron curtain A term used to describe the separation of certain E European countries from the rest of Europe by the political and military domination of the Soviet Union. First used in 1945, the term became widely known after Churchill used it in a speech in 1946.

iron lung *respirator*

Irons, Jeremy (John) [iyonz] (1948–) Actor, born in Cowes, Isle of Wight. He became well known after his role in *The French Lieutenant's Woman* (1981) and the television series *Brideshead Revisited* (1981). Later films include *Reversal of Fortune* (1990, Oscar), *Stealing Beauty* (1996), and *Eragon* (2006).

Ironside, William Edmund Ironside, Baron (1880–1959) British field marshal, born in Ironside, Aberdeenshire. He was Chief of the Imperial General Staff at the outbreak of World War 2, and placed in command of the home defence forces (1940). The 'Ironsides', fast light-armoured vehicles, were named after him.

Iroquois [irokwoy] A North American Indian people concentrated in the Great Lakes area. They speak Iroquoian languages of the Hokan–Siouan family, c.80 000 (2000 census).

Iroquois Confederacy [irokwoy] A confederation of Iroquois groups during the 17th–18th-c in upper New York State: the Mohawk, Oneida, Onondaga, Cayuga, and Seneca, later joined by the Tuscarora; also known as the **Iroquois League** or the 'Six Nations'. The League broke up during the American Revolution.

irradiance *radiometry*

irrational numbers *numbers*

Irrawaddy, River *Ayeyarwady, River*

irrigation The application of water to soil and crops. In dry areas water may be applied by flooding or through inter-row channels. More general application techniques include rain guns, sprinklers, and, more expensively, drip lines, which provide water to plants and trees on an individual basis.

irritable bowel syndrome A common condition involving abdominal discomfort and altered bowel habit. Not serious, it may be related to an increased spontaneous movement of the intestines, though there is almost certainly a psychological element; there are no obvious abnormal findings and it is exacerbated by emotional stress. Changes in diet, such as increased dietary fibre, may help to reduce symptoms, and measures to reduce anxiety may also be successful.

Irtysh, River [irtish] Chief tributary of the R Ob in Kazakhstan and Russia; rises in N China; length, 4248 km/2640 mi.

Irvine (of Lairg), Alexander Andrew Mackay Irvine, Baron (1940–) Judge, born in Inverness, Highland, N Scotland. He was called to the bar in 1967, and became a QC (1978) and a deputy judge in the High Court (1987). Appointed shadow Lord Chancellor (1992–7), he then served as Lord Chancellor (1997–2003). He was made a life peer in 1987.

Irving, David (1938–) Historian, born in Essex. His Holocaust revisionist agenda began with his best-selling 1977 book, *Hitler's War*, and was followed by a number of publications in which he denied the exterminationist nature of German anti-Semitism. In 2000 he sued the publisher, Penguin Books Ltd, and the American historian, Deborah Lipstadt, for libel and falsification of history in her book, *Denying the Holocaust* (1993), but the verdict went against him. In 2005 he was arrested in Austria to face charges linked to speeches he made in 1989 denying the existence of gas chambers at Auschwitz, and was jailed for three years (Feb 2006).

Irving, Sir Henry, originally **John Henry Brodribb** (1838–1905) Actor and theatre manager, born in Keinton-Mandeville, Somerset. He gained a reputation as the greatest English actor of his time, and in 1878 began a theatrical partnership with Ellen Terry which lasted until 1902.

Irving, John (Winslow) (1942–) Novelist, born in Exeter, NH. His first three novels received little attention, but he made his name with *The World According To Garp* (1978, filmed 1982). Later books include *The Hotel New Hampshire* (1981, filmed 1984), *The Cider House Rules* (1985, filmed 1999, Oscar), *A Prayer for Owen Meany* (1989), and *Until I Find You* (2005).

Irving, Washington, pseudonym **Geoffrey Crayon** (1783–1859) Man of letters, born in New York City. Under his pseudonym he wrote *The Sketch Book* (1819–20), a miscellany containing such items as 'Rip Van Winkle' and 'The Legend of Sleepy Hollow'.

Irwin, Steve, popular name of **Stephen Robert Irwin** (1962–2006) Naturalist, environmentalist, and television presenter, born in Melbourne, Victoria, Australia. He spent his childhood in Queensland, where his parents ran a reptile and fauna wildlife park. In 1991 he took over management of the park, renaming it Australia Zoo, and made the *Crocodile Hunter* series for television (1992–5). Though often making headlines for his daring stunts with crocodiles, lizards, sharks and snakes, he was a committed conservationist and created International Crocodile Rescue and the Steve Irwin Conservation Foundation (later renamed Wildlife Warriors Worldwide). He was killed by a stingray while filming a documentary at the Great Barrier Reef off Australia's NE coast.

Isaac [iyzak] Biblical character, son of Abraham by Sarah, through whose line of descent God's promises to Abraham were seen to continue. He was nearly sacrificed by Abraham at God's command (*Gen* 22).

Isabella I (of Castile), also known as **Isabella the Catholic** (1451–1504) Queen of Castile (1474–1504), born in Madrigal de las Altas Torres, the daughter of John II, King of Castile and León. In 1469 she married Ferdinand V of Aragon, with whom she ruled jointly from 1479. During her reign, the Inquisition was introduced (1478) and the Jews expelled (1492). She sponsored the voyage of Columbus to the New World.

Isabella of France (1292–1358) Daughter of Philip IV of France, who in 1308 married Edward II of England at Boulogne. She became the mistress of Roger Mortimer, with whom she overthrew and murdered the king (1327).

Isaiah [iyziya], Heb **Jeshaiah** (8th-c BC) The first in order of the major Old Testament prophets, son of Amoz. A citizen of Jerusalem, he began to prophesy c.747 BC.

Isaiah or **Isaias, Book of** [iyziya] A major prophetic work in the

Hebrew Bible/Old Testament, ostensibly from the prophet Isaiah, active in Judah and Jerusalem in the latter half of the 8th-c BC. Many scholars doubt the unity of the contents.

ISBN *International Standard Book Numbering*

ischaemic / ischemic heart disease *coronary heart disease*

Isherwood, Christopher (William Bradshaw) (1904–86) Novelist, born in Disley, Cheshire. His best-known works, *Mr Norris Changes Trains* (1935) and *Goodbye to Berlin* (1939), were based on his experiences (1930–3) as an English tutor in Berlin, and later inspired *Cabaret* (musical, 1966; film, 1972). In collaboration with Auden, a school friend, he wrote three prose-verse plays with political overtones, and also *Journey to a War* (1939). In 1939 he emigrated to California to work as a scriptwriter, and where he also developed an interest in Hinduism.

Ishiguro, Kazuo [ishigooroh] (1954–) Novelist, born in Nagasaki, Japan. His third novel, *The Remains of the Day* (1989, filmed 1993), won the Booker Prize and established his reputation. Later books include *The Unconsoled* (1995) and *Never Let Me Go* (2005).

Ishmael [ishmayel] Biblical character, the son of Abraham by Hagar, his wife's maid; expelled into the desert with his mother Hagar from Abraham's household after the birth of Isaac. He is considered the ancestor of the Bedouin tribes of the Palestinian deserts (the Ishmaelites).

Ishtar [ishtah(r)] Originally a Mesopotamian mother-goddess of love and war; also known as **Astarte**; later the goddess of love, identified with the planet Venus.

Isidore of Seville, St [izidaw(r), sevil] (c.560–636) Ecclesiastic, encyclopedist, and historian, born either in Seville or Carthagena, Spain. A voluminous writer, his most influential work was the encyclopedia, *Etymologies*. He was canonized in 1598. Feast day 4 April.

isinglass [iyzingglahs] A pure gelatin found in fish. Its particular use is in the clarification of fermented beverages. The name is also applied to a form of mica, with similar appearance.

Isis [iysis] Ancient Egyptian goddess, wife of Osiris and mother of Horus, sometimes portrayed with horns and the Sun's disc. In Hellenistic and Roman times, she was a central figure in mystery religions.

Islam [izlahm] The Arabic word for 'submission' to the will of God (Allah), the name of the religion originating in Arabia during the 7th-c through the Prophet Mohammed. Followers of Islam are known as Muslims, or Moslems, and their religion embraces every aspect of life. They believe that individuals, societies, and governments should all be obedient to the will of God as it is set forth in the Qur'an, which they regard as the Word of God revealed to his Messenger, Mohammed. There are five essential religious duties known as the **Pillars of Islam**. (1) The *shahada* (profession of faith) is the sincere recitation of the twofold creed: 'There is no god but God' and 'Mohammed is the Messenger of God'. (2) The *salat* (formal prayer) must be performed at five points in the day (varying with time of sunrise and sunset) while facing towards the holy city of Mecca. (3) Almsgiving through the payment of *zakat* ('purification') is the duty of sharing one's wealth out of gratitude for God's favour, according to the uses laid down in the Qur'an. (4) There is a duty to fast (*saum*) during the month of Ramadan. (5) The *Hajj* or pilgrimage to Mecca is to be performed if at all possible at least once during one's lifetime. *Sharia* is the sacred law of Islam, and applies to all aspects of life, not just religious practices. There is an annual cycle of festivals, including the Feast of the Sacrifice (*Id al-Adha*), commemorating Abraham's willingness to sacrifice Isaac, which comes at the end of the Hajj pilgrimage, and the *Id al-Fitr*, marking the end of the month of fasting in Ramadan.

There are two basic groups within Islam. *Sunni Muslims* are in the majority, and they believe that correct religious guidance derives from the practice or *sunna* of the Prophet. They recognize the first four caliphs as Mohammed's legitimate successors. The *Shiites* comprise the largest minority group, and they believe that correct religious guidance obtains from members of the family of the Prophet, on which basis they recognize only the line of Ali, the fourth caliph and nephew and son-in-law of Mohammed as the Prophet's legitimate successors. There are a number of sub-sects of Islam, and in 2007 there were over 1500 million Muslims throughout the world.

Islamabad [islamabad] 33°40N 73°08E, pop (2000e) 329 000. Capital city of Pakistan, on the R Jhelum; a modern planned city, built since 1961; two universities (1965, 1974); centre of agricultural region.

Islamic law *Sharia*

Isle of Man *Man, Isle of*

Isle of Wight *Wight, Isle of*

Ismailis [izmayeeleez] Adherents of a secret Islamic sect, one of the main branches of the Shiites; also known as the **Seveners**. It developed from an underground movement (c.9th-c), reaching political power in Egypt and N Africa in the 10th–12th-c. Today, the Khojas are the largest Ismaili sect, numbering c.20 million.

Ismailiya or **Ismailia** [izmiyleea] 30°36N 32°15E, pop (2000e) 268 100. City in NE Egypt; on W bank of Suez Canal; founded in 1863; railway; market gardening in irrigated area.

Ismail Pasha [ismaeel] (1830–95) Khedive of Egypt, born in Cairo, the second son of Ibrahim Pasha. His massive development programme included the building of the Suez Canal, which was opened in splendour in 1869.

isobar 1 In meteorology, a line on a weather map joining places of equal barometric pressure. The closer the lines are together, the stronger the pressure gradient force, and therefore the stronger the winds.

2 In thermodynamics, a line of constant pressure on a graph, depicting the relationship between volume and temperature.

Isocrates [iysokrateez] (436–338 BC) Greek orator and prose writer, born in Athens. He became an influential teacher of oratory (c.390 BC), and presented rhetoric as an essential foundation of education.

isocynate *fulminate*

isohyet [iysohhiyet] A line on a weather map joining places receiving equal amounts of rainfall.

isolationism A foreign policy strategy of withdrawing from international affairs as long as the country's interests are not affected. It was practised most notably by the USA, which kept out of the League of Nations, World War 1, and World War 2 until attacked by the Japanese.

isoline [iysohliyn] A line on a map which joins places of equal value; also known as an **isopleth**. For example, on a temperature map, places recording the same temperature are joined by an isotherm.

isomers [iysohmerz] Substances having the same molecular formula but with the atoms connected differently.

isometrics [iysohmetriks] A form of physical exercise in which muscles are contracted, but not allowed to move the associated joints. Muscles are used in this way when exerting force on a closed door or fixed bar.

isopentane *pentane*

isopleth *isoline*

Isopoda [iysopoda] A diverse order of crustaceans characterized by a flattened body and seven similar pairs of thoracic legs; typically bottom-living in aquatic habitats, some (the woodlice), are highly successful in terrestrial habitats. (Class: Malacostraca.)

isoprene [iysohpreen] C_5H_8, IUPAC 2-methylbuta-1,3-diene, boiling point 34°C. A liquid, used in the production of synthetic rubber, it is also the basic unit from which terpene molecules are constructed.

Israel

□ International Airport   - - - Palestinian National Authority

Heb **Yisrael**, official name **State of Israel**, Heb **Medinat Yisrael**

Local names Yisra'el (Hebrew), Isrā'īl (Arabic)

Timezone GMT +2

Area 20 770 km²/8017 sq mi (within boundaries defined by 1949 armistice agreements)

Population total (2002e) 6 394 000 (excluding E Jerusalem and Israeli settlers in occupied territories)

Status Republic

Date of independence 1948

Capital Jerusalem

Languages Hebrew and Arabic (official), also European languages spoken

Ethnic groups Jewish (83%), Arab (11%)

Religions Jewish (85%), Muslim (11%), Christian and others (4%)

Physical features Extends 420 km/261 mi N–S; width varies from 20 km/12 mi to 116 km/72 mi; mountainous interior, rising to 1208 m/3963 ft at Mt Meron; mountains near Galilee (Lake Tiberius) and Samaria in the West Bank, dropping E to below sea-level in the Jordan-Red Sea rift valley; R Jordan forms part of E border; Dead Sea, between Israel and Jordan, 400 m/1286 ft below sea level, is the largest lake and has no outlet; Negev desert (S) occupies c.60% of the country's area.

Climate Mediterranean climate in N and C, with hot, dry summers and warm, wet winters; average annual temperature 9°C (Jan), 23°C (Jul) in Jerusalem; rainfall 528 mm/21 in.

Currency 1 New Israeli Shekel (ILS/NIS) = 100 agorot

Economy Over 90% of exports are industrial products; major tourist area, primarily to the religious centres; copper, potash, phosphates, citrus fruits, cotton, sugar beet, bananas, beef and dairy products; a world leader in agrotechnology, with areas of intensive cultivation; the kibbutz system produces c.40% of food output, but in recent years has turned increasingly towards industry.

GDP (2002e) $117·4 bn, per capita $19 500

Human Development Index (2002) 0·896

History Zionist movement founded by Theodor Herzl, end of 19th-c; thousands of Jews returned to Palestine, then part of the Ottoman Empire; Britain given League of Nations mandate to govern Palestine and establish Jewish national home there, 1922; British evacuated Palestine, and Israel proclaimed independence, 1948; invasion by Arab nations, resulting in armistice, 1949; Israel gained control of the Gaza Strip, Sinai Peninsula (as far as the Suez Canal), West Bank of the R Jordan (including E sector of Jerusalem), and the Golan Heights in Syria, during the Six-Day War, 1967; Camp David conference between Egypt and Israel, 1978; Israeli withdrawal from Sinai, 1979; invasion of Lebanon, forcing the PLO to leave Beirut, 1982–5; renewed tension with uprising of Arabs in occupied territories (the Intifada), 1988; peace agreement with PLO, and planned recognition of Palestine, 1993; withdrawal from Gaza and Jericho, 1994; conflict with Jordan formally ended, 1994; assassination of Yitzhak Rabin, 1995; Arafat elected President in first Palestine general election, Jan 1996; withdrawal from S Lebanon, 2000; escalating reprisal

---

isopropyl *propyl*

Isoptera [iysoptera] *termite*

ISO speed rating The sensitivity to light of photographic material expressed on a numerical scale defined by the International Standards Organization (ISO). It replaces both the former systems established by the American Standards Association (ASA) and a Deutsche Industrie Norm (DIN). A film speed is expressed in the form ISO 200/24°, the first set of digits referring to an arithmetical film speed, the second to a logarithmic system.

isotherm 1 In meteorology, a line on a weather map joining places of equal temperature.

2 In thermodynamics, a line of constant temperature on a graph, depicting the relationship between volume and pressure.

isotopes Species of the same element that are chemically identical, having the same proton number, but of different atomic

masses due to a differing number of neutrons in the nucleus. All elements have isotopes.

ISP *Internet Service Provider*

Israel *see panel*

Israel, tribes of In the Bible, a confederacy of 12 tribes generally traced to Jacob's 12 sons – six by Leah (Reuben, Simeon, Levi, Judah, Issachar, Zebulun), two by Rachel (Joseph, Benjamin), two by Rachel's maid Bilhah (Dan, Naphtali), and two by Leah's maid Zilpah (Gad, Asher). During the settlement of Canaan and the Transjordan, the tribes were allocated portions of land (*Josh* 13–19); but the Levites, a priestly class, had no allocation and possibly were never a 'tribe' as such, and Joseph's 'tribe' was actually two tribes, traced to his two sons Ephraim and Manasseh (*Gen* 48). The number of tribes was thereby maintained as 'twelve'.

issuing house A merchant bank which specializes in the issue of shares and bonds on the stock market.

attacks on Palestinian targets, 2001; siege of Bethlehem, 2002; conflict ongoing, 2003–4; Geneva Accord peace plan launched, Dec 2003; fresh talks with new Palestinian government following death of Arafat, 2005; army began evacuation of Jewish settlers from the Gaza Strip (Aug 2005) in line with Prime Minister Sharon's disengagement plan; Islamic militant group HAMAS won Palestine election (Jan 2006) posing serious threat to continuation of peace talks with Israel; Sharon suffered serious stroke in late 2005 and power transferred to vice premier Ehud Olmert; Olmert won election for the Kadima party, Mar 2006; air and sea blockade imposed on Lebanon in major offensive after hostile action from militant group Hezbollah (Jul 2006); fighting escalated, UN brokered ceasefire (Aug); air blockade lifted (Nov); national unity cabinet formed in Palestine (Mar 2007); a parliamentary democracy, with a Prime Minister, a Cabinet, and a unicameral Parliament (Knesset); President elected for a maximum of two five-year terms.

Head of State
1948–52 Chaim Weizmann
1952–63 Itzhak Ben-Zvi
1963–73 Zalman Shazar
1973–8 Ephraim Katzair
1978–83 Yitzhak Navon
1983–93 Chaim Herzog
1993–2000 Ezer Weizmann
2000 Avraham Burg *Interim*
2000–7 Moshe Katzav
2007– Dalia Itzik *Acting*

Head of Government
1948–53 David Ben-Gurion
1954–5 Moshe Sharett
1955–63 David Ben-Gurion
1963–9 Levi Eshkol
1969–74 Golda Meir
1974–7 Yitzhak Rabin
1977–83 Menachem Begin
1983–4 Yitzhak Shamir
1984–6 Shimon Peres
1986–92 Yitzhak Shamir
1992–5 Yitzhak Rabin
1995–6 Shimon Peres
1996–9 Binyamin Netanyahu
1999–2001 Ehud Barak
2001–6 Ariel Sharon
2006– Ehud Olmert

Istanbul [istanbul], or **Stamboul**, formerly **Byzantium** (c.660 BC–AD 330), **Constantinople** (330–1930) 41°02N 28°57E, pop (2000e) 7 862 000. Capital city in NW Turkey, on both sides of the Bosporus; seaport of Turkey; damaged in terrorist bomb attacks, 2003; founded and renamed by Constantine I in AD 330 on the site of ancient Byzantium, becoming the new capital of the Roman Empire; remains of ancient Constantinople are a world heritage site; see of the patriarch of the Greek Orthodox Church and of the Armenian Church; airport; railway; five universities (1453, 1773, 1863, 1883, 1911); suspension bridges (first in 1973) link European and Asian sections; Topkapi Palace (15th-c), Hagia Sophia Basilica (6th-c).

Istria [eestria], Serbo-Croatian **Istra** area 3160 km²/1220 sq mi. Peninsula at the N end of the Adriatic Sea, Yugoslavia; occupied by Croats, Slovenes, and Italians; formerly part of Italy; ceded to Yugoslavia, 1947 (apart from Trieste); chief town, Pula.

i.t.a. Abbreviation of **Initial Teaching Alphabet**, devised in 1959 by UK educationist Sir (Isaac) James Pitman (1901–85), to assist children in the early stages of reading. It is a lower-case system of 44 symbols in which each symbol represents a phoneme, giving a closer correlation between symbol and sound than in traditional English orthography, which it was to supplement. Its popularity declined after the 1970s.

Itaipú Dam [eetiypoo] A major earth- and rock-fill gravity buttress dam on the R Paraná at the Brazil–Paraguay frontier; completed in 1991; height 189 m/620 ft. It has the capacity to generate 12 600 megawatts of hydroelectricity, and is claimed to be the largest hydroelectric complex in the world.

Italian *Italian literature; Romance languages*

Italic languages The early languages spoken in the area of modern Italy. The major language of the group was *Latin*, the language of Rome, evidenced in inscriptions from the 6th-c BC; it is used now only in formulaic contexts of religion (in public (usually governmental) declamations. The modern Romance languages ultimately belong to the Italic family.

italic script A sloping style of handwriting introduced by Aldus Manutius of Venice in c.1500, which was later introduced into printing. Today, it has a wide range of functions, including the identification of foreign words, book titles, and emphatic utterance.

Italy *p.476*

ITAR-TASS The Russian state central information agency, with headquarters in Moscow. The successor to TASS, the Soviet news agency, it was renamed in 1992. The present names comprises two acronyms, ITAR: Informationoe Telegrafnoe Agentsvo Rossii (the Information Telegraph Agency of Russia) and TASS: Telegrafnoe Agentsvo Sovetskovo Soyuza (Telegraph Agency of the Soviet Union).

itch An irritating sensation in the skin, also known as **pruritus**, which may be extremely distressing. It may occur in one area as the result of a local irritant or skin disease (eg lice, scabies, dermatitis, psoriasis), or may also be a generalized symptom of an underlying disorder (eg lymphoma, jaundice).

Ito, Hirobumi [eetoh] (1841–1909) Japanese statesman and premier (1885–8, 1892–6, 1898, 1900–1), born in Choshu province. He drafted the Meiji constitution (1889), and played a major role in building up the modern state.

Itúrbide, Agustín de [eetoorbithay] (1783–1824) Mexican general, born in Morelia, Mexico. He became prominent in the movement for Mexican independence, and made himself emperor as Agustín I (1822–3). He was forced to abdicate, and was executed.

IUD *contraception*

IUPAC [yoopak] Acronym for **International Union of Pure and Applied Chemistry**, best known as the more-or-less acknowledged authority on chemical nomenclature. Its system attempts to provide clear rules for naming compounds unambiguously.

Iuppiter *Jupiter* (mythology)

Ivan III, known as **the Great** (1440–1505) Grand Prince of Moscow (1462–1505), born in Moscow. He succeeded in ending his city's subjection to the Tartars, and in 1472 assumed the title of 'Sovereign of all Russia'.

Ivan IV, known as **the Terrible** (1530–84) Grand prince of Moscow (1533–84), born near Moscow, the first to assume the title of 'tsar' (Lat *Caesar*). In 1564 the treachery of some of his counsellors led him to embark on a reign of terror, directed principally at the feudal aristocracy and the church. He nonetheless did much for Russian commerce.

Ivanisevic, Goran [ivaneesevich] (1971–) Tennis player, born in Split, W Croatia. Ranked world number 2 in 1992, he won a bronze medal at the Barcelona Olympics. He lost the Wimbledon final that year to Andre Agassiz, and was a losing finalist

Italy

□ International Airport ∴ World heritage site

Ital **Italia**, official name **Italian Republic**, Ital **Repubblica Italiana**

Local name Italia

Timezone GMT +1

Area 301 255 km²/116 314 sq mi

Population total (2002e) 57 988 000

Status Republic

Capital Rome

Languages Italian (official), with German spoken in the Trentino-Alto Adige, French in Valle d'Aosta, and Slovene in Trieste-Gorizia

Ethnic groups Homogeneous (98%), with German-Italian, French-Italian, and Slovene-Italian minorities

Religions Roman Catholic (83%), non-religious (14%)

Physical features Comprises the boot-shaped peninsula extending south into the Mediterranean Sea, as well as Sicily, Sardinia, and some smaller islands; Italian peninsula extends c.960 km/600 mi SE from the Lombardy plains; Apennines rise to peaks above 2900 m/9000 ft; Alps form a border in N; broad, fertile Lombardo-Venetian plain in basin of R Po; several lakes at foot of the Alps, including Maggiore, Como, Garda; flat and marshy on Adriatic coast (N); coastal mountains descend steeply to the Ligurian Sea on the Riviera (W); Mt Vesuvius, 1289 m/4230 ft, and Vulcano, 502 m/1650 ft, are active volcanoes; island of Sicily separated from the mainland by the 4 km/2.5 mi wide Strait of Messina; the island includes the volcanic cone of Mt Etna, 3390 m/11 122 ft.

Climate Warm and temperate in S; hot and sunny summers, short cold winters; average annual temperatures 7°C (Jan), 25°C (Jul); average annual rainfall 657 mm/26 in;cold, wet, often snowy in higher peninsular areas; Mediterranean climate in coastal regions; Adriatic coast colder than the W coast, and receives less rainfall.

Currency 1 euro (EUR) = 100 cents (previous to February 2002, 1 Italian Lira (ITL) = 100 centesimi).

Economy Industry largely concentrated in N; machinery, iron and steel; tourism; poorer agricultural region in S; Po valley a major agricultural region, with wheat, maize, sugar, potatoes, rice, beef, dairy farming; foothills of the Alps produce apples, peaches, walnuts, wine; further S, citrus fruits, vines, olives, tobacco.

GDP (2002e) $1.455 tn, per capita $25 100

Human Development Index (2002) 0.913

History Inhabited by the Etruscans (N), Latins (C), and Greeks (S) in pre-Roman times; most regions part of the Roman Empire by 3rd-c BC; invaded by barbarian tribes, 4th-c AD; last Roman emperor deposed, 476; ruled by the Lombards and by the Franks under Charlemagne, crowned Emperor of the Romans, 800; part of the Holy Roman Empire under Otto, 962; conflict between popes and emperors throughout Middle Ages; dispute between Guelphs and Ghibellines, 12th-c; divided among five powers, 14th–15th-c (Kingdom of Naples, Duchy of Milan, republics of Florence and Venice, the papacy); major contribution to European culture through the Renaissance; numerous republics set up after the French Revolution; Napoleon crowned King of Italy, 1804; upsurge of liberalism and nationalism (Risorgimento) in 19th-c; unification achieved under Victor Emmanuel II of Sardi-

---

twice more (1994, 1998). After a disappointing season in 2001, he entered Wimbledon on a wild card, and went on to win the title, defeating Pat Rafter.

Ivanovo [eevahnovo], formerly **Ivanovo-Voznesensk** (1871–1932) 57°00N 41°00E, pop (2000e) 480 000. City in C European Russia; on R Uvod; founded, 1871; railway; historic centre of Russia's cotton-milling.

Ives, Charles E(dward) (1874–1954) US composer, born in Danbury, CT. His compositions are firmly based in the American tradition, and include four symphonies, chamber music, and many songs.

Iviza *Ibiza*

Ivor Novello Awards British awards given annually since 1955 for the best songs, and musical scores in various categories, and for services to popular music.

Ivory, James (Francis) (1928–) Film director and writer, born in

Berkeley, CA. With Ismail Merchant he formed Merchant-Ivory Productions in 1961, which became one of the most enduring and productive of independent film associations. International success came with *Shakespeare Wallah* (1965), which he wrote with Ruth Jhabvala. He went on to direct a series of films based on major works in English literature, such as *Howard's End* (1992, BAFTA Best Film). In 2002 Merchant and Ivory were awarded a BAFTA Fellowship for outstanding contribution to world cinema.

ivory Pieces of walrus and elephant tusk, regarded as precious material by many societies throughout the world. Carved ivory ornaments, jewellery and religious objects were produced in China from about the 15th-c BC. Modern concern for wildlife conservation has now strictly curtailed its supply.

Ivory Coast *Côte d'Ivoire*

ivy An evergreen woody climber (*Hedera helix*), growing to nia, aided by Cavour and Garibaldi, by 1870; fought alongside Allies in World War I; Fascist movement brought Mussolini to power, 1922; conquest of Abyssinia, 1935–6, and Albania, 1939; alliance with Hitler in World War 2 led to the end of the Italian Empire; institution of monarchy abolished and became a democratic republic, 1946; founder member of the European Union (formerly EC), 1958; parliament consists of a Chamber of Deputies and a Senate; the President of the Republic is Head of State and appoints a Prime Minister; continued political instability, with some 50 governments in power since the formation of the republic; Romano Prodi's centre-left opposition party won a narrow victory in 2006 elections.

Head of State

1946–8 Enrico de Nicola
1948–55 Luigi Einaudi
1955–62 Giovanni Gronchi
1962–4 Antonio Segni
1964–71 Giuseppe Saragat
1971–8 Giovanni Leone
1978–85 Alessandro Pertini
1985–92 Francesco Cossiga
1992–9 Oscar Luigi Scalfaro
1999–2006 Carlo Ciampi
2006– Giorgio Napolitano

Head of Government

1970–2 Emilio Colombo
1972–4 Giulio Andreotti
1974–6 Aldo Moro
1976–8 Giulio Andreotti
1979–80 Francisco Cossiga
1980–1 Arnaldo Forlani
1981–2 Giovanni Spadolini
1982–3 Amintore Fanfani
1983–7 Bettino Craxi
1987 Amintore Fanfani
1987–8 Giovanni Goria
1988–9 Ciriaco de Mita
1989–92 Giulio Andreotti
1992–3 Giuliano Amato
1993–4 Carlo Azeglio Ciampi
1994–5 Sylvio Berlusconi
1995–6 Lamberto Dini
1996–8 Romano Prodi
1998–2000 Massimo D'Alema
2000–1 Giuliano Amato
2001–6 Silvio Berlusconi
2006– Romano Prodi

30 m/100 ft, native to Europe and W Asia; adhesive aerial roots; flowers greenish-yellow, 5-petalled; fruits berry-like, black, ribbed, poisonous. (Family: Araliaceae.)

Ivy League A group of long-established and prestigious colleges in NE USA. The league was formally established in 1956 to oversee inter-collegiate sports.

Iwo Jima [eewoh jeema] area c.21 km^2/8 sq mi. The most important and largest of the Volcano Is; in the W Pacific Ocean, 1222 km/759 mi S of Tokyo; 8 km/5 mi long; maximum width 4 km/2$\frac{1}{2}$ mi; scene of major battle of World War 2 (1944–5); returned to Japan, 1968.

Ixion [ikseeon] In Greek mythology, a king of Thessaly, the first murderer; also the father of the Centaurs. He was bound to a wheel of fire, usually located in the underworld.

iz(z)ard [izah(r)d] *goat*

Izhevsk [izhefsk], formerly **Ustinov** (1985–7) 56°49N 53°11E, pop (2000e) 690 000. Capital city of Udmurtia, Russia; founded, 1760; renamed in honour of Soviet armaments politician, Dmitri Fedorovich Ustinov (1908–84); airfield; railway; university; cultural and educational centre.

Izmir [eezmeer], formerly **Smyrna** 38°25N 27°10E, pop (2000e) 2 115 000. Port and third largest city in Turkey; severely damaged by earthquakes, 1928, 1939; airfield; railway; two universities (1955, 1982).

Izzard, Eddie [izah(r)d] (1962–) British comedian, born in Aden, Yemen. His family moved to the UK, where he worked in street theatre and comedy clubs before devising a theatre act as a stand-up comic. He became nationally known through live videos of his major shows at the Ambassadors (1993) and the Albery (1995) in London, and won two Emmy awards for *Eddie Izzard: Dressed to Kill* (2000). His film appearances include *Circus* (2000) and *Blueberry* (2004), and his television work includes *40* (2003). In 2007 he starred in the US television drama series *The Riches*.

jabiru [jabiroo] A name used for several species of stork; especially *Jabiru mycteria* of Central and South America.

Jabneh [jabne], or **Jamnia** An ancient city on the coastal plain S of modern Tel Aviv. Famous Jewish scholars gathered there to lay the foundations for the Mishnah.

jacamar [jakamah(r)] A bird native to the New World tropics; long bill and tail; iridescent plumage; nests on ground in burrow. (Family: Galbulidae, 15 species.)

jacana [jakana], Port **jaçaná** [jasanah] A bird native to the tropics worldwide; inhabits freshwater lakes and ponds; toes extremely long; walks on floating vegetation; also known as **lily-trotter** or **lotus bird**. (Family: Jacanidae, 8 species.)

jacaranda A small deciduous tree (*Jacaranda mimosifolia*) growing to 12 m/40 ft; flowers drooping, funnel-shaped, blue. Native to Argentina, it has been widely planted in warm regions as an ornamental and street tree. (Family: Bignoniaceae.)

jacinth [jasinth] A rare red, orange, or yellow gemstone variety of the mineral zircon.

jackal A member of the dog family, resembling a large fox in appearance and habits; three African species; also, the **golden jackal** (*Canis aureus*) from N Africa to SE Asia. (Family: Canidae.)

jackass *kookaburra*

jackdaw Either of two species of bird of the genus *Corvus*: the omnivorous jackdaw (*Corvus monedula*) from N Africa, Europe, and W Asia; and the insect-eating **daurian jackdaw** (*Corvus dauuricus*) from E Asia. Both nest in holes. (Family: Corvidae.)

Jacklin, Tony, popular name of **Anthony Jacklin** (1944–) Golfer, born in Scunthorpe, North Lincolnshire. He won the 1969 Open at Royal Lytham, and in 1970 won the US Open at Hazeltine (the first British winner for 50 years). He was captain of the European Ryder Cup team 1983–9. He retired from the professional tournament circuit in 1999, and was elected to the World Golf Hall of Fame in 2002.

jackrabbit *hare*

Jack Russell A small terrier, developed in Britain by Rev John Russell (1795–1883); sent into foxes' burrows.

Jackson 32°18N 90°12W, pop (2000e) 184 300. Capital of state in C Mississippi, USA, on the Pearl R; established as a trading post, 1792; state capital, 1822; named after President Andrew Jackson; much of the city destroyed by Sherman's forces during the Civil War, 1863; airfield; railway; university; many civil rights demonstrations in the 1960s.

Jackson, Andrew, nickname **Old Hickory** (1767–1845) US statesman and seventh president (1829–37), born in Waxhaw, SC. In the war of 1812 against Britain, he was given command of the South, and became famous for his defence of New Orleans (1815). His election as president was the result of a campaign in which he gained the support of the mass of voters – a new development in US politics which came to be called 'Jacksonian democracy'.

Jackson, Betty (1949–) Fashion designer, born in Backup, Lancashire. She became chief designer with Quorum (1975–81), and is now design director of Betty Jackson Ltd. In 1985 she was British Designer of the Year and won the British Fashion Council award.

Jackson, Colin (Ray) (1967–) Athlete, born in Cardiff, S Wales. His achievements in the 110 m hurdles include World Championship gold medals (1993, 1999), silver medals (1987, 1997), and Olympic silver (1988). He also held the European Championship title four times (1990, 1994, 1998, 2002). In the Commonwealth Games he won gold (1990, 1994) and silver medals (1986, 2002). He retired in 2003 and became a BBC television commentator.

Jackson, Glenda (1936–) Actress and politician, born in Birkenhead, Merseyside. She became a leading member of the Royal Shakespeare Company before appearing in films in 1967, winning Oscars for *Women in Love* (1969) and *A Touch of Class* (1973). Later films include *Beyond Therapy* (1985) and *Business as Usual* (1986). She became a Labour MP in 1992.

Jackson, Helen (Maria) Hunt, *née* **Fiske** (1830–85) Writer and campaigner for American Indian rights, born in Amherst, MA. Her foremost works were the non-fiction *A Century of Dishonor* (1881) and the novel *Ramona* (1884).

Jackson, Jesse (Louis) (1941–) Clergyman and politician, born in Greenville, NC. An active participant in the civil rights movement, in 1984 and 1988 he sought the Democratic nomination for the presidency, the first African-American to mount a serious candidacy for the office. Active in a wide variety of public domains, and frequently controversial, he remained one of the more striking figures in American public life in the late 20th-c. In 2001 he decided to withdraw temporarily from public life following revelations of an extra-marital affair.

Jackson, Mahalia (1911–72) Gospel singer, born in New Orleans, LA. The daughter of a clergyman, her strong religious background and the influence of contemporary blues music were unmistakeably evident in her singing style. Two notably successful records were 'Move On Up a Little Higher' and 'Silent Night'.

Jackson, Michael (1958–) Pop singer, born in Gary, IN. With his brothers in the pop group The Jacksons, he knew stardom from the age of 11, and sang on four consecutive Number One hits. His first major solo album was *Off The Wall* (1979), and he consolidated his career with *Thriller* (1982), which sold over 35 million copies, and *HIStory* (1995). *Number Ones* appeared in 2003. He developed a reclusive lifestyle in adulthood, though continuing to tour widely. Worldwide publicity surrounded him in 1993, when allegations about his sexual life caused the cancellation of an international tour on health grounds. In 2003 he was arrested on child molestation charges and released on bail pending a court hearing in January 2004. His trial was delayed until January 2005 and he was cleared of all charges in June of that year. He married Lisa Marie Presley in 1994, but they divorced in 1996. Later that year he married Debbie Rowe (divorced, 1999); they have two children. He was inducted into the Rock and Roll Hall of Fame in 2001, and the newly established UK Music Hall of Fame in 2004.

Jackson, Peter (1961–) Film director, writer, and producer, born in Pukerua, North Island, New Zealand. He began making amateur short films, eventually producing a science fiction cult classic called *Bad Taste* (1987). Later successes include *Braindead* (1992), *Heavenly Creatures* (1994), *The Frighteners* (1996), and *Contact* (1997). His next project was the multi-award winning *The Lord of the Rings* trilogy: *The Fellowship of the Ring* (2001) and *The Two Towers* (2002). *The Return of the King* (2003) won Golden Globes for Best Picture and Best Director, a BAFTA for Best Film, and 11 Oscars including Best Picture and Best Director. In 2005 he directed a remake of the 1933 film, *King Kong*.

Jackson, Thomas Jonathan, nickname **Stonewall Jackson** (1824–63) Confederate general in the American Civil war, born in Clarksburg, WV. During the Civil War, he commanded a brigade at Bull Run, where his firm stand gained him his byname, and showed tactical superiority in the campaign of the Shenandoah valley (1862). He was accidentally killed by his own troops.

Jack the Ripper Unidentified English murderer who, between August and November 1888, murdered and mutilated at least seven prostitutes in the East End of London. The murderer was never discovered, but speculation about the murderer's identity was still continuing at the start of the 21st century.

Jacob Biblical character, son of Isaac, patriarch of the nation Israel. He supplanted his elder brother Esau, obtaining his father Isaac's special blessing and thus being seen as the inheritor of God's promises. He fathered 12 sons, to whom Jewish tradition traces the 12 tribes of Israel.

Jacobean Style A form of English Renaissance architecture from the period 1603–25. The name derives from King James I of that period. The style is characterized by large windows and a symmetry of facades.

Jacobi, Sir Derek (George) [jakohbee] (1938–) Actor, born in London. He made his professional theatrical debut in 1961, and worked with both the National Theatre and the Royal Shakespeare Company. His roles include *I, Claudius* (1977) and *Cadfael* for television, and the films *Dead Again* (1991), *Gladiator* (2000), and *Bye Bye Blackbird* (2004); but his main work continues to be in the theatre. From 1995 to 1997 he was associate director of the Chichester Festival Theatre (1995–7). He was knighted in 1994.

Jacobins (French history) [jakobinz] A radical political group in the French Revolution, based at the premises of the Dominican or 'Jacobin' fathers in Paris (1789). It became the instrument of the Reign of Terror (1793–4), the name being associated thereafter with left-wing extremism.

Jacobins (religion) *Dominicans*

Jacobites Those who supported the claim of the Catholic James II, and his successors, to the British throne. The Jacobites launched two rebellions, in 1715 and 1745, against the Protestant Hanoverian succession.

Jacobson, Dan (1929–) Novelist and short-story writer, born in Johannesburg, South Africa. He settled in Britain in 1958 and began writing in the 1950s, with *The Trap* (1955). Later novels include *The Beginners* (1966), *Her Story* (1987), *The God-Fearer* (1993), *All For Love* (2005).

Jacopo della Quercia [yakohpoh dela kwairchia] (c.1374–1438) Sculptor, born in Siena, Italy. His greatest works include the city's fountain (the 'Fonte Gaia', executed 1414–19) and the reliefs on the portal of San Petronia, Bologna.

Jacopone da Todi [yakopohnay da tohdee], originally **Iacopo di Iacobello dei Benedetti** (c.1236–1306) Religious poet, born in Todi, Italy. To him is ascribed the authorship of the *Stabat Mater*; and he wrote *laudi spirituali* ('spiritual praises'), important in early Italian drama.

Jacquard, Joseph Marie [zhakah(r)] (1752–1834) Silk-weaver, born in Lyon, France. His invention (1801–8) of the Jacquard loom enabled an ordinary workman to produce highly intricate weaving patterns.

Jacquerie [zhakuhree] (1358) A serious peasant rebellion in NE France, noted for its savagery. Started by mercenaries following the English victory at Poitiers (1356), it ended when the insurgents were massacred.

jade A semi-precious stone, either of two distinct mineral species: the relatively rare *jadeite* (a green pyroxene) which is often translucent, and *nephrite* (a variety of amphibole) which has a waxy lustre. Commonly green or white in colour, it is often used in ornamental carvings.

jaeger *skua*

Jaffa *Tel Aviv–Yafo*

Jagiellons [yagyelonz] The ruling dynasty of Poland–Lithuania, Bohemia, and Hungary, which dominated EC Europe from the Baltic to the Danube in the 15th–16th-c. It was founded when Jagiello, Grand Duke of Lithuania, became King of Poland (1386–1434).

jaguar A big cat (*Panthera onca*), found from S USA to N Argentina; coat with rings of dark blotches surrounding dark spots; some individuals almost black.

jaguarundi or **jaguarondi** [jagwarundee] A member of the cat family (*Felis yagouaroundi*), found from S USA to Paraguay; short legs; long body; grey or reddish-brown.

Jainism [jiynizm] An indigenous religion of India which regards Vardhamana Mahavira (599–527 BC), said to be the last Tirthankara, as its founder. Jains believe that salvation consists in conquering material existence through adherence to a strict ascetic discipline, thus freeing the 'soul' from the working of karma for eternal all-knowing bliss. Liberation requires detachment from worldly existence, an essential part of which is the practice of *Ahimsa*, non-injury to living beings. They numbered over 4·3 million in 2007.

Jaipur [jiypoor] 26°53N 75°50E, pop (2000e) 1 708 000. Capital of Rajasthan state, NW India; founded, 1727; railway; university (1947); known as the 'pink city' since 1875, when Sawai Ram Singh had all the buildings of the bazaar painted pink.

Jakarta or **Djakarta** [jakah(r)ta], formerly **Batavia** 6°08S 106°45E, pop (2000e) 10 069 000. Seaport capital of Indonesia; on NW coast of Java; largest Indonesian city; developed as a trading post, 15th-c; headquarters of Dutch East India Company, 17th-c; capital, 1949; airport; railway; 11 universities (1950–60); much of city submerged by floodwater (Feb 2007).

Jakobson, Roman (Osipovich) [yahkobson] (1896–1982) Linguist, born in Moscow. The founder of the Moscow Linguistic Circle (which generated Russian formalism), he moved in 1920 to Czechoslovakia (starting the Prague Linguistic Circle), and finally in 1941 to the USA.

Jalalabad [jalalabad] 34°26N 76°25E, pop (2001e) 100 000. Capital of Nangarhar province, E Afghanistan; on Kabul R, near Khyber Pass; founded c.1570 by Akbar the Great; nearest Afghan city of importance to the Pakistan border; university and medical school; airfield; in the 1990s, a Taliban stronghold with many guerilla training camps; camps targeted in US-led attack in campaign against the Taliban, 2001.

Jamaica *p.480*

James I (of England) (1566–1625) The first Stuart king of England (1603–25), also King of Scotland (1567–1625) as **James VI**, born in Edinburgh Castle, the son of Mary, Queen of Scots, and Henry, Lord Darnley. When he began to govern for himself, he ruled through his favourites, which caused a rebellion, and a period of imprisonment. On Elizabeth's death, he ascended the English throne as great-grandson of James IV's English wife, Margaret. At first well received, his favouritism again brought him unpopularity.

James II (of England) (1633–1701) King of England and Ireland (1685–8), also King of Scotland, as **James VII**, born in London,

Jamaica

☐ International Airport

Local name Jamaica
Timezone GMT -5
Area 10 957 km²/4229 sq mi
Population total (2002e) 2 630 000
Status Independent state within the Commonwealth
Date of independence 1962
Capital Kingston
Languages English (official), with Jamaican Creole widely spoken
Ethnic groups African (76%), Afro-European (15%), East Indian and Afro-Indian (3%), white (3%), Chinese and Afro-Chinese (1%)

Religions Christian (Protestant 56%, Roman Catholic 5%), non-religious (17%)

Physical features Third largest island in the Caribbean; maximum length, 234 km/145 mi; width, 35–82 km/22–51 mi; mountainous and rugged, particularly in the E, where the Blue Mt Peak rises to 2256m/7401 ft; over 100 small rivers, several used for hydroelectric power.

Climate Humid, tropical climate at sea-level; more temperate at higher altitudes; average annual temperature 24°C (Jan), 27°C (Jul); mean annual rainfall 1980 mm/70 in; virtually no rainfall on S and SW plain; lies within the hurricane belt.

Currency 1 Jamaican Dollar (JMD) = 100 cents

Economy Plantation agriculture (still employs about a third of workforce); sugar, bananas, citrus fruits, coffee, cocoa, ginger, coconuts; bauxite (world's second largest producer); cement, fertilizer, textiles, rum, chemical products; tourism.

GDP (2002e) $10·8 bn, per capita $3800

Human Development Index (2002) 0·742

History Visited by Columbus in 1494; settled by Spanish, 1509; West African slave labour imported for work on sugar plantations from 1640; British occupation, 1655; self-government, 1944; independence, 1962; Governor-General appoints Prime Minister and Cabinet; bicameral Parliament consists of a House of Representatives and a Senate; Portia Simpson Miller sworn in as first woman prime minister, Mar 2006.

Head of State
(British monarch represented by Governor-General)
1973–91 Sir Florizel Glasspole
1991–2006 Sir Howard Cooke
2006– Kenneth Octavius Hall

Head of Government
1989–1992 Michael Norman Manley
1992–2006 Percival Patterson
2006– Portia Simpson Miller

the second son of Charles I. After he became a convert to Catholicism, several unsuccessful attempts were made to exclude him from the succession. His actions in favour of Catholicism raised general indignation, and William, Prince of Orange, was formally asked to invade (1688). James escaped to France, where he was warmly received by Louis XIV. He made an ineffectual attempt to regain his throne in Ireland, which ended in the Battle of the Boyne (1690).

James IV (1473–1513) King of Scots (1488–1513), the eldest son of James III. In 1503 he married Margaret Tudor, the eldest daughter of Henry VII – an alliance which led ultimately to the union of the crowns. However, he adhered to the French alliance when Henry VIII joined the League against France, and invaded England. He was killed at the Battle of Flodden, Northumberland.

James, St ('brother' of Jesus), also known as **St James the Just** (1st-c) Listed with Joseph, Simon, and Judas (*Matt* 13.55) as a 'brother' of Jesus of Nazareth, and identified as the foremost leader of the Christian community in Jerusalem (*Gal* 1.19, 2.9; *Acts* 15.13). Feast day 1 May.

James, St (son of Alphaeus), also known as **St James the Less** (1st-c) One of the 12 apostles. He may be the James whose mother Mary is referred to at the crucifixion of Jesus. Feast day 3 May.

James, St (son of Zebedee), also known as **St James the Great** (1st-c) One of Jesus's 12 apostles, often listed with John (his brother) and Peter as part of an inner group closest to Jesus. According to *Acts* 12.2, he was martyred under Herod Agrippa I (c.44). Feast day 25 July.

James, Clive (Vivian Leopold) (1939–) Writer, satirist, broadcaster, and critic, born in Sydney, New South Wales, Australia. His television programmes have been a combination of chat, humour, and commentary, and include *Saturday Night Clive*, as well as a series of 'documentaries' set in cities around the world.

James, Harry (Hagg) (1916–83) Jazz trumpeter and bandleader, born in Albany, GA. He played with Benny Goodman before forming and leading his own band in 1938, and enjoyed success through the 1940s and 1950s.

James, Henry (1843–1916) Novelist, born in New York City. His work as a novelist falls into three periods. In the first, he is mainly concerned with the impact of American life on the older European civilization, as in *Roderick Hudson* (1875), *Portrait of a Lady* (1881), and *The Bostonians* (1886). From 1869 he made his home in England, chiefly in London and in Rye, Sussex. His second period is devoted to purely English subjects, such as *The Tragic Muse* (1890) and *The Spoils of Poynton* (1897). He reverted to Anglo-American attitudes in his last period, which includes *The Wings of a Dove* (1902) and his masterpiece, *The Ambassadors* (1903). The acknowledged master of the psychological novel, he was a major influence on 20th-c writing.

James, Jesse (Woodson) (1847–82) Wild West outlaw, born in Centerville, MO. He and his brother **Frank James** (1843–1915) led numerous bank, train, and stagecoach robberies before Jesse was murdered for a reward by Robert Ford, a gang member.

James, Dame Naomi (Christine) (1949–) Yachtswoman and writer, born in New Zealand. She became the first woman to sail solo around the world, and first woman solo around Cape Horn (Sep 1977–Jun 1978) on her yacht *Express Crusader*. In 1980 she entered the Observer Transatlantic Race on *Kriter Lady*, winning the Ladies' Prize and achieving the women's record for a single-handed Atlantic crossing.

James, P D, pseudonym of **Phyllis Dorothy White, Baroness James of Holland Park** (1920–) Detective-story writer, born in Oxford, Oxfordshire. Her novels include *Shroud for a Nightingale* (1971), *Original Sin* (1994), and *A Certain Justice* (1997). The futuristic novel *Children of Men* (1992, filmed 2006) represents a new departure, and later books include *Time to be in Earnest* (1999), *The Murder Room* (2003), and *The Lighthouse* (2005).

James, William (1842–1910) Psychologist and philosopher, born in New York City, the brother of the novelist Henry James. His books include *The Principles of Psychology* (1890) and *The Varieties of Religious Experience* (1902). He helped found the American Society for Psychical Research.

Jameson Raid An expedition against the South African Republic (Dec 1895–Jan 1896), to help topple the government of President Kruger. Leander Starr Jameson (1853–1917), administrator for the South Africa Company at Fort Salisbury, led a detachment of British South Africa Police into the Transvaal, but they were easily defeated. The German kaiser, Wilhelm II, sent a telegram of congratulation to Kruger, and the incident caused a major government crisis in Britain as well as precipitating the resignation of Cecil Rhodes as Cape premier and contributing to the tensions that led to the Boer War.

James Tait Black Memorial Prize Annual literary prize awarded in two categories: best work of fiction and best biography first published in Britain in the previous 12 months. The award was established in memory of a partner at A & C Black Publishers Ltd (founded 1807 in Edinburgh by Adam Black), and is administered by the University of Edinburgh, Department of English Literature. The prize is £3000 for each category.

Jamestown (St Helena) 15°56S 5°44W, pop (2000e) 1500. Seaport capital and only town on the British island of St Helena in the S Atlantic; passenger and cargo services.

Jamestown (USA) A deserted town, 24 km/15 mi inland from Chesapeake Bay, Virginia, USA, the site of the first successful British settlement in America. It was founded in 1607 by 105 settlers as James Fort.

Jammu–Kashmir [jamoo kashmeer] pop (2001e) 10 069 900; area 101 283 km²/39 095 sq mi. State in the extreme N of India; part of the Mughal Empire, 1586; Afghan rule, 1786; annexed to the Sikh Punjab, 1819; Kashmir asked for agreements with both India and Pakistan at independence, 1947; attacked by Pakistan, and acceded to India; further hostilities, 1965, 1972, 2002; separatist violence escalated (Mar 2003); ceasefire agreed (Nov 2003); opening (Apr 2005) of first bus service across divided Kashmir in nearly 60 years; summer capital, Srinagar; winter capital, Jammu; governed by a Legislative Council and Legislative Assembly; manufacturing industry largely in Jammu; horticulture widespread in Kashmir; devastation caused by earthquake, destroying much of Muzaffarabad, Oct 2005.

Jamnia *Jabneh*

Janáček, Leoš [yanachek] (1854–1928) Composer, born in Hukvaldy, Czech Republic (formerly Moravia, Austrian Empire). Devoted to the Czech folksong tradition, he wrote several operas, a Mass, instrumental chamber pieces, and song cycles.

Jane, Frederick Thomas (1865–1916) Writer, journalist, and artist, born in Upottery, Devon. He founded and edited *Jane's Fighting Ships* (1898) and *All the World's Aircraft* (1909), the annuals by which his name is best known.

JANET *Joint Academic Network*

janissaries [janisareez] An elite force of Turkish soldiers established in the 14th-c. Throughout their history they mutinied several times, and were finally suppressed.

Jan Mayen [yahn miyen], formerly Eng **Hudson's Tutches** area 380 km²/147 sq mi. Norwegian volcanic island in the Arctic Ocean; length 53 km/33 mi; highest point, Beerenberg (2277 m/7470 ft); discovered by Henry Hudson in 1608; annexed to Norway, 1929; radio and meteorological stations.

Jansen, Cornelius (Otto) [jansen], Dutch [yahnsen] (1585–1638) Roman Catholic theologian, founder of the reform movement known as **Jansenism**, born in Acquoi, The Netherlands. His four-volume work, *Augustinus* (published 1640) sought to prove that the teaching of St Augustine on grace, free will, and predestination was opposed to the teaching of the Jesuit schools. The book was condemned by Pope Urban VIII in 1642, but the controversy raged in France for nearly a century, when a large number of **Jansenists** emigrated to the Netherlands.

Jansky, Karl (Guthe) [yanskee] (1905–50) Radio engineer, born in Norman, OK. His fundamental discovery (1932) was of radio waves from outer space, which allowed the development of radio astronomy during the 1950s.

Januarius, St [janyuahrius], Ital **San Gennaro** (?–c.305) Christian martyr, whose body is preserved in Naples Cathedral, with two phials supposed to contain his blood. The solid matter in the phials is said to liquefy on his feast day, and at several other times during the year. Feast day 19 September.

Janus (astronomy) [jaynuhs] The 10th natural satellite of Saturn, discovered in 1966; distance from the planet 151 000 km/94 000 mi; diameter 200 km/120 mi.

Janus (mythology) [jaynuhs] An ancient Roman divinity who guards the 'gate' or the door. He became the god of beginnings, and is the god of the first month (January). He is always depicted in art with two faces, one at the back of the head.

Japan *p.482*

Japan, Sea of *East Sea*

Japanese The language of Japan, spoken by c.122 million in Japan, and a further 2 million elsewhere, mainly in the USA and Brazil. It has written records from the 8th-c in Chinese characters (*kanji*), still used in one of the Japanese writing systems.

Japanese tosa *mastiff*

japanning A European substitution for Oriental lacquer, produced with layers of copal varnish. Japanned tinwares were produced commercially in Britain in the late 18th-c.

Japheth [jayfeth] Biblical character, one of the sons of Noah who survived the Flood, the brother of Shem and Ham. He is portrayed as the ancestor of peoples in the area of Asia Minor and the Aegean (*Gen* 10).

Japonaiserie A term used for the imitation of Japanese motifs, patterns, and compositions by European artists from the mid-19th-c to the early 20th-c.

japonica [japonika] A deciduous, sometimes spiny shrub (*Chaenomeles speciosa*), native to E Asia; flowers 5-petalled, bowl-shaped, usually scarlet, produced on old wood; also known as **flowering quince** or **Japanese quince**. (Family: Rosaceae.)

Jaques-Dalcroze, Emile [zhak dalkrohz] (1865–1950) Music teacher and composer, born in Vienna. He originated eurhythmics, a method of expressing the rhythmical aspects of music by physical movement.

Jardine, Al(an) *Beach Boys, The*

Jardine, Douglas (Robert) [jah(r)din] (1900–58) Cricketer, born in Mumbai (Bombay), India. He was captain of England during the controversial 'bodyline' tour of Australia (1932–3), where he employed Harold Larwood to bowl extremely fast at the batsman's body, the first use of intimidatory bowling in the game. The event almost caused England and Australia to sever diplomatic relations.

Jarrow March (Oct 1936) A march to London by unemployed workers in the Co Durham shipbuilding and mining town and port, to put the unemployed case. It alerted the more prosperous South and Midlands to the problems of depressed areas.

Japan

☐ International Airport

Jap **Nippon** or **Nihon**

Local name Nihon (Nippon)

Timezone GMT +9

Area 377 728 km²/145 803 sq mi

Population total (2002e) 127 347 000

Status Monarchy

Capital Tokyo

Language Japanese (official)

Ethnic groups Japanese (99%), with Korean minorities

Religions Shintoist (40%), Buddhist (39%), Christian (4%)

Physical features Island state comprising four large islands (Hokkaido, Honshu, Kyushu, Shikoku) and several small islands; consists mainly of steep mountains with many volcanoes; Hokkaido (N) central range runs N–S, rising to over 2000 m/6500 ft, falling to coastal uplands and plains; Honshu, the largest island, comprises parallel arcs of mountains bounded by narrow coastal plains, and includes Mt Fuji, 3776 m/12 388 ft; heavily populated Kanto plain in E; Shikoku and Kyushu (SW) consist of clusters of low cones and rolling hills, mostly 1000–2000 m/3000–6000 ft; Ryukyu chain of volcanic islands to the S, largest Okinawa; frequent earthquakes notably in Kanto (1923), Kobe (1995).

Climate Oceanic climate, influenced by the Asian monsoon; heavy winter rainfall on W coasts of Honshu and in Hokkaido; short, warm summers in N, and severe winters, with heavy snow; variable winter weather throughout Japan, especially in N and W; typhoons in summer and early autumn; mild and almost subtropical winters in S Honshu, Shikoku, and Kyushu; average annual temperatures 5°C (Jan), 25°C (Jul) in Tokyo.

Currency 1 Yen (JPY) = 100 sen

Economy Limited natural resources (less than 20% of land under cultivation); intensive crop production (principally of rice); tim-

ber, fishing, engineering, shipbuilding, textiles, chemicals; major industrial developments since 1960s, especially in computing, electronics, and vehicles.

GDP (2002e) $3·651 tn, per capita $28 700

Human Development Index (2002) 0·933

History Originally occupied by the Ainu; developed into small states, 4th-c; culture strongly influenced by China, 7th–9th-c; ruled by feudal shoguns until power passed to the emperor, 1867; limited contact with the West until the Meiji Restoration, 1868; successful war with China, 1894–5; gained Formosa (Taiwan) and S Manchuria; formed alliance with Britain, 1902; war with Russia, 1904–5; Russia ceded southern half of Sakhalin; Korea annexed, 1910; joined allies in World War 1, 1914; received German Pacific islands as mandates, 1919; war with China; occupied Manchuria, 1931–2; renewed fighting, 1937; entered World War 2 with surprise attack on the US fleet at Pearl Harbor, Hawaii, 1941; occupied British and Dutch possessions in SE Asia, 1941–2; pushed back during 1943–5; atomic bombs dropped on Hiroshima and Nagasaki by allied forces in 1945, ending World War 2 with Japanese surrender; allied control commission took power, and Formosa and Manchuria returned to China; Emperor Hirohito became figurehead ruler, 1946; full sovereignty regained, 1952; joined United Nations, 1958; strong economic growth in 1960s; regained Bonin, Okinawa, and Volcano Islands, 1972; a constitutional monarchy with Emperor as Head of State; government consists of a Prime Minister, Cabinet, and bicameral Diet (Kokkai), with a House of Representatives and a House of Councillors; co-location (with South Korea) of the FIFA 2002 World Cup.

Head of State (Emperor)
1867–1912 Mutsuhito (Meiji)
1912–26 Yoshihito (Taisho)
1926–89 Hirohito (Showa)
1989– Akihito (Heisei)

Head of Government (Prime Minister)
1945 Naruhiko Higashikuni
1945–6 Kijuro Shidehara
1946–7 Shigeru Yoshida
1947–8 Tetsu Katayama
1948 Hitoshi Ashida
1948–54 Shigeru Yoshida
1954–6 Ichiro Hatoyama
1956–7 Tanzan Ishibashi
1957–60 Nobusuke Kishi
1960–4 Hayato Ikeda
1964–72 Eisaku Sato
1972–4 Kakuei Tanaka
1974–6 Takeo Miki
1976–8 Takeo Fukuda
1978–80 Masayoshi Ohira
1980–2 Zenko Suzuki
1982–7 Yasuhiro Nakasone
1987–9 Noburu Takeshita
1989 Sasuke Uno
1989–91 Toshiki Kaifu
1991–3 Kiichi Miyazawa
1993–4 Morihiro Hosokawa
1994–4 Tsutomu Hata
1994–5 Tomiichi Murayama
1995–8 Ryutaro Hashimoto
1998–2000 Keizo Obuchi
2000–1 Yoshiro Mori
2001–6 Junichiro Koizumi
2006– Shinzo Abe

Jarry, Alfred [zharee] (1873–1907) Writer, born in Laval, France. His satirical play, *Ubu-Roi*, was first written when he was 15; later rewritten, and first performed in 1896. Now considered the founding play of the avant-garde theatre, it was a seminal influence on French Surrealism and on the Theatre of the Absurd. He went on to write short stories, poems, and other plays in a Surrealist style, inventing an anarchic logic of the absurd which he called *pataphysique*.

Jaruzelski, General Wojciech (Witold) [yaruzelskee] (1923–) Polish general, prime minister (1981–5), head of state (1985–9), and president (1989–90), born near Lublin, Poland. As premier, in 1981, in an attempt to ease the country's economic problems and to counteract the increasing influence of *Solidarity*, he declared a state of martial law, which was lifted in 1982.

jasmine A slender shrub or woody climber, sometimes evergreen; flowers tubular with spreading lobes; fruit a berry. **Winter jasmine** (*Jasminum nudiflorum*), an evergreen shrub native to China, has bright yellow flowers in winter. **Summer jasmine** (*Jasminum officinale*), a deciduous climber native to Asia, has fragrant white flowers in summer. (Genus: *Jasminum*, 300 species. Family: Oleaceae.)

Jason [jaysn] In Greek legend, the son of Aeson, King of Iolcos. He was sent on the quest of the Golden Fleece, leading the Argonauts to Colchis; there he obtained the fleece with Medea's assistance.

Jason, Sir David, popular name of **David White** (1940–) Actor, born in Edmonton, Greater London. Best known as a television actor, his many series include *Open All Hours* (1976, 1981–5), *Only Fools and Horses* (several series), *A Touch of Frost* (1992–), and *Diamond Geezer* (2005, 2007). He received BAFTAs for best actor (1988), best light entertainment performer (1990), and best comedy actor (1997), and in 2003 was honoured with a BAFTA Fellowship. He was knighted in 2005.

jasper A red variety of chalcedony.

Jaspers, Karl (Theodor) [yasperz] (1883–1969) Philosopher, born in Oldenburg, Germany. His main work is the three-volume *Philosophie* (1932), a systematic exposition of existential philosophy. With the advent of Nazism, he had his work banned, but stayed in Germany, and for his uncompromising stand was awarded the Goethe Prize in 1947.

Jataka [jahtaka] Stories of the Buddha's previous births, contained in the Buddhist Sutra literature.

jaundice A condition in which there is a rise in the amount of bile pigments (bilirubin and biliverdin) in the blood. These stain the skin and other tissues, including the whites of the eyes, a greenish-yellow colour. Jaundice arises as a result of excessive breakdown of the blood pigment, haemoglobin, severe liver disease, or obstruction in the bile duct, such as a gallstone.

Jaurès, (Auguste Marie Joseph) Jean [zhohres] (1859–1914) Socialist leader, writer, and orator, born in Castres, France. The main figure in the founding of the French Socialist Party, he was assassinated in Paris.

Java (country), Indonesian **Jawa** pop (2000e) 128 516 000; area 132 187 km²/51 024 sq mi. Island of Indonesia, in the Greater Sunda group; one of the most densely populated islands in the world; major cities include Jakarta, Bandung, Surabaya; mountainous, rising to 3371 m/11 059 ft at Gunung Sumbung; covered with dense rainforest; 115 volcanic peaks; Mt Merapi active in 2006, followed by severe earthquake with over 6000 deaths; tsunami hit Pangandaran area with over 500 deaths (Jul 2006); eruption of hot mud and gas near Surabaya (May 2006), still uncontrollable by Feb 2007; noted for its batik method of cloth decoration.

JAVA (computing) Trade-name of a programming language devised to create machine-independent networking applications; the name derives from Java coffee, whose strong, rich properties were thought by its devisers to be just as applicable to their new language. It has proved to be of special value to designers of pages of the World Wide Web, where special effects on the page can be created by embedding the name of a short program (*applet*) which downloads and runs when the page is accessed.

Java Man The first known fossil of *Homo erectus*, found in Java in 1891 by the Dutch anatomist Eugène Dubois (1858–1940). It was long known by the name he gave it: *Pithecanthropus erectus*. Subsequent discoveries show specimens to date from ?0·8–0·3 million years ago.

Javanese The largest ethnic group of Java, Indonesia. Their language (Javanese), a member of the Austronesian family, has a literary tradition dating from the 8th-c. The people are Muslim with some Hindu traditions.

Java Sea area 430 000 km²/165 000 sq mi. Sea of SE Asia, bounded N by Borneo, S by Java, and W by Sumatra.

javelin throw An athletics field event of throwing a spear-like javelin. The men's javelin is 2·6–2·7 m/8·6–8·10 ft in length, and weighs 800 g/1 lb 12 oz; the women's javelin is 2·2–2·3 m/7 ft 3 in in length, and weighs at least 600 g/1·5 lb. The current world record for men is 98·48 m/324 ft, achieved by Jan Zelezny (1966–) of the Czech Republic in 1996 at Jenna, Germany; for women it is 71·70 m/235 ft 2·60 in, achieved by Osleidys Menendez (1979–) of Cuba, in 2005 at Helsinki, Finland.

jaw The upper and lower bones surrounding the mouth, which contain the teeth. The upper jaw (**maxilla**) is usually firmly fixed to the face, while the lower jaw (**mandible**) moves against it.

Jay, John (1745–1829) US statesman and jurist, born in New York City. He became secretary for foreign affairs (1784–9), Chief Justice of the Supreme Court (1789–95), and Governor of New York (1795–1801). He is especially remembered for the American–British treaty of 1794, which has been given his name.

jay A name used for many birds, usually of the crow family (Corvidae, 42 species), especially the **common jay** (*Garrulus glandiarus*) from N areas of the Old World.

Jayawardene, Junius Richard [jayawah(r)denay] (1906–96) Sri Lankan statesman and president (1978–89), born in Colombo. He became minister of finance (1947–53), opposition leader (1970–7), prime minister (1977–8), and finally president.

jazz A type of music developed from ragtime and blues in the S states of the USA during the second decade of the 20th-c, originating among black musicians. Prominent features of the earliest New Orleans jazz included *syncopation* (strongly accented rhythms which conflict with the basic pulse of the music), collective *improvisation*, and the exploitation of unusual timbres and extreme ranges in an ensemble which consisted typically of clarinet, trumpet (or cornet), trombone, piano, double bass (played pizzicato), guitar, and drums.

jazz dance North American form of vernacular dancing performed to the rhythms of jazz. It is a popular dance style, used in musical shows on Broadway and in the UK (eg *Cats*).

Jean de Meung [zhã duh mõe], or **Jean Clopinel** (c.1250–1305) Poet, born in Meung-sur-Loire, France. His great work is the lengthy continuation (18 000 lines) of the *Roman de la Rose*.

Jeans, Sir James (Hopwood) [jeenz] (1877–1946) Astrophysicist and popularizer of science, born in Ormskirk, Lancashire. He made important contributions to the theory of gases, quantum theory, and stellar evolution, and became widely known for his popular exposition of physical and astronomical theories.

jebeer *dorcas gazelle*

Jedda or **Jeddah** 21°29N 39°16E, pop (2000e) 2 278 000. Seaport in WC Saudi Arabia; on the E shore of the Red Sea; Saudi Arabia's commercial capital and largest port; airport; university (1967).

jeep The name given to a general purpose (GP) light vehicle developed in World War 2 for the United States Army. It became renowned for its exceptional sturdiness and capability for operating on rough terrain, because of its high clearance and four-wheel drive. Its design led to the manufacture of such types as the Range Rover.

Jefferson, Thomas (1743–1826) US statesman and third president (1801–9), born in Shadwell, VA. He took a prominent part in the first Continental Congress (1774), and drafted the Declaration of Independence (1776). Events of his administration included the Louisiana Purchase (1803) and the prohibition of the slave trade.

Jefferson City 38°34N 92°10W, pop (2000e) 39 600. Capital of state in C Missouri, USA, on the Missouri R; city status, 1839; railway; university (1866).

Jeffreys (of Wem), George Jeffreys, Baron, known as **Judge Jeffreys** (1648–89) Judge, born in Acton, Wrexham, N Wales. His journey to the West Country to try the followers of Monmouth earned the name of *the Bloody Assizes* for its severity. He was Lord Chancellor (1685–8), but on James II's flight was imprisoned in the Tower, where he died.

Jeffries, John (1744–1819) Balloonist and physician, born in Boston, MA. He settled in England, and in 1785 made the first balloon crossing of the English channel with Jean Pierre Blanchard (1753–1809).

Jehovah [jehohva] Term used since the 11th-c as a form of the Hebrew name for Israel's God, **Yahweh**. It is formed from a combination of the Latinized consonants of the Hebrew word *YHWH* with the vowels of the Hebrew word *Adonai* ('Master, Lord').

Jehovah's Witnesses A millenarian movement organized in the USA in 1884 under Charles Taze Russell (1852–1916). They believe in the imminent second coming of Christ, and refuse to obey any law which they see as a contradiction of the law of God – refusing, for example, to take oaths, enter military service, or receive blood transfusions. They numbered over 6 million in 2007.

Jellicoe, John Rushworth Jellicoe, 1st Earl [jelikoh] (1859–1935) British admiral, born in Southampton, Hampshire. Commander-in-chief at the outbreak of World War 1, his main engagement was the Battle of Jutland (1916). He later organized defences against German submarines.

jellyfish A typically bell-shaped, marine coelenterate with a ring of marginal tentacles containing stinging cells and a central mouth on the undersurface; body displays a 4-part radial symmetry. (Phylum: Cnidaria. Class: Scyphozoa.)

Jenkins (of Hillhead), Roy (Harris) Jenkins, Baron (1920–2003) British statesman, born in Abersychan, Torfaen, S Wales. His posts included minister of aviation (1964–5), home secretary (1965–7, 1974-6), and Chancellor of the Exchequer (1967–70). He resigned as an MP in 1976 to take up the presidency of the European Commission (1977–81). He co-founded the Social Democratic Party (1981), and became its first leader, standing down after the 1983 election in favour of David Owen. Defeated in the 1987 election, he was given a life peerage and also became Chancellor of Oxford University.

Jenkins' Ear, War of A war between Britain and Spain starting in 1739, and soon merging into the wider War of the Austrian Succession (1740–8). The name derives from Captain Robert Jenkins, who claimed to have had an ear cut off by Spanish coastguards in the Caribbean.

Jenner, Edward (1749–1823) Physician, born in Berkeley, Gloucestershire. In 1796 he inoculated a child with cowpox, then two months later with smallpox, and the child failed to develop the disease. This led to the widespread use of vaccination.

Jennings, Elizabeth (Joan Cecil) (1926–2001) Poet and writer, born in Boston, Lincolnshire. A Roman Catholic, her verse is intensely personal, with themes of childhood, age, religion, and art. Her work includes *A Way of Looking* (1955, Somerset Maugham Award), *Collected Poems 1967* (1967), and *Selected Poems* (1980).

Jennings, Pat(rick) (1945–) Footballer, born in Newry, Co Down, Northern Ireland. A goalkeeper, he played for Watford, Tottenham Hotspur, and Arsenal, making 747 League appearances. He is Britain's most capped footballer, playing for Northern Ireland 119 times. He retired in 1986. Since 1993 he has been goalkeeping coach at Tottenham Hotspur.

Jennings, Waylon (1937–2002) Country-rock singer and songwriter, born in Littlefield, TX. In the 1970s he and Willie Nelson championed the 'outlaw movement' of country music, breaking away from the commercialism of Nashville; their *Wanted! The Outlaws* (1976) was the first country album to sell a million copies.

Jepson, Willis (Linn) (1867–1946) Botanist, born near Vacaville, CA. He spent his career at the University of California, Berkeley (1899–1937), and his works include the classic *A Manual of the Flowering Plants of California* (1925). He founded the California Botanical Society (1913) and the Save the Redwoods League (1918). A genus of flowering plants, *Jepsonia*, is named after him.

jerboa A mouse-like rodent; moves by jumping; hind legs at least four times as long as front legs; ears large; long tail, with long hairs at tip; does not drink; also known as **desert rat**. (Family: Dipodidae, 31 species.)

Jeremiah or **Jeremias, Book of** [jeremiya] A major prophetic work of the Hebrew Bible/Old Testament, attributed to the prophet Jeremiah, who was active in Judah c.627–587 BC. The work is notable for its record of the prophet's inner struggles, persecution, and despair.

Jeremais *Jeremiah, Book of*

Jerez (de la Frontera) [hereth], also **Xeres** 36°41N 6°07W, pop (2000e) 185 000. Picturesque town in Andalusia, S Spain, giving its name to *sherry*; airport; noted centre for sherry, wine, and brandy.

Jericho [jerikoh], Arabic **Eriha**, Heb **Yeriho** 31°51N 35°27E, pop (2000e) 29 000. Oasis town in Israeli-occupied West Bank, W Jordan; focus of the state of Palestine (area 62 km²/24 sq mi), following Israeli–PLO peace agreement, 1993); 95% Sunni Muslim, 5% Christian; farming, tourism; site of the world's earliest known town, continuously occupied c.9000–1850 BC; scene of famous siege during the Israelite conquest of Canaan, when it is said that the walls fell down at the shout of the army under Joshua.

Jerome, St [jerohm], originally **Eusebius Hieronymus** (c.342–420) Christian ascetic and scholar, born in Stridon, Croatia. He made the first translation of the Bible from Hebrew into Latin (the *Vulgate*). Feast day 30 September.

Jerome, Jerome K(lapka) [jerohm] (1859–1927) Humorous writer, novelist, and playwright, born in Walsall, Staffordshire. His *Three Men in a Boat* (1889) established itself as a humorous classic.

Jersey pop (2000e) 90 000; area 116 km²/45 sq mi. Largest of the Channel Is, lying W of Normandy; chief languages, English with some Norman-French; airport; ferries to UK and France; capital, St Helier; noted for its dairy farming (Jersey cattle) and potatoes; tourism; Jersey Zoological Park founded by Gerald Durrell in 1959.

Jerusalem, Hebrew **Yerushalayim** 31°47N 35°15E, pop (2000e) 686 000. Capital city of Israel; a holy city of Christians, Jews, and Muslims; old city is a world heritage site, surrounded by a fortified wall and divided into four quarters (Armenian, Muslim, Christian, Jewish); ancient holy city, frequently referred to in Biblical sources; part of Roman Empire (1st-c BC); under Muslim rule until conquered by Crusaders, and Kingdom of Jerusalem established, 1099; retaken by Saladin, 1187; ruled by Ayyubids and Mamluks from Cairo until conquered by the Ottomans in 1516 (ruled until 1917); capital of Palestine,

1922–48; divided between Israel and Jordan by 1949 armistice; declared capital of Israel, 1950, but lacks international recognition; E Jerusalem annexed after Six-Day War, 1967; airfield; railway; Hebrew University (1925); 12th-c Cathedral of St James, Temple Mount, El Aqsa Mosque (705–15), Dome of the Rock (685–705), Western Wall, Church of the Holy Sepulchre (1099), Garden of Gethsemane, Mount of Olives; Holocaust History Museum (2005).

Jerusalem artichoke A large perennial growing to 2·8 m/9·2 ft (*Helianthus tuberosus*), a native of North America; numerous underground shoots with potato-like tubers; flower-heads yellow; cultivated for its edible tubers. (Family: Compositae.)

Jespersen, (Jens) Otto (Harry) [yespersen] (1860–1943) Philologist, born in Randers, Denmark. He wrote several major works on grammar, and contributed to the development of phonetics and linguistics. He also invented an international language, 'Novial'.

Jesuits A religious order, the **Society of Jesus** (**SJ**), founded in 1534 by Ignatius de Loyola. A non-contemplative order, it demands strict obedience, compliance with Ignatius's Spiritual Exercises, and special loyalty to the pope. Jesuits have been leading apologists for the Roman Catholic Church.

Jesus Christ (c.6 /5 BC–AD c.30 /33) The central figure of the Christian faith, whose nature as 'Son of God' and whose redemptive work are traditionally considered fundamental beliefs for adherents of Christianity. 'Christ' became attached to the name 'Jesus' in Christian circles in view of the conviction that he was the Jewish Messiah ('Christ'). Jesus of Nazareth is described as the son of Mary and Joseph, and is credited with a miraculous conception by the Spirit of God. He was apparently born in Bethlehem c.6–5 BC (before the death of Herod the Great in 4 BC), but began his ministry in Nazareth. After having been baptized by John the Baptist in the Jordan, he gathered a group of 12 apostles, and began his public ministry. The main records of his ministry are the New Testament Gospels, which show him proclaiming the coming of the kingdom of God, and in particular the acceptance of the oppressed and the poor into the kingdom. He was mainly active in the villages and country of Galilee, where he performed many healings, exorcisms, and other miracles. The duration of his ministry is uncertain, but was probably a 3-year period. He was executed by crucifixion under the order of Pontius Pilate, the Roman procurator, perhaps because of the unrest Jesus's activities were causing. The date of death is uncertain, but is usually considered to be in 30 or 33. Accounts of his resurrection from the dead and later events are preserved in the Gospels, Pauline writings, and Acts of the Apostles.

jet A resinous, hard, black variety of lignite, formed from wood buried on the sea floor. It is often polished, and used in jewellery.

jet engine An engine that accelerates a fluid into its surrounding environment to form a fast-moving jet. The reaction felt by the engine to this expulsion is the *thrust force*, which acts in the opposite direction to the jet. This reactive thrust force is the propulsion force of the engine.

jetfoil A hydrofoil with a waterjet form of propulsion. Water is sucked in from the sea and expelled at great pressure through the after foils.

jet lag Unpleasant mental and bodily sensations of fatigue, inability to concentrate, and impaired judgment, induced by rapid air travel through several time-zones. The condition is due to a disturbance in biological circadian rhythms, and usually subsides within a few days.

jew's harp A simple musical instrument held between the player's lips and teeth. A flexible metal tongue is set in motion with the hand, and the pitch and timbre of its vibrations are controlled by the mouth.

Jhabvala, Ruth [jabvahla], *née* **Prawer** (1927–) Writer, born in Cologne, Germany. Significant novels include *To Whom She Will* (1955), *The Householder* (1960), *Heat and Dust* (1975, Booker) and *Shards of Memory* (1995). The short-story collection *My Nine Lives* appeared in 2004. Among her screenplays are *Shakespeare Wallah* (1965), *A Room with a View* (1986, Oscar), and *Le Divorce* (2003).

Jhelum, River [jayluhm] River in Asia, the most westerly of the five rivers of the Punjab, Pakistan; rises in the Himalayas, meets the R Chenab SW of Jhang Maghiana; length 725 km/450 mi.

Jiang Jieshi [jiang jieshee], or **Chiang Kai-shek** [chang kiy shek] (1887–1975) Leader of the Chinese government and the Guomindang (Nationalist Party) in mainland China (1925–49), then in Taiwan. Born in Zhejiang, in 1918 he joined the separatist revolutionary government of Sun Yixian (Sun Yatsen), and in 1925 launched an expedition against the Beijing government, entering Beijing in 1928. Defeated by communist forces in the civil war, he retreated to Taiwan (1949) where, under US military protection, he maintained unyielding hostility to the new People's Republic. His son, **Jiang Jingguo** (Chiang Chingkuo, 1918–88), became prime minister in 1971 and president in 1978.

Jiang Qing [jiang ching], also spelled **Chiang Ch'ing** (1914–91) Third wife of Mao Zedong, born in Zhucheng, Shandong Province, China. An actress in Shanghai, she met Mao Zedong, and became his wife in 1939. Active in revolutionary propaganda, she attacked alleged bourgeois penetration of the arts, and was a leader of the Cultural Revolution (1965–9). After Mao's death (1976) she was arrested with three others, and sentenced to death, though the sentence was later commuted.

Jiang Zemin (1926–) Chinese president (1993–2003), born in Yangzhou, Jiangsu Province, China. A cautious reformer, loyal to the party, he was inducted into the Politburo in 1987, and became party leader (1989) and chairman of the Central Military Commission (1990–2004).

Jiddah *Jedda*

jig A dance of Great Britain and Ireland, the **Irish jig** involving rapid footwork, a rigidly-held body and vigorous leaps. Several different types are recorded. Jig music is usually in 6/8 time, with some varieties (the **hop** or **slip jig**) in 9/8 time.

jihad [jeehad] (Arabic 'struggle') The term used in Islam for 'holy war'. According to the Qur'an, Muslims have a duty to oppose those who reject Islam, by armed struggle if necessary, and jihad has been invoked to justify both the expansion and defence of Islam.

Jilong [jeelung], also **Keelung** or **Chi-lung**, formerly Span **Santissima Trinidad** 25°06N 121°34E, pop (2000e) 385 000. Second largest seaport in Taiwan; occupied by the Spanish and Dutch, 17th-c; destroyed by earthquake, 1867; occupied by the Japanese, 1895–1945; naval base.

Jim Crow Laws A nickname for statutes enacted by Southern states and municipalities in the USA, beginning in the 1880s, to keep black people in a segregated condition. They were abolished in the mid-20th-c.

Jiménez, Juan Ramón [himayneth] (1881–1958) Lyric poet, born in Moguer, Spain. He made his birthplace famous by his delightful story of the young poet and his donkey, *Platero y yo* (1914, Platero and I), one of the classics of modern Spanish literature. He was awarded the Nobel Prize for Literature in 1956.

jimson weed *thorn apple*

Ji'nan [jeenahn], **Tsinan**, or **Chi-nan**, nickname **City of Springs** 36°41N 117°00E, pop (2000e) 2 680 000. Capital of Shandong province, E China; founded in 8th-c BC; commercial centre in the Tang dynasty, 618–907; airfield; railway.

Jinja [jinja] 0°27N 33°14E, pop (2000e) 71 000. Second largest city in Uganda; on the N shore of L Victoria; airfield; railway.

Jinnah, Muhammad Ali [jina] (1876–1948) Indian Muslim politician, born in Karachi, Pakistan (formerly India). His advocacy of a separate state for Muslims led to the creation of Pakistan in 1947, and he became its first governor-general.

jinni (plural **jinn**), or **genie** In Arab mythology a supernatural creature that could take human or animal form and then interfered, often vengefully, in human affairs. They are frequently mentioned in the Qur'an and in the collection of oriental tales called *The Arabian Nights*.

jird *gerbil*

Joachim of Fiore or **Joachim of Floris** [johakim] (c.1135–1202) Mystic, born in Calabria. Abbot of the Cistercian monastery of Corazzo, he is known for his mystical interpretation of history, recognizing three ages of increasing spirituality.

Joad, C(yril) E(dwin) M(itchinson) [johd] (1891–1953) Writer and controversialist, born in Durham. He wrote 47 highly personal books, notably *Guide to Philosophy* (1936), and was a fashionable atheist until his last work, *Recovery of Belief* (1952). He is also remembered for his BBC Brains Trust intervention, 'It all depends what you mean by ...'.

Joan, Pope (9th-c) Fictitious personage long believed to have been, as John VII, pope (855–58). One legend claims she was born at Mainz, and elected pope while in male disguise. Her reign is said to have ended abruptly when she died on giving birth to a child during a papal procession.

Joan of Arc, St, Fr **Jeanne d'Arc**, known as **the Maid of Orléans** (c.1412–31) French patriot and martyr, born into a peasant family in Domrémy, France. At the age of 13 she heard saints' voices bidding her rescue France from English domination. Clad in a suit of white armour and flying her own standard, she entered Orleans (1429), forced the English to retire, and took the Dauphin to be crowned Charles VII at Rheims. Later captured and sold to the English, she was put on trial (1431) for heresy and sorcery, and burned. She was canonized in 1920. Feast day 30 May.

Job, Book of [johb] A major book of the wisdom literature of the Hebrew Bible/Old Testament, probably drawing on old popular traditions. Job persists in his struggles until presented with the inscrutable majesty of God directly.

Jobs, Steven [jobz] (1955–) Computer inventor and entrepreneur, born in San Francisco, CA. He studied at Reed College, Portland, and with engineer **Stephen Wozniak** (1950–), founded the Apple Computer Co in a garage in 1976. Their brainchild, the Apple II computer (1977), helped launch the personal computer and made their company the fastest growing in US history. In 1985 he left Apple and founded a new company, NeXT Inc, but he returned to Apple in 1997 as CEO and later released the iMac, iTunes, and the iPod.

Jocasta [johkasta] In Greek legend, the wife of King Laius of Thebes and mother of Oedipus, later unwittingly becoming the wife of her son; she is called **Epikaste** in Homer. She killed herself when she discovered her incest.

Jockey Club The controlling body for horse racing in Britain, founded c.1750 at the Star and Garter Coffee House, Pall Mall, London. In 1968 the Jockey Club and National Hunt Committee amalgamated.

Jodl, Alfred [yohdl] (1890–1946) German general, born in Aachen, Germany. He became the planning genius of the German High Command and Hitler's chief adviser. He was found guilty of war crimes at Nuremburg (1946) and executed.

Jodrell Bank 53°13N 2°21W. Observatory station in Cheshire, NWC England; leading radio astronomy centre.

Joel, Billy (1949–) Singer, songwriter, and pianist, born in Long Island, NY. He earned a gold disc with the album *Piano Man* (1974); later albums include *Stormfront* (1989), *River of Dreams* (1993), and *Movin' Out* (2002).

Joel, Book of One of the 12 so-called 'minor' prophetic writings of the Hebrew Bible/Old Testament, attributed to Joel, of whom

nothing is known, but who is today usually assigned to the post-exilic period (c.400–350 BC).

Joffre, Joseph Jacques Césaire [zhofruh] (1852–1931) French general, born in Rivesaltes, France. As French chief-of-staff (1914) and commander-in-chief (1915), he carried out a policy of attrition against the German invaders of France.

Johanan ben Zakkai, Rabban [yohhanan ben zakiy] (1st-c) Prominent Jewish teacher and leader of the reformulation of Judaism after the fall of Jerusalem (AD 70), who helped to found rabbinic Judaism.

Johannesburg [johhanizberg], Afrikaans [yohhanuhsberkh], abbreviated **Jo'burg** 26°10S 28°02E, pop (2000e) 1 837 000 (metropolitan area). Largest city in South Africa, and capital of Gauteng province; altitude 1665 m/5462 ft; founded in 1886 after the discovery of gold in the Witwatersrand; airport; railway; two universities (1922, 1966).

Johansson, Scarlett (1984–) Actress, born in New York City. She made her film debut in *North* (1994), and gained recognition for her role in *The Horse Whisperer* (1998). Later films include *Girl with a Pearl Earring* (2003), *Lost in Translation* (2003, BAFTA Best Actress), *Match Point* (2005), and *The Black Dahlia* (2006).

John (of England), also known as **John Lackland** (1167–1216) King of England (1199–1216), the youngest son of Henry II, born in Oxford, Oxfordshire. He tried to seize the crown during Richard I's captivity in Germany (1193–4), but was forgiven and nominated successor by Richard, who thus set aside the rights of Arthur, the son of John's elder brother Geoffrey. After Arthur was murdered on John's orders (1203), Philip II of France marched against him and conquered all but a portion of Aquitaine (1204–5). In 1206 John refused to receive Stephen Langton as Archbishop of Canterbury, and in 1208 his kingdom was placed under papal interdict. He was then excommunicated (1209), and finally conceded (1213). His oppressive government led to demands for constitutional reform. The barons met the king at Runnymede, and forced him to grant the Great Charter (Magna Carta) (Jun 1215). His repudiation of the Charter precipitated the first Barons' War (1215–17).

John, St, also known as **John, son of Zebedee** and **John the Evangelist** (1st-c) One of the 12 apostles, son of Zebedee, and the younger brother of James; one of the inner circle of disciples who were with Jesus at the Transfiguration and Gethsemane. He spent his closing years at Ephesus, after having written the Apocalypse, the Gospel, and the three Epistles which bear his name (though his authorship has been disputed). Feast day 27 December.

John XXIII, originally **Angelo Giuseppe Roncalli** (1881–1963) Pope (1958–63), born in Sotto il Monte, Italy. He convened the Second Vatican Council (1962–5) to renew the religious life of the Church, with the aim of eventual unity of all Christians.

John, Augustus (Edwin) (1878–1961) Painter, born in Tenby, Pembrokeshire. His favourite themes were gipsies, fishing folk, and naturally regal women, as in 'Lyric Fantasy' (1913/14), and he painted portraits of several political and artistic contemporary figures.

John, Sir Elton (Hercules), originally **Reginald Kenneth Dwight** (1947–) Rock singer and pianist, born in Pinner, Greater London. He was one of the top pop stars of the 1970s, known for such songs as 'Rocket Man' and 'Goodbye Yellow Brick Road', and for his clownish garb that included huge glasses, sequinned and fringed jump suits, and ermine boots. His recording of 'Candle in the Wind '97', sung at the funeral of Princess Diana, became the largest-selling single in history within a month of its release. He has produced many hit albums and also composed the music for the successful West End musical *Billy Elliot* (2005). He was knighted in 1998. In 2005, he was joined in an official civil partnership with his long-time companion, David Furnish.

John of Austria, Don, Span **Don Juan** (1547–78) Spanish soldier, the illegitimate son of the Emperor Charles V, born in Regensburg, Germany. He defeated the Moors in Granada (1570) and the Turks at Lepanto (1571). In 1573 he took Tunis, and was then sent to Milan and (1576) to Holland as viceroy.

John of Damascus, St, also called **St John Damascene** (c.675–c.749) Theologian and hymn writer of the Eastern Church, born in Damascus. He defended the use of images in church worship during the iconoclastic controversy. Feast day 4 December.

John of Gaunt (1340–99) Duke of Lancaster, the fourth son of Edward III, born in Ghent, Belgium. He became highly influential as a peacemaker during the troubled reign of Richard II. On his second wife's death (1394) he married his mistress, Catherine Swynford, by whom he had three sons; from the eldest descended Henry VII.

John of Leyden (1509–36) Anabaptist leader, born in Leyden, The Netherlands. He went to Münster, became head of the movement, and set up a 'kingdom of Zion', with polygamy and community of goods. In 1535 the city was taken, and John and his accomplices were executed.

John of the Cross, St, originally **Juan de Yepes y Álvarez** (1542–91) Christian mystic, the founder with St Teresa of the Discalced Carmelites, born in Fontiveros, Spain. Imprisoned at Toledo (1577), he wrote a number of poems, such as *Canto espiritual* (The Spiritual Canticle), highly regarded in Spanish mystical literature. He was canonized in 1726. Feast day 14 December.

John the Baptist, St (1st-c) Prophetic and ascetic figure referred to in the New Testament Gospels, the son of a priest named Zechariah; roughly contemporary with Jesus of Nazareth. Seen as a forerunner of Christ, he baptized Jesus and others at the R Jordan. He was executed by Herod Antipas. Feast day 24 June.

John Birch Society A moderately sized, extreme right-wing pressure group in the USA which promotes conservative ideas and policies, and is strongly patriotic and anti-communist. Founded in 1958, the name derives from a US missionary and intelligence officer, killed by Chinese communists on 25 August 1945, who was seen by the Society as the first hero of the Cold War.

John Bull A personification of the typical Englishman, or of England itself, first depicted in *The History of John Bull* by Arbuthnot. In many political cartoons of the 18th-c and 19th-c, he is drawn as a short stocky figure, often wearing a waistcoat showing the British flag.

John Henry The hero of an American ballad, who pits himself against a steam drill, and succeeds in crushing more rock than the machine, but dies from the effort.

John o'Groats [jonuhgrohts] Locality in NE Highland, NE Scotland; 'from Land's End to John o'Groats', a common phrase for the length of Britain (970 km/603 mi apart); named after Dutchman John de Groot, who settled in Scotland in the 16th-c.

John Paul I, originally **Albino Luciani** (1912–78) Pope (Aug–Sep 1978), born in Forno di Canale, Italy. The first pope to use a double name (from his two immediate predecessors, John XXIII and Paul VI), he died after only 33 days in office, the shortest pontificate of modern times.

John Paul II, originally **Karol Jozef Wojtyła** (1920–2005) Pope (1978–2005), born in Wadowice, S Poland, the first non-Italian pope in 450 years. He studied in Poland, was ordained in 1946, and became professor of moral theology at Lublin and Kraków. Archbishop and Metropolitan of Kraków (1964–78), he was created cardinal in 1967. Noted for his energy and analytical ability, his pontificate saw many foreign visits, in which he preached to huge audiences. In 1981 he survived an assassination attempt, when he was shot in St Peter's square by a Turkish national, Mehmet Ali Agca, the motives for which have

remained unclear. A champion of economic justice and an outspoken defender of the Church in Communist countries, he was uncompromising on moral issues. Although in failing health, he joined in the celebrations for his silver jubilee in 2003. His papacy became the third longest in the history of the Catholic Church in 2004. Greatly mourned on his death, his body lay in state at St Peter's Basilica where over two million people queued to pay their last respects. The process for his beatification began soon after.

Johns, Jasper (1930–) Painter, born in Augusta, GA. Attracted by the Dadaist ideas of Marcel Duchamp, he chose to paint flags, targets, maps, and other pre-existing images in a style deliberately clumsy and banal. He was one of the founders of Pop Art.

Johns, W(illiam) E(arl) (1893–1968) Writer, born in Hertford, Hertfordshire. He served in the Royal Flying Corps and RAF, and after 1930 edited *Popular Flying*, where he first wrote his stories featuring Captain James Bigglesworth ('Biggles'). He went on to write over 70 novels.

Johnson, Amy (1903–41) Aviator, born in Hull, NE England. She flew solo from England to Australia (1930), to Japan via Siberia (1931), and to Cape Town (1932), making new records in each case.

Johnson, Andrew (1808–75) US statesman and 17th president (1865–9), born in Raleigh, NC. Made vice-president in 1865, on Lincoln's assassination (1865) he became president. A Democrat, his conciliatory policies were opposed by Congress; he vetoed the congressional measures, was impeached, and acquitted.

Johnson, Dame Celia (1908–82) Actress, born in Richmond, Greater London. Well established on the stage, she is best remembered on film for her performance in *Brief Encounter* (1945).

Johnson, James Weldon (1871–1938) Writer and diplomat, born in Jacksonville, FL. He became secretary of the National Association for the Advancement of Colored People (1916–30), and from 1930 was professor of creative literature at Fisk University.

Johnson, Lyndon B(aines), also known as **LBJ** (1908–73) US statesman and 36th president (1963–9), born in Stonewall, TX. Vicepresident in 1960, he was made president after Kennedy's assassination, and was returned to the post in 1964 with a huge majority. His administration passed the Civil Rights Act (1964) and the Voting Rights Act (1965), which helped the position of African-Americans in US society. The escalation of the war in Vietnam led to unpopularity, and he retired in 1969.

Johnson, Magic, popular name of **Earvin Johnson** (1959–) Basketball player; born in Lansing, MI. He played 12 years as a guard for the Los Angeles Lakers (1980–91), was named to the All-NBA (National Basketball Association) team nine times (1983–91), and was voted the league's Most Valuable Player three times (1987, 1990, 1991). He retired from the NBA in 1992 when he tested positive for the HIV virus, but returned to play for the Lakers in 1996. His autobiography was called, simply, *Magic* (1983). He was inducted into the Basketball Hall of Fame in 2002.

Johnson, Michael (1967–) Track athlete, born in Dallas, TX. Fourtimes world champion at 400 m (1993, 1995, 1997, 1999), he achieved the 200 m/400 m double at the 1995 championships, and an unprecedented male double of 200 m and 400 m gold medals at the 1996 (Atlanta) Olympics.

Johnson, Pamela Hansford (1912–81) Writer, born in London. Best known for her portrayal of her native post-war London, her books include *An Avenue of Stone* (1947), *A Bonfire* (1981), and several works of non-fiction, such as *On Iniquity* (1967). In 1950 she married the novelist C P Snow.

Johnson, Samuel, known as **Dr Johnson** (1709–84) Lexicographer, critic, and poet, born in Lichfield, Staffordshire. From

1747 he worked for eight years on his *Dictionary of the English Language*, started the moralistic periodical, *The Rambler* (1750), and wrote his philosophical romance of Abyssinia, *Rasselas* (1759). In 1762 he was given a crown pension, which enabled him to figure as arbiter of letters and social personality, notably in The Literary Club, of which he was a founder member (1764). In 1773 he went with Boswell on a tour of Scotland. His chief later work is *Lives of the Most Eminent English Poets* (1779–81). His reputation as man and conversationalist outweighs his literary reputation.

Johnston, Bruce *Beach Boys, The*

Johor or **Johore** [johaw(r)] pop (2000e) 2 622 000; area 18 985 km²/7328 sq mi. State in S Peninsular Malaysia, occupying the entire S tip of the peninsula; capital, Johor Baharu.

joint The region of contact between bones of the body. **Fibrous joints** allow almost no movement, because the two bones are held firmly together by fibrous tissue. These include the joints between the skull bones, and between the roots of the teeth and the alveolar bone. **Cartilaginous joints** unite two bones by a continuous plate of cartilage, such as those between the bodies of the vertebrae. **Synovial joints** are specialized to allow free movement, and constitute the majority of permanent joints with the limbs.

Joint Academic Network (JANET) A computer network provided in the UK to link computer centres in higher education and research establishments, providing electronic mail, file transfer, and the ability for a user at one computer centre to log into the facilities at another. Gateways are provided to other networks.

Joint European Torus (JET) A research facility in nuclear fusion comprising a large doughnut-shaped experimental fusion reactor, which became operational in 1983 at Abingdon, Oxfordshire, UK. It stands c.9 m/30 ft high, and weighs c.3000 tonnes.

Joinville, Jean, sieur de (Lord of) [zhwĩveel] (c.1224–1317) Historian, born in Joinville, France. He took part in the Crusade of Louis IX (1248–54), in which the army was defeated, and he and Louis were imprisoned at Acre, and ransomed. He later wrote up these events in his *Histoire de Saint Louis* (completed by 1309).

Jolie, Angelina [johlee], in full **Angelina Jolie Voight** (1975–) Actress, born in Los Angeles, CA, the daughter of actor Jon Voight. She gained her first film lead role in *Hackers* (1995), and later films include *Gia* (1998, Best Actress Golden Globe), *Girl, Interrrupted* (1999, Golden Globe; Best Supporting Actress Oscar), *Lara Croft: Tomb Raider* (2001, sequel 2003), *Alexander* (2004), and *The Good Shepherd* (2006). She has a daughter (born 2006) with actor Brad Pitt.

Joliot-Curie, Irène [zholioh kyooree], *née* **Curie** (1897–1956) Physical chemist, the daughter of Pierre and Marie Curie, born in Paris. In 1934 she and her husband **Frédéric** (1900–58) succeeded in producing radioactive elements artificially, for which they received the 1935 Nobel Prize for Chemistry.

Jolson, Al [johlson], originally **Asa Yoelson** (1886–1950) Actor and singer, born in Srednike (now Seredzius), Lithuania, and raised in Washington and New York. His sentimental songs, such as 'Mammy', 'Sonny Boy', and 'Swanee', delivered on one knee, arms outstretched, brought tears to the eyes of vaudeville audiences in the 1920s.

Jonah or **Jonas, Book of** One of the 12 so-called 'minor' prophetic writings of the Hebrew Bible/Old Testament. It emphasizes Israel's role in addressing the heathen nations.

Jonas *Jonah, Book of*

Jonathan (c.11th-c BC) Biblical character, the son and heir of Saul (the first King of Israel) and loyal friend of David. He was killed in the battle of Gilboa against the Philistines.

Jones, Bobby, popular name of **Robert (Tyre) Jones** (1902–71)

Golfer, born in Atlanta, GA. He won the (British) Open three times (1926–7, 1930) and the US Open four times (1923, 1926, 1929–30). In 1930 he took the Amateur and Open titles of both countries.

Jones, Daniel (1881–1967) Phonetician, born in London. He compiled the *English Pronouncing Dictionary* (1917), and produced several influential textbooks. His 'cardinal vowels' act as a reference system for the description of the vowels of real languages.

Jones, (Alfred) Ernest (1879–1958) Psychoanalyst, born in Llwchwy, S Wales. A lifelong disciple and friend of Freud, he introduced psychoanalysis to the UK and USA, founding the British Psychoanalytical Society in 1913.

Jones, Henry, pseudonym **Cavendish** (1831–99) Writer on whist and other games, born in London. The author of manuals on several games, he is mainly remembered for his codification of the rules of whist (1862).

Jones, Inigo (1573–1652) The first of the great English architects, born in London. He studied landscape painting in Italy, and from Venice introduced the Palladian style into England. His designs include the Queen's House at Greenwich (1635) and the Banqueting House in Whitehall (1622), both in London.

Jones, Jack, popular name of **James (Larkin) Jones** (1913–) Trade unionist, born in Liverpool, Merseyside. He was general secretary of the Transport and General Workers Union (1969–78), favouring the decentralization of trade-union power to the local branch.

Jones, John Paul, originally **John Paul** (1747–92) American naval officer, born in Kirkbean, Dumfries and Galloway. He joined the navy at the outbreak of the War of Independence, and performed a number of daring exploits off the British coast, capturing and sinking several ships.

Jones, Marion (1975–) Track and field athlete, born in Los Angeles, CA. A sprinter and jumper, she won the 100 m World Championship in 1997. The International Athletics Federation Woman Athlete of the Year in 1998, she headed the rankings for 100 m, 200 m and long jump. She became the first woman in history to win five athletics medals at a single Olympic Games (2000).

Jones, Mary Harris, known as **Mother Jones** (1830–1930) US labour agitator, born in Co Cork, Ireland. She devoted herself to the cause of labour, travelling to areas of labour strife, especially in the coal industry.

Jones, Sir Tom, originally **Thomas Jones Woodward** (1940–) Singer, born in Pontypridd, S Wales. He became known following his hit single, 'It's Not Unusual' (1965). His version of 'Green Green Grass of Home' (1966) was his biggest selling single, other hits including 'What's New Pussycat?' (1965), 'Delilah' (1968), and 'She's a Lady' (1971). Later albums include *Reload* (1999) and *Mr Jones* (2002). In 2003 he received a Brit Award for Outstanding Contribution to Music. He was knighted in 2006.

Jones, Sir William (1746–94) Orientalist, born in London. He devoted himself to Sanskrit, whose startling resemblance to Latin and Greek he pointed out in 1787.

Jongkind, Johan Barthold [yongkint] (1819–91) Painter, born in Lattrop, The Netherlands. He exhibited with the Barbizon painters, and was an important precursor of Impressionism.

Jönköping [yoenchoeping] 57°45N 14°10E, pop (2000e) 117 000. Industrial town in S Sweden; charter, 1284; railway; focus point for agriculture and forestry.

Jonson, Ben(jamin) (1572–1637) Playwright and poet, born in London. He joined Henslowe's company, where he killed a fellow player in a duel. His *Every Man in His Humour*, with Shakespeare in the cast, was performed in 1598. His four chief plays are *Volpone* (1606), *The Silent Woman* (1609), *The Alchemist* (1610), and *Bartholomew Fair* (1614), and he also produced several masques. A major influence on 17th-c poets (known as 'the tribe of Ben'), he was appointed poet laureate in 1617.

Joplin, Scott (1867/8–1917) Composer and pianist, born in Texarkana, AR. His 'Maple Leaf Rag' (1899) made ragtime music a national craze, and was the first of his several popular rags. Ragtime experienced a revival in the 1970s, and Joplin's music (especially 'The Entertainer') became more widely known.

Jordaens, Jakob [yawdahns] (1593–1678) Painter, born in Antwerp, Belgium. He painted several altarpieces, and became known for his scenes of merry peasant life, such as 'The King Drinks' (1638, Brussels).

Jordan *p.490*

Jordan, River River in the Middle East; rises in the Anti-Lebanon mountains; flows over 320 km/200 mi S through L Tiberias and El Ghor to the Dead Sea; S half separates the East Bank of Jordan from the Israeli-occupied West Bank; many biblical associations, especially with the life of Jesus.

Jordan, Dorothea, *née* **Bland** (1762–1816) Actress, born near Waterford, Ireland. For nearly 30 years she kept her hold on the public mainly in comic tomboy roles. In 1790 commenced her connection with the Duke of Clarence, afterwards William IV, which endured until 1811, and by whom she had 10 of her 15 children.

Jordan, Michael (Jeffrey), nickname **Air Jordan** (1963–) Basketball player, born in New York City. He played with the Chicago Bulls from 1984, holds the record for most points in an NBA play-off game (63), and was a member of the USA Olympic gold medal-winning team in 1984 and 1992. He announced his retirement in 1993, turned to baseball, but rejoined the Bulls in 1995, and in 1996 took the NBA scoring title for the eighth time to break Wilt Chamberlain's record, and won it again in 1997. In 1998 he won his sixth NBA title with the Chicago Bulls. He retired in 1999, but made a brief comeback with the Washington Wizards (2001–3).

Jordan, (Ernst) Pascual (1902–80) Physicist, born in Hanover, NC Germany. He was professor of theoretical physics at the universities of Rostock (1928–44), Berlin (1944–51), and Hamburg (after 1951). In the late 1920s he helped to found quantum mechanics and quantum electrodynamics. He also discovered an important class of non-associative algebras known as **Jordan algebras**.

Jordan, Vernon E(ulion), Jr (1935–) Attorney and civil rights leader, born in Atlanta, GA. President of the National Urban League (1971–81), in 1980 he was wounded in a racially-motivated sniper attack. He became an influential Washington lobbyist with strong ties to the Democratic Party. His efforts to find a job for Monica Lewinsky in 1997–8 brought him directly into the obstruction of justice charges in the impeachment proceedings against the president.

Joseph, St (1st-c BC) Husband of the Virgin Mary, a carpenter in Nazareth, who last appears in the Gospel history when Jesus is 12 years old. Feast day 19 March.

Joseph Biblical character and subject of many stories in *Gen* 37–50; the 11th son of Jacob, but the first by his wife Rachel. He is depicted as Jacob's favourite son (marked by the gift of a multicoloured coat) who was sold into slavery by his jealous brothers, yet who by prudence and wisdom rose to high office in Pharaoh's court. Eventually he is reconciled with his brothers.

Joseph (of Portsoken), Keith (Sinjohn) Joseph, Baron (1918–94) British Conservative statesman, born in London. A former secretary of state for social services (1970–4) and industry (1979–81), he then held the education and science portfolio (1981–6).

Joseph, Père, known as **l'Eminence grise** ('Grey Eminence'), originally **François Joseph le Clerc du Tremblay** (1577–1638) French diplomat and mystic, born in Paris. He became Cardinal Richelieu's secretary in 1611. His nickname derives from his contact with Richelieu (the 'Red Eminence'), for whom he went on several important diplomatic missions.

Joseph of Arimathea, St [arimatheea] (1st-c) A rich Israelite, a secret disciple of Jesus, and a councillor in Jerusalem. He went to Pontius Pilate and begged the body of Jesus, burying it in his own rock-hewn tomb. According to tradition, he brought the Holy Grail to England. Feast day 17 March (W), 31 July (E).

Joséphine de Beauharnais, *née* **Marie Josèphe Rose Tascher de la Pagerie** (1763–1814) First wife of Napoleon Bonaparte, and French empress, born in Trois-Ilets, Martinique. She married Napoleon in 1796, accompanied him on his Italian campaign, and in Paris attracted round her the most brilliant society of France. The marriage, being childless, was annulled in 1809.

Josephson, Brian (David) (1940–) Physicist, born in Cardiff. In 1962 he deduced the existence of **Josephson effects** used in certain superconducting devices. He shared the Nobel Prize for Physics in 1973.

Josephson constant The international standard of voltage measurement; symbol K_J, defined as $2e/h$, where e is the electron charge and h is Planck's constant; based on the Josephson effect (discovered by Brian Josephson).

Josephus, Flavius [johseefus], originally **Joseph ben Matthias** (c.37–?) Jewish historian and soldier, born in Jerusalem. In Rome he produced several writings on Jewish history and religion, including *History of the Jewish War* (75–9) and *Antiquities of the Jews* (93).

Joshua or **Josue, Book of** A book of the Hebrew Bible/Old Testament named after its main hero, Joshua (originally Hoshea, but renamed by Moses). It continues the stories of the Pentateuch, beginning with the death of Moses.

Josiah [johsiya] (7th-c BC) Biblical character, King of Judah (c.639–609 BC). He is credited with destroying pagan cults and attempting to centralize worship in Jerusalem and the Temple.

Jospin, Lionel [zhospī] (1937–) Prime minister of France (1997–2002), born in Meudon, France. Elected to the National Assembly in 1981, he became first secretary of the Socialist Party (1981–8), then held posts in education (1988–92) and foreign affairs (1992–7), before being elected prime minister. He retired from politics in 2002.

Josquin des Prez or **Prés** [zhoskī day pray] (c.1440–1521) Composer, probably born in Condé, France, possibly a pupil of Jean d'Okeghem. One of the greatest masters of Renaissance polyphony, he left about 20 Masses and numerous motets.

Jotunheimen [yohtoonhiymn] or **Jotunheim** Highest range of mountains in Europe, SC Norway; rises to 2470 m/8104 ft at Glittertind.

Joule, James (Prescott) [jool] (1818–89) Physicist, born in Salford, Greater Manchester. He showed that heat is a form of energy, established the mechanical equivalent of heat, and formulated the absolute scale of temperature.

joule [jool] SI unit of energy, work done, and quantity of heat; symbol J; named after James Joule; defined as the work done by a force of one newton applied over a distance of 1 metre in the direction of the force.

Joule–Thomson effect The change in temperature of a gas when passed through a nozzle and allowed to expand; named after James Joule and William Thomson (Lord Kelvin). For a gas already at low temperature, the expansion produces further cooling. For a gas above a certain temperature, the effect causes warming.

Jovian [johvian], in full **Flavius Claudius Jovianus** (c.331–64) Roman emperor (363–4), appointed by the army in Mesopotamia on Julian's death in battle. He was immediately forced to make a humiliating peace with Shapur II, ceding great tracts of Roman territory to Sassanian Persia.

Jordan

☐ International Airport   ∴ World heritage site

official name **Hashemite Kingdom of Jordan**, Arabic **Al-Mam-laka al-Urduniya al-Hashemiyah**

Local name al'Urdun

Timezone GMT +2

Area 89 544 km²/34 564 sq mi

Population total (2002e) 5 260 000

Status Hashemite kingdom

Date of independence 1946

Capital Amman

Language Arabic (official)

Ethnic groups Arab (99%), Circassian, Armenian, Turkish, Kurd minorities

Religions Muslim (Sunni 95%), Christian (including Roman Cath-olic, Anglican, Coptic, Greek Orthodox, and Evangelical Lutheran) (5%)

Physical features Located in Middle East; divided N–S by Red Sea-Jordan rift valley, much lying below sea level; lowest point, -400 m/-1312 ft at the Dead Sea; highest point, Jebel Ram, 1754 m/5754 ft; land levels out to the Syrian desert (E); c.90% of Jordan is desert.

Climate Mediterranean; hot, dry summers, cool, wet winters; desert area uniformly hot, sunny; rainfall below 200 mm/8 in; average annual temperatures 7·5°C (Jan), 24·9°C (Jul) in Amman.

Currency 1 Jordanian Dinar (JOD) = 1000 fils

Economy Oil, cement, potash, phosphate (world's third largest exporter), light manufacturing; cereals, vegetables, citrus fruits, olives.

GDP (2002e) $22·63 bn, per capita $4300

Human Development Index (2002) 0·717

History Part of Roman Empire; Arab control, 7th-c; part of Turk-ish Empire, 16th-c until World War 1; area divided into Palestine (W of R Jordan) and Transjordan (E of R Jordan), administered by Britain; independence as Hashimite Kingdom of Jordan, 1946; British mandate over Palestine ended, 1948, with newly-created Israel fighting to control West Bank area; armistice in 1949 left Jordan in control of West Bank; Israeli control of West Bank after Six-Day War, 1967; civil war, following attempts by Jordanian army to expel Palestinian guerrillas from West Bank, 1970–1; claims to the West Bank ceded to the Palestine Liberation Organ-ization, 1974; links with the West Bank cut, and PLO established a government in exile, 1988; martial law formally abolished by King Hussein in 1992, and ban on political parties lifted; conflict with Israel formally ended, 1994; Monarch is Head of State and appoints a Prime Minister, who selects a Council of Ministers; Parliament consists of a Senate and a House of Representatives.

Head of State (Monarch)
1949–51 Abdullah I
1951–2 Talal I
1952–99 Hussein I
1999– Abdullah II

Head of Government
1989 Sharif Zaid bin Shaker
1989–91 Mudar Badran
1991 Taher al-Masri
1991–3 Sharif Zaid bin Shaker
1993–6 Abdul Salam Majali
1996–7 Abdul Karim Kabariti
1997–8 Abdul Salam Majali
1998–9 Fayez Tarawneh
1999–2000 Abdul-Raouf Rawabdeh
2000–3 Ali Abu al-Ragheb
2003–5 Faisal al-Fayez
2005 Adnan Badran
2005– Marouf Bakhet

Jowell, Tessa (Jane Helen Douglas) (1947–) British stateswoman, born in London. Before becoming a Labour MP in 1992, she was active in the voluntary sector. Following a number of shadow posts, she became minister for public health in 1997, and employment minster. She was appointed secretary of state for culture, media and sport (2001–).

Joyce, James (Augustine Aloysius) (1882–1941) Writer, born in Dublin. His early work includes short stories, *Dubliners* (1914), and *A Portrait of the Artist as a Young Man* (1916). His best-known book, *Ulysses*, based on one day in Dublin (16 Jun 1904), appeared in Paris in 1922, but was banned in the UK and USA until 1934. *Work in Progress* began to appear in 1927, and finally emerged as *Finnegans Wake* (1939). His work revolutionized the novel form, partly through the abandonment of ordinary plot for *stream of consciousness*, but more fundamentally through his unprecedented exploration of language. A letter he sent to his wife in 1909 fetched £240 800 at auction in 2004, the high-est price ever paid for a 20th-century autographed letter.

Joyce, William, nickname **Lord Haw-Haw** (1906–46) British Nazi propagandist, born in New York City. Throughout World War 2, he broadcast from Radio Hamburg propaganda against Britain, gaining his nickname from his upper-class drawl. He was cap-tured by the British, convicted of treason, and executed in London.

joystick A computer peripheral, similar to a mouse, which controls the movement of a cursor on a visual display terminal. Like the joystick of an aeroplane, it can indicate movement in any direction.

JPEG [jaypeg] *digital media*

Juan Carlos I [hwan kah(r)los] (1938–) King of Spain (1975–), born in Rome, the grandson of Spain's last ruling monarch, Alfonso XIII (1886–1941). In 1962 he married **Princess Sophia of Greece** (1938–), and they have three children. In 1969 Franco named him as his successor, and he was proclaimed king on Franco's death in 1975. He presided over Spain's democratization, helping to defeat a military coup (1981).

Juan Fernández Islands [hwan fernandez] Group of three Chilean islands in the Pacific Ocean, 640 km/398 mi W of mainland; total area 181 km²/70 sq mi; Alexander Selkirk shipwrecked on Robinson Crusoe (1704–9) (basis of Defoe novel, *Robinson Crusoe*).

Juárez, Benito Pablo [hwahres] (1806–72) Mexican national hero and president (1861–72), born in San Pablo Guelatao, Mexico. During the civil war of 1857–60, he assumed the presidency, and was elected to that office on the Liberal victory (1861). He successfully resisted the French invasion under Maximilian.

Jubilees, Book of An account purporting to be an extended revelation to Moses during his 40 days on Mt Sinai, a book of the Old Testament Pseudepigrapha, perhaps from the mid-2nd-c BC. It has also been called the *Little Genesis* or the *Testament of Moses*.

Judah, Kingdom of [jooda] An ancient Jewish state established when the united monarchy split into the kingdoms of Judah (in the S) and Israel (in the N) in the late 10th-c BC. Jerusalem was in the kingdom of Judah.

Judaism The religion of the Jews, central to which is the belief in one God, the transcendent creator of the world who delivered the Israelites out of their bondage in Egypt, revealed his law (*Torah*) to them, and chose them to be a light to all humankind. The Hebrew Bible is the primary source of Judaism. Next in importance is the *Talmud*, which consists of the *Mishnah* (the codification of the oral Torah) and a collection of extensive early rabbinical commentary. Various later commentaries and the standard code of Jewish law and ritual (*Halakhah*) produced in the late Middle Ages have been important in shaping Jewish practice and thought. The family is the basic unit of Jewish ritual. The Sabbath, which begins at sunset on Friday and ends at sunset on Saturday, is the central religious observance. The synagogue is the centre for community worship and study. Its main feature is the 'ark' containing the hand-written scrolls of the Pentateuch. The rabbi is primarily a teacher and spiritual guide. There is an annual cycle of religious festivals and days of fasting. The first of these is Rosh Hashanah, New Year's Day; the holiest day in the Jewish year is Yom Kippur, the Day of Atonement. Other annual festivals include Hanukkah and Pesach, the family festival of Passover. Today most Jews are the descendants of either the *Ashkenazim* or the *Sephardim*, each with their marked cultural differences. There are also several religious branches of Judaism. *Orthodox* Judaism (19th-c) seeks to preserve traditional Judaism. *Reform* Judaism (19th-c) represents an attempt to interpret Judaism in the light of modern scholarship and knowledge – a process carried further by *Liberal* Judaism. *Conservative* Judaism attempts to modify orthodoxy through an emphasis on the positive historical elements of Jewish tradition. In 2007 there were some 14·5 million Jews.

Judas Iscariot [iskaryot] (1st-c) One of the 12 apostles of Jesus. He is the one who betrayed Jesus for 30 pieces of silver by helping to arrange for his arrest at Gethsemane by the Jewish authorities (*Mark* 14.43–6).

Judas tree A deciduous tree (*Cercis siliquastrum*) growing to 10 m/30 ft, native to the Mediterranean region; pea-flowers pink, usually appearing before the leaves; pods up to 10 cm/4 in long. By tradition, this is the tree from which Judas Iscariot hanged himself. (Family: Leguminosae.)

Jude, St or **Thaddeus** (1st-c) One of the 12 apostles, probably the Judas who was one of the 'brethren of the Lord', the brother of James. A New Testament letter is named after him, but the authorship of the work is disputed. Feast day 28 October (W), 19 June or 21 August (E).

Judea [joodeea] Roman–Greek name for S Palestine, area now occupied by SW Israel and W Jordan; chief town, Jerusalem; since 1967, West Bank and E Jerusalem occupied by Israel.

judge A public officer with authority to adjudicate in both civil and criminal disputes; in some jurisdictions (eg the USA) this authority is limited to a single branch of law. In the UK, judges are appointed by the Crown on the advice of the prime minister, in the case of the Court of Appeal and House of Lords; and on the advice of the Lord Chancellor, in the case of High Court and circuit judges. Judges are usually appointed from the ranks of experienced barristers. In the USA, state and local judges are often appointed subject to election or confirmation by the public after a fixed time. Federal judges are appointed for life.

Judges, Book of A book of the Hebrew Bible/Old Testament, with 'judges' referring to the tribal heroes (such as Deborah, Gideon, and Samson) whose acts of leadership are described. Its stories probably underwent editing at several stages of Israel's history.

judicial review In England and Wales, a legal means of obtaining remedies in the High Court against inferior courts, tribunals, and administrative bodies. A similar procedure is available in other jurisdictions.

Judith, Book of Book of the Old Testament Apocrypha, possibly dating from the Maccabean period (mid-2nd-c BC). It tells the story of how Judith saved the city of Bethulia from siege by the Assyrian army.

judo An unarmed combat sport, developed in Japan, and useful in self-defence. Contestants wear a *judogi* (loose fitting suit) and compete on a mat to break their falls. They are graded in their abilty from 5th to 1st *Kyu*, and then 1st *Dan* to the highest, 12th *Dan*. Different coloured belts indicate a fighter's grade.

Jugendstil *Art Nouveau*

Juggernaut [juhgernawt] (Sanskrit 'protector of the world') A Hindu deity equated with Vishnu. His temple is at Puri in E India, and is noted for its annual festival. The modern English sense of a massive, irresistible force (and its application to a large, heavy vehicle) is related to the belief that devotees of the god threw themselves beneath the wheels of the cart bearing his image during the festival procession.

Jugoslavia *Yugoslavia*

jugular veins Blood vessels draining the structures of the head and neck. The **internal jugular vein** returns blood from the brain, face, and much of the neck (particularly the deeper structures). The **external jugular vein** returns blood from the scalp and superficial aspects of the neck.

Jugurtha [jugoortha] (c.160–104 BC) King of Numidia (118–105 BC), after whom the **Jugurthine War** (112–104 BC) is named. His surrender to Marius's deputy, Sulla, ended the war, but was the starting point of the deadly feud between Marius and Sulla which plunged Rome into civil war 20 years later.

Juilliard School [jooliah(r)d] Music conservatory at Lincoln Center, New York City. Founded in 1905 as the Institute of Musical Art, it is now named after US financier Augustus D Juilliard, following a bequest made upon his death in 1919.

jujitsu The Japanese art of offence and self-defence without weapons, used by the Samurai. Jujitsu forms the basis of many modern forms of other combat sports, such as judo, aikido, and karate.

jujube [joojoob] A deciduous shrub (*Ziziphus jujuba*) growing to

9 m/30 ft, native to the E Mediterranean region; characteristic zig-zag stem and paired spines, one hooked, one straight; flowers yellow; olive-like edible fruits black. (Family: Rhamnaceae.)

Julia The name of numerous ladies of the Julian family (*gens*), notably: **1** the wife of Marius and aunt of Julius Caesar; **2** the daughter of Augustus by his first wife Scribonia (39 BC–AD 14), banished for adultery in 2 BC; **3** the daughter of **2** and Agrippa (c.19 BC–AD 28).

Julian, in full **Flavius Claudius Julianus**, known as **Julian the Apostate** (332–63) Roman emperor (361–3), the son of a half-brother of Constantine the Great. He publicly proclaimed himself a pagan, and initiated a vigorous policy of reviving the old pagan cults.

Julian or **Juliana of Norwich** (c.1342–1413) English mystic who probably lived in isolation outside St Julian's Church, Norwich. Her work, *Sixteen Revelations of Divine Love*, has been a lasting influence on theologians stressing the power of the love of God.

Juliana, in full **Juliana Louise Emma Marie Wilhelmina** (1909–2004) Queen of the Netherlands (1948–80), born in The Hague. On the German invasion of Holland (1940), she escaped to Britain and later resided in Canada. She later became Queen on the abdication of her mother, Wilhelmina, and herself abdicated in favour of her eldest daughter, Beatrix.

Julian calendar A calendar established in 46 BC by Julius Caesar, further modified in AD 8, when leap years were correctly implemented, then used in Catholic Europe until 1582, when it was replaced by the Gregorian calendar. Caesar inserted an extra 67 days into 43 BC, and decreed a year of 365 days, with an extra day every fourth year.

Julian date The number of days that have elapsed since 1200 GMT on 1 January 4713 BC, giving a calendar independent of month and year used for analysing periodic phenomena, especially in astronomy. The Julian day beginning at noon on 1 January 2000 was 2 451 544. Devised in 1582 by Joseph Justus Scaliger (1540–1609), it has no connection with the Julian calendar.

July Days (2–5 Jul 1917) Anti-government demonstrations in Petrograd marking a decisive stage in the Russian Revolution. Lenin judged the time for a proletarian-socialist revolution to be premature, and urged restraint.

July Revolution (1830) A three-day revolt in Paris which ended the Bourbon Restoration, forcing the abdication of the reactionary Charles X (r.1824–30). It resulted in the establishment of a more liberal regime under Louis Philippe.

Jumblat, Kemal (1919–77) Lebanese Socialist statesman and hereditary Druze chieftain, born in the Chouf Mts, Lebanon. He founded the Progressive Socialist Party in 1949. Following his assassination in an ambush, his son **Walid Jumblat** became leader of the Druze.

Jumna, River *Yamuna, River*

jumping bean A seed of *Sebastiania pringlei*, a Mexican shrub of the spurge family Euphorbiaceae. It provides food for the larva of the small moth *Carpocapsa solitaris*, which occupies the seed. Warmth intensifies movement of the larva, causing the 'bean' to jump or jerk erratically.

Juneau [joonoh] 58°18N 134°25W, pop (2000e) 30 700. Seaport capital of state in SE Alaska, USA; developed as a gold-rush town after 1880; airport; trade centre, with an ice-free harbour.

June War *Arab–Israeli Wars*

Jung, Carl (Gustav) [yung] (1875–1961) Psychiatrist, born in Kesswil, Switzerland. He met Freud in Vienna in 1907, became his leading collaborator, and was president of the International Psychoanalytic Association (1911–14). Increasingly critical of Freud's approach, his *Wandlungen und Symbole der Libido* (1911–12, trans The Psychology of the Unconscious) caused a break in 1913. He then developed his own theories, which he called 'analytical psychology', that included a description of psychological types ('extraversion/introversion'); the exploration of the 'collective unconscious'; and the concept of the psyche as a 'self-regulating system' expressing itself in the process of 'individuation'.

Jungfrau [yungfrow] 46°33N 7°58E. Mountain peak in the Bernese Alps, SC Switzerland; height 4158 m/13 642 ft.

jungle fowl A pheasant native to India and SE Asia; inhabits forest and scrub; ancestral to the domestic fowl. (Genus: *Gallus*, 4 species.)

Juninho [zhooneenyo], popular name of **Osvaldo Giroldo Jr** (1973–) Footballer, born in Brazil. A midfielder, he joined Middlesbrough in 1995 from São Paulo, moving to Atletico Madrid in 1997, and Vasco da Gama, Brazil in 2000. He was Footballer of the Year in 1994, and scored on his international debut for Brazil in 1995. He rejoined Middlesbrough (2002), moved to Scottish club Celtic (2004–5), then returned to Brazil, signing for Palmeiras.

junior high school *high school*

juniper An evergreen coniferous tree or shrub native to most of the N hemisphere; leaves needle- or scale-like, in some species on the same tree; cones fleshy, berry-like. The foliage yields an oil used in perfume, and the berries are used to flavour gin. (Genus: *Juniperus*, 60 species. Family: Cupressaceae.)

junk bonds The debt of firms whose creditors are doubtful whether they will be paid, on time or at all. The debt of any one such firm is very risky, so cautious lenders regard it as junk and refuse to hold it. However, such bonds pay high rates of interest, and lenders can hold a mixture of the debts of many different borrowers, of whom only a proportion can be expected to default. Thus while junk bonds always present a risk, the rewards may be sufficient to induce less risk-averse lenders to take it.

Junkers [yungkerz] Prussian aristocrats whose power rested on their large estates, and on their traditional role as army officers and civil servants. Their position came increasingly under threat in late 19th-c Germany, but they jealously safeguarded their privileges and power.

Juno (astronomy) The third asteroid to be discovered, in 1804. Its diameter is 248 km/154 mi.

Juno (mythology) In Roman mythology, the supreme goddess, and the wife of Jupiter. She was later identified with Hera.

Jupiter (astronomy) The fifth major planet from the Sun, and the innermost of the giant outer planets. It has been observed in close-up by five space probes: Pioneer 10 and 11, Voyagers 1 and 2, and Galileo. Its basic characteristics are: mass 1.90×10^{27} kg; equatorial radius 71 492 km/44 423 mi; polar radius 66 854 km/41 541 mi; mean density 1.33 g/cm^3; rotational period 9 h 55 min 41 s; orbital period 11.9 years; inclination of equator to orbit 3.1°; mean distance from the Sun 5.203 AU. It is made primarily of hydrogen (82%) and helium (17%). The face of the planet is covered by clouds, organized into bands, called *belts* and *zones*. Zones are light, and cold (−130°C) because they are high in the atmosphere; belts are darker and warmer clouds (−40°C) at a lower elevation; and a third, warmer level of clouds has also been observed (20°C). The uppermost clouds are inferred to be solid ammonia, the middle clouds ammonium hydrosulphide, and the lowest clouds water. The rotation period in the equatorial region is 5 min faster than that of the rest of the planet – a differential which contributes to the formation of a richly coloured banded structure in the cloudy atmosphere. Complex currents and vortices are observed within the bands, including a long-lived atmospheric storm called the *Great Red Spot*. The known Jovian moons (as of 2006) number 63. A dark ring of dust around the planet was discovered by Voyager.

Jupiter (mythology) or **Iuppiter** The chief Roman god, equivalent to Greek Zeus, originally a sky-god with the attributes of thunder and the thunderbolt.

Jura Mountains [joora] Limestone mountain range in E France and W Switzerland, forming a plateau 250 km/155 mi long by 50 km/31 mi wide; highest point in France, Crêt de la Neige (1718 m/5636 ft).

Jurassic period [jurasik] A geological period of the Mesozoic era extending from c.213 to 144 million years ago; characterized by large reptiles on land, sea, and air, with shallow seas rich in marine life (eg ammonites), and the appearance of the first birds; mammals still primitive.

jurisprudence The science or philosophy of law. It has some claim to be regarded as a science of law, in that it seeks to ascertain regularities in human behaviour: judicial behaviourists claim good success rates in predicting the outcome of legal decision-making.

jury A group of lay persons of varying numbers who decide, on the basis of evidence, matters of fact in criminal or civil cases. They are usually 12 in number, although in Scotland 15 jurors sit in criminal trials. In the USA certain juries also have a role in deciding whether a person should be prosecuted for a particular crime; these juries, known as **Grand Juries**, have up to 23 people sitting on them. In England and Wales jurors are chosen from the electoral roll, and must be aged between 18 and 65. In the USA great effort is taken to ensure that jurors are selected randomly from the general population. In England and Wales a majority verdict (10 to 2) is now permitted, and many US states allow majority verdicts; in Scotland, jurors have in addition to guilty or not guilty, a third verdict of not proven; all that is required is a simple majority of 8 to 7. Certain people are ineligible for jury service (eg members of the Judiciary, the clergy, and the mentally ill) or may be excused (eg MPs, doctors), or disqualified (eg if previously convicted of certain types of offence). Many countries including Italy, France, and Germany have abandoned the institution altogether.

Jussieu [zhüsyoe] The name of a family of French botanists, notably **Bernard de Jussieu** (c.1699–1777), who created the botanical garden at Trianon for Louis XV, and adopted a system which has become the basis of modern natural botanical classification.

justice of the peace (JP) A judicial appointment, also known as a **magistrate**. Their principal function is to preside in the *magistrates' courts*, administering immediate (or *summary*) justice in the majority of cases, and committing the most serious cases for further trial elsewhere. A legally qualified clerk advises on the law. When trying cases, a JP in Scotland may sit alone, but in England and Wales sits with at least one other colleague. In the USA, JPs are usually elected but sometimes appointed. Magistrates now receive basic training, but no salary. American JPs also have an important role in the performing of marriages.

Justin (Martyr), St (c.100–c.165) One of the Fathers of the Church, born in Sichem, Samaria. He founded a school of Christian philosophy at Rome, where he is said to have been martyred. Feast day 1 June.

Justinian [justinian], in full **Flavius Petrus Sabbatius Justinianus** (c.482–565) Roman emperor (527–65), the protégé of his uncle, the Byzantine Emperor, Justin (r.518–27). Through his generals, Belisarius and Narses, he recovered N Africa, Spain, and Italy, and carried out a major codification of the Roman law (the **Justinian Code**), begun in 529.

jute An annual (*Corchorus capsularis*) growing to 3·5 m/11½ ft, native to S Asia; flowers yellow. The stems are used in hessian and sacking. (Family: Tiliaceae.)

Jutes A Germanic people whose original homeland was the N part of the Danish peninsula (Jutland). They participated in the 5th-c Germanic invasions of Britain and settled in Kent and the Isle of Wight.

Juvenal, in full **Decimus Junius Juvenalis** (c.55–c.130) Roman lawyer and satirist, born in Aquinum, Italy. His 16 verse satires (c.100–127) deal with a wide range of subjects, notably the corruption and immorality of the times.

juvenile court A court specifically concerned with the interests of children and young persons, where the emphasis is on rehabilitation and treatment rather than punishment. Some juvenile courts deal both with those children who have committed offences and with those who are believed to be in need of care and protection as a result of acts committed against them, while others deal solely with young offenders.

juvenilia The very early works of writers who later become well-known. Jane Austen's *Minor Works* (published 1932) contain extensive entertaining examples.

Kaba, Kaaba, or **Kabah** [kaba] The most sacred site in Islam, situated within the precincts of the Great Mosque at Mecca, Saudi Arabia. It is a small cube-shaped building, unadorned except for the sacred Black Stone, a meteorite, set into the E corner of its walls. The stone, or *qibla*, is the focus-point to which Muslims turn when they pray.

Kabbalah [kabahla] (Heb 'tradition') Jewish religious teachings originally transmitted orally, predominantly mystic in nature, and ostensibly consisting of secret doctrines. Adherents aimed to discover mysteries hidden in the Jewish Scriptures using special methods of interpretation.

Kabuki [kabookee] Originally a city entertainment in Japan, particularly popular from 1650 to 1850, designed to last from dawn to dusk. Modern performances present selected acts or highlights from the traditional repertoire.

Kabul [kahbul] 34°30N 69°10E, pop (2000e) 2 375 000. Capital city of Afghanistan; in a high mountain valley, commanding the approaches to the Khyber Pass; capital of Mughal Empire, 1504–1738; modern state capital in 1773; US-led military attack on Taliban controlled stronghold (Oct 2001) in response to government's refusal to give up Osama bin Laden, chief suspect in terrorist attack on New York and Washington (Sep 2001); university (1931); airport.

Kabyle [kabeel] A Berber people of Algeria. They speak Kabyle, an Afro-Asiatic language, and are predominantly Muslims.

Kádár, János [kahda(r)] (1912–89) Hungarian statesman, premier (1956–8, 1961–5) and first secretary (1956–88), born in Kapoly, Hungary. When the anti-Soviet uprising broke out in 1956, he was a member of the 'national' government of Imre Nagy, but then formed a puppet government which repressed the uprising.

Kaddish [kadeesh] (Aramaic 'holy') An ancient Jewish congregation prayer, mostly in Aramaic, which marks the closing parts of daily public worship, praising the name of God and seeking the coming of the kingdom of God.

Kafka, Franz [kafka] (1883–1924) Novelist, born in Prague. His three unfinished novels were published posthumously (against his wishes): *Der Prozess* (1925, The Trial), *Das Schloss* (1926, The Castle), and *Amerika* (1927). He has influenced many authors with his vision of society (often called 'Kafkaesque') as a pointless, rational organization, with tortuous bureaucratic and totalitarian procedures, into which the bewildered individual has strayed. A collection of his notebook writings was published in 2006: *The Zürau Aphorisms*.

Kahlo, Frida [kahloh] (1907–54) Artist, born in Coyoicoán, Mexico City. She began painting while convalescing from a serious road accident at the age of 18, and sent her work to the painter Diego Rivera, whom she later married (1928). Characterized by vibrant imagery, many of her pictures were striking self-portraits. Pain, which dogged her all her life, and the suffering of women, are recurring and indelible themes in her Surrealistic and often shocking pictures.

Kahn, Oliver (1969–) Footballer, born in Karlsruhe, Germany. He joined Bayern Munich for the 1994–5 season for €2·5 million, a record fee for a goalkeeper at the time. In 2000 he was voted German Footballer of the Year and Best European goalkeeper. In the 2002 World Cup finals in Korea/Japan, he won the Lev Yashin Award for Best Goalkeeper and the Golden Ball Award for the best player, the first goalkeeper to win the award. Following his appearance in the 2006 World Cup held in Germany, he retired from international football with 86 caps.

Kahneman, Daniel Economist, born in Tel Aviv, Israel. A researcher at Princeton University, he shared the 2002 Nobel Prize for Economics for having integrated insights from psychological research into economic science, especially concerning human judgment and decision-making under uncertainty.

Kaieteur Falls [kiyuhtoor] Waterfall in C Guyana, on the R Potaro; nearly five times the height of Niagara, with a sheer drop of 226 m/742 ft.

Kaikoura Ranges [kiykohra] Mountain ranges in NE South Island, New Zealand; length 40 km/25 mi; highest peak, Mt Tapuaenuku (2885 m/9465 ft).

Kairouan [kayrwan] 35°42N 10°01E, pop (2000e) 94 000. City in NE Tunisia; founded in 671; capital of the Aglabite dynasty, 9th-c; an important Muslim holy city.

Kaiser [kiyzer] (Lat *caesar*) The title assumed (Dec 1870) by the Prussian king, William (Wilhelm) I, following the unification of Germany and the creation of the German Second Empire. It was used until 1918.

Kaiser, Georg [kiyzer] (1878–1945) Playwright, born in Magdeburg, Germany. His plays established him as a leader of the Expressionist movement, such as *Von Morgens bis Mitternachts* (1916, From Morn to Midnight), *Gas I* (1918), and *Gas II* (1920).

kakapo [kahkapoh] A flightless, ground-dwelling parrot (*Strigops habroptilus*), native to New Zealand, also known as an **owl parrot**; face with owl-like array of radiating feathers; nocturnal; seriously endangered. (Family: Psittacidae.)

kakee *persimmon*

Kakopetria [kakohpetria] 34°59N 32°54E. Summer resort town in Cyprus; tomb of Archbishop Makarios III.

kakuro [kakooroh], abbreviation of Jap **kasan** ('addition') + **kurosu** ('cross') A grid game marketed in 2005 to take advantage of the interest generated by su doku; also known as **cross sums** (in the US) and **kakro** (in Japan). The game has a playing area of black and empty cells, arranged horizontally and vertically in the manner of a crossword puzzle. Some of the black cells contain a diagonal slash: a number above the slash acts as an 'across' clue; one below the slash as a 'down' clue. The aim is to place numbers one to nine, without repetition, into the empty cells so that the total matches the one given in the associated clue. Dell Magazines published the first such puzzles, under the name of Cross Sums, in the early 1950s.

kala-azar [kahla azah(r)] *leishmaniasis*

Kalahari [kalahahree] Desert region of Africa, in SW Botswana, SE Namibia and N Cape Province, South Africa; area c.260 000 km²/100 000 sq mi; elevation generally 850–1000 m/2800–3280 ft; annual average rainfall over whole area, 150–500 mm/6–20 in; sparsely inhabited by nomads.

kale A very hardy mutant of cabbage (*Brassica oleracea*, variety *acephala*) with dense heads of plain or curled, green or purple leaves; widely grown as a vegetable and fodder crop. The leaves are sometimes called *borecole*. (Family: Crucifereae.)

Kalevala [kahlevahla] The name given to a compilation of Finnish legends, published by Elias Lönnrot in 1835, and now regarded as the Finnish national epic. The poem is in a trochaic metre, imitated by Longfellow in *Hiawatha*.

Kalgoorlie [kalgoorlee], or **Kalgoorlie–Boulder** 30°49S 121°29E, pop (2000e) 27 600. Gold-mining town in Western Australia; gold discovered here, 1893; 60% of Australia's gold mined in the suburb of Boulder; airfield; railway; Flying Doctor centre.

Kali [kahlee] The Hindu goddess of destruction, who is also represented as the Great Mother, the giver of life. She is the consort of Shiva.

Kalidasa [kalidahsa] (c.5th-c) Indian poet and dramatist, best known through his drama *Abhijnana-Sakuntala* (The Recognition of Sakuntala).

Kalimantan [kalimantan] pop (2000e) 9 529 000. Group of four provinces in the Indonesian part of Borneo: **Kalimantan Berat**, **West Kalimantan**, or **West Borneo**, pop (2000e) 3 806 000, area 146 760 km²/56 649 sq mi, capital, Pontianak; **Kalimantan Selatan**, **South Kalimantan**, or **South Borneo**, pop (2000e) 3 053 000, area 37 660 km²/14 537 sq mi, capital, Banjarmasin; **Kalimantan Tengah**, **Central Kalimantan**, or **Central Borneo**, pop (2000e) 465 000, area 152 600 km²/58 904 sq mi, capital, Palangkaraya; **Kalimantan Timur**, **East Kalimantan**, or **East Borneo**, pop (2000e) 2 205 000, area 202 440 km²/78 142 sq mi, capital, Samarinda; an active guerrilla separatist movement.

Kalinin, Mikhail Ivanovich [kaleenin] (1875–1946) Soviet statesman, born in Tver, Russia. He was formal head of state after the 1917 Revolution and during the years of Stalin's dictatorship (1919–46).

Kaliningrad [kaliningrad], formerly **Königsberg, Prussia** 54°40N 20°30E, pop (2001e) 424 800. Capital of Kaliningrad region, W Russia; on the R Pregel at the point where it flows into the Vistula Lagoon, an inlet of the Baltic Sea; founded (1255) as a fortress of the Teutonic Knights; renamed (1946) after E Prussia was ceded to Russia; major ice-free Baltic seaport and naval base; birthplace of Frederick I, Immanuel Kant, Regiomontanus; university (1967); railway; airfield; cathedral; Institute of Oceanography.

Kalmar or **Calmar** 56°39N 16°20E, pop (2000e) 59 000. City in SE Sweden; railway; castle (11th-c).

Kalmar Union The dynastic union of Denmark, Norway, and Sweden achieved at Kalmar, Sweden, where in 1397 Eric of Pomerania was crowned king of all three kingdoms. In 1523 Sweden broke away from the Union, but Norway was united with Denmark until 1814.

Kama [kahma] The Hindu god of love; also, one of the four ends of life in Hindu tradition. In this view, the pursuit of love or pleasure is necessary for life, but should be regulated by considerations of dharma.

Kamchatka [kamchatka] area 270 033 km²/104 233 sq mi. Large peninsula in E Siberian Russia, separating the Sea of Okhotsk (W) from the Bering Sea (E); extends c.1200 km/750 mi S; width, 130–480 km/80–300 mi.

Kamerlingh-Onnes, Heike [kamerling awnes] (1853–1926) Physicist, born in Groningen, The Netherlands. He was the first to produce liquid helium, and discovered the phenomenon of superconductivity. In 1913 he was awarded the Nobel Prize for Physics.

kamikaze [kamikahzee] (Jap 'divine wind') A term identifying the volunteer suicide pilots of the Japanese Imperial Navy, who guided their explosive-packed aircraft onto enemy ships in World War 2. They emerged in the last year of the Pacific War, when 1465 pilots died in the battle for Okinawa, destroying 26 US warships and damaging 164. Other kamikaze tactics (eg using boats and submarines) were also employed.

Kampala [kampahla] 0°19N 32°35E, pop (2000e) 739 000. Capital of Uganda; founded, late 19th-c; capital, 1963; airport at Entebbe; railway; Makerere University (1922); two cathedrals.

Kampuchea *Cambodia*

kana *syllabary*

Kananga [kanangga], formerly **Luluabourg** (to 1966) 5°53S 22°26E, pop (2000e) 462 300. City in WC Democratic Republic of Congo, on R Lulua; scene of a mutiny by Congo Free State troops, 1895; airfield; railway.

Kanarese *Kannada*

Kanchenjunga *Kangchenjunga*

Kandahar [kandahah(r)] 31°36N 65°47E, pop (2000e) 409 200. City in Afghanistan; capital of Afghanistan, 1748–73; Taliban stronghold attacked by US-led military forces in October 2001 in response to the Taliban government's refusal to give up Osama bin Laden, implicated in the terrorist attack on New York and Washington, (Sep 2001); airfield; agricultural market.

Kandel, Eric (1929–) Neurophysiologist, born in Vienna. In the 1970s he joined the Center for Neurobiology and Behaviour at Columbia University. He shared the 2000 Nobel Prize for Physiology or Medicine for discoveries concerning signal transduction in the nervous system.

Kandinsky, Wassily [kandinskee] or **Vasily Vasilyevich** (1866–1944) Russian painter, born in Moscow. In 1911 he co-founded the Expressionist group *Der Blaue Reiter* (The Blue Rider) with Franz Marc, and later taught at the Weimar Bauhaus in Dessau, Germany (1922–33). He is regarded as the founder of abstract art.

Kandy [kandee], known as **City of the Five Hills** 7°17N 80°40E, pop (2000e) 116 000. City in Sri Lanka; royal city until 1815; commercial centre for tea-growing area; focal point of the Buddhist Sinhalese culture; Dalada Maligawa (Temple of the Tooth).

kangaroo A marsupial, usually with long hind legs used for hopping, short front legs, and a long stiff tail; young (a *joey*) develops in a pouch on the mother's abdomen; large species tend to be called *kangaroos*, smaller species *wallabies*. (Family: Macropodidae, 50 species.)

kangaroo rat A squirrel-like rodent, native to North America; hind legs longer than front legs; long tail with long hairs at tip; moves by hopping. (Genus: *Dipodomys*, 22 species. Family: Heteromyidae.)

Kangchenjunga or **Kanchenjunga, Mount** [kanchenjungga], Tibetan **Gangchhendzönga**, Nepali **Kumbhkaran Lungur** 27°42N 88°09E. Mountain in the Himalayan range; third highest mountain in the world; five peaks, the highest at 8586 m/28 169 ft; scaled by the Charles Evans British Expedition in 1955.

Kang de *Puyi*

KaNgwane [kahngwahnay] Former national state or non-independent black homeland in Natal province, South Africa; self-governing status, 1971; incorporated into KwaZulu Natal following the South African constitution of 1994.

kanji [kanjee] A character in Chinese writing, as used in Japan. Kanji are slightly simpler than the Chinese originals, and are pronounced differently.

Kankan [kankan] 10°22N 9°11W, pop (2000e) 122 000. Town in E Guinea; second largest town in Guinea; railway terminus; commercial and transportation centre.

Kannada [kanada] A Dravidian language of S India; also known as **Kanarese**, spoken mainly in the state of Karnataka. It has about 25 million speakers, and has written records from the 5th-c.

Kano [kahnoh] 12°00N 8°31E, pop (2000e) 853 000. City in N Nigeria; ancient Hausa settlement; modern city founded in the 19th-c; city walls nearly 18 km/11 mi long; airport; railway; university (1975).

Kanpur [kahnpoor], formerly **Cawnpore** 26°35N 80°20E, pop (2000e) 2 300 000. City in Uttar Pradesh, N India; on R Ganges; ceded to the British, 1801; entire British garrison massacred during the Indian Mutiny, 1857; airfield; railway; university (1966); major trade and industrial centre.

Kansas [kanzas] pop (2000e) 2 688 400; area 213 089 km²/ 82 277 sq mi. State in C USA; the 'Sunflower State'; part of the Louisiana Purchase, 1803; 34th state admitted to the Union (as a free state), 1861; highest point, Mt Sunflower (1227 m/4025 ft); land rises steadily from prairies (E) to semi-arid high plains (W); suffered severe land erosion in the 1930s (part of the Dust Bowl); capital, Topeka; nation's leading wheat producer; major cattle state.

Kansas City (Kansas) [kanzas] 39°07N 94°38W, pop (2000e) 146 900. River-port city in E Kansas, USA; port at the junction of the Kansas and Missouri Rivers, adjacent to Kansas City, Missouri; settled by Wyandotte Indians, 1843; sold to the US government, 1855; railway; market for surrounding agricultural region.

Kansas City (Missouri) [kanzas] 39°06N 94°35W, pop (2000e) 456 000. River-port city in W Missouri, USA; on the S bank of the Missouri R, adjacent to its sister city, Kansas City, Kansas; established, 1838; city status, 1853; present name, 1889; airport; railway; university (1929); nation's leading winter-wheat market; jazz centre in the 1930s–40s; professional teams (representing the two Kansas Cities), Royals (baseball), Chiefs (football).

Kant, Immanuel [kant] (1724–1804) Philosopher, born in Königsberg, Prussia (now Kaliningrad, Russia). His main work is the *Kritik der reinen Vernunft* (1781, Critique of Pure Reason), in which he provided a response to the empiricism of Hume. He also wrote critiques of ethics and aesthetics. His thought exerted great influence on subsequent philosophy.

Kanto earthquake The worst Japanese earthquake of modern times, occurring in E Japan in 1923. Old Tokyo and Yokohama were destroyed.

Kanuri [kanuree] A Nilo-Saharan-speaking people of Bornu, NE Nigeria, and SE Niger. Muslim since the 11th-c, they have a highly stratified social organization.

kaolin [kayolin] A pure clay composed chiefly of the mineral *kaolinite*, a hydrous aluminium silicate; also known as **china clay**. It is used in the manufacture of fine porcelain, and as a filler in paper making and paints.

Kapil Dev, Nihanj (1959–) Cricketer, born in Chandigarh, India. An all-rounder, he led India to victory in the 1983 World Cup, and became the youngest player (at 24 years 68 days) to perform a Test double of 2000 runs and 200 wickets. In 1994 he broke Sir Richard Hadlee's record of 431 Test wickets by taking 432 wickets in his 130th Test match.

kapok tree [kaypok] One of various members of the baobab family, with fruits containing seeds embedded in cotton-like fibres, used as filling for cushions, etc. (Family: Bombacaceae.)

Kapoor, Anish [kapoor] (1954–) Artist and sculptor, born in Mumbai (Bombay), India, moving to London in 1973. He has exhibited at major venues around the world, and his awards include the Premio Duemila Venice Biennale (1990) and the Turner Prize (1991). In 2003 he won a competition to create the centrepiece for a planned memorial garden to British victims of the 11 September 2001 terrorist attacks in New York City.

Karachi [karahchee] 24°51N 67°02E, pop (2000e) 8 345 000. Provincial capital of Sind province, SE Pakistan; Pakistan's principal seaport; founded, 18th-c; under British rule from 1843; former capital, 1947–59; airport; railway; university (1951).

Karadžić, Radovan [karajich] (1945–) Militant leader of the Bosnian Serbs within Bosnia and Herzegovina, born in the village of Petnijca in Montenegro, former Yugoslavia. In the 1990s' upsurge of nationalism, he founded and became president of the Serbian Democratic Party. When Bosnia and Herzegovina declared independence, Bosnia's Serbs, led by Karadžić, sought union with Serbia, and he declared himself president of the self-styled 'Serb Republic'. A period of purges followed. He accepted the Dayton peace accord (1995) under considerable Serb pressure. In the face of international efforts to bring him before the UN war crimes tribunal in The Hague, he resigned his presidency (1996). Since 1997 he has been in hiding.

Karageorge, Turkish **Karadjordje** ('Black George'), also **Czerny George**, nickname of **George Petrović** (1766–1817) Leader of the Serbians in their struggle for independence, born in Viševac, Serbia. He led a revolt against Turkey, and in 1808 was recognized as Prince of Serbia by the Sultan. When Turkey regained control of Serbia (1813) he was exiled, and on his return was murdered.

Karajan, Herbert von [kara-yan] (1908–89) Conductor, born in Salzburg, Austria. In 1955 he was made principal conductor of the Berlin Philharmonic, with which he was mainly associated until his resignation in 1989.

karakul [karakl] A breed of sheep native to Asia; also known as **caracul**. The name is also used for the skin of a young lamb of this breed, and for cloth which resembles this fur.

Kara-Kum [kara koom], Russ **Peski Karakumy** area c.300 000 km²/120 000 sq mi. Extensive desert in Turkmenistan, E of the Caspian Sea (W).

Karamanlis, Konstantinos [karamanlees], also spelled **Caramanlis** (1907–98) Greek statesman, prime minister (1955–63, 1974–80), and president (1980–5, 1990–5), born in Próti, Greece. During his administration, Greece signed a Treaty of Alliance with Cyprus and Turkey. As premier in 1974, he supervised the restoration of civilian rule.

karat *carat*

karate [karahtay] A martial art of unarmed combat, dating from the 17th-c, which was developed in Japan in the 20th-c. The aim is to be in total control of the muscular power of the body, so that it can be used with great force and accuracy at any instant. In fighting an opponent, blows do not actually make physical contact. Levels of prowess are symbolized by coloured belts.

Karelia [kareelia], Russ **Karelskaya** pop (2000e) 796 000; area 172 400 km²/66 560 sq mi. Constituent republic of Russia; in mediaeval times, an independent state with strong Finnish associations; under Swedish domination, 17th-c; annexed by Russia, 1721; constituted as a Soviet Socialist Republic, 1923; heavily forested.

Karen Sino-Tibetan-speaking, ethnically-diverse groups of S Myanmar. Sometimes divided into White Karen and Red Karen, they have united in common opposition to Burmese control.

Kariba Dam A major concrete arch dam on the Zambezi R at the Zambia–Zimbabwe border, impounding L Kariba; completed in 1959; height 128 m/420 ft; length 579 m/1900 ft.

Karloff, Boris, originally **William Henry Pratt** (1887–1969) Film star, born in London. After several silent films he made his name as the monster in *Frankenstein* (1931), and spent his career mostly in popular horror films.

Karlovy Vary [kah(r)lovee varee], Ger **Karlsbad** 50°14N 12°53E, pop (2000e) 60 200. Town in Czech Republic; airport; railway; famous health resort with hot alkaline springs.

Karlsbad *Karlovy Vary*

Karlsruhe [kah(r)lzroouh] 49°03N 8°23E, pop (2000e) 284 000. City in Germany; port on R Rhine; former capital of Baden; railway; university (1825); palace (1752–85).

karma [kah(r)ma] (Sanskrit 'action' or 'work') In Indian tradition, the principle that a person's actions have consequences meriting reward or punishment. Karma is the moral law of cause and effect by which the sum of a person's actions are carried foward from one life to the next.

Karnataka [kah(r)nataka], formerly **Mysore** pop (2001e) 52 734 000; area 191 773 km²/74 024 sq mi. State in SW India; formed as Mysore in 1956, bringing the Kannada-speaking population of five states together; renamed Karnataka, 1973; bicameral legislature comprises a Legislative Council and a Legislative Assembly; capital, Bangalore.

Karoo [karoo] Dry steppe country in South Africa, from the Orange R down to the Cape.

Kárpathos [kah(r)pathos], Ital **Scarpanto**, ancient **Carpathus** pop (2000e) 5040; area 301 km²/116 sq mi. Mountainous island of the Dodecanese group, E Greece; length 48 km/30 mi; rises to 1216 m/3989 ft; capital, Pigadhia.

Karpov, Anatoly Yevgenyevich [kah(r)pof] (1951–) Chess player and world champion (1975–85), born in Zlatoust, Russia. He became world champion by default after Bobby Fischer refused to defend his title (1975), and successfully defended the title until losing to Kasparov in a controversial match (1985). He defeated Jan Timman of Belgium in an official world championship match in 1993. He successfully defended the FIDE title in 1996 and 1998, but lost it in 1999 when he refused to accept the tournament format.

Karski, Jan, original surname **Kozielecki** (1914–2000) Polish resistance hero, born in Lodz, Poland. During World War 2, he gathered evidence of Nazi atrocities against Polish Jews, and was the first to present documented proof of Hitler's extermination policy to Allied leaders in Britain and the USA. After discovery by German intelligence, he emigrated to the USA in 1942. He was made an honorary citizen of Israel in 1994.

Karst, Slovenian **Kras**, Ital **Carso** Barren, stony limestone plateau in the Dinaric Alps of SW Slovenia; notable caves at Postojna; the name has come to be used in geography to describe limestone topography of this kind.

karting Motor racing of small four-wheeled vehicles, usually with single-cylinder and two-stroke engines. They are raced in categories dependent on engine size.

karyology [kariolojee] The branch of cytology dealing with the study of nuclei inside cells, especially with the structure of chromosomes.

Karzai, Hamid (1957–) Afghan head of state (2001–), born in Kandahar, Afghanistan. He served as deputy foreign minister in the Mujahideen administration (1992), then sided with the Taliban. By 1994 he had become disillusioned with the movement, and went into exile in Pakistan, where he began organizing anti-Taliban resistance. He travelled repeatedly to the USA to lobby for support, and secretly returned to Afghanistan to recruit anti-Taliban fighters in October 2001. At the UN Bonn conference on Afghanistan (Dec 2001), he was named leader of the interim government and became head of state in 2002.

Kashmir Jammu–Kashmir

Kasparov, Gary (Kimovich) [kasparhof] (1963–) Chess player, born in Baku, Azerbaijan. When he beat Anatoly Karpov for the world title (Nov 1985) he became the youngest world champion, at the age of 22 years 210 days. He became the highest-ranked active player, with a rating of 2812 (in 2006). Long-term friction between him and the international chess organization, FIDE, resulted in his establishing the Grandmasters' Association in 1987, and arranging a World Championship match in 1993 without FIDE involvement, in which he defeated Nigel Short of Britain. In 1996 he competed against Deep Blue, the world's best chess-playing computer, winning four of the six games, but was decisively beaten in a rematch the following year. At the FIDE Man–Machine $1 million match held in New York City early in 2003, he drew three games all with the Deep Junior

program. He announced his retirement from competitive chess in 2005. In April 2007 he was arrested and fined for attending a banned anti-Kremlin rally.

Kassel or **Cassel** 51°19N 9°32E, pop (2000e) 201 000. Cultural, economic, and administrative centre in Germany; on the R Fulda; an important traffic junction; badly bombed in World War 2; railway; university (1971).

Kästner, Erich [kestner] (1899–1974) Writer, born in Dresden, Germany. He is best known for his children's books, which include *Emil und die Detektive* (1928, Emil and the Detectives).

Katanga [katangga] The southernmost province of Democratic Republic of Congo, rich in minerals. In 1960, when the Congo (Zaire) achieved independence, Katanga (known as Shaba, 1971–97) attempted to secede under the leadership of Moise Tshombe (1919–69). The unitary state was later recreated under the military leadership of President Mobutu (1930–97).

Kathmandu or **Katmandu** [katmandoo], formerly **Kantipur** 27°42N 85°19E, pop (2000e) 587 000. Capital of Nepal; altitude 1373 m/4504 ft; built in its present form, 723; Gurkha capital, 1768; British seat of administration, 18th-c; university (1959); commercial centre, religious centre, tourism; the Vale of Kathmandu is a world heritage site.

Katowice [katoveetse], Ger **Kattowitz** 50°15N 18°59E, pop (2000e) 370 000. City in S Poland; centre of the Upper Silesian Industrial Region; airport; railway; two universities (1945, 1968); cathedral.

katydid [kaytidid] A large, grasshopper-like insect in which sound communication is well-developed. (Order: Orthoptera. Family: Tettigoniidae, c.5000 species.)

Katyn massacre [katin] A massacre of 14 000 Polish army officers in May 1940 in the Katyn forest near Smolensk, Belarus. Their mass graves were discovered by German occupying forces in 1943. In 1989 the Soviet–Polish historical commission reported that the crime was most probably committed by the Soviet security service (NKVD).

Kauai [kowiy], formerly **Kaieiewaho** pop (2000e) 58 500; area 1692 km²/653 sq mi. Island of the US state of Hawaii; chief town, Lihue.

Kaufman, George S(imon) [kowfman] (1889–1961) Playwright and director, born in Pittsburgh, PA. With Moss Hart he wrote *You Can't Take It With You* (1936, Pulitzer) and *The Man Who Came to Dinner* (1939). Other works include *The Solid Gold Cadillac* (with Howard Teichmann, 1953) and many musicals.

Kaufman, Philip [kawfman] (1936–) Film director and screenwriter, born in Chicago, IL. His films include *Invasion of the Body Snatchers* (1978), *The Unbearable Lightness of Being* (1988), *China: The Wild East* (1995), and *Twisted* (2004). He also wrote the stories for *The Outlaw Josey Wales* (1975) and *Raiders of the Lost Ark* (1981).

Kaunas [kownas], formerly **Kovno** (to 1917) 54°52N 23°55E, pop (2000e) 431 000. Ancient town and river port in Lithuania; on the R Neman; capital of independent Lithuania, 1918; airfield; railway; castle (13th–17th-c).

Kaunda, Kenneth (David) [kaoonda] (1924–) Zambian statesman and president (1964–91), born in Lubwa, Zambia. He founded the Zambian African National Congress (1958), played a leading part in his country's independence negotiations, and became the country's first president. After a failed military coup in 1990, he agreed to multi-party elections in 1991, but lost the presidency. In 1997 he was put under house arrest following a failed coup attempt, though he denied any involvement.

Kaunitz(-Rietberg), Wenzel Anton, Fürst von (Prince of) [kownits reetberg] (1711–94) Austrian statesman and chancellor (1753–92), born in Vienna. As chancellor, he instigated the Diplomatic Revolution, and directed Austrian politics for almost 40 years under Maria Theresa and Joseph II.

kauri pine An evergreen conifer, native to SE Asia and Australsia. It is the source of an important resin as well as timber. One species, *Agathis australis*, is an important forest tree in New Zealand. (Genus: *Agathis*, 20 species. Family: Araucariaceae.)

kava A Polynesian beverage made by fermenting chewed or grated, peeled roots of *Piper methysticum*, a relative of black pepper. The drink is narcotic and sedative as well as intoxicating.

Kawasaki [kawasakee] 35°32N 139°41E, pop (2000e) 1 192 000. Port city in E Honshu, Japan; railway.

kayak [kiyak] A small double-ended craft of Eskimo design, similar to a canoe, but enclosed except for a very small cockpit. It is usually propelled with a double-ended paddle.

Kaye, Danny, originally **David Daniel Kaminski** (1913–87) Comic actor and entertainer, born in New York City. *Wonder Man* (1944) made his reputation as a film comedian. Later films include *The Secret Life of Walter Mitty* (1946), *The Inspector General* (1950), and *Hans Christian Andersen* (1952). Well known for his fundraising activities for UNICEF, he received an Honorary Oscar in 1955.

Kazakh or **Kazak** [kazak] A Turkic-speaking Mongoloid people of Kazakhstan and adjacent areas in China. Traditionally nomadic pastoralists, they are now on collective cattle farms, though many are still nomadic.

Kazakhstan *p.499*

Kazan [kazan] 55°45N 49°10E, pop (2000e) 1 100 000. River-port city in E European Russia; founded, 13th-c; airport; railway; university (1804); cathedral (19th-c); important industrial and cultural centre of the Volga region.

Kazan, Elia [kazan], originally **Elias Kazantzoglou** (1909–2003) Stage and film director, born in Istanbul. He began as a film director in 1944, and won Oscars for *Gentleman's Agreement* (1948) and *On the Waterfront* (1954). He co-founded the Actors' Studio in 1947. A lifetime achievement award at the 1999 Oscars ceremony was given a mixed response, with opponents recalling that Kazan had given the names of communists in the film industry to the Un-American Activities Committee in the 1950s.

Kazantzakis, Nikos [kazanzakis] (1883–1957) Writer, born in Heraklion, Crete, Greece. He is best known for the novel *Vios kai politia tou Alexi Zormpa* (1946, trans Zorba the Greek, filmed 1964) and the long autobiographical narrative poem, *Odissia* (1938, The Odyssey, a Modern Sequel).

kazoo or **bazouka** A child's musical instrument, consisting of a short metal tube flattened at one end, with a hole in the top covered by a disc of membrane. This imparts a buzzing edge to the tone when the player sings or hums into the flattened end.

Kean, Edmund (c.1789–1833) Actor, born in London. A highly successful tragic actor, his irregularities lost him public approval, his reputation being finally ruined when he was successfully sued for adultery in 1825.

Keating, Paul (John) (1944–) Australian statesman and prime minister (1991–6), born in Sydney, New South Wales, Australia. As treasurer (1983–91), he was the main architect of the government's economic policies. Elected leader by the Labor Party in 1991, he retired from parliament following the election defeat of 1996. He declined the award of Companion to the Order of Australia in 1997 – the first living former prime minister not to accept the honour.

Keating, Tom (1918–84) Artist and forger, born in London. A self-confessed 'art imitator', he claimed to have produced some 2000 fakes in 25 years. His activity came to light in 1976. He was arrested, but charges were dropped when his health declined.

Keaton, Buster, popular name of **Joseph Francis Keaton** (1895–1966) Film comedian, born in Piqua, KS. Renowned for his 'deadpan' expression, he starred in and directed such classics as *The Navigator* (1924) and *The General* (1927). His reputation

went into eclipse with the advent of talking films until the 1950s, when many of his silent films were re-released. He received a special Academy Award in 1959.

Keaton, Diane [keeton] (1946–) Film actress and director, born in Los Angeles, CA. She became known through her roles in several of Woody Allen's films, such as *Annie Hall* (1977, Oscar), *Manhattan* (1979), and *Manhattan Murder Mystery* (1993). Other films include *Reds* (1981), *Marvin's Room* (1996), *Something's Gotta Give* (2003, Oscar nomination), and *Because I Said So* (2007), and she directed and acted in *Hanging Up* (2000).

Keaton, Michael (1951–) Actor, born in Caraopolis, PA. His breakthrough came with the film *Mr Mom* (1983), and five years later, after *Beetlejuice* (1988) and *Clean and Sober* (1988), he was named best actor by national film critics. Other films include *Batman* (1989), *Batman Returns* (1992), *Multiplicity* (1996), and *Cars* (2006).

Keats, John (1795–1821) Poet, born in London. His first book of poems (1817) was fiercely criticized, but he was nonetheless able to write *Lamia and Other Poems* (1820), a landmark in English poetry, which contains his major odes. Seriously ill with tuberculosis, he died in Rome.

Keble, John [keebl] (1792–1866) Anglican churchman and poet, born in Fairford, Gloucestershire. His sermon on 'National Apostasy' (1833) began the *Oxford Movement*, encouraging a return to High Church ideals. Keble College, Oxford, was erected in his memory.

keck cow parsley; hogweed

Kedah [kaydah] pop (2000e) 1 758 000; area 9425 km²/3638 sq mi. State in NW Peninsular Malaysia; governed by Thailand from early 19th-c until 1909, when it came under British rule; capital, Alor Setar.

Keeling Islands *Cocos Islands*

Keelung *Jilong*

keeshond [kayshond] A small, sturdy spitz breed of dog from The Netherlands; grey with dark tinges; head dark with pale rings around eyes; coat very thick, especially around neck; tail tightly curled.

kefir [kefeer] A fermented milk originating in the Caucasus. Traditionally made from camel's milk, it is now made from cow's milk.

Keflavik [keflavik, kyeplaveek] 64°01N 22°35W, pop (2000e) 8100. Fishing port in SW Iceland; important trade centre since the 16th-c; airport.

Keillor, Garrison [keeler], pseudonym of **Gary Edward Keillor** (1942–) Humorous writer and radio performer, born in Anoka, MN. In 1974 he began to host the live radio show, 'A Prairie Home Companion', delivering a weekly monologue set in the quiet, fictional mid-western town of Lake Wobegon. His books include *Lake Wobegon Days* (1985), *We Are Still Married* (1989), *Me: by Jimmy (Big Boy) Valente* (1999), and *Love Me* (2003). In 2006 he co-wrote and starred in Robert Altman's film *A Prairie Home Companion*.

Keitel, Wilhelm [kiytl] (1882–1946) German field marshal, born in Helmscherode, Germany. He was made chief of the Supreme Command of the Armed Forces (1938), and in 1945 was one of the German signatories of surrender in Berlin. He was convicted of war crimes at Nuremberg, and executed.

Kelantan [kelantan] pop (2000e) 1 519 000; area 14 796 km²/5711 sq mi. State in NE Peninsular Malaysia; governed by Thailand from early 19th-c until 1909, when it came under British rule; capital, Kota Baharu.

Keldysh, Mstislav (Vsevoldvich) (1911–78) Mathematician and space programme leader, born in Riga. He was a leading figure in the development of the theory of rocketry and in the emergence of the USSR in space exploration.

Keller, Helen (Adams) (1880–1968) Writer, born in Tuscumbia, AL. She lost her sight and hearing after an illness at 19 months, but

Kazakhstan

RUSSIAN FEDERATION

Petropavlovsk

Irtysh

INDIA

AFRICA

Kustanay
Ishim
Kokchetav
Pavlodar
Volga
Ural
Atbasar
■ Astana
Semey
Uralsk
Precaspian
Depression
Aktyubinsk
Lake Tengiz
Turgay Valley
Karaganda
Ateransk
Chelkar●
Aktogay
●Kulsary
ARAL
SEA
Space Launch
Station
Balkhash
Druzhba●
□ ●Baikonur
Lake
Balkhash
Taldy-Kurgan
Aktau
Ustyurt
Syr Darya
Ili
Plateau
CASPIAN SEA
Chimkent
Pik Khan
Tengri 6398m
UZBEKISTAN
KYRGYZSTAN
CHINA
500 km
250 mi
TURKMENISTAN

KAZAKHSTAN

□ International Airport

[kazakstahn], official name **Republic of Kazakhstan**, Kazakh **Qazaqstan Respublikasï** , Russ **Kazakhskaya**

Local name Kazakstan

Timezone GMT +5/6

Area 2 717 300 km²/1 048 878 sq mi

Population total (2002e) 14 888 000

Status Republic

Date of independence 1991

Capital Astana (from 1998), formerly Almaty (Alma-Ata)

Languages Kazakh (official), Russian, German

Ethnic groups Kazakh (53.4%), Russian (30%), Ukrainian (3.7%), Uzbek 2.5%, German (2.4%)

Religions Muslim (Sunni), Christian (Russian Orthodox, Protestant)

Physical features Bounded E by China and W by Caspian Sea; second largest republic in former USSR; mountain ranges in E and SE; steppeland (N) gives way to desert (S); lowest elevation near E shore of the Caspian Sea, 132 m/433 ft below sea-level; main rivers, Irtysh, Syr Darya, Ural, Ili; largest lake, L Balkhash; space launch centre at Tyuratam, near Baikonur.

Climate Continental; hot summers, extreme winters; wide range of temperatures, from -17°C in N and C ranges, to -3°C in S (Jan), 20°C in N, 29°C in S (Jul); strong, dry winds common in NW.

Currency (1992) 1 Tenge (KZT) = 100 kopecks

Economy Petroleum, natural gas, coal, iron ore, bauxite, zinc, gold, uranium; oil refining, metallurgy, heavy engineering, chemicals, leatherwork, footwear, food processing; cotton, fruit, grain, sheep.

GDP (2002e) $120 bn, per capita $7200

Human Development Index (2002) 0·750

History Under the control of the Mongols, 13th-c; gradually under Russian rule, 1730–1853; became constituent republic of USSR, 1936; independence movement, 1990–1; independence declared in 1991, and joined Commonwealth of Independent States; governed by a President, Prime Minister, and Supreme Soviet.

Head of State
1991– Nursultan A Nazarbayev

Head of Government
1991–4 Sergei Tereshchenko
1994–7 Kazhageldin Akezhan Magzhan Ulu
1997–9 Nurlan Balgimbayev
1999–2002 Kasymzhomart Tokayev
2002–3 Imangali Tasmagambetov
2003–7 Daniyal Akhmetov
2007– Karim Masimov

Anne Sullivan taught her to speak, read, and write, and became her companion until her death in 1936. Keller received communications by lipreading, braille, and finger-spelling using a manual alphabet, and she expressed herself through finger-spelling, typewriting, and speech. She obtained a degree in 1904, and became distinguished as a lecturer and a writer. Her autobiography, *The Story of My Life* (1902), was dramatized by William Gibson in *The Miracle Worker* (1959, Pulitzer, filmed 1962).

Kellogg, W(illie) K(eith) (1860–1951) Cereal manufacturer and philanthropist, born in Battle Creek, MI. During the 1980s he worked with his brother, Dr **John H Kellogg** to develop breakfast cereals, and after their first success with flaked wheat, they developed corn flakes. In 1906 Will founded the Battle Creek Toasted Corn Flake Co (later the W K Kellogg Co), and revolutionized the world's breakfast-eating habits. In 1930 he established the W K Kellogg Foundation, which became one of America's richest philanthropic organizations.

Kellogg–Briand Pact A proposal made in 1927 by French foreign minister Aristide Briand (1862–1932) to US secretary of state Frank B Kellogg (1856–1937) that the two countries should sign a pact renouncing war as an instrument of national policy. In 1928 the pact was signed by 65 states (the **Pact of Paris**).

Kellow, Kathleen Hibbert, Eleanor

Kells Ceanannus Mòr

Kelly, David (Christopher) (1944–2003) British microbiologist and consultant on arms control, born in the Rhondda Valley, S Wales. He studied at Oxford, and specialized in biological pesticides, joining the chemical research centre at Porton Down, Wiltshire, where he became head of microbiology (1984). He was the Ministry of Defence's chief scientific officer and senior adviser to the proliferation and arms control secretariat, and was also senior adviser on biological warfare for the UN in Iraq (1994–9). In 2003 he became a key figure in the row between the government and the BBC over claims that Downing Street 'sexed up' a dossier on Iraq's weapons capability. Having been identified by the press, he became the centre of media attention, and he committed suicide soon after. The circumstances surrounding his death became the subject of an enquiry chaired by Lord Hutton later that year. The Hutton Report (Jan 2004) criticised the BBC, said that Dr Kelly had broken the rules governing civil servants talking to journalists, and attached no blame to the government for naming him.

Kelly, Gene, popular name of **Eugene Curran Kelly** (1912–96) Actor, dancer, and film director, born in Pittsburgh, PA. His stage success in Pal Joey led to a Hollywood debut in For Me and My Gal (1942), followed by a long series of musicals, such as An American in Paris (1951), and Singin' in the Rain (1952). In 1951 he received a special Academy Award for his versatility.

Kelly, Jude, professional name of **Judith Pamela Kelly** (1954–) Theatre director, born in Liverpool, Merseyside. She founded the Solent People's Theatre in 1976, later becoming artistic director of the Battersea Arts Centre, assistant director at the Royal Shakespeare Company (1986), and artistic director of the West Yorkshire Playhouse (1988–2002). She then set up METAL in West Hampstead, London, a centre for research and experiment in the arts.

Kelly, Ned, popular name of **Edward Kelly** (1855–80) Outlaw, born in Beveridge, Victoria, Australia. He was a horse-thief who (from 1878) became a bushranger in Victoria and New South Wales, working with a gang whose daring robberies received widespread publicity. His trademark was his home-made armour. He was hanged at Melbourne.

keloid [keeloyd] The overgrowth of scar tissue (fibroblasts and collagen) in response to a surgical or accidental wound of the skin. It appears as a raised, warm, reddened, tender lump along the line of the wound.

kelp A large brown seaweed common in lower inter-tidal and subtidal zones in colder seas. (Division: Phaeophyceae. Order: Laminariales.)

kelpie A breed of dog developed in Australia as a sheepdog; medium size with thick, coarse coat and bushy tail; muzzle pointed; ears erect; also called **Australian kelpie**.

Kelvin (of Largs), William Thomson, 1st Baron (1824–1907) Mathematician and physicist, born in Belfast. He carried out fundamental research into thermodynamics, helping to develop the law of the conservation of energy, and the absolute temperature scale (now given in kelvin). He also presented the dynamical theory of heat, and developed notions in electricity and magnetism, and hydrodynamics.

kelvin Base SI unit of thermodynamic temperature; symbol K; defined as the fraction $1/273 \cdot 16$ of the thermodynamic temperature of the triple point of water; named after Lord Kelvin; always written K, not $°$K.

Kemble The name of a famous British acting family of the 18th-c.

The founding member was **Roger** (1721–1802), a travelling manager. His granddaughter, **Frances Ann**, known as **Fanny** (1809–93), became one of the leading actresses of the 19th-c.

Kempe, Margery [kemp], née **Brunham** (c.1373–c.1440) English religious mystic, wife of a burgess of Lynn. She wrote a spiritual autobiography, The Book of Margery Kempe (c.1432–6).

Kempe, Rudolf [kempuh] (1910–76) Conductor, born near Dresden, Germany. He appeared frequently at Covent Garden, London, and was principal conductor of the Royal Philharmonic Orchestra (1961–75).

Kempe, William [kemp] (c.1550–c.1603) Comic actor and dancer, who was famous in the Elizabethan theatre, and a leading member of Shakespeare's company in the last decade of the 16th-c. In 1600 he performed a 9-day morris dance from London to Norwich.

Kempis, Thomas à [kempis], originally **Thomas Hemerken** (1379–1471) Religious writer, so called from his birthplace, Kempen, Germany. An Augustinian monk, his many writings include the influential devotional work Imitatio Christi (c.1415–24, The Imitation of Christ).

Kenai bear brown bear

kendo The Japanese martial art of sword fighting, now practised with shiani, or bamboo swords. **Kendokas** (participants) wear traditional dress of the Samurai period, including face-masks and aprons.

Kendrew, Sir John (Cowdery) (1917–97) Biochemist, born in Oxford, Oxfordshire. For his discovery of the structure of myoglobin, he shared the Nobel Prize for Chemistry in 1962.

Keneally, Thomas (Michael) [keneelee] (1935–) Novelist, born in Kempsey, New South Wales, Australia. His novels are frequently historical, and include Schindler's Ark (1982, Booker; filmed in 1993 as Schindler's List), the story of an industrialist who saved the lives of Polish Jews during the early 1940s. Memoirs from a Young Republic (1993) expresses his passionate support for the Australian republican cause. Later works include The Great Shame (1999) and The Tyrant's Novel (2003).

Kennedy, A(lison) L(ouise) (1965–) Novelist and short-story writer, born in Dundee, Scotland. Her first collection of short stories was the prize-winning Night Geometry and the Garscadden Trains (1990). Her first novel was Looking for the Posssible Dance (1994, Somerset Maugham Award), followed by So I Am Glad (1995, Encore Award), Everything You Need (1999), and Paradise (2004).

Kennedy, Charles (1959–) British politician, born in Inverness, N Scotland. He worked as a journalist before being elected a Social Democratic MP (1983–) and becoming the youngest MP in the Commons. A supporter of merger with the Liberal Party, he was elected president of the new Liberal Democrat Party in 1990, and leader upon Paddy Ashdown's resignation in 1999. He quit as leader at the start of 2006 after admitting an alcohol problem.

Kennedy, Edward M(oore) (1932–) US politician, born in Brookline, MA, the youngest son of Joseph Kennedy. A lawyer, he was elected a Democratic senator for his brother John's Massachusetts seat in 1962. In 1969 he became the youngest-ever majority whip in the US Senate, but his involvement the same year in a car accident at Chappaquiddick, in which a woman companion (Mary Jo Kopechne) was drowned, dogged his subsequent political career, and caused his withdrawal as a presidential candidate in 1979.

Kennedy, Jackie Onassis, Jacqueline Kennedy

Kennedy, John F(itzgerald), also known as **JFK** (1917–63) US statesman and 35th president (1961–3), born in Brookline, MA, the son of Joseph P Kennedy. He was the first Catholic, and the youngest person, to be elected president. His 'New Frontier' in social legislation involved a federal desegregation policy in education, and civil rights reform. He displayed firmness and moderation in foreign policy, in 1962 inducing Russia to withdraw its missiles from Cuba, and achieving a partial nuclear test-ban treaty with Russia in 1963. On 22 November, he was assassinated by rifle fire while being driven in an open car through Dallas, TX. The alleged assassin, **Lee Oswald**, was himself shot two days later during a jail transfer.

Kennedy, Joseph P(atrick) (1888–1969) US businessman and diplomat, born in Boston, MA. The grandson of an Irish Catholic immigrant, he became a multimillionaire in the 1920s. In 1914 he married **Rose Fitzgerald**, and had nine children, including four sons, at whose political disposal he placed his fortune. The eldest, **Joseph Patrick** (1915–44), was killed in a flying accident while on naval service in World War 2. The others achieved international political fame.

Kennedy, Nigel (Paul), professional name (from 1997) **Kennedy** (1956–) Violinist, born in Brighton, East Sussex. He studied at the Yehudi Menuhin School, London, and the Juilliard School, New York City. He made his debut as a concert soloist in 1977, and has since played with many of the world's major orchestras. His recording of Vivaldi's *Four Seasons* held the number 1 spot in the UK Classical Chart for over a year (1989–90).

Kennedy, Robert F(rancis) (1925–68) US politician, born in Brookline, MA, brother of John F and Edward M Kennedy. An efficient manager of his brother John's presidential campaign, he became an energetic attorney general (1961–4), notable in his dealings with civil rights problems. After winning the 1968 Californian Democratic presidential primary election, he was shot, and died the following day. His assassin, Sirhan Bishara Sirhan, a 24-year-old Jordanian-born immigrant, was sentenced to the gas chamber in 1969, but was not executed.

Kennedy Space Center, John F US space centre situated on Merrit I and Cape Canaveral (known as Cape Kennedy 1963–73) off the E coast of Florida. It is the principal launch site for the US space exploration programme conducted by NASA.

kennel cough An infection of the upper respiratory tract in dogs, resulting in a characteristic, harsh, non-productive cough. Bacteria (*Bordetella bronchiseptica*) and various viruses are the main agents involved. The disease is highly infectious, and evidence of up-to-date vaccination is usually required by boarding establishments before accepting dogs at risk.

Kenneth I, known as **Kenneth MacAlpin** (?–858) King of the Scots of Dal Riata (from 841) and King of the Picts (from c.843). He combined the territories of both peoples in a united kingdom of Scotia (Scotland N of the Forth–Clyde line).

Kensington and Chelsea 51°30N 0°12W, pop (2001e) 158 900. Borough of C Greater London, UK; N of R Thames; Kensington granted the designation 'Royal Borough' by Edward VII in 1901; railway; Kensington Palace, Kensington Gardens, Victoria and Albert Museum, Science Museum, British Museum (Natural History).

Kent pop (2001e) 1 329 700; area 3731 km²/1440 sq mi. County in SE England; rises to 251 m/823 ft in the North Downs; The Weald in the SW; high chalk cliffs, especially at Dover; county town, Maidstone; principal cross-Channel ports, Dover, Folkestone, Ramsgate, Sheerness; Medway a unitary authority from 1998; known for its fruit and hops ('the Garden of England').

Kent, Edward (George Nicholas Paul Patrick), Duke of (1935–) British prince, the eldest son of Duke George Edward Alexander Edmund (1902–42), who was the fourth son of King George V and Queen Mary. He was commissioned in the army in 1955, and in 1961 married **Katharine Worsley**. They have three children: **George Philip Nicholas, the Earl of St Andrews** (1962–), **Helen Marina Lucy, Lady Helen Windsor** (1964–), and **Nicholas Charles Edward Jonathan, Lord Nicholas Windsor** (1970–).

Kent, Prince Michael of (1942–) British prince, the younger brother of Edward, Duke of Kent. He married in 1978 **Baroness Marie-Christine von Reibniz**, and their children are **Frederick**

Michael George David Louis, Lord Frederick Windsor (1979–) and **Gabriella Marina Alexandra Ophelia, Lady Gabriella Windsor** (1981–).

Kent, William (1685–1748) Painter, landscape gardener, and architect, born in Bridlington, East Riding. The principal exponent of the Palladian style of architecture in England, his best-known work is the Horse Guards block in Whitehall.

Kentucky pop (2000e) 4 041 800; area 104 658 km²/40 410 sq mi. State in EC USA; the 'Bluegrass State'; part of the territory ceded by the French, 1763; explored by Daniel Boone from 1769; first permanent British settlement at Boonesborough, 1775; originally part of Virginia; admitted to the Union as the 15th state, 1792; highest point, Mt Black (1263 m/4144 ft); C plain known as Bluegrass country; capital, Frankfort; famous for the distilling of bourbon whiskey (still the country's leading producer), and for its thoroughbred racehorses; nation's leading coal producer.

Kentucky and Virginia Resolutions (1798) Declarations by two state legislatures that the Alien and Sedition laws violated the US Constitution. They were written by Thomas Jefferson (Kentucky) and James Madison (Virginia).

Kenya, Mount 0°10S 37°18E. Extinct volcano cone in C Kenya; second highest mountain in Africa; highest peak, Batian (5199 m/17 057 ft).

Kenya p.502

Kenyatta, Jomo [kenyata], originally **Kamau Ngengi** (c.1889–1978) Kenyan statesman and president (1964–78), born in Mitumi, Kenya. Charged in 1952 with leading the Mau Mau terrorist organization (a charge he denied), he was exiled. In 1960, while still in detention, he was elected president of the new Kenya African National Union Party, became prime minister in 1963, then president.

Kenzo, in full **Kenzo Takada** (1940–) Fashion designer, born in Kyoto, Japan. He creates clothes with both Oriental and Western influences, and is a trend-setter in the field of knitwear.

Kepler, Johannes (1571–1630) Astronomer, born in Weil-der-Stadt, Germany. He showed that planetary motions were far simpler than had been imagined.

Kepler's laws of planetary motion Fundamental laws deduced by Kepler from Tycho Brahe's data. (1) Each planet travels an elliptical orbit with the Sun at one focus. (2) For a given planet radius, the vector to the Sun sweeps equal areas in equal times. (3) For any two planets, the squares of the periods are proportional to the cubes of the distances from the Sun.

Kerala [kerala] pop (2001e) 31 838 600; area 39 000 km²/15 000 sq mi. State in S India, capital, Trivandrum; governed by a unicameral legislature; created out of the former state of Travancore–Cochin under the 1956 States Reorganization Act.

keratin [keratin] A tough, fibrous protein synthesized by the outer layer of the skin (*epidermis*) of vertebrates. It is the major component of hair, nails, claws, horns, feathers, scales, and the dead outer layers of cells of skin.

keratosis [keratohsis] Small dark scaly lesions on exposed parts of the skin, commonly found in individuals over 60 years of age and in younger white-skinned residents in sunny climates.

Kerensky, Alexander Fyodorovich [kerenskee] (1881–1970) Russian socialist, born in Simbirsk, Russia. He took a leading part in the 1917 Revolution, becoming premier in the provisional government. Deposed by the Bolsheviks, he fled to France.

Kerkuane Carthaginian town in N Tunisia, founded in the 5th-c BC and abandoned c.140 BC after the destruction of Carthage; a world heritage site.

Kermode, Sir (John) Frank [kermohd] (1919–) Literary critic, born in the Isle of Man. His works include *Romantic Image* (1957), *Forms of Attention* (1985), *Uses of Error* (1991), *Shakespeare's*

Kenya

□ International Airport   – – Border dispute

[kenya], formerly [keenya], official name **Republic of Kenya**
Local name Kenya
Timezone GMT +3
Area 580 367 km²/224 081 sq mi
Population total (2002e) 31 139 000
Status Republic
Date of independence 1963
Capital Nairobi

Languages English and Swahili (official), with many local languages spoken

Ethnic groups Kikuyu (21%), Luhya (13%), Luo (11%), Kamba (11%), Kalejin (6%) Kisii (6%), Meru (6%)

Religions Christian (66%) (Roman Catholic 28%, Protestant 38%), local beliefs (26%), Muslim (6%)

Physical features Crossed by the Equator; SW plateau rises to 600–3000 m/2000–10 000 ft; includes Mt Kenya, 5200 m/17 058 ft; Great Rift Valley (W) runs N–S; dry, arid semi-desert in the N, generally under 600 m/2000 ft; rivers include Tana and Athi; L Turkana in NW.

Climate Tropical climate on coast, with high temperatures and humidity; average annual temperature 18°C (Jan), 16°C (Jul) in Nairobi; average annual rainfall 958 mm/38 in; national disaster declared (May 2003) following prolonged heavy rains and flooding, particularly in the W.

Currency 1 Kenyan Shilling (KES) = 100 cents

Economy Agriculture (accounts for c.35% of national income); coffee, tea, cashew nuts, rice, wheat, maize, sugar cane; textiles, chemicals, cement, oil refining, tobacco, rubber; reserves of soda ash, salt, limestone, lead, gemstones, silver, gold; 14 national parks attract large numbers of tourists; national disaster declared (Jun 2004) following 80 deaths and 180 casualties from consuming contaminated maize.

GDP (2002e) $32·89 bn, per capita $1100

Human Development Index (2002) 0·513

History Very early fossil hominids found in the region by anthropologists; coast settled by Arabs, 7th-c; Portuguese control, 16th–17th-c; British control as East African Protectorate, 1895; British colony, 1920; independence movement led to Mau Mau rebellion, 1952–60; independence within the Commonwealth, 1963; declared Republic of Kenya, 1964; first leader, Jomo Kenyatta; multi-party elections, 1992, gave Arap Moi a fourth term of office; result condemned by opposition parties; Moi defeated (Dec 2002) after 24 years rule; governed by a president elected for a 5-year term, with a unicameral National Assembly of 224 members; all UK flights temporarily suspended (May–Jul 2003) after Kenyan security alert; in referendum (Nov 2005) voters rejected proposed change to constitution including new post of prime minister.

Head of State/Government
1978–2002 Daniel Arap Moi
2002– Mwai Kibaki

Language (2000), and *The Age of Shakespeare* (2004). He was knighted in 1991.

Kern, Jerome (David) (1885–1945) Songwriter, born in New York City. He wrote a string of successful Broadway shows, notably *Show Boat* (1927, book and lyrics by Hammerstein). *Roberta* (1933) included three of his finest songs: 'Smoke Gets in Your Eyes', 'Yesterdays', and 'The Touch of Your Hand'.

kerosene or **paraffin** A petroleum distillation product, with larger molecules and consequently less volatility than the fraction used for gasoline (petrol). It is now an important source of domestic heating, and is the main fuel for jet engines.

Kerouac, Jack [kerooak], popular name of **Jean Louis Libris Kerouac** (1922–69) Writer, born in Lowell, MA. He is best known for *On the Road* (1957), a spontaneous work expressing the youthful discontent of the 'beat generation'. Later works in this vein, all autobiographical in character, include *The Subterraneans* (1958) and *Big Sur* (1962). A play, *Beat Generation*, written in 1957 was rediscovered in 2004 and published the next year.

Kerr, John [kair] (1824–1907) Physicist, born in Ardrossan, North

Ayrshire. He carried out valuable research on polarized light in magnetic and electric fields, and the **Kerr effects** which result.

Kerr, Sir John (Robert) [kair] (1914–91) Lawyer and administrator, born in Sydney, New South Wales, Australia. As Governor-General of Australia (1974–7) he made Australian constitutional history when he resolved a political impasse by exercising the regal 'reserve powers', sacking the elected prime minister, Gough Whitlam, and asking leader of the Liberal opposition, Malcolm Fraser, to form a caretaker government and call a general election.

Kerry, Ir **Chiarraighe** pop (2000e) 123 000; area 4701 km²/1815 sq mi. County in Munster province, SW Ireland; capital, Tralee; includes Killarney and Listowel.

Kerry, John (Forbes) (1943–) US politician, born in Denver, CO. He studied at Yale University, and then served with the US Navy in the Vietnam War winning several awards for bravery. He embarked on a career in law and worked as a prosecutor in Massachusetts before going into politics. In 1982 he was voted lieutenant governor for Massachusetts, and has been senator since 1984. In 2004 he secured the Democrat nomination for the US presidential election but was defeated by incumbent President George W Bush in a closely fought contest.

Kertész, Imre [kertesh] (1929–) Writer, born in Budapest, Hungary. Of Jewish descent, in 1944 he was deported to Auschwitz and Buchenwald. He became a translator of German authors and an independent writer. His first novel, *Sorstalanság* (1975, trans Fateless, 1992), based on his experiences in the camps, was followed by *A kudarc* (1988, trans Fiasco) and *Kaddis a meg nem születetett gyermekért* (1990, trans Kaddish for a Child not Born, 1997). Other works include a diary in fictional form, *Gályanapló* (1992, trans title Galley Diary), and collections of essays, such as *A száműzött nyelv* (2001, The Exiled Language). He was awarded the 2002 Nobel Prize for Literature.

Kesey, Ken (Elton) [keezee] (1935–2001) Writer, born in La Junta, CO. His best-known work is *One Flew Over the Cuckoo's Nest* (1962; filmed, 1975). The novel *Sailor Song* appeared in 1993.

Kesselring, Albert [keslring] (1885–1960) German air commander in World War 2, born in Markstedt, Germany. He led the Luftwaffe attacks on France and on Britain, and in 1943 was made commander-in-chief in Italy. He was released from a sentence of life imprisonment in 1952.

kestrel A falcon of the worldwide genus *Falco* (13 species), especially *Falco tinnunculus*; inhabits open country; catches prey on ground after hovering. (Family: Falconidae.)

ketch A two-masted fore-and-aft-rigged sailing vessel. The shorter (after-) mast, called the *mizzen*, is placed in position forward of the rudder post. By contrast, in a **yawl**, this mast is placed aft of the rudder post.

ketones [keetohnz] IUPAC **alkanones**. Organic compound containing a carbonyl (C=O) group bonded to two other carbon atoms. The simplest example is acetone (CH_3COCH_3).

Kettering, Charles F(ranklin) (1876–1958) Engineer, born in Loudonville, OH. He invented the electric starter motor for cars, discovered the cause of 'knocking' in car engines, and invented the refrigerant known as Freon.

Ketterle, Wolfgang [keterlay] (1957–) Physicist, born in Heidelberg, Germany. A researcher at the Massachusetts Institute of Technology, he shared the 2001 Nobel Prize for Physics for the achievement of Bose–Einstein condensation in dilute gases of alkali atoms, and for early fundamental studies of the properties of the condensates.

kettledrum *timpani*

Kevorkian, Jack [kuhvaw(r)kian], media nickname **Dr Death** (1928–) Physician, born in Pontiac, MI. An advocate of euthanasia, he has been charged with murder and assisting suicide, but found not guilty. In 1998 he became internationally known when a video showing the death of one of his clients was shown on national television, a strategy he had chosen to bring the public debate on euthanasia to a head. He was again charged, and found guilty of second-degree murder, receiving a prison sentence.

Kew Gardens The Royal Botanical Gardens at Kew, Surrey, England. The gardens, inherited by George III from his mother, were given to the nation in 1841 and occupy 120 ha/300 acres. It was designated a world heritage site in 2003.

key *tonality*

keyboard instrument A musical instrument in which the different pitches are controlled by means of a keyboard, ie a succession of levers arranged in two rows. The front row produces the notes of the diatonic C major scale, the rear the pitches in between; played in order from left to right, they produce an ascending 12-note chromatic scale. The term **keyboards** is also often used as a collective term for all the electronic keyboard instruments (electric pianos, electronic organs, and synthesizers) in a pop group.

key grip *grip*

Keynes (of Tilton), John Maynard Keynes, Baron [kaynz] (1883–1946) Economist, born in Cambridge, Cambridgeshire. In both World Wars he was an adviser to the Treasury. The unemployment crises inspired his two great works, *A Treatise on Money* (1930) and the revolutionary *General Theory of Employment, Interest and Money* (1936).

Keynesian [kaynzian] A follower of the economic concepts propounded by economist J M Keynes in the 1930s. The 'Keynesian revolution' changed the view of how economies should be managed, arguing that economies could be in equilibrium at less than full employment. Unless demand in the economy is stimulated, growth and therefore full employment are not possible. Keynesian theories were subject to critical appraisal in the 1960s and 1970s by Monetarists.

Keystone A US film production company of silent films (1912–19), founded by Mack Sennett. It specialized in knockabout comedy shorts, especially those featuring the **Keystone Kops** troupe.

KGB Abbreviation of **Komitet Gosudarstvennoy Bezopasnosti** ('Committee for State Security'), after 1953 one of the Soviet Union's two secret police organizations with joint responsibility for internal and external order and security. It underwent radical reform, following glasnost and the failure of the 1991 coup in the USSR, and is now known as the Ministry of State Security.

Khama, Sir Seretse [kahma] (1921–80) African statesman and president of Botswana (1966–80), born in Serowe, Bechuanaland (now Botswana). He was the first prime minister of Bechuanaland in 1965, and first president of Botswana.

Khamsin [kamsin] A hot, dry dust-laden SE wind which blows from desert areas in N Africa and Arabia. The word means '50', as it regularly blows for a 50-day period.

Khan, Mohammad Ayub *Ayub Khan, Mohammad*

Kharkov [khah(r)kof], Ukrainian **Kharkiv** 50°00N 36°15E, pop (2000e) 1 596 000. City in Ukraine; founded as a fortress, 1655–6; badly damaged in World War 2; airport; railway junction; Donets Basin coalfield nearby; university (1805); two cathedrals (1689, 1821–41).

Khartoum [kah(r)toom] or **El Khartûm** 15°33N 32°35E, pop (2000e) 764 000. Capital of Sudan; founded, 1820s; garrison town in 19th-c; scene of the British defeat by the Mahdi, 1885; city regained by Lord Kitchener, 1898; major communications and trade centre; regarded as the economic link between the Arab countries (N) and the African countries (S); airport; railway; university (1955); three cathedrals.

khat [kaht] A shrub (*Catha edulis*) growing in E Asia and the SW part of the Arabian peninsula, whose leaves are chewed for their stimulant effect. The active principle is *cathinone*. Early results from a study in 2004 suggest that its medical usage could boost male fertility.

Khatami, (Hojjatoleslam Seyed) Mohammed [katamee] (1943–) President of Iran (1997–2005), born in Ardakan, Iran. Following the revolution, he became head of the Hamburg Islamic Centre in Germany before being elected to the first Iranian parliament in 1980. He served twice as minister for culture and Islamic guidance (1982, 1989–92), was appointed cultural adviser to the president (1992–6), and went on to win the 1997 presidential election.

Khatchaturian, Aram [kachatooryan] (1903–78) Composer, born in Tiflis, Georgia. His compositions include three symphonies, concertos, ballets, instrumental music, and film scores.

khedive [kedeev] An ancient Persian title acquired from the Ottoman Sultan by the autonomous Viceroy of Egypt, Ismail, in 1867. It was used until Egypt became a British protectorate (1914).

Khmer [kmair] An Austro-Asiatic language, spoken by over 7 million people; also known as **Cambodian**. Inscriptions date from the 6th–7th-c.

Khmer Empire [kmair] An empire in SE Asia, founded in the 6th-c, with its capital at Angkor Thom from 802 onwards. Angkor was abandoned in 1431, and the Khmer Empire had collapsed by 1460.

Khmer Rouge [kmair roozh] A Cambodian communist guerrilla force. It gained control in 1975 and, led by Pol Pot, set about a drastic transformation of 'Democratic Kampuchea', involving mass forced evacuation from the towns to the countryside, the creation of agricultural co-operatives, and the execution of thousands of 'bourgeois elements'. More than 90% of Cambodia's traditional artists, performers, and scholars were murdered. In 1979, Vietnam invaded, and the Khmer Rouge withdrew to Thai border region. They mounted a fresh offensive following Vietnamese withdrawal in 1989. The Paris Conference on Cambodia brought about a ceasefire (1991) and an international peace plan launched by the UN, which led to elections in 1993. However, the Khmer Rouge refused to take part in the elections or to become part of the new political system, and tension remained, with continued fighting between government troops and guerrillas. The organization was banned in 1994.

Khoisan [koysan] A collective term for the San (Bushmen) and Khoi (Hottentot) peoples of S Africa. They now live mainly in the Kalahari Desert of Botswana and in Namibia.

Khomeini, Ayatollah Ruhollah [homaynee] (1900–89) Iranian religious and political leader, born in Khomeyn, Iran. A Shiite Muslim opposed to the pro-Western regime of Shah Mohammed Reza Pahlavi, he was exiled in 1964. He returned to Iran amid great popular acclaim in 1979 after the collapse of the Shah's government, and became virtual head of state. Under his leadership, Iran underwent a turbulent 'Islamic Revolution' in which a return was made to the strict observance of Muslim principles and traditions.

Khrushchev, Nikita Sergeyevich [khrushchof, khrushchof] (1894–1971) Soviet statesman, first secretary of the Soviet Communist Party (1953–64), and prime minister (1958–64), born in Kalinovka, Ukraine. He became First Secretary soon after the death of Stalin, and three years later denounced Stalinism. Among the events of his administration were the Poznan riots and Hungarian uprising (1956), and the failed attempt to install missiles in Cuba (1962). He was replaced by Brezhnev and Kosygin, and went into retirement.

Khyber Pass [kyiber] A defile through the Safed Koh mountain range on the frontier between Pakistan and Afghanistan. It is 45 km/28 mi long, and reaches heights of 1280 m/3518 ft.

kiang [kiang] ass

kibbutz, plural **kibbutzim** (Heb 'gathering', 'collective') A Jewish co-operative settlement in Israel which was self-supporting in terms of food supplies and many other goods. Kibbutzim spread in the 1950s as part of Israeli attempts at self-sufficiency. One of their distinctive features was the collective responsibility members took for child-rearing. Since c.1970, however, the movement to include children within the nuclear family has grown, and is now the norm.

Kidd, William, known as **Captain Kidd** (c.1645–1701) Privateer and pirate, probably born in Greenock, Inverclyde. In 1696 he was commissioned to suppress piracy, but turned pirate himself. He was hanged in London.

Kiddush [kidush] (Heb 'sanctification') A prayer usually recited by the head of the family over a cup of wine at the start of a meal in the home on the eve of a Sabbath or festival. It is sometimes used also in synagogues to consecrate the Sabbath or a festival.

Kidman, Nicole (Mary) (1967–) Film actress, born in Honolulu, HI. While living in Australia, she made her film debut in *Bush*

Christmas (1983). Later films include *Eyes Wide Shut* (1999), in which she co-starred with husband Tom Cruise (divorced, 2001), *Moulin Rouge* (2000, Golden Globe), *The Hours* (2002, Golden Globe; BAFTA; Oscar), *Cold Mountain* (2003), and *Margot at the Wedding* (2007).

kidney bean *haricot bean*

kidney dialysis The artificial control of blood electrolyte levels and the removal of waste products from the body when the kidneys are not functioning in patients with kidney failure. *Haemodialysis* involves removing blood through a specially created vein in the forearm (an *arterio-venous fistula*) and circulating it through a machine where diffusion of solutes occurs between the blood and a dialysis solution. *Peritoneal dialysis* is performed by introducing dialysis solution into the abdominal cavity through a catheter, to allow diffusion of solutes to occur across the membrane lining the cavity, before waste products and excess water are drained out of the abdomen.

kidney machine *dialysis*

kidneys The urine-producing organs of vertebrates. In humans the symmetrical, bean-shaped kidneys are situated in the upper rear part of the abdominal wall, one each side of the vertebral column. Each kidney weighs about 130 g/4·6 oz, and consists of approximately 1 million *nephrons* (the functional units) and supporting tissue. Medical problems affecting the kidneys include glomerulonephritis, kidney failure, pyelonephritis, urinary stones, and uraemia.

Kiel [keel] 54°02N 10°08E, pop (2000e) 251 000. Port city in Germany; Kiel Canal (1877–95), 98 km/61 mi between North Sea and Baltic Sea; badly bombed in World War 2; railway; ferry service to Scandinavia; naval base; university (1665); castle (13th-c).

Kielder Water [keelder] Reservoir in Northumberland, NE England; one of the largest artificial lakes in Europe, supplying water to the industrial NE; built 1974–82 by damming R North Tyne.

Kierkegaard, Søren (Aabye) [keerkuhgaw(r)d] (1813–55) Philosopher and religious thinker, born in Copenhagen. He is regarded as one of the founders of existentialism. In *Afsluttende uvidenskabelig Efterskrift* (1846, Concluding Unscientific Postscript), he attacked all philosophical system building.

Kiesinger, Kurt Georg [keesinger] (1904–88) West German Conservative statesman and chancellor (1966–9), born in Ebingen, Germany. Long a supporter of Adenauer's plans for European unity, he formed with Brandt a government combining the Christian Democratic Union and the Social Democrats, until in 1969 he was succeeded as chancellor by Brandt.

Kiev [kee-ef], Ukrainian **Kiyiv**, also **Kiyev** 50°28N 30°29E, pop (2000e) 2 587 000. Capital city of Ukraine, on R Dnepr; founded, 6th–7th-c; capital of mediaeval Kievan Russia, 9th-c; capital of Ukraine, 1934; besieged and occupied by Germany in World War 2; airport; railway; major industrial, cultural, and scientific centre; university (1834); cathedral (1037).

Kikuyu [kikooyoo] A Bantu-speaking agricultural people of the C highlands of Kenya, and the country's largest ethnic group. After Kenya's independence (1963) they provided many of the country's political leaders.

Kilby, Jack St Clair (1923–2005) Electrical engineer, born in Jefferson City, MO. He joined Texas Instruments (1958–70), where his inventions included the first hand-held calculator. In 2000 he shared the Nobel Prize for Physics for his invention of the integrated circuit.

Kildare [kildair], Ir **Cill Dara** pop (2000e) 124 000; area 1694 km²/654 sq mi. County in Leinster province, E Ireland; low-lying C plain known as the Curragh; capital, Naas; national stud at Tully, racecourse at the Curragh.

Kilimanjaro, Mount [kilimanjahroh] (Chagga 'glittering mountain') 3°02S 37°20E. Mountain on the frontier between Tanzania and Kenya, E Africa; height 5895 m/19 340 ft; highest point on the African continent; first climbed in 1889.

Kilkenny (county) [kilkenee], Ir **Cill Choinnigh** pop (2000e) 75 000; area 2062 km²/796 sq mi. County in Leinster province, SE Ireland; fertile county watered by R Nore; Slieve Ardagh Hills rise W; capital, Kilkenny, pop (2000e) 18 000.

Killarney [kilah(r)nee] Ir **Cill Airne** 52°03N 9°30W, pop (2000e) 10 000. Resort town in Kerry county, Munster, SW Ireland; centre of scenic lakeland area; railway.

killer whale A toothed whale (*Orcinus orca*), found worldwide in cool coastal waters; length, 9–10 m/30–33 ft; black with white underparts; white patches on head; dorsal fin narrow and vertical. (Family: Delphinidae.)

Killy, Jean-Claude [keelee] (1943–) Alpine skier, born in Val d'isère, France. He won all three alpine skiing titles at the 1968 Olympics, and was combined world champion in 1966 and 1968.

kilobyte *byte*

kilocalorie *calorie*

kilogram Base SI unit of mass; symbol *kg*; defined as equal to the international prototype of the kilogram, a platinum–iridium bar kept at the International Bureau of Weights and Measures; commonly used as **gram** (*g*, 1/1000 kg) and **tonne** (*t*, 1000 kg); 1 kg = 2·205 pounds.

kilohm *ohm*

kilometre *metre* (physics)

kiloparsec *parsec*

kiloton (TNT) A measure of explosive power; symbol *kT*; one kiloton equivalent to the explosive power of 1000 tons of TNT; used to describe the destructive power of nuclear weapons; one **megaton**, MT, equals 1000 kT.

kilowatt *watt*

kilowatt-hour The total energy consumed by a device of power 1 kilowatt operating for 1 hour; symbol *kWh*; equal to $3 \cdot 6 \times 10^6$ J (joule, SI unit); standard unit for the electricity supply industry.

Kilvert, (Robert) Francis (1840–79) Clergyman, born in Hardenhuish, Wiltshire. His notebooks (1870–9), giving a vivid picture of rural life in the Welsh marches, were discovered in 1937 and published as *Kilvert's Diary*, in three volumes (1938–40).

Kim, Dae-jung [day-jung] (1925–) South Korean president (1997–2003), born in Ha Eui, South Korea. He made a fortune in shipping, and was elected to the National Assembly in 1962. He ran for president in 1971, 1987, and 1992 before finally being elected. An opponent of South Korea's military governments, he was sentenced to death in 1980 before being reprieved after the intervention of US President Reagan. He was awarded the Nobel Peace Prize in 2000 for his efforts to achieve reconciliation with North Korea.

Kimberley 28°45S 24°46E, pop (2000e) 195 000. City in Northern Cape province, South Africa; major diamond-mining centre since its foundation, 1871 (mining ceased in 2005); under siege in the Boer War, 1899–1900; airfield; railway; two cathedrals.

Kimberley, Siege of (1899–1900) One of the three sieges of the second Boer War, in which Boer forces attempted to pen up their British opponents. The town was relieved by General French.

Kim Il-sung [kim ilsung], originally **Kim Song-ju** (1912–94) North Korean soldier, statesman, prime minister (1948–72), and president (1972–94), born near Pyongyang, North Korea. He founded the Korean People's Revolutionary Army in 1932, proclaimed the Republic in 1948, and became effective head of state. He established a unique personality cult wedded to an isolationist, Stalinist political-economic system, and named his son, **Kim Jong-il** (1942–), as his successor.

kimono [kimohnoh] Japanese traditional costume, today mostly worn for special occasions, such as weddings and the tea cere-

mony, or informally. Plain colours are for men; bright for girls and young women. The *obi* (waist sash) for women is frequently of an expensive material.

kinaesthesis / kinesthesis [kinuhstheesis] Perceived sensations of position and movement of body and limbs, and of the force exerted by muscles. *Proprioception* also includes information about posture and movement not consciously perceived, as well as the senses of balance, rotation, and linear acceleration.

kindergarten A nursery school for children under the age at which they must legally attend school. In many countries the kindergarten is organized on informal lines, with the emphasis on social development as well as on preparation for formal schooling.

kinematics *dynamics*

kine pox *cow pox*

kinescoping [kineeskohping] A US term for the recording of a television or video programme on cinematograph film.

kinesiology [kiyneeziolojee] A system of diagnosis and treatment which uses assessment of a patient's muscle responses to manual pressure to detect and locate blockage and imbalance of energy flow; developed by US chiropracter George Goodheart. Diagnosis is based on the belief that each group of muscles is related to other distant parts of the body, and generally follows the principles of traditional Chinese medicine.

kinetic To do with motion; in chemistry, to do with the speed of reactions. Mixtures which reach equilibrium quickly are called *labile*; those which react slowly *inert*.

kinetic art A term applied to certain types of modern art, especially sculptures, which move. Examples include the hanging mobiles of the US sculptor Alexander Calder (1898–1976), all the parts of which revolve separately to create changing patterns in space.

kinetic energy Energy associated with an object's motion; a scalar quantity; symbol K, units J (joule). For an object of mass m moving with velocity v, kinetic energy $K = Mv^2/2$.

kinetic energy weapons Weapons which achieve their destructive effect by the sheer force of their impact; distinguished from those which do damage by blast and heat (**chemical energy** or **explosive weapons**) on arrival at the target. An arrow fired from a bow or a bullet fired from a gun is a kinetic energy weapon.

kinetic theory of gases A classical theory of gases in which a gas is assumed to comprise large numbers of identical particles which undergo elastic collisions and obey Newtonian mechanics.

King, Billie Jean, *née* **Moffat** (1943–) Tennis player, born in Long Beach, CA. Between 1961 and 1979 she won a record 20 Wimbledon titles, including the singles in 1966–8, 1972–3, and 1975. She also won 13 US titles (including four singles), four French titles (one singles), and two Australian titles (one singles). In 1987 she was elected to the International Tennis Hall of Fame.

King, Cecil (Harmsworth) (1901–87) Newspaper proprietor, born in Totteridge, Hertfordshire. He became chairman of Daily Mirror Newspapers Ltd and Sunday Pictorial Newspapers Ltd (1951–63), and chairman of the International Publishing Corporation and Reed Paper Group (1963–8).

King, Larry, originally **Lawrence Harvey Zeiger** (1933–) Talk-show host, born in New York City. He joined CNN in 1985, taking *Larry King Live* to the top of the ratings by 1992, widely watched for its commentary and debate on contemporary events.

King, Martin Luther, Jr (1929–68) Clergyman, born in Atlanta, GA. A leader of the black Civil Rights movement, in 1964 he received the Kennedy Peace Prize and the Nobel Peace Prize. His greatest successes came in challenging the segregation laws of the South. He was assassinated in Memphis, TN, by **James Earl Ray**. A national holiday in King's honour has been recognized in many states since 1986.

King, Stephen (Edwin) (1947–) Novelist, born in Portland, ME. He achieved success with his first novel, *Carrie* (1974), and became known for his vivid treatment of horrific and supernatural themes, later books (many of which have been filmed) including *The Shining* (1976), *It* (1986), *Bag of Bones* (1998), and *Cell* (2006). His short story collections include *Hearts in Atlantis* (1999).

King, W(illiam) L(yon) Mackenzie (1874–1950) Canadian Liberal statesman and prime minister (1921–6, 1926–30, 1935–48), born in Berlin (modern Kitchener), Ontario, Canada. His view that the dominions should be autonomous communities within the British Empire resulted in the Statute of Westminster (1931).

King Charles spaniel A breed of dog developed in Britain, popular under Charles II; small active spaniel with short legs, long lowset ears, and large round frontal eyes; in original paintings, with a long face and flat skull; by 19th-c bred to a completely flat face, undershot jaw, and domed skull; in the USA also called **English Toy Spaniel**; during 1920s, breeders worked to restore the original apprearance, eventually producing the **Cavalier King Charles spaniel**.

king cobra The world's largest venomous snake (*Ophiophagus hannah*), native to India and SE Asia; (length, up to 5·5 m/18 ft): also known as **hamadryad**.

kingcup A perennial (*Caltha palustris*) growing in wet marshy places throughout the N hemisphere; leaves glossy, kidney-shaped; flowers cup-shaped, golden-yellow, up to 5 cm/2 in across; also called **marsh marigold**. (Family: Ranunculaceae.)

kingdom (biology) The highest category into which organisms are classified. Modern systems recognize five kingdoms: *Monera* (comprising the procaryotes such as bacteria and blue-green algae), *Protoctista* (comprising the eucaryotic protozoans and some flagellated algae and fungi), *Fungi* (the eucaryotic fungi that lack flagella at all stages of their life-cycle), *Plantae* (plants), and *Animalia* (animals).

kingfisher A bird found almost worldwide (especially Old World tropics); short-tailed, with large head; bill usually long, straight; bright blue-green back. (Family: Alcedinidae, c.85 species.)

King James Bible *Authorized Version of the Bible*

Kingman, Sir John (Frank Charles) (1939–) Academic, born in Beckenham, Kent. He chaired the Committee of Inquiry into the Teaching of the English Language (1987–8), which produced the *Kingman Report*, a major influence on changing practices in English language teaching in British schools in the 1990s.

Kings, Books of A pair of books of the Hebrew Bible/Old Testament, a compilation of stories about the kings and prophets of Judah and Israel from the enthronement of Solomon to the fall of the kingdom of Israel in c.721 BC, and the final collapse of Judah and Jerusalem in c.587/6 BC.

king's evil *scrofula*

Kingsley, Sir Ben, originally **Krishna Bhanji** (1943–) Actor, born in Snainton, North Yorkshire. He joined the Royal Shakespeare Company (1970–80, 1985–6), and achieved fame for his title role in the film *Gandhi* (1980, Oscar). Other films include *Schindler's List* (1993), *House of Sand and Fog* (2003), and *You Kill Me* (2007). Notable stage performances include the 1997 production of *Waiting for Godot* at the Old Vic, London.

Kingsley, Charles (1819–75) Writer, born in Holne vicarage, Dartmoor, Devon. A 'Christian Socialist', his social novels, such as *Alton Locke* (1850), had great influence at the time. His best-known works are *Westward Ho!* (1855), *Hereward the Wake* (1866), and his children's book, *The Water Babies* (1863).

Kingston (Canada) 44°14N 76°30W, pop (2000e) 63 400. City in SE Ontario, Canada; founded, 1784; Canadian naval base in War of 1812; capital of United Canada, 1841–4; railway; Royal Military College (1876); Queen's University (1841).

Kingston (Jamaica) 17°58N 76°48W, pop (2000e) 690 000. Capital city of Jamaica; founded, 1693; capital, 1870; airport; railway; Institute of Jamaica (1879); University of the West Indies (1948); severely damaged by Hurricane Ivan (Sep 2004).

Kingston-upon-Hull *Hull* (UK)

Kingston-upon-Thames [temz] 51°25N 0°17W, pop (2001e) 140 400. Borough of SW Greater London, on R Thames; said to have been the coronation place of Anglo-Saxon kings; railway; Kingston University (1992, formerly Polytechnic).

Kingstown 13°12N 61°14W, pop (2000e) 21 300. Capital and main port of St Vincent, Windward Is; airfield; cathedral.

King William's War (1689–97) The first of the great wars between France and England for the control of North America. Known in Europe as the **War of the League of Augsburg**, it was settled by the Treaty of Ryswick (1697).

kinkajou [kingkajoo] A nocturnal mammal (*Potos flavus*) native to Central and South America; superficially monkey-like, with a round head, small rounded ears, short face, large eyes, and long clasping tail; also known as **honey bear** or **potto**. (Family: Procyonidae.)

Kinkakuji [kinkakujee] or **Golden Pavilion** A three-tiered gilded pavilion built in 1394 by Ashikaga Yoshimitsu (1358–1408) at Kyoto, Japan. The present building dates from 1955; it is a faithful reconstruction of the original which was burnt down.

Kinnock (of Bedwellty), Neil (Gordon) Kinnock, Baron (1942–) British Labour politician, born in Tredegar, Blaenau Gwent, Wales. He became an MP in 1970, and was chief Opposition spokesman on education (1979–83). A skilful orator, he was elected party leader in 1983, and resigned after the 1992 general election. He became a European Commissioner (with responsibility for transport) in 1994. In 1999 he was appointed to the position of vice president for administrative reform under the new president, Romano Prodi, stepping down at the end of 2004, when he became chair of the British Council. He was made a life peer in 2004.

kinnor A musical instrument of the ancient Hebrews – a type of lyre plucked with the fingers or a plectrum.

Kinsey, Alfred (Charles) (1894–1956) Zoologist and social scientist, born in Hoboken, NJ. He is best known for his controversial studies *Sexual Behavior in the Human Male* (1948) and *Sexual Behavior in the Human Female* (1953).

Kinshasa [kinshasa], formerly Belgian **Léopoldville** (to 1964) 4°18S 15°18E, pop (2000e) 4 221 600. River-port capital of Democratic Republic of Congo; on the R Congo opposite Brazzaville; founded by Stanley, 1887; capital of Belgian colony, 1926; airport; railway; university (1954).

Kinski, Klaus, originally **Nikolaus Gunther Naksznski** (1926–91) Film actor, born in Sopot, Poland. He played minor parts in spaghetti Westerns, then became known for his leading roles in the films of Werner Herzog, such as *Aguirre, the Wrath of God* (1972) and *Fitzcarraldo* (1982). He was also acclaimed for his role in *Nosferatu, the Vampyre* (1979).

Kintyre [kintiy(r)] Peninsula in Argyll and Bute, SWC Scotland; runs S to the **Mull of Kintyre** from a narrow isthmus; 64 km/40 mi long; average width 13 km/8 mi.

Kipling, (Joseph) Rudyard (1865–1936) Writer, born in Mumbai (Bombay), India. His verse collections *Barrack Room Ballads* (1892) and *The Seven Seas* (1896) were highly successful, as were the two *Jungle Books* (1894–5), which have become classic animal stories, *Kim* (1901), and the *Just So Stories* (1902). He was awarded the Nobel Prize for Literature in 1907.

Kirchhoff, Gustav (Robert) [keerkhhohf] (1824–87) Physicist, born in Königsberg, Prussia (now Kaliningrad, Russia). He investigated electrical networks, heat, and optics, and with Robert Wilhelm Bunsen (1811–99) developed the technique of spectroscopy, with which they discovered caesium and rubidium.

Kirchner, Ernst Ludwig [keerkhner] (1880–1938) Artist, born in Aschaffenburg, Germany. He became the leading spirit in the

Kiribati

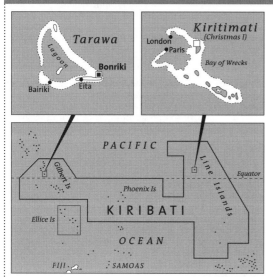

Timezone GMT -12

Area 717 km²/277 sq mi

Population total (2002e) 90 600

Status Republic

Date of independence 1979

Capital Bairiki (on Tarawa Atoll)

Languages English (official) and Gilbertese

Ethnic groups Micronesian, small Polynesian and non-Pacific minorities

Religions Roman Catholic (54%), Kiribati Protestant (39%), Baha'i (2%), Seventh-day Adventist (2%), Mormon (2%)

Physical features Group of 33 low-lying islands scattered over c.3 000 000 km²/1 200 000 sq mi of the C Pacific Ocean; comprises the Gilbert Is Group, Phoenix Is, and 8 of the 11 Line Islands, including Christmas I; islands seldom rise to more than 4 m/13 ft and usually consist of a reef enclosing a lagoon.

Climate Maritime equatorial climate in central islands, tropical further N and S; periodic drought in some islands; wet season (Nov–Apr); subject to typhoons; average annual temperatures 28°C (Jan), 27°C (July) in Tarawa; average annual rainfall 1977 mm/78 in.

Currency 1 Australian Dollar (AUD) = 100 cents

Economy 50% of land under permanent cultivation; main exports include fish, particularly tuna; phosphates; copra, coconuts, bananas, pandanus, breadfruit, papaya; sea fishing.

GDP (2001e) $79 mn, per capita $800

History Gilbert and Ellice Is proclaimed a British protectorate, 1892; became a Crown Colony, 1916; occupied by Japan during World War II, but driven out by US forces; Ellice Is severed links with Gilbert Is to form separate dependency of Tuvalu, 1975; Gilbert Is independence as Kiribati, 1979; a sovereign and democratic republic, with a President and an elected House of Assembly.

Head of State/Government
1979–91 Ieremia T Tabai
1991–4 Teatao Teannaki
1994–2003 Teburoro Tito
2003– Anote Tong

☐ International Airport

[kiribas], formerly **Gilbert Islands**, official name **Republic of Kiribati**

Local name Kiribati

---

formation of the Expressionist group, *die Brücke* (1905–13). Many of his works were confiscated by the Nazis in 1937.

Kirghizia *Kyrgyzstan*

Kiribati *see panel*

Kiritimati [krismas], Eng **Christmas Island** 2°00N 157°30W; pop (2000e) 3000; area 390 km²/150 sq mi. Largest atoll in the world, one of the Line Is, Kiribati; visited by Captain Cook, 1777; annexed by the British, 1888; used as an air base; nuclear testing site in late 1950s.

Kirkpatrick, Jeane (Duane Jordan) (1926–2006) US stateswoman and academic, born in Duncan, OK. She became Georgetown University's professor of government in 1978, and was appointed America's first woman ambassador to the United Nations by President Reagan (1981–5).

Kirkwall 58°59N 2°58W, pop (2000e) 6800. Port capital of Orkney, N Scotland; on island of Mainland; airport; cathedral (1137–1200).

Kirov, Sergey Mironovich [kirof] (1886–1934) Russian revolutionary and politician, born in Urzhum, Russia. He played an active part in the October Revolution and Civil War, and in 1934 became a secretary of the Central Committee. He was assassinated at his Leningrad headquarters, possibly at the instigation of Stalin, and his death served as the pretext for a widespread campaign of reprisals.

Kirov Ballet, officially, the **Mariinsky Theatre of Opera and Ballet** One of the two major ballet companies of Russia, based in St Petersburg. Originally the **Imperial Russian Ballet**, it was founded in 1738 as an academy to train dancers for the imperial court. In the late 19th-c the company moved to the Mariinsky Theatre, whose name it adopted. From 1867 to 1903 Petipa was principal ballet master, staging elaborate performances for the aristocracy and court. In 1935 the company was renamed the Kirov Ballet, and in 1991 the *Kirov–Mariinsky Ballet*. Valery Gergiev (1953–) became artistic and executive director in 1996.

Kisangani [keesangahnee], formerly **Stanleyville** (to 1966) 0°33N 25°14E, pop (2000e) 426 600. City in NC Democratic Republic of Congo; on the R Congo; founded by Stanley, 1882; airport; university (1963).

Kissinger, Henry (Alfred) [kisinjer] (1923–) US secretary of state (1973–6) and academic, born in Fürth, Germany. He became President Nixon's adviser on national security affairs in 1969, was the main American figure in the negotiations to end the Vietnam War (for which he shared the 1973 Nobel Peace Prize), and became secretary of state under Nixon and Ford. His 'shuttle diplomacy' was aimed at bringing about peace between Israel and the Arab states. He published *Diplomacy* (1994).

Kistna, River *Krishna, River*

kit A small violin, usually with four strings and a narrow body, in use from the 16th-c to the 19th-c, especially by dancing masters.

Kita-Kyushu [keeta kyushoo] 33°52N 130°49E, pop (2000e) 1 044 000. City in N Kyushu, Japan; airport; railway; Japan's leading centre for chemicals and heavy industry.

Kitano, Takeshi [kitahnoh] (1947–) Actor, comedian, director, and writer, born in Tokyo. He made his film debut in *Danpu Watari-dori* (1981) and received international attention for his role in *Merry Christmas Mr Lawrence* (1983). Later films include *Johnny Mnemonic* (1995) and *Gonin* (1995). He made his directorial debut in 1989 with the thriller *Violent Cop*. He is a prolific writer of both books and magazine columns.

Kit-Cat Club A political and literary club that flourished in London during 1700–20. Its membership comprised leading Whig politicians, writers, and painters, and included Robert Walpole, Joseph Addison, William Congreve, Richard Steele, John Vanbrugh, and artist Godfrey Kneller – who painted portraits of the members.

kit-cat portrait A life-size half-length portrait painted on a canvas 36 × 28 in (c.90 × 70 cm). The term derives from Kneller's series of portraits painted c.1700–17 of the members of the Kit-Cat Club in London (now in the National Portrait Gallery).

Kitchener (of Khartoum and of Broome), (Horatio) Herbert Kitchener, 1st Earl (1850–1916) British field marshal, born near Ballylongford, Co Kerry, Ireland. By the final rout of the Khalifa at Omdurman (1898), he won back the Sudan for Egypt. Commander-in-chief in South Africa (1900–2), he brought the Boer War to an end. He then became commander-in-chief in India (1902–9), and secretary for war (1914), when he organized manpower on a vast scale ('Kitchener armies').

kite (ornithology) A hawk of the subfamily Milvinae (**true kites**) or Elaninae (**white-tailed kites**), found worldwide; the most varied and diverse group of hawks. (Family: Accipitridae, c.27 species.)

kite (recreation) A frame covered with a light fabric or paper, flown on a long string. It was first documented in China (AD 549) in relation to military communications. They are popular as a leisure activity, and have practical applications in meteorology and surveying.

kithara A musical instrument of classical antiquity, resembling a lyre. The strings were plucked with a plectrum.

Kitt, Eartha (Mae) (1927–) Entertainer and singer, born in North, SC. Her vocal vibrancy, fiery personality, and cat-like singing voice made her a top international cabaret attraction and recording artiste. She received the Golden Rose of Montreux for *Kaskade* (1962), and was appropriately cast as Catwoman in the television series *Batman* (1966).

kittiwake Either of two species of marine bird of the genus *Rissa*: the **black-legged kittiwake** (*Rissa tridactyla*) from N areas of the N oceans; and the **red-legged kittiwake** (*Rissa brevirostris*) from the Bering Sea. (Family: Laridae.)

Kitwe [keetway] 12°48S 28°14E, pop (2000e) 633 200. Modern mining city in Copperbelt province, Zambia; Zambia's second largest town; railway.

Kitzbühel [kitzbüel] 47°27N 12°23E, pop (2000e) 8500. Winter sports resort in C Austria; railway; health resort, tourism, casino.

Kivu, Lake [keevoo] area 4750 km²/1800 sq mi. Lake in EC Africa; length, c.95 km/60 mi; width, 50 km/30 mi; altitude, 1460 m/4790 ft.

Kiwanis International *service club*

kiwi A flightless nocturnal bird; native to New Zealand; small eyes; acute sense of smell (rare in birds); long curved bill with nostrils at tip; strong legs. (Genus: *Apteryx*, 3 species. Family: Apterygidae.)

kiwi fruit A woody climber (*Actinidia chinensis*), native to China, and also called **Chinese gooseberry**, but cultivated in New Zealand, hence the better-known name; flowers creamy, 6-petalled; fruit oblong-oval, furry with reddish-green hairs, flesh green, sweet, surrounding black seeds. (Family: Actinidiaceae.)

Kjölen Mountains [kyoeluhn] or **Kolen Mountains** Mountain range along the boundary between NE Norway and NW Sweden; rises to 2111 m/6926 ft at Kebnekaise.

Klaproth, Martin Heinrich [klaproht] (1743–1817) Chemist, born in Wernigerode, Germany. He devised new analytical methods, and discovered zirconium, uranium, strontium, and titanium.

Klaus, Václav [klows, vatslav] (1941–) Czech politician, prime minister (1992–7), and president (2003–), born in Prague. A leading figure in the Civil Forum movement (1989), he became minister of finance in the Government of National Accord. In 1991 he became deputy prime minister and then prime minister, but resigned in 1997 after allegations of financial scandals. He then won re-election as leader of his centre-right Civic Democratic Party.

Klee, Paul [klay] (1879–1940) Artist, born in Münchenbuchsee, Switzerland. A member of the *Blaue Reiter* group (1911–12), he taught at the Bauhaus (1920–32). His early work consists of bright watercolours, but after 1919 he worked in oils, producing small-scale, mainly abstract pictures, as in his 'Twittering Machine' (1922, New York).

Klein, Calvin (Richard) [kliyn] (1942–) Fashion designer, born in New York City. He became known for the simple but sophisticated style of his clothes, including 'designer jeans'. He later added designer accessories, cosmetics, and homeware.

Klein, Melanie [kliyn] (1882–1960) Austrian child psychoanalyst. A student of Sigmund Freud, she was the first to use the content and style of children's play to understand their mental processes.

Kleist, (Bernd) Heinrich (Wilhelm) von [kliyst] (1777–1811) Playwright and poet, born in Frankfurt an der Oder, Germany. His best plays are still popular, notably *Prinz Friedrich von Homburg* (1821). His novellas, such as *Michael Kohlhaas* (1810–11), also became well known.

Klemperer, Otto (1885–1973) German conductor, born in Wrocław, Poland (formerly Breslau, Prussia). In his later years, he concentrated mainly on the German classical composers, and was particularly known for his interpretation of Beethoven. He also composed six symphonies, a Mass, and Lieder.

Klimt, Gustav (1862–1918) Painter, born in Vienna, the leading master of the Vienna *Sezession*. His murals for the University of Vienna (1900–3) used a Symbolist style which caused great controversy.

Kline, Kevin (Delaney) [kliyn] (1947–) Film actor, born in St Louis, MO. Though known for his dramatic abilities, it was his comic role in *A Fish Called Wanda* (1988) that earned him an Oscar as Best Supporting Actor. Later films include *Chaplin* (1992), *Wild, Wild West* (1999), and *The Pink Panther* (2006).

Klinger, Friedrich Maximilian von (1752–1831) Playwright and romance writer, born in Frankfurt, Germany. The *Sturm-und-Drang* school was named after one of his tragedies.

Klinsmann, Jürgen (1964–) Footballer, born in Göppingen, W Germany. He joined Vfb Stuttgart, and in 1988 was German Player of the Year. Among later clubs are Inter Milan, Monaco, and Bayern Munich. He had two successful spells with Tottenham Hotspur (1994–5, 1997–8), and was English Player of the Year in 1995. He captained Germany to win the 1990 World Cup and the 1996 European Championship, retiring after the 1998 World Cup. He was appointed coach of Germany (2004–6) and took the team to the semi-finals of the 2006 World Cup.

Klippel, Robert Edward (1920–2001) Sculptor, born in Sydney, New South Wales, Australia. His sculptures are intricate and complex, often made of metal 'found objects' welded together (hence the name 'junk sculpture'), though he did also work with wood, plaster, and bronze.

Klitzing *von Klitzing*

Klondike gold rush A flood of prospectors (largely US) when gold was discovered in Canada Yukon Territory in 1896. The rush lasted for five years.

Klopstock, Friedrich Gottlieb (1724–1803) Poet, born in Quedlinburg, Germany. Regarded in his own time as a great religious poet, he helped to inaugurate the golden age of German literature, especially by his lyrics and odes.

Klosters [klohsterz] 46°54N 9°54E, pop (2000e) 3800. Alpine winter skiing resort in E Switzerland; comprises the villages of Platz, Dörfli, and Brücke.

Kluane National park in SW Yukon territory, Canada; established in 1972; along with the Wrangell–St Elias park, forms the world's largest nature reserve; a world heritage site.

klystron A device for amplifying microwave beams. It is used in particle accelerators and radar, and may also be used as a producer of microwaves.

knapweed The name for many species of *Centaurea*, mostly perennials; hard rounded flower-heads surrounded by many closely overlapping bracts; florets purple or yellow. (Genus: *Centaurea*. Family: Compositae.)

knee Commonly used to refer to the region around the knee-cap (*patella*); more specifically, in anatomy, the largest joint in the human body, being the articulation between the femur and the tibia. It allows a wide range of movement.

Kneller, Sir Godfrey [kneler], originally **Gottfried Kniller** (1646–1723) Portrait painter, born in Lübeck, Germany. His best-known works are his 48 portraits of members of the Whig 'Kit-Cat Club' (1700–17, National Portrait Gallery, London), and of nine sovereigns.

Knesset [kneset] The Israeli parliament and state legislature. Its term of office is four years, and the country's president is elected by the Knesset for five years.

Knievel, Evel [kneevel, eevel], professional name of **Robert Craig Knievel** (1938–) Motorcycle stunt performer, born in Butte, MT. He began carrying out motorcycle stunts as a teenager, eventually forming Evel Knievel's Motorcycle Devils in 1965, becoming known for his spectacular and dangerous performances. He later managed the stunt career of his son, **Robbie Knievel**.

Knight, Dame Laura, *née* **Johnson** (1877–1970) Artist, born in Long Eaton, Derbyshire. She produced a long series of oil paintings of the ballet, the circus and gypsy life, in a lively and forceful style.

knight In the UK, a title of honour granted as a reward for services, permitting the use of *Sir* with one's name; originally (in the Middle Ages) men who formed an elite cavalry. The ideal of knighthood involved the maintenance of personal honour, religious devotion, and loyalty to one's lord.

knight bachelor (KB) In the UK, the lowest, but most ancient, form of knighthood, originating in the reign of Henry III. A KB is not a member of any order of chivalry.

Knightley, Keira (Christina) (1985–) Actress, born in London. Born into a showbusiness family, she began acting at an early age and made her film debut at the age of nine in *A Village Affair* (1994). Her first major part came in *Star Wars: Episode 1 – The Phantom Menace* (1999), and later films include *Bend It Like Beckham* (2002), *Pirates of the Caribbean* (2003, sequel 2006), *King Arthur* (2004), and *Pride and Prejudice* (2005, Oscar nomination).

Knights Hospitallers / of Jerusalem / of Malta / of Rhodes *Hospitallers*

Knights Templars *Templars*

knitting An ancient craft used for making fabric by linking together loops of yarn using two, three, or four hand-held needles. The first knitting machine was invented in England by William Lee (c.1550–c.1610). The manufacture of knitted fabrics in tubular form is known as *circular knitting*; such fabrics are often used in underwear and sportswear.

knocking An audible shuddering sound produced by an engine, because of the uneven burning of its air/fuel mixture. To overcome the problem, antiknocking fuels are used.

Knossos [knosos] An Aegean Bronze Age town at Kephala, NC Crete, flourishing c.1900–1400 BC, and covering c.50 ha/125 acres. Its Minoan palace was discovered in 1899, and later partly reconstructed by Sir Arthur Evans.

knot (ornithology) Either of two species of sandpiper; the widespread **knot** or **red knot** (*Calidris canutus*); and the **eastern knot** or **great knot** (*Calidris tenuirostris*) from E regions of the Old World.

knot (physics) A unit of speed equivalent to one nautical mile (1·85 km) per hour. It is used especially of ships, aircraft, and winds.

knotgrass A spreading annual (*Polygonum aviculare*), a widespread weed; each node of the stem enclosed in a silvery sheath; leaves small, elliptical, with small pink or white flowers. (Family: Polygonaceae.)

knowledge-based system A computer system which operates on knowledge, organized as a set of rules, rather than on data. It is used to mirror human decision-making processes, such as medical diagnosis or actuarial assessments.

Knowles, William S (1917–) Chemist, born in the USA. He studied at Columbia University, later joining the Monsato Co in St Louis. He shared the 2001 Nobel Prize for Chemistry for work on chirally catalysed hydrogenation reactions.

Know-Nothing movement (1856) The popular name for the anti-immigrant American Party in 19th-c USA. It was so called from the response members were instructed to give to questioning: 'I know nothing'.

Knox, John (c.1513–72) Protestant reformer, born near Haddington, East Lothian. A Catholic priest, he was influenced by George Wishart to work for the Lutheran reformation. After Wishart was burned (1546), Knox joined the reformers defending the castle of St Andrews, and became a minister. He was kept a prisoner until 1549, then became a chaplain to Edward VI. On Mary's accession (1553), he fled to Geneva, where he was much influenced by Calvin. After returning to Scotland he founded the Church of Scotland (1560).

Knox, Ronald (Arbuthnott) (1888–1957) Theologian and essayist, born in Birmingham, West Midlands. A convert to Catholicism, he wrote an influential translation of the Bible, as well as several works of apologetics, as well as detective novels.

Knox-Johnston, Robin, popular name of **Sir William Robert Patrick Knox-Johnston** (1939–) Yachtsman, born in London, the first person to circumnavigate the world non-stop and single-handed, 14 June 1968–22 April 1969. He is also holder of the British Sailing Trans Atlantic Record (1986: 10 days, 14 h, 9 min), and he co-skippered *Enza* achieving the world's fastest circumnavigation under sail (1994: 74 days, 22 h, 17 min, 22 s). In 2006 he came out of retirement to compete in the 30 000 mile solo round-the-world race aboard yacht *Saga Insurance*.

koala [kohahla] E Australian marsupial (*Phascolarctos cinereus*); thick soft grey or grey-brown fur with white chest; round head with small eyes, erect fluffy ears, large dark nose pad; also known (incorrectly) as a **koala bear**. (Family: Phascolarctidae.)

koatimundi *coati*

Kobe [kohbay] 34°40N 135°12E, pop (2000e) 1 500 000. Port in C Honshu, Japan; Japan's international leading commercial port; railway; 15 universities; badly damaged by earthquake, January 1995; Kobe Wing Stadium (2001).

Koblenz [kohblents], Eng **Coblenz**, ancient **Confluentes** 50°21N 7°36E, pop (2000e) 113 000. City in Germany; seat of Frankish kings, 6th-c; badly bombed in World War 2; largest garrison town in former West Germany; railway; major centre of Rhine wine trade.

Koch, (Heinrich Hermann) Robert [kokh, rohbert] (1843–1910) Bacteriologist, born in Clausthal-Zellerfeld, Germany. He discovered the tuberculosis bacillus (1882), and later the cholera bacillus (1883), and received the Nobel Prize for Physiology or Medicine in 1905.

Köchel, Ludwig Ritter von [koekhel] (1800–77) Musicologist, born in Stein, Austria. He is known as the compiler of the catalogue of Mozart's works, which he arranged in chronological order, giving them the numbers (K1, etc) commonly used to identify them today.

Kocher, Emil [kokher] (1841–1917) Surgeon, born in Bern. He gained his doctorate in Bern in 1865, and from 1872 he was professor of surgery and director of the University Surgical Clinic at Bern. He won the 1909 Nobel Prize for Physiology or Medicine for his work on the physiology, pathology, and surgery of the thyroid gland.

Kodály, Zoltán [kohdiy] (1882–1967) Composer, born in Kecskemét, Hungary. Among his best-known works are the *Háry János* suite (1926) and several choral compositions, especially his *Psalmus Hungaricus* (1923) and *Te Deum* (1936).

Kodiak Island 57°20N 153°40W, pop (2002e) 12 000. Island in the Gulf of Alaska, USA; 160 km/100 mi long; scene of the first settlement in Alaska (by the Russians, 1784); till 1804 the centre for Russian interests in the USA; home of the Kodiak brown bear (grizzly), the largest living carnivore.

Koechlin, Pat *Smythe, Pat*

Koestler, Arthur [kestler] (1905–83) Writer and journalist, born in Budapest. His masterpiece is the political novel *Darkness at Noon* (1940). His non-fiction books and essays deal with politics, scientific creativity, and parapsychology, notably *The Act of Creation* (1964). He became a British citizen in 1948. He and his wife were active members of the Voluntary Euthanasia Society, and, after he developed a terminal illness, they committed suicide.

Kofun [kohfuhn] The burial-mounds characteristic of early historic Japan, which have given their name to the archaeological period AD c.300–700.

Koheleth *Ecclesiastes, Book of*

Koh-i-noor [koheenoor] (Persian 'mountain of light') A famous Indian diamond with a history dating back to the 14th-c. It was presented to Queen Victoria in 1850, and is now among the British crown jewels.

Kohl, Helmut (1930–) German statesman and chancellor (1982–98), born in Ludwigshafen-am-Rhein, SW Germany. After the collapse of the Schmidt coalition in 1982, he was installed as interim chancellor, and in the elections of 1983 formed a government which adopted a central course between political extremes. He presided over the unification of Germany in 1990. In 1998 Kohl lost power to Schröder, ending the longest period of chancellorship since Kaiser Wilhelm's rule, and he resigned his leadership of the Christian Democrats.

kohlrabi [kohlrabee] A variety of cabbage (*Brassica oleracea*, variety *caulorapa*) with a very short, swollen, green or purple stem. It is eaten as a vegetable. (Family: Cruciferae.)

Kohn, Walter [kohn] (1923–) Chemist, born in Vienna. He became the founding director of the Institute of Theoretical Physics at the University of California, Santa Barbara. He shared the 1998 Nobel Prize for Chemistry for his contribution to studies of the properties of molecules and the chemical processes in which they are involved – specifically, for his development of the density-functional theory.

Kok, Willem, known as **Wim Kok** (1938–) Trade Union official, politician, and Dutch prime minister (1994–2002), born in Bergambacht, The Netherlands. After holding various posts in the Netherlands Association of Trade Unions, he became chairman

of the Federation of Dutch Trade Unions in 1981. In 1985 he entered parliament, representing the PvdA (Partij van de Arbeid) from 1986. He served as finance minister and vicepremier (1989–94) before becoming prime minister.

Kokoschka, Oskar [kokoshka] (1886–1980) Artist, born in Pöchlarn, Austria. He travelled widely, and painted many Expressionist landscapes in Europe.

kola or **cola** An evergreen tree native to tropical Africa. The woody fruits contain glossy nuts high in caffeine, which is released when the nuts are chewed. (Genus: *Cola*, 125 species. Family: Sterculiaceae.)

Kola Peninsula [kola], Russ **Kol'skiy Poluostrov** Peninsula in NW European Russia, forming the NE extension of Scandinavia; length, 400 km/250 mi; width, 240 km/150 mi.

Kolbe, St Maximilian (Maria) [kolbuh] (1894–1941) Franciscan priest, born near Łódź, Poland. He was arrested by the Gestapo in 1941, and imprisoned in Auschwitz, where he gave his life in exchange for one of the condemned prisoners, Franciszek Gajowniczek. He was canonized in 1982. Feast day 14 August.

Kolchak, Alexander Vasilevich (1874–1920) Russian admiral and leader of counter-revolutionary (White) forces during the Russian Civil War, born in the Crimea. He established an anti-Bolshevik government in Siberia, and proclaimed himself 'Supreme Ruler' of Russia. He was captured and shot by Red Army forces in Irkutsk.

Kolekole *Haleakala Crater*

Kolen Mountains *Kjölen Mountains*

Kolkatta *Calcutta*

Köln *Cologne*

Kolyma, River [kolima] River in E Russia, rising in the Khrebet Cherskogo; enters the E Siberian Sea; length, 2513 km/1562 mi.

Komodo [komohdoh] 8°35S 119°30E. Small island in Indonesia; part of the Lesser Sunda Is.

Komodo dragon A rare SE Asian monitor lizard (*Varanus komodoensis*), native to the islands of Komodo, Flores, Pintja, and Padar (Indonesia); the world's largest lizard (length, up to 3 m/10 ft); occasionally attacks and kills people; also known as **Komodo lizard** or **ora**.

Kompong Som or **Kampong Saom** 10°38N 103°30E. Seaport in S Cambodia; a new city, completed in 1960; chief deepwater port and commercial centre of Cambodia; airfield; railway.

Komsomol [komsomol] The All-Union Leninist Communist League of Youth, founded in 1918, incorporating almost all persons between the ages of 14 and 28. It served as a recruiting ground for party membership during the communist years, and disbanded in 1991.

kongoni *hartebeest*

Konstanz *Constance*

Kon Tiki [kon teekee] A balsa-wood raft built in 1947 by Thor Heyerdahl. He and five others sailed 6000 km/3800 mi from South America to Polynesia in the 13·7 m/45 ft-long raft to prove his theories on the migration of early man.

Konya [konya], ancient **Iconium** 37°51N 32°30E, pop (2000e) 618 000. Holy city in SC Turkey; visited by St Paul; order of the Whirling Dervishes founded here by Islamic mystical poet, Jalal al-Din Rumi, known as Mevlana ('our lord'); airfield; railway; trade centre of a rich agricultural region.

kookaburra Either of two species of bird of the kingfisher family: the **laughing kookaburra** or **laughing jackass** (*Dacelo novaeguinae*) from Australia; and the **blue-winged kookaburra** or **howling jackass** (*Dacelo leachii*) from Australia and New Guinea. They inhabit dry forest and savannah, and have loud laugh-like cries. (Family: Alcedinidae.)

Kópavogur [kopavogur] 64°06N 21°56W, pop (2000e) 17 600. Second largest town in Iceland; developed since 1945 to house people working in Reykjavík.

kopje *tor*

Koran *Qur'an*

Korda, Sir Alexander, originally **Sándor Laszlo Korda** (1893–1956) Film producer, born in Puszta, Hungary. His many films as producer include *The Private Life of Henry VIII* (1932), which he also directed, *The Third Man* (1949), and *Richard III* (1956).

Kordestan *Kurdistan*

Korea, North *p.512*

Korea, South *p.513*

Korean A language of uncertain origin, showing resemblances to the Altaic family and to Japanese. It is spoken by over 50 million people in N and S Korea, China, Japan, and Russia.

Korean War (1950–3) A war between Communist and non-Communist forces in Korea, which had been partitioned along the 38th parallel in 1945 after Japan's defeat. The Communist North invaded the South in 1950, and a United Nations force intervened, driving the invaders back to the Chinese frontier. China then entered the war, and together with the N Koreans occupied Seoul. The UN forces counter-attacked, and by 1953, when an armistice was signed, had retaken all territory S of the 38th parallel.

Koresh, David [koresh] (1960–93) Cult leader, born in Texas, USA. He was the charismatic leader of a heavily armed group of Branch Davidians (a sect which had split away from the Seventh Day Adventist Church in 1959) who were put under siege by federal agents at a ranch in Mount Carmel, Waco, TX, in 1993. The siege ended after a devastating fire in which Koresh and many of his followers were killed.

Kórinthos *Corinth*

Kornberg, Arthur (1918–) Biochemist, born in New York City. In 1959 he shared the Nobel Prize for Physiology or Medicine for showing how DNA molecules are duplicated in bacterial cells, and replicating this process in the test-tube.

Kornberg, Roger D (1947–) Biochemist, born in St Louis, MO. The son of Nobel prizewinner Arthur Kornberg, he studied at Harvard (1967) and Stanford (1972) universities, conducted postdoctoral research at Cambridge, and joined Harvard Medical School as an assistant professor in the department of biological chemistry in 1976. Since 1978 he has been professor of structural biology at Stanford. In 2006 he was awarded the Nobel Prize for Chemistry for his studies of the molecular basis of eukaryotic transcription.

Korolyov, Sergey (Pavlovich) [korolyof], also spelled **Korolev** (1907–66) Rocketry pioneer, aerospace engineer, and space programme leader, born in Zhitomir, Ukraine. He developed the first Soviet intercontinental ballistic missile, and was leader of the Soviet space programme.

Koror [kohraw(r)] 7°21N 134°31E, pop (2000e) 12900. Capital town of Belau, W Pacific Ocean, on Koror I; airport on neighbouring island of Babeldoab.

Kós *Cos*

Kościuszko or **Kościusko, Thaddeusz (Andrzej) Bonawentura** [koshchooshkoh] (1746–1817) Polish general and patriot, born near Slonim, Belarus (formerly Lithuania). In 1776 he volunteered to serve in the American Revolution, and fought in several campaigns, returning to Poland in 1784. His defeat of the Russians at Raclawice was followed by a rising in Warsaw; he established a provisional government, but was defeated at Maciejowice (1794) and taken prisoner until 1796.

Kosciuszko, Mount [koseeuhskoh] 36°28S 148°17E. Highest mountain in Australia (2228 m/7310 ft); in the Snowy Mts of the Australian Alps, New South Wales.

kosher [kohsher] Food fulfilling the requirements of Jewish Law, including the manner of preparation. In orthodox Judaism, only certain animals, which must be ritually slaughtered, may be eaten.

Koshiba, Masatoshi (1926–) Physicist, born in Toyohashi, Honshu, Japan. A researcher at the International Center for Elementary Particle Physics in Tokyo, he shared the 2002 Nobel Prize for Physics for his pioneering contributions to astrophysics, in particular for the detection of cosmic neutrinos.

Košice [koshitsuh], Ger **Kaschau**, Hung **Kassa** 48°43N 21°14E, pop (2000e) 240 000. Industrial city in Slovak Republic; on R Hornád; formerly part of Hungary; airport; railway; technical university (1952); cathedral (13th-c).

Kosovo [kosuhvuh] (Serbian), **Kosova** (Albanian) pop (2002e) 2 400 000; area 10 887 km²/4200 sq mi. Province of S Serbia; capital, Pristina; 90% of population Albanian (Kosovars, mostly Muslim); agricultural region; central part of Serbian kingdom, 11th–14th-c; under Ottoman rule, 14th-c–1912; annexed by Serbia, 1912; incorporated into Kingdom of Serbs, Croats, and Slovenes, 1918 (Yugoslavia from 1929); part of Greater Albania under Italian occupation, 1941–3; autonomous province of Serbia to 1989; declared independence in 1990, with president and parliament elected in 1992, but implementation disallowed by Serbian authorities; conflict between Serbia and ethnic Albanian armed resistance movement (Kosovo Liberation Army) since late 1997; NATO observers introduced, 1998; focus of international concern in early 1999, following escalation of conflict, with fresh reports of war crimes and violations of human rights; failure of peace talks at Rambouillet chateau near Paris (Feb); increase of Serbian incursions into Kosovo (Mar), with displacement of Kosovar Albanians; onset of NATO air-strikes campaign (Operation Allied Force) against targets in Yugoslavia (Mar); massive escalation in numbers of refugees forced to leave Kosovo, with over a million displaced by mid-April, burning of Albanian villages, and reports of widespread atrocities; further build-up of NATO forces in the region; President Milosevic accepted peace terms (Jun), followed by deployment of NATO troops into Kosovo (Operation Joint Guardian), and the departure of Serb forces; attempts to establish a multicultural policy marred by ongoing ethnic (Albanian/Serb) conflict; following its separation from Montenegro, Serbia approved new constitution (Oct 2006) defining Kosovo as a significantly autonomous province.

Kosrae [kozray], formerly **Kusaie** pop (2000e) 8900; area 100 km²/40 sq mi. Island group, one of the Federated States of Micronesia, W Pacific; capital, Lelu; airport on Kosrae I.

Kossoff, David (1919–2005) Actor, writer, and illustrator, born in London. He became known for his portrayal of Jewish characters on stage and film, and became popular with his short stories based on Jewish traditions and culture and for his Bible story-telling programmes on radio and television.

Kossuth, Lajos [kosooth, loyosh], also Hung [koshut] (1802–94) Hungarian statesman, a leader of the 1848 Hungarian Revolution, born in Monok, Hungary. He was appointed provisional governor of Hungary (1849), but internal dissensions led to his resignation, and he fled to Turkey, and then to England.

Kosygin, Alexey Nikolayevich [koseegin] (1904–80) Russian statesman and premier (1964–80), born in St Petersburg, Russia. First deputy prime minister (with Mikoyan) from 1960, he succeeded Khrushchev as chairman of the Council of Ministers. He resigned in 1980 because of ill health.

koto A Japanese zither, about 1·85 cm/6 ft long, with 13 silk strings stretched across movable bridges which allow a variety of tunings. It is placed on the floor; the player sits cross-legged or kneels before it, and plucks the strings using plectra.

Kotor [kotuh(r)] A region of both natural and culturo-historical interest, located on the Montenegrin coast; a world heritage site.

Kotzebue, August (Friedrich Ferdinand) von [kotzebyoo] (1761–1819) Playwright, born in Weimar, Germany. He wrote about 200 poetic dramas, notably *Menschenhass und Reue* (1789–90,

Korea, North

☐ International Airport

official name **Democratic People's Republic of Korea**, Korean **Choson Minjujuui In'min Konghwaguk**

Local name Ch-oson Minjujuüi In'min Konghwaguk

Timezone GMT +9

Area 122 098 km²/47 130 sq mi

Population total (2002e) 22 224 000

Status Democratic people's republic

Date of independence 1948

Capital Pyongyang

Language Korean (official)

Ethnic groups Korean (99·8%), Chinese (0·2%)

Religions Atheist or non-religious (68%), Buddhist (2%), Christian (1%)

Physical features Located in E Asia, in the N half of the Korean peninsula; separated from South Korea to the S by a demilitarized zone of 1262 km²/487 sq mi; volcanic peak of Mount Paek-tu rises 2744 m/9003 ft in NE; Yalu river valley marks Korean-Chinese border in NW; fertile Chaeryong and Pyongyang plains in SW; 74% of land forested, 18% arable.

Climate Temperate; warm summers, severely cold winters; often rivers freeze for up to 3–4 months in winter; average annual temperatures -8°C (Jan), 24°C (Jul); average annual rainfall 916 mm/26 in.

Currency 1 North Korean Won (KPW) = 100 chon

Economy Agriculture (employs c.48% of workforce, generally on large-scale collective farms); rice, maize, vegetables, livestock, wheat, barley, beans, tobacco; timber, fishing; severely affected during the Korean War, but rapid recovery with Soviet and Chinese aid; machine building, mining, chemicals, textiles.

GDP (2004e) $22·83 bn, per capita $1000

History (*see* Korea, South history); formally annexed by Japan, 1910; N area occupied by Soviet troops following invasion by US and Russian troops and the dividing of the country into N and S, 1945; Democratic People's Republic of Korea declared, 1948; Korean War, 1950–3; demilitarized zone established, 1953; friendship and mutual-assistance treaty signed with China, 1961; unsuccessful reunification talks in 1980; non-aggression agreement signed with S Korea, 1991; became a member of UN, 1991; death of Kim Il-sung, 1994; withdrawal from the 1970 Nuclear Non-Proliferation Treaty, 2003; first road link to be opened between North and South Korea since the Korean War, inaugurated, 2003; international condemnation of the country's first nuclear test, 2006; agreed to close main nuclear reactor in exchange for overseas aid, 2007; governed by a President and a Supreme People's Assembly.

Head of State

1948–57 Kim Doo-bong
1957–72 Choi Yong-kun
1972–94 Kim Il-sung
1994– Kim Jong-il

Head of Government

1948–76 Kim Il-sung
1976–7 Park Sung-chul
1977–84 Li Jong-ok
1984–6 Kang Song-san
1986–8 Yi Kun-mo
1988–92 Yon Hyong-muk
1992–7 Kang Song-san
1997–2003 Hong Song-nam
2003– Pak Pong-ju

---

trans The Stranger), as well as tales, satires, and historical works. He was assassinated at Mannheim as an alleged spy.

Koulouri *Salamis* (Greece)

koumiss or **kumiss** A fermented drink obtained from ass's or mare's milk. Originally made by nomadic peoples of C Asia, it has been used both as medicine and beverage.

Koussevitsky, Serge [koosevitskee], originally **Sergei Alexandrovich Koussevitsky** (1874–1951) Conductor, born in Vishni-Volochok, Russia. He was conductor of the Boston Symphony Orchestra (1924–49), and established a Music Foundation which commissioned works from several major composers.

Kowloon [kowloon], also **Jiulong** area 11 km²/4 sq mi. Peninsula and region of Hong Kong; railway link to Guangzhou (Canton); site of Hong Kong's airport.

Kozhikode [kohzhuhkohd], formerly **Calicut** 11°15N 75°43E, pop (2000e) 941 000. Port city in Kerala, SW India; trade centre since the 14th-c; railway; university (1968); gave its name to calico cotton.

Krafft-Ebing, Richard, Freiherr von (Baron) [kraft ebing] (1840–1902) Psychiatrist, born in Mannheim, Germany. A specialist in nervous diseases, he was an early investigator of sexual disorders.

krait [kriyt] A venomous Asian snake of genus *Bungarus* (several species); related to the cobra, but smaller and lacks a 'hood'; causes many deaths each year in India.

Krajina [krajina] Serbian enclave in SW Croatia; proclaimed autonomy as Serbian Autonomous Region (SAR), 1990; administrative base, Knin; unilaterally declared status as republic, 1991.

Krakatoa [krakatoha] Volcanic island in the Sunda Strait between Java and Sumatra. Active for the last million years, it erupted catastrophically in 1883. Several tsunamis were generated, causing the deaths of 36 000 people in the coastal areas of Java and Sumatra.

Kraków or **Cracow** [krakuf], Ger **Krakau**, ancient **Cracovia** 50°04N 19°57E, pop (2000e) 757 000. Industrial city in S

Korea, South

NORTH KOREA

Demilitarized Zone

Kangnung

Inchon ■ **Seoul**

Han

Chungju

Taebaek Sanmaek Mts

S O U T H

K O R E A

Naktong

YELLOW
SEA

Kunsan

Taegu

Chonju

Chirisan
1915m △

Kyongju

Kwangju

Masan

Pusan

Mokpo

Tsushima
(Japan)

Cheju

Cheju do

△ Hallasan
1950m

CHINA

EAST CHINA SEA

200 km

100 mi

☐ International Airport

or **Korea,**
official name **Republic of Korea**, Korean **Tae Han Minguk**

Local name Taehan-Min'guk

Timezone GMT + 9

Area 98 913 km²/38 180 sq mi

Population total (2002e) 47 640 000

Status Republic

Date of independence 1948

Capital Seoul

Language Korean (official)

Ethnic groups Korean (99·9%), Chinese (0·1%)

Religions Buddhist (18%), Christian (Protestant 41%, Roman Catholic 3%), Confucianist (1%)

Physical features Occupies the S half of the Korean peninsula; bordered N by North Korea, from which it is separated by a demilitarized zone at 38°N; Taebaek Sanmaek Mt range runs N–S along the E coast; descends to broad, undulating coastal lowlands; rivers include Naktong and Han; c.3000 islands off the W and S coasts; largest island is Cheju do, which contains Korea's highest peak, Hallasan, 1950 m/6398 ft.

Climate Extreme continental climate, cold winters, hot summers; average annual temperatures -5°C (Jan), 25°C (Jul); average annual rainfall 1250 mm/49 in.

Currency 1 South Korean Won (KRW) = 100 chon

Economy Light consumer goods, with a shift towards heavy industries; petrochemicals, textiles, electrical machinery, steel, ships, fish; one of the world's largest deposits of tungsten; only a fifth of land suitable for cultivation; rice, wheat, barley, grain, pulses, tobacco.

GDP (2002e) $941·5 bn, per capita $19 600

Human Development Index (2002) 0·882

History Originally split into three rival kingdoms, united in 668 by the Silla dynasty; succeeded by the Koryo dynasty, 935; Yi dynasty, 1392–1910; independence recognized by China, 1895; annexation by Japan, 1910; entered by Russia (from N) and USA (from S) to enforce the Japanese surrender, dividing the country in N and S at the 38th parallel, 1945; declared Republic of Korea, 1948; North Korean forces invaded, 1950; UN forces assisted South Korea in stopping the advance, 1950–3; military coup, 1961; assassination of Park Chung Hee, 1979; non-aggression pact signed with N Korea, 1991; President Roh Moo-hyun impeached (Mar 2004) but reinstated two months later; governed by a President, a State Council, and a National Assembly; co-location (with Japan) of the 2002 FIFA World Cup; first road link between North and South Korea since the Korean War, inaugurated Feb 2003.

Head of State

1980–8 Chun Doo-hwan
1988–93 Roh Tae-woo
1993–98 Kim Young-sam
1998–2003 Kim Dae-jung
2003– Roh Moo-hyun

Head of Government

1995–7 Lee Soo-sung
1997–8 Goh Kun
1998–2000 Kim Jong-pil
2000 Park Tae-joon
2000–2 Lee Han-dong
2002–3 Kim Suk-soo
2003–4 Goh Kun
2004–6 Lee Hae-chan
2006 Han Duk Soo *Acting*

Poland, on R Vistula; third largest city in Poland; capital, 1305–1609; airport; railway; includes Nowa Huta industrial centre; Jagiellonian University (1364); technical university (1945); cathedral (14th-c); royal castle; Market Square (14th-c), a world heritage site.

Kramer, Dame Leonie (Judith) [kraymer] (1924–) Academic, writer, and administrator, born in Melbourne, Victoria, Australia. Chancellor of Sydney University (1991), she is a prominent member of the group 'Australians for Constitutional Monarchy', founded in 1992 in response to growing republican sentiment.

Krasnoyarsk [krasnoyah(r)sk] 56°08N 93°00E, pop (2000e) 918 000. Fast-growing river-port capital in W Siberian Russia, on the R Yenisey; founded as a fortress, 1628; airport; on the Trans-Siberian Railway; university (1969).

Kray brothers Convicted British murderers, twin brothers who ran a criminal Mafia-style operation in the East End of London in the 1960s: **Ronald Kray** (1933–95) and **Reginald Kray** (1933–2000). Following a series of increasingly violent activities, they were tried at the Old Bailey in 1969, and sentenced to life imprisonment of not less than 30 years.

Krebs, Sir Hans (Adolf) (1900–81) Physiologist, born in Hildesheim, Germany. He shared the Nobel Prize for Physiology or Medicine in 1953 for his work on the nature of metabolic processes.

Krebs cycle A sequence of biochemical reactions in biological systems which results in the release of large amounts of energy; named after Hans Adolf Krebs, and also called the **citric acid cycle**.

Kreisler, Fritz [kriysler] (1875–1962) Violinist, born in Vienna. He became internationally known as a violinist, and also composed violin pieces, a string quartet, and an operetta, *Apple Blossoms* (1919), which was a Broadway success.

Kremlin The mediaeval citadel of a Russian town, generally used with reference to the Kremlin at Moscow, which was originally constructed of wood in the 12th-c, subsequently rebuilt in brick in the 14th-c, and later embellished so that its palaces and cathedrals reflect a variety of architectural styles. It was the residence of the tsars until 1712, and in 1918 became the political and administrative headquarters of the USSR.

Kreutzer, Rodolphe [kroytzer] (1766–1831) Violinist, born in Versailles, France. From 1784 until 1810 he was one of the leading concert violinists in Europe. He became friendly with Beethoven, who dedicated a sonata to him.

krill A typically oceanic, shrimp-like crustacean, length up to 50 mm/2 in; often migrates to surface, massing into vast aggregations that form the main food source of baleen whales. (Class: Malacostraca. Order: Euphausiacea.)

Krishna [krishna] According to Hindu tradition, the eighth incarnation, in human form, of the deity Vishnu. A great hero and ruler, the Mahabharata tells the story of his adventures. Disguised as a charioteer in an eve-of-battle dialogue with Arjuna, he delivers the great moral discourse of the Bhagavadgita.

Krishna or **Kistna, River** [krishna] River in S India; rises in the Western Ghats; enters the Bay of Bengal; length 1300 km/800 mi; its source is sacred to Hindus.

Krishna Menon, V(engalil) K(rishnan) [krishna menon] (1896–1974) Indian politician and diplomat, born in Kozhikode (formerly Calicut), Malabar. He was India's first high commissioner in London (1947), and the leader of the Indian delegation to the United Nations (1952).

Krishnamurti, Jiddu [krishnamoortee] (1895–1986) Theosophist, born in Chennai (Madras), India. He was educated in England by Annie Besant, who in 1925 proclaimed him the Messiah. Later he rejected this persona, and travelled the world advocating a way of life unconditioned by the narrowness of nationality, race, and religion.

Kristiansen, Ingrid, *née* **Christensen** (1956–) Athlete, born in Trondheim, Norway. A former cross-country skiing champion, she becamne an outstanding long-distance runner, and is the only person to hold world best times for the 5000 m, 10 000 m, and marathon, which she achieved in 1985–6. She was the world cross-country champion in 1988.

Kristianstad [kristyanstad] 56°02N 14°10E, pop (2000e) 75 000. Seaport in S Sweden, on R Helge; founded by Denmark, 1614; ceded to Sweden, 1658; taken by the Danes, 1676–8.

Kroc, Ray(mond A) (1902–84) Restaurateur, born in Chicago, IL, the founder of the McDonald's chain of fast-food restaurants. A manufacturer of milk-shake machines in the 1950s, he was impressed by the standards of one of his customers, Mac and Dick McDonald, who sold hamburgers, French fries, and milkshakes from a stand. He bought the rights to operate similar stands, set out strict standards of quality, hygiene, service, and value, and a franchise arrangement of individual restaurant owners. He opened the 100th US store in 1959, and by 2007 this number had reached 30 000 restaurants in 122 countries.

Kroemer, Herbert [kroemer] (1928–) Physicist, born in Germany. He joined the University of California, Santa Barbara in 1976, and in 2000 shared the Nobel Prize for Physics for his groundbreaking work in the development of semiconductor heterostructures.

Kropotkin, Pyotr Alexeyevich, Knyaz (Prince) [kropotkin] (1842–1921) Geographer and anarchist, born in Moscow. In 1872 he associated himself with the extremist section of the International, and was imprisoned (1874–6, 1883–6). Settling in England, he wrote on anarchism, social justice, and many other topics. He returned to Russia in 1917.

Kroto, Sir Harold [krohtoh] (1939–) Chemist, born in Wisbech, Cambridgeshire. He shared the Nobel Prize for Chemistry in 1996 for his contribution to the discovery of fullerenes (1985). He was knighted in 1996.

Kru A Kwa-speaking people of Liberia and Côte d'Ivoire. The largest settlement is now in Monrovia.

Kruger, Paul [krooger], in full **Stephanus Johannes Paulus Kruger**, nickname **Oom** ('Uncle') **Paul** (1825–1904) Afrikaner statesman and president (1883–1902) of the South African Republic, born in Colesberg, South Africa. He became leader of the independence movement when Britain annexed Transvaal (1877). During the second Boer War (1899–1902), he came to Europe to seek (in vain) alliances against Britain, making his headquarters at Utrecht.

Krugerrand A gold coin of the Republic of South Africa, 1 ounce in weight, named after the Boer statesman Paul Kruger (the *rand* being the unit of South African currency). They are bought for investment, and are not part of the everyday currency of South Africa.

Krupp, Gustav, originally **Gustav von Bohlen und Halbach** (1870–1950) Industrialist, born in The Hague. A Prussian diplomat who married **Bertha Krupp** (1886–1957), heiress to the Krupp industrial empire, a special imperial edict allowed him to adopt his wife's surname. During World War 1, his firm manufactured the long-range gun for the shelling of Paris, nicknamed 'Big Bertha'. He later gave financial support to Hitler, and connived in secret rearmament. After World War 2, the Krupp empire was split up by the Allies.

krypton Kr, element 36, the fourth of the noble gases. It liquefies at −150°C, and makes up about 0·0001% of the atmosphere.

K2 or **Mount Godwin-Austen** 35°53N 76°30E. Second highest mountain in the world and highest in the Karakoram range, NE Pakistan; height 8611 m/28 250 ft; named for English topographer Henry Godwin-Austen (1834–1923); the second peak to be measured in this range (hence, K2).

Kuala Lumpur [kwahla lumpoor] 3°08N 101°42E, pop (2000e) 1 534 000. Capital of Malaysia; large Chinese and Indian population; former capital of Selangor; capital of Federated Malay States, 1895; designated a Federal Territory, 1974; airport; railway; university (1962); technical university (1954); commercial centre; Petronas Twin Towers (1996), in 2000 the tallest building in the world (451·9 m/1483 ft).

Kubitschek (de Oliveira), Juscelino [kubshek] (1902–76) Brazilian statesman and president (1956–61), born in Diamantina, Minas Gerais, Brazil. His government sponsored rapid economic growth and the dramatic building of a new capital, Brasília.

Kublai Khan [koobliy kahn] (1214–94) First emperor (1279–94) of the Yuan dynasty in China, the grandson of Genghis Khan. He was acclaimed Great Khan in 1260, with suzerainty from the Pacific to the Black Sea. The splendour of his court was legendary.

Kubrick, Stanley [koobrik] (1928–99) Screen writer, film producer, and director, born in New York City. His films include *Spartacus* (1960), *Lolita* (1962), *Dr Strangelove* (1964), *2001: A Space Odyssey* (1968), *A Clockwork Orange* (1971), and *The Shining* (1980). His last film was *Eyes Wide Shut* (1999).

Kudelka, James [kudelka] (1955–) Ballet dancer, choreographer, and director, born in Newmarket, Ontario, Canada. He joined the National Ballet of Canada, then Les Grands Ballets Canadiens in Montreal. Artist in residence at the National Ballet of Canada from 1992, he took over as director in 1996.

Kudrow, Lisa [kudroh] (1963–) Actress, born in Encino, CA. She became known for her role as Ursula in *Mad About You* (1992), then achieved a major success as Phoebe Buffay (Ursula's 'twin sister') in the acclaimed television series *Friends* (1994–2004). Her feature films include *Romy and Michelle's High School Reunion* (1997) and *Kabluey* (2007).

Kuei-yang *Guiyang*

Kuhn, Thomas (Samuel) [koon] (1922–96) Philosopher and historian of science, born in Cincinnati, OH. His book *The Structure of Scientific Revolutions* (1962) challenged the idea of cumulative, unidirectional scientific progress. His theory of 'paradigms', as sets of related concepts which compete for acceptance in times of rapid scientific change or revolution, has been influential in many fields of enquiry.

Kuiper, Gerard (Peter) [kiyper] (1905–73) Astronomer, born in Harencarspel, The Netherlands. He pioneered the spectroscopy of planetary atmospheres, and laid the groundwork for early exploration missions of the space age.

Kuiper Belt [kiyper] A region in the Solar System beyond the planet Neptune where a swarm of icy asteroids orbits the Sun. Its existence was predicted in 1951 by Dutch-born US astronomer Gerard Kuiper; the first was found in 1992. It is thought to be the source of most comets with orbital periods shorter than a century or two.

Ku Klux Klan The name of successive terrorist organizations in the USA, thought to derive from Greek *kyklos* 'circle'. The first was founded after the Civil War (1861–5): the members, disguised in robes and hoods, terrorized blacks and their sympathizers in the South. It faded after Federal measures were passed against it, but was re-established in a stronger form after World War 1, attacking Catholics, foreigners, Jews, and organized labour, as well as blacks. It was revived again by the fear of communism in the 1950s, then by opposition to the civil rights movements in the 1960s, but strong measures from the federal government (under President Johnson) imposed some control. The organization is still sporadically active in various parts of the USA.

kulaks The most progressive stratum of the late 19th-c and early 20th-c Russian peasantry. They developed after the emancipation of the serfs, and engaged in capitalist farming and entrepreneurial activities. During the collectivization of agriculture in the 1930s, Stalin 'liquidated' the kulaks as a class.

kulan [koolan] ⊳⊳ *ass*

Kulturkampf [kultoorkampf] In the German Second Empire, a 'cultural conflict' between the Prussian state and the Roman Catholic Church. It was inspired by Bismarck's suspicion of Catholics' extra-German loyalties. Most intense during 1870–8, it effectively ended by 1886.

Kumasi [koomahsee], known as **Garden City**, **City of the Golden Stool** 6°45N 1°35W, pop (2000e) 537 000. Second largest city in Ghana; centre of the Ashanti kingdom since the 17th-c; airfield; railway; university (1951); large market centre for cocoa-growing region.

kumquat or **cumquat** [kuhmkwot] A spiny evergreen shrub closely resembling citrus, native to E and SE Asia; fruits look and taste like tiny oranges, and are often candied. (Genus: *Fortunella*, 6 species. Family: Rutaceae.)

Kun, Béla (1886–c.1939) Hungarian Communist leader, born in Szilágycseh, Hungary. In 1919 he set up a Soviet republic in Hungary, but his policy of nationalization alienated much of the population, and his regime was overthrown.

Kundera, Milan [kundaira] (1929–) Novelist, born in Brno, Czech Republic. In 1975 he fled to Paris, where he has lived ever since. He came to prominence in the West with *Kniha smichu a zapomneni* (1979, The Book of Laughter and Forgetting). *Nesnesitelna lehkost byti* (The Unbearable Lightness of Being) appeared in 1984, and was filmed in 1987. Later works include *Identity* (1998), and *La Ignorancia* (2001), and a collection of essays, *Le Rideau* (2005, The Curtain).

Küng, Hans (1928–) Roman Catholic theologian, born in Sursee, Switzerland. A professor at Tübingen from 1960, his questioning of received interpretations of Catholic doctrine and Christianity aroused controversy, and the Vatican withdrew his licence to teach as a Catholic theologian in 1979.

kung fu A form of Chinese unarmed combat dating from the 6th-c, when it was practised at the Shaolin Temple. The best known form is **wing chun**, popularized by the actor Bruce Lee (1940/1–73) in several films.

Kunlun Shan [kunlun shahn] or **K'un-lun Shan** Mountain range in W China; length 2500 km/1500 mi; rises to 7723 m/25 338 ft at Muztag peak.

Kunming or **K'un-ming** 25°04N 102°41E, pop (2000e) 1 797 000. City in S China, on Yunnan plateau; altitude 1894 m/6214 ft; major market and transport centre from 279 BC; spring-like weather and scenery ('City of Eternal Spring'); airfield; railway; university (1934); agricultural university.

Kuomintang *Guomindang*

Kurchatov, Igor (Vasilevich) [koorchatof] (1903–60) Physicist, born in Sim, Russia. He was the leading figure in the building of Russia's first atomic (1949) and thermonuclear (1953) bombs.

Kurdistan or **Kordestan** [koordistahn] pop (2000e) 1 312 000; area 24 998 km²/9649 sq mi. Province in NW Iran, bounded W by Iraq; capital, Sanandaj; inhabited by Kurds, who also occupy parts of NE Iraq, SE Turkey, and NE Syria; in 1920 a Kurdish autonomous state was agreed at the Treaty of Sèvres, but the terms were never carried out; new Kurdish Council formed after elections, 1992, not recognized by central government.

Kurds A W Iranian-speaking ethnic group settled in neighbouring mountainous areas of Turkey, Iraq, Iran, Syria, and the former Soviet Union, an area which they themselves call **Kurdistan**, and numbering 25 million. They have been Sunni Muslims since the 7th-c AD. They form the world's largest ethnic group without their own state and their aim is to achieve independence or autonomy within their own national area. Their host countries have suppressed Kurdish independence movements, Turkey has been particularly severe in repressing them. They suffered religious persecution in Iran. In Iraq, their failure to achieve autonomous status for Kurdistan has resulted in hostilities between Kurds and government forces. Following the Gulf War (1991), there was an Iraq offensive against Kurdish rebels. Many sought refuge in Turkey and Iran, while UN troops tried to maintain safe havens in Iraq. It was only Anglo–US surveillance flights over North Iraq that prevented further Iraqi attacks. In Turkey, an armed separatist movement, the Kurdistan Workers' Party (PKK), has been active since the mid-1980s. Its leader, Abdullah Ocalan, was captured in Kenya (Feb 1999) and imprisoned in Turkey, triggering widespread international protests by Kurdish supporters.

Kurgan culture The semi-nomadic population of the S Russian steppes in the fourth millennium BC, characterized archaeologically by burials sprinkled with red ochre beneath a barrow mound or *kurgan*.

Kuril Islands [kureel], Russ **Kurilskiye Ostrova** area 15 600 km²/6000 sq mi. Archipelago off the N Japanese coast; extends c.1200 km/750 mi from the tip of Kamchatka Peninsula to the NE coast of Hokkaido I, Japan; over 50 islands, actively volcanic, with hot springs; visited in 1634 by the Dutch; divided between Russia and Japan, 18th-c; all ceded to Japan, 1875; occupied by Soviet troops, 1945; part of the USSR, 1947; claimed by Japan.

Kurosawa, Akira [kurohsahwa] (1910–98) Film director, born in Tokyo. He was renowned for his adaptation of the techniques of the Noh theatre to film-making, in such films as *Rashomon* (1951), which won the Venice Film Festival prize, and *The Seven Samurai* (1954). Also characteristic were his literary adaptations, such as *The Lower Depths* (1957, from Dostoyevsky) and *Ran* (1985, from *King Lear*). His last film was *Madadayo* (1993).

kuru [kuroo] A prion disease endemic to the Fore peoples of Papua New Guinea in the early part of the 20th-c. It involves progressive degeneration of the central nervous system, leading to dementia, inco-ordination, and paralysis. Abnormal pro-

Kuwait

80 km
40 mi

IRAN

IRAQ

Umm Qasr

Bubiyan Island

Zor Ridge

Wadi al Batin

Sabiyah

Failakah I.

Al Jahrah

Shuwaikh

■ **Kuwait City**

☐ Kuwait International Airport

KUWAIT

Al Ahmadi

Mina al Ahmadi

Shuaiba

PERSIAN GULF

Mina Saud

ASIA

AFRICA

SAUDI ARABIA

☐ International Airport

[koowayt], official name **State of Kuwait**, Arabic **Dowlat al-Kuwait**

Local name Dowlat al-Kuwait (Arabic)

Timezone GMT +3

Area 17 818 km²/6878 sq mi

Population total (2002e) 2 253 000

Status Independent state

Date of independence 1961

Capital Kuwait City

Language Arabic (official)

Ethnic groups Kuwaiti (52%), non-Kuwaiti Arab (45%), Asian (3%)

Religions Muslim (90%), Christian (8%), Hindu (2%)

Physical features Consists of mainland and nine offshore islands; terrain flat or gently undulating, rising SW to 271 m/889 ft; Wadi al Batin on W border with Iraq; low ridges in NE generally stony with sparse vegetation.

Climate Hot and dry climate; summer temperatures very high, often above 45°C (Jul–Aug); humidity often over 90%; sandstorms common all year; average annual temperature 14°C (Jan) to 37°C (Jul) in Kuwait City; average annual rainfall 111 mm/4 in.

Currency 1 Kuwaiti Dinar (KWD) = 1000 fils

Economy Oil discovered, 1938, providing 95% of government revenue; active programme of economic diversification; petrochemicals, fertilizers, construction materials, asbestos, batteries; agriculture gradually expanding; dates, citrus fruits, timber, livestock.

GDP (2002e) $36·85 bn, per capita $17 500

Human Development Index (2002) 0·813

History Port founded in 18th-c; British protectorate, 1914; full independence from Britain, 1961; invasion and annexation by Iraq (Aug 1990), leading to Gulf War (Jan–Feb 1991), with severe damage to Kuwait City; Kuwait liberated with the aid of UN forces in 1991, and government returned from exile; large refugee emigration; major post-war problems, including burning of Kuwaiti oil wells by Iraq and pollution of Gulf waters by oil; Emir is Head of State, governing through an appointed Prime Minister and a Council of Ministers.

Head of State (Emir)
1965–77 Sabah Ill al-Salim
1977–2006 Jaber al-Ahmad al-Jaber
2006 Saad al-Abdullah al-Salim al-Sabah
2006– Sabah al-Ahmad al-Jaber al-Sabah

Head of Government (Prime Minister)
1962–3 Abdallah al-Salem
1963–5 Sabah al-Salem
1965–78 Jaber al-Ahmed al-Jaber
1978–2003 Saad al-Abdallah al-Salim al-Sabah
2003–6 Sabah al-Ahmad al-Jaber al-Sabah
2006– Nasser al-Muhammad al-Ahmad al-Sabah

tein deposits known as **kuru plaques** are present in the brain. It is thought to be transmitted by cannibalistic funerary rites. Changes in these practices have led to a marked reduction in incidence.

Kurzweil, Raymond C [kertzviyl] (1948–) Computer scientist, a pioneer of reading technology, born in New York City. Since the 1970s he has led the development of the optical character recognition device, the text-to-speech synthesizer, the flat-bed scanner, the orchestral music synthesizer, and a large vocabulary automatic speech recognizer. He has formed then sold-on a number of successful companies based on his inventions. In a joint venture with the American Board of Family Practice in 1997 he formed the Medical Learning Company based on his Medical Synthesizer System. He was given the Lemelson-MIT Award in 2001.

Kush An independent kingdom on the Nile which emerged from the Egyptian province of Nubia in the 11th-c BC. In the 8th-c BC Kush conquered Egypt, and established the XXVth dynasty which ruled until the Assyrian conquest in 671–666 BC.

Kutab Minar *Qutb Minar*

Kutch, Rann of [kuch], also spelled **Kachch**, or **Cutch** area 9000 km²/3474 sq mi. Region of salt marsh in the Indian state of Gujarat and Sind province, Pakistan; once a shallow arm of the Arabian Sea; scene of Indo-Pakistani fighting in 1965.

Kuti, Fela Anikulapo [kootee], born **Fela Ransome Kuti** (1938–97) Singer, musician, composer, and dissident, born in Abeokuta, SW Nigeria. The pioneer of 'Afro-beat', he successfully took his music to Europe and America, and in Nigeria used it as a form of political protest and championing African identity. His saxophonist son **Femi Kuti** continues the family tradition of music combined with political activism.

Kutuzov, Mikhail Ilarionovich, Knyaz (Prince) [kutoozof] (1745–1813) Russian field marshal, born in St Petersburg, Russia. In 1812, he fought Napoleon obstinately at Borodino, and obtained a major victory over Davout and Ney at Smolensk.

Kuwait *see panel*

Kuwait City, Arabic **al-Kuwayt**, formerly **Qurein** 29°20N 48°00E, pop (2000e) 45 000. Capital city of Kuwait, on S shore of Kuwait Bay; developed in the late 1940s after discovery of oil; suburban port of Shuwaikh, SW; airport; university (1966); severely damaged during Gulf War (1991).

Kuybyshev [kooibishef] *Samara*

Kyrgyzstan

□ International Airport

[keergizstahn], official name **Republic of Kyrgyzstan**, also spelled **Kirgizstan**, Kyrgyz **Kyrgyz Respublikasy**, Russ **Kirgiziya**

Local name Kyrgyzstan
Timezone GMT +5
Area 198 500 km²/76 621 sq mi
Population total (2002e) 5 002 000
Status Republic

Date of independence 1991
Capital Bishkek (formerly Frunze)
Language Russian (official), Kyrgyz
Ethnic groups Kyrgyz (52%), Russian (21%), other (27%)
Religion Sunni Muslim (chief religion)
Physical features Located in C Asia, bounded SE and E by China; largely occupied by the Tien Shan Mts; highest point within the republic at Pik Pobedy, 7439 m/24 406 ft; chief river, the Naryn. Largest lake, L Issyk-Kul.
Climate Typical desert climate in N, W, and SE; hot, dry summers in valleys; mean annual temperature -18°C (Jan), 28°C (Jul).
Currency 1 Kyrgyzstani Som (KGS) = 100 tyiyn
Economy Metallurgy; machines; coal; natural gas; textiles, food processing, gold; wheat, cotton, tobacco, animal husbandry.
GDP (2002e) $13·88 bn, per capita $2900
Human Development Index (2002) 0·712
History Part of an independent Turkestan republic, 1917–24; proclaimed a constituent republic of the USSR, 1936; declaration of independence, 1991, and joined Commonwealth of Independent States; governed by a president, prime minister, and Supreme Assembly; President Akayev deposed in popular coup, Mar 2005; new constitution, Nov 2006.

Head of State
1991–2005 Askar Akayev
2005– Kurmanbek Bakiev

Head of Government
2002–5 Nikolai Tanayev
2005 Kurmanbek Bakiev *Acting*
2005–7 Felix Kulov
2007– Azimbek Isabekov

Kuznets Basin [kuznets] Basin of the Tom R in Russia; a major industrial zone, with rich deposits of coal and iron ore.

Kuznetsov, Alexander Vasilievich [kuznetsof] (1929–79) Writer, born in Kiev. He is best known for *Babi Yar* (1966), a novel about the massacre of Ukrainian Jews by the German SS in 1941. He defected to England in 1969, changing his name to **A Anatoli**.

Kwakiutl [kwakiootl] A N Pacific Coast American Indian group living on the coast of British Columbia as fishermen and traders. They were famed for their woodwork, frequently painted in bright colours, and for their elaborate dances and ceremonies, including the potlatch.

KwaNdebele [kwahndebelay] Former national state or non-independent black homeland in Transvaal province, NE South Africa; self-governing status, 1981; incorporated into Mpumalanga following the South African constitution of 1994.

Kwang-chow *Guangzhou*

kwashiorkor [kwashiaw(r)ker] A nutritional disorder of young children, stemming from an inadequate intake of protein in the diet. In Africa, it frequently begins after weaning.

KwaZulu Natal [kwahzooloo natahl] pop (2000e) 8 071 000; area 91 481 km²/35 312 sq mi. One of the nine new provinces established by the South African constitution of 1994, in E South Africa, on the Indian Ocean; comprises former areas of Natal and KwaZulu; Natal, annexed to Cape Colony, 1844; separate colony, 1856; joined Union of South Africa, 1910; KwaZulu, former national state or non-independent black homeland; self-governing status, 1971; provincial status, 1994; capital, alternating between Ulundi and Pietermaritzburg; Durban, business port and second largest city in South Africa; chief languages, Zulu (80%), English, Afrikaans; 'the garden province'.

Kyd or **Kid, Thomas** (1558–94) Playwright, born in London. His tragedies early brought him reputation, especially *The Spanish Tragedy* (c.1592), and he has been credited with a share in several plays.

Kydland, Finn E (1943–) Economist, born in Norway. A member of the Tepper School of Business, Carnegie Mellon University, Pittsburgh, in 2004 he was appointed to the Chair in Economics at the University of California, Santa Barbara. He shared the 2004 Nobel Prize for Economics for contributions to dynamic macroeconomics, specifically the time consistency of economic policy and the driving forces behind business cycles.

Kyoto [kyohtoh] 35°02N 135°45E, pop (2000e) 1 491 000. City in C Honshu, Japan; founded, 8th-c; capital of Japan, 794–1868; railway; 22 universities, including university of industrial arts and textiles (1949); over 2000 temples and shrines; Nijo-jo Castle (1603), containing the Imperial Palace; Kinkakuji, the Golden Pavilion (1394).

Kyoto Protocol An addendum to the 1992 Rio Earth Summit agreement on climate change, initiated when delegates from the world's industrialized nations met in Kyoto in December 1997 and agreed to reduce their combined emissions by about 5 per cent between 1990 and 2012. The USA withdrew in 2001, thereby attracting much international criticism. By the end of 2002 the Protocol had been ratified by 100 countries, but in 2003 Russia announced it would not ratify it in its present form, putting its future in serious doubt. In 2004 the Russian government finally gave its approval, the treaty coming into force on 16 February 2005 with 141 ratifications. In December 2005, the signatories agreed to extend the treaty on emissions reductions beyond its 2012 deadline.

Kyrgyzstan *p.517*

Kyushu [kyushoo] pop (2000e) 13 597 000; area 42 084 km²/ 16 244 sq mi. Island region in Japan; southernmost and most densely populated of the four main islands; rising to 1935 m/ 6348 ft at Mt Miyanoura-dake; subtropical climate; crops damaged and 50+ deaths from successive typhoons (Chaba, Megi, Songda), Sep 2004; heavily forested apart from the NW; major industrial towns include Fukuoka, Kagoshima, Nagasaki.

Kyzyl-Kum [kizil kum], Russ **Peski Kyzylkum** area 300 000 km²/ 115 000 sq mi. Extensive desert in Kazakhstan and Uzbekistan; extends SE from the Aral Sea; rises to 922 m/3025 ft in the C.

l

La (in place name) *also under initial letter of the following word*

Laban, Rudolf von [laybn] (1879–1958) Dancer, choreographer, and dance theoretician, born in Pozsony (now Bratislava, Slovak Republic). As the leader of the C European dance movement he was instrumental in the development of modern dance as a theatre form. He also developed an influential notation system (**Labanotation**).

labelling theory The view, developed primarily during the 1950s and 1960s in American criminology, that certain people and their behaviour come to be 'labelled' by law enforcement agencies as in some way 'deviant' or 'criminal'. Labelling theorists argue that one must look at those doing the labelling – the lawmakers and community at large – and not just the law-breakers.

Labiche, Eugène [labeesh] (1815–88) Playwright, born in Paris. He wrote over 100 comedies, farces, and vaudevilles, such as *Le Chapeau de paille d'Italie* (1851, The Italian Straw Hat).

labile [laybiyl] *kinetic*

Labor Day *Labour Day*

labor union *trade union*

Labour / Labor Day A day of celebration, public demonstrations, and parades by trade unions and labour organizations, held in many countries on 1 May, or the first Monday in May; in the USA, Canada, and Bermuda it is the first Monday in September, and in New Zealand the fourth Monday of October.

Labour Party (UK) A socialist/social democratic political party in Britain, originally formed in 1900 as the Labour Representation Committee to represent trade unions and socialist societies. Twenty-six MPs were elected in 1906, and the name changed to the Labour Party. The first minority Labour government was elected in 1924. The first majority Labour government (1945–51) established the welfare state and carried out a significant nationalization programme. Since then Labour have been in office 1964–70, 1974–9, 1997–2001, and 2001– . The leader and deputy leader are elected annually when in opposition by an electoral college composed of trade unions, constituency parties, and the Parliamentary Labour Party. In the 1990s, the party developed a policy of combining traditional socialist values with a concern to respond to the new ideals and aspirations of the individual (**New Labour**).

labour / labor relations *industrial relations*

Labrador area 285 000 km²/110 000 sq mi. Mainland part of Newfoundland, Canada; mainly a barren plateau, part of Canadian Shield; many lakes; interior region awarded to Newfoundland, 1927, disputed by Quebec.

Labrador retriever A breed of dog, developed in Britain from imported Newfoundland dogs and local breeds; large, with muscular legs and body; long tail and muzzle; short, pendulous ears; thick fawn or black (occasionally brown) coat; also known as **labrador**.

Labrador Sea Arm of the Atlantic Ocean between Newfoundland and Greenland; cold SE-flowing Labrador Current brings icebergs.

La Bruyère, Jean de [brooyair] (1645–96) Writer, born in Paris. His major work is the satirical *Caractères de Théophraste* (1688, Characters of Theophrastus), which gained him a host of implacable enemies as well as an immense reputation.

laburnum A deciduous tree (*Laburnum anagyroides*) growing to 7 m/23 ft, native to S and C Europe; pea-flowers yellow, numerous, in pendent leafy clusters; pods up to 6 cm/2½ in long, hairy when young; seeds black; also called **golden rain** or **golden chain**. All parts but especially the seeds are extremely poisonous. (Family: Leguminosae.)

Lacaille, Nicolas Louis de [lakiy] (1713–62) Astronomer, born in Rumigny, France. He travelled to South Africa (1750–5) to draw up the first reliable catalogue of S hemisphere stars, and named 14 new constellations.

Laccadive Islands *Lakshadweep Islands*

lace An ornamental fabric in which a large number of separate threads are twisted together into a decorative network, such as for the edges of items of clothing or furnishing. Hand-made lace is still widely produced, but machines have been used for making lace since 1808.

lacecap *hydrangea*

Lacerta [laserta] (Lat 'lizard') A smallish, faint N constellation. It includes the object BL Lacertae, the prototype of a class of quasar-like objects.

lacewing A medium to large insect possessing two pairs of similar, membranous wings, each with a lacework of veins; adults and larvae predatory, with simple, biting mouthparts. (Order: Neuroptera.)

Lachesis *Moerae*

Lachlan River [laklan] River in New South Wales, Australia; rises in the Great Dividing Range, N of Canberra; flows 1484 km/922 mi to join the Murrumbidgee R.

lac insect A bug that lives in clusters on twigs of trees; females legless, with reduced antennae; body enclosed in a protective shell of resinous secretion from which shellac is made. (Order: Homoptera. Family: Kerridae.)

Laclos, Pierre (Ambroise François) Choderlos de [lakloh] (1741–1803) Soldier, novelist, and politician, born in Amiens, France. He is remembered for his masterpiece, *Les Liaisons dangereuses* (1782, Dangerous Liaisons), a novel in letter form. It has been successfully adapted for the theatre and in several films.

lacquer A hard waterproof substance made from the resin of the lacquer tree. A very ancient Chinese invention, it can be coloured, polished, carved, and used to decorate wooden vessels and furniture.

lacquer tree A deciduous tree (*Rhus vernicifera*) growing to c.9 m/30 ft, native to China and Japan; flowers tiny, 5-petalled, yellowish, in drooping clusters; also called **varnish tree**. A resin obtained from cuts in the stem is a major constituent of Chinese and Japanese lacquer. (Family: Anacardiaceae.)

Lacroix, Christian [lakrwah] (1951–) Fashion designer, born in Arles, France. In 1981 he joined Jean Patou, which showed his first collection in 1982. In 1987 he opened the House of Lacroix in Paris, making his name with ornate and frivolous clothes. He now has shops in a number of countries.

lacrosse A stick-and-ball field game derived from a North American Indian game, so called because French settlers thought the stick resembled a bishop's crozier (*crosse*). It is a team game usually played with 10 on each side on a pitch measuring 100–110 m/110–120 yd by 55–75 m/60–85 yd. The object is to score goals by throwing the ball into the goal using the lacrosse stick, or *crosse*. The crosse is at least 0·9 m/3 ft in length with a triangular net attached to the end in which to catch the ball.

lactation The process of suckling a newborn infant. During pregnancy, milk-producing glands in the breasts proliferate, and at birth hormones from the pituitary gland stimulate the secretion of milk, which is further augmented when the infant suckles.

lactic acid CH_3–$CH(OH)$–$COOH$, IUPAC **2-hydroxypropanoic acid**. An acid which takes its name from milk, where it is formed on souring. It is an important stage in the breakdown of carbohydrates during respiration.

lactose $C_{12}H_{22}O_{11}$. A sugar occurring in the milk of all mammals. It is a disaccharide, a combination of glucose and galactose, and only slightly sweet-tasting.

ladies' fingers *okra*

Ladoga, Lake, Russ **Ozero Ladozhskoye**, Finnish **Laatokka** area 17 700 km^2/6800 sq mi. Largest lake in Europe, in European Russia, close to the Finnish border; length, 219 km/136 mi; maximum depth, 230 m/755 ft.

ladybird A rounded, convex beetle usually red, black, or yellow with a pattern of spots or lines; adults and larvae feed mostly on aphids and other plant pests; also known as a **ladybug**. (Order: Coleoptera. Family: Coccinellidae.)

ladybug *ladybird*

Lady chapel A chapel dedicated to the Virgin Mary. It is usually built behind the main altar, and forms an extension to the main building.

Lady Day *Annunciation*

Ladysmith, Siege of (1899–1900) A siege of the second Boer War in which Boer forces attempted to pen up their British opponents. General Sir Redvers Buller (1839–1908) succeeded in raising the siege on 28 February 1900.

laetrile [laytriyl] The trade name of the drug *Amygdalin* (bitter almond), which can be extracted from some fruit stones (eg apricot). Formerly known as vitamin B_{17}, it was recommended as a cancer cure. It was never recognized as effective by orthodox medical opinion, and was banned from use as being potentially dangerous.

Lafayette, Marie Joseph (Paul Yves Roch Gilbert Motier), marquis de [lafiyet] (1757–1834) French soldier and politician, born in Chavaniac, Auvergne, France. He fought in America against the British during the War of Independence (1777–9, 1780–2), and in the National Assembly of 1789 presented a draft of a declaration of the Rights of Man. Hated by the Jacobins for his moderation, he defected to Austria, returning to France during the Consulate. He later became a radical leader of the Opposition (1825–30).

La Fayette, Marie Madeleine (Pioche de la Vergne), comtesse de (Countess of) [lafiyet], known as **Madame de La Fayette** (1634–93) Novelist and reformer of French romance writing, born in Paris. Her major novel is *La Princesse de Clèves* (1678), a vivid picture of the court life of her day.

La Fontaine, Jean de [fonten] (1621–95) Poet, born in Château-Thierry, France. His major work is the collection of over 200 verse stories, *Fables choisies mises en vers* (1668, Selected Fables in Verse), in translation usually called 'La Fontaine's Fables'.

lager *beer*

Lagerfeld, Karl [lahgervelt] (1939–) Fashion designer, born in Hamburg, Germany. He was design director at Chanel, and updated the Chanel look. Known for his high quality ready-to-wear clothing, he showed the first collection under his own label in 1984.

Lagerkvist, Pär (Fabian) [lahgerkvist] (1891–1974) Writer, born in Växjö, Sweden. His works include *Bödeln* (1934, The Hangman), *Dvärgen* (1944, The Dwarf), and *Barabbas* (1951). He received the Nobel Prize for Literature in 1951.

Lagerlöf, Selma (Ottiliana Lovisa) [lahgerloef] (1858–1940) Novelist, born in Mårbacka, Sweden. Her fairy tales and romances earned her the 1909 Nobel Prize for Literature – the first woman to receive the distinction.

lagomorph [lagoma(r)wf] An order of mammals comprising rabbits, hares, and pikas; virtually worldwide; long soft fur, long ears, short tails, fully furred feet, slit-like nostrils which can be closed. (Order: Lagomorpha, 58 species.)

Lagos [laygos] 6°27N 3°28E, pop (2000e) 1 642 000. Chief port of Nigeria, settled c.1700; occupied by the British, 1851; colony of Lagos, 1862; part of the S Nigeria protectorate, 1906; capital of Nigeria, 1960–82; airport; university (1962); tanker terminal.

Lagrange, Joseph Louis, comte de l'Empire (Count of the Empire) [lagrãzh], originally **Giuseppe Luigi Lagrangia** (1736–1813) Mathematician and astronomer, born in Turin, Italy. In 1766 he became director of the Berlin Academy, where he worked on number theory, mechanics, the Solar System, and algebraic equations. His major work was the *Mécanique analytique* (1788, Analytical Mechanics).

lagrangian [lagronjian] The difference between kinetic energy K and potential energy V; symbol L, units J (joule); $L = K - V$. It is the fundamental expression of the properties of a mechanical system.

lagrangian points [lagronjian] Five points in the plane of revolution of two bodies where gravitational forces balance so as to allow a small third body to remain in equilibrium. For example, the Trojan asteroids are found in stable orbits at L-4 and L-5 points, forming an equilateral triangle with the Sun and Jupiter.

La Guardia, Fiorello H(enry) [la gah(r)dia] (1882–1947) US politician and lawyer, born in New York City, where he spent most of his career. A popular mayor (1933–45), he initiated housing and labour safeguards schemes. One of the city airports is named after him.

Lahore [lahaw(r)] 31°34N 74°22E, pop (2000e) 4 777 000. Second largest city in Pakistan; taken in 1849 by the British, who made it the capital of Punjab; railway; two universities (1882, 1961); trade and communications centre; considered the cultural capital of Pakistan.

laissez-faire [laysay fair] (Fr 'let do') An economic doctrine advocating that commerce and trade should be permitted to operate free of controls of any kind. It was a popular view in the mid-19th-c.

lake A body of water surrounded by land, and lying in a hollow which may be caused by Earth movement, glaciation, volcanic craters, or the collapse of the roof of limestone caves. Saltwater lakes may be parts of seas or oceans cut off by Earth movement, or formed in areas of low rainfall where mineral salts can accumulate due to evaporation. (*see panel p.521*)

Lake District Part of Cumbria, NW England; area of c.1800 km^2/700 sq mi noted for its scenery; a system of glaciated valleys and ribbon lakes; lakes include Windermere, Derwent Water, Ullswater, Bassenthwaite, Thirlmere, Buttermere, and Coniston Water; mountains include Scafell, Skiddaw, Helvellyn.

lake dwellings *Glastonbury lake village; Swiss lake dwellings*

Lakeland terrier A medium-sized terrier developed in the English Lake District to hunt foxes; coarse coat, very thick on the legs, forehead, and muzzle.

Lake Placid 44°18N 74°01W, pop (2000e) 2600. Resort in N New

Largest Lakes

Name/location	Area*	
	km²	sq mi
Caspian Sea, Iran/Russia	371 000	143 200[1]
Superior, USA/Canada	82 260	31 760[2]
Victoria, E Africa	62 940	24 300
Aral Sea, Kazakhstan	62 000	24 180[1]
Huron, USA/Canada	59 580	23 000[2]
Michigan, USA	58 020	22 400
Tanganyika, E Africa	32 000	12 350
Baikal, Russia	31 500	12 160
Great Bear, Canada	31 330	12 100
Great Slave, Canada	28 570	11 030
Erie, USA/Canada	25 710	10 030[2]
Winnipeg, Canada	24 390	9 420
Malawi/Nyasa, E Africa	22 490	8 680
Balkhash, Kazakhstan	17 000–	6 500–
	22 000	8 500[1]
Ontario, Canada/USA	19 270	7 440[2]
Ladoga, Russia	18 130	7 000
Chad, W Africa	10 000–	4 000–
	26 000	10 000
Maracaibo, Venezuela	13 010	5 020[3]
Patos, Brazil	10 140	3 920[3]
Onega, Russia	9 800	3 800
Rudolf, Kenya	9 100	3 500
Eyre, Australia	8 800	3 400[3]
Titicaca, Peru/Bolivia	8 300	3 200

[1]Salt lakes
[2]Average of areas given by Canada and USA
[3]Salt lagoons
*Areas are given to the nearest 10 km²/sq mi. The Caspian and Aral Seas, being entirely surrounded by land, are classified as lakes. Pollution is reducing the size of many lakes, notably the Aral Sea, which may now be less than half its original size.

York State, USA; in the Adirondack Mts; scene of Winter Olympic events (1932, 1980).

Lake poets A phrase used for the poets who took up residence in the English Lake district in the early 19th-c. Wordsworth and Coleridge were the best known.

Laker, Sir Freddie, popular name of **Sir Frederick Alfred Laker** (1922–2006) Business entrepreneur, born in Kent. In 1966 he headed the successful Laker Airways Ltd, but was severely set back by the failure of the 'Skytrain' fares-buster project (1982), the first low-cost transatlantic operation.

Laker, Jim, popular name of **James Charles Laker** (1922–86) Cricketer, born in Saltaire, Yorkshire. He made test cricket history at Old Trafford in 1956 when he took 19 Australian wickets for 90 runs. During his career (1946–64) he took 1944 wickets.

Lakshadweep Islands [lahkshadweep], formerly **Laccadive Islands** (to 1973) pop (2001e) 60 600; area 32 km²/12 sq mi. Union territory of India, comprising 10 inhabited and 17 uninhabited coral islands in the Arabian Sea 300 km/190 mi off the Malabar Coast of Kerala; ruled by British, 1792; ceded to India, 1956; population mainly Muslim.

Lakshmi [lakshmee] The Hindu goddess of prosperity and good fortune, the consort of Vishnu, sometimes called 'the lotus-goddess'. She is associated with Diwali, the autumn festival of lights.

Lalić, Susan (Kathryn) [lalich], *née* **Walker** (1965–) British chess player. Her achievements include the British Ladies Championships (1986, 1990–2, 1998), and the Commonwealth Ladies

Championships (1988–92). She gained the woman international master title in 1985, and is the first British-born woman to achieve the woman grandmaster title (1988).

Lalique, René [laleek] (1860–1945) Jeweller and glassware designer, born in Ay, France. His glass designs, decorated with relief figures, animals, and flowers, were an important contribution to the Art Nouveau and Art Deco movements.

Lamaism [lahmaizm] The religion of Tibet, a form of Mahayana Buddhism, dating from the 8th-c. The Dalai Lama is the traditional spiritual and temporal ruler of Tibet. Upon the death of a reigning Lama, a search is conducted to find an infant who is his reincarnation.

Lamarck, Jean Baptiste (Pierre Antoine) de Monet, Chevalier de [lamah(r)k] (1744–1829) Naturalist and pre-Darwinian evolutionist, born in Bazentin, France. His major work was the *Histoire des animaux sans vertèbres* (1815–22, Natural History of Invertebrate Animals).

Lamartine, Alphonse (Marie Louis) de [lamah(r)teen] (1790–1869) Poet, statesman, and historian, born in Mâcon, France. His best-known work was his first volume of lyrical poems, *Méditations poétiques* (1820, Poetic Meditations). He was a member of the provisional government in the 1848 Revolution.

Lamb, Charles, pseudonym **Elia** (1775–1834) Essayist and poet, born in London. He achieved a success through the joint publication with his sister of *Tales from Shakespear* (1807). His best-known works are the essays he wrote under the pen name of **Elia**.

lamb *sheep*

Lambert, Constant (1905–51) Composer, conductor, and critic, born in London. His best-known composition is the choral work in jazz idiom, *The Rio Grande* (1927).

Lambert, Johann Heinrich (1728–77) Mathematician, born in Mülhausen, Alsace, NE France. He first showed how to measure scientifically the intensity of light (1760). The unit of light intensity is named after him.

Lambert, John (1619–84) English general, born in Calton, Yorkshire. In the English Civil War, he commanded the cavalry at Marston Moor (1644). He headed the cabal which overthrew Richard Cromwell (1659), and at the Restoration was imprisoned (1661) until his death.

Lambeth Conferences Gatherings of bishops of the Anglican Communion throughout the world for consultations, but without legislative powers. The first conference was held in 1867 at Lambeth Palace, the London house of the Archbishop of Canterbury. It is normally convened every 10 years.

lamellibranch [lamelibrangk] *bivalve*

Lamentations (of Jeremiah) A book of the Hebrew Bible/Old Testament, probably dated shortly after the Babylonian conquest of Jerusalem (c.587/586 BC), attributed in tradition to the prophet Jeremiah. It consists of five poems lamenting the destruction of Jerusalem.

Lamian War [laymian] (323–322 BC) The unsuccessful revolt of the Greek states from Macedon after the death of Alexander the Great.

Laminaria [laminairia] *kelp*

Lammas [lamas] In the UK, a former church festival (1 Aug); the name means 'loaf-mass', the festival originally being held in thanksgiving for the harvest, with the consecration of loaves made of flour from the newly harvested wheat.

lammergeier [lamergiyer] An Old World vulture (*Gypaetus barbatus*), native to S Europe, Africa, India, and Tibet; also known as the **bearded vulture**; grey back; reddish head and underparts; white chest; dark 'beard' of stiff feathers. (Family: Accipitridae.)

Lamont (of Lerwick), Norman Lamont, Baron [lamont] (1942–) British politician, born in Lerwick, Shetland Is. He was appointed financial secretary to the Treasury in 1986, and in 1990 managed John Major's successful campaign for the Conservative Party leadership and was rewarded with the post of Chancellor of the Exchequer. Following his replacement in the 1993 Cabinet reshuffle, he launched an attack on Major's policies.

Lampedusa, Giuseppe Tomasi, duca di (Duke of) **Palma** [lampedooza] (1896–1957) Writer, born in Palermo, Sicily. His only complete work, *Il gattopardo* (The Leopard), was published in 1958.

lamprey Primitive jawless fish (*Petromyzon marinus*) found in marine and adjacent fresh waters of the N Atlantic; length up to 90 cm/36 in; mouth sucker-like with rasping teeth; may be a serious pest to local fisheries. (Family: Petromyzonidae.)

lamp shell An unsegmented, marine invertebrate possessing a bivalve shell and a long stalk; feeds using an array of tentacles around the mouth; contains c.350 living species; over 12 000 fossil species described. (Phylum: Brachiopoda.)

LAN *local area network*

Lancashire pop (2001e) 1 135 000;area 3063 km²/1182 sq mi. County of NW England; county town, Preston; Blackpool and Blackburn unitary authorities from 1998; ports at Heysham, Fleetwood; world centre for cotton manufacture in 19th-c.

Lancaster (UK) 54°03N 2°48W, pop (2001e) 133 900. Town in Lancashire, NW England; on R Lune; chartered, 1193; city status, 1937; university (1964); railway; 12th-c castle, on site of Roman fort.

Lancaster (USA) *Lincoln* (USA)

Lancaster, Burt(on Stephen) (1913–94) Film actor, born in New York City. Cast early on in a succession of tough-guy roles, he increasingly found opportunities to show his dramatic abilities, notably in *From Here to Eternity* (1953), *Elmer Gantry* (1960, Oscar), and *Birdman of Alcatraz* (1962). Later films include *Local Hero* (1983) and *Field of Dreams* (1989).

Lancaster, Sir Osbert (1908–86) Cartoonist and writer, born in London. He began drawing cartoons for the *Daily Express* in 1939, creating Maudie Littlehampton and other characters.

Lancaster, Duchy of *Duchy of Lancaster*

Lancaster, House of The younger branch of the Plantagenet dynasty, founded by Edmund 'Crouchback', the younger son of Henry III and first earl of Lancaster (1267–96), whence came three kings of England: Henry IV (1399–1413); Henry V (1413–22); and Henry VI (1422–61, 1470–1).

lancehead viper *fer-de-lance*

lancelet *amphioxus*

Lancelot, Sir or **Launcelot du Lac** The most famous of King Arthur's knights, though a relatively late addition to the legend. He was the courtly lover of Guinevere, and the father of Galahad by Elaine.

lancet A sharp pointed arch in a building, mainly used in Early English architecture of the 13th-c. It may also refer to a tall and narrow pointed-arch window of the same period.

Lanchow *Lanzhou*

Land, Edwin (Herbert) (1909–91) Inventor and physicist, born in Bridgeport, CT. His 'Land Polaroid' camera (1947) was a system of instant photography, with developing agents incorporated in the film itself.

Landers, Ann, pseudonym of **Esther Pauline Friedman Lederer** (1918–2002) Journalist, born in Sioux City, IA. In 1955 she inherited her job as a Chicago-based advice columnist from a previous 'Ann Landers', creating an international institution, and won many public service awards for her open discussions of medical issues.

Land League An association formed in Ireland in 1879 by Michael Davitt to agitate for greater tenant rights, in particular the '3 Fs': *fair rents*; *fixity of tenure* while rents were paid; and *freedom* for tenants to sell rights of occupancy. Gladstone conceded the essence of these demands in the 1881 Land Act.

Landor, Walter Savage (1775–1864) Writer, born in Warwick, Warwickshire. He wrote poems, plays, and essays, but is mainly remembered for his prose dialogues, *Imaginary Conversations* (1824–9).

Landowska, Wanda (Louise) [landofska] (1877–1959) Pianist, harpsichordist, and musical scholar, born in Warsaw. In 1927 she established in Paris her Ecole de Musique Ancienne, where she gave specialized training in the performance of old works.

landrace A type of domestic pig; long, pale body with large pendulous ears; bred mainly for bacon; three varieties.

landrail *corncrake*

land registration A legal procedure in which ownership of land (*title*) is officially registered. In England and Wales, this is with the **Land Registry**. Registration is now compulsory in all areas on transfer, though there is no compulsion on existing owners to register. It simplifies the procedure whereby land is transferred from vendor to purchaser. In the USA, all states have recording systems for instruments affecting the title to land.

landscape gardening The art of laying out gardens and estates for aesthetic or spiritual effect. A variety of techniques are used, including terracing, the use of artificial mounds, still and running water, walls, and trees. In 18th-c Europe, formal landscaping (as in the work of Le Nôtre, who made heavy use of symmetry, topiary, and artificial ornament) gave way to an artfully informal naturalism, seen particularly in the work of Kent, Repton, and Capability Brown.

landscape painting The representation of natural history in art. The depiction of unified landscape for its own sake, frequently with a moral dimension, dates only from the 16th-c in Europe, though 600 years earlier in China.

Landseer, Sir Edwin (Henry) (1802–73) Artist, born in London. Dogs and deer were his main subjects, and several of his pictures are located in the highlands of Scotland. His paintings include 'Monarch of the Glen' (1851), and his most famous sculptures are the bronze lions in Trafalgar Square (1867).

Land's End, ancient **Bolerium** 50°03N 5°44W. A granite headland in Cornwall, SW England; the W extremity of England.

Lane, Sir Allen, originally **Allen Lane Williams** (1902–70) Publisher and pioneer of paperback books, born in Bristol, SW England. In 1935 he formed Penguin Books Ltd, a revolutionary step in the publishing trade.

Lang, Fritz (1890–1976) Film director, born in Vienna. His films include *Metropolis* (1926) and, after moving to the USA, *Fury* (1936) and *The Big Heat* (1953).

Langdon, Harry (Philmore) (1884–1944) Film comedian, born in Council Bluffs, IA. He appeared in several popular feature films, notably *Tramp Tramp Tramp* (1926), *The Strong Man* (1926), and *Long Pants* (1927), and is remembered for his character as a baby-faced innocent, bemused by the wider world.

Lange, David (Russell) [longee] (1942–) New Zealand statesman and prime minister (1984–9), born in Auckland, New Zealand. A lawyer by profession, he became leader of the Labour Party in 1983, and prime minister in the fourth Labour government.

Langland, William, also spelled **Langley** (c.1332–c.1400) Poet, probably born in Ledbury, Herefordshire. He is credited with the authorship of the great mediaeval alliterative poem on the theme of spiritual pilgrimage, *Piers Plowman* (written over an uncertain period from c.1360).

Langley, Samuel (Pierpont) (1834–1906) Astronomer and aeronautics pioneer, born in Roxbury (now part of Boston), MA. He invented the bolometer for measuring the Sun's radiant heat, and was the first to build a heavier-than-air flying machine – a steam-powered model aircraft.

Langmuir, Irving [langmyoor] (1881–1957) Physical chemist, born in New York City. He received the Nobel Prize for Chemistry in 1932 for his work on solid and liquid surfaces. His many inventions include the gas-filled tungsten lamp and atomic hydrogen welding.

Langobards *Lombards*

Langton, Stephen (c.1150–1228) Theologian, born (possibly) in Lincolnshire. He studied at the University of Paris. He became a cardinal in 1206, and Archbishop of Canterbury in 1207. He sided warmly with the barons against King John, and his name is the first of the subscribing witnesses of Magna Carta.

Langtry, Lillie, popular name of **Emilie Charlotte Langtry**, *née* **Le Breton**, nickname **the Jersey Lily** (1853–1929) Actress, born in Jersey, Channel Is. One of the most noted beauties of her time, she made her first important stage appearance in 1881, and managed the Imperial Theatre. She was also known for her close friendship with Edward VII.

language 1 A species-specific communicative ability, restricted to humans, which involves the use of sounds, grammar, and vocabulary, according to a system of rules. Though other animals can communicate vocally and by gesture, they are restricted to a particular set of messages, genetically given, which cannot be creatively varied. **2** An individual manifestation of **1**, found within a particular community. The designation of 'language' status is dependent on a wide variety of social, linguistic, and political considerations, and as a result, estimates of the number of living languages in the world (usually ranging between 5000 and 7000) are uncertain.

language laboratory A room made up of banks of booths, each one containing a cassette recorder for a student's use, connected to a central console. At the console, a language instructor monitors the performance of students as they listen to taped exercises and record their responses to them. Its great advantage is that the students are able to advance at their own pace. Modern laboratories are now often equipped with video recorders and various kinds of computational aids.

Languedoc [lãguhdok] Former province in S France; name derived from the local variety of language, *langue d'oc* (Provençal); centre of wine production.

langur [langgoor] An Old World monkey, native to S and SE Asia; prominent dark 'eyebrows'; slender hand with short thumb; long tail; inhabits forests; two genera: **langur** or **leaf monkey** (*Presbytis*, 15 species) and **snub-nosed langur** (*Pygathrix*, 4 species).

Lanier, Sidney [laneer] (1842–81) Poet, born in Macon, GA. Among his writings are a novel and several works of criticism, but he is best remembered for his poems, which broke away from traditional metrical techniques.

lanolin [lanolin] A waxy material occurring naturally in wool. It is a mixture of esters of cholesterol with stearic, palmitic, and oleic acids. It forms strong emulsions with water, and is used in toilet preparations and ointments.

Lansbury, George (1859–1940) British politician, born near Lowestoft, Suffolk. Active as a radical, he founded and edited the *Daily Herald* (1912–22), and became leader of the Labour Party (1931–5).

L'Anse aux Meadows [lahnsee medohz] An isolated Norse settlement of nine turf-built houses in Newfoundland, Canada, discovered in 1961. Built AD c.970–1000, the settlement proves that the Vikings reached North America in pre-Columbian times. It is a world heritage site.

Lansing 42°44N 84°33W, pop (2000e) 119 100. Capital of state in SC Michigan, USA, on the Grand R; railway; car and truck manufacturing centre.

lanternfish Any of the small deep-sea fishes of family Myctophidae (6 genera), widely abundant in the world's oceans; length up to 15 cm/6 in; head blunt, eyes large, body with numerous light organs in characteristic patterns.

lanthanides [lanthaniydz] or **rare earth elements** Elements with atomic numbers from 58–72 inclusive. They have very similar chemistry, mainly forming compounds in which they show oxidation state +3.

Lanza, Mario, originally **Alfredo Arnold Cocozza** (1921–59) Tenor, born in Philadelphia, PA. Discovered while working in the family's grocery business, he went on to Hollywood to appear in several musicals. His most famous role was in *The Great Caruso* (1951).

Lanzhou [lahnjoh], **Lan-chou**, or **Lanchow** 36°01N 103°19E, pop (2000e) 1 803 000. Capital of Gansu province, NC China, on the upper Yellow R; airfield; railway; university (1946); centre for China's atomic energy industry since 1960.

Laoighis, Laois [layish], or **Leix** [layks], formerly **Queen's County** pop (2000e) 53 000; area 1720 km²/664 sq mi. County in Leinster province, SC Ireland; capital, Portlaoighise.

Laos *p.524*

Laozi [lautsee], also spelled **Lao-tzu** or **Lao-tse** ('Old Master') (?6th-c BC) A sage and recluse, the reputed founder of Taoism, probably a legendary figure. The *Tao Te Ching* or the *Lao Tzu*, the most venerated of the three classical texts of Taoism, is attributed to him, though it dates from much later.

La Paz [la pas] 16°30S 68°10W, pop (2000e) 1 244 000. Capital of Bolivia, altitude 3636 m/11 929 ft; founded by Spanish, 1548; airport; railway; university (1830); cathedral.

lapis lazuli [lapis lazyuliy, lazyulee] A deep-blue ornamental stone, principally lazurite (a silicate of sodium and aluminium), found in metamorphosed limestones.

Laplace, Pierre Simon, Marquis de [laplas], also known as **Comte de** (Count of) **Laplace** (1749–1827) Mathematician and astronomer, born in Beaumont-en-Auge, France. His 5-volume *Mécanique céleste* (1799–1825, Celestial Mechanics) is a landmark in applied mathematics.

Lapland, Swed **Lappland**, Finn **Lapin Lääni** pop (2000e) 207 000, area 98 938 km²/38 190 sq mi. Province of N Finland, mainly within Arctic Circle; largely tundra (N), forest (S), and mountains (W); occupies c.30% of total area of Finland; provincial capital, Rovaniemi. The area generally called Lapland also includes large parts of Norway, Sweden, and Russia.

La Plata [la plahta] 34°52S 57°55W, pop (2000e) 610 200. Port on the R Plate, SE of Buenos Aires; founded in 1882; three universities (1884, 1965, 1968); named **Eva Perón** (1946–55); railway; main outlet for produce from the pampas.

Lapp A people living in the sparsely populated N areas of Finland, Sweden, Norway, and Russia, with more than half in Norway. Most are fishermen, while others farm, breed reindeer, are foresters, and work in factories.

laptop computer A small lightweight computer, usually powered by internal batteries, which can easily be carried around and used comfortably on the user's lap. They became generally available in the mid-1980s.

lapwing A plover, especially the **common lapwing** (*Vanellus vanellus*); inhabits grassland, cultivation, water edges, and swamps. (Genus: *Vanellus*, 10 species. Family: Charadriidae.)

Lara, Brian (1969–) Cricketer, born in Cantaro, Trinidad, West Indies. He came to prominence in the 1994 season, when he broke several cricketing records, including a world record Test innings of 375 for the West Indies against England. He became the world's first batsman to score over 500 runs in one innings in first-class cricket. He captained the West Indies between 1997–9 and 2003–5. In 2005 he became the highest run-scorer in Test cricket history when he surpassed Allan Border's record of 11 174 runs.

larch A deciduous conifer native to colder parts of the N hemisphere; long shoots rough-textured with persistent bases of fallen leaves; short shoots with tufts of needles; widely planted for timber. (Genus: *Larix*, 10–12 species. Family: Pinaceae.)

lard A fat produced from pigs, widely used in cooking and baking, and also in the preparation of certain perfumes and ointments. **Lard oil** is used as a lubricant and in soap manufacture.

Lardner, Ring(gold Wilmer) (1885–1933) Writer, born in Niles, MI.

Laos

□ International Airport

[lows], official name **Lao People's Democratic Republic**, Lao **Sathalanalat Paxathipatai Paxaxôn Lao**
Local name Lao
Timezone GMT +7
Area 236 800 km²/91 405 sq mi
Population total (2002e) 5 777 000
Status Republic

Date of independence 1949
Capital Vientiane
Languages Lao (official), French, and tribal languages
Ethnic groups Laotian (60%), hill tribes (35%)
Religions Buddhist (58%), animist (largely the Lao-Theung) (34%), Christian (2%)
Physical features Landlocked country on the Indo-Chinese peninsula; dense jungle and rugged mountains (E), rising to 2751 m/9025 ft on Vietnamese border, and 2820 m/9252 ft at Phou Bia on the Xieng Khouang plateau; Mekong R flows NW–SE, fertile Mekong floodplains in W; 4% of land arable, 58% forested.
Climate Monsoonal climate; average annual rainfall 1715 mm/67·5 in; (heaviest, May–Sep); average annual temperature 14°C (Jan), 34°C (Jul) in Vientiane.
Currency (1992) 1 Kip (LAK) = 100 at
Economy Agricultural economy suffered severely in the civil war; rice, coffee, tobacco, cotton, spices, opium; tin, iron ore, potash; forestry (1991 logging ban to halt deforestation), rubber, cigarettes, matches; textiles.
GDP (2002e) $10·4 bn, per capita $1800
Human Development Index (2002) 0·485
History Visited by Europeans, 17th-c; formed French Indo-Chinese Union with Cambodia and Vietnam, 1887; French protectorate, 1893; occupied by Japanese in World War 2; independence from France, 1949; civil war, 1953–75, between the Lao government, supported by the USA, and the communist-led Patriotic Front (Pathet Lao), supported by North Vietnam; monarchy abolished and communist republic established, 1975; draft constitution approved, 1991 provides for a directly elected National Assembly and executive President.

Head of State
1991–2 Kaysone Phomvihane
1992–8 Nouhak Phoumsavan
1998–2006 Khamtay Siphandon
2006– Choummaly Sayasone

Head of Government
1991–8 Khamtay Siphandon
1998–2001 Sisavat Keobounphanh
2001–6 Boungnang Vorachith
2006– Bouasone Bouphavanh

He wrote prolifically in a variety of forms: novels, plays, satirical verse (*Bib Ballads*, 1915), and an autobiography, *The Story of a Wonder Man* (1927), but is mainly appreciated for his short stories.

lark A small, dull-coloured songbird, found mainly in the Old World, especially Africa; nests on ground. (Family: Alaudidae, 75 species.)

Larkin, Philip (Arthur) (1922–85) Poet and novelist, born in Coventry, West Midlands. His collections of poems include *The Less Deceived* (1955) and *High Windows* (1974). *Collected Poems* was published posthumously (1988) and became a best seller. His *Letters* appeared in 1992. He also edited the *Oxford Book of Twentieth Century English Verse* (1973). In 2004, hundreds of unpublished works were discovered in the library archives at Leicester University.

larkspur An annual native to the N hemisphere; related to delphiniums; flowers blue, pink, or white, borne in short spikes. (Genus: *Consolida*, 40 species. Family: Ranunculaceae.)

Larnaca [lah(r)naka], Gr **Larnax**, Turkish **Larnaka**, **Iskele** 34°55N 33°36E, pop (2000e) 68 400. Port in S Cyprus; airport; old Turkish fort (1625), now a museum.

La Rochefoucauld, François, duc de (Duke of) [la roshfookoh] (1613–80) Writer, born in Paris. He was an active member of the opposition to Cardinal Richelieu, and fought in the Fronde revolts (1648–53). His major works were written while in retirement: *Mémoires* (1664) and the epigrammatic collection commonly known as the *Maximes* (1665, Maxims).

Larousse, Pierre (Athanase) [laroos] (1817–75) Lexicographer and encyclopedist, born in Toucy, France. He wrote several grammars, dictionaries, and other textbooks, notably his *Grand dictionnaire universel du XIXe siècle* (15 vols, 1865–76).

larva A general term for a stage in an animal's development between hatching and the attainment of the adult form, or maturity. Larval stages are often typical of the group, such as the caterpillar larva of butterflies.

laryngitis [larinjiytis] Acute or chronic inflammation of the larynx, with swelling of the vocal cords. It often accompanies infection elsewhere in the respiratory tract.

larynx That part of the air passage lying in humans between the trachea (below) and the laryngopharynx (above), situated in the middle of the front of the neck; also called the 'voice box', because it contains the *vocal cords*. It consists of a framework of cartilages joined together by a number of ligaments and moves upwards on swallowing. The prominent hard projection in the front of the neck, especially in males (the *Adam's apple*), is part of the thyroid cartilage.

La Salle, René Robert Cavelier, sieur de (Lord of) [la **sal**] (1643–87) Explorer, born in Rouen, France. He settled in Canada in 1666, and descended the Ohio and Mississippi to the sea (1682), naming the area Louisiana (after Louis XIV of France).

La Scala [la **skahla**], or **Teatro Alla Scala** (Ital 'theatre at the stairway') The world's most famous opera house, built (1776–8) on the site of the Church of Santa Maria della Scala in Milan, Italy. It closed in 2001 for extensive renovations and reopened in 2004.

Las Campanas Observatory An astronomical observatory on Cerro Las Campanas, Chile. Instruments include the 2·5 m/100 in du Pont reflector and the 1 m/39 in Swope reflector. The first of two 6·5 m/256 in telescopes, called Magellan, was completed in 2000 (named after Walter Baade); the second (named after Landon Clay) was completed in 2002.

Las Casas, Bartolomé de [las **kahsas**], known as **the Apostle of the Indians** (1474–1566) Missionary priest, born in Seville, Spain. He sailed in the third voyage of Columbus (1502) to Hispaniola, and travelled to Cuba (1513). His desire to protect the natives from slavery led him to visit the Spanish court on several occasions.

Lascaux [**laskoh**] A small, richly-decorated Palaeolithic cave of c.15 000 BC near Montignac, Dordogne, SW France, renowned for its naturalistic mural paintings and engravings of animals. It was closed in 1963, when humidity changes threatened the paintings, and a replica was opened nearby.

laser A device which produces light, infrared, or ultraviolet radiation with special properties, for example using a system of excited atoms; the name is an acronym of *light amplification by the stimulated emission of radiation*. The first laser was built in 1960 by physicist Theodore Maiman. Laser action depends on the choice of special atomic systems for which an energy supply is able to raise large numbers of atoms to excited states, ready to emit photons when stimulated. Mirrors at either end of the laser reflect light end-to-end inside the laser to maintain its action. At one end, the mirror is partially transparent, allowing a portion of the light to escape to produce a laser beam. Laser light is monochromatic (all one colour), coherent (in step), produced as a beam which does not spread, and travels large distances undiminished in intensity. The many uses of lasers include supermarket bar code scanners, welding, surveying, phototherapy in medicine, eye surgery, hologram production, compact disk systems, and directed energy weapons.

laser printer A type of printer which uses a small laser to generate characters. It generally operates using xerographic principles, and is capable of producing very high quality typescript and graphics.

laser typesetter A form of typesetting used by printers in which the characters are drawn by a computer-controlled laser onto a bromide film. The bromide film is then used to etch a lithographic plate from which the required documents are printed.

Laski, Harold J(oseph) (1893–1950) Political scientist and socialist, born in Manchester, Greater Manchester. The development of his political philosophy, a modified Marxism, can be seen in his many books, such as *Authority in the Modern State* (1919).

Laski, Marghanita (1915–88) Writer and critic, born in Manchester, Greater Manchester, the niece of Harold Laski. Her first novel, *Love on the Supertax*, appeared in 1944. She wrote extensively for newspapers and reviews, and published a number of critical works.

Las Palmas (de Gran Canaria) [**palmas**] pop (2000e) 760 000; area 4072 km²/1572 sq mi. Spanish province in the Canary Is, comprising the islands of Gran Canaria, Lanzarote, and Fuerteven-

tura; capital, Las Palmas (de Gran Canaria), pop (2000e) 347 000, resort and seaport (Puerto de la Luz); airport; cathedral.

Lassa fever An infectious disease caused by a virus confined at the present time to sub-Saharan W Africa. It is highly contagious, and causes fever, vomiting, chest pain, and haemorrhage. It carries a high mortality.

Lassus, Orlandus, also known as **Orlando di Lasso** (c.1532–94) Composer, born in Mons, Belgium. He wrote several Masses, motets, and psalms, and also a large number of madrigals and songs in French and German.

Last Supper In the New Testament Gospels, the last meal of Jesus with his disciples on the eve of his arrest and crucifixion. It is considered significant for Jesus's words over the bread and cup of wine, where he declares 'This is my body' and 'This is my blood' (*Mark* 14.22–4). The event is commemorated in the sacrament of Holy Communion.

Las Vegas [las **vaygas**] (Span 'the meadows') 36°10N 115°09W, pop (2000e) 478 400. Largest city in Nevada, USA; settled by Mormons, 1855–7; city status, 1911; airport; railway; university (1957); noted for its gaming casinos and 24-hour entertainment.

La Tène [la **ten**] A prehistoric site on the shores of L Neuchâtel, Switzerland, excavated from 1858. Its name is commonly used to describe the later European Iron Age that succeeded Hallstatt culture c.500 BC.

latent heat Heat absorbed or released when a substance undergoes a change of state at a constant temperature, such as solid to liquid (*latent heat of fusion*) or liquid to gas (*latent heat of vaporization*); symbol *L*, units J (joule).

laterality or **lateralization** A characteristic of the human brain, in which the left and right cerebral hemispheres are specialized for different functions; also known as **hemispheric specialization**. In the majority of people, the left hemisphere is specialized for language functions, and the right for the perception of complex patterns, both visual (eg faces) and tactile.

Lateran Church of St John The oldest of the four patriarchal basilicas of Rome, the episcopal seat of the pope as Bishop of Rome. The present building dates from the 16th-c.

Lateran Councils A series of councils of the Church held at the Lateran Palace, Rome, between the 7th-c and the 18th-c. The Fourth or Great Council (1215) defined the doctrine of the Eucharist (*transubstantiation*).

Lateran Treaty (1929) An agreement between the Italian fascist state and the papacy, ending a church-state conflict dating from 1870. Italy recognized the sovereignty of Vatican City, and Catholicism as the country's only religion; the papacy recognized the Italian state, and accepted the loss of other papal territories as irreversible.

laterite Tropical soil in which seasonal fluctuations of groundwater have concentrated aluminium and iron oxide, forming a thick, hard, reddish layer. It is often used as roadstone.

latex A milky fluid found in special cells or ducts (*lactifers*) and present in many different plants. It is usually white, but can be colourless, yellow, orange, or red, and contains various substances in solution or suspension, such as starch and rubber.

lathe A common machine tool used to shape workpieces of various materials. The tools for boring, threading, cutting, or facing the workpiece are brought into contact with it either manually or under machine control.

Latimer, Hugh (c.1485–1555) Protestant reformer and martyr, born in Thurcaston, Leicestershire. He was one of the divines who examined the lawfulness of Henry VIII's marriage, and declared on the king's side; but he opposed the Six Articles of Henry VIII, for which he was imprisoned in 1536, 1546, and 1553. He was tried for heresy under Mary and burned at Oxford.

Latin *Italic / Romance languages; Latin literature*

Latin America The 18 Spanish-speaking republics of the W hemi-

latitude and longitude

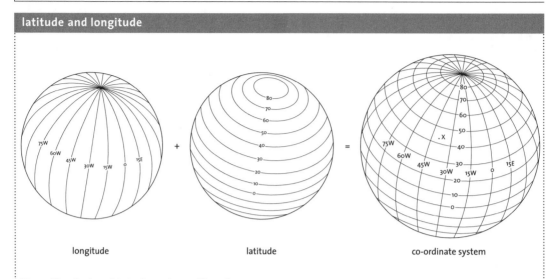

longitude   latitude   co-ordinate system

Lines of longitude and latitude on the Earth's surface, measured in degrees °, minutes ', and seconds ". The point x would have the following co-ordinate locations: 44°10'10"N, 39°25'40"W.

sphere, together with Portuguese-speaking Brazil (the largest Latin-American country) and French-speaking Haiti.

latitude and longitude Two dimensions used in mapping. The **latitude** of a point on the Earth's surface is the angular distance, N or S from the Equator (at latitude 0°); the Poles are at latitude 90°; lines (*parallels*) of latitude are parallel circles running E–W joining points of equal latitude. Important lines of latitude are the Tropic of Cancer (23.5° N), Tropic of Capricorn (23.5° S), the Arctic Circle (66.5° N), and the Antarctic Circle (66.5° S). Lines (*meridians*) of **longitude** are great circles running N–S and meeting at the Poles; the longitude is measured as an angular distance from the Greenwich meridian defined as 0° up to 180° E or W. (*see panel*)

Latium [layshium] In antiquity, the area SE of Rome between the Apennine Mts and the sea. Densely populated in early Roman times, by the imperial period it had become the recreation area of the Roman rich, who filled it with luxurious villas.

La Tour, Georges de (1593–1652) Artist, born in Vic-sur-Seille, France. Only 14 of his paintings have been found, the best known being candle-lit religious scenes, such as 'St Jerome' and 'St Joseph' (Louvre).

La Tour, Maurice Quentin de [latoor], also spelled **Latour** (1704–88) Pastellist and portrait painter, born in St Quentin, France. His portraits include those of Louis XV, Madame de Pompadour, Voltaire, and Rousseau.

Latrobe, Benjamin (Henry) [latrohb] (1764–1820) Architect and civil engineer, born in Fulneck, West Yorkshire. He emigrated to the USA in 1795, where he introduced the Greek Revival style and was surveyor of public buildings in Washington, DC (1803–17). His most notable work is the Basilica of the Assumption of the Blessed Virgin Mary, Baltimore (begun 1805).

Latter-Day Saints (LDS) *Mormons*

Latvia *p.527*

Latynina, Larisa Semyonovna [lateenina] (1934–) Gymnast, born in Kherson, Ukraine. In 1956 and 1964 she collected 18 Olympic medals, a record for any sport, winning nine golds.

Laud, William [lawd] (1573–1645) Archbishop of Canterbury, born in Reading, S England. He became a Privy Councillor (1626), Bishop of London (1628), and Archbishop of Canterbury (1633). With Strafford and Charles I, he worked for absolutism in Church and state. In Scotland, his attempt (1635–7) to anglicize the Church led to the Bishops' Wars. In 1640 the Long Parliament impeached him, and he was executed.

Lauda, Niki [lowda], popular name of **Nikolas Andreas Lauda** (1949–) Motor-racing driver, born in Vienna. He was three times world champion, in 1975, 1977 (both Ferrari), and 1984 (Marlboro–McLaren), despite a horrific crash in 1976. He finally retired in 1985 after 25 career wins, and became the proprietor of Lauda-Air.

laudanum [lawdanum] A preparation of opium introduced by Paracelsus in the early 16th-c. Addiction to laudanum was socially acceptable until the early 19th-c.

Lauder, Estée [lawder], *née* **Mentzer** (1908–2004) Businesswoman, born in New York City. She co-founded cosmetics company Estée Lauder Inc with her husband **Joseph Lauder** in 1946, and had great success with the fragrance 'Youth Dew' in the 1950s. She retired in 1995 and the role of head of the family business passed to her daughter-in-law, **Evelyn Lauder** (1937–).

Lauder, Sir Harry (MacLennan) [lawder] (1870–1950) Singer, born in Edinburgh. Originally a music hall comedian, he made his name as a singer of Scots songs, many of which he wrote himself, such as 'Roamin' in the Gloamin''.

Lauderdale, John Maitland, Duke of [lawderdayl] (1616–82) Scottish statesman, born in Lethington, East Lothian. He was taken prisoner at Worcester (1651), and imprisoned. At the Restoration (1660) he became Scottish secretary of state. A privy councillor, he was a member of the Cabal, advisers to Charles II.

laughing gas *nitrous oxide*

laughing jackass / kookaburra *kookaburra*

Laughlin, Robert B (1950–) Physicist, born in Vesalia, CA. He graduated from MIT in 1979, joining Stanford University, and shared the 1998 Nobel Prize for Physics for his contribution to

Latvia

☐ International Airport

official name **Republic of Latvia**, Latvian **Latviya**, Russ **Latviskaya**

Local name Latvija (Latvian)

Timezone GMT +2

Area 64 600 km²/24 900 sq mi

Population total (2002e) 2 331 000

Status Republic

Date of independence 1991

Capital Riga

Language Latvian (official)

Ethnic groups Latvian (52%), Russian (34%), Belorussian (5%), Ukrainian (4%), Polish (2%), Lithuanian (1%)

Religions Predominantly Evangelical Lutheran, with Orthodox and Roman Catholic minorities

Physical features Flat, glaciated region; highest point, central Vidzeme (Livonia) elevation, 312 m/1024 ft; over 40% forested; coastline ranges over 472 km/293 mi; wooded lowland, marshes, lakes; NW coast indented by the Gulf of Riga; chief river, Daugava.

Climate Mild climate, with high humidity; only c.30–40 days of sunshine annually; summers cool and rainy; average mean temperature -2°C (Jan), 17°C (Jul); average annual rainfall 700–800 mm/28–31 in.

Currency (1991) 1 Latvian Lat (LVL) = 100 santims

Economy Machine-building, metalworking, electrical engineering, electronics, chemicals, furniture, food processing, fishing, timber, paper and woollen goods, meat and dairy products.

GDP (2002e) $20·99 bn, per capita $8900

Human Development Index (2002) 0·800

History Incorporated into Russia, 1721; independent state, 1918–40; proclaimed a Soviet Socialist Republic, 1940; occupied by Germany in World War 2; USSR regained control, 1944; coalition government elected, 1989; declared independence, 1991; governed by a President, Prime Minister and Congress of Latvia; joined European Union, 2004.

Head of State
1991–3 Anatolijs Gorbunovs
1993–9 Guntis Ulmanis
1999– Vaira Vike-Freiberga

Head of Government
1997–8 Guntar Krasts
1998–9 Vilis Kristopans
1999–2000 Andris Skele
2000–2 Andris Berzins
2002–4 Einars Repse
2004 Indulis Emsis
2004– Aigars Kalvitis

the discovery of a new form of quantum fluid with fractionally charged excitations.

Laughton, Charles [lawtn] (1899–1962) Actor, born in Scarborough, North Yorkshire. He began to act in films in 1932, and portrayed a wide range of memorable roles, such as Henry VIII in *The Private Life of Henry VIII* (1932, Oscar) and Captain Bligh in *Mutiny on the Bounty* (1935).

Launceston [lonsestn] 41°25S 147°07E, pop (2000e) 73 200 (Greater Launceston). Second largest city in Tasmania, Australia; airfield; railway.

launch vehicle A rocket-propelled vehicle used to carry aloft spacecraft from the Earth's surface, generally consisting of several 'stages' which separate sequentially as fuel in each is consumed. The thrust is provided by the controlled explosive burning of liquid fuels (eg kerosene and oxygen, hydrogen and oxygen) or solid propellants (typically a synthetic rubber fuel mixed with an oxidizer powder).

Laurasia The name given to the N 'supercontinent' comprising present-day North America, Europe, and Asia, excluding India, which began to break away from the single land mass Pangaea about 200 million years ago.

laurel A name applied to various unrelated trees and shrubs which have glossy, leathery, evergreen leaves, but mainly to members of the large family Lauraceae, in which the tissues contain numerous oil cavities and are aromatic.

Laurel and Hardy Comedians who formed the first Hollywood film comedy team. The 'thin one', **Stan Laurel** (1890–1965), originally **Arthur Stanley Jefferson**, was born in Ulverston, Lancashire. He went to the USA in 1910, and worked in silent films from 1917. The 'fat one', **Oliver Hardy** (1892–1957), born near Atlanta, GA, joined a troupe of minstrels before drifting into the film industry. They came together in 1926. They made many full-length feature films, but their best efforts are generally thought to be their early (1927–31) shorts.

Lauren, Ralph [loren], originally **Ralph Lifschitz** (1939–) Fashion designer, born in New York City. He is famous for his American styles, such as 'prairie look' and 'frontier fashions'.

Laurentian Shield *Canadian Shield*

Laurie, (James) Hugh (Calum) (1959–) Actor and writer, born in Oxford, Oxfordshire. He studied at Cambridge University (1978) where he met Stephen Fry, with whom he formed a prolific comedy writing partnership, producing the television series *A Bit of Fry and Laurie* (1986–95). He appeared in the series *Blackadder* (1986–9) and *Jeeves and Wooster* (1990–3), and his feature films include *Sense and Sensibility* (1995) and *Stuart Little* (1999, sequels 2002, 2003). In 2004 he was cast as Dr Gregory House in the popular US drama series *House M.D.* for which he won a Golden Globe Best Actor award in 2007.

Laurier, Sir Wilfrid [loryay] (1841–1919) Canadian statesman and prime minister (1896–1911), born in St Lin, Quebec, Canada. Leader of the Liberal Party (1887–1919), he was the first French-Canadian to be prime minister of Canada.

laurustinus [loruhstiynuhs] A dense evergreen shrub or small tree (*Viburnum tinus*), growing to 7 m/23 ft, native to S Europe; flowers 5-petalled, white, in clusters; fruit berry-like, dark, metallic blue. (Family: Caprifoliaceae.)

Lausanne [lohzan] 46°32N 6°39E, pop (2000e) 129 000. Tourist resort and convention centre in W Switzerland; seat of the Federal Supreme Court; on N shore of L Geneva; railway junction; university (1891); seat of the International Olympic Committee; cathedral (1275).

Lauterbur, Paul C [lowterboor] (1929–2007) Chemist, born in Sidney, OH. He became professor of chemistry at New York University, Stony Brook (1969–85), and was then appointed director of the Biomedical Magnetic Resonance Laboratory at the University of Illinois, Urbana-Champaign. In 2003 he shared the Nobel Prize for Physiology or Medicine for discoveries concerning magnetic resonance imaging.

lava Hot molten rock erupted onto the Earth's surface from a volcano. On solidification it forms volcanic igneous rocks such as rhyolite, andesite, or basalt.

Laval, Pierre (1883–1945) French statesman and prime minister (1931–2, 1935–6), born in Châteldon, France. In the Vichy government he was Pétain's deputy (1940), then his rival. As prime minister (1942–4), he openly collaborated with the Germans. After the war he was executed in Paris.

lavallier *microphone*

La Vallière, Louise-Françoise de La Baume le Blanc, duchesse de (Duchess of) [la valyair] (1644–1710) Mistress of Louis XIV of France (1661–7), born in Tours, France. She bore the king four children, and remained at court reluctantly after Mme de Montespan superseded her (1667).

lavender A small aromatic shrub, native mainly to Mediterranean regions and Atlantic islands, typical of dry scrub; flowers 2-lipped, lavender or mauve, in dense spikes. (Genus: *Lavandula*, 28 species. Family: Labiatae.)

Laver, Rod(ney George) [layver], nickname **the Rockhampton Rocket** (1938–) Tennis player, born in Rockhampton, Queensland, Australia. The first person to achieve the Grand Slam twice (1962, 1969), he won four singles titles at Wimbledon (1961–2, 1968–9).

Lavoisier, Antoine Laurent [lavwazyay] (1743–94) Chemist, born in Paris, regarded as the founder of modern chemistry. In 1788 he showed that air is a mixture of gases which he called oxygen and nitrogen, thus disproving the earlier theory of phlogiston. His major work is the *Traité élémentaire de chimie* (1789). He also devised the modern method of naming chemical compounds. Politically a liberal, and despite his many reforms, he was guillotined in Paris on a contrived charge of counter-revolutionary activity.

Law, (Andrew) Bonar [law, boner] (1858–1923) British statesman and prime minister (1922–3), born in New Brunswick, Canada. In 1911 he succeeded Balfour as Unionist leader. He acted as colonial secretary (1915–16), Chancellor of the Exchequer (1916–18), and Lord Privy Seal (1919), before serving for a short time as premier.

Law, (David) Jude (1972–) Actor, born in London. His feature films include *Wilde* (1997), *The Talented Mr Ripley* (1999), *Cold Mountain* (2003), *Alfie* (2004), and *Breaking and Entering* (2006). He was married (1997–2003) to actress Sadie Frost.

Law, William (1686–1761) Clergyman, born in Kingscliffe, Northamptonshire. He wrote several treatises on Christian ethics and

mysticism, notably the *Serious Call to a Devout and Holy Life* (1729), which influenced the Wesleys.

law Specifically, a rule of conduct laid down by a controlling authority; generally, the whole body of such rules, recognized and enforced by society in the courts. In common law systems, the courts are particularly influential in developing the law, through the accretion of case decisions. In states with a written constitution, such as the USA, the Supreme Court may have the power to declare particular laws unconstitutional.

Law Commission Body established by the Law Commissions Act (1965) for England and Wales (with a separate commission for Scotland), appointed by the Lord Chancellor from the judiciary and from practising and academic lawyers. Its function is to examine the law with a view to reform and codification.

Lawler, Ray(mond Evenor) (1921–) Playwright and actor, born in Melbourne, Victoria, Australia. He achieved international fame with his play about the outback, *Summer of the Seventeenth Doll* (1955), in which he took the leading role.

Lawrence D(avid) H(erbert Richard) (1885–1930) Poet and novelist, born in Eastwood, Nottinghamshire. He achieved fame with *Sons and Lovers* (1913), but was prosecuted for obscenity after publishing *The Rainbow* (1915). He left England in 1919, living in Italy, Australia, the USA, and Mexico, and returning to Italy for health reasons in 1921. Other major novels include *Women in Love* (1921), *The Plumed Serpent* (1926), and *Lady Chatterley's Lover* (1928). He also wrote many short stories, short novels, and travel books. His letters are an important part of his output.

Lawrence, Ernest (Orlando) (1901–58) Physicist, born in Canton, SD. He constructed the first cyclotron for the production of high-energy atomic particles, and was awarded the Nobel Prize for Physics in 1939.

Lawrence, Stephen (1974–93) Victim of racist murder, born in London. The five white youths suspected of killing the black student claimed their right to silence and refused to answer questions at the inquest. Criminal charges against them were dropped by the police 'for lack of sufficient evidence', and a private prosecution brought by Lawrence's parents also collapsed for the same reason. An official inquiry into the case led by Sir William Macpherson concluded that the police investigations had been marred by professional incompetence and institutional racism.

Lawrence, T(homas) E(dward), known as **Lawrence of Arabia** (1888–1935) British soldier and writer, born in Tremadoc, Gwynedd. In 1916 he was appointed the British liaison officer to the Arab Revolt, and was present at the taking of Aqaba in 1917 and of Damascus in 1918. His account of the Arab Revolt, *Seven Pillars of Wisdom*, became one of the classics of war literature, and his exploits received so much publicity that he became a legendary figure.

Law Society The professional body for solicitors in England and Wales; a separate Law Society exists for Scotland and another for Northern Ireland. It has disciplinary powers relating to solicitors' conduct, and prescribes the rules governing their admission to practice.

Lawson, Henry (1867–1922) Poet, born in Grenfell, New South Wales, Australia. His bush ballads and stories, published by *The Bulletin* from 1888, were immensely popular, and many now see him as the national poet. He was given a state funeral when he died.

Lawson, Louisa (1848–1920) Suffragist and social reformer, born in Mudgee, New South Wales, Australia. In 1888 she founded *Dawn*, Australia's first feminist journal, which elevated women's affairs and promoted women's suffrage.

Lawson (of Blaby), Nigel, Baron (1932–) British Conservative statesman, born in London. Elected to parliament in 1974, he became financial secretary to the Treasury (1979–81), energy secretary (1981–3), and Chancellor of the Exchequer (1983–9).

Lawson, Nigella (1960–) Journalist and cookery writer, born in London. The daughter of politician Nigel Lawson, she studied at Oxford (1979) and entered journalism, becoming deputy literary editor of *The Sunday Times*. Her first book *How to Eat* (1998) was the basis for her Channel 4 television series, *Nigella Bites*, with an accompanying book (2001). Other bestsellers include *How to be a Domestic Goddess* (2000, Guild of Food Writers Award), *Forever Summer* (2002), and *Feast* (2004).

laxative A drug which causes emptying of the bowels; also known as a **purgative**. Examples include castor oil and diphenylmethane.

Laxness, Halldór (Gujónsson Kiljan) (1902–98) Writer, born in Reykjavík. His works include *Salka Valka* (1934), a story of Icelandic fishing folk, and the epic *Sjálfstaet folk* (1934–5, Independent People). He was awarded the Nobel Prize for Literature in 1955.

Layamon [layamon] (13th-c) English priest and poet, who lived at Areley Kings, on the R Severn, Worcestershire. He wrote one of the first poems in Middle English, recounting the history of England from the arrival of a legendary Trojan, Brutus, down to the 7th-c AD.

Lazarists A religious order, founded in France at the priory of St Lazare, Paris, in 1625 by St Vincent de Paul; properly known as the **Congregation of the Mission** (**CM**); also called the **Vincentians**.

L-dopa or **levodopa** A drug used very effectively in the treatment of Parkinson's disease. It reduces symptoms in more than two-thirds of patients.

Leach, Bernard (Howell) (1887–1979) Studio potter, born in Hong Kong. He studied in Japan (1911–19), then established a pottery at St Ives, Cornwall, where he made earthenware and stoneware. He played a crucial role in promoting handmade pottery which could be appreciated as art. His elder son, **David Leach** (1911–2005), became a renowned potter and teacher, and was also manager of the Leach Pottery.

Leach, Johnny, popular name of **John Leach** (1922–) Table tennis player, born in Romford, Essex. He won the world singles title in 1949 and 1951, and represented his country 152 times.

Leacock, Stephen (Butler) (1869–1944) Economist and humorist, born in Swanmore, Hampshire. His family emigrated to Canada when he was six. His popular short stories, essays, and parodies include *Literary Lapses* (1910) and *Nonsense Novels* (1911).

lead Pb (from Lat *plumbum*) element 82, a soft, dense (11·5 g/cm^3) metal, melting point 328°C. Its main natural source is the sulphide (PbS). Its good corrosion resistance and easy workability led to its early use in plumbing and for corrosive liquids containers, with considerable toxic results, as it is slowly oxidized in the presence of air and water.

leaf The main photosynthetic organ of green plants, divided into a blade (*lamina*) and a stalk (*petiole*). The lamina is usually broad and thin, to present maximum surface area to sunlight and allow easy diffusion of gases and water vapour to and from the leaf. It is composed of several distinct layers of tissues: the *epidermis* protects the inner tissues – the *palisade layer*, which is the primary site of photosynthesis, and the *spongy mesophyll*, which has large air spaces and is the primary site of gas exchange. A network of vascular tissues, the *veins*, transports water and sap to and from the leaf. The epidermis secretes a waxy cuticle, mostly impervious to water and gases which enter and leave via pores (stomata) concentrated in the lower surface of the leaf. Leaves range from a few mm to 20 m/65 ft in length, exhibit a great variety of shapes, and may be entire, toothed, lobed, or completely divided into separate *leaflets*. Leaves may also have specialized functions, such as water-storage in succulents, traps in carnivorous plants, and tendrils in climbers.

leaf beetle A robust, often brightly coloured beetle; most are surface feeders on plant leaves. (Order: Coleoptera. Family: Chrysomelidae, c.35 000 species.)

leaf hopper A small, hopping insect that feeds by sucking sap or cell contents of plants; causes damage by direct feeding, by toxic secretions, and by transmitting viral diseases. (Order: Homoptera. Family: Cicadellidae, c.20 000 species.)

League of Nations An international organization whose constitution was drafted at the Paris Peace Conference in 1919. The main aims were to preserve international peace and security by the prevention or speedy settlement of disputes and the promotion of disarmament. It became increasingly ineffective in the later 1930s, and after World War 2 transferred its functions to the United Nations.

League of Rights An Australian populist right-wing organization, founded in 1960 by Eric Butler (1916–2006). The League, which operates on the fringe of conservative politics, supports God, the Queen, the Commonwealth of Nations, apartheid, and private enterprise.

Leakey, L(ouis) S(eymour) B(azett) [leekee] (1903–72) Anthropologist, born in Kabete, Kenya. His great discoveries took place in E Africa, where in 1959 he and his wife **Mary Leakey** (1913–96, *née* Nicol) unearthed the skull of *Zinjanthropus*. In 1964 they found the remains of *Homo habilis* and in 1967 of *Kenyapithecus africanus*. Their son, **Richard Leakey** (1944–), has continued to make further important finds in the area.

Lean, Sir David (1908–91) Film director, born in Croydon, Greater London. In the 1950s–60s he produced three great epics: *The Bridge Over the River Kwai* (1957), *Lawrence of Arabia* (1962), and *Doctor Zhivago* (1965). Later films were *Ryan's Daughter* (1970) and *A Passage to India* (1984). In 1990, he became the first non-American to receive a life achievement award from the American Film Institute.

Leander *Hero and Leander*

Leaning Tower Ital **Torre Pendente** Marble belltower in Pisa, W Italy, 54 m/177 ft high, begun in 1173, completed in 1372. The ground beneath the tower began to sink after three storeys had been built, and the tower was 5·2 m/17 ft out of line in 1997. Closed to visitors in 1990, a programme of strengthening work stopped the process of tilting by 2000, and it was reopened in 2001.

leap year In the Gregorian calendar, a year of 366 days, with a day added to the month of February. Any year whose date is a number exactly divisible by four is a leap year, except years ending in 00, which must be divisible by 400 to be accounted leap years. The extra day is added every 4 years to allow for the difference between a year of 365 days and the actual time it takes the Earth to circle the Sun (approximately 365$\frac{1}{4}$ days).

Lear A legendary king of Britain, first recorded in Geoffrey of Monmouth, though his name resembles that of the Celtic god of the sea. Leicester is named after him.

Lear, Edward (1812–88) Artist and writer, born in London. He is remembered for his illustrated books of travels, and for his books of nonsense verse, beginning with *A Book of Nonsense* (1846).

lease A legal arrangement; also known as a **tenancy**, whereby the **lessor** (or landlord) grants the **lessee** (or tenant) the right to occupy land for a defined period of time.

leaseback An economic operation where a business sells an asset (such as property), the buyer renting (ie leasing) the asset back to the business. The firm continues to have use of the asset, but also has cash from the proceeds of the sale which it can use in other ways.

leasehold *freehold*

leather Animal skin rendered durable and resistant to wear and degeneration by tanning. The cleaned skin is soaked in solutions which contain tannins (tannic acids widely distributed in nature) or chrome salts. The properties of leather are due to its fibrous and porous structure, and to its resistance to deterioration on repeated wetting and drying.

leatherback turtle A sea-turtle (*Dermochelys coriacea*), worldwide in warm seas; the largest turtle (length, over 1·5 m/5 ft); no shell (adult has only small bony plates embedded in leathery skin); long front limbs (over 2·5 m/8 ft tip to tip); no claws; also known as **leathery turtle**. (Family: Dermochelyidae.)

leatherhead *friarbird*

leatherjacket *cranefly*

Leavis, F(rank) R(aymond) [leevis] (1895–1978) Critic, born in Cambridge, Cambridgeshire. He edited the journal *Scrutiny* (1932–53), and wrote several major critical works, such as *The Great Tradition* (1948) and *The Common Pursuit* (1952). Throughout his work (much of it shared with his wife Q D Leavis, 1906–81) he stresses the moral value of literary study.

Lebanon *p.531*

Lebed, Alexander (Ivanovich) [ljebed] (1950–2002) General and politician, born in Novocherkassk, Russia. He served in Afghanistan (1981–2) and the Caucasus (1988–90), and became Commander of the 14th Army in Moldova in 1992. After retiring from the army in 1995, he entered politics, coming to international attention during the 1996 presidential elections. He then gave his support to Yeltsin, was appointed National Security Advisor, and acted as chief negotiator in the Chechen conflict. After what many observers saw as a power struggle within the Kremlin, Yeltsin dismissed him. He then formed the Russian Popular Republican Party, and announced the continuation of his presidential aspirations. He died from injuries sustained in a helicopter crash.

LeBlanc, Matt(hew Steven) (1967–) Actor, born in Newton, MA. He played a range of television roles before achieving success as Joey Tribbiani in the acclaimed series *Friends* (1994–2004), and continued this role in a spin-off series *Joey* (2004–6). His feature films include *Lookin' Italian* (1994), *Lost in Space* (1998), and *Charlie's Angels: Full Throttle* (2003).

Lebowa [leboha] Former national state or non-independent black homeland in NE South Africa; self-governing status, 1972; incorporated into Northern Province in the South African constitution of 1994.

Le Brun, Charles [luh brõe] (1619–90) Historical painter, born in Paris. He helped to found the Academy of Painting and Sculpture in 1648, and was employed by Louis XIV in the decoration of Versailles (1668–83).

Le Carré, John [luh karay], pseudonym of **David John Moore Cornwell** (1931–) Novelist, born in Poole, Dorset. His first published novel, *Call for the Dead* (1961) introduced his 'anti-hero' George Smiley, who appears in most of his stories. Among his later books are *Tinker, Tailor, Soldier, Spy* (1974), *Smiley's People* (1980), *The Russia House* (1989), *The Constant Gardener* (2000), and *The Mission Song* (2006). Many of his novels have been filmed or televised.

lecithin [lesuhthin] *choline*

Leconte de Lisle, Charles Marie René [luhkõt duh leel] (1818–94) French poet, born in Saint-Paul, La Réunion. After travels in India and the East he settled in Paris. He exercised a profound influence on younger poets, was a member of the anti-Romantic school called *Parnassiens*, and succeeded to Victor Hugo's chair at the Academy in 1886. His works include *Poésies complètes* (1858), *Poèmes barbares* (1862), and *Poèmes tragiques* (1884).

Le Corbusier [luh kaw(r)büsyay], pseudonym of **Charles Edouard Jeanneret** (1887–1965) Architect and city planner, born in La Chaux-de-Fonds, Switzerland. He published, with Amédée Ozenfant (1886–1966), the Purist manifesto, and developed a theory of the interrelation between modern machine forms and architectural techniques. His first building, based on the

technique of the *Modulor* (a system using units whose proportions were those of the human figure), was the *Unité d'habitation* ('Living unit'), Marseille (1945–50). His city planning designs include those proposed for Algiers (1932–42), several other cities, and realized at Chandigarh in India (1951).

LED *light-emitting diode*

Leda (astronomy) [leeda] The 13th natural satellite of Jupiter, discovered in 1974; distance from the planet 11 100 000 km/6 900 000 mi; diameter 16 km/10 mi.

Leda (mythology) [leeda] In Greek mythology, the wife of Tyndareus, and mother, either by him or Zeus, of Castor and Pollux, Helen, and Clytemnestra. A frequent subject in art is Zeus courting Leda in the form of a swan.

LED printer A form of computer printer, similar to a xerographic printer, where the ionization of the drum is carried out using a row of light-emitting diodes (LEDs) rather than a laser beam.

Lee, Ang (1954–) Film director, producer, and screenwriter, born in Taipei, Taiwan. He earned Academy Award nominations for *The Wedding Banquet* (1993) and *Eat Drink Man Woman* (1994). Later films include *Sense and Sensibility* (1995, Best Picture Oscar nomination), *The Ice Storm* (1997), *Crouching Tiger, Hidden Dragon* (2000, four Oscars, four BAFTA Awards, Best Director Golden Globe), and *Brokeback Mountain* (2005, Oscar, four Golden Globes, BAFTA).

Lee, Ann, known as **Mother Ann** (1736–84) Religious mystic, born in Manchester, Greater Manchester. In 1758 she joined the 'Shaking Quakers', or 'Shakers', who saw in her the second coming of Christ. She emigrated with her followers to the USA in 1774, and founded the parent Shaker settlement.

Lee, Christopher (1922–) Film actor, born in London. His gaunt appearance and sinister image led to acclaimed performances in *Dracula* (1958) and its sequels, as well as in a range of other horror movies. Later films include *The Three Musketeers* and its sequel (1973, 1989), *The Stupids* (1996), and he played the role of Saruman in parts one and two of the *Lord of the Rings* trilogy (2001–2).

Lee, David M(orris) (1931–) Physicist, born in Rye, NY. He worked at Cornell University, where he contributed to the discovery of the superfluidity of helium-3. He shared the Nobel Prize for Physics in 1996.

Lee (of Ashridge), Jennie Lee, Baroness (1904–88) British stateswoman, born in Lochgelly, Fife. A dedicated socialist, she became the youngest elected woman MP (1929–31), and married Aneurin Bevan in 1934. Re-elected to parliament in 1945, as minister for the arts (1967–70) she established the Open University.

Lee, (Nelle) Harper (1926–) Novelist, born in Monroeville, AL. Her first and only novel, *To Kill a Mockingbird* (1960, filmed 1962), a story of racial prejudice set in a Southern town, received a Pulitzer Prize.

Lee, Laurie (1914–97) Writer, born in Stroud, Gloucestershire. He was best known for his autobiographical stories of childhood and country life, *Cider With Rosie* (1959), *As I Walked Out One Midsummer Morning* (1969), and *I Can't Stay Long* (1975). *A Moment of War* (1991) recalls his experiences during the Spanish Civil War.

Lee, Robert E(dward) (1807–70) Confederate general, born in Stratford, VA. He was in charge of the defences at Richmond, and defeated Federal forces in the Seven Days' Battles (1862). His strategy in opposing General Pope, his invasion of Maryland and Pennsylvania, and other achievements are central to the history of the Civil War. In 1865, he surrendered his army to General Grant at Appomattox Courthouse, VA.

Lee, Spike, popular name of **Shelton Jackson Lee** (1957–) Filmmaker, born in Atlanta, GA. *She's Gotta Have It* (1986) established him internationally. Other films, centred around African-American culture, include *Mo' Better Blues* (1990), *Get on*

Lebanon

☐ International Airport

Fr **Liban**, official name **Republic of Lebanon**, Arabic **Al-Jumhouriya al-Lubnaniya**

Local names al-Lubnān (Arab), Liban (French)

Timezone GMT +2

Area 10 452 km²/4034 sq mi

Population total (2002e) 3 678 000

Status Republic

Date of independence 1943

Capital Beirut

Languages Arabic (official), French, English, and Armenian also spoken

Ethnic groups Arab (93%), with several minorities

Religions Muslim (c.75%), Christian (c.25%), also many religious sects including Armenian, Greek, Roman Catholic, Alawite, Druze, and Jewish

Physical features Narrow coastal plain rises gradually E to the Lebanon Mts (Jebel Liban) reaching 3087 m/10 128 ft at Qornet es Saouda; arid E slopes fall abruptly to the fertile Beqaa plateau, average elevation 1000 m/3300 ft; Anti-Lebanon range (Jebel esh Sharqi) in the E; R Litani flows S between the two ranges.

Climate Mediterranean climate, varying with altitude; hot, dry summers, warm, moist winters; average annual temperatures 13°C (Jan), 27°C (Jul); average annual rainfall 920 mm/36 in; much drier and cooler in the Bekaa valley.

Currency 1 Lebanese Pound/Livre (LBP) = 100 piastres

Economy Commercial and financial centre of the Middle East until the civil war, which severely damaged economic infrastructure and reduced industrial and agricultural production; oil refining, textiles, chemicals, food processing; citrus fruits, apples, grapes, bananas, sugar beet, olives, wheat; tourism virtually collapsed, but began to revive in the mid-1990s.

GDP (2002e) $17·61 bn, per capita $4800

Human Development Index (2002) 0·755

History Part of the Ottoman Empire from 16th-c; after the massacre of (Catholic) Maronites by (Muslim) Druzes in 1860, Maronite area around Jabal Lubnan granted special autonomous status; Greater Lebanon, based on this area, created in 1920 under French mandate; Muslim coastal regions incorporated, despite great opposition; constitutional republic, 1926; independence, 1943; Palestinian resistance units established in Lebanon by late 1960s despite government opposition, including the Palestine Liberation Organization (PLO); several militia groups developed in the mid-1970s; following terrorist attacks, Israel invaded S Lebanon, 1978 and 1982; heavy Israeli bombardment of Beirut forced the withdrawal of Palestinian forces, 1982; unilateral withdrawal of Israeli and Syrian forces from Lebanon brought clashes between the Druze (backed by Syria) and Christian Lebanese militia; ceasefire announced in late 1982, broken many times; Syrian troops entered Beirut, 1988 in an attempt to restore order; release of Western hostages taken by militant groups began in 1990; timetable for militia disarmament introduced, 1991; Israeli withdrawal from South Lebanon border area, 2000; former Lebanese prime minister Rafiq al-Hariri killed in bombing, 2005; Syrian troops withdrawn in line with UN demands, 2005; Israel impose air and sea blockade in major offensive after hostile action by militant group Hezbollah (Jul 2006), fighting escalates; UN broker ceasefire (Aug); air blockade lifted (Nov); mass anti-government protests by pro-Syrian factions (Dec); constitution provides for a Council of Ministers, a President (a Maronite Christian), Prime Minister (a Sunni Muslim), a Cabinet, and a Parliament, equally divided between Christians and Muslims.

Head of State

1970–6 Suleiman Frenjieh
1976–82 Elias Sarkis
1982 Bachir Gemayel
1982–8 Amin Gemayel
1988–9 *No President*
1989 Rene Muawad
1989–98 Elias Hrawi
1998– Emile Lahoud

Head of Government

1973 Amin al-Hafez
1973–4 Takieddine Solh
1974–5 Rashid Solh
1975 Noureddin Rifai
1975–6 Rashid Karami
1976–80 Selim al-Hoss
1980 Takieddine Solh
1980–4 Chafiq al-Wazan
1984–8 Rashid Karami
1988–90 Michel Aoun/Selim al-Hoss
1990 Selim al-Hoss
1990–2 Umar Karami
1992 Rashid al-Solh
1992–8 Rafiq al-Hariri
1998–2000 Selim al-Hoss
2000–4 Rafiq al-Hariri
2004–5 Omar Karameh
2005 Najib Mikati *Interim*
2005– Fouad Siniora

the Bus (1996), *Summer of Sam* (1998), and *Inside Man* (2006). He received a BAFTA special achievement award in 2002. In 2006 appeared *When the Levees Broke: A Requiem in Four Acts*, a documentary about life in New Orleans in the aftermath of Hurricane Katrina.

leech A specialized ringed worm related to the earthworms; body highly contractile, usually with a sucker at each end; many are blood-feeders on vertebrate hosts. One species was used in early medicine for 'bleeding' patients suffering from various illnesses. (Phylum: Annelida. Subclass: Hirudinea.)

leechee *litchi*

Leeds 53°50N 1°35W, urban area pop (2001e) 715 400. City in West Yorkshire, N England; in the 18th-c an important centre of cloth manufacture; universities (1904, 1992); major industrial and cultural centre; railway (important early freight and passenger centre); Town Hall (1858), Kirkstall Abbey (1147); Leeds Music Festival (every 3 years, Apr); International Pianoforte Competition (every 3 years, Sep); football league team, Leeds United (Peacocks).

leek A perennial with strap-shaped, sheathing leaves in two rows, and white flowers sometimes mixed with bulbils. It is now cultivated as a vegetable (*Allium porrum*). (Family: Liliaceae.)

Leeuwarden [layvah(r)dn], Frisian **Liouwert** 53°12N 5°48E, pop (2000e) 90 000. City in N Netherlands, on the R Ee; railway; economic and cultural capital of Friesland; major cattle market; Grote Kerk (13th–16th-c).

Leeuwenhoek, Antonie van [layvenhook] (1632–1723) Scientist, born in Delft, The Netherlands. He became a renowned microscopist, the first to observe bacteria, protozoa, spermatozoa, and features of the blood.

Leeward Islands (Caribbean), Span **Islas de Sotavento** Island group of the Lesser Antilles in the Caribbean Sea; from the Virgin Is (N) to Dominica (S); sheltered from the NE prevailing winds.

Leeward Islands (French Polynesia), Fr **Iles sous le Vent** pop (2000e) 29 200; area 507 km²/196 sq mi. Island group of the Society Is, French Polynesia; chief town, Uturoa (Raiatea).

Le Fanu, (Joseph) Sheridan [lefuhnyoo] (1814–73) Writer and journalist, born in Dublin. His novels include *The House by the Churchyard* (1863) and *Uncle Silas* (1864). He also wrote short stories, mainly of the supernatural.

Lefkosia *Nicosia*

Left Bank The S bank of the R Seine in Paris, an area occupied by numerous educational establishments, including the University of Paris and the Ecole des Beaux Arts. It is noted as a haunt of writers and intellectuals.

leg A term commonly used to refer to the whole of the lower limb, primarily used for support and movement; more precisely, in anatomy, the region between the knee and ankle joints. The bones are the *femur* in the thigh, the *tibia* and *fibula* in the leg, and the *tarsals*, *metatarsals*, and *phalanges* in the foot.

legacy *property*

Legal Aid A scheme which provides those with limited financial means with advice and assistance from solicitors, barristers or advocates, and aids with representation at civil and criminal trials and certain tribunals. In the UK, civil legal aid is administered by the Law Society; help is means-tested, and a contribution may be required. A person seeking criminal aid applies to the court, when the offence carries a possible penalty of 6 months or more, and may be granted if the person's financial circumstances requires it, and if, in the case of summary offences, the interest of justice is served. In serious offences, Legal Aid is granted by the relevant Legal Aid Board, once granted no contribution from the applicant is required. In the USA, there is a constitutional right in criminal cases to

be represented by a lawyer appointed by the court, where someone has insufficient means to pay privately. The Legal Services Corporation provides financial assistance for legal help in non-criminal proceedings for those unable to afford such help. Similar schemes exist in many other countries.

legal tender Forms of money that a creditor is bound to accept in settlement of a debt. Some money, such as coin or small denomination notes, may be legal tender only for amounts up to a limit. Other money, such as large denomination notes, is not legal tender for smaller amounts, as nobody is legally required to give change. The vast majority of actual transactions in a modern economy are in fact carried out by the use of cheques, credit or debit cards, or electronic transfer, none of which are legal tender. This, however, is for convenience and at the recipient's discretion; nobody is legally obliged to accept a cheque.

Léger, Fernand [layzhay] (1881–1955) Painter, born in Argentan, France. He helped to form the Cubist movement, but later developed his own 'aesthetic of the machine', as in 'Contrast of Forms' (1913, Philadelphia).

Leggett, Sir Anthony J (1938–) Physicist, born in London. Working at the University of Illinois at Urbana-Champaign (from 1983), he became recognized as a world leader in the theory of low-temperature physics. He shared the 2003 Nobel Prize for Physics for his pioneering work on superfluidity. He was knighted in 2004.

Leghorn *Livorno*

leghorn A small breed of domestic fowl; named after Legorno (now Livorno) in Italy.

legion The principal unit of the Roman army. It was made up of 10 cohorts, each one of which was divided into six centuries.

Légion d'Honneur [layzhõ donoe(r)] (Legion of Honour) In France, a reward for civil and military service created by Napoleon I in 1802. The five grades are chevalier, officer, commander, grand officer, and grand cross.

legionnaire's disease A serious form of pneumonia caused by *Legionella pneumophilia*. The bacteria live in warm water and are transmitted by water droplets from contaminated shower heads, humidifiers, and particularly from hot-water systems. When the cooling towers of air-conditioning plants are affected, larger numbers of people tend to be involved. The disease is so named because the first outbreak in 1976 affected members of the American Legion in Philadelphia.

Legion of Mary An organization founded in Ireland in 1921 to enable lay members of the Roman Catholic Church to engage in apostolic (missionary and charitable) work. It was inspired by writings devoted to the Virgin Mary by St Louis Marie Grignon de Montfort (1673–1716).

legitimacy The legal status of a child at birth. A child is legitimate if born when its parents are validly married to each other, and the child is the biological issue of the couple, though most jurisdictions presume legitimacy where the child is born to a married woman living with her husband who is not impotent. A person born illegitimate may be legitimized by the subsequent marriage of his or her parents.

legume A dry, 1-many-seeded fruit of the pea family (*Leguminosae*). When ripe it splits into two valves, each bearing alternate seeds. Many kinds are eaten as vegetables.

Lehár, Franz [luhhah(r)] (1870–1948) Composer, born in Komárom, Hungary. His works include two violin concertos, but he is best known for his operettas, which include *The Merry Widow* (1905) and *The Count of Luxembourg* (1909).

Le Havre [luh hahvr], formerly **Le Havre-de-Grace** 49°30N 0°06E, pop (2000e) 205 000. Commercial seaport in NW France; Allied base in World War 1; largely rebuilt since heavy damage in World War 2; chief French port for transatlantic passenger liners; ferry service to UK.

Lehmann, Lilli [layman] (1848–1929) Soprano, born in Würzburg, Germany. She took part in the first performance of Wagner's *Ring* cycle (1876) at Bayreuth.

Lehmann, Lotte [layman] (1888–1976) Soprano, born in Perleberg, Germany. She was noted particularly for her performances in operas by Richard Strauss, including two premieres.

Leibniz, Gottfried Wilhelm [liybnits] (1646–1716) Philosopher and mathematician, born in Leipzig, Germany. He visited London in 1673, becoming involved in a controversy over whether he or Newton was the inventor of the infinitesimal calculus. His great influence, especially upon Russell, was primarily as a mathematician and as a pioneer of modern symbolic logic.

Leicester [lester], Lat **Ratae Coritanorum** 52°38N 1°05W, pop (2001e) 279 900. City and county town of Leicestershire, C England; unitary authority from 1997; an important royal residence in mediaeval times; charter granted by Elizabeth I, 1589; two universities (1957, 1992); railway; many Roman remains; cathedral (14th-c), Guildhall (14th-c); football league team, Leicester City.

Leicester, Robert Dudley, Earl of [lester], also known as **Baron Denbigh** and **Sir Robert Dudley** (c.1532–88) English nobleman, the favourite and possibly the lover of Elizabeth I. He continued to receive favour in spite of his unpopularity at court and two secret marriages. Although unwell, in 1588 he successfully commanded the forces against the Spanish Armada, but died shortly afterwards.

Leicester (of Holkham), Thomas William Coke, Earl of [lester, holkam] (1752–1842) Agriculturalist, the 'father of experimental farms', born in London. People visited his estate from all over the world, and special meetings were held at sheep-clipping time – called 'Coke's Clippings' – the last of which took place in 1821.

Leicestershire [lestersheer] pop (2001e) 609 600; area 2553 km²/985 sq mi. County of C England; Leicester and Rutland new unitary authorities from 1997; administrative centre, Leicester.

Leiden *Leyden*

Leif Eriksson [layv erikson] (fl.1000) Icelandic explorer, the son of Eric the Red, the first European to reach America. c.1000 he discovered land which he named Vinland after the vines he found growing there.

Leigh, Janet, originally **Jeanette Helen Morrison** (1927–2004) Actress, born in Merced, CA. She studied music and psychology at the University of the Pacific until 'discovered' by actress Norma Shearer. This led to a starring role in *The Romance of Rosy Ridge* (1947). Many successful films followed, including *Little Women* (1949), *My Sister Eileen* (1955), *Touch of Evil* (1958), *Psycho* (1962, Golden Globe, Oscar nomination), *The Manchurian Candidate* (1962), and *The Fog* (1980). Married four times, her third husband (1951–62) was actor Tony Curtis.

Leigh, Mike [lee] (1943–) Playwright and film director, born in Salford, Greater Manchester. He has scripted a distinctive genre based on actors' improvizations around given themes. His most successful work for the theatre has had a second life on film, as in *Bleak Moments* (1970), and on television, as in *Abigail's Party* (1977). Later films include *Secrets and Lies* (1996) and *Vera Drake* (2004, Venice Golden Lion; BAFTA Best Director). His stage play *Two Thousand Years* premiered in London in 2005.

Leigh, Vivien [lee], originally **Vivian Hartley** (1913–67) Actress, born in Darjeeling, India. She was put under contract by Alexander Korda, playing in *Fire Over England* (1937) against Laurence Olivier, whom she subsequently married (1940–60). Her star role of Scarlett O'Hara in *Gone With the Wind* (1939) brought her an Oscar, as did her role in *A Streetcar Named Desire* (1951).

Leinster [lenster] pop (2000e) 1 884 000; area 19 633 km²/7578 sq mi. Province in E Ireland; capital, Dublin.

leiomyoma *fibroid*

Leipzig [liypzig], ancient **Lipsia** 51°20N 12°23E, pop (2000e) 528 000. City in SE Germany; airport; railway; Karl Marx University (1409); college of technology; centre for commerce, education, and music (associations with Bach and Mendelssohn).

Leipzig, Battle of [liypzig] (1813) The overwhelming defeat of Napoleon's forces by the armies of the Fourth Coalition, also called the **Battle of the Nations**. He was heavily outnumbered by the Allied force of Austrians, Prussians, Russians, and Swedes.

leishmaniasis [leeshmaniyasis] A group of conditions caused by the protozoan *Leishmania*, conveyed by sandflies, occurring on the Mediterranean shores, Africa, and S Asia; also known as **kala-azar**. The *skin form* of the disease occurs as pimples which enlarge and ulcerate. The *visceral form* affects the liver, spleen, and lymph nodes.

Leitrim [leetrim], Ir **Liathdroma** pop (2000e) 24 000; area 1526 km²/589 sq mi. County in Connacht province, Ireland; capital, Carrick-on-Shannon.

Lely, Sir Peter [leelee], originally **Pieter van der Faes** (1618–80) Painter, born in Soest, The Netherlands. Court painter to Charles II, his 13 Greenwich portraits of English admirals (1666–7) are among his best works.

Lemaître, Georges (Edouard) [luhmaytruh] (1894–1966) Astronomer, born in Charleroi, Belgium. His most important paper led to the concept of the 'big bang' theory of the universe.

Léman, Lac *Geneva, Lake*

Le Mans [luh mã], ancient **Oppidum Suindinum** 48°00N 0°10E, pop (2000e) 152 000. Commercial city in NW France; ancient capital of Maine; fortified by the Romans, 3rd–4th-c; railway junction; cathedral (11th–15th-c); annual 24-hour motor race (Jun).

Lemieux, Mario [luhmyoe] (1965–) Ice hockey player, born in Montreal, Canada. A member of the Pittsburgh Penguins from 1984, in 834 National Hockey League matches he scored 683 goals and 966 assists. He retired in 1997, but returned in 1999 after buying the Pittsburgh team, finally retiring in 2006.

lemma *theorem*

lemming A mouse-like rodent of the tribe Lemmini (9 species); large powerful head, long fur, short tail. The **Norway lemming** (*Lemmus lemmus*) undergoes a population 'explosion' every 3–4 years. When this happens there is a mass migration. The direction of migration appears random, and sometimes groups reaching large bodies of water will swim offshore and drown in large numbers. There is no basis for the popular belief that lemmings march suicidally into the sea.

Lemnos [leemnos], Gr **Límnos** pop (2000e) 17 000; area 476 km²/184 sq mi. Greek island in the N Aegean Sea, off the NW coast of Turkey; length 40 km/25 mi; rises to 430 m/1411 ft; airfield; capital, Kastron.

lemon A citrus fruit (*Citrus limoni*) 6–12·5 cm/2½–4¾ in diameter; ovoid, with thick, bright yellow rind and sour pulp. (Family: Rutaceae.)

lemon sole Common European flatfish (*Microstomus kitt*) found in shelf waters from N Norway to the Bay of Biscay; body oval, length up to 65 cm/26 in; mouth small; brown with a mosaic of yellow and green patches; valuable food fish. (Family: Pleuronectidae.)

lemur [leemer] A primitive primate from Madagascar; large eyes and pointed snout; most species with long tail; 27 species in three families: **lemur** (*Lemuridae*), **mouse** (or **dwarf**) **lemur** (*Cheirogaleidae*), and **leaping lemur** (*Indriidae*).

Le Nain [nã] A family of French painters: three brothers, **Antoine** (c.1588–1648), **Louis** (c.1593–1648), and **Mathieu** (c.1607–77). All were born in Laon and were foundation members of the Académie in 1648. Louis is considered the best, with his large genre-scenes of peasant life.

Lena, River [lyena] River in Siberian Russia; rises in the Baykalskiy Khrebet, enters the Laptev Sea; length, 4400 km/2700 mi.

Lenclos, Ninon de [lãkloh], popular name of **Anne de Lenclos** (1620–1705) Courtesan of good family, born in Paris. Her lovers included several leading members of the aristocracy, as well as political and literary figures.

Lendl, Ivan [lendl] (1960–) Tennis player, born in Ostrava, Czech Republic. He became a US citizen in 1992. He dominated male tennis in the 1980s, winning the singles title at the US Open (1985–7), French Open (1984, 1986–7), and Australian Open (1989), and becoming the Masters champion (1986–7). He won 94 singles titles, but failed to win at Wimbledon. He was forced to retire in December 1994 because of a spinal condition.

Lend-Lease Agreement The means by which the USA lent or leased war supplies and arms to Britain and other countries during World War 2. Up to the end of August 1945, the UK received about £5000 million worth of materials.

L'Enfant, Pierre Charles [lãfã] (1754–1825) Architect and city planner, born in Paris. He moved to America in 1777, where he fought the British in the Revolutionary War. At Washington's invitation, in 1791 he submitted a plan for the new federal capital in the District of Columbia, which became an influential model of urban planning.

Lenin, Peak, Russ **Lenina, Pik**, formerly **Mt Kaufmann** 39°21N 73°01E. Highest peak in the Alayskiy Khrebet, and second highest in Russia; height, 7134 m/23 405 ft; first climbed in 1928.

Lenin, Vladimir Ilyich, originally **Vladimir Ilyich Ulyanov** (1870–1924) Marxist revolutionary and politician, born in Simbirsk, Russia. From 1897 to 1900 he was exiled to Siberia for participating in underground revolutionary activities. At the Second Congress of the Russian Social Democratic Labour Party (1903) he caused the split between the Bolshevik and Menshevik factions. In October he led the Bolshevik revolution and became head of the first Soviet government. With Trotsky, he brought it successfully through the ensuing Civil War (1918–21), after which he introduced the New Economic Policy, which his critics in the Party saw as a 'compromise with capitalism' and a retreat from strictly Socialist planning. His birthplace was renamed Ulyanovsk in his honour (1924–91).

Leningrad *St Petersburg*

Leninism *Marxism-Leninism*

Lenin Mausoleum Burial vault, designed by Aleksey V Shchusev and built in 1930 in Red Square, Moscow, where Lenin's embalmed body may be viewed by the public.

Lennon, John (Winston) (1940–80) Pop star, composer, songwriter, and recording artist, born in Liverpool, Merseyside. He was the Beatles rhythm guitarist, keyboard player, and vocalist, and a partner in the Lennon–McCartney song-writing team. He married Japanese artist Yoko Ono – his second marriage – in 1969. Together they invented a form of peace protest by staying in bed while being filmed and interviewed, and the single recorded under the name of The Plastic Ono Band, 'Give Peace a Chance' (1969), became the 'national anthem' for pacifists. On the birth of his son, **Sean** (1975–), he retired from music to become a house-husband. He was shot and killed by an obsessed schizophrenic, Mark Chapman, but continues to be revered by new generations of fans. His son **Julian** (1963–) has had some success as a singer/musician.

Leno, Dan [leenoh], originally **George Galvin** (1860–1904) Comedian and music-hall star, born in London. He appeared for many years in the annual pantomime at Drury Lane.

Le Nôtre, André [luh nohtr] (1613–1700) The creator of French landscape gardening, born in Paris. He designed the gardens at Versailles, and laid out St James's Park in London.

lens A transparent optical element comprising two refracting surfaces, at least one of which is curved; parallel light rays passing through the lens may converge (and focus at a point) or diverge, depending on the lens shape. Lenses are characterized by their *focal length* (the distance at which the image of a distant object is most sharply defined) and their *aperture* or *f-number* (the light transmission).

Lent In the Christian Church, the weeks before Easter, observed as a period of prayer and penance in commemoration of Christ's 40-day fast in the wilderness; in the Western Churches, Lent begins on Ash Wednesday; in the Eastern Churches, it begins eight weeks before Easter.

lenticel A small pore in a stem or root, with a similar role to that of stomata in leaves, allowing the passage of gases to and from tissues.

lentil An annual growing to c.40 cm/15 in (*Lens culinaris*); peaflowers white, veined with lilac, borne 1–3 on a long stalk; pods rectangular with 1–2 disc-shaped seeds. The seeds (lentils) are rich in protein. (Family: Leguminosae.)

Lenya, Lotte [laynya], originally **Karoline Wilhelmine Blamauer** (1900–81) Singer, born in Vienna. She married Kurt Weill in 1926, and made an international reputation as Jenny in Weill's *Die Dreigroschenoper* (1928, The Threepenny Opera).

Leo III, known as **Leo the Isaurian** (c.680–741) Byzantine Emperor (717–41), born in Syria. In 726 he prohibited the use of images in public worship, which led to more than a century of controversy.

Leo I, St, known as **the Great** (c.390–461) Pope (440–61), and one of the most eminent of the Latin Fathers. He summoned the Council of Chalcedon in 451. Feast day 10 November (W), 18 February (E).

Leo III, St (c.750–816) Pope (795–816), born in Rome. He crowned Charlemagne Emperor of the West (800), thus initiating the Holy Roman Empire. He was canonized in 1673. Feast day 12 June.

Leo X, originally **Giovanni de' Medici** (1475–1521) Pope (1513–21), born in Florence, Italy. His vast project to rebuild St Peter's, and his permitting the preaching of an indulgence in order to raise funds, provoked the Reformation.

Leo (Lat 'lion') A N constellation of the Zodiac, lying between Cancer and Virgo. **Leo Minor** ('little lion') is a hard-to-see constellation N of Leo.

León (Mexico) [layon] 21°06N 101°41W, pop (2000e) 1 050 000. City in SC Mexico; altitude, 1804 m/5919 ft; railway; commercial centre.

León (Spain) [layon] 42°38N 5°34W, pop (2000e) 146 000. City in NW Spain; bishopric; capital of a mediaeval kingdom; railway; cathedral (13th–14th-c).

Leonard, 'Sugar' Ray (1956–) US boxer, born in Wilmington, DE. He fought 12 world title fights, and became WBC world welterweight champion in 1979, adding the WBA light middleweight crown in 1981. He is one of only two boxers to have been world champion at five weights.

Leonardo da Vinci [leeonah(r)doh da veenchee] (1452–1519) Painter, sculptor, architect, and engineer, born in Vinci, Rome. In 1482 he settled in Milan, where he painted his 'Last Supper' (1498) on the refectory wall of Santa Maria delle Grazie. In 1500 he entered the service of Cesare Borgia in Florence as architect and engineer, and with Michelangelo decorated the Sala del Consiglio in the Palazzo della Signoria with historical compositions. About 1504 he completed his most celebrated easel picture, 'Mona Lisa' (Louvre). His notebooks contain original remarks on most of the sciences, including biology, physiology, hydrodynamics, and aeronautics.

Leoncavallo, Ruggero [leeonkavaloh] (1857–1919) Opera composer, born in Naples, Italy. He wrote a number of operas, of which only *I Pagliacci* (1892) achieved lasting success.

Leonidas [leeonidas] (?–480 BC) King of Sparta (c.491–480 BC), hero of the Persian Wars. He perished at Thermopylae, fighting to check the Persian advance into C Greece.

Leonids [leeuhnidz] A meteor shower due around 17 November each year that is spectacular at 33-year intervals. Particularly spectacular sightings occurred in 1966 and 2001.

Leontief, Wassily [layontyef, vasilee] (1906–99) Economist, born in St Petersburg, Russia. In 1973 he was awarded the Nobel Prize for Economics for developing the input–output method of economic analysis used for planning and forecasting.

leopard A member of the cat family (*Panthera pardus*), found from Siberia to Africa; solitary; reddish- or yellowish-brown with small empty rings of dark blotches; black individuals (**black panthers**) sometimes found in dense forests.

Leopardi, Giacomo, conte (Count) [layohpah(r)dee] (1798–1837) Poet and scholar, born in Recanati, Italy. He was a gifted, congenitally handicapped child whose afflicted life was lived in hopeless despondency and unrequited love. Among his most noted works are those collected under the title *I canti* (1831).

Leopold I (Emperor) (1640–1705) Holy Roman Emperor (1658–1705), born in Vienna. Committed throughout his long reign to the defence of the power and unity of the House of Habsburg, he faced constant external threats from the Ottoman Turks and the King of France, in addition to the hostility of the Hungarian nobility.

Leopold I (of Belgium) (1790–1865) First king of the Belgians (1831–65), born in Coburg, Germany, son of Francis, Duke of Saxe-Coburg and uncle of Queen Victoria. He was an influential force in European diplomacy prior to Bismarck's ascendancy.

Leopold II (of Belgium) (1835–1909) King of the Belgians (1865–1909), born in Brussels, the son of Leopold I. In 1885 he became king of the Congo Free State, which became a Belgian colony in 1908.

Leopold III (1901–83) King of the Belgians (1934–51), born in Brussels. He is especially known for his brave decision in 1940 to prolong the resistance of the Belgian army to the German invasion for a further two days, thus enabling the British evacuation at Dunkirk to succeed.

Léopoldville *Kinshasa*

Lepanto, Battle of [lepantoh] (1571) The defeat of the Turkish navy in the Gulf of Corinth, ending the Turks' long-standing domination of the E Mediterranean. It was inflicted by the Christian forces of Spain and the Italian states in coalition.

Le Pen, Jean-Marie [luh pen] (1928–) French politician. He formed the National Front in 1972, and this party, with its extreme right-wing policies, emerged as a new 'fifth force' in French politics in the 1986 Assembly elections. A controversial figure and noted demagogue, he unsuccessfully contested the presidency in 1988 and 1995. His success in the first round of the 2002 presidential election caused widespread demonstrations across France. In 2007 he contested the presidential election and finished fourth.

Lepenski Vir [lepenskee veer] A small prehistoric settlement on the banks of the R Danube in the Iron Gates Gorge, Serbia and Montenegro, dating from c.6500–5500 BC. It includes the earliest monumental sculpture in Europe.

Lepidoptera [lepidoptera] A large order of insects comprising the 165 000 species of butterflies and moths; adults have two pairs of membranous wings covered with scales; forewings and hindwings coupled together; mouthparts typically modified as a slender sucking proboscis.

Lepidus, Marcus Aemilius [lepidus] (?–13/12 BC) Roman statesman of the civil war era (49–31 BC), who first rose to prominence under Caesar, becoming his deputy at Rome. He reached the high point of his career in 43 BC, when he formed the Second Triumvirate with Antonius and Octavian.

leprechaun [leprekawn] A fairy of Irish folklore, traditionally a tiny old man occupying himself with cobbling, and the possessor of a crock of gold whose whereabouts he could be persuaded to reveal by threats of violence.

leprosy *Hansen's disease*

Leptis Magna or **Lepcis Magna** 32°59N 14°15E. An ancient seaport of N Libya, the site of spectacular Roman remains; now a world heritage site. It was founded by the Phoenicians as a trading post perhaps as early as the 7th-c BC.

lepton In particle physics, a collective term for all those particles of half integer spin (ie fermions) not affected by strong interactions. The leptons are electrons, muons, and taus, and their respective neutrinos.

Lepus [leepus] (Lat 'hare') A constellation in the S sky, easy to see S of Orion.

Lermontov, Mikhail Yuryevich [lermontof] (1814–41) Writer, born in Moscow. He is best known for his novel *Geroy nashego vremeni* (1840, A Hero of Our Time).

Leroux, Gaston (Louis Alfred) [leroo] (1868–1927) Writer, born in Paris. His first novel, *The Seeking of the Morning Treasures* (trans, 1903) was followed by a series of detective stories. His best-known work, *The Phantom of the Opera* (1911), attracted little attention in its early days, but became a hit following a Lon Chaney film in 1924.

Lerwick [lerwik] 60°09N 1°09W, pop (2000e) 8100. Capital of Shetland, N Scotland; airfield; ferry terminus; Fort Charlotte (1665).

Lesage, Alain René [luhsahzh], also spelled **Le Sage** (1668–1747) Novelist and playwright, born in Sarzeau, France. He is best known for his picaresque 4-volume novel *Histoire de Gil Blas de Santillane* (1715–35, The Adventures of Gil Blas of Santillane).

lesbianism A sexual attraction and expression between women, which may or may not involve the complete exclusion of men as potential sexual partners. As with male homosexuality, lesbianism became increasingly politicized in the latter part of the 20th-c.

Lesbos, Gr **Lesvos** or **Mitilini** pop (2000e) 108 000; area 1630 km²/629 sq mi. Greek island in the E Aegean Sea; third largest island of Greece; length 61 km/38 mi; hilly, rising to 969 m/3179 ft; in classical times, a centre of Greek lyric poetry; chief town, Mitilini.

Lescot, Pierre [leskoh] (c.1515–78) Renaissance architect, born in Paris. His masterpiece was the Louvre, one wing of which he completely rebuilt.

Lesotho *p.536*

less developed countries (LDCs) The majority of the world's countries, typically characterized by poverty, low levels of nutrition, health, and literacy, poorly developed industry, transport, and communications, and the export of agricultural products and minerals. The notion includes a very wide variety. Many countries, while still on average underdeveloped, have growing industrial sectors. The most backward LDCs, however, especially in Africa, continue to be poor.

Lesseps, Ferdinand (Marie), vicomte de (Viscount of) [leseeps] (1805–94) Engineer, born in Versailles, France. In 1854 he began to plan the Suez Canal, finally built 1859–69. In 1880 work began on his scheme for a Panama Canal.

Lessing, Doris (May), *née* **Tayler** (1919–) Writer, born in Kermanshah, Iran. She was brought up in Southern Rhodesia, the setting for her first novel, *The Grass is Singing* (1950). Her later works include the five-book sequence *Children of Violence*, and the novels *The Golden Notebook* (1962), *The Good Terrorist* (1985), *Mara and Dann* (1999), and its sequel *The Story of General Dann and Mara's Daughter, Griot and the Snow-Dog* (2005).

Lessing, Gotthold (Ephraim) (1729–81) Playwright and man of letters, born in Kamenz, Germany. *Laokoon* (1766) is a critical treatise defining the limits of poetry and the plastic arts. *Minna von Barnhelm* (1767) is the first German comedy on the grand scale.

Lester, Dick, popular name of **Richard Lester** (1932–) Film director, born in Philadelphia, PA. He came to Britain and gained

Lesotho

☐ International Airport

[lesootoo], official name **Kingdom of Lesotho**

Local name Lesotho

Timezone GMT +2

Area 30 355 km²/11 720 sq mi

Population total (2002e) 2 208 000

Status Independent kingdom within the Commonwealth

Date of independence 1960

Capital Maseru

Languages Lesotho (Sesotho) and English (official), Zulu, Afrikaans, French, Xhosa also spoken

Ethnic groups Basotho (99%), Zulu, Tembu, and Fingo tribes, European and Asian minorities

Religions Roman Catholic (44%), Protestant (mostly Lesotho Evangelical) (30%), Anglican (12%), other Christian (8%), traditional beliefs (6%)

Physical features S African kingdom completely bounded by South Africa; Drakensberg Mts in NE and E, highest peak Thabana-Ntlenyana, 3482 m/11 424 ft; serious soil erosion, especially in W; main rivers, the Orange and the Caledon; mountainous land, particularly in SW with the Maloti Mountain range.

Climate Mild, dry winters; warm summer season (Oct–Apr); average annual temperatures 15°C (Jan), 25°C (Jul); average annual rainfall 725 mm/28·5 in (Oct–Apr).

Currency 1 Loti (plural Maloti) (LSL) = 100 lisente; 1 South African Rand (ZAR) = 100 cents

Economy Economy based on intensive agriculture and contract labour working in South Africa; wheat, peas, beans, barley, cattle; diamonds, textiles, pharmaceuticals; jewellery, crafts, wool, mohair.

GDP (2002e) $5·106 bn, per capita $2700

Human Development Index (2002) 0·535

History Originally inhabited by hunting and gathering bushmen; Bantu arrived 16th-c, and Basotho nation established; incorporated in Orange Free State, 1854; under British protection as Basutoland, 1869; independence, 1960; declared Kingdom of Lesotho in 1966, as a hereditary monarchy within the Commonwealth; constitution suspended and country ruled by Council of Ministers, 1970–86; Prime Minister deposed by coup and political activity banned, 1986, with Military Council as effective ruling body; King Moshoeshoe dethroned by military council in 1990, and replaced by eldest son; elections (first since 1970) to restore civilian rule, 1993; Moshoeshoe returned to the throne, 1994, but died in a car accident, 1996; status of the monarchy a continuing issue; new electoral system introduced, 2002.

Head of State (Monarch)

1966–90 Moshoeshoe II
1990–4 Letsie III (abdicated)
1994–6 Moshoeshoe II
1996– Letsie III

Head of Government

1966–86 Leabua Jonathan

Chairman of Military Council

1986–91 Justin Metsing Lekhanya
1991–3 Elias Tutsoane Ramaema

Head of Government

1993–4 Ntsu Mokhehle
1994 Hae Phoofolo (Chairman of Transitional Council)
1994–8 Ntsu Mokhehle
1998– Bethuel Pakalitha Mosisili

---

success with two feature films starring The Beatles, *A Hard Day's Night* (1964) and *Help!* (1965). Later film credits include *Superman II* and its sequel (1980, 1983), *The Return of the Musketeers* (1989), and *Get Back* (1991).

Lethe [leethee] In the Greek and Roman Underworld, the name of a slow-moving river. When the souls of the dead drank from it, they forgot their lives on Earth.

Letterman, David (1947–) Television talk-show host, born in Indianapolis, IN. He became well-known following guest-host appearances on the Johnny Carson Show during 1979 and 1980. He hosted a late-night show for MBC from 1982, then in 1993 joined CBS as presenter of 'Late Night with David Letterman'.

letter of credit A document issued by a bank or other body in which the issuer undertakes to substitute its financial strength for that of the beneficiary, when presented with a draft (bill of exchange) or other demand for payment along with other specified documents. They are especially used abroad, as a means of paying for foreign goods.

letterpress A form of printing in which the image to be communicated is placed on a relief surface of metal or wood, and transferred as an inked impression to the printing foundation, usually paper. To be read correctly on the paper, the printing image has to be reversed from left to right. Letterpress has now been largely superseded by offset lithography.

lettuce An annual or perennial, very widespread but mostly N temperate; leaves often with prickly margins; flower-heads small, often in clusters, yellow or blue. It is an important salad plant, its numerous cultivars being divided into two main groups: *cos*, with upright heads of crisp oblong leaves, and the round-headed *cabbage* types, with broadly rounded leaves. (Genus: *Lactuca*, 100 species. Family: Compositae.)

leucocytes [lyookohsiyts] Blood cells without respiratory pigments, also known as **white blood cells**, whose function is to combat injury and bacterial, parasitic, and viral infection. In vertebrates the major types are *granulocytes*, sometimes called *polymorphs* (neutrophils, eosinophils, basophils) and *agranulocytes* (lymphocytes, monocytes).

leucotomy *psychosurgery*

leukaemia / leukemia [l(y)ookeemia] A group of malignant disorders of the bone marrow, with abnormal proliferation of the cells that develop into white blood cells. The disease may be rapid in onset and highly aggressive (eg *acute lymphoblastic* and *myeloblastic leukaemia*) or slow and prolonged (eg *chronic lymphocytic* and *myelocytic leukaemia*). Patients become anaemic and vulnerable to infection, and blood clotting is impaired. The cause is unknown, but some cases occur in clusters, and have been associated with ionizing radiation, industrial chemicals such as benzene and toluene, electromagnetic fields, and viruses. Some cases have been treated successfully with bone marrow transplantation.

Leuven [loeven], Fr **Louvain**, Ger **Lowen** 50°53N 4°42E, pop (2000e) 87 000. University town in Belgium; centre of cloth trade in Middle Ages; largely destroyed in World War 1; Catholic University (1425), reorganized into French- and Flemish-speaking divisions since 1970; railway.

Levant, The [levant] A general name formerly given to the E shores of the Mediterranean Sea, from W Greece to Egypt. The **Levant States** were Syria and Lebanon, during the period of their French mandate, 1920–41.

Le Vau or **Levau, Louis** [luh voh] (1612–70) Architect, born in Paris. His design of Vaux-le-Vicomte (1657–61), in which he collaborated with the landscape gardener Le Nôtre and the painter Le Brun, was a milestone in French architecture. The team went on to work at Versailles (from 1661), where Le Vau designed the garden facade.

Levellers A radical political movement during the English Civil War and the Commonwealth. It called for the extension of manhood franchise to all but the poorest, religious toleration, and the abolition of the monarchy and the House of Lords.

Leverhulme (of the Western Isles), William Hesketh Lever, 1st Viscount [leeverhyoom], also known as **Baron Leverhulme of Bolton-Le-Moors** (1851–1925) Soap manufacturer, born in Bolton, Lancashire. In 1884 he began to turn a small soap works into a national business, and developed Port Sunlight as a model industrial village.

Leverrier, Urbain Jean Joseph [luhveryay] (1811–77) Astronomer, born in St Lô, France. Interested in planetary motions, he correctly predicted the existence of Neptune in 1846.

Levesque, Rene [luhvek] (1922–87) Canadian politician and premier of Quebec (1976–85), born in Campbellton, New Brunswick, Canada. Elected to the Quebec National Assembly as a Liberal in 1960, in 1968 he founded the separatist *Parti Québecois*.

Levi, Primo [layvee] (1919–87) Writer, born in Turin, Italy. All of his writings attempt to understand the nature of Nazi barbarity and the variety of responses to it. They include *Se questo è un Uomo* (1947, If this is a Man) and its sequel, *La tregua* (1963, The Truce).

Leviathan [leviyathan] A rare Hebrew loan-word of uncertain derivation, apparently used to refer to a kind of sea or river monster. It may have been a mythical supernatural figure, perhaps symbolic of chaos or evil.

Levinson, Barry (1942–) Film director and producer, born in Baltimore, MD. His directorial debut, *Diner* (1982), earned him an Oscar nomination for Best Screenplay. Other films include *Good Morning, Vietnam* (1987) and *Rain Man* (1988, Oscar). He later produced *Donnie Brasco* (1997), and directed *Liberty Heights* (1999) and *Man of the Year* (2006).

levirate A marriage custom or law which expects a widow to marry a brother (either real or a close relative classified as such) of her deceased husband. A **sororate** is a custom whereby a man has the right to marry his wife's sister, though this normally applies only if the wife is childless or dies young.

Lévi-Strauss, Claude [layvee strows] (1908–) Social anthropologist, born in Brussels. A major influence on contemporary anthropology, his four-volume study *Mythologiques* (1964–72) studied the systematic ordering behind codes of expression in different cultures.

Levites [leeviyts] Descendants of the Biblical character Levi (one of Jacob's sons), who apparently formed a class of auxiliary ministers dedicated to the care of the Tabernacle and eventually the Jerusalem Temple (*Num* 3.5–10).

Leviticus, Book of [levitikus] A book of the Hebrew Bible/Old Testament, the third book of the Pentateuch, the English title referring to the priestly traditions of the Levites. It was probably compiled from earlier materials during the exile.

levodopa *L-dopa*

Levy, Andrea (1956–) Writer, born in London. Born to Jamaican parents, her first three novels, *Every Light in the House Burnin'* (1994), *Never Far From Nowhere* (1996), and *Fruit of the Lemon* (1999), explore the problems faced by black British-born children of Jamaican emigrants. Later novels include *Small Island* (2004), which won the Orange Prize and the Whitbread Best Novel and Book of the Year.

Lewinsky, Monica [luhwinskee] (1973–) Former White House intern, born in San Francisco, CA. She joined the White House in 1995, moving to the Pentagon the following year. She became known in 1998 during the official investigation into claims of sexual harrassment made by Paula Jones against President Clinton (a claim later dismissed). In 1999 she was called to give evidence in the impeachment trial against the president. It was alleged that Lewinsky had had a sexual relationship with the president, and that he had persuaded her to deny the affair in her deposition to lawyers acting for Jones. Clinton subsequently denied the affair himself, while under oath (a denial he was forced by circumstantial evidence to retract during his impeachment trial). The enquiries were fuelled by a series of covert tape recordings of conversations made with her by her confidante Linda Tripp (1950–), a former White House aide. Lewinsky continued to maintain a high national and international profile after the impeachment. Her memoir, *Monica's Story* (1999), became a best-seller.

Lewis, (Frederick) Carl(ton) (1961–) Athlete, born in Birmingham, AL. He won four gold medals at the 1984 Olympic Games, two at the 1988 Olympics, two more at the 1992 Olympics, and another at the 1996 Olympics .

Lewis, C Day *Day-Lewis, C*

Lewis, C(live) S(taples) (1898–1963) Mediaevalist and Christian apologist, born in Belfast. His best-known book is *The Screwtape Letters* (1942), one of several works which expound issues of Christian belief and practice. He is also known for his children's stories of the land of Narnia, beginning with *The Lion, the Witch, and the Wardrobe* (1950, filmed 2005).

Lewis, Edward B (1918–2004) Developmental biologist, born in Wilkes-Barre, PA. He shared the Nobel Prize for Physiology or Medicine in 1995 for his research into how genes control early development of the human embryo. Using the fruit fly, he investigated how genes could control development of body segments into specialized organs.

Lewis, Jerry Lee (1935–) Rock singer, country singer, and pianist, born in Ferriday, LA. His 1957 recordings 'Whole Lotta Shakin' and 'Great Balls of Fire' became classics of rock, copied by successive generations of musicians.

Lewis, John L(lewellyn) (1880–1969) Labour leader, born near Lucas, IA. President of the United Mine Workers (1920–60), he was active in creating the Congress of Industrial Organizations in 1935, and served as its president until 1940.

Lewis, Lennox (1965–) Heavyweight boxer, born in London.

Awarded the World Boxing Council (WBC) heavyweight title in 1993, he lost it in 1994 to Oliver McCall, but regained it from McCall in 1997. In 1999 he drew a unification bout with World Boxing Association champion Evander Holyfield, but a rematch was called for after protests over the scoring. Lewis won the rematch but was stripped of the title by a New York court in 2000. In 2001 he lost the WBC and the International Boxing Federation heavyweight titles but regained them the same year, and successfully defended them against Mike Tyson in 2002. He retained the WBC title following a controversial match with Vitali Klitschko in 2003, and announced his retirement from professional boxing in 2004.

Lewis, Martyn (John Dudley) (1945–) British television journalist, presenter, and newsreader. He worked with BBC Belfast, HTV Wales, and ITN, becoming newsreader and foreign correspondent on *News at Ten* and *News at 5.45* (1978–86). He became well known as presenter of the BBC's *Nine O'Clock News* (1987–94) and *Six O'Clock News* (1994–9). His books include *Go For It* (annual, 1993–) and *Reflections on Success* (1997).

Lewis, Meriwether (1774–1809) Explorer, born in Charlottesville, VA. With William Clark he was joint leader of the first overland transcontinental expedition to the Pacific coast and back (1804–6).

Lewis, M(atthew) G(regory), nickname **Monk Lewis** (1775–1818) Novelist, born in London. His best-known work is the Gothic novel *The Monk* (1795).

Lewis, (Harry) Sinclair (1885–1951) Novelist, born in Sauk Center, MN. *Main Street* (1920) was the first of a series of best-selling novels satirizing the materialism and intolerance of American small-town life. Other works include *Babbitt* (1922), *Elmer Gantry* (1927), and *Dodsworth* (1929). He received the 1930 Nobel Prize for Literature.

Lewis, (Percy) Wyndham [windam] (1882–1957) Artist, writer, and critic, born in Nova Scotia, Canada. With Ezra Pound he founded *Blast*, the magazine of the Vorticist school. His writings include the satirical novel *The Apes of God* (1930) and the multi-volume *The Human Age* (1955–6), as well as literary criticism and autobiographical books.

Lewis and Clark Expedition *Clark, William; Lewis, Meriwether*

Lewis with Harris area 2134 km²/824 sq mi. Island in the Western Isles, NW Scotland; largest and northernmost of the Hebrides; Lewis (N) linked to Harris (S) by a narrow isthmus.

lexicography *dictionary*

Lexington 42°27N 71°14W, pop (2000e) 30 400. Town in NE Massachusetts, USA; flashpoint of the American War of Independence.

Lexington (Virginia) 37°47N 79°26W, pop (2000e) 6900. Historic town in Rockbridge Co, VA; birthplace of Sam Houston; Washington and Lee university; Virginia Military Institute houses the George C Marshall Museum; Stonewall Jackson House; Virginia Horse Centre.

Leyden [liydn], Dutch **Leiden** 52°09N 4°30E, pop (2000e) 118 000. University city in W Netherlands; charter, 1266; famous for its weaving, 14th-c; besieged for a year by the Spaniards, 1573; as a reward for their bravery the citizens were given Holland's first university, 1575; birthplace of several painters, notably Rembrandt.

Leyden jar [liydn] The earliest device for storing electric charge, named after the University of Leyden, where it was invented in 1746. A glass jar was coated inside and outside with metal foils, which were connected by a rod passing the insulating stopper.

ley lines [lay] Visible lines that connect ancient sites and features (eg burial mounds, standing stones) across the countryside. They have been interpreted as ancient trading tracks, as 'energy lines' which can be detected by dowsing, and as 'spirit lines' which begin and end in cemeteries.

Lhasa [lahsa], Chin **Lasa**, known as **The Forbidden City** 29°41N 91°10E, pop (2000e) 156 000. Capital of Tibet (Xizang), SW China; altitude 3600 m/11 800 ft; airfield; ancient centre of Tibetan Buddhism, with many temples and holy sites; closed to foreigners in 19th-c; Chinese occupation, 1951; many monks have fled (including the Dalai Lama), especially after uprising in 1959.

liane [liahn], or **liana** [liahna] A woody climber growing from the ground to the top of the tree canopy, where it branches out and produces flowers.

Libby, Willard (Frank) (1908–80) Chemist, born in Grand Valley, CO. He received the Nobel Prize for Chemistry in 1960 for his part in the invention of the carbon-14 method of dating.

libel A defamatory statement published in permanent form. In many jurisdictions this is extended to include broadcast by wireless telegraphy (radio, television), and words spoken during the public performance of a play; also, the libel need not involve words – a sculpture or painting may be libellous. The expression is not used in this technical sense in Scottish law, being subsumed under defamation. In the USA, defamation on radio and television is usually classified as slander.

Liberace [libuhrahchee], also known as **Walter Busterkeys**, originally **Wladziu Valentino Liberace** (1919–87) Entertainer, born in Milwaukee, WI. His television series, *The Liberace Show* (1952–7), won him an Emmy as Best Male Personality. His enduring career rested on his live performances and a flamboyant lifestyle, full of piano-shaped swimming pools, glittering candelabra, and sartorial excess.

Liberal Democrats *Liberal Party* (UK); *Social Democratic Party*

liberalism A political philosophy developed largely in the 18th–19th-c associated with the rise of the new middle classes, challenging the traditional monarchical, aristocratic, or religious views of the state. Classical liberalism argues for limited government, and the values traditionally espoused are those of freedom – of the individual, religion, trade and economics (expressed in terms of *laissez faire*), and politics. In the 20th-c, liberalism in most countries was overtaken by socialism as the major radical challenge to conservative parties, and came to occupy a position in the centre ground, finding it difficult to establish a firm electoral base.

Liberal Party (Australia) Australia's largest conservative political party, formed by R G Menzies in 1944 from existing conservative groups. Under Menzies (prime minister, 1949–66), the party followed policies of economic growth and conservative pragmatism, espousing private enterprise. It is the main alternative to the Australian Labor Party, achieving success under John Howard in 1996.

Liberal Party (Canada) A Canadian national and provincial political organization that grew out of 19th-c reformism. At the federal level, it regained power in the general election of 1993.

Liberal Party (UK) A British political party, originating in the mid 19th-c, whose electoral appeal was to the new middle classes and working-class elite of skilled artisans. The Liberals and Conservatives were the two major parties until 1922, since when it has become a centrist minority party. After the formation of the Social Democratic Party (SDP) in 1980, the Liberal Party entered into an electoral 'Alliance', and in 1987 voted to merge with the SDP, subsequently forming the **Social and Liberal Democratic Party**, from 1988 known as the **Liberal Democrats**.

liberation theology A style of theology originating in Latin America in the 1960s. Accepting a Marxist analysis of society, it stresses the role and mission of the Church to the poor and oppressed in society, of which Christ is understood as liberator. Its sympathy for revolutionary movements led to clashes with established secular and religious authorities.

Liberia *p.539*

Liberia

SIERRA LEONE

GUINEA

AFRICA

Voinjama

Wologisi Mts

Mano

Mt Nimba 1752m

Sanniquellie

Gbarnga • Ganta

Robertsport

St John

CÔTE D'IVOIRE

LIBERIA

Monrovia

• Buchanan

Cess

Zwedru

Duoubé

ATLANTIC OCEAN

Grain Coast

Niete Mts

Greenville

Kru Coast

200 km
100 mi

Harper

□ International Airport

[liybeeria], official name **Republic of Liberia**

Local name Liberia

Timezone GMT

Area 111 370 km²/43 760 sq mi

Population total (2002e) 3 288 000

Status Republic

Date of independence 1847

Capital Monrovia

Languages English (official) with many dialects/languages of Niger-Congo spoken

Ethnic groups Indigenous tribes (including Kpelle, Bassa, Gio, Kru, Gola, Kissi, Vai, and Bella) (95%), Americo-Liberians (repatriated slaves from the USA) (5%)

Religions Traditional animist beliefs (70%), Muslim (20%), Christian (10%)

Physical features Low coastal belt with lagoons, beaches, and mangrove marshes; land rises inland to mountains, reaching 1752 m/5748 ft at Mt Nimba; rivers include Mano, Moro, St Paul, St John, Cess, Duoubé, Cavalla.

Climate Equatorial climate; high temperatures, abundant rainfall; high humidity during rainy season (Apr–Sep), especially on coast; average annual temperatures 26°C (Jan), 24°C (Jul); average annual rainfall 5138 mm/202 in.

Currency 1 Liberian Dollar (LRD) = 100 cents

Economy Based on minerals, especially iron ore; two-thirds of the population rely on subsistence agriculture; rubber, timber, palm oil, rice, cassava, coffee, cocoa, coconuts; large merchant fleet, including the registration of many foreign ships.

GDP (2002e) $3·116 bn, per capita $1000

History Mapped by the Portuguese in 15th-c; created as a result of the activities of several US philanthropic societies, wishing to establish a homeland for former slaves; founded in 1822; constituted as the Free and Independent Republic of Liberia, 1847; military coup and assassination of President, 1980, established a People's Redemption Council, with a chairman and a Cabinet; new constitution in 1986, with an elected Senate and a House of Representatives; 200 000 die in civil war, followed by arrival of West African peacekeeping force, 1990; interim Government of National Unity installed; transitional Council of State, 1994; peace accord signed, 1995; elections held, 1997; rebels of the Liberians United for Reconciliation and Democracy (LURD) launched a large-scale offensive in the NW (Feb 2003), later agreeing to government talks, but fighting continued; rebels attack Monrovia (Jul 2003), leading to the exile of President Taylor, arrival of US troops to help Nigerian-led UN peacekeepers, and a new power-sharing government; UN mission launched disarmament process, Dec 2003; Liberia's first woman president, Ellen Johnson-Sirleaf, elected Nov 2005.

Head of State/Government
1986–90 Samuel Kanyon Doe
1990–4 Amos Sawyer *Acting*

Council of State – Chairman
1994–5 David Kpormakor
1995–6 Wilton Sankawulo *Transitional*
1996–7 Ruth Perry

Head of State/Government
1997–2003 Charles Taylor
2003 Moses Blah *Interim*
2003–5 Gyude Bryant
2005– Ellen Johnson-Sirleaf

Liberty, Statue of The representation of a woman holding aloft a torch, which stands at the entrance to New York harbour; a world heritage site. It was designed by the French sculptor Bartholdi, and assembled in 1886. The statue is 40 m/152 ft high.

Liberty Bell *Independence Hall*

Libra [leebra] (Lat 'scales') An inconspicuous S constellation zodiac, lying between Virgo and Scorpius.

librarianship *library science*

Library of Congress The US depository and largest library in the world, founded in 1800 in Washington, DC. Its functions include the provision of reference materials for the US Congress.

library program A computer program which carries out a specific function and which can be incorporated into another program doing a more sophisticated task. For example, a library program to print a current debit can be incorporated into a program to print a credit-card customer's statement.

library science The study of all aspects of library functions. It covers such topics as selection and acquisition policy, classification systems, and cataloguing, as well as bibliography and administration. As a discipline in its own right, library science, or **librarianship**, is a late 19th-c development.

Libreville [leebruhveel] 0°30N 9°25E, pop (2000e) 448 000. Capital of Gabon, W Africa; founded in 1849 as a refuge for slaves freed by the French; occupied by the British and Free French, 1940; airport; railway; university (1970); cathedral; first Central African Games held here, 1976.

Librium *benzodiazepines*

Libya

□ International Airport   ∴ World heritage site

official name **Socialist People's Libyan Arab Jamahiriya**

Local name Lībiyā

Timezone GMT +1

Area 1 758 610 km²/678 823 sq mi

Population total (2002e) 5 369 000

Status Republic

Date of independence 1951

Capital Tripoli

Languages Arabic (official), with English and French widely spoken

Ethnic groups Berber and Arab (97%), Greek, Maltese, Italian, Egyptian, Pakistani, Turk, Indian, and Tunisian minorities (3%)

Religions Sunni Muslim (96%), Christian (Roman Catholic, Anglican, Coptic Orthodox) (3%), Jewish (1%)

Physical features Mainly low-lying Saharan desert or semi-desert; 93% of land is contained in the arid Saharan plateau; land rises (S) to over 2000 m/6500 ft in the Tibesti massif; highest point, Pic Bette, 2286 m/7500 ft; comparatively fertile region in Gefara plain and Jabal Nafusah plateau in Tripolitania region.

Climate Mediterranean climate on coast; rainy season (Oct–Mar) in NW and NE upland regions; average annual temperature 11°C (Jan), 27°C (Jul) in Tripoli; average annual rainfall 385 mm/15 in.

Currency 1 Libyan Dinar (LYD) = 1000 dirhams

Economy Former agricultural economy; barley, olives, fruit, dates, almonds, tobacco; relatively poor until economy transformed by discovery of oil and natural gas, 1959; petroleum processing; iron, steel, aluminium; textiles; nomadic farming in S.

GDP (2002e) $33·36 bn, per capita $6200

Human Development Index (2002) 0·773

History Controlled by Phoenicians, Carthaginians, Greeks, Vandals, and Byzantines; Arab domination during 7th-c; Turkish rule from 16th-c; Italians gained control, 1911; named Libya by the Italians, 1934; heavy fighting during World War 2, followed by British and French control; independent Kingdom of Libya, 1951; military coup established a republic under Muammar al-Gaddafi, 1969; governed by a Revolutionary Command Council; foreign military installations closed down in early 1970s; Libyan troops occupied Aozou Strip, 1973 (returned to Chad, 1994); strained relations with other countries due to controversial activities, including alleged organization of international terrorism; diplomatic relations severed by UK after the murder of a policewoman in London, 1984; Tripoli and Benghazi bombed by US Air Force in response to alleged terrorist activity, 1986; alleged base of terrorist operation which caused the Lockerbie air disaster (1988), suspects extradicted to stand trial in The Netherlands (1999), followed by suspension of international sanctions; responsibility for the disaster formally accepted, 2003; international inspection of nuclear sites allowed, 2003; US resumed partial relations and lifted trade embargo, 2004; EU lifted arms embargo, 2004; US restored full diplomatic relations, 2006; a socialist state, governed by a chief-of-state, a General People's Committee, and a 750-member General People's Congress.

Monarch
1951–69 Mohammed Idris al-Mahdi al-Senussi

Revolutionary Command Council
Chairman
1969–77 Muammar al-Gaddafi (Qaddifi)

General Secretariat
Secretary General (Prime Minister)
1977–9 Muammar al-Gaddafi
1979–84 Abdul Ati al-Ubaidi
1984–6 Mohammed az-Zaruq Rajab
1986–90 Omar al-Muntasir
1990–7 Abu Zaid Omar Dourda
1997–2000 Muhammad Ahmad al-Mangoush
2000–3 Mubarak Abdullah as-Shamikh
2003– Shukri Mohammed Ghanim

Leader of the Revolution (Head of State)
1969– Muammar al-Gaddafi

Libya *see panel*

lice *louse*

lichen [liykn, lichn] A type of composite organism formed as an association between a fungus and an alga or blue-green bacterium. The body may be encrusting, scale-like, leafy, or even shrubby, according to species. The fungal partner typically belongs to the Ascomycetes.

Lichtenstein, Roy [likhtenstiyn] (1923–97) Painter, born in New York City. From the early 1960s he produced many of the best-known images of American Pop Art, especially frames from comic books complete with speech balloons, enlarged onto canvases and painted in primary colours.

licorice *liquorice*

Lie, Trygve (Halvdan) [lee, trigvuh] (1896–1968) Lawyer, the first secretary-general of the United Nations, born in Oslo. Elected secretary-general in 1946, he resigned in 1952 over Soviet opposition to his policy of intervention in the Korean War.

Liechtenstein

GERMANY

50 km
25 mi

Lake Constance

St Gallen •
Bregenz

S W I T Z E R L A N D

Säntis •

Rhine

Vaduz
LIECHTENSTEIN

A U S T R I A

Davos •

S W I T Z E R L A N D

I T A L Y

EUROPE

☐ International Airport

[likhtnshtiyn], official name **Principality of Liechtenstein**, Ger **Fürstentum Liechtenstein**

Local name Liechtenstein

Timezone GMT +1

Area 160 km²/62 sq mi

Population total (2002e) 33 300

Status Independent principality

Date of independence 1719

Capital Vaduz

Language German (official)

Ethnic groups Liechtensteiner (64%), Swiss (16%), Austrian (8%), German (4%)

Religions Roman Catholic (87%), Protestant (9%)

Physical features Alpine principality, located in C Europe; fourth smallest country in the world; land boundary 76 km/47 mi; bounded W by the R Rhine; mean altitude, 450 m/1475 ft; forested mountains rise to 2599 m/8527 ft in the Grauspitz; Samina River flows N.

Climate Mild, equable climate; temperatures range from 15°C (Jan), 20–8°C (Jul); average annual rainfall 1050–1200 mm/41–47 in.

Currency 1 Swiss Franc (CHF) = 100 centimes

Economy Industrial sector developing since 1950s; export-based, centred on specialized and high-tech production; metal-working, engineering, chemicals, pharmaceuticals; international banking and finance; tourism.

GDP (1999e) $825 mn, per capita $25 000

History Became a sovereign state in 1342; independent principality within Holy Roman Empire, 1719; part of Holy Roman Empire until 1806; adopted Swiss currency, 1921; united with Switzerland in a customs union, 1923; became a member of UN, 1990; joined European Free Trade Association (EFTA), 1991; constitutional monarchy ruled by hereditary princes of the House of Liechtenstein; day-to-day running of the principality transferred by Hans-Adam II to his son, Prince Alois, 2004; governed by a Prime Minister, four Councillors, and a unicameral Parliament; referendum for constitutional reforms was approved in 2003, including the granting of extensive new powers to the reigning prince.

Head of State (Monarch)
1858–1929 Johann II
1929–38 Franz von Paula
1938–89 Franz Josef II
1989– Hans Adam II

Head of Government
1928–45 Franz Josef Hoop
1945–62 Alexander Friek
1962–70 Gérard Batliner
1970–4 Alfred J Hilbe
1974–8 Walter Kieber
1978–93 Hans Brunhart
1993 Markus Büchel
1993–2001 Mario Frick
2001– Otmar Hasler

Liechtenstein *see panel*

Lied [leet] plural **Lieder** A song with German words. It generally refers to the solo songs with piano of the great German Romantic composers.

lie detector An instrument supposed to indicate whether a person to which it is applied is responding truthfully to questions; also known as a **polygraph**. Involuntary physiological reactions detected by electrodes attached to the subject's skin indicate stresses. Its validity is not universally acknowledged nor accepted judicially.

Liège [lyezh], Flemish **Luik**, Ger **Lüttich** 50°38N 5°35E, pop (2000e) 199 000. River port in E Belgium, at confluence of Ourthe and Meuse rivers; bishopric; fifth largest city in Belgium; railway; centre of former coal-mining area; university (1817); cathedral.

lifeboat A vessel designed specifically for saving life at sea; also, a craft carried by seagoing vessels to save the lives of personnel in the event of abandoning ship. Lionel Lukin is believed to have been the first to build a lifeboat, in 1786, basing it at Bamburgh Head, Northumberland, UK. The first mechanically powered lifeboat was launched, equipped with a steam engine,

in 1890. Several countries now run lifeboat services; some are government controlled, and others are voluntary.

life insurance Insurance designed to provide protection against financial hardship for dependents following the death of the insured person; also (especially in the UK) called **life assurance**. *Whole life policies* run for the whole of a person's life, accumulating a cash value which is paid when the policy matures (or is surrendered), but which is less than the policy's face value. *Endowment policies* run for a specified period of time, and pay the full face value when the policy matures. *Term policies* run for a specified number of years, but when the policy expires there is no cash sum remaining. Policies may be for a fixed money amount or *with profits*, where the amount payable is related to the profits the life company has been able to make by investing the premium.

Liffey, River [lifee] River in E Ireland, rising in N Wicklow county; flows through Dublin to the Irish Sea; length 80 km/50 mi.

ligament A tough band of tissue connecting bones (eg across joints) or supporting internal organs (eg peritoneal ligaments). Ligaments act to prevent mechanical disruption at joints, and as sensory organs for the perception of movement and joint position.

ligand [ligand] A molecule or ion bonded to another. It is most often used to describe species bonded to the central metal ion in a co-ordination compound.

liger [liyger] A member of the cat family, resulting from the mating of a male lion with a female tiger. The offspring produced when a male tiger mates with a female lion is called a **tigon.**

Ligeti, György (Sándor) [ligetee] (1923–2006) Composer, born to Hungarian parents in Dicsöszent-Márton (now Târnarveni) in Transylvania, Romania. He developed an experimental approach to composition, as seen in his first large orchestral work, *Apparitions* (1958–9), and in *Aventures* (1962). His music appeared in the Stanley Kubrick film *2001: A Space Odyssey* (1968).

light The visible portion of the electromagnetic spectrum, corresponding to electromagnetic waves ranging in wavelength from approximately 3.9×10^{-7} m (violet) to 7.8×10^{-7} m (red) (corresponding frequencies 7.7×10^{14} Hz and 3.8×10^{14} Hz, respectively). Different wavelengths of light are perceived by humans as different colours. *White light* is composed of light of different wavelengths (colours), as may be seen by dispersing the beam through a prism. Light of a single colour is called *monochromatic*, as in the laser. Light as an electromagnetic wave was deduced by James Clerk Maxwell: light can also be viewed as composed of particles (*photons*) of definite energy. The modern description of light is as particles whose behaviour is governed by wave principles according to the rules of quantum theory. In geometrical optics (eg lens systems), light is thought of as rays, travelling in straight lines, causing shadows for opaque objects.

light-emitting diode (LED) A tiny semiconductor diode which emits light when an electric current is passed through it. It is used in electronic calculator displays and digital watch readouts.

lighthouse A tower or other structure erected to give guidance and warning to ships and aircraft by either visible or radio-electrical means. The first man-made lighthouse was the Pharos of Alexandria (3rd-c BC). Early lighthouses were erected on land and burnt mainly wood, coal, or oil. The Eddystone lighthouse built by Henry Winstanley (1644–1703) was the first structure (1699) fully exposed to the open sea, while the masonry tower, built by John Smeaton (1724–94) on the same site in 1756–9, embodied an important new construction principle, using masonry blocks dovetailed together in an interlocking pattern. Modern lighthouses are generally built of concrete and steel, standing on submerged caissons or steel-piled structures similar to those used for offshore oil and gas rigs. Equipment within the lighthouse includes rotating paraboloid mirrors to create a pattern of flashes. Lights are beamed on and off by an electrical code unit using modern lens equipment driven by an electric motor. Most lighthouses are now automated and self-sustaining.

lightning A visible electric discharge in the form of a flash of light which results from charge separation in a thundercloud. The reflection of lightning on surrounding clouds, in which the illumination is diffused, is known as **sheet lightning**.

lightning bug *firefly*

lightning conductor A means of protecting buildings and tall structures from lightning strikes; also called a **lightning rod**. It consists of a metal rod or strip, usually made of copper, placed at the highest point of a building. The lower end of the rod is connected to earth by a low-resistance cable.

lightpen A computer input device used in conjunction with a visual display unit (VDU). The pen is held against the screen of the VDU, and its position can be used to generate or to alter information on the screen.

Lights, Feast of *Hanukkah*

light year The distance travelled through empty space in one tropical year by any kind of electromagnetic radiation: 9.4607×10^{12} km/5.8788×10^{12} mi. It is not normally used by astronomers, who prefer the parsec.

lignite *coal*

lignum vitae [lignum viytee] An evergreen tree (*Guaiacum officinale*) growing to c.10 m/30 ft, native to W Indies; bark pale, smooth; flowers blue, 5-petalled. It is a source of durable timber. (Family: Zygophyllaceae.)

Ligurian Sea [liygyurian] Arm of the Mediterranean Sea, bounded N and E by NW Italy and S by Corsica and Elba.

lilac A deciduous shrub or small tree (*Syringa vulgaris*), native to the Balkans; growing to 3–7 m/10–23 ft, flowers lilac or white, fragrant; fruit a pointed capsule. (Family: Oleaceae.)

Lilburne, John (c.1614–57) English revolutionary, born near London, who became a leading figure in the Levellers during the English Civil War. He was repeatedly imprisoned for his pamphlets.

Lilienthal, Otto [leelyentahl] (1849–96) Aeronautical inventor, born in Anklam, Germany. He studied bird flight in order to build heavier-than-air flying machines resembling the birdman designs of Leonardo da Vinci.

Lilith [lilith] In Jewish legend, the first wife of Adam; or, more generally, a demon woman.

Lille [leel], formerly Flemish **Lisle** or **Ryssel**, ancient **Insula** 50°38N 3°03E, pop (2000e) 177 900. Industrial and commercial city in N France; badly damaged in both World Wars; road and rail junction; part of the main industrial centre of N France; university (1560); cathedral (begun, 1854), 16th-c citadel.

Lillie, Beatrice (Gladys) (1898–1989) Revue singer, born in Toronto, Ontario, Canada. She became renowned from 1914 in music hall and the new vogue of 'intimate revue'. Her film appearances include *Thoroughly Modern Millie* (1967).

Lilongwe [leelonggway] 13°58N 33°49E, pop (2000e) 319 000. Capital of Malawi, SE Africa; altitude 1100 m/3600 ft; capital since 1975; airport; railway.

lily A perennial with a bulb formed from swollen, overlapping, scale-like leaves, native to N temperate regions; flowers with six segments, large, terminal, often hanging; mostly white, yellow to red, purple, and often spotted; stamens long, protruding. (Genus: *Lilium*, 80 species. Family: Liliaceae.)

lily-of-the-valley A perennial growing to 20 cm/8 in (*Convallaria majalis*), native to Europe and Asia; flowers drooping, globular bells with six short lobes, white, fragrant; berries red; cultivated for ornament, and as a source of perfume. (Family: Liliaceae.)

lily-trotter *jacana*

Lima [leema] 12°06S 77°03W, pop (2000e) 7 721 000. Federal capital of Peru; founded by Pizarro, 1535; chief city of Spanish South America until independence; devastated by earthquake, 1746; airport; railway; 10 universities; cathedral (16th-c).

Limassol [limasol], Gr **Lemesos**, Turkish **Limasol** 34°41N 33°02E, pop (2000e) 148 000. Port in S Cyprus; airfield; wine-making; export of fruit and vegetables; castle (14th-c).

Limbaugh, Rush H(udson) [limbaw] (1951–) Conservative talk-radio host and activist, born in Cape Girardeau, MO. He devised a radio programme in San Diego, CA, at the end of the 1980s, blending political commentary and satire. His growing popularity led him to New York City, where he built a national audience for his daytime show. He was given credit for rousing conservative sentiment that contributed to the Republican capture of the House of Representatives in 1994.

limbo In mediaeval Christian theology, the abode of souls excluded from the full blessedness of the divine vision, but not condemned to any other punishment. They included unbaptized infants and Old Testament prophets.

lime (botany) **1** A deciduous N temperate tree; flowers fragrant, white, 5-petalled, in pendulous clusters; fruits rounded, the whole cluster with a wing-like bract which aids in dispersal; also called **liden**. (Genus: *Tilia*, 50 species. Family: Tiliaceae.) **2** A citrus fruit resembling lemon, but smaller and more globose. *Citrus limetta*, the sweet lime, is possibly a mutant of lemon. (Family: Rutaceae.)

lime (chemistry) Mainly calcium oxide or hydroxide, produced by heating limestone above 800°C, expelling carbon dioxide. The dry product is called **quicklime**; the addition of water converts the oxide to hydroxide or 'slaked' lime.

Limerick (county), Ir **Luimneach** pop (2000e) 164 000; area 2686 km²/1037 sq mi. County in Munster province, SW Ireland; capital, Limerick, pop (2000e) 75 000 founded, 1197; scene of major sieges by Cromwell and William III; railway; two cathedrals (12th-c, 19th-c).

limerick 'The limerick, it would appear,/ Is a verse form we owe Edward Lear:/ Two long and two short/ Lines rhymed, as was taught,/ And a fifth just to bring up the rear'. Lear, in fact, popularized the form, which is known from the 11th-c. It is especially used with the opening: 'There was a ...' (young man from Dundee, young lady of Cheam, etc).

limestone A sedimentary rock consisting mainly of carbonates, primarily calcite (calcium carbonate, $CaCO_3$) or dolomite ($CaMg(CO_3)_2$), with detrital sand or clay as impurities. Most limestones are organically formed from the secretions, shells, or skeletons of plants and animals such as corals and molluscs. Inorganic limestones are formed by precipitation from water containing dissolved carbonates. Limestone is of economic importance as a building material, and as a source of lime and cement.

limner A painter of portraits 'in little', ie in miniature. Nicholas Hilliard's treatise *The Art of Limning* (c.1600) describes the highly specialized techniques required.

Limoges [leemohzh], ancient **Augustoritum Lemovicensium**, later **Lemovic** 45°50N 1°15E, pop (2000e) 140 000. Ancient town in C France; Gallic tribal capital, destroyed 5th-c; sacked by the English, 1370; road and rail junction; famed for manufacture of enamels and porcelain since 18th-c; university (1808); meteorological observatory; cathedral (begun, 1273).

Limousin or **Limosin, Léonard** [limoozĩ] (c.1505–77) Painter in enamel, born in Limoges, France. He was appointed head of the royal factory at Limoges by Francis I.

limpet A primitive snail with a simple, flattened, conical shell; lives attached to rocks by its muscular foot; found in the intertidal zone or shallow seas. (Class: Gastropoda. Order: Archaeogastropoda.)

Limpopo *Northern Province*

Limpopo, River [limpohpoh], also **Crocodile River** River in SE Africa; length c.1600 km/1000 mi. rises in the S Transvaal and flows into the Indian Ocean.

Linacre, Thomas (c.1460–1524) Humanist and physician, born in Canterbury, Kent. He was king's physician to Henry VII and Henry VIII, and founded the Royal College of Physicians.

Lin Biao or **Lin Piao** [lin byow] (1907–71) A leader of the Chinese Communist Party, born in Hupeh province, China. He became minister of defence in 1959, and in 1968 replaced the disgraced Liu Shaqi as heir apparent to Mao Zedong. After differences with Mao and an abortive coup, he was killed in a plane crash in Mongolia, apparently while fleeing to the USSR.

Lincoln (UK) [lingkn] 53°14N 0°33W, pop (2001e) 85 600. County town of Lincolnshire, EC England; important centre of the wool trade in the Middle Ages; railway; parts of 3rd-c Roman wall remain; Lincoln Castle; cathedral (1073); football league team, Lincoln City (Imps).

Lincoln (USA) [lingkn], formerly **Lancaster** (to 1867) 40°49N 96°41W, pop (2000e) 225 600. Capital of state in SE Nebraska, USA; state capital in 1867, when it was renamed after President Lincoln; railway; two universities (1867, 1887); trade in grain and livestock.

Lincoln, Abraham (1809–65) US Republican statesman and 16th president (1861–5), born near Hodgenville, KY. He was elected president on a platform of hostility to slavery's expansion. When the Civil War began (1861), he defined the issue in terms of national integrity, a theme he restated in the Gettysburg Address of 1863, and in the same year proclaimed freedom for all slaves in areas of rebellion. On 14 April 1865 he was shot at Ford's Theater, Washington, DC, by an actor, John Wilkes Booth, and died next morning.

Lincoln Center for the Performing Arts A group of theatres, recital halls, etc erected to the W of Broadway, New York City. The complex was completed in 1969.

Lincoln Memorial A monument in Washington, DC, dedicated in 1922 to President Abraham Lincoln. The building, designed on the plan of a Greek temple by Henry Bacon (1866–1924), houses the statue of Lincoln (6 m/19 ft high) by Daniel Chester French (1850–1931).

Lincolnshire [lingknsheer] pop (2001e) 646 600; area 5915 km²/2284 sq mi. Flat agricultural county in EC England; county town, Lincoln; North Lincolnshire and North East Lincolnshire unitary authorities from 1996; Fens drained in 17th-c.

Lincoln's Inn *Inns of Court*

Lind, Jenny, originally **Johanna Maria Lind**, known as **the Swedish Nightingale** (1820–87) Soprano, born in Stockholm. She made her debut in Stockholm in 1838, and attained great popularity everywhere. After 1856 she lived in England.

Lindbergh, Charles A(ugustus) [lindberg] (1902–74) Aviator, born in Detroit, MI. He made the first solo non-stop transatlantic flight (New York–Paris, 1927), in the monoplane *The Spirit of St Louis*. His young son was kidnapped and murdered in 1932, the most publicized crime of the 1930s. His grandson, Erik Lindbergh, successfully duplicated the 1927 Atlantic solo flight in 2002.

Lindemann, Frederick Alexander *Cherwell, Viscount*

linden *lime* (botany)

Lindisfarne [lindisfah(r)n] area 10 km²/3³⁄₄ sq mi. An island off the NE coast of England, renowned for its monastery founded from Iona by St Aidan in AD 634; also known as **Holy Island**. The Lindisfarne Gospels were illuminated here, probably in the 690s, by Eadfrith (Bishop, 698–721). The island is accessible from the mainland at low water by a causeway.

Lindow Man *bog burials*

Lindrum, Walter (1898–1960) Billiards player, born in Kalgoorlie, Western Australia. In 1932 he set the current world break record of 4137 while playing Joe Davis.

Lindsay, Norman (1879–1969) Artist, born in Creswick, Victoria, Australia. He became chief cartoonist for the Sydney *Bulletin*, and in 1912 settled in Springwood, New South Wales. A prolific artist, he produced vigorous drawings, etchings, oil paintings, and watercolours. He also wrote poems, novels, and the children's book *The Magic Pudding* (1918), now regarded as an Australian classic.

Lindsay, Robert, popular name of **Robert Lindsay Stevenson** (1949–) Actor, born in Ilkeston, Derbyshire. He studied at the Royal Academy of Dramatic Art in London (1968–70), and became well known as 'Wolfie' in the popular sitcom *Citizen Smith* (1977). He has gone on to a prolific career in television, films, and on the stage. In musical theatre, his award-winning performances include *Me and My Girl* (1987) and *Oliver!* (1997). Later television work includes the series *Hornblower* (1998–2003), *My Family* (2001–), and *Jericho* (2005).

Linear A A system of writing found throughout Minoan Crete. It was used mainly by administrators in the compilation of inventories.

Linear B A system of writing found on clay tablets at Mycenaean palace sites. Deciphered in the 1950s by Michael Ventris, it is (unlike Linear A) an early form of Greek.

line-engraving A method of intaglio printing, the metal plate being cut with a *burin*. The technique originated in 15th-c Germany.

Lineker, Gary (Winston) [lineker] (1960–) Footballer, journalist, and broadcaster, born in Leicester, Leicestershire. He played for Leicester City, Everton, Barcelona, Tottenham Hotspur, and Grampus 8, Nagoya, Japan. He made his England debut in 1984 (captain 1990–2), playing in the 1986 and 1990 World Cups, and gaining 80 caps. He won Player of the Year awards in 1986 and 1992. Retiring in 1994, he became a presenter of sports programmes for the BBC, including TV's *Match of the Day* (from 1999), and is a familiar figure on television commercials.

linen Yarn and fabrics made from flax fibres, probably the earliest textile made from plants. Linen fabrics and yarns are fine, strong, and lustrous, and still fashionable, despite their poor easy-care properties.

line printer A type of printer, usually associated with larger computer systems, which prints a complete line of information at a time. It is very fast, especially when compared with printers that print one character at a time.

ling (botany) *heather*

ling (zoology) Slender-bodied fish (*Molva molva*) of the cod family, abundant in offshore waters of the NE Atlantic from Norway to the Bay of Biscay; length up to 2 m/6½ ft; mottled brownish-green on back. (Family: Gadidae.)

lingam [linggam] The principal symbolic representation of the Hindu deity Shiva, a phallic-shaped emblem. The female equivalent is the **yoni**, the shaped image of the female genitalia.

lingua franca [linggwa frangka] An auxiliary language used for routine and often restricted purposes by people who speak different native languages. English and French are frequently used for this purpose in many parts of the world.

linguistic philosophy A movement within 20th-c English-language analytic philosophy, associated particularly with the later work of Wittgenstein and with Ryle and Austin. The main methodological assumption is that traditional philosophical problems arise from a misuse of language.

linguistics The scientific study of language. The discipline is concerned with such matters as providing systematic descriptions of languages, investigating the properties of language structures as communicative systems, exploring the possibility that there are universals of language structure, and accounting for the historical development of linguistic systems. It began with the publication of Ferdinand de Saussure's *Cours de Linguistique Générale* (1916, Course in General Linguistics), which introduced the distinction between *diachronic* (historical) linguistics, and *synchronic* (descriptive) linguistics, and laid the foundation for the era of **structural linguistics**, which dominated the first half of the 20th-c. The major development in the second half of the 20th-c was the emergence of generative grammar, originally proposed by linguist Noam Chomsky in *Syntactic Structures* (1957), and since elaborated in a wide range of works.

Linklater, Eric (Robert Russell) (1899–1974) Novelist, born in Dounby, Orkney. While in the USA (1928–30) he wrote *Poet's Pub* (1929), the first of a series of satirical novels which include *Juan in America* (1931) and *Private Angelo* (1946).

Linnaeus, Carolus [linayus], Swed **Carl von Linné** (1707–78) Botanist, the founder of modern taxonomy, born in Råshult, Sweden. Two of his books, *Species plantarum* (1753) and *Systema*

naturae (10th edition, 1758–9), are the official starting-point for the current system of binomial Latin names for plants and animals. In many other books he described schemes of classification, grouping plants and animals into genera, classes, and orders.

linnet Any of three species of finch of the genus *Carduelis*, especially the **Eurasian linnet** (*Carduelis cannabina*); native to Europe, N Africa, and W Asia. (Family: Fringillidae.)

Linz [lints] 48°18N 14°18E, pop (2000e) 211 000. Industrial town in N Austria; on R Danube, centre of a rich agricultural region; extensive port installations; third largest city in Austria; University of Social and Economic Sciences (1966); many historical buildings, including early 16th-c castle.

lion A member of the cat family (*Panthera leo*), native to Africa and NW India; brown; male with mane of long dark hair; inhabits grassland and open woodland; often territorial; lives in 'prides' averaging 15 individuals; the only cat that hunts in groups.

Lions Clubs, International Association of *service club*

Lipchitz, Jacques [lipshitz], originally **Chaim Jacob Lipchitz** (1891–1973) Sculptor, born in Druskininkai, Lithuania. An exponent of Cubism, in the 1930s he developed a more dynamic style which he applied to bronze figure and animal compositions.

Lipizzaner [lipitsahner] A breed of horse, developed at Lipizza in Austria, now in Slovenia, in the 16th-c from the Andalusian horse; height, 15–16 hands/1·5–1·6 m/5 ft–5 ft 4 in; grey or pale brown.

Li Po [lee poh], also found as **Li Bo** and **Li T'ai Po** (c.700–762) Poet, born in Szechwan Province, China. A Taoist, interested in nature, mountains, and alchemy, he wrote over 1000 imaginative and rhapsodic free-style poems. Many were about drinking, such as 'Wine Song'.

Lippershey, Hans or **Jan** [lipers-hay], also spelled **Lippersheim** (c.1570–1619) Dutch lens grinder, born in Wesel, Germany. He has been called the inventor of the telescope, but this is unproven. Certainly, in 1608 he offered the government of The Netherlands what we would now call a refracting telescope, and shortly afterwards others, such as Galileo, constructed similar devices.

Lippi, Filippino [lipee] (c.1458–1504) Painter, born in Prato, nr Florence, Italy, the son of Filippo Lippi. He completed c.1484 the frescoes in the Brancacci Chapel in the Carmine, Florence, left unfinished by Masaccio.

Lippi, Fra Filippo [lipee], known as **Lippo** (c.1406–69) Religious painter, born in Florence. Italy. His greatest work was on the choir walls of Prato cathedral, begun in 1452. His later works are deeply religious and include a series of 'Nativities'.

Lippmann, Walter (1889–1974) Journalist, born in New York City. A special writer for the *Herald Tribune*, his daily columns became internationally famous, and he won many awards, including the Pulitzer Prize for International Reporting (1962).

liqueur A spirit, usually distilled from grain, mixed with syrup, and with the addition of fruits, herbs, or spices to infuse a strong aroma and taste. Liqueurs have a high alcohol content, and are usually drunk in small quantities after a meal. Examples include Cointreau, Bénédictine, and Chartreuse (France), Tia Maria (Jamaica), and Drambuie (Scotland).

liquid A dense form of matter which is able to flow but unable to transmit twisting forces; density typically a few per cent less than the corresponding solid. It is virtually incompressible; the atoms are constantly changing position in a random way.

liquidation *bankruptcy*

liquid crystals Organic materials, crystalline in the solid state, which form a partially ordered state (the **liquid crystal state**) upon melting, and become true liquids only after the temperature is raised further. Their optical transparency can be reduced by applying electric fields, a property extensively exploited in displays for watches, calculators, and other electronic devices.

liquidity In business and banking, actual money, or assets that are easily convertible into money. **Liquid assets** are cash, short-term investments, and debtors (ie amounts due from customers).

liquorice or **licorice** A perennial growing to 1 m/3¼ ft (*Glycyrrhiza glabra*), native to SE Europe and W Asia; pea-flowers whitish-violet. Its roots are a source of liquorice, used medicinally and as a confectionery ingredient. (Family: Leguminosae.)

Lisbon, Port **Lisboa**, ancient **Olisipo** or **Felicitas Julia** 38°42N 9°10W, pop (2000e) 672 000. Seaport and capital of Portugal, on N bank of R Tagus; settlement in Roman Empire; occupied by Moors, 8th-c; Portuguese capital, 1256; devastated by earthquake, 1755; Chiado shopping district of old town destroyed by fire, 1988; archbishopric; airport; railway; university (1911); 16th-c Tower of Belém and Jerónimos Monastery, a world heritage site; Belém Cultural Centre, cathedral (1150).

Lisdoonvarna [lishdoonvah(r)na] 53°02N 9°17W, pop (2000e) 850. Spa town in Clare county, Munster, W Ireland; leading sulphurspring health centre; Lisdoonvarna fair (Oct).

LISP [lisp] Acronym for **LISt Processing**, a high-level computer programming language designed for use with non-numeric data. It is widely used in artificial intelligence applications.

Lissitsky, El(iezer) [lisitskee], also spelled **Lissitzky** (1890–1941) Painter, born in Smolensk, Russia. He painted in a totally abstract style, based on arrangements of simple lines, planes, and cubes, and became a leading Constructivist.

Lister (of Lyme Regis), Joseph Lister, Baron (1827–1912) Surgeon, born in Upton, Essex. His great work was the introduction (1865) of the use of antisepsis, which revolutionized modern surgery.

Listeria [listeeria] A genus of typically rod-shaped bacteria, motile by means of flagella and exhibiting a tumbling motion. It grows best in the presence of small quantities of oxygen; some strains cause food poisoning.

Liszt, Franz (1811–86) Composer and pianist, born in Raiding, Hungary. From 1835 to 1839 he lived with the Comtesse d'Agoult, by whom he had three children. He gave concerts throughout Europe, and in 1847 met Princess Carolyne zu Sayn-Wittgenstein with whom he lived until his death. His works include 12 symphonic poems, Masses, two symphonies, and a large number of piano pieces.

litany A form of prayer used in public or private worship. Supplications or invocations are made by the priest or minister, to which the congregation replies with a fixed formula.

litchi, litchee, leechee, or **lychee** [liychee] An evergreen tree (*Litchi chinensis*) native to China; flowers white, starry; edible fruit 2·5–4 cm/1–1½ in long, ovoid with thin, horny, red-brown rind enclosing a single seed surrounded by sweet, white pulp. (Family: Sapindaceae.)

literacy The ability to read and write in a language. Discussion of the problem of **illiteracy**, both within a country and on a world scale, is complicated by the difficulty of measuring the extent of the problem in individuals. Defining even minimal levels is difficult, especially today, with increasing demands being made on people to be literate in a wider range of contexts. Current world estimates suggest that c.900 million adults are illiterate to a greater or lesser extent. National literacy campaigns in several countries have raised public awareness, and standards are slowly rising.

literary agent A person who sells the various rights in a book to publishers and other potential purchasers (eg film companies) on behalf of the author, and represents the author in negotiations. The agent retains a percentage of the author's earnings as commission.

litharge [lithah(r)j] Lead(II) oxide (PbO); a bright yellow pigment used in paints.

lithium Li, element 3, melting point 181°C. The lightest of the alkali metals; not common, but found widely in several minerals. Its compounds are used in organic synthesis; its salts have found application as anti-depressants in psychiatry.

lithography A method of printing, invented by Aloys Senefelder in 1796, based on the principle that grease (ie ink) and water do not mix. A flat surface is treated so that the image area alone will attract ink. Ink and water are then applied to the surface; ink adheres to the image area and water to the non-image area. Paper is then brought into contact with the printing surface. In **offset lithography**, the image to be printed is created photographically and the printing plate is wrapped round a cylinder. When the plate cylinder has been inked and dampened, the image is transferred ('offset') to a rubber 'blanket' cylinder and then transferred again to the printing substrate (normally paper, but also metal and plastic).

lithosphere Part of the Earth, consisting of the crust and the solid outermost layer of the upper mantle, extending to a depth of around 100 km/60 mi.

lithotripsy *urinary stones*

Lithuania *p.546*

litmus A complex vegetable dye traditionally used as a pH indicator. It is red in acid solutions and blue in alkaline ones.

litre Unit of volume; symbol *l*. The litre is no longer considered to be a precisely defined unit of volume. Officially the term may be used as a name for the cubic decimetre, but should not be used for high accuracy measurements. The precise unit of volume is the cubic metre, approximately 1000 litres.

Little Bighorn, Battle of the, also known as **Custer's Last Stand** (25 Jun 1876) The engagement between US cavalry, under Lieutenant-Colonel Custer, and the Sioux and Cheyenne, under Sitting Bull and Crazy Horse. The Indians destroyed Custer's force.

Little Richard, popular name of **Richard Wayne Penniman** (1932–) Rock-and-roll singer and pianist, born in Macon, GA. 'Tutti Frutti' (1955) brought him international popularity. Most of his recordings from 1958 to 1964 were of Gospel songs, but he later made a comeback with his album *The Rill Thing* (1970).

Little Rock 34°45N 92°16W, pop (2000e) 183 100. City in C Arkansas, USA; largest city in the state, and a port on the Arkansas R; settled, 1821; railway; university; in 1957 Federal troops were sent to the city to enforce a 1954 US Supreme Court ruling against segregation in schools.

Littlewood, (Maudie) Joan (1914–2002) Theatre director, born in London. She pioneered work in left-wing, popular theatre, forming the Theatre Workshop in 1945. After settling at the Theatre Royal Stratford East in 1953, her productions included *The Hostage* (1958) and *Oh! What A Lovely War* (1963).

liturgy (Gr *leitourgia*, 'duty, service') The formal corporate worship of God by a Church. It includes words, music, actions, and symbolic aids, and in Christian form is derived from Jewish ritual.

Liupanshui or **Liu-p'an-shui** [liopahnshway] 25°45N 104°40E, pop (2000e) 2 056 000. City in Guizhou province, S China; railway.

Liu Shaoqi [lyoo showchee], also spelled **Liu Shao-ch'i** (1898–1969) Leading figure in the Chinese Communist revolution, born in Hunan, China. In 1943 he became Party secretary, and succeeded Mao Zedong in 1959. After the Cultural Revolution (1966), the extreme left made Liu their principal target, and in 1968 he was stripped of all his posts.

Live Aid *Geldof, Bob*

Live 8 *Geldof, Bob*

liver In vertebrates, a large, unpaired gland with digestive functions, situated in the upper part of the left-hand side of the abdominal cavity under cover of the ribs. It secretes bile, facilitates the digestion and absorption of fats, and deals with the

Lithuania

□ International Airport

official name **Republic of Lithuania**, Lithuanian **Lietuvos Respublika**

Local name Lietuva

Timezone GMT +2

Area 65 200 km²/25 167 sq mi

Population total (2002e) 3 473 000

Status Republic

Date of independence 1991

Capital Vilnius

Language Lithuanian (official)

Ethnic groups Lithuanian (80%), Russian (9%), Polish (7%), Belorussian (2%)

Religions Roman Catholic, small minority of Evangelical Lutherans and Evangelical Reformists

Physical features Glaciated plains cover much of the area; central lowlands with gentle hills in W and higher terrain in SE; highest point, Jouzapine in the Asmenos Hills, 294 m/964 ft; 25% forested; some 3000 small lakes mostly in E and SE; complex sandy dunes on Kursiu Marios lagoon; chief river, the Nemunas.

Climate Continental climate, affected by maritime weather of W Europe and continental E; Baltic Sea influences a narrow coastal zone; average annual temperatures -5°C (Jan), 16°C (Jul); average annual rainfall 630 mm/25 in.

Currency 1 Litas (LTL) = 100 centas

Economy Electrical engineering, computer hardware, instruments, machine tools, ship building; synthetic fibres, fertilizers, plastics, food processing, oil refining; cattle, pigs, poultry, grain, potatoes, vegetables.

GDP (2002e) $30·08 bn, per capita $8400

Human Development Index (2002) 0·808

History United with Poland, 1385–1795; intensive russification led to revolts in 1905 and 1917; occupied by Germany in both World Wars; proclaimed a republic, 1918; annexed by the USSR, 1940; growth of nationalist movement in the late 1980s; declared independence in 1990, but not recognized until 1991; President Paksas impeached for violating the constitution, April 2004, later dismissed; governed by a President, Prime Minister and Supreme Council; joined European Union, 2004.

Head of State

1991–3 Vytautas Landsbergis
1993–8 Algirdas Brazauskas
1998–2003 Valdas Adamkus
2003–4 Rolandas Paksas
2004 Arturas Paulauskas *Acting*
2004– Valdas Adamkus

Head of Government

1991–2 Gediminas Vagnorius
1992 Aleksandras Abisala
1992–3 Bronislovas Lubys
1993–6 Adolfas Šleževičius
1996 Gediminas Vagnorius
1999 Irena Degutiene *Acting*
1999 Rolandas Paksas
1999 Irena Degutienë *Acting*
1999–2000 Andrius Kubilius
2000–1 Rolandas Paksas
2001 Eugenijus Gentvilas *Acting*
2001–6 Algirdas-Mykolas Brazauskas
2006– Gediminas Kirkilas

newly absorbed products of digestion. It also manufactures the anticoagulant heparin and other plasma proteins, stores glycogen, fat, iron, copper, and the vitamins A, D, E, and K, detoxifies harmful substances, and destroys red blood cells. Medical problems affecting the liver include cirrhosis, infectious hepatitis, jaundice, and Reye's syndrome.

liver fluke A leaf-like, parasitic flatworm (*Fasciola hepatica*), with a mouth sucker on its cone-shaped front end; can be a serious pest of domesticated animals. (Phylum: Platyhelminthes. Class: Trematoda.)

Liverpool 53°25N 2°55W, pop (2001e) 439 500. Seaport in Merseyside, NW England; on the right bank of the R Mersey estuary; founded in the 10th-c, became a borough in 1207 and a city in 1880; importance enhanced in the 18th-c by the slave trade and the Lancashire cotton industry; major world trading centre and the UK's most important seaport for Atlantic trade; railway; container terminal (1972); linked to Birkenhead under the R Mersey by road and rail tunnels (1934, 1971); John Lennon Airport; universities (1903, 1992); Catholic cathedral, modern design by Frederick Gibberd on earlier classical foundation by Edward Lutyens (consecrated 1967); Anglican cathedral, designed by Giles Gilbert Scott (begun 1904, completed 1980); Royal Liver Building (landmark at Pier Head), St George's Hall, Albert Dock redevelopment, Maritime Museum, Tate in the North (1987), Walker Art Gallery; Royal Liverpool Philharmonic Orchestra; home of the Beatles (museum, 1984), and many other pop groups; football league teams, Liverpool (Reds) and Everton (Toffeemen); International Garden Festival held here in 1984; Grand National steeplechase at Aintree (Apr); nominated European Capital of Culture for 2008.

Liverpool, Robert Banks Jenkinson, 2nd Earl of (1770–1828) British statesman and Tory prime minister (1812–27), born in London. He became foreign secretary (1801–4), home secretary (1804–6, 1807–9), and secretary for war and the colonies (1809–12). As premier, he oversaw the final years of the Napoleonic Wars and the War of 1812–14 with the USA.

Liverpool poets A group of poets writing out of Liverpool, beginning in the 1960s. The best known are Adrian Henri (1932–2000), Roger McGough (1937–), and Brian Patten (1946–).

liverwort A small, spore-bearing, non-vascular plant of the Class Hepaticae, closely related to mosses and hornworts. They are divided into two types: **thalloid** liverworts have a flattened, often lobed or branched body (the *thallus*); **foliose** or leafy liverworts have slender, creeping stems with three rows of leaves, of which usually only two develop fully. They are found almost everywhere, but are restricted to damp, shady habitats.

livery companies In the UK, charitable and professional associations in the City of London, which have developed from the City Craft Guilds of the Middle Ages. The 12 'great' companies (nominated in 1514) are the mercers, grocers, drapers, fishmongers, goldsmiths, merchant taylors, skinners, haberdashers, salters, ironmongers, vintners, and clothworkers.

Livia Drusilla (58 BC–AD 29) Augustus's wife (39 BC–AD 14) and key backroom figure in the early days of the Roman Empire. The mother of Tiberius by her first husband, Tiberius Claudius Nero, she plotted strenuously to ensure his succession.

Livingstone, David (1813–73) Missionary and traveller, born in Blantyre, South Lanarkshire. He worked for several years in Bechuanaland, then travelled N (1852–6), discovering L Ngami and the Victoria Falls (1855). He led an expedition to the Zambezi (1858–63), and discovered L Shirwa and L Nyasa. He later disappeared while searching for the sources of the Nile, and was found in 1871 by Stanley, sent to look for him by the *New York Herald*.

Livingstone, Ken(neth Robert) (1945–) British politician, born in London. Elected a member of Lambeth Council in 1971 and then of Camden (1978–82) he was also a member of the Greater London Council (GLC) (1973–86). He was elected leader of the GLC in 1981 and fought a long battle to prevent its abolition by Magaret Thatcher. Following the GLC's demise, he became Labour MP for Brent East in 1987. He was an unsuccessful Labour candidate for the newly established position of Mayor of London in 2000, but nonetheless stood as an independent and was elected. He was subsequently expelled from the Labour Party but readmitted in 2004. Later that year he was re-elected as Mayor of London.

Living Theater / Theatre A theatre begun by Judith Malina (1926–) and Julian Beck (1925–85) in 1947 as an Off-Broadway venture. Its main feature was a conscious refusal to separate the art of theatre from the art of living.

Livius *Livy*

Livorno [leevaw(r)noh], Eng **Leghorn** 43°33N 10°18E, pop (2000e) 183 000. Port in W Tuscany, Italy; railway; ferries to Corsica; cathedral (17th-c).

Livy [livee], in full **Titus Livius** (c.59 BC–AD 17) Roman historian, born in Patavium, Italy. His history of Rome, from its foundation to the death of Drusus (9 BC), comprised 142 books, of which 35 have survived.

lizard A reptile, found worldwide except in the coldest regions. Some have no obvious limbs and resemble snakes; but most differ from snakes in having eyelids and an obvious ear opening. (Suborder: Sauria or Lacertilia. Order: Squamata, c.3750 species.)

Lizard Point 49°56N 5°13W. Promontory in Cornwall, SW England; the most S point on the UK mainland, near Lizard Town.

Ljubljana [lyooblyahna], Ital **Lubiana**, ancient **Emona** 46°00N 14°30E, pop (2000e) 292 000. Capital of Slovenia; founded, 34 BC; capital of the former Kingdom of Illyria, 1816–49; badly damaged by earthquake, 1895; ceded to Yugoslavia, 1918; airport; railway; university (1595); education and convention centre; cathedral.

llama A member of the camel family (*Lama glama*), found in the

C Andes; domesticated c.4500 years ago; used mainly as a beast of burden; long flat-backed body with long erect neck and long ears; dense coat.

Llandudno [hlandidnoh] 53°19N 3°49W, pop (2001e) 20 000. Seaside resort town in Gwynedd, NW Wales, on a small peninsula terminating in the Great Orme's Head; Great Orme country park; railway; Oriel Mostyn, North Wales Theatre and Conference Centre, Alice in Wonderland Centre; Victorian Extravaganza weekend (May), October Festival.

Llanfairpwllgwyngyll [hlanviyrpulhgwingihl], in full **Llanfairpwllgwyngyllgogerychwyrndrobwllllantysiliogogogoch** ('St Mary's Church in the hollow of the white hazel near a rapid whirlpool and the Church of St Tysilio by the red cave') 53°13N 4°12W. Village in Anglesey, NW Wales, UK; gained notoriety through the extension of its name (to 58 letters) by a poetic cobbler in the 18th-c; first Women's Institute in Britain founded here, 1915.

Llangefni [hlangevnee] 53°16N 4°18W, pop (2000e) 4800. Town in Anglesey, NW Wales, UK; administrative centre for the island; Oriel Môn.

Llangollen [hlangolhen] 52°58N 3°10W, pop (2000e) 3200. Town in Denbighshire, NE Wales, UK; on the R Dee; site of annual international musical eisteddfod since 1947.

Llano Estacado [lahnoh estakahdoh] ('staked plain') Area 78 000 sq km/30 000 sq mi. Vast semi-arid S portion of the Great Plains, in E New Mexico and W Texas, USA.

llanos [lyahnos] The savannah grasslands of the plains and plateaux of the Orinoco region (Colombia, Venezuela), N South America, traditionally an important livestock farming area.

Llewellyn, Richard [hlooelin], pseudonym of **Richard Dafydd Vivian Llewellyn Lloyd** (1906–83) Writer, born in St David's, Pembrokeshire. He became a best-selling novelist with *How Green Was My Valley* (1939).

Lleyn Peninsula [hleen] Peninsula in Gwynedd, NW Wales, UK; chief towns, Pwllheli, Porthmadog.

Llosa, (Jorge) Mario (Pedro) Vargas [hohsa] (1936–) Novelist, born in Arequipa, Peru. His novels include *Pantaleon y las visitidores* (1973, Captain Pantoja and the Special Service), *Aunt Julia and the Scriptwriter* (1977), *The Notebooks of Don Rigoberto* (1998), and *The War at the End of the World* (1985). Critics acclaim *La fiesta del chivo* (2000, trans The Feast of the Goat) as his finest novel. Later novels include *The Way to Paradise* (2003). In 1990 he ran unsuccessfully for the Peruvian presidency, having declined an offer of the premiership in 1984.

Lloyd, Harold (Clayton) (1893–1971) Film comedian, born in Burchard, NE. He made hundreds of short, silent comedies, adopting from 1917 his character of the unassuming 'nice guy' in horn-rimmed glasses and a straw hat. He received an honorary Academy Award in 1952.

Lloyd, Marie, originally **Matilda Alice Victoria Wood** (1870–1922) Music-hall entertainer, born in London. Among her most famous songs were 'Oh, Mr Porter' and 'My Old Man Said Follow the Van'.

Lloyd-George (of Dwyfor), David Lloyd George, 1st Earl (1863–1945) British Liberal statesman and prime minister (1916–22), born in Manchester, Greater Manchester, of Welsh parentage. He was President of the Board of Trade (1905–8), Chancellor of the Exchequer (1908–15), minister of munitions (1915), secretary for war (1916), and superseded Asquith as coalition prime minister, carrying on a forceful war policy. He negotiated with Sinn Féin, and conceded the Irish Free State (1921) – a measure which brought his downfall.

Lloyd's An international market for insurance, based in London. It originated in Edward Lloyd's coffee house in Tower Street in the City of London, from 1688. All kinds of insurance are now handled worldwide. The members (*underwriters*) of Lloyd's are organized into syndicates, and risks are spread among the members of the syndicate so that no single individual (or 'name') carries too large a risk personally. There is, however, no limit to a member's liability, and large losses made by some syndicates in 1990 and 1991 gave rise to controversy concerning the management of Lloyds, and limited liability has been proposed. *Lloyd's Shipping Index* gives daily information about the worldwide movements of over 20 000 merchant vessels.

Lloyd's Register of Shipping A publication which catalogues information about the construction and characteristics of individual vessels, to help insurance underwriters. 'A1 at Lloyd's' refers to the top grade of the classification made by the Register, indicating that the vessel is in first-class order.

Lloyd-Webber, Andrew Lloyd Webber, Baron (1948–) Composer, born in London. He met Tim Rice in 1965, and together they wrote a 'pop oratorio' *Joseph and the Amazing Technicolour Dreamcoat* (1968) which was extended and staged in 1972. Their greatest success was the 'rock opera' *Jesus Christ Superstar* (staged 1971, filmed 1973). His later musicals include *Evita* (1978), *Cats* (1981), *Starlight Express* (1983), *The Phantom of the Opera* (1986), *Sunset Boulevard* (1993), and *The Woman in White* (2004).

Lloyd Webber, Julian (1951–) Cellist, born in London, the brother of Andrew Lloyd Webber. He made his UK debut in 1972, and has since performed with all the major British orchestras, appeared internationally, and made many recordings.

Llull or **Lull, Ramón** [lul], Eng **Raymond Lully**, known as **the Enlightened Doctor** (c.1235–1315) Franciscan theologian and philosopher, born in Palma, Majorca. His major work is the *Ars magna* (The Great Art), condemned in 1376 for its attempt to link faith and reason, but later viewed more sympathetically. His followers, known as **Lullists**, combined religious mysticism with alchemy.

Llywelyn [hlooelin] The name of two Welsh princes. **Llywelyn ap Iorwerth** or **Llywelyn the Great** (?–1240) successfully maintained his independence against King John and Henry III, and gained recognition of Welsh rights in the Magna Carta (1215). **Llywelyn ap Gruffydd** (?–1282) helped the English barons against Henry III, and opposed Edward I, who forced his submission.

loach Slender-bodied freshwater fish of the family Cobitidae (7 genera), found in rivers and lakes throughout Europe and Asia; length commonly less than 10 cm/4 in; mouth fringed with barbels.

Lobachevsky, Nikolay Ivanovich [lobachefskee] (1792–1856) Mathematician, born in Nizhni Novgorod, Russia. In 1829 he published the first geometry on non-Euclidean principles.

lobefish Any of the mainly fossil bony fishes belonging to the Sarcopterygii, but including also the extant lungfishes (Dipnoi) and the coelacanth (Crossopterygii).

lobelia [lohbeelia] A member of a large and very diverse genus, ranging from small annuals to shaggy, columnar perennials reaching several metres high; found almost everywhere, but mostly tropical and subtropical, especially in the New World; flowers usually red, blue, or violet, with five fused petals forming a curved, 2-lipped tube. (Genus: *Lobelia*, 200–300 species. Family: Campanulaceae.)

lobotomy *psychosurgery*

lobster A large marine crustacean with a well-developed abdomen and the front pair of legs modified as pincers (*chelipeds*), one for crushing and one for cutting; length up to 60 cm/2 ft; edible, caught commercially using pots or wickerwork traps (*creels*). (Class: Malacostraca. Order: Decapoda.)

local area network (LAN) A system which allows communication between computers situated within a well-defined geographical area, and which does not use the public telephone system. By contrast, a **wide area network** or **long distance network**

allows computer communication over a large geographical area, generally using the telephone system.

local education authority (LEA) A regional government organization responsible for education in its area. In the UK, this is usually a city or county council. The elected members of the LEA are local politicians; professional officers are responsible for the day-to-day running of the education system in their area.

local government A set of political institutions constitutionally subordinate to the national, provincial, or federal government, with delegated authority to perform certain functions within territorially defined parts of the state. Some of the services most commonly provided by local government include education, public transport, roads, social services, housing, leisure and recreation, public health, and water.

Locarno Pact [lokah(r)noh] A series of international agreements reached in 1925 at an international conference held at Locarno, Switzerland, guaranteeing post-1919 frontiers between France, Belgium, and Germany, and the demilitarization of the Rhineland. The treaty was signed by France, Germany, and Belgium, and guaranteed by Britain and Italy.

Lochner, Stefan [lokhner] (c.1400–1451) Painter, born in Meersburg, Germany. He became the principal master of the Cologne School, marking the transition from the Gothic style to Naturalism.

Loch Ness Monster *Ness, Loch*

lock (canal) A means of altering the height of a canal waterway while allowing the passage of boats. A **pound lock** has a chamber which can be filled and emptied of water by opening and closing paddles, to bring the level to the upper or the lower height. The lower gates are usually double, pointing upstream so as to be pressed together by the water.

Locke, John (1632–1704) Philosopher, born in Wrington, Somerset. His major work, the *Essay Concerning Human Understanding* (1690), accepted the possibility of rational demonstration of moral principles and the existence of God, but its denial of innate ideas, and its demonstration that 'all knowledge is founded on and ultimately derives itself from sense...or sensation', was the real starting point of British empiricism.

Lockerbie 55°07N 3°22W, pop (2000e) 3040. A town in Dumfries and Galloway, SW Scotland, the scene of Britain's worst air disaster, when a Pan Am Boeing 747 flying from Frankfurt to New York via London crashed on 21 December 1988, killing 270, including several townspeople. The explosive device which led to the disaster was thought to have been taken on board at Frankfurt. Efforts to extradite suspected Libyan terrorists to stand trial were finally successful in early 1999, the trial taking place at a Scottish court at Camp Zeist in The Netherlands. In January 2001, one of the two people charged, Abdelbaset ali Mohmed al-Megrahi, was found guilty and jailed for life; an appeal was rejected in March 2002. In August 2003, Libya formally accepted responsibility for the bombing and agreed to pay compensation to the bereaved families.

lockjaw *tetanus*

Lockwood, Margaret (1916–90) English actress, born in Karachi, Pakistan (formerly India). She made her film debut in *Lorna Doone* (1935), and starred in the Alfred Hitchcock film *The Lady Vanishes* (1938). In the late 1940s she was Britain's most popular leading lady, appearing regularly in theatre productions.

locomotive The vehicle that provides the tractive force to haul trucks and carriages on a railway. The world's first locomotive was built by Richard Trevithick in 1801, and although some famous locomotives (such as 'Puffing Billy' and 'Locomotion') were used on railways to haul coal after that time, it was not until 1829 that the 'Rocket' won the Rainhill trials and inaugurated the full-time carriage of passengers. By the mid-19th-c, the steam locomotive had developed into a form which did not change substantially thereafter. During the 20th-c the steam locomotive was progressively displaced as the main type of locomotive by diesel, diesel-electric, and electric motive power. New types of propulsion are currently under test, such as the use of linear electric motors for propulsion coupled with magnetic levitation.

locust Any of several species of grasshoppers, with a 2-phase life cycle. At low population density they are solitary in behaviour, but at high density they become gregarious, swarming and migrating, often causing massive destruction of vegetation. (Order: Orthoptera. Family: Acrididae.)

locust tree *carob; false acacia*

lodestone *magnetite*

Lodge, David (John) (1935–) Novelist and critic, born in Dulwich, Greater London. His novels include *Changing Places* (1975), *Nice Work* (1988), *Therapy* (1995), *Thinks* (2001), and *Author, Author* (2004). Among his critical works is *The Practice of Writing* (1996).

Lodge, Henry Cabot (1850–1924) US Republican senator, historian, and biographer, born in Boston, MA. He prevented the USA joining the League of Nations in 1920. His grandson, **Henry Cabot Lodge, Jr** (1902–85), was US representative at the United Nations (1953–60) and participated in the Vietnam peace talks in 1969.

Lodge, Thomas (c.1558–1625) Playwright, romance writer, and poet, born in London. His best-known work is the pastoral romance, *Rosalynde* (1590), which was the source of Shakespeare's *As You Like It*.

Łódź [wudzh, lodz] 51°49N 19°28E, pop (2000e) 858 000. Industrial city in C Poland; second largest city in Poland; charter, 500; development since 1820 through the textile industry; railway; two universities (1945).

loerie *turaco*

Loesser, Frank (Henry) [lerser] (1910–69) Songwriter and composer, born in New York City. He achieved international fame with the music and lyrics for *Guys and Dolls* (1950). Later musicals included *The Most Happy Fella* (1956) and *How to Succeed in Business Without Really Trying* (1961).

Loess Region [lohis] NC Chinese highlands; area 400 000 km^2/ 150 400 sq mi; altitude 800–2000 m/2600–6500 ft; covered with a layer of wind-blown loamy deposit (*loess*); site of China's oldest anthropoid remains (700 000 years ago) and principal Palaeolithic to Neolithic sites; location of first historical Chinese dynasty (16th-c BC), and the power-centres of all later dynasties until 12th-c AD.

Loewe, Frederick [loh] (1901–88) Composer, born in Berlin. He went to the USA in 1924, and worked as a composer on a number of Broadway musicals, in collaboration with Alan Jay Lerner (1918–86), including *My Fair Lady* (1956).

Lofoten Islands [lohfohtn] area 1425 km^2/550 sq mi. Mountainous island group in the Norwegian Sea, off the NW coast of Norway.

Lofty–Flinders Ranges, Mount Mountain ranges in South Australia state, Australia; extending 800 km/500 mi; Mt Lofty Ranges in the S, comparatively low, rising to Mt Lofty (727 m/2385 ft); Flinders Ranges in the N rising to St Mary Peak (1166 m/3825 ft); tourist area.

Logan, Mount 60°34N 140°24W. Highest mountain in Canada, and second highest in North America; rises to 5950 m/19 521 ft in the St Elias Mts, SW Yukon territory.

loganberry An accidental hybrid between raspberry and blackberry which arose in the garden of Judge Logan of California, after whom it was named. The fruits, which resemble raspberries, are much larger and more tart than either parent. (Family: Rosaceae.)

logarithm The power *n* to which a number *a* must be raised to equal another number *b*, ie 'the logarithm to the base *a* of *b*': $a^n = b \Rightarrow \log_a b = n$; for example, since $10^2 = 100$, $\log_{10} 100 = 2$.

Logarithms were used extensively as calculating aids before the advent of computers.

loggia [lohjia] A gallery in a building, behind an open arcade or colonnade, and facing onto a garden, street, or square. It is sometimes a separate structure.

logic The formal, systematic study of the principles of valid inference and correct reasoning. **Deductive logic** is the study of inferences that are valid (or invalid) in virtue of their structure, not their content. 'If A then B; A; therefore B' is valid whatever the value of A and B; and any inference with that structure is valid. There are two main parts of elemental deductive logic. **Propositional logic** deals with the inferences involving simple sentences in the indicative mood joined by such connectives as *not* (negation), *and* (conjunction), *or* (disjunction), and *if...then* (conditional). **Predicate logic** deals with sentences in the indicative mood involving such quantifying terms as *some*, *all*, and *no*. Thus, 'All cats are mammals, and no mammals are worms; therefore no cats are worms' is a (valid) inference in predicate logic. The investigation of deductive inference has also been extended beyond propositional and predicate logic to include: **modal logic**, which treats the notion of necessity and possibility; **epistemic logic**, the logic of knowledge and belief; **many-valued logic**, which allows some sentences to be assigned a designation other than true or false; **tense logic**, which analyses inferences involving such temporal notions as past, present, and future; and **deontic logic** which deals with imperatives, practical reasoning, and expressions of obligation. **Inductive logic** is the study of inferences which are not deductively valid, but are such that the premises, if true, would increase the likelihood of the truth of the conclusion, and this leads naturally to probability theory and statistics. Aristotle wrote the first systematic treatises on logic; Boole and others evolved a rigorous mathematical logic in the 19th-c.

logical positivism A philosophical movement beginning with the Vienna Circle in the 1920s and 1930s under the leadership of Moritz Schlick and Rudolf Carnap, and associated in Britian with A J Ayer. Most of metaphysics, ethics, and religious discourse was said to be literally meaningless, since its propositions could not be verified by observation and experiment nor by logical deduction.

logography The study of writing systems in which the symbols (**logographs** or **logograms**) represent whole words, or, in some cases, components of words. A few logographs are found in European languages, such as & ('and'), and £ ('pound'); but Chinese and Japanese are the most famous examples of a logographic writing system.

Lohengrin [lohengrin] In Germanic legend, the son of Parsifal. He leaves the temple of the Grail and is carried to Antwerp in a boat drawn by swans. There he saves Princess Elsa of Brabant, and is about to marry her; but she asks forbidden questions about his origin, and he is forced to leave her.

Loire, River [lwah(r)], ancient **Liger** River in E France, rising in the Massif Central; empties into the Bay of Biscay; length 1020 km/ 634 mi; valley known for its vineyards.

Loki [lohkee] A mischievous Norse god; originally a Giant, he was later accepted into the company of the gods. Although he plays tricks on them, he is also able to save them from danger by his cleverness.

Lollards A derisive term applied to the followers of the English theologian John Wycliffe (14th-c). The movement, responsible for the translation of the Bible into the vernacular, was suppressed.

Lombard, Peter, known as **Magister Sententiarum** ('Master of Sentences') (c.1100–60) Theologian, born near Novara, Italy. His work was the standard textbook of Catholic theology down to the Reformation.

Lombard League A coalition of N Italian cities, established in 1167 to assert their independence as communes (city-republics) against the German emperor, Frederick I Barbarossa.

Lombardo, Pietro [lombah(r)doh] (c.1435–1515) Sculptor and architect, born in Carona, Italy. He ran the most important workshop in Venice, specializing in tomb sculpture. The Church of Santa Maria dei Miracoli (1481–9) was his design.

Lombards A Germanic people settled in Hungary – their name deriving from the long beards (*langobardi*) they traditionally wore – who invaded N Italy in AD 568 under their king, Alboin. Their kingdom was annexed by Charlemagne in 774.

Lombardy [lombah(r)dee], Ital **Lombardia** pop (2000e) 8 931 000; area 23 835 km²/9200 sq mi. Region of N Italy; capital, Milan; highly developed industrial and agricultural region in the S; tourism important in the mountains.

Lomé [lohmay] 6°10N 1°21E, pop (2000e) 589 000. Seaport capital of Togo; important market centre, noted for its marble, gold, and silver crafts; airport; railway junction; university (1965).

Lomé Convention A series of conventions governing the European Union's trading relationship with 71 developing countries in Africa, the Caribbean, and the Pacific (the 'ACP countries'). The first convention was signed in 1975, with follow-up conventions every five years (1979, 1984). The 1989 convention was for a 10-year period. The system was replaced by a new treaty, the **Suva Convention**, in 2000, expected to run for 20 years.

Lomond, Loch [lohmond] Largest lake in Scotland; area 70 km²/27 sq mi; 34 km/21 mi long; narrow in the N, opening out to 8 km/5 mi in the S; up to 190 m/625 ft deep; major tourist area; Loch Lomond and the Trossachs National Park designated 2002.

Lomu, Jonah [lohmoo] (1975–) Rugby union player, born in Mangere, New Zealand, of Tongan parents. Selected for the New Zealand All Blacks in 1994, he became internationally known as a member of the World Cup squad, his massive physique making him an awesome opponent. A kidney disorder kept him out of the game for over a year, but he returned to international rugby at the end of 1997. He struggled to maintain fitness because of the side-effects of his treatment, and in 2003 was forced to retire. He underwent a succesful kidney transplant operation in 2004 and returned to competitive rugby in late 2005.

London, Lat **Londinium** (in the 4th-c, **Augusta**) 51°30N 0°10W, pop (2001e) 7 172 000 (Greater London), 3300 (City of London). Capital city of England and the UK; on the R Thames in SE England; **Greater London** consists of 32 boroughs and the City of London, area 1579 km²/610 sq mi; from 1st–5th-c, a Roman town (AD c.43), situated where the Thames narrowed to its lowest convenient crossing; sacked by Boudicca, c.61; later surrounded by a defensive wall, fragments of which remain (c.350); received charter privileges, 1067; mayoralty established, 1191; major building programmes in Middle Ages; extended W, especially in 16th-c; Great Plague (1665), Great Fire (1666), followed by major reconstruction; in 17th-c developed into a major trade centre; severe damage especially to City and East End in World War 2 (the Blitz), with much subsequent rebuilding; administered by London County Council, 1888–1963, and by the Greater London Council until 1986, its functions then transferring to the boroughs and other bodies; **City of London**, occupying site of the old mediaeval city N of the Thames, is the financial and business centre; **City of Westminster** is the administrative and judicial centre, including the Houses of Parliament, Buckingham Palace, and government departments; the **West End** is the main shopping and entertainment centre, around Oxford Street, Piccadilly, and Regent Street; extensive dockland, much now scheduled for redevelopment; headquarters of Port of London Authority; extensive underground system (known as 'the Tube'); main airports at Heathrow (W) and Gatwick (S), also at London City, Luton (N), and Stansted (E); markets (Billingsgate, Smithfield; Nine Elms at Vauxhall, replacing Covent Garden, now a tourist centre); parks (Battersea / Hyde / Regent's / St James's Parks, Kensington Gardens); zoological gardens at Regent's Park; leading cultural centre, with many theatres, museums (British / London / Natural History / Science / Victoria and Albert), galleries (National / National Portrait / Tate Galleries, Courtauld Institute), concert halls (Albert / Queen Elizabeth / Royal Festival / Wigmore Halls, Barbican Centre), churches and cathedrals (Saint Paul's / Westminster Cathedrals; Westminster Abbey and St Margaret's Church, a world heritage site); London Eye; South Bank development includes (from W to E) Royal Festival Hall, National Theatre, National Film Theatre, Tate Modern, Shakespeare's Globe; London University (from 1836); polytechnics gained University status in 1992; football league teams, Arsenal (Gunners), Charlton Athletic (Valiants), Chelsea (Blues), Crystal Palace (Eagles), Fulham (Cottagers), Leyton Orient ('O's), Millwall (Lions), Queens Park Rangers ('R's'), Tottenham Hotspur (Spurs), Watford (Hornets), West Ham United (Hammers); new Wembley Stadium completed in 2007 after several delays.

London, Jack, pseudonym of **John Griffith Chaney** (1876–1916) Novelist, born in San Francisco, CA. His books include *The Call of the Wild* (1903), *Sea-Wolf* (1904), and *The Iron Heel* (1907).

London Bridge A bridge over the R Thames linking Southwark with the City of London. The 1831 5-arch bridge was dismantled and sold to Lake Havasu City, Arizona in 1968. It was replaced by a concrete structure.

Londonderry *Derry* (county)

London Eye An observation wheel, the largest in the world, located on the South Bank of the R Thames, London, UK, opened in 2000 as part of the millennium celebrations; originally called the **Millennium Wheel**. Sponsored by British Airways, it was designed by London architects David Marks and Julia Barfield, and is operated by the Tussauds Group; height 135 m/443 ft; weight 1500 tons. Its 32 capsules carry passengers on a 30-minute journey, offering views up to 25 miles.

London Festival Ballet *English National Ballet*

London Group A society of British artists founded in 1913 by Nash, Epstein, Fry, and others. It held regular exhibitions for half a century.

London Missionary Society (LMS) Formed in London in 1795 by evangelical Protestants to undertake missionary work in the Pacific islands. It later operated in other parts of the world, including Africa.

London Museum A museum at London Wall in the City of London, created from the former London and Guildhall museums and opened in 1975.

London University A federation of colleges, medical schools, and research institutions established as a university in London in 1836. *(see panel p.551)*

Long, Crawford Williamson (1815–78) Physician, born in Danielsville, GA. He was the first to use ether to relieve pain during a surgical procedure. In 1842 he painlessly removed a tumour from the neck of a patient after administering ether by dropping the liquid on a cloth; however, he did not make his work public until 1849, and the delay in reporting his findings prevented him from being recognized as the pioneer anaesthetist for many years.

Long, Huey (Pierce), nickname **Kingfish** (1893–1935) US Democratic politician, born near Winnfield, LA. After 1930 he was both Governor of Louisiana and a US senator. He enjoyed virtually total control of his state until his assassination by Carl Weiss.

Long Beach 33°47N 118°11W, pop (2000e) 461 500. City in SW California, USA; developed rapidly after the discovery of oil,

LONDON UNIVERSITY

College	Founded
Wye College (Ashford) (controlled by London University since 1900)	1447
Royal Veterinary College	1791
Birkbeck College	1823
University College London	1826
King's College London (merged with Queen Elizabeth College and Chelsea College 1985)	1829
School of Pharmacy	1842
Goldsmith's College (controlled by London University since 1904)	1891
London School of Economics and Political Science	1895
Institute of Education (controlled by London University since 1932; school of London University since 1987)	1902
Imperial College of Science Technology and Medicine	1907
School of Oriental and African Studies	1916
Royal Holloway and Bedford New College (Egham) (founded through merger of Bedford College and Royal Holloway College)	1985
Queen Mary and Westfield College (founded through merger of Queen Mary College and Westfield College)	1989

1921; railway; university (1949); location for the British cruise liner *Queen Mary*, now a museum-hotel-convention centre.

longbow An English bow with a shaft of yew-wood 1·5 m/5 ft long, which could shoot an arrow capable of penetrating plate armour at 400 yd (365 m). It dominated the battlefield for 200 years from 1300, proving decisive at the Battles of Crécy, Poitiers, and Agincourt.

Longchamp *Bois de Boulogne*

long-distance network *local area network*

Longfellow, Henry Wadsworth (1807–82) Poet, born in Portland, ME. *Voices of the Night* (1839), his first book of verse, made a favourable impression, and this was followed by several other works, notably *Evangeline* (1847) and *The Song of Hiawatha* (1855).

Longford (county), Ir **Longphort** pop (2000e) 31 000; area 1044 km²/403 sq mi. County in NW Leinster province, C Ireland; capital, Longford, pop (2000e) 6900.

Longinus [lonjiynus], also called **Dionysius Longinus** and **Pseudo-Longinus** (fl. 1st-c) Name assigned to the Greek author of the surviving portion of a treatise on excellence in literature, *On the Sublime*, which influenced many Neoclassical writers.

Long Island area 3600 km²/1400 sq mi, length 190 km/118 mi. Island in SE New York State, USA, bounded N by Long Island Sound; separated from the Bronx and Manhattan by the East River, and from Staten I by the Narrows; settled by the Dutch in 1623, and by the English, c.1640; site of the Battle of Long Island (1776) in the US War of Independence, when British forces under Howe defeated American forces under Washington.

longitude *latitude and longitude*

long jump An athletics field event in which the competitors leap for distance into a sandpit after running up to a take-off board. It is sometimes called the **running broad jump**. The current world record for men is 8·95 m/29 ft 4¼ in, achieved by Mike Powell (USA) in 1991 at Tokyo; and for women is 7·52 m/24 ft 8¼ in, achieved by Galina Chistyakova (USSR) in 1988 at St Petersburg, Russia.

Longman, Thomas (1699–1755) Publisher, born in Bristol, SW England. He bought a bookselling business in Paternoster Row, London, in 1724, and was the founder of the British publishing house that still bears his name.

Long March The epic of Chinese communist revolutionary history. In 1934 the Red Army was blockaded in SE China by Jiang Jieshi's forces. In October, Mao Zedong, Zhu De, and Lin Biao broke out with 100 000 troops to lead a 13 000 km/8000 mi evacuation westwards then north. The march ended in Shaanxi, N China, the following October. The Long March established Mao's supremacy in the party.

Long Parliament An English parliament called (Nov 1640) by Charles I after his defeat by the Scots in the second Bishops' War. It was legally in being 1640–60, but did not meet continuously. It attacked prerogative rights and alleged abuses of power by the king and his ministers. Moderates were eliminated in Pride's Purge (Dec 1648), and the remaining Rump was dismissed by Cromwell in 1653.

long-range navigation system *loran*

longship A vessel used by the Vikings in their voyages of exploration, plunder, and conquest. The largest were 45 m/150 ft in length, very strong, and propelled by both oars and sail.

long-sightedness *eye*

Lonsdale Belt In boxing, a championship belt awarded to a fighter who wins a British title fight. It is named after the 5th Earl of Lonsdale, who presented the first belt to the National Sporting Club in 1909.

loofah An annual climbing vine with tendrils (*Luffa cylindrica*), native to the tropics; flowers yellow, funnel-shaped; fruit marrow-like, up to 30 cm/12 in long, roughly cylindrical. The sponge-like item used in bathrooms is the fibrous vascular tissue of the fruit left when the soft parts are removed. (Family: Cucurbitaceae.)

look-and-say A method of teaching reading through whole-word recognition. The aim is to teach words as meaningful entities, rather than as sequences of phonic syllables.

loon *diver*

Lope de Vega *Vega, Lope de*

Lopez, Jennifer [lohpez], popularly known as **J-Lo** (1970–) Actress and pop singer, born in the Bronx, New York City. She trained as a dancer and gained a part in the TV series *In Living Color* (1990–3). She went on to star in *Selena* (1997), and among later films are *The Wedding Planner* (2001), *Shall We Dance?* (2004), *Monster-in-Law* (2005), and *Bordertown* (2007). Her albums include *J-Lo* (2001) and *Rebirth* (2005).

loquat [lohkwat] A small evergreen tree (*Eriobotrya japonica*) with very hairy twigs, native to China; leaves coarse, reddish, hairy beneath; flowers white, fragrant, in terminal clusters; fruits 3–6 cm/1¼–2½ in, round, yellowish-orange, flesh sweet and edible. (Family: Rosaceae.)

loran Acronym for **long-range navigation system**. Radio pulses emitted at fixed intervals by pairs of transmitters define a grid pattern, over a very large area. The timing of the reception of these paired pulses by an aircraft or ship indicates its position on the network.

Lorca, Federico García [law(r)ka, gah(r)seea] (1898–1936) Poet, born in Fuente Vaqueros, Spain. His best-known works are his gypsy songs, *Canciones* (1927, Songs) and *Romancero Gitano* (1928, 1935, The Gypsy Ballads). He also wrote several successful plays. He was assassinated in the Spanish Civil War at Granada.

Lord Chancellor The head of the judiciary of England and Wales, a member of the cabinet, and the Speaker of the House of Lords. He appoints, and may dismiss, magistrates and circuit judges. It was abolished in 2003, its powers being taken over by a Department of Constitutional Affairs. In the Constitutional Reform Bill (2005), the decision to abolish the office of Lord Chancellor was reversed. However, its judicial powers were greatly reduced, the office-holder would no longer automatically be Speaker of the House of Lords, and the appointment could be made from either House.

Lord Chief Justice The president or head of the Queen's Bench Division of the High Court in England and Wales, and of the Criminal Division of the Court of Appeal.

Lord Howe Island 31°33S 159°04E, pop (2000e) 600. Volcanic island in the Pacific Ocean, 702 km/436 mi NE of Sydney; part of New South Wales; area 16·6 km²/6·4 sq mi; rises to 866 m/2841 ft; discovered, 1788; a world heritage site.

Lord-Lieutenant [leftenant] In the UK, the sovereign's permanent representative in a county or county borough of England, Wales, or Northern Ireland, or in a part of one of the Scottish regions. The lordly prefix is by custom only, and the office is now primarily one of honour.

Lords, House of Its membership formerly included both hereditary peers and life peers (including judicial members – the *Lords of Appeal in Ordinary*), as well as the two archbishops and certain bishops of the Church of England; but in 1999 the hereditary component was abolished (though a group of 92 hereditaries would continue to sit in an interim chamber, pending the results of a Royal Commission). Membership of 1330 was thereby reduced to 670. Its functions are mainly deliberative, its authority being based on the expertise of its membership. It also constitutes the most senior court in the UK. Government proposals for the second stage of reform were made in November 2001. Voting in February 2003 failed to achieve parliamentary agreement on the method of constituting a reformed House.

lords-and-ladies A perennial native to Europe and N Africa (*Arum maculatum*), with glossy dark-green arrowhead-shaped leaves and poisonous scarlet berries; also called **cuckoo-pint**. (Family: Araceae.)

Lord's Cricket Ground A cricket ground founded by Thomas Lord (1755–1832) in 1814 in NW London. It is the home of the Marylebone Cricket Club (MCC) and the Middlesex County Cricket Club, and the recognized home of cricket.

Lord's Prayer A popular prayer of Christian worship, derived from *Matt* 6.9–13 and (in different form) *Luke* 11.2–4; also known as the **Pater Noster** ('Our Father'). It is a model for how Jesus's followers are to pray.

Lorelei [loreliy] The name of a precipitous rock on the Rhine, dangerous to boatmen and celebrated for its echo. The story of the siren of the rock whose songs lure sailors to their death originates in Heine's poem *Die Lorelei* (1827).

Loren, Sophia [loren], originally **Sofia Scicolone** (1934–) Film actress, born in Rome. She became the protégée, and later the wife, of the producer Carlo Ponti (1912–2007), and gained the lead in *The Pride and the Passion* (1957). Her performance under the direction of De Sica in *La Ciociara* (1961, Two Women) won her an Oscar.

Lorentz, Hendrik Antoon [lohrents] (1853–1928) Theoretical physicist, born in Arnhem, The Netherlands. He shared the Nobel Prize for Physics in 1902 with Pieter Zeeman (1865–1943) for their work on electromagnetic radiation, which prepared the way for Einstein's theory of relativity.

Lorenz, Konrad (Zacharias) [lohrents] (1903–89) Zoologist, a founder of the science of ethology, born in Vienna. His work in the late 1930s favoured the investigation of animal behaviour in the wild. He shared the Nobel Prize for Physiology or Medicine in 1973.

Lorenzetti, Ambrogio [lorenzetee] (c.1280–c.1348) Artist, born in Siena, Italy. He is best known for his allegorical frescoes in the Palazzo Pubblico at Siena. His brother, **Pietro** (c.1280–c.1348), also belonged to the Sienese School.

Lorenzo [lorenzoh], known as **il Monaco** ('the Monk'), originally **Piero di Giovanni** (c.1370–c.1425) Painter, born in Siena. Italy.

His major work is the 'Coronation of the Virgin' (1413, Florence).

lorikeet *lory*

loris A primitive primate, native to forests in S and SE Asia; no tail; pale face with dark rings around large eyes; three species. (Family: Lorisidae.)

Lorrain, Claude *Claude Lorrain*

Lorraine [loren], Ger **Lothringen** pop (2000e) 2 417 000; area 23 547 km²/9089 sq mi. Region and former province of NE France, duchy since the 10th-c; part of France, 1766; ceded to Germany as part of Alsace-Lorraine, 1871; returned to France after World War 1; chief towns, Metz, Nancy.

Lorraine, Cross of [lorayn] A cross with two horizontal crosspieces. The symbol of Joan of Arc, it was adopted by the Free French forces leader (Charles de Gaulle) in 1940.

Lorris, Guillaume de *Guillaume de Lorris*

lory [lawree] A parrot of the subfamily Loriinae (c.60 species), found from SE Asia to Australia; tongue has brush-like tip. Smaller species are called **lorikeets**. (Family: Psittacidae.)

Los Alamos [los alamos] 35°52N 106°19W, pop (2000e) 11 900. Community in N New Mexico, USA; a nuclear research centre since 1943; the first nuclear weapons were developed here during World War 2.

Los Angeles 34°04N 118°15W, pop (2000e) 3 694 800. Seaport in California, USA; founded by the Spanish, 1781; originally called **Nuestra Señora Reina de Los Angeles**; captured from Mexico by the US Navy, 1846; established, 1850; second largest US city; three airports; railway; five universities; harbour on San Pedro Bay, 40 km/25 mi S of city centre; major industrial and research centre; high density of road traffic; smog a major problem; professional teams, Dodgers (baseball), Clippers, Lakers (basketball), Raiders, Rams (football), Kings (ice hockey); district of Hollywood a major centre of the US film and television industry; Hollywood Bowl; Universal Film Studios; Disneyland; new Cathedral of Our Lady of the Angels (dedicated 2002); scene of summer Olympic Games, 1984.

Losey, Joseph (Walton) [lohsee] (1909–84) Film director, born in La Crosse, WI. His films include *The Servant* (1963) and *The Go-Between* (1971), as well as the quite untypical *Modesty Blaise* (1966).

Lossiemouth [loseemowth] 57°43N 3°18W, pop (2000e) 7800. Port town in Moray, NE Scotland; air force base nearby; birthplace of Ramsay MacDonald.

Lot Biblical character, portrayed in Genesis as the nephew of Abraham. Stories describe his rescue from the wickedness of Sodom by Abraham and two angels. Lot's wife is described as looking back during this escape and being turned into 'a pillar of salt'.

Lothian [lohthian] pop (2000e) 755 500; area 1755 km²/677 sq mi. Former region in E Scotland (1975–96); replaced in 1996 by North Lanarkshire, Falkirk, West Lothian, Midlothian, East Lothian, and City of Edinburgh councils.

Lots, Feast of *Purim*

lottery A way of raising money through the sale of chances (tickets) and the use of a random procedure to decide the prize-winners. Very large numbers of people take part, producing a correspondingly large sum of money which (after deduction of taxes and organizational expenses) is available for prizes. Many countries now organize state lotteries, which provide an attractive extra source of government income, as well as offering a promise of vast wealth for a few. They have also been used to finance major projects, such as roads, buildings, and universities, as well as projects to do with the arts, the environment, and all forms of charity. Famous lotteries include those of Italy, Ireland (the Irish Hospitals' Sweepstake), and Australia (where a lottery helped finance the Sydney Opera House). Britain's national lottery began in 1994.

lotus A name given to three different plants. The sacred lotus of Egypt (*Nymphaea lotus*) is a species of waterlily. The sacred lotus of India and China (*Nelumbium nuciferum*), traditionally associated with the Buddha, has circular leaves with the stalks attached in the centre of the blade, and pink and white flowers. The lotus of classical times (*Ziziphus lotus*) is a type of jujube from the Mediterranean region.

lotus bird *jacana*

Lotus 123 A popular computer package to enable the user to work on a spreadsheet. It is a registered trade mark of Lotus Development Corporation.

Louangphrabang or **Luang Prabang** [luangprabang] 19°53N 102°10E, pop (2000e) 68 000. Town in W Laos; former capital, 1946–75; centre of agricultural region.

loudspeaker or **speaker** A device which converts electrical energy into sound waves. The loudspeaker is fed a current having frequencies and amplitudes proportionate to some original sound waves. It reconverts these signals, radiating a new set of sound waves which reproduce at a listener's ears as nearly as possible the acoustic experience of the original performance. The majority of loudspeakers use the electromagnetic principle. An alternating signal current passes through one or more voice coils set in powerful permanent magnetic fields. The alternating magnetic fields which result cause the coils (and the diaphragm or cone to which each one is fixed) to move to and fro in vibration, and it is this mechanical vibration that regenerates the sound waves.

Louis IX, St (1215–70) King of France (1226–70), born in Poissy, France. He led the Seventh Crusade (1248), but was defeated in Egypt, and ransomed. He embarked on a new Crusade in 1270, and died of plague at Tunis. He was canonized in 1297. Feast day 25 August.

Louis XIV, known as **le Roi soleil** ('the Sun King') (1638–1715) King of France (1643–1715), born in St Germain-en-Laye, the son of Louis XIII. During his minority (1643–51) France was ruled by his mother, Anne of Austria, and her Chief Minister, Cardinal Mazarin. In 1660 Louis married the Infanta Maria Theresa, elder daughter of Philip IV of Spain, through whom he was later to claim the Spanish succession for his second grandson. His obsession with France's greatness led him into aggressive foreign and commercial policies, particularly against the Dutch. His patronage of the Catholic Stuarts also led to the hostility of England after 1689, but his major political rivals were the Austrian Habsburgs, particularly Leopold I. His attempt to create a Franco–Spanish Bourbon bloc led to the formation of the Grand Alliance of England, the United Provinces, and the Habsburg Empire, and resulted in the War of the Spanish Succession (1701–13). His determination to preserve the unity of the French state and the independence of the French Church led him into conflict with the Jansenists, the Huguenots, and the papacy, with damaging repercussions. His long reign nonetheless marked the cultural ascendancy of France within Europe, symbolized by the Palace of Versailles.

Louis XV, known as **Louis le Bien-Aimé** ('Louis the Well-Beloved') (1710–74) King of France (1715–74), born in Versailles, France, the great-grandson of Louis XIV. His reign coincided with the great age of decorative art in the Rococo mode (dubbed the Louis XV style). Until he came of age (1723) he was guided by the regent, Philippe d'Orléans, and then by the Duc de Bourbon. In 1726 Bourbon was replaced by the king's former tutor, the elderly Fleury, who skilfully steered the French state until his death (1744). Thereafter Louis allowed the government to drift into the hands of ministerial factions, while indulging in secret diplomatic activity through his own network of agents – a system which brought confusion to French foreign policy. France was drawn into a trio of continental wars which culminated in the loss of the French colonies in America and India (1763).

Louis XVI (1754–93) King of France (1774–93), born in Versailles, France, the grandson of Louis XV. He was married in 1770 to the Archduchess Marie Antoinette, daughter of the Habsburg Empress Maria Theresa, to strengthen the Franco–Austrian alliance. He failed to give consistent support to ministers who tried to reform the outmoded financial and social structures of the country, such as Turgot (1774–6) and Necker (1776–81). To avert a crisis, he agreed in 1789 to summon the States General. However, encouraged by the queen, he resisted demands from the National Assembly for sweeping reforms, and in October was brought with his family from Versailles to Paris as hostages to the revolutionary movement. Their attempted flight to Varennes (Jun 1791) branded them as traitors. In August an insurrection suspended Louis's constitutional position, and in September the monarchy was abolished. He was tried for conspiracy and guillotined in Paris.

Louis (Charles) XVII (1785–95) Titular King of France (1793–5), born in Versailles, France, the second son of Louis XVI and heir to the throne from June 1789. After the execution of his father (Jan 1793) he remained in the Temple prison in Paris until his death.

Louis XVIII, originally **Louis Stanislas Xavier, comte de** (Count of) **Provence** (1755–1824) King of France in name from 1795 and in fact from 1814, born in Versailles, France, the younger brother of Louis XVI. He fled from Paris in June 1791, finally taking refuge in England, becoming the focal point for the Royalist cause. His restoration was interrupted by Napoleon's return from Elba, but after Waterloo (1815) he again regained his throne.

Louis, Joe [loois], popular name of **Joseph Louis Barrow**, nickname **the Brown Bomber** (1914–81) Boxer, born in Lafayette, AL. He beat James J Braddock (1905–74) for the world heavyweight title in 1937, and held the title for a record 12 years, making a record 25 defences.

Louisiade Archipelago [looeeziahd] pop (2000e) 25 000; area 1550 km²/600 sq mi. Mountainous island group in Papua New Guinea, SE of New Guinea; named in 1768 after Louis XIV of France.

Louisiana [loozeeana] pop (2000e) 4 469 000; area 123 673 km²/47 752 sq mi. State in S USA; the 'Pelican State'; named after Louis XIV of France, claimed for France by La Salle, 1682; most of the E region ceded to Spain in 1763, then to the USA in 1783; W region acquired by the USA in the Louisiana Purchase, 1803; admitted to the Union as the 18th state, 1812; seceded from the Union, 1861; re-admitted, 1868; Mississippi large delta area in the S; highest point Mt Driskill (162 m/532 ft); capital, Baton Rouge; over half the land area forested, supporting a major lumber and paper industry; highly productive in agriculture; a major source of pelts, especially muskrat; second only to Texas in oil and natural gas production (mainly offshore); leads the nation in salt and sulphur production; world famous for the jazz music which grew up in and around New Orleans; special population groups of Creoles (French descent) and Cajuns (descendants of French Acadians driven from Canada by the British in the 18th-c); areas devastated by Hurricane Katrina (notably New Orleans) in 2005.

Louisiana Purchase (1803) The sale by France to the USA of an area between the Mississippi R and the Rocky Mts for $15 000 000. The purchase gave the USA full control of the Mississippi Valley.

Louis Napoleon *Napoleon III*

Louis-Philippe [fileep], known as **the Citizen King** (1773–1850) King of the French (1830–48), born in Paris, the eldest son of the Duke of Orléans, Philippe Egalité. At the Revolution he entered the National Guard, and with his father renounced his titles to demonstrate his progressive sympathies. He lived in exile from 1793 to 1814. In 1830 he was elected lieutenant-general of the kingdom, and after the July Revolution was given the title of King of the French. Political corruption and economic depression caused discontent, and he abdicated at the onset of the 1848 revolution.

Louisville [looeevil] 38°15N 85°46W, pop (2000e) 256 200. City in NW Kentucky, USA; port at the Falls of the Ohio R; settled, 1778; named after Louis XVI of France; city status, 1828; largest city in the state; university (1798); a major horse breeding centre; important shipping point for coal.

Lourdes [loordz], Fr [loord] 43°06N 0°00W, pop (2000e) 17 400. Town and important site of Roman Catholic pilgrimage in Hautes-Pyrénées department, S France; Bernadette Soubirous was led by a vision of the Virgin Mary to the springs at the Grotte de Massabielle in 1858; since then, the scene of many reputed miraculous cures.

lourie *turaco*

louse A secondarily wingless insect, parasitic on warm-blooded vertebrates. **Sucking lice** (Order: Anoplura) suck blood of mammals; length up to 6 mm/$\frac{1}{4}$ in; bodies flattened, legs with claws for attaching to host; c.300 species. They include two varieties of human louse: **head lice** (*Pediculus humanus capitis*) and **body lice** (*Pediculus humanus humanus*), both transmitted by direct contact; lay eggs (*nits*) on hair and clothing. **Biting lice** (Order: Mallophaga) live mostly on birds; c.2700 species.

Louth [lowth], Ir **Lughbhaidh** pop (2000e) 92 000; area 821 km^2/317 sq mi. County in NE Leinster province, Ireland; capital, Dundalk.

Louvain [loovĩ] *Leuven*

L'Ouverture, Toussaint *Toussaint L'Ouverture*

Louvois, François Michel le Tellier, marquis de [loovwah] (1641–91) French statesman and secretary of state for war under Louis XIV, born in Paris. He was recognized as a brilliant administrator and the king's most influential minister in the years 1683–91.

Louvre [loovr] The national museum of art in Paris, and one of the finest art collections in the world. It was built for Francis I in 1546.

lovage A strong-smelling perennial (*Levisticum officinale*) growing to 2·5 m/8 ft, native to Iran; flowers small, greenish-yellow; fruit ellipsoid with narrowly winged ribs. (Family: Umbelliferae.)

Love, Mike *Beach Boys, The*

love apple *tomato*

lovebird A small parrot native to Africa and Madagascar; female sometimes larger than male; a popular cagebird. They preen one another, hence the name. (Genus: *Agapornis*, nine species. Family: Psittacidae.)

Lovecraft, H(oward) P(hillips) (1890–1937) Short-story writer, born in Providence, RI. His reputation as a skilful practitioner of the tale of horror is almost entirely posthumous, based on *The Outsider and Others* (1939).

love-in-a-mist An annual native to Europe and W Asia (*Nigella damascena*); finely divided, feathery leaves and bracts; large, pale blue flowers; a globular, papery capsule. (Family: Ranunculaceae.)

Lovelace, Richard (1618–58) Cavalier poet, probably born in Woolwich, Greater London. In 1642 he wrote 'To Althea, from Prison' ('Stone walls do not a prison make...'), and in 1649 published his best-known work, *Lucasta*.

Lovell, Sir (Alfred Charles) Bernard (1913–) Astronomer, born in Oldham Common, Gloucestershire. Director of the Nuffield Radio Astronomy Laboratories at Jodrell Bank (1951–81), he is distinguished for his pioneering work in radio telescope design, space research, and the physics of radio sources.

Low, Sir David (Alexander Cecil) (1891–1963) Political cartoonist, born in Dunedin, New Zealand. In 1927 he joined the *Evening Standard*, for which he drew some of his most successful cartoons, including the notable Colonel Blimp.

Iowan *mallee fowl*

Low Countries A term used to refer to The Netherlands and Belgium. It derives its name from the low-lying coastal plain of both countries.

low Earth orbit (LEO) A spacecraft orbit about the Earth typically used for manned missions and for Earth remote-sensing missions; the minimum altitude above the surface is c.200 km/125 mi to minimize drag effects of the Earth's atmosphere. Typical orbital periods are c.100 min; circular velocity c.7·8 km/s (4·9 mi/s)

Lowell, Amy (Lawrence) (1874–1925) Imagist poet, born in Brookline, MA. She produced volumes of free verse which she named 'unrhymed cadence' and what she called 'polyphonic prose', as in *Sword Blades and Poppy Seed* (1914).

Lowell, Percival (1855–1916) Astronomer, born in Boston, MA. He is somewhat notorious for his observations alleging canals on Mars, but he correctly predicted the existence of Pluto.

Lowell, Robert (Traill Spence), Jr (1917–77) Poet, born in Boston, MA. He is especially known for his poems on painfully autobiographical subjects, giving rise to the style of 'confessional' poetry, as in *Notebook* (1969), *History* (1973), and *Day by Day* (1977).

Lowestoft [lohistoft] 52°29N 1°45E, pop (2000e) 65 800. Port town and resort in Suffolk, E England; railway; known for its fishing industry.

Lowry, L(aurence) S(tephen) [lowree] (1887–1976) Artist, born in Manchester, Greater Manchester. From the 1920s he produced many pictures of the Lancashire industrial scene, mainly in brilliant whites and greys, peopled with scurrying stick-like men and women.

Lowry, (Clarence) Malcolm [lowree] (1909–57) Novelist, born in Liscard, Merseyside. His reputation is based on *Under the Volcano* (1947), a novel set in Mexico, where he lived 1936–7.

Lowry Centre [lowree] Arts centre in Salford Quays, 2·5 km/1·5 mi from Manchester city centre in NW England; named after artist L S Lowry. Opened in 2000, the steel and glass structure houses a Lowry exhibition, contemporary art works, theatre, conference room, and restaurants. In 2001 it was named building of the year by the Royal Fine Art Commission Trust.

Loy, Myrna [loy] (1905–93) Film actress, born in Helena, MT. She made her debut in *Pretty Ladies* (1925), went on to play a series of exotic female roles, then developed a bright and witty persona in such films as *The Great Ziegfeld* (1936) and *Too Hot to Handle* (1938). Known as the 'Queen of Hollywood', she continued to appear in films until the early 1980s, and received an honorary Oscar in 1991.

Loyalists Refugees from the 13 British American colonies who fled to Britain, New Brunswick, Nova Scotia, Prince Edward Island, and Canada (1783) as a result of the American War of Independence (1765–88).

Loyalty Islands, Fr **Iles Loyauté** pop (2000e) 22 000; area 1981 km^2/765 sq mi. Group of coral islands in the SW Pacific Ocean; dependency of the Territory of New Caledonia; capital, We (Lifu I).

Loyola, Ignatius of, St [loyohla], originally **Iñigo López de Recalde** (1491 or 1495–1556) Theologian, born in his ancestral castle of Loyola in Guipúzcoa, Spain. In 1534 he founded with six associates the Society of Jesus. The author of the influential *Spiritual Exercises*, he was canonized in 1622. Feast day 31 July.

LSD or **lysergic acid diethylamide** A hallucinogen which was a popular drug of abuse in the 1960s and early 1970s, taken as 'microdots' and known as 'trips', 'tabs', or simply 'acid'. The cult of LSD-taking was promoted by Dr Timothy Leary (1920–96), who was dismissed from his post as clinical psychologist at Harvard in 1963.

LSI *very large scale integration*

Luanda [lwanda], formerly also **Loanda**, Port **São Paulo de**

Loanda 8°50S 13°15E, pop (2000e) 2 460 000. Seaport capital of Angola; founded in 1575; the centre of Portuguese administration from 1627; a major slave trading centre with Brazil in 17th–18th-c; airport; railway; university (1962); cathedral.

Luang Prabang *Louangphrabang*

Luba-Lunda Kingdoms A succession of African states occupying territory in what is now Democratic Republic of Congo. They were powerful in the 17th–18th-c, involved in slave and ivory trading.

Lübeck [lübek] 53°52N 10°40E, pop (2000e) 222 000. Commercial and manufacturing seaport in NE Germany; major city in the Hanseatic League; railway; birthplace of Thomas Mann; cathedral (1173); noted for its red wine trade and its marzipan; the Hanseatic City is a world heritage site.

Lubitsch, Ernst [loobich] (1892–1947) Film director, born in Berlin. He established himself as the creator of witty sophisticated light comedies, such as *The Love Parade* (1929) and *Ninotchka* (1939). He received a Special Academy Award in 1947.

Lublin [lubleen] 51°18N 22°31E, pop (2000e) 356 000. City in E Poland; a castle town, gaining urban status in 1317; railway; university (1918); cathedral (16th-c).

Lublin, Union of [lubleen] (1569) An Act uniting Poland and the Grand Duchy of Lithuania. The Union completed the formal unification of the two states begun in the 14th-c.

Lubumbashi [lubumbashee], formerly **Elisabethville** (to 1966) 11°40S 27°28E, pop (2000e) 862 500. City in SE Democratic Republic of Congo; founded, 1910; airport; railway; university (1955); copper mining and smelting; cathedral.

Lucan [lookn], in full **Marcus Annaeus Lucanus** (39–65) Roman poet, born in Córdoba, Spain. In 62 he published the first three books of his epic *Pharsalia* on the civil war between Pompey and Caesar. After Nero forbade him to write poetry, he joined a conspiracy against him, but was betrayed and compelled to commit suicide.

Lucan, Richard John Bingham, 7th Earl of [lookn], known as **Lord Lucan** (1934–?) British aristocrat, and alleged murderer. He disappeared in 1974, when police found the body of the Lucan family's nanny, Sandra Rivett. The police failed to trace him, and in 1975 a coroner's jury charged him with the murder. Speculation about his whereabouts continues to this day.

Lucas, George (Walton) (1944–) Film director, screenwriter, and producer, born in Modesto, CA. He is best known as producer of the Indiana Jones series and as director/writer of the *Star Wars* series (1977, 1980, 1983, 1999, 2002, 2005). In 1975 he started Industrial Light and Magic, a company that creates special visual and audio effects for film and television.

Lucas, Matt *Walliams, David*

Lucas, Robert E, Jr (1939–) Economist, born in Yakima, WA. He won the Nobel Prize for Economics in 1995 for developing and applying the hypothesis of rational expectations in macroeconomic analysis. He is known for his 'Lucas critique' (1976), showing that shifts in economic policy can produce unexpected outcomes if people adapt their expectations to new policy stances.

Lucas van Leyden [laydn], or **Lucas Jacobsz** (1494–1533) Painter and engraver, born in Leyden, The Netherlands. His masterpiece is the triptych, 'The Last Judgment' (1526, Leyden).

Luce, Clare Boothe, *née* **Boothe** (1903–87) Playwright, born in New York City. She wrote several successful plays, such as *The Women* (1936) and *Kiss the Boys Goodbye* (1938). She later became US ambassador to Italy (1953–7).

Luce, Henry R(obinson) (1898–1967) Magazine publisher and editor, born in Shandong province, China, to a missionary family. He co-founded and edited *Time* (1923), which aimed to present news in narrative style, and later founded *Fortune* (1930) and *Life* (1936).

Lucerne [loosern], Ger **Luzern** 47°03N 8°18E, pop (2000e) 62 000. Resort city in C Switzerland, on W shore of L Lucerne; railway junction; lake steamers; cathedral (17th-c).

Lucerne, Lake, Ger **Vierwaldstätter See** area 114 km²/44 sq mi. Fourth largest of the Swiss lakes; length 38 km/24 mi; maximum depth 214 m/702 ft.

lucerne A bushy perennial (*Medicago sativa*, subspecies *sativa*) growing to 90 cm/3 ft; leaves with three leaflets, broadest and toothed towards the tip; pea-flowers purple or blue; fruit a spiral pod with 1½–3 coils; also called **alfalfa**. (Family: Leguminosae.)

Lucian [looshan] (c.117–c.180) Greek rhetorician, born in Samosata, Syria. He devoted himself to philosophy, and produced a new form of literature – humorous dialogue. His satires include *Dialogues of the Gods* and *Dialogues of the Dead*.

Lucid, Shannon [loosid] (1943–) US astronaut and biochemist, who in 1996 set a new record for the longest US space mission (188 days) in orbit aboard the *Mir* space station. She became the first woman to be awarded the Congressional Space Medal of Honor.

Lucifer *Devil*

Lucknow [luhknow] 26°50N 81°00E, pop (2000e) 1 869 000. Capital of Uttar Pradesh, NC India; capital of the Kingdom of Oudh, 1775–1856; capital of the United Provinces, 1877; British garrison besieged for five months during the Indian Mutiny, 1857; airfield; railway; university (1921).

Lucretia [lookreesha] (6th-c BC) According to Roman legend, the wife of Collatinus. She was raped by Sextus, son of Tarquinius Superbus; after telling her story, she committed suicide.

Lucretius [lookreeshus], in full **Titus Lucretius Carus** (c.94–c.55BC) Latin poet and philosopher. His major work is the 6-volume hexameter poem *De rerum natura* (On the Nature of Things).

Lucullus, Lucius Licinius [lukuhlus] (c.110–57 BC) Roman politician and general, famous for his victories over Mithridates VI, and also for his enormous wealth and patronage of the arts.

Luddites The name given to groups of workers who in 1811–12 destroyed newly introduced textile machinery in the North of England, because they feared that many jobs would be lost; those involved claimed to be acting under the leadership of a certain 'Ned Ludd', although it is doubtful that such a person ever existed. The term has since been used to describe any resistance to technological innovation.

Ludendorff, Erich von [ludendaw(r)f] (1865–1937) General, born near Poznan, Poland. He became chief-of-staff under Hindenburg, defeated the Russians at Tannenberg (1914), and conducted the 1918 offensives on the Western front. In 1923 he was a leader in the unsuccessful Hitler putsch at Munich.

Luderitz [lüderits], formerly **Angra Pequena** 26°38S 15°10E, pop (2000e) 11 000. Seaport in SW Namibia; Diaz landed here in 1486; first German settlement in SW Africa, 1883; railway.

Ludlow 52°22N 2°43W, pop (2000e) 8500. Historic market town in Shropshire, WC England; developed in the 12th-c around a Norman fortress; Ludlow Castle (11th-c).

Ludwigshafen (am Rhein) [ludviks-hahfen] 49°29N 8°27E, pop (2000e) 167 000. Commercial and manufacturing river port in Germany; on W bank of the R Rhine.

Luftwaffe [luftvahfuh] (Ger 'air-weapon') The correct name for the German Air Force, re-established in 1935 under Göring, in contravention of the Treaty of Versailles. Dominant in the years of German victory in World War 2, the Luftwaffe had all but ceased to exist by 1945. The Federal Republic of Germany's air force, also known as the Luftwaffe, was re-established in 1956.

Lugano [loogahnoh] 46°01N 8°57E, pop (2000e) 27 000. Resort town in S Switzerland, on N shore of L Lugano; on road and rail route over the St Gotthard Pass; third largest financial centre in Switzerland; cathedral (13th-c).

Lugansk [lugansk], formerly **Voroshilovgrad** (1970–91) 48°35N 39°20E, pop (2000e) 491 000. City in E Ukraine; founded, 1795; airfield; railway; iron and steel.

lugeing [loozhing] Travelling across ice on a toboggan sled, usually made of wood with metal runners. The rider sits upright or lies back, as opposed to lying on the stomach in tobogganing. The luge is approximately 1·5 m/5 ft in length, and is steered by the feet and a hand rope.

lugworm A large annelid worm that burrows in soft inshore or estuarine sediments; breathes using external gills along body; widely used as fishing bait. (Class: Polychaeta. Order: Capitellida.)

Luik [loyk] Liège

Lukács, Georg or **György** [lookach] (1885–1971) Marxist philosopher and critic, born in Budapest. He was a prolific writer on literature and aesthetics, and wrote works on Hegel and existentialism. His books include Studies in European Realism (1948) and The Destruction of Reason (1955).

Luke, St (1st-c) New Testament evangelist, a Gentile Christian. He is first named as author of the third Gospel in the 2nd-c, and tradition has ever since ascribed to him both that work and the Acts of the Apostles. Feast day 18 October.

Lull, Ramón Llull, Ramón

Lully, Jean Baptiste [loolee], originally **Giovanni Battista Lulli** (1632–87) Composer, born in Florence, Italy. He composed many operas, in which he made the ballet an essential part, and also wrote church music, dance music, and pastorals.

Lully, Raymond Llull, Ramón

Luluabourg Kananga

lumbago [luhmbaygoh] An imprecise term used to indicate pain or discomfort in the back over the lumbar region, without identifying or defining a specific cause.

lumbar puncture The introduction of a needle between the vertebrae in the lower back (the lumbar region) into the narrow space lying between the inner two layers of membranes surrounding the spinal cord and its nerve roots. Its purpose is to obtain a sample of cerebrospinal fluid for examination in the diagnosis of infections or bleeding.

Lumbini [lumbeenee] Town and centre of pilgrimage in the W Terai of Nepal; the birthplace of Buddha; world heritage site.

lumen [loomin] SI unit of luminous flux; symbol lm; defined as the luminous flux emitted from a light source of intensity 1 candela into a solid angle of 1 steradian.

Lumière brothers [lümyair] Chemists, born in Besançon, France: **Auguste (Marie Louis) Lumière** (1862–1954) and **Louis (Jean) Lumière** (1864–1948). In 1893 they developed a cine camera, the cinématographe, and showed the first motion pictures using film projection in 1895.

luminescence The emission of light from a substance for reasons other than heating. **Photoluminescence** corresponds to a bombardment with light, exploited in zinc sulphide-based paints, which continue to glow after the external light source is removed. **Bioluminescence** is observed for example in fireflies, and results from chemical reactions. Solids which luminesce are called phosphors.

luminosity The intrinsic or absolute amount of energy radiated per second from a celestial object. Stars vary greatly in their observed luminosities, between about 1 million times more and 1 million times less than the Sun. In astronomy, luminosity is measured in magnitudes.

luminous flux The total flow of visible light available for illumination from some source, taking into account the source's ability to generate visible light; symbol Φ, unit lm (lumen).

luminous intensity The flow of visible light capable of causing illumination, emitted from a source per unit solid angle; symbol I, unit cd (candela). It is independent of distance from source. A related quantity is **luminance**, formerly called

brightness, symbol L, units cd/m², the luminous intensity per square metre.

lumpsucker Heavy-bodied fish (Cyclopterus lumpus) widespread in the N Atlantic and Arctic Oceans; length up to 60 cm/2 ft; body rounded, bearing rows of spiny plates and with a large underside sucker. (Family: Cyclopteridae.)

Lumumba, Patrice (Hemery) [lumumba] (1925–61) Congolese statesman, born in Katako Kombé, Democratic Republic of the Congo (formerly Zaire). He became the leader of the Congolese national movement, and premier when the Congo became an independent republic in 1960 (now Zaire). He was deposed after four months, and soon after assassinated.

Luna programme A highly successful evolutionary series of Soviet lunar missions carried out between 1959 and 1976. Luna 2 (1959) was the first spacecraft to impact the Moon; Luna 3 (1959) acquired the first pictures of the lunar far side; Luna 9 (1966) achieved the first soft landing, and returned first TV pictures from the surface.

Lunar Orbiter programme A series of US spacecraft used to survey the Moon at high resolution from a lunar orbit, prior to the crewed Apollo landings. Launched 1966–7, and equipped only with cameras, it provided the database for the selection of Apollo landing sites.

Lund 55°42N 13°10E, pop (2000e) 93 000. Ancient city in SW Sweden; bishopric; railway; university (1666); technical institute (1961); cathedral (1080).

Lunda Luba-Lunda Kingdoms

Lundy Island [luhndee] Island in the Bristol Channel, off the NW coast of Devon, SW England; two lighthouses; area 9·6 km²/ 3·7 sq mi; National Trust area, since 1969.

Lüneburger Heide [lüneberguh hiyduh] ('Luneburg Heath') A region of moorland and forest lying between the R Aller and R Elbe in W Germany, where Field Marshal Montgomery accepted the capitulation of the German Army (4 May 1945).

lungfish Any of a small group of freshwater fishes with a pair of lungs on the underside of the gut, connected to the oesophagus; gills much reduced; includes the African (Family: Protopteridae), Australian (Family: Ceratodontidae), and South American lungfish (Family: Lepidosirenidae).

lungs The organs of respiration, where the exchange of oxygen and carbon dioxide between the blood and air takes place. They are present in terrestrial vertebrates (reptiles, birds, mammals) and some fish (eg lungfish). In humans the paired lungs lie within the pleural cavities of the thorax. Each lung is highly elastic, and is divided into a number of lobes, each of which is further subdivided; each lobe receives a bronchus (bronchiole when the lobules become small) and blood vessels. The subdivisions continue until the respiratory bronchioles divide into a cluster of alveoli, where gaseous exchange occurs. At rest, the volume of air passing in and out of the lungs at each breath is about 500 ml: this can increase eight-fold during extreme exertion. Medical problems affecting the lungs include asphyxia, emphysema, empyema, pneumonia, and tuberculosis.

Lunt, Alfred (1892–1977) Actor, born in Milwaukee, WI. He studied at Carroll College, Waukesha, abandoned early plans to be an architect, and made his stage debut in 1912 with the Castle Square Theatre Company in Boston, MA. He met **Lynn Fontanne** in 1916, when they both appeared in A Young Man's Fancy. They were married in 1922, and from 1924 became a popular husband-and-wife team. Broadway's Lunt–Fontanne Theatre, opened in 1958, was named in the couple's honour, and in 1964 they received the US Medal of Freedom.

Luo [loooh] A Nilotic-speaking people of W Kenya. Mainly farmers and fishers, they are the second largest ethnic group in Kenya.

Luoyang or **Loyang** [lwohyahng] 34°47N 112°26E, pop (2000e) 1 341 000. City in NC China; capital of ancient China during the E Zhou dynasty, 770–256 BC; railway; Baimasi Temple (founded AD 75); Longmen Caves, with c.100 000 images and statues of Buddha (5th–7th-c) is a world heritage site.

Lupercalia [looperkaylia] An ancient festival of purification and fertility. It was held every year in ancient Rome (on 15 Feb) at a cave on the Palatine Hill called the Lupercal.

lupin A member of a large group of annual and perennial herbs or shrubs, native to America and the Mediterranean region; pea-flowers in long, terminal, often showy spikes, blue, pink, yellow, or white; pods splitting open explosively to release the seeds. (Genus: *Lupinus*, 200 species. Family: Leguminosae.)

Lupus (astronomy) [**loopus**] (Lat 'wolf') A small S constellation next to Centaurus, known since Greek times.

lupus erythematosus *systemic lupus erythematosus*

lupus vulgaris [loopus vulgahris] Tuberculosis of the skin, now rare in countries in which pulmonary tuberculosis is well controlled. It causes ulceration and scarring of the skin of the face or neck.

lurcher A cross-bred dog formerly kept by poachers for catching rabbits and hares; usually a cross between a greyhound and a collie.

Lusaka [loosaka] 15°26S 28°20E, pop (2000e) 1 150 300. Capital of Zambia; replaced Livingstone as capital of former N Rhodesia, 1935; capital of Zambia, 1964; airport; railway; university (1965); cathedral (1957).

Lusatians *Wends*

Lusitania [loositaynia] A Cunard passenger liner of 31 000 tonnes gross, sunk in the Irish Sea in 1915 by a German U-boat, with great loss of life. The Germans claimed she was carrying armaments, but this was officially denied by the British.

Lusophone Community, formally the **Comunidad dos Paises de Língua Portuguesa** An organization to facilitate social, cultural, and economic co-operation among Portuguese-speaking countries: Angola, Brazil, Cape Verde, Guinea-Bissau, Mozambique, Portugal, and São Tomé and Principe. It was formally created in 1996.

lute A European stringed instrument in use from the Middle Ages to the 18th-c, and revived in modern times for performing early music. It has a large pear-shaped body, a wide neck, and is plucked with the right hand.

Luther, Martin (1483–1546) Religious reformer, born in Eisleben, Germany. During a visit to Rome in 1510–11, he was angered by the sale of indulgences. In 1517 he drew up 95 theses on indulgences, which he nailed on the church door at Wittenberg, and publicly burned the papal bull issued against him. He was summoned to appear before the Diet at Worms, and was put under the ban of the Empire. In 1525 he married a former nun, Katharina von Bora. The drawing up of the Augsburg Confession marks the culmination of the German Reformation (1530). His translation of the Bible became a landmark of German literature.

Lutheranism Churches derived from the Reformation of Martin Luther, and the doctrine which they share. The doctrine emphasizes justification by faith alone, the importance of scripture, and the priesthood of all believers. Three sacraments are recognized: baptism, Eucharist, and penance. The Lutheran World Federation, a free association of Lutheran Churches, was founded in 1947.

Luthuli or **Lutuli, Albert (John Mvumbi)** [lutoolee] (c.1899–1967) Resistance leader, born in Zimbabwe (formerly Rhodesia). He became president-general of the African National Congress, and dedicated himself to a campaign of nonviolent resistance, for which he was awarded the Nobel Peace Prize in 1960.

Lutine Bell [looteen] A bell formerly rung at Lloyd's of London insurers' offices to announce the loss of a ship or other news of great importance to the underwriters. The bell belonged to a vessel (HMS *Lutine*), carrying gold bullion, which foundered off

the Dutch coast in 1799. Nowadays it is rung mainly on ceremonial occasions.

Luton [lootn] 51°53N 0°25W, pop (2001e) 184 400. Industrial town and unitary authority (from 1997) in Bedfordshire, SC England; railway; airport; football league team, Luton Town (Hatters).

Lutosławski, Witold [lootohslavskee] (1913–94) Composer, born in Warsaw. His works include the *Variations on a Theme of Paganini* (1941) for two pianos, three symphonies, concertos, songs, and chamber music.

Lutuli, Albert John *Luthuli, Albert*

Lutyens, Sir Edwin Landseer [lutyenz] (1869–1944) Architect, born in London. His best-known projects are the Cenotaph in Whitehall, London (1919–20), and the laying out of New Delhi, India (1912–30).

lux SI unit of illuminance; symbol *lx*; defined as 1 lumen of luminous flux incident on 1 square metre.

Luxembourg (city) [luhksmberg] 49°37N 6°08E, pop (2000e) 82 000. Capital of Luxembourg; also site of the Court of Justice of the European Communities, the General Secretariat of the European Parliament, and other bodies; airport; railway.

Luxembourg or **Luxemburg** *p.558*

Luxembourg, Palais du [pale dü lüksāboorg] Since 1958, the seat of the French Senate in Paris. The palace was built in 1613–14 by Salomon de Brosse (1565–1626).

Luxemburg, Rosa (1871–1919) German revolutionary, born in Poland. With the German politician, Karl Liebknecht (1871–1919), she formed the Spartacus League, which later became the German Communist Party. She was murdered during the Spartacus revolt in Berlin.

Luxor [luhksaw(r)], Arabic **al-Uqsor**, or **al-Uqsur** 25°41N 32°24E, pop (2000e) 191 800. Winter resort town in EC Egypt; known as Thebes to the Greeks; numerous tombs of pharaohs in Valley of the Kings.

Lu Xun [loo shün], also spelled **Lu-hsün** or **Lu-hsin** (1881–1936) Writer, born in Shaoxing, China. His short story, *Diary of a Madman* (1918), was an immediate success, as was his 1921 book, *The True Story of Ah Q*.

Luzon [loozon] pop (2000e) 35 813 000; area 108 130 km^2/ 41 738 sq mi. Largest island of the Philippines; Cordillera Central rises to 2929 m/9609 ft in the NW at Mt Puog; occupied by Japanese in World War 2; chief city, Manila.

Lvov [livof], Pol **Lwow**, Ger **Lemberg**, Ukrainian **Lwiw** 49°50N 24°00E, pop (2000e) 778 000. City in Ukraine; founded, 1256; part of Poland (1340–1772), then given to Austria; ceded to Poland after World War 1; ceded to USSR, 1939; airfield; railway junction; centre for Ukrainian culture; university (1661); cathedral.

Lyallpur *Faisalabad*

lycanthropy [liykanthropee] In popular belief, the assumption by humans of the shapes of other animals, typically the most dangerous beast of the area. In Europe and N Asia it is usually a wolf or bear.

Lyceum [liyseeum] The school of philosophy founded by Aristotle in 335 BC, in a gymnasium just to the E of the city walls of Athens. It rivalled the Academy of Plato as a research centre in the ancient world.

lychee *litchi*

Lycra® An artificial elastomeric fibre which has the ability to return to its original size and shape even after it has been stretched up to 600 times its starting length. Invented by Du Pont, it is a segmented polyurethane fibre which behaves as a single continuous thread but is actually made up of a bundle of tiny filaments. It is this segmented molecular structure which gives Lycra its stretch properties. It is always combined with other fibres in a material.

Lycurgus [liykergus] The name of various Greeks, including, in mythology, **1** The King of Thrace who opposed Dionysus and

Luxembourg

□ International Airport

Area 2586 km²/998 sq mi

Population total (2002e) 447 000

Status Grand Duchy

Date of independence 1867

Capital Luxembourg

Languages French (official), Letzeburgish, German

Ethnic groups Luxemburger (73%), Portuguese (9%), Italian (5%), French (3%), Belgian (3%), German (2%)

Religions Roman Catholic (97%), Protestant (2%), Jewish (1%)

Physical features Divided into the two natural regions of Ardennes (Ösling) (N); forest in N, and Gutland in S, flatter, average height 250 m/820 ft; principal rivers include the Sûre, Our, Moselle.

Climate Mild climate, influenced by warm S wind (Föhn); average annual temperatures 0·7°C (Jan), 18°C (Jul) in Luxembourg; average annual rainfall, 1050–1200 mm/41–7 in.

Currency 1 euro (EUR) = 100 cents (previous to February 2002, 1 Luxembourg Franc (LVF) = 100 centimes).

Economy Important international centre based in city of Luxembourg; iron and steel, food processing; chemicals, tyres, metal products; mixed farming, dairy farming; wine; forestry; tourism.

GDP (2002e) $21·94 bn, per capita $48 900

Human Development Index (2002) 0·925

History Made a Grand Duchy by the Congress of Vienna, 1815; granted political autonomy, 1838; recognized as a neutral independent state, 1867; occupied by Germany in both World Wars; joined Benelux economic union, 1948; neutrality abandoned on joining NATO, 1949; founder member of European Union (formerly EC), 1958; a hereditary monarchy with the Grand Duke as Head of State; Parliament consists of Chamber of Deputies and State Council; Head of Government is the Minister of State.

Head of State (Grand Dukes and Duchesses)
1919–64 Charlotte (in exile, 1940–4)
1964–2000 Jean
2000– Henri

Head of Government
1979–84 Pierre Werner
1984–95 Jacques Santer
1995– Jean-Claude Juncker

or **Luxemburg**

(country) [**luhks**mberg], official name **Grand Duchy of Luxembourg**, Fr **Grande-Duché de Luxembourg**, Ger **Grossherzogtum Luxemburg**, Letzeburgish **Grousherzogdem Lëtzebuerg**

Local names Lëtzebuerg (Letzeburgish), Luxembourg (French), Luxemburg (German)

Timezone GMT +1

---

was blinded. **2** The founder of the Spartan constitution, with its military caste-system.

Lydgate, John [lidgayt] (c.1370–c.1451) Poet, born in Lidgate, Suffolk. His major works are the narrative poems *The Troy Book* (1412–20), *The Story of Thebes* (1420), and *Falls of Princes* (1430–8).

Lydia [lideeuh] In antiquity, the area of W Asia Minor lying inland of Ionia. Its capital was Sardis. At the height of its power in the 7th-c and 6th-c BC, it was the centre of an empire which stretched from the Aegean to C Turkey.

Lyly, John [lilee] (c.1554–1606) Writer, born in the Weald of Kent, SE England. He is remembered for the style of his writing, as seen in his two-part prose romance *Euphues* (1578, 1580), which led to the term *euphuism* for artificial and extremely elegant language.

Lyme disease An infectious disease caused by the bacteria *Borrelia burgdorferi*, which is transmitted to humans in the bite of ticks that normally infest deer and other wild animals. A red skin lesion (*erythema migrans*) appears at the site of the bite and expands over a few days accompanied by fever, muscle pains, headaches, and inflammation of the joints. It can be cured completely with antibiotics.

lymph A clear, colourless tissue fluid comprising protein, water, and other substances derived from blood, and conveyed in an independent system of thin-walled vessels. It contains lymphocytes for destroying infective organisms.

lymphocyte [limfohsiyt] A type of white blood cell (*leucocyte*), present in blood and lymph vessels and in spleen and lymph nodes. Lymphocytes are classified as bone-marrow-derived B lymphocytes (*B cells*) and thymus-derived T lymphocytes (*T cells*). They have an essential role in the production of antibodies.

Lynam, Desmond (Michael) [liynam] (1942–) Sports broadcaster, born in Ennis, County Clare, Ireland. He joined the BBC in 1969 as a sports presenter and commentator, moving to television in 1978, where he became nationally known for his contributions to such programmes as *Grandstand*, *Sportsnight*, and *Match of the Day*. He joined Independent Television in 1999, retired from TV sports presenting in 2004, and later that year returned to the BBC with his own sports chat show, 'Des Meets...', on Radio 5 Live. He also became host (2005–6) of *Countdown*, the long-running Channel 4 quiz show.

Lynch, Jack, popular name of **John Lynch** (1917–99) Irish statesman and Fianna Fáil prime minister (1966–73, 1977–9), born in

Cork. He held ministerial posts in education (1957–9), industry and commerce (1959–65), and finance (1965–6), before becoming prime minister. A strong supporter of the Catholic minority in Ulster, he drew criticism from both Ulster and mainland Britain.

Lyngstad, Anni-Frid *Abba*

Lynn, Dame Vera, originally **Vera Welch** (1917–) British singer, born in London. A vocalist with Howard Baker's orchestra at the age of 15, she became highly popular during World War 2, hosting a BBC radio programme *Sincerely Yours*, and overseas servicemen voted her 'The Forces Sweetheart'. Her regular songs included 'White Cliffs of Dover' and 'We'll Meet Again'. She continued to perform into the 1970s, after which she saved her performances for nostalgic occasions.

Lynx A very faint N constellation near to Ursa Major.

lynx A nocturnal member of the cat family, native to the northern N Hemisphere; plain brown or with dark spots; very short tail; tips of ears tufted; cheeks with long 'whiskers'; two species: **lynx** (*Felis lynx*), and the rare **Spanish lynx** (*Felis pardina*).

Lyon [leeõ], Eng also **Lyons**, ancient **Lugdunum** 45°46N 4°50E, pop (2000e) 434 000. Manufacturing and commercial city in SC France; at confluence of Rhône and Saône Rivers; third largest city in France; Roman capital of Gaul; airport; road and rail junction; metro; archbishopric; two universities (1875, 1896); cathedral (12th–15th-c); leading centre of French textile industry, particularly silk production; international exhibition hall (Eurexpo).

Lyons, Sir John (1932–) Linguist, born in Manchester, Greater Manchester. A specialist in semantics and linguistic theory, his major publications include *Semantics* (1977), *Language, Meaning and Context* (1980), and *Linguistic Semantics* (1995).

Lyons, Joseph Aloysius (1879–1939) Australian statesman and prime minister (1932–9), born in Stanley, Tasmania, Australia. In 1931 he founded the United Australian Party, and became prime minister until his death.

lyophilization or **freeze drying** The process for the removal of solvent or adherent water from materials (eg blood plasma, foodstuffs, beverage bases) while in a frozen condition.

Lyra [liyra] ('harp') A small but obvious N constellation. It includes the fifth-brightest star, Vega, as well as the prototype variable RR Lyrae, and the Ring nebula.

lyre A musical instrument of great antiquity, with a resonator, two arms, and a crossbar. Gut strings, from 3 to 12 in number, were stretched from the front of the resonator to the crossbar, and plucked with a plectrum.

lyrebird Either of two species of a shy, ground-feeding, Australian bird of the genus *Menura*; long legs; flies poorly but runs well; tail of male shaped like lyre; spectacular display and song. (Family: Menuridae.)

Lysenko, Trofim Denisovich [lisengkoh] (1898–1976) Biologist and plant physiologist, born in Karlovka, Ukraine. Using political affiliation rather than scientific recognition for advancement, he became director of the Academy of Agricultural Sciences (1938–56, 1958–62) and in 1948 declared the accepted Mendelian theory erroneous, banishing many outstanding Soviet scientists.

Lysithea [liysitheea] The 10th natural satellite of Jupiter, discovered in 1938; distance from the planet 11 720 000 km/7 283 000 mi; diameter 36 km/22 mi.

lysosome [liysosohm] A membrane-bound sac which contains numerous enzymes capable of digesting a wide variety of substrates. They are involved in the digestion of food and in the destruction of bacteria in white blood cells.

lysozyme [liysohziym] An enzyme present in tears, saliva, sweat, milk, and nasal and gastric secretions; also known as *muramidase*. It destroys bacterial cell walls by digesting their polysaccharide component.

Lytham St Anne's [litham] 53°45N 3°01W, pop (2000e) 43 500. Resort town in Lancashire, NW England; railway; championship golf course.

Lyttelton, Humphrey [litltuhn] (1921–) Jazz trumpeter and bandleader, born in Windsor, S England. He formed a band in 1948, and became the leading figure in the British revival of traditional jazz, later presenting a range of more modern jazz styles. On BBC Radio he has hosted *The Best of Jazz* for many years, and has been chairman of the panel game *I'm Sorry I Haven't a Clue* since 1972. He was honoured with a Sony Gold Award (1993) for his contribution to radio.

Lytton (of Knebworth), Edward George Earle Bulwer-Lytton, Baron [litn] (1803–73) Writer and statesman, born in London. He wrote many popular novels, especially on historical themes, such as *The Last Days of Pompeii* (1834) and *Harold* (1843), as well as plays and essays.

Maasai *Masai*

Maastricht [mahstrikht], ancient **Traieclum ad Mosam** or **Traiectum Tungorum** 50°51N 5°42E, pop (2000e) 124 000. City in S Netherlands, on the R Maas; commercial hub of an area extending well into Belgium; railway junction; noted for its vegetable and butter markets; location of conference on European union, 1991.

Maastricht Treaty [mahstrikht, mahstrikht] An agreement reached in 1991 at Maastricht, The Netherlands, during a meeting of the heads of state and government of the European Community. It was the conclusion of a series of inter-governmental conferences on European political union and economic/monetary union which had been taking place since December 1990. The summit agreed a treaty framework for European union, incorporating political and economic agreements and setting a timetable for their implementation, and providing for new security/defence co-operation. The treaty required ratification by the 12 national governments: rejection by Denmark necessitated a revision of the ratification timetable, but by the end of 1992 all countries except Denmark and the UK had ratified, and these did so in mid-1993.

Maathai, Wangari (1940–) Environmentalist and human rights campaigner, born in Nyeri, Kenya. In 1977 she founded the Green Belt Movement, the largest tree-planting project in Africa, aimed at promoting biodiversity and giving women a stronger identity in society. In 2002 she entered parliament and was appointed Deputy Environment Minister the following year. She was awarded the 2004 Nobel Peace Prize for her contribution to sustainable development, democracy, and peace, the first African woman to win the honour.

Maazel, Lorin (Varencove) [mahzel] (1930–) Conductor, born in Neuilly, France. He was conductor of the Pittsburgh Symphony Orchestra (1986–96) and the Bavarian Radio Symphony Orchestra (1993–2002), and became music director of the New York Philharmonic Orchestra (from 2002) and the Arturo Toscanini Philharmonic (from 2004). In 2002 he conducted the premiere of John Adams' work, *The Transmigration of Souls*, commissioned to commemorate the terrorist attacks of 11 September 2001.

Mabinogion, The [mabinogion] The name widely given to a collection of 12 mediaeval Welsh stories, first translated by English diarist Charlotte Guest (1812–95), and published in three volumes (1838–49). It includes the tales of Branwen, Culhwch and Olwen, Geraint and Enid, Llud and Llefelys, Manawydan, Math, Owain, Peredur, Pwyll, Taliesin, the Dream of Macsen Wledig, and the Dream of Rhonabwy.

Mabo, Eddie Koiki [mahboh] (1940–92) Traditional leader of the Meriam people of Murray I in Torres Strait, Australia. In 1982, with four other Meriam people, he began legal proceedings against the Queensland government, seeking recognition of their traditional ownership of the island and its surrounding seas. In 1992 the High Court of Australia held that Australian common law recognizes a form of native title, making it a landmark case.

McAdam, John Loudon (1756–1836) Road builder, born in Ayr, South Ayrshire. His *Macadam surfaces* used crushed stone bound with gravel, and raised the carriageway to improve drainage. He was made surveyor (1816) to the Bristol Turnpike Trust, and later made surveyor-general of metropolitan roads.

macadamia nut [makadaymia] An evergreen tree (*Macadamia integrifolia*) growing to c.20 m/65 ft, native to NE Australia; flowers in long, drooping spikes, with four creamy segments; fruits green, splitting to reveal round, edible nut. (Family: Proteaceae.)

McAleese, Mary [makalees] (1951–) President of Ireland (1997–), born in Belfast. A professor of criminal law, in the 1980s she became known as a campaigner for many social causes. She was the first woman and Catholic pro-vice-chancellor at Queen's University, Belfast, in 1994. Despite her northern background, she became the presidential successor to Mary Robinson in the 1997 election. In 2004, she was elected for a second 7-year term.

Macao [makow], Chin **Aomen**, Port **Macáu** pop (2002e) 464 000; area 16 km²/6 sq mi. Special administrative region of China, and former overseas province of Portugal; flat, maritime tropical peninsula in SE China and the nearby islands of Taipa and Colôane; on the Pearl R delta, 64 km/40 mi W of Hong Kong; airport; capital, Nome de Deus de Macau; population largely Chinese (99%); official languages, Portuguese, Chinese (Cantonese generally spoken); chief religions, Buddhism, Roman Catholicism; unit of currency, the Pataca of 100 avos; ferry links with Hong Kong; occupied by Portugal from 1557, with official consent from 1678; ceded to Portugal, 1887; a Chinese territory under Portuguese administration, 1979; returned to Chinese rule in December 1999; governor appointed by China, with a 23-member Legislative Assembly; licensed gambling since the 19th-c; tourism, textiles, electronics, plastics, toys, banking, fishing; several fortresses, Jaialai Palace; grand prix racing.

macaque [makahk] An Old World monkey, native to S and SE Asia (18 species) and NW Africa (*Barbary ape*); legs and arms of equal length; tail often short; buttocks with naked patches. (Genus: *Macaca*, 19 species.)

macaroni *pasta*

MacArthur, Douglas (1880–1964) US general, born in Little Rock, AR. In 1941 he became commanding general of the US armed forces in the Far East, and from Australia directed the recapture of the SW Pacific (1942–5). In 1950 he led the UN forces in the Korean War.

MacArthur, Dame Ellen (1976–) Yachtswoman, born in Whatstandwell, Derbyshire. In 2000 she entered the gruelling Vendée Globe yacht race in *Kingfisher* and made history by becoming the fastest woman ever to sail solo around the world in a time of 94 days, 4 hrs, 25 min, 40 s, gaining second place in the race. In 2001 she was named female world sailor of the year by the International Sailing Federation. She won the Route du Rhum solo transatlantic race in record-breaking time of 13 days, 13 hrs, 31 min, 47 s aboard *Kingfisher* in 2002. In 2005 she sailed solo around the world in a record time of 71 days, 14 hrs, 18 min, 33 s, aboard trimaran *B & Q*, beating the previous record, set by Francis Joyon in 2004, by almost 33 hours. She was honoured with a damehood.

Macassar *Makassar Strait; Ujung Padang*

Macaulay, Dame (Emilie) Rose (1881–1958) Novelist, essayist, and poet, born in Rugby, Warwickshire. She won a considerable reputation as a social satirist, with such novels as *Dangerous Ages* (1921). Her best-known novel is *The Towers of Trebizond* (1956).

Macaulay (of Rothley), Thomas Babington Macaulay, Baron [muh-kawlee] (1800–59) Essayist and historian, born in Rothley Temple, Leicestershire. He became an MP (1830), established his powers as an orator in the Reform Bill debates, and became secretary of war (1839–41). He wrote the highly popular *Lays of Ancient Rome* (1842). His major work, the *History of England from the Accession of James II*, was published between 1848 and 1861, the fifth volume unfinished.

macaw A large parrot native to the Caribbean, and to Central and tropical South America; nests in holes. (Genera: *Ara, Anodorhynchus, Cyanopsitta*, c.16 species.)

Macbeth (c.1005–57) King of Scots (1040–57). The *mormaer* (provincial ruler) of Moray, he became king after slaying Duncan I in battle near Elgin. He was defeated and killed by Duncan's son, Malcolm Canmore. Shakespeare's version of events comes from the accounts of Holinshed and Boece.

MacBeth, George (Mann) (1932–92) Poet and novelist, born in Shotts, North Lanarkshire. A prolific poet, his *Collected Poems 1958–70* was published in 1971. His first novel, *The Transformation*, appeared in 1975, and he also produced several books for children and many anthologies.

McBride, Willie John, popular name of **William John McBride** (1940–) Rugby union player, born in Toomebridge, Co Antrim. A lock forward, he won 63 caps for Ireland, plus 17 British Lions caps – both records.

MacBride principles A code of conduct for Northern Ireland advocated by Irish statesman Sean MacBride (1904–88), and adopted in 1976, recommending that local firms should aim for balanced community representation in their staff recruitment. The code was created as part of a policy of creating jobs for the Catholic minority in Northern Ireland, and was initially focused on US companies which had branches in the region.

Maccabees [makabeez] An important Jewish family, and those of its party (also known as the **Hasmoneans**) who initially resisted the influences of Greek culture on Israel during Syrian rule over Palestine. **Judas Maccabeus** (or **ben Mattathias**) led a revolt in 168 BC, which was continued by his sons, resulting eventually in semi-independence from Syrian control.

Maccabees or **Machabees, Books of the** [makabeez] Four writings, the first two being part of the Old Testament Apocrypha and the last two being assigned to the Old Testament Pseudepigrapha.

McCarthy, Joseph R(aymond) (1909–57) US Republican politician and inquisitor, born in Grand Chute, WI. His unsubstantiated accusations that Communists had infiltrated the State Department led to his becoming chairman in 1953 of the powerful Permanent Subcommittee on Investigations. The anti-Communist witchhunt which ensued became known as **McCarthyism**.

McCarthy, Cormac (1933–) Novelist, born in Providence, RI, and raised in Tennessee. His first work, *The Orchard Keeper*, was published to great acclaim in 1965 (William Faulkner Foundation Award). His Border Trilogy comprises the best-selling *All The Pretty Horses* (1992), *The Crossing* (1994), and *Cities of the Plain* (1999).

McCarthy, Mary (Therese) (1912–89) Writer and critic, born in

Seattle, WA. Her novels include *The Company She Keeps* (1942), *The Group* (1963), and *Cannibals and Missionaries* (1979).

McCartney, Sir (James) Paul [muhkah(r)tnee] (1942–) Pop star, composer, songwriter, guitarist, and recording artist, born in Liverpool, Merseyside. The Beatles' bass guitarist, vocalist, and member of the Lennon–McCartney songwriting team, he made his debut as a soloist with the album *McCartney* (1970), heralding the break-up of the group. In 1971 he formed the band Wings with his wife, **Linda** (1942–98, *née* Eastman). 'Mull of Kintyre' (1977) became the biggest selling UK single (2·5 million). With Carl Davis he wrote the *Liverpool Oratorio* in 1991 and has continued to develop his interests as a classical composer in *Standing Stone* (1997), *Working Classical* (1999), and *Ecce Cor Meum* (2006). In 2004, he played his 3000th concert before 60 000 fans in the Russian city of St Petersburg. He married **Heather Mills** (1968–) in 2002 (separated 2006).

McCartney, Stella (1971–) British fashion designer, the daughter of Paul McCartney. She became chief designer at the French couture house Chloé in 1997, and received the Designer of the Year Award at the Vogue Fashion Awards in New York in 2000. She joined Gucci in 2001 and showed the first collection under her own label later that year. In 2003 she opened retail outlets in London and Los Angeles, and launched her first perfume. She received the Glamour Award for Best Designer of the Year in 2004.

McClellan, George B(rinton) (1826–85) US Union general in the Civil War, born in Philadelphia, PA. His Virginian campaign ended disastrously at Richmond (1862), and though he forced Lee to retreat at Antietam, he failed to follow up his advantage, and was recalled.

McClure, Sir Robert (John le Mesurier) [muhkloor] (1807–73) Explorer, born in Wexford, Ireland. He commanded a ship in Franklin's 1850 Artic expedition that penetrated E to the coast of Banks Land, where he was icebound for nearly two years. Rescued by another ship which had travelled from the W, he thus became the first person to accomplish the Northwest Passage.

McColgan, Liz [muhkolgan], popular name of **Elizabeth McColgan**, *née* Lynch (1964–) Athlete, born in Dundee, Scotland. Her athletic achievements in the 10 000 m include gold medals at the Commonwealth Games (1986, 1990), gold at the World Championships (1991), and silver at the Olympics (1988). She also won the silver for the 3000 m at the Indoor World Championships (1989), and was winner of the New York Marathon (1991) and the London Marathon (1996).

McCormack, John (Francis) (1884–1945) Tenor, born in Athlone, Ireland. He made his London debut in 1907, and sang at Covent Garden, appearing also in oratorio and as a *Lieder* singer. He later turned to popular sentimental songs.

McCormick, Cyrus (Hall) (1809–84) Inventor of the reaper, born in Rockbridge Co, VA. He manufactured more than six million harvesting machines during his lifetime.

McCourt, Frank [muhkaw(r)t] (1930–) Writer and teacher, born in Brooklyn, New York City. His family returned to their native Ireland when he was four, and settled in Limerick. His best-selling memoir, *Angela's Ashes* (1996, Pulitzer), chronicles the bitter years of an impoverished childhood until he left Ireland in 1949. A sequel, *Tis: A Memoir* (1999), follows his return to the USA, and *Teacher Man* (2005) relates his experiences as a teacher in New York.

McCoy, Tony, properly **Anthony Peter McCoy** (1974–) Jockey, born in Co Antrim, Northern Ireland. National Hunt Champion jockey since 1995, in 2002 he broke the record for the number of winners in a season (269 set on the flat by Sir Gordon Richards in 1947), finishing with a total of 289 winners. He rode his 1700th winner on Mighty Montefalco at Uttoxeter in 2002 to beat Richard Dunwoody's all-time British winners' record.

McCullers, (Lula) Carson, *née* **Smith** (1917–67) Writer, born in Columbus, GA. She is known for her realistic, tragic, and often symbolic novels, notably *The Heart is a Lonely Hunter* (1940) and *The Member of the Wedding* (1946, filmed 1952).

McCullough, Colleen [muhkuhluh] (1937–) Novelist, born in Wellington, New South Wales, Australia. Her books include *The Thorn Birds* (1977), which sold 20 million copies, and *The Grass Crown* (1991). Novels in the Masters of Rome series include *Caesar's Women* (1995), *Caesar: Let the Dice Fly* (1997), and *Queen of the Beast* (2007).

MacDiarmid, Alan G [muhkdermid] (1927–2007) Chemist, born in New Zealand. He joined the faculty at the University of Pennsylvania (1955) where he became professor of chemistry (1988). In 2000 he shared the Nobel Prize for Chemistry for the discovery and development of conductive polymers.

MacDiarmid, Hugh [muhkdermid], pseudonym of **Christopher Murray Grieve** (1892–1978) Poet, born in Langholm, Dumfries and Galloway. A founder-member of the Scottish National Party, he established himself as the leader of a vigorous Scottish Renaissance with *A Drunk Man Looks at the Thistle* (1926).

McDonagh, Martin [muhkdona] (1970–) Playwright, born in London. Brought up in London by Irish parents, much of his work is set in Ireland. In 1997 his first four plays were running simultaneously in London's West End: *The Leenane Trilogy* and *The Cripple of Inishmaan*. Later plays include *The Lieutenant of Inishmore* (2001) and *The Pillowman* (2003). He wrote and directed the Oscar-winning short film *Six Shooter* (2005).

Macdonald, Flora (1722–90) Scottish heroine, born in South Uist, Western Isles. After the rebellion of 1745, she conducted the Young Pretender, Charles Edward Stuart, disguised as 'Betty Burke', to safety in Skye. For this she was imprisoned in the Tower of London, but released in 1747.

Macdonald, Sir John A(lexander) (1815–91) Canadian statesman and prime minister (1857–8, 1864, 1867–73, 1878–91), born in Glasgow. He was instrumental in bringing about the confederation of Canada, and in 1867 formed the first government of the new Dominion.

MacDonald, (James) Ramsay (1866–1937) British statesman and prime minister (1924, 1929–31, 1931–5), born in Lossiemouth, Moray. He became an MP in 1906, and was prime minister and foreign secretary of the first British Labour government. He met the financial crisis of 1931 by forming a largely Conservative 'National' government.

McDonald, Sir Trevor (1939–) Television journalist and newscaster, born in Trinidad. He became a reporter for ITN in 1973, then a sports correspondent (1978), diplomatic correspondent (1980), and diplomatic editor (1987). He became nationally known after he joined ITN's *News at Ten* (1990–9), and began presenting *Tonight With Trevor McDonald* in 1999. He presented ITN's late night bulletin for many years until 2005. His awards include the BAFTA Richard Dimbleby Award (1999), a National Television Award for special achievement (2003), and a Royal Television Society journalism award for lifetime achievement (2005).

MacDonnell Ranges Mountain ranges in Northern Territory, C Australia; extend 320 km/200 mi W from Alice Springs; rising to 1524 m/5000 ft at Mt Liebig.

mace A spice obtained by grinding up the red, net-like aril which surrounds the seed of the nutmeg tree (*Myristica fragrans*). It is poisonous if consumed in large quantities.

Macedon [masedon] In antiquity, the territory to the N of Greece abutting on to the NW corner of the Aegean. Philip II (359–336 BC) transformed it into the most powerful state in Greece. It became a Roman province in 146 BC.

Macedonia (Greece) [masedohnia], Gr **Makedhonia** pop (2000e) 2 308 000; area 34 177 km²/13 192 sq mi. N region of Greece; capital, Thessaloniki; mountainous, with fertile plains.

Macedonia (republic) *p.563*

McEnroe, John (Patrick) [makenroh] (1959–) Lawn tennis player, born in Wiesbaden, Germany. He won the Wimbledon title three times (1981, 1983–4), the US singles four times (1979–81, 1984), and was World Championship Tennis champion in 1979, 1981, and 1983–4. His outbursts on court were the source of much adverse publicity. Since 1995 he has been a television commentator. An autobiography, *Serious*, appeared in 2002.

McFadden, Daniel L (1937–) Economist, born in Raleigh, NC. He joined the faculty at the University of California, Berkeley (1963), where he became professor of economics. In 2000 he shared the Nobel Prize for Economics for work in the field of microeconometrics.

Macgillycuddy's Reeks [makgilikuhdeez reeks] Mountain range in Kerry county, Munster, SW Ireland, rising to 1041 m/3415 ft at Carrantuohill, highest peak in Ireland.

McGonagall, William [muhgonagl] (1830–1902) Doggerel poet, born in Edinburgh, the son of an Irish weaver. He gave readings in public houses, published broadsheets of topical verse, and in Edinburgh was lionized by the legal and student fraternity.

McGough, Roger [muhgof] (1937–) Poet and performer, born in Liverpool, Merseyside. He became known as one of the 'Liverpool Poets' together with Adrian Henri (1932–2000) and Brian Patten (1946–). A poet of bizarre irony and wit, he is well-known for his public readings. Collections of poems include *Gig* (1973), *Waving at Trains* (1982), and *Everyday Eclipses* (2003). Other works include a book for children, *The Magic Fountain* (1995), a novel, *Defying Gravity* (1996), and an autobiography, *Said and Done* (2005). *A Poem for Bootle* (2007) was commissioned as a logo for his home town.

McGovern, George S(tanley) [muhguhvern] (1922–) US Democratic politician, born in Avon, SD. He sought the Democratic presidential nomination in 1968, and opposed Nixon in the 1972 presidential election, but was defeated. He tried again for the presidential nomination in 1984, but withdrew.

McGregor, Ewan (1971–) Actor, born in Crieff, Perthshire. His first important role was in the television series *Lipstick on Your Collar* (1993), and feature film success followed with *Shallow Grave* (1994) and *Trainspotting* (1996). Later films include three *Star Wars* episodes (1999, 2002, 2005), *Moulin Rouge* (2000), and *Miss Potter* (2006).

McGuffey, William (Holmes) [muhguhfee] (1800–73) Educator, born near Claysville, PA. He compiled the famous *McGuffey Readers*, six elementary schoolbooks (1836–57) that sold 122 million copies and became standard texts for generations of 19th-c US children.

McGuinness, Martin [muhginis] (1950–) Sinn Féin politician, born in Londonderry, Northern Ireland. A militant supporter of the IRA, who served two jail sentences in the Irish Republic, he developed a major role as a political strategist during the Northern Ireland peace process in the 1990s. He became an MP, and minister of education in the devolved Assembly in 1999. He was nominated as deputy first minister in the restored Assembly in 2007.

McGwire, Mark [muhgwiyuh] (1963–) Baseball player, born in Pomona, CA. A power-hitting first baseman, his final total of 70 homers passed the previous seasonal record of 61 set by Roger Maris in 1961. He was voted American League Rookie of the Year in 1987, after hitting 49 homers, the most ever by a rookie, for Oakland Athletics. In 1997 he was traded to the St Louis Cardinals, and retired in 2001.

Mach, Ernst [mahk] (1838–1916) Physicist and philosopher, born in Turas, Austria. He influenced aeronautical design and the science of projectiles. His writings also greatly influenced Einstein and laid the foundations of logical positivism.

Machabees *Maccabees, Books of the*

Machaut, Guillaume de *Guillaume de Machaut*

Macedonia

☐ International Airport

(republic) [masedohnia], Serbo-Croatian **Makedonija**, also called **Former Yugoslav Republic of Macedonia (FYROM)**

Local name Makedonija

Timezone GMT +2

Area 25 713 km²/9925 sq mi

Population total (2002e) 2 036 000

Status Republic

Date of independence 1991

Capital Skopje

Language Macedonian (status as language or dialect is a political issue with Greece), and Albanian

Ethnic groups Macedonian Slav (66%), Albanian (23%), with Turk

(4%), Serb (3%), and other minorities (but minority totals disputed as underestimates by Albanians and Serbs)

Religions Macedonian Orthodox Christian (autocephalous), Muslim

Physical features Landlocked, mountainous region, bordered by Serbia, Bulgaria, Greece, Albania; divided from Greek Macedonia by the Kožuf and Nidže ranges, highest point, Korab, 2764 m/ 9068 ft; main rivers, Struma and Vardar.

Climate Continental climate; average annual temperatures 0°C (Jan), 24°C (Jul); often heavy winter snowfalls; average annual rainfall 500 mm/20 in.

Currency 1 Macedonian Denar (MKD) = 100 paras

Economy Agriculture; wheat, barley, corn, rice, tobacco; sheep, cattle; mining of minerals, iron ore, lead, zinc, nickel; steel, chemicals, textiles.

GDP (2002e) $10·57 bn, per capita $5100

Human Development Index (2002) 0·772

History Part of Macedonian, Roman, and Byzantine Empires; settled by Slavs, 6th-c; conquered by Bulgars, 7th-c, and by Serbia, 14th-c; incorporated into Serbia after the Balkan Wars; united in 1918, in what later became Yugoslavia, but continuous demands for autonomy persisted; occupied by Bulgaria during World War 2, 1941–44; declaration of independence, 1991; international discussions continue over the name under which the country will be accorded international recognition (the adjacent province of Greece bears the name Macedonia); President Gligorov seriously injured in assassination attempt, 1995; received large numbers of refugees during the Kosovo crisis, 1999; peace agreement signed and NATO task force deployed, 2001; EU took over operations, Mar 2003 (the EU's first military operation); President Trajkovski killed in air crash, 2004; governed by a President, Prime Minister, and Assembly.

Head of State

1991–9 Kiro Gligorov
1999 Savl Klimovski *Interim*
1999–2004 Boris Trajkovski
2004 Ljubco Jordanovski
2004– Branko Crvenkovski

Head of Government

1991–2 Branko Crvenkovski
1992–6 Petar Gosev
1996–8 Branko Crvenkovski
1998–2002 Ljubco Georgievski
2002–4 Branko Crvenkovski
2004 Hari Kostov
2004–6 Vlado Buckovski
2006– Nikola Gruevski

Machel, Samora Moïsés [mashel] (1933–86) The leader of the guerrilla campaign (FRELIMO) against Portuguese rule in Mozambique, and first president (1975–86). Although a Marxist, he established warm relations with Western governments, and attempted an accommodation with the South African regime.

Machiavelli, Niccolò (di Bernardo dei) [makiavelee] (1469–1527) Italian statesman and political theorist, born in Florence, Italy. His masterpiece is *Il Principe* (1532, The Prince), whose main theme is that all means may be used in order to maintain authority. It was condemned by the pope, and its viewpoint gave rise to the adjective **machiavellian**.

machine An assembly of connected parts arranged to transmit or modify force to perform useful work. All machines are based on six types: (1) lever; (2) wheel and axle; (3) pulley; (4) inclined plane; (5) wedge; and (6) screw.

machine code The fundamental instructions which can be dir-

ectly understood and acted on by a computer, written in a hexadecimal system.

machine-gun A gun firing a rifle calibre bullet with an automated ammunition feed and firing cycle, allowing sustained automatic fire. In 1883 inventor Hiram Maxim hit on the principle of using the force of recoil to eject the spent cartridge, chamber a new one, close the breech block, and fire.

machine tools A variety of powered machines used in industry to work and shape components made of metal or other material. They include lathes, planes, saws, and milling machines. Finer tolerances and greater repeatability of product is possible with machine tools than with hand tools.

Mach number [mahk] Unit of velocity; symbol *Ma*; defined as the ratio of velocity of an object to that of sound in some medium, usually air; an aircraft travelling at Ma 1 has velocity 331·5 m/s, the velocity of sound in air.

Machu Picchu [machoo peechoo] 13°07S 72°34W. Ruined Inca city in SC Peru; a world heritage site; on the saddle of a high mountain; discovered in 1911 by US explorer Hiram Bingham.

Macintosh A model of personal computer known particularly for its use of windows and icons to communicate with the user. It is very popular among users involved in aspects of graphic design work. Macintosh is a trade mark of Apple Computer Inc of California.

Macintosh, Charles (1766–1843) Manufacturing chemist, born in Glasgow, who in 1823 patented a method of waterproofing fabric, to which he gave his name. The technique involved the use of rubber dissolved in a naphtha solution to cement two pieces of cloth.

McKay, Heather [muhkiy], *née* **Blundell** (1941–) Squash player, born in Queanbeyan, New South Wales, Australia. She won the British Open in 16 successive years (1962–77), 14 Australian titles (1960–73), and was World Champion in 1976 and 1979.

Macke, August [mahkuh] (1887–1914) Expressionist painter, born in Meschede, Germany. Profoundly influenced by Matisse, he and Franz Marc founded the *Blaue Reiter* group.

Mackenzie, Sir (Edward Montague) Compton (1883–1972) Writer, born in West Hartlepool, Co Durham. He wrote a large number of novels, notably *Sinister Street* (1913–14) and *Whisky Galore* (1947).

McKenzie, Kevin (1954–) Ballet dancer and choreographer, born in Burlington, VT. He danced with the Washington School of Ballet and the Joffrey Ballet, then joined the American Ballet Theatre as soloist (1979) and principal dancer (1980). He was appointed artistic director of the company in 1992.

Mackenzie, William Lyon (1795–1861) Canadian politician, born in Dundee, Scotland. In 1837 he published a declaration of Canadian independence, and headed a band of reform-minded insurgents, but was forced to flee to the USA. He returned to Canada in 1849, becoming a journalist and a member of the Legislative Assembly (1850–8).

Mackenzie Range Mountain range in Northwest Territories, NW Canada; extends c.800 km/497 mi SE–NW; rises to 2972 m/9750 ft at Keele Peak; named after Scottish explorer Sir Alexander Mackenzie (?1755–1820).

Mackenzie River River in Northwest Territories, NW Canada; issues from the Great Slave Lake; enters the Beaufort Sea; length 4241 km/2635 mi.

mackerel Surface-living fish (*Scomber scombrus*) widespread and locally abundant in the N Atlantic; length up to 60 cm/2 ft; body slender, rounded in section, tail deeply forked, small finlets between dorsal and anal fins; bright blue or green with dark blue or black bars, underside silvery white; important food fish. (Family: Scombridae.)

Mackerras, Sir (Alan) Charles (MacLaurin) [muhkeras] (1925–) Conductor, born in Schenectady, NY. He has been musical director of the Sadler's Wells (later English National) Opera (1970–9), of the Sydney Symphony Orchestra, and the Welsh National Opera (1987–92). He became principal guest conductor of the Scottish Chamber Orchestra (1992–5), the Czech Philharmonic (from 1996), and the London Philharmonia Orchestra (from 2004). A noted scholar of the music of Janáček, he was knighted in 1979 and made a Companion of Honour in 2003.

Mckillop, Mary Helen [muhkilop], known as **Mother Mary of the Cross** (1842–1909) Religious, born in Fitzroy, Melbourne, Australia. With Father Tenison-Woods she founded in 1866 the Society of the Sisters of St Joseph of the Sacred Heart in Penola, South Australia. Her beatification was approved in 1993.

McKinley, William (1843–1901) US Republican statesman and 25th president (1897–1901), born in Niles, OH. In his first term, the war with Spain (1898) took place, with the conquest of Cuba and the Philippines. He was shot by an anarchist at Buffalo.

McKinley, Mount 63°04N 151°00W. Mountain in SC Alaska, USA; highest peak in North America; consists of two peaks (6194 m/20 321 ft, 5934 m/19 468 ft).

MacKinnon, Roderick (1956–) Biochemist, born in Burlington, MA. Head of the Laboratory of Molecular Neurobiology and Biophysics at Rockefeller University, NY, he shared the 2003 Nobel Prize for Chemistry for discoveries concerning channels in cell membranes.

Mackintosh, Charles Rennie (1868–1928) Architect and designer, born in Glasgow. He became a leader of the *Glasgow Style*, a movement related to Art Nouveau. As well as interiors and furniture, his designs include the Glasgow School of Art (1896–1909). In 1924 he moved to Port-Vendres, S France, where in 2004 an exhibition opened as a prelude to the creation of a permanent centre devoted to his life and work.

MacLaine, Shirley, stage name of **Shirley Maclean Beaty** (1934–) Actress, born in Richmond, VA. An understudy on *The Pajama Game* (1954), she moved centre stage when the star broke her leg. She made her film debut in *The Trouble with Harry* (1955) and later films include *Irma La Douce* (1963), *Sweet Charity* (1969), *Terms of Endearment* (1983, Oscar), *Postcards from the Edge* (1990), and *Bewitched* (2005). An activist for liberal causes, she led the first US women's delegation to China.

McLaughlin, Audrey [muhgloklin] (1936–) Canadian politician, born in Dutton, Ontario, Canada. She was MP for the Yukon Territory (1987–97) and leader of the federal New Democratic Party (1989–95).

Maclean, Alistair [muhklayn] (1922–87) Writer, born in Glasgow. His first novel *HMS Ulysses* (1955) became an immediate bestseller. Later books included *The Guns of Navarone* (1957) and *Where Eagles Dare* (1967).

Maclean, Donald (Duart) [muhklayn] (1913–83) British diplomat and Soviet intelligence officer, born in London. He joined the diplomatic service in 1934, and from 1944 acted as a Soviet agent. In 1951 he disappeared with Burgess, reappearing in Russia in 1956.

MacLeish, Archibald [muhkleesh] (1892–1982) Poet, born in Glencoe, IL. He won Pulitzer Prizes for *Conquistador* (1932), *Collected Poems 1917–52* (1953), and his social drama in modern verse, *J.B.* (1959). He was assistant secretary of state (1944–5).

Macleod, Iain (Norman) [muhklowd] (1913–70) British Conservative statesman, born in Skipton, North Yorkshire. He became minister of health (1952–5), minister of labour (1955–9), secretary of state for the Colonies (1959–61), and chairman of the Conservative Party (1961–3). He died in office as Chancellor of the Exchequer.

Macleod, J(ohn) J(ames) R(ickard) [muhklowd] (1876–1935) British physiologist, born in Clunie, Perth and Kinross. In 1922 he was a member of the group who discovered insulin, for which he shared the 1923 Nobel Prize for Physiology or Medicine.

McLuhan, (Herbert) Marshall [muhklooan] (1911–80) Writer, critic, and cultural theorist, born in Edmonton, Alberta, Canada. He held controversial views on the effect of the communication media on the development of civilization, claiming that it is the media, not the ideas which they disseminate, that influence society. His books include *The Gutenberg Galaxy* (1962), *Understanding Media* (1964), and *The Medium is the Message* (with Q Fiore, 1967).

Macmahon, Marie Edme Patrice Maurice de, duc de (Duke of) **Magenta** [makmahon] (1808–93) Marshal and second president of the Third Republic, born in Sully, France, descended from an Irish Jacobite family. He suppressed the Commune (1871), and succeeded Thiers as president (1873). Failing to assume dictatorial powers, he resigned in 1879, thus ensuring the supremacy of parliament.

McMahon, Sir William [muhkmahn] (1908–88) Australian statesman and prime minister (1971–2), born in Sydney, New South

Wales, Australia. He took over the premiership when John Gorton lost a vote of confidence in 1971, and continued to lead his party until 1977.

Macmillan, (Maurice) Harold, 1st Earl of Stockton (1894–1986) British Conservative statesman and prime minister (1957–63), born in London. He was minister of housing (1951–4) and defence (1954–5), foreign secretary (1955), Chancellor of the Exchequer (1955–7), and succeeded Eden as premier. He gained unexpected popularity with his infectious enthusiasm, effective domestic policy ('most of our people have never had it so good'), and resolute foreign policy.

MacMillan, Sir Kenneth (1929–92) Ballet dancer, choreographer, and ballet company director. He became artistic director of the Royal Ballet (1970–7), becoming its principal choreographer in 1977.

McMurtry, Larry (Jeff) [muhkmertree] (1936–) Writer, bookseller, and academic, born in Wichita Falls, TX. His first novel *Horseman, Pass By* (1961, Jess H Jones Award) was filmed as the Academy Award-winning *Hud* (1963), and he wrote the screenplay for his novel *The Last Picture Show* (1966; Oscar Best Picture, 1972). His best-selling frontier epic *Lonesome Dove* (1985) won a Pulitzer Prize in 1986.

McNaghten rules [muhknawtn] A legal set of principles which state when a defendant who is believed to be insane should not be convicted of a crime or offence. The rules were developed subsequent to the 19th-c murder trial of Daniel McNaghten, a case in which insanity was proved.

McNamara, Robert S(trange) (1916–) US Democratic politician and businessman, born in San Francisco, CA. In 1961 he joined the Kennedy administration as secretary of defense, being particularly involved in the Vietnam War. In 1968 he resigned to become president of the World Bank (until 1981).

MacNeice, (Frederick) Louis [muhknees] (1907–63) Writer, born in Belfast. Closely associated with the British left-wing poets of the 1930s, his books include *Autumn Journal* (1939) and *The Burning Perch* (1963).

Mâcon [makõ], ancient **Matisco** 46°19N 4°50E, pop (2000e) 40 300. Manufacturing city in C France, on the R Saône; episcopal see from the 6th-c until the Revolution; road and rail junction; commercial centre of major wine area; remains of 12th-c cathedral.

McPhee, John (Angus) (1931–) Writer, born in Princeton, NJ. He became a television playwright for *Robert Montgomery Presents* (1955–7), co-editor of *Time* magazine (1957–64), and a staff writer for the *New Yorker* (from 1964). His non-fiction books include a series on geology beginning with *Basin and Range* (1981).

McPherson, Aimée Semple, *née* **Kennedy** (1890–1944) Religious leader, born near Ingersoll, Ontario, Canada. She founded the Church of the Foursquare Gospel and flourished as an evangelist, preaching a simple gospel of personal salvation.

Macquarie, Lachlan [muhkworee] (1761–1824) Soldier and colonial administrator, born on the I of Ulva, Argyll and Bute. He became Governor of New South Wales in 1810 after the deposition of Bligh. Known as 'the father of Australia' he has given his name to the Lachlan and Macquarie rivers, and to Macquarie I.

Macquarie Island 54°30S 158°56W, area 123 km²/47 sq mi. Island lying 1345 km/835 mi SW of Tasmania, Australia; rises to 425 m/1400 ft; nature reserve (1933); made world heritage site, 1997.

McQueen, (Terence) Steve(n) (1930–80) Actor, born in Beech Grove, IN, who gained a reputation as a tough unconventional rebel, both on and off the screen. Typical of his successes were *The Magnificent Seven* (1960), *Bullitt* (1968), and *An Enemy of the People* (1977).

macramé [makrahmee] A type of coarse lace produced by knotting and plaiting, which enjoyed a widespread revival in the mid-19th-c. It was used to make decorative fringed borders for costumes as well as furnishings.

Macready, William Charles [muhkreedee] (1793–1873) Actor and theatre manager, born in London. He was the leading English actor of his day, notable for his Shakespearean roles. He became manager of Covent Garden in 1837, and of Drury Lane in 1841.

macrobiotics A 'perfect diet', influenced by Zen Buddhist philosophy at the beginning of the 20th-c, thought to improve health and prolong life. All foods are seen as either *yin* (eg fruit) or *yang* (eg bread), and a strict balance of intake is prescribed.

macroeconomics The study of economic aggregrates and averages. These include levels of national income, employment and unemployment, price levels and inflation, short-term fluctuations, and long-term growth rates in the economy. This involves analyzing the behaviour of various sectors of the economy: the determinants of consumption, investment, and foreign trade and payments, and the policies followed by the government and monetary authorities.

macronutrients *nutrients*

macro-photography or **photomacrography** The photography of small objects or details using normal or special purpose camera lenses, in contrast to **photomicrography**, which uses two-stage magnification by objective and eyepiece lenses.

McVeigh, Timothy (James) [muhkvay] (1968–2001) Convicted bomber, born in Pendleton, NY. He joined the army in 1988, took part in Operation Desert Storm, and was discharged in 1991. He became internationally known when he was charged with the bombing of the Alfred P Murrah US government building in Oklahoma City in 1995, in which 168 people died. At his trial in 1997, a Denver jury found him guilty of conspiracy and murder. After a series of failed appeals, he was executed by lethal injection. Two other conspirators, Terry Nichols and Michael Fortier, were also later convicted.

Macy, William H (1950–) Actor, born in Miami, FL. He co-formed the *St Nicholas Company* with David Mamet and Steven Schachter, and during the 1970s–80s appeared in numerous productions. He became a household name in 1994 when he appeared in the television series *ER*, and in 2003 he won an Emmy for his role in the TV mini-series *Door to Door*. His films include *Fargo* (1996), *Magnolia* (1999), *Seabiscuit* (2003), and *Bobby* (2006).

Madagascar *p.566*

Madara Rider An 8th-c bas-relief, carved out of the sheer cliff face in the village of Madara, E Bulgaria; a world heritage monument. The near life-size sculpture depicts a man on horseback trampling a lion beneath his horse's hooves.

Madariaga (y Rojo), Salvador de [mathariahga] (1886–1978) Spanish diplomat and writer, born in La Coruña, Spain. An opponent of the Franco regime, he was in exile 1936–76. He was the author of many historical works, especially on Spain and Spanish-America.

mad cow disease *bovine spongiform encephalopathy*

madder An evergreen perennial (*Rubia tinctoria*), native to the Mediterranean; stems trailing or scrambling by means of small downwardly directed hooks; flowers small, yellow, 5-petalled; berries reddish-brown. The roots produce the dye alizarin. (Family: Rubiaceae.)

Madeira (Islands) *p.567*

Madeira, River [madayra] River in NW Brazil, the longest tributary of the Amazon; length with its headstream, the Mamoré, over 3200 km/2000 mi.

Maderna, Bruno [madairna] (1920–73) Composer and conductor, born in Venice, Italy. In 1954 he became involved with electronic music, founding with Berio the Studio di Fonologia Musicale of Italian Radio.

Madhya Pradesh [madya pradaysh] pop (2001e) 60 385 100; area

Madagascar

800 km
400 mi

AFRICA

Cap d'Ambre ● Antseranana

Nosy-Bé □

△ *Maromokotra*
2876m

MOZAMBIQUE
CHANNEL

● Mahajanga

Betsiboka

Nosy Boraha

Toamasina

■ **Antananarivo**

Ankaratra △ ●Vatomandry
2643m

Morondava● M A D A G A S C A R

●Ambohimanga

Fianarantsoa●

Mangoky

Isalo
Plateau

INDIAN

Toliara●

Tropic of Capricorn

Toalañaro●

OCEAN

Cap Ste Marie

☐ International Airport

[madagasker], official name **Republic of Madagascar**, Malagasy **Repoblikan'i Madagasikara**

Local name Madagasikara

Timezone GMT +3

Area 587 041 km²/226 658 sq mi

Population total (2002e) 16 473 000

Status Republic

Date of independence 1960

Capital Antananarivo

Languages Malagasy (official), with French widely spoken

Ethnic groups Malagasy (99%) (including Merina 26%, Betsimisaraka 15%, Betsileo 12%)

Religions Traditional animist beliefs (47%), Christian (48%) (Roman Catholic 26%, Protestant 23%), Muslim (5%)

Physical features World's fourth largest island, length (N–S) 1580 km/982 mi; dissected N–S by a ridge of mountains (Tsaratananan Range), rising to 2876 m/9436 ft at Maromokotra; cliffs (E) drop down to a coastal plain through tropical forest; terraced descent (W) through savannah to coast, heavily indented in N.

Climate Tropical, variable rainfall; average annual rainfall 1000–1500 mm/40–60 in, higher in tropical coastal region; average annual temperatures 21°C (Jan), 15°C (Jul).

Currency 1 Ariary (MGA) = 5 iraimbilanja (before 2005, 1 Malagasy Franc (MGF) = 100 centimes)

Economy Chiefly agricultural economy; rice, manioc, coffee, sugar, vanilla, cotton, peanuts, tobacco, livestock; food processing, tanning, cement, soap, paper, textiles, oil products; graphite, chrome, coal, ilmenite.

GDP (2002e) $12·59 bn, per capita $800

Human Development Index (2002) 0·469

History Settled by Indonesians in 1st-c AD and by African traders in 8th-c; visited by Portuguese, 16th-c; French established trading posts in late 18th-c; claimed as a protectorate by the French, 1895; autonomous overseas French territory (Malagasy Republic), 1958; independence, 1960; became Madagascar, 1977; new multi-party constitution, 1992; new constitution in 1998; governed by a President, who appoints a Council of Ministers and is guided by a Supreme Revolutionary Council; National People's Assembly is elected every five years; crisis followed 2001 elections, when President Ratsiraka refused to yield power; opposition leader Marc Ravalomanana appointed president, May 2002; legislative elections (Dec) followed by new cabinet, 2003.

Head of State
1993–6 Albert Zafy
1996 Norbert Ratsirahonana *Interim*
1997–2002 Didier Ratsiraka
2002– Marc Ravalomanana

Head of Government
1995–6 Emmanuel Rakotovahiny
1996–7 Norbert Ratsirahonana
1997–8 Pascal Rakotomavo
1998–2002 Tantely Andrianarivo
2002–7 Jacques Sylla
2007– Charles Rabemananjara

442 841 km²/170 937 sq mi. Largest state in India; ruled by the Gonds, 16th–17th-c, and Marathas, 18th-c; occupied by the British, 1820; called Central Provinces and Berar, 1903–50; formed under the States Reorganization Act, 1956; capital, Bhopal.

Madison 43°04N 89°24W, pop (2000e) 208 100. Capital of state in S Wisconsin, USA; state capital, 1836; city status, 1856; airfield; railway; university (1836); trading and manufacturing centre in agricultural region.

Madison, James (1751–1836) US statesman and fourth president (1809–17), born in Port Conway, VA. He played a major role in the Constitutional Convention of 1787, becoming known as 'the father of the Constitution'. Secretary of state under Jefferson, and president for two terms, his administration saw the Napoleonic Wars and the War of 1812.

Madison Avenue A street in Manhattan, New York City, extending N to the R Harlem from Madison Square. With its glittering skyscrapers and expensive boutiques, it is seen as the centre of the advertising industry.

Madonna, in full **Madonna Louise Ciccone** (1958–) Pop singer, born in Rochester, MI. Her first album, *Madonna* (1983), included five US hit singles. Later albums included *Like A Virgin* (1984), *True Blue* (1986), *Music* (2000), *American Life* (2003), and *Confessions on a Dancefloor* (2005). She has also acted in films, including *Desperately Seeking Susan* (1985) and *Shanghai Surprise* (1986). Her defiant and raunchy stage appearances were reinforced in several media in the early 1990s, with the publication of a controversial collection of erotic photographs of herself in *Sex* (1992), alongside an album, *Erotica*. Later films include *Body of Evidence* (1993) and *Evita* (1996).

Madras [madras], official name **Chennai** (Nov 1996) 13°08N 80°19E, pop (2000e) 6 296 000. Capital of Tamil Nadu, SE India; fourth largest city in India, and chief port of Tamil Nadu; founded by the British, 17th-c; airport; railway; university (1857); St Mary's Church (1680), thought to be the oldest Anglican church in Asia; Mount St Thomas nearby, traditional site of martyrdom of the apostle.

Madeira (Islands)

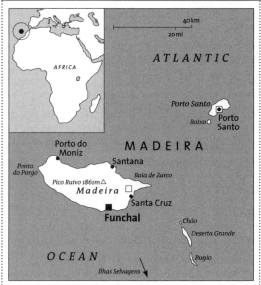

□ International Airport

[madeera], Port **Arquipélago da Madeira**
Local name Ilha de Madeira
Timezone GMT
Area 796km²/307 sq mi
Population total (2002e) 265 000
Status Semi-autonomous region of Portugal
Capital Funchal (on Madeira Island)
Physical features Main island in an archipelago off the coast of N Africa, 980 km/610 mi SW of Lisbon; consists of Madeira, Porto Santo and three uninhabited islands; highest point, Pico Ruivo de Santana, 1862 m/6111 ft on Madeira.
Economy Agriculture; sugar cane, fruit, fishing, Madeira (a fortified wine); embroidery, crafts; tourism.
History Occupied by the Portuguese, 15th-c; occupied by Britain, 1801, and 1807–14; gained partial autonomy, 1980, but remains a Portuguese overseas territory; locally-elected government, and Assembly.

Madrid [madrid] 40°25N 3°45W, pop (2000e) 2 948 000. Capital of Spain; altitude, 655 m/2149 ft, the highest capital city in Europe; archbishopric; airport; railway; metro; two universities (1508, 1968); site of a Moorish fortress until 11th-c; under siege for nearly three years in the Civil War; capital (replacing Valladolid), 1561; El Escorial, a world heritage site; Royal Palace (18th-c), Prado Museum, El Retiro Park; terrorist bombings at railway stations killed at least 200 people and injured more than 1400 (Mar 2004).

madrigal A polyphonic song, usually secular and without instrumental accompaniment. It was cultivated especially in Italy during the 16th-c, and is characterized by a mixture of contrapuntal and chordal style and by serious, Petrarchan, and usually amorous verses.

Madura foot *mycetoma*

Madurai [maduriy] 9°55N 78°10E, pop (2000e) 1 117 000. City in Tamil Nadu, S India; capital of the Pandyan kingdom and the Nayak dynasty; occupied by the British, 1801; airfield; railway;

university (1966); large Dravidian temple complex (14th–17th-c).

Maecenas, Gaius (Cilnius) [miyseenas] (?–8 BC) Roman politician who played a key role in the rise to power of Augustus. He was a patron of the arts, encouraging such poets as Horace and Virgil.

maenads [meenads] In Greek mythology, 'mad women', who followed Dionysus (Bacchus) on his journeys; also known as **Bacchae** or **Bacchantes**.

Maes, Nicholas [mays] (1634–93) Painter, born in Dordrecht, The Netherlands. He specialized in small genre subjects, especially kitchen scenes (eg 'Woman Scraping Parsnips', 1655, National Gallery, London), and old women praying.

Maes Howe [mayz how] A chambered tomb of the early 3rd millennium BC on Orkney, N Scotland. It is outstanding for its construction and preservation.

Maeterlinck, Maurice (Polydore Marie Bernard) [mahterlingk], also known as **comte** (Count) **Maeterlinck** (1862–1949) Writer, born in Ghent, Belgium. He became a disciple of the Symbolist movement, and in 1889 produced his first volume of poetry, *Les Serres chaudes* (trans Hot House Blooms). His plays include *Pelléas et Mélisande* (1892), on which Debussy based his opera. He was awarded the Nobel Prize for Literature in 1911.

Mafeking, Siege of (1899–1900) The most celebrated siege of the second Boer War. Colonel Robert Baden-Powell and a detachment of British troops were besieged by the Boers from October 1899 until May 1900. The news of their relief aroused public hysteria in Britain.

Mafia (Ital 'swank') A powerful criminal organization, originating as a secret society in 13th-c Italy. It developed (along with its modern name) in the 19th-c, and from Italy moved to the USA, where it became known as *Cosa Nostra* ('Our Affair'). There have been many attempts to suppress the Mafia, but its system of family loyalty and code of silence makes progress difficult. A widespread protest against the Mafia spread in Italy during 1993, following the murder of several senior people involved in anti-Mafia law enforcement, and a number of public figures were accused of corruption and forced to resign.

Magdalenian [magdaleenian] The last Upper Palaeolithic archaeological culture of W Europe, named after the cave of La Madeleine, Dordogne, SW France, excavated in 1863. Many sites dated c.17 000–12 000 BC are known, notably the painted caves of Lascaux and Altamira.

Magdeburg [mahkdeboorg] 52°08N 11°36E, pop (2000e) 289 000. River-port city in C Germany; on R Elbe; former capital of Saxony, and important mediaeval trading town; badly bombed in World War 2; railway; college of medicine; college of technology (1953); cathedral (13th–16th-c).

Magellan, Ferdinand [majelan] (c.1480–1521) Navigator, born near Villa Real, Portugal. He sailed from Seville (1519) around the foot of South America to reach the ocean which he named the Pacific (1520). He was killed by natives in the Philippines, but his ships continued back to Spain (1522), thus completing the first circumnavigation of the world. The Strait of Magellan is named after him.

Magellanic Clouds Two dwarf galaxies, satellites of the Milky Way, visible as cloudy patches in the S night sky, first recorded by Magellan in 1519, 52 and 58 kiloparsec away, and each containing a few thousand million stars.

Magellan project A US space mission which mapped Venus at sub-kilometre resolution using side-looking radar from a Venus orbit. A single spacecraft was launched in 1989, and images were returned to Earth in the latter half of 1990.

Magen David *Star of David*

Maggiore, Lake (Ital **Lago**) [majawray], ancient **Verbanus Lacus** area 212 km²/82 sq mi. Second largest of the N Italian lakes; N end in the Swiss canton of Ticino; length 65 km/40 mi; width 3–5 km/1¾–3 mi; maximum depth 372 m/1220 ft.

maggot The grub-like larval stage of many true flies. (Order: Diptera.)

Maghreb [magreb], Eng **Maghrib** area c.9 million km²/3·5 million sq mi. Area of NW Africa including the countries of Morocco, Algeria, and Tunisia; largely occupied by the Kabyle, Shluh, and Tuareg. In Arabic, it refers to Morocco only.

Magi [mayjiy] **1** Members of the priestly clan of the Persians. Classical Greek and Roman writers used the term in a derogatory sense to refer to sorcerers and 'quacks'.
2 A group of unspecified number guided by a mysterious star (*Matt* 2.1–12), who came from 'the East' and presented gifts to the infant Jesus in Bethlehem. Origen (3rd-c AD) suggested they were three because of the three gifts of gold, frankincense, and myrrh. Later Christian tradition named them as Caspar, Melchior, and Balthazar.

magic Beliefs and practices which promise a power to intervene in natural processes, but which have no scientific basis. Two common principles of magical belief are that 'like affects like' – that a cloud of smoke rising to the sky will bring rain, for example; and that 'part affects whole' – so that by burning a person's hair-cuttings, for instance, that person will be damaged.

magic mushroom A mushroom, chiefly the British liberty-cap mushroom *Psilocybe semilanceata*, which contains the hallucinogen *psilocybin*. Its use is cultish among young people, who take it as an infusion, adding it to boiling water.

magic realism or **magical realism** A type of post-modernist fiction that mixes elements of fantasy, fable, and folklore with realistic narrative, imbuing it with a fabulous or dreamlike quality. The term was first applied in the 1940s by the Cuban novelist Alejo Carpentier and introduced into the critical vocabulary by Alistair Reid. It is particularly associated with Latin-American writers such as Mario Vargas Llosa and Gabriel Garcia Márquez. Writers in English include Salman Rushdie and Angela Carter. The term is also applied to the work of a group of German painters in the 1920s known as the *Neue Sachlichkeit* (New Objectivity) movement, distinguished by their realistic, often cynical style of painting.

Maginot Line [mazhinoh] French defensive fortifications stretching from Longwy in Belgium to the Swiss border, named after André Maginot (1877–1932), French minister of defence (1924–31). The line was constructed (1929–34) to act as protection against German invasion, but Belgium refused to extend it along her frontier with Germany. The German attack of 1940 through the Low Countries largely bypassed it.

magistrate *justice of the peace; stipendiary magistrate*

Maglemosian [maglemohzian] A N European Mesolithic culture extending from Britain to S Scandinavia and NW Russia c.8000–5600 BC; its name derives from the Danish *Magle Mose* ('Great Bog') on Zeeland, where notable early finds were made.

magma Molten rock, formed by the partial melting of the Earth's mantle. Under certain geological conditions it may migrate upwards and solidify within the crust, or may reach the surface, where it is erupted as lava.

Magna Carta The 'Great Charter', imposed by rebellious barons on King John of England at Runnymede in June 1215, designed to prohibit arbitrary royal acts by declaring a body of defined law and custom which the king must respect in dealing with all his free subjects. It was the first systematic attempt to distinguish between kingship and tyranny, and was of fundamental importance to the constitutional development of England.

magnesia Magnesium oxide (MgO), also called **periclase**; a white solid, melting point 2850°C, obtained from heating magnesium carbonate, used as a heat-resisting material. **Milk of magnesia** is a suspension of hydrated magnesia used as a laxative.

magnesium Mg, element 12, melting point 649°C. A silvery metal, always found combined in nature, but mainly as the carbonate in magnesite ($MgCO_3$) and dolomite ($CaMg(CO_3)_2$). It is used in alloys for its lightness (density 1·7 g/cm³), and for flares and (in older cameras) flash bulbs because of the bright white light produced by its reaction with oxygen. Hydrated magnesium sulphate is known as *Epsom salts*.

magnet A source of magnetic field; always with two poles, named N (north) and S (south), since no isolated single pole exists; like poles repel; opposite poles attract. A permanent magnet is usually made from a ferromagnetic material which at some time has been exposed to a magnetic field. An **electromagnet** is some suitable core material around which is wrapped a current-carrying coil.

magnetic disk A disk coated with magnetizable material on one or both sides. Magnetic disks are an important type of computer storage medium. Data is written to or read from a set of concentric tracks on the disk by magnetic read/write heads. Two general classes exist: the so-called *hard* disks made of rigid material, and *floppy* disks, formerly made of flexible plastic. Disks may be removable from the disk drive or nonremovable.

magnetic field A region of magnetic influence around a magnet, moving charge, or current-carrying wire; denoted by *B*, the magnetic flux density, units T (tesla), and by *H*, the magnetic field strength, units A/m (amps per metre)

magnetic flux The flow of magnetic influence from the N to S poles of a magnet, or around a current-carrying wire; symbol Φ, units Wb (weber). It is the product of magnetic flux density *B* (sometimes called 'magnetic field') and area.

magnetic moment A property of magnets, currents circulating in loops, and spinning charged particles that dictates the strength of the turning force exerted on the system by a magnetic field, *B*; symbol μ, units A.m² (amp.metre-squared) or J/T (joules per tesla); a vector quantity; also called the **magnetic dipole moment**. Turning force (torque), Γ is $\Gamma = \mu B \sin\theta$, where θ is the angle between μ and *B* directions.

magnetic poles The two points on the Earth's surface to which a compass needle points. The N and S magnetic poles have geographical co-ordinates 78·5°N 69°W and 78·5°S 111°E, and move very slowly with time.

magnetic storm A disturbance in the Earth's magnetic field causing global disruption of radio signals and the occurrence of auroras. They are caused by the interaction of charged solar particles with the Earth's magnetic field.

magnetic susceptibility The ratio of magnetization *M* to magnetic field strength *H*; symbol , expressed as a pure number. It expresses the dependence of a magnetic field in a material on an external field which results only from current in the magnetizing coils.

magnetic tape 1 A clear plastic film coated with crystalline magnetic particles embedded in varnish, first demonstrated as an effective sound recording and reproducing medium in the 1930s. It was later extended to video recording, and to data storage for computers. Professional recording practice of the 1980s employed multiple-track open-reel tape, storing the sounds in digital form, while domestic use came to be dominated by the compact cassette introduced first by Philips in 1964. **2** A storage medium used on larger computers, the most common being 2400 ft (c.750 m) reels of 0·5 in (12·7 mm)-wide tape. In recent years, smaller format magnetic cartridge tape systems have been used as archiving ('back-up') systems for microcomputers, especially those employing Winchester disks. All magnetic-tape systems are relatively slow, compared to magnetic disks, since the access time required to obtain a particular piece of information depends on its position on the tape.

magnetic vector potential A vector quantity whose rate of change with distance is related to magnetic field in a complex way; symbol *A*, units Wb/m (webers per metre). Electric current is the source for *A*, as electric charge is for electrostatic potential.

magnetism Phenomena associated with magnetic fields and magnetic materials, and the study of such phenomena. All magnetic effects ultimately stem from moving electric charges, and all materials have magnetic properties.

magnetite or **lodestone** An iron oxide mineral (Fe_3O_4) with a very strong natural magnetism. It is a valuable ore of iron.

magnetization Magnetic moment per unit volume, resulting from the individual magnetic moments contributed by molecules of the material; symbol *M*, units A/m (amps per metre); expresses how much a material is magnetized.

magneto A simple machine which generates alternating current, using the principle that a current is generated when a conductor moves through a magnetic field. It is used with combustion engines to provide the power for the sparking plugs.

magnetometer A device for measuring the strength and direction of magnetic fields. Gauss built an early magnetometer in 1832. Modern magnetometers include the *fluxgate* magnetometer, in which paired electromagnets driven by an external alternating voltage generate an electrical signal in a coil surrounding the pair in response to the field under test, and *cryogenic* or *SQUID* magnetometers.

magnetosphere The region surrounding Solar System bodies having magnetic fields, in which the field is confined under the influence of the streaming solar wind. It is a teardrop-shaped region whose size and shape are constantly readjusting to the variations of the solar wind.

magnetron A device for generating microwaves. It comprises an evacuated chamber with a central cathode surrounded by a circular anode. Electrons expelled from the cathode circle it under the influence of electric and magnetic fields. Microwave production results from resonances between the moving electrons and cavities in the anode. It is today widely used in microwave ovens.

magnification A measure of an optical system's power to reduce or enlarge an image. It is approximately equal to the ratio of size of image to size of object.

Magnitogorsk [magnyitogaw(r)sk], formerly **Magnitnaya** 53°28N 59°06E, pop (2000e) 442 000. Industrial town in SW Siberian Russia, on the R Ural; built, 1929–31; airfield; railway; one of the largest centres of the metallurgical industry.

magnitude A measure of the brightness of a celestial object. The brightest stars visible to the human eye are said to be 'first magnitude' and the dimmest as 'sixth magnitude'; equal magnitude steps are in logarithmic progression. The **apparent magnitude** of a star is its brightness measured at the Earth, which depends on distance and luminosity. More useful physically is **absolute magnitude**; this is the observed apparent magnitude converted to what the object would have at an (arbitrary) distance of 10 parsec.

magnolia A deciduous or evergreen shrub or tree native to E North America and E Asia; leaves often glossy; flowers generally large, cup-shaped, with several whorls of white or pink segments. (Genus: *Magnolia*, 80 species. Family: Magnoliaceae.)

magnon In magnetic materials, oscillation in the relative orientations of atomic spins, which correspond to magnetization waves.

Magnusson, Magnus (1929–2007) Writer and broadcaster, born in Reykjavik, Iceland. He was brought to Edinburgh as an infant, where his father served as the Icelandic Consul-General. He studied at Oxford, became a journalist and broadcaster, and was chiefly known for presenting a wide range of radio and television programmes, notably the annual series of *Mastermind* (1972–97). His books included *Vikings!* (1980), *Treasures of Scotland* (1981), and *Fakers, Forgers and Phoneys* (2006).

Magog *Gog and Magog*

magot [magoh] *Barbary ape*

magpie A bird of the crow family (13 species); especially the **black-billed magpie** (*Pica pica*). The name is also used for black-and-white birds in several other families.

Magritte, René (François Ghislain) [magreet] (1898–1967) Painter, born in Lessines, Belgium. He was a leading member of the Belgian Surrealist group in the 1920s, and in the 1960s was acclaimed in the USA as an early innovator of Pop Art.

Magyar A Uralic language spoken as a national language by c.11 million people in Hungary, and by a further 3 million in the surrounding areas.

Mahabalipuram monuments [mahahbalipuram] A collection of Hindu temples at Mahabalipuram in Tamil Nadu, S India; a world heritage site. They date from the 7th–8th-c, and are noted for their rich carvings.

Mahabharata [mahabhahrata] A major epic of Hindu culture and history, and a holy book. Dating from the first millennium BC, its 110 000 couplets make it the longest epic in the world. It was orally transmitted and later printed versions were brought together and published in the 19th-c as the Mahabharata.

Maharashtra [mahahrashtra] pop (2001e) 96 752 000; area 307 762 km²/118 796 sq mi. State in W India; ruled by the Mughals, 14th–17th-c; British control, early 19th-c; became a state in 1960; capital, Mumbai (Bombay); governed by a Legislative Council and Legislative Assembly; industry largely in Mumbai, Pune (Poona), and Thana.

Maharishi [maharishee] (Sanskrit, 'great sage') The Hindu title for a guru or spiritual leader. In the West, the teaching of Transcendental Meditation by the Maharishi Mahesh Yogi is well known.

Mahayana [mahayahna] (Sanskrit, 'greater vehicle') The form of Buddhism commonly practised in China, Tibet, Mongolia, Nepal, Korea, and Japan. It dates from about the 1st-c, when it arose as a development within Buddhism in N India.

Mahdi (divine leader) [mahdee] (Arabic, 'divinely guided one') The name given by Sunni Muslims to those who periodically revitalize the Muslim community. Sunnis look forward to a time before the Last Day when a Mahdi will appear and establish a reign of justice on Earth.

Mahé [mah-hay] 4°41S 55°30E; pop (2000e) 72 000; area 153 km²/59 sq mi. Main island of the Seychelles, Indian Ocean; Victoria, capital of the Seychelles, on the NW coast; airport.

mah-jong or **mah-jongg** A Chinese game, usually played by four people using 144 small tiles divided into three suits and four sets of honour tiles. The aim is to collect sequences of tiles, in the manner of rummy card games. The name means 'sparrow', a bird of mythical great intelligence, which appears on one of the tiles.

Mahler, Gustav (1860–1911) Composer, born in Kalištĕ, Czech Republic (formerly Bohemia, Austrian Empire). His mature works consist entirely of songs and nine large-scale symphonies, with a tenth left unfinished. He is best known for the song-symphony *Das Lied von der Erde* (1908–9, The Song of the Earth).

mahogany An evergreen tree (*Swietenia mahagoni*) native to Central America and the Caribbean Is; flowers 5-petalled, yellowish, in loose clusters. It is one of several timbers commercially called mahogany, a reddish wood of high quality, heavy, hard, and easily worked. (Family: Meliaceae.)

Mahomet *Mohammed*

Mahratta *Maratha*

Maiden Castle A spectacular Iron Age hillfort near Dorchester, Dorset, UK, with multiple earthwork ramparts and ditches. The existing defences date to c.150 BC, their complex entrances remodelled c.70 BC.

Maidstone 51°17N 0°32E, pop (2001e) 139 000. County town in

Kent, SE England; on the R Medway; railway; birthplace of William Hazlitt.

Maier, Hermann [miyer], nickname **The Herminator** or **Hermannator** (1972–) Skier, born in Flachau, Salzburg, Austria. His parents ran a skiing school, and he took part in his first skiing races at the age of five. His achievements include the European Cup (1996) and World Cup (1998, 2000, 2001, 2004), and in March 2001 he equalled the World Cup season record of 13 wins. Later that year, a motorcycle accident badly damaged his right leg and kept him out of competition until 2003. He made a successful return and in 2004 received the Laureus World Sports Award for 'Comeback of the Year'.

Maier, Ulrike [miyer] (1965–94) Skier, born in Austria. She won the world Supergiant slalom skiing championship twice before her fatal accident during a practice run at Garmisch-Partenkirchen. She was the first woman skier to be killed in a World Cup race.

Mailer, Norman (Kingsley) [mayler], originally **Nachum Malech Mailer** (1923–) Writer, born in Long Branch, NJ. His best-known novels are *The Naked and the Dead* (1948), a panoramic World War 2 novel, and *American Dream* (1964). Identified with many of the US liberal protest movements, his political studies include *The Armies of the Night* (1968, Pulitzer). Later novels include *Harlot's Ghost* (1991) and *The Castle in the Forest* (2007).

Maillol, Aristide (Joseph Bonaventure) [mayol] (1861–1944) Sculptor, born in Banyuls-sur-Mer, France. He is particularly known for his representations of the nude female figure in a style of monumental simplicity and classical serenity.

mailmerge A word-processing facility which allows inserts to be placed in a standard document. It is widely used for the bulk mailing of circulars in letter form, as it gives these the semblance of having been individually produced.

Maiman, Theodore H(arold) [miyman] (1927–2007) Physicist, born in Los Angeles, CA. After working on the maser, by 1960 he devised the first working laser.

Maimonides, Moses [miymonideez], originally **Moses ben Maimon** (1138–1204) Jewish philosopher, born in Córdoba, Spain. A major influence on Jewish thought, he wrote an important commentary on the Mishna, and a philosophical work arguing for the reconciliation of Greek philosophy and religion.

Mainbocher [maynboshay], originally **Main Rousseau Bocher** (c.1890–1976) Fashion designer, born in Chicago, IL. He started his couture house in Paris in 1930, one of his creations being Mrs Wallis Simpson's wedding dress. He opened a salon in New York City in 1940, which continued until 1971.

Maine pop (2000e) 1 274 900; area 86 153 km²/33 265 sq mi. New England state in the NE corner of the USA; the 'Pine Tree State' or 'Lumber State'; explored by the Cabots in the 1490s; settled first by the French in 1604, and by the English in 1607; separated from Massachusetts in 1820, when admitted to the Union as 23rd state; crossed by the Appalachian Mts which rise to 1605 at Mt Katahdin; dotted with over 1600 lakes; N 80% forested; capital, Augusta; largest town, Portland; S coastal strip mainly arable; main industries agriculture, forestry, fishing.

mainframe computer A somewhat dated term still used to refer to very large capacity computers, and to distinguish them from the smaller computers now widely available. However, the distinction between mainframe and other computers is not always clear.

maintained school In the UK, a school which receives its money from a local education authority. It is often known popularly as a 'state school', though this term is inappropriate in a country where the state does not run schools.

maintenance A term used in England and Wales for money payments paid by one marriage partner to help support the other during or following legal separation or divorce. The payments

are often referred to as *alimony*, but terminology varies (eg it is *aliment* or *periodical allowance* in Scotland).

Maintenon, Françoise d'Aubigné, Marquise de (Marchioness of) [mĭtenõ], (1635–1719) Second wife of Louis XIV of France, born in Niort, France. In 1652 she married the crippled poet, Paul Scarron, and on his death was reduced to poverty. In 1669 she took charge of the king's two sons by Madame de Montespan. After the queen's death (1683) Louis married her secretly. She was accused of having great influence over him, especially over the persecution of Protestants.

Mainz [miynts], Fr **Mayence** 50°00N 8°16E, pop (2000e) 186 000. Old Roman city in Germany; on left bank of R Rhine; important traffic junction and commercial centre; railway; centre of the Rhine wine trade; Gutenberg set up his printing press here; university (1477); cathedral (mostly 11th–13th-c).

maiolica [mayolika], also (19th-c) spelled **majolica** Tin-glazed earthenware produced in Italy since before 1250. In the Renaissance period the decoration was often similar to the work of contemporary Italian painters.

maize The only cereal (*Zea mays*) native to the New World, originally tropical and developed as a major food crop by the Indians of Central America; also called **sweet corn** and **Indian corn**. It is a robust annual, its heads eaten ripe or unripe as a vegetable. The grains and foliage are used for animal fodder, and it also yields flour, starch, syrup, alcohol, and paper. (Family: Gramineae.)

majlis [majles] (Arabic 'council') Any of a number of political institutions in the Middle East, ranging from parliaments to advisory councils for rulers.

Major, Sir John (1943–) British statesman and prime minister (1990–7), born in London. He became an MP in 1976, and rose to become chief secretary to the Treasury. He was unexpectedly made foreign secretary in Margaret Thatcher's Cabinet reshuffle in 1989, and soon after replaced Nigel Lawson as Chancellor of the Exchequer. He won the leadership contest following Mrs Thatcher's resignation, and became prime minister in November 1990. He resigned as leader of the Conservative Party after they lost the 1997 general election. He was made a Companion of Honour in 1998 and was knighted in 2005. He retired from the House of Commons in 2001.

Majorca [mayaw(r)ka], Span **Mallorca**, ancient **Balearis Major** pop (2000e) 600 000; area 3640 km²/1400 sq mi. Largest island in the Balearics, W Mediterranean; chief town, Palma; Sierra del Alfabia rises to 1445 m/4741 ft; taken in 1229 by James I of Aragón; in the Middle Ages, famous for its porcelain (maiolica); popular tourist resort.

majuscule [majuhskyool] A form of writing in which the letters are of uniform height, as if contained within a pair of horizontal lines. Usually called CAPITAL letters, the Greek and Roman alphabets were originally written in this way. It is contrasted with the later system known as **minuscule**, in which parts of some letters extend above and below the horizontal lines ('small letters'), such as *h*, *g*.

Makale *Mekele*

Makarios III [makaryos], originally **Mihail Khristodoulou Mouskos** (1913–77) Archbishop and primate of the Orthodox Church of Cyprus, and president of Cyprus (1960–74, 1974–77), born in Ano Panayia. He reorganized the *enosis* (union) movement, was arrested in 1956, but returned to a tumultuous welcome in 1959 to become chief Greek-Cypriot Minister in the new Greek–Turkish provisional government.

Makassar *Ujung Pandang*

Makhmalbaf, Mohsen (1951–) Film director, born in Tehran, Iran. He founded the Centre for Propagation of Islamic Thought and Arts (1981) where he wrote short stories and scripts before his directorial film debut in 1982 with *Nassouh Repentant*. Later films include *Nun Va Goldoon* (1996, Moment of Innocence)

Malawi

□ International Airport

[malahwee], official name **Republic of Malawi**
Local name Malawi (Malaêi)
Timezone GMT +2

Area 118 484 km²/45 735 sq mi
Population total (2002e) 10 520 000
Status Republic
Date of independence 1964
Capital Lilongwe
Languages English and Chichewa (official)
Ethnic groups Maravi (including Nyanja, Chewa, Tonga, Tumbuka) (60%), Lomwe (18%), Yao (13%), Ngoni (7%), also Asian and European minorities
Religions Protestant (55%), Roman Catholic (20%), Muslim (20%), traditional animist beliefs (3%)
Physical features Crossed N–S by the Great Rift Valley; contains Africa's third largest lake, L Malawi; main river, Shire; Shire highlands (S) rise to nearly 3000 m/10 000 ft at Mt Mulanje.
Climate Tropical climate in S; high year-round temperatures, 28–37°C; average annual temperatures 23°C (Jan), 16°C (Jul) in Lilongwe; average annual rainfall, 740 mm/30 in; more moderate temperatures in central areas.
Currency 1 Kwacha (MWK) = 100 tambala
Economy Based on agriculture (employs 90% of population); tobacco, sugar, tea, cotton, groundnuts, maize; textiles, matches, cigarettes, beer, spirits, shoes, cement.
GDP (2002e) $6·811 bn, per capita $600
Human Development Index (2002) 0·400
History Visited by the Portuguese, 17th-c; European contact established by David Livingstone, 1859; Scottish church missions in the area; claimed as the British Protectorate of Nyasaland, 1891; British colony, 1907; in the 1950s joined with N and S Rhodesia to form the Federation of Rhodesia and Nyasaland; independence, 1964; republic, 1966; governed by a President, Cabinet and National Assembly.

Head of State/Government
1966–94 Hastings Kamuzu Banda
1994–2004 Bakili Muluzi
2004– Bingu wa Mutharika

---

and *Scream of the Ants* (2006). His daughter **Samira Makhmalbaf** (1980–), is also an internationally acclaimed director, her films include the award-winning semi-documentary feature film *Sib* (1998, The Apple), and *Takhte Siah* (2000, The Blackboard), scripted by Mohsen, which won the Jury Prize at the Cannes Film Festival.

Malabo [malaboh], formerly **Clarencetown** or **Port Clarence**, and **Santa Isabel** 3°45N 8°50E, pop (2000e) 14 000. Seaport capital of Equatorial Guinea, W Africa; on island of Bioko, Gulf of Guinea; founded by British in 1827; airfield.

malabsorption The failure of intestinal absorption of nutrients taken as food. In general, this results in diarrhoea, abdominal pain and distension, loss of weight, anaemia, and features of specific vitamin deficiencies. The most important cause in the UK is coeliac disease.

Malacca or **Melaka** [malaka] pop (2000e) 726 000; area 1657 km²/640 sq mi. State in SW Peninsular Malaysia; one of the former Straits Settlements; capital, Malacca, pop (1995e) 123 000; centre of a great trading empire since the 15th-c; held at various times by the Portuguese, Dutch, and British; large Chinese population.

Malacca, Strait of [muhlakuh] Channel between the Malaysia Peninsula and the Indonesian island of Sumatra; 800 km/

500 mi long by 50–320 km/30–200 mi wide; links the Andaman Sea to the S China Sea; joint naval operations to combat piracy begun by Indonesia, Singapore, and Malaysia, 2004.

Malachi or **Malachias, Book of** [malakhiy] The last of the 12 so-called 'minor' prophetic writings of the Hebrew Bible/Old Testament; probably anonymous, since *Malachi* in Hebrew means 'my messenger'; usually dated c.510–460 BC.

malachite [malakiyt] A hydrated copper carbonate mineral ($Cu_2CO_3(OH)_2$) found in weathered copper ore deposits. It is bright green in colour.

Málaga [malaga], ancient **Malaca** 36°43N 4°23W, pop (2000e) 519 000. Port in Andalusia, S Spain; founded by the Phoenicians, 12th-c BC; part of Spain, 1487; bishopric; airport; railway; car ferries to Casablanca, Tangier, Genoa; university (1972); Moorish Alcazaba, cathedral (16th–18th-c); birthplace of Picasso; Museu Picasso (2003).

Malagasy [malagasee] The peoples of the island of Madagascar, comprising about 50 ethnic groups; Malagasy languages are Austronesian. The traditional economy is based on agriculture.

Malamud, Bernard [malamuhd] (1914–86) Novelist and short-story writer, born in New York City. His novels reflect his keen interest in Jewish-American life, and include *The Natural* (1952), *The Fixer* (1966, Pulitzer), and *Dublin's Lives* (1979).

Malaysia

1. Langkawi	400 km
2. Pinang State	200 mi
3. Cameron Highlands	
4. Mt Tahaan 2189m	
5. Kuala Terengganu	
6. Petaling Jaya	
7. Melaka	
8. Johor Baharu	
9. Kuching	
10. Bintulu	
11. Labuan	
12. Kota Kinabalu	
13. Sandakan	

□ International Airport

[malayzha]

Local name Malaysia

Timezone GMT +8

Area 329 749 km²/127 283 sq mi

Population total (2002e) 24 370 000

Status Republic

Date of independence 1957

Capital Kuala Lumpur

Languages Bahasa Malaysia (Malay) (official), also Chinese, English, and Tamil widely spoken

Ethnic groups Malay (59%), Chinese (32%), Indian (9%)

Religions Muslim (53%), Buddhist (17%), Chinese folk-religionist (12%), Hindu (7%), Christian (6%)

Physical features Independent federation of states located in SE Asia, comprising 11 states and a federal territory in Peninsular Malaysia, and the E States of Sabah and Sarawak on the island of Borneo; mountain chain of granite and limestone running N–S, rising to Mt Tahan, 2189 m/7182 ft; peninsula length 700 km/435 mi, width up to 320 km/200 mi; mostly tropical rainforest

and mangrove swamp; Mt Kinabalu on Sabah, Malaysia's highest peak, 4094 m/13 432 ft.

Climate Tropical climate strongly influenced by monsoon winds; high humidity; average annual rainfall in the peninsula, 260 mm/10 in (S), 800 mm/32 in (N); average daily temperatures, 21–32°C in coastal areas, 12–25°C in mountains.

Currency 1 Malaysian Dollar/Ringgit (MYR) = 100 cents

Economy Discovery of tin in the late 19th-c brought European investment; rubber trees introduced from Brazil; minerals including iron ore, bauxite; oil, natural gas; electronic components, electrical goods; tourism.

GDP (2002e) $198·4 bn, per capita $8800

Human Development Index (2002) 0·782

History Part of Srivijaya Empire, 9th–13th-c; Hindu and Muslim influences, 14th–15th-c; Portugal, the Netherlands, and Britain vied for control from the 16th-c; Singapore, Malacca, and Penang formally incorporated into the British Colony of the Straits Settlements, 1826; British protection extended over Perak, Selangor, Negeri Sembilan, and Pahang, constituted into the Federated Malay States, 1895; protection treaties with several other states (Unfederated Malay States), 1885–1930; occupied by Japanese in World War 2; Federation of Malaya, 1948; independence, 1957; constitutional monarchy of Malaysia, 1963; Singapore withdrew from the Federation in 1965; governed by a bicameral Federal Parliament; Head of State is a Monarch elected for five years by his fellow sultans; advised by a Prime Minister and a Cabinet; coastal regions hit by tsunami, 2004.

Head of State (Yang di-Pertuan Agong)
1963–5 Sayyid Harun Putra Jamal-ul-Lail Perlis
1965–70 Ismail Nasir-ud-Din Shah Trengganu
1970–5 Abdul-Halim Muazzam Shah Kedah
1975–9 Yahya Petra Kelantan
1979–84 Ahmad Shah al-Mustain Pahang
1984–9 Mahmud Iskandar Shah Johore
1989–9 Azlan Muhibbuddin Shah Perak
1994–9 Ja'afar ibn Abdul Rahman
1999–2002 Salehuddin Abdul Aziz Shah
2002–6 Tuanku Syed Sirajuddin
2006– Mizan Zainal Abidin

Head of Government
1963–70 Abdul Rahman Putra al-Haj
1970–6 Abdul Razak bin Hussein
1976–9 Haji Hussein bin Onn
1979–97 Mahathir bin Mohamad
1997 Anwar Ibrahim *Acting*
1997–2003 Mahathir bin Mohamad
2003– Abdullah Ahmad Badawi

---

malamute [malamyoot] *Alaskan malamute*

Malan, Daniel (François) [malan] (1874–1959) South African statesman and prime minister (1948–54), born in Riebeek West, South Africa. In 1939 he founded with Hertzog the reunited Nationalist Party, and in 1948 became premier and minister for external affairs, introducing the controversial apartheid policy.

malaria A disease, endemic in tropical countries, caused by infection with one of four species of *Plasmodium*, a parasite transmitted by *Anopheles* mosquitoes. The parasites multiply in the liver and in red blood cells, which are destroyed with each life cycle, producing characteristic symptoms of high fever, shaking, and aches. Several drugs are available for treatment, but increasing resistance to these is now being seen. Travellers should consult an expert centre for provision of anti-malarial medication.

Malawi *p.571*

Malawi, Lake *Nyasa, Lake*

Malay (language) The language of the Malay Peninsula, which has provided the modern standard language, **Bahasa Indonesia**, known as **Bahasa Malaysia** in Malaysia. A pidginized form, **Bazaar Malay**, has been a lingua franca in the region for many centuries. A further variety, **Baba Malay**, is used by Chinese communities in Malaysia.

Malay (people) A cluster of Malay-speaking (Austronesian) peoples of the Malay Peninsula and neighbouring territory, including parts of Borneo and Sumatra. Hindu Indian influence on their culture is strong.

Malayalam [malayahlam] The Dravidian language associated with the S Indian state of Kerala. It has c.34 million speakers.

Malaysia see panel

Malcolm III, nickname **Malcolm Canmore** ('Big Head') (c.1031–

Maldives

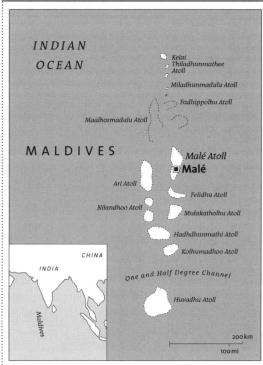

☐ International Airport

[moldiyvz], formerly **Maldive Islands**, official name **Republic of Maldives**, Dhivehi **Dhivehi Jumhuriya**

Local name Dhivehi Jumhuriya

Timezone GMT +5

Area 300 km²/116 sq mi

Population total (2002e) 281 000

Status Independent republic within the Commonwealth

Date of independence 1968

Capital Malé

Languages Dhivehi (official), Arabic, Hindi, and English widely spoken

Ethnic groups Sinhalese (Dravidian extraction mainly), also Arab, Negrito, African influences

Religion Almost 100% Sunni Muslim

Physical features Island archipelago in the Indian Ocean; comprises c.1190 islands (202 inhabited) in a chain of 20 coral atolls; many small and low-lying with sandy beaches fringed with coconut palms; none of the islands rising above 1·8 m/5 ft; 10% of land arable, 3% forested.

Climate Generally warm and humid; wet season created by SW monsoons (Apr–Oct), dry season by NE monsoon (Dec–Mar); average annual rainfall, 2100 mm/83 in; average daily temperature 22°C.

Currency 1 Rufiyaa (MVR) = 100 laaris

Economy Agriculture; breadfruit, banana, mango, cassava, sweet potato, millet; fishing, shipping, tourism.

GDP (2002e) $1·25 bn, per capita $3900

Human Development Index (2002) 0·743

History Former dependency of Ceylon (Sri Lanka); British protectorate, 1887–1965; became a Republic within the Commonwealth, 1953; Sultan restored, 1954; independence outside the Commonwealth, 1965; rejoined Commonwealth, 1982; state of emergency following pro-democracy protests, 2004; governed by a president, a ministers' Majlis (cabinet), and a citizens' Majlis of 48 members elected for five years; many areas strongly hit by tsunami, 2004.

Monarch (Sultan)

1954–68 Muhammad Farid Didi

Head of State/Government

1968–78 Ibrahim Nasir

1978– Maumoon Abdul Gayoom

---

93) King of Scots (1058–93), the son of Duncan I. He conquered S Scotland, but did not become king until he had defeated and killed Macbeth (1057). He launched five invasions of England.

Malcolm, George (John) (1917–97) Harpsichordist and conductor, born in London. He was Master of the Music at Westminster Cathedral (1947–59), and earned a wide reputation as a harpsichord soloist.

Malcolm X, originally **Malcolm Little** (1925–65) Political leader, born in Omaha, NE. He entered the Nation of Islam (Black Muslims) and became a leading spokesman for its separatist policies, but left the organization in 1964, and founded the Organization of Afro-American Unity. A factional feud ensued, culminating in his assassination by Black Muslim enemies during a rally in Harlem.

Maldives see panel

Malé [malee], Dhivehi **Daviyani** 4°00N 73°28E, pop (2000e) 76 000; area 2 km²/0·77 sq mi. Chief atoll and capital of the Maldives; airport.

Malebranche, Nicolas [malbrāsh] (1638–1715) Philosopher, born in Paris. His major work is *De la recherche de la vérité* (1674, Search after Truth), which defends many of Descartes' views.

maleic acid [malayik] $C_4H_4O_8$, IUPAC *cis*-**butenedioic acid**, melting point 139°C. A geometrical isomer of fumaric acid, but with a much lower melting point.

Malenkov, Georgiy Maksimilianovich [malyenkof] (1902–88) Soviet statesman and premier (1953–5), born in Orenburg, Russia. He was involved in the purges of the 1930s under Stalin, and succeeded Stalin as Party first secretary and premier. He was replaced by Khrushchev.

Malesherbes, Chrétien (Guillaume de Lamoignon) de [malzairb] (1721–94) French statesman, born in Paris. At Louis XVI's accession (1774) he was made secretary of state for the royal household, instituting prison and legal reforms, but resigned in 1776. Despite his reforming zeal, he was mistrusted as an aristocrat during the Revolution, and was guillotined.

Malevich, Kazimir (Severinovich) [malayevich] (1878–1935) Painter, born in Kiev. With Mondrian he was one of the earliest pioneers of pure abstraction, founding the Suprematist movement.

Mali *p.574*

malic acid HOOC–CH_2–CH(OH)–COOH, IUPAC **2-hydroxybutanedioic acid**, melting point 100°C. An acid found in unripe fruit, especially apples.

Malinke [malingkay] or **Mandingo** A cluster of autonomous Mande-speaking agricultural peoples of Mali, Guinea, Senegal, and neighbouring areas.

Malinowski, Bronislaw (Kasper) [malinofskee] (1884–1942) Anthropologist, born in Kraków, Poland. He was the pioneer

Mali

MOROCCO
ALGERIA
WESTERN SAHARA
AFRICA
Tropic of Cancer
Sahara Desert
ALGERIA
MAURITANIA
Adrar des Iforas
M A L I
Timbuktu
Niger
Gao
Macina Marshes
Kayes
Mopti
Bandiagara
NIGER
Ségou
Djénné
Bamako
Bani
BURKINA FASO
Sénégal
GUINEA
Sikasso
600 km
300 mi
CÔTE D'IVOIRE

☐ International Airport

[mahlee], official name **Republic of Mali**, Fr **République de Mali**

Local name Mali

Timezone GMT

Area 1 240 192 km²/478 714 sq mi

Population total (2002e) 11 340 000

Status Republic

Date of independence 1960

Capital Bamako

Languages French (official), local languages (including Bambara) widely spoken

Ethnic groups Mande (Bambara, Malinke, Sarakole) (50%), Peul (Fulani nomads) (17%), Voltaic (including Senufo, Bura, Senouto, Minianka) (12%), Songhai (6%), Tuareg and Moor (5%)

Religions Muslim (90%), traditional animist beliefs (9%), Christian (1%) (Roman Catholic 0·5%, Protestant 0·5%)

Physical features Landlocked country on the fringe of the Sahara; lower part of the Hoggar massif (N); arid plains 300–500 m/1000–1600 ft; mainly savannah land in the S; main rivers, Niger, Bani, Sénégal; featureless desert land (N).

Climate Subtropical in S and SW, with rainy season (Jun–Oct); average rainfall c.1000 mm/40 in; average annual temperatures 24°C (Jan), 27°C (Jul) in Bamako.

Currency 1 CFA Franc (XAF) = 100 centimes

Economy Mainly subsistence agriculture; crops severely affected by drought conditions; fishing, livestock, food processing, textiles, leather, cement; some tourism.

GDP (2002e) $9·775 bn, per capital $900

Human Development Index (2002) 0·386

History Mediaeval state controlling the trade routes between savannah and Sahara, reaching its peak in the 14th-c; governed by France, 1881–95; territory of French Sudan (part of French West Africa) until 1959; partnership with Senegal as the Federation of Mali, 1959; separate independence, 1960; under 1979 constitution (suspended, 1991) governed by a President elected every six years, and a National Assembly.

Head of State

1960–8 Modibo Keita
1969–91 Moussa Traoré
1991–2 Amadou Toumani Touré *Military Junta*
1992–2002 Alpha Oumar Konaré
2002– Amadou Toumani Touré

Head of Government

1986–8 Mamadou Dembelé
1988–91 *No Prime Minister*
1991–2 Soumana Sacko
1992–3 Younoussi Touré
1993–4 Abdoulaye Sekou Sow
1994–2000 Ibrahim Boubakar Keita
2000–2 Mande Sidibe
2002 Modibo Keita
2002–4 Mohammed Ag Amani
2004– Ousmane Issoufi Maïga

---

of 'participant observation' as a method of fieldwork (notably, in the Trobriand Is), and a major proponent of functionalism in anthropology.

Malipiero, (Gian) Francesco [malipyayroh] (1882–1973) Composer, born in Venice, Italy. He wrote symphonic, operatic, vocal, and chamber music, and edited Monteverdi and Vivaldi.

mallard A dabbling duck (*Anas platyrhynchos*) found near water throughout the N hemisphere; blue patch on wing; male with green head and thin white neck ring; the ancestor of nearly all domestic ducks. (Family: Anatidae.)

Mallarmé, Stéphane [malah(r)may] (1842–98) Symbolist poet, born in Paris. A leader of the Symbolist school, his works include *Hérodiade* (1864), and *L'après-midi d'un faune* (1865, published 1876), which inspired Debussy's prelude.

Malle, Louis [mal] (1932–95) Film director, born in Thumeries, France. The success of his second film *Les Amants* (1958, The Lovers) brought recognition, and he went on to receive critical acclaim for such works as *Calcutta* (1969), *Le Souffle au coeur* (1971, Dearest Love), *Au Revoir Les Enfants* (1987, Goodbye, Children), and *Damage* (1993).

mallee [malee] A scrubland vegetation zone in the semi-arid parts of SE and SW Australia. Dwarf eucalyptus shrubs dominate, growing to 2 m/6 ft in height.

mallee fowl A megapode bird (*Leipoa ocellata*) native to Australia; brown with white spots on wings; inhabits dry scrubland; also known as **lowan**. (Family: Megapodiidae.)

Mallon, Seamus (1936–) Northern Ireland politician, born in Markethill, Armagh, Northern Ireland. He was elected to Armagh District Council (1973–86) and the Northern Ireland Assembly (1973–4). A member of the Social Democratic and Labour Party, he became a UK MP in 1986. He was elected to the new Northern Ireland Assembly in 1998, becoming deputy first minister (1999–2001).

mallow N temperate annual and perennial herb; flowers with petals, rose, purple, or white, often with dark veins; stamens numerous, united into a central column; fruit a flat whorl of 1-seeded segments. (Genus: *Malva*, 40 species. Family: Malvaceae.)

Malmö [malmoe] 55°35N 13°00E, pop (2000e) 245 000. Fortified seaport in SW Sweden; third largest city in Sweden; under Danish rule until 1658; railway.

malnutrition A deficiency of one or more of the essential ingre-

Malta

official name **Republic of Malta**, Maltese **Repubblika ta' Malta**, ancient **Melita**

Local name Malta

Timezone GMT +1

Area 316 km²/122 sq mi

Population total (2002e) 386 000

Status Independent republic within the Commonwealth

Date of independence 1964

Capital Valletta

Languages English and Maltese (official)

Ethnic groups Maltese (mixed Arabic, Sicilian, Norman, Spanish, English, Italian racial origin) (95%), English (2%)

Religions Roman Catholic Apostolic (97%), Anglican Communion (2%)

Physical features Archipelago, comprising the islands of Malta (246 km²/95 sq mi), Gozo (67 km²/26 sq mi), and Comino (2·7 km²/1 sq mi), with the uninhabited islets of Cominotto, Filfla, and St Paul; highest point, 252 m/830 ft, on island of Malta; well-indented coastline with natural harbours, rocky coves; no rivers.

Climate Mediterranean, hot, dry summers, cool, rainy winters; rainy season (Oct–Mar); average annual rainfall 400 mm/16 in; average annual temperatures 13°C (Jan), 26°C (Jul) in Valletta.

Currency 1 Maltese Lira (MTL) = 100 cents

Economy Tourism; ship repair (naval dockyards now converted to commercial use); developing as a trans-shipment centre for the Mediterranean; tobacco, plastic and steel goods, paints, detergents; potatoes, tomatoes, oranges, grapes.

GDP (2002e) $6·818 bn, per capita $17 200

Human Development Index (2002) 0·875

History Controlled at various times by Phoenicia, Greece, Carthage, and Rome; conquered by Arabs, 9th-c; given to the Knights Hospitallers, 1530; British Crown Colony, 1815; important strategic base in both World Wars; for its resistance to heavy air attacks, the island was awarded the George Cross, 1942; achieved independence, 1964; republic, 1974; British military base closed, 1979; governed by a President, Prime Minister, Cabinet and House of Representatives; joined European Union, 2004.

Head of State
1994–9 Ugo Mifsud Bonnici
1999–2004 Guido de Marco
2004– Edward Fenech-Adami

Head of Government
1996–8 Alfred Sant
1998–2004 Edward Fenech-Adami
2004– Lawrence Gonzi

---

dients of a diet. Undernutrition occurs when insufficient food energy is taken and, when prolonged, may lead to profound weight loss. The insufficiency may involve one or several vitamin deficiencies.

Malory, Sir Thomas (?–1471) English writer, known for his work, *Le Morte Darthur* (The Death of Arthur). From Caxton's preface (1485), we are told that Malory was a knight, and that he finished his work in the ninth year of the reign of Edward IV (1461–70).

Malouf, David [maloof] (1934–) Writer, born in Brisbane, Queensland, Australia. His novels include *The Great World* (1991, Miles Franklin Award), *Remembering Babylon* (1993), and *The Conversations at Curlow Creek* (1997). Among his short-story collections are *Dream Stuff* (2000), and *Every Move You Make* (2007).

Malraux, André (Georges) [malroh] (1901–76) French statesman and novelist, born in Paris. Minister of cultural affairs (1960–9), he is known for his novels, notably *La Condition humaine* (1933, Man's Fate; Prix Goncourt) and *L'espoir* (1937, Man's Hope).

Malta see panel

Maltese (language) A language spoken by 300 000 people on the island of Malta, related to the W dialects of Arabic. It is the only variety of Arabic written in the Roman alphabet.

Maltese (zoology) A small toy spaniel developed in Italy (name probably derived from the Sicilian town of Melita); colour uniform; hair straight, coat very long and thick, reaching ground; legs short, hidden by coat.

Malthus, Thomas Robert (1766–1834) Economist, born near Dorking, Surrey. His *Essay on the Principle of Population* (1798) argued that the population has a natural tendency to increase faster than the means of subsistence, and that efforts should be made to cut the birth rate, either by self-restraint or birth control – a view which later was widely misrepresented under the name of **Malthusianism**.

maltose [mawltohs] $C_{12}H_{22}O_{11}$. A condensation dimer of two molecules of glucose which are produced when it is hydrolysed; also known as **malt sugar**. It is derived from the limited hydrolysis of starch.

malt sugar *maltose*

Malvern [mawlvern] or **Great Malvern** 52°07N 2°19W, pop (2000e) 31 700. Town in Worcestershire, WC England; popular health resort in the Malvern Hills; railway; Elgar lived and is buried here.

Malvinas [malveenas] *Falkland Islands*

mamba A venomous African snake of the family Elapidae; strong venom; two species: the **black mamba** (*Dendroaspis polylepis*), correctly the **black-mouthed mamba**, with body dark brown or grey, never black; and the **green mamba** (*Dendroaspis angusticeps*).

Mamet, David (Alan) [mamet], sometimes credited as **Richard Weisz** (1947–) Playwright, screenplay writer, and film director, born in Chicago, IL. His works include the plays *American Buf-*

falo (1976), *Speed the Plow* (1987), *The Cryptogram* (1994), and *Romance* (2005), the screenplays *The Postman Always Rings Twice* (1981), *The Untouchables* (1986), and *Hannibal* (2001), and the films (as director) *House of Games* (1986) and *State of Maine* (2000). In 2004 he wrote and directed *Spartan*. He received the 1984 Pulitzer Prize for Drama for *Glengarry Glen Ross*.

Mamluks or **Mamelukes** Slave soldiers who constituted the army of the Ayyubid sultanate established in Egypt by Saladin in the 1170s. Their commanders (*amirs*) created a professional army of high quality. They continued to rule in Egypt until their massacre by Mohammed Ali in 1811.

mammal An animal characterized by having mammary glands in the female, along with several other features, such as a covering of hair (very sparse in some mammals). Mammals are divided into **placental mammals**, in which the young develop in a womb (the *uterus*) and are born in an advanced stage of development; **marsupials**, in which the young are born in a very early stage and develop outside the mother's body, usually in a pouch; and **monotremes** (or **egg-laying mammals**), in which the young hatch from an egg outside the body of the mother. (Class: Mammalia, c.4000 species.)

mammary gland In female mammals, a gland responsible for the production and release of milk to feed their young. They are located on the surface of the chest or abdomen, and may be concentrated into an udder.

mammoth A specialized elephant originating in Africa, which spread in the early Pleistocene epoch through Eurasia and North America. The **woolly mammoth** was abundant in tundra regions, and had long hair and a thick fat layer for insulation. It died out c.12 000 years ago. (Order: Proboscidea.)

Mammoth Cave A system of subterranean passages and caverns created by limestone erosion and extending over 480 km/300 mi in W Kentucky. The area is a world heritage site.

mammoth tree A massive evergreen conifer (*Sequoiadendron giganteum*) confined to the W slopes of the Sierra Nevada Mts, California; also called **giant redwood**, **California big tree**, or **wellingtonia**. Age estimates range from 400–4000 years. (Family: Taxodiaceae.)

Man, Isle of *see panel*

Managua [managwa] 12°06N 86°18W, pop (2000e) 1 414 000. Commercial centre and capital city of Nicaragua; badly damaged by earthquake in 1931 and 1972, and by civil war in the late 1970s; airport; railway; university (1961).

manakin A small bird native to C and tropical South America; short bill, wings, and (usually) tail; toes partially joined; noted for its complex display. (Family: Pipridae, c.53 species.)

Manama [manama], Arabic **al-Manamah** 26°12N 50°38E, pop (2000e) 176 000. Seaport capital of Bahrain, a free trade port.

Manasseh, Prayer of [manase] Short, eloquent writing of the Old Testament Pseudepigrapha, ostensibly the work of Manasseh, a wicked king of Judah (c.687–642 BC), expressing his personal confession of sin and petition for pardon. Most scholars date the work from the 2nd-c BC to the 1st-c AD.

manatee [manatee] An aquatic mammal, found from Brazil to SE USA, and in W Africa; large rounded body; short head with square muzzle; front legs are flippers; no hind legs; tail ends in a flat horizontal disc. (Order: Sirenia. Family: Trichechidae, 3 species.)

Manaus or **Manáos** [manãos] 3°06S 60°00W, pop (2000e) 1 285 000. River-port city in N Brazil, on the N bank of the R Negro; the collecting point for produce of a vast area; founded, 1660; free zone established, 1967; airfield; university (1965); Teatro Amazonas opera house (1896, rebuilt 1929 and 1974).

Man Booker Prize *Booker Prize*

Manchester (UK), Lat **Mancunium** 53°30N 2°15W, pop (2001e) 392 800. Metropolitan district in Greater Manchester urban

Man, Isle of

☐ International Airport

(UK British Islands)

Timezone GMT

Area 572 km²/221 sq mi

Population total (2002e) 75 000

Status Crown dependency of the United Kingdom

Capital Douglas

Languages English (Manx survived as an everyday language until 19th-c)

Physical features Island in the Irish Sea; rises to 620 m/2036 ft at Snaefell.

Economy Tourism, agriculture, fishing, light engineering; used as a tax haven; not part of European Community. Annual Tourist Trophy motorcycle races held here.

History Ruled by the Welsh, 6th–9th-c; then by the Scandinavians, Scots, and English; purchased by the British Government between 1765 and 1828; the island has its own Parliament, the bicameral Court of Tynwald, which consists of the elected House of Keys and the Legislative Council; Acts of the British Parliament do not generally apply to Man.

area, NW England, on the R Irwell; Roman town: focal point of English cotton industry during the Industrial Revolution; became a city in 1853; railway; airport; connected to the Irish Sea by the 57 km/35 mi Manchester Ship Canal (1894); UK's second largest commercial centre; cultural centre for NW; Hallé Orchestra; three universities (1880, 1824, 1992): cathedral (15th-c): Free Trade Hall (1843); football league teams, Manchester City (Blues), Manchester United (Reds); location of the 2002 Commonwealth Games.

Manchester, Greater pop (2001e) 2 482 400; area 1287 km²/ 497 sq mi. Metropolitan county of NW England, consisting of 10 boroughs; metropolitan council abolished in 1986; county town, Manchester.

Manchester Ship Canal An artificial waterway in the UK linking Manchester with the Mersey estuary. The canal, which is 57 km/ 35 mi long, was opened in 1894.

Manchester United Football Club English Association football club, based in Manchester. Founded in 1878, it turned professional in 1885. The team has won the Premier League eight times and the FA Cup 11 times. In the 1998–9 season, they became the first British club to win the Premier League Championship, the FA Cup, and the European Cup.

Manchukuo or **Manzhouguo** [manchookwoh] A Japanese puppet-state established in 1932 in Manchuria. Puyi, the last Qing emperor, was its nominal head. The regime ended with the defeat of Japan in 1945.

Manchuria A region of NE China; mountainous area, sparsely populated by nomadic tribes; Manchus overthrew Ming dynasty to become the last Chinese emperors (Qing dynasty); vast natural resources of timber and minerals; Russian military control, 1900; captured by Japan, 1931, and part of puppet state of Manchukuo; Russian control re-asserted, 1945; Chinese sovereignty recognized, 1950, but border area with Russia a continuing focus of political tension.

Manchus A nomadic people of Jürchen stock in Manchuria who ruled all China from 1644 to 1912 under the Qing dynasty. There are now about 2·5 million Manchu people in China.

Mancini, Henry [manseenee], popular name of **Enrico Mancini** (1924–94) Composer, born in Cleveland, OH. His Oscar-winning compositions include the songs 'Moon River' (1961) and 'Days of Wine and Roses' (1962), and the film scores for *Breakfast at Tiffany's* (1961) and *Victor/Victoria* (1982). He composed more than 80 film scores, including the theme for the *Pink Panther* films, and won 20 Grammy Awards.

mandala [mandala] Circular designs in Hindu and Buddhist religious art, representing the universe or other aspects of their beliefs. They are used as a focus and aid to concentration in worship and meditation.

Mandalay [mandalay] 21°57N 96°04E, pop (2000e) 731 200. River-port city in C Myanmar; on R Ayeyarwady; airfield; railway; university (1964); commercial centre, tourism; Kuthodaw Pagoda.

Mandarin *Chinese*

mandarin A citrus fruit (*Citrus reticulata*) with yellow to deep orange-red fruits, very like small oranges but with thin, loose rind. Its species include satsumas and tangerines. (Family: Rutaceae.)

mandates A system under which former territories of the German and Ottoman Empires were administered by the victorious powers of World War 1 under supervision by the League of Nations. Britain and France acquired mandates in the Middle East and Africa, while Belgium acquired Rwanda-Urundi, South Africa acquired South-West Africa, and Australia and New Zealand acquired New Guinea and Western Samoa.

Mande [manday] A cluster of Mande-speaking agricultural peoples of W Sudan, Sierra Leone, Liberia, and Côte d'ivoire. They include the Bambara, Dyula, Malinke, Mende, and Soninke.

Mandela, Nelson (Rolihlahla) [mandela] (1918–) South African statesman and president (1994–99), born in Transkei, South Africa. He was a lawyer in Johannesburg, then joined the African National Congress in 1944. For the next 20 years he directed a campaign of defiance against the South African government, and in 1964 was sentenced to life imprisonment. The 1980s saw a co-ordinated international campaign for his release, finally successful in 1990. He was elected president of the African

National Congress in 1991, and was closely involved in constitutional negotiations with President de Klerk which led to South Africa's first all-race elections in 1994. In 1993 he shared the Nobel Peace Prize with de Klerk for their work towards dismantling apartheid, and in 1995 was awarded the Order of Merit. He retired from active politics at the 1999 general election and announced his formal retirement from public life in June 2004.

Mandela, Winnie [mandela], also **Madikizela-Mandela**, popular name of **Nomzano Zaniewe Winifred Mandela** (1934–) Former wife of Nelson Mandela, born in Bizana, South Africa. She married Mandela in 1958, and was subsequently banned, restricted, detained, and jailed a number of times. In 1990, after her husband was released from prison, she took an increasingly prominent role in the African National Congress (ANC), until her conviction on charges of kidnapping and assault. She continued to operate as a militant figure under ANC colours, making a political comeback in late 1993, and given a role in the 1994 government as deputy minister for arts, culture, science, and technology (dismissed in 1995). In 1996, the Mandelas divorced. She figured prominently in the proceedings of the Truth and Reconciliation Commission in 1997. In 2004, her conviction for theft and fraud in connection with bank loans was overturned on appeal.

Mandelbrot, Benoit (1924–) Mathematician, born in Warsaw. A central figure in the development of fractals, his book *The Fractal Geometry of Nature* (1982) was important in demonstrating the potential application of fractals to natural phenomena. His name is applied to a particular set of complex numbers which generate one type of fractal (the **Mandelbrot set**), whose visually attractive properties have captured public interest since the 1980s.

Mandelson, Peter [mandelson] (1953–) Politician, born in London. He became an MP in 1992, and in 1996 worked exclusively on the Labour Party election campaign. In 1998 he was appointed president of the Board of Trade and secretary of state for trade and industry. He resigned from the government following his failure to declare, in the Member's Register of Interests, a private mortgage loan from his cabinet colleague, Geoffrey Robinson (paymaster general). After 10 months without office, he was appointed Northern Ireland Secretary. He was forced to resign again from the cabinet in 2001, following a controversy over the passport application of Indian billionaire Srichand Hinduja, but made a second political comeback in 2004 when he was appointed European Commissioner for trade.

Mandelstam, Osip Emilevich [manduhlstam] (1891–1938) Poet, born in Warsaw. His early poems led to arrest (1934) by the Soviet authorities, and his death was reported from Siberia in 1938. His collected works were published in three volumes (1964–71).

Mandeville, Jehan de or **Sir John** [mandevil] (14th-c) The name assigned to the compiler of a famous book of travels, published apparently in 1366, and translated from the French into many languages.

Mandingo *Malinke*

mandolin A plucked string instrument, about 60 cm/2 ft long, developed in the 18th-c. It has a pear-shaped body somewhat like a lute's, a fretted fingerboard, and a pegbox set back at an angle. There are four pairs of steel strings, played with a plectrum.

mandrake A thick-rooted perennial (*Mandragora officinalis*) native to Europe; leaves in a rosette; flowers blue; berries yellow to orange. Once widely regarded for its medicinal and narcotic properties, it has been the subject of many superstitions. (Family: Solanaceae.)

mandrill A baboon (*Mandrillus sphinx*) native to W African forests; stocky with short limbs and thick coat; tail minute; buttocks red-blue; naked face with scarlet muzzle and bright blue, ridged cheeks (especially in male).

Manet, Edouard [manay] (1832–83) Painter, born in Paris. His 'Déjeuner sur l'herbe' (1863, Luncheon on the Grass) was rejected by the Salon, and although the equally provocative 'Olympia' was accepted in 1865, the Salon remained hostile to him. He exhibited in the *Salon des Refusés*, and helped to form the group out of which the Impressionist movement arose.

mangabey [manggabee] An Old World monkey, native to tropical Africa; slender with long tail, long coat; pronounced whiskers on sides of face. (Genus: *Cercocebus*, 4 species.)

manganese Mn, element 25, melting point 1244°C. A transition metal, density about 7·4 g/cm^3, always found combined in nature, but mainly as the dioxide, MnO_2. It is mainly used in alloy steels. Potassium permanganate is a convenient and strong oxidizing agent in aqueous solution.

mange [maynzh] A contagious skin disease of domestic animals. It results from infestation with several types of mites which burrow into the skin, causing itching and irritation.

mangel-wurzel *beet*

mangetout [māzh **too**] *pea*

mango An evergreen tree (*Mangifera indica*) growing to 18 m/60 ft, native to SE Asia; flowers tiny, white, with 4–5 petals; fleshy fruit 7–10 cm/2$\frac{3}{4}$–4 in, oval to kidney-shaped, yellow flushed with red. It is grown for the sweet-tasting, edible fruit. (Family: Anacardiaceae.)

mangrove Any of several unrelated tropical or subtropical trees, all sharing similar structure and biology, growing on coastal and estuarine mud-flats. All possess either aerial roots or *pneumatophores*, special breathing roots which help aerate the root system in swampy ground. (Main genera: *Rhizophora*, 7 species, and *Brugeria*, 6 species. Family: Rhizophoraceae. Also *Avicennia*, 14 species. Family: Avicenniaceae.)

Manhattan pop (2000e) 1 537 200; area 72 km^2/28 sq mi. An island forming one of the five boroughs of the City of New York, New York State, E USA; settled by the Dutch as part of New Netherlands in 1626; taken by the British in 1664; major financial and commercial centre based around Wall Street and the former World Trade Center (destroyed in terrorist attack on 11 Sep 2001); headquarters of the United Nations; Broadway, Empire State Building, Greenwich Village; six universities; named after a local tribe of Indians.

Manhattan project The codename for the most secret scientific operation of World War 2, the development of the atomic bomb, undertaken in the USA from 1942. The first atomic weapon was detonated at Alamogordo, New Mexico (16 Jul 1945).

Manichaeism [manikeeizm] or **Manichaeanism** A religious sect founded by the prophet Manes (or Mani) (c.216–76), who began teaching in Persia in 240. His teaching was based on a primaeval conflict between the realms of light and darkness. The purpose of religion is to release the particles of light imprisoned in matter, and Buddha, the Prophets, Jesus, and finally Manes have been sent to help in this task. The Zoroastrians executed Manes, but the sect survived in the West until the 10th-c.

Manila [manila] 14°36N 120°59E, pop (2000e) 1 961 000. Capital of the Philippines on Luzon I; founded, 1571; taken by the USA during the Spanish–American War, 1898; badly damaged in World War 2; airport; railway; several universities (earliest, 1611).

Manila hemp *abaca*

manioc *cassava*

Manipur [manipoor] pop (2001e) 2 388 600; area 22 356 km^2/8629 sq mi. State in NE India; British rule in 1891; administered from the state of Assam until 1947, when it became a union territory; became a state in 1972; capital, Imphal; governed by a Legislative Assembly.

Manitoba [manitohba] pop (2000e) 1 223 000; area 649 950 km^2/250 945 sq mi. Province in C Canada; known as the 'land of 100 000 lakes', the result of glaciation; land rises in W and S to 832 m/2730 ft at Mt Baldy; capital, Winnipeg; trading rights given to Hudson's Bay Company, 1670; French claims ceded to the British under the Treaty of Paris, 1763; settlement on the Red R from 1812; joined the confederation, 1870, provoking insurrection under Riel; major development of area after railway reached Winnipeg in the 1880s; governed by a lieutenant-governor and a Legislative Assembly; cereals (especially wheat), livestock, vegetables, fishing, timber, hydroelectric power, mining, tourism.

manitou [manitoo] A term used by the Algonkin Indians of the E Woodlands of North America to designate the supernatural world and to identify any manifestation of it.

Manizales [manisalays] 5°03N 75°32W, pop (2000e) 325 200. City in C Colombia; altitude 2153 m/7064 ft; founded, 1848; railway; centre of coffee area; university (1950); cathedral (unfinished).

Mankowitz, (Cyril) Wolf [mangkohvits] (1924–98) Writer, playwright, and antique dealer, born in London. His fiction includes the novel *A Kid for Two Farthings* (1953), the play *The Bespoke Overcoat* (1954), the films *The Millionairess* (1960) and *Casino Royale* (1967), and the musicals *Expresso Bongo* (1958–9), *Pickwick* (1963), and *Stand and Deliver!* (1972).

Mann, Thomas (1875–1955) Novelist, born in Lübeck, Germany. His works include *Buddenbrooks* (1901), *Der Tod in Venedig* (1913, Death in Venice; filmed, 1971), and *Der Zauberberg* (1924, The Magic Mountain), for which he won the Nobel Prize for Literature in 1929. His best-known work was a modern version of the mediaeval legend, *Doktor Faustus* (1947).

manna The name of several edible plant products, some of which have been proposed as the biblical food dropped from heaven during the Israelites' flight from Egypt. Lichen (*Lecanora esculenta*) from Asia Minor, the source of lichen bread and manna jelly, curls into balls when dry and blows in the wind.

Mannerism A form of art and architecture prevalent in France, Spain, and especially Italy during the 16th-c, characterized by overcrowded detail, and an irrational manipulation of classical elements, for playful or startling effect. In art, leading Mannerists included Giulio Romano, Pontormo, and Parmigiano, whose pictures are painted with jewel-like colours, and sculptors such as Cellini.

Mannheim [manhiym] 49°30N 8°28E, pop (2000e) 320 000. Commercial and manufacturing river port in Germany; on right bank of R Rhine; one of the largest inland harbours in Europe; seat of the Electors Palatine, 18th-c, when it became a cultural centre; badly bombed in World War 2; railway; university (1907); castle.

mannikin A small seed-eating bird, native to Africa S of Sahara, India, and SE Asia; inhabits forest, open country, and cultivation. (Genus: *Lonchura*, 23 species. Family: Estrildidae.)

Manning, Henry Edward, Cardinal (1808–92) Roman Catholic cardinal, born in Totteridge, Hertfordshire. At the Council of 1870, he was a zealous supporter of the infallibility dogma; and, named cardinal in 1875, he continued as a leader of the Ultramontanes.

manometer A device for measuring pressure exerted by or within a fluid (gas or liquid). It usually refers to various U-tube methods, pressure being shown by the difference in the height of the fluid (such as mercury) in the two arms of the tube, one arm being connected to the fluid whose pressure is being measured.

manorial system or **seignorial system** A basic feature of European society from the 11th-c to the 15th-c. The 'typical' manor used to be regarded as an agricultural estate coincident with the village, and comprising the lord's estate (demesne) or home farm, attached villein tenements providing labour services on the demesne, and free tenements owing rents. In reality, there was a pronounced lack of uniformity. Manors, which might be concentrated or dispersed, frequently cut across villages; some consisted solely or largely of demesne; others contained only peasant tenements; and labour dues varied widely.

Mansard or **Mansart, François** [māsah(r)] (1598–1666) Architect, born in Paris. He brought a simplified adaptation of the Baroque style into use in France, and made fashionable the high-pitched type of roof which bears his name.

Mansell, Nigel [mansl] (1953–) Motor-racing driver, born in Birmingham, West Midlands. He entered Formula 1 racing in 1980, retiring in 1992 after winning the driver's championship with eight wins. He joined the Haas–Newman Indy car-racing team in the USA, becoming Indy car champion in 1993, his first year, briefly returned to Formula 1 in 1995, driving for McLaren, then retired.

Mansfield, Katherine, pseudonym of **Kathleen Mansfield Murry**, *née* **Beauchamp** (1888–1923) Short-story writer, born in Wellington, New Zealand. She married John Middleton Murry in 1918. Her chief works are *Bliss* (1920), *The Garden Party* (1922), and *Something Childish* (1924).

Mansfield, Sir Peter (1933–) Physicist, born in London. Professor of physics at Nottingham University (1979), in 2003 he shared the Nobel Prize for Physiology or Medicine for discoveries concerning magnetic resonance imaging (MRI).

manslaughter An English legal term for a form of unlawful homicide which does not amount to murder, covering a wide spectrum of culpability, including behaving recklessly or negligently but without an intention to kill; known as *culpable homicide* in Scottish law. Mitigating factors, such as provocation, may reduce an offence from murder to manslaughter (often called **voluntary manslaughter** in the USA). Grossly negligent behaviour or omission, in certain circumstances, which results in unintended death may also constitute the offence (often called **involuntary manslaughter** in the USA). There is a separate statutory offence of causing death by reckless driving; this is often called *vehicular homicide* in the USA.

Manson, Charles (1934–) Cult leader, born in Cincinnati, OH. Members of his cult conducted a series of grisly murders in California in 1969, including that of actress Sharon Tate. He and his accomplices were spared the death penalty due to a Supreme Court ruling against capital punishment.

manta ray Largest of the devil rays, exceeding 6 m/20 ft in width and 1300 kg/2800 lb in weight; mouth broad, situated across front of head. (Genus: *Manta*. Family: Mobulidae.)

Mantegna, Andrea [mantenya] (c.1431–1506) Painter, born near Vicenza. In 1460 he settled in Mantua, where his major works included nine tempera pictures representing the 'Triumph of Caesar' (1482–92). He was also an engraver, architect, sculptor, and poet.

Mantel, Hilary (Mary) (1952–) Novelist, born in Hadfield, Derbyshire. Her books include *Fludd* (1989), *A Change of Climate* (1994), *The Giant, O'Brien* (1999), and *Beyond Black* (2005). In 1987 she won the first Shiva Naipaul Prize.

mantis A medium to large insect that has a well-camouflaged body and a mobile head with large eyes; waits motionless for insect prey to approach before striking out with its grasping, spiny forelegs; in some species, the female eats the male head-first during copulation. (Order: Mantodea, c.1800 species.)

Mantle, Mickey (Charles) (1931–95) Baseball player, born in Spavinaw, OK. A great centrefielder, baserunner, and hitter, he was a member of the renowned New York Yankees team of the 1950s and 1960s. The American League's Most Valuable Player in 1956, he once hit a home run measured at a record 177 m/565 ft. He was elected to the Baseball Hall of Fame in 1974.

Mantoux test [mantoo] Intradermal injection of an extract prepared from tuberculosis bacilli. The skin reaction measures the immune response to tuberculosis. When positive, the patient is known to suffer from or to have suffered from tuberculosis, or to have been vaccinated. It is named after French physician Charles Mantoux (1877–1947).

mantra [mantruh] In Hindu ritual, the belief that the repetition of a special phrase or word in meditation and devotion helps to concentrate the mind and aids in the development of spiritual power.

Mantua [mantyua], Ital **Mantova** 45°10N 10°47E, pop (2000e) 61 000. City in Lombardy, N Italy, on R Mincio; founded in Etruscan times; railway; ringed by ancient walls and bastions; cathedral (10th–18th-c).

Manu [manoo] In Hindu mythology, the forefather of the human race, to whom the Manu Smirti ('Lawbook of Manu') is attributed.

manure Organic material which is used to fertilize land. It usually consists of livestock excrement, generally mixed with straw or other litter used in the animals' housing. The generic term for dung mixed with straw is **farmyard manure**; animals housed in systems requiring little or no straw (commonly intensive systems) produce *slurry*, which is excrement plus water.

Manuzio, Aldo *Aldus Manutius*

Manx cat A breed of domestic cat, native to the Isle of Man; a British short-haired type; thick double-layered coat; no tail; also known as a **rumpy**.

Manzoni, Alessandro [mantsohnee] (1785–1873) Novelist and poet, born in Milan, Italy. He published his first poems in 1806, and spent the next few years writing sacred lyrics and a treatise on the religious basis of morality. The work which gave him European fame is his historical novel, *I promessi sposi* (1825–7, The Betrothed). He was a strong advocate of a united Italy, and became a senator of the kingdom in 1860. Verdi composed his *Requiem* in Manzoni's honour.

Maoism Specifically, the thought of Mao Zedong (Tse-tung), and more broadly a revolutionary ideology based on Marxism–Leninism adapted to Chinese conditions. Maoism shifted the focus of revolutionary struggle from the urban workers or proletariat to the countryside and the peasantry. There were three main elements: strict Leninist principles of organization, Chinese tradition, and armed struggle as a form of revolutionary activity. Since his death, his use of the masses for political purposes, his economic reforms, and his conception of political power have been increasingly criticized inside and outside China as seriously misguided and too rigid.

Maori [mowree] Polynesian people who were the original inhabitants of New Zealand. The first of them arrived, probably from the Marquesas Is, about AD 800, and by 1800 numbered over 100 000. In the 19th-c they came to be outnumbered and dominated by European (*pakeha*) settlers. By 1896 their population had shrunk to 42 200. There was some improvement in the 20th-c. Numbers rose (523 000 in the 1996 census), and after the 1970s they became politically more assertive. The Maori language has been officially encouraged, and they have obtained the return of some of their land.

Mao Zedong [mow dzuhdoong], also spelled **Mao Tse-tung** (1893–1976) Leader and leading theorist of the Chinese communist revolution, born in Hunan province, the son of a farmer. He took a leading part in the May Fourth Movement (1919), then became a Marxist and a founding member of the Chinese Communist Party (1921). After the break with the Nationalists in 1927, he evolved the guerrilla tactics of the 'people's war', and in 1934 led the Communist forces on the Long March to Shanxi. He increased the political and military power of his party, ousted the regime of Jiang Jieshi from the

Chinese mainland, and proclaimed the new People's Republic of China (1949) with Mao as both Chairman of the Chinese Communist Party and President of the Republic. In 1958 he launched his Great Leap Forward in rural and agricultural development, and in 1965 the Cultural Revolution. After his death, a strong reaction set in against 'cult of personality' and the excessive collectivism which had emerged, but his anti-Stalinist emphasis on rural industry and on local initiative was retained by his successors.

map The graphic representation of spatial information about a place on a plane surface through the use of symbols and signs. Maps are generally produced for specific purposes (eg *topographical* maps show relief and terrain features; *thematic* maps illustrate particular features, such as maps of population density). *see panel*

maple A member of a large genus of deciduous trees, native to N temperate regions; leaves variable in shape but typically palmately lobed with 3–13 toothed lobes; flowers in clusters, small, greenish, purple, or red; characteristic fruit of two winged seeds fused at base, eventually splitting apart, the wings acting as propellers. Many species produce striking autumn colours, especially reds and purples. Maple syrup is obtained from the sap of the **sugar maple** (*Acer saccharum*). (Genus: *Acer*, 200 species. Family: Aceraceae.)

Mappa Mundi [mapa mundee] (Lat 'map of the world') A celebrated 13th-c map of the world, owned by Hereford Cathedral, Hereford, UK. The map is on vellum, measuring 163 × 137 cm/ 64 × 54 in, and shows the world as a round plate, with Jerusalem centrally located. In 1988 there was a public outcry over proposed plans to sell the map, to help raise funds for the Cathedral. The proposal was subsequently withdrawn, following assistance given by the National Heritage Memorial Fund.

Mapplethorpe, Robert (1946–89) Photographer, born in New York City. He studied painting and sculpture, then concentrated on photography, mounting his first exhibition in 1976. A major retrospective of his often controversial work was presented by the Whitney Museum of American Art in 1988. He died of AIDS the following year.

map projection *see panel*

Maputo [mapootoh], formerly **Lourenço Marques** (to 1976) 25°58S 32°32E, pop (2000e) 1 329 000. Seaport capital of Mozambique, visited by the Portuguese, 1502; capital of Portuguese East Africa, 1907; airport; railway; university (1962); an outlet for several SE African countries.

Maquis [makee] The local name given to the dense scrub in Corsica; name adopted in German-occupied France by the resistance groups.

marabou A large stork (*Leptoptilos crumeniferus*) native to Africa S of Sahara; also known as the **marabou stork**; head and neck naked; nests in trees. (Family: Ciconiidae.)

Maracaibo [marakiyboh] 10°44N 71°37W, pop (2000e) 1 460 400. Second largest city in Venezuela, on NW shore of L Maracaibo; airport; two universities (1891, 1973); oil production and processing.

Maracaibo, Lake [marakiyboh] (Span **Lago de**) area 13 000 km²/ 5000 sq mi. Lake in NW Venezuela; length, c.210 km/130 mi; contains one of the world's greatest oilfields.

maracas [muhrakuhs] A pair of rattles, originally gourds filled with dried seeds, used as a rhythm instrument in Latin-American and occasionally Western orchestral music.

Maradona, Diego [maradona] (1960–) Footballer, born in Lanus, Argentina. In June 1982 he became the world's most expensive footballer when he joined Barcelona for £5 million. He captained Argentina to their second World Cup in 1986, only for his career to founder amid accusations of drug-taking. Following a 15-month ban, he returned by popular demand, though without a club, to the World Cup side as captain in 1994, but was

map projection

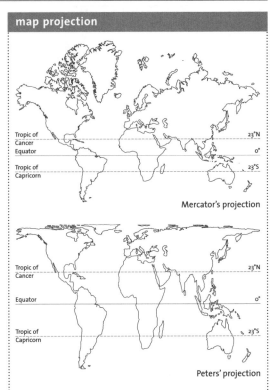

Mercator's projection

Peters' projection

The method of portraying the spherical surface of the Earth on a flat surface. Because a sphere is three-dimensional in form, and a map two-dimensional, there is inevitably some distortion: the representation of distance (true scale), direction (true bearing), area, and shape cannot be shown correctly together on the same map. Consequently different map projections have been developed, according to purpose, which show for example true distance, or true area. The greatest distortions occur when a large area, such as the whole of the Earth's surface, is being mapped. For the mapping of smaller areas, such as topographical maps, a compromise is made to minimize the distortion of all four properties.

again suspended from the team following a positive drug test. He signed for Santos in 1995 and announced his retirement in 1997. In 2000, he developed a severe heart condition following cocaine use, and his health remained an ongoing problem. In 2005 he began a new career as a TV chat-show host.

maral *red deer*

Marat, Jean Paul [mara] (1743–93) French revolutionary politician, born in Boudry, Switzerland. Elected to the National Convention, he became a leader of the Mountain, and advocated radical reforms. He was fatally stabbed in his bath by a Girondin supporter, Charlotte Corday; thereafter he was hailed as a martyr.

Maratha or **Mahratta** [marahta] A Marathi-speaking people of Maharashtra, W India. Historically they are famed as warriors and for promoting Hinduism.

marathon A long-distance running race, normally on open roads, over the distance 42 km 195 m/26 mi 385 yd. The race was introduced at the first modern Olympic Games in 1896 to commemorate the run of the Greek courier (according to legend, Phei-dippides) who ran the c.39 km/24 mi from Marathon to Athens in 490 BC with the news of a Greek victory over the Persian army. The current marathon distance was first used at the 1908 London Olympics. The distance was standardized in 1924. It is now a popular event for the non-competitive enthusiast, with many thousands taking part in the annual marathons in London, Boston, and New York City. It was supplemented in the 1980s by the **half-marathon**, run over the distance 21 km/13 mi 192½ yd.

Marathon, Battle of (490 BC) The decisive Athenian victory over the Persians on the E coast of Attica, which brought the First Persian War to an end.

Marbella [mah(r)baya] 36°30N 4°57W, pop (2000e) 78 000. Port and resort on the Costa del Sol, Andalusia, S Spain.

marble A metamorphic rock formed by the recrystallization of limestone and dolomite. It is white when pure, but its impurities give it a distinctive coloration.

Marburg [mah(r)boorg] 50°49N 8°36E, pop (2000e) 75 400. City in Germany; on the R Lahn; railway; university (1527); castle (15th–16th-c).

Marc, Franz (1880–1916) Artist, born in Munich, Germany. He helped to found the *Blaue Reiter* group in 1911. Most of his paintings were of animals (eg 'Tower of the Blue Horses', 1911, Minneapolis) portrayed in forceful colours.

marcasite [mah(r)kaseet] An iron sulphide mineral (FeS₂). It is found in sedimentary rocks, and also associated with major ore deposits of the Mississippi Valley.

Marceau, Marcel [mah(r)soh] (1923–) Mime artist, born in Strasbourg, France. His white-faced character, Bip, became famous from his appearances on stage and television throughout the world. Since 1978 he has been head of the *Ecole de Mimodrame Marcel Marceau*.

Marches, the, Ital **Marche** pop (2000e) 1 446 000; area 9693 km²/3741 sq mi. The area of EC Italy between the Apennines and the Adriatic Sea, centred on Ancona. Except for the narrow coastal plain, it is mostly mountainous.

marchioness *marquess*

March to the Sea *Sherman, William Tecumseh*

Marciano, Rocky [mah(r)siahnoh], originally **Rocco Francis Marchegiano**, nickname **the Rock from Brockton** (1923–69) Heavyweight boxing champion, born in Brockton, MA. He made his name by defeating the former world champion, Joe Louis, in 1951. When he retired in 1956 he was undefeated as world champion.

Marconi, Guglielmo [mah(r)kohnee] (1874–1937) Inventor, born in Bologna, Italy. He pioneered wireless telegraphy in Italy and England, sending signals across the Atlantic in 1901, and shared the Nobel Prize for Physics in 1909.

Marco Polo *Polo, Marco*

Marco Polo's sheep *argali*

Marcos, Ferdinand (Edralin) [mah(r)kos] (1917–89) Philippines statesman and president (1965–86), born in Ilocos Norte, Philippines. His regime as president was marked by increasing repression and political murders (notably, the assassination of Benigno Aquino in 1983). He was overthrown in 1986 by a popular front led by Corazon Aquino. He went into exile in Hawaii, where he and his wife, **Imelda**, fought against demands from US courts investigating charges of financial mismanagement and corruption. His body was returned for burial in 1993, and soon afterwards Imelda was convicted of corruption and sentenced to 18 years imprisonment. She was acquitted on appeal in 1998. Still commanding popular support, she was re-elected to congress for Leyte province in 1996.

Marcus Aurelius Antoninus (121–180) *Aurelius*

Marcuse, Herbert [mah(r)koozuh] (1898–1979) Marxist philosopher, born in Berlin. An influential figure of the Frankfurt

School, his books include *Reason and Revolution* (1941) and *Eros and Civilization* (1955).

Mar del Plata [mah(r) thel plata] 38°00S 57°30W, pop (2000e) 466 500. Port in E Argentina; founded in 1874; one of the prime holiday resorts of South America; railway; airfield; two universities (1958, 1962).

Mardi Gras [mah(r)dee grah] The French name (literally 'fat Tuesday') for Shrove Tuesday, the day before the beginning of Lent; Mardi Gras carnivals, beginning some time before Shrove Tuesday, are held in many places.

Marduk [mah(r)duk] Originally the patron deity of the city of Babylon. He later became the supreme god of Babylonia.

Marfan's syndrome [mah(r)fan] An inherited disease of connective tissue. The arms and legs grow to abnormal lengths, and the fingers and toes are long and spidery; also known as **arachnodactyly**. It is named after French paediatrician Bernard Jean Antonin Marfan (1858–1942).

Margaret (of Scotland), St (c.1046–93) Scottish queen, born in Hungary, sister of Edgar the Atheling. She married the Scottish king, Malcolm Canmore, and did much to assimilate the old Celtic Church to the rest of Christendom. She was canonized in 1250. Feast day 16 November or 19 June.

Margaret (Rose), Princess (1930–2002) British princess, second daughter of George VI and sister of Queen Elizabeth II, born in Glamis Castle, Angus. In 1960 she married **Antony Armstrong-Jones** (divorced, 1978), who was created Viscount Linley and Earl of Snowdon in 1961. The former title devolved upon their son, **David Albert Charles** (1961–), who married Serena Alleyne Stanhope in 1993; their children are **Charles Armstrong-Jones** (1999–) and **Margarita Armstrong-Jones** (2002–). Their daughter is **Sarah Frances Elizabeth** (1964–), who married Daniel Chatto in 1994; their children are **Samuel Chatto** (1996–) and **Arthur Chatto** (1999–).

Margaret of Anjou [ãzhoo] (1430–82) Queen Consort of Henry VI of England from 1445, born in Lorraine, France, the daughter of René of Anjou. During the Wars of the Roses, she was a leading Lancastrian. Defeated at Tewkesbury (1471), she was imprisoned in the Tower for four years, until ransomed by Louis XI.

Margaret Tudor (1489–1541) Queen of Scotland, born in London, the eldest daughter of Henry VII. She became the wife of James IV of Scotland (1503) and the mother of James V, for whom she acted as regent.

margarine A butter-substitute that does not contain dairy fat, usually made from vegetable oils and skimmed milk, and supplemented with vitamins A and D. The degree of hydrogenation of the original oil determines how much remains of the original polyunsaturates.

margay [mah(r)gay] A rare member of the cat family (*Felis wiedii*), found from N Mexico to N Argentina; pale with ring-like dark spots; rear feet adapted for climbing.

marguerite [mah(r)gereet] *ox-eye daisy*

Mari [mahree] The most important city on the middle Euphrates in the third and second millennia BC until its destruction c.1759 BC by the Babylonians. It was the centre of a vast trading network in NW Mesopotamia.

maria [mariya] (singular **mare** [mahray]) Dark regions mainly on the nearside of the Moon. They are flat plains of basalt formed 3–3·9 thousand million years ago. Dense concentrations of material beneath the maria are known as *mascons*.

Mariana Islands *p.582*

Marianas Trench An oceanic trench off the I of Guam and the N Marianas Is, Pacific Ocean. Its deepest point, Challenger Deep, 11 040 m/36 220 ft, is the Earth's maximum ocean depth.

Maria Theresa (1717–80) Archduchess of Austria, Queen of Hungary and Bohemia (1740–80), born in Vienna, the daughter of Emperor Charles VI. Her Habsburg claim led to the War of the Austrian Succession. In 1741 she received the Hungarian crown,

Mariana Islands

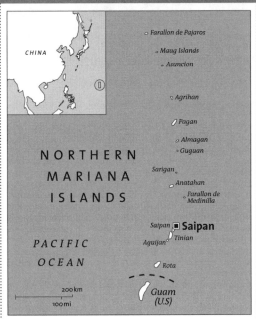

☐ International Airport

in full **Commonwealth of the Northern Mariana Islands** pop (2000e) 72 000; area 471 km²/182 sq mi. Group of 14 islands in the NW Pacific, c.2400 km/1500 mi E of the Philippines; capital, Saipan; mainly volcanic (three still active); includes Saipan, Tinian, Rota, Pagan, Guguan; held by the USA under UN mandate after World War 2 as part of the US Trust Territory of the Pacific Is, 1947–78; self-governing commonwealth of the USA, 1978–90; trusteeship ended 1990; tourism, sugar cane, coconuts, coffee.

and in 1745 her husband was elected Holy Roman Emperor. Military conflict was renewed in the Seven Years' War, and by 1763 she was finally forced to recognize the status quo of 1756.
mariculture The cultivation of marine fish, shellfish, and algae; distinguished from **aquaculture**, which includes both freshwater and saltwater organisms. Practices vary from raising fish, shellfish, and algae in protected enclosures to releasing salmon from hatcheries in the hope of catching them years later when they return to the same waters to spawn.
Marie Antoinette (Josèphe Jeanne) (1755–93) Queen of France, born in Vienna, the daughter of Maria Theresa and Francis I, and sister of Leopold II. She was married to the Dauphin, afterwards Louis XVI (1770), to strengthen the Franco-Austrian alliance, and exerted a growing influence over him. She aroused criticism by her extravagance and opposition to reform, and helped to alienate the monarchy from the people. After the king's execution, she was arraigned before the Tribunal and guillotined.
Marie Celeste An American 103-ft brigantine, found abandoned in the mid-Atlantic in 1872. She had left New York for Genoa, and was encountered by an English ship 400 miles off the Portuguese coast. There were plenty of supplies on board, as well as the crew's personal possessions, but the ship's lifeboat was missing, as were several navigational papers and instruments, suggesting that everyone had left anticipating some

danger, and had been unable to return. Several speculative accounts of the mystery were propounded, and the event continues to intrigue over a century later. The ship continued in service, despite its reputation, sinking off Haiti in 1885.
Marie de France (12th-c) Poet, born in Normandy, France. She spent much of her life in England, where she wrote several verse narratives based on Celtic stories.
Marie de Médicis [maydeesees], Ital **Maria de' Medici** [**may**dichee] (1573–1642) Queen Consort of Henry IV of France, born in Florence, Italy. After her husband's death (1610) she acted as regent for her son (later Louis XIII), but her capricious behaviour led to her confinement in Blois when Louis assumed royal power (1617). Further intrigues led to her exile in 1630.
Marie Louise (1791–1847) Empress of France, born in Vienna, the daughter of Francis I of Austria. She married Napoleon in 1810 (after his divorce from Joséphine), and in 1811 bore him a son, who was created King of Rome and who became Napoleon II.
marigold A name applied to several different species of the daisy family, Compositae.
Mariinsky Theatre of Opera and Ballet *Kirov Ballet*
marijuana or **marihuana** *cannabis*
marimba In modern orchestras and pop groups, a percussion instrument resembling a xylophone, but with a lower compass and played with soft beaters.
Mariner programme A series of spacecraft launched by NASA to begin the exploration of the inner and outer Solar System. The programme included the first planetary flyby (Mariner 2, Venus, Dec 1962), the first mission to Mercury (Mariner 10, Mar 1974, Sep 1974, and Mar 1975), and the first detailed observations of Jovian, Saturnian, and Uranian systems (Mariner *Jupiter-Saturn* – renamed *Voyager* – 1979–86). In 2004 the Mercury Messenger probe was launched successfully, the first US mission to Mercury for more than 30 years. After arriving in 2011 it will orbit the planet for a year to explore its atmosphere, composition, and structure.
Marines Soldiers, under naval command, who nevertheless are equipped and organized to make war on land. Marines have been used as combat forces in their own right, specializing in such operations as commando raiding and amphibious assault.
Marinetti, Filippo (Tommaso) Emilio [marinetee] (1876–1944) Italian writer, born in Alexandria, Egypt. He published the manifesto for Futurism in 1909, his ideas influencing several painters and sculptors.
Marini, Marino [mareenee] (1901–80) Sculptor, born in Pistoia, Italy. He worked mainly in bronze in a traditional figurative style, his favourite subjects including horses and riders, portraits, and dancers.
Marino, Dan [mareenoh] (1961–) Player of American football, born in Pittsburgh, PA. An outstanding quarterback with the Miami Dolphins, in the 1984 season he gained 5084 yards passing to create a National Football League record. He announced his retirement in 2000, and was elected to the NFL Hall of Fame in 2005.
marionettes *puppetry*
Maritain, Jacques [mareetĩ] (1882–1973) Catholic philosopher and diplomat, born in Paris. His philosophical writings include *Les degrés du savoir* (1932, The Degrees of Knowledge), but he is best known outside France for his many writings on art, politics, and history.
Maritime Trust A national organization in the UK to restore, maintain, and display ships of historic or technical importance. It was set up in 1969, on the initiative of Prince Philip.
Mariupol [mariupol], formerly **Zhdanov** 47°05N 37°34E, pop (2000e) 512 000. Seaport in Ukraine, at the mouth of R Kalmius; founded, 1779; airfield; railway; noted mud-bath resort.
Marius, Gaius (c.157–86 BC) Roman general and politician, born in Arpinum. Famous for his victories over Jugurtha (105 BC), the

Teutones (102 BC), and the Cimbri (101 BC), it was by his army reforms that he made his greatest impact on the state. His final years were dominated by his rivalry with Sulla.

Marivaux, Pierre (Carlet de Chamblain de) [mareevoh] (1688–1763) Playwright, born in Paris. He wrote many comedies on romantic themes, such as *Le Jeu de l'amour et du hasard* (1730, The Game of Love and Chance). His affected style, full of witty plays on words, came to be known as 'Marivaudage'.

marjoram [mah(r)joram] A somewhat bushy perennial (*Origanum vulgare*), native to Europe, the Mediterranean, and Asia; flowers small, 2-lipped, white or purplish-pink, in dense spikes. It is cultivated as a culinary herb, often under the name **oregano**. (Family: Labiatae.)

Mark, St, also called **John Mark** (fl.1st-c) Described in the New Testament as 'John whose surname was Mark' (*Acts* 12.12, 25), and a helper of the apostles Barnabas and Paul during their first missionary journey. He is often considered the Mark who is accredited in 2nd-c traditions with the writing of the second Gospel. Feast day 25 April.

Mark, Gospel according to The second book of the New Testament canon, the shortest of the four gospels; anonymous, but traditionally attributed to John Mark. It places relatively greater emphasis on Jesus's miracle-working, opposers, and death. The Gospel begins abruptly, and may have ended equally abruptly, since the disputed stories of the resurrection appearances in *Mark* 16.9–20 are likely to be a late addition.

Mark Antony *Antonius, Marcus*

Markarian galaxy *galaxy*

market economy An economic system where prices, wages, and what is made and sold are determined by market forces of supply and demand, with no state interference. The contrast is with a *command economy*, where the state takes all economic decisions.

market gardening The intensive production of horticultural crops on smallholdings, especially fruit and vegetables for local markets. It may incorporate pick-your-own enterprises, where labour is scarce.

marketing The management of a business with the customer in mind. It aims to identify a market where a potential exists for profitable business, and to take the necessary steps to satisfy that market by careful planning of the 'marketing mix' or the 'Four Ps': product, price, place, and promotion (including advertising).

marketing board A statutory body which has the power to control some aspect(s) of production, processing, or marketing for a specific commodity. Most frequently used for agricultural commodities, it is particularly common in North America.

market socialism A variant of socialism which seeks to marry the benefits of the market system with those of socialism and thus avoid the negative aspects of both. It is associated with the Polish economist Oskar Lange (1904–65).

markhor [mah(r)kaw(r)] A wild goat (*Capra falconeri*) native to the mountains of S Asia; the largest goat; long horns extremely thick, close (or joined) at base, with sharp spiral ridge around outside.

Markievicz, Constance (Georgine), Countess [mah(r)kyayvich], *née* **Gore-Booth** (1868–1927) Irish nationalist, born in London, married to the Polish **Count Casimir Markievicz**. She fought in the Easter Rising (1916), and was sentenced to death but reprieved. Elected the first British woman MP in 1918, she did not take her seat.

Markova, Dame Alicia [mah(r)kova], originally **Lilian Alicia Marks** (1910–2004) Ballerina, born in London. She joined Diaghilev's Ballets Russes company in 1924 and became well known for her appearances with Sadler's Wells (later, The Royal Ballet) and the London Festival Ballet (now the English National Bal-

let). She retired in 1963 and became a director of the Metropolitan Opera Ballet (1963–9).

Markov chain In mathematics, a chain of events in which the probability of moving from one state to another depends on the existing state. The notion is named after the Soviet mathematician Andrey Andreyevich Markov (1856–1922).

Markowitz, Harry M [mah(r)kovits] (1927–) Economist, born in Chicago, IL. He shared the 1990 Nobel Prize for Economics for developing the theory of the rational behaviour involved in portfolio selection under uncertainty.

Marks (of Broughton), Simon Marks, Baron (1888–1964) Businessman, born in Leeds, West Yorkshire. In 1907 he inherited the 60 Marks and Spencer 'penny bazaars', which his father Michael had built up from 1884. In collaboration with Israel (later Lord) Sieff (1899–1972), his brother-in-law, he developed Marks and Spencer into a major retail chain, the 'St Michael' brand label becoming a guarantee of high quality at a reasonable price.

marl Carbonate-rich clay deposits formed by the weathering of impure limestones.

Marlborough, John Churchill, 1st Duke of [mah(r)lbruh] (1650–1722) English general, born in Ashe, Devon. In 1678 he married Sarah Jennings (1660–1744), a close friend and attendant of Princess Anne, through whom he obtained advancement. He commanded the British forces in the War of the Spanish Succession, winning several great victories – Donauwörth and Blenheim (1704), Ramillies (1706), Oudenaarde and the capture of Lille (1708) – for which he was richly rewarded with Blenheim Palace and a dukedom. Forced by political interests to align himself with the Whig war party (1708), his influence waned with theirs after 1710. He was dismissed on charges of embezzling, and left England until the accession of George I (1714), when he was restored to his former offices.

Marley, Bob, popular name of **Robert Nesta Marley** (1945–81) Singer, guitarist, and composer of reggae music, born near Kingston, Jamaica. With his band, **the Wailers**, he popularized reggae in the 1970s. He was a disciple of Rastafarianism.

marlin Any of several large, fast-swimming, highly agile billfishes widespread in warm seas; length up to 4.5 m/14³⁄₄ ft; highly prized as sport fish. (Genera: *Makaira*, *Tetrapturus*. Family: Istiophoridae.)

Marlowe, Christopher (1564–93) Playwright and poet, born in Canterbury, Kent. He was the most significant of Shakespeare's predecessors in English drama. His *Tamburlaine the Great* (c.1587) shows his discovery of the strength and variety of blank verse, and this was followed by *The Jew of Malta* (c.1590), *The Tragical History of Dr Faustus* (c.1592), partly written by others, and *Edward II* (c.1592). He led an irregular life, and was fatally stabbed at Deptford in a tavern brawl.

Marmara [mah(r)mara] or **Marmora, Sea of**, Turkish **Marmara Denizi**, ancient **Propontis** area 11 474 km²/4429 sq mi. Sea in NW Turkey, between Europe (N) and Asia (S); connected (E) with the Black Sea through the Bosporus and (W) with the Aegean Sea through the Dardanelles; length, c.200 km/125 mi.

Marmes Man Prehistoric human remains found in 1965 on R J Marmes's ranch in Washington, USA. About 11 000 years old, they rank as early evidence for the peopling of North America from E Asia.

marmoset [mah(r)moset] A monkey-like primate, native to South America; thick fur, long tail; thumb not opposable; nails long, curved, pointed. (Family: Callitrichidae, 17 species.)

marmot [mah(r)mot] A large, ground-dwelling squirrel native to Europe, Asia, and North America; length, c.750 mm/30 in; lives in burrows; hibernates for up to 9 months. (Genus: *Marmota*, 11 species.)

Marne, Battle of the (1914) A battle early in World War 1, in which General Joffre's French armies and the British Expeditionary

Force halted German forces which had crossed the Marne, thus ending German hopes of a swift victory.

Marne, River, ancient **Matrona** River in C France rising in the Langres Plateau; meets the R Seine near Paris; length 525 km/ 326 mi; scene of two major battles in World War 1 (1914, 1918).

Maronite Church A Christian community originating in Syria in the 7th-c, claiming origin from St Maro (d.407). Condemned for its Monothelite beliefs in 680, the Church survived in Syria and elsewhere, and since 1182 has been in communion with the Roman Catholic Church.

Marprelate Tracts Seven pamphlets covertly published in London, 1587–9. The pseudonymous author, 'Martin Marprelate', satirized the Elizabethan Church and bishops, and favoured a Presbyterian system. The Tracts led to statutes against dissenting sects and sedition (1593).

Marquesas Islands [mah(r)kaysaz], Fr **Iles Marquises** pop (2000e) 9300; area 1189 km²/459 sq mi. Mountainous, wooded volcanic island group of French Polynesia, 1184 km/736 mi NE of Tahiti; includes Nuku Hiva (where Herman Melville lived), and Hiva Oa (where Gauguin painted); acquired by France, 1842; chief settlement, Taiohae (Hiva Oa).

marquess or **marquis** In the UK, a nobleman holding a title in the second rank of the peerage. The word (from Latin *Marchio*) originally denoted a commander of a march, or frontier area. The wife of a marquess is a **marchioness**.

marquetry Veneers (thin sheets of highly polished woods of different colours) applied to furniture in ornamental patterns. A popular technique throughout W Europe in the later 17th–18th-c, the finest examples were by French cabinetmakers of the reigns of Louis XIV, XV, and XVI. **Parquetry** is marquetry arranged in geometrical patterns, popular in England in the second half of the 17th-c.

Márquez, Gabriel (Gabo) García [mah(r)kes] (1928–) Novelist, born in Aracataca, Colombia. His best-known work is *Cien años de soledad* (1967, One Hundred Years of Solitude). Later works include *El amor en los tiempos del cólera* (1985, Love in a Time of Cholera) and *Memories of My Melancholy Whores* (2004). He received the Nobel Prize for Literature in 1982.

marquis *marquess*

Marr, Andrew (1959–) Journalist, broadcaster, and writer, born in Glasgow. He studied at Cambridge and joined *The Scotsman* newspaper as a trainee business reporter in 1981. He later became political editor at *The Economist* (1988–92), then joined *The Independent* as chief political commentator (1992) and was promoted to editor in 1996. In 1998 he became columnist for *The Express* and *The Observer* before being appointed BBC political editor (2000–5). He has presented *Start the Week* for Radio 4 since 2002, and in 2005 he became host of *Sunday AM* on BBC 1.

Marrakesh or **Marrakech** [marakesh] 31°49N 8°00W, pop (2000e) 640 000. Second largest city in Morocco; one of Morocco's four imperial cities, founded in 1062; airport; railway; university; Medina, a world heritage site.

marram grass A tough perennial (*Ammophila arenaria*) with creeping rhizomes, native to coasts of W Europe; leaf-blades inrolled, panicles spike-like. It is often planted on dunes as a sand-binder. (Family: Gramineae.)

marriage In anthropology, the legitimate long-term mating arrangement institutionalized in a community. If a union is called marriage, this implies that husband and wife have recognized claims over their partners; and it renders the children born of such a union legitimate heirs to both parents. Marriage also creates relationships of affinity between a person and his or her spouse's relatives. In many parts of the world a man may legitimately marry more than one wife (*polygyny*), but it is very unusual for a woman to be permitted more than one husband

(*polyandry*). Same-sex unions (*civil unions* or *partnerships*) are now legal in several European countries.

marrow (anatomy) *bone marrow*

marrow (botany) A trailing or climbing vine (*Cucurbita pepo*) native to America, long cultivated as a vegetable; flowers yellow, 12·5 cm/5 in diameter, funnel-shaped; fruit up to 90 cm/ 3 ft or more long, cylindrical, oval, or round; rind green or yellow, with thick flesh surrounding numerous seeds. (Family: Cucurbitaceae.)

Marryat, Frederick (1792–1848) Naval officer and novelist, born in London. He wrote a series of novels on sea life, notably *Peter Simple* (1833) and *Mr Midshipman Easy* (1836). He later wrote stories for children, notably *The Children of the New Forest* (1847).

Mars (astronomy) The fourth major planet from the Sun; the outermost of the terrestrial-type planets, with an eccentric orbit at a mean distance of 1·52 AU, and a diameter about half that of Earth. Its basic planetary characteristics are: mass $6·42 \times 10^{23}$ kg; equatorial radius 3397 km/2111 mi; mean density 3·93 g/cm³; equatorial gravity 372 cm/s²; day (sidereal) 24 h 37 min 22 s; year 687 days; obliquity 25°11'; orbital eccentricity 0·093. A characteristically red planet, it has been the subject of popular interest as a possible abode of life. There are two small natural satellites, Phobos and Deimos. Modern understanding dates back to the first spacecraft flyby of the planet in 1965 (NASA's Mariner 4) with later knowledge derived from Mariners 6 and 7, from the first planetary orbiter Mariner 9, from Viking landers and orbiters, and a series of orbiters and landers beginning with Mars Global Surveyor and the Pathfinder lander (with the Sojourner rover) which arrived in 1997, and continuing (after several failed missions) with the Mars Exploration Rovers (Spirit and Opportunity) in Jan 2004. It is a dry, cold planet with a thin, 95% carbon dioxide atmosphere. The atmospheric circulation is marked by annual episodes of violent dust-storm activity. There is a complex surface of cratered uplands, lowland plains, and massive volcanic regions. A variety of channel-like features (the 'canals') are observed. Viking lander soil analysis revealed no organic material, and indicates that the soil/atmospheric chemistry destroys organics. In 2004, the Mars Exploration Rover Opportunity revealed that rocks at its landing site were once in contact with substantial amounts of liquid water, suggesting that Mars had the right conditions to support life at some time in its history.

Mars (mythology) The Roman god of war, second only to Jupiter. The month of March is named after him.

Marseille [mah(r)say], also Eng **Marseilles**, ancient **Massilia** 43°18N 5°23E, pop (2000e) 837 000. Second largest city in France and leading port of the Mediterranean; founded c.600 BC by Greeks; Old Port (Vieux Port) on a rocky peninsula; airport; railway; metro; archbishopric; university; two cathedrals (11th–12th-c, 1852–93).

Mars Express mission A spacecraft mission to Mars undertaken by the European Space Agency launched by a Soyuz rocket in June 2003. The mission included a remote sensing orbiter and a small lander named Beagle 2. It had the goal of recovering some of the orbital science objectives of the Russian-European Mars '96 mission that was lost at launch. Beagle 2 was scheduled to reach Mars on 25 December 2003 but by February 2004 no signal had been received from the lander to indicate a successsful landing and it was classed as lost. The spacecraft is expected to orbit Mars until 2009 and deployed *Marsis*, a water-detecting radar array, in mid-2005.

Marsh, Dame Ngaio (Edith) [niyoh] (1899–1982) Detective-story writer, born in Christchurch, New Zealand. Her novels and short stories, featuring Superintendent Roderick Alleyn of Scotland

Yard, include *Vintage Murder* (1937), and *Black as he's Painted* (1974).

Marshall, Barry (1951–) Microbiologist, born in Kalgoorlie, Western Australia. He studied at the University of Western Australia (1968–74) and later held senior posts at the University of Virginia, USA (1986–96) before joining the University of Western Australia as clinical professor of medicine (1997) and microbiology (1999). In 2003 he was appointed NHMRC Senior Principal Research Fellow. In 2005 he shared the Nobel Prize for Physiology or Medicine with Robin Warren for their discovery of the bacterium *Helicobacter pylori* and its role in gastritis and peptic ulcer disease.

Marshall, George C(atlett) (1880–1959) US general and statesman, born in Uniontown, PA. He became secretary of state (1947–9) and originated the Marshall Aid plan for the postwar reconstruction of Europe. He was awarded the Nobel Peace Prize in 1953.

Marshall, John (1755–1835) Jurist, born in Germantown, VA, the foremost chief justice in the history of the US Supreme Court. He became Chief Justice of the USA (1801–35), during which time he dominated the Supreme Court, and established the US doctrine of judicial review of federal and state legislation.

Marshall, Thurgood (1908–93) Judge, born in Baltimore, MD. As an attorney he won a historic victory in the case of *Brown* v. *Board of Education of Topeka* (1954) which declared that racial segregation in public schools was unconstitutional. He served as US solicitor general (1965–7), before becoming the first African-American justice of the US Supreme Court (1967–91).

Marshall Islands *p.586*

marsh gas *methane*

marsh marigold *kingcup*

Mars Observer project A US Mars orbiter spacecraft launched in September 1992. Contact with the spacecraft was lost in August 1993, just before the scheduled Mars orbit insertion. It was followed by the Surveyor programme.

Mars programme A Soviet series of robotic Mars exploration projects (1962–74), including flybys, orbiters, and hard landers. It was less successful than other Soviet planetary missions. The Soviets resumed Mars exploration in 1988. Two more missions in the series were planned to continue by Russia after the breakup of the Soviet Union, but the programme suffered a serious set-back after a major failure during a launch in 1996.

Mars Surveyor programme A NASA-led programme of Mars exploration missions of relatively low cost and mass, initiated after the in-flight failure of Mars Observer, and intended to provide a decade-long series of orbital and landed spacecraft beginning with launches in 1996. Mars Odyssey entered orbit around Mars in October 2001, and Mars Express in December 2003. NASA's Mars Spirit rover landed on Mars in January 2004 and its twin rover, Opportunity, was deployed soon after. The Mars Reconnaissance Orbiter (MRO) was launched in August 2005 on a two-year mission to map and find water on the planet.

Marston, John (1576–1634) Playwright, born in Wardington, Oxfordshire. His plays include *The Malcontent* (1604), and *Eastward Ho!* (1605), a satirical comedy written in conjunction with Chapman and Jonson.

Marston Moor, Battle of (1644) A major conflict in the English Civil War, in which parliamentary forces under Oliver Cromwell defeated royalist forces led by Prince Rupert. The defeat led to the virtual collapse of Charles I's cause in the N.

marsupial A mammal, native to Australasia and the New World; young often develop in a pouch which opens forwards (climbing species) or backwards (burrowing species). (Order: Marsupialia, 266 species.)

Martello towers [mah(r)teloh] Small circular forts with thick walls. Many were erected on the S and SE coast of England in the early 19th-c to provide observation posts and defence against a projected French invasion. The name comes from Cape Mortella, Corsica, where such a tower was captured by a British Fleet in 1794.

marten A mammal of genus *Martes* (7 species), native to Europe, Asia, and North America; solid body with sharp nose and long bushy tail. (Family: Mustelidae.)

Martha's Vineyard Island in the Atlantic off the SE coast of Massachusetts, USA; area 280 km²/108 sq mi; chief town, Edgartown; summer resort; so called because the first English settlers found an abundance of wild grapes growing here.

Martial, in full **Marcus Valerius Martialis** (c.40–c.104) Latin poet and epigrammatist, born in Spain. He is remembered for his 12 books of epigrams, mainly satirical comments on contemporary events and society.

martial arts Styles of armed or unarmed combat developed in the East. In modern times most of these arts have developed into popular sports in the West.

martial law The imposition of military rule on the civilian population, either by the leader of an occupying army, or by a territory's own government. In the latter case, it most commonly occurs after there has been a military coup or during a period of colonial rule.

Martin, St (c.316–c.400) Patron saint of France, born in Sabaria, Pannonia. He founded the first monastery near Poitiers c.360, and in 371–2 was made Bishop of Tours. Feast day 11 (W) or 12 November (E).

Martin, Steve (1945–) Film actor, born in Waco, TX. He made his film debut in *The Absent Minded Waiter* (1977), which received an Oscar nomination for best short film. An inspired performance of lunacy in *All Of Me* (1984) brought him a New York Film Critics' Best Actor Award. Later films include *Parenthood* (1989), *Father of the Bride* and its sequel (1991, 1995), *Bringing Down the House* (2003), and *The Pink Panther* (2006).

martin A bird of the swallow family. Those with short tails are usually called 'martins', those with long tails 'swallows'. The names are not applied consistently. (Family: Hirundinidae 23 species.)

Martín de Porres, St [pohres] (1579–1639) South American saint, who spent his entire life in the Dominican Order in Lima, Peru, ministering to the sick and poor. He was canonized in 1962. Feast day 3 November.

Martin du Gard, Roger [mah(r)tī dü gah(r)] (1881–1958) Novelist, born in Neuilly, France. He is known for his 8-novel series *Les Thibault* (1922–40), dealing with family life during the first decades of the 20th-c. He was awarded the Nobel Prize for Literature in 1937.

Martini, Simone [mah(r)teenee] (c.1284–1344) Painter, born in Siena, Italy. The most important artist of the 14th-c Sienese School, his work is notable for its grace of line and use of colour, as in his 'Annunciation' (Uffizi).

Martinique [mah(r)tineek] pop (2000e) 416 000; area 1079 km²/416 sq mi. Island in the Windward group of the Lesser Antilles, E Caribbean; capital, Fort-de-France; timezone GMT -4; population mainly of African or mixed descent; chief religion, Roman Catholicism; official language, French, with creole widely spoken; unit of currency, the euro; length, 61 km/38 mi; width, 24 km/15 mi; highest point, Mt Pelée (1397 m/4583 ft); tropical climate with high humidity; visited by Columbus, 1502; French colony, 1635; overseas department of France, 1946; administered by a commissioner-general and a Regional Council; economy based largely on agriculture.

Martin Luther King Day In the USA, the third Monday in January; a federal public holiday in honour of the civil rights leader, commemorated in about half of the US states. The date of the celebration varies from state to state.

Martinmas In the UK, the feast of St Martin (11 Nov), a day on

Marshall Islands

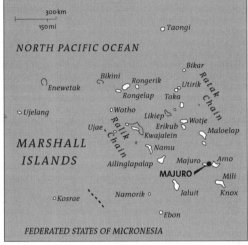

□ International Airport

Timezone GMT +12

Area c.180 km²/70 sq mi

Population total (2002e) 56 600

Status Republic

Date of independence 1986

Capital Delap-Uliga-Darrit (municipality on Majuro Atoll)

Languages Marshallese (Kajin-Majol) (official), English and Japanese also spoken

Ethnic group Micronesian (99%)

Religions Christian (Protestant 90%, Roman Catholic 8%)

Physical features Archipelago in C Pacific Ocean; comprising 34 islands, including Kwajalein and Jaluit, and 870 reefs; two parallel chains of coral atolls, Ratik (E) and Ralik (W), extending c.925 km/800 mi in length; volcanic islands, rise no more than a few metres above sea level.

Climate Hot and humid; wet season (May–Nov); typhoon season (Dec–Mar); average annual temperature 27°C.

Currency 1 US Dollar (USD) = 100 cents

Economy Farming; fishing; tropical agriculture; coconuts, tomatoes, melons, breadfruit.

GDP (2001e) $115 mn, per capita $1600

History Explored by the Spanish, 1529; part of UN Trust Territory of the Pacific, 1949–78, administered by the USA; US nuclear weapon tests held on Bikini and Eniwetak atolls, 1946–62; self-governing republic, 1979; compact of free association with the USA in 1986 with US recognizing independence; trusteeship ended, 1990; governed by a President elected by a Parliament.

Head of State/Government
1979–96 Amata Kabua
1996–7 Kunio Lemari *Acting*
1997–2000 Imata Kabua
2000– Kessia Note

which traditionally rents were paid, servants hired, and livestock slaughtered for winter salting.

Martinů, Bohuslav [mah(r)tinoo] (1890–1959) Composer, born in Polička, Czech Republic. A prolific composer, his music includes symphonies, concertos, ballets (notably *Ishtar*), and operas.

Marvell, Andrew [mah(r)vl] (1621–78) Poet, politician, and satirist, born in Winestead, Hull. He is remembered for his pastoral and love poems, notably 'To His Coy Mistress'.

Marx, Karl (Heinrich) (1818–83) Founder of modern international communism, born in Trier, Germany, the son of a Jewish lawyer. With Engels as his closest collaborator, he reorganized the Communist League, and in 1848 finalized the *Communist Manifesto*, which attacked the state as the instrument of oppression, and religion and culture as ideologies of the bourgeoisie. In 1849 he settled in London, where he wrote the first volume of his major work, *Das Kapital* (1867, two further volumes, compiled by Engels from Marx's drafts were added posthumously in 1884 and 1894). He died in London.

Marx Brothers Family of film comedians, born in New York City, comprising **Julius** (1895–1977), or **Groucho**; **Leonard** (1891–1961), or **Chico**; **Arthur** (1893–1961), or **Harpo**; and **Herbert** (1901–79), or **Zeppo**. Another brother, **Milton** (?1897–1977), known as **Gummo**, left the act early on. Their main reputation was made in a series of films, such as *Animal Crackers* and *Monkey Business* (both 1932). Zeppo retired from films in 1935. Each had a well-defined stencil: Groucho with his wisecracks; Chico, the pianist with his own technique; and Harpo, the dumb clown and harp maestro. The team broke up in 1949.

Marxism The body of social and political thought informed by the writings of Karl Marx. Much of his writing, especially *Das Kapital*, was concerned with the economic dynamics of capitalist societies, seeing the state as an instrument of class rule supporting private capital and suppressing the masses. This situation would eventually lead to revolution, whereby the working class would seize the state and establish a dictatorship of the proletariat, and class differences would disappear (socialism). This classless society would eventually lead to the withering away of the state, producing a communist society. It is generally recognized that Marx's writings regarding the transformation to socialism and the nature of socialism lacked detail. In consequence, Marxism has attracted a wide range of interpretations by political theorists.

Marxism–Leninism A distinct variant of Marxism formulated by Lenin, who prior to the Bolshevik revolution argued for direct rule by workers and peasants, and advocated direct democracy through the soviets (councils). Leninist principles of a revolutionary vanguard have become the central tenet of all communist parties. Lenin modified Marx's theory of historical materialism, contending that revolutionary opportunities should be seized when they arose, and not when the social and economic conditions of capitalist crisis leading to proletarian revolution existed.

Mary I, Tudor (1516–58) Queen of England and Ireland (1553–8), born in Greenwich, the daughter of Henry VIII by his first wife, Catherine of Aragon. A devout Catholic, on her accession she repealed anti-Catholic legislation, revived Catholic practices, and aimed to cement a Catholic union with Philip II of Spain. These aspirations provoked Wyatt's rebellion, followed by the execution of Jane Grey and the imprisonment of Mary's half-sister, Elizabeth. The burning at the stake of some 300 Protestants earned her the name of 'Bloody Mary' in Protestant hagiography. She died allegedly of cancer.

Mary, Queen of Scots (1542–87) Queen of Scotland (1542–67) and Queen Consort of France (1559–60), born at Linlithgow Palace, West Lothian, daughter of James V of Scotland by his second wife, Mary of Guise. In 1565 she married her cousin, Henry Stewart, Lord Darnley, a grandson of Margaret Tudor, but was soon alienated from him. The murder of Rizzio, her Italian secretary, by Darnley and a group of Protestant nobles in her presence (1566) confirmed her insecurity. The birth of a son, the future James VI, failed to bring a reconciliation. Darnley was mysteriously killed in an explosion at Kirk o' Field (1567); the chief suspect was the Earl of Bothwell, who underwent a mock trial and was acquitted. Mary's involvement is unclear, but she consented to marry Bothwell. The Protestant nobles rose against her; she surrendered at Carberry Hill, and was compelled to abdicate. Placing herself under the protection of Queen Elizabeth, she found herself instead a prisoner for life. Her presence in England gave rise to countless plots to depose Elizabeth and restore Catholicism. Finally, after the Babington conspiracy (1586), she was brought to trial for treason, and executed.

Mary (mother of Jesus), also known as **Our Lady** or **the Blessed Virgin Mary** (?–c.63) Mother of Jesus Christ. In the New Testament she is most prominent in the stories of Jesus's birth (Matthew and Luke), and only occasionally appears in Jesus's ministry. According to the Acts of the Apostles, she remained in Jerusalem during the early years of the Church, and a tradition places her tomb there. The belief that her body was taken up into heaven is celebrated in the festival of the Assumption, defined as Roman Catholic dogma in 1950. Her Immaculate Conception has been a dogma since 1854. Belief in the apparitions of the Virgin at Lourdes, Fatima, and in several other places attracts many thousands of pilgrims each year. In Roman Catholic and Orthodox Christianity, she holds a special place as an intermediary between humankind and God.

Maryland pop (2000e) 5 296 500; area 27 090 km²/10 460 sq mi. State in E USA; the 'Old Line' or 'Free State'; first settlement, 1634, at St Mary's (state capital until 1694); seventh of the original 13 states to ratify the Constitution, 1788; gave up territory for the establishment of the District of Columbia; abolished slavery, 1864; Chesapeake Bay stretches N through the state, almost splitting it in two; highest point Mt Backbone (1024 m/ 3360 ft); capital, Annapolis; major city, Baltimore (85% of the population live in this area); Eastern Shore noted for its scenic beauty.

Mary Magdalene, St [magdalen] (1st-c) New Testament character; *Magdalene* possibly means 'of Magdala', in Galilee. *Luke* 8.2 reports that Jesus exorcized seven evil spirits from her; thereafter she appears only in the narratives of Jesus's passion and resurrection. Feast day 22 July.

Mary Rose A warship built in 1511 for Henry VIII and rebuilt in 1536. In 1545, while in action against the French off Portsmouth, she capsized and sank with the loss of most of her crew. Her remains were salvaged in 1982 in a complex and much-publicized operation, and are now exhibited at Portsmouth.

Masaccio [masachio], originally **Tommaso de Giovanni di Simone Guidi** (1401–28) Painter, born in San Giovanni Valdarno, Italy. A pioneer of Renaissance painting, he worked in Florence, where he executed frescoes in collaboration with Masolino.

Masada [masahda] or **Mezada** A Roman hilltop fortress established 37–31 BC by the Palestinian ruler Herod in barren mountains W of the Dead Sea; within Israel since 1947. Seized by zealots during the First Jewish Revolt in AD 66–70, it was

taken by the Roman army in 73 after a lengthy siege which culminated in the mass suicide of all 400 defenders.

Masai or **Maasai** [masiy] A people of the Rift Valley area of Kenya and Tanzania, speaking a Nilotic language. They are nomadic and semi-nomadic cattle herders.

Masaryk, Tomáš (Garrigue) [masarik] (1850–1937) First president of the Czech Republic (1918–35), born in Hodonin, Czech Republic. While in exile during World War 1 he organized the Czech independence movement.

Mascagni, Pietro [maskanyee] (1863–1945) Composer, born in Livorno, Italy. He is best known for his one-act opera, *Cavalleria Rusticana* (1890).

Mascarene Islands [maskareen], Fr **Archipel des Mascareignes** Island group in the Indian Ocean, 700–800 km/450–500 mi E of Madagascar; named after the 16th-c Portuguese navigator, Mascarenhas.

mascon *maria*

Masefield, John (Edward) (1878–1967) Poet and novelist, born in Ledbury, Herefordshire. His sea poetry includes *Salt Water Ballads* (1902), and his narrative poetry *Reynard the Fox* (1919). He also wrote novels, plays, and works for children, such as *The Box of Delights* (1935). He became poet laureate in 1930.

maser A device which produces microwaves from excited atoms or molecules, devised in 1954 by US physicist Charles Townes and others; the name is an acronym of *microwave amplification by the stimulated emission of radiation*. Masers employ the same physical principles as lasers, but produce lower frequency radiation. They are used as sensitive low-noise amplifiers for radar and satellite communications.

Maseru [maseeroo] 29°19S 27°29E, pop (2000e) 148 000. Capital of Lesotho; on the R Caledon; altitude 1506 m/4941 ft; founded, 1869; airport; railway terminus; university (1964).

Mashhad [mashhad] or **Meshed** 36°16N 59°34E, pop (2000e) 2 021 000. Second largest city in Iran; industrial and trade centre; airport; railway; university (1956).

masochism *sadomasochism*

Masolino (da Panicale) [masohleenoh], originally **Tommaso di Cristoforo Fini** (1383–c.1447) Artist, born in Panicale, Italy. A distinguished early Renaissance painter, he collaborated with Masaccio in the Brancacci chapel.

Mason, James (1909–84) Actor, born in Huddersfield, West Yorkshire. He was nominated for an Oscar for *A Star Is Born* (1954), *Georgy Girl* (1966), and *The Verdict* (1982). Other respected performances from more than 100 films include *Lolita* (1962) and *The Shooting Party* (1984).

Mason–Dixon Line The border between Maryland and Pennsylvania, drawn in 1763–7 by British astronomer Charles Mason (1730–87) and Jeremiah Dixon (1733–79). It is regarded as the boundary between 'the North' and 'the South'.

Masoretes or **Massoretes** [masohreets] (Heb 'transmitters of tradition') Jewish scholars who preserved traditions regarding the text of the Hebrew Bible, especially creating a system of vowel signs to reflect the pronunciation of the Hebrew consonantal text in the 9th–10th-c (the Masoretic Text).

masque A courtly celebration composed of poetry, song, dance, and (usually) elaborate mechanical scenery, unified by a theme or emblematic story. The Royal masques of Tudor and Stuart England are best known for the collaboration of Ben Jonson and Inigo Jones.

mass An intrinsic property of all matter and energy, the source of gravitational field; symbol m, units kg (kilogram). It is perceived as an object's weight (the downward-acting force due to gravity) or its inertia (its reluctance to change its motion). The mass of an object increases with its velocity, according to special relativity.

Mass (Lat *missa*, from *missio* 'dismissal') The sacrament of the Eucharist (Holy Communion) in the Roman Catholic Church and some other churches. Masses perform different functions in the life of the Church, eg a Requiem Mass for the dead, a Nuptial Mass for a marriage.

Massachusetts pop (2000e) 6 349 000; area 21 455 km²/8284 sq mi. New England state in NE USA; the 'Bay State' or 'Old Colony'; third most densely populated state; one of the original states of the Union, sixth to ratify the Constitution, 1788; Pilgrim Fathers settled at Plymouth in 1620; colony of Massachusetts founded 1629; first shots of the War of Independence fired at Lexington in 1775; rises from an indented coastline to a stony, upland interior and gentle, rolling hills to the W; highest point Mt Greylock (1049 m/3442 ft); capital, Boston.

Massawa [masahwa] or **Mitsiwa** 15°37N 39°28E, pop (2000e) 58 900. Seaport in Eritrea; occupied by Italy, 1885; capital of Italian Eritrea until 1897; largely rebuilt after earthquake in 1921; railway; commercial centre; naval base.

Masséna, André [masayna] (1758–1817) Leading French general of the Revolutionary and Napoleonic Wars, born in Nice. He distinguished himself in Napoleon's Italian campaign (1796–7), and defeated the Russians at Zürich (1799). He was forced to retreat in the Iberian Peninsula by Wellington's forces.

mass–energy relation A relationship in physics, stated by Einstein, expressed as $E = mc^2$, where E is energy, c is the velocity of light, and m is mass, as measured for a moving object. It corresponds to the statement that all energy has mass.

Massenet, Jules (Emile Frédéric) [masenay] (1842–1912) Composer, born in Montaud, France. His operas include *Don César de Bazan* (1872) and *Manon* (1884), and he also wrote oratorios, orchestral suites, music for piano, and songs.

Massey, Raymond (Hart) (1896–1983) Actor, born in Toronto, Ontario, Canada. He is best known for his role as Dr Gillespie in the long-running *Dr Kildare* series during the 1960s.

Massif Central [maseef sõtral] Area of ancient rocks in SEC France, occupying about a sixth of the country; generally over 300 m/1000 ft; highest peak, Puy de Sancy in the Monts Dore (1885 m/6184 ft); Millau viaduct over the Tarn valley opened 2004.

Massine, Léonide [maseen], originally **Leonid Fyodorovich Miassin** (1896–1979) Dancer and choreographer, born in Moscow. He was principal dancer and choreographer with Diaghilev (1914–21, 1925–8) and the Ballets Russes de Monte Carlo (1938–43).

Massinger, Philip (1583–1640) Playwright, born near Salisbury, Wiltshire. Much of his work is a collaboration with others, particularly Fletcher. His comedies include *A New Way to Pay Old Debts* (1633).

mass media media

mass number nucleon number

mass spectrometer A machine for measuring the proportions and masses of the atomic species in some sample; invented in 1919 by British scientist Francis Aston (1877–1945). Ions formed from a gaseous sample are passed through a magnetic field, where they are deflected by an amount depending on their mass.

Massys or **Matsys, Quentin** [masees] (c.1466–c.1530) Painter, born in Louvain, Belgium. His pictures are mostly religious, with decided touches of realism. His many portraits include the notable 'Erasmus'.

mast cells Cells with granules containing histamine, heparin, and other chemicals. Tissue injury and infection causes the release of the granular contents, resulting in inflammatory and allergic responses.

mastectomy A surgical procedure involving the removal of all or part of the breast, sometimes including the excision of the associated lymph nodes under the arm. The operation is performed in the treatment of malignant breast tumours.

master An artistic status achieved within the mediaeval guild system. Artists and craftsmen followed several years' apprenticeship before becoming 'masters', through production of a 'masterpiece'. The term **Old Master** is used loosely to refer to any major painter from Giotto to Cézanne, regarded as a model of traditional excellence.

Masters, Edgar Lee (1869–1950) Writer, born in Garnett, KS. He is mainly remembered for his satirical *Spoon River Anthology* (1915), epitaphs in free verse dealing with the lives of people in the Midwest.

Masters, John (1914–83) Writer and soldier, born in Calcutta, India. After Indian independence he moved to the USA and wrote a series of novels about the Savage family in India. *Nightrunners of Bengal* (1951) and *Bhowani Junction* (1953) became immediate best-sellers. He also wrote a trilogy about World War 1, *Loss of Eden: Now God Be Thanked* (1979).

Masters The popular name for the **US Masters** golf tournament, played every April over four rounds of the course at Augusta, GA, USA. An invitational event, only the world's top players take part. The first Masters was in 1934.

Masters and Johnson Human sexuality researchers and authors: **William H(owell) Masters** (1915–2001), born in Cleveland, OH, and **Virginia E(shelman) Johnson** (1925–), born in Springfield, MO. In 1964 they established the Reproductive Biology Research Foundation, where the study of sexual intercourse was carried out using volunteer subjects under laboratory conditions. *Human Sexual Response* (1966), became an international best-seller. They married in 1971 and divorced in 1992.

mastic An evergreen shrub, sometimes a small tree (*Pistacia lentiscus*) growing to 8 m/26 ft, native to the Mediterranean region; flowers tiny, in dense heads; fruits round, red becoming black, very aromatic. The mastic resin is used both in medicine and as a varnish sealant. (Family: Anacardiaceae.)

mastiff A large domestic dog; originally any large dog, but now restricted to three breeds: the **Old English mastiff** (short pale coat, long legs and tail, heavy head with short pendulous ears, deep muzzle and jowls), the rare **Tibetan mastiff**, and the **Japanese tosa**.

mastodon A browsing, elephant-like mammal found in woodland savannahs during the Miocene epoch, almost worldwide in distribution; became extinct in the Pleistocene epoch. (Order: Proboscidea.)

mastoid process The large bony prominence behind the ear. It is part of the temporal bone, and contains air cells (**mastoid air cells**) which communicate with the middle ear cavity.

Mastroianni, Marcello [mastroyahnee] (1924–96) Film actor, born in Fontana Liri, Italy. His major films included *La dolce vita* (1959, The Sweet Life) and *Otto e Mezzo* (1963, 8½). He received Oscar nominations for *Divorzio all'italiano* (1962, Divorce, Italian Style), *Una giornata particolare* (1977, A Special Day), and *Oci ciornie* (1987, Dark Eyes).

Matabeleland [matabeeleeland] Region of W and S Zimbabwe; named after the Matabele Bantu; acquired by the British South Africa Company, 1889; part of Southern Rhodesia, 1923; chief town, Bulawayo.

Mata Hari [mahta hahree], (Malay 'sun'), pseudonym of **Margaretha Geertruide MacLeod**, *née* **Zelle** (1876–1917) Dancer and spy, born in Leeuwarden, The Netherlands. She became a dancer in Paris and adopted her stage name. Found guilty of espionage for the Germans during World War 1, she was shot by the French in Paris.

matamata [matamata] A side-necked turtle from South America; large head shaped like an arrowhead; shell with a jagged irregular surface. (*Chelus fimbriatus*. Family: Chelidae.)

materialism The philosophical view that everything is composed exclusively of physical constituents located in space and time. Materialists thus deny the independent existence of minds, mental states, spirit, or abstract entities such as universals and numbers.

materials science The study of the engineering properties of materials, as dictated by their microscopic structure. It has been responsible for the development of several new materials, such as conducting rubber, metallic glasses, and the fibreglass and carbon fibre composites used in sports equipment.

mathematical logic The application of mathematical rigour and symbolic techniques to the study of logic – for example, the development of formal languages and axiom systems for constructing logical proofs.

mathematics A systematic body of knowledge built on certain axioms and assumptions, principally relating to numbers and spatial relationships. Abstract ideas in mathematics may be classified as **pure mathematics**, and their applications as **applied mathematics**; but many abstract ideas (eg set theory) have had practical applications (eg electrical networks) and many practical problems (eg the fair distribution of lottery prizes) have stimulated abstract ideas (the concept of a random number).

Mather, Cotton [mather] (1663–1728) Colonial minister, born in Boston, MA. He reported on American botany, and was one of the earliest New England historians. His reputation suffered because of his involvement in the Salem witchcraft trials of 1692.

Mather, John C (1946–) Astrophysicist, born in Roanoke, VA. He studied at Swarthmore College (1968) and the University of California, Berkeley (1974), then later joined the NASA Goddard Space Flight Center in Greenbelt, MD, to head the Cosmic Background Explorer (COBE) mission. He has been a Goddard Fellow since 1994 and currently serves as senior project scientist and chair of the science working group for the James Webb Space Telescope (JWST) mission. In 2006 he shared the Nobel Prize for Physics with George Smoot for 'their discovery of the blackbody form and anisotropy of the cosmic microwave background radiation'.

Mathias, William (James) (1934–92) Composer, born in Whitland, Pembrokeshire. His works include an opera *The Servants* (1980), two symphonies, several concertos, and the anthem written for the wedding ceremony of the Prince and Princess of Wales (1981).

Matilda of Flanders (c.1031–83) Queen consort of William I of England, born in Flanders, France. She married William in 1050 in Normandy, and during his absences in England the duchy of Normandy was under her regency, with the aid of their son, Robert Curthose.

Matisse, Henri (Emile Benoît) [matees] (1869–1954) Painter, born in Le Cateau, France. The leader of the *Fauves*, his most characteristic paintings display a bold use of brilliant areas of primary colour, organized within a rhythmic two-dimensional design.

Matlock 53°08N 1°32W; pop (2000e) 14 500. County town in Derbyshire, C England; railway; formerly a spa town.

Mato Grosso [matoh grosoh], formerly **Matto Grosso** pop (2000e) 2 330 000; area 881 000 km²/340 000 sq mi. State in CW Brazil; half the area under forest; capital, Cuiabá.

matrilineal descent A descent system in which family or clan membership, inheritance, and succession is traced through the mother's daughters. One of the most famous examples was found on the Trobriand Is, New Guinea.

Matsys, Quentin *Massys, Quentin*

matter The substances of which everything in the universe is composed. At one level, this is taken to mean atoms bound together into bulk matter. At the ultimate level, matter means the spin $\frac{1}{2}$ particles such as electrons and quarks, bound together by spin 1 force particles such as photons and gluons.

Matterhorn, Fr **Mont Cervin**, Ital **Monte Cervino** 45°59N 7°39E. Mountain peak in Switzerland, in the Pennine Alps; height, 4478 m/14 691 ft; first climbed by British mountaineer Edward Whymper in 1865.

Matthau, Walter [matow], originally **Walter Matthow** (1920–2000) US film actor, born in New York City. The son of Russian-Jewish immigrants, he began working in Yiddish theatre, then gained recognition on Broadway. His films include *The Odd Couple* (1968), *Hello Dolly* (1969), *Cactus Flower* (1969), *The Odd Couple II* (1998), and *Hanging Up* (2000).

Matthew, St (1st-c) One of the 12 apostles, a tax gatherer before becoming a disciple of Jesus. According to tradition he was the author of the first Gospel, a missionary to the Hebrews, and suffered martyrdom. Feast day 22 July

Matthew Paris (c.1200–59) Chronicler and Benedictine monk. *Chronica Majora* gives the fullest available account of events in England between 1236 and 1259.

Matthews, Sir Stanley (1915–2000) Footballer, born in Hanley, Staffordshire. He played for Stoke City and Blackpool, and 54 times for England. He was twice Footballer of the Year (1948, 1963), and the inaugural winner of the European Footballer of the Year award in 1956.

Matthias I, known as **Matthew Corvinus**, Hung **Mátyás Corvin** (c.1443–90) King of Hungary (1458–90), born in Kolozsvár (Cluj-Napoca), Romania, the second son of János Hunyady. He drove back the Turks, and considerably extended his territory, capturing Vienna in 1485. He greatly encouraged arts and industry, and reformed finances and justice.

Maudling, Reginald (1917–79) British Conservative statesman, born in London. His posts included minister of supply (1955–7), paymaster-general (1957–9), President of the Board of Trade (1959–61), colonial secretary (1961–2), and Chancellor of the Exchequer (1962–4). He resigned as home secretary in 1972, implicated in the bankruptcy proceedings of architect John Poulson.

Maugham, W(illiam) Somerset [mawm] (1874–1965) Writer, born in Paris. He published his successful first novel, the lurid *Liza of Lambeth*, in 1897. Later works include the novels *Of Human Bondage* (1915), and the plays *The Moon and Sixpence* (1919), *Cakes and Ale* (1930), and *The Razor's Edge* (1945). He is best known for his short stories, several of which were filmed, such as *Quartet* (1949).

Maui [mowee] pop (2000e) 128 100; area 1885 km²/728 sq mi. Second largest island of the US state of Hawaii; chief town, Wailuku; rises to 3055 m/10 023 ft at Haleakala.

Mau Mau A secret society which led a revolt of the Kikuyu people of Kenya in the 1950s. British troops were deployed in its suppression, but the cost convinced Britain that decolonization was imperative.

Mauna Kea [mowna kaya] 19°50N 155°28W. Dormant volcano in NC Hawaii, USA; rises to 4201 m/13 783 ft; several large telescopes at the summit.

Mauna Loa [mowna loha] 19°28N 155°35W. Active volcano in C Hawaii, USA; rises to 4169 m/13 678 ft; last erupted 1984.

Maundy Thursday [mawndee] The Thursday before Easter, so called from Latin *mandatum*, 'commandment', the first word of the anthem traditionally sung on that day; in memory of Christ's washing his disciples' feet (*John* 13.4–10). In Britain, special money (**Maundy money**) is given by the sovereign to the same number of elderly poor people as there are years in the sovereign's age.

Maupassant, (Henri René Albert) Guy de [mohpasã] (1850–93) Novelist and short-story writer, born near Dieppe, France. He joined the Naturalist group led by Zola. His first success, *Boule de suif* (1880, Ball of Fat), was followed by a decade in which he wrote c.300 short stories, as well as such novels as *Une Vie* (1883, trans A Woman's Life) and *Bel-Ami* (1885).

Maupertuis, Pierre Louis Moreau de [mohpertwee] (1698–1759) Astronomer and mathematician, born in St Malo, France. He is best known for his 'principle of least action' in explaining the paths of moving bodies.

Mauresmo, Amelie [moresmoh] (1979–) Tennis player, born in Laye, France. She turned professional in 1997 and gained her first grand-slam singles title at the 2006 Australian Open. Later that year she became the first Frenchwoman for 81 years to win the Wimbledon singles crown when she beat number 1 seed Justine Henin-Hardenne. She began 2007 ranked world number 3.

Mauriac, François [mohriak] (1885–1970) Novelist, born in Bordeaux, France. He is regarded as the leading French Catholic novelist of the 20th-c, dealing with the themes of temptation, sin, and redemption. His main works include the novels *Le Baiser au lépreux* (1922, The Kiss to the Leper) and *Thérèse Desqueyroux* (1927), and his play *Asmodée* (1938). He received the 1952 Nobel Prize for Literature.

Maurice, Prinz van Oranje, Graaf van Nassau (Prince of Orange, Count of Nassau) (1567–1625) Stadtholder of the United Provinces of the Netherlands, born in Dillenburg, the son of William the Silent. He became captain-general of the armies of the United Provinces during their War of Independence from Spain. He checked the Spanish advance, and by his steady offensive (1590–1606) liberated the N provinces of the Netherlands.

Maurists [mawrists] A French Benedictine congregation of St Maur, founded in the early 17th-c. Suspected of being influenced by Jansenism, they were eventually dissolved in 1818.

Mauritania *p.591*

Mauritius *p.592*

Maurois, André [mohrwah], pseudonym of **Emile Herzog** (1885–1967) Writer and biographer, born in Elbeuf, France. His many works include studies of Shelley (1923), Disraeli (1927), Voltaire (1935), and Proust (1949).

mausoleum *Gur Amir; Lenin Mausoleum; Mausolus, Tomb of; Mount Li; Taj Mahal*

Mausolus, Tomb of [mowzolus] A huge, ornate tomb built at Halicarnassus in SW Asia Minor around 350 BC by Mausolus's widow, Queen Artemisia II of Caria (reigned c.353–350 BC).

Maxim, Sir Hiram (Stevens) (1840–1916) Inventor, born in Sangersville, ME. He is best known for the invention of the first fully automatic machine-gun (1883).

Maximilian, Ferdinand Joseph (1832–67) Emperor of Mexico (1864–7), born in Vienna, the younger brother of Emperor Francis Joseph I. In 1863, he accepted the offer of the crown of Mexico, supported by France; but when Napoleon III withdrew his troops, he refused to abdicate, and was executed.

Maxwell, James C(lerk) (1831–79) Physicist, born in Edinburgh. In 1873 he published his great *Treatise on Electricity and Magnetism*, which treats mathematically Faraday's theory of electrical and magnetic forces. His greatest work was his theory of electromagnetic radiation, which established him as the leading theoretical physicist of the century.

Maxwell, (Ian) Robert, originally **Ludvik Hoch** (1923–91) Publisher and politician, born in Slatinske Dòly, Czech Republic. He founded the Pergamon Press, became a Labour MP (1964–70), and had many business interests. Following his death in suspicious circumstances, it transpired that he had secretly siphoned large sums of money from two of his companies and from employee pension funds to preserve his financial empire.

Maxwell–Boltzmann distribution A description of the distribution of energy among the atoms or molecules of a (perfect) gas; made by British physicist James Clerk Maxwell and Austrian physicist Ludwig Boltzmann in 1868.

Maxwell Davies, Sir Peter *Davies, Sir Peter Maxwell*

may *hawthorn*

Mayakovsky, Vladimir (Vladimirovich) [miyakofskee] (1893–1930) Poet, born in Bagdadi, Georgia. Regarded as the leader of the Futurist school, during the Russian Revolution (1917) he emerged as the propaganda mouthpiece of the Bolsheviks.

Mayas [miyaz] The best-known civilization of the classic period of Middle America (AD 250–900). They developed astronomy, calendrical systems, hieroglyphic writing, and ceremonial architecture, including pyramid temples. Maya civilization started to decline c.900.

maybug *cockchafer*

Mayer, Louis B(urt) [mayer], originally **Eliezer Mayer** (1885–1957) Film mogul, born in Minsk, Belarus. His family emigrated to the USA, where in 1924 he became vice-president of Metro-Goldwyn-Mayer. He was in charge of the studios for more than 25 years.

Mayfair A district in London where throughout the 17th-c a fair was held in May. It became a fashionable residential area in the late 19th-c and early 20th-c, but is now largely given over to offices.

Mayflower A three-masted carrack in which the Pilgrims sailed from Plymouth to North America in 1620. The ship was only 27·5 m/90 ft in length, and the voyage took 66 days. Her 100 passengers, Puritan refugees from religious intolerance, became 101 by the end of the journey (there were two births and one death during the passage).

mayfly A winged insect with a short adult life. Mayflies live as aquatic larvae for up to four years, then emerge as non-feeding, flying adults that survive only 2–72 hours. (Order: Ephemeroptera, c.2000 species.)

May Fourth Movement A student demonstration in Beijing on 4 May 1919 which crystallized the aspirations of those who struggled for a new China. Originally a protest against the Japanese takeover of Germany's rights in Shandong, the movement spread nationwide.

mayhem A common-law crime and civil injury involving the intentional disfigurement of another person. The disfigurement has to be of a permanent, though not necessarily disabling character, such as cutting off an ear or a finger.

Maynooth 53°23N 6°35W, pop (2001e) 10 000. Historic town in Co Kildare, E Ireland; located 25 km/15 mi W of Dublin; railway; university; Maynooth College (1795) training seminary for priests; castle (1175) was home of the Fitzgeralds (earls of Kildare) and the political capital of the country during 15th–16th-c.

Mayo [mayoh], Ir **Mhuigheo** pop (2000e) 112 000; area 5398 km²/2084 sq mi. County in Connacht province, W Ireland; capital, Castlebar; Knock, scene of apparition of Virgin Mary in 1879, major place of pilgrimage, served by new airport; Croagh Patrick, Ireland's holy mountain, scene of annual pilgrimage (Jul).

Mayo, Charles Horace [mayoh] (1865–1939) Surgeon, born in Rochester, MN. In 1905 he helped his brother, William James Mayo (1861–1939), to organize the Mayo Clinic, within what is now St Mary's Hospital, Rochester, which their father William Worrall Mayo (1819–1911) had founded. The family were pioneers in the practice of group medicine.

mayor The political head of a town or city government. The name is used in a vast range of political systems, but the role and status of mayors vary considerably. In some cases the mayor can have significant executive powers, while in others the role is largely a ceremonial one.

Mayotte [mayot], Eng **Mahore** pop (2000e) 156 900; area 374 km²/144 sq mi. Small island group of volcanic origin, in the Mozambique Channel, W Indian Ocean; administered by France; two main islands; Grande Terre (area 360 km²/140 sq mi), rising to 660 m/2165 ft at Mt Benara; La Petite Terre or Ilot de Pamandzi (area 14 km²/5 sq mi); capital,

Mauritania

□ International Airport

[moritaynia], Fr **Mauritanie**, Arabic **Muritaniyah**, official name **Islamic Republic of Mauritania**, Fr **République Islamique de Mauritanie**
Local names Mūritāniyā (Arabic), Mauritanie (French)
Timezone GMT
Area 1 029 920 km²/397 549 sq mi

Population total (2002e) 2 656 000
Status Islamic republic
Date of independence 1960
Capital Nouakchott
Languages Arabic (official), French and local languages also spoken
Ethnic groups Moor (30%), black (30%), mixed (40%)
Religions Sunni Muslim (99%), Roman Catholic (1%)
Physical features Saharan zone in N comprises two-thirds of the country; coastal zone has minimal rainfall; Sahelian zone, with savannah grasslands; Sénégal R zone, the chief agricultural region; highest point, Kediet Ijill, 915 m/3002 ft in the NW.
Climate Dry, tropical climate, with sparse rainfall; average annual temperatures 22°C (Jan), 28°C (Jul) in Nouakchott; rainy season (May–Sep) in S, with occasional tornadoes; average annual rainfall 158 mm/6·2 in.
Currency 1 Ouguija (MRO) = 5 khoums
Economy Subsistence agriculture (employs 80% of population); crop success constantly under threat from drought; livestock, cereals, vegetables, dates; crops and pasture ravaged by locust plague, 2004; mining of iron ore, copper, gypsum;
GDP (2002e) $4·891 bn, per capita $1700
Human Development Index (2002) 0·438
History Visited by Portuguese, 15th-c; French protectorate within French West Africa, 1903; French colony, 1920; independence, 1960; military coup, 1979; new constitution, 1991; became a republic, 1992; military coup (Aug 2005); governed by an executive President (6-year term), Prime Minister, National Assembly, and Senate.

Head of State
1980–4 Mohammed Khouna Ould Haydalla
1984–2005 Moaouiya Ould Sid Ahmed Taya
2005–7 Ely Ould Mohammed Vall *Military Council*
2007– Sidi Ould Sheikh Abdullahi

Head of Government
1992–6 Sidy Mohammed Ould Boubacar
1996–7 Cheikh el Avia Ould Mohamed Khouna
1997–8 Mohamed Lemine Ould Guig
1998–2003 Cheikh el Avia Ould Mohamed Khouna
2003–5 Sghair Ould M'barek
2005– Sidy Mohamed Ould Boubacar *Military Council*

Dzaoudzi; chief languages, French, Mahorian; French colony, 1843–1914; attached with the Comoros Is to Madagascar; overseas territory of France; airport.

maypole Traditionally, a tall pole decorated with vegetation and ribbons on the first of May, and the focus of festivities on that day to welcome Spring and ensure fertility. Since the later 19th-c a shorter pole is sometimes substituted, around which children perform a plaited-ribbon dance.

Mays, Willie (Howard), nickname **the Say Hey Kid** (1931–) Baseball player, born in Westfield, AL. An outstanding batter, centerfielder, and baserunner with the San Francisco Giants and New York Mets (1951–73), he was the leading all-round player of the era.

Mazar-e-Sharif [mazah(r) ay shareef] 36°43N 67°05E, pop (2001e) 232 800. Capital of Balkh province, N Afghanistan; 56 km/35 mi S of Uzbekistan border; Blue Mosque and shrine mark the reputed site of the tomb of the caliph Ali, son-in-law of Mohammed; Taliban stronghold with many guerilla training camps; camps targeted by US-led attack (Oct 2001) in response to Taliban government's refusal to give up bin Laden.

Mazarin, Jules [mazarī], known as **Cardinal Mazarin**, originally **Giulio Raimondo Mazzarino** (1602–61) Neapolitan clergyman, diplomat, and statesman, born in Pescine, Italy. Through the influence of Richelieu he was elevated to cardinal, succeeding his mentor as first minister in 1642. Blamed by many for the civil disturbances of the Frondes, he twice fled the kingdom. He concluded the Peace of Westphalia (1648), and negotiated the Treaty of the Pyrenees (1659), ending the prolonged Franco–Spanish conflict.

Mazatlán [masatlan] 23°11N 106°25W, pop (2000e) 376 000. Seaport in W Mexico; airfield; railway; largest Mexican port on the Pacific; main industrial and commercial centre in the W.

mazurka A quick Polish dance in triple metre, with a strong accent on the second or third beat. Chopin wrote numerous examples for piano solos.

Mazzini, Giuseppe [matseenee] (1805–72) Patriot and republican, born in Genoa, Italy. He founded the Young Italy Association (1833), and in 1848 collaborated with Garibaldi in attempting to keep the patriot struggle alive in the Alps. During the events of 1859–60 he and his supporters worked strenuously but vainly to make the new Italy a republic.

Mbabane [mbabanay] 26°18S 31°06E, pop (2000e) 53 000. Cap-

Mauritius

□ International Airport

[morishuhs]
Local name Mauritius
Timezone GMT +4
Area 1 865 km²/720 sq mi
Population total (2002e) 1 211 000
Status Republic within the Commonwealth
Date of independence 1968
Capital Port Louis
Languages English (creole-English) (official), French, Hindi, Urdu, Bojpoori, and Hakka also spoken

Ethnic groups Indo-Mauritian (68%), Creole (27%), Sino-Mauritian (3%), Franco-Mauritian (2%)

Religions Hindu (53%), Roman Catholic (26%), Muslim (13%), Protestant (4%)

Physical features Comprises the main island, 20 adjacent islets and the dependencies of Rodrigues I, Agalega I, and Cargados Carajos Is (St Brandon Is); volcanic main island; highest peak, 826 m/2710 ft, Piton de la Petite Rivière Noire; dry, lowland coast with wooded savannah, mangrove swamp, and (E) bamboo; surrounded by coral reefs enclosing lagoons and sandy beaches.

Climate Humid tropical-maritime climate; average annual temperatures 23°C (Jan), 27°C (Jul) in Port Louis; average annual rainfall 1000 mm/39 in; lies within Indian cyclone belt.

Currency 1 Mauritian Rupee (MUR) = 100 cents

Economy Sugar-cane (employs over 25% of the workforce); clothing; diamond-cutting, watches, rum, fertilizer; tea, tobacco, vegetables; fishing; tourism.

GDP (2002e) $12·15 bn, per capita $10 100

Human Development Index (2002) 0·772

History Visited by the Portuguese and Dutch, 16th-c; settled by the French, 1715; ceded to Britain, 1814; governed jointly with Seychelles as a single colony until 1903; independent sovereign state within the Commonwealth, 1968; links with British monarchy broken, 1992, became a republic, remaining within the Commonwealth; President (ceremonial post) is elected by the National Assembly; Prime Minister appoints the Council of Ministers; a unicameral National Assembly.

Head of State
1992 Veerasamy Ringadoo
1992–2002 Cassum Uteem
2002 Angidi Chettiar
2002 Arianga Pillay
2002–3 Karl Offman
2003– Anerood Jugnauth

Head of Government
1982–95 Anerood Jugnauth
1995–2000 Navin Ramgoolam
2000–3 Anerood Jugnauth
2003–5 Paul Berenger
2005– Navin Ramgoolam

---

ital of Swaziland; capital, 1902; administrative and commercial centre; iron ore; casino.

MBE *British Empire, Order of the*

Mbeki, Thabo (Mvuyelwa) [mbekee] (1942–) Leader of the African National Congress (ANC), and president of South Africa (1999–), born in Idutywa, South Africa. Elected to the National Executive Committee of the ANC in 1975, he became one of its most influential leaders. After the organization was unbanned in 1990, he returned to South Africa, and played a major role in the negotiations for a new political dispensation. He was made first deputy president in the new administration (1994), and in 1997 succeeded Mandela as president of the ANC.

Mc surnames *as if spelled* **Mac**

MCC Abbreviation of **Marylebone Cricket Club**, whose headquarters are at Lord's Cricket Ground, N London. It was founded in 1787 by a group of noblemen, and retained responsibility for the making of cricket laws until 1969.

Meacher, Michael (Hugh) [meecher] (1939–) British statesman, born in Hemel Hempstead, Hertfordshire. He was a university lecturer before being elected Labour MP in 1970. He became a member of Labour's national executive committee (1983–8), and served as minister for the environment (1997–2003).

Mead, Margaret (1901–78) Anthropologist, born in Philadelphia, PA. She carried out field studies in the Pacific, writing academic and popular books such as *Coming of Age in Samoa* (1928) and *New Lives for Old* (1956). Increasingly she became a freelance media heavyweight, particularly well known for her views on educational and social issues.

mead An alcoholic beverage derived from fermented honey. It was widely drunk in Anglo-Saxon England, and was known as *hydromel* by the Romans.

Meade, Richard (John Hannay) (1938–) Equestrian rider, born in Chepstow, Monmouthshire. One of Britain's most successful Olympians, he won three gold medals – the three-day event team golds in 1968 and 1972, and the individual title in 1972 (on Laurieston).

meadow grass A perennial grass (*Poa pratensis*) with creeping, rooting stems forming rather stiff tufts; variable and widespread throughout the temperate N hemisphere. It is important as a pasture grass. (Family: Gramineae.)

meadowlark A bird native to the New World; plumage streaked and mottled on back; nests on ground. (Genus: *Sturnella*, 5 species. Family: Icteridae.)

mealybug A scale insect that infests all parts of its host plants;

adult female flattened, males enclosed in cocoon-like sac; distributed worldwide. (Order: Homoptera. Family: Pseudococcidae, c.1100 species).

mean In mathematics, the sum of n scores, divided by n; colloquially called the 'average'. The **arithmetic mean** is obtained by adding a set of scores and dividing the total by the number of scores; for example, the arithmetic mean of the scores 6, 2, 8, 4 is 5 $(6 + 2 + 8 + 4 = 20; 20 \div 4 = 5)$. The **geometric mean** of n scores is the nth root of the product of those scores; for example, the geometric mean of 2, 9, 12 is 6, since $2 \times 9 \times 12 = 216$, and $\sqrt[3]{216} = 6$.

mean free path The average distance travelled by some atom or molecule before colliding with another, typically about 60 nm in gases; symbol l, units m (metre).

mean life In atomic, nuclear, and particle physics, the average time taken for an excited atom to lose energy or for a particle to decay; symbol τ, units s (second).

means test A method of assessing an individual or family's eligibility for some kind of financial assistance, used by government agencies and local authorities. The 'means' refers to a person's income and other sources of money. Aid is given on a sliding scale, and above a certain level no help is given.

measles A viral childhood disease spread by airborne infected droplets. It begins with a cough and runny nose, followed by a generalized blotchy red rash and fever.

meat The edible muscle of animals, the most common forms including beef, pork, bacon, lamb, and poultry. The flesh of many other species is also eaten as meat, including the horse, buffalo, camel, dog, deer, rabbit, and monkey, though cultural practices vary.

Meath [meeth], Ir **na Midhe** pop (2000e) 107 000; area 2339 km²/903 sq mi. County in Leinster province, E Ireland; former kingdom; capital, Trim.

Mecca [meka], Arabic **Makkah**, ancient **Macoraba** 21°30N 39°54E, pop (2000e) 1 005 000. Islamic holy city in WC Saudi Arabia; birthplace of Mohammed; chief shrine of Muslim pilgrimage; city closed to non-Muslims; al-Harram Mosque with the Kaba and sacred Black Stone.

mechanical engineering The branch of engineering concerned with the design, construction, and operation of machines of all types. Mechanical engineers design, operate, and test engines that produce power from steam, petrol, nuclear energy, and other sources, and a wide range of associated equipment.

mechanics The study of the motion of objects as a result of the forces acting on them. Motion in a straight line is called *linear* or *rectilinear* motion, and is described using mass m, velocity v, acceleration a, momentum p, and force F; *rotational* motion is described using moment of inertia I, angular velocity ω, angular acceleration α, angular momentum L, and torque Γ. **Quantum mechanics** governs objects the size of atoms (10^{-10} m) or less. **Classical mechanics** corresponds to all other aspects of mechanics, and includes **Newtonian mechanics**, **celestial mechanics** (the motion of stars and planets), general relativity, **fluid mechanics**, and **relativistic mechanics** (for objects moving at high velocity).

Mecklenburg Declaration of Independence (1775) Resolutions adopted in Mecklenburg County, N Carolina, during the American Revolution, denying all British authority.

medal A piece of metal, often in the form of a coin or cross, bearing a device or inscription, struck or cast in commemoration of an event or as a reward for merit. Medals may be awarded for personal bravery, for participation in an event or battle, or for sports.

Medal of Honor (MH, MOH) In the USA, the highest decoration awarded for heroism, instituted in 1861; it is worn on a blue ribbon decorated with white stars.

Medawar, Sir Peter (Brian) [medawah(r)] (1915–87) Zoologist, born in Rio de Janeiro, Brazil. He shared the 1960 Nobel Prize for Physiology or Medicine for his discovery of acquired immunological tolerance. He is also well known for his general books on the nature of science.

Medea [medeea] In Greek mythology, a witch, the daughter of Aeetes, the King of Colchis, who assisted Jason in obtaining the Golden Fleece. When deserted by Jason at Corinth, she fled in her aerial chariot after killing her children.

Médecins Sans Frontières [maydsɪ sã frõtyair] ('Doctors Without Borders') An independent medical agency, founded in France in 1971. It is devoted to providing rapid professional help to victims of natural and human disasters wherever it is needed, and to raising public awareness of their plight. It received the Nobel Peace Prize in 1999 for its pioneering humanitarian work.

Medellín [medeyeen] 6°15N 75°36W, pop (2000e) 1 665 000. City in NW Colombia, and leading industrial centre; airport; railway; five universities; cathedral.

Medes [meedz] An ancient people living to the SW of the Caspian Sea. They were at their peak in the 7th-c and 6th-c BC.

media The means of producing and disseminating news information, and entertainment to a universal audience, typically through the press (both tabloid and broadsheet), magazines, cinema, radio and television, and even paperback publishing and pornography. The mass media have been hailed at times as bulwarks of democracy and key contributors to social cohesion and well-being, and at other times reviled as agents of repression, or as promoting anti-social behaviour and perverting cultural standards. The Internet poses a contemporary challenge by virtue of its freedom of access and interactive character.

median In mathematics, the middle score, when the scores are arranged in order of size; for example, the scores 1, 5, 3, 7, 2 are re-arranged 1, 2, 3, 5, 7, and the middle score is 3.

Medicaid and **Medicare** Two US schemes to provide health care, introduced by the federal government in 1965. **Medicaid** is operated by state governments, and provides financial assistance to low-income persons. **Medicare** is for persons over the age of 65. Similar schemes operate in several other countries, such as Australia.

medical ethics The branch of medicine that deals with the incorporation of an individual's interests, societal values, legal issues, and moral arguments into medical practice.

Medici [maydeechee], Fr **Médicis** A banking family which virtually ruled Florence from 1434 to 1494, though without holding formal office. They were overthrown by the republic in 1494, but restored to power in 1512, and from 1537 became hereditary dukes of Florence.

medicine The science and practice of preventing, alleviating, and curing human illness. Although the study of anatomy grew rapidly from the time of Aristotle and the Alexandrian medical school in 300 BC, physiology and ideas of organ function remained rudimentary. Chinese medicine is documented from 600 BC, and the first Chinese medical text was wrtten in 1st-c BC. The major contribution of Greek medicine was in the field of medical ethics, and the Hippocratic code of conduct is still invoked today. Roman medicine was pre-eminent in public health, with its emphasis on clean water, sewage disposal, and public baths. Arabian medicine made significant contributions to chemistry and drugs, and set up the first organized medical school in Salerno (c.900). In Padua, Vesalius corrected the anatomical misconceptions of Galen. The major medical discovery of the 17th-c was the circulation of the blood; 100 years later, oxygen and its relationship to blood. The value of post-mortem studies was demonstrated by Morgagni in Padua. New methods of examination were introduced, notably the stethoscope (by Laënnec) and percussion of the chest. Jenner showed the benefit of vaccination to prevent smallpox. The germ theory of disease dominated the 19th-c, and Pasteur virtually created the science of bacteriology, from which Lister was inspired to develop the concept of antisepsis. Progress in the 20th-c was unparalleled, being distinguished by the growth in modern technology and the development of rigorous experimental testing. Developments were stimulated rather than hindered by World Wars 1 and 2, in such areas as rehabilitation after injury, blood transfusion, anaesthesia, and chemotherapy, including the development of antibiotics and vitamins and the discovery of insulin and cortisone. New concepts have included genetic disease, the adverse effects of some lifestyles and environmental pollution, vaccination for a number of infectious diseases, artificial organ and life-support systems, organ transplantation, and the science of immunology.

medick An annual and perennial, native to Europe, W Asia, and N Africa; pea-flowers small, mostly yellow; fruit usually a spirally coiled pod, often spiny. (Genus: *Medicago*, 100 species. Family: Leguminosae.)

Medina [medeena], Arabic **Madinah, Al** 24°35N 39°52E, pop (2000e) 813 000. Islamic holy city in Saudi Arabia; contains the tomb of Mohammed; important pilgrimage trade; city closed to non-Muslims; airfield; Islamic university (1961); centre of a large date-growing oasis.

meditation Devout and continuous reflection on a particular religious theme, practised in many religions and serving a variety of aims, such as deepening spiritual insight, or achieving union with the divine will.

Mediterranean Sea, ancient **Mediterraneum** or **Mare Internum** area 2 516 000 km²/971 000 sq mi. World's largest inland sea, lying between Africa, Asia, and Europe; connected with the Atlantic by the Straits of Gibraltar; includes the Ligurian, Adriatic, Aegean, Ionian, and Tyrrhenian Seas; length, 3860 km/2400 mi; maximum width, 1610 km/1000 mi; maximum depth, 4405 m/14 452 ft; 'Mediterranean climate' of hot, dry summers and mild winters with rainstorms; seaboard highly favoured as holiday and health resort; maritime highway since ancient times, connecting Europe with the E; Suez Canal (1869) increased its importance; pollution a major problem.

medium (parapsychology) Especially in spiritualism, a person through whom spirits of the dead are claimed to demonstrate their presence by means of spoken or written messages, or apparently paranormal physical effects.

Medjugorje [medyoogorye] 43°20N 17°49E. Village in Bosnia and Herzegovina; since 1981, claimed to be the scene of regular appearances by the Virgin Mary to a group of local children; now a major site of pilgrimage; in the 1990s, number of pilgrims much reduced by civil war.

medlar A small deciduous tree or shrub (*Mespilus germanica*), growing to 6 m/20 ft, native to SE Europe; flowers solitary, white; fruit brown, becoming soft and edible when over-ripe. (Family: Rosaceae.)

Médoc [maydok] District in Gironde department, SW France; famous for its clarets, notably at Haut-Médoc.

medulla oblongata [meduhla oblonggahta] The lower part of the brain stem, continuous with the pons above and with the spinal cord below. It contains the 'vital centres' concerned with the reflex control of the cardiovascular and respiratory systems. It also helps to govern swallowing, sneezing, coughing, and vomiting.

medusa [medyooza] The free-swimming phase in the life-cycle of a coelenterate. The body is typically discoid or bell-shaped, with marginal tentacles and a centrally located mouth on the underside.

Medusa [medyooza] In Greek mythology, the name of one of the Gorgons, whose head is portrayed with staring eyes and snakes for hair.

Medway Towns Urban area in Kent, SE England; includes Gillingham and Rochester (merging as Medway unitary authority, 1998), Chatham, and Strood on the R Medway, E of London.

Mee, Arthur (Henry) (1875–1943) Journalist, editor, and writer, born in Stapleford, Nottinghamshire. He is most widely known for his *Children's Encyclopaedia* (1908).

Meech Lake Accord A Canadian constitutional package, put together by the government of Brian Mulroney in 1987 at a conference at Meech L, N of Ottawa. It proposed a fresh federal structure for Canada, giving the provinces more authority, and recognized Quebec as a 'distinct society'. The Accord died after it failed to receive the support of all 10 Provinces and First Nations leaders in 1990.

Meegeren, Han van *van Meegeren, Han*

meerschaum [meershuhm] or **epiolite** A hydrated magnesium silicate mineral, which forms fine, fibrous masses like white clay and is easily carved. It is used for pipe bowls.

megabyte *byte*

megalith (Gr *mega*, 'large' + *lithos*, 'stone') In European prehistory, a monument built of large, roughly-dressed stone slabs; sometimes called a **cromlech**. Most are of Neolithic date.

Megaloptera [megaloptera] *alderfly; dobsonfly*

megaparsec *parsec*

megapode An Australasian ground-living bird; sturdy body with large legs and feet; also known as **mound bird**, **mound builder**, or **incubator bird**. (Family: Megapodiidae, 12 species.)

Megatherium [megatheerium] The largest ground sloth, found in Central and South America during the Pleistocene epoch; a two-legged grazer; forelimbs large, hindlimbs short but massive. (Order: Xenarthra.)

megaton *kiloton* (TNT)

megavitamin therapy A form of nutritional therapy based on the work of Linus Pauling, who believed that very large doses of vitamin C could cure or prevent the common cold by having a direct anti-viral effect and also by enhancing the effect of the immune system. Large doses of various vitamins have been used to treat patients with a wide variety of disorders, such as schizophrenia and depression, on the assumption that these problems may be the result of vitamin deficiency. However, some vitamins taken in excessive amounts may cause toxic effects.

megawatt *watt*

Megiddo [megidoh] In antiquity, an important town in N Palestine controlling the main route from Egypt to Syria. Among its most impressive remains are the 9th-c stables of the Israelite kings.

megohm *ohm*

Mehta, Ved (Parkash) [mayta] (1934–) Writer, born in Lahore, Pakistan (formerly India). Blind from the age of four, he went to the USA when he was 15. He has had a distinguished career as a journalist, contributing chiefly to *The New Yorker. Continents of Exile* is an acclaimed series of autobiographical books (1972–89). Later works include *Remembering Mr Shawn's New Yorker* (1999) and *The Red Letters* (2004).

Mehta, Zubin [mayta] (1936–) Conductor, born in Mumbai (Bombay), India. His posts as conductor or musical director have included the Los Angeles Philharmonic (1962–78) and the New York Philharmonic (1978–91). In 1977 he was appointed musical director of the Israel Philharmonic Orchestra, and made director for life in 1981.

Meiji Restoration (1868) [mayjee] An important point in Japanese history, when the last Shogun was overthrown in a short civil war, and the position of the emperor (Meiji, the title of Mutsuhito, who ruled until 1912) was restored to symbolic importance.

Meiji Tenno *Mutsuhito*

meiosis [miyohsis] One of the principal mechanisms of nuclear division in living organisms, resulting in the formation of gametes (in animals) or sexual spores (in plants). A diploid nucleus (ie one possessing a double set of chromosomes) undergoes two successive divisions. The phases of meiosis are *leptotene* (the appearance of chromosomes as threads in the nucleus), *zygotene* (the pairing of chromosomes to form bivalents), *pachytene* (the separation of bivalents), and *diplotene* (the moving apart of chromosomes).

Meir, Golda [mayeer], originally **Goldie Myerson**, *née* **Mabovitch** (1898–1978) Israeli stateswoman and prime minister (1969–74), born in Kiev. As prime minister, her efforts for peace in the Middle East were halted by the fourth Arab–Israeli War (1973).

Meissen porcelain [miysn] Porcelain made at Meissen, near Dresden; the first factory in Europe to make true hard-paste porcelain. The secret was discovered in 1708 by Johann Friedrich Böttger (1682–1719).

Meissonier, (Jean Louis) Ernest [maysonyay] (1815–91) Painter, born in Lyon, France. His works were largely of military and historical scenes, including several of the Napoleonic era.

Meistersinger [miysterzinger] Members of German guilds of the 14th–16th-c devoted to the encouragement of poetry and music in strict traditional forms. Their activities form the basis for Wagner's opera *Die Meistersinger von Nürnberg* (1868).

Meitner, Lise [miytner] (1878–1968) Physicist, born in Vienna. In 1917 she shared with Hahn the discovery of the radioactive element protactinium, and became known for her work in nuclear physics. With her nephew O R Frisch she devised the idea of nuclear fission in late 1938.

Mekele or **Makale** [makalay] 13°32N 39°33E, pop (2000e) 94 200. Capital of Tigray region, NE Ethiopia; airport; major refugee centre during the severe drought of 1983.

Meknès [meknes] 33°53N 5°37W, pop (2000e) 465 000. City in N Morocco; one of Morocco's four imperial cities, founded in the 12th-c; capital until 1728; railway.

Mekong River [meekong], Chin **Lancang Jiang** River in Indo-China, SE Asia; rises on the Tibet Plateau, China; delta on the South China Sea; length c.4000 km/2500 mi.

Melaka *Malacca*

Melanchthon, Philipp [melangkthon], originally **Philipp Schwartzerd** (1497–1560) Religious reformer, born in Bretten, Germany; his *Loci Communes* (1521) is the first great Protestant work on dogmatic theology, and the Augsburg Confession (1530) was composed by him.

Melanesia One of the three broad geographical–cultural areas of the Pacific. It includes the islands of New Guinea, the Solomons, Vanuatu, and New Caledonia. The peoples of Melanesia typically have dark skin, kinky hair, large jaws, and a high incidence of blood group B.

melanins [melaninz] Dark brown pigments which in different concentrations give coloration (shades of yellow and brown) to the eyes, skin, hair, feathers, and scales of many vertebrates. In humans they help protect the skin against the damaging effects of sunlight.

melanoma [melanohma] A pigmented tumour due to overgrowth of melanin-producing cells in the basal cell layer of the skin. A proportion become malignant, and spread to other parts of the body.

Melba, Dame Nellie, professional name of **Helen Armstrong**, *née* **Mitchell** (1861–1931) Prima donna, born in Melbourne, Victoria, Australia; her professional name derives from the city. Her coloratura soprano voice won her worldwide fame. 'Peach Melba' and 'Melba toast' were named after her.

Melbourne 37°45S 144°58E, pop (2000e) 3 339 000. Port and state capital in Victoria, Australia; on the Yarra R; founded in 1835, named after the British prime minister, Lord Melbourne; state capital, 1851; capital of Australia when federal parliament sat here, 1901–27; two airports; railway; underground; Australia's

biggest cargo port; five universities (1855, 1958, 1964, 1991, 1992); two cathedrals; Flemington racecourse (holds the Melbourne Cup horse race); site of 1956 summer Olympic Games and 2006 Commonwealth Games.

Melbourne, William Lamb, 2nd Viscount (1779–1848) British statesman and Whig prime minister (1834, 1835–41), born in London. He formed a close relationship with the young Queen Victoria, but took little part in public affairs after his election defeat in 1841. His wife (1785–1828) wrote novels as **Lady Caroline Lamb**, and was notorious for her 9-months' devotion to Lord Byron.

Melchett, Baron *Mond, Alfred*

Melchites [melkhiyts] Christians who follow the Byzantine rite, and who belong to the Patriarchates of Alexandria, Antioch, and Jerusalem. During the 5th-c, they supported the Byzantine emperor in his opposition to the Monophysites.

Méliès, Georges [maylyes] (1861–1938) Illusionist and film maker, born in Paris. He was a pioneer in trick cinematography to present magical effects.

Melilla [mayleelya], ancient **Russadir** 35°21N 2°57W, pop (2000e) 67 000. Free port and modern commercial city on N coast of Morocco; with Ceuta, forms a region of Spain; founded as a port by the Phoenicians; free port since 1863; re-occupied by Spain in 1926; airport; car ferries to Málaga.

melilot [melilot] Typically an annual or biennial, native to Europe, Asia, and N Africa; pea-flowers small, yellow or white. It is used for fodder, and also for flavouring cheeses. (Genus: *Melilotus*, 20 species. Family: Leguminosae.)

Mello, Craig Cameron (1960–) Molecular biologist, born in Worcester, MA. He studied at Brown University (1982) and Harvard (1990), and was a postdoctoral fellow at the Fred Hutchinson Cancer Research Center. In 1994 he joined the University of Massachusetts Medical School in Worcester, where he is currently professor of molecular medicine. In 2006 he shared the Nobel Prize for Physiology or Medicine with Andrew Fire for 'their discovery of RNA interference – gene silencing by double-stranded RNA'.

Mellon, Andrew W(illiam) (1855–1937) Financier, philanthropist, and statesman, born in Pittsburgh, PA. He made a reputation for himself as an industrial magnate, and endowed the National Gallery of Art in Washington, DC. As secretary of the Treasury (1921–32), he controversially reduced taxation of the wealthy.

Mellor, David (John) (1949–) British statesman. A barrister, he was elected a Conservative MP in 1979, and held several ministerial portfolios during the late 1980s. He became minister for the arts in 1990, then chief secretary to the Treasury (1990–2) and secretary of state for national heritage (1992). He was forced to resign from the government in 1992 following revelations about an extra-marital affair. He failed to retain his seat in the 1997 election, but was later appointed head of a football task force (1997–9) by the Labour minister for sport.

melodrama A theatrical genre which became a mass entertainment in Europe and the USA throughout the 19th-c. It is a style which emphasizes the depiction of story, the creation of suspense, and the use of sensational episodes.

melody A basic constituent of music, being a succession of pitches arranged in some intelligible order. Between c.1675 and 1925, melodic inspiration (a gift for composing 'good tunes') became more and more highly prized as the token of a composer's originality. Since then, many composers have sought to express their musical personalities in other ways, through the use of texture, rhythm, etc.

melon A trailing or climbing vine (*Cucumis melo*) with tendrils, probably native to Africa; flowers yellow, funnel-shaped; fruit up to 25 cm/10 in long, round or ovoid; rind green or yellow, leathery; edible flesh thick, sweet, surrounding numerous seeds. (Family: Cucurbitaceae.)

Melos [meelos], Gr **Mílos** area 151 km²/58 sq mi. Southwestern-most island of the Cyclades, Greece; main town, Plaka.

Melpomene [melpominee] The Greek Muse of tragedy.

meltdown A catastrophic event in a nuclear reactor. The temperature of the reacting core rises to a point at which the fuel rods melt, and radioactive material may be released into the environment.

melting point The temperature at which a solid becomes liquid. If heat is applied to a solid, its temperature rises until the melting point is reached, when heat energy is then absorbed to form liquid from the solid.

Melville, Herman (1819–91) Novelist, born in New York City. His journeys on a whaling ship were the subject matter of his first novels, *Typee* (1846) and *Omoo* (1847), and his masterpiece *Moby-Dick* (1851). After 1857 he wrote only some poetry, leaving his long story, *Billy Budd, Foretopman*, in manuscript.

membranophone Any musical instrument in which the sound is generated by the vibrations of a stretched membrane. The most important are the various kinds of drum.

Memlinc or **Memling, Hans** [memling] (c.1435–1494) Religious painter, born in Seligenstadt, Belgium. His works include the triptych of the 'Madonna Enthroned' at Chatsworth (1468). He was also an original and creative portrait painter.

Memnon [memnon] In Greek mythology, a prince from Ethiopia, the son of Eos and Tithonus, who was killed at Troy by Achilles.

Memorial Day A national holiday in the USA, held on the last Monday in May in honour of American war dead; originally instituted as **Decoration Day** in 1868 in honour of soldiers killed in the American Civil War.

Memphis (Egypt) An important town in ancient Egypt on the W bank of the Nile. The capital of Lower Egypt under the pharaohs, it declined in importance under the Ptolemies.

Memphis (USA) [memfis] 35°08N 90°03W, pop (2000e) 650 000. Port in SW Tennessee, USA, on the Mississippi R; largest city in the state; site of military fort, 1797; city established, 1819; captured by Union forces during the Civil War (battle of Memphis, 1862); airfield; railway; two universities (1848, 1912); Martin Luther King Jr assassinated here (1968); Graceland, home of Elvis Presley; Beale Street, regarded as the birthplace of the blues.

Menai Strait [meniy] Channel separating Anglesey from the mainland of NW Wales, UK; length 24 km/15 mi; width varies from 175 m/575 ft to 3·2 km/2 mi; crossed by the Menai Suspension Bridge, built by Telford (1819–26), length 176 m/580 ft, and the Britannia railway/road bridge (1980), rebuilt after fire in 1970 seriously damaged the original tubular railway bridge of Robert Stephenson (1846–9).

Menander [menander] (c.343–291 BC) Greek comic dramatist, born in Athens. Only a few fragments of his work were known until 1906, and in 1957 the complete text of the comedy *Dyskolos* (The Bad-Tempered Man) was found in Geneva.

Menchik-Stevenson, Vera (Francevna), *née* **Menchik** (1906–44) Chess player, born in Moscow. Recognized as the finest of all female chess players, she held the world title from 1927 (the first champion) to 1944.

Mencius [menshius], Latin name **Meng-tzu** (Master Meng) (c.371–c.289 BC) Philosopher and sage, born in Shantung, China, who founded a school modelled on that of Confucius. After his death his disciples collected his sayings and published them as the *Book of Meng-tzu*.

Mencken, H(enry) L(ouis) (1880–1956) Philologist, editor, and satirist, born in Baltimore, MD. He greatly influenced the US literary scene in the 1920s. His major work, *The American Language*, was published in 1918, and in 1924 he founded the *American Mercury*, editing it until 1933.

Mendel, Gregor (Johann) (1822–84) Botanist, born in Heinzendorf, Austria. Abbot of the Augustinian monastery in Brno, he pursued research into plant breeding, and eventually established his 'laws' governing the nature of inheritance, which became the basis of modern genetics. Recognition came many years after his death.

Mendeleyev, Dmitri Ivanovich [mendelayef] (1834–1907) Chemist, born in Tobolsk, Russia. He devised the periodic classification (or table) by which he predicted the existence of several elements which were subsequently discovered. Element 101 (*mendelevium*) is named after him.

Mendelssohn(-Bartholdy), (Jakob Ludwig) Felix [mendlsuhn] (1809–47) Composer, born in Hamburg, Germany, the grandson of Moses Mendelssohn, and the son of a Hamburg banker who added the name Bartholdy. Among his early successes as a composer was the *Midsummer Night's Dream* overture (1826). A tour of Scotland in the summer inspired him with the *Hebrides* Overture and the *Scottish Symphony*. Other major works include his oratorios *St Paul* (1836) and *Elijah* (1846).

Mendelssohn, Moses [mendelsuhn] (1729–86) Philosopher and biblical scholar, born in Dessau, Germany. A zealous defender of enlightened monotheism, he was an apostle of deism.

Mendes, Sam(uel Alexander) [mendez] (1965–) Theatre and film director, born in Reading, England. He joined the Royal Shakespeare Company in 1992, then became artistic director of London's Donmar Warehouse (1992–2002), where he received Olivier Awards for his productions of *Company* (1996), *Uncle Vanya* (2002), and *Twelfth Night* (2002). He made his film debut in 1999 with *American Beauty* (Oscars for Best Director and Best Picture). Later films inlcude *Road to Perdition* (2002) and *Jarhead* (2005).

Mendès France, Pierre [mendez frãs] (1907–82) French statesman and prime minister (1954–5), born in Paris. As prime minister, he ended the war in Indo-China, but his government was defeated on its N African policy.

Mendicant Orders (Lat *mendicare*, 'to beg') Religious Orders in which friars were not permitted to hold property, either personally or in common.

Mendip Hills Hill range in SW England; extending 37 km/23 mi; rises to 326 m/1069 ft at Blackdown.

Mendoza [menthohsa] 32°48S 68°52W, pop (2000e) 135 300. City in W Argentina; altitude 756 m/2480 ft; belonged to Chile until 1776; destroyed by fire and earthquake in 1861; airport; railway; four universities (1939, 1959, 1960, 1968); centre of a large, irrigated agricultural area, dealing mainly in wine.

Menelaus [menilayus] In Greek legend, the younger brother of Agamemnon. He was King of Sparta, and married to Helen.

menhir [meneer] (Welsh *maen*, 'stone' + *hir*, 'long') In European prehistory, a single standing stone or megalith.

Ménière's disease [menyair, muhnyair] Repeated attacks of vertigo, usually abrupt in onset, accompanied by tinnitus and progressive deafness, and sometimes associated with nausea. It is a disorder of the inner ear of unknown cause, affecting mainly middle-aged and elderly persons. It is named after French physician Prosper Ménière (1799–1862).

meningitis [meninjiytis] An infection of the membranes (pia and arachnoid) covering the brain. **Viral meningitis** is usually short-lived and harmless; **bacterial meningitis** is more serious and may cause death. The onset is usually sudden, with headache, fever, stiffness of the neck on flexion, and dislike of the light.

meniscus [muhniskuhs] *surface tension*

Mennonites [menoniyts] Dutch and Swiss Anabaptists who later called themselves Mennonites after one of their Dutch leaders, Menno Simons (1496–1559). Most of their 1 million adherents live in the USA.

Menon, Krishna *Krishna Menon*

menopause Strictly defined as the cessation of menstruation, but more commonly used to refer to the period of time (up to eight years beforehand) when the menstrual cycle becomes less regular; also known as **climacteric**. The complete cessation of menstruation usually occurs between 45 and 50 years. It is often accompanied by physical and psychogenic disturbances.

menorah [menohra] A candelabrum of seven branches, with three curving upwards on each side of a central shaft. It is an ancient symbol of Judaism, and the official symbol of the modern State of Israel.

menorrhagia [menorayjia] Excessive menstrual bleeding. It commonly results from local abnormalities of the uterus, but also arises from disorders of the hormones controlling normal menstruation.

Menotti, Gian Carlo [menotee] (1911–2007) Composer, born in Cadegliano, Italy. He achieved international fame with a series of operas, notably *Amelia Goes to the Ball* (1937), *The Consul* (1950, Pulitzer), *The Saint of Bleecker Street* (1954, Pulitzer), and the television opera *Amahl and the Night Visitors* (1951).

Mensa (Lat 'table') An inconspicuous constellation in the S sky. It was named by Lacaille after Table Mountain, Cape Province, South Africa, where he had an observatory.

Mensa International An organization of people whose members are admitted only after they 'have established by some standard intelligence test, that their intelligence is higher than 98% of the population'. Founded in England in 1945, branches now exist in around 100 countries.

men's health A recent branch of medicine that deals with preventing and treating illnesses that particularly affect men, such as testicular and prostatic cancer, and encourages healthy lifestyles including exercise, good diet, and sensible alcohol consumption.

Mensheviks [mensheviks] (Russ 'minority-ites') Members of the moderate faction of the Marxist Russian Social Democratic Labour Party, which split with Lenin's Bolsheviks in 1903. The Mensheviks opposed Lenin's policies on party organization and his revolutionary tactics.

menstruation A periodic discharge from the vagina of blood, mucus, and debris from the disintegrating mucous membrane of the uterus, in response to hormone changes when the ovum is not fertilized. It lasts 3–5 days. In women of child-bearing age (13–50 years), it occurs at approximately 4-week intervals. The first menstrual period in life is known as *menarche*, the last as *menopause*.

mental disorders A group of conditions with psychological or behavioural manifestations which may be accompanied by impaired functioning. Examples include anxiety, dementia, drug addictions, eating disorders, schizophrenia, and sleep disorders.

mental handicap A condition in which people have an intelligence quotient of less than 70, with deficits in their ability to live independently, evidenced before age 18. Four types are generally recognized: **mild** (IQ 50–70), **moderate** (IQ 35–49), **severe** (IQ 20–34), and **profound** (IQ < 20). The cause is unknown in c.75% of cases.

mental underdevelopment The delay or premature arrest of a child's intellectual, behavioural, and social development. Intelligence quotient (IQ) is sometimes used to describe the degree of mental handicap, with scores below 50 indicating serious levels of handicap.

menthol $C_{10}H_{20}O$, a terpene alcohol, melting point 43°C. A waxy solid, the main constituent of oil of peppermint, it is used as a flavouring, a mild antiseptic, a decongestant, and a local anaesthetic.

menu (computing) A set of options presented to the user by a computer program. A program which communicates with the user solely by providing choices from interlinked menus is said to be **menu-driven**. The menu facility is used extensively, in addition to icons, in graphic user interfaces.

Menuhin, Yehudi Menuhin, Baron [menyooin] (1916–99) Violinist, born in New York City. At the age of seven he appeared as a soloist, and won international renown as a virtuoso violinist. In 1962 he founded a school for musically gifted children near London. He took British nationality in 1985. His sister **Hephzibah** (1920–81) was a gifted pianist.

Menzies, Sir Robert Gordon [menzees] (1894–1978) Australian statesman and prime minister (1939–41, 1949–66), born in Jeparit, Victoria, Australia. His first term as premier was as head of the United Australia Party, his second as head of the Liberal Party, which he formed in 1944.

Mercalli intensity scale [merkalee] A scale of 12 points, devised by Italian seismologist Giuseppe Mercalli (1850–1914), for measuring the intensity of an earthquake. The scale is based on the damage done, rather than on the total energy released, and so varies from place to place. It has been superseded by the Richter scale.

mercantilism The view that exports add to a country's wealth, and imports detract from it. This is allied to the view of international trade as a zero-sum game, in which one country's gain is another country's loss. This school of thought has led to protectionist policies in the past, and is by no means extinct. It contrasts with the free-traders' view that exports are a cost to an economy and imports a benefit, and that international trade is a source of potential gains to all parties.

Mercator's map projection [merkayter] A map projection devised in 1569 by Flemish cartographer Gerardus Mercator (1512–94), which was the first of real use for navigation purposes. It is based on parallels equal in length to that of the Equator. As a result, a line of constant bearing appears as a straight line rather than the curved line on a globe. The major distortion is that area is exaggerated at high latitudes.

Mercer, David (1928–80) Playwright, born in Wakefield, West Yorkshire. His plays include *Ride a Cock Horse* (1965) and *Cousin Vladimir* (1978). He also wrote screenplays (eg *Morgan*, 1965; *Family Life*, 1972) and many TV plays.

mercerizing The chemical treatment of cotton with strong alkalis, to make it stronger, lustrous, and more silk-like. The process was devised in 1844 by British chemist John Mercer (1791–1866).

Merchant, Ismail, originally **Ismail Noormohamed Abdul Rehman** (1936–2005) Film producer, born in Mumbai (Bombay), India. In 1961 he collaborated with James Ivory (1928–) in setting up a film production company, Merchant-Ivory Productions. Their films include *Shakespeare Wallah* (1965), the Oscar-nominated *A Room With A View* (1985), and *The Remains of the Day* (1993). In 2002 he was awarded, with James Ivory, a BAFTA Fellowship for outstanding contributions to world cinema.

Merchant Adventurers Local guilds exporting woollen cloth from 14th-c London. Formed in 1407, they increasingly dominated trade at the expense of smaller ports; from 1496, their headquarters were in Antwerp.

merchant bank A UK bank specializing in trading and company financial matters; similar to a US *investment bank*. The term is traditionally used to describe members of the Accepting Houses Committee, dealing primarily with bills of exchange.

Merchant Navy The commercial ships of a nation, a term first used by King George V in a speech in 1922. The mercantile marine was classed as an armed service throughout World War 2. In 1939 there were over 9000 ships in Britain's Merchant Navy, but by the 2000s the number had dwindled to under 1000.

Mercia A kingdom of the Anglo-Saxon heptarchy, with its main centres at Tamworth, Lichfield, and Repton. Mercian supremacy reached its height under Offa, but in 874 Mercia succumbed to the invading Danish army, and the E part became (886) a portion of the Danelaw, while the W part was controlled by Alfred of Wessex.

Merckx, Eddy [merks], nickname **the Cannibal** (1945–) Cyclist, born in Woluwe St Pierre, Belgium. He won the *Tour de France* five times (1969–72, 1974), the Tour of Italy five times, and all the major classics. He retired in 1978.

Mercosur (Span), **Mercosul** (Portuguese) ('Southern Common Market') A common market agreement, signed in 1991 between Argentina, Brazil, Paraguay, and Uruguay, which aimed to introduce free movement of goods and services; inaugurated on 1 January 1995. Venezuela joined in 2006. Its secretariat is in Montevideo, Uruguay. Chile and Bolivia joined as associate members in 1996. It is the world's fourth largest free trade grouping, with over 200 million people.

Mercouri, Melina [merkooree], originally **Anna Amalia Mercouri** (1923–94) Film actress and politician, born in Athens. She started in films in 1955, and found international fame in 1960 with *Never on Sunday*. Always politically involved, she was exiled from Greece (1967–74), returned to be elected to parliament in 1977, and became minister of culture (1981–9, 1993–4).

Mercredi, Ovide [mairkredee] (1946–) Canadian aboriginal affairs activist, born in Grand Rapids, Manitoba, Canada. A Cree Indian, he became a lawyer, and was made National Chief of the Assembly of First Nations in 1991. His book, *In the Rapids: Navigating the Future of First Nations*, appeared in 1993.

Mercury (astronomy) The innermost major planet of the Solar System; an airless, lunar-like body with the following characteristics: mass 3.30×10^{23} kg; radius 2439 km/1516 mi; mean density 5.4 g/cm^3; rotational period 58.65 days; orbital period 88 days; obliquity $0°$; orbital eccentricity 0.206; mean distance from the Sun 57.9×10^6 km/36.0×10^6 mi. The equatorial surface temperatures reach $430°C$, while on the night side temperatures may drop to $-180°C$. It has a weak magnetic field (c.1% of Earth's), and a very tenuous atmosphere. One hemisphere of the surface was mapped by Mariner 10 (1974–5), the other is still unknown. It has an apparently lunar-like crust, shaped by asteroidal bombardment and episodes of volcanic flooding.

mercury (chemistry) Hg (from Lat *hydrargyrum*), element 80, melting point $-39°C$, boiling point $357°C$. Silver in colour, unique among metals by being a liquid at normal temperatures; also known as **quicksilver**. A relatively unreactive metal, it is found free in nature, but is much more common as the sulphide (HgS), called *vermilion* when used as a pigment. It is used in both temperature- and pressure-measuring equipment. The vapour and soluble salts are toxic and cumulative.

Mercury (mythology) or **Mercurius** A Roman god, principally of trading, who was identifed with Hermes, and inherited his mythology.

Mercury Messenger *Mariner programme*

Mercury programme The first US crewed spaceflight programme, the precursor to the Gemini and Apollo programmes, using a one-man crew. The first suborbital flight (5 May 1961) was piloted by Alan Shepard; the first orbital flight (20 Feb 1962) by John Glenn. The spacecraft demonstrated a life-support system and the basic elements of recovery.

Meredith, George (1828–1909) Writer, born in Portsmouth, Hampshire. He achieved popularity with *The Egoist* (1879) and *Diana of the Crossways* (1885). His main poetic work is *Modern Love* (1862).

merganser [merganser] A sea duck native to the N hemisphere and SE Brazil; slender serrated bill; also known as **saw-bill**. (Genus: *Mergus*, 5 species. Subfamily: Anatinae. Tribe: Mergini.)

merger A business arrangement in which two companies bring together their operations and form a single company. The share capital of the two companies is replaced by an issue of shares in the new company, shareholders of the old companies receiving new shares on a formula basis.

meridian (astronomy) At any location, the great circle on the Earth at right angles to the Equator passing from N to S Poles. All celestial objects reach their highest point in the sky when they cross the celestial meridian, and the Sun is on the meridian at local noon.

Mérimée, Prosper [mayreemay] (1803–70) Writer, born in Paris. His novels include *Colomba* (1841) and *Carmen* (1843), the source of Bizet's opera.

merino A breed of sheep, originating in Spain, which produce a heavy thick white fleece of very high quality. Australia is by far the largest producer of merino wool.

Merionethshire *Gwynedd*

meristem A region of growth or potential growth in a plant, such as the tips of shoots and roots, or buds.

Merkel, Angela (Dorothea) [merkel], *née* **Kasner** (1954–) German stateswoman and chancellor (2005–), born in Hamburg, Germany. She studied physics at the University of Leipzig and later worked as a chemist. In 1990 she joined the Christian Democratic Union (CDU) political party and soon after was appointed to Helmut Kohl's cabinet as minister for women and youth. In 1998 she was named Secretary-General of the CDU, was chosen party leader in 2000, and ran unsuccessfully for chancellor in 2002. In the 2005 election she narrowly defeated Chancellor Gerhard Schröder, and after the CDU agreed a coalition deal with the Social Democrats (SPD), she was declared Germany' first female chancellor.

Merleau-Ponty, Maurice [mairloh pŏtee] (1908–61) Philosopher, born in Rochefort-sur-mer, France. His books include *La Structure du comportement* (1942, The Structure of Behaviour) and *Phénoménologie de la perception* (1945, The Phenomenology of Perception).

merlin A small falcon native to the N hemisphere (*Falco columbarius*); lacks white cheeks of other falcons; also known as **pigeon hawk**. (Family: Falconidae.)

Merlin In the Arthurian legends, a good wizard or sage whose magic was used to help King Arthur. He was the son of an incubus and a mortal woman, and therefore indestructible; but he was finally entrapped by Vivien, the Lady of the Lake, and bound under a rock for ever. He was famous for his prophecies.

Meroe *Kush*

meroplankton *plankton*

Merovingians [merohvinjianz] The original Frankish royal family, named after the half-legendary Merovech or Meroveus (the 'sea-fighter'). Clovis was the first Merovingian king to control large parts of Gaul.

Mersey, River [merzee] River in NW England; formed at junction of Goyt and Tame Rivers; flows 112 km/70 mi W into the Irish Sea at Liverpool Bay.

Merseyside pop (2001e) 1 362 000; area 652 km²/252 sq mi. County of NW England created in 1974 from parts of Lancashire and Cheshire; metropolitan council abolished in 1986; chief town, Liverpool.

Merthyr Tydfil [merther tidvil], Welsh **Merthyr Tudful** pop (2001e) 56 000; area 111 km²/43 sq mi. County (unitary authority from 1996) in S Wales, UK; administrative centre, Merthyr Tydfil.

Merton, Robert C (1944–) Economist, born in New York City. He worked at MIT, joining Harvard Business School in 1988. He shared the 1997 Nobel Prize for Economics for his contribution to a new method of determining the value of derivatives.

mesa [maysa] An area of high, flat land (tableland) with steep escarpments formed by the remnants of horizontal resistant rocks, and underlain by softer rock.

Mesa Verde [maysa verday] (Span 'green table') An area of precipitous canyons and wooded volcanic mesa in SW Colorado, USA; a world heritage site. It is renowned for its Anasazi Indian cliff-dwellings.

mescal *century plant*

mescal button *peyote*

mescaline [meskalin, -leen] A hallucinogenic drug from the Mexican cactus *Lophophora williamsi*, also known as *Anhalonium lewinii*. It was widely used during the 'psychedelic era' of the 1960s.

Meshed *Mashhad*

Mesmer, Franz Anton [mezmer] (1734–1815) Physician and founder of mesmerism, born near L Constance, Austria. He claimed that there exists a power, which he called 'magnetism', that could be used to cure diseases. In 1778 he went to Paris, where he created a sensation; but in 1785 a learned commission reported unfavourably, and he retired into obscurity in Switzerland.

Mesoamerica or **Middle America** The area covered by Central America and Mexico together. Because Mexico is geographically a part of North America, this term is often used to identify features of cultural or historical importance which both regions share.

meson [meezon] In particle physics, a collective term for strongly interacting subatomic particles having integer spin, each comprising a quark–antiquark pair. Mesons, especially pi-mesons (pions), are responsible for holding together protons and neutrons in atomic nuclei.

Mesopotamia [mesopotaymia] Literally, 'the land between the rivers'; the name in antiquity for the area between the Tigris and Euphrates. **Lower Mesopotamia** was the home of the Sumerian and Babylonian civilizations; **Upper Mesopotamia** was the home of the Assyrians. The world's first urban civilization emerged here during the fourth millennium BC; the Mesopotamian Empire was established c.2300 BC.

Mesosaurus A lightly built, aquatic reptile known from the late Carboniferous to the early Permian periods in South America and S Africa; up to $1\,m/3\frac{1}{4}\,ft$ long. (Class: Anapsida. Order: Mesosauria.)

mesosphere A region of the atmosphere from c.50–80 km/30–50 mi, between the stratosphere below and the thermosphere above. It is characterized by rapidly falling temperature with height, from around 0°C to −100°C.

Mesozoa [mezozoha] A small phylum of multicellular animals found as internal parasites of marine invertebrates such as cephalopod molluscs.

Mesozoic era [mezozohik] A major division of geological time extending from c.250 to 65 million years ago; subdivided into the Triassic, Jurassic, and Cretaceous periods. It was the age of the giant reptiles and the beginning of mammalian life.

Messager, André (Charles Prosper) [mesazhay] (1853–1929) Composer and conductor, born in Montluçon, France. He wrote several operettas and three ballets, notably *Les Deux pigeons* (1886, The Two Pigeons).

Messerschmitt, Willy [mesershmit], popular name of **Wilhelm Messerschmitt** (1898–1978) Aviation designer and production chief, born in Frankfurt, Germany. During World War 2 he supplied the Luftwaffe with its foremost types of combat aircraft.

Messiaen, Olivier (Eugène Prosper Charles) [mesiã] (1908–92) Composer and organist, born in Avignon, France. His music, which has evolved new methods of pitch organization and intricate mathematical rhythmic systems, is motivated by religious mysticism and a keen interest in birdsong.

Messiah [mesiya] (Heb 'anointed one') In Jewish writings from c.2nd-c BC onwards, one who would help deliver Israel from its enemies, aid in its restoration, and establish a worldwide kingdom. In Christian thought, the role is interpreted as fulfilled in Jesus of Nazareth.

Messier, Charles-Joseph [mesyay] (1730–1817) Astronomer, born in Badonviller, France. He is mainly remembered for the Messier Catalog of 103 star clusters, nebulae, and galaxies.

Messina, Strait of, ancient **Fretum Siculum** Channel between Sicily and the Italian mainland; minimum width (N) 5 km/3 mi; length 35 km/22 mi.

ME syndrome An abbreviation for **myalgic encephalomyelitis syndrome**; also known as **chronic fatigue syndrome**. It is characterized by persisting weakness, mild fever, diffuse muscle and joint pains, depression, visual disturbance, and headaches, which persist. The cause is unknown; precipitating factors include viral infections.

metabolism The complete range of biochemical processes taking place within living organisms. It comprises those processes which produce complex substances from simpler components, with a consequent use of energy (**anabolism**), and those which break down complex food molecules, thus liberating energy (**catabolism**). In nutrition, it refers to an efficient way of burning food calories to give the body the energy it needs for its various functions. **Basal metabolism** is the minimum energy expenditure needed to maintain all the vital functions of the body – the energy expended during sleep, or while the body is resting.

metal An element whose solid phase is characterized by high thermal and electrical conductivities. Pure metals are all lustrous, opaque, cold to the touch, and more or less malleable. Most elements are metals, and metallic properties increase from lighter to heavier elements in each group of the periodic table and from right to left in each row.

metal fatigue A weakness which develops in a metal structure that has been subjected to many repeated stresses, even though they may be intermittent. As a result, the structure may fail under a load which it could initially have sustained without fracture.

metallic glass Metal in an amorphous condition (ie the atoms of the metal have no regular or crystalline arrangement; first produced in 1960 by US materials scientist William Klement (1937–). Metallic glasses are useful for transformer cores, and for forming very strong components such as gears.

metallocene *ferrocene*

metallography The study of the structure of metals, usually implying the use of microscopy or X-ray diffraction. Various kinds of structure can be observed, arising from grain, crystalline structure, and the inclusion of impurities.

metalloids Elements midway between being metals and non-metals. They make a diagonal band across the periodic table, and are generally considered to include boron, silicon, germanium, arsenic, antimony, tellurium, and polonium.

metallurgy The technique and science of extracting metals from their ores, converting them into useful forms, and establishing the conditions for their fabrication. The changes undergone by metals are now important aspects of metallurgy, as are the physics and chemistry of corrosion prevention.

metamorphic rock Rock formed by the alteration of pre-existing rock by intense heat and/or pressure, and often accompanied by the action of hot fluids in the Earth's crust. Slates, schists, and gneisses are metamorphic rocks.

metamorphosis In biology, an abrupt structural change, as seen in the marked changes during the development of an organism, especially the transformation from larva to adult, or from one larval stage to the next.

metaphor (Gr 'carrying from one place to another') A figurative device in language where something is referred to, implicitly, in terms of something else: the Moon is a goddess, life a dark wood, the world a stage. An explicit comparison ('Life, like a dome of many-coloured glass') is a **simile**.

metaphysical poetry A term applied to some English poetry of the late 16th-c and early 17th-c, on account of its use of unusual and sometimes difficult ideas in relation to emotional states. Dr Johnson referred to the way in which in this poetry 'heterogeneous ideas [are] yoked by violence together'.

metaphysics A traditional branch of philosophy which deals at the most general level with the nature of existence – what it is, what sorts of things exist, of what categories, and in what structure. The origin of the term is a reference to the text Aristotle wrote 'after the Physics'.

Metastasio, Pietro [metastahzioh], originally **Pietro Armando Dominico Trapassi** (1698–1782) Poet, born in Rome. He wrote the libretti for 27 operas, including Mozart's *Clemenza di Tito*, and in 1729 became court poet at Vienna.

metastasis [metastasis] The occurrence of tumour tissue in organs distant from the site of the primary tumour. It is characteristic of malignant tumours, where cancer cells are transported by way of the bloodstream or lymphatics.

metazoan [metazohan] A multicellular animal with its body organized into specialized tissues and organs; a member of the subkingdom Eumetazoa.

meteor A piece of dust or rock which gives off a streak of light seen when it burns up in the Earth's atmosphere; popularly known as a *shooting star*. A **meteor shower** can be seen when the Earth passes through a trail of dust left by a comet in interplanetary space. *see panel*

Meteor Crater or **Barringer Crater** An impact crater 1·3 km/0·8 mi across near Flagstaff, AZ; estimated age 20 000 years. It is believed to be the result of the impact of a meteorite c.10 m/11 yd across.

meteorite A lump of interplanetary debris that survives a high-speed passage through the atmosphere and hits the ground. Meteorites mostly derive from asteroids, with a few from the Moon and some even from Mars. The types are stony, iron, and stony-iron; some have intriguing inclusions of organic material. A meteorite is known as a **meteoroid** while travelling in space.

meteoroid *meteorite*

meteorology The scientific study of global atmospheric processes: the receipt of solar radiation, evaporation, evapotranspiration, and precipitation, and the determination of, and changes in, atmospheric pressure (and, therefore, wind). Meteorology is generally concerned with the short-term processes (ie hours and days rather than months and seasons) operating in the troposphere and mesosphere.

methanal *formaldehyde*

methane [meethayn, methayn] CH_4. The simplest of the alkane or paraffin hydrocarbons. Formed by the anaerobic decomposition of organic matter, it is the main constituent of natural gas, and was originally called **marsh gas**.

methanogen *Archaebacteria*

methanoic acid *formic acid*

methanol [methanol] CH_3OH, also called **methyl** or **wood alcohol**, boiling point 65°C. A colourless, poisonous liquid, now synthesized from hydrogen and carbon monoxide. It is an important starting chemical in synthesis, a solvent, and a denaturing agent for ethyl alcohol.

Methicillin Resistant *Staphylococcus aureus* (MRSA) A bacterium strain of *Staphylococcus* which has become resistant to normal antibiotics; in the media often referred to as 'staph' or 'the superbug', and used with reference to any antibiotic-resistant strain of the bacterium. The organism is commonly found on the skin or in the nose of many individuals without causing problems, but if it enters the body, for example under the skin or into the lungs, it can cause infection. MRSA can develop in a person who has been on long-term antibiotic treatment using penicillin-type drugs, as the bacterium develops resistance to the antibiotic in an attempt to survive. The infection can also be acquired through direct contact with infected persons, though healthy people are not usually affected.

MRSA was rare before the 1980s, but is now found in many hospitals, where the bacterium readily spreads via health-care staff, if hygiene is lax, attacking patients already weakened by disease, and illnesses and deaths due to MRSA have risen sharply. It can be treated with higher doses of an antibiotic or with a different combination of drugs, but new strains of increasingly resistant bacteria are developing (such as VRSA, **vancomycin resistant *Staphylococcus aureus***), and there is concern over the undisciplined use of antibiotics in the community at large. The spread of infection can be prevented and controlled by following basic hygiene procedures – crucially, thorough hand washing after patient contact and maintaining a clean environment. Other measures are routine screening to identify those carrying the bacterium and carefully controlling which antibiotics are used.

Method, the Both a style of acting and a system of training for the working actor, developed in the USA by Lee Strasberg. The method stresses inner motivation and psychological truth. A well-known exponent of this style is Marlon Brando.

Methodism A Christian denomination founded in 1739 by John Wesley as an evangelical movement within the Church of England, becoming a separate body in 1795. The movement spread rapidly as he travelled the country on horseback and sent other evangelical leaders to the American colonies. The principal doctrines of the Church are laid down in Wesley's sermons, his notes on the New Testament, and his Articles of Religion. In 2006 there were c.34 million Methodists worldwide.

Methodius, St *Cyril, St*

Methuselah [mithoozela] The eighth and longest-lived of the Hebrew patriarchs, who lived before the Flood. His supposed 969 years makes him the paragon of longevity.

methyl alcohol *methanol*

methylated spirits Ethyl alcohol with additives to make it poisonous and unpalatable, and hence unsuitable for beverage use; also called **denatured alcohol**. Its major ingredients are methanol, pyridine, and benzene.

methylbenzene *toluene*

methylbutane *pentane*

Metis [meetis] A tiny natural satellite of Jupiter, discovered in 1979; distance from the planet 128 000 km/79 000 mi; diameter 40 km/25 mi.

Métis [maytee] The mixed blood offspring of primarily French-Canadian and native Indian marriages; in the west, the descendants of the *coureurs de bois*.

metre (UK) **/ meter** (US) (literature) (Gr *metron* 'measure') The recurrence of a rhythmic pattern in poetry, within the line and over larger units (*stanzas*). Different languages measure different things to establish metre. In the classical languages, it is length (or 'quantity'); in Chinese, it is pitch; in Germanic languages, stress. Some English metre works by stress count, some by counting both stressed and unstressed syllables (as in the traditional iamb, dactyl, etc).

Annual major meteor showers

Name	Dates of maximum	Hourly rate
Quadrantids	3–4 January	100
Lyrids	21–22 April	10
Eta Aquarids	5–6 May	35
Delta Aquarids	28–29 July	20
Perseids	12–13 August	75
Orionids	22 October	25
Taurids	4 November	10
Leonids	17–18 November	10
Geminids	13–14 December	75

Mexico

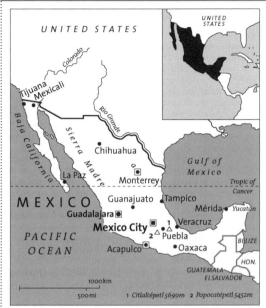

□ International Airport

Span **México** or **Méjico**, official name **United Mexican States**, Span **Estados Unidos Mexicanos**

Local name México
Timezone GMT -8 to -6
Area 1 978 800 km²/763 817 sq mi
Population total (2002e) 100 977 000
Status Republic
Date of independence 1821
Capital Mexico City
Languages Spanish (official), indigenous languages
Ethnic groups Indian-Spanish (mestizo) (60%), Amerindian (30%), white (9%)
Religions Roman Catholic (80%), Protestant (3%)

Physical features Narrow coastal plains; land rises steeply to C plateau, c.2400 m/7800 ft; volcanic peaks to S, notably Citlaltépetl, 5699 m/18 697 ft; limestone lowlands of the Yucatán peninsula stretch into the Gulf of Mexico (SE); region subject to earthquakes.

Climate Tropical climate in S; severe, arid conditions N and W; average annual temperatures 13°C (Jan), 16°C (Jul) in Mexico City; average annual rainfall 747 mm/29·4 in.

Currency 1 Mexican Peso (MXN) = 100 centavos

Economy Wide range of mineral exports; major discoveries of oil and natural gas in the 1970s (now world's fourth largest producer); fluorite and graphite (world's leading producer); large petrochemical industry; important trading relationship with USA, especially after free-trade-area agreement in 1993.

GDP (2002e) $924·4 bn, per capita $8900

Human Development Index (2002) 0·796

History Centre of Indian civilizations for over 2500 years; Gulf Coast Olmecs based at La Venta, Zapotecs at Monte Albán near Oaxaca, Mixtecs at Mitla, Toltecs at Tula, Maya in the Yucatán, Aztecs at Tenochtitlán; Spanish arrival in 1516; Vice-royalty of New Spain established; struggle for independence from 1810; federal republic, 1824; lost territory to the USA, 1836, and after the Mexican War, 1846–8; civil war, 1858–61; occupation of Mexico City by French forces, 1863–7; revolution, 1910–17; major earthquake in Mexicio City, 1985; revolt in S state of Chiapas by Zapatista National Liberation Army, 1994; negotiations over Indian rights in late 1990s, ongoing; major economic crises, 1994, followed by package of loan guarantees from the USA, 1995; governed by a President, Cabinet, and bicameral Congress with a Senate and a Chamber of Deputies.

Head of State/Government
1940–6 Manuel Avila Camacho
1946–52 Miguel Alemán
1952–8 Adolfo Ruiz Cortines
1958–64 Adolfo López Mateos
1964–70 Gustavo Díaz Ordaz
1970–6 Luis Echeverría
1976–82 José López Portillo
1982–8 Miguel de la Madrid Hurtado
1988–94 Carlos Salinas de Gortari
1994–2000 Ernesto Zedillo
2000–6 Vincente Fox
2006– Felipe Calderón

metre (UK) **/ meter** (US) (physics) Base SI unit of length; symbol *m*; defined as the length of the path travelled by light in a vacuum during an interval of 1/299 792 458 of a second; commonly used as **kilometre** (*km*, 1000 m), **centimetre** (*cm*, 1/100 m) and **millimetre** (*mm*, 1/1000 m).

metronome A device for indicating and determining the tempo of a musical work. The type in common use, patented in 1815 by Johann Nepomuk Maelzel (1770–1838), works like a pendulum clock; its rate of swing, and therefore of 'tick', is controlled by an adjustable weight on the upper extension of a pendulum arm.

Metternich, Klemens (Wenzel Nepomuk Lothar), Fürst von (Prince of) **[meternikh]** (1773–1859) Austrian statesman, born in Koblenz, Germany. He took a prominent part in the Congress of Vienna (1814), and between 1815 and 1848 was the most powerful influence for conservatism in Europe, contributing much to the tension that produced the upheaval of 1848.

Metz [mets], ancient **Divodurum Mediomatricum** 49°08N 6°10E, pop (2000e) 125 000. Fortified town in NE France; on R Moselle; strategic focus of crossroads; residence of Merovingian kings, 6th-c; later, part of Holy Roman Empire; taken by

France, 1552; part of Germany from 1871 until after World War 1; scene of major German defence in 1944 invasion; World War 1 military cemetery nearby; airport; bishopric; university (1971); Gothic cathedral (1250–1380); trade in coal, metals, wine.

Meung, Jean de *Jean de Meung*

Meuse, River [moez], Dutch **Maas**, ancient **Mosa** River in NE France, Belgium, and The Netherlands, rising on the Langres Plateau, NE France; enters the North Sea in the Rhine delta; length 950 km/590 mi.

Mexican War (1846–8) A war between Mexico and the USA, which began in territory disputed between Texas (annexed by the USA but claimed by Mexico) and Mexico. US troops invaded Mexico and forced a capitulation in which Mexico ceded most of the present-day SW United States.

Mexico *see panel*

Mexico, Gulf of area 1 543 000 km²/596 000 sq mi. Gulf on the SE coast of North America; deepest point, Sigsbee Deep (3878 m/12 723 ft); oil and natural gas resources on continental shelves.

Mexico City, Span **Ciudad de México** 19°25N 99°10W, pop (2000e) 11 431 000; 'Metromex' region, pop (2000e)

26 000 000. Federal district and capital of Mexico; in C Mexico, altitude 2200 m/7200 ft, area 50 km^2/20 sq mi; largest city in the world; built on the site of the Aztec capital, Tenochtitlán; city centre a world heritage site; airport; railway; seven universities; cathedral (16th–19th-c), National Palace (1692); location of 1968 summer Olympic Games; major earthquake (1985) killed c.20 000.

Meyerbeer, Giacomo [miyerbayer], originally **Jakob Liebmann Meyer Beer** (1791–1864) Operatic composer, born in Berlin. His operas include *Robert le Diable* (1831) and *Les Huguenots* (1836).

mezzanine [mezaneen] An intermediate floor in a building, placed between two main (usually lower) storeys; also known as an **entresol**.

Mezzogiorno [metzohjaw(r)noh] pop (2000e) 20 383 000. Geographical region comprising regions of S Italy and the islands of Sicily and Sardinia; a largely agricultural area; name ('midday') refers to the heat of the region; devastated by earthquake (1980).

mezzotint [metzohtint] A technique of engraving which gives tonal rather than linear effects. Invented c.1640, it was rendered obsolete by photography in the 19th-c.

Miami [miyamee] 25°47N 80°11W, pop (2000e) 362 500. Port city in SE Florida, USA; settled around a military post in the 1830s; since 1945, one of the country's most famous and popular resorts; airport; railway; major tourist industry with extensive recreational facilities; hub of a large agricultural region; large numbers of immigrants (nearly half the metropolitan population is Hispanic); professional teams, Dolphins (football), Heat (basketball), Marlins (baseball).

Miami Beach 25°47N 80°08W, pop (2000e) 87 900. Town in SE Florida, USA, on an island across Biscayne Bay from Miami; area developed in 1920s; railway; connected to Miami by four causeways; popular year-round resort, famous for its 'gold coast' hotel strip.

Miao [myow] A Sino-Tibetan-speaking mountain people of SE Asia and S China, constituting many different groups. Population more than 4 million, mostly in China.

Micah, Book of [miyka] or **Micheas, Book of** One of the 12 so-called 'minor' prophetic books of the Hebrew Bible/Old Testament, attributed to the prophet Micah of Moresheth-gath, a contemporary of Isaiah in Judah and active in the late 8th-c BC. Some parts may be of later date (6th–5th-c BC).

micas [miykaz] An important group of common rock-forming minerals characterized by a layer structure which gives the crystals a platy form and a perfect basal cleavage. Important members are *muscovite* (white mica), a light, silvery-coloured potassium aluminium silicate, and *biotite*, which is dark brown, and contains additional iron and magnesium.

Michael (of Romania) (1921–) King of Romania (1927–30, 1940–7), born in Sinaia, Romania, the son of Carol II (1893–1953). He first came to the throne on the death of his grandfather, his father having renounced his own claims in 1925. In 1930 he was supplanted by his father Carol (r.1930–40), then returned to the throne when the Germans gained control of Romania. In 1944 he helped to overthrow the dictatorship of Antonescu, but was later compelled to abdicate (1947), and has since lived in exile near Geneva.

Michael (angel) An angel described as the guardian of Israel (*Dan* 10, 12). He appears as a great patron, intercessor, and warrior in later Jewish non-canonical works.

Michael, George, originally **Yorgos Kyriatou Panayiotou** (1963–) Singer and songwriter, born in Finchley, Greater London. A partner with **Andrew Ridgeley** (1963–) of the band Wham!, he released his debut solo single 'Careless Whisper' in 1985, which reached number 1 in the UK charts. His debut solo album, *Faith* (1988), stayed in the US charts for over a year.

Later albums include *Ladies and Gentlemen* (1998) and *Patience* (2004).

Michaelmas [miklmas] In the Christian Church, the feast of St Michael and All Angels (29 Sep); a quarter-day in England and Wales.

Michaelmas daisy [miklmas] A member of a large group of perennial cultivars of aster, mostly derived from the North American *Aster novi-belgii*; flower-heads daisy-like; spreading outer florets blue, pink, red, or white; inner disc florets yellow. (Genus: *Aster*. Family: Compositae.)

Micheas (OT book) [mikayas] *Micah, Book of*

Michelangelo [miyklanjeloh], in full **Michelangelo di Lodovico Buonarroti Simoni** (1475–1564) Sculptor, painter, and poet, born in Caprese, Italy. His 'Cupid' was bought by Cardinal San Giorgio, who summoned him to Rome (1496). In Florence he sculpted the marble 'David', and the 'Pietà' in the cathedral. In 1503 Julius II summoned him back to Rome, where he was commissioned to design the pope's tomb, and decorated the ceiling of the Sistine Chapel with paintings (1508–12). His last pictorial achievement was 'The Last Judgment' (1537), and the next year he was appointed architect of St Peter's, to which he devoted himself until his death.

Michelin, André [michelin], Fr [meeshlĩ] (1853–1931) Tyre manufacturer, born in Paris. He and his younger brother **Edouard** (1859–1940) were the first to use demountable pneumatic tyres on motor cars. They also initiated the production of high-quality road maps and guide books.

Michelson, A(lbert) A(braham) [mikelsn] (1852–1931) Physicist, born in Strzelno, Poland. He is chiefly remembered for his experiment with US chemist **Edward Williams Morley** (1838–1923) to determine ether drift, the negative result of which set Einstein on the road to the theory of relativity. He was the first US scientist to receive a Nobel Prize (1907).

Michigan [mishigan] pop (2000e) 9 938 400; area 151 579 km^2/58 527 sq mi. State in NC USA; the 'Great Lake State' or the 'Wolverine State'; 26th state admitted to the Union, 1837; settled by the French, 1668; ceded to the British, 1763; handed over to the USA in 1783 and became part of Indiana Territory; Territory of Michigan established, 1805; 99 909 km^2/38 565 sq mi of the Great Lakes lie within the state boundary; highest point Mt Curwood (604 m/1982 ft); capital, Lansing; major tourist area; the S part of the state is highly industrialized; motor vehicles and parts, iron and steel (second in the country for iron ore production); corn and dairy products.

Michigan, Lake Third largest of the Great Lakes (area 58 020 km^2/22 400 sq mi) and the only one lying entirely within the USA; 494 km/307 mi long; maximum width 190 km/118 mi; maximum depth 281 m/922 ft; linked in the NE with L Huron via the Strait of Mackinac.

Michiko *Akihito*

Mickiewicz, Adam (Bernard) [mitskyayvich] (1798–1855) National poet of Poland, born near Navahrudak, Belarus (formerly Novogrodek). His masterpiece is the epic *Pan Tadeusz* (1834, Thaddeus). In 1853 he went to Italy to organize the Polish legion.

microbe *micro-organism*

microchip A tiny wafer of semiconductor material, such as silicon, processed to form an integrated circuit. With progress in circuit fabrication technology, the integration size of an IC (integrated circuit) chip was improved through **large-scale integration (LSI)**, which made it possible to pack thousands of transistors and related electronic components onto a single chip. Further advances led to the integration size being increased to **very large-scale integration (VLSI)**, in which hundreds of thousands of transistors and related electronic components are packed onto each IC chip. When memory and logic circuits are built in, the microchip becomes known as a microprocessor.

microcomputer A computer based on a single chip microprocessor plus necessary memory and input and output devices. The term (often abbreviated to **micro**) was first applied to the small desktop computers which first appeared in the 1970s.

microeconomics The study of decision-making by individuals and firms. This includes personal decisions about training, earning and spending income, and retirement. It includes decisions about setting up or closing down firms, what funds should be lent or borrowed, what investment to make in productive equipment, how many people to employ, what to produce, at what price and by what methods it can be sold, and what attitude is taken to risk. Much of microeconomics uses the assumption that individuals try to maximise utility, and firms try to maximise profits.

microelectronics A branch of electronics concerned with producing and using microcircuits – miniaturized electronic circuits consisting of tiny transistors, integrated circuits, and other electronic components often contained in one microchip. Microelectronic circuiting is used in computers, inertial guidance systems, and spacecraft.

microfarad *farad*

microfilm Black-and-white photographic material of extremely fine grain and high resolution for document copying on a greatly reduced scale. Microfilms are usually read by enlarged projection.

microfloppy disk *minidisk*

microgravity A state of free-fall weightlessness experienced in spacecraft. Gravitational effects of the spacecraft itself make it difficult to obtain less than one-millionth Earth gravity for experimentation. There are limited opportunities for microgravity experiments in the small space stations presently available.

microlight *hang glider*

micromachine A fully functional device, such as a tiny motor, or robot, which may be no bigger than a speck of sand. The tiny size of micromachines allows them to be used in locations where people are unable to operate, such as inside other working machines, in the heart of nuclear reactors, or in pipes full of poisonous substances. Fitted with cameras, they can be used inside the human body to give surgeons a unique insight into problems.

micrometre *micron*

micron Unit of length; symbol μ; defined as one micrometre or 10^{-6} m; commonly used in biological sciences.

Micronesia A collection of island groups in the N Pacific. Included are the Marianas, Carolines, Marshalls, Kiribati (Gilbert Is), and Nauru. Most are of atoll formation, and very small. The people are outwardly distinguishable from Melanesians and Polynesians, and analysis of their blood typing suggests that they are a distinctive racial grouping.

Micronesia, Federated States of *p.604*

micronutrients *nutrients*

micro-organism An organism of microscopic size, typically not visible to the unaided eye; also referred to as a **microbe**.

microphone A device that converts acoustic waves in air to electrical signals for transmission, recording, and reproduction. First developed by Bell and Edison in 1876–7 for telephony, microphones are widely employed in telecommunications, sound recording, and hearing aids. In all types, impinging sound waves cause corresponding oscillations of a diaphragm. These movements in their turn vary a resistance (**carbon microphones**, as in telephone receivers), capacitance (**condenser microphones**), electromagnetic field (**dynamic and coil microphones**), or the shape of a piezo-electric crystal (**crystal microphones**), each producing a variation in electrical output. A **lavallier** [la**val**yay] is a small personal microphone worn by the speaker on a neck-cord or coat lapel, allowing freedom of movement.

microprocessor *microchip; microcomputer*

micro-satellite DNA *satellite DNA*

microscope An optical instrument for producing enlarged images of minute objects. The compound microscope, in which a second lens further magnifies the image produced by a primary lens, was invented in the Netherlands in the late 16th-c. The effectiveness of compound light microscopes is limited by the resolving power of the lens; magnifications can be achieved up to a maximum of 2000. Electron microscopes allow magnifications of over 500 000.

Microscopium (Lat 'microscope') A small, faint S constellation, introduced in the 18th-c.

Microsoft A computer company which came into prominence with the design and supply of the operating system (MS-DOS) for the IBM personal computer. The system is supported by spreadsheet and word-processing packages and more recently by the Windows application software. During the 1990s, Microsoft became the world's leading computer company, and found itself having to defend its practices when the US government brought an initially successful anti-trust (monopoly) action against it in 1999, arguing that Microsoft unfairly used the dominance of its Windows computer operating system to squeeze out smaller rivals. In 2000 a judge ordered that Microsoft be split into two companies. This ruling was overturned in June 2001 by the US Court of Appeals, and later that year Microsoft and the Justice Dept. agreed on a settlement, though a group of states continued to press for tougher penalties. In 2003 Microsoft faced a European challenge in Brussels along similar lines, and in 2004 a record fine of €497.2 million was imposed on the company for unfairly using its near-monopoly dominance in European markets.

microteaching A technique used in the training of teachers which involves the trainee practising a specific teaching skill (such as questioning or explaining) for a short time with a small group of children, receiving feedback such as a tutor's comments, a written appraisal, or seeing a videotape of the mini-lesson.

microtone A musical interval smaller than a semitone. Microtones are indigenous to some musical cultures, especially in the East, and they occur naturally in the harmonic series.

microwave background radiation *cosmic background radiation*

microwave oven An oven, first constructed in 1947, which uses microwave radiation to heat food. The radiation penetrates inside food, where it is absorbed primarily by water molecules, causing heat to spread through the food. This penetration effect makes heating much faster than in conventional ovens.

microwaves Electromagnetic radiation of wavelength between 1 mm and 10 cm, less than radio waves and more than infrared. They are produced by klystrons and magnetrons, and used in radar, communications, and microwave ovens.

micturition *urine*

Midas [**miy**das] A legendary King of Phrygia. As a reward for helping the satyr, Silenus, Dionysus gave Midas a wish, and he asked that anything he touched should turn to gold. However, this caused so many difficulties (eg in eating) that he asked to be released; he was told to bathe in the River Pactolus, which thereafter had golden sands.

Middle Ages The period of European history between the collapse of the Roman Empire in the West and the Renaissance (c.500–c.1500); sometimes, however, the term is restricted in its use to the four or five centuries after the year 1000, characterized by such features as the emergence of national states, separate kingdoms, the development of forms of government, the foundation of universities, and the flowering of scholarship. In the 15th-c and 16th-c the Renaissance in Italy and humanism in N Europe marked a new spirit of sceptical inquiry which heralded the end of mediaevalism in much of Europe.

Micronesia, Federated States of

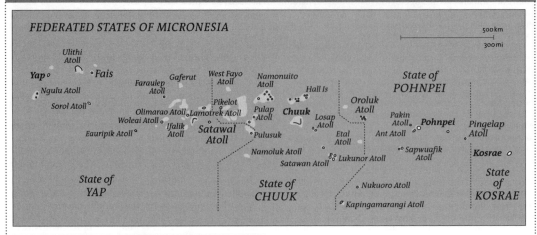

FEDERATED STATES OF MICRONESIA

500 km
300 mi

□ International Airport

Timezone GMT +11

Area 700 km²/270 sq mi

Population total (2002e) 109 000

Status Republic

Date of independence 1991

Capital Palikir (on Pohnpei Island)

Languages English (official), with several indigenous languages also spoken

Ethnic groups Trukese (41%), Pohnpeian (26%)

Religions Roman Catholic (50%), Protestant (47%)

Physical features Group of four states in the W Pacific Ocean (Yap, Truk, Pohnpei, Kosrae); comprises all the Caroline I except Belau; islands vary from high mountainous terrain to low coral atolls.

Climate Tropical climate, with occasional typhoons; heavy rainfall all year.

Currency 1 US Dollar (USD) = 100 cents

Economy Agriculture; farming and fishing; tropical fruits, coconuts, vegetables; few mineral resources.

GDP (2002e) $277 mn, per capita $2000

History Settled by Spanish seafarers, 1565; formally annexed by Spain, 1874; sold to Germany, 1899; control mandated to Japan by League of Nations, 1920; American Navy took control following Japan's defeat in World War 2, 1945; part of UN Trust Territory of the Pacific, 1947; compact of free association with the US, 1982; trusteeship ended, 1990; independent state, 1991, under Compact of Free Association, the US continues to control its defence and foreign relations; governed by a President and a National Congress.

Head of State/Government
1991–6 Bailey Olter
1996–9 Jacob Nena
1999–2003 Leo Falcam
2003– Joseph Urusemal

Middle America A geographical region encompassing Mexico, Central America, and the West Indies; includes the Gulf of Mexico and the Caribbean.

Middle East A loosely defined geographical region encompassing the largely Arab States to the E of the Mediterranean, together with Cyprus, Turkey, and the countries of North Africa. The region conventionally includes the countries of Syria, Lebanon, Israel, Jordan, Egypt, Iraq, Iran, Kuwait, Saudi Arabia, Bahrain, Qatar, Oman, United Arab Emirates, Yemen, Sudan, Libya, Tunisia, Algeria, and Morocco.

Middlesbrough [midlzbruh] 54°35N 1°14W, pop (2001e) 134 800. Port town and (from 1996) unitary authority, NE England; on the R Tees estuary; developed around the iron industry in the 19th-c; railway; university, 1992.

middle school A type of school in the UK for children aged 8–12 or 9–13. The former are regarded as primary, the latter as secondary schools.

Middlesex Former county of England, which lost its official iden-

tity after local government reorganization in 1965. Most of its area was subsumed under Greater London, with some districts transferred to Surrey and Hertfordshire. The name continues to be used by many local organizations.

Middle Temple *Inns of Court*

Middleton, Thomas (c.1580–1627) Playwright, born in London. His works include the satirical *A Game at Chess* (1624), and the tragedy *Women Beware Women* (?1621). He also collaborated in many plays, such as *The Changeling* (1622), with William Rowley (c.1585–c.1642).

Middle West or **Midwest** The region of the USA comprising the states between the Great Lakes and the upper Mississippi R valley: Illinois, Indiana, Iowa, Kansas, Minnesota, Missouri, Nebraska, Ohio, and Wisconsin.

Midgard [midgah(r)d] Middle Earth, the land in which human beings live, according to Norse mythology.

midge A small, delicate fly that gathers in vast swarms at dusk near standing water; adults gnat-like but non-biting, as mouthparts are poorly developed. (Order: Diptera. Family: Chironomidae, c.5000 species.)

midget *dwarfism*

Mid Glamorgan pop (2000e) 551 500; area 1018 km²/393 sq mi. Former county in S Wales, UK; created in 1974, and replaced in 1996 by Merthyr Tydfil, Caerphilly, Bridgend, and Rhondda Cynon Taff counties.

MIDI [midee] *digital media*

Midianites [midianiyts] An ancient semi-nomadic people dwelling in the desert area of the Transjordan. They are portrayed as enticing the Israelites into idolatry, but are overcome by Gideon (*Jud* 6–8).

Midland Canal *Mittelland Canal*

Midler, Bette [bet] (1945–) Comedienne and actress, born in Honolulu, HI. She developed a popular nightclub act with outrageously bawdy comic routines, and in 1974 received a Tony Award for a record-breaking Broadway show. Her performance in the film *The Rose* (1979) earned her an Oscar nomination. Later films include *The First Wives Club* (1996), *Get Bruce* (1999), and *The Stepford Wives* (2004).

midnight sun A phenomenon during the summer period within the Arctic and Antarctic circles, when the Sun remains continuously above the horizon. There is an equal period in winter when the Sun does not rise at all.

midrash [midrash] In general terms, teaching linked to a running exposition of scriptural texts, especially found in rabbinic literature. The term can also apply to the genre of rabbinic writings which consist of such interpretations.

midsummer The summer solstice or 'longest day', which falls in the northern hemisphere on 21 or 22 June, depending on the locality. **Midsummer Day**, a quarter-day in England and Wales, is 24 June. It is preceded by **Midsummer Night**, when supernatural beings are said to roam abroad.

Midway Islands 28°15N 177°25W; pop (2000e) 450; area 3 km²/1 sq mi. Circular atoll enclosing two small islands in the C Pacific Ocean 1850 km/1150 mi NW of Oahu, Hawaii; annexed by USA, 1867; submarine cable station since 1905; military airbase since 1941; Allied air victory in the Battle of Midway (1942) was a turning point in World War 2.

midwife toad A European frog of the family Discoglossidae; lives away from water; mates on dry land; male wraps eggs around his legs and carries them until they hatch, then puts tadpoles in water.

Mies van der Rohe, Ludwig [mees van duh rohuh], also spelled **Miës**, originally **Ludwig Mies** (1886–1969) Architect and designer, born in Aachen, Germany. He was director of the Bauhaus at Dessau and Berlin (1930–3), and moved to Chicago in 1938. Among his major works are the Seagram Building in New York City (1956–8) and the Public Library in Washington, DC (1967). He also designed tubular-steel furniture, particularly the 'Barcelona chair'.

mifepristone *contraception*

migraine A recurrent, severe, usually one-sided headache, often accompanied by vomiting and a visual disturbances. It tends to occur in young people, lasts a few hours, and lessens in severity and frequency with age. It is believed to arise from the constriction of small arteries within the brain followed by their dilation.

migration 1 In anthropology and sociology, a movement of population within or between countries. Migration within countries has been preponderantly towards urban centres, seen by migrants as attractive alternatives to rural overpopulation and its associated deprivation. International migration (*emigration*) may be a response to other factors, such as political threats against minority groups or warfare.

2 In biology, the movement of organisms or their dispersal stages (seeds, spores, or larvae) from one area to another; usu-ally the periodic two-way movements that take place over relatively long distances and along well-defined routes.

Mihailović, Dragoljub [mihiylohvich], nickname **Drazha** (1893–1946) Serbian soldier, born in Ivanjica, Serbia. He remained in Yugoslavia in 1941 after the German occupation, forming groups (*Chetniks*) to wage guerrilla warfare. He was executed in Belgrade by the Tito government for collaboration.

Mikonos or **Mykonos** [meekonos] pop (2000e) 5800; area 85 km²/33 sq mi. Island of the Cyclades, Greece; airfield; several noted resorts.

Mikoyan, Anastas Ivanovich [mikoyan] (1895–1978) Soviet statesman, born in Sanain, Armenia. He supported Stalin against Trotsky, and in 1926 became minister of trade, doing much to improve Soviet standards of living.

Milan, Ital **Milano** 45°28N 9°12E, pop (2000e) 1431000. Commercial city in Lombardy, N Italy, on R Olna; Gallic town, taken by the Romans in 222 BC; later the chief city of the Western Roman Empire; from 12th-c, ruled by the dukes of Milan; Duchy of Milan held by Spain, 16th-c; ceded to Austria, 1713; capital of Kingdom of Italy, 1797–1814; held by Austria, 1815–60; two airports; railway junction; underground; two universities (1920, 1923); Santa Maria delle Grazie (15th-c, with Leonardo da Vinci's 'Last Supper' on the wall of the adjoining monastery); a world heritage site; cathedral (14th-c), Palazzo dell'ambrosiana (1603–9), La Scala opera house (1775–8).

mildew Any fungal disease of a plant in which the thread-like fungal strands are visible on the leaves of the host plant as pale or white patches.

Milesians [miyleezhnz] A group of Presocratic philosopher-scientists who came from Miletus in Ionia and were active in the 6th-c BC. Thales, Anaximander, and Anaximenes are usually regarded as the first Greek philosophers, in the sense that they offered rational rather than supernatural accounts of cosmology.

Miletus [miyleetus] A prosperous Greek city-state in Ionia on the W coast of Asia Minor. It was the birthplace of the Milesians.

milfoil *yarrow*

Milhaud, Darius [meeoh] (1892–1974) Composer, born in Aix-en-Provence, France. For a time he was a member of *Les Six*. He was a prolific composer, writing several operas, ballets, and symphonies, and orchestral, choral, and chamber works.

Militant Tendency A British political group which came to prominence in the 1980s. (*Militant* is a newspaper published originally by Labour Party members espousing Marxist positions). Its supporters infiltrated a number of local Labour Parties and the Young Socialists (its youth wing). Fearing the adverse electoral publicity resulting from Militant activities, the Labour Party moved to expel members of Militant on the grounds that they were members of a separate political party. After this, Militant's influence in the Party declined. In 1996 it became the *Socialist Party*.

Military Cross (MC) A military award in the UK, instituted in 1914, awarded to captains, lieutenants, and warrant officers in the Army for acts of gallantry or devotion to duty. The ribbon has equal stripes: white, purple, white.

military intelligence The collection and evaluation of information relevant to military decision making. Intelligence can be gathered by many means, such as listening to enemy electronic emissions (electronic intelligence, or *elint*), monitoring signals traffic (*Sigint*), the use of surveillance satellites, and traditional espionage techniques. National agencies which collate information at a strategic level include the US Defense Intelligence Agency (DIA) and the British Secret Intelligence Service (SIS). The practice of resisting and frustrating hostile attempts to gain military, political, or scientific intelligence is known as **counter-intelligence**.

military science The theoretical study of warfare and of the strategic, tactical, and logistic principles behind it. It is concerned with such unchanging principles as the primacy of the objective, concentration of force, economy of force, surprise, and manoeuvre.

militia A military force raised (usually in times of emergency) for national defence, separate from the regular army. These national forces are raised by government decree, and can thus be distinguished from guerrilla forces.

milk A white or whitish liquid secreted by the mammary glands of female mammals to nourish their young. The milk of many species has been consumed by humans from earliest times, especially cow's milk, with goat's, ewe's, and buffalo milk also making a significant contribution in various parts of the world. Milk is about 88% water, 4·8% lactose, 3·2% protein, and 3·9% fat. *Cream* is the yellowish surface layer of fat which forms when milk is allowed to stand. This may be removed, leaving water emulsion and **skimmed milk**. Low-fat milk, which is increasing in popularity, is produced by partially removing the fat (by 50% – **semi-skimmed milk**).

milk of magnesia A suspension of magnesium hydroxide $(Mg(OH)_2)$ used as an antacid to sooth an acid stomach. It can also be used as a mild laxative.

milkwort A perennial herb or small shrub, found almost everywhere; flowers in spikes, five sepals, two inner large, often brightly coloured, enclosing three petals fused with eight stamens to form a tube. (Genus: *Polygala*, 500–600 species. Family: Polygalaceae.)

Milky Way A diffuse band of light across the sky, resulting from the combined light of thousands of millions of faint stars in our Galaxy. Strictly it means the belt of light seen in the night sky, but the term is used freely, as the name of the Galaxy to which our Sun belongs.

Mill, John Stuart (1806–73) Philosopher and social reformer, born in London. He was educated by his father, Scottish philosopher James Mill (1773–1836), and became an MP in 1865, supporting women's suffrage and liberalism. His major writings include *Principles of Political Economy* (1848), *On Liberty* (1859), and his most widely known work, *Utilitarianism* (1863).

Millais, Sir John Everett [milay] (1829–96) Painter, born in Southampton, Hampshire. He became a founder of the Pre-Raphaelite Brotherhood, his works in this style including the controversial 'Christ in the House of His Parents' (1850, Tate, London). He later became well known for his woodcut illustrations for magazines. He served as president of the Royal Academy in 1896.

Millay, Edna St Vincent [milay] (1892–1950) Poet, born in Rockland, ME. She received the Pulitzer Prize with *The Harp-Weaver* (1923).

millenarianism [milinaireeuhnizm] The belief held by some Christians that there will be a thousand-year (millennium) reign of the saints, either before or immediately after the return of Christ. The belief is usually based on an interpretation of *Rev* 20. 1–7. In recent decades, the term has been used more broadly by social scientists, referring to any religious group looking forward to a sudden and early transformation of the world.

Millennium Dome The centrepiece of the UK's millennial celebrations, opened on 31 December 1999, designed by the Richard Rogers Partnership, and built in Greenwich, at a cost of £758 million: diameter 320 m/1050 ft, height 50 m/164 ft, circumference 1 km/0·62 mi, floor space 8 hectares/20 acres. Its contents included 14 thematic areas devoted to the mind, the body (including the world's largest representation of the human form), spiritual belief, workplace skilling, the nature of learning, the financial world, relaxation and imagination, leisure and play, community, the environment, planet Earth, and the nature of British identity today. It closed at the end of 2000 with an uncertain future, but after development by the

Anschutz Entertainment Group it was renamed **The O2** and opened as an entertainment/sporting complex in mid-2007.

Millennium Stadium *Cardiff Arms Park*

Millennium Wheel *London Eye*

Miller, Arthur (1915–2005) Playwright, born in New York City. His major works include *All My Sons* (1947), *Death of a Salesman* (1949, Pulitzer), *A View from the Bridge* (1955), *The Crucible* (1953), and *Playing for Time* (1981). In 1956 he received considerable publicity from his marriage to Marilyn Monroe (divorced 1961), and in 1957 he was tried and found guilty of contempt of Congress for refusing to reveal to the House Un-American Activities Committee the names of a literary circle suspected of Communist affiliations. His autobiography *Timebends* was published in 1987. In 1999 he was awarded the Prix Molière. His autobiographical play, *Finishing the Picture* (2004), is based on Monroe's last film, *The Misfits* (1961).

Miller, (Alton) Glenn (1904–44) Bandleader and trombonist, born in Clarinda, IA. In 1938 he enjoyed phenomenal success with his 'sweet' ensemble sound, fox-trot rhythms, and well-drilled showmanship. During 1939–42, his hit records included 'Moonlight Serenade' (his theme song), 'Little Brown Jug', and 'In the Mood'. He joined the US Air Force in 1942, and assembled a large orchestra which he took to England, but was killed while travelling in an aircraft lost without trace over the English Channel.

Miller, Henry (Valentine) (1891–1980) Writer, born in New York City. His early books *Tropic of Cancer* (1934) and *Tropic of Capricorn* (1938), much of which is autobiographical and explicitly sexual, were not published in Britain and the USA until the early 1960s. Later work includes the series *Sexus* (1945), *Plexus* (1949), and *Nexus* (1960).

Miller, Sir Jonathan (Wolfe) (1934–) Actor and director, born in London. He qualified as a doctor, and his career has combined medical research with contributions to stage and television. He came to public attention as part of the *Beyond the Fringe* team (1961–4), and has since directed for several theatres, including the National Theatre, English National Opera, and the Old Vic. He is also known for his television work, notably the BBC series *The Body in Question* (1977) and *States of Mind* (1982).

Miller, Keith (Ross) (1919–2004) Cricketer, born in Melbourne, Victoria, Australia. In the great Don Bradman Test side of 1948, he established himself as the world's leading all-rounder of the time. During his career he scored 2958 runs in 55 Test matches, including seven centuries, and took 170 wickets.

Miller, Merton (1923–2000) Economist, born in Boston, MA. In 1990 he shared the Nobel Prize for Economics for his contributions in applying economic theory to the field of corporate finance.

miller's thumb *bullhead*

Millet, Jean François [meeay] (1814–75) Painter, born in Gruchy, France. After the 1848 Revolution he settled at Barbizon. His paintings of rustic life included 'Sower' (1850) and 'The Gleaners' (1857).

millet A small-grained, rather inferior cereal from the tropics and warm temperate regions, grown in poor areas or as emergency crops mainly for animal feed and bird seed. (*Panicum miliaceum*. Family: Gramineae.)

millibar *bar* (physics)

Milligan, Spike, popular name of **Terence Alan Patrick Sean Milligan** (1918–2002) Humorist, born in Ahmadnagar, India. He became known through co-writing and performing in *The Goon Show* (1951–9). His unique perspective on the world, allied to an irrepressible sense of the ridiculous, has been a major influence on British humour.

Millikan, Robert (Andrews) (1868–1953) Physicist, born in Morrison, IL. His oil drop experiment demonstrated that electric charge always occurs in multiples of a fixed electron charge, and measured the value of this charge. He was awarded the 1923 Nobel Prize for Physics. He also did important work on cosmic rays, showing them to come from space.

millilitre *litre*

millimetre *metre* (physics)

millipede A long-bodied, terrestrial arthropod; typically with double body segments, each bearing two pairs of walking legs. (Class: Diplopoda, c.10 000 species.)

Mills, Hayley (1946–) Film actress, born in London. She made her film debut in *Tiger Bay* (1959) with her father, John Mills. She won a special Oscar for her part in *Pollyanna* (1960), and went on to star in such films as *The Parent Trap* (1961), *Whistle Down The Wind* (1961), *Endless Night* (1971), and *Appointment With Death* (1988).

Mills, Sir John (Lewis Ernest Watts) (1908–2005) Actor, born in Felixstowe, Suffolk. Much in demand for typically English roles, his character parts were often outstanding, as in *Great Expectations* (1946) and *The History of Mr Polly* (1949). Later roles were in *Ryan's Daughter* (1978, Oscar), *Gandhi* (1982), and *Deadly Advice* (1994). He married Mary Hayley Bell (1914–2005) in 1941; their daughters, **Juliet** and **Hayley**, are both actresses.

Mills, Juliet (Maryon) (1941–) Film actress, born in London, the daughter of Sir John Mills. Her films include *Carry on Jack* (1964), *Oh! What a Lovely War* (1969), and *Jonathan Livingston Seagull* (1973), as well as several television movies, such as *Waxwork II* (1992) and *A Stranger in the Mirror* (1993).

Milne, A(lan) A(lexander) (1882–1956) Writer, born in London. In 1924 he achieved world fame with his book of children's verse, *When We Were Very Young*, written for his own son, Christopher Robin; further classics include *Winnie-the-Pooh* (1926) and *The House at Pooh Corner* (1928).

Milo of Croton [miyloh, meeloh] (6th-c BC) Greek athlete, from Crotona in Magna Graecia. He was twelve times victor for wrestling at the Olympic and Pythian games, and commanded the army which defeated the Sybarites (511 BC).

Milosevic, Slobodan [milosuhvich] (1941–2006) President of Serbia (1990–2000) and Yugoslavia (1997–2000), born in Pozarevac, Serbia. He studied law at Belgrade University, then began a career in management and banking before entering politics. He was the founder and president of the socialist party of Serbia. He became the focus of world attention during the Kosovo crisis and NATO confrontation in early 1999. In 2001 he was arrested and handed over to UN investigators to face a war crimes tribunal in The Hague. His trial began in February 2002 and was ongoing in 2006, with repeated delays due to his health, but everything came to a premature conclusion when he was found dead in his cell (Mar 2006).

Miłosz, Czeslaw [meewosh, chezhwof] (1911–2004) Poet, born in Szetejnie, Lithuania. His books include *Hymn of the Pearl* (1981), *Hymn of the Earth* (1986), and *Road-Side Dog* (1998) (trans titles). A selection of his wartime essays, *Legends of Modernity* (trans title), appeared in 1996. He was awarded the Nobel Prize for Literature in 1980.

Milstein, César [milstiyn] (1927–2002) Molecular biologist, born in Bahía Blanca, Argentina. His main research had been into the production of monoclonal antibodies. He shared the Nobel Prize for Physiology or Medicine in 1984.

Miltiades, the Younger [miltiyadeez] (c.550–489 BC) Athenian general, statesman, and the chief architect of the Greek victory at Marathon.

Milton, John (1608–74) Poet, born in London. His early works include *L'allegro* and *Il Penseroso* (1632), *Comus* (1633), and *Lycidas* (1637). Becoming involved in the Civil War with revolutionary ardour, he wrote very little poetry for the next 20 years. Instead, he published a series of controversial pamphlets, and became official apologist for the Commonwealth. Blind from 1652, after the Restoration he devoted himself wholly to poetry.

The theme of his epic sacred masterpiece, *Paradise Lost*, had been in his mind since 1641. He began to write it in 1658, and it was completed in 1665. It was followed by *Paradise Regained* and *Samson Agonistes* (both 1671). He is widely esteemed as a poet second only to Shakespeare.

Milton Keynes [keenz] 52°03N 0°42W, pop (2001e) 207 100. Industrial new town (since 1967) and unitary authority (from 1997) in Buckinghamshire, SC England; designed on a grid pattern; Open University (1969); railway.

Milwaukee [milwawkee] 43°02N 87°55W, pop (2000e) 597 000. City in SE Wisconsin, USA, on the W shore of L Michigan; largest city in the state; settled by German immigrants in the mid-19th-c; airfield; railway; two universities (1857, 1908); leading manufacturer of diesel and petrol engines; home of several breweries; professional teams, Brewers (baseball), Bucks (basketball).

Mimas [miymas] A natural satellite of Saturn, discovered in 1789; distance to the planet 186 000 km/116 000 mi; diameter 390 km/240 mi; orbital period 0·942 days.

mime In terms of ancient theatre, both a short dramatic sketch and a professional entertainer. In 20th-c theatre, it signified the art of silent corporeal expression as espoused by Etienne Decroux and popularized by Marcel Marceau.

MIME [mimee] *digital media*

mimosa *wattle*

mimulus An annual or perennial, found almost everywhere, many from North America; flowers usually yellow with red blotches. (Genus: *Mimulus*, 100 species. Family: Scrophulariaceae.)

Minas Gerais [meenas zheriys] pop (2000e) 18 159 000; area 587 172 km²/226 648 sq mi. State in SE Brazil; accounts for half of Brazil's mineral production (iron ore, gold, diamonds); capital, Belo Horizonte.

mind An entity usually contrasted with the body or matter, as the mental is with the physical, but variously understood in the history of thought. In its broadest sense (included in or conflated with the meaning of *soul*) it is taken to be the distinction between the animate and the inanimate; in a narrower sense it is taken to be the distinguishing feature of *persons*, and related to self-consciousness and identity. It has posed problems of definition and explanation for philosophers, psychologists, and cognitive scientists, who from their different standpoints have tried to relate it to the brain and to behaviour and have considered analogies with computer software.

Mindanao [mindanahoh] pop (2000e) 16 321 000; area 99 040 km²/38 229 sq mi. Island in the S Philippines; mountainous, rising to 2954 m/9691 ft at Mt Apo; chief towns, Davao, Zamboanga; Islamic secessionist movement since mid-1970s; Autonomous Region of Muslim Mindanao created, 1989; peace agreement, 1996.

Mindelo [meendayloo] 16°54N 25°00W, pop (2000e) 41 900. City and chief port (Porto Grande) of Cape Verde; important refuelling point for transatlantic ships.

Mindoro [mindohroh] pop (2000e) 1 003 000; area 9732 km²/3756 sq mi. Island of the Philippines; rises to 2585 m/8481 ft at Mt Halcon; chief town, Calapan.

Mindszenty, József, Cardinal [mindsentee], (1892–1975) Roman Catholic clergyman, born in Mindszent, Hungary. Primate of Hungary (1945), he became internationally known in 1948 when charged with treason by the Communist government in Budapest, and imprisoned (1949–55). He was then granted asylum in the US legation at Budapest (1956–71).

mine An explosive device hidden underground or in water to destroy vehicles, ship, or people as they pass over or near it. Mines are particularly effective in creating barriers against hostile naval or land forces. Over 500 types of mines have been developed, encased in metal, plastic, glass, or wood, and containing an explosive device such as trinitrotoluene (TNT). An estimated 100 million uncharted landmines in more than 60 countries are left over from post-World War 2 conflicts; they are now estimated to kill 10 times as many civilians as soldiers. In 1997 a treaty banning the production, use, transfer, and stockpiling of landmines was signed by 125 countries, but not the USA, Russia, and China.

mineralogy The study of the chemical composition, physical properties, and occurrence of minerals. Major aspects of the subject include identification, classification and systematics, crystallography, and mineral associations in rocks and ore deposits.

mineral oil A term used to distinguish lubricating oils of mineral origin from those of vegetable or animal origin. It is widely used for machinery.

minerals Naturally occurring substances, generally inorganic and crystalline, with a homogeneous structure and a chemical composition defined within specified limits; classified by chemical composition and crystal structure. They are the constituents of rocks in the Earth.

mineral waters Naturally occurring groundwaters rich in dissolved minerals derived from the rocks through which they flow. They are associated with medicinal properties, and may be used for bathing or as drinking water.

Minerva [minerva] The Roman goddess of handicrafts, identified with Athena.

minesweeper A small vessel designed or adapted to cut the moorings of mines, thus allowing them to float to the surface where they are destroyed by gunfire.

Ming dynasty (1368–1644) Major Chinese dynasty, established by Hongwu (r.1368–98) and consolidated by Yongle (r.1403–24). Its capital was shifted from Nanjing to Beijing in 1421. The period is known for its philosophical, historical, and literary writing, its porcelain, lacquer, and cloisonné, its opulent lifestyle, and its developments in manufacturing and medicine.

Minghella, Anthony [minggela] (1954–) Director and screenwriter, born in Ryde, Isle of Wight. His credits as film director/writer include *Truly, Madly, Deeply* (1991), *The English Patient* (1996, Oscars for Best Film and Best Director), *The Talented Mr Ripley* (1999), *Cold Mountain* (2003), and *Breaking and Entering* (2006).

miniature painting A term sometimes used for the small pictures in illuminated manuscripts, and (more often, and properly) for the 'portraits in little' that were so popular in Elizabethan England.

minicomputer *mainframe computer*

minidisk A very compact magnetic disk storage medium for microcomputers, sometimes known as a **microfloppy disk**. Four main sizes were designed, varying from about 1·5 in to 4 in (c.3·8 cm–10 cm) in diameter. Minidisks are enclosed in a rigid jacket.

minilab A device for the rapid production of colour prints. The film is developed in an automated machine and the negatives placed in an automatic printer/processor using a long roll of colour paper. The exposure paper is processed immediately, and dry finished prints emerge. Results are available in an hour or less.

Minimal Art A modern art movement that has flourished since the 1950s, mainly in the USA. Typical products are the monochrome canvases of US painter Ad Reinhardt (1913–67), and the prefabricated firebricks of US sculptor Carl André (1935–). In all cases the art content may be described as minimal.

minimalism In music, a style of composition, increasingly prominent since the 1960s, which abjures the complexities of many earlier 20th-c techniques in favour of simple harmonic and melodic units repeated many times, usually with phased modifications and superimpositions, in an unchanging, 'mechanical'

metre. The term is shared with several other art forms (eg painting, theatre) which make use of their medium in a reduced or simplified way.

minimum lending rate (MLR) Formerly the minimum rate of interest at which the Bank of England would lend to discount houses. It superseded the bank rate in 1973, and was itself superseded in 1981 by the *bank base rate*.

mining The extraction of useful mineral substances from the Earth. In surface, strip, and open-cast mining, the soil is stripped away, and the ore, coal, clay, or mineral is dug directly. At greater depths the deposits are approached by horizontal tunnels dug from vertical shafts (*drifts*).

mink A mammal of genus *Mustela*; thick dark brown coat important to the fur trade (other colours produced by captive breeding); two living species: most important commercially is the **American mink** from North America; also, the **European mink**. (Family: Mustelidae.)

Minneapolis [mineeapolis] 44°59N 93°16W, pop (2000e) 382 600. Largest city in Minnesota, USA; port on the Mississippi R to the W of its twin city, St Paul; part of Fort Snelling military reservation, 1819; later developed as a centre of the timber and flour milling industries; city status, 1867; airport; railway; university (1851); centre for enormous grain and cattle area; financial capital of the upper Midwest; professional teams, Minnesota Twins (baseball), Minnesota Vikings (football), Minnesota North Stars (ice hockey), Minnesota Timberwolves (basketball).

Minnelli, Liza (May) [minelee] (1946–) Singer and actress, born in Los Angeles, CA, the daughter of Vincente Minnelli (1910–86) and Judy Garland. She was the youngest-ever actress to win a Tony Award, for *Flora, the Red Menace* (1965). She won an Oscar for *Cabaret* (1972), and later appeared in *New York, New York* (1977) and with Dudley Moore in the *Arthur* films. Her work for television includes *West Side Waltz* (1995) and the comedy sitcom *Arrested Development* (2003). In 2002 she married her fourth husband, producer David Gest, but the marriage ended acrimoniously in 2003.

Minnesinger [minuhzinger] Aristocratic German minstrels who performed songs of courtly love in the 12th–14th-c.

Minnesota [minisohta] (Siouan 'watery cloud') pop (2000e) 4 919 500; area 218 593 km²/84 402 sq mi. State in N USA, the 'North Star State' or the 'Gopher State'; 32nd state admitted to the Union, 1858; permanently settled after the establishment of Fort Snelling, 1820; area became Minnesota Territory in 1849; settled by many Scandinavians in the 1880s; over 11 000 lakes scattered throughout the state; highest point Mt Eagle (701 m/ 2300 ft); glaciated terrain in the N; capital, St Paul; major tourist area; prairies in the S and W; agriculture the leading industry; nation's second biggest producer of dairy products, hay, oats, rye, turkeys.

minnow Small freshwater fish (*Phoxinus phoxinus*) widely distributed in lakes and streams of N Europe and Asia; length up to 13 cm/5 in; body slender, cylindrical, mouth small; variable greenish-brown above, underside yellowish. (Family: Cyprinidae.)

Minoan civilization [minohan] The brilliant Bronze Age culture which flourished in the Aegean area in the third and second millennia BC, reaching its zenith around the middle of the second millennium (1700–1450 BC). Its most impressive remains come from Crete, at Knossos, Phaestus, Mallia, and Zakron. The civilization came abruptly to an end c.1450 BC. The cause is unknown.

Minogue, Kylie [minohg] (1968–) Singer and actress, born in Melbourne, Victoria, Australia. She achieved worldwide fame for her role in the television soap opera, *Neighbours*. In 1987 she began a successful recording career, and her 1988 single 'I Should Be So Lucky', had huge sales. She topped the UK singles and album charts with 'Can't Get You Out Of My Head' (from

Fever, 2001), and made number one again with 'Slow' from the album *Body Language* (2003). Her world *Showgirl Homecoming Tour* began in 2005 but was halted when she was diagnosed with breast cancer. Following successful treatment, she resumed the tour in late 2006.

Minor, William Chester (1835–1920) Murderer and lexicographer, born in Ceylon (now Sri Lanka). He graduated from Yale Medical School, and fought in the American Civil War. In 1871 he moved to London, where in a fit of insanity he shot dead George Merritt, a brewery stoker. He spent the next 38 years in Broadmoor. Answering an appeal by James Murray in the 1880s for readers to help create the *New English Dictionary*, he became a prolific and scholarly contributor. His story is told in *The Surgeon of Crowthorne* (1998) by Simon Winchester.

minor In the UK, a person who has not yet reached the age of 18; in Scots law, a distinction is drawn between *pupils* (up to age 12 for girls, 14 for boys) and *minors* (from those ages to age 18); in the USA, the age of majority varies across jurisdictions and for different purposes. Minors cannot validly enter certain contracts, such as a contract for a loan.

Minorca [minaw(r)ka], Span **Menorca**, ancient **Balearis Minor** pop (2000e) 63 000; area 700 km²/270 sq mi. Second largest island in the Balearics, W Mediterranean, NE of Majorca; length, 47 km/29 mi; breadth, 10–19 km/6–12 mi; low-lying, rising to 357 m/1171 ft at Monte Toro; airport at Mahón, the island capital.

minor planet *asteroids*

Minos [miynos] A legendary King of Crete (or several kings). In Greek mythology, he was the son of Zeus and Europa. In the Underworld he became a judge of the dead.

Minotaur [miynotaw(r)] The son of Pasiphae and a bull from the sea, half bull and half human; the name means Minos's bull. He was kept in a labyrinth, and killed by Theseus with the help of Ariadne.

Minsk 53°51N 27°30E, pop (2000e) 1 653 000. Capital city of Belarus, on the R Svisloch; one of the oldest towns in the state, c.11th-c; under Lithuanian and Polish rule; part of Russia, 1793; badly damaged in World War 2; airport; railway junction; university (1921); cathedral (17th-c).

Mint *Royal Mint*

mint A perennial native to temperate regions, especially in the N hemisphere; whorls of small pale pink to purplish flowers. Its characteristic pungent scent is due to the presence of essential oils containing menthol. Mints are grown for their culinary value as herbs and flavourings. Many have distinctive odours, including peppermint (*Mentha* × *piperita*) and spearmint (*Mentha spicata*). (Genus: *Mentha*, 25 species. Family: Labiatae.)

Mintoff, Dom(inic) (1916–) Maltese Labour statesman and prime minister (1955–8, 1971–84), born in Cospicua, Malta. As premier, his demands for independence and accompanying political agitation led to the suspension of Malta's constitution (1959). He resigned in 1958 to lead the Malta Liberation Movement, and followed a policy of moving away from British influence.

Minton ceramics One of the principal British potteries of the 19th–20th-c, founded in 1796 by Thomas Minton (1765–1826). They produced pottery and porcelain, making large quantities of willow pattern.

minuet A French dance in triple metre and moderate tempo, popular among the European aristocracy in the 17th–18th-c. It became a standard movement in the symphony.

minuscule [minuhskyool] *majuscule*

Minutemen Militiamen, particularly in New England, who were prepared to take up arms at very short notice. They were important in the first months of the US War of Independence.

Miocene epoch [miyoseen] A geological epoch of the Tertiary period, from c.24 to 5 million years ago. It was characterized by great mountain-building episodes, which formed the Alps

and Himalayas, and the development of most modern mammalian groups.

MIPS [mips] Acronym for **millions of instructions per second**. It is a measure of the speed at which computers can operate.

Mira [miyra] (Lat 'the Wonderful') A star (*omicron Ceti*) in the constellation Cetus. It is a red giant, varying on a cycle of 331 days from 10th magnitude (minimum) to 2nd magnitude (maximum). It is the prototype for **Mira variables** – variable stars with long periods of months or more.

Mirabeau, Honoré Gabriel Riqueti, comte de (Count of) [meeraboh] (1749–91) French revolutionary politician and orator, born in Bignon, France. His political acumen made him a force in the National Assembly, while his eloquence endeared him to the people. He advocated a constitutional monarchy on the English model, but his views were rejected by the revolutionaries.

miracle play *mystery play*

mirage An optical illusion caused by the refraction of light through thin surface layers of air with different temperature and hence density, causing objects near the horizon to become distorted. It appears as a floating and shimmering image on the horizon, particularly in deserts, on very hot days.

Miranda A natural satellite of Uranus, discovered in 1948; distance from the planet 130 000 km/81 000 mi; diameter 480 km/300 mi. Its very complex surface, observed by Voyager 1 in 1986, suggests a history of almost total destruction and subsequent re-accretion.

Miranda warning *right to silence*

Miró, Joán [meeroh, hwan] (1893–1983) Artist, born in Barcelona, Spain. A founder of Surrealism, his paintings are predominantly abstract, and his humorous fantasy makes play with a restricted range of pure colours and dancing shapes, as in 'Catalan Landscape' (1923–4, New York).

Mirren, Dame Helen (1945–) Actress, born in London. She appeared in a wide range of classical theatre roles, and won the Best Actress award at Cannes for *Cal* (1984). Later films include *The Madness of King George* (1994), *Calendar Girls* (2003), and *The Queen* (2006, Best Actress Oscar and Golden Globe). Her role as DS Jane Tennison in the television series *Prime Suspect* (1991–2006) made her a household name in the UK. Other TV work includes *Elizabeth I* (2005, Golden Globe Best Actress). She was made a dame in 2003.

Mirrlees, James (Alexander) (1936–) Economist, born in Minnigaff, Dumfries and Galloway, Scotland. He shared the Nobel Prize for Economics in 1996 for his work in analyzing the consequences of incomplete financial information

mirror A smooth surface which reflects large amounts of light, usually made of glass with a highly reflective metal deposit on the front or back, or of highly polished metal. Large astronomical mirrors can be over 5 m/16 ft across, but mirrors of all sizes are used in optical instruments. Half-silvered mirrors are used as one-way mirrors between a well-lit and a dim room.

Mir (Russ 'peace') **space station** A Russian space station (launched Feb 1986) which evolved from Salyut, having more power (solar panels) and more docking ports (five) than previous spacecraft, allowing for the build-up of a modular station. It is used for long-duration spaceflight experience, and for biomedical, science, and applications experiments. The station was repaired in 1997, after an unmanned cargo ship collided with one of its modules. Mir was abandoned in 1999 and in a controlled destructive re-entry of the station in 2001, its remains plunged into the Pacific Ocean 1800 miles east of New Zealand.

MIRV [merv] Acronym for **Multiple, Independently-targeted Re-entry Vehicle**, a nuclear-armed warhead, numbers of which may be incorporated in the front end of a large ballistic missile to be dispensed over a target area.

miscarriage *abortion*

miscarriage of justice A criminal case where an injustice has or may have been committed, either in the preparation of the case or at trial, resulting in an innocent person being convicted or an 'unsafe and unsatisfactory' verdict of guilt being returned. There can be several reasons for such a miscarriage, including non-disclosure of evidence, inappropriate questioning, or the giving of partisan evidence by prosecution scientists.

misdemeanour / misdemeanor At common law, any offence other than treason or a felony; in most US jurisdictions, a criminal offence other than a felony, with a punishment of a fine or less than one year in a local prison. The felony/misdemeanour distinction in the UK was abolished by the Criminal Law Act of 1967.

Mishima, Yukio, pseudonym of **Hiraoka Kimitake** (1925–70) Writer, born in Tokyo. His great tetralogy, *Hojo no umi* (1965–70, Sea of Fertility), spanned Japanese life and events in the 20th-c. He became expert in the martial arts, and in 1968 founded the Shield Society, dedicated to the revival of *Bushido*. He committed ritual suicide in protest against modern Japanese decadence.

Mishnah [mishnuh], (Heb 'repetition', referring to the practice of learning by repetition) An important written collection of rabbinic laws, supplementary to the legislation in Jewish Scriptures. Its general arrangement can be traced to Rabbi Akiba (AD c.120), its final editing to Rabbi Judah the Prince (AD c.200).

Miskolc [meeshkolts] 48°07N 20°50E, pop (2000e) 192 000. Second largest city in Hungary; airfield; railway; technical university of heavy industry (1870); castle of Diósgyör.

Missal The liturgical book of the Roman Catholic Church, containing liturgies for the celebration of Mass throughout the year. It includes all the prayers, Biblical readings, ceremonial, and singing directions.

missile *guided missile*

Mississippi pop (2000e) 2 844 700; area 123 510 km²/47 689 sq mi. State in S USA, the 'Magnolia State'; held by France, Britain, and Spain in turn, becoming part of the USA in 1795; the 20th state to join the Union, 1817; seceded, 1861; re-admitted in 1870; highest black population of any state (35%); highest point Mt Woodall (246 m/807 ft); much of the S state covered in pine woods; fertile coastal plain; capital, Jackson; major cotton-producing area between Mississippi and Yazoo Rivers; petroleum, natural gas (over a third of the land given over to oil and gas development); fisheries prominent along the Gulf coast; the lowest per capita income in the USA; a centre of the civil rights movement in the 1960s; state severely damaged by Hurricane Katrina, 2005.

Mississippian period *Carboniferous period*

Mississippi River River in C USA; rises in N Minnesota; enters the Gulf of Mexico in SE Louisiana, near New Orleans; length estimates vary, because of the extensive delta; from its source in L Itasca, MN, to the delta, 3766 km/2340 mi; the **Upper Mississippi** runs from L Itasca to the confluence with the Missouri R, 1884 km/1171 mi; when the Missouri is considered part of the main stream, length from the Missouri's Upper Red Rock source to the delta is 6020 km/3740 mi; several artificial levees on the banks of the lower river help to cope with flooding; delta swampland dissected by numerous distributaries (*bayous*); navigable as far as Minneapolis; steamboat era in the 19th-c.

Missouri [mizooree] pop (2000e) 5 595 200; area 180 508 km²/69 697 sq mi. State in C USA, the 'Show Me State'; became part of USA with the Louisiana Purchase, 1803; a territory in 1812; admitted as the 24th state in 1821 under the Missouri Compromise; Ozark Plateau in the SW; highest point Mt Taum Sauk (540 m/1772 ft); split into two parts by the Missouri R; to the N, open prairie-land with corn and livestock, particularly hogs and cattle; to the S, foothills and the Ozarks, much of which is forested; capital, Jefferson City; more farms than any

other state except Texas; mines yield over 90% of the nation's lead; starting point for the pioneering advance W across the continent.

Missouri Compromise (1820) An agreement to admit Missouri, with slavery, and Maine (separated from Massachusetts), without it, to statehood simultaneously, in order to preserve a sectional balance in the US Senate.

Missouri River Major river in the USA, and chief tributary of the Mississippi; formed in SW Montana; joins the Mississippi just N of St Louis; length 3725 km/2315 mi (with longest headstream, 4125 km/2563 mi); navigation (as far as Fort Benton) is dangerous.

Mistinguett [meestīget], originally **Jeanne-Marie Bourgeois** (1875–1956) Dancer and actress, born in Enghien-les-Bains, France. She was the most popular French music-hall artiste for 30 years, reaching the height of success with Maurice Chevalier at the Folies Bergère.

Misti, Volcán El or **El Misti** [meestee] 16°18S 71°24W. Dormant volcano in S Peru, in the Andean Cordillera Occidental; height, 5843 m/19 170 ft; last eruption, 1600; observatory near its summit.

mistletoe A hemiparasitic evergreen shrub (*Viscum album*) native to Europe, N Africa, and Asia; stem growing to 1 m/3¼ ft, branches regularly forked; flowers small, in tight clusters of 3–5, greenish-yellow, males and females on separate plants; berries white. The plant, venerated by the druids, was widely held to cure sterility and counteract poisons. Nowadays it is used as a Christmas decoration. (Family: Loranthaceae.)

Mistral A strong, cool wind common in S France. It originates in the Massif Central, and blows down the Rhône Valley.

Mistral, Frédéric [meestral] (1830–1914) Poet, born in Maillane, France. He became a founder of the Provençal renaissance movement (the *Félibrige* school) and received the Nobel Prize for Literature in 1904.

Mistral, Gabriela [meestral], pseudonym of **Lucila Godoy de Alcayaga** (1889–1957) Writer, educationalist, and diplomat, born in Vicuña, Chile. Her works include *Sonetos de la muerte* (1914, Sonnets of Death) and *Desolación* (1922, Desolation). She was awarded the Nobel Prize for Literature in 1945.

Mitchell, George (John) (1933–) US lawyer and politician, born in Waterville, ME. Appointed senator for Maine in 1980, he achieved national prominence for his interrogation of Oliver North during the Iran-Contra investigation, and was elected Senate majority leader in 1989. He retired from the Senate in 1995, but became internationally known as the mediator in charge of the talks leading to the Good Friday agreement in April 1998, and again as the leader of the review of the peace process which led to the establishment of the devolved national Assembly in November 1999.

Mitchell, Joni, *née* **Roberta Joan Anderson** (1943–) Singer and songwriter, born in Fort McLeod, Alberta, Canada. She moved to the USA in the mid-1960s, and in 1968 recorded her first album, *Joni Mitchell*. Many of her songs, notably 'Both Sides Now', have been recorded by other singers.

Mitchell, Margaret (1900–49) Novelist, born in Atlanta, GA. Her only novel, *Gone with the Wind* (1936), sold over 25 million copies, was translated into 30 languages, and filmed (1939).

Mitchell, R(eginald) J(oseph) (1895–1937) Aircraft designer. He designed seaplanes for the Schneider trophy races (1922–31) and later the Spitfire, whose triumph he did not live to see.

Mitchum, Robert (1917–97) Film actor, born in Bridgeport, CT. A prolific leading man particularly associated with the post-war film noir thriller, his laconic, heavy-lidded manner disguised a potent screen presence. His major films included *Night of the Hunter* (1955), *The Sundowners* (1960), and *Farewell My Lovely* (1975).

mite A small, short-bodied arthropod with head and abdomen fused into a compact body; typically with four pairs of walking legs; mouthparts include a pair of fangs; c.30 000 described species. (Class: Arachnida. Order: Acari.)

Mitford, Nancy (Freeman) (1904–73) Writer, born in London. She established a reputation with such witty novels as *The Pursuit of Love* (1945) and *Love in a Cold Climate* (1949). In *Noblesse Oblige* (1956), she popularized the 'U' (upper-class) and 'non-U' classification of linguistic usage.

Mithr or **Mithras** A god worshipped in the early Roman Empire, of Persian origin, and identified with the sun. The cult was predominantly military, and restricted to males. The main story was of his fight with the bull, which he conquers and sacrifices.

Mithridates VI (Eupator) [mithridayteez], also spelled **Mithradates**, known as **the Great** (?–63 BC) King of Pontus (c.115–63 BC), a hellenized ruler in the Black Sea area, whose attempts to expand his empire led to a series of wars (the **Mithridatic Wars**) with Rome (88–66 BC). He was defeated by Sulla (c.86 BC), Lucullus (72–71 BC), and Pompey (66 BC), and later took his own life.

Mitla [meetla] 16°54N 96°16W. Ancient city in C Oaxaca, S Mexico; former centre of the Zapotec civilization.

mitochondrion [miytohkondrion] A typically oval-shaped structure, often about 2 μm long, found in large numbers in eucaryotic cells. It functions as a major site for metabolic activities that release energy by breaking down food molecules.

mitosis [miytohsis] The normal process of nuclear division and separation that takes place in a dividing cell, producing two daughter cells, each containing a nucleus with the same complement of chromosomes as the mother cell.

mitre / miter (Gr *mitra*, 'turban') The liturgical headwear of a bishop of the Western Christian Church. It takes the form of a shield-shaped, high, stiff hat, representing the 'helmet of salvation'.

MIT school In linguistics, a label applied to the group of US linguists associated with the Massachusetts Institute of Technology (MIT), who have developed the concept of generative grammar, under the influence of Noam Chomsky.

Mitsiwa *Massawa*

Mittelland Canal [miteland] (Ger 'Midland Canal') A system of German canals and rivers linking the Dortmund–Ems Canal with Magdeburg. The waterway was completed in the late 1930s. It is 325 km/202 mi in length.

Mitterrand, François (Maurice Marie) [meetuhrã] (1916–96) French statesman and socialist president (1981–95), born in Jarnac, France. For many years a stubborn opponent of de Gaulle, he became secretary of the Socialist Party in 1971. Following his victory in 1981, he embarked on a programme of nationalization and job creation in an attempt to combat stagnation and unemployment. During his retirement, revelations emerged of his friendship with wartime Vichy collaborators, political corruption, and extra-marital affairs.

mix; mixing *dissolve; dubbing*

mixed-ability groups *streaming*

mixed economy *market economy*

MMR Acronym for **measles mumps rubella**, a combined vaccination given to young children, introduced in 1972. Usually given in two doses, over 500 million doses of MMR vaccine have been used in 90 countries since its introduction. The vaccine became controversial in the UK after 1998, when British surgeon Andrew Wakefield published with colleagues a paper in *The Lancet* identifying a new inflammatory bowel disease linked with autism, which suggested an association with the vaccine. It was recommended that MMR be split into three single vaccines to reduce the impact on the immune system. During the ensuing controversy, several studies failed to confirm the link between the vaccine and autism, and the World Health Organisation said that MMR had an outstanding safety record. No country in fact recommends giving MMR as three single vaccines. By the end of 2004 vaccination rates had fallen to 80% in England, well below the 95% 'herd immunity' rate considered by the WHO needful to protect the population as a whole.

Mnemosyne [neemozinee] In Greek mythology, a Titan, daughter of Earth and Heaven, and mother of all the Muses. The name means 'Memory'.

Mo, Timothy (Peter) [moh] (1950–) Novelist, born in Kowloon, Hong Kong. He attracted attention with his first novel, *The Monkey King* (1978), set in Hong Kong. Later books include *The Redundancy of Courage* (1991), *Brownout on Breadfruit Boulevard* (1995), and *Renegade or Halo Squared* (1999).

moa An extinct bird native to New Zealand; a large ratite (up to 3 m/10 ft high) with long neck and legs, no wings; slow-moving. (Family: Dinornithidae, c.12 species.)

Moabites [mohabytes] An ancient Semitic people who in Old Testament times inhabited the area to the SE of the Dead Sea. They were believed to be descended from Lot.

Moabite Stone [mohabiyt] An inscribed basalt slab, discovered in 1868, which describes the successful revolt of Mesha, king of Moab, against the Israelites in the 9th-c BC.

Mobile [mohbeel] 30°41N 88°03W, pop (2000e) 198 900; Port in SW Alabama, USA; settled by the French, 1711; ceded to the British, 1763; city status, 1819; scene of a Federal victory at the naval battle of Mobile Bay, 1864; railway; university (1963); hit by Hurricane Katrina, 2005.

mobile A name first applied by Marcel Duchamp to the hanging wire-and-metal sculptures of Alexander Calder. They have been widely imitated.

mobile communications A system which provides a simple, convenient means of communication for people who wish to keep in touch when travelling. The first system was a ship-borne radio. In modern times the term also refers to personal communication systems such as CB radio, radio paging, and car and pocket phones which use cellular radio. Cellular radio employs local radio transmitters, covering small areas (*cells*), which receive and transmit calls in association with the telecommunications network.

mobile phone (UK) or **cellphone** (US) A portable telephone handset, used with a cellular radio or other mobile communication system, small enough to fit into the pocket. It enables users to make direct-dial telephone calls wherever they are.

Möbius strip *p.612*

Mobutu, Sese Seko [mobootoo], originally **Joseph Désiré Mobutu** (1930–97) Zairean soldier and president (1965–97), born in Lisala, Democratic Republic of Congo (formerly Zaire, and earlier, Belgian Congo). A sergeant-major in the Belgian colonial *force publique*, he came to power in a military coup in 1960. He was forced to stand down May 1997 following an uprising led by Laurent Kabila (1939–2001).

Mobutu Sese Seko, Lake *Albert, Lake*

mockingbird A bird native to the New World; thrush-like with sharp, slightly curved bill and long tail; sings well; excellent mimic; also known as **mocking-thrush**. (Family: Mimidae, 16 species.)

mock orange A deciduous, temperate shrub, mainly from E Asia; flowers fragrant, usually white, bowl-shaped, with four petals and numerous stamens; fruit a capsule. It is named for the resemblance of its flowers to those of the orange, but in horticulture it is sometimes called **syringa**, the botanical name for lilac. (Genus: *Philadelphus*, 75 species. Family: Hydrangeaceae.)

Mod The annual autumn musical and literary festival of Gaelic-speaking Scotland organized by An Comunn Gaidhealach (the Gaelic language society) on the model of the Welsh eisteddfod; first held in Oban in 1892.

mode In mathematics, the commonest of a set of scores; for example, the mode of 1, 2, 3, 4, 4, 5 is 4.

modello [modeloh] A small, but complete and detailed painting or drawing made to show to a patron before embarking on the full-size work. Superb oil *modelli* exist by Rubens and Tiepolo.

modem [mohdem] Acronym for **MOdulator/DEModulator**, a device which converts digital information from computers into electrical signals that can be transmitted over telephone lines and vice versa.

moderator A person who presides over Presbyterian Church courts, such as the kirk session, presbytery, synod, or General Assembly. In Reformed Churches generally, the term is applied to the chairman of official Church gatherings.

modern art A term used widely but imprecisely to refer to all the 'progressive' movements in 19th–20th-c art. Towards the end of the 19th-c a number of artists, including Cézanne, Gauguin, van Gogh, Ensor, and Munch, challenged in various ways the traditional approach to painting based on such notions as naturalistic figure-drawing and Renaissance perspective. Their innovations inspired the younger generation around 1904–5. Picasso and Braque developed Cubism (1906–8), the most widely influential of all modern movements. The *Blaue Reiter* group in Munich pushed further away from imitation (1912–14), and a purely abstract art emerged in the hands of Kandinsky and Klee. In Moscow in 1917 Malevich developed a totally abstract art which he called 'Suprematism'. By 1916 a nihilist reaction known as 'Dadaism' was already emerging in Zürich; it attacked all artistic values, but itself contributed to the ideas of the early Surrealists, who launched their first manifesto in Paris in 1924.

modern dance A theatre form of dance which began c.1910 and continues to evolve, rejecting the established form of dance, ballet. Greek myths, psychological states, political comment, the mechanization of life, and alienation have been common themes. Isadora Duncan and Ruth Saint Denis are often credited with originating the modern movement in the first two decades of the 20th-c, the former in returning to natural movements, the latter in using exotic Oriental influences. Later, Martha Graham and Doris Humphrey emerged as major figures. In Germany in the 1970s–80s, Pina Bausch's dramatic theatrical works continued the modern, expressionist movement.

Modernism A generic term which refers to experimental methods in different art forms in the earlier part of the 20th-c. These experiments were stimulated by a sharpened sense of the arbitrariness of existing artistic conventions, and doubts about the human place and purpose in the world. Dada, Surrealism, and various anti-genres are all manifestations of Modernism.

Modern Movement *Bauhaus; International Style* 2

Modigliani, Amedeo [mohdeelyahnee] (1884–1920) Painter and sculptor of the modern school of Paris, born in Livorno, Italy. In 1918, his first one-man show included some very frank nudes, and the exhibition was closed for indecency. He received recognition only after his death.

Modigliani, Franco [mohdeelyahnee] (1918–2003) US economist, born in Rome. He was awarded the Nobel Prize for Economics in 1985 for his work on personal saving and on corporate finance.

modulation (physics) The imposition of regular changes on some background, usually a beam of particles or radiation, and often as a means of conveying information via the beam. A broadcast signal is used to modulate the electron beam inside a television set to reproduce the picture.

module A unit measure of proportion in architecture used to regulate all the parts of a building. In classical architecture, this meant the diameter of the column at the base of the shaft. Since World War 2, it is particularly used as the common unit of measure that co-ordinates the sizes of all the components in a standardized or *modular* building, so that they may be fitted together with maximum ease and flexibility.

Moerae or **Moirai** [moyree, moyriy] In Greek mythology, the fates; a trio of goddesses who control human destiny and sometimes overrule the gods. **Lachesis** [lakesis] ('the distributor') allots the destinies of human beings; **Clotho** [klohthoh] ('the spinner') spins the thread of life; and **Atropos** [atropos] ('the inflexible') cuts it.

Mogadishu [mogadishoo], Somali **Muqdisho**, Ital **Mogadiscio** 2°02N 45°21E, pop (2000e) 633 000. Seaport capital of Somalia; founded, 10th-c; taken by the Sultan of Zanzibar, 1871; sold to Italy, becoming capital of Italian Somaliland, 1905; occupied by British forces in World War 2; airport; university (1954); mosques (13th-c), cathedral (1928).

Mogadon *benzodiazepines*

Mogollon [moguhyohn] A prehistoric culture of the American SW AD c.300–1350, artistically notable for its vigorous ceramics, extending from S Arizona and New Mexico to the Chihuahuan and Sonoran deserts of Mexico.

Mogul *Mughal*

mohair *Angora goat*

Mohammed or **Mahomet** (Western forms of Arabic **Muhammad**) (c.570–c.632) Prophet of Islam, born in Mecca, the son of Abdallah, a poor merchant. Orphaned at six, he was cared for first by his grandfather, then by his uncle, and earned his living by tending sheep. At 25 he led the caravans of a rich widow,

Möbius strip

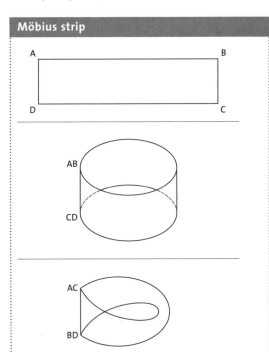

[moebius] In topology, a one-sided surface bounded by a single continuous line. Take a long, thin rectangle *ABCD*, and join *A* to *B*, and *C* to *D*. This forms a cylinder, with two surfaces, an inside and an outside. Now take a similar rectangle *ABCD*, and join *A* to *C*, *B* to *D*. Starting at any point *P* on the surface now formed, we can draw a continuous line over the surface to reach the point at the 'other' side of *P*.

whom he later married. When he was 40, the angel Gabriel appeared to him on Mt Hira, near Mecca, and commanded him in the name of God to preach the true religion. Four years later he was told to come forward publicly as a preacher. The basis of his teaching was the Qur'an, which had been revealed to him by God. At first dismissing him as a poet, the Meccans finally rose against him and his followers. He sought refuge at Medina in 622 (the date of the Mohammedan Era, the *Hijra* or *Hegira*), and assumed the position of highest judge and ruler of the city. He then engaged in war against the enemies of Islam. In 630 he took Mecca, where he was recognized as leader and prophet, and thus secured the new religion in Arabia. In 632 he undertook his last pilgrimage to Mecca, and there on Mt Arafat fixed the ceremonies of the pilgrimage (*Hajj*). He fell ill after his return, and died at the house of his favourite wife, Aïshah, the daughter of Abu-Bakr.

Mohammed II or **Mehmet II**, known as **the Conqueror** (1432–81) Ottoman sultan (1451–81), born in Adrianople. He took Constantinople in 1453, thus extinguishing the Byzantine Empire, and conquered Greece.

Mohammed Ahmed, known as **the Mahdi** (1844–85) African political and religious leader, born in Dongola, Sudan. A rebel against Egyptian rule in the E Sudan, he defeated Hicks Pasha and an Egyptian army. In 1885 his forces took Khartoum, resulting in the death of General Gordon.

Mohawk [mohhawk] An Iroquoian-speaking North American Indian group, living around L Champlain. A member of the Iroquois League, they were defeated by US troops in 1777, and crossed into Canada, settling in Ontario.

Mohenjo-daro [mohenjoh daroh] A prehistoric walled city on the R Indus, in Sind, Pakistan; a world heritage site. Occupied c.2300–1750 BC, it covered 100 ha/250 acres and held an ancient population of c.30–40 000.

Moholy-Nagy, László [mohhoy nodj] (1895–1946) Artist, born in Bàcsborsod, Hungary. He was an abstract painter, experimental photographer, theatrical designer, and pioneer constructivist, using translucent and transparent plastic materials. He founded in 1937 the New Bauhaus in Chicago.

Mohorovičić discontinuity [mohhorohvichich] (or **Moho**) The zone separating the Earth's crust from the mantle, lying at c.6 km/3·5 mi below the ocean floor but up to 70 km/45 mi below the surface of the continents. It is named after its discoverer, Croatian geophysicist Andrija Mohorovičić (1857–1936).

Mohs scale *hardness*

Moi, Daniel Arap [moy] (1924–) Kenyan politician and president (1978–2002), born in Rift Valley Province. He served as a minister from 1961, and became vice-president under Kenyatta in 1967. Despite an increasingly autocratic rule during the 1980s, he won multi-party elections in 1992. In late 2004 the High Court ruled that he would have to appear before a commission investigating corruption during his presidency.

Mojave or **Mohave Desert** [mohhahvee] Desert in S California, USA, part of the Great Basin; area c.65 000 km²/25 000 sq mi; annual rainfall c.120 mm/4·7 in.

molasses A brownish syrup, obtained as a by-product of the sugar-beet or sugar-cane industry; it is what remains once the sugar has been refined. It is widely used as an animal feed supplement, and in the production of rum and treacle.

Mold, Welsh **Yr Wyddgrug** 53°10N 3°08W, pop (2000e) 9500. Administrative centre of Flintshire, NE Wales, UK; on the R Alyn; railway; Theatre Clwyd.

Moldavia and Wallachia [moldayvia, wolaykia] Two independent Balkan principalities formed in the 14th-c: Moldavia in NE Romania; Wallachia in S Romania. In the 16th-c they were incorporated into the Ottoman Empire, but they gained autonomy by the Treaty of Adrianople (1829). In 1862 they merged to

form the unitary Principality of Romania; Russian Moldavia became a Soviet Socialist Republic in 1940, and declared independence as the Republic of Moldova in 1991.

Moldova *p.614*

mole (medicine) Usually a small flat congenital lesion in the skin resulting from the proliferation of small blood vessels and containing scattered pigment cells (*birthmarks*). Occasionally these are more extensive and form raised patches (*plaques*).

mole (physics) Base SI unit of amount of substance; symbol *mol*; defined as the amount of substance of a system which contains as many elementary entities as there are atoms in 0·012 kg of carbon-12.

mole (zoology) A mammal native to lowlands in Europe, Asia, and North America; an insectivore; dark with minute eyes; short tail; enlarged forelimbs used for digging. (Family: Talpidae, 27 species.)

molecular biology The study of the structure and function of the large organic molecules associated with living organisms, especially the nucleic acids (DNA and RNA) and proteins.

molecule A finite group of two or more atoms, which is the smallest unit of a substance having the properties of that substance. Molecular compounds include water, most organic compounds, globular proteins, and viruses. Non-molecular compounds include metals, ionic compounds, and diamond.

Molière [molyair], pseudonym of **Jean Baptiste Poquelin** (1622–73) Playwright, born in Paris. From the publication of *Les Précieuses ridicules* (1659, The Affected Young Ladies) no year passed without at least one major dramatic achievement, such as *Tartuffe* (1664), *Le Misanthrope* (1666, The Misanthropist), and *Le Bourgeois gentilhomme* (1670).

Molina, Luis de [mohleena] (1535–1600) Jesuit theologian, born in Cuenca, Spain. His main work was *Concordia liberi arbitrii cum gratiae donis* (1588, The Harmony of Free Will with Gifts of Grace), which presented the view (later known as **Molinism**) that predestination to eternal happiness or punishment depends on God's foreknowledge of the free determination of human will.

mollusc [moluhsk] An unsegmented invertebrate animal, typically with an underside muscular foot and a mantle above, covered by calcareous scales or a solid calcareous shell. A posterior cavity contains gills for respiration. Visceral organs are typically protected by a shell secreted by the mantle. There are c.80 000 species. (Phylum: Mollusca.)

molly Small, colourful, freshwater fish (*Poecilia sphenops*) found in Central America; length up to 12 cm/4³⁄₄ in; greenish-brown above, rows of orange spots along sides, dorsal fin with orange and black markings. (Family: Poeciliidae.)

Molly Maguires A secret organization of (primarily Irish) miners, involved in industrial disputes in Pennsylvania during the 1870s. The prosecution of their leaders led to hangings and imprisonments, which crushed the group.

Molnár, Ferenc [mohlnah(r), ferents] (1878–1952) Writer, born in Budapest. He is best known for his novel *A Pál utcai fiuk* (1907, The Paul Street Boys), and his plays *Az ördög* (1907, The Devil) and *Liliom* (1909).

Moloch [mohlok] In the Bible, a god of the Canaanites and other peoples, in whose cult children were sacrificed by fire. The name is used for any excessive and cruel religion.

moloch [mohlok] An agamid lizard (*Moloch horridus*) native to W Australia; entire body covered with large thorn-like spines; also known as **thorny devil** or **horny devil**.

Molokai [molokiy] area 670 km²/260 sq mi. Island of the US state of Hawaii; Kalaupapa leper settlement (pop 130) on the N coast.

Molotov, Vyacheslav Mikhailovich [molotof] (from Russ *molot*, 'hammer'), originally **Vyacheslav Mikhailovich Skriabin** (1890–1986) Russian statesman and premier (1930–41), born in Kukaida, Russia. He was Stalin's chief adviser at Teheran

Moldova

☐ International Airport

[moldohva], official name **Republic of Moldova**, formerly (to 1990) **Moldavian SSR**, Russ **Moldavskaya**
Local name Moldova
Timezone GMT +2
Area 33 700 km²/13 008 sq mi
Population total (2002e) 4 231 000

Status Republic
Date of independence 1991
Capital Chisinau (Kishinev)
Languages Moldovan (official), Ukrainian also spoken
Ethnic groups Moldovan (64%), Ukrainian (14%), Russian (13%), Gagauzi (4%), Jewish (2%)
Religions Christian (mainly Russian Orthodox, also Baptist and Roman Catholic)
Physical features Landlocked area consisting of hilly plains, average elevation of 147 m/482 ft, cut by river valleys, ravines, and gullies; uplands in C, Kodry Hills, reach highest point, Mt Balaneshty, 429 m/1409 ft; chief rivers, the Dnestr and Prut; level plain of Bel'tsy Steppe and uplands (N); eroded Medobory-Toltry limestone ridges border R Prut (N).
Climate Warm, moderately continental; long dry periods in S; average annual temperatures -5°C (N), -3°C (S) (Jan), 20°C (N), 23°C (S) (Jul); average annual rainfall 450–550 mm/18–22 in.
Currency 1 Moldovan Leu (MDL) = 100 bani
Economy Main exports include wine, tobacco, food-canning, machinery, electrical engineering, knitwear, textiles, fruit.
GDP (2002e) $11·51 bn, per capita $2600
Human Development Index (2002) 0·701
History Formerly part of Romania (the region known as Bessarabia); W part remained in Romania, Bessarabia in E became the Moldavian Soviet Socialist Republic in 1940; occupied by Romania, who allied with Germany in World War 2; recaptured by USSR, 1944; Moldavian language granted official status, 1989, leading to tension between ethnic Russians and Moldovans; declaration of independence, 1991, joined Commonwealth of Independent States; tension due to separatist pressure from Gagauz and Dnestr Russian minorities, 1990–1; new constitution, 1994; governed by a President, Prime Minister and Supreme Soviet.

Head of State
1991–6 Mircea Snegur
1996–2001 Petru Lucinschi
2001– Vladimir Voronin

Head of Government
1991–2 Valeriu Muravschi
1992– 7 Andrei Sangeli
1997–9 Ion Cebuc
1999 Ion Sturza
1999–2001 Dumitru Barghis
2001– Vasile Tarlev

---

and Yalta, and was present at the founding of the United Nations (1945). After World War 2, he emerged as the uncompromising champion of world Sovietism; his *nyet* ('no') at meetings of the UN became a byword, and fostered the Cold War.

Moltke, Helmuth (Karl Bernhard), Graf von (Count of) [moltkuh] (1800–91) Prussian field marshal, born in Parchim, Germany. His reorganization of the Prussian army led to the successful wars with Denmark (1863–4), Austria (1866), and France (1870–1).

Moluccas [moluhkas], Indonesian **Maluku**, or **Spice Islands** pop (2000e) 2 182 000; area 74 505 km²/28 759 sq mi. Island group and province of Indonesia; includes c.1000 islands, notably Halmahera, Seram, Buru; mostly volcanic and mountainous; visited by the Portuguese, 1512; under Dutch rule, early 17th-c; secession movement in the S Moluccas followed Indonesian independence (1949), still continuing in The Netherlands; over 5000 deaths in the region after sectarian conflict broke out 1999–2003; capital, Ambon; copra, spices, sago, coconut oil, tuna.

molybdenum [molibdenum] Mo, element 42, density 10·2 g/cm³, melting point 2610°C. A grey metal, occurring most commonly as the disulphide, MoS₂. It is an ingredient of several steel alloys.

Molyneux, Edward (Henry) [molinyoo] (1891–1974) Fashion designer, born in London. He was famous for the elegant simplicity of his tailored suits with pleated skirts, and for his evening wear.

Mombasa [mombasa] 4°04S 39°40E, pop (2000e) 697 000. Kenya's main port; capital of British East Africa Protectorate, 1888–1907; used as a British naval base in World War 2; airport; railway terminus.

moment In physics, a general term referring to a system's ability to rotate under the application of an external force. The moment of force in mechanics is called *torque*.

moment of inertia In mechanics, the notion that, for a rotating

Monaco

[monakoh], official name **Principality of Monaco**

Local name Monaco

Timezone GMT +1

Area 1·95 km²/0·75 sq mi

Population total (2002e) 32 000

Status Principality

Capital Monaco-Ville

Languages French (official), English, Italian, and Monegasque also spoken

Ethnic groups French (58%), Italian (16%), Monegasque (16%)

Religion Roman Catholic (95%)

Physical features Located on Mediterranean Riviera, close to the Italian frontier with France; surrounded landward by the French department of Alpes-Maritimes; steep and rugged landscape; area available for commercial development has been extended by land reclaimed from sea.

Climate Mediterranean; warm, dry summers, mild, wet winters; average annual temperatures 10°C (Jan), 23°C (Jul); average annual rainfall 758 mm/30 in.

Currency 1 euro (EUR) = 100 cents (previous to February 2002, 1 French Franc (FRF) = 100 centimes).

Economy Tourism; chemicals, printing, textiles, plastics.

GDP (1999e) $870 mn, per capita $27 000

History Under the protection of France since the 17th-c, apart from a period under Sardinia, 1815–61; 1911 constitution ended power of the Prince as an absolute ruler; constitution of 1911 suspended in 1959; new constitution adopted, 1962; governed by a Prince as Head of State, a Minister of State, heading a Council of Government, and a National Council.

Head of State (Prince)
1949–2005 Rainier III
2005– Albert II

Head of Government (Minister of State)
1986–91 Jean Ausseil
1991–4 Jacques Dupont
1994–7 Paul Dijoud
1997–2000 Michel Lévêque
2000– Patrick Leclerq

object, the turning force required to make the object turn faster depends on how the object's mass is distributed about the axis of rotation; symbol I, units kg.m². For a uniform disc of radius r and mass m spinning horizontally about its centre, $I = mr^2/2$.

momentum The product of mass and velocity; symbol p, units kg.m/s; a vector quantity. 'Force equals the rate of change of momentum with time' is the proper statement of Newton's second law. For a closed system on which no forces act, momentum is conserved – an essential principle in physics.

Mommsen, (Christian Matthias) Theodor (1817–1903) Historian, born in Garding, Germany. His greatest work is his *Römische Geschichte* (3 vols, History of Rome, 1854–5), in which he applied the new historical method of critical examination of sources. He was awarded the Nobel Prize for Literature in 1902.

Mon An agricultural people of Burma and Thailand, thought to have come originally from W China, establishing a kingdom in Burma in about the 9th-c. They speak an Austro-Asiatic language, also known as **Tailang**.

Monaco *see panel*

Monaghan (county) [monaghan], Ir **Mhuineachain** pop (2000e) 52 000; area 1290 km²/498 sq mi. County in Ulster province, Ireland; capital, Monaghan pop (2000e) 6300.

monarchy A political system in which a single person is a polit-

ical ruler, whose position normally rests on the basis of divine authority, backed by tradition. In Europe, the democratic revolutions of the 18th–20th-c saw an end to what was until then the most widely known form of government. A number of countries, however, maintained **constitutional monarchies**, where the sovereign acts on the advice of government ministers who govern on his or her behalf.

monasticism A form of religious life found in both Christianity and Buddhism, emphasizing the perfection of the individual either through a solitary ascetic existence or more often through life in a consecrated community. Members of such communities are known as **monks**. In Christianity the most significant early monastic legislation was the rule of Benedict (480–543), which became a standard in Western Christianity. In the 13th-c several new orders emerged, known as *friars* or *mendicant orders*, which combined monastic life with missionary preaching to those outside.

monazite [monaziyt] A phosphate mineral containing rare-earth metals (*lanthanides*) such as lanthanum, cerium, yttrium, and thorium, and important as the major source of these metals.

Monck, George *Monk, George*

Mond, Ludwig (1839–1909) Chemist and industrialist, born in Kassel, Germany. He perfected a sulphur recovery process, founded an alkali works, and devised a process for the extraction of nickel. His son, **Alfred Moritz Mond, Baron Melchett** (1868–1930), helped to form Imperial Chemical Industries (ICI).

Mondale, Walter F(rederick) (1928–) US Democratic politician, born in Ceylon, MN. He served under President Carter as vice-president (1977–81), and obtained the Democratic nomination in 1984, but lost to Reagan. President Clinton appointed him US ambassador to Japan (1993–97). He was defeated for a seat in the Senate (2002).

Mondrian, Piet [mondrian], originally **Pieter Cornelis Mondriaan** (1872–1944) Artist, born in Amersfoort, The Netherlands. He founded, with Theo van Doesburg, (1883–1931) the *De Stijl* movement in architecture and painting. His rectilinear abstracts in black, white, and primary colours have had considerable influence, and he is considered the leader of Neoplasticism.

Monet, Claude [monay] (1840–1926) Impressionist painter, born in Paris. He exhibited at the first Impressionist exhibition in 1874; one of his works, 'Impression: soleil levant' (Impression: Sunrise, 1872, Paris), gave the name to the movement.

monetarism An economic policy based on the control of a country's money supply. It assumes that the quantity of money in an economy determines its economic activity, and particularly its rate of inflation. If the money supply is allowed to rise too quickly, prices will rise, resulting in inflation. To curb inflationary pressures, governments therefore need to reduce the supply of money and raise interest rates. This view was a major influence on British and US economic policy in the 1980s.

Monetary Compensation Amount *green pound*

money A generally acceptable and convenient medium of exchange, in order to avoid the problems of barter; also a representation of value and a means of storing value. It is usually in the form of coins or notes, but it can be any generally accepted object. The first bank notes issued in Europe were by the Bank of Stockholm in 1661. Money is now increasingly not in tangible form, but consists of balances in accounts at banks, exchange being by means of cheques, credit-cards or charge-cards, and by *credit-transfer*, where one account is reduced (debited) and another increased (credited) by the same amount electronically. Many definitions of money are in use. In the UK, for example, the narrow definition, M0, refers to the stock of notes and coins in circulation, banks' till money, and bankers' balances at the Bank of England. Also in use are M1, M2, M3, and other measures, each containing additional items.

Mongolia

☐ International Airport

Mongolian **Mongol Uls**, formerly **Mongolian People's Republic** (1924–92)

Local name Mongol Ard Uls

Timezone GMT +7 (W), +8 (C), +9 (E)

Area 1 566 500 km²/604 800 sq mi

Population total (2002e) 2 457 000

Status State

Date of independence 1911

Capital Ulaanbaatar

Languages Khalka (official), Russian and Chinese spoken by respective minorities

Ethnic groups Mongol (Khalka, Dorbed, Buryat, Dariganga) (90%), Kazakh (4%), Russian (2%), other (4%)

Religions Formerly Tibetan Buddhist (now only a single monas-tery remains in Ulaanbaatar); unreliable data on current situation as a result of religious suppression in 20th-c.

Physical features Landlocked mountainous country; highest point, Tavan-Bogdo-Uli, 4373 m/14 347 ft; high ground mainly in W, with mountains lying NW–SE to form Mongolian Altai chain; lower SE area runs into the Gobi Desert; lowland plains; mainly arid grasslands.

Climate Extreme continental climate, with hard and long-lasting frosts in winter; arid desert conditions prevail in the S; average annual temperatures -26°C (Jan), 16°C (Jul); average annual rainfall 208 mm/18·2 in.

Currency 1 Tugrik (MNT) = 100 möngö

Economy Traditionally a pastoral nomadic economy; series of 5-year plans aiming for an agricultural-industrial economy; 70% of agricultural production derived from cattle raising; foodstuffs, animal products; coal, gold, uranium, lead.

GDP (2002e) $5·06 bn, per capita $1900

Human Development Index (2002) 0·655

History Originally the homeland of nomadic tribes, which united under Genghis Khan in the 13th-c to become part of the great Mongol Empire; assimilated into China, and divided into Inner and Outer Mongolia; Outer Mongolia declared itself an independent monarchy, 1911; changed name to Mongolian People's Republic, 1924, not recognized by China until 1946; governed by a people's Great Hural (unicameral legislature), a Council of Ministers, and a Presidium; chairman of Presidium is Head of State; changed name to State of Mongolia, 1992, and new constitution established.

Head of State
1990–7 Punsalmaagiyn Ochirbat
1997–2005 Natsagiyn Bagabandi
2005– Nambaryn Enkhbayar

Head of Government
1992–6 Puntsagiyn Jasray
1996–8 Mendsayhany Enhsayhan
1998 Tsakhiagiin Elbegdorj
1998–9 Janlaviyn Narantsatsralt
1999 Nyam-Osoriyn Tuyaa *acting*
1999–2000 Rinchinnyamiyn Amarjargal
2000–4 Nambaryn Enkhbayar
2004–6 Tsakhiagiin Elbegdorj
2006– Miyeegombo Enkhbold

money spider A small, dark-coloured spider that constructs a sheet-like web on vegetation; very abundant in N hemisphere. The name is derived from the folk belief that a spider on one's clothes was a sign of good luck or money coming. (Order: Araneae. Family: Liniphiidae.)

Monge, Gaspard, comte de (Count of) **Péluse** [mŏzh] (1746–1818) Mathematician, physicist, and inventor of descriptive geometry, born in Beaune, France. In 1795 he published his treatise on the application of geometry to the arts of construction.

Mongo A cluster of Bantu-speaking peoples of forested regions of C Democratic Republic of Congo, organized into many small chiefdoms.

Mongol *Altaic*

Mongolia *see panel*

mongolism *Down's syndrome*

Mongoloid *race*

Mongols Mongolian and S Siberian tribes who created the largest empire in ancient history (including C Asia, China, Korea, Russia, and Persia), of key importance in the process of cultural diffusion. United under Genghis Khan in 1206, they conquered China under his grandson Kublai, who ruled as first emperor of the Yuan dynasty (1271–1368).

mongoose A carnivorous mammal, native to S and SE Asia and Africa; adept at killing snakes and rats. (Family: Viverridae, 36 species.)

monism In philosophy, the metaphysical doctrine either that only one thing really exists in the universe; or that there is only one *kind* of thing, as in materialism (matter) and idealism (mind).

monitorial system A concept of early 19th-c British education, developed by British educationalists Andrew Bell (1753–1832) and Joseph Lancaster (1778–1838), to train young school leavers to act as teachers' assistants or 'monitors'.

Monk or **Monck, George, 1st Duke of Albemarle** (1608–70) General, born in Great Potheridge, Devon. He joined the Commonwealth cause and served successfully in Ireland, Scotland, and in the first Dutch War (1652–4). Fearing a return to Civil War, he was instrumental in bringing about the restoration of Charles II.

Monk, Thelonious (Sphere) (1917–82) Composer and pianist, born in Rocky Mount, NC. Although once called the 'High Priest of Bebop', and credited with helping to create the jazz style of the 1940s, his angular, idiosyncratic melodies stood apart from the main currents of the day.

monk *monasticism*

monkey A primate of the group Anthropoidea; two subgroups: the **Platyrrhine** or **flat-nosed monkeys** from the New World (includes New World monkeys and marmosets), and the **Catarrhine** or **downward-nosed monkeys** from the Old World.

monkey nut *peanut*

monkey-puzzle An evergreen conifer (*Araucaria araucana*) native to Chile and Argentina; branches in open whorls, covered with hard, sharp-pointed, triangular, overlapping leaves; also known as **Chile pine**. (Family: Araucariaceae.)

Monkey Trial *Scopes Trial*

monkfish Largest of the angelsharks (*Squatina squatina*) common in the E North Atlantic and Mediterranean; length up to 1·8 m/6 ft; head flattened, mouth anterior, gill openings lateral, pectoral fins very broad, tail slender; also called **angelfish**. (Family: Squatinidae.)

monkshood A perennial (*Aconitum napellus*) with blackish, tuberous roots, native to Europe and NW Asia; flowers mauve, with a cowl-shaped helmet or hood; also called **aconite**. It is used as a narcotic and painkiller, but is highly poisonous. (Family: Ranunculaceae.)

Monmouth, James Scott, Duke of (1649–85) Illegitimate son of Charles II of England, born in Rotterdam, The Netherlands. He had substantial popular support, and as a Protestant became a focus of opposition to James II. In 1685 he landed at Lyme Regis, and asserted his right to the crown. He was defeated at the Battle of Sedgemoor, and beheaded in London.

Monmouth, Battle of (1778) An engagement in New Jersey between British and American troops during the US War of Independence. It was notable for Washington's suspension of General Charles Lee (1731–82) from command.

Monmouthshire [monmuhthsheer], Welsh **Sir Fynwy** pop (2000e) 84 900; area 851 km²/328 sq mi. County (unitary authority from 1996) in SE Wales, UK; drained by R Wye and R Usk; Brecon Beacons in NW; administrative centre, Cwmbran; tourism, especially in Wye Valley; castles at Abergavenny, Caldicott, Chepstow, Monmouth, Raglan, Usk; Tintern Abbey (12th-c).

Monoceros [monoseros] (Gr 'unicorn') A N constellation in the Milky Way, next to Orion, containing several clusters and nebulae.

monoclonal antibody [monohklohnal antibodee] A pure antibody produced in bulk by artificial means, used in medicine for treating diseases (eg some cancers) and in scientific research. It is produced from animals which have been immunized with particular antigens.

monocotyledons [monohkotileednz] One of two major divisions of the flowering plants, often referred to simply as **monocots**; contrasting with *dicotyledons* (*dicots*). The seed embryo has only one cotyledon, and the primary root of the seedling soon withers, leaving only a fibrous root system. Monocots form a much smaller group than dicots, with about 60 families currently recognized, although some (eg grasses, palms, orchids, lilies) are among the largest families of flowering plants. (Subclass: Monocotyledonae.)

Monod, Jacques (Lucien) [monoh] (1910–76) Biochemist, born in Paris. He shared the Nobel Prize for Physiology or Medicine in 1965 for his work on the mechanisms governing the activity of genes.

monody In music, a single vocal or instrumental line, in contrast to polyphony. The term is often applied to the continuo-accompanied solo vocal music of the early 17th-c.

monomer [monomer] A simple molecule which can add to or

condense with itself to form a *polymer*. An amino acid is a monomer of a protein; ethylene ($CH_2=CH_2$) is the monomer of polyethylene ($-CH_2-CH_2-)_n$.

mononucleosis, infectious *glandular fever*

Monophysites [monofisiyts] (Gr 'one nature') Adherents to the doctrine that Christ did not have two natures after his Incarnation – one human and one divine – but rather had only one nature, which was effectively divine since the divine apparently dominated the human. The view was condemned by the Council of Chalcedon (451).

Monopolies Commission or **Monopolies and Mergers Commission** A UK government body set up in 1948 as the *Monopolies and Restrictive Practices Commission*. It has wide powers to investigate activities which may be against the public interest, particularly with respect to mergers, takeovers, and monopoly situations.

monopoly A business situation where there is only one supplier of a good or service. This is unusual except where there is only one possible source of supply (**natural monopoly**) or the state excludes competition (eg in postal services). In economics, the term refers to a lack of competition.

monorail A railway using a single rail for the support of the train. The rail may be above or below the train, and the train may be stabilized if necessary by guide wheels and gyroscopes. Considerable research has gone into investigating non-wheeled methods of support, such as using air cushions and magnetic levitation. Monorails are used almost exclusively for public transport, notably in Tokyo and Seattle.

monosaccharide [monosakariyd] A simple sugar, the monomer of a polysaccharide, formed from it by condensation polymerization.

monosodium glutamate (MSG) A flavouring agent used to enhance the meat flavour of many processed foods containing meat or meat extracts. It is commonly associated with the 'Chinese Restaurant Syndrome', an array of symptoms associated with eating a Chinese meal in which excess MSG has been used.

monotheism The belief that only one God exists. It developed within the Jewish faith, and remains a feature of Judaism, Christianity, and Islam. It is opposed to both polytheism and pantheism.

Monothelites [monotheliyts] A Christian group who believed that in the person of Jesus Christ there was only one will, not two (one human, one divine). They were condemned at the Council of Constantinople in 680.

monotreme [monohtreem] An egg-laying mammal; lays soft-shelled eggs which hatch after 10 days; suckles young for 3–6 months; no teeth as adults. (Order: Monotremata, 3 species.)

Monroe, James (1758–1831) US statesman and fifth president (1817–25), born in Westmoreland Co, VA. He recognized the Spanish American republics, and in 1823 promulgated the *Monroe Doctrine*, embodying the principle 'that the American continents ... are henceforth not to be considered as subjects for future colonization by any European power'.

Monroe, Marilyn, stage name of **Norma Jean Mortenson** or **Baker** (1926–62) Film star, born in Los Angeles, CA. After a childhood spent largely in foster homes, she became a photographer's model in 1946. She studied at Strasberg's Actors' Studio, and came to star as a sexy 'dumb blonde' in many successful films, such as *How to Marry a Millionaire* (1953), *Bus Stop* (1956) and *The Misfits* (1961), written for her by her third husband, Arthur Miller (divorced 1961). She died apparently from an overdose of sleeping pills, and has since become a symbol of Hollywood's exploitation of beauty and youth.

Monroe Doctrine A major statement of American foreign policy, proclaimed in 1823, attributed to President James Monroe, but written by secretary of state John Quincy Adams. It announced

(1) the existence of a separate political system in the Western hemisphere, (2) US hostility to attempts to extend European influence, and (3) non-interference with existing European colonies or in European affairs.

Monrovia [monrohvia] 6°20N 10°46W, pop (2000e) 741 000. Seaport capital of Liberia, W Africa; founded by the American Colonization Society, 1822; original name Christopolis, changed to Monrovia after the US president; airport; railway terminus; university (1862); Firestone rubber plantation and processing centre nearby.

Mons [mõs], Eng [monz], Flemish **Bergen** 50°28N 3°58E, pop (2000e) 93 800. Commercial and cultural city in S Belgium; built on site of one of Caesar's camps; often a battlefield, notably in World War 1 (Aug 1914); railway; university (1965); cathedral.

Monsarrat, Nicholas (John Turney) [monsarat] (1910–79) Novelist, born in Liverpool, Merseyside. During World War 2 he served in the navy, and then wrote his best-selling novel *The Cruel Sea* (1951), which was filmed.

monsoon climates Climates characterized by distinct wet and dry seasons, resulting from the seasonal migration of the intertropical convergence zone and changes in wind direction; they are found in tropical areas, especially Asia. Much of the agriculture of Asia is dependent on the monsoon, but the timing of its arrival is variable, and if it is late there is generally less rainfall.

monstera [monstera] A tall climber or liane (*Monstera deliciosa*) native to tropical America; leaves heart-shaped, developing deep notches and sometimes holes as tissue between veins ceases to grow; also called **Swiss cheese plant**. It is a popular house plant. (Family: Araceae.)

monstrance A liturgical vessel, usually of gold or silver frame with a glass window, used to display the Eucharistic host or consecrated bread. It enables the host to be venerated by worshippers.

montage [montahzh] 1 In art, a technique whereby illustrations or photographs are cut from papers or magazines, arranged in new ways, and mounted. A development of collage, it was used by the Dadaists and Surrealists.
2 In film editing, a sequence containing a series of rapidly changing images, often superimposed to convey a visually dramatic effect.

Montagu, Lady Mary Wortley [montagyoo], *née* **Pierrepont** (1689–1762) Writer, born in London, who gained a brilliant reputation among literary figures. While in Constantinople with her husband, she wrote her entertaining *Letters* describing Eastern life.

Montaigne, Michel (Eyquem) de [mõten] (1533–92) Essayist, born at the Château de Montaigne, Périgord, France. He is remembered for his *Essais* on the ideas and personalities of the time, which introduced a new literary genre, and provided a major contribution to literary history.

Montale, Eugenio [montahlay] (1896–1981) Poet, born in Genoa, Italy. He was the leading poet of the modern Italian *hermetic* school, his primary concern being with language and symbolic meaning. He received the 1975 Nobel Prize for Literature.

Montana [montana] pop (2000e) 902 200; area 380 834 km²/147 046 sq mi. State in NW USA; the 'Treasure State'; most of the state acquired by the Louisiana Purchase, 1803; border with Canada settled by the Oregon Treaty, 1846; became the Territory of Montana, 1864; gold rush after 1858 discoveries; ranchers moved into the area in 1866, taking over Indian land; six Indian reservations now in the state; 41st state to join the Union, 1889; fourth largest US state; crossed by the Missouri and Yellowstone Rivers; highest point Granite Peak (3901 m/12 798 ft); the Great Plains (E) largely occupied by vast wheat fields and livestock farms; W dominated by the Rocky Mts, covered in dense pine forests; capital, Helena; tourism a major state indus-

try; copper, silver, gold, zinc, lead, manganese in the mountainous W; petroleum, natural gas, large coalmines in the E.

Montana, Joe [montana], popular name of **Joseph C Montana, Jr** (1956–) Player of American football, born in New Eagle, PA. He joined the San Francisco 49ers in 1979, and led them to victories in four Super Bowls (1982, 1985, 1989, 1990). The League's most valuable player in 1989, he joined the Kansas City Chiefs 1993–5, before retiring.

Montand, Yves [mõtã, eev], originally **Ivo Livi** (1921–91) Actor-singer, born in Monsummano Alto, Italy. His films include *Le Salaire de La peur* (1953, The Wages of Fear), *Let's Make Love* (1960), and *Z* (1968). In the 1980s he became a distinguished elder statesman of the French film industry.

Montanism [montanizm] A popular Christian movement whose name derives from Montanus of Phrygia (AD c.170). Its ecstatic prophecies and literal expectation of the imminent end of the age won a wide following of churches in Asia Minor, though its austere ethical and spiritual ideals were opposed by the Catholic Church.

Mont Blanc [mõ blã] Highest alpine massif of SE France, SW Switzerland, and NW Italy; 25 peaks over 4000 m/13 000 ft; highest peak, Mont Blanc (4807 m/15 771 ft); frontiers of France, Switzerland, and Italy meet at Mt Dolent (3823 m/12 542 ft); road tunnel (12 km/7½ mi long) connects France and Italy; closed by fire which killed over 40 people, March 1999, reopened in 2002; first climbed in 1786 by J Balmat and M G Paccard; chief resort, Chamonix.

montbretia [monbreesha] A perennial (*Crocosmia × crocosmiiflora*) growing to 90 cm/3 ft; flowers orange, funnel-shaped, in one-sided sprays. (Family: Iridaceae.)

Montcalm (de Saint Véran), Louis Joseph de Montcalm-Grozon, marquis de [mõkalm] (1712–59) French general, born in Condiac, France. He took command of the French troops in Canada (1756), and defended Quebec, where he died in the battle against General Wolfe.

Monte Albán [montay alban] The ancient capital of the Zapotecs of S Mexico; a world heritage site. In use c.400 BC–AD 800, it occupied an area of 40 km²/15 sq mi at its peak (c.200–700), with a population of c.20 000.

Monte Carlo [montay kah(r)loh] 43°46N 7°23E. Resort town in Monaco; famous Casino, providing c.4% of national revenue, built in 1878; annual car rally, world championship Grand Prix motor race.

Montefiore, Sir Moses (Haim) [montefyohray] (1784–1885) Philanthropist, born in Livorno, Italy. From 1829 he was prominent in the struggle for the rights of Jews, making several journeys throughout Europe on their behalf.

Montego Bay [monteegoh], locally **Mobay** 18°27N 77°56W, pop (2000e) 89 000. Free port and principal tourist centre of Jamaica; airport; railway.

Montenegro *see p.619*

Montespan, Françoise Athenaïs de Rochechouart, marquise de (Marchioness of) [mõtespã] (1641–1707) Mistress of Louis XIV, born in Tonnay-Charente, France, the daughter of the Duc de Mortemart. She became the king's mistress in c.1667, and after her marriage was annulled (1674) was given official recognition of her position. She bore the king seven children.

Montesquieu, Charles Louis de Secondat, Baron de la Brède et de [mõteskyoe] (1689–1755) Philosopher and jurist, born near Bordeaux, France. His best-known work is the comparative study of legal and political issues, *De l'esprit des lois* (1748, The Spirit of Laws), which was a major influence on 18th-c Europe.

Montessori, Maria [montesawree] (1870–1952) Physician and educationalist, born in Rome. She opened her first 'children's house' in 1907, developing a system of education for children of three to six, based on freedom of movement, the provision of considerable choice for pupils, and the use of specially-

Montenegro

□ International Airport

[monteneegroh], official name (from 2006) **Republic of Montenegro**, formerly (2003–6) **Union of Serbia and Montenegro**, and (1992–2003) **Federal Republic of Yugoslavia**

Local name Crna Gora

Timezone GMT +1

Area 13 812 km²/5333 sq mi

Population total (2004e) 631 000

Status Republic

Capital Podgorica (administrative), Cetinje (state)

Languages Serbian (official), Albanian

Ethnic groups Montenegrin (43%), Serbian (32%), Bosniak (8%), Albanian (5%), other (12%)

Religions Orthodox Christian, Muslim, Roman Catholic

Physical features Highly indented coastline with narrow coastal plain, high limestone mountains and plateaus; highest peak Mt Durmitor 2522 m/8274 ft; Lake Skadar 391 km²/151 sq mi; Durmitor National Park, Tara River Gorge, and old city of Kotor are world heritage sites

Climate Mediterranean climate on coast, winter snow in mountains; average temperatures 5°C (Jan), 25°C (Jul)

Currency 1 euro (EUR) = 100 cents

Economy Aluminium, bauxite, coal, sea salt, hydroelectricity, steel-making, engineering, wood-processing, textiles, chemicals, leather, household appliances, construction and forestry machinery; grain, tobacco, potatoes, citrus fruits, olives, grapes; tourism

GDP (2002e) $23.15 bn, per capita $2200 (former Serbia and Montenegro)

History Use of name Montenegro began in 15th-c when the Crnojevic dynasty began to rule the Serbian principality of Zeta; maintained independence from the Ottoman Empire; theocratic state ruled by a series of bishop princes, 16th-c–19th-c; transformed into a secular principality, 1852; independent monarchy until 1918; became constituent republic of Yugoslavia, 1946; federated with Serbia as the Federal Republic of Yugoslavia, 1992; confrontation with Croatia over disputed border areas and status of Serbian minority led to civil war, 1991 (for history of civil war *see* Serbia); focus of NATO air-strikes, along with Serbia, in Kosovo crisis, 1999; Union of Serbia and Montenegro, 2003; referendum voted for independence from Serbia, 2006; governing coalition won general election (Sep 2006); governed by a President, Prime Minister, and 81-seat state assembly.

Republic of Montenegro
Head of State
2006– Filip Vujanovic

Head of Government
2006 Milo Djukanovic
2006– Zeljko Sturanovic

---

designed activities and equipment. **Montessori schools** were also later developed for older children.

Monteverdi, Claudio [montayvairdee] (1567–1643) Composer, born in Cremona, Italy. His works include eight books of madrigals, operas, and (his greatest contribution to church music) the Mass and Vespers of the Virgin (1610), which contained tone colours and harmonies well in advance of their time.

Montevideo [montevidayoh] 34°55S 56°10W, pop (2000e) 1 374 500. Capital of Uruguay, on the R Plate; founded, 1726; capital, 1830; airport; railway; university (1849); cathedral (1790–1804); German battleship *Graf Spee* scuttled offshore during the Battle of the River Plate (1939), and an operation to raise it from the mouth of the River Plate began in early 2004.

Montez, Lola [montez], originally **Marie Dolores Eliza Rosanna Gilbert** (1818–61) Dancer and adventurer, born in Limerick, Ireland. She became a dancer in London, and while in Munich (1846) gained influence over the eccentric artist-king, Ludwig I (1786–1868), who created her Countess of Landsfeld.

Montezuma II [montezooma] (1466–1520) Mexican emperor (1502–20), a distinguished warrior and legislator, who died at Tenochtitlán during the Spanish conquest.

Montfort, Simon de, Earl of Leicester (c.1208–1265) English statesman and soldier, born in Montfort, France. In 1238 he married Henry III's youngest sister, Eleanor. He was leader of the barons in their opposition to the king, defeated him at Lewes (1264), and became virtual ruler of England. The barons soon grew dissatisfied with his rule, and the king's army defeated him at Evesham, where he was killed.

Montgolfier brothers [mõgolfyay] Aeronautical inventors: **Joseph Michel Montgolfier** (1740–1810) and **Jacques Etienne Montgol-**fier (1745–99), born in Annonay, France. They constructed a balloon which in 1783 achieved a flight of 9 km/5½ mi over Paris.

Montgomery (Alabama) 32°23N 86°19W, pop (2000e) 201 600. Capital of state in C Alabama, USA, on the Alabama R; state capital, 1847; Confederate States of America formed here, 1861; occupied by Federal troops, 1865; railway; university (1874); important market centre for farming produce; scene of 1955 bus boycott by blacks protesting against segregation.

Montgomery (of Alamein), Bernard Law Montgomery, 1st Viscount (1887–1976) British field marshal, born in London. He gained renown as arguably the best British field commander since Wellington, establishing a remarkable rapport with his troops. He commanded the 8th Army in N Africa, defeated Rommel at El Alamein (1942), played a key role in the invasion of Sicily and Italy (1943), and was appointed commander-in-chief, ground forces, for the Allied invasion of Normandy (1944). In 1945, the German forces surrendered to him on Lüneberg Heath.

month The time for the Moon to orbit the Earth, relative to a reference point. The Moon orbits the Earth in 27.32 days (relative to the stars), passing through the familiar cycle of lunar phases. The lunar month of 29.53 days is the interval between successive new Moons. Twelve lunar months is less than one solar year, so the calendar months are arbitrarily longer than lunar months.

Montherlant, Henri (Marie Joseph Millon) de [mõtairlã] (1896–1972) Writer, born in Paris. His major work is a 4-novel cycle, beginning with *Les jeunes filles* and *Pitié pour les femmes* (1936, trans Pity for Women).

Montoneros [montonairos] Argentine urban guerrillas claiming allegiance to Peronism and (from 1970) staging terrorist actions

Montserrat

[montsuhrat], also **Emerald Isle** (UK British Overseas Territory)

Timezone GMT – 4

Area 106 km²/41 sq mi

Population (1997e) 11 000 (pre-disaster), (2002e) 4000

Capital Plymouth (abandoned in 1997), new buildings at Brades Estate, NW Montserrat

Physical features Volcanic island in the Leeward Is, E Caribbean; mountainous, heavily forested; highest point, Chance's Peak, 914 m/3000 ft; seven active volcanoes.

Climate Tropical climate, with low humidity; average annual rainfall 1500 mm/60 in; hurricanes occur (Jun-Nov).

Currency 1 East Caribbean Dollar (XCD) = 100 cents

Economy Tourism (accounts for 25% of national income); cotton, peppers, livestock, electronic assembly, crafts, rum distilling, postage stamps.

GDP (2002e) $29 mn, per capita $3400

History Visited by Columbus, 1493; colonized by English and Irish settlers, 1632; plantation economy based on slave labour; British Crown Colony, 1871; joined Federation of the West Indies, 1958–62; island severely damaged by hurricane Hugo, 1989; half the island, including the capital, destroyed by eruption of Soufriere Hills volcano, June 1997; 8000 people left the island, with returnees (from 1998) limited by lack of housing; British sovereign represented by a Governor, with an Executive Council and a Legislative Council.

---

against the military regime then in power. Repudiated by Perón himself (1974), they renewed their attacks on the regime installed in 1976, meeting with severe repression.

Montpelier [montpeelyer] 44°16N 72°35W, pop (2000e) 8000. Capital of Vermont, USA; on the Winooski R; settled, 1780; state capital, 1805; railway; Vermont College (1834).

Montpellier [mõpelyay] 43°37N 3°52E, pop (2000e) 217 000. Industrial and commercial city in S France; founded around a Benedictine abbey, 8th-c; airport; railway; bishopric; university (1289); cathedral (1364); Jardin des Plantes, France's first botanical garden (1593).

Montreal [montreeawl], Fr **Montréal** [mõrayal] 45°30N 73°36W, pop (2000e) 1 139 000. River-port city in Quebec, Canada; on Montreal I, on the St Lawrence R (ice-free May–Nov); largest city in Canada, and second largest French-speaking city in the world; first visited by Cartier, 1535; fort, 1611; developed as a fur-trading centre; surrendered to British, 1760; capital of Canada, 1844–9; British garrison withdrawn, 1870; two airports; railway; metro; four universities (1821, 1876, 1969, 1974); two cathedrals; major commercial centre; professional teams, Montreal Expos (baseball), Montreal Canadiens (ice hockey); location of 1967 World's Fair (Expo) and 1976 Olympic Games.

Montreux [mõtroe] 46°27N 6°55E, pop (2000e) 20 200. Winter sports centre and resort town in SW Switzerland; at E end of L Geneva; railway; casino; Golden Rose Television Festival (spring), International Jazz Festival (Jun–Jul).

Montrose, James Graham, 1st Marquess of (1612–50) Scottish general. He led the Royalist army to victory at Tippermuir (1644), but after the Royalist defeat at Naseby (1645), his remaining force was defeated at Philiphaugh. He fled to Europe, returning to Scotland after Charles's execution, but was defeated at Invercharron (1650) and hanged in Edinburgh.

Mont-Saint-Michel [mõ sī mishel] A rocky isle off the coast of Normandy, NW France, famous for its Gothic abbey; a world

---

heritage site. A Benedictine settlement was first established here in the 8th-c.

Montserrat *see panel*

Monty Python, in full **Monty Python's Flying Circus** An anarchic satirical series, shown on BBC television between 1969 and 1974, starring Graham Chapman (1941–89), John Cleese, Eric Idle, Terry Jones, and Michael Palin. The series changed the face of British television humour, with its inspired lunacy, surreal comedy, and animated graphics (by Terry Gilliam), and generated a cult following which was eventually international. The troupe later collaborated on such films as *Monty Python and the Holy Grail* (1975), *The Life of Brian* (1979), and *The Meaning of Life* (1983). A musical, *Spamalot*, written by Eric Idle, debuted on Broadway in 2005. The Tony award-winning show transferred to London in late 2006.

Monument, the A Doric column in C London, surmounted by a representation of a flame-encircled globe, designed by Wren and erected (1671–7) to commemorate the Fire of London. The structure is 61·5 m/202 ft high.

Moody, Dwight L(yman) (1837–99) Leading independent US evangelist, born in Northfield, MA. In 1870 he was joined by **Ira David Sankey** (1840–1908), who accompanied his preaching with singing and organ playing.

Moody, Helen (Newington) Wills (1905–98) Tennis player, born in Centerville, CA. She won the Wimbledon singles title eight times in nine attempts (1927–30, 1932–3, 1935, 1938). Between 1927 and 1932 she won all the major singles championships (except the Australian) without losing a set.

Moog synthesizer *synthesizer*

Moon *pp.622–3*

moonfish Large, midwater fish (*Lampris guttatus*) widespread in tropical and temperate seas; length up to 1·5 m/5 ft; body deep, compressed, fins well-developed, protruding mouth, lacking teeth; colour very characteristic, deep blue on back spotted with white, underside silver, fins deep red; also called **opah**. (Family: Lampridae.)

Moonies A derisive name applied to members of the religious movement founded in 1954 by Korean evangelist Sun Myung Moon (1920–). Known as the **Unification Church** (in full, the Holy Spirit Association for the Unification of World Christianity), the organization was founded in 1954 in South Korea, and moved to Tarrytown, NY, in the 1970s. Mass marriages are one of the movement's more public activities. The missionary activities of the Church have attracted a great deal of criticism, especially from parents who believe that their children have been brainwashed. The organization's financial affairs have also been the subject of investigation, and in 1982 Moon was fined and sentenced to 18 months imprisonment for US tax evasion. He has continued to live chiefly in the USA, where he owns several companies, but has encountered increasing opposition to his movement there, and also in several countries where he has tried to expand, especially in C and S America. In the late 1990s he began to develop a centre at Jardim, W Brazil, as a new 'garden of Eden'.

moonrat A SE Asian insectivorous mammal; resembles closely related hedgehogs, but lacks spines and has a longer tail; several species reputed to be the most evil-smelling animals; also known as **hairy hedgehog** or **gymnure**. (Family: Erinaceidae, 5 species.)

moonstone A semi-precious gemstone variety of the mineral potassium feldspar. It has a pale opalescent lustre because of its fine-scale oriented microstructure, which diffracts light.

Moore, Archie, originally **Archibald Lee Wright**, nickname **the Mongoose** (1913/16–98) Boxer, born in Benoit, MI. His actual date of birth is uncertain, but he was still the oldest man to hold a world title when he beat Joey Maxim for the light-heavyweight title in 1952 at the age of 39 (or 36).

Moore, Bobby, popular name of **Robert Frederick Chelsea Moore** (1941–93) Footballer, born in London. He had a long career with West Ham United (1958–74) and Fulham (1974–7), and was capped 108 times, 90 of them as captain, a total only surpassed by Peter Shilton. He led the victorious England side in the 1966 World Cup.

Moore, Brian (1921–99) Writer, born in Belfast. His first novel, *Judith Hearne*, appeared in 1955; later works include *The Doctor's Wife* (1976) and *Black Robe* (1985), both short-listed for the Booker Prize, and *The Magician's Wife* (1998).

Moore, Demi, originally **Demetria Guynes** (1962–) Film actress, producer, and director, born in Roswell, NM. She became well known following her role in *Ghost* (1990), later films including *Indecent Proposal* (1992), *G.I. Jane* (1997), *Charlie's Angels: Full Throttle* (2003), and *Bobby* (2006). She was married to actor Bruce Willis (1987–98).

Moore, Dudley (Stuart John) (1935–2002) British actor, comedian, and composer. He was one of the successful *Beyond the Fringe* team (1960–4), and joined Peter Cook for the TV series *Not only ... but also* (1964–70). He went on to star in several films including *10* (1979), *Arthur* (1981), and *Crazy People* (1990). An accomplished musician, he performed with his own jazz piano trio, and composed for several films and plays. In 1999 he was diagnosed with a degenerative brain disease, progressive supranuclear palsy.

Moore, G(eorge) E(dward) (1873–1958) Philosopher, born in London. His major ethical work was *Principia Ethica* (1903), in which he argued against the naturalistic fallacy, and he was also editor (1921–47) of *Mind*. He was a leading influence on the Bloomsbury group.

Moore, Henry (Spencer) (1898–1986) Sculptor, born in Castleford, West Yorkshire. He produced mainly figures and groups in a semi-abstract style based on the organic forms and rhythms found in landscape and natural rocks. His interest lay in the spatial quality of sculpture, an effect he achieved by the piercing of his figures. His major works include 'Madonna and Child' (1943–4) in St Matthew's Church, Northampton.

Moore, Sir John (1761–1809) British general, born in Glasgow. He is remembered for his command of the British army in Spain (1808–9), where he was forced to retreat to Coruña. There he was mortally wounded (as recounted in the poem by Charles Wolfe).

Moore, Julianne, originally **Julie Anne Smith** (1961–) Actress, born in Fayetteville, NC. She studied drama at Boston University's School of Performing Arts, and became known for her role in the TV soap *As The World Turns* (1985–8). Film credits include *The Hand That Rocks the Cradle* (1991), *The Hours* (2002), and *Children of Men* (2006). She has twice been nominated for a Best Actress Oscar, for *Boogie Nights* (1997) and *Far From Heaven* (2002).

Moore, Marianne (Craig) (1887–1972) Poet, born in St Louis, MO. Her *Collected Poems* appeared in 1951, and *Complete Poems* in 1967.

Moore, Michael (1954–) Film director, producer, and writer, born in Davison, Flint, MI. He worked as a newspaper journalist and editor, and began film-making with the groundbreaking documentary *Roger and Me* (1989). Later films include *Canadian Bacon* (1995) and *Bowling for Columbine* (2002, Oscar for Best Documentary). In 2004 the film studio Disney initially refused to give US distribution to his documentary *Fahrenheit 911*, which heavily criticized President Bush. Among his books are *The Awful Truth* (1999), the best-selling *Stupid White Men* (2001), *Dude, Where's My Country?* (2003), and *Will They Ever Trust Us Again?* (2004).

Moore, Sir Patrick (Alfred Caldwell) (1923–) Amateur astronomer, writer, broadcaster, and musician, born in Pinner, Greater London. He is best known as the enthusiastic and knowledgeable presenter of the long-running BBC television programme *The Sky at Night* (1957–). He has published over 60 books, and is an accomplished xylophone player and composer.

Moore, Sir Roger (George) (1927–) Film star, born in London. On television he won stardom as the action-man hero of such series as *Ivanhoe* (1958), and *The Saint* (1962–9). He brought a lightweight insouciance to the role of James Bond in seven films between *Live and Let Die* (1973) and *A View to a Kill* (1985).

Moores, Sir John (1896–1993) Businessman, born in Eccles, Greater Manchester. He founded Littlewoods football pools in 1923, established a mail-order business in Britain in 1932, and opened the first store in the Littlewoods chain in 1937. Liverpool John Moores University is named after him.

moorhen Either of two species of rail of genus *Gallinula*, especially the **moorhen**, **common gallinule**, or **Florida gallinule** (*Gallinula chloropus*), found worldwide; also the **lesser** or **little moorhen** (*Gallinula angulata*), found in sub-Saharan Africa.

Moors A nomadic people of the N seaboard of Africa, originally the inhabitants of Mauritania. They were chiefly of Berber and Arab descent. In the 8th-c the Moors were converted to Islam. They were killed or expelled in the Christian reconquest which began with the recovery of Toledo (1085), and during the height of the Inquisition were virtually exterminated.

Moors Murderers *Brady, Ian*

moose *elk*

moped [mohped] A small, lightweight motorcycle fitted with pedals, and capable of being pedalled if necessary. It was established as a means of personal transport before World War 2, but it was not until after the War that its economy made it attractive. This economy was achieved by lightness of design and the application of the two-stroke engine.

moraine A sedimentary deposit of poorly sorted rock and detritus transported by glaciers and ice-sheets. Different classes of moraine correspond to the different zones of glaciers where deposition occurs (eg terminal moraines, lateral moraines).

morality play A play which dramatizes a moral argument, presenting the opposition between good and evil, often with characters who personify virtues, vices, diseases, and temptations. It was popular in England, Scotland, France, and The Netherlands in the 15th-c and early 16th-c. Unlike the mystery play, it was not tied to religious festivals, and was performed by professional actors.

Moral Majority A US political action committee founded in 1979 which has played a leading part in the revival of the New Right. It is associated with Christian fundamentalists who in the 1980s came to play a prominent role in US politics.

Moral Rearmament A movement founded by Frank Buchman in 1938 to deepen the spirituality and morality of Christians. It succeeded the 'Oxford Group Movement' (founded 1921), and expanded its goals to include political and social concerns.

moral theology A theological discipline concerned with ethical questions considered from a specifically Christian perspective. In Roman Catholic teaching, it deals traditionally with God as the goal of human life, and provides instruction on spirituality and the means of grace. It has become increasingly ecumenical, and concerned with issues such as peace, justice, and bioethics.

Morar, Loch [morer] Loch in W Highland, W Scotland; 19 km/12 mi long; deepest loch in Britain (310 m/1017 ft).

Moravia [morayvia], Czech **Morava**, Ger **Mähren** Historic province of the Czech Republic; chief towns include Brno, Ostrava, Olomouc; early mediaeval kingdom (Great Moravia), 9th-c; part of Bohemia, 1029; under Habsburg rule from early 16th-c; province of Czechoslovakia, 1918; united with Silesia, 1927–49; political status under discussion, 1991.

Moravia, Alberto [morayvia], pseudonym of **Alberto Pincherle**

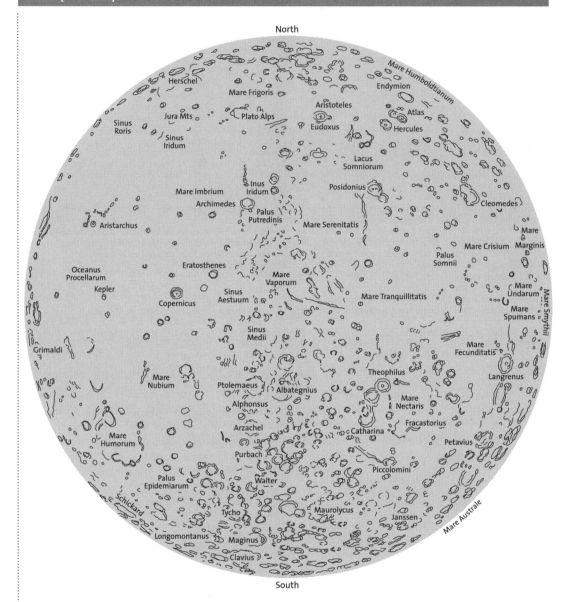

North

Mare Humboldtianum
Herschel
Mare Frigoris
Endymion
Aristoteles
Atlas
Jura Mts
Plato Alps
Sinus
Roris
Eudoxus
Hercules
Sinus
Iridum
Lacus
Somniorum
Inus
Iridum
Posidonius
Mare Imbrium
Cleomedes
Archimedes
Palus
Putredinis
Mare
Mare Serenitatis
Marginis
Aristarchus
Mare Crisium
Palus
Somnii
Oceanus
Procellarum
Eratosthenes
Mare
Undarum
Kepler
Mare
Vaporum
Mare
Spumans
Sinus
Aestuum
Mare Tranquillitatis
Copernicus
Mare
Fecunditatis
Sinus
Medii
Mare
Grimaldi
Theophilus
Langrenus
Mare
Nubium
Ptolemaeus
Albategnius
Mare
Nectaris
Alphonsus
Fracastorius
Arzachel
Catharina
Petavius
Mare
Humorum
Purbach
Piccolomini
Palus
Epidemiarum
Walter
Schickard
Maurolycus
Mare Australe
Tycho
Janssen
Longomontanus
Maginus
Clavius

South

The Earth's only natural satellite, lacking any atmosphere; about a quarter the size of the Earth, and treated as one of the family of terrestrial planets. It has the following characteristics: mass 0.073×10^{27} g; radius 1738 km/1080 mi; mean density 3.34 g/cm³; equatorial gravity 162 cm/s; rotational period 27.3 days; orbital period 27.3 days; average distance from Earth 384 400 km/238 850 mi. Overall density is low, because of a major iron deficiency. Apollo seismic measurements indicate that the interior is solid to a depth of c.1000 km/600 mi; the nature of the core is still uncertain. There is no global magnetic field, but evidence of past magnetization is contained in individual rock samples. The equality of rotational and orbital rates is due to tidal despinning of the Moon into a stable synchronous period, so that the same hemisphere of the Moon always faces the Earth.

The brighter surface regions (*highlands*) represent the original lunar crustal material shaped by saturation bombardment of meteoritic material. The dark surface regions (*mare* regions),

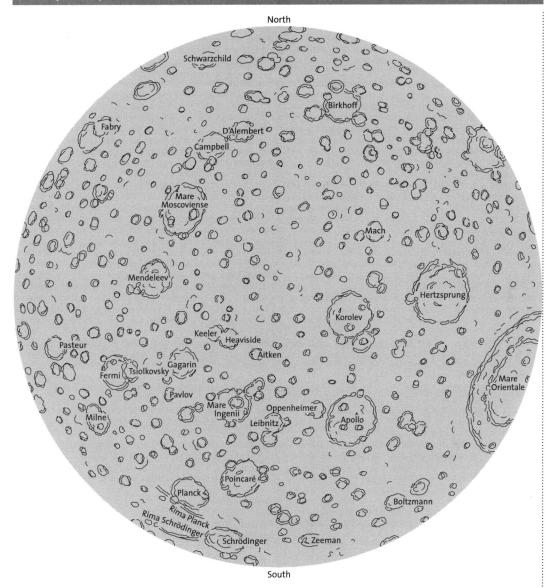

North

Schwarzchild

Birkhoff

Fabry

D'Alembert

Campbell

Mare
Moscoviense

Mach

Mendeleev

Hertzsprung

Korolev

Keeler
Heaviside
Pasteur
Aitken
Gagarin
Fermi Tsiolkovsky
Mare
Orientale
Pavlov
Mare
Ingenii
Oppenheimer
Milne
Leibnitz
Apollo

Poincaré
Planck
Rima Planck
Boltzmann
Rima Schrödinger
Schrödinger Zeeman

South

located mainly on the side observable from Earth, represent basaltic (volcanic) flooding of basins created by major asteroidal impacts. Apollo and Luna sample isotopic dating places mare basalts in the range of 3–4 thousand million years, in contrast to 4·2–4·5 thousand million for highland samples. Lunar evolution models based on Lunar Orbiter mapping of the Moon and on Apollo and Luna sample analyses suggest five principal episodes: accretion and large-scale melting; crustal separation and concurrent massive meteoritic bombardment; partial melting at depth; diminished bombardment with further melting at depth and emplacement of mare basalts; and cessation of volcanism and gradual internal cooling. The popular current theory for the creation of the Moon involves the impact of a Mars-sized object with the Earth, occasioning a catastrophic disruption of the Earth, and the accretion of the Moon in Earth orbit from debris torn from the Earth's mantle.

(1907–90) Novelist and short-story writer, born in Rome. His first novel was a major success, *Gli indifferenti* (1929, trans The Time of Indifference), portraying in a fatalistic way the pre-occupation with sex and money of bourgeois Roman society. Later works include *Racconti romani* (1954, Roman Tales).

Moravian Brethren A Protestant body descended from an association of Brethren formed in Bohemia in 1457, and driven out in 1722 by persecution. In 1734 the Moravian Church was established in North America, where most members live today.

Moray, James Stuart, Earl of [muhree] (1531–70) Regent of Scotland (1567–70), the illegitimate son of James V of Scotland, and half-brother of Mary, Queen of Scots. He acted as Mary's chief adviser (1560), but opposed her marriage to Darnley. He became regent for Mary's baby son when she abdicated (1567), and defeated her army at Langside (1568). He was killed at Linlithgow by one of Mary's supporters.

Morceli, Noureddine [maw(r)selee] (1970–) Athlete, born in Tenes, Algeria. World champion over 1500 m in 1991 – the youngest ever – he repeated his success in 1993 and 1995. During the latter year he held the world record for 1500 m, the mile, 2000 m and 3000 m, and in 1996 was Olympic 1500 m champion.

Mordecai [maw(r)dekiy] (c.5th-c BC) Biblical hero, described in the Book of Esther as a Jew in exile in Persia who gained the favour of King Xerxes, and used his influence to protect Jews from an edict issued against them. The event is commemorated by the annual Jewish feast of Purim.

More, Henry [moor] (1614–87) Philosopher and poet, born in Grantham, Lincolnshire. He was a leading member of the Cambridge Platonists. His works include the *Divine Dialogues* (1668).

More, Sir Thomas [moor], also **St Thomas More** (1478–1535) English statesman and scholar, born in London. On the fall of Wolsey (1529), he was appointed Lord Chancellor, but resigned in 1532 following his opposition to Henry's break with the Roman Catholic Church. On refusing to recognize Henry as head of the English Church, he was imprisoned and beheaded. A leading humanist scholar, as revealed in his Latin *Utopia* (1516) and many other works, he was canonized in 1935, and is the patron saint of politicians. Feast day 22 June.

Morecambe, Eric, originally **Eric Bartholomew** (1926–84) Comedian, born in Morecambe, Lancashire. He teamed up in 1943 with fellow entertainer, **Ernie Wise** (originally **Ernest Wiseman**) (1925–99), eventually becoming Britain's leading comedy double-act.

morel [morel] An edible fungus (*Morchella esculenta*); fruiting body consists of a pale stalk (*stipe*) and brownish, egg-shaped head with a pitted or ridged surface. (Subdivision: Ascomycetes. Order: Pezizales.)

Morgagni, Giovanni Battista [maw(r)ganyee] (1682–1771) Physician and pathologist, born in Forli, Italy. He correlated pathological lesions with symptoms in over 700 cases, and is traditionally considered to be the 'father of morbid anatomy'.

Morgan, Sir Henry (c.1635–88) Welsh buccaneer, born in Llanrumney, S Wales. He led many raids against the Spanish and Dutch in the West Indies and Central America. His most famous exploit was the sacking of Porto Bello and Panama (1671). He later became Deputy Governor of Jamaica.

Morgan, J(ohn) P(ierpont) (1837–1913) Banker, financier, and art collector, born in Hartford, CT. The son of the financier **John Spencer Morgan** (1813–90), he built his father's firm into the most powerful private banking house in the USA, providing US government finance, and developing interests in steel, railroads, and shipping.

Morgan, Thomas Hunt (1866–1945) Geneticist, born in Lexington, KY. Following experiments with the *Drosophila* fruit fly, he proved that Mendel's 'genetic factors' are the chromosomes, and showed the link between genes and chromosomes. He received the Nobel Prize for Physiology or Medicine in 1933.

Morgan le Fay In Arthurian legend, an enchantress, 'Morgan the Fairy', King Arthur's sister, and generally hostile towards him.

Morisot, Berthe (Marie Pauline) [morisoh] (1841–95) Painter, born in Bourges, France. She was the leading female exponent of Impressionism.

Morley, Robert (1908–92) Actor and writer, born in Semley, Wiltshire. In his film career, beginning with *Marie Antoinette* (1938, Best Supporting Actor Oscar nomination), he played many individual character parts, including the title role in *The Trials of Oscar Wilde* (1960). His books include *Robert Morley's Book of Bricks* (1979) and *Morley Matters* (1980). His son, the writer, broadcaster, and critic **Sheridan Morley** (1941–2007), published a biography *Robert, My Father* in 1994.

Mormons [mawmuhnz] A religious movement based on the visionary experiences of Joseph Smith, who organized it as the 'Church of Jesus Christ of Latter-Day Saints' in 1830 at Fayette, NY. Smith claimed to have been led to the Book of Mormon, inscribed on golden plates and buried 1000 years before in a hill near Palmyra, NY. It teaches Christ's future establishment of the New Jerusalem in America. Subjected to persecution, the Mormons moved W, and Brigham Young finally led most of them to the valley of the Great Salt Lake, Utah (1847). There were over 11 million worldwide in 2007.

morning-after pill *contraception; DES*

morning glory An annual (*Ipomoea tricolor*) growing to 3 m/10 ft, native to tropical America; climbing by means of twining stems; flowers up to 12·5 cm/5 in diameter, funnel-shaped, blue with yellow throat, sometimes purple or red. (Family: Convolvulaceae.)

morning sickness Nausea and vomiting during the first three months of pregnancy, which affects c.50% of women. It tends to subside thereafter, and is believed to result from associated hormonal changes.

Moro, Aldo [moroh] (1916–78) Italian statesman and prime minister (1963–4, 1964–6, 1966–8, 1974–6, 1976), born in Maglie, Italy. Red Brigade left-wing terrorists kidnapped him in Rome in 1978, and subsequently murdered him.

Morocco *p.625*

Moroni [morohnee] 11°40S 43°16E, pop (2000e) 26 300. Capital of Comoros; airport; pilgrimage centre at Chiouanda.

Morpeth 55°10N 1°41W, pop (2000e) 15 200. County town of Northumberland, on the R Wansbeck; railway; remains of Morpeth Castle (14th-c).

Morpheus [maw(r)fyoos] In Roman mythology, one of the sons of Somnus ('sleep') who sends or impresses images of people in the dreamer's mind.

morphine A drug derived from opium, used to ease severe pain. Because of its addictive potential, its use is controlled. In overdoses it causes death by suppressing respiration.

morphology (biology) The form and structure of an individual organism, with special emphasis on its external features.

morphology (linguistics) The study of **morphemes**, the smallest indivisible units of meaning in the structure of a word (eg *anti-lock-ing*, *horse-s*). It recognizes such notions as roots, inflections, and affixes.

Morris, Desmond (John) (1928–) Zoologist, writer, and painter, born near Swindon, Wiltshire. His study of human behaviour in *The Naked Ape* (1967) was a best-seller, and was followed by many television programmes on animal and social behaviour. His other books include *Manwatching* (1977), *Illustrated Babywatching* (1995), *Body Guards* (1999), *Peoplewatching* (2002), and *Watching: Encounters with Humans and Other Animals* (2006).

Morris, Estelle (1952–) British stateswoman, born in Manchester, Greater Manchester. A teacher, she was elected a Labour MP in

Morocco

□ International Airport

[muhrokoh], official name **The Kingdom of Morocco**, Arabic **al-Mamlakah al-Maghribiyah**

Local name al-Magrib

Timezone GMT

Area 409 200 km²/157 951 sq mi

Population total (2002e) 29 632 000

Status Kingdom

Date of independence 1956

Capital Rabat

Languages Arabic (official), Berber, Spanish, and French also widely spoken

Ethnic groups Arab-Berber (99%), non-Moroccan (0·7%), Jewish (0·2%)

Religions Sunni Muslim (98%), Christian (1%), Jewish (0·2%)

Physical features Dominated by a series of mountain ranges, rising in the Atlas Mts (S) to 4165 m/13 664 ft at Jebel Toubkal; broad coastal plain; main rivers, Drâ'ar (S and SW) and Moulouya (N) draining into the Mediterranean.

Climate Mediterranean climate on N coast; semi-arid in S; Sahara

virtually rainless; average annual temperatures 13°C (Jan), 22°C (Jul) in Rabat; average annual rainfall 564 mm/22·2 in.

Currency 1 Moroccan Dirham (MAD) = 100 Moroccan francs

Economy Agriculture (employs over 50% of population); largest known reserves of phosphate in world; fishing, textiles, cement, soap, tobacco, chemicals, paper, timber products; tourism centred on the four imperial cities and the warm Atlantic resorts.

GDP (2002e) $121·8 bn, per capita $3900

Human Development Index (2002) 0·602

History N coast occupied by Phoenicians, Carthaginians, and Romans since 12th-c BC; invasion by Arabs, 7th-c AD; conflicting French and Spanish interest in the region in 19th-c; Treaty of Fez in 1912, established Spanish Morocco (capital, Tétouan) and French Morocco (capital, Rabat); Tangier became an international zone, 1923–56; protectorates gained independence, 1956; became Kingdom of Morocco, 1957; Spanish withdrew from former Spanish Sahara (Western Sahara) in 1975; Morocco laid claim to this area using the 'Green March' as a gesture of peaceful occupation; Mauritania withdrew from southern third of territory in 1979, leaving Morocco fighting with the Polisario for the whole of Western Sahara; ceasefire agreement signed, 1990; 'constitutional' monarchy, but the King presides over his appointed Cabinet, which is led by a Prime Minister; a unicameral Chamber of Representatives.

Head of State (Monarch)

1957–61 Mohammed V
1961–99 Hassan II
1999– Mohammad VI

Head of Government

1955–8 Si Mohammed Bekkai
1958 Ahmad Balfrej
1958–60 Abdullah Ibrahim
1960–3 *As monarch*
1963–5 Ahmad Bahnini
1965–7 *As monarch*
1967–9 Moulay Ahmed Laraki
1969–71 Mohammed Ben Hima
1971–2 Mohammed Karim Lamrani
1972–9 Ahmed Othman
1979–83 Maati Bouabid
1983–5 Mohammed Karim Lamrani
1985–92 Azzedine Laraka
1992–4 Mohammed Karim Lamrani
1994–8 Abdellatif Filali
1998–2002 Abderrahmane el-Yousifi
2002– Driss Jettou

1992, and became minister of state for the Department for Education and Employment (1997–8), minister for school standards (1997–2001), secretary of state for education and skills (2001–2), and arts minister (2003–5). Following her resignation as an MP in 2005, she became pro-vice-chancellor of Sunderland University.

Morris, Robert L(yle) (1942–2004) Psychologist, born in Canonsburg, PA. In 1985 he was appointed the first Koestler professor of parapsychology at the University of Edinburgh.

Morris, Robert (1931–) Sculptor and mixed media artist, born in Kansas City, MO. He moved to San Francisco in 1950, becoming active as a painter and in improvisatory theatre. He settled in New York City in 1961, specializing in minimalist works, earthwork projects, and scatter pieces.

Morris, William (1834–96) Craftsman and poet, born near London. He associated with the Pre-Raphaelite Brotherhood, then specialized in the revival of handicrafts and the art of house decoration and furnishing. He organized the Socialist League, and in 1890 set up the Kelmscott Press, issuing his own works and reprints of classics.

morris dance A form of traditional dance found in England. Its distinctive features are stamping and hopping performed by files of performers usually dressed in white and always carrying some prop – a stick, handkerchief, or garland.

Morrison (of Lambeth), Herbert Stanley Morrison, Baron (1888–1965) British Labour statesman, born in London. He was minister of transport (1929–31), minister of supply (1940), and home secretary (1940–5). He served in the war cabinet from

1942, and became a powerful post-war figure, acting as deputy prime minister (1945–51).

Morrison, Toni, *née* **Chloe Anthony Wofford** (1931–) Novelist, born in Lorain, OH. Her early titles include *The Bluest Eye* (1970) and *Song of Solomon* (1977). Two later novels, *Tar Baby* (1981) and *Beloved* (Pulitzer, 1988), confirmed her as a leading novelist of her generation, and she received the Nobel Prize for Literature in 1993. Later books include *Jazz* (1993), *Paradise* (1998), and *Love* (2003).

Morrison, Van, popular name of **George Ivan Morrison** (1945–) Singer, musician, and songwriter, born in Belfast. His first solo hit was 'Brown-Eyed Girl' (1967) and a year later he released the highly acclaimed, surreal album *Astral Weeks*. Other successes of that period include the single 'Caravan' (1970). Later albums include *The Healing Game* (1996), *Down the Road* (2002), and *Pay the Devil* (2006).

Morse, Samuel F(inley) B(reese) (1791–1872) Artist and inventor, born in Charlestown, MA. He developed the magnetic telegraph (1832–5), which along with the **Morse code** (1838) brought him honours and rewards after the opening of the first telegraph line between Washington and Baltimore (1844).

Morse code A binary code for the transmission of verbal messages, devised during the 1830s by Samuel Morse. Each letter of the alphabet, numeral, and punctuation mark was assigned a distinctive combination of (short) dots and (long) dashes. Modern telegraphy has made greater use of the more economical **Baudot code**, devised in 1874 by French engineer Jean Maurice Emile Baudot. Although Morse code was officially replaced by the Global Maritime Distress and Safety System (GMDSS) in 1999, it will continue to be used by amateur radio enthusiasts and others.

mortar (building) Any one of many mixtures of lime and sand or (modern) cement and sand with water, which provide a bond between bricks, masonry, or tiles.

mortar (military) A weapon, used typically by infantry forces, which projects a small bomb at a high trajectory to fall on enemy forces at short range.

mortar and pestle A device known in various forms since ancient times for grinding granular material into powder. The **mortar** is a shallow bowl of abrasive stone. The **pestle** is a conical piece of the same material with a rounded end, with which the material to be ground is forced against the bowl.

Mortensen, Viggo (1958–) Actor, born in Manhattan, NY. He studied at St Lawrence University, NY and then took up acting, later moving to Los Angeles where he earned critical praise for his stage performance in *Bent*. His film debut was in *Witness* (1985), and further films include *The Indian Runner* (1991), *Portrait of a Lady* (1996), and *28 Days* (2000). He became well known for his role as the brave warrior Aragorn in *The Lord of the Rings* trilogy (2001–3). Later films include *Hidalgo* (2004) and *A History of Violence* (2005).

mortgage [mawgij] An arrangement whereby a lender (the **mortgagee**) lends money to a borrower (the **mortgagor**), the loan being secured on the mortgagor's land. Mortgages have played a significant role in permitting the spread of home ownership.

Mortimer, Sir John (Clifford) (1923–) Playwright and novelist, born in London. He came to prominence as a dramatist with his one-act play *The Dock Brief* (1957). Television plays and stories about the disreputable barrister Horace Rumpole began in 1978. Later novels include *Paradise Postponed* (1985) and *Summer of a Dormouse* (1999), and among other works are a volume of autobiography, *Clinging to the Wreckage* (1982), and *Where There's a Will* (2003), a collection of his observations on life.

Morton, H(enry) V(ollam) (1892–1979) Travel writer and journalist, born in Birmingham, West Midlands. The author of many informally written travel books, he is best known for *In Search of London* (1951), and others in the *In Search of...* series.

Morton, James Douglas, 4th Earl of (c.1516–81) Regent of Scotland (1572–8) for James VI. He was made Lord High Chancellor by Mary Stuart (1563); yet he was involved in the murders of Rizzio (1566) and Darnley (1567), and helped to overthrow the queen. He succeeded the Earl of Mar as regent, but his high-handed treatment of the nobles and clergy caused his downfall (1581), and he was executed at Edinburgh.

Morton, Jelly Roll, popular name of **Ferdinand Lemott** (1890–1941) Jazz composer, bandleader, and pianist, born in Gulfport, LA. His unaccompanied piano solos made best sellers of such tunes as 'King Porter Stomp' and 'Jelly Roll Blues', and he made powerful orchestral arrangements for his band, **The Red Hot Peppers**.

Morton, John Cameron (Andrieu Bingham Michael), pseudonym **Beachcomber** (1893–1979) British writer and journalist. He was best known for his regular humorous column in the *Daily Express* under his pseudonym.

mosaic The technique of making decorative designs or pictures by arranging small pieces of coloured glass, marble, or ceramic in a bed of cement. It was much used by the Romans for pavements, by the early Christians and Byzantines for murals in churches, and also by Islamic artists.

Mosaic Law *Torah*

mosasaurus [mohsasawrus] A very large, marine lizard abundant in Cretaceous seas around N Europe and America; swimming mainly by movements of tail; paddle-like limbs used for steering; head long, teeth long and sharp. (Order: Squamata.)

moschatel [moskatel] A perennial (*Adoxa moschatellina*) native to the N hemisphere, 5–10 cm/2–4 in high; flowers greenish-yellow, forming an almost square head, each face formed by a 5-petalled flower (hence the alternative name, **town hall clock**) plus a 4-petalled flower at the top. (Family: Adoxaceae.)

Moscow, Russ **Moskva** 55°45N 37°42E, pop (2000e) 9 400 000. Capital and largest city of Russia, on the R Moskva; known from the 12th-c; capital of the principality of Muscovy, 13th-c; invaded by Napoleon, 1812; capital of the Russian SFSR, 1918; capital of the USSR, 1922; airport; railway; underground; universities (1755, 1960); Academy of Sciences; Moscow Art Theatre, Bolshoi Theatre of Opera and Ballet, Moscow State Circus; Kremlin (1300); Uspenski (Assumption) Cathedral (1475–9), Cathedral of the Archangel (1333, rebuilt 1505–9), Blagoveshchenski (Annunciation) Cathedral, St Basil's Cathedral (16th-c); Red Square; Lenin Mausoleum; scene of the 1980 Olympic Games.

Moselle, River [mohzel], Ger **Mosel**, ancient **Mosella** River in Germany, Luxembourg, and NE France; rises in the French Vosges; flows N and NE to enter the R Rhine at Koblenz; length 514 km/319 mi; a major wine area.

Moses [mohziz] (c.13th-c BC) Major character of Israelite history, portrayed in the Book of Exodus as the leader of the deliverance of Hebrew slaves from Egypt and the recipient of the divine revelation at Mt Sinai. Stories about his early life depict his escape from death as an infant, his upbringing in the Egyptian court, and his prediction of a series of miraculous plagues to persuade the Pharaoh to release the Hebrews. Traditions then describe Moses' leadership of the Israelites during their 40 years of wilderness wanderings. He was traditionally considered the author of the five books of the Law, but this is doubted by modern scholars.

Moses, Ed(win Corley) (1955–) Athlete, born in Dayton, OH. The world's most successful hurdler over 400 m, he was the world champion in 1983, and Olympic champion in 1976 and 1984.

Moses, Grandma, popular name of **Anna Mary Robertson Moses** (1860–1961) Artist, born in Greenwich, NY. She began to paint childhood country scenes at about the age of 75, when arthritis made it difficult for her to sew, and achieved great popular success throughout the USA.

Moslem *Islam*

Mosley, Nicholas [mohzlee], Baron Ravensdale (1923–) Writer, born in London. He published his first novel, *Spaces of the Dark* in 1951. Later novels include *The Rainbearers* (1955), *Accident* (1964, filmed 1967), *Hopeful Monsters* (1990, Whitbread Prize), and *Look at the Dark* (2005).

Mosley, Sir Oswald (Ernald) [mohzlee] (1896–1980) Politician, born in London. In 1932 he founded the British Union of Fascists, remembered for its anti-Semitic violence in the East End of London and its support for Hitler. Detained under the Defence Regulations during World War 2, he founded another racialist party, the Union Movement, in 1948.

mosquito, also known as **gnat** A small, slender fly with a piercing proboscis; eggs laid in water; blood-feeding females act as intermediate hosts of malaria, yellow fever, filariasis, dengue, and other disease organisms; distributed worldwide. (Order: Diptera. Family: Culicidae, c.3000 species.)

Mosquito Coast Undeveloped lowland area in E Honduras and E Nicaragua, Central America, following the Caribbean coast in a 65 km/40 mi-wide strip of tropical forest, lagoons, and swamp; controlled by the British, 1665–1860.

Moss, Sir Stirling (1929–) Motor-racing driver, born in London. He won many major races in the 1950s, but never won a world title, though he was runner-up twice. A bad crash at Goodwood in 1962 ended his career.

moss A small, spore-bearing, non-vascular plant of the class Musci, related to liverworts and hornworts. Mat- or cushion-forming mosses are found almost everywhere, most often in damp, shady places. However, some species are better able to withstand drying out, and a few even inhabit very dry places such as walls.

Mosul [mohsool] 36°21N 43°08E, pop (2000e) 884 000. City in NW Iraq, on W bank of R Tigris; chief town of N Mesopotamia, 8th–13th-c; airfield; railway; university (1967); agricultural market centre.

motet A sacred musical work, originating in the 13th-c and cultivated during the Renaissance as an unaccompanied polyphonic piece, reaching its highest point of development in the works of such composers as Palestrina and Byrd. After 1600, motets often included instrumental accompaniment, but the term continued to distinguish sacred works in Latin from others (cantatas and anthems) in the vernacular.

moth An insect belonging to the order Lepidoptera, which comprises the butterflies and moths. Moths are distinguished from butterflies by being active mostly at night, by folding their wings flat over the body when at rest, and by having complex comb-like tips to their antennae; but there are exceptions.

mother-in-law's-tongue A perennial (*Sansevieria trifasciata*) native to W Africa; leaves to 1 m/3¼ ft, stiff, erect, sword-shaped, fleshy, dark green with pale bands; flowers greenish white; berries orange. It is a widely grown house plant, also called **sansevieria** and **snake plant**, from the patterning on its leaves. (Family: Agavaceae.)

Mother Lode The gold-mining region in the W foothills of the Sierra Nevada, California, USA. It was the centre of the Californian gold rush.

Mother's Day A day set apart in honour of mothers: in the UK, Mothering Sunday, the fourth Sunday of Lent; in Australia, Canada, and the USA, the second Sunday in May.

Motherwell 55°48N 4°00W, pop (2000e) 29 600. Administrative centre of North Lanarkshire, C Scotland; railway; engineering.

Motion, Andrew (1952–) Poet, born in London. He studied English at Oxford, and in 1995 became professor of creative writing at the University of East Anglia. His works include *Selected Poems 1976–1997* (1998) and *Public Property* (2002), and he is also a biographer and novelist. He was made poet laureate in 1999.

motion pictures *cinema; cinematography*

moto-cross A specialist form of motorcycle racing over a circuit of rough terrain, and taking advantage of natural hazards such as streams and hills. The first moto-cross was held at Camberley, Surrey, UK, in 1924. The sport is also often known as **scrambling**.

motorcycle A two-wheeled vehicle designed to carry a rider and frequently a passenger for transport and pleasure, using a two- or four-stroke internal combustion engine to drive the rear wheel, with steering being accomplished by the rider turning the front wheel. A sidecar was often fitted to provide extra passenger accommodation. They developed in the mid-1890s.

motorcycle racing The racing of motorcycles, first organized by the Automobile Club de France in 1906, from Paris to Nantes and back. The most famous races are held on the roads of the Isle of Man each June, and are known as the *TT* (*Tourist Trophy*) races; first held in 1907. Races are held for each of the following engine-size categories: 80 cc, 125 cc, 250 cc, 500 cc, and sidecar. Other forms of motorcycle racing include speedway moto-cross (scrambling), and motorcycle trials riding.

motorcycle trials One of the oldest forms of motorcycle competition. Trials riding is a severe test of the machine's durability, held over tough predetermined courses normally 50–60 km/30–40 mi in length.

motor insurance A system by which motorists pay premiums, often annual, to an insurance company, which will then pay costs arising from accident, damage, or theft. In many countries there is a legal requirement to have *third party* insurance before using public roads; this covers damage and injury except to the insured and to the insured's own vehicle and passengers. *Comprehensive* insurance is needed in order to cover damage and injury in these other cases.

motor neurone disease A rare disorder of the central nervous system in which the nerve cells responsible for muscular movement slowly degenerate. Affected persons have progressive difficulty in speaking and moving the limbs, and eventually breathing. The cause is unknown.

motor racing The racing of finely tuned motor cars, which can either be purpose-built or modified production vehicles. The most popular form of motor racing is Formula One grand prix racing for high-powered purpose-built cars which can average well over 240 kph/150 mph. A season-long world championship (Mar–Nov), involves usually 16 races at different venues worldwide. Other popular forms include Formula 3000, Formula Three, rallying, sports car, Indy car racing in the USA, Formula Ford, hill climbing, and production car races. The first race was in 1894, from Paris to Rouen; the first grand prix was the French, in 1906. Current famous races include the Le Mans 24-hour endurance race, the Monte Carlo Rally, and the Indianapolis 500.

Motown A black-owned record company, founded in 1959 by Berry Gordy (1929–) in Detroit, MI ('Motortown'). Early Motown hits by Smokey Robinson and the Miracles were followed by dozens more rhythm-and-blues and soul classics in the 1960s, recorded by the Supremes, the Jackson Five, the Temptations, the Four Tops, and others.

Mott, Lucretia, *née* **Coffin** (1793–1880) Abolitionist and feminist, born in Nantucket, MA. A Quaker, she became deeply involved in anti-slavery agitation in the 1830s, along with her husband James Mott. She helped organize the American Anti-Slavery Society (1833) and the Anti-Slavery Convention of American Women (1837).

motte and bailey A quickly constructed earth and timber fortification of Norman date. It consisted of an artificial mound or *motte* surrounded by a ditch, a separately defended outer court or *bailey* adjoining to one side.

mould Any fungus, particularly one with an abundant, woolly

Highest mountains

Name	Height*		Location
	m	ft	
Mt Everest	8 850	29 035	China/Nepal
K2 (Mt Godwin-Austen)	8 610	28 250	Kashmir–Jammu
Kangchenjunga	8 590	28 170	India/Nepal
Lhotse	8 500	27 890	China/Nepal
Kangchenjunga, S Peak	8 470	27 800	India/Nepal
Makalu I	8 470	27 800	China/Nepal
Kangchenjunga, W Peak	8 420	27 620	India/Nepal
Llotse E Peak	8 380	27 500	China/Nepal
Dhaulagiri	8 170	26 810	Nepal
Cho Oyu	8 150	26 750	China/Nepal
Manaslu	8 130	26 660	Nepal
Nanga Parbat	8 130	26 660	Kashmir–Jammu
Annapurna I	8 080	26 500	Nepal
Gasherbrum I	8 070	26 470	Kashmir–Jammu
Broad-highest	8 050	26 400	Kashmir–Jammu
Gasherbrum II	8 030	26 360	Kashmir–Jammu
Gosainthan	8 010	26 290	China
Broad-middle	8 000	26 250	Kashmir–Jammu
Gasherbrum III	7 950	26 090	Kashmir–Jammu
Annapurna II	7 940	26 040	Nepal
Nanda Devi	7 820	25 660	India
Rakaposhi	7 790	25 560	Kashmir
Kamet	7 760	25 450	India
Ulugh Muztagh	7 720	25 340	Tibet
Tirich Mir	7 690	25 230	Pakistan
Muz Tag Ata	7 550	24 760	China
Communism Peak	7 490	24 590	Tajikistan
Pobedy Peak	7 440	24 410	Kyrgyzstan
Aconcagua	6 960	22 830	Argentina
Ojos del Salado	6 910	22 660	Argentina/Chile

*Heights are given to the nearest 10 m/ft.

mycelium of thread-like strands, often with visible spore-bearing structures.

moulting The shedding of an external covering, such as the periodic loss of hair by mammals and feathers by birds. Feather shedding in birds is usually gradual and does not affect flight, but in some birds (eg ducks) all flight feathers are shed simultaneously, and the bird is temporarily flightless.

mound bird / builder *megapode*

Mountain, the A group of Jacobin extremist deputies in the French Convention, led by Robespierre, so-called because they sat high up at the back of the Assembly where they overlooked their political opponents, the Girondins, and the uncommitted majority who were known collectively as 'the Plain'.

mountain ash *rowan*

mountain avens [avinz] A dwarf, creeping, evergreen shrub to 8 cm/3 in (*Dryas octopetala*) native to arctic regions and high mountains; flowers 7–10-petalled, white, heliotropic; fruits with feathery plume. (Family: Rosaceae.)

mountain beaver A squirrel-like rodent (*Aplodontia rufa*) native to the Pacific coast of North America; not a true beaver; the most primitive living rodent; stocky with a minute hairy tail; also known as **sewellel**, **boomer**, or **whistler**. (Family: Aplodontidae.)

mountaineering The skill of climbing a mountain aided by ropes and other accessories, such as crampons. The most popular form in the UK is **rock climbing**; **snow and ice climbing** is practised on the higher peaks of the world. All the world's highest peaks have now been conquered, and present-day mountaineering expeditions aim to climb previously untried routes. *see panel*

mountain laurel An evergreen shrub or small tree (*Kalmia latifolia*) native to North America; flowers saucer-shaped, 5-lobed, white, pink, or red; also called **calico bush**. (Family: Ericaceae.)

Mount Athos, Gr **Ayíon Oros** pop (2000e) 1620; area 336 km²/130 sq mi. Autonomous administration in Macedonia region, Greece; Mt Athos, rising to 1956 m/6417 ft, is the 'Holy Mountain' of the Greek Church, associated with the monastic order of St Basil since the 9th-c; declared a theocratic republic in 1927.

Mountbatten (of Burma), Louis (Francis Albert Victor Nicholas) Mountbatten, 1st Earl (1900–79) British admiral of the fleet and statesman, born in Windsor, England, younger son of Prince Louis of Battenberg and Princess Victoria of Hesse, granddaughter of Queen Victoria. In World War 2 he became chief of Combined Operations Command (1942), and played a key role in preparations for D-Day. In 1943 he was appointed supreme commander, SE Asia, where he defeated the Japanese offensive into India (1944), worked closely with Slim to reconquer Burma (1945), and received the Japanese surrender at Singapore. In 1947 he became last Viceroy of India. He was assassinated by Irish terrorists near his summer home, Classiebawn Castle, Co Sligo.

Mountbatten, Prince Philip *Edinburgh, Duke of*

Mounties The popular name of the **Royal Canadian Mounted Police**, the federal police force of Canada. The organization was founded in 1873, and until 1920 was known as the North West Mounted Police. The red jacket and broad-brimmed hat worn by its officers are features of their distinctive uniform.

Mount Li The burial place of Qin Shihuangdi, the first Emperor of China (259–210 BC); a world heritage site. It is renowned for the discovery in 1974 of a life-size army of c.7500 painted terracotta figures deployed in military formation in chambers underground.

Mount of Olives *Olives, Mount of*

Mount Palomar Observatory *Palomar Observatory*

Mount Sinai *Sinai, Mount*

Mount Vernon The family home of George Washington on the Potomac R in Virginia. Washington and his wife, Martha, are buried there.

Mourne Mountains [mawn] Mountain range in SE Northern Ireland; length 24 km/15 mi; rises to 852 m/2795 ft at Slieve Donard.

mouse (computing) A computer input device which can be moved around on a flat surface causing a cursor to move around the computer screen in response. It can be used to choose options pointed to on the screen.

mouse (zoology) A name used for many small unrelated species in the rodent family, found worldwide, especially for members of genus *Mus* (36 species throughout Old World); **house mouse** (*Mus musculus*), from Asia, has dispersed globally in association with humans. (Family: Muridae.)

mousebird *coly*

Mouskouri, Nana [muskooree] (1934–) Singer, born in Chania, Crete, Greece. She made her first record in London in 1959, and went on to record 'The White Rose of Athens' (1962), which became a major European hit. She was a member of the European Parliament (1994–9).

Moussorgsky, Modest (Petrovich) [musaw(r)gskee], also spelled **Mussorgsky** or **Musorgsky** (1839–81) Composer, born in Karevo, Russia. A member of the Glinka-inspired nationalist group in St Petersburg, his masterpiece is the opera *Boris Godunov* (1874). His piano suite *Pictures from an Exhibition* (1874) has also kept a firm place in the concert repertoire.

Mousterian [moosteerian] A European archaeological culture of the Middle Palaeolithic Age (c.70 000–40 000 BC), named after

Mozambique

□ International Airport

[mohzam**beek**], official name (from 1991) **Republic of Mozambique**, Port **República de Moçambique**
Local name Moçambique
Timezone GMT +2
Area 799 380 km²/308 641 sq mi
Population total (2002e) 18 083 000
Status Republic
Date of independence 1975
Capital Maputo

Languages Portuguese (official)
Ethnic groups Makua/Lomwe (52%), Thonga (24%), Malawi (12%), Shona (6%), Yao (3%)
Religions Local animist beliefs (60%), Christian (majority Roman Catholic) (30%), Muslim (10%)
Physical features Located in SE Africa; main rivers, the Zambezi and Limpopo provide irrigation and hydroelectricity; savannah plateau inland, mean elevation 800–1000 m/2600–4000 ft; highest peak, Mt Binga, 2436 m/7992 ft; S of Zambezi is low-lying coast with sandy beaches and mangroves; low hills of volcanic origin inland, Zimbabwe plateau further N.
Climate Tropical with high humidity; rainy season (Dec–Mar); drought conditions in S; average annual temperatures 26°C (Jan), 18°C (Jul) in Maputo; average annual rainfall 560 mm/30 in.
Currency 1 Metical (MZM) = 100 centavos
Economy Badly affected by drought (1981–4), internal strife, and lack of foreign exchange; agriculture (employs 85% of population); cashew nuts, tea, cotton, sugar cane, copra, sisal, groundnuts, fruit, rice, cereals, tobacco; forestry; livestock; reserves of gemstones and minerals; Great Limpopo Transfrontier Park game reserve established, 2002.
GDP (2002e) $19·52 bn, per capita $1100
Human Development Index (2002) 0·322
History Originally inhabited by Bantu peoples from the N, 1st–4th-c AD; coast settled by Arab traders; visited by Portuguese explorers by late 15th-c; part of Portuguese Africa since 1751; Mozambique Portuguese East Africa in late 19th-c; overseas province of Portugal, 1951; independence movement formed in 1962, the Frente de Libertaçao de Moçambique (FRELIMO), with armed resistance to colonial rule; independence as the People's Republic of Mozambique, 1975; continuing civil war, with first peace talks in 1990; socialist one-party state, 1975–90; new constitution and change of name to Republic of Mozambique, 1990; peace accord signed between Chissanó (President of Mozambique) and Dhlakama (leader of the Renamo-Mozambique National Resistance), 1992; President (term of 5 years) rules with an Assembly of the Republic; new constitution adopted (Nov 2004).

Head of State
1975–86 Samora Moïses Machel
1986–2005 Joaquim Alberto Chissanó
2005– Armando Emilio Guebuza
Head of Government
1986–94 Mario de Graça Machungo
1994–2004 Pascoal Mocumbi
2004– Luisa Diogo

the cave at Le Moustier, Dordogne, SW France. Its stone tools are probably the work of Neanderthal peoples.
mouth The first part of the gastro-intestinal tract; in mammals one of its characteristic features is the movable muscular lips and cheeks, which are intimately related to chewing, and in humans to speech.
mouth organ *harmonica*
mouth-to-mouth respiration *artificial respiration*
movement In music, a self-contained section of a longer work, such as a concerto or symphony. It may be linked to the movement that precedes or follows it, with which it is usually contrasted in tempo or key (often both).
movies *cinema; cinematography*
Movietone The trade name for one of the first sound-on-film recording and reproducing systems, launched by Fox in 1927. It was used initially for newsreels, and subsequently for all their feature film production.

Mowlem, Mo [mohlem], popular name of **Marjorie Mowlem** (1949–2005) British stateswoman, born in Watford, Hertfordshire. She became a Labour MP (1987–2001), and was appointed secretary of state for Northern Ireland (1997–9), and minister for the cabinet office and chancellor of the Duchy of Lancaster (1999–2001). She played a key part in achieving the Good Friday Agreement and in the establishment of the Northern Ireland Assembly. Her political memoir, *Momentum*, appeared in 2002.
Moynihan, Daniel P(atrick) (1927–2003) Academic and politician, born in Tulsa, OK. He served in the administrations of Presidents Johnson and Nixon, acquiring notoriety as the author of *The Negro Family: The Case for National Action* (1965). In 1976 he won a Democratic seat in the US Senate and served four successive terms, retiring in 2001.
Mozambique *see panel*
Mozart, Wolfgang Amadeus [mohtsah(r)t] (1756–91) Composer,

born in Salzburg, Austria. A child prodigy, he made his first professional tour (as a pianist) through Europe when he was six. After some years in Salzburg as *Konzertmeister* to the archbishop, he resigned (1781) and settled in Vienna. His operas *The Marriage of Figaro* (1786) and *Don Giovanni* (1787) made it impossible for the court still to overlook the composer, and he was appointed court composer to Joseph II in 1787. He wrote over 600 compositions (indexed by Köchel), including 41 symphonies, and many concertos, string quartets, and sonatas. Celebrations marking his 250th birthday in 2006 were held around the world.

MPEG [empeg] *digital media*

Mpumalanga [mpumalangga] (Swati 'land of the rising sun') One of the nine new provinces established by the South African constitution of 1994, in NE South Africa, situated largely on high plateau grasslands; formerly constituted part of Transvaal; capital, Nelspruit, pop (2000e) 2 784 000; area 81 816 km²/ 31 581 sq mi; chief languages, Siswati (40%), Zulu (28%), Afrikaans; game reserves, including Kruger National park.

MS Access A computer package for data management, developed by Microsoft to run on the IBM personal computer. It is intended to interface to, and provide the data storage for, applications developed in Visual Basic.

MS-DOS An operating system developed by Microsoft for the IBM personal computer; it is a registered trade mark. This system has contributed largely to the success of the IBM product.

Mubarak, (Mohammed) Hosni (Said) [mubarak] (1928–) Egyptian statesman and president (1981–), born in al-Minufiyah, Egypt. Vice-president under Sadat (1975), he continued the same domestic and international policies, including firm treatment of Muslim extremists, and the peace process with Israel.

mucous membrane [myookuhs] A sheet of fibrous tissue that lines every cavity or canal of the body which opens to the exterior (eg the alimentary tracts). It provides a barrier between the cells that form the body and the external environment.

mudhopper Very distinctive fish (*Periophthalmus koelreuteri* and *Periophthalmodon schlosseri*) widespread in the Indo-Pacific; locally common on mud flats, living much of the time out of water; length 15–25 cm/6–10 in; eyes raised on top of head; paired fins used as props and for locomotion across the mud; also called **mudskipper**. (Family: Gobiidae.)

mudlark Either of two species of bird of the genus *Grallina*, also known as **mudnester** or **mudnest builder**: the black-and-white **magpie lark** (*Grallina cyanoleuca*), from open woodland in Australia; and the **torrent lark** (*Grallina bruijni*), from mountain streams in New Guinea. (Family: Grallinidae.)

mudpuppy A salamander from North America (*Fecturus maculosus*); spends entire life in water; brown-grey with feathery gills; limbs with four toes; deep narrow tail. (Family: Proteidae.)

mudskipper *mudhopper*

muesli [myoozlee] A popular breakfast cereal now available in a wide variety of mixtures, which include cereals, nuts, and fruits. These mixtures have been developed from the raw food diet of Dr Max Birchner-Brenner (1867–1939).

muezzin [mooezin] In Islam, an official of the mosque who issues the call to prayer to the faithful. The name means 'announcer'.

mufti In Islamic religion, a man trained in the *Sharia*, or Muslim divine law, and who can give a legal opinion (*fatwa*) on questions concerning Islamic practice.

Mufulira [mufuleera] 12°30S 28°12E, pop (2000e) 270 700. Mining city in Zambia; world's second largest underground copper mine nearby; railway.

Mugabe, Robert (Gabriel) [mugahbay] (1924–) Zimbabwean statesman, first prime minister (1980–), and president (1987–), born in Kutama, Zimbabwe. In 1963 he co-founded the Zimbabwe African National Union (ZANU). After a 10-year detention in Rhodesia (1964–74), he spent five years in

Mozambique preparing for independence (1980). Though he formerly espoused a pragmatic Marxism, and declared his intention of turning Zimbabwe into a one-party state, multiparty elections were held in 1990 (which he won), and his party dropped all references to 'Marxism-Leninism' and 'scientific socialism' from its constitution in 1991. He came to world attention in 2000 for initiating a land redistribution policy aimed at local white farmers, which resulted in intimidation, civil disturbance, some deaths, and much international condemnation. He won a fifth term in office in 2002, but controversy surrounding the election process led to Zimbabwe being suspended from the Commonwealth for a year, and following the decision to reaffirm the suspension in 2003 he announced that he would withdraw from the organization.

Mughal or **Mogul Empire** An important Indian Muslim state (1526–1857), founded by Babur (1526–30). Akbar (1556–1605), defeated the Afghan challenge at Panipat (1556) and extended the empire to include territory between Afghanistan and Deccan. Akbar was succeeded by Jehangir (1605–27) and Shah Jehan (1627–58). Its last great emperor was Aurangzeb (1658–1707), who extended the limits of the empire further south. The empire disintegrated under Maratha and British pressure. Its last emperor was exiled by the British after the 1857 uprising.

mugwort An aromatic perennial growing to 120 cm/4 ft, native to many temperate areas; leaves dark green above, silvery with woolly hairs below; flower-heads reddish-brown, crowded on long leafy stems. The young leaves are used as a condiment for goose, duck, and pork. (Genus *Artemisia*. Family: Compositae.)

mugwump (Alonkin Indian 'great chief') A name for Independent Republicans in the US election of 1884 who preferred reform to party discipline, particularly on the question of ending the spoils system. They included E L Godkin, George William Curtis, Carl Schurz, and Charles Francis Adams.

Muhammad *Mohammed*

Muharram [muharam] The first month of the Muslim year; also used as the name of a religious celebration culminating in Ashura.

Muir, Edwin [myoor] (1887–1959) Poet, born in Deerness, Orkney. His poems appeared in eight slim volumes, dating from 1925, notably in *The Voyage* (1946) and *The Labyrinth* (1949).

Mujahideen [moojahadeen] ('holy warriors') Muslim guerrillas who resisted the Soviet occupation of Afghanistan after the invasion (Dec 1979). After the Soviet withdrawal in 1989, they experienced much internal dissent over their role in the country's future. The term is also used more generally than in relation to the Afghan conflict, referring to any Muslim whose armed struggle can be said to be in the interest of the faith.

mujtahid [moojtahhid] A religious scholar who exercises personal interpretation of the *Sharia* or Muslim divine law. Shiism allows such interpretations, while Sunnism has usually refused them.

Mukden *Shenyang*

mulberry A deciduous tree, of oriental origin, but long cultivated; male and female flowers in separate catkin-like spikes; individual fruits juicy, coalescing so that the whole spike forms the 'berry'. (Genus: *Morus*, 10 species. Family: Moraceae.)

Muldoon, Sir Robert (David) [muhldoon] (1921–92) New Zealand statesman and prime minister (1975–84), born in Auckland, New Zealand. After 5 years as minister of finance, he became party leader in 1974.

mule (textiles) A spinning frame invented by Samuel Crompton in 1779, which fully mechanized the hand spinning process. It was regarded as a hybrid of two previous inventions, hence its name.

mule (zoology) An animal produced by the mating of a male donkey with a female horse. If a male horse mates with a female donkey the result is a **hinny**. Both are usually sterile.

Mulhouse [muhlooz], Ger **Mulhausen** 47°45N 7°21E, pop (2000e) 114 000. Industrial and commercial river port in NE France; second largest town in Alsace; imperial free city from 1308; allied with the Swiss, 1515–1648; independent republic until 1798, then voted to become French; under German rule in 1871, reverting to France in 1918; railway; university.

mullah [mula] (Arabic, 'master') In Islam, a scholar, teacher, or man of religious piety and learning. It is also a title of respect given to those performing duties related to Islamic Law.

mullein [muluhn] Typically a biennial or perennial, often very hairy, with a tall, erect stem, native to Europe and Asia; flowers in long dense spikes, 5-petalled, yellow, pink, purple, or white. (Genus: *Verbascum*, 360 species. Family: Scrophulariaceae.)

Mullen, Larry *U2*

mullet *grey mullet; red mullet*

Mulliken, Robert (Sanderson) (1896–1986) Chemist and physicist, born in Newburyport, MA. He was awarded the 1966 Nobel Chemistry Prize for his work on chemical bonds and the electronic structure of molecules.

Mullingar [muhlingah(r)], Ir **Muileann Cearr** 53°32N 7°20W, pop (2000e) 12 000. Market town and capital of Westmeath county, E Ireland; railway; cathedral.

Mulready, William [muhlreedee] (1786–1863) Painter, born in Ennis, Co Clare, Ireland. He specialized in genre paintings, becoming best known for his rural scenes, such as 'Interior of an English Cottage' (1828).

Mulroney, (Martin) Brian (1939–) Canadian politician and prime minister (1984–93), born in Baie Comeau, Quebec, Canada. He became leader of the Progressive Conservative Party in 1983, won a landslide election victory in 1984, and was re-elected in 1988, but forced to resign in 1993.

Multan [multan] 30°10N 71°36E, pop (2000e) 1 193 000. City in Punjab province, Pakistan; ruled by the emperors of Delhi 1526–1779, and by the Afghans until 1818; under British rule, 1849; airfield; railway.

multilateralism In economics, a system where a group of countries negotiate trade and payments arrangements, rather than dealing bilaterally. In trade, multilateralism is summed up by the 'most favoured nation' clause, whereby imports from any member country are to be treated no less favourably than those from any other member. In payments, multilateral settlement means that a country need only be concerned to balance its payments with other countries in total, and need not keep its payments in bilateral balance.

multimedia (computing) The tools and techniques used in computing to allow computer programs to handle sound, picture, and video components. In a multimedia system one could use the computer to select extracts from a piece of music which could then be broadcast with a full video picture of the orchestra and hi-fi sound, or could be broadcast in sound only with the video displaying the score.

multimedia (projection) The audio-visual presentation from groups of slide projectors programmed to show a complex sequence of images on a very wide screen with accompanying sound from tape recording.

multiple sclerosis A disease in which the normal coating of neurones (*myelin*) in the brain and spinal cord is lost. This affects the transmission of impulses along the nerves, impairing the function of the body systems that they control. It is found in 1 in 2000 people. The cause is uncertain, but it may be related to an auto-immune process. Clinical features include weakness of the limbs, double vision, vertigo, and inability to co-ordinate movements (*ataxia*), all of which can be transient but recurrent, and slowly become more severe.

multiple star Three or more stars gravitationally bound in complex orbits. The star complex Alpha Centauri is an example of such a system.

multiplexer A device in data communications which enables the inputs from a number of communication lines to be concentrated and fed down a single line.

Mumbai, official name (1995) of **Bombay** 18°55N 72°50E, pop (2000e) 12 500 000. Port capital of Maharashtra, W India; India's largest city built on a group of islands linked by causeways; ceded to Portugal, 1534; ceded to Britain, 1661; airport; railway; two universities (1916, 1957); film industry (Bollywood).

Mumford, Lewis (1895–1990) Sociologist and writer, born in Flushing, NY. He wrote on architecture and urbanization in such works as *The Story of Utopias* (1922) and *The City in History* (1961), stressing the unhappy effects of technology on society.

mummers English traditional actors providing entertainment at seasonal festivals. In the 18th-c the mummers' Christmas play evolved, based on a legend of St George, with a duel between champions ending in the death of one of them and his revival by a doctor.

mumps A viral infection spread by droplets, especially common among children and young adults. A characteristic feature is pain and swelling of one or both parotid glands near the angle of the jaw.

Munch, Edvard [mungk] (1863–1944) Painter, born in Löten, Norway. He was obsessed by subjects such as death and love, which he illustrated in an Expressionist Symbolic style, using bright colours and a tortuously curved design, as in 'The Scream' (1893, Oslo). In 2004, a rendition of 'The Scream' and 'Madonna' were snatched from the Munch Museum in Oslo, Norway.

Münchhausen, (Karl Friedrich Hieronymus), Freiherr von (Baron) [munchhowzen] (1720–97) Soldier, born in Bodenwerder, Germany. He served in Russian campaigns against the Turks, and became proverbial as the narrator of ridiculously exaggerated exploits.

Münchhausen's syndrome [münshhowzn] The falsification of illness in order to attract attention and sympathy, but not for immediate financial or personal gain. Typically, individuals feign or even self-induce symptoms, and present themselves to health-care providers for investigation and treatment. In **Münchhausen's syndrome by proxy**, an individual falsifies illness in another person, usually a child. It is named after an 18th-c baron, notorious for his tales and romances.

Muncie [muhnsee] 40°12N 85°23W, pop (2000e) 67 400. City in E Indiana, USA, on W fork of the White R; settled, 1824; city status, 1865; railway; university (1918); represented as the 'average American town' in the 1929 sociological study *Middletown* by R & H Lynd.

Munda An Austroasiatic-speaking people settled in hilly and forested regions of E and C India.

Mundell, Robert A(lexander) (1932–) Economist, born in Ontario, Canada. His posts include professorships at the universities of Chicago (1966–71) and Columbia, New York (from 1974). He was awarded the 1999 Nobel Prize for Economics for his analysis of monetary and fiscal policy under different exchange rate regimes and his analysis of optimal currency areas.

Munich [myoonikh], Ger **München** 48°08N 11°35E, pop (2000e) 1 270 000. Capital of Bavaria province, Germany, on the R Isar; founded, 1158; capital of Bavaria, from 1506; badly bombed in World War 2; railway; university (1471); technical university (1868); cathedral (15th-c), Nymphenburg Palace (17th-c); Pinakothek der Moderne (opened 2002); Oktoberfest (beer festival); site of summer Olympic Games (1972).

Munich Agreement An agreement endorsed (29 Sep 1938) at a conference in Munich by the British prime minister Chamberlain, the French prime minister Daladier, Mussolini, and Hitler. It ceded the Sudeten area of Czechoslovakia to Germany.

Munich Putsch The abortive attempt by Hitler to overthrow the state government of Bavaria in 1923, as a prelude to the establishment of the Nazi regime in Germany. Hitler was tried for treason, and sentenced to five years' imprisonment.

Munnings, Sir Alfred (1878–1959) Painter, born in Mendham, Suffolk. A specialist in the painting of horses and sporting pictures, he was well known for his forthright criticism of modern art.

Munro, H(ector) H(ugh) [muhnroh], pseudonym **Saki** (1870–1916) Writer, born in Akyab, Myanmar. He is best known for his humorous and macabre short stories, such as *Reginald* (1904) and *The Chronicles of Clovis* (1911). He was killed on the Western front in World War 1.

Munsell Color System A system for measuring and naming colours, devised by US painter Albert H Munsell (?–1918). The Munsell Book of Colour contains 1200 samples grouped according to hue, saturation, and brilliance.

Munster [muhnster] pop (2000e) 1 022 000; area 24 127 km²/ 9313 sq mi. Province in S Ireland; comprises the counties of Clare, Cork, Kerry, Limerick, Tipperary, and Waterford; a former kingdom.

Münster [munster] 51°58N 7°37E, pop (2000e) 268 000. City in Germany; on the R Aa; member of the Hanseatic League; capital of former province of Westphalia; bishopric; railway; university (1780); cathedral (1225–65).

muntjac or **muntjak** A true deer, native to India and SE Asia; face with 'V'-shaped ridge; arms of 'V' continued as freely projecting bony columns; projecting canine teeth; call resembles a dog barking; also known as **barking deer** or **rib-faced deer**. (Genus: *Muntiacus*, 5 species.)

Müntzer, Thomas [müntser], also spelled **Münzer** or **Monczer** (c.1489–1525) Anabaptist preacher, born in Stolberg, Germany. In 1525 he was elected pastor of the Anabaptists of Mühlhausen, where his communist ideas soon aroused the whole country. A leader of the Peasants' Revolt (1524–5), he was executed at Mühlhausen.

muon A fundamental particle, produced in weak radioactive decays of pions; symbol μ; mass 106 MeV; charge −1; spin ½. It behaves like a heavy electron, but decays to an electron and neutrinos.

Murad, Ferid (1936–) Pharmacologist, born in Whiting, IN. He worked at the universities of Virginia, Stanford, and (from 1997) Texas at Houston, and shared the 1998 Nobel Prize for Physiology or Medicine for his contribution to the discovery of nitric oxide as a signalling molecule in the cardiovascular system.

mural A painting or carving on a wall. Murals, representing human and animal motifs as well as pure pattern, have existed since prehistoric times. A great deal survives from the Ancient Near East: the Egyptians, for instance, used distemper or gouache for decorating their tombs, while the Babylonians and Assyrians made extensive use of stone low-relief sculpture. Roman wall decoration is seen from the excavations at Pompeii, Herculaneum, and Stabiae (2nd-c BC–AD 79). Mosaic was much favoured during the Byzantine period in Italy, fresco during the later Middle Ages and Renaissance.

muramidase *lysozyme*

Murasaki, Shikibu [murasahkee] (978–c.1031) Court lady and writer, born in Kyoto, Japan. She wrote the saga *Genji Monagatari* (The Tale of Genji), a classic of Japanese literature, and considered to be the world's earliest novel.

Murat, Joachim [mürah] (1767–1815) French marshal and king of Naples (1808–15), born in La Bastide-Fortunière, France. He married Napoleon's sister, Caroline, after helping him become First Consul. After failing to gain the Spanish crown (1808), he was proclaimed King of the Two Sicilies. He fought at Leipzig, but concluded a treaty with the Austrians, hoping to save his kingdom. On Napoleon's return from Elba, he recommended war against Austria, but was defeated, and executed.

Murcia, Eng [mersha], Span [**moorthya**] pop (2000e) 1 046 000; area 11 313 km²/4367 sq mi. Region and province of SE Spain;

thinly populated, except in the river valleys; capital, Murcia, pop (1995e) 321 000; former capital of Moorish kingdom; airport; railway; university (1915); cathedral (14th-c).

murder Unlawful homicide other than manslaughter, infanticide (where separately recognized), or causing death by reckless driving. In England and Wales, a person can be convicted of murder only where the crime was committed with malice aforethought. In many US jurisdictions (and also in Scotland), the notion of 'malice aforethought' is not relevant: murder is the intentional killing of another without justification, excuse, or mitigating circumstances, or in the perpetration of a felony (US). In the UK, the sentence on conviction is life imprisonment, but several countries provide for capital punishment.

Murdoch, Dame (Jean) Iris (1919–99) Novelist and philosopher, born in Dublin. Her books include *Under the Net* (1954), *The Sea, The Sea* (1978, Booker), *The Philosopher's Pupil* (1983), and *Jackson's Dilemma* (1995). She also wrote plays and several philosophical and critical studies.

Murdoch, Lachlan (Keith) (1971–) Media executive, born in London, the son of Rupert Murdoch. In 1995 he became publisher of *The Australian* newspaper, and by 1997 was executive chairman of News Limited. One of a trio of possible heirs to Rupert, Lachlan is the only sibling who took up a seat on News Corporation's board.

Murdoch, (Keith) Rupert (1931–) Media proprietor, born in Melbourne, Victoria, Australia. He built a substantial newspaper and magazine publishing empire in Australia, the USA, Hong Kong, and the UK, including the *Sun*, the *News of the World*, and *The Times* and its related publications in Britain. He also has major business interests in other media industries, especially television, films, and publishing. He is owner of the Twentieth Century Fox film studio and the Fox television network in the US, and satellite broadcaster BSkyB in the UK.

Murdock, William (1754–1839) Engineer and inventor of coal gas for lighting, born near East Ayrshire, Strathclyde. His distillation of coal to make coal gas began at Redruth in 1792.

Murillo, Bartolomé Esteban [mooreelyoh] (1618–82) Painter, born in Seville, Spain. His pictures naturally fall into two groups: scenes from low society, mostly executed early in his life, and religious works.

Murmansk [moormansk], formerly **Romanov-na-Murmane** (to 1917) 68°59N 33°08E, pop (2000e) 470 000. Seaport in Russia; founded, 1916; most important Russian fishing port (ice-free); airfield; railway.

Murphy, Eddie, popular name of **Edward Reagan Murphy** (1961–) Comic performer and film director, born in New York City. His films include *Trading Places* (1983), *Beverly Hills Cop* and its sequel (1984, 1987), *Dr Dolittle* (1998), *Bowfinger* (1999), *Daddy Day Care* (2003), and *Dreamgirls* (2006, Golden Globe Best Supporting Actor; Best Supporting Actor Oscar nomination). He made his directorial debut with *Harlem Nights* (1989).

Murphy, Lionel (Keith) (1922–86) Lawyer and politician, born in Sydney, New South Wales, Australia. A lawyer, he was elected as Labor senator for New South Wales in the 1962 Federal Parliament, became opposition leader in 1967, and was appointed attorney-general in 1972. He oversaw several items of landmark legislation, and in 1975 was appointed to the High Court of Australia. A controversial figure who challenged political and legal boundaries, the impact of his reforms on Australian society is widely acknowledged.

Murphy-O'Connor, Cormac, Cardinal (1932–) Roman Catholic cardinal, born in Reading, England. He worked in Portsmouth and Southampton before his appointment to the English College as rector (1971–7). In 1977 he became Bishop of Arundel and Brighton and in 2000 Archbishop of Westminster (2000). He was made a cardinal in 2001.

Murray, Andy (1987–) Tennis player, born in Dunblane, Perthshire. In 2004 he won the junior men's singles title at the US Open and turned professional in 2005. In March that year he became Britain's youngest Davis Cup player and later gained world attention at the Wimbledon championships when he knocked out 14th seed Radek Stepanek in the first round. In 2006 he won the San Jose Open, becoming the youngest Briton to win an ATP tour event, and later that month he became Britain's number 1 when his world ranking rose to 42; this had risen to 17 at the start of 2007.

Murray, Bill, popular name of **William James Murray** (1950–) Actor, born in Wilmette, IL. He began his career on the 1970s US TV comedy show *Saturday Night Live*, and became known for his film role in *Ghostbusters* (1984). Later films include *Groundhog Day* (1993), *The Royal Tenenbaums* (2001), *Lost in Translation* (2003, Best Actor BAFTA; Golden Globe; Oscar nomination), and *Broken Flowers* (2005).

Murray, (George) Gilbert (Aimé) (1866–1957) Classical scholar, writer, and lifelong Liberal, born in Sydney, New South Wales, Australia. His work as a classical historian and translator of Greek dramatists brought him world acclaim.

Murray, Sir James (Augustus Henry) (1837–1915) Philologist and lexicographer, born in Denholm, Scottish Borders. His major project was the editing of the New English Dictionary, begun in 1879. He edited about half the work himself, and created the organization for its completion (in 1928).

Murray, Len, popular name of **Baron Lionel Murray of Telford** (1922–2004) Trade unionist, born in Shropshire. He became general secretary of the Trades Union Congress (1973–84), and was made a life peer in 1985.

Murray River Longest river in Australia; rises in the Australian Alps; length 2570 km/1600 mi; enters the Southern Ocean SE of Adelaide; receives the Darling R 640 km/400 mi from its mouth (the Murray–Darling is 3750 km/2330 mi long); used extensively for irrigation and hydroelectric power.

Murrow, Ed(ward Roscoe), originally **Egbert Roscoe Murrow** (1908–65) Journalist and broadcaster, born in Greensboro, NC. Joining CBS in 1935, he became a compassionate conveyor of the wartime spirit in Britain. In 1946 he was appointed CBS vice-president and director of public affairs, producing and presenting hard-hitting current affairs programmes.

Murrumbidgee River [muhruhmbee] River in New South Wales, Australia; rises in the Snowy Mts; flows 1759 km/1093 mi to join the Murray R on the Victoria border.

Murry, John Middleton (1889–1957) Writer and critic, born in London. His poetry, essays, and criticism had a strong influence on the young intellectuals of the 1920s. He was the husband of Katherine Mansfield.

Mururoa [mururoha] 139°00W 22°00S, pop (2000e) 3500. Remote atoll in French Polynesia, used by France as a nuclear testing site.

Musca (Lat 'fly') A small S constellation near Crux.

muscarine [muhskarin, -reen] A substance isolated from the poisonous mushroom *Amanita muscaria*. In W Europe, extracts were used as fly-killing agents (the common name for the mushroom is *fly agaric*).

Muscat [muhskat], Arabic **Masqat** 27°37N 58°36E, pop (2000e) 423 000. Seaport capital of Oman; occupied by the Portuguese, 1508–1650; airport; residence of the Sultan.

muscle A contractile tissue consisting of fibres bound together by connective tissue and specialized to convert chemical energy into mechanical energy for movement. **Skeletal muscle** is generally attached to bone and, being under central nervous control, is principally concerned with voluntary movement. **Smooth muscle** is present mainly in the walls of hollow structures (eg the gut, uterus, blood vessels, ducts). **Cardiac muscle** is present only in the heart, where it is in continuous rhythmical contraction. Medical problems affecting muscle include convulsions, cramp, fibrositis, muscular dystrophy, myasthenia gravis and rheumatism.

muscovite *micas*

muscovy duck A large duck (*Cairina moschata*) native to Central and tropical South America; wild male black/green with white patches on wing; dark bare skin on face. Domestic breeds are grey, white, or speckled, with a scarlet skin patch. (Family: Anatidae.)

muscular dystrophy A group of genetically determined disorders in which muscle fibres undergo progressive degeneration and are replaced by fibrous tissue (*fibrosis*). The condition appears early in life, and causes symmetrical weakness and wasting of groups of muscles.

Musée d'Orsay [müzay daw(r)say] A museum in Paris, developed on the site of the former railway station and hotel, the Gare d'Orsay, and incorporating several of its architectural features. Originally designed by French architect Victor Laloux (1850–1937), the building was converted into a museum in 1984–5. It contains a wide range of artistic works produced chiefly between 1848 and 1914.

Muses In Homer, the nine daughters of Zeus and Mnemosyne, who inspire the bard: **Calliope**, epic poetry; **Clio**, history; **Erato**, lyric poetry, hymns; **Euterpe**, flute; **Melpomene**, tragedy; **Polyhymnia**, acting, music, dance; **Terpsichore**, lyric poetry, dance; **Thalia**, comedy; **Urania**, astronomy.

Museum of Modern Art (New York City) Museum founded (1929) in New York City by three private citizens, Lillie P Bliss, Mary Quinn Sullivan, and Abby Aldrich Rockefeller, as the first US museum to devote its collections entirely to the modern art movement. It covers architecture and design, drawings, film and video, painting and sculpture, photography, and prints and illustrated books. To mark its 75th anniversary in 2004, the museum underwent major renovation and expansion.

Museveni, Yoweri Kaguta [moosevaynee] (1945–) Ugandan statesman and president (1986–). He became head of the Front for National Salvation against Idi Amin (1971–9). As president, he has been responsible for the reconstruction of the country after its civil war. He was re-elected for a third term (Feb 2006) in his country's first multi-party elections for 26 years.

Musgrave Ranges [muhzgrayv] Mountain ranges in South Australia; extend 80 km/50 mi; rise to 1440 m/4724 ft at Mt Woodroffe.

Musharraf, Pervez [musharaf] (1943–) Pakistani military leader and president (1999–), born in New Delhi, India. He emigrated to Pakistan in 1947, and became a career soldier, appointed army chief in 1998. He supported the Pakistani invasion of the Indian-held territory of Jammu–Kashmir (1999). Angered by the decision to withdraw from the territory, he seized power after learning that he had been sacked as army chief. In 2001, he played a major role in relation to the international movement against terrorism, focused on adjoining Afghanistan, and in 2002 was again at the centre of international attention, during the renewed confrontation between Pakistan and India over Jammu–Kashmir. He survived an assassination attempt by Islamic extremists in 2002 and again in December 2003.

mushroom The cultivated mushroom (*Agaricus bisporus*); fruiting body comprises a short white stalk (*stipe*) and rounded cap with brownish gills on the underside; also used as a general name for any similar-shaped fungus. (Subdivision: Basidiomycetes. Order: Agaricales.)

Musial, Stan(ley Frank) [myoozial], nickname **Stan the Man** (1920–) Baseball player, born in Donora, PA. He topped the National League's batting list seven times (1943–57) and retired in 1963 with a National League record of 3630 hits to his credit.

music An orderly succession of sounds of definite pitch, whose constituents are melody, harmony, and rhythm. Almost as fundamental to a perception of the nature of music, however, is *articulation*, which embraces not only the phrasing, dynamics, etc that breathe life into a musical performance, but also the composer's creative use of silence. Virtually all musical structures entail a degree of audible repetition, even if this cannot always be fully grasped at a first hearing. Music is therefore a kind of aural patterning rather than aural painting – abstract rather than representational. This is not to deny its capacity to elicit a strong emotional response, but the essential nature of music is possibly closer to mathematics than to any of its sister arts.

musical A distinctive genre of musical theatre, where a strong story is fused with a musical score and professional choreography, found in both theatre and cinema. Feature films with spectacular show-business song-and-dance themes followed rapidly on the introduction of sound-film.

musical glasses An instrument, also known as the **glass harmonica**, consisting of glass vessels of various sizes and pitches which were struck or stroked to produce musical, bell-like sounds. Various types were popular in the 18th-c.

musical instruments Devices for producing musical sounds, among the oldest cultural artefacts known. The instruments of the modern symphony orchestra are commonly divided into four types: *woodwind*, *brass*, *percussion*, and *strings*. Another classification is according to the method of playing them: whether they are bowed, blown, struck, plucked, strummed, or (as with keyboard instruments) touched. The classification now generally regarded as standard was devised by musicologists Erich von Hornbostel (1877–1935) and Kurt Sachs (1881–1959), and published in 1914. They divided instruments into four main classes according to the physical characteristics of the sound source (ie the vibrating agent): *aerophones* (in which the sound is generated by air), *chordophones* (by one or more strings), *idiophones* (by the body of the instrument itself), and *membranophones* (by a stretched membrane). To these a fifth class has since been added: *electrophones*, in which the sound is produced by electromagnets, oscillators, or other non-acoustic devices.

music hall Mass entertainment of the Victorian era which developed in the music rooms of London taverns. Itinerant performers perfected short turns with stage business and comic songs to suit their individual style.

musicology The scientific and scholarly study of music, including the recovery and evaluation of source material, the study of music's historical context, and the analysis of particular works and repertories. Modern musicologists need to command many specialized skills, including a knowledge of palaeography, paper-types, watermarks, and rastrology (the study of how music staves are drawn).

Musil, Robert (Elder von) [moosil] (1880–1942) Novelist, born in Klagenfurt, Austria. His masterpiece is a very long, unfinished novel *Der Mann ohne Eigenschaften* (The Man without Qualities), written between 1930 and 1942.

musique concrète [müzeek kõkret] Music composed of 'natural' (ie non-electronic but not necessarily musical) sounds, which are then mixed and manipulated on tape and heard through loudspeakers. The technique originated with French composer Pierre Schaeffer (1910–95) in the 1940s.

musk A species of mimulus (*Mimulus moschatus*) with yellow flowers, native to North America from British Columbia to the California region. It was formerly cultivated for its scent, but the plants are nowadays scentless. (Family: Scrophulariaceae.)

musk deer A deer native to wet mountain forests in E Asia; kangaroo-like head has no antlers; male with gland on abdomen, producing a pungent oily jelly (*musk*), used in perfumes to make the scent longer-lasting. (Genus: *Moschus*, 3 species. Family: Moschidae.)

muskeg The poorly drained sphagnum moss peat-bog and marshland found in the tundra and taiga areas of N Canada. It is underlain by permafrost.

muskellunge [muhskeluhnj] Largest of the pike fishes (*Esox masquinongy*) in the Great Lakes of North America and associated rivers; length up to 2·4 m/8 ft. (Family: Esocidae.)

musket A heavy firearm, the most important infantry weapon from the late 17th-c to the mid-19th-c. Smooth-bored and muzzle-loading, the musket required a high degree of training to operate.

Muskie, Edmund S(ixtus) (1914–96) US lawyer and statesman, born in Rumford, ME. Secretary of state under President Carter, he was Democratic candidate for the vice-presidency in 1968.

musk ox A large goat-antelope (*Ovibos moschatus*) native to the Arctic tundra of North America; very thick long shaggy dark-brown coat; head large, with flat horns meeting in mid-line.

muskrat A large nocturnal water rat (*Ondatra zibethicus*) native to North America; thick fur exploited commercially; has a musky smell; also known as **musquash**.

Muslim *Islam*

Muslim Brotherhood An Islamic movement, founded in Egypt in 1928 by an Egyptian schoolteacher, Hasan al-Banna. Its original goal was the reform of Islamic society by eliminating Western influences and other decadent accretions.

musquash *muskrat*

mussel A sedentary bivalve mollusc found in estuaries and shallow seas, attached to a substrate by means of tough filaments; commonly used for human consumption. (Class: Pelecypoda. Order: Mytiloida.)

Musset, (Louis Charles) Alfred de [müsay] (1810–57) Poet and playwright, born in Paris. In 1833 he met the novelist George Sand, and there began the stormy love affair which coloured much of his work after that date, notably in his autobiographical novel *La Confession d'un enfant du siècle* (1835, The Confession of a Child of the Age).

Mussolini, Benito (Amilcare Andrea), known as **il Duce** ('the Leader') (1883–1945) Dictator and prime minister of Italy (1922–43), born in Predappio, Romagna. In 1919 he helped found the *Fasci di Combattimento* as a would-be revolutionary force, and in 1922 became prime minister, his success symbolized by the March on Rome (Oct 1922). His rule saw the replacement of parliamentarism by a totalitarian system; the establishment of the Vatican state (1929); the annexation of Abyssinia (1935–6) and Albania (1939); and the formation of the Axis with Germany. His declaration of war on Britain and France was followed by a series of defeats in Africa and the Balkans. Following the Allied invasion of Sicily (1943), he was overthrown and arrested (Jul 1943). Rescued from imprisonment by German paratroopers, he was placed in charge of the puppet Italian Social Republic, but in 1945 he was captured by the Italian Resistance and shot.

Mussorgsky, Modest *Moussorgsky, Modest*

mustang A breed of horse, developed naturally in North America as a wild horse; descended from Spanish horses introduced by the Conquistadors; height, 14–15 hands/1·4–1·5 m/4 ft 8in–5 ft.

Mustapha Kemel Atatürk *Atatürk, Mustapha Kemal*

mustard An erect annual growing to 1 m/3¼ ft; yellow, cross-shaped flowers. Commercial mustard is produced from ground seeds of two of the species. (Family: Cruciferae.)

mustard gas A light-yellow, oily liquid which becomes a gas above 14°C, acting as a powerful vesicant (producer of blisters) that attacks the human skin, eyes, and lungs. It was used as a poison gas at Ypres by the Germans in July 1917. Chemically, it is

2,2'-dichlorodiethylsulphide, (Cl–CH$_2$–CH$_2$)$_2$S, boiling point 216°C.

Muste, A(braham) J(ohn), originally **Abraham Johannes Muste**, known as **A J** (1885–1967) Labour leader and pacifist, born in Zierikzee, The Netherlands. His family moved to the USA in 1891, where he became a minister. As director of Brookwood Labor College (1921–33), he helped train labour activists ('Musteites'). A mystical experience brought him back to Christian pacifism, and during the 1950s he was active in civil rights and world peace movements. Sometimes called 'America's Gandhi', he was a leading influence on 20th-c social movements in the USA.

Mustelidae [muhstelidee] A family of carnivorous mammals (67 species), found worldwide except in Australasia and Madagascar; usually with long thin body, short legs, long tail.

mutation An abrupt change in the genetic characteristic of an organism. In **chromosomal** mutations there is a deletion, breakage, or re-arrangement of large amounts of chromosomal material. In **molecular mutation**, there is an alteration in the DNA sequence of a gene which can adversely affect one or more codons, or the splicing of the primary transcript, or the non-coding genetic control elements (eg promoter) which allows the gene to be transcribed into mRNA.

Mutsuhito [mutsuheetoh], **Meiji Tenno** (1852–1912) Emperor of Japan who became the symbol of Japan's modernization. He is commemorated by the Meiji Shrine in Tokyo.

muttonbird The alternative name for the **short-tailed shearwater** (*Puffinus tenuirostris*) from S Australia and the Pacific, or the **sooty shearwater** (*Puffinus griseus*) from New Zealand.

mutual fund *open-ended investment company*

Muzorewa, Abel (Tendekayi) [muzoraywa] (1925–) Zimbabwean politician and clergyman, born in Umtali (now Mutare), Zimbabwe. In 1971 he became president of the African National Council, and prime minister of 'Zimbabwe Rhodesia' in 1979. After independence his party was defeated by the Patriotic Front of Mugabe and Nkomo.

MX missile An abbreviation used for **Missile Experimental**, the codename of a US third-generation land-based intercontinental ballistic missile. It was eventually deployed as the 'Peacekeeper' missile from 1987 onwards in land-based silos in the US Mid-west.

Myanmar *p.636*

myasthenia gravis [miyastheenia grahvis] A condition characterized by the inability to sustain a contraction of voluntary (*somatic*) muscles. The muscles become rapidly fatigued, but recover temporarily after a period of rest.

Mycenae [miyseenee] A fortified town in the Argolid, associated in Greek tradition with Agamemnon, the conqueror of Troy. It has extensive Bronze Age remains.

Mycenaean / Mycenean civilization [miyseneean] A brilliant Bronze Age culture which flourished in Greece and the Aegean in the second millennium, reaching its high point in Greece in the 13th-c BC.

mycetoma [miysetohma] A painless mass arising from a fungal infection produced when the fungus grows within the body and becomes matted together with the body's tissues. Fungi such as *Actinomyces* can enter the skin through wounds. The lesion commonly affects the lower limbs, and is also known as **Madura foot**.

mycology [miykolojee] The identification, description, and classification of the great diversity of fungi. Fungi are usually identifiable only when they are fruiting, as their vegetative bodies consist of a mass of filamentous threads (*hyphae*), and are similar in appearance in the majority of species.

Mycoplasma The smallest, self-replicating micro-organisms, usually 150–300 nm in diameter. A distinct nucleus is lacking, as are cell walls. There are c.60 species, all except one being

parasitic on vertebrates, plants, and insects. (Kingdom: Monera. Class: Mollicutes.)

mycorrhiza [miykoriyza] A common symbiotic association formed between a fungus and the roots of a plant. Mycorrhizal systems have enhanced absorption abilities, and infected plants compete better than non-infected ones, while the fungus benefits from nutrients supplied by the plant.

myelin [miyelin] A soft, white substance (a complex of protein lipids) forming a multilayered insulating sheath around the large-diameter axons of vertebrate and crustacean neurones. This increases the speed of conduction of the action potential along the axon.

myeloma [miyelohma] A malignant proliferation of antibody-producing cells derived from type B lymphocytes (plasma cells) in the bone marrow. Patients become anaemic and vulnerable to infection, and blood clotting is impaired. The bones are weakened and prone to fractures. Production of large quantities of abnormal antibody can damage the kidneys.

Myers, F(rederic) W(illiam) H(enry) (1843–1901) Psychical researcher, born in Keswick, Cumbria. In 1882 he helped found the Society for Psychical Research.

Myers, Mike (1963–) Actor, comedian, writer, and director, born in Scarborough, Ontario, Canada. In 1988 he became a comedian on the television programme *Saturday Night Live*, where he introduced the character 'Wayne Campbell'. He took the character to the big screen in the film *Wayne's World* (1992) which proved a hit. Later films include three *Austin Powers* movies (1997, 1999, 2002), and the voice of Shrek (*Shrek*, 2001, 2004).

Mykonos *Mikonos*

My Lai incident [mee liy] The massacre of several hundred unarmed inhabitants of the S Vietnamese village of My Lai by US troops during the Vietnam War (Mar 1968), an incident exposed by *Life* magazine photos in 1969. The officer responsible, Lieutenant Calley, was court-martialled in 1970–1.

mynah / myna A bird of the starling family (13 species), native to India and SE Asia; good imitator of sounds and speech.

myocardial infarction [miyohkah(r)dial] The death of muscle cells of the heart, occurring when they are deprived of oxygen. The cardinal symptom is severe pain over the chest, which unlike that of angina persists for several hours. It may cause little bodily disturbance beyond a few days of tiredness, but it may lead to heart failure, cardiac arrhythmias, and cardiac arrest. Uncomplicated cases can recover fully.

Myolodon [miyolodon] The last of the ground sloths, surviving in Patagonia until recent times, now extinct. (Order: Xenarthra.)

myopia *eye*

Myrdal, (Karl) Gunnar [mürdahl] (1898–1987) Economist, politician, and international civil servant, born in Gustafs Dalecarlia, Sweden. He shared the Nobel Prize for Economics in 1974, principally for his work on the application of economic theory to Third World countries.

Myriapoda [miriapoda] A diverse group of terrestrial arthropods containing the millipedes (Class: Diplopoda), centipedes (Class: Chilopoda), and two small classes, Symphyla and Pauropoda. All have a segmented trunk that is not differentiated into thorax and abdomen.

Myrmidons [mermidnz] In Greek legend, a band of warriors from Thessaly who went to the Trojan War with Achilles.

Myron [miyron] (fl.c.480–440 BC) Sculptor, born in Eleutherae, Greece. He worked in bronze, and is known for the celebrated 'Discobolos' (Discus Thrower).

myrrh 1 A spiny, deciduous shrub, native to Africa and W Asia. Several species exude the aromatic resin myrrh used in incense and perfume. (Genus: *Commiphora*, 185 species. Family: Burseraceae.)

2 *sweet cicely*

Myanmar

□ International Airport

[myanmah(r)], formerly (to 1989) **Burma**, official name **Union of Myanmar**, Burmese **Pyidaungzu Myanma Naingngandaw**

Local name Pyidaungzu Myanma Naingngandaw

Timezone GMT +6·5

Area 678 576 km²/261 930 sq mi

Population total (2002e) 42 238 000

Status Union

Date of independence 1948

Capital Pyinmana (from 2005, formerly Yangon (Rangoon))

Languages Burmese (official), also tribal languages spoken

Ethnic groups Burman (Tibeto-Chinese) (72%), Shan (9%), Karen (7%), Chinese (3%), Indian (2%)

Religions Theravada Buddhist (85%), animist, Muslim, Hindu, Christian minorities (15%)

Physical features Bordered in the N, E, and W by mountains rising (N) to Hkakabo Razi, 5881 m/19 294 ft; located on Chinese frontier, forming part of Kumon Range; Chin Hills (W) descend into upland forests of the Arakan-Yoma range (S); principal rivers, Ayeyarwady (Irrawaddy), Thanlwin (Salween), and Sittang.

Climate Tropical monsoon climate; equatorial on coast; humid temperate in extreme N; SW monsoon season (Jun–Sep); cool, dry season (Nov–Apr); hot, dry season (May–Sep); average annual temperatures 23°C (Jan), 27°C (Jul) in Yangon; average annual rainfall 2616 mm/103 in;.

Currency 1 Kyat (MMK) = 100 pyas

Economy Largely dependent on agriculture; rice, pulses, sugar cane; forestry (hardwoods); textiles, pharmaceuticals, petroleum refining, and mining of minerals.

GDP (2002e) $73·69 bn, per capita $1700

Human Development Index (2002) 0·552

History First unified in the 11th-c by King Anawrahta; invasion by Kubla Khan, 1287; second dynasty established under King Tabinshweti in 1486, but plagued by internal disunity and wars with Siam from 16th-c; new dynasty under King Alaungpaya, 1752; annexed to British India following Anglo-Burmese wars (1824–86); separated from India, 1937; occupied by Japanese in World War 2; independence as Union of Burma under Prime Minister U Nu, 1948; military coup under U Ne Win, 1962; single-party socialist republic, 1974; army coup in 1988, leading to formation of a State Law and Order Restoration Council, headed by a Chairman; name changed to Union of Myanmar in 1989 and renamed capital Yangon; capital moved to centrally located Pyinmana, 2005; Aung San Sun Kyi (Nobel Peace Prize, 1991), main opposition leader, placed under house arrest in 1989–95, 2000–2, 2003–; constitutional conference ongoing since 1992; rebel separatist groups causing unrest but peace talks held Jan 2004; coastal regions strongly hit by tsunami, 2004.

Union of Burma
President
1948–52 Sao Shwe Thaik
1952–7 Agga Maha Thiri Thudhamma Ba U
1957–62 U Wing Maung
1962 Sama Duwa Sinwa Nawng

Revolutionary Council – Chairman
1962–74 Ne Win (Maung Shu Maung)

State Council – Chairman
1974–81 Ne Win (Maung Shu Maung)
1981–8 U San Yu
1988 U Sein Lwin
1988 Maung Maung
1988–9 Saw Maung

Union of Myanmar
1989–92 Saw Maung
1992– Than Shwe

Prime Minister
1947–56 Nu U (Thakin Nu)
1956–7 U Ba Swe
1957–8 U Nu
1958–60 Ne Win (Maung Shu Maung)
1960–2 U Nu
1962–74 Ne Win (Maung Shu Maung)
1974–7 U Sein Win
1977–8 U Maung Maung Ka
1988 U Tun Tin
1988–92 Saw Maung
1992–2003 Than Shwe
2003–4 Khin Nyunt
2004– Soe Win

myrtle An evergreen shrub of the family Myrtaceae, found mainly in South America, but also in other warm locations; common myrtle grows to over 5 m/16 ft; leaves thick, oil-bearing; solitary white flowers, c.1·8 cm/0·7 in long; purple-black berries; oil formerly used as an antiseptic. (Genus: *Myrtus*, c.16 species.)

Mysore [miysaw(r)] 12°17N 76°41E, pop (2000e) 564 000. City in Karnataka state, SW India; formerly the dynastic capital of

Mysore state; founded, 16th-c; railway; university (1916); known as 'the garden city of India' because of its wide streets and numerous parks.

mystery play A mediaeval play based upon a Biblical episode. Cycles of plays (notably, those of York and Wakefield) tell a continuous story, often portraying the Christian vision from the Creation to the Day of Judgment. These plays, and the later **miracle plays** on the Virgin and saints' lives, represent an important phase in the evolution of secular drama from religious ritual. The Chester cycle is re-enacted every five years (most recently in 2003) with hundreds of volunteers working under professional direction.

mystery religions Religious cults of the Graeco-Roman world, full admission to which was restricted to those who had gone through certain secret initiation rites or mysteries. The most famous were those of Demeter at Eleusis in Greece.

mysticism The spiritual quest in any religion for the most direct experience of God. Characteristically, mysticism concentrates on prayer, meditation, contemplation, and fasting, so as to produce the attitude necessary for what is believed to be a direct encounter with God. Notable Christian mystics include such diverse figures as St Augustine, St Francis of Assisi, and St Teresa of Ávila.

mythology The traditional stories of a people, often orally transmitted. The subject-matter of myths is either the gods and their relations with human or other beings, or complex explanations of physical phenomena. Until recently *mythology* meant Greek mythology, distinct in its concentration on stories of heroes and heroines. Recent scholarship has found unexpected parallels in myths from widely different sources, showing their function in determining social behaviour.

myxoedema / myxedema [miksuh**dee**ma] The deposition of a substance (*mucopolysaccharide*) under the skin, producing thickening, swelling, and pallor, and a characteristic puffy facial appearance.

myxomatosis [miksoma**toh**sis] A contagious viral disease of rabbits, characterized by the presence of jelly-like tumours (*myxomata*); devastated wild rabbit populations in Europe in the 1950s.

Naas [nays], Ir **Nás na Riogh** 53°13N 6°39W, pop (2000e) 11 300. Market town and capital of Kildare county, Ireland; former capital of the kings of Leinster; noted horse-racing area.

Nabis, Les [nabee] A small group of artists working in Paris c.1890–c.1900 under the influence of Gauguin.

Nablus [nabloos] 32°13N 35°16E, pop (2000e) 120 000. Town in Israeli-occupied West Bank, NW Jordan; market centre for an agricultural region; Great Mosque (rebuilt, 1167, as Crusader church).

Nabokov, Vladimir [nabohkof] (1899–1977) Writer, born in St Petersburg, Russia. A considerable Russian author, he established himself also as a novelist in English, notably with his controversial book *Lolita* (1955), dealing with the desire of a middle-aged intellectual for a 12-year-old girl.

Nadal, Rafael, in full **Rafael Nadal-Parera**, nickname **Rafa** (1986–) Tennis player, born in Manacor, Mallorca. He began playing tennis at age four with his uncle **Toni Nadal**, who remains his coach. He turned professional in 2001 and earned the ATP Newcomer of the Year award in 2003. His achievements to date include the Monte Carlo Masters (2005), Rome Masters (2005, 2006), and the French Open (2005, 2006), and in 2006 he reached the Wimbledon singles final, losing to Roger Federer. He began 2007 ranked world number 2. He was named Laureus World Sports Newcomer of the Year in 2006.

Nader, Ralph [nayder] (1934–) Lawyer and consumer activist, born in Winsted, CT. His best-seller about the automobile industry, *Unsafe at Any Speed* (1965), led to the passage of improved car safety regulations in 1966. He became head of the Public Citizen Foundation in 1980. In 2000 he ran unsuccessfully for the US presidency as a Green Party candidate.

nadir [naydeer] A point on the celestial sphere immediately below an observer, therefore unobservable. Its opposite, the point vertically above the observer, is the **zenith**.

Naevius, Gnaeus [neevius] (c.264–c.194 BC) Poet and playwright, probably born in Campania. Fragments of an epic on the Punic War, *De bello Punico*, are extant.

naevus *birthmark*

Nagaland [nahgaland] pop (2001e) 1 988 600; area 16 527 km²/6379 sq mi. State in NE India; administrative centre, Kohima; governed by a State Assembly; former territory of Assam; became a state in 1961; strong movement for independence among Naga tribesmen.

Nagarjuna [nagah(r)juna] (c.150–c.250) Indian Buddhist monk–philosopher. He was the founder of the Madhyamika or Middle Path school of Buddhism.

Nagasaki [nagasakee] 32°45N 129°52E, pop (2000e) 455 000. City in W Kyushu, Japan; visited by the Portuguese, 1545; centre for Jesuit missionaries from 16th-c; target for the second atomic bomb of World War 2 (9 Aug 1945), destroying over a third of the city; airport; railway; university (1949); Peace Park.

Nagorno-Karabakh [nagaw(r)noh karabakh], Russ **Nagorno-Karabakhskaya** area 11 400 km²/4400 sq mi. Autonomous region in Azerbaijan, established in 1923 after the reversal of a decision to unite the region with Armenia; administrative centre, Stepanakert; in Karabakhsky and Murovdag ranges of the Caucasus; majority of population Armenian, leading to claims by Armenia for its incorporation into that republic; opposed by Azerbaijan and former Soviet Union, leading to military conflict from 1988 onwards; ceasefire agreement signed, 1994.

Nagoya [nagoya] 35°08N 136°53E, pop (2000e) 2 154 000. Port in C Honshu, Japan; founded as a castle, 17th-c; fourth largest city of Japan; heavily bombed in World War 2; airport; railway; two universities (1939, 1950); Nagoya Castle (rebuilt, 1959), Atsuta Shrine (c.1st-c).

Nagpur [nahgpoor] 21°08N 79°10E, pop (2000e) 1 905 000. City in Maharashtra, WC India; founded, 18th-c; former capital of Berar and Madhya Pradesh states; airfield; railway; university (1923).

Nagy, Imre [noj, imray] (1895–1958) Hungarian statesman and prime minister (1953–5), born in Kaposvar, Hungary. When Soviet forces began to put down the 1956 revolution, he was displaced by the Soviet puppet János Kádár, and executed.

Nahum, Book of [nayhum] One of the 12 so-called 'minor' prophetic writings of the Hebrew Bible/Old Testament, attributed to a prophet named Nahum, about whom little else is known.

naiad [niyad] In Greek mythology, a nymph who inhabits springs, rivers, and lakes.

Naidoo, Jay (Jayaseelan) [niydoo] (1954–) South African labour leader and opponent of apartheid, born in Durban, South Africa. When the Congress of South African Trade Unions (COSATU) was founded in 1985, he was elected general secretary. From 1990 he was active in the negotiations for a new political dispensation in South Africa.

nails Rectangular plates of horny tissue found on the back of the end bones (*terminal phalanges*) of each digit. They grow at c.1 mm/0·04 in per week, faster in summer than in winter.

Naipaul, Sir V(idiadhar) S(urajprasad) [niypawl] (1932–) Novelist, born in Chaguanas, Trinidad. He has lived in England since 1950. A sequence of comic novels set in Trinidad concluded with *A House for Mr Biswas* (1961). Later novels include *The Enigma of Arrival* (1987), *A Way in the World* (1994), *Half a Life* (2001), and *Magic Seeds* (2004). He received the Nobel Prize for Literature in 2001.

Nairobi [niyrohbee] 1°17S 36°50E, pop (2000e) 1 833 000. Capital of Kenya; largest city in E Africa; airport; railway; centre of communications and commerce; university (1956); cathedral (1963).

Nakasone, Yasuhiro [nakasohnay] (1918–) Japanese statesman, and prime minister (1982–8), born in Takasaki, E Japan. As premier, he supported the renewal of the US–Japan Security Treaty, and maintained close relations with US President Reagan.

Namaqualand [namakaland], Afrikaans [namakwalant] Region in S Namibia and W South Africa; N and S of the Orange R; European presence since 1665; indigenous peoples known as Namaquas or Nama.

Namibia

ANGOLA
ZAMBIA
Cunene Ruacaná Dam
Cubango Caprivi Strip Zambezi
OVAMBOLAND
Z.M.
Etosha Pan
Tsumeb
Grootfontein
Okavango
Delta
N A M I B I A
Brandberg△
Karibib Gobabis
BOTSWANA
3606m
Swakopmund
Walvis Bay
■ Windhoek
Tropic of Capricorn
Mariental Kalahari
Desert
300 km
150 mi
Keetmanshoop
Lüderitz
Fish
AFRICA
Karasburg
Oranjemund
Orange
ATLANTIC
OCEAN
SOUTH
AFRICA
Skeleton Coast
Namib Desert

□ International Airport

[namibia], formerly **Southwest Africa** (to 1968), earlier **German South-West Africa**

Local name Namibia

Timezone GMT +2

Area 824 292 km²/318 261 sq mi

Population total (2002e) 1 837 000

Status Republic

Date of independence 1990

Capital Windhoek

Languages English (official), Afrikaans, German, local languages

Ethnic groups African (chiefly Ovambo) (85%), white (7%), mixed (8%)

Religions Christian (Lutheran, Roman Catholic, Dutch Reformed, and Anglican) (90%), traditional animist beliefs (10%)

Physical features Located in SW Africa; Namib Desert runs parallel along the Atlantic Ocean coast; inland plateau, mean elevation 1500 m/5000 ft; highest point, Brandberg, 2606 m/8550 ft; Kalahari Desert to the E and S; Orange R forms S frontier with South Africa.

Climate Arid, continental tropical climate; average maximum daily temperature, 20–30°C; 49°C (Nov–Apr) in coastal desert (Namib); average annual rainfall 360 mm/14 in at Windhoek.

Currency 1 Namibian Dollar (NAD) = 100 cents; 1 South African Rand (ZAR) = 100 cents

Economy Agriculture (employs c.60% of population); indigenous subsistence farming in N; major world producer of diamonds and uranium; fishing; brewing; textiles; plastics.

GNP (2002e) $13·15 bn, per capita $6900

Human Development Index (2002) 0·610

History Visited by British and Dutch missionaries from late 18th-c; German protectorate, 1884; mandated to South Africa by the League of Nations, 1920; UN assumed direct responsibility in 1966, changing name to Namibia, 1968, and recognizing the Southwest Africa People's Organization (SWAPO) as representative of the Namibian people, 1973; South Africa continued to administer the area as Southwest Africa; SWAPO commenced guerrilla activities, 1966; bases established in S Angola, involving Cuban troops in 1970s; interim administration installed by South Africa, 1985; full independence, 1990; governed by a President, Prime Minister and Cabinet, and an elected National Assembly.

Head of State
1990–2004 Sam Daniel Nujoma
2004– Hifikepunye Pohamba

Head of Government
1990–2002 Hage Geingob
2002–5 Theo-Ben Gurirab
2005– Nahas Angula

Namatjira, Albert [namatjeera] (1902–59) Artist, born in Hermannsburg Lutheran mission, near Alice Springs, Northern Territory, Australia. A member of the Aranda Aboriginal people, he achieved wide fame for his European-influenced watercolour landscapes.

Namen [namen] *Namur*

Namib Desert [namib] Desert in W Namibia; length, c.1300 km/800 mi; width, 50–160 km/30–100 mi.

Namibia *see panel*

Namier, Sir Lewis (Bernstein) [naymyer], originally **Ludwik Bernstein Niemirowski** (1888–1960) Historian, born near Warsaw. He created a school of history in which the emphasis was on detailed analysis of events and institutions, particularly parliamentary elections.

Namur [namür], Eng [namoor], Flemish **Namen** 50°28N 4°52E, pop (2000e) 105 500. City in Belgium, at confluence of Sambre and Meuse Rivers; conquered by the Germans in 1914 and 1940; railway; university (1831); cathedral (1751–67).

Nanak [nanak], known as **Guru Nanak** (1469–1539) Religious leader, the founder of Sikhism, born at Talwandi, near Lahore, Pakistan (formerly India). A Hindu by birth, he left his home at around the age of 30, and spent 20 years travelling widely in search of spiritual truth. He eventually settled in Kartarpur, in the Punjab, where he attracted many followers. He was a revolutionary in his thought, denouncing many contemporary reli-

gious practices as idolatrous, speaking out against caste and discriminatory rituals, and preaching equality for all. His doctrine was set out later in the *Adi-Granth*.

Nana Sahib [nana saheeb], originally **Brahmin Dundhu Panth** (c.1820–c.1859) Indian rebel, who became known as the leader of the Indian Mutiny in 1857. After the collapse of the rebellion he escaped into Nepal.

Nanchang or **Nan-ch'ang** [nanchang] 28°38N 115°56E, pop (2000e) 1 527 000. Industrial city in SE China; founded 201 BC; centre of abortive uprising (1927) led by pro-communist Guomindang officers; airfield; railway; university; distribution centre for kaolin clay.

Nancy [nāsee] 48°42N 6°12E, pop (2000e) 104 000. Manufacturing city in NE France, on R Meurthe; former capital of Lorraine; part of France, 1766; road and rail junction; university (1572); cathedral (1703–42); noted for its 18th-c Baroque architecture, a world heritage site.

nandu *rhea* (ornithology)

Nanjing [nahnjing] or **Nanking** 32°03N 118°47E, pop (2000e) 2 987 000. City in SE China, on the Yangtze R; founded, 900 BC; capital of China 220–589, 907–79, 1356–68; centre of Taiping Rebellion (1850–64); river port and trade centre; open port after the Opium War (1842); airfield; railway; university (1902).

Nanking *Nanjing*

Nanning or **Nan-ning** 22°50N 108°06E, pop (2000e) 1 298 000.

City in S China; founded during the Yuan dynasty; closed to foreigners until 1977; airfield; railway; agricultural trade.

nanotechnology The science of construction in which dimensions of the components are less than 100 nanometres (nm; 10^{-9} of a metre); this is c.100 000 times thinner than a human hair. The term was introduced by Nomo Taniguchi in 1974 to refer to mechanical machining methods. *Top-down* nanotechnology concentrates on manufacturing on this very small scale, such as the use of photolithography to make transistors for integrated circuits. *Bottom-up* nanotechnology builds with individual atoms: a **scanning tunnelling microscope** is used to manipulate and arrange individual atoms exactly as required. Another development is the **nanomanipulator**, which senses the electric fields of the atoms; this uses 3-D computer graphics and virtual reality technology to allow scientists to 'see' and 'feel' the atoms as they move them. The application of nanotechnology may result in revolutionary methods of atom-by-atom manufacturing and surgery on a cellular scale, as well as the creation of computers of great compactness and power.

Nansen, Fridtjof [frityof] (1861–1930) Explorer, scientist, and statesman, born near Oslo. His greatest scheme was to reach the N Pole by letting his specially built ship, the *Fram*, get frozen into the ice N of Siberia and drift towards Greenland. In this way he reached in 1895 the highest latitude till then attained, 86°14N. In 1922 he was awarded the Nobel Peace Prize for Russian relief work.

Nantes [nãt], Breton **Naoned**, ancient **Condivincum**, later **Namnetes** 47°12N 1°33W, pop (2000e) 256 000. Manufacturing and commercial seaport in W France; at head of Loire estuary; seventh largest city in France; France's leading port in 18th-c; major bomb damage in World War 2; railway; university (1962); Gothic cathedral; birthplace of Jules Verne.

Nantes, Edict of [nãt] (1598) A law promulgated by Henry IV of France at Nantes granting religious and civil liberties to his Protestant Huguenot subjects at the end of the Wars of Religion. It was revoked by Louis XIV in 1685.

Nantucket (Algonquian 'narrow-tidal-river-at') pop (2002e) 9000. Island in the Atlantic off the SE coast of Massachusetts, USA; area 122 km^2/47 sq mi; formerly an important whaling centre; now a summer resort.

napalm [naypahm] A munition (usually air-launched in canisters by aircraft) containing petroleum gel which uses flame for its destructive effects. It is an aluminium soap of naphthenic and palmitic acids (which give the substance its name).

naphtha [naftha] A mixture of hydrocarbons obtained either from coal tar or from petroleum, used mainly as a solvent. It has a boiling range of about 100–180°C.

naphthalene [nafthaleen] $C_{10}H_8$, melting point 80°C. A white, waxy solid, containing two fused benzene rings; obtained from the distillation of coal tar. Important as a starting material in the synthesis of dyestuffs and plastics, it is familiar as the main ingredient of mothballs.

Napier [naypyer] 39°29S 176°58E, pop (2000e) 57 000. Seaport in North Island, New Zealand; largely destroyed by earthquake in 1931; airfield; railway; centre of a rich farming area.

Napier, John [naypyer] (1550–1617) Mathematician, the inventor of logarithms, born near Edinburgh. He devised a calculating machine, using a set of rods called **Napier's bones**.

Naples, Ital **Napoli**, Lat **Neapolis** 40°50N 14°15E, pop (2000e) 1 205 000. Seaport in SW Italy; founded c.600 BC; capital of Napoleon's Parthenopean Republic, 1799, and of the Sicilian kingdom, 1806; joined Kingdom of Italy, 1860; severely damaged in World War 2, and by earthquakes, 1980; archbishopric; airport; railway; university (1224); cathedral (13th–15th-c).

Napoleon I, Fr **Napoléon Bonaparte**, Ital **Napoleone Buonaparte** (1769–1821) French general, consul, and emperor (1804–15), born in Ajaccio, Corsica. He commanded the artillery at the siege of Toulon (1793), and in 1796 married Joséphine, widow of the Vicomte de Beauharnais. In Italy, he defeated the Piedmontese and Austrians, and made several gains through the Treaty of Campo Formio (1797). Intending to break British trade by conquering Egypt, he captured Malta (1798), and entered Cairo; but after the French fleet was destroyed by Nelson at the Battle of the Nile in 1798 (also known as The Battle of Aboukir Bay), he returned to France (1799). The *coup d'état* of 18th Brumaire followed (9 Nov 1799) in which Napoleon assumed power as First Consul, instituting a military dictatorship. He then routed the Austrians at Marengo (1800), and consolidated French domination by the Concordat with Rome and the Peace of Amiens with Britain (1802).

Elected consul for life, he assumed the hereditary title of emperor in 1804. War with Britain was renewed, and extended to Russia and Austria. Forced by Britain's naval supremacy at Trafalgar (1805) to abandon the notion of invasion, he attacked the Austrians and Russians, gaining victories at Ulm and Austerlitz (1805). Prussia was defeated at Jena and Auerstadt (1806), and Russia at Friedland (1807). After the Peace of Tilsit, he became the arbiter of Europe. He then tried to cripple Britain with the Continental System, and sent armies into Portugal and Spain, which resulted in the unsuccessful Peninsular War (1808–14).

In 1809, wanting an heir, he divorced Joséphine, who was childless by him, and married the Archduchess Marie Louise of Austria, a son being born in 1811. Believing that Russia was planning an alliance with Britain, he invaded, defeating the Russians at Borodino (1812), before entering Moscow, but he was forced to retreat. In 1813 his victories over the allied armies continued at Lützen, Bautzen, and Dresden, but he was routed at Leipzig, and France was invaded. Forced to abdicate, he was given the sovereignty of Elba (1814). The unpopularity of the Bourbons motivated him to return to France in 1815. He regained power for a period known as the Hundred Days, but was defeated at Waterloo. He fled to Paris, abdicated, and was banished to St Helena, where he died.

Napoleon II, in full **François Charles Joseph Bonaparte** (1811–32) Son of Napoleon I by the Empress Marie Louise, born in Paris. Styled King of Rome at his birth, after his father's abdication he was brought up in Austria, though allowed no active political role.

Napoleon III, until 1852 **Louis Napoleon**, originally **Charles Louis Napoleon Bonaparte** (1808–73) President of the Second French Republic (1848–52) and emperor of the French (1852–70), born in Paris, the third son of Louis Bonaparte (the brother of Napoleon I) and Hortense Beauharnais. He made two abortive attempts on the French throne (1836, 1840), for which he was imprisoned, but after the 1848 Revolution he was elected president, and assumed the title of emperor. His reign coincided with the Crimean War (1854–6), the expeditions to China (1857–60), the annexation (1860) of Savoy and Nice, and the ill-starred intervention in Mexico (1861–7). He unwisely declared war on Prussia in 1870 and suffered humiliating defeat. He went into exile in England, living in Kent until his death.

Napoleonic Wars (1800–15) The continuation of the Revolutionary Wars, fought to preserve French hegemony in Europe. The wars began with Napoleon's destruction of the Second Coalition (1800). After a peaceful interlude (1802–3) Britain resumed hostilities, prompting Napoleon to prepare for invasion, and encouraging the formation of a Third Coalition (1805–7). While Britain retained naval superiority (1805), Napoleon established territorial domination, resulting in the invasions of Spain (1808) and Russia (1812). Gradually the French were overwhelmed by the Fourth Coalition (1813–14); the Hundred Days' epilogue ended with Waterloo (1815).

Nara [nahra] 34°41N 135°49E, pop (2000e) 359 000. City in S Honshu, Japan; first urban capital of Japan, 710; centre of Japanese Buddhism; railway; women's university (1908); Daibutsuden (Great Buddha Hall) in Todaiji (East Great Temple, founded 743); housing bronze statue of Buddha (22 m/72 ft tall).

Narayan, R(asipuram) K(rishnaswami) [nariyan] (1906–2001) Novelist and short-story writer, born in Chennai (Madras), India. His novels include *Swami and Friends* (1935), *Mr Sampath* (1949), *The World of Nagaraj* (1990), and *The Grandmother's Tale* (1993).

Narayanganj [narayangganj] 23°36N 90°28E, pop (2000e) 557 300. City in SE Bangladesh, on R Meghna; river port for Dhaka; collection centre for jute, hides, and skins; major industrial region.

narcissism A condition of self-infatuation. It may manifest as exhibitionism, indifference to criticism, and fantasies of unlimited sexual prowess, intelligence, or attractiveness.

Narcissus [nah(r)sisus] In Greek mythology, a beautiful youth who fell in love with his reflection in a pool; he pined away and was changed into a flower.

narcissus [nah(r)sisuhs] A bulb native to Europe, the Mediterranean region, and W Asia; flowers solitary or several on a long stalk, central trumpet or cup (the *corona*), surrounded by six spreading perianth segments, white, yellow, or pink. Horticulturally a division is made into *daffodils*, with the corona equalling or longer than the perianth, and *narcissi*, with the corona shorter than the perianth. (Genus: *Narcissus*, 60 species. Family: Amaryllidaceae.)

narcolepsy An extreme tendency towards excessive sleepiness often associated with cataplexy, in which sleep onset is accompanied by dreaming. Sleep paralysis and hallucinations are accompanying features.

narcotics Drugs related to morphine which, in the literal sense, induce *narcosis* or stupor. In common parlance the term has been adopted to include all addictive drugs.

Narmada [nah(r)mada] or **Narbada, River** River of India, rising in the Maikala range; enters the Gulf of Cambay; length 1245 km/774 mi; a sacred river to Hindus.

Narnia [nah(r)nia] A mythical country, the scene of a sequence of novels by C S Lewis, beginning with *The Lion, The Witch, and The Wardrobe* (1950).

Narses [nah(r)seez] (c.478–573) Famous general of the Emperor Justinian, born in Armenia. He reasserted Byzantine control over Rome and Italy by his victories over the Ostrogoths (550–4).

Narvik [nah(r)vik] 68°26N 17°25E, pop (2000e) 19 400. Seaport in N Norway; airfield; ice-free harbour; occupied by Germany, 1940; scene of World War 2 naval battles.

narwhal [nah(r)wuhl] A small, toothed whale (*Monodon monoceros*) native to the Arctic seas; mottled brown; no dorsal fin; two teeth (at front of upper jaw); in male, left tooth grows forwards forming a long straight tusk. (Family: Monodontidae.)

NASA (National Aeronautics and Space Administration) An independent agency of the US Government responsible for the civil space programme, established in 1958 by President Eisenhower, with its headquarters in Washington DC. Individual projects are implemented at different field centres: *Ames Research Center* (Mountain View, CA) for astrobiology and information systems; *Dryden Flight Research Center* (Edwards, CA) for aeronautic flight research; *Goddard Space Flight Center* (Greenbelt, MD) for astronomy and Earth sciences; *Jet Propulsion Laboratory* (Pasadena, CA) for Solar System exploration; *Johnson Space Center* (Houston, TX) for manned missions; *Kennedy Space Center* (Cape Canaveral, FL) for launch operations; *Langley Research Center* (Norfolk, VA) for aeronautics; *Glenn* (formerly *Lewis*) *Research Center* (Cleveland, OH) for space technologies; and *Marshall Space Flight Center* (Huntsville, AL) for launch vehicles and space science.

Naseby, Battle of [nayzbee] (14 Jun 1645) A major conflict of the English Civil War in the E Midlands. The Royalist forces of Charles I were defeated by Parliament's New Model Army led by Fairfax.

Nash, John (1752–1835) Architect and city planner, born in London. He designed Regent's Park and Marble Arch, recreated Buckingham Palace, and laid out Trafalgar Square and St James's Park.

Nash, John F (1928–) Economist, born in Bluefield, WV. He shared the Nobel Prize for Economics in 1994 for his contribution to the analysis of equilibria in the theory of non-co-operative games.

Nash, (Frederic) Ogden (1902–71) Humorous writer, born in Rye, NY. His subject matter was the everyday life of middle-class America, which he described in a witty and acute manner in such books as *Hard Lines* (1931) and *Marriage Lines* (1964).

Nash, Paul (1889–1946) Painter, born in London. He won renown as a landscape painter, and also as a war artist, with such pictures as 'Battle of Britain' and 'Totes Meer' (1940–1, Tate, London).

Nash, Richard, nickname **Beau Nash** (1674–1762) Dandy, born in Swansea, S Wales. In 1705 he became master of ceremonies at Bath, which he transformed into a leading fashionable centre.

Nashe or **Nash, Thomas**, pseudonym **Pasquil** (1567–1601) Playwright and satirist, born in Lowestoft, Suffolk. He plunged into the Martin Marprelate controversy, attacking the Puritans in *Pierce Penilesse* (1592). Other works include the satirical masque, *Summer's Last Will and Testament* (1592), and the picaresque tale, *The Unfortunate Traveller or the Life of Jacke Wilton* (1594).

Nashville–Davidson, commonly **Nashville**, nickname **Music City, USA** 36°10N 86°47W, pop (2000e) 556 000. Capital of state in N Tennessee, USA; port on the Cumberland R; settled as Nashborough, 1779; renamed Nashville, 1784; state capital, 1843; merged with Davidson, 1963; airfield; railway; three universities (1867, 1872, 1909); famed for its music industry (country and western); Country Music Hall of Fame.

Nasik [nahsik] 20°02N 75°30E, pop (2000e) 848 000. City in WC India; a holy place of Hindu pilgrimage.

Nassau (Bahamas) [nasaw] 25°05N 77°20W, pop (2000e) 14 400. Capital of the Bahamas on New Providence I; airport; a popular winter tourist resort.

Nassau (European history) [nasow] A Burgundian noble family, who rose as servants of the Habsburgs, then rebelled against their authority in the Low Countries. William of Orange (1533–84), and his brother Louis (1538–74), Count of Nassau, supported and led the Dutch Revolt (1566–1648).

Nasser, Gamal Abdel (1918–70) Egyptian statesman, prime minister (1954–6), and president (1956–70), born in Alexandria. Dissatisfied with the corruption of the Farouk regime, he was involved in the military coup of 1952. As president, he nationalized the Suez Canal, which prompted Britain and France, in collaboration with Israel, to seek his forcible overthrow. In 1958 he created a federation with Syria (the United Arab Republic), but Syria withdrew in 1961.

Nasser, Lake, Arabic **Buheiret en-Naser** Lake in S Egypt; length 500 km/310 mi; area c.5000 km²/1930 sq mi; created after building the Aswan High Dam (1971).

nasturtium [nastershuhm] An annual or perennial, trailing or climbing by twining leaf-stalks, native to Mexico and temperate South America; flowers large, roughly trumpet-shaped with five petals and a backward-projecting spur, in shades of yellow, orange, and scarlet. (Genus: *Tropaeolum*, 90 species. Family: Balsaminaceae.)

Natal (Africa) *KwaZulu Natal*

Natal (Brazil) [natahl] 5°46S 35°15W, pop (2000e) 692 200. Port in NE Brazil; airfield; railway; university (1958); cathedral; 16th-c fort.

Natchez Trace A road built by the US Army in the early 19th-c to link Nashville, TN, with the then pioneer outpost of Natchez in Mississippi, 725 km/450 mi distant.

Nation, Carry (Amelia), *née* **Moore** (1846–1911) Temperance agitator, born in Garrard Co, KY. A large, powerful woman of volcanic emotions, she went on hymn-singing, saloon-smashing expeditions with a hatchet in many US cities, attacking what she considered to be illegal drinking places.

National Academy of Design The main official academy of art in the USA. Founded in 1826, it still exists as an exhibiting society for the more traditionally-minded artists.

national accounts A set of accounts showing how much a nation has produced and consumed during some period, normally a year. This will include the composition of goods and services produced, by sector; the division of expenditures between consumption, investment, government, imports, and exports; and the division of incomes between wages, profits, rents, interest, taxes, and transfer payments.

National Aeronautics and Space Administration *NASA*

National Assembly for Wales *Welsh Assembly*

National Association for the Advancement of Colored People (NAACP) A group which aims to extend awareness among the country's African-American population of their political rights. It was founded in the USA in 1909.

National Audubon Society [awduhbon] A US private conservation organization named after the US artist and naturalist, John James Audubon. It manages more than 60 wildlife sanctuaries in the USA.

National Bureau of Standards *National Institute of Standards and Technology*

National Council of the Churches of Christ in the USA An association of Protestant, Eastern Orthodox, and National Catholic Churches formed in 1950 in the USA. It is committed to the principle of manifesting the oneness of the Church of Christ.

national curriculum A curriculum for all the schools in a country. Some countries (eg France) have had one for many years; some (eg the USA) do not have one at all. England and Wales introduced one in 1988, consisting of three 'core' subjects (English, maths, science), and seven 'foundation' subjects (art, geography, history, music, physical education, technology, and, in secondary schools only, a modern language). Some variation in practice is allowed (eg to take account of the status of Welsh in Wales).

National Economic Development Council (NEDC), nickname **Neddy** A UK forum set up in 1962 where government, industry, and unions could meet to discuss economic affairs. Many 'little Neddies' were created, relating to specific industries. NEDC was closed in 1992.

National Front (NF) A strongly nationalist political party in Britain which centres its political programme on opposition to immigration, and calls for the repatriation of ethnic minorities even if they were born in the UK. The party was created in 1960. Its political appeal declined with the election of a Conservative government in 1979. Many of the Front's leaders are avowedly racist and anti-semitic.

National Gallery An art gallery in London housing the largest collection of paintings in Britain. It was opened in 1824, and moved to its present premises in Trafalgar Square in 1838. The Sainsbury Wing opened in 1991. The first phase of a major redevelopment scheme opened in 2004 with the addition of two new entrances to the gallery.

National Gallery of Art A gallery endowed by Andrew W Mellon and opened in Washington, DC in 1941. It is a branch of the Smithsonian Institution.

National Gallery of Australia An art gallery on the shores of L Burley Griffin in Canberra, opened in 1982. It houses a permanent collection showing the history of Australian art, including Aboriginal art, and has several other collections.

National Geographic Society In the USA, a scientific and educational organization, founded in 1888. It publishes a monthly journal, *National Geographic*. It had over 10 million members in 2007.

National Grid Reference System A unique grid reference for mapping purposes for any part of the UK. The country has been divided by the Ordnance Survey into a number of grid squares, 100 × 100 km (62·14 mi), each with its own identifying letters. Each square is further subdivided into numbered 1 km (0·62 mi) squares.

national guard A militia or reserve military force. The US National Guard is organized on a state-by-state basis, its members voluntarily enlisting for military training and for service in aiding the civil power when called upon by the state governor.

National Health Service (NHS) A system of health care established in the UK in 1948. It is largely a free service available to the whole population, funded out of general taxation, and the largest single employer of labour in the UK.

National Heritage Memorial Fund A fund set up in 1980 as a memorial to those who have died in service for the UK. It is used to help acquire and preserve land, buildings, and objects of outstanding scenic, historic, architectural, artistic, and scientific interest.

National Hockey League The pre-eminent association of professional ice hockey teams in Canada and the USA. Established in 1917 at Montreal, it was originally composed of four teams from Ontario and Quebec, and later expanded to include larger numbers of teams from American cities. A championship series is played annually for the Stanley Cup.

national hunt racing *horse racing*

national income A measure of the aggregate level of economic activity in a country. **Gross domestic product** (GDP) is the total value of production in a country, before allowing for depreciation of its capital stock. **Gross national product** (GNP) is GDP plus net property income from abroad. To get from GDP to GNP the profits of foreign firms operating domestically and interest paid abroad are deducted, and the profits of domestic firms operating abroad and interest received from abroad are added. National income as a technical term is GNP minus depreciation of the capital stock. In considering national welfare, the aggregate national income needs to be divided by the population, to get national income per capita.

National Institute of Standards and Technology (NIST) A US government facility, established by Congress in 1901, researching and developing measurement methods, standards, and technology in support of industry, commerce, scientific institutions, and government; formerly known as the **National Bureau of Standards**. Its laboratories are located mainly at Boulder, CO, or at the NIST headquarters in Gaithersburg, MD.

national insurance A system whereby the state insures all its residents against illness, disability, unemployment, and old age. In the UK, for example, a National Insurance Scheme is funded by compulsory contributions on all workers above a low exemption limit and their employers. The contributions cover only a small part of the total cost of the scheme, the remainder coming from central government revenues.

nationalism A political doctrine which views the nation as the principal unit of political organization. A primary aim of nationalists, therefore, is to secure the right to belong to an independent state based on a particular national grouping. With the exception of anti-colonial movements, nationalism is based around a conservative, and sometimes romantic political philosophy that emphasizes the nation's past.

nationalization Taking into public ownership an entire industry, normally a public utility. The main reasons for nationalization are that an industry is crucial to the economy and in need of government direction, has suffered a period of decline which needs to be reversed, or is important to national defence. There is also the view, based on a socialist ideology, that public ownership is desirable to prevent the concentration of economic power in private hands.

National Library of Wales The library was established by Royal Charter in 1907 and opened on its present site in Aberystwyth, W Wales, UK, in 1916; the main building was not completed until 1955. It is a Copyright Library, with the right to claim any work published in the British Isles.

National Lottery *lottery*

National Museum of Photography, Film, and Television A museum which explores the world of the media, part of the National Museum of Science and Industry, founded in 1983, and located in Bradford, W Yorkshire, UK. Its collection includes over 3 million items of social, historical, and cultural value in photography and film making. These include the world's first negative, the earliest television footage, and what is regarded as the world's first example of moving pictures – Louis Le Prince's 1888 film of Leeds Bridge.

National Park According to the United Nations, an area of educational and scientific importance for habitat and wildlife, of great beauty, and of recreational value, but which has suffered little human impact, so remaining a relative wilderness. It should also be protected from resource development and be relatively unpopulated. National parks date back to 19th-c USA, where the first was established around the Yellowstone R, WY, in 1872. The first parks in England and Wales were designated in 1951, and there were 12 in 2006. The New Forest was designated a national park in 2005. The first Scottish park was established in 2002.

National Party (Australia) The third largest party in Australia since 1920, originally named the **Country Party**. It is conservative in social matters, generally favours policies of free trade and low tariffs, and supports government public expenditure. Since 1923 it has been in coalition with the Conservative Party.

National Physical Laboratory A state laboratory established in 1900 at Teddington, near London, to research and develop industrial and scientific standards of measurement.

National Portrait Gallery A gallery of portraits of distinguished people in British history. Opened in London in 1859, it was moved to its present position adjoining the National Gallery in 1895.

national product *gross domestic product*

National Radio Astronomy Observatory (NRAO) The principal radio astronomy observatory of the USA, with powerful telescopes at Green Bank, WV and headquarters at Charlottesville, VA. Instruments at Green Bank include a 100 × 110 m dish, the world's largest fully steerable radio telescope, completed in 1999.

National Road A road built in the early 19th-c from Cumberland, MD, to Vandalia, IL, and eventually to St Louis, MO. It played an important role in the expansion of the West.

National Savings A range of financial instruments provided by the UK government for use by small savers. All have full state guarantees for both capital and interest, are available at post offices without fees in small quantities, and are repayable on sight or relatively short notice. National Savings tend to have yields lower than the best obtainable by larger investors, but their safety, at least in money terms, makes them attractive to small savers whose funds and information are both limited.

National Security Adviser A member of staff who is responsible for advising the US president on security matters. He is regarded as a senior figure in the White House.

National Security Council A body created by Congress in 1947 to advise the US president on the integration of domestic, foreign, and military policies relating to national security. It is composed of the president, vice-president, secretary of state, secretary of defense, and director of the Office of Emergency Planning.

national service *conscription*

National Socialism *Nazi Party*

National Socialist German Worker's Party *Nazi Party*

National Society for the Prevention of Cruelty to Children (NSPCC) A child welfare society, founded in 1884. It has over 200 inspectors in England, Wales, and Northern Ireland who investigate reports of cruelty to, or neglect of, children.

national theatre A theatre which is endowed by the state and is usually situated in the national capital. In Britain, a National Theatre was not inaugurated until 1962, and since 1976 has occupied its own building on the South Bank. In 1999 the first National Theatre Ensemble Company was formed.

National Trust In the UK, a charity founded in 1895 with the full name 'The National Trust for Places of Historic Interest and Natural Beauty'. Its membership stands at 3.4 million, making it the largest and most influential conservation body in Britain.

Nation of Islam *Black Muslims*

Nations, Battle of the *Leipzig, Battle of*

Nativity, the The story of the miraculous birth of Jesus of Nazareth to Mary. The year of Jesus's birth is usually fixed at c.6 BC. The festival of Christmas has been celebrated since the 4th–5th-c on 25 December throughout most of Christendom.

NATO [naytoh] Acronym for **North Atlantic Treaty Organization**. An organization established by a treaty signed in 1949 by Belgium, Canada, Denmark, France, Iceland, Italy, Luxembourg, The Netherlands, Norway, Portugal, the UK, and the USA; Greece and Turkey acceded in 1952, West Germany in 1955, and Spain in 1982. Poland, the Czech Republic, and Hungary formally joined in 1999. NATO was established as a military alliance to defend W Europe against Soviet aggression. Its institutions include a Council, an International Secretariat, and the Supreme Headquarters Allied Powers, Europe (SHAPE). After the 1989 changes in E Europe, a NATO summit in London (1990) began the process of redefining NATO's military and political goals, and in 1997 NATO and Russia signed a Founding Act on Mutual Relations, allowing for NATO's eastward expansion. In 1999, NATO authorized air-strikes in Yugoslavia, in response to Serbian measures against the ethnic Albanian population in Kosovo. In 2002 Russia became a strategic partner when the NATO–Russian Council (NRC) was formed. Estonia, Latvia, Lithuania, Bulgaria, Romania, Slovenia, and the Slovak Republic formally joined in 2004. NATO's first peacekeeping role outside Europe took place in 2003, when it assumed control of the International Security Assistance Force in Afghanistan.

natterjack A European true toad (*Bufo calamita*); rough green skin with thin yellow line along spine; the loudest European toad (croak may be heard 2 km/1¼ mi away).

Natufian [natoofian] A Mesolithic culture of SW Syria, Lebanon, and Palestine (c.12 800–10 500 BC), named after the Palestinian site of Wadi en-Natuf.

natural childbirth Successful labour entirely without or with minimal use of drugs or outside assistance. It is facilitated by a full awareness of the nature of childbirth, developing psychological attitudes which reduce anxiety and fear, and increase pain tolerance.

natural gas Gas which occurs in subterranean accumulations, often in association with petroleum deposits. It mainly consists of simple hydrocarbons, mostly methane, with some propane. It is one of the most widely used and versatile of fuels, and a source of other chemicals. When used as a gas supply, it is adulterated with other gases to give it an odour.

Nauru

[naooroo], official name **Republic of Nauru**
Local name Naeoro (Nauruan)
Timezone GMT +12
Area 21·3 km²/8·2 sq mi
Population total (2002e) 12 300
Status Republic

Date of independence 1968
Capital Yaren District (No official capital)
Languages Nauruan (official), English
Ethnic groups Nauruans (62%), Pacific islanders (26%), Asian (9%), Caucasian (3%)
Religions Christian (Nauruan Protestant, Roman Catholic)
Physical features Small isolated island in WC Pacific Ocean, 4000 km/2500 mi NE of Sydney, Australia; ground rises from sandy beaches to give fertile coastal belt, c.100–300 m/300–1000 ft wide, the only cultivable soil; central plateau inland, highest point 65 m/213 ft; mainly phosphate-bearing rocks.
Climate Tropical, hot, and humid; average annual temperatures 27°C (Jan), 28°C (Jul); average annual rainfall 1520 mm/60 in; monsoon season (Nov–Feb).
Currency 1 Australian Dollar (AUD) = 100 cents
Economy Based on phosphate mining, now limited reserves; coconuts, some vegetables; tourism; tax haven.
GDP (2001e) $60 mn, per capita $5000
History Under German administration from 1880s to 1914; after 1919, League of Nations mandate, administered by Australia; occupied by Japan, 1942–5; independence movement, 1960s; self-government, 1966; full independence, 1968; unicameral Parliament, elects a President, who appoints a Cabinet.

Head of State/Government
1999–2000 René Harris
2000–1 Bernard Dowiyogo
2001–3 René Harris
2003 Bernard Dowiyogo
2003 Derog Gioura
2003 Ludwig Scotty
2003–4 René Harris
2004– Ludwig Scotty

Natural History Museum The popular name for the British Museum (Natural History), housed since 1881 in S Kensington, London.

Naturalism A term used in art criticism for the faithful copying of nature, with no attempt to 'improve' or idealize the subject; used in this sense in 1672 by Giovanni Pietro Bellori (1615–96) to characterize the work of Caravaggio and his followers. It later became used to describe the incorporation of scientific method into art, especially literature.

naturalistic fallacy A term in ethics, coined by G E Moore: the mistake of thinking that goodness is some natural or empirical property of things, such as their capacity to produce pleasure; more generally, the alleged mistake of inferring normative conclusions from factual premises – an 'ought' from an 'is'.

natural selection The complex process by which environmental factors determine the differential reproduction of genetically different organisms. It is viewed as the force which directs the course of evolution by preserving those traits best adapted to survive.

Nature Conservancy Council *English Nature*

Nature Reserve A protected area for the conservation and management of wildlife and habitat. In the UK these range from National Nature Reserves, in the care of English Nature, to reserves managed by the National Trust, local authorities, and county naturalist trusts.

naturopathy [natyuropathee] A holistic approach to health care which aims to create favourable conditions in which the body's own natural powers of healing will eliminate any illness and then continue to maintain health. The symptoms of an illness are seen as part of the healing process, so these are not sup-

pressed; instead, the body is encouraged to correct its own disturbed equilibrium.

Naughtie, (Alexander) James [nokhtee] (1951–) Journalist and broadcaster, born in Milltown of Rothiemay, Aberdeenshire. He became presenter of the BBC's *The World At One* (1988–94), and joined the team of *Today* in 1994. He has also presented several documentary series, such as *The Thin Blue Line* (1993).

Naukratis [nawkratis] A Greek town in the Delta of Egypt, established by the Milesians c.675 BC. It was the commercial centre of the Greeks in Egypt until the foundation of Alexandria (c.331 BC).

Nauru *see panel*

Nausicaa [nawsikaya] In Homer's *Odyssey*, the daughter of King Alcinous. She welcomed Odysseus when he landed in Phaeacia.

nautilus [nawtilus] A primitive cephalopod mollusc with an external spiral shell; numerous tentacles present around mouth; four gills; eyes like a pinhole camera in design, without lenses; only a single living genus known. (Class: Cephalopoda. Subclass: Nautiloidea.)

Navajo or **Navaho** [navahoh] Athapascan-speaking North American Southwest Indians, the second largest Indian group in the USA, numbering c.269 000 (2000 census). They settled in 1888 on a reservation in Arizona (presently 15 million acres).

Navaratri [navarahtree] A Hindu festival held in the autumn (Asvina S 1–10) in honour of the goddess Durga, and also commemorating the victory of Rama over Ravana, the Demon King; also known as **Durga Puja** [doorguh poojuh].

Navarre [navah(r)], Span **Navarra** pop (2000e) 523 000; area 10 421 km²/4022 sq mi. Region and former kingdom of N Spain; united with Castile, 1515; capital, Pamplona.

nave The W part of a church open to the laity, as opposed to the chancel or choir; more specifically, the middle section of the W limb between the side aisles.

navel *umbilical cord*

navigation The means of finding the way from one place to another in safety. *Celestial navigation* is the oldest and most traditional type of navigation. Navigators could calculate their craft's latitude from the angle of the sun or other stars above the horizon, measured using a sextant. Longitude was calculated by knowing the local time exactly compared to that at 0° longitude, at Greenwich, London. Time is based on the time of rotation of the Earth, and is measured aboard ship using a very accurate chronometer. The simplest form of navigation is called *dead reckoning* (from the term *deduced reckoning*): the position of a ship or aircraft is simply calculated by knowing its speed (measured in knots), the direction it is heading from a compass reading (the bearing), and the time it has been travelling. Navigators can improve on this if they take account of effects of wind and tide pushing their craft off course. Another type of navigation, known as *piloting*, uses features along the route as landmarks (eg tall buildings, hills). The disadvantage of these systems is that they do not work in poor visibility conditions. *Electronic navigation* can be used in all weather conditions. *Satellites* are also increasingly being used for navigation, sending out signals which can be received and used as position finders. The Global Positioning System (GPS) gives an almost instant fix of position in latitude and longitude. *Radar navigation* works by sending out signals and representing the reflection from obstacles on a display. *Inertial navigation* is a completely self-contained system, unaffected by weather, magnetic fields, electric storms, etc. It uses the outputs from three gyroscopes and three accelerometers to measure changes in rotation and position accurately in three dimensions (roll, pitch, and yaw).

Navigation Acts Protective legislation in Britain passed between 1650 and 1696, designed to increase England's share of overseas carrying trade. The laws stated that all imports to England had to be in English ships or in those of the country of origin. They were not repealed until 1849.

Navratilova, Martina [navratilohva] (1956–) Tennis player, born in Prague. The winner of a record-equalling nine singles titles at Wimbledon (1978–9, 1982–7, 1990), she won 167 singles titles (including 18 Grand Slam events) and 165 doubles titles with her partner Pam Shriver (including 37 Grand Slam events), becoming the most prolific winner in women's tennis. In 1994 she retired from competitive singles tennis. In 2003 she secured a record-equalling 20th Wimbledon title when she won the mixed doubles final. In 2004 she competed in the Wimbledon singles once more and became the oldest person to win a singles match there in the modern era. She retired from professional tennis after competing at Wimbledon in 2006. She has become known as a spokeswoman on social issues, as well as those concerning the status of women and young players in tennis. She became a US citizen in 1981.

navy The branch of the armed forces whose main function is the projection of military power at and by sea. The role of naval forces is manifold, primarily the protection of lines of communication for the safe transport of troops and supplies (and its converse, denying the enemy the freedom of the seas). In the two World Wars, naval power was of critical importance, with the added dimensions of submarine, amphibious, and carrier warfare.

Naxos [naksos] pop (2000e) 15 300; area 428 km²/165 sq mi. Largest island of the Cyclades, Greece, in the S Aegean Sea; length 35 km/22 mi; width 26 km/16 mi; rises to 1002 m/3287 ft; chief town, Naxos.

Nazareth, Hebrew **Nazerat** 32°41N 35°16E, pop (2000e) 70 000.

Town in N Israel; mainly Christian population; home of Jesus for most of his life; Church of the Annunciation.

Nazca [naska] A pre-Columbian culture located along the S Peruvian coast, and flourishing between c.200 BC and AD 500. It was noted for its distinctive style of pottery and large-scale 'lines' (best seen from the air) on the desert surface.

Naze, the, Norwegian **Lindesnes** 57°59N 7°03E. Cape on the S extremity of Norway, projecting into the North Sea at the entrance to the Skagerrak.

Nazi Party A German political party which originated as the German Worker's Party, founded in 1919 to protest against the German surrender of 1918, and renamed the *Nationalsozialistische Deutsche Arbeiterpartei* (National Socialist German Worker's Party, or Nazi Party) in 1920. Adolf Hitler became the party's leader the following year. Its ideology was extremely nationalist, imperialist, and racist, maintaining that the world was divided into a hierarchy of races: Aryans, of whom Germans were the purest example, were the supreme culture-bearing race, while the Jews were the lowest. In 1933 Hitler was appointed chancellor in a coalition government, a position from which he, aided by the party, was able to build up a personal dictatorship, through legal measures, terror, and propaganda. Once in power, the Nazis ruthlessly crushed opposition, and in the late 1930s invaded Austria and the Sudetenland, which according to the ideology was necessary for obtaining land for the 'master race'. During World War 2, their actions included slave labour, plunder, and mass extermination. Nazism as a political ideology is now viewed very much as the expression of extreme inhumanity and fanatical nationalism.

Ndebele [nduhbeelee] or **Matabele** A Bantu-speaking people of SW Zimbabwe and N South Africa. In the 1890s they resisted white pioneers' encroachment on their land, but were ruthlessly suppressed.

N'djamena [njameena], formerly **Fort Lamy** 12°10N 14°59E, pop (2000e) 791 000. Capital of Chad, NC Africa; founded by French, 1900; bombed by Italians, 1942; airport; university (1971).

Ndola [ndohla] 13°00S 28°39E, pop (2000e) 514 900. Capital of Copperbelt province, C Zambia; airport; railway; technical college; commercial centre of a major mining area.

Neagh, Lough [lokh nay] area 396 km²/153 sq mi. Large lake in C Northern Ireland; length, 29 km/18 mi; width, 18 km/11 mi; largest lake in the British Isles.

Neanderthal Man [neeandertahl] *Homo sapiens neanderthalensis*. A distinctive form of archaic *Homo sapiens*, with a long, flat, braincase (capacity 1200–1800 cm), a retreating frontal, heavy brow ridge, and projecting face with a large nose; fully upright with a stocky, muscular body build (height 1·55–1·8 m/5 ft 1 in–5 ft 10 in). Fossil evidence indicates Neanderthal characters evolved slowly from about 0·5 million years ago, but the full set of features only occur after c.0·1 million years ago in Europe, S Russia, and S W Asia. In W Europe they disappeared c.33 000 years ago with the arrival of anatomically modern humans (*H. sapiens sapiens*); in SW Asia the two subspecies coexisted for c.60 000 years.

neap tide An especially small tidal range occurring twice monthly, produced by the tidal forces of the Sun and Moon acting in opposition. They occur when the Moon is in its first and third quarters.

near-death experience (NDE) A striking experience sometimes reported by those who have recovered from being close to death. It generally includes an out-of-the-body experience in which one travels through a dark void or tunnel towards a bright light, and then may encounter religious figures or deceased loved ones. It is often accompanied by strong feelings of peacefulness.

Near Earth Object (NEO) An asteroid or comet in the Solar System with an orbit that brings it close to the Earth, presenting a potential collision hazard. There are estimated to be approximately 2000 NEOs larger than 1 km/0·6 mi in diameter, and more than a million larger than 50 m/165 ft in diameter, the size above which they would penetrate the Earth's atmosphere. From this size up to about 1 km in diameter, an NEO impact on Earth would cause immense local damage. The impact of an NEO larger than about 2 km/1·2 mi (energy greater than a million megatons) would produce severe environmental damage around the globe. Still larger impacts can cause mass extinctions, such as the one (15 km/9 mi diameter and c.100 million megatons) that ended the age of the dinosaurs 65 million years ago.

nearsightedness *eye*

Neath and Port Talbot, Welsh **Castell-Nedd a Phort Talbot** pop (2001e) 134 500; area 442 km²/171 sq mi. County (unitary authority from 1996) in SC Wales, UK; drained by R Neath and R Avan; administrative centre, Port Talbot, known for its steelworks; castle, abbey and Roman fort at Neath.

Nebraska [nebraska] pop (2000e) 1 711 300; area 200 342 km²/77 352 sq mi. State in C USA; the 'Cornhusker State'; part of the Louisiana Purchase, 1803; became a territory in 1854; the 37th state admitted to the Union, 1867; capital, Lincoln; highest point Johnson Township (1654 m/5426 ft); E region undulating fertile farmland, growing corn; further W, on the Great Plains, grass cover helping to stabilize eroded land; agriculture dominates the economy; cattle (second largest producer in the country), corn, hogs, wheat, sorghum.

Nebuchadnezzar II [nebookadnezer], also spelled **Nebuchadrezzar** (c.630–562 BC) King of Babylon (605–562 BC). Under him, Babylonian civilization reached its height, and its empire extended as far as the Mediterranean. In the West, he is remembered chiefly for his deportation of the Jews to Babylonia (586 BC).

nebula A cloud of gas and dust in space, appearing either light or dark. Some nebulae are areas where stars form; others are produced by the death of stars. **Star-forming nebulae** include the Orion Nebula. **Dark nebulae** examples are the Coalsack and the Horsehead Nebula. Other nebulae are produced by supernova explosions, such as the Crab Nebula.

neck That part of the body which connects the head and the thorax as well as the upper limbs to the trunk. It contains the continuations of many structures: the vertebral column, alimentary and respiratory tracts, blood vessels and their branches, lymph nodes and lymphatic vessels, groups of muscles, and several cranial and cervical nerves.

Necker, Jacques (1732–1804) Statesman and financier, born in Geneva, Switzerland. As director-general of finances in France, he attempted reforms, but was dismissed (1781). Recalled to deal with the impending financial crisis (1788), he summoned the States General, but his proposals aroused royal opposition, and he was again dismissed.

necropsy *post mortem*

nectar A sugary fluid secreted by specialized glands (*nectaries*) usually found in flowers, and used to attract insect pollinators.

nectarine A smooth-skinned variety of peach. (*Prunus persica*, variety *nectarina*. Family: Rosaceae.)

Neddy *National Economic Development Council*

Nederlands *Dutch*

needlefish Slender-bodied fish with very long jaws forming a narrow bill; widespread in tropical and warm temperate seas; length up to 1·2 m/4 ft; also called **garfish**. (Family: Belonidae.)

Ne'eman, Yuval (1925–2006) Physicist and politician, born in Tel Aviv, Israel. He became a member of the Israeli Knesset in 1981, and held ministerial posts in the areas of science and development (1982–92). In physics he worked on the role of symmetry in particle physics, and co-authored the influential book *The Eight-Fold Way* with Murray Gell-Mann.

Neer, Aernout or **Aert van der** (1603/4–77) Painter, born in Amsterdam. He specialized in wintry river scenes, the emphasis almost always on the effect of the Moon peering through ragged clouds.

Neeson, Liam (1952–) Film actor, born in Ballymena, Northern Ireland. He received an Oscar nomination for his role as Schindler in *Schindler's List* (1993), and went on to play the title roles in *Rob Roy* (1995) and *Michael Collins* (1996). Later films include *Star Wars Episode 1: The Phantom Menace* (1999), *Batman Begins* (2005), and *The Chronicles of Narnia: The Lion, the Witch and the Wardrobe* (2005).

Nefertiti [neferteetee] (14th-c BC) Egyptian queen, the consort of Akhenaton. She is immortalized in the sculptured head found at Amarna in 1912, now in the Berlin museum.

negative An image in which the tonal scale of the original scene is inverted, light areas being reproduced as dark and vice versa. In a **colour negative** the hues of the original are also represented in their complementary colours.

Negeri Sembilan [negree sembilahn] pop (2000e) 900 000; area 6643 km²/2564 sq mi. State in SW Peninsular Malaysia; capital, Seremban.

Negev [negev] area 12 200 sq km/4700 sq mi. Hilly desert region of S Israel; hilly in the S, reaching 1935 m/6348 ft at Har Ramon; increasing kibbutz settlement.

negligence A tort (or delict, in Scotland) applicable to a very wide range of situations. To succeed in negligence, the plaintiff must prove that the defendant owed him or her a duty of care; that the duty was breached in this instance; and that the breach caused damage to the plaintiff (known as *actual* or *proximate cause* in the USA). Road accidents are a common source of negligence claims.

Negro, River (Brazil) [negroh] (Port **Rio**) Important N tributary of the Amazon, N Brazil; rises in SE Colombia; length c.2250 km/1400 mi.

Nehemiah, Book of [neehemiya] A book of the Hebrew Bible/Old Testament, named after a Jewish official of the King of Persia, who apparently led a return to Judea by Jewish exiles.

Nehru, Jawaharlal [nairoo], known as **Pandit** ('Teacher') **Nehru** (1889–1964) Indian statesman and prime minister (1947–64), born in Allahabad, India. Imprisoned several times by the British, in 1929 he was elected president of the Indian National Congress. As India's first prime minister, he introduced a policy of industrialization, reorganized the states on a linguistic basis, and brought the dispute with Pakistan over Kashmir to a peaceful solution.

nekton Swimming marine organisms, capable of locomotion at speeds greater than those of ocean currents; distinct from plankton, which are drifters. Nekton range in size from tiny fish to giant sperm whales.

Nelson, Horatio (1758–1805) British admiral, born in Burnham Thorpe, Norfolk. In 1794 he commanded the naval brigade at the reduction of Bastia and Calvi where he lost the sight of his right eye, and in an action at Santa Cruz had his right arm amputated. In 1798 he followed the French fleet to Egypt, destroying it at Aboukir Bay. On his return to Naples, he fell in love with Emma, Lady Hamilton, and began a liaison with her which lasted until his death. In 1805 he gained his greatest victory, against the combined French and Spanish fleet at Trafalgar. During the battle he was mortally wounded on his flagship, HMS *Victory*.

Nelson, Willie (1933–) Country singer, songwriter, and guitarist, born in Abbott, TX. After writing and recording many country-music hits in the 1960s, he later gained a wider audience with such albums as *Shotgun Willie* (1972) and *Stardust* (1978).

nematode An unsegmented worm, typically circular in section;

body covered with cuticle; head end with terminal mouth, surrounded by lips and three rings of sense organs; c.12 000 species described; also known as **eelworms**, **roundworms**, or **pinworms**. (Phylum: Nematoda.)

Nemertea [nemertia] *ribbon worm*

nemesia [nemeezha] An annual (*Nemesia strumosa*) growing to 60 cm/2 ft, native to S Africa; flowers with 2-lobed upper lip and large, spreading 3-lobed lower lip, in a range of colours. (Family: Scrophulariaceae.)

Nemesis [nemesis] In Greek mythology, the goddess of retribution. She primarily represents the penalty the gods exact for human folly, excessive pride, or too much good fortune.

Nemirovich-Danchenko, Vladimir (Ivanovich) [nemirohvich danchengkoh] (1858–1943) Theatre director, writer, and teacher, born in Ozurgety. Co-founder with Stanislavsky of the Moscow Art Theatre, he became sole director.

Nenets A Uralic-speaking ethnic group living in N Russia, originally known as **Samoyed** or **Yurak**. Formerly nomadic, they are now settled in villages.

Nennius (fl.796) Writer, from Wales, the reputed author of *Historia Britonum*. The book gives the mythical account of the origins of the Britons, the Roman occupation, and the settlement of the Saxons, and closes with the historical Arthur's 12 victories over the Saxons.

NEO *Near Earth Object*

Neoclassicism (art and architecture) A classical revival affecting all the visual arts, including architecture and the decorative arts, which flourished from c.1750 onwards, lasting well into the 19th-c. A reaction against the decorous excesses of Baroque and Rococo, it began in Rome, but spread throughout W Europe and North America. In painting, the style reached its peak in the works of David, eg 'Oath of the Horatii' (1784, Louvre). Buildings are usually characterized by pure geometric form, restrained decoration, unbroken contours, an overall severe appearance, and sometimes monumental proportions.

Neoclassicism (music) A 20th-c music movement which sought to restore the ideals, and to some extent the style and vocabulary, of the 18th-c classical period. It is associated particularly with Stravinsky's middle-period works (c.1920–30).

Neoexpressionism A vague term sometimes used for all forms of abstract art which are regarded as conveying strong emotions, or which seem to have been produced by the artist in a heightened emotional state. Examples include Kandinsky's work after c.1920, or US Action Painting.

neofascism Fascist ideas and movements that have continued after the demise of the inter-war fascist dictatorships. Neofascism in W Europe has been especially opposed to immigration from former colonial and Balkan countries, and has used this as a major campaigning platform.

Neoimpressionism *Divisionism*

Neo-Keynesianism or **new Keynesianism** [kaynzianizm] A term introduced in 1982, related to the economic theories of J M Keynes, but modified to apply to the economic situation of the time. It recognizes three government economic targets: growth, balance of payments equilibrium, and adequate investment. These aims can be met by tax policy, exchange rates, and interest rates.

neologism [neeolojizm] A term referring to any newly coined word, usually identifying a new concept. In the 1980s, English neologisms included *stagflation* and *yuppie*; in the 1990s, *spam* and *texting*; and in the 2000s, *blogging* and *podcasts*.

Neo-Marxism The doctrines of Marxists who draw upon Marx's early writings, which had a more utopian emphasis than his later works concerned with economics and historical materialism. A key feature is its self-critical approach, which accepts the need for a review of theory, rather than a rigid acceptance of dogma.

neon Ne, element 10. The second noble gas, forming c.0·002% of the atmosphere, and obtained by the fractional distillation of liquid air. It is used mainly in gas discharge tubes and gas lasers, where it emits a characteristic red glow.

neopentane *pentane*

neoplasm *tumour*

Neoplasticism A term invented c.1917 by Mondrian to describe his own particularly severe form of abstract art. He permitted only primary colours, black, white, and grey, and restricted his shapes to squares or rectangles defined by vertical and horizontal lines.

Neoplatonism A school of philosophy founded by Plotinus (205–70), lasting into the 7th-c, which attempted to combine doctrines of Plato, Aristotle, and the Pythagoreans.

Nepal *p.648*

nephanalysis (Gr *nephos* 'cloud') A meteorological term for the study of clouds, in particular the amount and frequency of different cloud forms.

nephrite *jade*

nephritis *glomerulonephritis*

nephrons *kidneys*

Neptune (astronomy) The eighth major planet from the Sun, the outermost of the four 'gas giant' planets; discovered in 1846 as a result of a prediction by Leverrier to explain anomalies in the observed orbit of Uranus; encountered by Voyager 2 (24 Aug 1989); 13 known moons; mass $1·02 \times 10^{26}$ kg; equatorial radius 24 766 km/15 389 mi; mean density $1·7 \mathrm{g/cm^3}$; rotational period 16·11 hours; orbital period 164·8 years; inclination of equator 28·3°; eccentricity of orbit 0·010; mean distance from Sun 30·07 AU. It is an apparent twin of Uranus internally, composed of hydrogen and helium, but with much more carbon, nitrogen, and oxygen than Jupiter and Saturn. Its bluish-green coloration is produced by methane in the upper atmosphere. There are five rings between 42 000 km/26 000 mi and 63 000 km/39 000 mi from Neptune's centre.

Neptune (mythology) The Roman water-god. He was later identified with Poseidon, whose characteristics and mythology he acquired.

Nereid [neereeid] A natural satellite of Neptune, discovered in 1949; distance from the planet 5 510 000 km/3 424 000 mi; diameter c.340 km/210 mi.

nereid [neereeid] In Greek mythology, a sea-nymph, one of the 50 or (in some accounts) 100 daughters of Nereus and Doris. They lived with their father in the depths of the sea.

Nereus [neeryoos] In Greek mythology, a sea-god, the wise old man of the sea who always tells the truth. Heracles had to wrestle with him to find the location of the Golden Apples.

Nergal [nergahl] The Mesopotamian god of the Underworld; at first, a solar deity capable of killing enormous numbers of people in the heat of noon-day.

Neri, St Philip [nairee] (1515–95) Founder of the Oratory, born in Florence, Italy. In 1551 he became a priest, and gathered around him a following of disciples which in 1563 became the Congregation of the Oratory. He was canonized in 1622. Feast day 26 May.

Nero [neeroh], in full **Nero Claudius Caesar**, originally **Lucius Domitius Ahenobarbus** (37–68) Emperor of Rome (54–68), the son of Gnaeus Domitius Ahenobarbus and the younger Agrippina, daughter of Germanicus. His mother engineered his adoption by the Emperor Claudius, her fourth husband. Initially his reign was good, thanks to his three main advisers: his mother, the philosopher Seneca, and the Praetorian Prefect Burrus. But after her murder (59), and their fall from favour, Nero neglected affairs of state, and corruption set in. He was blamed for the Great Fire of Rome (64), despite assiduous attempts to make scapegoats of the Christians. He was toppled from power by the army, and forced to commit suicide.

Nepal

400 km
200 mi

CHINA

Indus

Tsangpo

Silgarhi

Dhaulagiri
8167m

Karnali

Kangchenjunga
8598m

Mt Everest
8848m

Pokhara

NEPAL

Kathmandu Patan

Bhadgaon

Dhankuta

BHUTAN

INDIA

Ghaghara

Gandak

BANGLADESH

Ganges

☐ International Airport

[nepawl, naypal], official name **Kingdom of Nepal**, Nepali **Nepal Adhirajya**

Local name Nepāl

Timezone GMT +5¾

Area 145 391 km²/56 121 sq mi

Population total (2002e) 23 692 000

Status Kingdom

Capital Kathmandu

Languages Nepali (official), Maithir, Bhojpuri

Ethnic groups Nepalese (58%), Bihari (19%), Tamang (4%), Tharu (3%), Newar (3%)

Religions Only official Hindu state in the world: Hindu (90%), Buddhist (5%), Muslim (3%), Christian (0·2%)

Physical features Landlocked, rises steeply from the Ganges basin in India; high fertile valleys in the 'hill country' at 1300 m/4300 ft, notably the Vale of Kathmandu (a world heritage site); dominated by the Himalayas (glaciated), highest peak, Mt Everest, 8848 m/29 028 ft.

Climate Varies from subtropical lowland with hot, humid summers and mild winters, to an alpine climate over 3300 m/10 800 ft, with permanently snow-covered peaks; average annual temperatures 0°C (Jan), 24°C (Jul) in Kathmandu; monsoon season (Jun–Sep); average annual rainfall 1428 mm/56 in.

Currency 1 Nepalese Rupee (NPR) = 100 paise/pice

Economy Agriculture (employs 90% of population); rice, jute, cereals, sugar cane; agricultural and forest-based goods; carpets; garments, handicrafts; hydroelectric power developing; tourism increasingly important.

GDP (2002e) $37·32 bn, per capita $1400

Human Development Index (2002) 0·490

History Originally a group of independent hill states, united in 18th-c; parliamentary system introduced, 1959; replaced by village councils (panchayats), 1960; a constitutional monarchy ruled by hereditary king; period of unrest in 1990, followed by reduction of king's powers, a new constitution and fresh elections, 1991; king now rules with a Council of Ministers, a bicameral Parliament consisting of an elected House of Representatives and a National Council; Crown Prince Dipendra allegedly murdered 10 members of his immediate family, including his father King Birendra and his mother Queen Aishwarya, before killing himself, 2001; state of emergency following new conflict with Communist Party rebels, 2001; peace-talks break down, 2003; King Gyanendra sacked cabinet and assumed direct power, 2005; unrest led to reinstatement of parliament, which then voted to curtail king's political powers, 2006; landmark peace agreement between government and Maoist rebels (Nov 2006) formally ended 10-year insurgency; rebels to join transitional government; interim constitution (Dec) transferred all constitutional powers from the king to the prime minister.

Head of State (Monarch)

1972–2001 Birendra Bir Bikram Shah Deva
2001 Dipendra Bir Bikram Shah
2001– Gyanendra Bir Bikram Shah

Head of Government

1970–1 *As king*
1971–3 Kirti Nidhi Bista
1973–5 Nagendra Prasad Rijal
1975–7 Tulsi Giri
1977–9 Kirti Nidhi Bista
1979–83 Surya Bahadur Thapa
1983–6 Lokendra Bahadur Chand
1986–90 Marich Man Singh Shrestha
1990 Lokendra Bahadur Chand
1990–1 Krishna Prasad Bhattarai
1991–4 Girija Prasad Koirala
1994–5 Man Mohan Adhikari
1995–7 Sher Bahadur Deupa
1997 Lokendra Bahadur Chand
1997–8 Surya Bahadur Thapa
1998–9 Girija Prasad Koirala
1999–2000 Krishna Prasad Bhattarai
2000–1 Girija Prasad Koirala
2001–2 Sher Bahadur Deuba
2002–3 Lokendra Bahadur Chand *Interim*
2003–4 Surya Bahadur Thapa
2004–5 Sher Bahadur Deuba
2005–6 *No prime minister*
2006– Girija Prasad Koirala

Neruda, Pablo [neroo**th**a], pseudonym of **Neftali Ricardo Reyes y Basualto** (1904–73) Poet and diplomat, born in Parral, Chile. He made his name with *Veinte poemas de amor ya una canción desesperada* (1924, Twenty Love Poems and a Song of Despair). His other works include *Residencia en la tierra* (1925–31, Residence on Earth) and *Canto General* (1950, General Song). He received the Nobel Prize for Literature in 1971.

nerve (cell) *neurone*

nerve gas An agent of chemical warfare, whose deadly effects are

achieved by attacking the human body's central nervous system. Paralysis and death come within seconds of absorption.

Nervi, Pier Luigi [nairvee] (1891–1979) Architect, born in Sondrio, Italy. He achieved an international reputation by his designs for the Olympic Games in Rome (1960). He also designed San Francisco Cathedral (1970).

nervous system That part of the body concerned with controlling and integrating the activity of its various parts. It is composed of nerves (*neurones*) and supporting cells. The transfer of information between nerve cells (at *synapses*) is usually by the release of small quantities of *transmitter substances*. In all activities involving the nervous system, there are three components involved: a *receptive* or *sensory* component, an integrative component and an *effector* or *motor* component. In higher animals the integrative component has undergone the greatest development, and forms the major part of the nervous system. In mammals the nervous system is divided into **central** and **peripheral** parts, both parts working together as a functioning unit: the central part comprises the brain and spinal cord, while the peripheral part comprises the remainder. Disorders, diseases, and infections of the nervous system include neuralgia, paralysis, prion disease, and tetanus.

Nesbit, E(dith), maiden name and pseudonym of **Mrs Hubert Bland** (1858–1924) Writer, born in London. She is best remembered for her children's stories, such as *The Wouldbegoods* (1901) and *The Railway Children* (1906).

Nesselrode, Karl (Robert) Vasilyevich, Graf (Count) [neselrohduh] (1780–1862) Russian diplomat, born in Lisbon, Portugal. He became foreign minister in 1822, and dominated Russian foreign policy for 30 years.

Ness, Loch Loch in Highland, N Scotland; 38 km/24 mi long; average width 2 km/1$\frac{1}{4}$ mi; maximum depth 230 m/755 ft; part of the Caledonian Canal; said to be inhabited by a 12–15 m/40–50 ft-long 'monster'; no clear results from scientific investigations.

nest A domicile or home constructed, typically by birds, for the purpose of containing and protecting eggs and young. Young birds that remain in the nest for a prolonged period after hatching are known as *nidicolous*; those that leave soon after hatching are known as *nidifugous*.

Nestor [nestaw(r)] A senior Greek leader in the Trojan War, the son of Neleus. In the *Iliad*, Homer portrays him as a longwinded sage, whose advice is often not taken.

Nestorians Followers of Nestorius, Bishop of Constantinople (died c.451), who is alleged to have taught the doctrine, later declared heretical, of two persons (one human, one divine) as well as two natures in the incarnate Christ.

Netanyahu, Benjamin [netanyahoo], nicknamed in Israel **Bibi** (1949–) Israeli prime minister (1996–9), born in Tel Aviv, Israel. He was elected to the Israeli parliament in 1988, becoming leader of the Likud Party in 1993. A hard-liner on security issues, he campaigned on a platform of peace with security, and defeated Shimon Peres by a narrow margin in the 1996 elections.

netball A women's seven-a-side court game, invented in the USA in 1891 and developed from basketball. The court is 100 ft (30·5 m) long and 50 ft (15.25 m) wide. The object is to score goals by throwing the ball through the opponent's net, which is attached to a circular hoop suspended on a post 10 ft (3·05 m) high.

Netherlands, Austrian and Spanish Ten provinces in the S of the Low Countries, predominantly Catholic, and united to Spain through Emperor Charles V. They were ceded to the Austrian Habsburgs by the Treaty of Utrecht (1713), and achieved independence from Austria (1794) in the French Revolutionary Wars.

Netherlands Antilles *p.650*

Netherlands East Indies The name applied to Indonesia until 1945, when Dr Sukarno declared independence. The Dutch recognized Indonesia's independence in 1948.

Netherlands, The *p.651*

nettle *dead-nettle; stinging nettle*

nettle rash *urticaria*

network *local area network*

Neuchâtel [noeshatel], Ger **Neuenburg** 44°60N 6°56E, pop (2000e) 34 500. Town in W Switzerland, on W shore of L Neu-

châtel; railway; university (1909); research centre for the Swiss watch industry.

Neuchâtel, Lake [noeshatel] (Fr **Lac de**) area 218 km²/84 sq mi. Largest lake to lie wholly within Switzerland; major wine-growing area.

Neumann, (Johann) Balthasar [noyman] (1687–1753) Architect, born in Cheb, Czech Republic (formerly Eger, Bohemia). He designed many outstanding examples of the Baroque style, notably Würzburg Palace and Schloss Bruchsal.

Neumann, John Von [noyman] *Von Neumann, John*

neuralgia [nyooraljia] Pain arising from a sensory nerve, and felt over the surface of the body supplied by the affected nerve. In the most common type, **trigeminal neuralgia**, pain, usually severe and paroxysmal, is felt over the forehead, face, or jaw supplied by one or more of the branches of the trigeminal (Vth cranial) nerve. The cause is unknown.

neural network An arrangement of computers linked together in a way which attempts to mimic the activity of the brain. The individual computers undertake specific tasks and relate the outcome of those tasks to other computers in the network.

Neurath, Otto [noyraht] (1882–1945) Philosopher and social theorist, born in Vienna. A member of the influential Vienna Circle of logical positivists, he wrote on sociology, education, and social policy.

neuritis *neuropathy*

neuroanatomy *anatomy*

neurolinguistic programming (NLP) A system of training which aims to develop the ability to communicate, to achieve rapid learning, to improve behaviour patterns, and to change destructive habits in oneself and others. The system is based on the work of the psychotherapists Milton Erickson, Fritz Perls, and Virginia Satir.

neurolinguistics The study of the neurological basis of language use: in particular, how the brain controls the processes of speech and comprehension.

neurology The branch of medicine which deals with the study of the central nervous system (the brain and spinal cord) and its peripheral nerves, in health (*neurophysiology*) and disease (*neuropathology*).

neurone / neuron [nyoorohn, -ron] The functional unit of the nervous systems of animals; also known as a **nerve cell**. Neurones process and transmit information to target tissues, usually through the mediation of chemicals (*neurotransmitters*). Vertebrate neurones typically consist of a cell body (with a well-developed nucleus surrounded by a mass of cytoplasm), an *axon* (with terminal branches specialized to carry information to target tissues), and *dendrites* (receiving information from axon terminals of other neurones). Most invertebrate neurones lack dendrites.

neuropathology The study of the disease processes which affect the nervous system. These include diseases of the brain, degenerative disorders such as Parkinsonism and prion disease, neuropathies, and demyelinating disorders such as multiple sclerosis.

neuropathy [nyooropathee] A term which covers all pathological processes that affect peripheral somatic and autonomic nerves. When there is widespread involvement of many nerve fibres, the condition is known as **polyneuropathy**.

neurophysiology The study of the functions of the nervous systems of animals. Common techniques of study are the electrical stimulation of nerve cells using electrodes, and techniques borrowed from other disciplines (eg autoradiography).

neuropsychology The study of psychological phenomena in the light of what is known about brain organization and function. Neuropsychologists are often concerned with brain damage, the aim being to identify disabilities, discover methods of

Netherlands Antilles

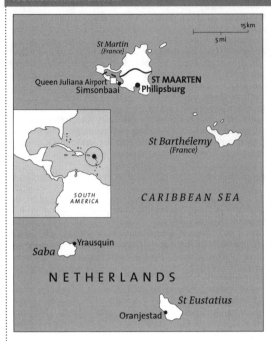

[antileez], Dutch **Nederlandse Antillen**

Local name Nederlandse Antillen

Timezone GMT -4

Area 993 km²/383 sq mi

Population total (2002e) 221 000

Status Self-governing region of The Netherlands

Capital Willemstad (on Curaçao Island)

Languages Dutch (official), Papiamento, English, and Spanish widely spoken

Ethnic groups Large majority of mixed European/Caribbean Indian descent

Religions Christian (mainly Roman Catholic)

Physical features Islands in the Caribbean Sea, comprising the Southern group (Leeward Is) of Curaçao and Bonaire, 60–110 km/37–68 mi N of the Venezuelan coast, and the Northern group (Windward Is) of St Maarten, St Eustatius, and Saba; terrain generally hilly, with volcanic interiors.

Climate Tropical maritime climate; average annual temperature 27·5°C; average annual rainfall varies from 500 mm/20 in (S) to 1000 mm/40 in (N); Northern group subject to hurricanes (Jul–Oct).

Currency 1 Netherland Antilles Guilder/Florin (ANG) = 100 cents

Economy Based on refining of crude oil imported from Venezuela; aim of industrial diversification; ship repairing; tourism.

GDP (2002e) $2·4 bn, per capita $11 400

History Visited by Columbus, initially claimed for Spain; small-scale Spanish colonization in Curaçao, 1511; occupied by Dutch settlers, 17th-c; acquired full internal self-government within Kingdom of the Netherlands, 1954; Aruba separated from the other islands, 1986; Sovereign of The Netherlands is Head of State, represented by a Governor, a Council of Ministers and a unicameral legislature.

Head of State
(Dutch monarch represented by Governor-General)
1983–90 Rene Romer
1990–2002 Jaime Saleh
2002– Fritz Goedgedrag

Head of Government
1988–94 Maria Liberia Peters
1994–8 Suzie Rommer
1998–2002 Miguel Pourier
2002–3 Etienne Ys
2003 Ben Komproe *Acting*
2003–4 Mirna Louise-Godett
2004–6 Etienne Ys
2006– Emily de Jongh-Elhage

rehabilitation, and use this information to make inferences about the normal mind and brain.

Neuroptera [nyooroptera] An order of primitive winged insects, including the snakeflies, lacewings, and antlions; typically two pairs of similar wings with lace-like veins; mouthparts of a simple, biting type.

neurosis A mental illness often associated with high levels of anxiety and representing exaggerated and/or unconscious ways of dealing with conflicts. The condition is enduring, and reality remains intact. Examples include obsessive-compulsive disorders and phobic disorders.

neurotoxins Naturally occurring or synthetic substances which specifically or predominantly affect the nervous system. Examples are aconitum (from aconite), and toxins of bacterial origin such as tetanus.

neurotransmitter A chemical substance (eg acetylcholine, noradrenaline) released as a messenger from nerves. It enables the transmission of a nervous impulse across the narrow gap (*synapse*) between a nerve ending and a muscle, gland, or another nerve.

neutralization In acid–base reactions, the mixing of chemically equivalent amounts of acid and base to give a solution near pH 7.

neutrino A fundamental particle; symbol v; mass not known exactly, but small, possibly zero; charge 0; spin ½, with spin direction always opposing the direction of motion; senses only gravitational and weak nuclear forces; produced in weak radioactive decays; three species known, corresponding to the electron, muon, and tau.

neutron A component particle of the atomic nucleus; symbol n; mass $1·675 \times 10^{-27}$ kg (939·6 MeV), charge 0, spin ½; held in the nucleus by strong nuclear force. Free neutrons decay to protons, electrons, and antineutrinos.

neutron bomb More precisely an **enhanced radiation (ER)**

Netherlands, The

☐ International Airport

or **Holland**, Dutch **Nederland**, official name **Kingdom of the Netherlands**, Dutch **Koninkrijk der Nederlanden**

Local name Nederland

Timezone GMT +1

Area 33 929 km²/13 097 sq mi

Population total (2002e) 16 142 000

Status Kingdom

Date of independence 1830

Capital Amsterdam

Language Dutch (official)

Ethnic groups Dutch (Germanic/Gallo-Celtic descent) (99%), Indonesian/Surinamese (1%)

Religions Roman Catholic (38%), Protestant (Dutch Reformed Church and other Protestant churches) (30%)

Physical features Generally low and flat, except SE where hills rise to 321 m/1053 ft; much of coastal area below sea-level, reaching lowest point -6·7 m/-19·7 ft N of Rotterdam; protected by coastal dunes and artificial dykes; highest point, Vaalserberg, in SE; 27% of land area is below sea level, an area inhabited by c.60% of population.

Climate Cool, temperate maritime climate, with continental influences. Average annual temperatures 1·7°C (Jan), 17°C (Jul); average annual rainfall exceeds 700 mm/27 in, evenly distributed throughout the year.

Currency 1 euro (EUR) = 100 cents (previous to February 2002, the Guilder (NLG)/ Florin (DFL) = 100 cents)

Economy Rotterdam and newly-constructed Europort are the major European ports of transshipment, handling goods for EC member countries; Amsterdam is a world diamond centre; world's largest exporter of dairy produce; highly intensive agriculture; horticulture; engineering, chemicals, oil products, natural gas, high technology and electrical goods; fishing; tourism.

GDP (2002e) $437·8 bn, per capita $27 200

Human Development Index (2002) 0·935

History Part of Roman Empire to 4th-c AD; part of Frankish Empire by 8th-c; incorporated into the Holy Roman Empire; lands passed to Philip II, who succeeded to Spain and the Netherlands, 1555; attempts to stamp out Protestantism led to rebellion, 1572; seven N provinces united against Spain, 1579; United Provinces independence, 1581; overrun by the French, 1795–1813, who established the Batavian Republic; united with Belgium as the Kingdom of the United Netherlands until 1830, when Belgium withdrew; neutral in World War 1; occupied by Germany, World War 2, with strong Dutch resistance; joined with Belgium and Luxembourg to form the Benelux economic union, 1948; conflict over independence of Dutch colonies in SE Asia in late 1940s; joined NATO, 1949; independence granted to former colonies, Indonesia, 1949, with the addition of W New Guinea, 1963, and Suriname, 1975; founder member of European Union (formerly EC), 1958; a parliamentary democracy under a constitutional monarchy; government led by a Prime Minister; States General (Staten-Generaal) consists of a 75-member First Chamber, and a 150-member Second Chamber; resignation of entire cabinet, 2002, following critical report on Dutch peace-keeping role in Bosnia in 1995; referendum rejected European constitution (Jun 2005).

Head of State (Monarch)
1890–1948 Wilhelmina
1948–80 Juliana
1980– Beatrix

Head of Government
1939–40 Dirk J de Geer
1940–5 Pieter S Gerbrandy (in exile)
1945–6 Willem Schemerhorn/ Willem Drees
1946–8 Louis J M Beel
1948–51 Willem Drees/Josephus R H van Schaik
1951–8 Willem Drees
1958–9 Louis J M Beel
1959–63 Jan E de Quay
1963–5 Victor G M Marijnen
1965–6 Joseph M L T Cals
1966–7 Jelle Zijlstra
1967–71 Petrus J S de Jong
1971–3 Barend W Biesheuvel
1973–7 Joop M den Uyl
1977–82 Andreas A M van Agt
1982–94 Rudd Lubbers
1994–2002 Wim Kok
2002– Jan-Peter Balkenende

weapon, a nuclear munition small enough to be used on the battlefield, fired as an artillery shell or short-range missile warhead, which on detonation produces radiation effects rather than blast and heat. The destructive effect is therefore aimed against living things rather than vehicles and buildings.

neutron star A star that has collapsed so far under gravity that it consists almost entirely of neutrons. Stars of more than 1·5 solar masses shrink until pressure between the neutrons balances the inward pull of gravity. They are observed as pulsars.

Nevada [nevahda] pop (2000e) 1 998 300; area 286 341 km²/

110 561 sq mi. State in W USA; the 'Sage Brush State', 'Battle Born State', or 'Silver State'; part ceded by Mexico to the USA in the Treaty of Guadalupe Hidalgo, 1848; separate territory, 1861; joined the Union as the 36th state, 1864; highest point Boundary Peak (4006 m/13 143 ft); mainly within the Great Basin, a large arid desert interspersed with barren mountain ranges; capital, Carson City; the driest of all the states; mostly unpopulated and uncultivated, with a few oases of irrigation; Hoover Dam creates L Mead; mining (mercury, barite, and several other minerals); a major gold supplier; oil discovered, 1954; agriculture not highly developed; tourism, notably Death Valley National Monument (partly in Nevada), and the gambling resorts of Las Vegas and Reno (gaming taxes a primary source of state revenue); very rapid population growth (50% increase between 1980 and 1990).

Nevado (mountain) *Ampato / Illampu / Ruiz / Salcantay, Nevado (de/del)*

Never Never Land Area of Northern Territory, Australia, SE of Darwin; featured in Mrs Aeneas Gunn's book, *We of the Never Never* (1908).

nevus *birthmark*

New Age A period of time recognized as our Solar System passes through one sign of the Zodiac to the next. It takes c.2000 years to travel through each star sign, each of which constitutes an 'age'. The Piscean age (represented by water) started with the beginning of the Roman Empire, and we entered the new age of Aquarius (an air sign) in 1997. In the early 1990s, various groups of people united chiefly by their unattached lifestyle came to be called 'new age travellers' by the UK media.

New Amsterdam *New York City*

Newark (UK) [nyooah(r)k], properly **Newark-on-Trent** 53°05N 0°49W, pop (2000e) 33 400. Town in Nottinghamshire, England; railway; Newark Castle place of King John's death.

Newark (USA) [nyooerk], locally [nooerk] 40°44N 74°10W, pop (2000e) 273 500. Largest city in NE New Jersey, USA; port on Newark Bay; an important road, rail, and air centre; settled by Puritans from Connecticut, 1666; city status, 1836; airport; railway; university (1934); cathedral; insurance and financial centre; linked to New York City by underground rail.

Newbery, John (1713–67) Publisher and bookseller, born in Berkshire. He was the first to publish books specifically for children, and was part-author of some of the best of them, notably *Goody Two-Shoes*. Since 1922 the **Newbery Medal** has been awarded annually for the best American children's book.

New Britain, formerly **Neu-Pommern** pop (2000e) 318 000; area 37 800 km²/14 600 sq mi. Largest island of the Bismarck Archipelago, Papua New Guinea; length, 480 km/298 mi; width, 80 km/50 mi; capital, Rabaul.

New Brunswick pop (2000e) 810 200; area 73 440 km²/28 355 sq mi. Province in E Canada; capital, Fredericton; forested, rocky land, generally low-lying, rising in the NW; several rivers and lakes; first settled by French fur traders; 'Acadia' ceded to Britain by the Treaty of Utrecht, 1713; many United Empire Loyalist immigrants, and separation from Nova Scotia, 1783; joined confederation, 1867; governed by a lieutenant-governor and Legislative Assembly.

Newbury 51°25N 1°20W, pop (2001e) 34 800. Town in W Berkshire, S England, UK; on R Kennet, 27 km/17 mi SW of Reading; two English Civil War battles fought here (1643, 1644); racecourse; Greenham Common nearby; controversial by-pass opened, 1998; Vodafone headquarters.

New Caledonia, Fr **Nouvelle Calédonie** pop (2000e) 200 500; area 18 575 km²/7170 sq mi. Territory in the SW Pacific Ocean, 1100 km/680 mi E of Australia, comprising New Caledonia, Loyalty Is, Isle des Pins, Isle Bélep, and the uninhabited Chesterfield and Huon Is; capital, Nouméa; timezone GMT +11; chief ethnic groups, Melanesians (43%), Europeans (37%); chief religion,

Roman Catholicism; official language, French, with English widely spoken; unit of currency, the French Pacific franc; long, narrow main island, 400 km/250 mi in length; rises to 1639 m/5377 ft at Mt Panie; C mountain chain; mild Mediterranean-type climate; warm and humid; visited by Captain Cook, 1774; annexed by France as a penal settlement, 1853; French Overseas Territory, 1946; governed by a high commissioner and Territorial Council; serious disturbances in the mid-1980s when indigenous Melanesians began their struggle for independence; decision to stay part of France after referendum of voters, 1987; agreement (Noumea Accord, 1998) provides for referendum on independence within 15–20 years, and gradual transfer of powers; nickel (world's third largest producer).

Newcastle (Australia) [nyookahsl] 32°55S 151°46E, pop (2000e) 472 300. City and major port in New South Wales, Australia, on the E coast; founded as a penal settlement, 1804; scene of Australia's biggest earthquake (1989); airfield; railway; university (1965).

Newcastle (UK) [nyookahsl], locally [nyookasl], in full **Newcastle upon Tyne**, Lat **Pons Aelii** 54°59N 1°35W, pop (2001e) 259 600. Administrative centre of Tyne and Wear, NE England; on R Tyne; cultural, commercial, and administrative centre for the NE of England; founded 11th-c; city status 1882; railway; underground; ferries to N Europe; two universities (1963, 1992); two cathedrals (15th-c, 1844); 12th-c castle keep; football league team, Newcastle United (Magpies).

Newcastle, Duke of *Cavendish, William; Pelham, Thomas*

Newcastle disease *fowl pest*

Newcomen, Thomas [nyookuhmen] (1663–1729) Inventor, born in Dartmouth, Devon. By 1698 he had invented the atmospheric steam engine, and from 1712 this device was being used for pumping water out of mines.

New Criticism A critical theory which concentrates on the text itself, the 'words on the page', to the exclusion of extrinsic information. It was developed by such critics as Cleanth Brooks (1906–94) and John Crowe Ransom (1888–1974) in the USA in the 1930s and 1940s, and in its turn provided a basis for the technique of *practical criticism*.

New Deal The administration and policies of US President Roosevelt, who pledged a 'new deal' for the country during the campaign of 1932. He embarked on active state economic involvement to combat the Great Depression. Historians often distinguish the **first New Deal** (1933–4), concerned primarily with restarting and stabilizing the economy, from the **second New Deal** (1935–9), aimed at social reform.

New Delhi *Delhi*

New Democratic Party (NDP) A Canadian political party which succeeded the Co-operative Commonwealth Federation as Canada's social democratic political party in 1961. Formally supported by the Canadian Labour Congress, the NDP has formed provincial governments in several provinces, but never risen above third party status nationally.

New English Bible An English translation of the Bible from the original languages undertaken by an interdenominational committee of scholars under the auspices of the University Presses of Cambridge and Oxford since 1948. The first edition of the New Testament was completed in 1961, and the first complete Bible was produced in 1970. It was substantially revised in 1989 under the title of the **Revised English Bible**.

New Forest An area of heath, woodland, and marsh covering c.37 300 ha/92 200 acres of S Hampshire, England; a popular tourist area. William the Conqueror appropriated the area for his new 'forest' (royal hunting land) in 1079. Administered by 10 Verderers, it was designated a national park in 2005.

New Forest pony A breed of horse, developed naturally in the New Forest, Hampshire, England; classed as two types: **Type A** (height, 12–13·2 hands/1·2–1·4 m/4 ft–4 ft 6 in) and the more solid **Type B** (height, 13·2–14·2 hands/1·4–1·5 m/4 ft 6 in–4 ft 10 in).

Newfoundland (Canada) [**nyoof**nland] pop (2000e) 636 200; area 405 720 km²/156 648 sq mi. Province in E Canada, consisting of the island of Newfoundland and the coast of Labrador, separated by the Strait of Belle Isle; capital, St John's; a roughly triangular island, rising to 814 m/2671 ft (W); mainly a rolling plateau with low hills; Vikings visited Labrador AD c.1000; coastline explored by Cabot, 1497; British sovereignty declared, 1583 (Britain's first colony); self-governing colony, 1855; voted to unite with Canada, 1949; governed by a lieutenant-governor and a House of Assembly.

Newfoundland (zoology) [**nyoof**nland] A breed of dog, developed in Newfoundland; large, very thick-set, with an enormous heavy head; broad deep muzzle and small ears and eyes; very thick, black, double-layered, water-resistant coat; webbed feet.

Newfoundland and Labrador (Canada) *Labrador; Newfoundland*

New France North American colonies claimed by France from the 16th-c, including Canada, Acadia, and Louisiana. Canada and Acadia were lost to the British incrementally up to 1763; Louisiana was sold to the USA in 1803.

New Frontier The administration and policies of US President Kennedy (1961–3). It was characterized by a high international profile and a liberal domestic stance.

Newgate From the 13th-c to 1902, the main prison of the City of London, whence many convicted criminals were taken to Tyburn for hanging.

New General Catalogue (NGC) An astronomical catalogue published in 1888 by J L E Dreyer, Armagh Observatory, Northern Ireland, listing 7840 nebulae, galaxies, and clusters.

New Granada, Span **Nueva Granada** The official name in the Spanish-American Empire for the area now covered by the Republic of Colombia.

New Grange A megalithic passage grave of c.3200 BC in the Boyne R valley, Ireland. The ornament of the kerb, passage, and chamber is among Europe's finest prehistoric art.

New Guard In Australian history, an extreme right-wing organization formed in New South Wales in 1932. Its principal achievement was the disruption of the official opening of Sydney Harbour Bridge (1932). The Guard was defunct by 1935.

New Hampshire pop (2000e) 1 235 800; area 24 032 km²/9279 sq mi. State in NE USA; the 'Granite State'; explored by Champlain and Pring, 1603–5; ninth of the original 13 states to ratify the Federal Constitution, 1788; forested mountains in the N (White Mts), highest point Mt Washington (1917 m/6289 ft); S largely devoted to arable farming and grazing; capital, Concord; chief agricultural products dairy and greenhouse products, maple syrup, hay, apples, eggs; diverse manufacturing industries.

New Haven, formerly **Quinnipiac** (to 1640) 41°18N 72°55W, pop (2000e) 123 600. Port town in S Connecticut, USA; on Long Island Sound; founded by Puritans, 1638; joint capital of state with Hartford, 1701–1875; railway; Yale University (1701); diverse industrial development.

New Hebrides *Vanuatu*

New Horizons mission A mission to Pluto, launched by NASA on 19 January 2006, the first ever mission to the dwarf planet. Lifting off from Cape Canaveral, the spacecraft, propelled by an Atlas 5 rocket, began a 9-year journey to the planet where it will gather information on Pluto and its moons before continuing on to explore other objects in the outer Solar System. It made its rendevous with Jupiter in February 2007, and is due to arrive for its closest approach to Pluto in July 2015.

New Ireland, formerly **Neu-Mecklenburg** pop (2000e) 107 000; area 8647 km²/3338 sq mi. Second largest island in the Bismarck Archipelago, Papua New Guinea; length, 480 km/298 mi; average width, 24 km/15 mi; capital, Kavieng.

New Jersey pop (2000e) 8 414 300; area 20 168 km²/7787 sq mi. State in E USA; the 'Garden State'; one of the original states of the Union, third to ratify the Federal Constitution, 1787; colonized after the explorations of Verrazano (1524) and Hudson (1609); Appalachian Highlands fall down through Piedmont Plateau to low coastal plains, broken by ridges of the Palisades; highest peak Mt High Point (550 m/1804 ft); 40% of the land forested, mostly in the SE; capital, Trenton; NE highly industrialized and densely populated; the rest mainly arable and grazing; a major industrial and commercial area; many tourist centres.

New Jerusalem, Church of the A religious sect based on the teachings of the Swedish scientist and seer, Emanuel Swedenborg. Through visionary experiences he saw that a first dispensation of the Christian Church had ended and a new one was beginning, the 'New Jerusalem'. His first church was organized in London in 1783.

New Labour A movement in the UK Labour Party which accepts a policy of combining traditional socialist values with a concern to respond to the new ideals and aspirations of the individual. It is associated with the approach of Tony Blair, especially in his concern to develop a 'stakeholder economy', where each member of society has an interest in the state's economic progress. It involved a rethinking of several traditional principles, such as the rewriting of Clause Four of the Labour Party constitution, which had affirmed the commitment to common ownership of industry and services. Those who do not share these views are sometimes referred to as 'Old Labour'.

New Left A Neo-Marxist movement which espoused a more libertarian form of socialism compared to orthodox Marxism. The movement had some influence in the 1960s, particularly in student politics and in opposition to the Vietnam War, but it never became an effectively organized political force.

newly industrialized countries The formerly less developed countries which have built up considerable industrial production and exports over recent decades. This group includes the four 'Asian Tigers', Hong Kong, Singapore, South Korea, and Taiwan, and also countries such as China, India, Malaysia, and Thailand in Asia, and Brazil and Mexico in Latin America. They account for an increasing proportion of world trade.

Newman, John Henry, Cardinal (1801–90) Theologian, born in London. He became a vigorous member of the Oxford Movement, composing a number of its tracts. A convert to Catholicism in 1845, he joined the Oratorians, later publishing his spiritual autobiography, *Apologia pro vita sua* (1864). A moderate in the controversies of the Vatican Council, he was made a cardinal in 1879.

Newman, Paul (Leonard) (1925–) Film actor, born in Cleveland, OH. His good looks and rugged individualism have brought continued success in a wide range of parts, as in *Cool Hand Luke* (1967), *Butch Cassidy and the Sundance Kid* (1969), *The Sting* (1973), and *Road to Perdition* (2002). In addition to winning several Oscars, he was given an Honorary Academy Award in 1986.

Newman, Randy, popular name of **Randall Stuart Newman** (1943–) Singer and songwriter, born in Los Angeles, CA. He established himself as a major songwriter, with something of a cult following, before his debut vocal album *Randy Newman* (1968). Later albums included *Sail Away* (1972), *Little Criminals* (1978), *Land of Dreams* (1988), and *Bad Love* (1999), and among his film scores is *The Paper* (1994).

new mathematics A term used to denote mathematical topics introduced into the school curriculum later than other more traditional activities, and which are thus usually less familiar to parents and the general public. The actual mathematics is not in itself 'new'.

New Mexico pop (2000e) 1 819 000; area 314 914 km²/121 593 sq mi. State in SW USA; the 'Land of Enchantment'; first explored by the Spanish in the early 1500s; first white settlement at Santa Fe, 1609; governed by Mexico from 1821; ceded to the USA in the Treaty of Guadalupe Hidalgo, 1848; organized as a territory (1850), including Arizona and part of Colorado; admitted to the Union as the 47th state, 1912; over a third of the population Hispanic; highest point Wheeler Peak (4011 m/ 13 160 ft); mainly broad deserts, forested mountain wildernesses, and towering barren peaks; forests mainly in the SW and N; mostly semi-arid plain with little rainfall; capital, Santa Fe; farming in the well-irrigated valley of the Rio Grande; nation's chief producer of uranium, potash, perlite; tourism important (warm, dry climate and striking scenery); several military establishments and atomic energy centres; Los Alamos atomic research centre built, 1943; first atomic bomb explosion at White Sands, 1945; several mountain Indian reservations.

New Model Army An English army established by Parliament (1645) to strengthen the Roundheads' forces in the Civil War against the Royalists. The county and regional armies of Essex, Manchester, and Waller were merged into a successful national force.

New Netherland A Dutch colony in the valley of the Hudson R. The first settlement was Fort Orange (Albany), founded in 1617, Nieuw Amsterdam followed in 1624; it was conquered by the English and named New York in 1664.

New Orleans [aw(r)leenz] 29°58N 90°04W, pop (2000e) 407 000; following Hurricane Katrina, c.200 000. City in SE Louisiana, USA; 'Crescent City', located on a bend in the Mississippi; founded by the French, 1718; capital of French Louisiana, 1722; ceded to Spain, 1763; passed to the US in the Louisiana Purchase 1803; French influence still evident today; prospered in the 19th-c as a market for slaves and cotton; gained a lasting reputation for glamour and wild living; industrial growth in the 20th-c after the discovery of oil and natural gas in the region; New Orleans musicians contributed to the early development of jazz, late 19th-c; airport; railway; streetcar system (1835); five universities; cathedral; oil and petrochemical industries; shipbuilding yards; professional team, Saints (football); French Quarter; Mardi Gras (Feb–Mar); severely damaged by Hurricane Katrina, 2005.

Newport (Isle of Wight) 50°42N 1°18W, pop (2000e) 21 800. River port, market town, and administrative centre of Isle of Wight, S England; on the R Medina; Parkhurst prison nearby; 12th-c Carisbrooke Castle.

Newport (Rhode Island) 41°29N 71°19W, pop (2000e) 26 500. Port in SE Rhode Island, USA; settled, 1639; city status, 1853; haven for religious groups; railway; several US Navy establishments; Newport Jazz Festival held here, 1954–71; yachting (including America's Cup races).

Newport (Wales), Welsh **Casnewydd** pop (2001e) 137 000; area 191 km²/74 sq mi. County (unitary authority from 1996) in SE Wales, UK; administrative centre, Newport, on R Usk; steel, aluminium, electronics, chemicals, market gardening; Roman fort at Caerleon.

New Providence pop (2000e) 199 000; area 207 km²/80 sq mi. Island in the NC Bahamas; length 32 km/20 mi; capital, Nassau; airport; popular tourist resort.

New Right A wide-ranging ideological movement associated with the revival of conservatism in the 1970s and 1980s, particularly in the UK and USA. It is strongly in favour of state withdrawal from ownership, and a free-enterprise system. There is also a strong moral conservatism – an emphasis on respect for authority, combined with a strong expression of patriotism and support for the idea of the family. In the USA it has been associated with the emergence of Christian fundamentalism.

New River Gorge Bridge Longest single arch steel span bridge in the world, on the New River N of Fayetteville, West Virginia; length 923 m/3030 ft; arch span 518 m/1700 ft; height 267 m/ 876 ft; completed in 1977.

New Ross, Ir **Baile Nua** 52°24N 6°56W, pop (2000e) 6100. Mediaeval town and river port in Wexford county, SE Ireland; home of the Kennedy family in Dunganstown, 8 km/5 mi S.

news agency An organization providing a general or specialized news service. Agencies range from large, publicly-quoted companies (eg Reuters) and state-owned concerns (eg Xinhua) to small private operations.

newsgroup *USENET*

New Siberian Islands, Russ **Novosibirskiye Ostrova** area 28 250 km²/10 900 sq mi. Uninhabited archipelago in the Arctic Ocean; rises to 374 m/1227 ft.

New South Wales pop (2000e) 6 333 000; area 801 428 km²/ 309 400 sq mi. State in SE Australia; first British colony, named by Captain Cook, who landed at Botany Bay, 1770; first settlement at Sydney, 1788; coastal lowlands give way to tablelands, formed by the Great Dividing Range (highest point Mt Kosciuszko, 2228 m/7310 ft); fertile irrigated plains further W comprise two-thirds of the state; capital, Sydney; the most populous and most heavily industrialized state in Australia.

New Spain, Span **Nueva España** The formal title of the Spanish viceroyalty covering the area of modern Mexico.

newspaper A regularly published account of recent events. Modern newspapers are printed, usually by offset lithography, on large sheets, folded once and inserted one within another, and published at daily, weekly, or (occasionally) monthly frequencies. The modern newspaper can be traced back to the British publications, the *Corante* (1621) and *Weekly Newes* (1622). The first daily paper was the *Daily Courant* (1702), and the first true evening paper the *Courier* (1792). Technical developments include mechanized metal typesetting, photoengraved illustrations, phototypesetting, offset lithography, and facsimile transmission of text and pictures. The revolution in news gathering and editorial preparation has equalled the technical advances. In the mid-2000s, c.18 000 newspapers were being published around the world, with over 200 million printed daily.

New Style date The dating system which followed the adoption of the Gregorian calendar by Great Britain and its American colonies (14 Sep 1752); previous dates are referred to as **Old Style** dates. The new system eliminated 11 days to get in step with Europe, and moved the day on which the count of years changes from the Feast of the Annunciation (25 Mar) back to 1 January.

New Sweden A Swedish colony, founded at Fort Christina (Wilmington) on the Delaware R in 1633, with Dutch investment and involvement. It was absorbed by New Netherland in 1655.

newt An amphibian of order Urodela; breeds in water; young (called the *eft* stage) live on land for 1–7 years. (Family: Salamandridae.)

New Territories area 950 km²/367 sq mi. Region of Hong Kong; includes part of the mainland and over 200 islands.

New Testament Along with the Old Testament, the sacred literature of Christianity. It is called 'New Testament' because its writings are believed to represent a new covenant of God with his people, centred on the person and work of Jesus Christ, as distinct from the old covenant with Israel which is described in the 'Old Testament'. The 27 New Testament writings were originally composed in Greek, mainly in the 1st-c AD, unlike the Old Testament writings which are primarily in Hebrew and from earlier centuries.

Newton, Sir Isaac (1642–1727) Physicist and mathematician, born in Woolsthorpe, Lincolnshire. In 1665–6 the fall of an apple is said to have suggested the train of thought that led to the law of gravitation. He studied the nature of light, and devised the first reflecting telescope. His *Philosophiae naturalis principia mathematica* (1687, Mathematical Principles of Natural Philosophy) established him as the greatest of all physical scientists. He was appointed master of the Mint from 1699 till the end of his life, and he also sat in parliament on two occasions. During his life he was involved in many controversies, notably with Leibniz over the question of priority in the discovery of calculus.

newton SI unit of force; symbol N; named after Isaac Newton; defined as the force which causes an acceleration of 1 m/s^2 for an object of mass 1 kg.

Newton's laws The basic expression of Newtonian mechanics; formulated in 1687 by Isaac Newton. *First law*: the velocity of an object does not change unless a force acts on it. *Second law*: a force F applied to an object of mass m causes an acceleration a according to $F = ma$. *Third law*: every action has an equal and opposite reaction.

new town A British solution to problems of city growth: a planned, self-contained settlement designed to relieve urban congestion. Dating from the 1946 New Towns Act, 14 were designated between 1947 and 1950, and seven more since then. Examples include Cumbernauld, Cwmbran, Harlow, and Milton Keynes.

new universities Universities built to accommodate the expanding numbers entering higher education in Britain during the post-war period: Keele (1949); Sussex (1961); Essex (1961); York (1963); Lancaster (1964); East Anglia (1964); Kent (1965); Warwick (1965); Stirling (1967); Open (1969). The term has also come to be applied to polytechnics in Britain which acquired university status in 1992.

New Wave *Nouvelle Vague*

New World monkey A monkey inhabiting Central and South America; nostrils wide apart and opening to the side (unlike Old World monkeys); some species with prehensile (grasping) tails. (Family: Cebidae, 32 species.)

New Year's Day The first day of the year (1 Jan) in countries using the Gregorian calendar. Communities using other calendars celebrate New Year on other dates: the Jewish New Year, for example, is Rosh Hashanah (1 Tishri), which falls in September or October.

New York (state) pop (2000e) 18 976 500; area 127 185 km²/ 49 108 sq mi. State in NE USA; the 'Empire State'; second most populous state; one of the original states of the Union, 11th to ratify the Federal Constitution, 1788; explored by Hudson and Champlain, 1609; Dutch established posts near Albany, 1614, settled Manhattan, 1626; New Netherlands taken by the British, 1664; Adirondack Mts rise in the N, Catskill Mts in the S; highest point, Mt Marcy (1629 m/5344 ft); state contains 11 334 km²/4375 sq mi of the Great Lakes; extensive woodland and forest in the NE, elsewhere a mixture of cropland, pasture, and woodland; capital, Albany; New York City the chief ethnically mixed centre of population in the USA.

New York City or **New York** 40°43N 74°00W, pop (2000e) 8 008 300. Largest city in the USA and largest port, at the mouth of the Hudson R; with 1200 km/750 mi of waterfront; trading post established in 1624 by Henry Hudson; colonized by the Dutch and named New Amsterdam 1625; captured by the British in 1664 and named New York after the king's brother, the Duke of York; Washington inaugurated here as first US president; rapid commercial and industrial growth after the opening of the Erie Canal, 1825; divided into five boroughs – Bronx (Bronx Co), Brooklyn (Kings Co), Manhattan (New York Co), Queens (Queens Co), Staten Island (Richmond Co); eight universities; railway; two airports; major world financial centre, with Stock Exchange in Wall Street; professional teams, Mets, Yankees (baseball), Knickerbockers (basketball), Giants, Jets (football), Islanders, Rangers (ice hockey); the country's centre for fashion, arts, and entertainment, with many museums and galleries; Central Park. A New York landmark, the World Trade Center, collapsed after two aircraft were deliberately flown at the 1360-ft twin towers in a terrorist attack on 11 September 2001.

New York City Ballet Resident ballet company of the New York State Theater at the Lincoln Center for the Performing Arts and the Saratoga Performing Arts Center, both in New York, USA. First named the **Ballet Company**, it was founded in 1946 by George Balanchine and Lincoln Kirstein as a private subscription organization. In 1948 it was renamed the New York City Ballet, and in 1964 it moved to its present home.

New Zealand *p.656*

Ney, Michel, duc d' (Duke of) Elchingen [nay] (1769–1815) French marshal, born in Saarlouis, France. He distinguished himself at Jena (1806), Eylau, and Friedland (1807), and commanded the third corps of the Grand Army in the Russian campaign (1813), for which he received the title of Prince of Moskowa. He accepted the Bourbon restoration, but deserted to Napoleon, and led the centre at Waterloo. He was condemned for high treason, and shot in Paris.

Ngorongoro Crater [nggohronggohroh] Crater in N Tanzania, in the Rift Valley; its rim is at an altitude of c.2100 m/6900 ft, and its floor lies c.600 m/2000 ft below this level; area, c.260 km²/ 100 sq mi; centre of a conservation region, and a world heritage site.

Nguni [ngoonee] A cluster of Bantu-speaking peoples of S Africa. The main groups today include the Zulu, Swazi, and Xhosa of South Africa and Swaziland; the Ndebele of Zimbabwe; and the Ngoni of Zambia, Malawi, and Tanzania.

nhandu *rhea* (ornithology)

niacin *nicotinic acid*

Niagara Falls Two waterfalls in W New York, USA and S Ontario, Canada; between L Erie and L Ontario, on the international border; American Falls 55·5 m/182 ft high, 328 m/1076 ft wide; Canadian Falls, known as Horseshoe Falls, 54 m/177 ft high, 640 m/2100 ft wide; world-famous tourist attraction since early 19th-c; twin resort towns of Niagara Falls in New York (visited by Louis Hennepin 1678) and Ontario; scene of many daredevil exploits, such as the tightrope crossing by Blondin (1859).

Niamey [neeamay] 13°32N 2°05E, pop (2000e) 569 000. River-port capital of Niger; airport; railway terminus; university (1971).

Niarchos, Stavros (Spyros) [nyah(r)khos] (1909–96) Shipowner, born in Athens. He became the controller of one of the largest independent fleets in the world, pioneering the construction of supertankers.

Nias [neeas] Island in the Indian Ocean, 125 km/78 mi off the W coast of Sumatra, Indonesia; 240 km/159 mi long by 80 km/ 50 mi wide; airfield; chief town, Gunungsitoli; severely damaged by earthquake, Mar 2005.

Nibelungen [neebelungen] In mediaeval German legends, a race of dwarfs who live in Norway and possess a famous treasure. The *Nibelungenlied* recounts how Siegfried obtained the treasure and his later misfortunes.

Nicaea, Council of [niyseea] **1** (325) The first ecumenical Council of the Church, called by Emperor Constantine to settle the doctrinal dispute between the Arians and the Orthodox on the person of Christ.

2 (787) A Council of the Church called to deal with the question of the veneration of images.

NICAM An acronym for **near instantaneously companded** [ie compressed and expanded] **audio multiplex**, a digital system

New Zealand

North Cape

AUSTRALIA

Whangarei

Auckland

Hamilton
Waikato

*North
Island*

300 km

150 mi

L. Taupo

△2   △1

T A S M A N
S E A

Wanganui • Napier

Palmerston North

■ **Wellington**

Nelson

*South
Island*

**N E W
Z E A L A N D**

Mt Cook △
3753 m

■ Christchurch

Bank's Peninsula

Queenstown

Timaru

*S O U T H
P A C I F I C
O C E A N*

*Lake
Wakatipu*

Dunedin

Invercargill

Stewart I

Key
1. Mt Ruapehu 2797m
2. Mt Egmont 2158m

☐ International Airport

Maori **Aotearoa**

Local name Aotearoa (Maori)

Timezone GMT +12

Area 268 812 km²/103 761 sq mi

Population total (2002e) 3 893 000

Status Independent member of the Commonwealth

Date of independence 1947

Capital Wellington

Languages English and Maori (official)

Ethnic groups European (mainly British, Australian and Dutch) (87%), Maori (9%)

Religions Christian (59%) (Anglican 25%, Presbyterian 18%, Roman Catholic 16%)

Physical features Consists of two principal islands (North and South) separated by the Cook Strait, and several minor islands; North Island mountainous in the centre with many hot springs; peaks rise to 2797 m/9176 ft at Mt Ruapehu; South Island mountainous for its whole length, rising in the Southern Alps to 3753 m/12 313 ft at Mt Cook, New Zealand's highest point; many glaciers and mountain lakes; largest area of level lowland is the Canterbury Plain, E side of South Island; L Taupo, largest natural lake, occupies an ancient volcanic crater; major lakes include Te Anau and Wakatipu.

Climate Cool, temperate climate, almost subtropical in extreme N; Mean temperature range, 18°C in N, 9°C in S; lower tempera-

tures in South Island; highly changeable weather, all months moderately wet; average daily temperature 16–23°C (Jan), 8–13°C (Jul) in Auckland; average annual rainfall 1053 mm/41 in; subject to periodic sub-tropical cyclones.

Currency 1 New Zealand Dollar (NZD) = 100 cents

Economy Farming, especially sheep and cattle; one of the world's major exporters of dairy produce; third largest exporter of wool; kiwi fruit, venison; textiles; timber, food processing; substantial coal and natural gas reserves; hydroelectric power; tourism.

GDP (2002e) $78·4 bn, per capita $20 100

Human Development Index (2002) 0·917

History Settled by Maoris from E Polynesia by c.1000 AD; first European sighting by Abel Tasman in 1642, named Staten Landt; later known as Nieuw Zeeland, after the Dutch Province; visited by Captain Cook, 1769; first European settlement, 1792; dependency of New South Wales until 1840; annexed by Britain 1840; outbreaks of war between immigrants and Maoris, 1860–70; Dominion of New Zealand, 1907; independent within the Commonwealth, 1947; governed by a Prime Minister, a Cabinet and a unicameral, 97-member House of Representatives; elections every 3 years.

Head of State

(British monarch represented by Governor-General)
1996–2001 Michael Hardie Boys
2001–6 Dame Silvia Cartwright
2006– Anand Satyanand

Head of Government

1906 William Hall-Jones *Lib*
1906–12 Joseph George Ward *Lib/Nat*
1912 Thomas Mackenzie *Nat*
1912–25 William Ferguson Massey *Ref*
1925 Francis Henry Dillon Bell *Ref*
1925–8 Joseph Gordon Coates *Ref*
1928–30 Joseph George Ward *Lib/Nat*
1930–5 George William Forbes *Un*
1935–40 Michael Joseph Savage *Lab*
1940–9 Peter Fraser *Lab*
1949–57 Sidney George Holland *Nat*
1957 Keith Jacka Holyoake *Nat*
1957–60 Walter Nash *Lab*
1960–72 Keith Jacka Holyoake *Nat*
1972 John Ross Marshall *Nat*
1972–4 Norman Eric Kirk *Lab*
1974–5 Wallace Edward Rowling *Lab*
1975–84 Robert David Muldoon *Nat*
1984–9 David Russell Lange *Lab*
1989–90 Geoffrey Palmer *Lab*
1990 Michael Kenneth Moore *Lab*
1990–7 James Brendan Bolger *Nat*
1997–9 Jenny Shipley *Nat*
1999– Helen Clark *Lab*

Lab Labour *Ref* Reform *Lib* Liberal *Un* United *Nat* National

Overseas territories

Name / Area (km²/sq mi) / Capital / Population
Cook Islands / 238/92 / Avarua / (2002e) 18 000
Niue / 263/101 / Alofi / (2002e) 2000
Ross Dependency / 413 550 /159 600 / uninhabited
Tokelau / 10/4 / Nukunonu / (2002e) 2000

used in television transmissions which provides high-quality stereophonic sound. First used by the BBC in 1986, it is now found in several other countries. A decoder attached to a television set enables the viewer to receive stereo sound along with any television programme which has recorded it.

Nicaragua p.657

Nice [nees], Ital **Nizza**, ancient **Nicaea** 43°42N 7°14E, pop (2000e) 358 000. Fashionable coastal resort in SE France; fifth largest city in France; airport; railway; university (1965); cathedral (1650); leading tourist centre; palm-lined Promenade des Anglais.

Nicaragua

□ International Airport

[nikaragwa], official name **Republic of Nicaragua**, Span **República de Nicaragua**

Local name Nicaragua

Timezone GMT -6

Area 148 000 km²/57 128 sq mi

Population total (2002e) 5 024 000

Status Republic

Date of independence 1821

Capital Managua

Languages Spanish (official), indigenous Indian languages and English (creole-English)

Ethnic groups Mestizo (69%), white (17%), black (9%), Indian (Sumu, Mikito, Ramaguie peoples) (5%)

Religions Roman Catholic (95%), Protestant (5%)

Physical features Mountainous W half, with volcanic ranges rising to over 2000 m/6500 ft (NW); two large lakes, L Nicaragua and L Managua, behind the coastal mountain range; rolling uplands and forested plains to the E; many short rivers flow into the Pacific Ocean and the lakes.

Climate Tropical climate; average annual temperatures, 26°C (Jan), 30°C (Jul) at Managua; rainy season (May–Nov), high humidity; average annual rainfall 1140 mm/45 in; country devastated by hurricane Mitch in 1998.

Currency 1 New Córdoba (NIC) = 100 centavos

Economy Agriculture (accounts for over two-thirds of total exports); cotton, coffee, sugar cane, rice, corn, tobacco; oil, natural gas. Gold, silver, chemicals, textiles.

GDP (2002e) $11·16 bn, per capita $2200

Human Development Index (2002) 0·635

History Colonized by Spaniards, early 16th-c; independence from Spain, 1821; left the Federation of Central America in 1838; dictatorship under Anastasio Somoza, 1938; Sandinista National Liberation Front seized power in 1979, and established a socialist junta of national reconstruction; under the 1987 constitution (revised in 1994), a President and a Constituent Assembly are elected for 6-year terms; former supporters of the Somoza government (the Contras), based in Honduras and supported by the USA, carried out guerrilla activities against the junta from 1979; ceasefire and disarmament agreed in 1990.

Head of State/Government

1950–6 Anastasio Somoza García
1956–63 Luis Somoza Debayle
1963–6 René Schick Gutiérrez
1966–7 Lorenzo Guerrero Gutiérrez
1967–72 Anastasio Somoza Debayle
1972–4 *Triumvirate*
1974–9 Anastasio Somoza Debayle
1979–84 *Government junta of National Reconstruction*
1984–90 Daniel Ortega Saavedra
1990–6 Violeta Barrios de Chamorro
1996–2001 Arnoldo Aleman Lacayo
2001–6 Enrique Bolaños Geyer
2006– Daniel Ortega

Nicene Creed [niyseen] An expanded formal statement of Christian belief, based on the creed of the first Council of Nicaea (325). It is still publicly recited in Eucharistic liturgies.

Nichiren Buddhism [nichiren] A sect founded by the Japanese Buddhist reformer Nichiren (1222–82); sometimes called the **Lotus** sect, because of his claim that the Lotus Sutra contained the ultimate truth.

Nicholas II (1868–1918) The last tsar of Russia (1895–1917), born near St Petersburg, Russia. He took command of the Russian armies against the Central Powers in 1915. Forced to abdicate at the Revolution, he was executed with his family at Ekaterinburg. The Russian Orthodox Church bestowed sainthood on Nicholas, his wife and five children in 2000.

Nicholas, St (4th-c) Bishop of Myra, Lucia, and patron saint of Russia. He is the patron of youth, merchants, sailors, travellers, and thieves. His identification with Father Christmas began in Europe, and spread to America, where the name was altered to *Santa Claus*. The tradition of exchanging gifts on Christmas Day derives from a legend of his benevolence. Feast day 6 December.

Nicholas or **Nicolaus of Cusa** [kyooza] (1401–64) Cardinal and philosopher, born in Cusa, Germany. A Renaissance scientist in advance of his time, he wrote on astronomy, mathematics, philosophy, and biology.

Nicholson, Ben (1894–1982) Artist, born in Denham, Buckinghamshire. Although he produced several purely geometrical paintings and reliefs, he generally used as a starting point conventional still-life objects. His second wife was Barbara Hepworth.

Nicholson, Jack (1937–) Film actor, scriptwriter, and director, born in Neptune, NJ. He has created a versatile range of anti-heroes, winning Oscars for *One Flew over the Cuckoo's Nest* (1975), *Terms of Endearment* (1984), and *As Good As It Gets* (1997). Other films include *The Shining* (1980), *The Witches of Eastwick* (1986), *Batman* (1989), *About Schmidt* (2002, Golden Globe; Oscar nomination), and *The Departed* (2006).

nickel Ni, element 28, density 8 g/cm³, melting point 1450°C. A silvery metal, most commonly obtained from pentlandite, a complex sulphide of nickel and iron. The metal forms a protective oxide coating, is used in coinage and cutlery, and is an ingredient of many stainless steels.

Nicklaus, Jack (William) [niklows] (1940–) Golfer, born in Columbus, OH. He has won all the world's major tournaments: the (British) Open (1966, 1970, 1978), the US Open (1962, 1967, 1972, 1980), the US Professional Golfers Association tournament a record-equalling five times (1963, 1971, 1973, 1975, 1980), and the US Masters a record six times (1963, 1965–6, 1972, 1975, 1986). His 18 professional majors is a world record. He retired from professional golf in 2005.

Nicobar Islands *Andaman and Nicobar Islands*

Nicolai, (Carl) Otto (Ehrenfried) [nikoliy] (1810–49) Composer and conductor, born in Königsberg, Prussia (now Kaliningrad, Russia). His opera *The Merry Wives of Windsor* was produced in Berlin just before his death.

Nicolaus *Nicholas of Cusa*

Nicomedia [niykohmeedia] In antiquity, the capital first of the kingdom and then of the Roman province of Bithynia. Under Emperor Diocletian (AD 284–316), it was the capital of the E half of the Roman Empire.

Nicosia [nikoseea], proposed new name **Lefkosia** (1995), Gr **Levkosia**, Turkish **Lefkosa**, ancient **Ledra** 35°11N 33°23E, pop (2000e) 187 300. Capital city of Republic of Cyprus; on R Pedias; capital since 12th-c; 'Green Line' divides the city into northern (Turkish) and southern (Greek) sectors; agricultural trade centre; old city surrounded by Venetian-built walls (late 16th-c); technical institute (1968); cathedral.

nicotine $C_{10}H_{14}N_2$. An alkaloid derived from pyridine, found in the leaves of the tobacco plant. It is a poisonous and addictive material, usually indulged in for its relaxing properties.

nicotinic acid A B vitamin found usually in plants and animals, important in the production of energy inside cells. It generally exists in the form of **nicotinamide**. In cereals, nicotinic acid is present as **niacytin**.

Niebuhr, Barthold Georg [neeboor] (1776–1831) Historian, born in Copenhagen. His main work, the *Römische Geschichte* (1811–32, History of Rome), marked him out as a founder of the 19th-c school of German historical scholarship.

Nielsen, Carl (August) [neelsen] (1865–1931) Composer, born in Nørre-Lyndelse, Denmark. He is particularly known for his six symphonies, and he also wrote concertos, choral and chamber music, the operas *Saul and David* (1902) and *Masquerade* (1906), and a huge organ work, *Commotio* (1931).

Niemöller, (Friedrich Gustav Emil) Martin [neemoeler] (1892–1984) Lutheran pastor, born in Lippstadt, Germany. He publicly opposed the Nazi regime, and was placed in concentration camps until 1945. He was then responsible for the 'Declaration of Guilt' by the German Churches for not opposing Hitler more strenuously.

Niepce, (Joseph) Nicéphore [nyeps] (1765–1833) Chemist, born in Chalon-sur-Saône, France. He succeeded in producing a permanent photographic image on metal (1822), said to be the world's first.

Nietzsche, Friedrich (Wilhelm) [neechuh] (1844–1900) Philosopher and critic, born in Röcken, Germany. He determined to give his age new values, Schopenhauer's 'will to power' serving as the basic principle. His major work, *Also sprach Zarathustra* (1883–5, Thus Spake Zarathustra) develops the idea of the 'overman'. Much of his esoteric doctrine appealed to the Nazis, and he was a major influence on existentialism.

Niger *p.659*

Niger, River [niyjer] River in W Africa; length c.4100 km/2550 mi; third longest river in Africa; rises 280 km/175 mi from the Atlantic coast; enters the Gulf of Guinea through a wide delta; first explored by Mungo Park, 1795–6.

Niger–Congo languages The largest language family in Africa, with 1000 languages spread over almost the entire continent S of the Sahara. It is usually divided into six sub-groups of languages: Adamawa-Eastern, Benue–Congo, Kwa, Mande, Voltaic, and West Atlantic. Among the important Niger–Congo languages are Igbo, Swahili, Wolof, Yoruba, and Zulu. The largest group is the Benue–Congo, which comprises c.700 languages; of these, c.500 belong to the *Bantu* group.

Nigeria *p.660*

night blindness Reduced ability to adapt to the dark and to see in dim light, resulting from deficiency of vitamin A (retinol). This vitamin is an essential component of rhodopsin, a retinal pigment responsible for colour vision.

Nightingale, Florence, known as **the Lady of the Lamp** (1820–1910) Hospital reformer, born in Florence, Italy. After the Battle of Alma (1854) she led a party of 38 nurses to organize a nursing department at Scutari, where she soon had 10 000 under her care. She was later involved in army sanitary reform, the improvement of nursing, and public health in India.

nightingale Either of two species of thrush of the genus *Luscinia*, native to Europe, Asia, and N Africa; mid-brown with paler breast; male renowned for its song; often sings at night. (Family: Turdidae.)

nightjar A nocturnal bird of the widespread family Caprimulgidae (c.70 species); mottled brown with short bill.

Night of the Long Knives The event which took place in Germany (29–30 Jun 1934) when the SS, on Hitler's orders, murdered Röhm and some 150 other leaders of the Sturmabteilung (SA 'storm troopers'). It has been estimated that up to 1000 of Hitler's political rivals were killed.

nightshade *deadly nightshade; woody nightshade*

Nighy, Bill [nye] (1949–) Actor, born in Caterham, Surrey. He studied at the Guildford School of Dance and Drama and later joined the National Theatre, where he met his long-time partner, actress **Diana Quick** (1946–). On television he gained recognition with his role in the drama series *The Men's Room* (1991), and later work includes *The Lost Prince* (2003), *State of Play* (2003, BAFTA Best Actor), and *Gideon's Daughter* (2006, Golden Globe Best Actor). Among his feature films are *Love Actually* (2003, BAFTA Best Supporting Actor), *The Constant Gardener* (2005), *Pirates of the Caribbean: Dead Man's Chest* (2006), and *Pirates of the Caribbean: At World's End* (2007).

nihilism (Lat, literally 'nothing-ism') A term invented by Turgenev in connection with his character, the revolutionary Bazarov, in *Fathers and Sons*, and later applied to other members of the Russian radical intelligentsia. It popularly denotes the disillusioned rejection of conventional moral values and institutions.

Niigata [neegata] 37°58N 139°02E, pop (2000e) 490 000. Port in N Honshu, Japan; airport; railway; three universities; leading producer of *sake* (rice wine); Niigata Stadium Big Swan (2001).

Nijinska, Bronislava [nizhinska] (1891–1972) Ballet dancer and choreographer, born in Minsk, Belarus, the sister of Vaslav Nijinsky. She danced with the Diaghilev company in Paris and London (1909–14), then joined Diaghilev in 1921 as principal choreographer. After 1938 she lived and worked mainly in the USA.

Nijinsky, Vaslav [nizhinskee] (1890–1950) Dancer, born in Kiev, brother of Bronislava Nijinska. Diaghilev encouraged his choreography, which foreshadowed the development of modern ballet. In 1913, his *Le sacre du printemps* (The Rite of Spring) was regarded as outrageous in its subversion of ballet and its use of Stravinsky's rhythmically complex score.

Nijmegen or **Nimeguen** [niymuhkhn, niymaygn], Ger **Nimwegen**, ancient **Noviomagus** 51°50N 5°52E, pop (2000e) 153 000. City in E Netherlands; on the R Waal, Roman fort, AD 69; former residence of the Carlovingian kings; member of the Hanseatic League; railway; university (1923).

Nijo-jo Castle [nijohjoh] A stronghold built in 1603 in Kyoto, Japan, by Tokugawa Ieyasu. The complex is set in fine landscaped gardens and surrounded by a moat.

Niger

□ International Airport   - - - - Disputed border

[niyjer], official name **Republic of Niger**, Fr **République du Niger**

Local name Niger

Timezone GMT +1

Area 1 267 000 km²/489 191 sq mi

Population total (2002e) 10 640 000

Status Republic

Date of independence 1960

Capital Niamey

Languages French (official) with Hausa, Songhai, Fulfulde, Tamashek, and Arabic widely spoken

Ethnic groups Hausa (54%), Djerma and Songhai (22%), Fulani (9%), Tuareg (8%), Beriberi (4%), Arab (2%)

Religions Muslim (80%), traditional beliefs and small Christian minority (primarily Roman Catholic) (20%)

Physical features Occupies S fringe of Sahara Desert, on a high plateau; Hamada Mangueni plateau (far N); Aïr Massif (C); Ténéré du Tafassasset desert (E); W Talk desert (C and N); water in quantity found only in the SW (R Niger) and SE (L Chad).

Climate One of the hottest countries in the world; average annual temperature 16°C (Jun-Oct), 41°C (Feb-May); rainy season in S (Jun-Oct); rainfall decreases N to almost negligible levels in desert areas; average annual rainfall at Niamey, 554 mm/22 in.

Currency 1 CFA Franc (XAF) = 100 centimes

Economy Dominated by agriculture and mining; production badly affected by severe drought conditions in 1970s; uranium, tin, phosphates, coal, salt, natron; building materials, textiles, food processing.

GDP (2002e) $8·713 bn, per capita $800

Human Development Index (2002) 0·277

History Occupied by the French, 1883–99; territory within French West Africa, 1904; independence, 1960; military coup, 1974; governed by a Higher Council for National Orientation led by a President who appoints a Council of Ministers; elected National Assembly, 1989; constitution suspended, 1991; multi-party constitution adopted, 1992; in 2005 international aid effort begun to help 2·5 million people in the S affected by famine.

Head of State
1993–6 Mahamane Ousmane
1996–9 Ibrahim Barre Mainassara
1999 Daouda Malam Wanke
1999– Mamadou Tandjo

Head of Government
1990–1 Aliou Mahamidou
1991–3 Amadou Cheiffou *Interim*
1993–4 Mahamoudou Issoufou
1994–5 Abdoulaye Souley
1995–6 Hama Amadou
1996 Boukary Adji
1996–7 Amadou Boubacar Cisse
1997–2000 Ibrahim Assane Mayaki
2000– Hama Amadou

Nike [niykee, neekay] The Greek goddess of Victory, either in war or in an athletic contest. She is the frequent subject of sculpture, often shown as a winged figure. The Roman equivalent was Victoria.

Nile, River *p.661*

Nile, Battle of the *Aboukir Bay, Battle of* 1

nilgai [nilgiy] An Indian spiral-horned antelope (*Boselaphus tragocamelus*), the largest Indian antelope; male bluish with short slightly curved horns, tuft of dark hairs on throat; female brown without horns; also known as **blue bull** or **bluebuck**.

Nilgiri Hills [neelgiree] Hills linking the Eastern Ghats with the Western Ghats, Tamil Nadu state, S India; highest point, Doda Betta (2636 m/8648 ft).

nimbostratus clouds [nimbohstratuhs] Dark-grey, rain-producing clouds of the stratus family. They are found at relatively low layers of the atmosphere, c.1000–3000 m/3000–9000 ft. Cloud symbol: Ns.

nimbus Another word for the halo, circular or square, which surrounds the heads of sacred persons in much religious art. It is common in Roman art, and was taken over by the early Christians.

nimbus clouds Clouds which produce rain or snow. For example,

cumulonimbus clouds form from convectional cooling and are associated with thunderstorms, while nimbostratus clouds give more or less continuous rain.

Nîmes [neem], ancient **Nismes** or **Nemausus** 43°50N 4°23E, pop (2000e) 134 000. Ancient town in S France; principal city of Roman Gaul; Protestant stronghold in 16th-c; airport; railway; bishopric; cathedral (11th-c); centre of silk industry (cloth 'de Nîmes', name later contracted to 'denim'); Roman buildings and monuments.

Nimitz, Chester W(illiam) [nimits] (1885–1966) US admiral, born in Fredericksburg, TX. In World War 2 he commanded the US Pacific Fleet, his conduct of naval operations being a major factor in the defeat of Japan.

Nimoy, Leonard [nimoy] (1931–) Actor, director, producer, and writer, born in Boston, MA. He came to be identified with the half-Vulcan/half-human character of Spock in the *Star Trek* series (1966–9). When the series was reprised as feature films (1979–91), he produced the third and fourth instalments, and scripted the fourth. His work as a director includes *Three Men and a Baby* (1987) and *Holy Matrimony* (1994).

Nimrod In the Table of Nations (*Gen* 10), purportedly the son of Cush and great-grandson of Noah. He was a legendary warrior

Nigeria

☐ International Airport · ---- Disputed border

official name **Federal Republic of Nigeria**

Local name Nigeria

Timezone GMT +1

Area 923 768 km²/356 669 sq mi

Population total (2002e) 129 935 000

Status Republic

Date of independence 1960

Capital Abuja

Languages English (official), Hausa, Yoruba, Ibo, and other Niger-Congo dialects widely used

Ethnic groups Over 250 tribal groups, notably Hausa and Fulani, Yoruba and Ibo (65%); Kanuri, Tiv, Edo, Nupe, and Ibidio (25%)

Religions Muslim (50%), Christian (34%), indigenous animist beliefs (10%)

Physical features Long, sandy shoreline with mangrove swamp, dominated by R Niger delta; undulating area of tropical rainforest and oil palm bush behind a coastal strip; open woodland and savannah further N; numerous rivers, notably the Niger and the Benue; Gotel Mts on SE frontier, highest point, Mt Vogel, 2024 m/6640 ft.

Climate Tropical; uniformly high temperatures; average annual temperatures 21–7°C (Jan), 25–6°C (Jul); dry season in the N (Oct–Apr); average annual rainfall 1836–2497 mm/54–98 in; subject to influence of the Saharan Harmattan in N.

Currency 1 Naira (NGN) = 100 kobos

Economy Oil (provides c.90% of exports); agriculture (employs 50% of population); palm oil, groundnuts, cotton, cassava, rice, sugar cane, tobacco; fishing, livestock, forestry; natural gas, tin, iron ore, columbite, tantalite, limestone; pulp, paper, textiles, rubber; locust swarms devastated crops in N (Aug 2004).

GDP (2002e) $112·5 bn, per capita $900

Human Development Index (2002) 0·462

History Centre of the Nok culture, 500 BC- AD 200; Muslim immigrants, 15th–16th-c; British colony at Lagos, 1861; protectorates of N and S Nigeria, 1900; amalgamated as the Colony and Protectorate of Nigeria, 1914; federation, 1954; independence, 1960; federal republic, 1963; military coup, 1966; E area formed Republic of Biafra, 1967; civil war, and surrender of Biafra, 1970; military coups 1983 and 1985; major civil and religious unrest, 1992; presidential elections held, then annulled, 1993; military coup, 1993; restoration of civilian rule, 1999; governed by a President, a 360-seat House of Representatives, and a 109-seat Senate.

Military Government
1966–75 Yakubu Gowon
1975–6 Murtala R Mohamed
1976–9 Olusegun Obasanjo

Head of State/Government
1979–83 Alhaji Shehu Shagari

Military Government
1985–93 Ibrahim B Babangida
1993 Ernest Adegunle Shonekan *Interim*
1993–8 Sani Abacha
1998–9 Abdusalam Abubakar

Head of State/Government
1999–2007 Olusegun Obasanjo
2007– Umaru Yar 'Adua

and hunter, allegedly one of the first to rule over a great empire after the Flood.

Nin, Anaïs [neen, anaees] (1903–77) Novelist and short-story writer, born in Neuilly, France. Her early work includes novels and short stories, but her reputation as an artist and seminal figure in the new feminism of the 1970s rests on her *Journals* (1966–83).

ninety-five theses A series of points of academic debate with the pope, posted by Martin Luther on the church door at Wittenberg in 1517. They attacked many practices of the Church, including indulgences and papal powers. This act is generally regarded as initiating the Protestant Reformation.

Nineveh [ninevuh] One of the most important cities of ancient Assyria, located E of the Tigris, and the site of royal residences from c.11th-c BC. It was at its height in the 8th–7th-c BC under Sennacherib, but fell in 612 BC to the Medes and Persians.

Ningbo or **Ning-po** [ningboh] 29°54N 121°33E, pop (2000e) 1 274 000. Port city in E China; traditional outlet for silk and porcelain; designated a special economic zone; railway; Tianyi Ge Library (1561).

ninjutsu An armed Japanese martial art, whose origins are obscure because of the secrecy surrounding the *Ninja*, who were assassins. In the 1980s it became popular as a cult in the cinema and video world.

Niño, El El *Niño*

Niobe [niyohbee] In Greek mythology, the daughter of Tantalus and the wife of Amphion. She had twelve children (or more) and said she was better than any mother, including Leto. This provoked Leto's children, Apollo and Artemis, who killed her children, and turned the weeping Niobe into a weeping rock on Mt Sipylos.

Nirvana [neervahna] In Buddhism, the attainment of supreme bliss, tranquillity, and purity, when the fires of desire are extinguished.

Niš or **Nish** [neesh], ancient **Naisus** 43°20N 21°54E, pop (2000e) 178 000. Industrial town in SEC Serbia, on R Nišava; occupied by Bulgaria until 1918; airfield; railway; university (1965).

nit An egg laid by a louse of the order Phthiraptera, especially used of eggs of the human head and body lice.

Niterói [neeteroy] 22°54S 43°06W, pop (2000e) 553 300. Port in SE Brazil, opposite Rio de Janeiro; founded 1573; former state capital; connected to Rio by a bridge, length 14 km/9 mi; railway; university (1960).

nitinol An elastic type of metal wire containing nickel and titanium.

nitrate A salt of nitric acid, containing the NO_3^- ion. Potassium and sodium nitrates occur in nature (*saltpetre* or *Chile saltpetre*), and are used in food preservation, fertilizers, and explosives.

nitre [niyter] *potassium*

nitric acid HNO_3, melting point −42°C. A strong, oxidizing acid, made commercially by the oxidation of ammonia. It is important in the manufacture of agricultural chemicals and explosives.

nitrite A salt of nitrous acid (HNO_2), containing the ion NO_2^-. Nitrites are the most effective means of reducing the growth of the bacteria causing botulism.

nitro- The name for the group $-NO_2$, isomeric with the nitrite group, but bonded through nitrogen. Most organic nitro-compounds are explosive, such as trinitrotoluene (TNT).

nitrocellulose A chemical compound formed by the action of nitric acid on cellulose; first made in 1845. Its explosive properties proved unmanageable until it was turned into the form known as **gun-cotton**. Some forms of cellulose nitrate, less explosive but still highly inflammable, were for many years used in plastics and as a film base.

nitrogen N, element 7, boiling point −196°C. In the form of diatomic molecules (N_2), it is the most abundant gas in the atmosphere, of which it makes up 78%. Conversion of nitrogen to water-soluble forms, such as ammonia and nitrates, is called **nitrogen fixation**. This can be carried out by soil bacteria, and industrially by the Haber process. The main uses of its compounds are in agricultural fertilizers and in explosives.

nitrogen cycle The dynamic system of changes in the nature of nitrogen-containing compounds circulating between the atmosphere, the soil, and living organisms. It includes the fixation of gaseous molecular nitrogen into nitrogenous compounds by micro-organisms, lightning, or other processes; the oxidation of ammonia to nitrite and nitrite to nitrate by aerobic organisms (*nitrification*); the decomposition of organic matter by putrefaction; and the eventual release of gaseous nitrogen by the reduction of nitrates and nitrites, typically by anaerobic micro-organisms (*denitrification*).

nitrogen mustard *cyclophosphamide*

nitroglycerine An explosive liquid made by the action of nitric acid (mixed with sulphuric acid) on glycerol. At first considered impossibly dangerous, from 1867 Nobel made its use more general by mixing it with moderators. It is a constituent of several mixed explosives (eg gelignite).

nitrous oxide Boiling point −88°C. Dinitrogen oxide, N_2O, isoelectronic with carbon dioxide; also called **laughing gas**. It has a slightly sweet odour, and is used as a general anaesthetic for short periods, especially in dentistry.

Niue [nyooay] 19°02S 169°55W; pop (2000e) 2100; area 259 km²/ 100 sq mi. Coral island in the S Pacific Ocean, 2140 km/1330 mi NE of New Zealand; main settlement, Alofi; timezone GMT +12; chief religion, Christianity; official language, English; New Zealand currency used; mainly coral, with a flat, rolling interior and porous soils; highest point, 70 m/230 ft; subtropical and damp climate; visited by Captain Cook, 1774; European missionaries in mid-19th-c; British protectorate, 1900; annexed to New Zeal-

Nile, River

□ International Airport

[niyl], Arabic **Nahr en-Nil** River in E and NE Africa; longest river in the world; length from its most remote headstream (Luvironza R), 6695 km/4160 mi; Luvironza rises in SC Burundi, and flows generally NE and N under various names, entering L Victoria in W; Victoria Nile flows N through L Kyoga into NE end of L Albert; Albert Nile flows N through NW Uganda, becoming known as the White Nile at the Sudanese frontier; joined by the Blue Nile at Khartoum, to become the Nile proper, c.3000 km/1900 mi from its delta on the Mediterranean Sea; joined (E) by R Atbara, the only significant tributary; on entering Egypt, flows into L Nasser, created by the Aswan High Dam; opens out into a broad delta N of Cairo, from Alexandria (W) to Port Said (E), 250 km/155 mi E–W and 160 km/100 mi N–S; flows through two mouths (Rosetta and Damietta), both c.240 km/150 mi long; Egypt's population and cultivated land almost entirely along the floodplain; European discovery of Blue Nile's source made by James Bruce, 1768–73; L Victoria established as Nile's main reservoir by J H Speke, 1858.

and, 1901; since 1974, internal self-government in free association with New Zealand, which still maintains responsibility for defence and foreign affairs; governed by a Legislative Assembly, headed by a premier; mainly agricultural economy; severely damaged by cyclone Heta, Jan 2004.

Niven, David, popular name of **James David Graham Nevins** (1909–83) Film actor, born in Kirriemuir, Angus. He became established in urbane romantic roles with an English style, his films including *Around the World in 80 Days* (1956), *Separate Tables* (1958, Oscar), *The Guns of Navarone* (1961), and *55 Days at Peking* (1963).

Nixon, Richard (Milhous) (1913–94) US Republican statesman and 37th president (1969–74), born in Yorba Linda, CA. He lost the

1960 election to Kennedy, but won in 1968, and was re-elected in 1972. He resigned in 1974 under the threat of impeachment, after several leading members of his government had been found guilty of involvement in the Watergate affair, but was given a full pardon by President Ford.

Nizhni Novgorod [nizhnee novgorod], formerly **Gorky** (1929–91) 56°20N 44°00E, pop (2000e) 1 430 000. River-port in E European Russia; founded as a frontier post, 1221; famous for its annual trade fairs (1817–1930); earlier name in honour of Maxim Gorky; airport; railway; university (1918).

Nkomo, Joshua (Mqabuko Nyongolo) [nkohmoh] (1917–99) Zimbabwean statesman, born in Semokwe, Zimbabwe. President of the Zimbabwe African People's Union (ZAPU), in 1976 he formed the Popular Front with Robert Mugabe to press for black majority rule in an independent Zimbabwe, and was given a cabinet post in the Mugabe government in 1980. However, tension between his party and Mugabe's led to his dismissal in 1982.

Nkrumah, Kwame [nkrooma] (1909–72) Ghanaian statesman, prime minister (1957–60), and president (1960–6), born in Nkroful, Ghana. Called the 'Gandhi of Africa', he was a significant leader both of the movement against white domination and of Pan-African feeling. Economic reforms led to political opposition and the formation of a one-party state in 1964. His regime was overthrown by a military coup during his absence in China.

Noah [nohuh] Biblical character, depicted as the son of Lamech; a 'righteous man' who was given divine instruction to build an ark in which he, his immediate family, and a selection of animals were saved from a widespread flood over the Earth (*Gen* 6–9). Noah's sons (Japheth, Ham, and Shem) are depicted as the ancestors of all the nations on Earth.

Nobel, Alfred Bernhard [nohbel] (1833–96) Inventor and manufacturer, born in Stockholm. In 1866 he invented a safe and manageable form of nitroglycerine he called *dynamite*, and later, smokeless gunpowder and (1875) gelignite. He amassed a huge fortune, much of which he left to endow annual prizes (first awarded in 1901).

Nobel Prizes [nohbel] Prizes awarded each year from the income of a trust fund established by the will of Alfred Nobel to those who, in the opinion of the judges, have contributed most in the fields of physics, chemistry, physiology or medicine, literature, and peace. The first prizes were awarded in 1901. A sixth prize, for economics, was established by the Swedish National Bank in 1968, and awarded for the first time in 1969.

Nobile, Umberto [nohbilay] (1885–1978) Engineer and aviator, born in Lauro, Italy. He built the airships *Norge* and *Italia*, but was wrecked in *Italia* when returning from the North Pole (1928).

noble gases The final or zeroth group of the periodic table; also called the **rare** or **inert gases**. They are all gases at normal temperatures, and were called 'noble' because they were long thought to form no chemical compounds.

noble metals Metals which are intrinsically unreactive and not readily subject to corrosion. Gold, silver, and the 'platinum metals' are the best examples. Metals such as aluminium and chromium, whose corrosion resistance is due to an adhering coat of oxide, are called *passive*.

Noctiluca [noktilooka] An unusually large, single-celled marine organism; a dinoflagellate, moving by means of whip-like flagella; bioluminescent, producing flashes of light when disturbed. (Class: Dinophyceae.)

noctilucent cloud Very high altitude (80 km/50 mi) dusty clouds visible as a rippled or veiled structure after sunset from about May to August in the N hemisphere. They consist of water ice frozen onto a dust core.

noctuid moth [noktyooid] Any of a large family, the Noctuidae, of typically drab, nocturnal moths (Order: Lepidoptera); c.21 000 species, many of which cause serious damage to crops; also known as the **owlet moth**.

nocturne A piece of music, usually in a meditative, languid style. The title has been used for piano pieces by John Field (its inventor), Chopin, and Fauré, and for orchestral pieces by Mendelssohn and Debussy.

noddy *tern*

Noel-Baker (of the City of Derby), Philip (John) Noel-Baker, Baron (1889–1982) British Labour statesman, born in London. He was secretary of state for air (1946–7), and of Commonwealth Relations (1947–50), and minister of fuel and power (1950–1). He was awarded the Nobel Peace Prize in 1959.

Noether, (Amalie) Emmy [noeter] (1882–1935) Mathematician, born in Erlangen, Germany. She emigrated to the USA in 1933. One of the leading figures in the development of abstract algebra, the theory of **Noetherian rings** has been an important subject of later research.

Noh Classical theatre of Japan in which imitation, gesture, dance, mask-work, costume, song, and music are fused in a concise stage art. Five schools of Noh exist, and most of the plays they perform were written before 1600.

Nolan, Sir Sidney (Robert) (1917–92) Painter, born in Melbourne, Victoria, Australia. He made his name with a series of 'Ned Kelly' paintings, begun in 1946, following this with an 'explorer' series. He was also a theatrical designer and book illustrator.

Nolan Committee (Committee on Standards in Public Life) A committee chaired by Lord Nolan (1928–2007) and established by UK prime minister John Major in 1994, in the wake of accusations of sleaze involving members of the government and others in public life. It published its first report in 1995 and laid down seven principles by which those involved in public life should conduct themselves: selflessness, integrity, objectivity, accountability, openness, honesty, leadership.

Nolde, Emil [nolduh], pseudonym of **Emil Hansen** (1867–1956) Artist, born in Nolde, Germany. He was one of the most important Expressionist painters, his powerful style being summed up by the phrase 'blood and soil'.

Nollekens, Joseph [nolekenz] (1737–1823) Neoclassical sculptor, born in London. He executed likenesses of most of his famous contemporaries, such as Goldsmith, Johnson, Fox, Pitt, and George III.

nomadism A way of life characterized by moving from one place to another, with no fixed residence. Most nomadic people (eg the Bedouin, the Kirghiz) are either hunter-gatherers or pastoralists. Some are described as **semi-nomadic** (eg the Fulani), as they remain settled in one area for a span of time and cultivate crops. As various governments have restricted movements of people, nomadism has declined in recent decades.

nominalism In metaphysics, the view that only individual things exist in the full sense. Universals and properties (eg 'redness') have no independent reality, but are just names.

non-aligned movement A movement of states which espoused the position of not taking sides in the major division within world politics between the USA and USSR. A number of recently de-colonized countries have favoured non-alignment as a mark of their independence. A formal Non-Aligned Movement, begun in 1961, holds conferences every three years; there were 116 members in 2005.

Nonconformists Originally, those Protestants in England and Wales in the 17th-c who dissented from the principles of the Church of England. It now generally refers to Christians who refuse to conform to the doctrine and practice of an established or national Church.

Non-Co-operation Movement An unsuccessful nationalist campaign (1919–22) led by Gandhi and Congress to force the British to grant Indian independence. The movement involved the boycott of Government institutions and foreign goods, and was abandoned when the protest became violent.

non-Euclidian geometries *geometries, non-Euclidian*

nonjurors Those who refused to swear an oath of loyalty to William III and Mary II in 1689, since to do so would infringe the divine right of monarchical succession. Most were clerics, who were then deprived of their offices.

Nono, Luigi [nohnoh] (1924–90) Composer, born in Venice, Italy. He was a leading composer of electronic, aleatory, and serial music. *Il canto sospeso* (1956, The Suspended Song), based on the letters of victims of wartime oppression, brought him to international notice.

Non-Proliferation Treaty (NPT) A treaty signed in 1968 by the USA, Soviet Union, UK, and an open-ended list of over 100 other countries. It seeks to limit the spread of nuclear weapons, and for states to pursue only peaceful uses of nuclear energy.

non-renewable resources Resources (ie objects of material or economic use to society, such as minerals, timber, and fish) which have evolved or formed over such long time periods that their exploitation is not sustainable. Examples include fossil fuel deposits (coal, oil, gas) and mineral deposits (iron, gold).

nonsense verse Verse which is written in defiance of sense and logic to satisfy the ear and the spirit rather than the intelligence. Edward Lear wrote famous examples, as did Lewis Carroll in the two *Alice* books.

non-sporting dog A category of domestic dog; name used for breeds bred as pets/companions (except very small such breeds, which are called **toy dogs**); includes dogs formerly bred for sport (eg bulldog, some poodles); sometimes includes **working dogs** (eg collies).

non-tariff barriers Barriers to international trade other than tariffs. Tariffs, or taxes on imports, have been greatly reduced during successive rounds of negotiation under the General Agreement on Tariffs and Trade (GATT). On some trade flows, especially industrial exports from less developed countries (LDCs), tariffs have been replaced by the growth of non-tariff barriers (NTBs), such as import quotas and voluntary export restraint agreements. The limitation or elimination of NTBs should provide work for many future rounds of negotiation under the World Trade Organization (WTO).

non-verbal communication (NVC) Those forms of interpersonal communication beyond the spoken or written word; often referred to as body language. The messages communicated may be deliberate (eg winking or bowing), or unintentional (eg blushing or shivering).

Noonuccal, Oodgeroo [nunuhkl, ujuhroo], originally **Kath(leen Jean Mary) Walker** (1920–93) Poet and Aboriginal rights activist, born in Brisbane, Queensland, Australia. She was the first Aboriginal writer to be published in English, with her collection of poems *We are Going* (1964).

Nootka An American Indian group of the Northwest Pacific Coast. They were famous as whalers, and became wealthy during the late 18th-c through the fur trade.

Norbertines *Premonstratensians*

Nordenskjöld, Nils (Adolf Erik), Baron [naw(r)denshoel] (1832–1901) Arctic navigator, born in Helsinki. He accomplished (1878–9) the navigation of the Northeast Passage, from the Atlantic to the Pacific along the N coast of Asia.

Nördliche Kalkalpen [nerdlikhuh kalkalpen] Mountain range of the E Alps in C Austria, rising to 2995 m/9826 ft at Hoher Dachstein.

Norfolk (UK) [naw(r)fuhk] pop (2001e) 796 700; area 5368 km²/ 2073 sq mi. County in E England; low-lying, with fens in W; Norfolk Broads in E; county town, Norwich; offshore natural gas; Sandringham royal residence, Shrine of Our Lady of Walsingham.

Norfolk (USA) [nawfuhk] 36°51N 76°17W, pop (2000e) 234 400. Seaport and independent city, SE Virginia, USA, on the Elizabeth R; settled, 1682; city status, 1845; centre of fighting in the American Revolution and the Civil War; largest city in the state; airfield; railway; Norfolk State College (1935); headquarters of the US Atlantic Fleet, largest naval base in the world.

Norfolk Island [naw(r)fuhk] 29°04S 167°57E; pop (2000e) 2200; area 35 km²/13 sq mi; length 8 km/5 mi. Fertile, hilly island in the W Pacific Ocean, 1488 km/925 mi NE of Sydney, Australia; a British penal settlement in 1788–1806 and 1826–55; an Australian external territory since 1913; English and Tahitian spoken.

Noriega, Manuel (Antonio) [noriayga] (1938–) Panamanian soldier and politician, born in Panama City. He became the ruling force behind the Panamanian presidents (1983–9). Alleging his involvement in drug trafficking, the US authorities ordered his arrest in 1989: 13 000 US troops invaded Panama to support the 12 000 already there. He surrendered in January 1990, and was taken to the USA for trial. Found guilty in 1992, he was sentenced to 40 years imprisonment.

Norma (Lat 'level') A small, faint S hemisphere constellation.

Norman, Barry (Leslie) (1933–) Writer and television film critic, born in London. In 1973 he joined BBC television as host of *Film '73*, then wrote and presented the show (1973–81, 1983–97) until joining Sky television in 1998. Other work includes the series *The Hollywood Greats* (1977–9, 1984–5) and *Talking Pictures* (1988).

Norman, Greg(ory John), nickname **the Great White Shark** (1955–) Golfer, born in Mount Isa, Queensland, Australia. Rated the world's top player in 1986, he has won the (British) Open (1986, 1993), and the World Matchplay Championship (1980, 1983, 1986).

Norman, Jessye (1945–) Soprano, born in Augusta, GA. She made her operatic debut in *Tannhäuser* at Berlin in 1969, and in *Aïda* at both La Scala and Covent Garden in 1972. She has since toured widely at music festivals and concerts.

Norman Conquest A fundamental watershed in English political and social history. It not only began the rule of a dynasty of Norman kings (1066–1154), but entailed the virtual replacement of the Anglo-Saxon nobility by Normans, Bretons, and Flemings, many of whom retained lands in N France.

Normandy, Fr Normandie Former duchy and province in NW France; leading state in Middle Ages; William Duke of Normandy conquered England in 1066; focus of English–French dispute in 12th–14th-c, until became part of France in 1449; scene of Allied invasion, 1944.

Normandy Campaign (1944) A World War 2 ('Operation Overlord') campaign which began on D-Day (6 Jun 1944). Allied forces under the overall command of General Eisenhower began the liberation of W Europe from Germany by landing on the Normandy coast. Heavy fighting ensued for three weeks before Allied troops captured Cherbourg (27 Jun).

Normans By the early 11th-c, a name (derived from 'Northmen', ie Vikings) applied to all the people inhabiting Normandy, a duchy (and later province) in N France. They completed the conquest and aristocratic colonization of England and a large part of Wales, established a kingdom in S Italy and Sicily, and founded the Norman principality of Antioch.

norm-referenced test A test which compares candidates with each other, usually spreading marks over a normal distribution, with most in the middle and few at each extreme. Most conventional tests which give percentages of A to E grades are of this kind.

Norns In Norse mythology, the equivalent of the Fates, three sisters who sit under the tree Yggdrasil and spin the web of Destiny. Their names are Urd (who knows the past), Verlandi (the present), and Skuld (the future).

North, Frederick, 8th Baron North (1732–92) British statesman

ASIA

ARCTIC OCEAN

Ellesmere
Island

Greenland
(to Denmark)

Bering Strait

Beaufort
Sea

Baffin
Bay

Bering
Sea

Brooks Range

UNITED STATES
OF AMERICA

Victoria Island

Baffin Island

Davis Strait

Aleutian Islands

Aleutian Range

Mackenzie

Foxe
Basin

Great Bear Lake

Gulf of
Alaska

Mackenzie Mountains

Hudson Strait

Great Slave
Lake

Queen
Charlotte
Islands

C A N A D A

Lake Athabasca

Hudson
Bay

Reindeer Lake

Vancouver
Island

R o c k y   M o u n t a i n s

Lake Winnipeg

Lake Superior

Lake Huron

P A C I F I C   O C E A N

Great Salt Lake

Lake Michigan

Lake
Ontario

Lake Erie

U N I T E D   S T A T E S

Missouri

O F   A M E R I C A

Appalachian Mountains

Colorado

Ohio

Arkansas

Mississippi

Gulf of California

Rio Grande

Mississippi
Delta

Gulf of
Mexico

Lower California

Cayman Islands
(to UK)

Yucatan
Peninsula

M E X I C O

BELIZE

HONDURAS

GUATEMALA

EL SALVADOR

NICARAGUA

Lake
Nicaragua

COSTA RICA

Labrador
Sea

ATLANTIC OCEAN

Newfoundland
St Pierre & Miquelon
(to France)

BAHAMAS

West Indies
Virgin Islands (to US)
British Virgin
Islands
(to UK)
Anguilla (to UK)
Turks & Caicos
Islands (to UK)
Puerto Rico
(to US)
ANTIGUA & BARBUDA
DOMINICAN
REPUBLIC
Guadeloupe (to France)
CUBA
HAITI
ST KITTS & NEVIS
Montserrat (to UK)
DOMINICA
Martinique (to France)
ST LUCIA
Navassa Island (to US)
ST VINCENT &
THE GRENADINES
BARBADOS
JAMAICA
Greater Antilles
Lesser Antilles
GRENADA
TRINIDAD & TOBAGO

Caribbean
Sea
Aruba
(to Neth.)
Netherlands Antilles
(to Neth.)

SOUTH
AMERICA

NAMA

and prime minister (1770–82), born in London. He was widely criticized both for failing to avert the Declaration of Independence by the North American colonies (1776) and for failing to defeat them in the subsequent war (1776–83).

North, Oliver (1943–) US soldier, born in San Antonio, TX. Appointed a deputy-director of the National Security Council by President Reagan in 1981, he played a key role in a series of controversial military and security actions. Implicated in the Irangate scandal, he was forced to resign in 1986.

North, Sir Thomas (1523–?1601) English translator, born in London. He is known for his translation of Plutarch's *Lives of the noble Grecians and Romans* (1579), which Shakespeare used in many of his plays.

North America Third largest continent, extending 9600 km/6000 mi from 70°30N to 15°N; area c.24 million km²/9¼ million sq mi; separated from Asia by the Bering Strait; includes Canada, USA, and Mexico; numerous islands, including Baffin I, Newfoundland, and the West Indies; ranges include the Rocky Mts, Alaska Range (including Mt McKinley, highest point), and Appalachian Mts; major lake system, the Great Lakes; major rivers include the Mississippi, Missouri, Rio Grande, and St Lawrence. *see map*

North American Free Trade Agreement (NAFTA) An association of the USA, Canada, and Mexico, established in 1992 to create a free-trade area covering all of North America, eliminating over a period of time customs duties and other restrictions. Finally ratified in late 1993, the bloc is now the second largest free-trade area in the world, with c.360 million customers.

Northampton 52°14N 0°54W, pop (2001e) 194 500. County town in Northamptonshire, C England; on R Nene; originally a Saxon town; destroyed by fire in 1675; designated a 'new town' in 1968; railway; football league team, Northampton Town (Cobblers).

Northamptonshire pop (2001e) 629 700; area 2367 km²/914 sq mi. Agricultural county in C England; county town, Northampton.

North Atlantic Treaty Organization *NATO*

North Carolina pop (2000e) 8 049 300; area 136 407 km²/52 669 sq mi. State in SE USA; the 'Tar Heel State' or 'Old North State'; unsuccessful settlement on Roanoke I in the 1580s; part of the Carolina grant given by Charles II, 1663; named North Carolina, 1691; a royal province, 1729; location of Mecklenburg Declaration of Independence (1775); twelfth of the original 13 states to ratify the Constitution, 1789; withdrew from the Union, 1861; slavery abolished, 1865; re-admitted to the Union, 1868; highest point Mt Mitchell (2037 m/6683 ft); chain of coastal islands with constantly shifting sand dunes, enclosing several lagoons; low land gives way to the rolling hills of the Piedmont; fast-flowing rivers provide hydroelectric power for manufacturing industries; in the W the Blue Ridge and Great Smoky Mts; capital, Raleigh; major tourist area; provides 40% of all US tobacco; industrial growth greatest of any Southern state since World War 2.

Northcliffe, Lord *Harmsworth, Alfred*

North Dakota [dakohta] pop (2000e) 642 400; area 183 111 km²/70 702 sq mi. State in NC USA; 'Sioux State', 'Flickertail State'; became part of USA in the Louisiana Purchase, 1803; included in Dakota Territory, 1861; separated from South Dakota to become the 39th state admitted to the Union, 1889; sparsely populated; highest point, White Butte (1069 m/3507 ft); semi-arid conditions in the W; E region a flat, fertile plain, covered almost entirely by crops, chiefly spring wheat, barley, sunflowers, and flaxseed (nation's leading producer of all these crops); capital, Bismarck; major cattle state; oil (NW) and lignite coal (W); several Indian reservations.

North Downs Way Long-distance footpath in S England; length 227 km/141 mi; follows the crest of the North Downs from Farnham to Dover.

Northeast Passage A shipping route through the S Arctic Ocean along the N coast of Europe and Asia, connecting the Atlantic and Pacific Oceans. It was not successfully travelled until 1878–9.

Northern Cape One of the nine new provinces established by the South African constitution of 1994, in W South Africa; formerly part of Cape Provinces; largely semi-arid; NW frontier with Namibia formed by the Orange R; largest province, smallest population; pop (2000e) 785 000; area 363 389 km²/140 268 sq mi; capital, Kimberley; chief languages, Afrikaans (65%), Setswana (22%), Xhosa; Kalahari-Gemsbok National Park.

Northern Ireland p.667

Northern Ireland Assembly A 108-member governing body for Northern Ireland, established (following a referendum) as part of the Good Friday Agreement. It has responsibility for the policy areas of agriculture, economic development, education, environment, and health and social services. Elections (by proportional representation) to the body were held in 1998 with 10 parties represented, the largest being the Ulster Unionist Party (28 members), the Social and Democratic Labour Party (24), the Democratic Unionist Party (20), and Sinn Féin (18). The assembly, meeting in Stormont Castle, Belfast, is overseen by a presiding officer appointed by the secretary of state for Ireland, and elects its own officers and executive committee. David Trimble (UUP) was elected the inaugural first minister and Seamus Mallon (SDLP) the inaugural deputy minister. The full establishment of the Assembly was delayed by disagreement over the participation of Sinn Féin in the executive committee before the decommissioning of weapons held by republican paramilitaries, but the Assembly came into effect in December 1999; however, a perceived lack of progress on the decommissioning issue led to the reimposition of UK rule in February–May 2000, and there was a further suspension of devolution in October 2002. Negotiations aimed at restoring devolved government began in September 2004 and by December a power-sharing agreement had been reached, though its implementation remained in doubt following the IRA's refusal to produce photographic evidence of decommissioning. In July 2005 the IRA formally announced its intention to end its armed campaign and to continue through exclusively peaceful means. In 2006, a Transitional Assembly paved the way for restoration of the Northern Ireland Assembly, following elections, in May 2007.

northern lights aurora (astronomy)

Northern Province, renamed **Limpopo** (Feb 2002) One of the nine new provinces established by the South African constitution of 1994, in N South Africa; Limpopo R to the N; formerly part of Transvaal, and includes former homelands of Lebowa and Gazankulu; capital, Polokwane (formerly, Pietersburg); pop (2000e) 4 343 000; area 119 606 km²/46 168 sq mi; chief language, Pedi (56%), Shangaan (22%), Venda; largely bushveld, with some mountains and forests; lowest per capita income in the country.

Northern Territory pop (2000e) 194 400; area 1 346 200 km²/520 000 sq mi. One of the two mainland territories of Australia, covering about a sixth of the continent; part of New South Wales, 1824; annexed by South Australia, 1863; transferred to Federal Government control, 1911; achieved self-government, 1978; mainly within the tropics; land rises S to the Macdonnell Ranges, reaching 1524 m/5000 ft at Mt Liebig; good pasture land in the N (Barkly Tableland), largely flat and arid in the S (Simpson Desert); Ayers Rock in Uluru national park; capital and chief port, Darwin; many Aboriginal settlements.

Northern War Great Northern War

North German Confederation The state system and constitutional arrangement created in 1866 by Bismarck, chancellor of Prussia, following the Prussian defeat of Austria and the dissolution of the German Confederation. It was dissolved with the creation of the German Empire in 1871.

northing A grid line which runs W to E on a map, but which is numbered northwards. It is related to the **easting**, a grid line which runs N to S, and which is numbered eastwards. The northing number associated with a place is always given after the number of the easting when citing a grid reference.

North Korea Korea, North

North Pole Poles

North Sea area 520 000 km²/201 000 sq mi. Arm of the Atlantic Ocean between continent of Europe (E) and UK (W), from Shetland Is (N) to Straits of Dover (S); length c.950 km/600 mi; maximum width 650 km/400 mi; generally shallow, lying on wide continental shelf, with banks running across from Yorkshire coast (eg Dogger Bank); important fishing grounds; extensive offshore oil and gas exploitation; some land reclamation in the Dutch polder area.

North Sea oil Oil and gas deposits in the sedimentary rocks below the North Sea, first discovered in 1969 in Norwegian waters (the Ekofisk field) and in 1975 in the UK sector. Reserves are estimated at 12 thousand million barrels.

Northumberland pop (2001e) 307 200; area 5032 km²/1943 sq mi. County in NE England; Pennines in the W; rises in the N to 755 m/2 477 ft at The Cheviot; Holy I and the Farne Is lie off the coast; Kielder Water (artificial lake, 1982); county town, Morpeth; many Roman remains, especially Hadrian's Wall; castles at Alnwick and Bamburgh.

Northumberland, Dukes of Percy

Northumbria The largest kingdom of the Anglo-Saxon heptarchy. In the 7th-c it established a broad dominance in Britain both N and S of the Humber, while in the 8th-c the Northumbrian monasteries gained a European-wide reputation for sanctity and learning. The kingdom came to an end in 876.

North West One of the nine new provinces established by the South African constitution of 1994, in NW South Africa; completely land-locked; capital Mmabatho; pop (2000e) 3 201 000; area 118 710 km²/45 822 sq mi; resort complex at Sun City.

Northwest Coast Indians North American Indians living along the Pacific coastline from Alaska to NW California. They consisted of a number of different groups, who were wealthy, hierarchical, and had highly developed artistic traditions.

North West Company A trading partnership based in Montreal and Fort William, Canada, from the 1780s to 1821. It merged into the Hudson's Bay Company in 1821.

Northwest Frontier pop (2000e) 18 085 000; area 74 521 km²/28 765 sq mi. Federal province in Pakistan; bounded W and S by Afghanistan and N by India; linked to Afghanistan by the Khyber Pass; inhabited mainly by the Pathans, renowned for their warlike character; capital, Peshawar.

Northwest Ordinance Ordinance of 1787

Northwest Passage A route through the S Arctic Ocean, N Canada, and along the N coast of Alaska. From the 16th-c attempts were made to find it, but not until 1903–6 was it first traversed by Amundsen.

Northwest Territories pop (2000e) 64 600; area 1 346 106 km²/519 597 sq mi. Canadian territory consisting of the Arctic islands, the islands in Hudson and Ungava Bays, and the land N of 60°N, between Hudson Bay and the Yukon territory; sparsely populated, two-thirds Athapaskan-speaking peoples and Inuit; capital, Yellowknife (since 1967); formerly called Rupert's Land and North West Territory; entered Canadian federation, 1870; governed by a commissioner and a Legislative Assembly; the new Canadian territory of Nunavut was created in 1999 from a region formerly in E Northwest Territories.

Northern Ireland

☐ International Airport   ∴ World heritage site

also **Ulster** (UK)

Area 14120 km²/5450 sq mi

Population total (2001e) 1685300

Status Constituent division of the United Kingdom

Capital Belfast

Languages English, Irish Gaelic

Religions Christian (Roman Catholic 28%, Presbyterian 23%, Church of Ireland 19%)

Physical features Occupies the NE part of Ireland, centred on Lough Neagh; Mourne Mts in SE; highest point, Slieve Donard, 847 m/2786 ft, in the former Co. Down; R Mourne, 82 km/51 mi in length.

Economy Agriculture; service industries, shipbuilding, engineering, chemicals; linen, textiles; economy badly affected by the sectarian troubles since 1969.

History Separate Parliament established in 1920, with a 52-member House of Commons and a 26-member Senate; Protestant majority in the population, generally supporting political union with Great Britain; many of the Roman Catholic minority look for union with the Republic of Ireland; violent conflict between the communities broke out in 1969, leading to the establishment of a British army peace-keeping force; sectarian murders and bombings continued both within and outside the province; as a result of the disturbances, Parliament was abolished in 1972; powers are now vested in the UK secretary of state for Northern Ireland; formation of a 78-member Assembly, 1973; replaced by a Constitutional Convention, 1975; Assembly reformed in 1982, but Nationalist members did not take their seats; under the 1985 Anglo-Irish agreement, the Republic of Ireland was given a consultative role in the government of Northern Ireland; all Northern Ireland MPs in the British Parliament resigned in protest, 1986; continuing controversy in the late 1980s; fresh talks between all main parties and the Irish government, 1992; breakthrough in December 1993 with the Downing Street Declaration; IRA and loyalist ceasefires, 1994; joint Irish/British Framework Document, February 1995; new IRA campaign, 1996; start of all-party talks (initially with Sinn Féin excluded), 1996; Good Friday agreement, 1998, introduced Northern Ireland Assembly; problems over arms decommissioning by the IRA hindered implementation of the agreement; review of the peace process by US senator George Mitchell announced (Jul 1999), leading to a compromise formula and the inauguration of the Assembly in December; reimposition of UK rule (Feb–May 2000); further suspension of devolution (Oct 2002); multiparty peace talks to restore devolution resumed (Mar 2003) but suffered setback as scheduled elections (May) to the Assembly postponed; elections reset (Nov) with success for the anti-Agreement Democratic Unionist Party; post-election talks began; IRA formally announced an end to its armed campaign (Jul 2005) and NI secretary Peter Hain set out a 2-year plan on demilitarization; Transitional Assembly established, 2006; elections (March 2007), with restoration of full Assembly, May 2007.

Districts of Northern Ireland

Name / Area (km²/sq mi) / Population total (2000e) / Admin

Antrim / 563 / 217 / 44700 / Antrim
Ards / 369 / 142 / 67900 / Newtownards
Armagh / 672 / 259 / 52100 / Armagh
Ballymena / 638 / 246 / 57800 / Ballymena
Ballymoney / 419 / 162 / 25500 / Ballymoney
Banbridge / 444 / 171 / 34600 / Banbridge
Belfast / 140 / 54 / 285800 / Belfast
Carrickfergus / 87 / 34 / 35000 / Carrickfergus
Castlereagh / 85 / 33 / 53600 / Belfast
Coleraine / 485 / 187 / 52100 / Coleraine
Cookstown / 623 / 240 / 31800 / Cookstown
Craigavon / 383 / 147 / 77800 / Craigavon
Down / 646 / 249 / 63000 / Downpatrick
Dungannon / 779 / 301 / 49900 / Dungannon
Fermanagh / 1876 / 715 / 54100 / Enniskillen
Larne / 338 / 131 / 30400 / Larne
Limavady / 587 / 227 / 23700 / Limavady
Lisburn / 444 / 171 / 103000 / Lisburn
Londonderry (Derry) / 382 / 147 / 102000 / Londonderry (Derry)
Magherafelt / 573 / 221 / 37500 / Magherafelt
Moyle / 495 / 191 / 15000 / Ballycastle
Newry and Mourne / 895 / 346 / 75600 / Newry
Newtownabbey / 152 / 59 / 77900 / Newtownabbey
North Down / 73 / 28 / 74500 / Bangor
Omagh / 1129 / 436 / 47900 / Omagh
Strabane / 870 / 336 / 37400 / Strabane

Norway

□ International Airport

Norwegian **Norge**, official name **Kingdom of Norway**, Norwegian **Kongeriket Norge**

Local name Norge
Timezone GMT +1
Area 323 895 km²/125 023 sq mi
Population total (2002e) 4 537 000
Status Kingdom
Date of independence 1905
Capital Oslo
Languages Norwegian (official) (in the varieties of Bokmål and Nynorsk), Lappish- and Finnish-speaking minorities
Ethnic groups Germanic (Nordic, Alpine, Baltic descent) (97%), Sami/Lapp minority in far N

Religions Evangelical Lutheran (95%), Baptist, Pentecostalist, Methodist, and Roman Catholic (5%)

Physical features Mountainous country; Kjölen Mts form the N part of the boundary with Sweden; Jotunheimen range in SC Norway; much of the interior over 1500 m/5000 ft; numerous lakes, the largest being L Mjøsa, 368 km²/142 sq mi; irregular coastline with many small islands and long deep fjords.

Climate Arctic winter climate in interior highlands, snow, strong winds and severe frosts; comparatively mild conditions on coast; average annual temperatures -4°C (Jan), 17°C (Jul) in Oslo; average annual rainfall 683 mm/27 in; rainfall heavy on W coast.

Currency 1 Norwegian Krone (NOK) = 100 øre

Economy Based on extraction and processing of raw materials, using plentiful hydroelectric power; oil and natural gas from North Sea fields; land under cultivation, less than 3%; productive forests covered 21% of land area in 1985.

GDP (2002e) $149·1 bn, per capita $33 000

Human Development Index (2002) 0·942

History A united kingdom achieved by St Olaf in the 11th-c, whose successor, Cnut, brought Norway under Danish rule; united with Sweden and Denmark, 1389; annexed by Sweden as a reward for assistance against Napoleon, 1814; growing nationalism resulted in independence, 1905; declared neutrality in both World Wars, but occupied by Germany, 1940–5, after heavy resistance; Free Norwegian government based in London; joined NATO, 1949; joined European Free Trade Association, 1960; a limited, hereditary monarchy; government led by a Prime Minister; Parliament (Storting) comprises upper (Lagting) and lower (Odelsting) chambers.

Head of State (Monarch)
1872–1905 Oscar II *Union with Sweden*
1905–57 Haakon VII
1957–91 Olav V
1991– Harald V

Head of Government
1973–6 Trygve Bratteli
1976–81 Odvar Nordli
1981 Gro Harlem Brundtland
1981–6 Kåre Willoch
1986–9 Gro Harlem Brundtland
1989–90 Jan P Syse
1990–6 Gro Harlem Brundtland
1996–7 Thorbjoern Jagland
1997–2000 Kjell Magne Bondevik
2000–1 Jens Stoltenberg
2001–5 Kjell Magne Bondevik
2005– Jens Stoltenberg

North York Moors National park chiefly in North Yorkshire, England; area 1432 km²/553 sq mi; established in 1952.
North Yorkshire *Yorkshire, North*
Norway *see panel*
Norway spruce The most common species of spruce (*Picea abies*) native to Europe and planted on a vast commercial scale. It is a source of timber, pitch, spruce beer, and, in Britain, Christmas trees. (Family: Pinaceae.)
Norwegian *Germanic languages; Scandinavian languages*
Norwegian Sea area 1 383 000 km²/534 000 sq mi. N Atlantic sea bounded by NW coast of Norway and E coast of Iceland; generally ice-free.
Nor-wester *Föhn / Foehn wind*
Norwich (UK) [norich] 52°38N 1°18E, pop (2001e) 121 600. County town in Norfolk, E England; provincial centre for the largely

agricultural East Anglia; major textile centre in 16th–17th-c; railway; University of East Anglia (1964); cathedral (1096); football league team, Norwich City (Canaries).
Norwich School A group of provincial English landscape painters, in oil and watercolour, working in Norwich 1803–34.
nose The protrusion from the front of the face above the mouth and below the eyes. Part of the respiratory tract, it consists of an external part (with a skeleton of bone and cartilage) and an inner cavity. The functions of the nasal cavity are olfaction (smell) and changing the nature of the inspired air. The rich vascular network also warms the air. Because of this network, the nose has a tendency to bleed profusely if it is hit.
Nostradamus [nostradahmus], Latin name of **Michel de Notredame** (1503–66) Astrologer, born in St Rémy, France. He became a doctor of medicine in 1529, and set himself up as a prophet

c.1547. His *Centuries* of predictions in rhymed quatrains (1555–8), expressed generally in obscure and enigmatical terms, brought him a great reputation.

notebook A very compact form of personal computer which can be accommodated inside a briefcase. Even so, most notebooks offer the same facilities as a desk-top personal computer.

nothosaur [nothosaw(r)] A long-necked, marine reptile; flourished during the Triassic period, but extinct by the early Jurassic period; limbs well adapted for swimming. (Order: Sauropterygia. Suborder: Nothosauria.)

notochord [nohtohkaw(r)d] A rod-like structure which extends almost the entire length of the body in larvae and some adult chordates. It lies behind the gut but below the nerve cord, providing flexible support for the body. It is replaced by the vertebral column in most vertebrates.

Notre Dame (de Paris) [notruh dam duh paree] An early Gothic cathedral on the Ile de la Cité in Paris. It was commissioned by Maurice de Sully, Bishop of Paris, in 1159 and constructed over a period of two centuries (1163–1345).

Nottingham, Anglo-Saxon **Snotingaham** or **Notingeham** 52°58N 1°10W, pop (2001e) 267 000. City and (from 1998) unitary authority in Nottinghamshire, England; on the R Trent; founded by the Danes; became a city in 1897; Civil War started here in 1642; railway; two universities (1948, 1992); castle (17th-c); football league teams, Nottingham Forest (Reds), Nottingham County (Magpies).

Nottinghamshire pop (2001e) 748 500; area 2164 km²/836 sq mi. County in the R Trent basin of C England; Pennines in W, remains of Sherwood Forest in SW; county town, Nottingham (unitary authority from 1998).

Notungulata [notuhngyoolahta] A large order of extinct, South American, plant-eating mammals, known from the late Palaeocene to the Pleistocene epochs.

Nouadhibou [nooadeeboo], Fr **Port Etienne** 20°54N 17°00W, pop (2000e) 83 000. Mauritania's main seaport; linked by rail to the iron ore mines near Zouîrât; airport.

Nouakchott [nwakshot] 18°09N 15°58W, pop (2000e) 553 000. Capital of Mauritania; founded on an important caravan route, 1960; airport.

Nouméa [noomaya], formerly **Port de France** 22°16S 166°26E, pop (2000e) 79 000. Seaport capital of New Caledonia; capital, 1854; US air base in World War 2; airport; cathedral.

nouveau roman [noovoh rohmã] (Fr 'new novel') A term used to describe a type of novel written (and theorized) by a group of French novelists of the 1950s in reaction against established fictional forms. The new novelists claimed that any authorial interpretation was arbitrary, and that there is no ultimate meaning behind existence apart from the subjective experience of the individual. Writers include Michel Butor, Alain Robbe-Grillet, and Nathalie Sarraute.

nouvelle cuisine [noovel kwizeen] A movement away from the elaborate food of classical cuisine to a simpler, more natural presentation. The approach began in the 1970s, and was given emphasis by the French chef Michel Guérard (1933–). The first consideration is the quality of the fresh produce, with the aim of achieving lightness by using less fat and no flour in sauces.

nouvelle vague [noovel vahg] (Fr 'new wave') The 'New Wave' group of young French film directors of the late 1950s and 1960s, who wished to discard many of the conventional formulae of the current cinema. They used the freedom of lightweight hand-held cameras outside the studio, with unconventional editing and sound.

nova In a binary star system near the end of its life, the phenomenon where one star becomes a giant, and its atmosphere spills over to its companion, a white dwarf. A nuclear explosion is triggered on the white dwarf, whose luminosity increases by 10 000 times for a few months.

Novak, Kim, originally **Marilyn Pauline Novak** (1933–) Film actress, born in Chicago, IL. She became a leading box-office attraction of the 1950s – perhaps the last of the 'sex goddesses' produced by the Hollywood star system. Her films include *The Man With The Golden Arm* (1955), *Pal Joey* (1957), *Vertigo* (1958), *The Mirror Crack'd* (1980), and *Liebestraum* (1991).

Novak, Michael [nohvak] (1933–) Lay Roman Catholic theologian, economist, and political philosopher, born in Johnstown, PA. A former priest, he taught at various US universities, and in 1981 he was appointed US ambassador for the UN Human Rights Commission. His books include *The Experience of Nothingness* (1970) and *The Spirit of Democratic Capitalism* (1982). In 1994 he received the Templeton Prize for Progress in Religion.

Novalis [nohvalis], pseudonym of **Friedrich Leopold von Hardenberg** (1772–1801) Romantic poet, born in Oberwiederstedt, Germany. Known as the 'prophet of Romanticism', he is best known for his *Geistliche Lieder* (1799, Sacred Songs) and *Hymnen an die Nacht* (1800, Hymns to the Night).

Nova Scotia [nohva skohsha] pop (2000e) 1 050 000; area 55 490 km²/21 424 sq mi. Province in SE Canada; includes Cape Breton I to the NE, connected by causeway; capital, Halifax; deeply indented coastline, low hill ranges, many lakes and small rivers; probably first visited by Vikings and European fishermen; settled by the French as Acadia, 1604–5; mainland assigned to Britain in the Treaty of Utrecht, 1713, Cape Breton I remaining French until seized in 1758; many United Empire Loyalists settled here after the American Revolution; Cape Breton I a separate province from 1784, re-incorporated into Nova Scotia, 1820; joined the Canadian federation, 1867; governed by a lieutenant-governor and a House of Assembly.

Novaya Zemlya [novaya zimlya] area 81 279 km²/31 374 sq mi. Archipelago in the Arctic Ocean, between the Barents Sea (W) and Kara Sea (E), NW Russia; two large islands separated by a narrow strait; length, 960 km/596 mi; rises to heights above 1000 m/3000 ft; some settlement on W coast; formerly used for thermonuclear testing.

novel A work of fiction, most often in prose. The term (literally meaning 'new' or 'news') came into general use in the 18th-c to describe that form of fiction which centred on the life of an individual, as in *Robinson Crusoe* and *Tom Jones*. The novel quickly became the dominant literary form in the West; and such writers as Dickens and George Eliot, Balzac and Zola, Dostoevsky and Tolstoy, helped create the moral and imaginative climate of their age. In the 20th-c the novel was developed by (among others) Joyce, Proust, Virginia Woolf, and Nabokov. An important contribution to the evolution of the novel was made in the second half of the 20th-c by Latin-American writers such as Carlos Fuentes, Mario Vargas Llosa, and Gabriel Garcia Marquez.

novella (Ital 'tale', 'news') Originally a short story, as in Boccaccio's *Decameron*. The term is now used to define (if somewhat precariously) a prose fiction which is longer than a short story but shorter than a novel.

Novello, Ivor [noveloh], originally **David Ivor Davies** (1893–1951) Actor, composer, songwriter, and playwright, born in Cardiff. His most successful works were the 'Ruritanian' musical plays such as *The Dancing Years* (1939) and *King's Rhapsody* (1949).

Novgorod [nofgorod] 58°30N 31°20E, pop (2000e) 232 000. City in NW European Russia; on R Volkhov; one of the oldest cities in Russia, known in the 9th-c; badly damaged in World War 2; railway; centre of an important agricultural area; cathedral (1045–50).

Novi Sad [novee sahd], Ger **Neusatz** 45°15N 19°51E, pop (2000e) 181 000. Commercial and industrial city in N Serbia; on R Danube; railway; university (1960); Petrovaradin castle; cathedral.

Novosibirsk [novosyibyeersk], formerly **Novonikolaevsk** (1903–

25) 55°00N 83°05E, pop (2000e) 1 440 000. River port in S Siberian Russia, on the R Ob; founded, 1893; on the Trans-Siberian Railway; university (1959); leading economic centre of Siberia; Kuznetsk Basin coal and iron deposits nearby.

Noyori, Ryoji (1938–) Chemist, born in Kobe, Japan. A researcher at the Research Center for Materials Science at Nagoya University, he shared the 2001 Nobel Prize for Chemistry for work on chirally catalysed hydrogenation reactions.

NTSC (National Television Systems Commission), responsible for the coding system for colour television introduced in the USA in 1954. It has since then been generally adopted throughout the Americas and Japan for all 525-line 60 Hz transmission.

Nu, U [noo] ('uncle'), originally **Thakin Nu** (1907–95) Burmese statesman and prime minister (1948–56, 1957–8, 1960–2), born in Wakema, Myanmar (Burma). The first prime minister of the independent Burmese Republic, he was overthrown by a military coup in 1962, and imprisoned, but released in 1966.

Nubian Desert [nyoobian] area c.400 000 km²/155 000 sq mi. Desert in NE Sudan; a sandstone plateau between the Red Sea and the R Nile.

Nubian monuments [nyoobian] A group of world heritage monuments around L Nasser in Egypt, many of which were rescued from flooding during the construction of Aswan High Dam. They include the 13th-c BC temples of Ramses II at Abu Simbel.

nuclear disarmament A political movement which emerged soon after the advent of nuclear weapons, demanding their control and eventual abolition. Although the US and Soviet governments had some success in reaching arms limitation treaties, such as the Intermediate range Nuclear Forces (INF) agreement (1987), mass political movements such as the British Campaign for Nuclear Disarmament (CND) have continued to attract support.

nuclear fission The splitting of a heavy atomic nucleus into two approximately equal portions, with the emission of free neutrons and energy; discovered by Otto Hahn in 1938. Fission in uranium and plutonium forms the basic mechanism of nuclear power and atomic bombs.

nuclear fusion The fusing together of two lightweight atomic nuclei, typically isotopes of hydrogen or lithium, having a total rest mass which exceeds that of the products. The mass difference is made up by energy released in the fusion. Such fusions are possible in the high-temperature environments of the Sun and nuclear explosions. Fusion reactors attempt to reproduce such conditions in a controlled way. The chief experimental fusion reactors are the Joint European Torus (JET) in the UK, the Tokamak Fusion Test Reactor at Princeton, USA and JT60 near Tokyo in Japan. In 1991, JET scientists achieved a breakthrough, combining hydrogen and tritium to produce over a million watts of energy in a reaction which was sustainable for two minutes.

nuclear magnetic resonance (NMR) An analytic technique, important in chemistry, which relies on magnetic resonance involving protons. It is an important imaging technique in medicine, complementary to X-ray imaging, known as **magnetic resonance imaging (MRI)**.

nuclear physics The study of the properties and composition of the atomic nucleus. Early nuclear physics experiments include the study of natural radioactivity, and the demonstration of the existence of the nucleus in 1911. The nucleus is probed using X-rays, neutrons, mesons, and electrons. The applications of nuclear physics include nuclear power, nuclear weapons, and radio-isotopes in medicine.

nuclear power *nuclear fission / fusion / reactor*

nuclear reactor A device for producing a continuous supply of heat energy from controlled radioactivity. Certain radioactive atomic nuclei, on being struck by neutrons, generate additional neutrons. This is self-sustaining if the speed of the neutrons is not too great. A nuclear reactor therefore has (i) a 'fuel', which may be uranium 235 or 238, or plutonium 239; (ii) a moderator, to control the speed and number of neutrons; and (iii) a heat exchange system, to utilize the heat generated (generally by operating the steam-driven turbines of a conventional electric power station). A **boiling water reactor** uses the cooling water itself as the source of steam for the turbines. In a **pressurized water reactor**, the coolant is water under such pressure that it reaches a high temperature without evaporation, and is used to heat boiler water via a heat exchanger. A **gas-cooled reactor** uses carbon dioxide or some other gas as a coolant, heating turbine water via a heat exchanger. A **fast reactor** has no moderator, and generally uses liquid sodium as a coolant. A **breeder reactor** uses uranium 238 enriched with plutonium 239; it produces more Pu 239, and is the type of reactor used to generate material for atomic weapons.

Nuclear Test-Ban Treaty A 1963 treaty prohibiting the testing of nuclear weapons on or above the surface of the Earth, originally put forward by the USA, USSR, and UK. The impact of the treaty was somewhat diminished by its boycott by two nuclear nations, France and China. All five nations signed a Comprehensive Test Ban Treaty in 1996.

nuclear weapons Weapons of mass destruction employing the energy-liberating nuclear phenomena of fission or fusion for their effects. According to their size and the means of delivery, they may be classified as **tactical short-range weapons** for use against enemy battlefield forces; **theatre medium-range weapons** for use against deep military targets; and **strategic long-range weapons** for use against enemy cities and command centres.

nucleic acids Large molecules which store genetic information, produced by living cells, and composed of a chain of nucleotides. Two forms are found: deoxyribonucleic acid (DNA) and ribonucleic acid (RNA), which may be either single- or double-stranded.

nucleonics The technology associated with nuclear reactors and their functioning. It entails the study of the techniques of assembling the radioactive material, the transfer of heat energy to boilers and turbines for the production of electricity, and the installation of all these units in structures which will be safe. It is also concerned with the design and use of instruments which monitor and control radioactivity, as well as with the disposal of radioactive waste material.

nucleon number The total number of protons plus neutrons in an atomic nucleus; symbol A; also called the **mass number**. This total differs for different isotopes, and so is useful for labelling them.

nucleosome The basic unit into which the DNA is packed in the chromatin of eucaryotes. A nucleosome contains an octomer of proteins consisting of two copies each of histones H2A, H2B, H3, and H4, around which is wrapped two-and-a-half turns (146 base pairs) of DNA. Other proteins will be involved in the packing; these will vary according to whether the DNA is active or silent.

nucleosynthesis The creation of chemical elements by nuclear reactions in stars and other cosmic explosions. Hydrogen burning in stars, and nuclear explosions at the end of a star's life, have formed all other elements by transmutation.

nucleotide A portion of a nucleic acid consisting of a purine or pyrimidine base, a sugar molecule, and a phosphate group bonded together. There are four principal nucleotides in DNA.

nucleus (astronomy) **1** The central core of a comet, about 1–10 km/½–6 mi across, consisting of icy substances and dust. **2** The central part of a galaxy or quasar, possibly the seat of unusually energetic activity within the galaxy.

nucleus (biology) The chromosome-containing structure found in the great majority of non-dividing eucaryotic cells;

delimited from the surrounding cytoplasm by a double membrane; typically ovoid or spherical, sometimes irregularly shaped.

nucleus (physics) The core of an atom, comprising various numbers of protons and neutrons, making up c.99·975% of an atom's mass. The number of protons equals the total positive charge of the nucleus, and equals the number of electrons in a complete atom. The nuclear components are bound together by strong nuclear force. The nucleus diameter is approximately 10^{-14} m.

Nudibranchia [nyoodibrangkia] *sea slug*

Nuesslein-Volhard, Christiane [nüsliyn folhaht] (1942–) Developmental biologist, born in Magdeburg, Germany. She shared the Nobel Prize for Physiology or Medicine in 1995 for her research into how genes control early development of the human embryo. Using the fruit fly, her contribution, in collaboration with Wieschaus, was to identify a number of genes which determine the body plan and formation of body segments.

Nuffield, William Richard Morris, 1st Viscount (1877–1963) Motor magnate and philanthropist, born in Worcester, Worcestershire. He became the first British manufacturer to develop the mass production of cheap (Morris) cars. In 1943 he established the Nuffield Foundation for medical, scientific, and social research.

Nuffield Radio Astronomy Laboratories An institution at Jodrell Bank, Cheshire, UK, founded in 1945, operated by the University of Manchester. It contains the first fully steerable radio telescope (76 m/250 ft), completed in 1957, now called the Lovell telescope.

Nujoma, Sam Daniel [nujohma] (1929–) Namibian nationalist leader, and first president of independent Namibia (1990–2004), born in Ongandjera, Namibia. He founded the South-West Africa People's Organization (SWAPO), and led the Namibian armed struggle against South Africa from 1966. He returned from exile in 1989 to win the presidential election.

Nuku'alofa [nookualohfah] 21°09S 175°14W, pop (2000e) 23 500. Port and capital town of Tonga, S Pacific; on Tongatapu I; university; royal palace (1867).

Nullarbor Plain [nuhlabaw] Vast plateau in SW South Australia and S Western Australia; extends for 480 km/300 mi; maximum height 305 m/1000 ft; crossed by the Trans-Australian Railway, the world's longest straight stretch of railway (478 km/297 mi).

numbat An Australian marsupial (*Myrmecobius fasciatus*); narrow pointed head with horizontal black line through eye; hindquarters with grey and white hoops; long bushy grey tail; female without a pouch; eats termites; also known as **banded anteater** or **marsupial anteater**. (Family: Myrmecobiidae.)

numbers A concept used initially in counting, to compare the sizes of groups of objects. **Natural numbers** (or *cardinal numbers*) are the numbers used in counting, 1,2,3,4,5.... These are always *whole numbers*. The set of *integers* comprises all the natural numbers (the *positive integers*), zero, and the *negative numbers*...–3,–2,–1. The **rational numbers** are all the numbers that can be expressed in the form m/n, where m and n are two integers, positive or negative. Rational numbers include *proper fractions* (those whose numerator is less than their denominator, eg $3/8$) and *improper fractions* (those whose numerator is greater than their denominator, eg $8/3$). **Mixed numbers** are the sum of an integer and a proper fraction, eg $2\frac{1}{2}$. *Decimal fractions* are those with denominator a power of 10, written as 0·3, 0·345, etc. **Irrational numbers** are all real numbers that are not rational. Some can be expressed as the roots of algebraic equations with rational coefficients, eg $\sqrt{3}$ is a root of $x^2 = 3$. Those that cannot be so expressed are called **transcendental numbers**, eg π, e, e^2. **Real numbers** are all numbers that do not contain an **imaginary number** (a square root of a negative

number). The positive square root of –1 is denoted by i (occasionally j). **Complex numbers** have a real and an imaginary part, eg $3 + 4i$.

Numbers, Book of A book of the Hebrew Bible/Old Testament, the fourth book of the Pentateuch; called 'Numbers' in Greek tradition because of the census of the tribes recorded in the first chapters. It describes the wanderings of Israel after the Exodus.

number theory The abstract study of the relationship between numbers, by which is meant positive rational numbers. An example of an early problem is one solved by Diophantus: 'Find three numbers such that their sum is a perfect square, and the sum of any two is a perfect square' (41, 80, 320). In the 17th-c Fermat proved many results in number theory.

numeral In mathematics, the symbol used to represent a number. The commonest system of numerals today is the Hindu–Arabic, possibly invented by the Hindus and brought to Europe by the Arabs. This uses the symbols 0, 1, 2, 3,...9 and the idea of place-value to represent each whole number. Other systems of numerals include the Roman and the Greek.

numerology The mystical study of numbers, derived mainly from Hindu and Arabic teaching, but also from Jewish and Chinese traditions. Each number has a size, quality, vibration, and mystical value, and the study of their symbolism can be used as a method of divination.

Numidia [nyumidia] The Roman name for the region in N Africa to the W and S of Carthage. It roughly corresponds to modern Algeria.

numismatics The study and collecting of coins, notes, and other similar objects, such as medals. The first known coins were issued by the Lydians of Anatolia in the 7th-c BC. Coin collectors worldwide were brought together in 1936, when the International Numismatics Foundation was set up.

nun A member of a religious order of women living under vows of poverty, chastity, and obedience. The term includes women living in enclosed convents, as well as sisters devoted to service of the sick or poor.

Nunavut [noo nah voot] (Inuktitut, 'Our land') A Canadian territory (area 2 093 190 km²/807 971 sq mi) created from a region formerly in E Northwest Territories, Canada, stretching from Manitoba to the North Pole; capital, Iqaluit. Its establishment was agreed in 1991 following negotiations between the federal government of Canada and Inuit leaders, and it was officially created on 1 April 1999. The population of c.29 000 is mainly Inuit (Eskimo).

Nunn, Sir Trevor (Robert) (1940–) Stage director, born in Ipswich, Suffolk. He became the Royal Shakespeare Company's artistic director (1968–87), and also directed the musicals *Cats* (1981), *Starlight Express* (1984), and *Aspects of Love* (1989). He was appointed director of the Royal National Theatre (1997–2003).

Nuremberg [nyooremberg], Ger **Nürnberg** 49°27N 11°05E, pop (2000e) 511 000. Commercial and manufacturing city in Germany; on the R Pegnitz; second largest city in Bavaria; scene of Mastersingers' contests during the Renaissance; annual meeting place of Nazi Party after 1933; badly bombed in World War 2; scene of German war criminal trials (1945–6); railway; birthplace of Albrecht Dürer; Imperial Castle (12th–16th-c).

Nuremberg Laws [nyooremberg] A series of racial laws promulgated in Nuremberg in 1935 during a Nazi Party rally. The two main ones deprived of German citizenship those not of 'German or related blood' and made marriage or extra-marital relations illegal between Germans and Jews.

Nuremberg Trials [nyooremberg] Proceedings held by the Allies at Nuremberg after World War 2 to try Nazi war criminals. An International Military Tribunal sat from November 1945 until October 1946. Twenty-one Nazis were tried in person.

Nureyev, Rudolf (Hametovich) [noorayef] (1938–93) Ballet dancer, born in Irkutsk, Russia. While touring with the Kirov Ballet in

1961, he obtained political asylum in Paris. He made his debut at Covent Garden with the Royal Ballet in 1962, and became Fonteyn's regular partner, his virtuosity making him one of the greatest male dancers of the 1960s. He became ballet director of the Paris Opéra in 1983.

Nurmi, Paavo (Johannes) [noormee] (1897–1973) Athlete, born in Turku, Finland. He won nine gold medals at three Olympic Games (1920–8), and set 22 world records at distances ranging from 1500–20 000 m. His statue stands outside the Helsinki Olympic Stadium.

Nürnberg *Nuremberg*

Nurse, Sir Paul (M) (1949–) Biochemist and cell biologist, born in London. He headed the Cell Cycle Laboratory of the Imperial Cancer Research Fund in London (1984–7) and returned to it in 1993 after a period holding a chair at Oxford. He shared the 2001 Nobel Prize for Physiology or Medicine for his contributions to understanding the key regulators of the cell cycle. He was knighted in 1999.

nursery rhymes Traditional rhymes, essentially adult-inspired, passed on from parent to child as nursery entertainment. Most date from no earlier than the 18th-c; the earliest printed collection appeared in 1744. A major collection of nursery rhymes and children's books, made by Iona Opie (1923–) and Peter Opie (1918–82), is housed in the Bodleian Library, Oxford.

nursery school A school for children under the age at which schooling becomes compulsory. The teachers are usually trained, by comparison with *playgroups*, which make greater use of volunteer helpers.

nursing The branch of medicine which provides care for the sick and injured, and assumes responsibility for the patients' physical, social, and spiritual needs that encourage recovery. Nurses comprise the largest single group of health workers. They are responsible for monitoring therapies, and increasingly have the authority to prescribe specific medical or surgical remedies or drugs, as well as assisting doctors and surgeons in carrying out treatment.

nut A dry, non-splitting fruit with a woody shell, often seated in a cup-like structure and containing several seeds, only one of which develops fully. In non-specialist use, the term is often applied to any woody fruit or seed.

nutcracker Either of two species of crow of the genus *Nucifraga*: the **nutcracker** (*Nucifraga caryocatactes*) of Europe and Asia; and **Clark's nutcracker** (*Nucifraga columbiana*) of W North America. (Family: Corvidae.)

nuthatch A small bird of the family Sittidae (c.23 species), inhabiting rocks or woodland in the N hemisphere; short tail, sharp straight bill; eats insects (sometimes nuts).

nutmeg An evergreen tree (*Myristica fragrans*) growing to 9 m/ 30 ft, native to the Moluccas, Indonesia; flowers waxy, yellow, 3-lobed bells; fruit fleshy, pear-shaped, containing a single, large seed (the nutmeg) surrounded by a red outgrowth from which mace is made. Both spices contain a narcotic, and are poisonous in large quantities. (Family: Myristicaceae.)

nutria *coypu*

nutrients All components of foods and all diet supplements. **Macronutrients** are energy proteins, carbohydrates, and fats;

micronutrients are minerals, vitamins, and various chemical substances present in tiny quantities (the *trace elements*).

nutrition The scientific study of all aspects of what organisms eat. It involves the analysis of what people eat, the psychology of why they eat, what happens to food in the body, and how the balance of food affects health. An expert in nutrition is known as a **nutritionist**.

nutritional medicine The study of the interaction of nutritional factors within the human body to find ways of treating disease and maintaining health. It includes the study of the properties of the nutrients themselves, and the physiology of digestion, absorption, and biochemical utilization.

nutritional minerals Elements found in all cells and fluids of the body that are essential in the diet, though only in very small quantities. Examples include: calcium, required to build bones and teeth and for the process of transmitting nervous impulses to muscles; and iron, used by the body to make haemoglobin, an oxygen-carrying pigment in the blood.

nyala An African spiral-horned antelope; greyish-brown with thin vertical white lines; two species: **nyala** (*Tragelaphus angasi*), found in SE Africa; and **mountain nyala** (*Tragelaphus buxtoni*), from high forest in Ethiopia.

Nyasa [niasa] or **Malawi, Lake**, Mozambique **Niassa** area 28 500 km²/11 000 sq mi. Lake in SEC Africa; third largest lake in Africa, in the S section of the Great Rift Valley; altitude, 437 m/1434 ft; sometimes known as the 'Calendar Lake' because it is 365 miles long and 52 miles across, at its widest point; a world heritage site.

Nyerere, Julius (Kambarage) [nyerairay] (1922–99) Tanzanian statesman and president (1962–85), born in Butiama, Tanzania. He was premier when Tanganyika was granted internal self-government (1961), and president on independence (1962). In 1964 he negotiated the union of Tanganyika and Zanzibar, as Tanzania.

nylon A generic term for the most widely-produced type of synthetic fibre, used commercially since 1938. It is a polyamide whose lightness and elasticity make it available for use both in fibre and solid form. It is also an extremely strong and hard-wearing material. Its uses are therefore varied, including ropes, tyre cords, engineering components, furnishings, and apparel.

Nyman, Michael [niyman] (1944–) Pianist and composer, born in London. He formed the Michael Nyman Band in 1977, for which he composed several works in which his own piano playing is a driving force. His compositions include scores for the films of Peter Greenaway, and for the films *The Piano* (1993), *Carrington* (1995), *The Libertine* (2004), and *A Cock and Bull Story* (2005). Operatic works include *The Man Who Mistook His Wife for a Hat* (1986), *Facing Goya* (2000), and *Love Counts* (2006).

nymph (mythology) In Greek mythology, one of the 'young women', nature-spirits, who live in streams (*naiads*), trees (*hamadryads*), the sea (*nereids*), as well as rocks and mountains. They are long-lived but not immortal.

nymphalid butterfly A butterfly of the family Nymphalidae; typically colourful, with long hair-like scales; c.8200 species, including admirals, emperors, fritillaries, and tortoiseshell butterflies. (Order: Lepidoptera.)

nymphomania *satyriasis*

O

Oahu [ohahhoo] pop (2000e) 920 000; area 1526 km²/589 sq mi. Third largest island of the US state of Hawaii; chief town, Honolulu; naval base at Pearl Harbor.

oak A member of a large genus of often massive and long-lived trees and also small shrubs, native to the N hemisphere; leaves deciduous or evergreen; flowers tiny, 4–7-lobed; fruit an acorn seated in a scaly cup. It is a traditional source of excellent timber, and also of cork and bark for tanning. (Genus: *Quercus*, 450 species. Family: Fagaceae.)

Oakland 37°49N 122°16W, pop (2000e) 399 500. Port in W California, USA, on the E shore of San Francisco Bay; founded, 1850; two airports; railway; observatory; professional teams, A's (baseball), Golden State Warriors (basketball).

Oakley, Annie, popular name of **Phoebe Anne Oakley Moses** (1860–1926) Sharpshooter and Wild West performer, born near Woodland, OH. She won fame in Buffalo Bill's Wild West Show, but her career ended when she was injured in a train crash in 1901.

OAS 1 Abbreviation of **Organisation de l'armée Secrète** ('Secret Army Organization'), the clandestine organization of French Algerians, active (1960–2) in resisting Algerian independence. It caused considerable violence until thrown into rapid decline by Algerian independence (Jul 1962).
2 Organization of American States

Oates, Lawrence (Edward Grace) (1880–1912) Explorer, born in London. In 1910 he joined Scott's Antarctic Expedition, and was one of the party of five to reach the S Pole in 1912. Lamed by severe frostbite, and convinced that his condition would fatally handicap his companions' prospect of survival, he walked out into the blizzard, sacrificing his life.

Oates, Titus (1649–1705) English conspirator and perjurer, born in Oakham, Leicestershire. In 1677 he fabricated a 'Popish Plot', supposedly directed at the life of Charles II. When the plot was made public, he became the hero of the day; but two years later he was found guilty of perjury, and imprisoned. He was freed at the Revolution of 1688.

oath A solemn expression from a person giving evidence in court or making a sworn written statement. The traditional wording is 'I swear by Almighty God that the evidence which I shall give shall be the truth, the whole truth, and nothing but the truth'. Alternatively, it is possible to *affirm*, that is to solemnly promise to tell the truth. Other traditional or religious practices may be recognized.

oats A cereal (*Avena sativa*), probably native to the Mediterranean basin, and cultivated in temperate regions, especially in the N hemisphere, tolerating a wide climatic range, and growing where other cereals fail. It is an important human and animal food, though less so in recent times. (Family: Gramineae.)

Ob, River [op] Chief river of the W Siberian Lowlands, C Russia; enters the Kara Sea; length, 3650 km/2268 mi; with the R Irtysh, its chief tributary, length 5570 km/3461 mi, the world's fourth longest river; frozen for 5–6 months of the year.

Obadiah, Book of [ohbadiya] One of the 12 so-called 'minor' prophetic writings of the Hebrew Bible/Old Testament; named after the otherwise unknown prophet, whose name means 'Servant of God'; sometimes called **Book of Abdias**. The work may have originated soon after the fall of Jerusalem in 587/6 BC.

Obelia [ohbeelia] A genus of marine invertebrate animals; hydroids, living in colonies, commonly found growing on seaweeds in the inter-tidal zone on shores. (Phylum: Cnidaria. Class: Hydrozoa.)

obelisk A tall pillar, usually made of granite, square in section, tapering upwards, and ending in a small pyramid. Well-known examples are Cleopatra's Needles (c.1475 BC), one of which is now located on the Victoria Embankment, London, the other in Central Park, New York City.

Oberammergau Passion Play [ohberamergow] A dramatization every 10 years of the Passion of Christ, performed by villagers of Oberammergau in Bavaria, Germany. It is performed in fulfilment of a vow made in 1663, when the village was saved from plague.

Oberon (astronomy) [ohberon] The second-largest satellite of Uranus, discovered in 1787 by Herschel; distance from the planet 583 500 km/362 600 mi; diameter 1524 km/947 mi.

Oberon (mythology) [ohberon] In European literature, the name of the king of the fairies, as in Shakespeare's *A Midsummer Night's Dream* and Wieland's *Oberon*.

obesity [ohbeesitee] Extreme overweight, with an excessive amount of body fat. It may be related to genetic factors, or to hormonal disorders such as hypothyroidism, or Cushing's syndrome. However the majority of cases are a consequence of excessive food intake and inadequate physical exercise.

obo [ohboh] A term derived from 'oil/bulk ore', a vessel designed to carry oil and bulk ore either together or separately. This is a relatively new class of vessel, first built in the mid-1960s. By 2000, total obo tonnage was 20 million gross tonnes, over 37 million deadweight tonnes.

oboe A musical instrument made of wood in three jointed sections, opening to a small bell; it is fitted with a double reed. It first appeared in recognizable form in the mid-17th-c and was widely used in the 18th-c. In the orchestra it is normally the oboe that sets the pitch for the other instruments.

Obote, (Apollo) Milton [obohtay] (1924–2005) Ugandan nationalist leader, prime minister (1962–6) and president (1967–71, 1981–5), born in Lango, Uganda. He founded the Uganda People's Congress (1960), and became leader of the opposition (1961–2). At independence in 1962 he became the new nation's first prime minister. He ruled Uganda both before and after the dictatorship of Idi Amin. He was deposed in 1985, and fled into exile in Zambia where he remained until his death. His body was returned to Uganda for burial.

O'Brien, (Josephine) Edna (1930–) Novelist, born in Tuamgraney, Co Clare, Ireland. Her novels include *The Country Girls* (1960), *House of Splendid Isolation* (1994), *Wild Decembers* (1999), and

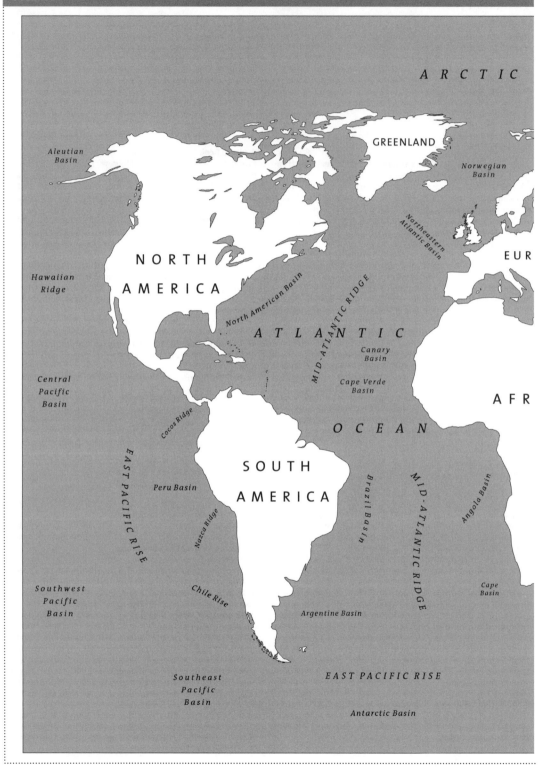

A R C T I C

GREENLAND

Aleutian
Basin

Norwegian
Basin

Northeastern
Atlantic Basin

NORTH

AMERICA

EUR

Hawaiian
Ridge

North American Basin

A T L A N T I C

MID-ATLANTIC RIDGE

Canary
Basin

Cape Verde
Basin

AFR

Central
Pacific
Basin

Cocos Ridge

O C E A N

EAST PACIFIC RISE

SOUTH

AMERICA

Peru Basin

Nazca Ridge

Brazil Basin

MID-ATLANTIC RIDGE

Angola Basin

Southwest
Pacific
Basin

Chile Rise

Argentine Basin

Cape
Basin

Southeast
Pacific
Basin

EAST PACIFIC RISE

Antarctic Basin

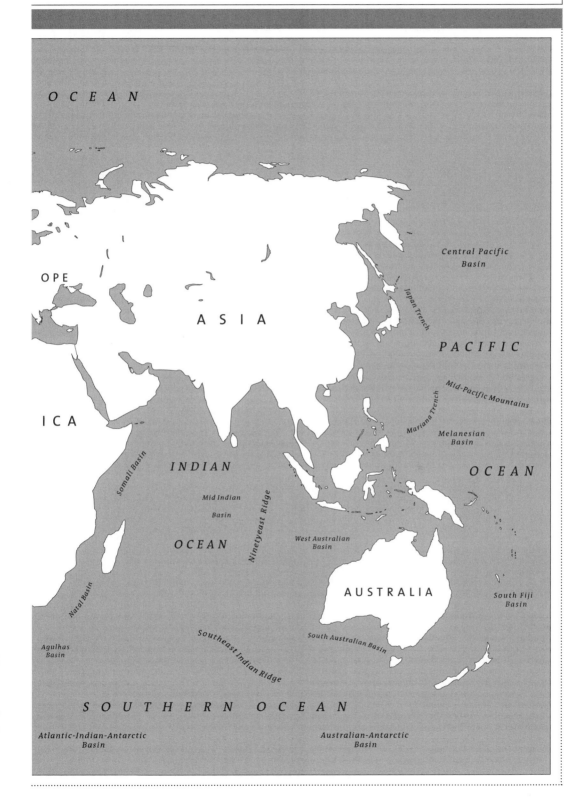

OCEAN

OPE

ICA

ASIA

Central Pacific
Basin

Japan Trench

PACIFIC

Mid-Pacific Mountains

Mariana Trench

Melanesian
Basin

OCEAN

INDIAN

Somali Basin

Mid Indian

Basin

Ninetyeast Ridge

West Australian
Basin

OCEAN

AUSTRALIA

South Fiji
Basin

Natal Basin

Agulhas
Basin

Southeast Indian Ridge

South Australian Basin

SOUTHERN OCEAN

Atlantic-Indian-Antarctic
Basin

Australian-Antarctic
Basin

The Light of Evening (2006). Her short stories are also highly regarded; the best from several collections appear in *The Fanatic Heart* (1985).

O'Brien, Flann, pseudonym of **Brian O'Nolan**, also known as **Myles na Gopaleen** (1911–66) Writer, born in Strabane, Co Tyrone, Ireland. As 'Myles na Gopaleen' he made regular satirical contributions to the *Irish Times*. His novels include *At Swim-Two-Birds* (1939), *The Hard Life* (1960), and *The Dalkey Archive* (1964).

observatory The instruments and associated buildings for conducting astronomical research. This broad definition includes the structures of native proto-astronomers, such as the builders of Stonehenge and Meso-American pyramids, the great mountain observatories of professionals in Hawaii, Australia, and Chile, the backyard shed of the keen amateur, and satellites carrying telescopes far above the atmosphere. Modern optical observatories are situated on mountain-tops to get above cloud and atmospheric pollution, with oceanic islands being particularly satisfactory.

obstetrics [obstetriks] The medical and surgical care of pregnancy and childbirth. It involves the prenatal care and assessment of the woman's ability to undergo labour, the assessment of the size and health of the fetus in the womb, the detection of diseases related to pregnancy, the diagnosis of the position of the fetus in the uterus, and the conduct of the delivery. Also important are the control of pain and the diagnosis and treatment of complications.

ocarina [okareena] A simple, egg-shaped musical instrument belonging to the flute family, with a protruding mouthpiece, six fingerholes, and two thumbholes. It is made from terracotta.

O'Casey, Sean, originally **John Casey** (1880–1964) Playwright, born in Dublin. His early plays, such as *Juno and the Paycock* (1924), were written for the Abbey Theatre. He was awarded the Hawthornden Prize in 1926. His later work includes *Cock-a-doodle Dandy* (1949) and *The Bishop's Bonfire* (1955).

occultism Activities purporting to achieve communication with the supernatural. The term includes magic, divination, certain types of spiritualism, and witchcraft.

occupational diseases Diseases which arise in the course of employment; also known as **industrial disease**, in the context of industrial work. For example, many chemicals and dyes induce dermatitis. Inhalation of industrial products affects the lungs, and may lead to pneumoconiosis or asbestosis. Ionizing radiation may cause leukaemia. Compressed-air workers suffer damage to their ears and fingers, and welders may damage their eyes. Such events have led to the development of *industrial medicine*.

occupational therapy A range of treatments designed to minimise the impact of physical and psychiatric conditions on life in order to help people reach their maximum level of function and independence. It includes provision of physical aids, such as stair rails, and activities such as vocationally orientated workshops and arts and crafts classes.

oceanarium *aquarium*

Oceania [ohshiahnia], also **Oceanica** A general name applied to the isles of the Pacific Ocean, including Polynesia, Melanesia, Micronesia, Australasia, and sometimes the Malaysian islands.

oceanic ridges Giant undersea mountain ranges, rising above the surrounding sea floor 1–4 km/½–2½ mi, which wind their way around the globe for over 80 000 km/50 000 mi and cover 35% of the sea floor. The Mid-Atlantic Ridge is the best-known ridge system. Large areas of the sea floor which rise more than several hundred metres above the level of the ocean basin floor are **oceanic rises**.

Oceanides [ohseeanideez] In Greek mythology, the innumerable nymphs who inhabit the ocean and other watery places. They are the daughters of Oceanus and Tethys.

oceanography The study of the oceans, also referred to as **oceanology**. **Geological oceanography** deals with the structure and origin of the ocean floor, and the processes which operate along the shoreline. **Chemical oceanography** deals with the chemical properties of seawater, and the reactions which take place in the ocean. **Physical oceanography** covers the physical processes in the ocean, including ocean currents, waves, tides, and the interaction between the atmosphere and the ocean. **Biological oceanography** deals with marine organisms and their relationship with their environment. *pp.674–5*

Oceanus [ohseeanus] In Greek mythology, a Titan, the son of Uranus and Gaia. He is a benign god who personifies the stream of Ocean which was assumed to surround the world.

ocelot [oselot] A rare member of the cat family (*Felis pardalis*), found from S USA to N Argentina; pale with dark spots and lines; sometimes reared as pets; also known as **painted leopard** or **tigrillo**.

ochre Earth consisting of a mixture of hydrated iron oxides and clay, light yellow to brown in colour. It is ground to a powder and used as a pigment.

Ockham, William of *William of Ockham*

O'Connell, Daniel, known as **the Liberator** (1775–1847) Irish Catholic political leader, born near Cahirciveen, Co Kerry, Ireland. In 1823 he formed the Catholic Association, which successfully fought elections against the landlords. His election as MP for Co Clare precipitated a crisis in Wellington's government, which eventually granted Catholic Emancipation (1829), enabling him to take his seat in the Commons.

O'Connor, Feargus Edward (1794–1855) Chartist leader, born in Connorville, Co Cork, Ireland. His Leeds *Northern Star* (1837) became the most influential Chartist newspaper. He attempted, without great success, to unify the Chartist movement via the National Charter Association (1842).

O'Connor, Sandra Day, *née* **Day** (1930–) Jurist, born in El Paso, TX. In 1981 President Reagan named her as the first woman justice of the US Supreme Court. She retired in 2005.

octadecanoic acid *stearic acid*

octane number The measure of ability of a fuel to resist knocking (premature ignition) in the cylinder of an internal combustion engine.

Octans (Lat 'octant') An inconspicuous S constellation.

October Revolution (1917) The overthrow of the Russian provisional government by Bolshevik-led armed workers (Red Guards), soldiers, and sailors (25–26 Oct 1917). The members of the provisional government were replaced by the Soviet of People's Commissars, chaired by Lenin – the first Soviet government.

October War *Arab–Israeli Wars*

octopus A carnivorous marine mollusc with a short, sac-like body and eight arms largely connected by webbing; reaches 5·4 m/18 ft in length, and with a maximum outstretched armspan of nearly 9 m/30 ft; when alarmed, may eject a cloud of ink. (Class: Cephalopoda. Order: Octopoda.)

octopush A form of hockey played underwater, first introduced in South Africa in the 1960s. Teams consist of six players who use miniature hockey sticks and a puck replacing the ball.

ode (Gr 'song') A lyric poem, usually of some length and formal complexity. Pindar in Greek, Horace in Latin, and Keats in English were notable practitioners.

Odense [ohdensuh] 55°24N 10°25E, pop (2000e) 182 600. Port and chief town on Fyn I, Denmark; third largest city of Denmark; railway; university (1964); birthplace of Hans Christian Andersen.

Oder, River [ohder], Czech, Polish **Odra**, ancient **Viadua** River in C

Europe rising in E Sudetes Mts of Czech Republic; enters the Baltic Sea; length 854 km/531 mi; canal links to W and E Europe.

Oder–Neisse Line [ohder niysuh] The Polish–German border, drawn by the Allies (1944–5), and involving the transfer to Poland of large areas of pre-war Germany.

Odessa [ohdesa] 46°30N 30°46E, pop (2000e) 1 095 000. Seaport in Ukraine, on NW shore of the Black Sea; centre of the battleship *Potemkin* mutiny in the 1905 Revolution; naval base; leading Black Sea port; large health resorts nearby; railway; university (1865); cathedral (1855–69).

Odets, Clifford [ohdets] (1906–63) Playwright and actor, born in Philadelphia, PA. A leading author of the 1930s, his works include *Waiting for Lefty* (1935) and *Golden Boy* (1937).

Odette, popular name of **Odette Hallowes**, formerly **Churchill** (to 1955) and **Sansom** (to 1946), née **Brailly** (1912–95) French wartime resistance heroine, born in Amiens, France. Brought up in France, she married an Englishman in 1931 and moved to London. Sent to France as an agent, she was arrested by the Germans in 1943, and sent to Ravensbruck concentration camp. Her wartime exploits were retold in a successful film, *Odette* (1950), starring Anna Neagle.

Odin [ohdin] In Norse mythology, the All-Father, the god of poetry and the dead; also known as **Woden** (English) or **Wotan** (German). He gave one eye to the Giant Mimir in exchange for wisdom.

Odo [ohdoh] (c.1036–97) Bishop of Bayeux (1049–97) and Earl of Kent, the half-brother of William the Conqueror. He may have commissioned the Bayeux tapestry.

Odoacer [ohdohayser], also found as **Odovacar** (?–493) Germanic warrior who destroyed the W Roman Empire, and became the first barbarian king of Italy (476–93). He was challenged and overthrown by the Ostrogothic King Theodoric (489–93).

Odonata [ohdonata] *damselfly; dragonfly*

Odysseus [odisyoos] A Greek hero, known in Latin as **Ulixes**, from which **Ulysses** is derived. The son of Laertes, King of Ithaca, he took part in the Trojan War. He took 10 years to return from Troy, encountering many romantic adventures, described in Homer's *Odyssey*.

Oe, Kenzaburo [ohay] (1935–) Novelist and short-story writer, born in Shikoku, Japan. His major books include *A Personal Matter* (1964, trans 1968), *The Silent Cry* (1967, trans 1974, Tanizaki Prize), and *A Healing Family* (trans 1996). Later works include *Grand Street 55* (trans 1999). He received the Nobel Prize for Literature in 1994.

oedema / edema [eedeema] The accumulation of excess amounts of body fluids (water and salts) within the tissues of the body. The most common causes are heart, kidney, and liver failure.

Oedipus [eedipus] In Greek legend, a Theban hero of whom it was foretold that he would kill his father and marry his mother. He fled from his adoptive parents when an oracle revealed his destiny, but on the way to Thebes he killed his father Laius by chance, was made the new ruler of the city and married its queen, Jocasta. When all was revealed, he blinded himself.

Oedipus complex [eedipus] A psychoanalytic term describing the erotic feelings of a son for his mother, and an associated sense of competitiveness towards the father. The female equivalent is the **Electra complex**. Both terms were coined by Freud.

Oersted *Ørsted, Hans Christian*

oesophagus / esophagus [eesofaguhs] A long, muscular tube passing from the lower part of the pharynx through the thorax to the stomach; also known as the **gullet**. In adult humans it is c.24 cm/9·5 in long.

oestrogens / estrogens [eestrojenz] Steroid sex hormones (eg *oestradiol, oestriol, oestrone*) produced in the ovary, placenta, testis, and adrenal cortex. They are responsible for the development of female secondary sexual characteristics in humans.

They are also used in oral contraceptives and in the treatment of certain cancers (eg of the prostate).

oestrus / estrus [eestruhs] The period of maximum sexual receptivity, or heat, in female mammals. It is usually also the time of release of the egg from the ovary.

'Of'- (organizations) *regulator*

Offa (?–796) King of Mercia (757–96). He was the greatest Anglo-Saxon ruler in the 8th-c, treated as an equal by Charlemagne. His reign represents an important but flawed attempt to unify England, with the Mercian supremacy collapsing soon after his death.

offal All the organs of slaughtered animals other than muscles and bones. Several of these organs (such as the liver and kidneys) are eaten; others (such as the gut) are discarded.

Offaly [ofalee], Ir **Ua bhFailghe** pop (2000e) 59 000; area 1997 km²/771 sq mi. County in C Ireland; Slieve Bloom Mts rise in the SW; capital, Tullamore; large tracts of peat used as fuel for power stations.

Offa's Dyke An interrupted linear earthwork 130 km/80 mi long linking the R Dee near Prestatyn, N Wales, with the Severn Estuary at Chepstow. Erected in the late 8th-c AD by Offa, King of Mercia, to define the W boundary of his kingdom, it marks the traditional boundary between England and Wales.

Off-Broadway *Broadway*

Offenbach, Jacques [ofenbahkh], originally **Jacob Eberst** (1819–80) Composer, born in Cologne, Germany. He composed many light, lively operettas, such as *Orphée aux enfers* (1858, Orpheus in the Underworld). He also produced one grand opera, *Les contes d'hoffmann* (Tales of Hoffmann), which was not produced until 1881. A handwritten copy of the original score was discovered in the Paris Opera library in 2004.

Office, Divine or **Holy** In the pre-Reformation Western Church and in the Roman Catholic Church, prayers which must be said by priests and religious every day, originally at fixed hours.

Office of Fair Trading A non-ministerial government department in England and Wales, headed by the Director-General of Fair Trading. It keeps under review commercial activities which supply goods or services to the consumer, and collects information about these activities. The director-general also monitors commercial activities which relate to monopoly situations.

Office of Management and Budget (OMB) The office which the US president uses to control the financial operations of government, created in 1970 out of the Bureau of the Budget. It is an important political arm of the presidency.

offset lithography *lithography*

O'Flaherty, Liam (1897–1984) Writer, born in the Aran Is, Co Galway, Ireland. His novels include *The Informer* (1925), which was a great popular success, *The Assassin* (1928), and *Land* (1946).

Ogaden [ogaden] Geographical area in SE Ethiopia; dry plateau; part of Abyssinia, 1890; part of Italian East Africa, 1936–41; largely inhabited by Somali-speaking nomads; area claimed by Somalia in 1960s; Somali invasion in 1977 repulsed by Ethiopian forces; fighting continued throughout the 1980s.

Ogam or **Ogham** [ogam] A writing system used from around the 4th-c AD for writing Irish and Pictish. The alphabet has 20 letters composed of sets of parallel straight lines, cut to and across the vertical corners of stone monuments.

Ogden, C(harles) K(ay) (1889–1957) Linguistic reformer, born in Fleetwood, Lancashire. In the 1920s he conceived the idea of Basic English, a simplified form of English with only 850 words, to provide a practical means of international communication.

Ogdon, John (Andrew Howard) (1937–89) Pianist, born in Mansfield Woodhouse, Nottinghamshire. In 1962 he was joint prize-winner in the Tchaikovsky Competition in Moscow. Illness forced him to give up playing for several years.

Ogham *Ogam*

Ogilvy, Mrs Angus *Alexandra, Princess*

O'Hara, John (Henry) (1905–70) Writer, born in Pottsville, PA. Several of his novels were made into successful films, such as *Butterfield 8* (1935; filmed, 1960) and *Ten North Frederik* (1955; filmed, 1958). *Pal Joey* (1940) was adapted into a celebrated musical comedy. His short-story collections include *The Doctor's Son* (1935) and *Waiting for Winter* (1967).

O. Henry Henry, O

O'Higgins, Bernardo, known as **the Liberator of Chile** (1778–1842) Chilean revolutionary, born in Chillán, Chile. The son of an Irish-born Governor of Chile, he played the major role in the Chilean struggle for independence. He became the first leader of the new Chilean state in 1817, but was deposed in 1823.

Ohio [ohhiyoh] pop (2000e) 11 353 000; area 107 040 km²/ 41 330 sq mi. State in E USA; the 'Buckeye State'; visited by La Salle in 1669; 17th state to join the Union, 1803; part of the Allegheny plateau; capital, Columbus; grain, livestock, coal (E and SE Appalachian coalfield); major industrial centre.

Ohio River River in EC USA; formed at Pittsburgh; flows to join the Mississippi at Cairo, IL; length 2101 km/1306 mi (including the Allegheny).

Ohlin, Bertil (Gotthard) (1899–1979) Economist and politician, born in Klippan, Sweden. He is best known for the **Heckscher–Ohlin theorem**, which states that countries will export goods that are produced with their relatively abundant factors of production, and import those goods produced with their scarce factors. He shared the 1977 Nobel Prize for Economics.

Ohm, Georg Simon (1787–1854) Physicist, born in Erlangen, Germany. His main discoveries were in the field of electricity.

ohm SI unit of electrical resistance; symbol Ω; a resistance of 1 ohm exists between two points of a conductor if a potential difference of 1 volt causes a current of 1 amp to flow between them; named after Georg Ohm; commonly used as **kilohms** ($k\Omega$, 10^3 ohms) and **megohms** ($M\Omega$, 10^6 ohms); resistance is measured using an **ohmmeter**.

Ohm's law In electrical circuits, the result that potential difference U and current I satisfy $U = IR$ for resistance R; for alternating current circuits, $U = IZ$, where Z is impedance; stated by Georg Ohm in 1827.

Ohrid [okhrid], Ital **Ohrida** 41°06N 20°49E, pop (2000e) 69 000. Town in the SW of the Former Yugoslav Republic of Macedonia; on the shores of L Ohrid; airfield; tourism; old town, a world heritage site; cathedral; castle.

oil (botany) A fluid secreted by special glands in many plants, often forming food reserves in fruits and seeds such as olives, palms, rape, and flax. Volatile *essential oils* are produced by aromatic plants, especially in dry regions. *Edible oils* are obtained from many plants, including soy beans, maize, olives, sunflowers, coconut, and rapeseed.

oil (earth sciences) A fossil fuel that is chemically a complex mixture of hydrocarbons, formed from organic remains by the action of heat and pressure over millions of years; known as *natural* or *crude* oil. It occurs together with natural gas and solid hydrocarbons (collectively termed *petroleum*) as well as water. When refined it is used as a primary fuel for industry, and hence has great economic importance.

oilbird A nightjar-like bird (*Steatornis caripensis*) native to N South America and Trinidad; uses echolocation; also known as the **guacharo** or **diablotin**. Its fledglings are very fat, and were formerly boiled to extract oil, used for cooking. (Family: Steatornithidae.)

oil painting A method of painting which employs drying oils (such as linseed oil) in the medium. In use since Roman times, the technique was perfected and adapted to painting pictures in the 15th-c.

oil palm A tree (*Elaeis guineensis*) reaching 15 m/50 ft, native to tropical Africa; leaves 4.5 m/15 ft, feathery. The numerous oval, orange fruits are rendered down for oil. (Family: Palmae.)

oil rig An artificial platform set up above deposits of oil and gas at sea to support drilling equipment. The tall towers are known as *jackets*, which are made on land and towed out to sea on their sides before being erected. *Shallow-water rigs* are built on barges which are towed into position and then sunk to provide a steady base for the derrick and drilling gear. In deep water, *fixed-leg rigs* stand on the seabed and are held by steel pins; these are so heavy and strong that they can withstand almost all rough weather conditions. *Compliant rigs* are designed to sway slightly in storms, and are less likely to fall over; they stand on narrow columns on the seabed, and are held upright by guy ropes. The drill bit which cuts through the rock to the oil deposit is made of hard material such as diamond or tungsten. It is at the end of a long pipe called the *drill string*, which is made up of sections 9 m (30 ft) long. By steering the drill bit, an oil rig platform can drill up to 40 wells under the seabed at different angles, allowing more access to the oil deposit.

Oireachtas [erakhtas] An annual Irish gathering organized, on the lines of the Welsh eisteddfod, by the Gaelic League; first held in 1898.

Oistrakh, David (Fyodorovitch) [oystrak] (1908–74) Violinist, born in Odessa, Ukraine. He made several concert tours in Europe and the USA, and was awarded the Stalin (1945) and Lenin (1960) Prizes.

Ojibwa [ohjibwa] An Algonkin North American Indian group originally concentrated around L Superior and L Huron; called **Chippewa** by the Europeans; c.150 000 (2000 census).

Ojos del Salado, Cerro [ohkhohs thel salathoh] 27°05S 68°35W. Andean peak rising to 6908 m/22 664 ft on the Argentina–Chile border; second highest peak in the W hemisphere, after Aconcagua; world's highest active volcano.

okapi [ohkahpee] A mammal of the giraffe family (*Okapia johnstoni*) native to Democratic Republic of Congo; reddish-brown with long neck, large ears, and extremely long tongue; face and lower legs pale; upper legs and hindquarters with thin horizontal stripes; male with two blunt 'horns'.

Okavango, River [ohkavanggoh] Third largest river in S Africa; rises in C Angola; drains into the Okavango delta (c.15 000 km²/ 6000 sq mi), containing forest, swamp, marsh, and lagoon, a major wildlife area, where all the water evaporates; length 1600 km/1000 mi.

Okayama [ohkayama] 34°40N 133°54E, pop (2000e) 610 000. Port in SW Honshu, Japan; railway; university (1949); dominated by 'Castle of the Crow' (16th-c).

Okeechobee, Lake [ohkeechohbee] Lake in SC Florida, USA; largest lake in S USA; area 815 km²/315 sq mi.

O'Keeffe, Georgia (1887–1986) Painter, born in Sun Prairie, WI. As early as 1915 she pioneered abstract art in the USA (eg 'Blue and Green Music', 1919), but later moved towards a more figurative style, painting flowers and architectural subjects frequently with a Surrealist flavour, and with New Mexico settings (where she lived after 1949). She married photographer Alfred Stieglitz in 1924.

Okefenokee Swamp [ohkefenohkee] (Muskogean 'water-shaking') Area of swamp land in SE Georgia and NE Florida, USA; important wildlife refuge.

Okhotsk, Sea of, Russ **Okhotskoye More** area 1 528 000 km²/ 590 000 sq mi. NW arm of the Pacific Ocean, bounded E by the Kamchatka Peninsula, W by the island of Sakhalin and the far E coast of Russia; maximum depth 3365 m/11 039 ft; ice-bound (Nov–Jun) and subject to heavy fogs.

Okinawa [ohkinawa] pop (2000e) 1 278 000; area 2263 km²/ 874 sq mi. Region of Japan comprising the S part of the Ryukyu group; island of Okinawa is the largest in the group (area

1176 km²/454 sq mi); taken by the USA in World War 2; returned to Japan, 1972; capital, Naha.

Oklahoma [ohklahohma] (Muskogean 'red people') pop (2000e) 3 450 700; area 181 083 km²/69 919 sq mi. State in SW USA; the 'Sooner State'; mostly acquired by the USA in the Louisiana Purchase, 1803; Indians forced to move here in the 1830s (Indian Territory); Indians then lost the W region to whites (Oklahoma Territory, 1890); merged Indian and Oklahoma territories admitted to the Union as the 46th state, 1907; Ouachita Mts in the SE; Wichita Mts in the SW; highest point, Black Mesa (1516 m/4974 ft); in the W, high prairies part of the Great Plains; capital, Oklahoma City; major agricultural products livestock and wheat; large oil reserves and associated petroleum industry.

Oklahoma City 35°30N 97°30W, pop (2000e) 506 000. State capital in C Oklahoma, USA, on the N Canadian R; settled around a railway station, 1889; state capital, 1910; developed rapidly after oil discovered, 1928; largest city in the state; airport; railway; university (1911); terrorist bomb destroyed federal office block, April 1995; oil production; processing centre for livestock, grain, cotton.

okra [ohkra, okra] A vegetable crop (*Hibiscus esculentis*), originating in tropical Africa, and producing cylindrical edible fruits up to 20 cm/8 in long which are eaten immature, either cooked or fresh; also known as **ladies' fingers** or **gumbo**. The crop is widely cultivated in the tropics and sub-tropics. (Family: Malvaceae.)

Olah, George A [ola] (1927–) Chemist, born in Budapest. He left Hungary in 1956 for Canada, then the USA. He received the 1994 Nobel Prize for Chemistry for the study of hydrocarbons, and of new ways to use them, identifying an intermediate stage of short-lived compounds ('carbocations') in organic chemical reactions.

Öland [oeland] pop (2000e) 26 500; area 1344 km²/519 sq mi. Elongated Swedish island in the Baltic Sea, off the SE coast of Sweden; length, 136 km/84 mi; largest island in Sweden; chief town, Borgholm; castle (12th–13th-c). The southern part of the island is a world heritage site.

Olav V [ohlaf] (1903–91) King of Norway (1957–91), born near Sandringham, Norfolk, the only child of Haakon VII and Maud, daughter of Edward VII. In 1929 he married **Princess Martha** (1901–54) of Sweden, and had two daughters and a son, **Harald** (b.1937), King of Norway (1991–). His son, **Crown Prince Haakon**, married **Mette-Marit Tjessem Hoiby** in 2001 and they have a daughter, **Ingrid Alexandra** (2004–).

Old Bailey A street in the City of London, and, by association, the Central Criminal Court located there. The present building dates from 1907; the bronze statue of Justice surmounting its dome is a notable London landmark.

Oldcastle, Sir John, nickname **Good Lord Cobham** (c.1378–1417) Lollard leader and knight of England, born in Hereford, Herefordshire. An intimate of Henry V when Prince of Wales, he was convicted on charges of heresy in 1413. He conspired with other Lollards to take control of London, but was caught and executed. Shakespeare's Falstaff is based partly on him.

Old Catholics A group of Churches separated at various times from the Roman Catholic Church, including the Church of Utrecht (separated 1724), and German, Austrian, and Swiss Catholics who refused to accept papal infallibility (1870); also some former Poles and Croats in North America.

Old Church Slavonic *Slavic languages*

Old Comedy Athenian comic theatre of the 5th-c BC. The only complete plays extant are by Aristophanes.

Oldenburg, Claes (Thure) (1929–) Sculptor, born in Stockholm. He blends Surrealism and Pop Art, especially in his giant models of everyday objects made of canvas stuffed with foam rubber and painted in bright colours.

Old English The language of the Anglo-Saxons in England, in the period before the Norman Conquest; also known as **Anglo-Saxon**. Glosses to Latin texts survive from the 8th-c; the epic poem *Beowulf* (composed in the 8th-c) is preserved in an 11th-c manuscript. Anglo-Saxon was written in an Irish form of the Latin alphabet, introduced by monks.

Old English sheepdog A breed of dog, developed in Britain in the 18th-c to protect cattle; long, untidy coat, often hiding ears and eyes; usually white with large dark patches; short tail.

Oldfield, Bruce (1950–) Fashion designer, born in London. He showed his first collection in London in 1975. His designs include evening dresses for royalty and screen stars, and ready-to-wear clothes.

Old High German *Germanic languages*

Oldman, Gary (1959–) Film actor, producer, and director, born in London. He became known following his portrayal of punk rocker Sid Vicious in the film *Sid and Nancy* (1986). Later films include *Prick up Your Ears* (1987), *Bram Stoker's Dracula* (1992), *Lost in Space* (1998), and *Batman Begins* (2005).

Old Masters *master*

Old Persian *Iranian languages*

Old Style date *New Style date*

Old Testament The sacred literature of Judaism, in which the corpus of writings is known simply as the Jewish Scriptures or Hebrew Bible, or even sometimes the Torah; it was also adopted by Christians as part of their sacred writings, and they began to call it the 'Old Testament' as distinct from the Christian writings that constitute the 'New Testament'. The canon of the Jewish religious community, which was fixed AD c.100, was arranged into three parts – the **Law**, the **Prophets**, and the **Writings** – although the precise arrangement and divisions of the books have varied through the centuries. The Law consists of the five books of the Pentateuch (Genesis, Exodus, Leviticus, Numbers, Deuteronomy). The Prophets have been divided since about the 8th-c AD into the *former* and *latter* prophets: the former prophets consist of the narratives (presumed written by prophets) found in Joshua, Judges, Samuel, and Kings, and the latter prophets consist of Isaiah, Jeremiah, Ezekiel, and the Book of the Twelve Prophets (Hosea, Joel, Amos, Obadiah, Jonah, Micah, Nahum, Habakkuk, Zephaniah, Haggai, Zechariah, Malachi). The Writings contain all remaining works: Psalms, Proverbs, Job, Song of Songs, Ruth, Lamentations, Ecclesiastes, Esther, Daniel, Ezra-Nehemiah, and Chronicles.

Olduvai Gorge [olduviy] 2°58S 35°22E. A gorge within the Ngorongoro conservation area of the Rift Valley, N Tanzania. It is of great archaeological importance as the source of some of the oldest known 'human' remains.

Old Vic Theatre Theatre in London, UK, first opened in 1818 as the Royal Coburg Theatre and renamed the Royal Victoria Theatre in 1833. After 1880 it became the Royal Victorian Music Hall, popularly known as the Old Vic. Under the management of Lilian Mary Baylis from 1912, the theatre was devoted to the production of opera and the plays of Shakespeare. It became the home of the new National Theatre in 1963 until that theatre's South Bank venue was established in 1976. In 1946 the Bristol Old Vic was established as a permanent repertory company, and the London-based Young Vic was created in 1973. The Old Vic is now owned by a charitable trust, The Old Vic Theatre Trust 2000, established in 1998 in response to public pleas to save the theatre, when it was put onto the open market for sale. Kevin Spacey was appointed its artistic director in 2003.

Old World monkey A monkey of family Cercopithecidae (76 species); nostrils close together and opening downwards or forwards (unlike New World monkeys); tails never grasping, sometimes short; buttocks may have naked patches of skin.

oleander [oliander] An evergreen shrub (*Nerium oleander*) growing to 5 m/16 ft, native to the Mediterranean region; leaves leathery; flowers tubular with five spreading lobes, pink or white. All parts are poisonous. (Family: Apocynaceae.)

oleaster [oliaster] A deciduous, sometimes thorny, shrub or tree (*Elaeagnus angustifolia*) growing to 13 m/42 ft, native to W Asia; leaves dull green above, covered with minute silvery scales beneath; flowers tubular with four spreading lobes, silver outside, yellow inside, fragrant; berries silvery-yellow. (Family: Eleagnaceae.)

olefin(e)s [ohluhfinz] *alkenes*

Oléron, Ile d' [eel dolayrõ], ancient **Uliarus** Wooded fertile island in E Bay of Biscay, W France; France's second largest off-shore island (after Corsica); 3 km/1¾ mi from mainland; area 157 km²/68 sq mi; length 30 km/19 mi; linked by modern toll-bridge.

oligarchy In ancient Greece, the term applied to city-states such as Corinth and Thebes, where political power was in the hands of a minority of its male citizens. They contrasted with democracies such as Athens and Argos, where power was held by the majority.

Oligocene epoch [oligoseen] A geological epoch of the Tertiary period from c.37 to 25 million years ago, and characterized by colder climate, the general retreat of the seas, and the evolution of many modern mammals.

oligomer [oligomer] A small polymer, generally consisting of three to ten monomer units; examples include oligopeptides and oligosaccharides.

oligopoly [oligopolee] An economic situation where an industry is dominated by a few suppliers. In economic theory, it constitutes one type of imperfect competition.

Olivares, Gaspar de Guzman y Pimental, conde-duque de (Count-Duke of) [olivahrez] (1587–1645) Spanish statesman, favourite and chief minister of Philip IV (1623–43), born in Rome. He took Spain into renewed conflict with the United Provinces and challenged France over the Mantuan Succession (1628–31) and in the Thirty Years' War (1635–48). After Spanish defeats, he was dismissed in 1643, and died in exile.

olive A long-lived evergreen tree (*Olea europaea*) native to the Mediterranean region, growing to 15 m/50 ft; trunk silvery, gnarled with numerous cavities; leaves leathery, dark green above, pale beneath; flowers small, white, four petals; fruit succulent, oily, green, ripening over one year to black. The cultivated olive (variety *europaea*) has been grown since early times as an important source of olive oil. (Family: Oleaceae.)

Oliver, King, popular name of **Joseph Oliver** (1885–1938) Cornettist, composer, and bandleader, born in Abend, LA. He moved to Chicago, where in 1922 he formed his Creole Jazz Band, and is remembered for his discovery of Louis Armstrong. His compositions, such as 'Dippermouth Blues' and 'Dr Jazz', have become part of the standard traditional repertoire.

Oliver, Jamie (Trevor) (1975–) Chef, born in Clavering, Essex. He joined Antonio Carluccio's London restaurant before moving to the River Café Restaurant as a sous-chef. In 1999 he made the popular cooking series *The Naked Chef* for BBC television, with an accompanying cookbook. Several more successful books followed, including *Jamie's Dinners* (2004) and *Cook with Jamie* (2006). In 2005 the Channel 4 series *Jamie's School Dinners* (BAFTA, 2006) documented his 'crusade' to improve the standard of school dinners in England, an initiative which received widespread public and political support.

Olives, Mount of or **Mount Olivet** [olivet] A rocky outcrop overlooking the Old City of Jerusalem across the Kidron Valley, a traditional Jewish burial ground. It is the supposed location of the ascension of the risen Jesus.

Olivier (of Brighton), Laurence (Kerr) Olivier, Baron (1907–89) Actor, producer, and director, born in Dorking, Surrey. He played all the great Shakespearean roles, while his versatility was underlined by his virtuoso display in *The Entertainer* (1957)

as a broken-down low comedian. His films include *Henry V*, *Hamlet*, and *Richard III*. Divorced from his first wife, **Jill Esmond** in 1940, in the same year he married English actress **Vivien Leigh** (1913–67), whose film career included the role of Scarlett O'Hara in *Gone With the Wind*. They were divorced in 1961, and he then married English actress **Joan Plowright** (1929–). In 1962 he became director of the Chichester Theatre Festival and (1963–73) of the National Theatre. After 1974 he appeared chiefly in films and on television, notably in *Brideshead Revisited* (1982) and *King Lear* (1983).

olivine [olivyn] A silicate mineral ranging in composition from Fe_2SiO_4 (*fayalite*) to Mg_2SiO_4 (*forsterite*); glassy, hard, and typically olive-green in colour. Its gem quality crystals are termed *peridot*.

Olmecs Members of a highly elaborate Middle American Indian culture on the Mexican Gulf Coast, at its height 1200–600 BC. The Olmecs influenced the rise and development of the other great civilizations of Middle America. They were probably the first people in the area to devise glyph writing and the 260-day Mesoamerican calendar.

Olmsted, Frederick (Law) (1822–1903) Landscape architect, born in Hartford, CT. He was architect-in-chief of the improvement scheme for Central Park, New York City, and later designed other important public park schemes, including the grounds surrounding Washington, DC, and the campus at Berkeley, CA.

Olympia (Greece), Gr **Olímbia** 37°38N 21°39E. Village and national sanctuary in S Greece, on R Alfios; chief sanctuary of Zeus, from c.1000 BC; site of the Panhellenic religious festival held every 4 years from 776 BC; railway; major excavations in 19th-c; Temple of Zeus (5th-c BC).

Olympia (USA) 47°03N 122°53W, pop (2000e) 42 500. Seaport capital of Washington State, USA; at the S end of Puget Sound; founded at the end of the Oregon Trail, 1850; capital of Washington Territory, 1853; railway.

Olympians In Greek mythology, a collective name for the major gods and goddesses, who were thought to live on Mt Olympus.

Olympic Games A sports gathering held every 4 years by athletes from all over the world, each celebration taking place at a different venue. They evolved from the ancient Greek games, held at Olympia, which go back at least to the 8th-c BC. They were banned in AD 393 by the Christian Emperor Theodosius I, probably because of their pagan practices, and were revived in 1896 by French educator Pierre de Fredi, Baron de Coubertin (1863–1937), with Athens as the first venue. In the 2004 games more than 11 000 competitors from 201 nations competed, in 28 different sports. Since 1924 a separate Winter Olympic Games has been staged, and held in the same year as the Summer Games, until 1992, when it was decided to stage it midway between the Summer Games.

Olympus, Mount (Cyprus) [olimpuhs] 34°56N 32°52E. Mountain in the Troödos range of C Cyprus, rising to 1951 m/6401 ft; highest peak on the island.

Olympus, Mount (Greece) [olimpus], Gr **Olimbos** Range of mountains between Macedonia and Thessalia regions, N Greece; highest point, Mitikas (2917 m/9570 ft); traditionally the abode of the dynasty of gods headed by Zeus.

Om [om, ohm] A mystical and sacred monosyllable in Hindu tradition, the sound of which was believed to have a divine power. It was used at the beginning and end of prayers, as a mantra for meditation, and as an invocation itself.

Omagh [ohmah], Ir **An Omaigh** 54°36N 7°18W, pop (2000e) 18 100. County town of Tyrone, WC Northern Ireland, on R Strule; inside the 19th-c Catholic parish church is the Black Bell of Drumragh (9th-c); town centre badly damaged by bomb-attack (Aug 1998), which killed 29, the worst incident of the Northern Ireland troubles since the 1960s.

Omaha (Indians) [ohmaha] A Siouan-speaking North American

Oman

Status Sultanate

Date of independence 1951

Capital Muscat

Languages Arabic (official), English, Baluchi (and other Mahri languages), Urdu and Indian dialects also spoken

Ethnic groups Arab, with small Baluchi, Iranian, Indian, Pakistani, and W European minorities

Religions Ibadhi Muslim (75%), Sunni Muslim, Shi'a Muslim and Hindu (25%)

Physical features Located on the SE corner of the Arabian peninsula; the tip of the Musandam peninsula in the Strait of Hormuz is separated from the rest of the country by an 80 km/50 mi strip belonging to the United Arab Emirates; several peaks in the Hajjar Mt range, Jabal Akhdar ridge rises to 3000 m/10 000 ft; vast sand desert in NE; Dhofar uplands in SW.

Climate Desert climate, hot and arid; hot, humid on coast (Apr–Oct); average annual temperature 22°C (Jan), 33°C (Jul); light monsoon rains in S (Jun–Sep); average annual rainfall 99 mm/3·9 in.

Currency 1 Omani Rial (OMR) = 1000 baizas

Economy Oil discovered, 1964, now provides over 90% of government revenue; natural gas an important source of industrial power; c.70% of the population relies on agriculture; alfalfa, wheat, tobacco, fruit, vegetables, fishing.

GDP (2002e) $22·4 bn, per capita $8300

Human Development Index (2002) 0·751

History Dominant maritime power of the W Indian Ocean in 16th-c; independent from UK, 1951; separatist tribal revolt in Dhofar, 1964, led to a palace coup that installed the present Sultan in 1970; opened airbases to Western forces, following Iraqi invasion of Kuwait, 1990; independent state ruled by a Sultan who is both Head of State and Premier, and who appoints a Cabinet and a 59-member Consultative Council.

Head of State/Government (Sultan)
1888–1913 Faisal Bin Turki
1913–32 Taimur Bin Faisal
1932–70 Said III bin Taimur
1970– Qaboos bin Said

☐ International Airport   – – – Border awaiting demarcation

[ohman], formerly **Muscat and Oman**, official name **Sultanate of Oman**

Local name 'Umān

Timezone GMT +4

Area 300 000 km²/115 800 sq mi

Population total (2002e) 2 522 000

Plains Indian group, originally from the Atlantic seaboard. They now live on reservations in Nebraska.

Omaha (Nebraska) [ohmaha] 41°17N 96°01W, pop (2000e) 390 000. City in E Nebraska, USA; a port on the Missouri R; fur-trading post, 1812; city status, 1867; largest city in the state; airport; railway; two universities (1878, 1908); major livestock market and meat-processing centre; centre for medical treatment and research; air force base.

Oman see panel

Oman, Gulf of NW arm of the Indian Ocean, lying between Oman and Iran; linked to the Persian Gulf by the Strait of Hormuz, and (SE) to the Arabian Sea; 480 km/300 mi long.

Omar or **Umar I** [ohmah(r)] (c.581–644) The second caliph (634–44), the father of one of Mohammed's wives, who succeeded Abu-Bakr. He was assassinated at Medina by a slave.

Omar Khayyám [kayam], also spelled **Umar Khayyám** (c.1050–c.1122) Astronomer-poet, born in Nishapur, Persia. He was known to the Western world as a mathematician, until in 1859 Edward FitzGerald published a translation of his *Rubáiyát* ('Quatrains'). The original work is now regarded as an anthology of which little or nothing may be by Omar.

OMB *Office of Management and Budget*

ombudsman [ombudzman] (Swed 'agent' or 'representative') An official who investigates complaints regarding administrative action by governments – so-called 'mal-administration'. The findings do not have the force of law, and are put in the form of reports from which it is hoped remedial action will result. The first such institution was created in Sweden at the beginning of the 19th-c, and today most countries have followed the lead.

Omdurman [omdoorman] 15°37N 32°29E, pop (2000e) 816 000. Major suburb of Khartoum, C Sudan; military headquarters of Mohammed Ahmed (the Mahdi), 1884; captured by the British under Kitchener, 1898; university (1961).

OMNIMAX *IMAX*

omnivore Any animal, or human, whose diet includes both the flesh of animals and vegetable material; there may be specialized teeth to deal with the varied foodstuffs.

Omri (9th-c BC) King of Israel (c.886 BC–c.875 BC). An army commander, he was made king after Zimri assassinated Elah and seized the throne. He is the first Israelite monarch found to be mentioned in historical records other than the Bible itself. He was succeeded by his son Ahab.

Omsk 55°00N 73°22E, pop (2000e) 1 161 000. River port in W

Siberian Russia; at the confluence of the Irtysh and Om Rivers; founded as a fortress, 1716; airport; on the Trans-Siberian Railway; university (1974).

onager [onajer] *ass*

Onassis, Aristotle (Socrates) [ohnasis] (1906–75) Greek millionaire shipowner, born in Smyrna, Turkey. He built up one of the world's largest independent fleets, and became a pioneer in the construction of supertankers. In 1968 he married **Jacqueline Bouvier Kennedy**.

Onassis, Jacqueline Kennedy, *née* Jacqueline Lee Bouvier, popularly known as **Jackie Kennedy** (1929–94) US first lady (1961–3), born in Southampton, NY. She married John F Kennedy in 1953. Her stoic behaviour after Kennedy's death enhanced her standing with the public, but she stunned the world when in 1968 she married the Greek millionaire shipping magnate, Aristotle Onassis. After Onassis's death (1975), she worked in publishing.

oncology [ongkolojee] The branch of medicine concerned with the nature and origin of tumours, including the study of their natural history and response to treatment by drugs, surgery, or ionizing radiation (radioactive substances or X-rays).

Ondaatje, Michael [ondahchee] (1943–) Poet, novelist, and editor, born in Colombo, Sri Lanka. He moved to Canada in 1962, becoming a university lecturer. His novel *The English Patient* was co-winner of the Booker Prize in 1992 (filmed 1996), and later novels include *Anil's Ghost* (2000) and *Divisadero* (2007).

ondes Martenot [ôd mah(r)tenoh] An electronic musical instrument invented in 1928 by Maurice Martenot; the name derives from Fr *ondes* '[musical] waves'. A keyboard, capable of producing a vibrato, is played by the right hand; the left operates the controls for timbre and dynamics.

O'Neal, (Patrick) Ryan (1941–) Film actor, born in Los Angeles, CA. He became well known as Rodney Harrison in the television series *Peyton Place*, a character he played for nearly five years. His films include *Love Story* (1970), *Paper Moon* (1973), *Hacks* (1997), and *People I Know* (2002).

Onega, Lake [onyega], Russ **Ozero Onezhskoye** area 9720 km²/3752 sq mi. Second largest lake in Europe, NW European Russia; length, 250 km/155 mi; maximum depth, 120 m/394 ft; numerous islands (N).

Oneida [ohniyda] An Iroquoian-speaking North American Indian agricultural group, the smallest tribe of the Iroquois League, originally based in C New York State.

O'Neill, Eugene (Gladstone) (1888–1953) Playwright, born in New York City. He joined the Provincetown Players in 1915, for whom *Beyond the Horizon* (1920, Pulitzer) was written. His best-known works are *Desire Under the Elms* (1924), *The Iceman Cometh* (1946), and *Long Day's Journey into Night* (1957, Pulitzer). He was the first US dramatist to receive the Nobel Prize for Literature, in 1936.

O'Neill (of the Maine), Terence (Marne) O'Neill, Baron (1914–90) Northern Ireland statesman and prime minister (1963–9), born in Co Antrim, Northern Ireland. A member of the Northern Ireland parliament (1946–70), he became minister for home affairs (1956) and finance (1956–63), and then prime minister. He was a supporter of closer cross-border links with the Republic.

One Nation Australian political party, formed in 1997 by Pauline Hanson, an Australian businesswoman elected as an independent MP in 1996. It advocates curbs on Asian immigration, the removal of Aboriginal welfare programmes, and a protectionist economic policy. It received strong support in the 1998 Queensland state elections, but increasing nationwide condemnation of its policies brought a major setback in the 1998 federal elections, with Hanson losing her Queensland seat.

onion Any of several species of the genus *Allium*, probably originating in Asia, and all grown as vegetables. The ordinary onion (*Allium cepa*) has solitary, globular, or flask-shaped bulbs, often of great size, and inflated stalks bearing white flowers. **Spanish onion** is a variety with white-skinned bulbs; the **shallot** a variety with clusters of small, oval bulbs. (Family: Liliaceae).

on-line processing The use of computers to undertake tasks where transactions are initiated and data entered from terminals located in the users' offices. Common examples are the booking of airline tickets, holidays, hotels, and car hire, and transactions in building societies and some banks.

Ono, Yoko (1933–) Multimedia artist, born in Tokyo. At age 18 she moved with her family to Scarsdale, NY. She studied at Sarah Lawrence College but left to elope with her first husband, Toshi Ichiyanagi. Settling in Greenwich Village, she developed her interest in art and poetry and gained recognition after working with American jazz musician/film producer Anthony Cox, who became her second husband. In the early 1960s she joined Fluxus, a group of avante-garde artists, and while attending their exhibition in London in 1967, she met future husband **John Lennon**. They collaborated on art, film, and musical projects, and became famous for their series of 'conceptual events' to promote world peace, including the 'bed-in' held in an Amsterdam hotel room during their honeymoon in 1969. After Lennon's death in 1980 she continued her career and has recorded albums, performed concert tours, and composed two off-Broadway musicals. She inaugurated the Lennon Ono Grant for Peace prize in 2002.

onomastics [onohmastiks] The study of the history, development, and geographical distribution of proper names. All categories of names are included, such as people's first names and surnames, place names, home names, and the names of boats, trains, and pets.

onomatopoeia [onomatopeea] (Gr 'name-making') The imitation of a natural (or mechanical) sound in language. This may be found in single words (*screech, babble, tick-tock*) or in longer units. It is especially heard in poetry.

Ontario pop (2000e) 11 293 000; area 1 068 580 km²/412 578 sq mi. Province in SE Canada; capital, Toronto; rocky Canadian Shield in N, with clay belt suitable for farming; many lakes; N area sparsely populated, densely wooded; most populated and second largest province; widely explored by French fur traders and missionaries, 17th-c; British territory, 1763; many United Empire Loyalist immigrants after the American War of Independence; constituted as Upper Canada, 1791; separatist rebellion, 1837–8; joined to Lower Canada, 1840; modern province established at time of confederation, 1867; governed by a lieutenant-governor and a 125-member legislature.

Ontario, Lake Smallest of the Great Lakes, North America, on US–Canadian border; length 311 km/193 mi; breadth 85 km/53 mi; maximum depth 244 m/800 ft; area 19 011 km²/7338 sq mi, just over half in Canada; connected (SW) with L Erie via the Niagara R and the Welland Ship Canal; outlet, the St Lawrence R (NE); never ice-bound.

ontological argument One of the traditional arguments for the existence of God, first developed by Anselm. God is defined as the being than which nothing greater can be conceived; something which exists must be greater than something which does not; therefore God must exist.

ontology A central part of metaphysics: the theory of what sorts of things really exist. A materialist will argue that matter is the only fundamental existent, in terms of which everything else must be explained.

Onychophora [onikofora] A sub-phylum of primitive arthropods, comprising the velvet worms; sometimes classified as a separate phylum.

onyx *agate*

oolite [ohuhliyt] A limestone composed of *ooliths*, ie rounded grains made of concentric layers of radiating fibres of carbonate, usually aragonite or calcite. Coarser oolites (> 3 mm/$^1/_8$ in diameter) are termed *pisolites*.

Oort cloud [aw(r)t] A hypothesized source of the long-period comets; a spherical 'halo' about the Sun at a distance of c.50 000 AU; named after Dutch astronomer Jan Hendrik Oort (1900–92), who first noted the clustering of aphelia of new comets in this region.

Oostende [ohstenduh] *Ostend*

opah [ohpa] *moonfish*

opal A natural form of amorphous (non-crystalline) silica (SiO_2). It is usually white, but gems have a characteristic play of rainbow colours.

Op Art An abbreviation for **Optical Art**, a modern art movement of the 1960s which exploits the illusionistic effects of abstract spiral or wavy patterns, stripes, spots, etc. Hungarian-born French painter Victor Vasarely and British painter Bridget Riley were leading exponents.

OPEC (Organization of Petroleum Exporting Countries) [ohpek] An international economic organization set up in 1960 with its headquarters in Vienna, originally consisting of 13 oil-producing countries (now 11). The founder members were Iran, Iraq, Kuwait, Saudi Arabia, and Venezuela; and they were later joined by Algeria, Ecuador (withdrew, 1992), Gabon (withdrew, 1996), Indonesia, Libya, Nigeria, Qatar, and the United Arab Emirates (formerly Abu Dhabi). Its purpose is to co-ordinate the petroleum policy of members to protect their interests.

open-cast mining *mining*

open-ended investment company An investment company which pools the funds of its shareholders, and invests in a diversified portfolio of stocks and shares. Such a company contrasts with a **closed-end investment company**, which has a fixed amount of share capital.

open-hearth process A steel-making process devised in 1860 by William Siemens (1823–83) and first successfully operated in 1864 by Pierre Emile Martin (1824–1915). The molten pig iron from which the steel is to be made is not in direct contact with the fuel providing the heat, but only with the hot flames from combustion which play on a shallow hearth containing pig-iron, scrap, and a flux.

open plan An arrangement of rooms in a building in which the internal doors and walls have been reduced to a minimum, or even omitted altogether. It is particularly associated with the International Style architecture of the 1920s and 1930s, and with offices and private housing after World War 2.

open shop *closed shop*

open systems interconnection (OSI) An international standard for the definition of connections between computers, which allows computers of different makes and architectures to communicate with each other for the transfer of data. The organization committed to the establishment of software and standards to enable computers to fulfil these requirements is the **Open Software Foundation (OSF)**.

Open University An institution of higher education which enables students to study for a degree without attendance. Courses are usually based on a credit system, and the student graduates when sufficient credits have been amassed. The teaching is frequently carried out through correspondence units and broadcast or recorded supporting programmes.

opera A stage work in which music plays a continuous or substantial role. The genre originated in China from the 10th-c, and in Europe at Florence c.1600. In Italy, opera, whether serious or comic, has usually been sung throughout; elsewhere other types have developed which alternate songs with spoken dialogue (*semi-opera* in England, *opéra comique* in France, *Singspiel* in Germany). Wagner's music dramas aimed at a

Gesamtkunstwerk which united the arts of music, poetry, gesture, and painting.

opera buffa Italian comic opera, especially of the 18th-c, with dialogue in recitative. Mozart's *Le nozze di Figaro* (1786, The Marriage of Figaro) is an outstanding example of the genre.

opéra comique French opera, with spoken dialogue, originally comic but later including such dramatic operas as Bizet's *Carmen* (1875).

opera seria Italian serious opera of the 18th-c and early 19th-c, exhibiting a rigid separation of aria and recitative. It reached its highest point of development in Mozart's *Idomeneo* (1781) and *La clemenza di Tito* (1791).

operating system A computer program which supervises the running of all other programs on a computer. Common microprocessor operating systems are CP/M, MS DOS, and Microsoft Windows.

operetta Light opera, with spoken dialogue and usually dancing, exemplified in the stage works of Offenbach, Strauss, and Sullivan.

Ophir [ohfer] A land of unknown location, mentioned in the Bible as famous for its resources of gold; it is variously placed in Arabia, India, or E Africa.

Ophiuchus [ofyookus] (Gr 'serpent bearer') A large constellation on the celestial equator.

ophthalmia [op-, ofthalmia] Inflammation of the conjunctival membrane covering the eye in the newborn, or arising in one eye as a consequence of injury to the other eye.

ophthalmology [op-, ofthalmolojee] The branch of medical practice concerned with disorders and diseases of the eyes. It includes general or systemic diseases that may affect the eye, and their medical or surgical treatment.

Ophuls or **Opüls, Max** [opüls], originally **Max Oppenheimer** (1902–57) Film director, born in Saarbrücken, Germany. His major films include *La Ronde* (1950, The Round) and *Lola Montez* (1955).

Opie, John [ohpee] (1761–1807) Portrait and historical painter, born near St Agnes, Cornwall. His portraits interested his teacher John Wolcot (1738–1819), by whom he was taken to London to become the 'Cornish Wonder', producing such works as 'The Murder of Rizzio' (1787).

opinion poll The taking of opinions from a sample of the electorate regarding their voting intentions, their views of political leaders, and wider political attitudes. They are also used to assess consumer preferences. Polls originated in the USA in the 1930s, and today are commonplace both at and between elections.

opioid peptides [ohpioyd peptiydz] A family of chemical substances (peptides), including *enkephalins*, *endorphins*, and *dynorphins*, which are found in the brain, spinal cord, pituitary gland, gastro-intestinal tract, and adrenal medulla; also known as **endogenous opioids**. In the brain and spinal cord they appear to be involved in pain perception.

Opitz (von Boberfeld), Martin (1597–1639) Poet, born in Bolesławiec, Poland (formerly Bunzlau, Germany). He wrote in a scholarly style which influenced German poetry for 200 years, and introduced Renaissance poetic thinking into Germany.

opium The dried extract of the unripe seed capsules of the opium poppy, *Papaver somniferum*, which contains several narcotic alkaloids, including morphine. It was used by many ancient cultures for its properties of relieving pain, inducing sleep, and promoting psychological effects of peace and well-being.

Opium Wars Two wars (1839–42, 1856–60) between China and the Western powers, especially Britain, fought over the question of commercial rights in China. When the Chinese attempted to stop opium imports (1839), a British force besieged Guangzhou (Canton), and imposed the Treaty of Nanjing (Nanking) in 1842.

This opened Guangzhou, Nanjing, Shanghai, Fuzhou (Foochow), and Xiamen (Amoy) to Western trade. The Second Opium War, or **Arrow War**, began when Chinese boarded a Hong Kong ship (*The Arrow*), flying a British flag but suspected of piracy (1856). British troops occupied Guangzhou, and an Anglo–French army marched on Beijing. The Treaties of Tianjin (Tientsin) in 1858 opened 10 more ports and legalized the opium traffic. These treaties established a strong Western influence in China, and helped stir up nationalist sentiments which led to the 1911 revolution.

Oporto [opaw(r)toh], Port **Porto** 41°08N 8°40W, pop (2000e) 307 000. City in N Portugal, on R Douro; second largest city in Portugal; bishopric; railway; university (1911); cathedral (12th-c).

opossum [oposm] A marsupial of family Didelphidae (75 species), native to the New World; hind foot with opposable 'thumb', and lacking the 'comb' of many Australian marsupials; New World marsupials called opossums; Australian marsupials of similar appearance called **possums**.

Oppenheimer, J(ulius) Robert [openhiymer] (1904–67) Nuclear physicist, born in New York City. He became director of the atom bomb project at Los Alamos (1943–5). Opposing the hydrogen bomb project, in 1953 he was suspended from secret nuclear research as a security risk, but was awarded the Enrico Fermi prize in 1963.

opposition (astronomy) The moment when a planet is opposite the Sun, as observed in our sky. It crosses the meridian at local midnight, which is therefore the best time for observing.

opposition (politics) The right of parties and political movements not holding government office to criticize the government and seek to replace it by offering alternative policies. In democratic systems the **Opposition** normally consists of those parties which oppose the government through parliamentary channels, their activities being recognized in electoral procedures.

Ops The Roman goddess of plenty, the consort of Saturn, identified with Rhea.

optical character reader (OCR) A machine which can read standard texts into a computer using a combination of optical and computer techniques.

optical fibres Fibres of transparent optical material, usually glass, for transmitting images or data. Each fibre consists of a core and an outer cladding of lower refractive index: light travels through the core and is contained within it by refraction. In telecommunications, optical fibres transmit data very long distances (up to 50 km/30 mi at one stretch). The technique is also used in medicine for viewing inaccessible parts of the body (*endoscopy*).

optics The study of light and of instruments using light. Modern optical developments include optical fibres and their use in communications, optical logic elements and potentially optical computers, spatial filtering (eg allowing the removal of unwanted horizontal lines from photographs), the mass production of plastic lenses with complicated curved surfaces, lasers, and holography.

opting out (education) *grant-maintained school*

options market A market in which traders can buy the right to buy or sell shares or commodities at a pre-agreed 'exercise price' at some future date or within some future period. Options markets exist only for a few widely traded shares and commodities.

optoelectronics The study of the production and control of light by electronic devices, such as semiconductor lasers, liquid crystals, and light-emitting diodes. It provides the technology for electronic displays in watches and calculators.

optometry [optometree] The assessment of the function of the eye, with special reference to errors of refraction, and the provision of appropriate corrective lenses and spectacles. It also now includes the specialized examination of the eye to diagnose a wide range of defects. These assessments are carried out by *optometrists*.

opuntia [opuhnsha] A large genus of cacti with stems made up of flattened, spiny, pear-shaped segments; native to the Americas, but widely introduced elsewhere. (Genus: *Opuntia*, 250 species. Family: Cactaceae.)

Opus Dei [ohpus dayee] (Lat 'work of God') The title of a Roman Catholic society, founded in 1928, to promote the exercise of Christian virtues by individuals in secular society. In some countries and at certain periods (eg Spain in the mid-20th-c) it acquired a measure of political power.

ora *Komodo dragon*

orache [orich] A member of a genus of annuals or perennials, found almost everywhere, some forming small shrubs; the whole plant often mealy white; flowers tiny, green. (Genus: *Atriplex*, 200 species. Family: Chenopodiaceae.)

oracle Divine prophetic declarations about unknown or future events, or the places (such as Delphi) or inspired individuals (such as the Sibyls) through which such communications occur. In ancient Greek stories, these revelations were usually given in response to questions put to the gods.

Oracle (telecommunications) The teletext system operated by the UK Independent Broadcasting Association (later, the Independent Television Commission) as a commercial service since 1981. The name is an acronym of *Optional Reception of Announcements by Coded Line Electronics*. In 1993 it was renamed *Teletext on 3*, and later became known as *ITV-text* or just *Teletext*.

oracle bones Inscribed shoulder blades of pig, ox, and sheep (later tortoise shells) used for divination by the Shang monarchs of N China, 16th–11th-c BC. The patterns of cracks made by hot brands applied to the bones were read as guidance from royal ancestors.

oracy The ability to express oneself coherently and to listen with good comprehension. The fostering of these skills has come to be seen as an important goal of childhood education, alongside the traditional focus on reading and writing.

oral contraceptives *contraception*

oral history The means of discovering information about the past by interviewing subjects. The technique has been increasingly used since the 1970s to augment the written record, especially in areas where 'orthodox' sources are deficient or unobtainable.

oral surgery *dentistry*

Oran [orahn] or **Wahran** 35°45N 0°38W, pop (2000e) 850 900. Seaport in N Algeria; founded 8th-c; first ruled by Arabs, then Spaniards (1509–1708), Turks (1708–32), and French (1831–1962); airport; railway; university (1965); fortress (16th-c).

Orange (France) [orāzh] 44°08N 4°48E, pop (2000e) 29 400. Town in SE France, on the R Rhône; developed around a group of Roman monuments, now a world heritage site.

Orange, Princes of *William I* (of the Netherlands); *William III* (of Great Britain)

orange A citrus fruit 7–10 cm/2$\frac{3}{4}$–4 in diameter, globular with thick, often rough rind. The familiar edible fruit is the **sweet orange** (*Citrus sinensis*). **Bergamot orange** (*Citrus bergamia*) is grown as a source of bergamot oil. (Genus: *Citrus*. Family: Rutaceae.)

Orange Free State *Free State*

Orange Order An association that developed from the Orange Society, which had been formed in 1795 to counteract growing Catholic influence in Ireland. The name was taken from the Protestant Dutch dynasty represented by William III. Organized in 'Lodges', it has operated as a force for conservative Protestantism in Northern Ireland since partition.

Orange Prize A literary prize established in 1996, given annually to fiction written by women and published in the UK. Worth £30 000, it is the UK's largest annual literary award for a single novel. The winner also receives a bronze figurine known as a 'Bessie'.

Orange River, Afrikaans **Oranjerivier** River in Lesotho, South Africa, and Namibia; rises in the Drakensberg Mts in NE Lesotho; enters the Atlantic Ocean; length 2100 km/1300 mi; dammed in several places as part of the **Orange River Project** (begun 1963) to provide irrigation and power.

orang-utan An ape (*Pongo pygmaeus*) native to forests of Sumatra and Borneo; height, 1·5 m/5 ft; sparse covering of long shaggy red-brown hair; armspan up to 2·25 m/7½ ft; adult male with large naked fatty folds around face; endangered species due to hunting, habitat destruction, and illegal logging.

Oratorians Priests of the French Oratory, or **Oratory of Jesus Christ**, founded in 1611 and following a modified form of the rule established by St Philip Neri (16th-c), living together without vows, and devoted to prayer, preaching, and attractive services of worship. Dissolved in 1791, they were re-established in 1852, and now flourish in many countries outside France. The **English Oratorians** were introduced into England by Cardinal Newman in 1847; their home in London is Brompton Oratory.

oratorio A non-liturgical, quasi-dramatic sacred work, usually for solo voices, chorus, and orchestra. It takes its name from the Italian 'prayer-hall' in which the earliest oratorios were performed in the mid-17th-c. Examples include Handel's oratorios, originally performed in the London theatres, Haydn's *The Creation* (1798), and works by Mendelssohn and Elgar.

oratory The art and practice of public speaking. Effective oratory requires that the choice of language, its style, and mode of delivery should be appropriate for a given audience, location, and occasion. Its major forms (legal, political, ceremonial) can be traced back to earliest times, notably to the Greek orators of the 4th-c BC (eg Demosthenes), and the Roman orators of the 1st-c BC (eg Cicero). In modern times, oratory has been effectively practised, as can be seen in the speeches of Hitler, Churchill, John F Kennedy, and Martin Luther King Jr, and the radio or television debates and 'fireside chats' used by leading politicians.

orbit In astronomy, the path followed by any celestial object or satellite moving through a gravitational field. A **geostationary orbit** is one followed by a satellite above the Equator at 35 900 km/22 300 mi, where it keeps in exact step with the Earth's rotation and is thus always in the same part of the sky.

Orcagna [aw(r)kanya] originally **Andrea de Cione** (c.1308–c.1368) Painter, sculptor, and architect, born in Florence, Italy. His greatest paintings are frescoes, an altarpiece in Santa Maria Novella, Florence, and 'Coronation of the Virgin' (National Gallery, London).

orchestra Originally the name for the semi-circular space in front of a stage, later extended to the body of instrumentalists that performed there; today, a regular constituted body of string players, with additional woodwind, brass, and percussion as required. The advent of the concerto in the late 17th-c stimulated the formation of four-part string orchestras, and by the end of the 18th-c the standard orchestra for the symphonies of Haydn and Mozart included also pairs of flutes, oboes, bassoons, horns, trumpets, timpani, and (sometimes) clarinets. The modern symphony orchestra consists of about 100 players.

orchid A monocotyledonous plant belonging to the family Orchidaceae, one of the largest and most advanced flowering-plant families, containing some 17 000 species. Orchids are found in virtually all parts of the world except Antarctica, but are especially abundant in the tropics. They are best known for their complex, often spectacular and exotic flowers, and for their highly developed pollination mechanisms. They exert a strong

fascination for many people, and numerous species are now commonly cultivated, with whole societies devoted to their study and care.

Orczy, Emma (Magdalena Rosalia Marie Josepha Barbara), Baroness [awtsee, awksee] (1865–1947) Writer, born in Tarna-Eörs, Hungary. *The Scarlet Pimpernel* (1905) was her first success, followed by many popular adventure romances.

Order in Council In British government, legislation made by the Monarch in Council allowed by act of parliament, but which does not need to be ratified by parliament. In practice the decisions are taken by government ministers, not by the monarch.

Order of Merit (OM) In the UK, a decoration for those who have provided pre-eminent service to the country. Instituted by Edward VII in 1902 and limited to 24 members, it comprises a military and a civil class. The ribbon is blue and scarlet.

Orders, Holy Grades of ministry in Orthodox, Roman Catholic, and Anglican Churches. **Major Orders** consist of ordained ministers, bishops, priests, and deacons (and, in the Western Church, subdeacons). **Minor Orders** include, in the Western Church, lectors, porters, exorcists, acolytes; in the Eastern Church, subdeacons. Major Orders constitute the hierarchy of the Church, to be distinguished from the laity. A distinction is also drawn between **First Orders** (fully professed men), **Second Orders** (fully professed women), and **Third Orders** (those affiliated usually to one of the Mendicant Orders).

orders of architecture *pp.686–7*

Ordinance of 1787 An Act of the American Continental Congress establishing procedures by which newly-settled Western territories could enter the American union on the basis of full political equality with the original states.

Ordnance Datum (OD) The mean sea level in the UK, used as a fixed reference from which the elevations of all points in the country are surveyed. The equivalent in the USA is the **Sea Level Datum**.

Ordnance Survey of Great Britain The survey and mapping agency established by the 1841 Ordnance Survey Act, although founded initially in 1791 as the Trigonometrical Survey. Maps were originally produced at a scale of 1 in to the mi. The basic scales are 1 : 1250 (1 cm to 1250 cm or 1 in to 1250 in, ie 50 in to the mi), 1 : 2500 (or c.50 in to the mi), and 1 : 10 000, which supersedes the 1 : 10 350 (c.6 in to the mi).

Ordovician period [aw(r)dovishian] The second of the geological periods of the Palaeozoic era, extending from c.505 to 438 million years ago. All animal life was restricted to the sea; numerous invertebrates flourished, and the first vertebrates appeared (jawless fish).

ore A mineral deposit from which metallic and non-metallic constituents can be extracted. Ores may be formed directly from crystallizing magma, precipitated from hydrothermal fluids associated with igneous activity, or concentrated in alluvial deposits after weathering.

oregano [origahnoh, oreganoh] *marjoram*

Oregon [origuhn] pop (2000e) 3 421 400; area 251 409 km²/ 97 073 sq mi. State in NW USA; the 'Beaver State'; established as a fur-trading post, 1811; occupied by both Britain and the USA, 1818–46, when the international boundary was settled on the 49th parallel; became a territory, 1848; joined the Union as the 33rd state, 1859; population grew after 1842 with settlers following the Oregon Trail; split by the Cascade Range; fertile Willamette R valley in the W, with the Coast Ranges beyond; High Desert in the E, a semi-arid plateau used for ranching and wheat-growing; highest point, Mt Hood (3424 m/11 234 ft); about half the area forested; capital, Salem; produces over a quarter of the USA's softwood and plywood; major tourist region; Crater Lake National Park in the SW.

Oregon boundary dispute A disagreement between the British and US governments over the frontier between respective pos-

orders of architecture

The arrangement of the parts of a column and an entablature in classical architecture according to one of five accepted principles, or orders: Tuscan, Doric, Ionic, Corinthian, Composite. Originally developed by the ancient Greeks, the earliest surviving codification is by the 1st-c Roman Vitruvius, subsequently analysed in much greater detail by European architectural theorists from the Renaissance onwards.

Greek Doric   Ionic   Corinthian

A. Entablature	D. Frieze	G. Shaft	1. Guttae	4. Abacus	7. Fluting
B. Column	E. Architectural	H. Base	2. Metope	5. Echinus	8. Dentils
C. Cornice	F. Capital	I. Plinth	3. Triglyph	6. Volute	9. Fascia

sessions on the W coast of North America. The Oregon Treaty (1846) settled on the 49th parallel, dipping S at Juan de Fuca Strait to maintain British claims to Vancouver Island.

Oregon Trail The main route for emigration to the far W of the USA in the 1840s. The trail began at Independence, Missouri, crossed the Rockies at South Pass in Wyoming, and terminated at the mouth of the Columbia R.

Orestes [oresteez] In Greek legend, the son of Agamemnon and Clytemnestra. After his father's murder he went into exile, but returned to kill Aegisthus and his mother, for which he was pursued by the Erinyes.

orfe [aw(r)f] Freshwater fish (*Leuciscus idus*) widespread in lowland rivers and lakes of E Europe and C Russia; length up to 40 cm/16 in; greenish-brown on back, sides silver, underside white; also known as **ide**. (Family: Cyprinidae.)

Orff, Carl (1895–1982) Composer, born in Munich, Germany. He is best known for his secular oratorio based on a 13th-c poem, *Carmina Burana* (1937); later works include *Oedipus* (1959) and *Prometheus* (1966).

organ The name of various types of musical instruments, but without further qualification referring to an instrument in which air from a windchest, fed by bellows, is released under pressure into metal or wooden pipes of various lengths and bores by the action of keys operated by the player's fingers or feet. The ranks of pipes are brought into action by means of drawknobs (or *stops*). The **cinema organ**, with its distinctive 'voicing' and its special effects (train hooter, telephone bell, etc) was developed in the early 20th-c, especially by the Wurlitzer Company in the USA, to accompany silent films and to play popular medleys during intervals. In **electronic organs**, an

Tuscan   Roman Doric   Composite

invention of the 1920s, the pipes are replaced by other means of tone production, such as electromagnets and oscillators.

organic chemistry That part of chemistry which deals specifically with the structures and reactions of the compounds of carbon. These compounds are much more numerous than those of the other elements.

organic farming Farming without synthetic chemical fertilizers, sprays, or pharmaceuticals. Fertility is maintained through the addition of animal manures and composts, and through rotations which include nitrogen-fixing plants such as clover. In some countries there is a premium market for certified organic produce.

Organisation de l'Armée Secrète *OAS* 1

Organization for Economic Co-operation and Development (OECD) An international organization set up in 1961 to assist member states to develop economic and social policies aimed at high sustained economic growth with financial stability. In 2007 it had 30 members. It is located in Paris.

Organization for International Economic Co-operation *COMECON*

Organization for Security and Co-operation in Europe (OSCE), formerly known as **Conference on Security and Co-operation in Europe (CSCE)** A political grouping first established in 1975 and which came to prominence after the European political revolution of 1989–90. Its purpose is conflict prevention, crises management, and post-conflict rehabilitation. It embraces Europe, USA, and Canada, (with Albania the only European non-participant). Its secretariat opened in Prague in 1991. There were 56 members in 2007.

Organization of African Unity *African Union*

Organization of American States (OAS) A regional agency established in 1948 for the purpose of co-ordinating the work of a variety of inter-American agencies, recognized within the terms of the United Nations Charter. All 35 independent countries of the Americas have ratified the OAS Charter, but Cuba remains excluded (since 1962).

Organization of Arab Petroleum Exporting Countries (OAPEC) An organization formed under the umbrella of the Organization of Petroleum Exporting Countries (OPEC) in 1968 by Saudi Arabia, Kuwait, and Libya, with its headquarters in Kuwait. By 1972 all the Arab oil producers had joined.

Organization of Central American States An agency established in 1951 by Costa Rica, El Salvador, Guatemala, Honduras, and Nicaragua (Panama refused to join) to promote economic, social, and cultural co-operation. In 1965 this was extended to include political and educational co-operation.

Organization of Petroleum Exporting Countries *OPEC*

Organization of the Islamic Conference An organization of sovereign Muslim states, formed in 1969, with the aims of promoting Islamic solidarity, safeguarding Muslim holy places, and promoting the rights of all Muslim peoples. It had 57 members and five observer states in 2007.

oribi [oribee] A dwarf antelope (*Ourebia ourebi*) native to Africa S of the Sahara; pale brown with tufts of long hairs on the knees; males with short spike-like horns.

orienteering A form of cross-country running with the aid of a map and compass. The sport was devised by Swedish youth leader Ernst Killander in 1918, and based on military training techniques. Popular in the Nordic countries, it developed as an international sport in the 1960s.

origami [origahmee] The art of making models of animals or other objects by folding sheets of paper into shapes with the minimum use of scissors or other implements. It originated in the 10th-c in Japan, where it is widely practised.

Origen [orijen] (c.185–c.254) Christian Biblical scholar and theologian of Alexandria, Egypt, who became head of the catechetical school in Alexandria. His views on the unity of God and the salvation of the devil were condemned by Church Councils in the 5th–6th-c.

Original Dixieland Jazz Band The first band to make a jazz record. It consisted of Nick LaRocca (1889–1961), cornet; Eddie Edwards (1891–1963), trombone and violin; Larry Shields (1893–1953), clarinet; Henry Ragas (1890–1919), piano; and Tony Sbarbaro (1897–1969), drums; all were born in New Orleans, LA. Their recordings in 1917 launched jazz as an international phenomenon.

original sin The traditional Christian doctrine that, by virtue of the Fall, every human being inherits a 'flawed' or 'tainted' nature in need of regeneration and with a disposition to sinful conduct.

oriole A bird of the Old World family Oriolidae (**Old World orioles**, 28 species) or the New World family Icteridae (**American orioles**, c.90 species).

Orion (astronomy) [oriyon] Perhaps the most conspicuous of all constellations, although only 26th in size. Equatorial, and thus visible in both hemispheres, its brightest stars Rigel, the seventh-brightest star in our sky, and Betelgeuse, a red supergiant. The **Orion nebula** is found in the 'sword' of Orion. It is the nearest and brightest emission nebula, 500 parsec away.

Orion (mythology) [oriyon] In Greek mythology, a gigantic hunter, beloved by Eos and killed by Artemis. He was changed into a constellation.

Orissa [orisa] pop (2000e) 37 009 000; area 155 782 km²/ 60 132 sq mi. State in E India; ceded to the Marathas, 1751; taken by the British, 1803; subdivision of Bengal until 1912, when province of Bihar and Orissa created; separate province, 1936; became a state, 1950; capital, Bhubaneswar; governed by a

Legislative Assembly; 65% of population depend on agriculture; major flooding caused by cyclone (Oct 1999).

Orkney [aw(r)knee] pop (2000e) 20 400; area 976 km²/377 sq mi. Group of islands off NE Scotland; 15 main islands (especially Mainland, South Ronaldsay, Sanday, Westray, Hoy); capital, Kirkwall, on Mainland; Norse dependency from 9th-c; annexed by Scotland from Norway and Denmark, 1472; fishing, farming, weaving; North Sea oil terminal on Flotta; oil service bases on Mainland and Hoy; Neolithic village at Skara Brae; isolated stack (height 137 m/449 ft), Old Man of Hoy (NW of Hoy); Scapa Flow, sea area within the islands, used in World Wars 1 and 2 as a major naval anchorage; German Fleet surrendered there in 1918.

Orlando 28°33N 81°23W, pop (2000e) 186 000. City in C Florida, USA; settled c.1844; airfield; railway; tourism, aerospace, and electronic industries; Walt Disney World.

Orleans [aw(r)leeanz], Fr **Orléans**, ancient **Aurelianum** 47°54N 1°52E, pop (2000e) 110 000. Ancient town in C France; on R Loire; associated with Joan of Arc, 'The Maid of Orleans', who raised the English siege here in 1429; road and rail junction; bishopric; centre of fruit and vegetable region; university (1309); cathedral (13th–16th-c).

Orléans, Charles, duc d' (Duke of) [aw(r)layā] (1391–1465) Poet, born in Paris. In 1406 he married his cousin Isabella, widow of Richard II of England. He commanded at Agincourt (1415), was taken prisoner, and carried to England, where he lived for 25 years, composing courtly poetry in French and English.

Orléans, Louis Philippe Joseph, duc d' (Duke of) [aw(r)layā], known as **Philippe Egalité** ('equality') (1747–93) French Bourbon prince, born in Saint-Cloud, the cousin of King Louis XVI and father of Louis Philippe. At the Revolution he supported the Third Estate, and in 1792 renounced his title of nobility for his popular name. At the Convention he voted for the king's death but was arrested after the defection of his eldest son to the Austrians (1793), and guillotined.

Orléans, House of The junior branch of the Valois and Bourbon dynasties in France; Philippe de Valois was created the first duke in 1344, and Ferdinand Philippe (1810–42) was the last to hold the ducal title.

Ormandy, Eugene [aw(r)mandee], originally **Jenö Ormandy** (1899–1985) Conductor, born in Budapest. He conducted the Minneapolis Symphony Orchestra (1931–6) and the Philadelphia Orchestra (1936–80).

ormer *abalone*

ormolu or **ormulu** A gilded metal alloy of copper, zinc, and tin used in France since the 17th-c for candelabra, clocks, and other decorative luxury objects.

Ornithischia [aw(r)nithiskia] The bird-hipped dinosaurs, characterized by the backward-pointing pubis bone in the pelvic girdle, similar to that of birds. They comprise exclusively plant-eating groups.

Ornitholestes [aw(r)nitholesteez] *Coelurus*

ornithology The study of birds. It includes observations on the evolutionary relationships of the different groups, the distribution of species and populations, ecology, conservation, migration, behaviour of individuals, birdsong, anatomy, physiology, biochemistry, and genetics.

orogeny [orojenee] A period of mountain-building involving intense deformation and subsequent uplift of rocks when crustal plates collide. The plate boundaries define an **orogenic belt** which forms a fold-mountain chain. Examples include the Himalayas, which resulted from the collision of the Indian and Asian continental plates.

Oromo A cluster of Cushitic-speaking peoples of Ethiopia and N Kenya; the largest group in Ethiopia, their former name **Galla** (Amharic: 'slave') is no longer in official use. Traditionally pastoralists, the groups in N Ethiopia are farmers, while the S Oromo are still cattle herders.

Orozco, José Clemente [oroskoh] (1883–1949) Painter, born in born in Ciudad Guzmán (formerly Zapotlán), Mexico. He was one of the greatest mural painters of the 20th-c, decorating public buildings in Mexico and the USA, in a powerful realistic style, verging on caricature. His best-known works include 'Soldadero' (c.1917) and 'Juárez Reborn' (1948).

Orpheus [aw(r)fyoos] A legendary Greek poet from Thrace, able to charm beasts and even stones with the music of his lyre. In this way he obtained the release of his wife Eurydice from Hades.

Orphism A modern art movement which flourished c.1912, experimenting with pure colour in ways that heralded abstract painting. The leading exponent was Delaunay.

orris A white-flowered species of iris (*Iris germanica*, variety *florentina*), with fleshy rhizomes which provide **orris root**, used in perfumery. (Family: Iridaceae.)

Ørsted, Hans Christian [oe(r)sted], also spelled **Oersted** (1777–1851) Physicist, born in Rudkøbing, Denmark. In 1820 he discovered the magnetic effect of an electric current. The unit of magnetic field strength used to be named after him.

Ortega y Gasset, José [aw(r)tayga ee gaset] (1883–1955) Philosopher and existentialist humanist, born in Madrid. His critical writings on modern authors made him an influential figure, and his *La rebelión de las masas* (1930, The Revolt of the Masses) foreshadowed the Civil War.

Ortelius [aw(r)teelius], Lat name of **Abraham Ortels** (1527–98) Cartographer, born in Antwerp. His *Theatrum Orbis Terrarum* (1570, Epitome of the Theatre of the World) was the first great atlas.

orthoclase [aw(r)thoklayz] A form of the mineral potassium feldspar; usually pink and a primary constituent of granite.

orthodontics *dentistry*

Orthodox Church or **Eastern Orthodox Church** A communion of self-governing Churches (with adherents estimated at over 220 million in 2007) recognizing the honorary primacy of the Patriarch of Constantinople. It includes the patriarchates of Alexandria, Antioch, Constantinople, and Jerusalem, and the Churches of Russia, Bulgaria, Cyprus, Serbia, Georgia, Romania, Greece, Poland, Albania, and the Czech and Slovak Republics.

orthopaedics / orthopedics [aw(r)thopeediks] The branch of surgery concerned with injuries and disorders affecting the skeleton. It includes the treatment of fractures and dislocations, the correction of deformities of posture, and the surgical replacement of damaged joints by artificial prostheses.

Orthoptera [aw(r)thoptera] An order of medium-to-large insects found in all terrestrial habitats; hindlegs usually modified for jumping; many produce sound by rubbing their limbs or wings (*stridulation*).

ortolan [aw(r)tohlan] A bunting found from Europe to Mongolia (*Emberiza hortulana*) (winters in N Africa); also known as the **ortolan bunting** or **garden bunting**.

Orton, Joe, popular name of **John Kingsley Orton** (1933–67) Playwright, born in Leicester, Leicestershire. He is known for his erotic and anarchic farces, among them *Loot* (1964–5) and *What the Butler Saw* (1969). He was murdered by his male lover in London. *The Orton Diaries* (1986) contain startling revelations.

Orwell, George, pseudonym of **Eric Arthur Blair** (1903–50) Novelist and essayist, born in Motihari, Bengal, India. He developed his own brand of socialism in *The Road to Wigan Pier* (1937) and many essays. He is best known for his satire of totalitarian ideology in *Animal Farm* (1945), and for the prophetic novel *Nineteen Eighty-Four* (1949).

oryx [oriks] A grazing antelope with very long slender horns; pale with striking white and dark markings on face and underparts;

three species in genus *Oryx*, two from Africa, one from the Middle East.

Osaka [ohsaka], formerly **Naniwa** 34°40N 135°30E, pop (2000e) 2 672 000. Port city in S Honshu, Japan; developed around a castle, built 16th-c; city almost completely destroyed in World War 2; now third largest city in Japan; airport; railway; subway; several universities; part of the Osaka–Kobe industrial area; Nagai Stadium (1996).

Osama bin Laden, also **Usama bin Ladin** [usama bin laden] (1958–) Wealthy Saudi guerrilla leader, born in Riyadh of a Yemeni family. After succeeding in business he moved to Afghanistan, where he supported and supplied the Mujahideen fighting against the Soviet occupation. He then founded al-Qaeda (see separate entry) and called for a jihad against the 'Judao-Christian alliance occupying Islamic sacred land in Palestine and the Arabian Peninsula'. In 1991 he moved to the Sudan, from where he was expelled in 1996 for organizing bombing and assassination campaigns. He was accused by the USA of being behind the 1998 bomb attacks on their embassies in Kenya and Tanzania, and the bombing of the USS *Cole* warship in the port of Aden, Yemen in 2000. Subsequently he conducted his terrorist campaigns under the protection of the Taliban in Afghanistan. He was named as the chief suspect in the assaults on the World Trade Center, New York, and the Pentagon, Washington, in September 2001, with subsequent events clarifying his role in the event, but his whereabouts became unknown as the US-led attack on the Taliban progressed later that year. Since 2002 occasional tape-recordings purporting to come from him have been made public.

Osborne, John (James) (1929–94) Playwright and actor, born in London. *Look Back in Anger* (1956) and *The Entertainer* (1957), established him as the leading younger exponent of British social drama. The 'hero' of the first, Jimmy Porter, became the prototype 'Angry Young Man'.

Osbourne, Ozzie, popular name of **John Michael Osbourne** (1948–) Rock musician and television entertainer, born in Birmingham, West Midlands. He formed the rock group Rare Breed, which eventually developed into Black Sabbath. He achieved international recognition following the success of a weekly MTV show, *The Osbournes* (2002), a mixture of reality television and family sitcom chronicling events in the life of himself and his family. The show was co-produced by his wife and manager, **Sharon Osbourne** (1952–). His single 'Changes', performed with daughter Kelly, topped the UK charts in 2003.

Oscar The familiar name for the statuettes awarded annually by the American Academy of Motion Picture Arts and Sciences for outstanding performances and creative and technical achievement in films shown during the preceding year. There are many accounts of the origin of the name, all speculative: in one account, it arose when a secretary at the Academy said that the figure reminded her of her Uncle Oscar.

oscillation A repetitive periodic change. Electrical currents in radio receivers oscillate, for example. Mechanical oscillations, such as those in a building caused by passing traffic, are usually called **vibrations**.

oscillator A circuit for converting direct current (DC) into alternating current (AC), of a required frequency. Part of the output is returned via a feedback circuit to the input.

Osee *Hosea, Book of*

O'Shane, Pat(ricia) June (1941–) Magistrate, born in Mossman, Queensland, Australia. In 1978 she was the first person of Aboriginal descent to be called to the bar. She has made a number of progressive, well-publicized decisions concerning women and Aboriginal people.

Osheroff, Douglas D [osherof] (1945–) Physicist, born in Aberdeen, WA. He studied at Cornell University, working under Lee and Richardson as part of the team which in 1972 discovered the superfluidity of helium-3. He shared the Nobel Prize for Physics in 1996.

osier A species of willow forming a shrub or small tree (*Salix viminalis*), growing to 3–5 m/10–16 ft; native to Europe and Asia; often grown as a source of *withies* – long pliant stems used, for example, in basketwork.

Osiris [ohsiyris] Ancient Egyptian god, the husband of Isis. He became king of the Underworld, and was seen as the judge of the soul after death.

Oslo [ozloh], formerly **Christiania** or **Kristiania** 59°55N 10°45E, pop (2000e) 483 000. Capital city of Norway; founded, 11th-c; under the influence of the Hanseatic League, 14th-c; destroyed by fire, 1624; rebuilt by Christian IV and renamed Christiania; capital, 1905; renamed Oslo, 1925; bishopric; airports; railway; largest port in Norway, the base of a large merchant shipping fleet; university (1811); cathedral (17th-c), royal palace (1825–48), castle (13th-c).

osmiridium [ozmiridium] A naturally occurring alloy of osmium and iridium in which the iridium content is less than 35%; *iridosmine* has osmium greater than 35%. It occurs with platinum ores.

osmosis *osmotic pressure*

osmotic pressure [ozmotik] The pressure that must be exerted on a solution containing a given concentration of solute separated from a sample of the pure solvent by a membrane which prevents the solvent's passage. Exerting a pressure greater than the osmotic pressure causes the solvent to pass from the solution to the solvent; this 'reverse osmosis' is a method of purifying water. Osmosis is an important process in living organisms, especially aquatic organisms.

Osnabrück [ohznabrük] 52°17N 8°03E, pop (2000e) 168 000. Manufacturing city in Germany; badly bombed in World War 2; railway; bishopric; university (1973); cathedral (13th-c).

osprey A large bird of prey (*Pandion haliaetus*), inhabiting sea coasts or inland waters worldwide; also known as **fish hawk** or **fish eagle**; dives on fish, grasping them in its talons. (Family: Pandionidae.)

Ossa, Mount 41°54S 146°01E. Highest mountain in Tasmania (1617 m/5305 ft).

Ossian or **Oisín** Legendary Irish poet and warrior, the son of the 3rd-c hero Fingal or Fionn MacCumhail. The Scottish poet **James Macpherson** (1736–96) professed to have collected and translated his works, though it was later shown that the poems were largely of his own devising.

Ostade, Adriaen van [ostahduh] (1610–85) Painter and engraver, born in Haarlem, The Netherlands. His subjects are taken mostly from everyday peasant life. His brother, **Isaak** (1621–49), treated similar subjects, but excelled at winter scenes and landscapes.

Ostend, Flemish **Oostende**, Fr **Ostende** 51°13N 2°55E, pop (2000e) 69 700. Seaport in W Belgium; principal ferry port for UK (Dover and Folkestone); largest seaside resort in Belgium; headquarters of the Belgian fishing fleet; railway.

osteoarthritis A common disease of joints of both humans and other animals; also known as **osteoarthrosis**. Over 80% of those over middle age are affected. The condition is a primary degeneration and disintegration of the articular cartilage, which tends to affect the weight-bearing joints such as the hips; but no joint is immune. The cause is unknown, though wear and tear is often invoked.

osteogenesis imperfecta *brittle bone syndrome*

osteology The scientific study of bone and bones. It is used in anthropology for species identification and carbon dating, in clinical medicine for the assessment of development in the individual, and in forensic medicine for the reconstruction and sexing of victims.

osteomalacia [ostiohmalaysha] A metabolic disorder of bone caused by a lack of vitamin D. In children and adolescents, normal growth is retarded, and the condition is called *rickets*.

osteomyelitis [ostiohmiyeliytis] Infection within bone. It arises either as a result of blood-borne infection or, less commonly, following direct injury.

osteopathy [ostiopathee] A system of treatment originally based on the belief that abnormalities in the skeletal system are responsible for a wide range of diseases by interfering with the blood supply to the region affected. Osteopaths use such techniques as massage and manipulation, stretch various joints, and apply high-velocity thrusts.

osteoporosis [ostiohporohsis] Thinning and weakening of bones because of a loss of tissue substance. It is common in elderly women, and is related to a reduction in the level of sex hormones. Affected women develop a characteristic stooping posture due to collapse of the vertebrae, and are prone to fractures.

Ostia [ostia] The ancient town situated at the mouth of the Tiber in W Italy. It was Rome's main naval base during the Punic Wars.

Ostpolitik [ostpoliteek] The policy initiated in West Germany in the 1960s to normalize relations with communist countries which recognized the German Democratic Republic and to reduce hostility between West Germany and its Eastern neighbours. Largely masterminded by Willy Brandt, the policy can be viewed as a forerunner of detente.

ostracism In ancient Athens, the means whereby unpopular citizens could be banished for up to 10 years without loss of property or citizenship.

ostracod A small, short-bodied crustacean with a hinged bivalve shell that completely encloses the body; legs typically adapted for walking over substrate; over 10 000 fossil species and 5700 living species. (Class: Ostracoda.)

Ostrava [ostrava] 49°50N 18°13E, pop (2000e) 333 000. Industrial city in Czech Republic; airport; railway.

ostrich The largest living bird (*Struthio camelus*) (height up to 2·75 m/9 ft); unable to fly; fastest animal on two legs (c.70 kph/45 mph); largest egg of any living bird; inhabits dry areas of Africa. (Family: Struthionidae.)

Ostrogoths A Germanic people, forming one of the two great Gothic tribes, who entered Italy in 489 and established a kingdom under Theodoric. The kingdom collapsed in the mid-6th-c, but was revived by the Lombards.

O'Sullivan, Ronnie, popular name of **Ronald Antonio O'Sullivan** (1975–) Snooker player, born in Wordsley, Wolverhampton. He turned professional in 1992, and his achievements to date include the British Open (1994), two World Championship titles (2001, 2004), the European Open (2003), and the Masters (1995, 2005, 2007). Nicknamed 'the Rocket', he also compiled the fastest-ever 147 maximum break (5 min 20 sec), completed during the 1997 World Championships.

Oswald, St (c.605–642) Anglo-Saxon King of Northumbria (633–41). He established Christianity in Northumbria with St Aidan's help. Feast day 5 August.

Oswald, Lee Harvey (1939–63) The alleged killer of President Kennedy, born in New Orleans, LA. Two days after the assassination, he was killed at Dallas by nightclub owner Jack Ruby (1911–67), before he could stand trial. The Warren Commission (1964) held him to be responsible for the assassination, although the belief that he was part of a conspiracy still persists.

Oswega / Oswega tea [osweeguh] *bergamot 1*

Otaka, Tadaaki [ohtaka] (1947–) Japanese conductor. He made his professional debut in 1971, and went on to become conductor of the Tokyo Philharmonic Orchestra (1971–91, laureate 1991), and principal conductor of the BBC National Orchestra of Wales (1987–95, laureate 1996) and the Kioi Sinfonietta, Tokyo (1995–2003, laureate 2003).

Otis, Elisha (Graves) [ohtis] (1811–61) Inventor, born in Halifax,

VT. In 1852, he designed and installed the first lift to incorporate an automatic brake, thus paving the way for the development of the skyscraper.

O'Toole, Peter (Seamus) (1932–) Actor, born in Connemara, Co Galway. His performance in *Lawrence of Arabia* (1962) made him an international film star. Nominated eight times for an Oscar, his later films include *The Lion in Winter* (1968), *Goodbye Mr Chips* (1969), *The Last Emperor* (1987), *Troy* (2004), and *Venus* (2006). He received an honorary Oscar in 2003.

Ottawa 45°25N 75°43W, pop (2000e) 351 300. Capital of Canada, in E Ontario on the Ottawa R; founded as Bytown, 1826; present name, 1854; capital of United Provinces, 1858; national capital, 1867; two-thirds English-speaking, one-third French; airport; railway; two universities (1848, 1942); Peace Tower in parliament buildings, 88 m/289 ft high; Eternal Flame on Parliament Hill, lit 1967; professional teams, Ottawa Senators (ice hockey), Ottawa Rough Riders (football).

Ottawa River, Fr **Rivière des Outaouais** Canadian river, the largest tributary of the St Lawrence; rises in the Canadian Shield; length 1270 km/780 mi.

otter A mammal of family Mustelidae; streamlined, with a flattened muzzle; brown with paler underparts; tail thick at base; feet usually webbed; inhabits streams and lakes; 12 species in genera *Lutra* (**river otters**), *Aonyx* (**clawless otters**), and *Pteronura* (the **giant otter**).

Otto, Nikolaus (August) (1832–91) Engineer, born near Schlangenbad, Germany. In 1876 he invented the four-stroke internal combustion engine, the sequence of operation of which is named the **Otto cycle** after him.

otto *attar*

Ottoman Empire A Muslim empire founded c.1300 by Sultan Osman I (1259–1326), and originating in Asia Minor. Ottoman forces entered Europe in 1345, conquered Constantinople in 1453, and by 1520 controlled most of SE Europe, including part of Hungary, the Middle East, and N Africa. Following the 'golden age' of Sulaiman the Magnificent, the empire began a protracted decline. It joined the Central Powers in 1914, and collapsed with their defeat in 1918.

Otway, Thomas (1652–85) Playwright, born in Trotton, West Sussex. His best-known works are the tragedies *The Orphan* (1680) and *Venice Preserved, or a Plot Discovered* (1682).

O2, The *Millennium Dome*

Ouagadougou [wagadoogoo] 12°20N 1°40W, pop (2000e) 725 300. Capital of Burkina Faso, W Africa; part of the Ivory Coast until 1947; capital of Mossi empire from 15th-c; captured by French, 1896; airfield; terminus of railway line from Abidjan (Nigeria); university (1969); cathedral.

Oudenaarde [oodenah(r)d], Fr **Audenarde** 50°50N 3°37E, pop (2000e) 27 400. Town in W Belgium; site of defeat of French by Marlborough and Prince Eugene (1708); railway; traditional centre for carpet-weaving and tapestries.

Ouija board [weeja, weejee] A board bearing letters, words, and numbers, upon which an indicator such as an upturned glass is placed. Several people rest their fingers on the indicator, which then moves without their conscious volition across the board. It can then purportedly spell out messages which provide information about events or situations unknown to the people present. The word originates from the French and German words for *yes* (*oui* and *ja*).

Oulu [ohloo], Swed **Uleåborg** 65°00N 25°26E, pop (2000e) 104 000. Seaport in W Finland, established, 1605; destroyed by fire, 1822; airfield; railway; university (1958).

ounce (zoology) *snow leopard*

Our Lady *Mary* (mother of Jesus)

Ouro Prêto [ohroh praytoh], formerly **Vila Rica** Town founded in 1711 in Minas Gerais, the mining area of NE Brazil; a world heritage site; centre of gold and diamond trading during the colonial era, with wealth reflected in its architecture.

Ouse, River (S England) [ooz] **1** River in East Sussex, S England; length 48 km/30 mi; enters the English Channel at Newhaven. **2** River in Yorkshire, NE England; length 96 km/60 mi; enters the R Trent where it becomes the Humber estuary. **3** River in Northamptonshire, C England; length 256 km/159 mi; enters the Wash; also known as the **Great Ouse**. **4** Tributary of the Great Ouse river; length 38 km/24 mi; also known as the **Little Ouse**.

ousel *ouzel*

out-of-the-body experience (OOBE or OBE) An experience in which people have the sensation that their consciousness exists in a separate location from their body. The experience often feels as real to them as normal everyday life reality.

ouzel or **ousel** A thrush (*Turdus torquatus*) native to Europe, N Africa, and SW Asia; dark with pale wings and white crescent on breast; also known as the **ring ouzel**.

ouzo [oozoh] A traditional Greek spirit flavoured with aniseed, and usually drunk with water.

Oval, the One of the largest cricket grounds in England, located at Kennington, S London. It is the headquarters of Surrey County Cricket Club.

Ovamboland [ohvambohland] Region in N Namibia; chief indigenous peoples, the Ovambo.

ovarian follicle A structure within the mammalian ovary, part of which may develop into a mature ovum to be released at ovulation; also known as **Graafian follicle**, named after the Dutch physiologist, Reinier de Graaf (1641–73).

ovary The reproductive organ in a female animal in which the eggs are produced, and which may also produce hormones. Ovaries are typically paired, and release their eggs down *oviducts* or uterine tubes. In plants the term refers to the hollow base of the carpel, containing the ovules.

Overland Telegraph A telegraph line crossing Australia and linking it with the outside world; opened in 1872. The line covered 3175 km/1972 mi between Port Augusta (South Australia) to Darwin (Northern Territory).

over-the-counter drugs (OTCs) Those drugs which may be purchased directly from a pharmacy without a prescription, such as aspirin. Some problems arise with OTCs, such as their inappropriate use (eg an overdose) and their dangerous interactions with some prescription drugs.

over-the-counter (OTC) trading Trading in stocks and shares other than via the stock exchange. Over-the-counter shares are issued by companies too small for Stock Exchange listing; they are often considered to be a very risky investment.

overture An orchestral prelude to an opera or other work, or (since the early 19th-c) an independent, usually descriptive, concert piece of similar length.

Ovett, Steve [ohvet], popular name of **Steven Michael James Ovett** (1955–) Athlete, born in Brighton, East Sussex. Gold medallist in the 800 m at the 1980 Olympics, he also won a bronze in the 1500 m. He broke the world record at 1500 m (three times), at one mile (twice) and at two miles.

Ovid [ovid], in full **Publius Ovidius Naso** (43 BC–AD 17) Latin poet, born in Sulmo, Italy. His major poems are the three-book *Ars Amatoria* (Art of Love) and the 15-book *Metamorphoses*, a collection of stories in which a transformation (metamorphosis) plays some part.

Oviedo [ovyaythoh] 43°25N 5°50W, pop (2000e) 197 000. City in NW Spain; former capital of Asturias; bishopric; airport; railway; university (1608); cathedral (14th-c).

Ovimbundu [ovimbundoo] A Bantu-speaking agricultural people of the Benguela Highlands of Angola, comprising some 20 indigenous chiefdoms.

ovo-lacto vegetarians *vegetarianism*

ovulation *ovarian follicle*

ovule The female sex-cell of seed plants which, after fertilization, forms the seed. In gymnosperms the ovules lie exposed on the scales of the female cone; in flowering plants they are enclosed within an ovary.

ovum *egg*

Owen, Alun (Davies) (1926–94) Playwright, born in Liverpool, Merseyside. A prolific writer for television and radio, his works include *The Rough and Ready Lot* (1958), *Progress to the Park* (1959), and a musical collaboration with Lionel Bart, *Maggie May* (1964).

Owen (of the City of Plymouth), David (Anthony Llewellyn), Baron (1938–) British politician, born in Plymouth, Devon. He was secretary for health (1974–6), and foreign secretary in the Labour government (1977–9). One of the so-called 'Gang of Four' who formed the Social Democratic Party (SDP) in 1981, he became its leader in 1983. In 1988, after the SDP voted to accept merger, Owen led the smaller section of the party to an independent existence. Retiring from the commons in 1992, he became (with Cyrus Vance) a UN peace envoy in war-torn former Yugoslavia. He was made a Companion of Honour in 1994.

Owen, Michael (James) (1979–) Footballer, born in Chester, Cheshire. A centreforward, he joined Liverpool FC in 1996, was voted FA Young Player of the Year (1997–8), and in 1998 became the youngest player in the 20th-c to receive an England cap. In 2003 he notched up his 100th goal for Liverpool. He joined Real Madrid in 2004, transferring to Newcastle United in 2005. He was a member of the 1998 and 2002 World Cup teams, and Euro 2000 and 2004 competitions. During the 2006 World Cup he sustained a serious knee injury early in the competition. He was voted Sports Personality of the Year in 1998, and European Footballer of the Year in 2001.

Owen, Robert (1771–1858) Social reformer, born in Newtown, Powys. In 1800 he became manager and part owner of the New Lanark cotton mills, Lanarkshire, where he set up a social welfare programme, and established a 'model community'.

Owen, Wilfred (Edward Salter) (1893–1918) Poet, born in Oswestry, Shropshire. His poems, expressing a horror of the cruelty and waste of war, were edited by his friend Siegfried Sassoon in 1920. He himself was killed in action on the Western Front.

Owens, Jesse, popular name of **James** or **John Cleveland** (1913–80) Athlete, born in Danville, AL. Within 45 min on 25 May 1935 at Ann Arbor, MI, he set five world records (100 yd, long jump, 220 yd, 220 yd hurdles, 200 m hurdles). His long jump record stood for 25 years.

owl A predatory nocturnal bird, found worldwide; large head and broad flat face; forwardly directed eyes; acute sight and hearing. There are two families: **typical owls** (Strigidae, c.120 species) and **barn owls**, **grass owls**, and **bay owls** (Tytonidae, 11 species). Tytonidae differ in having smaller eyes, long slender legs, a serrated middle claw, and a heart-shaped face. (Order: Strigiformes.)

ox A ruminant mammal of genus *Bos* (5 species); an artiodactyl. The name is used especially for the domestic bullock used as a draught animal.

oxalic acid [oksalik] IUPAC **ethanedioic acid**, HOOC–COOH, colourless crystals; melting point of the dihydrate is 101°C. It occurs in many plants, especially rhubarb, and is poisonous.

oxalis A perennial, sometimes an annual, found almost everywhere; leaves clover-like with three (sometimes more) leaflets; flowers 5-petalled, funnel-shaped; fruits with catapult mechanism for dispersing seeds. (Genus: *Oxalis*, 800 species. Family: Oxalidaceae.)

Oxenstierna or **Oxenstern, Axel Gustafsson, Greve** (Count) [oksensherna, oksenstern] (1583–1654) Swedish statesman, born near Uppsala, Sweden. From 1612 he served as chancellor, and during most of the minority of Queen Christina he was

effective ruler of the country (1636–44). He brought the Thirty Years' War to a successful conclusion at the Peace of Westphalia (1648).

ox-eye daisy A variable clump-forming perennial (*Leucanthemum vulgare*), growing to 1 m/40 in, native to Europe; flower-heads up to 5 cm/2 in or more across, long-stalked, solitary; spreading outer florets white, inner disc florets yellow; also called **marguerite** and **dog** or **moon daisy**. It was formerly used as a medicinal herb. (Family: Compositae.)

OXFAM A British charity based in Oxford, dedicated to alleviating poverty and distress throughout the world; an abbreviated form of **Oxford Committee for Famine Relief**. Founded in 1942, most of its funds provide long-term development aid to Third World countries.

Oxford (UK), Lat **Oxonia** 51°46N 1°15W, pop (2000e) 115 100. County town of Oxfordshire, SC England; on Thames and Cherwell Rivers; university (12th-c); Oxford Brookes University, 1992; Royalist headquarters in Civil War; airfield; railway; industry located in the suburb of Cowley (notably vehicles); cathedral (12th-c); football league team, Oxford United ('U's').

Oxford, Provisions of (1258) A baronial programme imposing constitutional limitations on the English crown. Henry III had to share power with a council of barons, parliaments, and other officers. In 1261 the pope absolved Henry from his oath to observe the Provisions.

Oxford Movement A movement within the Church of England, beginning in 1833 at Oxford, which sought the revival of high doctrine and ceremonial; also known as **Tractarianism**. Initiated by 'tracts' written by Keble, Newman, and Pusey, it led to Anglo-Catholicism and ritualism.

Oxfordshire pop (2001e) 605 500; area 2608 km²/1007 sq mi. County in the S Midlands of England; county town, Oxford.

Oxford University The oldest university in Britain, having its origins in informal groups of masters and students gathered in Oxford in the 12th-c. Prestigious university institutions include the Bodleian Library, the Ashmolean Museum, and the Oxford University Press (founded in 1585). *p.693*

oxidation The loss of electrons, always accompanied by reduction (the gain of the same electrons). Chemical reactions in which electrons are transferred from one atom to another are called **oxidation–reduction** or **redox** reactions. Elements in compounds are conveniently given an **oxidation state** or **oxidation number** which relates to their redox properties. This is expressed using Roman numerals, as in manganese(VII) or Mn^{VII}.

oxides *oxygen*

oxlip A perennial with a rosette of crinkled leaves, with drooping flowers at the tip of a common stalk. The true oxlip (*Primula elatior*), from C and N Europe, has pale yellow flowers all hanging on one side of the stalk. (Family: Primulaceae.)

oxopropanoic acid *pyruvic acid*

Oxus, River *Amudarya, River*

oxyacetylene welding A technique much used in cutting metal and in joining two pieces of metal by melting them together at the point of contact (*welding*). The temperature obtained by burning acetylene with oxygen is the highest obtainable by any gas–oxygen flame (over 3200 °C).

oxygen O, element 8, boiling point −183°C. By far the commonest element in the Earth's crust, of which it makes up nearly 50%; in various combined forms it also constitutes 21% of the atmosphere as diatomic molecules (O_2). All higher forms of life depend on oxygen. The element boils at 13°C higher than nitrogen, and is isolated by the fractional distillation of air. Oxygen occurs widely in organic and inorganic compounds (**oxides**), mainly showing oxidation state −2.

oxygen cycle The dynamic system of changes in the nature of

Oxford University

College	Founded
University College	1249
Balliol	1263
Merton	1264
St Edmund Hall	1278
Exeter	1314
Oriel	1326
Queen's	1340
New College	1379
Lincoln	1427
All Souls	1438
Magdalen	1458
Brasenose	1509
Corpus Christi	1517
Christ Church	1546
Trinity	1554
St John's	1555
Jesus	1571
Wadham	1612
Pembroke	1624
Worcester	1714
St Catherine's	1868
Keble	1870
Hertford	1874
Lady Margaret Hall	1878
Somerville	1879
St Hugh's	1886
St Hilda's[1]	1893
St Peter's	1929
Nutfield[2]	1937
St Antony's[2]	1950
St Anne's	1952
Linacre	1962
Wolfson[2]	1965
St Cross[2]	1965
Green[2]	1979
Rewley House[3]	1990

[1]Women's college until 2008 [2]Graduate colleges
[3]Continuing and part-time education college

oxygen-containing compounds circulating between the atmosphere, the soil, and living organisms. The main biological phase involves the use of gaseous oxygen during respiration in animals and plants, with the consequent production of water and carbon dioxide, and the use of these products by green plants during photosynthesis, resulting in the liberation of gaseous oxygen.

oyster Bivalve mollusc with unequal valves, the left valve typically being cemented to a hard substrate; often cultivated for human consumption (in oyster farms), regarded as a delicacy; some species used for the production of pearls. (Class: Pelecypoda. Order: Ostreoida.)

oystercatcher A large plover-like bird; black or black-and-white; long reddish bill and legs; eats invertebrates, especially bivalve shellfish; also known as the **sea pie**. (Genus: *Haematopus*, 4 species. Family: Haematopodidae.)

Oz, Amos, originally **Amos Klausner** (1939–) Novelist, born in Jerusalem. His novels describe the tensions of life in modern Israel, and include *Ma'kom aher* (1966, Elsewhere, Perhaps) and *Po y-sham be-Erets Yisre'el bis-setary* (1982, In the Land of Israel). Among later books are *The Same Sea* (2001). *A Tale of Love and Darkness*, chronicling his early life, was published in 2004. Among his awards are the Israel Prize for Literature in 1998 and the 2005 Goethe cultural prize for his life's work.

ozalid process *photocopying*

Ozark Mountains [ohzahk] (Fr *aux arks*, 'at the arks') Highlands in SC USA; area c.129 500 km^2/50 000 sq mi, altitude generally 300–360 m/1000–1200 ft.

ozone A form of oxygen having molecules O_3. It is formed by the action of ultraviolet radiation on ordinary oxygen, and is a gas, boiling point −112°C.

ozone layer The part of the stratosphere at a height of c.22 km/14 mi in which the gas ozone (O_3) is most concentrated. It is produced by the action of ultraviolet light from the Sun on oxygen (O_2) in the air. The ozone layer shields the Earth from the harmful effects of solar ultraviolet radiation, but can be decomposed by complex chemical reactions, notably involving chlorofluorocarbons (CFCs), used as the pressurized propellant in some aerosol sprays, in refrigerating systems, and in the production of foam packaging. An area of 50–75% depletion of total ozone has been called an **ozone hole**, defined geographically as the area in which the total ozone amount is less than 220 Dobson Units. (1 Dobson Unit is defined as 0.01 mm thickness at standard temperature and pressure of 0°C and 1 atmosphere pressure.) During the 1980s, reports of holes above the Arctic and Antarctic led to renewed efforts in Europe to reach agreement on an accelerated reduction in CFC consumption. The main focus of attention was in the Antarctic, where the hole, steadily increasing since the 1980s, was estimated to be c.27 million km² in September 2005. In 1987 the Montreal Protocol was signed by around 40 countries to limit the use of ozone-depleting substances (in force from 1990, since ratified by 180 countries), with the intention that consumption of CFCs would be frozen by 1999, reduced by 50% by 2005, and eliminated by 2010. Between 1986 and 1999, world global consumption of CFCs was reduced from 1·1 million to 150 000 tons, raising hopes that ozone levels would now begin to recover. In 2006 it was reported that the hole above the Antarctic appeared to have stopped widening and it is hoped that the area will recover fully over the next 60 years. The thinning over the Arctic is expected to recover sooner, sometime between 2030 and 2040.

p

paca [paka] A cavy-like rodent native to Central and South America. (Genus: *Cuniculus*, 2 species. Family: Dasyproctidae.)

pacemaker A cell or object that determines the rhythm at which certain events occur. In vertebrates, pacemaker cells are present in the heart and in the longitudinal muscle of the stomach and ureter. In patients with heart block, artificial pacemakers (usually battery-operated and implanted under the skin) stimulate the heart electrically to maintain higher rates of cardiac contraction.

Pachelbel, Johann [pakhelbel] (c.1653–1706) Composer and organist, born in Nuremberg, Germany, whose works profoundly influenced J S Bach. His best-known composition is the *Canon in D Major*.

pachinko [pachingkoh] The Japanese game of pinball, the word coming from the sound of a steel ball running round a pinball machine. It is Japan's most popular relaxation.

pachyderm [pakiderm] A mammal of the (now obsolete) group Pachydermata ('with thick skin'). The name was used for those ungulates which do not 'chew the cud', especially the elephants, but also other perissodactyls.

Pacific Community, formerly **South Pacific Commission** (to 1997) An organization set up in 1947 by Western states then exercising colonial rule in the S Pacific. The purpose was to advance the economic and social interests of the peoples under their control within a framework of regional co-operation. The S Pacific nations also joined, from the 1960s, as they became independent.

Pacific Islands *United States Trust Territory of the Pacific*

Pacific Islands Forum *South Pacific Forum*

Pacific Ocean area c.181 300 000 km²/70 000 000 sq mi. Ocean extending from the Arctic to the Antarctic, between North and South America (E) and Asia and Oceania (W); covers a third of the Earth and almost half the total water surface area; S part sometimes known as the South Sea; rim of volcanoes ('Pacific Ring of Fire'), deep open trenches, and active continental margins; greatest known depth, Challenger Deep in the Marianas Trench, 11 040 m/36 220 ft; ocean floor largely a deep sea-plain, average depth 4300 m/14 100 ft; many islands, either volcanic (eg Hawaii) or coral, mainly in the E section.

pacifism The doctrine of opposition to all wars, including civil wars. Its most obvious feature is the personal commitment to non-participation in wars, except possibly in a non-combatant role. Pacifists also advocate efforts to maintain peace and support disarmament.

Pacino, Al(fredo) [pacheenoh] (1940–) Film actor, born in New York City. His first main role came as Michael in *The Godfather* (1972), which he followed with acclaimed performances in *Serpico* (1973) and *The Godfather, Part II* and *III* (1974, 1990). Later films include *Scent of a Woman* (1992, Oscar), *The Devil's Advocate* (1997), *Insomnia* (2002), and *Two for the Money* (2005). His TV work includes the drama mini-series *Angels in America*, for which he won a Best Actor Emmy in 2004. In 2001 he received the Cecile B DeMille Award for his outstanding contribution to entertainment.

packet switching A service provided by Posts, Telegraph and Telephones Authorities which allows one computer to send a message to a second computer in the form of a set of packets which are transmitted over specially dedicated telephone lines. Packets from different subscribers are all sent down the same line in sequence. This removes the need for the telephone line to be dedicated to the two computers for the whole of the time that they are communicating and is, therefore, much cheaper for the users than a continuous link would be.

Pact of Paris *Kellogg–Briand Pact*

Padang [padang] 1°00S 100°21E, pop (2000e) 865 000. Main seaport on the W coast of Sumatra, Indonesia; third largest city in Sumatra; airfield; railway; university (1956).

Padania [padania] Area in N Italy declared to be an independent republic by the secessionist Northern League (led by Umberto Bossi) in 1996. It comprises over a third of the country, including all the land around the R Po, and extending to the S of Florence, from coast to coast. The declaration received widespread publicity, but limited support, and was condemned by the Italian government.

paddlefish Archaic sturgeon-like freshwater fish of family Polyodontidae, with only two living representatives; head has a long, flattened snout (or rostrum); known as fossils from the Eocene and Upper Cretaceous periods.

Paderewski, Ignacy (Jan) [paduhrefskee] (1860–1941) Pianist, composer, and patriot, born in Kurylowka, Poland. In 1919 he served briefly as the first premier of Poland and was elected president of Poland's provisional parliament in 1940.

Padua [padyooa] Ital **Padova**, ancient **Patavium** 45°24N 11°53E, pop (2000e) 217 000. City in NE Italy; on the R Bacchiglione; railway junction; 16th-c university; tomb of St Antony of Padua, a pilgrimage site; cathedral (16th-c); botanical garden (Orto Botanico) a world heritage site.

paediatrics / pediatrics [peediatriks] The medical care of infants and children, and the study of the diseases which affect them. It encompasses the care of the newborn child, including problems such as failure to breathe, jaundice, failure to thrive, congenital malformations, and special care units.

paedophilia / pedophilia A sexual interest in children (of either sex). Active interference is illegal, and there is often long-term psychological trauma experienced by the child.

Paestum [peestum] An ancient Greek town in SW Italy in the region of Naples, founded c.600 BC by Sybaris. It was renowned for its Doric temples.

Páez, José Antonio [paez] (1790–1873) Venezuelan general and president (1831–5, 1839–43, 1861–3), born in Aragua, Venezuela. He commanded forces of *llaneros* ('cowboys') in the war of independence as principal lieutenant of Simón Bolívar, and became president after the break-up of Gran Colombia.

Paganini, Niccolo [paganeenee] (1782–1840) Violin virtuoso, born in Genoa, Italy. He revolutionized violin technique, his innovations including the use of stopped harmonics. His compositions include six violin concertos.

Page, Sir Frederick Handley (1885–1962) Pioneer aircraft designer and engineer, born in Cheltenham, Gloucestershire. In 1909 he founded the firm of aeronautical engineers which bears his name. His Hampden and Halifax bombers were used in World War 2.

PageMaker® A desk-top publishing package in which page composition, including full graphics, is the principal objective.

pager A small radio receiver used in one-way communication to alert an individual or deliver a short message; not normally used with voice transmission. It works within a small area using one low-power transmitter, or over larger areas using multiple transmitters.

Paget's disease [pajet] A chronic disorder of the adult skeleton, of unknown origin, in which normal bone growth and replacement is disturbed; named after English surgeon James Paget (1814–99), and also known as **osteitis deformans**.

pagoda [pagohda] A Buddhist reliquary cairn or mound (*stupa*), modified by Chinese architectural principles, found throughout E Asia. It is a multi-storied tower, with each storey having a roof of glazed tiles.

Pahang [pahang] pop (2000e) 1 313 000; area 35 965 km²/ 13 882 sq mi. State in E Peninsular Malaysia; formerly part of the kingdom of Malacca; capital, Kuantan.

Pahlavi, Mohammad Reza [pahlavee] (1919–80) Shah of Persia, born in Tehran, Iran, who succeeded on the abdication of his father, Reza Shah, in 1941. His reign was marked by social reforms, but protest at western-style 'decadence' grew among the religious fundamentalists, and he was forced to leave Iran in 1979.

Paige, Elaine (1951–) Actress and singer, born in London. It was her performances in *Jesus Christ Superstar* (1972) and *Billy* (1974) that established her as a musical actress. She starred as *Evita* in 1978, and later shows include *Cats* (1981), *Chess* (1986), *Sunset Boulevard* in London (1994–5) and New York (1996), *The King and I* (2000), and *The Drowsy Chaperone* (2007).

pain An unpleasant sensation – in the simplest case, the stimulation of nerve endings by a strong stimulus, such as heat, pressure, or tissue damage. Pain receptors are located over most of the body surface and at many internal sites. When stimulated, they initiate reflex responses within the spinal cord, and convey information to the brain. The degree of pain is determined not only by the intensity of the stimulus, but also by psychological factors which can increase or decrease the release of pain-killing peptides (endorphins and enkephalins) within the brain and spinal cord.

Paine, Thomas (1737–1809) Radical political writer, born in Thetford, Norfolk. In 1774 he sailed for Philadelphia, where his pamphlet *Common Sense* (1776) argued for complete independence. In 1787 he returned to England, and wrote *The Rights of Man* (1791–2), in support of the French Revolution. Arraigned for treason, he fled to Paris, where he wrote *The Age of Reason*, in favour of deism.

paint A colouring substance consisting of two basic elements, pigment and medium. Pigments have been derived from earths (eg yellow ochre), minerals (eg malachite), and dyes (organic and, since the mid-19th-c, synthetic). These are reduced to powder, and dispersed in whatever medium (eg oil) the artist is using.

painted lady A medium-sized butterfly; wings brick-red with black patches, and white patches on point of forewings. (Order: Lepidoptera. Family: Nymphalidae.)

painting An art which originated in prehistoric times; but the modern sense of the word, the skilful arrangement of colours

on a surface to create an independent work, has been current only since the Renaissance.

Paisley, Rev Ian (Richard Kyle) [payzlee] (1926–) Militant Protestant clergyman and politician, born in Armagh, Northern Ireland. He founded the Protestant Unionist Party, and since 1974 has been the Democratic Unionist Party (DUP) MP for North Antrim. A rousing orator, he is fiercely opposed to the IRA, Roman Catholicism, and the unification of Ireland. He led the DUP to success in the Assembly elections in 2003. Following Assembly elections in March 2007, he became first minister of a new power-sharing executive.

Paiute [piyoot] Two separate Numic-speaking American Indian groups, traditionally hunter-gatherers, divided into the S Paiute (Utah, Arizona, Nevada, California) and the N Paiute (California, Nevada, Oregon).

Pakistan *p.696*

PAL [pal] Acronym for **Phase Alternating Line**, the coding system for colour television developed in Germany and the UK from 1965, and widely adopted for 625-line 50 Hz transmission in Europe and many other parts of the world.

pala [pahla] An altarpiece consisting of a single large picture, instead of several small ones; also known as a **pala d'altare**. The type first appeared in Florence c.1430.

Palach, Jan [palakh] (1948–69) Czech philosophy student, who as a protest against the invasion of Czechoslovakia by Warsaw Pact forces (1968) burnt himself to death in Wenceslas Square, Prague.

Palaeocene / Paleocene epoch [paliohseen] The first of the geological epochs of the Tertiary period, from c.66 to 55 million years ago. The vast majority of dinosaurs had disappeared, and mammals suddenly diversified.

palaeography / paleography The study of the styles of handwriting used by scribes in ancient and mediaeval times. The aim is to establish the provenance or authenticity of specific texts, by relating the hand of a particular scribe, in a particular document, to the styles prevailing in the relevant historical period.

Palaeolithic / Paleolithic art The art of the Old Stone Age, created c.30 000 years ago, the oldest known. Preserved in limestone caves in France and Spain are impressive murals representing hunting scenes. Small sculptures were also made.

palaeontology / paleontology The study of fossils; especially, the reconstruction of the organism from its fossil remains and the study of the processes of fossilization.

Palaeozoic / Paleozoic era [paleeohzohik] A major division of geological time extending from c.590 to 250 million years ago; subdivided into the Cambrian, Ordovician, and Silurian periods (the **Early Palaeozoic** era), and the Devonian, Carboniferous, and Permian periods (the **Late Palaeozoic** era).

palantype [palantiyp] The UK trade name of a shorthand typewriter known by the trade name **stenotype** in the USA. Using a silent keyboard, the operator produces on bands of paper a phonetic version of ongoing utterances. The output is later transcribed to produce a normal typescript.

palate A structure forming the roof of the mouth and the floor of the nasal cavity. It is divided into the **hard palate**, towards the front (formed by bone) and the mobile fibro-muscular **soft palate**, towards the back (which is continuous with the hard palate). The soft palate hangs downwards into the pharynx (separating its nasal and oral parts), and consists mainly of muscle attached to a fibrous base. It may be tensed and raised to close off the nasopharynx, as in swallowing or when producing certain sounds.

Palatinate, the A German Rhenish principality; capital, Heidelberg. It was elevated to an imperial Electorate in 1356, and became the leading Protestant German state and head of the

Pakistan

- □ International Airport · ∴ World heritage site
- -- India/Pakistan line of control

official name **Islamic Republic of Pakistan**

Local name Pākistān

Timezone GMT +5

Area 803 943 km²/310 322 sq mi

Population total (2002e) 145 960 000

Status Republic

Date of independence 1947

Capital Islamabad

Languages Urdu and English (official), Punjabi, Sindhi, Pashto, Urdu, Baluchi, and Brahvi mainly spoken

Ethnic groups Punjabi (66%), Sindhi (13%), Baluchi (3%), Pathan and Muhajir minorities, also Afghan refugees in W Pakistan

Religions Muslim (97%) (Sunni 77%, Shi'a 20%), Christian, Hindu, Parsee, Buddhist minorities

Physical features R Indus flows from Himalayas to Karachi, forming a vast, fertile, densely populated alluvial floodplain in E; bounded N and W by mountains rising to 8611 m/28 250 ft at K2, and 8126 m/26 660 ft at Nanga Parbat; mostly flat plateau, low-lying plains and arid desert to the S; major rivers include Jhelum, Chenab, Indus, Sutlej.

Climate Continental, with many temperature and rainfall variations; dominated by the Asiatic monsoon; severe winters in mountainous regions; average annual temperatures 10°C (Jan), 32°C (Jul) in Islamabad; average annual rainfall in Punjab, 250 mm/10 in in SW, 635 mm/25 in in NE; rainy season (Jun–Oct).

Currency 1 Pakistan Rupee (PKR) = 100 paisa

Economy Agriculture (employs 55% of labour force); cotton production important, supporting major spinning, weaving, and processing industries; sugar cane; textiles; natural gas; tobacco; salt; uranium.

GDP (2002e) $295.3 bn, per capita $2000

Human Development Index (2002) 0.499

History Remains of Indus Valley civilization over 4000 years ago; Muslim rule under the Mughal Empire, 1526–1761; British rule over most areas, 1840s; separated from India to form a state for the Muslim minority, 1947; consisted of West Pakistan (Baluchistan, North-West Frontier, West Punjab, Sind) and East Pakistan (East Bengal), physically separated by 1610 km/1000 mi; occupied Jammu and Kashmir, 1949 (disputed territory with India, and the cause of wars in 1965 and 1971); proclaimed an Islamic republic, 1956; differences between E and W Pakistan developed into civil war, 1971; E Pakistan became an independent state (Bangladesh); military coup by General Zia ul-Haq, 1977, with execution of former prime minister Bhutto in 1979; new constitution (1985) strengthened Zia's powers; Benazir Bhutto elected prime minister, 1988, deposed 1990, re-elected 1993; deposed 1996; ethnic (Muslim/Sindh) violence, especially in Karachi, 1994, and ongoing; military coup, 1999; coup leader, General Musharraf, declared president in 2001; sensitive border area with Afghanistan, following the US-led anti-Taliban campaign, 2001, focusing on Afghan refugees, Pakistani pro-Taliban fighters, and Taliban escapees; ongoing tension with India over Kashmir, with some fighting, 2001, escalating into a major crisis, mid-2002; ceasefire announced (Nov 2003) and diplomatic ties and transport links resumed; full membership of the Commonwealth restored (May 2004); earthquake in N killed over 87 000 (Oct 2005); governed by an elected President and a bicameral Federal Parliament.

Head of State
1988–93 Ghulam Ishaq Khan
1993–7 Farooq Ahmed Leghari
1997–2001 Mohammad Rafiq Tarar
2001– Pervez Musharraf

Head of Government
1973–7 Zulfikar Ali Bhutto
1977–85 *No Prime Minister*
1985–8 Mohammad Khan Junejo
1988 Mohammad Aslam Khan Khattak
1988–90 Benazir Bhutto
1990 Ghulam Mustafa Jatoi
1990–3 Mian Mohammad Nawaz Sharif
1993–6 Benazir Bhutto
1996–7 Malik Meraj Khalid
1997–9 Mian Mohammad Nawaz Sharif
1999–2001 Pervez Musharraf (Chief Executive Officer)
2002–4 Zafarullah Khan Jamali
2004– Shaukat Aziz

Protestant Union (1608). In the 18th-c it lost significance, and was finally absorbed into the German Reich (1871).

Palau *Belau*

Palawan [palahwan], formerly **Paragua** (1902–5) pop (2000e) 467 000; area 11 780 km²/4547 sq mi. Island of the W Philippines; rises in the S to 2054 m/6739 ft at Mt Mantalingajan; chief town, Puerto Princesa.

Pale The 'land of peace' where English rule prevailed in late mediaeval times on the edges of English territory around Calais (until its loss in 1558), Scotland, and a large part of E Ireland. It was defined as the four counties of Dublin, Kildare, Louth, and Meath in 1464, but the Act of 1495 showed a smaller area.

Palembang [palembang] 2°59S 104°45E, pop (2000e) 1152 000. River-port city on S Sumatra I, Indonesia; former capital of the Srivijaya Empire (7th–12th-c); airfield; university (1960).

Palenque [palengke] A Mayan city of AD 600–800 on the slopes of the Chiapas Mts, S Mexico, celebrated for its beauty and distinctive architecture: a world heritage site.

Paleo-, paleo- *see under Palaeo-, palaeo-*

Palermo [palermoh] 38°08N 13°23E, pop (2000e) 733 000. Port on N coast of Sicily, Italy; founded by Phoenicians, 7th–8th-c BC; archbishopric; airport; railway; ferries; university (1777); cathedral (12th-c).

Palestine (Middle East) A country in the Middle East whose boundaries were transformed by political considerations across the 20th-c. Following the break-up of the Ottoman Empire in the settlement after World War 1, Palestine was created as a British mandate in 1922. Britain had pledged its support for Zionist national aspirations in the 1917 Balfour Declaration, prior to the formation of Palestine and in disregard of the interests of the 88% Arab majority. These competing national aspirations made Britain's position in Palestine untenable, and in 1947 it relinquished control to the UN, which voted in November to partition the territory and impose a two-state solution, one Jewish and one Arab, with Jerusalem under international control. Rejected by the Arabs and accepted by the Zionists, partition ultimately was superseded by the outcome of the 1948 Arab–Israeli War, which left the new state of Israel in possession of 77% of the mandated territory. As Jordan annexed the West Bank, including East Jerusalem (1948), and Egypt administered the small Gaza Strip, Palestine effectively disappeared from the map. Israel occupied East Jerusalem, the West Bank, and the Gaza Strip in the June 1967 War, since which time these regions have been collectively referred to as the **Occupied Territories**.

In July 1988, King Hussein of Jordan severed administrative and legal ties to the West Bank in deference to the claim by the Palestine Liberation Organization (PLO) to be the legitimate representative of the Palestinian people. At the 19th meeting of the Palestine National Council in Algiers (Nov 1988), the PLO proclaimed the State of Palestine. The boundaries of that state were never specified, the declaration amounting to PLO recognition of the principle of partition rejected in 1947, although the PLO Charter still denied Israel's right to exist. Over 100 states have since recognized the State of Palestine, and PLO offices in those countries are recognized as embassies.

In 1993, a historic peace agreement was signed in Washington between the PLO and Israel, which provided for an Israeli withdrawal from the Gaza Strip and the West Bank town of Jericho. These two areas would be under full Palestinian authority, and a degree of self-rule would be allowed in parts of the rest of the West Bank. The agreement was internationally acclaimed (though greeted with hostility by many Israelis and Palestinians), but was only haltingly implemented by Israel. Yasser Arafat, the chairman of the Palestine National Authority (see separate entry), became president in 1996. A period of stalemate was broken by the US-brokered Wye agreement (1998), by which Israel would redeploy its forces from further West Bank areas, and the Palestinians would strengthen anti-terrorist measures and cancel anti-Israel provisions in their national charter. However, disagreement over troop withdrawals, Israeli settlements, the return of Palestinian refugees, and the status of Jerusalem continued to hinder peace negotiations, and threatened the projected deadline for the declaration of an independent state (Sep 2000).

Violent clashes between Israeli troops and Palestinian police and civilians intensified in 2001. Israeli Prime Minister Ariel Sharon maintained a hard-line approach to the crisis, and the conflict escalated when he ordered Israeli troops into the territory controlled by the Palestinian National Authority. Following a wave of attacks on Israel by suicide-bombers, further incursions took place, 2002–4. US President Bush published (Apr 2003) a peace initiative, known as the 'road map', for a phase-by-phase route to ending conflict in the Middle East and to full Palestinian statehood. Palestinian and Israeli moderates launched an alternative peace plan, the Geneva Accord (Dec 2003). In 2002 Israel began building a 640 km/440 mi security barrier to seal off the West Bank (ruled illegal by the World Court). Tension increased again in 2004 following further Israeli proposals to build settlements within disputed areas, and following the death of President Yasser Arafat later that year. Mahmoud Abbas was elected to succeed Arafat in January 2005. At a summit meeting the next month, hopes for peace were renewed when he and Sharon declared a truce to end the violence, with an immediate ceasefire. In August 2005 the army evacuated Jewish settlers from the Gaza Strip in line with Sharon's disengagement plan. In January 2006, in the first parliamentary elections for a decade, the ruling Fatah party suffered a shock defeat by Islamic militant group HAMAS. A resurgence of factional violence led to the formation of a national unity cabinet (Mar 2007), with independents holding key ministerial posts.

Palestine Liberation Organization *PLO*

Palestine National Authority (PNA) pop (2002e) West Bank 2 164 000; Gaza Strip 1 226 000 Autonomous authority created by charter in 1968 and established in May 1994 to give self-government to the Palestinians of Gaza and certain areas on the West Bank (by 1997, Jericho, Jenin, Tulkarem, Nablus, Qalqiliya, Bethlehem, Ramallah, and 80% of Hebron); chief ethnic groups: Palestinian Arab and other 99.4% (West Bank), 83% (Gaza), Jewish 0.6% (West Bank), 17% (Gaza); religions: Muslim 98.7 (Gaza), 75% (West Bank), Jewish 0.6% (West Bank), 17% (Gaza), Christian and other 0.7% (West Bank), 8% (Gaza); GDP (2002) $2.1 bn (West Bank), $750 mn (Gaza); headquarters, Ramallah; governed by a cabinet and Legislative Council, with security maintained by an army and police force; first cabinet resigned in 1997 facing charges of corruption; foreign financial aid allowed PNA to develop industry, trade, and communications; opening of Gaza airport, 1998; avowed aim of PNA to declare a Palestinian state (see separate entry). Head of state (president): Mahmoud Abbas (Abu Mazen) (2005–); Head of government (prime minister): Ismail Haniya (2006–).

Palestrina, Giovanni Pierluigi da [palestreena] (c.1525–94) Composer, born in Palestrina, Italy. The most distinguished composer of the Renaissance, he composed over 100 Masses, motets, hymns, and other church pieces.

palette In art, a term with two main senses: **1** A flat wooden plate on which painters arrange their colours. **2** The range of colours used by an artist. By extension, this sense has come to be used in computing, referring to the range of colours available using computer graphics.

Palgrave, Francis Turner [palgrayv] (1824–97) Poet and critic, born in Great Yarmouth, Norfolk. He is best known as the editor of the *Golden Treasury of Songs and Lyrical Poetry* (1861), which influenced poetic taste for many years.

Palin, Michael (Edward) [paylin] (1943–) Scriptwriter and actor, born in Sheffield, UK. He joined the team in *Monty Python's Flying Circus* (1969–74), co-wrote and acted in the Monty Python films, and won a BAFTA Award for his role in *A Fish Called Wanda* (1988). He went on to present a popular series of travel documentaries for BBC TV, including *Around the World in Eighty Days* (1989), *Pole to Pole* (1992), *Full Circle* (1997), *Michael Palin's Hemingway Adventure* (1999), and *Himalaya* (2004). In 2005 he received a BAFTA award for outstanding contribution to television.

palindrome A word or phrase which reads the same backwards as forwards, such as 'madam', 'radar', and 'Draw, o coward!'.

Palladianism [palaydianizm] An architectural style of the 17th-c and 18th-c derived from the Renaissance buildings and writing of the Italian architect, Andrea Palladio (1508–80), and characterized by the use of symmetrical planning and the application of Roman architectural forms. Especially popular in England, it was first used by Inigo Jones for the Banqueting House, London (1619–22).

Pallas The second asteroid to be found (1802), 540 km/335 mi across.

palm A woody plant found throughout the tropics, typical of oceanic islands, with a few species reaching warm temperate regions. Palms are monocotyledons. Most species are trees, achieving their full diameter as seedlings, subsequent growth increasing only their height. Leaves are mostly fan- or feather-shaped, with numerous, pleated segments, and can reach 20 m/ 65 ft in length. The fruits are 1-seeded berries, dry, fleshy or fibrous, oily rather than starchy, often brightly coloured, and showing a great size range. Palms are of immense economic importance, especially in the tropics, where they provide a range of basic products, including vegetables, starch, fruits and nuts, timber, fibre, sugar, alcohol, and wax. (Family: Palmae.)

Palma (de Mallorca) [palma] 39°35N 2°39E, pop (2000e) 300 000. Seaport and chief city of Majorca I, Balearic Is; bishopric; airport; university (1967); castle (14th-c), cathedral (13th–16th-c).

palmate In botany, the shape of a leaf in which four or more leaflets arise from the same point, and spread like the fingers of a hand.

Palmer, Arnold (Daniel) (1929–) Golfer, born in Latrobe, PA. His wins include the (British) Open (1961–2), the US Open (1960), and the US Masters (1958, 1960, 1962, 1964).

Palmerston (Australia) *Darwin* (Australia)

Palmerston (of Palmerston), Henry John Temple, 3rd Viscount (1784–1865) British statesman and Liberal prime minister (1855–8, 1859–65), born in Broadlands, Hampshire. He served as secretary of war (1809–28), and was three times foreign secretary (1830–4, 1835–41, 1846–51). His robust defences of British interests abroad secured him the name of 'Firebrand Palmerston'. A more comfortable nickname was **Pam**, and his frequently xenophobic foreign policy won him substantial popular support in Britain. He is associated with 'Gunboat Diplomacy', whereby Britain employed, or threatened to employ, its unchallengeable naval supremacy to resolve overseas differences in its favour. As premier in 1855, he vigorously prosecuted the Crimean War with Russia.

Palmerston North 40°20S 175°39E, pop (2000e) 77 000. City in North Island, New Zealand; airfield; railway; university (1926); agricultural research centre.

palmitic acid [palmitik] $C_{15}H_{31}COOH$, IUPAC **hexadecanoic acid**, a saturated fatty acid, melting point 63°C. It is obtained from many animal and plant sources, especially milk and palm oil (from which the name is derived).

palm oil A major edible oil, obtained from the fruit of several types of palm tree. It is widely used for the manufacture of margarine, as well as in soap, candles, and lubricating grease.

Palm Springs 33°50N 116°33W, pop (2000e) 42 800. Resort city in S California, USA; founded, 1876; developed as a luxurious desert resort in the early 1930s; airfield; hot springs.

Palm Sunday In the Christian Church, the Sunday before Easter, commemorating the entry of Jesus into Jerusalem, when the crowd spread palm branches in front of him.

Palmyra (Pacific Ocean) [palmiyra] 5°52N 162°05W. Uninhabited atoll enclosing 50 small islets in the Pacific Ocean 1600 km/ 1000 mi S of Honolulu; annexed by USA, 1912; site for nuclear waste disposal since 1986.

Palmyra (Roman history) [palmiyra] In Roman times, a flourishing oasis town controlling the desert trade routes between N Syria and Babylonia. At the height of its power in the 3rd-c AD, it briefly gained independence before being destroyed by the Romans in 273.

Palomar Observatory An observatory on Mount Palomar near San Diego, CA, the site of the 5 m/200 in Hale reflector tele-

scope (1948), which has made numerous contributions to observational astronomy and cosmology. The first Palomar Observatory Sky Survey in the 1950s is a primary database used by all observatories.

palomino [palomeenoh] A horse with a distinctive type of colouring, found in various breeds; pale golden brown with white mane and tail; also known as **California sorrel**.

Palouse *Appaloosa*

Paltrow, Gwyneth [paltroh] (1972–) Film actress, born in Los Angeles, CA. Her films include *Seven* (1995), *Emma* (1996), *Shakespeare in Love* (1998, Oscar), *The Talented Mr Ripley* (1999), *Sky Captain and the World of Tomorrow* (2004), and *The Good Night* (2007). She made her London West End stage debut in *Proof* in 2002, and reprised the role in the 2005 film version.

palynology [paylinolojee] The analysis of pollen grains preserved in ancient sediments and soils to reconstruct variations in vegetation over time.

pampa(s) The extensive grassland (prairie) region of Argentina and Uruguay around the R Plate estuary. It is a major centre for cattle ranching.

Pamplona [pamplohna], Lat **Pampeluna** or **Pompaelo** 42°48N 1°38W, pop (2000e) 182 000. City in N Spain; on R Arga; archbishopric; capital of the Kingdom of Navarre, 10th-c; airport; railway; university (1952); cathedral (14th–15th-c); Fiesta of San Fermin (Jul), with bull-running in the streets.

Pamuk, Orhan (1952–) Novelist and writer, born in Istanbul, Turkey. He studied architecture at the Istanbul Technical University but left to join the University of Istanbul Institute of Journalism, graduating in 1976. He became a visiting scholar at Columbia University, USA (1985–8) and visiting fellow at the University of Iowa, and in 2006 took up a position as visiting professor at Columbia. His books include *Cevdet Bey and His Sons* (1982), *The New Life* (1995), *My Name is Red* (1998), *Snow* (2002), and *Istanbul* (2003). He was awarded the Nobel Prize for Literature in 2006.

Pan (astronomy) The 18th natural satellite of Saturn, discovered in 1990 from photographs taken nine years earlier by the Voyager 2 space probe; distance from the centre of Saturn 133 600 km/83 000 mi; diameter 20 km/12 mi; orbital period 0·58 days.

Pan (mythology) A Greek god, the 'nourisher' of flocks and herds, depicted with goat-like ears, horns, and legs. His pan-pipe is made of reeds.

Pan-Africanist Congress (PAC) A black political party in South Africa which broke away from the African National Congress in 1958 under the leadership of Robert Sobukwe (1924–78). It pursued a distinctly black and radical policy, its campaign of resistance leading to the Sharpeville massacre. It was one of the political parties unbanned by President de Klerk.

Panama *p.699*

Panama Canal A canal bisecting the Isthmus of Panama and linking the Atlantic and Pacific Oceans. It is 82 km/51 mi long, and 150 m/490 ft wide in most places; built by the US Corps of Engineers (1904–14). Panama guaranteed the neutrality of the waterway when it took over operational control of the canal in 2000.

Panama City, Span **Panamá** 8°57N 79°30W, pop (2000e) 713 000. Capital city of Panama; founded, 1673; airport; railway; two universities (1935, 1965); on the Pan-American Highway; historic district and Salón Bolivar, a world heritage site.

Pan-American Games A multi-sport competition for athletes from North, South, and Central American nations. First held at Buenos Aires, Argentina, in 1951, they now take place every four years.

Pan-American Highway A network of designated roads extending 27 000 km/17 000 mi across the Americas from Alaska to Chile.

Pan-American Union An organization founded in 1890 to foster

Panama

□ International Airport ∴ World heritage site

Span **Panamá**, official name **Republic of Panama**, Span **República de Panamá**

Local name Panamá

Timezone GMT -5

Area 77 082 km²/29 753 sq mi

Population total (2002e) 2 915 000

Status Republic

Date of independence 1903

Capital Panama City

Languages Spanish (official), English and indigenous languages (including Cuna, Chibchan, Choco)

Ethnic groups Mestizo (mixed Spanish-Indian) (70%), West Indian (14%), white (10%), Indian (6%)

Religions Christian (Roman Catholic 93%, Protestant 6%), Jewish, Muslim, and Baha'i minorities

Physical features Mostly mountainous; Serranía de Tabasará (W) rises to 3475 m/11 401 ft at Volcán Baru; Azuero peninsula (Peninsula de Azuero) in the S; lake-studded lowland cuts across the isthmus; dense tropical forests on the Caribbean coast; Panama Canal, 82 km/51 mi long, connects Pacific and Atlantic oceans.

Climate Tropical, with uniformly high temperatures; average annual temperature 26°C (Jan), 27°C (Jul) in Panama City; dry season (Jan–Apr) only; average annual rainfall 1770 mm/69.7 in.

Currency 1 Balboa (PAB) = 100 cents; 1 US Dollar (USD) = 100 cents

Economy Canal revenue (accounts for 80% of country's wealth); great increase in banking sector since 1970; attempts to diversify include oil refining, cigarettes, paper products; tourism; copper, gold, silver; bananas, coffee, cacao, sugar cane.

GDP (2002e) $18·06 bn, per capita $6200

Human Development Index (2002) 0·787

History Visited by Columbus, 1502; under Spanish colonial rule until 1821; joined the Republic of Greater Colombia; separation from Colombia after a US-inspired revolution, 1903; assumed sovereignty of the 8 km/5 mi-wide Canal zone, previously administered by the USA, 1979; military rule under Manuel Noriega, 1983–9; US invasion in 1989, deposed Noriega; governed by a President, Cabinet, and unicameral Legislative Assembly.

Head of State/Government

1960–4 Roberto Francisco Chiari
1964–8 Marco A Robles
1968 Arnulfo Arias Madrid
1968 *Military junta*
1968–9 Omar Torrijos Herrera
1969–78 Demetrio Basilio Lakas
1978–82 Aristides Royo
1982–4 Ricardo de la Espriella
1984 Jorge Enrique Illueca Sibauste
1984–5 Nicolás Ardito Barletta
1985–8 Eric Arturo Delvalle
1988–9 Manuel Solís Palma
1989–94 Guillermo Endara
1994–9 Ernesto Pérez Balladares
1999–2004 Mireya Moscoso de Gruber
2004– Martin Torrijos

political and economic co-operation among American states, and to draw North and South America closer together; first called the **International Bureau for American Republics**. In 1948 it became part of the wider Organization of American States.

Pancake Day *Shrove Tuesday*

Panchen Lama [panchen lahma] A spiritual leader and teacher in Tibetan Buddhism, second in importance to the Dalai Lama, and said to be the reincarnation of the Buddha Amitabha.

pancreas [pangkrias] A soft gland made up of small lobes associated with the alimentary canal of vertebrates with jaws. In humans it is c.12–15 cm/4·5–6 in long. One part produces an alkaline mixture of digestive enzymes (the **pancreatic juices**); another (the islets of Langerhans) synthesizes hormones involved in carbohydrate metabolism.

panda A mammal of the family Ailuropodidae; inhabits bamboo forests in mountains; two species: **giant panda** (*Ailuropoda melanoleuca*) from China; bear-like with large round head; white with black legs, shoulders, chest, ears, and area around eyes; also the **red panda**, **lesser panda**, or **cat bear** (*Ailurus fulgens*) found from S China to N Myanmar; red-brown with

black underparts and tail tip; dark rings around tail; white markings on face. One of the world's most endangered species, the number of known giant pandas in the wild has been rising, from 1114 before 2000 to 1596 by 2005. A record 30 giant pandas were born in captivity in China in 2006, bringing the total there to 217.

Pandit, Vijaya Lakshmi, *née* **Swarup Kumari Nehru** (1900–90) Indian politician and diplomat, born in Allahabad India, the sister of Nehru. In 1953, she became the first woman president of the UN General Assembly, and Indian High Commissioner in London (1954–61).

Pandora [pandawra] In Greek mythology, the first woman, adorned by the gods with special qualities. Zeus gave her a box from which all the evils which plague mankind came out; only Hope was left in the bottom of the box.

panegyric [panejirik] A speech, poem, or song of praise addressed to an individual, group, or institution. An example is Mark Antony's oration on Caesar in Shakespeare's *Julius Caesar*.

Pangaea [panjeea] The name given to the hypothesized 'supercontinent' comprising Gondwanaland and Laurasia which made up the Earth's continental crust before the Jurassic period.

Papua New Guinea

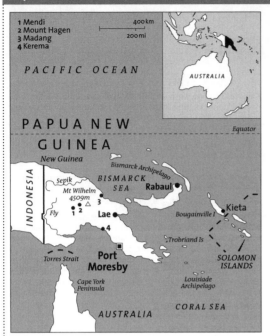

1 Mendi
2 Mount Hagen
3 Madang
4 Kerema

400 km
200 mi

PACIFIC OCEAN

AUSTRALIA

PAPUA NEW GUINEA

Equator

New Guinea

Bismarck Archipelago

INDONESIA

Sepik

BISMARCK SEA

Rabaul

Mt Wilhelm 4509m

Fly

Lae

Bougainville I

Kieta

Trobriand Is

Torres Strait

Port Moresby

SOLOMON ISLANDS

Cape York Peninsula

Louisiade Archipelago

AUSTRALIA

CORAL SEA

□ International Airport

official name **Independent State of Papua New Guinea**

Local name Papua New Guinea

Timezone GMT +10

Area 462 840 km²/178 656 sq mi

Population total (2002e) 5 426 000

Status Independent state within the Commonwealth

Date of independence 1975

Capital Port Moresby

Languages Pidgin English and Hiri Motu (official parliamentary languages), Tok Pisin, and c.750 indigenous languages spoken

Ethnic groups Papuan (80%), Melanesian (15%), Polynesian, Chinese, and European minorities

Religions Christian (Protestant 64%, Roman Catholic 33%), local beliefs

Physical features Island group in SW Pacific Ocean, comprising E half of the island of New Guinea, the Bismarck and Louisiade archipelagos, the Trobriand and D'Entrecasteaux Is, and other off-lying groups; complex system of mountains, highest point, Mt Wilhelm, 4509 m/14 793 ft; mainly covered with tropical rainforest; vast mangrove swamps along coast; archipelago islands are mountainous, mostly volcanic and fringed with coral reefs; in 2006, many previously unknown plants and animals discovered in the Foja Mountains region.

Climate Typical monsoon, with temperatures and humidity constantly high; average annual temperature 28°C (Jan), 26°C (Jul); average annual rainfall 2000–2500 mm/80–100 in.

Currency 1 Kina (PGK) = 100 toea

Economy Farming, fishing, and forestry (engages c.75% of workforce); vegetables, sugar, peanuts; natural gas; brewing; tourism.

GDP (2002e) $10·86 bn, per capita $2100

Human Development Index (2002) 0·535

History British protectorate in SE New Guinea, 1884; some of the islands under German protectorate, 1884; German New Guinea in NE in 1899; German colony annexed by Australia in World War I; Australia mandated to govern both British and German areas, 1920; combined as the United Nations Trust Territory of Papua and New Guinea, 1949; independence within the Commonwealth, 1975; a Governor-General represents the British Crown; governed by a Prime Minister and a Cabinet, with a unicameral National Parliament.

Head of State
(British monarch represented by Governor-General)
1991–7 Wiwa Korowi
1997–2003 Sir Silas Atopare
2003–4 Bill Skate *Acting*
2004– Sir Paulias Matane

Head of Government
1975–80 Michael Thomas Somare
1980–2 Julius Chan
1982–5 Michael Thomas Somare
1985–8 Paias Wingti
1988–92 Rabbie Namiliu
1992–4 Paias Wingti
1994–7 Julius Chan
1997 John Giheno (*caretaker*)
1997–9 Bill Skate
1999–2002 Mekere Morauta
2002– Michael Thomas Somare

pangamic acid A component of many seeds, whose chemical name is n-di-isopropyl-glucuronate. Although it is promoted as a vitamin (B_{15}), it serves no known nutritional function.

pangolin [panggohlin] A mammal native to Africa and S and SE Asia; pointed head with small eyes; long broad tail; long tongue and no teeth; eats ants and termites; covered in large overlapping horny plates; the only member of the order Pholidota; also known as **scaly anteater**. (Genus: *Manis*, 7 species.)

Panhandle Any territory comprising a narrow strip of land running out from a large area in the shape of a pan handle; in the USA, applied to areas in (1) NW Texas, (2) NW Oklahoma, (3) N Idaho, (4) NE West Virginia, (5) N West Virginia, (6) SE Alaska, (7) Nebraska, and (8) an extension of the Golden Gate Park in San Francisco.

panicle A branched, racemose type of inflorescence. The term is often used for any complexly-branched inflorescence.

Paninari [paninahree] An Italian youth cult of the 1980s named

from the sandwich bars where its members gathered. They wore expensive 'designer' clothes presenting a tough militaristic image.

Panjabi *Indo-Aryan languages*

Pankhurst, Emmeline, *née* **Goulden** (1858–1928) Suffragette, born in Manchester, Greater Manchester. In 1905 she organized the Women's Social and Political Union, and fought for women's suffrage by violent means, on several occasions being arrested and going on hunger strike.

panpipes A musical instrument made of various lengths of hollowed cane or wood joined together in a row. The player blows across the top to sound a different pitch from each pipe.

pansy Any of several species or varieties of violet, in which the flat, 5-petalled flowers are held in a vertical plane and often resemble a face. The cultivated pansy has large flowers with overlapping petals in a wide range of colours. (Genus: *Viola*. Family: Violaceae.)

parabola

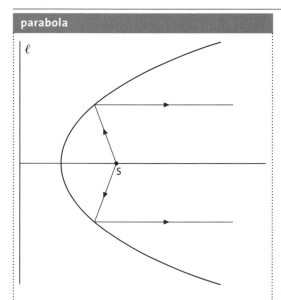

In mathematics, the locus of a point whose distance from a fixed point *S* (the *focus*) is equal to its distance from a fixed line *l* (the *directrix*). It is one of the classical conic sections. The parabola has the property that the tangent at any point *P* is equally inclined to the line *PS*, and the line through *P* parallel to the *x*-axis of the parabola. Thus rays emitted from *S* and reflected by the curve will be parallel. This notion underlies the technique for obtaining parallel rays of light, and for transmitting parallel radio waves.

pantheism The belief that God and the universe are ultimately identical. It is a characteristic feature of Hinduism and certain schools of Buddhism.

pantheon A temple in Rome dedicated to all the gods, begun by Agrippa in 27 BC and rebuilt by Hadrian (AD 100–125), and now S Maria Rotonda. The name is more generally used for any burial place or Temple of Fame.

panther A member of the cat family, but not a distinct species. The name is used for the black form of the leopard (especially in the combination **black panther**) or as an alternative name for the cougar.

pantomime In most European languages the term denotes what in English is usually referred to as a mime. In England the term signifies a specific form of entertainment developed from the harlequinade in the 19th-c. It is performed during the Christmas season as a mixture of songs, dances, slapstick, topical jokes, male and female impersonations, magic, and spectacle, with a storyline that is loosely connected to a fairy-tale or nursery-rhyme.

pantothenic acid A B vitamin which acts as a co-factor in several enzyme reactions. It is found widely in nature.

Panzer (Ger 'armour') A term used in the German armed forces, applied particularly to armoured fighting vehicles. The Panzer divisions (essentially tank forces) were the most important component of the German army during World War 2.

papacy *pope*

Papa Doc *Duvalier, François*

Papago [papagoh] A Uto-Aztecan-speaking group of North American Indians, originally semi-nomadic wild food gatherers. They live chiefly on reservations in Arizona.

Papal States The 'States of the Church', straddling rural, mountainous areas of C Italy, comprising territories received by treaties and donations in the Middle Ages. They were annexed by Italy in 1870, but the papacy refused to recognize their loss until the Lateran Treaty (1929), which established the Vatican papal state.

papaw [papaw] A small, unbranched tree (*Carica papaya*) growing to 6 m/20 ft, with very soft wood and copious latex; a crown of long-stalked leaves up to 75 cm/30 in wide; flowers yellow; fruit up to 30 cm/12 in long, oval, yellow; also called **papaya** and **pawpaw**. It is widely cultivated throughout the tropics for its juicy but bland fruits. (Family: Caricaceae.)

papaya *papaw*

Papeete [papayaytay] 17°32S 149°34W, pop (2000e) 99 300. Capital and chief port of French Polynesia, on NW coast of Tahiti; airport.

Papen, Franz von [papen] (1879–1969) German politician, born in Werl, Germany. He was Hitler's vice-chancellor (1933–4), and ambassador to Austria (1936–8) and Turkey (1939–44). Taken prisoner in 1945, he was acquitted at the Nuremberg Trials.

paper Material in sheet form used for a wide range of functions, notably writing, drawing, printing, and packaging. Invented in China in AD 105, it was originally produced from pulped rags or plant fibres. From the 19th-c, wood pulp and cellulose have largely been used in its manufacture, but plant fibres (eg esparto grass) and rags continue to be used, and the recycling of waste paper is increasingly practised on ecological grounds. The world uses some 200 million tons of paper each year.

paper-bark birch A species of birch with peeling white bark (*Betula papyrifolia*), which is used to make canoes. It is native to North America. (Family: Betulaceae.)

paper nautilus [nawtilus] An octopus-like marine mollusc (*Argonauta*); female c.30 cm/12 in long, male only 1 cm/0·4 in long; widely distributed in tropical and subtropical seas. (Class: Cephalopoda.)

Paphos [pafos] 34°45N 32°23E, pop (2000e) 31 700. Resort town in SW Cyprus; capital of Cyprus during Roman times; old city founded probably in Mycenaean period, a world heritage site; 7th-c Byzantine castle.

papilionid butterfly [papilyonid] A butterfly of the family Papilionidae; medium to very large, and often brightly coloured; c.550 species. (Order: Lepidoptera.)

papilloma [papilohma] Localized overgrowths of cells on epithelial surfaces such as the skin, intestinal lining, or bladder lining.

papillon [papilon] A toy breed of dog developed in France several centuries ago; small with long fine coat; ears with fringes of hair, resembling a butterfly's wings.

Pappus of Alexandria (4th-c) Greek mathematician, whose eight-book *Synagoge* (Collection) is extant in an incomplete form.

paprika *pepper 1*

Papua New Guinea *p.700*

papyrus [papiyruhs] An aquatic perennial (*Cyperus papyrus*) native to N Africa; stems growing to 4 m/13 ft; leaves grass-like; flowers tiny, yellowish. The ancients made paper by pressing wet strips of the pithy stems side by side. (Family: Cyperaceae.)

parable A metaphor in narrative form with the purpose not so much of imparting propositional truths or general moral lessons as challenging the perspective of the hearer. In the Bible, parables are frequently used by Jesus in his preaching about the kingdom of God.

parabola *see panel*

Paracelsus [paraselsus], originally **Philippus Aureolus Theophrastus Bombastus von Hohenheim** (1493–1541) Alchemist and physician, born in Einsiedeln, Switzerland. He travelled widely and acquired great fame as a medical practitioner, intro-

Paraguay

☐ International Airport

[paragwiy], official name **Republic of Paraguay**, Span **República del Paraguay**

Local name Paraguay
Timezone GMT -4
Area 406 750 km²/157 000 sq mi
Population total (2002e) 5 774 000
Status Republic
Date of independence 1811
Capital Asunción
Languages Spanish (official), but Guaraní also spoken

Ethnic groups Mestizo (mixed Spanish-Guaraní Indian) (91%), Amerindian, black, European, and Asian minorities
Religions Roman Catholic (96%), Mennonite, Baptist/Anglican minorities
Physical features Landlocked, in C South America; divided into two regions by the R Paraguay; Gran Chaco in the W, mostly cattle country or scrub forest; more fertile land in the E; Paraná plateau at 300–600 m/1000–2000 ft, mainly wet, treeless savannah.
Climate Tropical NW, with hot summers, warm winters; temperate in SE; average annual temperatures 27°C (Jan), 18°C (Jul) in Asunción; average annual rainfall 1316 mm/52 in.
Currency 1 Guaraní (PYG) = 100 céntimos
Economy Agriculture (employs 43% of the labour force); oilseed, cotton, wheat, tobacco, corn, rice, sugar cane; pulp, timber, textiles, cement, glass.
GDP (2002e) $25·19 bn, per capita $4300
Human Development Index (2002) 0·740
History Originally inhabited by Guaraní Indians; arrival of the Spanish, 1537; arrival of Jesuit missionaries, 1609; independence from Spain, 1811; War of the Triple Alliance against Brazil, Argentina, and Uruguay, 1865–70; Chaco War with Bolivia, 1932–5; civil war, 1947; General Alfredo Stroessner seized power, 1954, forced to stand down following a coup in 1989; new constitution, creating post of Vice-President, 1992; dengue fever outbreak led to a state of emergency (Mar 2007); governed by a President, an appointed Council of Ministers, and a bicameral National Congress.

Head of State/Government
1940–8 Higinio Moríñigo
1948 Juan Manuel Frutos
1948–9 Juan Natalicio González
1949 Raimundo Rolón
1949 Felipe Molas López
1949–54 Federico Chaves
1954 Tomás Romero Pareira
1954–89 Alfredo Stroessner
1989–93 Andres Rodriguez
1993–8 Juan Carlos Wasmosy
1998–9 Raúl Cubas Grau
1999–2003 Luis Gonzalez Macchi
2003– Nicanor Duarte Frutos

ducing laudanum, sulphur, lead, and mercury into Western therapeutics.
paracetamol [parasetamol] A mild painkiller commonly used for headache, menstrual pain, etc. It will also reduce body temperature during fever.
parachuting The act of jumping out of an aircraft and eventually landing with the aid of a parachute. French aeronaut André-Jacques Garnerin (1769–1823) made the first recorded descent over Paris in October 1797, when he was released from a balloon.
paradox In logic, a contradictory or implausible conclusion which seems to follow by valid argument from true premisses. 'This sentence is false' appears to be true if false, and false if true. Such paradoxes played an important role in the work of Russell and Frege on the foundations of mathematical logic.
paraffin *kerosene*
paraffin wax Solid hydrocarbon wax, originally produced from shale c.1850, but now made from petroleum. It is used for candles, waterproofing, textile conditioning, polishes, and ointments.
Paraguay *see panel*
Paraguay, River [paragwiy] (Span **Río**), Port **Rio Paraguai** River in

C South America; a chief tributary of the R Paraná; rises in Brazil; length 2300 km/1450 mi.
Paraguayan War *Triple Alliance, War of the*
parakeet The name used for some small parrots with long pointed tails (c.37 species).
paraldehyde [paraldehiyd] $(C_2H_4O_3)_3$. An oligomer containing three molecules of acetaldehyde; a liquid boiling at 128°C.
Paralipomenon [paralipomenon] *Chronicles, Books of*
parallax In astronomy, an apparent displacement in the position of any celestial object caused by a change in the position of the observer; specifically, a change because of the motion of the Earth around the Sun.
parallel distributed processing *connectionism*
parallel processing The use of two or more processors simultaneously to carry out a single computing task, each processor being assigned a particular part of the task at any given time. This differs from conventional computing, where the whole task is carried out sequentially by one processor. The approach promises greatly increased computing speeds for certain types of task.
Paralympics (an abbreviation of 'Parallel Olympics') The equiva-

lent of the Olympic Games for disabled people, inaugurated in 1960, and held every four years where possible in the same city or country as the Olympic Games. The major events of the Summer Games include archery, basketball, boccia, cycling, fencing, judo, power/weight lifting, shooting, soccer, swimming, table tennis, tennis, and volleyball; Winter Games have been held since 1976.

paralysis Loss of movement resulting from interference with the nerve supply to a muscle or muscles. It may arise from destruction of the motor nerve cells in the brain (eg *hemiplegia*, following a stroke in which muscles on one side of the body are affected) or in the spinal cord (eg poliomyelitis). *Paraplegia* refers to the loss of muscle power affecting both lower limbs. In *quadriplegia* all four limbs are affected.

Paramaribo [paramareeboh] 5°54N 55°14W, pop (2000e) 261 000. Federal capital and chief port of Suriname; capital of British Suriname, 1651; under Dutch rule, 1814–1975; airport; university (1968); cathedral (19th-c).

Paramecium [parameesium] A genus of single-celled microorganisms, ovoid in shape, length up to 0·33 mm/0·013 in; cells contain two types of nucleus; hair-like processes (*cilia*) arranged uniformly over cell surface; common in aquatic habitats. (Phylum: Ciliophora.)

paramedic A medical specialist responsible for collecting injured or unwell people (eg from the site of an accident), administering life-saving procedures where necessary, and initiating emergency treatment while transporting the casualty to a hospital.

Paraná, River [parana] (Span **Río**), in Brazil **Alto Parana** Major river of South America; rises in SEC Brazil and joins the R Uruguay after 3300 km/2000 mi to form the R Plate estuary on the Atlantic.

parana pine *araucaria*

paranoia An excessive tendency to suspiciousness and sensitivity to being rebuffed. Paranoid individuals may presume by merely seeing a police car, for example, that there is an elaborate plot to put them in jail, and that the plot has been directed by an unknown authority.

paranormal Beyond the bounds of what can be explained in terms of currently held scientific knowledge. The use of the term allows for the possibility that new discoveries in physics may account for events which are now classified as paranormal. This is in contrast with the term *supernatural*, which implies a non-physical explanation for events.

paraplegia *paralysis*

parapsychology The scientific study of certain aspects of the paranormal, primarily those in which an organism appears (i) to receive information from its environment through some means not presently understood (also known as **extrasensory perception** or **ESP**), or (ii) to exert an influence on its environment through some means not presently understood (also known as **psychokinesis** or **PK**).

parasitic plant A plant which obtains some or all of its food and/or shelter from another plant. Many fungi and some plants have adopted this lifestyle. Among flowering plants total parasites include broomrapes, rafflesias, and dodders. A much larger group are the semi-parasitic plants, which possess green leaves and are able to manufacture at least some nutrients, but which supplement their food supply from a host. They are termed **hemiparasites**, and include mistletoe and eyebrights.

parasitology [parasitolojee] The study of organisms which live on and at the expense of another living creature (the *host*) and of their interactions.

parasympathetic nervous system *autonomic nervous system*

parathyroid glands In humans a set of glands, usually four in number, closely associated with the back of the thyroid

gland. Their removal in mammals causes death within a few days.

paratyphoid fever A disease caused by a species of *Salmonella*. It is similar to but less serious than typhoid fever.

Parcae [pah(r)see, pah(r)kiy] The Fates. The name originally referred to a Roman birth-goddess. She was later trebled, and identified with the Moerae.

parchment A prepared but untanned animal skin, usually of a sheep, goat, or calf, developed by the Greeks c.2nd-c BC as a medium of writing. In mediaeval Europe parchment was used for manuscripts and later for printed books. A high quality, fine-grained parchment is known as *vellum*.

parchment-bark *pittosporum*

pardalote *diamondbird*

Pareto, Vilfredo [paraytoh] (1848–1923) Economist and sociologist, born in Paris. His *Trattato di sociologica generale* (1916, trans The Mind and Society), with its theory of governing elites, anticipated some of the principles of fascism.

Paretsky, Sara [paretskee] (1947–) Writer of detective fiction, born in Ames, IA. Most of her books feature V I Warshawski, a female private detective. Her first novel, *Indemnity Only*, appeared in 1982. Later novels include *Blood Shot* (1988), *Burn Marks* (1990), *Blacklist* (2004), and *Fire Sale* (2006). She is a founder of Sisters in Crime, which promotes the work of women writers of detective fiction. She received the Diamond Dagger Award of the Crime Writers Association of Great Britain in 2002.

Paricutín [pareekooteen] 19°29N 102°17W. Active volcano in WC Mexico; height 2774 m/9101 ft.

Paris (France), ancient **Lutetia** 48°50N 2°20E, pop (2000e) 2 251 000. Capital of France, on R Seine; originally a Roman settlement; capital of Frankish kingdom, 6th-c; established as capital, 987; R Seine spanned here by 37 bridges, oldest the Pont Neuf (1578–1604), Pont Simone de Beauvoir opened in 2006; tourist river boats ('bateaux mouches'); bounded by Bois de Boulogne (W), Bois de Vincennes (E); divided into 20 arrondissements; 'Left Bank' (formerly associated with the aristocracy, later with writers and artists) and 'Right Bank' (formerly associated with the middle class); headquarters of many international organizations (notably UNESCO); airports at Orly (S), Charles de Gaulle (Roissy), and Le Bourget (NE); métro; Sorbonne University (13th-c); one of the world's main fashion centres; world centre of high fashion and production of luxury goods; wide range of heavy and light industry in suburbs; *Right Bank*: Arc de Triomphe, Champs Elysées, Place de la Concorde, Centre Pompidou (1977), Louvre, Montmartre, L'opéra (1861–75), Tuileries gardens; *Left Bank*: Eiffel Tower (1889), Hôtel des Invalides, Palais du Luxembourg, Musée d'orsay, Notre Dame Cathedral (1163), Montparnasse and Latin Quarter; Euro Disney Theme Park.

Paris (mythology) In Greek mythology, a prince of Troy, the son of Priam and Hecuba; also called **Alexander**. Called upon to decide which of Hera, Aphrodite and Athene was the fairest and should be awarded Eris's golden apple ('the judgment of Paris'), he chose Aphrodite, who had offered him Helen, the most beautiful woman in the world, as an inducement. He then abducted Helen, and so caused the Trojan War.

Paris, Matthew *Matthew Paris*

Paris, Treaties of 1 (1761–3) The peace settlement ending the Seven Years' War (1756–63), signed by Britain, France, and Spain. British gains from France included Canada, and America E of the Mississippi, and led to British colonial supremacy. **2** (1814–15) Successive peace settlements involving France and the victorious coalition of Britain, Austria, Prussia, Russia, Sweden, and Portugal, restoring the Bourbon monarchy to France in place of the Napoleonic Empire, before and after the Hundred Days (1815).

3 (1951) *European Coal and Steel Community*

Paris, University of A university founded c.1208 on the left bank of the R Seine in Paris. In the 14th-c it was pre-eminent among European universities. As a result of student demands for educational reform in 1968, the university was re-organized into 13 independent faculties, known as *Universités de Paris I à XIII*.

parish council The smallest unit of local elective government in the UK, dating from the 16th-c and originally based on an area covered by one church. It is not normally elected along party political lines, but has close links with the local community.

Paris Opéra Ballet The oldest national ballet company in the world. It was established in France in 1661 by Louis XIV as the Académie Royale de Danse, and amalgamated with the Académie Royale de Musique in 1672. Its first great director was Lully, who pioneered the opera-ballet form in which dancers became as important a part of the performance as the virtuoso singers. As part of the Théâtre National de l'Opéra, the company exercised great influence over European theatrical dance of the 18th and early 19th-c. In 1875 the Paris Opéra Ballet moved to the purpose-built Palais Garnier. Brigitte Lefèvre was appointed director of dance in 1995.

Paris Peace Conference 1 (1919–20) A meeting of 32 'allied and associated powers' who met in Paris to draw up a peace settlement after World War 1.

2 (1946) A meeting of the five members of the Council of Foreign Ministers (UK, France, USA, Russia, China) and 16 other nations involved in the war against the Axis Powers. It drew up peace treaties with Bulgaria, Finland, Hungary, Romania, and Italy.

parity (economics) A term used when central banks undertake to limit fluctuations in exchange rate; abbreviated as **par**; the **par rate** is that around which the margin of fluctuation is measured. A security stands at par if its market price is equal to its face value.

parity (physics) In quantum mechanics, a quantity which monitors the behaviour of a system under change from left- to right-handed co-ordinates; symbol *P*.

parity check A simple means of detecting errors in transmitted binary data. Each byte contains a **parity bit** which is set to indicate whether the byte contains an odd or even number of 1s. This bit is then checked on reception to ensure that it is consistent. This system will not detect all errors, and more complex systems such as Hamming Codes are now in general use.

Park, Mungo (1771–1806) Explorer, born in Fowlshiels, Scottish Borders. In 1795–6 he made a journey along the Niger R, and was killed during a second journey a decade later.

Park, Nick, popular name of **Nicholas Wulstan Park** (1958–) Film animator and director, born in Preston, Lancashire. He studied at Sheffield Hallam University (1980), and at the National Film and Television School near London. In 1985 he joined Aardman Animations in Bristol where his work included *A Grand Day Out* (1989, BAFTA), introducing the plasticine characters of Wallace and his dog Gromit. His later Oscar-winning films (with Steve Box) featuring Wallace and Gromit are *The Wrong Trousers* (1993), *A Close Shave* (1995), and *Wallace and Gromit in the Curse of the Were-Rabbit* (2005).

Parker, Sir Alan (1944–) Film director and actor, born in London. He made his feature-length cinema debut with *Bugsy Malone* (1976). Later films include *Midnight Express* (1978), *Birdy* (1985), *Evita* (1996), *Angela's Ashes* (1998), and *The Life of David Gale* (2002).

Parker, Charlie, popular name of **Charles (Christopher) Parker**, nickname **Bird** or **Yardbird** (1920–55) Jazz alto saxophonist, born in Kansas City, KS. In New York, he joined Dizzy Gillespie and other musicians in expanding the harmonic basis for jazz.

The new music, called *bebop*, developed an adventuresome young audience at the end of World War 2.

Parker, Matthew (1504–75) The second Protestant Archbishop of Canterbury, born in Norwich, Norfolk. Deprived of his preferments by Queen Mary, he was made Archbishop of Canterbury by Elizabeth I (1559). He was in charge of the formulation of the Thirty-nine Articles (1562).

Parker Bowles, Camilla *Cornwall, Duchess of*

Parkes, Sir Henry (1815–96) Australian statesman, born in Stoneleigh, Warwickshire. Five times premier of New South Wales, in 1891 he helped draft a constitution for a federated Australia.

Parkinson, C(yril) Northcote (1909–93) Writer, historian, and political scientist, born in Barnard Castle, Co Durham. He is especially known for his serio-comic tilt at bureaucratic malpractices in *Parkinson's Law: the Pursuit of Progress* (1958). **Parkinson's Law** – that work expands to fill the time available for its completion, and subordinates multiply at a fixed rate, regardless of the amount of work produced – has passed into the language.

Parkinson, Michael (1935–) Journalist and broadcaster, born in Cudworth, nr Barnsley, South Yorkshire. He has produced and presented several television programmes, and is best known as the host of his own chat show *Parkinson* (BBC, 1971–82, 1998–2004). He joined ITV in 2004 where he continues to present the show. His many sporting publications include *Sporting Profiles* (1995), and in the same year he was voted Sports Feature Writer of the Year.

Parkinson's disease A disorder of the central nervous system, named after British physician James Parkinson (1755–1824); also known as **paralysis agitans**. It affects the basal ganglia, the part of the brain that controls the co-ordination of movements. Neurones in this area become depleted of dopamine, the chemical that they use to transmit nerve impulses. Muscles become rigid, and it is difficult to initiate movements. Facial expression is lost, and there is a characteristic 'pill-rolling' tremor of the hands. Relief is obtained by providing dopamine as a drug, or by transplanting dopamine-secreting brain tissue.

parliament The general term in most English-speaking countries for the national legislative body, normally elected by popular vote. Its role is to pass legislation and keep a check on the activities of the government or executive. In the UK, the national parliament is constituted by the House of Lords and the elected House of Commons. Proposed laws must go through a defined procedure in both Houses and receive the royal assent, before becoming statutes.

Parliamentary Commissioner for Administration The British ombudsman for central administration, established in 1967, who examines complaints of maladministration. The commissioner works closely with a House of Commons select committee.

Parma [pah(r)ma] 44°48N 10°19E, pop (2000e) 181 000. City in N Italy; on R Parma; chief cultural centre in Middle Ages; railway; university (13th-c); cathedral (12th-c).

Parmenides [pah(r)menideez] (c.515–c.445 BC) Greek philosopher, a native of the Greek settlement of Elea in S Italy, and founder of the Eleatic school.

Parmigianino [pah(r)mijianeenoh], also called **Parmigiano**, originally **Girolamo Francesco Maria Mazzola** (1503–40) Painter of the Lombard School, born in Parma, Italy. At Bologna he painted his famous Madonna altarpiece for the nuns of St Margaret.

Parnell, Charles Stewart [pah(r)nel, pah(r)nel] (1846–91) Irish politician, born in Avondale, Co Wicklow, Ireland. In 1879 he was elected president of the Irish National Land League, and in 1886 allied with the Liberals in support of Gladstone's Home Rule Bill. He remained an influential figure until 1890, when he was cited as co-respondent with Katharine O'Shea in a divorce case, and was forced to retire.

parole A conditional release given to a prisoner who still has part of a sentence left to serve. In England and Wales, parole has now been abolished for prisoners serving four years or less. They are automatically released on licence after serving one half of their sentence. Prisoners with longer sentences, except life, must be paroled after serving two thirds of their sentences, and may be paroled after serving half their sentences. Release is conditional, and those paroled are supervised by a probation officer. In the USA, a parole board considers release, based on extensive guidelines, usually after a fixed portion of the sentence has been served.

Paros [pahros] area 195 km²/75 sq mi; pop (2000e) 8470. Third largest island of the Cyclades, Greece; chief town, Parikia; famous for its marble and churches.

Parque Nacional de Los Glaciares [glasyarays] Andean national park in Patagonia, Argentina; area 4459 km²/1721 sq mi; established in 1937; a world heritage site.

parquetry *marquetry*

Parr, Catherine (1512–48) Sixth (and surviving) wife of Henry VIII, the daughter of Sir Thomas Parr of Kendal. As queen (1543), she persuaded Henry to restore the succession to his daughters. Very soon after Henry's death (1547) she married a former suitor, Lord Thomas Seymour of Sudeley, and died in childbirth the following year.

parrot A colourful bird, native to warm regions worldwide; bill large, hooked; good at mimicking human voice. (Family: Psittacidae, c.330 species.)

parrot disease *psittacosis*

parrotfish Colourful fish belonging to the family Scaridae (4 genera), in which jaw teeth are fused into a parrot-like beak; body compressed, length 20–100 cm/8–40 in.

Parry, Sir (Charles) Hubert (Hastings) (1848–1918) Composer, born in Bournemouth, Dorset. He wrote oratorios, symphonies, and many other works, but is best known for his unison chorus 'Jerusalem' (1916), sung at the end of each season of Promenade Concerts in London.

Parry, Joseph (1841–1903) Musician, born in Merthyr Tydfil, S Wales. He composed oratorios, operas, and songs, and became one of the leading hymn-writers in the Welsh tradition.

parsec (pc) A unit of length, used for distances beyond the Solar System. The term is a contraction of **parallax second**, and is the distance at which the astronomical unit (AU) subtends one second of arc; it equals 206 265 AU, 3·086 × 10¹³ km/ 1·918 × 10¹³ mi, 3·26 light years. The larger units **kiloparsec (kpc)** and **megaparsec (Mpc)** for 1000 and 1 000 000 pc respectively are also widely used.

Parseeism [pah(r)seeizm] The religion of the descendants of the ancient Zoroastrians, who fled Persia after its conquest and settled in India in the 8th-c. They live mainly in the region round Mumbai, and preach a rule of life conforming to the purity of Ahura Mazda.

Parsifal *Perceval, Sir*

parsing The analyzing and labelling of the grammatical components of a sentence, according to their function within some grammatical framework, such as 'subject', 'verb', and 'object'. Introduced in schools during the 19th-c, parsing fell into disfavour during the 1950s because of its uninspiring techniques. During the 1980s a move to re-introduce some form of parsing, as an antidote to the perceived widespread ignorance of grammar, received increasing support.

parsley A biennial or perennial (*Petroselinum crispum*), growing to 75 cm/30 in, but usually smaller; leaves triangular, shining, divided into wedge-shaped segments; flowers yellowish, petals notched; fruit ovoid. It is widely cultivated as a flavouring. (Family: Umbelliferae.)

parsnip A biennial growing to 1·5 m/5 ft, but usually smaller, native to Europe and W Asia; flowers yellow; fruit ellipsoid, broadly winged. It is grown commercially for the sweet, fleshy tap-roots, which are eaten as a vegetable and used as fodder for livestock. (*Pastinaca sativa*. Family: Umbelliferae.)

parson bird *tui*

Parsons, Talcott [tawlcot] (1902–79) Sociologist, born in Colorado Springs, CO. He developed a functionalist analysis of social systems through his principal publications, *The Structure of Social Action* (1939) and *The Social System* (1951).

Parsons, Tony (1953–) Journalist and novelist, born in Romford, ·Essex. During the 1990s he became a newspaper columnist and a regular panellist on BBC 2's *Late Review* programme. His novel, *Man and Boy* (1998), won Book of the Year at the British Book Awards, and later novels include *One for My Baby* (2001) and *Stories We Could Tell* (2005).

parthenocarpy *fruit*

parthenogenesis [pah(r)thenohjenesis] The development of an individual from an egg without fertilization by a male gamete (*sperm*). Eggs that develop parthenogenetically are usually diploid (possessing two chromosome sets) and genetically identical with the mother.

Parthenon The principal building of the Athenian Acropolis, a Doric temple of Pentelic marble dedicated to Athena *Parthenos* ('the Maiden'); a world heritage site. Built 447–433 BC to the plans of Ictinus and Callicrates under the supervision of Phidias, in 1687 it was reduced to a shell by an explosion while housing a powder magazine during the Turkish–Venetian war.

Parthians The inheritors of the E territories of the Seleucids, from the 3rd-c BC ruling an empire that stretched from the Euphrates to the Indus. They were Rome's main rivals for power in the east.

particle accelerators Machines for accelerating charged subatomic particles, usually electrons or protons, to high velocity. The basic configurations are straight (linear accelerators) or circular (synchrotrons). In the latter, magnetic fields control the beam path. Both use radiofrequency electric fields to provide acceleration.

particle beam weapons The use of high-energy subatomic particles, generated in nuclear accelerators and turned into a directable beam, as a practical weapon. One of the goals of late 20th-c military research was to prove the technology of this approach, which would be used, for example, to shoot down missiles in space.

particle detectors Devices for detecting and identifying subatomic particles in particle physics experiments. They are designed to measure total energy, charge to mass ratio, velocity, position, and time.

particle physics The study of the fundamental components of matter and the forces between them; also called **high energy physics** or **elementary particle physics**. Most particle physics experiments involve the use of large particle accelerators, necessary to force particles close enough together to produce interactions. All theories in particle physics are quantum theories, in which symmetry is of central importance. Atoms are viewed as comprising a central nucleus surrounded by electrons, the nucleus being composed of protons and neutrons. These protons, neutrons, the particles from which they are made, and other related objects are the entities studied in particle physics. Subatomic particles thought to be indivisible into smaller particles are known as *fundamental particles*: these are the matter particles (quarks, neutrinos, electrons, muons, and taus) and the force particles (gluons, photons, W and Z bosons). The important forces acting between these particles are the electromagnetic, strong nuclear, and weak nuclear forces. During the 1950s, studies revealed other particles of various masses, some exhibiting unusual or 'strange' behaviour. A new quantum number called *strangeness*, conserved in strong but not in weak interactions, was invented to explain these results. Other quantum numbers have subsequently been introduced to account for observed particle interactions. Current research focuses on resolving difficulties in existing theories, constructing unified theories of strong, weak, and electromagnetic forces, and incorporating gravity to give a complete theory of the physical universe.

Parti Québecois (PQ) [kaybekwah] A separatist political party in Canada, established in 1968. Led by René Lévesque until 1985, the *péquistes* formed the government in Quebec in 1976, and were elected for a second term in 1981.

partita [pah(r)teeta] In music of the Baroque period, **1** one of a set of instrumental variations (*partite*); **2** a set of instrumental dances.

Partition of Ireland (1949) The division of Ireland between an independent Irish Republic and Northern Ireland (Ulster), where the Protestant majority wanted to remain British. The Ulster Plantation in the 17th-c had established a Protestant ascendancy over the native Catholic population. A partition movement arose during the 1880s series of Home Rule Bills. The Anglo-Irish Treaty (1921) established an Irish Free Sate that excluded the six counties of Ulster. The formation of an independent Republic of Ireland in 1949 led to Britain guaranteeing Northern Ireland the status of a self-governing province of the UK, as long as this was supported by a majority vote in the Northern Ireland parliament.

partnership A form of business organization where the owners share all the profits – or take all the losses – according to some predetermined formula. There are usually not more than 20 partners, though larger partnerships do exist.

Parton, Dolly (Rebecca) (1946–) Country singer, songwriter, and actress, born in Locust Ridge, TN. She took country-based music into the pop mainstream, her hits including 'Jolene' (1974) and 'Islands In The Stream' (1984). From 1982 she had success as a film actress, and also began to operate her own theme park, 'Dollywood'.

Partridge, Eric (Honeywood) (1894–1979) Lexicographer, born near Gisborne, New Zealand. He became a freelance author and lexicographer, specializing in studies of style, slang, and colloquial language, such as his *Usage and Abusage* (1947).

partridge A drab, plump, short-tailed bird of the pheasant family; found from Europe to SE Asia, and in Africa. (Family: Phasianidae, 84 species.)

par value *parity* (economics)

parvovirus A group of small, single-stranded DNA viruses that can infect animals or humans. Animal parvoviruses are responsible for commonly occurring blood disorders in cats and dogs, and the B19 parvovirus causes disease in humans. Infection during pregnancy may lead to severe damage or death of the fetus.

Pasargadae [pasah(r)gadiy] The site in S Iran chosen by Cyrus the Great in 546 BC to be the capital of the new Achaemenid empire.

Pascal, Blaise [paskal] (1623–62) Mathematician, physicist, theologian, and man-of-letters, born in Clermont-Ferrand, France. In 1647 he invented a calculating machine, and later the barometer, the hydraulic press, and the syringe. He defended Jansenism against the Jesuits in *Lettres provinciales* (1656–7). Fragments jotted down for a case book of Christian truths were discovered after his death, and published as the *Pensées* (1669, Thoughts).

PASCAL A high-level computer programming language, named after the French mathematician, Blaise Pascal, which was developed from ALGOL in the late 1960s.

pascal SI unit of pressure; symbol *Pa*; named after French mathematician Blaise Pascal; defined as the pressure due to a force of 1 newton acting on an area of 1 square metre.

Pascua, Isla de *Easter Island*

Pashtun or **Pathan** [patahn] A cluster of Pashto-speaking agricultural and herding people of NW Pakistan and SE Afghanistan. They are the most numerous group in Afghanistan, numbering 6·2 million; 6·7 million live in Pakistan.

Pasiphae (astronomy) [pasifayee] The eighth natural satellite of Jupiter, discovered in 1908; distance from the planet 23 500 000 km/14 603 000 mi; diameter 50 km/30 mi.

Pasiphae (mythology) [pasifayee] In Greek mythology, the daughter of Helios, and wife of Minos, King of Crete. She loved a bull sent by Poseidon, and became the mother of the Minotaur.

Pasmore, (Edwin John) Victor (1908–98) Artist, born in Chelsham, Surrey. One of the founders of the Euston Road School (1937), he developed a highly abstract style, in which colour is often primarily used to suggest relief.

Pasolini, Pier Paolo [pasohleenee] (1922–75) Film director, born in Bologna, Italy. He became known for such films as *Il Vangelo secondo Matteo* (1964, The Gospel According to St Matthew) and *The Canterbury Tales* (1972).

passacaglia [pasakahlya] A musical structure in which a continuously repeated bass line or harmonic progression provides the basis for a set of uninterrupted variations.

Passchendaele, Battle of [pashendayl] (1917) The third battle of Ypres during World War 1; a British offensive notable for appallingly muddy conditions, minimal gains, and British casualties of at least 300 000. In the final action, Canadians captured the village of Passchendaele, NE of Ypres.

passerine Any bird of the worldwide order Passeriformes ('perching birds'); includes the **songbirds** (Suborder: Oscines); comprises more than half the living species of birds; four toes, one pointing backwards and opposing the others; wing has 9–10 primary feathers; tail usually with 12 main feathers.

passion flower A member of a large genus of climbers with twining tendrils, native to America, a few to Asia and Australia; flowers large, showy, with five coloured sepals alternating with five petals, said to symbolize the crucifixion, with the inner corona of filaments representing the crown of thorns, and the styles the cross and nails; yellow or purple edible berry (known as **passion fruit** or **granadilla**), up to 10 cm/4 in long. (Genus: *Passiflora*, 500 species. Family: Passifloraceae.)

passion fruit *passion flower*

Passionists A religious order, founded in Italy in 1720 by St Paul of the Cross; properly known as the **Congregation of the Barefooted Clerics of the Most Holy Cross and Passion of our Lord Jesus Christ**. Their declared objective is to maintain the memory of Christ's sufferings and death.

passive smoking Inhalation by non-smokers of tobacco smoke introduced into the atmosphere by smokers. It increases the risk of lung cancer and coronary heart disease.

Passover An annual Jewish festival, occurring in March or April (15–22 Nisan), commemorating the exodus of the Israelites from Egypt; named from God's passing over the houses of the Israelites when he killed the first-born children of the Egyptians (*Ex* 13); also known as **Pesach** [paysakh].

pasta A mixture of water, wheat flour (hard), and occasionally egg, originating in Italy. The dough is extruded through dies of various shapes, and dried to provide a wide variety of types (eg cannelloni, spaghetti, lasagne, macaroni, and ravioli).

pastel Powdered pigment mixed with a little gum or resin and shaped into sticks like crayons. The artist works directly onto the paper.

Pasternak, Boris (Leonidovich) [pasternak] (1890–1960) Lyric poet, novelist, and translator, born in Moscow. His major work, *Dr Zhivago*, caused a political furore, and was banned in the USSR, but was an international success after its publication in Italy in 1957. Expelled by the Soviet Writers' Union in 1958, he was compelled to refuse the Nobel Prize for Literature. The ban was lifted in 1988 and his entire works began publication in his home country in 2004.

Pasteur, Louis [paster] (1822–95) Chemist and microbiologist, born in Dôle, France. He established that putrefaction and fermentation were caused by micro-organisms, and in 1881 showed that sheep and cows 'vaccinated' with the attenuated bacilli of anthrax received protection against the disease.

pasteurization A mild heat treatment used to kill micro-organisms in milk. The process heats the milk at 63–66°C for 30 minutes or 72°C for 15 seconds. It was discovered by the French chemist, Louis Pasteur.

pastoral (Lat 'pertaining to shepherds') A poem or other work expressing love of and longing for an idealized rural existence. Deriving from Theocritus, the pastoral mode has been much imitated and adapted.

pastoralism A way of life characterized by keeping herds of animals, such as cattle, sheep, camels, reindeer, goats, and llamas. It is common in dry, mountainous, or severely cold climates not suitable for agriculture. Many pastoralists are nomadic, and some have become important long-distance traders.

pastoral staff A crook-shaped stick carried by bishops; otherwise called a **crozier**. It represents the rod of correction and the crook of care.

Patagonia [patagohnia] area 489 541 km²/188 963 sq mi. Region of S Argentina; a semi-arid tableland rising in terraces from the Atlantic coast to the base of the Andes; many immigrants in 19th-c, especially from Wales.

Patan [patan], also **Lalitpur** 27°40N 85°20E, pop (2000e) 245 000. City in C Nepal, 5 km/3 mi SE of Kathmandu; founded, 7th-c; capital of the Nepali kingdom, 17th-c; captured by the Gurkhas, 1768; known as the 'city of artists'.

Patchett, Ann (1963–) Writer, born in Los Angeles, CA. Appointed Tennessee Williams fellow in creative writing at the University of the South, Nashville (1997), her novels include *The Patron Saint of Liars* (1992), *Taft* (1994), and *Bel Canto* (2001, PEN/ Faulkner Award, Orange Prize). *Truth and Beauty*, a non-fiction work, appeared in 2004.

patchouli A shrubby aromatic perennial (*Pogostemon cablin*) growing to 1 m/3¼ ft or more, native to the tropics and subtropics of SE Asia; flowers white, tubular, 2-lipped, in whorls. It yields an aromatic essential oil used in perfumery. (Family: Labiatae.)

paten [patn] In Christian liturgy, a circular metal plate, often of silver or gold, on which bread is placed at the celebration of the Eucharist.

patent A formal document which gives inventors the exclusive right for a period of years to exploit the product or process they have created, either by operating it themselves or by licensing others to use it. Patents have the disadvantage of restricting the diffusion of new techniques, but the merit of increasing the incentive to spend on research and development.

Pater, Walter (Horatio) [payter] (1839–94) Critic and essayist, born in London. He became known with his *Studies in the History of the Renaissance* (1873), and exercised considerable influence on the aesthetic movements of his time.

Pater Noster [pahter noster] *Lord's Prayer*

Paterson, A(ndrew) B(arton), nickname **Banjo Paterson** (1864– 1941) Journalist and poet, born at Narambla, New South Wales, Australia. He wrote several books of light verse, but is best known as the author of 'Waltzing Matilda' (1895).

Paterson, Don (1963–) Poet, writer, and musician, born in Dundee. In 1993 he was appointed writer-in-residence at the University of Dundee and became poetry editor for London

publishers Picador (from 1995). His poetry collections include *Nil Nil* (1993), *God's Gift to Women* (1997, T S Elliot Prize), and *Landing Light* (2003, T S Elliot Prize, Whitbread Poetry Award). He is also editor of *101 Sonnets: From Shakespeare to Heaney* (1999), and has written plays for radio and theatre. An accomplished jazz guitarist, he works solo and with the jazz-folk ensemble Lammas.

Pathan *Pashtun*

Pathé, Charles [pathay], Fr [patay] (1863–1957) Film pioneer, born in Paris. In 1896 he founded Société Pathé Frères with his brothers, which by 1912 had become one of the largest film production organizations in the world. They introduced the newsreel in 1909.

pathology The scientific study of disease in humans and other living organisms. It includes the detection of micro-organisms and of chromosome and enzyme defects, the microscopic study of cells and tissues, and microchemical analyses.

Patmore, Coventry (Kersey Dighton) (1823–96) Poet, born in Woodford, Essex. His major work, *The Angel in the House* (1854–62), was followed by his conversion to Catholicism. Thereafter he wrote mainly on mystical or religious themes.

Patmos area 34 km²/13 sq mi; pop (2000e) 2700. Island of the Dodecanese, Greece; chief town, Hora; St John the apostle lived here for two years.

Patna [patna] 25°37N 85°12E, pop (2000e) 1 077 000. Winter capital of Bihar, E India; on S bank of R Ganges; French trading post, 1732; university (1917); major rice-growing region; noted for its handicrafts.

Paton, Alan (Stewart) [paytn] (1903–88) Writer and educator, born in Pietermaritzburg, South Africa. From his deep concern with the racial problem in South Africa sprang several novels, notably *Cry, the Beloved Country* (1948) and *Too Late the Phalarope* (1953).

patriarch 1 The head of a family or tribe. In Biblical literature, usually applied either to the 10 purported ancestors of the human race prior to the Flood, or more commonly to Abraham, Isaac, Jacob, and Jacob's 12 sons.
2 An ecclesiastical title used since about the 6th-c for the bishops of the five important ecclesiastical centres of the early Christian Church: Alexandria, Antioch, Constantinople, Jerusalem, and Rome.

patricians In ancient Rome, the members of a select number of aristocratic clans or *gentes*, such as the Julii. The precise origins of this elite are obscure and still much debated.

Patrick, St (c.385–461) Apostle of Ireland, born (perhaps) in S Wales. Ordained a bishop at 45, he became a missionary to Ireland (432), and fixed his see at Armagh (454). Feast day 17 March.

patristics *Fathers of the Church*

patron saint A saint who, by tradition or otherwise, has been chosen as the special intercessor and advocate in heaven of a particular place, person, occupation, or organization. The custom of having patron saints for churches arose from the practice of building churches over the tombs of martyrs. *p.708*

Patten, Chris(topher Francis) (1944–) British politician, born in London. He became minister for overseas development (1986), secretary of state for the environment (1989), and party chairman (1991). Credited with master-minding the Tory victory in the 1992 election, he lost his own seat and was appointed Governor of Hong Kong (1992–7). He served as a European Commissioner (1999–2004), and was elected Chancellor of Oxford University in 2003. He was made a life peer in 2004.

pattern recognition *character recognition*

Patterson, James (1949–) Novelist, born in New York City. His detective novels featuring FBI Agent Alex Cross include *Kiss The Girls* (1995; filmed 1997), *Pop Goes the Weasel* (1999), *Violets are Blue* (2001), *Mary, Mary* (2005), and *Cross* (2006).

Patron Saints Of Occupations

Accountants	Matthew	Lawyers	Ivo, Thomas More
Actors	Genesius, Vitus	Librarians	Jerome, Catherine of Alexandria
Advertisers	Bernadino of Siena	Merchants	Francis of Assisi
Architects	Thomas (Apostle)	Messengers	Gabriel
Artists	Luke, Angelico	Metalworkers	Eligius
Astronauts	Joseph (Cupertino)	Midwives	Raymond Nonnatus
Astronomers	Dominic	Miners	Anne, Barbara
Athletes	Sebastian	Motorists	Christopher
Authors	Francis de Sales	Musicians	Cecilia, Gregory the Great
Aviators	Our Lady of Loreto	Nurses	Camillus de Lellis, John of God
Bakers	Honoratus	Philosophers	Thomas Aquinas, Catherine of Alexandria
Bankers	Bernardino (Feltre)	Poets	Cecilia, David
Barbers	Cosmas and Damian	Policemen	Michael
Blacksmiths	Eligius	Postal workers	Gabriel
Bookkeepers	Matthew	Priests	Jean-Baptiste Vianney
Book trade	John of God	Printers	John of God
Brewers	Amand, Wenceslaus	Prisoners	Leonard
Builders	Barbara, Thomas (Apostle)	Radio workers	Gabriel
Butchers	Luke	Sailors	Christopher, Erasmus, Francis of Paola
Carpenters	Joseph	Scholars	Thomas Aquinas
Chemists	Cosmas and Damian	Scientists	Albert the Great
Comedians	Vitus	Sculptors	Luke, Louis
Cooks	Lawrence, Martha	Secretaries	Genesius
Dancers	Vitus	Servants	Martha, Zita
Dentists	Apollonia	Shoemakers	Crispin, Crispinian
Doctors	Cosmas and Damian, Luke	Singers	Cecilia, Gregory
Editors	Francis de Sales	Soldiers	George, Joan of Arc, Martin of Tours, Sebastian
Farmers	Isidore		
Firemen	Florian	Students	Thomas Aquinas
Fishermen	Andrew, Peter	Surgeons	Luke, Cosmas and Damian
Florists	Dorothy, Thérèse of Lisieux	Tailors	Homobonus
Gardeners	Adam, Fiacre	Tax collectors	Matthew
Glassworkers	Luke, Lucy	Taxi drivers	Fiacre
Gravediggers	Joseph (Arimathea)	Teachers	Gregory the Great, John Baptist de la Salle
Grocers	Michael	Theologians	Augustine, Alphonsus Liguori Thomas Aquinas
Hotelkeepers	Amand, Julian the Hospitaler		
Housewives	Martha	Television workers	Gabriel
Jewellers	Eligius	Undertakers	Dismas, Joseph of Arimathea
Journalists	Francis de Sales	Waiters	Martha
Labourers	James, John Bosco	Writers	Lucy

Patton, George (Smith), Jr (1885–1945) US general, born in San Gabriel, CA. He played a key role in the Allied invasion of French N Africa (1942), led the US 7th Army in its assault on Sicily (1943), commanded the 3rd Army in the invasion of France, and contained the German counter-offensive in the Ardennes (1944).

Pau [poh] 43°19N 0°25W, pop (2000e) 88 000. City in SW France; on right bank of R Gave de Pau; former capital of Béarn province, 1464; health resort, winter sports centre; road and rail junction; castle (12th–15th-c).

Paul, St, originally **Saul of Tarsus** (?10–65/67 AD) Apostle to the Gentiles and important theologian of the early Christian Church, born of Jewish parents at Tarsus, Cilicia. A persecutor of Christians, on his way to Damascus (c.34–35) he was converted to Christianity by a vision of Christ, and began to preach the Christian message. His missionary journeys included visits to Asia Minor and through Galatia and Phrygia to Macedonia and Achaia, where in Corinth he was especially successful. An extensive mission was also undertaken in Ephesus. On his return to Jerusalem, he was apparently imprisoned for 2 years, transferred to Rome, and according to later tradition was executed by Nero (c.64). Thirteen New Testament letters are traditionally attributed to him. Feast day 29 June.

Paul VI, originally **Giovanni Battista Montini** (1897–1978) Pope (1963–78), born in Concesio, Italy. He travelled more widely than any previous pope, and initiated important advances in the move towards Christian unity.

Pauli, Wolfgang [powlee] (1900–58) Theoretical physicist, born in Vienna. In 1924 he formulated the 'exclusion principle' in quantum physics (that no two electrons, or other fermions, may occupy exactly the same quantum state), and in 1931 postulated the existence of an electrically neutral particle called the neutrino. He was awarded the 1945 Nobel Prize for Physics.

Paulin, Tom [pawlin] (1949–) Poet, born in Leeds, West Yorkshire. His books include *A State of Justice* (1977), *Seize the Fire* (1990), and *The Invasion Handbook* (2002). He edited the Faber books of political (1986) and vernacular verse (1990), and his critical works include *The Day-Star of Liberty* (1999) and *Crusoe's Secret* (2005). He is also known in the UK as a contributor to television discussion programmes on the arts.

Pauline Letters or **Pauline Epistles** A set of New Testament writings ascribed to the apostle Paul, usually numbering 13. Modern scholars are confident of Paul's authorship in only seven cases (Romans, 1 and 2 Corinthians, Galatians, Philippians, 1 Thessalonians, and Philemon), and debate the authenticity of 2 Thessalonians, Colossians, Ephesians, and the Pastoral Letters.

Pauling, Linus (Carl) [pawling] (1901–94) Chemist, born in Portland, OR. He applied quantum theory to chemistry, and was awarded the Nobel Prize for Chemistry in 1954 for his contributions to the theory of valency. He became a controversial figure from 1955 as the leading scientific critic of US nuclear deterrent policy. Awarded the Nobel Peace Prize in 1962, he was the first person to have received two full Nobel Prizes.

pavane [pavan] A stately dance of the 16th–17th-c, probably of Italian origin. It was often linked to a livelier dance, generally in triple time, known as a *galliard* (from Fr 'merry').

Pavarotti, Luciano [pavarotee] (1935–) Tenor, born in Modena, Italy. He won the international competition at the Teatro Reggio Emilia in 1961, and made his operatic debut there the same year. He made his US debut in 1968, and is internationally known as a concert performer.

Pavese, Cesare [pavayzay] (1908–50) Writer, born in Cuneo, Italy. He is best known for his novel *La luna e i falò* (1950, The Moon and the Bonfires). His work exerted a strong influence on later Italian fiction and film making.

Pavia [paveea], ancient **Ticinum** 45°12N 9°09E, pop (2000e) 86 000. City in N Italy, on R Ticino; railway; university (1361); cathedral (begun 1487).

Pavlov, Ivan Petrovich [pavlov] (1849–1936) Physiologist, born in Ryazan, Russia. From 1902 he studied what later became known as Pavlovian or classical conditioning in animals. A major influence on the development of behaviourism in psychology, he was awarded the Nobel Prize for Physiology or Medicine in 1904.

Pavlova, Anna [pavlova] (1881–1931) Ballerina, born in St Petersburg, Russia. In 1909 she travelled to Paris with the Ballets Russes, and after 1913 danced with her own company in reduced versions of the classics in many parts of the world.

Pavo [pahvoh] (Lat 'peacock') A constellation in the S hemisphere.

pawnbroking A system of money-lending in which an article, usually personal property, is deposited with an agent (the **pawnbroker**) as security for the loan. The article can be redeemed within a given time on repayment of the loan plus interest. Articles unredeemed at the end of the period become the property of the pawnbroker.

pawpaw *papaw*

Paxman, Jeremy (Dickson) (1950–) British television presenter and journalist, born in Leeds, West Yorkshire. He joined the BBC 1 *Tonight* team in 1977, and later joined BBC 2's *Newsnight* (1989), on which he developed a reputation as a tough but fair interviewer. He became presenter of *University Challenge* in 1994. His books include *The English: A Portrait of A People* (1999), *The Political Animal* (2002), and *On Royalty* (2006).

Paxton, Sir Joseph (1801–65) Gardener and architect, born near Woburn, Bedfordshire. He designed a building for the Great Exhibition of 1851 (nicknamed the 'Crystal Palace'), which he re-erected in Sydenham (destroyed by fire in 1936).

PAYE An abbreviation of **pay as you earn**, a UK taxation system whereby income tax is deducted from a worker's pay by an employer before handing over the wage. The amount to be collected is determined by reference to each person's *tax code*, calculated at the start of each fiscal year. Several other countries have a payroll deduction plan of this kind.

Payton, Walter (1954–99) Player of American football, born in Columbia, MS. In his career with the Chicago Bears (1975–88), he rushed for 16 726 yards, a National Football League record.

pay TV The non-broadcast distribution of video entertainment to a restricted audience of subscribers who pay for the programmes viewed. The programmes are received either by individual cable connection or by scrambled microwave or satellite transmission requiring a rented decoder.

Paz, Octavio (1914–98) Poet, born in Mexico City. He was a writer of great energy and versatility, with 30 volumes from 1933; his *Collected Poems* (1957–87), in Spanish and English, were pub-lished in 1988. He received the Nobel Prize for Literature in 1990.

Paz, La *La Paz*

Paz Estenssoro, Victor [pahs estensawroh] (1907–2001) Bolivian revolutionary and politician, born in Tarija, Bolivia. Following the 1952 Revolution he served as president (1952–6, 1960–4). Ousted by a military coup, he later served again as president (1985–9).

PC *personal computer*

PCBs Abbreviation of **polychlorobiphenyls**, usually a mixture of compounds in which chlorine is substituted for many of the hydrogen atoms in biphenyl, $C_{12}H_{10}$, a molecule in which two phenyl groups are joined to one another. Their stability makes them excellent flame retardants and electrical insulators, but their eventual degradation products are toxic.

PCP *angel dust*

pea A botanical term used as a suffix, referring to several plants of the family Leguminosae, but especially to members of the genus *Pisum*. The best-known species are **sweet pea** (*Lathyrus odoratus*) and **garden pea** (*Pisum sativum*), a climbing annual growing to 2 m/$6\frac{1}{2}$ ft, native to S Europe and N Africa; flowers up to 3·5 cm/$1\frac{1}{2}$ in long, white, pink or purplish, in small clusters of 1–3; pods up to 12 cm/$4\frac{3}{4}$ in long, oblong, containing up to 10 seeds. It has been cultivated since prehistoric times for the edible seeds (*peas*) eaten as a vegetable, fresh, dried, frozen, or canned. Many cultivars are also widely grown, including the smaller-seeded *petit pois*, and also *mangetout*, where the whole pod is consumed.

Peace Corps An agency of volunteers funded by the US government, established in 1961. Volunteers numbered more than 10 000 in 52 countries in 1966, but in the 1980s the corps was asked to leave some countries hostile to US policies. There were more than 7800 volunteers in 75 countries in 2007.

Peace River River in W Canada, rising in British Columbia as the Finlay R; enters the Slave R; length 1923 km/1195 mi to the head of Finlay R.

peace studies Educational courses designed to explore the role of the military in society, international strategic relationships, and those conditions that most promote peace and human welfare in society.

peach A small deciduous tree (*Prunus persica*), growing to 6 m/20 ft; flowers pink, rarely white, appearing before leaves; fruit globular, velvety 4–8 cm/$1\frac{1}{2}$–3 in, yellow flushed red with thick sweet flesh, stone grooved. (Family: Rosaceae.)

Peacock, Thomas Love (1785–1866) Novelist, born in Weymouth, Dorset. His satirical romances include *Headlong Hall* (1816), *Melincourt* (1817), and *Nightmare Abbey* (1818). In each case a company of humorists meet in a country house, and the satire arises from their conversation rather than from character or plot.

peacock Either of two species of pheasant (Genus: *Pavo*) from the forests of India and SE Asia: especially the **Indian peafowl** (*Pavo cristatus*); alternatively known as **peafowl**; the female sometimes called **peahen**. The peacock is known for its resplendent train (extending to some 1·5 m/5 ft), in which each feather ends with a brightly coloured, ring-shaped feature (the 'eye'). The peacock displays his tail by raising it above and behind his head. Males are mainly blue-green or green-bronze; females green or brown, and lack a train. The birds are known for their ill temper.

peafowl *peacock*

Peak District National park in NC England; area 1404 km²/542 sq mi; established in 1951; mainly in Derbyshire; limestone caves, notably at Peak Cavern, near Castleton; highest point, Kinder Scout, 727 m/2088 ft.

Peake, Mervyn (Laurence) (1911–68) Writer and artist, born in Kuling, China. He is best known for his Gothic fantasy trilogy of novels: *Titus Groan* (1946), *Gormenghast* (1950), and *Titus Alone* (1959), and his novel *Mr Pye* (1953).

peanut An annual (*Arachis hypogaea*), growing to 50 cm/20 in, native to South America; pea-flowers yellow; also called **groundnut** or **monkey nut**. It is widely grown for the edible seeds (*peanuts*), used in confectionery and as a source of peanut oil. (Family: Leguminosae.)

pear A deciduous, usually thorny tree or shrub, native to Europe and Asia; flowers white or pinkish, in flat-topped clusters; fruit round or top-shaped as well as pear-shaped. (Genus: *Pyrus*, 30 species. Family: Rosaceae.)

Pearce, Stuart (1962–) Footballer, born in London. A left back, he played for Coventry City before moving to Nottingham Forest (1985–97), where he also acted for a time as player/manager, Newcastle United (1997–9), West Ham (1999), and Manchester City (2001), where he later became assistant coach, and manager (2005–7). He won 78 caps for England (including several as captain from 1992).

pearlfish Elongate and very slender fish widespread in tropical and warm temperate seas, living inside sea cucumbers, sea urchins, and other marine invertebrates; length up to 30 cm/ 12 in. (Family: Carapidae, 2 genera.)

Pearl Harbor US deep-water naval base on the island of Oahu in the US Pacific Ocean state of Hawaii, adjacent to Honolulu, established in 1908. The bombing of the base by the Japanese (7 Dec 1941), brought the USA into World War 2.

pearlite A type of steel formed by an intimate intergrowth of iron with iron carbide. It has a lustrous sheen.

Pearl River *Zhu Jiang*

Pears, Sir Peter (Neville Luard) [peerz] (1910–86) Tenor, born in Farnham, Surrey. In 1946 he helped Britten found the English Opera Group, and was co-founder with him of the Aldeburgh Festival (1948).

Pearse, Patrick (or **Pádraic**) **Henry** [peers] (1879–1916) Writer, educationist, and nationalist, born in Dublin. He commanded the insurgents in the Easter Rising of 1916, and was proclaimed president of the provisional government. After the revolt had been quelled, he was court-martialled and shot.

Pearson, Lester B(owles) (1897–1972) Canadian statesman and prime minister (1963–8), born in Newtonbrook, Ontario, Canada. Secretary of state for external affairs (1948–57), his efforts to resolve the Suez Crisis were rewarded with the Nobel Peace Prize in 1957.

Peary, Robert (Edwin) [peeree] (1856–1920) Naval commander and explorer, born in Cresson Springs, PA. He made eight Arctic voyages to the Greenland coast, in 1891–2 arriving on the E coast by crossing the ice. In 1909 he led the first expedition to the North Pole, reaching it on 6 April.

Peary Land Region of N Greenland on the Arctic Ocean, forming a mountainous peninsula; not covered by ice; explored by Peary in 1892 and 1900.

Peasants' Revolt An English popular rising of June 1381, among townsmen as well as peasants, based in Essex, Kent, and London. Precipitated by the three oppressive poll taxes of 1377–81, it was quickly suppressed.

Peasants' War (1524–5) Probably the largest peasant uprising in European history, raging through Germany. It was denounced by Luther, and suppressed by the princes.

peat The partially decomposed remains of plants which accumulate and are preserved in waterlogged conditions in areas of cool, humid climate. It is the first stage in the formation of coal, and is widely used as a form of fuel (eg in Ireland and Russia).

pecan A deciduous tree (*Carya pecan*) growing to 45 m/150 ft, native to E North America; flowers small, green, lacking petals; nut 4–5 cm/1½–2 in, roughly oblong, reddish-brown, edible. (Family: Juglandaceae.)

peccary [pekaree] A mammal native to forest and dry scrubland in Central and South America; a New World equivalent of the Old World pig, but smaller, with three toes on each hind foot; tusks grow downwards. (Family: Tayassuidae, 3 species.)

Peck, (Eldred) Gregory (1916–2003) Film star, born in La Jolla, CA. He received an Oscar for his portrayal of a liberal Southern lawyer in *To Kill a Mockingbird* (1962). Among his other films were *Spellbound* (1945), *Twelve O'clock High* (1949), and *The Omen* (1976). In 1999 he received the American film industry's Lifetime Achievement Award.

Peckinpah, Sam [pekinpah] (1925–84) US film director, born in Fresno, CA. He portrayed a harshly realistic view of the lawless US West, accentuating the inherent violence, as in *Major Dundee* (1965) and *The Wild Bunch* (1969).

Pecos River [paykohs] River in S USA; rises in the Sangre de Cristo Mts; flows S to join the Rio Grande; length 1490 km/925 mi.

Pécs [paych], Ger **Fünfkirchen**, Lat **Sopianae** 46°05N 18°15E, pop (2000e) 166 000. Industrial city in S Hungary; bishopric; university (1367, refounded 1922), university of medicine (1923); centre of a noted wine-producing area.

pectin A complex molecule (a homopolysaccharide) especially rich in galacturonic acid. It functions as a cement-like material in plant cell walls, and is abundant in fruits such as apples.

pediatrics *paediatrics*

pediment In classical architecture, a triangular section of wall above the entablature and enclosed by the sloping cornices, ie a low-pitched gable.

pedology The study of soil as a natural phenomenon. It embraces soil mapping, the study of soil formation and development, and the subdisciplines of soil chemistry, soil physics, and soil microbiology.

pedometer A device for counting the number of paces taken by the wearer. It usually consists of a free pendulum, operating a ratchet, which moves a toothed wheel one tooth per pace; this is then connected to a dial counter.

pedophilia *paedophilia*

Pedra Furada [pedra furahda] Rock shelter in Piaui region, Brazil, the earliest human settlement yet known in the Americas. It suggests that early modern humans reached the New World more than 30 000 years ago, around the time they arrived in Europe and Australia, and much earlier than previously thought.

Peel, John, popular name of **John Robert Parker Ravenscroft** (1939–2004) Radio disc jockey and presenter, born in Heswall, Merseyside. He worked as a disc jockey and joined pirate radio station Radio London where he championed British underground bands such as Pink Floyd. In 1967 he began a long career with Radio 1, hosting many shows including *Top Gear*. From 1998 to 2004 he presented Radio 4's popular *Home Truths*, which won four Sony Radio awards in 1999. At the time of his death, while on holiday in Peru, he was working on his autobiography. The book, *John Peel: margrave of the marshes*, was completed by his wife and family and published in 2005. In October that year, John Peel Day marked the first anniversary of his death with over 300 concerts taking place around the world in his honour.

Peel, Sir Robert (1788–1850) British statesman and prime minister (1834–5, 1841–6), born near Bury, Greater Manchester. As home secretary (1822–7, 1828–30), he carried through the Catholic Emancipation Act (1829) and reorganized the London police force (whose members became known as 'Peelers' or 'Bobbies'). As prime minister, his decision to phase out agricultural protection by repealing the Corn Laws (1846) split his party, and precipitated his resignation.

Peele, George (c.1558–96) Playwright and poet, born in London. His best-known works are the pastoral *The Arraignment of Paris* (1584) and the historical play *Edward I* (1593).

peepul A species of strangler fig (*Ficus religiosa*) native to SE Asia, and regarded as sacred in India; also called **pipal** or **bo-tree**. (Family: Moraceae.)

peerage In the UK, holders of the title of duke, marquess, earl, viscount, or baron, who make up, in that order of precedence, the titled nobility. Their privileges have been much reduced in recent years, especially after the 1999 reform of the House of Lords, but they remain exempt from jury service.

peewit An alternative name for the lapwing (*Vanellus vanellus*); also known as **pewit**. It was formerly an alternative name for the **black-headed gull** (*Larus ridibundus*).

Pegasus (astronomy) (Lat 'winged horse') The seventh largest constellation, conspicuous in the N hemisphere.

Pegasus (mythology) In Greek mythology, a winged horse, which sprang from the body of the Medusa after her death. Bellerophon caught it with Athene's assistance.

pegmatite [**peg**matiyt] Very coarse-grained igneous rocks with varied and sometimes exotic mineralogy due to concentrations of the rarer elements. They are the source of many gem-quality and uncommon minerals.

Pei, I(eoh) M(ing) [pay] (1917–) Architect, born in Canton, China. He emigrated to the USA in 1935. His projects include Mile High Center, Denver, the 60-storey John Hancock Tower, Boston, the glass pyramids at the Louvre, Paris, the Miho Museum, Kyoto, Japan (1998), the Arts Center at Christopher Newport University, Newport News, VA (2005), and the Suzhou Museum, E China (2006).

Peierls, Sir Rudolph (Ernest) [pairlz] (1907–95) Theoretical physicist, born in Berlin. He applied quantum theory to solids and to magnetic effects, and then turned to nuclear physics, working on the atomic bomb project throughout World War 2.

Peirce, Charles Sanders [peers] (1839–1914) Philosopher, logician, and mathematician, born in Cambridge, MA. A pioneer in the development of modern formal logic and the logic of relations, he is best known as the founder of pragmatism. His theory of meaning helped establish the field of semiotics.

pekan *fisher*

Pekinese or **Pekingese** A toy breed of dog, developed in China 2000 years ago; long body with short legs; tail curved over back; long, pendulous ears; flat face, muzzle virtually non-existent; coat very long, fine; also known as **peke**.

Peking *Beijing*

Pelagianism *Pelagius*

Pelagius [pe**lay**jius] (c.360–c.420) A British or Irish monk, who settled in Rome c.400. His view that salvation can be achieved by the exercise of human powers (**Pelagianism**) was condemned as heretical by Councils in 416 and 418.

pelargonium An annual or perennial, native mainly to S Africa; flowers in a range of colours in clusters. They include the so-called 'geraniums' of horticulture. (Genus: *Pelargonium*, 250 species. Family: Geraniaceae.)

Pelasgians [pe**lazg**ianz] The name given by the Greeks to the indigenous, pre-Greek peoples of the Aegean region.

Pelau *Belau*

Pelé [pe**lay**], popular name of **Edson Arantes do Nascimento** (1940–) Footballer, born in Três Corações. Widely held to be the best player in the game's history, he played in Brazil's winning team in the 1958, 1962, and 1970 World Cup finals. His first-class career was spent at Santos (1955–74) and with the New York Cosmos (1975–7), scoring 1281 goals. He is a national hero in Brazil. He was appointed a sports minister in the Brazilian cabinet in 1994. In 2005 he was honoured with the FIFPro Legend Award.

Pelecypoda [pele**sipo**da] *ark shell; bivalve*

Pelée, Mount [pe**lay**], Fr **Montagne Pelée** 14°18N 61°10W. Active volcano on Martinique I, E Caribbean; height, 1397 m/4583 ft; erupted in 1902 killing over 26 000 people in the town of St Pierre.

Peleus [**peely**oos] In Greek mythology, the King of Phythia in Thessaly, who had to capture Thetis, a nereid, before he could marry her. He was the father of Achilles.

Pelevin, Victor (1962–) Writer, born in Moscow, considered the leading Russian novelist of his generation. His first book, *Omon Ra* (1992), was followed by *The Blue Lantern and Other Stories* (1993), and a novel, *The Yellow Arrow* (1994), both of which were awarded literary prizes in Russia. Later books include *Babylon* and *Clay Machine Gun* (both 2000), and *The Helmet of Horror* (2006).

Pelham (-Holles), Thomas, 1st Duke of Newcastle [**pel**am] (1693– 1768) British statesman and prime minister (1754–6, 1757–62). A Whig and a supporter of Walpole, in 1724 he became secretary of state, and held the office for 30 years. He succeeded his brother, **Henry Pelham** (c.1696–1754) as premier, and was extremely influential during the reigns of George I and II.

pelican A large aquatic bird from warm regions worldwide; bill long, with lower part sack-like; eats fish and crustaceans. (Genus: *Pelecanus*, 8 species. Family: Pelecanidae.)

pellagra [pe**layg**ra] A nutritional disease which results from a deficiency of niacin (a vitamin of the B group). It is common in Africa due to a combination of a low niacin diet and malabsorption of food.

Pelopidas [pe**lopi**das] (c.410–364 BC) Theban general and statesman who, with Epaminondas, established the short-lived Theban hegemony over Greece in the 360s BC. He played a prominent part in the Theban victory over Sparta at Leuctra (371 BC).

Peloponnese [pelo**ponee**z], Gr **Pelopónnisos** pop (2000e) 1 125 000; area 21 379 km²/8252 sq mi. Peninsular region of Greece, the most southerly part of the Greek mainland, to which it is linked by the Isthmus of Corinth; a popular holiday region.

Peloponnesian War [pelo**ponee**shan] (431–404 BC) The war waged throughout the Greek world on land and sea by the Spartans and their allies. The underlying cause was Athenian imperialism. Following Persian intervention on the side of the Spartans, the Athenians were defeated.

pelota [pe**loh**ta] The generic name for various hand, glove, racket, or bat-and-ball court games which all developed from the French *jeu de paume* ('palm [of hand] game'). It is one of the world's fastest games.

pelvic inflammatory disease An infection of the uterus, uterine tubes, ovaries, and surrounding tissues. It is usually caused by bacteria spreading from the lower genital tract (vagina and cervix) and may occur during delivery of a baby or insertion of contraceptive intrauterine devices, but is most commonly due to sexually transmitted organisms, especially *chlamydia trachomatis* and *neisseria gonorrhoea*. It can be treated with antibiotics, but if left untreated can seriously and permanently damage the organs of the upper genital tract, reducing fertility, and increasing the risk of ectopic pregnancy if pregnancy does occur.

pelvis 1 The region of the trunk that lies below the abdomen. It contains part of the gastro-intestinal tract, part of the urinary system, and some of the genital organs. **2** A ring of bone which serves to transmit forces from the lower limbs to the trunk. It consists of the two hip bones, the sacrum, and the coccyx.

pelycosaur [**pelikosaw**(r)] A carnivorous fossil reptile known from the Carboniferous to the late Permian periods, mostly in North America; skull mammal-like; typically with expanded sail along back. (Subclass: Synapsida. Order: Pelycosauria.)

Pemba pop (2000e) 354 000; area 981 km²/379 sq mi. Island region of Tanzania, in the Indian Ocean; capital, Chake Chake; cloves (world's largest producer).

Pembrokeshire, Welsh **Sir Penfro** pop (2001e) 112 900; area

1590 km²/614 sq mi. County (unitary authority from 1996) in SW Wales, UK; administrative centre, Haverfordwest; ferries to Ireland (Rosslare) from Fishguard; Caldy I priory and monastery; castles at Pembroke, Cilgerran, Carew; St David's Cathedral.

PEN Initials standing for 'poets, playwrights, editors, essayists, novelists', an international association, founded by C A Dawson Scott in 1921, to promote understanding between writers, and to defend freedom of expression.

penance (Lat *poena*, 'punishment') Both the inner turning to God in sorrow for sin, and the outward discipline of the Church in order to reinforce repentance by prayer, confession, fasting, and good works. In the Orthodox and Roman Catholic Churches, penance is a sacrament.

Penang [penang], also **Pulau Pinang** pop (2000e) 1 421 000; area 1044 km²/403 sq mi. State in NW Malaysia; first British settlement in Malaya; capital, Pinang (formerly George Town).

Penates [penayteez, penahteez] In Roman religion, the guardians of the storeroom; 'Lares and Penates' were the household gods.

pencil In art, originally a brush, a meaning still found in the 18th-c. Drawing sticks of graphite encased in wood were in use by the 17th-c, but modern hard and soft pencils, in which the graphite is mixed with clay and fired in a kiln, were first devised in France c.1790 by French inventor Nicholas-Jacques Conté (1755–1805). The hardness of a pencil depends on the amount of clay used along with the graphite, and is indicated by a hardness rating, such as 8B (very soft) to 10H (very hard).

Penda (c.575–655) King of Mercia (c.632–55). He established mastery over the English Midlands, and was frequently at war with the kings of Northumbria.

Penderecki, Krzysztof [pendreskee] (1933–) Composer, born in Debica, Poland. His works include *Threnody for the Victims of Hiroshima* (1960), the opera *The Devils of Loudun* (1969), and a St Luke Passion.

Pendleton, Don(ald Eugene) (1927–95) Writer, born in Little Rock, AR. He is best known for his series of 38 'Executioner' novels, starring Mack Bolan. Launched in 1969 with *War Against the Mafia*, the series led to the emergence of a new genre of 'action/adventure' writing in the 1970s, especially popular in North America.

pendulum In its simplest form, a weight, suspended by a wire or rod from a firm support, allowed to swing freely to and fro under the influence of gravity. The swing period does not depend on the weight of the bob nor on the size of the swing (for small swings), which is why pendulums are used in clocks.

Penelope In Greek legend, the wife of Odysseus, who faithfully waited 20 years for his return from Troy. She tricked her suitors by weaving a shroud for Odysseus' father (which had to be finished before she could marry), and undoing her work every night.

Penghu Qundao [punghoo] or **P'eng-hu Ch'ün-tao**, Span, Port **Pescadores** pop (2000e) 103 000; area 127 km²/49 sq mi. Island archipelago of Taiwan; 85% of the population lives on the largest island, Penghu.

penguin A flightless seabird, native to S hemisphere; wings modified as flippers. (Family: Spheniscidae, 18 species.)

penicillin An antibiotic produced by the mould *Penicillium*. In 1928, Fleming first noted its activity against the bacterium *Staphylococcus* when his culture plate accidentally became contaminated with the mould. Several types are now used, such as ampicillin and benzylpenicillin (penicillin G).

Peninsular Campaign (1862) In the American Civil War, an extended attempt by the Union army under General McClellan to take Richmond, Virginia (the Southern capital), by moving up the peninsula between the James and York Rivers. The effort failed, but Confederate troops were unable to drive the Northerners off the peninsula.

Peninsular War (1808–14) The prolonged struggle for the Iberian peninsula between the occupying French and a British army under Wellington (formerly Wellesley), supported by Portuguese forces. British troops repulsed Masséna's Lisbon offensive (1810–11) and advanced to liberate Spain. Wellington's army then invaded SW France (1813–14).

penis A part of the male urogenital system composed mainly of erectile tissue and traversed by the *urethra*. The skin over the body of the penis is thin, delicate, freely mobile, and largely free from hairs. Towards the base of the glans penis it forms a free fold (the *foreskin*) which overlaps the glans to a variable extent (the foreskin is surgically removed in circumcision so that the glans is always visible). The size of the penis varies with the amount of blood present within the erectile tissue.

Penn, Sean (Justin) (1960–) Actor, writer, producer, and director, born in Santa Monica, CA. Born into a show business family, he gained his first feature-film role in *Taps* (1981). Later films include *Dead Man Walking* (1995), *The Thin Red Line* (1998), *Mystic River* (2003, Best Actor Oscar), and *All the King's Men* (2006). His first wife was Madonna (1985–9).

Penn, William (1644–1718) Quaker leader and founder of Pennsylvania, born in London. He was imprisoned for his writings (1668), and while in the Tower wrote the most popular of his books, *No Cross, no Crown*. In 1681 he obtained a grant of land in North America, which he called Pennsylvania in honour of his father. He sailed in 1682, and governed the colony for two years.

Penney, William (George) Penney, Baron (1909–91) Physicist, born in Gibraltar. Director of the Atomic Weapons Research Establishment at Aldermaston, Berkshire (1953–9), he was the key figure in the UK's success in producing its own atomic (1952) and hydrogen bombs (1957).

Pennines or **Pennine Chain**, nickname **the backbone of England** Mountain range in N England; extends S from Northumberland to Derbyshire; fold of carboniferous limestone and overlying millstone grit, worn into high moorland and fell; rises to 893 m/2930 ft at Cross Fell; **Pennine Way** footpath extends 402 km/250 mi from Derbyshire to the Scottish Borders.

Pennsylvania [pensilvaynia] pop (2000e) 12 281 000; area 117 343 km²/45 308 sq mi. State in E USA; the 'Keystone State'; one of the original states of the Union, second to ratify the Federal Constitution, 1787; first settled by the Swedish, 1643; taken by the Dutch, and then by the British in 1664; region given by King Charles II to William Penn, 1681; scene of many battles in the American Revolution and Civil War; capital, Harrisburg; major industrial state, noted for its coal mining.

Pennsylvanian period *Carboniferous period*

pennyroyal A species of mint (*Mentha pulegium*) native to Europe and the Mediterranean, and also found in N America, with pale green leaves, mauve flowers, and strong, slightly peppermint, scent. It is used for soups and stuffings. As a mildly spicy tea, it is sometimes recommended for its physiological effects or as a herbal remedy. However, its oils contain pulegone, which is extremely toxic, and in some circumstances (eg when used in an attempt to induce abortion) it has proved lethal. (Family: Labiatae.)

Penrose, Sir Roger (1931–) Mathematical physicist, born in Colchester, Essex. He held posts at several universities before taking up an appointment at Oxford (1973). His research interests span topology and gravitation. His work with Stephen Hawking showed that general relativity predicates a 'big bang' creation of the universe (1970). He invented *twistors*, geometrical entities that can be used to describe space-time. The *Penrose triangle* is an impossible figure that inspired M C Escher's 'Ascending and descending'. He was knighted in 1994.

pension A payment made to an individual who has retired from work, on a weekly or monthly basis, related to the wage or salary being earned before retirement. **Company pension**

schemes operate by receiving contributions from employees and employers; the funds are invested, and the pensions are paid from the proceeds of the investment. In the UK, a **state pension scheme** (SERPS, or State Earnings Related Pension Scheme) is available for individuals without a company pension. The state also pays a basic old-age pension (introduced 1909).

Pentagon The central offices of the US military forces and the Defense Department, in Arlington, VA. The complex was built in 1941–3, and covers 14 ha/34 acres. It is composed of five 5-storey, pentagonal buildings. A section of the complex was destroyed on 11 Sep 2001 when an aircraft was deliberately flown into it in a terrorist attack.

pentane C_5H_{12}, an alkane hydrocarbon which has five carbon atoms. There are three structural isomers: **n-pentane**, $CH_3CH_2CH_2CH_2CH_3$ (boiling point 36°C); **isopentane** (IUPAC **methylbutane**), $CH_3CH_2CH(CH_3)CH_3$ (boiling point 28°C); and **neopentane** (IUPAC **dimethylpropane**), $CH_3C(CH_3)_2CH_3$ (boiling point 10°C).

Pentateuch [pentatyook] The five Books of Moses in the Hebrew Bible/Old Testament, comprising Genesis, Exodus, Leviticus, Numbers, and Deuteronomy; also called the *Torah*. The works are now believed by modern scholars to be composed of several strands of traditions from various periods. Together they trace Israel's origins from the earliest times.

pentathlon A five-event track-and-field discipline for women, seldom contested, having been replaced in 1981 by the seven-event heptathlon. The events were the 100 m hurdles, shot put, high jump, long jump, and 800 m. The **modern pentathlon** is a five-sport competition based on miltary training. The events are cross-country riding on horseback, épée fencing, pistol shooting, swimming, and cross-country running.

pentatonic scale A musical scale with five notes in the octave, most commonly equivalent to the first, second, third, fifth, and sixth degrees of the major scale.

Pentecost [pentekost] 1 The Jewish feast of Shabuoth. 2 A festival day in the Christian calendar, some 50 days after the death and resurrection of Jesus, commemorating the event when the Holy Spirit was said to have come upon Jesus's apostles in Jerusalem, enabling them to 'speak in other tongues' to those present.

Pentecostal Churches *Pentecostalism*

Pentecostalism [pentikostalizm] A modern Christian renewal movement inspired by the descent of the Holy Spirit experienced by the Apostles at the first Christian Pentecost, and marked by speaking in tongues, prophecy, and healing. Pentecostal churches are characterized by a literal interpretation of the Bible, informal worship during which there is enthusiastic singing and spontaneous exclamations of praise, and the exercise of the gifts of the Holy Spirit. There are over 22 million Pentecostals worldwide.

pentyl *amyl*

penumbra 1 An area of partial shadow. A partial eclipse of the Sun is visible from within the penumbra of the Moon's shadow when it falls on the Earth. 2 The lighter periphery of a sunspot, surrounding the umbra.

Penzance [penzans] 50°07N 5°33W, pop (2000e) 21 100. Town in Cornwall, SW England; chief resort town of 'the Cornish Riviera'; railway; ferry and helicopter services to Scilly Is.

Penzias, Arno (Allan) [penzias] (1933–) Astrophysicist, born in Munich, Germany. His research detected residual radiation from the 'big bang' at the origin of the universe. He shared the Nobel Prize for Physics with Robert W(oodrow) Wilson (1936–) in 1978.

peony A perennial herb or shrub, native to Europe (especially Greece), Asia, and W North America; flowers large, showy, ranging in colour from white or yellow to pink or red, up to 15 cm/

6 in across, with 5–10 petals and numerous stamens. (Genus: *Paeonia*, 33 species. Family: Paeoniaceae.)

People's Liberation Army *Red Army* (China)

Pepin III, known as **Pepin the Short** (c.714–68) King of the Franks (751–68), the founder of the Frankish dynasty of the Carolingians, the father of Charlemagne. He was chosen king after the deposition of Childeric, the last of the Merovingians.

pepper 1 An annual native to the New World tropics. It has white flowers and large, fleshy, edible berries in a variety of shapes and colours. Its hot, spicy flavour is due to the chemical *capsaicin*. Used whole or ground into powder, peppers include paprika, chillies, cayenne pepper, and red pepper; the familiar green peppers are simply unripe red peppers. (Genus: *Capsicum*, 50 species. Family: Solanaceae.)
2 A tropical shrub or climber (*Piper nigrum*) with long, slender spikes of minute flowers and small hard fruits. The dried, unripe fruits are called *black peppercorns*. Removal of the outer layer yields *white peppercorns*. Both are used whole or ground as spice or condiment. (Family: Piperaceae.)

pepperidge *tupelo*

peppermint *mint*

pepsin A digestive enzyme, present in the gastric juice of vertebrates, which breaks down dietary protein into polypeptides of various sizes. It is active only in the acid environment of the stomach.

peptic ulcer The ulceration of a small part of the lining of either the stomach or the duodenum, caused by erosion by gastric acid.

peptide A molecule obtained by the partial hydrolysis of proteins, a short chain (oligomer) of amino acids. Longer polymers (generally 50 or more amino acids) are called **polypeptides** or proteins.

Pepys, Samuel [peeps] (1633–1703) Naval administrator and diarist, born in London. His diary runs from 1 January 1660 to 31 May 1669 – a detailed personal record and a vivid picture of contemporary life. It was written in shorthand, and not decoded until 1825.

Perak [perak] pop (2000e) 2 765 000; area 21 005 km²/8108 sq mi. State in W Peninsular Malaysia; capital, Ipoh; one of the wealthiest states in Malaysia since the discovery of tin in the 1840s.

Perceval, Sir, or **Parsifal** In the Arthurian legends, a knight who went in quest of the Holy Grail.

Perceval, Spencer (1762–1812) British statesman, and prime minister (1809–12), born in London. He was shot while entering the House of Commons by a bankrupt Liverpool broker, John Bellingham.

perch Name used for many of the freshwater fish in the families Percidae and Centropomidae; deep-bodied, length up to 50 cm/ 20 in; green and brown with dark vertical bands.

Percheron [pershuhron] A heavy breed of horse, developed in France; height, 15·2–17 hands/1·6–1·7 m/5 ft 2 in–5 ft 5 in; black or grey; deep, solid body with strong neck and short, very muscular legs; the most popular heavy draught horse worldwide.

perching duck A duck of the tribe Cairinini (8 species), including the genera *Aix*, *Nettapus*, *Callonetta*, *Cairina*, *Chenonetta*, and *Sarkidiornis*. They nest in holes or (**muscovy duck**) in hollows. The tribe also includes four species of geese, called **perching geese**.

percussion A category of musical instruments, essentially idiophones and membranophones, which are played by being struck or shaken.

Percy A noble N England family, whose founder, **William de Percy** (c.1030–96), travelled to England with the Conqueror. The most famous member of the family was **Henry** (1364–1403), the famous 'Hotspur', who fell fighting against Henry IV at Shrewsbury.

peregrine falcon A fast, agile falcon (*Falco peregrinus*), found virtually worldwide; dives vertically on prey, or chases in flight; also known as **duck hawk**.

perennial A plant which lives for at least several years. **Herbaceous perennials** die back to ground level each year, surviving as underground organs such as bulbs or rhizomes. **Woody perennials** retain their aerial stems, which put out further growth each year.

Peres, Shimon [perez], originally **Shimon Perski** (1923–) Israeli statesman and prime minister (1984–6, 1995–6), born in Valozhyn, Belarus (formerly Wolożyn, Poland). He entered into a unique power-sharing agreement with the leader of the Consolidation Party (Likud), Yitzhak Shamir, becoming prime minister for two years, when Shamir took over. Peres was replaced as Labour Party leader by Yitzhak Rabin in 1992, and shared the Nobel Peace Prize with him in 1994. He served a second term as prime minister (1995–6), became minister of foreign affairs (2001–2), interim Labour leader in opposition (2003–4), and vice premier (2005–).

perestroika [perestroyka] The process of 'reconstructing' Soviet society through a programme of reforms initiated from 1985 by General Secretary Gorbachev. The reforms were directed at relaxing state controls over the economy, eliminating corruption from the state bureaucracy, and democratizing the Soviet communist party.

Pérez de Cuellar, Javier [peres duh kwayah(r)] (1920–) Peruvian diplomat, born in Lima. He became a representative to the United Nations in 1971, and served as secretary-general (1982–91). He played a prominent role in the Falklands Crisis, and in the negotiations for the release of the hostages from Lebanon in 1991. He was briefly prime minister and foreign minister (2000–1) in the Peruvian transitional cabinet following President Fujimori's resignation.

Pérez Galdós, Benito [peres galdos] (1843–1920) Writer, born in Las Palmas, Canary Islands. He is regarded as Spain's greatest novelist after Cervantes. His series of 46 short novels, *Episodios nacionales* (1873–1912), gives a vivid picture of 19th-c Spain from the viewpoint of the people.

perfect numbers In mathematics, a number where the sum of its divisors is equal to the number itself. Thus the divisors of 6 are 1, 2, 3, and 1 + 2 + 3 = 6; the divisors of 28 are 1, 2, 4, 7, 14, and their sum is 28; the next perfect number is 496. In Euclid's *Elements* a formula is given for finding perfect numbers: if $2^n - 1$ is prime, then $2^{n-1}(2^n - 1)$ is a perfect number.

Pergamum (Asia Minor) [pergamum] or **Pergamon** An ancient city in NW Asia Minor, which in Hellenistic times was the capital of the Attalids. Under their patronage it became a major centre of art and learning.

Pergamum (Berlin) A branch of the Staatliche (state) museum in Berlin, housing one of the world's finest collections of Greek, Roman, and Eastern art and antiquities.

Pergolesi, Giovanni Battista [pergolayzee] (1710–36) Composer, born in Jesi, Italy. His comic intermezzo *La serva padrona* (1732) influenced the development of *opera buffa*. He wrote much church music, notably his great *Stabat Mater*.

Perham, Michael (1993–) Yachtsman, born in Potters Bar, Hertfordshire. He began sailing at age seven, encouraged by his father, and completed Royal Yachting Association courses in dinghy sailing and windsurfing. At the age of 14, he became the youngest person to sail solo across the Atlantic. On 18 November 2006 he left Gibraltar aboard his yacht *Cheeky Monkey* on the 3500-mile voyage to the Caribbean island of Antigua, arriving there on 3 January 2007.

peri [peeree] In Persian mythology, the generic name given to a good fairy or genie.

perianth The two outer whorls of floral parts (sepals and petals)

taken together. When the whorls are not clearly distinguishable, the individual parts are referred to as **perianth segments**.

periapsis The closest point of approach of an orbiting body (planet, comet, spacecraft, etc) to the primary body; contrasted with **apoapsis**, the furthest point. For orbits about the Sun, **perihelion** is the point of closest approach; **aphelion** the furthest distance. For orbits about the Earth, the closest point is **perigee**; the furthest distance **apogee**.

pericarditis Inflammation of the pericardium, the sac of fibrous tissue that surrounds the heart. It may arise due to infections, especially viruses, connective tissue diseases such as systemic lupus erythematosus, as a complication of heart attack, or with no obvious cause. The predominant clinical feature is a sharp chest pain, aggravated by inspiration, and accompanied by fever.

periclase *magnesia*

Pericles [perikleez] (c.495–429 BC) General and statesman of the aristocratic Alcmaeonid family, who presided over the 'Golden Age' of Athens, and was virtually its uncrowned king (443–429 BC). His unremitting hostility to Sparta brought about the Peloponnesian War (431–404 BC).

peridot *olivine*

peridotite [peridohtiyt] A coarse-grained igneous rock rich in the mineral olivine together with pyroxene and other ferromagnesian minerals. It is thought to be a major constituent of the Earth's mantle.

perigee *periapsis*

Périgord [payreegaw(r)] Part of the former province of Guyenne, SW France; chief town, Périgueux; Palaeolithic (Perigordian) caves.

perihelion *periapsis*

perinatology The study of disorders of the newborn that occur in the perinatal period, between 24 weeks of gestation and one week of life. It includes the care of such disorders as distressed breathing, bleeding, and birth injuries.

period (geology) *geological time scale*

period (physiology) *menstruation*

periodic motion Any motion which repeats itself in a regular way, such as the swing of a pendulum, a weight bouncing on a spring, or wave motion.

periodic table *p.715*

periodontics *dentistry*

Peripatus [peripatus] A genus of velvet worm typically found in humid forest litter; body segmented, length up to 150 mm/6 in; head with a pair of antennae and jaws. (Phylum: Arthropoda. Subphylum: Onychophora.)

peripheral nervous system (PNS) That part of the nervous system arranged into a large number of nerves, which connects the central nervous system with other tissues of the body. It is divided into an **autonomic** part, involved in voluntary (automatic) responses, and a **somatic** part, comprising in humans the 12 pairs of *cranial nerves* and some 31 pairs of *spinal nerves*, which are involved in voluntary acts and in monitoring the external and (in part) the internal environments of the body.

periscope An optical instrument for viewing an object concealed from view by a barrier. The basic principle is the use of two mirrors, parallel but separated by some distance: light from the object being observed reaches the first mirror, is reflected downwards, then reflected again at the second mirror, its whole path being somewhat in the form of a Z.

perissodactyl [perisohdaktil] ('odd-toed ungulate') A hoofed mammal of order Perissodactyla (16 species); foot with one or three functional toes (the first absent on all feet, the fifth absent on hindfeet).

peristyle [peristiyl] A series of columns surrounding an open court, temple, or other building. It is particularly used in clas-

periodic table

Transition series

under investigation

1	2	3	4	5	6	7	8	9	10	11	12	13	14	15	16	17	18
1 H Hydrogen 1.00794																	2 He Helium 4.00260
3 Li Lithium 6.941	4 Be Beryllium 9.01218											5 B Boron 10.81	6 C Carbon 12.011	7 N Nitrogen 14.0067	8 O Oxygen 15.9994	9 F Flourine 18.998403	10 Ne Neon 20.179
11 Na Sodium 22.98977	12 Mg Magnesium 24.305											13 Al Aluminium 26.98154	14 Si Silicon 28.0855	15 P Phosphorus 30.97376	16 S Sulphur 32.066	17 Cl Chlorine 35.453	18 Ar Argon 39.948
19 K Potassium 39.0983	20 Ca Calcium 40.08	21 Sc Scandium 44.9559	22 Ti Titanium 47.88	23 V Vanadium 50.9415	24 Cr Chromium 51.996	25 Mn Manganese 54.9380	26 Fe Iron 55.847	27 Co Cobalt 58.9332	28 Ni Nickel 58.69	29 Cu Copper 63.546	30 Zn Zinc 65.38	31 Ga Gallium 69.72	32 Ge Germanium 72.59	33 As Arsenic 74.9216	34 Se Selenium 78.96	35 Br Bromine 79.904	36 Kr Krypton 83.80
37 Rb Rubidium 85.4678	38 Sr Strontium 87.62	39 Y Yttrium 88.9059	40 Zr Zirconium 91.22	41 Nb Niobium 92.9064	42 Mo Molybdenum 95.94	43 Tc Technetium (98)	44 Ru Ruthenium 101.07	45 Rh Rhodium 102.9055	46 Pd Palladium 106.42	47 Ag Silver 107.8682	48 Cd Cadmium 112.41	49 In Indium 114.82	50 Sn Tin 118.69	51 Sb Antimony 121.75	52 Te Tellurium 127.60	53 I Iodine 126.9045	54 Xe Xenon 131.29
55 Cs Caesium 132.9054	56 Ba Barium 137.33	57–71 Lanthenide series (rare earth elements) ★	72 Hf Hafnium 178.49	73 Ta Tantalum 180.9479	74 W Tungsten 183.85	75 Re Rhenium 186.207	76 Os Osmium 190.2	77 Ir Iridium 192.2	78 Pt Platinum 195.08	79 Au Gold 196.9665	80 Hg Mercury 200.59	81 Tl Thallium 204.383	82 Pb Lead 207.2	83 Bi Bismuth 208.9804	84 Po Polonium (209)	85 At Astatine (210)	86 Rn Radon (222)
87 Fr Francium (223)	88 Ra Radium 226.0254	89–103 Actinide series (radioactive rare earth elements) ☆	104 Rf Rutherfordium (261)	105 Db Dubnium (262)	106 Sg Seaborgium (263)	107 Bh Bohrium (262)	108 Hs Hassium (265)	109 Mt Meitnerium (266)	110 Uun Ununnilium (269)	111 Uuu Unununium (272)	112 Uub Unununbium (277)						

★	57 La Lanthanum 138.9055	58 Ce Cerium 140.12	59 Pr Praseodymiurm 140.9077	60 Nd Neodymium 144.24	61 Pm Promethium (145)	62 Sm Samarium 150.36	63 Eu Europium 151.96	64 Gd Gadolinium 157.25	65 Tb Terbium 158.9254	66 Dy Dysprosium 162.50	67 Ho Holmium 164.9304	68 Er Erbium 167.26	69 Tm Thulium 168.9342	70 Yt Ytterbium 173.04	71 Lu Lutetium 174.967
☆	89 Ac Actinium 227.0278	90 Th Thorium 232.0381	91 Pa Protactinium 231.0359	92 U Uranium 238.0289	93 Np Neptunium 237.0482	94 Pu Plutonium (244)	95 Am Americium (243)	96 Cm Curium (247)	97 Bk Berkelium (247)	98 Cf Californium (251)	99 Es Einsteinium (254)	100 Fm Fermium (257)	101 Md Mendelevium (258)	102 No Nobelium (259)	103 Lr Lawrencium (260)

atomic number — symbol

86 Rn Radon (222)

element name

atomic weight (most stable isotope of radioactive elements in parenthesis)

The method of listing the chemical elements in terms of increasing atomic number, so that the rows represent increasing occupancy of an electron subshell, and the columns represent equivalent numbers of valence electrons. The original table of Mendeleyev (1869) was based on atomic weight, but had several successes in predicting the existence and chemical properties of undiscovered elements.

sical architecture, such as the Lincoln Memorial, Washington, DC (dedicated, 1922).

peritoneum [peritoneeum] The fluid-secreting lining of the abdominal cavity and part of the pelvic cavity. Inflammation of the peritoneum caused by infection or by irritant substances is known as **peritonitis**.

periwinkle (botany) An evergreen, creeping herb (Family: Apocynaceae), originally native to Madagascar, now found in Europe, W Asia, and N Africa; flowers white, mauve, or blue-purple, tubular with five flat, asymmetric lobes; widely known as **myrtle** in the USA. Main species: **common periwinkle** (Genus: *Catharanthus roseus*) and **lesser periwinkle** (Genus: *Vinca*).

periwinkle (zoology) A marine snail commonly found in the inter-tidal zone on shores; aperture closed off by a horny plate on the foot. (Class: Gastropoda. Order: Mesogastropoda.)

perjury A crime committed by a person who, when giving evidence in a court under oath (or having affirmed or declared), deliberately makes a false statement. The crime is essentially one of disregarding the oath: someone who makes several such false statements during a single case may be convicted of only a single perjury.

Perkins, Anthony (1932–92) Actor, born in New York City. After several early films, he achieved international fame as the maniacal Norman Bates in Hitchcock's *Psycho* (1960), with its three sequels (1983, 1986, 1990).

Perkins, Charles (Nelson) (1936–2000) Bureaucrat and activist, born in Alice Springs, Australia of Arunta and European descent. He was a leader of the Aboriginal movement in the 1960s, his 'freedom rides' bringing injustice to Aboriginal people to public attention. He later became chairman of the Aboriginal Development Commission (1981–4) and head of the Department of Aboriginal Affairs (1984–9).

Perkins, Kieren (John) (1973–) Swimmer, born in Brisbane, Queensland, Australia. He set four world records in the year leading up to the 1992 Barcelona Olympics, where he won the 1500 m freestyle final, breaking the Games record in the process, and regaining the title at the Atlanta Olympic Games in 1996.

Perl, Martin (Lewis) (1927–) Physicist, born in Brooklyn, NY. His study of elementary particles led to his detection of the tau lepton – a short-lived, heavy-weight cousin of the electron, and one of the fundamental building blocks of matter. He shared the Nobel Prize for Physics in 1995.

Perlis [perlis] pop (2000e) 233 000; area 818 km²/316 sq mi. State in NW Peninsular Malaysia; smallest state in Malaysia; Langkawi Is lie offshore; capital, Kangar.

Perm, formerly **Molotov** (1940–57) 58°01N 56°10E, pop (2000e) 1 092 000. Industrial city in NE European Russia, on R Kama; founded, 1723; airfield; railway; university (1916).

permafrost Perennially frozen ground in low temperature regions of the Earth. It is underlain at depth by unfrozen ground, and also overlain by an active surface layer which thaws in summer and refreezes in the autumn.

permalloy An alloy of iron and nickel, which is easily magnetized and demagnetized. The high magnetic permeability of permalloys is very useful for parts of electrical machinery subject to rapidly alternating magnetic fields. Their importance was realized in 1920 by the communication and telephone industry to make deep-sea communication telegraph cables capable of handling large numbers of messages.

permeability The ratio of magnetic flux density B in some material to the applied magnetic field strength H; symbol μ, units H/m (henrys per metre); $B = \mu H$.

Permian period A geological period of the Upper Palaeozoic era, extending from c.286 to 250 million years ago. It was marked by the extinction of many groups of marine invertebrate animals and the diversification of reptiles.

permittivity A measure of the degree to which molecules of some material polarize (align) under the influence of an electric field; symbol ε, units F/m (farad per metre).

permutational art A form of modern art in which certain features of the work are subject to change. Such changes may be predetermined by the artist (as in computer graphics) or left to chance.

Perón, (Maria) Eva (Duarte de) [peron], known as **Evita** (1919–52) The second wife of Argentine President Juan Perón, born in Los Toldos, Argentina. An actress before her marriage in 1945, she became a powerful political influence and a mainstay of the Perón government. The successful musical *Evita* (1979) was based on her life.

Perón, Isabelita [peron], popular name of **Maria Estela Perón** *née* **Martínez Cartas** (1931–) President of Argentina (1974–6), born in La Rioja province, Argentina. A dancer who became the third wife of Juan Perón (1961), she was made vice-president when he returned to Argentina in 1973. She took over the presidency at his death in 1974, but after a military coup in 1976 she was imprisoned for five years. On her release, she settled in Madrid.

Perón, Juan (Domingo) [peron] (1895–1974) Argentinian soldier and president (1946–55, 1973–4), born in Lobos. He took a leading part in the army coup of 1943, gaining widespread support through his social reforms. Deposed and exiled in 1955, he returned in triumph in 1973, and won an overwhelming electoral victory, but died the following year.

Peronism [peronizm] A heterogeneous Argentine political movement formed in 1945–6 to support Juan Domingo Perón and his government. The movement later underwent division, but it survived Perón's death (1974), and made a good showing in the congressional elections of 1986. Its ideology is an amalgam of nationalism and social democracy, strongly coloured by loyalty to the memory of Perón.

Perot, (Henry) Ross [peroh] (1930–) Businessman and politician, born in Texarkana, TX. He founded the Electronic Data Systems Corporation Inc, Dallas, in 1962, and was its chairman and chief executive (1982–6). He became internationally known when he stood as an independent candidate in the 1992 and 1996 US presidential elections.

peroxide A compound containing the ion O_2^{2-} or the group –O–O–. **Hydrogen peroxide** (H_2O_2) is an important oxidizing agent and bleach.

Perpignan [perpeenyã] 42°42N 2°53E, pop (2000e) 111 000. Market town and resort in S France; settled in Roman times; capital of former province of Roussillon; chartered, 1197; scene of Church Council, 1408; united to France, 1659; road and rail junction; university (14th-c); cathedral (14th–17th-c).

Perrault, Charles [peroh] (1628–1703) Writer, born in Paris. He is best known for his fairy tales, the *Contes de Ma Mère l'Oye* (1697, trans Tales of Mother Goose), which included 'The Sleeping Beauty' and 'Red Riding Hood'.

Perry, Fred(erick John) (1909–95) Tennis and table tennis player, born in Stockport, Greater Manchester. He won the world table tennis title in 1929, the men's lawn tennis singles title at Wimbledon in 1934–6, and was the first man to win all four major titles.

Perry, Matthew (1969–) Actor, born in Williamstown, MA. He became known for his role as Chandler Bing in the acclaimed television series *Friends* (1994–2004). Roles in feature films include *Fools Rush In* (1997) and *The Whole Nine Yards* (2000, sequel 2004).

perry An alcoholic beverage made from fermenting pears. It is produced commercially in the UK, Germany, and France, and is very popular in the UK.

Perseids [perseeidz] A major meteor shower visible for a week or so before and after peaking on 12 August each year, the date on which the Earth crosses the orbit.

Persephone [persefonee] In Greek mythology, the daughter of Demeter and Zeus, originally called Kore ('maiden'); known as **Proserpine** in Latin. Hades abducted her and made her queen of the Underworld.

Persepolis [persepolis] The site in the mountains of Iran of the palaces and graves of the Achaemenid rulers of Persia; a world heritage site. It was sacked by Alexander the Great in 331 BC.

Perseus (astronomy) [persyoos] A N hemisphere constellation, in the Milky Way. It includes a double cluster of stars visible to the naked eye.

Perseus (mythology) [persyoos] In Greek mythology, the son of Zeus and Danae. He killed the Gorgon, and used its head to rescue Andromeda and save his mother.

Pershing, John J(oseph), nickname **Black Jack** (1860–1948) US general, born in Laclede, MO. In 1917 he was made commander-in-chief of the US Expeditionary Force in Europe, and later became chief-of-staff of the US army (1921–4).

Pershing missile A medium-range, land-based missile with a nuclear warhead, deployed by the US Army in West Germany from 1983 onwards.

Persia *Iran*

Persian *Iranian languages*

Persian cat A type of long-haired domestic cat; round head and short face; many breeds. The name is still used in the USA for breeds which in Britain are called *long-hairs* (eg *blue Persian = blue long-hair*).

Persian Empire An empire created by the Achaemenids in the second half of the 6th-c BC, extending from NW India to the E Mediterranean. It was overthrown by Alexander the Great in the 330s BC.

Persian Gulf, also **The Gulf**, **Arabian Gulf**, Lat **Sinus Persicus** area 238 800 km²/92 200 sq mi. Arm of the Arabian Sea, connected to it via the Gulf of Oman and the Strait of Hormuz; bounded N by Iran, NW by Iraq and Kuwait, W by Saudi Arabia and Qatar, and S by the United Arab Emirates; length 885 km/550 mi; maximum width 322 km/200 mi; average depth 100 m/325 ft; important source of oil; scene of great tension during the Iran–Iraq War (1980s) and the Gulf War; suffered major oil pollution during the Gulf War (Feb 1991).

Persian Wars The name given to the two punitive expeditions launched by the Persian kings, Darius I and Xerxes, against Greece in 490 and 480–479 BC. The first ended in catastrophe for the Persians at Marathon; the second ended in the twin defeats for the Persians at Plataea and Mycale.

persimmon [persimon] Any of several species of ebony, widely cultivated for their fleshy berries, which are edible but very astringent until fully ripe; also called **date plums**. (Family: Ebonaceae.)

personal computer (PC) A term used to describe microcomputers in general, and also used by the firm of IBM in its range of microcomputers.

personal electronic organizer A hand-held electronic device which typically functions as a filing and indexing system for personal information, such as would be found in an address book, diary, or task list. It usually has a small screen for displaying the information, and keys for entering alphanumeric characters, although some devices use a pointer or pen-like device.

perspective In art, any method whereby the illusion of depth is achieved on a flat surface. Most methods are based on the fact that objects appear smaller in proportion to their distance from the beholder, and that receding parallel lines appear to meet on the horizon at what is called the *vanishing point*. The Greeks developed scientific perspective as a by-product of their interest in optics and geometry perspective.

Perspex The proprietary name for a flat sheet form of polymethylmethacrylate resin, of notably high transparency.

perspiration *sweat*

Perth (Australia) 31°58S 115°49E, pop (2000e) 1 263 000. State capital of Western Australia, near the mouth of the Swan R; the commercial, cultural, and transportation centre on the W coast; founded, 1829; city status, 1856; rapid development after the discovery of gold, 1897; fourth largest city in Australia; airport; railway; four universities (1911, 1975, 1987, 1990); two cathedrals; gold and diamond mining; tourism; scene of the Commonwealth and Empire Games, 1962.

Perth (Scotland) 56°24N 3°28W, pop (2000e) 42 900. Administrative centre of Perth and Kinross council, E Scotland; on R Tay; scene of assassination of James I, 1437; railway; castle.

perturbation In astronomy, any small deviation in the equilibrium motion of a celestial object caused by a change in the gravitational field acting on it. Perturbations in the orbit of Uranus led directly to the discovery of Neptune in 1846.

perturbation theory A mathematical technique frequently used to obtain approximate solutions to equations describing physical systems that are too complicated to solve exactly. The problem is rewritten in two portions: one which can be solved exactly, and a smaller part (the **perturbation**) which allows the calculation of corrections to the first answer.

pertussis *whooping cough*

Peru *p.718*

Perugia [payroojia] 43°07N 12°23E, pop (2000e) 145 000. Town in Umbria, Italy; founded by Etruscans; taken by Romans, 295 BC; archbishopric; railway; university (1276); cathedral (15th-c).

Perugino [perujeenoh] (Ital 'the Perugian'), originally **Pietro di Cristoforo Vannucci** (c.1445–1523) Italian painter, born in Città della Pieve, Italy. He painted several frescoes in the Sistine Chapel at Rome, notably 'The Giving of the Keys to St Peter' (1489).

Pesach *Passover*

Peshawar [peshahwa(r)] 34°01N 71°40E, pop (2000e) 907 000. Capital of North-West Frontier province, Pakistan; city of the Pathan people; under Sikh rule, early 19th-c; occupied by the British, 1849; airfield; railway; university (1950); major trade centre on the Afghan frontier.

Pestalozzi, Johann Heinrich [pestalotsee] (1746–1827) Educationalist, a pioneer of mass education for poor children, born in Zürich, Switzerland. His method sees the process of education as a gradual unfolding, prompted by observation, of the child's innate faculties. *Pestalozzi International Children's Villages* have been established at Trogen, Switzerland (1946) and Sedlescombe, Surrey, UK (1958).

pesticide Any substance used to kill insects, rodents, weeds, fungi, or other living things which are harmful to plants, animals, or foodstuffs.

Pétain, (Henri) Philippe (Omer) [paytĩ] (1856–1951) French soldier and statesman, born in Cauchy-à-la-Tour, France. When France collapsed in 1940, he negotiated the armistice with Germany and Italy, and became chief-of-state, establishing his government at Vichy. After the liberation, he was tried in the French courts for collaboration with Germany, his death sentence for treason being commuted to life imprisonment. His role remains controversial, and some still regard him as a patriot rather than a traitor.

petal One of the second whorl of flower parts, collectively termed the *corolla*. It is usually large and brightly coloured to attract pollinators.

Peter I (of Russia), known as **the Great** (1672–1725) Tsar of Russia (1682–1721) and emperor (1721–5), born in Moscow. He embarked on a series of sweeping military, fiscal, administrative, educational, cultural, and ecclesiastical reforms, many of them based on W European models. He fought major wars with the Ottoman Empire, Persia, and in particular Sweden, which Russia defeated in the Great Northern War (1700–21). This victory

Peru

Equator
COLOMBIA
ECUADOR
Putumayo
Napo
Tumbes
Iquitos
Solimões
Talara
Marañón
Juruá
Chiclayo • Cajamarca
P E R U
BRAZIL
Trujillo
Ucayali
Mt Huascarán
6768m
PACIFIC
OCEAN
Callao ■ Lima
Macchu Picchu
Ayacucho • Cuzco
Ica
Nazca
Lake
Titicaca
Puno
SOUTH
AMERICA
Arequipa
Mollendo
Tacna
CHILE

600 km
300 mi

□ International Airport   ∴ World heritage site

official name **Republic of Peru**, Span **República del Peru**

Local name Perú

Timezone GMT -5

Area 1 284 640 km²/495 871 sq mi

Population total (2005e) 27 925 000

Status Republic

Date of independence 1821

Capital Lima

Languages Spanish and Quechua (official), Aymará also spoken

Ethnic groups South American Indian (45%), Mestizo (mixed Indian and European) (37%), white (15%), black, Japanese, and Chinese (3%)

Religions Roman Catholic (90%), Anglican, Methodist, Peruvian Baha'i minorities

Physical features Arid plains and foothills on the coast, with areas of desert and fertile river valleys; Central Sierra, average altitude 3000 m/10 000 ft, contains 50% of the population; highest peak, Mt Huascarán, 6768 m/22 204 ft, in W; forested Andes and Amazon basin (E), with major rivers flowing to the Amazon.

Climate Mild temperatures all year on coast; dry, arid desert in the S; typically wet, tropical climate in Amazon basin; average annual temperatures 23°C (Jan), 17°C (Jul) in Lima; average annual rainfall 48 mm/1.9 in.

Currency 1 New Sol (PEN) = 100 céntimos

Economy One of the world's leading producers of silver, zinc, lead, copper, gold, iron ore; 80% of Peru's oil extracted from the Amazon forest; cotton, potatoes, sugar, olives; tourism, especially to ancient sites.

GDP (2004e) $155.3 bn, per capita $5600

Human Development Index (2002) 0.747

History Highly developed Inca civilization; arrival of Spanish, 1531; Vice-royalty of Peru established; independence declared, 1821; frequent border disputes in 19th-c (eg War of the Pacific, 1879–83); several military coups; terrorist activities by Maoist guerrillas; bicameral Congress consists of a Senate and a National Chamber of Deputies; an elected President appoints a Council of Ministers.

Head of State
1985–90 Alan García Pérez
1990–2000 Alberto Keinya Fujimori
2000–1 Valentin Paniagua Corazao *Interim*
2001–6 Alejandro Toledo
2006– Alan García Pérez

Head of Government
1999 Victor Joy Way
1999–2000 Alberto Bustamante Belaúnde
2000 Frederico Salas Guevara
2000–1 Javier Pérez de Cuellar *Transitional*
2001–2 Roberto Danino
2002–3 Luis Maria Solari de la Fuente
2003 Beatriz Merino
2003–5 Carlos Ferrero Costa
2005–6 Pedro Pablo Kuczynski
2006– Jorge del Castillo Gálvez

established Russia as a major European power, and gained a maritime exit on the Baltic coast, where Peter founded his new capital, St Petersburg (1703).

Peter, St, originally **Simon** or **Simeon bar Jona** ('son of Jona') (1st-c) One of the 12 apostles of Jesus, a fisherman living in Capernaum, who was renamed by Jesus as **Cephas** or Peter (meaning 'rock') in view of his leadership among the disciples. Immediately after Jesus's ascension, Peter appears as the leader of the Christian community in Jerusalem. Tradition says that he was executed with his head downward in Rome (c.64), and he is regarded by the Roman Catholic Church as the first Bishop of Rome. Two New Testament letters bear his name, but the authenticity of both is often disputed. Feast day 29 June.

Peter the Hermit (c.1050–c.1115) Monk, a preacher of the first Crusade, born in Amiens, France. He led the second army, which reached Asia Minor, but was defeated by the Turks at Nicaea. He then accompanied the fifth army in 1096, which reached Jerusalem.

Peter and Paul Fortress A stronghold founded in 1703 by Peter the Great on a small island in the Neva R delta, and around which the city of St Petersburg sprang up. It has been a museum since 1922.

Peter Lombard *Lombard, Peter*

Peterloo Massacre (1819) The name given to the forcible break-up of a mass meeting about parliamentary reform held at St Peter's Fields, Manchester. The Manchester Yeomanry charged into the crowd, killing eleven people. 'Peterloo' was a pun on the Waterloo victory of 1815.

Peterson, Oscar (Emmanuel) (1925–) Jazz pianist, born in Montreal, Quebec, Canada. In 1949 he became an international star when he joined a concert tour called 'Jazz at the Philharmonic' in New York. He is especially known for his extraordinary keyboard facility, and has probably recorded more than any other jazz musician.

Petipa, Marius [peteepa] (1818–1910) Dancer, ballet master, and choreographer, born in Marseille, France. He went to St Petersburg in 1847 to join the Imperial Ballet, and as ballet master created 46 original ballets, the most famous being *The Sleeping Beauty* (1890) and *Swan Lake* (1895).

Petit, Roland [puhtee] (1924–) Choreographer and dancer, born in Paris. In 1948 he founded Les Ballets de Paris de Roland Petit, and in 1972 the Ballet de Marseille.

petit mal [petee mal] *epilepsy*

petit pois [petee pwah] *pea*

Petra [petra], Arabic **Wadi Musa** 30°20N 35°26E. Ancient rock-cut city in SW Jordan; capital of the Nabataean Arabs until their conquest by Rome in the early 2nd-c AD; a world heritage site.

Petrarch [petrah(r)k], in full **Francesco Petrarca** (1304–74) Poet and scholar, born in Arezzo, Italy. In 1327 at Avignon he first saw Laura, who inspired him with a passion which has become proverbial for its constancy and purity. The earliest of the great Renaissance humanists, he wrote widely on the classics, but he is best known for the series of love poems addressed to Laura, the *Canzoniere*. His writing proved to be a major influence on many authors, notably Chaucer.

petrel A seabird of the order Procellariiformes (tubenoses): small species called *petrels*; larger species called *albatrosses*. They include fulmars, prions, shearwaters, gadfly petrels (all from the family Procellariidae), storm petrels (*Hydrobatidae*), and diving petrels (*Pelecanoididae*).

Petrie, Sir (William Matthew) Flinders [peetree] (1853–1942) Archaeologist and Egyptologist, born in Charlton, Kent. He surveyed Stonehenge (1874–7), but turned from 1881 entirely to Egyptology, beginning by surveying the pyramids and temples of Giza, and excavating the mounds of Tanis and Naucratis.

petrified forest The results of a fossilizing process in which wood is gradually replaced by silica, through the infiltration of mineral-rich water. The fine structural detail may be perfectly preserved during the process, as in the Petrified Forest National Park in Arizona, USA.

petrochemicals Organic chemicals made from products of the petroleum industry or from natural gas. Simple chemical reactions on distillates provide materials for conversion to plastics, fibres, detergents, etc.

petrogenesis; petrography *petrology*

petrol (UK) or **gasoline** (US) A liquid fuel for use in those internal combustion engines in which the fuel–air mixture is ignited by a spark. It consists of a mixture of many volatile hydrocarbons derived from petroleum. It normally contains additives such as lead compounds (to improve performance) or rust inhibitors. In the 1980s, environmental concern led to a rapid increase in the use of unleaded petrol, but criticisms of reduced performance led to the development of a *super-unleaded* petrol, with the addition of benzene and other compounds. Debate continues over the environmental impact of these additives.

petroleum Crude oil, probably of biological origin, occurring as accumulations under impervious rock. Normally liquid, it ranges from being light and mobile to very viscous, and is often associated with gas or water. Its main constituents are a variety of hydrocarbons.

petrology The study of rocks: their composition, mineralogy, mode of occurrence, and origin. **Petrography** is concerned with the textural and mineralogical description of rocks, often studied by optical microscopy of thin slices, while **petrogenesis** is concerned with their origin.

Petronas Twin Towers Between 1998 and 2004, the tallest building in the world (each tower is 451·9 m/1483 ft), completed in Kuala Lumpur in 1996. It has 88 storeys, and was designed by Cesar Pelli and Associates. Taipei 101, Taiwan, is higher (509 m/1670 ft).

petunia A bushy, free-flowering annual (*Petunia × hybrida*) native to South America, with large, funnel-shaped flowers. It is a popular garden plant grown for its brightly coloured, often striped flowers. (Family: Solanaceae.)

Peul *Fulani*

Pevsner, Antoine (1886–1962) Sculptor, born in Oryol, Russia. In Moscow he helped to form the Suprematist group, but in 1920 broke away to issue the *Realist Manifesto* with his brother, Naum Gabo. Exiled from Russia, he migrated to Paris.

Pevsner, Sir Nikolaus (Bernhard Leon) (1902–83) Art historian, born in Leipzig, Germany, an authority on English architecture. His best-known works are *An Outline of European Architecture* (1942), and the 50-volume Penguin series, *The Buildings of England* (1951–74).

pewit *peewit*

pewter A grey alloy consisting mainly of tin with other constituents, such as antimony. It is traditionally used in candlesticks, drinking vessels, and other utensils.

peyote or **peyot** [payohtee] A small cactus (*Lophophora williamsii*) native to Mexico and Texas; also called **mescal button**. It was used by American Indians to produce a drug containing the hallucinogen *mescalin*, used in religious rites. (Family: Cactaceae.)

Pfeiffer, Michelle [fiyfer] (1958–) Film actress, born in Santa Ana, CA. She played several film and television roles before gaining recognition in *The Witches of Eastwick* (1987) and *Dangerous Liaisons* (1988). Other films include *Frankie and Johnny* (1991), *Batman Returns* (1992), *Up Close and Personal* (1996), *What Lies Beneath* (2000), and *I Could Never Be Your Woman* (2007).

pH A measure of the acidity of a solution; it is approximately the negative of the common logarithm of the concentration of hydrogen ions in a solution. It varies between 0 (strongly acidic) and 14 (strongly basic). A neutral solution has pH = 7.

Phaeophyceae [feeohfiysee-ee] The class of seaweeds comprising the brown algae; also known as the Phaeophyta.

Phaethon [fayithohn] or **Phaeton** [fayiton, fayton] In Greek mythology, the son of Helios the sun-god and Clymene. He asked to drive the chariot of the Sun, but swung it too near the Earth, so Zeus destroyed him with a thunderbolt.

phagocyte [fagosiyt] Any cell which engulfs and usually digests particles, micro-organisms (bacteria), or harmful cells. Many unicellular animals are phagocytic. In most multicellular animals, phagocytes fulfil a protective and cleansing role.

phalanger [falanjer] An Australasian nocturnal marsupial; thick fur, small ears, large forward-facing eyes, long grasping tail; inhabits trees; also known as **cuscus**. (Genus: *Phalanger*, 10 species. Family: Phalangeridae.)

phalarope [falerohp] A sandpiper of the genus *Phalaropus* (3 species); widespread; breeds in N hemisphere, winters in S tropics; adapted for swimming.

Phanerozoic time [fanerozohik] A geological term used to describe the period of c.590 million years from the end of the Precambrian era to the present.

pharaoh The title applied to the god-kings of ancient Egypt from the New Kingdom (c.1500 BC) onwards. Pharaohs were the chief mediators between their mortal subjects and the gods, and after death were believed to become gods themselves. Best known are Tutankhamun (c.1352 BC), Rameses II (the pharaoh of the Exodus), and Rameses III (the conqueror of the Sea Peoples).

Pharisees [fariseez] An influential minority group within Palestinian Judaism before AD 70, mainly consisting of laymen. They were noted for their punctilious observance of written and oral laws regarding ritual purity, cleansings, and food laws. In the New Testament Gospels, they are often portrayed as the opponents of Jesus.

pharmacology A branch of medical science which studies the actions, uses, and undesirable side-effects of drugs. The first descriptions of remedies from plant sources were made by the ancient Greeks and Chinese. Dioscorides' *De materia medica* (AD c.60) was the first basic Western pharmacopoeia. The subject became a scientific discipline in the 19th-c.

pharmacopoeia [fah(r)makopeea] A book of standards for drugs, advising on identity, purity, and identification. In most countries there is an official pharmacopoeia, and any dispensed drug must comply with its standards.

pharmacy Originally the science of preparing, compounding, and dispensing medicines. Since more potent drugs have become available (mid-1940s), the scope of pharmacy has become increasingly concerned with more clinical functions, such as the checking of doses and drug interactions.

Pharos of Alexandria [fairos] A marble watch tower and lighthouse on the island of Pharos in the harbour of Alexandria, built by Ptolemy II (285–246 BC). It was the first of its kind.

pharyngitis [farinjiytis] A sore throat; one of the commonest medical complaints, usually the result of bacterial or viral infection of the lining tissues of the pharynx.

pharynx A space formed by mucous membrane-covered muscle situated behind and communicating with the nose, mouth, and larynx. The upper areas contain accumulations of lymphoid tissue (the tonsils) which, it is thought, help to guard against airborn infection.

phase In wave motion, the fraction of a wave cycle completed by a time variable, where one complete cycle corresponds to 2π radians; alternatively, an argument of a function describing a wave. The phase difference, ϕ radians, represents the degree to which one wave leads or lags behind another; for $\phi = 0$ or 2π, the waves are in phase; for $\phi = \pi$, the waves are antiphase.

phases of matter The three possible states of matter: solid, liquid, and gas. The phase of a particular substance depends on temperature and pressure. A change from one phase to another, as in boiling or melting, is called a **phase transition**.

Phasmida [fazmida] An order of large insects with either elongate bodies and limbs (stick insects) or flattened, leaf-like bodies and limbs (leaf insects); length up to 30 cm/1 ft; c.2500 species, all of which are foliage feeders, mostly tropical or subtropical in distribution.

pheasant A large, plump, ground-feeding bird, native to Africa (1 species) and Asia; short wings and fast, low flight; male brightly coloured with long tail; many species bred for sport. (Family: Phasianidae, 48 species.)

Pheloung, Barrington (1954–) Composer and conductor, born in Sydney, New South Wales, Australia. He became principal conductor to the London Contemporary Dance Theatre (1979–90) and has also composed for ballet, dance, and theatre. His work for TV includes *Inspector Morse* (1986) and *Dalziel and Pascoe* (1995), and among his film scores are *Truly, Madly, Deeply* (1990), *Hilary and Jackie* (1998), and *Shopgirl* (2006).

Phelps, Edmund Strother (1933–) Economist, born in Evanston, IL. He studied at Amherst College (1951–5) and Yale (1959), and in 1961 took up a research position at the Cowles Foundation, where his work focused on neo-classical growth theory. In 1966 he joined the University of Pennsylvania and then Columbia University (1971), where he has been professor of political economy since 1982. He was awarded the Nobel Prize for Economics in 2006 for his analysis of intertemporal trade-offs in macroeconomic policy.

Phelps, Michael (1985–) Swimmer, born in Baltimore, MD. He made his mark at the 2001 World Championships where he won the 200 m butterfly in record time. He competed at the 2003 World Championships in Barcelona where he won three gold medals and set new record times in the 200 m butterfly, 200 m individual medley, and the 400 m individual medley. At the 2004 Olympic Games in Athens, he won gold medals in the butterfly (100 m and 200 m), and the individual medley (200 m and 400 m), setting a new record for the 400 m event. At the

2005 World Championships in Montreal his gold medals in the 200 m freestyle and 200 m individual medley brought his individual world titles to six. He bettered his own world records in the 200 m butterfly (1:53.80) and 200 m individual medley (1:55.84) at the 2006 World Championships in British Columbia.

phenanthrene [fenanthreen] $C_{14}H_{10}$, melting point 101°C. A crystalline solid, an aromatic hydrocarbon containing three fused benzene rings. It occurs in coal tar, and is suspected of being carcinogenic.

phencyclidine *angel dust*

phenobarbitone *barbiturates*

phenol [feenol, fenohl] C_6H_5OH, IUPAC **hydroxybenzene**, also called **carbolic acid**, used as an antiseptic where its corrosive properties are not a problem. A major constituent of coal tar, it is also synthesized in large quantities, as it has applications in the manufacture of fibres, resins, dyes, drugs, and explosives.

phenology [fenolojee] The branch of biology which studies the timing of natural phenomena. Examples include seasonal variations in vegetation, and their relationship with weather and climate.

phenomenalism In philosophy, the theory that statements about physical objects are in the end equivalent to statements about factual or possible perceptual experiences.

phenomenology A philosophical movement begun by Husserl, in its broadest sense it is a descriptive philosophy of experience. Its central method is to describe carefully one's conscious processes, concentrating on subjective experiences and suspending all beliefs and assumptions about their 'external' existence and causation. The result is supposed to be a nonempirical, intuitive enquiry into the real essences or meanings that are common to different minds.

phenothiazines [feenohthiyazeenz] A class of drugs introduced in the 1950s and used in the treatment of psychiatric disorders such as schizophrenia and mania.

phenyl [feeniyl, fenil] $C_6H_5–$. A group derived by the removal of one hydrogen atom from a benzene ring.

phenylamine *aniline*

phenylketonuria [fenilkeetonyooria] A rare inherited disorder due to a defect in the metabolism of phenylalanine (an amino acid contained in protein). Phenylalanine accumulates in the body, and may cause mental deficiency.

phenylmethanal *benzaldehyde*

phenylmethyl *benzyl*

pheromone [feromohn] A chemical substance secreted to the outside by an animal, which has a specific effect on another member of the same species, such as mating or aggression. Pheromones are common in insects, and are also found in rodents and monkeys.

Phidias [fiydias] (5th-c BC) Sculptor, born in Athens. He constructed the Propylaea and the Parthenon, carving the gold and ivory Athena there and the Zeus at Olympia.

Philadelphia 39°57N 75°10W, pop (2000e) 1 517 500. Major deepwater port in SE Pennsylvania, USA, at the confluence of the Schuylkill and Delaware Rivers; noted centre for culture, education, and medical research; fifth largest city in the USA; first settled by Swedes in the 1640s; birthplace of the nation, where the Declaration of Independence was signed, 1776; Constitutional Convention met here, 1787; US capital, 1790–1800; heavily involved in the anti-slavery movement and the Civil War; airport; railway; four universities (1740, 1851, 1884, 1891); service economy supplanting the dwindling manufacturing industry; naval dockyard; professional teams, Phillies (baseball), 76ers (basketball), Eagles (football), Flyers (ice hockey); Liberty Bell (Independence Hall).

philadelphus [filadelfuhs] *mock orange*

philately filatelee] The collecting and study of stamps and related matter, popularly known as **stamp collecting**. The

Philippines

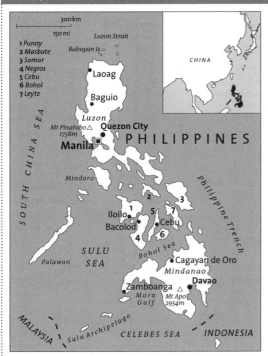

1 Punay
2 Masbate
3 Samar
4 Negros
5 Cebu
6 Bohol
7 Leyte

□ International Airport

[filipeenz], official name **Republic of the Philippines**, Pilipino **Republika ng Pilipinas**

Local name Filipinas

Timezone GMT +8

Area 299 679 km²/115 676 sq mi

Population total (2002e) 79 999 000

Status Republic

Date of independence 1946

Capital Manila

Languages Tagalog (Pilipino), and English (official), over 87 local languages, including Cebuano, Ilocano, Bicol, and Samar-Leyte

Ethnic groups Filipino, with Chinese, Spanish, and American minorities

Religions Roman Catholic (83%), Protestant (9%), Muslim (5%), Buddhist (3%)

Physical features An archipelago of more than 7100 islands and islets, NE of Borneo; largest island, Luzon 108 172 km²/41 754 sq mi; Mindanao, 94 227 km²/36 372 sq mi, has active volcano Apo, 2954 m/9690 ft, and mountainous rainforest; Mount Pinatubo volcano, 1758 m/5770 ft, situated 90 km/56 mi NW of Manila; largely mountainous islands.

Climate Tropical, maritime; warm and humid throughout year; average annual temperature 25°C (Jan), 28°C (Jul) in Manila; average annual rainfall 2083 mm/82 in; frequent typhoons and occasional earth tremors and tsunamis (tidal waves); 1000+ deaths from Typhoon Nanmadol, Dec 2004.

Currency 1 Philippine Peso (PHP) = 100 centavos

Economy Farming (employs c.50% of workforce); rice, pineapples, mangos, vegetables, livestock, sugar, tobacco, rubber, coffee; oil, copper, gold; textiles; vehicles; tourism.

GDP (2002e) $379.7 bn, per capita $4600

Human Development Index (2002) 0.754

History Claimed for Spain by Magellan, 1521; ceded to the USA after the Spanish-American War, 1898; became a self-governing Commonwealth, 1935; occupied by the Japanese in World War 2; independence, 1946; Communist guerrilla activity in N; Muslim separatist movement in S; martial law following political unrest, 1972–81; exiled political leader Benigno Aquino assassinated on returning to Manila, 1983; coup in 1986 ended the 20-year rule of President Ferdinand Marcos; new constitution, 1987; attempted coup, 1989, with continuing political unrest; eruption of Mount Pinatubo, 1991; governed by a President and a bicameral legislature, comprising a Senate and a House of Representatives.

Head of State/Government

First Republic
1946–8 Manuel A Roxas
1948–53 Elpidio Quirino
1953–7 Ramon Magsaysay
1957–61 Carlos P Garcia
1961–5 Diosdado Macapagal
1965–72 Ferdinand Edralin Marcos

Martial Law
1972–81 Ferdinand Edralin Marcos

Second Republic
1981–6 Ferdinand Edralin Marcos
1986–92 (Maria) Corazon Aquino
1992–8 Fidel Ramos
1998–2001 Joseph Arap Estrada
2001– Gloria Macapagal Arroyo

first stamp-collector is thought to have been John Tomlynson, who started collecting stamps on 7 May 1840, the day after the issue of the world's first postage stamp, the penny black.

Philby, Kim, popular name of **Harold Adrian Russell Philby** (1912–88) Double agent, born in Ambala, India. Already recruited as a Soviet agent, he was employed by the British Secret Intelligence Service (MI6), from 1944–6 as head of anti-communist counter-espionage. In 1963 he disappeared to Russia, where he was granted citizenship.

Philemon and Baucis [fiyleemon, bawsis] An old couple, man and wife, who were the only ones to offer hospitality to the Greek gods Zeus and Hermes when they visited the Earth. They were made priest and priestess, and allowed to die at the same time, when they were changed into trees.

Philemon, Letter to [fiyleemon] The shortest of Paul's letters, usually accepted as genuinely from the apostle to an individual

Christian named Philemon. It probably dates from the late 50s or the early 60s AD.

Philip II (of Macedon) (382–336 BC) King of Macedon (359–336 BC), the father of Alexander the Great. He created a powerful unified state at home (359–353 BC), then made himself master of the whole of independent Greece, with his decisive victory at Chaeronea (338 BC).

Philip II (of Spain) (1527–98) King of Spain (1556–98) and Portugal (as Philip I, 1580–98), born in Valladolid, Spain. Following the death of his first wife, Maria of Portugal, he married Mary I (1554), becoming joint sovereign of England. Before Mary's death (1558) he had inherited the Habsburg possessions in Italy, the Netherlands, Spain, and the New World. To seal the end of Valois–Habsburg conflict, he married Elizabeth of France (1559). As the champion of the Counter-Reformation, he sought to crush Protestantism, first in the Low Countries

An A To Z Of Phobias

Technical term	Everyday term	Technical term	Everyday term	Technical term	Everyday term	Technical term	Everyday term
acero-	sourness	claustro-	closed spaces	hypno-	sleep	ourano-	heaven
achulo-	darkness	cnido-	stings	ideo-	ideas	pan- (panto-)	everything
acro-	heights	cometo-	comets	kakorraphia-	failure	partheno-	girls
aero-	air	crystallo-	crystals	katagelo-	ridicule	patroio-	heredity
agora-	open spaces	cyno-	dogs	keno-	void	penia-	poverty
aichuro-	points	demo-	crowds	kineso-	motion	phasmo-	ghosts
ailouro-	cats	demono-	demons	klepto-	stealing	phobo-	fears
akoustico-	sound	dermato-	skin	kopo-	fatigue	photo-	light
algo-	pain	dike-	justice	kristallo-	ice	pnigero-	smothering
amaka-	carriages	dora-	fur	lalo-	stuttering	poine-	punishment
amatho-	dust	elsoptro-	mirror	linono-	string	poly-	many things
andro-	men	elektro-	electricity	logo-	words	poto-	drink
anemo-	wind	enete-	pins	lysso- (-mania-)	insanity	pterono-	feathers
angino-	narrowness	entomo-	insects	mastigo-	flogging	pyro-	fire
anthropo-	man	eoso-	dawn	mechano-	machinery	rypo-	soiling
antlo-	flood	eremo-	solitude	metallo-	metals	Satano-	Satan
apeiro-	infinity	ergo-	work	meteoro-	meteors	sela-	flash
arachno-	spiders	erythro-	blushing	miso (myso-)-	contamination	sidero-	stars
astheno-	weakness	geno-	sex	mono-	one thing	sito-	food
astra-	astral	geuma- (geumato-)	taste	musico-	music	sperma- (spermato-)	germs
ate-	ruin	grapho-	writing	muso-	mice	stasi-	standing
aulo-	flute	gymno- (gymnoto-)	nudity	necro-	corpses	stygio- (hadeo-)	hell
Auroro-	Northern Lights	gyno-	women	nelo-	glass	syphilo-	syphilis
bacillo-	microbes	hamartio-	sin	neo-	newness	thalasso-	sea
baro-	gravity	hapto-	touch	nepho- (nephelo-)	clouds	thanato-	death
baso-	walking	harpaxo-	robbers	noso- (patho-)	disease	thasso-	sitting
batracho-	amphibians	hedono-	pleasure	ocho-	vehicles	theo-	God
belone-	needles	hemato-	blood	odonto-	teeth	thermo-	heat
bronto- (tonitro-)	thunder	helmintho-	worms	oiko-	home	toxi-	poison
cheima- (cheimato-)	cold	hodo-	travel	olfacto-	smell	tremo-	trembling
chiono-	snow	homichlo-	fog	ommato-	eyes	triskaideka-	thirteen
chrometo- (chremato-)	money	horme-	shock	oneiro-	dreams	xeno-	strangers
chromo-	colour	hydro-	water	ophidio-	snakes	zelo-	jealousy
chrono-	duration	hypegia-	responsibility	ornitho-	birds	zoo-	animals

(from 1568), then in England and France, but his Armada (1588) was destroyed, and he was unable to subdue the Netherlands.

Philip III (of Burgundy), known as **Philip the Good** (1396–1467) Duke of Burgundy (1419–67), born in Dijon, France, the grandson of Philip the Bold. He at first recognized Henry V of England as heir to the French crown, but concluded a separate peace with the French in 1435. He created one of the most powerful states in later mediaeval Europe, and was a committed crusader against the Ottoman Turks.

Philip V (1683–1746) First Bourbon king of Spain (1700–46), born in Versailles, France, the grandson of Louis XIV and Maria Theresa. He gained the throne at the Peace of Utrecht (1713), but lost the Spanish Netherlands and Italian lands.

Philip VI (1293–1350) First Valois king of France (1328–50). His right to the throne was denied by Edward III of England, leading to the Hundred Years' War with England. In 1346 Edward III defeated Philip at Crécy.

Philip, St (1st-c) One of the disciples of Jesus, listed among the 12. Traditions suggest he was martyred on a cross. Feast day 3 May (W) or 14 November (E).

Philip, Prince *Edinburgh, Duke of*

Philippi, Battle of [filipiy] (42 BC) The decisive battle in N Greece in which Antony and Octavian (later the Emperor Augustus) defeated Brutus and Cassius, and thus avenged the murder of Julius Caesar.

Philippians, Letter to the [filipianz] New Testament writing, widely accepted as genuinely from the apostle Paul to a Christian community that he had founded earlier at Philippi in Macedonia.

philippic A denunciation in speech or writing, direct and often abusive. The term derives from Demosthenes' orations (c.350 BC) attacking Philip of Macedon.

Philippines *p.721*

Philistines The ancient warlike inhabitants of the coastal area of the SE Mediterranean between present-day Jaffa and Egypt.

Everyday term	Technical term	Everyday term	Technical term	Everyday term	Technical term	Everyday term	Technical term
air	aero-	feathers	pterono-	meteors	meteoro-	smothering	pnigero-
amphibians	batracho-	fire	pyro-	mice	muso-	snakes	ophidio-
animals	zoo-	flash	sela-	microbes	bacillo-	snow	chiono-
astral	astra-	flogging	mastigo-	mirrors	eisoptro-	soiling	rypo-
birds	ornitho-	flood	antlo-	money	chrometo-	solitude	eremo-
blood	hemato-	flute	aulo-	motion	kineso-	sound	akoustico-
blushing	erythro-	fog	homichlo-	music	musico-	sourness	acero-
carriages	amaka-	food	sito-	narrowness	angino-	spiders	arachno-
cats	ailouro-	fur	dora-	needles	belone-	standing	stasi-
closed spaces	claustro-	germs	sperma- (spermato-)	newness	neo-	stars	sidero-
clouds	nepho- (nephelo-)	ghosts	phasmo-	Northern Lights	Auroro-	stealing	klepto-
cold	cheima- (cheimato-)	girls	partheno-	nudity	gymno- (gymnoto)-	stings	cnido-
colour	chromo-	glass	nelo-	one thing	mono-	strangers	xeno-
comets	cometo-	God	theo-	open spaces	agora-	string	linono-
contamination	miso-, myso-	gravity	baro-	pain	algo-	stuttering	lalo-
corpses	necro-	heat	thermo-	pins	enete-	syphilis	syphilo-
crowds	demo-	heaven	ourano-	pleasure	hedono-	taste	geuma- (geumato-)
crystals	crystallo-	heights	acro-	points	aichuro-	teeth	odonto-
darkness	achulo-	hell	stygio- (hadeo-)	poison	toxi-	thirteen	triskaideka-
dawn	eoso-	heredity	patroio-	poverty	penia-	thunder	bronto- (tonitro-)
death	thanato-	home	oiko-	punishment	poine-	touch	hapto-
demons	demono-	ice	kristallo-	responsibility	hypegia-	travel	hodo-
disease	noso-, patho-	ideas	ideo-	ridicule	katagelo-	trembling	tremo-
dogs	cyno-	infinity	apeiro-	robberies	harpaxo-	vehicles	ocho-
dreams	oneiro-	insanity	lysso- (-mania)	ruin	ate-	void	keno-
drinks	poto-	insects	entomo-	Satan	Satano-	walking	baso-
duration	chrono-	jealousy	zelo-	sea	thalasso-	water	hydro-
dust	amatho-	justice	dike-	sex	geno-	weakness	astheno-
electricity	elektro-	light	photo-	shock	horme-	wind	anemo-
everything	pan- (panto-)	machinery	mechano-	sin	hamartio-	women	gyno-
eyes	ommato-	man	anthropo-	sitting	thasso-	words	logo-
failure	kakorraphia-	many things	poly-	skin	dermato-	work	ergo-
fatigue	kopo-	men	andro-	sleep	hypno-	worms	helmintho-
fears	phobo-	metals	metallo-	smell	olfacto-	writing	grapho-

They were constantly at odds with the Israelites of the hinterland.

Phillip, Arthur (1738–1814) Admiral, founder and first governor of New South Wales, born in London. He joined the merchant navy at 16, and the Royal Navy at 23, saw service in the Mediterranean, and was at the taking of Havana. In 1787 he was appointed commander of the 'First Fleet' carrying convicts to Australia, and founded a penal colony settlement at Sydney in 1788. The site and foundations of his Government House still exist in Bridge Street, Sydney, the oldest piece of colonial heritage in the country.

Phillips, William D (1948–) Physicist, born in Wilkes-Barre, PA. He graduated in 1976 from MIT, joining the National Institute of Standards and Technology in Gaithersburg, MD. In 1997 he shared the Nobel Prize for Physics for his contribution to the development of methods to cool and trap atoms with laser light.

Philoctetes [filokteeteez] A Greek hero, the son of Poeas, who inherited the bow of Heracles and its poisoned arrows. It was prophesied that only with the arrows of Heracles could Troy be taken. He entered the battle, killing Paris.

philodendron [filodendron] An evergreen plant native to warm regions of the New World; many species are popular house plants. (Genus: *Philodendron*, 275 species. Family: Araceae.)

Philo Judaeus [fiyloh judayus] (c.20 BC–c.AD 40) Hellenistic Jewish philosopher, born in Alexandria. His work brought together Greek philosophy and the Hebrew scriptures.

Philomela and Procne [filuhmeela, proknee], or **Philomel, Progne** In Greek mythology, the daughters of Pandion, King of Athens. Procne married Tereus, King of Thrace, who raped Philomela and removed her tongue; but she was able to tell Procne by a message in her embroidery.

Philosophes [filozof] The leaders of the French Enlightenment – political commentators, writers, and propagandists. Their great collective work was the *Encyclopédie* (1751–80).

philosophy Literally the love of wisdom, a subject which deals with some of the most general questions about the universe and our place in it. Philosophy differs from science, in that its questions cannot be answered empirically, by observation or experiment; and from religion, in that its purpose is entirely intellectual, and allows no role for faith or revelation. Philosophy tends to proceed by an informal but rigorous process of conceptual analysis and reasoning. The major branches are *metaphysics*, the inquiry into the most general features, relations, and processes of reality; *epistemology*, the investigation of the possibility, types, and sources of knowledge; *ethics*, the study of the types, sources, and justification of moral values and principles; and *logic*, the analysis of correct and incorrect reasoning. Philosophical issues can arise concerning other areas of inquiry, for example, in art, law, religion, and science.

philosophy of science A branch of philosophy, often approached through the history of science, which studies the nature of scientific theories, explanations, and descriptions, and relates them to general philosophical issues in epistemology, logic, or metaphysics.

Phiz *Browne, Hablot Knight*

phlebitis [flebiytis] Inflammation of a vein, commonly associated with varicose veins. It often arises in association with thrombosis of the blood within veins, when it is referred to as **thrombophlebitis**. The most important complication is embolism, especially to the lung.

phloem [flohem] Tissue which transports sap from the leaves to other parts of a plant. It is either located in the vascular bundles or forms the inner bark of woody plants.

phlogiston theory [flojistn] A theory, popular in the 18th-c, whereby a material undergoing combustion was held to lose a substance (*phlogiston*) to the atmosphere. The theory became increasingly untenable as it became clear that the products of combustion always weigh more than the material burnt.

phlox A mat-forming or erect annual or perennial, almost exclusively native to North America and Mexico; flowers tubular with five notched lobes, often white, pink, or blue, sometimes fragrant, in dense terminal heads. (Genus: *Phlox*, 67 species. Family: Polemoniaceae.)

Phnom Penh [(p)nom pen] 11°35N 104°55E, pop (2000e) 1 122 000. River port capital of Cambodia, at the confluence of Mekong R and Tonlé Sap (lake); founded by the Khmers, 1371; capital, 1434; under Japanese occupation in World War 2; railway; several universities; current population uncertain, because of continuing refugee problem.

phobia A reaction of extreme fear to an object or situation not ordinarily considered dangerous. Avoidance behaviour may occur. The major forms of phobia are **simple phobia** (in which people are afraid of a specific object or situation) and **social phobia** (in which they are concerned about their behaviour in front of others). *pp.722–3*

Phobos [fohbos] The larger of the two natural satellites of Mars, discovered in 1877; distance from the planet 937 800 km/582 700 mi; diameter 27 km/17 mi; orbital period 7 h 39 min.

Phocis [fohkis] The region in C Greece to the W of Boeotia, in which Delphi was situated.

Phoebe (astronomy) [feebee] The ninth natural satellite of Saturn, discovered in 1898; distance from the planet 12 950 000 km/8 047 000 mi; diameter 220 km/137 mi; orbital period 550·5 days.

Phoebe (mythology) [feebee] In Greek mythology, a Titaness, identified with the Moon. Later she was confused with Artemis.

Phoenicia [fuhneesha] The narrow strip in the E Mediterranean between the mountains of Lebanon and the sea, where the cities of Arad, Byblos, Sidon, and Tyre were located. It derived its name from the Phoenicians, who dominated the area from the end of the second millennium BC. From here came their most important contribution to Western culture – the alphabet.

Phoenix, Joaquin (Rafael), also known as **Leaf Phoenix** (1974–) Film actor, born in San Juan, Puerto Rico. He travelled with his family in South America before settling in Los Angeles. He made his feature film debut in *Space Camp* (1986), and success came with *To Die For* (1995). Later films include *Return to Paradise* (1998), *Gladiator* (2000), and *Hotel Rwanda* (2004). In 2005 he received an Oscar nomination for his role as Johnny Cash in the biopic *Walk the Line*.

Phoenix, River (1970–93) Film actor, born in Madras, OR. He made his film debut in *Explorers* (1985), and received a Best Actor Oscar nomination for his role in *Running on Empty* (1988). Later films included *Indiana Jones and the Last Crusade* (1989) and *Love You To Death* (1990). His early death was due to a drugs overdose.

Phoenix (USA) [feeniks] 33°27N 112°04W, pop (2000e) 1 321 000. State capital in SC Arizona, USA, on the Salt R; largest city in the state; settled, 1870; state capital, 1889; airport; railway; hub of the rich Salt River Valley; important centre for data-processing and electronics research; popular winter and health resort; professional teams, Suns (basketball), Cardinals (football).

Phoenix (astronomy) [feeniks] A S hemisphere constellation.

phoenix / phenix (mythology) [feeniks] A legendary bird, which lives a long time. It kills itself on a funeral pyre, but is then reborn from the ashes. The idea of resurrection appealed to Christian allegorists.

Phoenix Park murders The murder in Dublin on 6 May 1882 of the recently appointed chief secretary for Ireland, Lord Frederick Cavendish (1836–82), and his under-secretary, Thomas Henry Burke (1829–82), by a terrorist nationalist group called 'The Invincibles'. Five of the murderers were arrested and hanged.

phoneme The smallest unit in the sound system of a language, capable of signalling a difference of meaning between words. For example, the English words *pail* and *tail* are distinguished by the initial consonant phonemes /p/ and /t/. The number of phonemes in a language varies greatly, from less than a dozen to well over 80.

phonetics The study of the range of sounds which can be produced by the human vocal organs. *Articulatory phonetics* studies the movements of the vocal organs (such as the tongue, lips, and larynx); *acoustic phonetics*, the physical properties of the sound waves produced in speech; and *auditory phonetics*, the way in which the listener uses ear and brain to decode sound waves.

phonics A general method of teaching children to read by recognizing the relationship between individual letters and sounds. It builds up the pronunciation of new words by saying them sound by sound, as with the one-to-one correspondences between *cat* and [k-a-t].

phonograph The first practical device for recording and reproducing sounds stored as grooves cut in cylinders, mainly of wax, rotated beneath a stylus by hand or clockwork. Demonstrated by Edison in 1877, it came to be widely applied in home musical entertainment during the next half-century.

phonology The study of the sound system of a language, and of the general properties of sound systems. Phonologists study the way the sound segments (or **phonemes**) are organized in languages, and also the patterns of pitch, loudness, and other voice qualities.

phosphates Salts of phosphoric acid. Phosphates occur in various minerals, especially apatite, and are mined for use as fertilizers.

phospholipid A special category of fats, the main component of all biological membranes. Phospholipids also store arachidonic acid.

phosphor *luminescence*

photometry

Photometric Quantities	Symbols	Units	Corresponding Radiometric Quantities
luminous flux		lumen (lm)	radiant power
luminous intensity	I	candela (cd)	radiant intensity
luminance	L	cd/m²	radiance
illuminance	E	lux (lx)	irradiance

phosphorescence Light produced by an object excited by a means other than heat, where the light emission continues after the energy source has been removed; a type of luminescence. An example is the long after-glow on a television screen, after the television has been switched off.

phosphoric acid H_3PO_4. A tribasic acid, with three series of salts. Dehydration gives phosphorus pentoxide (P_2O_5), an excellent drying agent.

phosphorus P, element 15, the second element of the nitrogen group. It is not found free in nature, but may be prepared both as a very reactive, molecular, white form (P_4), melting point 44°C, and as a variety of less reactive, high-melting polymeric solids with colours ranging from red to black. It is found in many minerals, particularly apatite, mainly as calcium phosphate. Phosphorus is essential to life, being required for DNA and RNA. Industrial uses include matches and agricultural fertilizers.

photino *supersymmetry*

photocell *photoelectric cell*

photochemistry The study of chemical reactions brought about by the absorption of visible and ultraviolet light, and of those reactions that produce light. The decomposition or dissociation of molecules by exposure to light is known as **photolysis**.

photoconductivity The increase in conductivity of a material (usually a semiconductor, such as silicon) resulting from the exposure to light. The effect is exploited in light-sensitive detectors and switches, and in television cameras.

photocopying The photographic reproduction of written, printed, or graphic work. In **xerography** an image of the original is focused on to a photosensitive surface (a selenium plate or cylinder), which converts light into electric charge. This electrostatic image attracts charged ink powder, and the image is then transferred to paper or other support, and permanently fixed by heating. The **ozalid process** (also called the **diazo process**) uses paper coated with diazonium compounds. This is exposed to ultraviolet light through a transparent original. Only the diazo in the shadows of the original is developed by ammonia vapour to give a positive print.

photoelectric cell, also known as **photocell** A device sensitive to light which responds to radiation with an electrical effect. It is generally based on a semiconductor (eg selenium, germanium). They are used in light meters (eg in photography), light detectors (eg in burglar alarms), and spacecraft power supplies.

photogrammetry The use of photographic records to determine precise measurements. It is principally applied in map-making by aerial survey, but is also used for medical, forensic, and architectural purposes.

photography The recording and reproduction of images on light-sensitive materials by chemical processes. In 1816 Nicéphore Niepce in France tried to record the optical image formed in a camera obscura, and in 1822 succeeded in obtaining a photographic copy of an engraving superimposed on glass. By 1839 Daguerre had established a reliable process. About the same time in England, Fox Talbot discovered the process of developing and fixing the exposed image as a negative and making a positive print. Scott Archer (1813–57) in 1851 invented the collodion 'wet plate', and dry plates coated with sensitized emulsion were produced commercially in the mid-1870s, followed by celluloid-based film from 1889.

photoluminescence *luminescence*

photolysis *photochemistry*

photomacrography *macro-photography*

photometry The measurement of light and its rate of flow. Photometric quantities are measured using **photometers**. The technique is important in photography and lighting design. *see panel*

photomicrograph A photograph of an object as observed through a microscope. Optical means can provide magnifications up to about × 2000. For an electron microscope, magnifications of × 10⁶ or more can be achieved.

photo-montage An assembly of selected images achieved either by physically mounting cut-out portions of prints on a backing, or by combination printing from several separate negatives in succession. It is widely used in the preparation of advertising display material.

photon The quantum or particle of light. Light and all other electromagnetic radiation comprises a stream of photons, each of which has energy $E = h\nu$, where h is Planck's constant and ν is frequency. Photons have no (rest) mass and are spin 1. In quantum theory they transmit electromagnetic force.

photonic crystal An artificial crystal composed of regularly spaced light-reflecting elements, eg a square lattice of reflecting columns spaced about a micron apart. Light waves entering the side of the lattice are reflected from different columns and interfere, blocking the transmission of light of certain frequencies. Missing columns or missing rows of columns serve to trap light, so photonic crystals can be used to manipulate very fine light beams. Three-dimensional photonic crystals operating in the visible part of the spectrum have been produced, and may provide the means of 'wiring' for optical microcircuits for use in telecommunications applications. A much larger scale photonic crystal blocks the transmission of sound, and has been proposed as a soundproofing technique.

Photorealism A style of modern painting, also called *Hyperrealism* or *Superrealism*. Pictures are meticulously painted in a style of extreme naturalism like a sharply-focused coloured photograph.

photosphere The visible surface of the Sun or a star. About 500 km/300 mi thick, it is the zone from which the light we see actually comes. The temperature is about c.6000 K.

photosynthesis The complex process in which light energy is used to convert water and carbon dioxide into simple carbohydrates. Light-absorbing pigments, notably chlorophyll, are essential to the process, which can be carried out only by green plants and photosynthetic bacteria.

phototherapy Body exposure to cool blue light (420–480 nm), free of ultraviolet light. It is used in the treatment of jaundice occurring in the newborn.

phototypesetter A machine for composing type and creating an image of the composed type on film or paper, ready for exposure to a plate for printing. The individual characters may be stored in the machine either as images on film, or digitally within the machine's computer memory.

photovoltaic effect The production of electrical current by light falling on some material, usually a semiconductor. The effect is the basic mechanism of solar cells.

phreaker A term applied to a hacker who uses hacking expertise to gain entry to telephone company computer systems. The aim is usually to make free telephone calls.

phrenology [frenolojee] The analysis of mind and character by the study of the shape and contours of the skull. It is based on the erroneous belief that this reflects the degree of development of the underlying regions of the brain. It was popular in Europe during the early 19th-c.

Phrygia [frijia] The name of the kingdom in antiquity with which the legendary Midas is associated. At its widest extent around the beginning of the first millennium, it consisted of the C plateau of Asia Minor and its W flank.

phylloxera [filokseera] A dwarf, aphid-like insect that can kill grape vines. (Order: Homoptera. Family: Phylloxeridae.)

phylogeny [fiylojenee] The relationships between groups of animals as determined by their evolutionary history. Groups are linked together on the basis of the recency of common ancestry.

phylum [fiyluhm] In animal classification, one of the major groupings, forming the principal category below *kingdom*, and comprising classes and lower categories. Phyla represent the major types of animals.

physalis [fisalis] A soft-leaved annual or perennial; found almost everywhere; salver-shaped, 5-petalled flowers. (Genus: *Physalis*, 100 species. Family: Solanaceae.)

physical chemistry The study of the dependence of physical properties on chemical composition, and of the physical changes accompanying chemical reactions.

physical fitness The conditioning of the body so that it is able to endure longer and more strenuous periods of aerobic exercise. The capacity of the lungs, heart, and muscles to absorb oxygen, pump it round the body, and use it to generate energy are increased. It is important to health because it is protective against illness.

physics The study of matter and forces, at the most basic level. Physics as a discernible discipline began during the Renaissance, with Copernicus' model of planetary motion and Galileo's mechanics. Astronomy and mechanics continued to dominate the field, with the work of Newton, Kepler, and others. Newton's theories dominated physics for two centuries, and was in part responsible for a philosophy that attempted to explain all phenomena in terms of mechanics. The physicists' view of the world has changed dramatically due to two major developments in the early part of the 20th-c. The first was Einstein's theory of special relativity; the second was the development of quantum theory and atomic theory, made possible by work in thermodynamics, electromagnetism, and the new radiations. It has led to modern solid state physics, as well as atomic, nuclear, and particle physics.

physiology An experimental science concerned with the study of the functions of living things. It includes studies of the processes that go on in cells (eg photosynthesis); of how tissues or organs work; and of how living things respond to their environment.

physiotherapy A process of physical rehabilitation to help restore normal bodily function after injury, surgery, or disease. Treatment varies widely, but includes active and passive exercises, massage, and the application of heat by diathermy.

phytic acid A store of phosphorus present in most cereals and legumes; also called *inositol hexaphosphate*. This acid can bind such minerals as calcium, iron, and zinc, and reduce their bioavailability.

phytogeography The study of the factors responsible for the past and present distribution of plants on the Earth's surface. It is part of the larger discipline of biogeography.

phytoplankton *plankton*

phytosaur [fiytosaw(r)] An extinct reptile with a crocodile-like body; teeth inserted in sockets (*thecodontic*); known from the late Triassic period of North America, Europe, and Asia. (Subclass: Archosauria.)

phytotherapy *herbalism*

pi (π) [piy] In mathematics, the ratio of a circle's circumference to its diameter (3·14159...). Archimedes proved that $223/71 < \pi < 22/7$, ie $3·1408 < \pi < 3·14285$. It is now known to over 10 million decimal places.

Piacenza [pyachentsa], ancient **Placentia** 45°03N 9°41E, pop (2000e) 111 000. City in N Italy, on R Po; railway; cathedral (12th–13th-c); well-preserved circuit of 16th-c walls.

Piaf, Edith [peeaf], popular name of **Edith Giovanna Gassion** (1915–63) Singer and actress, born in Paris. Known as *Piaf* (Parisian argot 'little sparrow'), she is mainly remembered for her songs, such as 'Non, je ne regrette rien'.

Piaget, Jean [pyahzhay] (1896–1980) Psychologist, born in Neuchâtel, Switzerland. He is best known for his research on the development of cognitive functions in children, in such pioneering studies as *La Naissance de l'intelligence chez l'enfant* (1948, The Origins of Intelligence in Children).

piano The most important domestic and recital instrument for over 200 years, first made by Cristofori in Florence in the last years of the 17th-c. The main difference between its mechanism and that of the earlier clavichord is that the hammers (tipped with felt) rebound after they have struck the string, and this made possible the dynamic contrasts from which the instrument derived its full name (**pianoforte** = quiet/loud). The modern piano is fitted with a mechanism operated by two pedals: the left ('soft') pedal makes the tone quieter; the other sustains it after the keys have been released.

pianola A trade name for a type of player piano manufactured by the Aeolian Corporation in the USA.

piapiac [peeapeeak] A crow native to C Africa (*Ptilostomus afer*); black with thick black bill and very long tail. (Family: Corvidae.)

pica [piyka] The consumption of non-food items, including in particular the consumption of soil, known as *geophagia* or *geophagy*. Among humans, geophagy is especially common in W Africa.

Picabia, Francis [pikahbia] (1879–1953) Painter, born in Paris. He was one of the most anarchistic of modern artists, involved in Cubism, Dadaism, and Surrealism. His anti-art productions, often portraying senseless machinery, include many of the cover designs for the American magazine *291*, which he edited.

Picardy [pika(r)dee], Fr **Picardie** pop (2000e) 1 893 000; area 19 399 km²/7488 sq mi. Region and former province of N France; flat landscape, crossed by several rivers (eg Somme, Oise) and canals; scene of heavy fighting during World War 1.

picaresque novel (Span *picaro* 'rogue') A novel which dealt originally with the comic misfortunes of a low-life character; now applied more loosely to the adventures of any character living on his or her wits, and often on the road.

Picasso, Pablo [pikasoh] (1881–1973) Artist, born in Málaga, Spain. He was the dominating figure of early 20th-c art. His 'blue period' (1902–4), a series of striking studies of the poor, gave way to the gay, life-affirming 'pink period' (1904–6), full of harlequins, acrobats, and the incidents of circus life. He then turned to brown, and began to work in sculpture. His break with tradition came with 'Les Demoiselles d'avignon' (1906–7, New York), the first exemplar of analytical Cubism, a movement which he developed with Braque (1909–14). His major creation is 'Guernica' (1937, Madrid), expressing in synthetic Cubism his horror of the bombing of this Basque town during the Civil War. The Museu Picasso was opened in Málaga in 2003.

Piccard, Auguste (Antoine) [peekah(r)] (1884–1962) Physicist, born in Basel, Switzerland. In 1932 he ascended in a balloon 16 940 m/55 563 ft into the stratosphere, and in 1948, explored the ocean depths off W Africa in a bathyscaphe of his own design. His twin brother, **Jean (Felix) Piccard** (1884–1963) also made pioneer balloon ascents.

piccolo A small transverse flute pitched one octave higher than the standard instrument.

Pichincha [peecheencha] 0°10S 78°35W. Andean volcano in NC Ecuador; rises to 4794 m/15 728 ft; last eruption, 1981; site of decisive battle (1822) in fight for independence.

Pickering, William H(ayward) (1910–2004) Rocket scientist, born in Wellington, New Zealand. As director of the Jet Propulsion Laboratory in the USA (1954–76), he oversaw the first orbit of the Earth by a US satellite (1958), the first US soft landings on the Moon, and the first missions to Mars (Mariner IX), Venus, and Mercury (Mariner X).

picketing The action by a trade union in an industrial dispute to try to persuade fellow-workers and others not to go to work, or do business with the company involved in the dispute. Pickets stand outside the gates of the factory or offices, and lobby all who would go in. Trade union legislation in the UK now limits picketing to the place where the picket actually works, and requires that it be carried out peacefully. Picketing was formerly illegal in the USA, but is now allowed under a variety of state regulations.

Pickford, Mary, originally **Gladys Mary Smith** (1893–1979) Actress, born in Toronto, Ontario, Canada. She made her first film in 1913, and quickly gained the title of 'America's sweetheart', playing an innocent heroine in many silent films. She founded United Artists Film Corporation in 1919.

Pico della Mirandola, Giovanni, comte (Count) [peekoh, miran-dola] (1463–94) Renaissance philosopher, born in Mirandola, Italy. He wrote Latin epistles and elegies, a series of Italian sonnets, and a major study of free will.

Pico de Orizaba *Citlaltépetl*

picofarad *farad*

picric acid $C_6H_2(NO_2)_3OH$, 2,4,6-trinitrophenol, melting point 122°C. A yellow solid, made by nitrating phenol. A weak acid, it is a yellow dye and an explosive.

pictography The study of writing systems, which make use of symbols called **pictographs** or **pictograms** – direct, stylized representations of objects in the real world, drawn in outline. Pictographic writing is the oldest form of writing known, and occurs very widely throughout the world; the earliest discovered in Egypt is dated to c.3000 BC.

Pictor (Lat 'easel') A small, inconspicuous S constellation, near the Large Magellanic Cloud.

Picts (Lat *picti* 'painted people') A general term coined by the Romans in the 3rd-c for their barbarian enemies in Britain N of the Antonine Wall. The name derives from the local custom of body tattooing.

piculet *woodpecker*

pidgin A language with a highly simplified grammar and vocabulary, the native language of no one, which develops when people who lack a common language attempt to communicate. Pidgins flourish in areas of trade contact. Some have developed into important systems of communication, such as Tok Pisin in Papua New Guinea.

Piedmont [peedmont], Ital **Piemonte** pop (2000e) 4 334 000; area 25 400 km²/9800 sq mi. Region of N Italy; centre of Italian unification in 19th-c; capital, Turin.

Pied Piper of Hamelin In German legend a 13th-c piper who charmed Hamelin's rats out of the city with his pipe-music. He was refused his fee, and in revenge lured all the children away from the city.

Pierce, Franklin (1804–69) US statesman and 14th President (1853–7), born in Hillsboro, NH. As president he tried unsuccessfully to bridge the widening chasm between the South and the North.

Pierce, Mary [peers] (1975–) French tennis player, born in Montreal, Canada. Her tournament victories include the Australian Open in 1995, the first Frenchwoman to win this title since 1967, and the French Open in 2000. She reached the Masters semifinal in 1993 and the Roland-Garros final in 1994. At the start of

2006 she had a world ranking of number 5 but this had fallen to 79 by 2007.

Piero della Francesca [pyayroh, franchayska] (c.1420–92) Painter, born in Borgo San Sepolcro, Italy. He is known especially for his series of frescoes, 'The Legend of the True Cross' (1452–66), at the church of San Francesco in Arezzo.

Piero di Cosimo [pyairoh di kohzimoh], originally **Piero di Lorenzo** (c.1462–c.1521) Painter, born in Florence, Italy. His later work is largely devoted to mythological scenes, such as 'Death of Procris' (c.1500, National Gallery, London).

Pierre [pyayr] 44°22N 100°21W, pop (2000e) 13 900. Capital of state in C South Dakota, USA, on the Missouri R; founded as a railway terminus, 1880; state capital, 1889; centre of a grain and dairy region.

Pierrot Originally **Pedrolino**, a servant role in the *commedia dell' arte*. Pierrot gained his white face and white floppy costume on the French stage. His childlike manner and his pathos, dumb and solitary, was the creation of the great 19th-c pantomimist Deburau.

pietà [peeuhta] (Ital 'pity') In art, the representation of the dead Christ mourned by angels, apostles, or holy women. A famous example is Michelangelo's marble 'Pietà' (c.1500) in St Peter's, Rome.

Pietermaritzburg [peetermaritzberg] or **Maritzburg** 30°33S 30°24E, pop (2000e) 266 000. City in KwaZulu Natal province, E South Africa; founded by Boers, 1838; capital of former province of Natal; railway; university (1910); centre of rich farming area.

Pietism [piyetizm] Originally, a movement within Lutheranism in the 17th-c and 18th-c stressing good works, Bible study, and holiness in Christian life. It was a reaction against rigid Protestant dogmatism.

piezo-electric effect [piyeetzoh] The appearance of an electric field in some material as a result of the application of stress, as in quartz and bone. The effect is exploited in gas cooker lighters, load sensors, and transducers.

pig A mammal native to woodland in Europe, S Asia, and Africa; an artiodactyl; stout body with short legs and coarse hair; short thin tail; face in front of ears and small eyes very long; snout muscular, flattened, disc-like; male called *boar*, female called *sow*, young called *piglets*; also known as **hog** or **swine**. (Family: Suidae, 9 species.)

pigeon A bird of the widespread family Columbidae (c.255 species); plump with round bill; many domestic breeds.

Piggott, Lester (Keith) (1935–) Jockey, born in Wantage, Oxfordshire. During his career he rode 4493 winners in Britain (1948–85), and was champion jockey 11 times. After retiring, he took up training at Newmarket, but was imprisoned (1987–8) for tax offences. He resumed his career as a jockey in 1990 and retired in 1995.

pig-iron The product of the blast furnace. The molten iron is run into channels which have moulds led off them, fancifully likened to pigs in a litter. This cast-iron has a high proportion of carbon (c.4%) which has to be reduced to under 1% to form steel.

pigweed *amaranth*

pika [peeka, piyka] A mammal of order Lagomorpha, native to C and NE Asia and W North America; resembles a small rabbit, with short legs, short rounded ears, and minute tail; also known as **cony**. (Family: Ochotonidae, 14 species.)

pike Any of the large predatory freshwater fish of the family Esocidae; distinguished by an elongate body with dorsal and anal fins set close to the tail; snout pointed, jaws large; length up to 1·5 m/5 ft; mottled greenish-brown.

pikeperch *zander*

piket *skunk*

pilaster [pilaster] A rectangular pillar that projects only slightly from the wall of a building. In classical architecture it is usually designed according to one of the five orders.

Pilate, Pontius [ponshus], Lat **Pontius Pilatus** (1st-c) Roman appointed by Tiberius in AD c.26 as prefect of Judea, having charge of the state and the occupying military forces. Although based in Caesarea, he also resided in Jerusalem, and is known for his order to execute Jesus of Nazareth at the prompting of the Jewish authorities.

Pilates [pilahteez] An exercise-based system that aims to develop the body's 'centre' in order to create a stable core for all types of movement; named after its deviser, German gymnast Joseph Pilates (1880–1967). Originally referred to as *contrology*, the method tones, stretches, and mobilizes the body through regular sessions, so that the body's structure realigns and a balance is achieved within the muscular-skeletal system.

pilchard Small herring-like surface-living fish (*Sardina pilchardus*) widespread in the E North Atlantic and Mediterranean; length up to 25 cm/10 in; greenish-blue above, underside silver; important commercial fish, usually canned for marketing; also called **sardine**. (Family: Clupeidae.)

piles *haemorrhoids*

Pilgrimage of Grace (Oct 1536–Jan 1537) A major Tudor rebellion in N England directed against the policies and ministers of Henry VIII. It was led by Lord Thomas Darcy (1467–1537), Robert Aske (?–1537), and 'pilgrims' carrying banners of the Five Wounds of Christ. The leaders and over 200 others were executed.

Pilgrims or **Pilgrim Fathers** The English religious dissenters who left to establish Plymouth Colony in America in 1620, after crossing the Atlantic aboard the *Mayflower*. They originally came from Lincolnshire.

Pilgrims' Way A long-distance footpath in Surrey and Kent, S England, opened in 1972. Its name derives from the popular belief that it was used by mediaeval pilgrims travelling from Winchester to Canterbury.

pill *contraception*

Pillars of Hercules The ancient mythological name for the promontories flanking the Strait of Gibraltar: the Rock of Gibraltar and Cueta, N Africa.

pillars of Islam *Islam*

pilotfish Marine fish (*Naucrates ductor*) which derives its name from the behaviour of juveniles that swim alongside ships or larger fish such as sharks; length up to 60 cm/2 ft; greyish-blue on back with banding on sides. (Family: Carangidae.)

pilotis [pilotee, piloteez] Posts or columns used on the ground floor of a building to raise most of the main body to first-floor level, leaving unenclosed space below. They are particularly associated with the work of Le Corbusier.

pilot whale A toothed whale of family Delphinidae; black with bulbous overhanging snout; two species.

Pilsen *Plzeň*

Piłsudski, Józef (Klemens) [pilsudskee] (1867–1935) Polish marshal and statesman, born in Zulow, Poland. He declared Poland's independence in 1918, and served as president until 1922. He returned to power in 1926 by means of a military coup, and established a dictatorship.

Piltdown Man A supposed early fossil man found in 1912 near Piltdown, Sussex, England; named *Eoanthropus* ('Dawn Man'). Later study proved the find a forgery.

pimento *allspice*

pi-meson *pion*

pimpernel A sprawling annual weed (*Anagallis arvensis*); flowers on long slender stalks, five petals. Scarlet and blue pimpernels are different coloured forms of the same plant. (Family: Primulaceae)

PIN [pin] Acronym for **Personal Identification Number**; a unique number allocated to the users of computer-based

equipment which allows the identity of each user to be established. It is often used in modern banking systems.

Pinakothek, Alte [altuh peenakohtek] A museum founded in 1836 in Munich, Germany, housing one of the finest collections of German, Dutch, Flemish, and Spanish paintings. The adjacent **Neue** [noyuh] **Pinakothek** was established in 1853.

Pinang (city) [pinang], or **Penang**, formerly **George Town** 5°26N 100°16E, pop (2000e) 379 000. Capital of Pinang state, W Peninsular Malaysia; named after King George III of Great Britain; Malaysia's chief port; railway.

pinchbeck An alloy of copper and zinc, but with less zinc than in brass. It is named after London watchmaker Christopher Pinchbeck (1670–1732) who used it to simulate gold.

Pinckney, Charles (Cotesworth) (1746–1825) US statesman, born in Charleston, SC. He was Washington's aide-de-camp at the Brandywine and Germantown, and a member of the convention that framed the US constitution (1787).

Pincus, Gregory (Goodwin) (1903–67) Physiologist, born in Woodbine, NJ. Impressed by the work of the birth-control campaigner, Margaret Sanger, he began research into the nature of reproduction. He found that some of the new synthetic hormones controlled fertility effectively, and this led to the development of the contraceptive pill.

Pindar (518–438 BC) The chief lyric poet of Greece, born near Thebes. He became famous as a composer of odes for people in all parts of the Greek world. Only his *Epinikia* (Triumphal Odes) have survived entire.

Pindus Mountains, Gr **Píndhos Oros** Mountain range in WC and NW Greece; length c.500 km/310 mi; highest peak, Smolikas (2633 m/8638 ft).

pine A member of a large genus of evergreen conifers widespread throughout the N hemisphere. The leaves are of three kinds: (1) seedling leaves, narrow, toothed; (2) adult scale leaves, borne on long shoots but soon falling; (3) adult needle leaves in bundles of 2, 3, or 5, according to species, borne on short shoots in the axils of the scale leaves. The cones are woody, at least two years old when ripe. Pines are of great commercial importance, and are planted on a vast scale. The timber is resistant to decay because of a high content of resin, rich in oil of turpentine. (Genus: *Pinus*, 70–100 species. Family: Pinaceae.)

pineal gland [pinial] A small gland of vertebrates situated above the third ventricle of the brain. It synthesizes the hormone *melatonin*, and has an important role in determining seasonal breeding patterns in some mammals.

Pinero, Sir Arthur (Wing) [pinairoh] (1855–1934) Playwright, born in London. He wrote several farces, but is best known for his social dramas, notably *The Second Mrs Tanqueray* (1893).

pink An annual, biennial, or perennial herb, native to the temperate N hemisphere; flowe˙˙ with five petals, pink, also red or white, often scented. The genus includes the well-known carnations and sweet williams of horticulture. (Genus: *Dianthus*, 300 species. Family: Caryophyllaceae.)

Pinkerton, Allan (1819–84) Detective, born in Glasgow. He settled in Illinois, USA (1842) and founded the Pinkerton National Detective Agency (1850). During the Civil War he headed a Federal intelligence network.

pinnate The shape of a leaf divided into several lobes or leaflets arranged in two opposite rows along the stalk. In **bi-pinnate** leaves, the leaflets are themselves pinnate.

Pinochet (Ugarte), Augusto [peenohshay] (1915–2006) Chilean dictator, born in Valparaíso, Chile. He led the military coup overthrowing the Allende government (1973), and in 1980 enacted a constitution giving himself an eight-year presidential term (1981–9). He stood down as president in 1990 following the democratic election of Patricio Aylwin. In October 1998 he became the centre of international attention when he was arrested in London, following a request from Spain for his extradition to stand trial for 'crimes of genocide and terrorism', in which some of the victims had been Spanish nationals. The arrest caused tension between UK and Chile, and civil unrest in Chile between Pinochet supporters and opponents. At the beginning of 2000, Pinochet remained under house arrest in the UK, pending the outcome of legal procedures, but the UK government returned him to Chile on the grounds of ill health. Chile's Supreme Court decided to strip Pinochet of immunity from prosecution, and he was later ordered to stand trial but an appeals court voted in favour of suspending proceedings against him on the grounds that he was mentally unfit to stand, and in 2002 the Chilean Supreme Court ruled that proceedings against him be suspended for good. However, he was later again stripped of immunity from prosecution, thus paving the way for a trial on charges of human rights abuses during his rule. The case was ongoing at the time of his death from a heart attack.

pinochle [peenuhkl] A card game derived from *bézique*. Two packs of 24 cards are used, all cards from 2–8 having been discarded. The object is to win tricks, and to score points according to the cards won.

Pinsent, Sir Matthew (Clive) (1970–) Rower, born in Dorset. In 1990 he teamed up with Steve Redgrave for the coxless pairs. His many honours include eight gold medals in the World Championship Coxless Pairs (1991, 1993–5, 1997–9, 2002) and Olympic gold Coxless Pairs (1992, 1996) and Coxless Fours (2000, 2004). He announced his retirement in 2004. He served as a member of the International Olympic Committee (2002–4), and was knighted in 2005.

pint *litre*

pintail A dabbling duck of the genus *Anas* (3 species): two are native to South America and the Caribbean; one to the N hemisphere (*Anas acuta*). The male has long central tail feathers.

Pinter, Harold (1930–) Playwright, born in London. His first major play, *The Birthday Party* (1957), was badly received, but was revived after the success of *The Caretaker* (1960). Other plays include *The Homecoming* (1965), and *No Man's Land* (1975), and he has written many television and film scripts. His work is highly regarded for the way it uses the unspoken meaning behind inconsequential everyday talk to induce an atmosphere of menace. Later works include the plays *Moonlight* (1993), *Ashes to Ashes* (1996), and *Various Voices* (1998), and the poetry collection 'War' (2004). He received the Nobel Prize for Literature in 2005.

Pintupi A people of Australia's Western Desert. Most now live in or around the communities of YaiYai, Docker River, and Haast's Bluff. Pintupi artists were influential early members of the art school which developed at Papunya in the 1970s.

pinworm *nematode*

pin-yin *Chinese*

pion [piyon] A strongly interacting subatomic particle of the meson family; symbol π; spin zero; also called a **pi-meson**. Charged pions decay to muons and neutrinos; neutral pions decay to gamma rays. Discovered in 1947, pions are carriers of strong nuclear force.

Pioneer programme A series of relatively simple spin-stabilized spacecraft launched by the USA 1958–78. Pioneers 10 and 11 (launched in 1972 and 1973) achieved the first flybys of Jupiter and of Saturn. Pioneer 12 was the first US Venus orbiter, and Pioneer 13 explored Venus's atmosphere (1978).

pipa A Chinese lute with a pear-shaped body, short neck, fretted soundboard, and four silk strings plucked with the fingernails.

pipal *peepul*

pipefish Distinctive fish with a very slender segmented body, small mouth on a tubular snout, and delicate fins; with seahorses and seadragons comprises the family Syngnathidae (11 genera); length up to 60 cm/2 ft, typically much smaller.

Piper, Billie (Paul) (1982–) Pop-singer and actress, born in Swindon, Wiltshire. She studied at the Sylvia Young Theatre School in London, and at age 15 was signed by record company Innocent Records. Her debut single, 'Because We Want To' (1998), made number 1 in the UK charts. She later focused on an acting career and in 2003 starred in BBC TV's drama series *The Canterbury Tales*. She was cast (2005–6) as Rose Tyler, travelling companion to the Doctor in the revived cult BBC television series *Doctor Who*, and later work for television includes *The Ruby and the Smoke* (2006) and *Mansfield Park* (2007).

Piper, John (1903–92) Artist, born in Epsom, Surrey. He is known for his pictures of war damage, and his topographical pictures, notably the watercolours of 'Windsor Castle' commissioned by the Queen in 1941–2. He also created the stained-glass designs in Coventry Cathedral.

Piper Alpha An oil-drilling platform in the North Sea, off the coast of Scotland, which was destroyed by an explosion in July 1988. The disaster killed 167.

pipes of Pan *panpipes*

pipistrelle [pipistrel] A bat of family Vespertilionidae; genus *Pipistrellus* (46 species), found worldwide except South America.

pipit A wagtail of the worldwide genus *Anthus* (34 dull-coloured species), or the more colourful African genera *Tmetothylacus* (1 species) and *Macronyx* (8 species, the 'longclaws').

Piquet, Nelson [peekay], originally **Nelson Souto Maior** (1952–) Motor-racing driver, born in Rio de Janeiro, Brazil. He was world champion in 1981, 1983 (both Brabham), and 1987 (Williams). He won 23 grand prix between 1978 and a serious accident in 1991.

Piraeus [piyreeus], Gr **Piraiéus** 37°57N 23°42E, pop (2000e) 212 000. Major port in Greece; 8 km/5 mi SW of Athens; rail terminus; ferries to the Greek islands.

Pirandello, Luigi [pirandeloh] (1867–1936) Writer, born in Girgenti (now Agrigento), Sicily. He became a leading exponent of the 'grotesque' school of contemporary drama. Among his plays are *Six Characters in Search of an Author* (1921). In 1934 he was awarded the Nobel Prize for Literature.

Piranesi, Giambattista [piranayzee], or **Giovanni Battista** (1720–78) Architect and copper-engraver of Roman antiquities, born in Venice, Italy. He developed original techniques of etching, and was a major influence on Neoclassicism.

piranha [pirahna, pirahnya] Any of several voracious predatory freshwater fishes widespread in rivers of South America; length up to 60 cm/2 ft; strong jaws and sharp interlocking teeth; extremely aggressive flesh-eating fish, often feeding in large shoals.

Pire, Dominique (Georges) [peer] (1910–69) Dominican priest and educator, born in Dinant, Belgium. He was awarded the 1958 Nobel Peace Prize for his scheme of 'European villages' for elderly refugees and destitute children.

Pisa [peeza] 43°43N 10°24E, pop (2000e) 107 000. City in Tuscany, W Italy, on the R Arno; archbishopric; airport; railway; university (1338); birthplace of Galileo; cathedral (11th–12th-c); campanile (the 'Leaning Tower', 1173–1372); Piazza del Duomo is a world heritage site.

Pisanello, Antonio [peesaneloh], originally **Antonio Pisano** (c.1395–1455) Medallist and painter, born in Pisa, Italy. Little of his painting survives, but numerous drawings attest to his mastery of the International Gothic style.

Pisano, Andrea [peesahnoh], also known as **Andrea da Pontedera** (c.1270–1349) Sculptor, born in Pontedera, Italy. He settled in Florence, where he completed the earliest bronze doors of the baptistery (1336).

Pisano, Nicola [peesahnoh] (c.1225–78/84) Sculptor, probably born in Apulia, Italy. His works include the pulpit of the baptistery at Pisa (1260) and the pulpit of Siena cathedral (1268).

Pisces [piyseez] (Lat 'fishes') A large N constellation of the zodiac

Pitcairn Islands

(UK British Dependent Territory)

Timezone GMT -9

Area 27 km²/10 sq mi

Population total (2003e) 48

Capital Adamstown

Physical features Volcanic island group in the SE Pacific Ocean, E of French Polynesia; comprises Pitcairn Island, 4.5 km²/1.7 sq mi, and the uninhabited islands of Ducie, Henderson, and Oeno; Pitcairn Island rises to 335 m/1099 ft.

Climate Equable climate; average annual temperatures 24°C (Jan), 19°C (Jul); average annual rainfall 2000 mm/80 in.

Currency 1 New Zealand Dollar (NZD) = 100 cents

Economy Postage stamps; tropical and subtropical crops; crafts, forestry.

History Visited by the British, 1767; occupied by nine mutineers from HMS Bounty, 1790; overpopulation led to emigration to Norfolk I, 1856; some returning in 1864; transferred to Fiji, 1952; now a UK Dependent Territory, governed by the High Commissioner in New Zealand; in 2004 six men tried under British law were convicted of sex crimes against women and under-age girls committed over the past 40 years; in 2005 the seven-member island council unanimously elected Brenda Christian as the island's first female mayor.

---

which lacks bright stars, and so is hard to identify. It lies between Aquarius and Aries.

Piscis Austrinus [piy̱sis ostriy̱nus] (Lat 'southern fish') A small S hemisphere constellation, which includes the first magnitude star Fomalhaut.

Pisistratus [piy̱sistratus], also spelled **Peisistratos** (c.600–527 BC) Tyrant of Athens (561–c.556 BC, 546–527 BC). A patron of the arts, he invited the leading Greek poets of the day to settle in Athens, where he set about fostering a sense of national unity by instituting or expanding great religious and cultural festivals.

Pissarro, Camille [peesaroh] (1830–1903) Impressionist artist, born in St Thomas, Danish West Indies. He was the leader of the original Impressionists, and the only one to exhibit at all eight of the Group exhibitions in Paris (1874–86).

pistachio [pistahshioh] A small deciduous tree (*Pistacia vera*) growing to 6 m/20 ft, native to W Asia; flowers greenish, in long, loose heads; fruit 2–2.5 cm/³⁄₄–1 in, red-brown, nut-like. It is widely cultivated for its edible seeds, used in confectionery. (Family: Anacardiaceae.)

pistil *carpel*

pistol A hand-held firearm first developed from 'hand-cannons' in the 14th-c. The application of the revolver principle in the 1830s made the pistol a multi-shot weapon, followed by the development of 'automatic' weapons c.1900 (such as the Luger and Browning).

pit bull terrier *bull terrier*

Pitcairn Islands *see panel*

pitch (acoustics) An aspect of auditory sensation which makes listeners judge a sound as relatively 'high' or 'low'. The pitch at which a musical note sounds, and to which instruments are tuned, is *a'* = 440 Hz, adopted in 1955.

pitch (chemistry) The black, semi-solid residue left after the distillation of tar, used in bitumen and road-surfacing. It contains a complex mixture of hydrocarbons and resins.

pitchblende or **uraninite** Uranium oxide (UO_2), the chief ore of uranium; hard, very dense, and radioactive.

pitcher plant Any of the members of three separate families of carnivorous plants, in which the leaves are modified to form lidded pitcher traps containing water and enzymes. Insect prey drown in the fluid-filled base, and are digested by the plant. The Sarraceniaceae are native to E North America, California, and tropical South America; the Nepenthaceae are native to the tropics of SE Asia, Australia, and Madagascar; the Cephalotaceae contain a single species, the **flycatcher plant** (*Cephalotus follicularis*), native to W Australia.

Pitești [peetesht] 44°51N 24°51E, pop (2000e) 160 000. City in Romania, on R Argeș; railway junction.

Pithecanthropus [pithekanthropus] A name formerly used for the fossil ape-man, *Homo erectus*, which includes Java Man and Peking Man.

Pitjantjatjara The principal Aboriginal language of Australia's Western Desert, spoken by several thousand people. An active literacy programme has resulted in it becoming one of the most widely-used written Aboriginal languages.

Pitman, Sir Isaac (1813–97) Inventor of a shorthand system, born in Trowbridge, Wiltshire. He was also interested in the development of spelling reform. In 1842 he brought out the *Phonetic Journal*.

Pitney, Gene (1941–2006) Singer and songwriter, born in Hartford, CT. His hits as a writer included 'Rubber Ball' and 'Hello Mary Lou' (both 1961). Among his hits as a singer were '24 Hours From Tulsa' (1963) and 'Something's Gotten Hold Of My Heart' (1967). He died suddenly while on tour in the UK.

Pitot tube [peetoh] An instrument for measuring the velocity of a flowing fluid; named after French engineer Henri Pitot (1695–1771). The pressure observed by an attached manometer is a function of velocity.

Pitt, Brad (1963–) Film actor, born in Shawnee, OK. He became known after his appearance in *Thelma & Louise* (1991), and later films include *Legends of the Fall* (1994), *Interview with the Vampire* (1994), *Ocean's Eleven* (2001, sequels 2004, 2007), and *Babel* (2006). He was married to actress Jennifer Aniston (2000–5). He has a daughter (born 2006) with actress Angelina Jolie.

Pitt, William, 1st Earl of Chatham, also known as **Pitt the Elder** (1708–78) British statesman and orator, born in London. He led the young 'Patriot' Whigs, and in 1756 became nominally secretary of state, but virtually premier. The king's enmity led him to resign in 1757, but public demand caused his recall. He was again compelled to resign when his cabinet refused to declare war with Spain (1761). He formed a new ministry in 1766, but ill health contributed to his resignation in 1768. His second son, William, was twice prime minister.

Pitt, William, also known as **Pitt the Younger** (1759–1806) British statesman and prime minister (1783–1801, 1804–6), born in Hayes, Kent, the second son of the Earl of Chatham (William Pitt, the Elder). His first ministry lasted for 18 years, during which he carried through important reforms, his policy being influenced by the political economy of Adam Smith. He negotiated coalitions against France (1793, 1798), and after the Irish rebellion of 1798, proposed a legislative union which would be followed by Catholic emancipation. The union was effected in 1800, but Pitt resigned office rather than contest George III's hostility to emancipation.

Pitti Palace [pitee] A palace in Florence, Italy, designed by Brunelleschi in the 15th-c, originally the residence of the Grand Dukes of Tuscany. The palace now houses museums of silverware and of modern art, and the Palatine Gallery.

pittosporum [pitosporum] An evergreen shrub or small tree, mostly native to Australasia but also to parts of Africa and Asia; flowers 5-petalled, purple, white, or greenish-yellow, and often fragrant; also called **parchment-bark**. (Genus: *Pittosporum*, 150 species. Family: Pittosporaceae.)

Pittsburgh 40°26N 80°01W, pop (2000e) 334 600. City in W Pennsylvania, USA; Fort Duquesne built here by the French;

taken by the British and renamed Fort Pitt, 1758; city status, 1816; airport; railway; three universities (1787, 1878, 1900); city's traditional steel industry largely replaced by service industries; third largest US corporate headquarters; professional teams, Pirates (baseball), Steelers (football), Penguins (ice hockey).

pituitary gland [pityooitree] A vertebrate endocrine gland situated within the skull; also known as the **hypophysis**. It acts mainly by controlling the activities of all the other endocrine glands.

pit viper A viper of the subfamily Crotalinae (142 species), sometimes treated as a separate family (Crotalidae, with the remaining vipers called *true vipers*); front of face with small heat-sensitive pit on each side.

Pius V, St, originally **Michele Ghislieri** (1504–72) Pope (1566–72), born near Alessandria, Italy. He implemented the decrees of the Council of Trent (1545–63), excommunicated Queen Elizabeth I (1570), and organized the expedition against the Turks (1571). He was canonized in 1712. Feast day 30 April.

Pius IX, known as **Pio Nono**, originally **Giovanni Maria Mastai-Ferretti** (1792–1878) Pope (1846–78), born in Senigallia, Papal States. He decreed the dogma of the Immaculate Conception in 1854, and called the Vatican Council (1869–79), which proclaimed papal infallibility. His pontificate is the longest in papal history. His beatification was announced in 2000.

Pius XI, originally **Ambrogio Damiano Achille Ratti** (1857–1939) Pope (1922–39), born in Desio, Italy. He signed the Lateran Treaty (1929), which brought into existence the Vatican State.

Pius XII, originally **Eugenio Maria Giuseppe Giovanni Pacelli** (1876–1958) Pope (1939–58), born in Rome. During World War 2 the Vatican did much humanitarian work, notably for prisoners of war and refugees; but there has been continuing controversy over his attitude to the treatment of the Jews in Nazi Germany, critics arguing that he could have used his influence with Catholic Germany to prevent the massacres, others that any attempt to do so would have proved futile and might have worsened the situation.

pixel From *pic*ture *el*ement, the smallest resolved unit of a video image which has specific luminance and colour. Its proportions are determined by the number of lines making up the scanning raster and the resolution along each line.

Pizarro, Francisco [peethahroh] (c.1478–1541) Conquistador, born in Trujillo, Spain. In 1526 he and Almagro sailed for Peru, and in 1531 began the conquest of the Incas. Dissensions between Pizarro and Almagro led to the latter's execution. In revenge, Almagro's followers assassinated Pizarro at Lima.

PK *psychokinesis*

placebo [plaseeboh] An inactive substance given as a drug to a patient, who may benefit from the belief that the drug is active. Because patients can improve under this illusion, new drugs are usually tested for clinical efficacy in trials where a placebo is given to one group.

placenta (anatomy) [plasenta] An organ which develops in the uterus of all pregnant mammals, except monetremes. It is attached to the uterus of the mother, and connected to the fetus by the umbilical cord. It secretes a number of hormones essential for pregnancy.

placenta (botany) [plasenta] Tissue to which the ovules or spores of plants are attached. The arrangement of ovules is termed **placentation**, and is an important diagnostic character in many plants.

Placid, Lake *Lake Placid*

Placodermi [plakodermee] An extinct class of primitive, jawed fishes known primarily from the Devonian period; large head covered by shield composed of bony plates; body heavily armoured.

plagioclase [playjioklayz] *feldspar*

plague The most notorious epidemic disease of all time, caused by infection with *Yersinia* (formerly *Pasteurella*) *pestis*, carried by fleas that infest rats and squirrels, which then bite humans. **Bubonic plague** is a severe illness with the development of 'buboes', swollen pus-filled lymph nodes. Untreated, it is fatal in over 50% of cases. **Pneumonic plague** is rare but almost always fatal. It can also be spread by inhalation of infected respiratory secretions. In the 14th-c, outbreaks of plague (*black death*) killed half the population of Europe. It can now be treated with antibiotics.

plaice Common European flatfish (*Pleuronectes platessa*) widespread in continental shelf waters from N Norway to the Mediterranean; length up to 90 cm/3 ft; both eyes on right side; upper surface brown with orange spots, underside white; important food fish. (Family: Pleuronectidae.)

Plaid Cymru [pliyd kuhmree] The Welsh National Party, founded in 1925, with the aim of achieving independence for Wales. It finds support mainly in the N of the country. In 2006 it formed the second largest political party in the Welsh Assembly. It changed its name to **The Party of Wales** in 2006.

Plaidy, Jean *Hibbert, Eleanor*

Plain, the, known as the *Marais* The majority of deputies in the French Revolutionary Convention, politically uncommitted to a particular faction, although broadly aligned with the Girondins.

plainchant The unaccompanied, single-strand music to which the Mass and other parts of the Roman liturgy were sung (and to some extent still are). It is notated, without precise indications of rhythm, on a four-line staff.

Plains Indians North American Indian groups who lived on the Great Plains between the Mississippi R and the Rocky Mts in the USA and Canada. Most were nomadic or semi-nomadic buffalo hunters living together in small bands. White settlers finally destroyed their power, placing the surviving Indians in reservations.

plainsong *plainchant*

plaintiff *defendant*

Planck, Max (Karl Ernst Ludwig) (1858–1947) Theoretical physicist, born in Kiel, Germany. His work on thermodynamics and black-body radiation led him to abandon classical principles and introduce the quantum theory (1900), for which he was awarded the Nobel Prize for Physics in 1918.

Planck's constant A fundamental constant which appears in all equations of quantum theory; symbol h, value 6.626×10^{-34} J.s (joule.second); introduced by Max Planck in 1900. It relates the energy E of a quantum of light to its frequency v by $E = hv$.

plane In mathematics, a surface such that if any two points in that surface are joined by a straight line, all the points on the straight line lie on the surface. The equation of a general plane in rectangular Cartesian co-ordinates is $ax + by + cz + d = 0$.

planet A nonluminous body gravitationally bound to the Sun or a star, and rotating in orbit in a prograde direction (ie counter-clockwise, viewed from N). The theory of planetary formation suggests that they condense from material left over during primary star formation. They should therefore be common, but they are extremely hard to detect. The first extrasolar planet, 51 Pegasi B, was detected in 1995, and 115 such planets had been detected by 2004, including the oldest and most distant (in the M4 star cluster in the constellation Scorpius, c.12·7 thousand million years old). In the Solar System there are eight major (classical) planets, four dwarf planets (plutons), and innumerable minor planets, or *asteroids*. The major planets comprise the *inner* terrestrial planets (Mercury, Venus, Earth, Mars) and the giant gaseous *outer* planets (Jupiter, Saturn, Uranus, Neptune). All except Mercury and Venus have associated moons or, for the giant planets, systems of moons. All are believed to have been formed about 4·6 thousand million years ago. Jupiter is by far the most massive

Planetary Data

Planet	Distance from sun maximum		minimum		Sidereal period	Axial rotation (equatorial)	Diameter (equatorial)	
	million km	million mi	million km	million mi			km	mi
Mercury	69.4	43.0	46.8	29.0	88 d	58 d 16 h	4 878	3 032
Venus	109.0	67.6	107.6	66.7	224.7 d	243 d	12 104	7 520
Earth	152.6	94.6	147.4	91.4	365.26 d[1]	23 h 56 m 4 s	12 756	7 926
Mars	249.2	154.5	207.3	128.5	687 d	24 h 37 m 22 s	6 794	4 222
Jupiter	817.4	506.8	741.6	459.8	11.86 y	9 h 55 m 41 s	142 984	88 846
Saturn	1 512	937.6	1 346	834.6	29.46 y	10 h 14 m	120 536	74 898
Uranus	3 011	1 867	2 740	1 699	84.01 y	17.2 h[2]	51 118	31 764
Neptune	4 543	2 817	4 466	2 769	164.79 y	16.11 h[2]	49 532	30 778
Pluto	7 364	4 566	4 461	2 766	248.5 y	6.387 d	2 274	1 412

[1]365 d 5 h 48 m 46 s.
[2]Different latitudes rotate at different speeds.
y:years d:days h:hours m:minutes s:seconds km:kilometres mi:miles

planet, containing over two-thirds of the material in the Solar System apart from the Sun. Searches continue for further planets in our Solar System, with new proposals regularly made (eg Quaoar in 2002, Sedna in 2004). *see panel*

planetarium A special building with a dome in which a projector produces an impression of the stars in the night sky. A famous example is the London Planetarium.

planetary nebula A shell of glowing gas surrounding an evolved star, from which it was ejected. There is no connection with planets: the name derived from the visual similarity between the disc of such a nebula and the disc of a planet.

plane tree A tall, long-lived deciduous tree, native to S Europe, Asia, and especially North America; distinctive flaking bark, revealing large creamy or pink patches. (Genus: *Platanus*, 10 species. Family: Platanaceae.)

planimeter A mathematical instrument for measuring the area enclosed by an irregular curve. A pointer moved around the perimeter is connected by lever arms to an integrating mechanism.

plankton Organisms without effective means of locomotion; drifters. They have been subdivided into plant (**phytoplankton**) and animal (**zooplankton**) types. Most are microscopic in size.

planographic printing *printing*

plant An organism which typically uses sunlight as an energy source via photosynthetic pathways involving the green pigment chlorophyll (Kingdom: Plantae). Plants are mostly nonmotile and lack obvious excretory and nervous systems, and sensory organs. They are eucaryotic, and typically possess cell walls composed largely of cellulose.

Plantagenets The name of the royal dynasty in England from Henry II to Richard II (1154–1399), then continued by two rival houses of younger lines, Lancaster and York, until 1485. The dynasty was so called because, allegedly, Henry II's father Geoffrey, Count of Anjou, sported a sprig of broom (Old Fr, *plante genêt*) in his cap.

plantain 1 Typically an annual or perennial, sometimes a shrub, often a weed; very widespread; a rosette of narrow, strongly veined leaves; flowers tiny, with four brownish or green petals, packed into a dense, erect spike. (Genus: *Plantago*, 265 species. Family: Plantaginaceae.)
2 *banana*

Plantation of Ulster *Ulster Plantation*

plant breeding The improvement of agriculturally or horticul-

turally important plants, either by selecting improved varieties from mixtures or by hybridization followed by the selection of desirable genotypes. Once a simple *ad hoc* process largely based on the laws of inheritance established by Gregor Mendel and involving hybrids within or between related species or genes, plant breeding developed in the second half of the 20th-c into an increasingly sophisticated science which may involve the introduction of characters from widely differing plants or even animals. The moral and ecological aspects of the genetic modifications involved have given rise to great controversy, particularly when the new products are used in human or animal food.

plant hopper A small, hopping insect that feeds by sucking sap or cell contents of plants; species include pests of economically important crops, such as rice and sugar cane. (Order: Homoptera. Family: Delphacidae, c.1300 species.)

plasma (physics) A fourth state of matter comprising a fluid of ions and free electrons, formed for example by the extreme heating of a gas, and characterized by powerful electrical forces between the particles. Plasma properties are studied in **plasma physics**. The main interest is the creation of controlled nuclear fusion, with the ultimate aim of power generation.

plasma (physiology) [plazma] The fluid portion of whole blood, in which the blood cells are suspended. It transports nutrients, waste products, and chemicals involved in the clotting process, as well as hormones and drugs, to their target cells.

plasmapheresis [plazmaferesis] or **plasma exchange** The circulation of whole blood outside the body, during which centrifugal force separates the cells and plasma, which is replaced by fresh plasma or plasma albumin. The purpose is to remove a damaging plasma component such as an abnormal antibody.

plasma screen A form of flat panel display which uses the excitation of plasma to produce light, used for television and other display screens.

Plasmodium [plazmohdium] A genus of parasitic protozoans containing the micro-organisms that cause malaria in humans; life-cycle involves stages in an intermediate host, the mosquito, and stages in the blood or other organs of a final vertebrate host. (Phylum: Apicomplexa. Class: Sporozoa.)

Plassey, Battle of [plasee] (1757) A decisive British victory under Clive over Siraj ud Daula, Nawab of Bengal, India. The victory was an important step in the British acquisition of Bengal.

plaster *gypsum*

plastics Originally any soft, formable material; now commonly used for synthetic organic resins which can be softened by heating, and then shaped or cast. Some (called *thermoset*, eg phenol-formaldehyde resin) are then resistant to softening on further heating; others (called *thermoplastic*, eg polyethylene and polystyrene) may be repeatedly softened. Plastics may be designed with almost any desired property, ranging from great heat stability to rapid natural decomposition in soil, and from good electrical insulators to conductors.

plastic surgery The grafting of skin and subcutaneous tissue from a healthy site on the body to one that has suffered damage from disease, trauma, or burns. It also includes surgical operations undertaken for cosmetic purposes, such as face-lifting, reshaping noses, breast augmentation, and removing unsightly fat.

Plataea [plateea] **1** A Greek city-state in Boeotia, which shared with Athens the honour of defeating the Persians at Marathon. **2** The site in 479 BC of a decisive Greek victory over the Persians.

Plate, River, Span **Río de la Plata** A wide, shallow estuary of the Paraná and Uruguay Rivers on the E coast of South America, between Argentina (S and W shore) and Uruguay (N shore); area 35 000 km²/13 510 sq mi; length 320 km/200 mi; width 220 km/140 mi at its mouth and 45 km/28 mi at Buenos Aires; scene of a naval engagement (Dec 1939) between three out-gunned British cruisers and the formidable German pocket-battleship *Graf Spee* (**Battle of the River Plate**); the *Graf Spee* inexplicably disengaged, and was trapped in the neutral port of Montevideo, to be scuttled a few days later. An operation to raise it from the mouth of the River Plate began in early 2004 and was ongoing in 2007.

Plateau Indians North American Indian groups who lived on the plateau between the Rocky Mts and the Cascade Range. Most groups lived in camps during the summer, hunting and fishing; during the severe winters, they sheltered in villages located along the rivers. During the 19th-c European settlers fought with the Indians over land, forcing the survivors into reservations.

platelets Small disc-like structures (2–4 μ in diameter) found in the blood of all mammals, produced in bone marrow. They contain factors important in the arrest of bleeding and in wound healing.

plate tectonics A model of the structure and dynamics of the Earth's crust, developed in the 1960s to explain such observations as continental drift, mid-ocean ridges, the distribution of earthquakes, and volcanic activity. The theory proposes that the Earth's lithosphere is made up of a number of relatively thin, rigid plates which may include both continental and ocean crust and which move relative to one another. Plate boundaries are defined by major earthquake zones and belts of volcanic activity. Plate collisions result in the formation of mountain belts such as the Alps and Himalayas.

platform tennis A variation of paddle tennis, a cross between lawn tennis and squash. It is a popular outdoor winter sport in the USA.

Plath, Sylvia (1932–63) Poet, born in Boston, MA. She married Ted Hughes in 1956. Her first collection *The Colossus* appeared in 1960, and a novel *The Bell Jar* in 1963, shortly before she committed suicide in London. Her *Collected Poems*, edited by Ted Hughes, appeared in 1981.

platinum Pt, element 78, density 21·5 g/cm³, melting point 1772°C. A precious metal, which occurs occasionally uncombined but more importantly as a sulphide. Similar to gold in its unreactivity, it is used for jewellery and for laboratory vessels.

platinum metals A series of elements which occur together in nature, and have similar properties: ruthenium (Ru), rhodium (Rh), palladium (Pd), osmium (Os), iridium (Ir), and platinum (Pt).

Plato (c.428–347 BC) Greek philosopher, probably born in Athens

of an aristocratic family. He became a disciple of Socrates, who appears in most of Plato's 35 dialogues, then before 368 BC founded his own Academy at Athens. In the *early* dialogues, the main interlocutor is Socrates, and the main interest is the definition of moral concepts (eg courage in *Laches*). In the *middle* dialogues, Plato increasingly outlines his own doctrines (eg the theory of forms in the *Republic*). The *later* dialogues express his rigorous self-criticism (eg the *Sophist*). Taken as a whole, his philosophy has been so enormously influential that the whole subsequent Western tradition was described by Whitehead as a series of 'footnotes to Plato'.

Platonic solids In mathematics, solids whose faces are congruent regular polygons. There are five such solids: the *tetrahedron* (four faces, each an equilateral triangle); the *cube* (six faces, each a square); the *octahedron* (eight faces, each a pentagon); the *dodecahedron* (12 faces, each a hexagon); and the *icosahedron* (20 faces, each an equilateral triangle). All five were described by Plato.

Platt, David (Andrew) (1966–) Footballer, born in Chadderton, Greater Manchester. A midfielder, he played for Crewe Alexandra, Aston Villa, Bari, Juventus, Sampdoria, and Arsenal, and won 62 caps for England (captain, 1994–6). Retiring as a player in 1998, he became coach of Sampdoria, but resigned in 1999. He was coach of the England Under-21 side 2001–4.

Platyhelminthes [plateehelminths] A phylum of flattened, worm-like animals comprising parasitic groups, such as the tapeworms (Class: Cestoda) and flukes (Class: Trematoda), and free-living groups, such as the planarians (Class: Tricladida).

platypus *duck-billed platypus*

Plautus, Titus Maccius [plawtus] (c.250–184 BC) Comic playwright, born in Sarsina, Italy. About 130 plays have been attributed to him, but many are thought to be the work of earlier playwrights which he revised. Varro limited the genuine comedies to 21, and these 'Varronian comedies' are the ones which have survived.

Player, Gary (Jim) (1935–) Golfer, born in Johannesburg, South Africa, whose major wins span four decades (1950s–1980s). His successes include the (British) Open (1959, 1968, 1974), the US Open (1965), and the US Masters (1961, 1974, 1978).

player piano A mechanism attached to a piano (or a piano fitted with such a mechanism) in which a perforated roll passes over a brass 'tracker bar' and causes those keys to be depressed to which the perforations correspond. The mechanism is driven by suction generated by pedals operated by the player's feet.

playing cards Small rectangular cards used for playing card games. A standard pack contains 52 cards divided into four *suits*; hearts, clubs, diamonds, and spades. Each suit is subdivided into 13 cards numbered as follows: ace, 2–10, and the court (or picture) cards, jack, queen, and king. Most packs also contain two cards known as jokers, which can be given any value, but they are used in very few games. The earliest playing cards were used in China in the 10th-c. The pack was standardized at 52 in the 15th-c.

plea bargaining A controversial administrative device of resolving criminal cases, in which the defendant pleads guilty to a lesser offence or one carrying a lighter punishment, with the consent of the court and the prosecution, in order to conserve resources by moving cases through the system more quickly. It is controversial, because there is concern that the innocent might plead guilty to secure lesser sentences, to avoid long trials, or under pressure from their lawyers; conversely, when cases are disposed of without a complete disclosure of all the facts, defendants may escape with lighter sentences.

Pleasence, Sir Donald [plezuhns] (1919–95) Actor, born in Worksop, Nottinghamshire. He scored a huge success as the malevolent tramp, Davies, in Harold Pinter's *The Caretaker* (1960), and appeared in many films, often as a villain, such as *Dr Crippen* (1962) and *Cul-de-Sac* (1966).

plebeians [plebeeanz] or **plebs** In early Rome, citizens other than the patricians, who were the ruling elite. By the late Republic, some plebeian clans (such as the Claudians) had come to be part of the ruling aristocracy.

plebiscite *referendum*

Plecoptera [plekoptera] *stonefly*

plectrum A short length of metal, tortoise-shell, ivory, plastic, or other material worn on the fingers or held between them, to pluck a string instrument such as the guitar and mandolin.

Pléiade, La [playad] (Fr 'the Pleiades') A group of French poets of the 16th-c who sought to emancipate the French language (and literature) from mediaevalism by introducing Greek and Latin models. The best known were Ronsard and du Bellay (1522–60).

Pleiades (astronomy) [pleeadeez, pliyadeez] An open cluster of stars in Taurus, familiarly known as the **Seven Sisters**. Distance: 116 parsec.

Pleiades (mythology) [pliyadeez] In Greek mythology, the seven daughters of Atlas and Pleione: Maia, Taygete, Elektra, Alkyone, Asterope, Kelaino, and Merope.

Pleistocene epoch [pliystoseen] The earlier of the two geological epochs of the Quaternary period, from 2 million years ago to 10 000 years ago; termed the *Ice Age* in the N hemisphere. It was marked by the evolution of man and familiar mammalian life.

Plekhanov, Georgiy Valentinovich [plekahnof] (1856–1918) Marxist philosopher, historian, and journalist, 'the father of Russian Marxism', born in Gundalovka, Russia. He was a major intellectual influence on the young Lenin, but denounced the October Revolution.

plesiosaur [plesiosaw(r)] A marine reptile known from the Mesozoic era; body broad and compact, with large limbs developed as paddles; neck typically long, head small with a long snout bearing sharp teeth. (Order: Sauropterygia.)

pleurisy [ploorizee] Inflammation of membranes in the chest cavity (*pleura*) by micro-organisms, especially bacteria or viruses. It induces sharp pain on one or other side of the chest, aggravated by breathing.

Plimsoll, Samuel (1824–98) Social reformer, 'the sailors' friend', born in Bristol. He caused the Merchant Shipping Act (1876) to be passed. Every owner was ordered to mark upon the side of a ship a circular disc (the **Plimsoll line**), with a horizontal line drawn through its centre, down to which the vessel might be loaded.

Pliny (the Elder), in full **Gaius Plinius Secundus** (23–79) Roman scholar, born in Novum Comum (Como), Gaul. He wrote a 37-volume encyclopedia, the *Historia Naturalis* (77, Natural History), his only work to survive.

Pliny (the Younger), in full **Gaius Plinius Caecilius Secundus** (c.62–c.114) Roman writer and administrator, born in Novum Comum (Como), Gaul, who became the adopted son of Pliny the Elder. He was the master of the epistolary style, his many letters providing an insight into the life of the upper class in the 1st-c.

Pliocene epoch [pliyoseen] The last of the geological epochs of the Tertiary period, from 5 to 2 million years ago and immediately preceding the Pleistocene epoch.

pliosaur [pliyosaw(r)] A powerfully built plesiosaur known from Mesozoic seas; short neck and enormous head. (Order: Sauropterygia.)

PLO (Palestine Liberation Organization) An umbrella organization for the diverse factions which sought the creation of a Palestinian state in part or the whole of British Mandated Palestine. **Fatah**, the Movement for the Liberation of Palestine, founded by Yasser Arafat (1929–2004), is the largest of the groups. After its withdrawal from Beirut during the Israeli

siege of 1982, the PLO was based in Tunis. In 1988 the PLO accepted Israel's right to exist and renounced terrorism. Since the established of the Palestine National Authority, the PLO has largely been superseded and remains mainly as a negotiator.

Ploieşti [ployesht] 44°57N 26°01E, pop (2000e) 246 000. City in SC Romania; railway; major centre for the petroleum industry.

Plotinus [plotiynus] (c.205–70) The first systematic philosopher of Neoplatonism, probably born in Lycopolis in Egypt. His 54 works were edited by his pupil, Porphyry, who arranged them in six groups of nine books, or *Enneads*.

plough An implement used for turning over the soil into ridges and furrows, so that surface vegetation is buried and seed-bed preparation can begin. Modern ploughs are made of steel and are tractor-drawn.

Plough, the A familiar pattern of seven bright stars within Ursa Major; also called the **Big Dipper** (chiefly US) and **Charles's Wain**. The two stars furthest from the handle (the Pointers) point almost directly to Polaris, the North Star.

Plough Monday The Monday after Twelfth Night, traditionally the time when ploughmen and others resumed work after the Christmas festivities.

Plovdiv [plovdif], formerly **Philippopoli**, Lat **Evmolpia**, Thracian **Pulpudeva** 42°08N 24°25E, pop (2000e) 352 000. City in C Bulgaria; on the R Maritsa; airport; railway; second largest city in Bulgaria; Roman amphitheatre.

plover A small to medium-sized bird, found worldwide; short tail, long legs; bill straight, same length as head; includes lapwings and dotterels. (Family: Charadriidae, 63 species.)

plum Any of various species of the genus *Prunus*. The widely grown plum of orchards (*Prunus domestica*) is a small deciduous tree or shrub; ovoid yellow, red, purplish, or black fruit; sweet flesh enclosing a large stone. (Family: Rosaceae.)

pluralism (philosophy) Any metaphysical theory which is committed to the ultimate existence of two or more kinds of things. For example, mind–body dualists, such as Descartes, are pluralists.

Plutarch [plootah(r)k], Gr **Ploutarchos** (c.46–c.120) Historian, biographer, and philosopher, born in Chaeronea, Boeotia, Greece. His extant writings comprise a series of essays on ethical, political, religious, and other topics, and several historical works, notably *Bioi paralleloi* (Parallel Lives), a gallery of 46 portraits of the great characters of preceding ages. North's translation of this work into English (1579) was the source of Shakespeare's Roman plays.

Pluto (astronomy) Dwarf planet, smaller than our Moon, discovered in 1930 by Clyde Tombaugh after an extensive search. It was known as the ninth planet until downgraded to pluton status in 2006. It is accompanied by a relatively large moon, Charon, discovered in 1978. The two objects may be escaped satellites of Neptune. Pluto's known characteristics are: mass 0.125×10^{23} kg; radius 1137 km/706 mi; mean density 2.0 g/cm^3; inclination of equator 122°; rotational period 6·387 days; orbital period 248·0 years; eccentricity of orbit 0·249; mean distance from the Sun 39·48 AU. There is a thin atmosphere of methane gas.

Pluto (mythology) In Greek mythology, originally the god of wealth, **Plutos**. The name later became a synonym for Hades.

plutonium Pu, element 94, essentially a synthetic element, density 19·8 g/cm^3, melting point 641°C. First prepared by a deuteron bombardment of uranium, its most important isotope (^{239}Pu) has a half-life of nearly 25 000 years. It is mainly important as a fissile nuclear fuel.

Plymouth (Montserrat) [plimuhht] 16°44N 62°14W, pop (1997e) 3500 (pre-disaster). Port capital of Montserrat, E Caribbean; abandoned after 1997 volcano eruption, with new buildings at Brades Estate, NW Montserrat.

Plymouth (UK) [plimuhth] 50°23N 4°10W, pop (2001e) 240 700. Seaport and (from 1998) unitary authority in Devon, SW England; at the confluence of the Tamar and Plym Rivers; Pilgrim Fathers set out from here in the *Mayflower*, 1620; severe bombing in World War 2; major base for the Royal Navy; ferry links to Santander, Roscoff, and St Malo; railway; airfield; university, 1992; Plymouth Hoe, where Drake is said to have finished his game of bowls before leaving to fight the Spanish Armada; Eddystone Lighthouse 22 km/14 mi offshore; football league team, Plymouth Argyle (Pilgrims).

Plymouth (USA) [plimuhth] 41°57N 70°40W, pop (2000e) 51 700. Town in SE Massachusetts, USA; first permanent European settlement in New England, founded by Pilgrims in 1620; railway; 'living history' community at Plimouth Plantation.

Plymouth Brethren A religious sect founded by a group of Christian evangelicals in 1829 in Dublin, Ireland. It spread to England, where in 1832 a meeting was established at Plymouth, Devon. Millenarian in outlook, the sect is characterized by a simplicity of belief, practice, and style of life based on the New Testament.

Plynlimon Fawr [plinlimon vowr] 52°28N 3°47W. Mountain rising to 752 m/2467 ft on the Cardiganshire–Powys border, C Wales, UK.

Plzeň [puhlzen], Ger **Pilsen** 49°40N 13°10E, pop (2000e) 176 000. Industrial city in Czech Republic; railway.

pneumococcus [nyoomohkokus] A common name for the bacterium *Streptococcus pneumoniae*, one of the causative agents of pneumonia. (Kingdom: Monera. Family: Streptococcaceae.)

pneumoconiosis [nyoomohkonyohsis] A lung disease caused by the inhalation of air containing fine particles. A common industrial disorder, it occurs among coal and other miners and those working with silica and asbestos.

pneumonia [nyoomohnia] Inflammation of the lungs from infection by micro-organisms, usually bacteria or viruses. In contrast to bronchitis, the infection involves the alveoli deep in the lungs, where oxygen exchange normally takes place. It is usually an acute illness of sudden onset, with shortness of breath, fever, and pleurisy.

pneumothorax [nyoomohthawraks] The presence of air in the space between the two layers of membrane covering each lung (the *pleural space*). The resulting increase in pressure around the lung prevents it from expanding properly, and may cause it to collapse. The air may enter the pleural space from the lung through an area of weakness or be introduced from the outside through a wound in the chest wall.

Po, River [poh], ancient **Padus**, Gr **Eridanos** River in N Italy, rising in the Cottian Alps; enters the Adriatic Sea; length 652 km/ 405 mi; longest river in Italy; its valley is the most fertile agricultural region in the country.

Pocahontas [pohkahontas], personal name **Matoaka** (1595–1617) American-Indian princess, the daughter of an Indian chief, Powhatan, who twice saved the life of Captain John Smith, leader of a group of colonists who settled in Chesapeake Bay in 1607. She embraced Christianity, was baptised Rebecca, married an Englishman, John Rolfe (1585–1622), and went to England with him in 1616.

pochard [pohcherd] A duck of the worldwide tribe, Aythyini (15 species), comprising the diving-duck genera *Aythya* and *Netta*. It nests on the ground.

pocket borough British parliamentary boroughs, especially before the First Reform Act (1832), where the electorate was so small that the local landed proprietor was able to return his own nominee.

Podgorica [podgoritsa], formerly **Titograd** (1946–92) 42°28N 19°17E, pop (2000e) 120 000. Capital of Montenegro on R Morava; badly damaged in World War 2; originally named after Marshal Tito; airfield; railway; university (1973).

podiatry [podiyatree] *chiropody*

Poe, Edgar Allan (1809–49) Poet and story writer, born in Boston, MA. He became known with *Tales of the Grotesque and Arabesque* (1840), and several short stories, notably 'The Murders in the Rue Morgue' (1841), the first detective story. His weird and fantastic stories, dwelling by choice on the horrible, were both original and influential. His poem 'The Raven' (1845) won immediate fame.

poetic licence The poet's practice of taking liberty with known facts in the interests of telling a more interesting or more effective story. The historical Hotspur was 20 years older than Prince Henry; in *Henry IV*, for dramatic purposes, Shakespeare makes them the same age.

Poet Laureate A poet appointed by the British sovereign with the duty (no longer obligatory) of writing verse upon significant royal and national occasions. The first was John Dryden, who held office 1668–88. The post is now also recognized in the USA.

poetry (Gr *poiein* 'to make') Originally, any creative literary work; the term is still so defined in Shelley's *Defence of Poetry* (1821). With the development and diversification of literary forms, 'poetry' came to be used for metrical composition in any mode, as distinct from writing in prose. But the weakening of such distinctions (with the prose poem and the poetic novel) has meant that a strict separation is not maintainable. The theory and practice of poetry, concerning itself with such fundamental questions as what poetry is, what it does, and how it should be written, is known as **poetics**.

Pohnpei *Ponape*

poikilotherm [poykilohtherm] An animal that has no internal mechanism for regulating body temperature, so that it fluctuates with changes in ambient temperatures. It is often termed *cold-blooded*, but body temperatures may be maintained at a high level as a result of activity, or by behaviour patterns such as basking.

Poincaré, (Jules) Henri [pwīkaray] (1854–1912) Mathematician, born in Nancy, France. He created the theory of automorphic functions, using new ideas from group theory, non-Euclidean geometry, and complex function theory. In a 1889 paper he originated the theory of chaos, and contributed many of the basic ideas to such fields as topology, triangulation, and homology.

Poincaré, Raymond (Nicolas Landry) [pwīkaray] (1860–1934) French statesman, prime minister (1912–13, 1922–4, 1926–9), and president (1913–20), born in Bar-le-Duc, France. His national union ministry averted ruin in 1926.

poinsettia [poynsetia] A deciduous shrub native to Mexico (*Euphorbia pulcherrima*). The flower is in fact a specialized inflorescence (*cyathium*) with large vermilion bracts resembling petals. (Family: Euphorbiaceae.)

Pointe-à-Pitre [pwīt a peetruh] 16°14N 61°32W, pop (2000e) 105 000. Seaport and capital town of Guadeloupe, on SW coast of island of Grande-Terre; airport.

Pointe-Noire [pwīt nwah(r)] 4°48S 11°53E, pop (2000e) 552 800. Seaport in SW Congo, W Africa; W terminus of railway from Brazzaville; airfield; centre of Congo's oil industry.

pointer A sporting dog belonging to one of several breeds developed to detect game; stands rigidly, like a statue, with the muzzle pointing towards the prey animal.

Pointers *Plough, the*

Pointillism *Divisionism*

point-to-point An event featuring horse races for amateur riders over a cross-country course, normally on farmland. Original courses went from one point to another, hence the name, but are now often over circular or oval courses with a mixture of artificial and natural fences.

poise [pwahz] *viscosity*

poison A chemical substance that is harmful to the body if ingested, inhaled, or inoculated. The poison may be an artificial

Poland

☐ International Airport ∴ World heritage site

Polish **Polska**, official name **The Republic of Poland**

Local name Polska

Timezone GMT +1

Area 312 683 km²/120 695 sq mi

Population total (2002e) 38 644 000

Status Republic

Date of independence 1918

Capital Warsaw

Language Polish (official)

Ethnic groups Polish (99%), Ukrainian, Belorussian, and Jewish minorities

Religions Roman Catholic (94%), small Jewish and Muslim minorities

Physical features Part of the great European plain, with the Carpathian and Sudetes Mts (S) rising in the High Tatra to 2499 m/8199 ft at Mt Rysy; Polish plateau in N, cut by the Bug, San, and Wisła (Vistula) rivers; richest coal basin in Europe in the W (Silesia); flat Baltic coastal area; forests cover 20% of land.

Climate Continental climate, with severe winters, hot summers; average annual temperatures -4°C (Jan), 19°C (Jul) in Warsaw; average annual rainfall 550 mm/22 in.

Currency 1 Złoty (PLN) = 100 groszy

Economy Nearly 50% of the land under cultivation; major producer of coal; zinc, lead, sulphur; shipbuilding, machinery, vehicles, electrical equipment; textiles.

GDP (2002e) $373·2 bn, per capita $9700

Human Development Index (2002) 0·833

History Emergence as a powerful Slavic group in 11th-c; united with Lithuania, 1569; divided between Prussia, Russia, and Austria, 1772, 1793, 1795; semi-independent state after Congress of Vienna, 1815; incorporated into the Russian Empire; after World War 1, declared an independent Polish state, 1918; partition between Germany and the USSR, 1939; invasion by Germany, 1939; major resistance movement, and a government in exile during World War 2; People's Democracy established under Soviet influence, 1944; rise of independent trade union, Solidarity, 1980; state of martial law imposed, 1981–3; loss of support for communist government and major success for Solidarity in 1989 elections; proclaimed Polish Republic, 1989, and constitution amended to provide for a bicameral National Assembly; joined European Union, 2004; Lech Kaczynski appointed president, 2005; twin brother Jaroslaw Kaczynski appointed prime minister, 2006.

Head of State

1989–90 Wojciech Jaruzelski
1990–5 Lech Wałęsa
1995–2005 Alexander Kwasniewski
2005– Lech Kaczynski

Head of Government

1989–91 Tadeusz Mazowiecki
1991 Jan Krzysztof Bielecki
1991–2 Jan Olszewski
1992 Waldemar Pawlak
1992–3 Hanna Suchocka
1993–5 Waldemar Pawlak
1995–6 Jozef Oleksy
1996–7 Wlodzimierz Cimoszewicz
1997–2001 Jerzy Buzek
2001–2004 Leszek Miller
2004–5 Marek Belka
2005–6 Kazimierz Marcinkiewicz
2006– Jaroslaw Kaczynski

---

chemical, a naturally occurring element, or an organic substance derived from a bacterium, animal, or plant. Many drugs that are therapeutic at the correct dose are poisonous at high doses. Examples include paracetamol, which in high doses damages the liver; and lead, which causes a variety of adverse effects in children with prolonged exposure.

poison-arrow frog *arrow-poison frog*

poison gas Chemical munitions fired in artillery shells or released from containers which spread toxic or disabling gases onto the battlefield. Such gases (used in World War 1) included mustard, phosgene, and chlorine.

poison ivy A shrub or woody vine, native to North America (*Rhus toxicodendron*); leaves with three leaflets, sometimes resembling oak leaves, hence the alternative name, **poison oak**,

regarded as a separate species by some authorities; flowers white. All parts produce a resin containing the chemical urushinol, which is poisonous to the touch, causing severe dermatitis. (Family: Anacardiaceae.)

poison oak *poison ivy*

Poisson, Siméon Denis [pwasō] (1781–1840) Mathematician, born in Pithiviers, France. He is known for his research into celestial mechanics, electromagnetism, and also probability, where he established the law governing the distribution of large numbers (the **Poisson distribution**).

Poitier, Sidney [pwatyay] (1924–) Actor and director, born in Miami, FL. His films include *Lilies of the Field* (1963, Oscar), *In the Heat of the Night* (1967), and *One Man One Vote* (1997). He has also directed a number of lowbrow comedies, such as *Stir*

polarization

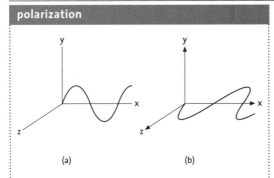

(a)   (b)

A property of (transverse) waves in which wave oscillations occur in a direction which is either constant or varies in a well-defined way. Illustration (a) shows a wave moving in x direction along a rope, polarized in the y direction, and illustration (b) in the z direction. These are both linear polarizations, since each portion of rope moves up and down in straight lines. General linear polarization can be represented as a sum of x and z polarizations, not necessarily in equal amounts. The x and z polarized waves may be combined such that they are not in step, ie their phases differ. The y polarized wave may lead the x wave by a phase difference of $\pi/2$, corresponding to elliptical polarization, ie when looking back along the direction of motion, the rope traces out an ellipse. The precise shape of the ellipse depends on the phase difference and amplitudes of the two waves. A special case is equal amplitude linear waves, differing in phase by $\pi/2$, which gives circular polarization. If, when looking back along the direction of motion, the rope appears to move clockwise, the polarization is described as right circular; if anticlockwise, it is left circular. A plate with a slit cut in it placed in the path of a wave will allow that portion of the wave in the direction of the slit to pass; the slit acts as a polarizer. Corresponding polarization effects to those oberved in the rope can be seen elsewhere. Polarization in electromagnetic radiation (including light) is dictated by the electric part of the wave. Skylight, reflected light, and scattered light are all (partially) polarized.

Crazy (1980) and *Ghost Dad* (1990). In 2002 he received an honorary Oscar.

Poitiers [pwatyay] 46°35N 0°20E, pop (2000e) 86 300. Market town in W France; Roman settlement; former capital of Poitou; site of French defeat by English, 1356; road and railway junction; bishopric; university (1431); 4th-c Baptistry (France's oldest Christian building), cathedral (12th–13th-c).

Poitou [pwatoo] Former province in W France; chief town, Poitiers; held by England until 1369.

poker A gambling card game for two to eight players which started in the USA in the 19th-c. The object is to get (or convince your opponents that you have) a better hand than theirs. There are several varieties.

Pokhara Valley [pohkara] Valley in Nepal, C Asia; town of Pokhara at an altitude of 913 m/2995 ft; road and air flights from Kathmandu.

Poland *p.736*

Polanski, Roman [polanskee] (1933–) Film director, scriptwriter, and actor, born in Paris of Polish parents. He made his first Hollywood film *Rosemary's Baby* in 1968, exploring the nature of evil and personal corruption. After the murder of his wife in the Manson killings in 1969, he went through a troubled period

and left the USA under a cloud. Later films include *Frantic* (1988), *The Ninth Gate* (1999), *The Pianist* (2002, BAFTA; Oscar), and *Oliver Twist* (2005).

Polanyi, Michael [polanyee] (1891–1976) Physical chemist and social philosopher, born in Budapest. He did notable work on reaction kinetics and crystal structure, and wrote much on the freedom of scientific thought, philosophy of science, and social science.

polar bear A bear native to the Arctic ice pack and surrounding seas (*Thalarctos maritimus*); white with long neck and small head; swims well; by 2007 under threat, due to effects of global warming on habitat.

Polar Circle *Arctic Circle*

Polaris [polahris] The brightest star in the constellation Ursa Minor, currently lying (by chance) within 1° of the N celestial pole; also called the **Pole Star**. This star was much used for simple navigation.

Polaris missile [pohlahris] A first-generation US submarine-launched ballistic missile under development from the mid-1950s. It is no longer operational with the US Navy, but a modified version continued with the Royal Navy's four Polaris-equipped submarines, until the Trident system began to replace them during the 1990s.

polarity therapy A form of therapy devised by Randolph Stone (1890–1983), who taught that the body has five energy centres corresponding to the five elements (earth, water, fire, air, and ether), and that most illnesses are caused by a blockage in the flow of energy between these centres.

polarization see panel

Polaroid 1 A trade name for doubly refracting material; developed by US physicist Edwin Land in 1938. A plastic sheet is strained so as to align its molecules, thus making it refract light preferentially, ie linearly polarized in one direction, otherwise it is absorbed. It is familiar in sun-glasses to reduce the glare from light polarized on reflection.

2 The trade name of an instant photography system developed by Land for black-and-white (1948) and colour (1963). The film is processed with viscous chemical reacting substances applied in the camera immediately after exposure.

polder [polder] A Dutch term for a flat area of land reclaimed from the sea or a river flood-plain, and protected from flooding by dykes (eg the partial reclamation of the Zuider Zee in The Netherlands).

Pole, Reginald, Cardinal (1500–58) Roman Catholic archbishop, born at Stourton Castle, Staffordshire. He opposed Henry VIII on divorce, lost all his preferments, and went to Italy, where he was made a cardinal (1536). In the reign of the Catholic Queen Mary, he returned to England as papal legate, became one of her most powerful advisers, returned the country to Rome, and became Archbishop of Canterbury.

pole *magnetic poles; Poles*

polecat A mammal of family Mustelidae; resembles a large weasel (length, 60 cm/24 in); dark with pale marks on face and ear tips. (Genus: *Mustela*, 2 species.)

Poles The two diametrically opposite points at which the Earth's axis cuts the Earth's surface; known as the **geographical poles**. The North Pole is covered by the Arctic Ocean, and the South Pole by the land mass of Antarctica. The **magnetic poles** are the positions towards which the needle of a magnetic compass will point. The South Pole was first reached by Amundsen on 14 December 1911, a month before the British team, led by Scott, which arrived on 17 January 1912; the North Pole was first reached by Robert E Peary on 6 April 1909.

Pole Star *Polaris*

pole vault An athletics field event; a jumping contest for height using a fibreglass pole for leverage to clear a bar. The current world record for men is 6·14 m/20 ft 1·68 in, achieved by Sergey Bubka (Ukraine) in 1994; for women it is 5 m/16·4 ft achieved by Yelena Isinbayeva (Russia) in 2005 in London, UK.

Poliakoff, Stephen [polyakof] (1952–) Playwright and film director, born in London. He made his debut as a playwright in 1974 with *Clever Soldiers*; later works include *Breaking the Silence* (1984), *Blinded by the Sun* (1989), and *Sweet Panic* (2003). He wrote and directed the film *Close My Eyes* (1991), and his television plays include *Caught on a Train* (1980), *Shooting the Past* (1999), *Perfect Strangers* (2001), and *Friends & Crocodiles* (2006).

police The body of civilian officers responsible for and concerned with the enforcement of law and maintenance of civil order. The police receive their authority from the legislature and act in the public interest. In addition to national forces, there are a number of specialized police forces concerned with riot control or the security and protection of particular areas, such as military establishments or railway stations.

policy unit A small group of officials in a government department, or other public agency, whose role is to supply information, advice, and analysis to policy-makers, normally politicians.

Polignac, Auguste Jules Armand Marie, prince de [poleenyak] (1780–1847) French statesman, born in Versailles, France. He became in 1829 head of the last Bourbon ministry, which promulgated the Saint-Cloud Ordinances that cost Charles X his throne (1830).

poliomyelitis [pohliohmiyeliytis] A disease due to a virus transmitted in contaminated food and water, particularly affecting children; formerly known as **infantile paralysis**. It initially infects cells lining the intestine, causing a diarrhoeal illness. In 1% of cases, it then migrates to motor neurone cells in the spinal cord, the nerves that supply muscles. Destruction of these cells leads to paralysis that may affect a limb or the respiratory muscles, resulting in death. The disease has now been virtually eliminated by improved sanitation and the use of vaccines.

polis [polis, polays] (plural **poleis**) Conventionally translated 'city-state', the principal political and economic unit of classical Greece (eg Athens, Corinth, Thebes, Sparta). Always self-governing, they were usually economically self-sufficient as well.

Polish *Polish literature; Slavic languages*

Polish Corridor An area of formerly German territory granted to Poland by the Treaty of Versailles (1919). It divided E Prussia from the rest of Germany, and its recovery was one of Hitler's aspirations during the late 1930s.

Politburo [politbyooroh] The Political Bureau of the Central Committee of the Communist Party of the Soviet Union; at various times, known as the **Presidium**. It was the highest organ of the party. Elected by the Central Committee, there were 12 members plus seven candidate members who had no votes, but in practice membership was decided by the politburo itself under the General Secretary, who presided over it.

political action committee A non-party organization in the USA, which contributes money to candidates for public office. The committees are created by various organized interests, such as unions, trade associations, and groups with strong political beliefs.

political correctness A pejorative term for the view which demands that all instances of real or perceived linguistic discrimination against social groups should be eradicated. The movement, espoused especially by US political liberals, has focused on those aspects of language which seem to preserve demeaning attitudes towards disadvantaged or oppressed groups, such as the use of *black* with negative overtones (as in the idiom *be in my black books*). The most sensitive domains are to do with race (racism), gender (sexism), sexual affinity,

ecology, and (physical or mental) personal development. The view was at first supported by many concerned with the rights of minorities, but by attracting extremists it has attracted increasing antagonism and ridicule (eg people who are less than beautiful might be described as 'aesthetically challenged'). The inflexible condemnation of 'incorrect' vocabulary has itself been condemned for its intolerance, reminding some of the 'thought police' of futuristic novels.

political economy The name given to economics in the late 18th-c and early 19th-c. The term has not been much used in modern times, reflecting the fact that the scope of economics is today much wider, dealing with many more issues than national economic affairs and the role of government.

political philosophy The philosophical study both of the concepts, values, and arguments used in political science and of the substantive issues involved in the exercise and distribution of political power. It addresses such issues as the nature of the state, the relations between Church and state, individual rights, democracy, and law and freedom.

political science The academic discipline which describes and analyses the operations of government, the state, and other political organizations, and any other factors which influence their behaviour, such as economics. A major concern is to establish how power is exercised, and by whom, in resolving conflict within society. **Political theory** (of which **political philosophy** is a sub-branch) has two principal concerns: the clarification of values in order to demonstrate the purpose of political activity, and thereby the way in which society 'ought' to proceed (eg in allocating resources); and the testing of theories drawn from empirical research.

politics *political science*

Politzer, David (1949–) Theoretical physicist, born in New York City. He joined the California Institute of Technology in 1974, becoming professor of theoretical physics (1979–). In 2004 he shared the Nobel Prize for Physics for work contributing to the discovery and exploration of the force that binds particles inside an atomic nucleus.

Polk, James K(nox) (1795–1849) US statesman and 11th president (1845–9), born in Mecklenburg Co, NC. During his presidency, Texas was admitted to the Union (1845), and after the Mexican War (1846–7) the USA acquired California and New Mexico.

polka A quick dance of Bohemian origin, in duple metre, with an accent on the second beat. It was a favourite 19th-c ballroom dance.

poll *opinion poll*

Pollack, Sydney (1934–) Film director and producer, born in South Bend, IN. He made his debut as a feature film director with *Slender Thread* (1965). Later films include *They Shoot Horses Don't They?* (1969), *Tootsie* (1982), *Out of Africa* (1985, 2 Oscars), *Sabrina* (1995), and *The Interpreter* (2005).

pollack Cod-like fish (*Pollachius pollachius*) found in inshore waters of the N Atlantic from Norway to the Mediterranean; length up to 1·3 m/4¼ ft; lower jaw protrudes beyond upper; greenish-brown on back, sides pale yellow, underside white. (Family: Gadidae.)

pollen The male sex-cells of seed plants, produced in large numbers in the anthers of flowering plants and the pollen-sacs of gymnosperms. Wind-borne pollen is smooth and light; that carried by insects is often heavier and sticky. The outer coat of the grain is very resistant to decay, and fossilized pollen can be used to investigate the vegetation of prehistoric times.

pollen analysis *palynology*

Pollock, (Paul) Jackson (1912–56) Artist, born in Cody, WY. The first exponent of Action Painting in America, his art developed from Surrealism to abstract art and the first drip paintings of 1947. This technique he continued with increasing violence and often on huge canvases, as in *One* (1950), which is 17 ft long.

pollock *saithe*

poll tax *community charge*

pollution The direct or indirect introduction of a harmful substance into the environment. Different categories include air pollution (eg acid rain), freshwater pollution (eg discharge of chemical effluent from industry into rivers), marine pollution (eg oil spills from tankers), noise pollution (eg from aircraft), land pollution (eg the burial of toxic waste), and visual pollution (eg the intrusion of industry into an area of scenic beauty).

Pollux *Gemini*

Polo, Marco (1254–1324) Merchant and traveller, born in Venice. He is commonly believed to have given Europe the first eyewitness account of Chinese civilization. His *Il milione* (The Million, trans The Travels of Marco Polo) claimed that his father and uncle, having visited Kublai Khan (1260–9), took him on their second visit (1271–5). He stayed in China until 1292 in Kublai Khan's service, becoming Governor of Yangzhou, before returning home. His account, printed in 1477, helped incite the voyages of Western discovery; but the historicity of his account has been questioned.

polo A stick-and-ball game played on horseback by teams of four. The playing area measures 300 yd/274 m by 160 yd/146 m making it the largest of all ball games. The object is to strike the ball with a hand-held mallet into the opposing goal, which measures 8 yd/7·3 m wide by 10 ft/3 m high. Each game is divided into 7-minute periods known as *chukkers*.

polonaise A Polish dance in a moderate triple metre. Chopin wrote some famous examples for piano, but the dance itself dates from the 16th-c or earlier.

Pol Pot [pol pot], also called **Saloth Sar** (1926–98) Cambodian politician, born in Kompong Thom Province. He became leader of the Khmer Rouge guerrillas, defeating Lon Nol's military government in 1976. As prime minister, he set up a totalitarian regime which caused the death, imprisonment, or exile of around 2 million. Overthrown in 1979, he withdrew to the mountains to lead the Khmer Rouge forces. He defected from the Khmer Rouge in 1996, was captured by his former comrades in 1997, and after a show trial deep in the Cambodian jungle, he died while still in captivity having been condemned to life imprisonment.

Poltava [poltahva] 49°35N 34°35E, pop (2000e) 314 000. Industrial city in Ukraine, on R Vorskla; known since the 7th-c; site of Swedish defeat by Peter the Great, 1709; railway; cathedral (1689–1709).

poltergeist Unusual apparently paranormal physical disturbances, such as movement and/or breakage of objects, which seem to depend upon the presence of a particular living person. This individual is often referred to as the 'agent' or 'focus'.

Polunin, Slava [poloonin] (1950–) Mime artist and clown, born in Orel, Russia. In the early 1980s he founded the Theatre of the Art of Modern Clowning. He has travelled around the world performing *Snowshow* (1993), a popular family entertainment which has received several awards.

polyamides Large molecules formed by the condensation polymerization of diamines with dicarboxylic acids. These complementary molecules give the same type of amide linkage as that found in natural protein fibres, such as silk and wool.

polyanthus [polianthuhs] A garden hybrid (*Primula* × *polyanthus*) derived mainly from the primrose and the cowslip, with the large flowers of the former, borne in heads like the latter. (Family: Primulaceae.)

Polybius [polibius] (c.200–c.120 BC) Greek politician, diplomat, and historian from Megalopolis in the Peloponnese, who wrote of the rise of Rome to world-power status (264–146 BC). Only five of the original 40 books survive.

polycarbamates *polyurethanes*

Polycarp, St (c.69–c.155) Greek Bishop of Smyrna, who bridges the little-known period between the age of his master, the apostle John, and that of his own disciple Irenaeus. His only extant writing is the *Epistle to the Philippians*. Feast day 23 February.

polychlorobiphenyls *PCBs*

Polyclitus or **Polycleitos** [polikliytus] (5th-c BC) Greek sculptor from Samos, a contemporary of Phidias, known for his statues of athletes. One of his greatest works is the bronze 'Doryphorus' (Spear Bearer, Naples).

Polycrates [polikrateez] (6th-c BC) Tyrant of Samos (540–522 BC), who turned Samos into a major naval power, and made her the cultural centre of the E Aegean.

polyesters Large molecules formed by the condensation polymerization of dialcohols with dicarboxylic acids. Synthetic fibres include Terylene (ICI) and Dacron (Du Pont): they impart crease-resistant and easy-care properties to domestic textiles. Their high strength, abrasion resistance, and chemical inertness are also exploited industrially.

polyethylene A family of thermoplastics of a waxy nature, made by subjecting ethene (ethylene) to high pressures at moderate temperatures; commonly known as **polythene**. Valuable as an insulator, it is easy to work into vessels with high chemical resistance.

polygamy A form of marriage where a person has more than one spouse at the same time. The concept includes *polygyny*, the most common, where a man has more than one wife, and *polyandry*, where a woman has more than one husband.

polygon In mathematics, a plane figure whose boundaries are segments of straight lines. A **regular polygon** has sides equal in length, and all the interior angles at the vertices are equal. There is an infinite number of regular figures.

polyhedron In mathematics, a solid completely bounded by plane surfaces. There are only five regular polyhedra, those bounded by congruent regular polygons. Polyhedra are of great importance in crystallography and mineralogy.

Polyhymnia [poleehimnia, polimnia] In Greek mythology, one of the Muses, associated with dancing or mime.

polymerization The forming of a large molecule, a **polymer**, by the combination of smaller ones (*monomers*). Combinations of two molecules are called **dimers**; of three, **trimers**. Small polymers (usually of three to ten monomers) are known as **oligomers**. Polymers may contain anything from 100 to over 10 000 monomer residues.

polymethylmethacrylate *Perspex*

Polynesia A large triangular area in the EC Pacific extending from Hawaii in the N to New Zealand in the S and to Easter I in the E. It includes Tuvalu (Ellice Is), Tokelau, Samoa, Tonga, Cook Is, Marquesas, and Society Is (Tahiti). Polynesians are typically of medium height, stocky build, with light-to-medium skin colour, and little body hair; there is a high rate of blood group N, a low rate of B, and an absence of Rh-negative.

polyneuropathy *neuropathy*

Polynices or **Polyneices** [poliniyseez] A Greek hero, the second son of Oedipus, who led the Seven against Thebes.

polynomial An algebraic expression containing several terms added to or subtracted from each other, eg $a + 2b - 3c$.

polyp (medicine) A small tumour growing from the lining surface of an organ, such as the large intestine, nose, or larynx. It may need surgical removal.

polyp (zoology) The individual, soft-bodied, sedentary form of a coelenterate; body consists of a cylindrical trunk with an apical mouth surrounded by tentacles. (Phylum: Cnidaria.)

polypeptide *peptide*

Polyphemus [polifeemus] In Greek mythology, one of the Cyclopes, who imprisoned Odysseus and some of his companions in his cave. They blinded his one eye, and told Polyphemus that 'No one' had hurt him. As a result, when he called on the other Cyclopes for help, and they asked who had attacked him, they did not understand his answer.

polyphony [polifonee] Music in more than one part. In general usage the term implies counterpoint, rather than simple chordal texture (homophony). One might thus talk of 'Renaissance polyphony' with reference to the Masses, motets, and madrigals of the 16th-c, but not of 'Romantic polyphony' with reference to 19th-c music.

polypody [polipodee] A perennial fern with creeping rhizomes, found almost everywhere; often epiphytic; fronds solitary, deeply lobed, or divided. (Genus: *Polypodium*, 75 species. Family: Polypodiaceae.)

polypropylene A thermoplastic made by passing propene (propylene) over a phosphoric acid catalyst at a moderately high temperature, or by passing propene into heptane with a catalyst. It is useful as a moulding material.

polysaccharides [poleesakariydz] Large carbohydrate molecules resulting from the condensation polymerization of sugars. Common polysaccharides include starch and cellulose, both polymers of glucose.

polystyrene *styrene*

polytechnic An institution of higher education devoted to the teaching of many subjects. What distinguishes it from a university is that more of its courses have a strong vocational bias, often involving actual work experience during the course. However, it is not exclusively devoted to vocational work, and may offer liberal studies as well. Research is also undertaken, especially in conjunction with industry. In Britain, polytechnics were given university status in 1992.

polytetrafluorethylene (PTFE) A thermosetting plastic polymer with important surface-modifying properties. PTFE has a low coefficient of friction which makes it valuable in non-lubricated bearings, ski-surfaces, etc. Its anti-stick properties make it useful in cooking utensils.

polytheism The belief in or worship of many gods, characteristic not only of primitive religions but also of the religions of classical Greece and Rome.

polythene *polyethylene*

polyunsaturated fatty acids Dietary fats largely comprised of glycerol combined with three fatty acids, the whole molecule being a *triglyceride*. Fatty acids can be **saturated**, **mono-unsaturated**, or **polyunsaturated**, depending on the number of carbon-to-carbon bonds which are not fully saturated with hydrogen atoms. An adequate intake of these fats can contribute to the maintenance of acceptable levels of blood cholesterol. All marine oils, and most vegetable oils (but not palm and coconut oils) are polyunsaturated fats. The main such fat in nature is linoleic acid, an essential component of the human diet (one of the **essential fatty acids**).

polyurethanes [poliyoorethaynz] or **polycarbamates** Large molecules formed from the addition polymerization of butane-1,4-diol and hexane-1,6-di-isocyanate, which give lightweight, flexible or rigid foams. They are widely used in coatings and adhesives, and the flexible form is found in swimsuits and corsets.

polyuria *diabetes mellitus*

polyvinylacetate [poliviynilasetayt] A polymer of vinyl acetate monomer ($CH_2COO.CH=CH_2$) used in adhesives, plasticizers, and concrete additives.

polyvinylchloride (PVC) [poliviynilklawriyd] A family of polymers of vinyl chloride ($CH_2 = CHCl$). It is generally mixed with additives or fillers to give materials useful for their limited flexibility, such as floor coverings, luggage, furnishing, and electric wire coating.

pomegranate A deciduous, sometimes spiny, shrub or tree (*Punica granatum*) growing to 9 m/30 ft, native to SW Asia; fruit 5–8 cm/2–3 in, globose with yellow or reddish, leathery skin; seeds numerous, each embedded in translucent, purplish, juicy and sweet flesh. (Family: Punicaceae.)

Pomerania [pomeraynia], Ger **Pommern**, Polish **Pomorze** Region of NC Europe along the Baltic Sea from Stralsund (Germany) to the R Vistula in Poland; a disputed territory, 17th–18th-c; divided among Germany, Poland, and the free city of Danzig, 1919–39; divided between East Germany and Poland, 1945.

Pomeranian A toy breed of dog developed from spitz breeds in Britain during the 19th-c; thick double-layered coat; tail curled only at tip, carried across the back.

Pomona [pomohna] Roman goddess of fruit-trees and their fruit, especially apples and pears.

Pompadour, Jeanne Antoinette Poisson, marquise de (Marchioness of) [pompadoor], known as **Madame de Pompadour** (1721–64) Mistress of Louis XV, born in Paris. A woman of remarkable grace, beauty, and wit, she assumed the entire control of public affairs, and for 20 years swayed state policy, appointing her own favourites. She was a lavish patroness of architecture, the arts, and literature.

pompano [pompanoh] Any of several large deep-bodied marine fish which with jacks and scads comprise the family Carangidae (11 genera); head with steep profile, tail deeply forked; widespread in open oceanic waters, especially warm seas.

Pompeii [pompayee], Ital **Pompei** [pompay] 40°45N 14°27E, pop (2000e) 24 000. Ruined ancient city in SW Italy, at the S foot of Vesuvius, 20 km/12 mi SE of Naples; world heritage site; an important port and agricultural, wine, and perfume centre in Roman times; damaged by a violent earthquake in AD 63; great eruption of Vesuvius in AD 79 covered the whole city with a layer of ashes and pumice-stone 6–7 m/20–23 ft deep; systematic excavation since 18th-c with many buildings well-preserved by the volcanic ash; two-fifths of the city still remains buried; modern town lies to the E.

Pompey [pompee], in full **Gnaeus Pompeius Magnus**, known as **Pompey the Great** (106–48 BC) Roman politician and general of the late Republic, whose military talents led to his victories over the Marians (83–82 BC), Sertorius (77 BC), Spartacus (71 BC), the pirates (67 BC), and Mithridates VI (66 BC). Consistently outmanoeuvred in the 50s BC by Julius Caesar, he was finally defeated by him in the Battle of Pharsalus (48 BC), and was assassinated in Egypt shortly after.

Pompidou, Georges (Jean Raymond) [pōpeedoo] (1911–74) French statesman, prime minister (1962, 1962–6, 1966–7, 1967–8), and president (1969–74), born in Montboudif, France. He helped to draft the constitution for the Fifth Republic (1958), and negotiated a settlement in Algeria (1961) and in the student-worker revolt of 1968. The Pompidou Centre in Paris is named after him.

Pompidou Centre *Centre Beaubourg*

Ponape or **Pohnpei** [ponpay] pop (2000e) 41 100; area 345 km²/133 sq mi. One of the Federated States of Micronesia, W Pacific; comprises the island of Ponape (303 km²/117 sq mi) and eight outlying atolls; capital, Kolonia.

Ponce de León, Juan [ponthay thay layon] (1460–1521) Explorer, born in San Servas, Spain. He was a member of Columbus's second expedition (1493), explored Puerto Rico (1510), and was the first European to discover Florida (1513).

Pondicherry [pondicheree] pop (2001e) 973 800; area 492 km²/190 sq mi. Union territory in S India; founded, 1674, the chief French settlement in India; transferred to India, 1954; union territory, 1962; capital, Pondicherry; governed by a Council of Ministers responsible to a Legislative Assembly.

pond skater An aquatic bug which lives and moves over water surface, supported by surface tension. (Order: Heteroptera. Family: Gerridae, c.400 species.)

pondweed An aquatic perennial, native to freshwater habitats everywhere; submerged leaves translucent; floating leaves, if present, opaque, green. (Genus: *Potamogeton*, 100 species. Family: Potamogetonaceae.)

Ponta Delgada [pōta delgahda] 37°29N 25°40W, pop (2000e) 21 000. Largest town in the Azores, on S coast of São Miguel I.

Pontedera, Andrea da *Pisano, Andrea*

Ponte Vecchio [pontay vekyoh] A bridge across the R Arno at Florence, completed in 1345 by Taddeo Galli. The lower walkway is lined with jewellers' shops above which an upper corridor, built by Vasari, links the Pitti Palace with the Uffizi.

Pontiac's Conspiracy or **Rebellion** (1763) An unsuccessful attempt by American Indians of the Ohio and Great Lakes country to drive whites out of the area W of Niagara. It was led by Pontiac (c.1720–69), chief of the Ottawa tribe.

pontoon A popular card game which is a variation of blackjack. The object is to try to obtain a total of 21 with your cards, and is thus also known as *vingt-et-un* (Fr '21').

pontoon bridge A floating bridge supported by pontoons. The structure may be temporary, as for military usage, or permanent, where deep water and adverse ground conditions make piers expensive. Typically the pontoons consist of flat bottomed boats, hollow metal cylinders, or concrete rafts.

Pontormo, Jacopo da [pontaw(r)moh], originally **Jacopo Carrucci** (1494–1557) Painter, born in Pontormo, Italy. His masterpiece is the 'Deposition' (c.1525), a chapel altarpiece in Santa Felicità, Florence.

Pontypridd [pontiprith] 51°37N 3°22W, pop (2000e) 32 300. Valley town in Rhondda Cynon Taff, S Wales, UK; on the R Taff; railway; Glamorgan University (1992, formerly Polytechnic of Wales).

pony *Dales / Dartmoor / Exmoor / Highland / New Forest / Shetland / Welsh pony; horse*

Pony Club A worldwide organization with the aim of establishing good horsemanship among children through championships and rallies. It was established in 1929.

pony express A rapid mail service from St Joseph, MO, to San Francisco, CA, using relays of riders and horses. Established in 1860, the service was withdrawn after the completion of the first transcontinental telegraph line a year later.

poodle A French breed of dog, developed originally for hunting; three sizes: *standard* (taller than 38 cm/15 in), *miniature*, and *toy* (less than 28 cm/11 in); narrow head with pendulous ears; thick coat often clipped for ornamental effect.

pool An American table game played in many forms. It uses 16 balls, and a cue similar to that used in snooker. The most popular form is the variation known as **8-ball pool**. The object is to sink all balls of a certain design, and then finally the black ball (the No. 8 ball, hence the name).

Poona or **Pune** 18°34N 73°58E, pop (2000e) 1 831 000. Industrial city in Maharashtra state, W India; former capital of the Marathas; under British rule, 1818; important colonial centre; airfield; railway; university (1949).

Poopó, Lake [pohohpoh] (Span **Lago**) Lake in W Bolivia; length 97 km/60 mi; width 32–48 km/20–30 mi; c.2·5 m/8·2 ft deep.

Poor Clares *Franciscans*

Poor Laws Legislation in Britain originally formulated in 1598 and 1601, whereby relief of poverty was the responsibility of individual parishes. As the population grew and rates rose at the end of the 18th-c, the poor laws were increasingly criticized. The Poor Law Amendment Act of 1834 radically changed the system.

Pop Art A modern art form based on the commonplace and ephemeral aspects of 20th-c urban life, such as soup cans, comics, movies, and advertising. Leading contributors include Eduardo Paolozzi (1924–2005), Jasper Johns, Andy Warhol, and Roy Lichtenstein.

Popayán [popayan] 2°27N 76°22W, pop (2000e) 171 900. Historic city in SW Colombia; founded, 1536; serious earthquake, 1983; cathedral; university (1827).

Pope, Alexander (1688–1744) Poet, born in London. He became well known as a satirical poet, and a master of the heroic couplet. His major works include *The Rape of the Lock* (1712), *The Dunciad* (1728, continued 1742), the *Epistle to Doctor Arbuthnot* (1735), the philosophical *Essay on Man* (1733–4), and a series of satires imitating the epistles of Horace (1733–8).

pope (Lat *papa*, Gk *papas*, 'father') The title of the Bishop of Rome as head or Supreme Pontiff of the Roman Catholic Church. He is elected by a conclave of the College of Cardinals, his authority deriving from the belief that he represents Christ in direct descendancy from the Apostle Peter, said to be the first Bishop of Rome. The claim to infallibility was formalized at the First Vatican Council in 1870. *pp.742–3*

Popish Plot An apocryphal Jesuit conspiracy in 1678 to assassinate Charles II of England, slaughter Protestants, and place James, Duke of York, on the throne. It was invented by Titus Oates and Israel Tonge (1621–80).

poplar A deciduous, N temperate tree; flowers tiny, in pendulous catkins appearing before leaves; seeds with cottony white hairs, which give rise to the American name **cottonwood**. (Genus: *Populus*, 35 species. Family: Salicaceae.)

Pople, Sir John Anthony (1925–2004) Chemist, born in Burnham-on-Sea, Somerset. He graduated from Cambridge in mathematics in 1951, and taught at Northwestern University, IL. He shared the 1998 Nobel Prize for Chemistry for his contribution to methods that can be used for theoretical studies of the properties of molecules and the chemical processes in which they are involved – specifically, for his development of computational methods in quantum chemistry. He was knighted in 2003.

pop music Popular commercial music, with its audience mainly among the young, current since the late 1950s. Inaugurated by rock and roll, it has since diversified to include elements from a diverse range of musical sources, including soul, reggae, country and western, and various ethnic styles. Pop music is generally played, presented, and marketed for a teenage audience, with success measured in terms of the various pop charts (particularly in the UK the Music Week/Gallup/BBC chart, and in the USA the Billboard chart), which list records in order of sales attained. From 2007, the UK singles charts also included EP and computer download sales.

Popocatépetl [popohkataypetl] 19°01N 98°38W. Dormant volcano in C Mexico, height 5452 m/17 887 ft; erupts intermittently, last eruption, 2005.

Poppaea Sabina [popaya sabeena] (?–65) Roman society beauty and voluptuary who before her marriage to the Emperor Nero (62) had been the wife of his playboy friend, the future Emperor Otho.

Popper, Sir Karl (Raimund) (1902–94) Philosopher, born in Vienna. His major contributions to scientific methodology include *Die Logik der Forschung* (1934, The Logic of Scientific Discovery). He left Vienna during Hitler's rise to power, later becoming professor of logic and scientific method at London (1949–69).

poppy The name given to many members of the family Papaveraceae. All produce latex, are often brightly coloured, and have flowers with two sepals and four overlapping petals. Red poppies, which grew wild in the fields of Flanders, are used in November as a symbol of remembrance of those who died in the two World Wars.

Popski's Private Army A British fighting unit in World War 2. It was raised in October 1942 by Lt-Col Vladimir Peniakoff (1897–1951), known as 'Popski', and engaged in intelligence-gathering and hit-and-run attacks behind enemy lines in N Africa and Italy.

population density A measure of the number of people living within a standard unit of area, useful for comparative purposes.

Popes

Antipope refers to a pontiff set up in opposition to one asserted to be canonically chosen.

until *c.* 64	Peter	535–6	Agapetus I
c. 64–*c.* 76	Linus	536–7	Silverius
c. 76–*c.* 90	Anacletus	537–55	Vigilius
c. 90–*c.* 99	Clement I	556–61	Pelagius I
c. 99–*c.* 105	Evaristus	561–74	John III
c. 105–*c.* 117	Alexander I	575–9	Benedict I
c. 117–*c.* 127	Sixtus I	579–90	Pelagius II
c. 127–*c.* 137	Telesphorus	590–604	St Gregory I 'the Great'
c. 137–*c.* 140	Hyginus	604–6	Sabinianus
c. 140–*c.* 154	Pius I	607	Boniface III
c. 154–*c.* 166	Anicetus	608–15	Boniface IV
c. 166–*c.* 175	Soter	615–18	Deusdedit *or* Adeodatus I
175–89	Eleutherius	619–25	Boniface V
189–98	Victor IV	625–38	Honorius I
198–217	Zephyrinus	640	Severinus
217–22	Calixtus I	640–2	John IV
217–*c.* 235	Hippolytus *Antipope*	642–9	Theodore I
222–30	Urban I	649–55	St Martin I
230–5	Pontian	654–7	St Eugenius I[1]
235–6	Anterus	657–72	Vitalian
236–50	Fabian	672–6	Adeodatus II
251–3	Cornelius	676–8	Donus
251–*c.* 258	Novatian *Antipope*	678–81	Agatho
253–4	Lucius I	682–3	Leo II
254–7	Stephen I	684–5	Benedict II
257–8	Sixtus II	685–6	John V
259–68	Dionysius	686–7	Cono
269–74	Felix I	687	Theodore *Antipope*
275–83	Eutychianus	687–92	Paschal *Antipope*
283–96	Caius	687–701	Sergius I
296–304	Marcellinus	701–5	John VI
308–9	Marcellus I	705–7	John VII
310	Eusebius	708	Sisinnius
311–14	Miltiades	708–15	Constantine
314–35	Sylvester I	715–31	St Gregory II
336	Mark	731–41	St Gregory III
337–52	Julius I	741–52	St Zacharias
352–66	Liberius	752	Stephen II (*not consecrated*)
355–65	Felix II *Antipope*	752–7	Stephen II (III)
366–84	Damasus I	757–67	Paul I
366–7	Utsinus *Antipope*	767–9	Constantine II *Antipope*
384–99	Siricius	768	Philip *Antipope*
399–401	Anastasius I	768–72	Stephen III (IV)
402–17	St Innocent I	772–95	Adrian I
417–18	St Zosimus	795–816	Leo III
418–22	Boniface I	816–17	Stephen IV (V)
418–19	Eulalius *Antipope*	817–24	Paschal I
422–32	Celestine I	824–7	Eugenius II
432–40	Sixtus III	827	Valentine
440–61	Leo I 'the Great'	827–44	Gregory IV
461–8	Hilarus	844	John *Antipope*
468–83	Simplicius	844–7	Sergius II
483–92	Felix III (II)	847–55	Leo IV
492–6	St Gelasius I	855–8	Benedict III
496–8	Anastasius II	855	Anastasius Bibliothecarius *Antipope*
498–514	(Coelius) Symmachus	858–67	St Nicholas I 'the Great'
498, 501–5	Laurentius *Antipope*	867–72	Adrian II
514–23	Hormisdas	872–82	John VIII
523–6	John I	882–4	Martin II (Marinus I)
526–30	Felix IV (III)	884–5	Adrian III
530–2	Boniface II	885–91	Stephen V (VI)
530	Dioscorus *Antipope*	891–6	Formosus
533–5	John II		

896	Boniface VI	1045	Sylvester III
896–7	Stephen VI (VII)	1045	Benedict IX (*second reign*)
897	Romanus	1045–6	Gregory VI
897	Theodore II	1046–7	Clement II
898–900	John IX	1047–8	Benedict IX (*third reign*)
900–3	Benedict IV	1048	Damasus II (Poppo)
903	Leo V	1048–54	Leo IX (Bruno of Toul)
903–4	Christopher *Antipope*	1055–7	Victor II (Gebhard of Hirschberg)
904–11	Sergius III	1057–8	Stephen IX (X) (Frederick of Lorraine)
911–13	Anastasius III		
913–14	Lando	1058–9	Benedict X (John of Tusculum) *Antipope*
914–28	John X		
928	Leo VI	1059–61	Nicholas II (Gerard of Burgundy)
928–31	Stephen VII (VIII)		
931–5	John XI	1061–73	Alexander II (Anseim of Lucca)
936–9	Leo VII		
939–42	Stephen IX	1061–72	Honorius II (Peter Cadalus) *Antipope*
942–6	Martin III (Marinus II)		
946–55	Agapetus II	1073–85	Gregory VII (St Hildebrand)
955–64	John XII (Octavian)		
963–5	Leo VIII	1080, 1084–1100	Clement III (Guibert of Ravenna) *Antipope*
964–6	Benedict V		
965–72	John XIII	1086–7	Victor III (Desiderius)
973–4	Benedict VI	1088–99	Urban II (Odo of Chatillon)
974, 984–5	Boniface VII *Antipope*	1099–1118	Paschal II (Raneiro da Bieda)
974–83	Benedict VII		
983–4	John XIV		
985–96	John XV		
996–9	Gregory V		
997–8	John XVI *Antipope*		
999–1003	Sylvester II		
1003	John XVII		
1004–9	John XVIII		
1009–12	Sergius IV		
1012–24	Benedict VIII		
1012	Gregory *Antipope*		
1024–32	John XIX		
1032–44	Benedict IX		

---

[1] Elected during the banishment of Martin I   [2] Different individuals   [3] There was no John XX

1100–2	Theodoric *Antipope*
1102	Albert *Antipope*
1105–11	Sylvester IV *Antipope*
1118–19	Gelasius II (John of Gaeta)
1118–21	Gregory VIII (Maurice of Braga) *Antipope*
1119–24	Callistus II (Guy of Burgundy)
1124–30	Honorius II (Lamberto dei Fagnani)
1124	Celestine II *Antipope*
1130–43	Innocent II (Gregory Parareschi)
1130–8	Anacletus II *Antipope*
1138	Victor IV² *Antipope*
1143–4	Celestine II (Guido di Castello)
1144–5	Lucius II (Gherardo Caccianemici)
1145–53	Eugenius III (Bernardo Paganelli)
1153–4	Anastasius IV (Corrado della Subarra)
1154–9	Adrian IV (Nicholas Breakspear)
1159–81	Alexander III (Orlando Bandinelli)
1159–64	Victor IV² (Ottaviano di Monticelli) *Antipope*
1164–8	Paschal III (Guido of Crema) *Antipope*
1168–78	Calixtus III (John of Struma) *Antipope*
1179–80	Innocent III (Lando da Sessa)
1181–5	Lucius III (Ubaldo Allucingoli)
1185–7	Urban III (Uberto Crivelli)
1187	Gregory VIII (Alberto di Morra)
1187–91	Clement III (Paolo Scolari)
1191–8	Celestine III (Giacinto Boboni-Orsini)
1198–1216	Innocent III (Lotario de' Conti)
1216–27	Honorius III (Cancio Savelli)
1227–41	Gregory IX (Ugolino di Segni)
1241	Celestine IV (Goffredo Castiglione)
1243–54	Innocent IV (Sinibaldo de' Fieschi)
1254–61	Alexander IV (Rinaldo di Segni)
1261–4	Urban IV (Jacques Pantaléon)
1265–8	Clement IV (Guy le Gros Foulques)
1271–6	Gregory X (Tebaldo Visconti)
1276	Innocent V (Pierre de Champagni)
1276	Adrian V (Ottoboni Fieschi)
1276–7	John XXI³ (Pietro Rebuli-Giuliani)
1277–80	Nicholas III (Giovanni Gaetano Orsini)
1281–5	Martin IV (Simon de Brie)
1285–7	Honorius IV (Giacomo Savelli)
1288–92	Nicholas IV (Girolamo Masci)
1294	Celestine V (Pietro di Morrone)

1294–1303	Boniface VIII (Benedetto Caetani)
1303–4	Benedict XI (Niccolo Boccasini)
1305–14	Clement V (Raymond Bertrand de Got)
1316–34	John XXII (Jacques Duèse)
1328–30	Nicholas V (Pietro Rainalducci) *Antipope*
1334–42	Benedict XII (Jacques Fournier)
1342–52	Clement VI (Pierre Roger de Beaufort)
1352–62	Innocent VI (Étienne Aubert)
1362–70	Urban V (Guillaume de Grimoard)
1370–8	Gregory XI (Pierre Roger de Beaufort)
1378–89	Urban VI (Bartolomeo Prignano)
1378–94	Clement VII (Robert of Geneva) *Antipope*
1389–1404	Boniface IX (Pietro Tomacelli)
1394–1423	Benedict XIII (Pedro de Luna) *Antipope*
1404–6	Innocent VII (Cosmato de' Migliorati)
1406–15	Gregory XII (Angelo Correr)
1409–10	Alexander V (Petros Philargi) *Antipope*
1410–15	John XXIII (Baldassare Cossa) *Antipope*
1417–31	Martin V (Oddone Colonna)
1423–9	Clement VIII (Gil Sanchez Muños) *Antipope*
1425–30	Benedict XIV (Bernard Garnier) *Antipope*
1431–47	Eugenius IV (Gabriele Condulmer)
1670–6	Clement X (Emilio Altieri)
1439–49	Felix V (Amadeus VIII of Savoy) *Antipope*
1447–55	Nicholas V (Tommaso Parentucelli);
1455–8	Calixtus III (Alfonso de Borja)
1458–64	Pius II (Enea Silvio de Piccolomini)
1464–71	Paul II (Pietro Barbo)
1471–84	Sixtus IV (Francesco della Rovere)
1484–92	Innocent VIII (Giovanni Battista Cibo)
1492–1503	Alexander VI (Rodrigo Borgia)
1503	Pius III (Francesco Todoeschini-Piccolomini)
1503–13	Julius II (Giuliano della Rovere)
1513–21	Leo X (Giovanni de'Medici)
1522–3	Adrian VI (Adrian Dedel)
1523–34	Clement VII (Giulio de'Medici)
1534–49	Paul III (Allessandro Farnese)
1550–5	Julius III (Gianmaria del Monte)
1555	Marcellus II (Marcello Cervini)
1555–9	Paul IV (Giovanni Pietro Caraffa)

1559–65	Pius IV (Giovanni Medici)
1566–72	Pius V (Michele Ghislieri)
1572–85	Gregory XIII (Ugo Buoncompagni)
1585–90	Sixtus V (Felice Peretti)
1590	Urban VII (Giambattista Castagna)
1590–1	Gregory XIV (Niccolo Sfondrati)
1591	Innocent IX (Gian Antonio Facchinetti)
1592–1605	Clement VIII (Ippolito Aldobrandini)
1605	Leo XI (Alessandro de' Medici-Ottaiano)
1605–21	Paul V (Camillo Borghese)
1621–3	Gregory XV (Alessandro Ludovisi)
1623–44	Urban VIII (Maffeo Barberini)
1644–55	Innocent X (Giambattista Pamfili)
1655–67	Alexander VII (Fabio Chigi)
1667–9	Clement IX (Julio Rospigliosi)
1670–6	Clement X (Emilio Altieri)
1676–89	Innocent XI (Benedetto Odescalchi)
1689–91	Alexander VIII (Pietro Vito Ottoboni)
1691–1700	Innocent XII (Antonio Pignatelli)
1700–21	Clement XI (Gian Francesco Albani)
1721–4	Innocent XIII (Michelangelo dei Conti)
1724–30	Benedict XIII (Pietro Orsini)
1730–40	Clement XII (Lorenzo Corsini)
1740–58	Benedict XIV (Prospero Lambertini)
1758–69	Clement XIII (Carlo Rezzonico)
1769–74	Clement XIV (Lorenzo Ganganelli)
1775–99	Pius VI (Giovanni Braschi)
1800–23	Pius VII (Luigi Barnaba Chiaramonti)
1823–9	Leo XII (Annibale della Genga)
1829–30	Pius VIII (Francesco Saven Castiglioni)
1831–46	Gregory XVI (Bartolomeo Alberto Capellari)
1846–78	Pius IX (Giovanni Maria Mastai Ferretti)
1878–1903	Leo XIII (Vincenzo Gioacchino Pecci)
1903–14	Pius X (Giuseppe Sarto)
1914–22	Benedict XV (Giacomo della Chiesa)
1922–39	Pius XI (Achille Ratti)
1939–58	Pius XII (Eugenio Pacelli)
1958–63	John XXIII (Angelo Roncalli)
1963–78	Paul VI (Giovanni Montini)
1978	John Paul I (Albino Luciani)
1978–2005	John Paul II (Karol Jozef Wojtyła)
2005–	Benedict XVI (Joseph Ratzinger)

For example, the population density of The Netherlands (2001) was 384·5 per km²/996 per sq mi, and for Australia (2001) 2·5 per km²/6·5 per sq mi. These measurements take no account of the area of habitable land, and density is often calculated to relate population to cultivable land or some other economic indicator.

porcelain A hard, vitreous, translucent material, contrasting with thicker, more porous pottery. Porcelain was first manufactured by the Chinese in the Tang dynasty (7th–10th-c). The first European attempts to make it were at the Medici factory in Florence in the 1570s, but real success was only achieved at Meissen in the early 18th-c.

porcupine A cavy-like rodent; some hairs modified as long sharp spines; 22 species in two families: ground-dwelling family Hystricidae (**Old World porcupines**) from Africa and S Asia, and tree-climbing family Erithizontidae (**New World porcupines**), widespread in the New World.

porcupine-fish Large bottom-living fish (*Diodon hystrix*) widespread in shallow waters of tropical seas; length up to 90 cm/3 ft; body covered with long sharp spines; inflates body as a defence to become almost spherical with spines erect. (Family: Diodontidae.)

porgy *sea bream*

Porifera [porifera] *sponge*

porky *filefish*

pornography The presentation of erotic behaviour intended to cause sexual arousal, typically using film, graphic, or written media. It is widely considered to be a demeaning representation of sexuality and the body. Most authorities distinguish between 'soft' and illegal 'hard core' pornography, but many, especially feminists, argue that the 'softer' version should be banned as well. Pornography is now a major industry; difficulties of definition and changing social attitudes have led to problems of control and law enforcement.

porosity A mechanical property of solids, a measure of their ability to allow the passage of a fluid. The narrow channels that make a material porous allow it to absorb fluid via capillarity, as a sponge absorbs water.

porphyria [paw(r)firia] A group of inherited disorders involving the excess production of chemical substances known as *porphyrins*. They cause a wide range of abnormalities, including pigmentation of the skin, abdominal pain, and mental confusion. It entered the British royal family, and was most acutely displayed in the supposed 'madness' of George III. It is sometimes called 'the royal malady', not because of its royal connections, but due to the production of purple urine.

Porphyry [paw(r)fuhree] (c.233–304) Neoplatonist philosopher, born in Tyre or Batanea. His most influential work was the *Isagoge*, a commentary on Aristotle's *Categories*, widely used in the Middle Ages.

porpoise *dolphin*

Porres, St Martín de *Martín de Porres, St*

Porsche, Ferdinand [paw(r)shuh] (1875–1951) Automobile designer, born in Hafersdorf, Germany. In 1934 he designed a revolutionary type of cheap car with the engine in the rear, to which the Nazis gave the name *Volkswagen* ('people's car'). The Porsche sports car was introduced in 1950.

port A sweet, fortified wine, first produced in the upper Douro valley, N Portugal. The wine used to be transported down the fast-flowing river to Oporto (hence the name), but is today taken by road.

Port Augusta 32°30S 137°27E, pop (2000e) 16 100. Town in South Australia; airfield; railway; base for the flying doctor service.

Port-au-Prince [paw(r)t oh prīs] 18°33N 72°20W, pop (2000e) 859 000. Seaport capital of Haiti; on the W coast of Hispaniola I; railway; archbishopric; university (1944); cathedral (18th-c).

Port Elizabeth 33°58S 25°36E, pop (2000e) 846 000 (metropol-

itan area). Seaport in Eastern Cape province, South Africa, on the Indian Ocean; Fort Frederick, 1799; founded, 1820; airfield; railway; university (1964).

Porter, Cole (1891–1964) Composer, born in Peru, IN. He composed lyrics and music for many stage successes, such as *Kiss Me Kate* (1948) and *Can-Can* (1953). His songs include 'Night and Day' (1932) and 'Begin the Beguine' (1935).

Porter, (of Luddenham), Sir George Porter, Baron (1920–2002) Physical chemist, born in Stainforth, North Yorkshire. He studied very fast reactions in gases, using a combination of electronic and spectroscopic techniques, and was awarded the Nobel Prize for Chemistry in 1967.

Porter, Katherine Anne (Maria Veronica Callista Russell) (1890–1980) Writer, born in Indian Creek, TX. Apart from short stories, she is best known for a long allegorical novel, *The Ship of Fools* (1962). *The Collected Stories of Katherine Anne Porter* (1965) received both the Pulitzer Prize and the National Book Award.

Porter, Peter (Neville Frederick) (1929–) Poet, born in Brisbane, Queensland, Australia. He emigrated to England in 1951. His works include *Collected Poems* (1983), *Dragons in their Pleasant Palaces* (1997), *Missing Max* (2002), and *Afterburner* (2004). In 2002 he won the Queen's Gold Medal for Poetry and the Forward Poetry Prize. He edited the *Oxford Book of Modern Australian Verse* (1998).

porter *beer*

portfolio theory The analysis of how investors allocate their wealth between the various types of asset available. It assumes that all would prefer the best available return for any given degree of risk, and the lowest degree of risk for any expected rate of return. Different investors choose between expected profits and safety differently, to suit their own wealth and temperament.

Port Harcourt [hah(r)kert] 4°43N 7°05E, pop (2000e) 452 000. Nigeria's second largest port; on R Bonny; established in 1912; airport; railway link to the Enugu coalfields; university (1975).

portico [paw(r)tikoh] A colonnaded and roofed space attached to a building and forming an entrance way. It is usually classical in style, with detached or attached columns and a pediment above.

Portillo, Michael (Denzil Xavier) [paw(r)tiloh] (1953–) British Conservative statesman, born in London. He became an MP in 1984 and was appointed minister of state for transport (1988–90) and the environment (1990–2), chief secretary for the Treasury (1992–4), secretary of state for employment (1994–5), and defence secretary (1995–7). He lost his seat in the 1997 general election, but won a by-election for Kensington and Chelsea in 1999, and became shadow chancellor in 2000. He was defeated in the Conservative leadership contest in 2001, and left politics after the 2005 general election.

Portland (Maine) 43°39N 70°16W, pop (2000e) 64 200. Business capital and chief port of Maine, USA; established, 1632; city status, 1832; state capital, 1820–32; railway; Westbrook Junior College (1831); birthplace of Longfellow.

Portland (Oregon) 45°32N 122°37W, pop (2000e) 529 100. Freshwater port in NW Oregon, USA, on the Willamette R; largest city in the state; laid out, 1845; airport; railway; university (1901); professional team, Trail Blazers (basketball).

Portland, Isle of Rocky peninsula on Dorset coast, S England; connected to the mainland by a shingle ridge (Chesil Beach); area 12 km²/4·6 sq mi; naval base at Portland Harbour; Portland Stone (limestone); Portland Castle built by Henry VIII (1520).

Portland, Duke of *Bentinck, William Henry Cavendish*

Portland Cement *cement*

Portlaoighise [paw(r)tlayish] or **Port Laoise**, formerly **Maryborough** 53°02N 7°17W, pop (2000e) 8500. Capital of Laoighis county, Leinster, Ireland; railway.

Port Louis [loois] 20°18S 57°31E, pop (2000e) 159 000. Seaport capital of Mauritius; established, 1735; university (1965); two cathedrals; handles almost all of the trade of Mauritius.

Port Moresby [maw(r)zbee] 9°30S 147°07E, pop (2000e) 240 000. Seaport capital of Papua New Guinea; Allied base in World War 2; airport; university (1965).

Port Natal *Durban*

Port of Spain 10°38N 61°31W, pop (2000e) 50 000. Seaport capital of Trinidad and Tobago, NW coast of Trinidad; capital of Trinidad, 1783; airport; principal commercial centre in the E Caribbean; two cathedrals.

Porton Down A research centre established by the Ministry of Defence in Wiltshire, S England, for the investigation of biological and chemical warfare.

Porto Novo 6°30N 2°47E, pop (2000e) 341 300. Seaport capital of Benin, W Africa; settled by the Portuguese, centre for slave and tobacco trading; though the official capital, there is little political and economic activity, this taking place in Cotonou; railway.

Portree 57°24N 6°12W, pop (2000e) 1970. Port in Highland region, NW Scotland; largest town on Skye.

Port Royal [royal] A French religious and intellectual community occupying the former convent of Port-Royal-des-Champs, near Paris. It was associated with the Jansenist movement, and founded by the Abbé de Saint-Cyran (1637). The community was dispersed in 1665.

Portrush, Ir **Port Rois** 55°12N 6°40W, pop (2000e) 5800. Town in Antrim, NE Northern Ireland, on the N coast; railway; tourist centre for the Giant's Causeway.

Port Said [saeed], Arabic **Bur Said** 31°17N 32°18E, pop (2000e) 551 500. Seaport in NE Egypt; on Mediterranean coast at N end of Suez Canal; founded, 1859.

Port San Carlos 51°30S 58°59W. Settlement on the W coast of East Falkland, Falkland Is; British Task Force landed near here in May 1982, during the Falklands War.

Portsmouth (UK) 50°48N 1°05W, pop (2001e) 186 700. Seaport city and (from 1997) unitary authority in Hampshire, S England; on Portsea I; major naval base; railway; university, 1992; ferries to the Channel Is, France, and the I of Wight; birthplace of Charles Dickens; Nelson's flagship HMS *Victory*; Tudor warship, *Mary Rose*; Royal Navy Museum; Southsea Castle; Spinnaker Tower (2005); football league team, Portsmouth (Pompey).

Portsmouth (Virginia) 36°50N 76°18W, pop (2000e) 100 600. Port city, SE Virginia, USA, on the Elizabeth R; founded, 1752; evacuated and burned by Union troops during the Civil War, 1861, then retaken, 1862; part of a US naval complex; railway.

Port Sudan [soodan] 19°38N 37°07E, pop (2000e) 319 000. Sudan's main port; founded, 1906; airfield; railway; handles most of the country's trade.

Port Talbot *Neath and Port Talbot*

Portugal *p.746*

Portuguese *Portuguese literature; Romance languages*

Portuguese man-of-war A jellyfish-like coelenterate which floats at the ocean surface, held up by a gas-filled float; lives as a colony; long stinging tentacles hang down from the float; can inflict painful stings on swimmers. (Phylum: Cnidaria. Order: Siphonophora.)

Porvoo [paw(r)voh], Swed **Borgå** 60°24N 25°40E, pop (2000e) 20 900. Picturesque town in SE Finland; established, 1346; bishopric; boat service to Helsinki; home of national poet, Johan Runeberg; cathedral (15th-c).

Poseidon [posiydn] In Greek mythology, the brother of Zeus, god of water and the sea, depicted with a trident in his hand. He is responsible for earthquakes and similar destructive forces.

positivism In philosophy, the position that all genuine knowledge is derived from and validated by science. Developed from the British empiricist tradition, it was first explicitly formu-

lated in the 19th-c, and taken up by those optimistic about the benefits of scientific progress for humanity and who were hostile to theology and metaphysics.

positron The antiparticle partner to the electron; symbol e^+; mass and spin same as electron, but charge +1; discovered in 1932 by US physicist Carl Anderson (1905–91) and British physicist Patrick Blackett (1897–1974), by observing tracks left in cloud chambers by cosmic rays.

possum An Australian marsupial of family Burramyidae (**pygmy possum**, 7 species), family Pseudocheiridae (**ringtail possum**, 16 species), family Phalangeridae (**scaly-tailed possum** plus 3 species of **brushtail possum**), or family Petauridae (**Leadbetter's possum** plus 2 species of **striped possum**). The name is commonly used for **opossum** in the USA.

postage stamp An adhesive printed or embossed stamp or label indicating the prepayment of a fee for the conveyance of letters, postcards, parcels etc. The first postage stamps were issued in England in the 1840s, but soon became a global phenomenon. Definitive stamps are those which are normally available for purchase, while commemorative stamps are issued periodically to mark special occasions. The latter in particular have become a design specialism.

postal service The collection, sorting, and delivery of mail. National postal services have existed since the early 19th-c, using a network of post offices and post boxes for the collection of letters, cards, parcels, and other missives. In some countries, private operators now provide competition for the former monopoly state suppliers. Post offices may also offer a range of additional counter services, such as savings accounts and currency exchange.

post and lintel / lintol A form of architectural construction consisting of vertical, loadbearing posts supporting horizontal lintels to create openings. It is typified by Greek architecture. The technique is also known as **trabeated** construction.

Postimpressionism An imprecise term coined by the art critic Roger Fry c.1910 to cover the more progressive forms of French painting since c.1880. The painters included van Gogh, Gauguin, Cézanne, and Matisse.

postmodern dance Originally, a chronological label to describe dance forms that rejected the theories and practices of modern dance. The term was first coined to describe the reaction against the formalized systems of codified movement in dance. It was based on a rejection of stylized techniques, introducing in their stead 'natural' movements such as walking, running, and breathing. As the century advanced, the notion became so diffuse as to lose its definition.

Postmodernism A term used in architecture to describe a style or concept that supersedes 20th-c modernism and the International Style in particular. It is generally applied to buildings which draw upon an eclectic range of stylistic precedents, especially classical. In recent years the term has been increasingly used to identify a basic rejection of previously widely-held architectural beliefs, and has also emerged in relation to such fields as literature and cinema.

post mortem The dissection of a body after death in order to determine the cause of death; also known as **necropsy**. A post mortem is carried out whenever the cause of death is uncertain, particularly when death has occurred in suspicious circumstances.

post-natal depression A disturbance in a mother's mood during the period following delivery of a baby. It is related to sudden drops in hormone levels, fatigue, and a reaction to the momentous events of childbirth. Mild emotional upset is common, usually limited tearfulness and irritability lasting a few days. More serious depression may occur, particularly in cases where social support is poor, with feelings of anxiety and groundless fears about the baby; a few mothers even react with revulsion,

Portugal

☐ International Airport

official name **Republic of Portugal**, Port **República Portuguesa**, ancient **Lusitania**
Local name Portugal
Timezone GMT
Area 91 630 km²/35 370 sq mi
Population total (2002e) 10 384 000
Status Republic
Capital Lisbon
Languages Portuguese (official), with many dialectal variations

Ethnic groups Homogeneous (Mediterranean stock), with small African minority
Religions Roman Catholic (97%), Protestant (1%), Muslim minority
Physical features Located on W side of Iberian peninsula; includes semi-autonomous Azores and Madeira Is; chief mountain range, the Serra da Estrêla (N), rising to 1991 m/6532 ft; main rivers, Douro, Tagus, Guadiana, are the lower courses of rivers beginning in Spain.
Climate Cool, maritime climate in N; warmer Mediterranean type in S; most rainfall in winter; average annual temperature 11°C (Jan), 22°C (Jul) in Lisbon; average annual rainfall 686 mm/ 27 in; record temperatures caused widespread forest fires in C and S regions (Aug 2003); serious forest fires in S (Jul 2004), C and N regions (Aug 2005), C region (Jul 2006).
Currency 1 euro (EUR) = 100 cents (previous to 2002, 1 Escudo (PTE) = 100 centavos)
Economy Several labour-intensive areas, including textiles, leather, wood products, cork, ceramics; timber; wine, fish; chemicals, electrical machinery, steel, shipbuilding; minerals, cereals, pulses, fruit, olive oil; c.20% of land is forested.
GDP (2002e) $195·2 bn, per capita $19 400
Human Development Index (2002) 0·880
History Became a kingdom under Alfonso Henriques in 1140; major period of world exploration and beginning of Portuguese Empire in 15th-c; under Spanish domination, 1580–1640; invaded by the French, 1807; island of Azores granted semiautonomy, 1895; monarchy overthrown and republic established, 1910; dictatorship of Dr Salazar, 1928–68; military coup in 1974, followed by 10 years of political unrest under 15 governments; island of Madeira gained partial autonomy, 1980; Macao still administered by Portugal; joined European Union (formerly EC), 1986; governed by a President, elected for five years, a Prime Minister and Council of Ministers, and a unicameral Assembly of the Republic.
Head of State
1976–86 António dos Santos Ramalho Eanes
1986–96 Mário Alberto Nobre Lopez Soares
1996–2006 Jorge Sampaio
2006– Anibal Cavaco Silva
Head of Government
1980–1 Francisco de Sá Carneiro
1981–3 Francisco Pinto Balsemão
1983–5 Mário Alberto Nobre Lopez Soares
1985–95 Aníbal Cavaco Silva
1995–2001 António Guterres
2002–4 Jose Manuel Durao Barroso
2004–5 Pedro Santana Lopes
2005– José Socrates

forming the notion that their baby is not their own. Rarely, a severe mental illness develops (*puerperal psychosis*), with a manic depressive or schizophrenic-type episode that requires treatment on a psychiatric ward.
post office *postal service*
postpartum haemorrhage / hemorrhage Bleeding in the mother in excess of 500 ml (c.1 pt) occurring in the first 24 hours after the birth of the baby. It has many causes.
post-production The completion stages of a film after shooting up to the first public showing. The picture is finally edited to the director's satisfaction, and the original negative cut to conform; music and sound effects are recorded and mixed with the actors' dialogue in dubbing the final track. Corresponding stages are followed for a video production.

PostScript A computer language which has been developed to provide a uniform means of describing pages of text and/or graphics. It is widely used in desk-top publishing.
post-traumatic stress disorder A severe anxiety reaction that occurs in some people exposed to a traumatic event involving witness to, threat of, or experience of death or serious harm; it often affects war veterans. The traumatic event is re-experienced in the form of images or thoughts ('flashbacks'), accompanied by sweating, a rapid heart beat, and a feeling of fear. The condition also predisposes to depression and addiction. It may be prevented by offering counselling or other psychiatric interventions.
potash Potassium oxide, K_2O. The term is generally used for any potassium compounds used as fertilizers whose potassium

content is reported in terms of the equivalent amount of K_2O, or about 1·2 times the percentage by weight of potassium.

potassium K (Lat *kalium*), element 19, melting point 63°C. One of the most reactive metals, and the third of the alkali metal group. It is not found free in nature, but obtained chiefly from mineral deposits of the chloride (KCl) and the nitrate (KNO_3, also known as *nitre* or *saltpetre*). Its compounds are important mainly as agricultural chemicals and explosives.

potassium–argon dating A radiometric method for dating rocks more than 100 000 years old. It uses the fact that radioactive isotope potassium-40 decays with a known half-life to yield argon-40, and hence the amount of each isotope in a rock can be used to determine its age.

potato A well-known tuber-producing plant and staple crop throughout temperate regions of the world; an erect to somewhat sprawling perennial. The tubers vary greatly in size, shape, colour, and taste. The skins can be white, yellow to brown, pink, red, or purplish-black, and the flesh white to yellow, pink, or purple. The 'eyes' on a potato are dormant buds, which in favourable conditions give rise to new stems. There are thousands of varieties, all regarded as belonging to a single species, *Solanum tuberosum*. The potato is native to South America, and probably first arrived in Spain c.1565, and separately in England towards the end of the 16th-c (though not, as legend would have it, brought by Sir Walter Raleigh). Potatoes are susceptible to a number of diseases, including viruses and potato blight. Production of higher-yielding and disease-resistant strains is a priority for crop breeders. (Family: Solanaceae.)

potato blight A widespread disease of potato and related plants caused by the fungus *Phytophthora infestans*, especially in wet weather. A severe outbreak in Ireland in the 1840s caused the great Irish potato famine. (Class: Oomycetes. Order: Peronosporales.)

Potemkin, Grigoriy Alexandrovich [potyomkin] (1739–91) Russian field marshal, born near Smolensk, Russia. He entered the Russian army, attracted the notice of Catherine II, and became her intimate favourite, heavily influencing Russian foreign policy. There is some reason to believe they were secretly married.

potential A scalar quantity associated with a force whose rate of change with distance is proportional to the strength of that force; symbol *V*. In a gravitational field, it is the potential energy of an object of mass 1 kg; in an electric field it is the potential energy of a charge of 1 C.

potential difference A quantity in physics, often called **voltage**; symbol *U*, units V (volt). A potential difference is said to exist between two points if work must be done against an electric field to carry a charge from one point to the other. The potential difference between the terminals of a battery indicates the battery's ability to drive current around a circuit.

potential energy The energy stored by an object by virtue of its position in the region of influence of some force; symbol *V*, units J (joule). For example, work done in compressing a spring is stored as elastic potential energy in the spring.

potentilla A member of a large genus of annuals or perennials, sometimes creeping, rarely small shrubs, native to N temperate regions; **cinquefoils** with 5-petalled flowers, and **tormentils** with 4-petalled flowers. (Genus: *Potentilla*, 500 species. Family: Rosaceae.)

potentiometer An instrument for the accurate measurement or control of electrical potential. Potentiometers are used in electronic circuits, especially as volume controls in transistor radios.

potholing *speleology*

pot marigold An annual to perennial (*Calendula officinalis*), growing to 70 cm/27 in; slightly sticky to the touch; flower-heads solitary, up to 7 cm/2¾ in across; outer ray florets orange or yellow; fruit boat-shaped. (Family: Compositae.)

Potomac River [potohmak] River in West Virginia, Virginia, and Maryland, USA; rises in the Allegheny Mts; flows through Washington, DC, into Chesapeake Bay; length 460 km/286 mi.

Potosí [potohsee] 19°34S 65°45W, pop (2000e) 136 400. City in SW Bolivia; altitude 4070 m/13 353 ft; founded by Spanish in 1545; major silver-mining town in 17th–18th-c; railway; chief industrial centre of Bolivia; university (1892); cathedral; nearby mint (Casa Real de Moneda), founded 1542, rebuilt 1759, now a museum and world heritage site.

Potsdam 52°23N 13°04E, pop (2000e) 145 000. City in Germany; on R Havel; former residence of German emperors and Prussian kings; badly bombed in World War 2; railway; Academy of Political Science and Law; Central Meteorological Centre; Sans Souci palace and park (1745–7).

Potsdam Conference A conference which met during the final stages of World War 2 (17 Jul–2 Aug 1945). Churchill (and later Attlee), Stalin, and Truman met to discuss the post-war settlement in Europe. It was agreed that Poland's W frontier should run along the Oder–Neisse line, and the decision was made to divide Germany into four occupation zones. The **Potsdam Declaration** (26 July 1945) demanded from Japan the choice between unconditional surrender or total destruction.

Potter, (Helen) Beatrix (1866–1943) Writer, born in London. She wrote many books for children, which she illustrated herself, creating such popular characters as Peter Rabbit (1900) and Benjamin Bunny (1904).

Potter, Dennis (Christopher George) (1935–94) Playwright, born in the Forest of Dean, Gloucestershire. His first success was *Vote, Vote, Vote for Nigel Barton* (1965). Later works include *Pennies from Heaven* (1978), *Blue Remembered Hills* (1979, BAFTA), *Cream in my Coffee* (1982, Prix Italia), and *Lipstick on Your Collar* (1993). He completed *Karaoke* and *Cold Lazarus* just before his death.

Potter, Paul (1625–54) Painter and etcher, born in Enkhuizen, The Netherlands. His best pictures are small pastoral scenes with animal figures, but he also painted large pictures, notably the life-size 'Young Bull' (1647, The Hague).

Potter, Stephen (Meredith) (1900–69) British writer and radio producer. He is best known for his humorous studies of the art of demoralizing the opposition, such as *Gamesmanship* (1947), *Lifemanship* (1950), and *One-Upmanship* (1952).

Potteries, The NW Midlands urban area in the upper Trent valley of Staffordshire, C England; extends c.14 km/9 mi (NW–SE) by 5 km/3 mi (W–E); railway; since the 18th-c, the heart of the English china and earthenware industry.

pottery Vessels made out of fired clay, produced by mankind since the earliest civilizations. They can be hand-built, moulded, or in more sophisticated societies thrown on a wheel. Pottery tends to be soft and rather porous, and is therefore normally protected by a **glaze**, which also gives a shiny decorative appearance.

potto A primitive primate (*Perodicticus potto*) native to Africa; resembles the slow loris, but has a dark face and short tail; four spines on back of neck. (Family: Lorisidae.) The name **golden potto** is used for the related angwantibo.

Poulenc, Francis [poolãk] (1899–1963) Composer, born in Paris. He became a member of *Les Six*, and was prominent in the reaction against Impressionism. He is best known for his considerable output of songs, such as *Fêtes galantes* (1943).

Pound, Ezra (Weston Loomis) (1885–1972) Poet, born in Hailey, ID. He was an experimental poet, whom T S Eliot regarded as the motivating force behind modern poetry. His main work is *The Cantos*, a loosely-knit series of poems, which he began during World War 1, and which were published in many instalments (1930–59).

pound (economics) The unit of currency of the UK (the **pound sterling**), and certain other countries. The symbol £ is derived from letter *L* for *libra*, a measure of weight. It was formerly divided into 20 shillings and 240 pence; but since decimalization in 1971 it is divided into 100 pence (*new pence*). In 1983 the British government introduced a one-pound coin to replace the one-pound note.

pound (physics) *kilogram*

Poussin, Nicolas [poosĩ] (1594–1665) Painter, born near Les Andelys, France. The greatest exponent of French classicism, deeply influenced by Raphael and the Antique, his masterpieces include two sets of the 'Seven Sacraments'.

poverty trap An anomaly in a social welfare and taxation system which occurs when individuals, previously unemployed and claiming various social benefits, obtain work, and find that they are taxed, so ending up with less net income than before.

POW Abbreviation of **prisoner-of-war**, whose treatment was first codified by International Treaty at the Hague Conference of 1899. This stated that POWs must be humanely treated, and not obliged to divulge military information other than name, rank, and number.

powder metallurgy Making metal shapes by compressing powdered metal into a finished or near-finished shape. First used for tungsten lamp filaments, it is now used for such products as tungsten carbide cutting tools and self-lubricating bearings.

Powell, Anthony (Dymoke) (1905–2000) Novelist, born in London. After World War 2, he wrote a major series of satirical social novels, *A Dance to the Music of Time* (1951–75; televised, 1997) – 12 volumes covering 50 years of British upper-middle-class life and attitudes.

Powell, Colin (Luther) [kohlin] (1937–) US army general, born in New York City. He studied at the City College of New York, and took an army commission, later serving in Vietnam (1962–3, 1968–9). After holding a series of senior commands, he was appointed head of the National Security Council by President Reagan (1987–9), took over the Army Forces Command, and was made chairman of the joint chiefs-of-staff by President Bush (1989–93), the first African-American officer to receive this distinction. He had overall responsibility for the US military operation against Iraq in 1990–1. Britain awarded him an honorary knighthood in 1993. He retired from the army in 1993, and wrote a best-selling autobiography, *My American Journey* (1995), emerging as a popular and high-profile national figure. A Republican, he announced he was not interested in running for president in 1996. George W Bush appointed him secretary of state (2001–4).

Powell, (John) Enoch (1912–98) British Conservative statesman, born in Birmingham, West Midlands. His outspoken attitude on the issues of non-white immigration and racial integration came to national attention in 1968, and as a consequence he was dismissed from the shadow cabinet. He was elected as an Ulster Unionist MP in 1974, losing his seat in 1987.

Powell, Michael (1905–90) Film director, scriptwriter, and producer, born near Canterbury, Kent. With Emeric Pressburger (1902–88) he formed The Archers company in 1942, and for more than 10 years made a series of unusual and original features, such as *Black Narcissus* (1947), *The Red Shoes* (1948), and *The Tales of Hoffman* (1951).

Powell, Robert (1944–) Actor, born in Salford, Lancashire. He became widely known through his role in *Jesus of Nazareth* (1977), later films including *Frankenstein* (1984) and *The Mystery of Edwin Drood* (1993). His television work includes *The Detectives* (1989, 1993–7), *The First Circle* (1991), and *Holby City* (2005–).

power (physics) The rate of change of work with time; symbol *P*, units W (watt). To lift an object some distance into the air requires a fixed amount of work, but to do the job more quickly requires more power.

power boating The sport or pastime of travelling over water in a craft powered by an engine. Craft range in size and type from 'personal water craft' or 'aquabikes', to motor yachts. Propulsion is provided by inboard engines concealed within the craft and mainly diesel in type, or outboard engines mounted externally at the stern of the vessel, normally two- or four-stroke petrol engines, but some electric outboards are available. The engines usually drive propellors but increasing use is being made of water-jets where the engine drives pumps that draw in and eject water at high pressure. Power boats are raced in a number of classes and configurations, the most popular being inboard-engined hydroplanes that skim the surface at speeds up to 275 kph/170 mph. The sport is governed by Union Internationale Motonautique (UIM).

powerboat racing The racing of boats fitted with high-powered and finely-tuned engines. A boat was first fitted with a petrol engine in 1865, by Frenchman Jean Joseph Lenoir (1822–1900). The first race was c.1900.

Powhatan Confederacy [powuhtan] A group of North American Algonkin Indian tribes inhabiting the Tidewater region of Virginia at the time of the first white contact; named after chief Powhatan. Initially receptive, the Indians grew suspicious of the newcomers, and in 1622 and 1644 launched massive (but unsuccessful) attacks on them.

Powys [powis] pop (2001e) 126 300; area 5077 km²/1960 sq mi. Mountainous county in E Wales, UK; created in 1974, and status reaffirmed in 1996; Lake Vyrnwy (reservoir); administrative centre, Llandrindod Wells; Brecon Beacons National Park.

Powys, John Cowper [powis] (1872–1963) Writer and critic, born in Shirley, Derbyshire. He is best known for his long novels on West Country and historical themes, such as *A Glastonbury Romance* (1932) and *Owen Glendower* (1940). His brothers **Llewelyn** (1884–1939) and **T(heodore) F(rancis)** (1875–1953) were also writers.

Poznań [poznan], Ger **Posen** 52°25N 16°53E, pop (2000e) 595 000. City in W Poland, on R Warta; capital of Poland until 13th-c; bishopric; airfield; railway; noted for its choirs and the Polish Theatre of Dance; two universities (1918, 1919); castle (13th-c), cathedral (18th-c, largely rebuilt).

PR *public relations*

Prado [prahdoh] The Spanish national museum in Madrid, housing the world's finest collection of Spanish art. The gallery was opened to the public in 1819.

Praesepe [priyseepee] *Cancer*

Praetorian Guard [pritawrian] An elite corps in imperial Rome – effectively, the emperor's bodyguard. Their real influence dates from the 20s AD, when they were concentrated in a single barracks in Rome itself.

Praetorius, Michael [pritawrius] (1571–1621) Composer, born in Creuzburg, Germany. As well as being one of the most prolific composers of his time (especially of church music), he wrote an important treatise *Syntagma musicum* (1614–20).

praetors [preeterz] In ancient Rome, the chief law officers of the state, elected annually, second only to the consuls in importance. The office could not be held before the age of 33.

pragmatics In linguistics, the study of the way context influences the use and understanding of language, particularly in interactive situations such as in addressing, being polite, or being persuasive. This includes the study of speech acts; for example, *I promise*, used in appropriate circumstances, *is* to promise.

Prague, Czech **Praha** 50°05N 14°25E, pop (2000e) 1 219 000. Industrial and commercial capital of Czech Republic, on R Vltava; important trading centre since 10th-c; capital of newly-created Czechoslovakia, 1918; occupied by Warsaw Pact troops, 1968; historical centre declared a conservation area,

1971; archbishopric; airport; railway; metro; Charles University (1348); technical university (1707); Hradčany Castle, two cathedrals.

Praia [prahya] 14°53N 23°30W, pop (2000e) 43 000. Port and capital of the Republic of Cape Verde; airport; naval shipyard.

prairie The extensive grassland and treeless region of N USA and Canada. Its fertile soils encouraged ploughing and cultivation, and the prairies are now a major arable area. Cattle ranching is also important.

prairie chicken A grouse native to C USA (*Tympanuchus cupido*); upright tail; long upright feathers on head; inflatable orange neck sacs; inhabits prairie.

prairie dog A North American squirrel; length, up to 45 cm/18 in, with short tail; digs extensive burrow systems. (Genus: *Cynomys*, 5 species.)

prairie schooner A type of wagon used by emigrants making the journey W across the USA in the 19th-c, with cloth covers stretched over hoops. They were commonly known as **covered wagons**, and also as **Conestoga wagons**, from the place in Pennsylvania where they were originally manufactured.

prairie wolf *coyote*

Pramoedya, Ananta Toer [pramudya], also spelled **Pramudya Ananta Tur** (1925–2006) Novelist, born in Blora, Java, Indonesia. He is Indonesia's most celebrated writer, best known for his 'Buru Quartet', named after the prison island where he was incarcerated in 1965 as a political prisoner. In the early 1960s, as a communist sympathizer, he had become a key member of the Institute for People's Culture in which he denounced other writers. This tarnished his reputation, and there were protests when, in 1995, he was awarded the Magsaysay prize.

Prasad, Rajendra [prasad] (1884–1963) Indian statesman and president (1950–62), born in Zeradei, Bihar, India. He was president of the Indian National Congress on several occasions between 1934 and 1948, and became India's first president in 1950.

Pratchett, Terry (1948–) Writer, born in Beaconsfield, Buckinghamshire. He is best known for his series of fantasy novels, Discworld, which began in 1983 with *The Colour of Magic* and which had reached a 33rd novel in 2007. *The Science of Discworld* appeared in 1999, with a second volume in 2002. Other works include the 'Truckers' trilogy (called the 'Bromeliad' trilogy in the USA), and a series of Johnny Maxwell novels.

pratincole [pratingkohl] A bird of the Old World family Glareolidae, subfamily Glareolinae (8 species); long wings, short tail; short black bill with reddish base; short legs (*Glareolus*, 7 species) or long legs (*Stiltia*).

prawn A general name for many shrimp-like crustaceans. *Prawn* and *shrimp* are interchangeable common names, with usage varying according to local tradition. (Class: Malacostraca. Order: Decapoda.)

Praxiteles [praksiteleez] (4th-c BC) Sculptor, a citizen of Athens. His works have almost all perished, but several of his statues are known from Roman copies.

praying mantis A large, green mantis which lies motionless in wait for its prey, holding its grasping forelegs in an attitude suggestive of prayer; found in Europe. (Order: Mantodea. Family: Mantidae.)

Precambrian era A geological time before the Phanerozoic, from the formation of the Earth (c.4600 million years ago) to c.590 million years ago; subdivided into the Archean and the Proterozoic eons.

precedent 1 A doctrine of law, present in most legal systems, whereby an earlier court's decision or judgment on the same point of law involving similar facts is followed by another court at a later date. Precedent is sometimes referred to as 'judgemade law', as opposed to statute law; but precedent can be overruled by statute, and where any conflict exists the statute takes precedence. **2** A copy of a legal document, such as a will or a deed, which is used or adapted as a model or style for drafting other documents.

precession In rotational mechanics, the progressive change in orientation of the axis of rotation. For example, a child's spinning top spins about its own axis, but also wobbles or precesses about the vertical. The Earth precesses in a complicated way.

precious stones *gemstones*

precipitate Insoluble material formed during a chemical reaction in solution. Examples include the deposition of scale in a kettle and the formation of soap scum by hard water.

precipitation A climatic term covering rainfall, drizzle, snow, sleet, hail, and dew. As rising air cools, it condenses around dust particles to form water droplets and clouds. If the droplet grows to a critical size, it will fall as precipitation; the type reaching the ground depends on the air temperature between the cloud and the ground.

Precise Positioning Service *Global Positioning System*

predestination In Christian theology, the doctrine that the ultimate salvation or damnation of each human individual has been ordained beforehand. It was first fully articulated by Augustine during his controversy with the Pelagians. The Protestant Reformers Luther and Calvin defended the doctrine, though in varying degrees. Jakob Arminius (1560–1609) rejected the Calvinist view of predestination, and argued that the divine sovereignty was compatible with human free will.

pre-eclampsia [pree-eklampsia] A potentially serious, abnormal condition of late pregnancy, with high blood pressure, protein in the urine, and swelling (*oedema*) of the limbs; also known as **pregnancy induced hypertension**. It is an uncommon condition, of unknown cause.

prefabrication In architecture, the manufacture of parts or the whole of a building in a factory or other place away from the construction site. First considered in earnest during the 1920s, it was subsequently put into practice on a wide scale during the post-war years. Since the 1960s, the practice has been increasingly referred to as **systems building**.

preference shares Shares issued by a company, without voting rights, which carry a fixed rate of dividend (or interest). The holders have a prior claim on the profits of the company over ordinary shareholders.

pregnancy A physiological process in which female, live-bearing mammals nurture their developing young within the uterus; also known as **gestation**. It begins when the fertilized ovum embeds itself in the uterine wall (*implantation*), and ends with the birth of the offspring (*parturition*). The duration of pregnancy is species-specific: smaller animals with large litters generally have short gestation periods (eg hamsters, 16 days). *p.750*

prelude A piece of instrumental music which precedes a longer work, or is coupled with another of comparable length, especially a fugue. Until the 17th-c, independent preludes were often written, or improvised, to test an instrument's tuning.

premenstrual syndrome / tension (PMS, PMT) A condition in which a variety of symptoms occur in relation to menstruation which interfere with normal life. It is of variable duration, has components that are both physical (eg abdominal pain, sleep disturbance) and mental (eg irritability, depression), and does not usually commence at the very beginning of puberty. The causes are unknown.

premier *prime minister*

Premier Division The name of the English football league first division, comprising the top 20 English sides, established as a separate organization in the 1992–3 season. The three lower divisions (2, 3, and 4) were renamed 1, 2, and 3, respectively;

Length Of Pregnancy In Some Mammals

Animal	Gestation period*	Animal	Gestation period*
camel	406	kangaroo	40
cat	62	lion	108
chimpanzee	280	mink	50
cow	237	monkey, rhesus	164
dog	62	mouse	21
dolphin	276	opossum	13
elephant, African	640	orangutan	245–275
ferret	42	pig	113
fox	52	rabbit	32
giraffe	395–425	rat	21
goat	151	reindeer	215–245
guinea pig	68	seal, northern fur	350
hamster	16	sheep	148
hedgehog	35–40	skunk	62
horse	337	squirrel, grey	44
human	266	tiger	105–109
hyena	110	whale	365

*average number of days

in 2004 these were renamed the Championship, division 1, and division 2.

Preminger, Otto [preminjer] (1906–86) Film director and producer, born in Vienna. He emigrated to the USA in 1935, and after some years of directing on the Broadway stage, made *Laura* (1944), often considered his best film. Later films included *Porgy and Bess* (1959), *Exodus* (1960), and *The Human Factor* (1979).

premiss A sentence which is explicitly assumed in an argument. In *Paris is larger than London; therefore London is smaller than Paris*, 'Paris is larger than London' is the only premiss.

premium bond A UK government security, introduced in 1956, and issued in numbered units of one pound. The accumulated interest on bonds sold is distributed through a lottery in the form of weekly and monthly tax-free cash prizes. Winning numbers are selected by a computer known as ERNIE (Electronic Random Number Indicator Equipment).

Premonstratensians [preemonstratensianz] A religious order founded by St Norbert at Prémontré, France, in 1120; also known as the **Norbertines** or **White Canons**. They are noted for parish education and mission work.

preparatory school In the UK, an independent fee-paying school for children up to the age when they might move to a public school, or to a maintained secondary school if parents no longer wish to pay fees. It usually caters for pupils up to the age of 13. In the USA, a preparatory school is one which prepares students for college, equivalent to the British public school.

Pre-Raphaelite Brotherhood (PRB) A group of artists formed in London in 1848 with the aim of revolutionizing early Victorian art; their preference was for the styles of the 15th-c (ie pre-Raphael). PRB pictures are recognizable by their bright colours, hard-edged forms, shallow picture-space, and meticulous attention to detail.

presbyopia *eye*

presbyter *elder* (religion)

Presbyterianism The conciliar form of Church government of the Reformed Churches, deriving from the 16th-c Reformation led by John Calvin in Geneva and John Knox in Scotland. Government is by courts at local congregational (eg kirk session), regional (presbytery), and national (General Assembly) levels.

Elders (ordained laymen) as well as ministers play a leading part in all courts.

presbytery 1 The E part of the chancel of a church, behind the choir.

2 The traditional name for the dwelling-house of priests in the Roman Catholic Church.

3 In Presbyterianism, a church court composed of equal numbers of elders and ministers, presided over by a moderator, and overseeing a geographical grouping of congregations.

preschool education The provision of education for children under the statutory school age. This can either be in nursery or kindergarten, where there will usually be trained personnel, or in playgroups, where parent volunteers work with playgroup leaders.

Prescott, Edward C (1940–) Economist, born in Glen Falls, NY. In 2003 he joined the W P Carey School of Business at Arizona State University, Tempe, and was appointed senior monetary advisor at the Federal Reserve Bank of Minneapolis. He shared the 2004 Nobel Prize for Economics for contributions to dynamic macroeconomics, specifically the time consistency of economic policy and the driving forces behind business cycles.

Prescott, John (Leslie) (1938–) British politician, born in Prestatyn, Denbighshire. He was elected to the European Parliament in 1975, and became deputy leader of the Labour group (1976–9). He became deputy prime minister and secretary of state for the environment, transport and the regions (1997–2001), secretary of state at the cabinet office and chancellor of the Duchy of Lancaster (2001–2), and in 2002 was given responsibility for local government and the regions. Following a cabinet reshuffle in 2006, he remained as deputy prime minister but lost his department.

prescription An order for drugs written by a physician to a pharmacist, who will supply the correct medicine to the patient. Until the 1940s prescriptions were written entirely in Latin.

president The name used by a head of state who is not appointed on a hereditary basis. Some presidents perform a largely formal and ceremonial role, ensuring that a government is formed (eg Ireland). Others share constitutionally in governing with the prime minister, cabinet, and legislature (eg France). Yet others effectively act as head of the government (eg the USA).

Presidential Medal of Freedom The highest American award for civilians in peacetime, given for contributions to the interests of the USA, or to world peace, or for cultural achievements.

presiding officer The name given to the officer who oversees the conduct and business of a legislative chamber. It is used in the Scottish Parliament, and in the Northern Ireland and Welsh Assemblies.

Presidium *Politburo*

Presley, Elvis (Aaron) (1935–77) Rock singer, born in Tupelo, MS. In 1953 he recorded some sides for Sun Records in Memphis, TN, then in 1956 'Heartbreak Hotel' sold millions of copies. His performances, featuring much hip-wriggling and sexual innuendo, incited hysteria in teenagers. He made many records that sold in the millions, including 'Hound Dog', 'Love Me Tender', and 'Jailhouse Rock'. His Hollywood films such as *Loving You* (1957), *King Creole* (1958), and *GI Blues* (1960) became enormous moneymakers. He died at Graceland, his Memphis mansion, which is now a souvenir shrine for his many fans. A remix of an earlier song 'A Little Less Conversation' topped the UK charts in 2002, giving Elvis his 18th number one hit in Britain. In January 2005, 'Jailhouse Rock' was re-released to commemorate what would have been his 70th birthday and topped the UK charts. Later the same month his single 'One Night' made history by becoming the 1000th UK number one.

Presocratics The first Greek (and therefore Western) philosophers, who came 'before Socrates' in the 6th-c and 5th-c BC. They sought natural rather than mythological explanations for phenomena.

Pressburg *Bratislava*

press freedom The right claimed by newspapers, journals, etc to disseminate such information, news, and opinions as they judge to be in the public interest. Specific press freedoms include the right to found a newspaper free from licensing restraints; editorial freedom; the right of access to public institutions; and the confidentiality of the journalist's sources. The concept is regarded as an essential feature of modern democracies. In democratic countries, press freedom may conflict with other rights, such as the individual's right to privacy or the right to reply to adverse comments made by the press. In repressive societies and totalitarian states, press freedom is non-existent; its denial is characterized by censorship and the punitive treatment of independently minded editors and journalists. However, even in democratic countries press freedom is usually limited by legal constraints, proprietors' interests, economic factors, and professional codes.

pressure Force per unit area; symbol *p*, units Pa (pascal). It is measured using barometers or pressure gauges.

pressure gauge A gauge which measures pressure, consisting of a hook-shaped tube called the *Bourdon tube*. When the pressure inside exceeds that outside, the tube straightens. This movement is transferred through levers and gears to move a pointer around a calibrated dial.

pressure group A voluntary organization formed to articulate a particular political or commercial interests or causes; also called an **interest group**; sometimes known as **lobbyists**. It differs from a political party in that it does not seek political office.

pressurized water reactor *nuclear reactor*

Prestel An interactive computer-based information system provided over the telephone network in the UK by British Telecom. It provides access to a wide variety of information sources.

Prester John A mythical Christian priest-king of a vast empire in C Asia. The story almost certainly related to the Christian kingdom of Ethiopia, which had been cut off by the Islamic conquest of Egypt.

Preston 53°46N 2°42W, pop (2001e) 129 600. City and county town of Lancashire, NW England; on the R Ribble; site of Royalist defeat in the Civil War (1648); 19th-c centre of the cotton industry; city status, 2002; railway; university (1994); football league team, Preston North End (Lillywhites).

Prestonpans [prestnpanz] 55°57N 3°00W, pop (2000e) 8080. Town in East Lothian, E Scotland; railway; site of Scottish victory over the English (1745).

Prestwick 55°30N 3°12W, pop (2000e) 13 700. Town in South Ayrshire, SW Scotland; airport (the official international gateway for Scotland); railway.

Pretoria [pritawria], known as **Tshwane** ('we are the same') from 2005. 25°45S 28°12E, pop (2000e) 613 000 (metropolitan area). Administrative capital of South Africa, and alternative capital of Gauteng province; altitude 1369 m/4491 ft; founded, 1855; capital of South African Republic, 1881; railway; two universities (1873, 1908); in 2005 the city council voted to change name of municipality of Pretoria to Tshwane, but retain Pretoria for city centre.

Pretorius, Andries (Wilhelmus Jacobus) [pretawrius] (1799–1853) Afrikaner leader, born in Graaff-Reinet, South Africa. He joined the Great Trek of 1836 into Natal, where he was chosen commandant-general, and later trekked again across the Vaal. Pretoria was named after him.

Pretorius, Marthinus (Wessel) [pretawrius] (1819–1901) Afrikaner soldier and statesman, born in Graaff-Reinet, South Africa, the son of Andries Pretorius. He was elected president of the South

African Republic (1857–71) and of the Orange Free State (1859–63).

preventive medicine A branch of medical practice concerned with the prevention of disease. This is achieved by measures that (1) control the environment, such as clean air legislation, (2) ensure a hygienic and suitable food and water supply, (3) promote mass medication (eg schemes of immunization), (4) organize programmes for the eradication of disease (eg smallpox, diphtheria), and (5) promote safer lifestyles largely by education (eg the promotion of condoms to reduce the possibility of AIDS).

Previn, André (George) [previn] (1929–) Conductor and composer, born in Berlin. He spent some years as a jazz pianist, and became musical director of symphony orchestras at Houston, (1967–9), London (1968–79), Pittsburgh, (1976–86), and Los Angeles (1986–9). He became composer laureate of the London Symphony Orchestra in 1991, and conductor laureate the following year. He has composed musicals, film scores, and orchestral works, and done a great deal to bring classical music to the attention of a wide public.

Prévost, (Antoine François), l'Abbé [prayvoh] (1697–1763) Novelist, born in Hesdin, France. He is best known for *Manon Lescaut* (1731), originally published as the final part of a seven-volume novel.

Priam [priyam] In Greek legend, the King of Troy. He was son of Laomedon, and husband of Hecuba, and is presented in the *Iliad* as an old man. At the sack of Troy, he was killed by Neoptolemus.

Pribilof Islands [pribilof] Group of four islands in the Bering Sea, Alaska, USA; two inhabited (St Paul, St George); area 168 km²/ 65 sq mi; centre of seal fur trade.

Price, (Mary Violet) Leontyne (1927–) Soprano, born in Laurel, MS. A notable Bess (1952–4) in Gershwin's *Porgy and Bess*, she was the first black opera singer on television, in *Tosca* for NBC (1955).

Price, Nick, popular name of **Nicholas Raymond Leige Price** (1957–) Golfer, born in Durban, South Africa. His family moved to Zimbabwe, where he turned professional in 1977. His wins include the PGA World Series (1983), the United States PGA Championship (1992, 1994), and the (British) Open (1994).

Price, Vincent (Leonard) (1911–93) Actor and writer, born in St Louis, MO. Known for his distinctive, low-pitched, creaky, atmospheric voice, and his quizzical, mock-serious facial expressions, he went on to star in a series of acclaimed Gothic horror movies, such as *The Pit and the Pendulum* (1961) and *The Abominable Dr Phibes* (1971).

price index *retail price index*

prices and incomes policy An attempt by government to control inflation by acting directly on prices and wages, either by persuasion or by law. This contrasts with the view that inflation should be controlled by monetary or fiscal policies to influence demand, or supply-side measures to improve productivity. The correct structure of prices and wages is controversial, and the government's power to control prices and wages is uneven. It is impossible for governments to avoid prices and incomes policy entirely, as they are themselves major purchasers of goods and employers of labour. Efforts at prices and incomes policy have been sporadic, in the UK in the 1960s and 1970s, and in France in the early 1980s.

prickly heat A common generalized skin disorder in tropical countries that may also affect local areas of skin in temperate climates. Obstruction to the ducts of sweat glands results in a crop of small red pimples associated with itching.

prickly pear A species of opuntia (*Opuntia vulgaris*) often cultivated for its reddish, juicy, edible fruits. (Family: Cactaceae.)

Pride, Sir Thomas (?–1658) English parliamentarian during the Civil War, born (possibly) near Glastonbury. When the House of

Commons betrayed a disposition to effect a settlement with Charles I, he was appointed by the army (1648) to expel its Presbyterian Royalist members (**Pride's Purge**).

priest The person authorized to sacrifice. In Christianity, the term derives from the Old Testament sacrificial system. Now, mainly in Roman Catholic and Orthodox usage, it refers to an ordained officer authorized to administer the sacraments, in particular the Eucharist (the sacrifice of the Mass).

Priestley, J(ohn) B(oynton) (1894–1984) Writer, born in Bradford, West Yorkshire. In 1929 his novel *The Good Companions* (1929) gained him wide popularity. He established his reputation as a playwright with *Dangerous Corner* (1932), *Time and the Conways* (1937), and other plays on space-time themes, as well as popular comedies, such as *Laburnum Grove* (1933). His wife, **Jacquetta Hawkes** (1910–96), was an archaeologist and writer.

Priestley, Joseph (1733–1804) Chemist and clergyman, born in Fieldhead, West Yorkshire. He is best known for his research into the chemistry of gases, and his discovery of oxygen. His controversial views on religion and political theory (he was a supporter of the French Revolution) led him in 1794 to leave in fear of his life for America, where he was well received.

primary In politics, an election to choose the candidates for an election to public office. It differs from other forms of candidate selection in that the primary election is not organized by political parties, but by the government authority for which the election is to be held. The procedure is commonly associated with the USA.

primary education The first phase of statutory education, usually covering the years from 5 or 6 up to 11 or 12. In most countries, the emphasis is on the coverage of a wide range of subjects and themes usually taught by the class teacher. There is also emphasis on social and personal development in the primary phase, and on 'learning by doing'.

primate (religion) The most senior bishop of a given area; for example, in the Church of England the Archbishop of Canterbury is primate of All England.

primate (zoology) A mammal of the order Primates (c.180 species); most inhabit tropical forests; both eyes face forwards; hands and (usually) feet with grasping 'opposable thumb', used for climbing; cerebral hemispheres of brain well developed. Living species are usually placed in two suborders: the Strepsirhini (**prosimians**) and the Haplorhini (**tarsiers** and **Anthropoidea**).

prime minister The leader of and usually head of a government; also known as a **premier**. In general, prime ministers have to work through collective decision-making in a *cabinet*, although they can enjoy certain separate powers. In electoral systems, they are usually the leader of the largest party or coalition in parliament.

prime number In mathematics, a positive integer greater than 1 that has no divisors other than 1 and itself. Number theorists have tried to devise functions $f(n)$ which produce only prime numbers for positive integer values of n, but so far all have failed.

prime rate The US bank base lending rate, at which the bank will lend to its best ('prime') customers. This rate applies to only 50 or so large US corporations, all others paying higher rates.

Primo de Rivera (y Orbaneja), Miguel [preemoh thay rivera] (1870–1930) Spanish general, born in Jerez de la Frontera, Spain. In 1923 he led a military coup, inaugurating a dictatorship which lasted until 1930. His son, **José Antonio Primo de Rivera** (1903–36) founded the Spanish Fascist Party, *Falange Española* in 1933, and was executed by the Republicans in 1936.

primrose A stemless perennial (*Primula vulgaris*) native to Europe, W Asia, and N Africa; flowers long-stalked with spreading, pale yellow, rarely pink petals. (Family: Primulaceae.)

Prince, stage name by which **Prince Roger Nelson** is most widely known (1958–) Pop-singer and composer, born in Minneapolis, MN. Named after the Prince Roger Trio, a jazz band in which his father was a pianist, he began singing as a teenager, and released *For You* in 1978. International success followed the release of *1999* (1982), the film and album *Purple Rain* (1984), and *Batman* (1989). He changed his name to the unpronounceable glyph O(+> in 1993–2000, and also adopted the designation of **The Artist (formerly known as Prince)**.

Prince Edward Island pop (2000e) 145 600; area 5660 km²/ 2185 sq mi. Province in E Canada; island in the Gulf of St Lawrence; rises to 142 m/466 ft; capital, Charlottetown; visited by Cartier, 1534; French claim as Île St Jean; settled by Acadians; captured by British, 1758; annexed to Nova Scotia, 1763; separate province, 1769; modern name, after Queen Victoria's father, 1798; joined Canada, 1873; governed by a lieutenant-governor and Legislative Assembly.

Prince of Wales In the UK, the title conferred (by custom, not law) on the sovereign's eldest son. Wales was ruled by a succession of independent princes from the 5th-c; the first to be acknowledged by an English king was Llewelyn ap Gruffudd (r.1246–82) in 1267. Tradition holds that after the death of Llewelyn in battle (against the English), Edward I presented his own infant son to the Welsh people at Caernarfon Castle as their prince. The title has been used since that time.

Princess Royal A title sometimes bestowed on the eldest, or only, daughter of a sovereign. George V's daughter Mary was Princess Royal until her death in 1965; the title was conferred by the Queen on Princess Anne in 1987.

Princeton 40°21N 74°40W, pop (2000e) 14 200. Borough in WC New Jersey, USA, on the Millstone R; founded by Quakers, 1696; scene of a British defeat by George Washington, 1777; a noted centre for education and research; university (1746); Institute for Advanced Study.

printed circuit A technique which replaces individual wiring between components in electronic circuits. It is made by depositing a network of thin, metallic connections on to a board, the electronic components usually being soldered to pins on the other side of the board. Printed circuit boards can be mass-produced, and their use enables circuit assembly to be easily automated.

printer *computer printer*

printing A set of techniques for placing an image on a foundation in a controlled sequence of identical copies; the foundation is generally paper, and the colouring agent is generally ink. The techniques include *relief*, *planographic* (surface), and *intaglio* (recess) printing. The principal forms of relief printing are *letterpress* and *flexography*; those of planographic printing, *lithography* and the obsolescent *collotype*. Intaglio printing is typified by *gravure*, but most of the techniques used by artists in printmaking (engraving, drypoint, mezzotint, and etching) also fall into this category.

Printing probably originated in 6th-c China (a text survives from 594), and newspaper was first printed c.860. Printing with metal plates developed in the 11th-c; movable metal type c.1050. The first European block printing dates from 1375. Gutenberg began printing in 1436, and Caxton in 1475. The oldest form of printing, letterpress, depends upon pressure for the satisfactory transfer of ink to paper. Later design improvements included the 'Dutch' press developed in Amsterdam and introduced into N America in 1639. The wooden handpress was superseded in 1795 by the first all-metal press, the Stanhope. The 19th and 20th-c saw the development of increasingly elaborate mechanical presses. Offset lithography developed at the beginning of the 20th-c, and came into widespread use. Techniques of typesetting can now create the typographic image direct, either on film or on paper, thus cutting out the need for typesetters to set and store metal type.

prion disease [priyon] An unusual category of disease, thought to be transmitted by infectious agents composed of protein; the name is derived from **proteinaceous infectious particles**. It is found in humans (eg Creutzfeldt-Jakob disease, kuru) and animals (eg bovine spongiform encephalopathy in cows, scrapie in sheep). There is progressive degeneration of the central nervous system, with characteristic pathological changes including small holes (vacuoles) in the cells, which has led to the term *spongiform ecephalopathy*, and deposits of an abnormal, highly folded protein. All the functions of the brain are affected, most obviously resulting in movement disorders and dementia. The disease can be inherited or occur sporadically, and may be transmitted within and possibly between species. Hereditary cases have a genetic mutation that causes them to produce the prion. Infectious transmission is thought to occur as a result of inoculation or ingestion of tissue from an infected source. The possibility of transmission from cattle to humans has raised major anxieties.

Prior, Matthew (1664–1721) Diplomat and poet, born in Wimborne, Dorset. He is best known for his light occasional verse, collected as *Poems on Several Occasions* (1709).

Priscian [prishian], Lat **Priscianus** (6th-c) Latin grammarian, born in Caesarea. His 18-volume *Institutiones grammaticae* (Grammatical Foundations) was highly regarded in the Middle Ages.

prism In mathematics, a solid geometrical figure: its section is a rectilinear figure, with parallel edges. In optics, it is a transparent object used to produce or study the refraction and dispersion of light.

prison That part of the penal system where criminals are held in custody for varying lengths of time determined by the courts as punishment for offences. Prisons developed rapidly from the early 19th-c; before then, banishment and corporal or capital punishment were the main ways of dealing with offenders. Conditions in the earliest municipal prisons were usually atrocious, and were improved only through the work of penal reformers such as Elizabeth Fry. Problems of overcrowding still dog many prisons today.

Priština [preeshtina] 42°39N 21°10E, pop (2001e) 190 500. Capital town of Kosovo autonomous province, S Serbia; former capital of Serbia; airfield; railway; university (1976); population decimated by forced removal of ethnic Albanian population (Mar–Apr 1999); severely damaged in the ensuing Yugoslavia/NATO conflict.

Pritchett, Sir V(ictor) S(awdon) (1900–97) Writer and critic, born in Ipswich, Suffolk. He became known for his critical works, such as *The Living Novel* (1946), short stories (2 vols, 1982, 1983), and travel books.

Pritzker Architecture Prize Architecture prize established by Jay A Pritzker in 1979. Worth $100 000, the prestigious prize is awarded annually by the Chicago-based Hyatt Foundation to honour the achievements of a living architect.

private enterprise An economic system where individuals may engage in a business venture using their own resources and without needing state approval, as long as the venture does not contravene existing laws. It contrasts with **public enterprise**, where the activity is carried out by a state-owned or -controlled organization.

privateering *buccaneers*

privatization The return to private ownership of organizations formerly owned by the state. The government issues shares in the company to be privatized, and offers them for sale to the public. Several cases of privatization took place in Britain in the 1980s, including British Telecom and British Gas.

privet A mostly temperate, evergreen or deciduous shrub or small tree; leaves leathery; flowers tubular with four spreading lobes, creamy, fragrant; berries black or purple, poisonous. Several species are commonly used for garden hedges. (Genus: *Ligustrum*, c.40 species. Family: Oleaceae.)

Privy Council A body which advises the British monarch, appointed by the crown. In previous times, particularly the Tudor period, it was a highly influential group; today its role is largely formal. Its membership is over 300.

Prix de l'Arc de Triomphe [pree duh lahk duh treeöf] The richest horse race in Europe, held at the end of the season over 2400 m/2625 yd at Longchamp, near Paris, on the first Sunday in October. First run in 1920, it is the leading race in Europe for horses at least three years old.

Prix Goncourt France's most prestigious literary prize for fiction, given annually since 1903 by the Académie Goncourt (founded by Edmond de Goncourt). The award carries a symbolic prize of 50 francs but guarantees huge sales for the author.

Prizren [preezren] 42°12N 20°43E, pop (2001e) 114 900. Town in Kosovo autonomous province, SW Serbia; on R Prizrenska Bistrica; built on the site of a Roman town (Theranda); important mediaeval trade centre; part of Albania, 1941–4; railway.

probability theory The mathematical study of relative probabilities in processes involving uncertainty, for example tossing a coin or rolling dice. The foundations of the subject were laid by Pascal and Fermat in the 17th-c.

probate The official proving of a will. The executor of the will applies to the court for a certificate confirming the validity of the will and the authority of the executor to administer the estate of the deceased. The term is not used in all jurisdictions (eg in Scotland).

probation A method of dealing with offenders over the age of 16 where, instead of a sentence of imprisonment, a court may order the offender to be supervised for a fixed period by a **probation officer**. Offenders must agree to be placed on probation after the obligations under the order are explained to them.

proboscis monkey [probosis] An Old World monkey (*Nasalis larvatus*) native to Borneo; pale with darker 'cap' on head, and dark back; long tail; protruding nose, which in adult males becomes bulbous and pendulous.

procaryote or **prokaryote** [prohkarioht] An organism that lacks an organized nucleus separated from the surrounding cytoplasm by a nuclear membrane. They are predominantly single-celled micro-organisms, such as the bacteria and blue-green algae, or infectious agents of cells, such as the viruses.

Proclus [prohklus] (c.412–85) Greek Neoplatonist philosopher, born in Constantinople. The last head of Plato's Academy, his approach combined the Roman, Syrian, and Alexandrian schools of thought in Greek philosophy into one theological metaphysic.

Proconsul *Dryopithecus*

Procop(ius) *Prokop*

Procopius [prokohpius] (c.499–565) Byzantine historian, born in Caesarea, Palestine. He accompanied Belisarius on his campaigns against the Persians, the Vandals in Africa, and the Ostrogoths in Italy. His principal works are histories of the wars, and of the court of Justinian.

Procrustes [prohkruhsteez] In the legend of Theseus, a robber, living in Attica, who made travellers lie on his bed, and either cut or lengthened them to fit it; his name means 'the stretcher'. Theseus gave him the same treatment, and killed him.

procurator fiscal A public offical in Scotland who is responsible for pursuing the prosecution of crimes and offences in the sheriff court and the district court. The 'fiscal' is also responsible for reporting serious crimes to the Crown Office, which may merit prosecution in the High Court, as well as for investigating all cases of sudden, accidental, or suspicious deaths.

Prodi, Romano [prodee] (1939–) Italian prime minister (1996–8,

2006–), and president of the European Commission (1999–2004), born in Scandiano, Reggio Emilia, Italy. Minister for industry in 1978–9, he left to head a centre-left coalition *L'Ulivo*, which was successful in the 1996 elections and he became prime minister. He was appointed president of the European Commission following the mass resignation of the commissioners over a report detailing maladministration, and introduced a new code of conduct. In 2006 he led Italy's centre-left party to a narrow victory in the parliamentary elections.

producer In the film industry, the person who brings the initial concept to practical reality, organizing budgetary control, choosing the director, and holding the balance between the director and other important members of the production team. Producers are also concerned with distribution for the international market, and exploitation on television and video. In major television organizations, one producer is often in charge of a series of programmes, working with several different directors or presenters. In radio broadcasting, the producer has a dual role, being also the person who actually controls the making of the programmes (the province of the *director*, in other media).

productivity The ratio of output to input in an industrial context. It usually refers to the quantity of goods or commodities produced in relation to the number of employees engaged in the operation (**labour productivity**). **Total productivity** includes the input of capital also. The notion is important in wage negotiations: **productivity bargaining** balances a proposed increase in wages with an anticipated rise in productivity.

profit The difference for a company between its sales revenue and the costs attributable to those sales. Profit may be calculated before or after deducting interest payments, and before or after deducting taxation charges. The surplus may be paid out to shareholders as a dividend, or retained by the business (as *reserves*) to finance capital expenditure. **Profit sharing** is a scheme whereby a percentage of the profits of a company is given to staff in the form of an additional bonus payment. **Profitability** is the measurement of how effectively a company has used the resources available to it. There are also many **non-profit-making** companies, where a surplus is ploughed back into the company, or (as in the case of charities) used for charitable purposes.

Profumo, John (Dennis) [profyoomoh], popularly known as **Jack Profumo** (1915–2006) British Conservative statesman. Secretary of state for war in 1960, he resigned in 1963 after deceiving the House of Commons about the nature of his relationship with Miss Christine Keeler, who was at the time also involved with a Russian diplomat. He then dedicated his life to social and charitable work, and was chairman (1982–5) then president of Toynbee Hall, London. He married actress **Valerie Hobson** (1917–98) in 1954.

progesterone [prohjesterohn] A steroid present in both sexes of all vertebrates. In female mammals it acts to prepare the uterus for implantation of the embryo, inhibits ovulation during pregnancy, and prepares the breasts for lactation.

prognosis In medicine, an assessment of the likely outcome of a disease and its treatment. A good prognosis implies that the patient is likely to recover completely; a poor prognosis implies that the disease is likely to prove terminal within a short period.

program; programmer *computer program*

programmed learning A form of learning developed in the 1960s, based on the behaviourist learning theories of US psychologist B F Skinner. He stressed the need for short frames of information to be given, followed by an active response and the immediate reinforcement of correct answers. Programmed-learning principles have been influential in the development of microcomputer software and the interactive video disk.

programme music Music which paints a scene or tells a story. Among early examples are the violin concertos by Vivaldi called *The Four Seasons*, but it was in the 19th-c, with the increased resources of the symphony orchestra, that composers most effectively gave musical expression to literary and other extra-musical ideas, notably in the concert overture and the symphonic poem.

programming language An artificial language which allows people to instruct computers to carry out specific tasks. Many programming languages have been developed; among the relatively common high-level languages are ADA, APL, ALGOL, BASIC, COBOL, CORAL, FORTH, FORTRAN, LISP, PASCAL, PROLOG, and JAVA (*see separate entries*).

Progressive Conservative (PC) Party A Canadian political party, mainly active at the federal level, but with branches in most provinces and territories. It originated in C Canada in the 1850s, though with roots going back to 18th-c Toryism. The PCs have formed the government nationally five times since the 1940s, but were resoundingly defeated in the general election in 1993.

progressive education A term used to denote teaching which places greater emphasis on the wishes of the child. It usually involves greater freedom of choice, activity, and movement than traditional forms of teaching.

Progress spacecraft An uncrewed version of the Soviet Soyuz crewed spacecraft, modified as a resupply vehicle for the Salyut and Mir space stations. After unloading, the spacecraft is separated and removed from orbit to burn up in the atmosphere.

Prohibition (1920–33) An attempt to stop the sale of all alcoholic drinks in the USA, authorized by the Eighteenth Amendment to the Constitution (1919) and the Volstead Act (1920). Prohibition met great resistance, and generated a large bootlegging industry. It was ended in 1933.

projection television A television system in which images are projected through special wide-aperture lenses on a large external screen, usually using three high-brightness cathode ray tubes in the component colours red, green, and blue. The limited brightness output limits the width of an external high-reflection screen to c.4 m/13 ft.

projective tests In psychology, a number of somewhat contentious procedures for assessing personality. Their use involves the presentation of ambiguous or unstructured material onto which the testee is assumed to project his/her personality. The most famous is the Rorschach Psychodiagnostic Technique, which requires subjects to describe what they see in 10 bilaterally symmetrical inkblots.

projector An apparatus for presenting an enlarged image on a screen from a transparency such as a photographic slide or film. In a film projector, each frame is held stationary at an illuminated aperture for a brief period, and then advanced by an intermittent sprocket or reciprocating claw, the light being cut off by a rotating shutter during the movement. The sound track on the film is reproduced at a separate sound head where the film is moved continuously at constant speed.

prokaryote *procaryote*

Prokofiev, Sergey Sergeyevitch [prohkofief] (1891–1953) Composer, born in Sontsovka, Ukraine. His works have a vast range, including seven symphonies, nine concertos, ballets, operas, suites, cantatas, sonatas, and songs, and his most popular work, *Peter and the Wolf* (1936).

Prokop or **Procop(ius)** [prohkop, prokohpius], known as **the Bald** or **the Great** (c.1380–1434) Bohemian Hussite leader, a follower of Žižka, and on his death, the leader of the Taborites. He repeatedly defeated German armies, but fell in battle at Lipany, Hungary.

prolactin [prohlaktin] A hormone secreted by the front part of the pituitary gland which initiates lactation in mammals and stimulates the production of progesterone.

prolapsed intervertebral disc A condition which arises when the nucleus of the disc situated between the bodies of the vertebrae is forced outwards through the surrounding joint capsule; commonly known as a **slipped disc**. It is caused by an excessive load being placed on the joints between the bodies of the spinal vertebrae, such as in heavy or awkward lifting, and is followed by back pain or sciatica.

proletariat In radical and socialist philosophy, a term coined to denote the **working class**, ie those who live by their labour and do not own property. *Lumpenproletariat* was coined by Marx to refer to those in big cities from whom class identification could not be expected.

pro-life movement Organized opposition to the legality of induced abortion, and to laboratory experiments on human embryos. There are a number of national organizations and pressure groups, such as Operation Rescue in the USA, the Society for the Protection of the Unborn Child (SPUC), and LIFE. Active support comes from members of several religions, notably Roman Catholics, but also Muslims and Jews.

PROLOG A high-level programming language based on mathematical logic, widely used in artificial intelligence applications. PROLOG has, to some extent, replaced LISP.

PROM [peerom] An acronym of **programmable read-only memory**, a special type of integrated circuit read-only memory (ROM) into which the user can write data after manufacture. Once written, the data cannot be altered.

promenade concert A musical performance, especially by an orchestra, during which some at least of the audience are offered floor space, without seats, at reduced prices. The London 'proms' were started at the Queen's Hall by Sir Henry Wood in 1895; they transferred to the Royal Albert Hall in 1941.

Prometheus [prohmeethyoos] In Greek mythology, a Titan; his name means 'the foreseeing'. He stole fire from heaven to help mankind, whom Zeus wished to destroy, and was punished by being chained to a rock in the Caucasus; every day an eagle fed on his liver, which grew again in the night. Heracles shot the eagle and set Prometheus free.

promissory note A signed document containing a written promise to pay a sum of money on or by a specific date. The document is legally binding and is signed, for example, when a bank customer takes out a loan.

promoter (genetics) The non-coding region immediately next to the start of a gene which acts as a 'switch' to allow transcription. Various proteins (known as *transcription factors*) bind to the promoter DNA sequences which ultimately have the effect of recruiting the enzyme RNA polymerase. This begins the process of transcription of the gene.

prongbuck *pronghorn*

pronghorn A North American antelope (*Antilocapra americana*); male called **prongbuck**; pale brown with prominent eyes; male horns with frontal 'prong' and backward-curving tips.

proof spirit *alcohol strength*

propane C_3H_8, boiling point $-42°C$. The third in the alkane series of hydrocarbons; a gas obtained from petroleum and natural gas, used as a fuel and a refrigerant.

propanone *acetone*

propeller A device used principally by ships and aeroplanes to transform the rotational energy of an engine into directed thrust. To accomplish this, the propeller is fitted with blades radiating from a central hub, each blade being of aerofoil cross section. As the propeller rotates, the water or air is accelerated backwards, producing a reactive force in the forward direction.

Propertius, Sextus [propershius] (c.48–c.15 BC) Latin elegiac poet, probably born in Asisium (Assisi), Italy. The central figure of his inspiration was his mistress, to whom he devoted the first of his four surviving books, *Cynthia*.

property Something owned or possessed – a notion whose pre-

cise definition varies greatly between different jurisdictions. In Anglo–US law, **real property** includes lands and buildings; other kinds of property are known as **personal property**. **Chattels** are movable goods, classed as personal property. A gift of personal property made by will is a **legacy**; a gift of real property made by will is a **devise**. **Intellectual property** is a general term covering intangible rights in the product of intellectual effort. It includes copyright in published work, and patents granted to protect new inventions.

propfan An aircraft propeller designed for a turbo-engine, enabling large amounts of power to be delivered by increasing the number and area of the blades in comparison with a conventional aircraft propeller.

prophet One who is inspired to reveal a message from a divine being; an important figure in many religious traditions, sometimes a lone figure opposing the established cult or social order (eg Jeremiah, Amos, and Hosea in the Old Testament). Their messages usually address a specific situation or problem.

proportional representation Any system of voting designed to ensure that the representation of voters is in proportion to their numbers. In the *list system* the number of candidates on a party's list who are elected depends on the proportion of votes they receive in national elections. In the *single transferable vote*, votes are cast in multi-member constituencies and an ordered preference for all the candidates can be expressed on the ballot paper, votes being transferred from one candidate to another to enable them to gain the necessary quota to be elected. Most European countries use proportional representation. The case against it is that it produces unstable coalitions, and breaks the bond between MPs and their constituencies.

proprioception *kinaesthesis*

propyl [prohpiyl, -pil] $CH_3CH_2CH_2-$. A group derived from propane. **Isopropyl** is the isomeric $(CH_3)_2CH-$. Propyl and isopropyl alcohols (propan-1-ol and propan-2-ol) are both used as solvents and as substitutes for ethanol in non-beverage applications.

propylaeum or **propylaea** [prohpileeum, prohpileea] An important entrance gateway or vestibule. It is usually in front of a sacred building, as on the Acropolis, Athens (437–432 BC).

proscenium An arch and opening of a stage wall separating the auditorium of a theatre from the acting and scenic area. Its development, linked to a concept of theatrical illusion, dominated Western drama until the early 20th-c, becoming a 'fourth wall' through which the audience, sitting in darkness, could see and eavesdrop.

prosecution The initiation and pursuance of criminal proceedings against an individual in a criminal court. Common law systems are *accusatorial*, with the burden of proof normally resting with the prosecution to prove the offence beyond reasonable doubt. Civil law systems, such as France and Germany, are *inquisitorial*, whereby the prosecutor presents the case to court, but it is the responsibility of the judge to investigate the facts of the case and if necessary to call and question witnesses.

Proserpine *Persephone*

prosimian A primate of the suborder Strepsirhini (40 species); wet nose with slit-like nostrils; tip of nose, between nostrils, with an obvious vertical groove; also known as **primitive primate**.

prosody The pitch, loudness, tempo, and rhythm of speech. A particular application of prosodic study is in relation to poetry, where it provides a means of analyzing the rhythmical properties of lines (*metrics*), as part of the study of versification.

Prost, Alain [prost], nickname **the Professor** (1955–) Motor-racing driver and team owner, born in St Chamond, France. The first Frenchman to win the world title, he won in 1985–6 (both for Marlboro–McLaren), was runner-up in 1983–4 and 1988, and won again in 1989 (for Maclaren–Honda) and 1993, when he announced his retirement. His 51 wins and 798·5 championship points is a world record. He was less successful as an F1 team owner with Team Prost (1997–2001).

prostaglandins [prostaglandins] A family of unsaturated fatty acids produced by virtually every tissue of the body in response to particular stimuli. Their physiological role is unclear, but they are implicated in platelet function, the natural prevention of ulcers, and the causes of inflammation.

prostate gland A partly muscular, partly glandular, accessory male sex organ in mammals, lying within the pelvis below the bladder, encircling part of the urethra. During sexual arousal it contributes an alkaline fluid to semen, accounting for approximately one-third of its volume. After age 50 the gland may atrophy; however, an excessive increase in the size of the side and middle lobes may also occur, compressing the urethra, and adversely affecting the functioning of the kidneys. Treatment involves the removal of part or all of the gland.

prosthesis [prostheesis] An artificial substitute for a part of the body. Examples include a mechanical arm or leg, artificial heart valves, dentures, and tooth implants.

Protagoras [prohtagoras] (c.490–421 BC) Greek philosopher, born in Abdera, Greece. He taught a system of practical wisdom based on the doctrine that 'man is the measure of all things'.

protea [prohtia] A shrub or small tree, native to tropical and especially S Africa, where they are very diverse. The spectacular 'flowers' are actually inflorescences containing numerous small true flowers in the centre, surrounded by petal-like bracts. (Genus: *Protea*, 130 species. Family: Proteaceae.)

protectionism A government policy of protecting domestic industries against foreign competition. Devices used include tariffs, quotas on imports, subsidies for domestic firms, and preference in state purchasing. Protection is supposed to be checked by international treaties.

Protectorate A regime established by the Instrument of Government, the work of army conservatives, England's only written constitution. The Lord Protectors, Oliver Cromwell (ruled 1653–8) and his son Richard (ruled 1658–9), issued ordinances and controlled the armed forces, subject to the advice of a Council of State and with Parliament as legislative partner. It failed to win support, and its collapse led to the Restoration.

protectorate A territory over which the protecting state enjoys power and jurisdiction short of full sovereignty; not formally annexed, it can come about by treaty, grant, or usage. The commonest types were the 19th–20th-c colonial protectorates, such as Botswana, all of which have now achieved independence.

protein One of the three essential types of energy foods. It is a natural condensation polymer of amino acids occurring mainly as structural tissue in animals but also as enzymes in both animals and plants. Nearly all proteins are derived from 20 amino acids.

Proterozoic eon The later of the two geological eons into which the Precambrian era is divided; the period of time from 2500 million years ago until the beginning of the Cambrian period 590 million years ago.

Protestantism The generic term for expressions of Christian faith originating from the 16th-c Reformation as a protest against Roman Catholicism. Common characteristics include the authority of scripture, justification by faith alone, and the priesthood of all believers. There were over 350 million Protestants in 2007.

Proteus [prohtyoos] A genus of typically rod-shaped bacteria that move by means of flagella. They are found primarily in the intestines and faeces of humans and other animals. (Kingdom: Monera. Family: Enterobacteriaceae.)

Proteus [prohtyoos] In Greek mythology, a sea god, associated with seals, and a shape-changer; he will give answers to questions after a wrestling match.

protista *Protoctista*

Protoceratops [prohtohseratops] A primitive ceratopsian dinosaur, known from the Upper Cretaceous period of E Asia; rear frill on skull well developed; teeth for shearing. (Order: Ornithischia.)

protochordate [prohtohkaw(r)dayt] An informal name for any of the chordates (phylum: Chordata) that lack a vertebral column.

Protoctista [prohtoktista] A kingdom of relatively simple, eucaryotic organisms, comprising the single-celled protozoans and those algae and fungi that possess flagellated spores. They vary greatly in size, from the smallest micro-organisms (eg *Chlorella*) to the giant kelps. The smallest members of this kingdom, generally composed of a single cell, or only a few cells, are known as **protists**, in some classifications.

Proto-Indo-European *Indo-European languages*

proton A component particle of the atomic nucleus; symbol p; mass $1·673 \times 10^{-27}$ kg (938·3 MeV), charge +1, spin $1/2$. It is held in the nucleus by strong nuclear force.

proton number The number of protons in an atomic nucleus, equal to the number of electrons in an atom; symbol Z; also called **atomic number**. Each element has a unique proton number.

protoplasm The complex, translucent substance that makes up every living cell. In eucaryotes, protoplasm is divisible into *nucleoplasm* (the protoplasm in the nucleus) and *cytoplasm* (the protoplasm in the rest of the cell).

Protozoa A diverse group of unicellular micro-organisms found free-living, as consumers of organic matter, in all kinds of habitats, and as parasites or associates of other organisms; typically possess a single nucleus, sometimes two or more; usually reproduce by splitting in two (binary fission).

Protura [protyoora] An order of small, primitively wingless insects that lack eyes and antennae; use forelegs as feelers; possess three pairs of rudimentary limbs on abdominal segments; c.120 species.

Proudhon, Pierre Joseph [proodõ] (1809–65) Socialist and political theorist, born in Besançon, France. His first important book, *Qu'est-ce que la propriété?* (1840, What is Property?), affirmed the bold paradox 'property is theft', because it involves the exploitation of the labour of others. His greatest work was the *Système des contradictions économiques* (1846, System of Economic Contradictions).

Proulx, (Edna) Annie [proo] (1935–) Novelist, born in Norwich, CT. In 1988 her collected stories were published as *Heart Songs and Other Stories*. She turned to novel writing with *Postcards* (1992), and won the Pulitzer Prize for her second book, *The Shipping News* (1994). Later works include *Accordion Crimes* (1996) and *That Old Ace in the Hole* (2002), and the story *Brokeback Mountain* (1997, filmed 2005).

Proust, Marcel [proost] (1871–1922) Novelist, born in Auteuil, France. In 1912 he produced the first part of his 13-volume masterpiece, *A la recherche du temps perdu* (trans Remembrance of Things Past). The second volume won the Prix Goncourt in 1919. His massive novel, exploring the power of the memory and the unconscious, as well as the nature of writing itself, has been profoundly influential.

Provence [provãs], Lat **Provincia** Former province in SE France; part of France, 1481; distinctive Romance dialect; tourism (especially on Riviera).

Proverbs, Book of A book of the Hebrew Bible/Old Testament, attributed in the opening title to Solomon, but probably consisting of collected wisdom traditions from several centuries.

Providence 41°49N 71°24W, pop (2000e) 173 600. Capital of Rhode Island, USA; port at the head of Providence R; established, 1636; city status, 1832; an early haven for religious dissenters; airport; railway; Brown University (1764); popular sailing resort.

Provincetown Players A US theatre group (1915–29) remembered for the work of its leading playwright Eugene O'Neill and designer Robert Edmond Jones.

Provisional IRA *IRA*

Provisional Sinn Féin *Sinn Féin*

Provisions of Oxford *Oxford, Provisions of*

Proxima Centauri [proksima sentawree] *Centaurus*

Prozac *antidepressants*

Prudhoe Bay [proodoh] Bay on N coast of Alaska, USA, on the Beaufort Sea; pipeline links Arctic oil fields with Valdez on the Gulf of Alaska.

Prud'hon, Pierre Paul [prüdō] (1758–1823) Painter, born in Cluny, France. Patronized by the empresses of Napoleon, he was made court painter, and among his best work is a portrait of Joséphine.

prunus A tree or shrub of a large temperate genus containing many well-known ornamentals and orchard fruits; fruit a single stony seed surrounded by a fleshy outer layer. (Genus: *Prunus*, 400 species. Family: Rosaceae.)

Prusiner, Stanley B (1942–) Neurologist, born in Des Moines, IA. He graduated from the University of Pennsylvania in 1968, then worked at the University of California, Berkeley and San Francisco. He shared the 1998 Nobel Prize for Physiology or Medicine for his discovery of prions.

Prussia A N European state, originally centred in the E Baltic region as a duchy owing suzerainty to Poland. The kingdom of Prussia was founded in 1701; under Frederick William I (1713–40) and Frederick II ('the Great') (1740–86) it acquired W Prussia and Silesia, and gained considerable territory in W Germany at the Congress of Vienna (1815). During the 19th-c it emerged as the most powerful German state, and ultimately the focus of German unification. Within the German Empire (1871–1918) and the Weimar Republic (1919–33), it retained considerable autonomy and influence. As a legal entity, Prussia ceased to exist with the post-1945 division of Germany.

prussic acid *cyanide; hydrocyanic acid*

Prynne, William [prin] (1600–69) Puritan pamphleteer, born in Swanswick, Somerset. In 1633 appeared his *Histrio-Mastix: the Players Scourge*, which contained an apparent attack on the queen, for which he was imprisoned. Released in 1640 by the Long Parliament, he prosecuted Laud (1644), and became an MP (1648). After Cromwell's death he returned to parliament as a Royalist, for which he was made Keeper of the Tower Records.

Psalms, Book of A book of the Hebrew Bible/Old Testament; also known as the **Psalter**. It consists of 150 hymns or poems of various types, representing material from several centuries. It was the most important type of mediaeval illustrated book.

Psalter *Psalms, Book of*

psephology [sefolojee] The study of elections and voting. It is popularly associated with the analysis of voting figures and the forecasting of outcomes, but covers all aspects of elections and electoral systems.

Pseudepigrapha [syoodepigrafa] An ancient Jewish (and sometimes Christian) body of literature which is not part of the Jewish Scriptures or of major Christian versions of the Old Testament or of the Apocrypha, but which is similar to the Old Testament in character. It spans roughly the period 200 BC–AD 200, and includes apocalypses (eg 1 Enoch, 4 Ezra), testaments (eg Testaments of the 12 Patriarchs), wisdom literature, prayers, and psalms (eg Prayer of Manasseh, Psalms of Solomon), and additions to Old Testament stories (eg Life of Adam and Eve).

pseudopodium [syoodohpohdium] A lobe-like protrusion, usually temporary, of the cell body of amoeboid cells, brought about by cytoplasmic streaming. Pseudopodia function as a means of locomotion, and also as a way of feeding (by engulfing food particles).

psi [psiy, siy] A parapsychological term for certain paranormal processes, embracing both extrasensory perception and psychokinesis. This letter of the Greek alphabet was felt to be most appropriate to stand for things considered as psychic.

psittacosis [(p)sitakohsis] A disease caused by infection with *Chlamydia psittaci*, transmitted to humans in infected bird droppings; also known as *parrot disease*. There is a flu-like illness with pneumonia, often severe.

psoriasis [(p)soriyasis] A common persisting or recurring skin disorder, in which small red scaly itching patches form in the superficial layers of the skin, particularly affecting the elbows, knees, scalp, and nails. The cause is unknown.

Psyche [siykee] In Greek mythology, 'the soul', usually represented by a butterfly. In the story told by Apuleius, she was beloved by Cupid.

psychedelic drugs *hallucinogens*

psychiatry A branch of medicine concerned with the study, diagnosis, prevention, and treatment of mental and emotional disorders. Within psychiatry, there is a range of sub-specialties including **child psychiatry**, **forensic psychiatry** (the study and treatment of patients who have broken the law), and **psychotherapy**. The range of conditions treated by psychiatrists is wide, and includes patients suffering from psychoses (in which there is a loss of contact with reality), neuroses (in which anxiety is a major component), eating disorders, mental retardation, and sleep disorders.

psychical research *parapsychology*

psychic healing A form of therapy in which the healer uses a patient's aura to diagnose the problem or illness that has brought about the consultation, and then transmits to the patient the energy that is needed for healing. In **psychic surgery**, healers work upon a patient by moving their hands over the diseased parts.

psychoanalysis The theory and clinical practice of a form of psychology which emphasizes unconscious aspects of the mental life of an individual. The treatment, pioneered by Freud, is a form of therapy which attempts to eliminate conflict by altering the personality in a positive way. The study of dreams was used as a way of understanding people's deeper emotions.

psychokinesis (PK) One of the two major categories of allegedly paranormal phenomena (the other being extrasensory perception). It is defined as the influencing by a living agent of a physical system or object by means other than those currently understood by the physical sciences. The phenomenon was earlier referred to as **telekinesis**.

psycholinguistics The study of the psychology of language. Psycholinguists are variously concerned with first and second language acquisition, language production and comprehension, and linguistic deficits such as aphasia and dyslexia.

psychology The science of mental life – a succinct definition used by US psychologist William James in 1890. Modern psychology began with the great advances in science and medicine of the 19th-c, including work on comparative studies of behaviour, human abilities, the functions of the nervous system, 'irrational' behaviour, intelligence, and the nature of learning. Contemporary psychology has seen a revival of interest in cognitive processes, with new interpretations using concepts from communication theory and computer systems. The application of psychological methods pervades many aspects of everyday life, such as the investigation of opinions and prejudices, the design of work and leisure environments, personnel management, counselling, and therapy.

psychometrics A branch of psychology concerned with the measurement of psychological characteristics, especially intelligence, abilities, personality, and mood states.

psychopathology A term used in psychiatry and clinical psychology, referring to any form of mental illness or aberration.

psychopharmacology The science of the mechanisms, uses, and side-effects of drugs that modify psychological function and behaviour.

psychophysics Methods originated by Gustav Fechner in 1860 as an attempt to quantify, as psychophysical laws, the relationships between physical stimulation and sensations. Measures of *sensitivity* describe the constraints on perception provided by the sensory apparatus. *Scaling* methods assess the magnitude of the effect of different amounts of stimulation.

psychosis A psychiatric term with a variety of uses. It is most clearly used when referring to psychiatric illnesses in which there is a loss of contact with reality, in the form of delusions or hallucinations. It is also used with reference to two main groups of psychiatric illnesses: **organic psychoses** are caused by diseases affecting the brain; **functional psychoses** do not have a known physical cause.

psychosomatic disorder A set of real physical symptoms (eg headaches, high blood pressure) which have been caused, maintained, or exacerbated by emotional factors; also called a **psychophysiological disorder**.

psychosurgery A procedure in which there is surgery on a brain regarded as histologically normal, with the intention of influencing the course of a behaviour disorder. The intention is to create a lesion in the brain to remove pathological thoughts and feelings with the preservation of normal functions. These procedures were initially referred to as **lobotomy** in the USA and **leucotomy** in Europe.

psychotherapy The treatment of emotional problems by a trained therapist, with the object of removing or modifying maladaptive feelings or behaviours and the promotion of what is referred to as 'personal growth and development'. There are various styles of treatment, including individual psychotherapy, marital counselling, family psychotherapy, and group psychotherapy.

psychotomimetic drugs *hallucinogens*

psyllid [silid] A jumping plant louse; feeds by sucking sap; distributed worldwide. (Order: Homoptera. Family: Psyllidae, c.1300 species.)

Ptah [tah, ptah] An early Egyptian god associated with Memphis, and represented in human shape. Originally the creator of the world, he is later the god of craftsmanship.

ptarmigan [tah(r)migan] A grouse of the N hemisphere, inhabiting the high-altitude Alpine zone and tundra; plumage mottled grey in summer, white in winter, with thickly feathered feet and toes acting as snowshoes. (Genus: *Lagopus*, 3 species.)

Pteranodon [teranodon] A huge pterosaur from the late Cretaceous period of North America; wingspan up to 7 m/23 ft; long toothless beak counterbalanced by a bony crest arising at neck joint; tail reduced to short stump. (Order: Pterosauria.)

Pteraspis [teraspis] A fossil jawless vertebrate; known from the late Ordovician to the Devonian periods; body eel-like, without paired fins. (Class: Pteraspidimorphi.)

pteridophyte [teridohfiyt] Any spore-bearing vascular plant, in some classifications forming the division Pteridophyta.

pterodactyl [terodaktil] *pterosaur*

pterosaur [terosaw(r)] An extinct, flying reptile known from the late Triassic to the end of the Cretaceous period; ranged in size from sparrow-like to a wingspan of 15 m/50 ft; narrow, leathery wings supported by elongated fourth finger; formerly known as **pterodactyls**. (Subclass: Archosauria. Order: Pterosauria.)

Ptolemaic system [tolemayik] The planetary system described in the 2nd-c AD by Claudius Ptolemaeus of Alexandria. It is Earth-centred, with the planets moving in circular orbits. It was widely used as the definitive description of the Solar System until overthrown by Copernicus in 1543.

Ptolemy I Soter [tolemee] ('Saviour') (c.366–c.283 BC) Macedonian general, in the army of Alexander the Great, who became ruler of Egypt after Alexander's death (323 BC). In 304 BC he adopted the royal title, and thus founded the Ptolemaic dynasty. In 285 BC, he was succeeded by his son, **Ptolemy II Philadelphus**, the greatest of the Ptolemaic kings. Alexandria (with its royally founded museum and library) became the chief centre for learning in the Mediterranean world.

Ptolemy [tolemee], in full **Claudius Ptolemaeus** [tolemayus] (fl.127–145) Greek astronomer and geographer, who worked in the great library in Alexandria. His book *Almagest* is the most important compendium of astronomy produced until the 16th-c.

puberty The period of change from childhood to adulthood, characterized by the attainment of sexual maturity and full reproductive capacity. It begins earlier in girls (about age 11) than in boys (about age 13), and lasts between 3 and 5 years. In both sexes there is an accelerated growth of the body and the development of secondary sexual characteristics: the development of breasts, appearance of pubic hair, and onset of menstruation in girls; the appearance of pubic and facial hair, enlargement of the penis, and deepening of the voice in boys.

public debt The total amount of government borrowings, both short-term, such as treasury bills, and long-term bonds; also known as the **government debt** or the **national debt**.

public health *community medicine*

public prosecutor *district attorney*

Public Record Office (PRO) The British national depository of government papers, selected archives, and legal documents to be permanently preserved – for example, the Magna Carta, Domesday Book, and Shakespeare's will. Established in 1838, it is now housed in Kew, Surrey.

public relations (PR) The practice of managing reputation and of building goodwill on behalf of organizations, both externally and internally. It developed as a management and, later, academic discipline in the USA and in the UK in the early 20th-c, but is now practised worldwide in the commercial and public sectors. PR is commonly associated with ploys to ensure positive media coverage. In reality, public relations today is a multifaceted activity, which includes crisis management, political lobbying, dealings with the financial world, community involvement, and internal communications. Each of these recognizes a specific 'public' with which an organization has a key relationship.

Public Safety, Committee of A French Revolutionary political body, set up in the war crisis (Apr 1793) to organize defence against internal and external enemies. Its members came to exercise dictatorial powers during the Reign of Terror.

public school In England, a fee-paying school for pupils of secondary age, often over 11 for girls and over 13 for boys; famous examples include Charterhouse, Eton, Harrow, Rugby, and Westminster. In the USA, it is the exact opposite: a school run by public authorities where fees are not paid.

public sector borrowing requirement (PSBR) The amount of money a government needs to raise in a fiscal year by borrowing. The need arises from tax revenues and other income being less than the total expenditure budgeted by the various government departments. Reducing the PSBR has been seen in the UK as important in restricting the growth of the money supply, and thus for the control of inflation.

public switched telephone network (PSTN) The conventional telephone network provided by the Posts, Telegraph and Telephones Authorities for normal voice communication. It is of particular interest to computer specialists since, by using modems, data communication between computers can be effected over a public telephone line. The line is in use, and has to be paid for, for the whole of the time of transmission.

Puccini, Giacomo (Antonio Domenico Michele Secondo Maria) [pucheenee] (1858–1924) Operatic composer, born in Lucca,

Puerto Rico

□ International Airport

[pwairtoh reekoh], formerly **Porto Rico** (to 1932), official name **Commonwealth of Puerto Rico** (USA Formal Dependencies) Local name Puerto Rico

Timezone GMT -4

Area 8897 km²/3434 sq mi

Population total (2002e) 3 879 600

Status Commonwealth

Capital San Juan

Languages Spanish (official), with English widely spoken

Religion Roman Catholic

Physical features Easternmost island of the Greater Antilles; almost rectangular in shape; crossed W–E by mountains, rising to 1338 m/4389 ft at Cerro de Punta; coastal plain belt in N; islands of Vieques and Culebra also belong to Puerto Rico.

Climate Tropical maritime climate; average annnual temperature 25°C; high humidity.

Currency 1 US Dollar (USD) = 100 cents

Economy Manufacturing the most important sector of the economy; food processing, petrochemicals, electrical equipment, pharmaceuticals, textiles, clothing; livestock, tobacco, sugar, pineapples, coconuts; tourism.

GDP (2002e) $43·01 bn, per capita $11 100

History Originally occupied by Carib and Arawak Indians; visited by Columbus, 1493; remained a Spanish colony until ceded to the US, 1898; high levels of emigration to the US from 1940s–50s; became a semi-autonomous Commonwealth in association with US, 1952; executive power exercised by a Governor; a bicameral Legislative Assembly consists of a Senate and House of Representatives.

Italy. His first great success was *Manon Lescaut* (1893), but this was eclipsed by *La Bohème* (1896), *Tosca* (1900), and *Madama Butterfly* (1904). His last opera, *Turandot*, was left unfinished at his death.

Pucelle, Jean [püsel] or **Pucello, Johan** (c.1300–c.1355) French painter. He ran an important workshop in Paris from the 1320s onwards, specializing in illuminated manuscripts.

Pucello, Johan *Pucelle, Jean*

puddling process 1 A process for converting pig iron (high car-

bon) into wrought iron (very low carbon) by melting it in a small furnace in which it is worked to remove carbon (by exposure to oxidation by air) and the slag. **2** The agitation of a concrete mix to promote settling and uniformity of texture.

Pudovkin, Vsevoled (Illarianovich) [pudofkin] (1893–1953) Film director and writer, born in Penza. His films include the silent classics *Mat* (1926, Mother), *Konets Sankt-Peterburga* (1927, The End of St Petersburg) and *Potomok Chingis-Khan* (1928, trans Storm Over Asia).

Puebla [pwaybla] or **Heróica Puebla de Zaragoza** 19°03N 98°10W, pop (2000e) 1 269 000. City in SC Mexico; altitude 2150 m/7054 ft; damaged by earthquake, 1973; railway; two universities (1937, 1940); famous for its glazed tiles which cover the domes of many of its 60 churches; cathedral (17th-c); historic centre now a world heritage site.

Pueblo (Indians) [p웨bloh] North American Indians of SW USA, living in settlements called *pueblos* in multi-storied, permanent houses made of clay. Culturally and linguistically diverse, they include the Hopi and Zuni.

puerperal fever [pyooerperal] A fever greater than 38°C arising in a mother in the first 14 day after childbirth. It was formerly a serious complication of childbearing.

Puerto Rico *see panel*

puff adder A viper which inhabits grassland; two species: the **puff adder** (*Bitis arietans*) from Africa and the Middle East; length, up to 2 m/6½ ft; very thick mottled brown body; puffs up the body with air when alarmed; the **dwarf puff adder** (*Bitis peringueyi*) from SW Africa; length, 30 cm/12 in.

puffball A globular, often spherical fruiting body of certain fungi (the Gasteromycetes); spores released when the wall of the puffball ruptures. (Subdivision: Basidiomycetes. Order: Lycoperdales.)

puffer Any of several stout-bodied marine and freshwater fish which can inflate the body with air or water to become almost spherical; widespread in shallow warm seas; some organs and tissue extremely poisonous. (Family: Tetraodontidae, 7 genera.)

puffin Any of four species of auk of the genus *Fratercula* (2 species), *Cerorhinca* (1 species), or *Lunda* (1 species); bill large, deep, multicoloured; nests in burrows or rock crevices. *Cerorhinca* is nocturnal.

pug A toy breed of dog developed in China; similar origins to the Pekinese, but with a short coat; now taller and heavier than the Pekinese, but face still flat, and tail carried over back.

Pugachev, Yemelyan Ivanovich [pugachef], also spelled **Pugachov** (1726–75) Russian Don Cossack, pretender to the Russian throne and leader of a mass rebellion against Catherine II (1773–5), proclaiming himself to be Peter III, Catherine's murdered husband. Pugachev's name later became a byword for the spirit of peasant revolution in Russia. He was captured in 1774 and executed.

Pugin, Augustus (Welby Northmore) [pyoojin] (1812–52) Architect, born in London. He designed a large part of the decoration and sculpture for the new Houses of Parliament (begun 1840), and did much to revive Gothic architecture in England.

Pugwash Conference A series of conferences first held in Pugwash, Nova Scotia, in 1957, which brought together scientists concerned about the impact on humanity of nuclear weapons. It owed much to the initiative of Bertrand Russell, and along with its president, Joseph Rotblat, it received the Nobel Peace Prize in 1995.

Pula [poola], Ital **Pola**, Lat **Pietas Iulia** 44°52N 13°52E, pop (2000e) 60 100. Seaport and resort town in W Croatia, on the Adriatic coast; built on the site of a former Roman colony; airport; railway; car ferries to Italy; Roman amphitheatre, temple; cathedral; castle (17th-c).

puli [poolee] A medium-sized breed of dog developed in Hungary for hunting and as a sheepdog; ears pendulous; tail curls over back; coat thick and long, often reaching the ground.

Pulitzer, Joseph [poolitser] (1847–1911) Newspaper proprietor, born in Makó, Hungary. In 1864 he emigrated to the USA, and made his fortune in newspapers. In his will he established annual **Pulitzer Prizes** in the fields of literature, drama, history, music, and journalism.

pulley A simple machine: a wheel with a grooved rim in which a rope can run. This changes the direction of force applied to the rope, and so can be used to raise heavy weights by pulling downwards.

Pullman, George (Mortimer) (1831–97) Inventor and businessman, born in Brocton, NY. He designed the Pullman railroad sleeping-car (1865), and later introduced dining-cars (1868).

Pullman, Philip (1946–) Novelist, born in Norwich, Norfolk. He worked as a teacher and lecturer, then turned to writing. Publishing works mostly for children, he gained success with his trilogy for young adults, *His Dark Materials*, comprising *Northern Lights* (1995, aka *The Golden Compass*), *The Subtle Knife* (1997), and *The Amber Spyglass* (2000; Whitbread Book of the Year, 2002). Later books include *The Scarecrow and his Servant* (2004). The *Dark Materials* trilogy was given a National Theatre production in 2004.

pulmonary embolism The passage of an *embolus* (an abnormally circulating body in the blood) into the arteries to the lungs. It may lodge in the main pulmonary artery and cause sudden death.

pulsar A cosmic source of rapid and regular bursts of radio waves. Pulsars are collapsed neutron stars, having a mass similar to the Sun, and a diameter of only 10 km/6 mi or so.

pulse (botany) A general name applied to peas, beans, and lentils, the edible ripe seeds of several plants of the pea family. (Family: Leguminosae.)

pulse (physiology) A pressure wave generated by the ejection of blood from the left ventricle into the vascular system. The number of pulsations per minute reflects heart rate, which in humans is between 70 and 90 at rest.

puma *cougar*

pumice A very light and porous igneous rock, usually granitic in chemical composition, formed by solidifying the froth caused by vigorous degassing of volatile substances from a lava during eruption. It is used as an abrasive.

pump A machine for moving a fluid or gas from one place to another; commonly used to move fluids, often water, through pipes. *Pressure pumps* are used to blow up tyres, footballs, and other containers. *Evacuation pumps* suck air from sealed containers to make a partial vacuum.

pumpkin A trailing or climbing vine (*Cucurbita maxima*) native to America; flowers 12·5 cm/5 in diameter, funnel-shaped; fruit usually globular, often reaching great size and weight; rind and flesh orange, rather fibrous, surrounding numerous seeds; cultivated as a vegetable. It is often used to make Hallowe'en lanterns by placing a candle in the hollowed out centre, and carving a face in the rind, through which the light shines. (Family: Cucurbitaceae.)

Punch and Judy A glove-puppet show – named after the man and wife who are its central characters – which developed in Britain from the marionette plays based on Pulcinella, the impudent hunchback of the *commedia dell' arte*. Punch, operated by the right hand, is a constant figure, while the challenges of the left hand introduce character after character to be defeated by Punch's anarchic vigour.

punctuation The part of a language's writing system which provides clues to the way a text is organized. Early writing systems made little or no use of punctuation. Some conventions organize the text into grammatical or semantic units, such as paragraphs and words (spaces), sentences, clauses and phrases (full-stop, comma, colon, semi-colon). Other conventions carry meaning of their own: the question mark identifies a sentence type, while the apostrophe marks possession (*John's*) and contractions (*I'm, must've*).

Pune *Poona*

Punic Wars [pyoonik] The three wars fought and won in the 3rd-c and 2nd-c BC by Rome against the Phoenician (Punic) city, Carthage. The first (264–241 BC) resulted in Rome's acquisition of her first overseas province, Sicily, hitherto a Carthaginian territory. The second (218–201 BC) saw Carthage surrender to Rome all her remaining overseas possessions. The third (149–146 BC) ended in the capture and total destruction of Carthage itself.

Punjab (India) [punjahb] pop (2001e) 24 289 300; area 50 362 km²/19 440 sq mi. State in NW India, bounded W and NW by Pakistan; capital (jointly with Haryana), Chandigarh; population c.60% Sikh in Indian Punjab, mainly Muslim in Pakistani Punjab; part of the Mughal Empire until end of 18th-c; annexed by the British after the Sikh Wars (1846, 1849); autonomous province, 1937; partitioned between India and Pakistan into East and West Punjab on the basis of religion, 1947; Indian state renamed Punjab, reformed as a Punjabi-speaking state, 1956 and 1966; governed by a Legislative Assembly; Alkai Dai Party campaigns for Sikh autonomy.

Punjab (Pakistan) [punjahb] pop (2000e) 77 280 000; area 205 334 km²/79 259 sq mi. Province in Pakistan, bounded E and S by India; chiefly Muslim population; capital, Lahore.

Punjabi *Indo-Aryan languages*

punk rock A type of anarchistic rock music, originating in the late 1970s with such groups as Generation X and The Sex Pistols. Their very loudly amplified performances were characterized by the public use of swear words, outrageous behaviour, and clothes and hairstyles which sought to challenge establishment values.

Punt, land of In antiquity, the area to the S of Egypt near the mouth of the Red Sea. From the third millennium BC, it was the source for the Egyptians of incense, myrrh, gold, and ivory.

Punta Arenas [punta araynas] 53°09S 70°52W, pop (2000e) 141 000. Most southerly city in Chile, on the Straits of Magellan; airfield; sheep-farming trade, exporting wool, skins, and frozen meat.

pupa The life-cycle stage of an insect during which the larval form is reorganized to produce the definitive adult form. It is commonly an inactive stage, enclosed in a hard shell (*chrysalis*) or silken covering (*cocoon*).

pupil *eye*

puppetry The art and craft of manipulating inanimate figures for performance. There are three major means of manipulation: from above, by strings, as with **marionettes**; from below, behind or beside, by inserting a hand into the puppet, as with **glove puppets**; and from below or behind, by supports activating the head, body, and limbs, as with **rod-puppets**. Puppet shows have become highly popular on television in recent years, both to provide children's entertainment and for political satire.

Puppis [pupis] (Lat 'ship's stern') A S constellation, partly in the Milky Way, which includes many notable star clusters.

Purcell, Henry [persel], earlier [persel] (1659–95) Composer, born in London. Though his harpsichord pieces and his trio-sonatas for violins and continuo have retained their popularity, he is best known for his vocal and choral works. He also wrote an opera, *Dido and Aeneas* (1689). Of his many songs, 'Nymphs and Shepherds' is probably the best known.

purchase tax An excise tax levied on consumer goods, and added to the price paid by the customer; the rate varied with the type of goods. In the UK it was replaced by value-added tax in 1973.

purgative *laxative*

purgatory In Roman Catholic and some Orthodox teaching, the place and state in which the souls of the dead suffer for their sins before being admitted to heaven.

Purim [pyurim, pureem] The Jewish Feast of Lots, celebrated on 14 or 15 Adar (about 1 Mar), commemorating the deliverance of the Jews from a plot to have them massacred, as related in the Book of Esther.

purines [pyooreenz] A group of organic bases, the most important of which are adenine and guanine, part of the nucleotide chains of DNA and RNA.

Puritanism The belief that further reformation was required in the Church of England under Elizabeth I and the Stuarts. It arose in the 1560s out of dissatisfaction with the 'popish elements', such as surplices, which had been retained by the Elizabethan religious settlement. It included the separatist churches that left England for Holland and America from 1590 to 1640, and several 'presbyterian', 'independent', and more radical groups.

Purkinje, Johannes (Evangelista) [poorkinyay] (1787–1869) Histologist and physiologist, born in Libochovice, Czech Republic. An early user of the improved compound microscope, he discovered a number of microscopic anatomical structures, some of which are named after him.

Purple Heart In the USA, a decoration instituted in 1782 as an award for gallantry; it was revived in 1932, since when it has been awarded for wounds received in action. The ribbon is purple with white edges.

purpura [perpyoora] A condition in which there is spontaneous bleeding into the skin or mucous membranes, giving rise to small scattered areas of bruising.

purslane A name applied to several different plants. **Common purslane** (*Portulacca oleracea*), a weed very widespread in warm regions, is a fleshy-leaved annual with yellow, 4–6-petalled flowers. The related **pink purslane** (*Claytonia sibirica*), native to W North America, is an annual or perennial with long-stalked leaves and white or pink 5-petalled flowers. (Family: Portulaccaceae.)

pus Yellow liquid formed after localized inflammation, such as an abscess, or on the surface of a wound, produced by infection with certain bacteria (known as *pyogenic* bacteria).

Pusan or **Busan** [poosahn] 5°05N 129°02E, pop (2000e) 4 170 000. Seaport and second largest city in Korea; airport; railway; international ferry; hydrofoil; two universities (1946–7); UN Memorial Cemetery from the Korean War; Pusan Stadium (2001).

Pusey, E(dward) B(ouverie) [pyoozee] (1800–82) Theologian, born in Pusey, Oxfordshire. He joined Newman in the Oxford Movement (1833), contributing several tracts, notably those on baptism and the Eucharist.

Pushkin, Alexander Sergeyevich [pushkin] (1799–1837) Poet, born in Moscow. Hailed in Russia as its greatest poet, his first success was the romantic poem *Ruslan and Lyudmila* (1820), followed by the verse novel *Eugene Onegin* (1828), the historical tragedy *Boris Godunov* (1831), and several other large-scale works.

Putin, Vladimir (Vladimirovich) (1952–) Russian president (1999–), born in Leningrad (now St Petersburg), Russia. He began his career in the KGB as an intelligence officer stationed mainly in East Germany (1975–89). Following the collapse of the Soviet Union in 1991, he retired from the KGB, and became first deputy mayor of Leningrad (1994), moving to Moscow in 1996. In 1998 he was appointed deputy head of management in Boris Yeltsin's administration, then head of the Federal Security and of Yeltsin's Security Council, and was promoted prime minister in August 1999. In December 1999 Yeltsin resigned as president, appointing Putin acting president until official elections were held (in early 2000). He was re-elected in 2004. In April 2005 he made a historic visit to Israel, the first by any Kremlin leader.

Puttnam (of Queensgate), David (Terence) Puttnam, Lord (1941–) Film-maker and educationist, born in London. Following his first feature film *S.W.A.L.K.* (1969), he became known for such successful productions as *Bugsy Malone* (1976) and *Chariots of Fire* (1981, four Oscars). In 1986 he became chief executive of Columbia Pictures, but returned to Britain after a year. Later films include *Memphis Belle* (1990), *Being Human* (1994), and *My Life So Far* (1997). He received a life peerage in 1997. He now works principally in the field of education.

putty A cement made of fine, powdered chalk or white lead, mixed with linseed oil, which hardens on being exposed to air. It is used for filling wood, and for fixing glass in frames. **Putty powder** is a fine, tin oxide powder used for polishing glass and granite.

Puvis de Chavannes, Pierre (Cécile) [püvee duh shavan] (1824–98) Painter, born in Lyon, France. He is best known for his murals on public buildings, notably the life of St Geneviève in the Panthéon, Paris.

Puyi, Pu Yi, or **P'u-i** [pooyee], personal name of the **Xuantong Emperor** (1906–67) Last emperor of China (1908–12) and the first of Manchukuo (1934–5), born in Beijing. Known in the West as Henry Puyi, in 1932 he was called from private life by the Japanese to be provincial dictator of Manchukuo, under the name of **Kangde**. Taken prisoner by the Russians in 1945, he was tried in China as a war criminal (1950), pardoned (1959), and became a private citizen. The story of his life was made into a successful film, *The Last Emperor*, in 1988.

PVC *polyvinylchloride*

Pycnogonida [piknuhgonida] *sea spider*

pyelitis *pyelonephritis*

pyelonephritis [piyelohnefriytis] A bacterial inflammation of the kidney, usually associated with infection in the lower urinary tract, such as the bladder. Infection is accompanied by high fever and back pain and needs treatment with appropriate antibiotics, since persisting or recurrent infection may lead to renal failure.

Pygmalion [pigmaylion] In Greek mythology, a king of Cyprus, who made a statue of a beautiful woman. He prayed to Aphrodite, and the sculptured figure came to life.

Pygmies A small-statured people living in C Africa (averaging 1·50 m/4·9 ft in height). The best known are the forest-dwelling Mbuti of the Democratic Republic of Congo and the Twa of the Great Lakes savannahs.

Pym, Barbara (Mary Crampton) (1913–80) Novelist, born in Oswestry, Shropshire. She is best known for her series of satirical novels on English middle-class society, including *Excellent Women* (1952) and *Quartet in Autumn* (1977).

Pym, John [pim] (1584–1643) English politician, born in Brymore, Somerset. In 1641 he took a leading part in the impeachment of Strafford, and helped to draw up the Grand Remonstrance.

Pynchon, Thomas (Ruggles) [pinchon] (1937–) Writer, born in Glen Cove, NY. His novels include *V* (1963), *The Crying of Lot 49* (1966), *Gravity's Rainbow* (1973), *Mason and Dixon* (1997), and *Against the Day* (2006).

Pyongyang [pyuhngyang], Jap **Heijo** 39°00N 125°47E, pop (2000e) 2 906 000. Capital of North Korea; Korea's oldest city, founded allegedly in 1122 BC; capital of Choson kingdom, 300–200 BC; colony of China, 108 BC; capital of North Korea since 1948; rebuilt after the Korean War; airport; railway; university (1946).

pyorrhoea / pyorrhea [piyoreea] *dentistry*

pyracantha *firethorn*

pyralid moth [piralid] A moth of the family Pyralidae; adults often slender with long hindlimbs; c.20 000 species, many pests of crops and dried vegetable products. (Order: Lepidoptera.)

pyramid An architectural structure on a triangular, square, or

Pythagoras's theorem

$$c^2 = a^2 + b^2$$

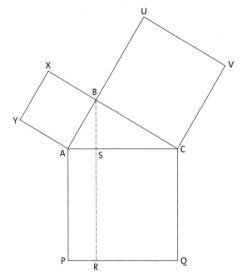

$$AC^2 = AB^2 + BC^2$$

[piythagoras] A mathematical proposition advanced by Pythagoras, that in any right-angled triangle, the square on the hypotenuse is equal to the sum of the squares on the other two sides. The converse of the theorem is also true: in any triangle in which the square on the longest side is equal to the sum of the squares on the other two sides, the angle opposite the longest side is a right angle. Although known to the Babylonians, tradition ascribes to Pythagoras himself the first proof, probably based on the first diagram. The commoner proof (the second diagram), proving first that the area of square *ABXY* is equal to that of the rectangle *APRS*, was given by Euclid. Pythagorean triples – three integers (eg 3,4,5) that can be the sides of right-angled triangles – have long fascinated people. The formula 2k*mn*, k($m^2 + n^2$), k($m^2 - n^2$) generates all Pythagorean triples. The theorem was probably independently conceived and proved in 2nd-c AD China.

polygonal base, with triangular sides meeting in a single point. In Egyptian architecture, it is a sepulchral stone monument with a square base. The phrase **the Pyramids** usually refers to the Fourth Dynasty pyramids of the Giza plateau on the SW outskirts of modern Cairo. The Great Pyramid of Cheops (c. 2589–2566 BC) is 146 m/480 ft high, 230 m/755 ft square, and 2 352 000 cu m/27 688 000 cu ft in volume, made up of 2.5 million limestone blocks each of 2.5 tonnes.

pyramid healing A form of healing which uses the electromagnetic energy thought to be mystically concentrated within the dimensions of a pyramid. The height of the Great Pyramids is the radius of a circle whose circumference is the same as the circumference of the square base.

Pyramus and Thisbe [piramus, thizbee] Two lovers, kept apart by their parents, who conversed through a crack in the wall between their houses, and agreed to meet at Ninus's tomb outside the city of Babylon. Finding Thisbe's blood-stained cloak, Pyramus thought she had been killed by a lion, and committed suicide. When she found him, Thisbe killed herself on his sword.

Pyrenean mountain dog A breed of dog developed in the Pyrenees several centuries ago to protect sheep; large powerful body with heavy head; thick, usually pale-coloured, coat.

Pyrenees [pireneez], Fr **Pyrénées**, Span **Pirineos** Mountain range extending W–E from the Bay of Biscay to the Mediterranean Sea, separating the Iberian Peninsula from the rest of Europe; stretches 450 km/280 mi along the French–Spanish frontier; includes Andorra; highest point, Pic de Aneto (3404 m/ 11 168 ft); Gouffre de la Pierre St Martin, one of the deepest caves in the world.

Pyrenees, Treaty of the (1659) A treaty between France and Spain ending the hostilities of the Thirty Years' War. It marked the end of Spanish military and political dominance in W Europe.

pyrethrum [piyreethruhm] A perennial, growing to 45 cm/18 in (*Tanacetum cinerariifolium*), native to parts of the Balkan peninsula, but extensively cultivated, especially in E Africa and South America; flower-heads solitary, daisy-like, spreading outer florets white. An insecticide is prepared from the extracts of the powdered and dried flower-heads. (Family: Compositae.)

Pyrex® A trade name for a borosilicate glass with a high silica content, some boron, and some aluminium. It has high mechanical strength, resistance to strong alkalis and acids, and a low coefficient of thermal expansion. These properties favour its extensive domestic and scientific use.

pyrexia *fever*

pyridine [pirideen] C_5H_5N, boiling point 115°C. An organic base with a vile odour. It occurs in a fraction of coal tar, and is carcinogenic.

pyridoxine A B vitamin (B_6) which acts as a co-enzyme involved in the metabolism of amino acids. Although a deficiency is rare, B_6 is frequently used as a vitamin supplement for the treatment of mild depression, although its efficacy is disputed.

pyrimidines [pirimideenz] A group of organic bases, the most important of which are cytosine, thymine, and uracil, part of the nucleotide chains of DNA and RNA.

pyrite A metallic yellow iron sulphide (FeS_2) mineral, common and widespread; also termed 'fool's gold' because of its colour. It is used as a source of sulphur and in the manufacture of sulphuric acid.

pyroclastic rock A general name given to rocks formed from fragments of lava ejected from a volcano into the atmosphere.

pyrolysis The decomposition of a substance by heating in the absence of oxygen. The most important example is the pyrolysis or 'cracking' of petroleum, by which alkanes are converted into shorter alkanes and alkenes, eg propane may be converted to ethene and methane.

pyrometer A type of thermometer for measuring high temperatures. In the optical pyrometer, the heat colour of the hot object is compared to that of a heated filament through which a controlled current is passed.

pyrope [piyrohp] *garnet*

pyroxenes [piyrokseenz] A large group of silicate minerals including many important rock-forming minerals; important members of the group are enstatite, diopside, augite, pigeonite, and jadeite.

Pyrrho [piroh] (c.360–c.270 BC) Philosopher, born in Elis, Greece. He established the philosophical tradition later called *scepticism*. He recommended that since we know nothing we should 'suspend judgment' and thus achieve 'an imperturbable peace of mind'.

Pyrrhus [pirus] (c.318–272 BC) King of Epirus (modern Albania) (307–303 BC, 297–272 BC), an ambitious ruler whose aim was to revive the empire of his second cousin, Alexander the Great. Unsuccessful in this goal (283 BC), he came into conflict with Rome. Though he won two battles against her (280–279 BC), his losses, particularly at Asculum (279 BC), were so great that they gave rise to the phrase 'Pyrrhic victory'.

pyruvic acid [piyroovik] CH_3–CO–COOH, IUPAC **2-oxopropanoic acid**. The non-chiral oxidation product of lactic acid.

Pythagoras [piythagoras] (6th-c BC) Philosopher and mathematician, born in Samos, Greece. About 530 BC he established a religious community in S Italy. Pythagoreanism was a way of life, of moral abstinence and purification; its teaching included the doctrine of the transmigration of souls between successive bodies. The school is best known for its studies of the relations between numbers.

Pythagoras's theorem *p.762*

Pythian Games [pithian] In ancient Greece, one of the main Pan-Hellenic festivals, held every four years in the sanctuary of Apollo Pythios at Delphi. 'Pythios' or 'python slayer' was the name under which Apollo was worshipped there.

Pythias (of Syracuse) *Damon and Pythias*

python A snake of family Pythonidae (27 species), sometimes included in the boa family; native to Africa, S and SE Asia, Australasia, and (a single species) Central America; a constrictor; eye with vertical slit-like pupil; females lay eggs and often incubate these until they hatch.

pyx A small metal box used in the Roman Catholic Church for carrying the Blessed Sacrament to the sick; also a larger receptacle for exposing the host or consecrated bread.

q

Qaddafi, Muammar *Gaddafi, Muammar*

Qaeda, al- *al-Qaeda*

Qatar *p.765*

Qin dynasty or **Ch'in dynasty** [chin] (221–206 BC) The first dynasty to rule over a united China, founded by Qin Shihuangdi. Its achievements included the standardization of Chinese script, weights, and measures, and the construction of the Great Wall.

Qingdao, Tsingtao, or **Ch'ing-tao** [chingdow] 36°04N 120°22E, pop (2000e) 2 343 000. Resort seaport city in E China, on the Yellow Sea; occupied by Japan in World War 1; airfield; railway.

Qing dynasty [ching] (1644–1912) The last imperial Chinese dynasty. They took the appellation Manchu in 1635, and the dynastic title Qing in 1636. Building a power base in Manchuria, Mongolia, and Korea, they subsequently extended supremacy over all China. The dynasty was overthrown by revolutionaries in 1911.

Qinghai–Tibet Plateau *Tibet Plateau*

Qinhuangdao or **Ch'in-huang-tao** [chinhwahngdow] 39°55N 119°37E, pop (2000e) 581 400. Port in N China; designated a special economic zone in 1985; linked by pipeline to the Daqing oil field; railway.

Qin Shihuangdi [chin shihwangdee], also spelled **Ch'in Shih Huang-ti** (259–210 BC) First true emperor of China, who forcibly unified much of modern China following the decline of the Zhou dynasty. He consolidated N defences into a Great Wall, and drove the Huns from S of the Yellow R. He conquered the S, built canals and roads, divided China into 36 military prefectures, destroyed feudalism, and disarmed nobles. He was buried in a starry mausoleum with c.7500 life-size terracotta guards.

Qoheleth [kohheleth] *Ecclesiastes, Book of*

Qom [koom] 34°39N 50°57E, pop (2000e) 761 000. Industrial town in Iran; on R Anarbar; road and rail junction; gas pipeline; pilgrimage centre for Shiite Muslims; shrine of Fatima.

Quadragesima [kwodrajesima] In the Western Christian Church, the first Sunday in Lent, so called from its being approximately 40 days before Easter (Lat *quadragesimus*, 'fortieth').

quadratic equations *equations*

quadrature The position of a planet or the Moon when the angular distance from the Sun, as measured from the Earth, is 90°.

quadrille A popular 19th-c dance, performed to music (often arranged from contemporary tunes) in a lively duple time.

quadriplegia *paralysis*

quadrivium (Lat 'the place where four roads meet') The four scientific disciplines of astronomy, geometry, arithmetic, and music, which together with the *trivium* of grammar, rhetoric, and logic constituted the university curriculum of the seven liberal arts in the Middle Ages.

quadrophonic sound A system attempting greater authenticity in reproducing concert-hall musical performances by the use of four signal channels and four loudspeakers placed in a square around the listener. Unconvincing results, additional equipment costs, and no single industry standard restricted this to being an episode of the 1970s.

Quadruple Alliance 1 (1718) A treaty signed by Britain, France, and the Habsburg emperor, to which the Dutch were expected to accede, to ensure the principle of collective security in W Europe.

2 (1815) A treaty signed initially by Austria, Prussia, Russia, and Britain, and acceded to by France in 1818, confirming the 1815 Paris and Vienna provisions for 20 years.

quaestors [kweesterz] Junior, annually elected, financial officers at Rome. The quaestorship was the lowest rank in the hierarchy of offices, the *cursus honorum*, and could not be held before the age of 25.

quagga [kwaga] An extinct zebra native to S Africa (*Equus quagga*); stripes only on head and shoulders; brown body, white legs and tail; last individual died in 1883.

Quaid, Dennis [kwayd] (1954–) Film actor, born in Houston, TX. His films include *Innerspace* (1987), *Postcards from The Edge* (1990), *Any Given Sunday* (1999), and *American Dreamz* (2006). His TV work includes the highly rated *Bill* and its sequel (1981, 1983).

Quai d'Orsay [kay daw(r)say] The embankment on the left bank of the R Seine in Paris, and by association the French Foreign Ministry located there. In 2004, amid much controversy, the foreign minister Michel Barnier proposed to sell the Ministry building and transfer it to a site in the suburbs.

quail A small, short-tailed bird of the pheasant family Phasianidae; native to the New World (29 species) and the Old World (10 species). The name is also used for several other species.

Quakers *Friends, Society of*

quango A shortened form of the term **quasi-non-governmental organization**, a type of organization which became common in the USA, being established by the private sector but largely or entirely financed by the federal government. In the UK the term has been applied to non-departmental bodies that are neither part of a central government department nor part of local government, such as the Monopolies Commission. Many are merely advisory bodies.

Quant, Mary [kwont] (1934–) Fashion designer, born in London. Her clothes were particularly fashionable in the 1960s, when the geometric simplicity of her designs, especially the mini-skirt, and the originality of her colours became a feature of the 'swinging Britain' era.

quantity theory of money An economic theory stating that money supply (M) and its velocity of circulation (V) – how fast it changes hands – is more or less equal to the aggregate of prices (P) and the quantity of goods etc (Q) available. So, $MV = PQ$.

quantum chromodynamics A widely accepted theory of strong nuclear force in which quarks are bound together by gluons; proposed in 1973; also known as **QCD**. Quarks interact because of a 'colour' quantity on each in a way analogous to the interaction between charged particles.

quantum computer A computer which makes explicit use of the rules of quantum mechanics. Pioneered by David Deutsch in

Qatar

PERSIAN GULF

BAHRAIN

Ruwais

Ras Laffan

Hawar Is

Al Khawr

•Dukhan

QATAR ■ Doha

SAUDI ARABIA

•Umm Bab Al Wakrah•

Umm Sai'd •

Salwah

AFRICA

30 km
15 mi

U.A.E

Gulf of Bahrain

Dukhan Heights

□ International Airport

[katah(r)], official name **State of Qatar**, Arabic **Dawlat al-Qatar**
Local name Qatar
Timezone GMT +3
Area 11 437 km²/4415 sq mi
Population total (2002e) 606 000
Status Independent state

Date of independence 1971
Capital Doha
Languages Arabic (official), English
Ethnic groups Arab (40%), Pakistani (18%), Indian (18%), Iranian (10%)
Religion Sunni Muslim (95%)
Physical features Low-lying state on the E coast of the Arabian Peninsula, comprising the Qatar Peninsula and numerous small offshore islands; peninsula, 160 km/100 mi long and 55–80 km/34–50 mi wide, slopes gently from the Dukhan Heights 98 m/321 ft, to the E shore; barren terrain, mainly sand and gravel; coral reefs offshore.
Climate Desert climate; average temperatures 23°C (Jan), 35°C (Jul); high humidity; sparse rainfall; average annual rainfall 62 mm/2·4 in.
Currency 1 Qatar Riyal (QAR) = 100 dirhams
Economy Based on oil; offshore gas reserves thought to be an eighth of known world reserves; oil refineries, petrochemicals, liquefied natural gas, fertilizers, steel, cement, ship repairing, engineering; fishing.
GDP (2002e) $15·91 bn, per capita $20 100
Human Development Index (2002) 0·803
History British protectorate after Turkish withdrawal, 1916; independence, 1971; palace coup brought Khalifah bin Hamad to power, 1972; long-standing territorial dispute with Bahrain over Hawar Is, awarded to Bahrain, 2001; a hereditary monarchy, with an Emir who is both Head of State and Prime Minister; Council of Ministers is assisted by a Consultative Council; country's first constitution approved in a national referendum (Apr 2003), provides for establishment of 45-member Advisory Council, of whom 30 members to be elected by Qatari citizens and 15 appointed by the Amir.

Head of State/Government (Emir)

Family name: al-Thani
1960–72 Ahmad bin Ali
1972–95 Khalifah bin Hamad
1995– Hamad bin Khalifa

Head of Government
1996– Abdulla bin Khalifa

1985, it relies on quantum entanglement to achieve a highly parallel operation in which many manipulations are effectively processed simultaneously, offering greatly improved speed over conventional computers, including parallel computers, for certain types of calculation. Elementary calculations and simple logic circuits have been demonstrated, but a complete quantum computer has not yet been built.

quantum electrodynamics A modern theory of electromagnetic interactions, developed during the 1940s; also called **QED**. Charged subatomic particles interact via photons, the quantum of electromagnetic radiation.

quantum entanglement A fundamental property of quantum systems, first described by Erwin Schrödinger, in which two quantum systems can become correlated in a way which is impossible in classical physics. The two systems retain this correlation such that, under certain circumstances, subsequent action on one system can then have implications for the outcome of a measurement on the other. Explicitly verified by experiment, its applications include quantum computing and secure telecommunications via quantum cryptography.

quantum field theory The most sophisticated form of quantum theory, in which all matter and force particles are expressed as sums over simple waves. It is essential for understanding the processes in which particles are created or destroyed.

quantum gravity Gravitation acting at submicroscopic length scales where quantum effects are important. Theories of quantum gravity seek to combine features of quantum mechanics and general relativity, but no consistent theory has yet been developed.

quantum mechanics A system of mechanics applicable at distances of atomic dimensions, 10^{-10} m or less, and providing for the description of atoms, molecules, and all phenomena that depend on properties of matter at the atomic level. The basic concept derives from the work of Max Planck, who proposed that light is composed of photons – minute packets (*quanta*) of light. The development of quantum mechanics applicable to particles moving at high speed is known as **relativistic quantum mechanics**. A further development of quantum theory, incorporating the creation and destruction of particles, took place during the 1940s and is called **quantum field theory**. The wave-like nature of electrons and other particles is expressed by wavefunctions, the most fundamental way of describing either simple particles or other more complicated quantum systems. Particles such as electrons are no longer considered as point-like objects, but are spread out in a way governed by wavefunctions. Quantum mechanics necessarily means dealing with a probabilistic description of nature, and thus contrasts with classical mechanics, in which the precise properties of every object are in principle calculable.

quantum numbers Simple numbers or vectors that specify the state of a quantum system and the results of observations performed on that system. Subatomic particles and atomic states are classified by quantum numbers.

quantum teleportation A way of transferring quantum information from one place to another. It was proposed by US physicist Charles Bennett and collaborators in 1993, and first demonstrated by Anton Zeilinger and others in 1996. Teleportation involving photons can impose the state of a 'message' photon, for example its spin orientation, on to a distant 'recipient' photon. The state of the original message photon is destroyed. Quantum teleportation offers reliable movement of quantum information from point to point, avoiding problems caused by fragility of quantum states, but it does not imply the ability to move large objects from place to place. In 2004, scientists working independently in the US and Austria performed successful teleportation on atoms by transferring qubits from one atom to another with the help of a third auxiliary atom.

quarantine A period during which people or animals suspected of carrying a contagious disease are kept in isolation. Originally quarantine was an attempt to prevent the spread of plague in the 14th-c: ships arriving at port were kept offshore for 40 days. Later the principle was applied to many infectious diseases, and the time shortened to relate to the incubation period of the particular infection. The practice is still applied to dogs and other animals imported from overseas to the UK, as a defence against the spread of rabies; a 6-month period is normal. In 2000, *pet passports* were introduced in the UK, allowing pet owners to take their dogs and cats to EU countries without the animals having to spend time in quarantine upon return.

quark A fundamental component of matter; symbol q. Though there is experimental support for quarks, none has been observed directly. Six quark types are known, identified by their 'flavours': *up, down, strange, charm, top,* and *bottom*. Each flavour quark carries one of three possible 'colours'. Quarks have spin $\frac{1}{2}$, and charges of $\pm\frac{1}{3}$ or $\pm\frac{2}{3}$. According to current theory, subatomic particles composed of quarks are bound together by gluons.

Quark XPress® A desk-top publishing package which offers facilities for both text and graphic manipulation.

Quarles, Francis [kwaw(r)lz] (1592–1644) Religious poet, born near Romford, Essex. His best-known work is the emblem book (a series of symbolic pictures with verse commentary), *Emblems* (1635), and a prose book of aphorisms, *Enchyridion* (1640).

quarter-day Any of the four days in the year (ie one every quarter-year) on which rents and similar charges are traditionally paid; in England and Wales, the quarter-days are Lady Day (25 Mar), Midsummer Day (24 Jun), Michaelmas (29 Sep) and Christmas Day (25 Dec); Scottish quarter-days are Candlemas (2 Feb), Whitsunday (15 May), Lammas (1 Aug) and Martinmas (11 Nov). They are different in the USA (1 Jan, 1 Apr, 1 Jul, 1 Oct).

quartz The crystalline form of silicon dioxide (SiO_2), one of the most common minerals in the Earth's crust. The clear crystals are known as *rock crystal*, but it is commonly white and translucent. Semi-precious varieties (eg amethyst) may be coloured. It is very important industrially because of its piezo-electric properties.

quartzite A rock produced by the recrystallization of sandstone by metamorphism, and consisting of interlocking crystals of quartz (**metaquartzite**). It is also a sandstone with purely siliceous cement (**orthoquartzite**).

quasar [kwayzah(r)] A distant, compact object far beyond our Galaxy, which looks starlike on a photograph, but has a redshift characteristic of an extremely remote object. The word is a contraction of **quasi-stellar object**. The distinctive features of quasars are an extremely compact structure and high redshift corresponding to velocities approaching the speed of light. They are the most distant and luminous objects in the universe.

Quasimodo, Salvatore [kwazeemohdoh] (1901–68) Poet, born in Syracuse, Sicily, Italy. His early work was Symbolist in character, as in *Ed é subito sera* (1942, And Suddenly it's Evening), and he became a leader of the *hermetic* poets. After World War 2 his poetry dealt largely with social issues.

quassia [kwoshia] A shrub or small tree (*Quassia amara*) native to tropical America; flowers tubular, red. The bitter wood containing the chemical *quassiin* is used medicinally to counter dysentery. (Family: Simaroubaceae.)

Quaternary period [kwaternaree] A geological period of the Cenozoic era extending from 2 million years ago to the present day; subdivided into the Pleistocene and Holocene epochs. It is characterized by extensive glaciations in the N Hemisphere and the emergence of mankind.

quaternions In algebra, a set of four ordered real numbers subject to certain laws of composition. Developed by William Hamilton (1803–65), they provide an example of a non-commutative algebra, as multiplication is not commutative.

Quayle, (James) Dan(forth) [kwayl] (1947–) US politician, born in Indianapolis, IN. He worked as a lawyer, journalist, and public official, becoming a Republican member of the Congress (1977–81) and Senate (1981–8). He was elected vice-president under George Bush (1989–92), and announced in 1999 that he would run for president in 2000, but later withdrew.

qubit [kyoobit] The basic element of information in quantum computing; an abbreviation of **quantum bit**. In conventional computing, the basic element of information is the bit, having values of either '0' or '1'. In quantum computing, information is also encoded using two states, but the quantum system is not restricted to existing merely in one or other, and can exist as a combination of both simultaneously. The qubit is in a superposition of two quantum states, a '0' state and a '1' state. Reading a qubit gives a certain probability of finding a '0' state, and a certain probability of finding a '1' state, and in the process destroys the special character of the qubit.

Quebec (city) [kwebek], Fr **Québec** [kaybek] 46°50N 71°15W, pop (2000e) 187 800. Capital of Quebec province, Canada, on the St Lawrence R; built on Cape Diamond, cliff rising 100 m/328 ft; 92% French-speaking; French colony founded, 1608; captured by the British under Wolfe, 1759; ceded to Britain, 1763; capital of Lower Canada (1791) and Quebec (1867); airport; railway; two universities (1852, 1968); professional team (ice hockey), Quebec Nordiques; Citadel fortress (a world heritage site).

Quebec (province) [kwebek], Fr **Québec** [kaybek] pop (2000e) 7 722 000; area 1 540 680 km²/594 856 sq mi. Largest province in Canada; capital, Quebec; Canadian Shield in N four-fifths, a rolling plateau dotted with lakes; rises to 1588 m/5210 ft at Mont d'iberville; S part intensely cultivated; most population in St Lawrence valley; claimed for France by Cartier, 1534; province of New France, 1608; captured by British, 1629; restored to France, 1632; transferred to Britain by Treaty of Paris, 1763; constituted as Lower Canada, 1791; province of Quebec, 1867, with English and French as official languages; strong separatist movement emerged in 1960s, but 1980 referendum decided against sovereignty-association, and a further referendum was narrowly defeated in 1995; governed by a lieutenant-governor and Legislative Assembly.

Quechua [kechwa] A South American Indian language of the Andean–Equatorial group. The official language of the Incas, it is now spoken by 8 million from Colombia to Chile, and is widely used as a lingua franca.

Queen Anne's lace *cow parsley*

Queen Anne Style The architecture, furniture, and silver designed during the reign of Queen Anne (1702–14), notable for carefully calculated proportions and a lack of applied ornament. The style was revived in English architecture in the last third of the 19th-c, characterized by mullioned windows, handsome brickwork, and imposingly grouped chimneys.

Queen Anne's War (1702–1713) The second of the four intercolonial wars waged by Britain and France for control of colonial North America, known in Europe as the **War of the Spanish Succession**. Settled by the Treaty of Utrecht (1713), the war resulted in British control of Newfoundland, Acadia, and Hudson Bay.

Queen Charlotte Islands, Haida **G'waii** pop (2000e) 5900; area 9790 km²/3779 sq mi. Archipelago of c.150 islands off the W coast of British Columbia, W Canada; extend over c.100 km/60 mi.

Queen Elizabeth Islands area over 390 000 km²/150 000 sq mi. Northernmost islands of the Canadian Arctic Archipelago, situated N of latitude 74°N; named in 1953.

Queen Maud Land, Norwegian **Dronning Maud Land** Main part of Norwegian Antarctic Territory (between 20°W and 45°W and S of 60°S), extending to the S Pole; claimed by Norway in 1939.

Queens pop (2000e) 2 229 400; area 283 km²/109 sq mi. Borough of New York City, USA; connected to Manhattan by the Queensboro Bridge; contains the two New York airports.

Queen's Award In the UK, an award given annually on the Queen's birthday (21 Apr). Established in 1965, there are now two separate awards, one for export achievement, and the other for technological achievement.

Queensberry, Sir John Sholto Douglas, 8th Marquess of (1844–1900) British aristocrat, a keen patron of boxing, who supervised the formulation in 1867 of new rules to govern that sport, since known as the **Queensberry Rules**.

Queen's Counsel (QC) A senior member of the English or Scottish Bar, when the monarch is a queen; the equivalent term under a king is **King's Counsel (KC)**. A practising barrister of 10 years' standing may apply to become a Queen's Counsel (or 'take silk' – a reference to the gowns which they wear).

Queensland pop (2000e) 3 290 000; area 1 727 200 km²/666 900 sq mi. Second largest state in Australia; established as a penal colony, 1824; open to free settlers, 1842; part of New South Wales until 1859; Cape York Peninsula in the N; the Great Dividing Range runs N–S, separating a fertile coastal strip to the E from dry plains to the W; tropical climate in the N; most population in the SE; capital, Brisbane; provides 22% of Australia's agricultural production, with sugar the main export crop; Great Barrier Reef runs parallel to the Pacific coast; major resort areas with fine surfing beaches.

Queneau, Raymond [kenoh] (1903–76) Novelist and poet, born in Le Havre, France. The best of his poetry is contained in *Les Ziaux* (1943) and *Si tu t'imagines* (1952, If you suppose). His novels include *Zazie dans le métro* (1959, Zazie in the Metro, filmed 1960).

Quercia, Jacopo della *Jacopo della Quercia*

Querétaro [keraytaroh] 20°38N 100°23W, pop (2000e) 547 000. City in C Mexico; altitude, 1865 m/6119 ft; important in the 1810 independence rising; railway; university (1618).

Quesnay, François [kenay] (1694–1774) Physician and economist, born in Mérey, France, known for his essays in political economy. He became a leader of the *Economistes*, also called the Physiocratic School.

Quetta [kweta] 30°15N 67°01E, pop (2000e) 465 000. Capital of Baluchistan province, W Pakistan; altitude 1650 m/5500 ft;

strategic location between Afghanistan and the Lower Indus valley; acquired by the British, 1876; badly damaged by earthquake, 1935; airfield; railway; centre of a fruit-growing area.

quetzal A Central American bird (*Pharomachrus mocinno*), inhabiting mountain forests; male with red underparts, green head and back, and very long trailing tail; also known as the **resplendent quetzal** or **resplendent trogon**. Revered by the Mayans and Aztecs, it is the national bird of Guatemala.

Quetzalcoatl [ketzlkohatl] The feathered serpent god of the pre-Columbian Aztec and Mayan cultures of Central America. He is represented variously as a culture hero, as a deity and creator, and as the Aztec high priest. He is associated with the invention of the calendar and the re-creation of human life.

Quezon City [kayson] 14°39N 121°01E, pop (2000e) 2 044 000. Residential city in the Philippines; on Luzon I; former capital, 1948–76; university (1908).

quicklime *calcium*

quicksilver *mercury* (chemistry)

quickthorn *hawthorn*

quill A pen made from the tapered stem of a bird's feather, especially the outer wing feathers of geese. Quills were the chief writing implement from the 6th-c AD until the advent of steel pens in the mid-19th-c.

Quiller-Couch, Sir Arthur (Thomas) [kwiler kooch], pseudonym **Q** (1863–1944) Man of letters, born in Bodmin, Cornwall. He edited the *Oxford Book of English Verse* (1900) and other anthologies, and published several volumes of essays and criticism. He also wrote poems, short stories, and humorous novels of Cornwall and the sea, often under his pseudonym.

quillwort A spore-bearing vascular plant related to clubmosses, mostly aquatic pteridophytes distributed throughout the world. (Genus: *Isoetes*, 75 species. Family: Isoetaceae.)

Quimper [kīpair] or **Quimper Corentin** 48°00N 4°09W, pop (2000e) 65 400. Manufacturing and commercial town in NW France; on estuary of R Odet; railway; pottery (Quimper or Brittany ware) since 16th-c; cathedral (13th-c).

quince A deciduous shrub or small tree (*Cydonia oblonga*) reaching 1·5–7·5m/5–25 ft, native to Asia; flowers pale pink, bowl-shaped, resembling apple blossom; fruit apple- or pear-shaped, fragrant but hard when ripe, mainly used in preserves. (Family: Rosaceae.)

Quine, Willard Van Orman [kwiyn] (1908–2000) Philosopher and logician, born in Akron, OH. His books include *The Logic of Sequences* (1990), and *From Stimulus to Science* (1995).

quinine A drug used in the prevention of malaria, and sometimes in its treatment. It is present in the bark of various *Cinchona* trees native to the Andes, but it is also cultivated in Sri Lanka, India, and Java.

Quinnipiac *New Haven*

quinoline [kwinolin] C_9H_7N, boiling point 238°C. An organic base, related to pyridine. Both it and the isomeric **isoquinoline** are oily liquids, constituents of coal-tar. Quinine and other alkaloids are derivatives of quinoline.

quinone $C_6H_4O_2$. One of two isomers derived from benzene (*benzoquinones*) or derivatives of these. They are highly coloured, and a quinone group is often a chromophore of a dyestuff.

Quinquagesima [kwinkwajesima] In the Western Christian Church, the Sunday before Lent, so called from its being 50 days before Easter, counting inclusively (Lat *quinquagesimus*, 'fiftieth').

quinsy [kwinzee] The formation of an abscess in and around the tonsils. It is a complication of severe tonsillitis caused by a bacterial infection.

Quintero, Serafin Alvarez *Alvarez Quintero, Serafin*

quipu [keepoo] An accounting system of knotted cords

developed by the Peruvian Incas and others. The system was a complex one, with strings and knots of various lengths, shapes, and colours.

Quirinal One of the seven hills of Rome, NE of Capitoline Hill, the site of several ancient shrines. A papal palace was built in Quirinal Square (begun c.1585). Later known as the Quirinal palace, it became the residence of the kings of Italy (1870–1946), and from 1947 it has been the home of the presidents of Italy.

Quirk, (Charles) Randolph, Baron (1920–) Grammarian and writer on the English language, born in the Isle of Man. Major grammars in which he was involved are *A Grammar of Contemporary English* (1972) and *A Comprehensive Grammar of the English Language* (1985).

Quisling, Vidkun (Abraham Lauritz Jonsson) [kwizling] (1887–1945) Diplomat and fascist leader, born in Fyresdal, Norway. He founded the *Nasjonal Samling* ('National Unity') in imitation of the German National Socialist Party (1933), and became puppet prime minister in occupied Norway. Executed in 1945, his name has since become synonymous with 'traitor'.

Quit India Movement A campaign launched (Aug 1942) by the Indian National Congress calling for immediate independence from Britain. Gandhi and other Congress leaders were arrested, and the movement quickly suppressed.

Quito [keetoh] 0°14S 78°30W, pop (2000e) 1 358 000. Capital of Ecuador; altitude 2850 m/9350 ft; former Inca capital (old city designated a world heritage site); captured by Spanish, 1534; airport; railway; three universities (1769, 1869, 1946); cathedral.

Qumran, community of [kumran] (c. 2nd-c BC–1st-c AD) An exclusive Jewish sect, located near the NW corner of the Dead Sea. They were destroyed during the Jewish revolt of AD 66–70, but many of their writings were discovered in 1947 as part of the Dead Sea Scrolls.

quoits An outdoor game demanding great accuracy, which

involves the throwing of a metal ring at a peg. It has been a popular sport in England since the middle of the 14th-c.

quota (IMF) The share of a member country in the International Monetary Fund (IMF). Its quota determines the amount of its own and other currencies a member has to subscribe on joining. The voting power of a member on decisions by the IMF, and the amount it can borrow if necessary, are both proportional to its quota. A large quota for a rich country such as the USA implies a large subscription and a large say in decisions. A larger quota for a poor country means larger access to various forms of loan if it encounters balance of payments problems. IMF quotas are revised periodically, by negotiation between members.

quota (OPEC) The maximum quantity of oil that a member of the Organization of Petroleum Exporting Countries (OPEC) is supposed to sell in a given period. OPEC sets quotas by periodical negotiation in order to maintain world crude oil prices. As any individual member of a cartel can gain by selling more than its quota while others stick to theirs, there is some suspicion that OPEC quotas are not fully effective.

quotas, import A means of restricting imports of a commodity or product by limiting the quantity that can be imported in a particular period. The aim is to protect domestic industry and preserve foreign currency reserves.

Qur'an or **Koran** [korahn] The sacred book of Islam. It is held to be the direct word of God, revealed piecemeal to the Prophet Mohammed as a message for all humanity.

Qutb Minar or **Kutab Minar** [kutb minah(r)] A famous city landmark in Delhi, India. Built in 1199 as a Muslim tower of victory, the Qutb Minar is 72·5 m/263 ft high.

QwaQwa [kwakwa] Former national state or non-independent black homeland in South Africa; self-governing status, 1974; incorporated into KwaZulu Natal following the new South African constitution of 1994.

r

Rabat (Malta) [rabat] 35°53N 14°25E, pop (2000e) 14 000. Town in SWC Malta; St Paul lived in a cave here after shipwreck, AD 60.

Rabat (Morocco) [rabat] 34°02N 6°51W, pop (2000e) 756 000. Capital of Morocco, one of Morocco's four imperial cities; founded, 12th-c; French colonialists established a Residency-General, 1912; airport; railway; university (1957); fortress (14th-c).

rabbi (Heb 'my lord', or 'my master/teacher') In Judaism after AD 70, a title for accredited Jewish teachers or sages; prior to 70, used less technically as a form of respectful address. The teachings of these early sages are preserved in the Mishnah, the Talmud, and many other forms of rabbinic literature. Today rabbis also have pastoral functions and a role in worship, much like ministers of other faiths.

rabbit A mammal of the order Lagomorpha, family Leporidae (23 species); differs from the closely related **hare** in several respects (different skull features, smaller, gives birth to naked young, lives in groups, burrows to produce complex warrens, lacks black ear tips); also called **con(e)y** – a name often used for rabbit skin.

rabbitfish *chimaera* (zoology)

Rabelais, François [rabelay], pseudonym (an anagram of his name) **Alcofribas Nasier** (?1494–1553) Satirist, physician, and humanist, born in or near Chinon, France. He is remembered for his comic and satirical *Pantagruel* (1533) and *Gargantua* (1535), published under his pseudonym, though condemned by the Church.

rabies [raybeez] A virus infection that affects a wide range of animals, such as dogs, cats, foxes, skunks, and vampire bats; also known as **hydrophobia**. It is transmitted to humans by bites, or by licks on skin abrasions or intact mucous membranes. The central nervous system is affected, leading to delusions and hallucinations. The alternative name stems from the violent contractions of the larynx and inspiratory muscles induced by drinking. Death is almost invariable.

Rabin, Yitzhak [rabeen] (1922–95) Israeli soldier, statesman, and prime minister (1974–7, 1992–5), born in Jerusalem. He was appointed chief-of-staff in 1964, heading the armed forces during the Six-Day War (1967). He became Labour Party leader and prime minister, resigning in 1977 when involved in a scandal over accounts he kept in the USA. He later served as defence minister (1984–90), and became prime minister again in 1992. He shared the Nobel Peace Prize in 1994. He was assassinated by a right-wing Israeli law student.

raccoon A mammal of genus *Procyon* (7 species), native to North and Central America; grey with dark bands around tail; face pale with black band across eyes. (Family: Procyonidae.)

RACE [rays] Acronym for **Research in Advanced Communications in Europe**, a European special programme of research in telecommunications particularly related to data communications.

race A biologically distinctive major division of a species, in which the differences between recognized races exceed the variation within them. While useful in describing variation in many plants and animals, where race is often equated with subspecies, the concept has little or no value for describing human biological diversity. In the past 500 years, contacts between all human groups have been intensive; gene pools are in constant flux; and the biological differences between populations are slight. The familiar 'racial' classifications typically emphasize superficially obvious features, such as skin colour or hair type, but other genetically transmitted features, such as blood groupings, tend to cross-cut the classical categories. There is no evidence for biologically-determined differences between populations in such ability or character traits, nor any consistent relationship with cultural systems or institutions.

racehorse *thoroughbred*

raceme *inflorescence*

Rachmaninov, Sergey Vasilyevich [rakhmaninof], also spelled **Rachmaninoff** and **Rakhmaninov** (1873–1943) Composer and pianist, born in Nizhni Novgorod. He wrote operas, orchestral works, and songs, but is best known for his piano music, which includes four concertos, the popular *Prelude in C Sharp Minor*, and his last major work, the *Rhapsody on a Theme of Paganini* (1934) for piano and orchestra.

racial discrimination Treating someone in a particular way because of their race or ethnicity. The term is usually understood to mean negative discrimination, that is, treating people in a way which will disadvantage them relative to other social groups.

Racine, Jean (Baptiste) [raseen] (1639–99) Dramatic poet, born in La Ferté-Milon, France. His major verse tragedies include *Andromaque* (1667), *Britannicus* (1669), *Bérénice* (1679), *Bajazet* (1672), and *Phèdre* (1677). He later wrote two religious plays on Old Testament subjects, *Esther* (1689) and *Athalie* (1691).

racism An ideology that claims to explain an alleged inferiority of certain racial or ethnic groups in terms of their biological or physical characteristics. Racist beliefs have been used to justify genocide and the maintenance of systems of inequality (such as apartheid).

rackets (UK) / **racquets** (US) A racket-and-ball game played on a walled court by two or four players. Thought to have originated in the Middle Ages, it is regarded as the forerunner of many modern games.

Rackham, Arthur [rakam] (1867–1939) Artist, born in London. A watercolourist and book illustrator, he was well known for his typically Romantic and grotesque pictures in books of fairy tales, such as *Peter Pan* (1906).

racoon *raccoon*

rad In radioactivity, an old unit for absorbed dose; symbol rad; 1 rad is equivalent to 0·01J/kg, or 0·01 Gy (gray, SI unit); an abbreviation of **radiation**.

radar Acronym for **radio detection and ranging**, a system developed in the 1930s whereby the position and distance of objects can be determined by measuring the time taken for radio waves to be reflected and returned. It is used in navigation, air traffic control, fire control, detection and location of underground objects, and speed control by police.

radar astronomy The use of pulses of radio waves to detect the distances and map the surfaces of objects in the Solar System. It has been applied with great success to Venus.

Radcliffe, Ann, *née* **Ward** (1764–1823) Novelist, born in London. She became well known for her Gothic novels, notably *The Romance of the Forest* (1791), *The Mysteries of Udolpho* (1794), and *The Italian* (1797).

Radcliffe, Daniel (Jacob) (1989–) Actor, born in London. He began performing in school productions as a boy and gained his first TV role in *David Copperfield* (1999). His film debut was in *The Tailor of Panama* in 2001, and later that year he was cast as Harry Potter in *Harry Potter and the Philosopher's Stone*. He continued the role in *Harry Potter and the Chamber of Secrets* (2002), *Harry Potter and the Prisoner of Azkaban* (2004), and later films (2005, 2007).

Radcliffe, Paula (1973–) Athlete, born in Northwich, Cheshire. She won the world junior cross-country title in 1992, and later achievements include the 5000 m gold at the 2002 Commonwealth Games, 10 000 m gold at the 2002 European Championships, three times women's winner of the London Marathon (2002, 2003, 2005), and winner of the Chicago Marathon (2002) where she set a new women's world record. After a disappointing performance at the 2004 Olympic Games in Athens, she went on to win the New York Marathon later that year, and at the 2005 World Championships she won the women's marathon. She was named female athlete of the year by the International Association of Athletics Federations in 2002. An autobiography, *Paula: The Story So Far*, appeared in 2004.

Radhakrishnan, Sir Sarvepalli [rahdakrishnan] (1888–1975) Indian philosopher, statesman, and president (1962–7), born in Tiruttani, Chennai (Madras), India. He was professor of Eastern religions and ethics at Oxford (1936–52), before becoming vice-president of India (1952–62), and president.

radian SI unit for measuring angles in a plane: symbol *rad*; 1 radian is the angle subtended at the centre of a circle by an arc along the circumference equal in length to the circle's radius; thus π radians = 180°.

radiance; radiant intensity / power *radiometry*

radiation A general term for the processes by which energy is lost from a source without physical contact. It refers to various radioactive and electromagnetic emissions.

radiation sickness An acute affect on the body of high doses of ionizing radiation, which may be a complication of radiotherapy for the treatment of cancer. It results in weakness, nausea, vomiting, and diarrhoea, and damage to epithelial surfaces with hair loss, red patches on the skin (*erythema*), and mouth ulcers.

radical An unstable molecule containing unpaired electrons (eg CH_3, methyl). The term is also used as a synonym for 'group' in the sense of 'part of a molecule'.

radicalism Any set of ideas, of either left or right, which argues for more substantial social and political change than is supported in the political mainstream. What is radical is a matter of judgment, and so the term is very widely applied.

radiesthesia [raydiestheezha] The use of dowsing as a method of diagnosing disease and selecting a suitable treatment, usually in the form of a herbal or homeopathic remedy. One method uses a pendulum: diagnosis is made by comparing the response of the pendulum to that observed with reference samples taken in various disease states.

radio The transmission of sound signals through space by means of radio-frequency electromagnetic waves. In 1888 the German physicist Heinrich Hertz produced and detected radio waves. Guglielmo Marconi constructed a device to translate radio

waves into electrical signals, and in 1901 transmitted signals across the Atlantic Ocean. Radio broadcasting became routinely available during the 1920s, when such institutions as the BBC came into being.

radioactive dating *radiocarbon dating*

radioactive fallout The radioactive substances produced by a nuclear explosion, carried away from the site by winds, and deposited (either from dry air as particles, or dissolved in rain) causing contamination. Fallout from the Chernobyl accident in 1986 included caesium-134, caesium-137, iodine-131, plutonium-239, and strontium-90.

radioactive tracer A radioactive isotope of an element substituted specifically in a compound in order to 'tag' it. Much has been learned about the mechanisms of reactions in this way, as the reactant supplying a specific atom to a product can be identified.

radioactive waste A byproduct of the many processes involved in the generation of nuclear power. *Low-level* and *intermediate-level* waste is generally buried in pits. *High-level* waste is generally stored in stainless steel tanks, and continually cooled. One possibility for storage is vitrification (solidification in glass), to reduce the volume of waste. Proposals exist for the burial of high-level waste either under the seabed or deep underground on land. The production and storage of radioactive waste is a major international environmental issue.

radioactivity The spontaneous decay of atomic nuclei, resulting in the emission of particles and energy; discovered by Antoine Henri Becquerel in 1896. The possible emissions are alpha particles, beta particles, and gamma rays. Radioactivity is detected and measured using Geiger counters.

radioactivity units The activity of a radioactive source expressed in **becquerels** *Bq*, where 1 Bq is one decay per second. The **gray**, *Gy*, measures the energy deposited in some object by the radiation: the *absorbed dose*. Different types of radiation cause different degrees of biological damage; for example, 1 Gy of alpha radiation causes 20 times as much damage as 1 Gy of beta radiation. This potential for causing harm is expressed as *dose equivalent*, units **sievert**, *Sv*, which is the product of absorbed dose in Gy and a *relative biological effectiveness* (RBE) factor. Radiation limits for working places and the environment are expressed in Sv. *see panel*

radio astronomy The exploration of the universe by detecting radio emission from celestial objects. The frequency range is very great, from 10 mHz to 300 gHz. A variety of antennas are used, from single dishes to elaborate networks of telescopes.

radio beacon A fixed radio transmitting station, sending out a coded signal characteristic of that station. This helps aircraft

Radioactivity Units

Name	Definition	Unit	Old Unit
activity	rate of disintegrations	Bq	Ci (curie)
absorbed dose	energy deposited in object divided by mass of object	Gy	rad
dose equivalent	absorbed dose x RBE	Sv	rem

RBE	Radiation
20	alpha
10	neutron
1	beta, gamma, X-ray

Radiometry

Radiometric quantity	Symbol	Units
radiant power	Φ	W
radiant intensity	I	W/sr
radiance	L	W/sr.m²
irradiance	E	W/m²

pilots and ships' captains to navigate safely, especially in bad weather conditions.

radiobiology The branch of biology concerned with the effects of radioactive materials on living organisms, and with the use of radioactive tracers to study metabolic processes.

radiocarbon dating A radiometric method for measuring the decay of the radioactive isotope carbon-14 in organic material up to 80 000 years old, developed in 1948–9 by Willard Libby. Living animals and plants take in carbon, which contains some radioactive carbon-14. When the organism dies, it stops taking in carbon, and as the carbon-14 decays, its proportion to the total amount of carbon decreases in a way which is directly related to the time elapsed since death.

radiochemistry The production and use of radioisotopes to study chemical compounds and their reactions. An example is the synthesis of compounds incorporating radioactive atoms in specific sites, to see whether those atoms are present in a product of a subsequent chemical reaction.

radio galaxy A galaxy which is an intense source of cosmic radio waves. In such objects, an active galactic nucleus (almost certainly a black hole) is producing immense quantities of electrons travelling at almost the speed of light. When these encounter a magnetic field, they spiral around the field lines, emitting synchrotron radiation as radio waves.

radiogram A single device capable of both receiving radio broadcasts and playing gramophone records. It was developed during the 1930s, and incorporated a record player which made use of the radio's amplifier and speaker.

radiography Producing a photographic image (actually a shadow-image) of a structure which is penetrated by X-rays, gamma-rays, or electrons. The first radiograph was made by Röntgen in 1895, and the technique is now highly developed for medical diagnosis and for non-destructive industrial testing.

radio-immunoassay A method using radioactively labelled material corresponding to a substance to be measured, together with a specific antibody to the substance. The degree of binding of the antibody to the labelled substance can be used to calculate the amount of substance present in a biological fluid, such as blood.

radioisotope An isotope which spontaneously undergoes radioactive decay. It may be naturally occurring or artificially produced. All isotopes of all elements with an atomic number above 83 are radioisotopes.

Radiolaria [raydiohlairia] An informal grouping of marine single-celled organisms (protozoans). They have a typically spherical cell body, with an elaborate skeleton consisting of radiating spikes of silica. (Class: Actinopoda.)

radiometric dating A method for determining the absolute age of a rock by measuring the amount of radioactive element present and comparing it to the amount of stable element into which it decays.

radiometry The measurement of radiated electromagnetic energy, especially infrared; see table for symbols and units. *Radiant power* is the total power from a source; *radiant intensity* is radiant power per unit solid angle, and is used to describe sources that do not radiate uniformly in all directions; *radiance*

is radiant intensity per unit area; *irradiance* is total power per unit area. *see panel*

radiosonde (radiosounding) balloon [raydiohsond] A package of instruments sent up with a weather balloon to measure pressure, temperature, and humidity as the balloon rises to high altitudes (20 000 m/65 000 ft). Information is transmitted back to ground-receiving stations by radio signals. A **rawindsonde** (radar wind sounding) balloon is a version of radiosonde which also measures wind speed and direction.

radio telescope *telescope*

radiotherapy The use of radiation (especially X-rays) to treat disease, especially malignant tumours, which are more sensitive to certain kinds of radiation than are normal tissues. Radioactive materials can also be used (eg a tiny pellet), implanted directly into the tumour to give a carefully calculated total dose. The technique has proved particularly successful in the treatment of cancer.

radio waves Electromagnetic radiation of wavelength greater than about 10 cm. It is produced by oscillating electric currents in antennas, and travels at the velocity of light.

radish An annual or biennial (*Raphanus sativus*) with a tuberous root, irregularly lobed leaves, and cross-shaped, white to purplish flowers. Its origin is unknown, but it has been used as a vegetable since Ancient Egyptian times. (Family: Cruciferae.)

radium Ra, element 88, melting point 700°C. A metal, with all its isotopes radioactive. The most stable isotope, ^{226}Ra, has a half-life of only 1620 years, and occurs in uranium ores as a product of radioactive decay. It is a source of α-particles, and combined with beryllium, a neutron source. Radium salts exhibit fluorescence.

radius (anatomy) *arm*

radon Rn, element 86, boiling point −62°C. The heaviest of the noble gases. It has several isotopes: that with the longest half-life (4 days) is ^{222}Rn, formed with radium. It is continuously liberated to the atmosphere by natural radioactive decay; its primary use is in radiotherapy.

Raeburn, Sir Henry [rayburn] (1756–1823) Portrait painter, born near Edinburgh. He painted the leading members of Edinburgh society in a typically bold, strongly-shadowed style.

Raeder, Erich [rayder] (1876–1960) German grand admiral, born in Wandsbek, Germany. In 1928 he was made commander-in-chief of the navy, and in 1943 head of an anti-invasion force. At the Nuremberg Trials (1946), he was sentenced to life imprisonment, but released in 1955.

RAF *Royal Air Force*

raffia palm A tree growing to 7·5 m/25 ft, native to Africa; leaves 18 m/60 ft, feathery. The surface of the young leaflets is stripped to provide raffia fibre. (Genus: *Raffia*, 30 species. Family: Palmae.)

Raffles, Sir (Thomas) Stamford (1781–1826) Colonial administrator, born at sea, off Port Morant, Jamaica. He became Lieutenant-Governor of Java (1811–16), and as Lieutenant-Governor of Benkoelen (1818–23) established a settlement at Singapore (1819). A famous Singapore hotel carries his name.

rafflesia The best-known member of an entirely parasitic family of flowering plants from the tropics and subtropics. Native to Malaysia, it parasitizes woody vines and has enormous flowers. The flowers of *Rafflesia arnoldii* are the largest in the world, reaching 1 m/3¼ ft in diameter. They are typical carrion flowers, the whole structure being coloured to resemble rotting meat, and producing a strong putrid smell which attracts flies to pollinate them. (Genus: *Rafflesia*, 12 species. Family: Rafflesiaceae.)

Rafsanjani, Ali Akbar Hashemi [rafsanjahnee] (1934–) Iranian president (1989–97), born in Rafsanjan, Iran. After the 1979 revolution, he helped to found the ruling Islamic Republican Party, and in 1980 he was chosen as Speaker of the Majlis (Lower House). He was the most influential figure in Iran after Khomeini, and succeeded him as president.

raga In Indian music, the equivalent of the Western 'mode', but with broader connotations of melodic contour, performance style, ornamentation, etc.

Raglan (of Raglan), Lord Fitzroy James Henry Somerset, Baron (1788–1855) British general, born at Badminton, Gloucestershire. In 1854 he led an ill-prepared force against the Russians in the Crimea, his ambiguous order leading to the Charge of the Light Brigade (1854) at Balaclava. His name was given to the **raglan sleeve**, which came into use in the 1850s.

Ragnarök [ragnaroek] In Norse mythology, the final battle between the gods and the monstrous forces hostile to them. Though gods and monsters die, a new world will arise.

ragtime A type of syncopated US music popular from c.1890 to c.1920, when it yielded to (and influenced) the new jazz style. 'Rags' were composed mainly for piano, and ragtime was popularized by Scott Joplin and other pianist–composers. It had a revival in the 1970s.

ragwort A robust biennial or perennial (*Senecio jacobaea*), growing to 1·5 m/5 ft, native to Europe and W Asia; flower-heads numerous, bright golden yellow and daisy-like, in dense flat-topped clusters. It is poisonous to livestock if eaten in quantity. (Family: Compositae.)

Rahman, Shaikh Mujibur [rahman] (1920–75) First prime minister (1972–5) and president (1975) of Bangladesh, born in Tongipara, Bangladesh (formerly East Bengal). In 1966 he was arrested and imprisoned for two years for provoking separatism. In 1970 he launched a non-co-operation campaign which escalated into civil war and the creation of Bangladesh. He was overthrown and killed in a coup in Dacca.

Rahner, Karl (1904–84) Leading Roman Catholic theologian, born in Freiburg, Germany. In his voluminous writings (such as his multivolume *Theological Investigations*), he uses insights from existentialism while remaining true to the tradition of Aquinas. He played a major role as consultant at the Second Vatican Council (1962–6).

Raikes, Robert [rayks] (1735–1811) Philanthropist, born in Gloucester, Gloucestershire. He pioneered the Sunday School movement in 1780.

rail A bird of the worldwide family Rallidae (c.130 species), possibly the most widespread group of terrestrial birds; large legs, short rounded wings, and short tails.

rail gun 1 A heavy artillery piece mounted on a railway carriage. **2** A proposed component of the Strategic Defense Initiative, a land-based, short-range system for the last-ditch defence of individual land targets. It uses electrical energy to accelerate kinetic energy munitions to very high velocities.

railway The general name given in the UK to a transport system that has as its central feature the operation of a locomotive hauling passenger carriages or freight trucks on specially mounted tracks or rails, called the **permanent way**. The geographical area covered by the rails forms a **rail network**, and the operation of all trains on the network together with their scheduling, control, and engineering support services form a **railway system**. North American usage retains the historical name of **railroad** to describe the above definition of railway, and uses the term **railway** to describe the permanent way, ie the rails, their fixings, and associated engineering. The world's first railway, the Stockton and Darlington, was opened in 1825, and was used mainly for the carriage of coal and other goods, and some passengers, employing both steam locomotives and horses for traction. It was not until 1830, and the opening of the Liverpool and Manchester Railway, that a full passenger-carrying railway, solely dependent on steam locomotives, became operational. The 'Best Friend of Charleston' pulled the first train on US soil in 1830, and by 1869 it was possible to cross the USA by rail.

rainbow An arc of light comprising the spectral colours, formed when the Sun's rays are refracted and internally reflected by raindrops acting as prisms or lenses. It is visible when the Sun is behind the observer and the rain is in front.

Rainbow Snake In Australian aboriginal religion, the great fertility spirit, both male and female, creator and destroyer; known as **Julunggul**. It is associated with streams and waterholes, from which it emerges in the creation-story and leaves special markings on the ground.

Raine, Craig (Anthony) (1944–) Poet, born in Shildon, Co Durham. Poetry editor at Faber and Faber (1981–91), his books include *The Onion, Memory* (1978), *Selected Poetry* (1992), *Clay: Whereabouts Unknown* (1996), and *A la recherche du temps perdu* (2000).

rainfall A type of precipitation in which water droplets reach the ground in liquid state. When water droplets are small, rain may be called *drizzle*. In temperate and humid regions, rainfall may form the major contribution to annual precipitation totals.

rainforest The vegetation type found in wet equatorial regions and other areas of high precipitation. Tropical rainforests are characterized by a great diversity of plant and animal species, a closed canopy layer which allows little light to reach the forest floor, and rapid nutrient cycling within the forest. Many of the trees have considerable commercial value, and large areas are being cleared. Deforestation is also occurring to create new agricultural areas (cattle ranching) and industry (mining). The United Nations Food and Agricultural Organization estimates that c.100 000 km²/c.40 000 sq mi are cleared each year. This rate of disappearance is alarming many conservationists, because of the extinction of unique plant and animal species. Tropical rainforests also play an important role in the global climate system, which could also be disrupted by clearance.

rain gauge A meteorological instrument used to measure the amount of rainfall for a given period. It is commonly in the form of a bucket, with an opening of known size, which funnels rain into a measuring cylinder below.

Rainier, Mount [raynyer] 46°51N 121°46W. Dormant volcano in WC Washington, USA; height 4395 m/14 419 ft; highest point in the Cascade Range; the largest single-peak glacier system in the USA.

Rainier III [raynyay], in full **Rainier Louis Henri Maxence Bertrand de Grimaldi** (1923–2005) Prince of Monaco (1949–2005), born in Monaco. In 1956 he married US film actress Grace Kelly. They had two daughters, **Princess Caroline Louise Marguerite** (1957–) and **Princess Stephanie Marie Elisabeth** (1965–). He was succeeded by his son, **Prince Albert Alexandre Louis Pierre** (1958–).

Rais or **Raiz, Baron** *Retz, Baron*

raisins Black or white grapes, dried naturally or artificially. They have a high sugar content, and are used widely in cake- and bun-making to impart sweetness.

Rajasthan [rahjastahn] pop (2001e) 56 473 100; area 342 214 km²/132 095 sq mi. State in NW India, formed in 1948; capital, Jaipur; governed by a Legislative Assembly; Thar desert in the W.

Rakhmaninov, Sergei *Rachmaninov*

Raleigh [rahlee] 35°46N 78°38W, pop (2000e) 276 100. Capital of state in EC North Carolina, USA; established, 1788; named after Sir Walter Raleigh; airfield; railway; two universities (1865, 1887).

Raleigh, Sir Walter [rawlee, ralee], also spelled **Ralegh** (1552–1618) Courtier, explorer, soldier, and writer, born in Hayes Barton, Devon. He was a rival of the Earl of Essex for Queen Elizabeth's favours. In 1584 he sent the first of three expeditions to America, and in 1588 he took part in the victory over the Spanish Armada. He forfeited Elizabeth's favour by his marriage to one of her maids-of-honour, Bessy Throckmorton, and was committed to the Tower (1592). Released, he led an abortive expedition to Guiana in search of El Dorado, the legendary land of gold, instead he helped introduce the potato plant and tobacco use in England and Ireland. Elizabeth's successor, James I, had him charged with treason and condemned him to death, but commuted the sentence to imprisonment (1603). While in the Tower, he wrote his *History of the World* (1614), and several other works. He was released in 1616 to search for gold in South America, but when this failed he was arrested on his return to England, the original death sentence for treason was invoked, and he was executed.

rally A form of motor racing which demands skill and endurance from driver and navigator. Rallies are raced over several days (sometimes weeks) using modified production cars. Famous rallies include the Monte Carlo Rally, the RAC Lombard Rally, and the Safari Rally.

RAM [ram] Acronym for **random access memory** (sometimes **read-and-write memory**), a type of computer memory, usually integrated circuits, which can be read from and written to. RAM is used in all computers; data contained in RAM is lost when the electrical power is removed.

ram *sheep*

Ramadan [ramadahn] The ninth month of the Muslim year, observed as a month of fasting during which Muslims abstain from eating and drinking between sunrise and sunset; the Ramadan fast is one of the five 'pillars', or basic duties, of Islam.

Ramadan War *Arab–Israeli Wars*

Ramakrishna [ramakrishna], originally **Gadadhar Chatterjee** (1836–86) Hindu religious teacher, born in Hooghly, Bengal, India. He formed a religious order which bore his name, and established its headquarters in Calcutta. His most noteworthy disciple was Swami Vivekananda.

Raman, Sir Chandrasekhara (Venkata) [rahman] (1888–1970) Physicist, born in Trichinopoly, now Tiruchchirappalli, India. In 1930 he was awarded the Nobel Prize for Physics for his discoveries relating to the scattering of light.

Ramaphosa, Cyril (Matamela) [ramapohza] (1952–) South African politician and trade unionist, born in Johannesburg, South Africa. He played a prominent part in the protest politics of the 1980s, and in 1991 became the secretary-general of the African National Congress, resigning in 1996.

Ramapithecus [ramapithekus] A fossil ape, known from the Miocene epoch of E Europe, Asia, and E Africa; ground-dwelling, walked on all fours; jaws robust; canine teeth low as in early hominids. (Family: Pongidae.)

Ramayana [ramayahna] One of the two great Sanskrit epics of ancient India, which tells the story of Rama, his wife Sita, and the evil forces ranged against them. Though ascribed to the sage Valmiki, it derives from oral tradition. Its 24 000 couplets make it one-quarter the length of the *Mahabharata*.

Rambert, Dame Marie [rombair], originally **Cyvia Rambam** (1888–1982) Ballet dancer and teacher, born in Warsaw. In 1913 she worked with Diaghilev's Ballets Russes. In 1935 she formed the Ballet Rambert, and remained closely associated with it through its change to a modern dance company in the 1960s.

Ramblers' Association A British federation of local rambling clubs, established in 1935. It campaigns for access to open countryside, defends outstanding landscape and rights-of-way, and is one of the main advocates of long-distance footpaths.

Rameau, Jean Philippe [ramoh] (1683–1764) Composer, born in Dijon, France. His *Traité de l'harmonie* (1722, Treatise on Harmony) is a work of fundamental importance in the history of musical style. He wrote many operas, as well as ballets, harpsichord pieces, and vocal music.

Rameses or **Ramses II** [ram(e)seez], known as **the Great** (13th-c BC) King of Egypt (1304–1237 BC), whose long and prosperous reign marks the last great peak of Egyptian power. He has left innumerable monuments, among them the great sandstone temples at Abu Simbel.

Rameses or **Ramses III** [ram(e)seez] (12th-c BC) King of Egypt (1198–1166 BC), famous primarily for his great victory over the Sea Peoples. Tradition identifies him with the pharaoh who oppressed the Hebrews of the Exodus.

ramjet A type of jet engine in which fast-moving air is slowed down by a diffuser, which produces a corresponding increase in the air's pressure. This high-pressure air then has fuel injected into it, and the mixture is continuously burned. The resulting hot gases are ejected rearwards in the form of a jet of gas. This method of jet propulsion is practical up to speeds of eight times the speed of sound.

Ramos-Horta, José [ramos haw(r)ta] (1949–) Political activist, prime minister (2006–7), and president (2007–) of East Timor, born in Dili, East Timor. He studied at the Hague Academy of International Law (1983), Antioch University (1984), and the International Institute of Human Rights in Strasbourg (1983). A former guerilla member of the independence movement in East Timor (Fretilin), he withdrew to Australia following the 1975 Indonesian invasion, became East Timor's international spokesman for a peaceful solution, and was jointly awarded the Nobel Peace Prize in 1996. East Timor gained independence in 2002 and he served as the first foreign minister until his appointment as prime minister in 2006 and president in 2007.

Ramsay, Allan (c.1685–1758) Poet, born in Leadhills, South Lanarkshire. His works include the pastoral comedy, *The Gentle Shepherd* (1725), and an edited collection of Scots poetry, *The Evergreen* (1724).

Ramses *Rameses*

Ramsey (of Canterbury), (Arthur) Michael Ramsey, Baron (1904–88) Archbishop of Canterbury (1961–74), born in Cambridge, Cambridgeshire. He was Bishop of Durham (1952–6) and Archbishop of York (1956–61). As Archbishop of Canterbury he worked for Church unity, making a historic visit to Pope Paul VI in the Vatican in 1966.

Ramsgate 51°20N 1°25E, pop (2000e) 38 700. Port town in Kent, SE England; railway; hovercraft service to France; yachting, fishing, tourism; Celtic cross marks the spot where St Augustine is thought to have landed in 597.

Ramus, Petrus [ramü], Lat name of **Pierre de la Ramée** (1515–72) Humanist, born in Cuts, France. His attempts to reform the science of logic excited much hostility among the Aristotelians, and his *Dialectic* (1543) was suppressed. He later became a Protestant (c.1561), and was murdered in the massacre of St Bartholomew's Day.

rancidity The reaction of atmospheric oxygen with fats, which reduces vitamin A and E levels in foods. Antioxidants are commonly added to foods to prevent the development of rancidity.

Rand *Witwatersrand*

Randolph, A(sa) Philip (1889–1979) Labour leader and civil rights activist, born in Crescent City, FL. He built the first successful African-American trade union, the Brotherhood of Sleeping Car Porters (1925). The founder of the Negro American Labor Council in 1960, he directed the civil rights march on Washington in 1963.

randomized controlled trial A scientific method used in medicine to determine whether a new drug or other medical intervention is effective. It is designed to ensure that therapies are thoroughly evaluated before being widely used. A group of people is allocated at random to receive either the active treatment or a dummy treatment (*placebo*). The proportion of people in each group who benefit is then compared to see whether the active treatment has a statistically greater beneficial effect than the dummy treatment.

Randstad Urban conurbation of settlements in NW Netherlands, forming a horse-shoe shape around a central agricultural zone; contains most of the Dutch population; chief cities, Amsterdam, Rotterdam, Utrecht, The Hague.

Ranger programme The first US series of lunar spacecraft missions, designed to study the surface characteristics of the Moon prior to the Apollo manned landings. The spacecraft were targeted to impact the Moon after telemetering images of increasingly high resolution. The first successful mission was Ranger 7 (Aug 1964).

Rangoon *Yangon*

Ranjit Singh [ranjit sing], known as **the Lion of the Punjab** (1780–1839) Sikh ruler, born in Budrukhan, Pakistan (formerly India). Succeeding his father as ruler of Lahore, he fought to unite all the Sikh provinces, and became the most powerful ruler in India.

Rank (of Sutton Scotney), J(oseph) Arthur Rank, Baron (1888–1972) Film magnate, born in Hull. He became chairman of many film companies, and did much to promote the British film industry.

Rankine temperature *temperature*

Ransome, Arthur (Michell) (1884–1967) Writer, born in Leeds, West Yorkshire. He wrote critical and travel books before making his name with books for young readers, notably *Swallows and Amazons* (1930).

ransoms A perennial growing to 45 cm/18 in (*Allium ursinum*), native to Europe and Asia; narrow bulb consisting of a single leaf base, 2–3 broadly elliptical leaves, and white, star-shaped flowers; smells strongly of garlic. (Family: Liliaceae.)

Rantzen, Esther (Louise) (1940–) Television presenter and producer, born in Berkhamsted, Hertfordshire. During 1973–94 she produced and presented *That's Life*, a populist consumer programme. In 1988 she received the Richard Dimbleby Award for her contributions to factual television. She began presenting the talk-show *Esther* for BBC2 in 1995, and a new series of issue-based journalism for ITV in 1998. In 1986 she founded the charity 'Childline'.

rape (botany) A biennial herb (*Brassica rapus*, variety *arvensis*) growing to 1 m/3¼ ft; bluish-green leaves; yellow, cross-shaped flowers. It is grown for fodder and, increasingly, as a source of rape-oil, obtained from crushed seeds, and rape-seed cake, made from the residue. (Family: Cruciferae.)

rape (law) The crime committed when a person forces a male or female to have sexual intercourse without consent. The maximum sentence is life imprisonment. The law now recognizes rape by a husband against his wife. **Statutory rape** occurs when sexual advantage is taken of someone deemed unable to understand the nature of sexual intercourse, such as a severely mentally-handicapped person or someone below the age of consent.

Raphael [rafael], in full **Raffaello Sanzio** (1483–1520) Painter, born in Urbino, Italy. In Florence he completed several sweet Madonnas, as well as such works as 'The Holy Family' (Madrid). In 1508 he went to Rome, where he produced his greatest works, including the frescoes in the papal apartments of the Vatican, and the cartoons for the tapestries of the Sistine Chapel. In 1514 he succeeded Bramante as architect of St Peter's.

Raphael, Frederic (Michael) (1931–) Novelist, playwright, screenwriter, and biographer, born in Chicago, IL. He has adapted several of his novels for the screen, including *The Glittering Prizes* (1976), which became a popular television series. In 1966 he won an Oscar for the screenplay of his novel *Darling* (1965). *Eyes Wide Open* (1999) is about the writing of the screenplay for Stanley Kubrick's *Eyes Wide Shut* (1999).

rap music A musical style which started in the streets of New York with inner-city high-school students chanting crude incantations over rock records customized by reversing the turntable and distorting the amplification. In 1983, 'It's Like That' by Run DMC, a trio of schoolmates from the borough of Queens, sold 500 000 copies, heralding the music conquest of the suburbs. The main effect comes from a tortuous backbeat. The lyrics went unnoticed until increasingly flagrant advocacy of drug use, promiscuity, authority-bashing, and rioting led to bans and legal threats.

rare earths *lanthanides*

rare gases *noble gases*

Ras al-Khaimah [ras al khiyma] pop (2000e) 119 900; area 1690 km²/652 sq mi. Northernmost of the United Arab Emirates; capital, Ras al-Khaimah; offshore oil production began in 1984.

Rasmussen, Knud (Johan Victor) [razmusen] (1879–1933) Explorer and ethnologist, born in Jacobshavn, Greenland. From 1902 he directed several expeditions to Greenland, in 1910 established Thule base on Cape York, and in 1921–4 crossed by dog-sledge from Greenland to the Bering Strait.

raspberry A deciduous shrub (*Rubus idaeus*) growing to c.2 m/6½ ft, native to Europe and Asia; straight, slender prickles; woody, biennial stems from buds on the roots; flowers 5-petalled, white; red berry. It is cultivated for fruit. (Family: Rosaceae.)

Raspe, Rudolf Erich *Münchhausen, Baron von*

Rasputin, Grigoriy Yefimovich [raspyootin] (?1871–1916) Peasant and self-styled religious 'elder', born in Pokrovskoye, Russia. He gained the confidence of the emperor (Nicholas II) and empress (Alexandra of Hesse) by his ability to control through hypnosis the bleeding of the haemophiliac heir to the throne. He created a public scandal through the combination of his sexual and alcoholic excesses, and was murdered by a group of right-wing patriots, led by Prince Felix Yusupov.

Ras Shamra texts [rahs shahmra] Some 350 texts, inscribed on tablets, found 1928–60 on the site of ancient Ugarit in NW Syria, many written in a previously unknown cuneiform script now described as 'Ugaritic', and others in Babylonian.

Rastafarianism A religious movement from the West Indies, followed by about a million people. It largely derives from the thought of Jamaican political activist Marcus Garvey (1887–1940), who advocated a return to Africa as a means of solving the problems of black oppression. When Haile Selassie was crowned Emperor of Ethiopia in 1930, he came to be viewed as the Messiah, with Ethiopia seen as the promised land. Rastafarians follow strict taboos governing what they may eat (eg no pork, milk, coffee); ganja (marijuana) is held to be a sacrament; they usually wear their hair in long dreadlocks; and they cultivate a distinctive form of speech.

rat A mouse-like rodent of family Muridae; name used generally for many unrelated species in this family, especially for members of genus *Rattus* (c.80 species throughout the Old World). It can spread human diseases (bubonic plague was spread by fleas of the black rat).

ratel A badger-like mammal (*Mellivora capensis*) native to Africa and S Asia, dark brown with top of head and centre of back pale yellowish-grey; fearless, with very tough skin; eats small animals, carrion, and vegetation; follows honeyguides to beehives and takes the honey; also known as **honey badger**. (Family: Mustelidae.)

rates The system of local taxation in use in the UK up to 1990 (for England and Wales; up to 1989 for Scotland). The **rateable value** of properties was decided by public valuers, and the rate per pound was set by the local authority. Because rates were paid only by occupiers of property, this system was regarded as unfair, since other residents had votes for the bodies determining the level of rates, but did not pay for the cost of the policies. Rates were therefore replaced by the community charge, though rating valuations stayed as the basis for charges by water companies. However, after much opposition, in 1993 there was a return to the system of basing local taxation on property values.

ratfish *chimaera* (zoology)

Rathenau, Walther [rahtenow] (1867–1922) German statesman and industrialist, born in Berlin. He organized German war industries during World War 1, and later dealt with reparations. His attempts to negotiate with the Allies, and the fact that he was Jewish, made him extremely unpopular in nationalist circles, and he was murdered.

Rather, Dan (Irvin) [rather] (1931–) Television news presenter and writer, born in Wharton TX. He became a television journalist, then White House correspondent and London bureau chief (1963–74). His national profile grew as co-editor of *60 Minutes* (1975–81), and he went on to become anchor of *CBS Evening News* (1981–2005).

Rathlin Island area 14 km²/5½ sq mi. Island in N Antrim, N Northern Ireland; length, 8 km/5 mi; up to 5 km/3 mi wide; rises to 137 m/449 ft; St Columba founded a church here, 6th-c.

rationalism (architecture) A 20th-c conception of architecture which pursued the most logical possible solution to every aspect of building. It is particularly associated with the work of most of the Bauhaus and International Style architects of the 1920s and 1930s.

rationalism (philosophy) In philosophy, the tradition represented by the 17th-c figures Descartes, Leibniz, and Spinoza, who believed that the general nature of the world could be established by reason alone, through *a priori* knowledge independent of sense-experience; it is usually contrasted with *empiricism*. In a popular sense, the term expresses a commitment to reason as opposed to faith, convention, or emotion, and is therefore contrasted with *irrationalism*.

rational number *numbers*

Ratitae [ratiytee] (Lat *ratis* 'raft') An obsolete term for flightless running birds, such as the ostrich and emu (which are still referred to as **ratites**). The breastbone in these birds has lost its keel and become flat (or 'raft-like').

rattan palm [ratan] A member of a large genus of tropical climbing palms with slender, extremely long stems up to 180 m/ 500 ft. The stems are stripped to make rattan canes, widely used for furniture, baskets, and other items; also the very strong malacca cane used for walking sticks. (Genus: *Calamus*, 375 species. Family: Palmae.)

Rattigan, Sir Terence (Mervyn) (1911–77) Playwright, born in London. His plays include *French Without Tears* (1936), *The Winslow Boy* (1946), *The Browning Version* (1948), and *Ross* (1960).

Rattle, Sir Simon (Denis) (1955–) Conductor, born in Liverpool, Merseyside. After winning the International Conductors' Competition in 1974, he worked with orchestras in Bournemouth, Liverpool, and the BBC. He became widely acclaimed as the principal conductor of the City of Birmingham Symphony Orchestra (1990–98). Since 1981 he has been principal guest conductor of the Los Angeles Philharmonic, and joined the Berlin Philharmonic orchestra as chief conductor and artistic director in 2002.

rattlesnake A New World pit viper of genus *Crotalus* (28 species); tail with a segmented rattle (except in the **Santa Catalina rattlesnake**, *Crotalus catalinensis*); rattle made from modified scales (one segment added at each moult, but old segments are lost); venom attacks blood cells.

Rau, Johannes [row] (1931–2006) German president (1999–2004), born in Wuppertal-Barmen, W Germany. First elected to the North Rhine–Westphalia state parliament in 1957, he became a member of the Social Democratic Party Executive (1968–99). He was minister for science and research in the state government (1970–8), and then minister president (1978–98), before being elected federal president.

Rauschenberg, Robert [rowshenberg] (1925–) Avant-garde artist, born in Port Arthur, TX. One of the most aggressive US modernists, his collages and 'combines' incorporate a variety of rubbish (rusty metal, old tyres, fragments of clothing, etc) splashed with paint.

Ravel, Maurice [ravel] (1875–1937) Composer, born in Ciboure, France. His works include *Pavane pour une infante défunte* (1899, Pavane for a Dead Princess), *Rapsodie espagnole* (1908), the 'choreographic poem' *La Valse* (1920), and *Boléro* (1928), intended as a miniature ballet.

raven A large crow, especially the **great raven** (*Corvus corax*) of the N hemisphere; omnivorous; territorial; does not nest in colonies. (Genus: *Corvus*, 9 species.)

Ravenna [ravena] 44°25N 12°12E, pop (2000e) 142 000. Town in NE Italy; capital of W Roman Empire in AD 402, and of later Ostrogothic and Byzantine rulers; archbishopric; railway; cathedral (18th-c).

Ravi [rahvee], **River**, ancient **Hydraotes** River in NW India and Pakistan; one of the five rivers of the Punjab; rises in the SE Pir Panjal range; joins the R Chenab; length 765 km/475 mi.

Rawalpindi [rahwalpindee] 33°40N 73°08E, pop (2000e) 1 300 000. City in Punjab province, Pakistan; strategically important location controlling routes to Kashmir; occupied by the British, 1849; interim capital, 1959–69; airfield; railway; military and commercial centre.

rawindsonde [raywinsond] *radiosonde balloon*

Rawsthorne, Alan (1905–71) Composer, born in Haslingden, Lancashire. He wrote a wide range of works, including three symphonies, eight concertos, choral and chamber music, and several film scores.

Ray, John (1627–1705) Naturalist, born in Black Notley, Essex. His classification of plants, with its emphasis on the species as the basic unit, was a foundation of modern taxonomy.

Ray, Man, originally **Emanuel Rudnitsky** (1890–1976) Painter, sculptor, photographer and film-maker, born in Philadelphia, PA. He became a major figure in the development of Modernism, founding the New York Dadaist movement. He became interested in films, and during the 1930s produced many photographs and 'rayographs' (photographic montages).

Ray, Satyajit [riy] (1921–92) Film director, born and educated in Kolkata (Calcutta), India. India's leading film maker, his films include the trilogy *Pather Panchali* (1954, On the Road), *Aparajito* (1956, The Unvanquished), *Apur Sansar* (1959, The World of Apu), and *An Enemy of the People* (1989). He received an Academy Lifetime Achievement Award in 1991.

ray Any of the numerous small to large bottom-dwelling cartilaginous fishes in families Anacanthobatidae, Pseudorajidae, Rajidae (skates and rays), Gymnuridae (butterfly ray), Rhinopteridae, Mobulidae (devil rays), Torpedinidae (electric rays), and Myliobatidae (eagle rays); front part of the body strongly flattened with broad pectoral fins; mouth and gill openings on underside.

Rayleigh scattering The scattering of light by objects which are small compared to the wavelength of light; described by British physicist Lord Rayleigh (1842–1919). The Rayleigh scattering of sunlight by air molecules makes the sky appear blue, since blue light is scattered more than other frequencies.

rayon A textile fibre formed from cellulose (a constituent of wood pulp), first produced late in the 19th-c. Improvements in manufacturing methods have made modern rayon fibres important as domestic and industrial materials.

Razi *Rhazes*

razorbill An auk native to the N Atlantic (*Alca torda*); black bill, with vertical white stripe near tip.

razor shell A burrowing marine bivalve with two similar elongate shell valves; shell closed by two muscles. (Class: Pelecypoda. Order: Veneroida.)

Re [ray] or **Ra** [rah] In Egyptian religion, the ancient Sun-god of Heliopolis. He is depicted as a falcon with the Sun's disc on his head.

reactance In alternating current circuits containing inductors and capacitors, the factor which determines the phase relationship between current and voltage; symbol X, units Ω (ohms).

reactive armour A form of protection for military vehicles such as tanks against the kind of 'hollow-charge' warhead typically used in infantry-fired antitank missiles; also known as **Chobham armour**. Reactive armour itself detonates locally, neutralizing the attacking weapon's effects.

Read, Sir Herbert (Edward) (1893–1968) Poet and art critic, born near Kirby Moorside, North Yorkshire. He became known as a poet and a writer on aesthetics in such works as *The Meaning of Art* (1931).

Reading (UK) [reding] 51°28N 0°59W, pop (2001e) 143 100. Unitary authority (from 1998) and former county town of Berkshire, S England, on the R Thames; unitary authority from 1998; railway; university (1926); rapidly developing commercial centre; 12th-c Benedictine abbey, burial place of Henry I; football league team, Reading (Royals).

readymade In modern art, any object not made by the artist but chosen by him or her and exhibited as a 'work of art'. Thus Duchamp exhibited a bottle-rack in 1914 and (most notoriously) a urinal, which he entitled 'Fountain' in 1917.

Reagan, Ronald (Wilson) [raygn] (1911–2004) US Republican statesman and 40th president, born in Tampico, IL. He went to Hollywood in 1937 and made over 50 films, beginning with *Love Is On the Air* (1937). He became Governor of California in 1966, stood unsuccessfully for the Republican presidential nomination in 1968 and 1976, but in 1980 defeated Jimmy Carter, and won a second term in 1984, defeating Walter Mondale. He introduced a major programme of economic change, took a strong anti-communist stand, especially in the Middle East and Central America, and introduced the Strategic Defense Initiative. In 1981 he was wounded in an assassination attempt. During his second term, he reached a major arms-reduction accord with Soviet leader Gorbachev.

Realism (art and literature) In art criticism, a term (especially with a capital R) referring to the deliberate choice of ugly or unidealized subject-matter, sometimes to make a social or political point. Realism with a small 'r' is often used rather vaguely as the opposite of 'abstract'. More generally, in literature and art, the term refers to the advocacy of verisimilitude, as encountered in the Realist movement of mid-19th-c France, which flourished (as Naturalism) in the revolutionary scientific confidence of that era.

realism (philosophy) **1** The theory supporting the common-sense view that the world and its contents do not depend for their existence on the fact that some mind (whether human or divine) is aware of them. It is opposed to *idealism* and *phenomenalism*.
2 The theory held by Plato and others that universals (eg 'redness') or abstract entities (eg numbers) have a real existence outside the mind and apart from their instances. It is opposed to *nominalism*.

Real Madrid [rayal madrid] Spanish football club, based in Madrid. Founded in 1902, it has been champion of the Spanish League a record 29 times and cup winners 17 times. It won the first five European Cup finals between 1956 and 1960, and its total of nine victories – subsequent wins in 1966, 1998, 2000, and 2002 – is still a record. They were named 'Team of the Century' by FIFA in 1998, and later that year won the International Cup, to become World Club Champions.

real numbers *numbers*

real tennis An indoor racket-and-ball game played on a walled court, similar to rackets, but containing specifically designed hazards. A minority sport, it is also known as 'royal' or 'court' tennis.

real-time computing A notion which applies to those computing systems where near-simultaneous response to input data is a necessary requirement; examples include air-traffic control, point-of-sale terminals, and vehicle control.

Reardon, Ray(mond) [reerdn] (1932–) Snooker player, born in Tredegar, Blaenau Gwent, Wales. The first of the great snooker players of the modern era, he was dominant in the 1970s, being world professional champion six times (1970, 1973–6, 1978).

reasoning Mental activity in which the reasoner moves from given information to a novel conclusion, in a series of steps that the reasoner can justify. Reasoning may be **deductive**, arriving at a conclusion from a set of premises (eg proving a theorem in mathematics), or **inductive**, when we try to create a new generalization based on available evidence.

Réaumur, René Antoine Ferchault de [rayohmür] (1683–1757) Polymath, born in La Rochelle, France. His thermometer (with spirit instead of mercury) has 80 degrees between the freezing and boiling points.

Rebecca Riots A popular protest movement by Welsh peasants and agricultural labourers in W Wales in the late 1830s and early 1840s. The rioters took their text from *Genesis* 24:60: 'And they blessed Rebecca and said unto her, let thy seed possess the gates of those which hate thee'. Each band of rioters had a Rebecca for a leader – often a man disguised as a woman.

rebirthing A form of psychotherapy based on the idea that traumatic experiences at birth may result in negative thoughts and attitudes in later life. Regression back to birth and reliving the experience may allow these attitudes to be corrected. **Water rebirthing** for example, involves being submerged in a bath of water.

Rebuck, Gail (Ruth) [reebuhk], married name **Gould** (1952–) Publisher, born in London. Appointed publishing director at Century Publishing in 1982, she stayed with the company when it became Century Hutchinson (1985) and also when this was taken over by Random House (1989), and in 1991 became chair and chief executive of Random House UK.

rebus [reebuhs] The enigmatic representation in visual form of the sounds of a name or word. As a form of visual pun, rebuses are often used to puzzle or amuse, such as a drawing of a ray-gun (= 'Reagan'), or the letters CU (= 'see you'). They are an ancient means of communication, being found in early forms of picture-writing.

Récamier, (Jeanne Françoise) Julie (Adélaide) [ruhkamyay], *née* **Bernard** (1777–1849) Hostess, born in Lyon, France. Her salon became a fashionable meeting-place, especially for former Royalists and those opposed to Napoleon.

receptacle In flowering plants, the area at the tip of the flower-stalk to which the floral parts are attached. Usually convex, it may become swollen or expanded to enclose the carpels, and plays an important role in fruit formation.

receptors In physiology, specialized sites, usually within the cell membrane, which have evolved to bind and mediate the effects of neurotransmitters and hormones, but which also mediate the effects of many substances foreign to the body (such as drugs); also known as **binding sites**.

recession An economic situation where demand is sluggish, output is not rising, and unemployment is on the increase. Not as severe a downturn as a depression, it is usually identified when gross domestic product declines for two successive quarters.

Recife [reseefay] 8°06S 34°53W, pop (2000e) 1 586 000. Port in NE Brazil, at the mouth of the R Capibaribe; most important commercial and industrial city in the NE; airport; two universities (1951, 1954); Forte do Brum (1629).

recitative A type of musical declamation which allows the words to be delivered naturally and quickly, and is therefore indispensable in those types of all-sung opera, oratorio, and cantata in which dialogue and narrative are interrupted by long or numerous arias.

RECONSAT An abbreviation of *reconnaissance satellite*, a military space system placed into Earth orbit. It is equipped with sensors capable of recording objects (such as military units) and activities on the ground, and relaying that information to Earth stations for analysis.

Reconstruction The period after the American Civil War when the South was occupied by Northern troops, while major changes went forward in its way of life. These included the destruction of slavery and the attempted integration of the freed black people. Resistance to it among white southerners resulted in the founding of the Ku Klux Klan in 1866.

recorder (law) In the legal system of England and Wales, a part-time judge. Those appointed are barristers or solicitors. Recorders sit mainly in the Crown Court.

recorder (music) A type of end-blown duct flute in two or three jointed sections, with seven fingerholes and a thumbhole. It is made of wood or (in recent times) plastic in various sizes, the most common being the **descant** and the **treble**. It was revived in the 20th-c as a school instrument and for playing early music.

recording *sound recording*

record player The successor to the gramophone. It was essentially a turntable, pick-up, and arm which reproduced the music or other sounds recorded on discs (gramophone records), usually through its own amplifier and speaker.

rectifier A device that changes alternating current (AC), which continuously reverses direction, into direct current (DC), by allowing it to flow in one direction only. Most electronic equipment needs direct current.

rectilinear motion *mechanics*

rector In the Church of England, the parish priest receiving full tithe rents; in other Anglican churches, generally a parish priest; in Roman Catholicism, the priest in charge of a religious house, college, or school; in some countries (eg Scotland), the senior officer of a university, elected by students.

rectum That part of the gastro-intestinal tract between the sigmoid colon and the anal canal. When gastro-intestinal contents enter the rectum, the individual has the urge to defaecate.

recycling Putting waste substances back into productive use. It is a means of reducing the demand on non-renewable resources, and of preventing problems of pollution and waste disposal. Examples include the pulping of waste paper to make recycled paper, the existence of bottle banks to collect used glass, and the smelting of metals from scrap.

red admiral A large butterfly found widely in the N hemisphere; upperside of wings black with scarlet bands and patches of white and blue. (Order: Lepidoptera. Family: Nymphalidae.)

Red Army (China) Communist army built up by Zhu De at Mao Zedong's Jiangxi soviet after 1927. It was distinguished by more egalitarian command, disciplined treatment of civilians, the dissemination of political ideas, and the use of guerrilla tactics. In the civil war after 1945, it defeated the Nationalist forces, having been reorganized as the **People's Liberation Army (PLA)** in 1946. It now numbers three million troops, and is a significant political as well as military force.

Red Army (USSR) The Red Army of Workers and Peasants (*RKKA, Rabochekrest'yanshi Krasny*), the official name of the army of the Soviet Union (1918–45).

red-brick universities Those English universities founded in the late 19th-c or first half of the 20th-c in the provincial cities: Manchester (1880; new charter 1903), Liverpool (1903; affiliated to Manchester, 1884–1903), Leeds (1904; affiliated to Manchester, 1887–1904), Birmingham (1900), Sheffield (1905), Bristol (1909), Reading (1926), Southampton (1952, University College 1902), Exeter (1955, University College, 1922), and Leicester (1957, University College 1918).

Red Brigade, Ital **Brigate Rosse** A left-wing Italian terrorist group which began operating in 1974 as a response to the failure of the New Left, involved in bombings and killings. Its activities were largely directed at the kidnapping and killing of Italian judges, politicians, and businessmen, such as the former Italian premier Aldo Moro in 1978.

red cedar 1 A species of *arbor vitae* (*Thuja plicata*), native to North America, which yields red timber. (Family: Cupressaceae.) **2** The commercial name for timber from the American species of juniper, *Juniperus virginiana*, often used for pencils.

Red Crescent *Red Cross*

Red Cross An international agency founded by the Geneva Convention (1864) to assist those wounded or captured in war. All branches use the symbol of the red cross on a white ground, except Muslim branches, which use the red crescent, Israel, which uses a red Star of David, and Iran, which uses a red lion and sun.

red currant A species of currant (*Ribes rubrum*) native to W Europe. It produces edible red berries on old wood. The **white currant** is merely a white-berried form. (Family: Grossulariaceae.)

red deer A true deer (*Cervus elephas*) widespread in the temperate N hemisphere (introduced in Australia and New Zealand); also known as the **Bactrian deer**, **Yarkand deer**, **maral**, **shou**, **hangul**, or (in North America) **wapiti** or **elk**. Each antler usually has five tines (the *Swedish* form); if each has six, the stag is a *Royal*; if each has seven, it is a *Wilson*.

red dwarf A small, cool star, 0·5–0·1 the mass and diameter of the Sun, and 100–100 000 times fainter than the Sun. Red dwarfs are probably the most abundant type of star, but are difficult to see because they are so dim. Two of the nearest stars to the Sun, Proxima Centauri and Barnard's Star, are red dwarfs.

Redford, (Charles) Robert (1937–) Actor and director, born in Santa Barbara, CA. His films include *Butch Cassidy and the Sundance Kid* (1969), *The Sting* (1973), *Up Close and Personal* (1996), and *An Unfinished Life* (2005). As a director, his films include *Ordinary People* (1980, Oscar), and *The Horse Whisperer* (1998), in which he also starred.

red giant A cool red star, 10–100 times the radius of the Sun, but of similar mass. It develops in a late stage of stellar evolution, after the main sequence. Hydrogen in the core is exhausted, and the outer layers expand.

Redgrave, Sir Michael (Scudamore) (1908–85) Actor, born in Bristol. His notable stage performances included Richard II (1951), Prospero (1952), and Antony (1953), and he also had a distinguished film career, starting with Hitchcock's *The Lady Vanishes* (1938). He married the actress **Rachel Kempson** (1910–2003) in 1935, and their three children are all actors; **Vanessa**, **Corin** (1939–), and **Lynn** (1944–).

Redgrave, Sir Steve(n Geoffrey) (1962–) Rower, born in Marlow, Buckinghamshire. His main event is the heavyweight coxless pairs. He was the winner of five consecutive gold Olympic medals from 1984 to 2000, and also of six World Championship gold medals and three Commonwealth Games gold medals, more than any other rower. He received a knighthood in 2001, and in 2003 received the Golden Personality award at the 50th anniversary BBC Sports Personality of the Year awards.

Redgrave, Vanessa (1937–) Actress, born in London, the daughter of Michael Redgrave. Her films include *Morgan, a Suitable Case for Treatment* (1966), *Julia* (1977, Oscar), and *The White Countess* (2005). Other work includes *The Gathering Storm* (2002) for television, and in 2003 she won a Tony Award for her performance in *Long Day's Journey into Night*. She is well known for her active support of left-wing causes.

Redgrove, Peter (William) (1932–2003) Poet and writer, born in Kingston, Surrey. A founder member of an association of poets, the Group, his books include *The Moon Disposes: Poems 1954–87*

(1987). He also wrote novels, plays, and non-fiction works, including a pioneering work with his second wife, **Penelope Shuttle** (1947–), *The Wise Wound* (1978). In 1996 he was awarded the Queen's Medal for Poetry.

Red Guards Young radical Maoist activists (mostly students) who spread the 1966 Cultural Revolution across China, destroying whatever was 'old', and rebelling against all 'reactionary' authority.

red-hot poker A perennial native to S Africa (*Kniphofia uvaria*); flowers tubular, downward-angled, red, turning orange then yellow with age, in dense, poker-shaped spikes on stems up to 2 m/6½ ft high. (Family: Liliaceae.)

red mullet Colourful marine fish widespread in tropical and warm temperate seas; mouth with pair of large chin barbels; also called **goatfish**. (Family: Mullidae, 3 genera.)

Red River (China), Chin **Yuan Jiang**, Vietnamese **Song Hong** River rising in C Yunnan province, China; flows into the Gulf of Tongking in a large delta; length, c.800 km/500 mi.

Red River (USA) River in S USA; rises in N Texas in the Llano Estacado; flows S to the Gulf of Mexico; length 1966 km/1222 mi.

Red River Colony A British colony founded by the Earl of Selkirk in Rupert's Land (Manitoba) on the Assiniboine and Red Rivers in 1812. It was the focus of ethnic, racial, and commercial rivalries.

Red River Rebellion A movement for self-determination in 1869–70 by the resident Métis population of Red River Colony, Canada (now Manitoba), led by Louis Riel. Canada agreed to the terms of the rebels (in the Manitoba Act, 1870).

red salmon *sockeye*

Red Sea, ancient **Sinus Arabicus** area c.453 000 km²/175 000 sq mi. NW arm of the Indian Ocean, between the Arabian Peninsula and Egypt, Sudan, and Ethiopia; connected to the Mediterranean Sea by the Suez Canal; divided into the Gulfs of Suez and Aqaba by the Sinai Peninsula (NW); a narrow sea, up to 360 km/225 mi wide, 2335 km/1450 mi long; name probably derives from reddish seaweed found here; major trade route.

red setter *Irish setter*

redshift The displacement of features in the spectra of astronomical objects, particularly galaxies and quasars, towards the longer wavelengths. This is generally interpreted as a result of the Doppler effect resulting from the expansion of the universe.

Red Spot, Great *Jupiter* (astronomy)

Red Square The central square of Moscow. Its Russian name (*Krasnaya Ploshchad*) derives from the Old Slavonic *krasny* ('beautiful' or 'red'). The translation of 'red' became established only in the 20th-c.

red squirrel A small tree-dwelling squirrel; coat reddish-brown; four species: the **European red squirrel** (*Sciurus vulgaris*) from Europe and Asia, and the **North American red squirrels** or **chickarees** of genus *Tamiasciurus*.

Red Terror (1918–21) The Bolshevik campaign of terror and anarchy that followed the Russian Revolution of 1917. It was carried out systematically by the Cheka (Secret Police) and loosely-organized Red Army forces during and after the Russian Civil War (1918–20) against potential political opponents and 'class enemies' – especially the bourgeoisie, former aristocracy, and peasants who resisted the seizing of grain for the war. The tsar and his family were executed along with 200 000 other Russians.

reduction A chemical process involving the gain of electrons, always accompanied by oxidation, the loss of electrons. It often involves the gain of hydrogen or the loss of oxygen by a compound.

redundancy Dismissal of employees whose work is no longer needed. This may occur through a fall in the demand for their products, or through technical progress leading to automation of production. If the need for labour falls slowly, adjustment may be possible through natural wastage, ie not replacing those who leave. If demand falls quickly, redundancies occur. Employers often prefer to offer sufficiently favourable terms to induce voluntary redundancy, to preserve the morale of their remaining workforce; where this fails, compulsory redundancies may occur.

redwing A thrush native to Europe, Asia, and N Africa (*Turdus iliacus*); speckled breast, red sides, and cream 'eyebrow'; migrates S in autumn, often with fieldfares.

redwood *coast redwood; dawn redwood*

Redwood, John (1951–) British politician, born in Dover, Kent. Elected a Conservative MP in 1987, he became secretary of state for Wales (1993–5). He was a strong but ultimately unsuccessful contender for leadership of his party, following Major's resignation in 1997. He became shadow secretary of state for trade and industry (1997–2000) and deregulation spokesman (2004).

Reed, Sir Carol (1906–76) Film director, born in London. He produced or directed several major films, such as *Kipps* (1941), *The Fallen Idol* (1948), and *Oliver!* (1968, 2 Oscars), but is best known for *The Third Man* (1949).

reed A tall grass found (*Phragmites australis*) almost everywhere; stout, erect stems 2–3 m/6–10 ft high. It forms vast beds in swamps or shallow water, and is used for good-quality thatch. (Family: Gramineae.)

reedbuck An African grazing antelope of genus *Redunca*; pale brown with white underparts; male with horns curving forward at tip; female without horns; three species.

reed instrument Any woodwind instrument whose sound is produced by a stream of air causing a 'reed' (which may be of cane, metal, or plastic) to vibrate. The reed may be single (as in the clarinet) or double (as in the oboe); it may vibrate freely (as in the harmonica and the crumhorn) or be controlled by the player's lips (as in all orchestral reed instruments).

reedmace An aquatic perennial (*Typha latifolia*), more or less cosmopolitan; stems robust, growing to 2·5 m/8 ft leaves grass-like; also called **cat's-tail**, **false bulrush** and, erroneously, **bulrush**. It often forms extensive reed-swamps. (Family: Typhaceae.)

reed organ A musical instrument in which reeds, brought into play by means of one or more keyboards, are made to vibrate freely by air under pressure from bellows. Reed organs were at one time popular as domestic instruments and also in small churches.

reef *atoll*

reefer A vessel designed to carry refrigerated cargoes in specially cooled and insulated compartments. Modern cargoes include carcases of beef, dairy produce, and most kinds of fruit.

Reeve, Christopher (1952–2004) Film actor, born in New York City. He had various stage and television roles before becoming universally known as the star of *Superman* and its sequels (1978, 1980, 1983, 1991). In 1995 he became wheel-chair bound following an accident, but acted again in films and in a TV production of *Rear Window* (1998). He was much involved in campaigns supporting handicapped children and paraplegics, and founded the Christopher Reeve Paralysis Foundation in 1998 to promote research into spinal cord injuries.

reeve *ruff*

Reeves, Keanu [keeahnoo] (1964–) Film actor, born in Beirut, Lebanon. *Bill and Ted's Excellent Adventure* (1989), and its sequel (1991), brought him international recognition. Later films include *Much Ado About Nothing* (1993), *Speed* (1994), *The Matrix* (1999) and its sequels, *The Matrix Reloaded* and *Matrix Revolutions* (both 2003), and *The Lake House* (2006).

referendum A device of direct democracy whereby the electorate can pronounce, usually for or against, on some measure put before it by government; also known as a **plebiscite**. Most commonly referenda are held on constitutional changes, rather than on government policy.

reflation In economics, government action designed to stimulate an economy which is in a period of recession. Strategies include increasing government expenditure, lowering taxes, and reducing interest rates.

reflectance *reflection*

reflecting telescope *telescope*

reflection In physics, the bouncing off from a suitable surface of a beam of light, sound, or other wave at an angle equal to that of the incident beam. **Reflectance** is the measured ratio of incident intensity to reflected intensity.

reflex A rapid, involuntary, and stereotyped action made by an animal in response to a particular stimulus involving the central nervous system. An example is the rapid withdrawal of the hand after touching a very hot surface.

reflex camera A camera in which an image of the scene being photographed is shown on the viewfinder screen by way of a mirror. In **single-lens reflex** (**SLR**) types, the mirror is at 45° behind the camera lens and is automatically swung out of the way immediately before exposure. The **twin-lens reflex** has two matched lenses coupled for focusing.

reflexology An ancient system of diagnosis and treatment, dating from c.3000 BC, based on the belief that an image of the entire body, including the internal organs, is represented on the surface of the foot. Palpation of the feet locates sites of blocked energy flow, and treatment is given by pressure and massage to disperse the blockages and stimulate the internal organs.

Reform Acts Legislation in Britain which altered parliamentary constituencies and increased the size of the electorate. The main Acts were: **1832** (known as the **Great Reform Act**), which gave the vote to almost all male members of the middle classes, introduced a uniform £10 franchise in the borough and enfranchised the new industrial towns; **1867**, which gave the vote to all settled tenants in the boroughs, thus creating a substantial working-class male franchise for the first time; **1884**, which extended a similar franchise to rural and mining areas and to domestic servants; **1885**, which aimed to create parliamentary constituencies of broadly equal size; **1918**, which created a universal male suffrage and gave the vote to propertied, educated women of 30 years and over; **1928**, which gave universal suffrage to everyone over 21; and **1969**, which lowered the minimum voting age from 21 years to 18.

Reformation The Protestant reform movements in the Christian Church, inspired by and derived from Martin Luther, John Calvin, and others in 16th-c Europe. Various factors are common to all reforms: a Biblical revival and translation of the Word of God into the vernacular; an improvement in the intellectual and moral standards of the clergy; emphasis on the sovereignty of God; and insistence that faith and scriptures are at the centre of the Christian message. In Germany, Luther's 'ninety-five theses' (1517) questioned the authority of the Church and led to his excommunication. The Lutheran Church then spread rapidly, in Switzerland under Zwingli and later under Calvin, neither of whom allowed any form of worship or devotion not explicitly warranted by scripture. In England, Henry VIII declared that the king was the supreme head of the English Church, and appropriated Church property; in 1549 the Book of Common Prayer, embodying Reformation doctrine, was published, and under Elizabeth I a strong anti-papal stance was taken. In Scotland, under the influence of Calvin and the leadership of John Knox, the Presbyterian Church of Scotland was established in 1560, and remains the national Church.

Reformation, Catholic *Counter-Reformation*

Reformed Churches Churches deriving from Calvin's Reforma-

tion in 16th-c Geneva, adopting a conciliar or presbyterian form of Church government. They are now worldwide in extent.

Reformed Church in America A Christian denomination established in 1628 with the organization of the Collegiate Church for the early Dutch Reformed settlers. It adopted its current name in 1867.

Reform Judaism A movement beginning in early 19th-c Germany for the reform of Jewish worship, ritual, and beliefs in the light of modern scholarship and knowledge.

Reform Party A Canadian political party, established to articulate discontent in the W of the country. It captured the third largest number of seats in the 1993 general election, almost all from Alberta and British Columbia.

refracting telescope *telescope*

refraction *p.780*

refractive index A measurement of the ratio of velocity of light (or other electromagnetic wave) in a vacuum to that in matter; symbol n; always greater than 1; $n(air) = 1.0003$, $n(water) = 1.33$, so the velocity of light in water is about 75% of that in air.

refractories Materials which are neither deformed nor chemically changed by exposure to high temperatures. This makes them suitable for containers, structural materials, and components, particularly in metallurgical operations, such as furnace linings. Naturally occurring refractories include silica, fireclay, and alumina. Synthetic refractories include the high-melting carbides and nitrides used in nuclear power plant.

refrigerator An insulated enclosed space, with a cooling mechanism to reduce its temperature, which preserves foodstuffs for short periods. The earlier *ice-house* used ice as a coolant, but from c.1875 mechanical means were introduced, compressing a coolant outside to allow it to expand inside and thus absorb heat. From c.1910 domestic models were available, now running at 4°C. A colder-running version (at c.−20°C) is the *deep freeze*, which can store food for some months.

Regency Style An elegant Neoclassical style current in England for about the first quarter of the 19th-c. Like the Empire Style in France, it made bold use of Greek motifs and Egyptian devices.

Regensburg [raygnzboorg], Fr **Ratisbon**, ancient **Castra Regina** 49°01N 12°07E, pop (2000e) 126 000. Commercial city in Germany; at confluence of R Regen and R Danube; Imperial Diets held here, 1663–1806; bishopric; railway; river harbour; university (1962); cathedral (13th–16th-c).

regent The person appointed to act for the monarch if he/she is incapacitated, unavailable, or under 18. In the UK, it is customary for the next heir to the throne to be regent.

reggae [regay] A type of popular music, of Jamaican origin but drawing on Afro-American traditions and influenced by rock. Among prominent reggae artists were Bob Marley and the Wailers.

Reggio di Calabria [rejioh dee kalabria] 38°06N 15°39E, pop (2000e) 182 000. Seaport in S Italy; founded by Greek colonists, 8th-c BC; archbishopric; airfield; railway; ferry to Sicily.

Reggio nell'Emilia [rejioh nelaymeelia] 44°42N 10°37E, pop (2000e) 135 000. City in N Italy; founded by the Romans; railway; cathedral (13th-c).

Regina [rejiyna] 50°30N 104°38W, pop (2000e) 188 800. Capital of Saskatchewan province, SC Canada; founded, 1882 as capital of Northwest Territories; named in honour of Queen Victoria; capital, 1905; centre of grain, potash, and oil industries; airport; railway; university (1917); professional team, Saskatchewan Rough Riders (football).

Regiomontanus [rejiohmontaynus], Lat name of **Johannes Müller** (1436–76) Mathematician and astronomer, born in Königsberg (Lat *Mons Regius*, hence his pseudonym), Prussia (now Kaliningrad, Russia). He established the study of algebra and trigonometry in Germany.

regolith The layer of fine, powdery material on the Moon pro-

refraction

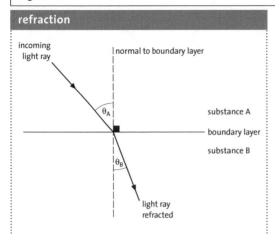

incoming light ray

normal to boundary layer

θ_A

substance A

boundary layer

substance B

θ_B

light ray refracted

A change in the direction of a wave as it passes from one medium to another in which the wave velocity is different, for example a sound wave passing from hot to cold air. It is expressed by Snell's law, $\sin \theta_A / \sin \theta_B$ = constant. The illustration shows a wave having a velocity in substance B which is less than its velocity in substance A. If the wave was light and substance A was a vacuum, $\sin \theta_{vac} / \sin \theta_B = n_B$, the refractive index of substance B. Light passing into a substance of higher refractive index is bent towards normal. The distortion of partially submerged objects, rainbows, and mirages are all caused by the refraction of light.

duced by the repeated impact of meteorites. It is up to 25 m/80 ft thick.

regression One of many defence mechanisms in which the individual returns to behaviour more suitable to an earlier age. This can be a component of a psychotherapy process and can also occur in physical illness.

regulator The non-ministerial head of a government department which controls privatized industries in England and Wales. In the 1980s and 1990s, a large number of state-owned enterprises were sold off as monopolies, in some cases without any real competition. Many of these corporations provided essential services to the public, so control and accountability were not transferred to the purchasers. These functions are vested in independent regulators who head **regulatory agencies** such as the Office of Telecommunications (OFTEL), the Office of Gas Supply (OFGAS), and the Office of the Rail Regulator (OFRAIL). They are responsible for protecting the consumer interest and obtaining redress for grievances, as well as setting standards and monitoring prices.

Regulus, Marcus Atilius [regyulus] (3rd-c BC) Roman general and statesman of the First Punic War, whose heroic death at the hands of the Carthaginians earned him legendary status.

rehabilitation In medicine, the process of helping a patient return to normal life or attain the best possible lifestyle following a serious illness or injury. It may involve physiotherapy and occupational therapy to help the body regain its optimal level of functioning.

Reich [riykh] The term used to describe the German Empire. The Holy Roman Empire (962–1806) was regarded as the **First Reich**, and unified Germany after 1870 was referred to as the **Second Reich** (**Kaiserreich**). After 1933, the enlarged Germany envisaged in Hitler's plans was known as the **Third Reich**.

Reich, Wilhelm [riykh] (1897–1957) Psychoanalyst, born in Dobrz-

cynica, Austria-Hungary (part of modern Poland). He broke from the Freudian school, developing a theory in which neuroses resulted from repressed, undissipated feelings or sexual energy. He emigrated to the USA in 1939, and established the pseudo-scientific 'Orgone' Institute, but died in gaol after being prosecuted for promoting a fraudulent treatment. During the sexual revolution of the 1960s, he was a cult figure in the USA.

Reichenbach, Hans [riykhenbakh] (1891–1953) Philosopher of science, born in Hamburg, Germany. An early associate of the logical positivists, he made important technical contributions to probability theory and the philosophy of science in such works as *Philosophie der Raum-Zeit-Lehre* (1927–8, Philosophy of Space and Time), and *The Rise of Scientific Philosophy* (1951).

Reichstag fire [riykhstag] The deliberate burning down of Germany's parliament building (27 Feb 1933), shortly after the Nazi accession to power. A deranged Dutch ex-communist, van der Lubbe, was accused of arson and executed. The new Nazi government used the situation to ban and suppress the German Communist Party.

Reign of Terror (1793–4) The extreme phase of the French Revolution, characterized by the systematic execution of political opponents of the Jacobins and supposed sympathizers of the Counter-Revolution. 40 000 people are thought to have been killed in Paris and the provinces.

Reims *Rheims*

reincarnation The belief that, following death, some aspect of the self or soul can be reborn in a new body (human or animal), a process which may be repeated many times. This belief is fundamental to many Eastern religions, such as Hinduism and Buddhism.

reindeer A true deer (*Rangifer tarandus*) native to high latitudes of the N hemisphere; the only deer in which females have antlers; long coat of hollow hairs; hooves broad; also known as **caribou** ('shoveller').

Reiner, Rob [riyner] (1947–) Film actor, director, and producer, born in New York City. He became known for his role in *All in the Family* (1971–8, 2 Emmys), later roles including *Sleepless in Seattle* (1993), *The First Wives Club* (1996), and *EDtv* (1999). He has produced and directed several films, notably *When Harry Met Sally* (1989) and *Ghosts of Mississippi* (1996), and directed *The Story of Us* (1999) and *Rumor Has It* (2005).

Reines, Frederick (1918–98) Physicist, born in Paterson, NJ. For his discovery of the neutrino, one of the fundamental particles of the universe, he shared the Nobel Prize for Physics in 1995.

Reinhardt, Django [riynhah(r)t], popular name of **Jean Baptiste Reinhardt** (1910–53) Jazz guitarist, born in Liverchies, Belgium. He played in the Quintet of the Hot Club of France with Stephane Grapelli, and became the first European jazz musician to influence the music.

Reisz, Karel [riys] (1926–2002) Film and theatre actor, director, and producer, born in Ostrava, Czechoslovakia (now Czech Republic). As a child he was sent to England in 1938. His film credits include *Saturday Night and Sunday Morning* (1959), *Night Must Fall* (1963), and *The French Lieutenant's Woman* (1981). In later years he worked mainly as a theatre director.

Reith (of Stonehaven), John (Charles Walsham) Reith, Baron [reeth] (1889–1971) British statesman and engineer, born in Stonehaven, Aberdeenshire. He became the first general manager of the BBC in 1922 and its director-general (1927–38). The BBC inaugurated the *Reith Lectures* in 1948 in honour of his influence on broadcasting.

relational database A form of organizing data in a computer in which each entity type is stored separately as a table, and the relationships between entities are stored as another table. In the database for the present encyclopedia, for example, the individual entries are stored in one file, and the relationships between entries (such as the indexing of the words in the entries, which controls the alphabetical order) are stored separately.

relative atomic mass The mass of atoms, expressed in atomic mass units u, eg carbon-12 is 12·0000 u by definition, nitrogen-14 is 14·0031 u; symbol A_r; formerly called **atomic weight**.

relative density Density measured relative to some standard, typically water at 20°C; symbol d, expressed as a pure number; measured using hydrometers; formerly called **specific gravity**. For example, for alcohol, density $\rho = 789$ kg/m^3, $d = 0·791$.

relativistic quantum mechanics Quantum mechanics consistent with special relativity, and thus applicable to fast-moving systems; originally developed by British physicist Paul Dirac in 1928.

relativity *general relativity; special relativity*

relay An electrical or solid-state device, operated by changes in input, which is used to control or operate other devices connected to the output. They have a range of applications in telephone exchanges, switches, and automation systems.

relics Material remains (eg bones, skin) of, or objects which have been in contact with, a saint or person worthy of special religious attention. In many religions they are objects of veneration.

relief printing A print, made from a block (usually wood or lino) which has been cut away in those parts intended to be left white; the method contrasts with intaglio or surface prints. The ink adheres to the raised (relief) parts only.

relief sculpture A type of sculpture in which the forms are raised above the background, but not shaped fully. In **low relief** (or **bas-relief**) the design is hardly raised above the surface, as on a coin, while in **high relief** the forms may be almost free-standing.

religion A concept which encompasses varied sets of traditions, practices, and ideas. Some religions involve the belief in and worship of a god or gods, but this is not true of all. Christianity, Islam, and Judaism are theistic religions, while Buddhism does not require a belief in gods, and where it does occur, the gods are not considered important. There are theories of religion which construe it as wholly a human phenomenon, without any supernatural or transcendent origin and point of reference, while others argue that some such reference is the essence of the matter. Boundary disputes exist; for example, debate continues as to whether Confucianism is properly to be considered a religion; and some writers argue that Marxism is in important respects a religion.

Religion, Wars of (1562–98) A series of religious and political conflicts in France, caused by the growth of Calvinism, noble factionalism, and weak royal government. Civil wars were encouraged by Philip II of Spain's support of the Catholic Guise faction and by Elizabeth I's aid to the Huguenots. They ended when Henry of Navarre returned to Catholicism and crushed the Guise Catholic League (1589–98).

rem In radioactivity, an old measure of dose equivalent; symbol *rem*; equal to absorbed dose in rad multiplied by relative biological effectiveness, 1 rem = 0·01 Sv (sievert, SI unit); an abbreviation of **röntgen equivalent in man**.

Remarque, Erich Maria [ruhmah(r)k], originally **Erich Paul Remark** (1898–1970) Novelist, born in Osnabrück, Germany. His first novel, *Im Westen nichts Neues* (1929, trans All Quiet on the Western Front), was an immediate success, and was filmed in 1930.

Rembrandt (Harmenszoon van Rijn) [rembrant] (1606–69) Painter, born in Leyden, The Netherlands. His early works include religious and historical scenes, unusual in Protestant Holland. He settled in Amsterdam (1631), where he ran a large studio and took numerous pupils. 'The Anatomy Lesson of Dr Nicolaes Tulp' (1632, The Hague) assured his reputation as a portrait painter. In 1634 he married Saskia van Ulenburgh

(1613–42), and in the year of her death produced his masterpiece, 'The Night Watch' (Amsterdam). His extravagance, especially as a collector, led to bankruptcy in 1656. His preserved works number over 650 oil paintings, 2000 drawings and studies, and 300 etchings.

Remembrance Sunday In the UK, the Sunday nearest 11 November, on which are commemorated those who died in the two world wars; formerly Armistice Day. A two-minute silence is observed at 11 am.

Remington, Eliphalet (1793–1861) US firearms manufacturer and inventor, born in Suffield, CT. He pioneered several improvements in small arms manufacture, including the first successful cast steel rifle barrel in the USA.

Remington, Frederic (Sackrider) (1861–1909) Painter, sculptor, and illustrator, born in Canton, NY. He became a painter of the American West, illustrating Geronimo's Apache campaign (1882) and the Indian Wars of 1890–1. He also wrote and illustrated several books on his adventures.

Remonstrants Christians adhering to the Calvinistic doctrine of Jacobus Arminius (17th-c Holland), whose followers were also known as **Arminians**. They were named after the 'Remonstrance', a statement of Arminian teaching dating from 1610.

remora [remuhra] Slender-bodied fish (*Remora remora*) widespread in warm seas; large sucking disc on head, with which it attaches firmly to other fish, especially sharks; length up to 45 cm/18 in; also called **shark-sucker**. (Family: Echeneidae.)

remote sensing A method of measuring the characteristics of an object without touching it. The term is usually applied to images of the Earth taken by satellites, and to cameras in aircraft which can be used to map different phenomena.

Renaissance From the French for 'rebirth', referring to the revival of classical literature and artistic styles at various times in European history. Such renaissances occurred in the 8th-c and 9th-c, in the 12th-c, and from the 14th-c to the 16th-c. The first, or **Carolingian Renaissance**, centred upon the recovery of classical Latin texts in cathedral schools; the second, or **Twelfth-century Renaissance**, was marked by the foundation of universities and the rediscovery of Aristotle's ethical and philosophical works; and the third (usually called **the Renaissance**) was distinguished for the development of naturalistic works of art, the study of ancient Greek authors, above all Plato, and the critical study of Christian texts. This third revival is often said to mark the beginnings of modern times.

Renault, Mary [renoh], pseudonym of **Eileen Mary Challans** (1905–83) Novelist, born in London. Her first novel, *Purposes of Love* (1939), was a frank account of heterosexuality and lesbianism. In 1948 she emigrated to South Africa where she wrote *The Charioteer* (1953) and *Last of the Wine* (1956), the first of eight accounts of life in Ancient Greece.

Rendell (of Babergh), Ruth Rendell, Baroness [rendl], originally **Ruth Barbara Grasemann**, occasional pseudonym **Barbara Vine** (1930–) Detective-story writer, born in London. Her detective stories featuring Chief Inspector Wexford (eg *Harm Done*, 1999), and mystery thrillers (eg *A Judgement in Stone*, 1977) have formed the basis of a successful TV series, *The Ruth Rendell Mysteries*. Later novels include *The Rottweiler* (2003) and *The Water's Lovely* (2006). She received a life peerage in 1997.

renewable resources Resources with a yield which is sustainable and which may be used without danger of exhaustion, such as solar power, wind energy, and hydroelectric power. Some renewable resources (eg crops, timber, fish) are sustainable in the long term only through careful management.

Renfrew (of Kaimsthorn), (Andrew) Colin Renfrew, Baron (1937–) Archaeologist, born in Stockton-on-Tees, Durham. Since 1981 he has been professor of archaeology at Cambridge. He has contributed to several pioneering archaeological programmes on BBC television, notably in the *Chronicle* series.

Reni, Guido [raynee] (1575–1642) Baroque painter, born near Bologna, Italy. The fresco painted for the Borghese garden house in Rome, 'Aurora and the Hours' (1613–14), is usually regarded as his masterpiece.

Renner, Karl (1870–1950) Austrian statesman, chancellor (1918–20, 1945), and president (1945–50), born in Unter-Tannowitz, Austria. He became the first chancellor of the Austrian Republic, and first president of the new republic.

Rennes [ren], Breton **Roazon**, ancient **Condate** 48°07N 1°41W, pop (2000e) 207 000. Industrial and commercial city in NW France; capital of Brittany, 10th-c, and now its economic and cultural centre; largely rebuilt after major fire, 1720; badly bombed in World War 2; airport; road and rail junction; archbishopric; university (1461); cathedral (largely rebuilt, 19th-c).

rennet An extract from the stomach of most young animals, but particularly the calf and the lamb, which contains the enzyme *rennin*. It causes the main milk protein *casein* to precipitate, thus allowing the milk to clot. It is sometimes used in recipes and the manufacture of cheese.

Rennie, John (1761–1821) Civil engineer, born in Phantassie, East Lothian. He became famous as a bridge-builder, constructing several bridges over the R Thames. He also designed London docks.

Reno [reenoh] 39°31N 119°48W, pop (2000e) 180 500. City in W Nevada, USA, on the Truckee R; settled, 1859; airport; university (1874); noted for its casinos.

Reno, Janet [reenoh] (1938–) US attorney general (1993–2001), born in Miami, FL, the first woman to become US attorney general and the longest serving occupant of that cabinet post. She became one of the most respected members of the Clinton administration in its first term, known for her innovative programmes. The anti-trust suit against Microsoft, Inc (1998–9) was the most publicized policy action of her tenure.

Renoir, Jean [renwah(r)] (1894–1979) Film director, born in Paris, the son of Pierre Auguste Renoir. His major works include his antiwar masterpiece, *La Grande Illusion* (1937, Grand Illusion) and *La Règle du jeu* (1939, The Rules of the Game). He received an honorary Academy Award in 1975.

Renoir, Pierre Auguste [ruhnwah] (1841–1919) Impressionist artist, born in Limoges, France. In 1874–9 and 1882 he exhibited with the Impressionists. His picture of sunlight filtering through leaves – 'Le Moulin de la Galette' (1876, Louvre) – epitomizes his colourful, happy art.

reparations Payments imposed on the powers defeated in war to cover the costs incurred by the victors. For example, they were levied by the Allies on Germany at the end of World War 1.

repetitive strain injury (RSI) A term used to describe a variety of types of soft tissue injury caused by repetitive motion, poor posture, or excessive stress of a body part. It includes tendinitis, carpal tunnel syndrome (affecting the thumb and hand), and some sports injuries such as tennis elbow. Injuries may be work-related, due to typing or using tools, and may be prevented by a suitable working environment, eg correct seating and avoiding long periods spent at repetitive tasks.

Representatives, House of *House of Representatives*

reproduction The act or process of producing offspring; one of the essential properties of a living organism. Reproduction in its simplest form is an asexual process involving the division of an organism into two or more parts by fission, budding, spore formation, or vegetative propagation. Sexual reproduction involves the formation of specialized gametes (such as sperm and egg) by meiosis, and the fusion of a pair of gametes to form a zygote.

reptile An animal of the class Reptilia (6547 species), which evolved from primitive amphibians; most live on land; breathe with lungs, not gills; dry waterproof skin with horny scales (not separated, like those of a fish, but folds of skin); classified in four orders: Squamata (lizards and snakes), Chelonia (Testudinata or Testudines – tortoises and turtles), Crocodilia (or Loricata – crocodiles, alligators, etc), and Rhyncocephalia (the tuatara); many extinct species, including dinosaurs, pterodactyls, plesiosaurs, and ichthyosaurs.

Repton, Humphry (1752–1818) Landscape gardener, born in Bury St Edmunds, Suffolk. He completed the change from the formal gardens of the early 18th-c to the 'picturesque' types favoured later.

republic A form of state and government where, unlike a monarchy (which is hereditary), the head of state and leader of the government are periodically appointed under the constitution. It thus covers most modern states. Republics now vary considerably in form, ranging from liberal democratic states to personal dictatorships.

Republican Party One of the two main parties in US politics, created in 1854 out of the anti-slavery movement that preceded the Civil War. It found almost immediate success when Lincoln was elected president in 1860, and held the presidency except for four terms until Roosevelt in 1933. Since then there has been a period of split party control, with the Republicans often winning the presidency, and the Democrats holding the majority in Congress. Traditionally supported by voters with high income, education, and social status, its largest support is in NE industrial and W farming areas. It is identified with big business rather than unions, and with white Anglo-Saxons rather than ethnic minorities. In the 1980s, it became much more conservative in outlook. During the 1990s the party regained control of the House of Representatives, but lost the 1992 and 1996 presidential elections. It won the presidential election in 2000. In 2006 it lost control of the House of Representatives and the Senate in mid-term elections.

requiem [rekwee-em] (Lat 'rest') In the Roman Catholic Church, a Mass for the dead. In addition to its liturgical use, it has become a musical form; composers who have written requiems include Mozart, Fauré, and Britten.

requirements engineering A branch of computer science which studies business requirements as part of an overall computer system development process. It addresses the investigation and analysis stages of the systems development life cycle rather than the design and construction stages, and incorporates examination of the social and cultural aspects of the system as well as the functional and data aspects.

reredos [reeredos] *altarpiece*

resale price maintenance (RPM) The action of manufacturers in fixing the prices at which their products may be resold by retailers. RPM was stopped in the UK by the Restrictive Trade Practices Act (1956) and the Retail Prices Act (1964), except for a few special cases, such as the (now abandoned) Net Book Agreement. Manufacturers can now set only a 'recommended' resale price.

reserve currency A currency which countries choose to hold as foreign exchange reserves. In theory this could be issued by an international institution such as the International Monetary Fund, but historically national currencies have been used, such as the US dollar. A country needs two things to make its currency appear attractive to others to hold as reserves. Its currency must be expected to maintain its value relative to others, which implies having stable prices, or relatively low inflation. The country must also be sufficiently large and wealthy that there is enough of its currency available to hold.

reserves Gold and convertible currency held by countries as a result of receiving payment for exports. Falling reserves occur as a result of imports being greater than exports. In banking, the term refers to the notes and coins banks must hold in case of a sudden demand (a 'run on the bank'). In accountancy, it refers to the profits which have been ploughed back into a company.

resin A natural or synthetic polymer which softens on heating. The term is loosely used to include any polymer, as in 'ion-exchange resins'.

resistance A measure of the potential difference U needed to produce direct current I in an electrical circuit component; symbol R, units Ω (ohm); $R = U/I$ by definition. It measures a component's ability to restrict current flow. I/R is called conductance.

Resistencia [reseestensia] $27°28S\ 58°59W$, pop (2000e) 243 900. Agricultural, commercial, and industrial capital of Chaco province, N Argentina; on the R Barranqueras; founded as a Jesuit mission, mid-18th-c; airport; railway.

resistivity The electrical resistance of a metre cube of material, constant for a given material at a specific temperature; symbol ρ, units Ω.m (ohm.metre). $1/\rho$ is conductivity.

resistor A component in an electrical circuit designed to introduce a known resistance to the flow of current. Resistance changes with temperature rise, increasing in metals, and falling in semiconductors.

Resnais, Alain [ruhnay] (1922–) Film director, born in Vannes, France. His first feature film was *Hiroshima mon amour* (1959, Hiroshima my Love), and this was followed by the controversial *L'année dernière à Marienbad* (1961, Last Year at Marienbad), hailed as a surrealistic and dreamlike masterpiece by some, as a confused and tedious failure by others. Later films include *On Connaît la Chanson* (1997, Same Old Song) and *Coeurs* (2006).

Respighi, Ottorino [respeegee] (1879–1936) Composer, born in Bologna, Italy. His works include nine operas, the symphonic poems, *Fontane di Roma* (1916, Fountains of Rome) and *Pini di Roma* (1924, Pines of Rome), and the ballet *La Boutique fantasque*, produced by Diaghilev in 1919.

respiration A physiological term with a range of related meanings: (1) the act of breathing, whereby terrestrial animals move air in and out of their lungs, and aquatic animals pump water through their gills; (2) the uptake of oxygen from and the release of carbon dioxide to the environment; and (3) the metabolic processes by which organisms derive energy from foodstuffs by utilizing oxygen (**aerobic respiration**) or without the involvement of oxygen (**anaerobic respiration**); often referred to as **tissue** or **cell respiration**.

respirator A mechanical method of delivering oxygen to and removing carbon dioxide from patients who are unable to breathe for themselves. It expands the lungs intermittently through a tube introduced into the trachea.

Restoration The return of Charles II to England (Jun 1660) at the request of the Convention Parliament, following the collapse of the Protectorate regime. Parliament took the lead in passing the Clarendon Code (1661–5) outlawing dissent from the Book of Common Prayer (1662).

restrictive practices Agreements between firms which restrict competition. Such agreements may refer to prices, division of markets, or collusion over matters such as selling practices or the granting of credit. Many countries have laws forbidding restrictive practices and procedures for regulating them. For example, resale price maintenance (RPM), by which producers could dictate the prices at which distributors sold their products to the public, was forbidden in the UK in the 1960s, subject to a few exceptions such as the now-lapsed Net Book Agreement.

resurrection A form of re-animation of a person after death, the belief in which can be traced to late Biblical Judaism and early Christianity. Christian faith affirms the resurrection of Jesus Christ in particular, signifying God's vindication of Jesus.

retable *altarpiece*

Retail Price Index (RPI) A means of calculating the general trend of prices of goods and services; popularly known as **the cost of living index**. It is used as the main indicator of inflation, and is calculated each month by identifying the prices that an average household will have paid for a basket of goods and services.

Reticulum [retikyulum] (Lat 'net') A small S constellation near the Large Magellanic Cloud.

retina The innermost lining of the vertebrate eyeball, which transmits information about the visual world to the brain. It consists of an outer pigmented layer and an inner (cerebral) layer of photosensitive cells (*rods* and *cones*) and neurones. The cerebral layer radiates out from the *optic disc* (the region where the nerve fibres leave the eyeball to form the optic nerve) to the periphery. The optic disc is nonpigmented and insensitive to light, and is known as the *blind spot*. Light focused by the lens forms an inverted image on the retina. This stimulates the rods and cones to generate impulses which are transmitted via the optic nerve to the visual areas of the cortex.

retinol The active form of vitamin A. In the diet, retinol is found in margarine, oily fish, and dairy fats. It acts to maintain the integrity of skin and lung and is also involved in the synthesis of visual purple, which determines our ability to adapt vision to darkness. Retinol can be synthesized from dietary carotene found in carrots and green leafy vegetables – hence the belief that carrots help eyesight.

retriever A sporting dog belonging to one of several breeds developed to assist hunters. When game has been shot, the retriever is sent to the point where it fell to collect it and bring it to the hunter.

retrovirus A virus c.100 nm in diameter, with an outer envelope enclosing the core. The genetic information is stored in a molecule of single-stranded ribonucleic acid. (Family: Retroviridae.)

Returned Services League In Australia, an organization recruited from men and women with military service overseas. Its functions are social (welfare care and clubs) and political: it forms a major pressure group, with direct access to the cabinet.

Retz (Jean François Paul de Gondi), Cardinal de (1614–79) Prelate, born in Montmirail, France. He plotted against Mazarin, and exploited the Parlementary Fronde (1648) to further his own interests and the power of the Church. In his last years he wrote his *Mémoires*, a classic in 17th-c French literature.

Réunion [rayoonyon], formally **Bourbon** pop (2000e) 730 000; area 2512 km²/970 sq mi. Island in the Mascarenes archipelago, Indian Ocean; capital, St-Denis; timezone GMT +4; established as a French penal colony, 1638; overseas department, 1946; part of an administrative region, 1973; governed by a commissioner, a General Council, and a Regional Council.

Reuter, Paul Julius, Freiherr (Baron) **von** [royter], originally **Israel Beer Josaphat** (1816–99) Founder of the first news agency, born in Kassel, Germany. He developed the idea of a telegraphic news service, and in 1851 moved his headquarters to London.

revelation Generally, the disclosure of what was previously unknown, usually by divine or preternatural means. In religion, it is used to refer to disclosures by God or the divine as distinguished from that attained by the human processes of observation and reason.

Revelation, Book of or **the Apocalypse of St John** The last book in the New Testament, whose author is named as 'John', an exile on the island of Patmos (1.9), although scholars differ about his precise identity. Chapters 4–22 consist of symbolic visions about future tribulations and judgments marking the End times and the return of Christ.

Revere, Paul [reveer] (1735–1818) US patriot, born in Boston, MA. On 18 April 1775, the night before Lexington and Concord, he started for Concord, where arms were secreted. He was turned back by a British patrol, and his mission was completed by Dr

Samuel Prescott. It was Revere, however, whom the poet Longfellow immortalized for the 'midnight ride'.

Revised English Bible *New English Bible*

revisionism A doctrinal deviation from the ideological stance of a communist party or state; also, the critical re-assessment of Marxist theories. In general, the term has polemical overtones, and is applied to those thought to have broken with Marxist–Leninist orthodoxy.

Revolt of the Netherlands (1568–1648) Uprisings and wars against Spanish Habsburg rule by 17 provinces in the Low Countries, also called the **War of Independence**, the **Eighty Years' War**, and the **Dutch Revolt**. The rebels were led by William of Orange and his Protestant naval force of 'sea beggars' (*Watergeuzen*). Independence was recognized by Spain in 1648.

Revolution of 1905 A series of nationwide strikes, demonstrations, and mutinies in Russia, sparked off by the massacre of peacefully demonstrating workers by imperial soldiers in St Petersburg on *Bloody Sunday* (9 Jan 1905). Faced with continuing popular unrest, Nicholas II was forced to make concessions.

Revolutions of 1848 A succession of popular, violent uprisings in various W and C European countries during 1848–9. In France the abdication of Louis Philippe was followed by the Second Republic; liberal constitutions were granted in Austria and in many German states; Britain experienced Chartism. The revolutions collapsed from internal weakness or military suppression, and aroused reaction.

revolver A single-barrelled pistol with a revolving breech containing chambers for cartridges (usually six), which automatically brings a new cartridge into alignment for firing after each shot. The first practical example was produced by Samuel Colt in 1835.

rex A domestic cat with an unusually thin curly coat; a *foreign short-haired* variety; three forms: **Cornish**, **Devon**, and **German**. The name is also used for a rabbit with a short outer coat.

Reykjavík [raykjaveek] 64°09N 21°58W, pop (2000e) 106 000. Capital and chief port of Iceland; founded, 874; chartered, 1786; seat of Danish administration, 1801; capital, 1918; seat of Icelandic parliament; Lutheran bishopric; airport; university (1911); heating system uses nearby hot springs.

Reynaud, Paul [raynoh] (1878–1966) French statesman, born in Barcelonnette, France. He was premier for a short time during the fall of France in 1940, and was imprisoned by the Germans during World War 2.

Reynolds, Burt(on Leon, Jr), nickname **Buddy** (1936–) Actor and director, born in Lansing, MI. He studied at Florida State University (1958) where a promising career in football ended after he sustained a knee injury. He then took up acting and gained recognition with his role in the 1972 film *Deliverance*. His many later films include *Smokey and the Bandit* and its sequels (1977, 1980, 1983), *Sharky's Machine* (1981, also director), *Boogie Nights* (1997, Best Actor Golden Globe; Oscar nomination), and *The Dukes of Hazzard* (2005).

Reynolds, Sir Joshua [renuhldz] (1723–92) Portrait painter, born in Plympton, Devon. His works include 'Dr Samuel Johnson' (c.1756, National Portrait Gallery, London) and 'Sarah Siddons as the Tragic Muse' (1784, San Marino, CA). He produced over 2000 works, from which 700 engravings have been executed.

Reza Pahlavi, Mohammed *Pahlavi, Mohammed Reza*

Rhadamanthus or **Rhadamanthys** [radamanthus] In Greek mythology, a Cretan, son of Zeus and Europa. He did not die but was taken to Elysium, where he became the just judge of the dead.

Rhaetian [reeshn] *Romance languages*

rhapsody A piece of music in which the composer allows his imagination to range more or less freely over some theme, story, or idea, without regard for any prescribed structure. Lizst's Hungarian Rhapsodies are examples of what is essentially a Romantic genre.

Rhätikon [raytikon] Mountain range of the E or Rhaetian Alps, rising to 2965 m/9728 ft at Schesaplana.

Rhazes or **Razi** [rayzeez, rayzee], in full **Abu Bakr Muhammad ibn Zakariya ar-Razi** (10th-c) Persian physician and alchemist, who lived in Baghdad. His encyclopedia had considerable influence on medical science in the Middle Ages.

Rhea (astronomy) [reea] The fifth natural satellite of Saturn, discovered in 1672; distance from the planet 527 000 km/327 000 mi. It is the second largest moon in its system, diameter 1530 km/950 mi; orbital period 4.518 days.

Rhea or **Rheia** (mythology) [reea] In Greek mythology, a Titan, sister and wife of Cronus. She was the mother of Zeus and other Olympian gods.

rhea (ornithology) [reea] A South American ratite, resembling the ostrich, but smaller (up to 1·5 m/5 ft), duller plumage, and larger wings; can swim; also known as the **ema**, **nandu** (**nhandu**), or **American ostrich**. (Family: Rheidae, 2 species.)

Rhee, Syngman (1875–1965) Korean statesman, born near Kaesong, Korea. After the unsuccessful rising of 1919, he became president of the exiled Korean Provisional Government. On Japan's surrender (1945) he returned to become the first elected president of South Korea (1948–60).

Rheims [reemz], Fr **Reims** [rīs], ancient **Durocortorum**, later **Remi** 49°15N 4°02E, pop (2000e) 189 000. Historic town in NE France; on right bank of R Vesle; port on Aisne–Marne Canal; bishopric since 4th-c, now an archbishopric; former coronation site of French kings; extensive damage in World War 1; scene of German surrender, 1945; road and rail junction; major wine-producing centre (especially champagne); university (1967); Gothic cathedral (13th-c).

Rhenish Slate Mountains, Ger **Rheinisches Schiefergebirge** Extensive plateau of Germany, dissected by the Rhine and its tributaries; highest peak, the Grosser Feldberg (879 m/2884 ft).

rheology [reeolojee] The study of the deformation and flow of materials subjected to force. It includes the viscosity of liquids and gases, strain and shear due to stresses in solids, and plastic deformation in metals.

rhesus factor A series of closely related but distinct antigens (*agglutinogens*) usually present in the plasma membranes of human red blood cells. Individuals with the factor are **Rh+**; those without are **Rh–**. An Rh– woman carrying her first Rh+ child may produce anti-Rh antibodies after the birth. During the next pregnancy, these antibodies may cross the placenta, and if the fetus is Rh+ they may cause *haemolytic disease of the newborn*. The ratio of Rh+ to Rh– differs between ethnic populations.

rhesus monkey A macaque (*Macaca mulatta*) native to S Asia from Afghanistan to Indochina; stocky; sandy-brown; used widely for medical research; also known as **rhesus macaque**.

rhetoric The spoken and written language of persuasion. In the classical and mediaeval world, it was a formal branch of learning concerned with the techniques and devices required to persuade or convince an audience. Aristotle, Cicero, and Quintilian developed theories of successful speech-making. Subsequently it came to signify elaborate and pompous language, which is nonetheless empty and insincere. In recent years, there has been a renewed interest in presenting a message in the most effective way.

rheumatic fever A common disease of children and adolescents in Asia and Africa, arising from an immunological reaction to preceding infection with certain strains of *Streptococcus* (eg scarlet fever). Serious rheumatic heart disease can produce incompetence of the valves of the heart.

rheumatism A non-specific name given to aches and pains in muscles, particularly in the shoulders and back, and common in older people.

Rhine, River *p.785*

Rhine, River

Key
1 Rotterdam
2 Bonn
3 Koblenz
4 Mainz
5 Mannheim
6 Strasbourg
7 Basel

Ger **Rhein**, Dutch **Run**, Fr **Rhin**, ancient **Rhenus** River in C and W Europe, rising in SE Switzerland, in the Rheinwaldhorn glacier; flows N to L Constance, W to Basel, then generally N, forming part of the Germany–France border; divides into two major branches in The Netherlands, the Lek and Waal, before entering the North Sea; length, 1320 km/820 mi; main waterway of W Europe, flowing through major industrial areas; widely connected by canals to other rivers; tourism in the Rhine Valley and on the Rhine itself.

Rhine, J(oseph) B(anks) (1895–1980) Psychologist, a pioneer of parapsychology, born in Juniáta, PA. His experiments involving packs of specially designed cards attempted to establish the phenomena of extrasensory perception and telepathy on a statistical basis.

rhinitis Inflammation of the lining of the nose, leading to a discharge, and producing a stuffy, running nose. It may be caused by allergic conditions such as hay fever, or by infections such as the common cold.

rhinoceros The second largest land animal (after the elephant), native to S and SE Asia and Africa; a perissodactyl mammal of the family Rhinocerotidae; skin tough, usually with few hairs; long head with small eyes placed well forward; nose with 'horn(s)' made from fibrous outgrowths of the skin; five species: also known as **rhino**.

rhizoid A uni- or multicellular thread-like structure found in algae, mosses, liverworts, and ferns. Rhizoids anchor the plant to the substrate and absorb water, but unlike true roots are not differentiated into separate tissues.

rhizome A horizontally growing underground stem. It is either slender and fast-growing, allowing the plant to spread vegetatively, or fleshy and acting as a food store.

Rhizopoda [riyzopoda] A large group of protozoans distinguished on the basis of their types of pseudopodia; includes the amoebae and foraminiferans.

Rhode Island pop (2000e) 1 048 300; area 3139 km²/1212 sq mi. New England state in NE USA; 'Little Rhody' or the 'Ocean State'; smallest US state, but the second most densely populated; one of the original states, 13th to ratify the Federal Constitution, 1790; gave protection to Quakers in 1657 and to Jews from the Netherlands in 1658; rises from the Narragansett Basin in the E to flat and rolling uplands in the W; highest point, Jerimoth Hill (247 m/810 ft); capital, Providence.

Rhodes, Gr **Ródhos**, Ital **Rodi** pop (2000e) 95 400; area 1398 km²/540 sq mi. Largest island of the Dodecanese, Greece; length 72 km/45 mi; maximum width 35 km/22 mi; fourth largest Greek island; ridge of hills rise to 1215 m/3986 ft; originally settled by Mycenean Greeks, 1400 BC; Knights of the Order of St John settled here, 1309–1522; held by Italy, 1912–47; capital, Rhodes, pop (2000e) 45 600; airfield; Temple of Aphrodite (3rd-c BC).

Rhodes, Cecil (John) (1853–1902) British colonial statesman, born in Bishop's Stortford, Hertfordshire. He secured the charter for the British South Africa Company (1889), whose territory was later to be named after him as Rhodesia. In 1890 he became prime minister of Cape Colony, but was forced to resign in 1896. He was a conspicuous figure during the Boer War of 1899–1902, when he organized the defences of Kimberley. His will founded scholarships at Oxford for Americans, Germans, and colonials (*Rhodes scholars*).

Rhodes, Wilfred (1877–1973) Cricketer, born in Kirkheaton, West Yorkshire. He played for Yorkshire and England, and during his career (1898–1930) took a world record 4187 wickets and scored 39 722 runs. He performed the 'double' of 1000 runs and 100 wickets 16 times.

Rhodes, Zandra (1940–) Fashion designer, born in Chatham, Kent. She showed her first collection in 1969, and is noted for her distinctive, exotic designs in floating chiffons and silks.

Rhodesia Zambia; Zimbabwe

rhododendron An evergreen shrub or small tree, native to N temperate regions but found only on acid soils; flowers in clusters at tips of main branches, funnel or bell-shaped; 5–10 petals and stamens. Several hundred cultivars are known, with flowers varying greatly in size and colour. (Genus: *Rhododendron*, c.1200 species. Family: Ericaceae.)

Rhodope Mountains [rodopee], Bulgarian **Rhodopi** Range of mountains stretching NW–SE in SW Bulgaria and NE Greece, rising to 2925 m/9596 ft at Musala; length 290 km/180 mi.

Rhondda, Cynon, Taff [rontha, kuhnon, taf] pop (2001e) 232 000; area 126 km²/49 sq mi. County (unitary authority from 1996) in S Wales, UK; administrative centre, Clydach Vale; former major coal mining area; Royal Mint at Llantrisant.

Rhône, River River in C and SW Europe, rising in S Switzerland, and flowing to its delta on the Mediterranean; length, 812 km/504 mi; joined at Lyon by its largest tributary, the Saône.

rhubarb A long-lived perennial herb (*Rheum rhaponticum*), related to dock, and native to Siberia; basal leaves large, heart-shaped, wavy, with edible green or red stalks; flowers small, white, 6-petalled; leaves can be poisonous. (Family: Polygonaceae).

Rhyl [ril] 53°19N 3°29W, pop (2000e) 24 400. Seaside resort town in Denbighshire, NE Wales, UK; railway; funfair, promenade.

rhyme The repetition of the same or a similar syllable, for rhetorical effect, typically at the end of a poetic line. There is a limitless variety of rhyme schemes. Several 20th-c poets explored half-rhyme, as in Wilfred Owen's 'Strange Meeting', where *friend/frowned* and *killed/cold* are rhymes.

rhyolite [riyoliyt] A silica-rich volcanic igneous rock with a composition approximately equivalent to granite. It is fine-grained or glassy.

Rhys, Jean [rees], pseudonym of **Ella Gwendolen Rees Williams** (1894–1979) Novelist, born in Roseau, Dominica. Her best-known novel is *Wide Sargasso Sea* (1966), a 'prequel' to Charlotte Bronte's *Jane Eyre*.

Rhys-Jones, Sophie *Edward, Prince*

rhythm A pattern marked by the regular recurrence of elements, found in speech, music, dance, and other forms of behaviour, and more generally in the cyclical changes of nature. In speech, rhythm is most noticeable in the metrical patterns of poetry. In music, it is the constituent that has to do with metre, note-lengths, and accent rather than with pitch. Music is said to be 'strongly rhythmic' when the basic pulse is firmly emphasized or when a rhythmic pattern is insistently repeated; but rhythmic subtlety in music depends more on the play between an established pulse and the melodic or harmonic accents that disturb it, or between one rhythmic pattern and another (**cross-rhythm**).

rhythm and blues A type of popular music dating from the 1940s and 1950s which combined melodic and textual features of the blues with the rhythm section of a pop group (electric guitars, keyboards, and drum set). It was an important forerunner of rock and roll, and was itself superseded by soul.

rhythm method *contraception*

Rialto Bridge [reealtoh] A bridge spanning the Grand Canal in Venice. It was built in 1588–92 by Antonio da Ponte.

rib A curved, twisted strip of bone passing around the thorax from the vertebral column to articulate indirectly with the sternum. There are twelve pairs in humans, of which the eleventh and twelfth are not attached at the front (**floating ribs**). They provide protection for the lungs, heart, and great vessels.

Ribbentrop, Joachim von [ribentrop] (1893–1946) German statesman, born in Wesel, Germany. He became ambassador to Britain (1936) and foreign minister (1938–45). Captured in 1945, he was executed at Nuremberg.

Ribble, River River rising in the Pennine Hills of North Yorkshire, N England; flows 120 km/75 mi to meet the Irish Sea in a broad estuary.

ribbon worm An unsegmented, bilaterally symmetrical worm found mainly on or in shallow marine sediments, occasionally in fresh water; may reach lengths of over 20 m/65 ft. (Phylum: Nemertea.)

Ribera, José or **Jusepe de** [reevera], known as **Lo Spagnoletto** ('the Little Spaniard') (1588–1652) Painter and etcher, born in Játiva, Spain. He is noted for the often gruesome realism with which he treated religious and mythological subjects, such as the martyrdom of the saints.

riboflavin A B vitamin (B$_2$), an essential active component (*coenzyme*) involved in energy transfers in cells, found especially in green vegetables, milk, eggs, liver, and yeast.

ribonucleic acid *RNA*

ribose [riybohs] C$_5$H$_{10}$O$_5$. A pentose or 5-carbon sugar, occurring in the structure of ribonucleic acids (RNA).

ribosome A complex of RNA (**ribosomal RNA** or **rRNA**) and several proteins which exist in bacteria and the cytoplasm of nucleated (eucaryotic) cells. Ribosomes occur both as free particles within the cell and as particles attached to the membranes of the endoplasmic reticulum in eucaryotic cells. They account for a large proportion of the total RNA in a cell. In combination with other molecules (in particular, transfer RNA or tRNA), they function as the machinery that decodes the genetic information present in mRNA, converting this into the amino acid sequence of protein molecules through the process known as *translation*.

Ricardo, David [rikah(r)doh] (1772–1823) Political economist, born in London. In 1817 appeared the work on which his reputation chiefly rests, *Principles of Political Economy and Taxation*.

Ricci, Nina, originally **Maria Nielli** (1883–1970) Fashion designer, born in Turin, Italy. She joined Raffin in 1908, and stayed with him for 20 years, eventually becoming his business partner.

She showed her first collection in 1932, and her fragrances in 1941, and developed a wide range of further products in cosmetics, furs, and fashion accessories.

Ricci, Sebastiano [reechee] (1659–1734) Painter, born in Belluno, Italy. He worked throughout Europe, becoming one of the leading decorative painters of his day.

Riccio, David *Rizzio, David*

Rice, Condoleezza [kondoleetsa] (1954–) US academic and Republican politician, born in Birmingham, AL. She started political life as a Democrat, but changed parties in 1982 as a result of Jimmy Carter's Afghanistan policy. She joined Stanford University in 1981, becoming a professor in the political science department (1985–6, 1991–3), and was the first woman and first African-American to become a Stanford provost (1993–9). She was director of Soviet and East European affairs with the National Security Council (1989), and special assistant to George Bush. In 2001 she was appointed national security adviser by George W Bush, and made secretary of state in 2004.

Rice, Tim, popular name of **Sir Timothy Miles Bindon Rice** (1944–) Lyricist, writer, and broadcaster, born in Buckinghamshire. He is best known for writing the lyrics for *Joseph and the Amazing Technicolour Dreamcoat* (1968), *Jesus Christ Superstar* (1971), and *Evita* (1978). Later work includes the lyrics for *Chess* (recorded, 1984), *Starmania* (1991), and *Beauty and the Beast* (1997).

rice An important cereal grass (*Oryza sativa*), with open panicles, drooping with numerous grains. The premier food plant of Asia, it is cultivated in flooded paddy fields, with many varieties adapted to different water-levels. Recent breeding programmes have produced successful, high-yielding, semi-dwarf varieties. (Family: Gramineae.)

Richard I, known as **Richard Coeur de Lion** or **Richard the Lion-heart** (1157–99) King of England (1189–99), born in Oxford, the third son of Henry II and Eleanor of Aquitaine. Of his 10-year reign, he spent only five months in England, devoting himself to crusading, and defending the Angevin lands in France. He took Messina (1190), Cyprus, and Acre (1191) during the Third Crusade, and advanced to within sight of Jerusalem. On the return journey, he was arrested at Vienna (1192), and remained a prisoner of the German Emperor Henry VI until he agreed to be ransomed (1194). He was killed while besieging the castle of Châlus, Aquitaine.

Richard II (1367–1400) King of England (1377–99), born in Bordeaux, France, the younger son of Edward the Black Prince. He succeeded his grandfather, Edward III, at the age of 10. He displayed great bravery in confronting the rebels during the Peasants' Revolt (1381); but already parliament was concerned about his favourites, and the reign was dominated by the struggle between Richard's desire to act independently, and the magnates' concern to curb his power. He exiled several lords, including Henry Bolingbroke (later Henry IV). Having failed to restrain the king by constitutional means, the magnates resolved to unseat him from the throne. Bolingbroke invaded England unopposed, and Richard was deposed in his favour (Sep 1399). He died in Pontefract Castle, Yorkshire, possibly of starvation.

Richard III (1452–85) King of England (1483–5), born in Fotheringhay Castle, Northamptonshire, the youngest son of Richard, Duke of York. He was created Duke of Gloucester by his brother, Edward IV, in 1461. When Edward died (1483) and was succeeded by his under-age son, Edward V, Richard acted first as protector; but within three months, he had himself proclaimed and crowned as the rightful king. Young Edward and his brother were probably murdered in the Tower on Richard's orders (though not all historians agree). His rival, Henry Tudor (later Henry VII), confronted him in battle at Bosworth Field, where Richard was killed. Though ruthless, he was not the absolute monster Tudor historians portrayed him to be. Nor is there proof he was a hunchback.

Richard, Cliff, popular name of **Sir Harry Roger Webb** (1940–) Pop-singer, born in Lucknow, India. He moved to England at the age of eight, and formed his own band in 1958. Originally called The Drifters, the group changed its name to The Shadows, and after the success of 'Living Doll' (1959) it was hailed as Britain's answer to American rock. He made a series of family musical films during the 1960s, including *The Young Ones* (1961) and *Summer Holiday* (1962), and played the leading role in the musical *Heathcliff* (1996). Following his conversion to Christianity, his clean-cut image damaged his reputation with rock fans, but he has nevertheless become a British entertainment institution. His albums include *Love Songs* (1981), *Silver* (1983), *Mistletoe and Wine* (1988), *Cliff at Christmas* (2003), and *Somethin's Goin' On* (2004). He became the UK's top selling singles artist in 2004 with 21 million records, overtaking The Beatles.

Richard Alston Dance Company Britain's largest independent dance company. Founded by its artistic director Richard Alston in 1994, it focuses on new choreography but combines this with the re-creation of seminal past works from Alston's career. It is resident at The Place, London.

Richards, Emma (1975–) Yachtswoman, born in Helensburgh, Argylle and Bute. In her 18 m/60 ft yacht *Pindar*, she became the first woman and youngest person to complete the 29 000-mile Around Alone solo race. She departed from New York (Sep 2002) and after 135 days at sea crossed the finishing line at Newport, RI (May 2003) in fourth place.

Richards, Frank, pseudonym of **Charles (Harold St John) Hamilton** (1875–1961) Children's writer, born in London. He wrote for boys' papers, particularly for *Gem* (1906–39) and *Magnet* (1908–40), and became known as the author of the 'Tom Merry', 'Billy Bunter', and other school-story series.

Richards, Sir Gordon (1904–86) Jockey and trainer, born in Oakengates, Shropshire. Between 1921 and 1954 he rode a record 4870 winners in Britain, and was champion jockey a record 26 times between 1925 and 1953.

Richards, I(vor) A(rmstrong) (1893–1979) Literary critic and scholar, born in Sandbach, Cheshire. He pioneered the detailed critical study of literary texts in the 20th-c. With C K Ogden he wrote *The Meaning of Meaning* (1923), followed by the influential *Principles of Literary Criticism* (1924).

Richards, Viv, popular name of **Sir Isaac Vivian Alexander Richards** (1952–) Cricket player, born in Antigua. In 1976 he scored a record 1710 Test runs in one calendar year. He captained the West Indies (1985–91), and scored 8540 runs in 121 Test matches, including 24 centuries.

Richardson, Miranda (1958–) Actress, born in Southport, Lancashire. Her films include *Empire of The Sun* (1987), *Damage* (1992, BAFTA Best Supporting Actress), *Tom and Viv* (1994), *Sleepy Hollow* (1999), and *Puffball* (2007). She also appeared as Queen Elizabeth in the BBC TV comedy series *Blackadder* (1990).

Richardson, Sir Ralph (David) (1902–83) Actor, born in Cheltenham, Gloucestershire. His association with the Old Vic company commenced in 1930, and he was asked to lead its postwar revival. His films included *The Fallen Idol* (1948) and *Doctor Zhivago* (1965).

Richardson, Robert C (1937–) Physicist, born in Washington, DC. At Cornell he contributed to the discovery of the superfluidity of helium-3, and shared the Nobel Prize for Physics in 1996.

Richardson, Samuel (1689–1761) Novelist, born in Mackworth, Derbyshire. His novels include *Pamela* (1740), *Clarissa* (1748), published in seven volumes, and *Sir Charles Grandison* (1754). In using the epistolary method, he helped to develop the dramatic scope of the novel, then little regarded as a literary form.

Richelieu, Armand Jean du Plessis, Cardinal, duc de (Duke of) [reeshlyoe] (1585–1642) French statesman and first minister of France (1624–42), born in Richelieu, near Chinon, France. A protégé of the queen mother, Marie de' Medicis, he became minister of state (1624), and as chief minister was the effective ruler of France. His principal achievement was to check Habsburg power, ultimately by sending armies into the Spanish Netherlands, Alsace, Lorraine, and Roussillon.

Richler, Mordecai (1931–2001) Writer, born in Montreal, Quebec, Canada. His best-known novel is *The Apprenticeship of Duddy Kravitz* (1959), which was later filmed, although *St Urbain's Horseman* (1971) is a more ambitious work. Later books include *Barney's Version* (1997). He wrote a memoir, *This Year in Jerusalem* (1994).

Richmond (UK), properly **Richmond-upon-Thames [temz]** 51°28N 0°19W, pop (2001e) 172 300. Borough of SW Greater London, England; on the R Thames; railway; Hampton Court Palace, Royal Botanic Gardens (Kew Gardens).

Richmond (Virginia) 37°33N 77°27W, pop (2000e) 197 800. Port and capital of state in E Virginia, USA, on the James R; trading post (Fort Charles), 1645; state capital, 1779; Confederate capital during the Civil War; captured by Union forces, 1865; airfield; railway; three universities (1804, 1832, 1865); corporate headquarters centre.

Richter, Hans (1843–1916) Conductor, born in Raab, Hungary. He was an authority on the music of Wagner, with whom he was closely associated in the Bayreuth festivals.

Richter, Johann Paul (Friedrich), pseudonym **Jean Paul** (1763–1825) Novelist and humorist, born in Wunsiedel, Germany. He produced a wide range of works, achieving success with such romances as *Die unsichtbare Loge* (1793, The Invisible Lodge), *Hesperus* (1795), and the four-volume *Titan* (1800–3).

Richter, Sviatoslav (Teofilovich) (1915–97) Pianist, born in Zhitomir, Ukraine. Winner of the Stalin Prize in 1949, he made extensive concert tours, and had been associated with the music festivals at Aldeburgh and Spoleto.

Richter scale A logarithmic scale, devised in 1935 by US geophysicist Charles Richter (1900–85), for representing the energy released by earthquakes. A figure of two or less is barely perceptible, while eight or more is a major earthquake.

Richthofen, Ferdinand (Paul Wilhelm), Baron von [rikhthohfn] (1833–1905) Geographer, geologist, and traveller, born in Karlsruhe, Germany. His research helped to develop the field of geomorphology.

ricin [riysin, risin] An extremely toxic protein present in the castor bean (*Ricinus communis*) of the family Euphorbiaceae). It has been proposed as a chemical warfare agent.

rickets A disorder of infants and growing children resulting from a deficiency of vitamin D. There is a failure to calcify the growing ends of long bones, and the soft bones are prone to deformities. Swelling and enlargement of the ends of the ribs in front of the chest is known as the 'rickety rosary'.

Rickettsia [riketsia] A genus of typically rod-shaped micro-organisms with bacteria-like cell walls. Rickettsias multiply inside or in close association with cells of animal hosts. They include the causative agents of trench fever and other human diseases. (Kingdom: Monera. Family: Rickettsiaceae.)

Rickman, Alan (1946–) Actor, born in London. He played a wide range of theatre roles during the 1980s, then became known for his film work, including *Truly, Madly, Deeply* (1991), *Robin Hood, Prince of Thieves* (1991, BAFTA Best Supporting Actor), *Michael Collins* (1996), *Rasputin* (1996, Emmy), *Harry Potter and the Philosopher's Stone* (2001), and *Perfume* (2006).

riddle An utterance, often cast in a traditional form, whose intention is to mystify or mislead; a linguistic guessing game. In Europe, riddles tend to be short questions, generally restricted to children's games and conversation. In ancient Greece, they had a serious purpose, being used by judges, oracles, and others to test a person's wisdom.

Ridgeley, Andrew *Michael, George*

Ridgeway A long-distance footpath in England running 137 km/ 85 mi from Beacon Hill, Buckinghamshire, to Overton Hill, Wiltshire.

Ridgway, Matthew (Bunker) (1895–1993) US soldier, born in Fort Monroe, VA. He commanded the 82nd Airborne Division in Sicily (1943) and Normandy (1944), the 18th Airborne Corps in the North West Europe campaign (1944–5) and the US 8th Army in UN operations in Korea (1950).

Riding for the Disabled The organized riding of horses and ponies to enrich the lives of seriously disabled people, especially children. People with Down's syndrome, cerebral palsy, spina bifida, and other such disabilities are taught to ride suitable mounts under careful supervision.

riding the marches A Scottish ritual, also called **common riding**, the equivalent of English *beating the bounds*. It is performed on horseback, chiefly in the towns of S Scotland.

Ridley, Nicholas (c.1500–1555) Protestant martyr, born near Haltwhistle, Northumberland. An ardent reformer, he became Bishop of London (1550), and helped Cranmer prepare the Thirty-nine Articles. On the death of Edward VI he espoused the cause of Lady Jane Grey, and was executed at Oxford.

Rie, Dame Lucie [ree] (1902–95) Studio potter, born in Vienna. In the 1940s and 1950s she made ceramic buttons and tableware, but later concentrated on stoneware or porcelain bowls and vases with a variety of textured and coloured glazes.

Riefenstahl, Leni [reefenshtahl], popular name of **Berta Helene Amalie Riefenstahl** (1902–2003) Film-maker, born in Berlin. Her films include *Triumph des Willens* (1935, Triumph of the Will), a compelling record of a Nazi rally at Nuremberg, and *Olympiad* (1938), an epic two-part documentary of the Berlin Olympic Games.

Riel, Louis [ree-el] (1844–85) Canadian political leader, born in Red River Settlement, Rupert's Land. He headed the Red River Rebellion in 1869–70, and became president of the provisional government. Following a second uprising (1885) in what is now Saskatchewan, he was arrested and executed.

Riemann, (Georg Friedrich) Bernhard [reeman] (1826–66) Mathematician, born in Breselenz, Germany. His early work was on the theory of functions, but he is best remembered for his development of non-Euclidian geometry.

Rienzi, Cola di [rienzee], also spelled **Rienzo** (1313–54) Italian patriot, born in Rome. In 1347 he incited the citizens to rise against the rule of the nobles, but was killed in a reaction against him.

Rievaulx Abbey [reevoh] A ruined 12th-c Cistercian abbey, located in a deep valley in the North Yorkshire Moors National Park, Ryedale district, UK. The monastery was founded during the Christianizing mission of St Bernard of Clairvaux in N England.

Rif or **Riff** A cluster of Berber agricultural and herding groups of NE Morocco. Famed as warriors, in the 1920s they defeated the Spanish, but were eventually conquered by combined French and Spanish forces.

Rifkind, Sir Malcolm (Leslie) (1946–) British Conservative statesman, born in Edinburgh. Elected an MP in 1974, he became secretary of state for Scotland (1986–90), transport (1990–2), defence (1992–5), and foreign secretary (1995–7). He lost his seat in the 1997 general election but was re-elected in 2005 and briefly served as shadow secretary of state for work and pensions. That year he entered the Conservative leadership race to succeed Michael Howard but later withdrew. He was knighted in 2005.

rifle A type of firearm developed into a practical weapon in the mid-19th-c in which the barrel of the gun is internally grooved in a spiral form. The bullet is spun as it passes down the bore, the spin stabilizing it in flight and thus increasing its accuracy.

Today's military **assault rifles** are lightweight, fully automatic weapons with great range and accuracy.

rift valley An elongated trough in the Earth's crust bounded by normal faults; also termed a **graben**. It is a region of tension in the Earth's crust arising from crustal plates moving apart.

Rift Valley or **Great Rift Valley** Major geological feature running from the Middle East S to SE Africa; from Syria to Mozambique; contains the Sea of Galilee, Dead Sea, Gulf of Aqaba, and Red Sea; W branch (also known as the Albertine Rift), along the edge of the Congo basin, includes lakes Albert, Edward, Kivu, and Tanganyika.

rig(ging) *sailing rig*

Riga [reega] 56°53N 24°08E, pop (2000e) 836 000. Seaport capital of Latvia; on the R Daugava; trading station, 1201; member of the Hanseatic League, 1282; capital of independent Latvia, 1918–40, and from 1991; occupied by Germany in World War 2; airport; railway; military base; cultural centre and seaside resort; university (1919); castle (1330), cathedral (13th-c, rebuilt 16th-c); historic centre, a world heritage site.

Rigel [riyjuhl] A supergiant in Orion, the seventh brightest star in our sky, and also one of the most luminous of all stars. Distance: 320 parsec.

Rigg, Dame Diana (1938–) Actress, born in Doncaster, S Yorkshire. She played Emma Peel in the popular *The Avengers* television series, then joined the National Theatre (1972). Among her films are *Evil Under the Sun* (1982), *A Good Man in Africa* (1994), and *Heidi* (2005). Her TV work includes *Mother Love* (1990, BAFTA), *The Mrs Bradley Mysteries* (2000), and *King Charles II: The Power and the Passion* (2003). She received a Tony award for *Medea* (1994).

rightsizing A strategy for organizing the use of mainframe, mini, and personal computers in an organization, in such a way that data is held on the type of computer and at the location for which it is most suited.

right to silence In most legal jurisdictions, a right which protects criminal suspects from answering questions put to them by the relevant authority or from giving any evidence. In the UK, police are required to *caution* suspects about their right to silence and right to legal advice. In the USA, police are required to give all suspects a *Miranda warning*, based on the United States Supreme Court case *Miranda v. Arizona* (1966), in which the court held that prosecutors may not use incriminating statements of suspects unless strict procedural safeguards are followed to guarantee the suspect's awareness of the constitutional right to remain silent and to have an attorney.

right wing One end of the political continuum, originally identifying those who supported the institutions of the monarchy during the French Revolution. In the 19th-c the term was applied to those who were conservative in their view, supporting authority, the state, tradition, property, patriotism, and institutions such as the Church and family. In the 20th-c, the right also developed a radical, non-conservative side.

rigidity *shear modulus*

rigor mortis [riger maw(r)tis] A temporary stiffening of the body after death because of the depletion of adenosine triphosphate and phosphoryl creatinine within skeletal muscle fibres. It usually begins 3 hours after death and is completed by 12 hours. The effects persist for 3–4 days, after which flaccidity returns.

Rijeka [riyeka], Ital **Fiume** 45°20N 14°27E, pop (2000e) 172 900. Seaport town in W Croatia; on R Rečina; Croatia's largest port; former Roman base (Tarsatica); occupied by the Slavs, 7th-c; naval base of the Austro–Hungarian Empire until 1918; ceded to Italy, 1924; ceded to Yugoslavia, 1947; airfield; railway; ferries; university (1973); castle, cathedral.

Rijksmuseum [riyksmoozayum] ('state museum') The national art gallery in Amsterdam, The Netherlands. The present building was designed by Petrus Cuypers and erected in 1877–85.

Rila Mountain [reela], Bulgarian **Rila Planina** Mountain in W Bulgaria; highest range in the Balkan peninsula, rising to 2925 m/9596 ft at Musala.

Riley, Bridget (1931–) Artist, born in London. She is a leading practitioner of Op Art (eg 'Fall' 1963, Tate, London), and was the first English painter to win the major painting prize at the Venice Biennale (1968). A major retrospective of her work was held at Tate Britain in 2003.

Rilke, Rainer Maria [rilkuh] (1875–1926) Lyric poet, born in Prague. Among his major works are *Die Sonnette an Orpheus* (Sonnets to Orpheus) and *Duineser Elegien* (Duino Elegies), both written in 1923.

rille [ril] A straight or winding valley, with a U-shaped cross-section, found in the lunar maria. Rilles mark places where molten lava has flowed in the past.

Rimbaud, (Jean Nicolas) Arthur [rĩboh] (1854–91) Poet, born in Charleville, France. His most famous work is *Le Bateau ivre* (1871, The Drunken Boat). In 1871 Verlaine invited him to Paris, where they led together a life of ill repute. Before the relationship ended (1873), Rimbaud wrote *Les Illuminations*, which show him to be a precursor of Symbolism, and which were published by Verlaine in 1876, when he believed Rimbaud to be dead.

rime A form of precipitation in which surfaces are coated in opaque ice. It forms when ice accretes on objects through the freezing, on impact, of supercooled water droplets.

Rimet, Jules [reemay] (1873–1956) French football administrator. He was president of the French football league (1910) and French Football Federation (1919–49). He promoted the Fédération Internationale de Football Association (FIFA), becoming president (1921–56), and founded the World Cup competition (1930), his name being added to the title in 1946.

Rimington, Dame Stella (1935–) Administrator, born in South Norwood, London. She studied at Edinburgh and Liverpool before working in the Worcester County Record Office and the India Office Library in London. In 1965, she moved to New Delhi, where she joined the Security Service (MI5). She returned to the UK in 1969 becoming successively director of counter-subversion, counter-espionage, and counter-terrorism. In 1992, she became director-general of MI5, the first woman to be appointed and the first to be publicly named while in office. Her book, *At Risk* (2004), is based on her own experiences in the service. She retired in 1996, and was made a dame that year.

Rimini, Lat **Arminium** 44°04N 12°34E, pop (2001e) 131 400. City in Emilia-Romagna, N Italy, on the Riviera del Sole of the Adriatic; at the junction of the Roman Aemilian Way and Flaminian Way; under Papal States control (1509); annexed to the Kingdom of Italy (1860); railway; Roman Arch of Augustus (c.27 BC); amphitheatre; Palazzo dell'Arengo (1204); castle (1446); popular beach resort.

Rimsky-Korsakov, Nikolai (Andreyevich) [rimskee kaw(r)sakof] (1844–1908) Composer, born in Tikhvin, Russia. In 1887–8 he produced his three great orchestral masterpieces – *Capriccio Espagnol*, *Easter Festival*, and *Scheherazade*. Ever conscious of his bygone technical shortcomings, he rewrote almost all his early work.

rinderpest [rinderpest] An infectious disease of ruminant mammals; also known as **cattle plague**. It is characterized by blood in the faeces, fever, and swelling of the mucous membranes.

ring (chemistry) In chemistry, a closed group of atoms. For carbon compounds, rings of five or six atoms are the most stable.

Ring nebula *Lyra*

ring of fire A belt of major earthquake and volcanic activity around the Pacific Ocean, defining the boundary between crustal plates.

ringworm A common skin disease resulting from a fungal infec-

tion of the outer layers of the skin. It usually affects the scalp, groin, and the clefts of the toes.

Rinzai Zen *Zen Buddhism*

Rio de Janeiro [reeoh duh zhaneeroh], known as **Rio** 22°53S 43°17W, pop (2000e) 6 968 000. Port city in SE Brazil; Pão de Açucar (Sugar Loaf Mountain) rises to 396 m/1299 ft; discovered, 1502; first settled by the French, 1555; taken by the Portuguese, 1567; seat of the Viceroy, 1763; capital of Brazil, 1834–1960; trade in coffee, sugar, iron ore; major international tourist centre, with famous beaches at Copacabana, Ipanema, Leblon; airport; two airfields; railway; metro; three universities (1920, 1940, 1950); many colonial and 19th-c buildings; figure of Christ on the highest peak, Corcovado (690 m/2264 ft); world-famous Carnival, on the days preceding Lent.

Rio Grande (Mexico) [reeoh grand, granday] **Río Bravo**, **Río Bravo del Norte**. River in SW USA and N Mexico; rises in the Rocky Mts, SW Colorado; enters the Gulf of Mexico; length 3033 km/ 1885 mi.

Rioja [reeohkha] pop (2000e) 265 000; area 5034 km²/1943 sq mi. Region of N Spain; major wine-producing area; capital, Logroño.

Río Muni [reeoh moonee] area 26 016 km²/10 042 sq mi. Mainland territory of Equatorial Guinea, WC Africa; chief town, Bata.

Riot Act Legislation in Britain concerned to preserve public order, first passed in 1714. When 12 or more people were unlawfully assembled and refused to disperse, they were, after the reading of a section of this Act by a person in authority, immediately considered felons having committed a serious crime. It was repealed in 1911.

Ripken, Cal, popular name of **Calvin James Ripken Jr** (1960–) Baseball player, born in Havre de Grace, MD. The Baltimore Orioles 'Iron Man' shortstop, he is famed for his all-time record of 2632 consecutive major league games from 1982 to 1999. He was the American League's Most Valuable Player in 1983 and 1991, winning the Golden Gloves in 1991 and 1992. He retired from major league baseball in 2001.

Ripon [ripn] 54°08N 1°31W, pop (2000e) 13 700. Town in North Yorkshire, N England; reckoned to be England's second oldest town; racecourse; cathedral.

risk analysis A technique used in insurance and in business which attempts to calculate the effect of the 'worst possible' outcome of a venture. Risk analysis looks at all possible outcomes, assigning probabilities to each so that all the options are quantified.

Risorgimento [rizaw(r)zhimentoh] (It 'resurgence', 'rebirth') The 19th-c movement by which Italy achieved unity and nationhood. It began with the 1830 revolutions and, after failure in 1848–9, reached fruition under the leadership of Piedmont/Sardinia during 1859–70. In 1859–61 the Austrians were expelled from Lombardy, and the C Italian duchies, the Papal States, and Naples/Sicily united with Sardinia to form the Kingdom of Italy.

river A body of flowing water restricted to a relatively narrow channel by banks. It typically originates as a stream in high ground, and moves downhill, eroding a channel which grows as tributaries join the flow, and often carving out major valleys. In its middle stages the river flows more slowly, and meanders begin to form; while in its mature stages deposition of sediment and the formation of broad flood-plains and deltas is characteristic. *p.790*

Rivera, Diego [rivayra] (1886–1957) Painter, born in Guanajuato, Mexico. In 1921 he began a series of murals in public buildings depicting the life and history of the Mexican people. His art is a blend of folk art and revolutionary propaganda. He married artist Frida Kahlo in 1928.

river blindness An infection endemic in Africa caused by the filaria *Onchocerca volvulus*; also known as **onchocerciasis**.

Eye involvement causes itching, inflammation, glaucoma, and blindness.

Rivers, Joan, professional name of **Joan Alexandra Molinsky** (1933–) Comedienne and writer, born in Larchmont, NY. The regular guest host of *The Tonight Show* (1983–6), she went on to host *The Late Show* (1986–7) and her own daytime talk show in 1989. She has also worked as a film director and recording artist, and her books include *Bouncing Back* (1997).

Riviera The Mediterranean coast between Toulon, France, and La Spezia, Italy. It is a narrow coastal strip bordered by the Alps to the N, and includes many holiday resorts.

Riyadh [riyad], Arabic **Ar Riyad** 24°41N 46°42E, pop (2000e) 3 044 000. Capital city of Saudi Arabia; formerly a walled city; airport; railway; communications centre; three universities (1950, 1957, 1984); over 1000 mosques; target of terrorist suicide bomb attacks, May 2003.

Rizzio, David [ritsioh], also spelled **Riccio** (?1533–1566) Courtier and musician, born in Pancalieri, Italy. He entered the service of Mary, Queen of Scots in 1561, and was made her French secretary in 1564. He negotiated her marriage with Darnley (1565), who became jealous of his influence, and plotted his death.

RNA or **ribonucleic acid** A nucleic acid found throughout the cell, distinguished from DNA by the substitution of the pyrimidine base (uracil) for thymidine, and the sugar component (ribose) for deoxyribose. RNA is involved in many crucial cellular processes, in particular the synthesis of proteins. It is synthesized as a complementary strand to a section of DNA base sequences by a class of enzymes known as **RNA polymerases**. RNA copies of protein coding genes are processed (introns being spliced out) to give **mature messenger RNA (mRNA)**, which is then transported through the nuclear membrane to the ribosomes in the cytoplasm. **Transfer RNA (tRNA)** is copied from tRNA genes and collects the free amino acids in the cytoplasm, transporting them to the ribosomes (which contain ribosomal RNA or rRNA copied from rRNA genes). The amino acids transported by the tRNA molecules are joined in a sequence dictated by the mRNA. Therefore, once the mRNA is attached to the ribosomes, it serves as a template for the production of protein polypeptide chains. Another class of RNAs, known as **small nuclear RNA (snRNA)**, forms part of complexes with proteins called snRNPs, which are involved in the removal of introns (splicing) to produce mRNA.

Roach, Hal, popular name of **Harald Eugene Roach** (1892–1992) Film producer, born in Elmira, NY. In 1914 he formed a production company to make short silent comedies, whose players included Harold Lloyd and Will Hays, and after 1928 continued with sound. In 1984 he was given a Special Academy Award for his achievements.

roach Freshwater fish (*Rutilus rutilus*) found in rivers and lakes of Europe; body moderately deep, length up to 45 cm/18 in; greenish-brown on back, sides silver, pelvic and anal fins red. (Family: Cyprinidae.)

road rage Aggressive behaviour while driving a motor vehicle on a public highway. There is no specific road rage offence in many jurisdictions, but such behaviour may involve a breach of other laws. If the aggressor causes injury, he or she may face conviction for murder, causing death by reckless driving, battery, or some other offence.

roadrunner A ground-dwelling cuckoo, native to SW USA and Central America; long tail and legs; head with short crest. (Genus: *Geococcyx*, 2 species.)

Road Town 18°26N 64°32W, pop (2000e) 3600. Seaport and capital of the British Virgin Is, E Caribbean.

Roanoke [rohanohk] 37°16N 79°56W, pop (2000e) 94 900. City in SW Virginia, USA, on the Roanoke R; settled, 1740; airfield; railway.

Roaring Forties *westerlies*

Robards, Jason, Jr [rohbah(r)dz] (1922–2000) Actor, born in Chicago, IL. The son of **Jason Robards Sr** (1892–1963), he won acclaim as a stage actor in *The Iceman Cometh* (1956) and *Long Day's Journey Into Night* (1957). He won Best Supporting Actor Oscars for *All the President's Men* (1976) and *Julia* (1977). He was awarded the National Medal of Arts in 1997.

Robbe-Grillet, Alain [rob greeyay] (1922–) Novelist, born in Brest, France. After his first novel, *Les Gommes* (1953, The Erasers), he emerged as the leader of the *nouveau roman* group, contributing to the form such novels as *La Jalousie* (1959, Jealousy). Later novels include *Un Régicide* (1978) and *La Belle Captive* (1995). He also wrote film scenarios, notably *L'année dernière à Marienbad* (1961, Last Year at Marienbad).

robber fly An active, predatory fly commonly found in open sunny habitats; forelegs robust, armed with strong bristles for gripping insect prey caught in flight. (Order: Diptera. Family: Asilidae, c.5000 species.)

Longest Rivers

Name	Outflow	Length[*]	
		km	mi
Nile-Kagera-Ruvuvu-Ruvusu-Luvironza	Mediterranean Sea (Egypt)	6 690	4 160
Amazon-Ucayali-Tambo-Ene-Apurimac	Atlantic Ocean (Brazil)	6 570	4 080
Mississippi-Missouri-Jefferson-Beaverhead-Red Rock	Gulf of Mexico (USA)	6 020	3 740
Chang Jiang (Yangtze)	E China Sea (China)	5 980	3 720
Yenisey-Angara-Selenga-Ider	Kara Sea (Russia)	5 870	3 650
Amur-Argun-Kerulen	Tartar Strait (Russia)	5 780	3 590
Ob-Irtysh	Gulf of Ob, Kara Sea (Russia)	5 410	3 360
Plata-Parana-Grande	Atlantic Ocean (Argentina/Uruguay)	4 880	3 030
Huang Ho (Yellow)	Yellow Sea (China)	4 840	3 010
Congo (Zaire)-Lualaba	Atlantic Ocean (Angola-D.R. Congo)	4 630	2 880
Lena	Laptev Sea (Russia)	4 400	2 730
Mackenzie-Slave-Peace-Finlay	Beaufort Sea (Canada)	4 240	2 630
Mekong	S China Sea (Vietnam)	4 180	2 600
Niger	Gulf of Guinea (Nigeria)	4 100	2 550

*Lengths are given to the nearest 10 km/mi, and include the river plus tributaries comprising the longest watercourse.

robbery The taking of personal property from the person or immediate presence of another against his or her will through the use of violence or intimidation. A threat of violence is sufficient.

Robbia, Luca della (c.1400–82) Sculptor, born in Florence, Italy. He executed 10 panels of figures for the cathedral there (1431–40), and later made a bronze door with ten panels of figures in relief for its sacristy (1448–67). He is also known for his figures in terracotta.

Robbins, Frederick C(hapman) (1916–2003) Physiologist and paediatrician, born in Auburn, AL. He joined the Children's Hospital, Boston, where he helped devise techniques for cultivating the poliomyelitis virus. Professor of paediatrics at Case Western Reserve University, Cleveland (1952–80), he shared the 1954 Nobel Prize for Physiology or Medicine.

Robbins, Jerome (1918–98) Dancer, choreographer, and director, born in New York City. His collaboration with Leonard Bernstein resulted in his most famous musical, *West Side Story* (1957).

Robbins (of Clare Market), Lionel Charles Robbins, Baron (1898–1984) Economist and educationist, born in Sipson, Greater London. Professor of economics at the London School of Economics (1929–61), he chaired the **Robbins Committee** on the expansion of higher education in the UK (1961–4).

Robbins, Tim (1958–) Film actor, director, and writer, born in West Govina, CA. He wrote, directed, and composed the songs for the critically acclaimed *Bob Roberts* (1992). His films include (as actor) *The Shawshank Redemption* (1994), *Arlington Road* (1999), *Mystic River* (2003), and *War of the Worlds* (2005), and (as producer/director/writer) *Dead Man Walking* (1995) and *Cradle Will Rock* (1999). He wrote and directed the controversial play *Embedded* (2004), satirizing journalistic involvement in US military operations.

Robert I *Bruce, Robert*

Robert II (1316–90) King of Scots (1371–90), the son of Walter, hereditary steward of Scotland. He founded the Stuart royal dynasty.

Robert, Duke of Normandy *Henry I* (of England)

Roberts (of Kandahar, Pretoria, and Waterford), Frederick Sleigh Roberts, 1st Earl (1832–1914) British field marshal, born in Cawnpore, India. He served as supreme commander in South Africa during the Boer War, relieving Kimberley (1900).

Roberts, John Glover, Jr (1955–) Lawyer and jurist, born in Buffalo, NY. He studied at Harvard University (1976) and Harvard Law School (1979). His later posts include special assistant to the US Attorney General (1981–2) and associate counsel to President Reagan (1982–6). He entered private law practice in 1986 but left to serve in the George H W Bush administration as deputy solicitor general (1989–93). In July 2005, President George W Bush nominated him as Associate Judge to the US Supreme Court, and in 2006 he succeeded William Rehnquist as Chief Justice.

Roberts, Julia, originally **Julie Fiona Roberts** (1967–) Film actress, born in Smyrna, GA. She made her screen debut in 1988, and became well known following *Steel Magnolias* (1989) and *Pretty Woman* (1990). Later films include *Notting Hill* (1999), *Erin Brockovich* (2000), *Ocean's Eleven* (2001, sequel 2004), and *Closer* (2004).

Roberts, Tom (1856–1931) Painter, born in Dorchester, Dorset. His best work, which deals with pioneering life in the bush, was produced in Australia in the late 1880s and 1890s.

Robertson (of Port Ellen), George (Islay MacNeill) Robertson, Baron (1946–) British statesman, born on the island of Islay, Scotland. He was elected an MP in 1978, rising to be spokesman on Scotland in the shadow cabinet (1993–7). He became defence secretary (1997–9) in the Labour government, and was appoin-

ted secretary-general of NATO in 1999, stepping down at the end of 2003.

Robertson, Pat popular name of **Marion Gordon Robertson** (1930–) Religious broadcaster and politician, born in Lexington, VA. He founded the Christian Broadcast Network in 1960 and began his popular religious talk show, the '700 Club', in 1968. He realized early the possibilities of cable television for reaching a targeted audience, and became one of the most influential 'televangelists' of the 1980s.

Robeson, Paul (Bustill) [rohbsn] (1898–1976) Singer and actor, born in Princeton, NJ. He appeared in works ranging from *Show Boat* to *Othello*, gave song recitals, notably of Negro spirituals, and appeared in numerous films. In the 1950s, his left-wing views caused him to leave the USA for Europe (1958–63), and he retired after his return.

Robespierre, Maximilien François Marie Isidore de [rohbspyair] (1758–94) French revolutionary leader, born in Arras. He became a prominent member of the Jacobin Club, and emerged in the National Assembly as a popular radical, known as 'the Incorruptible'. In 1793 he became a member of the Committee of Public Safety and for three months dominated the country, introducing the Reign of Terror and the cult of the Supreme Being. But as his ruthless exercise of power increased, his popularity waned. He was guillotined on the orders of the Revolutionary Tribunal.

Robey, Sir George [rohbee], originally **George Edward Wade** (1869–1954) Comedian, born in Herne Hill, Kent. Dubbed 'the Prime Minister of Mirth', he was famous for his bowler hat, black coat, hooked stick, and thickly painted eyebrows.

robin A bird of the thrush family Turdidae (44 species), usually with a red breast; especially the Eurasian/N African robin (*Erithacus rubecula*); traditionally seen as a symbol of Christmas.

Robin Goodfellow In English 16th-c and 17th-c popular belief, a mischievous fairy, also called **Puck** or **Hobgoblin**. His characteristic activities are listed in Shakespeare's *A Midsummer Night's Dream* (2.i).

Robin Hood A legendary 13th-c outlaw, known for his archery, who lived in Sherwood Forest in the English N Midlands, celebrated in ballads dating from the 14th-c. He protected the poor, and outwitted, robbed, or killed the wealthy and officials, notably the Sheriff of Nottingham.

Robinson, Anne (1944–) Journalist and television presenter, born in Liverpool, Merseyside. A journalist for several newspapers, she also presented the BBC consumer programme *Watchdog* (1993–2001). In 2000 she became known as the formidable presenter of the quiz game *The Weakest Link*.

Robinson, Edward G, originally **Emanuel Goldenberg** (1893–1973) Film actor, born in Bucharest, Romania. He became famous as the gangster Rico in *Little Caesar* (1930), a typecasting which dogged him for many years. He was posthumously awarded a special Academy Award in 1973.

Robinson, Edwin Arlington (1869–1935) Poet, born in Head Tide, ME. He received Pulitzer Prizes for his *Collected Poems* (1922), *The Man Who Died Twice* (1924), and *Tristram* (1927).

Robinson, (William) Heath (1872–1944) Artist, cartoonist, and book illustrator, born in London. His fame rests mainly on his humorous drawings satirizing the machine age, displaying 'Heath Robinson' contraptions of absurd and complicated design but with highly practical and simple aims, such as the raising of one's hat.

Robinson, Jackie, popular name of **Jack Roosevelt Robinson** (1919–72) The first black player to play major league baseball, born in Cairo, GA. He became a star infielder and outfielder for the Brooklyn Dodgers (1947–56), and led them to six National League pennants and one World Series, in 1955.

Robinson, Joan V(iolet), *née* **Maurice** (1903–83) Economist, born in Camberley, Surrey. She was one of the most influential economic theorists of her time, and a leader of the Cambridge School, which developed macro-economic theories of growth and distribution, based on the work of Keynes.

Robinson, Mary, *née* **Bourke** (1944–) Constitutional lawyer, politician, and president of the Irish Republic (1990–7), born in Ballina, Mayo, Ireland. She left the Labour Party in protest against the Anglo-Irish Agreement (1985), which she argued did not represent the rights of Unionists in Northern Ireland. In 1990 she became the first woman to hold the office of President of the Republic and the first successful candidate to be nominated from outside the two largest parties in the state. She was the UN High Commisioner for Human Rights, 1997–2002.

Robinson, Sugar Ray, originally **Walker Smith** (1921–89) Professional boxer, born in Detroit, MI. He turned professional in 1940, and was never knocked out in 201 contests. He held the world welterweight title (1946–51) and the world middleweight title (1950–1).

roble beech A tree similar to the beech, and replacing that genus in the S hemisphere; also called **southern beech**. It differs chiefly by having nuts in threes, enclosed in a spiny or scaly case. (Genus: *Nothofagus*, 35 species. Family: Fagaceae.)

robotics (cybernetics) The application of automatic machines (*robots*) to perform tasks traditionally done by humans. Robots are widely used in industry to perform simple repetitive tasks accurately and without tiring, and to work in environments which are dangerous to human operators. They can also be used as sensors, equipped for artificial vision, touch, and temperature sensing. If the robots are in human form, they are called *androids*.

robotics (dance) *street dance*

Rob Roy (Gaelic 'Red Robert'), nickname of **Robert MacGregor** or **Campbell** (1671–1734) Outlaw, born in Buchanan, Stirling, Scotland. After his name were seized by the Duke of Montrose, he gathered his clansmen and became a brigand. His career gave rise to many stories about his brave exploits. His life was romanticized in the novel by Sir Walter Scott.

Robson, Dame Flora (McKenzie) (1902–84) Actress, born in South Shields, Tyne and Wear. She became famous for her historical roles in plays and films, such as Queen Elizabeth in *Fire over England* (1931).

Rochas, Marcel [rosha] (1902–55) Fashion designer, born in Paris. He set up a couture house in Paris in 1925, launching his first fragrances in 1931, and the sheepskin jacket in 1942. The couture house closed upon his death in 1955, but his wife Hélène took over the perfume department until she left the company in 1989.

Rochdale 53°38N 2°09W, pop (2001e) 205 200. Town in Greater Manchester, NW England; railway; textiles (especially cotton); Co-operative Society founded here in 1844; football league team, Rochdale.

Rochester (UK), ancient **Durobrivae** 51°24N 0°30E, pop (2000e) 25 500. Town in Kent, SE England; railway; cathedral (12th-c); castle (11th-c).

Rochester (USA) 43°10N 77°37W, pop (2000e) 219 800. City in W New York, USA; port on Genesee R; first settled, 1811; city status, 1834; airfield; railway; university (1850).

rock A naturally occurring material which comprises the solid Earth. Rocks are an assemblage of minerals, and are classified according to origin.

rock ape *Barbary ape*

rock art *Palaeolithic / Paleolithic art*

Rockefeller, John D(avison) [rokuhfeler] (1839–1937) Industrialist and philanthropist, born in Richford, NY. In 1875 he founded with his brother **William Rockefeller** (1841–1922) the Standard Oil Company, securing control of the US oil trade. He gave over $500 million in aid of medical research, universities, and churches, and established in 1913 the **Rockefeller Foundation** 'to promote the wellbeing of mankind'. His son, **John D Rockefeller, Jr** (1847–1960) built the Rockefeller Center in New York City. His third son, **Nelson A(ldrich) Rockefeller** (1908–79), became Republican Governor of New York State (1958–73), and was vice-president (1974–7) under President Ford.

Rockefeller Center A complex of 14 skyscrapers commissioned by John D Rockefeller Jr (1874–1960) and built (1931–40) in Manhattan, New York City. The centre includes the Radio City Music Hall.

rocket A self-propelling device in which the fuel substances needed to produce the propulsion are carried internally. The term most commonly refers to space vehicles, although it can also apply to distress rockets and fireworks. In addition, rockets are used to power missiles, and for supersonic and assisted-take-off aeroplane propulsion. **Solid fuel rockets** commonly use a mixture of nitrocellulose and nitroglycerin as the fuel source. The more efficient **liquid fuel rockets** use kerosene (fuel) and liquid oxygen (oxidant).

Rockhampton 23°22S 150°32E, pop (2000e) 65 600. City in Queensland, Australia, on the Fitzroy R; railway; university (1992); centre of Australia's largest beef-producing area.

Rockingham, Charles Watson Wentworth, 2nd Marquess of (1730–82) British statesman and prime minister (1765–6, 1782). He repealed the Stamp Act, affecting the American colonies, and opposed Britain's war against the colonists. He died soon after taking office in 1782.

rock music A type of popular music, originally called **rock and roll**, which spread throughout the USA and Europe in the 1950s. It began as a basically simple musical style, dominated by a strong dance beat and by the use of the electric guitar. It developed out of country and western, and more particularly from rhythm and blues – a style which previously had been played almost exclusively by US black artists. The term 'rock and roll' was popularized by Cleveland disc jockey Alan Freed. The music gained widespread popularity during the late 1950s, when major artists included Bill Haley, Elvis Presley, and Chuck Berry. Primarily aimed at and enjoyed by a young audience, it became an important symbol of teenage rebellion. Since then, rock music has diversified into a distinct series of subgenres – such as **hard rock** in the late 1960s and early 1970s and **punk rock** in the late 1970s – most of which have been characterized not only by musical differences but by their own associated features in dress, lifestyle, and (from the 1980s onwards) video publicity.

rockrose A small evergreen shrub, mostly native to the Mediterranean region and parts of Asia; flowers 5-petalled, white, yellow, or red. (Genus: *Helianthemum*, 100 species. Family: Cistaceae.)

rock salt *halite*

Rocky Mountain goat A wild goat (*Oreamnos americanus*) native to the mountains of North America; thick shaggy white coat and short backward-curved horns; also known as **mountain goat**, **goat antelope**, or **antelope goat**.

Rocky Mountains or **Rockies** Major mountain system of W North America, extending from C New Mexico generally NNW through the USA, into W Canada and N Alaska and reaching the Bering Strait N of the Arctic Circle; about 4800 km/3000 mi long; forms the continental divide, separating the Pacific drainage from the Atlantic and Arctic; highest point in the USA Mt Elbert (4399 m/14 432 ft), in Canada Mt Robson (3954 m/12 972 ft) important source of mineral wealth; several national parks.

Rocky Mountain sheep *bighorn*

Rococo [rokohkoh] (Fr *rocaille*, 'rock-work') In art history, the period following the late Baroque in European art and design. It flourished especially in France and S Germany c.1700–50, until superseded by the Neoclassical taste spreading from Rome. Rococo sought effects of charm and delicacy on a small scale – surface effects rather than bold masses. It was therefore most successful as a style of interior decoration.

Roddenberry, Gene, popular name of **Eugene Wesley Roddenberry** (1921–91) Writer, and film and television producer, born in El Paso, TX. A former pilot and policeman, he became a full-time writer in the 1950s. He is best known as the creator and producer of *Star Trek*.

Roddick, Andy, popular name of **Andrew Stephen Roddick** (1982–) Tennis player, born in Omaha, NE. A junior number 1 world champion in 2000 (the youngest American to achieve this position since rankings began), he turned professional and won the US Open that year. He went on to reach the semi-finals (2003) and final (2005) at Wimbledon, and in 2006 he claimed the Cincinnati Masters title and reached the final of the US Open. At the beginning of 2007 he had a world ranking of 6.

Roddick, Dame Anita (Lucia) (1943–) Retail entrepreneur, born in Brighton, East Sussex. In 1976 she opened a small shop in Brighton selling beauty products made from natural products, not tested on animals, and supplied in refillable containers. Her growing commitment to ecology and the Third World brought great success to the Body Shop chain in the 1980s. She resigned in 2002 but remained as consultant, and launched her own publishing company the following year. Body Shop was acquired by French cosmetics company L'Oreal in 2006.

rodent A mammal of worldwide order Rodentia (3 suborders, 30 families, 1702 species); 40% of all living mammal species are rodents; chisel-like upper and lower incisor teeth grow continuously, kept short by gnawing.

rodeo A US sport, consisting mainly of competitive riding and a range of skills which derive from cowboy ranching practices. The events include bronco riding, with and without saddle, bull riding, steer wrestling, calf roping, and team roping.

Rodin, (René François) Auguste [rohdĩ] (1840–1917) Sculptor, born in Paris. The great 'La Porte de l'enfer' (The Gate of Hell) was commissioned for the Musée des Arts Décoratifs in 1880. Among his other works is 'Le Penseur' (1904, The Thinker), in front of the Panthéon in Paris.

Rodman, Dennis (Keith), nickname **The Worm** (1961–) Basketball player, born in Trenton, NJ. He started with the Detroit Pistons, winning two championships (1989–90) with them before joining the Chicago Bulls, winning championships in 1996–8. He signed for the LA Lakers in 1998, but was waived by the club after less than three months. He is the author of *Bad As I Wanna Be* (2003) and *Walk On the Wild Side* (1997).

Rodrigues Island [rohdreegez] 19°45S 63°20E, pop (2000e) 42 900. Island in the Indian Ocean; part of the Mascarene Is; a dependency of Mauritius; rises to 396 m/1299 ft at Mt Limon; chief town, Port Mathurin.

rods and cones Photoreceptor cells of the vertebrate retina, so called because of their shapes. Rods are sensitive to dim light (*scotopic*) and function at twilight. Cones are sensitive to bright light (*photopic*) and function in daylight.

Roentgen, Wilhelm Konrad von *Röntgen*

Rogation Days In the Christian Church, the three days before Ascension Day, once observed with fasting, processions, and prayers to God for a successful harvest (**rogation**, Lat *rogare*, 'to ask').

Rogers, Carl R(ansom) (1902–87) Psychotherapist, born in Oak Park, IL. His book *Client-centered Therapy* (1951) developed the notion of open therapy sessions and encounter groups in which patients talk out their problems under the supervision of a passive therapist.

Rogers (of Riverside), Richard Rogers, Lord (1933–) British architect, born in Florence, Italy. He studied at the Architectural Association, London, and was a founder member of Team 4 with Norman Foster. Two notable and controversial works are the Beaubourg or Pompidou Centre, Paris (1971–9), with Renzo Piano, and Lloyds of London (1979–85). Later projects include the Millennium Dome, London (2000), the Welsh Assembly building, Cardiff (2006), and Terminal 4 of Barajas Airport, Madrid, winner of the 2006 Stirling Prize. He was created a life peer in 1996.

Roget, Peter Mark [rozhay] (1779–1869) Scholar and physician, born in London. He is best known for his *Thesaurus of English Words and Phrases* (1852).

Röhm, Ernst [roem], also spelled **Roehm** (1887–1934) German soldier, politician and Nazi leader, born in Munich, Germany. The organizer and commander of the stormtroopers ('Brownshirts'), his plans to increase the power of this force led to his execution on Hitler's orders.

Rolfe, Frederick William (Serafino Austin Lewis Mary), pseudonym **Baron Corvo** (1860–1913) Novelist, historian, and essayist, born in London. He converted to Roman Catholicism, but failed in his efforts to join the priesthood. His best-known novel is *Hadrian the Seventh* (1904).

Rolland, Romain [rolã] (1866–1944) Writer, born in Clamecy, France. He published several biographies and a 10-volume novel, *Jean-Christophe* (1904–12), and in 1915 was awarded the Nobel Prize for Literature.

roller A crow-like bird of the widespread Old World family Coraciidae (11 species); usually blue and brown; somersaults in flight when displaying (hence its name).

roller skating A pastime first seen in Liège, Belgium, in 1760. The modern four-wheeled skate was introduced by the US inventor James L Plymton in 1863. Competitions exist as for ice skating: individual, pairs, dancing, and speed skating. Blade-type skates are now replacing the corner-wheel model.

Rolling Stones, The Rock group, with members **Mick Jagger** (1943–) vocals, **Keith Richards** (1943–) guitar, **Bill Wyman** (1936–) bass, **Charlie Watts** (1942–) drums, **Ron Wood** (1947–) guitar, former member **Brian Jones** (1944–69) guitar, one of the most successful popular music groups to emerge in the 1960s. They first performed together in 1962. Among their hits were 'Satisfaction' and 'Jumpin' Jack Flash'. Still recording after four decades, they released the album *A Bigger Bang* in 2005.

Rollo, originally **Hrolf** (c.860–c.932) Viking leader who secured from Charles III of France in 911 a large district on condition of being baptized and becoming Charles's vassal. This grant was the nucleus of the duchy of Normandy.

Rolls, C(harles) S(tewart) (1877–1910) Motorist and aeronaut, born in London. From 1895 he experimented with the earliest motor cars, and combined with Henry Royce for their production.

Rolls-Royce A major British firm of car engine and aero-engine manufacturers, founded in 1906. In the 1970s the firm was split into two separate companies, following financial problems caused by the high cost of aero-engine research and development.

ROM [rom] Acronym of **read-only memory**, a type of computer memory which can only be read from; the data is fixed during the manufacture of the chip. ROM is used where the data does not have to be altered.

Rom A travelling people whose origins lie in the subcontinent of India, now concentrated in S Europe, but found throughout the world; popularly called **Gypsies**, but not by the people themselves. 'Traveller' is generally the preferred term in Britain. There are an estimated 9–12 million Rom today, worldwide.

Romains, Jules [romĩ], pseudonym of **Louis Henri Jean Farigoule** (1885–1972) Writer, born in Saint-Julien-Chapteuil, France. His poems *La Vie unanime* (1908) brought about the Unanimist school, devoted to a belief in universal brotherhood and group consciousness. His best-known works are the comedy *Knock, ou le triomphe de la médecine* (1923, Dr Knock, or the triumph of medicine) and the 27-volume cycle of novels, *Les Hommes de bonne volonté* (1932–46, Men of Good Will).

Roman Catholicism The doctrine, worship, and life of the Roman Catholic Church (1120 million members in 2007). A direct line of succession is claimed from the earliest Christian communities, centring on the city of Rome, where St Peter (claimed as the first bishop of Rome) was martyred. The Church was the only effective agency of civilization in Europe, and after the 11th-c schism with the Byzantine or Eastern Church, it was the dominant force in the Western world, the Holy Roman Empire. The Protestant Reformation of the 16th-c inspired revival, the most dramatic reforms being enacted by the two Vatican Councils of the 19th-c and 20th-c. The Second Vatican Council (1962–5) signalled a new era, with a new ecumenical spirit pervading the Church. Great emphasis was placed on the Church as the 'people of God', with the laity being given a much more active part in liturgy. Doctrine is declared by the pope, or by a General Council with the approval of the pope, and is summarized in the Nicene Creed. Scripture and the tradition of the Church are both accepted as authoritative. Principal doctrines are similar to those of mainstream Protestant and Orthdox Churches – God as Trinity, creation, redemption, the person and work of Jesus Christ, and the place of the Holy Spirit – the chief doctrinal differences being the role of the Church in salvation, and its sacramental theology. Ancient traditional practices such as the veneration of the Virgin Mary and the Saints, or the Stations of the Cross, are still regarded as valuable aids to devotion.

Romance languages The languages which developed from the 'vulgar' or spoken form of Latin used throughout the Roman Empire. The major ones are Italian, French, Spanish, Portuguese, and Romanian, all of which are official languages in their respective states. There are also several other varieties, such as Sardinian, Rhaetian (dialectal variants in N Italy and Switzerland), and Catalan, used mainly in NE Spain. Over 700 million people now speak a Romance language or a creole based on one. French is spoken by c.72 million as a mother-tongue, and is used as a second language by a further 200 million; Spanish is spoken by over 270 million; Portuguese by c.175 million; and Italian by c.63 million.

Roman Curia (Lat *curia*, 'court') An organization in the Vatican (Rome) which administers the affairs of the Roman Catholic Church under the authority of the pope. It is comprised of congregations (administrative), tribunals (judicial), and offices (ministerial).

Roman history The Monarchy (753–509 BC). Founded, according to tradition, in 753 BC, Rome was initially ruled by kings, of whom Romulus was the first and Tarquinius Superbus the seventh and last.

The Republic (509–31 BC). Brought into being with the overthrow of the monarchy, the Republican system of government was designed to prevent a tyrant ever ruling Rome again. Executive power was entrusted to two annually elected officials (*consuls*); their advisory council, the Senate, provided the necessary elements of experience and continuity. The system brought stability, and Rome grew rapidly from a small city-state into an empire. The Republic perished at Actium after decades of civil war.

The Empire (31 BC–AD 476 in the W, AD 1453 in the E). The Roman Empire was the creation of one man, Augustus. Pretending that he had restored the Republic, in reality he and his successors were absolute monarchs. Abroad, the expansionism of Republican days was abandoned, and territorial limits were set – the Rhine and Danube in Europe, the Euphrates in Asia. Subsequent modifications were few; Britain (43), Dacia, and

Arabia (both annexed by Trajan in 106) were the only significant later additions. The Rhine–Danube frontier was the hardest to hold, and in the 5th-c, hordes of tribesmen (eg Huns, Vandals, Ostrogoths) poured into the W provinces carrying all before them. The last emperor, Romulus Augustulus, was deposed in 476. The E provinces proved more resilient; here the barbarian challenge was contained for another thousand years, until the E capital Constantinople fell to the Ottoman Turks in 1453.

Romani The language of the Rom, of Indo-Aryan origin, earlier spelled **Romany**. There are now many dialects, which have taken on features of the languages with which they have come into contact in various parts of the world.

Romania *p.795*

Romanian *Romance languages*

romanization The use of the Roman alphabet to replace a language's writing system constructed on a different principle. This procedure has been very common in language planning, especially in countries where the native script is non-alphabetic in character, as in Chinese logographic writing.

Roman numerals The Roman symbols for numbers, which have a fixed value, and do not use the concept of place-value. The symbols generally used are I = 1, V = 5, X = 10, L = 50, C = 100, D = 500, and M = 1000. A symbol may be repeated up to three times (eg XVIII = 18).

Romanovs [rohmanofs] The second (and last) Russian royal dynasty (1613–1917). The first Romanov tsar (Mikhail) was elected in 1613. The Romanovs ruled as absolute autocrats, allowing no constitutional or legal checks on their political power. The dynasty ended with the execution of Nicholas II and his immediate family in 1918.

Roman roads *p.796*

Romans, Letter to the A New Testament book, written by the apostle Paul in c.55–8, which presents his understanding of salvation for both Gentiles and Jews, and warns against libertine and legalistic interpretations of the Christian message.

Romanticism (literature) A large-scale movement of the mind in the late 18th/early 19th-c, which affected the whole of human understanding and experience. Romanticism placed the individual at the centre of his/her own world, and permitted the free expression of feeling and emotion. Writers associated with Romanticism are, in England, Wordsworth, Coleridge, Blake, Keats, Shelley, and Byron; in Germany, Goethe and Schiller; in France, Rousseau and Hugo. Artists included Turner, Constable, and Goya. In music, the period saw the growth of the modern symphony orchestra, and a general expansion of the inherited genres of opera, symphony, concerto, etc, in which composers could express a response to literature and the other arts. The works of the major Romantic composers (eg Beethoven, Mahler, Wagner) form the staple repertory of modern concert halls and opera houses.

Romany *Rom; Romani*

Romberg, Sigmund (1887–1951) Composer of operettas, born in Nagykanizsa, Hungary. He settled in the USA in 1909. Of more than 70 works, his most famous were *Blossom Time* (1921), *The Student Prince* (1924), *The Desert Song* (1926), and *The New Moon* (1928).

Rome, Ital **Roma** 41°53N 12°30E, pop (2000e) 2 820 000. Capital city of Italy; on the R Tiber; on the left bank are the Seven Hills of Rome – the Capitoline (50 m/165 ft), Quirinal (52 m/172 ft), Viminal (56 m/185 ft), Esquiline (53 m/175 ft), Palatine (51 m/168 ft), Aventine (46 m/152 ft), and Caelian (50 m/165 ft) – on which the ancient city was built during the 8th-c BC; centre of the Roman Empire; sacked by Germanic tribes, 5th-c; ecclesiastical centre from 6th-c; Vatican City on W bank; capital of unified Italy, 1871; two airports; railway; metro; university (1303); important centre of fashion and film; headquarters of

Romania

300 km
150 mi

☐ International Airport ∴ World heritage site

Roumania, or **Rumania**, official name **Republic of Romania**, Romanian **Republica România**

Local name România

Timezone GMT +2

Area 237 500 km²/91 675 sq mi

Population total (2002e) 21 667 000

Status Republic

Date of independence 1918

Capital Bucharest

Languages Romanian (official), with French, Hungarian, and German widely spoken

Ethnic groups Romanian (89%), Hungarian (7%), German (2%), Ukrainian, Serb, Croat, Russian, Turk, and Gypsy (2%)

Religions Eastern Orthodox Christian (80%), Roman Catholic (6%), Calvinist, Lutheran, Baptist (4%)

Physical features Carpathian Mts form the heart of the country; highest peak, Negoiul, 2548 m/8359 ft; crossed by many rivers; c.3500 glacial ponds, lakes, and coastal lagoons; over 25% of land forested.

Climate Continental, with cold, snowy winters and warm summers; winters can be severe; mildest along the Black Sea coast; average annual temperatures range from 7°C (N), to 11°C (S), -3°C (Jan), 24°C (Jul); average annual rainfall 579 mm/22·8 in.

Currency 1 Leu (plural lei) (ROL) = 100 bani

Economy Gradual change from agricultural to industrial economy (since World War 2); state owns nearly 37% of farm land, mainly organized as collectives and state farms; wheat, maize, sugar beet, fruit, potatoes; livestock; oil, natural gas; iron and steel, metallurgy, engineering, chemicals, textiles, electronics, timber; tourism.

GDP (2002e) $169·3 bn, per capita $7600

Human Development Index (2002) 0·775

History Formed from the unification of Moldavia and Wallachia, 1862; monarchy created, 1866; Transylvania, Bessarabia, and Bucovina united with Romania, 1918; support given to Germany in World War 2; occupied by Soviet forces, 1944; monarchy abolished and People's Republic declared, 1947; Socialist Republic declared, 1965; increasingly independent from the USSR from the 1960s; leading political force was the Romanian Communist Party, led by dictator Nicolae Ceaușescu; popular uprising due to violent repression of protest led to the overthrow of the Ceaușescu regime, 1989; new constitution, 1991; joined EU 2007; governed by a President, Prime Minister, Chamber of Deputies, and Senate.

Republic

Head of State

1947–8 Mihai Sadoveanu *Interim*
1948–52 Constantin I Parhon
1952–8 Petru Groza
1958–61 Ion Georghe Maurer
1961–5 Georghe Gheorghiu-Dej
1965–7 Chivu Stoica
1967–89 Nicolae Ceausescu
1989–96 Ion Iliescu
1996–2000 Emil Constantinescu
2000–4 Ion Iliescu
2004– Traian Basescu

Head of Government

1980–3 Ilie Verdet
1983–9 Constantin Dascalescu
1989–91 Petre Roman
1991–2 Theodor Stolojan
1992–6 Nicolae Vacaroiu
1996–8 Victor Ciorbea
1998–9 Radu Vasile
1999–2000 Mugur Isarescu
2000–4 Adrian Nastase
2004– Calin Tariceanu

many cultural and research institutions; centre of Rome is a world heritage site; Palazzo Venezia (15th-c), Forum Romanum (AD 113), Colosseum (from AD 75), Pantheon (27 BC), Trevi Fountain (1762); replica of London's Globe Theatre (2003); numerous churches, notably St Peter's (in the Vatican), St John Lateran (Rome's cathedral).

Rome, Treaties of *EURATOM; European Community*

Romero (y Galdames), Oscar (Arnulfo) [rohmayroh] (1917–80) Roman Catholic clergyman, born in Ciudad Barrios, El Salvador. He studied at the Gregorian University in Rome, was ordained in 1942, and became bishop in 1970 and archbishop in 1977. An outspoken critic of the government, he was shot down while celebrating Mass a year after he was nominated for the Nobel Peace Prize. In March 2005, 25 years after his death, the Roman Catholic Church moved to bestow sainthood on him, beginning with the process of beatification.

Rommel, Erwin (Johannes Eugen) (1891–1944) German field marshal, born in Heidenheim, Germany. He led a Panzer division during the 1940 invasion of France, then commanded the Afrika Korps, where he achieved major successes, but was eventually driven into retreat. He condoned the plot against Hitler's life, and after its discovery committed suicide.

Romney, George [romnee, ruhmnee] (1734–1802) Painter, born in Dalton-in-Furness, Lancashire. His reputation rivalled that of

Roman roads

Chief Roman roads in Britain

CALEDONIA

Antonine Wall

Firth of Forth

Firth of Clyde

Hadrian's Wall

Carlisle
Luguvallium

Wallsend

Solway Firth

HIBERNIA

Dere Street

York
Eboracum

Chester
Deva

Lincoln
Lindum

Watling Street

Wroxeter
Viroconium

Ermine Street

London
Londinium

Colchester
Cumulodunum

Bath
Aquae Sulis

Richborough
Rutupiae

Dover
Dubris

Exeter
Isca

Chichester
Noviomagus

A network of over 80 000 km/50 000 mi of usually straight roads radiating from ancient Rome. Built primarily for military purposes, the roads also served an important commercial function. Main routes were constructed on an earth footing with a layer of small stones in mortar above, on top of which was a hard filling surfaced with stone slabs. The first roads were built with a slope and ditches, allowing water to drain away. The Appian Way, built in the 3rd-c BC and linking Rome with present-day Capua, was the first great Roman road. The Aurelian Way connected Rome with present-day Pisa, while the Flaminian Way served as the main northern route.

Reynolds, his many pictures of Lady Hamilton being particularly well known.

Romulus and Remus [romyulus, reemus] In Roman legend, the twin sons of Mars and the Vestal Virgin Rhea Silvia. They were thrown into the Tiber, which carried them to the Palatine, where they were suckled by a she-wolf. In building the wall of Rome, Remus was killed by Romulus. Having founded Rome, Romulus was later carried off in a thunderstorm.

Romulus Augustulus [romyulus awguhstyulus] (5th-c AD) The last Roman emperor of the West, deposed by Odoacer in 476.

Ronaldinho (1980–) Footballer, born in Porto Alegre, Brazil. He began his career in 1997 with Gremio de Porto Alegre, moving to French side Paris Saint-Germain in 2001. In his Brazilian national team debut in 1999 he scored his first international goal, against Venezuela, to win the Copa America, and was a key player in his team's victory in the 2002 World Cup. In 2003 he

signed for Barcelona, his honours with the club including FIFA World Player of the Year (2004, 2005), European Footballer of the Year (2005), and FifPro Player of the Year (2005, 2006).

Ronaldo (Luiz Nazario de Lima) [ronaldoh], nickname **Ro-Ro** (1976–) Footballer, born in Itaguai, Brazil. A forward, he played for Cruzeiro, Brazil, then PSV Eindhoven and Barcelona, moving to Inter Milan (1997–2002), Real Madrid (2002–7), and AC Milan (2007–). While at Barcelona he scored a Spanish league record of 34 goals in a season, his team also winning the European Cup Winners' Cup and the Spanish cup final. He has been FIFA World Footballer of the Year three times (1996, 1997, 2002) and European Player of the Year twice (1997, 2002). By mid-July 2006 he had won 97 caps.

Ronay, Egon [ronay, eegon] (1920–) Gastronome and writer, born in Hungary. He emigrated to England in 1946 and opened his own restaurant in London (1952–5). He founded his first annual guide, *Egon Ronay's Guide to Hotels and Restaurants*, in 1956.

roncey *cob*

rondo A musical structure in which restatements of the initial theme are separated by contrasting episodes, eg on the pattern A–B–A–C–A–B–A, perhaps with an introduction and a coda.

Ronsard, Pierre de [rõsah(r)] (1524–85) Renaissance poet, born in La Possonière, France. A leader of the *Pléiade* group, his early works include *Odes* (1550) and *Amours* (1552), and he later wrote reflections on the state of the country.

Röntgen, Wilhelm Konrad von [roentguhn], also spelled **Roentgen** (1845–1923) Physicist, born in Lennep, Germany. In 1895 he discovered the electromagnetic rays which he called X-rays, for which he was awarded the first Nobel Prize for Physics in 1901.

röntgen or **roentgen** [rontguhn, -juhn] The unit of exposure to ionizing radiation; symbol R; named after Wilhelm Röntgen.

Röntgen rays *X-rays*

rook A crow (*Corvus frugilegus*) native to Europe, Asia, and N Africa; black with pale bare patch on face; forms dense nesting colonies in trees (*rookeries*).

Roon, Albrecht (Theodor Emil), Graf (Count) **von** (1803–79) Prussian army officer, born near Kolberg, Poland (formerly Germany). He became war minister (1859–73), and effectively reorganized the army, which helped make possible Prussian victories in the wars of the 1860s and 1870s.

Rooney, Mickey, originally **Joe Yule, Jr** (1920–) Film actor, born in New York City. He became known for his child roles in the Mickey McGuire (1927–33) and Andy Hardy (1937–8) series, later films including *Boy's Town* (1938, Special Oscar), *Babes in Arms* (1939), *Summer Holiday* (1948), and *Breakfast at Tiffany's* (1961). He was married eight times, including once to film actress Ava Gardner. He returned to the stage in 1979 with the musical *Sugar Babes*, and won an Emmy for his television role in *Bill* (1982). He wrote and acted in *The Legend of O B Taggart* (1995).

Rooney, Wayne (1985–) Footballer, born in Liverpool, Merseyside. He joined Everton Football Club as a youth, and in 2002 made his premiership debut at age 16. In 2003 he became the youngest ever senior England international (17 yrs 111 days) when he debuted as a substitute in a friendly match against Australia. His first full appearance was against Turkey in a qualifying match for the Euro 2004 competition, and in a later round of the same competition he became England's youngest goal scorer. He joined Manchester United at the start of the 2004–5 season. He recovered from a broken metatarsal to join the 2006 World Cup squad, bringing his caps to 33. He was voted BBC Young Sports Personality of the Year in 2002, and his awards include Best Young Player in Europe (2004), PFA Young Player of the Year (2005, 2006), and FIFPro's World Young Player of the Year (2005).

Roosevelt, (Anna) Eleanor [rohzuhvelt, roozvelt] (1884–1962) Diplomat and humanitarian, born in New York City, the wife of Franklin D Roosevelt, whom she married in 1905, and the niece of Theodore Roosevelt. An independent activist, she had a strong part in shaping her husband's New Deal administration. During her widowhood she was a major figure in Democratic Party politics, and was much involved with the UN.

Roosevelt, Franklin D(elano) [rohzuhvelt, roozvelt], nickname **FDR** (1882–1945) US Democratic statesman and 32nd president (1933–45), born in Hyde Park, NY. He met the economic crisis with his *New Deal* for national recovery (1933), and became the only president to be re-elected three times. He strove in vain to ward off war, and was brought in by Japan's action at Pearl Harbor (1941). He met with Churchill and Stalin at Teheran (1943) and Yalta (1945).

Roosevelt, Theodore [rohzuhvelt, roozvelt], known as **Teddy Roosevelt** (1858–1919) US statesman and 26th president (1901–9), born in New York City. Elected Republican vice-president in 1900, he became president on the death (by assassination) of McKinley, and was elected in 1904 in his own right. An 'expansionist', he insisted on a strong navy, and introduced a *Square Deal* policy for social reform.

Root, Elihu (1845–1937) Jurist and statesman, born in Clinton, NY. He became US secretary of war (1899–1904) and secretary of state (1905–9), and was awarded the Nobel Prize for Peace in 1912 for his promotion of international arbitration.

root (botany) The part of a plant's axis which usually lies underground, absorbing water and nutrients, and anchoring the plant in the soil; also commonly serving as a storage organ. It develops either by repeated branching to form a mass of fibrous **lateral roots** or by forming a central **taproot** with relatively few laterals. Roots can be modified in various ways to add to their functions. **Pneumatophores** are specialized breathing roots developed in swampy, oxygen-poor ground. Roots which develop above ground are called **aerial roots**; they grow from stems or leaves, and absorb moisture direct from the atmosphere. Other types of aerial root include **buttress** or **prop roots**, which help support the stem or trunk, and **climbing** and **adhesive** roots, which help to elevate the plant.

root (linguistics) The basic element of a word, to which affixes can be added to give derived forms. For example, from the root *kind*, we may derive *un-kind*, *kind-ly*, *kind-ness*, etc. A root to which other elements have been added, so that the form can serve as the basis for inflections, is known as a **stem**.

rope A length of thick fibre used to secure objects together. The fibres are twisted or plaited for added strength, and can be natural (eg hemp, sisal, flax, jute, cotton) or synthetic (eg nylon, polyester). Wire ropes are also used as cables on suspension bridges.

Roraima, Mount [roriyma] 5°12N 60°43W. Highest peak (2875 m/ 9432 ft) in the Guiana Highlands; a giant table mountain, total area 67 km²/26 sq mi.

ro-ro [rohroh] A term derived from 'roll on, roll off', a vessel designed to permit vehicles to drive on and off the ship under their own power.

rorqual [raw(r)kwal] A baleen whale of worldwide family Balaenopteridae (6 species); longitudinal furrows on throat; small dorsal fin near tail; comprises **blue**, **sei**, **fin**, **minke**, **Bryde's**, and **humpback** whales.

Rorschach, Hermann [raw(r)shahkh] (1884–1922) Psychiatrist and neurologist, born in Zürich, Switzerland. He devised a diagnostic procedure for mental disorders based upon the patients' interpretation of a series of standardized ink blots (the **Rorschach test**).

Rosa, Salvator [rohza] (1615–73) Painter, born near Naples, Italy. He owes his reputation mainly to his landscapes of wild and savage scenes.

Rosario [rosarioh] 33°00S 60°40W, pop (2000e) 1 214 000. Third largest city in Argentina; on the R Paraná; Argentina's largest inland port, founded in 1725; airport; railway; university (1968);

cathedral; distribution outlet for local agricultural provinces; racecourse.

rosary A form of religious meditation, in which a sequence of prayers is recited using a string of beads or a knotted cord, each bead or knot representing one prayer in the sequence. In Christianity, it most commonly refers to the Rosary of the Blessed Virgin Mary, which probably dates from the 13th-c.

Roscius [roshius], in full **Quintus Roscius Gallus** (c.134–62 BC) Roman comic actor, a slave by birth. He became the greatest comic actor in Rome, and was freed from slavery by the dictator, Sulla.

Roscommon, Ir **Ros Comáin** pop (2000e) 53 000; area 2463 km²/ 951 sq mi. County in Connacht province, WC Ireland; capital, Roscommon, pop (2000e) 1500; 13th-c abbey and castle.

Rose, Irwin (1926–) Biologist, born in New York City. He worked in Yale Medical School's biochemistry department (1954–63) before becoming emeritus professor at the College of Medicine at the University of California, Irvine. In 2004, he shared the Nobel Prize for Chemistry for the discovery of ubiquitin-mediated protein degradation.

Rose, Pete(r Edward) (1942–) Baseball player, born in Cincinnati, OH. In his career (1963–86), spent mainly with the Cincinnati Reds, he had a record 4256 base hits. He was banned from baseball in 1989 after an investigation into alleged gambling offences.

rose A member of a genus of shrubs or scrambling perennials, nearly all native to the N hemisphere. They are semi-evergreen, many retaining at least some leaves throughout the winter. The flowers of wild species are 5-petalled, flat or shallowly dish-shaped, white or yellow to red or purple, and often fragrant. Cultivated forms show a greater range of colours. The orange, red, or black fruit (*hip* or *hep*) is attractive to birds and animals, and a rich source of vitamin C. Prized for centuries for their beauty and as a source of perfume, roses are probably the world's most widely cultivated ornamental plants. They are very hardy, tolerate most growing conditions, and provide a profusion of forms and colours. Several distinct types have been developed by horticulturists, and there are now over 20 000 named cultivars. The rose has been extensively used as both a decorative and a heraldic symbol, for example by the Royal Houses of York and Lancaster, and is the national emblem of England. (Genus: *Rosa*, 250 species. Family: Rosaceae.)

Roseanne, popular name of **Roseanne Barr** (1952–) Actress and producer, born in Salt Lake City, UT. After hosting a number of television specials and series, she became known for her realistic, unglamorized sitcom *Roseanne* (1988–97). Her film credits include *She-Devil* (1989) and *Blue in the Face* (1995).

Roseau [rozoh], formerly **Charlotte Town** 15°18N 61°23W, pop (2000e) 15 000. Seaport and capital town of Dominica, Windward Is; cathedral (1841); trade in tropical fruit and vegetables; badly damaged by hurricane, 1979.

Rosebery, Archibald Philip Primrose, 5th Earl of (1847–1929) British statesman and Liberal prime minister (1894–5), born in London. He became foreign secretary (1886, 1892–4) under Gladstone, whom he succeeded as premier. He was noted for his racehorse stables, and in his later years as a biographer of British statesmen.

rosemary A dense, aromatic, evergreen shrub (*Rosmarinus officialis*), growing to 2 m/6½ ft, native to the Mediterranean; flowers pale blue; widely cultivated for ornament and as a culinary herb. (Family: Labiatae.)

Rosenberg [rohzenberg] Alleged spies: **Julius Rosenberg** (1918–53) and **Ethel Rosenberg** (1915–53), husband and wife, both born in New York City. They joined the Communist Party, and were part of a transatlantic spy ring uncovered after the trial of Klaus Fuchs in Britain. They became the first US civilians to be executed for espionage. They had many supporters who claimed that the couple were the victims of the witch-hunt atmosphere of the early 1950s.

Roses, Wars of the (1455–85) A series of civil wars in England, which started during the weak monarchy of Henry VI; named from the emblems of the two rival branches of the House of Plantagenet, York (white rose) and Lancaster (red rose) – a symbolism which was propagated by the Tudor dynasty (1485–1603), which united the two roses. The wars began when Richard, Duke of York, claimed the protectorship of the crown after the king's mental breakdown (1453–4), and ended with Henry Tudor's defeat of Richard III at Bosworth (1485).

Rose Theatre A London playhouse built c.1587 by Philip Henslowe on land he had leased on the S bank of the Thames. Rebuilt in 1592, the Rose was where Marlowe's plays were first performed, as well as some of the early plays of Shakespeare. The foundations were discovered in 1989.

Rosetta Stone A black basalt slab with a trilingual inscription in Greek and Egyptian hieroglyphic and demotic, found in 1799 on the Rosetta branch of the R Nile; now in the British Museum. It allowed hieroglyphs to be deciphered for the first time.

rose window A round window with mullions or tracery radiating outwards from the centre, filled with stained or painted glass. Commonly associated with Gothic architecture, it is also known as a **wheel window**.

rosewood A high-quality wood scented like roses, because of the presence of aromatic gum. It is obtained from various trees of the genus *Dalbergia*, native to the tropics and subtropics. (Family: Leguminosae.)

Rosh Hashanah [rosh hashahna, hashanah] The Jewish New Year (1 Tishri), which falls in September or October.

Rosicrucianism [rohzikrooshnizm] An esoteric movement which spread across Europe in the early 17th-c. In 1614–15 two pamphlets appeared in Germany and were attributed to Christian Rosenkreutz (1378–1484), who claimed to possess occult powers. He founded the Order of the Rosy Cross, and the pamphlets invited men of learning to join. No trace of the Order has been found, but many occult organizations claim Rosicrucian origins.

rosin A resin obtained as the residue from the distillation of turpentine, melting point c.120°C; also called **colophony**. It is used as a flux in soldering.

Roskilde [rohskilduh] 55°39N 12°07E, pop (2000e) 51000. Port and ancient town in Zealand, Denmark; capital of Denmark, 10th-c–1443; Peace of Roskilde, 1658; railway; university (1970); cathedral (12th-c); museum, including 1000-year-old Viking longboats.

Ross, Sir James Clark (1800–62) Polar explorer, born in London. He discovered the N magnetic pole in 1831, then commanded an expedition to the Antarctic seas (1839–43), where Ross Barrier, Sea, and Island are named after him.

Ross, Jonathan (1960–) Television and radio presenter, born in London. His prolific career as a presenter includes BBC TV's long-running *Film Night* (from 1999) and *It's Only TV...But I Like It* (from 1999). In 2000 he joined the panel of the sports quiz show *They Think It's All Over*, and also began a Saturday morning show for Radio 2. His talk-show *Friday Night With Jonathan Ross* (2001–) has won a string of awards: British Comedy Award for best comedy entertainment programme (2003), BAFTA for best entertainment programme (2004), and BAFTA for best entertainment performance (2004, 2006).

Ross, Nick, popular name of **Nicholas David Ross** (1947–) British broadcaster and journalist. He became a BBC reporter on several radio and television programmes, becoming nationally known for his investigative reporting in *Call Nick Ross* (from 1987). He has also presented a wide range of news and discussion television programmes, notably *Crimewatch UK* (from 1984).

Ross Dependency Land area 413500 km²/159600 sq mi; permanent shelf ice area 337000 km²/130000 sq mi. Antarctic territory administered by New Zealand (since 1923), including all the land between 160°E and 150°W and S of 60°S; no permanent inhabitants.

Rossellini, Roberto [roseleenee] (1906–77) Film director, born in Rome. His films include *Roma, città aperta* (1945, Rome, Open City), made with hidden cameras in a style which came to be known as 'neo-Realism', *Paisà* (1946, Paisan) and *Il generale della Rovere* (1959, General della Rovere).

Rossetti, Christina (Georgina) [rozetee] (1830–94) Poet, born in London, the sister of Dante Gabriel Rossetti. A devout Anglican, and influenced by the Oxford Movement, she wrote mainly religious poetry.

Rossetti, Dante Gabriel [rozetee] (1828–82) Poet and painter, born in London. He trained at the Royal Academy in London, and c.1850 helped to form the Pre-Raphaelite Brotherhood. His early work was on religious themes, such as 'The Annunciation' (1850, Tate); his later manner became more secular, and more ornate in style.

Rossini, Gioacchino (Antonio) [roseenee] (1792–1868) Composer, born in Pesaro, Italy. Among his early successes were *Tancredi* (1813) and *L'Italiana in Algeri* (1813, The Italian Girl in Algiers), and in 1816 he produced his masterpiece, *Il Barbiere di Siviglia* (The Barber of Seville). His overtures have continued to be highly popular items in concert programmes.

Rosslare [roslair], Ir **Ros Láir** 52°17N 6°23W, pop (2000e) 850. Port town in Wexford county, SE Ireland; ferry links with Fishguard and Milford Haven.

Ross Sea Extension of the Pacific Ocean in Antarctica; McMurdo Sound (W) generally ice-free in late summer, an important base point for exploration; main islands, Roosevelt (E) and Ross (W).

Rostand, Edmond [rostã] (1868–1918) Poet and playwright, born in Marseille, France. He achieved international fame with *Cyrano de Bergerac* (1897), the story of the nobleman with the enormous nose.

Rostock or **Rostock-Warnemünde** 54°04N 12°09E, pop (2000e) 258000. Industrial port in N Germany; on the Baltic Sea; founded, 12th-c; former Hanseatic League port; badly bombed in World War 2, rebuilt in the 1950s; university (1419); 15th-c town hall.

Rostov-na-Donu [rostof na donoo], Eng **Rostov-on-Don** 47°15N 39°45E, pop (2000e) 1020000. Port in SE European Russia; on R Don; major grain-exporting centre in the 19th-c; airport; railway; university (1917).

Rostropovich, Mstislav Leopoldovich [rostropohvich] (1927–2007) Cellist and conductor, born in Baku, Azerbaijan. In 1975, while in the USA, he and his wife decided not to return to the USSR; he then became musical director and conductor of the National Symphony Orchestra, Washington (1977–94).

Rotary International *service club*

Rotblat, Sir Joseph (1908–2005) Physicist and anti-nuclear weapons activist, born in Warsaw. He moved to the UK in 1939, and after the war devoted himself to the peaceful application of nuclear physics. He helped to found the annual series of conferences on arms control in Pugwash, Nova Scotia, in 1957 (the Pugwash Conferences), acting first as secretary-general (1957–73) and later as president (from 1988). He received the Nobel Peace Prize, shared with the Conferences, in 1995, and was knighted in 1998.

Roth, Henry (1906–95) Novelist, born in Tysmenytsya, Ukraine (formerly Tysmenica, Austria–Hungary). He moved to New York in 1907. His only novel, *Call It Sleep* (1934), is a classic treatment of Jewish immigrant life and childhood.

Roth, Philip (Milton) (1933–) Novelist, born in Newark, NJ. His books include *Portnoy's Complaint* (1969), *My Life as a Man* (1974), the trilogy *Zuckerman Bound* (1989), *American Pastoral*

(1998, Pulitzer), *The Human Stain* (2000, filmed 2003), and *Exit Ghost* (2007). He was married to Claire Bloom (dissolved, 1995).

Rotherham [rotheram] 53°26N 1°20W, pop (2001e) 248 200. Town in South Yorkshire, N England; on the R Don; railway.

Rothermere, Viscount *Harmsworth, Harold Sydney*

Rothko, Mark, originally **Marcus Rothkowitz** (1903–70) Painter, born in Dvinsk, Russia (now Daugavpils, Latvia). His family emigrated to the USA in 1913. During the 1940s he was influenced by Surrealism, but by the early 1950s had evolved his own meditative form of Abstract Expressionism. A previously unknown book, *The Artist's Reality*, was published in 2004.

Rothschild, Meyer (Amschel), Eng [rothschiyld], Ger [rohtshilt] (1743–1812) Financier, born in Frankfurt, Germany. Having studied as a rabbi, he became the financial adviser to the Landgrave of Hesse-Kassel. His five sons continued his firm, establishing branches in other countries, and negotiated many of the great government loans of the 19th-c.

rotifer [rohtifer] A microscopic aquatic animal with an unsegmented body; swims by means of a ring of beating hair-like structures that resembles a spinning wheel; group contains c.1800 species; also known as **wheel animalcules**. (Phylum: Rotifera.)

Rotorua [rohtorooa] 38°07S 176°17E, pop (2000e) 58 000. Health resort in North Island, New Zealand; in a region of thermal springs, geysers, and boiling mud.

rotten borough The name given to certain British parliamentary boroughs before the Great Reform Act of 1832, which had few voters and were usually controlled by a landowner or by the Crown. Examples were Gatton, Dunwich, and Old Sarum.

Rotterdam 51°55N 4°30E, pop (2000e) 617 000. Industrial city and chief port of The Netherlands; at the junction of the R Rotte with the Nieuwe Maas, 24 km/15 mi from the North Sea; major commercial centre of NW Europe since the 14th-c; city centre almost completely destroyed by German bombing, 1940; Europort harbour area inaugurated, 1966; railway; underground; university (1973); shipbuilding (largest shipyard in Europe); petrochemicals (largest plant on the Continent of Europe); birthplace of Erasmus; philharmonic orchestra.

rottweiler [rotviyler] A German breed of dog, developed around the Alpine town of Rottweil to protect cattle; agile, with heavy muscular body and neck; powerful muzzle and short soft ears; short black and tan coat; tail docked short; popular guard dogs; attracted adverse publicity in the late 1980s, following reports of fatal attacks on children.

Rouault, Georges (Henri) [roo-oh] (1871–1958) Painter and engraver, born in Paris. He was apprenticed to a stained-glass designer in 1885, and retained the art's glowing colours, outlined with black, in his paintings of clowns, prostitutes, and Biblical characters.

Roubaix [roobay] 50°42N 3°10E, pop (2000e) 103 000. Industrial town in NW France; chartered in 1469; centre of N France textile industry.

Roubillac, Louis François [roobeeyak], also spelled **Roubiliac** (1702–62) Sculptor, born in Lyon, France. His statue of Handel for Vauxhall Gardens (1738) first made him popular, and he completed statues of Newton, Shakespeare and others.

Rouen [rooā], Lat **Rotomagus** 49°27N 1°04E, pop (2000e) 108 000. River-port in NW France; on right bank of R Seine; fifth largest port in France; former capital of Upper Normandy; scene of trial and burning of Joan of Arc, 1431; badly damaged in World War 2, but reconstructed largely as a Ville Musée (museum town); road and rail junction; university (1967); birthplace of Flaubert; restored Gothic cathedral (13th–16th-c); Gros Horloge (clock tower).

Rouget de Lisle, Claude Joseph [roozhay duh leel] (1760–1836) French army officer, born in Lons-le-Saunier, France. He

wrote and composed the *Marseillaise* when stationed in 1792 at Strasbourg.

roughage *dietary fibre*

Rough Riders The nickname for the First US Volunteer Cavalry Regiment, commanded during the Spanish-American War (1898) by Colonel Leonard Wood (1860–1927) and Lieutenant-Colonel Theodore Roosevelt.

roulette A casino game played with a spinning wheel and ball. The wheel is divided into 37 segments numbered 0–36, but not in numerical order. All numbers are alternately either red or black except the 0. Punters bet, before and during the spin of the wheel, on the landing place of the ball after the wheel has stopped spinning. Bets can also be placed as to whether the winning number will be odd or even, or red or black.

Roumania *Romania*

rouncy *cob*

rounders An outdoor bat-and-ball game from which baseball probably derived. Each team consists of nine players, and the object, after hitting the ball, is to run around the outside of three posts before reaching the fourth and thus scoring a rounder.

Roundheads *Cavaliers*

roundworm infestation A condition in which roundworms (*nematodes*) live within the body of their hosts, many without causing disease.

Rous, (Francis) Peyton [rows] (1879–1970) Pathologist, born in Baltimore, MD. The **Rous chicken sarcoma**, which he discovered in 1911, remains the best-known example (as well as the first) of a cancer produced by a virus. In 1966 he shared the Nobel Prize for Physiology or Medicine.

Rousseau, Henri Julien Félix [roosoh], known as **le Douanier** ('the Customs Officer') (1844–1910) Primitive painter, born in Laval, France. He produced painstaking portraits, exotic imaginary landscapes, and dreams, such as 'Sleeping Gypsy' (1897, New York).

Rousseau, Jean-Jacques [roosoh] (1712–78) Political philosopher, educationist, and essayist, born in Geneva, Switzerland. His *Discourse sur l'origine et les fondements de l'inégalité parmi les hommes* (1755, Discourse on the Origin and Foundations of Inequality Amongst Men) emphasized the natural goodness of human beings, and the corrupting influences of institutionalized life. His masterpiece, *Du contrat social* (1762, The Social Contract), had a great influence on French revolutionary thought, introducing the slogan 'Liberty, Equality, Fraternity'. The same year he published his major work on education, *Emile*, in novel form. In England he wrote most of his *Confessions* (published posthumously, 1782).

Rousseau, (Pierre Etienne) Théodore [roosoh] (1812–67) Landscape painter, born in Paris. During the 1840s he settled at Barbizon, where he worked with a group of other painters, becoming leader of the Barbizon School.

Roux, (Pierre Paul) Emile [roo] (1853–1933) Bacteriologist, born in Confolens, France. In 1894 he helped to discover diphtheria antitoxin, and he also worked on rabies and anthrax.

Rovaniemi [rovanyaymee] 66°29N 25°40E, pop (2000e) 34 800. City in Finland; established, 1929; airfield; railway; centre for timber trade; largely destroyed by fire, 1944–5, and rebuilt by Alvar Aalto.

Rovno [rovno], Polish **Rowne**, Ger **Rowno** 50°39N 26°10E, pop (2000e) 236 000. City in Ukraine, on R Uste; formerly in Poland; railway.

rowan [rohan] A slender deciduous tree (*Sorbus aucuparia*), growing to 20 m/65 ft, native to Europe; flowers creamy, in large clusters; berries red, rarely yellow; also called **mountain ash**. (Family: Rosaceae.)

Rowe, Nicholas [roh] (1674–1718) Poet and playwright, born in Little Barford, Bedfordshire. Three of his plays became very popular: *Tamerlane* (1702), *The Fair Penitent* (1703), and *Jane Shore* (1714). In 1715 he was appointed poet laureate.

rowing A sport or pastime in which a boat is propelled by oars as opposed to mechanical means. If there is only one rower with two oars it is known as **sculling**. Rowing involves two or more people, each rower having one oar. Famous races include the Oxford and Cambridge Boat Race (began 1829), and the Diamond Sculls and Grand Challenge Cup, both contested at the Henley Royal Regatta every year.

Rowland, Tiny, originally **Rowland W Furhop** (1917–98) Financier, born in India. He joined Lonrho (the London and Rhodesian Mining and Land Company) in 1961, and became its chief executive and managing director. In 1983 he became chairman of *The Observer* newspaper, which he sold to *The Guardian* in 1993. He stepped down from Lonrho in 1994, following a bitter battle for control of the company with German property tycoon Dieter Bock.

Rowlandson, Thomas (1756–1827) Caricaturist, born in London. Some of his best-known works are his illustrations to the 'Dr Syntax' series (1812–21) and 'The English Dance of Death' (1815–16).

Rowley, Thomas [rohlee] *Chatterton, Thomas*

Rowling, J(oanne) K(athleen) (1965–) Writer, born in Chipping Sodbury, Gloucestershire. A former teacher, her life changed following the publication of *Harry Potter and the Philosopher's Stone* (1997; filmed 2001, US title *Harry Potter and the Sorcerer's Stone*). It was followed by *Harry Potter and the Chamber of Secrets* (1998; filmed 2002), *Harry Potter and the Prisoner of Azkaban* (1999; filmed 2004), *Harry Potter and the Goblet of Fire* (2000; filmed 2005), *Harry Potter and the Order of the Phoenix* (2003), *Harry Potter and the Half Blood Prince* (2005), and *Harry Potter and the Deathly Hallows* (2007). Her numerous awards include the British Book Awards' Children's Book of the Year, and the Whitbread Children's Book of the Year.

Rowntree Foundation A charity founded by Joseph Rowntree, a Quaker chocolate manufacturer. The *Joseph Rowntree Memorial Trust* (1959) was renamed the *Joseph Rowntree Foundation* in 1990, and is the UK's largest independent social policy research and development charity.

Royal Academy of Arts A British academy founded in 1768 under royal patronage, with the aim of holding annual exhibitions (which are still held). Its premises are at Burlington House, London.

Royal Academy of Dramatic Art (RADA) A London theatre school founded in 1904 by Beerbohm Tree, and granted its Royal Charter in 1920. It is located in Chenies Street. Major refurbishment of its Malet Street premises began in 1997 (completed 2001).

Royal Academy of Music A London conservatory founded in 1822, opened in 1823, and granted its royal charter in 1830. It moved to its present location in Marylebone in 1912.

Royal Air Force (RAF) Britain's air force, established in 1918. Today the RAF comprises three Commands: Strike, Support, and RAF Germany.

Royal Albert Hall, popularly known as the **Albert Hall** Concert hall built (1867–71) in memory of Prince Albert, consort of Queen Victoria of Great Britain, located S of Kensington Gardens, London. Designed by British army engineer, Major General H Y D Scott, the hall is an oval arena with a domed roof constructed of iron and glass, and seats c.8000. The South Porch extension opened in 2003.

Royal and Ancient Golf Club of St Andrews (R & A) The ruling body of the game of golf in the eyes of most countries (the USA being a notable exception). The R & A was formed in 1754 and adopted its present name in 1834.

royal assent A legal stage through which a bill has to pass in the UK before it becomes law. The monarch's approval is a formality; it has never been withheld in modern times.

Royal Australian Air Force (RAAF) Australia's air force, established in 1921. It saw service in all theatres of World War 2.

Royal Australian Navy (RAN) Australia's Navy, established in 1911. Based on the British Royal Navy, it had an early success in 1914 in sinking the German raider *Emden*, and saw action in the Atlantic, Mediterranean, and the Pacific.

Royal Ballet, The Britain's national ballet company, the inspiration of Dame Ninette de Valois. It gave its first performances in 1931, became Sadler's Wells Ballet and, in 1936, the Royal Ballet. Its famous dancers have included Margot Fonteyn, Alicia Markova, and Anthony Dowell.

Royal British Legion An organization for all ex-servicemen and women, and serving members of HM Forces. Formed in 1921, its aim is to provide social and welfare services for its members and to perpetuate the memory of those who died in the service of their country. It provides poppies for the Remembrance (or Poppy Day) Appeal each November.

Royal Canadian Mounted Police *Mounties; police*

Royal College of Music A London conservatory founded by royal charter in 1883. It moved to its present location in Prince Consort Road in 1894.

Royal Commission In the UK, a body appointed by the sovereign on the prime minister's recommendation to investigate and report on the operation of laws which it is proposed to change. It may also deal with social, educational, or other matters about which the government wishes to make general, long-term policy decisions.

Royal Court Theatre Theatre in Sloane Square, London, founded in 1888. A grade II listed building, it was closed in 1996 for major refurbishment and reopened in early 2000. The theatre is known for its support of the works of new writers and as a platform for emerging talent.

Royal Family, British *Anne, Princess; Charles, Prince; Diana, Princess; Edinburgh, Duke of; Edward, Prince; Elizabeth II; Gloucester, Duke of; Kent, Duke of; Margaret, Princess; York, Duke of*

royal garden parties In the UK, four summer gatherings held in June/July by the Queen, three in the grounds of Buckingham Palace, and the other at the Palace of Holyroodhouse, Edinburgh. Up to 10 000 people are invited to each party.

Royal Greenwich Observatory An observatory founded by Charles II of England in 1675. Its role in the preparation of calendars and time-keeping was of major importance until the mid-20th-c. Its transit circle has been used since 1851 for the accurate measurement of time; and in 1884 it was agreed to take the axis of this telescope as the prime meridian of longitude. Its headquarters moved to Cambridge in 1990.

Royal Horticultural Society A society founded in the UK in 1804. An experimental garden is maintained at Wisley, Surrey; shows and competitions, notably the Chelsea Flower Show, are held annually.

Royal Institution In the UK, a learned scientific society founded in 1799 by the physicist, Count Rumford. Lectures are still given at its headquarters in Albemarle Street, London, notably the Christmas lectures for young people.

royal jelly A highly nutritious substance produced by the salivary glands of the worker bees to nourish the queen bee and those larvae that are destined to become queens. There are many anecdotal reports of its beneficial effects on humans. It is usually taken in the form of a rather expensive dietary supplement, but it has also been incorporated into some cosmetic products, where it is claimed to have a rejuvenating action on the skin.

Royal Marines (RM) Britain's Marine force, which can trace its origin to the Lord High Admiral's Regiment first raised in 1664. The first RM Commando units were raised in 1942.

Royal Military Academy, popularly known as **Sandhurst** Military academy in Sandhurst, Berkshire. It developed from the Royal

Military Academy (founded 1799) at Woolwich, London, and the Royal Military College which was established (1802) by royal warrant at Great Marlow, and moved to Sandhurst in 1812. The present academy was formed in 1947.

Royal Mint The British government department responsible for manufacturing metal coins. The London mint probably dates from AD 825. It is now situated in Llantrisant, S Wales.

Royal National Lifeboat Institution (RNLI) In the UK, a rescue organization manned by volunteers and financed by voluntary contributions, founded in 1824. The modern RNLI operates over 200 lifeboat stations and maintains over 250 active vessels.

Royal Navy (RN) The naval branch of the British armed forces. Originating in the time of Henry VIII, it reached its peak at the end of World War 2, when it had more than 500 warships. It has been responsible for the operation of Britain's nuclear deterrent since 1969.

Royal Observatory, Edinburgh An observatory at Edinburgh, Scotland, UK, founded in 1818. It houses the UK Astronomy Technology Centre, responsible for developing instrumentation for UK astronomers.

Royal Opera House The home of the Royal Ballet and the Royal Opera in Bow Street, London. The present building, by Edward Middleton Barry (1830–80), opened in 1858. It was closed for major refurbishment, 1997–9.

Royal Shakespeare Company An English theatre company based in Stratford-upon-Avon and London. It was developed out of the Shakespeare Memorial Theatre by Peter Hall between 1960 and 1968. Trevor Nunn took over as artistic director in 1968, followed by Adrian Noble (1999–2003), and Michael Boyd (2003–).

Royal Society (RS) In the UK, a prestigious scientific institution – the oldest in the world to have enjoyed continuous existence. Its inaugural meeting was held in London in 1660 and the Society was granted a royal charter in 1662.

Royal Society for Nature Conservation, also known as the **Wildlife Trusts** A British conservation society which co-ordinates the work of county naturalist trusts and urban wildlife groups. It was founded in 1912, and now manages over 2000 reserves.

Royal Society for the Prevention of Cruelty to Animals *RSPCA*

Royal Society for the Protection of Birds *RSPB*

Royal Victorian Order An order of knighthood instituted in 1896 by Queen Victoria, designed to reward distinguished service to the sovereign. The motto is 'Victoria' and the ribbon blue with red and white edges.

Royce, Sir (Frederick) Henry (1863–1933) Engineer, born in Alwalton, Cambridgeshire. He made his first car in 1904, and his meeting with C S Rolls in that year led to the formation (1906) of Rolls-Royce, Ltd.

RSI *repetitive strain injury*

RSPB In the UK, an abbreviation of **Royal Society for the Protection of Birds**, a society founded in 1889. It was originally formed to protest against the killing of birds for their plumage, especially for use in ladies' hats. It is now one of the major conservation bodies, owning over 100 nature reserves.

RSPCA In the UK, an abbreviation of **Royal Society for the Prevention of Cruelty to Animals**, the main animal welfare society, founded in 1824. In the USA there are several animal societies. The oldest is the American Society for the Prevention of Cruelty to Animals (1866), but the Animal Protection Society of America (1968) has a larger membership.

Ruapehu, Mount [rooapayhoo] 39°18S 175°40E. Active volcano and highest peak on North Island, New Zealand; rises to 2797 m/9176 ft; last eruptions, 1995–6, 1999.

rubber A resilient, elastic substance obtained from a variety of unrelated, latex-producing, tropical trees. Raw rubber, or **caoutchouc**, is obtained from the milky latex exuded by the trees as a response to injury. The latex is collected by making a series of spiral cuts halfway around the circumference of the trunk, allowing the fluid to collect in cups. It is is congealed using acid, pressed, and sometimes smoked, before undergoing manufacture into final products. Initially, rubber was collected solely from wild trees in Brazil, but from c.1900 they were introduced as plantation trees to other tropical countries, notably Malaysia, which has become the world's largest producer. **Synthetic rubbers**, made by the polymerization of isoprene or substituted butadienes, exceed natural rubber in the quantity used.

rubber plant / tree *indiarubber tree; rubber*

Rubbia, Carlo (1934–) Physicist, born in Gorizia, Italy. From 1960 he headed the proton–antiproton collider team at CERN, Geneva. He shared the Nobel Prize for Physics in 1984 for work leading to the discovery of the W and Z sub-atomic particles.

Rubbra, Edmund (1901–86) Composer, born in Northampton, Northamptonshire. He wrote 11 symphonies, chamber, choral and orchestral music, songs, and solo instrumental works.

rubella A highly infectious disease, caused by a virus, that affects older children and young adults; also called **German measles**. Although a trivial short-lived illness, limited to fever and a rash, it is important because women who are infected in the first 18 weeks of pregnancy are likely to have children with congenital abnormalities. A vaccine to prevent the disease is available, and is given to infants and children.

Rubens, (Peter Paul) [roobenz] (1577–1640) Painter, born in Siegen, Germany. In 1608 he settled in Antwerp, becoming court painter to the Archduke Albert. His triptych 'The Descent from the Cross' (1611–14) in Antwerp Cathedral is one of his early masterpieces. In 1622 he was invited to France by Marie de Médicis, for whom he painted 21 large subjects on her life and regency (Louvre). In 1628 he was sent on a diplomatic mission to Spain, and there executed some 40 works. The following year he became envoy to Charles I of England, where his paintings included 'Peace and War' (National Gallery, London).

rubidium–strontium dating A method of radiometric dating for rocks more than 10 million years old. It uses the fact that the radioactive isotope rubidium-87 decays with a known half-life to yield strontium-87, and hence the amount of each isotope in a rock or mineral can be used to determine its age.

Rubik's Cube A mathematical puzzle named after its inventor, Hungarian architect Ernö Rubik (1944–). A coloured cube is divided into 26 small incomplete cubes, each of which will pivot. There are $c.4 \cdot 3 \times 10^{22}$ combinations, but only one possible way of getting all six sides to form a different colour. It became a world craze in the late 1970s.

Rubin, Robert E [roobin] (1938–) US statesman, born in New York City. He became a lawyer, then joined the White House as assistant to the president for economic policy (1993–5). He became secretary of the Treasury in 1995, and was reappointed to this post in 1997, serving until 1999.

Rubinstein, Artur [roobinstiyn] (1887–1982) Pianist, born in Łódź, Poland. He moved to the USA during World War 2, becoming a US citizen in 1946. He continued to perform there with enormous success, making over 200 recordings.

Rubinstein, Helena [roobinstiyn] (1870–1965) Beautician and business executive, born in Kraków, Poland. She moved in the 1890s to Australia, where she opened the country's first beauty salon in Melbourne (1902). In 1915 she emigrated to New York City and launched an international business empire. Her success was spiced by a 50-year feud with arch-rival Elizabeth Arden.

Ruby, Jack L, originally **Jacob Rubenstein** (1911–67) Assassin, born in Chicago, IL. Two days after the assassination of President John F Kennedy, he shot and killed Lee Harvey Oswald, the alleged assassin of the president. He was sentenced to death in 1964, but died while awaiting a second trial.

ruby A gem variety of corundum, coloured deep crimson to pale red by the presence of minor impurities of chromium.

rudbeckia A biennial or perennial, native to North America; large flower-heads, characterized by the conical receptacle in the centre, giving rise to the alternative name of **coneflower**; outer ray florets red, yellow, or orange. (Genus: *Rudbeckia*, 15 species. Family: Compositae.)

rudd Freshwater fish (*Scardinius erythrophthalmus*) widespread in European rivers and lakes; length up to 40 cm/16 in; greenish-brown on back, sides yellow, fins reddish. (Family: Cyprinidae.)

Rudolf I (1218–91) German king (1273–91), the founder of the Habsburg sovereign and imperial dynasty, born in Schloss Limburg, Germany. Chosen king by the electors, he was recognized by the pope in 1274.

Rudolf, Lake *Turkana, Lake*

rue A small aromatic evergreen shrub (*Ruta graveolens*) with acrid scent and taste, native to the Balkans; leaves bluish-green; flowers with 4–5 rather dirty yellow petals curved up at the tips. It is cultivated as a culinary and medicinal herb. (Family: Rutaceae.)

ruff A sandpiper (*Philomachus pugnax*) native to Europe, Asia, and Africa; breeding male with naked face and large ruff of feathers around neck.

Rugby 52°23N 1°15W, pop (2000e) 60 700. Town in Warwickshire, C England; on R Avon; famous boys' public school (1567); railway.

rugby football *football, Rugby League; football, Rugby Union*

Ruhr, River [roor] River in Germany; rises N of Winterberg; flows W to the R Rhine at Duisburg; length 213 km/132 mi; its valley is an important mining and industrial area; cities include Essen, Bochum, Dortmund.

Ruiz, Nevado del [rooees] 4°53N 75°22W. Active Andean volcanic peak in WC Colombia; rises to 5399 m/17 713 ft; erupted in 1985, with loss of many lives.

rum A spirit distilled either from sugar cane, freshly crushed, or from the fermentation of molasses, a by-product of the West Indian sugar-cane industry. The British navy gave rum a special status by providing a daily tot to all serving sailors.

Rumania *Romania*

rumba A dance of Cuban origin which became popular as a ballroom dance in the 1930s. Its distinctive rhythm, often played on maracas or bongos, is the *tresillo*, a bar of eight quavers/eighth-notes divided 3 + 3 + 2.

Rumford, Count *Thompson, Benjamin*

ruminant A mammal of suborder Ruminantia, comprising the *traguloids* (chevrotains) and *pecorans* (other deer, giraffes, and Bovidae), and suborder Tylopoda (the camel family); an artiodactyl; many-chambered stomach breaks down coarse plant material; camels and chevrotains have three chambers, pecorans have four; regurgitates mouthfuls (*cud*), chews them thoroughly, then reswallows; also known as a **cud-chewer**.

rummy A large family of domestic card games. In one popular version, each player has seven cards, and the object is to form them into two hands, one of three cards and one of four (or one hand of seven) by taking and discarding cards from the pack. The hand obtained must be three (or four) cards of the same denomination, or a sequence of three (or four) cards of the same suit. A variation popular in the USA is **gin rummy**, in which hands (of three or four) are laid face upwards, and can be added to by players in certain circumstances during the game. Points are deducted according to which cards are left in the hand when one of the players wins the game by disposing of all his or her cards.

Rump Parliament The members of the British Long Parliament who were left after Pride's Purge of 'presbyterian' elements (1648), numbering about 60. It abolished the monarchy and the House of Lords. When it fell out with the army, Cromwell dismissed it (1653). It was recalled in 1659, and dissolved itself in 1660.

Rum Rebellion In Australian history, an uprising in Sydney which deposed the governor of New South Wales, Captain William Bligh (1808). It occurred because of personal antagonisms, and Bligh's attempt to end the use of rum as a currency.

Rumsfeld, Donald (1932–) US Republican politician, born in Chicago, IL. He served three terms in the House of Representatives (1962–9), then joined the Nixon administration as an assistant to the president (1969–72). He was chief-of-staff under Gerald Ford (1974–5), who also appointed him defence secretary (1975–7). He then held various business posts. Appointed defence secretary (2001–6) by George W Bush, he was responsible for the US campaign during the Iraq War (2003).

Runcie (of Cuddesdon), Robert (Alexander Kennedy) Runcie, Baron [ruhnsee] (1921–2000) British Anglican churchman, born in Crosby, Lancashire. He was Bishop of St Albans for 10 years before becoming Archbishop of Canterbury (1980–91). He presided at the Lambeth Conference in 1987.

Rundstedt, (Karl Rudolf) Gerd von [rundshtet] (1875–1953) German field marshal, born in Aschersleben, Germany. In 1939 he directed the attacks on Poland and France. Checked in the Ukraine in 1941, he was relieved of his command, but in 1942 was given a new command in France. He was recalled after the success of the 1944 Allied invasion, but returned to direct the Ardennes offensive.

Runeberg, Johan Ludvig [roonuhberg] (1804–77) Finnish poet, writing in Swedish, born in Jakobstad, Finland. His major work is the verse romance based on Scandinavian legend, *King Fjala* (1844). One of his poems became Finland's national anthem.

runes The letters of the earliest Teutonic alphabet; widely known as the *futhark*, from the names of its first six symbols (*f, u, th, a, r, k*). Used mainly by the Scandinavians and the Anglo-Saxons, it comprised 24 basic symbols, though there was considerable regional variation both in the overall number of symbols and the symbol shapes used. Runes are preserved in c.4000 inscriptions and a few manuscripts, dating from the 3rd-c AD.

runner bean A twining perennial (*Phaseolus coccineus*) growing to 5 m/16 ft, native to tropical America; pea-flowers scarlet or less commonly white, in stalked clusters; pods up to 40 cm/16 in long, containing large red, kidney-shaped seeds. It is a common garden vegetable. (Family: Leguminosae.)

running *athletics; cross-country running*

Runnymede A meadow on the S bank of the R Thames, Surrey, SE England; here, or on Magna Carta Island in the river, King John signed the Magna Carta in 1215.

Runyon, (Alfred) Damon (1884–1946) Writer, born in Manhattan, KS. He is best known for his short stories about underworld New York life. His collection *Guys and Dolls* (1931) was adapted for a musical revue (1950) and film (1955).

Rupert, Prince, also known as **Rupert of the Rhine** (1619–82) Royalist commander in the English Civil War, born in Prague, the third son of the Elector Palatine Frederick V and Elizabeth, daughter of James I of England. A notable cavalry leader, he won several victories, but was defeated at Marston Moor (1644) and dismissed by Charles I. Banished by parliament, he led the small Royalist fleet until it was routed by Blake (1650).

rupture *hernia*

Rusedski, Greg(ory) [ruzetskee] (1973–) Tennis player, born in Montreal, Quebec, Canada. He became a British subject in 1995. A left-handed player, known for his very fast serves, he moved ahead of Tim Henman to become British number 1 in 1997, and by the end of 1999 was ranked 10th in the world. A variety of injuries kept him off the circuit for much of 2002–3. In 2006 he briefly held the British number 1 spot, but finished the year disappointingly, and retired from professional tennis in April 2007. In recent years he has worked as a newspaper columnist and as a tennis commentator for British Eurosport.

rush A densely tufted annual or evergreen perennial; typically found in cold and wet places; flowers with six segments, brownish, in dense heads. (Genus: *Juncus*, 300 species. Family: Juncaceae.)

Rush, Geoffrey (1951–) Actor, born in Toowoomba, Queensland, Australia. Known as a theatre actor in Australia, he received international recognition for his role as David Helfgott in the 1996 film *Shine* (Oscar, Golden Globe, BAFTA). He won a BAFTA in 1999 for Best Supporting Actor in *Shakespeare in Love*. Later work includes the films *Mystery Men* (1999) and *Candy* (2005), and the TV mini-series *The Life and Death of Peter Sellers* (2004, Emmy).

Rush, Ian (1961–) Footballer, born in St Asaph, Denbighshire. He played for Liverpool (1981–6), scoring 110 goals in 182 league matches, then played for Juventus, returning to Liverpool in 1988, joined Leeds United in 1996, moving to Newcastle United (1997–8), to Wrexham as coach (1998–2000), and then to Sydney Olympic (Australia). In 2004 he took over as manager of Chester City, resigning in 2005. He was a regular member of the Welsh international team from 1980.

Rushdie, (Ahmed) Salman (1947–) Writer, born in Mumbai (Bombay), India, of Muslim parents. He became widely known after the publication of his second novel, *Midnight's Children* (1981, Booker, James Tait Black). *The Satanic Verses* (1988) caused worldwide controversy because of its treatment of Islam from a secular point of view, and in 1989 he was forced to go into hiding because of a sentence of death passed on him by Ayatollah Khomeini of Iran for blasphemy (officially lifted in 1998, but renewed by Ayatollah Khamenei in 2005). Later books include the novels *The Moor's Last Sigh* (1995, Whitbread), *Fury* (2001), and *Shalimar the Clown* (2005).

Rushmore, Mount 43°53N 103°28W. Mountain in W South Dakota, USA, in the Black Hills; a national memorial; height 1943 m/6375 ft; famous for the gigantic sculptures of four past US presidents (Washington, Jefferson, Roosevelt, Lincoln); each head 18 m/60 ft high; constructed 1927–41 under the direction of Gutzon Borglum.

Rusk, (David) Dean (1909–94) US statesman, secretary of state 1961–9, born in Cherokee Co, GA. As secretary of state under Kennedy, he played a major role in the Cuban crisis of 1962. He retained the post under the Johnson administration.

Ruska, Ernst (1906–88) Physicist, born in Heidelberg, Germany. For his development of the electron microscope, he was awarded the 1986 Nobel Prize for Physics.

Ruskin, John (1819–1900) Writer and art theorist, born in London. His critical works, such as *Modern Painters* (1843–60) and *The Stones of Venice* (1851–3) made him the most influential critic of the day, and his social criticism gave him the status of a moral guide or prophet.

Russell, Bertrand (Arthur William) Russell, 3rd Earl (1872–1970) Philosopher and mathematician, born in Trelleck, Monmouthshire. His major works were *Principles of Mathematics* (1903), and (with A N Whitehead) *Principia mathematica* (1910–13). In 1907 he offered himself as a Liberal candidate, but was turned down for his 'free-thinking'. In 1918 his pacifism led to his serving six months in prison. Later works included *An Enquiry into Meaning and Truth* (1940) and *Human Knowledge* (1948). After 1949 he became a champion of nuclear disarmament. The single most important influence on 20th-c analytic philosophy, he was awarded the 1950 Nobel Prize for Literature.

Russell, Henry Norris (1877–1957) Astronomer, born in Oyster Bay, NY. Independently of Ejnar Hertzsprung (1873–1967), he discovered the relationship between stellar absolute magnitude and spectral type, and represented the results in the Hertzsprung–Russell diagram (1913).

Russell, Jack, popular name of **John Russell** (1795–1883) 'Sporting parson', born in Dartmouth, Devon. He became curate of Swymbridge near Barnstaple (1832–80), and master of foxhounds. The **Jack Russell terrier** was named after him.

Russell, (Ernestine) Jane (Geraldine) (1921–) Film actress, born in Bemidji, MN. Known for her striking looks, she became one of the leading Hollywood sex symbols of the 1950s, her major films including *Paleface* (1948) and *Gentlemen Prefer Blondes* (1953).

Russell (of Kingston Russell), John Russell, 1st Earl, known as **Lord John Russell** (1792–1878) British statesman and Whig–Liberal prime minister (1846–52, 1865–6), born in London. He became prime minister after the Conservative Party split over the repeal of the Corn Laws (1846). In Aberdeen's coalition of 1852 he was foreign secretary, but lost popularity over alleged incompetent management of the Crimean War, and retired in 1855 (though recalled as foreign secretary in 1859 and as premier after Palmerston's death).

Russell, Ken, popular name of **Henry Kenneth Alfred Russell** (1927–) Film director, born in Southampton. He produced experimental studies of Debussy, Isadora Duncan, Delius, and Richard Strauss, which gradually abandoned naturalism. His feature films include *Women in Love* (1969), *The Devils* (1971), and *The Rainbow* (1989), and for TV *Lady Chatterley* (1993) and *Treasure Island* (1995).

Russell, William, Lord (1639–83) English Whig politician. A leading member of the movement to exclude James II from the succession, he was arrested with others for participation in the Rye House Plot (1683), and beheaded in London.

Russell, Willy, popular name of **William Martin Russell** (1947–) Playwright, born in Whiston, Lancashire. Among his best-known plays are *Educating Rita* (1979), *Blood Brothers* (1983), and *Shirley Valentine* (1986).

Russia pp.804–5

Russian *Russian literature; Slavic languages*

Russian blue A breed of domestic cat; *foreign short-haired* variety; thick blue-grey coat, each hair often with a silver tip; large thin ears and green eyes; also known as an **Archangel cat**.

Russian Civil War (1918–22) A war which took place in Russia following the October 1917 Revolution. Anti-Bolshevik forces (Whites) led by tsarist generals mounted a series of military and political campaigns against the new Soviet regime. They were opposed by the Soviet Red Army, created by Trotsky, which successfully fought back against the Whites between 1918 and 1922.

Russian Orthodox Church A Church originating from missionary activity of the see of Constantinople of the Orthodox Church, with a community organized at Kiev in the 9th-c. The contemporary Russian Church retains fidelity in doctrine and liturgy to its Orthodox inheritance, but is also developing its national character.

Russian Revolution (1917) The revolution which overthrew the Russian imperialist regime and set up the first Marxist proletarian state. Mass demonstrations of revolutionary workers and soldiers in Petrograd led to the abdication of Nicholas II and the overthrow of the imperial government in February 1917. There followed a period of power-sharing between a provisional government and the Petrograd Soviet, known as 'dual power'. Lenin's Bolsheviks refused to collaborate, and in October led an insurgency of armed workers, soldiers, and sailors, seizing political power and establishing the first Soviet government.

Russian Space Agency An agency established in 1992 to administer the civilian and commercial space programme of the Russian Federation. It is based on the principal assets and ongoing

Russia

☐ International Airport   ∴ World heritage site

official name **Russian Federation**, formerly (1917–91) the **Russian SFSR (Soviet Federal Socialist Republic)**, Russ **Rossiyskaya**

Local name Rossiyskaya (Rossiyskaya Federatsiya)

Timezone GMT ranges from +2 to +12

Area 17 075 400 km²/6 591 100 sq mi

Population total (2002e) 143 673 000

Status Republic

Date of independence 1991

Capital Moscow

Languages Russian (official), and c.100 different languages

Ethnic groups Russian (82%), Tatar (3%), Ukrainian (3%)

Religions Christian (Russian Orthodox 25%), non-religious (60%), Muslim

Physical features Occupying much of E Europe and N Asia; consists of c.75% of the area of the former USSR and over 50% of its population; vast plains dominate the W half; Ural Mts separate the E European Plain (W) from the W Siberian Lowlands (E); E of the R Yenisey lies the C Siberian Plateau; N Siberian Plain further E; Caucasus on S frontier; Lena, Ob, Severnaya Dvina, Pechora, Yenisey, Indigirka, and Kolyma rivers flow to the Arctic Ocean; Amur, Argun, and rivers of the Kamchatka Peninsula flow to the

projects of the former Soviet space programme, most of which were carried out within Russian territory. Earlier the Soviet space programme had been a dominant element in the exploration of space since the launch of Sputnik in 1957. Military and civilian programmes were administered by a complex organization whose characteristic secrecy increasingly diminished in the 1980s as the programme took on an international emphasis. Three principal launch sites (cosmodromes) are Biakonur (or Tyuratam), Plesetsk, and Kaputstin Yar, which in the past have launched about 100 spacecraft per year. The mission control facility is located in Kaliningrad (near Moscow).

Russian wolfhound borzoi

Russo–Finnish War (1939–40) A war between the USSR and Finland during the winter of 1939–40 (the **Winter War**). Soviet forces invaded Finland to secure Finnish territory from which to defend Leningrad against German attack. Finland was forced to cede territory to the Soviet Union.

Russo–Japanese War (1904–5) A war between the Russian Empire and Japan over rival territorial claims and imperial ambitions in N China and Korea. The war ended in Japanese victory with the Treaty of Portsmouth (1905).

Russo–Turkish Wars A series of wars between the Russian and

Ottoman Empires from the 17th-c to the 19th-c, principally for domination of the Black Sea and adjacent regions. Many areas gained their independence or were incorporated into the Russian Empire.

rust The product of corrosion, especially of iron-containing materials. It consists mainly of iron(III) oxide (Fe_2O_3) or hydrated forms.

rust fungus A parasitic fungus that occurs as a thread-like network (*mycelium*) between cells of the host plant; includes the genus *Puccinia*, containing over 4000 species. (Subdivision: Basidiomycetes. Order: Uredinales.)

Rutanzige, Lake Edward, Lake

Ruth, Babe, popular name of **George Herman Ruth**, nicknames **the Babe, the Bambino, the Sultan of Swat** (1895–1948) Baseball player, born in Baltimore, MD. He joined the New York Yankees in 1920, and when he retired in 1935 had scored 714 home runs, a figure not bettered until 1974. *The Babe Ruth Story* was filmed in 1984; *The Babe* in 1991.

Ruth, Book of A book of the Hebrew Bible/Old Testament, usually dated c.5th–4th-c BC, presenting a popular story ostensibly set in the time of Israel's tribal judges. Ruth became the mother of Obed, grandfather of David.

Pacific Ocean; Caspian Sea basin includes the Volga and Ural rivers; over 20 000 lakes, the largest being the Caspian Sea, L Taymyr, L Baikal.

Climate Half of country covered by snow for 6 months of year; coldest region, NE Siberia, average annual temperature -46°C (Jan), 16°C (Jul); summers in rest of country generally short and hot; average annual temperature -18–9°C (Jan), 16–24°C (Jul) in Moscow; average annual rainfall 500–750 mm/20–30 in.

Currency 1 Rouble (RUR) = 100 kopeks

Economy Oil fields in W Siberia (provide 50% of country's petroleum); series of 5-year plans since 1928 promoted industry; heavy-industry products include chemicals, construction materials, machine tool, and steel-making; mining, major producer of iron ore, manganese, natural gas, nickel, and platinum, also coal, copper, gold, zinc, tin, lead; agriculture, primarily wheat, fruit, vegetables, tobacco, cotton, sugar beet; textiles; timber.

GDP (2002e) $1·409 tn, per capita $9700

Human Development Index (2002) 0·781

History Conquered by Mongols in 13th-c; Ivan IV (the Terrible) became first ruler to be crowned Tsar, 1547; Time of Trouble, 1604–13; under Peter the Great, territory expanded to the Baltic Sea and St Petersburg founded as capital, 1703; Napoleon invasion failed, 1812; Crimean War, 1853–6; emancipation of the serfs, 1861; assassination of Alexander II, 1881; Balkan War with Turkey, 1877–8; Russo-Japanese War, 1904–5; establishment of a parliament (Duma) with limited powers, 1906; Russia allied with Britain and France, World War I; revolution overthrew Nicholas II, Bolsheviks (Communists) seized power under the dictatorship of Lenin, 1917; Russia forced to withdraw from War; renamed the Russian Soviet Federated Socialist Republic, 1918, and Moscow reinstated as capital; Russia became part of the Union of Soviet Socialist Republics (USSR), 1922; death of Lenin, 1924; Trotsky deported in 1928, by which time Stalin acquiring dictatorial power; USSR fought with the Allies against Germany in World War II; from 1946 development of the Cold War between East and West; troops intervened in Afghanistan, 1979; radical reform of the system under the leadership of Gorbachev, 1985–91; first contested elections in Soviet history held, and the end of the Cold War announced, 1989; troops withdrawn from Afghanistan, 1989; USSR dissolved, 1991; Russian Republic became independent and a founder member of the Commonwealth of Independent States, 1991; war in Chechnya, 1994–6; further invasion of Chechnya, 1999; conflict ongoing into 2006; governed by a president, prime minister, and Federal Assembly, consisting of a State *Duma* and a Federation Council.

Soviet Union
Head of State
1917 Lev Borisovich Kamenev
1917–19 Yakov Mikhailovich Sverlov
1919–46 Mikhail Ivanovich Kalinin
1946–53 Nikolai Mikhailovich Shvernik
1953–60 Kliment Yefremovich Voroshilov
1960–4 Leonid Ilyich Brezhnev
1964–5 Anastas Ivanovich Mikoyan
1965–77 Nikolai Viktorovich Podgorny
1977–82 Leonid Ilyich Brezhnev
1982–3 Vasily Vasiliyevich Kuznetsov *Acting*
1983–4 Yuri Vladimirovich Andropov
1984 Vasily Vasiliyevich Kuznetsov *Acting*
1984–5 Konstantin Ustinovich Chernenko
1985 Vasily Vasiliyevich Kuznetsov *Acting*
1985–8 Andrei Andreevich Gromyko
1988–90 Mikhail Sergeyevich Gorbachev

Executive President
1990–1 Mikhail Sergeyevich Gorbachev

Russian Federation
Head of State
1991–9 Boris Yeltsin
1999– Vladimir Putin

Head of Government
1991–2 Yegor Gaidar *Acting*
1992–8 Viktor Chernomyrdin *Interim*
1998 Sergei Kiriyenko
1998–9 Yevgeny Primakov
1999 Sergey Stepashin
1999–2000 Vladimir Putin
2000– 4 Mikhail Kasyanov
2004 Viktor Khristenko *Acting*
2004– Mikhail Fradkov

Rutherford (of Nelson), Ernest Rutherford, 1st Baron (1871–1937) Physicist, a pioneer of subatomic physics, born near Nelson, New Zealand. With Frederick Soddy he proposed that radioactivity results from the disintegration of atoms (1903), and later he developed the modern concept of the atom. He received the Nobel Prize for Chemistry in 1908.

Rutherford, Dame Margaret (1892–1972) Theatre and film actress, born in London. She gained fame as a character actress and comedienne, played Agatha Christie's 'Miss Marple' in a series of films from 1962, and won an Oscar for her role in *The VIPs* in 1964.

Ruthwell Cross A runic stone cross at Ruthwell, near Dumfries, S Scotland, dating from the 7th-c. It is carved with scenes from the New Testament and stands 5 m/18 ft high.

rutile [rootiyl, -teel] A titanium dioxide (TiO_2) mineral, usually red-brown to black due to impurities of iron oxide, widespread in igneous and metamorphic rocks and in veins with quartz. It is a source of titanium and is also used as a gemstone.

Rutland County in the UK, known as the smallest in England, incorporated into Leicestershire in 1974, then made a unitary authority in 1997. It has given its name to a reservoir, Rutland Water.

Ruysdael, Jacob van [roysdahl], also spelled **Ruïsdael** (c.1628–82)

Landscape painter, born in Haarlem, The Netherlands. His best works are country landscapes, and he also excelled in cloud effects, particularly in his seascapes.

Ruyter, Michiel Adriaanszoon de [royter] (1607–76) Dutch admiral, born in Vlissingen, The Netherlands. He gave distinguished service in the three Anglo-Dutch Wars (1652–4, 1665–7, 1672–8), winning notable victories in the Four Days' Battle off Dunkirk (1666) and a daring raid up the Rivers Medway and Thames (1667), in which much of the English fleet was destroyed. In the third war, his victories prevented a seaborne invasion of the United Provinces, but he was mortally wounded in a battle against the French off Sicily.

Rwanda p.806

Ryan, Meg (1961–) Film actress, born in Fairfield, CT. She became well known after *When Harry Met Sally* (1989), later films including *Sleepless in Seattle* (1993), *French Kiss* (1995), *City of Angels* (1998), and *In the Land of Women* (2007).

Ryan, (Lynn) Nolan (1947–) Baseball player, born in Refugio, TX. One of the fastest pitchers ever seen in major league baseball, he played with the New York Mets, the California Angels, the Houston Astros, and the Texas Rangers, retiring in 1993 with a record 5714 strikeouts.

Rwanda

□ International Airport

Religions Christian (65%), local indigenous beliefs (25%), Muslim (9%)

Physical features Landlocked in C Africa; mountainous, with many of the highest mountains formed by volcanoes; highest point Karisimbi, 4507 m/14 787 ft, in the Virunga range; W third drains into L Kivu and then the R Congo, remainder drains towards the R Nile; L Kivu and R Ruzizi form W border as part of Africa's Great Rift Valley.

Climate Tropical climate, influenced by high altitude; average annual temperature 19°C (Jan), 21°C (Jul) in Kigali; average annual rainfall 1000 mm/40 in in Kigali; two wet seasons (Oct–Dec, Mar–May); highest rainfall in the W, decreasing in the C uplands and to the N and E.

Currency 1 Rwanda Franc (RWF) = 100 centimes

Economy Based largely on agriculture; coffee, tea, pyrethrum, maize, beans, livestock; minerals; plastic goods, textiles.

GDP (2002e) $8·92 bn, per capita $1200

Human Development Index (2002) 0·403

History In the 16th-c the Tutsi tribe moved into the country and took over from the Hutu, forming a monarchy; German protectorate, 1899; mandated with Burundi to Belgium as the Territory of Ruanda-Urundi, 1919; United Nations Trust Territory administered by Belgium, after World War 2; unrest in 1959 led to a Hutu revolt and the overthrow of Tutsi rule; independence, 1962; military coup, 1973; return to civilian rule, 1980s; rebellion by (mainly Tutsi) Rwandan Patriotic Front, 1990; new constitution, 1991; peace accord with rebels, 1993; unprecedented outbreak of inter-ethnic violence, with over half a million deaths, 1994; governed by a President, Prime Minister, Council of Ministers, and National Development Council; elections scheduled for 1999, but transitional government rule extended to 2003; new elections, Aug 2003.

Head of State

1962–73 Grégoire Kayibanda
1973–94 Juvenal Habyarimana
1994–5 Théodore Sindikubwabo *Interim*
1995–2000 Pasteur Bizimunga
2000– Paul Kagame

Head of Government

1991–2 Sylvestre Nsanzimana
1992–3 Dismas Nsengiyaremye
1993–4 Agathe Uwilingiymana
1994–5 Jean Kambanda *Acting*
1995–2000 Pierre-Celestin Rwigyema
2000– Bernard Makuza

[rooanda], official name **Republic of Rwanda**

Local name Rwanda

Timezone GMT +2

Area 26 338 km²/10 169 sq mi

Population total (2002e) 7 398 000

Status Republic

Date of independence 1962

Capital Kigali

Languages French, Kinyarwanda, and English (official), with Kiswahili widely used in commerce

Ethnic groups Hutu (84%), Tutsi (14%), Pygmoid Twa (1%)

Ryazan [ryazan] 54°37N 39°43E, pop (2000e) 524 000. City in W Russia; on R Oka; founded, 1095; railway.

Ryder, Winona [winohna] (1971–) Film actress, born in Winona, MI. Her films include *Beetlejuice* (1988), *Edward Scissorhands* (1990), *Girl, Interrupted* (1999), and *The Darwin Awards* (2006). She received a Best Supporting Actress Oscar nomination for *The Age of Innocence* (1993), and a Best Actress nomination for her role as Jo in *Little Women* (1995).

Ryder Cup A golf tournament played every 2 years between professional male golfers from the USA and Europe. First played at Worcester, MA, in 1927, the Cup was donated by English businessman Samuel Ryder (1859–1936).

rye A cereal (*Secale cereale*) resembling barley, but with longer, narrower ears. It succeeds on poor soils, and is cultivated mainly in cold regions such as North America and E Europe. It is used to make black bread, crispbreads, alcohol, and straw for hats and thatching. (Family: Gramineae.)

Rye House Plot An alleged plot by Whigs (1683) to murder Charles II of England and James, Duke of York, at Rye House near Hoddesdon, Hertfordshire. The conspirators were betrayed and captured; two of them, Algernon Sidney and William, Lord Russell, were executed.

Rykov, Alexey Ivanovich [reekof] (1881–1938) Russian revolutionary and politician, born in Saratov, Russia. He helped organize the October Revolution in Petrograd (1917) and was appointed People's Commissar for Internal Affairs in the first Soviet government. In 1928 after opposing Stalin's economic policies, he was arrested and shot.

Rylance, Mark (1960–) Actor and director, born in Kent. In 1994 he received an Olivier Award for Best Actor in Thelma Holt's production of *Much Ado About Nothing*. In 1995 he was appointed founding artistic director of Shakespeare's Globe Theatre in London, stepping down in 2005. His performances there include *Henry V* (1997), *Anthony and Cleopatra* (1999, as Cleopatra), *Hamlet* (2000), *Twelfth Night* (2002, as Olivia), and

Richard II (2003). His film work includes *Prospero's Books* (1991) and *Intimacy* (2000).

Ryle, Gilbert (1900–76) Philosopher, born in Brighton, East Sussex. He is best known for his book *The Concept of Mind* (1949), which argued against the mind/body dualism ('the ghost in the machine') proposed by Descartes.

Ryle, Sir Martin (1918–84) Radio astronomer, born in Brighton, East Sussex, the nephew of Gilbert Ryle. His development of interferometers enabled him to survey the most distant radio sources, and his work paved the way for renewed support of the 'big bang' theory. He was appointed Astronomer Royal in 1972, and shared the Nobel Prize for Physics in 1974.

Ryukyu Islands [ryukyoo], Jap **Nansei-shoto**, also called **Luchu Islands** pop (2000e) 1 273 000; area 2255 km^2/871 sq mi. Archipelago of over 50 islands SW of Kyushu, Japan, extending in a long chain for c.650 km/400 mi towards Taiwan; chief island Okinawa; became part of Japan, 1879; under US control, 1945; islands gradually returned to Japan in 1953, 1972.

S

Saar, River [zah(r)], Fr **Sarre** River in France and Germany; r'ises in the Vosges; enters the R Moselle; length 240 km/150 mi; its valley is a noted wine area.

Saarbrücken [zah(r)brükn], Fr **Sarrebruck** 49°15N 6°58E, pop (2000e) 198 000. City in Germany; on the R Saar; economic and cultural centre of Saarland; railway; university (1948); noted for its trade fairs.

Saarinen, Eero (1910–61) Architect, born in Kirkkonummi, Finland. His designs for Expressionist modern buildings include the Trans-World Airlines Kennedy Terminal, New York City (1956–62).

Saatchi & Saatchi [sahchee] Advertisers: **Charles Saatchi** (1943–) and **Maurice Saatchi** (1946–), both born in Iraq. They immigrated to England in 1947, set up an advertising agency in 1970, and were engaged by the Conservative Party in 1978 to create election posters and slogans. They became the world's largest agency, but suffered badly in the stock market crash at the end of the decade. In 1995, following a controversial share option package, chairman Maurice Saatchi left the company, and with his brother set up a new agency, M&C Saatchi. Maurice became a Lord in 1996 and in 2003 was appointed co-chairman of the Conservative Party.

Sabah [sabah], formerly **North Borneo** pop (2000e) 1 829 000; area 73 711 km²/28 452 sq mi. State in E Malaysia, on the N tip of Borneo; highest peak, Mt Kinabalu, 4094 m/13 432 ft; British protectorate, 1882; member of the Federation of Malaysia, 1963; capital, Kota Kinabalu.

Sabbath or **Shabbat** (Heb 'cessation', 'rest') The seventh day of the week, which in Jewish belief is designated a day of rest and cessation from labour, beginning just before sunset on Fridays.

Sabin, Albert (Bruce) [saybin] (1906–93) Microbiologist, born in Białystok, Poland. He is best known for his research into a live virus as a polio vaccine, which has replaced the Salk vaccine, as it gives longer-lasting immunity, and is capable of being given orally.

Sabines [sabiynz] A people of ancient Italy, inhabiting the mountainous country NE of Rome. Often at war with the Romans, they were ultimately absorbed by them.

sable An Asian marten (*Martes zibellina*) with a thick and silky winter coat valuable to the fur trade. The fur of the **American pine marten** (*Martes americana*) is known as *American sable* or *Hudson Bay sable*.

Sabra and Chatila Palestinian refugee camps on the outskirts of Beirut, Lebanon, developed in the 1950s and 1960s. They were the scene of a massacre of Palestinians by Christian Phalangists in 1983.

Sabratha Phoenician colony founded in the 8th-c BC on the NW coast of present-day Libya; the ruins are a world heritage site.

sabretooth A fossil cat, often referred to as **sabretooth tiger**, but not closely related to the tiger; upper canine teeth enlarged, sabre-like; became extinct in the late Pleistocene epoch. (Genus: *Smilodon*. Family: Felidae.)

saccharin [sakarin] $C_7H_5NO_3S$, melting point 229°C. A white solid which has more than 400 times the sweetening power of sucrose. It is used as an artificial sweetener.

Sacco and Vanzetti [sakoh, vanzetee] **Nicola Sacco** (1891–1927) and **Bartolomeo Vanzetti** (1888–1927) Italian immigrants to the USA, executed for murders which they were said to have committed during a payroll robbery in 1920. There was considerable protest about the justice of the verdict, as it was widely felt that they had been convicted for their anarchist beliefs.

Sachs, Hans [zaks] (1494–1576) Poet and playwright, born in Nuremberg, Germany. He headed the Meistersingers of Nuremberg in 1554, and in that role was idealized in Wagner's opera.

sackbut *trombone*

Sacks, Oliver (Wolf) (1933–) Neurologist, born in London. In New York City, he worked with patients who had contracted a form of sleeping sickness, and became known following his account of the brief cure they experienced after receiving treatment with L-dopa, *Awakenings* (1973; filmed, 1990). His insights into unusual syndromes, along with an appealing literary style, resulted in a series of best-selling books, such as *The Man who Mistook his Wife for a Hat* (1986) and *The Island of the Colorblind* (1998).

Sackville, Thomas, 1st Earl of Dorset (1536–1608) Poet and statesman, born in Buckhurst, Sussex. He collaborated with Thomas Norton (1532–84) in the tragedy *Gorboduc* (1561), the first English play in blank verse.

Sackville-West, Vita, popular name of **Victoria Mary Sackville-West** (1892–1962) Poet and novelist, born in Knole, Kent. Her best-known novels are *The Edwardians* (1930) and *All Passion Spent* (1931). In 1913 she married diplomat and critic **Harold (George) Nicolson** (1886–1968). Her intimate relationship with Virginia Woolf occasioned the latter's *Orlando* (1928).

sacrament A Christian rite understood as an outward and visible sign of an internal and spiritual grace. Orthodox and Roman Catholic Churches recognize seven sacraments: baptism, confirmation, the Eucharist (Mass), penance, extreme unction, holy orders (ordination), and matrimony. Protestant Churches recognize only baptism and the Eucharist (Communion) as sacraments.

Sacramento 38°35N 121°29W, pop (2000e) 407 000. Capital of state, C California, USA, on the E bank of the Sacramento R; settled, 1839; state capital, 1854; airport; railway; university (1947); professional team, Kings (basketball).

Sacramento River Longest river in California, USA; rises in the Klamath Mts; flows 615 km/382 mi S to Suisin Bay; joins with the San Joaquin to form the Central Valley Project for flood-control, irrigation, and hydroelectricity.

Sacré Coeur Cathedral [sakray koer], Fr **Basilique du Sacré Coeur**, Eng **Church of the Sacred Heart** Roman Catholic church in the Montmartre district of Paris. Designed by Paul Abadie in Romano-Byzantine style (1876–1912), it was consecrated in 1919. The interior contains one of the world's largest mosaics, depicting Christ with outstretched arms.

sacrum A triangular-shaped bone at the lower end of the vertebral column, formed by fusion of the five sacral vertebrae. It gives attachment to the muscles of the back.

Sadat, (Mohammed) Anwar el- [sadat] (1918–81) Egyptian statesman and president (1970–81), born in the Tala district. He sought settlement of the conflict with Israel, meeting the Israeli premier in Jerusalem (1977) and at Camp David, USA (1978), in which year he and Begin were jointly awarded the Nobel Peace Prize. Following criticism by hard-line Muslims, he was assassinated in Cairo by extremists.

Saddam Hussein *Hussein, Saddam*

saddle-bill stork *jabiru*

Sadducees [sadyuseez] A major party within Judaism (c.2nd-c BC–AD 70), the name probably deriving from the priest Zadok, whose descendants held priestly office from Solomon's times. They were mainly aristocrats, associated with the Jerusalem priesthood.

Sade, Marquis de [sahd], popular name of **Donatien Alphonse François, comte** (Count) **de Sade** (1740–1814) Writer, born in Paris. Condemned to death at Aix for his cruelty and sexual practices, he escaped, but was later imprisoned at Vincennes (1777) and in the Bastille (1784), where he wrote *Les 120 Journées de Sodome* (c.1784, The 120 Days of Sodom). His name has provided the language with the word **sadism**.

Sadler's Wells Theatre A popular London dance and opera theatre, so-called because in 1683 Richard Sadler discovered a medicinal well in his garden and established a music house there. Light entertainment was provided, and the theatre became famous for pantomimes, harlequinades, and burlesques. In the 19th-c it fell into disrepair, but in 1931 was reopened under Lilian Baylis and became one of the leading theatres in London for the production of ballet and opera, now housing the Sadler's Wells Royal Ballet. The old theatre was demolished in 1966 and a new building was opened in 1998; directors Stephen Remington (1998–2004) and Alistair Spalding (2004–).

sadomasochism Sexual behaviour in which gratification is based on the infliction (**sadism**) or receipt (**masochism**) of pain or humiliation; often abbreviated as **SM**.

Safavids [safahweedz] A Persian dynasty (1501–1736) which laid down the foundations of the modern Iranian state. It made Shiism the official religion, and saw a flowering of the arts.

safety lamp A device used by miners to detect explosive methane gas in mines (*firedamp*), invented in 1815 by Sir Humphry Davy. Any methane present would cause a change in the appearance of the flame, but a double layer of wire gauze surrounding it prevented the gas igniting.

safflower An annual growing to $1\,m/3\frac{1}{4}\,ft$ (*Carthamus tinctorius*); flower-heads thistle-like, up to $3\,cm/1\frac{1}{4}\,in$ across, the florets bright red-orange; probably native to W Asia. Formerly a dye plant, it is now grown mainly for the seeds, which yield a useful oil. (Family: Compositae.)

saffron An autumn-flowering species of crocus (*Crocus sativus*), native to S Europe and Asia, with lilac flowers. It is a source of saffron, used as a food dye and as flavouring. (Family: Iridaceae.)

Safin, Marat (1980–) Tennis player, born in Moscow. He turned professional in 1997 and won his first ATP title in 1999. Further achievements include the US Open and two Masters Series titles in 2000, and the Paris Masters in 2002. Twice runner-up in the Australian Open (2002, 2004), he won the title in 2005. At the start of 2007 he had a world ranking of 26.

Safire, William [safiyr] (1929–) Journalist, born in New York City. A former public relations writer, he became a Washington-based columnist for the *New York Times* in 1973. He won the Pulitzer Prize for commentary in 1978, and went on to become a national figure known for his weekly column devoted to language matters.

saga (Old Norse 'saying') A mediaeval Icelandic or Scandinavian prose narrative, transcribed from oral tradition after 1100, and later composed in writing. The term is also more generally used of any extended narrative, in fact or fiction.

Sagan, Carl (Edward) [saygn] (1934–96) Astronomer and writer, born in New York City. He worked on planetary atmospheres and surfaces, the origin of life on Earth, and the possibility of extraterrestrial intelligence, and did much to popularize astronomy and other aspects of science.

Sagan, Françoise [sagã], pseudonym of **Françoise Quoirez** (1935–2004) Novelist, born in Paris. At 18 she wrote the best-selling *Bonjour tristesse* (1954, Good Morning, Sadness). *Aimez-vous Brahms?* (Do You Like Brahms?) appeared in 1959. She also wrote several plays, a ballet, *La Chamade* (1966), and in 1993 appeared *Oeuvres*, a volume of collected works.

sage An aromatic shrub (*Salvia officinalis*) growing to $0.5\,m/1\frac{1}{2}\,ft$, native to S Europe; flowers purplish, 2-lipped, the upper lip hooded. It is widely cultivated as a culinary and medicinal herb. (Family: Labiatae.)

sagebrush The name applied to certain North American species of *Artemisia*, including **big sagebrush** (*Artemisia tridentata*), a much-branched aromatic shrub growing to $3\,m/10\,ft$; flower-heads small, greenish, and inconspicuous; also called **sagebush**. (Genus: *Artemisia*. Family: Compositae.)

sagebush *sagebrush*

Sagitta [sajita] (Lat 'arrow') The third-smallest constellation, lying in the Milky Way near Cygnus.

Sagittarius [sajitairius] (Lat 'archer') A S constellation of the zodiac, lying between Scorpius and Capricornus.

sago palm A small tree with large feathery leaves, native to SE Asia and the Pacific. Its trunk provides sago, a primary source of carbohydrate in the tropics. (Genus: *Metroxylon*, 15 species. Family: Palmae.)

saguaro [sagwahroh] The largest of the cacti (*Carnegiea gigantea*), slow-growing, reaching 21 m/70 ft, with a thick stem, candelabra-like branches, and white flowers; found only in Arizona, S California, and Mexico. (Family: Cactaceae.)

Sagunto [sagoontoh], Arabic **Murviedro** (to 1877), ancient **Saguntum** 39°42N 0°18W, pop (2000e) 56 000. Town in E Spain; on R Palancia; Roman theatre, fortress.

Sahara Desert (Arabic 'wilderness') Desert in N Africa; the largest desert in the world, area 7·7 million km^2/3 million sq mi; average width, 1440 km/895 mi across N Africa from the Atlantic to the Libyan Desert, in which it continues unbroken to the Nile, and beyond that in the Nubian Desert to the Red Sea; areas of drift sand, rock, or gravel and pebbles; scattered outlets of surface water at oases, where agriculture is possible; generally void of vegetation; climate arid since the glacial epoch, when the region was relatively humid with a park savannah vegetation; camel caravans follow routes marked by oases; oil exploration near the Algeria–Libya frontier; phosphates in Morocco and Western Sahara; first crossed by Europeans in the 1820s.

sahel [sahel] A vegetation zone intermediate between desert and savannah conditions where rainfall is irregular and unpredictable. The vegetation is a transitional scrubland. The name is most commonly applied to the area S of the Sahara (**the Sahel**), which frequently suffers from drought and famine.

saiga [sayga] A goat-antelope native to Asia (*Saiga tatarica*); thick pale brown coat; eyes protruding; nose grotesquely swollen with large downward-facing nostrils at tip; male with short yellow horns; inhabits cold steppelands.

Saigon *Ho Chi Minh City*

Sailer, Toni (Anton) [ziyler] (1935–) Alpine skier, born in Kitzbühel, Austria. In 1956, he became the first man to win all three Olympic skiing titles (downhill, slalom, giant slalom), and was the world combined champion in 1956 and 1958.

sailfish Large agile billfish (*Istiophorus platypterus*) widely distributed in open ocean surface waters; length up to 3·5 m/11½ ft; blue-grey above, underside silver; long tall dorsal fin. (Family: Istiophoridae.)

sailing A term used to describe the sport or pastime of travelling over water in a suitable craft, using wind power acting on sails. Craft range in size from the 2·3 m/7·75 ft long *Optimist* dinghy with a single sail of 10·7 m²/35 sq ft area, which is sailed and raced at national and international levels by young children, to the 117·5 m/385 ft four-masted square-rigged barque *Sedov* (the world's largest sailing vessel) with more than 28 sails totalling over 4000 m²/13123 sq ft sail area, and a crew of 70. The sport has two main divisions, *racing*, where craft, grouped into different classes depending on size, type of rig, and whether mono or multi-hull, compete on waters ranging from an inland lake or river to the oceans of the world; and *cruising*, where vessels have accommodation enabling the crew to live aboard for extended periods. Many cruising yachts are also used for racing, and a handicap system is applied to enable vessels of different size and configuration to compete fairly against each other.

Saimaa [siymah] Lake system extending over the Finnish Lake Plateau, SE Finland; total area 4400 km²/1700 sq mi; fifth largest lake system in Europe.

sainfoin [sanfoyn] A perennial growing to 80 cm/30 in (*Onobrychis viciifolia*), possibly native to C Europe; pea-flowers bright pink veined with purple; pods 1-seeded; widely cultivated for fodder. (Family: Leguminosae.)

saint In Roman Catholic and Orthodox teaching, a man or woman recognized as being in heaven because of their special qualities. Veneration of saints (often martyrs) began in the 2nd-c, and individual saints were eventually looked to for intercession and devotion. An elaborate procedure is required before canonization may go forward.

St Albans [awlbnz], Lat **Verulamium** 51°46N 0°21W, pop (2001e) 129 000. Town in Hertfordshire, England; on R Ver; named after the first Christian martyr to be executed in Britain; royal charter, 1553; city status (1887); railway; cathedral (1115, founded as Benedictine abbey, 793); Roman theatre.

St Andrews 56°20N 2°48W, pop (2000e) 15 400. Town in Fife, E Scotland; university (oldest in Scotland, founded 1412); remains of castle (1200) and cathedral (12th–13th-c); St Andrews Royal and Ancient Golf Club; British Amateur Golf Championships (Jun).

St Anthony's fire *ergotism*

St Anton am Arlberg 47°08N 9°52E, pop (2000e) 2400. Winter sports resort in the Lechtal Alps (Arlberg massif), W Austria; major skiing centre.

St Bartholomew's Day Massacre (24 Aug 1572) The slaughter of French Huguenots in Paris, ordered by King Charles IX and connived at by the Queen Mother, Catherine de' Medici, to coincide with celebrations for the marriage of Marguerite de Valois and Henry of Navarre (18 Aug).

St Basil's Cathedral Part of the Historical Museum in Moscow. It was built (1555–61) as the Cathedral of the Intercession of the Virgin. The present title was adopted after 1588, when a chapel was added to house the remains of the ascetic Basil the Blessed.

St Bernard The heaviest breed of dog (up to 100 kg/220 lb), developed at the Hospice of St Bernard in Switzerland to track people lost in the mountain snow; orange-brown and white; large with broad head, deep muzzle, pendulous ears; also known as **Great St Bernard**.

St Bernard's Passes Two transalpine frontier passes: the **Great St Bernard**, which crosses the Pennine Alps between Martigny in Switzerland and Aosta in Italy, and the **Little St Bernard**, which crosses the Graian Alps between Aosta and Bourg St Maurice in France. St Bernard of Menthon founded hospices in both passes in the 10th-c.

St Catharines 43°10N 79°15W, pop (2000e) 144 500. Town in SE Ontario, S Canada; founded, 1784; at entrance to Welland Ship Canal; railway; university (1964); heart of Canada's fruit belt and major wine-growing region.

St Christopher-Nevis *St Kitts-Nevis*

St Croix [saynt kroy], formerly **Santa Cruz** pop (2000e) 56 200; area 218 km²/84 sq mi. Largest of the three main US Virgin Is, Caribbean; main towns, Christiansted (former capital of the Danish West Indies) and Frederiksted.

St-Cyr, Ecole de [aykol duh sī seer] A French military academy founded by Napoleon at Fontainebleau but transferred to St-Cyr in 1808. The school was moved to Coetquidan in Brittany after World War 2, but retained the name of its former home.

St David's, Welsh **Tyddewi** 51°54N 5°16W, pop (2000e) 1860. Village city in Pembrokeshire, SW Wales; episcopal seat; 12th-c cathedral honours the 6th-c Welsh patron saint, Dewi (David); mediaeval place of pilgrimage; city status, 1994.

St-Denis (France) [sī duhnee] 48°56N 2°21E, pop (2000e) 95 000. Modern industrial town and railway centre in NC France; N suburb of Paris; 12th-c Gothic Basilica of St-Denis, with tombs of several French monarchs.

St-Denis (Réunion) [sī duhnee] 20°52S 55°27E, pop (2000e) 145 000. Capital of Réunion, on the N coast; airport.

St Denis, Ruth, originally **Ruth Dennis** (1879–1968) Dancer, director, choreographer, and teacher, born in Somerville, NJ. With Ted Shawn, whom she married in 1914, she founded the Denishawn school and company (1915), and became known for her exotic, colourful, Eastern dances.

Sainte-Beuve, Charles Augustin [sīt boev] (1804–69) Literary critic, born in Boulogne, France. He produced several volumes of poetry, critical articles on French literature, and several books of 'portraits' of literary contemporaries. His speeches in favour of liberty of thought earned him great popularity.

St Elias, Mount [eliyas] 60°17N 140°55W. Mountain in St Elias Mts, on the Yukon–Alaska border, USA; rises to 5489 m/18 008 ft; second highest peak in the USA.

St Elmo's fire A blue-green-coloured electrical discharge which occurs during thunderstorm weather around the masts of ships, weather-vanes, and aircraft wing tips.

St-Etienne [sītaytyen] 45°27N 4°22E, pop (2000e) 208 000. Manufacturing town in SW France; railway; university; school of mining (1816); centre of metallurgical industry since 16th-c.

Saint-Exupéry, Antoine (Marie Roger) de [sīt egzüpayree] (1900–44) Airman and writer, born in Lyon, France. His philosophy of 'heroic action' is found in such novels as *Vol de nuit* (1931, Night Flight). He is also known for his popular children's fable for adults, *Le Petit Prince* (1943, The Little Prince). Fighting as an officer in the Free French air force, he was declared missing after a flight to North Africa in World War 2. The wreckage of his plane was found off the coast of France in 1999, but the French government did not confirm the discovery until 2004. The circumstances surrounding his death have been the subject of much controversy, amid speculation that he may have committed suicide.

St Gallen [sankt galen], Fr **St Gall** [sī gal] 47°25N 9°23E, pop (2000e) 77 000. Ancient abbey town in NE Switzerland; developed around the abbey founded by St Gall, 7th-c; a world heritage site; university; cathedral (18th-c).

St George's 12°03N 61°45W, pop (2000e) 8460. Port and capital town of Grenada, on SW coast; founded, 1650; airport.

St George's Channel Stretch of sea between the SE of Ireland (W) and Wales (E), connecting the Atlantic Ocean with the Irish Sea; at its narrowest between Carnsore Point (Ireland) and St David's Head (Wales), 74 km/46 mi across.

St Germain-en-Laye [sī zhairmī ã lay] 48°54N 2°05E, pop (2001e) 37 600. Historic city in NC France; founded, 1020; birthplace of Louis XIV, Charles IX, Claude Debussy; famous chateau built by Louis VI (1124) contains the National Antiquities Museum.

St Helena

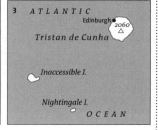

□ International Airport

[heleena] (UK British Dependent territory)

Timezone GMT

Area 122 km²/47 sq mi

Population total (2002e) 5000

Capital Jamestown (on St Helena Island)

Physical features Volcanic group of islands in the S Atlantic, 1920 km/1200 mi from the SW coast of Africa; includes St Helena, Ascension, Gough I, Inaccessible I, Nightingale I, and Tristan da Cunha; rugged, volcanic terrain; highest point, Diana's Peak, 823 m/2700 ft.

Climate Tropical marine; mild, tempered by SE 'trade' winds.

Currency 1 St Helena Pound (SHP) = 100 pence

Economy Fish (mostly tuna); agriculture, coffee; postage stamps; heavily subsidized by the UK.

GDP (1998e) $18 mn, per capita $2500

History Discovered by the Portuguese on St Helena's feast day, 1502; annexed by the Dutch, 1633; annexed by the East India Company, 1659; Napolean exiled here, 1815–21; Ascension and Tristan da Cunha made dependencies, 1922; evacuated between 1961–3, following volcanic eruption; governed by an executive council and 12-member elected Legislative Council.

St Gotthard Pass [gotah(r)d] 46°34N 8°31E. Mountain pass and tunnel (road and rail, 15 km/10 mi) between Andermatt and Airolo, in the Lepontine Alps, SC Switzerland; height, 2108 m/6916 ft; pass open between June and October; St Gotthard Hospice (14th-c).

St Helena *see panel*

St Helens 53°28N 2°44W, pop (2001e) 176 800. Industrial town in Merseyside, NW England; railway.

St Helens, Mount 46°12N 122°12W. Volcano in SW Washington, USA, in the Cascade Range; rises to 2549 m/8363 ft; major eruption in 1980; eruptions occurred again in 1986 and 2005.

St Ives 50°12N 5°29W, pop (2000e) 10 800. Resort town in Cornwall, SW England; railway.

St James's Palace Until the mid-19th-c, one of the principal royal palaces in London. Only parts of the original Tudor palace built for Henry VIII remain.

Saint John (Canada) 45°16N 66°03W, pop (2000e) 84 000. Seaport in S New Brunswick, Canada, at mouth of St John R; harbour ice-free all year; French fort, 1631–5; taken by British, 1758; largely destroyed by fire, 1877; airfield; railway.

Saint John (US Virgin Is) pop (2000e) 3030; area 52 km²/20 sq mi. Smallest of the three main US Virgin Is, Caribbean.

St John Ambulance Brigade A worldwide charitable organization that provides medical and nursing help to the aged, sick, and injured. It derives its inspiration from the Hospitallers, a military and religious order founded in the 11th-c (the Knights of Saint John of Jerusalem).

Saint John's 47°34N 52°41W, pop (2000e) 107 600. Port and provincial capital of Newfoundland, E Canada; Cabot landed here, 1497; British possession, 1583; held by the French, taken by the British, 1762; airport; railway; university (1925); two cathedrals.

St John's wort An annual or perennial, sometimes a shrub, native throughout temperate regions and tropical mountains; flowers often large and showy, yellow, 5-petalled with numerous stamens; fruit a capsule or berry. (Genus: *Hypericum*, 400 species. Family: Guttifereae.)

Saint-Just, Louis (Antoine Léon Florelle) de [sī zhüst] (1767–94) French revolutionary, born in Decize, France. He was elected to the National Convention (1792), became a devoted follower of Robespierre and was made president of the Convention (1794). He was guillotined with Robespierre in the Thermidorian Reaction.

St Kilda 57°49N 8°34W. A group of small volcanic islands in the Atlantic Ocean, 100 km/62 mi W of Scotland; abandoned in 1930, having been inhabited for 2000 years; major bird colonies; a world heritage site.

St Kitts-Nevis *p.812*

Saint-Laurent, Yves (Henri Donat Mathieu) [sī lohrã] (1936–) Fashion designer, born in Oran, Algeria. In 1962 he opened his own house, and launched the first of his 160 Rive Gauche boutiques in 1966, selling ready-to-wear clothes, a trend which many other designers were to follow.

St Lawrence River, Fr **St Laurent** A principal river of North America, in E Canada, the chief outlet for the Great Lakes; issues from NE end of L Ontario and flows NE to the Gulf of St Lawrence; forms part of border between Canada and USA; total length 1197 km/744 mi; increases gradually in width to c.145 km/90 mi; formerly navigable for ocean-going vessels only as far as Montreal; St Lawrence Seaway (1955–9) between L Ontario and Montreal now allows passage to Great Lakes; often partly unnavigable in winter months.

Saint Leger, Barry [selinjer, saynt lejer] (1737–89) British army colonel. He fought in the American Revolution, and founded horse-racing stables at Doncaster in 1776. The **St Leger** race was named for him in 1778.

St-Lô [sī loh], ancient **Briovera**, later **Laudus** 49°07N 1°05W, pop (2000e) 23 900. Market town in NW France; fortified by Charlemagne; almost completely destroyed in World War 2, but mediaeval part of town largely preserved; railway.

St-Louis (Senegal) [sī looee] 16°01N 16°30W, pop (2000e) 136 000. Seaport in Senegal; built in 1658 as a French trading company fort, and prospered with the slave trade; capital of French West Africa, 1895–1902; airfield; railway terminal.

St Louis (USA) [saynt loois] 38°37N 90°12W, pop (2000e) 241 000. City and port in E Missouri, USA, on the Mississippi R; settled by the French, 1764; under Spanish control, 1770–1800; ceded to the USA, 1804; city status, 1822; largest city in the state; busiest inland port on the Mississippi; a major land transport hub; railway; three universities (1818, 1853, 1960); professional

St Kitts-Nevis

☐ **International Airport**

official name **Federation of St Kitts and Nevis**, with **Christopher** a former alternative for **Kitts**

Local name Saint Christopher (Kitts) and Nevis

Timezone GMT -4

Area 269 km²/104 sq mi

Population total (2002e) 46 200

Status Independent state within the Commonwealth

Date of independence 1983

Capital Basseterre

Languages English (official), with creole-English widely spoken

Ethnic groups Black African descent (94%), mulatto (3%), White (1%)

Religions Christian (Anglican 36%, Methodist 32%, other Protestant 8%, Roman Catholic 11%)

Physical features Located in the N Leeward Is, E Caribbean; comprises the islands of St Christopher (St Kitts), Nevis, and Sombrero; volcanic origin with mountain ranges rising to 1156 m/3793 ft at Mt Liamuiga; Nevis dominated by a central peak rising to 985 m/3232 ft.

Climate Tropical, warm climate; average annual temperature 26°C; average annual rainfall 1375 mm/54 in; low humidity, modified by sea winds; hurricanes possible (Jul-Oct).

Currency 1 East Caribbean Dollar (XCD) = 100 cents

Economy Sugar and its products (supply 60% of total exports); copra, cotton, electrical appliances, footwear, garments, tourism.

GDP (2002e) $339 mn, per capita $8800

Human Development Index (2002) 0·814

History St Kitts was the first British colony in the W Indies, 1623; control disputed between France and Britain, 17th-18th-c; ceded to Britain, 1783; St Kitts and Nevis united, 1882; area gained full internal self-government, 1967; Anguilla declared itself independent from the control of St Kitts, which led to British troops intervention, 1969; island reverted to being a British dependent territory, 1971, and was formally separated from St Kitts-Nevis, 1980; independence of St Kitts-Nevis, 1983; British monarch represented by a Governor-General; governed by a Prime Minister and two legislative chambers; island of Nevis has its own legislature (the Nevis Island Assembly), and executive, which has exclusive responsibility for the island's internal administration; Nevis I voted in favour of secession, 1997.

Head of State
(British monarch represented by Governor-General)
1983–96 Sir Clement Athelston Arrindell
1996– Sir Cuthbert Montroville Sebastian

Head of Government
1983–95 Kennedy Alphonse Simmonds
1995– Denzil Douglas

teams, Cardinals (baseball), Blues (ice hockey); Gateway Arch, 192 m/630 ft high.

St Lucia *p.813*

St-Malo [sī mahloh] 48°39N 2°00W, pop (2000e) 51 600. Old port in W France; at mouth of R Rance; badly damaged in World War 2; birthplace of Chateaubriand.

St Mark's Cathedral, Ital **San Marco** A church constructed in 1063–71 on the site of a 9th-c shrine which housed the relics of St Mark, in Venice. It became a cathedral in 1807.

St Michael and St George, Most Distinguished Order of In the UK, an order of chivalry for those who have rendered distinguished service abroad. There are three classes: Knights and Dames Grand Cross (GCMG), Knights and Dames Commanders (KCMG/DCMG), and Companions (CMG). The motto is *Auspicium melioris aevi* (Lat 'a pledge of better times').

St Moritz [morits], Ger **Sankt Moritz**, Fr **Saint** [sī] **Moritz**, Romansch **San Murezzan** 46°30N 9°51E, pop (2000e) 5700. Resort town in SE Switzerland; altitude 1853 m/6079 ft; railway; spa; winter sports resort, home of the 1928 and 1948 Winter Olympics; Cresta Run (bobsledding).

St-Nazaire [sī nazair] 47°17N 2°12W, pop (2000e) 69 100. Seaport and industrial town in W France; on right bank of R Loire; major debarkation port for American Expeditionary Force in World War 1; German submarine base in World War 2, in which the town was largely destroyed.

St Paul 44°57N 93°06W, pop (2000e) 287 200. Capital of state in SE Minnesota, USA; a port on the Mississippi River E of its twin city Minneapolis; founded, 1838; capital of Minnesota Territory, 1849; city status, 1854; state capital, 1858; railway; university (1854); major industrial and commercial centre for a vast agricultural region.

saintpaulia *African violet*

St Paul's Cathedral A Baroque cathedral on Ludgate Hill, London, built by Wren to replace the mediaeval cathedral destroyed by the Fire of London in 1666. It is surmounted by a central lantern dome which still dominates the C London skyline.

St Peter's Basilica The largest Christian church, started in 1506 in Rome on the site of the 4th-c basilica built by Emperor Constantine. The present building was designed by Bramante on a Greek cross plan, but in 1605 Maderna was instructed to extend the nave, thereby changing the plan to that of a Latin cross. The immense dome, designed by Michelangelo and completed by Giacomo della Porta and Domenico Fontana, has a diameter of 42 m/137 ft.

St Petersburg, Russ **Sankt Peterburg**, formerly **Petrograd** (1914–24), **Leningrad** (1924–91) 59°55N 30°25E, pop (2000e) 4 994 000. Port in NW European Russia; on the R Neva, at the head of the Gulf of Finland; largest Russian Baltic port (frozen, Jan–Apr) and second largest Russian city; former capital of the Russian Empire, 1712–1918; founded by Peter the

St Lucia

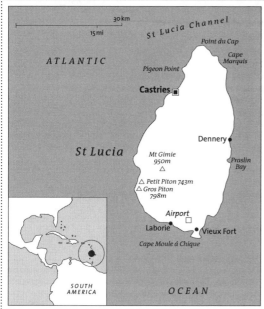

30 km
15 mi

ATLANTIC

St Lucia Channel

Point du Cap

Cape Marquis

Pigeon Point

Castries ■

St Lucia

Mt Gimie 950m △

Dennery ●

Praslin Bay

△ Petit Piton 743m
△ Gros Piton 798m

Airport □

Laborie ● ● Vieux Fort

Cape Moule á Chique

SOUTH AMERICA

OCEAN

□ International Airport

[loosha]
Local name Saint Lucia
Timezone GMT -4
Area 616 km²/238 sq mi
Population total (2002e) 160 000
Status Independent state within the Commonwealth

Date of independence 1979
Capital Castries
Languages English (official), with French patois widely spoken
Ethnic groups African descent (90%), mixed (6%), East Indian (3%), Caucasian (1%)
Religions Christian (Roman Catholic 90%, Protestant 7%, Anglican 3%)
Physical features Second largest of the Windward Is, E Caribbean. Volcanic island; forested mountainous centre rising to 950 m/3117 ft at Mt Gimie; sulphurous springs of Qualibou and twin peaks of Gros and Petit Pitons (SW).
Climate Tropical climate; average temperature 26°C; wet season (Jun–Dec), dry season (Jan–Apr); average annual rainfall 1500 mm/60 in (lowlands), 3500 mm/138 in (mountainous zone).
Currency 1 East Caribbean Dollar (XCD) = 100 cents
Economy Tourism (fastest-growing sector of the economy); bananas, cocoa, copra, citrus fruits, coconut oil; garments, textiles, electronic components; oil refining and transshipment.
GDP (2002e) $866 mn, per capita $5400
Human Development Index (2002) 0·772
History Reputedly visited by Columbus, 1502; disputed ownership between England and France, 17th-18th-c; British Crown Colony, 1814; full internal autonomy, 1967; independence, 1979; British monarch represented by a Governor-General; House of Assembly, elected every five years, and a Senate; constitutional amendment approved (Jul 2003) to replace oath of allegiance to Queen Elizabeth II with an oath to St Lucia and its people.
Head of State
(British monarch represented by Governor-General)
1997– Pearlette Louisy
Head of Government
1997– Kenny Anthony
2006– Sir John George Melvin Compton

Great, 1703; scene of a major siege by Germany in World War 2, 1941–4; airport; railway junction; university (1819); Academy of Sciences (1726); Winter Palace (1754–62, rebuilt 1839), St Isaac Cathedral (19th-c), Kazan Cathedral (1801–11), Fortress of Peter and Paul (1703), St Nicholas Navy Cathedral (1753–62).

St Pierre et Miquelon [sĩ pyair ay meeklõ] pop (2000e) 7000; area 240 km²/93 sq mi. Two islands comprising a French overseas department, S of Newfoundland; main town, St Pierre; settled by Breton and Basque fishermen, 16th–17th-c; disputed between UK and France, 19th-c; confirmed as French territory, 1946.

St-Quentin [sĩ kãtĩ] 49°51N 3°17E, pop (2000e) 65 000. Industrial town in N France, on R Somme; railway; centre of woollen industry in Middle Ages; surrounded by battlefields throughout World War 1; 12th–15th-c basilica.

Saint-Saëns, (Charles) Camille [sĩ sãs] (1835–1921) Composer and music critic, born in Paris. His works include five symphonies; 13 operas; symphonic poems; piano, violin, and cello concertos; the popular *Carnaval des animaux* (1886, Carnival of the Animals); and church music, including his *Messe solennelle* (1855).

Saint-Simon, Claude Henri de Rouvroy, comte de (Count of) [sĩ seemõ] (1760–1825) Social reformer, the founder of French socialism, born in Paris. His writing was a reaction against the savagery of the revolutionary period, and proclaimed a brotherhood of man in which science and technology would become a new spiritual authority.

Saint-Simon, Louis de Rouvroy, duc de (Duke of) [sĩ seemõ] (1675–

1755) Writer, born in Paris. He joined the court of Louis XIV, and from the 1690s kept a journal, published as his *Mémoires* (1752), giving impressions and descriptions of court life up to 1723.

St Swithin's Day *Swithin, St*

St Thomas pop (2000e) 53 600; area 72 km²/28 sq mi. One of the three main US Virgin Is, Caribbean; length, 21 km/13 mi; rises to 474 m/1555 ft at Crown Mt; capital, Charlotte Amalie; airport.

St-Tropez [sĩ trohpay] 43°16N 6°39E, pop (2000e) 6100. Fashionable resort on the Mediterranean coast, SE France; former small fishing port now frequented by yachtsmen, artists, and tourists.

St Valentine's Day (14 Feb) A day on which special greetings cards (**valentine cards** or **valentines**) are sent, usually anonymously, to a person or people to whom one feels attracted. The saint ostensibly commemorated on this day was an obscure 3rd-c Roman priest, and none of the traditions connected with 14 February have anything to do with him. There is a traditional English belief that birds choose their mates on this day.

St Vincent *p.814*

St Vincent, Cape, Port **Cabo de São Vicente** 37°01N 8°59W. Rocky headland 60 m/200 ft above sea-level on the Atlantic coast, Portugal; SW extremity of Portugal; in the 12th-c a ship bearing the body of St Vincent came ashore here; scene of a British naval victory over the Spanish fleet in 1797.

St Vitus' dance *chorea*

Saipan [siypan] pop (2000e) 48 300; area 122 km²/47 sq mi. Largest of the N Mariana Is, W Pacific; length 23 km/14 mi; airport.

saithe [sayth] Commercially important codfish (*Pollachius virens*) widely distributed in inshore waters of the N Atlantic;

St Vincent

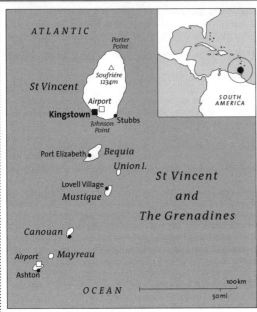

□ International Airport

official name **Saint Vincent and the Grenadines**
Local name Saint Vincent and the Grenadines
Timezone GMT -4
Area 390 km²/150 sq mi
Population total (2002e) 113 000

Status Independent state within the Commonwealth
Date of independence 1979
Capital Kingstown
Languages English (official), with French patois widely spoken
Ethnic groups Black African descent (82%), mixed (14%), White, Asian, and Amerindian minorities
Religions Christian (Anglican 42%, Methodist 21%, Roman Catholic 12%)
Physical features Island group of the Windward Is, E Caribbean, comprising the island of St Vincent and the N Grenadine Is; St Vincent volcanic in origin; highest peak, Soufrière, active volcano 1234 m/4048 ft (N), most recent eruption, 1979.
Climate Tropical climate, average annual temperature, 25°C; average annual rainfall 1500 mm/60 in (coast), 3800 mm/150 in (interior).
Currency 1 East Caribbean Dollar (XCD) = 100 cents
Economy Based on agriculture; bananas, arrowroot (world's largest producer), coconuts, spices, sugar cane; food processing, textiles; tourism.
GDP (2002e) $339 mn, per capita $2900
Human Development Index (2002) 0.733
History Visited by Columbus, 1498; British control in 1763; part of West Indies Federation, 1958–62; achieved internal self-government, 1969; independence, 1979; British sovereign represented by a Governor-General; a Prime Minister leads a unicameral National Assembly.

Head of State
(British monarch represented by Governor-General)
1996–2002 Charles Antrobus
2002– Sir Freddy Ballantyne

Head of Government
2000–1 Arnhim Eustace
2001– Ralph Gonsalves

---

length up to 1·2 m/4 ft; dark green on back, sides and underside silvery grey; also called **coalfish**, **coley**, or **pollock**. (Family: Gadidae.)

Saka Era [sahka] An era of dating in India calculated from AD 78. It has been used alongside Gregorian dates by the Indian Government since 1957.

Sakai [sakaee] 34°35N 135°28E, pop (2000e) 825 000. City in SC Honshu, Japan; formerly an important port.

saké [sakay] A Japanese rice wine, brewed in Japan for centuries, and very popular in winter. It is generally warmed in small bottles and drunk from small cups.

Sakhalin [sakaleen], Jap **Karafuto** area 74 066 km²/28 589 sq mi. Island in the Sea of Okhotsk, E Russia; length, 942 km/585 mi; maximum width, 160 km/100 mi; first Russian visit, 1644; colonized by the Japanese, 18th-c; ceded to Russia in exchange for the Kuril Is, 1875; Japan gained control of S area, 1905; ceded to the USSR, 1945; severe climate; largely forested.

Sakharov, Andrey [sakarof] (1921–89) Physicist, born in Moscow. He is credited with a critical role in developing the Soviet hydrogen bomb. In 1958 he opposed nuclear weapon tests, thereafter supporting East–West co-operation and human rights, and in 1975 was awarded the Nobel Peace Prize. Exiled to Nizhni Novgorod (formerly Gorky) in 1980 as a leading dissident, he lived under poor conditions until restored to favour in 1986.

Sakhmet or **Sekmet** [sakmet] An ancient Egyptian goddess of Memphis, depicted with the head of a lioness; her name means 'powerful'. She is associated with savage cruelty.

Saki *Munro, H H*

saki [sakee] A New World monkey; coat long, especially around face; tail long; broad mouth turns downwards at sides. (Genus: *Pithecia*, 4 species.)

Sakigake and Suisei project [sakeegakay, sooisay] The first Japanese interplanetary spacecraft, launched to intercept Halley's comet. *Sakigake* ('forerunner') was launched (Jan 1985) as a test spacecraft for *Suisei* ('comet', launched Aug 1985). They made highly successful encounters (11 and 8 Mar 1986 respectively).

Saladin [saladin], in full **Salah al-Din Yussuf ibn Ayub** (1137–93) Sultan of Egypt and Syria, the leader of the Muslims against the crusaders in Palestine, born in Tekrit, Mesopotamia. He defeated the Christians in 1187, recapturing almost all their fortified places in Syria, but a further crusade captured Acre in 1191, and he was defeated.

Salamanca [salamangka], ancient **Helmantica** or **Salmantica** 40°58N 5°39W, pop (2000e) 165 000. City in W Spain; on R Tormes; scene of British victory over the French in the Peninsular War, 1812; bishopric; railway; university (1218), a leading centre of learning until the end of the 16th-c; old and new cathedrals.

salamander An amphibian widespread in the temperate N hemisphere and tropical South America; slim body with long tail. (Order: Urodela, 358 species.)

Salamis (Cyprus) [salamis] The principal city of prehistoric and classical Cyprus, founded c.1075 BC. It flourished particularly during the 8th–4th-c BC, but was destroyed by earthquake in AD 332–42.

Salamis (Greece) [salamis] or **Koulouri** 37°58N 23°30E, pop (2000e) 22100. Town in Greece, on the W coast of Salamis I; to the E, scene of a decisive Greek naval victory over the Persians, 480 BC.

sal ammoniac [sal amohniak] *ammonium*

Salazar, António de Oliviera [salazah(r)] (1889–1970) Portuguese dictator (1932–68), born near Coimbra, Portugal. As premier, in 1932 he introduced a new, authoritarian regime, the *Estado Novo* ('New State'). He was also minister of war (1936–44) and of foreign affairs (1936–47) during the delicate period of the Spanish Civil War, in which he supported Franco.

Salem (Massachusetts) [saylem] 42°31N 70°53W, pop (2000e) 40400. Residential suburb of Boston on Massachusetts Bay; settled, 1626; 20 people executed as witches here, 1692; railway; birthplace of Nathaniel Hawthorne.

Salem (Oregon) [saylem] 44°56N 123°02W, pop (2000e) 136900. State capital in NW Oregon, USA; on the Willamette R; founded by Methodist missionaries, 1841; capital of Oregon Territory, 1851; state capital, 1859; railway; university (1842).

Salerno [salairnoh] 40°40N 14°46E, pop (2000e) 162000. Industrial town in Campania, Italy; founded by the Romans, 197 BC; one of the earliest universities in Europe; scene of major World War 2 fighting, after Allied landing, 1943; archbishopric; railway; new university (1970); cathedral (11th-c).

Sales, Francis of *Francis of Sales, St*

sales tax A tax levied on goods sold, usually a percentage of the price. It is levied in the USA by most states, at differing rates, and on most products.

Salford [sawlferd] 53°30N 2°16W, pop (2001e) 216100. City in Greater Manchester, NW England; on the R Irwell and Manchester Ship Canal; chartered in 1230; designated a city in 1926; railway; docks for Manchester; university (1967); cathedral (1848); Lowry Centre at Salford Quays.

Salians *Franks*

salicylic acid [salisilik] A drug first prepared from an extract of meadowsweet (*Spirea ulmaria* – hence the word *aspirin*), and in 1838 from an extract of willow bark; its salt, *sodium salicylate*, was first used therapeutically in 1875. It was superseded in 1899 by the more potent *acetylsalicylic acid* (aspirin).

Salieri, Antonio [salyayree] (1750–1825) Composer, born in Verona, Italy. He wrote over 40 operas, an oratorio, and Masses, and became a famous rival of Mozart.

Salinger, J(erome) D(avid) [salinjer] (1919–) Novelist and short-story writer, born in New York City. His fame rests on the novel *The Catcher in the Rye* (1951); other books include *Franny and Zooey* (1961) and, after a long period of silence, *Hapworth 16, 1924* (1997). He has become a recluse in his later years.

salinity The saltiness of seawater, ie the total amount of dissolved substances in seawater, usually reported in parts per thousand (‰), grams of solute per kilogram of sea water. The average salinity of ocean water is about 35‰.

Salisbury (Rhodesia) [sawlzbree] *Harare*

Salisbury (UK) [sawlzbree], sometimes called **New Sarum** 51°05N 1°48W, pop (2001e) 114600. City in Wiltshire, S England; Old Sarum (3 km/1¾ mi N), Iron Age hill fort, later the centre of settlement, but abandoned when New Sarum was founded in 1220 (though continued to return two members to parliament until the passing of the Reform Bill, 1832); railway; 13th-c cathedral, with the highest spire in Britain, contains one of four copies of the Magna Carta.

Salisbury, Marquess of [sawlzbree] *Cecil, Robert*

Salisbury Plain [sawlzbree] A chalk plateau of open downs in Wiltshire, S England, rising to an average of 140 m/450 ft and covering some 77700 ha/192000 acres. Much of the area is now either under cultivation or used for army training, but it remains remarkable for a number of prehistoric sites, particularly Stonehenge.

Salish [saylish] North American Indian groups, part of the Plateau Indian culture, who originally settled between the Rocky Mts and the Cascade Mts. Today they are mostly settled on small reservations, working as farmers and labourers.

saliva A secretory product of insect and terrestrial vertebrate salivary glands. In the latter it is a clear, often sticky solution of salts and proteins. It includes *mucin*, which binds food together and lubricates the throat to facilitate swallowing.

Salk, Jonas (Edward) [sawlk] (1914–95) Virologist, discoverer in 1953 of the first vaccine against poliomyelitis, born in New York City. In 1953–4 he prepared inactivated poliomyelitis vaccine, given by injections, which (after some controversy) was successfully tested.

sallow Any of several species of willow with broad, greyish leaves, and catkins (the 'pussy willows' of hedgerows) appearing before the leaves. (Family: Salicaceae.)

salmon Large anadromous (ascending rivers to breed) fish (*Salmo salar*), widespread and locally common in the N Atlantic (**Atlantic salmon**) and in NW North America (**Pacific salmon**); length up to 1·5 m/5 ft; greatly prized as game fish; with the trouts and charrs, comprise the very important family Salmonidae.

Salmonella [salmonela] A genus of rod-shaped, typically motile bacteria that can grow with or without oxygen. Two species cause typhoid and paratyphoid fever respectively; other species cause food poisoning. (Kingdom: Monera. Family: Enterobacteriaceae.)

Salome [salohmee] (1st-c) The traditional name of the daughter of Herodias. She danced before Herod Antipas, and was offered a reward. At her mother's instigation, she was given the head of John the Baptist.

Salon [salō] In France, an exhibition of art by members of the French Royal Academy, originating in 1667 and held then in the *Salon d'apollon* of the Louvre Palace, Paris. In the 19th-c the selection jury refused to hang many of the Impressionist and Postimpressionist painters, whose work was then shown (1863 and 1883) in the **Salon des Refusés**. The **Salon des Indépendents** is an annual art exhibition first held in Paris in 1884. In recent years, the term has come to be applied to other kinds of exhibition, such as the book-fair, **Salon du Livre**.

Salonica *Thessaloníki*

Salote Tupou III [salohtay] (1900–65) Queen of Tonga, remembered in Britain for her colourful and engaging presence during her visit for the coronation of Elizabeth II (1953).

salp *tunicate*

salsa A type of popular music of Cuban origin, taken to the E USA in the 1940s and 1950s, since when it has both merged with jazz and absorbed other influences, while retaining its distinctive rhythm.

salsify A plant, usually biennial (*Tragopogon porrifolius*), growing to 125 cm/50 in, native to the Mediterranean region; flowerheads violet-purple; fruit with a large feathery parachute of hairs. It is widely grown for its edible fleshy root. (Family: Compositae.)

SALT [sawlt] Acronym for **Strategic Arms Limitation Talks**, held between the USA and USSR. There were two rounds of talks. The first began in Helsinki in 1969, designed to place a numerical limit on intercontinental nuclear weapons. An agreement (SALT 1) was reached in 1974. After this there was a hardening of attitudes in the West against the intentions of the USSR, partly because of its refusal to allow on-site verification. In consequence, SALT 2 (1979) was not ratified by the US Senate, and it was withdrawn. Both sides have, however, kept to the limitations set. With the end of the Cold War, the USA and Russia moved to reduce rather than merely limit nuclear weapons and the focus shifted to the Strategic Arms Reduction Talks (START).

salt An ionic compound derivable in principle from the reaction of an acid with a base. Most salts are solids at normal temperatures, and dissolve in water. Common salt is sodium chloride (NaCl).

Salta [salta] 24°46S 65°28W, pop (2000e) 416 400. City in NW Argentina; on the R Arias; altitude 1190 m/3904 ft; founded, 1582; airport; railway; site of battle in which Spanish royalists were defeated (1813); university (1967); commercial and trade centre for extensive agricultural and mining area; cathedral.

Saltillo [salteeyoh] 25°30N 101°00W, pop (2000e) 530 000. Resort city in N Mexico; altitude 1609 m/5279 ft; founded, 1575; railway; university (1867, refounded 1957); cathedral (18th-c).

Salt Lake City 40°45N 111°53W, pop (2000e) 181700. State capital in N Utah, USA; on the Jordan R, near the S end of the Great Salt Lake; settled by Mormons, 1847; world centre of the Mormon Church (60% of the population are Mormons); railway; university (1850); processing centre for irrigated agricultural region; professional team, Jazz (basketball).

saltpetre *potassium*

saltwort A prickly, much-branched annual (*Salsola kali*), native to the N hemisphere; stems red-striped; flowers tiny, green. It is salt-tolerant, growing on sandy shores. (Family: Chenopodiaceae.)

saluki [salookee] The fastest breed of dog, developed in Arabia to hunt in the desert with Bedouin; oldest of the greyhound group; also known as **Arabian hound** or **gazelle hound**.

Salut, Iles du [eel dü salü] Island archipelago c.13 km/8 mi off the coast of French Guiana, NE South America; includes Ile du Diable (Devil's I); housed notorious French penal colonies from 1898 until 1940s.

Salvador [salvadaw(r)], also known as **Bahia** 12°58S 38°29W, pop (2000e) 2 364 000. Port capital of Bahia state, NE Brazil; founded, 1549; capital of Brazil until 1763; airfield; railway; university (1946); older parts of the upper city are a national monument and world heritage site.

Salvador, El *El Salvador*

salvage Compensation paid to someone (the **salvor**) who saves life or maritime property (a ship or its cargo) from loss or damage. The service must be rendered at sea or in tidal waters. A salvor may claim an award in the courts, where he or she has acted voluntarily. Salvage may also be the subject of prior agreement between the salvor and the property owner.

Salvation Army A non-sectarian Christian organization founded in the East End of London by William Booth in 1865, dedicated to minister to the poor and needy. It retains a military-style structure and evangelical atmosphere, and its members, both men and women, wear distinctive uniform. In 2007 it was working in some 111 countries.

salvia A member of a large genus of tropical and temperate annual or perennial herbs and shrubs; flowers 2-lipped, the upper often hooded. Popular garden plants include the scarlet-flowered annual *Salvia splendens*. (Genus: *Salvia*, 700 species. Family: Labiatae.)

sal volatile [sal volatilee] *ammonium*

Salween, River *Thanlwin, River*

Salyut (Russ 'salute') **space station** [salyoot] The first-generation Soviet space station, capable of docking with the Soyuz crew ferry and Progress resupply vehicle; it provided 100 m³/3500 cu ft of living space for up to five cosmonauts. Two versions have been flown – the first in 1971, the last (Salyut 7) in 1982. The station's orbit eventually decayed, with the vehicle re-entering the atmosphere and burning up.

Salzburg [zahltsboorg] 47°25N 13°03E, pop (2000e) 150 000. City in C Austria; on the R Salzach; railway; university (re-opened 1962); archbishopric; cathedral (1614–28); fortress of Hohensalzburg (1077) dominates the town; birthplace of Mozart, a fame

reflected in the Mozarteum (musical academy) and the Mozart Festival (Jan).

Salzkammergut [zaltskamergut] E Alpine region in C Austria; popular tourist area with many lakes; name originally applied to a salt-mining area around Bad Ischl.

Samara [samahra], formerly (1935–91) **Kuybyshev** 53°10N 50°10E, pop (2000e) 1 250 000. River-port city in EC European Russia; on the R Volga; founded as a fortress, 1586; Soviet government transferred here in World War 2, 1941–3; airport; railway; university (1969).

Samaranch, Juan Antonio [samaranch] (1920–) Seventh president of the International Olympic Committee (IOC), born in Barcelona, Spain. He was elected president of the IOC in 1980, and on his retirement in 2001 he was made honorary life president.

Samaria [samairia] The site in C Palestine of the ancient capital of the N kingdom of the Hebrews, Israel. Destroyed by the Assyrians c.722 BC, Herod the Great rebuilt and enlarged it in the 20s BC. It is now in the Israeli-occupied West Bank.

Samaritans 1 A sect of Jewish origin, living in Samaria, who were in tension with the Jews of Judea well into New Testament times. A small remnant survives today.
2 A group founded in London in 1953 by an Anglican priest, Chad Varah (1911–), providing a telephone counselling service to support those who are depressed or contemplating suicide. It is named after the 'Good Samaritan' in the parable of Jesus. A free, confidential, and anonymous service is offered 24 hours a day.

Samarkand [samah(r)kand] 39°40N 66°57E, pop (2000e) 430 300. City in Uzbekistan; a major industrial, scientific, and cultural centre; Abbasid capital, 9th–10th-c; ruled by the Uzbeks, 16th–19th-c; airfield; railway; university (1933).

samba A Brazilian dance which existed in various rural and urban forms, always accompanied by singing, before it was taken up as a ballroom dance in the 1930s.

samizdat [samizdat] (Russian *sam*, 'self' + *izdatelstvo*, 'publishing') Privately circulated editions of book-length and shorter texts not authorized for publication in the former USSR. The publishing of such work abroad was known as **tamizdat** (Russian *tam*, 'there').

Samoa *p.817*

Samos [saymos] pop (2000e) 43 800; area 476 km²/184 sq mi. Wooded island in the E Aegean Sea, Greece; rises to 1440 m/4724 ft in the W; birthplace of Pythagoras.

Samothrace [samohthrays], Gr **Samothráki** pop (2000e) 4250; area 178 km²/69 sq mi. Greek island in the NE Aegean Sea; rises to 1600 m/5249 ft.

Samoyed (anthropology) *Nenets*

Samoyed (zoology) [samoyed] An active spitz breed of dog, developed in Siberia; medium-sized with an extremely thick coat of straight pale hairs; tail carried over back only when alert, loosely curled.

samphire A fleshy, much-branched perennial (*Crithmum maritimum*), growing to 30 cm/12 in, native to coastal areas of Europe, the Mediterranean, and the Black Sea; flowers yellowish. The fleshy leaves are sometimes made into a pickle. (Family: Umbelliferae.)

Sampras, Pete (1971–) Tennis player, born in Washington, DC. He turned professional in 1988, and went on to become the youngest men's US Open champion (1990), which he subsequently won in 1993, 1995, 1996, and 2002. His wins include the Association of Tennis Professionals Tour World Championship title (1991, 1994, 1996–7), and Wimbledon a record seven times (1993–5, 1997–2000), setting a world record of 14 Grand Slam titles in the process. He retired in 2003.

Samson (c.11th-c BC?) A legendary hero of the tribe of Dan, purportedly the last of Israel's tribal leaders ('judges') prior to Samuel. Stories tell of his great strength, and his fatal infatu-

Samoa

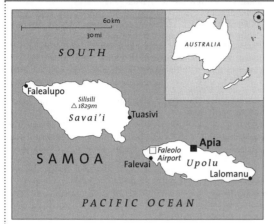

Religions Christian (99%) (Protestant 70%, Roman Catholic 20%, other 9%)

Physical features Two large (Upolu, Savai'i) and seven small islands in the South Pacific Ocean, 2600 km/1600 mi NE of Auckland, New Zealand; formed from ranges of extinct volcanoes, rising to 1829 m/6001 ft on Savai'i; last volcanic activity, 1905–11; thick tropical vegetation; several coral reefs along coast.

Climate Tropical climate; cool, dry season (May–Nov), average temperature 22°C; rainy season (Dec–Apr) with temperatures reaching 36°C; average annual rainfall, 2775 mm/109 in; frequent hurricanes.

Currency 1 Tala (SAT) = 100 sene

Economy Largely agricultural subsistence economy; taro, yams, breadfruit, pawpaws, coconuts, cocoa, bananas; tourism increasing; internal transportation system depends largely on roads and ferries; charter air service operates between the two main islands.

GDP (2002e) $1 bn, per capita $5600

Human Development Index (2002) 0·715

History Visited by the Dutch, 1772; 1889 commission divided Samoa between Germany (which acquired Western Samoa) and the US (which acquired Tutuila and adjacent small islands, now known as American Samoa); New Zealand granted a League of Nations mandate for Samoa, 1919; UN Trust Territory under New Zealand, 1946; independence, 1962; became a member of the Commonwealth, 1970; from 2007 governed by a Head of State for a 5-year term, a Prime Minister, and a 49-member Legislative Assembly (Fono).

Head of State (O le Ao O le Malo)
1963–2007 Malietoa Tanumafili II

Head of Government
1982 Tupuola Taisi Efi
1982–6 Tofilau Eti
1986–8 Va'ai Kolone
1988–98 Tofilau Eti Alesana
1998– Tuila'epa Sa'ilele Malielegaoi

(Western) [samoha], formerly (to 1997) **Western Samoa**, official name **The Independent State of Samoa**

Local name Samoa i Sisifo (Samoan)

Timezone GMT -11

Area 2842 km²/1097 sq mi

Population total (2002e) 178 000

Status Independent state within the Commonwealth

Date of independence 1962

Capital Apia

Languages Samoan and English (official)

Ethnic groups Polynesian, with Pacific Islanders, Euronesian, Chinese, and European minorities

---

ation with Delilah. When she cut his hair, breaking his Nazirite vow, he lost his strength, and was held by the Philistines until his hair grew back and he pulled down their temple upon them.

Samsova, Galina (1937–) Ballet dancer and director, born in Russia. She joined the Kiev Opera House (1956–60), and became principal dancer with the National Ballet of Canada (1961–4), the London Festival Ballet (1964–73), the New London Ballet (1973–8), and Sadlers Wells Royal Ballet (1980–90). She was appointed artistic director of the Scottish Ballet (1991–7).

Samuel (Heb probably 'name of God') (11th-c BC) In the Hebrew Bible/Old Testament, the last of the judges and first of the prophets. He presided over Saul's election as the first king of Israel, but finally anointed David as Saul's successor, rather than Saul's own son, Jonathan.

Samuel, Books of Two books of the Old Testament; also called **1** and **2 Kings**, in some Catholic versions. They are probably a compilation from several, partially-overlapping sources.

Samuel Johnson Prize Literary prize established in 1999 to celebrate the variety and originality of contemporary non-fiction published in the UK. It is worth £30 000 to the winner, with the other shortlisted authors receiving £2500 each. The annual prize is open to works in the areas of current affairs, history, politics, science, sport, travel, biography, autobiography, and the arts.

samurai [samuriy] Japanese warrior-gentry. An elaborate military feudal system: knights (*samurai*) held land from lords (*daimyo*) for military service. They were expected to display such virtues as loyalty, self-sacrifice, and valour, and to avoid dishonour by ritual suicide. They became involved in administration under the Tokugawas (17th–19th-c). Shinto bushido developed from samurai ethics under the later Tokugawas, influencing the Japanese army's officer class pre-1945.

San *Khoisan*

Sana [sanah] 15°27N 44°12E, pop (2000e) 638 400. Political capital of Republic of Yemen; former capital of North Yemen; altitude 2170 m/7119 ft; walled city, a world heritage site; university (1970).

San Andreas Fault A major fault in the Earth's crust running for about 950 km/600 mi through NW California to the Colorado Desert. It marks the boundary between the Pacific and American crustal plates, which are slipping past each other at an average rate of 1 cm/⅜ in a year. Sudden movements can cause earthquakes, the most notable of which devastated San Francisco in 1906. Serious movement also occurred in 1989, 1993, and 1994.

San Antonio 29°25N 98°30W, pop (2000e) 1144 600. City in SC Texas, USA, on the San Antonio R; eighth largest city in the USA; settled by the Spanish, 1718; captured by the Texans in the Texas Revolution, 1835; scene of the Mexican attack on the Alamo, 1836; airport; railway; two universities (1852, 1869); military aviation centre; industrial, trade, and financial centre for a large agricultural area; professional team, Spurs (basketball); the Alamo, Tower of the Americas (229 m/750 ft high).

sanction In international law, penalties imposed by one state against another. *Retorsion* is a lawful act designed to injure another state, such as the withdrawal of economic aid. *Reprisals* are acts ordinarily illegal, but which are made lawful on account of a prior unlawful act committed by the other state.

Sand, George [sã, zhaw(r)zh], pseudonym of **(Amandine) Aurore (Lucile) Dudevant**, *née* **Dupin** (1804–76) Writer, born in Paris. The companion of those poets, artists, philosophers, and politicians whose work she found inspiring, she wrote over 100 books, the most successful being those describing rustic life, such as *François le champi* (1848).

sand Grains of rock and mineral with sizes between 63 μm and 2 mm (0·0025–0·079 in), formed by the physical weathering of rocks, and composed of resistant minerals (usually quartz) not destroyed during weathering. Many shorelines consist of sandy beaches.

sandalwood A hemiparasitic tree (*Santalum album*) native to SE Asia. A fragrant timber is obtained from the white outer wood, used for carvings, incense, and joss sticks. Sandal oil is made from the yellow heartwood, and the roots are used for perfume and soap. (Family: Santalaceae.)

Sandburg, Carl (August) (1878–1967) Poet, born in Galesburg, IL. His books include *Cornhuskers* (1918) and *Good Morning, America* (1928). Interested in folksongs, he published a collection in *The American Songbag* (1927), and also wrote a vast *Life of Abraham Lincoln* (6 vols, 1926, 1939).

sanderling A pale sandpiper (*Calidris alba*) native to the N hemisphere; inhabits tundra and (in winter) coasts.

sandfly A small, hairy fly commonly found in moist, shady habitats; may act as carriers of diseases, such as leishmaniasis. (Order: Diptera. Families: Psychodidae and Phlebotamidae.)

sandgrouse A bird native to Africa, Asia, and S Europe; resembles a plump pigeon. (Family: Pteroclididae, 16 species.)

sand hopper A semiterrestrial crustacean, with a flattened body, capable of vigorous jumping; also known as a **beach flea**. (Class: Malacostraca. Order: Amphipoda.)

Sandhurst *Royal Military Academy, Sandhurst*

San Diego [san deeaygoh] 32°43N 117°09W, pop (2000e) 1 223 400. Seaport in SW California; sixth largest city in the USA; naval and marine base; airport; railway; four universities; cultural, convention, and research centre; professional teams, Padres (baseball), Chargers (football); San Diego de Alcalá mission.

Sandino, Augusto César [sandeenoh] (1895–1934) Nicaraguan revolutionary, born in Niquinohomo (or La Victoria), Nicaragua. He led guerrilla resistance to US occupation forces after 1926, and was later murdered near Managua. The Nicaraguan revolutionaries of 1979 (later known as **Sandinistas**) took him as their principal hero.

Sandjak of Novi Pazar, Serbo-Croat **Sandžak**, Turkish **Sancak** Historical province of the Ottoman Empire, comprising 8000 km²/3000 sq mi on both sides of the border between Serbia and Montenegro. By 1992 it was a potential flashpoint in the wars of Yugoslav succession, with more than half of its 400 000 population composed of Slav Muslims.

Sandown 50°39N 1°09W, pop (2000e) 17 200 (with Shanklin). Town in Isle of Wight, S England; home of the poet Swinburne; railway.

sandpiper A wading bird, widespread, mostly native to the N hemisphere, migrating to the S during the N winter; long legs and bill. (Family: Scolopacidae, c.86 species.)

sandstone A sedimentary rock composed of grains of sand (usually quartz) cemented together by a matrix, usually silica or calcium carbonate. It is quarried as a building stone.

Sandwich, John Montagu, 4th Earl of (1718–92) British politician, remembered as the inventor of **sandwiches**, which he devised in order to eat while playing around the clock at a gaming-table.

He was First Lord of the Admiralty under both Henry Pelham and Lord North (1748–51, 1771–82).

Sandwich Island *Efate*

San Francisco 37°47N 122°25W, pop (2000e) 776 700. City in W California, USA; connected to Marin county (N) by the Golden Gate Bridge, one of the longest single-span suspension bridges in the world (1280 m/4200 ft, excluding the approaches); mission and pueblo founded by the Spanish, 1776 (named Yerba Buena); Mexican control, 1821; taken by the US Navy, 1846; renamed San Francisco, 1848; terminus of the first transcontinental railway, 1869; devastated by earthquake and fire, 1906; several areas seriously damaged by earthquake, 1989; tram (cable-car); railway; airport; four universities; financial and insurance centre of W coast; major tourist, cultural, and convention centre; professional teams, Giants (baseball), 49ers (football); largest Chinatown in the USA; Fisherman's Wharf, Nob Hill mansions; Alcatraz I in San Francisco Bay, site of a Federal prison (1934–63).

Sangay [sangiy] 2°00S 78°20W. Active Andean volcano, EC Ecuador; rises to 5230 m/17 159 ft.

Sanger, Frederick (1918–) Biochemist, born in Rendcombe, Gloucestershire. He revealed the full sequence of the 51 amino acids in insulin, for which he was awarded the Nobel Prize for Chemistry in 1958. He then worked on the problems of the nucleic acids, and devised new methods to elucidate molecular structures for these also. His Nobel Prize for Chemistry in 1980 made him the first to receive two such awards.

Sanger, Margaret (Louise), *née* **Higgins** (1879–1966) Social reformer and founder of the birth control movement, born in Corning, NY. She started the first US birth-control clinic in New York City in 1916, but was charged with creating a 'public nuisance', and imprisoned for 30 days. After a world tour, she founded the American Birth Control League in 1921.

Sanhedrin [sanhedrin] (Gr 'council', also called by Josephus the *gerousia*, Gr 'senate') A Jewish council of elders meeting in Jerusalem, which during the Graeco-Roman period acquired internal administrative and judicial functions over Palestinian Jews, despite foreign domination.

sanicle A perennial (*Sanicula europaea*) growing to 60 cm/2 ft, native to woods in Europe, Asia, and Africa; flowers white or pink; fruit thickly covered with hooked bristles. (Family: Umbelliferae.)

San Joaquin River [san wakeen] River in C California, USA; rises in the Sierra Nevada; joins the Sacramento R; 510 km/317 mi long.

San José (Costa Rica) [san hohzay] 9°59N 84°04W, pop (2000e) 355 900. Capital city of Costa Rica; altitude 1150 m/3773 ft; founded, 1737; capital, 1823; airport; railway; university (1940); cathedral.

San Jose (USA) [san hohzay] 37°10N 121°53W, pop (2000e) 894 900. City in W California, USA; first city in the state, 1777; state capital, 1849–51; railway; university.

San Juan [san hwan] 18°29N 66°08W, pop (2000e) 422 000. Seaport capital of Puerto Rico; founded, 1510; airport; two universities (1912, 1950); El Morro (1591, old Spanish fortress), cathedral (16th-c).

Sankara [sangkara, shangkara] (?700–?750) Hindu philosopher and theologian, born in Kerala, India. The most famous exponent of Advaita (the Vedanta school of Hindu philosophy), he is the source of the main currents of modern Hindu thought.

Sankey, Ira David *Moody, Dwight Lyman*

Sankt Gallen *St Gallen / St Moritz (under Saint)*

San Luis Potosí [san looees potosee] 22°10N 101°00W, pop (2000e) 633 000. City in NC Mexico; altitude 1877 m/6158 ft; founded as a Franciscan mission; railway; university (1826); cathedral.

San Marino *p.819*

San Martín, José de [san mah(r)teen] (1778–1850) South American

San Marino

(state) [san mareenoh], official name **Most Serene Republic of San Marino**, Ital **Serenissima Repubblica di San Marino**

Local name San Marino

Timezone GMT +1

Area 61 km²/23 sq mi

Population total (2002e) 27 700

Status Republic

Capital San Marino

Language Italian (official)

Ethnic groups Sanmarinesi (San Marino citizens) (87%), Italian (12%)

Religion Roman Catholic (95%)

Physical features Landlocked in C Italy; smallest republic in the world, land boundaries, 34 km/21 mi; ruggedly mountainous, centred on the limestone ridges of Monte Titano, 793 m/2602 ft and the valley of the R Ausa.

Climate Temperate climate, with cool winters, warm summers; average annual temperatures -6°C (Jan), 26°C (Jul); moderate rainfall; average annual rainfall 880 mm/35 in.

Currency 1 euro (EUR) = 100 cents (previous to February 2002, 1 Italian Lira (ITL)/1 San Marino Lira = 100 centesimi).

Economy Wheat, grapes, cheese, livestock; postage stamps, tourism, textiles, pottery; chemicals, paints, wine.

GDP (2001e) $940 mn, per capita $34 600

History Founded by a 4th-c Christian saint as a refuge against religious persecution; treaty of friendship with the Kingdom of Italy, preserving independence, 1862; in World War 2, followed Italy and declared war on Britain, 1940; declared neutrality shortly before Italian surrender, 1943; governed by an elected unicameral Parliament (the Grand and General Council) a Congress of State; parliament elects two of its members every six months to act as Captains-Regent (Capitani Reggenti), with the functions of Head of State.

Head of State/Government (Captains-Regent)
2005 Fausta Morganti/Cesare Gasperoni
2005–6 Claudio Muccioli/Antonello Bacciocchi
2006 Gianfranco Terenzi/Loris Francini
2006–7 Antonio Carattoni/Roberto Giorgetti
1986–2002 Gabriele Gatti
2002–3 Fiorenzo Stolfi
2003– Fabio Berardi

patriot, born in Yapeyú, Argentina. He played a major role in winning independence from Spain for Argentina, Chile, and Peru, defeating the Spanish at Chacubuco (1817) and Maipó (1818), and became Protector of Peru (1821–2).

San Miguel de Tucumán or **Tucumán** [san meegel thay tukuman] pop (2000e) 563 400. City in NW Argentina; on the R Salí; founded, 1565; site of defeat of Spanish royalists in 1812; airport; railway; two universities (1914, 1965); cathedral.

San Salvador [san salvadaw(r)] 13°40N 89°18W, pop (2000e) 591 300. Capital city of El Salvador, on the R Acelhuate; altitude, 680 m/2230 ft; founded, 1525; destroyed by earthquake, 1854; capital, 1839; railway; cathedral.

San Salvador de Jujuy or **Jujuy** [san salvathor thay khookhooee] 24°10S 65°48W, pop (2000e) 138 500. Resort city in N Argentina; on the R Grande de Jujuy; founded, 1561; airport; railway; cathedral (18th-c).

sans-culottes [sã külot] (Fr, literally 'without breeches') The French name for the mass of the working populace in French towns at the time of the Revolution, but more specifically applied to small-time Parisian shopkeepers, craftsmen, wage-earners, and unemployed who were politically active.

San Sebastián, Span [san sayvastyan], Basque **Donostia** 43°17N 1°58W, pop (2000e) 172 000. Fortified Basque seaport and fashionable resort in N Spain; on R Urumea; bishopric; airport; railway.

sansevieria [sansiveeria] *mother-in-law's-tongue*

Sanskrit The name given to the early forms of Indo-Aryan, at c.1000 BC, in which the sacred Hindu texts known as the Vedas were written. Their grammatical form and pronunciation have been scrupulously preserved as a matter of religious observance.

Sansom, William (Norman Trevor) (1912–76) Writer, born in London. His many novels include the much acclaimed *The Body* (1949). In addition to many collections of stories, he also wrote travel books, children's stories, essays, and songs.

Sansovino, Jacopo [sansoveenoh], originally **Jacopo Tatti** (1486–1570) Sculptor and architect, born in Florence, Italy. He was responsible for bringing the High Renaissance style from Florence to Venice. From 1529 he was chief architect in Venice, where he is noted for several buildings, notably the Library of St Mark (1537–54).

Sans Souci [sã soosee] A Rococo palace built (1745–7) at Potsdam, Germany, for Frederick II of Prussia. It has been preserved in its original state, and houses several picture galleries.

Santa Ana 14°00N 79°31W, pop (2000e) 286 000. City in NW El Salvador; second largest city in the country; railway; on the Pan-American Highway; cathedral.

Santa Anna, Antonio López de (1794–1876) Mexican soldier, president (1833–6), and dictator (1839, 1841–5), born in Jalapa, Mexico. Following the Texas revolt (1836), he defeated Texan forces at the Alamo, but was then routed at San Jacinto R. He returned to power on two occasions (1846, 1853).

Santa Barbara 34°25N 119°42W, pop (2000e) 92 300. Resort in SW California, USA; founded, 1782; railway; university (1891); Santa Barbara Mission (established 1786).

Santa Claus A name derived from *Sinte Klaas*, a Dutch dialect form of St Nicholas, the patron saint of children, on whose feast day (6 Dec) presents were traditionally given to children; also known as **Father Christmas**. The English of New York took over from the Dutch the name and the present-giving custom, now transferred to Christmas Day. Countries vary greatly in the way they act out these traditions.

Santa Cruz [kroos] or **Santa Cruz de la Sierra** 17°45S 63°14W, pop (2000e) 678 700. City in E Bolivia; country's second largest city; founded in 1561 by Spanish; airport; railway; university (1880); cathedral.

Santa Cruz de Tenerife [santa krooth thay tenereefay] 28°28N 16°15W, pop (2000e) 192 000. Seaport in Canary Is, on N coast of Tenerife I; airport.

Santa Fe (Argentina) [santa fay] 31°38S 60°43W, pop (2000e) 494 200. River-port city in NEC Argentina; at the mouth of the R Salado; founded, 1573; airfield; railway; two universities (1919, 1959).

Santa Fe (USA) [santa fay] 35°41N 105°57W, pop (2000e) 62 200. State capital in NC New Mexico, USA; founded by the Spanish, 1609; after Mexican independence, 1821, centre of trade with the USA; occupied by US troops, 1846; territorial capital, 1851; railway; noted for Indian wares; cathedral.

Santa Marta [santa mah(r)ta] 11°18N 74°10W, pop (2000e) 201 500. Caribbean port in N Colombia; at mouth of R Manzanares; founded, 1525; Bolívar died here (1830); airport; railway; leading seaside resort.

Santander [santandair] 43°27N 3°51W, pop (2000e) 192 000. Seaport and resort in N Spain; bishopric; airport; railway; car ferries to Plymouth, Gijón; university (1972); cathedral (13th-c).

Santander, Francisco de Paula [santandair] (1792–1840) Colombian statesman, born in Rosario de Cúccuta, Colombia. He acted as vice-president of Grancolombia (1821–7) during Bolívar's campaigns, and was president of New Granada (modern Colombia) in 1832–7.

Santarém (Brazil) [santarem] 2°26S 54°41W, pop (2000e) 279 800. River-port in N Brazil, at the junction of the Tapajós and Amazon Rivers; founded, 1661; third largest town on the Amazon; airfield.

Santarém (Portugal) [santarã], ancient **Scalabis** or **Praesidium Julium** 39°12N 8°42W, pop (2000e) 23 500. Walled town in C Portugal; railway.

Santa Rosa de Copán *Copán*

Santa Sophia *Hagia Sophia*

Santayana, George [santayahna], originally **Jorge Augustín Nicolás Ruiz de Santayana** (1863–1952) Philosopher, poet, and novelist, born in Madrid. He became known as a philosopher and stylist, in such works as *The Life of Reason* (5 vols, 1905–6), *Realms of Being* (4 vols, 1927–40), and his novel *The Last Puritan* (1935).

Santer, Jacques [sãtair] (1937–) European statesman, born in Wasserbillig, Luxembourg. He studied law, entered politics in 1966, and went on to serve three successive terms as prime minister of Luxembourg (1984–95). In 1975 he became a member of the European Parliament, and in 1995 was elected president of the European Commission, but resigned in 1999 in the light of a damning report on corruption and maladministration within the European bureaucracy. In the same year he was elected to the European Parliament.

Santiago [santyahgoh], **Gran Santiago**, or **Santiago de Chile** 33°27S 70°38W, pop (2000e) 6 037 000. Capital of Chile, crossed E–W by R Mapocho; founded, 1541; capital, 1818; often damaged by floods, fires, and earthquakes; airport; railway; three universities (1738, 1888, 1947); cathedral; Avenida O'higgins (the Alameda) stretches for more than 3 km/1¾ mi; Santa Lucía Hill, site of first fort.

Santiago (de los Caballeros) [santyahgoh] 19°30N 70°42W, pop (2000e) 565 900. City in Dominican Republic; second largest city in country; airfield; most important trading centre in N; scene of decisive battle of Dominican struggle for independence, 1844; cathedral, fort.

Santiago de Compostela [santyahgoh thay kompostayla], ancient **Campus Stellae**, Eng **Compostella** 42°52N 8°37W, pop (2000e) 106 000. City in Galicia, NW Spain, on R Sar; former capital of the Kingdom of Galicia; world-famous place of pilgrimage in the Middle Ages (shrine of St James); airport; railway; university (1501); old town is a world heritage site; cathedral (11th–12th-c).

Santiago de Cuba [santyahgoh thay kooba] 20°00N 75°49W, pop (2000e) 433 500. Cuba's second largest city; founded, 1514; formerly capital of the republic; scene of Castro's 1953 revolution; rail terminus; university (1947); cathedral (1528); San Pedro de la Roca Castle, a world heritage site.

Santiago del Estero [santyahgoh thel estayroh] 27°48S 64°15W, pop (2000e) 224 700. City in N Argentina; on the R Dulce; oldest Argentinian town, founded in 1553; university; railway; airfield; agricultural trade and lumbering centre; cathedral; convent of Santo Domingo contains one of two copies of the Holy Shroud of Turin.

Santo Domingo, formerly (1936–61) **Ciudad Trujillo** 19°30N 70°42W, pop (2000e) 2 710 000. City in S Dominican Republic, on R Ozama; founded, 1496; airport; harbour; highway junction; university (1538); cathedral (1514–40), castle (1514).

Santorini [santoreenee], Gr **Santorin**, ancient **Thera** or **Thíra** pop (2000e) 7600; area 75 km²/29 sq mi. An island in the S Cyclades. The last great eruption of its volcano (c.1470 BC) has been held responsible (probably mistakenly) for the rapid decline of Minoan civilization.

Santos [santohs] 23°56S 46°22W, pop (2000e) 561 800. Port in SE Brazil; founded in 1534; the most important Brazilian port; major industrial area around the oil refinery and hydroelectric plant at Cubatão; railway.

São Francisco, River [sõw franseeskoh] (Port **Río**) River in E Brazil; rises in the Serra de Canastra; enters the Atlantic; length 2900 km/1800 mi.

Saône, River [sohn], ancient **Arar** River in E France rising in the Mts Faucilles (Vosges); meets the R Rhône at Lyon; length 480 km/298 mi.

São Paulo [sõw powloh] 23°33S 46°39W, pop (2000e) 12 834 000. City in SE Brazil, on the R Tietê; founded by Jesuits, 1554; airport; airfield; railway; three universities (1934, 1952, 1970); cathedral; leading commercial and industrial centre in South America; fastest-growing South American city.

São Tomé and Príncipe *p.821*

sapi-utan or **sapi-outan** *anoa*

sapodilla plum *chicle*

Sapor II *Shapur II*

Sapper, pseudonym of **Herman Cyril McNeile** (1888–1937) Novelist, born in Bodmin, Cornwall. He achieved fame as the creator of 'Bulldog' Drummond, the aggressively patriotic hero of a series of thrillers written between 1920 and 1937, of which *The Final Count* (1926) is a typical example.

sapphire A gem variety of corundum, coloured by the addition of minor amounts of impurity. It occurs in a variety of colours (except red, when it is termed *ruby*), but blue is the most valuable.

Sappho [safoh] (c.610–c.580 BC) Greek poet, born in Lesbos. The most celebrated female poet of antiquity, she wrote lyrics unsurpassed for depth of feeling, passion, and grace. Only two of her odes are extant in full.

Sapporo [sapohroh] 43°05N 141°21E, pop (2000e) 1 724 000. City in WC Hokkaido, Japan; founded, 1871; railway; subway; university (1876); Snow Festival (Jan–Feb); scene of 1972 Winter Olympics; Sapporo Dome Stadium (2001).

saprophyte [saprohfiyt] A plant which feeds on the products of decay. It includes many fungi. A few flowering plants are saprophytic; they have reduced leaves, lack chlorophyll, and form symbiotic associations with mycorrhizal fungi.

Saqqarah [sakara] The large necropolis of Memphis in Egypt, where several pharaohs and many noble Egyptians were buried. The most famous surviving monument is the stepped pyramid of Zozer (c.2630 BC), designed by Imhotep.

sarabande A 16th-c dance of Spanish or Latin-American origin in triple time. In a different form and slower tempo it became a standard movement of the Baroque suite.

Saragossa [saragosa], Span **Zaragoza**, ancient **Salduba** 41°39N 0°53W, pop (2000e) 594 000. Industrial city in NEC Spain; on R Ebro; scene of a long siege against the French in the Peninsular War, 1808–9; archbishopric; airport; railway; university (1553); two cathedrals.

Sarah or **Sarai** (Heb 'princess') Biblical character, wife and half-sister of Abraham, who is portrayed as having accompanied him from Ur to Canaan. Long barren, she is said to have eventually given birth to Isaac in her old age as God promised.

Sarajevo [sarayayvoh] 43°52N 18°26E, pop (2000e) 400 000. Capital of Bosnia and Herzegovina; on R Miljacka; governed by Austria, 1878–1918; scene of the assassination of Archduke Francis Ferdinand and his wife (28 Jun 1914); under siege and badly damaged in civil war, 1992–3; airport; railway; university (1946); educational and cultural centre; site of 1984 Winter Olympic Games; two cathedrals; annual film festival.

Saramago, José [saramahgoh] (1922–) Writer, born in Azinhaga, Portugal. A former technician, journalist and translator, since 1979 he has worked as a writer, his major works including *O Evangelho Segundo Jesus Christo* (1991, The Gospel According to

São Tomé and Príncipe

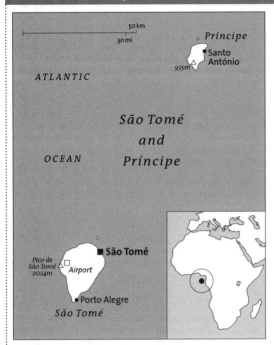

[sōw tomay, preensipe], Port **São Tomé e Príncipe**, official name **Democratic Republic of São Tomé and Príncipe**

Local name São Tomé e Príncipe

Timezone GMT

Area 1001 km²/387 sq mi

Population total (2002e) 147 000

Status Democratic republic

Date of independence 1975

Capital São Tomé

Languages Portuguese (official), with a number of creoles spoken

Ethnic groups Portuguese-African descent, African minority

Religions Roman Catholic (80%), Seventh Day Adventist, and Evangelical Protestant

Physical features Equatorial volcanic islands in the Gulf of Guinea, off the coast of Equatorial Guinea, W Africa; comprise São Tomé, Príncipe, and several smaller islands; São Tomé (area 845 km²/326 sq mi), greatest height, 2024 m/6640 ft, Pico de São Tomé in central volcanic uplands; heavily forested.

Climate Tropical climate; average annual temperature 27°C (coast), 20°C (mountains); rainy season (Oct–May); annual average rainfall 500–1000 mm/20–40 in.

Currency 1 Dobra (STD) = 100 centimos

Economy Based on agriculture (employs c.70% of population); cocoa, copra, palm kernels, coffee, wine, fishing; restructured economy since 1985, with greater involvement in commerce, banking, and tourism.

GDP (2002e) $200 mn, per capita $1200

Human Development Index (2002) 0·632

History Visited by the Portuguese, 1469–72; Portuguese colony, 1522; resistance to Portuguese rule led to riots in 1953, and the formation of an overseas liberation movement based in Gabon; independence, 1975; sole legal party was the Movement for the Liberation of São Tomé and Príncipe, until new constitution in 1990 approved multi-party democratic system; bloodless coup by army rebels (Jul 2003) when President Fradique de Menezes was visiting Nigeria; he returned when agreement to restore democratic rule was reached; governed by a President, a Prime Minister, and a National Assembly.

Head of State
1975–91 Manuel Pinto da Costa
1991–2001 Miguel Trovoada
2001– Fradique de Menezes

Head of Government
1992–4 Norberto José d'Alva Costa Alegre
1994 Evaristo do Espiritu Santo Carvalho
1994–5 Carlos da Graça
1995–6 Armindo Vaz d'Almeida
1996–9 Raul Bragança Neto
1999–2001 Guilherme Posser da Costa
2001–2 Evaristo de Carvalho
2002 Gabriel Costa
2002–4 Maria das Neves de Sousa
2004–5 Damiao Vaz d'Almeida
2005–6 Maria do Carmo Silveira
2006– Tomé Soares da Vera Cruz

Jesus Christ), *Todos os Nomes* (1997, All the Names), and *El Hombre Duplicado* (2002, The Double). He was awarded the Nobel Prize for Literature in 1998.

Sarandon, Susan [sarandon], originally **Susan Abigail Tomalin** (1946–) Film actress, born in New York City. She began her screen career in 1970, and became well known after her role in *The Rocky Horror Picture Show* (1975). Later films include *The Witches of Eastwick* (1987), *Thelma and Louise* (1991), *Dead Man Walking* (1995, Oscar), *Alfie* (2004), and *Irresistible* (2006).

Saransk [saransk] 54°12N 45°10E, pop (2000e) 318 000. City in C European Russia, on R Insar; founded as a fortress, 1641; railway; university (1957).

Saratoga, Battle of [saratohga] (Oct 1777) One of the most important engagements of the US War of Independence. Actually fought near modern Schuylerville, New York, the battle brought the defeat of a large British army under John Burgoyne by American troops under Horatio Gates.

Saratov [saratof] 51°30N 45°55E, pop (2000e) 905 000. River port in E European Russia, on R Volga; founded as a fortress, 1590; airport; railway; university (1909); cathedral (1689–95).

Sarawak [sarahwak] pop (2000e) 2 076 000; area 124 449 km²/48 037 sq mi. State in E Malaysia, on NW coast of Borneo; narrow coastal strip, and highly mountainous forested interior; highest peak, Mt Murud (2423 m/7949 ft); given by the Sultan of Brunei to James Brooke, the 'white raja' in 1841, and governed by the Brooke family until World War 2; British protectorate, 1888; Crown Colony, 1946; capital, Kuching.

Sarcodina [sah(r)kodiyna] A subphylum of protozoans, all of which possess some kind of pseudopodia; cell body typically naked, sometimes with a shell; reproduces by splitting in two (binary fission).

sarcoma [sah(r)kohma] A malignant tumour in connective tissue, bone, or muscle. Sarcomas are much less common than **carcinomas**, which arise from the lining tissues of the skin and internal organs.

Sardanapalus [sah(r)danapalus] (7th-c BC) Legendary Assyrian king, notorious for his effeminacy and sensual lifestyle. He probably represents an amalgam of at least three Assyrian rulers, one of them being Assurbanipal.

sardine *pilchard*

Sardinia, Ital **Sardegna** pop (2000e) 1 644 000; area 24 000 km²/ 9300 sq mi. Region and island of Italy; settled by Phoenicians; formed part of Kingdom of Sardinia, 18th-c; capital and chief port, Cagliari; length 272 km/169 mi; width 144 km/89 mi; largely hilly, rising to 1835 m/6020 ft in the Monti del Gennargentu; mineral-bearing SW; fertile alluvial plain of Campidano.

Sardinia, Kingdom of An Italian kingdom created 1718–20 through the Duchy of Savoy's acquisition of Sardinia, in compensation for the loss of Sicily. In 1861, Victor Emmanuel II of Sardinia became the first King of Italy.

Sardinian *Romance languages*

Sardis [**sah(r)**dis] The capital of Lydia and the political centre of Asia Minor in the pre-Hellenistic period. It was a flourishing city in Roman imperial times.

sardonyx [**sah(r)**doniks] A white and brown variety of onyx.

Sardou, Victorien [**sah(r)**doo] (1831–1908) Playwright, born in Paris. His plays include *Les Pattes de monde* (1860, trans A Scrap of Paper), *La Tosca* (1887), and over 60 others.

Sargasso Sea [**sah(r)**gasoh] Sluggish area of the Atlantic Ocean, between the Azores and the West Indies within the 'Horse Latitudes'; a still sea, allowing great biological activity; abundance of surface gulfweed.

Sargent, John Singer [**sah(r)**jnt] (1856–1925) Painter, born in Florence, Italy. Most of his work was done in England, where he became the most fashionable portait painter of his age, but he also worked on decorative paintings for public buildings in the USA.

Sargent, Sir (Harold) Malcolm (Watts) [**sah(r)**jnt] (1895–1967) Conductor, born in Ashford, Kent. He conducted the Royal Choral Society from 1928, the Liverpool Philharmonic Orchestra (1942–8), and the BBC Symphony Orchestra (1950–7). From 1948 he was in charge of the London Promenade Concerts.

Sark, Fr **Sercq** pop (2000e) 640; area 4 km²/1½ sq mi. Smallest of the four main Channel Islands, lying between Guernsey and the Cotentin Peninsula, France; consists of Great and Little Sark, connected by an isthmus; separate parliament (the Chief Pleas); Seigneurie of Sark established by Elizabeth I; ruler known as the Seigneur (male) or Dame (female) until 2006, when the islanders voted to abolish the feudal system and establish an elected governing council; no cars allowed on the island.

Sarmatia [**sah(r)**maysha] In Roman times, the area to the N of the Black Sea and the middle and lower Danube occupied by the Sarmatians, a nomadic people closely related to the Scythians.

saros [**sah**ros] The natural cycle over which sequences of lunar and solar eclipses repeat themselves. The period is 6585·32 days (c.18 years): over this cycle the Earth, Sun, and Moon return to the same relative positions.

Saroyan, William [**saroyan**] (1908–81) Writer, born in Fresno, CA. His first work, *The Daring Young Man on the Flying Trapeze* (1934), a volume of short stories, was followed by a number of highly original novels, such as *The Human Comedy* (1943), and plays, such as *The Time of Your Life* (1939).

Sarraute, Nathalie [**saroht**], *née* **Nathalie Ilyanova Tcherniak** (1902–99) Writer, born in Ivanovo, Russia. A leading exponent of the *nouveau roman*, her books include *Tropismes* (1939, Tropisms), *Portrait d'un inconnu* (1947, Portrait of a Man Unknown), and *Entre la vie et la mort* (1968, Between Life and Death). Later works include *ICI* (1995).

sarrusophone [**saroozofohn**] A musical instrument made of brass in various sizes, with a double reed. It was designed by a French bandmaster, W Sarrus, in 1856 as a substitute for oboes and bassoons in military bands, but enjoyed only brief success.

SARS Acronym for **severe acute respiratory syndrome**, a highly contagious viral infection first recorded in November 2002 in Guandong province, China, which subsequently began to spread around the world through air travel. By the end of 2003, the virus had killed 818 people worldwide and infected over 8000, with China and Hong Kong most affected. Known symptoms are similar to those of influenza and may progress to pneumonia. The incubation period is thought to be between two to seven days. The World Health Organization announced that SARS was a new strain of coronavirus, the family of viruses that are a cause of the common cold, and this was later confirmed. Efforts to develop a safe and effective human vaccine against the disease are ongoing. By the start of 2005 the virus had been effectively contained and is considered eradicated outside laboratories.

sarsaparilla [**sasparila**] A climbing, prickly perennial, native to tropical and subtropical regions; flowers greenish or yellowish; berries red or black. The berries are used to make a type of soft drink, and the dried roots yield a drug used to treat rheumatism. (Genus: *Smilax*, 350 species. Family: Smilacaceae.)

Sarto, Andrea del [**sah(r)**toh], originally **Andrea d'Agnolo**, or **Andrea Vannucchi** (1486–1531) Painter, born in Florence, the son of a tailor (*sarto*, 'tailor'). Many of his most celebrated pictures are in Florence.

Sartre, Jean-Paul [**sahtr**] (1905–80) Existentialist philosopher and writer, born in Paris. His novels include the trilogy, *Les Chemins de la liberté* (1945–9, The Roads to Freedom), and he also wrote a large number of plays, such as *Huis clos* (1944, trans In Camera/No Exit). His philosophy is presented in *L'etre et le néant* (1943, Being and Nothingness). In 1964 he was awarded (but declined) the Nobel Prize for Literature. In the later 1960s he became heavily involved in opposition to US policies in Vietnam.

SAS Abbreviation of **Special Air Service**, a British army unit specializing in clandestine and anti-terrorist operations. First formed in 1941 as a special commando unit to parachute behind enemy lines, the SAS (motto 'Who Dares Wins') was revived as a regular unit of the British Army in 1952 for special operations.

sashimi [**sasheemee**] Japanese sliced raw fish, considered a delicacy, and served in many special restaurants. Slices of raw fish on small portions of boiled seasoned rice are called *sushi*.

Saskatchewan [**saska**chuan] pop (2000e) 1 108 000; area 652 380 km²/251 883 sq mi. Province in W Canada; capital, Regina; fertile plain in S two-thirds; rises to 1392 m/4567 ft in the Cypress Hills (SW); many lakes; Hudson's Bay Company land, acquired by Canada in 1869 to become part of Northwest Territories; land disputes led to North West-Rebellion, 1885; province of Canada, 1905; governed by a Lieutenant-Governor and an elected Legislative Assembly; wheat (about two-thirds of Canada's production), potash (largest fields in the world).

Saskatchewan River [**saskachuan**] River in S Canada; rises in the Rocky Mts; flows E into L Winnipeg; length 1300 km/800 mi.

Saskatoon [**saskatoon**] 52°10N 106°40W, pop (2000e) 207 800. Town in Canada, on the S Saskatchewan R; settled in 1882 as a temperance colony; airfield; railway; university (1907); centre of large grain-growing area.

Sasquatch *Bigfoot*

sassafras [**sas**afras] A name applied to several different plants. True sassafras (*Sassafras albidum*), is a large shrub or tree, growing to 30 m/100 ft, native to E North America; aromatic foliage; inconspicuous greenish flowers; blue-grey, berry-like fruits. **Oil of sassafras**, chiefly a flavouring, is distilled from the bark, twigs, and roots. (Family: Lauraceae.)

Sassanids [**sas**anidz] The aggressive Persian dynasty that overthrew the Parthian Empire in AD 224. They were driven from Mesopotamia by the Arabs in AD 636.

Sassoon, Siegfried (Loraine) [sasoon] (1886–1967) Poet and novelist, born in Brenchley, Kent. World War 1, in which he served, gave him a hatred of war, fiercely expressed in his *Counter-attack* (1918) and *Satirical Poems* (1926). His later poetry was increasingly devotional, and he became a Catholic in 1957.

SAT 1 In the United States an abbreviation for **Scholastic Aptitude Test**, a general examination of verbal and mathematical skills not related to specific course work, taken in the USA by high-school pupils wishing to attend university.
2 In England and Wales the term is an abbreviation for **Standard Assessment Task**, a test administered to children at the ages 7, 11, 14, and 16 to discover what level of the national curriculum they have reached.

Satan *Devil*

Satanism The worship of Satan or other figures of demonology. It may include the perversion of religious rituals (eg the black Mass), the practice of witchcraft, and other practices associated with the occult.

satellite 1 A spacecraft orbiting the Earth or some other heavenly body. The first artificial satellite was Sputnik 1, launched by the USSR on 4 October 1957, and there are now more than 3000 satellites orbiting the Earth for remote sensing, military surveillance, communications, and space astronomy.
2 The moons of the planets in our Solar System. Jupiter and Saturn have extensive systems.

satellite television Television transmission using super-high-frequency beam linkage by way of an artificial satellite followed in its elliptical terrestrial orbit; commenced in 1962 with Telstar. Shortly after, satellites in fixed geostationary orbit above the Equator were introduced, providing continuous communication without tracking. In direct broadcasting from satellite (DBS), programmes are relayed at sufficient power to serve domestic TV receivers within a specific territory, known as the 'footprint', using small individual dish antennae of 60 cm/23 in diameter or less.

sati or **suttee** [satee] A custom which led Indian widows to burn themselves alive on their husbands' funeral pyres. It was prohibited during Mughal times, and suppressed by the British in 1828.

Satie, Erik (Alfred Leslie) [satee] (1866–1925) Composer and pianist, born in Honfleur, France. He wrote ballets, lyric dramas, and whimsical pieces in violent revolt against musical orthodoxy.

satinwood A deciduous tree (*Chloroxylon swietenia*) growing to 25 m/80 ft, native to S India and Sri Lanka; leaves to 60 cm/2 ft; flowers 5-petalled, creamy-white, in clusters. It provides very hard, heavy, yellow wood, valued for its satin-like lustre. (Family: Flindersiaceae.)

satisficing [satisfiysing] In economics, an alternative theory to the view that human activities can be seen as choosing between known alternatives with the aim of maximizing something, usually profits for firms. Satisficing argues that uncertainty makes maximizing very difficult. Instead, activities proceed by trial and error. Any policy, such as price-setting, is continued as long as it produces results which are up to some acceptable level. If the results fall below this level, trial and error starts again. This theory owes much to the US economist H A Simon (1916–2001).

satsuma [satsooma] A citrus fruit (*Citrus reticulata*); a variety of mandarin with an easily detachable rind. (Family: Rutaceae.)

saturated In chemistry, a term describing a hydrocarbon containing no multiple bonds. The name derives from the fact that these compounds contain the maximum amount of hydrogen for their carbon content. Alkanes are saturated hydrocarbons; alkenes and alkynes are **unsaturated**.

saturated fatty acids *polyunsaturated fatty acids*

Saturn (astronomy) The sixth major planet from the Sun, notable for its ring system – first seen by Galileo in 1610, and first identified by Huygens in 1656. It has 57 known moons (in 2007), 9 of which are not yet named; the largest, Titan, has a dense atmosphere. Its main characteristics are: mass $5.68 \times 10_2{}^6$ kg; mean density $0.69\,\text{g/cm}^3$; equatorial radius 60 268 km/ 37 449 mi; polar radius 54 364 km/33 780 mi; rotational period 10 h 14 m; orbital period 29.5 years; inclination of equator 26.7°; mean distance from the Sun 9.54 AU. Like Jupiter, it is a hydrogen/helium planet with a presumed innermost core of rocky composition and several Earth masses, an outer core of metallic hydrogen and helium, a liquid mantle of hydrogen/helium, and an atmosphere about 1000 km/600 mi deep. It is believed to have several cloud layers: solid ammonia (the highest), ammonium hydrosulphide, water ice, and water/ammonia. The rings were observed by Voyager to have particle sizes ranging up to several metres. Their infrared signature suggests that they are made of water ice – possibly created by break-up of a moon or captured comet whose orbit decayed inside the Roche limit.

Saturn (mythology) or **Saturnus** A Roman god. At his festival (**Saturnalia**, 17 Dec) slaves had temporary liberty, and presents were exchanged.

saturniid moth [saterneeid] A moth of the family Saturniidae; large, with wingspan up to 30 cm/12 in; conspicuous eyespots and banded markings present on wings; c.1300 species, including the *atlas* and *emperor moths*. (Order: Lepidoptera.)

satyr In Greek mythology, a minor deity associated with Dionysus; usually depicted with goat-like ears, tail, and legs. Rural, wild and lustful, the satyrs were said to be the brothers of the nymphs.

satyriasis [satiriyasis] Pathological exaggerated sexual drive or excitement in a male. The corresponding drive in females is known as **nymphomania**.

Saudi Arabia *p.824*

sauerkraut [sowerkrowt] A popular German food, produced by layering alternately shredded white cabbage and salt in a wooden box. Air is expelled by placing a weight on top. The cabbage salt layers are left for 3–4 weeks to ferment.

Saul [sawl] (11th-c BC) In the Hebrew bible, the first king to be elected by the Israelites. He became jealous of David, his son-in-law, and was ultimately at feud with the priestly class. Saul fell in battle with the Philistines on Mt Gilboa.

Saul of Tarsus *Paul, St*

Sault Sainte Marie [soo saynt maree], Fr [soh sĩt maree] 46°32N 84°20W, pop (2000e) 91 300. Town in SW Ontario, Canada, on N shore of St Mary's R; opposite Sault Ste Marie, Michigan; fort, 1751, taken by the British, 1762; Soo canals link L Superior and L Huron (177 m/581 ft); airport; railway.

Saunders, Jennifer (1958–) Comedy writer and actress, born in Sleaford, Lincolnshire. She teamed up with Dawn French in a comedy act, making a breakthrough into television with 'The Comic Strip Presents ...' (1990), and six series of 'French and Saunders'. She became internationally known following the success, as writer and actress, of her comedy series *Absolutely Fabulous* (1993–5, 2001; Emmy, 1993). In 2006 she wrote the series *Jam and Jerusalem* (featuring French).

Saurischia [sawriskia] The reptile-hipped dinosaurs; characterized by a forward-pointing pubis bone in the pelvic girdle, as in modern reptiles. They comprise the Theropoda, including the two-legged flesh-eaters such as *Tyrannosaurus*; and the giant plant-eating forms belonging to the Sauropodomorpha, including *Diplodocus*.

saury [sawree] Agile, slender-bodied fish, widespread and locally common in temperate ocean surface waters; head pointed or forming a narrow beak; body length up to 45 cm/18 in. (Family: Scomberosocidae, 2 genera, 4 species.)

sausage A cylindrical portion of minced meat, usually blended with breadcrumbs and herbs, and enclosed in an edible casing.

Saudi Arabia

☐ International Airport   − − Boundary awaiting demarcation

[sowdee araybia], official name **Kingdom of Saudi Arabia**, Arabic **Al-Mamlaka al-Arabiya as-Saudiya**

Local name al-'Arabīyah as-Sa'ūdīyah (Arabic)

Timezone GMT +3

Area 2 331 000 km²/899 766 sq mi

Population total (2002e) 23 370 000

Status Kingdom

Capital Riyadh (Ar-Riy-ad)

Language Arabic (official)

Ethnic groups Arab (90%), Afro-Asian (10%)

Religions Muslim (Sunni 85%, Shi'ite 15%), small Christian minority

Physical features Comprises four-fifths of the Arabian peninsula; Red Sea coastal plain bounded E by mountains; highlands in SW contain Jebel Abha, Saudi Arabia's highest peak, 3133m/ 10 279 ft; Arabian peninsula slopes gently N and E towards oil-rich al-Hasa plain on the Persian Gulf; interior comprises two extensive areas of sand desert, the An Nafud (N) and Rub' al-Khali (the Great Sandy Desert) (S); salt flats numerous in E lowlands; large network of wadis drains NE; 95% of land is arid or semi-arid desert.

Climate Hot, dry climate; average temperatures 21°C (N), 26°C (S), rise to 50°C in the interior; night frosts common in N and highlands; Red Sea coast hot and humid; average annual temperatures 14°C (Jan), 33°C (Jul) in Riyadh; average annual rainfall 100 mm/0·4 in.

Currency 1 Saudi Arabian Riyal (SAR) = 100 halalah

Economy Oil discovered in 1930s; now the world's leading oil exporter (reserves account for c.25% of world's known supply); rapidly-developing construction industry; large areas opened up for cultivation in 1980s; agriculture; wheat, dates, livestock; pilgrimage trade.

GDP (2002e) $268·9 bn, per capita $11 400

Human Development Index (2002) 0·759

History Famed as the birthplace of Islam, a centre of pilgrimage to the holy cities of Mecca, Medina, and Jedda; modern state founded by Ibn Saud who by 1932 united the four tribal provinces of Hejaz (NW), Asir (SW), Najd (C), and al-Hasa (E); governed as an absolute monarchy based on Islamic law and Arab Bedouin tradition; King (official title: Custodian of the Two Holy Mosques (Mecca and Medina)) is Head of State and Prime Minister, assisted by a Council of Ministers; there is no parliament; royal decree, 1992, provided for the creation of a Consultative Council.

Head of State/Government (Monarch)

Family name: al Saud

1932–53 Abdulaziz ibn Abdur-Rahman ibn Saud
1953–64 Saud IV ibn Abdulaziz
1964–75 Faisal II ibn Abdulaziz
1975–82 Khalid (II) ibn Abdulaziz
1982–96 Fahd ibn Abdul-Aziz
1996 Abdullah ibn Abdul Aziz *Acting*
1996–2005 Fahd ibn Abdul-Aziz
2005– Abdullah Bin-Abd-al-Aziz al Saud

Originally, the casing came from prepared animal intestine; today it is made from edible carbohydrate polymers.

sausage dog dachshund

Saussure, Ferdinand de [sohsür] (1857–1913) Linguist, born in Geneva, Switzerland, often described as the founder of modern linguistics. *Cours de linguistique générale* (1916, Course in General Linguistics) was compiled from the lecture notes of his students after his death. His focus on language as an 'underlying system' inspired a great deal of later semiology and structuralism.

Savannah 32°05N 81°06W, pop (2000e) 131 500. City in E Georgia, USA; port near the mouth of the Savannah R; founded, 1733; during the War of Independence, held by the British, 1778–82; captured by Sherman during Civil War, 1864; airfield; railway; city's historic district designated a national historic landmark.

savannah The grassland region of the tropics and subtropics, located between areas of tropical rainforest and desert. The length of the arid season prevents widespread tree growth; the scattered trees which do exist, such as acacia and baobab, are adapted to reduced precipitation levels.

Save the Children Fund In the UK, the largest international children's charity, founded in 1919, and having as its president the Princess Royal. It is concerned with the rescue of children from disaster and the longer-term welfare of children in need. Together with the US **Save the Children Federation**, it is a member of the **International Save the Children Alliance**.

Savile, Jimmy [savil], popular name of **Sir James Wilson Vincent Savile** (1926–) Television and radio personality, born in Leeds, West Yorkshire. A former miner, he achieved fame as a disc jockey, and presented BBC television's *Top of the Pops* regularly from 1964, and also hosted *Jim'll Fix It* from 1975. In 2006 he joined fellow veteran disc jockeys to present the final *Top of the Pops* show. He has used his nationwide prominence and popularity to raise huge sums of money for deserving causes.

savings and loan associations *building society*

Savonarola, Girolamo [savonarohla] (1452–98) Religious and political reformer, born in Ferrara, Italy. His eloquent preaching began to point towards a political revolution as the means of restoring religion and morality. When a republic was established in Florence (1494), he was its guiding spirit, fostering a Christian commonwealth. Accused of heresy, he was burned in Florence.

savory Either of two related species of culinary herbs. **Summer savory** (*Satureja hortensis*) is a slender, bushy annual native to the Mediterranean. **Winter savory** (*Satureja montana*) is a woody perennial native to S Europe. (Genus: *Satureja*. Family: Labiatae.)

Savoy, House of Rulers of the duchy of Savoy, a transalpine area in present-day Switzerland and France, from the 11th-c to the 19th-c. Its heyday in European politics was from the mid-14th-c to the mid-15th-c.

saw, musical A common handsaw used as a musical instrument by pressing it towards the thigh and drawing a violin bow across the straight edge. The pitch is controlled by the curve of the blade.

saw-bill *merganser*

Sawchuk, Terry, popular name of **Terrance (Gordon) Sawchuck** (1929–70) Ice hockey player, born in Winnipeg, Manitoba, Canada. One of the game's greatest goalminders, he appeared in 971 games 1950–70, a record for a goalminder.

sawfish A very large and distinctive ray, with a greatly prolonged snout, armed on each side with a regular row of strong blunt teeth; widespread in tropical seas; length up to 7·5 m/25 ft. (Family: Pristidae, 1 genus.)

sawfly A wasp-like insect which lacks a constricted waist; egg-laying tube large, saw-like, and used for depositing eggs deep into plant tissues. (Order: Hymenoptera. Suborder: Symphyta.)

Saxe, (Hermann) Maurice, comte de (Count of), usually called **Marshal de Saxe** (1696–1750) Marshal of France, born in Goslar, Germany, the illegitimate son of Augustus II, King of Poland. In the War of the Austrian Succession (1740–8) he invaded Bohemia, taking Prague by storm, and later won victories at Fontenoy (1745), Raucoux (1746), and Lauffeld (1747).

Saxe-Coburg-Gotha [saks kohberg gotha] The name of the British royal family, 1901–17. King Edward VII inherited it from his father, Prince Albert, the second son of the Duke of Saxe-Coburg-Gotha. The obviously Germanic name was changed to Windsor during World War 1.

saxhorn A musical instrument, made from brass tubing, resembling a small tuba, with the mouthpiece set at right angles and an upright bell. It was patented in 1843 by French instrument-maker Adolphe Sax (1814–94), and manufactured in various sizes.

saxifrage [saksifrij] A member of a large, varied genus of annuals or perennials, native to N temperate regions and South America, mainly in arctic or alpine regions; flowers usually 5-petalled, white, yellow, through pink to purple; fruit a capsule. (Genus: *Saxifraga*, 370 species. Family: Saxifragaceae.)

Saxo Grammaticus (Lat 'the Scholar') (c.1140–1206) Chronicler, born in Zealand. He wrote the *Gesta Danorum*, a Latin history of the Danes, in 16 books.

Saxons A Germanic people from the N Danish plain. With the Angles and Jutes, they formed the bulk of the invaders who conquered and colonized most of what became Anglo-Saxon England. They were especially prominent in Essex, Sussex, and Wessex.

Saxony A German ducal and electoral state which experienced many changes of fortune. Prominent from the 9th–11th-c, and again in the 16th–17th-c, it was finally merged in the North German Confederation (1866) and the German Second Reich (1871).

saxophone A single-reed musical instrument, made of metal with a wide conical bore. It was patented in 1846 by French instrument-maker Adolphe Sax (1814–94), and made in a variety of sizes and pitches, the most frequently used being the alto and tenor instruments. These are usually joined by the soprano and baritone instruments to form the saxophone quartet; bass and contrabass sizes are also in use.

Sayers, Dorothy L(eigh) (1893–1957) Writer, born in Oxford, Oxfordshire. She became a celebrated writer of detective stories, introducing her hero Lord Peter Wimsey in various accurately observed milieux – such as advertising in *Murder Must Advertise* (1933) or bell-ringing in *The Nine Tailors* (1934).

SBS Abbreviation of **Special Boat Service**, the naval arm of British Military Special Forces responsible for all non-conventional maritime operations. It provided the blueprint for the formation of the American SEALS (Sea, Air, Land teams).

scabies [skaybeez] A common but harmless itchy skin infestation with a mite (*Sarcoptes scabei*), which burrows below the skin surface.

scabious A perennial growing to 70 cm/27 in (*Scabiosa columbaria*), native to Europe, W Asia, and N Africa; flowers bluish-lilac, with five unequal petals, in heads 1·5–3·5 cm/$\frac{1}{2}$–1$\frac{1}{2}$ in across. (Family: Dipsacaceae.)

Scafell Pike [skawfel], also spelled **Scawfell** 54°28N 3°12W. Mountain in Lake District of Cumbria, NW England; highest peak in England, rising to 977 m/3205 ft.

scalar In mathematics, a physical quantity which can be represented by a real number, having magnitude but not direction, such as mass, time, and temperature.

scald *burn*

scale In music, the notes forming the basic vocabulary of a melodic or harmonic system, arranged in a succession of upward or downward steps. Scales in traditional Western music consist of seven notes, made up of a starting note (*tonic*) and six others related by a mathematical rule.

scale insect A plant-sucking bug; wingless adult females usually protected by a scale-like wax covering secreted over the body; males non-feeding, with one pair of wings; c.4000 species, including many pests. (Order: Homoptera. Family: Coccidae.)

Scalfaro, Oscar (Luigi) [skalfahroh] (1918–) Italian politician and president (1992–9), born in Novara, Piedmont, Italy. He was a leader of the Azione Cattolica (Catholic Action) movement, a member of the Constituent Assembly (1946), then a deputy. He served as minister for transport (1966–8, 1972), education (1972–3), and the interior (1983–7), before becoming president.

Scaliger, Julius Caesar [skalijer], originally **Benedetto Bordone** (1484–1558) Italian humanist scholar, born in Riva, Italy. After studying medicine he settled in France where he wrote on grammar, philosophy, botany, zoology, and literary criticism, his best-known work being *Poetice* (1561). His third son, **Joseph Justus Scaliger** (1540–1609), became one of the most erudite scholars of his day.

scallop A marine bivalve mollusc with unequal shell valves; lives unattached to a substrate, and is able to swim by clapping its valves together; fished commercially for human consumption. (Class: Pelecypoda. Order: Ostreoida.)

scampi The Italian culinary term for large Gulf shrimps or Dublin Bay prawns, usually fried in batter.

Scandinavian languages The languages of the N Germanic branch of Indo-European, including Norwegian (c.5 million in Norway and the USA), Swedish (c.9 million in Sweden, Finland, and the USA), Danish (c.5 million in Denmark, Germany, and the USA), Icelandic (c.0·5 million in Iceland and the USA), and Faroese (c.40 000 in the Faroe Is). These languages are mutually intelligible to varying degrees.

scanner An input device in a computer system which scans documents and transfers a map of the document into the memory of the computer. The document is represented by an array of pixels, with the number of pixels per square inch of document signifying the quality of the scanner. Low-quality scanners scan only black and white at 300 pixels per inch; high-quality ones scan in full colour at 1200 pixels per inch. In each element of the array a value is stored to represent the colour and brightness of that pixel.

scanning The exploration of a picture area along a systematic series of lines, providing information in sequential form. For TV broadcasting, two sets of interlaced alternate scanning lines are employed, giving a total picture coverage of 525 lines 30 times a second for American NTSC and 625 lines 25 times a second for European PAL. Optical scanning at a much slower rate is also employed for the transmission of facsimile documents and pictures over land lines.

scanning probe microscopy A general term for a variety of microscope techniques in which a sample surface is studied using a probe tip which scans relative to the sample surface. The *scanning tunnelling microscope* (STM) uses an electron tunnelling current to image a conducting surface. The *atomic force microscope* (AFM) measures the force on the tip to map a conducting or non-conducting surface. Magnetic and electrical surface properties can be characterized using coated tips, for example in *scanning electrical potential microscopy* (SEPM) which uses a platinum-coated probe to simultaneously map the surface and its charge. The *scanning near-field optical microscope* (SNOM), creates optical images with a resolution of tens of nanometres using light from a fine fibre scanning the surface, evading the diffraction limit applicable to normal microscopes because the light leaves the fibre very close to the sample surface. The applications of scanning probe microscopy are limitless, ranging from checking semiconductor wafers and optical disks during manufacture, to observing cells, proteins, bacteria, and viruses in situ.

Scapa Flow The area of open water in the Orkney Is, Scotland, surrounded by the islands of Mainland, Hoy, Flotta, S Ronaldsay, and Burray. It was a British naval base in both World Wars. In 1919 the German naval fleet was scuttled there.

scapula A triangular bone on each side of the body over the upper part of the back (second to seventh ribs). With the clavicle it forms the *pectoral girdle*. It moves in conjunction with the shoulder joint to increase the total range of movement of the upper limb.

Scarborough [skah(r)bruh] 54°17N 0°24W, pop (2001e) 106 200. Coastal resort town in North Yorkshire, N England; England's oldest spa town; railway; castle (12th-c); football league team, Scarborough.

Scardino, Marjorie (Morris) [skah(r)deenoh] (1947–) Businesswoman, born in Texas. She trained as a lawyer, later becoming president of the Economist Newspaper Group in New York (1985–92), and its chief executive in London (1992–6). In 1997 she joined the Pearson group as its chief executive, becoming chair of the company in 1999. She was named businesswoman of the year in 1998.

Scarfe, Gerald (1936–) Cartoonist, born in London. His cartoons, based on extreme distortion in the tradition of Gillray (eg Mick Jagger's lips are drawn larger than the rest of his face), have appeared in *Punch*, *Private Eye*, and elsewhere, especially *The Sunday Times* since 1967. Appointed artist to the *New Yorker* from 1993, he has also worked as a theatrical designer and animated film director, notably with *Hercules* (1997).

Scargill, Arthur (1938–) Trade unionist, born in Leeds, West Yorkshire. He became president of the National Union of Mineworkers in 1981, and is primarily known for his strong defence of British miners through a socialist politics that has often brought his union into conflict with government. This was most notable during the miners' strike of 1984–5, and again

in 1990 as a result of British Coal's plans to close most deep-mine collieries.

Scarlatti, (Pietro) Alessandro (Gaspare) [skah(r)latee] (1660–1725) Composer, born in Palermo, Sicily, Italy. He reputedly wrote over 100 operas, of which 40 survive complete, including *Tigrane* (1715). He also wrote 10 Masses, c.700 cantatas, and oratorios, motets, and madrigals.

Scarlatti, (Giuseppe) Domenico [skah(r)latee] (1685–1757) Composer, born in Naples, Italy, the son of Alessandro Scarlatti. He was a skilled harpsichordist, and is mainly remembered for the 555 sonatas written for this instrument.

scarlet fever An acute infectious disease of children caused by haemolytic streptococci. A sore throat is followed by a generalized red skin rash. It responds rapidly to antibiotics.

scarlet pimpernel *pimpernel*

Scarron, Paul [skaroh] (1610–60) Writer, born in Paris. He is best known for his realistic novel, *Le Roman comique* (1651–7, The Comic Novel). In 1652 he married Françoise d'Aubigné (later, Madame de Maintenon).

scat singing Wordless or meaningless improvisatory jazz singing, often imitating rapid instrumental solos. It was made popular by Louis Armstrong, Ella Fitzgerald, and many others. Armstrong's 'Heebie Jeebies' (1926) was the first recorded example; dubious legend has it that he dropped the song-sheet or forgot the words.

scattering In physics, the redirection of a beam of light or sound, or a stream of particles resulting from a collision. Scattering experiments are an important source of information in atomic, nuclear, particle, and solid state physics.

Scawfell *Scafell Pike*

scepticism / skepticism A philosophical tradition which casts doubt on the possibility of human knowledge, either in general or in some particular sphere. Pyrrho is usually credited as the founder, and from 280–80 BC it was the official philosophy of the Academy.

Schaffhausen [shafhowzn], Fr **Schaffhouse** 47°42N 8°38E, pop (2000e) 36 000. Industrial town in NE Switzerland; on the R Rhine; well-preserved mediaeval town; railway; Minster (1087–1150).

Scharnhorst, Gerhard Johann David von [shah(r)nhaw(r)st] (1755–1813) Prussian general and military reformer, born in Bordenau, Germany. He worked with Gneisenau to reform the Prussian army after its defeat by Napoleon. He was fatally wounded fighting the French at Lützen.

Schawlow, Arthur (Leonard) [showloh] (1921–99) Physicist, born in Mount Vernon, NY. With his brother-in-law Charles Townes he devised the laser, although the first working model was made by Maiman in 1960. He shared the Nobel Prize for Physics in 1981.

Scheel, Walter [shayl] (1919–) West German statesman and president (1974–9), born in Solingen, Germany. He was minister for economic co-operation (1961–6) and foreign minister (1969–74), and in 1970 negotiated treaties with the USSR and Poland.

scheelite [sheeliyt] A mineral calcium tungstate ($CaWO_4$) occurring in hydrothermal veins and pegmatites. It is an important ore of tungsten.

Schelde or **Scheldt, River** [skelduh, skelt], Fr **Escaut** River rising in N France; meets the North Sea through two estuaries (East and West Schelde) in The Netherlands; length 435 km/270 mi.

Schelling, Friedrich (Wilhelm Joseph) von [sheling] (1775–1854) Philosopher, born in Leonberg, Germany. His early work culminated in his *System des transzendentalen Idealismus* (1800, System of Transcendental Idealism).

Schelling, Thomas Crombie (1921–) Economist, born in Oakland, CA. He studied at the University of California, Berkeley (1944) and Harvard (1951). His posts include professorships at Yale (1953–8), Harvard (1958–60), and the John F Kennedy School of Government, Harvard (1969–90). He later joined the Department of Economics and School of Public Policy, University of Maryland, College Park. In his influential book *The Strategy of Conflict* (1960) he pioneered the study of bargaining and strategic behaviour and introduced the concept of the *Schelling point*. In 2005 he shared the Nobel Prize for Economics with Robert J Aumann for their work on game-theory analysis.

scherzo [skairtsoh] A lively musical piece, though not necessarily a 'joke', as the Italian name suggests. Haydn and Beethoven established it as an alternative to the minuet in the classical symphony and sonata.

Schiaparelli, Elsa [skyaparelee] (1890–1973) Fashion designer, born in Rome. Her designs were inventive and sensational, and she was noted for her use of colour, including 'shocking pink', and her original use of traditional fabrics.

Schiaparelli, Giovanni (Virginio) [skyaparelee] (1835–1910) Astronomer, born in Savigliano, Italy. He discovered the asteroid Hesperia, and termed vague linear features on Mars as 'canali' (1877).

Schick Test A test of the susceptibility to diphtheria, in which a small amount of diphtheria toxin is injected into the skin. It is named after the Austrian paediatrician, Bela Schick (1877–1967).

Schiele, Egon [sheeluh] (1890–1918) Painter, born in Tulln, Austria. He developed a powerful form of Expressionism in which figures, often naked and emaciated, fill the canvas with awkward, anguished gestures.

Schiller, (Johann Christoph) Friedrich (von) [shiler] (1759–1805) Playwright, poet, and historian, born in Marbach, Germany. His works include the poem *An die Freude* (Ode to Joy), later set to music by Beethoven in his choral symphony. His last decade was highly productive, including the dramatic trilogy, *Wallenstein* (1796–9), held to be the greatest German historical drama, *Maria Stuart* (1800), and *Wilhelm Tell* (1804).

Schinkel, Karl Friedrich [shingkl] (1781–1841) Architect, born in Neuruppin, Germany. He designed a wide range of buildings, in classical style, and introduced new streets and squares in Berlin.

schipperke [shiperkee, skiperkee] A breed of dog, developed in Belgium, originally used as a watchdog on barges; small, lively; erect pointed ears, pointed muzzle, no tail; thick, usually black, coat; also known as **little boatman**, **little captain**, or **little corporal**.

schist [shist] A medium-grade regional metamorphic rock characterized by a foliated texture, resulting from the alignment of layers of mica minerals.

schistosomiasis [skistosomiyasis] A common cause of illness in tropical countries, resulting from infestation with *Schistosoma*, a fluke; also known as **bilharziasis**. Once inside the body the flukes spread in the blood and cause disease of the lungs, liver, brain, and kidney.

schizophrenia A major psychiatric disorder characterized by an alteration of thinking and perception, including a loss of contact with reality. In addition there may be a basic change in personality, a loss of normal emotional responsiveness, and considerable withdrawal. The causes are not fully understood, but there is a major genetic component. Management includes drug treatment, skilful counselling, and rehabilitation.

Schlegel, August Wilhelm von [shlaygl] (1767–1845) Poet and critic, born in Hanover, Germany. He is famous for his translations of Shakespeare and other authors, and for founding Sanskrit studies in Germany. His brother, **Karl Wilhelm Friedrich Schlegel** (1772–1829), also born in Hanover, became the greatest critic produced by the German Romantics, writing widely on comparative literature and philology.

Schleiermacher, Friedrich (Ernst Daniel) [shliyermahkher] (1768–1834) Theologian and philosopher, born in Wrocław, Poland (formerly Breslau, Prussia). He was a leader of the movement

which led to the union in 1817 of the Lutheran and Reformed Churches in Prussia, and is widely held to be the founder of modern Protestant theology.

Schlesinger, Arthur M(eier), Jr [shlezinjer] (1917–2007) Historian, born in Columbus, OH. Special assistant to President Kennedy (1961–3), his publications include *The Age of Jackson* (1945) and *A Thousand Days: John F Kennedy in the White House* (1965), both Pulitzer prizewinners.

Schlesinger, John (Richard) [shlezinjer] (1926–2003) Actor and director, born in London. His early films, of contemporary social realism, were *A Kind of Loving* (1962) and *Billy Liar* (1963). Later films display a considerable range, as seen in *Midnight Cowboy* (1969, Oscar), *Marathon Man* (1976), *Honky Tonk Freeway* (1980), *Madame Sousatzka* (1989), and *The Next Best Thing* (2000). His work for television included *An Englishman Abroad* (1983) and *Cold Comfort Farm* (1996).

Schleswig [shlezvig] A breed of heavy horse, developed in Germany; height, 15.2–16 hands/1·5–1·6 m/5 ft 2 in–5 ft 4 in; usually pale brown with yellow mane; short powerful legs; also known as **Schleswig heavy draught**.

Schleswig-Holstein [shlezvig holshtiyn] pop (2000e) 2 700 000; area 15 721 km²/6068 sq mi. Northernmost province of Germany; includes the North Frisian Is; capital, Kiel; coast includes an extensive swimming and sailing resort area; focus of a dispute between Denmark and Prussia in the 19th-c, leading to annexation by Prussia, 1866.

Schlick, Moritz [shlik] (1882–1936) Philosopher, born in Berlin. One of the leaders of the 'Vienna Circle' of logical positivists, he was shot down on the steps of the university by a deranged student.

Schlieffen, Alfred, Graf von (Count of) [shleefn] (1833–1913) Prussian field marshal, born in Berlin. He advocated the plan which bears his name (1895), on which German tactics were unsuccessfully based in World War 1. He envisaged a German breakthrough in Belgium and the rapid defeat of France by a movement through Holland.

Schliemann, Heinrich [shleeman] (1822–90) Archaeologist, born in Neubukow, Germany. He hoped to find the site of the Homeric poems by excavating the tell at Hisarlik in Asia Minor, the traditional site of Troy. From 1871 he discovered nine superimposed city sites, one containing a considerable treasure (found 1873) which he over-hastily identified as Priam's.

Schmidt, Helmut (Heinrich Waldemar) [shmit] (1918–) West German statesman and chancellor (1974–82), born in Hamburg, Germany. He was minister of defence (1969–72) and of finance (1972–4), and succeeded Brandt as chancellor in 1974, describing his aim as the 'political unification of Europe in partnership with the United States'.

schnauzer [shnowtser] A German breed of dog; terrier-like with thick wiry coat; marked eyebrows, moustache, and beard; top of head flat, with short pendulous ears.

Schneider Trophy [shniyder] A flying trophy for seaplanes presented by French armaments magnate Jacques Schneider in 1913. After being won outright by Great Britain in 1931 the contest ceased, but the races were revived in the 1980s.

Schnitzler, Arthur [shnitsler] (1862–1931) Playwright and novelist, born in Vienna. His highly psychological, often strongly erotic works include his one-act play cycles *Anatol* (1893) and *Reigen* (1900, Merry-go-round, filmed as *La Ronde*, 1950).

Schoenberg, Arnold [shoenberg], also spelled **Schönberg** (1874–1951) Composer, born in Vienna. His *Chamber Symphony* caused a riot at its first performance in 1907 through its abandonment of the traditional concept of tonality. He became known for his concept of '12-note' or 'serial' music, used in most of his later works.

scholastic aptitude test *SAT 1*

scholasticism The Catholic philosophical tradition dominant in the mediaeval universities of the 12th–14th-c in Western Europe. It is characterized by its use of philosophy in the service of theology, and its use of ancient authorities such as Aristotle and St Augustine.

Scholes, Myron Samuel (1941–) Economist, born in Timmins, Ontario, Canada. He studied at the University of Chicago (1962), went on to gain a PhD from MIT (1968), and joined the faculty at Stanford University in 1983. He shared the 1997 Nobel Prize in Economics for his contribution to a new method of determining the value of derivatives.

Schönberg, Arnold *Schoenberg, Arnold*

Schönbrunn Palace [shoenbrun] A Baroque palace in Vienna, designed (1696–1730) by Fischer von Erlach for Emperor Leopold I, and converted for Maria Theresa's use in the 1740s.

School of the Air A two-way radio educational service for Australian children living in isolated areas; begun in South Australia in 1951 to supplement correspondence teaching and reduce feelings of isolation.

schooner A sailing vessel with more than one mast, each fore-and-aft-rigged. The masts are usually of equal height, but when two-masted the forward one is often shorter.

Schopenhauer, Arthur [shohpenhower] (1788–1860) Philosopher, born in Gdańsk, Poland (formerly Danzig, Germany). His chief work, *Die Welt als Wille und Vorstellung* (1819, The World as Will and Idea), emphasizes the central role of human will as the creative, primary factor in understanding.

Schreiner, Olive (Emilie Albertina) [shriyner], pseudonym **Ralph Iron** (1855–1920) Writer, born in Wittebergen, South Africa. *The Story of an African Farm* (1883) was the first sustained, imaginative work to come from Africa. In her later work she became a passionate propagandist for women's rights, pro-Boer loyalty, and pacifism.

Schrock, Richard (1945–) Chemist, born in Berne, IN. He studied at the University of California (1967) and at Harvard (1971) after which he spent a year as a postdoctoral fellow at Cambridge University. He later joined the Massachusetts Institute of Technology faculty (1975) and was named the Frederick G Keyes Professor of Chemistry in 1989. In 2005 he shared the Nobel Prize for Chemistry with Robert Grubbs and Yves Chauvin for his work on the development of the metathesis method in organic synthesis.

Schröder, Gerhard [shroeder] (1944–) German statesman and chancellor (1998–2005), born in Mossenberg, Germany. He qualified as a lawyer, and entered parliament as a social democrat in 1980. He became minister president of Lower Saxony in 1990, and defeated Helmut Kohl to become chancellor in 1998, he won a second term in 2002. He lost his position following the 2005 election which gave Christian Democrat (CDU) leader, Angela Merkel, victory after the CDU agreed a coalition deal with the Social Democrats (SPD).

Schrödinger, Erwin [shroedinger] (1887–1961) Physicist, born in Vienna. He originated the study of wave mechanics as part of the quantum theory with his celebrated wave equation, for which he shared the Nobel Prize for Physics in 1933.

Schubert, Franz (Peter) [shoobert] (1797–1828) Composer, born in Vienna. His major works include the 'Trout' piano quintet (1819), his C major symphony (1825), and his B minor symphony (1822), known as the 'Unfinished'; but he is particularly remembered as the greatest exponent of German songs (*Lieder*), which number c.600. He also wrote a great deal of choral and chamber music.

Schumacher, Michael [shoomaker] (1969–) Motor-racing driver, born in Hürth-Hermuhlheim, Germany. He made his Formula One debut with Jordan in 1990, then joined Benetton, with whom he became world champion in 1994 and 1995. He joined Ferrari in 1996, and achieved second place in the 1997 championship, but lost this position following an enquiry into a

driving incident. During the 1999 British Grand Prix at Silverstone he broke a leg which ended his challenge for the season. He won the world championship for Ferrari three years in succession (2000–2), gaining a record sixth title in 2003, and achieved a seventh title in 2004. He retired in 2006. His brother, **Ralf Schumacher** (1975–), is also a F1 motor-racing driver.

Schuman, Robert [shooman] (1886–1963) French statesman and prime minister (1947–8), born in Luxembourg. As foreign minister (1948–52) he proposed the **Schuman plan** (1950) for pooling the coal and steel resources of W Europe.

Schumann, Clara (Josephine) [shooman], *née* **Wieck** (1819–96) Pianist and composer, born in Leipzig, Germany. Her compositions include chamber music, songs, and many piano works, including a concerto. She married Robert Schumann in 1840.

Schumann, Elisabeth [shooman] (1885–1952) Operatic soprano and *Lieder* singer, born in Merseburg, Germany. She made her debut in Hamburg in 1909, and in 1919 was engaged by Richard Strauss for the Vienna State Opera, later specializing in *Lieder*.

Schumann, Robert (Alexander) [shooman] (1810–56) Composer, born in Zwickau, Germany. He produced a large number of compositions, until 1840 almost all for the piano. He then married Clara Wieck, and under her influence began to write orchestral works, notably his A minor piano concerto (1845) and four symphonies. He also wrote chamber music and a large number of songs (*Lieder*).

Schuman Plan A plan to unify Europe formulated in 1950 by the French foreign minister, Robert Schuman. He proposed that W European countries should allow their coal and steel industries to be run by a common authority, with free movement of capital and labour. This plan led to the European Coal and Steel Community (1952), the first step towards a European Community.

Schuschnigg, Kurt von [shushnik] (1897–1977) Austrian statesman and chancellor (1934–8), born in Riva, Italy (formerly Austria–Hungary). His attempt to prevent Hitler occupying Austria led to his imprisonment until 1945. He then lived in the USA.

Schwann, Theodor [shvahn] (1810–82) Physiologist, born in Neuss, Germany. He discovered the enzyme pepsin, investigated muscle contraction, and extended the cell theory from plants to animal tissues.

Schwarzenberg, Felix (Ludwig Johann Friedrich) [shvah(r)tsenberg] (1800–52) Austrian statesman, born in Krummau, Austria. During the 1848 Revolution, he was made prime minister, and created a centralized, absolutist, imperial state. His bold initiatives temporarily restored Habsburg domination of European affairs.

Schwarzenegger, Arnold [shwaw(r)tseneger] (1947–) US film actor, born near Graz, Austria. He won several body-building titles, and in the 1980s became the leading figure in muscular action films, beginning with *Conan the Barbarian* (1982), which became increasingly technological and violent with *The Terminator* (1984) and *Total Recall* (1990). A more humane side emerged in such films as *Twins* (1988) and *Junior* (1994). Later films include *End of Days* (1999) and *Terminator 3* (2003). He became an American citizen in 1983. A supporter of the US Republican Party, in 2003 he successfully ran for governor of California. In 2006 he successfully negotiated a deal to cut greenhouse gas emissions, making California the first US state to legislate on the expulsion of carbon dioxide and other gases.

Schwarzkopf, Dame (Olga Maria) Elisabeth (Friederike) [shvah(r)tskopf] (1915–2006) Soprano, born in Janotschin, near Posen, Germany (now Poznan, Poland). She made her debut at Berlin in 1938, first specializing in coloratura roles and later appearing more as a lyric soprano, especially in recitals of *Lieder*. She was made a dame in 1992.

Schwarzkopf, H Norman [shvah(r)tskopf], nickname **Stormin' Norman** (1934–) US army officer, born in Trenton, NJ. He commanded US and allied forces against Iraq during 'Operation Desert Storm' in 1991, then retired from the army.

Schwarzschild, Karl [shvah(r)tsshild] (1873–1916) Theoretical astrophysicist, born in Frankfurt, Germany. He computed exact solutions of Einstein's field equations in general relativity. The **Schwarzschild radius** is the critical radius at which an object becomes a black hole if collapsed or compressed indefinitely.

Schweitzer, Albert [shviytser] (1875–1965) Medical missionary, theologian, musician, and philosopher, born in Kaysersberg, NE France (formerly Germany). In 1896 he made his famous decision that he would live for science and art until he was 30, and then devote his life to serving humanity. His religious writing includes *Von Reimarus zu Wrede* (1906, trans The Quest of the Historical Jesus), and major works on St Paul. True to his vow, despite his international reputation in music and theology, he began to study medicine in 1905, and after qualifying (1913) set up a hospital to fight leprosy and sleeping sickness at Lambaréné, French Equatorial Africa, where he remained for the rest of his life. He was awarded the Nobel Peace Prize in 1952.

Schwerin [shvayreen] 53°37N 11°22E, pop (2000e) 132 000. City in N Germany; former capital of Mecklenburg state; railway; cathedral (13th-c).

Schwimmer, David [shwimer] (1966–) Actor and director, born in New York City. He played several small roles in television series, eventually becoming known for his role as Ross Geller in the acclaimed television series *Friends* (1994–2004). Feature films include *The Pallbearer* (1996), *Uprising* (2001), and *Big Nothing* (2006).

Schwitters, Kurt [shviterz] (1887–1948) Artist, born in Hanover, Germany. He joined the Dadaists, developing a form of collage (*merz*) using such everyday detritus as broken glass, tram tickets, and scraps of paper picked up in the street.

Schwyz [shveets] 47°02N 8°39E, pop (2000e) 13 300. Town in C Switzerland; the town and canton gave their name to the whole country; railway.

sciatica [siyatika] Pain in the distribution of the sciatic nerve (ie over the buttocks and the back of the leg as far as the foot). It is commonly due to pressure on the lumbosacral nerve roots of the sciatic nerve.

science fiction Fiction that focuses on the technical possibilities and human effects of scientific advance. The first novelist to explore this theme systematically was Jules Verne, with four novels (1863–73) including *20 000 Leagues under the Sea* (1870). H G Wells's novels include *The Time Machine* (1895) and *The First Men in the Moon* (1901). Major authors, such as Ray Bradbury (eg *Fahrenheit 451*, 1954), Arthur C Clarke (eg *Childhood's End*, 1954), and Isaac Asimov (eg *Foundation Trilogy*, 1957–63), did not emerge until after World War 2.

Science Museum A museum in S Kensington, London, housing the most important British collection of scientific and technological exhibits.

science park A concentration of scientific and high technology industries and businesses on one site. The term includes research parks established by universities to promote academic and business links in science, and technology parks designed for the commercial exploitation of high technology. Science parks began in the USA in the 1930s.

Scientology® (Latin, *scio* 'know' + Greek *logos* 'study') An applied religious philosophy and non-denominational religion, founded in the USA by L Ron Hubbard in 1952. The Church of Scientology was formed by Scientologists in 1954. It holds man to be an intrinsically spiritual being of unlimited ability and beneficence, its goal the achievement of complete certainty of one's spiritual existence and relationship to the Supreme Being. A central technique is **Dianetics®** (Greek *dia* 'through' + *nous* 'soul'), a spiritual healing technology aimed at the improvement of mental ability and the alleviation of psychosomatic ills.

Scilly, Isles of [silee] pop (2001e) 2200 area 16 km²/6 sq mi. A group of c.140 islands and islets W of Land's End, Cornwall, SW England; administered by Duchy of Cornwall; includes the five inhabited islands of St Mary's (chief town, Hugh Town), St Martin's, Tresco, St Agnes, Bryher.

scintillation counter A device for detecting the passage of charged particles, using materials such as sodium iodide, or special plastics which emit light (**scintillate**) when charged particles pass through them. The technique is an important means of timing the passage of particles in particle physics experiments.

Scipio Africanus [skipioh], in full **Publius Cornelius Scipio Africanus**, also called **Scipio Africanus Major** (236–c.183 BC) Roman general of the Second Punic War. His victory at Ilipa (206 BC) forced the Carthaginians out of Spain, and his defeat of Hannibal at Zama (202 BC) broke the power of Carthage altogether.

Scipio Aemilianus [skipioh aymiliahnus], in full **Scipio Aemilianus Publius Cornelius**, also called **Scipio Africanus Minor** (185–129 BC) Roman statesman, general, and orator, the adopted grandson of Scipio Africanus Major. He was famous primarily for the sack of Carthage in the Third Punic War (146 BC), the destruction of Numantia (133 BC), and his patronage of the arts.

scirocco Sirocco

scissorbill skimmer

scoliosis [skoliohsis] *vertebral column*

Scopes Trial (1925) A trial of a high-school teacher, John Thomas Scopes, in Tennessee, who instructed his biology students in the evolutionary theory of creation in violation of a Tennessee state law mandating that only the literal account of the creation as told in the Book of Genesis should be taught. He was arrested and charged with violating the statute. The trial was broadcast on the radio and became a media event. Many accepted the view that monkeys and humans had common ancestors, and so the Scopes case was sometimes called the 'Monkey Trial'. Scopes was found guilty and paid a small fine of $100, and the Tennessee law remained in effect until 1967.

scorpion A terrestrial arthropod; body typically elongate, up to 18 cm/7 in long, including a long tail bearing a conspicuous terminal sting; c.1200 species, mostly tropical in distribution. (Class: Arachnida. Order: Scorpiones.)

scorpionfish Robust, bottom-living, marine fish with well-developed fin and body spines, frequently armed with venom glands; widespread in tropical to cool temperate seas; length up to 40 cm/16 in. (Family: Scorpaenidae, 11 genera.)

Scorpius (Lat 'scorpion') Constellation in the S sky; often wrongly called **Scorpio**. It is a constellation of the zodiac, lying between Libra and Sagittarius. The brightest star is Antares. Distance: 185 parsec.

Scorsese, Martin [skaw(r)sayzee] (1942–) Film director, born in Flushing, Long Island, NY. His many films include *Taxi Driver* (1976), *Raging Bull* (1980), *GoodFellas* (1990), *Gangs of New York* (2002, Golden Globe Best Director; Oscar nomination), *The Aviator* (2004, Golden Globe Best Film), and *The Departed* (2006, Best Director BAFTA, Golden Globe, Oscar). In 2004 he was honoured with the Directors Guild of America lifetime achievement award.

Scotch whisky A spirit distilled from malted barley, either **single malt**, the product of one distillery, or **blended** whiskies. Grain whisky, distilled from barley and maize in continuous stills, is now used as the base for much of the blended whisky.

Scotland

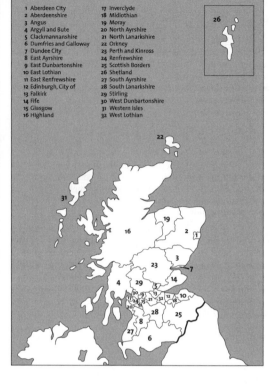

1	Aberdeen City	17	Inverclyde
2	Aberdeenshire	18	Midlothian
3	Angus	19	Moray
4	Argyll and Bute	20	North Ayrshire
5	Clackmannanshire	21	North Lanarkshire
6	Dumfries and Galloway	22	Orkney
7	Dundee City	23	Perth and Kinross
8	East Ayrshire	24	Renfrewshire
9	East Dunbartonshire	25	Scottish Borders
10	East Lothian	26	Shetland
11	East Renfrewshire	27	South Ayrshire
12	Edinburgh, City of	28	South Lanarkshire
13	Falkirk	29	Stirling
14	Fife	30	West Dunbartonshire
15	Glasgow	31	Western Isles
16	Highland	32	West Lothian

☐ International Airport

(UK)

Area 78 742 km²/30 394 sq mi

Population total (2001e) 5 062 000

Status Constituent part of the United Kingdom

Capital Edinburgh

Languages English, Scots Gaelic (Gallic) (known or used by c.80 000 residents)

Physical features Comprises the N part of the UK, and includes the island groups of Outer and Inner Hebrides, Orkney and Shetland; divided into Southern Uplands, rising to 843 m/2766 ft at Merrick; Central Lowlands (most densely populated area); and Northern Highlands, divided by the fault line following the Great Glen, and rising to 1344 m/4409 ft at Ben Nevis; W coast heavily indented; several wide estuaries on E coast, primarily Firths of Forth, Tay and Moray; many freshwater lochs in the interior, largest being Loch Lomond, 70 km²/27 sq mi, and deepest Loch Morar, 310 m/1020 ft.

Economy Based on coal, but all heavy industry declined through the 1980s, with closure of many pits; oil services on E coast; tourism, especially in Highlands; shipbuilding, steel, whisky, textiles, agriculture, forestry.

Scotland see panel

Scotland Yard, officially **New Scotland Yard** The headquarters of the Metropolitan Police at Westminster in London. Its name derives from its original site by Great Scotland Yard.

Scott, George C(ampbell) (1927–99) Film actor, born in Wise, VA. His early roles included *The Hustler* (1961) and *Dr Strangelove* (1963). He won an Oscar for *Patton* (1969), but refused to accept it (the first actor to do so), and also refused the Emmy he won for *The Price* (1970). Later films included *Dick Tracy* (1989), *Malice* (1993), and *Country Justice* (1997).

Scott, Sir George Gilbert (1811–78) Architect, born in Gawcott, Buckinghamshire. He became the leading practical architect of the British Gothic revival, as seen in the Albert Memorial (1862–3), St Pancras Station and Hotel in London (1865), and Glasgow University (1865).

Scott, Paul (Mark) (1920–78) Novelist, born in London. His reputation is based on four novels collectively known as the *Raj Quartet* (1966–74), in which he gave an exhaustive account of the British withdrawal from India.

Scott, Sir Peter (Markham) (1909–89) Artist, ornithologist, and broadcaster, born in London. He began to exhibit his paintings of bird scenes in 1933, and after 1945 led several ornithological expeditions. His writing and television programmes helped to popularize natural history.

Scott, R(obert) F(alcon) (1868–1912) Antarctic explorer, born near Devonport, Devon. In 1910 he led an expedition to the South Pole (17 Jan 1912), only to discover that the Norwegian expedition under Amundsen had beaten them by a month. All members of his party died.

Scott, Ronnie, originally **Ronald Schatt** (1927–96) Jazz saxophonist and night club owner, born in London. In 1959 he opened a jazz club in London's Soho district, which became an international landmark.

Scott, Sir Walter (1771–1832) Novelist and poet, born in Edin-

History Roman attempts to limit incursions of N tribes marked by Antonine Wall and Hadrian's Wall; beginnings of unification, 9th-c; wars between England and Scotland in Middle Ages; Scottish independence declared by Robert Bruce, recognized 1328; Stuart succession, 14th-c; crowns of Scotland and England united, 1603; parliaments united under Act of Union, 1707; unsuccessful Jacobite rebellions, 1715 and 1745; devolution proposal rejected, 1979; vote for Scottish parliament, 1997; in 1974, divided into 12 regions (including three islands councils); local government reorganization, 1996, replaced this two-tier system by a single tier of 29 mainland councils, plus the three islands councils; successful referendum for Scottish parliament, 1997; devolved Scottish parliament, 1999.

Name / Area (km² / sq mi) / Population total (2000e) / Admin centre

Aberdeen City / 186 / 72 / 221 000 / Aberdeen
Aberdeenshire / 6318 / 2439 / 227 000 / Aberdeen
Angus / 2181 / 842 / 113 000 / Forfar
Argyll and Bute / 6930 / 2675 / 92 000 / Lochgilphead
Clackmannanshire / 157 / 61 / 49 000 / Alloa
Dumfries and Galloway / 6439 / 2485 / 150 000 / Dumfries
Dundee City / 65 / 25 / 156 000 / Dundee
East Ayrshire / 1252 / 483 / 126 000 / Kilmarnock
East Dunbartonshire / 172 / 66 / 112 000 / Kirkintilloch
East Lothian / 6778 / 2616 / 87 000 / Haddington
East Renfrewshire / 173 / 67 / 88 000 / Giffnock
Edinburgh, City of / 262 / 101 / 448 000 / Edinburgh
Falkirk / 229 / 115 / 145 000 / Falkirk
Fife / 1323 / 511 / 134 000 / Glenrothes
Glasow, City of / 175 / 68 / 633 000 / Glasgow
Highland / 25 284 / 9953 / 210 000 / Inverness
Inverclyde / 162 / 63 / 91 000 / Greenock
Midlothian / 356 / 137 / 81 000 / Dalkeith
Moray / 2238 / 864 / 87 000 / Elgin
North Ayrshire / 884 / 341 / 141 000 / Irvine
North Lanarkshire / 474 / 183 / 331 000 / Motherwell
Orkney / 992 / 383 / 20 000 / Kirkwall
Perth and Kinross / 5311 / 2050 / 132 000 / Perth
Renfrewshire / 261 / 101 / 179 000 / Paisley
Scottish Borders / 4734 / 1827 / 107 000 / Newton St Boswells
Shetland / 1438 / 555 / 23 000 / Lerwick
South Ayrshire / 1202 / 464 / 116 000 / Ayr
South Lanarkshire / 1771 / 684 / 311 000 / Hamilton
Stirling / 2196 / 848 / 83 000 / Stirling
West Dunbartonshire / 161 / 63 / 99 000 / Dunbarton
Western Isles / 3133 / 1209 / 30 000 / Stornaway
West Lothian / 425 / 164 / 149 000 / Livingston

burgh. His narrative poems made him the most popular author of the day. His historical novels fall into three groups: those set in the background of Scottish history, from *Waverley* (1814) to *A Legend of Montrose* (1819); a group which takes up themes from the Middle Ages and Reformation times, from *Ivanhoe* (1819) to *The Talisman* (1825); and his remaining books, from *Woodstock* (1826) until his death. His last years were spent in immense labours for his publishers, much of it hack editorial work, in an attempt to recover from bankruptcy following the collapse of his publishing ventures in 1826. His journal is an important record of this period of his life.

Scottish Borders pop (2000e) 106 100; area 4672 km²/1803 sq mi. Council in SE Scotland, formerly the region of **Borders**; crossed E–W by Southern Uplands; capital, Newtown St Boswells, near Melrose.

Scottish National Heritage A British governmental agency, set up by the 1991 National Heritage (Scotland) Act, which came into

effect in 1992. The Act merged into a single body the Nature Conservancy Council for Scotland, set up in 1991, with the Countryside Commission for Scotland.

Scottish National Party (SNP) A political party formed in 1928 as the National Party of Scotland, which merged with the Scottish Party in 1933. Its principal policy aim is independence for Scotland from the UK.

Scottish Parliament A legislative body tracing its origins to the groups of advisors to Scottish monarchs in the 12th-c. Following the uniting of the crowns of Scotland and England in the persons of James VI (Scotland) and I (England), Scotland retained its parliament unil 1707, when the Act of Union was passed. The Scottish parliament was re-established as a result of a 1997 referendum, and re-assembled in 1999. A new parliament built at Holyrood was completed in 2004. It has responsibility for all matters apart from basic economic policy, defence, social security, foreign policy, immigration and nationality, and employment. It is made up of 129 MSPs (Members of the Scottish Parliament) elected to 4-year terms, led by a presiding officer (a post first held by Lord Steel). The political leader of the parliament and head of the Scottish Executive is known as the first minister, a post first held by Donald Dewar, then by Henry McLeish (2000–1) and Jack McConnell (2001–).

Scottish reel A form of stepping dance performed to music in 4/4 time and showing French aristocratic connections. The feet are in balletic positions with the weight on the balls of the feet. In higland reels men's costume is the kilt; women wear dresses with a tartan sash.

Scottish terrier A breed of dog; long body with very short legs; short erect tail; long head, with eyebrows, moustache, and beard; short erect ears; coat black, thick and wiry, almost reaching the ground; also known as **Scottie**. The coarser-haired form is called the **Aberdeen terrier**.

scouting The practice of teaching the young to become good citizens and leaders, based on the principles laid down by Robert Baden-Powell, founder of the Boy Scout movement in 1908. The Scout Association operates in over 100 nations, and has over 14 million members, classified into *Beaver Scouts* (aged 6–8), *Cub Scouts* (aged 8–11), *Scouts* (11–16), and *Venture Scouts* (16–29). Their motto is 'Be prepared'. The corresponding association for girls, known as *Girl Scouts* or *Girl Guides*, was founded in 1910 by Baden-Powell and his sister, Agnes. In the UK, its four classes of membership are *Rainbow Guides* (aged 5–7), *Brownie Guides* (aged 7–10), *Guides* (10–16), and *Ranger Guides* (14–20); in the USA, the groups are *Brownies* (7–8), *Juniors* (9–11), *Cadettes* (12–14), and *Seniors* (15–17). There are around 7 million Guides throughout the world.

scrambling *moto-cross*

scrambling circuit A circuit or device used to protect the security of voice, data, or video signals in communication systems. The original signal is coded by the scrambler before transmission, and reconstituted into its original form at the receiver.

scramjet A special ramjet designed for operation at very high speeds (c.6–25 times the speed of sound) where the performance of a conventional ramjet becomes impracticable. The gases flowing through the engine's combustion chamber move at supersonic rather than subsonic speed.

scrapie [skraypee] A progressive degenerative disease of the central nervous system of sheep and goats worldwide. There are two forms of the disease: in one, there is uncontrollable itching, the animal scraping itself against objects (hence the name); in the other, there is drowsiness, trembling of the head and neck, and paralysis of the legs. The animals usually die within six months of the first symptoms appearing.

scree Loose, angular fragments of rock debris, formed by the action of rain and frost, which accumulate on hill slopes; also termed **talus**.

screen The surface on which an image is displayed, reflective for front projection, translucent for back projection. In the cinema theatre, the screen is perforated with a pattern of small holes so that sound from loudspeakers behind is not seriously attenuated.

screening A system which prevents the pick-up or transmission of stray electrical signals; also known as **shielding**. Grids in the front of microwave ovens shield users from harmful microwaves. Conducting enclosures and meshes shield electrical signals.

screening tests Investigations that are carried out on apparently well persons in order to identify unrecognized disease. *Prescriptive* screening is carried out solely for the benefit of the individual, to detect disease at an early stage in its development, as in blood pressure measurement and chest radiography.

screen-process printing A form of printing in which ink is forced through the mesh of a screen (originally – but less frequently today – made of silk). It is used for a wide range of commercial printed work in which large areas of solid colour are required, such as posters and showcards, and in the decoration of fabrics.

screw pine A member of a large genus of evergreen trees and shrubs, native to Old World tropics, superficially resembling palms; fruit pineapple-shaped, starchy, in some species edible like breadfruit. (Genus: *Pandanus*, 600 species. Family: Pandanaceae.)

Scriabin, Alexander Nikolayevich [skryahbyin] (1872–1915) Composer and pianist, born in Moscow. His compositions include three symphonies, two tone poems, and 10 sonatas.

scribe In general, a writer of documents or copyist; more specifically, in post-exilic and pre-rabbinic Judaism, a class of experts on the Jewish law (the *sopherim*).

Scribner, Charles, originally **Charles Scrivener** (1821–71) Publisher, born in New York City. In 1846 he co-founded the New York publishing firm bearing his name, *Scribner's Magazine*, dating from 1887.

scrofula [skrofyula] Tuberculosis of the lymph nodes of the neck, with abscess formation and ulceration of the overlying skin. Now a rare condition, it was formerly known as 'the King's evil', because of the popular belief that the sovereign's touch would cure it.

scrotum The pouch which in most male mammals holds the testes. It is necessary for normal germ cell production because the temperature of the deeper part of the body is high enough to damage the developing germ cells.

scuba diving A form of underwater swimming with the aid of a *self-contained underwater breathing apparatus* (abbreviated as *scuba*), or *aqualung*. The first such device was developed by Jacques Yves Cousteau and Emil Gagnan in 1943.

sculling *rowing*

sculpin *bullhead*

Sculptor A small, faint S constellation, but including several galaxies.

sculpture Traditionally, modelling in a soft material such as clay or wax, the result sometimes being cast in metal, or carving from some hard material such as stone or wood. In the 20th-c much work joined together prefabricated pieces, a technique known as *assemblage*. Early Greek bronzes were cast from wooden models, using the 'lost wax' process, but most Renaissance and modern bronzes are cast from clay originals. An alternative process involves firing the clay model in a kiln, to produce a terracotta. Since the Renaissance the preference has been for displaying the natural surface of the material used. Marble, the most prestigious stone, has normally been given a high polish.

scumbling A technique in painting whereby one colour is dragged or rubbed across another to give a rich, rough texture.

The effect depends upon allowing the underneath layer to show through in irregular patches.

scurvy A nutritional disorder which results from a lack of vitamin C. Bleeding occurs into the skin, around teeth and bones, and into the joints.

scurvy-grass A N temperate annual or perennial; flowers white, cross-shaped. The sharp-tasting leaves, rich in vitamin C, were used by 17th-c sailors to combat scurvy. (Genus: *Cochlearia*, 25 species. Family: Cruciferae.)

Scutari, Lake [skutahree], Albanian **Ligen i Shkodrës**, Serbo-Croatian **Skadarsko Jezero**, ancient **Lacus Labeatis** Lake in SW Montenegro and NW Albania; area 370 km²/143 sq mi.

Scutum (Lat 'shield') A small S constellation in the Milky Way.

Scylla [sila] In Greek mythology, a sea-monster usually located in the Straits of Messina opposite to Charybdis. Originally a woman, she was changed into a snake with six heads.

Scyphozoa [skiyfozoha] A class of jellyfish with gastric tentacles derived from the stomach wall and 4-radial body symmetry. (Phylum: Cnidaria.)

Scythians [sithianz] In Graeco-Roman times a nomadic people of the Russian steppes who migrated to the area N of the Black Sea in the 8th-c BC, displacing the Cimmerians.

SDI Abbreviation of **Strategic Defense Initiative**, the controversial proposal first made by President Reagan in 1983 (dubbed by the press 'Star Wars') that the US should develop the technologies for a defensive layered 'shield' of weapons based primarily in space, able to shoot down incoming ballistic missiles.

SDP *Social Democratic Party*

sea A part of an ocean which is generally shallower and defined by somewhat loosely drawn boundaries related to the surrounding landmasses. Large inland lakes may also be called seas, such as the Caspian Sea and the Dead Sea. *p.833*

sea, law of the A branch of international law, which divides the sea into three zones. *Internal waters* include ports, rivers, lakes, and canals. *Territorial waters* include the width of sea adjacent to a coastal state, which legally belongs to that state. The width has traditionally been 5 km/3 mi, generally measured from the low water line, although many states now claim a greater width. Foreign ships have a right of innocent passage through territorial waters. Outside the territorial waters are the *high seas*, which may be used freely by all shipping. Many states claim exclusive economic zones extending beyond territorial waters; for example, exclusive fishery rights extending for 320 km/200 mi are now claimed by most coastal states.

sea anemone [anemonee] A typically solitary, marine coelenterate with a cylindrical body attached at its base to a substrate, and bearing a circle of tentacles at the top around its mouth; c.800 species known. (Phylum: Cnidaria. Order: Actiniaria.)

sea bass Any of a large number of fishes of the order Perciformes (Family: Serranidae), length up to 1·8 m/6 ft. Especially popular amongst anglers and fished commercially in some areas; found in inshore waters along the Pacific coast of North America.

sea bream Any of several deep-bodied fish widespread in tropical to temperate seas; length up to 50 cm/20 in; head bluntly rounded; pinkish red, with a large dark spot above the pectoral fin; also called **porgy**. (Family: Sparidae.)

sea canary *beluga* (mammal)

sea cow A term used for any mammal of the order Sirenia (manatees and the dugong); formerly used also for the walrus and the hippopotamus.

sea cucumber A typically sausage-shaped, soft-bodied marine invertebrate (echinoderm); mouth at one end surrounded by up to 30 tentacles; found on or in the seabed. (Class: Holothuroidea.)

sea elephant *elephant seal*

seagull *gull*

Largest Seas

Name	Area*	
	km²	sq mi
Coral Sea	4 791 000	1 850 200
Arabian Sea	3 863 000	1 492 000
S China (Nan) Sea	3 685 000	1 423 000
Caribbean Sea	2 515 000	971 000
Mediterranean Sea	2 510 000	967 000
Bering Sea	2 304 000	890 000
Bay of Bengal	2 172 000	839 000
Sea of Okhotsk	1 590 000	614 000
Gulf of Mexico	1 543 000	596 000
Gulf of Guinea	1 533 000	592 000
Barents Sea	1 405 000	542 000
Norwegian Sea	1 383 000	534 000
Gulf of Alaska	1 327 000	512 000
Hudson Bay	1 232 000	476 000
Greenland Sea	1 205 000	465 000
Arafura Sea	1 037 000	400 000
Philippine Sea	1 036 000	400 000
Sea of Japan	978 000	378 000
E Siberian Sea	901 000	348 000
Kara Sea	883 000	341 000
E China Sea	664 000	256 000
Andaman Sea	565 000	218 000
North Sea	520 000	201 000
Black Sea	508 000	196 000
Red Sea	453 000	175 000
Baltic Sea	414 000	160 000
Celebes Sea	280 000	110 000
Persian Gulf	240 000	93 600
St Lawrence Gulf	238 300	92 000

Oceans are excluded. *Areas are rounded to nearest 1000 km²/sq mi.

sea horse A distinctive small fish, widely distributed; body with segmented armour and slender prehensile tail, length 4–30 cm/1½–12 in; snout prolonged into a horse-like head; swims upright in water, using delicate membranous fins. (Genus: *Hippocampus*. Family: Syngnathidae.)

seakale A perennial (*Crambe maritima*) native to the Atlantic coasts of Europe; fleshy root; large, bluish, cabbage-like leaves; white, cross-shaped flowers. The shoots are eaten as a vegetable. (Family: Cruciferae.)

seal (communications) A blob of wax, or other adhesive substance, bearing an impression, and attached to a document as evidence of its authenticity; also the engraved or carved object (the *matrix* or *die*) used to make the impression. The study of seals, which are found from the oldest times, is known as **sigillography**.

seal (zoology) A marine mammal of the family Phocidae, called the **true seal**, **earless seal**, or **hair seal** (19 species); has fur and a thick layer of blubber; no external ears; cannot turn rear flippers forwards; moves on land by shuffling body horizontally along the ground.

sea level datum *Ordnance Datum*

sea-lion A marine mammal of the family Otariidae, called **eared seals** (14 species); resembles the true seal, but has small external ears and, on land, turns long hind flippers forwards under its body, and moves rapidly with body raised from the ground; some (**fur seals**) have a thick undercoat of soft fur, and have been hunted commercially.

SEALS *SBS*

Sealyham terrier [seeliam] A breed of dog, developed in the 19th-c on the Sealyham estate, Haverfordwest, Wales; long body with short legs; short erect tail; long head with eyebrows, moustache, and beard; short pendulous ears; thick pale wiry coat.

Seaman, David (Andrew) (1963–) Footballer, born in Rotherham, South Yorkshire. A goalkeeper, he played for Peterborough, Birmingham, and Queens Park Rangers, before joining Arsenal in 1989. He established himself as the England goalkeeper under Terry Venables, playing in the teams for Euro 96, World Cup (1998, 2002), and Euro 2000, and by the end of the 2003 season had won 75 caps. He moved to Manchester City for the 2003–4 season but announced his retirement in January 2004.

seance A meeting of one or more persons, generally with a spiritualist medium, for the purpose of contacting the deceased. A seance, sometimes referred to as a 'sitting', may involve apparently paranormal phenomena, such as the medium supposedly receiving communications from deceased people, or the apparent control of the medium by an alleged spirit (a *spirit guide* or *control*). Seances may also involve physical mediumship, such as materializations, and psychokinetic activity (raps, movement of objects, etc). They are also frequently associated with the fraudulent production of phenomena of this kind.

sea otter A mammal native to N Pacific coasts (*Enhydra lutris*); lives mostly in the water; broader body than freshwater otters; front feet small, not webbed; floats on its back with a stone on its chest, and breaks prey open on the stone. (Family: Mustelidae.)

Sea Peoples An assortment of marauders, probably from the Mycenaean world, who destroyed the Hittite empire in Anatolia c.1200 BC. They penetrated as far south as Egypt before being checked and dispersed.

sea perch Small, deep-bodied fish (*Morone americana*) found in fresh, brackish, and coastal marine waters of the W North Atlantic; length up to 35 cm/14 in; silver with greenish-grey upper surface. (Family: Serranidae.)

seaplane An aircraft capable of taking off and landing upon water using a specially shaped body or floats. The most famous seaplanes were those that took part in the Schneider Trophy races of the late 1920s and early 1930s, when the trophy was finally won by a British Supermarine S6B at a speed of 655 kph/407 mph.

search engine A resource on the World Wide Web, accessible via a browser, which helps a user to find sites and information. Search engines (eg Google, Yahoo, Lycos, Ask Jeeves) continually traverse the Web, following links that are built into documents, and building up indexes of material – for example, recovering titles, headings, and subheadings, important words, and the first few lines from documents. Manipulation of the indexes is carried out using standard techniques of information retrieval, and the continual traversal ensures that the indexes are routinely updated. The indexes enable search engines to locate many of the documents related to a particular search topic. However, most searches retrieve large numbers of irrelevant documents, within which relevant 'hits' can be lost, and a great deal of effort is currently being devoted to finding ways of improving search results.

Search for Extraterrestrial Intelligence (SETI) A NASA research programme, aimed at using large radio telescopes to detect artificially generated radio signals coming from interstellar space. The search is conducted in the quiet region of the electromagnetic spectrum – the 'microwave window' between 1000 and 10 000 mHz frequency. First proposed in 1959, a new programme was initiated in 1992 and was cancelled by the US Congress in 1993, but work has continued under private sponsorship. In May 1999 the SETI@home project was set up to harness the power of millions of home computers to analyze signal data picked up by Serendip IV, a detector placed on the Arecibo radio telescope.

Searle, Ronald (William Fordham) [serl] (1920–) Artist, born in Cambridge, Cambridgeshire. After the war he became widely known as the creator of the macabre schoolgirls of 'St Trinian's'.

Sears Tower The national headquarters of Sears, Roebuck and Co in Chicago, IL, USA; the second tallest office building in the world (as of 2004). Built in 1970–4, it has 110 storeys and reaches a height of 443 m/1454 ft.

seascape painting A genre of painting which flourished in the Netherlands in the 17th-c, reflecting the importance of overseas trade for the Dutch economy. A later master was Turner, whose great shipwrecks are among the highest achievements of 19th-c English art.

seasickness *travel sickness* 1

sea slug A marine slug-like mollusc, often brightly coloured and of an elaborate shape, with various projections along its body; shell absent. (Class: Gastropoda. Order: Nudibranchia.)

sea snake A venomous snake of family Hydrophiidae (50 species), sometimes included in family Elapidae; inhabits warm coastal waters in the Pacific and Indian oceans; small head, thick body, tail flattened from side to side; eats fish and fish eggs; venom very powerful.

seasonal affective disorder (SAD) A form of 'winter depression', due to lack of light, which is accompanied by fatigue and lethargy, with a craving for carbohydrates which often results in weight gain. People are often affected during winter months, since light affects the body's biological rhythms through substances released by the pineal gland. The best cure for SAD is natural sunlight, but sitting for 4–6 hours per day in front of a high intensity artificial 'light box' relieves symptoms for many patients.

sea spider A long-legged, small-bodied marine arthropod, found on the seabed; most are predators; contains c.1000 species. (Subphylum: Chelicerata. Class: Pycnogonida.)

SEATO *South East Asia Treaty Organization*

Seattle [seeatl] 47°36N 122°20W, pop (2000e) 563 400. City in WC Washington, USA; industrial, financial, and cultural centre of the Pacific NW; founded, 1851; developed rapidly after the 1897 Alaskan gold rush and the opening of the Panama Canal; main port serving Alaska; airport; railway; monorail; two universities (1861, 1892); Space Needle, a tower 183 m/600 ft high with a revolving restaurant and observation deck; professional teams, Mariners (baseball), Supersonics (basketball), Seahawks (football).

sea urchin A typically hollow, globular, marine invertebrate (echinoderm); body formed by fused skeletal plates bearing movable spines; anus usually on upper surface, mouth on lower surface; complex jaw apparatus known as 'Aristotle's lantern'; contains c.5000 fossil and 950 living species. (Phylum: Echinodermata. Class: Echinoidea.)

seaweed A common name for any large marine alga belonging to families Chlorophyceae (**green seaweeds**), Phaeophyceae (**brown seaweeds**), and Rhodophyceae (**red seaweeds**).

sebaceous glands *skin*

Sebald, W(infried) G(eorg) [zaybalt] (1944–2001) Novelist, born in Germany. He became professor of European Literature at the University of East Anglia. His books include *The Emigrants* (1996), *The Rings of Saturn* (1998), *Vertigo* (1999), and *Austerlitz* (2001, *The Independent* Foreign Fiction Prize).

Sebastian, St (?–288) Martyr, a native of Narbonne, France. He was a captain of the praetorian guard, and secretly a Christian. When his belief was discovered, Diocletian ordered his death. Feast day 20 January.

Sebastiano del Piombo [pyomboh], originally **Sebastiano Luciano** (c.1485–1547) Venetian painter, called *del Piombo* ('of

the Seal') from his appointment in 1523 as sealer of briefs to Pope Clement VII. His masterpiece is 'The Raising of Lazarus' (1519, National Gallery, London).

Sebastopol [sebastopol], Russ **Sevastopol** 44°36N 33°31E, pop (2000e) 358 000. Port in Ukraine; founded, 1783; besieged in the Crimean War (1854); rail terminus; naval base; seaside resort; health resorts nearby.

seborrhoea [sebuhreea] Excessively oily skin due to overactive *sebaceous glands*, the glands in the skin that secrete a natural oil called *sebum*. The skin appears shiny and can feel greasy and unpleasant. *Seborrheic dermatitis* may develop – reddened, flaky patches of skin, usually appearing on the scalp and producing dandruff as the scales are shed.

SECAM [seekam] Acronym for **Séquentiel Couleur à Mémoire**, a coding system for colour television developed in France in the 1960s and later adopted in the USSR, Eastern Europe, and some Middle East countries. The two colour difference signals are not phase-separated, but transmitted on alternate lines of the picture.

Secombe, Sir Harry (Donald) [seekm] (1921–2001) Comedian, singer, and media personality, born in Swansea. An exuberant comic, he achieved fame as a member of *The Goons* (1951–9). His stage appearances include *Humpty Dumpty* (1959) and *Pickwick* (1963), and his films include *Oliver!* (1968) and *Song of Norway* (1970). A professional singer with dozens of albums to his credit, he hosted the religious television series *Highway* (1983–93).

second Base SI unit of time; symbol *s*; defined as the duration of 9 192 631 770 periods of the radiation corresponding to the transition between the two hyperfine levels of the ground state of the caesium-133 atom. Formerly defined as 1/86 400 of the mean solar day, the atomic definition is now the basis of universal time.

secondary education The phase of education following the primary stage, beginning in most countries at the age of 11 or 12. Usually the style of education moves towards more specialized work in key subjects. Secondary education usually ends at some point between the age of 15 and 19, this varying in different countries, and culminates in most cases in some kind of public leaving-examination.

secondary modern school A school in those parts of the UK which operate a selective system. Intake consists of those children who were not successful in gaining entry to a grammar school, or who did not wish to attend it.

secondary store *backing store*

second-generation computers *computer generations*

Second World *Three Worlds theory*

Second World War *World War 2*

Secretariat, UN *United Nations*

secretary bird A large, ground-dwelling bird of prey (*Sagittarius serpentarius*) native to S Africa; long stilt-like legs; head with an untidy crest of long feathers (resembling pens held behind the ear of a secretary). (Family: Sagittariidae.)

secretary of state The title of most UK government ministers who preside over a department, as distinct from junior ministers. It has increasingly replaced the title of *minister*. In the USA, the term refers to the head of the state department in charge of foreign affairs, a senior member of the administration.

secret service *intelligence service*

sect A separately organized group, usually religious, which rejects established religious or political authorities, and claims to adhere to the authentic elements of the wider tradition from which it has separated itself. It is distinctive and exclusive, claiming to possess true belief, correct ritual, and warranted standards of conduct. Membership takes precedence over all other allegiances.

section (pathology) A thin slice of material mounted for inspection under a microscope. The technique is chiefly used in biology and medical pathology.

section (technology) A term used to describe a two-dimensional view in an architectural or engineering drawing, which reveals the internal structure of the subject of the drawing. The object is drawn as if cut through by an imaginary plane with the part between the observer and the cutting plane removed.

secular Christianity A mid-20th-c theology which acknowledged the secularization of W civilization and sought to present a 'religionless' Christianity, with the emphasis on human freedom and responsibility.

securities A general term for financial assets, such as stocks, shares, and bonds.

Securities and Exchange Commission (SEC) A body set up in 1934 in the USA during the Great Depression to regulate and control the issue of shares by corporations. It generally regulates the way US stock markets operate.

Securities and Investments Board (SIB) An agency set up in 1985 to regulate the activities of investment business in the UK. It has power, under the Financial Services Act (1986), to oversee the activities of various self-regulatory organizations which have been set up to control aspects of the UK's financial markets, such as the Investment Management Regulatory Board (IMRO).

Security Council *United Nations*

sedative A drug used to calm anxious patients without actually causing sleep; also known as **tranquillizer**. *Phenobarbitone* was previously the most commonly used sedative, but it has been replaced for this purpose by drugs such as the safer *benzodiazepines* (eg *diazepam*).

Seddon, Richard John, nickname **King Dick** (1845–1906) New Zealand statesman and prime minister (1893–1906), born in Eccleston, Lancashire, UK. As prime minister he led a Liberal Party government remembered for its social legislation, such as introducing old-age pensions.

sedge A name applied to many members of the family Cyperaceae, but especially to *Carex*, a huge genus (1500–2000 species) found almost everywhere, but especially common in alpine and marshy, subarctic habitats; perennial; tufts of grass-like leaves; flowers tiny; males and females usually in separate spikes which resemble those of grasses; characteristic fruit oval, 3-sided. (Family: Cyperaceae.)

sedimentary rock Consolidated deposits composed of material laid down by water, wind, ice, or gravity, or by chemical precipitation.

sedimentation The process of deposition of rock fragments suspended in water on to the floor of an ocean, sea, lake, or river floodplain. The unconsolidated sediment may become compacted, dewatered, and cemented together, ultimately forming a sedimentary rock.

seed The mature, fertilized ovule of a plant, containing the embryo and a food store to sustain the seedling during germination, enclosed within a protective coat, the *testa*. In gymnosperms the seeds lie exposed on the cone scales; in flowering plants they are protected within the ovary. Some seeds are very large and are produced in small numbers (eg the coconut); others are very small and are produced in prodigious numbers (eg the orchid).

seed plant Any plant reproducing by seeds. All flowering plants and gymnosperms are included. In some classifications these together form the division Spermatophyta.

Seeger, Pete(r) (1919–) Folk singer, songwriter, guitarist, and banjo player, born in New York City. In 1940 he started the 'protest' movement in contemporary folk-music. With his group, the Weavers, his best-known songs include 'Where

Have All the Flowers Gone?', 'If I Had a Hammer', and 'Little Boxes'.

Seghers, Hercules [saygerz] (c.1589–c.1635) Painter, born in Haarlem, The Netherlands. He was author of some of the most romantic mountain landscapes of the 17th-c (influencing Rembrandt, who collected his work), yet fewer than 15 pictures survive.

segmented worm *annelid*

Segovia [segohvia] 40°57N 4°10W, pop (2000e) 55 000. City in NWC Spain; altitude c.1000 m/3000 ft; bishopric; railway; Roman aqueduct and old town, a world heritage site; cathedral (16th-c).

Segovia, Andrés [segohvia] (1894–1987) Guitarist, born in Linares, Spain. He evolved a revolutionary guitar technique permitting the performance of a wide range of music, and many modern composers wrote works for him.

segregation The cultural, political, organizational, and typically geographical separation of one group of people from another. It is often based on perceived ethnic or racial divisions, an extreme example being apartheid (literally 'separateness') in South Africa, where physical segregation between whites and blacks was most apparent (eg in public transport, washrooms, housing, sport).

Seiber, Mátyás [shiyber] (1905–60) Composer, born in Budapest. He gained only belated recognition as a composer, his works including chamber music, piano pieces, and songs.

seiche [saysh] An oscillation or sloshing of water in a partially confined body of water such as a bay or an estuary. The period of time required for the oscillation is determined by the physical size and shape of the basin.

Seifert, Jaroslav [siyfert] (1901–86) Poet, born in Prague. His major works include *Postovni holub* (1929, The Carrier Pigeon) and *Zhasnête svêtla* (1938, Put out the Lights), and with his postwar volume *Prílba hlíny* (1945, A Helmet of Earth) he was established as the national poet. He was awarded the Nobel Prize for Literature in 1984.

Seine, River [sen] River in NC France, rising in the Langres plateau; flows past Paris and Rouen to enter the English Channel; length 776 km/482 mi; third longest river in France.

Seinfeld, Jerry [siynfeld] (1954–) Comedian, actor, and writer, born in Brooklyn, New York City. He began working in Manhattan comedy clubs, later becoming a household name with his successful long-running TV sit-com series *Seinfeld* (1990–9). He continues his career as a touring stand-up comic and is a regular television host. His book of comic observations, *SeinLanguage* (1993), became a best-seller.

seismic zone A belt of intense earthquake activity which occurs at the boundaries between crustal plates.

seismograph The data collected by a **seismometer**, an instrument that records and measures the arrival of seismic waves from distant earthquakes, or from movement caused by explosions in the Earth's crust.

seismology The study of earthquakes and the propagation of seismic waves through the Earth. By studying the velocity of seismic waves, the structure of the Earth and the discontinuities which define its core, mantle, and crust have been discovered.

seismometer *seismograph*

Sejanus [sejaynus] (?–31) Prefect of the Praetorian Guard (14–31), and all-powerful at Rome after the Emperor Tiberius's retirement to Capri (26). When his ambitions were made known to Tiberius, his fall from grace was sudden and spectacular.

Sekmet *Sakhmet*

Sekondi-Takoradi 4°59N 1°43W, pop (2000e) 134 000. Major seaport in S Ghana; founded by the Dutch, 16th-c; Sekondi expanded after construction of railway to Tarkwa (1898–

1903), and merged with Takoradi, 1946; important supply base during World War 2.

selaginella [selajinela] A member of a large genus of mostly tropical spore-bearing plants related to clubmosses and quill-worts. It is one of the few living members of the ancient class Lycopsida. (Genus: *Selaginella*, 700 species. Family: Selaginellaceae.)

Selangor [saylanggaw(r)] pop (2000e) 2 461 000; area 7997 km²/3087 sq mi. State in W Peninsular Malaysia; British protectorate, 1874; capital, Shah Alam.

Selcraig, Alexander *Selkirk, Alexander*

select committee Members of a legislature whose task is to inquire into matters that come within its competence, usually as prescribed by the government. Two main types may be distinguished: *ad hoc*, which normally ceases to exist when its task is completed; and *permanent* or *standing*, which normally lasts for an electoral term and which investigates particular policy areas or the actions of government departments. Membership is usually based on party composition in the legislature.

selective school *comprehensive school; grammar school; grant maintained school*

Selene [seleenee] In Greek mythology, the goddess of the Moon. She was depicted as a charioteer.

selenium [seleenium] Se, element 34. A metalloid in the oxygen group, found as a minor constituent of sulphide ores, and mainly produced from the residue of copper refinement. Mainly important for its electrical properties, selenium can be used to convert light to electric current (in photocells) and alternating current to direct current (in rectifiers).

Seles, Monica [selesh] (1973–) Tennis player, born in Novi Sad, Serbia and Montenegro (former Yugoslavia). In 1990 she became the youngest woman to win a 'Grand Slam' singles title in the 20th-c, winning the French Championship at 16 years 169 days (a record broken by Hingis in 1997). Before she reached 18 she had won three Grand Slam singles titles. In 1993 she was unable to play for some months following an incident on court in which she was stabbed by a deranged fan of Steffi Graf. Later successes include the 1996 Australian Open title. She became a US citizen in 1994.

Seleucids [seloosidz] The Greek dynasty descended from Alexander the Great's general, Seleucus (c.358–281 BC). They ruled a vast empire stretching from Asia Minor to NW India, but were suppressed by Rome in 63 BC.

self-regulatory organization (SRO) A body which manages its own affairs and has its own rules of conduct, eliminating the need for government legislation. Lloyd's and the London Stock Exchange are two such bodies.

Selfridge, Harry Gordon (c.1864–1947) Merchant, born in Ripon, WI. While visiting London in 1906, he bought a site in Oxford Street, and built upon it the large store which bears his name (opened 1909).

Seljuqs / Seljuks A family of Turkish mercenary soldiers that rose to prominence and conquered much of Asia Minor in the 11th–12th-c. They were converted to the Muslim faith, and became established as sultans in the area of present-day Syria and E Turkey.

Selkirk, Alexander, also spelled **Selcraig** (1676–1721) Sailor, born in Largo, Fife, whose story suggested that of Defoe's Robinson Crusoe. He joined the South Sea buccaneers, quarrelled with his captain, and at his own request was put ashore on Juan Fernández I, (1704). He lived there alone until 1709, when he was discovered and brought back to Britain.

Sellafield, formerly **Windscale** 54°38N 3°30W. Nuclear power plant in Cumbria, NW England; processes nuclear waste; process of decommissioning begun, 2005; nearby Calder Hall gas-cooled, moderated nuclear reactors, operational 1956–2003.

Sellers, Peter (1925–80) Actor and comedian, born in Southsea,

Hampshire. His meeting with Spike Milligan heralded *The Goon Show* (1951–9), which revolutionized British radio comedy. One of the stalwarts of British film comedy, *Lolita* (1962) and *Dr Strangelove* (1963) established his international reputation. His popularity was unrivalled as the incompetent Inspector Clouseau in a series of films that began with *The Pink Panther* (1963). He received an Oscar nomination for *Being There* (1980).

Selten, Reinhard [zelten] (1930–) Economist, born in Wrocław, Poland (formerly Breslau, Prussia). He shared the Nobel Prize for Economics in 1994 for his contribution to the analysis of equilibria in the theory of non-co-operative games.

selva The Portuguese term for the tropical rainforest of the Amazon Basin. Its use has been extended to cover similar vegetation types elsewhere.

Selwyn-Lloyd, (John) Selwyn (Brooke) Lloyd, Baron [selwin loyd] (1904–78) British Conservative statesman, born in Liverpool, Merseyside. His posts include minister of defence (1955); foreign secretary (1955–60), defending Eden's policy on Suez; Chancellor of the Exchequer, introducing the 'pay pause' (1960–2); and Speaker of the House of Commons (1971–6).

Selznick, David O(liver) (1902–65) Film producer, born in Pittsburgh, PA. He founded his own company in 1937, which at its peak made *Gone with the Wind* (1939). Among the stars he created was Jennifer Jones, to whom he was married from 1949.

semantics The study of the meaning system of a language. The word *meaning* has itself many meanings, and semantic approaches vary widely. In one view, meaning is the relationship between language and the external world (*referential* or *denotative* meaning), or between a word and the concept it stands for. In another, it involves the mental state of the speaker, as reflected in a range of personal and emotional overtones (*affective* or *connotative* meaning). A considerable part of the present-day subject is devoted to the study of the meanings of expressions in terms of formal systems of analysis, or calculi (**formal semantics**).

semaphore A code and signalling apparatus for visual communication. It consists of one or two mechanically-operated arms attached to an upright post, or two hand-held flags at arm's length, which are moved in a vertical plane to a sequence of positions. Each position represents a different letter of the alphabet, numeral, or punctuation feature. The system was widely used in visual telegraphy, before the advent of electricity.

Semele [semilee] In Greek mythology, the daughter of Cadmus, and mother by Zeus of Dionysus. She asked Zeus to appear in his glory before her, and was consumed in fire, but it made her son immortal.

semen Yellow-white fluid ejaculated from the penis at orgasm. It consists of spermatozoa, and secretions from the accessory sex glands which assist in the nourishment and motility of the spermatozoa.

semicircular canals *vestibular apparatus*

semiconductor A substance whose electrical conductivity is between that of an insulator and a conductor at room temperature. The conductivity can be made to vary with temperature and the impurities in the semiconductor crystal. Typical semiconductor devices such as diodes and transistors have different arrangements of impurities in the crystal.

semiconductor laser A tiny laser, crucial to optical fibre communications and compact disk players. A current flowing across the junction between two regions of semiconductor (eg gallium arsenide) doped in different ways causes electron transitions in the material.

Seminole [seminohl] A Muskogean-speaking North American Indian group of SE USA. They eventually moved to reservations in Oklahoma, now numbering c.12 000 (2000 census).

semiology *semiotics*

semiotics The study of signs, sign systems, and the social production of meaning, also known as **semiology**. A fundamental notion is the arbitrary nature of communication systems (written and spoken language, gestures, dress, etc). Meaning is largely produced by relationships and differences between individual signs, organized in codes, rather than by simple reference to external reality.

Semipalatinsk [semipalatinsk], formerly **Semipalatka** 50°26N 80°16E, pop (2000e) 356 000. River port in Kazakhstan, on R Irtysh; founded as a fortress, 1718; airport; railway.

semi-precious stones *gemstones*

Semiramis [semiramis] (9th-c BC) In Greek mythology, the daughter of the goddess Derceto, who became Queen of Assyria. She founded many cities, including Nineveh and Babylon, and is probably based on the historical Sammu-ramat (c.810–805 BC).

Semites A group of peoples found in SW Asia. In antiquity they included the Ammonites, Amorites, Assyrians, Babylonians, Canaanites, and Phoenicians; today the most prominent Semitic peoples are the Jews and the Arabs.

Semitic alphabets The writing systems of the Semitic languages spoken in the Middle East, in which only consonants are registered, the vowels being optionally marked by diacritics. The earliest known alphabet was North Semitic, developed from the second millennium BC in Palestine and Syria.

Semitic languages *Afro-Asiatic languages*

semolina A heated solution of the flour of hard wheat. It is used to make pasta and milk puddings.

Senate (Roman) An advisory body, first to the kings, then the consuls, finally the emperor. By the end of the Republic its resolutions had come to have the force of law.

Senate (USA) One of the two houses of the US Congress, consisting of two senators from each State (100 in all), chosen by the people to serve for six years; a third are chosen every two years. It has powers of 'advice and consent' on presidential treaties and appointments. Much of its work is done through committees rather than on the floor.

Sendai [sendaee] 38°16N 140°52E, pop (2000e) 952 000. City in NE Honshu, Japan; airport; railway; university (1907); Miyagi Stadium (2001).

Sendero Luminoso [sendairoh loominohsoh] (Span 'Shining Path') A rural guerrilla movement of uncompromisingly revolutionary character, which began operating in the Peruvian C Andes during the 1980s.

Seneca, Lucius Annaeus [seneka], known as **the Elder** (c.55 BC–c.AD 40) Roman rhetorician, born in Córdoba, Spain. Besides a history of Rome, now lost, he wrote several works on oratory.

Seneca, Lucius Annaeus [seneka], known as **Seneca the Younger** (c.5 BC–AD 65) Roman philosopher, statesman, and author, born in Córdoba, Spain, the son of Seneca the Elder. He was the tutor of Nero, but his high moral aims gradually incurred the emperor's displeasure. Drawn into conspiracy, he was condemned, and committed suicide. The publication of his *Tenne Tragedies* in 1581 was a major influence on Elizabethan drama.

Seneca [seneka] An Iroquois-speaking North American Indian group, who settled in present-day W New York State and E Ohio. A member of the Iroquois League, they supported the British during the American Revolution. They were settled on reservations in 1797.

Senefelder, Aloys [zaynefelder, alohis] (1771–1834) Inventor, born in Prague. He accidentally discovered the technique of lithography by using a grease pencil on limestone (1796).

Sénégal, River River in W Africa; rises in the Fouta Djallon massif (Guinea); enters the Atlantic Ocean; length, 1635 km/1016 mi.

Senegal *p.838*

Senegambia, Confederation of [senegambia] An association between The Gambia and Senegal, begun in 1982, designed to integrate military, economic, communications, and foreign policies, while preserving independence and sovereignty. It was ended by mutual agreement in 1989.

senescence A series of changes in the body which are related to increasing mortality with increasing age. Modern views hold that it is essentially a continuing and increasing failure of adaptability to environmental variations, due ultimately to errors in the replication of DNA in cell division and/or errors in the production of proteins and enzymes by cells.

senile dementia *dementia*

Senna, Ayrton, in full **Ayrton Senna da Silva** (1960–94) Motor racing driver, born in São Paulo, Brazil. He became World Formula One champion 1988, 1990, and 1991, and had 41 Grand Prix victories (second only to Alain Prost). He was killed during the 1994 San Marino Grand Prix.

senna A drug obtained from the pods and dried leaves of certain species of *Cassia*, a large group of trees and shrubs native to Africa and Arabia. It is noted for its laxative properties. (Genus: *Cassia*. Family: Leguminosae.)

Sennacherib [senakerib] (8th–7th-c BC) King of Assyria (704–681 BC), the son of Sargon II. His fame rests mainly on his conquest of Babylon (689 BC) and his rebuilding of Nineveh.

Sennett, Mack, originally **Michael** or **Mikall Sinnott** (1880–1960) Film producer, born in Richmond, Quebec, Canada. He made hundreds of shorts, establishing a tradition of knockabout slapstick under the name of Keystone Komics (1912) and later the Sennett Bathing Beauties (1920). He was given a special Academy Award in 1937.

sensitive plant A perennial, prickly-stemmed herb (*Mimosa pudica*), growing to 90 cm/3 ft, native to South America; a common weed in tropical areas, and in cooler climates often cultivated as a novelty in hothouses. It is exceedingly sensitive, exhibiting nastic movement, closing up at night. This response can also be triggered at greater speed by a shock stimulus such as a touch. (Family: Leguminosae.)

sentence In law, the decision of a court imposed on a person convicted of a crime, such as a fine, a period of imprisonment, a period of supervision, the death sentence in certain jurisdictions, or an absolute discharge.

Seoul or **Sul** [sohl] 37°30N 127°00E, pop (2000e) 11 670 000. Capital of Korea; founded, 14th-c; called Hanyang until the 20th-c; seat of the Yi dynasty government 1392–1910; badly damaged in Korean War; airport; railway; 17 universities; Kyongbok-kung Palace (14th-c, rebuilt 1867); Ch'angdŏ-kung palace (1405, rebuilt 1611); location of 1988 Olympic Games; Seoul World Cup Stadium (2001).

sepal [sepl] One of the outermost whorl of flower parts, collectively termed the *calyx*. Usually green, free, or sometimes fused together, they protect the flower in bud.

separation, judicial An order granted by a court in the UK where either marriage partner presents a petition supported by one of the facts necessary for a divorce. The parties remain married, however. In the USA, legal separation also changes the parties' financial obligations to each other, especially in community property jurisdictions.

separatism The demand by a particular group or area for separation from the territorial and political sovereignty of the state of which they are a part. Examples of separatist movements are the Basques in Spain and the Tamils in Sri Lanka.

Sephardim [sefah(r)dim] Descendants of Jews who lived in Spain and Portugal before 1492, but who were then expelled for not accepting Christianity. They migrated to N Europe and the Americas, where during the 16th–17th-c they kept distinct from other Jews.

sepiolite *meerschaum*

septicaemia / septicemia [septiseemia] The occurrence and

Senegal

□ International Airport   ∴ World heritage site

[senegawl], **Sénégal**, official name **Republic of Senegal**, Fr **République du Sénégal**

Local name Sénégal (French)

Timezone GMT

Area 196 790 km²/75 729 sq mi

Population total (2002e) 9 905 000

Status Republic

Date of independence 1960

Capital Dakar

Languages French (official), with various ethnic languages spoken

Ethnic groups Wolof (36%), Serer (19%), Fulani (13%), Toucouleur (9%), Diola (9%), Mandingo (9%), European and Lebanese (1%)

Religions Sunni Muslim (91%), Roman Catholic (5%), local beliefs (3%)

Physical features Located in W Africa; extensive low-lying basin of savannah and semi-desert vegetation to the N; sand dunes along coastline; dunes and mangrove forests in S, where land rises to around 500 m/1640 ft; lowland savannah and semi-desert regions of N drain into R Sénégal, which forms the N and NE boundary with Mauritania and Mali.

Climate Tropical climate; rainy season (Jun–Sep); high humidity levels and high night-time temperatures, especially on the coast. Average temperature, 22–8°C; average annual rainfall 541 mm/21 in at Dakar.

Currency 1 CFA Franc (XAF) = 100 centimes

Economy Agriculture (employs c.75% of workforce); groundnuts, cotton, sugar, millet, sorghum, maize, livestock; minerals, iron ore, gold; oil, natural gas; fishing, timber; textiles, chemicals; shipbuilding and repairing; tourism; maritime disaster (Sep 2002) when Senegalese ferry capsized killing 1200 people.

GDP (2002e) $15·64 bn, per capita $1500

Human Development Index (2002) 0·431

History Part of the Mali Empire, 14th–15th-c; French established a fort at Saint-Louis, 1658; incorporated as a territory within French West Africa, 1902; autonomous state within the French community, 1958; joined with French Sudan as independent Federation of Mali, 1959; withdrew in 1960 to become a separate independent republic; joined with The Gambia to form the Confederation of Senegambia, 1982–9; Confederation collapsed, 1989, following violent clashes between Senegalese and Mauritanians; governed by a President (elected for a 5-year term), Prime Minister, a Senate and National Assembly.

Head of State
1981–2000 Abdou Diouf
2000– Abdoulaye Wade

Head of Government
1991–8 Habib Thiam
1998–2000 Mamadou Lamine Loum
2000–1 Moustapha Niasse
2001–2 Madior Boyé
2002–4 Idressa Seck
2004– Macky Sall

---

multiplication of bacteria in the blood stream; more commonly known as **blood poisoning**. If untreated, the condition progresses rapidly to septic shock and death.

Septuagesima [septyuajesima] In the Western Christian Church, the third Sunday before Lent, apparently so called by analogy with *Quinquagesima* which is two Sundays later. (Latin *septuagesimus*, 'seventieth'.)

Septuagint [septyuajint] A translation into Greek of the Hebrew Bible, obtaining its name (meaning 'translation of the 70') from a legend in the *Letter of Aristeas* (2nd-c BC) about its composition as the work of 72 scholars, six from each of the 12 tribes of Israel. The translation was begun c.3rd-c BC to meet the need of Greek-speaking Jews in the Diaspora. When it was adopted by Christians as their preferred version of the Old Testament, it lost favour among the Jews.

sequence (music) **1** From c.850 to c.1000, a non-biblical Latin text added to a long portion of chant originally sung to one syllable at the end of the Alleluia; later, a similar syllabic chant specially composed.

2 A musical phrase immediately repeated at a different pitch. The opening of Beethoven's Fifth Symphony furnishes a familiar example.

Sequoia (California) [sekwoya] National park in E California, USA, in the Sierra Nevada; contains the enormous, ancient sequoia trees; area 1631 km²/630 sq mi.

Sequoia or **Sequoyah** (Cherokee) [sekwoya], also known as **George Gist** or **Guest** (c.1770–1843) Cherokee Indian leader, born in Taskigi, NC. Probably the son of Nathaniel Gist, a British trader, and a Cherokee mother, he was a major figure behind the decision of the Cherokee to adopt as much as possible of the white culture, while retaining their own identity.

sequoia [sekwoya] *coast redwood*

seraphim [serafim] Heavenly beings mentioned in Jewish Scriptures only in the vision in *Isa 6*, where they are described as having six wings and being stationed above the throne of God.

Serapis [seraypis, serapis] A compound deity, combining the names and aspects of two Egyptian gods, Osiris and Apis, to which were further added features of major Greek gods, such as

Zeus and Dionysus. The god was introduced to Alexandria by Ptolemy I in an attempt to unite Greeks and Egyptians in common worship.

Serbia *p.840*

serenade Originally, music to be played or sung in the evening, especially for courting. The term is now most widely applied to works for full or string orchestra in several movements, which are lighter in style and less ambitious than a symphony.

Serengeti [serenggetee] area 14 763 km²/5698 sq mi. National park in N Tanzania; a world heritage site; established in 1951; average elevation c.1500 m/5000 ft; noted for its wildlife.

serfdom The condition of peasants lacking personal freedom, especially of movement and the disposal of property, and liable to uncertain or arbitrary obligations; an intermediate position between slavery and freedom. Characteristic of mediaeval times, the condition persisted in E Europe – in Russia until 1861.

sergeant at arms In the UK, the officer of the House of Commons responsible for maintaining order and for internal administration. He also has certain ceremonial functions, particularly that of carrying the Speaker's mace in procession to the Chair at the beginning of the day's business.

serialism A method of composing music in which a series (or 'row' or 'set') of different notes is used, in accordance with certain strict practices, as the basis of a whole work. The most common type is 12-note serialism, in which the 12 pitches of the chromatic scale are re-ordered to form one of a possible 479 001 600 different series. Schoenberg arrived at 12-note serialism in 1923, as a means of structuring atonal music; his method was adopted, in very different ways, by his pupils Berg and Webern. Some later composers have applied serial methods to such other elements of composition as rhythm, dynamics, and articulation.

serial killing A class of murder which, though known to have existed for centuries, became increasingly prominent during the latter part of the 20th-c. Serial killing involves a succession of at least two but usually more murders committed as discrete episodes over a substantial period of time, often months or years. This is in contrast to a mass murder or mass killing, where a number of people are killed over a short period of time, such as a few hours, as part of a single continuous act.

serin *canary*

Serious Organised Crime Agency (SOCA) Britain's first non-police law-enforcement agency, launched in 2006. It is an amalgamation of the National Crime Squad, the National Criminal Intelligence Service, and investigators from Customs and the Home Office's Immigration Service. With a staff of more than 4000, the agency's role is to target the international gangs behind such crimes as people trafficking, drug smuggling, fraud, and global paedophile networks.

serjeanty [sah(r)juhntee] or **sergeantry** The name for a wide range of tenures in mediaeval times, by which men held land on condition of performing some definite personal service, other than knight-service, to the superior lord. The services demanded were weighty or frivolous, but the distinction made in England between grand and petty serjeanties is an invention of legal antiquarians.

Sermon on the Mount or **Plain** A collection of Jesus's ethical teaching, depicted in *Matt* 5–7 as preached on a mountain early in Jesus's ministry. It contains the Beatitudes, teaching about true adherence to God's law.

serology [serolojee] A branch of medicine which specializes in the analysis of serum. In particular it looks for evidence of infection, by the detection of antibodies or micro-organisms.

serotine bat [serotiyn] A bat found from Europe to SE Asia and N Africa (*Eptesicus serotinus*); brown with pale tips to the hairs; slow flying; eats mainly large moths and beetles. (Family: Vespertilionidae.)

serotonin [serotohnin] A widely distributed chemical substance (a monoamine), particularly found in the blood, brain, and certain cells of the gut; it is also known as **5-hydroxytryptamine (5-HT)**. It is involved in sleep, emotional disposition (mood), prolactin secretion, and circadian rhythms.

Serpens (Lat 'serpent') A constellation of the equatorial region of the sky. It is unique, because it is bisected (by Ophiuchus) into two distinct sections: **Serpens Caput** ('head') and **Serpens Cauda** ('body').

serpent *snake*

serpentine A hydrous magnesium silicate ($Mg_3Si_2O_5(OH)_4$) occurring in two main forms: **chrysotile** (an asbestos variety) and **antigorite**. It is soft, green to black, and used in decorative carving.

SERPS *pension*

serpulid [serpyulid] A tube-building bristleworm; reduced head, bearing a crown of gills; body retractable inside a calcareous tube; aperture closed by a flap (*operculum*); found in the intertidal zone in shallow waters. (Phylum: Annelida. Class: Polychaeta.)

serum The residue of any animal liquid after the separation and removal of the more solid components. It is specifically used to refer to human blood serum, which is a clear, yellowish fluid separated from clotted blood plasma. Serum with appropriate antibodies protects against specific diseases.

serum sickness The repeated administration of an antigenic substance (a foreign protein), such as in immunization, which sometimes gives rise to an acute severe reaction. These reactions include fever, urticaria, arthritis, and inflammation of the heart and kidneys.

serval [servl] A nocturnal member of the cat family (*Felis serval*) native to S Africa; slender, with long neck and short tail; pale with small or large dark spots (small-spotted type formerly called **servaline cat**).

Servetus, Michael [servaytus] (1511–53) Theologian and physician, born in Tudela, Spain. His theological writings denied the Trinity and the divinity of Christ, and he was burnt at Geneva for heresy. While studying medicine he discovered the pulmonary circulation of the blood.

service club A group of men and women organized to perform volunteer community service. The first such club, for business and professional men, was formed in 1905 by US lawyer Paul Harris (1868–1947) in Chicago, IL, using the name *Rotary* (because the meetings took place at each member's office in turn). This grew into Rotary International, whose motto 'Service above Self' embodies the ideals of all service clubs. Women were admitted for the first time in 1987. *Kiwanis International* began in 1915 in Detroit, MI, and the *International Association of Lions Clubs* was formed in Dallas, TX in 1917.

service industry An industry which does not manufacture a product, but provides a service. It is a fast-growing sector in most Western nations; activities range from banking and other financial services to tourism, hotels, and catering.

service tree The name given to two species of *Sorbus*, native to Europe, both deciduous trees with white flowers in large, flat clusters. The wild service tree or **chequerberry** (*Sorbus torminalis*) has lobed leaves and brown berries, used for preserves and drinks. (Family: Rosaceae.)

Servile Wars The collective name for the official attempts to suppress the slave uprisings of the late 2nd-c and early 1st-c BC in Sicily and S Italy. The most serious was the revolt led by Spartacus (73–71 BC).

servo system A system controlled by a servomechanism: a high-power output device is controlled with a command signal from a low-input device. Power-assisted braking or steering are servo systems.

sesame [sesamee] An annual (*Sesamum indicum*) growing to

Serbia

☐ International Airport

[serbia], formerly spelled **Servia**; official name (from 2006) **Republic of Serbia**, formerly (2003–6) **Union of Serbia and Montenegro**, and (1992–2003) **Federal Republic of Yugoslavia**

Local name Srbija

Timezone GMT +1

Area 88 361 km²/34 107 sq mi

Population total (2002e) 7 500 000 (excluding Kosovo)

Status Republic

Capital Belgrade

Languages Serbian (official)

Ethnic groups Serbian (83%), Hungarian (4%), Bosniak (2%), Roma (1·5%), Yugoslavs (1%), many others under 1%

Religions Serbian Orthodox, Muslim, Roman Catholic, other Christian

Physical features Landlocked country located in central Balkan Peninsula; mainly flat in N, mountainous in C and S areas; land rises to Dinaric Alps (W) and Stara Planina (E); fertile Danubian plain in NE; chief river, R Danube, also Morava, Sava, Tisza; linked to Adriatic Sea and Montenegro via Belgrade–Bar railway

Climate Moderate, continental climate, average annual temperatures 0°C (Jan), 22°C (Jul) in Belgrade; average rainfall 610 mm/24 in

Currency 1 New Yugoslav Dinar (YUM) = 100 paras (in Kosovo 1 euro (EUR) = 100 cents also legal)

Economy Manufactured goods, machinery, transport equipment; food products, wheat, maize, vines, livestock; ore and stone mining

GDP (2002e) $23·15, per capita $2200 (former Serbia and Montenegro)

History Serbia absorbed by Ottoman Empire during 15th-c–18th-c, becomes autonomous principality, 1817; Serbian independence recognized by international treaties, 1878; Kingdom of Serbs, Croats, and Slovenes formed 1918, renamed Kingdom of Yugoslavia, 1929; together with Slovenia, Macedonia, Croatia, Bosnia and Montenegro, becomes a republic in new Socialist Federal Republic of Yugoslavia under Josip Tito, 1945; revised constitution in 1974, instituted a rotating leadership, with the Prime Minister elected annually; governed by a bicameral Federal Assembly, comprising a Federal Chamber and a Chamber of Republics and Provinces; following a break with the USSR in 1948, the country followed an independent form of communism and a general policy of non-alignment; at the end of the 1980s political disagreement between the federal republics increased; ethnic unrest in Serbia (Kosovo); Slovenian unilateral declaration of independence, 1990, followed by Macedonian and Croatian declarations, 1991, considered illegal by central government; inter-republic talks on Yugoslavia's future, but confrontation between Croatia and Serb-dominated National Army developed into civil war, 1991; Serbian support of Serb guerrillas in Bosnia resulted in UN sanctions, mid-1992; arrival of UN Protection Force, 1992; Federal Republic of Yugoslavia declared, 1992, consisting of Montenegro and Serbia; fighting between ethnic groups in Bosnia continued until 1995, when peace accord signed in Dayton, Ohio; conflict in Kosovo between Serbia and ethnic Albanian resistance movement (Kosovo Liberation Army), 1997; escalation of conflict (early 1999) led to Serbian incursions into Kosovo and displacement of Kosovar Albanians; NATO airstrikes campaign against Yugoslav targets; President Milosevic accepted peace terms, with deployment of NATO troops into Kosovo and the departure of Serb forces; Milosevic ousted after elections, 2000, and arrested for crimes against humanity, 2001 (died while awaiting trial, 2006); new accord led to a Union of Serbia and Montenegro, 2002, new constitution, 2003; referendum in Montenegro voted for independence from Serbia, 2006; Serbia declared itself an independent sovereign state (5 Jun 2006); new constitution (Oct 2006) defined Kosovo as autonomous province; UN International Court of Justice found Serbia not guilty of genocide as a nation (Feb 2007), a landmark charge brought by Bosnia and Herzegovina over events in Srebrenica (1995).

Republic of Serbia

Head of State

2006– Boris Tadic

Head of Government

2006– Vojislav Kostunica

---

60 cm/2 ft, probably native to SE Asia; flowers white, usually marked with purple or yellow; fruit an oblong capsule. It is cultivated in warmer countries for its seeds, which are used for baking and as a source of oil in margarine, soap manufacture, and cosmetics. (Family: Pedaliaceae.)

Sessions, Roger (Huntingdon) (1896–1985) Composer, born in New York City. His compositions include eight symphonies, a violin concerto, piano and chamber music, and operatic works.

Set or **Seth** An ancient Egyptian god, depicted with the head of an animal with a long muzzle. The brother and enemy of Osiris, he was associated with evil forces and rebellion.

set In mathematics, a well-defined class of elements, ie a class where it is possible to tell exactly whether any one element does or does not belong to it. We can have the set of all even numbers, as every number is either even or not even, but we cannot have the set of all large numbers, as we do not know what is meant by 'large'. The **empty set** is the set with no elements. The **universal set** or is the set of all elements. The **intersection** of two sets A and B (written $A \cap B$) is the set of all elements in both A and B. The **union** of two sets A and B (written $A \cup B$) is the set of all elements in either A or B or both.

Seth, Vikram (1952–) Novelist, poet, and travel-writer, born in

Calcutta, India. He became widely known after his novel *A Suitable Boy* (1993), one of the longest works of fiction in English. His other writing includes the travel book *From Heaven Lake* (1983), the poetry collection *Mappings* (1980), and the novel *An Equal Music* (1999). *Two Lives*, a memoir, appeared in 2005.

SETI *Search for Extraterrestrial Intelligence*

Seton, St Elizabeth Ann [seetn], *née* **Bayley** (1774–1821) The first native-born saint of the USA, born in New York City. In 1809 she founded the USA's first religious order, the Sisters of Charity. She was beatified by Pope John XXIII in 1963, and canonized in 1975. Feast day 4 January.

setter A long-haired sporting dog which belongs to one of several breeds performing the same function as a pointer; probably developed by breeding spaniels with pointers.

Settlement, Act of An important British statute of 1701 which determined the succession of the English throne after the death of Queen Anne and her heirs, if any. It excluded the Catholic Stuarts from the succession, which was to pass to the Protestant Electress Sophia of Hanover, descendant through the female line of James I.

Setúbal [setoobal] 38°30N 8°58W, pop (2000e) 83 000. Industrial seaport in S Portugal; at the mouth of R Sado; railway.

Seurat, Georges (Pierre) [soerah] (1859–91) Artist, born in Paris. He became known for such works as 'Une Baignade, Asnières' (Bathers at Asnières, 1883–4, National Gallery, London), painted in a Divisionist style. His main achievement was the marrying of an Impressionist palette to classical composition.

Seuss, Dr, pseudonym of **Theodor Seuss Geisel**, other pseudonyms **Theo LeSieg** and **Rosetta Stone** (1904–91) Writer and illustrator of children's books, born in Springfield, MA. His famous series of 'Beginner Books' started with *The Cat in the Hat* (1957) and *Yertle the Turtle* (1958). By 1970, 30 million copies had been sold in the USA, and Seuss had become synonymous with learning to read.

Seven against Thebes In Greek legend, seven champions who attacked Thebes to deprive Eteocles of his kingship, led by his brother Polynices. They were defeated by another seven champions at the seven gates of Thebes. Later the sons of the Seven, the Epigoni, succeeded in destroying the city.

Seven Days' Battles (26 Jun–2 Jul 1862) The final conflict in the Peninsular Campaign during the American Civil War, fought below Richmond. The battles ended with a Confederate withdrawal.

seven deadly sins The fundamental vices thought, in Christian tradition, to underlie all sinful actions. They are pride, covetousness, lust, envy, gluttony, anger, and sloth.

Seven Sisters *Pleiades* (astronomy)

Seven Sleepers of Ephesus In mediaeval legend, seven persecuted Christians who fled into a cave at the time of the Emperor Decius (AD 250); they slept for 200 years, emerging in 447 at the time of Theodosius II.

Seven Wonders of the Ancient World The most renowned artificial structures of the ancient world: the Pyramids of Egypt; the Hanging Gardens of Babylon; the Tomb of Mausolus at Halicarnassus; the Temple of Artemis at Ephesus; the Colossus of Rhodes; the Statue of Zeus at Olympia; and the Pharos of Alexandria.

Seven Years' War (1756–63) A major European conflict rooted in the rivalry between Austria and Prussia and the imminent colonial struggle between Britain and France in the New World and the Far East. Hostilities in North America (1754) pre-dated the Diplomatic Revolution in Europe (1756), which created two opposing power blocs: Austria, France, Russia, Sweden, and Saxony against Prussia, Britain, and Portugal. British maritime superiority countered Franco-Spanish naval power, and prevented a French invasion.

severe acute respiratory syndrome *SARS*

Severn, River River in SE Wales and W England; rises on Plynlimon, C Wales; wide estuary into the Bristol Channel; length 354 km/220 mi; known for the **Severn bore** (tidal wave c.2 m/6 ft); railway tunnel (completed 1885); **Severn Bridge**, suspension bridge carrying M4 motorway (988 m/3240 ft), completed 1966; **Severn Bridge II** (456 m/1496 ft) completed 1996.

Severnaya Zemlya [sayvernaya zemlya], formerly **Zemlya Imperatora**, Eng **North Land** or **Nicholas II Land** area 37 000 km²/14 300 sq mi. Uninhabited archipelago in the Arctic Ocean.

Severus, Lucius Septimius [seveerus] (c.146–211) Roman emperor (193–211) and founder of the Severan dynasty (193–235). He proved to be an able administrator, effecting many reforms. His final years were spent in Britain, trying unsuccessfully to restore order in the N of the province.

Sévigné, Madame de [sayveenyay], *née* **Marie de Rabutin-Chantal** (1626–96) Writer, born in Paris. Her letters, lasting over 25 years, recount the inner history of her time in great detail, and in a natural, colloquial style.

Seville [sevil], Span **Sevilla**, ancient **Hispalis** 37°23N 6°00W, pop (2000e) 667 000. River-port in Andalusia, SW Spain; on R Guadalquivir; Moorish cultural centre, 8th–13th-c; archbishopric; airport; railway; university (1502); birthplace of Velásquez and Murillo; cathedral (15th-c), largest Gothic church in the world, with tomb of Columbus; Moorish citadel and Archivo de Indias, a world heritage site.

Sèvres porcelain [sevr] The French royal porcelain factory, founded c.1745 to produce soft- and hard-paste luxury porcelain. The factory's speciality became items with exquisitely painted vignettes against richly coloured plain grounds with elaborate gilding.

sewage Waste matter, especially human excrement, carried away from houses by special conduits (**sewers**). The use of water-borne sewage disposal became established in the 1870s, the sewers being linked either directly to the sea through an outfall, if a suitable one was available, or to a **sewage farm**. A sewage farm uses beds of sand to grow and support a gelatinous bacterial film which develops as the true filter, removing almost all solids. Other precipitation treatments remove substances in solution.

Seward Peninsula Peninsula in Alaska, USA; the most W point of the North American continent.

Sewell, Anna [syooel] (1820–78) Novelist, born in Yarmouth, Norfolk. Her *Black Beauty* (1877), the story of a horse, was written as a plea for the more humane treatment of animals.

sewellel [sewelel] *mountain beaver*

Sexagesima [seksajesima] The second Sunday before Lent, apparently so called by analogy with *Quinquagesima*, the following Sunday. (Lat *sexagesimus*, 'sixtieth'.)

sex discrimination Unfavourable treatment, whether direct or indirect, or victimization of a person because of sex or marital status. In many jurisdictions, dismissal on the grounds of pregnancy, or discrimination when taking on staff or affording access to promotion is also unlawful, as is victimization of someone claiming discrimination. European Communities law calls for member states to apply the principle that men and women shall receive equal pay for equal work. In England and Wales, the relevant Acts are the Sex Discrimination Acts of 1975 and 1986.

sex hormones Steroid hormones produced and secreted mainly by the gonads, necessary for sexual development and the control of reproductive function. In humans the most important are certain androgens (testosterone and dihydrotestosterone) found predominantly in males, and progestogens (progesterone) and certain oestrogens (oestradiol, oestrone, and oestriol) found predominantly in females.

sexism A set of preconceived assumptions about the 'proper' roles, attitudes, and characteristics (especially physical) that men and women should have, typically working to the advantage of men over women; for example, the assumption that 'a woman's place is in the home'.

Sextans (Lat 'sextant') A very faint equatorial constellation between Leo and Hydra.

sextant An optical instrument for measuring angular distances; in particular, the elevation of the Sun above the horizon at noon, for determining latitude. The observer views the horizon through a telescope, and simultaneously (through a mirror attached to an arm on a graduated arc) the Sun.

sex therapy Treatment for sexual problems of psychological origin, which may arise as a result of a mental reaction to physical illness by the affected individual or partner, or to psychological attitudes themselves, either of which imperil normal sexual relations. An assessment of the individual or couple's problem is followed by simple counselling or, in the event of failure, by referral to specially trained sex therapists, who generally advise a graduated programme of tasks which the couple pursue at home.

sexually transmitted diseases AIDS; gonorrhoea; syphilis; venereal disease

Seychelles p.843

Seyfert, Carl (Keenan) [sayfert] (1911–60) US astronomer, who first drew attention (1943) to the existence of galaxies with brilliant nuclei.

Seymour, Jane [seemoor] (c.1509–37) Third queen of Henry VIII, the mother of Edward VI, and the sister of Protector Somerset. She was a lady-in-waiting to Henry's first two wives, and married him 11 days after the execution of Anne Boleyn. She died soon after the birth of her son.

Sezession [setsesyohn] (Ger 'secession') The name adopted by a number of groups of modern artists in Germany between c.1890 and World War 1, who seceded from the orthodox academic bodies to form their own exhibiting societies.

Sfax [sfaks] 34°45N 10°43E, pop (2000e) 303 000. Seaport in E Tunisia; second largest city of Tunisia; built on the site of Roman and Phoenician settlements; occupied by Sicilians (12th-c) and Spaniards (16th-c); airfield; railway.

SGML Standard Generalized Mark-up Language

sgraffito or **graffito** A technique in art in which one colour is laid over another and a design scratched through. Mediaeval and Renaissance buildings were sometimes decorated with two layers of plaster – one white, one coloured – and scratched decoration applied.

Shabbat Sabbath

Shabuoth or **Shavuot(h)** [shavoo-oth, -ot] The Jewish Feast of Weeks, observed in May or June (6 or 7 Sivan) in commemoration of God's giving of the Law to Moses on Mount Sinai (Ex 19); also known as **Pentecost**.

Shackleton, Sir Ernest Henry (1874–1922) Explorer, born in Kilkee, Co Kildare, Ireland. He was a junior officer in Scott's National Antarctic Expedition (1901–3), and nearly reached the South Pole in his own expedition of 1909. In 1915 his ship Endurance was crushed in the ice. He died at South Georgia during a fourth expedition.

shad Small herring-like fish (Alosa sapidissima) native to the Atlantic seaboard of North America but now widespread on the Pacific coast also; live in large schools; length up to 75 cm/30 in; silver with greenish-blue upper surface. (Family: Clupeidae.)

shaddock A citrus fruit (Citrus grandis) resembling grapefruit, 10–25 cm/4–10 in diameter; globose or pear-shaped, with greenish-yellow rind and sweet pink or yellow pulp. It is grown mainly in the tropics. (Family: Rutaceae.)

shadow-mask tube A cathode-ray tube for the display of colour video images. Electron beams from three separate guns modulated by the red, green, and blue signals are deflected by a scanning system through holes in a plate to fall on minute phosphor dots of the appropriate colour comprising the screen. These dots glow according to the intensity of the beam reaching them and appear as additive colour hues.

shadow puppets Puppets which are manipulated in performance so as to cast a shadow on a screen. There are two major traditions. In one, the sticks operating the two-dimensional figures are worked from below, as with Balinese and Javanese shadow theatre. In the other, the sticks are operated from behind, as with Chinese and Turkish shadow theatre.

Shadwell, Thomas (c.1642–92) Playwright, born in Brandon, Norfolk. He found success with his first satirical comedy, The Sullen Lovers (1668), and such later 'comedies of manners' as Epsom-Wells (1672). He succeeded Dryden as poet laureate in 1689.

Shaftesbury, Anthony Ashley Cooper, 1st Earl of [shahftsbree] (1621–83) English statesman, born in Wimborne St Giles, Dorset. He became a member of the Short Parliament (1640) and of the Barebones Parliament (1653), and was made one of Cromwell's Council of State, but from 1655 was in opposition. At the Restoration he became Chancellor of the Exchequer (1661–72), a member of the Cabal (1667), and Lord Chancellor (1672–3).

Shaftesbury, Anthony Ashley Cooper, 3rd Earl of [shahftsbree] (1671–1713) Moral philosopher, born in London, the grandson of the 1st Earl of Shaftesbury. He is best known for his essays, collected as Characteristics of Men, Manners, Opinions, Times (1711). He was one of the leading English deists.

Shaftesbury, Anthony Ashley Cooper, 7th Earl of [shahftsbree] (1801–85) Factory reformer and philanthropist, born in London. He became the main spokesman of the factory reform movement, and a leader of the evangelical movement within the Church of England.

shag cormorant

Shah Jahan [jahahn] (1592–1666) Mughal Emperor of India (1628–58), born in Lahore, Pakistan. His reign saw two wars in the Deccan, 1636, 1655, the subjugation of Bijapur and Golconda, 1636, and attacks on the Uzbegs and Persians. His buildings included the Taj Mahal (1632–54).

Shaka [shahka] (c.1788–1828) African ruler, born near Melmoth, KwaZulu Natal, South Africa. He was a highly successful military ruler, who intensified the centralization of Zulu power, adapted the weapons and tactics of local warfare, and set about the incorporation of neighbouring peoples. He was killed by his half-brother, Dingane.

Shakers The popular name for members of the United Society for Believers in Christ's Second Appearing, founded in England under the leadership of Ann Lee (1736–87), who led them to America in 1774. They are communitarian and pacifist, and their ecstatic dancing gave rise to their popular name. Their acceptance of strict celibacy has led to their decline, and by 2000 only the Sabbathday Lake Shaker community remained active, with a total of seven members.

Shakespeare, William (1564–1616) Playwright, actor, and poet, the greatest English writer, born in Stratford-upon-Avon, Warwickshire, the son of **John Shakespeare**, a glover, and **Mary Arden**, of farming stock. He married **Anne Hathaway**, from a local farming family, in 1582, who bore him a daughter, Susanna, in 1583, and twins Hamnet and Judith in 1585. He moved to London, possibly in 1591, and became an actor. His sonnets, known by 1598, though not published until 1609, fall into two groups: 1 to 126 are addressed to a fair young man, and 127 to 154 to a 'dark lady' who holds both the young man and the poet in thrall. The first evidence of his association with the stage is in 1594, when he was acting with the Lord Chamberlain's company of players. When the company built the Globe Theatre S of the Thames in 1597, he became a partner. He returned to Stratford c.1610, living as a country gentleman at his house, New Place. His will was made in March 1616, and he was buried at Stratford. The modern

Seychelles

[**sayshelz**], official name **Republic of Seychelles**

Local name Seychelles

Timezone GMT +4

Area 455 km²/175 sq mi

Population total (2002e) 83 400

Status Republic

Date of independence 1976

Capital Victoria (on Mahé Island)

Languages Creole French (official since 1981), and English

Ethnic groups Seychellois (Asian, African, and European admixtures), Malagasy (3%), Chinese (2%), English (1%)

Religions Roman Catholic (95%)

Physical features Island group in SW Indian Ocean, N of Madagascar, comprising 115 islands; main islands include Mahé (largest), Praslin, and La Digue; islands fall into two main groups, a compact group of 41 mountainous islands rising steeply from the sea, highest point 906 m/2972 ft on Mahé; and a group of low-lying coralline islands and atolls to the SW, flat, waterless and mostly uninhabited.

Climate Tropical climate; average annual temperature 27°C (Jan), 26°C (Jul); wet humid season (Dec–May); average annual rainfall 2375 mm/93.5 in.

Currency 1 Seychelles Rupee (SCR) = 100 cents

Economy Agriculture; fruit, vegetables, livestock, cinnamon, copra; brewing, plastics, steel fabricated goods, fishing; tourism.

GDP (2002e) $626 mn, per capita $7800

Human Development Index (2002) 0·811

History Colonized by the French, 1768; captured by Britain, 1794; incorporated as a dependency of Mauritius, 1814; separate Crown Colony, 1903; independent republic within the Commonwealth, 1976; constitution, 1979, established a one-party state; governed by a President, elected for a 5-year term, a Council of Ministers, and a unicameral National Assembly; legislation legalizing the activity of opposition parties adopted, 1991.

Head of State/Government

1976–7 James R Mancham

1977–2004 France-Albert René

2004– James Michel

era of Shakespeare scholarship has been marked by an enormous amount of investigation into the authorship, text, and chronology of the plays, in particular the different quarto editions, and the first collected works, the First Folio of 1623. The authorship of such plays as *Titus Andronicus*, *The Two Noble Kinsmen*, and *Henry VI*, part I, is still a matter of controversy, as is Shakespeare's part in the writing of *Timon of Athens*, *Pericles*, *Henry VIII*, and (the latest proposed addition to the canon) *King Edward III*. It is conventional to group the plays into early, middle, and late periods, and to distinguish comedies, tragedies, and histories, recognizing other groups that do not fall neatly into these categories. *p.844*

shale Sedimentary rock predominantly formed from consolidated and compacted clay deposits. Oil shale contains sufficient decayed organic matter that an oil can be extracted from it by destructive distillation.

shallot [**shalot**] A variety of onion with clusters of small, oval bulbs, widely grown as a vegetable.

shaman [**shay**man, **shah**man] A person thought to possess special powers to communicate with and influence the spirits by dissociating his soul from his body. Shamans are found among Siberian and Asian peoples; similar practitioners are found in many other religions, under other names.

Shamir, Yitzhak [**shameer**], originally **Yitzhak Jazernicki** (1915–) Zionist leader and prime minister of Israel (1983–4, 1986–92), born in Ruzinoy, Poland. He was foreign minister (1980–3), before taking over the leadership of the right-wing Likud Party, and becoming prime minister. From 1984 he shared an uneasy coalition with the Labour leader Shimon Peres, and was re-elected in 1988, but lost his position when Labour under Yitzhak Rabin won the 1992 election.

Shammai [**shamiy**] (c.1st-c BC–AD 1st-c) A Jewish scholar and Pharisaic leader, head of a famous school of Torah scholars, whose interpretation of the Law was often in conflict with the equally famous school led by Hillel. Both are often referred to in the Mishnah.

shamrock The name applied to several different plants with leaves divided into three leaflets, including **wood sorrel** (*Oxalis acetosella*) and various species of **clover** (*Trifolium*). It has been adopted as the national emblem of Ireland, and is worn each year on 17 March to commemorate St Patrick. It is a slender annual growing to 25 cm/10 in; flowers yellow, petals later turning dark brown; native to Europe, N Africa, and the W African islands (Macaronesia). (Family: Leguminosae.)

Shang or **Yin dynasty** (1523–1028 BC) The earliest historical Chinese dynasty (the dates are disputed). Evidence is found in the Zhou and Han periods, and in 200 000 Shang period oracle bones which yield detail of daily life, as well as royal and ministerial chronologies. Its capital (from 1300 BC) was at Anyang, N of the Yellow River.

Shanghai 31°13N 121°25E; pop (2000e) 9 158 000; administrative region 13 876 000; municipality area 5800 km²/2239 sq mi. Port in E China, on Huangpu and Wusong Rivers; largest city in China; developed in the Yuan period as a cotton centre; trading centre in the 17th–18th-c; opened to foreign trade, 1842; two airports; two airfields; rail and sea links to other cities; university (1895) and several other higher education institutions; Longhua Temple (c.7th-c); Yu Yuan (Garden of Happiness), 1577, the basis for 'willow pattern' chinaware.

Shankar, Ravi [**shangkah(r)**] (1920–) Sitar player, born in Benares, India. Through his foreign tours and recordings, he has done much to make Indian classical music better known abroad.

Shanklin *Sandown*

Shankly, Bill, popular name of **William Shankly** (1913–81) Footballer and manager, born in Glenbuck, East Ayrshire. As a manager, he found fame with Liverpool (1959–74), creating a team which was highly successful in Britain and Europe.

Shakespeare: The Plays

Early comedies	Written	Well-known characters
The Comedy of Errors	1590–94	Antipholus, Dromio, Adriana
Love's Labour's Lost	1590–94	Armado, Berowne, Costard
The Two Gentlemen of Verona	1592–3	Proteus, Valentine, Julia, Sylvia
The Taming of the Shrew	1592	Petruchio, Katharina, Sly
Histories		
Henry VI Part I (with other authors)	1589–90	Henry, Talbot, Joan of Arc
Henry VI Part II	1590–91	Henry, Margaret, Jack Cade
Henry VI Part III	1590–91	Henry, Margaret, Richard of Gloucester
King Edward III (with other authors)	1590–5	Edward, Philippa, Prince Edward, Countess of Salisbury
Richard III	1592–3	Richard, Margaret, Clarence, Anne
King John	1595–7	John, Constance, Arthur, Bastard
Richard II	1595	Richard, John of Gaunt, Bolingbroke
Henry IV Part I	1596	Henry, Hal, Hotspur, Falstaff
Henry IV Part II	1597	Henry, Hal, Falstaff, Mistress Quickly
Henry V	1599	Henry (formerly Hal), Pistol, Nym, Katherine
Henry VIII (with John Fletcher)	1613	Henry, Katherine, Wolsey
Middle comedies		
A Midsummer Night's Dream	1595	Oberon, Titania, Puck, Bottom
The Merchant of Venice	1596–8	Bassanio, Portia, Shylock, Jessica
The Merry Wives of Windsor	1597	Falstaff, Mistress Quickly, Shallow
As You Like It	1599	Rosalind, Orlando, Touchstone, Jaques
Twelfth Night	1600–2	Orsino, Olivia, Viola, Malvolio, Feste, Sir Andrew Aguecheek
Dark comedies		
Much Ado About Nothing	1598	Beatrice, Benedick, Dogberry, Verges
All's Well That Ends Well	1602–3	Bertram, Helena, Parolles
Measure for Measure	1604–5	Duke, Angelo, Isabella, Mariana
Tragedies		
Romeo and Juliet	1595–6	Romeo, Juliet, Mercutio, the Nurse
Hamlet	1600–1	Hamlet, Ophelia, the Ghost, the Grave-Digger
Othello	1604	Othello, Desdemona, Iago, Cassio
King Lear	1605–6	Lear, Cordelia, the Fool, Kent, Edgar/Poor Tom
Macbeth	1605–6	Macbeth, Lady Macbeth, Banquo, the Three Witches
Greek and Roman plays		
Titus Andronicus	1590–94	Andronicus, Aaron, Lavinia
Julius Caesar	1599	Caesar, Brutus, Cassius, Antony
Troilus and Cressida	1601–2	Troilus, Cressida, Pandarus
Timon of Athens (with Thomas Middleton)	1605–9	Timon, Apemantus
Antony and Cleopatra	1606–7	Antony, Cleopatra, Enobarbus
Coriolanus	1607–8	Coriolanus, Volumnia, Menenius
Late plays		
Pericles (with George Wilkins)	1607–8	Pericles, Marina, Gower
Cymbeline	1609–10	Innogen, Iachimo, Posthumus
The Winter's Tale	1611	Leontes, Perdita, Florizel, Autolycus
The Tempest	1613	Prospero, Miranda, Ferdinand, Ariel, Caliban
The Two Noble Kinsmen (with John Fletcher)	1613	Arcite, Palamon, Emilia, Theseus

Shannon, Ir **Rineanna** 52°42N 8°57W, pop (2000e) 8000. Town in Clare county, W Ireland; duty-free airport.

Shannon, River River in Ireland, rising in Co Cavan, Ulster, and flowing c.385 km/240 mi to Limerick Bay.

SHAPE NATO

Shapur or **Sapor II** [shapoor], known as **the Great** (309–79) King of Persia (309–79), who ruled with the help of regents until the age of 16. Under him the Sassanian Empire reached its zenith.

Sharapova, Maria [sharapohvuh] (1987–) Tennis player, born in Nyagan, Siberia, Russia. She began playing tennis as a young child, and at age nine was taken by her father to Florida, USA, where she enrolled at a tennis academy. She turned professional at 14, and in 2003 reached the fourth round at Wimbledon. Success came in 2004 when she won the singles title there, becoming Russia's first woman Wimbledon champion. Further achievements include the WTA Championship title (2004) and the US Open (2006). She began 2007 ranked world number 2.

sharefarming A form of tenure in which the landlord provides the land, fixed equipment, and often a proportion of the variable inputs, in exchange for an agreed proportion of the final crop.

shares Certificates of part ownership of a company, which represent equal amounts of money invested in the company. The **shareholders** provide the original capital for the company and are its residual owners. They are entitled to any profits made, either as dividends or as a capital distribution if the company is sold or wound up. If the company makes losses they may lose their money, hence the term **risk capital**, though if the company has limited liability they cannot lose more than they put in.

Sharia [shareea] The sacred law of Islam, embracing all aspects of a Muslim's life. It has four sources: the *Qur'an*, the *sunna* or 'practice' of the Prophet Mohammed, *ijma* or 'consensus of opinion', and *qiyas* or 'reasoning by analogy'.

Sharif, Omar [shareef], originally **Michael Shalhouz** (1932–) Film actor, born in Alexandria, Egypt. He attracted international attention following his role in *Lawrence of Arabia* (1962), and starred in *Doctor Zhivago* (1965). Later films include *Funny Girl* (1968), *The Tamarind Seed* (1974), *The Mirror has Two Faces* (1996), and *One Night With the King* (2005). In 2003, he received the Venice Film Festival's Golden Lion award for his achievement in film. He is also a renowned bridge player.

Sharjah [shah(r)ja], or **Shariqah** pop (2000e) 385 900; area 2600 km²/1000 sq mi. Third largest of the United Arab Emirates; capital, Ash Sharjah; offshore oil production began in 1974.

shark Any of a large group of active, predatory, cartilaginous fishes belonging to 19 separate families, such as the Alopiidae (thresher sharks), Cetorhinidae (basking sharks), and Chlamydoselachidae (frilled sharks).

Sharman, Helen (Patricia) (1963–) Britain's first astronaut, born in Sheffield, South Yorkshire. In 1989 she responded to an advertisement for trainee astronauts, and was eventually selected to be the British member of the Russian scientific space mission, Project Juno (1991), spending eight days in space. She has since become known as a lecturer in science education; her book *The Space Place* appeared in 1997.

Sharon, Ariel [sharon] (1928–) Prime minister of Israel (2001–6) and soldier, born in Kfar Maalal, a communal farm in W Palestine. He won a seat in the Knesset (1973), becoming minister of defence (1981–3) during the war in Lebanon, but was forced to resign when he was found indirectly responsible for the massacre of civilians at refugee camps. Re-elected to the Knesset (1999), he became chairman of the Likud after the resignation of Binyamin Netanyahu, and replaced Ehud Barak as prime minister in 2001. He won a second term in 2003. In late 2005, Sharon quit the Likud and formed his own party named Kadima (Hebrew for 'Forward'). He suffered a massive stroke at the beginning of 2006 and remained in a coma in hospital. In the interim, power was transferred to vice premier Ehud Olmert who succeeded him following elections in March 2006.

Sharpe, Tom, popular name of **Thomas Ridley Sharpe** (1928–) Novelist, born in London. He was a lecturer in history (1963–71) before turning to full-time writing, beginning with *Riotous Assembly* (1971). Later novels include *Indecent Exposure* (1973), *Porterhouse Blue* (1974), a series introducing the character of Wilt (from 1976), *The Midden* (1996), and *Wilt in Nowhere* (2004).

Sharpe, William F (1934–) Economist, born in Cambridge, MA. He shared the 1990 Nobel Prize for Economics for his contributions to the corporate finance field.

Sharpeville [shah(r)pvil] 26°40S 27°52E, pop (2000e) 143 000. Black African township in NE South Africa; scene of the Sharpeville massacre (1960); inauguration of the new constitution took place here in December 1996.

Sharpeville massacre (21 Mar 1960) A major incident in the black African township of Sharpeville in South Africa, when police opened fire on a crowd demonstrating against the laws restricting non-white movements and requiring non-whites to carry identification (the *pass laws*); 69 people were killed and 180 wounded. The massacre produced an international outcry and made black nationalism in South Africa increasingly radical.

Sharpless, Barry K (1941–) Chemist, born in Philadelphia, PA. A researcher at the Scripps Research Institute at La Jolla, CA, he shared the 2001 Nobel Prize for Chemistry for work on chirally catalysed hydrogenation reactions.

Shastri, Lal (Bahadur) [shastree] (1904–66) Indian statesman and prime minister (1964–6), born in Mughalsarai, Uttar Pradesh, India. He succeeded Nehru as premier, but died of a heart attack in Tashkent, Uzbekistan, the day after signing a 'no war' agreement with Pakistan.

Shatner, William (1931–) Actor and director, born in Montreal, Canada. He became internationally known following the cult success of the *Star Trek* television series (1966–9), in which he played Captain James T(iberius) Kirk. He reprised the role in several feature film sequels, directing as well as acting in *Star Trek V: The Final Frontier* (1989). Later TV work includes the drama series *Boston Legal* (2005, Emmy).

Shatt al-Arab [shat al arab] Tidal river formed by the union of the Tigris and Euphrates Rivers, SE Iraq; flows 192 km/119 mi to enter the Persian Gulf; part of the Iraq–Iran border in its lower course; wide delta, containing the world's largest date-palm groves; international commission in 1935 gave control to Iraq, but disputes over navigational rights were one of the issues that led to the outbreak of the Gulf War.

Shavuot(h) *Shabuoth*

Shaw, Anna Howard (1847–1919) Minister and feminist, born in Newcastle upon Tyne, Tyne and Wear. Her family emigrated to the USA in 1851, and in 1880 she became the first woman to be ordained as a Methodist preacher. She was president of the National American Woman Suffrage Association (1904–15).

Shaw, Fiona (1958–) Actress, born in Cork, Co Cork, Ireland. Throughout her career she has worked consistently with the Royal Shakespeare Company. She often collaborates with the director Deborah Warner, most notably with *Richard II* (1995), in which she played the title role. Film work includes *My Left Foot* (1988), *Butcher Boy* (1996), and *Harry Potter and the Prisoner of Azkaban* (2004).

Shaw, George Bernard (1856–1950) Playwright, essayist, and pamphleteer, born in Dublin. In 1882 he turned to Socialism, joined the committee of the Fabian Society, and became known as a journalist. He began to write plays in 1885, and among his early successes were *Arms and the Man* (1894), *Candida* (1897), and *The Devil's Disciple* (1897). Later plays included *Man and Superman* (1905), *Major Barbara* (1905), *The Doctor's Dilemma* (1906), *Pygmalion* (1913, adapted as a musical play, *My Fair Lady*, in 1956, filmed in 1964), and *Saint Joan* (1923). He wrote over 40 plays, and continued to write them even in his 90s. He was also passionately interested in the question of spelling reform. In 1925 he was awarded the Nobel Prize for Literature.

Shawnee [shawnee] North American Algonkin Indians who originally settled in Ohio, but were pushed out of the area by the Iroquois. They eventually settled in Oklahoma.

Shearer, Alan (1970–) England footballer, born in Newcastle-upon-Tyne, Tyne & Wear. He played for Southampton (1988–92), then transferred to Blackburn Rovers (1992–6) at a then record British fee of £3·2 million. He transferred to Newcastle United in 1996 for a world record fee of £15 million. He joined the England squad in 1992, becoming captain in 1996, and by mid-2000 (when he announced his retirement from international play) had won 62 caps. His honours include Footballer of the Year (1994) and Professional Footballers' Association Player of the Year (1995), and in 2003 he received the Domestic

Player of the Decade award. In 2005 he achieved his 250th Premiership goal. In early 2006 he broke Jackie Milburn's record of 200 goals for Newcastle, and retired at the end of the season.

Shearing, Sir George (Albert) (1919–) Jazz pianist, bandleader, and composer, born in London. Blind from birth, he moved to New York in 1947 and led a trio and quartet before forming the quintet (1949) that brought him international fame. He maintained a widespread touring schedule thereafter while making many guest appearances with symphony orchestras. He was knighted in 2007.

shear modulus A measure of a material's resistance to twisting; symbol *G*, units Pa (pascal); also called the **modulus of rigidity** or **torsion modulus**. It is defined as shear stress divided by shear strain, and is applicable only to solids.

shearwater A petrel with a long slender bill; plumage dark above, dark or pale beneath. The name is also used for skimmers.

sheathbill A white, pigeon-like shorebird, native to the Antarctic and sub-Antarctic; short, stout bill with horny cover at base; the only native Antarctic bird without webbed feet. (Family: Chionididae, 2 species.)

Sheba, Queen of [sheeba] (c.10th-c BC) Monarch mentioned in the Bible (1 *Kings* 10 and 2 *Chron* 9). She is said to have journeyed to Jerusalem to test the wisdom of Solomon and exchange gifts.

Sheene, Barry (Stephen Frank) (1950–2003) Motorcycle racer, born in East London. He made his professional debut at age 18 and went on to win the British (1970) and European (1973) 750 cc titles. With Suzuki he won two successive 500 cc World Championships (1976, 1977). In 1982 he was seriously injured in a practice race at Silverstone and surgeons rebuilt his legs using metal plates. He later retired to Australia (1987) where he became a popular TV commentator for motorsports.

sheep A grazing mammal of family Bovidae; eight species in genus *Ovis* (seven wild species and the domestic sheep, *Ovis aries*); male with large spiralling horns; female with small or absent horns; wild sheep have a coarse outer coat and a fleecy underlayer which grows only in winter; domesticated breeds have only the underlayer, which is thick and grows continuously; male called a *ram* or *tup*, female a *ewe*, young a *lamb*.

sheepdog Any working dog used to guard sheep from wild animals or to assist in herding; also any dog belonging to a breed formerly used for this purpose.

Sheffield 53°23N 1°30W, urban area pop (2001e) 513 200. City in South Yorkshire, N England; on the R Don; developed as a cutlery-manufacturing town in the early 18th-c and as a steel town in the 19th-c; city status in 1893; major rebuilding after World War 2 bombing; universities, (1905, 1992); railway; cathedral (12th-c); Crucible Theatre; football league teams, Sheffield United (Blades), Sheffield Wednesday (Owls).

Sheffield Shield A silver trophy purchased from a donation of £150 by Lord Sheffield to promote Australian cricket. It has been the object of annual cricket competitions between the colonies (to 1900) and the states (after 1900) since 1892–3.

Shelburne, William Petty Fitzmaurice, 2nd Earl of (1737–1805) British statesman and prime minister (1782–3), born in Dublin. Made premier on the death of Rockingham, he resigned when outvoted by the coalition between Fox and North.

sheldgoose A South American goose of the genus *Chloephaga* (5 species); eats grass (4 species) or seaweed (the **kelp goose**, *Chloephaga hybrida*); nests on ground. (Subfamily: Anatinae. Tribe: Tadornini.)

sheldrake *shelduck*

shelduck A goose-like duck, native to the Old World (except the far N); nests in burrows or holes; also known as a **sheldrake**. (Genus: *Tadorna*, 7 species. Subfamily: Anatinae. Tribe: Tadornini.)

shell The mineralized outer covering of a variety of invertebrate animals, such as molluscs and brachiopods; usually containing a large amount of calcium. The calcareous shell of a bird's egg is a secondary egg membrane secreted by the genital duct of the mother bird.

shellac A resin generally obtained from a secretion from the insect *Tachardia lacca*. Solutions of shellac are used as varnishes and French polish.

Shelley, Mary (Wollstonecraft), *née* **Godwin** (1797–1851) Writer, born in London, the daughter of William Godwin and Mary Wollstonecraft. She eloped with Shelley in 1814, and married him two years later. She wrote several novels, notably *Frankenstein, or the Modern Prometheus* (1818).

Shelley, Percy Bysshe [bish] (1792–1822) Poet and political thinker, born in Horsham, West Sussex. He married Harriet Westbrook in London, and settled in Keswick, where he wrote his revolutionary poem *Queen Mab* (1813). He formed a liaison with Mary Godwin, with whom he eloped (1814) and whom he later married. From 1818 he lived in Italy, where he wrote the bulk of his poetry, including the verse drama *Prometheus Unbound* (1818–19). He was drowned near Livorno.

shellfish An informal name for edible molluscs and crustaceans collectively; includes groups such as shrimps, crabs, lobsters, clams, bivalves, whelks, and mussels.

Shelter (National Campaign for the Homeless) In the UK, a charity founded in 1966 to provide help for the homeless and to campaign on their behalf. Its income comes principally from donations.

Sheltie *Shetland pony; Shetland sheepdog*

Shem Biblical character, the eldest son of Noah, brother of Ham and Japheth. He is depicted as the legendary father of 'Semitic' peoples, meant to include the Hebrews.

Shema [shemah] (Heb 'hear') A well-known ancient Jewish prayer, beginning 'Hear, O Israel: the Lord our God, the Lord is one'. It introduces the Jewish morning and evening prayers.

Shenandoah River [shenuhndohuh] River in West Virginia and Virginia, USA; formed at the junction of the North Fork and South Fork Rivers; flows 88 km/55 mi NE to meet the Potomac R.

Shenyang [shuhnyahng], formerly **Mukden** 41°50N 123°26E, pop (2000e) 5 206 000. Largest industrial city in NE China; capital of Manchu state, 1625; taken by Japanese, 1931, which led to the establishment of Manchukuo; occupied by Nationalists, 1945; taken by Communists, 1948; renamed, 1949; airfield; railway; university; Imperial Palace (1625–36).

Shepard, Alan (Bartlett), Jr (1923–98) The first US astronaut, born in East Derry, NH. His sub-orbital flight in a Mercury space capsule ('Freedom 7') took place on 5 May 1961, reached an altitude of 185 km/116 mi, and lasted 15 min. He was also commander of the Apollo 14 crew which landed on the Moon in 1971.

Shepherd, Cybill (1950–) Film actress, born in Memphis, TN. She made an acclaimed film debut in *The Last Picture Show* (1971), following this with *The Heartbreak Kid* (1973) and *Taxi Driver* (1976). Television work includes the series *Moonlighting* (1985–9), with Bruce Willis, and *Cybill* (1995–8).

shepherd moons Small natural moons whose gravitational fields serve to confine narrow rings around some of the outer planets. For example, the 'F' Ring of Saturn discovered by Pioneer 11 is a ribbon c.100 km/60 mi wide; its 'braided' structure was observed by Voyager spacecraft.

Shepparton 36°25S 145°26E, pop (2000e) 27 900. City in N Victoria, Australia; railway; International Village, featuring worldwide tourist information.

sherardizing [sherah(r)diyzing] A steel protection process named after English inventor Sherard Osborn Cowper-Coles (1866–1935). The outermost layer of the finished product is zinc, which grades into an adherent iron/zinc alloy. It is very corrosion resistant, and good for surface painting.

Sheraton, Thomas (1751–1806) Cabinet-maker, born in Stockton-on-Tees, Durham. He produced a range of Neoclassical designs which had a wide influence on contemporary taste in furniture.

Sheridan, Philip H(enry) (1831–88) US general, born in Albany, NY. In 1864 he was given command of the Army of the Shenandoah, defeating General Lee, and was active in the final battles which led to Lee's surrender.

Sheridan, Richard Brinsley (Butler) (1751–1816) Playwright, born in Dublin, Ireland. In 1775 appeared the highly successful comedy of manners, *The Rivals*, and this was followed by several other comedies, notably *The School for Scandal* (1777).

sheriff Originally, the monarch's representative in the English shires responsible for legal, administrative, and military matters. Since the Middle Ages the office has largely declined in importance in England and Wales, and the sheriff's duties are now largely ceremonial and administrative. In Scotland, however, since 1825, sheriffs have been legally qualified judges with a wide civil and criminal jurisdiction. In the USA, sheriffs are generally elected in each of the 3000 or more counties. They are responsible for law enforcement principally in rural areas, though many of their duties have been transferred to local or state police.

Sheringham, Teddy, popular name of **Edward Paul Sheringham** (1966–) Footballer, born in Highams Park, London. A forward, he played for Millwall, Aldershot, Nottingham Forest, and Tottenham Hotspur, signing for Manchester United in 1997, and returning to Tottenham in 2001. He was an England team member in the 2002 World Cup campaign, winning 51 caps by the end of his international career. He joined Portsmouth (2003–4) and then West Ham (2004–).

Sherman, William Tecumseh (1820–91) US general in the Union army during the Civil War, born in Lancaster, OH. His most famous campaign was in 1864, when he captured Atlanta, and commenced his famous 'March to the Sea', which divided the Confederate forces.

Sherpa A mountain people of Sikkim State, India, and Nepal. They are famous as mountain traders and porters in the Himalayas.

Sherrington, Sir Charles Scott (1857–1952) Physiologist, born in London. His research on the nervous system constituted a landmark in modern physiology, and he shared the Nobel Prize for Physiology or Medicine in 1932.

sherry A white wine, fortified with brandy; named after Jerez de la Frontera in the Andalusian region of Spain. *Fino* is dry, light-coloured, of a high quality, and usually drunk young; *amontillado* is darker and moderately dry; *oloroso* is fuller and dark, the sweetest available.

Sherwood Forest An area of heath and woodland, mainly in Nottinghamshire, UK, where mediaeval kings hunted deer. It is famed for being the home of Robin Hood. In 2002 it was designated a national nature reserve.

Shetland, also called **The Shetlands**, formerly **Zetland** pop (2000e) 23 100; area 1433 km²/553 sq mi. Group of c.100 islands off coast of NE Scotland; 80 km/50 mi NE of Orkney Is; c.20 inhabited; chief islands, Mainland, Unst, Yell, Fetlar, Whalsay; low-lying, highest point Ronas Hill in N Mainland (450 m/1476 ft); capital, Lerwick, on Mainland; annexed by Norway in 9th-c; annexed by Scotland, 1472; cattle and sheep raising, knitwear, fishing, oil services at Lerwick and Sandwick, oil terminal at Sullom Voe; several prehistoric remains.

Shetland pony The strongest of all breeds of horse (can pull twice its own weight), developed on the Scottish Shetland and Orkney Is; height, 9 hands/0·9 m/3 ft; stocky, with short legs; long mane and tail; also known as **Sheltie** or **Shelty**.

Shevardnadze, Eduard Amvrosiyevich [shevernadze] (1928–) Georgian head of state (1992–2003) and former Soviet statesman, born in Mamati, Georgia. A member of the USSR Polit-

buro, in 1985 he was appointed foreign minister. He resigned in 1990, expressing concern over some of Gorbachev's decisions, and warning of dictatorship. He was elected Chairman of the State Council of Georgia in 1992, but was unable to prevent the country's slide into civil war. Stability was eventually restored, and he was elected president in 1995 and 2000. But growing public discontent mounted after allegations of irregularities in the parliamentary elections of November 2003 and forced his resignation.

shiatsu [sheeatsoo] (Jap 'finger pressure') A form of massage in which pressure is applied to acupuncture points and meridians using the fingers, thumbs, and sometimes elbows, knees, hands, and feet. It is designed to release blockages and balance the flow of energy, and healing energy may also be transmitted from the practitioner to the patient.

shield A geological term for a large region of stable continental crust, usually Precambrian in age and forming the core of a continental land mass.

shield bug A typically shield-shaped true bug; c.5000 species, including some pests of economically important crops. (Order: Heteroptera. Family: Pentatomidae.)

shielding *screening*

Shields, Carol (Ann Warner) (1935–2003) Novelist, born in Oak Park, IL. She studied at Hanover College, IN, Exeter University in England, and the University of Ottawa, and later became professor of literature and chancellor of the University of Winnipeg. Her first novel, *Small Ceremonies* (1976), received the Canadian Authors Association Award for best novel. Later books include *The Stone Diaries* (1993, Pulitzer) and *Larry's Party* (1997, Orange Prize). Her final novel, *Unless* (2001), was short-listed for the Booker and Orange prizes. She was made a Companion of the Order of Canada in 2002.

Shih-chia-chuang *Shijiazhuang*

Shih Tzu [shee tsoo] A toy breed of dog of Tibetan or Chinese origin; similar to the Pekinese in shape; thick straight coat; hair cascades to cover eyes and ears.

Shiites [sheeiyts] A minority division, representing c.10% of Islam, which holds that legitimacy derives from the descendants of the Prophet Mohammed. Shiites venerate the lineal descendants of Ali, the fourth caliph, as infallible *imams*. Three main groups are distinguished: the Zaydis of Yemen; the Ismailis of India and East Africa; and the Imamis, or 'twelvers', who recognize twelve *imams*, the last of which disappeared in the 9th-c and whose return as the *Mahdi* is expected to usher in an age of justice. Shiism is the state religion of the Islamic Republic of Iran.

Shijiazhuang or **Shih-chia-chuang** [shoejiahjwahng] 38°04N 114°28E, pop (2000e) 1 550 000. City in N China; a major railway junction; mining (coal, iron ore, limestone, marble); China's largest pharmaceutical plant.

Shikoku [shikohkoo] pop (2000e) 4 330 000; area 18 795 km²/7255 sq mi. Smallest of the four main islands of Japan; subtropical climate; mountainous and wooded interior; chief towns, Matsuyama, Takamatsu.

Shilluk An E Sudanic-speaking people living along the Nile S of Khartoum in the Sudan Republic. They are farmers, with many cattle.

Shiloh [shiyloh] The site of an ancient city in C Palestine; noted as the central sanctuary of the tribes of Israel during the settlement of Palestine under the tribal judges. It was destroyed c.1050 BC.

Shiloh, Battle of [shiyloh] (1862) An engagement in the American Civil War in SW Tennessee between Union forces under General Grant and Confederate forces under Albert Sidney Johnston (1803–62). Losses were heavy on both sides.

Shilton, Peter (1949–) Footballer, born in Leicester, Leicestershire. Starting his career with Leicester City at the age of 16, he also played for Stoke City, Nottingham Forest, Southampton, and Derby County. He made his international debut for England in 1970, and became the first England goalkeeper to gain 100 caps. He has won all the major honours in the game, including League championship and European Cup medals. On his retirement he had gained a record 125 caps.

shingles A condition arising from the re-activation of the chickenpox virus which lies latent in the ganglia of sensory somatic nerves; also known as **herpes zoster**. It causes pain and a blister-like rash over the segmental distribution of the affected nerve.

Shinkansen [shingkansen] The Japanese New Tokaido Line, a standard gauge line from Tokyo to Osaka for high speed trains (commonly known as 'bullet trains'), completed in 1964. The network is being extended to cover all main Honshu routes.

Shinto [shintoh] The indigenous religion of Japan. It emerged from the nature-worship of Japanese folk religions, reflected in ceremonies appealing to the mysterious powers of nature for protection. By the 8th-c, divine origins were ascribed to the imperial family, and in time it became the basis for State Shintoism and its obedience to the Emperor. There were nearly 2·7 million Shintoists in 2007.

shinty A twelve-a-side stick-and-ball game originating in Ireland more than 1500 years ago, and now popular in the Scottish Highlands. The playing pitch is up to 155 m/170 yd long and 73 m/80 yd wide. The object is to score goals by using the stick to propel the ball.

Shinwell, Emmanuel Shinwell, Baron, popularly known as **Manny Shinwell** (1884–1986) British statesman, born in London. In the post-war Labour government he was minister of fuel and power (1946), secretary of state for war (1947), and minister of defence (1950–1). Well known for his party political belligerence, in his later years he mellowed into a backbench 'elder statesman'.

ship A sea-going vessel of considerable size. At the time of Queen Hatshepsut (c.1500 BC) an expedition to E Africa was mounted using vessels of about 20 m/60 ft in length. These are the first sea-going ships of which there are reliable pictorial records. Greeks and Romans built galleys relying on oars, a square sail coming into use when the wind was favourable. Chinese ships were making voyages of over a year by the 1st-c AD. Roman merchant vessels 28–56 m/90–180 ft long were propelled by a large square sail hung from a single mast. Viking ships varied in length from 20 m/70 ft to 40 m/120 ft, and were propelled by a large square-rigged sail and oars. By the 15th-c the Portuguese had developed the lateen-rigged caravel into a three- or four-masted ocean-going craft. Out of this grew the carrack, where lateen sails gradually gave way to square sails. US influence dates from 1845, with the clipper ship.

In 1802 the first viable steamship, the *Charlotte Dundas*, was used as a tug on the Forth–Clyde canal. The first continuous steam crossing of the Atlantic was achieved by the British-owned packet vessel, the 700-ton *Sirius*, in 1838. Brunel's *Great Britain* (1844) was the first screw-propelled, double-bottomed, iron-hulled transatlantic passenger ship. The diesel engine, patented in 1892, won ocean-going acceptance in the 5000-gross-ton *Selandia* in 1912. Nuclear-fuelled vessels provide an alternative means of generating the heat to provide steam to drive turbines. This method is used in government vessels such as ice-breakers, aircraft carriers, and missile-carrying submarines, but it has proved to be uneconomical for merchant vessels.

Shipman, Harold (Frederick) (1946–2004) Doctor and serial murderer, born in Nottingham, Nottinghamshire. Fined for making out drug prescriptions to himself (to feed a pethidine addiction), he received treatment, and became a GP again in Hyde, Greater Manchester. After falling out with his partners, he set up his own practice. Arrested in 1998, he was sentenced to life imprisonment in 2000 for the murder of 15 of his elderly patients by injecting them with diamorphine. A public inquiry reported in 2002 that there had been 215 victims in all, dating from 1975, with another 45 likely, and a further 38 uncertain, making him Britain's worst ever serial killer. All the killings were carried out by injecting drugs, usually at a patient's home, but sometimes at his own surgery. No clear conclusion was reached about his motivation. He committed suicide in prison. In 2005, a report on Shipman's actions as a junior doctor suggested that the real total of his victims was around 250.

Ship of Cheops [keeops] An ancient Egyptian funeral ship found dismantled at Giza in 1954 in one of five boat pits around the Pyramid of Cheops (2551–2528 BC). Reconstructed, the ship measures 44 m/143 ft long with a beam of 6 m/19 ft, and carried six pairs of oars 6·5–8·5 m/21–28 ft long.

Shirakawa, Hideki (1936–) Chemist, born in Tokyo. He became professor of chemistry at the University of Tsukuba (1979). He shared the 2000 Nobel Prize for Chemistry for the discovery and development of conductive polymers.

Shiraz [sheeraz] 29°38N 52°34E, pop (2000e) 1 171 000. City in SW Iran; capital of Persia, 1750–79; fifth largest city in Iran; airfield; university (1945).

shire The largest breed of horse, developed in England from war-horses used to carry knights in armour; used for farm work; height, 17–18 hands/1·7–1·8 m/5 ft 8 in–6 ft; black or brown and white; long legs with hair covering hooves.

Shiva [sheeva] One of the three principal deities of the Hindu triad (*Trimurti*) – a god of contrasting features: creation and destruction, good and evil, fertility and asceticism.

Shkodër [shkohder], Ital **Scutari**, ancient **Scodra** 42°05N 19°30E, pop (2000e) 93 500. Market town in NW Albania; former capital of Albania; railway; citadel (14th-c), cathedral.

shock A term used by the lay public to denote the psychological state of fear or grief that follows a sudden accident, calamity, or bereavement. Its medical use refers to a clinical state in which the blood pressure and circulation is insufficient to maintain the functioning of the brain or other organs.

Shockley, William B(radford) (1910–89) Physicist, born in London. In 1947 he helped to devise the point-contact transistor, then devised the junction transistor, which heralded a revolution in radio, TV, and computer circuitry. He shared the Nobel Prize for Physics in 1956.

shock therapy A term sometimes used as a synonym for **electroconvulsive therapy**, but also for **electrosleep**, in which a weak rhythmically-repeated pulse of electric current is applied to the brain for the treatment of anxiety, insomnia, and a variety of other medical conditions with a psychological component.

shoddy Products made from reprocessed old wool. Strictly the term applies only to the loose fibre, but it is commonly used to describe the products made from shoddy.

shoebill A large, grey, stork-like bird with a large head (*Balaeniceps rex*); bill extremely wide and deep, shaped like a broad shoe; inhabits marshes in C Africa; nocturnal; also known as the **shoe-billed stork** or **whale-headed stork**. (Family: Balaenicipidae.)

Shoemaker, Willie, popular name of **William Lee Shoemaker**, nickname **the Shoe** (1931–2003) Jockey and trainer, born in Fabens, TX. He won more races than any other jockey – 8833 winners between 1949 and his retirement in 1989.

Shoemaker–Levy 9 [shoomaker-leevee] The name given to a comet (estimated to have been c.2 km/1·2 mi in diameter) which crashed into the planet Jupiter in 1994; jointly discovered by US astronomer Carolyn (Spellman) Shoemaker (1929–), her husband, astrogeologist Eugene (Merle) Shoemaker (1928–97), and amateur astronomer David Levy

(1948–). Over 20 fragments made spectacular impacts into the planet during the period 16–22 July, leaving dark markings observable by telescopes on Earth.

shogi [shohgee] A Japanese form of chess, believed to have originated in India. It is played on a squared board, each player having 20 pieces.

shogun [shohgn] A Japanese general, the head of a system of government which dates from 1192. Most important were the Tokugawa Shoguns (1603–1868), who ruled as military dictators, the emperor remaining a figurehead, without power. The system ended in 1868.

Sholem Aleichem [alaykhem], also spelled **Sholom** or **Shalom** (Hebrew, 'peace unto you'), pseudonym of **Solomon J Rabinowitz** (1859–1916) Writer, born in Pereyaslev, Ukraine. The pogroms of 1905 drove him to the USA, where he worked as a playwright for the Yiddish theatre. The musical *Fiddler on the Roof* is based on his stories.

Sholes, Christopher Latham [shohlz] (1819–90) Inventor, born in Mooresburg, PA. A printer in his early years, he went on to develop the typewriter (1868).

Sholokhov, Mikhail Alexandrovich [sholokhof] (1905–84) Novelist, born near Veshenskaya, Russia. Best known for his novel tetralogy *Tikhy Don* (1928–40, trans Quiet Flows the Don), he received the Nobel Prize for Literature in 1965.

Shona [shona] A cluster of Bantu-speaking agricultural peoples of E Zimbabwe who formed a powerful state during the 13th–15th-c. Their members dominate ZANU, the ruling party of Zimbabwe.

shooting The use of firearms for pleasure, hunting, sport, or in battle. The first reference to the gun was in 1326, and it soon became the chief weapon of war. It developed as a sport in the 15th-c, the first shooting club being formed at Lucerne, Switzerland, in 1466. In competitive shooting, the most popular weapons are the standard pistol, small bore rifle, full bore rifle, air rifle, and air pistol. Several tournaments are held, such as those organized by the National Rifle Association (founded, 1871) in the USA.

shooting star *meteor*

shop stewards Workers appointed by their fellows within a trade union to represent them on matters relevant to their pay and conditions. In some instances the post is a full-time job.

Short, Clare (1946–) British stateswoman, born in Birmingham, West Midlands. She became an MP in 1983, joined the shadow cabinet in 1995, and was spokesperson on transport (1995–6) and overseas development (1996–7). She served as secretary of state for international development in the Labour government (1997–2003). In 2006 she resigned from the Labour Party but decided to remain as an independent MP until the next general election.

Short, Nigel (1965–) Chess player, born in Atherton, Lancashire. He became the UK's youngest ever grandmaster in 1984, and in 1993 the first UK grandmaster to qualify for a World Championship match, but was defeated by Gary Kasparov. He resigned from FIDE (the international chess organization) in 1993 and with Kasparov formed the Professional Chess Association.

shorthand A method of writing at speed to take verbatim records of speech, also known as **stenography**. Shorthand systems variously use symbols which are abbreviations of words (as in *speedwriting*), representations of speech sounds, or arbitrary symbols which the user has to memorize. Much used in commerce and industry, and in courts of law, in recent years its popularity has lessened with the advent of dictating machines.

shorthorn A type of domestic cattle with short horns. In 18th-c England, Charles and Robert Colling improved the type, leading to such breeds as the **Durham** (the *shorthorn* of the American ranchers) and the **Teeswater**.

short-sightedness *eye*

short story A prose fiction of not more than some 10 000 words. Beyond this lie the similarly imprecise categories 'long short story', 'novella', and 'short novel'. There are many rudimentary forms of short story, including myths, fables, legends, and parables; but the modern short story began in the mid-19th-c with Edgar Allan Poe, and was confirmed as a major genre by Maupassant in France and Turgenev and Chekhov in Russia.

Short Take-Off and Landing *STOL*

Shoshoni [shohshohnee] North American Indians who once lived in California, Nevada, Utah, and Wyoming; semi-nomadic hunter-gatherers. They now live mainly on reservations.

Shostakovich, Dmitri Dmitriyevich [shostakohvich] (1906–75) Composer, born in St Petersburg, Russia. His music was at first highly successful, but his operas and ballets were later criticized by the government for some years for a failure to observe the principles of 'Soviet realism'. He wrote 15 symphonies; violin, piano, and cello concertos; chamber music; and choral works.

shotgun A smooth-bore weapon firing cartridges filled with small lead or steel pellets (*shot*), which spread in flight to broaden their destructive effects; widely used by farmers and sportsmen.

shot put An athletics field throwing event. The shot is a brass or iron sphere weighing 7·3 kg/16 lb for men and 3·6 kg/8 lb 13 oz for women. It is propelled, using only one hand, from a starting position under the chin. The thrower must not leave the 2·1 m/7 ft diameter throwing circle. The current world record for men is 23·12 m/75 ft 10 in, achieved by Randy Barnes (USA) in 1990 at Los Angeles, CA; for women it is 22·63 m/74 ft 3 in, achieved by Natalya Lisovskaya (Russia) in 1987 at Moscow.

shou *red deer*

shoulder Commonly used to refer to the rounded region at the top of the arm passing towards the neck and upper back; more specifically, in anatomy, the articulation between the humerus and the scapula. It is an extremely mobile joint, at the expense of some joint stability.

shove-halfpenny; shovelboard *shuffleboard*

shoveller / shoveler A dabbling duck, native to South America (1 species), S Africa (1 species), Australia and New Zealand (1 species), and the N hemisphere (1 species); nests in reed beds; also known as the **spoonbill**. (Genus: *Anas*, 4 species.)

Showa Tenno ('Emperor') **Hirohito** [shoha tenoh hirohheetoh] (1901–89) Emperor of Japan (1926–89), the 124th in direct lineage, born in Tokyo. His reign was marked by rapid militarization and the aggressive wars against China (1931–2, 1937–45) and Britain and the USA (1941–5).

showboat A paddle-wheel river steamer complete with theatre and its own repertory company. They were mainly used along the Mississippi in the 19th-c.

show jumping Horse jumping over a course containing a variety of strategically placed fences. Those who clear the fences and incur no penalty points are then involved in a 'jump-off' against the clock, where speed as well as accuracy is important. Points are incurred for knocking down a fence, or for refusing to jump a fence.

show trials Originally a series of trials held in Moscow in the late 1930s under Stalin. It refers to any political trial where the accused make a public confession of their 'crimes', although their guilt is often open to doubt.

Shrapnel, Henry (1761–1842) British artillery officer. In c.1793 he invented the **shrapnel shell**, an anti-personnel device which exploded while in flight, scattering lethal lead shot and other material.

shrew A widespread mammal of family Soricidae (246 species); an insectivore; mouse-like with a longer pointed snout and small eyes.

Shrewsbury [shrohzbree, shroozbree], Anglo-Saxon **Scrobesbyrig** 52°43N 2°45W, pop (2000e) 63 200. County town of Shropshire, England; on the R Severn; Roman city of Uriconium to the E; site of Battle of Shrewsbury (1403); railway; castle (11th-c; football league team, Shrewsbury Town (Shrews).

shrike A bird mainly of the Old World, especially Africa; strong bill with hooked tip; grasping, clawed feet. The **red-backed shrike** (*Lanius collurio*) is also called the **butcherbird**. (Family: Laniidae, c.72 species.)

shrimp An aquatic crustacean; females typically carry eggs on abdominal legs until ready to hatch into swimming larvae (*zoeae*); many species of economic importance as food. (Class: Malacostraca. Order: Decapoda.)

shrimp plant A bushy perennial (*Beloperone guttata*) growing to 1 m/3¾ ft, native to Mexico, named for the flower spikes which fancifully resemble crustacea; flowers hooded, white. (Family: Acanthaceae.)

Shropshire, sometimes abbreviated **Salop** pop (2001e) 283 200; area 3490 km²/1347 sq mi. County in England; county town, Shrewsbury; Wrekin a unitary authority from 1998; Ironbridge Gorge open-air museum.

Shroud of Turin *Holy Shroud*

Shrove Tuesday In the UK, the day before the beginning of Lent, so called because traditionally on that day Christians went to confession and were 'shriven' (absolved from their sins). Shrove Tuesday is often known as **Pancake Day** from the custom of making pancakes on that day.

shrub A woody perennial plant, usually differentiated from a **tree** by being smaller and having a trunk which produces branches at or near the base; but the distinction is far from clear-cut, and some large shrubs are essentially small trees.

shuffleboard A game in which discs are sent moving by hand or with an implement along a board or court, so that they come to a halt within a predetermined area. Today, a version of the game, also called **shovelboard**, is a popular deck sport aboard ship. Another version of the game, known as **shove-halfpenny**, is played on a small board in English pubs, where coins or small discs must be pushed so as to stop between narrowly ruled lines.

Shull, Clifford G(lenwood) (1915–2001) Physicist, born in Pittsburgh, PA. He shared the Nobel Prize for Physics in 1994 for his work in the field of neutron scattering.

Shultz, George P(ratt) (1920–) US secretary of state (1982–9), born in New York City. He was named secretary of labor by President Nixon (1969), and went on to hold a number of high governmental posts before returning to private life in 1974. In 1982 President Reagan made him secretary of state.

Shute, Nevil, pseudonym of **Nevil Shute Norway** (1899–1960) Writer, born in Ealing, Greater London. After World War 2, he emigrated to Australia, which became the setting for most of his later books, notably *A Town Like Alice* (1949), and *On the Beach* (1957).

shuttle 1 In spinning, a spindle-shaped device holding a bobbin, used to carry the crosswise threads (*weft*) through the lengthwise threads (*warp*) during weaving.

2 *space shuttle*.

Shwe Dagon Pagoda An important Buddhist pilgrimage site in Yangon (Rangoon), Myanmar. It consists of a magnificent goldplated shrine (*stupa*) 98 m/326 ft high.

Shwezigon Pagoda A pagoda erected in the 11th-c near Pagan, Myanmar, as a reliquary shrine for a tooth and a bone of the Buddha.

sial [siyal] The silica and alumina-rich upper part of the Earth's crust which makes up the bulk of the continents and overlies the sima.

Sialkot [syalkoht] 32°29N 74°35E, pop (2000e) 494 000. City in E Pakistan; railway; mausoleum of Sikh apostle Nanak.

Siam *Thailand*

siamang [siyamang] A gibbon (*Hylobates syndactylus*) native to Malaysia and Sumatra; the largest gibbon (armspan of 1·5 m/ 5 ft); throat with large red balloon-like vocal sac.

Siamese cat A domestic cat of the *foreign short-haired* variety; many breeds, some called **Siamese** in Britain, **short-hair** in the USA; lean, with a triangular face and blue eyes; coat pale with darker *points* (ie face, legs, and tail).

Siamese twins A fault in embryological development in which identical twins are born physically joined together. The deformity ranges from one in which the twins may merely share one umbilical cord to one in which heads or trunks are joined together. The latter presents a particular challenge in separation surgery because the twins may share organ systems. The name derives from the first twins in whom the condition was recognized in modern times, Chang and Eng (1811–74), born in Siam (modern Thailand). Only a few hundred pairs of conjoined twins are born each year worldwide.

Sian *Xian*

Sibelius, Jean (Julius Christian) [sibaylius] (1865–1957) Composer, born in Tavastehus, Finland. A passionate nationalist, he wrote a series of symphonic poems based on episodes in the Finnish epic *Kalevala*. His major works include seven symphonies (he destroyed his eighth), symphonic poems – notably *Finlandia* (1899) – and a violin concerto.

Siberia area c.7 511 000 km²/2 900 000 sq mi. Vast geographic region of Asiatic Russia, comprising the N third of Asia; **W Siberian Lowlands** stretch over 1500 km/1000 mi from the Ural Mts (W) to the R Yenisey (E); **C Siberian Plateau** lies between the R Yenisey (W) and the R Lena (E); **E Siberian Highlands**, including the Altay Mts, rise to 4506 m/14 783 ft at Gora Belukha; rivers include the Ob, Yenisey, Lena; extreme continental climate; average winter temperatures generally below −18°C; tundra extends c.320 km/200 mi inland along the Arctic coast; chief cities (Novosibirsk, Omsk, Krasnoyarsk, Irkutsk, Khabarovsk, Vladivostok) lie on the Trans-Siberian Railway; used as a penal colony and place of exile for political prisoners; dramatic economic development under the 5-year plans, relying heavily on forced labour and population resettlement to establish mining, industrial, and agricultural installations.

Sibyl or **Sibylla** In Roman legend, a prophetess who uttered mysterious wisdom. The **Sybilline Books** were nine books of prophecy offered by the Sybil to Tarquinus Priscus.

Sicilian Vespers The wholesale massacre of the French in Sicily which began the Sicilian revolt against Charles of Anjou. It was so called because the first killings occurred in a church outside Palermo at vespers (evensong) on Easter Monday, 1282.

Sicily, Ital **Sicilia** pop (2000e) 5 000 000; area 25 708 km²/ 9923 sq mi. Largest and most populous island in the Mediterranean, separated from the mainland of Italy by the narrow Strait of Messina; length 288 km/179 mi; width 192 km/119 mi; settled by the Greeks, 8th-c BC; province of Rome, 2nd-c BC; Norman conquest, 11th-c; conquest by Aragon, 1282; Kingdom of the Two Sicilies, 1815; conquest by Garibaldi, 1860, and unification with Italy; capital, Palermo; mountainous, average height 450 m/1450 ft; large earthquake zone on E coast, culminating in Mt Etna (3390 m/11 122 ft), highest point; an underdeveloped area, with considerable poverty; intensive vegetable growing, fruit, wine in fertile coastal areas; arable and pastoral farming in dry interior.

Sickert, Walter (Richard) (1860–1942) Artist, born in Munich, Germany. The Camden Town Group (later the London Group) was formed under his leadership c.1910, and he became a major influence on later English painters.

sickle cell disease An inherited chemical abnormality of haemoglobin (the oxygen-carrying pigment in red blood cells), affecting people from sub-Saharan Africa. It is caused by the inheritance of an abnormal gene. The red cells contain haemoglobin S instead of the normal haemoglobin A. As a result they become sickle-shaped in place of their normal bi-concave circular form, making them more fragile and less flexible; they do not survive long in circulation, leading to chronic anaemia. This is punctuated by a series of crises, often precipitated by infections, in which red cells block small blood vessels, preventing oxygen supply to the tissues.

Siddons, Sarah, *née* **Kemble** (1755–1831) Actress, born in Brecon, Powys, the eldest child of Roger Kemble. A member of her father's theatre company from childhood, she became the unquestioned queen of tragedy, renowned for her beauty, dignity, and rich, resonant voice.

side drum A shallow drum with a skin at each end, the upper one struck with a pair of wooden sticks, the lower fitted with *snares* (strings of metal or gut) which, when engaged, give the tone a rasping edge. It is worn slightly to one side when marching (hence the name).

sidereal time Time measured by considering the rotation of the Earth relative to the distant stars (rather than to the Sun, which is the basis of civil time).

sidewinder A snake which moves by pushing its head forward onto the ground, then winding the body forwards and sideways until it lies stretched out to one side; meanwhile the head is moved forward again. Repeating this behaviour allows the snake to move rapidly over soft sand. *Crotalus cerastes* (the North American horned rattlesnake) usually uses sidewinding, and is commonly called the **sidewinder**.

Sidi bel Abbès [sidee bel abes] 35°15N 0°39W, pop (2000e) 250 800. Town in N Algeria; headquarters of the French Foreign Legion until 1962; railway.

Sidmouth (of Sidmouth), Henry Addington, 1st Viscount [sidmuhth] (1757–1844) British Tory statesman and prime minister (1801–4), born in London. His administration negotiated the Peace of Amiens (1802). He later became home secretary under Liverpool (1812–21).

Sidney, Algernon (1622–83) English Whig politician, born in Penshurst, Kent. An extreme Republican, he fought in the Civil War, and after the Restoration lived on the Continent for some years. In 1683, he was implicated in the Rye House Plot, and beheaded.

Sidney, Sir Philip (1554–86) Poet, born in Penshurst, Kent. His literary work, written 1578–82, was not published until after his death. It includes the unfinished pastoral romance *Arcadia*, the *Defence of Poesie*, and a sonnet cycle, *Astrophel and Stella*.

Sidon [siydon] 33°32N 35°22E, pop (2000e) 31 000. Seaport in W Lebanon; founded in the third millennium BC; once noted for its glass and purple dyes; railway; Crusader castle.

Siegfried Line [zeegfreed] Name given by the Allies in World War 2 to a 600 km/373 mi line of defensive fortifications constructed in 1936–40 along the W frontier of Germany. It provided respite to retreating German forces in 1944, but was breached by the Allies in 1945, and largely dismantled after the war. All remains were demolished during 2003 to mark the 40th anniversary of the Franco-German friendship treaty (1963).

Siemens, (Ernst) Werner von [zeemens] (1816–92) Engineer, born in Lenthe, Germany. He developed the telegraphic system in Prussia, devised several forms of galvanometer, and determined the electrical resistance of different substances. His brother **(Karl) Wilhelm Siemens** (1823–83, known as **(Charles) William**, upon moving to England in 1844), invented a new steel-making technique in 1861.

siemens [seemnz] SI unit of electrical conductance; symbol S; defined as 1 divided by resistance as measured in ohms.

Siena [syayna], ancient **Suene Julia** 43°19N 11°19E, pop (2000e) 64 500. City in Tuscany, Italy; founded by the Etruscans; centre of the Ghibelline faction and a rival of Florence, 12th-c; influ-

ential centre of mediaeval art; archbishopric; university (1240); major tourist city; cathedral (12th–14th-c); town hall (13th-c) with tower, Torre del Mangia (14th-c).

Sienese School A school of art which flourished in Siena in the 14th-c and early 15th-c. It has deep roots in the Gothic and Byzantine traditions.

Sierra Club A US private, non-profit conservation organization. It was founded by the US naturalist and writer, John Muir (1838–1914) in 1892.

Sierra Leone *p.852*

Sierra Nevada (Spain) [syera nayvahtha] Mountain range in Andalusia, S Spain, rising to 3478 m/11 411 ft at Mulhacén, the highest peak in continental Spain.

Sierra Nevada (USA) [syera nevahda] Mountain range in W USA, mainly in E California; extends 725 km/450 mi between the Cascade and Coastal Ranges; highest point in the USA outside Alaska, Mt Whitney (4418 m/14 495 ft).

Sierra Nevada de Mérida [syeruh nayvahthuh thay mayreethuh] Mountain range in W Venezuela; length, 500 km/300 mi; rises to 5007 m/16 427 ft at Pico Bolívar, highest peak in Venezuela.

sievert [seevert] In radioactivity, the SI unit of dose equivalent, equal to absorbed dose multiplied by the relative biological effectiveness; symbol Sv; it is used in radiation safety measurements.

Sieyès, Emmanuel Joseph, comte de (Count of) [syayes], also known as **Abbé Sieyès** (1748–1836) French political theorist and clergyman, born in Fréjus, France. He became a member of the National Convention, the Committee of Public Safety (1795) and the Directory. In 1799, he helped to organize the revolution of 18th Brumaire, becoming a member of the Consulate. He was exiled at the Restoration (1815), returning to Paris after the July Revolution.

sifaka [sifaka] A leaping lemur; long silky hair and long tail; small gliding membranes from arms to sides of body; can leap 10 m/33 ft between trees. (Genus: *Propithecus*, 2 species.)

sigillography *seal* (communications)

Signac, Paul [seenyak] (1863–1935) Artist, born in Paris. With Seurat he developed Divisionism (but using mosaic-like patches of pure colour rather than Seurat's pointillist dots), mainly in seascapes.

sign language A communication system in which manual signs are used to express a corresponding range of meanings to those conveyed by spoken or written language. The most widely used are those which have developed naturally in a deaf community, such as the American, British, French, and Swedish Sign Languages. Contrary to popular belief, such languages are not mutually intelligible, as they use different signs and rules of sentence structure.

Signorelli, Luca [seenyawrelee], also known as **Luca da Cortona** (c.1441–1523) Painter, born in Cortona, Italy. The cathedral at Orvieto contains his greatest work, the frescoes of 'The Preaching of Anti-Christ' and 'The Last Judgment' (1500–4).

Sigurd [seegoord] In Norse mythology, the son of Sigmund the Volsung, who kills Fafnir the dragon and wins Brunhild. Virtually the same story is told of **Siegfried** [zeegfreed] in German legends.

Sihanouk, Prince Norodom [seeanook] (1922–) Cambodian leader, born in Phnom Penh. He was King of Cambodia (1941–55), chief of state (1960–70, and of the Khmer Republic 1975–6), prime minister on several occasions between 1952 and 1968, president of the government in exile (1970–5, 1982–91), president (1991–3), and once again king (1993–2004). His return to Cambodia in 1991 followed the signing of the peace treaty ending 13 years of civil war, and he was crowned king under the new constitution in 1993. He abdicated in 2004 and was succeeded by his son, Norodom Sihamoni (1953–).

sika [seeka] A true deer (*Cervus nippon*) native to E Asia; brown

Sierra Leone

□ International Airport

[syera leeohn], official name **Republic of Sierra Leone**
Local name Sierra Leone
Timezone GMT
Area 71 740 km²/27 692 sq mi
Population total (2002e) 4 823 000
Status Republic
Date of independence 1961
Capital Freetown
Languages English (official), with Krio widely spoken
Ethnic groups African origin (99%) (including Mendes, Temnes, Limbas, Korankos, and Lokos)

Religions Local beliefs (30%), Sunni Muslim (60%), Christian (Protestant 6%, Roman Catholic 2%)

Physical features Low narrow coastal plain in W Africa; rises to an average height of 500 m/1600 ft in the Loma Mts (E), highest point, Loma Mansa, 1948 m/6391 ft; Tingi Mts rise to 1853 m/6079 ft (SE); principal rivers include the Great Scarcies, Rokel, Gbangbaia, Jong, and Sewa.

Climate Equatorial climate; temperatures uniformly high throughout the year; average annual temperature 27°C; rainy season (May–Oct); highest rainfall on coast; average rainfall 3436 mm/135 in at Freetown.

Currency 1 Leone (SLL) = 100 cents

Economy Mining (most important sector of the economy); diamonds (represent c.60% of exports); bauxite, gold, titanium, iron ore, and other mineral and metal ores; subsistence agriculture (employs over 70% of population); rice, coffee, cocoa, citrus fruits; timber; food processing.

GDP (2002e) $2·826 bn, per capita $500

Human Development Index (2002) 0·275

History First visited by Portuguese navigators and British slave traders; land bought from local chiefs by English philanthropists who established settlements for freed slaves, 1780s; British Crown Colony, 1808; hinterland declared a British protectorate, 1896; independence declared within the Commonwealth as a constitutional monarchy, 1961; period of military rule, 1967–8; became a republic, 1971; established as a one-party state, 1978; new constitution, 1991, allowing for multi-party politics, and interim government formed until general elections; interrupted by military coup in 1992, House of Representatives dissolved, and Supreme Council of State (SCS) and Civilian Council of State Secretaries (Cabinet) established; further military coup, 1997, overturned 1998; renewed fighting in early 1999, followed by Lomé (Togo) peace agreement (Jul) and establishment of UN peacekeeping force; UN troops attacked and abducted by rebels (Apr 2000), leading to UK-sponsored military assistance plan within the country, and arrival of UN reinforcements; peace declared, 2002.

Head of State/Government
1971 Christopher Okero Cole
1971–85 Siaka Probin Stevens
1985–92 Joseph Saidu Momoh
1992–6 Valentine Strasser
1996 *Military rule*
1996–7 Ahmad Tejan Kabbah
1997–8 Johnny Paul Koroma
1998– Ahmad Tejan Kabbah

(with pale spots in summer) with white rump; white spot halfway down rear leg; long antlers; also known as **Japanese deer**.

Sikhism [seekizm] A religion founded by the Guru Nanak (1469–1539) in the Punjab area of N India. It is called a religion of the gurus, and seeks union with God through worship and service. God is the true Guru, and his divine word has come to humanity through the 10 historical gurus. The line ended in 1708, since when the Sikh community is called guru. The Adi Granth, their sacred scripture, is also called a guru. There were some 24 million Sikhs in 2007.

Sikh Wars [seek] Two campaigns (1845–6, 1848–9) between the British and the Sikhs which led to the British conquest and annexation of the Punjab, NW India (Mar 1849).

Sikkim [sikim] pop (2001e) 540 500; area 7300 km²/2817 sq mi. State in NE India, in the E Himalayas; part of British Empire, 1866–1947; protectorate of India, 1950; voted to become a state, 1975; capital, Gangtok; governed by an Assembly; inhabited mostly by Lepchas, Bhutias, and Nepalis; state religion, Mahayana Buddhism, but many of the population are Hindu.

Sikorski, Władysław (Eugeniusz) [sikaw(r)skee] (1881–1943) Polish general, statesman, and prime minister (1922–3), born in Galicia. In World War 2, he became commander of the Free Polish forces and from 1940 premier of the Polish government in exile in London. A national hero, his body was returned to Poland in 1993, and given a state funeral.

Sikorsky, Igor (Ivan) [sikaw(r)skee] (1889–1972) Aeronautical engineer, born in Kiev. He built and flew the first four-engined aeroplane (1913), and in 1939 produced the first successful helicopter.

silage A fodder made from grass, maize, or other leafy material, and preserved in an airtight tower-silo or silage pit. Initial fermentation creates organic and amino acids, which act as preservatives.

Silbury Hill An artificial chalk mound, 40 m/130 ft high, erected c.2700 BC near Avebury, Wiltshire, in S England. Probably pre-historic Europe's largest barrow, it was an estimated 18 million man-hours in construction.

Silchester One of the three main Belgic towns of pre-Roman Britain, situated SW of Reading, S England. It was a prosperous place in Roman times until its mysterious abandonment at an unknown date.

Silenus [siyleenuhs] In Greek mythology, a demi-god, who fostered and educated Dionysus. He is represented as a festive old man, usually quite drunk.

Silesia [sileezha], Czech **Slezsko**, Polish **Ślusk**, Ger **Schlesien** Region of EC Europe on both banks of the R Oder in SW Poland, N Czech Republic, and SE Germany; disputed area between Austria and Prussia, 17th–18th-c; divided into Upper and Lower Silesia, 1919; greater part granted to Poland, 1945; a largely industrial region.

silhouette A technique of paper cut-out picture popularized by French finance minister Etienne de Silhouette (1709–67) and used for cheap miniature portraits until the rise of photography in the mid-19th-c. The term is often extended to cover any type of dark image against a light background, or light on dark, as in Greek vase-painting.

silica Silicon dioxide (SiO_2), the main constituent of the Earth's crust, occurring in nature as pure minerals or combined with other elements in silicate minerals.

silicate minerals A group of minerals constituting about 95% of the Earth's crust, and containing silicon and oxygen combined with one or more other elements. They are classified according to the degree of polymerization, from silicates containing isolated SiO_4 groups (eg olivines, garnets) to rings (eg beryl) to chain silicates (eg pyroxenes), sheets (eg micas, clays), and three-dimensional frameworks (eg quartz, feldspars).

silicon Si, element 14, melting point 1410°C. A grey solid non-metal, the second most common element, 26% by weight, it is the second element in the carbon group, and like carbon it forms mainly covalent compounds, with a valence of 4. It does not occur uncombined in nature. Very pure silicon is widely used in electronic devices. It is also doped with controlled amounts of aluminium, phosphorus, and other elements to alter its conductivity. Silicates are the main constituents of brick, stone, cement, and glass.

silicon carbide SiC. A compound produced by fusing a mixture of carbon and silica; also known as **carborundum**. It is high-melting and hard, and is used mainly as an abrasive.

silicon chip A very small slice of silicon, a few millimetres square, on which many electronic circuits containing many components are built; also called an **integrated circuit**. Silicon chips are reliable and cheap to produce in large numbers, and they are now used in computers, calculators, many modern programmed household appliances, and in most electronic applications.

silicone An open-chain or cyclic polymer containing the repeating unit $-SiR_2-O-$. Odourless, colourless, insoluble in and unreactive with water, and having high flashpoints, silicones are used in high-temperature lubricants, hydraulic fluids, and varnishes.

Silicon Valley Santa Clara County, W California, USA, between Palo Alto and San José; a world centre since the 1970s for electronics, computing, and database systems.

silicosis [silikohsis] An industrial disease of occupations such as coal mining, stone dressing, and sand blasting, and of the ceramics industry. It is caused by inhalation of fine particles of silica which induce scarring of the lungs.

silk A very fine fibre obtained from the cocoons of silkworms. The rearing of silkworms (**sericulture**) originated in China before 1100 BC; and Japan and China now provide most of the high-quality cultivated silk. The fabrics are renowned for their lustre, drape, and handle.

Silk Road *p.854*

silk-screen *screen-process printing*

silkworm The larva of the common silk moth, *Bombyx mori*, which spins the silk cocoon from which commercial silk is derived. The cocoon is unwound mechanically, after softening, and each may contain up to 3 km/2 mi of silk. (Order: Lepidoptera. Family: Bombycidae.)

sill A sheet-like body of igneous rock that has been intruded between layers of sedimentary rock. It is usually composed of medium-grained rock, typically dolerite. Examples include the Whin Sill in N England.

Sillitoe, Alan [silitoh] (1928–) Novelist, born in Nottingham, Nottinghamshire. His first and most popular novel was *Saturday Night and Sunday Morning* (1958), followed by *The Loneliness of the Long Distance Runner* (1959, filmed 1962). Later novels include *Leonard's War* (1991), *The German Numbers Woman* (1999), and *A Man of His Time* (2004). An autobiography, *Life Without Armour*, appeared in 1995.

Silone, Ignazio [silohnay], pseudonym of **Secondo Tranquilli** (1900–78) Novelist and journalist, born in Aquilo, Italy. His books include *Fontamara* (1933), *Pane e vino* (1937, Bread and Wine), and *Il seme sotto la neve* (1941, The Seed Beneath the Snow).

silt The aggregate of fine mineral particles produced by the erosion and weathering of rock, in size intermediate between clay and sand. Silt deposits are laid down by water, and may consolidate to form the sedimentary rock **siltstone**.

Silurian period [siyloorian] The third of the geological periods of the Palaeozoic era, extending from c.435 to 408 million years ago. The earliest land plants appeared.

Silvanus or **Sylvanus** [silvaynus, silvahnus] In Roman religion, the god of uncultivated land, especially woodland. He was therefore strange, and dangerous, like Pan.

silver Ag (Lat *argentum*), element 47, melting point 961°C. A lustrous transition metal, relatively rare, but occurring uncombined in nature. Of all elements, it is the best conductor of electricity. Long used extensively in coinage, it has now become too expensive for that purpose. Much used in jewellery and medals, its compounds are also used in photography.

silver birch A slender, elegant, short-lived species of birch (*Betula pendula*) reaching 15–18 m/50–60 ft, with distinctive silvery-white bark. Native to Europe, it is often planted for ornament. (Family: Betulaceae.)

silver fir An evergreen conifer native to the temperate N hemisphere; foliage often silvery or bluish; needles leathery; widely grown for timber and as ornamentals; its resin yields *Canada balsam*. (Genus: *Abies*, 50 species. Family: Pinaceae.)

silverfish A tapering, primitively wingless insect covered with silvery white scales; tail 3-pronged; commonly found in houses; active at night, moves swiftly. (Order: Thysanura. Family: Lepismatidae.)

silver fox *red fox*

silver Persian *chinchilla cat*

silver plate A term applied to goods made of silver of sterling standard, established by law in England in the 13th-c. Hallmarking was introduced from 1300. It should not be confused with the various 19th-c techniques of **silver plating**, which involved a thin skin of sterling silver applied to base metal.

silverpoint A technique used by artists for drawing on paper, popular in the Renaissance, but afterwards superseded by the invention of the graphite pencil. The paper is coated with Chinese white paint and the drawing made with a slim metal point (silver, gold, copper, or lead).

Silves [seelvish] 37°11N 8°26W, pop (2000e) 10 500. Town in the

Silk Road

Ancient trade route from E China to C Asia and Europe. From the 2nd-c AD, the best-known route ran from Xian through the Hexi Corridor to the E Mediterranean coast. During the Sui dynasty (581–618), a route further N ended at Istanbul. In exchange for silk, China received grapes, cotton, chestnuts, lucerne, and pomegranates; Chinese techniques for silkworm breeding, iron-smelting, paper-making, and irrigation spread W. The route also brought Buddhism to China. The silk trade had a serious economic impact on the Roman Empire. Payment was in precious metals, and by AD 10 China's gold reserves exceeded those of much later mediaeval Europe. The situation possibly contributed to the fall of Rome.

Algarve, S Portugal; on R Arade; former Moorish capital; Moorish castle, cathedral (12th–13th-c).

sima [siyma] The silica and magnesia-rich lower part of the crust which underlies the sial of the continents and forms the bulk of the oceanic crust.

Simbirsk [simbirsk], formerly **Ulyanovsk** (1924–91) 54°19N 48°22E, pop (2000e) 665 000. River port in WC European Russia; founded as a fortress, 1648; airfield; railway; birthplace of Lenin; renamed after his family name, Ulyanov.

Simenon, Georges (Joseph Christian) [seemenō] (1903–89) Crime novelist, born in Liège, Belgium. He revolutionized detective fiction with his tough, morbidly psychological Inspector Maigret series, beginning in 1933.

Simeon Stylites, St [stiyliyteez] (387–459) The earliest of the Christian ascetic 'pillar' saints. Revered as a miracle-worker, he separated himself from the people c.420 by establishing himself on top of a pillar c.20 m/70 ft high at Telanessa, near Antioch, where he spent the rest of his life preaching to crowds. He had many imitators, known as *stylites*. Feast day 5 January (W), 1 September (E).

simile *metaphor*

Simla [simla] 31°07N 77°09E. Hill station in N India; altitude c.2200 m/7100 ft; established in 1819 as former summer capital of British India.

Simmons, Jean (1929–) Film actress, born in London. She made her film debut in 1942, and moved to Hollywood in 1950. Her films include *The Robe* (1953), *Guys and Dolls* (1955), *Spartacus* (1960), and *How to Make an American Quilt* (1995). During the 1980s she appeared in several television productions, including *The Thorn Birds* (1983).

Simnel, Lambert (c.1475–c.1535) English imposter, a joiner's son, who in 1487 was set up in Ireland, first as a son of Edward IV, and then as the Duke of Clarence's son, Edward, Earl of Warwick (1475–99), who was imprisoned in the Tower. Crowned at Dublin as 'Edward VI' (1487), he landed in Lancashire with 2000 German mercenaries, and was defeated at Stoke, Nottinghamshire.

Simon, Claude (Eugène Henri) [seemō] (1913–2005) Novelist, born in Tananarive, Madagascar. His novels include *Le Vent* (1957, The Wind), *L'herbe* (1958, The Grass), *Le Palace* (1962, The Palace), and *Le tramway* (2001, The Trolley). He received the Nobel Prize for Literature in 1985.

Simon (of Stackpole Elidor), John (Allsebrook) Simon, 1st Viscount (1873–1954) British Liberal statesman and lawyer, born in Manchester, Greater Manchester. He was home secretary (1915–16), before resigning in opposition to conscription. He formed the Liberal National Party, supporting MacDonald's coalition governments, and became foreign secretary (1931–5), home secretary (1935–7), Chancellor of the Exchequer (1937–40), and Lord Chancellor (1940–5).

Simon, (Marvin) Neil (1927–) Playwright, born in New York City. His first Broadway Show, *Catch a Star!*, opened in 1955, and a series of long-running successes followed in the 1960s, including *The Odd Couple* (1965). His later work includes *Biloxi Blues* (1985, Tony), *Lost in Yonkers* (1991, Pulitzer, Tony), *London Suite* (1995), and *Laughter on the 23rd Floor* (1996).

Simon, Paul (1941–) Singer, songwriter, and guitarist, born in

Forest Hills, NY. He teamed up with Art Garfunkel at the age of 15. Their first big hit, 'The Sound Of Silence' (1964), was followed in 1968 by the film *The Graduate*, with songs written by Simon, and they had a major success with the album *Bridge Over Troubled Water* (1970). His solo career, using Third-World choirs and percussionists, led to one of the most successful albums of the 1980s, *Graceland* (1986). *You're the One*, appeared in 2000, and he was inducted into the Rock and Roll Hall of Fame in 2001. In 2004 he reunited with Garfunkel for their successful Old Friends tour, performing across America and Europe.

Simond, Paul Louis [seemō] (1858–1947) Bacteriologist, born in Beaufort-sur-Gervanne, Drôme, France. He joined the Pasteur Institute in Paris (1895–7) where he showed that plague is primarily a disease of rats spread by rat fleas which transmit the disease to humans.

Simon Magus [maygus], Eng **Simon the Magician** (1st-c) Practitioner of magic arts, who appears in Samaria c.37 well known for his sorceries. His offer to buy the gift of the Holy Ghost was condemned by Peter. The term *simony* derives from his name.

Simon Peter *Peter, St*

simony [simonee] The practice of giving or acquiring some sacred object, spiritual gift, or religious office for money, or carrying on a trade in such matters. The practice was most notorious in the mediaeval practice of trading in indulgences.

Simplon Pass, Ital **Passa del Sempione** Mountain pass between Brig, Switzerland and Domodossola, Italy, over the S Bernese Alps; height, 2006 m/6581 ft; built on the orders of Napoleon, 1801–5; rail tunnel (20 km/12 mi) opened in 1906.

Simpson, N(orman) F(rederick) (1919–) Playwright, born in London. The success of *A Resounding Tinkle*, a zany disruption of middle-class normality, brought him to prominence. His absurdist approach is also seen in *One-Way Pendulum* (1959).

Simpson Desert Desert in SE Northern Territory and SW Queensland, C Australia; area c.77 000 km²/30 000 sq mi; first crossed in 1939 by Cecil Madigan.

simulator A mechanical, electromechanical, or computer device for producing a realistic representation of an event or system. It is used where the real thing is very expensive and inaccessible, and to train operators (eg aircraft pilots) in safety. Computers are also used to simulate complex phenomena where there are many variables, such as in atmospheric circulation studies.

simultaneity *special relativity*

sin A religious term signifying purposeful disobedience to the known will of God or an action offensive to God. The Hebrew Bible represents sin as a constant element in the experience of Israel. There is an emphasis upon human responsibility, and this is carried over into Christian doctrine, where it is joined with the idea of the inevitability of sin in the concept of **original sin**. Islam identifies two types of sin: inadvertent or accidental sins and wilful transgressions. Unlike Christianity, Islam does not have a concept of original sin.

Sinai [siyniy] pop (2000e) 246 300; area 60 174 km²/23 227 sq mi. Desert peninsula in NE Egypt; bounded by Israel and Gulf of Aqaba (E) and Egypt and Gulf of Suez (W); N coastal plain rises S to mountains reaching 2637 m/8651 ft at Mt Catherine, Egypt's highest point, and Mt Sinai, 2286 m/7500 ft; capital, al-Arish; taken by Israel, 1967; returned to Egypt following the peace agreement, 1984.

Sinai, Mount [siyniy] Mountain of uncertain location, traditionally placed in the S Sinai peninsula, but sometimes located in Arabia E of the Gulf of Aqaba; also called **Horeb** in the Hebrew Bible. According to the Book of Exodus, this is where God revealed himself to Moses, and made a covenant with Israel by giving him the Ten Commandments on tablets of stone.

Sinanthropus [sinanthropus] *Zhoukoudian*

Sinatra, Frank, popular name of **Francis Albert Sinatra** (1915–98) Singer and actor, born in Hoboken, NJ. One of the greatest singers of popular songs, he began in the 1940s, made several hit records, and starred on radio and in movies. His appeal disappeared for some years, then was revived by his appearance *From Here to Eternity* (1953, Oscar); later films include *High Society* (1956), and *The Manchurian Candidate* (1962). He produced his masterworks in a series of recordings (1956–65), notably the albums *Songs for Swinging Lovers* (1956) and *Come Fly With Me* (1959), and the songs 'That's Life' (1966) and 'My Way' (1969). His personal life always proved noteworthy, with turbulent marriages to Ava Gardner and Mia Farrow, among others, and alleged Mafia connections.

Sinclair, Upton (Beall) (1878–1968) Novelist and social reformer, born in Baltimore, MD. He found success with his novel exposing meat-packing conditions in Chicago, *The Jungle* (1906). Later novels, such as *King Coal* (1917), became increasingly moulded by his socialist beliefs. His 11-volume series about 'Lanny Budd' included *Dragon's Teeth* (1942, Pulitzer).

Sind pop (2000e) 31 112 000; area 140 914 km²/54 393 sq mi. Province in SE Pakistan; capital, Karachi; fertile land dissected by the R Indus; arrival of Islam, 8th-c; part of the Chandragupta Ganges Empire and the Delhi Empire; under British rule, 1843; autonomous province, 1937; province of Pakistan, 1947; agricultural economy.

sinfonietta An orchestral piece, usually in several movements but on a smaller scale than a symphony. The term is also used for a chamber orchestra, such as the London Sinfonietta (founded 1968).

Singapore *p.856*

Singapore City 1°20N 103°50E. Seaport capital of Singapore; one of the world's busiest ports; third largest oil refining centre; distribution base for many international companies; first container port in SE Asia, 1972; airport; railway; two universities (1953, 1964).

Singer, Isaac Bashevis (1904–91) Yiddish writer, born in Radzymin, Poland. He sets his books among the Jews of Poland, Germany, and America, such as *The Family Moskat* (1950) and *The Magician of Lublin* (1960). He was awarded the Nobel Prize for Literature in 1978.

Singer, Isaac M(erritt) (1811–75) Inventor and manufacturer of sewing machines, born in Pittstown, NY. At Boston in 1852 he devised an improved single-thread, chain-stitch sewing machine. His company became the largest producer of sewing machines in the world.

Singer, Peter (Albert David) (1946–) Philosopher, born in Melbourne, Victoria, Australia. His writing focuses on ethics, particularly in relation to animals and the environment. Also known as a political activist, his best known works, *Animal Liberation* (1977) and *Practical Ethics* (1979), were still exercising influence in the 1990s.

Single European Market A market created by the removal of internal trade barriers within the European Community during the 1980s. The Single European Act was introduced in 1985 to help speed up the process of implementing a single European market. The European Parliament was given greater voice and influence, and member states agreed to adopt common policies and standards on matters ranging from taxation and employment to health and the environment.

single lens reflex (SLR) A popular and versatile design of camera, with a surface-silvered mirror behind the lens angled at 45° to reflect the image onto a focusing screen. The camera lens is used both for the viewfinder system and for taking the photograph. Focusing is precise, and framing is free from parallax, so that 'what you see is what you get' in the picture.

Singspiel [zingshpeel] A German opera with spoken dialogue. Mozart's *Die Zauberflöte* (The Magic Flute) is a famous example.

Sinhalese [singgaleez] The dominant ethnic group (74%) of Sri

Singapore

Johor
Baharu
MALAYSIA
MALAYSIA
Woodlands
Kranji
Seletar
S I N G A P O R E
Changi □
Airport
Bukit Panjang● Serangoon●
△ *Bukit Timah*
177m
Katong
●Tuas Jurong
Singapore
City
Sentosa
CHINA
Straits of Singapore
20 km
10 mi
AUSTRALIA

official name **Republic of Singapore**
Local name Singapore
Timezone GMT +8
Area 618 km²/238 sq mi
Population total (2002e) 4 000 000
Status Republic
Date of independence 1965
Capital Singapore City
Languages English, Malay, Chinese, and Tamil (official)
Ethnic groups Chinese (77%), Malay (15%), Indian (6%)

Religions Chinese population mainly Buddhists, Malay mainly Muslim, also Taoist, Christian, and Hindu minorities
Physical features Located at the S tip of the Malay Peninsula, SE Asia; consists of the island of Singapore and c.50 adjacent islets; linked to Malaysia by a causeway across the Johor Strait; Singapore Island is low-lying, rising to 177 m/581 ft at Bukit Timah; Selatar River drains N-E; deep-water harbour (SE).
Climate Equatorial climate; high humidity; no clearly defined seasons; average annual temperature range, 21–34°C; average annual rainfall, 2438 mm/96 in.
Currency 1 Singapore Dollar/Ringgit (SGD) = 100 cents
Economy Major transshipment centre (one of world's largest ports); oil refining; rubber, food processing, chemicals, electronics; ship repair; financial services; fishing; tourism (affected by the SARS outbreak, 2003).
GDP (2002e) $112·4 bn, per capita $25 200
Human Development Index (2002) 0·885
History Originally part of the Sumatran Srivijaya kingdom; leased by the British East India Company, on the advice of Sir Stamford Raffles, from the Sultan of Johore, 1819; Singapore, Malacca, and Penang incorporated as the Straits Settlements, 1826; British Crown Colony, 1867; occupied by the Japanese, 1942–5; self-government, 1959; part of the Federation of Malaya from 1963 until its establishment as an independent state in 1965; governed by a President, a Prime Minister, and a unicameral Parliament.
Head of State
1959–70 Yusof bin Ishak
1970–81 Benjamin Henry Sheares
1981–5 Chengara Veetil Devan Nair
1985–93 Wee Kim Wee
1993–9 Ong Teng Cheong
1999– Sellapan Ramanathan Nathan
Head of Government
1959–90 Lee Kuan Yew
1990–2004 Goh Chok Tong
2004– Lee Hsien Loong

Lanka; descended from N Indians who came to the area in the 5th-c BC. They are predominantly Buddhist.

Sining *Xining*

Sinitic languages *Chinese*

Sinn Féin [shin fayn] (Gaelic 'Ourselves Alone') An Irish political party founded in 1900 by Arthur Griffith in support of Irish independence from Britain. It formed a separate assembly from the UK parliament, and succeeded in creating the Irish Free State (1922). It split to form the two main Irish parties, and in 1970 it split again into official and provisional wings. It remained active in Northern Ireland, and had close contacts with the Irish Republican Army. Sinn Féin obtained a high profile for its role in relation to the IRA ceasefire (1994), but conflict with the UK government over its attitude to the resumption of the IRA campaign (1996) led to its being excluded from all-party talks later that year. The party was eventually invited to join the talks following the resumption of the IRA ceasefire (1997), and in 1999 took its place in the Northern Ireland Assembly. In 2005 the IRA announced its intention to end its armed campaign. In January 2007 Sinn Féin members voted to support policing and criminal justice policies in Northern Ireland, and in March joined a power-sharing executive in the restored Assembly.

Sino–Japanese War 1 (1894–5) A longstanding conflict between Chinese and Japanese interests in Korea. China suffered a humiliating defeat.

2 (1937–45) A war which broke out in 1937 with the Japanese invasion of Tianjin and Beijing, but this was only the ultimate phase of Japan's territorial designs on China, following the occupation of Manchuria in 1932. Most of N China came under Japanese control. The war ended with Japan's surrender in 1945.

Sinope [siynohpee] The outermost natural satellite of Jupiter, discovered in 1914; distance from the planet 23 700 000 km/ 14 727 000 mi; diameter 36 km/22 mi.

Sino–Tibetan languages A family of languages spoken in China, Tibet, and Myanmar (Burma). There are some 300 languages in the family.

sintering One of the techniques of powder metallurgy. Metal parts are made by forming a shape in metal powder and then holding it for several hours just below the melting point of the metal. It is an economical process for making small parts, and is necessary for metal which has so high a melting point that it cannot easily be cast.

Sintra [seentra], formerly **Cintra** 38°47N 9°25W, pop (2000e) 20 600. Small resort town in C Portugal; former summer residence of the Portuguese royal family; railway; National Palace (14th–15th-c), Moorish castle.

sinus [siynuhs] In anatomy, a space within the head or elsewhere in the body. The air-filled **paranasal sinuses** all communicate with the nasal cavity, at the front of the face. The blood-filled **intracranial sinuses** are generally found between the layers of the outer membrane which surrounds the brain (the *dura mater*).

sinusitis [siynyusiytis] Infection of the lining of one or more sinuses around the nose and in the bones of the face. It sometimes arises from infection of the upper respiratory passages, and results in severe pain over the sinus, headache, and fever.

Sion (Jerusalem) [ziyon] *Zion*

Sion (Switzerland) [syŏ], Ger **Sitten** 46°14N 7°22E, pop (2000e) 26 500. Town in SW Switzerland; bishopric since the 6th-c; market town for the Rhône valley; brewing; railway; former cathedral (10th–13th-c), bishop's fortress (1294).

Sioux [soo] or **Dakota** A cluster of Siouan-speaking North American Indian groups belonging to the Plains Indian culture. They were involved in clashes with advancing White settlers, and were finally defeated at Wounded Knee (1890). They now number c.108 000 (2000 census), living mostly on reservations.

Sioux Falls [soo] 43°33N 96°44W, pop (2000e) 154 000. City in SE South Dakota, USA, on Big Sioux R; largest city in the state; established, 1857; city status, 1883; airfield; railway; commercial centre in a livestock farming region.

siphon / syphon A means of transferring liquid from one level to a lower level, relying on a liquid-filled tube, the siphon. Liquid moves through the pipe under the influence of gravity at a rate proportional to the difference in levels.

Siphonaptera [siyfonaptera] *flea*

Siraj-ud-Daula [siraj ud dowla], originally **Mirza Muhammad** (c.1732–57) Ruler of Bengal under the nominal suzerainty of the Mughal Empire. He forced the British to surrender at Calcutta, which led to the infamous Black Hole, for which he was held responsible. Defeated at Plassey in 1757, he was captured and executed.

siren A salamander native to SE North America; dark, eel-like body; length, up to 90 cm/36 in; no hind legs; tiny front legs; feathery gills. (Family: Sirenidae, 3 species.)

Sirens In Greek mythology, deceitful creatures, half-woman and half-bird, who lured sailors to death by their singing. Odysseus was able to sail past their island by stopping the ears of his crew with wax; and by having himself bound to the mast, was restrained when he heard their song.

si-rex [siyreks] *rex*

Sirius [sirius] The brightest star in our sky, and ninth nearest; also known as the **dog star**. It has a faint companion star, which was the first white dwarf star to be recognized as such.

Sirocco / Scirocco [sirokoh] A wind similar to the Khamsin in origin, blowing from the Sahara Desert. As it crosses the Mediterranean Sea it picks up moisture, and arrives in S Europe as a moist, oppressive, warm wind.

Sirte, Gulf of [seertay], Arabic **Khalij Surt** Gulf in the Mediterranean Sea off the coast of N Libya; access is an area of dispute between Libya and the USA.

siskin A finch, found worldwide; eats seeds and insects. (Genus: *Carduelis*, 16 species, or *Serinus*, 2 species. Family: Fringillidae.)

Sisley, Alfred [seeslay] (1839–99) Impressionist painter and etcher, born in Paris. He painted landscapes almost exclusively, particularly in the valleys of the Seine, Loire, and Thames.

Sistine Chapel [sisteen] A chapel in the Vatican, built in 1475–81 for Pope Sixtus IV. It is remarkable for a series of frescoes executed on its ceiling and altar wall by Michelangelo.

Sisyphus [sisifus] In Greek mythology, a Corinthian king who was a famous trickster. In the Underworld he was condemned to roll a large stone up a hill from which it always rolled down again.

sitar [sitah(r)] A large Indian lute, with a gourd resonator and a long fretted neck. The modern concert sitar is about 122 cm/4 ft long, with usually seven strings plucked with a wire plectrum.

Sites of Special Scientific Interest (SSSIs) Areas designated by English Nature for the purposes of conservation, including some of the UK's best examples of particular wildlife habitats,

interesting geological features, and habitats for rare plants and animals.

Sitka National monument on W Baranof I, SE Alaska, USA; Indian stockade, totem poles, Russian blockhouse; established, 1910; town and naval base of Sitka nearby.

Sitting Bull, Sioux name **Tatanka Iyotake** (1834–90) Chief of the Dakota Sioux, born near Grand River, SD. He was a leader in the Sioux War of 1876–7, and led the defeat of Custer and his men at the Little Bighorn (1876). He escaped to Canada, but surrendered in 1881. He later toured with Buffalo Bill's Wild West Show. He returned to his people, and was killed when the army suppressed the 'ghost dance' religious movement.

Sitwell, Dame Edith (Louisa) (1887–1964) Poet and critic, born in Scarborough, North Yorkshire, the sister of Osbert and Sacheverell Sitwell. Her recital of some of her own poems under the title *Façade* (1922), to music by William Walton, was given a stormy public reception in London. She became a Catholic in 1955, after which her works reflect a deeper religious symbolism, as in *The Outcasts* (1962).

Sitwell, Sir (Francis) Osbert (Sacheverell) (1892–1969) Writer, born in London, the brother of Edith and Sacheverell Sitwell. He acquired notoriety with his satirical novel of the Scarborough social scene, *Before the Bombardment* (1927). He is best known for his five-volume autobiographical series, beginning with *Left Hand: Right Hand* (1944).

Sitwell, Sir Sacheverell [sasheverel] (1897–1988) Poet and art critic, born in Scarborough, North Yorkshire, the brother of Edith and Osbert Sitwell. His books on art and architecture include *Southern Baroque Art* (1924). His many volumes of poetry cover a period of over 30 years, from *The People's Palace* (1918) to *An Indian Summer* (1982).

SI units *units* (scientific)

Six, Les [lay sees] A group of composers united for about six years after 1917 to further the cause of modern French music. It comprised Germaine Tailleferre (1892–1983), Georges Auric, Louis Durey (1888–1979), Arthur Honegger, Darius Milhaud, and François Poulenc.

Six Day War *Arab–Israeli Wars*

sixth-form college A college in the UK for pupils over the age of 16 and up to 18 or 19. It specializes in A-level work, but other forms of examination and qualification may also be offered.

Sizewell Nuclear power station in Suffolk, E England; gas-cooled, graphite-moderated reactors (**Sizewell A**) (operational 1966–2006); also site of the first UK pressurized light-water-moderated and cooled reactor (**Sizewell B**), opened in 1995.

Sjælland [shelahn] area 7500 km²/2900 sq mi. Group of islands in Danish territorial waters, between Jutland and S Sweden.

ska The Jamaican popular music of the early 1960s, drawing on American rhythm and blues and 'jump' music, and Jamaica's own 'mento', a form of calypso. Ska with a slower beat became 'rocksteady' in the later 1960s. A UK ska revival in the 1970s was driven by 'two-tone' bands such as Madness and Bad Manners.

Skagerrak [skagerak] Arm of the Atlantic Ocean linking the North Sea with the Baltic Sea; bounded (N) by Norway and (S) by Denmark; 240 km/150 mi long and 135 km/84 mi wide.

skaldic poetry (Old Norse *skaldr* 'poet') Poetry composed and recited by recognized individuals in Iceland and the Scandinavian countries between 800 and 1100. After this time, written versions made the *skaldr* redundant.

Skanda [skahnda] The Hindu god of War, the 'Attacker'. He is also responsible for the demons who bring diseases.

Skanderbeg [skanderbek], nickname of **George Castriota** or **Kastrioti** (1405–68) Albanian patriot. In 1443 he drove the Turks from Albania, and for 20 years maintained Albanian independence.

Skara Brae [skahra bray] An exceptionally preserved Neolithic village of c.3100–2500 BC on the Bay of Skaill, Orkney, Scotland.

skeleton

1 skull, displaying the frontal bone, and the front parts of the parietal and temporal bones.
2 maxilla
3 mandible
4 clavicle
5 scapula (obscured in this view by the upper ribs).
6 sternum
7 humerus
8 ribs
9 vertebral column, displaying (from above to below) cervical, thoracic, lumber, sacral and coccygeal vertebrae.
10 illium
11 5th lumbar vertebra
12 ulna
13 radius
14 coccyx
15 bones of the hand, comprising the eight carpels, the five metacarpels, the three phalanges in each finger, and the two phalanges in the thumb.
16 femur
17 patella
18 tibia
19 fibula
20 bones of the foot, comprising the seven tarsals, the five metatarsals, the two phalanges in the big toe, and the three phalanges in the other toes.

The hardened tissues forming the supporting framework of plants and animals. In vertebrates it usually refers to the assembly and arrangement of bones. The **appendicular skeleton** comprises the bones of the limbs and the pelvic and pectoral girdles, while the **axial skeleton** comprises the bones of the vertebral column, skull, ribs, and sternum. A total of 208 bones are usually recognized in the skeleton: skull (22), ears (6), vertebrae (26), vertebral ribs (24), sternum (3), throat (1), pectoral girdle (4), arms (60), hips (2), legs (60). Medical problems affecting the skeleton include fracture, osteoarthritis, Paget's disease, and scoliosis.

It was exposed below sand dunes by storms in 1850. A world heritage site.

skate Any of several bottom-living rays of the family Rajidae; includes the large European species, *Raja batis*; length up to 2·5 m/8 ft, upper surface greenish-brown with lighter patches; fished commercially.

skateboarding Riding on land on a single flexible board, longer and wider than the foot, fixed with four small wheels on the underside. It developed as an alternative to surfing, and became very popular in the USA during the 1960s and in the UK during the 1970s and late 1980s.

skating *ice hockey; ice skating; roller skating*

Skegness [skegnes] 53°10N 0°21E, pop (2000e) 19 000. Resort town in Lincolnshire, EC England; railway.

skeleton *see panel*

Skelton, John (c.1460–1529) Satirical poet, born in Norfolk. Court poet to Henry VII, and tutor to Prince Henry (VIII), he became known for his satirical vernacular poetry, such as *Colyn Cloute* (1522).

skepticism *scepticism*

sketchphone A system, linked to the telephone network, by which line drawings and sketches can be transmitted long distances to suitable receiving equipment. An electronic touch-sensitive screen sends sketches via a computer and the telephone line to a receiver.

Skiathos [skeeathos] area 48 km²/18 sq mi. Island of the N Dodecanese, Greece; chief town, Skiathos; a popular holiday resort.

Skiddaw [skidaw] 54°40N 3°08W. Mountain in the Lake District of Cumbria, NW England; rises to 928 m/3045 ft.

skiffle A type of popular music of the 1950s in which the washboard provided a distinctive timbre. It emanated from the USA, but the best-known singer was the Scot, Lonnie Donegan (1931–2002).

skiing The art of propelling oneself along on snow while standing on skis, and with the aid of poles, named from the Norwegian word *ski*, 'snow shoe'. **Alpine skiing** consists of the downhill and slaloms (zig-zag courses through markers), which are races against the clock. **Nordic skiing** incorporates cross-country skiing, the biathlon, and ski jumping.

skimmer A bird inhabiting tropical freshwater and coasts; lower bill longer and narrower than upper; catches fish by flying low with lower bill cutting water surface; also known as the **shearwater**, **sea-dog**, or **scissorbill**. (Family: Rhynchopidae, 3 species.)

skin The tough, pliable, waterproof covering of the body, blending with the mucous membranes of the mouth, nose, eyelids, and urogenital and anal openings. It is the largest single organ in the body – approximately 1·8 sq m/19·4 sq ft in the adult human and 1–2 mm/0·04–0·08 in thick. As well as a surface covering, it is also a sensory organ providing sensitivity to touch, pressure, changes in temperature, and painful stimuli. Its waterproofing function prevents fluid loss from the body, but it also has an absorptive function when certain drugs, vitamins, and hormones are applied to it in a suitable form. It is usually loosely applied to underlying tissues, so that it is easily displaced. When subjected to continuous friction, it responds by increasing the thickness of its superficial layers. When wounded, it responds by increased growth and repair. Skin is composed of a superficial layer (the *epidermis*) and a deeper layer (the *dermis*). The epidermis consists of many cell layers, many sensory nerve endings, but no blood vessels. The dermis is the deeper interlacing feltwork of collagen and elastic fibres containing blood and lymphatic vessels, nerves and sensory nerve endings, a small amount of fat, hair follicles, sweat and sebaceous glands, and smooth muscle. It is firmly anchored to the subcutaneous connective tissue. Skin colour depends on the presence of pigment (*melanin*) and the vascularity of the dermis. In response to sunlight, skin increases its degree of pigmentation, making it appear darker.

skin cancer *keratosis; melanoma*

skin-diving A form of underwater swimming, popularized in the 1930s. Until the advent of the scuba, skin-divers used only goggles, face mask, flippers, and a short breathing tube, or *snorkel*.

skink A lizard of the family Scincidae (1275 species), worldwide in tropical and temperate regions; usually with a long thin body and short legs (some species without legs); head often with large flat scales.

Skinner, B(urrhus) F(rederic) (1904–90) Psychologist, born in Susquehanna, PA. A leading behaviourist, he was a proponent of operant conditioning and inventor of the *Skinner box* for facilitating experimental observations. His main scientific works included *The Behavior of Organisms* (1938) and *Verbal Behavior* (1957).

skipjack Small species of tuna fish (*Katsuwonus pelamis*) widespread in offshore waters of tropical to temperate seas; body length up to about 1 m/3¼ ft; upper surface blue, sides silver with darker banding. (Family: Scombridae.)

skipper A butterfly with relatively short wings and a large head and body; antennae often club-shaped. (Order: Lepidoptera. Family: Hesperiidae, c.3100 species.)

Skiros [skeeros] pop (2000e) 3000; area 209 km²/81 sq mi. Largest island of the N Dodecanese, Greece; length 36 km/22 mi; maximum width 14 km/9 mi; tourism.

skittles A game played in several different forms, all of which have the same objective: to knock down nine pins with a ball. The most popular forms are **alley skittles**, played in long alleys, and **table skittles**, played indoors on a specially constructed table with a swivelled ball attached to a mast by means of a chain. The pins are much smaller than those used in ten-pin bowling.

Skopje [skopye], or **Skoplje**, Turkish **Usküp**, ancient **Scupi** 42°00N 21°28E, pop (2000e) 587 000. Industrial capital of the Former Yugoslav Republic of Macedonia, on R Vardar; capital of Serbia, 14th-c; largely destroyed by earthquake, 1963; airport; railway; university (1949).

Skorzeny, Otto [skaw(r)tsaynee] (1908–75) Soldier, born in Vienna. He was noted for his commando-style operations in World War 2. He freed Mussolini from internment in a mountain hotel on the Gran Sasso Range (1943), abducted Horthy, the Regent of Hungary (1944), but failed to capture Tito. He was tried at Nuremberg as a war criminal, but was acquitted (1947).

Skou, Jens C [skoh] (1918–) Chemist, born in Denmark. He studied at Aarhus University, where he went on to teach. He shared the 1997 Nobel Prize for Chemistry for the discovery of an ion-transporting enzyme, Na+, K+-ATPase.

Skraelings [skraylingz] (Old Norse *skraeling* 'pitiful wretch') The name given by the Vikings to the native peoples – principally Beothuk Indians and Inuit – they encountered in Greenland and North America.

skua A large, gull-like seabird; usually dark plumage, fleshy band at base of bill; central tail feathers longest; also known as the **jaeger** or **bonxie**. (Family: Stercorariidae, 7 species.)

skull The skeleton of the head and face, composed of many individual bones closely fitted together. It consists of a large cranial cavity, which encloses the brain; and the bones of the face, which complete the walls of the *orbits* (eye sockets), nasal cavity, and roof of the mouth. The lower jaw (*mandible*) may also be included as part of the skull. The top of the skull is relatively smooth and rounded, while the underside is irregular, having many openings for the passage of nerves and vessels. The major bony parts (the number present is shown in parentheses) are the *frontal* (1), *parietal* (2), *occipital* (1), *temporal* (2), *maxillary* (2), *ethmoid* (1), and *zygomatic* (2) bones.

skull-cap A very widespread perennial; flowers 2-lipped, often with upturned tube. Many species have brightly coloured flowers, and are cultivated for ornament. Others are medicinal, used for nerve tonics. (Genus: *Scutellaria*, 300 species. Family: Labiatae.)

skunk A mammal of family Mustelidae, native to the New World; long black and white coat; squirts foul-smelling fluid as defence.

skydiving Falling from an aircraft and freefalling down to a height of 600 m/2000 ft, when the parachute must be opened, before gliding to the ground. The sport is often called simply **freefalling**.

Skye Island in Highland, W Scotland; largest island of the Inner Hebrides, area 1665 km²/643 sq mi; pop (2000e) 12 300; Cuillin Hills in SW, rising to 1008 m/3307 ft at Sgurr Alasdair; chief towns, Portree, Broadford, Dunvegan; Dunvegan castle, Dunsgiath castle; Skye Bridge completed, 1995.

Skylab project The first US space station, launched on a Saturn V vehicle in May 1973. It was operated in low Earth orbit for 171 days by three successive three-man crews. The station re-entered the atmosphere in July 1979, the source of worldwide attention because there were fears of debris impacting Earth's surface (some pieces were in fact recovered from the Australian desert).

skylark A lark native to the Old World N hemisphere; inhabits grassland, farmland, salt marshes, and sand dunes; sings during ascending and descending fluttering flight. (Genus: *Alauda*, 2 species.)

skyscraper A multi-storey building of great height, typically using a steel frame and curtain wall construction, the floors being accessed via high-speed lifts. The term was first used in the USA at the end of the 19th-c. At 451·9 m/1483 ft, the Petronas Twin Towers (1996) was the world's tallest building at the beginning of 2004, but several taller buildings are scheduled, such as the Freedom Building, designed to replace the World Trade Center. Perhaps the most famous skyscrapers are those of the 1920s, such as the Empire State Building (1930–1).

Slade, Felix (1790–1868) Antiquary and art collector, born in Halsteads, Yorkshire. The Slade School of Fine Art, London, is named after him.

slander A defamatory statement made in some transient form – sounds (not necessarily words) or gestures. The term is not recognized by all jurisdictions (eg in Scotland).

slate A fine-grained metamorphic rock having a perfect cleavage because of the parallel alignment of mica crystals. Split into thin sheets it is used for roofing, being durable and light. Well-known occurrences are in N Wales and the Vosges, France.

slavery A system of social inequality in which some people are treated as items of property belonging to other individuals or social groups. At one extreme, slaves might be worked to death, as in the Greek mining camps of the 5th-c and 4th-c BC. At the other, slaves were used less as chattels and more as servants, working in households, and to an extent even administering them, and acting as tutors to young children.

slave trade A trade in Africa which started in ancient times. The scale of the trade built up with the arrival of the Portuguese in Africa and the development of the labour-intensive plantation system in the colonies. The Portuguese dominated the trade in the 16th-c, the Dutch in the early 17th-c, while the late 17th-c was a period of intense competition with the French, British, Danes, and Swedes joining the early practitioners. The British abolished the slave trade in 1807, and the institution of slavery in 1833. There have been various estimates of the number of slaves removed from Africa, the most reliable figure being c.12·5 million between 1650 and 1850.

Slavic or **Slavonic languages** The NE branch of the Indo-European languages, normally divided into **South Slavic** (eg Bulgarian), **West Slavic** (eg Polish), and **East Slavic** (eg Russian). There are written records of Old Church Slavonic from the 9th-c, and its modern form, Church Slavonic, is used as a liturgical language in the Eastern Orthodox Church. The Baltic and Slavic languages between them have c.300 million mother-tongue speakers, more than half of whom speak Russian. Russian is also spoken by a further 120 million as a second language, throughout the republics of the former USSR. Polish is spoken by c.40 million in Poland and surrounding areas, as well as by emigrants in several parts of the world. Serbian (7.5 million) and Croatian (4.8 million) are spoken chiefly in Yugoslavia and Croatia, respectively. Czech is spoken in the Czech Republic by c.12 million. All the East Slavic languages, and some others, are still written in Cyrillic script.

Slavs The largest group of European peoples sharing a common ethnic and linguistic origin, consisting of Russians, Ukrainians, Byelorussians, Poles, Czechs, Slovaks, Bulgarians, Serbs, Croats, Montenegrins, and Macedonians.

sleep An unconscious state where the subject shows little responsiveness to the external world. There are two phases of sleep which alternate throughout the night. In deep sleep, the brain activity (EEG) shows slow delta waves (**slow wave sleep**, or **SWS**). This is interrupted every 90 minutes or so by 30 minutes of **rapid eye movement** (**REM**) **sleep**. Here the muscles are completely relaxed, but the closed eyes show rapid movements. Dreaming occurs in REM sleep, and perhaps also in SWS.

sleep apnoea/apnea [apneea] The periodic reduction or cessation of breathing during sleep due to narrowing of the upper airways. It is caused by relaxation of the muscles of the soft palate and uvula, allowing the soft tissues of these structures to partially occlude the airway and also to vibrate, producing snoring. The condition leads to disturbed sleep and daytime drowsiness.

sleeping sickness *trypanosomiasis*

sleep-walking or **somnambulism** A state in which a sleeping individual rises from the bed and walks about for a variable period. It is unrelated to dream activity, and occurs particularly when an individual is subject to stress. It is most common in children. The most important aspect of management is ensuring that the sleep-walker has a safe environment (eg blocking off access to a flight of stairs).

sleet A form of precipitation found in near-freezing surface air. In the UK the term is used for partially melted snow which reaches the ground, or a mixture of snow and rain. In the USA it describes raindrops which have frozen into ice pellets, and then partially thawed before reaching the ground.

slepton *supersymmetry*

slide A still picture transparency mounted for projection. The modern form is a colour photograph 36 × 24 mm in a standard mount 50 mm/2 in square. Slides are widely used as illustrations in educational and commercial presentations, in audiovisual shows, and as inserts in television news and current affairs programmes.

Sliema [sleema] 35°55N 14°31E, pop (2000e) 14 500. Residential and resort town on N coast of main island of Malta; largest town in Malta.

Sligo (county) [sliygoh], Ir **Sligeach** pop (2000e) 55 000; area 1795 km²/693 sq mi. County in Connacht province, W Ireland; Ox Mts to the W; capital, Sligo, pop (2000e) 18 000; associated with W B Yeats.

Slim (of Yarralumia and of Bishopston), William (Joseph) Slim, 1st Viscount (1891–1970) British field marshal, born in Bristol. In World War 2, his greatest achievement was to lead his reorganized forces, the famous 14th 'Forgotten Army', to victory over the Japanese in Burma. He was also Governor-General of Australia (1953–60).

slime mould A primitive micro-organism resembling a fungus,

but with an amoeba-like colony stage in its life cycle. (Class: Myxomycota.)

slipped disc *prolapsed intervertebral disc*

Sloane, Sir Hans (1660–1753) Physician, born in Killyleagh, Co Down. His museum and library of 50 000 volumes and 3560 manuscripts formed the nucleus of the British Museum.

sloe *blackthorn*

sloop A single-masted, fore-and-aft rigged sailing vessel with only one headsail. In World War 2, it referred to an anti-submarine vessel superior to a corvette in speed and equipment.

sloth A South American mammal of family Megalonychidae (**two-toed sloths**, 2 species) or of family Bradypodidae (**three-toed sloths**, 3 species); two-toed sloths actually have two fingers (all sloths have three toes); an edentate; hangs upside down in trees using huge claws.

Slough [slow] 51°31N 0°36W, pop (2001e) 119 100. Town and unitary authority (from 1998) in S England; railway; London Heathrow airport nearby.

Slovakia *Slovak Republic*

Slovak Republic *p.861*

Slovenes A Slavonic people, concentrated in the NW corner of the Balkan peninsula; overwhelmingly Roman Catholic. Most live in the republic of Slovenia, though c.100 000 continue to inhabit Italy and c.80 000 Austria.

Slovenia *p.862*

Slovo, Joe [slohvoh] (1926–95) South African political leader, born in Lithuania. He moved to South Africa as a child, and became one of the most influential white South Africans associated with the national liberation movement. He held high office in both the Communist Party and the African National Congress, and played a major role in the negotiations for a new dispensation. In 1994 he was appointed minister for housing in Mandela's first cabinet.

slow-worm A legless lizard (*Anguis fragilis*) native to Europe, NW Africa, and SW Asia; grey or brown; also known as **blindworm**. (Family: Anguidae.)

slug (zoology) A terrestrial snail with an elongate body and usually a small external shell, or no shell at all; typically two pairs of tentacles on its head, the upper pair bearing the eyes; common in moist environments. (Class: Gastropoda. Subclass: Pulmonata.)

slump *depression* (economics); *recession*

slurry *manure*

Sluter, Claus or **Claes** [slooter] (c.1350–c.1405) Sculptor, probably born in Haarlem, The Netherlands. His chief works are the porch sculptures of the Carthusian house of Champmol near Dijon, and the tomb of Philip the Bold.

Smalley, Richard Erret (1943–2005) Chemist, born in Akron, OH. He shared the Nobel Prize for Chemistry in 1996 for his contribution to the discovery of fullerenes (1985).

smallpox A highly infectious viral disease. As a result of a World Health Organization programme including vaccination, smallpox was declared in 1979 to have been completely eradicated.

smart bomb *bomb*

smart card A plastic card, similar to a credit card, which has a micro-computer embedded in the card rather than a magnetic strip. The micro-computer has contacts which can be used for input and output, and the card can be used to process information held in the memory. Current uses for the card include identification, holding medical data in case of emergency, building up credits in reward schemes, storing credits to use in telephone boxes, buses, and underground railways, and as a substitute for cash (*electronic cash*).

smart material A substance which responds in a specific mechanical way to a given trigger. The trigger can be a change in pressure, temperature, electric field, or magnetic field. The response can be a change in size, shape, rigidity, transpar-

Slovak Republic

☐ International Airport

or **Slovakia**, Slovak **Slovenská Republika**
Local name Slovenská republiká
Timezone GMT +1
Area 49 035 km²/18 927 sq mi
Population total (2002e) 5 383 000
Status Republic
Date of independence 1993
Capital Bratislava
Languages Slovak (official), with Czech and Hungarian widely spoken
Ethnic groups Slovak (87%), Hungarian (11%), Czech (1%), with German, Polish, and Ukrainian minorities
Religions Roman Catholic (70%), Protestant (6%)

Physical features Dominated by the Carpathian Mountains, consisting of a system of E–W ranges separated by valleys and basins; ranges include the Low Tatras of the Inner Carpathians, 1829 m/6000 ft, and the highest point, Gerlachovsky, 2655 m/8711 ft in the Tatra Mts (N); main rivers include the Danube, Vah, Hron; National parks at Pieniny, Low and High Tatra.

Climate Continental climate; warm humid summers, cold dry winters; snow remains on the mountains for 130 days of the year; average annual temperature -4°C (Jan), 18°C (Jul) in Bratislava; average annual rainfall 500–650 mm/20–30 in.

Currency 1 Slovak Koruna (SKK) = 100 halers

Economy Agricultural region, especially cereals, wine, fruit; steel production in Košice; heavy industry suffering since previously dependent on state subsidies.

GDP (2002e) $67·34 bn, per capita $12 400

Human Development Index (2002) 0·835

History Settled in 5th–6th-c by Slavs; part of Great Moravia, 9th-c; part of Magyar Empire from 10th-c; became part of Kingdom of Hungary, 11th-c; united with Czech lands to form the separate state of Czechoslovakia, 1918; under German control, 1938–9; Slovakia became a separate republic under German influence, 1939; Czechoslovakia regained its independence, 1945; under Communist rule following 1948 coup; attempt at liberalization by Dubček terminated by intervention of Warsaw Pact troops, 1968; from 1960s, Slovaks revived efforts to gain recognition for Slovak rights; fall from power of Communist party, 1989; 1992 agreement to divide Czechoslovakia into its constituent republics led to declaration of independence of Slovak Republic, 1993; governed by a President, Prime Minister, Council of Ministers, and National Council; joined European Union, 2004.

Head of State
1993–8 Michal Kovac
1999–2004 Rudolf Schuster
2004– Ivan Gasparovic

Head of Government
1993–4 Vladimir Mečiar
1994–7 Jozef Moravcik
1997–8 Vladimír Mečiar
1998–2006 Mikuláš Dzurinda
2006– Robert Fico

---

ency, colour, or electric potential. *Shape memory alloys* (SMA) are metals which return to their manufactured shape when they are heated. Spacecraft aerials, for example, have been made from SMAs; these unfurl when an electric current passes through them. *Smart crystals*, which produce electric signals when they are deformed, are used as sensors; others change colour with temperature and can be used for warnings. *Smart ceramics* expand or contract in response to an electric signal; these are being used as synthetic muscles. *Smart liquids* which set when exposed to a magnetic field can be used to dampen vibrations in machines, or as protection in earthquake areas.

Smart 1 A lunar probe launched by the European Space Agency (ESA) in August 2003. In Europe's first mission to the Moon, the Smart 1 solar-powered spacecraft was designed to enter orbit around the Moon and produce an X-ray map of the surface. In November 2004 the probe successfully entered orbit and began its descent towards the surface. After reaching its final orbit in February 2005, deployment of an X-ray spectrometer called D-Cixs began to comprehensively map chemical elements on the Moon's surface. The data will help scientists test theories of its birth and evolution. The probe ended its mission

in September 2006 by crashing onto the Moon's surface in a controlled collision.

smelt Slender-bodied marine and freshwater fish belonging to either the N hemisphere family Osmeridae or the Australasian family Retropinnidae; several species migrate into fresh water to breed.

smelting Obtaining a metal from its ore by heating, using fuel which will simultaneously remove other components of the ore, and a flux to promote the removal of impurities. Copper was probably the first metal to be obtained from an ore, and tin, lead, and silver were also smelted in early times. Charcoal was the universal fuel and reducing agent until the use of coke in the 18th-c.

Smetana, Bedřich [smetana] (1824–84) Composer, born in Litomyšl, C Czech Republic (formerly Bohemia, Austrian Empire). His compositions, intensely national in character, include nine operas, notably *Prodaná nevěsta* (1866, The Bartered Bride), and many chamber and orchestral works, including the series of symphonic poems *Má vlast* (1874–9, My Country).

smew A small bird, a species of merganser (*Mergus albellus*) native to the N Old World; untidy crest on back of head; male white with black back and tail; female mainly brown.

Slovenia

□ International Airport

[slohveenia], Slovene **Slovenija**
Local name Slovenija
Timezone GMT +1
Area 20 251 km²/7817 sq mi
Population total (2002e) 1 948 000
Status Republic
Date of independence 1991

Capital Ljubljana
Languages Slovene, Croatian
Ethnic group Slovene (90%)
Religions Roman Catholic, Protestant, some Eastern Orthodox
Physical features Mountainous republic between Austria and Croatia; Slovenian Alps (NW) rise to 2863 m/9393 ft at Triglav in the Julian Alps (Julijske Alpe); rivers include Sava, Savinja, and Drava; chief port, Koper.
Climate Continental climate; more Mediterranean in W; average annual temperature -1°C (Jan), 19°C (Jul) in Ljubljana; average annual rainfall 1600 mm/63 in.
Currency 1 euro (EUR) = 100 cents (previous to Jan 2007, 1 Slovene Tolar (SIT) = 100 paras)
Economy Agriculture; maize, wheat, sugar beet, potatoes, livestock, wine, timber, lignite; textiles; large iron and steel plants; vehicles; coal, lead, mercury mining in W.
GDP (2002e) $37·06 bn, per capita $19 200
Human Development Index (2002) 0·879
History Settled by Slovenes, 6th-8th-c; later controlled by Slavs and Franks; part of the Austro-Hungarian Empire until 1918; people's republic within Yugoslavia, 1946; declaration of full sovereignty, 1990; declaration of independence from Yugoslavia as the Republic of Slovenia, 1991; opposed by central government, brief period of fighting upon the intervention of the federal army who withdrew in Aug 1991; tricameral legislature replaced by a bicameral National Assembly, consisting of a Chamber of Deputies and a State Council; joined European Union, 2004.
Head of State
1991–2002 Milan Kučan
2002– Janez Drnovšek
Head of Government
1991– Lozje Peterle
1992–2000 Janez Drnovšek
2000 Andrej Bajuk
2000–2 Janez Drnovšek
2002–4 Anton Rop
2004– Janez Jansa

Smiles, Samuel (1812–1904) Writer and social reformer, born in Haddington, East Lothian, Scotland. His main work was a guide to self-improvement, *Self-Help* (1859), with its short lives of great men and the admonition 'Do thou likewise'.

Smiley, Jane (1952–) Novelist, born in Los Angeles, CA. An early short story, *Lily*, won the O Henry Award, later appearing in a collection *The Age of Grief* (1987). *A Thousand Acres* (1992), a modern retelling of the *King Lear* story set in a farming community in Iowa, won a Pulitzer Prize and the National Book Critics Award. Later novels include *Horse Heaven* (2000) and *Ten Days in the Hills* (2007).

Smith, Adam (1723–90) Economist and philosopher, born in Kirkcaldy, Scotland. In 1776 he published *An Inquiry into the Nature and Causes of the Wealth of Nations* (1776), the first major work of political economy.

Smith, Bessie, nickname **Empress of the Blues** (c.1895–1937) Blues singer, born in Chattanooga, TN. She recorded her first sides in New York City in 1923, and received her nickname after highly successful sales of her early songs.

Smith, Delia (1941–) Television chef and writer, born in Woking, Surrey. After working as a journalist, she published her first cookery book, *How to Cheat at Cooking*, in 1973, and her popularity increased with the many highly successful television series that followed. Later best-selling books include *Delia Smith's*

Christmas (1990), *Summer Collection* (1993), *Winter Collection* (1995), and *How to Cook* (1999). A new series of books, *The Delia Collection*, began in 2003.

Smith, Dodie, in full **Dorothy Gladys Smith**, pseudonym **C L Anthony** (1896–1990) Playwright, novelist, and theatre producer, born in Whitefield, Greater Manchester. Among her best known works are the play *Dear Octopus* (1938) and the children's book *The Hundred and One Dalmatians* (1956, filmed 1961, 1996).

Smith, Florence Margaret *Smith, Stevie*

Smith, Ian (Douglas) (1919–) Prime minister of Rhodesia (1964–79), born in Selukwe, Zimbabwe. As premier, in 1965 he unilaterally declared independence, which resulted in the imposition of increasingly severe economic sanctions. After formal independence (1980), he continued to be a vigorous opponent of the one-party state under Mugabe's government.

Smith, John (1580–1631) Adventurer, born in Willoughby, Lincolnshire. He joined an expedition to colonize Virginia (1607), where his energy in dealing with the Indians led to his being elected president of the colony (1608–9).

Smith, John (1938–94) British politician, born in Dalmally, Scotland. He held various posts in government and in Opposition, becoming shadow Chancellor of the Exchequer in 1988. He succeeded Neil Kinnock as Labour leader after the 1992 general election. A highly respected figure, his unexpected death after a heart attack in May 1994 caused an unusually strong sense of national loss.

Smith, Joseph (1805–44) Founder of the Church of Jesus Christ of Latter-day Saints (the Mormons), born in Sharon, VT. He received his first 'call' as a prophet in 1820, and in 1827 received the *Book of Mormon* on a hill near Palmyra, NY. He founded Nauvoo, IL in 1840, becoming mayor. Imprisoned for conspiracy, he was killed by a mob which broke into Carthage jail.

Smith, Maggie, popular name of **Dame Margaret Natalie Smith** (1934–) Actress, born in Ilford, Greater London. Her Oscar-winning roles include the films *The Prime of Miss Jean Brodie* (1969) and *California Suite* (1978), and she won BAFTA awards for *A Private Function* (1984), *A Room With a View* (1986), and *The Lonely Passion of Judith Hearne* (1987). Among many later films are *Gosford Park* (2001) and *Ladies in Lavender* (2004). In 2003 she won an Emmy for her role in the TV mini-series *My House in Umbria*.

Smith, Stevie, pseudonym of **Florence Margaret Smith** (1902–71) Writer, born in Hull, England. She acquired a reputation principally as an eccentrically humorous poet on serious themes, illustrated by 'Not Waving but Drowning' (1957).

Smith, Vernon L (1934–) Economist, born in Wichitaw, KS. A researcher at the Interdisciplinary Center for Economic Science in Fairfax, VA, he shared the 2002 Nobel Prize for Economics for having established laboratory experiments as a tool in empirical economic analysis, especially in the study of alternative market mechanisms.

Smith, Will, popular name of **Willard Christopher Smith Jr** (1968–) Film actor and rapper, born in Philadelphia, PA. His first major film role was in *Six Degrees of Separation* (1993), and later films include *Independence Day* (1996), *Men in Black* (1997, sequel 2002), *Ali* (2001), *I, Robot* (2004), and *In Pursuit of Happyness* (2006, Best Actor Oscar nomination).

Smithfield An area just outside the walls of the City of London, in former times the scene of tournaments, trials, fairs, and cattle markets. The main London meat market has been located here since the mid-19th-c.

Smithsonian Institution A foundation for the promotion of knowledge, endowed in 1826 by the English scientist James Smithson (1765–1829), and opened in Washington, DC in 1855. It administers a number of art, history, and science museums, and scientific research centres.

smog A form of air pollution with several sources. In Britain before the mid-20th-c, the smogs of industrial cities were a form of radiation fog, in which soot and smoke acted as condensation nuclei, and gases such as sulphur dioxide (SO_2) and carbon monoxide (CO) were unable to escape. At lower latitudes, photochemical smogs (*heat hazes*) occur. Emissions of hydrocarbons and oxides of nitrogen from industrial processes and vehicle exhausts react with sunlight.

smoked foods The preservation of food using the ancient method of exposing it over a period of time to wood smoke. The preservation is achieved partly through drying and partly through the effects of chemicals in the smoke.

smoking The practice of inhaling the fumes from burning tobacco leaves, generally using cigarettes, cigars, or pipes, introduced into Europe from the Americas by early explorers. The practice is habit-forming, and is known to be a causative factor in the development of several diseases, notably lung cancer, throat cancer, coronary heart disease, and respiratory conditions. Since 2003 a number of countries have banned smoking in several public places. In 2005 the World Health Organization's tobacco control treaty came into force. The document sets out a programme to reduce the number of people smoking across the world.

Smolensk [smolensk] 54°49N 32°04E, pop (2000e) 348 000. River port in WC European Russia, on the upper Dnepr R; part of Russia, 1654; severely damaged in World War 2; railway; cathedral (12th-c).

Smollett, Tobias (George) (1721–71) Novelist, born in Cardross, Scotland. He achieved success with his first works, the picaresque novels *The Adventures of Roderick Random* (1748) and *The Adventures of Peregrine Pickle* (1751). His masterpiece was *The Expedition of Humphry Clinker* (1771).

Smoot, George Fitzgerald, III (1945–) Astrophysicist, born in Yukon, FL. He joined the Lawrence Berkeley Laboratory, University of California, Berkeley in 1971 and became professor of astrophysics in 1994. He led a study of cosmic background radiation that in 1992 resulted in a picture of the universe shortly after the 'big bang' some 12 thousand million years ago. In 2006 he shared the Nobel Prize for Physics with John C Mather for 'their discovery of the blackbody form and anisotropy of the cosmic microwave background radiation'.

Smuts, Jan (Christiaan) (1870–1950) South African general, statesman, and prime minister (1919–24, 1939–48), born in Malmesbury, Cape Colony. A member of the Imperial War Cabinet in World War 1, he was a significant figure at Versailles, and was instrumental in the founding of the League of Nations in 1919. His coalition with the Nationalists in 1934 produced the United Party, and he became premier again in 1939.

Smyrna *Izmir*

Smythe, Pat(ricia), married name **Koechlin** (1928–96) Show jumper, born in London. She won the European championship four times on 'Flanagan' (1957, 1961–3), and in 1956 was the first woman to ride in the Olympic Games.

Snagge, John (Derrick Mordaunt) (1904–96) British broadcaster. He became a BBC announcer in 1928, especially known for his commentary on the Oxford and Cambridge Boat Race (1931–80). He retired in 1965, his voice having come to represent the traditional values of the BBC.

snail A common name for many types of gastropod mollusc, but sometimes used more specifically for members of subclass Pulmonata; predominantly terrestrial or freshwater forms; usually possess a spirally coiled external shell. (Class: Gastropoda.)

snake A reptile believed to have evolved c.135 million years ago; also known as **serpent**; c.2400 living species, found worldwide except in very cold regions and on some islands; separate jaw bones connected by ligaments; these bones can move apart, allowing prey much wider than the snake's head to be swallowed; eats animals (or eggs); cannot chew (swallows prey whole); long cylindrical scaly body; no limbs or eyelids; skin moulted several times each year; c.300 venomous species; more than 50 dangerous to humans. (Suborder: Serpentes or Ophidia. Order: Squamata.)

snake-necked turtle A side-necked turtle, native to South America and Australasia; very long slender neck; called *tortoise* in Australia; also known as **long-necked turtle**. (Family: Chelidae, 36 species.)

snake plant *mother-in-law's-tongue*

Snake River River in NW USA; rises in NW Wyoming; joins the Columbia R; length c.1600 km/1000 mi.

snapdragon A short-lived, slightly bushy perennial (*Antirrhinum majus*), growing to 80 cm/30 in, native to Europe; flowers have two lips, with a projection forming a landing platform for bumble-bees, the only insects with sufficient strength to part the lips and reach the nectar within. The flowers of the wild plants are reddish-purple, with cultivars in a range of colours. (Family: Scrophulariaceae.)

snapper Deep-bodied fish of the family Lutjanidae (4 genera, 300 species), widespread and locally common in tropical seas; name derives from the long conical front teeth and highly mobile jaws.

snare drum *side drum*

Snead, Sam(uel Jackson), nickname **Slammin' Sam** (1912–2002) Golfer, born in Hot Springs, VA. He won the (British) Open in 1946, and was three-times winner of the US PGA Championship (1942, 1949, 1951) and the US Masters (1949, 1952, 1954). His six Senior Championships (1964–5, 1967, 1970, 1972–3) are a record.

Snicket, Lemony, pseudonym of **Daniel Handler** (1970–) Writer, born in San Francisco, CA. He became well known for his series of novels for children entitled *A Series of Unfortunate Events*, featuring the Baudelaire siblings, Violet, Klaus and Sunny. Books in the series include *The Bad Beginning* (1999), *The Vile Village* (2001), *The Slippery Slope* (2003), and *The End* (2006). A film, *Lemony Snicket's A Series of Unfortunate Events*, appeared in 2004.

snipe A sandpiper, found worldwide; mottled brown plumage; shortish legs and long straight bill. (Genus: *Gallinago*, 17 species, or *Coenocorypha*, 1 species.)

snooker A popular indoor game played with cues on a standard English billiards table by two (sometimes four) players. 22 balls are placed at specific positions on the table: one white, 15 reds, and six coloured balls (yellow, green, brown, blue, pink, and black). The object is to use the cue to hit the white ball to send ('pot') the other balls into any of six pockets around the table, according to certain rules. The coloured balls have an ascending points value of 2–7, while each red is worth one point. The game ends when the black is finally potted; and the winner is the player with most points. Snooker was invented by army officers serving in the Devonshire Regiment in India in 1875, who developed it from Black Pool.

Snorri Sturluson *Sturluson, Snorri*

Snow, C(harles) P(ercy) Snow, Baron (1905–80) Novelist and physicist, born in Leicester, Leicestershire. He was the author of a cycle of successful novels portraying English life from 1920 onwards, starting with *Strangers and Brothers* (1940), and including *Corridors of Power* (1964). His controversial *Two Cultures and the Scientific Revolution* (Rede lecture, 1959) discussed the dichotomy between science and literature. He married the novelist Pamela Hansford Johnson in 1950.

Snow, Peter (John) (1938–) Broadcaster and writer, born in Dublin. He became a newscaster and reporter for ITN (1962–6), and a diplomatic and defence correspondent (1966–79), joining the BBC as presenter of *Newsnight* in 1979. He also became known as the co-presenter of the general elections (1974–2005).

snow A type of solid precipitation which forms at temperatures below the freezing point of water. At very cold temperatures, single ice crystals may fall as snow. At higher temperatures, ice crystals aggregate into geometrical forms called **snow flakes**.

snowboarding A popular recreation and sport that developed in the 1970s, using a single board (a relative of the skateboard) on snow. It is an official sport of the Winter Olympics for both men and women, with slalom racing and acrobatic displays in a specially built 'half-pipe'.

Snowdon, Welsh **Yr Wyddfa** 53°04N 4°05W. Mountain with five peaks rising to 1085 m/3560 ft in Gwynedd, NW Wales, UK; highest peak in England and Wales; rack railway from Llanberis to main peak.

Snowdon, Antony Armstrong-Jones, 1st Earl of (1930–) Photographer and designer, who married Princess Margaret in 1960 (divorced 1978). A freelance photojournalist since 1951, he designed the Aviary of the London Zoo in 1965, and in recent years has worked a great deal with the handicapped. In 2003 he published *Snowdon on Russia*.

snowdrop A bulb often flowering in late winter (*Galanthus nivalis*) native to Europe and W Asia; flowers on long stalks, solitary, drooping, white. (Family: Amaryllidaceae.)

snow leopard A rare big cat (*Panthera uncia*) native to the mountains of SC Asia, living near the snow line; thick pale grey coat with dark rings (sometimes enclosing small spots); also known as **ounce**.

Snowy Mountains Scheme A massive construction project in SE Australia carried out 1949–72. The object was to divert the Snowy R inland into the Murrumbidgee R to provide hydroelectricity and irrigation.

snuff Any drug prepared as a fine powder which is administered by sniffing; it is absorbed through the nasal mucous membranes. More commonly, snuff is synonymous with tobacco snuff, taken for its nicotine content.

Snyders, Frans (1579–1657) Painter, born in Antwerp. He specialized in still life and animals, and is well known for his hunting scenes.

Soane, Sir John (1753–1837) Architect, born in Goring, Oxfordshire. His designs include the Bank of England (1792–1833, now rebuilt) and Dulwich Picture Gallery (1811–14).

soap The salt of a fatty acid, usually stearic (octadecanoic) or palmitic (hexadecanoic) acids. Commercial soaps for toilet use are usually the sodium or potassium salts; insoluble calcium soaps are used as lubricants.

soapstone *talc*

Sobers, Gary [sohberz], popular name of **Sir Garfield St Aubrun Sobers** (1936–) Cricketer, born in Barbados. A great all-rounder, he is the only man to score 8000 Test runs and take 200 wickets. During his career (1953–74) he scored 28 315 runs in first-class cricket (average 54·87) and took 1043 wickets (average 27·74).

Sobukwe, Robert Mangaliso [sohbookway] (1924–78) African nationalist leader, born in Graaff-Reinet, South Africa. He was co-founder and first president of the Pan African Congress, the main rival to the African National Congress (ANC) as opponent of the apartheid regime. He was jailed in 1960, and detained on Robben I (1963–9) under legislation (nicknamed the 'Sobukwe clause') used only against him.

soca [sohka] Caribbean (originally Trinidadian) dance music, developed in the 1970s from calypso; the word may be a portmanteau of *soul* and *calypso*. Soca is generally faster than calypso, with a more varied instrumentation. **Parang soca** is a popular fusion with **parang**, a Trinidadian Christmas music, and **chutney soca** adds Indian flavourings.

SOCA *Serious Organised Crime Agency*

soccer *football, Association*

soccerene *buckminsterfullerene*

Social and Liberal Democratic Party (SLDP) *Liberal Party* (UK)

social anthropology *anthropology*

social contract or **social compact** The voluntary, unwritten agreement between a society's members to act in a mutually responsible manner, accepting the authority of the state which in turn guarantees certain moral principles. This philosophy was first propounded by Hobbes, Locke, and Rousseau, and has been an important feature of much liberal political theory in recent years. The concept was also seen in the UK in 1975, when the Labour government under Wilson arrived at a consensus with the Trades Union Council on the broad social and economic policies that the government should pursue. However, in 1978 no agreement could be reached, and the system lapsed.

Social Darwinism A school of thought which developed within 19th-c sociology based on the belief that social evolution depended on society adapting most efficiently to its environment.

social democracy A section of the socialist movement which emerged in the late 19th-c after the break-up of the First International, and which advocates achieving social change through reformist rather than revolutionary means. Some political parties that adopted the social democratic label in the latter part of the 20th-c were, however, moderate centrist parties.

Social Democratic Party (SDP) A UK political party formed in 1981 by a 'gang of four', comprising David Owen, Shirley Williams, Roy Jenkins, and Bill Rogers (1928–). They broke away from the Labour Party, forming an electoral pact with the Liberals in 1981, but failed to break the two-party 'mould' of British politics. The SDP merged with the Liberal Party in 1988, becoming the **Social and Liberal Democratic Party** (later known as the **Liberal Democrats**), although a rump, led by David Owen, continued in existence as the SDP until 1990.

socialism A wide-ranging political doctrine which first emerged in Europe during industrialization in the 18th-c. Most socialists would agree that social and economic relationships play a major part in determining human possibilities, and that the unequal ownership of the means of production under capitalism creates an unequal and conflictive society. The removal of property employed in the production process or some means of counterbalancing its power, it is held, will produce a more equal society where individuals enjoy greater freedom and are able to realize their potential more fully. Possibly the major division within socialism is between those who believe that to bring it about revolution is necessary, and those who believe change can be achieved through reforms within democratic politics.

Socialist Labor Party The longest-lasting socialist party in the USA. It nominated its first presidential candidate in 1892 and has existed ever since.

Socialist Party (UK) *Militant Tendency*

Socialist Realism In literature and art, the officially approved style of the former Soviet Union and of other socialist states, intended to appeal to the masses, and typically representing ordinary workers going about their mundane tasks. The Hungarian Marxist critic Georg Lukács was a major proponent, and Russian self-exile Andrei Sinyavsky (1925–97) a noted antagonist.

Socialist Revolutionary (SR) Party A neo-populist revolutionary party in Russia, founded in 1902 and led by Victor Chernov (1873–1952). Their 'fighting detachments' carried out a number of spectacular political assassinations between 1902 and 1918.

social medicine *community medicine*

social psychology The study of the behaviour of groups of individuals. Social psychologists might record anything from fine-grained details of the body posture of an individual to large-scale characteristics of crowd behaviour. They are also concerned with concepts that necessarily involve more than one individual, such as leadership, friendship, and persuasion.

social realism A term current in art criticism since World War 2, referring to pictures which treat 'real life' subjects in a way that challenges the values of 'bourgeois' society. Courbet's 'Stonebreakers' (1849) may have been the first great social realist picture.

social science A general term designating a number of disciplines, such as sociology, economics, political science, and geography, which have explored various aspects of society – such as social structure, the market, power, and spatial relations – through methods which are conventionally understood to be 'scientific'. There is still debate over whether these disciplines can be truly 'scientific', given that they are measuring patterns of human behaviour rather than the material of the natural and physical sciences.

social security 1 In the USA, a tax on wages and salaries imposed to pay for retirement benefits, disability insurance, and hospital insurance. The tax is an important part of all Federal revenues (around 40%), and is the equivalent of British **national insurance**.
2 In the UK, the provision of financial aid by the state to reduce poverty, financed out of taxation. It comprises a wide range of benefits (covering such matters as housing and family allowances) which are available to those in need.

social stratification A system of social inequality in which social groups occupy different positions (or *strata*) based on their unequal access to and ownership of material, political, and cultural (eg educational) resources.

social studies A range of disciplines within the arts, humanities, and social sciences, including sociology, history, economics, and geography, whose principal concern is the study of various aspects of society. The term is less favoured today and more likely to be replaced by **social sciences**.

social work A term which is usually understood to refer to the occupational activities of the social-work profession, ie the provision of social services to the 'needy', including counselling, care, and the general administration of the benefits of the state.

Society Islands, Fr **Archipel de la Société** pop (2000e) 193 000; area 1535 km²/592 sq mi. One of the five archipelagoes of French Polynesia, comprising the Windward Is (including Tahiti) and the Leeward Is; two clusters of volcanic and coral islands in a 720 km/450 mi chain stretching NW–SE; visited by Captain Cook in 1769, and named by him after the Royal Society; French protectorate, 1844; French colony, 1897; capital, Papeete (on Tahiti).

Socinus, Laelius [sosiynus], Ital **Lelio (Francesco Maria) Sozini** (1525–62) Protestant reformer, born in Siena, Italy. His anti-Trinitarian views were developed by his nephew **Faustus Socinus** (1539–1604) into a doctrine known as **Socinianism**.

sociobiology The integrated study of the biological basis of social behaviour, based on the assumption that all behaviour is adaptive. Emphasis is placed on social systems as ecological adaptations, and explanations are given in terms of evolutionary theory.

sociogram *sociometry*

sociolinguistics The study of the relationships between language and the society which uses it. The subject has a wide range, encompassing the use of standard and non-standard forms; the language of different social class and caste groups; the differences between male and female speech; and the character of multilingual societies.

sociology The study of patterned social behaviour which constitutes a social system or society, a term originally coined by French social theorist Auguste Comte. Sociologists explore the way in which social structures are continually modified as a result of social interaction, and thereby seek to explain the development of new institutions or new types of society. Certain areas of study have gained most attention, such as crime, the family, gender, the media, science and technology, medicine, and systems of inequality.

sociometry A technique for mapping social networks. The networks are based on respondents ranking those people they find more and those less desirable. A graphical representation of a network of social relationships is known as a **sociogram**.

sockeye Species of salmon (*Oncorhynchus nerka*), widespread in the N Pacific Ocean and adjacent rivers; length up to 80 cm/32 in; also known as **red salmon**. (Family: Salmonidae.)

Socrates [sokrateez] (469–399 BC) Greek philosopher, born in Athens. By Plato's account, he devoted his last 30 years to convincing the Athenians that their opinions about moral matters could not bear the weight of critical scrutiny. His technique, the so-called **Socratic method**, was to ask for definitions of such morally significant concepts as piety and justice, and to elicit contradictions from the responses, thus exposing the ignorance of the responder and motivating deeper enquiry into the concepts. He was tried on charges of impiety and corruption of the youth by zealous defenders of a restored democracy in Athens. Found guilty, he was put to death by drinking hemlock. His personality and his doctrines were immortalized in Plato's dialogues.

soda *sodium*

soda bread A type of bread which uses sodium bicarbonate to provide the necessary carbon dioxide. In contrast to yeast-risen bread, it is easier and quicker to prepare.

Soddy, Frederick (1877–1956) Radiochemist, born in Eastbourne, East Sussex. In 1913 he discovered forms of the same element with identical chemical qualities but different atomic weights (*isotopes*), for which he received the Nobel Prize for Chemistry in 1921.

Soderbergh, Steven [sohderberg] (1963–) Director, producer, and screenwriter, born in Atlanta, GA. He gained recognition with his directorial debut, *sex, lies, and videotape* (1989), which was nominated for an Academy Award and won the Palme d'Or at Cannes. Later films include *Kafka* (1991), *Erin Brockovich* (2000), *Traffic* (2000, Oscar, Best Director), *Ocean's Eleven* (2001, sequels 2004, 2007), and *Solaris* (2002).

sodium Na (Lat *natrium*), element 11, melting point 97·8°C. A very soft and reactive alkali metal, not found free in nature, but always in the form of one of its salts. These occur in salt deposits, but **sodium chloride** (common salt, or NaCl) can also be extracted from ocean water, of which it makes up about 3·5%. The metal is a very strong reducing agent, widely used in organic reactions and for the production of **sodium cyanide** (NaCN) and **sodium cyanamide** (Na_2CN_2), used in metallurgy and fertilizers. **Sodium carbonate** and **bicarbonate** (Na_2CO_3 and $NaHCO_3$), also called *washing soda* and *baking soda*, are important industrial chemicals, as is **sodium hydroxide** (NaOH), also called *caustic soda* or *lye*, used in soap making.

Sodom and Gomorrah [sodom, gomohra] Two of five 'cities of the plain' in ancient Palestine, perhaps now submerged under the S end of the Dead Sea or located to the SE of the Dead Sea. The people were legendary for their wickedness, especially their sexual perversity.

Soekarno, Achmad *Sukarno*

Sofia [sofeea], Bulgarian **Sofiya**, Lat **Serdica** 42°40N 23°18E, pop (2000e) 1 223 000. Capital of Bulgaria since 1878; Roman town 1st–4th-c; under Byzantine rule 6th–9th-c; under Turkish rule 1382–1878; airport; railway; university (1888); Alexander Nevsky memorial cathedral.

softball A smaller version of baseball, played on a diamond-shaped infield with bases 60 ft (18·3 m) apart. The object, as in baseball, is to score runs by completing a circuit of the diamond before being put out. The principal differences between the two sports are that the softball field is smaller, the ball is bigger, the pitcher throws the ball underarm, and the game lasts seven innings (not nine). Slow-pitch softball is played ten (not nine) a side.

software The suite of all computer programs, including operating system, compilers, packages, and user programs, which enable a particular computer centre to operate. The notion is contrasted with the **hardware** and the **liveware**. **Software engineering** is a methodology for developing computer software with the objective of ensuring that the software is efficient, does the job for which it is intended, and is produced within cost and on time.

Sogne Fjord [songnuh fyaw(r)d], Norwegian **Sognefjorden** Inlet on W coast of Norway; extends 204 km/127 mi; largest Norwegian fjord; average width, 5 km/3 mi.

SOHO *Solar and Heliospheric Observatory project*

soil The top layer of the Earth's surface, comprising a mixture of fine weathered rock particles and organic matter. The finest particles form clay; the less fine, silt; and the coarsest, sand. Provided moisture is available, soils generally support vegetation, and provide a habitat for a wide range of soil flora and fauna.

soil management The application of scientific management to agricultural land, including the maintenance of soil structures, the supply of nutrients, and the control of soil pollution and erosion. Good physical conditions in the soil are achieved by the maintenance and balance of organic matter through crop rotation and fertilization. The maintenance of specific soil acidities is important in order to encourage the adaptation of high-yielding crops to different soils. Soil pollution is now recognized to have adverse effects on plant growth and on animal and human health. It is caused by the presence of toxic compounds, chemicals, salts, radioactive materials, or disease-causing agents that enter the soil through industrial waste and pesticides.

soil science The study of soil, its information, and its management as a medium for plant growth. It includes both the physical management of soil, through cultivation, drainage, and irrigation, and the chemical management of soil, through the control of nutrient status, acidity, and salinity.

soja *soya bean*

Solar and Heliospheric Observatory (SOHO) project A co-operative project between the European Space Agency (ESA) and NASA to study the Sun from its deep core to its outer corona and, also, to study the solar wind, launched by an Atlas vehicle in December 1995, and subsequently inserted into a 'halo' orbit around the L1 Lagrangian point, it is located about 1·5 million km/900 000 mi sunward from the Earth.

solar cell A device for converting light directly into electrical power. Commercial cells using single crystals of silicon are efficient (converting c.14% of incident energy to electricity) but expensive; other materials are cheaper, such as germanium arsenide and amorphous silicon. Solar cells are used to provide electrical power in remote places, such as buoys and space satellites.

solar constant The total radiation falling on the Earth from the Sun, as measured for an average Earth–Sun distance; symbol *S*, value 1365 W/m² (watt per metre squared). A more accurate term is **total solar irradiance**, because the amount continually changes by as much as 1%.

solar flare A violent release of energy in the vicinity of an active region on the Sun, emitting energetic particles, X-rays, and radio waves. It causes notable auroral displays in our upper atmosphere.

solar power Energy radiating from the Sun, exploited to provide energy for heat and electricity generation. **Solar panels** or **collectors** (a black metal absorber) can be used to extract heat from the warmth of sunshine to heat water or air in pipes contained in or beneath the panels. Collectors can also be focused onto a small area of water to heat it, producing steam for electricity generation. In many developing countries solar power has great potential, especially as it is a renewable energy resource. By the early 1980s, solar collectors were producing energy equivalent to 0·01% of the world's total oil consumption.

solar prominence Flame-like clouds of matter in the solar chromosphere, sometimes triggered by solar flares, reaching heights of 1 000 000 km/600 000 mi at extremes.

Solar System The Sun and its associated, gravitationally bound, system of eight classical planets, their 100+ numbered satellites, four dwarf planets, the c.75 000 numbered asteroids, the comets, and interplanetary dust. The classical planets – Mercury, Venus, Earth, Mars (the four 'inner planets') and Jupiter, Saturn, Uranus, Neptune (the four outer 'gas giants') – and asteroids orbit approximately in the plane of the Sun's equator, and rotate about the Sun in the same direction (counter-clockwise when viewed from a N polar direction). The inner planets are comparatively small and dense, and are composed of high-temperature condensates (chiefly iron and metal silicates), while the four outer planets are much larger, and mainly composed of low-temperature condensates (chiefly gases and ices). The dwarf planets, or plutons, – Eris, Pluto, Charon, Ceres – are small distant planets that take more than 200 years to orbit the sun. It is thought that the planetary system was formed 4·6 thousand million years ago as a by-product of the Sun's formation, which resulted from the gravitational collapse of an accumulation of gas and dust in this region of the Milky Way galaxy.

solar time Time measured by considering the rotation of the Earth relative to the Sun. **Mean solar time** is established by reference to the mean Sun, and was established as the fundamental measure of clock time before it was realized that the Earth has variable rotation. **Apparent solar time** is time shown by a sundial.

solar wind A stream of charged particles (*plasma*) emanating from the upper atmosphere (corona) of the Sun and expanding continuously into the interplanetary medium with a velocity of 300–800 km/s (200–500 mi/s). The plasma interacts with planetary environments as it flows by them, notably by shaping the magnetospheres of those planets with magnetic fields.

solder An alloy which will melt easily at a moderate temperature, and so provide a bond between two metal surfaces. It usually consists of tin and lead, when used for joining copper, brass, or iron with tin-plate. As distinct from **welding**, soldering only fills in interstices in the juxtaposed metals, and does not fuse into them.

soldier beetle An elongate beetle; wing cases usually parallel-sided; adults commonly found on flowers and vegetation. (Order: Coleoptera. Family: Cantharidae, c.5000 species.)

sole Any of the flatfish in the family Soleidae, widespread in shallow continental shelf waters of tropical to temperate seas; includes the common European sole, or **Dover sole** (*Solea solea*); length up to 50 cm/20 in; both eyes on right side of body; very popular food fish.

Solemn League and Covenant An alliance between the English Parliament and the Scottish Covenanters against Charles I, agreed in September 1643. The pact facilitated parliamentary victory in the first Civil War, but although it was part of the bargain, Presbyterianism was never fully implemented in England.

solenodon [soleenodon] A mammal native to Cuba, Haiti, and the Dominican Republic; an insectivore, resembling a very large shrew (length, up to 33 cm/13 in), with longer legs; has a venomous bite. (Family: Solenodontidae, 2 species.)

solenoid A coil of wire, usually cylindrical, partially surrounding a movable iron core. When a current flows in the coil, a magnetic field is produced which makes the core move. A solenoid converts electrical energy into mechanical energy, as in operating a switch or circuit breaker.

Solent, the A channel separating the I of Wight from mainland England; a major shipping route from Southampton; yacht racing.

sol-fa, tonic tonic sol-fa

solicitor A lawyer whose responsibilities involve giving legal advice to clients. In order to practise, solicitors in the UK require a practising certificate from the appropriate Law Society. Most are concerned with advice on criminal law, family law, landlord and tenant law, and debt disputes. Solicitors also instruct barristers or advocates appearing for a client in either the lower or superior courts. The distinction between solicitors and barristers does not exist in the USA. A hybrid form of lawyer, termed a **solicitor advocate**, who can appear in the superior courts, was introduced in Scotland in 1993.

solicitor general In the UK, one of the government's law officers, who is a member of the House of Commons and junior to the

attorney-general. There is also a solicitor general for Scotland, who holds a similar position.

solid A dense form of matter characterized by its ability to transmit twisting forces and its inability to flow; virtually incompressible; tends to retain shape when stressed; described as rigid, the atoms generally not being free to move from point to point. Solids are divided into *crystals*, comprising ordered arrays of atoms; *amorphous solids*, which are disordered arrays; and *polymers* and *rubbers*, which comprise long chain-like molecules.

Solidarity (Polish *Solidarność*). An organization established in Poland (Sep 1980) as the National Committee of Solidarity to co-ordinate the activities of the emerging independent trade union following protracted industrial unrest, notably in the Lenin shipyard in Gdańsk. Its first president was Lech Wałęsa. It organized a number of strikes in early 1981 for improved wages and conditions, and became a force for major political reform. It was made illegal, but came back into the political arena in mid-1988. Following its successes in the 1989 elections, Solidarity entered into a coalition government with the communists, with one of its members (Tadeusz Mazowiecki) eventually becoming prime minister.

solid-state device A device in which an electric signal flows through a solid material rather than a vacuum. Most of the components (transistors, resistors, capacitors, and diodes), are made from a single solid piece of semiconductor material, such as silicon. They are much smaller and lighter than the traditional vacuum tubes and electrical components, and use less power, last longer, are more dependable, and cost less.

solid-state physics The study of all properties of matter in the solid state; a sub-branch of condensed matter physics, which includes liquids and solids. Traditionally it focuses on crystal structure, more recently embracing more complex systems such as alloys, ceramics, amorphous solids, and surfaces.

Solihull [solihuhl] 52°25N 1°45W, pop (2001e) 199 500. Town in West Midlands, C England; a suburb of SE Birmingham; National Exhibition Centre; railway.

soliloquy A stage device whereby a character talks aloud but alone, as it were confiding in the audience. The soliloquies of Richard III and Hamlet are famous examples in Shakespeare. There are similarities with the interior monologue or 'voice-over' in film.

Solingen [zohlingn] 51°10N 7°05E, pop (2000e) 168 000. Industrial city in Germany; in the Ruhr valley; badly bombed in World War 2.

solipsism In philosophy, the theory that 'I' alone exist and that the 'outside world' exists only in my consciousness. The thesis proves hard to refute from within theories such as Descartes', which makes introspection and immediate experience the ultimate source of factual knowledge.

solitaire An extinct dodo-like bird. The name is also used for the **Hawaian honeycreeper** (*Viridonia sagittirostris*) and New World thrushes of the genera *Myadestes* (7 species) and *Entomodestes* (2 species).

soliton A moving, solitary, stable wave having a well-defined position and constant amplitude. They can be observed in water in shallow channels, such as tidal bore waves.

solo One of the family of trick-taking card games, similar to bridge. Players have to declare how many tricks they will win before each game. Tricks are won as in whist, but the declarer plays without a partner (hence the name), and there is an auction.

Solomon (Hebrew Bible) (10th-c BC) King of Israel, the second son of David and Bathsheba. His outwardly splendid reign saw the expansion of the kingdom and the building of the great Temple in Jerusalem. He was credited with extraordinary wisdom, and

Solomon Islands

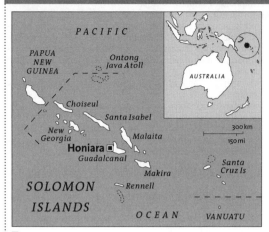

☐ International Airport

Local name Solomon Islands
Timezone GMT +11
Land area 27 556 km²/10 637 sq mi
Population total (2002e) 439 000
Status Independent state within the Commonwealth
Date of independence 1978
Capital Honiara
Languages English (official), with pidgin English and c.80 local languages also spoken
Ethnic groups Melanesian (93%), Polynesian (4%), Micronesian (1.5%), European (1%), Chinese (0.5%)
Religions Christian (95%) (Protestant 41%, Anglican 34%, Roman Catholic 19%)
Physical features Archipelago of several hundred islands in the SW Pacific Ocean, stretching c.1400 km/870 mi, between Papua New Guinea (NW) and Vanuatu (SE); six main islands, Choiseul, Guadalcanal, Malaita, New Georgia, San Cristobal (now Makira), Santa Isabel; highest point, Mt Makarakomburu, 2477 m/8126 ft, on Guadalcanal (largest island); large islands have forested mountain ranges and coastal belts; Anuta, Fataka, and Tikopia

islands are volcanic; Tikopia and Anuta struck by Cyclone Zoë (Dec 2002).
Climate Equatorial climate; high humidity; average annual temperature 27°C; maximum rainfall Nov–Apr; average annual rainfall, c.3500 mm/138 in; periodic cyclones.
Currency 1 Solomon Islands Dollar (SBD) = 100 cents
Economy Based on agriculture; forestry, livestock, fisheries, taro, rice, bananas, yams, copra, oil palm, rice; milling, fish processing; crafts.
GDP (2001e) $800 mn, per capita $622
Human Development Index (2002) 0.622
History Visited by the Spanish, 1568; S Solomon Is placed under British protection, 1893; outer islands (Santa Cruz group) added to the protectorate, 1899; scene of fierce fighting in World War 2; achieved internal self-government, 1976; independence, 1978; British monarch represented by a Governor-General; Prime Minister leads a unicameral National Parliament; fighting between two rival militias led to military coup (Jun 2000) and the resignation of Bartholomew Ulufa'alu; peace treaty brokered by Australia (Oct 2000); continued ethnic unrest, with departure of prime minister Kemakeza from the capital and arrival of Australian-led peace-keeping force (Jul 2003); rioting in Honiara following election of Snyder Rini as prime minister (Apr 2006), arrival of Australian troops, Rini's resignation after 3 weeks in office.

Head of State
(British monarch represented by Governor-General)
1999–4 Sir John Ini Lapli
2004– Nathaniel Waena

Head of Government
1978–82 Peter Kenilorea
1982–4 Solomon Mamaloni
1984–6 Peter Kenilorea
1986–9 Ezekiel Alebua
1989–93 Solomon Mamaloni
1993–4 Frances Billy Hilly
1994–7 Solomon Mamaloni
1997–2000 Bartholomew Ulufa'alu
2000–2001 Manasseh Sogavare
2001–6 Sir Allan Kemakeza
2006 Snyder Rini
2006– Manasseh Sogavare

---

his name became attached to several Biblical and extra-canonical writings.

Solomon (music), professional name of **Solomon Cutner** (1902–88) Pianist, born in London. He won a high reputation as a performer of the works of Beethoven, Brahms, and some of the modern composers.

Solomon, Psalms of A book of the Old Testament Pseudepigrapha, consisting of 18 psalms, probably written c.1st-c BC in response to the Roman occupation of Jerusalem.

Solomon Islands *see panel*

Solomon Sea *Coral Sea*

Solon [sohlon] (7th–6th-c BC) Athenian statesman, law-giver, and poet. As chief archon, he enacted many reforms, and paved the way for the development of democracy at Athens, and her emergence as a great trading state.

solstice An event when the Sun is at its furthest point from the Equator, resulting in the longest day and shortest night (the **summer solstice**) in one hemisphere and the shortest day and longest night (the **winter solstice**) in the other. In the N hemisphere, the summer solstice is on 21 or 22 June and the winter solstice on 21 or 22 December.

Solti, Sir Georg [sholtee] (1912–97) Conductor, born in Budapest. He became director at the Munich Staatsoper (1946–52) and later at Frankfurt (1952–61) and Covent Garden, London (1961–71). He was also artistic director of the Salzburg Easter Festival (1992–3).

solubility The extent to which one substance dissolves in another. It is expressed as the mass/number of moles of a solute which will dissolve in a given volume/mass/number of moles of solvent.

solution A uniform phase, generally liquid, containing more than one component. When one component is present in excess, it is called the **solvent**; minor components are called **solutes**.

Solutrian [solyutreean] In European prehistory, a short division of the Upper Palaeolithic Age, named after the site at La Solutré, Saône et Loire, C France, discovered in 1866.

Solvay process or **ammonia–soda process** A technique for the production of sodium carbonate (an important industrial alkali), devised in 1865 by Belgian chemist Ernest Solvay (1838–1922), and improved by Ludwig Mond in 1870. Sodium chloride is treated with ammonia and then with carbon dioxide.

Somalia

□ International Airport

[sohmahleeuh], official name **Somali Democratic Republic**, Arabic **Jamhuriyadda Dimugradiga Somaliya**
Local name Somaliya
Timezone GMT +3
Area 637 357 km²/246 201 sq mi
Population total (2002e) 7 753 000
Status Republic
Date of independence 1960
Capital Mogadishu
Languages Somali, Arabic (official)
Ethnic groups Somali (85%), Bantu (15%), with Arab, European, and Asian minorities
Religions Sunni Muslim (99%), small Christian minority
Physical features Occupies the E Horn of Africa, where dry

coastal plain broadens to the S, and rises inland to a plateau c.1000 m/3300 ft; forested mountains on the Gulf of Aden coast rise to 2416 m/7926 ft at Mt Shimbiris; main rivers, Jubba and Webi Shabeelle.

Climate Predominantly arid; average daily maximum temperatures 28–32°C in Mogadishu; average annual rainfall 490 mm/ 19·3 in; heavier rainfall (Apr–Sep) on E coast; serious, persistent threat of drought; NE coastal regions strongly hit by Indian Ocean tsunami, 2004.

Currency 1 Somali Shilling (SOS) = 100 cents

Economy Agriculture (c.50% nomadic people raising cattle, sheep, goats, camels); khat (qat), bananas, sugar, spices, cotton, rice, citrus fruits, tobacco, iron ore; textiles; fishing.

GDP (2001e) $4·27 bn, per capita $600

History Settled by Muslims, 7th-c; Italian, French, and British interests after the opening of the Suez Canal, 1869; after World War 2, Somalia formed by the amalgamation of Italian and British protectorates; independence, 1960; from the 1960s, territorial conflict with Ethiopia over Ogaden which has a large Somali population; military coup, 1969; peace agreement with Ethiopia, 1989; governed by a President, Council of Ministers, and People's Assembly; new constitution approved, 1990; NW region seceded as Somaliland Republic, 1991; civil war, 1991–2, forced UN troops to intervene to safeguard food supplies for starving population, 1992; gradual withdrawal of forces, 1993-5; National Salvation Council formed, 1997; peace accord, signed in Cairo by 26 of the country's 28 factions, 1997, but discord ongoing into 2000; transitional government formed, 2000; further peace agreement signed by 42 of the main factions, Jan 2004; members of first parliament for 13 years sworn in, Aug 2004; President Abdullahi Yusuf elected, Oct 2004; fragile peace broken when Islamists gained control of much of S, including Mogadishu (2006); backed by Ethiopian troops, forces loyal to the interim administration defeated Islamists (Dec 2006); violence ongoing in 2007.

Head of State
1980–91 Mohammed Siad Barre
1991–2000 Ali Mahdi Muhammed *Interim*
2000–4 Abdiqassim Salad Hassan (elected by the parliament-in-exile)
2004– Abdullahi Yusuf Ahmed

Head of Government
1987–90 Mohammed Ali Samater
1990–1 Mohammed Hawadie Madar
1991–8 Umar Arteh Ghalib
1998–2000 Hussein Mohamed Aidid
2000–1 Ali Khalif Galaid
2001–3 Hasan Abshir Farah
2003–4 Abdi Yusuf Mohammed *Interim*
2004– Ali Mohamed Ghedi

---

solvent The major component of a solution. Water is often described as the 'universal solvent', but the term is also applied specifically to volatile organic materials such as acetone and ethyl acetate, used in paints and adhesives.

Solway Firth Inlet of the Irish Sea, separating Cumbria, England, from Dumfries and Galloway, Scotland; length c.65 km/40 mi; width at mouth, c.40 km/25 mi.

Solzhenitsyn, Alexander (Isayevich) [solzhenitsin] (1918–) Writer, born in Kislovodsk, Russia. His first novel, *Odin den iz zhizni Ivana Denisovicha* (1962, One Day in the Life of Ivan Denisovich), set in a prison camp, was acclaimed both in the USSR and the West; but his denunciation of Soviet censorship led to the banning of his later, semi-autobiographical novels, *Rakovy kor-*

pus (1968, Cancer Ward) and *V kruge pervom* (1968, The First Circle). He was awarded the Nobel Prize for Literature in 1970 (received in 1974). His later books include *Arkhipelag Gulag* (1973–8, The Gulag Archipelago), a factual account of the Stalinist terror, for which he was arrested and exiled (1974). He lived in the USA for 20 years, returning to Russia in 1994.

Somali [somahlee] A Cushitic-speaking people of Somalia and parts of Kenya, Ethiopia, and Djibouti. Roughly two-thirds are transhumant herders (the Samaal) living inland, with farmers and traders along the coast (the Saab).

Somalia see panel

Somaliland Republic Somalia

somatic gene therapy The notion that a particular gene might be inserted into the body (somatic) cells of individuals who are born with a defective or absent gene. The therapeutic gene may be delivered directly to the body 'in vivo'. Alternatively, an 'ex vivo' procedure may be used where cells are first removed, genetically modified and corrected, then returned to the patient. Although having great promise, technical difficulties with regard to efficiency in gene delivery and function are delaying its introduction into clinical medicine.

Somers (of Evesham), John Somers, Baron [suhmerz] (1651–1716) English Whig statesman, born in Worcester, Worcestershire. He held several posts under William III, culminating as Lord Chancellor (1697), and was president of the Privy Council under Anne (1708–14).

Somerset [suhmerset] pop (2001e) 498100; area 3451 km²/ 1332 sq mi. County of SW England; uplands in the W include Exmoor and the Brendon and Quantock Hills; Mendip Hills in NE, Blackdown Hills in S; county town, Taunton; N Somerset, and Bath & NE Somerset, separate unitary authorities from 1996; Cheddar Gorge.

Somme, River [som] River in N France, rising near St-Quentin; enters the English Channel; length 245 km/152 mi; scene of some of the worst fighting in World War 1 (1916).

Somme, Battle of the [som] (1916) A major British offensive against German troops in NW France (1 Jul–19 Nov) which developed into the bloodiest battle in world history, with more than a million casualties.

somnambulism *sleep-walking*

Somoza (García), Anastasio [somohza] (1896–1956) Nicaraguan dictator, born in San Marcos, Nicaragua. He established himself in supreme power in the early 1930s, and retained power until assassinated. His sons **Luis Somoza Debayle** (1923–67) and **Anastasio Somoza Debayle** (1925–80) continued dynastic control of Nicaragua until the 1979 revolution.

sonar Acronym for **sound navigation and ranging**, a means of detecting underwater vessels and objects, shoals of fish, and seabed features. The device emits pulsed bursts of sound underwater and listens for reflected echoes (**active sonar**), or simply listens for the sounds that a target may itself make (**passive sonar**).

sonata A musical composition, usually for keyboard (harpsichord, piano, organ) or for another instrument with keyboard. The main Baroque type, however, was the trio sonata for two solo instruments (usually violins) and continuo. The 550 or so keyboard sonatas of Domenico Scarlatti are nearly all single-movement works, but the classical sonatas of Haydn, Mozart, and Beethoven are mostly in three or four movements.

sonatina A sonata of modest proportions, often not difficult to play.

Sonderbund [zonderbunt] A political and military league of seven Swiss Catholic cantons formed in 1845 to resist liberal plans for centralization. The 25-day Sonderbund War (1847) ended with their defeat, and the creation of a Federal State (1848).

Sondheim, Stephen (Joshua) [sondhiym] (1930–) Composer and lyricist, born in New York City. He earned his first success with his lyrics for *West Side Story* (1957) and Jule Styne's *Gypsy* (1959). His own highly successful musicals include *A Funny Thing Happened on the Way to the Forum* (1962), *Follies* (1971), *Sweeney Todd* (1979), and *Sunday in the Park with George* (1984, Pulitzer). Later works include *Passion* (1994).

songbird A bird of the passerine sub-order Oscines. This sub-order includes most birds renowned for their singing ability.

song cycle A sequence of separate songs united by some common theme or narrative thread. The earliest was perhaps Beethoven's *An die ferne Geliebte* (1816, To the Distant Beloved).

Song or **Sung dynasty** (960–1279) A Chinese dynasty established by Taizu (r.960–76), which re-unified China after post-Tang confusion. The period is famed for its art, literature, and historical writing, besides important agrarian, financial, industrial, scientific, and technological progress. There were two dynastic phases: the Northern Song (960–1126) had its capital at Kaifeng on the Yellow River; later all N China was lost, and the Southern Song relocated to Hangzhou, S of the Yangtze. The dynasty fell to the Mongols under Kublai Khan.

Songhai [songgiy] A W African state which rose to power in the second half of the 15th-c, commanding the trade routes of the Sahara. Songhai peoples still control much of the Saharan caravan trade.

Song of Solomon, Song of Songs, or **Canticles** A book of the Hebrew Bible/Old Testament, probably a collection of love songs, although sometimes considered a single poem or drama. The collection is usually dated c.3rd-c BC on linguistic grounds.

sonic boom A pressure shock wave created by aircraft travelling at supersonic speeds. The shock wave is produced continually, and travels outwards from the aircraft. Where it meets the ground it is perceived as a loud bang. A sonic boom was also produced when the British car *ThrustSSC* broke the land speed sound barrier in 1997.

sonnet (Ital *sonnetto* 'little song') A poem of 14 lines, usually in iambic pentameter, and with a structural balance between the first 8 lines (*octave*) and the last 6 (*sestet*). It was introduced in 13th-c Italy.

Soper, Donald (Oliver) Soper, Baron [sohper] (1903–98) Methodist minister, born in London. Widely known for his open-air speaking on London's Tower Hill, he wrote many books on Christianity and social questions.

sopherim *scribe*

Sophists [sofists] Itinerant teachers (literally 'experts') in 5th-c Greece who, for a fee, offered professional training in rhetoric, and other skills to aspiring public figures. They are vividly portrayed in the dialogues of Plato, usually as dialectical opponents of Socrates. Among the best known was Protagoras.

Sophocles [sofokleez] (c.496–406 BC) Greek tragic playwright, born in Colonus Hippius. He wrote 123 plays, of which only seven survive: *Ajax, Electra, Women of Trachis, Philoctetes*, and his three major plays *Oedipus Rex, Oedipus at Colonus*, and *Antigone*.

Sophonias [sofoniyas] *Zephaniah, Book of*

Sopwith, Sir Thomas (Octave Murdoch) (1888–1989) Aircraft designer and sportsman, born in London. He built many of the aircraft used in World War 1, such as the Sopwith Camel.

sorbic acid A permitted food preservative which can inhibit the growth of moulds. It is obtained from the unripe fruits of the mountain ash.

Sorbonne [saw(r)bon] *Paris, University of*

Sorbs *Wends*

sorcery *witchcraft*

Sorenstam, Annika [sorenstam] (1970–) Golfer, born in Stockholm. A promising tennis player, at age 16 she turned instead to golf. In 1990 she won a sports scholarship to study at the University of Arizona, USA, winning several collegiate titles and the 1992 World Amateur Team Championship. Turning professional, she debuted with the LPGA Tour in 1994 and was named Rookie of the Year. Her achievements to date include the British Women's Open (2003), and three-times winner of the Women's US Open (1995, 1996, 2006).

sorghum [saw(r)guhm] A cereal resembling maize in general appearance, but with dense heads of small grains. The most important is *Sorghum vulgare*, also called **kaffir corn** or **guinea corn**, cultivated as a staple food in much of Africa and parts of Asia, and in America and Australia for animal feed. (Genus: *Sorghum*, 60 species. Family: Gramineae.)

sororate *levirate*

sorority *fraternity and sorority*

Soros, George [sawros] (1930–) Financier and philanthropist, born in Budapest. He joined a merchant bank in London, then worked as a financial analyst in New York City. In 1969 he set up the Quantum and Quota groups of hedge funds, which grew rapidly from his daring speculations, and in 1979 he began to establish a network of Soros Foundations, mainly in E and C Europe, to advance opportunities in education and business. In 1992 his currency speculation earned him about $1 billion (£625 million) after betting that the British government would be forced to devalue sterling and leave the European Exchange Rate Mechanism. In 2000 the Soros funds were badly affected by misguided speculations on internet and telecommunications stocks that failed to pay off.

sorrel Any of several species of dock, native to Europe, usually with spear-shaped, acid-tasting leaves used as vegetables or in salads. (Genus: *Rumex*. Family: Polygonaceae.)

sort and merge A computer package designed to sort or re-sort files of computer data, and to combine two distinct files into a single sorted file.

sorus [sawruhs] A plant structure formed from a number of sporangia. It is usually associated with ferns, where they are arranged in distinctive patterns on the undersides of the fronds. The lid-like flap of tissue protecting the sorus in some ferns is known as the *indusium*.

Sotheby, John [suhthebee] (1740–1807) Auctioneer and antiquarian. In 1780 he became a director of the the first sale room in Britain exclusively for books, manuscripts, and prints.

Sotho–Tswana A cluster of Sotho-speaking peoples of Botswana, Lesotho, the Transvaal, Orange Free State, and N Cape.

soul (music) A strongly emotional type of popular music which followed on from rhythm and blues in the 1960s, and drew on other types of pop music. It is associated primarily with black US singers, such as Aretha Franklin.

soul (religion) Usually, the principle of life, the ultimate identity of a person, or the immortal constituent of the self. In Christian thought, the concept is fused with the idea of the resurrection of the body.

Soult, Nicolas Jean de Dieu [soolt] (1769–1851) French marshal, born in Saint-Amans-La-Bastide, France. He led the French armies in the Peninsular War (1808–14), and was Napoleon's chief-of-staff at Waterloo. Exiled until 1819, he presided over three ministries of Louis Philippe (1832–4, 1839–4, 1840–7).

Sound, The, Danish **Øresund** Strait between Zealand I, Denmark, and S Sweden, connecting the Kattegat with the Baltic Sea; width of narrowest section, 6 km/4 mi; a bridge connecting Copenhagen to Malmö in Sweden was opened in 2000.

sound A wave motion comprising a sequence of pressure pulses passing through some medium, typically air. The source of sound is a mechanical oscillator in a medium. It can be detected aurally, or using microphones or transducers. The speed of sound in air is 332 m/s.

sound barrier *aerodynamics*

sound film Cinema pictures with synchronized sound. A photographic sound record is printed by the side of the picture as a continuous track in which sound modulations are represented by variations of either its density or its width. By 1930, sound film had become universal in cinemas.

sound intensity level Symbol L_I, units db (decibel); noise level relative to the faintest audible sound, which is rated as 0 db. It is related to sound intensity I, units W/m², the power per unit area of the sound wave.

sound navigation and ranging *sonar*

sound recording The conversion of sound into a storage medium from which it can later be reproduced. At first, sound signals were stored by direct mechanical conversion into grooves in a cylinder or disc, and reproduced using a phonograph or gramophone. In **digital recording**, the signal converted into corres-

ponding electrical vibrations is represented numerically. With the *compact disk*, these digits are then directly decoded in the reproducing device, giving a recording that suffers no distortion as a result of the transmission process.

Sousa, John Philip [sooza] (1854–1932) Composer and bandmaster, born in Washington, DC. He became known as the composer of over 100 rousing military marches, and the inventor of the sousaphone.

sousaphone [soozafohn] A musical instrument resembling a tuba, but with the tubing encircling the player's body. It was designed by John Philip Sousa to be played while marching, and was first made in 1898.

souslik [sooslik] or **suslik** [suhslik] A squirrel native to Asia, Europe, and North America; coat may be striped or spotted; also known as **ground squirrel**. (Genus: *Spermophilus*, 32 species.)

Sousse [soos] 35°50N 10°38E, pop (2000e) 109 000. Port in NE Tunisia; founded by the Phoenicians, 9th-c BC; destroyed by the Vandals, AD 434; railway.

South Africa *pp.872–73*

South African Native National Congress *African National Congress*

South America The fourth largest continent, extending c.7500 km/5000 mi from 12°25N to 56°S; area c.18 million km²/7 million sq mi; linked to North America (NW) by the isthmus of Panama; bounded N by the Caribbean Sea, E by the Atlantic Ocean, and W by the Pacific Ocean; includes Argentina, Bolivia, Brazil, Chile, Colombia, Ecuador, Guyana, Paraguay, Peru, Suriname, Uruguay, and Venezuela; outlying islands include the Falkland Is, Galápagos Is, and Tierra del Fuego; the Andes run almost the full W length, rising to 6969 m/22 834 ft at Aconcagua; largest lake, Titicaca; major river basins, the Orinoco, Paraná, and Amazon (containing the world's largest tropical rainforest); considerable evidence of early Indian kingdoms, notably the Incas, destroyed by Spanish and Portuguese invaders during the 16th-c; most countries achieved independence following wars in the early 19th-c. (*see map p.874*)

Southampton, Lat **Clausentum**, Anglo-Saxon **Hamwih** 50°55N 1°25W, pop (2001e) 217 500. Port city and (from 1997) unitary authority in Hampshire, S England; on Southampton Water; major UK port handling container traffic and passenger ships; four tides daily; site of both Roman and Saxon settlements; city status (1964); railway; ferries to the I of Wight and N Europe; university (1952); St Michael's Church (1070); 15th-c Guildhall; football league team, Southampton (Saints).

Southampton, Henry Wriothesley, 3rd Earl of [rothslee] (1573–1624) Courtier, born in Cowdray, Sussex. He was known as a patron of poets, notably of Shakespeare, who dedicated to him both *Venus and Adonis* (1593) and *The Rape of Lucrece* (1594).

South Australia pop (2000e) 1 548 000; area 984 000 km²/379 900 sq mi. State in S Australia; established as a British Crown Colony 1836; became a state, 1901; included most of Northern Territory, 1863–1901; largely desert, notably the Great Victoria Desert and Nullarbor Plain; fertile land in the SE corner irrigated by the Murray R; dry salt lakes inland; Flinders and Mt Lofty Ranges in the E; highest point, Mt Woodroffe (1440 m/4724 ft); Woomera Prohibited Area (weapons-testing range); 9600 km/6000 mi-long Dingo Fence protects S grazing sheep; capital, Adelaide; supplies 95% of world's opals; oranges and other citrus fruit; almost half of Australia's wine produced from the Barossa Valley N of Adelaide.

South Carolina pop (2000e) 4 012 000; area 80 580 km²/31 113 sq mi. State in SE USA; the 'Palmetto State'; settled by the French at Port Royal, 1562; included in the Carolina grant in 1663, but returned to the Crown in 1729; brought under American control after the battle of Guilford Courthouse, 1781; eighth of the original 13 states to ratify the Constitution, 1788; the first state to secede from the Union, 1860; slavery abolished, 1865; re-admitted to the Union, 1868; capital, Columbia; Blue Ridge Mts in the extreme NW; highest point Mt Sassafras (1085 m/3560 ft); flat and (in the S) swampy coastland, cut by numerous rivers and creeks to form the Sea Islands, a major tourist centre; ground rises inland towards the rolling Piedmont, the agricultural and manufacturing centre; textiles and clothing, using the large cotton crop.

South China Sea area c.3 685 000 km²/1 423 000 sq mi. W arm of the Pacific Ocean; subject to violent typhoons; main arms, Gulfs of Tongkin and Kompong; deep basin in NE, reaching 5490 m/18 012 ft.

Southcott, Joanna (c.1750–1814) Religious fanatic, born in Dorset. In c.1792 she declared herself to be the woman in *Rev* 12 who would give birth to the second Prince of Peace. She obtained a great following, but died soon after the predicted date of the birth.

South Dakota [dakohta] pop (2000e) 754 800; area 199 723 km²/77 116 sq mi. State in NC USA; the 'Coyote State'; part of the USA as a result of the Louisiana Purchase, 1803; included in Dakota Territory, 1861; population swelled when gold was discovered in the Black Hills, 1874; separated from North Dakota and became the 40th state of the Union, 1889; capital, Pierre; the Black Hills rise in the SW corner of the state; highest point, Mt Harney Peak (2207 m/7241 ft); W of Missouri R is a semi-arid, treeless plain, one-third owned by Sioux Indians; severe erosion has formed the barren Bad Lands; E of the R Missouri are rich, fertile plains; town of Lead in the Black Hills is the nation's leading gold-mining centre; second largest gold and beryllium producer in the USA; Mt Rushmore (in the Black Hills).

South Downs Way Long-distance footpath following the South Downs of East and West Sussex, S England; stretches from Eastbourne to Harting; length 130 km/80 mi.

South East Asia Treaty Organization (SEATO) An organization founded mainly to provide collective defence in the case of an attack against any one of the eight signatories to the treaty: Australia, France, New Zealand, Pakistan, the Philippines, Thailand, UK, and USA. SEATO's headquarters is in Bangkok. By 1992 it was inactive.

Southend [sowthend], in full **Southend-on-Sea** 51°33N 0°43E, pop (2001e) 160 300. Resort town and unitary authority (from 1998) in Essex, SE England; on the R Thames estuary; famous pier, 2 km/1¼ mi long; railway; airfield; football league team, Southend United (Shrimpers).

Southern Alps Mountain range in WC South Island, New Zealand; length c.320 km/200 mi NE–SW; contains New Zealand's highest peaks, Mt Cook (3764 m/12 349 ft), Mt Tasman (3497 m/11 472 ft), and Mt Dampier (3440 m/11 286 ft).

Southern Cross *Crux*

Southern Ocean *Antarctic Ocean*

southernwood An aromatic shrub (*Artemisia abrotanum*) growing to 1 m/3½ ft; flower-heads globular, florets dull yellow. Its sweetly aromatic leaves are used for flavouring. (Family: Compositae.)

Southey, Robert [suhthee] (1774–1843) Writer, born in Bristol. Although made poet laureate in 1813, his poetry did not become as well known as his prose works, such as his life of Nelson, and his letters.

South Georgia 54°30S 37°00W; area c.3750 km²/1450 sq mi. Barren, mountainous, snow-covered island in the S Atlantic, about 500 km/300 mi E of the Falkland Is; a British Overseas Territory administered from the Falkland Is; length, 160 km/100 mi; discovered by the London merchant De la Roche, 1675; landing by Captain Cook, 1775; British annexation, 1908 and 1917; invaded by Argentina and recaptured by Britain, April 1982; sealing and whaling centre until 1965; burial place of Ernest Shackleton.

South Glamorgan pop (2000e) 419 200; area 416 km²/161 sq mi.

South Africa

☐ International Airport

official name **Republic of South Africa**, Afrikaans **Republiek van Suid-Afrika**

Local name South Africa

Timezone GMT +2

Area 1 233 404 km²/476 094 sq mi

Former county in S Wales, UK; created in 1974, and replaced in 1996 by Cardiff and Vale of Glamorgan counties.

South Korea *Korea*

South Orkney Islands, Span **Orcadas del Sur** area 620 km²/239 sq mi. Group of islands in the S Atlantic; used by British and US whalers since 1821; uninhabited, apart from scientific research; claimed by Argentina.

South Pacific Commission *Pacific Community*

South Pacific Forum An organization founded in 1971 to provide a setting where the heads of government of independent and self-governing Pacific island states could meet to discuss their common political concerns with each other and with Australia and New Zealand; also known as the **Pacific Islands Forum**. It had 16 members in 2007.

South Pole *Poles*

Southport 53°39N 3°01W, pop (2000e) 89 700. Coastal resort town in Merseyside, NW England; the original 'garden city'; a notable golfing area (Birkdale); railway; annual flower show.

South Sandwich Islands 56°18S–59°25S 26°15W. Group of small, uninhabited islands in the S Atlantic, c.720 km/450 mi SE of South Georgia; a British Overseas Territory administered from the Falkland Is; discovered by Captain Cook, 1775; annexed by Britain, 1908 and 1917.

Population total (2002e) 45 172 000

Status Republic

Date of independence 1961

Capitals Cape Town (legislative); Pretoria (administrative); Bloemfontein (judicial)

Languages (co-official) Afrikaans, English, Ndebele, Pedi, Sotho, Swazi, Tsonga, Tswana, Venda, Xhosa, Zulu

Ethnic groups Black African (70%), White (18%), Asian (3%), Coloured (9%)

Religions Christian (most whites and Coloureds and c.60% Africans), traditional beliefs, Hindu, Muslim, and Jewish minorities

Physical features Occupies the S extremity of the African plateau; fringed by fold mountains and a lowland coastal margin to the W, E, and S; N interior comprises the Kalahari Basin, scrub grassland, and arid desert; Great Escarpment rises E to 3482 m/ 11 424 ft at Thabana Ntlenyana; Orange R flows W to meet the Atlantic; chief tributaries, Vaal and Caledon rivers.

Climate Subtropical in E; average annual temperature 4°C (Jan), 17°C (Jul) in Cape Town; average annual rainfall 1008 mm/39·7 in Durban; dry moistureless climate on W coast; desert region further N, annual average rainfall less than 30 mm/1·2 in.

Currency 1 Rand (ZAR) = 100 cents

Economy Industrial growth as a result of 19th-c gold (c.50% of export income) and diamond discoveries; grain, wool, sugar, tobacco, cotton, citrus fruit, dairy products, livestock, fishing; motor vehicles, machinery, chemicals, fertilizers, textiles, clothes, metal products, electronics, computers, tourism.

GDP (2002e) $427·7 bn, per capita $10 000

Human Development Index (2002) 0·695

History Originally inhabited by Khoisan tribes; Portuguese reached the Cape of Good Hope in late 15th-c; settled by Dutch, 1652; arrival of British, 1795; British annexation of the Cape, 1806; Great Trek by Boers NE across the Orange R to Natal, 1836; first Boer republic founded, 1839; Natal annexed by the British in 1843, but the Boer republics of Transvaal (founded 1852) and Orange Free State (1854) were recognized; Zulu War, 1879; South African Wars, 1880–1, 1899–1902; Transvaal, Natal, Orange Free State, and Cape Province joined as the Union of South Africa, a dominion of the British Empire, 1910; sovereign state within the Commonwealth, 1931–61; independent republic, 1961; independence granted by South Africa to Transkei (1976), Bophuthatswana (1977), Venda (1979) and Ciskei (1981), not recognized internationally; politics dominated by treatment of non-White majority following the apartheid (racial segregation) policy after 1948; continuing racial violence and strikes led to a state of emergency in 1986, and several countries imposed economic and cultural sanctions; progressive dismantling of apartheid system by F W de Klerk from 1990; Black Nationalist leader Nelson Mandela freed after more than 27 years in prison, and the African National Congress unbanned, 1990; readmitted into international sport, USA lifted trade and investment sanctions, 1991; most remaining apartheid legislation abolished, 1991; new constitution, 1996; governed by a President, Cabinet, National Assembly and Senate; elections in May 1994 brought victory to the ANC.

Head of State/Government

1961–7 Charles Robberts Swart
1967 Theophilus Ebenhaezer Dönges
1967–8 Jozua François Naudé
1968–75 Jacobus Johannes Fouché
1975–8 Nicolaas Diederichs
1978–9 Balthazar Johannes Vorster
1979–84 Marais Viljoen
1984–89 Pieter Willem ('P W') Botha
1989–94 Frederick Willem de Klerk
1994–9 Nelson Rolihlahla Mandela
1999– Thabo Mbeki

South African Provinces

Name / Area (km² / sq mi) / State capital
Eastern Cape / 170 616 / 65 858 / Bisho
Mpumalanga / 81 816 / 31 581 / Nelspruit
KwaZulu Natal / 91 481 / 35 312 / Pietermaritzburg (Ulundi)
North-West / 118 710 / 45 822 / Mmabatho
Northern Cape / 363 389 / 140 268 / Kimberley
Limpopo / 119 606 / 46 168 / Pietersburg
Free State / 129 437 / 49 963 / Bloemfontein
Gauteng / 18 760 / 7 241 / Johannesburg (Pretoria)
Western Cape / 129 386 / 49 943 / Cape Town

South Sea Bubble A financial crisis in Britain (1720) arising out of speculation mania generated by Parliament's approval of the South Sea Company's proposal to take over three-fifths of the National Debt. Many investors were ruined in the aftermath.

South Shetland Islands area 4622 km²/1784 sq mi. Group of mountainous islands in the S Atlantic; discovered in 1819; occasionally used for scientific bases.

Southwark [suhtherk] 51°30N 0°06W, pop (2001e) 244 900. Borough of C Greater London, UK; S of the R Thames; formerly famous for its inns and Elizabethan theatres (site of Globe Theatre); railway; 13th-c Southwark Cathedral, Dulwich College (1621), Guy's Hospital (1721), Imperial War Museum, Shakespeare's Globe, Tate Modern.

Southwell, Robert (1561–95) Poet and martyr, born in Horsham, Norfolk. Beatified in 1929, he is known for his devotional lyrics, and for several prose treatises and epistles.

Southwest Africa *Namibia*

Southwest Africa People's Organization (SWAPO) A nationalist organization in Southwest Africa (Namibia), which opened a guerrilla campaign against South African rule in Namibia in 1969. Frontline states and the Organization of African Unity gave their support, and Angola provided bases for its liberation movement. At the end of 1988, an international agreement was reached in Geneva linking arrangements for the future independence of Namibia with the withdrawal of Cuban troops from Angola, and the cessation of South African attacks on that country and its support for the UNITA rebels.

Southwest Indians North American Indian groups living in the SW states of New Mexico, Utah, Colorado, and Texas, and in Mexico. Many prehistoric remains provide evidence of early settlement, dating back to possibly 10 000 years ago. The largest Indian groups in North America currently live in the area.

South Yorkshire *Yorkshire, South*

Soutine, Chaim [sooteen, khiym] (1893–1943) Artist, born in Smilovich, Belarus. He became known for his paintings of carcasses, and for his series of 'Choirboys' (1927). He was later recognized as a leading Expressionist painter.

sovereign A British gold coin originally worth £1, but since the abolition of the gold standard worth considerably more. Sovereigns can now be purchased, their price varying with the price of gold.

sovereignty The capacity to determine conduct within the territory of a nation-state without external legal constraint. Where legal limits are placed upon the organs of government by the constitution, as in the USA, sovereignty is claimed to reside with the people.

Caribbean Sea

ATLANTIC OCEAN

TRINIDAD
& TOBAGO

Gulf of
Venezuela

Lake
Maracaibo

Gulf of
Darien

Orinoco

Venezuelan
territorial
claim

Gulf of
Panama

PANAMA

Llanos

VENEZUELA

GUYANA

SURINAME

French
Guiana
(to France)

Kaluta

Magdalena

COLOMBIA

Guiana Highlands

Rio Negro

Branco

Surinamese
territorial
claim

Equator

Equator

Caqueta

Japurá

Amazon

Represa
Balbina

Putumayo

Amazon

Amazon

Amazon

Basin

Maranón

Juruá

Purus

Madeira

Tapajós

Tocantins

Xingu

Araguaia

Tocantins

PERU

A
n
d
e
s

Ucayali

BRAZIL

Represa de
Sobradinho

Madre de Dios

BOLIVIA

Planalto de
Mato Grosso

São Francisco

Brazilian Highland

Lake
Titicaca

Lago
Poopó

PACIFIC OCEAN

Atacama Desert

Pilcomayo

PARAGUAY

Gran Chaco

Paraná

Paraná

Tropic of Capricorn

Tropic of Capricorn

C
H
I
L
E

A
n
d
e
s

A
R
G
E
N
T
I
N
A

Paraná

Uruguay

URUGUAY

Salado

Pampas

Río de la Plata

Colorado

PACIFIC OCEAN

Rio Negro

ATLANTIC OCEAN

P
a
t
a
g
o
n
i
a

Chico

Lago
Colhué Huapí

Gulf of
San Jorge

Deseado

Golfo de
Penas

Bahía
Grande

Falkland
Islands
(to UK)

Strait of Magellan

Tierra del Fuego

Beagle Channel

Cape Horn

soviet Originally, a workers' council established in Russia after the 1905 revolution. They re-appeared as workers' and soldiers' councils, important instruments of the 1917 revolution. Members of soviets were elected by popular vote.

Soviet space programme A dominant element in the exploration of space after the launch of Sputnik in 1957 until the demise of the Soviet Union in 1990. It was formally replaced by the Russian Space Agency in 1992.

Soviet Union, official name **Union of Soviet Socialist Republics (USSR)**, Russ **Soyuz Sovyetskikh Sotsialisticheskikh Republik** (Cyrillic alphabet, **CCCP**) pop (1990) 290 122 000; area 22 402 076 km²/8 647 201 sq mi. Former federation of 15 republics, comprising most of E Europe and N and C Asia, which until its dissolution (1991) jointly formed the world's largest sovereign state; capital, Moscow; ethnic groups included Russian (52%), Ukrainian (16%), and over 100 others; chief religion, Russian Orthodox (18%), with 70% atheist; official language, Russian; unit of currency, the rouble of 100 kopeks; Union Republics were usually known as **Soviet Socialist Republics (SSR)**; there were in addition 20 **Autonomous Soviet Socialist Republics (ASSR)**, and several smaller divisions (6 *krays*, 123 *oblasts*, 8 *autonomous oblasts*, 10 *autonomous okrugs*); formed in 1922 following the October Revolution (1917) and the subsequent Civil War; first Soviet government headed by Lenin; vigorous socialist reform begun by Stalin in the 1920s, including the collectivization of agriculture and rapid industrialization; territories extended to the W after World War 2, with a corridor of communist-dominated countries between USSR and W Europe; period of Cold War following World War 2; intervention to suppress Hungarian uprising (1956) and Czech programme of liberalization (1968); invasion of Afghanistan, 1979–88; series of disarmament agreements in 1980s, with new approach to international relations under Gorbachev; constitutional reforms implemented in 1989 instituted a new Congress of the USSR People's Deputies, which elected from its ranks a 542-member Supreme Soviet; major internal changes in 1991, following the emerging independence of several republics and the reduced role of the Communist Party; failure of an attempted coup (Aug 1991), with resistance led by Yeltsin, resulted in the process of radical reform, liberalization, and recognition of independence movements in the constituent republics; recognition of Estonia, Latvia, and Lithuania (1990–1) was followed by the abolition of the Communist Party and ultimately the country's dissolution (Dec 1991); most of the constituent republics then formed the Commonwealth of Independent States.

sow *pig*

Soweto [sohwetoh] 26°15S 27°52E, pop (2000e) 1 073 000. Black African township in South Africa; the name derives from the official title of South-West Township; linked by rail (8 km/5 mi) to industrial W Johannesburg; student riots in 1976, when several hundred people were killed.

soya bean A bushy, reddish-haired annual (*Glycine max*), growing to 2 m/6¼ ft; pea-flowers rather inconspicuous, violet, pink, or white; pods up to 8 cm/3 in long, hairy; also called **soja** or **soy bean**. The edible seeds (**soya beans**), rich in protein, are eaten as a vegetable and used in the production of flour, margarine and cooking oils, artificial meat, and food for livestock. There are also numerous industrial uses, such as in enamels, paints, and varnishes. (Family: Leguminosae.)

Soyinka, Wole [soyingka, wolay], popular name of **Akinwande Oluwole Soyinka** (1934–) Writer, born near Abeokuta, Nigeria. His writing is deeply concerned with the tension between old and new in modern Africa. His poetic collection *A Shuttle in the Crypt* (1972) appeared after his release in 1969 from two years of political detention. His first novel, *The Interpreters* (1965), was called the first really modern African novel. Later works include

The Open Sore of a Continent (1996), *The Burden of Memory, the Muse of Forgiveness* (1998), a verse collection, *Samarkand & Other Markets I Have Known* (2002), and a memoir, *You Must Set Forth at Dawn* (2006). He was awarded the Nobel Prize for Literature in 1986.

Soyuz (Russ 'union') spacecraft A Soviet basic space capsule, consisting of three modules, and carrying a crew of one to three. It has been flown on several dozen missions, and is capable of precision targeting to soft-land in C Asia. The first flight was in 1967, when its pilot, V Komarov, was killed in a landing accident. Soyuz 19 docked with the Apollo spacecraft in Earth orbit after its rendezvous (1975). The Soyuz spacecraft is being used for crew return and transfer to the International Space Station.

Spaak, Paul Henri (1899–1972) Belgian statesman and prime minister (1938–9, 1946, 1947–9), born in Schaerbeek, Belgium. He became president of the first General Assembly of the United Nations (1946), foreign minister (1954–7, 1961–8), and secretary-general of NATO (1957–61).

spacecraft Vehicles designed to operate in the vacuum–weightlessness–high radiation environment of space; used to convey human crew, to acquire scientific data, to conduct utilitarian operations (eg telecommunications), and to conduct research (eg microgravity experiments). The first spacecraft (Sputnik 1) was launched by the USSR in 1957 (4 Oct).

space exploration An era which began with the first artificial satellite (Sputnik, 1957) and the first manned flight (Gagarin, 1961), with subsequent rapidly evolving capabilities in Earth orbit and Solar System exploration (initiated by Mariner 2, 1962). There has been reconnaissance as far as Neptune, in-depth exploration of Mars and Venus, and detailed study of the Moon. Human activity has been demonstrated to the point of crewed lunar landings (Apollo programme, 1969–72) and continuing space station occupancy (Skylab, Salyut, Mir, International), but remains dangerous and costly. Launch vehicle advances have achieved a re-usable crewed orbiter (US space shuttle), but inexpensive, reliable transportation is still in the future. The USA has retained its dominance, with Europe and Japan increasingly influential; China launched its first spacecraft capable of carrying a human in 1999. In 2004, SpaceShipOne became the first private manned spacecraft to fly to the edge of space and back, winning the Ansari X Prize for the Mojave Aerospace Ventures LLC team led by aviation pioneer Burt Rutan. Space physiological effects and the costliness of launch vehicles are likely to limit the rate at which future exploration proceeds.

Spacelab A research facility flown in the cargo bay of the NASA space shuttle; designed by the European Space Agency. It consists of a pressurized experiment module for scientist–astronaut activities, and one or more pallets upon which telescopes and Earth remote-sensing experiments are mounted.

space shuttle A re-usable crewed launch vehicle. The first-generation US shuttle launched in April 1981; it carries up to seven crew, and is capable of launching a 27 000 kg/60 000 lb payload into low Earth orbit; missions are up to 9 days' duration. It comprises a delta-winged lifting body orbiter with main engines, a jettisonable external fuel tank, and two auxiliary solid rocket boosters. The fleet comprised four vehicles: *Columbia* (first launched 1981), *Challenger* (1983), *Discovery* (1984), and *Atlantis* (1985). The *Challenger* explosion on the 25th flight (28 Jan 1986) 73 sec after launch caused the loss of the crew. The first reflight took place in September 1988, and a replacement fourth orbiter, *Endeavour*, became operational in 1992. A disaster on re-entry in February 2003 destroyed *Columbia* with loss of the crew. The launch in 2005 of *Discovery*, the sister ship to Columbia, was the first since NASA grounded all shuttle flights following the disaster. Once docked with the International Space Station, an astronaut carried out a pioneering six-hour spacewalk to the orbiter's underside to effect repairs to the heatshield. Loss of foam insulation from *Discovery's* tanks during launch led to further shuttle launches being placed on hold until the problems were resolved. The shuttle was re-launched in July 2006 on a successful mission to the ISS, and in September that year *Atlantis* completed a 12-day mission to re-start ISS construction.

space station A long-lived crewed spacecraft in low Earth orbit; examples are US Skylab and the Russian Mir. It is used for biomedical research, astronomy, Earth observations, and microgravity experiments. Eventually, it will be used as a transportation node for human planetary missions. The US space station programme underwent a major redesign in 1993 to incorporate substantial participation by Russia. The first launches to begin the construction of this International Space Station were carried out in 1998 and the first crew arrived in 2000.

space–time A fundamental concept in the special and general theories of relativity. Einstein showed that a complete description of relative motion required equations including time as well as the three spatial dimensions. The form in which time is expressed gives it the mathematical property of a fourth co-ordinate, or dimension.

space tourism *Tito, Dennis*

Spacey, Kevin [spaysee], stage name of **Kevin Spacey Fowler** (1959–) Actor, born in South Orange, NJ. His film work includes *LA Confidential* (1997), *American Beauty* (1999, Oscar), *Beyond the Sea* (2004), and *Superman Returns* (2006). Notable stage performances include *Lost in Yonkers* (1991) and *The Iceman Cometh* (1998). In 2003 he became artistic director of the Old Vic Theatre, London.

spadefoot toad A frog native to Europe, Asia, and North America; sharp projections (*spades*) on hind feet; burrows in dry sandy areas. (Family: Pelobatidae, 54 species.)

spadix [spaydiks] A specialized type of inflorescence in which the usually tiny flowers are crowded on a fleshy, cylindrical axis, generally enveloped by a large bract – the *spathe*. It is typical of the arum family (Araceae).

spaghetti Western A film drama following the themes and settings of the American 'Western', but cheaply produced by European companies on locations in Spain and Italy. The first of this genre was *A Fistful of Dollars* (1964), directed by Sergio Leone and starring Clint Eastwood.

Spain *p.877*

spaniel A sporting dog belonging to one of several breeds originally developed to assist hunters; usually small, affectionate, with long pendulous ears; now popular pets.

Spanish *Romance languages; Spanish literature*

Spanish–American War (1898) A brief conflict growing out of US intervention in the Cuban revolution for independence, effectively ended by the destruction of the Spanish fleet. The war resulted in Cuban independence under US suzerainty, and in US acquisition of Puerto Rico and the Philippines.

Spanish–American Wars of Independence (1810–26) Wars fought in South America, following Napoleon's invasion of Spain (1808): reformers in the major South American colonies set up semi-independent governments (1810). The ensuing wars were fought in two main theatres: Venezuela, New Granada and Quito, where Simón Bolívar was the leading patriot general, and Argentina and Chile, from where General José de San Martín mounted an invasion of the Viceroyalty of Peru (1820–1). The final liberation of Peru was effected in 1824 by Bolívar. The last Spanish garrisons in South America surrendered in 1826.

Spanish Armada A fleet of 130 Spanish ships sent by Philip II of Spain to invade England in 1588. The invasion was in retaliation for English support of Protestant rebels in the Netherlands, the execution of Mary, Queen of Scots (1587), and raids on Spanish shipping. The fleet was routed by English attacks off Gravelines (7–8 Aug); 44 ships were lost in battles and during the flight home around Scotland and Ireland.

Spanish Civil War (1936–9) The conflict between supporters and opponents of the Spanish Republic (1931–6). The 'Republicans' included moderates, socialists, communists, and Catalan and Basque regionalists and anarchists. The 'Nationalist' insurgents included monarchists, Carlists, conservative Catholics, and fascist Falangists. The armed forces were divided. The Nationalist victory was due to the balance of foreign aid; to 'non-intervention' on the part of the Western democracies; and to greater internal unity, achieved under the leadership of General Franco. The Nationalists initially (Jul 1936) seized much of NW Spain and part of the SW, then (autumn 1936) advanced upon but failed to capture Madrid. They captured Málaga (Mar 1937) and the N coast (Mar–Oct 1937); advanced to the Mediterranean, cutting Republican Spain in two (Apr 1938); overran Catalonia (Dec 1938–Feb 1939); and finally occupied Madrid and SE Spain (Mar 1939).

Spanish fly A slender, metallic-green beetle which exudes acrid yellow fluid from its joints; wing cases formerly collected as a source of blistering agent (*cantharidin*) and as a counter-irritant; more popularly (but spuriously) used as an aphrodisiac, where its high toxicity has led to many cases of fatal poisoning. (Order: Coleoptera. Family: Meloidae.)

Spanish Main The mainland area of Spanish South America, known until the 19th-c for its pirates. It extends from Panama to the Orinoco R estuary in Venezuela.

Spanish Riding School A school of classical horsemanship situated in Vienna, founded in the late 16th-c. The school is famous for its Lipizzaner horses, bred especially for *haute école* (Fr 'high school') riding, and originally imported from Spain.

Spanish Succession, War of the (1701–13) A conflict fought in several theatres – the Netherlands, Germany, Spain, the Mediterranean, and the Atlantic – between the Grand Alliance (headed by Britain, the Dutch, and the Habsburg emperor) and Louis XIV of France, supported by Spain. Hostilities arose after the death of the last Habsburg King of Spain, Charles II. The war was concluded by the Treaties of Utrecht.

Spanish Town 17°59N 76°58W, pop (2000e) 99 000. Second largest city in S Jamaica; on the R Cobre; capital, 1535–1872; railway; serves a rich agricultural area; cathedral (1655).

Spark, Dame Muriel (Sarah), *née* **Camberg** (1918–2006) Writer, born in Edinburgh. She was best known for her novels, notably *Memento Mori* (1959), *The Prime of Miss Jean Brodie* (1961), *The Mandelbaum Gate* (1965, James Tait Black), *The Driver's Seat* (1970), *Reality and Dreams* (1996), and *The Finishing School* (2004).

spark ignition engine An internal combustion engine which initiates the combustion of its air/fuel mixture by means of a spark, usually generated by a sparking plug. This type of engine is most commonly found in motor cars.

sparrow A small songbird, native to the Old World; plumage usually brown/grey. (Family: Ploceidae, c.37 species; but some authorities place the sparrow in a separate family Passeridae.)

sparrowhawk A hawk (Genus: *Accipiter*, 24 species), native to the Old World, and to Central and South America; eats birds, other small vertebrates, and insects.

sparrow-weaver *weaverbird*

Sparta (Greece) [spah(r)ta], Gr **Spartí** 37°05N 22°25E, pop (2000e) 16 200. Town in S Greece; on the R Evrotas; refounded on an ancient site in 1834.

Sparta (Greek history) [spah(r)ta] One of the two leading city-states of ancient Greece, the other being Athens. Her defeat of Athens in 404 BC put her centre stage, but she played her role

Spain

□ International Airport

Span **España**, ancient **Iberia**, Lat **Hispania**, official name **Kingdom of Spain**, Span **Reino de España**

Local name España (Spanish)

Timezone GMT +1

Area 504 750 km²/194 833 sq mi

Population total (2002e) 40 998 000

Status Kingdom

Capital Madrid

Languages Spanish (official) with Catalan, Galician, and Basque also spoken in their respective regions

Ethnic groups Spanish (Castilian, Valencian, Andalusian, Asturian) (73%), Catalan (16%), Galician (8%), Basque (2%)

Religions Roman Catholic (99%), other Christian (including Anglican, Baptist, Evangelical, Mormon, Jehovah's Witnesses) and Muslim minorities

Physical features Located in SW Europe, occupying four-fifths of the Iberian peninsula; includes the Canary Is, Balearic Is, several islands off the coast of N Africa, as well as the Presidios of Ceuta and Melilla in N Morocco; mostly a furrowed C plateau (the Meseta, average height 700 m/2300 ft) crossed by mountains; Andalusian or Baetic Mts (SE) rise to 3478 m/11 411 ft at Mulhacén; Pyrénées (N) rise to 3404 m/11 168 ft at Pico de Aneto; rivers run E–W, notably the Tagus, Ebro, Guadiana, Miñho, Duero, Guadalquivir, Segura, Júcar.

Climate Continental climate in the Meseta and Ebro Basin, with hot summers, cold winters, low rainfall; highest rainfall in the mountains; S Mediterranean coast has warmest winter temperatures on European mainland; average annual temperatures 5°C (Jan), 25°C (Jul) in Madrid; average annual rainfall 419 mm/16·5 in.

Currency 1 euro (EUR) = 100 cents (previous to February 2002, 1 Peseta (ESP) = 100 céntimos).

Economy Traditional agricultural economy gradually being supplemented by varied industries; textiles, iron, steel, shipbuilding, electrical appliances, cars, wine; forestry; fishing; tourism; zinc and other mineral ores; cereals, olives, almonds, pomegranates.

GDP (2002e) $850·7 bn, per capita $21 200

Human Development Index (2002) 0·913

History Early inhabitants included Iberians, Celts, Phoenicians, Greeks, and Romans; Muslim domination from the 8th-c; Christian reconquest completed by 1492; a monarchy since the unification of the Kingdoms of Castile, León, Aragón, and Navarre, largely achieved by 1572; 16th-c exploration of the New World, and the growth of the Spanish Empire; period of decline after the Revolt of the Netherlands, 1581, and the defeat of the Spanish Armada, 1588; War of the Spanish Succession, 1701–14; Peninsular War against Napoleon, 1808–14; war with the USA in 1898 led to the loss of Cuba, Puerto Rico, and remaining Pacific possessions; dictatorship under Primo de Rivera (1923–30), followed by exile of the King and establishment of the Second Republic, 1931; military revolt headed by Franco in 1936 led to civil war and a Fascist dictatorship; Prince Juan Carlos of Bourbon nominated to succeed Franco in 1969; acceded, 1975; joined European Union (formerly EC), 1986; terrorist bombings at railway stations in Madrid killed at least 200 people and injured more than 1400 (Mar 2004); under 1978 constitution, the Kingdom of Spain is a constitutional monarchy; Monarch appoints the Prime Minister; governed by a bicameral Parliament (Cortes Generales) comprising a Congress of Deputies and a Senate; moved towards local government autonomy with the creation of 17 self-governing regions.

Second Republic
President
1931–6 Niceto Alcalá Zamora y Torres
1936 Diego Martínez Barrio *Acting*

Civil War
1936–9 Manuel Azaña y Díez
1936–9 Miguel Cabanellas Ferrer

Nationalist Government
Chief of State
1936–75 Francisco Franco Bahamonde

Kingdom of Spain
Head of State (Monarch)
1975– Juan Carlos I

Head of Government
1973 Torcuato Fernández Miranda y Hevía *Acting*
1973–6 Carlos Arias Navarro
1976–81 Adolfo Suárez
1981–2 Calvo Sotelo
1982–96 Felipe González Márquez
1996–2004 José Maria Aznar
2004– José Luis Rodríguez Zapatero

so badly that the other city-states combined against her. Thebes delivered the final blow at Leuctra in 371 BC.

Spartacists A left-wing revolutionary faction (the *Spartakusbund*), led by Rosa Luxemburg and Karl Liebknecht (1871–1919) in 1917, which supported the Russian Revolution, and advocated a German socialist revolution. Luxemburg and Liebknecht were murdered in disturbances in Berlin during the period following the Kaiser's abdication in 1918.

Spartacus [spah(r)takus] (?–71 BC) Thracian-born slave and gladiator at Capua, who led the most serious slave uprising in the history of Rome (73–71 BC). With a huge army of slaves and dispossessed, he inflicted numerous defeats on the Roman armies sent against him, until defeated and killed by Crassus.

Spartakiad [spah(r)takiad] Sporting games held every four years in the former Soviet Union, until 1979 for nationals only. They were named after the ancient Greek city of Sparta, which placed great emphasis on physical fitness.

spasm A sudden intense contraction of a muscle due to stimulation by the nerve that supplies it.

spastic *cerebral palsy*

spathe [spayth] A large sheathing bract which surrounds the specialized inflorescence called a *spadix*. The spathe is often brightly coloured.

Speaker The officer who presides over a legislative chamber. The post originated in 14th-c England, where one member of the House of Commons was designated to speak to the king. In the UK, the Speaker presides over the House of Commons, maintains order, and interprets its rules and practice. He or she is a constituency MP elected by fellow members, but must sever party connections and be entirely impartial. In the US House of Representatives, the Speaker is a leader of the majority party, and expected to assist in securing the passage of his or her party's legislation.

spearmint *mint*

Spears, Britney (Jean) (1981–) Pop singer and actress, born in Kentwood, LA. She attended the Professional Performing Arts School in New York City during school vacations and at age 11 joined the cast of the popular TV show *The All New Mickey Mouse Club*. The title track of her first album, *Baby One More Time* (1999), became a number 1 hit. Later albums include *Britney* (2001), *In the Zone* (2003), and *Greatest Hits: My Prerogative* (2004). She made her film debut in *Crossroads* (2002).

Special Air Service *SAS*

Special Boat Service *SBS*

Special Branch A branch of the British police force principally responsible for investigating offences against public order, including terrorism, sedition, treason, and contravention of the Official Secrets Act. It was formed in 1883.

special education The provision of education to children who have special educational needs. They may be pupils who suffer from some kind of physical or mental handicap, who have learning or emotional difficulties, or whose needs cannot otherwise be catered for within the normal provision. In many cases the pattern is to provide special schools, but the trend in some countries has been for such children to be taught in ordinary schools.

Special Operations Executive (SOE) An organization set up with British war cabinet approval in July 1940 in response to Churchill's directive to 'set Europe ablaze'. It promoted and co-ordinated resistance activity in enemy-occupied territory until the end of World War 2.

special relativity A system of mechanics applicable at high velocities (approaching the velocity of light) in the absence of gravitation; a generalization of Newtonian mechanics, due almost entirely to Albert Einstein (1905). Its fundamental postulates are that the velocity of light, c, is the same for all observers, no matter how they are moving; that the laws of physics are the same in all inertial frames; and that all such frames are equivalent. On this basis, no object may have a velocity in excess of the velocity of light; and two events which appear simultaneous to one observer need not be so for another. The system gives laws of mechanics which reproduce those of 'common sense' Newtonian mechanics at low velocities, and is well supported experimentally, especially in particle physics. Generalized special relativity, incorporating gravitation, is called **general relativity**.

species A group of organisms, minerals, or other entities formally recognized as distinct from other groups. In biology, the species is a group of actually or potentially interbreeding natural populations, reproductively isolated from other similar groups such that exchange of genetic material cannot occur (the **species barrier**).

specific gravity *relative density*

specific heat capacity *heat capacity*

speckle interferometry A technique used in optical and infrared astronomy to produce high-resolution images. It processes numerous short exposures in a way which removes the effects of erratic motions (twinkling) caused by turbulence in the Earth's atmosphere.

spectacles A frame which supports lenses held in front of each eye, designed to correct abnormalities of refraction, such as long or short sight, and *astigmatism* (asymmetry of the cornea). **Bifocal spectacles** have lenses where the upper and lower parts have different curvatures, enabling the wearer to focus on distant and near objects respectively.

Spector, Phil (1940–) Record producer, born in New York City. In the 1960s he developed a distinctive 'wall of sound' style using echo-effects and other innovative recording techniques, with hits by such groups as the Ronettes and the Crystals. His *Christmas Album* remains a festive classic. In 2004 he was arrested and charged with murdering actress Lana Clarkson. After repeated delays, his trial began in 2007.

spectroscopy The study of energy levels in atoms or molecules, usually using absorbed or emitted electromagnetic radiation. Inner atomic electrons give spectra in the X-ray region; outer atomic electrons give visible light spectra; the rotation and vibration of molecules give infrared spectra; the precession of nuclear magnetic moments gives radio-wave spectra.

spectrum The distribution of electromagnetic energy as a function of wavelength or frequency. A common example is the spectrum of white light dispersed by a prism to produce a rainbow of constituent colours. For white light the colours are red, orange, yellow, green, blue, and violet in order of decreasing wavelength. Individual atoms can emit and absorb radiation only at particular wavelengths corresponding to the transitions between energy levels in the atom. The spectrum of a given atom (or element) therefore consists of a series of emission or absorption lines. The device for displaying a spectrum is called a **spectrograph**.

speech pathology The study and treatment of all forms of clinically abnormal linguistic behaviour; also known as **(speech and) language pathology**. In several countries (eg the USA), the designation **speech pathologist** applies to professionals concerned with the treatment of language-handicapped people; in others (eg the UK) the equivalent profession is that of **speech and language therapist**.

speech therapy *speech pathology*

Speed, John (1552–1629) Antiquary and cartographer, born in Cheshire. He published his 54 *Maps of England and Wales* in 1608–10.

speed (pharmacology) *amphetamine*

speed (physics) The rate of change of distance with time; symbol v, units m/s; a scalar quantity. Speed is the magnitude of velocity, but unlike velocity specifies no direction.

speed of light *velocity of light*

speedometer An instrument fitted in a vehicle to show its speed. Usually a cable from the vehicle road-drive rotates a magnet, which induces an eddy current in a non-magnetic conductor attached to a pointer.

speedway A form of motorcycle racing on machines with no brakes and only one gear. Other forms include **long track**

racing and **ice speedway**. The sport originated in the USA in 1902.

speedwell An annual or perennial, some agricultural weeds, native to N temperate regions; flowers solitary or in spikes, blue or white, with a short tube and four petals, upper largest, lower smallest. (Genus: *Veronica*, 300 species. Family: Scrophulariaceae.)

Speenhamland system [speenuhmland] The most famous of many local expedients in Britain to improve the operation of the old poor laws at a time of crisis. The name was taken from the Berkshire parish whose magistrates in 1795 introduced scales of relief for labourers dependent both on the prevailing price of bread and the size of labourers' families.

Speer, Albert [shpeer] (1905–81) Architect and Nazi government official, born in Mannheim, Germany. He became minister of armaments in 1942. Always more concerned with technology and administration than ideology, he openly opposed Hitler in the final months of the war. He was imprisoned for 20 years in Spandau.

Speke, John Hanning (1827–64) Explorer, born in Bideford, Devon. He and Burton discovered L Tanganyika (1858), then Speke travelled on alone, finding the lake he named Victoria. His claims to have discovered the source of the Nile were doubted, so a second expedition set out (1860–3). He died before he was able to defend his discovery.

speleology / spelaeology The scientific exploration and study of caves and other underground features, surveying their extent, physical history and structure, and natural history. When cave-exploring is taken up as a hobby, it is known as **spelunking** (US) or **potholing** (UK), where people descend through access points (potholes) to follow the course of underground rivers and streams.

spelling reform A movement to regularize a language's spelling system. In English, for example, the spelling system is widely perceived as being irregular, because of a relatively small but frequently used number of striking inconsistencies between sounds and letters. This has led to calls for reform – sometimes for the complete replacement of existing symbols (as in Shaw's proposal for a new alphabet), more usually for a 'standardizing system', in which the existing alphabet is used in a way which more consistently reflects the correspondence between sound and symbol. The vested interests of the publishing world, allied to general public conservatism, have so far militated against the widespread adoption of any new system.

spelunking *speleology*

Spence, Sir Basil (Urwin) (1907–76) Architect, born in Mumbai (Bombay), India. He emerged as the leading post-war British architect; examples of his work include the pavilion for the Festival of Britain (1951) and the new Coventry Cathedral (1951).

Spence, Michael A(ndrew) (1943–) Economist, born in Montclair, NJ. He became dean of the business school at Harvard University in 1990. His principal contributions include work on the economics of information and in the dynamic aspects of competition. He shared the Nobel Prize for Economics in 2001 for the analysis of markets with asymmetric information.

Spencer, Herbert (1820–1903) Evolutionary philosopher, born in Derby, Derbyshire. His main work is the nine-volume *System of Synthetic Philosophy* (1862–93). He was a leading advocate of 'Social Darwinism'.

Spencer, John (1935–2006) Snooker player, born in Radcliffe, Greater Manchester. He turned professional in his early 30s and became a key figure in the game's rise in popularity during the 1960s and 1970s. He went on to win the world championship three times (1969, 1971, 1977) and was the first winner of the Benson & Hedges Masters in 1975. Following his retirement in 1991, he became a snooker commentator for BBC television.

Spencer, Sir Stanley (1891–1959) Artist, born in Cookham, Windsor and Maidenhead. He produced many purely realistic landscapes, but his main works interpret the Bible in terms of everyday life, such as 'Resurrection: Port Glasgow' (1950, Tate, London).

Spencer-Churchill, Baroness *Churchill, Winston*

Spender, Sir Stephen (Harold) (1909–95) Poet and critic, born in London. He became in the 1930s one of the group of 'modern poets' with Auden and Day-Lewis. His *Collected Poems, 1928–85* were published in 1985.

Spengler, Oswald [shpenggler] (1880–1936) Philosopher of history, born in Blankenburg, Germany. *Der Untergang des Abendlandes* (1918–22, 2 vols, The Decline of the West) argues that all cultures are subject to the same cycle of growth and decay in accordance with predetermined 'historical destiny'.

Spenser, Edmund (?1552–99) Poet, born in London. His first original work was a sequence of pastoral poems, *The Shepheards Calendar* (1579). His major work, *The Faerie Queene*, uses a nine-line verse pattern which later came to be called the 'Spenserian stanza'.

sperm The male gamete of animals; also called **spermatozoa**. It is typically a small motile cell which locates and penetrates the female gamete (*ovum*). It contains little cytoplasm.

spermaceti [spermaseetee] A waxy oil found in the head of sperm whales (almost 2000 litres/440 UK galls/530 US galls per whale in *Physeter catodon*); solidifies in air; function unclear; formerly used as a lubricant, and in ointments and candles.

sperm whale A toothed whale, widespread in tropical and temperate seas; bulbous head contains spermaceti organ; three species; **sperm whale** or **cachalot** (*Physeter catodon*) is the largest toothed mammal (length up to 20 m/65 ft), grey-black, head up to one-third length of body. (Family: Physeteridae.)

sphalerite [sfaleriyt] A zinc sulphide (ZnS) mineral, also known as **zinc blende**. It is the principal ore of zinc.

sphere In mathematics, the locus in space of all points equidistant from a fixed point (the centre). The distance of each point from the centre is the radius r of the sphere. The surface area of a sphere is $4\pi r^2$; the volume of a sphere is $\frac{4}{3}\pi r^3$.

sphinx [sfingks] In ancient Greece a mythological monster with a human head and a recumbent animal body (usually a lion's). Originating in the east, probably Egypt, it is found throughout the Levant and E Mediterranean.

sphygmomanometer [sfigmomanomiter] A device for measuring blood pressure. An inflatable rubber cuff is placed round a limb (usually the arm), and inflated until the pulse (heard through a stethoscope) can no longer be detected. The cuff is then slowly deflated until the sound of the pulse can be heard again. The first sound heard reflects the pressure of blood in the arteries as the heart actively contracts (*systole*). As the deflation of the cuff continues, a second sound is heard, reflecting the resting pressure (*diastole*) within the arteries. The pressure is read off either electronically or direct from a column of mercury.

Spica [spiyka] *Virgo*

spice A pungent-tasting plant used to flavour or preserve food. The term is used particularly when referring to hard parts, such as dry fruits and seeds, but it can include parts such as flower buds.

Spice Islands *Moluccas*

spider A predatory, terrestrial arthropod; body divided into head (*prosoma*) and abdomen (*opisthosoma*) joined by slender waist; prosoma with 2–8 simple eyes, four pairs of slender legs, and a pair of fangs used to inject poison into prey; opisthosoma bears respiratory organs and usually three pairs of silk-spinning organs. (Class: Arachnida. Order: Araneae, c.35 000 species.)

spider crab A slow-moving crab with a small slender body and long legs; leg span up to 4 m/13 ft in the giant species. (Class: Malacostraca. Order: Decapoda.)

spider monkey A New World monkey; slender with extremely long legs and tail; thumbs small or absent. (Genus: *Ateles*, 4 species.)

Spielberg, Steven [speelberg] (1947–) Film director, born in Cincinnati, OH. He achieved success with *Jaws* (1975, three Oscars), and followed this with science fiction in *Close Encounters of the Third Kind* (1977, two Oscars) and *ET* (1982, four Oscars). Among his many films are *Indiana Jones and the Temple of Doom* (1984, Oscar), *The Color Purple* (1986), *Jurassic Park* (1993, sequel 1997), *Schindler's List* (1993, seven Oscars, two BAFTAs), *Saving Private Ryan* (1998, Oscar), *AI: Artificial Intelligence* (2001), and *Munich* (2005, Oscar nomination). In 1994 he formed a new studio, Dreamworks SKG (bought by Paramount Pictures in 2005), followed in 1995 by Dreamworks Interactive, to produce interactive games, videos, and teaching material. In 2004 he received the Directors Guild of America Lifetime Achievement Award, and the French Legion of Honour in recognition of his work. He received an honorary British knighthood in 2001.

spikelet A structure peculiar to the inflorescence of grasses, consisting of one or several reduced flowers enclosed in a series of small bracts. The spikelets can be arranged in several ways to form the inflorescence.

Spillane, Mickey [spilayn], pseudonym of **Frank Morrison Spillane** (1918–2006) Detective fiction writer, born in Brooklyn, NY. He wrote a series of successful novels featuring detective Mike Hammer. *Kiss Me Deadly* (1952, filmed 1955) typified his work, in its representation of sadism, cheap sex, and casual violence. Later novels included *The Last Cop Out* (1973) and *Black Alley* (1996).

spin A vector attribute of sub-atomic particles, having a precise meaning only in quantum theory, but modelled on classical mechanical spin; symbol *S*. It may be thought of as a particle spinning on its axis, with a higher spin number corresponding to a faster rotation. In the quantum case, only certain values of spin are possible. Electrons and protons have spin $\frac{1}{2}$; photons have spin 1.

spina bifida [spiyna bifida] A congenital defect of one or more vertebrae, in which the arch of a vertebra fails to develop. The condition varies in severity. In serious cases, a *meningocele* or *myelomeningocele* may develop, in which the spinal cord and/or its covering membrane protrude out of the back; the unprotected spinal cord is then vulnerable to damage. The cause is unknown, but it may be related to a deficiency of folic acid in the developing fetus, and pregnant women are sometimes given folic acid supplements to prevent the condition.

spinach beet *beet*

spinal cord That part of the vertebrate central nervous system contained within and protected by the vertebral column, continuous with the medulla oblongata of the brain. It is essentially a long, thick cable formed by thousands of parallel-running axons surrounding a central H-shaped core of grey matter. It has a minute central canal (containing cerebrospinal fluid) which is continuous with the ventricles of the brain. In the human adult it is approximately 45 cm/18 in long; it gives rise to 31 pairs of spinal nerves, which process motor and sensory information.

spin doctors *agenda setting*

spine *vertebral column*

spinel [spinel] The name given to a group of minerals which are double oxides of divalent and trivalent metals. Its principal members are *chromite* ($FeCr_2O_4$), the chief source of chromium, *magnetite* (Fe_3O_4), and *spinel* ($MgAl_2O_4$), which may be valuable as a gemstone.

spinet A keyboard instrument resembling a harpsichord, but with a single set of strings running diagonally to the keyboard. It was particularly popular in 17th-c England.

spinifex A coarse, spiny-leaved grass, native to E Asia and Australasia. The spikelets are massed to form globular heads which break off and act as tumbleweeds before breaking up. (Genus: *Spinifex*, 3 species. Family: Gramineae.)

Spinks, Leon (1953–) Boxer, born in St Louis, MO. He won a gold medal in the light heavyweight division at the 1976 Olympic Games, and went on to briefly hold the world heavyweight title in a split decision over Muhammad Ali in 1978. His brother **Michael Spinks** (1956–) also won the heavyweight title (1983), making them the only brothers to hold world boxing titles. Leon's son, **Cory Spinks** (1978–), became IBF light-middleweight champion in 2006.

spinning The conversion of fibres into yarns. Two main types of yarn were traditionally produced: in *woollen* yarns, the fibres are randomly arranged; in *worsted* types, the fibres lie parallel to the length of the yarn.

Spinoza, Baruch or **Benedictus de** [spinohza] (1632–77) Philosopher and theologian, born in Amsterdam. His major works include the *Tractatus theologico-politicus* (1670), and *Ethica* (published posthumously, 1677). He is regarded as one of the great Rationalist thinkers of the 18th-c.

spiraea / spirea [spiyreea] A deciduous, sometimes suckering shrub, native to the temperate N hemisphere; flowers 5-petalled, white or pink, in dense clusters. (Genus: *Spiraea*, 100 species. Family: Rosaceae.)

spirit control *seance*

spiritism *spiritualism*

spirits Alcoholic beverages produced by distilling ethanol from a fermentation of mash from various sources, such as barley for whisky, sugar cane for rum, and potatoes for vodka. Some are blended with wines to produce such drinks as port, a blend of brandy and wine.

spiritualism An organized religion which believes that spirits of the deceased survive bodily death and communicate with the living, usually via a medium by means of messages, or apparently paranormal physical effects. While many different cultures believe in **spiritism** (the ability of spirits of the deceased to communicate with the living), spiritualism is primarily a Western religion, most commonly found in North America and in Europe, arising in the mid-1800s. It maintains that, through communications with the deceased, people may come to better understand the laws of God. It is frequently criticized for having at least some members who use trickery to produce its phenomena.

spirochaete [spiyrohkeet] A motile, spiral-shaped bacterium. Spirochaetes include the causative agents of such diseases as syphilis and relapsing fever. (Kingdom: Monera. Family: Spirochaetaceae.)

Spirogyra [spiyrojiyra] A genus of filament-like green algae found in freshwater; chloroplast a spiral, ribbon-like band extending along the cell. (Class: Chlorophyceae. Order: Zygnematales.)

spiroplasm A motile, spiral-shaped mycoplasm, parasitic in insects and plants. It includes the causative agent of yellow disease in plants. (Kingdom: Monera. Class: Mollicutes.)

spit A ridge of sand and gravel stretching out along a coastline, deposited by longshore drift and often forming a lagoon on the landward side. A spit which links an island to the mainland is termed a **tombolo**.

Spitalfields An area in the East End of London, which flourished as a centre of silk-weaving from the late 17th-c until the late 19th-c. It lies on the site of a 12th-c spittle-house, or hospital, from which its name derives.

Spitsbergen *Svalbard*

spittlebug *froghopper*

Spitz, Mark (Andrew) (1950–) Swimmer, born in Modesto, CA. He earned worldwide fame at the 1972 Olympics by winning seven gold medals, all in world record time.

spitz [spits] (Ger 'pointed') A dog belonging to a group of breeds, characterized by a curled tail usually held over the back, pointed ears and muzzle, and (usually) a thick coat.

spleen A soft, delicate, relatively mobile organ which is responsible for clearing the body of bacteria, protozoa, and non-living particles; the destruction of red blood cells; and the metabolism of iron, fats, and proteins. It is situated under cover of the rib-cage on the left side of the body towards the midline. It can be ruptured by severe blows to the lower left part of the thoracic cage. In adults, the loss of the spleen does not cause any ill effects.

spleenwort A member of a large and widespread genus of perennial ferns, found especially in the temperate N hemisphere. (Genus: *Asplenium*, 650 species. Family: Polypodiaceae.)

Split, Ital **Spalato** 43°31N 16°28E, pop (2000e) 195 000. Seaport and city in W Croatia; railway; car ferries to Italy and Turkey; university (1974); Diocletian's palace (3rd-c), a world heritage site; cathedral.

Spock, Benjamin (McLane), popular name **Dr Spock** (1903–98) Paediatrician, born in New Haven, CT. In 1946 he published his best-selling *Common Sense Book of Baby and Child Care*. He was a People's Party candidate for the US presidency in 1972 and the vice-presidency in 1976.

Spode, Josiah [spohd] (1755–1827) Potter, born in Stoke-on-Trent, Staffordshire. In 1770 he founded a firm which manufactured pottery, porcelain, and stoneware, and became the foremost china manufacturer of his time.

Spohr, Louis [shpohr], originally **Ludwig Spohr** (1784–1859) Composer, violinist, and conductor, born in Brunswick, Germany. He is remembered chiefly as a composer for the violin, for which he wrote 17 concertos.

spoils system The US practice of filling public offices on the basis of loyalty to the party in power: 'to the victors belong the spoils'. It was said to have originated with De Witt Clinton, governor of New York (1817–23), and was in common use during the 19th-c.

Spokane [spohkan] 47°40N 117°24W, pop (2000e) 195 600. City in E Washington, USA, on the Spokane R; founded, 1872; city status, 1891; airfield; railway; university (1887); commercial centre for inland farming, forestry, and mining areas; two cathedrals.

Spoleto [spolaytoh], Lat **Spoletium** 42°44N 12°44E, pop (2000e) 20 000. Town in Umbria, C Italy; cathedral (11th-c), basilica (4th-c), Roman remains; Festival of Two Worlds (Jun–Jul).

spondylosis [spondilohsis] Degeneration of the vertebral bodies and of the joints between them. It especially affects the cervical and lumbar vertebrae (ie the spine in the neck and lower back).

sponge A multicellular animal with a body that lacks organization into tissues and organs; body perforated by a complex system of internal canals through which flagellate cells propel water; mostly marine, found from inter-tidal zone to deep sea; sometimes freshwater. (Phylum: Porifera.)

spoonbill An ibis-like bird, native to Old World (Genus: *Platalea*, 5 species) or Central and South America (*Ajaia ajaia*); bill straight and broadly flattened at tip. (Family: Threskiornithidae.)

Spooner, William Archibald (1844–1930) Anglican clergyman and educationist. His name is associated with a nervous tendency to transpose initial letters or half-syllables in speech, the **spoonerism** (eg 'a half-warmed fish' for 'a half-formed wish').

spoonworm An unsegmented, soft-bodied marine worm; body cylindrical or sac-like, bearing an extendable tube (*proboscis*) used for food collection and respiration. (Phylum: Echiura, c.140 species.)

sporangium [sporanjium] The organ in which spores are formed in certain types of plant. In algae and fungi they are unicellular; in bryophytes and ferns they are multicellular.

spore A plant reproductive cell which is capable of developing into a new individual, either directly or after fusion with another spore. Spores typically function as a means of dispersal. A spore does not contain an embryo, and is thus distinct from a **seed**.

sporophyte [spohrofiyt] The asexual (spore-producing or *diploid*) generation in the life cycle of a plant, produced by the fusion of two haploid gametes. In ferns and flowering plants it is the dominant part of the life cycle.

Sporozoa [sporozoha] A class of parasitic protozoans found in animal hosts. Several species cause serious diseases in humans and domesticated animals. (Phylum: Apicomplexa.)

sporting dog A dog belonging to a group of breeds developed to assist in field sports; includes pointers, setters, retrievers, spaniels (these four also called **gundogs**); used occasionally to include terriers and hounds.

sports injuries Damage to the body occurring during the course of physical activity and exercise, including bruises, fractures, sprains, and repetitive strain injuries. They may occur due to trauma or overuse. Minor injuries can be treated with rest, ice, compression, and elevation; more serious injuries require medical attention.

sprain Injury to a joint without fracture or displacement of bones. It is usually the result of a twisting movement, in which ligaments and tendons are torn.

sprat Small, slender-bodied fish (*Sprattus sprattus*) widespread and locally common in large shoals in coastal waters from Norway to the Mediterranean; length up to 15 cm/6 in; silver with upper surface green; young fish sold as whitebait. (Family: Clupeidae.)

spreadsheet A computer program which allows data, numbers, or text to be presented in a rectangular matrix. Data can be manipulated in a variety of different ways defined by the user; for example, columns or rows of numbers can be added, interchanged, or multiplied by constants. Spreadsheets provide a powerful means of analyzing numeric data, and are widely used in the commercial world.

springbok or **springbuck** A gazelle (*Antidorcas marsupialis*) native to S Africa; reddish-brown with white rump and thick dark line along side; short lyre-shaped horns with inturned tips; may leap 3.5 m/11½ ft into the air when alarmed.

Springboks The name used by South African sports teams, particularly in cricket and rugby. Adopted by the first South African rugby team touring Great Britain (1906–7), the 1912 team adopted the tradition of taking springbok heads with them to present to teams who beat them. The name's association with apartheid led to many teams, including cricket (which adopted the name Proteas) dropping it in the post-apartheid era. It was retained by rugby union following its victory in the 1995 World Cup.

Springer, Jerry, popular name of **Gerald N Springer** (1944–) Television presenter, lawyer, and politician, born in London. His parents fled Nazi Germany to London, and in 1949 they emigrated to Queens, NY. He began practising law in Cincinnati where he was elected mayor (1977–81). Also pursuing a career in broadcasting, he has hosted the controversial *Jerry Springer Show* since 1991. A show about his life, *Jerry Springer – The Opera*, opened in London's West End in 2003, winning several awards, but its content attracted controversy.

springer spaniel A medium-sized spaniel with thick coat; ears shorter and more highly set than in cocker spaniels; two breeds, white and brown (or black) **English springer spaniel**, and older, shorter-eared, white and red-brown **Welsh spaniel** or **Welsh springer spaniel**.

Springfield, Dusty, originally **Mary O'Brien** (1939–99) Pop singer, born in London. Originally part of The Springfields, her debut solo single 'I Only Want To Be With You' (1964) was a UK hit, as was her debut album, *A Girl Called Dusty* (1964). In the 1990s she acquired something of a cult following, as part of the renewed interest in music of the 1960s.

Springfield (Illinois) 39°48N 89°39W, pop (2000e) 111 500. Capital of state in C Illinois, USA; settled, 1818; city status, 1840; home and burial place of President Lincoln; railway; major commercial centre.

Springfield (Massachusetts) 42°06N 72°35W, pop (2000e) 152 100. City in SW Massachusetts, USA, on the Connecticut R; railway; game of basketball devised at Springfield College.

Springfield (Missouri) 37°13N 93°17W, pop (2000e) 148 000. City in SW Missouri, USA; established, 1829; railway; university; industrial, trade and shipping centre; tourist centre for Ozark Mts.

springhaas [springhahs] A nocturnal squirrel-like rodent (*Pedetes capensis*), native to S Africa; superficially resembles a small kangaroo (length, less than 1 m/3¼ ft) with bushy black-tipped tail; digs burrows; also known as **springhare** or **jumping hare**. (Family: Pedetidae.)

Springsteen, Bruce (1949–) Rock singer, guitarist, and songwriter, born in Freehold, NJ. In 1976, he released a hit in 'Born to Run', and by the mid-1980s had become the world's most popular white rock star. His albums include *Born in the USA* (1985), *The Ghost of Tom Joad* (1995), *The Rising* (2002), and *Devils and Dust* (2005).

springtail A blind, primitively wingless insect often extremely abundant in soils or leaf litter; leaps by means of a forked spring organ folded up on underside of abdomen. (Order: Collembola, c.2000 species.)

spring tide An especially large tidal range occurring twice monthly, produced by the tidal forces of the Sun and Moon acting in conjunction. These maximum monthly tides occur during new and full moon.

spruce An evergreen conifer native to the temperate N hemisphere, especially E Asia; leaves needle-like; cones pendulous, ripe after one year. It is a widespread forestry tree, grown for timber and for its turpentine-yielding resin. (Genus: *Picea*, 50 species. Family: Pinaceae.)

sprue *malabsorption*

spurge A member of a large worldwide genus of diverse, latex-producing plants, annuals or perennials, sometimes shrubs. Some from arid regions look like cacti, and when not in flower can be distinguished from cacti only by the presence of latex. (Genus: *Euphorbia*, 2000 species. Family: Euphorbiaceae.)

Sputnik [sputnik] (Russ 'travelling companion') The world's first artificial satellite. **Sputnik 1** was launched by the USSR (4 Oct 1957) from Tyuratam launch site; weight 84 gk/185 lb; it transmitted a radio signal for 21 days. **Sputnik 2** was launched in November 1957; weight 508 kg/1120 lb; it carried the dog 'Laika', killed by injection after 7 days of returning biomedical data.

squall A sudden increase in wind speed. For at least one minute, minimum velocity must increase by at least 8 m/s (26 ft/s), and reach 11 m/s (36 ft/s) before declining rapidly.

Square Deal The popular name for the domestic policies of US President Theodore R Roosevelt, especially the enforcement of the Antitrust Acts. The term was coined by him during a speaking tour in the summer of 1902.

squark *supersymmetry*

squash (botany) Any of several species of the cucumber family (*Cucurbita maxima / mixta / moschata / pepo*), native to America; all trailing or climbing vines with tendrils; large, yellow, funnel-shaped flowers; fruits of various shapes and colours. **Summer squashes** are eaten before becoming ripe and fibrous; **winter squashes** are eaten ripe and can be stored through winter. (Family: Cucurbitaceae.)

squash rackets (UK) / **squash racquets** (US) A popular indoor racket-and-ball court game, usually called **squash**. It is played by two players on an enclosed court 32 ft (9·75 m) long by 21 ft (6·4 m) wide. Each hits the ball against a front wall alternately. The object is to play a winning shot by forcing your opponent to fail to return the ball.

squid A carnivorous marine mollusc with a streamlined body bearing fins towards the back; eight arms and two tentacles around mouth, used to catch prey. (Class: Cephalopoda. Order: Teuthoidea.)

squill A perennial native to Europe, Asia, and S Africa; flowers star- or bell-shaped, sometimes drooping, blue or purple. (Genus: *Scilla*, 80 species. Family: Liliaceae.)

squint A defect in the alignment of the eyes, most commonly affecting movement in the horizontal plane; also known as **strabismus**. It is usually congenital in origin, and may be associated with an abnormality in focusing.

squirrel A rodent of family Sciuridae (267 species), virtually worldwide except Australasia; fine fur and bushy tail; range from small tree-dwelling squirrels to cat-sized ground-dwelling squirrels, which live in extensive burrows, and may hibernate for up to nine months.

squirrel monkey A New World monkey; small, lively, with long black-tipped tail; white face with black tip to muzzle; coat short, greyish. (Genus: *Saimiri*, 2 species.)

Sri Jayawardenapura-Kotte [sree jiyahwah(r)dnapoora] 6°55N 79°52E, pop (2000e) 122 000. Capital of Sri Lanka since 1983; located in an E suburb of Colombo; relocation ongoing during the 1990s.

Sri Lanka *p.883*

Srinagar [sreenagah(r)] 34°08N 74°50E, pop (2000e) 700 000. Summer capital of Jammu–Kashmir state, N India, on R Jhelum; founded, 6th-c; capital status, 1948; airfield.

SS Abbreviation of **Schutzstaffel** (Ger 'protective squad'), a Nazi organization founded in Germany in 1925 as Hitler's personal bodyguard. Within the Third Reich it became an independent organization, controlling a dominant repressive apparatus, and responsible for concentration camps and racial policy.

stabilizers (shipping) A device which limits rolling in a ship, usually in the form of movable fins. They were first fitted successfully in the P & O liner *Chusan* in 1950.

Staël, Madame de [stahl], popular name of **Anne Louise Germaine Necker, Baroness of Staël-Holstein** (1766–1817) Writer, born in Paris, the daughter of the financier Jacques Necker. Both before and after the French Revolution, her *salon* became a centre of political discussion. She is known for her *Lettres* (1788, Letters) on Rousseau, her romantic novel, *Corinne* (1807), and her major work, *De L'allemagne* (1810, Germany).

Stafford 52°48N 2°07W, pop (2001e) 120 700. County town of Staffordshire, C England; railway; 11th-c castle, destroyed in the Civil War; birthplace of Izaak Walton.

Staffordshire pop (2001e) 806 000; area 2716 km²/1049 sq mi. County in C England; county town, Stafford; Stoke-on-Trent a new unitary authority from 1997; Potteries.

Staffordshire bull terrier A medium-sized terrier developed in Britain as a fighting dog or guard dog; thick-set muscular body with a short coat, broad head, long muzzle, soft ears.

stag beetle A large, dark-coloured beetle; males up to 66 mm/ 2½ in long, typically with large, antler-like processes on head, formed from mandibles. (Order: Coleoptera. Family: Lucanidae, c.1200 species.)

stagecoach A type of horse-drawn coach that appeared c.1640 offering carriage to the public on predetermined routes and stages, usually running between provincial towns and London. The coming of the railways in the 1830s and 1840s ended the dominating role of stagecoaches within public transport. In the USA, the first mail stagecoaches ran between Boston and New York in 1784, but the main period of their use was from 1800 to 1840.

staghound *deerhound*

Sri Lanka

□ International Airport

[sree **langka**], formerly **Ceylon**, official name **Democratic Socialist Republic of Sri Lanka**

Local name Sri Lanka

Timezone GMT +5·5

Area 65 610 km²/25 325 sq mi

Population total (2002e) 18 870 000

Status Republic

Date of independence 1972

Capital Sri-Jayawardenapura (since 1983); (former capital, Colombo)

Languages Sinhala, Tamil (official), English also spoken

Ethnic groups Sinhalese (74%), Tamil (18%), Muslim (7%), Burgher, Malay, and Veddha (1%)

Religions Buddhist (69%), Hindu (15%), Christian (8%), Muslim (8%)

Physical features Island state in the Indian Ocean; separated from the Indian sub-continent by the Palk Strait, linked by a series of coral islands known as Adam's Bridge; low-lying areas in N and S, surrounding SC uplands; highest peak, Pidurutalagala, 2524 m/8281 ft; coastal plain fringed by sandy beaches and lagoons; c.50% of land is tropical monsoon forest or open woodland.

Climate Equatorial, tropical climate; modified temperatures in interior according to altitude; average annual temperature 27°C in Sri-Jayawardenapura; average annual rainfall 2527 mm/99·5 in; greatest rainfall on SW coast and in the mountains; monsoon season (Dec–Feb) in NE, dry, semi-arid for rest of year; severe flooding in SC districts (May 2003) with 200 000 made homeless.

Currency 1 Sri Lanka Rupee (LKR) = 100 cents

Economy Agriculture (employs 52% of labour force); rice, rubber, tea, coconuts, spices, sugar cane; timber, fishing; graphite, coal, precious and semi-precious stones; electricity produced largely by water power; textiles, chemicals, paper.

GDP (2002e) $73·7 bn, per capita $3700

Human Development Index (2002e) 0·741

History Visited by the Portuguese, 1505; taken by the Dutch, 1658; British occupation, 1796; British colony, 1802; Tamil labourers brought in from S India during colonial rule, to work on coffee and tea plantations; Dominion status, 1948; changed former name of Ceylon and became the independent republic of Sri Lanka, 1972; acute political tension between the Buddhist Sinhalese majority and the Hindu Tamil minority, who wish to establish an independent state in the N and E (Liberation Tigers of Tamil Eelam, LTTE); considerable increase in racial violence in the area during the 1980s; state of emergency declared, 1983; ceasefire agreed, 1994, but conflict soon resumed; President Kumaratunga wounded in bomb attack at election rally (1999), but re-elected; suicide attack by Tamil Tigers on international airport (2001); ceasefire agreed (Dec 2001) with mediation by Norway; conflict ongoing; ceasefire and a political agreement reached between government and rebels in late 2002 raised hopes for a lasting peace; Tamil Tigers issued power-sharing proposals (Nov 2003); political crisis after suspension of parliament (Nov 2003); President Kumaratunga dissolved parliament (Feb 2004); Mahinda Rajapakse led minority government (from Apr 2004), president from 2005; renewed violence and conflict with Tamil Tigers, ongoing in 2007; governed by a President, Prime Minister, and National State Assembly; E coastal regions devastated by tsunami, Dec 2004.

Head of State

1978–89 Junius Richard Jayawardene
1989–93 Ranasinghe Premadasa
1993–4 Dingiri Banda Wijedung
1994–2005 Chandrika Bandaranaike Kumaratunga
2005– Mahinda Rajapakse

Head of Government

1989–93 Dingiri Banda Wijedunga
1993–4 Ranil Wickremasinghe
1994 Chandrika Bandaranaike Kumaratunga
1994–2000 Sirimavo R D Bandaranaike
2000–1 Ratnasiri Wickremanayake
2001–4 Ranil Wickremesinghe
2004–5 Mahinda Rajapakse
2005– Ratnasiri Wickremanayake

---

stained glass Pieces of different coloured glass mounted in lead framing to form a pictorial image. It was introduced from Byzantine art for the windows of European buildings in the late 12th-c, and flourished most splendidly in Western Romanesque and Gothic churches. It was revived in the 19th-c.

stainless steels A group of steels which resist rusting and chemical attack through the addition of nickel and chromium. They are used to make utensils, cutlery, and chemical reaction vessels.

stakeholder economy *New Labour*

stalactites and stalagmites Icicle-like deposits of limestone formed by precipitation from slowly dripping water from the ceilings of caves. **Stalactites** grow from the ceiling, while **stalagmites** form on the floor and grow upwards at a rate of less than half a millimetre per year.

Stalin, Joseph, originally **Joseph Vissarionovich Djugashvili** (1879–1953) Georgian Marxist revolutionary and later virtual dictator of the Soviet Union (1928–53), born in Gori, Georgia. As a leading Bolshevik he played an active role in the October Revolution (1917), and in 1922 became general secretary of the Party Central Committee, a post he held until his death. After Lenin's death (1924) he pursued a policy of building 'socialism in one country', and gradually isolated and disgraced his political rivals, notably Trotsky. In 1928 he launched the campaign for the collectivization of agriculture during which millions of peasants perished, and the first 5-year plan for the forced industrialization of the economy. Between 1934 and 1938 he inaugurated a massive purge of the party, government, armed forces, and intelligentsia in which millions of so-called 'enemies of the people' were imprisoned, exiled, or shot. He took part in the conferences of Teheran, Yalta, and Potsdam which resulted in Soviet military and political control over the liberated countries of post-war E and C Europe. From 1945 his foreign policies contributed to the Cold War between the Soviet Union and the West. He was posthumously denounced by Khrushchev at the 20th Party Congress (1956) for crimes against the Party and for building a 'cult of personality'. Under Gorbachev many of Stalin's victims were rehabilitated, and the whole phenomenon of 'Stalinism' officially condemned.

Stalingrad, Battle of (1942–3) One of the great battles of World War 2, fought between Nazi German and Soviet troops in and around Stalingrad (now Volgograd) on the R Volga during the winter of 1942–3. The Germans alone suffered over 300 000 casualties, many of whom were taken as prisoners-of-war. The city was almost totally destroyed. The battle is regarded as a major turning-point in the Allied victory over Germany.

Stalinism A label used pejoratively outside the former USSR to refer to the nature of the Soviet regime 1928–53. It refers to a tightly disciplined and bureaucratic system, with the party hierarchy having a monopoly of political and economic power. It also encompasses the total subservience of society and culture to political ends, suppression of political opponents, terrorism, and the acceptance of dogmas in the communist movement of Stalin's time.

Stallone, Sylvester [stalohn] (1946–) Film actor, born in New York City. He became known as an action-film hero through the success of his first film *Rocky* (1976, 2 Oscars), which he also wrote. He went on to write and direct its sequels (1979, 1982, 1985, 1990), and brought his hero out of retirement for *Rocky Balboa* in 2006. Other films include *Rambo* and sequel (1985, 1988), *The Hunter* (1997), *Get Carter* (2000), and *D-Tox* (2002).

stamen The male organ of a flower, consisting of a stalk-like *filament* bearing sac-like *anthers* containing pollen. The number and arrangement is often diagnostic for plant families.

Stamitz, Johann (Wenzel Anton) [shtamits] (1717–57) Violinist and composer, born in Havlíčkův Brod, Czech Republic. His works include 74 symphonies, several concertos, chamber music, and a Mass. His school of symphonists had a profound influence on Mozart.

stammering *stuttering*

Stamp Act A British Act passed in 1765 by the administration of George Grenville (1712–70), which levied a direct tax on all papers required in discharging official business in the American colonies. It was the first direct tax levied without the consent of the colonial assemblies, and caused much discontent in the colonies. It was withdrawn in 1766.

Standard Generalized Mark-up Language (SGML) A standard for coding documents so that they can be stored in a document database and presented on an output medium in the correct form for that medium. For example, if the output were to be printed it would appear in one form; if it were to be presented on a computer screen it would be in a different form; but in each case the presentation would be what was appropriate for that document. A development in the 1990s for generating World Wide Web pages is the **HyperText Mark-up Language (HTML)**.

standard language The variety of a language which has greatest social and political prestige within a speech community. It cuts across regional differences in usage, and functions as a linguistically 'neutral' norm for use in the media and education.

standard of living The level of welfare achieved by a nation or group; usually measured in terms of food, clothing, housing, and other material benefits. A simple measure for comparative purposes is gross national product per head of population. This shows a very fast rate of growth in W Europe, the USA, and Japan, and a very wide gap between the richest nations and the poorest.

Standard Positioning Service *Global Positioning System*

standard time The officially established local time adopted by a region or country, + or − so many hours from Greenwich Mean Time. The Earth can be divided into 24 time zones each based on sections of 15° of longitude. In each of these, standard time is calculated from the position of the Sun at a central point within the zone. In the USA there are seven standard time zones and in continental Europe two (+1 hour and +2 hours from GMT). Zones differ generally by a whole hour, although there are a few cases of half-hour zones (eg South Australia, India). The system was mainly the creation of the railroad engineer Sir Sandford Fleming; it officially came into existence in 1884.

Standish, Myles (c.1584–1656) Colonist, probably born in Ormskirk, Lancashire. He sailed with the *Mayflower* in 1620, and became military head of the first American settlement at Plymouth, MA, and treasurer of the colony (1644–9).

Stanford, Sir Charles (Villiers) (1852–1924) Composer, born in Dublin. He wrote several major choral works, six operas, seven symphonies, and a great deal of chamber music, songs, and English church music.

Stanhope, James Stanhope, 1st Earl [stanuhp] (1675–1721) British soldier and statesman, born in Paris. He commanded in Spain during the War of the Spanish Succession (1701–13), was secretary of state for foreign affairs under George I, and became his chief minister in 1717.

Stanislavsky [stanislavskee], originally **Konstantin Sergeyevich Alexeyev** (1863–1938) Actor, theatre director, and teacher, born in Moscow. In 1898 he helped to found the Moscow Arts Theatre. His teaching on acting remains the basis of much Western actor-training and practice.

Stanisław I Leszczyński [stanislav leshinskee] (1677–1766) King of Poland (1704–9, 1733–5), born in Lvov, Ukraine (formerly Poland). After his election in 1704, he was driven out by Peter the Great. Re-elected in 1733, he lost the War of the Polish Succession, and formally abdicated in 1736.

Stanley 51°45S 57°56W, pop (2000e) 1600. Port and capital of the Falkland Is, on the E coast of East Falkland; airport.

Stanley, Sir Henry Morton, originally **John Rowlands** (1841–1904) Explorer and journalist, born in Denbigh, Denbighshire. In 1867 he joined the *New York Herald*, and in 1869 was told to 'find Livingstone' in Africa. In 1871 he left Zanzibar for Tanganyika and encountered Livingstone at Ujiji. In later expeditions, he explored L Tanganyika, traced the Congo to the sea, founded the Congo Free State, and went to the aid of Emin Pasha in the Sudan.

Stanleyville *Kisangani*

Stannaries Former tin-mining districts of Cornwall, UK, lying within the lands of the Duchy of Cornwall. The tin miners of the Stannaries held special privileges, including the right to send representatives to the Stannary Parliament and to administer their own courts.

Stanton, Elizabeth, *née* **Cady** (1815–1902) Social reformer and women's suffrage leader, born in Johnstown, NY. She involved herself in the anti-slavery and temperance movements, and was personally responsible for the emergence of women's suffrage as a public issue. In 1848 she helped to organize the first women's rights convention, and with Susan B Anthony founded the National Woman Suffrage Movement in 1869.

stapelia [stapeelia] A perennial native to arid areas of tropical and S Africa, superficially resembling cacti, and similarly drought-adapted; fleshy, green stems swollen with water-storage tissue; large carrion flowers mottled red or maroon produce an overpowering smell of rotten meat. (Genus: *Stapelia*, 75 species. Family: Asclepiadaceae.)

Staphylococcus [stafilohkokus] A spherical bacterium c.1 micron in diameter, commonly occurring in clusters, and requiring oxygen for growth. It can cause superficial abscesses, and chronic to fatal systemic infections. (Kingdom: Monera. Family: Micrococcaceae.)

Staples, The *Farne Islands*

star (astronomy) A sphere of matter held together entirely by its own gravitational field, and generating energy by means of nuclear fusion reactions in its deep interior. The important distinguishing feature of a star is the presence of a natural nuclear reactor in its core, where the pressure of the overlying mass of material is sufficient to cause nuclear reactions, principally the conversion of hydrogen to helium. (*see panel*)

starch $(C_6H_{10}O_5)_n$. A carbohydrate; a condensation polymer of glucose, and isomeric with cellulose, found as a reserve material in living cells. Its non-food uses include adhesives, pill fillers, and paper sizing.

Star Chamber, Court of the The royal prerogative court in Britain for hearing subjects' petitions and grievances, increasingly prominent under the Tudors and early Stuarts. It became notorious for its oppressive methods, and was abolished by the Long Parliament in 1641.

star cluster A group of stars physically associated in space. Dense, globular clusters are spherical, have hundreds of thousands of stars distributed in a halo around a galaxy, and are very old, of similar age to the Galaxy itself.

starfish A typically 5-armed, star-shaped marine invertebrate (echinoderm); most species omnivorous, feeding as scavengers or predators; contains c.1500 living species; also called **sea star**. (Phylum: Echinodermata. Subclass: Asteroidea.)

starling A songbird, native to the Old World, with some introduced to the Americas; plumage often with metallic sheen, usually dark but sometimes colourful; flocks often a major nuisance on city buildings and large structures. (Family: Sturnidae, 92 species.)

Star of Bethlehem A star mentioned in *Matt* 2.1–12, depicted as heralding Jesus's birth and guiding magi from the East to the birthplace in Bethlehem. Although sometimes considered a comet (Halley's comet, c.11 BC), a supernova, or a conjunction of Jupiter and Saturn in the constellation Pisces (c.7 BC), it is doubtful that these can explain the sustained presence or movement that is described.

star-of-Bethlehem A perennial with a small bulb (*Ornithogalum umbellatum*), native to S Europe and the Mediterranean region; leaves narrow, grooved, with a white stripe down the centre; six narrow petals, white with a green stripe on the back. (Family: Liliaceae.)

Star of David or **Magen David** ('Shield of David') A six-pointed star, consisting of two crossed equilateral triangles, which in the last two centuries has come to symbolize Judaism. It appears on Israel's national flag today as a blue design against white.

Starr, Kenneth (1946–) Lawyer, born in Vernon, TX. He rose rapidly as a Republican lawyer, becoming solicitor general. He became nationally known as the Independent Prosecutor chosen to investigate the alleged misdeeds of President Clin-

The Nearest Stars

Star	Distance (light years)
Proxima Centauri	4·24
Alpha Centauri A	4·34
Alpha Centauri B	4·34
Barnard's Star	5·97
Wolf 359 (CN Leonis)	7·80
Lalande 21185	8·19
UV Ceti A	8·55
UV Ceti B	8·55
Sirius A	8·67
Sirius B	8·67
Ross 154	9·52
Ross 248 (HH Andromedae)	10·37
Epsilon Eridani	10·63
Ross 128 (FI Virginis)	10·79
L 789-6	11·12
GX Andromedae	11·22
GQ Andromedae	11·22
61 Cygni A	11·22
61 Cygni B	11·22
HD 173739	11·25
Epsilon Indi	11·25
Tau Ceti	11·41

ton, first with reference to the Whitewater scandal, then in relation to Paula Jones and Monica Lewinsky. The 'Starr Report' into the latter appeared in the autumn of 1998, and he himself gave evidence before a Congressional judiciary committee set up to consider the question of impeachment.

START [stah(r)t] Acronym for **Strategic Arms Reduction Talks**, held between the USA and USSR in 1982 and 1983, adjourned, then resumed at the end of the decade between Presidents Reagan and Bush and General Secretary Gorbachev. **START 1** (the first **Strategic Arms Reduction Treaty**) was signed in 1991, and aimed to cut the overall number of nuclear warheads held by the two super-powers by between 25% and 30%. In 1992, a second treaty (**START 2**) was agreed between Presidents Bush and Yeltsin, by which the USA and Russia agreed to cut by two-thirds their stocks of long range, land-based missiles with multiple warheads. The treaty was ratified by the USA in 1996 and by Russia in 2000, opening the way forward for talks on a **START 3**.

Star Trek US science-fiction television series created by Gene Roddenberry. Although only 72 episodes were made before its withdrawal by NBC because of poor ratings in 1969, the adventures of the starship *Enterprise*, boldly going where no man had gone before, and led by Captain James T Kirk (William Shatner) and the half-Vulcan/half-human Mr Spock (Leonard Nimoy) inspired great loyalty and affection among thousands of fans (*Trekkies*). Three other series were produced in the 1990s: *Star Trek: The Next Generation* and *Deep Space Nine*, with Captain Jean-Luc Picard (Patrick Stewart); and *Star Trek: Voyager*, with Captain Kathryn Janeway (Kate Mulgrew). A new 'prequel' series entitled *Enterprise* appeared in 2002 and starred Scott Bakula as Captain Jonathan Archer. By 2003 there had been 10 *Star Trek* feature films.

Star Wars *SDI*

Stasi *German reunification*

State Department The oldest department of the US government, established by the fourth Act of Congress (Jul 1789), responsible to the president for the conduct of foreign affairs. It is headed by a secretary of state, and is regarded as the most senior department of government.

Staten Island [statn] pop (2000e) 443 700; area 153 km²/59 sq mi. Borough of New York City, USA; separated from Long Island by the Narrows; first settled in 1641; named by early Dutch settlers after the *Staaten* or States General of 17th-c Holland.

states' rights A US Constitutional doctrine that the separate states enjoy areas of self-control which cannot be breached by the federal government. The doctrine flourished among white Southerners between Reconstruction and the Civil Rights Movement, and amounted to a code term for white supremacy.

static electricity Electric charge which does not flow. Objects can acquire a static charge by rubbing against one another (eg by combing hair or rubbing a toy balloon on wool), which transfers electrons from one object to the other.

statics *disequilibrium*

Stations of the Cross A popular form of devotion in the Roman Catholic and some Anglican Churches. It consists of meditating on a series of 14 pictures or carvings recalling the passion of Christ from his condemnation to his burial.

statistical mechanics A branch of physics which provides a link between large-scale phenomena involving many atoms or molecules, and the microscopic properties and interactions of individual atoms and molecules. The subject is essential in understanding critical phenomena and the thermodynamic properties of solids.

statistics The branch of mathematics which deals with the collection and analysis of numerical data. Numbers commonly found useful are those representative of a set of data – 'averages', such as *mean*, *median*, and *mode*, and those indicating variation in the data, describing the spread or dispersion, such as *range* and *standard deviation*.

Statue of Liberty *Liberty, Statue of*

status The social position a person occupies, and the rank or esteem it enjoys. Systems of social stratification may be based on a strong status order, as in traditional caste systems, or status may be just one dimension of a more complex social hierarchy.

statute A particular law passed by the legislature, such as an act of parliament. A statute has a short title by which it is generally known, eg the Housing Act (1985).

Stauffenberg, Claus, Graf von (Count of) [shtowfnberg] (1907–44) German soldier, born in Jettingen, Germany. A colonel on the German general staff in 1944, he placed the bomb in the unsuccessful attempt to assassinate Hitler at Rastenburg (20 Jul 1944). He was shot next day.

Stavanger [stavanger] 58°58N 5°45E, pop (2000e) 103 000. Seaport in SW Norway; founded, c.8th-c; airport; rail terminus; important North Sea oil centre; cathedral (12th-c).

Steadman, Alison (1946–) Actress, born in Liverpool, Merseyside. Major roles include *Abigail's Party* (1977, Best Actress, Evening Standard Awards), and *The Rise and Fall of Little Voice* (1992, Best Actress, Olivier Awards). Television work includes *The Singing Detective* (1986), *Pride and Prejudice* (1995), *Fat Friends* (2000–5), and the series *The Worst Week of My Life* (2004–).

steady-state theory One of two rival theories of cosmology (the other is the 'big bang'), proposed in 1948. It asserts that the universe is infinitely old, and contains the same density of material (on average) at all points and at all times. From the mid-1960s this model fell out of favour.

steam The vapour phase of water (H_2O); also called **live steam**, to distinguish it from **dead steam**, visible droplets of recondensed vapour.

steam engine An external combustion engine, in which the engine's working fluid (steam) is generated in a boiler outside the engine. The steam is brought into the engine by valves, and through its pressure and expansive properties a piston is made to oscillate within a cylinder. This oscillatory motion is then converted into rotary motion by means of a crankshaft mechanism.

steamship *ship*

stearic acid [steearik] $C_{17}H_{35}COOH$, IUPAC **octadecanoic acid**, melting point 71°C. A waxy solid, the commonest of the fatty acids obtained from the saponification of animal fat. It is used in soap and candle manufacture.

stearin(e) [steearin] The name used to describe fats derived from stearic acid, and also for a mixture of stearic and palmitic acids used in candle manufacture.

steatite [steeuhtiyt] *talc*

Steel, Danielle (Fernande Schuelein) (1947–) Writer, born in New York City. A best-selling writer of romantic fiction, she achieved success with her fourth novel, *The Promise* (1978). She has also published several works of non-fiction, including *Having a Baby* (1984), *His Bright Light* (1998), and the Max and Martha series of children's books (1989).

Steel (of Aikwood), David (Martin Scott), Lord (1938–) British politician and leader of the Liberal Party (1976–88), born in Kirkcaldy, Fife. He sponsored a controversial bill to reform the laws on abortion (1966–7), and was active in the anti-apartheid movement. In 1981 he led the party into an Alliance with the Social Democratic Party, and following successful merger negotiations between the two parties (1987–8) was the last leader of the Liberal Party. He was elected to the Scottish Parliament in 1999.

steel The chief alloy of iron, and the most used of all metals. It consists of iron hardened by the presence of a small proportion of carbon. Most steel used today is a simple **carbon steel**, but there exist many special steels formed by the addition of other metals, such as high alloy steels for tools, and **stainless steel** (with nickel and chromium).

steel band An ensemble, native to Trinidad, consisting mainly of steel drums – tuned percussion instruments made from used oildrums. Steel bands are typically heard at West Indian Carnivals and other community festivities.

Steele, Sir Richard (1672–1729) Essayist, playwright, and politician, born in Dublin. He is best known for the satirical, political, and moral essays which formed much of the content of the new periodicals *The Tatler* (1709–11), which he founded, and *The Spectator* (1711–12), which he co-founded with Addison.

Steen, Jan (Havickszoon) [stayn] (1626–79) Painter, born in Leyden, The Netherlands. His best works were genre pictures of social and domestic scenes depicting the everyday life of ordinary folk, as in 'The Music Lesson' (National Gallery, London).

steenbok or **steinbok** A dwarf antelope (*Raphicerus campestris*) native to Africa S of the Sahara; reddish-brown with white underparts; large ears with white insides; short vertical horns.

steeplechase 1 A form of National Hunt horse racing in which the horses have to negotiate fixed fences normally 3–4 ft (0·9–1·2 m) high. The first steeplechase was in Ireland in 1752, between Buttevant Church and St Mary's, Doneraile. **2** A track athletics event over 3000 m. The competitors have to negotiate 28 hurdles and seven water jumps. Each obstacle is 3 ft (0·9 m) high.

Stegodon [stegodon] An extinct, elephant-like mammal known from the Pliocene epoch of India; upper tusks long and very closely placed together. (Order: Proboscidea.)

Stegosaurus [stegosawrus] A large dinosaur attaining a length of 9 m/30 ft; characterized by two rows of plates along back from skull to tail; four-legged, but forelimbs shorter than hindlimbs; known from the Upper Jurassic period of Colorado. (Order: Ornithischia.)

Steiger, Rod(ney Stephen) [stiyger] (1925–2002) Film actor, born in Westhampton, NY. An exponent of the Method, he became known following his role in *On the Waterfront* (1954). Later films include *Al Capone* (1958), *Dr Zhivago* (1965), *The Pawnbroker* (1965), *In the Heat of the Night* (1967, Oscar), and *End of Days* (1999).

Stein, Gertrude [stiyn] (1874–1946) Writer, born in Allegheny, PA. Her main works include *Three Lives* (1908), *Tender Buttons* (1914), and her most widely-read book, *The Autobiography of Alice B Toklas* (1933). Her Paris home became a salon for artists and writers between the two World Wars.

Stein, (Heinrich Friedrich) Karl, Freiherr (Baron) **von** [shtiyn] (1757–1831) Prussian statesman and reformer, born in Nassau, WC Germany. He entered the service of Prussia in 1780, becoming secretary for trade (1804–7). As chief minister (1807–8), he carried out important reforms in the army, economy, and government. In 1812 he went to St Petersburg, and built up the coalition against Napoleon. He was later adviser to Alexander I (1812–15).

Steinbeck, John (Ernst) [stiynbek], pseudonym **Amnesia Glasscock** (1902–68) Novelist, born in Salinas, CA. His first novel of repute was *Tortilla Flat* (1935), and soon after came his major work, *The Grapes of Wrath* (1939, Pulitzer; filmed 1940). Other books include *Of Mice and Men* (1937), *East of Eden* (1952), and the humorous *Cannery Row* (1945). He received the Nobel Prize for Literature in 1962.

steinbok *steenbok*

Steiner, (Francis) George [stiyner] (1929–) Critic and scholar, born in Paris. He is a leading exponent of comparative literature, his publications including *The Death of Tragedy* (1961), *After Babel* (1975), *No Passion Spent* (1996), and *Lessons of the Masters* (2003).

Steiner, Rudolf [shtiyner] (1861–1925) Social philosopher, the founder of anthroposophy, born in Kraljevec, Croatia. In 1912 he established his first 'school of spiritual science', at Dornach in Switzerland. His aim was to integrate the psychological and the practical dimensions of life into an educational, ecological, and therapeutic basis for spiritual and physical development. Many schools and research institutions arose from his ideas, notably the **Rudolf Steiner Schools**, focusing on the development of the whole personality of the child.

Steinway, Henry (Engelhard) [stiynway], originally **Heinrich Engelhardt Steinweg** (1797–1871) Piano-maker, born in Wolfshagen, Germany. He established a piano factory in Brunswick in 1835, later transferring the business to the USA.

stele [steelee, -liy] (plural **stelae**) In ancient Greece, a carved or inscribed upright rectangular stone which could be used as a gravestone, a boundary marker on property, or a permanent display board for public laws and documents.

stem (botany) The main axis of a plant, usually but not always above ground, and bearing the buds, leaves, and reproductive organs. It contains a vascular system: this conducts water and nutrients from the roots to the leaves, and the products of photosynthesis from the leaves to all other parts of the plant. In woody species, the stem is strengthened with additional supporting tissues, and protected by bark and cork layers.

stem (linguistics) *root* (linguistics)

stem cells Primitive cells that have the potential to develop into different types of cells. In embryos, these master cells develop into the 200 or so distinct cell types in the body; in adults they replenish existing cells when they wear out or are destroyed. Three types are recognized. Cells which have a total potential for body development (**totipotent** cells) are found in a fertilized egg. **Pluripotent** cells are a possible source of every type of cell or tissue in the body, apart from those needed to develop a foetus. **Multipotent** cells have restricted capabilities. Pluripotent stem cells exist in a natural state in the embryo, but are also found in the foetus and umbilical cord. Certain multipo-

tent stem cells are present in the adult body, such as the blood-forming cells in bone marrow.

Stem cell research offers fresh prospects for progress in treating a wide range of diseases, such as cancer, diabetes, spinal-cord injury, heart and brain disorders, and joint replacements. Adult stem cells have already been used successfully to treat some patients suffering from diabetes or heart disease. Stem cells from an individual, kept in storage, would be available for future use by that person if required, and thus could act as a natural 'body repair system'. Research using embryonic stem cells is highly controversial as it involves the creation and destruction of human embryos; such research is banned in some countries, and in permissive countries is subject to strict controls. There are also difficult scientific questions to be answered, notably the effects of cell multiplication ('colonization') in different parts of the body, and exactly how the process works – whether stem cells form new tissue or improve the functioning of existing tissue.

Stendhal [stendahl], pseudonym of **Marie-Henri Beyle** (1783–1842) Writer, born in Grenoble, France. He is best known for his novels, notably *Le Rouge et le noir* (1830, Scarlet and Black) and *La Chartreuse de Parme* (1839, The Charterhouse of Parma).

Sten gun The standard submachine-gun of the British Army from 1942 onwards. Its name derives from its designers Stephard and Turpin, and the Enfield factory where it was made.

Stenmark, Ingemar (1956–) Swedish skier, born in Tärnaby, Sweden, 100 mi S of the Arctic Circle. Overall champion three times (1976–8), he won 15 slalom/giant slalom titles, and five world titles. He retired in 1989.

Steno, Nicolaus [steenoh], Lat name of **Niels Steensen** (1638–86) Anatomist and geologist, born in Copenhagen. He discovered the duct of the parotid gland and explained the function of the ovaries. He was also the first to explain the structure of the Earth's crust.

stenography *shorthand*

stenotype *palantype*

stephanotis [stefanohtis] A twining, evergreen perennial (*Stephanotis floribunda*), native to Madagascar; a clustered waxy flower; stems to 3 m/10 ft or more; flowers tubular with five spreading lobes, white, strongly fragrant; also called **Madagascar jasmine**. (Family: Asclepiadaceae.)

Stephen (c.1090–1154) Last Norman king of England (1135–54), and son of Stephen-Henry, Count of Blois, and Adela, daughter of William the Conqueror. He had sworn to accept Henry I's daughter, Empress Matilda, as queen, but seized the English crown and was recognized as Duke of Normandy on Henry's death in 1135. After 18 years of virtually continuous warfare, he was forced in 1153 to accept Matilda's son, the future Henry II, as his lawful successor.

Stephen I, St (c.975–1038) The first king and spiritual patron of Hungary (997–1038). He received from Pope Sylvester II the title of 'Apostolic King' and, according to tradition, St Stephen's Crown, now a Hungarian national treasure. He was canonized in 1083. Feast day 16 August.

Stephen, St (1st-c) According to the Acts of the Apostles (6–7), the first Christian martyr. He was charged by the Jewish authorities for speaking against the Temple and the Law, and stoned to death by the crowds in Jerusalem. Feast day 26 December.

Stephen, Sir Ninian (Martin) (1923–) Judge, born in England. Appointed Governor-General of Australia (1982–9), he gave up the position to become Australia's first ambassador for the environment, a non-political role from which he retired in 1991. He was later judge on the International Criminal Tribunals for Yugoslavia (1993) and Rwanda (1995).

Stephenson, George (1781–1848) Railway engineer, born in Wylam, Northumberland. His most famous engine, the *Rocket*, running at 58 km/36 mi an hour, was built in 1829 in collaboration with his son Robert.

Stephenson, Robert (1803–59) Civil engineer, born in Willington Quay, Northumberland, the son of George Stephenson. They collaborated on the design of the famous engine the *Rocket* for the Rainhill Trials of 1829. Robert attained independent fame through his tubular design for the Britannia Bridge over the Menai Strait in Wales (1846–9), and for bridges at Conwy, Newcastle upon Tyne, Montreal (Canada), and elsewhere.

Stephenson, Sir William, known as **Intrepid** (1896–1989) Secret intelligence chief, born in Point Douglas, near Winnipeg, Canada. In 1940 he was appointed British intelligence chief in North and South America. The novelist Ian Fleming, a member of his wartime staff, is said to have adopted Stephenson as the model for the character 'M' in the James Bond books.

steppe The extensive grassland, treeless region of Eurasia. It extends from the Ukraine through SE European and C Asian Russia to the Manchurian plains. Large areas are important for wheat growing.

steradian [steraydian] SI unit of solid angle; symbol *sr*; an area drawn on the surface of a sphere equal to the square of the radius of the sphere subtends a solid angle of 1 steradian at the centre of the sphere; the total area of a sphere subtends a solid angle of 4π sr at the centre.

stereochemistry The study of the spatial relationships between atoms in molecules, especially the configuration of the atoms bonded to a central atom and the occurrence of geometrical and optical isomers.

stereolithography *lithography*

stereophonic sound The recording and transmission of sound which, when reproduced, appears to the listener to come from different directions and to reproduce a sound field similar to that where the sound was originally recorded. It normally uses two microphones, and two loudspeakers to reproduce the sound which has been recorded on two separate channels. Two-track stereo tape recordings appeared in 1954.

stereoscopic photography, also termed **3-D** (three-dimensional) **films** The recording and presentation of paired images to give the viewer an impression of solidity and depth. The basic system, developed from 1845, is to photograph the scene with two cameras whose lenses are 65 mm/2½ in apart, the normal separation of human eyes, and view the results in a device (such as a pair of special spectacles) which allows each eye to see only its appropriate right-eye or left-eye record.

sterilization 1 A surgical operation to render the individual unable to conceive. In the male the simplest procedure is to sever each vas deferens, a procedure known as *vasectomy*. In the female, the approach is to sever or obliterate the uterine tubes.

2 *asepsis*

sterling The name of the currency of Britain, usually used to distinguish the British pound from other currencies (**pound sterling**). The name derives from the Norman coin known as a *steorling*, which had a star on one face.

Stern, Howard (1954–) Radio disc jockey and television talk-show host, born in New York City. He built a reputation as a 'shock jock', developing a flamboyant style and explicit programme content, in various 'Howard Stern' shows on radio and television during the 1990s. His best-selling book *Private Parts* (1993) was later issued as a recording and filmed (both 1997).

Sternberg, Josef von [shternberg], originally **Jonas Stern** (1894–1969) Film director, born in Vienna. He went to Germany to make his most famous film, *Der blaue Engel* (1930, The Blue Angel), starring Marlene Dietrich, and then made several Hollywood features.. His autocratic methods and aloof personality made him unpopular in the studios, and his later career was erratic.

Sternberg, Sir Sigmund (1921–) Businessman and religious ecumenist, born in Budapest. Brought up in the Orthodox Jewish tradition in Hungary, he left the country for England in 1939, where he created the Sternberg group of companies. He became chair of the International Council of Christians and Jews (1979), and in the 1990s set up the Three Faiths Forum (including Muslims). Knighted in 1976, he was awarded the Templeton Prize for Progress in Religion in 1998 for his interfaith work worldwide.

Sterne, Laurence (1713–68) Novelist, born in Clonmel, Co Tipperary, Ireland. In 1759 he wrote the first two volumes of his comic novel, *The Life and Opinions of Tristram Shandy*, which was very well received in London, and the remaining volumes appeared between 1761 and 1767.

sternum An elongated, almost flat bone lying in the midline of the front wall of the thorax; also known as the **breastbone**. It articulates with the clavicle and the ribs, and gives some protection to the heart.

steroid Any of several natural products, including many hormones, bile acids, and the *sterols*, derived from the non-glyceride portion of fats, the best known of which is cholesterol. Steroids are responsible for maintaining many vital functions, including sexual characteristics, salt and water balance, and muscle and bone mass.

stethoscope A medical instrument used for detecting sounds within the body, invented by French physician René Laënnec (1781–1826) in 1816. It consists of a bell or diaphragm made of metal or plastic that is placed on the patient's body to pick up and amplify sound and conduct it via a flexible Y-shaped rubber tube to earpieces placed in the ears of the examiner.

Stevenage [steevnij] 51°55N 0°14W, pop (2001e) 79 700. Town in Hertfordshire, SE England; the first 'new town', 1946; railway.

Stevens, Wallace (1879–1955) Poet, born in Reading, PA. He was over 40 when his first volume, *Harmonium* (1923), was published. His *Collected Poems* appeared in 1954, and he is now regarded as a major if idiosyncratic poet in the Symbolist tradition.

Stevenson, Adlai (Ewing) [adliy] (1900–65) US Democratic politician, born in Los Angeles, CA. He helped to found the United Nations (1946), stood twice against Eisenhower as presidential candidate (1952, 1956), and was the US delegate to the UN in 1961–5.

Stevenson, Juliet (1956–) Actress, born in London. Her theatre performances include *Death and the Maiden* (1992, Olivier Award, Best Actress). Work in film includes *Drowning by Numbers* (1988), *Truly Madly Deeply* (1991, Evening Standard British Film Awards, Best Actress), *Emma* (1996), *Being Julia* (2004), and *Breaking and Entering* (2006).

Stevenson, Robert Louis (Balfour) (1850–94) Writer, born in Edinburgh. The romantic adventure story *Treasure Island* brought him fame in 1883, and entered him on a course of romantic fiction which included *Kidnapped* (1886), *The Strange Case of Dr Jekyll and Mr Hyde* (1886), *The Master of Ballantrae* (1889), and the unfinished *Weir of Hermiston* (1896), considered his masterpiece.

Stevenson screen A shelter for meteorological instruments, particularly thermometers, providing protection from solar radiation. It is a white, wooden box with louvred sides to give ventilation. It was invented by Thomas Stevenson (1818–87), the father of Robert Louis Stevenson.

Stewart, Alec (James) (1963–) Cricketer, born in Merton, Greater London. He began playing for Surrey in 1981, made his Test debut in 1990, and by the end of the 2003 season had played in a record 133 Tests, scoring 8463 runs and 15 centuries, and making 273 dismissals (a wicket-keeping record). He was England captain (1998–9), and retired from international and county cricket in 2003.

Stewart, Sir Jackie, popular name of **John (Young) Stewart** (1939–) Motor-racing driver, born in Milton, West Dunbartonshire. He won 27 world championship races between 1965 and 1973, and was world champion in 1969 (driving a Matra), 1971, and 1973 (both Tyrrell). He retired at the end of 1973. Since 1996 he has been chairman of Stewart Grand Prix.

Stewart, James (Maitland) (1908–97) Film actor, born in Indiana, PA. He won an Oscar for his role in *The Philadelphia Story* (1940, Oscar). Later films include a series of outstanding Westerns (1950–5), and two successes for Hitchcock, *Rear Window* (1954) and *Vertigo* (1958). Later films included *Fools' Parade* (1971) and *Right of Way* (1982). He received an honorary Oscar in 1985.

Stewart, Patrick (1940–) Actor and playwright, born in Mirfield, West Yorkshire. He is best known for his role as Captain Jean-Luc Picard in the follow-up series of *Star Trek: The Next Generation* (1987). Later films include *Star Trek: First Contact* (1996), *Star Trek: Insurrection* (1998), and *X-Men* (2000, sequel 2003).

Stewart, Rod(erick David) (1945–) Singer and songwriter, born in London. He began a career as a soloist, and also joined The Faces (1969–75). His numerous hit songs include 'Maggie May' (1971) and 'Sailing' (1975). Albums include *Every Picture Tells A Story* (1971), *Every Beat of My Heart* (1986), *When We Were The New Boys* (1998), and *As Time Goes By* (2003).

Stewart Island pop (2000e) 700; area 1735 km^2/670 sq mi. Island of New Zealand, to the S of South Island; highest point, Mt Anglem (977 m/3205 ft); a refuge for animal and bird life.

Stewarts *Stuarts*

stibine [stibeen] SbH$_3$. A highly poisonous gas formed by the reduction of antimony compounds.

stibnite An antimony sulphide (Sb$_2$S$_3$) mineral found in low-temperature hydrothermal veins, lead-grey in colour. It is the chief ore of antimony.

stick insect A large, twig-like insect with an elongate body and legs; up to 30 cm/12 in long; also known as **walking sticks**. (Order: Phasmida. Family: Phasmatidae, c.2000 species.)

stickleback Small marine or freshwater fish of the family Gasterosteidae (5 genera), common throughout the N hemisphere; body typically elongate with a number of strong dorsal spines; length up to 6 cm/2$\frac{1}{2}$ in.

Stieglitz, Alfred [steeglits] (1864–1946) Photographer, born in Hoboken, NJ. He founded in 1902 the American Photo-Secession Group with Edward Steichen (1879–1973) and consistently influenced the development of creative photography as an art form through his magazine *Camera Work* (1903–17) and his gallery of modern art in New York City.

Stiglitz, Joseph E (1942–) Economist, born in Gary, IA. He joined Princeton University in 1979, and became known for his highly technical analysis of the competitive process. He shared the Nobel Prize for Economics in 2001 for the analysis of markets with asymmetric information.

stigma In flowering plants, the part of the carpel receptive to pollen. Sticky secretions, corrugated surfaces, or hairs may help collect and retain pollen grains. The stigma, and often the style, may through physiological means operate a complex compatibility system which accepts only pollen of the correct type.

stigmata [stigmata, stigmahta] Marks or wounds appearing on the human body, similar to those of the crucified Jesus. They may be temporary (related to ecstasy or revelation) or permanent, and are alleged to be a sign of miraculous participation in Christ's passion.

stilbestrol / stilboestrol *DES*

Stilicho, Flavius [stilikoh] (?–408) Roman general who was virtual ruler of the W Roman Empire (395–408) under the feeble Emperor Honorius. His greatest achievements were his victories over Alaric and the Visigoths in N Italy at Pollentia (402) and Verona (403).

still life In art, the representation of objects such as books, candles, cooking utensils, musical instruments, fruit, flowers, etc. In W Europe it flourished above all in the Netherlands in the 17th-c.

Stilwell, Joseph W(arren), nickname **Vinegar Joe** (1883–1946) US general, born in Palatka, FL. In 1942 he commanded US forces in China, Burma, and India. Recalled after a dispute with Jiang Jieshi (Chiang Kai-shek) in 1944, he commanded the US 10th Army in the Pacific until the end of the war.

stimulants Drugs such as amphetamines, which produce feelings of wakefulness, alertness, elation, and an increased capacity to concentrate. Caffeine is a mild stimulant.

stimulated emission *laser*

Sting, originally **Gordon Matthew Sumner** (1951–) Singer, songwriter, and actor, born in Newcastle upon Tyne. Former vocalist and lyricist of The Police, his albums include *The Dream of the Blue Turtles* (1985), *Soul Cages* (1991), *Mercury Falling* (1996), *Sacred Love* (2003), and *Songs of the Labyrinth* (2006). His films include *Quadrophenia* (1978), *Dune* (1984), and *Lock, Stock and Two Smoking Barrels* (1999). He has also been much associated with campaigns concerning the environment and Amnesty International. The Police reformed in 2007 and began a reunion tour.

stinging nettle A perennial with creeping rhizomes (*Urtica dioica*) often forming large patches, native or introduced throughout temperate regions. The whole plant is covered in stinging hairs, each with a bulbous base containing acid, and a brittle, needle-like tip. When touched, the tip pierces the skin and breaks off, while pressure on the base injects acid, causing a sting and subsequent rash. The leaves are used as a vegetable and for tea; the stems yield tough fibres for cloth. (Family: Urticaceae.)

stingray Any of several bottom-living rays (Families: Dasyatidae, Potamotrygonidae, Urolophidae) in which the tail is whip-like and armed with one or more sharp poison spines; body length up to 2·5 m/8 ft.

stinkhorn The fruiting body of some fungi of the order Phallales; cap dissolves into putrid slime, containing spores that are dispersed by flies attracted over great distances by the fetid odour. (Subdivision: *Basidiomycetes*.)

stipendiary magistrate A salaried and legally qualified magistrate in England and Wales. Such magistrates may sit alone when trying cases, unlike lay magistrates, and are found in London and other large towns.

Stirling 56°07N 3°57W, pop (2000e) 30 300. City and capital of Stirling council, C Scotland, on S bank of R Forth; city status, 2002; railway; university (1967); Stirling castle (12th-c); scene of Bruce's parliament (1326).

Stirling Range Mountain range in SW Western Australia; extends 64 km/40 mi parallel with SW coast; rises to 1109 m/3638 ft at Bluff Knoll.

stitchwort Either of two species of bluish-green perennials with brittle stems native to woodlands in Europe, N Africa, and Asia Minor; flowers white, 5-petalled. (Genus: *Stellaria*. Family: Caryophyllaceae.)

stoat A mammal of family Mustelidae, native to Europe, Asia, and North America (*Mustela erminea*); in summer, resembles a large weasel (length, 50 cm/20 in) with black tip to tail; winter coat (*ermine*) white, with black tail tip.

stock An annual or perennial, growing to 80 cm/30 in, native to Europe and Asia; leaves greyish; flowers in spikes, purple, red or white, cross-shaped. It includes **garden stock** or **gilliflower** (*Matthiola incana*) and **night-scented stock** (*Matthiola bicornis*). (Genus: *Matthiola*, 55 species. Family: Cruciferae.)

stock-car racing A type of motor racing which takes different forms in the USA and UK. In the USA, highly supercharged production cars race around banked concreted tracks. In the

UK, 'bangers' (old cars) race against each other on a round or oval track with the intention of being the last car still moving at the end of the race.

stock exchange An institution through which stocks, shares, and bonds are traded under standard rules. The London Stock Exchange deals in some 7000 securities. Until 1986, business was carried out on 'the floor of the House', ie in the Stock Exchange itself. Individuals and institutions wishing to buy or sell securities would contact a *stockbroker*, who would place the order with a *jobber* (a trader on the floor). 27 October 1986 was the date of the 'Big Bang' when the distinction between brokers and jobbers was abolished and a computerized system was introduced for share trading. Most capital cities in the West have a stock exchange, Wall Street in New York City being the largest.

Stock Exchange Automated Quotations (SEAQ) A system introduced in 1986 in the London stock market for trading securities. It is a computerized market-making activity which enables member firms to buy and sell and quote prices for specific securities.

Stockhausen, Karlheinz [shtokhowzn] (1928–) Composer, born in Mödrath, Germany. In 1953 he helped to found the electronic music studio at Cologne. He has written orchestral, choral, and instrumental works, including some which combine electronic and normal sonorities, such as *Kontakte* (1960), and parts of a huge operatic cycle, *Licht* (Light), begun in 1977 and completed in 2002.

Stockholm 59°20N 18°03E, pop (2000e) 709 000. Seaport and capital of Sweden; on a group of islands and the adjacent mainland; founded, 1255; important trading centre of the Hanseatic League; capital, 1436; bishopric; airport; railway; underground railway; university (1878); Drottningholm Palace (royal family residence).

Stockholm syndrome The unnatural close relationship that occasionally develops between a hostage of a criminal or terrorist and his or her captor. It was first described in a woman held hostage in a bank in Sweden who remained faithful to the thief during his imprisonment.

stock market The system of buying and selling stocks and shares; also, a building in which these transactions take place (the *stock exchange*). A stock market 'crash' refers to a situation when the prices of stocks fall dramatically, resulting in many bankruptcies. The most famous case was the Wall Street crash of 1929; a less dramatic crash also occurred in October 1987 in most world stock markets.

Stockport 53°25N 2°10W, pop (2001e) 284 500. Town in Greater Manchester, NW England; railway; Manchester airport nearby; football league team, Stockport County.

stocks In economics, a term used in two main senses, both of which refer to amounts at a given moment; opposed to **flows**, which refer to changes over time. **1** Stocks of goods (or **inventories**): raw materials, fuels, or unsold products in store at a given date.
2 Financial assets: in the UK, for example, government debt is called **government stock**, and is traded on the stock exchange; in the USA, company shares are called **common stocks**.

Stockton *Macmillan, Harold*

Stockton-on-Tees 54°34N 1°19W, pop (2000e) 90 000. Town in NE England, on the R Tees estuary; unitary authority, 1996 (pop (2000e) 180 000); developed with the opening of the Stockton–Darlington railway in 1825; Saltholme Nature Reserve nearby.

Stoicism A philosophical movement which flourished in the Hellenistic Roman period from c.320 BC–AD 200, founded by Zeno of Citium. They believed in a rational, materialistic, and deterministic universe in which virtue consisted in understanding natural necessity and then cheerfully accepting it;

the individual soul is literally a part of a larger cosmos, into which it is absorbed.

Stoke-on-Trent 53°00N 2°10W, pop (2001e) 240 600. Industrial city and (from 1997) unitary authority in Staffordshire, C England; part of the Potteries urban area; on the R Trent; railway; University of Keele (1962) nearby, Staffordshire University (1992); clayware (largest producer in the world); birthplace of Josiah Wedgwood and Arnold Bennett; Alton Towers theme park nearby; football league teams, Stoke City (Potters), Port Vale.

Stoker, Bram, popular name of **Abraham Stoker** (1847–1912) Writer, born in Dublin. Among several books, he is remembered for the classic horror tale *Dracula* (1897), which has occasioned a whole series of film adaptations.

Stokes' law In physics, a law expressing the viscous drag force F acting on a spherical object of radius r moving with velocity v through a fluid of viscosity η as $F = 6\pi\eta rv$; stated in 1845 by British physicist George Stokes (1819–1903).

Stokowski, Leopold [stokofskee], originally **Antoni Stanislaw Boleslawowicz** (1882–1977) Conductor, born in London. He conducted the orchestras of Philadelphia (1912–36), New York (1946–50), and Houston (1955–60), and in 1962 founded the American Symphony Orchestra in New York City.

STOL [estol] Acronym used for a fixed-wing aircraft specially designed for **Short Take-Off and Landing**. These aircraft usually accomplish their function by special aerodynamic devices providing high lift.

stolon A long shoot which bends under its own weight to the ground, and roots at the tip or at the nodes to form new plants.

stomach A digestive pouch between the oesophagus and the duodenum, which stores food, secretes gastric juice and, by wave-like contractions, churns and releases its contents into the duodenum at a controlled rate. It is divided into the *cardiac* region around the *cardiac orifice* (where the oesophagus opens into the stomach), the *fundus* (the region above the level of the cardiac orifice), the *body*, and the *pylorus*, which opens into the duodenum at the *pyloric orifice*.

stomach cancer A cancer arising in the lining of the stomach. It usually affects people in late middle-age, and tends not to be recognized until a late stage, when it has invaded through the stomach wall and infiltrated adjacent organs. It also spreads in the blood to the liver. Surgical treatment requires the removal of all or part of the stomach, but the prognosis is poor.

Stone, Oliver (1946–) Film director, producer, and screenwriter, born in New York City. He fought in Vietnam (1967–8) then studied at New York University. His major films include *Midnight Express* (1978, Oscar), *Salvador* (1986), *Platoon* (1987, Oscars for best director and best picture), and *Born On The Fourth Of July* (1989, Oscar). Later films include the controversial *JFK* (1991), *Nixon* (1995), *Beyond Borders* (2000), and *World Trade Center* (2006).

Stone Age *Three Age System*

stonebass *wreckfish*

stone carving *sculpture*

stonechat A thrush (*Saxicola torquata*) native to most of the Old World; male with dark head, white neck spots and pale reddish breast.

stone circles Circular or near-circular rings of prehistoric standing stones found, particularly in Britain and Ireland, in the Late Neolithic and Early Bronze Age. They most probably functioned as temples in which celestial events, the passing of the seasons, and the fertility of the land and people could be celebrated.

stonecrop A member of a large genus of succulents, mostly perennials, native to N temperate regions; flowers 5-petalled, starry, mainly white, yellow, or red. (Genus: *Sedum*, 300 species. Family: Crassulaceae.)

stonefish Grotesque fish found in shallow inshore waters of the

Indo-Pacific region; body strongly camouflaged in shape and colour; length 30–60 cm/12–24 in; dorsal fin armed with sharp poison spines that can inflict extremely painful stings. (Genus: *Synanceia*. Family: Synanceiidae.)

stonefly A primitive, winged insect typically found among stones along river banks; adults are poor fliers that run and hide when disturbed. (Order: Plecoptera, c.2000 species.)

Stonehenge A prehistoric monument near Amesbury, Wiltshire, S England, 130 km/80 mi W of London; a world heritage site. It was constructed in three major phases within the Middle–Late Neolithic period: 2950–2900 BC, a circular ditch with low inner and outer banks, c.110 m/360 ft in diameter, and a circle of pits known as 'Aubrey Holes' which perhaps held timber posts; 2900–2400 BC, posts were set up inside the earthwork, and cremations were placed in the Aubrey Holes; the third phase, 2550–1600 BC, is that of the surviving stone monument, when a 30 m/100 ft diameter lintelled circle and inner horseshoe of 80 dressed sarsen (sandstone) blocks, each weighing 20–50 tonnes, were erected, and bluestones from South Wales were set up in a circle and horseshoe. Alignment on the midsummer sunrise/midwinter sunset implies prehistoric use for seasonal festivals, but the association with the druids dates only from 1905, and has no historical basis. The theory that the pillars had been transported by land on wooden rollers from South Wales to Salisbury Plain has now been superseded by the view that they were carried to the area by glaciers. In 2007, excavations at nearby Durrington Walls uncovered remains of the largest Neolithic village ever found in Britain, its dates corresponding with the construction of Stonehenge.

Stone Mountain Memorial A memorial carving on the exposed face of Stone Mountain in NW Georgia, USA. The work, which was completed in 1972, depicts Confederate leaders Jefferson Davis, Robert E Lee, and 'Stonewall' Jackson. It was executed by sculptors Gutzon Borglum, Augustus Lukeman, and Walter Kirtland Hancock, who worked on it in succession over a period of 50 years.

stoneware A type of ceramic midway between pottery and porcelain, made of clay and a fusible stone. It is fired to a point where partial vitrification renders it impervious to liquids, but unlike porcelain it is seldom more than slightly translucent.

Stooges, The Three Comedy trio, originally the **Horwitz** (later **Howard**) brothers, **Samuel** (b.1895), **Moses** (b.1897), and **Jerome (Jerry)** (b.1911), they were known by their respective nicknames of Shemp, Moe, and Curly (with the bald head). Shemp left for a career of his own, and the trio of Moe, Curly, and friend **Larry Fine** (originally **Feinberg**, with the wild wavy hair) went on to feature-film success. Their films were characterized by anarchic knockabout humour, with sound effects perfectly synchronized with their blows. Later, Shemp returned, replacing Curly (d.1952), and in turn was replaced by **Joe Besser**. In the late 1950s, **Joe de Rita** (b.1909) replaced Besser as the new Curly. Moe and Larry died in 1975, and Joe in 1993.

stoolball An 11-a-side bat-and-ball game resembling cricket and rounders. The batter defends his wicket, a 1 ft (30 cm) square wooden board 4 ft 8 in (1.4 m) from the ground, which the underarm bowler attempts to hit.

Stopes, Marie (Charlotte Carmichael) [stohps] (1880–1958) Pioneer advocate of birth control, suffragette, and palaeontologist, born in Edinburgh. Alarmed at the unscientific way in which men and women embarked upon married life, she wrote a number of books on the subject, of which *Married Love* (1918) caused a storm of controversy. She later founded the first birth control clinic in N London (1921).

stop–go policy A government economic policy in which action taken to boost the economy (**go**) results in inflation or exchange rate problems. Action is then taken to cure these problems, which results in a slow-down of the economy (**stop**).

Stoppard, Miriam, *née* **Stern** (1937–) British physician, writer, and broadcaster. She is well known for her television series, especially *Miriam Stoppard's Health and Beauty Show* (from 1988). Among her books are *The Baby and Child Medical Handbook* (1984) and *Defying Age* (2003). She married Tom Stoppard in 1972 (divorced, 1992).

Stoppard, Sir Tom, originally **Tomas Straussler** (1937–) Playwright, born in Zlín, Czech Republic. He made his name in 1967 with *Rosencrantz and Guildenstern are Dead*. Other plays include the philosophical satire *Jumpers* (1972), *Travesties* (1974), *The Real Thing* (1982), *The Invention of Love* (1997), and *Rock'n'Roll* (2006). Screenplays include *Shakespeare in Love* (1998). He was married to Miriam Stoppard (divorced, 1992).

Storey, David (Malcolm) (1933–) Novelist and playwright, born in Wakefield, West Yorkshire. His novels include *This Sporting Life* (1960), *Saville* (1976), and *Thin-Ice Skater* (2004); and his plays *The Changing Room* (1972) and *Stages* (1992).

stork A large bird, native to warm regions worldwide; long legs, neck, and long stout bill; flies with neck and legs outstretched. The **white stork** (*Ciconia ciconia*) is the stork of fable, a summer visitor to Europe, which prefers to nest on buildings. (Family: Ciconiidae, 17 species.)

storksbill An annual or perennial native to temperate regions; flowers white, pink, or purple; fruit with a long point resembling a bird's beak. (Genus: *Erodium*, 90 species. Family: Geraniaceae.)

storm An intense meteorological disturbance, categorized on the Beaufort scale as force 10 (storm) or force 11 (violent storm). Wind speeds range from 25–32 m/s (55–72 mph).

Störmer, Horst L(udwig) (1949–) Physicist, born in Frankfurt-am-Main, Germany. He graduated from Stuttgart University in 1977, joined Columbia University, NY, and shared the 1998 Nobel Prize for Physics for his contribution to the discovery of a new form of quantum fluid with fractionally charged excitations.

Stormont A suburb of Belfast, Northern Ireland, in which are situated Parliament House (built in 1932 to house the parliament of Northern Ireland, then the home of the Northern Ireland Assembly), Stormont House, and Stormont Castle.

storm petrel A petrel, worldwide, found at sea unless breeding. Some (Subfamily: Oceanitinae) 'walk' across the water surface in flight; others (Subfamily: Hydrobatinae) swoop over the water. (Family: Hydrobatidae, 22 species.)

storm surge A localized rise in sea level produced by on-shore winds and reduced atmospheric pressure caused by large storms. Much of the flood damage produced by hurricanes, typhoons, and other major storms is the result of storm surge.

Stornoway 58°12N 6°23W, pop (2000e) 8490. Port capital of Western Isles council, NW Scotland, on E coast of Lewis; airfield.

Stoss or **Stozz, Veit** [shtohs] (c.1447–1533) Woodcarver and sculptor, born in Nuremberg, Germany. He worked mainly in Kraków (1477–96), where he carved the high altar of the Marienkirche.

stout *beer*

Stowe, Harriet (Elizabeth) Beecher [stoh], *née* **Beecher** (1811–96) Novelist, born in Litchfield, CT. She became famous through her *Uncle Tom's Cabin*, which immediately focused anti-slavery sentiment in the North. Her other novels include *Dred* (1856) and *The Minister's Wooing* (1859).

Strabane [straban], Ir **An Srath Ban** 54°49N 7°27W, pop (2000e) 12 000. Market town in Tyrone, W Northern Ireland; on the Mourne and Finn Rivers; Irish border town.

strabismus *squint*

Strabo [strayboh] (Gr 'squint-eyed') (c.64 BC–c.AD 23) Geographer and historian, born in Amasia, Pontus. Only a few fragments remain of his 47-volume historical work, but his *Geographica* in 17 books has survived almost complete.

Strachey, (Giles) Lytton [straychee] (1880–1932) Biographer and

The Stratigraphical Column

The sequence of rock layers was established by stratigraphers during the 19th-c.

Holocene	Charles Lyell	1833
Pleistocene	Charles Lyell	1839
Pliocene	Charles Lyell	1833
Miocene	Charles Lyell	1833
Oligocene	Heinrich Ernst Beyrich	1854
Eocene	Charles Lyell	1833
Palaeocene	Wilhelm Philipp Schimper	1874
Cretaceous	Jesan Baptiste Julien d'Omalius d'Halloy	1822
Jurassic	Alexander von Humboldt	1799
Triassic	Friedrich August von Alberti	1834
Permian	Roderick Impey Murchison	1841
Carboniferous	William David Conybeare William Phillips	1822
Devonian	Roderick Impey Murchison Adam Sedgwick	1839
Silurian	Roderick Impey Murchison	1835
Ordovician	Charles Lapworth	1879
Cambrian	Adam Sedgwick	1835

critic, born in London. He began his writing career as a critic, but turned to biography, creating a literary bombshell with his *Eminent Victorians* (1918). Later works included *Queen Victoria* (1921) and *Elizabeth and Essex* (1928).

Stradivari or **Stradivarius, Antonio** [stradivahrius] (c.1644–1737) Violin maker, born in Cremona, Italy. His best instruments are thought to be unsurpassed in quality. He made over a thousand violins, violas, and violoncellos between 1666 and his death; about 650 of these still exist.

Strafford, Thomas Wentworth, 1st Earl of (1593–1641) English statesman, born in London. In 1632 he was Lord Deputy of Ireland, where he imposed firm rule, and in 1639 became the king's principal adviser. His suppression of the rebellion in Scotland failed, and he was impeached by the Long Parliament. Despite a famous defence at Westminster, he was executed.

strain The fractional change in the dimensions of some object subjected to stress, expressed as a number. For force acting along the axis of a rod, **linear strain** is the change in length divided by the original length. **Volume strain** is the fractional change in volume for an object pressured on all sides. **Shear strain** measures the effectiveness of a twisting force.

Straits Settlements The name given to the former British crown colony which consisted of Singapore, Malacca, the Dindings, Penang, and Province Wellesley. All became part of Malaysia in 1963, and Singapore became independent in 1965.

strangeness In particle physics, an internal additive quantum number conserved in strong and electromagnetic interactions, but not in weak interactions; symbol *S*. It was introduced during the 1930s to explain 'strange' reactions observed in cosmic ray experiments.

Stranraer [stranrah(r)] 54°54N 5°02W, pop (2000e) 10 100. Port in Dumfries and Galloway, SW Scotland; at the head of Loch Ryan; railway; ferries to N Ireland.

Strasberg, Lee, originally **Israel Strassberg** (1901–82) Theatre director, actor, and teacher, born in Budanov, Ukraine (formerly Budzanow, Austria). In 1931 he was involved in the formation of the Group Theatre, evolving a technique (influenced by Stanislavsky) which became known everywhere as 'the Method'. He exercised great influence as director of the Actors' Studio (1949–82), his pupils including Marlon Brando, Anne Bancroft, and Paul Newman.

Strasbourg [strazberg], Fr [strazboor], Ger **Strassburg** [shtrasboork], ancient **Argentoratum** 48°35N 7°42E, pop (2000e) 264 000. Industrial and commercial city in NE France; on the R Ill; sixth largest city and largest river-port in France; part of a bishopric since 1003; free imperial city in 13th-c; ceded to France, 1697; taken by Germany, 1871; returned to France, 1918; railway junction; university (founded 1537); seat of the Council of Europe, European Parliament, European Commission of Human Rights, and European Science Foundation; printing developed here by Gutenberg; tourist centre of Alsace; congress and conference centre; Gothic cathedral (begun 1015, with noted 14th-c astronomical clock).

Strategic Arms Limitation Treaty *SALT*

Strategic Arms Reduction Talks *START*

Strategic Defense Initiative *SDI*

strategic studies The academic study of the military, political, economic, and technological factors which affect the relations between nations. As distinct from military science, which concerns itself with the deployment of personnel and material in war, strategic studies looks at the continuous process of military relations between nations in war and peace.

Stratford-upon-Avon 52°12N 1°41W, pop (2001e) 111 500. Town in Warwickshire, C England; on the R Avon; birthplace of William Shakespeare; railway; Royal Shakespeare Theatre; Anne Hathaway's Cottage.

Strathclyde [strathkliyd] pop (2000e) 2 293 000; area 13 537 km²/5225 sq mi. Former region in W and C Scotland, established in 1975, and replaced in 1996 by 10 local councils: Argyll and Bute, West Dunbartonshire, East Dunbartonshire, Renfrewshire, Inverclyde, City of Glasgow, East Renfrewshire, North Ayrshire, East Ayrshire, South Ayrshire.

stratification A geological term for the formation of layers in sedimentary rock in which breaks in the deposition or changes in the nature of the deposited material define visible bedding planes.

stratigraphy A branch of geology concerned with the study of sequences of layers of rock, usually sedimentary. It aims to unravel changes in their depositional environment, and to correlate rocks of the same age in different places by their rock type and fossil content. (*see panel*)

Strato or **Straton of Lampsacus** [straytoh, strayton] (?–c.270 BC) Greek philosopher, the successor to Theophrastus as the third head of the Lyceum (from c.287 to c.269 BC). His writings are lost, but he seems to have worked mainly to revise Aristotle's physical doctrines.

stratocumulus clouds [stratohkyoomyuluhs] Low layer clouds with a distinct cumulus or rounded shape; layers of cloud are rolled into rounded forms. They are white or grey in colour, and are found at c.500–2000 m/1600–6500 ft. Cloud symbol: Sc.

stratosphere The layer of the Earth's atmosphere at a height of c.15–50 km/10–30 mi, separated from the troposphere below by the tropopause, and from the mesosphere above by the stratopause. It contains the ozone layer.

Stratton, Charles (Sherwood), nickname **General Tom Thumb** (1838–83) Midget showman, born in Bridgeport, CT. He stopped growing at 6 months of age, and stayed 63 cm/25 in until his teens, eventually reaching 101 cm/40 in. Barnum displayed him in his museum from the age of 5, under the name of **General Tom Thumb**, and he became famous throughout the USA and Europe.

stratus clouds [stratuhs] The lowest layer of clouds in the atmosphere. They are composed of water droplets, and result in dull, overcast, and often drizzly conditions associated with the warm sector of a depression. They are found up to c.500 m/1600 ft.

Strauss, Johann [strows], known as **the Elder** (1804–49) Violinist, conductor, and composer, born in Vienna. He founded, with

Josef Lanner, the Viennese Waltz tradition, and toured widely in Europe with his own orchestra. He composed several marches, notably the *Radetzky* (1848), and numerous waltzes.

Strauss, Johann [strows], known as **the Younger** (1825–99) Violinist, conductor and composer, born in Vienna, the son of Johann Strauss (the Elder). He wrote over 400 waltzes, notably *The Blue Danube* (1867) and *Tales from the Vienna Woods* (1868), as well as polkas, marches, several operettas, including *Die Fledermaus* (1874, The Bat), and a favourite concert piece, *Perpetuum Mobile*.

Strauss, Richard [strows] (1864–1949) Composer, born in Munich, Germany. He is best known for his symphonic poems, such as *Till Eulenspiegels lustige Streiche* (1894–5, Till Eulenspiegel's Merry Pranks) and *Also sprach Zarathustra* (1895–6, Thus Spoke Zarathustra), and his operas, notably *Der Rosenkavalier* (1911).

Stravinsky, Igor (Fyodorovich) [stravinskee] (1882–1971) Composer, born near St Petersburg, Russia. He became famous with his music for the Diaghilev ballets *The Firebird* (1910), *Petrushka* (1911), and *The Rite of Spring* (1913). Essentially an experimenter, after World War 1 he devoted himself to Neoclassicism, as in the opera-oratorio *Oedipus Rex* (1927) and the choral *Symphony of Psalms* (1930). Other major compositions include the *Symphony in C major* (1940), the opera *The Rake's Progress* (1951), and such later works as *Requiem Canticles* (1966), in which he adopted serialism.

Straw, Jack, popular name of **John Whitaker Straw** (1946–) British statesman, born in Buckhurst Hill, Essex. He became an MP in 1979, and went on to join the shadow cabinet as spokesman on education (1987–92), environment and local government (1992–3), local government (1993–4), and home affairs (1994–7). He became home secretary in the 1997 Labour government, secretary of state for foreign and Commonwealth affairs (2001–6), and Leader of the House of Commons (2006–).

strawberry A perennial with arching runners rooting at nodes to form new plants, native to North and South America, Europe (N as far as Ireland), and Asia; flowers 5-petalled, white; false fruit consisting of swollen, fleshy, red receptacle bearing brown, dry, achenes (the 'seeds') on the surface. (Genus: *Fragaria*, 15 species. Family: Rosaceae.)

strawberry tree An evergreen shrub or small tree (*Arbutus unedo*), native to the Mediterranean and W Europe north to Ireland; leaves reddish, leathery; flowers white, bell-shaped, in drooping clusters; fruits red, spherical, covered with soft warts. (Family: Ericaceae.)

streaming Putting children into higher or lower groups according to their general ability, as opposed to teaching them in *mixed ability* (also known as 'heterogeneous') groups, or *mixed age* (also called 'vertical' or 'family') groups. If this is done on the basis of their competence in a particular subject, the process is known as **setting** or (US) **tracking**.

streamlining A condition of fluid flow such that no turbulence occurs. Streamlining refers to the design of the shape of machinery or apparatus (eg automobiles, aircraft) so that turbulence is reduced to a minimum.

stream of consciousness A term introduced by William James in his *Principles of Psychology* (1890) to describe the continuous, random activity of the mind. It has been adopted by writers and critics to refer to the techniques used to register this inner experience in writing.

Streep, Meryl (Louise) (1949–) Actress, born in Summit, NJ. She made her film debut in *Julia* (1977). She gained Oscars for *Kramer v Kramer* (1979) and *Sophie's Choice* (1982), and critical acclaim for *The French Lieutenant's Woman* (1981), *Out of Africa* (1985), and *Postcards From the Edge* (1990). Later films include *The Hours* (2002), *Adaptation* (2002, Oscar nomination), and *The Devil Wears Prada* (2006, Golden Globe Best Actress, Oscar

nomination). Her television work includes the drama mini-series *Angels in America*, for which she won a Best Actor Emmy in 2004. The same year she was honoured with the American Film Institute lifetime achievement award.

street dance Forms of competitive dance that started in the early 1970s among gangs of youths in New York. **Break dancing** aims to develop control and co-ordination to perform acrobatic and athletic feats either solo, with a partner, or in a group. **Body popping** is a jerky articulation of isolated parts of the body creating a chain of movement. **Robotics** is a form where mime and puppet movements are important. A mechanical effect is created by tense muscles in a stiff body.

Street-Porter, Janet (1946–) British television executive, presenter, and journalist. A columnist and fashion writer, she entered independent television in 1975 as a presenter, later joining the BBC as head of Youth and Entertainment Features (1988–94). She was appointed editor of the *Independent on Sunday* (1999–2001), becoming its editor-at-large in 2001. She received the BAFTA Award for originality in 1988.

Streisand, Barbra [striysand], originally **Barbara Joan Streisand** (1942–) Actress and singer, born in New York City. She played the lead in the Broadway show *Funny Girl*, which she repeated in the 1968 film version to win an Oscar. Later films included *Hello, Dolly* (1969) and *A Star is Born* (1976). She scripted, composed, directed, and starred in *Yentl* (1983), and co-produced and directed *Prince of Tides* (1991), and *The Mirror Has Two Faces* (1996).

Streptococcus [streptohkokus] A spherical to ovoid bacterium which occurs in chains. Some species are useful in dairy fermentations; others are found in animal intestinal tracts and may be disease-causing. It includes the causative agents of scarlet fever and pneumonia. (Kingdom: Monera. Family: Streptococcaceae.)

streptomycin [streptomiysin] An antibiotic discovered in 1944 which became the first clinically effective drug for the treatment of tuberculosis. Although drug resistance developed during its first years of use, it is still occasionally used in a cocktail of several drugs for treating tuberculosis.

stress (physics) A force per unit area which acts on an object, attempting to deform it. A force F applied along the axis of a bar of cross section A produces a **linear stress** of F/A, units Pa (pascal). Such a force is involved in attempts to pull apart layers of atoms (**tensile stress**) or to push them together (**compressive stress**). A twisting force causes **shear stress**, which tries to slide layers of atoms over one another.

stress (psychology) In psychology, effects arising when certain external circumstances (**stressors**) lead to a stereotyped non-specific response from a person (the **stress response**). Stressors may be physical (noise, heat) or psychological (bereavement, unemployment), but their effect depends on their interpretation by the recipient. Response symptoms include attentional selectivity, memory loss, and autonomic activity (eg sweating).

stress analysis A means of predicting and monitoring stress within a structure. Stress is a measure of the deforming force applied to a body. The two main types are *normal* or *direct stress* (such as pulling (tension) or pressing (compression)) and *shear*, which is a sideways stress. Stress concentrates at points where the material changes shape. The more severe the change in shape, the higher will be the stress concentration. **Photoelastic stress analysis** is a means by which the stresses can be made visible.

strike (economics) A form of industrial action, where a group of workers stop work in protest at some action by their employer, or because of a failure of collective bargaining to achieve the desired results. An **official strike** is one which has been formally agreed by a majority of members of the union. Since the passing of the Trade Union Act (1984), unions in the UK have to hold a secret ballot of members before strike action is formally declared.

Strindberg, (Johan) August (1849–1912) Playwright and artist, born in Stockholm. He first achieved fame with the novel *Röda rummet* (1879, The Red Room), followed by several plays. His plays *Fadren* (1887, The Father) and *Fröken Julie* (1888, Miss Julie) brought him to the forefront as the exponent of naturalistic drama. He was also a pioneer of modern art, and anticipated the surrealism and abstract impressionism of the 20th-c.

string instrument 1 bowed Musical instruments in which the sound is produced by drawing a bow (made of horse-hair) across one or more taut strings. Gut, metal, and (more recently) nylon are the materials most often needed for the strings themselves. The bowed string instruments of the modern orchestra – violin, viola, cello, and double bass – all have four strings (some double basses have five). The strings can be plucked as well as bowed. *see* baryton; cello; chordophone; crwth; double bass; hurdy-gurdy; kit; string quartet; viola; viola da gamba; violin **2 non-bowed** Musical instruments in which the sound is produced by plucking or striking one or more strings. Many are fitted with keyboards; others are played with sticks or hammers, or are plucked or strummed with fingers or plectra. A large number are folk instruments, the only one commonly found in the modern orchestra being the harp.

string quartet An ensemble of two violins, viola, and cello; also, a piece of music for such an ensemble. The first important composer of string quartets was Haydn, who established the four-movement structure and wrote some of the earliest masterpieces in the form.

strobilus [strobiylus] A cone-shaped group of leaves or leaf-like structures bearing sporangia and found in spore-bearing vascular plants. In gymnosperms it has become the woody cone.

stroboscope A device for producing a succession of short pulses of light, usually using light from a mercury arc lamp. The pulse frequency is variable, with several thousand flashes per second possible. In photography, it may be used to produce several images of a moving object in a single picture.

Stroessner, Alfredo [stresner] (1912–2006) Paraguayan dictator, born in Encarnación, Paraguay. He became president in 1954, and was re-elected at regular intervals, but he was forced to stand down after a coup in 1989. He spent the rest of his life in Brazil.

Stroheim, Erich von [strohhiym], originally **Erich Oswald Stroheim** (1886–1957) Film director and actor, born in Vienna. His first success as film director was with *Blind Husbands* (1919), followed by the classic film *Greed* (1923). Later he returned to film acting, often playing the roles of German officers, as in *Desert Fox* (1951).

stroke A sudden interference with the blood supply to the brain which results in the death of nerve tissue followed by varying degrees of disability. If the part of the brain that controls vital functions is affected, death is the result. It may be caused by the rupture of an artery, by the clotting of blood within an artery (*thrombosis*), or by an embolism.

Strong, Sir Roy (Colin) (1935–) Art historian and museum director, born in London. He became assistant keeper (1959) and director (1967) of the National Portrait Gallery, London, and director of the Victoria and Albert Museum (1974–87). In 1992 he wrote and presented the BBC TV series *Royal Gardens*.

strong interaction The strong short-range force binding together protons and neutrons in atomic nuclei, and quarks in protons and neutrons; also called **strong nuclear force**. It is independent of and stronger than electromagnetic force, and governs nuclear fission, fusion, and alpha decay.

strong nuclear force *strong interaction*

strontium Sr, element 38, melting point 769°C. A very reactive metal, very similar to calcium, and also an alkaline earth element; not found uncombined. Its main importance is that it will replace calcium in most crystals. One isotope, strontium-90, is an important product of nuclear fission, with a half-life of 28 years.

structuralism A theory which attempts to define the general properties of cultural systems, including language, mythology, art, and social organization; the approach derives from the work of the Swiss linguist Ferdinand de Saussure and the French anthropologist Claude Lévi-Strauss. The fundamental thesis is that individual terms or phenomena can be understood only in relationship to other elements of the same system, and that each system is built up using a limited set of contrasts.

structure plan A requirement of UK planning law. Each planning authority has to produce a structure plan which is approved by the secretary of state for the environment. It forms the basis for policies of development (eg land use, traffic management) in the authority's area.

strychnine A poisonous alkaloid present in members of the genus *Strychnos*, thorny trees or climbing shrubs with hook-like tendrils, native to the tropics. *Strychnos nux vomica* was introduced into Germany in the 16th-c as a rat poison (and is still used for this purpose). (Genus: *Strychnos*, 200 species. Family: Loganiaceae.)

Stuart (Australia) *Alice Springs*

Stuart or **Stewart, Prince Charles Edward (Louis Philip Casimir)**, known as **the Young Pretender** and **Bonnie Prince Charlie** (1720–88) Claimant to the British crown, born in Rome, the son of James Francis Edward Stuart. In 1745, he landed with seven followers at Eriskay in the Hebrides (Jul 1745) and raised his father's standard. The clansmen flocked to him, Edinburgh surrendered, and he kept court at Holyrood. Victorious at Prestonpans, he invaded England, but was routed at Culloden Moor (1746). With the help of Flora Macdonald he escaped to the Continent. He then lived in France and Italy, where (after his father's death in 1766) he assumed the title of Charles III of Great Britain.

Stuart or **Stewart, Prince James (Francis Edward)**, also known as **the Old Pretender** (1688–1766) Claimant to the British throne, born in London, the only son of James II of England and his second wife, Mary of Modena. In 1715 he landed at Peterhead, Aberdeenshire during the Jacobite rising, but left Scotland some weeks later. Thereafter he lived mainly in Rome.

Stuart, John McDouall (1815–66) Explorer, born in Dysart, Fife. He accompanied Captain Charles Sturt's expedition (1844–6), and in 1860 traversed Australia from S to N. Mt Stuart is named after him.

Stuarts, earlier spelled **Stewarts** A Scottish royal family, commencing with Robert II (r. 1371–90), which succeeded to the English throne in 1603 with the accession of James VI and I, the great-grandson of Henry VIII's sister, Margaret. James I (1603–25) and Charles II (1649–85) were both successful politicians; but Charles I (1625–49) and James II (1685–8) were not, and both lost their thrones. The Stuart line ended in 1714 with the death of Queen Anne, although pretenders laid claim to the throne as late as 1745.

Stubbs, George (1724–1806) Anatomist, painter, and engraver, born in Liverpool, Merseyside. He was best known for his sporting pictures, and excelled in painting horses.

stucco [stukoh] A good quality plaster often used in classical architecture for low relief ornamental carvings and mouldings. It is also employed as an inexpensive render which can replace or resemble stone.

stump-jump plough An Australian-designed plough (patented 1881) with shears that work independently of each other, allowing the cultivation of land with roots or large stones. Ordinary ploughs break under such conditions.

stupa [stoopa] An Indian cairn or mound originally constructed over the ashes of an emperor or some other great person, such as the Buddha. Later they were used to house the ashes of Buddhist monks and holy relics.

sturgeon Any of a group of large, primitive fish found in the N hemisphere; body elongate, armed with rows of heavy bony scales; head tapering, underside mouth with long barbels; body length 1–5 m/3–16 ft; eggs sold as caviar. (Family: Acipenseridae, 4 genera, 25 species.)

Sturluson, Snorri [sturluson] (1179–1241) Icelandic poet and historian. His main works were the *Prose Edda* and *Heimskringla* ('the Circle of the World'), a series of sagas of the Norwegian kings down to 1177.

Sturm und Drang [shtoorm unt drang] (Ger 'storm and stress') A revolutionary literary movement in late-18th-c Germany, which rejected classical values in favour of subjective feeling and artistic creativity. An important tributary of the Romantic movement, it influenced Goethe, Schiller, and Herder.

Sturt, Charles (1795–1869) British explorer, born in Bengal, India. He went as an army captain to Australia, and headed three important expeditions (1828–45), discovering the Darling (1828) and the lower Murray Rivers (1830).

stuttering A disorder of fluency in the use of language; also called **stammering**. There is difficulty in controlling the rhythm and timing of speech, and a failure to communicate easily, rapidly, and continuously. Individual sounds may be abnormally repeated, lengthened, or fail to be released. The cause is unknown, but several physiological, genetic, and psychological factors have been implicated.

Stuttgart [shtutgah(r)t] 48°47N 9°12E, pop (2000e) 588 000. City in Germany; on the R Neckar; founded, 10th-c; former capital of the kingdom of Württemberg; badly bombed in World War 2; railway, airport; two universities (1967); notable mineral springs; major fruit and wine area; birthplace of Hegel; castle (originally 13th-c, much rebuilt).

Stuyvesant, Peter [stiyvesant] (1592–1672) Dutch administrator, born in Scherpenzeel, The Netherlands. In 1646 he directed the New Netherland colony, doing much for the commercial prosperity of New Amsterdam until his reluctant surrender to the English in 1664.

stye A localized infection in a gland or around a hair follicle in the eyelid. It causes a small, painful swelling in the eyelid, and is best treated by an appropriate antibiotic.

style (botany) In flowering plants, the upper part of the carpel, separating the ovary and stigma. It may be elongated in order to better present the stigma to receive pollen.

stylistics The systematic study of style, using the principles and procedures of linguistics. 'Style' here includes the features of language which identify an individual (as in 'Shakespeare's style') as well as those which identify major occupational groups (as in 'legal style', 'scientific style'). In **stylometry** or **stylostatistics**, a quantitative analysis is made of a text, to determine its statistical structure. Such studies are particularly important in plotting historical changes in style, or in investigating questions of disputed authorship.

Stylites, Simeon Simeon Stylites, St

stylometry stylistics

Styne, Jule (1905–94) Songwriter, born in London. For three decades he wrote dozens of memorable melodies for films and Broadway musicals, among them 'Diamonds are a Girl's Best Friend' (1949), 'Three Coins in the Fountain' (1954, Oscar), and 'People' (1964).

styrene C_6H_5–CH=CH_2, boiling point 145°C, **phenylethene** or **vinylbenzene**. A colourless liquid, which undergoes addition polymerization to a glassy resin called **polystyrene**. 'Expanded'

polystyrene, made porous with trapped gas, is widely used as a thermally-insulating packing material.

styrene butadiene rubber rubber

Styx [stiks] In Greek mythology, a principal river of the Underworld; the name means 'hateful'. It was also the name of a river in Arcadia, which passes through a gloomy gorge.

subatomic particles A general term for all particles smaller than atoms. It refers to electrons, protons, and neutrons, which directly constitute atoms, and to other particles including composite particles, resonances, and fundamental particles. All subatomic particles are either bosons (force particles) or fermions (matter particles).

subconscious unconscious

subduction zone A region in which one crustal plate of the Earth is forced down (**subducted**) beneath another, and moves down into the mantle where it is eventually assimilated. Present-day subduction zones occur around the margins of the Pacific Ocean at the sites of deep ocean trenches, and are associated with earthquake and volcanic activity and the formation of island arcs such as Japan and the Aleutian Is.

sublimation (chemistry) Passing directly from solid to vapour without an intermediate liquid phase. Substances which sublime at normal pressures include solid carbon dioxide ('dry ice') and iodine.

subliminal advertising Advertising designed to be imperceptible to the conscious mind of audiences. It mostly involves split-second projections of brand names or commands ('Eat Popcorn'), screened in the cinema or on television, or sound messages at frequencies beyond the range of human hearing. It is now banned in most countries, though its actual extent and effectiveness are still disputed.

submachine-gun A small-arm midway in size between a pistol and a rifle, capable of firing a burst of automatic fire. First developed around 1918, it was used extensively during World War 2, but has been replaced in most modern armies by the assault rifle.

submarine A vessel capable of remaining submerged for a considerable period of time. Since the advent of nuclear-armed, submarine-launched ballistic missiles, such as Polaris, submarines have become the most powerfully armed and strategically important of all warships, playing two distinct roles. They can act as an attack vessel, armed with torpedoes and missiles to attack other ships (including other submarines) at sea; and they can act as a floating platform for long-range missiles.

Subotica [soobotitsa], Hung **Szabadka** 46°04N 19°41E, pop (2000e) 101 000. Town in the autonomous province of Vojvodina, NW Serbia; railway.

subpoena [suhpeena] (Lat 'under penalty') An order to a person to attend court to give evidence or produce relevant documents. Failure to comply with the order is a contempt of court. The term is not used in Scottish law.

subsistence agriculture A form of farming where the land provides most of the necessities of life – food, fuel, and shelter. Tools and other items which cannot be generated in this way are acquired through trading surplus commodities.

succinic acid [suhksinik] HOOC–CH_2–CH_2–COOH, IUPAC **butanedioic acid**, melting point 188°C. A colourless solid, occurring in sugar cane, and also formed during fermentation.

Succoth Sukkoth

succubus [suhkyubuhs] incubus

succulent A plant in which the stems and leaves are fleshy and swollen with water-storage tissues. It is common in arid regions and other places where water is present, but not easily available.

Suchow Suzhou

sucker A shoot growing from a root, usually at some distance from the parent. It eventually develops its own root system and becoming independent of the parent plant.

Suckling, Sir John (1609–41) Poet and playwright, born in Whitton, Greater London. His plays (*Aglaura*, 1637) are austere, but his lyrics are acclaimed. They were published in *Fragmenta aurea* (1646).

Sucre [sookray], originally **Charcas**, also known as **Ciudad Blanca** 19°05S 65°15W, pop (2000e) 133 100. City in SC Bolivia; altitude 2790 m/9153 ft; official judicial and legal capital of Bolivia; founded 1538; revolutionary centre against Spain in 18th-c; airfield; railway; university (1624); cathedral (17th-c).

Sucre, Antonio José de [sookray] (1793–1830) South American soldier-patriot, born in Cumaná, Venezuela. He was Bolívar's lieutenant, who defeated the Spaniards at Ayacucho (1824), and became the first president (1826) of Bolivia.

sucrose [sookrohs] $C_{12}H_{22}O_{11}$, the best-known sugar – a disaccharide made up of a glucose molecule joined to a fructose molecule. It is digested in the small intestine to produce equal proportions of the monosaccharides glucose and fructose, which are then absorbed. Sucrose is the sugar of table sugar, icing sugar, and caster sugar, and may be obtained from either sugar beet or sugar cane.

Sudan *p.897*

sudden infant death syndrome (SIDS) The sudden, unexpected death of an infant for which no adequate cause can be found on clinical or post-mortem examination; also known as **cot death**. Current theories include the cessation of breathing (*apnoea*) as a result of an unusually prolonged spell of respiratory irregularity; an exaggerated neural response to the drawing up of a small amount of stomach contents into the respiratory tract; obstruction to the airways as a result of temporary closure of the structures below the pharynx; increased vulnerability to toxins of respiratory bacteria that are normally harmless; the presence of harmful chemicals in mattresses; and disturbance of body temperature control related to a cold environment or to excessive covering with bedding; it is more common among infants of parents who smoke. In 2006, research suggested that a brain abnormality, probably genetic in origin, may be responsible for SIDS. Studies of infant fatalities showed that they had a reduced ability to use and recycle the chemical serotonin. This subtle abnormality in the brainstem impairs a baby's ability to detect insufficient oxygen levels in the body, thus increasing the risk that a baby will become deprived of oxygen. It is hoped that a diagnostic test to identify babies with this condition will be developed.

Sudeten or **Sudetenland** [soodaytenland] Mountainous territory on Polish–Czech border, comprising the Sudetic Mts rising to 1603 m/5259 ft at Sněžka; during World War 2, the name also applied to the parts of Bohemia and Moravia occupied by German-speaking people; invaded by Germany in 1938, and restored to Czechoslovakia in 1945.

su doku or **sudoku** [soodohkoo], often capitalized, Jap **su** ('number') + **doku** ('single') A number logic game which became phenomenally popular in 2005. The puzzle has a nine-by-nine grid composed of nine three-by-three boxes, giving 81 squares, some of which are filled in with numbers. The goal is to fill in all the squares so that each row, column, and box contains the numbers one to nine once only. The concept of su doku appears to have originated with mathematician Leonhard Euler who, in 1783, devised a puzzle called 'Latin Squares'. A form of the game was published in the USA by Dell Magazines during the late 1970s (called Number Place), but in 1986 modifications were made to the puzzle by Japanese publisher Nikoli, who renamed it su doku. It was introduced into Britain at that time, but became mainstream only when it appeared in the *Daily Mail* towards the end of 2004. The game has since appeared in newspapers, magazines, books, television, the

Web, and on mobile phones. Spin-offs include a version using the first nine letters of the alphabet.

Sue, Eugène [sü], pseudonym of **Marie Joseph Sue** (1804–57) Novelist, born in Paris. He wrote a vast number of Byronic novels idealizing the poor, such as *Les Mystères de Paris* (1843, The Mysteries of Paris), which was a major influence on Hugo.

Suetonius [swetohnius], in full **Gaius Suetonius Tranquillus** (75–160) Roman biographer and antiquarian. His best-known work is *De vita Caesarum* (The Lives of the First Twelve Caesars). Only fragments survive of his other writings.

Suez [sooiz], Arabic **al-Suweis** 29°59N 32°33E, pop (2000e) 469 800. Seaport in E Egypt; at S end of Suez Canal; railway.

Suez Canal *p.898*

Suez Crisis A political crisis focused on the Suez Canal in 1956. When Egypt's President Nasser bought armaments from the Soviet block, the USA withdrew its support for the building of the Aswan Dam, whose financing collapsed. To remedy this, Nasser nationalized the Suez Canal, so that Canal revenues might pay for the Dam. Given the strategic interests of Britain and France in the Canal, they sought first to overturn Nasser's decision by appeal to the International Court, which instead confirmed the legality of the Egyptian government's move; thereafter, Britain and France worked to overthrow Nasser himself. Excluding the USA from their planning, they colluded with Israel to provoke a conflict which would serve as a pretext for Anglo-French intervention. Israel invaded the Sinai in October 1956, followed by French and British forces in the cities of the Canal Zone. Diplomatic action by the USA and the USSR forced Britain and France to withdraw, and Israel to relinquish the Sinai.

Suffolk [suhfuhk] pop (2001e) 668 500; area 3797 km²/1466 sq mi. County of E England; county town, Ipswich.

suffragette A woman identified with the late 19th–early 20th-c movement in the UK and USA to secure voting rights for women. The vote was won after the end of World War 1 in 1918, though it was limited to those women of 30 years of age or over. In England it was not until 1929 that women over 21 achieved the right to vote.

Sufism Islamic mysticism which represents a move away from the legalistic approach in Islam to a more personal relationship with God. The word comes from Arabic *suf* 'wool', because the early story-tellers from whom Sufism evolved wore woollen garments.

sugar beet *beet*

sugar cane A bamboo-like grass but with soft canes 3–8 m/10–26 ft high, 3.5–5 cm/1½–2 in diameter; white to yellowish-green, red, or purplish; cultivated in tropical and sub-tropical environments. The cane is cut, chopped, and soaked in water to extract the sugar (*sucrose*), and the sugary solution is filtered, clarified, and dried. Sucrose crystallizes out, leaving *molasses* behind. The raw sugar is brown, and can be further purified to yield white sugar. (*Saccharum officinarum*. Family: Gramineae.)

sugar palm A tree growing to 12 m/40 ft, native to Malaysia (*Arenga saccifera*); leaves 1–1.5 m/3¼–5 ft, feathery, silver beneath; also called **gomuti palm**. Sugar is obtained from the sap. (Family: Palmae.)

sugars A group of sweet-tasting carbohydrates, chemically classified into single-unit (*monosaccharide*) and double-unit (*disaccharide*) types. Most people take *sugar* to mean *sucrose*; however, many other sugars are present in our diet, although not to the same levels as sucrose. These include *lactose*, the sugar of milk, and free *glucose* and *fructose* in fruits and honey.

Suharto [soohah(r)toh] (1921–) Indonesian soldier, statesman, and president (1968–98), born in Kemusu, Java. Educated for service in the Dutch colonial army, in 1965 he became Indonesia's chief of the army staff. Following civil unrest under

Sudan

☐ International Airport — — Border in dispute

[soodan], official name **Republic of Sudan**, Arabic **Jamhuryat es-Sudan**

Local name As-Sūdān (Arabic)

Timezone GMT +2

Area 2 505 870 km²/967 243 sq mi

Population total (2002e) 37 090 000

Status Republic

Date of independence 1956

Capital Khartoum

Languages Arabic (official), local languages, including Darfurian, Nilotic, and Nilo-Hamitic, are also spoken

Ethnic groups Black (52%), Arab (39%), Beja (6%)

Religions Muslim (Sunni 70%), traditional animist beliefs (20%), Christian (5%)

Physical features Largest country on the African continent, astride the middle reaches of the R Nile; E edge formed by Nubian Highlands and an escarpment rising c.2000 m/6500 ft on the Red Sea; Imatong Mts (S) rise to 3187 m/10 456 ft at Kinyeti, highest point in Sudan; Darfur Massif in the W; White Nile flows N to meet the Blue Nile at Khartoum.

Climate Tropical, continental; desert conditions in NW, with temperatures rarely falling below 24°C; hottest months (Jul–Aug); sandstorms common; average annual temperature 23°C (Jan), 32°C (Jul) in Khartoum; average annual rainfall 157 mm/6·2 in.

Currency Sudanese Dinar (SDD) = 100 piastres

Economy Dominated by agriculture (employs c.75% of population); commercial farming (N) and livestock farming (S); large-scale irrigation schemes, fed by dams; major famines, especially 1984–5, 1990–1, and from 2005; gum arabic (80% of world supply); reserves of copper, lead, iron ore, chromite, manganese, gold; development hindered by poor transport system.

GDP (2002e) $52·9 bn, per capita $1400

Human Development Index (2002) 0·499

History Christianized in 6th-c; Muslim conversion from 13th–c; Egyptian control of N Sudan, early 19th-c; Mahdi unified W and C tribes in a revolution, 1881; fall of Khartoum, 1885; combined British-Egyptian offensive, 1898, leading to a jointly administered condominium; independence, 1956; period of military rule following coup in 1985; drought and N-S rivalry have contributed to years of instability and several coups; a transitional constitution of 1987 provided for a President, Prime Minister, Council of Ministers, and a Legislative Assembly; military coup, 1989, suspended constitution and dissolved National Assembly which was replaced by a Revolutionary Command Council; subsequent civil war between government and rebel Sudanese People's Liberation Army (SPLM); national constitutional conference to discuss reform, 1992; peace talks begun, 1993; new constitution, 1998; attacks by government-sponsored Janjaweed militia in Darfur led to over 30 000 deaths and the displacement of over a million people, 2004; peace accord signed (May 2004), but mass attacks on the black African population ongoing in Darfur; UN resolution called on the government to disarm the Janjaweed (Aug 2004); Sudan agreed to new UN Security Council resolution to end conflict (Sep 2004); talks to solve Darfur crisis ongoing; historic peace agreement between government and SPLM, Jan 2005; new government of national unity (Sep 2005) with members of SPLM and former ruling National Congress Party (NCP).

Chief of State

1956–8 Council of State
1958–64 Ibrahim Abboud
1964–5 Council of Sovereignty
1965–9 Ismail al-Azhari
1969–85 (Nemery) Gaafar Mohamad al-Nimeiri (President from 1971)

Chairman – Transitional Military Council

1985–6 Abd al-Rahman Siwar al-Dahab

Chairman – Supreme Council

1986–9 Ahmad al-Mirghani
1989–93 Omar Hassan Ahmed al-Bashir

Head of State/Government

1993– Omar Hassan Ahmad al-Bashir

Sukarno, he assumed power in 1967, becoming titular president the following year. He was forced to step down in 1998 following an economic crisis and civil disturbance. He was charged with embezzlement from the state but in 2000 judges ruled that he was medically unfit to stand trial for corruption, and the charges were dropped in 2006 for health reasons.

suicide The act of deliberate self-destruction. Up to 1961 in the UK, attempted suicide was considered to be a crime, and it is still illegal in some US states. Since then it has been accepted as a terminal symptom of an abnormal mental state. It is a rec-

ognized complication of severe depressive illness or psychosis in which the individual suffers from inconsolable moods of despair, guilt, and self-blame. In other cases death results unintentionally from a conscious attempt to manipulate a situation, or from an impulse to obtain redress of circumstances which cause distress. This act is sometimes referred to as **parasuicide**. In some societies, suicide in certain circumstances is socially acceptable, and in ancient Greece and Rome, it was offered to the privileged as an alternative to execution. Recent years have seen the emergence of such groups as the Hemlock

Suez Canal

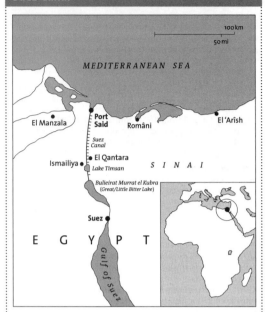

Canal connecting the Mediterranean and Red Seas, in NE Egypt; built by Ferdinand de Lesseps, 1859–69; length 184 km/114 mi, including 11 km/7 mi of approaches to Suez (S end) and Port Said (N end); minimum width, 60 m/197 ft; minimum draught, 16 m/52 ft; passes through L Timsah, and the Great and Little Bitter Lakes; by 1882 Convention, open to vessels of any nation (except in wartime); controlled by British, 1882–1956; nationalized by Egypt, 1956; blocked by Egypt during war with Israel, 1967; reopened, 1975; a major international waterway, and a substantial Egyptian economic asset.

Society in the USA, and other societies which represent the 'right to die'.

Sui dynasty [swee] (581–618) A two-reign dynasty which began the second great imperial phase of Chinese history (590–907). The crown was seized by Yang Jian, who took the reign name Wendi (590–604). He was followed by Yang Guang (Yangdi, 604–18). The Sui dynasty conquered the S and reunited China (590), fell to Northern insurrection, and was replaced by the Tang dynasty.

suite In Baroque music, a set of dances, all in the same key, perhaps preceded by a prelude; the terms *partita* and *ordre* are also used. Since the 19th-c the term has been used for a sequence of separate but connected pieces (as in Holst's *The Planets*) and for an orchestral selection from an opera, ballet, or other long work.

Sukarno or **Soekarno, (Achmed)** [sukah(r)noh] (1902–70) Indonesian statesman and first president of Indonesia (1945–66), born in Surabaya, Java. He formed the Indonesia National Party in 1927, and became president when Indonesia was granted independence in 1945. An abortive communist coup (1965) led to a takeover by the army, his powers gradually devolving onto General Suharto. Sukarno finally retired in 1968.

sukiyaki [sukeeyakee] A Japanese beef dish. Thinly sliced beef is cooked with suet in an iron pan in the middle of the table. Sauce is added, made of *shoyu*, beaten raw egg, sugar, and *mirin* (a type of sweet saké).

Sukkoth or **Succoth** [suhkohth, -koht] The Jewish Feast of Tabernacles or Booths, celebrated in September or October (15–21 Tishri) as a festival of thanksgiving. Light temporary shelters are constructed in homes and in synagogues, in memory of the tents used by the Israelites in the desert after leaving Egypt (*Exodus* 13).

Sukkur [sukoor], also **Sakhar** 27°42N 68°54E, pop (2000e) 315 000. City in Pakistan; on E bank of R Indus; Sukkur (Lloyd) Barrage built 1928–32 (dam 58 m/190 ft high); railway junction.

Sulaiman or **Suleyman I** [sülayman], known as **the Magnificent** (1494–1566) Ottoman Sultan (1520–66), who added to his dominions by conquest Belgrade, Budapest, Rhodes, Tabriz, Baghdad, Aden, and Algiers. His system of laws regulating land tenure earned him the name *Kanuni* ('law-giver'), and he was a great patron of arts and architecture.

Sulawesi [sulawaysee] Island in Indonesia, off E Borneo; formerly **Celebes**; pop (2000e) 14 715 000; area 189 216 km²/73 037 sq mi; chief towns Ujung Pandang, Palu, Kendari, Manado.

Suleyman *Sulaiman*

sulfur *sulphur*

Sulla, Lucius Cornelius, nickname **Felix** ('Lucky') (138–78 BC) Ruthless and enigmatic Roman politician of the late Republic, whose bitter feud with Marius twice plunged Rome into civil war in the 80s BC. Appointed 'Dictator' in 82 BC, he enacted a number of measures to boost the authority of the Senate.

Sullivan, Sir Arthur (Seymour) (1842–1900) Composer, born in London. From 1871 he was known for his collaboration with W S Gilbert in such comic operas as *HMS Pinafore* (1878) and *The Pirates of Penzance* (1879). He also composed a grand opera, *Ivanhoe* (1891), cantatas, ballads, a *Te Deum*, and hymn tunes.

Sullivan, Louis (Henry) (1856–1924) Architect, born in Boston, MA. His experimental, functional skeleton constructions of skyscrapers and office blocks, particularly the Gage building and stock exchange, Chicago, IL, earned him the title 'Father of Modernism'.

Sully, Maximilien de Béthune, duc de (Duke of) [sülee] (1560–1641) French Huguenot soldier, financier, and statesman, born in Rosny, France. Instrumental in arranging Henry of Navarre's marriage to Marie de Médicis (1600), he became the king's trusted counsellor. His major achievement was the restoration of the economy after the civil wars.

Sully-Prudhomme [sülee prüdom], pseudonym of **René François Armand Prudhomme** (1839–1907) Poet, born in Paris. A leader of the Parnassian movement, which tried to restore elegance and control to poetry in reaction against Romanticism, he was awarded the first Nobel Prize for Literature in 1901.

sulphonamides / sulfonamides [suhlfonamiydz] The first drugs to be used for the prevention and cure of bacterial infections in humans; their introduction in the late 1930s resulted in a sharp decline in deaths from infectious diseases.

sulphur / sulfur S, element 16, a non-metal occurring in nature in yellow molecular crystals of S₈, also called **brimstone**. The solid melts at 113°C and boils at 440°C. It shows a great variety of oxidation states, giving rise to compounds called **sulphides**, **sulphites**, and **sulphates**. By far the most important use is oxidation to sulphuric acid.

sulphuric / sulfuric acid H_2SO_4, boiling point 330°C. A strong dibasic acid, a colourless oily liquid, formerly known as **oil of vitriol** or simply **vitriol**. It is one of the most important industrial chemicals, used in the production of almost all other acids, and in the manufacture of fertilizers, fabrics, dyestuffs, and detergents.

Sulston, Sir John E (1942–) British microbiologist. A researcher at the Sanger Centre in Cambridge, UK, he shared the 2002 Nobel

Prize for Physiology or Medicine for discoveries concerning the genetic regulation of organ development and programmed cell death.

sumac or **sumach** [soomak] Any of several species of a genus which includes poison ivy and the turpentine tree, many causing skin damage or dermatitis. (Genus: *Rhus*. Family: Anacardiaceae.)

Sumatra [sumahtra], Indonesian **Sumatera** pop (2000e) 43 369 000; area 473 606 km²/182 812 sq mi. Island in W Indonesia, S of the Malay Peninsula; 1760 km/1094 mi long and 400 km/250 mi wide; centre of Buddhist kingdom of Sri Vijaya, 7th–13th-c; separatist movement followed Indonesian independence, 1949; growing civil unrest in Aceh province in support of independence, 1999; major cities include Medan, Padang, Bukit Barisan range (W) rises to 3805 m/12 483 ft at Gunung Kerinci; flash floods in N Medan area, 2003; major earthquake off NW coast caused tsunami devastation, especially in Aceh province, Dec 2004; further strong earthquake off NW coast, Mar 2005.

Sumer [soomer] The name given to the part of Lower Mesopotamia between Babylon and the Persian Gulf. It is the place where the world's first urban civilization evolved.

summary trial A trial in a court of summary jurisdiction, in England and Wales in the magistrates' court, and in Scotland in either the Sheriff Court without a jury or in district courts. A number of offences may be tried on either a summary or indictable basis and certain ones such as theft are regularly tried in courts of summary jurisdiction. The decision about mode of trial largely rests with the prosecutor, although in England and Wales the defence have a right in certain circumstances to demand a trial on indictment before a jury. Such a right does not exist in Scotland.

Summers, Anne (Fairhurst) (1945–) Academic, journalist, and bureaucrat, born in Deniliquin, New South Wales, Australia. In 1987 she became editor-in-chief of the influential American feminist magazine *Ms*, and was its editor-at-large (1990–2). Adviser on women's affairs to Prime Minister Paul Keating in 1992, she returned to journalism as editor of the *Sydney Morning Herald* and (until 1997) *The Age*'s colour supplement.

Summer Time *Daylight Saving Time*

summit diplomacy A term first used in the 1950s for negotiations between heads of state and governments with the intention of resolving disagreements; also known as **summitry**. Since the 1960s it has been applied to any special meeting between national leaders, with a symbolic and formal content.

sumo wrestling A Japanese national sport steeped in history and tradition. Competition takes place in a 12 ft (3·66 m) diameter circle, the object being to force one's opponent out of the ring or to the ground. Sumo wrestlers are very large and eat vast amounts of food to increase their weight and body size.

Sun The central object of our Solar System and the nearest star to the Earth. Its average distance from Earth is 150 million km/93 million mi, and on account of this proximity it is studied more than any other star. The source of its energy is nuclear reactions in the central core (temperature 15 million K, relative density 155) extending to a quarter of the solar radius and including half the mass. Our Sun is nearly 5000 million years old, and is about halfway through its expected life cycle.

sun bear The smallest bear (length, 1·3 m/4 ft), native to SE Asia; short black coat with pale snout and yellow crescent on chest; also known as **honey bear**, **Malay bear**, or **bruang**. (*Helarctos malayanus*.)

sunbird A small songbird, native to the Old World tropics and the Middle East; slender curved bill and tubular tongue. (Family: Nectariniidae, 106 species.)

sunburn Damage to the skin caused by strong sunlight, especially in people with fair complexions. Short exposure results

in redness and itch. More prolonged exposure causes pain, swelling of the skin, and blistering, accompanied by fever, headache, and nausea. Serious overexposure can cause skin cancers.

Sunda Islands [soonda] Island group in Indonesia, comprising the **Greater Sunda Is** of Java, Sumatra, Borneo, and Sulawesi, with their small adjacent islands, and **Nusa Tenggara**, formerly the **Lesser Sunda Is** of Bali, Lombok, Sumba, Sumbawa, Flores, and Timor, with their small islands.

Sun Dance An annual summer ceremony of the Plains Indians of North America. Participants are subject to a demanding discipline including ceremonial dancing while gazing at the Sun.

Sundance Kid, popular name of **Harry Longabaugh** or **Langbaugh** (1867–?1909) Outlaw, born in Phoenixville, PA. He teamed up with Butch Cassidy, and drifted throughout North and South America robbing banks, trains, and mines. His date and place of death is uncertain, but it is generally held that he was fatally shot by a cavalry unit in Bolivia.

Sundanese A people from the highlands of W Java, Indonesia, but now also living in other parts of Java and Sumatra. One of three main groups on the island, they converted to Islam in the 16th-c.

Sunday The day of the week set aside by the Christian religion for divine worship, mainly in commemoration of Christ's resurrection. In 1971 the UK ratified the recommendation of the International Standardization Organization that Monday replace Sunday as the first day of the week.

Sunday School Classes for the religious education of children, usually linked to worship services, in Protestant Churches. They derive from the Sunday charity school, instituted in London in 1780, for the basic education of children of the poor.

Sunday trading The opening of shops for trading on a Sunday. In England and Wales, as a result of a 20-year sustained campaign, the Shops Act (1950), which prohibited Sunday opening ('Keep Sunday Special'), was repealed by the Sunday Trading Act (1994). The Employment Rights Act (1996) contains regulations controlling Sunday trading. Larger shops may now open on a Sunday for a continuous period of six hours between 10 am and 6 pm, and small shops may open at any time.

Sunderland, formerly **Wearmouth** 54°55N 1°23W, pop (2001e) 280 800. Port city in Tyne and Wear, NE England; at the mouth of the R Wear; site of monastery (674); city status, 1992; railway; university (1992); football league team, Sunderland (Black Cats).

sundew A carnivorous plant, usually a small perennial, native in most tropical and temperate regions, especially Australasia and S Africa; flowers 5-petalled, in slender spikes. The long hairs of the leaves are tentacle-like, and secrete a sticky substance which traps insects. (Genus: *Drosera*, 100 species. Family: Droseraceae.)

sundial A device for showing the passage of time by the shadow cast on a graduated scale by a *gnomon* (some solid object, such as a rod or triangular plate attached to the dial). The earliest-known sundial dates from c.300 BC.

Sundsvall [sunsval] 62°22N 17°20E, pop (2000e) 98 200. Seaport and commercial town in SE Sweden; important trading centre from the 6th-c; charter, 1624; railway.

sunfish Large and very distinctive fish (*Mola mola*) widespread in open waters of tropical to temperate seas; body compressed, almost circular; length typically 1–2 m/3¹⁄₄–6¹⁄₂ ft, but up to 4 m/13 ft; mouth small, teeth fused into a sharp beak; also called **trunkfish**. (Family: Molidae.)

sunflower A large annual (*Helianthus annuus*) growing to 3 m/10 ft, a native of North America; usually a solitary drooping flower-head up to 30 cm/12 in across; outer ray florets golden yellow. Several varieties are cultivated for the edible and rich oil-yielding seeds. (Family: Compositae.)

Sung dynasty *Song* 1

sungrabe *finfoot*

Sung Tsu-wen *Song Ziwen*

Sun Microsystems A major company in the information technology field, specializing in the provision of hardware and software for the Internet and the World Wide Web. The company has developed, and currently markets, the JAVA programming language.

Sunnism [sunizm] The orthodox version of Islam, which bases its legitimacy on the sayings and actions, or *sunnah*, of the Prophet Mohammed. Sunnis represent c.85% of Muslims in the world.

sunscreen The use of barrier creams to reduce the penetration of ultraviolet rays to the skin. A number of substances are used, including para-aminobenzoic acid and zinc.

sun spider A long-legged, predatory arthropod found mostly in deserts and arid habitats; fangs massive; first pair of legs slender, used as feelers; also known as **wind scorpions**. (Class: Arachnida. Order: Solpugida, c.900 species.)

sunspot An apparently dark region on the solar photosphere, the central part termed the *umbra*. They are caused by an intense magnetic field erupting from within the Sun, and follow a cycle of growth and decay over c.11 years.

sunstroke *heat stroke*

Sun Yixian [sun yeeshan], or **Sun Yatsen**, originally **Sun Wen** (1866–1925) Founder and early leader of China's Nationalist Party, born in Xiangshan, Guangdong, China. He helped to organize risings in S China, but after the 1911 Wuhan rising, realized that he would not be widely acceptable as president, and voluntarily handed over the office to Yuan Shikai. Civil war ensued (1913), and he set up a separate government at Guangzhou (Canton). He was widely accepted as the true leader of the nation.

Super Bowl The annual championship of American football's National Football League, played in January between the champions of the American Football Conference and the champions of the National Football Conference. Held at a neutral ground, it was first played in 1967. The most successful teams are Dallas Cowboys, San Francisco 49ers, and Pittsburgh Steelers, with five championships each.

superconductivity The property of zero electrical resistance, accompanied by the expulsion of magnetic fields, exhibited by certain metals, alloys, and compounds when cooled to below some critical temperature, typically less than $-260°C$. An electrical current established in a superconducting ring of material will continue indefinitely while the low temperature is maintained. High temperature superconductivity, for temperatures in excess of $-250°C$, was first observed in 1986 by Swiss physicist K Alexander Müller (1927–) and German physicist Georg Bednorz, using a ceramic of copper oxide containing barium and lanthanum. Superconductors are currently used in large magnets, such as those required by nuclear magnetic resonance spectrometers and particle accelerators.

superfluidity The property of zero resistance to flow (ie zero viscosity), exhibited by liquid helium at temperatures below $-271°C$. Superfluid helium exhibits unusual properties, including the ability to creep out of a container apparently in defiance of gravity, and the inability to be set spinning in the way a solid object can.

supergiant A rare type of star, very massive, and the most luminous known. Examples include Polaris, Betelgeuse (in Orion), and Canopus. They are 10–60 solar masses, 10 000 times brighter than the Sun, and thus visible at great distances.

supergravity A speculative quantum theory incorporating gravity, electromagnetic force, and nuclear force. It is a gauge theory based on supersymmetry, postulating gravitons and gravitinos as carriers of the gravitational force. Theoretically attractive, it lacks experimental support.

superheavy elements Elements having an atomic number (number of protons, Z) greater than 112. Superheavy elements do not occur in nature, and it was once believed impossible to create them via collisions between smaller nuclei. In fact, several new elements have been created by exactly this method. The heaviest naturally occurring atom is uranium, Z=92. Elements 114 and 116 were discovered in 1999. It is not known if there is a maximum atomic number beyond which an element cannot be created.

superheterodyne [sooperheterodiyn] The most common technique used in radio reception. The incoming radio-frequency signal is converted into a lower intermediate frequency by mixing it with a signal generated inside the receiver, called the *local oscillator*.

Superior, Lake Largest of the Great Lakes, and the largest freshwater lake in the world; part of US–Canadian boundary; length 563 km/350 mi; breadth 257 km/160 mi; maximum depth 405 m/1329 ft; area 82 103 km²/31 692 sq mi, 35% in Canada; connected with L Huron (SE) via St Mary's R (the Soo canals).

supernatural *paranormal*

supernova A rare and spectacular explosion resulting in the destruction of a massive star. Light emission is temporarily 100 million times brighter than the Sun, and the star can be seen for up to two years. Well-known examples are the supernova of 1054 (Crab Nebula), 1604 (seen by Kepler), and 1987 in the Large Magellanic Cloud.

superovulation syndrome A condition which occasionally results when infertile women are given human gonadotrophic hormone and/or the synthetic drug clomiphene to stimulate ovulation. Several ova may be released simultaneously and then fertilized, with consequential multiple births.

superphosphates Fertilizers containing phosphate as the $H_2PO_4{}^{2-}$ ion. They are so called because, for a given weight, $Ca(H_2PO_4)_2$ contains more phosphorus than does $CaHPO_4$.

Superrealism *Photorealism*

supersonic In fluid mechanics, fluid flow which is faster than the velocity of sound in that fluid, either in the case of an object moving through the fluid, or a fluid moving around a stationary object. Supersonic aircraft fly faster than the speed of sound in air.

superstition A derogatory description of any behaviour, usually traditional in origin, that has lost its rationale though still betraying a fear of the unknown. An example is 'touching wood' when mentioning one's good fortune, a hidden reference to the cross on which Christ was crucified. In Ancient Roman religion, *superstition* referred to an act or attitude of excessive piety; the term was later applied by Christian clergy to religious or quasi-religious acts which they regarded as pagan or corrupt, such as ringing church bells to avert thunderstorms.

superstrings A speculative quantum theory, embracing all the forces of nature, which may avoid the difficulties encountered by early unification schemes involving gravity; proposed by British physicist Michael Green and US physicist John Schwartz in 1984. It is based on a fundamental extended submicroscopic string in place of the usual point particle, plus supersymmetry.

supersymmetry In particle physics, a symmetry relation linking particles of different spins. Theories incorporating supersymmetry predict particles that are partners to observed particles, having the same mass but different spin. No such supersymmetric partners (squark, slepton, photino, and others) have been observed.

supply and demand An economic concept which states that the price of an article (or 'good') will move to the level where the quantity demanded by purchasers equals the quantity that suppliers are willing to sell.

supply-side economics The view that the main contribution of policy to promoting the growth of incomes is through measures to improve the supply of goods and services and the working of markets. The approach contrasts with the Keynesian view, which puts more weight on managing the economy so as to increase demand.

suprarenal glands *adrenal glands*

Suprematism A form of modern art based on four simple shapes: rectangle, circle, triangle, and cross. The movement was started in Russia c.1913 by Kazimir Malevich (1878–1935).

Supreme Court In the USA, the highest federal court established under the constitution, members of which are appointed by the president with the advice and consent of the Senate. In addition to its jurisdiction relating to appeals, the court also exercises oversight of the constitution through the power of judicial review of the acts of state, federal legislatures, and the executive.

Supreme Headquarters Allied Expeditionary Force (SHAEF) An organization formally established (1944) in the UK in World War 2 under General Eisenhower, with Air Chief Marshal Tedder as deputy supreme commander, to mount the Allied invasion of occupied Europe and strike at the heart of Germany.

Supreme Soviet *soviet*

Surabaya [soorabahya] or **Surabaja** 7°14S 112°45E, pop (2000e) 2 930 000. Industrial seaport in E Java, Indonesia, at mouth of R Kali Mas; Indonesia's second largest city; important trading centre since the 14th-c; airfield; railway; university (1954); naval base.

Surat [soorat] 21°12N 72°55E, pop (2000e) 1 757 000. Port in Gujarat, W India; rich trading centre of Mughal Empire, 17th–18th-c; first English trading post in India, 1612; headquarters of British East India Company until 1687; railway; university (1967).

Sûreté [süruhtay], in full **Sûreté nationale** (Fr 'National Security') One of four police forces existing in France, which are largely independent of each other. Founded in the early 19th-c, it is responsible for criminal investigations, corresponding roughly to the CID in Britain and the FBI in the USA.

surf Wind-generated waves that have broken upon encountering shallow water. Waves become unstable and 'break' typically in water depth of about 1·3 times the wave height. Once a wave has broken, the water particles move laterally towards the shore, and are known as surf.

surface active agent *surfactant*

surface physics The study of the electronic and structural properties of the surface of matter, ie the outermost layer of atoms. Surface properties are important in several domains, including catalysis, corrosion, the emission of electrons from surfaces, optical properties, and friction.

surface tension A property of the surface of a liquid. It is a tensioning force due to the inward attraction of molecules at the surface. Because of surface tension, liquid surfaces appear elastic, as observed in bubbles and soap films.

surfactant Any substance that strongly influences the surface properties of a material; also called a **surface active agent**. It is often applied to soaps and detergents, whose cleaning powers depend on the surfactant's ability to increase the spreading and wetting power of water.

surgeonfish Any of the family Acanthuridae of colourful deep-bodied fish widespread in tropical seas; name refers to the sharp movable spine on sides of tail which can be erected for defence; body length typically 10–40 cm/4–16 in; also called **tang**.

surgery The branch of medicine which treats diseases and conditions by operating on the patient. Early surgical operations were limited to those near the surface of the body, such as hernia repair and amputation. With modern anaesthesia, all parts of the body have become accessible, and surgery is now routine in such areas as the lungs, heart, and brain. Organ transplantation, and the development of artificial body parts are major modern developments.

Suriname *p.902*

Surrealism (Fr 'over' or 'intense' realism) An important movement in modern art and literature which flourished between the World Wars, mainly in France. The first Surrealist manifesto of André Breton (1924) proposed the subversion of 19th-c Realism by the three related means of humour, dream, and counterlogic (the absurd). The basic idea was to free the artist from the demands of logic, and to penetrate beyond everyday consciousness to the 'super-reality' that lies behind. Freud's theory of the subconscious was appealed to, and many pictures by Dali, Magritte, and Tanguy seek to recreate the fantasy world of dreams. In literature, the movement is illustrated by the work of Ionesco, Beckett, and Genet. Luis Buñuel guaranteed its impact on the cinema.

Surrey pop (2001e) 1 059 000; area 1679 km²/648 sq mi. County in SE England; crossed E–W by the North Downs, rising to 294 m/964 ft at Leith Hill; county town, Guildford; largely residential; Box Hill, Runnymede, Royal Botanic Gardens (Kew).

Surrey, Henry Howard, Earl of (c.1517–47) Courtier and poet, born in Hunsdon, Hertfordshire. He is remembered for his love poetry, influenced by the Italian tradition, in which he pioneered the use of blank verse and the Elizabethan sonnet form.

Surrey, Earl of *Howard, Henry*

surrogate mother An arrangement whereby a woman agrees to bear a child for someone else and to hand over that child at birth to another person or persons, who are known as the *commissioning parents*. In England and Wales, for example, legislation provides that parental responsibility is given up in favour of the commissioning parents. Adoption procedures are sometimes used when the surrogacy agreement has gone wrong and the parties are in dispute.

Surtees, John (1934–) Racing driver and motor-cyclist, born in Westerham, Kent, the only man to win world titles on two and four wheels. He won the 350 cc motor cycling world title in 1958–60, and the 500 cc title in 1956, 1958–60 (all on an MV Augusta). He then won the 1964 world title driving a Ferrari.

Surtsey Island [sertsee] area 1·9 km²/0·7 sq mi. Volcanic island off S coast of Iceland; one of the Westman Is; erupted and formed in 1963.

surveying The accurate measurement and collection of data, such as relief, for a given area in order to make a map. It has traditionally been based on fieldwork, using equipment such as chains, plane tables, and theodolites, used to measure the distance, elevation, and angle of an object from an observation point. **Geodetic surveying** is the measurement of the size and shape of the Earth, and the determination of the position of places on its surface.

Surveyor programme A series of robotic soft-lander missions to the Moon undertaken by NASA (May 1966–Jan 1968) in preparation for the manned Apollo landings. It was highly successful, with five of the seven spacecraft landing as planned.

Surya [soorya] The Sun-god in Hindu mythology. He was the son of Indra, the pre-eminent god of the Rig-Veda.

Susa [sooza] The Greek name for **Shushan**, in antiquity, the main city of Elam and the capital of the Achaemenid empire under Darius I and his successors. It is the site of the world's best preserved ziggurat.

Susanna, Book of A book of the Old Testament Apocrypha, or Chapter 13 of the Book of Daniel in Catholic versions of the Bible; an addition of uncertain date or provenance.

suslik *souslik*

Suslov, Mikhail Andreyevich [suslof] (1902–82) Soviet politician, born in Shakhovskoye, Russia. He opposed Khrushchev's 'de-

Suriname

☐ International Airport

[soorinam], also **Surinam**, official name **Republic of Suriname**, **Republiek Suriname**

Local name Suriname
Timezone GMT -3
Area 163 265 km²/63 020 sq mi
Population total (2002e) 436 000
Status Republic
Date of independence 1975

Capital Paramaribo
Languages Dutch (official), Hindi and Javanese (native languages), Sranan Tongo, Chinese and Spanish also spoken
Ethnic groups Indo-Pakistan (37%), Creole (31%), Javanese (15%), Amerindian (3%), Chinese (2%), European (1%)
Religions Hindu (27%), Protestant (25%), Roman Catholic (23%), Muslim (20%), indigenous beliefs (5%)·
Physical features Located in NE South America; N natural regions, range from coastal lowland through savannah to mountainous upland; coastal strip covered by swamp; highland interior (S) overgrown with dense tropical forest; highest point, Juliana Top, 1230 m/4035 ft, in SC; seven major rivers including Marowijne (E), Corantijn (W), Suriname.
Climate Equatorial tropical, uniformly hot and humid; two rainy seasons (May-Jul, Nov-Jan); average annual temperatures 22–33°C in Paramaribo; average monthly rainfall 310 mm/12·2 in (N), 67 mm/2·6 in (S).
Currency 1 Suriname Dollar (SRD) = 100 cents (before 2004, 1 Suriname Guilder (SRG) = 100 cents)
Economy Based on agriculture and mining, but hindered by lack of foreign exchange; bauxite mining (provides c.80% of export income); sugar cane, rice, citrus fruits, coffee, bananas, oil palms, cacao, fishing; vast timber resources.
GDP (2002e) $1·469 bn, per capita $3400
Human Development Index (2002) 0·756
History Sighted by Columbus, 1498; first settled by the British, 1651; taken by the states of Zeeland, 1667; captured by the British, 1799; restored to the Netherlands, 1814 and remained part of Netherland West Indies as Dutch Guiana; independence as the Republic of Suriname, 1975; emigration of c.40% of population to the Netherlands, following independence; military coup, 1980; ban on political activities lifted, 1985; 1987 constitution provides for a National Assembly, and a President elected by the Assembly.

Head of State (President)
1988-90 Ramsewak Shankar
1990–1 Johan Kraag
1991–6 Ronald Venetiaan
1996–2000 Jules Wijdenbosch
2000– Ronald Ventiaan

Head of Government (Vice-President)
1988–90 Henck Arron
1990–1 Jules Wijdenbosch
1991–6 Jules Adjodhia
1996–2000 Pretaapnarain Radhakishun
2000– Jules Ajodhia

Stalinization' measures, economic reforms, and foreign policy, and was instrumental in unseating him in 1964.

suspended sentence A sentence of imprisonment which is not activated immediately, but may be imposed should the offender commit a further offence during the period of suspension, in addition to any penalty the later court imposes. Suspended sentences may operate in conjunction with supervision by a probation officer. They are not available in all jurisdictions (eg in Scotland).

suspension A mixture in which particles (of solid or liquid) are dispersed through another phase (liquid or gas) without dissolving in it. Suspensions are not indefinitely stable, and will eventually settle into separate phases.

Sussex Former county of England; divided into East Sussex and West Sussex in 1974, West Sussex gaining part of S Surrey.

Sussex, East pop (2001e) 492 300; area 1795 km²/693 sq mi. County of SE England; South Downs parallel to the coast,

part of the Weald to the N; county town, Lewes; Brighton and Hove a unitary authority (from 1997); major tourist area on S coast; castles at Bodiam, Hastings, Lewes, Pevensey; site of Battle of Hastings.

Sussex, Kingdom of A kingdom of the Anglo-Saxon heptarchy, situated between Kent and Wessex, and founded probably by c.500. It was annexed to Wessex in the 9th-c.

Sussex, West pop (2001e) 753 600; area 1989 km²/768 sq mi. County of S England; South Downs parallel to the coast; county town, Chichester; Arundel and Bramber castles.

sustainable agriculture A system of crop cultivation which does not impair the manurial or humus content of the soil. Such systems contrast with many systems of crop cultivation, particularly those used in the tropics, in which the mineral content and water-holding capacity of the soil is continually reduced.

Sutcliffe, Peter, known as **the Yorkshire Ripper** (1946–) Convicted murderer, born in Bingley, West Yorkshire. He murdered

13 women over five years in N England and the Midlands, the first body being found in 1975. A routine check on a car registration led to his arrest in 1981.

Sutherland, Donald (1934–) Film actor, born in St John, New Brunswick, Canada. He became known for his role in *The Dirty Dozen* (1967), following this with *M*A*S*H* (1970) and *Klute* (1971). Among his later films are *A Time To Kill* (1996), *Cold Mountain* (2003), *Pride & Prejudice* (2005), and *Puffball* (2007).

Sutherland, Graham (Vivian) (1903–80) Artist, born in London. He was an official war artist (1941–5), and later produced several memorable portraits, including 'Sir Winston Churchill' (1955). His large tapestry, 'Christ in Majesty', was hung in the new Coventry Cathedral in 1962.

Sutherland, Dame Joan (1926–) Operatic soprano, born in Sydney, New South Wales, Australia. She made her debut at Sydney in 1947, moved to London in 1951, and joined the Royal Opera, becoming resident soprano at Covent Garden. In 1990 she gave her final performance at the Sydney Opera House.

Sutlej, River [sutlej] River of Asia; the longest of the five rivers of the Punjab; rises in Tibet (Xizang); meets the Indus; length 1370 km/850 mi.

suttee *sati*

Sutton Hoo ship burial The grave of an Anglo-Saxon king, probably Raedwald of East Anglia (c.600–624/5), discovered beneath a barrow near Woodbridge, E England, in 1939. Amidships in a 40-oar open rowing boat (4·25 m/14 ft in beam and 27 m/89 ft long) stood a wooden burial chamber containing silver plate, gold jewellery, and coins, weapons, and domestic equipment (now in the British Museum).

Suva [soova] 18°08S 178°25E, pop (2000e) 81 100. Chief port and capital of Fiji, on SE coast of Viti Levu I; city since 1953; university (1968).

Suva Convention *Lomè Convention*

Suwon [soowuhn] or **Suweon** 37°16N 126°59E, pop (2000e) 722 000. Industrial city in NW Korea; subway from Seoul; agricultural college; reconstructed fortress walls and gates; Suwon World Cup Stadium (2001).

Suzhou [soojoh] or **Suchow** 31°21N 120°40E, pop (2000e) 983 800. Town in E China, on the banks of the Grand Canal; first settled c.1000 BC; capital, Kingdom of Wu, 518 BC; railway; over 150 ornamental gardens (a world heritage site); Suzhou Museum opened, 2006.

Suzman, Helen, *née* **Gavronsky** (1917–) South African politician, born in Germiston, Transvaal, South Africa. Elected to parliament in 1953, she gained the respect of the black community and, for years the sole MP of the Progressive Party, proved to be a fierce opponent of apartheid. In 1978 she received the UN Human Rights Award.

Svalbard [svalbah(r)d] pop (2000e) 3400; area 62 000 km²/ 23 900 sq mi. Island group in the Arctic Ocean, c.650 km/ 400 mi N of the Norwegian mainland; four large and several smaller islands; islands include Spitsbergen; discovered, 1596; formerly an important whaling centre; incorporated in Norway, 1925; administrative centre, Longyearbyen; wide range of minerals.

Sverdlovsk [sverdlofsk] *Yekaterinburg*

Svevo, Italo [zvayvoh], pseudonym of **Ettore Schmitz** (1861–1928) Novelist, born in Trieste, Italy. He had a considerable success with *La coscienza di Zeno* (1923, The Confessions of Zeno), a psychological study of inner conflicts.

Swabia, Ger **Schwaben** A SW mediaeval German duchy, extending from the R Rhine in the W to the Alps in the S, Bavaria in the E, and Franconia in the N, containing the cities of Strasbourg, Constance, and Augsburg.

Swabian League An alliance of 22 imperial German cities, clerical lords, and princes, with a league of knights of Swabia (1488), to support the Holy Roman Empire. It was active in suppressing rebellions in 1523–5, but declined because of religious divisions caused by the Reformation.

Swahili [swaheelee] A cluster of Bantu-speaking peoples of the coast and islands of E Africa, an amalgam of African groups and Arab immigrants entering the area continually since ancient times. By the 15th-c they were at the height of their power as a trading nation. The Swahili language probably replaced Arabic from about the 13th-c, and is today spoken by c.30 million as a lingua franca throughout E Africa.

swallow A small songbird, found worldwide; dark blue/green above, pale below; tail long, forked; inhabits open country near fresh water; eats small insects caught in flight; temperate populations migrate; nests in holes or mud nests on cliffs, buildings, etc. The name is also used for several unrelated birds. (Family: Hirundinidae, 57 species.)

swamp A permanently flooded area of land with thick vegetation of reeds or trees. **Mangrove swamps** are common along river mouths in tropical and subtropical areas. In the Carboniferous period, marine swamps were common, and are the origin of present-day coal deposits.

swamp cypress A deciduous or semi-evergreen conifer, native to the SE USA and Mexico; also called **bald cypress**. (Genus: *Taxodium*, 3 species. Family: Taxodiaceae.)

swan A large water-bird of the duck family; found worldwide; usually white; neck very long; male called *cob*, female *pen*. (Tribe: Anserini. Genus: *Cygnus*, 10 species, and *Coscoroba*, 2 species. Subfamily: Anserinae.)

Swank, Hilary (Ann) (1974–) Actress, born in Lincoln, NE. As a child she attended a local theatre group, and in 1990 moved to Los Angeles where she began acting professionally, gaining her breakthrough into films with *The Next Karate Kid* (1994). She received a Best Actress Oscar for *Boys Don't Cry* (1999) and *Million Dollar Baby* (2004, Golden Globe). Later films include *The Black Dahlia* (2006) and *Freedom Writers* (2007).

Swan River Major watercourse of SW Australia; rises in the hills near Corrigin; flows past Perth, entering the Indian Ocean at Fremantle; length 386 km/240 mi; the Swan River Settlement (1829) was the first colonial settlement in Western Australia.

Swanscombe skull The partial skull of an archaic form of *Homo sapiens* found at Swanscombe near London in 1935–6, and 1955. Its possible age is 250 000 years.

Swansea, Welsh **Abertawe** 51°38N 3°57W, pop (2001e) 223 300. Port city and (from 1996) unitary authority (pop (2000e) 233 000) in SC Wales, UK; at the mouth of the R Neath; chartered, 1158–84; airfield; railway; university college (1920); national vehicle licensing centre; Norman castle, National Waterfront Museum (2005); football league team, Swansea City (Swans).

swastika [swostika] A symbol consisting of a cross with its four arms bent at right angles, either clockwise or anticlockwise. Found in ancient Hindu, Mexican, Buddhist, and other traditions, possibly representing the Sun, it is now tainted since its appropriation by the Nazi party as its official emblem. The name derives from the Sanskrit *svasti + ka*, meaning a mystical cross used to denote good luck.

Swazi A Bantu-speaking agricultural and pastoral people living in Swaziland and adjoining parts of S Africa. They are one of the Nguni cluster of peoples, formed into a kingdom in the early 19th-c.

Swaziland *p.904*

sweat A dilute solution of salts (mainly sodium chloride) and other small molecules (eg urea, lactic acid, and ammonia) actively secreted by sweat (*sudoriferous*) glands present in the skin of mammals. It is particularly important in humans with respect to temperature regulation.

swede A biennial vegetable (*Brassica napus*, variety *napobras-*

Swaziland

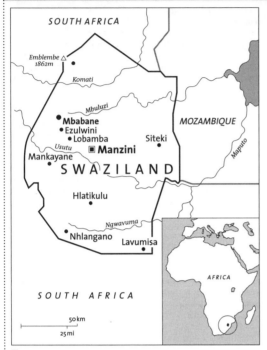

SOUTH AFRICA

Emblembe △ 1862m

Komati

Mbuluzi

● Mbabane
● Ezulwini
● Lobamba   Siteki ●
Usutu
Mankayane
S W A Z I L A N D
■ **Manzini**

MOZAMBIQUE

Maputo

Hlatikulu ●

Ngwavuma

● Nhlangano   Lavumisa ●

AFRICA

SOUTH   AFRICA

50 km
25 mi

☐ International Airport

[swahzeeland], official name **Kingdom of Swaziland**
Local name Swaziland
Timezone GMT +2
Area 17 363 km²/6702 sq mi
Population total (2002e) 1 124 000
Status Kingdom
Date of independence 1968
Capital Mbabane
Languages English and Siswati (official)
Ethnic groups Swazi (97%), European (3%)

Religions Christian (Roman Catholic, Anglican, Methodist, and Evangelical Lutheran) (57%), traditional animist beliefs (40%)
Physical features Landlocked, in SE Africa; divided into four topographical regions, mountainous Highveld (W), highest point Emblembe, 1862 m/6109 ft; heavily populated Middleveld (C), descending to 600–700 m/2000–2300 ft; rolling, bush-covered Lowveld (E), irrigated by river systems; Lubombo escarpment, covering 90% of the territory; main rivers, Komati, Usutu, Mbuluzi, flow W–E.
Climate Temperate; tropical in W, with relatively little rain, 500–890 mm/20–35 in; susceptible to drought; subtropical and drier in C; average annual temperature 15°C (Jul), 22°C (Jan) in Mbabane; average annual rainfall 1402 mm/55 in; rainy season (Nov–Mar).
Currency 1 Lilangeni (plural Emalangeni) (SZL) = 100 cents
Economy Agriculture (employs 70% of population); maize, groundnuts, beans, sorghum, cotton, tobacco, pineapples, citrus; sugar refining, several hydroelectric schemes; asbestos, iron ore, coal, textiles, cement, paper, chemicals.
GDP (2002e) $5·542 bn, per capita $4800
Human Development Index (2002) 0·577
History Arrival of Swazi in the area, early 19th-c; boundaries with the Transvaal decided, and independence guaranteed, 1881; British agreed to Transvaal administration, 1894; British High Commission territory, 1903; independence as a constitutional monarchy within the Commonwealth, 1968; all political parties are banned under 1978 constitution; governed by a bicameral Parliament consisting of a National Assembly and a Senate; the King has considerable executive power, appointing a Cabinet and Prime Minister.

Head of State (Monarch)
1899–1982 Sobhuza II (Chief from 1921)
1983 Dzeliwe *Queen Regent*
1983–6 Ntombi *Queen Regent*
1986– Mswati III
Head of Government
1967–78 Prince Makhosini
1978–9 Prince Maphevu Dlamini
1979–83 Prince Mbandla Dlamini
1983–6 Prince Bhekimpi Dlamini
1986–9 Sotsha Dlamini
1989–93 Obed Dlamini *Acting*
1993–6 Jameson Mbilini Dlamini
1996–2003 Sibusiso Barnabus Dlamini
2003– Absalom Themba Dlamini

---

sica), related to rape, with a taproot and stem base forming a fleshy tuber. (Family: Cruciferae.)
Sweden *p.905*
Swedenborg, Emanuel [sweednbaw(r)g], originally **Emanuel Swedberg** (1688–1772) Mystic and scientist, born in Stockholm. In 1734 he published his monumental *Opera philosophica et mineralia* (Philosophical and Logical Works), a mixture of metallurgy and metaphysical speculation on the creation of the world. He expounded his spiritual doctrines in such works as *The New Jerusalem* (1758), and in 1787 his followers (known as Swedenborgians) formed the Church of the New Jerusalem.
Swedish *Germanic / Scandinavian languages; Swedish literature*
Sweet, Henry (1845–1912) Philologist, born in London. His works include Old and Middle English texts, primers, and dictionaries, and a historical English grammar. He was the probable source for Professor Higgins in Shaw's *Pygmalion* (1913).
sweet alyssum [alisuhm] A low, bushy annual or perennial (*Lobu-*

laria maritima) native to the Mediterranean; flowers very numerous, white or blue, cross-shaped. It is one of the most popular garden bedding plants, often referred to simply as 'alyssum'. (Family: Cruciferae.)
sweet bay An evergreen shrub or tree (*Laurus nobilis*), growing to 20 m/65 ft, but often less, native to the Mediterranean; male and female flowers yellow or white, 4-lobed; berry black; often referred to simply as **bay**. It is the 'laurel' of poets and victors in classical times. (Family: Lauraceae.)
sweet briar *eglantine*
sweet cherry *cherry*
sweet chestnut A deciduous tree (*Castanea sativa*) growing to 30 m/100 ft, native to the Mediterranean and W Asia; long catkins have green female flowers below yellow males; nuts shiny, brown, three enclosed in a densely spiny case; also called **Spanish chestnut**. The nuts are the familiar roast chestnuts. (Family: Fagaceae.)
sweet cicely A perennial (*Myrrhis odorata*) growing to 2 m/6½ ft,

Sweden

☐ International Airport

Swed **Sverige**, official name **Kingdom of Sweden**, Swed **Konungariket Sverige**

Local name Sverige (Swedish)

Timezone GMT +1

Area 411 479 km²/158 830 sq mi

Population total (2002e) 8 925 000

Status Kingdom

Capital Stockholm

Languages Swedish (official), Finnish and Lapp in N

Ethnic groups Swedish (91%), Finns, with Polish, Turkish, W German, Chilean, Iranian, and other minorities

Religions Lutheran Protestant (93%), Roman Catholic (2%), Scandinavian Jewish minorities

Physical features Occupies the E side of the Scandinavian peninsula; 15% of country lies N of the Arctic Circle; large amount of inland water (9%); chief lakes being Vänern, Vättern, and Mälaren. Many coastal islands, notably Gotland and Öland; c.57% forested; Kjölen Mts (W) form much of the boundary with Norway; highest peak, Kebnekaise, 2111 m/6926 ft; several rivers flow SE towards the Gulf of Bothnia.

Climate Continental, with cold winters and mild summers; rainfall lowest in NE; winters warmer in SW; enclosed parts of Baltic Sea often freeze in winter and can remain frozen for up to 6 months; continuous daylight in N during Arctic summer produces mean temperatures of -10°C (Jan), 15°C (Jul).

Currency 1 Swedish Krona (SEK) = 100 øre

Economy Gradual shift in the economy from the traditional emphasis on raw materials (timber and iron ore) to advanced technology; transportation equipment, electronics, electrical equipment, chemicals, engineering, steelmaking, non-ferrous metals; hydroelectricity provides 70% of power; wheat, barley, oats, sugar beet, cattle, fishing; tourism.

GDP (2002e) $230·7 bn, per capita $26 000

Human Development Index (2002) 0·941

History Formed from the union of the kingdoms of the Goths and Svears, 7th-c; Danes continued to rule in the extreme S (Skåne) until 1658; united with Denmark and Norway under Danish leadership, 1389; union ended in 1527, following revolt led by Gustavus Vasa; Sweden acquired Norway from Denmark, 1814; union with Norway dissolved, 1905; a neutral country since 1814; Social Democratic Party controlled government, 1932–76 and returned to power, 1982; a representative and parliamentary democracy, with a Monarch as Head of State; governed by a Prime Minister and a unicameral Parliament (Riksdag) elected every three years; joined European Union, 1995; Swedish Foreign Minister Anna Lindh murdered, Sep 2003.

Head of State (Monarch)
1973– Carl XVI Gustaf

Head of Government
1978–9 Ola Ullsten
1979–82 Thorbjörn Fälldin
1982–6 (Sven) Olof Palme
1986–91 Ingvar Carlsson
1991–4 Carl Bildt
1994–6 Ingvar Carlsson
1996–2006 Göran Persson
2006– Fredrik Reinfeldt

smelling strongly of aniseed, native to Europe; divided, fernlike leaves; tiny white flowers, in clusters; also called **garden myrrh**. It is cultivated as a seasoning. (Family: Umbelliferae.)

sweet corn *maize*

sweeteners *additives*

sweet gum A deciduous tree native to North America, Asia Minor, and China; leaves turning bright red in autumn; flowers tiny, in separate, globular heads. It yields storax, a fragrant amber-coloured gum used in adhesives and perfumes. (*Liquidambar*, 6 species. Family: Styracaceae.)

sweet pea An annual climber, a native of S Italy and Sicily; stems growing to 2 m/6½ ft or more; flowers sweetly scented. The wild plants are purple-flowered, but cultivars now exist in a wide range or combination of colours. (*Lathyrus odoratus*. Family: Leguminosae.)

sweet potato A tuberous perennial with trailing or climbing stems (*Ipomoea batatas*); flowers large, purple, funnel-shaped. It is unknown in the wild, but numerous different strains are cultivated throughout warm regions as a staple food. The edible tubers, sometimes wrongly called *yams*, resemble large potatoes. (Family: Convolvulaceae.)

sweet sop *custard apple*

sweet william A biennial (*Dianthus barbatus*) native to S Europe; flowers in dense, compact heads; five petals, dark red or pink, in garden forms also white, and often spotted or barred. (Family: Caryophyllaceae.)

Sweyn or **Svein** [svayn], known as **Forkbeard** (?–1014) King of Denmark (987–1014) and England (1013–14), the son of Harold Blue-tooth, and the father of Canute. He first attacked England in 994, and during his final campaign in 1013 established mastery over the whole country.

Swift, Graham (1949–) Novelist and short-story writer, born in London. His books include the novels *The Sweet Shop Owner* (1980), *Last Orders* (1996, Booker), *The Light of Day* (2003), and *Tomorrow* (2007), as well as two collections of stories (1982, 1985).

Swift, Jonathan (1667–1745) Clergyman and satirist, born in Dublin. He attacked religious dissension in *A Tale of a Tub* (1704), and produced a wide range of political and religious essays and pamphlets. His world-famous satire, *Gulliver's Travels*, appeared in 1726. In later years he wrote a great deal of light verse, and several essays on such topics as language and manners.

swift A swallow-like bird of the worldwide family Apodidae (**true swifts**, 78 species) or the SE Asian Hemiprocnidae (**crested swifts**, 4 species); spends most of its life flying.

swimming The act of propelling oneself through water without any mechanical aids. There are four strokes: the *breast stroke*, developed in the 16th-c, and the *front crawl* (freestyle), *backstroke*, and *butterfly*, developed in the 20th-c. In competitions there are also relays, involving four swimmers, and medley races, which are a combination of all four strokes. Race lengths range from 50 m/55 yd to 1500 m/1640 yd.

Swinburne, Algernon Charles (1837–1909) Poet and critic, born in London. He achieved success with his play *Atalanta in Calydon* (1865), and the first of his series of *Poems and Ballads* (1866) took the public by storm.

Swindon 51°34N 1°47W, pop (2001e) 180 100. Old market town in Thamesdown (unitary authority from 1997), Wiltshire, S England; developed into a modern industrial town with the arrival of the Great Western Railway in the 19th-c; Great Western Railway museum (1962); football league team, Swindon Town (Robins).

swine *pig*

swine fever The name used for two highly contagious viral infections of pigs. An infection of the intestines is called *hog cholera*, and an infection of the lungs is called *swine plague*.

swing music A term originally used to describe most forms of jazz-based popular music, but from the 1930s it was applied more specifically to 'big-band' dance music with a propulsive rhythm and strong solo instrumental lines, with or without the improvisatory element that is an essential of jazz. The best known band leaders were Benny Goodman, Duke Ellington, Count Basie, and Glenn Miller.

Swiss cheese plant *monstera*

Swiss Guards The papal police corps, originally instituted by Pope Julius II (r.1503–13) and recruited from the mercenaries of the cantons of the Swiss confederacy, whose reputation as infantrymen was established after their victories over the Burgundian cavalry in 1476.

Swiss lake dwellings Prehistoric settlements around the Swiss lakes, first identified in 1854 at Obermeilen, L Constance, by Swiss archaeologist Ferdinand Keller (1800–81). Over 200 comparable Neolithic sites preserved by waterlogging were subsequently revealed (1860–75).

Swithin or **Swithun, St** (?–862) English saint and theologian, adviser to Egbert. When in 971 the monks exhumed his body to bury it in the rebuilt cathedral of Winchester, the removal, which was to have taken place on 15 July, is said to have been delayed by violent rains. Hence the current belief that if it rains on that day, it will rain for 40 days more. Feast day 15 July.

Switzerland *p.907*

sword dance A ceremonial form of dance. In Scotland individuals or groups perform jigs over crossed swords placed on the floor. In England the dancers are linked by metal or wooden swords held in the hand, and perform intertwining figures without breaking the circle.

swordfish Large, agile, and very distinctive fish (*Ziphias gladius*) found worldwide in temperate and warm temperate seas; length up to 5 m/16 ft; upper jaw prolonged into a flattened blade or 'sword', teeth absent. (Family: Xiphiidae.)

swordtail Small, colourful, freshwater fish (*Xiphophorus helleri*) native to streams and swamps of Central America; length up to c.12 cm/5 in; green with orange side stripe; lower edge of tail fin in male prolonged to form the 'sword'; a popular aquarium fish. (Family: Poeciliidae.)

sycamore A spreading deciduous tree (*Acer pseudoplatanus*), growing to 35 m/115 ft, native to C and S Europe and W Asia; leaves palmately divided into five toothed lobes; flowers yellowish, lacking petals, in pendulous clusters; winged seeds fused in pairs. (Family: Aceraceae.)

Sydenham's chorea [sidnuhmz koreea] Irregular, jerking, and unpredictable movements of the limbs, and sometimes of the whole body, arising as a complication of streptococcal infections such as rheumatic fever and scarlet fever. It is named after English physician Thomas Sydenham (1624–89).

Sydney 33°55S 151°10E, pop (2000e) 3 909 000. Port and state capital of New South Wales, Australia; largest city in Australia; founded as the first British settlement, 1788; airport; railway; five universities (1850, 1949, 1964, 1989, 1990); two cathedrals; two major harbours (Sydney, Port Botany); commercial, cultural, and financial centre; State Parliament House; location of Olympic Games in 2000.

Sydney Harbour Bridge One of Australia's best-known landmarks, and the widest and heaviest arch bridge in the world, built 1923–32; length of main arch 503 m/1651 ft; highest point 134 m/440 ft above sea-level. A harbour tunnel was opened in 1992.

Sydney Opera House Australia's best-known contemporary building. Its imaginative design came from an international competition, won in 1956 by the Danish architect Joern Utzon (1918–). The roofs are made up of 2194 pre-cast concrete sections, each weighing up to 15.5 tonnes (15 tons) and are covered with 1 056 056 Swedish ceramic tiles arranged in 4253 pre-cast lids. Because no building with its features had been built before, costs mounted enormously (from the original A$7.5 million), and in the political controversy Utzon resigned in 1966 and went back to Denmark. Completed in 1973, it cost over A$100 million, much of this coming from a New South Wales government lottery. In 1999 Utzon agreed to be a consultant, with his architect son Jan, on future developments, and in 2006 the western foyers were opened to the harbour by a new glassed facade and loggia. Utzon received the Pritzker prize in 2003.

syenite [siyeniyt] A coarse-grained igneous rock containing feldspar and hornblende as essential minerals, with some biotite.

syllabary A writing system in which the basic units (*graphemes*) correspond to syllables, normally representing a sequence of consonant and vowel. An example is found in Japanese *kana*, where the graphemes correspond to such spoken sequences as *ka*, *ga*, and *no*.

syllogism In logic, a deductive argument containing two premisses. For example, 'Some dogs are chihuahuas, All chihuahuas are small; *therefore* Some dogs are small'.

Sylvanus *Silvanus*

symbiosis [simbiohsis] A general term for the living together of two dissimilar organisms, usually to their mutual benefit. It is commonly used to describe all the different types of relationship between the members of two different and interacting species.

Switzerland

□ International Airport

Fr **La Suisse**, Ger **Schweiz**, Ital **Svizzera**, ancient **Helvetia**, official name **Swiss Confederation**, Fr **Confédération Suisse**, Ger **Schweizerische Eidgenossenschaft**, Ital **Confederazione Svizzera**

Local names Schweiz (German), La Suisse (French), Svizzera (Italian)

Timezone GMT +1

Area 41 228 km²/15 914 sq mi

Population total (2002e) 7 282 000

Status Confederation

Date of independence 1291

Capital Bern (Berne)

Languages German, French, Italian, Romansch (official), Spanish and Turkish also spoken

Ethnic groups (of Swiss nationals) German (74%), French (20%), Italian (4%), Romansch (1%)

Religions Christian (Roman Catholic 49%, Protestant 48%), Jewish minority

Physical features Landlocked, with Alps running roughly E–W in the S; highest peak, Dufourspitze, 4634 m/15 203 ft; Pre-Alps (NW) average 2000 m/6500 ft; sparsely-forested Jura Mts run SW–NW; mean altitude of C plateau, 580 m/1900 ft, fringed with great lakes; chief rivers, Rhine, Rhône, Inn, and tributaries of the Po; c.3000 km²/1160 sq mi of glaciers, notably the Aletsch.

Climate Temperate climate, subject to Atlantic, Mediterranean and E and C European influences; warm summers, with considerable rainfall; perennial snow cover above 300 m/9842 ft; average annual temperature 0°C (Jan), 19°C (Jul) in Bern; average annual rainfall 1000 mm/40 in; the Föhn (warm wind) noticeable late winter and spring in the Alps.

Currency 1 Swiss Franc (CHF) = 100 centimes

Economy Increased specialization and development in high-technology products; machinery, precision instruments, watches, drugs, chemicals, textiles; a major financial centre; headquarters of many international organizations; all-year tourist area; dairy farming, wheat, potatoes, sugar beet, grapes, apples.

GDP (2002e) $233·4 bn, per capita $32 000

Human Development Index (2002) 0·928

History Part of the Holy Roman Empire, 10th-c; Swiss Confederation created, 1291; expanded during 14th-c; centre of the Reformation, 16th-c; Swiss independence and neutrality recognized under the Treaty of Westphalia, 1648; conquered by Napoleon, who instituted the Helvetian Republic, 1798; organized as a confederation of cantons in 1815; federal constitution, 1848; Red Cross founded, 1863; neutral in both World Wars; helped form European Free Trade Association, 1960; Jura became 23rd canton of Switzerland, 1979; became a full member of the UN, 2002; bicameral Federal Association comprising of a Council of States (Ständerat) and a National Council (Nationalrat); president elected annually by Federal Council.

Head of State/Government
1995 Kaspar Villiger
1996 Jean-Pascal Delamuraz
1997 Arnold Koller
1998 Flavio Cotti
1999 Ruth Dreifuss
2000 Adolf Ogi
2001 Moritz Leuenberger
2002 Kaspar Villiger
2003 Pascal Couchepin
2004 Joseph Deiss
2005 Samuel Schmid
2006 Moritz Leuenberger
2007 Micheline Calmy-Rey

symbolic logic *mathematical logic*

Symbolism In general terms, the belief that ideas or emotions may be objectified in terms which make them communicable, whether in words, music, graphics, or plastic forms. In the West, this belief may be traced back to Plato, and is clearly active in much Romantic poetry. The systematic invocation of a transcendental world in poetry was practised by several French poets in the mid-19th-c, who came to be known as Symbolists.

Symbolists A group of mid-19th-c French poets, including Baudelaire, Mallarmé, Verlaine, and Rimbaud. Their general aim was to invoke rather than to describe reality, by subliminal means. In art, there was a reaction against Realism and Impressionism; leading artists included Denis and Puvis de Chavannes.

sympathetic nervous system *autonomic nervous system*

symphonic poem A single-movement orchestral work in which a composer seeks to express the emotional, pictorial, or narrative content of a poem, story, painting, etc. It was developed by Liszt from the programmatic concert overture and taken up by other Romantic composers.

symphony An orchestral work originating in the 18th-c, although the term had been used earlier with different meanings. The classical symphony of Haydn, Mozart, Beethoven, and Schubert was mostly in four movements: a fast movement in sonata form; a slow movement; a minuet or scherzo; and a finale, often in sonata form like the first movement. In the 19th-c the structure was varied a good deal, and programmatic or descriptive intentions were often present, as in the five-movement *Symphonie fantastique* of Berlioz.

Symplegades [simplaygadeez] In Greek mythology, the Clashing

Rocks, situated at the entrance to the Black Sea, through which the *Argo* had to pass.

synagogue (Gr 'congregation', 'meeting') The local Jewish institution for instruction in the Torah and worship, the religious focal point of individual Jewish communities. At first applied to the congregation, the term was eventually used of the buildings in which the people met. In Orthodox synagogues, men and women have traditionally separated; but in non-Orthodox synagogues, they now sit together.

synapse [siynaps] The specialized junction between two neurones, present in the nervous system of all animals. Nerve impulses at the axon terminals of one neurone are transmitted across the junction either chemically (by neurotransmitters) or electrically (by local currents).

synchrotron A machine for accelerating subatomic particles, usually protons or electrons. The particles are guided through an evacuated pipe in a circular path by magnets, accelerated by radio-frequency (rf) electric fields. Synchrotrons are a major experimental tool in particle physics.

syncline A geological fold structure in the form of a trough or inverted arch, produced by the downfolding of stratified rocks. It is the opposite of an anticline.

syncope [singkopee] *fainting*

syndicalism A revolutionary socialist doctrine that emphasized workers taking power by seizing the factories in which they worked; developed in the 1890s, and common in France, Italy, and Spain in the early 20th-c. By 1914 it had lost its political force.

Synge, (Edmund) J(ohn) M(illington) [sing] (1871–1909) Playwright, born near Dublin. He lived for a while among the people of the Aran Is, who provided the material for his plays, notably *The Playboy of the Western World* (1907). He was a director of the Abbey Theatre from 1904.

synodic period The average time taken by a planet to return to the same position in its orbit relative to the Earth. For the Moon this is 29·53 days, the interval between successive new Moons.

synonym A word which is similar enough in meaning to another word for it to be usable as a substitute in some contexts, such as *illuminate* and *light*. An **antonym** is a word which has the opposite meaning to another, such as *light* and *dark*. A **hyponym** is a word whose meaning is included within that of another, such as *horse* and *animal*. The study of sense relations of this kind is part of the subject of semantics.

synoptic gospels A term applied to three New Testament Gospels (Matthew, Mark, Luke), so called because of the striking amount of common material that they contain. Most of Mark's Gospel, for example, is reproduced in Matthew and Luke, and the correspondence often extends to the order of passages and wording.

synovitis [siynoviytis] Inflammation of the synovial membranes that enclose tendons or cover surfaces within and around the joints. It arises from persistent injury (eg from sports), or from bacterial or immunological inflammation, when it takes the form of arthritis.

synroc [sinrok] An artificial ceramic material used to store high-level radioactive waste. The waste is added to mixed powdered metal oxides from which the ceramic is formed by heat and compression. It is under development as an alternative to storage using glass.

syntax In linguistics, the study of sentence structure; alternatively, the study of how words can be combined into larger grammatical units. A syntax for a language specifies a set of grammatical categories (such as verb, noun phrase, and sentence) and a set of rules which define the ways in which these categories relate to each other.

synthesizer An electronic apparatus for generating musical sounds, usually fitted with one or more keyboards and loud-speakers. One of the earliest and best known was developed in 1964 by Robert A Moog (1934–2005). Modern digital types, based on microprocessors, are virtually unlimited in the number and range of sounds they can produce.

syphilis [sifilis] A chronic sexually transmitted disease caused by *Treponema pallidum*. Initially, a primary lesion (a *chancre*) develops on the genitals or anus, followed several weeks later by features of a generalized infection, with fever and a rash. The condition may then remain dormant for years. Nodules then form in the skin and mucous membranes, and these may break down to form large ulcers. Thereafter the cardiovascular and nervous systems become affected, resulting in damage to the heart valves, swelling of the aorta, and a combination of incoordination, loss of sensation, and dementia known as *generalized paralysis of the insane*.

syphon *siphon*

Syracuse (Italy) [siyrakyooz, sirakyooz], Ital **Siracusa** 37°04N 15°18E, pop (2000e) 122 000. Seaport in Sicily, Italy; founded by Greek settlers, 734 BC; leading cultural centre, 5th-c BC; taken by the Romans, 212 BC; railway; birthplace of Archimedes, Theocritus; cathedral (640), Greek theatre (3th-c BC), Roman remains.

Syracuse (USA) [sirakyooz] 43°03N 76°09W, pop (2000e) 147 300. City in C New York, USA; developed during the 1780s; city status, 1848; airfield; railway; university (1870).

Syria *p.909*

Syriac *Aramaic*

syringa [siringga] *lilac; mock orange*

Syrinx [siringks] In Greek mythology, a nymph pursued by Pan. She called on the Earth to help, and so sank down into it and became a reed-bed. Pan cut some of the reeds, and made the panpipes.

syrinx [siringks] The voice-producing organ of birds; situated in the windpipe where this divides into two. Its structure and position has been used in bird classification to indicate the relationships of groups.

system Any biological, mechanical, or organizational entity which carries out a specific function, receiving inputs from its surroundings and sending outputs to its surroundings. In computing, the word is used to refer to a part of the information processing of an organization which might be appropriate for implementation by a computer, such as the handling of a payroll. Today, **systems analysts** are just as concerned about the human organizational systems as the clerical processing systems.

systematics The classification of organisms into a hierarchical series of groups which emphasizes their presumed evolutionary interrelationships. The main categories of modern classifications are (in order of increasing generality) species, genus, family, order, class, phylum (animals), division (plants), and kingdom.

systemic lupus erythematosus (SLE) [loopus erithematohsus] A chronic multi-system inflammatory disease affecting connective tissue throughout the body, ten times more common in women. The exact cause is unknown, but it is characterized by the presence of several auto-antibodies in the blood; onset is around 20–40 years, and is gradually progressive. It is treated with steroids and immunosuppressive drugs.

systems analysis In computing, the techniques involved in the intimate understanding, design, and optimization of computer systems. **Systems analysts** are responsible for the precise definition and implementation of a computer system in business, research, and other contexts.

systole [sistolee] Phases of the cardiac cycle when the atria (**atrial systole**) and especially the ventricles (**ventricular systole**) contract forcibly, ejecting the blood into the aorta (from the left ventricle) and pulmonary trunk (from the right ventricle).

Syria

TURKEY

Jarabulus
Al Hasakah
Halab
Euphrates
Latakia   Lake Assad
Hama   Dayr az Zawr
Tartüs
Homs   S Y R I A
Tadmur   Abu Kamal
MEDITERRANEAN SEA
LEBANON
Syrian   I R A Q
Damascus   Desert
Mt Hermon 2814m
GOLAN HEIGHTS
Dara
WEST BANK
J O R D A N
ISRAEL
SAUDI ARABIA
ASIA
AFRICA
200 km
100 mi

☐ International Airport

Arabic **Suriya**, official name **Syrian Arab Republic**, Arabic **Al-Jumhuriyah al-Arabiyah as-Suriyah**

Local name as-Suriyah (Arabic)

Timezone GMT +2

Area 185 180 km²/71 479 sq mi

Population total (2002e) 17 156 000

Status Republic

Date of independence 1946

Capital Damascus

Languages Arabic (official), Kurdish, Armenian, Aramaic, and Circassian also spoken

Ethnic groups Arab (90%), Kurd, Armenian, Turkish, Circassian, and Assyrian

Religions Muslim (Sunni Muslim 74%, Alawite, Druse, and other sects 16%), Christian (10%)

Physical features Narrow Mediterranean coastal plain; Jabal al Nusayriyah mountain range rises to c.1500 m/5000 ft; steep drop (E) to Orontes R valley; Anti-Lebanon range (SW) rises to 2814 m/9232 ft at Mt Hermon; open steppe and desert to the E.

Climate Coastal Mediterranean, hot, dry summers, mild, wet winters; desert or semi-desert climate in 60% of country; annual rainfall below 200 mm/8 in; Khamsin wind causes temperatures to rise to 43–9°C; average annual temperatures 7°C (Jan), 27°C (Jul) in Damascus.

Currency 1 Syrian Pound (SYP) = 100 piastres

Economy Oil (most important source of export revenue since 1974); Euphrates dam project (begun 1978) presently supplies 97% of domestic electricity; intended to increase arable land by 6400 km²/500 sq mi; food processing; textiles; tobacco; cement.

GDP (2002e) $63·48 bn, per capita $3700

Human Development Index (2002) 0·691

History Part of Phoenician Empire; Islam introduced in 7th-c; conquered by Turks, 11th-c; part of Ottoman Empire, 1517; brief period of independence in 1920, then made a French mandate; independence, 1946; merged with Egypt to form United Arab Republic, 1958; re-established itself as independent state under present name, 1961; Golan Heights region seized by Israel, 1967; after outbreak of civil war in Lebanon (1975), Syrian troops sent to restore order, and became much involved in the region's power struggle until withdrawn in Apr 2005; breaking of diplomatic relations with Great Britain, 1986; condemned Iraqi invasion of Kuwait and sent allied forces troops in Gulf War in 1990, restoring relations; accepted US proposals for terms of an Arab-Israeli peace conference, 1991; governed by a president, prime minister, and 250-member People's Council.

Head of State
1971–2000 Hafez al-Assad
2000– Bashar al-Assad

Head of Government
1971–2 Abdel Rahman Khleifawi
1972–6 Mahmoud bin Saleh al-Ayoubi
1976–8 Abdul Rahman Khleifawi
1978–80 Mohammed Ali al-Halabi
1980–7 Abdel Rauof al-Kasm
1987–2000 Mahmoud Zubi
2000–3 Muhammad Mustafa Miro
2003– Muhammad Naji al-Utri

syzygy [sizijee] An astronomical situation which occurs when the Sun, Earth, and Moon are roughly in a straight line. Eclipses are likely when the Moon is at syzygy.

Szczecin [shchecheen], Ger **Stettin** 53°25N 14°32E, pop (2000e) 419 000. Industrial river port in NW Poland; on R Oder; largest Baltic trading port; urban status, 1243; member of the Hanseatic League, 1360; Prussian rule, 1720–1945; badly damaged in World War 2; ceded to Poland, 1945; airfield; railway; maritime college; medical academy; technical university (1946); cathedral, castle (16th-c), 13th–14th-c city walls.

Szeged [seged] 46°16N 20°10E, pop (2000e) 171 000. River port in S Hungary, on R Tisza; railway; university (1872, refounded 1921); railway; cultural centre of the S Alföld; medicinal baths; castle (1242).

Székely [saykel] A Magyar-speaking people, since the 11th-c inhabiting the SE Transylvanian region of post-1918 Romania.

In both the interwar and the contemporary periods, the position of the Székely has given rise to disputes between the Romanian and Hungarian states.

Székesfehérvár [saykeshfeheervah(r)], Ger **Stuhlweissenburg**, ancient **Alba Regia** 47°15N 18°25E, pop (2000e) 106 000. City in WC Hungary; ancient capital of Hungarian kingdom; badly damaged in World War 2; market centre for tobacco, wine, fruit; cathedral.

Szell, George [sel] (1897–1970) Conductor and pianist, born in Budapest. He conducted many of the world's major orchestras, and from 1946 was musical director and conductor of the Symphony Orchestra in Cleveland, OH.

Szilard, Leo [silah(r)d] (1898–1964) Physicist, born in Budapest. Earlier than most physicists, he saw (in 1934) the possibility of large-scale energy generation by nuclear fission, and initiated the idea of an atomic bomb.

Szombathely [sombot-hay], Ger **Steinamanger**, ancient **Sabaria** 47°14N 16°38E, pop (2000e) 83 300. City in W Hungary, on R Gyöngyös; bishopric; railway; cathedral.

Szymborska, Wislawa [simbaw(r)ska] (1923–) Poet and critic, born in Bnin (now part of Kornik), Poland. Her first collections of poetry appeared in 1952 and 1954, but were subject to the censorship of the era, and she now recognizes only her work published after 1957. English-language collections include *People on a Bridge* (1990), *Sounds, Feelings, Thoughts* (1996), and *Poems New and Collected* (1998). She received the Nobel Prize for Literature in 1996.

Tabari, al- [tabahree], in full **Abu Jafar Mohammed Ben Jarir al-Tabari** (839–923) Historian, born in Amol, Persia. He wrote a major commentary on the Qur'an, and a history of the world from creation until the early 10th-c.

Tabarley, Eric (1931–98) French yachtsman. He was twice winner of the single-handed trans-Atlantic race, in 1964 in *Pen Duick II*, and in 1976 in *Pen Duick VI*.

tabasco sauce [tabaskoh] A red sauce rich in chillis and hot red peppers, originating in the Mexican state of Tabasco. It is made from the fruit of the plant *Capsicum frutescens*.

Tabernacle A movable sanctuary or tent; in early Israelite religion, the shelter for the Ark of the Covenant during the desert wanderings.

Tabernacles, Feast of *Sukkoth*

tablature A system of musical notation tailored to a particular instrument or group of instruments and indicating the keys, frets, etc to be used rather than the pitch to be sounded. It is used today for the ukulele and the guitar: the notation conveys a diagrammatic indication of finger-placings.

Table Mountain 33°58S 18°25E. Mountain in SW South Africa; height 1086 m/3563 ft; a flat-topped central massif; Cape Town at the foot.

table tennis An indoor bat-and-ball game played by two or four players on a table measuring 9 ft (2·75 m) by 5 ft (1·52 m). The centre of the table has a net 6 in (15·25 cm) high stretched across it. The ball must be hit over the net and into the opposing half of the table. The object is to force one's opponent not to return the ball successfully. The winner is the first to reach 11 points with at least a two-point lead. Known as **ping pong** in the early part of the 20th-c, it is very popular in China and Korea.

taboo A prohibited form of conduct; from a Polynesian word, *tapu*. A wide variety of actions may be *tapu* – for example, a chief's *tapu* may prevent him being allowed to carry burdens, or children may be prohibited from touching sea-going canoes. Breaching a *tapu* may result directly in sickness or death, or may provoke physical punishment. The term is now used more generally, especially with reference to any subject-matter (eg death, politics) or language (eg swearing, obscenity) which people on occasion avoid.

tabor A small double-headed side drum with snares, known from mediaeval times. It was often played with one stick, the player at the same time blowing a three-holed pipe to accompany dancing.

Tabriz [tabreez], ancient **Tauris** 38°05N 46°18E, pop (2000e) 1 373 000. Fourth largest city in Iran; often severely damaged by earthquakes; airport; railway; university (1949); industrial and commercial centre.

Tachisme *action painting*

tachometer [takometer] An instrument for measuring the speed of rotation. There are many methods; a typical modern device rotates a magnet near a non-magnetic conductor, exerting a force through the field produced by eddy currents. It is widely used to monitor the driving practices of lorry-drivers and bus-drivers.

tachycardia An abnormally fast heart rate. It may arise due to a normal physiological process, such as during exercise, the ingestion of drugs such as caffeine and amphetamine, or generalized disorders such as serious infections or hyperthyroidism. It may also be due to specific disorders of the heart that disrupt the normal electrical pathways of the heart muscle, in which case the heart rate may be irregular.

tachyon [takyon] A hypothetical elementary particle having imaginary mass (ie m^2 less than 0), and able to travel faster than the velocity of light without violating special relativity.

Tacitus [tasitus], in full **Publius** or **Gaius Cornelius Tacitus** (c.55–120) Roman historian. His major works are two historical studies, the 12-volume *Historiae* (Histories), of which only the first four books survive whole, and the *Annales* (Annals), of possibly 18 books, of which only eight have been completely preserved.

Tacoma [takohma] 47°14N 122°26W, pop (2000e) 193 600. Port in WC Washington, USA; settled, 1868; city status, 1875; railway; university (1888); air force base; major NW Pacific container port.

Tadmur or **Tadmor**, ancient **Palmyra** 34°36N 38°15E, pop (2000e) 28 000. Ancient city in C Syria, a world heritage site; financial capital of the E world, 1st–2nd-c; on ancient caravan route from Persian Gulf to Mediterranean Sea; rail terminus.

tadpole The larva of an amphibian, especially a frog or toad; largest 25 cm/10 in long; usually a short spherical body, feathery gills, large tail; with age, gills and tail shrink, legs appear, larvae become carnivorous.

Taegu or **Daegu** [tiygoo] 35°52N 128°36E, pop (2000e) 2 448 000. City in SE South Korea; largest inland city after Seoul; market town at centre of apple-growing area; railway; university (1946); Haeinsa temple (802); Daegu World Cup Stadium (2001).

Taejon or **Daejeon** [tiyjon] 36°20N 127°26E, pop (2000e) 1 167 000. City in C South Korea; badly damaged in Korean War; railway; university (1952); agricultural centre; Daejeon World Cup Stadium (2001).

taekwondo [tiykwondoh] A martial art developed in Korea by General Choi Hong Hi. The International Taekwondo Federation was founded in 1966.

Taft, William Howard (1857–1930) US statesman and 27th president (1909–13), born in Cincinnati, OH. He secured an agreement with Canada that meant relatively free trade until 1910. His son **Robert Alphonso Taft** (1889–1953) became a Republican leader (1939–53), but was defeated as a candidate for presidential nomination on three occasions.

Taganrog [taganrok] 47°14N 38°55E, pop (2000e) 293 000. Seaport in S European Russia; on the Sea of Azov; founded as a fortress and naval base, 1698; rail terminus; birthplace of Chekhov.

Tagore, Rabindranath [tagaw(r)] (1861–1941) Poet and philosopher, born in Kolkata (Calcutta), India. He is best known for his poetic works, notably *Gitanjali* (1912, Song Offering), and short stories, such as *Galpaguccha* (1912, A Bunch of Stories). He received the Nobel Prize for Literature in 1913, the first Asian writer to do so, and was knighted in 1915 – an honour which he resigned in 1919 as a protest against British policy in the Punjab.

Tagus, River [tayguhs], Span *Río Tajo*, Port *Río Tejo* River rising in the Sierra de Albarracín, Spain; enters Lisbon Bay; length, 1007 km/626 mi.

Tahiti [taheetee], Fr **Archipel de Tahiti** [taeetee] 17°37S 149°27W; pop (2000e) 164 000; area 1042 km²/402 sq mi. Largest island of French Polynesia; length, 48 km/30 mi; French colony, 1880; capital, Papeete; rises to 2237 m/7339 ft in the volcanic peak of Mt Orohena.

Tai, Mount [tiy], Chin **Taishan** The most revered of China's five sacred mountains, in Shandong province; a world heritage site. Evidence of settlement dates back 400 000 years.

tai chi chuan [tiy chee chwan] A Chinese martial art said to date from the 13th-c, when a Taoist monk, Chang San Feng, observed a fight between a snake and a crane and devised a series of postures based on the movements of these animals from which the present forms are developed. The foundation of the art is the practice of 'the form', a series of 108 movements in a slow, continuous sequence, which is used as a method of meditation to harmonize the mind, body, and spirit.

Taif, at- [at tiyf] 21°05N 40°27E, pop (2000e) 473 000. Summer resort town in WC Saudi Arabia; altitude, 1158 m/3799 ft; unofficial seat of government during the summer; airfield; centre of fruit-growing district.

taiga [tiyga] A Russian term for the open coniferous forest zone intermediate between the boreal forest and tundra regions. Open areas are usually poorly drained muskeg.

Tailang *Mon*

tailorbird An Old World warbler (Family: *Sylviidae*) native to India and SE Asia; nest formed by folding a large leaf and 'sewing' the edges together with separate stitches of wool, silk, or spider's web. (Genus: *Orthotomus*, 9 species).

Taimyr, Lake *Taymyr, Lake*

Tainan or **T'ai-nan** [tiynahn] 23°01N 120°14E, pop (2000e) 745 000. Oldest city in Taiwan; capital, 1684–7; university (1971); oldest Confucian temple in Taiwan (1665).

Taine, Hippolyte (Adolphe) [ten] (1828–93) Critic, historian, and positivist philosopher, born in Vouziers, France. His greatest work, *Les Origines de la France contemporaine* (1875–94, The Origins of Contemporary France) constituted a strong attack on the Revolution.

taipan [tiypan] A venomous snake (*Oxyuranus scutellatus*), native to NE Australia and New Guinea; one of the world's most deadly snakes; length up to 4 m/13 ft; brown with paler head. (Family: Elapidae.)

Taipei or **Taibei** [tiybay], also **T'ai-pei** 25°05N 121°32E, pop (2000e) 2 934 000. Capital of Taiwan; one of the fastest-growing cities in Asia; occupied by the Japanese, 1895–1945; seat of the Nationalist Government, 1949; airport; airfield; railway; three universities (1927, 1928, 1946).

Taiping Rebellion (1850–64) A major uprising against the Qing dynasty in China, led by Hong Xiuquan (1814–64). Its programme aimed at ushering in a 'Heavenly Kingdom of Great Peace' (*Taiping Tian Guo*). The rebels took Nanjing (Nanking) in 1853, but the Qing forces under Zeng Guofan (1811–72) eventually brought about the downfall of the movement.

Taiwan *p.913*

Taiyuan or **T'ai-yüan** [tiyyüan] 37°50N 112°30E, pop (2000e) 2 287 000. Capital of Shanxi province, NEC China; founded during W Zhou dynasty; railway.

Taizé [tayzay] An ecumenical community founded near Lyon, France, by Swiss-born pastor Roger Schutz (1915–2005) and members of the French Reformed Church in 1940. Members observe a rule similar to most monastic orders. Their aim is the promotion of Christian unity, particularly between Protestants and Catholics. Brother Roger died from stab-wounds inflicted by a woman visitor during a Taizé service.

Taizhong or **T'ai-chung** [tiychung] 24°09N 120°40E, pop (2000e) 839 000. Third largest city in Taiwan; economic, cultural, and commercial centre of C Taiwan; designated an export processing zone.

Tajikistan *p.914*

Taj Mahal [tahj mahahl] A renowned monument to love constructed (1632–54) at Agra in Uttar Pradesh, India, as a mausoleum for Mumtaz Mahal, the favourite wife of Shah Jahan. Built of white marble and inlaid with semi-precious stones and mosaic work, it is a masterpiece of Mughal architecture, and a world heritage site.

take all A parasitic disease (*Gauemannomyces graminis*) which attacks the roots of wheat, barley, and rye, causing severe losses when susceptible crops are grown successively on the same land. The disease causes death (*take all*) or premature ripening (*whiteheads*) of the crop. (Order: Ascomycetes.)

talapoin [talapoyn] The smallest Old World monkey, from W Africa (*Miopithecus talapoin*); greenish with pale underparts; round head and long tail; partly webbed hands and feet; swims well; also known as **pygmy guenon**.

Talbot, William Henry Fox (1800–77) Pioneer of photography, born in Melbury Abbas, Dorset. In 1838 he succeeded in making photographic prints on silver chloride paper, which he termed 'photogenic drawing', and later developed the Calotype process.

talc A hydrous magnesium silicate mineral $(Mg_3Si_4O_{10}(OH)_2)$, formed in metamorphic rocks as light-grey soft masses; also known as **steatite** or **soapstone**. It is used in cosmetics (talcum powder) and in the paper, paint, rubber, and textile industries.

Talca [talka] 35°25S 71°39W, pop (2000e) 208 800. City in C Chile; founded, 1692; destroyed by earthquake, 1742 and 1928, then completely rebuilt; Chilean independence declared here, 1818; railway; greatest wine-producing area in Chile.

Talcahuano [talka-hwanoh] 36°40S 73°10W, pop (2000e) 282 000. Industrial port in C Chile; best harbour in Chile, containing main naval base and dry docks; railway.

Taliban / Taleban [taliban] (Persian 'students of religion') An Islamic revolutionary movement in Afghanistan, founded in 1995 by a group of young men of conservative views who emerged from religious schools and who had known only war against the Soviet occupiers (1979–89). They organized an unofficial army which, during the civil war that followed the Soviet withdrawal, was able to capture Kabul in 1996 and to take control of most of the country. Using harsh measures, they introduced a strictly conservative Islamic government with uncompromising observance of Muslim *sharia* (law). Men were forced to grow beards and wear black; women were forbidden to work outside the home or receive education, and were made to wear heavy veiling (the *burqa*). In October 2001, the Taliban government refused to give up Osama bin Laden, following his suspected involvement in the World Trade Center terrorist attack the previous month, provoking a US-led military attack on Afghanistan, and the removal of their regime. Subsequent Taliban resistance was ongoing in 2007.

Taliesin [talyesin] (6th-c) Welsh bard, possibly mythical. He is known only from a collection of poems, *The Book of Taliesin*, written in the late 13th-c.

Tallahassee [talahasee] (Muskogean 'town-old') 30°27N 84°17W, pop (2000e) 150 600. Capital of state in NW Florida, USA; state capital, 1824; railway; two universities (1857, 1887).

Talleyrand (-Périgord), Charles Maurice de [talayrã] (1754–1838) French statesman, born in Paris. Elected to the States General, he was made president of the Assembly (1790), but lived in exile until after the fall of Robespierre. As foreign minister

Taiwan

□ International Airport

[tiywan], official name **Republic of China**, formerly **Formosa**

Local name T'aiwan

Timezone GMT +8

Area 36 000 km²/13 896 sq mi

Population total (2002e) 22 457 000

Status Republic

Date of independence 1949

Capital Taipei

Languages Mandarin Chinese (official), various dialects including Taiwanese and Hakka also spoken

Ethnic groups Han Chinese (98%), small (Polynesian) aboriginal minority

Religions Taoist, Buddhist, Christian (Protestant and Roman Catholic)

Physical features Consists of Taiwan I and several smaller islands c.130 km/80 mi off the SE coast of mainland China; mountain range runs N–S, covering two-thirds of the island; highest peak, Yu Shan 3997 m/13 113 ft; low-lying land mainly in the W; crossed by the Tropic of Cancer.

Climate Tropical monsoon-type climate; hot, humid summers, mild, short winters; wet season (May–Sep); typhoons common (Jul–Sep); average daily temperature 12–19°C (Jan), 24–33°C (Jul) in Taibei; average annual rainfall 2500 mm/98 in.

Currency 1 New Taiwan Dollar (TWD) = 100 cents

Economy Progressed from agriculture to industry since 1950s; high technology, textiles, electronics, plastics, petrochemicals, machinery; natural gas, limestone, marble, asbestos; sugar, bananas, pineapples, citrus fruits, vegetables, tea, fish; affected by SARS outbreak, 2003.

GDP (2001e) $386 bn, per capita $17 200

History Taiwan (Formosa) visited by the Portuguese, 1590; conquered by Manchus, 17th-c; ceded to Japan following Sino-Japanese War, 1895; returned to China, 1945; Nationalist government moved to Taiwan by Jiang Jieshi (Chang Kai-shek); government still maintains claim to legal jurisdiction over mainland China and continues to designate itself as the Republic of China; protected by US naval forces during Korean War, 1950–3; signed mutual defence pact with USA, 1954–79; end of state of civil war with People's Republic of China declared by President Lee Teng-hui, 1991; governed by a President, who appoints a premier, National Assembly and Legislative *Yuan*; elections held for a reformed National Assembly, 1991; *Yuan* voted in favour of major constitutional change, 2004.

Head of State
1950–75 Chiang Kai-shek
1975–8 Yen Chia-kan
1978–88 Chiang Ching-kuo
1988–2000 Lee Teng-hui
2000– Chen Shui-bian

Head of Government
1978–84 Sun Yun-suan
1984–9 Yu Kuo-hwa
1989–90 Lee Huan
1990–3 Hau Pei-tsun
1993–6 Lien Chan
1997–2000 Vincent Siew
2000 Tang Fei
2000–2 Chang Chun-hsiung
2002–5 Yu Shyi-kun
2005–6 Frank Hsieh
2006– Su Tseng-chang

under the Directory (1797–1807), he helped to consolidate Napoleon's position; but, alarmed by Napoleon's ambitions, he resigned in 1807. He became foreign minister under Louis XVIII, representing France with great skill at the Congress of Vienna (1814–15), and was Louis Philippe's chief adviser at the July Revolution.

Tallien, Jean Lambert [talyĩ] (1767–1820) French revolutionary politician, born in Paris. As president of the Convention (1794), he was denounced by Robespierre, but conspired with Barras and Fouché to bring about the former's downfall.

Tallinn [talin], formerly Ger **Revel** or **Reval** (to 1917) 59°22N 24°48E, pop (2000e) 456 000. Seaport capital of Estonia, on S coast of the Gulf of Finland; member of the Hanseatic League; taken by Russia, 1710; occupied by Germany in World War 2; airfield; railway; extensive military and naval installations;

citadel (13th-c), cathedral (13th–15th-c); old town a world heritage site.

Tallis, Thomas (c.1505–85) English musician, 'the father of English cathedral music'. One of the greatest contrapuntists of the English School, he wrote much church music, including a motet in 40 parts, *Spem in alium*.

Talmud [talmud] (Heb 'study') An authoritative, influential compilation of rabbinic traditions and discussions about Jewish life and Laws. It includes the Mishnah of Rabbi Judah (c.200), accompanied by a commentary (the *Gemara*), in versions dating from the 4th–5th-c.

talus *scree*

Tamale [tamale] 9°26N 0°49W, pop (2000e) 197 000. Capital of Northern region, Ghana; airfield; educational centre.

tamandua [tamandooa] *anteater*

Tajikistan

☐ International Airport

[tajikistahn], official name **Republic of Tajikistan**, also spelled **Tadzhikistan**, Tajik **Jumhurii Tojikistan**

Local name Tojikistan

Timezone GMT +3

Area 143 100 km²/55 200 sq mi

Population total (2002e) 6 327 000

Status Republic

Date of independence 1991

Capital Dushanbe

Languages Tajik (official), Russian

Ethnic groups Tajik (64%), Uzbek (24%), Russian (1.1%)

Religion Sunni Muslim

Physical features Republic in SE Middle Asia; Tien Shan, Gissar-Alai, and Pamir ranges cover over 90% of the area; highest peaks, Communism Peak, 7495 m/24 590 ft, and Lenin Peak, 7134 m/ 23 405 ft, located in N part of Pamirs; R Pyandzh flows E–W along the S border till it is joined by R Valksh to form R Amu Darya; lakes include L Kara-Kul (largest) and L Sarez.

Climate Continental; subtropical valley areas, hot, dry summers; annual mean temperature -0·9°C (Jan), 27°C (Jul); average annual rainfall 150–250 mm/6–10 in; in highlands, average mean temperature -3°C (Jan); average annual rainfall 60–80 mm/2–3 in.

Currency 1 Somoni (TJS) = 100 diram (before 2000, 1 Tajik Rouble (TJR) = 100 kopeks)

Economy Oil, natural gas, coal, lead, zinc, machinery, metalworking, chemicals, food processing; cotton, wheat, maize, vegetables, fruit; hot mineral springs and health resorts.

GDP (2002e) $8·476 bn, per capita $1300

Human Development Index (2002) 0·667

History Conquered by Persia, and Alexander the Great; invaded by Arabs in 8th-c; Turkish invasion, 10th-c; until mid 18th-c, part of the emirate of Bukhara, which in effect became a protectorate of Russia, 1868; following the Russian Revolution (1917), became part of Turkestan Soviet Socialist Autonomous Republic, 1918; scene of the Basmachi revolt, 1922–3; Tajik Autonomous Soviet Socialist Republic created as part of the Uzbek SSR, 1924; became a Soviet Socialist Republic, 1929; declaration of independence from the Soviet Union, 1991; joined Commonwealth of Independent States, 1991; Republican Communist Party remained in power until civil war, 1992; governed by a President, Prime Minister, and Supreme Assembly.

Head of State

1992– Emomali Rahmonov

Head of Government

1996–9 Yahya Azimov

1999– Oqil Oqilov

---

tamaraw or **tamarau** *water buffalo*

tamarin [tamarin] A marmoset of genus *Saguinus* (10 species); lower canine teeth longer than incisors; also known as **long-tusked marmoset**.

tamarisk A slender shrub or tree, native to the Mediterranean and Asia; deciduous small twigs with scaly leaves giving a feathery appearance; flowers in spikes, 4–5 petals, pink or white. (Genus: *Tamarix*, 54 species. Family: Tamaricaceae.)

Tambo, Oliver Reginald (1917–93) South African politician, born in Mbizana, South Africa. He became deputy president of the African National Congress (ANC) in 1958, and when the ANC was banned in 1960, he left South Africa to set up an external wing. He became acting ANC president in 1967, and president in 1977.

tambourine A small frame drum fitted with jingles, and covered on one side with parchment or plastic. It may be shaken, tapped, or stroked, to produce various effects, mostly while accompanying dancing.

Tambov [tambof] 52°44N 41°28E, pop (2000e) 333 000. City in SC European Russia; founded as a fortress, 1636; airfield; railway.

Tamburlaine *Timur*

Tamerlane *Timur*

Tamil A Dravidian-speaking people of S India and Sri Lanka, living as traders and seafarers. Predominantly Hindu, they were instrumental in diffusing Indian culture to many parts of SE Asia in the 11th-c. Tamil is now the major Dravidian language of S India, with written records dating from the 3rd-c BC.

Tamil Nadu [tamil nahdoo], formerly **Madras** pop (2001e) 62 110 800; area 130 069 km²/50 207 sq mi. State in S India; part of the Chola Empire, 10th–13th-c; first British trading settlement, 1611; boundaries of Mysore state altered in 1956 and 1960; renamed Tamil Nadu, 1968; capital, Chennai (Madras); governed by a Legislative Council and a Legislative Assembly; population mainly Hindu (c.90%); coastal region devastated by tsunami disaster, 2004.

Tamil Tigers A Tamil separatist guerrilla movement in Sri Lanka. It emerged in the early 1970s, protesting against the second-class status of Sri Lanka's minority Tamils, who represent 18% of its predominantly Singhalese population. By the mid-1980s, the 'Tigers' had several armies of liberation, with bases in the S Indian state of Tamil Nadu. Their relations with the Indian government deteriorated from 1987, when Rajiv Gandhi's peace accord with President Jayawardene brought the Indian army into Sri Lanka and thereafter into collision with the Tigers.

Tammany Hall The most powerful of the four Democratic Party Committees in New York City; originally a club (the Society of Tammany) founded in 1789, which in the late 19th-c and early 20th-c was notorious for its political corruption.

Tammerfors *Tampere*

Tammuz or **Thammuz** [tamuz] A Babylonian god of vegetation who was beloved by Ishtar (in Syria by Astarte). He returns from the dead and dies again each year.

tamoxifen [tamoksifen] A drug used in the treatment of breast cancer, first developed by the British pharmaceutical company ICI. In the 1980s it was shown to be helpful in the treatment of about half of all breast cancer cases. It works by blocking the action of the female sex hormone oestrogen on cancers whose growth is linked to oestrogen levels.

Tampa 27°57N 82°27W, pop (2000e) 303 400. Port in W Florida, USA; developed around a military post, 1824; later a cigar-making centre, then a resort; airport; railway; university (1931); processing and shipping centre for citrus fruit and phosphates; professional team, Buccaneers (football).

Tampere [tampere], Swed **Tammerfors** 61°32N 23°45E, pop (2000e) 177 700. Second largest city in Finland; established, 1779; developed as industrial centre in 19th-c; airfield; railway; university (1966); technological institute (1965); cathedral (20th-c).

Tampico [tampeekoh] 22°18N 97°52W, pop (2000e) 327 000. Seaport in NE Mexico; airport; railway.

tam-tam *gong*

Tana, Lake, Amharic **Tana Häyk** Lake in NWC Ethiopia; area 3600 km²/1400 sq mi; altitude 1830 m/6000 ft; source of the Blue Nile; notable for its 40 monasteries on islands in the lake.

tanager [tanajer] A songbird, native to the New World tropics; plumage usually brightly coloured; wings short, rounded. (Family: Thraupidae, c.239 species.)

Tanaka, Koichi (1959–) Chemist, born in Toyama, N Honshu, Japan. A researcher at the Shimadzu Corporation, he shared the 2002 Nobel Prize for Chemistry for the development of soft desorption ionization methods for mass spectrometric analyses of biological macromolecules.

Tananarive *Antananarivo*

Tancred [tangkred] (c.1076–1112) Norman crusader, the grandson of Robert Guiscard. He went on the First Crusade, and was given the principality of Tiberias (1099). He also ruled at Edessa and Antioch.

tang *surgeonfish*

Tanga [tangga] 6°10S 35°40E, pop (2000e) 250 000. Seaport in NE Tanzania; occupied the British, 1916; centre of an agricultural area.

Tanganyika, Lake [tangganyeeka] Freshwater lake in EC Africa; length, 645 km/400 mi NNW–SSE; the longest, deepest (over 1400 m/4600 ft), and second largest lake (after L Victoria) in Africa; width, 25–80 km/15–50 mi; altitude, 772 m/2533 ft; European discovery in 1858 by John Speke and Richard Burton.

Tang or **T'ang dynasty** (618–907) A Chinese dynasty founded by Li Yuan with its capital at Changan (modern Xian). It is generally regarded as the golden age of Chinese poetry. It was also a major period for printing, porcelain, technology (eg gunpowder), medicine, education, and science.

tangent A line (usually a straight line) which touches a curve at a point *P* with the same gradient as the curve at *P*. The tangent to a circle at a point *P* is perpendicular to the radius of the circle through *P*.

tangerine A citrus fruit (*Citrus reticulata*); a variety of mandarin with bright orange rind. (Family: Rutaceae.)

Tangier or **Tangiers** [tanjeer(z)], ancient **Tingis** 35°48N 5°45W, pop (2000e) 365 000. Seaport in N Morocco; at W end of the Strait of Gibraltar; occupied by the Portuguese in 1471, and later by the Spanish, English, and Moors; established as an international zone, 1923; Spanish occupation in World War 2; part of Morocco, 1959; free port status restored, 1962; airport; railway; university (1971); royal summer residence.

Tangshan or **T'angshan** 39°37N 118°05E, pop (2000e) 1 692 000. City in N China; railway; coal mining, heavy industry.

Tanizaki, Junichiro [tanizakee] (1886–1965) Novelist, born in Tokyo. He became known in the West only after the translation in 1957 of his long novel *Sasameyuki* (1943–8, The Makioka Sisters), a notable example of descriptive realism.

tank An armoured fighting vehicle, typically equipped with tracks enabling it to manoeuvre across broken ground, and armed by a high velocity gun in a rotating turret. The first practical tanks were used in action in 1916 by the British. In the years before 1939, they were developed into fast-moving, hard-hitting machines, and emerged as the most important land weapon of World War 2. Modern vehicles show a great deal of electronic sophistication, with advanced night vision devices, laser range-finders, and fire control computers.

tanker A vessel designed to carry liquid in bulk in a number of tanks, each of which is an integral part of the hull structure.The vessel with the largest gross tonnage is the Norwegian-registered oil tanker *Jahre Viking* of 260 851 gross tonnes and a deadweight capacity of 564 739 tonnes. Previously known as the *Seawise Giant*, she is the largest ship ever built.

tanning The process of turning raw animal hide or skin into a permanent, durable, flexible form. Cleaned skin is soaked in solutions of vegetable extracts containing tannins (eg oak bark) or, since the 19th-c, chrome salts.

tannins A mixture of derivatives of polyhydroxybenzoic acid from various plants, notably tea. They are water-soluble, with a bitter and astringent taste, and have long been used in the tanning of leather and in dyeing.

Tantalus [tantalus] In Greek mythology, a son of Zeus and Pluto. As king of Sipylos in Lydia, he committed terrible crimes. He stole the food of the gods, so becoming immortal. As punishment, he sits in a pool which recedes when he bends to drink, and the grapes over his head elude his grasp.

tantra [tantra] A type of Hindu or Buddhist ritual text, and the practice of its instruction. They include spells, mantras, meditative practices, and rituals to be performed.

Tanzania *p.916*

Taoism or **Daoism** [towizm] Chinese philosophical tradition, initially based on the ideas of 'Laozi' (Lao-tzu, ?6th-c BC) and Zhuangzi (Chuang-tzu, 369–286 BC). The *Tao* is the 'way' governing all human existence, which in Taoist terms lies in harmony between the individual and the natural world. Appropriate conduct arises from such harmony. From these origins as a life-philosophy, Taoism developed (1st-c BC) as a cult, its idealized dream-world readily absorbing primitive mystical and shamanistic beliefs. Favoured as a court religion under the Sui and Tang dynasties (590–906), Taoism came into conflict with Buddhism, and the latter was suppressed (845). In 1281, Taoism itself was suppressed by Kublai Khan, but rose again to favour under Ming emperors (1368–1644).

tape recorder Equipment for storing sound and other information on magnetic tape; also used to play back these recordings. The sound to be recorded is turned into an electrical signal by a microphone, and fed to the recording head. Magnetic tape passes over this head, and a record of the original sound is imprinted in magnetic signals on the tape.

tapestry A heavy decorative textile, hand-woven with multi-colour pictorial designs, and often of large size. Oriental in origin, tapestries were used for wall hangings, furniture, and floor coverings. Some tapestries were not woven but were embroidered – the Bayeux Tapestry being a famous example.

tapeworm A parasitic flatworm; adults commonly found in intestines of vertebrates; life cycle usually includes a larval stage found in a different intermediate host that is eaten by the final host. (Phylum: Platyhelminthes. Class: Cestoda.)

tapioca [tapiohka] A starchy preparation derived from the root crop cassava. It is used in puddings and as a thickening agent in liquid food.

Tanzania

☐ International Airport   ∴ World heritage site   **1** Pemba I   **2** Zanzibar I

[tanzaneea], official name **United Republic of Tanzania**
Local name Tanzania
Timezone GMT +3
Area 945 087 km²/364 900 sq mi
Population total (2002e) 34 902 000
Status Republic
Date of independence 1961
Capital Dodoma (formerly Dar es Salaam)
Languages Swahili and English (official), various tribal languages
Ethnic groups Bantu (99%) (including Nyamwezi and Sukuma 21%, Swahili 9%, Hehet and Bena 6%, Makonde 6%, Haya 6%), Arab, Asian, and European minorities
Religions Mainland: Christian (34%), Muslim (33%), traditional animist beliefs (33%); Zanzibar: Muslim (96%), Hindu (4%)

Physical features Largest E African country, just S of the Equator; includes the islands of Zanzibar, Pemba, and Mafia; coast fringed by long sandy beaches protected by coral reefs; rises towards a C plateau, average elevation 1000 m/3300 ft; Rift Valley branches round L Victoria (N), several high volcanic peaks, notably Mt Kilimanjaro, 5895 m/19 340 ft; extensive Serengeti Plain to the W; other main lakes, L Tanganyika and L Rukwa.

Climate Tropical; hot, humid climate on coast and offshore islands; average temperatures 27°C (Jan), 23°C (Jul); average annual rainfall 1000 mm/40 in; hot and dry on C plateau, average annual rainfall 250 mm/10 in; semi-temperate conditions above 1500 mm/5000 ft.

Currency 1 Tanzanian Shilling (TZS) = 100 cents

Economy Agriculture; rice, sorghum, coffee, sugar, cloves (most of world's market), coconuts, tobacco, cotton; reserves of iron, coal, tin, gypsum, salt, phosphate, gold, diamonds, oil; tourism.

GDP (2002e) $20·42 bn, per capita $600

Human Development Index (2002) 0·440

History Swahili culture developed, 10th–15th-c; Zanzibar became the capital of the Omani empire in 1840s; became a British protectorate, 1890; German East Africa established, 1891; British mandate to administer Tanganyika, 1919; first E African country to gain independence and become a member of the Commonwealth, 1961; republic, 1962; Zanzibar given independence as a constitutional monarchy with Sultan as Head of State; Sultan overthrown, 1964, and Act of Union between Zanzibar and Tanganyika led to the United Republic of Tanzania; a one-party state following 1965 constitution; legislation passed allowing for opposition parties, 1991, following a unanimous vote for a multi-party system; governed by a President, Cabinet, and National Assembly.

Head of State
1964–85 Julius Kambarage Nyerere
1985–95 Ndugu Ali Hassan Mwinyi
1995–2005 Benjamin Mkapa
2005– Jakaya Kikwete

Head of Government
1964–77 Rashid M Kawawa (Vice President to 1972)
1977–80 Edward M Sokoine
1980–3 Cleopa D Msuya
1983–4 Edward M Sokoine
1984–5 Salim A Salim
1985–90 Joseph S Warioba
1990–4 John Malecela
1994–5 Cleopa Msuya
1995–2005 Frederick Sumaye
2005– Edward Lowassa

---

tapir [tayper] A nocturnal mammal native to Central and South America and SE Asia; resembles a small, smooth-skinned, hornless rhinoceros, with a short smooth coat, and a snout extended as a short trunk; the only perissodactyl with four toes on front feet. (Family: Tapiridae, 4 species.)

tar The liquid product of heating coal in the absence of air (**coal tar**). It contains many important substances, useful in the chemical industry (benzene, phenol, pyridine, etc). **Wood tar** is the first product of the destructive distillation of wood. Further distillation yields *creosote* and a variety of organic compounds depending on the wood; for example, resinous woods yield turpentine. The residue is *pitch*.

Tara A prehistoric hillfort, 40 km/23 mi NW of Dublin. It is the supposed site of St Patrick's conversion of Lóegaire in the 5th-c, and the traditional seat of the kings of Ireland.

tarantella [tarantela] A lively folk-dance from S Italy, named after the town of Taranto. It was said to cure (or in some legends to be induced by) the bite of the tarantula.

Tarantino, Quentin (Jerome) [taranteenoh] (1963–) Film director, producer, actor, and screenwriter, born in Knoxville, TN. He sold his first screenplays, *True Romance* (1987, released 1993) and *Natural Born Killers* (released 1994), to enable him to start production of *Reservoir Dogs* (1992), in which he was director, screenwriter, and actor. The success of this film, and its successor *Pulp Fiction* (1994, Oscar), brought him celebrity status. Later films include *Four Rooms* (1995), *Jackie Brown* (1998), and *Kill Bill* (2003).

tarantula Any of the large hairy spiders of the family Therophosidae; rather sluggish spiders with a strong bite which may be venomous; hairs can cause rash when handled. (Order: Araneae.)

Tarawa 1°30N 173°00E, pop (2000e) 31 000. Capital town of Kiribati; airport; scene of US–Japanese battle in 1943.

Tarbes [tah(r)b], ancient **Bigorra** 43°15N 0°03E, pop (2000e) 52 600. Industrial and commercial city in S France; on left bank of R Adour; originally a Roman settlement; ancient capital of province of Bigorre; road and rail junction; cathedral (12th–14th-c).

Tardigrada [tah(r)digrada] *water bear*

tare *vetch*

targum [tah(r)gum] (Heb 'translation') An Aramaic translation of the Hebrew Scriptures or parts thereof, probably originally composed orally (c.1st-c BC) when the Torah was read aloud in the synagogues, then written in the rabbinic period. Best known is the *Targum Onkelos*.

tariff A tax on goods entering a country. Tariffs may be intended mainly to raise revenue, particularly in less developed countries. They may also be aimed at reducing imports in general, or designed to promote the domestic production of goods. Tariffs generally harm other countries, and are the subject of various international agreements.

Tarim Basin, Chin **Talimu Pendi** Largest inland basin in China; area 530 000 km²/205 000 sq mi; rich in salt and non-ferrous metals; nuclear testing in the region.

Tarkenton, Fran(cis Asbury) (1940–) Player of American football, born in Richmond, VA. He played for the Minnesota Vikings and New York Giants (1961–78), and gained 47 003 yds passing, a National Football League record.

taro [taroh] A perennial (*Colocasia esculenta*) native to SE Asia; also called **dasheen**. It is cultivated commercially in the tropics for its large corms. (Family: Araceae.)

tarot [taroh] A pack of playing cards used chiefly in fortune-telling. It consists of 22 picture cards of the *major arcana* (*arcana* 'secret') and 56 cards in suits of the *minor arcana* – staves (or wands), cups, swords, and coins. Their design was influenced by occult features, and some designs relate to ancient religions.

tarpan A wild horse native to the steppes of SE Europe; grey-brown with dark stripe along spine, occasionally with stripes on front legs; stiff, erect mane.

tarpon Large fish (*Tarpon atlanticus*) widespread in open waters of the Atlantic Ocean; length up to 2·4 m/8 ft; mouth oblique, lower jaw prolonged; dorsal fin small with long posterior fin ray. (Family: Megalopidae.)

Tarquinius Superbus, Lucius [tah(r)kwinius sooperbus] (6th-c BC) Tyrannical king of Rome, whose overthrow (510 BC) marked the end of monarchy at Rome, and the beginning of the Republic.

tarragon An aromatic perennial (*Artemisia dracunculus*) growing to 120 cm/4 ft, native to Asia; flower-heads globular, yellowish, drooping. It is widely cultivated as a culinary herb, and for seasoning vinegar. (Family: Compositae.)

Tarragona [taragona], Lat **Tarraco** 41°05N 1°17E, pop (2000e) 112 000. Port in Catalonia, NE Spain; archbishopric; airport; railway; cathedral (12th–13th-c); the archaeological excavations are designated a world heritage site.

Tarrant, Chris(topher John) (1946–) British television presenter, writer, and producer. He made programmes for Independent Television, such as *Tiswas* (1974), *OTT* (1981), and *Tarrant on Television* (from 1989), and in 1998 became a household name as presenter of the TV quiz show *Who Wants to be a Millionaire*. His many awards include the 2001 Sony Radio Academy's gold award.

tarsier [tah(r)sier] A nocturnal primate native to Indonesia and the Philippines; large eyes, long hind legs; long naked tail with tuft of hairs at the tip. (Family: Tarsiidae, 3 species.)

Tarski, Alfred (1902–83) Logician and mathematician, born in Warsaw. He made pioneering contributions to the study of formal semantics, especially to the definition of 'truth', and to several branches of mathematics and mathematical logic.

Tarsus [tah(r)suhs] 36°52N 34°52E, pop (2000e) 176 000. Town in S Turkey, on R Pamuk; important ancient city of Asia Minor; birthplace of St Paul; railway; agricultural trade centre.

tartan A fabric of a twill structure, made from variously coloured warp and weft yarns, using checkered designs which are almost always symmetrical. Tartans are mainly associated with the Scottish clans, in a tradition of dress dating from the 17th-c.

Tartar *Tatar*

tartaric acid [tah(r)tarik] IUPAC **2,3-dihydroxybutanedioic acid**, $C_4H_6O_6$. Potassium hydrogen tartrate is used as an acid in baking powder, and is called **cream of tartar**. **Tartar emetic** is a double salt of potassium and antimony.

Tartarus [tah(r)tarus] In Greek mythology, the name of the part of the Underworld where those who offended the gods were punished.

tartrazine An artificial yellow colouring permitted for use in foods. It has been associated with hypersensitivity reactions among urticaria sufferers and asthmatics.

Tashkent [tashkent] 41°16N 69°13E, pop (2000e) 2 457 000. Capital city of Uzbekistan; oldest city of C Asia, known in the 1st-c BC; taken by Russia, 1865; virtually rebuilt after earthquake damage, 1966; airport; railway; university (1920).

Tasman, Abel Janszoon [tazmn] (1603–c.59) Navigator, born near Groningen, The Netherlands. In 1642 he discovered the area he named Van Diemen's Land (now Tasmania) and New Zealand, followed by Tonga and Fiji (1643). He made a second voyage (1644) to the NW coast of Australia.

Tasmania, formerly **Van Diemen's Land** (to 1856) pop (2000e) 501 000; area 67 800 km²/26 200 sq mi. Island state of Australia, separated from the mainland by the Bass Strait; includes the main island of Tasmania, and several smaller islands; European discovery by Abel Tasman, 1642; first European settlement, 1803 (a British dependency of New South Wales); became a separate colony, 1825; mountainous interior, with a Central Plateau rising to 1617 m/5305 ft at Mt Ossa; temperate maritime climate; the most fertile regions along the NW and E coasts and along the river valleys; capital, Hobart; first Aborigines settled here 25 000 years ago; numerous unique plants and animals.

Tasmanian devil An Australian carnivorous marsupial (*Sarcophilus harrisii*); the largest dasyure (length up to 1·1 m/3·6 ft); bear-like in shape, with large powerful head and long bushy tail; threatened species.

Tasmanian tiger / wolf *thylacine*

Tasman Sea [tazmn] Part of the Pacific Ocean separating E Australia and Tasmania from New Zealand; named for the Dutch explorer Abel Tasman.

TASS *ITAR-TASS*

Tasso, Torquato (1544–95) Poet, born in Sorrento, Italy. His epic masterpiece on the capture of Jerusalem during the first crusade, *Gerusalemme Liberata* (1581, Jerusalem Liberated), was later rewritten, in response to criticisms, as *Gerusalemme Conquistata* (1593, Jerusalem Conquered).

taste buds Small sensory organs located on the tongue and palate, which recognize four primary tastes: sweet, sour, salt, and bitter. The tip of the tongue is sensitive to salt and sweet stimuli, the back to bitter stimuli, and the edges to sour and salt.

tatami [tatahmee] Traditional Japanese floor matting, made of layers of rushes, edged with narrow strips of black cloth. Tatami are standard size, equivalent to one sleeping space, and rooms are described as '6 mat, 8 mat', etc.

Tatar or **Tartar** A Turkic-speaking people living in Russia. Sunni Muslims since the 14th-c, they were a highly stratified mediaeval society. Their fierce reputation is the source of the modern word 'tartar'.

Tate, Ellalice *Hibbert, Eleanor*

Tate, Sir Henry (1819–99) Sugar magnate, art patron, and philanthropist, born in Chorley, Lancashire. He patented a method for cutting up sugar loaves (1872), and rapidly made a large fortune. The Tate Gallery was founded by him.

Tate, James (Vincent), originally **James Vincent Appleby** (1943–) Poet, born in Kansas City, MO. He has taught at the University of Massachusetts since 1971, publishing his first collection, *The Lost Pilot*, in 1967. In 1992 he won the Pulitzer Prize for his *Selected Poems* (1991), and later works include *Shroud of the Gnome* (1997), *Memoir of the Hawk* (2001), and *Return to the City of White Donkeys: Poems* (2004).

Tate, Nahum [nayuhm] (1652–1715) Poet and playwright, born in Dublin. He is known for his 'improved' versions of Shakespeare's tragedies, substituting happy endings to suit the popular taste. He became poet laureate in 1692.

Tate Gallery A London gallery housing the nation's chief collection of British art and modern foreign art. It was opened in 1897 as a branch of the National Gallery, and became fully independent in 1955. The Tate Modern gallery, on the site of the former Bankside power station, London, opened in May 2000. There is also a Tate Gallery at the Albert Dock development in Liverpool, and at St Ives, Cornwall.

Tati, Jacques [tatee], popular name of **Jacques Tatischeff** (1908–82) Actor and film director, born in Le Pecq, France. He made his reputation as the greatest film comedian of the post-war period, notably in *Les vacances de Monsieur Hulot* (1953, Mr Hulot's Holiday) and *Mon oncle* (1958, My Uncle), which won several awards.

Tatra Mountains [tahtra], Czech **Tatry** Mountain group in C Carpathian Mts, rising to 2655 m/8711 ft at Gerlachovský Štít.

Taung skull The partial skull and brain case of a young *Australopithecus africanus*, found at Taung, S Africa, in 1924. This was the first discovery of these small-brained early hominids.

Taunton [tawntn] 51°01N 3°06W, pop (2000e) 55 700. County town in Somerset, SW England; on the R Tone; founded in 705; Duke of Monmouth crowned king here, 1685; 12th-c castle hall, where Bloody Assizes held (1685); railway.

Taupo, Lake [towpoh] area 606 km²/234 sq mi. Lake in C North Island, New Zealand, filling an old volcanic crater; length 40 km/25 mi, width 27 km/17 mi; largest New Zealand lake.

tauraco *turaco*

Taurus [tawrus] (Lat 'bull') A prominent N constellation of the zodiac, including the Pleiades and Hyades clusters and the Crab Nebula. It lies between Aries and Gemini. Its brightest star is the red giant, Aldebaran. Distance: 20 parsec.

Taurus Mountains [tawrus], Turkish **Toros Dağlari** Mountain chain of S Turkey; highest peak, Ala Dağlari (3910 m/12 828 ft); its NW extension is called the **Anti-Taurus**.

Tautou, Audrey (1976–) Actress, born in Beaumont, Puy-de-Dôme, C France. She studied drama at the Cours Florent in Paris, and in 1999 won a César Best Actress award for the film *Vénus beauté (institut)*. She received further César nominations for *Amélie* (2001), which brought her international recognition, and *A Very Long Engagement* (2004). Later films include *The Da Vinci Code* (2006) in which she starred as special agent Sophie Neveu.

Tavener, Sir John (Kenneth) (1944–) Composer, born in London. His music is predominantly religious, and includes the cantata *The Whale* (1966), a sacred opera *Therese* (1979), and the choral work *A New Beginning* (1999). His *Song for Athene* (1993), written to commemorate the death of a family friend, Athene Hariades, in a cycling accident, became nationally known when it was chosen as part of the funeral ceremony for Princess Diana in 1997. Later works include *The Veil of the Temple* (2003).

tawny owl A typical owl (*Strix aluco*) native to Europe, Asia, and N Africa; mottled brown with black eyes and no ear tufts.

taxation The means by which a government raises money to finance its activities. **Direct taxes** are paid by individuals (eg income tax, national insurance contributions) and companies (eg corporation tax). **Indirect taxes** are those levied on goods and services (eg value-added tax, sales tax).

tax-haven A country where tax rates are particularly low. Companies or individuals may choose to reside there to avoid paying high rates of tax in their own home country. The Isle of Man, the Channel Is, and some West Indian countries are current examples.

taxis [taksis] A directed movement or orientation reaction of an organism to a stimulus. Taxis is usually used with a prefix to indicate the nature of the stimulus, for example *chemotaxis* (for a chemical stimulus), *phototaxis* (for a light stimulus), and *thermotaxis* (for a temperature stimulus).

taxol A substance which occurs naturally in the bark of the evergreen Pacific yew tree (*Taxus brevifolia*), and which has shown promising activity against certain forms of cancer. It requires the bark of 12 000 trees to produce 2·5 kg of taxol, and strenuous efforts are being made to synthesize it artificially.

taxonomy The theory and practice of describing, naming, and classifying organisms. It is divided into *alpha taxonomy*, the description and designation of species typically on the basis of morphological characters; *beta taxonomy*, the arrangement of species into hierarchical systems of higher categories; and *gamma taxonomy*, the study of the evolutionary relationships between groups (*taxa*) and of variation within and between populations.

Tay, River Longest river in Scotland; length 192 km/119 mi; rises on Ben Lui in the Grampians; enters the Firth of Tay.

Taylor, Elizabeth (Rosemond) (1932–) Film star, born in London. Her films include *Cat on a Hot Tin Roof* (1958), *Butterfield 8* (1960, Oscar), and *Cleopatra* (1962), which provided the background for her well-publicized romance with her co-star Richard Burton, with whom she made several films, including *Who's Afraid of Virginia Woolf?* (1966, Oscar). She has been married eight times, her husbands including the actor Michael Wilding, film producer Michael Todd, and Richard Burton (twice). In 1999 she received a BAFTA honorary fellowship and was made a dame. She announced her retirement in 2003.

Taylor, Zachary (1784–1850) US general, statesman, and 12th president (1849–50), born in Montebello, VA. In the Mexican War (1846–8) he won a major victory at Buena Vista, though heavily outnumbered. The main issue of his presidency was the status of the new territories, and the extension of slavery there.

Taymyr or **Taimyr, Lake** [tiymeer] area 4560 km²/1760 sq mi. Lake in N Siberian Russia; length, 250 km/155 mi.

Tayside pop (2000e) 405 000; area 7493 km²/2893 sq mi. Former region in E Scotland, created in 1975 and replaced in 1996 by Angus, Perth and Kinross, and Dundee City councils.

Tbilisi [tbileesee], formerly **Tiflis** (to 1936) 41°43N 44°48E, pop (2000e) 1 250 000. Capital city of Georgia, on the R Kura; founded, 5th-c; airport; railway junction; university (1918); cathedral (6th–7th-c).

TBS (Transmission Based Signalling) *train protection systems*

Tchad *Chad*

Tchaikovsky or **Tschaikovsky, Piotr Ilyich** [chiykofskee] (1840–93) Composer, born in Kamsko-Votkinsk, Russia. Among his greatest works are the ballets *Swan Lake* (1876–7), *The Sleeping Beauty* (1890), and *The Nutcracker* (1892), the last three of his six symphonies, two piano concertos, and several tone poems, notably *Romeo and Juliet* and *Capriccio Italien*.

tea A small evergreen tree (*Camellia sinensis*) growing to c.4 m/13 ft in the wild, but only a small shrub in cultivation; native to Myanmar and Assam, but cultivated in China since early times, with Japan, India, and Sri Lanka now also major producers. The shoot tips with the first two leaves are picked, allowed to wither, then rolled, fermented, and dried; when infused with boiling water they make the well-known beverage containing the stimulants tannin and caffeine. (Family: Theaceae.)

Teacher of Righteousness The religious leader and founder of the Qumran community, probably in the mid-2nd-c BC. He was apparently a Zadokite priest who opposed the Hasmoneans, and led his followers into exile near the Dead Sea.

Teagarden, Jack, popular name of **Weldon Leo Teagarden** (1905–64) Jazz trombonist and singer, born in Vernon, TX. He joined the orchestras of Ben Pollack and Paul Whiteman before leading his own orchestra (1939–46). He was also a member of Louis Armstrong's All Stars (1947–51).

teak A large evergreen tree (*Tectona grandis*), growing to 45 m/150 ft, native to S India and SE Asia; flowers small, white, 5-lobed bells. It is a source of high-quality, durable, water-resistant timber. (Family: Verbenaceae.)

teal A small dabbling duck (Genus: *Anas*, 16 species), found worldwide; eats water-weeds and invertebrates. (Subfamily: Anatinae.)

Teamsters' Union The **International Brotherhood of Teamsters, Chauffeurs, Warehousemen and Helpers of America**, the largest US labour union, with over 1·5 million members.

teasel A large, stiff, and prickly biennial (*Dipsacus fullonum*), growing to 2 m/6½ ft, native to Europe and the Mediterranean; flowers tiny, white or mauve, in heads the size and shape of an egg. The prickly heads of the cultivated **fuller's teasel** (subspecies *sativus*) were used for raising the nap on cloth (**teasing**). (Family: Dipsacaceae.)

Tebbit (of Chingford), Norman (Beresford) Tebbit, Baron (1931–) British Conservative statesman, born in Enfield, Greater London. He was employment secretary (1981–3), and secretary for trade and industry (1983–5), but his career was interrupted in 1984 when both he and his wife were badly hurt during the IRA bombing of the Grand Hotel at Brighton. In 1985 he became chairman of the party, but following policy disagreements with Mrs Thatcher he retired to the backbenches in 1987. He was made a life peer in 1992.

Technicolor The trademark of a colour cinematography process internationally dominant between 1935 and 1955. Shooting involved special three-strip cameras.

technology The use of tools, machines, materials, techniques, and sources of power to make work easier and more productive. Whereas science is concerned with understanding how and why things happen, technology deals with making things happen; it can be subdivided into many specializations, such as medical, military, and nuclear.

tectonics The study of the structure of the Earth's crust, particularly such processes as the movement of rocks during folding and faulting.

Tecumseh [tekumsuh], originally **Tecumtha** (c.1768–1813) Indian chief of the Shawnees, born in Old Piqua, OH. He joined his brother, 'The Prophet', in a rising against the whites, which was suppressed at Tippecanoe (1811), and commanded the Indian allies in the War of 1812.

Tedder (of Glenguin), Arthur William Tedder, Baron (1890–1967) Marshal of the Royal Air Force, born in Glenguin, Stirling, Scotland. He became deputy supreme commander of the Allied Expeditionary Force under Eisenhower (1943–5).

Tees, River [teez] River of NE England; rises on Cross Fell, Cumbria and flows 128 km/79 mi to the North Sea; upper river valley known as **Teesdale**; Cauldron Snout, Britain's highest waterfall (61 m/200 ft) located in Upper Teesdale.

Teesside Urban area surrounding the R Tees estuary in NE England; includes Stockton-on-Tees, Redcar, Thornaby, Middlesbrough.

teeth Small, bone-like structures of the jaws used for the biting and chewing of food. Each tooth consists of a core of *pulp* surrounded by *dentine*, which is covered in its upper part by

Human Teeth

	Eruption	Shedding
Milk		
incisor 1	6 months	6–7 years
incisor 2	8 months	7–8 years
canine 1	18 months	10–12 years
molar 1	1 year	9–11 years
molar 2	2 years	10–12 years
Permanent		
incisor 1	7–8 years	
incisor 2	8–9 years	
canine 1	10–12 years	
premolar 1	10–11 years	
premolar 2	11–12 years	
molar 1	6–7 years	
molar 2	12 years	
molar 3	17–21 years	

Note: the lower teeth usually appear before the upper equivalent teeth.

enamel and in its lower part by cement (the *root*). The *crown* is the enamel-covered part that projects beyond the gums; it may have one or more projections called *cusps*. In many mammals, different types of teeth can be identified: *incisors* for cutting, *canines* for cutting and tearing, and *premolars* and *molars* for grinding. In humans the first set of teeth (*deciduous* or *milk* teeth) usually appears between 6 and 24 months of age, there being 20 deciduous teeth in all (2 incisors, 1 canine, and 2 molars in each half-jaw). These gradually become replaced (from about age 6) by the *permanent* teeth, with the addition of 3 more teeth in each half-jaw giving a total complement of 32. The third molar is often referred to as the *wisdom tooth*, because of its time of eruption. Not all of the teeth may appear. *see panel*

tefillin [tefileen] Jewish phylacteries or frontlets, consisting of two black leather cubes with leather straps, bound over the head and arm, and worn during Jewish morning prayers, except on sabbaths and festivals. The cubes contain scriptural texts.

Tegucigalpa [taygoosigalpa] 14°05N 87°14W, pop (2000e) 817 000. Capital city of Honduras; founded, 1524; altitude 975 m/3200 ft; capital, 1880; university (1847); cathedral (18th-c); devastated by hurricane Mitch in 1998.

Tehran or **Teheran** [tairahn] 35°44N 51°30E, pop (2000e) 8 317 000. Capital city of Iran; altitude 1200–1700 m/4000–5500 ft; capital of Persia, 1788; airport; road and rail junction; six universities (oldest, 1935); Shahyad Tower, symbol of modern Iran.

Tehran Conference [tairahn] The first inter-allied conference of World War 2, attended by Stalin, Roosevelt, and Churchill, held at Tehran in 1943.

Teilhard de Chardin, Pierre [tayah duh shah(r)dĩ] (1881–1955) Geologist, palaeontologist, Jesuit priest, and philosopher, born in Sarcenat, France. His unorthodox ideas led to a Church ban on his teaching and publishing. His major work, *Le Phénomène humain* (written 1938–40, The Phenomenon of Man) was posthumously published; it argues that humanity is in a continuous process of evolution towards a perfect spiritual state.

Te Kanawa, Dame Kiri [tay kahnawa] (1944–) Operatic soprano, born in Gisborne, New Zealand. She made her debut with the Royal Opera Company in 1971, and has since taken a wide range of leading roles and made many recordings. In 1981 she sang at the wedding of the Prince and Princess of Wales. She retired from opera in 2004 but continues to perform concerts.

tektite A rounded, flat, and glassy meteorite ranging in diameter from submillimetre size up to c.10 cm/4 in.

Tel Aviv–Yafo 32°05N 34°46E, pop (2000e) 444 000. Twin cities in W Israel, a commercial port on the Mediterranean Sea; Tel Aviv founded in 1909 as a garden suburb of Yafo (Jaffa), today an artists' centre; former capital (to 1950) of Israel; airport; railway; two universities (1953, 1974).

telebanking A system which enables banking transactions to be carried out via a communications network. This is usually by telephone through a viewdata system or an interactive computer link.

telecine [teleesinee] Equipment for converting motion-picture film to video for broadcast television or videotape recording. Developments in digital scanning allow special effects to be introduced during transfer.

telecommunications The transmission of data-carrying signals, often between two widely separated points; it includes radio, telegraphy, telephones, television, and computer networks. Telecommunications in the modern sense began in the 19th-c: the Great Western Railway telegraph lines from Paddington to Slough, England, opened in 1843; telephones for commercial use were installed in Boston and Cambridge, MA, in 1877; radio telegraphy became a commercial success after Marconi founded the Wireless, Telegraph and Signal Co in London in 1897. During the 20th-c, first radio (from the 1920s) and then television (from the 1950s) became important for communication over distance. In 1962 the US Telstar 1 satellite was launched to relay communications signals, and large numbers of *geostationary* satellites now provide day-long international links for telephony and television transmissions. The use of optical fibre links in telephone cables enables hundreds of simultaneous conversations to be transmitted.

teleconferencing The connection of several locations by television links to provide continuous intercommunication of sound and sight. In some applications, the picture is presented as a rapidly changing series of stills, rather than in continuous motion, in order to reduce the bandwidth required in transmission.

telegraphy Communication at a distance of written, printed, or pictorial matter, by the transmission of electrical signals along wires. Modern examples of this are telex and fax. In **radiotelegraphy** the message is carried by radio waves rather than along a wire.

telekinesis *psychokinesis*

Tel el-Amarna [tel el amah(r)na] The ancient Akhetaten ('the horizon of Aten'), a short-lived Egyptian city on the E bank of the R Nile, founded c.1350 BC by the heretic pharoah Akhenaton and demolished after his death.

Telemachus [telemakus] In the *Odyssey*, the son of Odysseus and Penelope. He sets out to find his father, and helps Odysseus fight Penelope's suitors.

Telemann, Georg Philipp [tayleman] (1681–1767) Composer, born in Magdeburg, Germany. A prolific composer, his works include church music, 46 passions, over 40 operas, oratorios, many songs, and a large body of instrumental music.

telemarketing A marketing system which uses the telephone, handling responses to advertisements which carry telephone numbers. It also involves making calls to prospective clients on behalf of marketing outlets.

teleology A view which maintains that some phenomena can be explained fully only by citing the functions they perform ('a function of the liver is to secrete bile') or the purposes for which the activity was undertaken ('Iago lied in order to provoke Othello').

teleost [teliost, teeliost] Any of a large group of ray-finned fishes (Actinopterygii) in which the tail is symmetrical, without an upturned body axis; comprises the great majority of extant species of true bony fishes.

telephone A device for transmitting speech sounds over a distance. In 1876 Alexander Graham Bell was granted a patent to develop such an instrument, and his induction receiver, along with Thomas Edison's carbon transmitter, form the basis of the modern telephone. In the mouthpiece, a carbon microphone translates sound vibrations into a varied electric current which is relayed through wires to the receiver, where it is converted back into sound waves by a diaphragm and an electromagnet. Amplifiers (repeaters) placed at intervals along a line make long-distance telephoning possible. Modern telephone instruments are largely electronic, with keypads replacing dials, and the addition of such 'smart' features as last-number recall. Developments of the 1990s included the growth in use of cordless telephones, the worldwide introduction of mobile phones, and the first digital videophones.

telephoto lens A camera lens of long focal length but comparatively short overall dimensions, giving increased magnification for a limited angle of view. In 35 mm still cameras, focal lengths of 100–300 mm are usual, but for special purposes such as news work, sports, and natural history 500–1000 mm may be employed.

telerecording The transfer of a video programme to motion-picture film. Since the interval between successive video frames is very short, a film camera with extremely rapid movement from one frame to the next is essential.

telescope An optical instrument for producing magnified images of distant objects. The earliest known devices were made c.1608 by Lippershey and Galileo. **Refracting telescopes** use a lens to bring light rays to a focus, a technique first applied to astronomy by Galileo. **Reflecting telescopes** use a mirror to bring the light rays to a focus, a technique first applied to astronomy by Newton. The largest telescopes today are all reflectors. For special purposes, such as photography, there may be a combination of mirror and lens, as in the Schmidt camera. **Radio telescopes** collect and analyse cosmic radio emission from celestial sources. The basic type consists of a steerable, paraboloidal collecting dish with a central detector connected to amplifiers. Telescopes for other types of radiation (eg infrared, ultraviolet, X-rays) are also used, sometimes above the Earth's atmosphere.

Telescopium [teleskohpium] (Lat 'telescope') A small, faint S constellation delineated by Lacaille in honour of the astronomical telescope.

teleshopping A system for shopping from home, using a communications network such as the Internet or a public videotex system; also called **online shopping**. A list of food and goods available to the shopper is displayed on the computer or television screen, and these can be ordered directly over the communications link.

Telesto [telestoh] The 13th natural satellite of Saturn, discovered in 1980; distance from the planet 295 000 km/183 000 mi; diameter 30 km/19 mi.

Teletex A service, provided by a posts, telegraph and telephones authority, which offers computer-based facilities such as electronic mail to a subscriber.

teletext An information service of alpha-numerical data and simple diagrams transmitted as individual pages in digitally coded form during a TV broadcast signal. The constantly updated results, typically news headlines, football scores, weather maps, etc, can be displayed on any domestic receiver equipped with a decoder and page-selection keyboard. In the UK, the services Ceefax (BBC) and Oracle (IBA) were introduced in the 1970s.

teletype An old form of keyboard printer-based terminal used for linking into a computer. Teletypes were slow and unreliable, and came to be replaced by a combination of visual display unit and (where hard copy is required) attached printer.

television The transmission and reproduction of moving pictures and associated sound by electronic means; developed in the late 19th-c and early 20th-c, with the first pictures presented by Baird in 1926. The image of a scene in a TV camera is analysed by scanning along a series of horizontal lines, the variations of brightness along each line being converted into a train of electrical signals for transmission or recording. At the receiver the picture is reconstituted on the fluorescent screen of a cathode-ray tube by an electron beam scanning a precisely similar pattern. The number of scanning lines and the picture frequency vary in different systems, the American standard having 525 lines with 30 pictures per second (pps) and the European 625 lines at 25 pps.

television camera *camera*

telex An international telegraphic system in which telephone lines transmit printed messages, using devices which convert typed words into electrical signals and vice versa (*teleprinters*); the name is a contraction of 'teletypewriter exchange service'. Subscribers to the system have their own call sign and number. The system is relatively cheap, and has been much used by commercial organizations, but was largely overtaken by fax and e-mail.

Telford 52°42N 2°28W. A new town in Shropshire, WC England, designated in 1963, comprising three previous urban areas: **Telford Dawley**, pop (2000e) 30 600; **Telford North**, (2000e) 56 700; **Telford South**, pop (2000e) 24 900; Telford and Wrekin a unitary authority in 1998; on the R Severn; railway.

Telford, Thomas (1757–1834) Engineer, born near Langholm, Dumfries and Galloway. His works include the Ellesmere (1793–1805) and Caledonian (1803–23) canals, and the road from London to Holyhead, with the Menai Suspension Bridge (1826).

Tell, Wilhelm, Eng **William Tell** (13th–14th-c) Legendary Swiss patriot and crossbow marksman of Bürglen in Uri. According to tradition, he was compelled by the tyrannical Austrian governor to shoot an apple off his own son's head from a distance of 80 paces. Later, Tell slew the tyrant, and so initiated the movement which secured the independence of Switzerland.

tell An Arabic 'mound' or 'hill', in archaeological usage, an artificial mound formed through the long-term accumulation of mud brick from houses successively levelled and rebuilt.

Tellus *Gaea*

telomere The part of a chromosome further from the centromere in eucaryotes, containing G-rich repetitive DNA. Without telomeres chromosomes are unstable, and can combine with other chromosomes to give ring structures.

Telugu [teluhgoo] The Dravidian language associated particularly with the state of Andhra Pradesh in S India. It has some 73 million speakers.

Tempe [tempee] 33°25N 111°56W, pop (2000e) 158 600. Health resort in SC Arizona, USA; settled, 1872; railway; university (1885).

tempera [tempera] A method of painting with powdered pigment mixed with egg-yolk and water, usually on specially prepared wooden panels. This technique was normal in the Middle Ages.

temperance movement A response to the social evils caused by the alcoholism so widespread in the 18th-c and 19th-c. Temperance societies were organized first in the USA, then in Britain and Scandinavia.

temperature Measurement related to heat flow between objects. It is measured using thermometers, thermocouples, and pyrometers, and is controlled using thermostats. The Kelvin temperature scale is used in physics (an SI unit), fixed by the triple point of water, 273·16 K. Other temperature scales include the Celsius (°C), also called Centigrade, Fahrenheit (°F) and Rankine (°R).

Templars The Poor Knights of Christ and of the Temple of Solomon; an international religious–military order, whose members were subject to monastic vows. The order was founded c.1120 chiefly to protect pilgrims to the Holy Land; its name derives from the location of its headquarters – near the site of the Jewish Temple in Jerusalem. It developed into a great army, and was suppressed by Pope Clement V in 1312.

Temple A group of buildings, including the 12th-c Temple church, in Fleet St, London. They were established on land once owned by the Knights Templar.

Temple, Jerusalem The central shrine of Jewish worship and its priesthood since its establishment under Solomon. It was first destroyed by Nebuchadnezzar in c.587 BC, but rebuilt later in the 6th-c BC after the return from exile. Extended on an elaborate scale by Herod the Great, beginning c.20 BC, it was barely renewed before its destruction under Titus during the Jewish revolt of AD 70. Still unrestored today, its site is now partly occupied by the Muslim mosque, the Dome of the Rock, built in the late 7th-c.

Temple, Shirley, married name **Black** (1928–) Child film star, born in Santa Monica, CA. During 1934–8 she appeared in more than 20 feature films, such as *Stand Up and Cheer* (1934) and *Bright Eyes* (1934), and was consistently the top US movie star. She received an honorary Academy Award in 1934. Retiring from the screen, in her married status as **Mrs S T Black** she entered Republican politics, and was US Ambassador to Ghana (1974–6), and Czechoslovakia (1989–93).

Temple, Sir William (1628–99) Diplomat and essayist, born in London. He negotiated the Triple Alliance (1668) against France, and helped to bring about the marriage of the Prince of Orange to the Princess Mary. His essay style was a major influence on 18th-c writers, including Swift, who was his secretary.

Temple, William (1881–1944) Anglican churchman, born in Exeter, Devon. He became Archbishop of York (1929–42) and Archbishop of Canterbury (1942–4). An outspoken advocate of social and Church reform, he was a leader in the ecumenical movement.

Temple Bar A site at the junction of the Strand and Fleet St, London, where from 1301 a gateway marked the boundary of the Cities of London and Westminster. It is now marked by a statue of a griffin.

Temple of Heaven A group of buildings in Beijing, in which the emperors formerly conducted their devotions. The complex was laid out in 1406–20.

Temple of the Tooth The Dalada Maligawa, an important Buddhist pilgrimage site in Kandy, Sri Lanka. The shrine was built to house one of the Buddha's teeth.

Templeton, Sir John Marks (1912–) Businessman and philanthropist, born in Winchester, TN. He started on Wall Street in 1937, and went on to found several major investment funds. He is widely known for the establishment in 1972 of the Templeton Prize for Progress in Religion.

Templeton Prize A prize for progress in religion, created in 1972, and awarded annually by the Templeton Foundation, New York City. It is the world's largest money award, whose total passed $1 million dollars for the first time in 1992. Its aim is to increase sensitivity to the diversity of religious thought and work.

tempura [tempura] Japanese fritters, probably originating with the Portuguese in 16th-c Japan. They are served crisp, with diluted soy sauce mixed with grated radish to balance the oil.

tench Freshwater fish (*Tinca tinca*) native to slow rivers and lakes of Europe and W Asia, but now more widespread; length up to 60 cm/2 ft; body stout, fins rounded; mouth with pair of thin barbels; dark green to brown. (Family: Cyprinidae.)

Ten Commandments or **Decalogue** The fundamental laws of the Jews; in the Bible, said to have been given to Moses on Mt Sinai. One tradition declares that God inscribed them on two tablets of stone which were then deposited in the Ark of the Covenant (*Deut* 9). The well-known 'ethical' decalogue contains the commands: (1) the God of Israel shall be acknowledged as one and unique, (2) worship of images is prohibited, (3) misuse of the Lord's name is prohibited, (4) the Sabbath must be observed, (5) one's parents must be honoured, (6–10) murder, adultery, theft, false testimony, and coveting one's neighbour's goods are prohibited.

tendinitis Inflammation of a tendon, the fibrous cord attaching a muscle to a bone. It results in pain over the affected area, particularly on movement. It is often cause by repetitive strain on the tendon, and can be alleviated by rest.

tendon An extremely strong fibrous cord or sheet of connective tissue (bundles of collagen fibres), continuously attaching muscle to bone or cartilage.

tendril An organ with which climbing plants attach themselves to supports; most coil around the support but some end in sticky, sucker-like pads.

Tenerife *Canary Islands*

Teng Hsiao-p'ing *Deng Xiaoping*

Teniers, David [teneerz], known as **the Elder** (1582–1649) Baroque genre painter, born in Antwerp, Belgium. His son, **David Teniers the Younger** (1610–90), executed c.700 paintings, and is best known for his scenes of peasant life, in the tradition of Brueghel.

Ten Lost Tribes of Israel Ten tribes of Israel taken captive by Assyria in 721 BC and merged (hence 'lost') with the Assyrians.

Tennant Creek 19°31S 134°15E, pop (2000e) 3800. Town in Northern Territory, Australia; airfield; an important gold mining centre since the 1930s.

Tennessee pop (2000e) 5 689 300; area 109 149 km²/42 144 sq mi. State in SEC USA; the 'Volunteer State'; ceded by France, 1763; explored by Daniel Boone, 1769; temporary state of Franklin formed in 1784, after the War of Independence; Federal government created the Territory South of the Ohio, 1790; admitted as the 16th state to the Union, 1796; seceded, 1861; the scene of many battles during the Civil War; slavery abolished, 1865; readmitted to the Union, 1866; highest point, Clingmans Dome (2025 m/6644 ft); in the E lie the Great Smoky Mts, Cumberland Plateau; fertile 'bluegrass' country in the C, ideal for livestock and dairy farming; in the W is a rich floodplain where most of the state's cotton is grown; capital, Nashville; nation's largest producer of zinc and pyrites.

Tennessee River River in SE USA; formed by the confluence of the French Broad and Holston Rivers; joins the Ohio R at Paducah; length (including the French Broad) 1398 km/869 mi; used for irrigation, flood-control, and hydroelectric power (the Tennessee Valley Authority, 1933).

Tenniel, Sir John [teneel] (1820–1914) Artist, born in London. He became known as a book illustrator, notably in his work for *Alice's Adventures in Wonderland* (1865) and *Through the Looking-glass* (1872).

tennis *see panel*

tennis elbow Pain in the external aspect of the elbow following repetitive trauma, such as may occur in playing tennis. It may result from small tears in the muscles in the region.

Tennyson, Alfred Tennyson, 1st Baron [tenison], known as **Alfred, Lord Tennyson** (1809–92) Poet, born in Somersby, Lincolnshire. His major poetic achievement was the elegy mourning the death of his friend, Arthur Hallam, *In Memoriam* (1850); and in the same year he succeeded Wordsworth as poet laureate. In

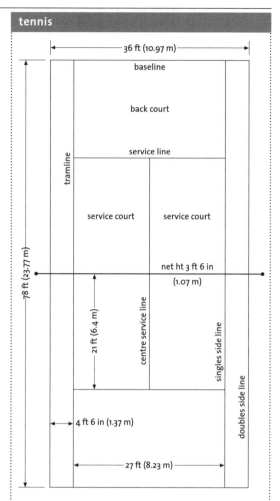

tennis

A racket-and-ball game for two or four players developed from real tennis; also known as **lawn tennis**. It is played on a rectangular court measuring 78 ft (23·77 m) long by 27 ft (8·23 m) wide for singles, or 36 ft (10·97 m) wide for doubles. A net 3 ft (0·9 m) high at the centre is stretched across the width of the court. Playing surface varies, and can be grass, clay, shale, concrete, wood, or other suitable artificial materials. The object is to play winning strokes by forcing one's opponent(s) to fail to return the ball successfully over the net. In doubles, players may hit the ball in any order, but must serve in rotation. The most famous lawn tennis championship is the All England Championships at Wimbledon each year. 'Field Tennis' was played in the 18th-c, but the game similar to the modern game was introduced by Major Walter Clopton Wingfield at a Christmas party at Nantclywd, Wales, in 1873. His game was called *sphairistike*.

1859–85 he published a series of poems on the Arthurian theme, *Idylls of the King* (1859).

Tenochtitlan [tenochtitlahn] The island capital of L Texcoco, now beneath Mexico City, from which the Aztecs dominated Mexico from c.1344–5 to the Spanish Conquest in 1519.

ten-pin bowling *bowling*

tenrec [tenrek] A mammal of family Tenrecidae (31 species), native to Madagascar; an insectivore; species can resemble hedgehogs, moonrats (but lack tails), shrews, or moles.

tensile strength The stretching stress at which a material breaks; symbol σ, units Pa (pascal).

Ten Years' War (1868–78) The name usually given to the unsuccessful Cuban insurrection against Spanish colonial rule.

Tenzing Norgay, known as **Sherpa Tenzing** (1914–86) Mountaineer, born in Tsa-chu near Makalu, Nepal. In 1953 he succeeded in reaching the Everest summit with Edmund Hillary, for which he was awarded the George Medal.

Teotihuacán [tayoteewakahn] A great city, 30 km/20 mi NE of Mexico City, flourishing c.450–650, but destroyed and burnt in c.700; a world heritage site.

tepal *perianth*

teratorn A condor-like vulture with a wingspan exceeding 4 m/ 13 ft; the largest flying bird ever to have lived, now extinct; known from Pleistocene fossils. (Genus: *Teratornia*.)

Terborch or **Terburg, Gerard** [terbaw(r)kh] (1617–81) Painter, born in Zwolle, The Netherlands. He worked mostly on a small scale, producing genre pictures and fashionable portraits, but is best known for his painting of 'The Peace of Munster' (1648, National Gallery, London).

Terbrugghen, Hendrik [tairbrookhen] (c.1588–1629) Painter, born in Deventer, The Netherlands. He excelled in chiaroscuro effects, and in the faithful representation of physiognomical details and drapery, as in his 'Jacob and Laban' (1627, National Gallery, London).

terebinth *turpentine tree*

Terence, in full **Publius Terentius Afer** (c.190–159 BC) Latin comic poet, born in Carthage, N Africa. His surviving six comedies are Greek in origin and scene, directly based on Menander. Many of his conventions were later used by European dramatists.

Terengganu [terenggahnoo] pop (2000e) 936 000; area 12 928 km²/4990 sq mi. State in NE Peninsular Malaysia; ceded to Britain, 1909; capital, Kuala Terengganu.

Teresa of Ávila, St (1515–82) Saint and mystic, born in Ávila, Spain. Famous for her ascetic religious exercises and sanctity, in 1562 she re-established the ancient Carmelite rule, with additional observances. She was canonized in 1622. Feast day 15 October.

Teresa (of Calcutta), Mother, originally **Agnes Gonxha Bojaxhiu** (1910–97) Christian missionary in India, born in Skopje, Former Yugoslav Republic of Macedonia. Her sisterhood, the Missionaries of Charity, started in 1950, and in 1957 she started work with lepers and in many disaster areas of the world. She was awarded the Pope John XXIII Peace Prize (1971), the Templeton Prize (1973), and the Nobel Peace Prize (1979). In 2003 she was beatified by Pope John Paul II.

Teresa of Lisieux *Theresa of Lisieux*

Tereshkova, Valentina [tereshkova] (1937–) Cosmonaut and the first woman to fly in space, born in Maslennikovo, Russia. She was a solo crew member of the 3-day Vostok 6 flight launched on 16 June 1963. She was made a hero of the Soviet Union, and married fellow cosmonaut Andrian Nikolayev later that year. She held many public positions in her later years, including presidency of the Soviet Women's Committee.

Terfel, Bryn [tervel, brin], originally **Bryn Terfel Jones** (1965–) Bass baritone, born in Pant-glas, Caernarfonshire, North Wales. He became known after winning the Lieder Prize in the Cardiff Singer of the World competition in 1989. In 1993 he received the Newcomer of the Year International Classic Music Award, and has since appeared at many of the world's leading opera houses. He is twice winner of best male artist at the Classical Brit Awards (2004, 2005). Among later albums is *Simple Gifts* (2005, Grammy). In 2000 he established the annual Bryn Terfel Faenol Festival held near Bangor, North Wales. He

became the second recipient of the Queen's Medal for Music in 2006.

Terkel, Studs, popular name of **Louis Terkel** (1912–) Writer and oral historian, born in New York City. He became a radio commentator and television host, and travelled worldwide conducting interviews with the famous and the anonymous. His publications include *The Good War: an Oral History of World War Two* (1984, Pulitzer) and *Will the Circle be Unbroken?* (2002).

Terme [tairmay] The national museum of Rome, containing one of the world's most important collections of Greek and Roman art. It is housed in the ancient Diocletian Baths.

terminal *computer terminal*

Terminus The Roman god of boundary marks, where his statue or bust was sometimes placed. His festival (**Terminalia**) was on 23 February.

termite A small, social insect that constructs nests in rotten wood or makes earth mounds which may measure several metres across; workers mostly sterile, blind, and with soft white cuticle (known as **white ants**); adults winged; c.2000 species, causing great economic problems in the tropics, damaging timber buildings and crops. (Order: Isoptera.)

tern A small, gull-like seabird, found worldwide; plumage usually pale with black cap and forked tail; head with partly erectile crest (**crested tern**) or smooth. (Family: Laridae, 42 species; some authors put the tern in a separate family, Sternidae.)

terpene A class of natural products, also known as **essential oils**, based upon the oligomerization of isoprene, having formulae closely related to $(C_5H_8)_n$. Common examples are pinene, limonene, menthol, and carotene.

Terpsichore [terpsikawree] In Greek mythology, one of the Muses, usually associated with dancing or lyric poetry.

terracotta Clay, modelled into sculpture or tiles and fired in a kiln, becoming hard and brittle but very permanent. Examples survive from ancient times and from all over the world.

Terracotta Army *Mount Li*

terrapin [terapin] A reptile of the family Emydidae, found in fresh or brackish water or on land; also known as **pond turtle**. (Order: Chelonia.)

terrier A small hardy domestic dog, bred for hunting (especially foxes); originally sent into burrows after prey; traditionally aggressive, tenacious, fearless; many modern breeds.

Territorial Army, in full **Territorial and Voluntary Reserve Army (TAVRA)** A British reserve military force, first formed in 1908, each battalion being attached to a battalion of the regular army. The 'Terriers' (known as the Territorial Force to 1920, the Territorials thereafter) fought with distinction in the two world wars. They receive continuous training on a part-time basis. The **Voluntary Reserve** consists of ex-regular soldiers who commit themselves to reserve service for a fixed period.

territory In US history, political status prior to the attainment of statehood. Hawaii and Alaska were the last two places to have territorial status.

terrorism Coercive and violent behaviour undertaken to achieve or promote a particular political objective or cause, often involving the overthrow of established order. Terrorist activity is designed to induce fear through its indiscriminate, arbitrary, and unpredictable acts of violence. It may be 'official', as under Stalin, or 'unofficial', as employed by various opposition or underground movements. Such movements are usually minority groups who feel there are no other means available to them of achieving their objectives. Terrorism may have an international dimension, manifest in hijackings and hostage-taking.

Terry, Dame (Alice) Ellen (1847–1928) Actress, born in Coventry, West Midlands, a member of a large family of actors. She became the leading Shakespearean actress in London, dominating the English and US theatre (1878–1902) in partnership with Henry Irving. In 1903 she went into theatre management.

Terry-Thomas, originally **Thomas Terry Hoar Stevens** (1911–90) Film actor, born in Finchley, Greater London. He was the gap-toothed villain in dozens of post-World War 2 comedies, satirizing and eventually personifying the upper-class bounder in such films as *I'm All Right Jack* (1959), *School for Scoundrels* (1960), and *Those Magnificent Men In Their Flying Machines* (1965).

Tertiaries Members of the Third Order of religious life. Normally, these are lay people striving after Christian perfection in life in the world under the guidance of a religious Order. A **Regular Tertiary** is a member of a community bound by vows.

tertiary education Post-secondary education. It is often used to refer to further and higher education, but in the UK it can also refer to attendance at a **tertiary college**, which is a college for all those over 16 wishing to pursue academic or vocational courses.

Tertiary period The earlier of the two geological periods of the Cenozoic era, extending from c.65 to 2 million years ago. It is divided into five epochs: the Palaeocene, Eocene, Oligocene, Miocene, and Pliocene.

Tertullian [tertulian], in full **Quintus Septimus Florens Tertullianus** (c.160–220) Christian theologian, born in Carthage. His opposition to worldliness in the Church culminated in his becoming a leader of the Montanist sect (c.207). He was the first to produce major Christian works in Latin.

Tesla, Nikola [tesla] (1856–1943) Physicist and electrical engineer, born in Smiljan, Croatia. His inventions included improved dynamos, transformers, electric bulbs, and the high-frequency coil which now bears his name. The unit of magnetic induction is named after him.

tesla SI unit of magnetic flux density; symbol *T*; defined as a magnetic flux of 1 weber per square metre; named after US inventor Nikola Tesla.

tessera *mosaic*

tessitura [tessitoora] That part of a vocal compass in which the most demanding passages in a piece of music are concentrated. An aria, operatic role, etc may be said to demand a high tessitura.

Test Act A British Act passed in 1673 by a parliament anxious to curb Catholic influence at Charles II's court. Every office holder had to take Oaths of Supremacy and Allegiance, and to take Communion according to the rites of the Church of England. The Act remained in force until 1828.

testis (plural **testes**) The essential reproductive gland (*gonad*) of male animals, producing spermatozoa; also known as the **testicle**. In vertebrates the testis also synthesizes and secretes sex hormones (*androgens*). In mammals (eg humans), there are usually two, lying suspended within the scrotum, oval and flattened in shape.

testosterone [testosterohn] The male sex hormone, produced in the testes, and responsible for the development of the primary sex organs, secondary sex characteristics (eg facial hair), and sexual behaviour.

test-tube baby The lay term to indicate *in vitro* **fertilization and embryo replacement** (**IVF**). Infertile women are given drugs that stimulate ovulation. Several ova are then retrieved from the surface of the ovaries by a technique known as *laparoscopy* and placed in a suitable culture medium to which spermatozoa are added. The fertilized ovum (4–8 cells in size) is transferred to the uterus via the vagina and cervix. Successful pregnancy occurs in about 10–20% of cases.

tetanus [tetanuhs] A disease resulting from infection with *Clostridium tetani*, which exists in the soil and in the gut of humans and other animals; also known as **lockjaw**. Infection enters the body through wounds in the skin caused by a nail or

splinter. The bacteria produce a toxin which affects motor nerve cells in the spinal cord, and induces convulsions and muscle spasms. The disease can be prevented by active vaccination.

tetany A state of neuromuscular hyperexcitability, usually associated with low blood calcium levels, but also induced by the toxin produced by the *clostridium tetani* bacteria. It leads to muscle cramps, high blood pressure, convulsions, and spasm of the larynx, which may result in life-threatening obstruction of the airway.

Tethys [teethis] The third natural satellite of Saturn, discovered in 1684; distance from the planet 295 000 km/183 000 mi; diameter 1060 km/660 mi; orbital period 1·888 days.

Tétouan or **Tetuán** [taytwahn] 35°34N 5°22W, pop (2000e) 291 000. City in NE Morocco; settled by Moorish exiles from Spain, 15th-c; captured by Spanish, 1860; airfield; Medina a world heritage site.

tetra Any of many small colourful freshwater fish (family Characidae), from South and Central America; length typically 3–4 cm/1-1¼ in.

tetracyclines [tetrasiyklinz] A class of antibiotics obtained from *Streptomyces*, a genus of organisms intermediate between bacteria and fungi, active against a broad spectrum of infections. The first was produced in 1948.

tetraethyl lead $Pb(C_2H_5)_4$. An organometallic compound made by the reaction of lead chloride with a Grignard reagent, used as an additive to petrol to control 'knocking'. Its hazardous properties have led to its disuse as a road fuel in most countries.

Tetragrammaton *Yahweh*

Teutonic Knights Members of the Order of St Mary of the Teutons, a religious-military order founded c.1190 and inspired by crusading ideals. By the 14th-c they controlled the E Baltic lands of the Livonian Knights, Prussia, and E Pomerania.

tex *count* (textiles)

Texas pop (2000e) 20 851 800; area 691 003 km²/266 807 sq mi. State in SW USA; the 'Lone Star State'; second largest state in the US; first settled by the Spanish in the late 1600s; first American settlement, 1821; declared independence, defeated by Santa Anna at the Alamo, 1836; Mexican army then defeated by Sam Houston at San Jacinto, 1836; independence of Texas recognized; admitted to the Union as the 28th state, 1845; US–Mexican War, 1846–8; joined the Confederate states in the Civil War; re-admitted to the Union, 1870; discovery of extensive oil deposits (1901) transformed the economy; Rio Grande forms the state's entire international border with Mexico; highest point, Guadalupe Peak (2667 m/8750 ft); Gulf coastal plains around Houston heavily industrialized; SC plains and Edwards Plateau have vast wheat and cotton farms and cattle ranches; capital, Austin; nation's leading producer of oil and natural gas; large Spanish-speaking population.

Thackeray, William Makepeace (1811–63) Novelist, born in Kolkata (Calcutta). His major novels were *Vanity Fair* (1847–8), *Pendennis* (1848), *Henry Esmond* (1852), and *The Newcomes* (1853–5), several published as monthly serials.

Thaddeus, St *Jude, St*

Thai [tiy] The official language of Thailand, spoken by c.30 million people. There is written evidence of the language from the 13th-c.

Thailand *p.925*

thalamus *diencephalon*

thalassaemia / thalassemia [thalaseemia] An inherited disease of the blood in which there is defective production of haemoglobin (the oxygen-carrying pigment in red blood cells), resulting in anaemia. It occurs in people of SE Asian and Mediterranean origin, and is caused by the inheritance of an abnormal gene. Treatment is with repeated blood transfusions.

Thales [thayleez] (c.620–c.555 BC) Greek natural philosopher,

Thailand

□ International Airport

[tiyland], Thai **Muang Thai**, formerly **Siam**, official name **Kingdom of Thailand**

Local name Muang Thai

Timezone GMT +7

Area 513 115 km²/198 062 sq mi

Population total (2002e) 63 430 000

Status Kingdom

Capital Bangkok (Krung Thep)

Languages Thai (official), Malay and English also spoken

Ethnic groups Thai (75%), Chinese (14%), Khmer and Mon minorities

Religions Theravada Buddhist (95%), Muslim, Hindu, Sikh and Christian (4%)

Physical features Agricultural region dominated by the floodplain of the Chao Phraya R; NE plateau rises above 300 m/1000 ft and covers a third of the country; mountainous N region rising to 2595 m/8514 ft at Doi Inthanon; narrow, low-lying S region separates the Andaman Sea from the Gulf of Thailand; covered in tropical rainforest, except sparsely vegetated Khorat plateau (NE).

Climate Equatorial climate in the S; tropical monsoon climate in the N and C; high temperatures and humidity; wet season (Jun–Oct); average annual temperature 26°C (Jan), 28°C (Jul) in Bangkok; average annual rainfall 1400 mm/55 in; coastal regions devastated by tsunami, Dec 2004.

Currency 1 Baht (THB) = 100 satang

Economy Agriculture: rice, maize, bananas, pineapple, sugar cane, rubber, teak; textiles, electronics, cement, chemicals, food processing, tourism; tin (world's third largest supplier), tungsten (world's second largest supplier), manganese, antimony, lead, zinc, copper, natural gas.

GDP (2002e) $445·8 bn, per capita $7000

Human Development Index (2002) 0·762

History Evidence of Bronze Age communities, 4000 BC; Thai nation founded, 13th-c; only country in S and SE Asia to have escaped colonization by a European power; revolution brought end to absolute monarchical rule, 1932; followed by periods of military rule interspersed with brief periods of democratic government; 1991 constitution (with amendments) provides for a National Legislative Assembly comprising a House of Representatives, an elected Senate, and a cabinet headed by a Prime Minister; King is Head of State; in Feb 2005 Thaksin Shinawatra became first democratically-elected prime minister to win a second consecutive term, 2005, but was ousted in a bloodless military coup, 2006.

Head of State (Monarch)
1946– Bhumibol Adulyadej (Rama IX)

Head of Government
1976–7 Thanin Kraivichien
1977–80 Kriangsak Chammanard
1980–8 Prem Tinsulanonda
1988–91 Chatichai Choonhavan
1991–2 Anand Panyarachun *Military Junta*
1992 Suchinda Kraprayoon
1992–5 Chuan Leekpai
1995–6 Banharn Silpa-Archa
1996–7 Chavalit Yongchaiyudh
1997–2001 Chuan Leekpai
2001–6 Thaksin Shinawatra
2006 Chidchai Vanasathidya *Acting*
2006 Thaksin Shinawatra *Restored*
2006– Surayud Chulanont *Interim*

---

traditionally regarded as the first philosopher, born in Miletus. None of his writings survive.

Thalia or **Thaleia** [thaliya] In Greek mythology, the Muse of comedy and idyllic poetry.

thalidomide A sedative introduced in West Germany in 1956, in the UK in 1958, and subsequently in some other countries. It became widely used because of its particular safety, but when it was found to cause congenital abnormalities, it was withdrawn; approximately 20% of babies whose mothers had taken thalidomide during early pregnancy suffered absence of limbs or part of limbs.

Thallophyta [thalofita] A collective name formerly used for all lower plant-like organisms that lack differentiation into root, stem, and leaf; sometimes treated as a subkingdom of plants

comprising the eucaryotic algae and fungi; also known as **Thallobionta**.

Thames, River [temz], Lat **Tamesis** River rising in the Cotswold Hills, SE Gloucestershire, England; flows 352 km/219 mi E and SE through Greater London to enter the North Sea in a long, wide estuary; navigable as far as London by large ships; Thames Conservancy Board established in 1857; tidal barrier built across approach to London to reduce risk of floods (completed 1983).

Thanet, Isle of Urban area in E Kent, SE England, originally an island; contains the towns of Margate, Broadstairs, and Ramsgate; railway.

Thanksgiving Day A day set apart for a public acknowledgment of God's goodness and mercy; in Canada the second Monday in October, and in the USA the fourth Thursday of November, both public holidays. The occasion dates from 1621, when the new American settlers celebrated their first harvest. In modern times, the day is especially important for family reunions.

Thanlwin, River, formerly **Salween** River in SE Asia, rising in SW China; enters the Andaman Sea; length 2815 km/1750 mi.

Thant, U [oo tant] (1909–74) Burmese diplomat, born in Pantanaw, Myanmar. As secretary-general of the UN (1962–71), he played a major diplomatic role during the Cuban crisis, formulated a plan to end the Congolese Civil War (1962), and mobilized a UN peace-keeping force in Cyprus (1964).

Thar Desert [tah] or **(Great) Indian Desert** area c.320 000 km²/ 125 000 sq mi. Arid region in NW India and E Pakistan, S Asia; 800 km/500 mi long and 400 km/250 mi wide.

Thatcher (of Kesteven), Margaret (Hilda) Thatcher, Baroness, née **Roberts** (1925–) British Conservative prime minister (1979–90), born in Grantham, Lincolnshire. She became minister of education (1970–4), and in 1975 replaced Edward Heath as Leader of the Conservative Party to become the first woman party leader in British politics. Her government instituted the privatization of nationalized industries and national utilities, tried to institute a market in state-provided health care and education, and reduced the role of local government as a provider of services. She resigned in 1990, following her opposition to full economic union with Europe, having become the longest serving premier of the 20th-c. She was created a life peer in 1992.

Thaw, John (Edward) (1942–2002) Actor, born in Manchester, Greater Manchester. Best known for his television work, which included *The Sweeney* (1974–8), *Inspector Morse* (1987–2000), and *Kavanagh QC* (1995–2000), he won a number of BAFTA awards and was honoured with a fellowship in 2001. He married actress **Sheila Hancock** (1933–) in 1973.

theatre / theater Derived from the Greek for 'seeing place', the term originally signified the area occupied by spectators. It now describes the whole building and the social art form it houses.

Theatre de Complicite [komplistay] An innovative international touring theatre company based in London, co-founded in 1983 by Simon McBurney (1957–), Annabel Arden (1959–), and Marcello Magni. Arising initially from the clown-based training of Jacques Lecoq, the company's work has always had strong physical and comedic elements, but it was its application of these principles to classic texts and literary adaptations that initially defined its style.

theatre / theater in the round, also called **arena theatre** A theatre in which the auditorium surrounds a central stage and both performer and audience share the same acoustic space. Also known as an **arena stage**, the form demands that the actors project in all directions simultaneously.

Theatre Workshop An English theatre company founded in Manchester by Joan Littlewood in 1945. From 1953 onwards it was based in London at the Theatre Royal, Stratford East, and is best remembered for its vigorous ensemble acting exemplified by such shows as *Oh, What a Lovely War* (1963).

Thebe [theebee] A tiny natural satellite of Jupiter, discovered in 1979 by Voyager 2; distance from the planet 222 000 km/ 138 000 mi; diameter 100 km/60 mi.

Thebes 1 The ancient capital of Upper Egypt, and the location of many magnificent temples and tombs, such as Tutankhamen's; a world heritage site. It was situated on the R Nile, where the town of Luxor now stands. **2** In ancient Greece, the most powerful city-state in Boeotia; now a market town for a rich agricultural region in SE Greece; pop (2000e) 20 000.

theft The taking or appropriation of property belonging to another person without consent, with the intention of permanently depriving that person of the property. Borrowing is not theft, but it may sometimes be the subject of another criminal sanction: the temporary taking of a motor-car without the owner's consent is a criminal offence. Most US jurisdictions divide theft into **petty theft** (usually involving thefts of property worth less than $400) and **grand theft** (all other property).

thegn or **thane** [thayn] (Old English 'one who serves') In Anglo-Saxon England, a member of the noble class. Until the Norman Conquest, thegns were indispensable to effective royal control of the localities.

theine [theein] *caffeine*

theism Belief in a single divine being, transcendent and personal, who created the world and, although involved with and related to the creation, is distinct from it. It is a feature of Jewish and Islamic as well as Christian faith.

theme park An entertainment centre based on a particular theme, the most popular being wildlife parks. Many are also amusement parks. The first theme park was Disneyland, at Anaheim, CA, USA, opened in 1955, based on the Walt Disney cartoon characters.

Themis [themis] In Greek mythology, the goddess of established law and justice. As a consort of Zeus, she is the mother of the Horae and the Moerae.

Themistocles [themistokleez] (c.523–c.458 BC) Athenian general and visionary politician. He made possible the great Athenian naval victory at Salamis (480 BC), and laid the foundations of their maritime empire.

Theocritus [theeokritus] (c.310–250 BC) Greek pastoral poet, probably born in Syracuse. His short poems dealing with pastoral subjects, and representing a single scene, came to be called 'idylls' (*eidullia*). Tennyson was deeply influenced by him.

theodolite [theeodoliyt] An optical surveying instrument for measuring vertical or (more importantly) horizontal angles. It is a small telescope, with cross wires, movable over horizontal and vertical graduated circular scales. It is usually seen mounted on a stable tripod.

Theodorakis, Mikis [thayodorahkees] (1925–) Composer, born in Khios, Greece. His prolific musical output includes oratorios, ballets, song cycles, and music for film scores, the best known of which was *Zorba the Greek* (1965).

Theodore of Mopsuestia (c.350–428) Christian theologian, born in Antioch. His views on the Incarnation were condemned by the fifth ecumenical council in 553.

Theodoric or **Theoderic** [theeodorik], known as **the Great** (?–526) King of the Ostrogoths (471–526), who invaded Italy in 489, defeating the barbarian ruler, Odoacer. His long reign secured for Italy tranquillity and prosperity.

Theodosius I [theeodohshus], known as **the Great** (c.346–95) Roman emperor of the East (379–95). His title comes from his vigorous championship of orthodox Christianity.

Theodosius II [theeodohshus] (401–50) Roman emperor (408–50), the grandson of Theodosius I and, like him, a staunch champion of orthodox Christianity. He is chiefly remembered for his codification of the Roman law in 438 (the **Theodosian Code**).

theology Literally, the science of the divine, or of discourse about God. In Christianity, it is understood as the systematic critical clarification of the historical beliefs of the Church. It has been divided into **natural theology**, that which can be known about God from nature or by reason alone, and **revealed theology**, that which can only be known through the self-disclosure of God.

Theophrastus [theeohfrastus] (c.372–286 BC) Greek philosopher, born in Eresus, Lesbos. He became head of the Peripatetic school after Aristotle's death.

theorbo [theeaw(r)boh] A large lute with six strings above a fretted fingerboard, and seven or eight additional bass strings which are not stopped and have a separate pegbox. It was widely used in the 17th-c as a continuo instrument.

theorem A proposition proved by logical deduction from one or more initial premises. Although geometrical theorems are the most widely known, theorems exist in all branches of mathematics. A theorem which has already been proved and is then used towards the proof of another theorem is known as a *lemma*.

theosophy [theeosofee] Any system of philosophical or theological thought based on the direct and immediate experience of the divine. It has been especially used to describe the principles of the Theosophical Society founded in 1875 by Madame Blavatsky (1831–91) and H S Olcott (1832–1907) in New York City.

Thera [theera] *Santorini*

Therapsida [therapsida] An order of fossil reptiles including the direct ancestors of the mammals; known mainly from the Permian and Triassic periods. (Subclass: Synapsida.)

Theravada [theravahda] The form of Buddhism commonly found in S Asia. It is generally distinguished from the later **Mahayana** Buddhism in its rejection of the theory of bodhisattvas.

Theresa, Mother *Teresa, Mother*

Theresa of Lisieux, St [leesyoe], originally (**Marie Françoise**) **Thérèse Martin**, also known as **the Little Flower** and **St Theresa of the Child Jesus** (1873–97) Saint, born in Alençon, France. She entered the Carmelite convent of Lisieux in Normandy at the age of 15, where she remained until her death from tuberculosis nine years later. Her account of her life was published posthumously as *Histoire d'une âme* (1898, Story of a Soul). She was canonized in 1925, and made a doctor of the Church in 1997. Feast day 1 October.

therm *British thermal unit*

thermal conduction The transfer of heat through a substance without bulk movement of the substance; thermal conductivity symbol k, units W/(m.K) (watt per metre.kelvin).

thermal efficiency In thermodynamics, the ratio of useful work derived from a heat engine to the heat absorbed by it; symbol e, a number between 0 and 1. It represents a theoretical maximum possible efficiency.

thermal insulation Shielding whose function is to reduce heat flow. Heat loss by conduction is stemmed using layers of material having low thermal conductivity. Loss by convection is reduced by preventing the movement of fluids around the object. Loss by heat radiation is reduced using reflective coatings.

thermal printer A type of printer which generally uses thermally sensitive paper and produces characters using a set of electrically heated wires. Although thermal printers are relatively inexpensive, the special paper they use is not.

thermic lance A torch-like cutting device for resistant steel and alloys, which depends on the fact that iron will burn in oxygen. A main nozzle for a jet of oxygen has a subsidiary nozzle for acetylene, which preheats the metal to the temperature at which it will begin to burn in the stream of oxygen.

Thermidor coup [thermidaw(r)] The *coup d'état* of 26–27 July 1794 (8–9 Thermidor Year II), when Robespierre and his supporters were overthrown, ending the most radical phase of the French Revolution.

thermionics The study of the processes involved in thermionic emission, ie the emission of electrons from a metal surface caused by applying heat to that surface. The effect was discovered by Thomas Edison in 1883.

thermionic valve An electronic device (an *electron tube*) containing two or more electrodes, which are used to regulate the flow of electrons in an electric current. Thermionic valves were used in all types of electronic circuit, but have now almost entirely been replaced by semiconductor devices such as the transistor.

thermistor A temperature sensor constructed from semiconductor material whose electrical resistance falls rapidly as the temperature rises; an abbreviation of **thermal resistor**. It

is used in electronic circuits measuring or controlling temperature, and in time-delay circuits.

thermite A mixture of aluminium and iron oxide which, if ignited, undergoes a fierce chemical reaction producing a high temperature (c.2400°C) and yielding molten iron. The process is useful for the preparation of intractable metals, or in welding, and has been used for incendiary bombs.

thermochemistry The study of the energy changes accompanying chemical reactions. These changes are widely used in determining the energy value of foods.

thermocouple A type of thermometer that allows the direct electronic monitoring of temperature.

thermodynamics The study of heat and heat-related phenomena, based on four fundamental laws. *Zeroth Law* If two systems are in thermodynamic equilibrium with a third, they will be in thermodynamic equilibrium with one another. For example, two objects left to stand a while in a still room will be the same temperature as the room and therefore as each other. *First Law* The sum of the energy changes occurring in some isolated process is zero, which is equivalent to the statement that total energy is conserved. For example, a battery may be used to raise the temperature of some water electrically, in which case chemical energy from the battery is converted into heat; but the total energy of the complete system before and after the circuit is switched on is the same. *Second Law* A law giving direction to thermodynamic processes in time, and thus forbidding some which would otherwise be allowed by the First Law. For example, no heat engine can have a thermal efficiency of 100%, ie it is impossible to convert heat totally into mechanical work. *Third Law* Absolute zero can never be reached. Expressing the thermodynamic properties of systems on the assumption that they are composed of large numbers of distinct atoms is termed *statistical mechanics*.

thermoelectric effects A general expression for temperature-dependent electrical properties of matter. Thermocouples use a potential difference resulting from the difference in temperature between two junctions of dissimilar metals – the **Seebeck effect**, discovered in 1821 by German physicist Thomas Seebeck (1770–1831). The **Peltier effect**, discovered in 1834 by French physicist Jean Peltier (1785–1845), is the reverse of the Seebeck effect, and may be used to make refrigerators having no moving parts.

thermography A detection technique which converts invisible heat energy into a visible picture. Objects radiate varying amounts of infrared (IR) heat energy, depending on their temperature. Inside a thermograph, a solid-state detector 'sees' the IR, even in the dark or smoke. TV-style pictures show temperatures by variations in brightness or colour.

thermoluminescence dating A method of dating ancient pottery by measuring the energy accumulated in the crystal lattice of its inclusions of quartz, through the breakdown over time of naturally occurring uranium.

thermometer A device for measuring temperature. In household alcohol and mercury thermometers, heat causes the liquid in a reservoir to expand, forcing some of the liquid up a graduated tube. The graduations are fixed by calibration against known markers of chosen temperature scale. The first reliable mercury-in-glass thermometer was invented by German physicist Gabriel Fahrenheit in 1714.

thermonuclear bomb *hydrogen bomb*

thermoplastic A class of resin which softens and hardens reversibly on heating and cooling any number of times.

Thermopylae [thermopilee] A pass between mountains and sea in C Greece. The failure of the Greeks to hold it in 480 BC enabled the Persians to capture Athens and sack the Acropolis.

thermoset A class of resin which sets irreversibly on heating. Examples include epoxy resins such as Araldite.

thermosphere The upper atmospheric layer above the mesopause (c.80 km/50 mi) in which atmospheric densities are very low. The lower part is composed mainly of nitrogen (N_2) and oxygen in molecular (O_2) and atomic (O) forms, whereas above 200 km/125 mi atomic oxygen predominates over N_2 and N.

Theroux, Paul (Edward) [theroo] (1941–) Novelist and travel writer, born in Medford, MA. He taught English in several parts of the world before settling in London. He first reached a wide public through his rail journeys, beginning with *The Great Railway Bazaar* (1975), later travel books including *Travelling the World* (1990). His novels include *Saint Jack* (1973, filmed 1979), *Picture Palace* (1978, Whitbread), *The Mosquito Coast* (1981, James Tait Black; filmed 1987), *The Pillars of Hercules* (1995), *Hotel Honolulu* (2001), and *Blinding Light* (2005).

Theseus [theesyoos] A legendary king and national hero of Athens. With Ariadne's help he killed the Minotaur. He conquered the Amazons, and married their queen; later, he married Phaedra.

Thessalonians, Letters to the New Testament writings of Paul to the church he founded in the capital of the Roman province of Macedonia, although his authorship of the second letter is disputed.

Thessaloníki [thesaloneekee], also **Salonika** or **Salonica** 40°38N 22°58E, pop (2000e) 1 021 000. Seaport and second largest city of Greece; founded, 315 BC; capital of Roman Macedonia, 148 BC; held by Turkey, 1430–1912; base for Allied operations in World War 1; airport; railway; two universities (1925, 1957); 5th-c and 9th-c basilicas.

Thessaly [thesalee], Gr **Thessalía** pop (2000e) 764 000; area 14 037 km²/5418 sq mi. Fertile agricultural region of E Greece; annexed by Greece, 1881; capital, Larisa; major cereal region.

Thetis [thetis] In Greek mythology, a nereid destined to bear a son greater than his father. This was the secret known to Prometheus. She was married to Peleus, and was the mother of Achilles.

thiamine A water-soluble vitamin (B_1) which acts as an enzyme co-factor in the oxidation of glucose. A deficiency leads to beriberi, a disease once common, especially in SE Asia.

thiazole [thiyazohl] C_3H_3NS, boiling point 117°C. A five-membered ring compound; a colourless liquid, the basis for a range of dyestuffs.

thickhead A songbird, native to E India, SE Asia, and Australia; rounded head and strong bill; also known as **whistler**. (Family: Pachycephalidae, 46 species.)

thick-knee A plover-like bird, widespread; legs with swollen ankles (not knees); plumage mottled; eyes large, yellow; mainly nocturnal. (Family: Burhinidae, 9 species.)

Thiers, (Louis) Adolphe [tyair] (1797–1877) French statesman, historian, and first president of the Third Republic (1871–3), born in Marseille, France. After the collapse of the Second Empire he became chief of the executive power in the provisional government, suppressed the Paris Commune, and was elected president. His most ambitious literary work was the 20-volume *L'histoire du consulat et de l'empire* (1845–62, History of the Consulate and the Empire).

Thimphu [thimpoo] or **Thimbu**, also **Tashi Chho Dzong** 27°32N 89°43E, pop (2000e) town, 14 400. Official capital of Bhutan, on R Raidak; founded, 1581; fortified town, a major monastery; capital since 1962; air strip.

Thingvellir [theengvetlir] 64°15N 21°06W. National shrine of Iceland, at the N end of Thingvalla Water; the Icelandic *Althing*, oldest parliament in the world, was founded here in 930; Thingvellir National Park a world heritage site.

Thíra [theera] *Santorini*

third-generation computers *computer generations*

third stream A type of music which aims to combine the styles of Western art music with those of jazz or various ethnic traditions. Among composers associated with it are John Lewis (1920–2001) and Günther Schuller (1925–).

Third World *Three Worlds theory*

Thirteen Colonies The American provinces that revolted against British rule and declared independence in 1776. From N to S they were New Hampshire, Massachusetts, Rhode Island, Connecticut, New York, New Jersey, Pennsylvania, Delaware, Maryland, Virginia, North Carolina, South Carolina, and Georgia. Fourteen states actually declared independence, because Vermont separated from New York at the same time.

thirty-eighth parallel The boundary line proposed for the partition of Korea at the Potsdam Conference in 1945, after the defeat of Japan (which had annexed Korea in 1910). It now forms the line of division between North and South Korea.

Thirty-nine Articles A set of doctrinal formulations for the Church of England, finally adopted by the Convocation of 1571. They do not comprise a creed, but rather a general Anglican view on a series of contentious matters in order to maintain the unity of the Anglican Communion. They concern matters such as the presence of Christ in the Eucharist and the authority of Scriptures and the Councils. Church of England clergy have been required since 1865 to affirm these principles in general terms.

Thirty Tyrants The Spartan-backed clique which seized power in Athens towards the end of the Peloponnesian War (404 BC), overthrew the democracy, and instituted a reign of terror. They were overthrown in 403 BC and democracy was restored.

Thirty Years' War (1618–48) A complex phase, specifically German in origin, of a long and intermittent power struggle between the kings of France and the Habsburg rulers of the Holy Roman Empire and Spain (1491–1715). With the Elector Frederick V's defeat (1620) and intervention by other powers, the conflict intensified, spreading to other theatres. Isolated as Spain collapsed, the emperor opened negotiations (1643–8) which ended the German war at the Peace of Westphalia.

thistle The name applied to several spiny plants of the daisy family, many belonging to the genera *Cirsium* and *Carduus*. All have leaves with spiny margins, flower heads often almost globular, solitary or in clusters; florets reddish, purple, or white; the national emblem of Scotland. (Family: Compositae.)

Thistle, Most Ancient and Most Noble Order of the A Scottish order of chivalry, probably instituted by James III of Scotland. There are 16 members under the sovereign (though royal knights may be additional to this number). The motto of the order is *Nemo me impune lacessit* (Lat 'No-one provokes me with impunity'); the ribbon is dark green.

Thomas, St (1st-c) A disciple of Jesus, most prominent in John's Gospel, where he is also called *Didymus* (Gr 'the Twin'), and where he is portrayed as doubting the resurrection until he touches the wounds of the risen Christ (*John* 20). Early church traditions describe him subsequently as a missionary to the Parthians or a martyr in India. Feast day 21 December.

Thomas, Clarence (1948–) Jurist, born in Savannah, GA. In 1992 he became the second black American to sit in the Supreme Court. His Senate confirmation hearings attracted widespread attention due to allegations of sexual misconduct brought by a former colleague.

Thomas, D(onald) M(ichael) (1935–) Novelist, poet, and translator, born in Redruth, Cornwall. A former teacher and lecturer, he became known after his controversial novel *The White Hotel* (1981). Other novels include his first, *The Flute Player* (1979), *Lying Together* (1990), *Flying into Love* (1992), and *Charlotte: the Final Journey* (2000). He has also translated major literary works from Russian.

Thomas, Dylan (Marlais) (1914–53) Poet, born in Swansea, S Wales. He established himself with the publication of *Eighteen Poems* in 1934. His *Collected Poems* appeared in 1953, and he then produced the radio 'play for voices', *Under Milk Wood* (1954). An alcoholic in later years, he died in New York City during a lecture tour. In 2004 the Swansea Dylan Thomas Book Prize was inaugurated in his memory.

Thomas, (Philip) Edward, pseudonym **Edward Eastaway** (1878–1917) Poet and critic, born in London. He wrote most of his work during active service between 1915 and his death at Arras, France.

Thomas, R(onald) S(tuart) (1913–2000) Poet, born in Cardiff. He was ordained in 1936 and became a rector in the Church of Wales. His collections include *Poetry for Supper* (1958), and *No Truth with the Furies* (1995).

Thomas, Terry *Terry-Thomas*

Thomas (à) Becket *Becket, Thomas*

Thomas à Kempis *Kempis, Thomas à*

Thomas Aquinas *Aquinas, St Thomas*

Thomism [tohmizm] In Christian philosophical theology, the name given to the doctrines of Thomas Aquinas, and to later schools claiming descent from him.

Thompson, Sir Benjamin, Graf (Count) **von Rumford**, known as **Count Rumford** (1753–1814) Administrator and scientist, born in Woburn, MA. In 1784 he entered the service of Bavaria, where he carried out military, social, and economic reforms, for which he was made a count of the Holy Roman Empire. He first showed the relation between heat and work, a concept fundamental to modern physics. In 1799 he returned to London, and founded the Royal Institution.

Thompson, Daley, popular name of **Francis Morgan Thompson** (1958–) Athlete, born in London. An outstanding decathlete, he was world champion (1983), European champion (1982, 1986), and Olympic champion (1980, 1984).

Thompson, Emma (1959–) Actress, born in London. In 1989 she appeared in the film of *Henry V*, directed by Kenneth Branagh whom she married the same year (divorced, 1996). With Branagh she went on to make *Dead Again* (1991) and *Much Ado About Nothing* (1993). Other films include *Howards End* (1992, Oscar), *Remains of the Day* (1993), *Sense and Sensibility* (1996, BAFTA), *Primary Colors* (1998), and *Nanny McPhee* (2005).

Thompson, Francis (1859–1907) British poet, born in Preston, Lancashire. His later work was mainly religious in theme; it includes the well-known 'The Hound of Heaven'.

Thompson, John T(alafierro) (1860–1940) US soldier and inventor, born in Newport, KY. In 1918 he originated the Thompson gun, one of the world's first effective submachine guns. The 'Tommy gun' became infamous as a favourite weapon of the gangsters of prohibition America.

Thomson, James (1700–48) Poet, born in Ednam, Scottish Borders. He is best known for his four-part work, *The Seasons* (1730), the first major nature poem in English; his ode 'Rule, Britannia' (1740); and the Spenserian allegory, *The Castle of Indolence* (1748).

Thomson, Sir J(oseph) J(ohn) (1856–1940) Physicist, born in Cheetham Hill, Greater Manchester. He showed in 1897 that cathode rays were rapidly moving particles, and deduced that these 'corpuscles' (electrons) must be nearly a 2000th smaller in mass than the lightest known atomic particle, the hydrogen ion. He received the Nobel Prize for Physics in 1906.

Thomson (of Fleet), Roy (Herbert) Thomson, Baron (1894–1976) Newspaper and television magnate, born in Toronto, Ontario, Canada. He started several radio stations, and bought many Canadian and US newspapers. He settled in Edinburgh on acquiring his first British paper, *The Scotsman* (1952), bought the Kemsley newspapers in 1959 (including the *Sunday Times*, to which he added the first colour supplement in 1962), and in 1966 took over *The Times*.

Thomson, Virgil (1896–1989) Composer and critic, born in Kansas City, MO. Best known for his operas with libretti by Gertrude Stein, *Four Saints in Three Acts* (1934) and *The Mother of Us All* (1947), he also wrote symphonies, ballets, and choral, chamber, and film music.

Thomson, Sir William *Kelvin, 1st Baron*

't Hooft, Gerardus [tohft] (1945–) Physicist, born in Den Helder, The Netherlands. He became professor at the University of Utrecht. He shared the 1999 Nobel Prize for Physics for his role in elucidating the quantum structure of electroweak interactions.

Thor In Norse mythology, the god of thunder, son of Odin and Frigga. His hammer is called Miolnir. He is the strongest of the gods, and protects them.

thorax That part of the body between the neck and the abdomen enclosed by the thoracic part of the vertebral column, the ribs, and the sternum, and separated from the abdomen by the diaphragm; also known as the **thoracic cage** or **chest**. Roughly cone-shaped, it surrounds and protects the lungs, heart, and great vessels.

Thoreau, Henry (David) [thoroh] (1817–62) Essayist and poet, born in Concord, MA. In c.1839 he began the walks and studies of nature which became his major occupation, recorded in a daily journal. His writings include *Walden, or Life in the Woods* (1854).

thorn-apple An evil-smelling annual weed (*Datura stramonium*) found throughout most of the N hemisphere; up to 1 m/3¼ ft high; flowers trumpet-shaped, white to blue; fruit a spiny, ovoid capsule containing poisonous seeds; also called **jimson weed**. (Family: Solanaceae.)

thornbill A warbler, native to Australia and New Guinea; also known as the **thornbill warbler**. (Genus: *Acanthiza*, 12 species. Family: Acanthizidae.)

Thorndike, E(dward) L(ee) (1874–1949) Psychologist, born in Williamsburg, MA. As a result of studying animal intelligence, he formulated his 'law of effect', which states that a given behaviour is learned by trial-and-error, and is more likely to occur if its consequences are satisfying.

Thorndike, Dame (Agnes) Sybil (1882–1976) Actress, born in Gainsborough, Lincolnshire. In 1924 she played the title role in the first performance of Shaw's *Saint Joan*, and during World War 2 was a notable member of the Old Vic Company. She married the actor Lewis Casson (1875–1969) in 1908.

Thornhill, Sir James (1675–1734) Baroque painter, born in Melcombe Regis, Dorset. He executed paintings for the dome of St Paul's Cathedral, Blenheim Palace, and other public buildings, and in 1718 was made history painter to the king.

thoroughbred The fastest breed of horse (over 65 kph/40 mph), developed in England for racing; height, 16 hands/1·6 m/5 ft 4 in; also known as **English thoroughbred** or **racehorse**.

Thorpe, Ian, known as **The Thorpedo** (1982–) Swimmer, born in Paddington, Sydney, Australia. In the 1998 World Championships he became the youngest male world champion in history by winning the 400 m freestyle. He won four gold medals at the Kuala Lumpur 1998 Commonwealth Games, and two gold medals at the 1998 World Swimming Championships. At the 2000 Sydney Olympics he won five medals (including three gold), and at the 2001 World Championships in Japan he won six gold. At the 2002 Manchester Commonweath Games he won a total of seven medals (six gold and a silver), and at the 2003 World Championships in Barcelona he won gold medals in the 200 m and 400 m freestyle. He won Olympic gold at Athens in 2004 in the 200 m and 400 m freestyle. He retired from competitive swimming in 2006.

Thorpe, (John) Jeremy (1929–) British politician, born in London. Elected Leader of the Liberal Party in 1967, he resigned the leadership in 1976 following allegations of a previous homosexual relationship with Norman Scott. In 1979 he was acquitted of charges of conspiracy and incitement to murder Mr Scott.

Thorvaldsen, Bertel [torvalsn] (c.1768–1844) Neoclassical sculptor, born in Copenhagen. His best-known pieces include 'Christ and the Twelve Apostles' at Copenhagen, and the Cambridge statue of Byron.

Thoth [thoht, toht] An ancient Egyptian Moon-god, sometimes depicted with the head of an ibis, sometimes as a baboon. The god of words, magic, and scribes, in the Underworld he records the souls of the dead.

Thothmes III *Thutmose III*

Thousand, Expedition of the (1860) A military campaign led by Garibaldi, originally involving 1146 men, which formed a crucial stage in the Italian Risorgimento. Sailing from Genoa, they seized Sicily, crossed to the mainland, and four months later had liberated the Kingdom of Naples.

Thrace [thrays], Gr **Thráki** pop (2000e) 353 000; area 8578 km²/3311 sq mi. NE region of Greece; area now divided between Turkey, Greece, and Bulgaria; capital, Komotini; region of fertile plains.

threadfin Any of the tropical marine and estuarine fish in the family Polynemidae (3 genera); long free pectoral fin rays which serve in part as sensitive feelers; body length may reach over 1·5 m/5 ft.

Three Age System The chronological division of Old World prehistory into three successive ages of **Stone**, **Bronze**, and **Iron**. The subdivision of the Stone Age into the **Palaeolithic** (**Old Stone Age**), characterized by chipped stone, and the **Neolithic** (**New Stone Age**), characterized by polished stone tools, was made in the 1860s, and the term **Mesolithic** (**Middle Stone Age**), covering the five millennia following the end of the last glaciation, also dates from then. The term **Chalcolithic** for the **Copper** or earliest Bronze Age belongs to more recent times.

three-day event A combined training competition comprising the three main equestrian disciplines: dressage, showjumping, and cross-country.

three-D (3-D) films *stereoscopic photography*

Three Emperors' League, Ger *Dreikaiserbund* An entente (1873) between emperors William I of Germany, Francis Joseph of Austria-Hungary, and Alexander II of Russia. It was designed by Bismarck to protect Germany by isolating France and stabilizing SE Europe. It lapsed in 1887.

Three Worlds theory A theory that sees the world as being divided into three main blocs of countries, defined by their economic status. These are the developed capitalist economies (the **First World**), the developed communist countries (the **Second World**), and underdeveloped countries (the **Third World**), covering most of Latin America and recently independent African and Asian states. Some (including the United Nations) recognize a 'Fourth World', of the 25 poorest nations. The collapse of the Communist states after 1989 makes the typology somewhat redundant, although the term *Third World* is likely to persist due to its extensive usage.

thresher shark Large surface-living shark (*Alopias vulpinus*), widespread in tropical to temperate seas; easily recognized by the long upper lobe of tail fin which may exceed half its body length; tail lobe used to round up shoals of fish by thrashing the water surface; body length up to 6 m/20 ft. (Family: Alopiidae.)

thrift A densely tufted perennial (*Armeria maritima*), woody at base, native to Europe; leaves grass-like, bluish-green; flowers pink, scented, in long-stalked, hemispherical heads; also called **sea pink**; a mainly coastal plant. (Family: Plumbaginaceae.)

thrip A minute insect in which the wings, when present, are slender with a long fringe of hairs; mouthparts specialized for piercing and sucking. (Order: Thysanoptera, c.5000 species.)

thrombophlebitis *phlebitis*

thrombosis [thrombohsis] The formation of a blood clot within a blood vessel, resulting in a partial or complete blockage. Its basis is the formation of the protein, fibrin, which forms a mesh in which platelets and red blood cells are trapped, and produces a plug to the flow of blood.

thrush (disease) *candidiasis*

thrush (ornithology) A medium-sized songbird, widespread, inhabiting diverse regions from tropical rainforests to deserts; some species called **chats**. (Family: Turdidae, c.300 species.)

ThrustSSC British jet-powered car, driven by Andrew Green, which broke the world land speed record at the Black Rock site, Great Basin, USA, in 1997, and became the first car to travel at supersonic speed. It achieved a speed of 1227·95 kph/763·035 mph (Mach 1·020).

Thucydides [thyoosidideez] **1** (c.460–c.400 BC) Athenian aristocratic historian of the Peloponnesian War.
2 (5th-c BC) Athenian politician, leader of the opposition to Pericles until ostracized in 443 BC.

Thuggee [thuhgee] An Indian cult which combined robbery and ritual murder (usually by strangling) in the name of Kali (the Hindu goddess of destruction). Vigorous steps were taken to eradicate the problem in the 19th-c.

thuja [thooja] *arbor vitae*

Thule [thyoolee] 77°30N 69°29W. Eskimo settlement in NW Greenland; founded as a Danish trading post in 1910; scientific installations; name also given by the ancients to the most northerly land of Europe, an island described c.310 BC by the Greek navigator, Pytheas.

Thumb, General Tom *Stratton, Charles*

Thummim *Urim and Thummim*

Thun [toon], Fr **Thoune** 46°46N 7°38E, pop (2000e) 40 000. Town in Switzerland, on the R Aare near L Thun; gateway to the Bernese Oberland; railway junction; castle (1191).

Thunder Bay 48°27N 89°12W, pop (2000e) 127700. Resort and port in S Ontario, Canada, on NW shore of L Superior; created in 1970 by the union of Fort William and Port Arthur; airfield; railway; university (1965); grain storage and shipping point.

thunderstorm A storm of heavy rain, thunder, and lightning which occurs when cumulonimbus clouds develop in unstable, humid conditions. As air rises, condensation releases latent heat, and this increases the available energy, reinforcing the rising tendency of the air. An electric charge builds up at the base of the cloud, and when large enough, is discharged in the form of lightning.

Thurber, James (Grover) (1894–1961) Writer and cartoonist, born in Columbus, OH. His drawings first appeared in his book *Is Sex Necessary?* (1929), and there are several anthologies of his work, such as *Thurber's Dogs* (1955). He was also the creator of the fantasizing character Walter Mitty.

Thuringia [thuringia] A historic area of Germany, including the Harz Mts and Thuringian Forest. It was divided between Saxony, Hesse-Kassel, and others 1485–1920, then became part of East Germany, and is now a province within united Germany.

Thurman, Uma (Karuna) (1970–) Film actress, born in Boston, MA. The daughter of an American father and Swedish mother, she left school at age 15 to pursue a modelling career. She then moved to New York to try her luck at acting, and gained recognition with her role in Quentin Tarantino's *Pulp Fiction* (1994). Later films include *Gattaca* (1997), *Batman and Robin* (1998), *Kill Bill: Vol.1* (2003; Vol.2, 2004), and *The Producers* (2005).

Thurso 58°35N 3°32W, pop (2000e) 8690. Port town in N Scotland; on N coast, at head of R Thurso; car ferry service to Orkney from Scrabster.

Thutmose III [thutmohsuh], also **Thothmes** or **Tuthmosis** (?–1450 BC) Egyptian pharaoh (c.1504–1450 BC), one of the greatest of Egyptian rulers, who re-established Egyptian control over

Syria and Nubia. He built the temple of Amon at Karnak, and erected many obelisks, including those now known as 'Cleopatra's Needle'.

Thyestes [thiyesteez] In Greek mythology, a son of Pelops, who inherited the curse upon that house. His brother Atreus set before him a dish made of the flesh of Thyestes' children.

thylacine [thiylasiyn] An Australian marsupial, probably extinct since the 1930s; length up to 1·6 m/5¼ ft; sandy brown with dark vertical stripes over back and hindquarters; female with short backward-facing pouch; also known as the **Tasmanian wolf** or **tiger**. (Family: Thylacinidae.)

thyme A small spreading aromatic shrub, often only a few cm high, native to Europe and Asia; flowers 2-lipped, usually pink or mauve, in crowded whorls forming spikes or heads. It is widely cultivated as a culinary herb. (Genus: *Thymus*, c.400 species. Family: Labiatae.)

thymine [thiymeen] $C_5H_6N_2O_2$. One of the pyrimidine bases in DNA, usually paired with adenine.

thymus A lymphoid gland of vertebrates, which in mammals lies in the upper part of the chest close to the great vessels and the heart. Its presence is essential in the newborn for the development of lymphoid tissue and immunological competence. In early life, cells migrate from bone marrow into the thymus, where they mature to become T-lymphocytes (*T-cells*) responsible for cellular immunity.

thyristor [thiyrister] A semiconductor device that acts as a switch; also often called a **silicon-controlled rectifier**. It is made of a sandwich of p-n-p-n semiconductor material.

thyroid gland An endocrine gland of vertebrates situated in the region of the neck, overlying the lower part of the larynx and the upper part of the trachea. It secretes thyroid hormone and calcitonin (from C-cells).

thyroid hormone A collective term for iodine-containing amine hormones secreted from vertebrate thyroid glands. In humans and other mammals, the principle hormones are thyroxine (T_4) and trilodothyronine (T_3), which have important roles in fetal development and throughout life in the control of metabolism.

Thysanoptera [thiysanoptera] *thrip*

Tiananmen Square [tianahnmen] or **T'ien-an-men Square** The largest public square in the world, covering 40 ha/98 acres and lying before the gate to the Imperial Palace in C Beijing. In June 1989, it was the scene of mass protests by students and others against the Chinese government, crushed by troops of the Chinese Army with an undisclosed number of dead.

Tianjin, Tientsin, or **T'ien-chin** [tianjin] 39°08N 117°12E; pop (2000e) 6 528 000; administrative region 9 136 000; municipality area 4000 km²/1500 sq mi. Port city in E China; China's largest artificial harbour, built during Japanese occupation, 1937–45, completed 1952; founded in Warring States period, 403–221 BC; attacked by British and French in 1860; badly damaged by earthquake, 1976; airport; railway; two universities; designated a special economic zone.

Tian Shan or **T'ien Shan** Mountain range in C Asia, on border of Russia and China; length, 2500 km/1500 mi; rises to 7439 m/24 406 ft at Tomur (Pobedy) peak.

Tiber, River [tiyber], Ital **Tevere** Third longest river of Italy, rising in the Etruscan Apennines; length 405 km/252 mi; enters the Tyrrhenian Sea near Ostia.

Tiberias [tiybeerias], Hebrew **Tevarya** 32°48N 35°32E, pop (2000e) 44 000. Holiday resort town in N Israel, on L Tiberias; named after the Roman emperor, Tiberius; medicinal hot springs; one of the four holy cities of the Jews.

Tiberias, Lake or **Sea of Galilee** [tiybeerias], Hebrew **Yam Kinneret**, ancient **Sea of Chinnereth** area 166 km²/64 sq mi. Lake in NE Israel, in the Jordan valley; 210 m/689 ft below sea-level; length 22·5 km/14 mi; width 12 km/7½ mi; maximum depth 46 m/150 ft; fed and drained by the R Jordan; Israel's largest

reservoir; many centres around the lake of historic and scriptural interest, especially connected with the life of Jesus.

Tiberius [tiybeerius], in full **Tiberius Julius Caesar Augustus** (42 BC–AD 37) Roman emperor (14–37), the son of Livia, and stepson and successor of the Emperor Augustus. The suspicious death of his heir Germanicus (19), followed by the excesses of his chief henchman, Sejanus, and the reign of terror that followed Sejanus's downfall (31), made him widely hated.

Tibesti Mountains [teebestee] Mountain range in NC Africa, largely in NW Chad; area 100 000 km²/38 600 sq mi, length 480 km/300 mi; highest peak, Emi Koussi (3415 m/11 204 ft).

Tibet, Chin **Xizang** [shitsang] pop (2000e) 2 448 000; area 1 221 600 km²/471 500 sq mi. Autonomous region in SW China; Tibet Plateau, average altitude 4000 m/13 000 ft; Himalayas in the S, rising to 8848 m/29 028 ft at Mt Everest; Kunlun Shan range in the N; major farming area in S valleys; capital, Lhasa; dominated by Buddhist lamas since 7th-c AD until departure of Dalai Lama into exile, 1959; conquered by Mongols, 1279–1368; controlled by Manchus, 18th-c; Chinese rule restored in 1951, and full control asserted after revolt in 1959; most monasteries and temples now closed or officially declared historical monuments, but many people still worship daily; further uprising in 1993; Qinghai–Tibet line linking Lhasa to the NW province of Qinghai, opened 2006.

Tibetan One of the major languages in the Sino-Tibetan group; probably 3–4 million speakers. Written records, mainly to do with the Buddhist religion, date from the 8th-c.

Tibet Plateau or **Qinghai–Tibet Plateau**, Chinese **Xizang Gaoyuan** Plateau in W and SW China; average altitude, 4000 m/13 000 ft; area 2·3 million km²/0·9 million sq mi; bounded S by the Himalayas; major farming region in S, with warm, humid climate; C and N are cold and dry.

tibia *leg*

Tibullus, Albius [tibulus] (c.54–19 BC) Latin poet, considered by Quintilian to be the greatest elegiac writer. He is known for his books of love poetry, but several works under his name are probably by other authors.

tic An involuntary non-rhythmic motor movement or vocal production which serves no apparent purpose. It occurs most famously in *Gilles de la Tourette syndrome*, where the patient may suddenly utter a sound like a bark, or swear without an intention to do so.

tick A large mite specialized as a blood-feeding, external parasite of terrestrial vertebrates; fangs modified for cutting skin; can transmit diseases of humans and domesticated animals. (Order: Acari. Family: Ixodidae.)

tidal wave The extremely long-period waves driven by the forces producing the tides. The term is often popularly used to refer to tsunamis, which are not related to tides.

tide The regular, periodic rise and fall of the surface of the sea. The tides are produced by differences in gravitational forces acting on different points on the Earth's surface, and affect all bodies of water to some extent. These so-called tidal forces are produced primarily by the Sun and Moon.

T'ien-ching *Tianjin*

Tientsin *Tianjin*

Tiepolo, Giovanni Battista [tyaypoloh] (1696–1770) Artist, born in Venice, Italy. The last of the great Venetian painters, he became renowned as a decorator of buildings throughout Europe.

Tiergarten [teergah(r)tn] A park covering 255 ha/630 acres in Berlin. Originally a royal hunting ground, it was landscaped in the 18th-c and opened to the public.

Tierra del Fuego [tyera thel fwaygoh] pop (2000e) 78 200; area 73 746 km²/28 473 sq mi. Island group at the extreme S of South America; E side (about one third) belongs to Argentina, remainder belongs to Chile; boundary agreed in 1881; highest point, Monte Darwin (2438 m/7999 ft); discovered by Magellan 1520;

capital (Argentina), Ushuaia; capital (on Chile mainland), Punta Arenas; dispute over islands at E end of Beagle Channel, resolved in 1985 in favour of Chile.

tiger A member of the cat family (*Panthera tigris*) native to S and SE Asia; reddish brown with dark vertical stripes; swims well; eats mainly large mammals; several subspecies: **Bengal, Indochinese, Chinese, Sumatran, Siberian** (the largest known cat), and possibly extinct **Caspian, Bali,** and **Javan** tigers.

tiger fish Large predatory freshwater fish with strong fang-like teeth, widespread in rivers and lakes of Africa; length up to 1·8 m/6 ft. (Genus: *Hydrocynus*. Family: Characidae.)

tiger-moth A medium-sized, typically colourful moth; may be an important pest causing damage to tree foliage. (Order: Lepidoptera. Family: Arctiidae.)

tiger shark Large and very dangerous shark (*Galeocerda cuvier*) widely distributed in tropical and warm temperate seas; length up to 5 m/16 ft; grey to brown, with darker vertical stripes and patches. (Family: Carcharhinidae.)

tigon [tiygn] *liger*

Tigray or **Tigre** [teegray] pop (2000e) 3 671 000; area 64 921 km²/ 40 575 sq mi. Region in NE Ethiopia; low-lying E half, with large section below sea-level at centre of Danakil Depression; capital, Mekele; one of the areas most severely affected by the drought in the 1980s, and a centre of resistance to the government; Tigray people are Semitic-speaking, mostly nomadic herders in the N, agriculturalists in the S.

tigrillo *ocelot*

Tigris, River [tiygris], Arabic **Shatt Dijla**, Turkish **Dicle** River in SE Turkey and Iraq; rises in EC Turkey; joins the Euphrates to form the Shatt al-Arab; length 1850 km/1150 mi; several ancient cities along its banks, eg Nineveh, Seleucia.

Tijuana [teehwahna] 32°32N 117°02W, pop (2000e) 894 000. Border town in NW Mexico; airfield; resort town with casinos and nightclubs.

Tikal [teekahl] An ancient Mayan city in N Guatemala, settled by 250 BC, at its peak in the 7th–8th-c AD, but abruptly abandoned c.900; a world heritage site.

Tilburg [tilberkh] 51°31N 5°06E, pop (2000e) 168 000. Industrial city in S Netherlands; railway; major business and cultural centre in the S.

Tilbury 51°28N 0°23E, pop (2000e) 12 100. Town in Essex, SE England; on the R Thames estuary; railway; major port and docks for London and the SE.

till or **boulder clay** A geological term for sediment or drift consisting of an unstratified and unsorted deposit of clay, sand, gravel, and boulders left behind after the retreat of glaciers and ice-sheets. **Tillite** is till which has consolidated into solid rock.

Tillett, Ben(jamin) (1860–1943) Trade union leader, born in Bristol. He achieved prominence as leader of the great dockers' strike (1889), and of the transport workers' strike in London (1911).

Till Eulenspiegel *Eulenspiegel, Till*

Tilley, Vesta, stage name of **Matilda Alice, Lady de Frece**, *née* **Powles** (1864–1952) Music-hall entertainer, born in Worcester, Worcestershire. She became a celebrated male impersonator, her many popular songs including 'Burlington Bertie'.

Tillich, Paul (Johannes) [tilikh] (1886–1965) Protestant theologian and philosopher, born in Starzeddel, Germany. A Lutheran pastor, he was dismissed by the Nazis in 1933, and moved to the USA. His main scholarly work was *Systematic Theology* (3 vols, 1951–63).

Tilly, Johann Tserclaes, Graf (Count) **von** (1559–1632) Flemish soldier, born in Tilly, Belgium. He successfully commanded the forces of the Catholic League in the Thirty Years' War, gaining decisive victories at the White Mountain and Prague (1620). He was routed by Gustavus Adolphus at Breitenfeld (1631).

timbre The sound quality of a voice or musical instrument, which depends on the prominence or otherwise of upper harmonics (*partials*) in the notes produced. The timbre of a flute or recorder, for example, is weak in upper harmonics compared with that of the much brighter violin or trumpet.

Timbuktu [timbuhktoo], Fr **Tombouctou** 16°49N 2°59W, pop (2000e) 32 000. Town in N Mali; settled in the 11th-c; a chief centre of Muslim learning; taken by the French, 1893; airfield; several mosques (13th-c–15th-c); world heritage site.

time That which distinguishes sequential events from simultaneous events; symbol *t*, units s (second); the fourth dimension, in addition to the three spatial dimensions. It allows the assignment of cause and effect, and, according to our perception, the assignment of past, present, and future. In Newtonian mechanics, time is absolute, meaning that a second as measured by one observer is the same as a second measured by any other observer in the universe. Relativity explains that this view of the nature of time is false.

time and motion study The technique of job analysis to discover how tasks are actually carried out; more usually known now as **work study** or **industrial engineering**. Its aim is to find the most efficient way of performing a task, in order to raise productivity.

time code A series of digitally coded signals appearing sequentially on the magnetic tape of a video or audio recording, and sometimes on film, to provide specific identification for each frame in editing and post-production. In its simplest form it denotes Hours, Minutes, Seconds, and Frames.

time-lapse photography A series of photographs taken at regular intervals from the same viewpoint to record the development of a subject, for example, plant growth or traffic flow. When filmed as successive single frames, projection at normal speed provides a rapid presentation of slow changes.

Time of Troubles, also known as the **Time of the Five Dmitris** A period of intense social and political turmoil in Russia (1598–1613), involving a series of successive crises, civil wars, famines, Cossack and peasant revolts, foreign invasions, and widespread material destruction. The political turmoil following the collapse of communism in the early 1990s was also referred to by the Russian people as 'The Time of Troubles'.

time-sharing (computing) A means of providing simultaneous access by several users to the same computer. Each user, in turn, is assigned full use of the central processing unit for a very small duration, making it appear that each user has continuous access.

time-sharing (leisure) The joint ownership of holiday accommodation by a consortium. Depending upon the number of shares acquired, each share holder is entitled to a specific period of use.

Times Square The area in New York City formed by the intersection of Broadway, 42nd Street, and 7th Avenue. It is at the centre of the city's theatre district.

Timişoara [timishwahra], Hung **Temesvár** 45°45N 21°15E, pop (2000e) 319 000. City in W Romania; ceded to Romania, 1919; violent suppression of a pro-Hungarian demonstration there in December 1989 sparked a more general uprising against the Ceauşescu regime; railway; university (1962); technical university (1920); fine arts academy; two cathedrals; Hunyadi Castle (15th-c).

Timor [teemaw(r)] pop (2000e) 1 905 000; area 33 912 km²/ 13 090 sq mi. Mountainous island in SE Asia, in the Sunda group; divided between Portugal and Holland, 1859; **West Timor** (former Dutch Timor) included in Indonesia at independence; capital, Kupang; former Portuguese territory of **East Timor** granted full independence, 2002 (*see* **East Timor**).

Timoshenko, Semyon Konstantinovich [timohshengkoh] (1895–1970) Russian general, born in Furmanka, Ukraine. In 1940 he smashed Finnish resistance during the Russo–Finnish War, then commanded in the Ukraine, but failed to stop the German advance (1942).

Timothy, Letters to Two of the Pastoral Letters in the New Testament, for which Pauline authorship is often disputed today. Both letters are purportedly addressed to Paul's close companion Timothy.

timpani [timpanee] (singular **timpano**) Drums made from large copper bowls (hence the English name **kettledrum**), with heads of calfskin or plastic, which can be tuned to various pitches by means of hand-screws or, in modern instruments, pedals. They are normally played with two felt-headed sticks.

Timur [timoor], known as **Timur Lenk** (Turkish 'Timur the Lame'), English **Tamerlane** or **Tamburlaine** (1336–1405) Tatar conqueror, born near Samarkand, Uzbekistan. He subdued nearly all Persia, Georgia, and the Tatar empire, conquered all the states between the Indus and the lower Ganges (1398), and defeated the Turks at Angora (1402), taking Sultan Bajazit prisoner.

tin Sn (Lat *stannum*), element 50, melting point 232°C, density 7·3 g/cm³. A white metal in the carbon group of elements, occurring in nature mainly as the oxide (SnO₂). It is used as a plating for other metals because of its corrosion resistance.

tinamou [tinamoo] A partridge-like bird, native to the New World tropics; eggs incubated by male. (Family: Tinamidae, c.50 species.)

Tinbergen, Jan [tinbergen] (1903–94) Economist, born in The Hague, the brother of Nikolaas Tinbergen. His major contribution was the econometric modelling of cyclical movements in socio-economic growth. In 1969 he shared the first Nobel Prize for Economics.

Tinbergen, Nikolaas [tinbergen] (1907–88) Ethologist, born in The Hague, the brother of Jan Tinbergen. His major concern was with the patterns of animal behaviour in nature, showing that many are stereotyped. He shared the Nobel Prize for Physiology or Medicine in 1973.

Tindale *Tyndale, William*

tineid moth [tineeid] A small, drab moth of the family Tineidae; c.3500 species, including the clothes moths, and other pests of stored products. (Order: Lepidoptera.)

Tinian [tinian] pop (2000e) 2500; area 101 km²/39 sq mi. One of the N Mariana Is; length 18 km/11 mi; four long runways built by the USA during World War 2.

tinnitus [tinitus] A ringing or hissing sound heard within the ear, which may arise from almost any disorder of the ear or its nerve supply. In many cases, the disorder is intractable.

Tin Pan Alley A nickname coined c.1900 for the popular music-publishing centre of New York City situated on 28th Street and 6th Avenue, and later on Broadway near 49th Street.

tinplate A thin steel sheet coated with tin by dipping or electrolytic deposition, used for light robust containers and protective constructions. After the invention of canning in the early 19th-c, it attained worldwide industrial importance.

Tintoretto [tintoretoh], originally **Jacopo Robusti** (1518–94) Venetian painters, probably born in Venice, the son of a dyer (*tintore*). His major works include 'The Last Supper' (1547, Venice), 'The Last Judgment' (c.1560, Venice) and the 'Paradiso' (1588, Venice), famous for its great size.

Tipperary [tipuhrairee], Ir **Thiobrad Arann** County in Munster province, SC Ireland; divided into **North Riding** (pop (2000e) 58500; area 1996 km²/770 sq mi) and **South Riding** (pop (2000e) 76000; area 2258 km²/872 sq mi); capital, Clonmel; rich dairy-farming area; centre for horse and greyhound breeding.

Tippett, Sir Michael (Kemp) (1905–98) Composer, born in London. His oratorio, *A Child of our Time* (1941), reflecting the problems of the 1930s and 1940s, won him wide recognition. His other works include the operas *The Midsummer Marriage* (1952) and

King Priam (1961), four symphonies, a piano concerto, and string quartets.

Tippoo Sultán [tipoo], also known as **Tippoo Sahib** (1749–99) Sultan of Mysore (1782–99), born in Devanhalli, India, the son of Haidar Ali. He continued his father's policy of opposing British rule, but was defeated by Cornwallis and had to cede half his kingdom.

Tiranë [teerahna], Ital **Tirana** 41°20N 19°50E, pop (2000e) 277200. Capital town of Albania; founded by Turks in the early 17th-c; made capital in 1920; university (1957); railway; airport.

Tiresias [tiyreezias] In Greek mythology, a blind Theban prophet, who takes a prominent part in Sophocles' plays about Oedipus and Antigone.

Tirol or **Tyrol** [tirohl] pop (2000e) 656300; area 12647 km²/4882 sq mi. Federal state of W Austria; capital, Innsbruck; leading state for tourism, especially winter sports.

Tirpitz, Alfred (Friedrich) von [teerpits] (1849–1930) German admiral, born in Kostrzyn, Poland (formerly Küstrin, Prussia). As secretary of state for the imperial navy (1897–1916), he raised a fleet to challenge British supremacy of the seas, and acted as its commander 1914–16.

Tirso de Molina [teersoh, moleena], pseudonym of **Gabriel Téllez** (c.1571–1648) Playwright, born in Madrid. He wrote many comedies and religious plays, but is best known for his treatment of the Don Juan legend in *El burlador de Sevilla* (1635, The Seducer of Seville).

Tirthankara [teertangkara] (Sanskrit, 'ford-maker') A title used by Jains of the 24 great heroes of their tradition who, by their teaching and example, taught them the way to cross the stream from the bondage of physical existence to freedom from rebirth.

Tiruchchirappalli [tiroochirapahlee] or **Trichinopoly** [trikinopolee] 10°45N 78°45E, pop (2000e) 835000. City in Tamil Nadu, S India, on the Kaveri R; airfield; railway; educational, religious, and commercial centre, noted for its gold, silver, and brass working.

Tiryns [teerinz] An ancient Greek town in the Argolid near Mycenae, famous for the remains of its fortified Bronze Age palace.

Tissot, James Joseph Jacques [teesoh] (1836–1902) Painter, born in Nantes, France. He painted highly accomplished scenes of Victorian life in London, and produced a series of the life of Christ in water-colour.

Tisza, River [tisa], Czech **Tisa**, Russian **Tissa** Longest tributary of the R Danube in E Europe; rises in the Carpathian Mts; enters the Danube SW of Belgrade; length 962 km/598 mi.

tit A small, lively, acrobatic songbird, native to the N hemisphere and Africa; also known as the **titmouse**; includes the **chickadees** of North America. (Family: Paridae, 46 species.)

Titan (astronomy) [tiytn] Saturn's largest satellite, discovered in 1655; distance from the planet 1222000 km/759000 mi; diameter 5150 km/3200 mi; orbital period 15·945 days. It is the second-largest moon in the Solar System, and the only satellite with a substantial atmosphere, principally composed of nitrogen and methane.

Titan (mythology) [tiytn] In Greek mythology, a member of the older generation of gods, the children of Uranus and Gaia. After Zeus and the Olympians took power, the Titans made war on them; but they were defeated and imprisoned in Tartarus.

Titania (astronomy) The largest satellite of Uranus, discovered in 1787 by Herschel; distance from the planet 436000 km/271000 mi; diameter 1580 km/980 mi. It has an icy, cratered surface.

Titania (mythology) In Greek mythology, a female Titan, identified with the Moon. In Shakespeare's *A Midsummer Night's Dream* she is the queen of the fairies.

Titanic [tiytanik] British 46329-gross-tonnes passenger liner, belonging to White Star Line, which collided with an iceberg in the N Atlantic on her maiden voyage in April 1912. Lifeboat capacity was inadequate, and just over 700 people were saved, while 1500 went down with the ship. The vessel was rediscovered in 1985, explored, and photographed on the seabed. An Oscar-winning film of the tragedy, directed by James Cameron, was released in 1997.

titanium Ti, element 22, melting point 1660°C. A lustrous, white metal, with a relatively low density of 4.5 g/cm^3. It is found widely distributed in nature, never uncombined, and usually as an oxide (TiO_2). The metal, produced by magnesium reduction, is used in some alloys, especially for aircraft.

titanothere [tiytanotheer] A medium to large plant-eating mammal; known as fossils from the early Tertiary period of North America and E Asia; some stood $2.5 \text{ m}/8 \text{ ft}$ at the shoulder. (Order: Perissodactyla.)

Titchmarsh, Alan (Fred) (1949–) Gardener, broadcaster, and writer, born in Ilkley, West Yorkshire. He became a BBC household name for his expert advice on gardening matters, in 1996 becoming presenter of the popular radio series, *Gardener's World*, and of TV's *Ground Force* (1997–2003). He has written almost forty gardening books, a number of novels, and is a regular newspaper columnist.

tithes Offerings of a proportion (literally 'the tenth part') of one's property or produce to God, often given to the priesthood of temples; customary among peoples since ancient times. Civil tithes were replaced in England by a rent charge in 1836, and even this was abolished in 1936.

titi or **tee-tee** [teetee] A New World monkey of genus *Callicebus* (3 species); thick coat and long tail; characteristically crouches on a branch with all four feet together, tail hanging vertically.

Titian [tishan], Ital **Tiziano Vecellio** (c.1490–1576) Venetian painter, born in Pieve di Cadore, Italy. For the Duke of Ferrara he painted three great mythological subjects, 'The Feast of Venus' (c.1515–18), 'Bacchanal' (c.1518, both Prado, Madrid), and the richly-coloured 'Bacchus and Ariadne' (c.1523, National Gallery, London). Later works include his famous 'Ecce Homo' (1543, Vienna) and 'Christ Crowned with Thorns' (c.1570, Munich).

Titicaca, Lake [teeteekakuh] Lake in SE Peru and W Bolivia; largest lake in South America (area 8290 km²/3200 sq mi) and highest large lake in world (3812 m/12 506 ft); length 177 km/110 mi; width 56 km/35 mi; maximum depth 475 m/1558 ft; steamers run from Guaqui (Bolivia) to Puno (Peru); hunting, fishing, yachting; statue of Virgin de Copacabana (1576) on SW shore, place of pilgrimage.

titmouse *tit*

Tito [teetoh], known as **Marshal Tito**, originally **Josip Broz** (1892–1980) Yugoslav president (1953–80), born in Kumrovec, Croatia. In 1941 he organized partisan forces against the Axis conquerors, and after the war became the country's first communist prime minister (1945). He broke with the Cominform in 1948, developing Yugoslavia's independent style of communism (**Titoism**).

Tito, Dennis (1941–) American multimillionaire businessman. On 28 April 2001, he made history as the world's first 'space tourist'. Paying a reputed $20 million (£14 million) to the Russians, he boarded a Soyuz spacecraft, along with two Russian cosmonauts, and had a 6-day stay aboard the International Space Station (ISS). The first woman tourist was Anousheh Ansari, a forty-year-old Iranian-born former telecom tycoon who took off from Baikonur on 18 Sep 2006 for a two-week stay at the ISS.

Titograd *Podgorica*

titration A technique for finding the volume of one solution chemically equivalent to a given volume of another, usually by adding the first solution slowly until equivalence is reached.

This can be detected by the addition of a small amount of an indicator material.

Titus [tiytus], in full **Titus Flavius Vespasianus** (39–81) Roman emperor (79–81), the elder son of Vespasian. Popular with the Romans, he is execrated in Jewish tradition for his destruction of Jerusalem (70) and suppression of the Jewish Revolt. His brief reign was marred by many natural calamities, notably the eruption of Vesuvius (79).

Titus, St [tiytus] (1st-c) In the New Testament, a Gentile companion of the apostle Paul. Ecclesiastical tradition makes him the first Bishop of Crete. Feast day 6 February (W), 23 August (E).

Titus, Letter to One of the Pastoral Letters in the New Testament, for which Pauline authorship is usually disputed today. The letter addresses problems of church order and false teachers.

Tiv An agricultural people of C Nigeria, living along the Benue R. They speak a Niger–Congo language.

Tiwi [teewee] The Aboriginal inhabitants of Melville and Bathurst Islands, off Darwin, Northern Territory, Australia. Cut off from the mainland for 5000 or more years, they developed a distinctive culture.

Tlapanek *Hokan languages*

Tlemcen [tlemsen], ancient **Pomaria** 34°53N 1°21W, pop (2000e) 333 700. Town in NW Algeria; capital of major Moroccan dynasties (12th–16th-c); railway; Almovarid Great Mosque (1135).

Tlingit A North American Indian group of the Pacific NW coast who lived mainly by fishing and hunting, c.14 000 (1990 census). They are famed for their art.

TNT (explosive) The abbreviation for **trinitrotoluene**, $C_7H_5N_3O_6$. A high explosive made by the nitration of toluene with nitric and sulphuric acids; a solid melting at 82°C. It is one of the most effective of the military high explosives.

toad *frog*

toadfish Robust bottom-living fish of the family Batrachoididae (6 genera), found in inshore waters of tropical to temperate seas; body typically elongate, tapering to a small tail, dorsal and anal fins long; eyes placed on top of flattened head, mouth large with strong teeth.

toadflax An annual or perennial, native to the N hemisphere, especially the Mediterranean region; flowers in a variety of colour combinations; tube spurred and 2-lipped, with a projection closing the tube, so that pollinators must part the lips to reach nectar held in the spur. (Genus: *Linaria*, 150 species. Family: Scrophulariaceae.)

toadstool An informal name for many typically umbrella-shaped fungal fruiting bodies, especially those that are poisonous or inedible.

Toamasina, also **Tamatave** 18°10S 49°23E, pop (2000e) 195 000. Port on the E coast of Madagascar, on the Indian Ocean; popular tourist resort; airfield; railway.

tobacco An annual or shrubby perennial, native to warm parts of the New World and Australasia; tubular flowers, greenish, yellow, pink, or reddish. The dried, slightly fermented leaves of various species, principally *Nicotiana tabacum*, are used for smoking, chewing, and snuff, and contain the powerful alkaloid *nicotine*. (Genus: *Nicotiana*, 66 species. Family: Solanaceae.)

Tobago [tobaygoh] pop (2000e) 48 000; area 300 km²/116 sq mi. Island in the West Indies; part of the Republic of Trinidad and Tobago; chief town, Scarborough; united with Trinidad in 1889; airport; luxury hotel-conference centre at Rocky Point; tourist complex at Minster Point.

Tobin, James [tohbin] (1918–2002) Economist, born in Urbana-Champaign, IL. Best known for his work on portfolio choice under uncertainty, in which he clarified the trade-off between risk and yield. He was awarded the Nobel Prize for Economics in 1981.

Tobit or **Tobias, Book of** [tohbit] A book of the Old Testament

Apocrypha named after its hero, Tobit, written perhaps c.3rd–2nd-c BC by an unknown author.

tobogganing *bobsledding*

Tobruk or **Tubruq** [tubruk] 32°06N 23°56E, pop (2000e) 142 000. Seaport in N Libya; occupied by the Italians, 1911; important battle site in World War 2; taken by Australians (Jan 1941), then changed hands several times until finally taken by the British (late 1942).

Toby jug A pottery jug in the form of a seated figure, usually a stout man smoking a pipe and wearing a tricorn hat which forms the pouring lip. Such jugs seem to have been introduced in N Staffordshire c.1770.

Toc H A Christian fellowship founded in 1915 as a club for British soldiers serving in Belgium. Its name derives from its location in Talbot House (named after Lt Gilbert Talbot (1891–1915)), the initials of which were 'pronounced' by army signallers as 'Toc H'. The club now engages in a wide range of social work in the English-speaking world.

tocopherols A small group of compounds having antioxidant properties; α-tocopherol (vitamin E) is the most active, inhibiting rancidity in oils rich in polyunsaturated fatty acids. It is widely distributed in foods, but its highest levels are found in vegetable oils.

Tocqueville, Alexis (Charles Henri Maurice Clérel) de [tokveel] (1805–59) Historian and political scientist, born in Verneuil, France. His political study, *De la Démocratie en Amerique* (1835, Democracy in America) gave him a European reputation. After Louis Napoleon's coup, he wrote the first volume of *L'ancien Régime et la Révolution* (1856, The Old Regime and the Revolution), but died before it could be completed.

Todaiji [tohdiyjee] Buddhist shrine at Nara, Japan. Founded in 743, it contains a huge Buddha, 16 m/53 ft high, made of 450 000 kg/1 million lb of bronze, on a base 20 m/68 ft across.

Todd, Mike, popular name of **Michael Todd**, originally **Avrom Hirsch Goldbogen** (1909–58) Showman, born in Minneapolis, MN. He sponsored the 'TODD-AO' wide-screen process, used for his greatest film, *Around the World in Eighty Days* (1956, Oscar). He married his third wife, Elizabeth Taylor, in 1957, but was killed the next year in an aircrash.

tog A unit for measuring the 'warmth' rating in bedding textiles. The tog rating is a measure of thermal resistance: the higher the value, the better its performance.

Togo *p.936*

Tojo, Hideki [tohjoh] (1885–1948) Japanese general, statesman, and prime minister (1941–4), born in Tokyo. During World War 2 he was minister of war (1940–1) and premier. He was hanged as a war criminal in Tokyo.

tokamak [tokamak] A machine used in nuclear fusion research. A helical system of magnetic fields confines the plasma of reactive charged particles in a hollow chamber, where it is then heated to temperatures in excess of $10^8°C$.

tokay gecko [tohkay gekoh] A large gecko (*Gekko gekko*) (length, almost 30 cm/12 in), native to India and SE Asia; mottled coloration; nocturnal; also known as **common gecko**.

Tokelau [tohkelow], formerly **Union Islands** 8–10°S 171–173°W; pop (2000e) 1000; area 10·1 km^2/3·9 sq mi. Island territory consisting of three small atolls in the S Pacific Ocean, c.3500 km/2200 mi N of New Zealand; chief settlement, Nukunonu; timezone GMT −11; ethnic group, Polynesian; chief languages, Tokelauan, English; inhabitants are citizens of New Zealand; Western Samoa and New Zealand currencies in use; British protectorate in 1877; annexed in 1916, and included with the Gilbert and Ellice Islands Colony; returned to separate status in 1925, under administrative control of New Zealand, but substantially self-governing at local level; principal revenue earners are copra, stamps, souvenir coins, and handicrafts.

tokonama [tokonahma] A Japanese alcove, in Japanese-style houses the place for scroll painting, flower arrangement, and art objects, especially at New Year. At home or in a restaurant the most honoured place for the guest is next to the tokonama.

Tok Pisin [tok pizhin] An English-based pidgin, spoken by c.3–4 million people in Papua New Guinea, mainly as a second language. It is now spoken by over 100 000 as a mother-tongue, and has thus become a creole.

Tokugawa, Ieyasu [tokugahwa] (1542–1616) The third of the three great historical unifiers of Japan; a noble from E Japan. He founded the Tokugawa shogunate (1603–1868), completed Edo Castle as his headquarters, and instituted a centralized control of Japanese life.

Tokyo 35°40N 139°45E, pop (2000e) 8 184 000 (metropolitan district). Seaport capital of Japan, E Honshu; on R Sumida; founded as village of Edo, 12th-c; headquarters of the Tokugawa shogunate, 1603; imperial capital, 1868; severe earthquake damage, 1923; heavily bombed in World War 2; airport; railway; over 100 universities; dense pollution and traffic congestion; Tokyo Tower (1958), tallest metal tower in the world; Ginza shopping district, 17th-c Imperial Palace, Meiji Shrine, Sensai Temple, Yasukuni Shrine; Disneyland (1983), 10 km/6 mi SE.

Toledo (Spain) [tolaytho], Lat **Toletum** 39°50N 4°02W, pop (2000e) 61 000. City in Spain, on R Tagus; former capital of Visigothic kingdom; railway; noted for its swords and knives; Moorish citadel, cathedral (13th–17th-c), El Greco's house; old city is a world heritage site.

Toledo (USA) [toleedoh] 41°39N 83°33W, pop (2000e) 313 600. Port in NW Ohio, USA, at the W end of L Erie; formed by the union of two settlements, 1833; involved in the 'Toledo War', 1835–6, a boundary dispute between Ohio and Michigan; railway; university (1872); one of the country's largest rail centres.

Tolkien, J(ohn) R(onald) R(euel) [tolkeen] (1892–1973) Philologist and writer, born in Bloemfontein, South Africa. His interest in language and saga led to his books about a fantasy world in which the beings have their own language and mythology, notably *The Hobbit* (1937), *The Lord of the Rings* (3 vols, 1954–5, filmed 2001–3), and *The Silmarillion* (1977).

Tolpuddle martyrs The name give to six agricultural labourers at Tolpuddle, Dorset, who were organized in 1833 into a local trade union by a Methodist preacher, George Loveless (1796–1874), convicted of taking illegal oaths, and transported. The action provoked substantial protests, and the labourers were eventually pardoned.

Tolstoy, Count Leo Nikolayevich (1828–1910) Russian writer, moralist, and mystic, born at Yasnaya Polyana, Russia. He became known for his short stories, then wrote his epic story of Russia during the Napoleonic Wars, *Voyna i mir* (1865–9, War and Peace), followed by *Anna Karenina* (1875–7). He experienced a spiritual crisis which culminated in such works as *Ispoved* (written 1879, A Confession) and *V chyom moya vera* (1883, What I Believe). He made over his fortune to his wife and lived poorly as a peasant under her roof. Leaving home secretly, he died of pneumonia some days later at Astopovo railway station. His doctrines founded a sect, and Yasnaya Polyana became a place of pilgrimage.

Toltecs [tolteks] A people (or peoples) who controlled most of C Mexico between AD c.900 and AD 1150; the last such dominant culture prior to the Aztecs. Their capital was at Tula, 80 km/50 mi N of Mexico City.

Toluca or **Toluca de Lerdo** [tolooka] 19°17N 99°39W, pop (2000e) 587 000. City in C Mexico; altitude 2675 m/8776 ft; founded, 1535; university (1956).

toluene [tolyooeen] $C_6H_5CH_3$, IUPAC **methylbenzene**, boiling point 111°C. A colourless liquid with a characteristic odour, widely used as an organic solvent, being substantially less toxic than benzene. It is obtained from coal tar.

Togo

100 km
50 mi

BURKINA FASO

AFRICA

Mango

White Volta

Oti

GHANA

Bassar

Sokodé

T O G O

Ouémé

Mono

B E N I N

Lake Volta

Atakpamé

Pic Baumann
986m

Kpalimé

Tsévié Vogan

Aného

Lome

Bight of Benin

☐ International Airport

[tohgoh], official name **Republic of Togo**, Fr **République Togolaise**

Local name République Togolaise (French)

Timezone GMT

Area 56 790 km²/21 921 sq mi

Population total (2002e) 5 286 000

Status Republic

Date of independence 1960

Capital Lomé

Languages French (official), local languages (Ewe, mostly in S, 47%), Hamitic people in N, mostly Voltaic speaking)

Ethnic groups Ewe (35%), Kabyè (22%), Mina (6%), with c.34 other ethnic groups, European and Syrian-Lebanese minorities

Religions Traditional animist beliefs (50%), Christian (35%), Muslim (10%)

Physical features Located in W Africa; land rises from the lagoon coast of the Gulf of Guinea, past low-lying plains to the Atakora Mts running NE–SW in the N; highest peak, Pic Baumann, 986 m/3235 ft; flat plains in NW; main rivers, Oti, Mono.

Climate Tropical, high temperatures and humidity; wet seasons (Mar–Jul, Oct–Nov); single rainy season in N (Jul–Sep); average annual temperature 27°C (Jan), 24°C (Jul) in Lomé; average annual rainfall 875 mm/34 in; dry Saharan Harmattan blows from NE (Oct–Apr).

Currency 1 CFA Franc (XAF) = 100 centimes.

Economy Largely agricultural economy; coffee, cocoa, cotton, cassava, maize, rice, timber; phosphates, bauxite, limestone, iron ore, marble; cement, steel, oil refining, food processing, crafts, textiles, beverages.

GDP (2002e) $7·594 bn, per capita $1400

Human Development Index (2002) 0·493

History Formerly part of the Kingdom of Togoland; German protectorate, 1884–1914; mandate of the League of Nations in 1922, divided between France (French Togo) and Britain (part of British Gold Coast); trusteeships of the United Nations, 1946; French Togo became an autonomous republic within the French Union, 1956; British Togoland voted to join the Gold Coast (Ghana), 1957; independence, 1960; military coups in 1963, 1967; return to civilian rule, 1980; National Conference, 1990, elected an interim Supreme Republican Council to supervise parliamentary elections in 1992; now governed by a president, prime minister, and 81-member National Assembly, elected for five years; constitution amended to allow Faure Gnassingbé to succeed his late father, President Eyadéma (Feb 2005) but international opposition forced his withdrawal; interim president installed pending elections (Apr 2005), Togo Constitutional Court confirmed Gnassingbé as winner.

Head of State

1960–3 Sylvanus Olympio
1963–7 Nicolas Grunitzky
1967–2005 Gnassingbé Eyadéma
2005 Faure Gnassingbé
2005 Abass Bonfoh *Interim*
2005– Faure Gnassingbé

Head of Government

1991–4 Joseph Kokou Koffigoh
1994–6 Edem Kodjo
1996–9 Kwasi Klutse
1999–2000 Koffi Eugene Adoboli
2000–2 Messan Agbeyome Kodjo
2002–5 Koffi Sama
2005–6 Edem Kodjo
2006– Yawovi Agboyibo

---

tomatillo An annual native to tropical America (*Physalis ixocarpa*); flowers bright yellow with dark basal spots; berry 5 cm/2 in, yellow to purple. It is a locally important food crop. (Family: Solanaceae.)

tomato A bushy annual (*Lycopersicon esculentum*) native to Pacific South America, but now cultivated on a commercial scale throughout the world; flowers in short sprays, yellow, with five reflexed petals; berry bright red, fleshy, edible; originally called **love apple** and regarded as an aphrodisiac. (Family: Solanaceae.)

Tombaugh, Clyde W(illiam) [tombow] (1906–97) Astronomer, born in Streator, IL. He discovered the planet Pluto in 1930 as a result of a systematic search, as well as galactic star clusters.

tombolo [tombohloh] *spit*

Tomlinson, Ray (1941–) Computer engineer, the inventor of e-mail, born in Vale Mills, NY. After graduating from Massachusetts Institute of Technology, he joined Bolt Beranek and Newman, a company that had a government contract to work on the US Department of Defense's Advanced Research Projects Agency Network (ARPANET), the precursor of the Internet. In 1971 he devised a method of sending a message from a user on one computer to a user on a remote machine. He selected the @

Tonga

official name **Kingdom of Tonga**, Tongan **Pule'anga Fakatu'i 'o Tonga**, formerly **Friendly Islands**

Local name Tonga

Timezone GMT +13

Area 646 km²/249 sq mi

Population total (2002e) 101 000

Status Independent kingdom within the Commonwealth

Date of independence 1970

Capital Nuku'alofa

Languages Tongan and English (official)

Ethnic groups Tongan (98%), other Polynesian, European minorities

Religions Christian (Free Wesleyan Methodists 47%, Roman Catholic 14%, Mormon 9%, Anglican minorities)

Physical features Island group in the SW Pacific Ocean, 2250 km/ 1400 mi NE of New Zealand; consists of 169 islands, 36 inhabited, divided into three main groups, Ha'apai, Tongatapu, and Vava'u; Tongatapu, largest island, inhabited by two-thirds of the population; W islands mainly volcanic, some still active; highest point, extinct volcano of Kao, 1014 m/3327 ft.

Climate Semi-tropical; average annual temperature 26°C (Jan), 21°C (Jul) in Nuku'alofa; average annual rainfall 1750 mm/69 in; occasional hurricanes in summer months.

Currency 1 Pa'anga/Tongan Dollar (TOP) = 100 seniti

Economy Largely based on agriculture; copra, coconuts, bananas, watermelons, yams, taro, cassava, groundnuts, rice, maize, tobacco, sugar cane; tourism and cottage handicrafts are small but growing industries.

GDP (2001e) $236 mn, per capita $2200

History Early settlers were Polynesians; visited by Dutch, early 17th-c; visited by the British explorer, James Cook, 1773; Methodist missionaries converted most of population to Christianity during early 19th-c; Chief Taufa'ahau united the islands and declared himself the first Monarch of Tonga, 1845; became a British protectorate, 1900, under its own monarchy; independence, 1970; King Taufa'ahau Tupou IV reigned 41 years (1965–2006) and was succeeded by his son Fiaofi Tupou V; governed by a Sovereign, a Privy Council, and a unicameral Legislative Assembly of Cabinet members, nobles, and elected people's representatives.

Head of State (Monarch)
1918–65 Salote Tupou III
1965–2006 Taufa'ahau Tupou IV
2006– Fiaofi Tupou V

Head of Government (Prime Minister)
1970–91 Fatafehi Tu'ipelehake
1991–2000 Baron Vaea
2000–6 Ulukalala Lavaka Ata
2006– Fred Sevele

---

symbol to separate the name of the user from the name of the machine to which the message was being sent.

Tommy gun *submachine-gun; Thompson, John T*

tomography [tohmografee] A technique using X-rays or ultrasound to produce an image of structures in the body.

Tompion, Thomas (c.1639–1713) Clock-maker, born in Northill, Bedfordshire. He made watches, table clocks, and long-case clocks with greatly improved timekeeping, and is acknowledged as the greatest English maker.

Tomsk 56°30N 85°05E, pop (2000e) 501 000. River port in WC Siberian Russia, on R Tom; founded, 1604; airfield; railway; university (1888).

Tom Thumb *Stratton, Charles*

tomtit *bluetit; great tit*

tom-tom A cylindrical, double-headed, high-pitched drum, played with sticks in sets of two or more in Western dance bands and jazz groups.

tonality The property of music which is written 'in a key', ie with a particular pitch as a point of aural reference towards which other key centres gravitate. The theoretical corner-stones of tonality are the diatonic major and minor scales, in which pitches are related to a **tonic**, or key note, so that the intervals between any two degrees of the scale remain the same whichever note serves as the tonic. Tonality admits only two modes (major and minor), but each of these may be expressed in 12 possible keys. Tonality gradually replaced modality in the 16th–17th-c, and served as the main structural basis for musical work of the next 250 years. In the 20th-c several alternatives were proposed.

Tone, (Theobald) Wolfe (1763–98) Irish nationalist, born in Dublin. He helped to organize the Society of United Irishmen, and had to flee to the USA and to France (1795). He induced France to invade Ireland, was captured, and committed suicide.

tone In music, **1** the interval (equal to two semitones) between, for example, the first two notes of a diatonic scale, or *doh* and *ray* in tonic sol-fa.
2 The timbre of a voice or instrument.
3 US usage for *note* (pitch) in such contexts as '12-tone music', 'tone cluster', and 'tone row'.

tone cluster *note-cluster; tone 3*

tone language A language in which the pitch level (**tone**) carried by a word is an essential signal of its meaning. In one variety of Chinese, for example, the word *ma* means 'mother' with a level tone, and 'horse' with a falling-rising tone.

tone poem *symphonic poem*

Tonga *see panel*

Tongariro [tonggareeroo] 39°08S 175°42E; area 765 km²/ 295 sq mi. Active volcano rising to 1968 m/6457 ft in SWC

North Island, New Zealand; winter skiing resort; many historical Maori sites.

Tongeren [tongeren], Fr **Tongres** 50°47N 5°28E, pop (2000e) 29 900. Rural market town in Belgium, on R Jeker; oldest town in Belgium, founded 1st-c AD; basilica of Our Lady.

Tongres [tõgr] *Tongeren*

tongue A highly mobile, muscular structure vital for the digestive functions of chewing, taste, and swallowing. In humans it is also important in speech, being essential for the production of all vowels and most consonants. It consists of a free front part within the mouth, containing numerous taste buds, and a more fixed back part in the oropharynx, which has accumulations of lymphoid tissue associated with it (the *lingual tonsil*). The two parts are separated by a V-shaped furrow on the upper surface, with its apex directed backwards. The muscles of the tongue are grouped into those which change its shape (the *intrinsic* muscles) and those which change its position within the mouth (the *extrinsic* muscles).

tonic sol-fa A system of musical notation devised by John Curwen, who based it on the solmization system of Guido d'arezzo, anglicizing the pitch names to *doh, ray, me, fah, soh, la, te.*

Tonkin or **Tongking, Gulf of** [tongkin] Gulf in Indo-China, situated E of Vietnam and W of Hainan I, China; an inlet of the South China Sea.

Tonlé Sap [tonlay sap], Eng **Great Lake** Freshwater lake in WC Cambodia; area 2850 km²/1100 sq mi during the dry season; linked to the Mekong R; area almost tripled during the wet season.

tonnage and poundage British mediaeval customs duties: tonnage was collected on tuns of imported wine; poundage at a rate of 3d (old pence) per £ of the value of imports. They were incorporated into the civil list in 1697.

tonne *kilogram*

tonsillitis Acute or chronic inflammation of the tonsils, usually due to infection with streptococci. Removal of the tonsils (**tonsillectomy**) is now rarely required, and only for repeated or serious infection.

tonsils Accumulations of lymphoid tissue found at the entrance to the respiratory and digestive tracts. The **palatine** tonsils (also referred to simply as 'the tonsils') are found at the entrance to the oropharynx. The **lingual** tonsils are under the back part of the tongue. The **tubal** tonsils are in the nasopharynx. The **pharyngeal** tonsils are behind the nasal cavity; they are also known as the **adenoids**. The four pairs of tonsils form a protective ring of tissue whose primary function is to combat airborne infections entering the body.

tonsure The shaving of all or part of the head, to denote clerical or monastic status. It is still compulsory for certain monks and priests.

Tony An annual award for theatrical achievement in New York City; named after US actress and director Antoinette Perry (1888–1946). It recognizes several categories within plays and musicals, including acting, direction, music, choreography, and design, as well as best play, best musical, and best revival.

Tooke, John Horne [tuk], originally **John Horne** (1736–1812) Radical politician, born in London. In 1771 he formed the Constitutional Society, supporting the American colonists and parliamentary reform. *The Diversions of Purley* (1786) was written while in prison for supporting the American cause.

tool Any implement which is used to carry out a task. Early man made the first axes by sharpening flint. Stone tools were replaced from around 4000 BC by bronze and then iron tools, which were later used to build instruments and simple machines. The Industrial Revolution saw the introduction of machine tools, and mass production of goods became a possibility.

Toole, John Kennedy (1937–69) Novelist, born in New Orleans, LA.

His novel *A Confederacy of Dunces* (1980), published 11 years after he committed suicide, won critical acclaim, and was awarded the 1981 Pulitzer Prize. *The Neon Bible* was published in 1989.

tooth *teeth*

toothwort A parasitic perennial (*Lathraea squamaria*), native to Europe and Asia; stem white; flowers tinged dull purple, forming a 1-sided spike. (Family: Scrophulariaceae.)

Toowoomba 27°35S 151°54E, pop (2000e) 89 500. City in Queensland, Australia; airfield; railway; university, 1989; commercial centre for the rich agricultural Darling Downs area.

topaz An aluminium silicate mineral ($Al_2SiO_4(OH,F)_2$), occurring in acid igneous rocks, pegmatites, and veins, with a colour range including colourless, yellow, and blue. It may be used as a gemstone.

tope [tohp] Slender-bodied grey shark common (*Galeorhinus galeus*) in inshore waters of the E North Atlantic; length up to c.2 m/6½ ft. (Family: Carcharhinidae.)

Topeka [topeeka] 39°03N 95°40W, pop (2000e) 122 400. Capital of state in E Kansas, USA, on Kansas R; settled by anti-slavery colonists, 1854; capital, 1861; railway; university (1865); marketing centre for agricultural products, particularly cattle and wheat; centre for psychiatric research.

topi [tohpee] An African ox-antelope (*Damaliscus lunatus*) with a long face; lyre-shaped horns ringed with ridges; coat with large dark patches on rich chestnut-red; fastest of all hoofed mammals (over 70 kph/40 mph).

topography The study of the physical characteristics of the Earth's surface (eg relief, soils, vegetation). A topographical map portrays information such as elevation and gradient through the use of symbols and special shading to show contours and spot heights.

topology A generalization of geometry which studies the properties of shapes and space that are independent of distance. The usual map of the London Underground is an example of a topological diagram, for it shows the lines joining various stations, yet is not to scale.

tor A mound of weathered, well-jointed, resistant, bare rocks. The rock is usually crystalline, and is exposed when surrounding and overlying rocks are stripped away by agents of erosion. Similar features in the tropics are known as **kopjes**.

Torah [tohra] (Heb 'instruction') The Jewish Law, most narrowly considered the Priestly Code found in the Pentateuch and said to have been given to Moses by God. The term was also often applied to the Pentateuch as a whole. This written Torah was eventually supplemented in Pharisaic and rabbinic tradition by the Oral Torah, an elucidation of the Written Torah by sages of various periods.

Torfaen [to(r)viyn] pop (2000e) 91 500; area 126 km²/49 sq mi. County (unitary authority from 1996) in SE Wales, UK; administrative centre, Pontypool; other chief town, Cwmbran.

Tories The British political party which emerged in 1679–80 as the group opposed to the exclusion of James, Duke of York, from succession to the throne. The name was taken from 17th-c Irish outlaws who plundered and killed English settlers. The party developed as the supporters of the divine right of monarchy, and had particular support from the country squirearchy and most sections of the Anglican church. It went into decline after the Hanoverian succession, but revived under the younger Pitt as the leading opposition to French Revolutionary ideology in the 1790s. Toryism developed into Conservatism under Peel, but survived as a nickname for the Conservatives.

torii [tohree] A Shinto gateway in Japan, the traditional arch at the entrance to the sacred grounds of Shinto shrines. It is generally orange-red in colour, but sometimes unpainted, giving the name of the deity.

tormentil [taw(r)mentil] Any of various species of *Potentilla*, with 4-petalled, yellow flowers. (Family: Rosaceae.)

tornado A column of air rotating rapidly (up to 100 m/s, c.225 mph) around a very low pressure centre. Over the Great Plains of the USA, they are common in spring and early summer, and resemble a dark funnel extending from the cloud base to the ground. Although short-lived, and usually only a few hundred metres in diameter, they can be very destructive in restricted areas.

Toronto 43°42N 79°25W, pop (2000e) 711 100, (metropolitan area) 3 358 000. Capital of Ontario province, Canada, on N shore of L Ontario, at the mouth of the Don R; largest city in Canada; French fort, 1749; occupied by the British, 1759; settled by migrants from the American Revolution, 1793; named York; capital of Upper Canada, 1796; city and modern name, 1834; capital of Ontario, 1867; two airports; railway; subway; two universities (1827, 1959); leading commercial and cultural centre; economy hit by SARS epidemic (2003); professional teams, Blue Jays (baseball), Maple Leafs (ice hockey); Toronto Symphony Orchestra; Fort York (1793, restored 1934).

torpedo A munition of naval warfare, in essence a guided underwater missile, equipped with a motor to propel it through the water and an explosive charge fused to detonate on impact with its target. The first practical torpedo dates from the middle of the 19th-c. Modern torpedoes are equipped with sonar-seeking heads which track underwater sounds, and computerized guidance systems.

torpedo ray *electric ray*

Torquay [taw(r)kee] 50°28N 3°30W, pop (2000e) 61 300. Resort town in Torbay unitary authority, Devon, SW England; centre for recreational sailing; railway; Torr Abbey (12th-c); football league team, Torquay United (Gulls).

torque In mechanics, the ability of a force to cause rotation. Torque equals the product of the force with the perpendicular distance between the rotation axis and the line of action of the force; symbol Γ, units Nm (newton.metre).

Torquemada, Tomás de [taw(r)kaymahtha] (1420–98) First Inquisitor-General of Spain, born in Valladolid, Spain. As Grand Inquisitor from 1483, he displayed great cruelty, and was responsible for an estimated 2000 burnings.

torr Unit of pressure; symbol *torr*; named after Evangelista Torricelli; defined via atmospheric pressure; 1 torr equals the pressure of a column of mercury 1 mm high; 1 torr = 133·3 Pa (pascal, SI unit).

Torrens, Lake Salt lake in SC South Australia, W of the Flinders Ranges; 240 km/150 mi long; 65 km/40 mi wide; area 5775 km²/2229 sq mi.

Torres Strait [torez] Channel to the N of Cape York, Queensland, Australia; c.130 km/80 mi wide; discovered by Spanish explorer Luis Vaez de Torres, 1606; contains **Torres Strait Islands**, which may be remains of a land bridge linking Asia and Australia; annexed by Queensland in 19th-c; pop (2000e) 6800.

Torricelli, Evangelista [torichelee] (1608–47) Physicist and mathematician, born in Faenza, Italy. He discovered the effect of atmospheric pressure on water in a suction pump, and gave the first description of a barometer, or 'Torricellian tube' (1643).

Tórshavn [tors-hown], also **Thorshavn** 62°02N 6°47W, pop (2000e) 16 300. Seaport capital of the Faeroe Is; on SE coast of Strømø I; commerce and fishing.

torsion The application of twisting force. *Torsional forces* cause shear strain. *Torsion balances* measure forces by detecting the degree of twist.

tort A wrong actionable in the civil courts of England and Wales. The usual remedies are damages and/or an injunction. Individual torts include negligence, trespass, and nuisance. The term is also used in the USA. **Delict** is the analogous term in Scots law.

Tortelier, Paul [taw(r)telyay] (1914–90) Cellist, born in Paris. He gained recognition as one of the leading soloists of the instrument. His son **Yan Pascal Tortelier** (1947–) and daughter **Maria de la Pau Tortelier** (1950–) are highly gifted players of the violin and piano respectively.

tortoise A land-dwelling reptile of order Chelonia; feet short, round, with short claws; toes not webbed; used especially for 41 species of family Testudinidae; native to tropical and subtropical regions (except Australasia); usually vegetarian.

tortoiseshell butterfly A colourful butterfly; wings reddish with dark patches, and with blue patches on both wings or on hindwings. (Order: Lepidoptera. Family: Nymphalidae.)

tortoiseshell cat A British short-haired domestic cat; mottled coat of black, dark red, and light red (with no white); also known as **calimanco cat** or **clouded tiger**.

torture In law, the infliction of severe physical or mental suffering, whether for punishment, intimidation, or to extract a confession for a crime. The Universal Declaration of Human Rights (1948) prohibits the use of torture, and it has been universally condemned. Banned since the 19th-c in Europe, it is still used in many parts of the world. International campaigns against torture are led by Amnesty International, and there are conventions which specifically outlaw its practice and provide for sanctions to enforce these, such as the United Nations Charter to the Convention Against Torture (1984).

Toruń [toroon], Ger Thorn 53°01N 18°35E, pop (2000e) 205 000. Industrial river port in NC Poland, on R Vistula; railway; university (1945); birthplace of Copernicus; Church of St John (13th-c), castle (13th-c); mediaeval town, a world heritage site.

torus *Joint European Torus*

Torvill and Dean Figure skaters **Jayne Torvill** (1957–) and **Christopher Dean** (1958–), both from Nottingham, Nottinghamshire. They were world ice dance champions 1981–4, and Olympic champions in 1984. They turned professional in 1984, but returned to international competition in 1993, winning the gold medal in the 1994 European Championships. However, after achieving only a bronze medal in the 1994 Winter Olympics, they once again retired.

Toscanini, Arturo [toskaneenee] (1867–1957) Conductor, born in Parma, Italy. He conducted at La Scala, Milan (1898–1908), the Metropolitan Opera House, New York (1908–15), and the New York Philharmonic (1926–36), and brought into being the Orchestra of the National Broadcasting Corporation of America (1937–53).

Tosefta or **Tosephta** [tohsefta] (Aramaic 'supplement') A large collection of rabbinic traditions and discussions which supplement the teachings of the Mishnah, but are usually considered of lesser authority. It was perhaps compiled AD c.4th–5th-c.

Toshack, John (1949–) Football player and manager, born in Cardiff. He began his career with Cardiff City Football Club (1966) and later signed for Liverpool (1970), where he formed a formidable striking partnership with Kevin Keegan. His honours with Liverpool include three league titles, two UEFA Cup wins, and one FA Cup. He moved to Swansea as player manager (1978–84), taking the club from the fourth division to the first division (now premiership). As manager, he was successful with a number of top European clubs during the 1980s and 1990s, including Real Madrid. Briefly in charge of Wales in 1994, he was appointed manager for a second time in 2004.

totalitarianism In its modern form, a political concept first used to describe the USSR's communist regime and Italy and Germany's fascist regimes during the period between the two World Wars. The leadership claims exclusive rights to govern, usually on behalf of the party and its ideology; all aspects of life are controlled by the state apparatus; political opposition is suppressed; and decision-making is highly centralized.

Totalizator A method of placing bets at horse race or greyhound meetings, commonly known as the **Tote**. All money invested is returned to winning punters, less expenses and taxes.

total solar irradiance *solar constant*

totem A word of North American Indian origin, widely used by social anthropologists and others to describe an animal or plant to which a particular clan or tribe has a special attachment. Attachment to the totem, or **totemism**, has been regarded as a key aspect of primitive religion.

totem pole An elaborately carved pole about 20 m/65 ft high, erected in front of houses, made by Pacific NW Coast American Indians. The tradition dates back to the mid-19th-c, when huge trees were cut down. It is a symbol of prestige, lacking any religious meaning.

toucan A largish bird with an enormous bill, native to the New World tropics; brightly coloured; bare coloured skin around eye; long tail. (Family: Ramphastidae, 42 species.)

touch-me-not *balsam*

touch screen A form of screen on a computer display which can sense any point at which it is touched and communicate the co-ordinates of that point to the computer. This is used in situations where the computer can display a set of options and the operator touches the screen at the option which is to be selected.

Toulon [toolō], Lat **Tilio Martius** 43°10N 5°55E, pop (2000e) 176 000. Fortified naval port in SE France; major naval station in World War 1; railway; episcopal see; cathedral (11th–12th-c).

Toulouse [toolooz], ancient **Tolosa** 43°37N 1°27E, pop (2000e) 376 000. City in S France; on R Garonne; capital of former province of Languedoc; fourth largest city in France; road and rail junction; archbishopric; cultural and economic centre of S France; university (1229); Catholic Institute of Toulouse (1877); Church of St-Sernin (11th–12th-c), cathedral (11th–17th-c).

Toulouse-Lautrec (-Monfa), Henri (Marie Raymond) de [toolooz lohtrek] (1864–1901) Painter and lithographer, born in Albi, France. Physically frail, at the age of 14 he broke both his legs, which then ceased to grow. He settled in Montmartre, where he painted and drew the cabaret stars, prostitutes, barmaids, clowns, and actors of that society, as in 'The Bar' (1898, Zürich) and 'At the Moulin Rouge' (1892, Chicago). He also depicted fashionable society, as in 'At the Races' (1899, Albi), and produced several portraits.

touraco *turaco*

Touraine [tooren] Former province in C France; known for its Huguenot silk-weaving trade; chief town, Tours.

Tour de France [toor duh frãs] The world's most gruelling bicycle race, first held in 1903. Riders have to cover approximately 3390 km/2106 mi of French countryside during a 3-week period each July. The Tour is broken into eleven flat stages, six mountain stages, two individual time-trials, and one team time-trial.

Tourette's syndrome A rare disorder of unknown cause characterized by repetitive muscle movements and vocal outbursts. Muscular tics usually affect the face and take the form of grimacing and blinking. They are accompanied by loud vocalizations, which may include grunts and noises, or uncontrollable use of obscenities and short phrases. The tics are made worse by emotional stress and are absent during sleep.

tourist industry The sector providing services for holiday makers. Tourism has become the major global economic activity, surpassing even the trade in oil and manufactured goods. For developed and underdeveloped countries alike, it has become a major source of foreign exchange earnings, a creator of employment, and a contributor to government revenues. In labour terms, it is probably the major source of employment in countries such as Italy, France, Spain, and the UK. For many developing countries, also, tourism has become one of the major features of economic and social development. However,

the benefits of tourism may be outweighed by the damage done to local communities and the environment, and the repatriation of profits by foreign investors. Increasingly, the development of **ecotourism** or **green tourism** has become linked to the concept of sustainability without degrading or depleting the resources which made development possible. 2002 was recognized by the UN as the International Year of Ecotourism.

tourmaline [toormaleen] A complex borosilicate mineral found in igneous and metamorphic rocks. It forms hard, dense, prismatic crystals, and may be used as a gemstone.

Tournai [toornay], Flemish **Doornik**, ancient **Tornacum** 49°52N 5°24E, pop (2000e) 68 800. Administrative and cultural town in Belgium, on the R Scheldt; bishopric; founded AD 275; railway; cathedral (11th–12th-c, restored 19th-c) is a world heritage site.

Tourneur, Cyril [terner] (c.1575–1626) English playwright. He is known for his two plays, *The Revenger's Tragedy* (1607, sometimes assigned to Webster or Middleton), and *The Atheist's Tragedy* (1611).

Tours [toor], ancient **Caesarodunum** or **Turoni** 47°22N 0°40E, pop (2000e) 135 000. Industrial and commercial city in WC France; episcopal see, 3rd-c; grew up around tomb of St Martin (died in 397), becoming a place of pilgrimage; Huguenot silk industry in 15th–16th-c; airport; road and rail junction; birthplace of Balzac; university (1970); cathedral (12th–16th-c).

Toussaint l'Ouverture [toosĩ loovertür], originally **François Dominique Toussaint** (1746–1803) Black revolutionary leader, born a slave in Saint Domingue (Haiti, from 1804). In 1791, he joined the insurgents, and by 1797 was effective ruler of the former colony. Following an expedition sent by Napoleon to restore slavery, he was arrested and died in a French prison. His surname comes from his bravery in once making a breach in the ranks of the enemy.

Tower Bridge The easternmost bridge on the R Thames, London, which can open to allow large ships in and out of the Pool of London. It was opened in 1894.

Tower of London A palace-fortress started by William I as a wooden fortification in 1067 and replaced by him with one in stone (c.1077–97). A state prison from the 12th-c to the 20th-c, it now houses the crown jewels. The ancient Ceremony of the Keys still takes place every night, conducted by the Chief Yeoman Warden, the sentries, and the Tower guards.

Townes, Charles H(ard) (1915–) Physicist, born in Greenville, SC. He shared the 1964 Nobel Prize for Physics for his work on the development of the maser, and later the laser. In 2005 he received the Templeton Prize for improving scientific understanding of religion.

town hall clock *moschatel*

Townsend, Sue (1946–) Novelist and playwright, born in Leicester, Leicestershire. She made her name through a series of novels introducing the character of Adrian Mole, beginning with *The Secret Diary of Adrian Mole Aged 13³/₄* (1982), later books including *The Cappuccino Years* (1999) and *Adrian Mole and the Weapons of Mass Destruction* (2004).

Townshend (of Rainham), Charles Townshend, 2nd Viscount [townzend], known as **Turnip Townshend** (1674–1738) British Whig statesman, born in Raynham, Norfolk. Made secretary of state by George I (1714–16, 1721–30), he acquired his nickname for his proposal to use turnips in crop rotation.

Townshend Acts (1767) Taxes imposed by the British parliament on five categories of goods imported into the American colonies. Following resistance, four categories were repealed in 1770. The fifth, on tea, remained in effect until the Boston Tea Party. The Acts are named after the British Chancellor of the Exchequer, Charles Townshend (1725–67), who sponsored them.

Townsville 19°13S 146°48E, pop (2000e) 96 500. Industrial port and resort in Queensland, Australia; founded, 1864; Australian Institute of Marine Science; airport; railway; university (1970); army and air-force bases.

toxicology The study of the adverse effects of chemicals on living systems. Toxicology allows prediction of the risks likely to be associated with a particular chemical or drug.

toxin A poison produced by a micro-organism, which causes certain diseases or disorders. Toxins from *Salmonella typhi* cause typhoid fever; toxins from *Pasteurella pestis* cause bubonic plague; toxins from *Shigella dysenteriae* cause dysentery.

toxocariasis [toksohkariyasis] Human infection with *Toxocara canis*, a roundworm carried by dogs. It affects a variety of organs, notably the eye leading to blindness.

toxoplasmosis [toksohplazmohsis] A disease caused by the protozoan *Toxoplasma gondi*, acquired by eating infected meat, or by contact with contaminated cat faeces. It is often harmless, but can be passed to the fetus during pregnancy, resulting in abortion or congenital toxoplasmosis in the child, with blindness and brain damage.

toy dog *non-sporting dog*

Toynbee, Arnold (Joseph) [toynbee] (1889–1975) Historian, born in London. Professor of modern Greek and Byzantine history at London (1919–24), his major work was the multi-volume *Study of History* (1933–61).

Toynbee, Polly, popular name of **Mary Louisa Toynbee** (1946–) British journalist and broadcaster. She became a reporter and feature writer with *The Observer* (1968–71, 1972–7), then a columnist on *The Guardian* (1977–88), BBC social affairs editor (1988–95), and associate editor and columnist on *The Independent* (from 1995).

Toynbee Hall The first university settlement (institutions through which universities provide support to deprived inner city communities), founded in E London in 1885. It was named after the social reformer and economist Arnold Toynbee (1852–83).

TPWS (Train Protection and Warning System) *train protection systems*

trabeated construction *post and lintel*

trace elements *nutrients*

tracer bullet A bullet containing a charge of chemical compound (such as phosphorus) which glows brightly as it flies through the air, indicating the 'trace' of the bullet's path, and thus its efficacy in reaching the target.

tracery The ornamental stone pattern work used in the upper part of a window, screen, panel, or other building element. It is usually associated with Gothic architecture.

trachea [trakeea] A tube connecting the larynx with the principal bronchi; also known as the **windpipe**. In the human adult it is 9–15 cm/3·5–6 in long. In cases of respiratory distress the trachea can be surgically opened between the cartilage rings within the lower part of the neck to provide a passage for air (**tracheostomy**).

trachoma [trakohma] An eye infection caused by the bacterium *Chlamydia trachomatis*. It is endemic in developing countries, and the world's leading preventable cause of blindness.

Tractarianism *Oxford Movement*

tractor A self-propelled vehicle found on farms or similar places of work, and normally used for towing and powering various agricultural machines. Tractors do not usually have a frame or springs, but use the engine and transmission housing to provide structural rigidity, with the tyres to provide cushioning.

Tracy, Spencer (Bonadventure) (1900–67) Actor, born in Milwaukee, WI. He received Oscars for *Captains Courageous* (1937) and *Boys' Town* (1938). In the 1940s and 1950s he played opposite Katherine Hepburn in eight outstanding comedies. Later films

included *Judgment at Nuremberg* (1961) and *Guess Who's Coming to Dinner* (1967), again with Hepburn.

trade association *employers' association*

trade cycle *business cycle*

trademark A symbol placed on an article to show that it has been made by a certain company. When the mark is registered, its unauthorized use is illegal. In the USA, trademarks often include the sign ®, signifying that the mark has been registered.

tradescantia [tradeskantia] A succulent perennial with jointed, often trailing stems, native to the New World; flowers 3-petalled, often white or blue, in small terminal clusters; named after John Tradescant, botanist to Charles I of England. (Genus: *Tradescantia*, 60 species. Family: Commelinaceae.)

Trades Union Congress (TUC) A voluntary association of trade unions in the UK, founded in 1868. It meets annually in September to decide policy, and representation at the Conference is based on one delegate per 5000 members. In 2007 there were 62 affiliated unions, representing nearly 6·5 million members.

trade union An association of people, often in the same type of business, trade, or profession, who have joined together to protect their interests and improve their pay, working conditions, and security of employment. In the UK, the trade union movement developed in the early years of the 19th-c, growing rapidly after the repeal of the Combination Acts (declaring unions illegal) in 1824–5. In the UK there are almost 100 such bodies, half of them supporting the Labour Party. They are often organized into branches, with local 'shop' representation in the form of a *shop steward*. In the 1930s, the Congress of Industrial Organizations (CIO) was formed in the US as a means of providing union membership for unskilled workers, such as in the steel and automobile industries. It merged with the American Federation of Labor in 1955.

trade winds Winds blowing from areas of high pressure, centred on the Tropics of Cancer (23·5°N) and Capricorn (23·5°S), towards the Intertropical Convergence Zone at the Equator.

traditional Chinese medicine (TCM) A system of medicine based on Taoist principles and texts, dating back more than 2000 years. It views health as a state in which the mind, body, and spirit are in harmony, and there is a perfect balance of yin and yang energy. Disease is due to an imbalance of energy, blockage of energy flow, and the influence of internal or external 'perverse energies', which are described according to the climatic conditions that they resemble (eg wind, heat, and damp).

Trafalgar, Battle of (21 Oct 1805) The most famous naval engagement of the Napoleonic Wars, which destroyed Napoleon's hopes of invading England. Fought off Cape Trafalgar, Spain, between the British and Franco-Spanish fleets, the British triumph was marred by the death of Nelson. In 2005, to mark the 200th anniversary of the battle, various celebrations took place throughout Britain.

traffic lights A set of coloured lights at a road junction whose function is to control the flow of traffic on main-road intersections. First used in the USA in 1914, traffic lights, suspended above or set alongside roads, have been adopted universally and follow a uniform pattern, using combinations of green, amber, and red (with countries showing some variation in the timing of amber). Today, the signalling systems are for the most part computerized.

tragedy In Western tradition, a play which presents the occurrence and the effects of a great misfortune suffered by an individual, and reverberating in society. Earlier, this required a great person as protagonist, but modern writers have attempted to confer tragic status on ordinary people. The fundamental purpose of tragedy (reminding us of its origins in religious ritual) was claimed by Aristotle to be the 'awakening of pity and fear', of a sense of wonder and awe at human potential, including the potential for suffering; it makes or implies an assertion of human value in the face of a hostile universe.

tragopan A pheasant, native to SE Asia; nests in tree. (Genus: *Tragopan*, 5 species.)

Traherne, Thomas [trahern] (c.1637–74) Mystical writer, born in Hereford, Herefordshire. The manuscripts of his *Poetical Works* (1903) and *Centuries of Meditations* (1908) were discovered by chance on a London street bookstall in 1896.

train protection systems Systems of railway signalling designed to prevent train collisions and derailments. The most basic form is the **Automatic Warning System** (AWS), which works by sounding a warning in the driver's cab if the line ahead is not clear. If the driver fails to acknowledge the warning by pressing a button, the brakes are automatically applied. Its effectiveness is not foolproof because frequent sounding can lead to driver desensitization, and the warning can be easily overridden. AWS is now supplemented by a **Driver Reminder Appliance (DRA)**, a device set by the driver whenever the train stops at a red signal. The train will not restart until the device is reset, which should remind the driver to check that the signal has cleared. Electronic technology has brought the development of more sophisticated systems, known collectively as **Automatic Train Protection (ATP)**. These systems monitor the speed of the train and calculate a safe speed based on a number of factors. If this calculated speed, indicated on the cab display, is exceeded by more than a set margin, automatic braking is applied until the train slows down sufficiently. The driver cannot override the system, and thus the system should eliminate most 'signals passed at danger' (SPADs), which have been factors in several collisions. The **Train Protection and Warning System** (TPWS) incorporates the existing AWS but provides a higher degree of protection. The system can initiate emergency braking if a train is either about to pass a red signal or has exceeded the maximum permitted speed. The driver cannot override the system. TPWS has been designed to enable simple installation to existing track and trains; however, it does not monitor the train continuously, and thus gives less complete protection than ATP. Other systems include **Automatic Train Control (ATC)**, used for example on the Docklands Light Railway in London, which dispenses with the need for a driver; 'trainstop' systems, such as that used on the London Underground, which automatically stop a train when it passes a red signal; and **Transmission Based Signalling (TBS)**, a new generation of signalling which uses radio transmission and in-cab signalling display.

Trajan [trayjn], in full **Marcus Ulpius Trajanus** (c.53–117) Roman emperor (98–117), the first after Augustus to expand the Roman Empire significantly. In Rome he constructed a new forum, library, and aqueduct.

Tralee [tralee], Ir **Tráighlí** 52°16N 9°42W, pop (2000e) 18 000. Capital of Kerry county, SW Ireland; railway; technical college.

tram A passenger vehicle normally propelled by an electric motor fed from overhead lines, designed to run on rails set into public roads. The tram is still a major means of transport in several US and European cities (eg New Orleans, Cologne); in the UK there is a tourist service in Blackpool, and in the 1990s new services began in Manchester and Sheffield.

trampolining The art of performing acrobatics on a sprung canvas sheet stretched across a frame, first used at the turn of the 20th-c as a circus attraction. It was developed into a sport in 1936.

tranquillizer *benzodiazepines*

transaction processing A form of computer processing of data, through the use of a terminal, in which the operation is carried out as a sequence of transactions. At each transaction the computer poses a question via the terminal, and the terminal operator gives a response. For example, to book an airline seat the computer asks which flight, then which class, then whether special meals are required, etc.

Transalpine Gaul *Gaul*

Transcaucasia Region extending S from the Greater Caucasus to the Turkish and Iranian frontiers; comprises the republics of Georgia, Azerbaijan, and Armenia, which in 1922–36 formed the Transcaucasian SFSR.

transcendentalism In philosophy, the theory, particularly associated with Kant, that the world of experience is conditioned by and logically dependent on the organizing structure of principles and concepts common to all rational minds. The term applies to a philosophical and literary movement in 19th-c New England led by Emerson and Thoreau, which exalted the ideals of self-knowledge, self-reverence, and individual autonomy.

transcendental meditation (TM) A meditation technique taught by Maharishi Mahesh Yogi, based in part on Hindu meditation. It has been widely practised in the West since the 1960s, when he 'converted' the Beatles.

transcription (genetics) The making of a complementary RNA copy of a gene in the DNA. Transcription requires the DNA or chromatin to be in an open configuration, allowing the binding of specific proteins (**transcription factors**) to the promoter of the gene being transcribed. Transcription is carried out by enzymes known as *RNA polymerases*.

transducer Any device which converts one form of energy into another. A microphone is an acoustic transducer, converting sound waves into electrical signals.

transept The part of a cruciform-planned church that projects out at right angles to the main body of the building, usually between nave and chancel.

transference In psychiatry, the unconscious attachment of feelings originally associated with significant early figures in one's life (eg parents) to others (particularly to the psychotherapist). In psychotherapy this allows for the exploration of a patient's early difficulties which have remained unresolved.

Transfiguration An event described in the synoptic gospels when Jesus was temporarily changed in appearance on a mountain in front of his disciples Peter, James, and John. The revelation of glory is described as accompanied by an appearance of Elijah and Moses, and a heavenly voice similar to that at Jesus's baptism. Feast day 6 August.

transformational grammar *generative grammar*

transformer A device which transfers an alternating current (AC) from one circuit to one or more other circuits by electromagnetic induction, usually with a change in voltage. There is no electrical connection between the two circuits. It is often used for converting the high voltage from AC power supplies to the normal domestic supply voltage.

transgenic Descriptive of an artificial organism containing extra copies or foreign DNA from the same or unrelated species. Transgenic organisms are made in the laboratory by inserting the DNA into zygotes or cells using various technologies, and then allowing them to develop normally. Genetically modified crops are examples of transgenic plants. The pigs developed for human heart transplants are transgenic for specific human proteins.

transhumance The transfer of livestock, usually cattle and sheep, between winter and summer pastures. It is characteristic of some mountainous regions, where whole families may move, with their flocks, up to the high-altitude pastures.

transistor A solid-state device, made from a sandwich of semiconductors, usually germanium or silicon, with different electrical characteristics, which can be used as an amplifier or a rectifier. Small, robust, and safe (since they need low voltage), transistors have replaced thermionic valves, and have revolutionized the construction of electronic circuits.

transition elements Chemical elements in which an incomplete electron shell other than the valence level is being filled. They are all metals, and include the elements with atomic numbers 21 (scandium) to 29 (copper) and their groups.

transition state In a chemical reaction, an unstable arrangement of atoms characteristic of the highest energy through which the atoms must pass during the reaction.

Transkei [tranzkiy] Former independent black homeland in SE South Africa; capital, Umtata; traditional territory of the Xhosa; self-government, 1963; granted independence by South Africa (not recognized internationally), 1976; military coup, 1987; incorporated into Eastern Cape province in the South African constitution of 1994.

translation (genetics) The making of a protein from a messenger RNA which takes place on a ribosome in the cytoplasm of the cell. Each three nucleotide bases of the mRNA represent a specific amino acid which are joined together in succession.

translation (language) The conversion of one language into another; often used specifically with reference to written texts, as opposed to the **interpretation** of spoken language. **Word-for-word translation**, in which each word is found an equivalent, often makes little sense; **literal translation** adheres to the linguistic structure of the original, but transposes it into the appropriate grammatical conventions of the target language; **free translation** translates the 'sense' of the text, and seeks an idiomatic equivalent.

transliteration The written representation of a word in the closest corresponding characters of a different language. The process is commonly seen at work in loan-words, as in the Welsh *miwsig* from 'music', *bws* from 'bus'.

transmission The system fitted to an engine that transmits the power generated by the engine to the point at which it is required. Normally this system is composed of mechanical components such as gears, shafts, clutches, and chains, but other methods using hydraulic and electrical means can also be used.

transpiration The loss of water vapour from a plant. The process cools and prevents damage to the leaves in hot weather, and helps draw water up from the roots to other parts of the plant.

transplantation The transfer of an organ or tissue from one person to another. Unless the recipient is an identical twin, such a graft sets up an immunological reaction of variable severity which may destroy the transplanted tissue. This reaction may be partially or completely controlled by the use of immunosuppressive drugs. Tissues that have been transplanted successfully include bone marrow, undertaken for leukaemia, and the kidney, liver, heart, and lungs, carried out for severe organ failure.

transportation Sentence of banishment from England for those convicted of certain offences, introduced in 1597. Increasingly large numbers of English convicts were shipped to North America in the 17th-c and 18th-c; but in 1788, after the US War of Independence, the inflow was stopped. As a result, the British government turned their attention to Australia: 162 000 convicts were transported to Australia from 1788 to 1868.

transposing instrument A musical instrument which sounds at a higher or lower pitch than that at which its music is notated. In the modern orchestra the main transposing instruments are as follows (sound level above/below written pitch is shown in parentheses): piccolo (one octave above), cor anglais (a perfect 5th below), clarinet in A (a minor 3rd below), clarinet in B♭ (a major 2nd below), horn in F (a perfect 5th below), trumpet in B♭ (a major 2nd below), celesta (one octave above), and double bass (one octave below).

Transputer A one-chip computer which has been designed specifically to allow parallel processing involving large numbers of Transputers working together. This technique can provide very fast, powerful computers.

transsexual A person who has changed behaviour, physical appearance, and body (by surgery and/or the consumption of hormones) to that of the opposite sex.

Trans-Siberian Railway *p.944*

transubstantiation The Roman Catholic doctrine of the Eucharist (Mass), affirming the belief that the bread and wine used in the sacrament are converted into the body and blood of Christ, who is therefore truly present. The doctrine, rejected by 16th-c Reformers, was reaffirmed by the Council of Trent.

transuranic elements [tranzyuranik] *actinides*

Transvaal [tranzvahl] Former province in South Africa; settled by the Boers after the Great Trek of 1836; independence, 1852, recognized by Britain; known as the South African Republic; annexed by Britain, 1877; Boer rebellion in 1880–1 led to restoration of the republic; annexed as a British colony, 1900; self-government, 1906; joined Union of South Africa, 1910; in the 1994 constitution, divided into Northern Province and Mpumalanga.

transverse wave *wave motion*

transvestism The recurrent practice of dressing in the clothes of the opposite sex, normally for sexual excitement. It usually begins in adolescence.

Transylvania [transilvaynia], Hung **Erdély**, Ger **Siebenbürgen** Geographical region and province of N and C Romania; a former Hungarian principality that became part of the Austro–Hungarian Empire; incorporated into Romania, 1918; chief towns, Cluj-Napoca and Braşov.

trapdoor spider A spider that lives in a silk-lined tube constructed in a burrow in the ground, closed off by a silk lid; passing insects are attacked and pulled into the tube with great speed; found in Africa, the Americas, and Australia. (Order: Araneae.)

Trapido, Barbara (1942–) Novelist, born in Cape Town, South Africa. Disenchanted with the South African political situation, she emigrated to the UK in 1963. Her novels include *Brother of the More Famous Jack* (1982, Whitbread), *Noah's Ark* (1984), *Temples of Delight* (1990), *The Travelling Hornplayer* (1999), and *Frankie & Stankie* (2003).

Trappists The popular name of the Cistercians of the More Strict Observance, centred on the monastery of La Trappe, France, until 1892. The Order continues throughout the world, devoted to divine office, and noted for its austerity (eg perpetual silence).

trap shooting *clay pigeon shooting*

travel sickness 1 Nausea and vomiting induced by the motion of ships, cars, and aeroplanes in some healthy individuals; also called **motion sickness**. The motion disturbs the function of the balance apparatus in the inner ear, and causes a reflex stimulation of the vomiting centre in the brain stem. Psychological factors play a part in some people. **2** A short attack of diarrhoea commonly affecting those who visit foreign countries. It sometimes arises due to food poisoning, but may be a result of ingesting unfamiliar food and water, or harmless (non-pathogenic) bacteria to which the traveller is not accustomed.

Traven, B [trayvn], pseudonym of **Albert Otto Max Frege** (?1882/90–1969) Writer of adventure stories, whose reclusive character left many details of his early life unclear. In Mexico in the 1920s he wrote several novels and short stories, notably *Der Schatz der Sierra Madre* (1927, The Treasure of the Sierra Madre), on which the celebrated film (1947) by John Huston is based.

Travers, Ben(jamin) (1886–1980) Playwright, born in London. He became famous for the farces which played in the Aldwych Theatre, London, continuously from 1922 until 1933. He was still writing in his nineties.

travertine [travertin] A type of limestone formed by precipitation from springs or streams rich in dissolved calcium carbo-

Trans-Siberian Railway

Key
1 Trans-Siberian Line
2 Trans-Manchurian Line
3 Trans-Mongolian Line
4 Baikal-Amur Magistral (BAM)

An important rail route extending across Siberia, originally between terminals at Chelyabinsk in the Urals and Vladivostok on the Pacific. It was constructed 1891–1905, with an extension around L Baykal completed in 1916. The line, which has played a major role in the development of Siberia, is now largely electrified; the journey from Moscow to Vladivostok (9311 km/5786 mi) takes 7 days. During the 1960s and 1970s a more northerly parallel line was built from N of L Baikal to Nikolaevsk-na-Amure: the Baikal–Amur Magistral (BAM).

nate. It is extensively mined in Tuscany, Italy, and used as a paving stone.

Travolta, John [travolta] (1954–) Film actor, born in Englewood, NJ. He joined the Broadway cast of *Grease*, and became well known for his role in the TV series *Welcome Back Koter*. His films include *Saturday Night Fever* (1977), *Grease* (1978), *Pulp Fiction* (1994), *Get Shorty* (1995, Golden Globe), and *Wild Hogs* (2007).

trawler A vessel designed to drag a large bag-shaped net along or near the bottom of the sea to catch fish. Modern trawlers, equipped with echo-sounder fish-finders and refrigeration to preserve their catch, may be as big as 4000 gross tonnes.

treacle A product obtained from molasses, used to sweeten and darken cakes and puddings. During the refining process, the molasses darkens from a richly golden syrup to a black treacle, also known as **blackstrap molasses** in the USA.

treason The crime of betrayal of the state or failing to pay proper allegiance to a government or monarch. In the UK, for example, it includes conspiring or inciting to kill the monarch, and levying war against the monarch in his or her realm (*insurrection*). In the USA, treason is defined and limited in Article III, section (3) of the Constitution, and conviction requires the testimony of at least two witnesses or a confession in open court as well as wrongful intent and an overt act.

treasury In business and accounting, the function of managing finance, especially its provision and use. In UK government terms, the **Treasury** is the name of the department responsible for managing the nation's finances, headed by the Chancellor of the Exchequer, who is responsible to the prime minister (the First Lord of the Treasury). In the USA, it is known as the **Department of Treasury**, and elsewhere usually as the **Ministry of Finance**.

treasury bills Bills sold at a discount over a three-month period by the Bank of England on behalf of the government. The bills are issued to discount houses at below their face value, and are redeemed at face value. These bills are frequently used by the government as a form of short-term borrowing.

treaty ports *Opium Wars*

Trebizond, Turkish **Trabzon** A city on the Black Sea coast of present-day Turkey, former capital of the Christian empire (1204–1461), It was founded by Alexius Comnenus.

Tree, Sir Herbert (Draper) Beerbohm (1853–1917) Actor-manager, born in London. He built His Majesty's theatre (1897), where he rivalled Irving's productions at the Lyceum. He founded the Royal Academy of Dramatic Art in 1904.

tree A large, perennial plant with a single, woody, self-supporting stem (the *trunk* or *bole*) extending to a considerable height above the ground before branching to form the leafy *crown*. Trees exhibit a wide variety of shapes, and may be evergreen or deciduous. Dicotyledonous and gymnosperm trees grow in height by extension of the shoots, and in girth by the addition of internal tissue layers; monocotyledonous trees achieve their full girth as seedlings, and subsequently increase in height only.

treecreeper Either of two families of songbirds of the N hemisphere: the **treecreeper** (US **creeper**) (Certhiidae, 6 species); and the **Australian treecreeper** (Climacteridae, 6 species), native to Australia and New Guinea.

tree fern The name applied to members of two fern families with a trunk-like stem reaching 25 m/80 ft, the fronds forming a crown. It is native to much of the tropics and subtropics. (Families: Cyatheaceae, Dicksoniaceae.)

tree frog A frog adapted to live in trees; flat with sucker-like discs on fingers and toes; two families: **true tree frogs** (Hylidae, 637 species) and **Old World tree frogs** (Rhacophoridaea, 184 species).

treehopper A small, hopping insect that feeds by sucking the sap of trees and shrubs; mainly in warm dry regions. (Order: Homoptera. Family: Membracidae, c.2500 species).

tree kangaroo A kangaroo of genus *Dendrolagus* (7 species); hind legs not longer than front legs; hands and feet with long claws; inhabits rainforests; may jump to ground from heights of 18 m/ 60 ft.

tree shrew A small SE Asian mammal, rodent-like with a long tail and long thin shrew-like muzzle; tail bushy or with tufted tip; lives in trees and on ground. (Order: Scandentia. Family: Tupaiidae, 16 species.)

trefoil A member of either of two groups of plants belonging to the pea family, Leguminosae. Genus *Trifolium* comprises yellow-flowered species of clovers. Genus *Lotus* includes a widely distributed group of annual or perennial herbs; pea-like flowers, small, often yellow or reddish-coloured.

Trekkies *Star Trek*

Tremain, Rose (1943–) [tremayn] Novelist and short-story writer, born in London. She published her first novel, *Sadler's Birthday*, in 1976. Later novels include *The Cupboard* (1981), *Sacred Country* (1992, James Tait Black), *The Colour* (2003), and *The Road Home* (2007). Her books of short stories include *Evangelista's Fan* (1994) and *The Darkness of Wallis Simpson* (2005).

Trematoda [trematohda] A class of parasitic flatworms; body flattened and covered with a horny layer (cuticle); contains c.8000 species, including the monogenetic and digenetic flukes. (Phylum: Platyhelminthes.)

tremor Involuntary shaking movements affecting any part of the body, but usually most obvious in the hands. It may be due to a variety of disorders including thyrotoxicosis, alcohol withdrawal, and Parkinson's disease, which produces a characteristic 'pill rolling' tremor.

Trenchard (of Wolfeton), Hugh Montague Trenchard, 1st Viscount (1873–1956) Marshal of the RAF, born in Taunton, Somerset. He commanded the Royal Flying Corps in World War 1, helped to establish the RAF (1918), and became the first Chief of Air Staff (1918–29).

trench mouth Severe, recurring infection of the teeth and surrounding tissues due to inadequate cleaning which allows plaque and bacteria to build up and invade the gum's and bones supporting them. Repeated infections in the bone leads to permanent holes, resulting in the teeth loosening and falling out, and painful abscesses developing.

trench warfare Fighting from long narrow ditches in which troops stood and were relatively sheltered from enemy fire. Trenches were used in the Crimean War, and on a far larger scale in World War 1. After the first Battle of the Marne (1914) the retreating Germans dug themselves in N of the R Aisne, setting the pattern for trench warfare on the Western Front. Thousands of miles of parallel trenches were dug, linked by intricate systems of communications and protected by barbed wire. Not until 1918, with an improved version of the tank (invented in 1915), was it possible to press forward over the trenches. Advances in land weaponry have made trench warfare obsolete.

Trent, Council of (1545–63) A Council of the Roman Catholic Church, held at Trento, Italy. It was called to combat Protestantism and to reform the discipline of the Church, and spearheaded the Counter-Reformation.

Trent, River River rising in N Staffordshire, C England; flows 275 km/171 mi to meet the Humber estuary.

Trento, Ger **Trent** 46°04N 11°08E, pop (2000e) 100 000. City in N Italy, on the left bank of the R Adige; archbishopric; railway; cathedral (11th–12th-c).

Trenton 40°14N 74°46W, pop (2000e) 85 400. State capital of New Jersey, USA, on the Delaware R; settled by English Quakers in the 1670s; city status, 1792; scene of a British defeat by George Washington, 1776; railway; research and development centre.

trepanning One of the earliest surgical operations: the removal of a rectangle or disc of bone from the vault of the skull, commonly to alleviate pressure on the brain caused by skull fracture; also known as **trephination**. The instrument involved (now called a **trephine**) is still commonly used in neurosurgical operations.

trephination *trepanning*

trespass Unlawful entry onto the property of another. It includes entry below the land (eg mining) and within a reasonable distance above the land (eg shooting a bullet). Historically, the notion includes any unlawful act which interferes with another's property or rights.

Tretyakov Gallery [tretyakof] One of the world's largest art galleries, located in Moscow, and housing exhibits of Russian painting and sculpture from the 11th-c to the present. The museum building was erected in 1901–2.

Treurnicht, Andries Petrus [troyernikht] (1921–93) South African politician, born in Piketberg, South Africa. He became Transvaal provincial National Party leader in 1978, and held a succession of posts in the cabinets of P W Botha from 1979. He and his colleagues resigned from the party in 1982 to form the new, right-wing Conservative Party.

Trevelyan, G(eorge) M(acaulay) [trevelyan] (1876–1962) Historian, born in Welcombe, Warwickshire. He is best known as a pioneer social historian. His *English Social History* (1944) was a companion volume to his *History of England* (1926).

Trèves *Trier*

Trevithick, Richard [trevithik] (1771–1833) Engineer and inventor, born in Illogan, Cornwall. In 1796–1801 he invented a steam carriage, which ran between Camborne and Tuckingmill, and which in 1803 was run from Leather Lane to Paddington by Oxford Street.

triad The Western name given to a Chinese secret society (because of the importance of the triangle, representing the harmony of Earth, Heaven, and Man, in the initiation ceremonies). These societies originated in response to Qing suppression of Ming loyalists in the later 17th-c, were active in revolutionary movements, and are now reputedly prominent in organized crime, especially international drug trafficking. They have similarities with the Chinese protection associations (*tongs*) which developed in the USA in the second half of the 19th-c.

triangle (mathematics) A plane figure bounded by three straight lines (*sides*). If all three are equal, the triangle is said to be *equilateral*; if two are equal, it is said to be *isosceles*. The sum of the angles of a triangle was proved by the Greeks to be equal to two right angles. If the largest angle in a triangle is less than a right angle, the triangle is called *scalene*; if the largest angle is greater than a right angle the triangle is *obtuse-angled*; if the largest angle is a right angle, the triangle is called *right-angled*, and the subject of Pythagoras's theorem.

triangle (music) A musical instrument of great antiquity, made from a steel rod in the form of a triangle, with one corner left open. It is struck with a short metal beater to produce a high, silvery sound of indefinite pitch.

Triangulum (Lat 'triangle') A small but distinctive N constellation between Aries and Andromeda. There is also a prominent S constellation **Triangulum Australe** ('southern triangle').

Trianon, Grand / Petit *Versailles*

Triassic period [triyasik] The earliest of the periods of the Mesozoic era, extending from c.248 to 213 million years ago. It was characterized by the first appearance of dinosaurs and small mammals.

triathlon A three-part sporting event consisting of sea swimming (3·8 km/2·4 mi), cycling (180 km/112 mi), and marathon running (42·2 km/26·2 mi). The events take place in sequence on a single occasion.

tribology [triybolojee] The study of phenomena involving the sliding of one surface over another. It includes friction, lubrication, and wear.

tribunal An official body exercising functions of a quasi-judicial nature. In the UK, tribunals frequently deal with matters where the citizen is in conflict with a government department. They tend to be specialized, governing such issues as employment rights, mental health, and taxation. The proceedings of a tribunal may be subject to judicial review.

tribunes In late Republican Rome, 10 annually elected officials whose function was to defend the lives and property of ordinary citizens. The office was part of the hierarchy of offices (the *cursus honorum*), coming between the quaestorship and praetorship.

Triceratops [triyseratops] The largest ceratopsian dinosaur, known from the Cretaceous period of North America; heavily built, reaching 9 m/30 ft in length; four-legged; bony frill at back of skull relatively short; paired nasal horns above eyes well developed; plant-eating. (Order: Ornithischia.)

Trichina [trikiyna] A small roundworm (*Trichinella spiralis*), parasitic in the small human intestine; infection usually results from eating raw or undercooked pork. (Phylum: Nematoda.)

Trichinopoly [trikinopolee] *Tiruchchirappalli*

trichinosis A foodborne disease caused by a microscopic parasite, *Trichinella spiralis*, acquired by eating the undercooked meat of infected animals, usually pork. The parasites spread throughout the body and become embedded in muscles, forming cysts, and provoking an inflammatory reaction. Involvement of the heart muscle can lead to cardiac failure and death.

trichomoniasis [trikomoniyasis] Infestation of the mucous membrane of the vagina with a flagellated protozoan. It causes irritation and vaginal discharge, and may be passed to the male urethra during sexual contact.

trick or treat *Hallowe'en*

Trident missile The US Navy's third-generation submarine-launched ballistic missile (SLBM) system, following on from the earlier Polaris and Poseidon missiles. The first version, Trident C-4, became operational in 1980. The larger Trident D-5 was tested with the US Navy in 1989, and entered service with the British Royal Navy in the mid-1990s. The missile has a very long range (11 000 km/7000 mi), and carries up to 14 individually targetable re-entry vehicles (MIRVs).

Trier [treer], Fr **Trèves**, Eng **Treves** [treevz], ancient **Augusta Treverorum** 49°45N 6°39E, pop (2000e) 101 000. River port in Germany; on the R Moselle; bishopric since the 4th-c; centre of wine production and trade; railway; university (1970); Roman Catholic Theological College; birthplace of Marx; Porta Nigra (2nd-c), cathedral (4th-c, 11th–12th-c), and Roman basilica, world heritage sites.

Trieste [tree-est] 45°39N 13°47E, pop (2000e) 255 000. Port in NE Italy, on the Adriatic coast; capital of Free Territory of Trieste, established by the United Nations in 1947, divided in 1954 between Italy and Yugoslavia; airport; railway; university (1938); cathedral (14th-c), castle (14th–17th-c).

triggerfish Deep-bodied fish with a spiny first dorsal fin; large front spine, locked in upright position by a second smaller spine, serving to wedge the fish in rock crevices. (Family: Balistidae, 5 genera.)

triglyceride The major chemical compound found in dietary fats

and in the storage fat in adipose tissue. A glycerol molecule ($C_3H_8O_3$) combines with three fatty acids, mostly of chain length 14–20.

trigonometry The branch of mathematics mainly concerned with relating the sides and angles of a triangle, based on triangles being similar if they have one right angle and one other angle equal. The **trigonometric functions** can be defined as the ratio of sides of a right-angled triangle, the commonest being

$$\text{sine} = \frac{\text{opposite}}{\text{hypoteneuse}}, \text{cosine} = \frac{\text{adjacent}}{\text{hypoteneuse}}, \text{tangent} = \frac{\text{opposite}}{\text{adjacent}}$$

trilobite An extinct primitive marine arthropod, characterized by two grooves along its body producing a tri-lobed appearance; diverse and widespread from the Cambrian to the Permian periods; ranged from minute to 1 m/3 ft long. (Phylum: Arthropoda. Class: Trilobita, c.4000 species.)

trimaran [triymaran] A vessel with a narrow hull and large outriggers or floats giving the appearance of a three-hulled craft. The design gives great stability, thus permitting a large sail area which produces relatively high speed.

Trimble (of Lisnagarvey), David, Lord (1944–) Northern Ireland politician, born in Bangor, Northern Ireland. A former university lecturer, he became MP for Upper Bann in 1990, and leader of the Ulster Unionist Party in 1995. He came to prominence for his role in the peace negotiations of the mid-1990s, and shared the 1998 Nobel Peace Prize with John Hume for his efforts. He became first minister of the new Northern Ireland National Assembly in 1998, and retained this position when devolution became a reality in December 1999. He resigned in 2001 but was re-elected later that year. In 2005 he resigned as leader of the UUP after losing his seat in the general election. He was made a life peer in 2006, and quit his Assembly seat in 2007.

Trimurti [trimoortee] (Sanskrit, 'having three forms') The Hindu triad, manifesting the cosmic functions of the Supreme Being, as represented by Brahma, Vishnu, and Shiva. Brahma is the balance between the opposing principles of preservation and destruction, symbolized by Vishnu and Shiva respectively.

Trincomalee or **Trinkomali** [tringkomalee] 8°44N 81°13E, pop (2000e) 55 000. Seaport in Sri Lanka; at the mouth of the R Mahaweli; taken by the British, 1795; principal British naval base during World War 2 after the fall of Singapore; ruins of Temple of a Thousand Columns (3rd-c BC).

Trinidad and Tobago *p.947*

trinitrotoluene [triyniytrotolyooeen] *TNT* (explosive)

Trinity A distinctively Christian doctrine that God exists in three persons, Father, Son, and Holy Spirit. The unity of God is maintained by insisting that the three persons or modes of existence of God are of one substance. The functions of the persons of the Trinity, and the relationship between them, has been the subject of much controversy (eg the split between Eastern and Western Churches on the *Filioque* clause), but the trinitarian concept is reflected in most Christian worship.

Trinity House The lighthouse authority for England and Wales, the Channel Islands, and Gibraltar. It is one of the principal pilotage authorities, and also supervises the maintenance of navigation marks carried out by local harbour authorities.

Trinity Sunday In the Christian Church, the Sunday after Whitsunday, observed in honour of the Trinity. It was introduced by Pope John XXII in 1334.

trio 1 An ensemble of three singers or instrumentalists, or a piece of music for such an ensemble. The **string trio** is normally composed of violin, viola, and cello; in the **piano trio**, a piano replaces the viola.

2 The central section of a minuet or scherzo, which in the earliest examples often employed a three-part texture.

triode An electronic valve having three electrodes; a positive anode, an electron-emitting cathode, and a negatively biased

Trinidad and Tobago

official name Republic of Trinidad and Tobago

Local name Trinidad and Tobago

Timezone GMT -4

Area 5128 km²/1979 sq mi

Population total (2002e) 1304000

Status Independent republic within the Commonwealth

Date of independence 1962

Capital Port of Spain

Languages English (official), Hindi, French, Spanish

Ethnic groups African (43%), East Indian (40%), mixed (14%), Chinese (1%)

Religions Christian (Roman Catholic 34%, Protestant 29%), Hindu (25%), Muslim (6%)

Physical features Southernmost islands of the Lesser Antilles, SE Caribbean; Trinidad, area 4828 km²/1864 sq mi, traversed by three mountain ranges (N, C and S), rising to 940 m/3084 ft at El Cerro del Aripo; drained by Caroni, Ortoire and Oropuche rivers; Tobago, area 300 km²/116 sq mi, Main Ridge extends along most of island, rising to 576 m/1890 ft.

Climate Tropical, hot and humid; average annual temperature 29°C; dry season (Jan–May); wet season (Jun–Dec); average annual rainfall 1270 mm/50 in (SW Trinidad), 2540 mm/100 in (Tobago mountains).

Currency 1 Trinidad and Tobago Dollar (TTD) = 100 cents

Economy Oil and gas (main industries); industrial complex, W coast of Trinidad; cement, oil refining, petrochemicals; cocoa, coffee, fruit; tourism.

GDP (2002e) $11·07 bn, per capita $10 000

Human Development Index (2002) 0·805

History Trinidad visited by Columbus in 1498; settled by Spain in 16th-c, and acquired by Britain in 1797; Tobago captured by French, 1781, and acquired by Britain, 1802; Tobago became a British colony, 1814; Trinidad and Tobago united as British Crown Colony, 1899; independent member of the Commonwealth, 1962; republic, 1976, governed by a President and bicameral Parliament, comprising a Senate and House of Representatives; also a 15-member Tobago House of Assembly; in 2005 government announced Spanish to become an official language by 2020.

Head of State

1976–87 Ellis Emmanuel Clarke

1987–97 Noor Mohammed Hassanali

1997–2003 Arthur Napoleon Raymond Robinson

2003– Max Richards

Head of Government

1962–81 Eric Williams

1981–6 George Chambers

1986–91 Arthur Napoleon Raymond Robinson

1991–5 Patrick Manning

1995–2001 Basdeo Panday

2001– Patrick Manning

---

control grid. A triode controls the flow of electrons from the cathode to the anode. It can be used as an amplifier or oscillator.

tripe The fore-stomach of a ruminant, used as food – both the rumen (*plain tripe*) and the reticulum (*honeycomb tripe*). In France and the UK it is traditionally stewed with onions, vegetables, and herbs, although recipes differ.

Triple Alliance, War of the or **Paraguayan War** (1864–70) A devastating war fought by Paraguay against the combined forces of Brazil, Argentina and Uruguay (the **Triple Alliance**). The eventual victory of the Allies was achieved at the cost of reducing the male population of Paraguay by nine-tenths.

Triple Crown A term used in many sports to describe the winning of three major events. In British horse racing it is the Derby, 2000 Guineas, and St Leger; in US racing, the Preakness Stakes, Kentucky Derby, and Belmont Stakes. In British Rugby Union it is the beating of the other three Home countries in the International Championship.

triple jump An athletics field event, which takes place in the same area as the long jump. Competitors, after completing their run-up, must take off and hop on the same foot. The second phase is a step onto the other foot, followed by a two-footed jump. The event was previously called the **hop,** **step, and jump**. The current world record for men is 18·29 m/60 ft 0 ¼ in, achieved by Jonathan Edwards of Great Britain, in 1995 at Gothenburg, Sweden; for women, it is 15·50 m/50 ft 10¼ in, achieved by Inessa Kravets (1966–) of Ukraine, in 1995 at Gothenburg, Sweden.

Tripoli (Lebanon) [tripolee], Arabic **Trablous**, Gr **Tripolis**, ancient **Oea** 34°27N 35°50E, pop (2000e) 219 000. Seaport in NW Lebanon; trade centre for N Lebanon and NW Syria; mostly occupied by Sunni Muslims; two Palestinian refugee camps nearby; railway; 12th-c Crusader Castle of St Gilles.

Tripoli (Libya) [tripolee], Arabic **Tarabulus** or **Tarabulus al-Gharb**, ancient **Oea** 32°54N 13°11E, pop (2000e) 808 000. Seaport capital of Libya; founded by the Phoenicians, and developed by the Romans; important Axis base in World War 2; bombed, 1941–2, and occupied by the British, 1943; bombed by US Air Force in response to alleged terrorist activities, 1986; airport; railway; university (1973); old city partly surrounded by Byzantine and mediaeval walls.

Tripolitania [tripolitaynia] Region of N Africa, lying between Tunis and Cyrenaica; under Turkish control from the 16th-c until 1911; under Italian control until 1943; British control until 1952.

Tripp, Linda *Lewinsky, Monica*

triptych *altarpiece*

Tripura [tripura] pop (2001e) 3 191 200; area 10 477 km²/ 4044 sq mi. State in E India; became a state of India, 1949; status changed to union territory, 1956; reverted to a state, 1972; capital, Agartala; governed by a Legislative Assembly; tribal shifting cultivation gradually being replaced by modern farming methods.

trireme [triyreem] A Mediterranean war galley of Greek origin propelled by three banks of oars. It was fitted with a square sail, and a strong projection fixed to the bow below the waterline, used to ram other ships.

Tristan da Cunha [tristan da kunya] 37°15S 12°30W; pop (2000e) 370; area 110 km²/42 sq mi. Small volcanic island in the S Atlantic; volcanic cone rises to 2060 m/6758 ft; inhabitants are the descendants of a British garrison established in 1816 during Napoleon's exile in St Helena; became a dependency of St Helena, 1922; chief settlement, Edinburgh; islanders evacuated in 1961 after a volcanic eruption, but returned in 1963.

Tristram or **Tristan** [tristram] In the Arthurian legends, a knight who was sent to woo Iseult the Fair (Isolde) on behalf of his uncle, King Mark of Cornwall. He fell in love with her himself, then fled to Brittany.

triticale [tritikaylee] An artificial hybrid (*Triticosecale*), derived from wheat (*Triticum*) and rye (*Secale*), giving yields and grain quality approaching those of wheat in cold climates where only rye could be grown previously. Its cultivation is expanding rapidly in Poland and Russia. (Family: Gramineae.)

tritium [tritium] A heavy isotope of hydrogen, in which the nucleus comprises one proton and two neutrons rather than a single proton (as for common hydrogen). It is radioactive, with a half-life of 12·3 years. It is an important ingredient of nuclear fusion reactions and hydrogen bombs.

Triton (astronomy) [triytn] The principal natural satellite of Neptune, discovered in 1846; distance from the planet 355 000 km/ 221 000 mi; diameter 2705 km/1681 mi, orbital period 5·9 days. Uniquely, for a large moon, its orbit is retrograde about Neptune. The encounter by Voyager 2 (Aug 1989) showed that it has a thin atmosphere of nitrogen.

Triton (mythology) [triytn] In Greek mythology, the son of Poseidon and Amphitrite. He is depicted in art as a fish from the waist down, and blowing a conch-shell.

triton shell [triytn] A large marine snail found in the Indo-Pacific region; one of the world's largest snails, length up to 36 cm/ 14 in. (Class: Gastropoda. Order: Mesogastropoda.)

triumvirate Literally Lat, 'a group of three men'; in ancient Rome **1** the name given to any publicly appointed administrative board of three; **2 First Triumvirate** the name commonly applied to the unofficial coalition between Caesar, Pompey, and Crassus in 60 BC; **3 Second Triumvirate** the name given to the joint rule from 43 BC of Antonius, Octavian (Augustus), and Lepidus.

Trivandrum or **Trivandram** [trivandruhm] 8°31N 77°00E, pop (2000e) 970 000. Capital of Kerala state, SW India; on the Malabar coast; airfield; railway; university (1937); commercial and cultural centre; noted for its wood and ivory carving.

trivium *quadrivium*

Trobriand Islander A Melanesian people of the scattered Trobriand Is, off New Guinea. They were studied by Malinowski from 1915, and their way of life described in several monographs.

trogon [trohgn] A bird native to the New World tropics, Africa, and SE Asia; plumage soft, brightly coloured; tail long. (Family: Trogonidae, c.40 species.)

Troilus [trohilus, troylus] In Greek legend, a prince of Troy, the son of Priam and Hecuba, who was killed by Achilles. In mediaeval stories, he is the lover of Cressida.

Trojan asteroids Asteroids which have orbits very similar to Jupiter, positioned 60° ahead or behind the planet, where they are trapped in a stable configuration. Nearly 500 are known.

Trojan Horse A huge wooden horse left behind on the beach by the Greeks, who had pretended to give up the siege of Troy. Told by Sinon that it was an offering to Athena, the Trojans broke down their city wall to bring it inside. At night, warriors emerged and captured the city.

Trojan War In Greek legend, the 10-year conflict between the Greeks and Trojans, which began when Paris carried off Helen, the wife of Menelaus, and ended in the sacking of Troy. The story was the subject of Homer's *Iliad*, and is tentatively dated on the basis of archaeology to c.1260 BC.

troll [trohl] In early Scandinavian mythology a huge ogre, in later tradition a mischievous dwarf, the guardian of treasure, inhabiting caves and mountains and skilled with his hands.

trolley bus A type of bus popular in the UK until the 1960s, using an electric motor rather than an internal combustion engine as its motive power. Electricity was provided by overhead cables, with the electricity being conducted from the wires by means of trailing wiper arms. The trolley bus differed from the tram in not running on tracks. They were used in the USA and several European cities, but were generally replaced by the motor bus, with its freer road movement. However, their avoidance of noise and air pollution renewed the attractiveness of the concept in the environmentally-aware 1990s.

Trollope, Anthony [troluhp] (1815–82) Novelist, born in London. His first novel in the 'Barsetshire' series, *The Warden*, appeared in 1855, and was followed by such successful books as *Barchester Towers* (1857). His later novels include *Phineas Finn* (1869) and *The Way We Live Now* (1875).

Trollope, Joanna (1943–) Writer and novelist, born in Minchinhampton, Gloucestershire. She became an English teacher and freelance writer, before publishing her first novel, *Eliza Stanhope* (1978). Later books include *The Rector's Wife* (1991), *Marrying the Mistress* (2000), and *Second Honeymoon* (2006). She has also written novels as **Caroline Harvey**, including *Legacy of Love* (1992) and *The Brass Dolphin* (1999).

trombone A musical instrument made from brass tubing, mainly cylindrical, which expands to a bell at one end and is fitted with a cup-shaped mouthpiece at the other. A slide is used to vary the length, and therefore the fundamental pitch, of the instrument. Its history dates back to the 15th-c; until c.1700 it was known as the **sackbut**.

Tromp, Maarten (Harpertszoon) (1598–1653) Dutch admiral, born in Brielle, The Netherlands. In 1639 he defeated a superior Spanish fleet off Gravelines, and won the Battle of the Downs. His encounter with Blake in 1652 started the first Anglo-Dutch War. Victorious off Dover, he was defeated off Portland, and finally off Terhejide, near Schevingen, where he was killed.

trompe l'oeil [trôp loeee] (Fr 'deceive the eye') A painting which may have little aesthetic value, but which is cleverly designed to trick the spectator into thinking the objects represented are really there.

Tromsø [tromsoe] 69°42N 19°00E, pop (2000e) 54 000. Seaport in N Norway; founded, 13th-c; charter, 1794; largest town in N Norway; base for expeditions to the Arctic; bishopric; university (1972).

Trondheim [trondhiym], formerly **Nidarøs** 63°36N 10°23E, pop (2000e) 145 000. Seaport in C Norway, at the mouth of the R Nidelv (Nea); former capital of Norway during the Viking period; occupied by the Germans, 1940–5; bishopric; airport; railway; university (1968); cathedral (1066–93).

Troödos Mountains [trohuhthos] Mountain range in C Cyprus; rises to 1951 m/6400 ft at Mt Olympus.

Troon 55°32N 4°40W, pop (2000e) 14 400. Town and golf resort in South Ayrshire, W Scotland; railway.

Trooping the Colour In the UK, originally the display of the regimental standard to the troops; now usually taken to refer to the annual ceremony on Horse Guards Parade, London, when the monarch reviews one of the five battalions of the Guards regiment and its flag, or **colour**, is presented. The ceremony takes place to mark the monarch's official birthday, and is currently in June.

tropical year or **solar year** The time taken for the Earth to complete one revolution round the Sun relative to the vernal equinox: 365·24219 mean solar days.

tropics A climatic zone located between the Tropics of Cancer (23·5°N) and Capricorn (23·5°S). The N tropic is so called because the Sun at the summer solstice (when it is vertically over that tropic) enters the zodiacal sign of Cancer; the S tropic is named for a similar reason. Temperatures are generally high, such as a mean monthly temperature greater than 20°C.

tropism [trohpizm] A plant response by directional movement towards (**positive tropism**) or away from (**negative tropism**) a sustained external stimulus. **Phototropism** is a response to light; **geotropism** to gravity; and **chemotropism** to chemicals.

troposphere The lowest layer of the Earth's atmosphere, within which the weather is active because of the continual motion of the air and a steadily decreasing temperature with height.

Trotsky, Leon, pseudonym of **Lev Davidovich Bronstein** (1879–1940) Russian Jewish revolutionary, born in Yanovka, Ukraine. He joined the Bolsheviks and played a major role in the October Revolution. In the Civil War he was Commissar for War, and created the Red Army. After Lenin's death (1924) he was ousted from the Party by Stalin, and expelled from the Soviet Union (1929). He finally found asylum in Mexico, but was assassinated there by Ramón Mercader, a Spanish Communist.

Trotskyism A development of Marxist thought by Leon Trotsky. Essentially a theory of permanent revolution, Trotskyism stressed the internationalism of socialism, avoided co-existence, and encouraged revolutionary movements abroad; this conflicted with Stalin's ideas of 'socialism in one country'.

troubadours [troobadoor] (Provençal, 'inventor') Court poet-musicians (some known by name, such as Guillaume d'Acquitaine) who flourished in the S of France 1100–1350. They wrote (in the S dialect *langue d'oc*) mainly love poems, and had an important influence on the development of the European lyric. Their equivalent in the N (writing in the N dialect *langue d'oil*) were the **trouvères**, who also wrote *chansons de geste*.

trout Any of several species of the family Salmonidae, existing in two forms: the **brown trout**, confined to fresh water, and the migratory and much larger **sea trout**; an excellent food fish.

Trowbridge [trohbrij] 51°20N 2°13W, pop (2000e) 30 800. County town of Wiltshire, S England; railway.

Troy, Turkish **Truva**, also ancient **Ilium** Ancient ruined city in W Turkey; the archaeological site lies S of the Dardanelles, near Hisarlik; from the Stone Age to Roman times, over a period of 4000 years, the city was rebuilt on the same site nine times; excavated by Heinrich Schliemann in the 1870s, the occupation level known as Troy VIIa is thought to be the city of the Greek legend.

Troyes [trwah], ancient **Augustobona Tricassium** 48°19N 4°03E, pop (2000e) 63 500. City in NEC France; on channel of the R Seine; bishopric, 4th-c; capital of old province of Champagne; railway; centre of hosiery trade; cathedral (13th–16th-c).

Trucial States The former name of the United Arab Emirates. The name derives from a truce signed between the ruling sheiks and Great Britain in 1820. In 1892 they accepted British protection.

Trudeau, Pierre (Elliott) [troodoh] (1919–2000) Canadian statesman and Liberal prime minister (1968–79, 1980–4), born in Montreal, Quebec, Canada. His term of office as prime minister saw the October Crisis (1970) in Quebec, the introduction of the

Official Languages Act, federalist victory during the Quebec Referendum (1980), and the introduction of Canada's constitution (1982).

Trueman, Freddy, popular name of **Frederick Sewards Trueman**, nickname **Fiery Fred** (1931–2006) Cricketer and broadcaster, born in Stainton, South Yorkshire. A Yorkshire fast bowler for 19 years (1949–68), he played in 67 Tests for England between 1952 and 1965, and was the first bowler to take 300 Test wickets. He worked as a cricket writer and commentator following retirement from first-class cricket in 1969.

Truffaut, François [troofoh] (1932–84) Film critic and director, born in Paris. In 1959 he made his first feature, *Les Quatre Cents Coups* (The 400 Blows), effectively launching the French 'Nouvelle Vague' movement, followed by *Tirez sur le Pianiste* (1960, Shoot the Pianist), *Jules et Jim* (1961), and *Fahrenheit 451* (1966). *La Nuit américaine* (1973, trans Day for Night) brought him an Oscar.

truffle The underground fruiting body of fungi belonging to the genus *Tuber*; may be fleshy or waxy; much sought after as a delicacy. (Subdivision: Ascomycetes. Order: Tuberales.)

Trujillo [trooheelyoh] 8°06S 79°00W, pop (2000e) 635 000. City in NW Peru; founded by Pizarro, 1536; airfield; railway; university (1824); cathedral.

Truk or **Chuuk** pop (2000e) 66 700; area 127 km²/49 sq mi. One of the Federated States of Micronesia, W Pacific, comprising 11 high volcanic islands and numerous outlying atolls; capital, Weno (formerly Moen).

Truman, Harry S (1884–1972) US Democratic statesman and 33rd president (1945–53), born in Lamar, MO. His decisions included the dropping of two atom bombs on Japan, the post-war loan to Britain, and the sending of US troops to South Korea. He promoted the policy of giving military and economic aid to countries threatened by Communist interference (the **Truman Doctrine**). At home, he introduced a *Fair Deal* of economic reform.

trumpet A musical instrument made from cylindrical brass (or other metal) tubing, fitted with a cup-shaped mouthpiece, and widening at the other end to a flared bell. It was traditionally used for signalling, and since the 17th-c as an orchestral and solo instrument. The modern trumpet has three valves and is a transposing instrument pitched in B♭.

Truro 50°16N 5°03W, pop (2000e) 20 700. City and county town of Cornwall, SW England; on R Truro; railway; cathedral (1880–1910), Pendennis Castle (1543).

Truss, Lynne (1955–) Writer, journalist, and broadcaster, born in Richmond, Greater London. She studied at University College, London, and worked as a columnist and sportswriter for *The Times*. She became well-known through her best-selling book *Eats, Shoots & Leaves: The Zero Tolerance Approach to Punctuation* (2003). In 2005 appeared *Talk to the Hand: The Utter Bloody Rudeness of Everyday Life*, her take on bad manners. Her novels include *With One Lousy Free Packet of Seed* (1994) and *Going Loco* (1999).

trust An arrangement whereby a person (the **trustee**) holds property for the benefit of another (the *beneficiary*). The terms of the settlement or will creating the trust are binding on the trustees.

Trusteeship *Trust Territory*

Trusteeship Council *United Nations*

Trust Territory A non-self-governing area, the administration of which is supervised by the United Nations established after World War 2. The origins of the system lay in the need to administer colonial territories taken from powers defeated in World War 1. Most such areas are now independent, with the exception of a small number of Pacific islands.

Truth, Sojourner, originally **Isabella Van Wagener** (c.1797–1883) Evangelist, abolitionist, feminist, and reformer, born a slave in

Ulster County, NY. She joined the abolitionist movement, became an effective anti-slavery speaker. Appointed counsellor to the freedmen of Washington by Lincoln, she continued to promote black and women's civil rights until her death.

Truth and Reconciliation Commission A committee established in South Africa in 1995 to investigate the abuses of the apartheid era. Its hearings, under the chairmanship of Archbishop Desmond Tutu, achieved an international profile, though the value of the exercise as a means of achieving better race relations was frequently questioned within the country. Its report was published in 1998.

trypanosomiasis [tripanohsomiyasis] Any of several diseases caused by infection with one of the trypanosomes, protozoa that infest domestic and wild animals and are transmitted to humans by insect vectors. **African trypanosomiasis** is transmitted to humans by bites from tsetse flies; it is also known as **sleeping sickness**. Symptoms are high fever, fatigue, headache, and joint pain; as the disease develops it leads to anaemia, and kidney and liver failure; finally extreme drowsiness is followed by coma and death. **American trypanosomiasis** occurs widely in South and Central America; also known as **Chagas' disease**, after the Brazilian physician Carlos Chagas (1879–1934).

tsar or **czar** The title used by the rulers of Russia from 1547 to 1721; derived from Latin *Caesar*. It remained in common use until the Revolution (1917), although the official title of the ruler from 1721 was *Emperor*.

Tschaikovsky, Piotr Ilyich *Tchaikovsky*

tsetse fly [tetsee, tseetsee] A small biting fly found in tropical Africa; feeds on blood of vertebrates; of great medical and veterinary importance as the carrier of sleeping sickness (in humans) and nagana (in cattle). (Order: Diptera. Family: Glossinidae.)

Tshwane *Pretoria*

Tsinan *Jinan*

Tsiolkovsky, Konstantin Eduardovich [tseeolkofskee] (1857–1935) Physicist and rocketry pioneer, born in Izhevsk, Russia. From 1911 he developed the basic theory of rocketry, and also multistage rocket technology (1929). Much earlier (1881), unaware of Maxwell's work, he independently developed the kinetic theory of gases.

Tsui, Daniel C [tsooee] (1939–) Physicist, born in Henan, China, but holding posts in the USA since the 1960s. He shared the 1998 Nobel Prize for Physics for his contribution to the discovery of a new form of quantum fluid with fractionally charged excitations.

tsunami [tsunahmee] Long-period ocean waves produced by movements of the sea floor associated with earthquakes, volcanic explosions, or landslides. Tsunamis may cross entire ocean basins at speeds as great as 800 km/500 mi per hour, and strike coastal regions with devastating force. Thousands of lives have been lost in regions of the Pacific subject to destructive tsunamis, which may reach heights in excess of 30 m/100 ft. They are also referred to as **seismic sea waves**, and in popular (but not technical oceanographic) use as **tidal waves**.

An unfamiliar phenomenon to many, the public's perception of tsunamis changed following the disaster that took place on 26 December 2004. The biggest earthquake for 40 years (magnitude 9.0) occurred between the Australian and Eurasian plates in the Indian Ocean and triggered a tsunami that spread over thousands of kilometres during several hours. The tsunami formed when energy from the earthquake vertically jolted the seabed by several metres, displacing hundreds of cubic kilometres of water. Large waves began racing away from the earthquake's epicentre, just north west of the Indonesian island of Sumatra, at a speed of 800 km/500 mi per hour. As it reached shallow water near coastal areas it slowed but increased in height, up to 10 m/32 ft. With no tsunami

detection equipment in place in the Indian Ocean, the coastal regions hit had no warning of its approach. Indonesia was worst hit, notably Aceh province on Sumatra, with whole towns destroyed and tens of thousands of lives lost. Eight more countries in S and E Asia were affected: India, Sri Lanka, Bangladesh, Myanmar (Burma), Thailand, Malaysia, Maldives, and Seychelles. Less severely hit were the East African coasts of Somalia, Kenya, and Tanzania. Within a week the total death toll was reported to be over 150 000, with thousands unaccounted for, and a massive international relief effort was launched. The final death toll was estimated at 300 000.

tsutsugamushi fever [tsutsugamushee] An infectious disease caused by a rickettsia, a bacterium that is spread to humans through the bites of *Leptotrombidium* mites that usually live in the ground, but can also infest humans. The disease was first recognized on Honshu I in Japan. A swollen, reddened area appears at the site of a bite, accompanied by headaches, fatigue, and a high fever. The bitten area later ulcerates and forms a characteristic black scab. If untreated by antibiotics, complications such as pneumonia, hepatitis, and cerebral haemorrhage can occur, and the disease is frequently fatal.

Tswana *Sotho–Tswana*

Tuamotu Archipelago [towmohtoo] 135–143°W 14–23°S; pop (2000e) 13 500; area 826 km^2/319 sq mi. Island group of French Polynesia; largest group of coral atolls in the world; area used for nuclear testing by the French since 1962.

Tuareg [twahreg] A Berber pastoral people of the C Sahara and the N Sahel zone of W Africa. About half the Tuareg population are no longer nomads, and demands for their own homeland increased during the early 1990s.

tuatara [tooatara] A rare lizard-like reptile (*Sphenodon punctatus*), native to islands off the coast of New Zealand; the only remaining member of the order Rhyncocephalia; green or orange-brown; length, up to 65 cm/26 in; male with crest of tooth-like spines along back; nocturnal.

tuba A musical instrument made from brass tubing curved elliptically, with usually three valves, a mouthpiece set at right angles, and a wide bell pointing upwards. It is the largest and lowest in pitch of all brass instruments.

tubenose A marine bird found worldwide; nostrils long and tubular on long, grooved, hooked bill; also known as **petrel**. (Order: Procellariiformes, or Tubinares.)

tuber An underground organ storing food for the next season's growth. **Stem tubers** are distinguished by the presence of buds or 'eyes'; **root tubers** bear no buds.

tuberculosis (TB) A chronic debilitating disease almost always caused in humans by *Mycobacterium tuberculosis*, characterized by deposits of infected granules (*tubercles*) throughout the body. It thrives in overcrowded and deprived conditions, and was the scourge of poor communities in the 19th-c. It remains a major health problem in the developing world, and is re-emerging in the West as a significant infectious threat. In 1998 the World Health Organization reported that TB is killing more people worldwide than any other infectious disease. People with suppressed immune systems, such as AIDS patients, are especially vulnerable. The micro-organisms are spread in the air, and enter the body via the respiratory tract, initially establishing a primary infection in the lung. Over months and years, the lesion gradually enlarges, resulting in the destruction of lung tissue and the formation of a cavity. The infection may spread locally, causing pneumonia, or elsewhere in the body to affect almost any organ. Treatment requires long courses of powerful antibiotics. However, new strains of antibiotic-resistant micro-organisms are emerging, causing considerable concern.

Tubifex [tyoobifeks] A genus of freshwater annelid worms, found part buried in mud on river beds; red in colour because of haemoglobin in blood; commonly used to feed aquarium fishes. (Class: Oligochaeta. Order: Haplotaxida.)

Tübingen [tübingen] 48°32N 9°04E, pop (2000e) 82 600. City in Germany; on R Neckar; railway; university (1477).

Tubman, Harriet, *née* **Ross** (c.1820–1913) Abolitionist and rescuer of slaves, born in Dorchester Co, MD. She escaped from slavery in Maryland (1849) and went north via the 'Underground Railway', a network of secret safe-houses. She returned to the South frequently to escort escaping slaves through this route.

Tubruq *Tobruk*

Tubuai Islands [toobwiy] or **Austral Islands**, Fr **Iles Tubuai** pop (2000e) 8900; area 137 km²/53 sq mi. Volcanic island group of French Polynesia; chief settlement, Mataura (on Tubuai).

tubular bells A set of metal tubes tuned to different pitches and suspended in a large frame. They are struck with a short mallet to produce bell sounds in orchestral and operatic music.

TUC *Trades Union Congress*

Tucana [tookahna] (Lat 'toucan') A faint S constellation, which includes the prominent Small Magellanic Cloud.

Tucker, Albert Lee (1914–99) Painter, born in Melbourne, Victoria, Australia. He was known as a pioneer of Surrealism in Australia, and for his paintings of harsh Australian landscape as well as for his self-portraits.

Tucson [tooson] 32°13N 110°58W, pop (2000e) 486 700. City in SE Arizona, USA, on the Santa Cruz R; founded, 1776; ceded to the USA, 1853; city status, 1883; state capital, 1867–77; airport; railway; university (1885); distributing centre for cotton, livestock, and nearby mines; major tourist and health resort.

Tucumán *San Miguel de Tucumán*

Tudjman, Franjo [tujman] (1922–99) Croatian president (1990–9), born in Veliko Trgvoisaeem Zagorie, NW Croatia. A professor of politics at Zagreb University (1962–7), he was expelled from the ruling Communist Party in 1967, lost his university post, and later spent several years in jail. In 1989 he founded the Croatian Democratic Union and became its president. Under his leadership, Croatia achieved full sovereignty, and he became a major figure in Balkan politics in the mid-1990s following the break-up of Yugoslavia.

Tudor, Owen *Catherine of Valois*

Tudors A N Wales gentry family, one of whose scions married a Plantagenet in the early 15th-c. The dynasty began when Henry, 2nd Earl of Richmond and son of Margaret Beaufort (a Lancastrian claimant to the crown) overthrew Richard III in 1485. It ended with the death of Elizabeth I in 1603.

tuff *pyroclastic rock*

tug of war An athletic event of strength involving two teams who pull against each other from opposite ends of a long, thick rope. A team normally consists of eight members. With sheer strength and determination they have to pull their opponents over a predetermined mark.

tui [tooee] A honeyeater (*Prosthemadera novaeseelandiae*) native to the New Zealand area; dark plumage with small knot of white feathers on throat, and collar of delicate white filaments; also known as **parson bird**.

Tuileries [tweeleree(z)] Formal gardens laid out in the 17th-c by Le Nôtre in Paris. They are all that remain of the former Tuileries Palace built for Catherine de' Medici in the 16th-c, and destroyed by fire in 1871.

Tula (Mexico) [toola] An ancient Meso-American city, from which the Toltecs dominated C Mexico AD c.900–1150. It developed from AD c.750, and was destroyed c.1168.

Tula (Russia) [toola] 54°11N 37°38E, pop (2000e) 541 000. Industrial city in NC European Russia; on R Upa; Imperial Small Arms Factory founded here by Peter the Great, 1712; railway; airfield; cathedral (1762–4).

tularaemia / tularemia A disease caused by infection with *Fran-*

cisella tularensis. The bacterium normally infects game animals but can remain alive for weeks in soil and water, and is highly infectious. It is acquired by humans by inhalation, direct skin contact, in the bites of ticks that infest wildlife, or by ingestion of contaminated meat and water. The disease is fatal if untreated, in c.10% of cases. The organism has been the subject of considerable research because of its potential as a biological warfare agent.

tulip A bulb native to Europe and Asia, especially the steppe regions; flowers solitary, occasionally 2–6, in a variety of shapes and colours but usually large and showy, with six segments. A huge industry is built around several thousand named cultivars, especially in Holland. (Genus: *Tulipa*, 100 species. Family: Liliaceae.)

tulip tree A deciduous tree (*Liriodendron tulipifera*) reaching 35 m/115 ft, native to North America; flowers with six greenish-yellow petals, resembling the tulip in size and shape. It is a valuable timber tree, known commercially as **Canary** or **American whitewood**; also called **tulip poplar** in North America. (Family: Magnoliaceae.)

Tull, Jethro (1674–1741) Agriculturist, born in Basildon, West Berkshire. He introduced several new farming methods, including the invention of a seed drill which planted seeds in rows (1701).

Tullamore [tuhlamaw(r)], Ir **Tulach Mhór** 53°16N 7°30W, pop (2000e) 9600. Capital of Offaly county, Leinster, C Ireland; railway; abbey at Durrow founded by St Columba.

Tulsa [tuhlsa] 36°10N 95°55W, pop (2000e) 393 000. City in NE Oklahoma, USA; port on the Arkansas R; settled in the 1830s; developed in the 1880s with the coming of the railway; airport; university (1894); major national centre of the petroleum industry.

tumbleweed The name given to various bushy plants which, at the end of the growing season, break off at ground level and are blown and rolled considerable distances by the wind, simultaneously scattering their seeds.

tumour A swelling of any kind in any part of the body. The literal definition refers to swellings of any origin, including infections and cysts. However the term is more often used to refer to benign or malignant growths (*neoplasms*).

tuna Any of several large fast-swimming predatory fish (especially the *Thunnus* species) found in surface ocean waters; belong to the mackerels in the family Scombridae; body adapted for power and speed; plans to halt overfishing adopted by 60 countries in 2007.

Tunbridge Wells or **Royal Tunbridge Wells** 51°08N 0°16E, pop (2000e) 60 300. Spa town in Kent, SE England; iron-rich springs discovered in 1606; fashionable health resort in 17th–18th-c; 'Royal' since 1909, a legacy of visits made by Queen Victoria; railway.

tundra The treeless vegetation zone found polewards of the taiga of North America, Europe, and Asia. Often underlain by permafrost, the vegetation is dominated by mosses, lichens, herbaceous perennials, dwarf shrubs, and grasses.

tungsten W (from Ger *wolfram*), element 74, density 20 g/cm³, melting point 3410°C. A grey metal, difficult to work, occurring mainly with other elements in oxide ores. The metal is used extensively for lamp filaments, because of its high melting point and general lack of reactivity. **Tungsten carbide** (WC), is very hard, and is used in cutting and grinding tools.

Tunguska event An explosion of enormous force low in the atmosphere over the Siberian wilderness area of Tunguska R valley (30 Jun 1908), thought to have resulted from the impact of a small comet nucleus or asteroid. It levelled 3000 km²/1200 sq mi of forest.

tunicate [tyoonikuht] A marine invertebrate chordate; may be solitary or in colonies, base-attached or free-swimming; adult body enclosed in leathery tunic; c.1250 species, including sea

Tunisia

□ International Airport   ∴ World heritage site

[tyoonizia], official name **Republic of Tunisia**, Arabic **al-Jum-huria at-Tunisia**

Local names Tunis (Arabic), Tunisie (French)

Timezone GMT +1

Area 164 150 km²/63 362 sq mi

Population total (2002e) 9 764 000

Status Republic

Date of independence 1956

Capital Tunis

Languages Arabic (official), French and Berber widely spoken

Ethnic groups Arab (98%), European (1%), small Jewish minority

Religions Sunni Muslim (98%), Christian (1%), small Jewish minority

Physical features Located in N Africa, on Mediterranean coast; Atlas Mts (NW) rise to 1544 m/5065 ft at Jebel Chambi; Majardah river valley is the most fertile area (N); from Tabussah range, land descends across a plateau to the Saharan desert (S) and a coastal plain (E).

Climate Mediterranean in N, with hot, dry summers, mild, rainy winters; extreme desert-continental conditions in S, with little rainfall; average annual temperature 9°C (Jan), 26°C (Jul); average annual rainfall 400 mm/15·7 in.

Currency 1 Tunisian Dinar (TND) = 1000 millimes

Economy Agriculture (employs c.50% of population, but of declining importance); wheat, barley, grapes; olive oil (world's fourth largest producer); phosphates (fifth largest producer).

GDP (2002e) $67·13 bn, per capita $6800

Human Development Index (2002) 0·722

History Ruled by Phoenicians, Carthaginians, Romans, Byzantines, Arabs, Spanish, and Turks; under the control of the Ottoman Empire, 1574; French protectorate, 1881; gained internal self-government in 1955; independence, 1956; monarchy abolished and republic declared, 1957; executive power held by President, who appoints the Prime Minister and Council of Ministers; unicameral legislature, National Assembly, elected every five years; new constitution, 2002, removed presidential term limits.

Head of State
1957–87 Habib Bourguiba
1987– Zine al-Abidine bin Ali

Head of Government
1970–80 Hadi Nouira
1980–6 Mohammed Mezali
1986–7 Rashid Sfar
1987 Zine al-Abidine bin Ali
1987–9 Hadi Baccouche
1989–99 Hamed Karoui
1999– Mohammed Ghannouchi

---

squirts, salps, and larvaceans. (Phylum: Chordata. Subphylum: Tunicata.)

tuning fork A two-pronged metal instrument, invented in 1711 by English trumpeter John Shore (c.1662–1752), which is made to vibrate and then pressed down on a wooden surface to produce a note (virtually free from upper harmonics) to which voices or instruments can adjust their pitch.

Tunis [tyoonis] 36°50N 10°13E, pop (2000e) 778 000. Seaport capital of Tunisia; Phoenician origin, later dominated by Carthage; capital status, 1236; captured by Turks, 1533; occupied by French, 1881; airport; railway; university (1960); Great Mosque of Zitouna (9th-c); Medina of Tunis is a world heritage site.

Tunisia *see panel*

Tunja [toonkha] 5°33N 73°23W, pop (2000e) 121 500. City in EC Colombia; altitude 2819 m/9249 ft; university (1953); one of the oldest cities in Colombia; refounded as a Spanish city, 1539; decisive battle of Boyacá, 1818.

tunnel An artificial underground passage constructed for a variety of purposes, such as roads, railways, canals, mining, or conducting water. Tunnels are constructed either by cutting away the material above and then covering the tunnel over (the *cut and cover* method), or by driving through the ground using hand tools, a tunnelling shield, or rock drills as appropri-

ate. The longest tunnel in the world is the Delaware Aqueduct in New York (169 km/105 mi), which is used for water supply.

tunny *tuna*

tup *sheep*

Tupamaros [toopamahros] An Uruguayan urban guerrilla movement founded by Raúl Sendic in 1963, named after the 18th-c Peruvian Indian rebel, Túpac Amaru. The movement was suppressed by the military-controlled government of 1972–85.

tupelo [tyoopeloh] A deciduous tree (*Nyssa sylvatica*) native to the swamps of eastern North America; inconspicuous flowers, small, greenish; edible fruit, oval, blue-black; also called **black gum** and **pepperidge**. (Family: Nyssaceae.)

Tupolev, Andrey Nikolayevich [toopolef] (1888–1972) Aircraft designer, born in Pustomezovo, Russia. He produced over 100 types of aircraft, including the first Soviet civil jet, the Tu-104 (1955), and in 1968 completed the first test flight of a supersonic passenger aircraft, the Tu-144.

Tupungato, Cerro [tupungahtoh] 33°22S 69°50W. Mountain on the border between Argentina and Chile, rising to 6800 m/22 309 ft.

tur *goat*

turaco [toorakoh] A large African bird; tail long; head usually with crest; also known as the **touraco**, **tauraco**, (in S Africa)

Turkey

☐ International Airport

Turkish **Türkiye**, official name **Republic of Turkey**, Turkish **Türkiye Cumhuriyeti**

Local name Türkiye Cumhuriyeti

Timezone GMT +2

Area 779 452 km²/300 868 sq mi

Population total (2002e) 69 359 000

Status Republic

Capital Ankara

Languages Turkish (Türkçe) (official), Kurdish and Arabic; Greek, Armenian, and Yiddish minorities

Ethnic groups Turkish (85%), Kurd (12%)

Religions Sunni Muslim (98%), Greek Orthodox, Armenian, and Jewish minorities

Physical features Lying partly in Europe and partly in Asia, W area (Thrace), E area (Anatolia); Turkish Straits (Dardanelles, Sea of Marmara, Bosporus) connect the Black Sea (NE) and Mediterranean Sea (SW); mountainous area, Taurus Mts, cover the entire S part of Anatolia; highest peak Mt Ararat, 5165 m/16 945 ft; earthquake region (major disasters in the NW, Aug and Nov 1999, E in May 2003); sources of rivers Euphrates and Tigris in E.

Climate Mediterranean climate on Aegean and Mediterranean coasts, with hot, dry summers, warm, wet winters; mean temperature 19°C (Jul); average annual temperatures 0·3°C (Jan), 23°C (Jul) in Ankara; average annual rainfall 723 mm/28 in.

Currency 1 New Turkish Lira (YTL) = 100 new kurus (before 2005, Turkish Lira (TRL))

Economy Agriculture (employs c.50% of workforce); cotton, tobacco, fruits, nuts, livestock; minerals, textiles, glass, and cement; many Turks find work elsewhere in Europe, especially Germany.

GDP (2002e) $489·7 bn, per capita $7300

Human Development Index (2002) 0·742

History Seljuk sultanate replaced by the Ottoman in NW Asia Minor in 13th-c; Turkish invasion of Europe, first in Balkans, 1375; fall of Constantinople, 1453; empire at its peak under Sulaiman the Magnificent, 16th-c; Young Turks seized power, 1908; Balkan War, 1912–13; allied with Germany during World War 1; Republic followed Young Turk revolution, led by Kemal Atatürk, 1923; policy of westernization and economic development; neutral throughout most of World War 2, then sided with Allies; military coups in 1960 and 1980; strained relations with Greece, and invasion of Cyprus, 1974; aided the allied forces during the Gulf War, 1991; constitution provides for a single-chamber National Assembly; a President appoints a Prime Minister and a Council of Ministers.

Head of State
1982–9 Kenan Evren
1989–93 Turgut Özal
1993–2000 Süleyman Demirel
2000– Ahmet Necdet Sezer

Head of Government
1980–3 Bülent Ulusu
1983–9 Turgut Özal
1989–91 Yildirim Akbulut
1991 Mesut Yilmaz
1991–3 Süleyman Demirel
1993–6 Tansu Çiller
1996 Mesut Yilmaz
1996–7 Necmettin Erbakan
1997–9 Mesut Yilmaz
1999–2002 Bulent Ecevit
2002–3 Abdullah Gul *Acting*
2003– Recep Tayyip Erdogan

---

lourie or **loerie**, and (in W Africa) **plantain-eater**. (Family: Musophagidae, 24 species.)

turbine A balanced wheel having at its rim a large number of small radiating blades of aerofoil cross section. When an axial flow of fluid is made to pass over the blades, the turbine rotates about its shaft. If the fluid is steam, the engine is called a **steam turbine**; if water, a **water turbine**. In a **turbo-jet** aircraft, the thrust is derived directly from the rearward expulsion of exhaust gases. In a **turbo-prop** aircraft, the exhaust gases drive a turbine fixed to a propeller.

turbo-jet; turbo-prop *turbine*

turbot European flatfish (*Scophthalmus maximus*) widespread on gravel bottoms of inshore waters of the E North Atlantic; length up to 1 m/3¼ ft; light brown with darker spots and patches. (Family: Scophthalmidae.)

Turenne, Henri de la Tour d'Auvergne, vicomte de (Viscount of) [türen] (1611–75) French marshal, born in Sedan, France. In the Thirty Years' War he fought with distinction for the armies of the Protestant alliance. In the Franco-Spanish war he conquered much of the Spanish Netherlands after defeating Condé at the Battle of the Dunes (1658), and won fame for his campaigns in the United Provinces during the Dutch War (1672–5).

Turgenev, Ivan (Sergeyevich) [toorgyaynyef] (1818–83) Novelist, born in Orel, Russia. His greatest novel, *Fathers and Sons* (1862), was badly received in Russia, but a particular success in England. He also wrote poetry, plays, short stories, and tales of the supernatural.

Turgot, Anne Robert Jacques [toorgoh] (1727–81) French statesman and economist, born in Paris. Appointed comptroller-general of finance by Louis XVI (1774), he embarked on a comprehensive scheme of national economic reform, but the opposition of the privileged classes to his Six Edicts led to his overthrow (1776), and his reforms were abandoned.

Turkmenistan

☐ International Airport

[terkmenistahn], official name **Republic of Turkmenistan**, formerly **Turkmenia**, Turkmen **Türkmenistan Jumhuriyäti**

Local name Turkmenostan

Timezone GMT +5

Area 488 100 km²/188 400 sq mi

Population total (2002e) 4 946 000

Status Republic

Date of independence 1991

Capital Ashkhabad (Ashgabad)

Languages Turkmenian (official), other Turkic languages, Russian

Ethnic groups Turkmen (72%), Russian (10%), Uzbek, Kazakh, Ukrainian minorities

Religion Sunni Muslim

Physical features Kara Kum (Black Sands) desert, area 310 800 km²/120 000 sq mi, covers c.80% of the country; Turan Plain covers four-fifths of Turkmenistan; foothills in the S; Kopet Dag mountain range is volcanic; other foothills are spurs of the Kugitangtau and Pamir-Alay ranges; Rivers Amu Darya and Murghab.

Climate Continental, great variation of temperatures; temperatures range from 50°C (Jul) in Kara Kum, to -33°C (Jan) in the Kushka; in the mountains; average annual rainfall 120–250 mm/5–10 in.

Currency 1 Manat (TMM) = 100 gapik

Economy Mineral resources of oil, natural gas, sulphur, potassium, and salt; oil, gas extraction (main industries); textiles; cotton production; agriculture; raising of Karakul sheep, Turkoman horses, and camels.

GDP (2002e) $31·34 bn, per capita $6700

Human Development Index (2002) 0·741

History Part of the ancient Persian empire; ruled by Seljuk Turks, 11th-c; conquered by Genghis Khan and the Mongols, 13th-c; Uzbeks invaded, 15th-c; divided into two: one part belonged to the Khanate of Khiva (which became part of the Russian empire), and the other to the Khanate of Bukhara; Turkistan Autonomous Soviet Socialist Republic formed, 1922; full Soviet Socialist Republic, 1924; declared sovereignty, 1990; independence and membership of Commonwealth of Independent States, 1991; governed by a President, who is both head of state and government, and parliament (*Majlis*); in 1999 parliament made Saparmurad Niyazov (president since 1991) president-for-life, but in 2005 he called for contested presidential elections to be held in 2009; following his sudden death (Dec 2006), Kurbanguly Berdymukhamedov was elected president (Feb 2007).

Head of State/Government

1991–2006 Saparmurad Niyazov

2006– Kurbanguly Berdymukhamedov

Turin [tyoorin], Ital **Torino**, ancient **Augusta Taurinorum** 45°04N 7°40E, pop (2000e) 991 000. City in Piedmont, NW Italy, on left bank of R Po; Roman colony under Augustus; capital of Kingdom of Sardinia, 1720; centre of the 19th-c Risorgimento; first capital of the Kingdom of Italy until 1865; airport; railway; archbishopric; university (1404); cathedral (15th-c).

Turin, Shroud of Holy Shroud

Turing, Alan (Mathison) [tooring] (1912–54) Mathematician, born in London. He provided a mathematical characterization of computability, and introduced the theoretical notion of an idealized computer (since called a **Turing machine**), laying the foundation for the field of artificial intelligence.

Turkana, Lake [toorkahna], formerly **Lake Rudolf** (to 1979) area 6405 km²/2472 sq mi. Lake in NW Kenya and Ethiopia, E Africa; length 290 km/180 mi; width 56 km/35 mi; depth c.70 m/230 ft; lake is surrounded by extensive Plio-Pleistocene deposits covering the last 3–4 million years. Many important hominid fossils have been recovered.

Turkestan Historical area of C Asia occupying parts of modern Kazakhstan, Kyrgyzstan, Tajikistan, Turkmenistan, Uzbekistan, and Xinjiang, including the great trading centres of Samarkand and Tashkent. It was traversed by the E–W Silk Road, and was

thus of great economic importance to China, especially from the 2nd-c BC onwards.

Turkey p.953

turkey A large pheasant-like bird, native to C and S North America; head naked; male with pendulous fold of skin at base of bill, and prominent spur on each leg; plumage dark, mottled; a popular poultry bird, especially in the USA at Thanksgiving and the UK at Christmas. (Family: Meleagrididae, 2 species.)

Turkish Altaic

Turkmenistan see panel

Turks and Caicos Islands p.955

Turku [toorkoo], Swed **Åbo** 60°27N 22°15E, pop (2000e) 163 000. Seaport in SW Finland; on R Aurajoki; third largest city in Finland; established, 11th-c; capital of Finland until 1812; airport; railway; ferries to Sweden and Åland Is; two universities (Swedish 1918, Finnish 1920).

turmeric [termerik] A perennial native to India (*Curcuma longa*), related to ginger and East Indian arrowroot; flowers with a yellow lip, borne in a dense spike with white and pink bracts. It is cultivated for the fleshy, aromatic rhizomes, ground to provide the distinctive smell and colour of curry powder. It also produces a yellow dye. (Family: Zingiberaceae.)

Turks and Caicos Islands

[kaykos] Timezone GMT -5

Area 500 km²/200 sq mi

Population total (2002e) 21 000

Capital Cockburn Town

Physical features Two island groups comprising c.30 islands and cays, forming the SE archipelago of the Bahamas chain, W Atlantic Ocean; Turk I and Caicos I are separated by 35 km/ 22 mi; only 6 of the other islands are inhabited.

Climate Subtropical climate; average annual temperatures 24– 7°C (Jan), 29–32°C (Jul); average annual rainfall 525 mm/21 in; occasional hurricanes.

Currency 1 US Dollar (USD) = 100 cents

Economy Tourism is a rapidly expanding industry; corn, beans, fishing, fish processing.

GDP (2000e) $231 mn, per capita $9600

History Visited by the Spanish, 1512; linked formally to the Bahamas, 1765; transferred to Jamaica, 1848; British Crown Colony, 1972; internal self-government, 1976; British sovereign represented by a Governor, who presides over a Council.

Turnbull, Malcolm (Bligh) (1954–) Merchant banker, lawyer, and republican, born in Sydney, New South Wales, Australia. He became known for successfully defending Peter Wright in the *Spycatcher* trial. In 1993 he was appointed chairman of the Republic Advisory Committee.

Turner, J(oseph) M(allord) W(illiam) (1775–1851) Landscape artist and watercolourist, born in London. He spent three years in collaboration with Girtin producing watercolours. He then took to oils, his early works including 'Frosty Morning' (1813) and 'Crossing the Brook' (1815). Later works include 'The Fighting Téméraire' (1839) and 'Rain, Steam and Speed' (1844), both in the National Gallery, London, and 'The Blue Rigi' (1842, Tate, London).

Turner, Kathleen (1954–) Actress, born in Springfield, MO. She made her film debut in *Body Heat* (1981), and among later films are *Romancing the Stone* (1984), *Peggy Sue Got Married* (1986), and *Prince of Central Park* (2000). She provided the husky voice for Jessica Rabbit in the film *'Who Framed Roger Rabbit?* (1988). Her West End stage performances include *The Graduate* (2000)

and *Who's Afraid of Virginia Woolf?* (2006, Evening Standard Theatre Award for best actress).

Turner, Nat (1800–31) Slave insurrectionist, born in Southampton Co, VA. Leading a force of eight, he succeeded in killing 51 whites, but the revolt quickly collapsed. Captured after six weeks in hiding, he was hanged at Jerusalem, VA.

Turner, Tina, originally **Annie Mae Bullock** (1939–) Pop singer, born in Nutbush, TN. She achieved considerable success in the rhythm-and-blues vocal duo, Ike and Tina Turner, before their marriage and professional partnership ended in 1976. Her solo hits include 'Let's Stay Together' (1983) and 'Private Dancer' (1985), and she recorded the title song for the James Bond film *Goldeneye* (1996).

Turner Prize Britain's most prestigious prize for contemporary art, awarded to a British artist under 50 for an outstanding exhibition in the previous year. An initiative of the Tate Gallery, London, it was first awarded in 1984, and has since attracted considerable controversy for its choice of winners, regularly forcing a public debate on the question of 'Is it art?'.

turnip An annual or biennial vegetable (*Brassica rapa*), 1 m/3¼ ft high; yellow, cross-shaped flowers. The cultivated turnip (subspecies *rapa*) has an edible tuberous taproot, and is widely grown as a vegetable and for fodder. (Family: Cruciferae.)

turnkey system A method of acquiring a system of computer hardware and software as a whole from a single supplier. Buying a turnkey system removes the need for carrying out a full systems analysis and design exercise.

turnover tax A tax levied at several stages in the progression from materials to finished goods, or when certain services are provided. For example, a miller pays turnover tax on wheat from the farmer; the baker pays it on the flour; and the customer pays it on the bread.

turnpike A gate across a road to stop the passage of vehicles or persons until a toll is paid. The roads were known as **turnpike roads**, and were common during the 18th–19th-c.

turpentine tree A deciduous shrub or small tree (*Pistacia terebinthus*), growing to 10 m/30 ft, native to the Mediterranean region and SW Asia; flowers tiny; fruits coral-red; also called **terebinth**. It produces a resin which yields turpentine. (Family: Anacardiaceae.)

Turpin, Dick, popular name of **Richard Turpin** (1706–39) Robber, born in Hempstead, Essex. He was hanged at York for horse stealing. His legendary ride to York upon Black Bess belongs (if to anyone) to 'Swift John Nevison', who in 1676 is said to have robbed a sailor at Gadshill at 4 am, and to have established an 'alibi' by reaching York at 7.45 pm.

turquoise A hydrated aluminium phosphate mineral formed by the surface alteration of aluminium-rich rock, with bright-blue to green-blue masses or veins, opaque with a waxy lustre. It is valued as a semi-precious stone.

turtle (computing) An electromechanical computer drawing device. The precise movements of the turtle are sent to it by the computer. The device is normally associated with the computer programming language LOGO, used in elementary educational environments.

turtle (zoology) A reptile of order Chelonia; in the USA, includes all species; in the UK, only the marine species with the legs modified as paddles (**sea turtles**, 7 species in families Chelonidae and Dermochelyidae).

turtle-dove A dove native to Europe, W Asia, and N Africa (*Streptopelia turtur*); eye with dark ring; breast pink, wing feathers with reddish edges.

Tuscan order The simplest of the five main orders of classical architecture, probably derived from Etruscan-type temples. It closely resembles the Doric order, but with a plain base, shaft, and entablature.

Tuvalu

Religions Christian (Protestant Church of Tuvalu, Roman Catholic, Baha'i) (97%), small Muslim minority

Physical features Island group in the SW Pacific, 1050 km/650 mi off Fiji; comprises nine low-lying coral atolls, running NW–SE in a chain 580 km/360 mi long; consists of the islands of Funafuti, Nukufetau, Nukulaelae, Nanumea, Niutao, Nanumanga, Nui, Vaitupu, and Niulakita; all low-lying, highest point, 4·6 m/15 ft, on Niulakita.

Climate Hot, humid climate; average annual temperatures 29°C (Jan), 27°C (Jul) in Funafuti; average annual rainfall 3535 mm/139 in.

Currency 1 Australian Dollar (AUD) = 100 cents; also, a Tuvaluan Dollar (TVD)

Economy Subsistence economy; agriculture, coconuts, copra, tropical fruit; fish; handcrafted products, postage stamps.

GDP (2002e) $12·2 mn, per capita $1100

History Invaded by Samoans, 16th-c; British protectorate, as the Ellice Is, 1892; administered as a colony jointly with Gilbert Is (now Kiribati), 1915; American soldiers occupied the Ellice Islands during World War 2, to counter the advance of the Japanese in 1942; separate constitution, following 1974 referendum; independence as a constitutional monarchy within the Commonwealth, 1978; Tuvalu Trust Fund set up by Britain, Australia, New Zealand, and South Korea, 1987; British monarch represented by a Governor-General; governed by a Prime Minister, Cabinet, and unicameral Parliament.

Head of State
(British monarch represented by Governor-General)
1998–2003 Sir Tomasi Puapua
2003–5 Sir Faimala Luka
2005– Filoimea Telito

Head of Government
1999–2000 Ionatana Ionatana
2001 Lagitupu Tuilimu *acting*
2001 Faimalaga Luka
2001–2 Koloa Talake
2002–4 Saufatu Sopoanga
2004–6 Maati Toafa
2006– Apisai Ielemia

[toovaloo], formerly **Ellice Is** (to 1976)
Local name Tuvalu
Timezone GMT +12
Area 26 km²/10 sq mi
Population total (2002e) 10 900
Status Independent state within the Commonwealth
Date of independence 1978
Capital Funafuti (Fongafale)
Languages Tuvaluan, English
Ethnic group Polynesian (96%)

Tuscany, Ital **Toscana** pop (2000e) 3 596 000; area 22 989 km²/8874 sq mi. Region of NW Italy; capital, Florence; mountainous with fertile valleys; industry mainly in the Arno valley; important agricultural area; home of Chianti wine; tourism focused on traditional centres of art, notably Florence, Siena, Pisa.

Tuskeegee Institute US institution dedicated to black education. It was founded by Booker T Washington in 1881, and since then has specialized in vocational and technical education.

Tussaud, Marie [tuhsawd], Fr [tüsoh], *née* **Grosholtz** (1761–1850) Modeller in wax, born in Strasbourg, France. She toured Britain with her life-size portrait waxworks, and in 1835 set up a permanent exhibition in London. The exhibition still contains her own handiwork, notably Marie Antoinette, Napoleon, and Burke and Hare in the Chamber of Horrors.

Tutankhamen or **Tut'ankhamun** [tootankahmen, tootangkamoon] (14th-c BC) Egyptian pharaoh of the XVIIIth dynasty (1361–1352 BC), the son-in-law of Akhenaton. He came to the throne at the age of 12, and is famous only for his magnificent tomb at Thebes, which was discovered intact in 1922 by Lord Carnarvon and Howard Carter.

Tuthmosis *Thutmose III*

Tutsi *Hutu and Tutsi*

Tutu, Desmond (Mpilo) (1931–) Anglican clergyman, born in Klerksdorp, South Africa. He became Bishop of Lesotho (1977), Bishop of Johannesburg (1984), and Archbishop of Cape Town (1986), retiring in 1996. A fierce critic of the apartheid system, he advocated international sanctions against South Africa, but condemned the use of violence by its opponents. He was awarded the Nobel Peace Prize in 1984, and was appointed chair of the Truth and Reconciliation Commission in 1995.

Tutuola, Amos [tutwohla] (1920–97) Novelist, born in Abeokuta, Nigeria. He was celebrated in the West as the author of *The Palm-Wine Drinkard* (1952), a transcription in pidgin English prose of an oral tale of his own invention.

Tuvalu *see panel*

Twain, Mark, pseudonym of **Samuel Langhorne Clemens** (1835–1910) Writer, born in Florida, MO. *The Innocents Abroad* (1869) established his reputation as a humorist. His two masterpieces, *Tom Sawyer* (1876) and *Huckleberry Finn* (1884), drawn from his own boyhood experiences, are firmly established among the world's classics. Widely known as a lecturer, he developed a great popular following.

twayblade An orchid (*Listera ovata*) native to cool and arctic regions of Europe and Asia; flowers green with a yellowish 2-lobed lip. Any insect visiting the flower triggers an explosion of sticky liquid which glues the pollen grains to the insect's head. (Family: Orchidaceae.)

Tweed, River River in SE Scotland and NE England; rises at Tweed's Well; enters the North Sea at Berwick-upon-Tweed; length, 155 km/96 mi.

tweed A coarse, heavy, wool, outerwear fabric, first made in S Scotland, manufactured in several distinctive weave patterns. Often mistakenly associated with the R Tweed, the name originates from *tweel*, a Scottish word for twill fabrics.

Tweed Ring US 19th-c political scandal. Led by William Magear 'Boss' Tweed (1823–78), the ring ruled New York City in the 1860s and 1870s. Its headquarters, Tammany Hall, became synonymous with urban corruption.

Twelfth Night The evening of 5 January, the last evening of the 12 days of the traditional Christmas festival. It was formerly marked by particularly boisterous and anarchic festivities before the return to sober normality on **Twelfth Day** (Epiphany, 6 Jan).

Twelve, the *apostle*

twelve-tone music Music based on the 12 notes of the chromatic scale arranged in a predetermined order.

Twickenham Rugby Union football ground in W London, UK. Opened in 1910, it has been the venue for almost all England internationals since then, as well as for the Rugby Football Union (RFU) Cup Final since 1972. Capacity: 78 000.

Twiggy, professional name of **Lesley Lawson**, *née* **Hornby** (1949–) Fashion model, actress, and singer, born in London. A modelling superstar almost overnight at the age of 17, she was a symbol of the 'swinging sixties' in London's Carnaby Street. Her films include *The Boy Friend* (1971) and *Blues Brothers* (1981).

twilight The interval of time shortly after sunset or just before sunrise. **Civil twilight** begins or ends when the Sun is 6° below the local horizon; **nautical twilight** 12° below the horizon; and **astronomical twilight** 18° below the horizon.

twill A type of woven fabric characterized by a pattern of diagonal lines. Many variations are possible, such as *herringbone* twills, where the pattern zigzags across the cloth. Twill weaves produce strong, hard-wearing fabrics, often employed in sports and work-wear situations.

twinning The linking of two towns or cities in different countries, so that they may have a 'special relationship' and foster cultural exchanges. For example, Edinburgh is twinned with Munich, Nice, Florence, Dunedin, Kiev, San Diego, Vancouver, Xian, and Aalborg.

twins A pair of offspring produced at the same birth. **Fraternal** (or *dizygotic*) twins are derived from two separate fertilized eggs. **Identical** (or *monozygotic*) twins are derived from a single fertilized egg, and are thus genetically identical.

twist The winding together of fibres, which gives added strength to yarns. The twist level affects other factors than strength, including stretch and softness.

twitch grass *couch grass*

two-stroke engine A practical engine cycle with one in two strokes of the piston being the power stroke. This type of engine is frequently used to drive light motorcycles.

Tyan Shan *Tian Shan*

Tyche [tiykee, tiykay] The Greek goddess of chance or luck, prominent in the Hellenistic period. She is usually depicted as blind.

Tyler, John (1790–1862) US statesman and 10th president (1841–5), born in Charles City Co, VA. He became president on the death of Harrison, only a month after his inauguration. His administration was marked by the annexation of Texas.

Tyler, Liv, originally **Liv Rundgren** (1977–) Actress, born in New York City. At age 14 she began a modelling career but later turned to acting. Her film debut was in *Silent Fall* (1994), and later work includes *Stealing Beauty* (1996), *Cookie's Fortune* (1999), *The Lord of the Rings* trilogy (2001–3), and *Reign Over Me* (2007).

Tyler, Wat (?–1381) English leader of the Peasants' Revolt (1381). The rebels of Kent, after taking Rochester Castle, chose him as captain, and marched to London. The Mayor of London, William Walworth, had him beheaded.

Tynan, Kenneth [tiynan] (1927–80) Theatre critic, born in Birmingham, West Midlands. He was drama critic for several publications, notably *The Observer* (1954–63), literary manager of the National Theatre (1963–9), and writer of the controversial revue *Oh! Calcutta* (1969).

Tyndale or **Tindale, William** [tindayl] (?–1536) Translator of the Bible, probably born in Slymbridge in Gloucestershire. He completed his translation of the New Testament into English in Cologne in 1525. In 1531 he went to Antwerp, where he continued to work on an Old Testament translation, but was accused of heresy, and executed.

Tyne, River [tiyn] River of NE England; formed by confluence of North Tyne and South Tyne; flows 48 km/30 mi E to meet the North Sea; South Tyne rises on Cross Fell, E Cumbria; North Tyne rises in the Cheviot Hills, and is dammed to form Kielder Water reservoir.

Tyne and Wear [weer] pop (2001e) 1 076 000; area 540 km²/208 sq mi. County of NE England, created in 1974; administrative centre, Newcastle upon Tyne; a highly industrialized area; now designated a special development area, with considerable diversification of industries; metropolitan council abolished in 1986.

Tyneside Urban area in NE England; towns include Newcastle upon Tyne, Gateshead, Jarrow, Wallsend, and North and South Shields; airport; railway; The Baltic, a centre for contemporary art, opened in Gateshead, 2002; Sage Gateshead concert venue opened on R Tyne quayside, 2004.

typewriter A hand-operated machine for producing printed letters and other symbols on paper. Traditionally, characters mounted on rods are made to hit an inked ribbon against paper by pressing on keys; the paper is automatically moved when a key is struck. The machine was invented by Christopher Sholes in 1867, and developed by the Remington firm soon after. Later developments include electric typewriters, in which the keys need only to be touched; the 'golf-ball' typewriter, using replaceable spheres with additional symbols and typefaces; and electronic typewriters, with memory, screen, fast printing, and many of the editing and storage features of word processors.

typhoid fever An infectious disease caused by *Salmonella typhi*, also known as **enteric fever**. It is acquired by ingesting food or liquids contaminated with faeces from an infected person, and is often spread in water supplies or during food preparation. Clinical features include a high fever, drowsiness, aches, diarrhoea, and an abdominal rash, progressing to delirium and coma. Immunization is desirable for people travelling to areas of the world, such as the Indian subcontinent, where the infection is endemic.

typhoon *hurricane*

typhus Any of several illnesses caused by infection with a strain of *Rickettsia*, carried by lice, fleas, and ticks; also known as **spotted fever**. A specific serological test, the Weil–Felix reaction, is the basis of diagnosis. The infections respond to the appropriate antibiotic.

typography The design of letterforms for use as typefaces, and the selection of typefaces for typeset documents. Typefaces are designed and used for a multitude of purposes (eg books, newspapers, handbills) and for use on various kinds of typesetting equipment, in both print and non-print media (such as film and television). Typefaces are chosen for their appeal, appropriateness, and legibility, and vary immensely in their appearance. They can be divided into two major classes: the *serif* faces, with short cross-strokes at the ends of the letters (eg Times), and the *sans-serif* faces, which lack these cross-strokes (eg Helvetica). Times New Roman, designed by Stanley Morrison in 1932 for the redesigned *Times* newspaper, has been called the most important type design of the 20th-c.

tyramine [tiyramin] A chemical compound derived from the amino acid tyrosine, which occurs in foods such as cheese and wine, sometimes in large quantities. Migraine headaches may be associated with excess amine production aggravated by a high intake of tyramine.

Tyrannosaurus rex [tiranosawrus reks] The largest terrestrial flesh-eating animal of all time; known from the Cretaceous period; a dinosaur reaching 12 m/40 ft in length; skull massive with short, deep jaws bearing dagger-like teeth; tail heavy and muscular; forelimbs tiny; slow-moving, with a top speed of about 4 kph/2½ mph. (Order: Saurischia.)

tyrant In Greek city-states of the 7th-c and 6th-c BC, a neutral term describing an absolute ruler who had seized power illegally. Only later (5th-c BC) did it acquire its present meaning – a cruel and oppressive ruler.

Tyre [tiyr], Arabic **Sour** 33°12N 35°11E, pop (2000e) 17 500. Mediterranean fishing port, SW Lebanon; railway; ancient city was the most important commercial centre in the E Mediterranean, noted for silk, glass, and Tyrean purple dye; several Roman remains; a world heritage site.

tyre / tire A circular cushion fixed to the rim of a wheel, which absorbs variations in the road surface, so providing an easier ride to the vehicle. Most tyres are *pneumatic*, being flexible tubes stiffened by high-pressure air, and are made of a combination of rubber compounded with other chemicals and fabric, usually nylon or polyester. The inventor of the pneumatic tyre was Robert William Thomson, who patented a design for application to coaches in 1845.

Tyrol *Tirol*

Tyrone [tiyrohn], Ir **Tir Eoghain** pop (2000e) 166 700; area 3136 km²/1210 sq mi. County in W Northern Ireland; hilly, with the Sperrin Mts rising (N) to 683 m/2241 ft at Mt Sawel; county town, Omagh.

Tyrrhenian Sea [tiyreenian] Arm of the Mediterranean Sea; bounded by the Italian Peninsula, Sicily, Sardinia, and Corsica.

Tyson, Mike, popular name of **Michael (Gerald) Tyson** (1966–) Boxer, born in New York City. He beat Trevor Berbick (1952–2006) for the World Boxing Council version of the world heavyweight title in 1987, when he beat James Smith (1954–). Later that year he became the first undisputed champion since 1978, when he beat Tony Tucker (1958–). He won 41 of 42 decisions before losing the title in 1990. He was later convicted of rape, and jailed (1992–5). He regained the WBC heavyweight title in 1996 but vacated it soon afterwards. In 2002 he unsuccessfully fought Lennox Lewis for the heavyweight title.

Tyumen [tyoomayn] 57°11N 65°29E, pop (2000e) 493 000. City in SW Siberian Russia, on R Tura; founded, 1585; formerly an important centre of trade with China; railway junction; university.

Tzu-po *Zibo*

U and non-U Terms coined by English linguist Alan Ross (1907–80) in an effort to capture the essentials of class-based variation in English usage. The features claimed to mark **upper-class** (U) and **non-upper-class** (non-U) usage are most noticeable in vocabulary, such as U *luncheon* and *pudding*, for non-U *dinner* and *sweet*.

Ubangi, River [oobanggee], Fr **Oubangui** Major tributary of R Congo, in N and WC Africa; length, including longest headstream (R Uele), 2250 km/1400 mi.

U-boat An abbreviation of *Unterseeboat* (Ger 'submarine'). The German Navy launched large-scale submarine offensives in both World Wars.

Ucayali, River [ookiyalee] River in E Peru; one of the Amazon's main headstreams; length c.1600 km/1000 mi.

Uccello, Paolo [oocheloh], originally **Paolo di Dono** (1397–1475) Painter, born in Pratovecchio, Italy. He applied the principles of perspective to his paintings, such as in 'The Flood' (1447–8, Florence), where his use of foreshortening gives a sternly realistic effect.

ud [ood] An Arabian lute, known since the 7th-c, with usually five courses of strings, played with a plectrum or with the fingers of both hands. It is the ancestor of the European lute.

udad *aoudad*

Udall, Nicholas [yoodal] (1504–56) Playwright, born in Southampton, Hampshire. He is chiefly remembered as the attributed author of the first major verse comedy in English, *Ralph Roister Doister* (c.1553, printed 1566).

Udine [oodeenay] 46°04N 13°14E, pop (2000e) 101000. Industrial town in NE Italy; suffered severe bombing in World War 2; archbishopric; railway; castle (16th-c), cathedral.

UEFA (Union of European Football Associations) [yooayfa] A football organization founded in 1954, which in 2007 consisted of 53 member associations. It is responsible for organizing the three major European club tournaments: the Champions' Cup, the Cup Winners' Cup, and the UEFA Cup. They also run their own European Championship.

Ufa [oofa] 54°45N 55°58E, pop (2000e) 1092000. City in E European Russia; in the Ural Mts, on the R Ufa; founded as a fortress, 1586; airport; railway; university (1957).

Uffizi [oofeetsee] A museum in Florence, Italy, housing one of the world's greatest collections of works by Italian masters. The Renaissance palace, designed by Vasari in 1560, was opened to the public in the 17th-c.

Uganda *p.960*

Uganda Martyrs A group of 22 African youths, converted to Roman Catholicism, killed for their faith in Uganda between 1885 and 1887. They were canonized in 1964.

Ugarit [oogareet] A flourishing Canaanite city on the coast of N Syria, which in the late Bronze Age (c.1450–1200 BC) enjoyed wide contacts with the Egyptians, the Hittites, and the Mycenaeans. It was destroyed by the Sea Peoples c.1200 BC.

UHT milk An abbreviation of **ultra-high-temperature milk**; milk heated to a temperature of 132°C for one second, and subsequently packed in an airtight container. It will then have a shelf-life of six months at room temperature.

Uighurs [weegoorz] One of China's national minorities, mostly settled in Xinjiang. They are a people of Turkic origin who emerged as an independent force in the 7th-c. They were brought into the Chinese empire in the 18th-c.

Ujung Pandang [oojoong pandang], formerly **Makassar** or **Macassar** (to 1973) 5°09S 119°28E, pop (2000e) 1108000. Seaport in Indonesia; in SW corner of Sulawesi I; important trade centre, established by the Dutch in 1607; free port, 1848; airfield; university (1956).

UK Athletics The governing body for athletics in England and Wales founded in 1998 to replace the British Athletic Federation, which went into liquidation. Ex-athlete David Moorcroft became its first chief executive.

ukiyo-e [ookeeyoh ay] (Jap 'pictures of the floating world') In Japanese painting and printmaking, a movement that flourished in the 16th–19th-c. Favourite themes included theatrical subjects, actors, prostitutes, and landscapes.

Ukraine *p.961*

ukulele [yookuhlaylee] A Hawaiian musical instrument, resembling a small guitar, with four gut or nylon strings that are strummed with the fingernails and fingertips. Since the 1920s it has been a favourite instrument for popular music in the USA.

Ulaanbaatar [oolahn bahtaw(r)], formerly **Ulan Bator**, **Urga** (to 1924) 47°54N 106°52E, pop (2000e) 674000. Capital of Mongolia; founded as Urga in 1639, centre of Lamaistic religion in Mongolia; trading centre on caravan routes between Russia and China, 18th-c; capital, 1921; university (1942).

Ulanova, Galina Sergeyevna [oolahnova] (1910–98) Ballerina, born in St Petersburg, Russia. She became the leading ballerina of the Soviet Union and was four times a Stalin prizewinner.

Ulan-Ude [oolan ooday], formerly **Verkhneudinsk** (to 1934) 51°45N 107°40E, pop (2000e) 358000. City in SE Siberian Russia; on R Selenga; founded, 1666; airfield; railway junction; cathedral (1741–85).

Ulbricht, Walter (Ernst Karl) [ulbrikht] (1893–1973) East German statesman, born in Leipzig, Germany. In 1945 he became deputy premier of the German Democratic Republic and general secretary of the Communist Party in 1950. He was largely responsible for the 'sovietization' of East Germany, and built the Berlin wall in 1961.

ulcer A break in the surface of the skin or mucous membrane, which may be acute in onset and short-lived or persistent. They may be caused by trauma (physical or chemical), infection, inadequate blood supply, or auto-immune disease. Ulcers may also occur in the mouth and gastro-intestinal tract.

Uleåborg *Oulu*

Ulfilas or **Wulfila** [ulfilas, wulfila] (c.311–83) Gothic missionary bishop. He devised the Gothic alphabet, and carried out the first translation of the Bible into a Germanic language (c.350).

Ullapool [uhlapool] 57°54N 5°10W, pop (2000e) 1360. Port town

Uganda

☐ International Airport

[yooganda], official name **Republic of Uganda**
Local name Uganda (Swahili)
Timezone GMT +3
Area 241 038 km²/93 040 sq mi
Population total (2002e) 24 378 000
Status Republic
Date of independence 1962
Capital Kampala

Languages English (official), Swahili, Luganda (Ganda), Ateso, and Luo are also spoken

Ethnic groups Bantu, with Nilotic and Hamitic minorities

Religions Christian (66%) (Roman Catholic 33%, Protestant 33%), traditional animist beliefs (18%), Muslim (6%)

Physical features Landlocked country in E Africa, mainly plateau, height 1200 m/4000 ft; dry savannah or semi-desert in the N; fertile L Victoria basin; highest point in Uganda and Zaïre, Margherita Peak, 5110 m/16 765 ft; main lakes, Victoria (SE), George and Edward (SW), Albert (W), Kwania and Kyoga (C), Bisina (formerly L Salisbury) (E); main rivers are the upper reaches of R Nile, the Victoria Nile, and the Albert Nile.

Climate Tropical climate; temperatures rarely rise above 29°C, or fall below 15°C (S); average annual temperature 23°C (Jan), 21°C (Jul); average annual rainfall 1150 mm/45 in.

Currency 1 Uganda Shilling (UGX) = 100 cents

Economy Agriculture; coffee (over 90% of exports), tea, sugar, cotton; bananas, plantains, cassavas, potatoes, sweet potatoes, maize, sorghum.

GDP (2002e) $30·49 bn, per capita $1200

Human Development Index (2002) 0·444

History Visited by Arab traders, 1840s; explored by Speke, 1860s; granted to the British East Africa Company, 1888; Kingdom of Buganda became a British protectorate, 1893; other territory included by 1903; independence, 1962; Dr Milton Obote assumed all powers, 1966; coup led by General Idi Amin Dada, 1971; Amin's regime overthrown, 1979; further coup in 1985, overthrew Obote; National Resistance Movement captured Kampala, 1986, and Museveni became president; elections to Constituent Assembly, 1994; new constitution, 1995; peace deal signed (Dec 2002) between government and the rebel Uganda National Rescue Front (UNRF II); President Museveni elected for third term (Feb 2006) in country's first multi-party elections for 26 years.

Head of State
1979–80 Godfrey Lukongwa Binaisa
1981–5 (Apollo) Milton Obote
1985–6 *Military Council* (Tito Okello Lutwa)
1986– Yoweri Kaguta Museveni

Head of Government
1985 Paulo Muwanga
1985–6 Abraham N Waliggo
1986–91 Samson B Kisekka
1991–4 George Cosmas Adyebo
1994–9 Kintu Musoke
1999– Apolo Nsimbabi

in Highland, NW Scotland; ferry service to Stornoway, I of Lewis; tourist resort.

Ullswater Second largest lake in England; length 12 km/7 mi; width 1 km/³/₄ mi; depth 64 m/210 ft.

Ulm [oolm] 48°24N 10°00E, pop (2000e) 114 000. Industrial and commercial city in Germany; on R Danube; scene of Napoleon's defeat of Austria, 1805; railway; university (1967); birthplace of Einstein; Gothic Minster (1377–1529), with the world's highest spire (161 m/528 ft).

ulna *arm*

Ulster [uhlster] One of the four ancient provinces of Ireland; comprising counties of Cavan, Donegal, and Monaghan in the republic of Ireland, and Antrim, Armagh, Down, Fermanagh, Londonderry, and Tyrone forming Northern Ireland, often referred to separately as Ulster (*see separate entry*); Donegal separated by part of Connacht, lying W of Northern Ireland; Cavan and Monaghan lie to the S of Northern Ireland; land

distributed to Protestant English and Scots settlers in the 17th-c; partitioned in 1921 into the present-day division.

Ulster Plantation The settlement of English and Scottish Protestants in Ulster during the reign of James I (ruled 1603–25); the direct cause of three centuries of conflict between the North and the South, Catholics and Protestants, and Ireland and England. Henry VIII put down a rebellion (1534–7), confiscated land, and established a Protestant 'Church of Ireland' (1537). The Irish rebelled three times during the reign of Elizabeth I and were brutally suppressed. Under James I, Ulster was settled by thousands of English and Scottish Protestants, and many of the Catholic Irish were driven off their lands. The policy led to rebellions by the native Irish and the Anglo-Irish aristocracy (1563–9, 1580–3, 1598–1603). A rebellion, begun in 1641, was crushed (1649–50) by Oliver Cromwell, in which possibly two-thirds of the Irish Catholics died. More land was confiscated, often given to absentee landlords, and more Protestants

Ukraine

□ International Airport

[yookrayn], official name **Republic of Ukraine**, Ukrainian **Ukrayina**

Local name Ukraina

Timezone GMT +2

Area 603 700 km²/233 028 sq mi

Population total (2002e) 48 120 000

Status Republic

Date of independence 1991

Capital Kiev

Languages Ukrainian (official), Russian

Ethnic groups Ukrainian (73%), Russian (22%), Moldovan, Bulgarian, and Polish minorities

Religions Orthodox (Autocephalous and Russian) (76%), Roman Catholic (14%), Jewish (2%), Baptist, Mennonite, Protestant, and Muslim (8%)

Physical features Most fertile area of former USSR, consisting largely of black soil steppes, forming a substantial part of the East European Plain; borders the Black Sea and Sea of Azov (S); Carpathian Mts, 2061 m/6762 ft at Mt Goverla (SW); Crimean Mts

(S); main rivers, Dnepr, Yuzhny, Bug; Donets coalfield, area 25 900 km²/10 000 sq mi.

Climate Moderate, mild winters, hot summers (SW); average annual temperatures -3°C (Jan), 23°C (Jul); average annual rainfall in Crimea 400–610 mm/16–24 in.

Currency 1 Hryvna (UAH) = 100 kopijka

Economy Important industrial bases for iron and steel manufacture, chemical and engineering bases; ship-building on Black Sea; agriculture (was the USSR's major wheat producer); wheat, corn, rye, potatoes, cotton, flax, sugar beet; coal and salt deposits in Donets basin.

GDP (2002e) $218 bn, per capita $4500

Human Development Index (2002) 0·748

History Conquered by Mongols, 1240; dominated by Poland, 13–16th-c; applied to Moscow for help fighting Poland in return for sovereignty, 1654; declared independence from Russia in 1918, after Russian Revolution; became a member of the USSR, 1922; suffered devastation during World War 2; Chernobyl the site of the world's worst nuclear accident, 1986; declared independence, 1991; ongoing disputes with Russia over control of the Black Sea Fleet and status of the Crimea; introduction of border controls and new currency, 1993, in contravention of CIS agreements; new constitution, 1996; governed by a President and Supreme Council; Viktor Yanukovych elected president (Nov 2004) amid allegations of vote-rigging; mass public protest in Kiev supporting opposition leader Viktor Yushchenko; poll result suspended by Ukraine's Supreme Court; Yushchenko won poll re-run (Dec 2004), gaining 52% of vote; Yanukovych approved as prime minister (Aug 2006).

Head of State

1991–4 Leonid M Kravchuk
1994–2004 Leonid Kuchma
2004– Viktor Yushchenko

Head of Government

1990–2 Vitold P Fokin
1992–3 Leonid Kuchma
1993 Yukhim Zvagilsky
1994–5 Vitalii Masol
1995–6 Yevhenii Marchuk
1996–7 Pavlo Lazarenko
1997 Vasyl Durdynets
1997–9 Valery Pustovoytenko
1999–2001 Viktor Yushchenko
2001–2 Anatoly Kinakh
2002–4 Viktor Yanukovich
2004–5 Mykola Azarov *Acting*
2005 Yulia Tymoshenko
2005–6 Yuri Yekhanurov
2006– Viktor Yanukovych

settled in Ireland. Successive generations of Ulster Protestants have wanted to remain part of Britain. Ulster Roman Catholics constitute two-fifths of the population and, along with many in the Republic, oppose partition.

Ultra A British security classification (the very highest) given during World War 2 to intelligence gathered from the breaking of the key German military codes used with their 'Enigma' encryption device. 'Ultra' intelligence was available to the British high command from the outset of the war.

Ultramontanism [uhltramontaynizm] Literally, 'beyond the mountains'; a movement, deriving from France, asserting the centralization of the authority and power of the Roman Catholic Church in Rome and the pope. It reached its high point with

the First Vatican Council (1870) and the declaration of papal infallibility.

ultrasound Sound of a frequency greater than 20 000 Hz; inaudible to humans, but certain animals such as dogs and bats can hear some ultrasonic signals. Pulses of very high frequency sound are reflected back to different extents by different materials. If such a 'sonar' device is connected to a computer, accurate representations of the structure of the material can be made. Ultrasound is widely used in medical scanning (eg in the examination of a fetus) and also in engineering (eg detecting cracks in railway lines).

ultraviolet astronomy The detection and analysis of radiation from celestial sources in the wavelength range 50–320 nm.

The hottest stars emit most of their radiation in this waveband, which is accessible only from rockets and satellites.

ultraviolet radiation Electromagnetic radiation of wavelength a little shorter than visible light, between 3.9×10^{-7} m and 10^{-8} m; discovered in 1801 by German physicist Johann Ritter (1776–1810). Invisible to the naked eye, it is produced by electron transitions in atoms, such as in mercury discharge lamps.

Uluru [oolooroo] National park in Northern Territory, C Australia; area c.1325 km²/500 sq mi; an area of cultural and religious significance to the Aboriginal people; a world heritage site.

Ulvaeus, Björn *Abba*

Ulysses *Odysseus*

Ulysses project A joint ESA–NASA space exploration mission, launched in 1990, to observe the Sun and solar wind from a high solar latitude perspective. It requires the spacecraft to fly on a trajectory which passes over the poles of the Sun, using a boost from Jupiter's gravity field.

U-matic The trade name for the first helical-scan videotape cassette recorder introduced by Sony in 1970, initially for the professional non-broadcast market. It used ¾-in (19 mm) tape at a speed of 9.53 cm/3¾ in per second in a large cassette with a playing time of up to 1 hour.

Umayyad Mosque [umiyad] The great mosque at Damascus in Syria, built (705–15) on the site of a Christian church to John the Baptist, and believed to incorporate the reliquary shrine of the saint's head.

Umayyads [umiyadz] A family of the Quraish tribe, beginning with Mu'awiya ibn Abi-Sufyan (c.605–80), successor to Ali, and ending with Marwan, who was beheaded in 750. The Umayyads originally ruled from Damascus, but when Marwan was killed the whole family perished with him except the grandson of Hisham, Abd-ar-Rahman, who escaped to Spain and founded the Spanish dynasty at Córdoba in 755, routing the Goths. The Umayyads of Spain reached their zenith in the reign of Abd-ar-Rahman III (912–61).

umbel A type of inflorescence, typical of the carrot family Umbelliferae, in which all the flower-stalks arise from the top of the stem, the outermost stalks longest, giving a flat-topped, umbrella-shaped cluster of flowers.

Umberto II [umbairtoh] (1904–83) Last king of Italy (1946), born in Racconigi, Italy. He succeeded to the throne after the abdication of his father, Victor Emmanuel III, but himself abdicated a month later, after a national referendum had declared for a republic. In 1947 he and his descendants were banished from Italy.

umbilical cord A solid flexible cord which connects the developing fetus of some mammals (eg humans and dogs) to the placenta within the uterus. The average length in humans is 60 cm/24 in. It allows the fetus to float freely in the fluid of the uterus (the *amniotic cavity*) and to obtain nutrition from the placenta, as well as to eliminate waste products, by the flow and return of blood through the vessels within it. At birth it is severed close to the infant's front abdominal wall, leaving a scar (the **umbilicus** or *navel*).

umbra *sunspot*

umbrella bird A large cotinga; males with dark plumage and umbrella-like crest covering head and bill; breast with inflatable air sac and pendant feathered fold of skin. (Genus: *Cephalopterus*, 3 species.)

Umbria [umbria] pop (2000e) 822 000; area 8456 km²/3265 sq mi. Region of C Italy; capital, Perugia; prosperous farming region; industry around Terni, Narni, and Foligno; textiles and crafts in Perugia and Spoleto; Umbrian school of painting during the Renaissance (eg Raphael); Basilica of St Francis in Assisi severely damaged by earthquake, 1997 is a world heritage site.

Umbriel [uhmbriel] The third-largest satellite of Uranus, discovered in 1851, distance from the planet 266 000 km/165 000 mi; diameter 1170 km/730 mi; orbital period 4.1 days.

Umeå [ümayaw] 63°50N 20°15E, pop (2000e) 97 000. Seaport in N Sweden; at the mouth of the R Ume; seat of the Provincial Appeal Court; railway; university (1963).

Umm al-Qaiwain [oom al kiywiyn] pop (2000e) 41 900; area 750 km²/290 sq mi. Member state of the United Arab Emirates; capital, Umm al-Qaiwain.

Un-American Activities Committee A committee of the House of Representatives established in 1938 to consider the loyalty of federal government employees. Supposedly concerned with identifying communists, it was notorious for harassing individuals whose political opinions offended committee members. It was abolished in 1975.

Unamuno (y Jugo), Miguel de [oonamoonoh] (1864–1936) Philosopher and writer, born in Bilbao, Spain. His main philosophical work is *Del sentimiento trágico de la vida en los hombres y en los pueblos* (1913, The Tragic Sense of Life in Men and Peoples). As rector of Salamanca, he defied the forces of Franco in the Civil War.

unconscious When used psychoanalytically, the collection of feelings, drives, memories, and emotional conflicts which individuals are not aware of, but which influence their mental processes and behaviour, such as dreams and slips of the tongue indicating true feelings. In contrast, the **subconscious** is used colloquially to describe memories about which an individual is only dimly aware, but which can be recalled if focused upon.

underground A complete railway system designed to operate underground in tunnels or tubes, also known as the **tube**, **subway**, or **metro**. Traction is supplied almost exclusively by electric motor. Due to their high cost of construction, undergrounds are normally used only for passenger traffic within large cities. The first practical underground railway was the City and South London Railway, which opened for traffic in 1890. The world's largest system (in terms of number of stations, 468) is the New York City subway (383 km/238 mi). London Underground in 2000 had 392 km/244 mi of track, with 274 stations, following the completion of the Jubilee Line extension in 1999. Three trains using the system were bombed by terrorists on 7 July 2005, killing over 50 people and injuring more than 700.

Underground Railroad A network of safe houses, hiding places, and routes to aid escaped American slaves to reach freedom in the N or Canada. It was active as early as 1786, but was most widespread after 1830.

underwriter In business or insurance, a person or company that guarantees payment if a certain event should occur. In insurance, the underwriter pays in the event of fire or theft. In finance, an underwriter of a share issue guarantees that they will buy at a pre-arranged price any shares not 'taken up' (ie bought) by others.

undulant fever *brucellosis*

unemployment A situation where a person able and willing to do work is not employed. **Demand-deficiency** or **Keynesian unemployment** is where there is simply insufficient demand. In **classical unemployment**, the lowest pay that workers will accept is above what employers think their labour is worth. **Frictional unemployment** is where workers and employers exist whose offers are mutually acceptable, but who are looking for and have not yet located each other. **Mismatch** occurs when the vacant jobs and unemployed workers differ in skill or location. Possible cures include expanding effective demand, lowering wages, improving the mechanics of matching workers and vacancies, and assisting mobility and the acquisition of skills.

UNESCO [yooneskoh] Acronym for **United Nations Educational, Scientific and Cultural Organization**, founded in 1946 with the objective of contributing to peace and security by promot-

United Arab Emirates

□ International Airport   – – Border awaiting demarcation

Arabic **al-Arabiyah al-Muttahida**, formerly **Trucial States**

Local name Ittih-ad al-Im-arat al-ʿArab-iyah

Timezone GMT +4

Area 83 600 km²/32 300 sq mi

Population total (2002e) 3 550 000

Status Federation of autonomous emirates

Date of independence 1971

Capital Abu Dhabi

Languages Arabic (official), English, Farsi, Urdu, and Hindi also spoken

Ethnic groups Emirian (19%), other Arab (23%), S Asian (50%)

Religions Muslim (Sunni 80%, Shiʿite 16%), Christian (4%), small Hindu minority

Physical features Seven states in EC Arabian peninsula on S shore (Trucial Coast) of the Persian Gulf; al-Fujairah has a coastline along the Gulf of Oman; salt marshes predominate on coast; barren desert and gravel plain inland; Hajar Mts in al-Fujairah rise to over 1000 m/3000 ft in E.

Climate Hot, dry desert climate, extreme summer temperatures exceeding 40°C and limited rainfall; frequent sandstorms; average annual temperatures 23°C (Jan), 42°C (Jul) in Dubai; average annual rainfall 60 mm/2·4 in.

Currency 1 United Arab Emirates Dirham (AED) = 100 fils

Economy Based on oil and gas (main producers, Abu Dhabi, Dubai); important commercial and trading centre; saline water supplies have restricted agriculture to oases and irrigated valleys of Hajar Mts; vegetables, fruits, dates, dairy farming; tourism.

GDP (2002e) $53·97 bn, per capita $22 100

Human Development Index (2002) 0·812

History Originally peopled by sea-faring tribes, converted to Islam in 7th-c; Mecca conquered by powerful sheikdom of Carmathians; upon its collapse piracy common, area known as the Pirate Coast; Portuguese explorers arrived, 16th-c; British East India Company arrived, 17th-c; British attacked the coastal ports, 1819–20 and exacted a pledge to renounce piracy in the General Treaty, 1820; became known as Trucial Coast after signing of Treaty of Maritime Peace in Perpetuity, 1853; administered by British India, 1873–1947, and thereafter by London Foreign Office; Trucial States Council formed, 1960; federated and became United Arab Emirates, 1971, comprising seven emirates: Abu Dhabi, Ajman, Dubai, al-Fujairah, Ras al-Khaimah, Sharjah, and Umm al-Qaiwain; Ras al-Khaimah joined federation, 1972; governed by Supreme Council of the seven emirate rulers (each of whom is an absolute Monarch in own state).

Head of State

1971–2004 Zayed bin Sultan al-Nahyan
2004– Khalifa bin Zayed al-Nahẏan

Head of Government

1971–9 Maktoum bin Rashid al-Maktoum
1979–90 Rashid bin Said al-Maktoum
1990–2006 Maktoum bin Rashid al-Maktoum
2006– Mohammed bin Rashid al-Maktoum

ing collaboration among nations through education, science, and culture. Its headquarters is in Paris. In the mid-1980s, there emerged serious concern among the non-communist industrialized countries over the organization's administrative inefficiency and its allegedly inappropriate political aims. In consequence the USA left in 1985, which had a major impact on UNESCO's finances. The UK and Singapore subsequently withdrew, and Yugoslavia was suspended in 1992, but the UK rejoined in 1997, newly constituted Yugoslavia (now Serbia and Montenegro) in 2000, and the USA in 2003. In 2007 there were 191 member states and 6 associate members.

Ungaretti, Giuseppe [unggaretee] (1888–1970) Poet, born in Alexandria, Egypt. His poems, characterized by symbolism, compressed imagery, and modern verse structure, became the foundation of the *hermetic* movement.

Ungava–Quebec Crater *Chubb Crater*

ungulate A mammal in which toes end in hooves rather than claws; includes *artiodactyls* (**even-toed ungulates**) and *perissodactyls* (**odd-toed ungulates**); also the **primitive ungulates** (elephant, hyrax, aardvark); usually large and herbivorous.

unicameral system A legislature which has only one chamber.

This uncommon system tends to be found in countries with relatively small populations, where there would be problems in maintaining a dual system of representation. New Zealand, Israel, and Denmark are examples.

UNICEF The **United Nations Children's Fund**, formerly known as the **United Nations International Children's Emergency Fund**, established in 1946 to provide help for children left destitute after Word War 2, and now concerned with children in need everywhere. It was given a permanent role within the UN in 1953. In 2007, UNICEF was supporting programmes in 191 countries in relation to child health, nutrition, water and sanitation, or education, and also providing emergency aid in many parts of the world. Funded entirely by voluntary contributions from the general public and governments, and with national committees in most industrialized countries, it is unique in the UN system.

unicorn A fabulous creature, a horse with a single horn on its forehead; probably based on stories of the rhinoceros.

Unification Church *Moonies*

Uniformity, Acts of A series of acts passed by the English parliament in 1549, 1552, 1559, and 1662. They sought to impose religious uniformity by requiring the use of the Church of England liturgy as contained in the Book of Common Prayer.

Uniform Resource Locator *World Wide Web*

union (economics) *trade union*

union (mathematics) *set*

Union, Acts of The Acts which joined England in legislative union with Scotland (1707) and Ireland (1800). The 1800 Act created the United Kingdom of Great Britain and Ireland, which came into effect in 1801, and lasted until 1922.

Union Islands *Tokelau*

Unionist *Conservative Party*

Union Movement A party formed by Sir Oswald Mosley in 1948 as a successor to his New Party (1931) and the British Union of Fascists (1932). The party's main plank was opposition to immigration. The movement died out by the end of the 1960s.

Union of European Football Associations *UEFA*

Union of Soviet Socialist Republics *Soviet Union*

Uniramia [yooniraymia] A group of arthropods characterized by their 1-branched (*uniramous*) limbs, and by jaws that bite transversely at the tip; comprises the insects (*Insecta*), centipedes (*Chilopoda*), millipedes (*Diplopoda*), and velvet worms (*Onychophora*); sometimes treated as a separate phylum at the arthropodan level of organization.

Unitarians A religious group which, although in many ways akin to Christianity, rejects the doctrines of the Trinity and the divinity of Christ. As an organized group, it dates back to the 16th-c Protestant Reformation, first in parts of S Europe, and from the 18th-c in Britain and America.

United Arab Emirates *p.963*

United Church of Christ A Christian denomination formed in the USA in 1961 by the union of the Congregational and Christian Churches with the Evangelical and Reformed Church.

United Fronts Two attempts to promote co-operation between the Chinese Communist and Nationalist Parties in the face of Japanese aggression in the late 1930s. Clashes between Nationalist and Communist forces led to its virtual disintegration by 1941.

United Irishmen, Society of A society formed in Belfast in 1791 by Protestant lawyer Wolfe Tone, which supported the French Revolution and espoused both religious equality and parliamentary reform. The Society was instrumental in organizing French support for the unsuccessful Irish rebellion of 1798, and afterwards went into decline.

United Kingdom (UK) *see panel*

United Kingdom Atomic Energy Authority An authority set up by the Atomic Energy Authority Act in 1954. It has prime responsibility for research and the development of nuclear power in the UK on behalf of the government.

United Nations (UN) An organization formed to maintain world peace and foster international co-operation, formally established on 24 October 1945 with 51 founder countries; there were 192 members in 2007. The **General Assembly** is the plenary body which controls much of the UN's work, and debates major issues of international affairs. The 15-member **Security Council** is dominated by the five permanent members (China, France, UK, Russia, and USA) who each have the power of veto over any resolutions; the remaining 10 are elected for 2-year periods. The primary role of the Council is to maintain international peace and security; its decisions, unlike those of the General Assembly, are binding on all other members. The **Secretariat**, under the secretary-general, employs some 25 000 (from 160 countries) worldwide. The secretary-general is often a significant person in international diplomacy and is able to take independent initiatives. The **International Court of Justice** consists of 15 judges appointed by the Council and the Assembly. As only states can bring issues before it, its jurisdiction depends on the consent of the states who are a party to a dis-

United Kingdom (UK)

UNITED KINGDOM
NORTH SEA
Shetland Is
Orkney Is
SCOTLAND ◉Aberdeen
◉Edinburgh
Glasgow ■
Newcastle
Belfast ■
Isle of Man
IRISH SEA
Leeds
IRELAND
Liverpool ■ Manchester
WALES
◉Birmingham
CELTIC SEA
Cardiff◉■ Bristol ■
LONDON
Plymouth
Isle of Wight
Isles of Scilly
English Channel
Channel Is
EUROPE
FRANCE
200 km
100 mi

□ International Airport

also **United Kingdom of Great Britain and Northern Ireland**

Local names United Kingdom of Great Britain and Northern Ireland, Great Britain, Britain

pute. The **International Criminal Court** (ICC), consisting of 18 judges elected by the States Parties, was inaugurated in 2003. The **Economic and Social Council** is elected by the General Assembly; it supervises the work of various committees, commissions, and expert bodies in the economic and social area, and co-ordinates the work of UN specialized agencies. The **Trusteeship Council** (suspended at the end of 1994) oversaw the transition of Trust Territories to self-government. In addition, there is a range of subsidiary agencies, many with their own constitutions and membership, and some pre-dating the UN. The UN had 192 members in 2007. Jointly, with secretary-general Kofi Annan, it was awarded the Nobel Peace Prize in 2001. *p.966*

United Nations Conference on Trade and Development (UNCTAD) An organ of the UN, established by the 1964 General Assembly, which meets irregularly to consider ways of increasing international trade and promoting economic development.

United Nations Educational, Scientific and Cultural Organization *UNESCO*

United Provinces of the Netherlands Seven sovereign states of the Dutch Republic, roughly comprising the present kingdom of

Timezone GMT

Area 244 755 km²/94 500 sq mi

Population total (2002e) 60 178 000

Status Kingdom

Capital London

Languages English, Irish Gaelic, Scots Gaelic (Gallic), Welsh

Ethnic groups English (81·5%), Scottish (9·5%), Irish (2·4%), Welsh (1·9%), West Indian, Asian, and African (2%), Arabic, Turkish, and Greek minorities

Religions Christian (90%) (Anglican 63%, Roman Catholic 14%, Presbyterian 4%, Methodist 3%, Baptist 1%, Orthodox 1%, other 6%), Muslim (3%), Sikh (1%), Hindu (1%), Jewish (1%), other (1%)

Physical features Varied landscape, comprising the mountainous Lake District in NW, rocky moors in SW, hilly downs of S and SE, and the low, marshy fenlands of C and E; Cheviot Hills separate Scotland and England; highest point, Ben Nevis in Scotland, 1342 m/4406 ft; the Pennines form a ridge down the middle of England, from Lake District to C; highest point in England and Wales, Mt Snowdon in Wales, 1085 m/3560 ft; in N Ireland, the Sperrin Mts and the granite Mourne Mts rise to heights over 610 m/2000 ft.

Climate Temperate maritime climate; SW airstream determines weather, bringing depressions (causing wet weather) or N winds (bringing drier and colder); some regional diversity, but no world climate systems' boundaries pass through the islands; on average, wetter and slightly warmer in W; rainfall evenly distributed throughout the year; average annual rainfall 1600 mm/60 in (W), 800 mm/30 in (C and E).

Currency 1 Pound Sterling (GBP) = 100 pence

Economy Service industries; agriculture, potatoes, wheat, barley, and sugar beets; livestock; large fishing industry; deposits of iron ore; oil and gas from N Sea; coal industry declining; highly developed financial systems; London the commercial and financial centre of Western world; UK one of the world's largest trading nations, relying heavily on imports; exports include machinery, transport equipment, petroleum, chemicals, textiles.

GDP (2002e) $1·528 tn, per capita $25 500

Human Development Index (2002) 0·928

History Migrations and settlements resulted in the insular Celtic nation; invaded by Rome, 1 AD; Romans withdrew, the 5th-c; constantly attacked by Scandinavian tribes; defeated by Alfred, 878; united under the kings of Wessex, 10th-c; Edward the Confessor died, 1066, leaving a disputed succession; Norman invasion under William, Duke of Normandy, 1066; Edward I conquered Wales, 1301; Hundred Years' War with France, 1337–1453; recurring plagues of Black Death, 1347–1400, wiped out one-third of population; Wars of the Roses, 1455–85, resulted in victory for House of Lancaster; establishment of Church of England and split from Church of Rome, 1533; union with Wales, 1536; coronation of Elizabeth I, 1558; execution of Mary Queen of Scots, 1587; defeat of the Spanish Armada, 1588; English Civil War, 1642–6 and 1648–9; execution of Charles I, 1649; England and Scotland joined by the Act of Union, 1707; 1714–60, development of parliamentary government under Hanoverian kings; revolt of the American colonies, 1775–81. Ireland officially joined to Great Britain, 1801; World War 1, 1914–18; became the United Kingdom of Great Britain and Northern Ireland following the establishment of the Irish Free State, 1922; General Strike, 1926; abdication of Edward VIII, 1936; World War 2, 1939–45; National Health system implemented, 1948; Indian independence, 1947; joined European Union (formerly EC), 1973; Falklands War with Argentina, 1982; involvement in Gulf War, 1991; involvement in Iraq War, 2003– ; a kingdom with the Monarch as Head of State; governed by a bicameral Parliament, comprising an elected 659-member House of Commons and a House of Lords; a Cabinet is appointed by the Prime Minister.

Head of State (Monarch)

1952– Elizabeth II

Head of Government

1951–5 Winston Leonard Spencer Churchill *Con*
1955–7 (Robert) Anthony Eden, 1st Earl of Avon *Con*
1957–63 (Maurice) Harold Macmillan, 1st Earl of Stockton *Con*
1963–4 Alexander Frederick (Alec) Douglas-Home, Baron Home of the Hirsel *Con*
1964–70 (James) Harold Wilson, Baron Wilson *Lab*
1970–4 Edward Richard George Heath *Con*
1974–6 (James) Harold Wilson, Baron Wilson *Lab*
1976–9 (Leonard) James Callaghan, Baron Callaghan *Lab*
1979–90 Margaret Hilda Thatcher *Con*
1990–7 John Major *Con*
1997–2007 Anthony Charles Lynton (Tony) Blair *Lab*
2007– (James) Gordon Brown *Lab*

Con Conservative *Lab* Labour *Lib* Liberal

The Netherlands, which achieved independence from the Spanish crown (1568–1609). The republic declined in the 18th-c, collapsing during the Revolutionary Wars (1795).

United Service Organizations (USO) Founded in the USA in 1941, it is an association of agencies, such as the YMCA, the YWCA, and the Salvation Army, whose aims are to care for the recreational needs of the Armed Forces.

United States military academies Federal training institutions for people who want to become officers in the US armed forces. The **United States Air Force (USAF) Academy** was formed by Act of Congress in 1948, and is located near Colorado Springs, CO. The **United States Military Academy** was founded in 1802, and is now at West Point on the Hudson R, NY. The **United States Naval Academy** was founded in 1845, and is at Annapolis, MD. The **United States Coast Guard (USCG) Academy** was founded in 1876, and has been located at New London, CT since 1936.

United States of America (USA) *pp.967–9*

United States Trust Territory of the Pacific Islands 1–22°N 142–172°E; pop (1990e), before devolution, 40 000; area 1854 km²/716 sq mi. Group of c.2000 islands in the W Pacific Ocean, N of Papua New Guinea; until 1990, comprised the Commonwealth of the N Mariana Is, the Federated States of Micronesia, the Republic of Belau, and the Marshall Is; population mostly Micronesian, with some Polynesian; official language, English; islands mainly of volcanic origin, few rising above 120 m/400 ft; administered by Japan in the inter-war years; placed under UN trusteeship, 1947; trust status ended, 1990, and for Belau, 1994; economy based on agriculture, fisheries, tourism.

United States Virgin Islands *Virgin Islands, United States*

units (scientific) Most quantities in science are expressed using the International System of units, abbreviated to **SI units**, introduced in 1960. The most fundamental are called **base units**: the metre, kilogram, second, ampere, kelvin, candela, and mole. All quantities of interest can be expressed in terms of these units. Certain combinations which appear often are called **derived units** and have special names, eg the newton. From 1995 the radian and steradian are also classed as derived units (previously, they were called supplementary units). Many other units exist, either for historical reasons or for convenience; examples are the parsec and calories. Other

United Nations Membership

Grouped according to year of entry.

1945	Argentina, Australia, Belgium, Belorussian SSR (Belarus, 1991). Bolivia, Brazil, Canada, Chile, China (Taiwan to 1971), Colombia, Costa Rica, Cuba, Czechoslovakia (to 1993). Denmark, Dominican Republic, Ecuador, Egypt, El Salvador, Ethiopia, France, Greece, Guatemala, Haiti, Honduras, India, Iran, Iraq, Lebanon, Liberia, Luxembourg, Mexico, Netherlands, New Zealand, Nicaragua, Norway, Panama, Paraguay, Peru, Philippines, Poland, Saudi Arabia, South Africa, Syria, Turkey, Ukrainian SSR (Ukraine, 1991), UK. Uruguay, USA, USSR, Venezuela, Yugoslavia (Union of Serbia and Montenegro, 2003–6)
1946	Afghanistan, Iceland, Sweden, Thailand
1947	Pakistan, Yemen (N)
1948	Burma (Myanmar, 1989)
1949	Israel
1950	Indonesia
1955	Albania, Austria, Bulgaria, Ceylon (Sri Lanka, 1970), Finland, Hungary, Ireland, Italy, Jordan, Kampuchea (Cambodia), Laos, Libya, Nepal, Portugal, Romania, Spain
1956	Japan, Morocco, Sudan, Tunisia
1957	Ghana, Malaya (Malaysia, 1963)
1958	Guinea
1960	Cameroon, Central African Republic, Chad, Congo, Córe d'Ivoire (formerly Ivory Coast), Cyprus, Dahomey (Benin, 1975), Gabon, Madagascar, Mali, Niger, Nigeria, Senegal, Somalia, Togo, Upper Volta (Burkina Faso, 1984), Zaïre (Democratic Republic of Congo, 1997)
1961	Mauritania, Mongolia, Sierra Leone, Tanganyika (within Tanzania, 1964)
1962	Algeria, Burundi, Jamaica, Rwanda, Trinidad and Tobago, Uganda
1963	Kenya, Kuwait, Zanzibar (within Tanzania, 1964)
1964	Malawi, Malta, Tanzania, Zambia
1965	Maldives, Singapore, The Gambia
1966	Barbados, Botswana, Guyana, Lesotho
1967	Yemen (S, to 1990)
1968	Equatorial Guinea, Mauritius, Swaziland
1970	Fiji
1971	Bahrain, Bhutan, China (Peoples' Republic), Oman, Qatar, United Arab Emirates
1973	Bahamas, German Democratic Republic (within GFR, 1990) German Federal Republic
1974	Bangladesh, Grenada, Guinea-Bissau
1975	Cape Verde, Comoros, Mozambique, Papua New Guinea, São Tomé and Principe, Suriname
1976	Angola, Seychelles, Western Samoa
1977	Djibouti, Vietnam
1978	Dominica, Solomon Islands
1979	St Lucia
1980	St Vincent and the Grenadines, Zimbabwe
1981	Antigua and Barbuda, Belize, Vanuatu
1983	St Kitts and Nevis
1984	Brunei
1990	Liechenstein, Namibia, Yemen (formerly N Yemen and S Yemen)
1991	Estonia, Federated States of Micronesia, Latvia, Lithuania, Marshall Islands, N Korea, Russia (formerly USSR), S Korea
1992	Armenia, Azerbaijan, Bosnia-Herzegovina, Croatia, Georgia, Kazakhstan, Kyrgysztan, Moldova, San Marino, Slovenia, Tajikistan, Turkmenistan, Uzbekistan
1993	Andorra, Czech Republic, Eritrea, Former Yugoslav Republic of Macedonia, Monaco, Slovak Republic
1995	Belau
1999	Nauru, Tonga, Kiribati
2000	Tuvalu, Serbia
2002	Switzerland, East Timor
2006	Montenegro

systems of units have been used in the past: these include the old FPS British system, based on foot, pound, and second; the CGS system, based on centimetre, gram, and second; and the MKSA system, based on metre, kilogram, second, and ampere. SI units are an extension of MKSA units.

unit trust A form of investment. The trust buys shares in a number of companies, and offers the public an opportunity to buy a unit of the portfolio. It is a means of spreading risk.

Universal Declaration of Human Rights An international declaration, adopted in 1948 by the General Assembly of the UN. It declares that all human beings are born free and equal in dignity and rights without discrimination of race, colour, sex, language, political opinion, or religion. The Declaration is not legally binding, but it has greatly influenced the activities of the UN, affecting both national and international law, and has widely influenced debate on human rights. The International Covenants on Civil and Political Rights and on Economic, Social and Cultural Rights (both 1966) bind countries which have signed them. The 1948 Declaration and these two Covenants are sometimes known as the **International Bill of Rights**.

universalism The religious belief that all people will be saved. It implies rejection of the traditional Christian belief in hell. A feature of much contemporary Protestant theology, it is motivated by moral doubts concerning eternal punishment, and by a recognition of the validity of other non-Christian world faiths.

universal time (UT) The precise system of time measurement used for all practical purposes. Formerly based on *mean solar*

time, it has since 1972 been based on *international atomic time*, a uniform time derived from the frequencies of selected transitions within atoms.

universe In modern astronomy, everything that is in the cosmos and that can affect us by means of physical forces. The definition excludes anything that is in principle undetectable physically, such as regions of space–time that were, are, or will be irreversibly cut off from our own space–time.

university An institution of higher education which offers study at degree level. Courses may be taken leading to bachelor, master, or doctoral level. Both academic and vocational courses are followed, leading to qualifications in such professions as medicine, teaching, engineering, and the law, sometimes in conjunction with professional bodies. Research is given a high priority. The earliest European universities are Bologna (10th-c), Paris (1170), Oxford (1249), and Cambridge (1284). The first Chinese university was established in 124 BC.

Unix An operating system developed by AT&T Laboratories in the USA which has become widely adopted, particularly in educational centres, and is seen as a suitable operating system to form the basis of open systems interconnection. The Open Software Foundation is seeking to develop Unix as a standard operating system for this purpose.

Unknown Soldier or **Warrior** An unnamed soldier, taken as representative of all those who died in World War 1, whose grave is a memorial to all war dead. Several countries have such a memorial: in France beneath the Arc de Triomphe; in the UK

United States of America (USA)

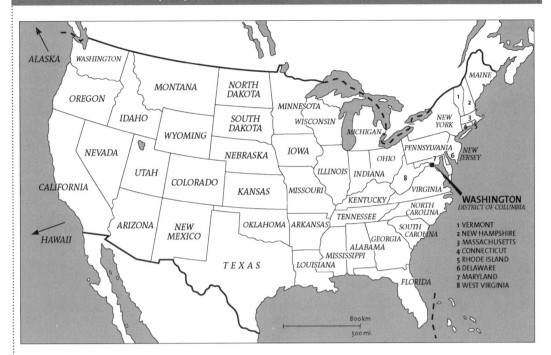

1 VERMONT
2 NEW HAMPSHIRE
3 MASSACHUSETTS
4 CONNECTICUT
5 RHODE ISLAND
6 DELAWARE
7 MARYLAND
8 WEST VIRGINIA

also called **United States**, and often **America**

Timezone GMT -5 (E coast) to -8 (Pacific coast)

Area 9 160 454 km²/3 535 935 sq mi

Population total (2002e) 287 602 000

Status Federal republic

Date of independence 1776

Capital Washington, DC.

Languages English, large Spanish-speaking minority

Ethnic groups European origin (including 9% Hispanic) (83·9%), African American (12·1%), Asian and Pacific (2·9%), Native American, Aleut, and Inuit (0·9%)

Religions Christian (70%) (Protestant 61%, Roman Catholic 25%), atheist (7%), other (5%), Jewish (2%)

Physical features Includes the separate states of Alaska (GMT -9) and Hawaii (GMT -10). E Atlantic coastal plain is backed by the Appalachian Mts from the Great Lakes to Alabama, a series of parallel ranges including the Allegheny, Blue Ridge, and Catskill Mts; plain broadens out (S) towards the Gulf of Mexico and into the Florida peninsula; Gulf Plains stretch N to meet the Great Plains from which they are separated by the Ozark Mts; further W, Rocky Mts rise to over 4500 m/14 750 ft; highest point in US, Mt McKinley, Alaska, 6194 m/20 321 ft; Death Valley, -86 m/-282 ft, is the lowest point; drainage N is into the St Lawrence R or the Great Lakes; in the E, the Hudson, Delaware, Potomac, and other rivers flow E to the Atlantic Ocean; central plains drained by the great Red River–Missouri–Mississippi system and by other rivers flowing into the Gulf of Mexico; main rivers

in W, Columbia and Colorado; deserts cover much of Texas, New Mexico, Arizona, Utah, Nevada.

Climate Climate varies from conditions found in hot, tropical deserts (SW), to those typical of Arctic continental regions on the northern Pacific Coast; continental climate on High Plains, with summer dust storms and winter blizzards; temperate continental on Central Plains; continental Mid West and the Great Lakes, with very cold winters; cool temperate in N Appalachians, warm temperate in S; subtropical to warm temperate on the Gulf Coast, with plentiful rainfall and frequent hurricanes and tornadoes; temperate maritime on the Atlantic coast, with heavy snowfall in N; cool temperate in New England, with warm summers and severe winters; mean annual temperatures range from 29°C in Florida, to -13°C in Alaska; average annual temperatures in Chicago, -3°C (Jan), 24°C (Jul); in Arizona, 11°C (Jan), 32°C (Jul); average annual rainfall in Alabama, 1 640 mm/65 in, in Arizona, 180 mm/7 in; hot and humid in Hawaii, with average annual rainfall 1524–5080 mm/60–200 in.

Currency 1 US Dollar (USD) = 100 cents

Economy One of the world's most productive industrial nations; highly diversified economy; vast mineral and agricultural resources; major exporter of grains, cereals, potatoes, sugar, fruit; livestock farming of beef, veal, pork; chief exports include aircraft, cars, machinery, chemicals, military equipment, non-fuel minerals; advanced system of communications and transportation; leader in space-exploration programme of the 1970s.

GDP (2002e) $10·45 tn, per capita $36 300

Human Development Index (2002) 0·939

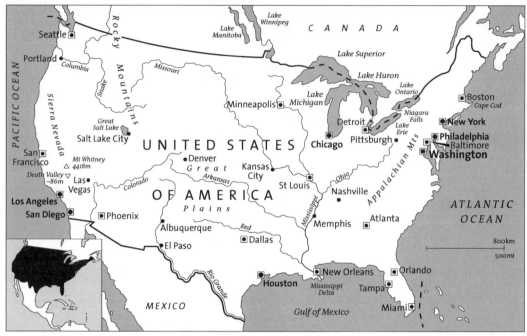

☐ International Airport

History First settled by groups who migrated from Asia across the Bering Straits over 25 000 years ago; explored by the Norse in 9th-c; and by the Spanish in 16th-c, who settled in Florida and Mexico; in the 17th-c, settlements by the British, French, Dutch, Germans, and Swedes; many Black Africans introduced as slaves to work on the plantations; British control during 18th-c after defeat of French in Seven Years' War; revolt of the English-speaking colonies in the War of Independence, 1775–83, resulted in the creation of the United States of America; Louisiana sold to the USA by France in 1803 (the Louisiana Purchase) and the westward movement of settlers began; Florida ceded by Spain in 1819, and further Spanish states joined the Union, 1821–53; 11 Southern states left the Union over the slavery issue and formed the Confederacy, 1860–1; Civil War, 1861–5, ended in victory for the North, and the Southern states later rejoined the Union; Alaska purchased from Russia, 1867; Hawaiian islands annexed, 1898; several other islands formally associated with the USA, such as Puerto Rico, American Samoa, and Guam; in the 19th-c, arrival of millions of immigrants from Europe and the Far East; more recent arrival of large numbers of Spanish-speaking people, mainly from Mexico and the West Indies; entered World War 1 on the side of the Allies, 1917, and again in World War 2 in 1941; became the chief world power opposed to communism, a policy which led to involvement in the Korean War (1950–3) and Vietnam (1956–75); campaign for Black civil rights developed, 1960s, and eventually led to Civil Rights Act (1964); invasion of Grenada, 1983; mid 1980s rapprochement of US and USSR; invasion of Panama, 1989; involvement in Gulf War, 1991; military intervention in Somalia, 1993; following the Al-Qaeda attack on the World Trade Center in New York (11 Sep 2001), and earlier terrorist attacks (notably, the 1998 bomb attacks on US embassies in

Kenya and Tanzania, and the bombing of the USS *Cole* warship in the port of Aden, Yemen in 2000), the USA led the successful campaign to remove the Taliban from power in Afghanistan; further campaign against international terrorism, 2002; Iraq's apparent failure to comply with a UN resolution to eliminate its weapons of mass destruction led to invasion by US-led military coalition forces and the removal of Saddam Hussein (Mar–Apr 2003), followed by handover of power to an interim Iraqi government (Jun 2004) overseeing of elections (Jan 2005); ongoing terrorist threats against the USA, both within the country and abroad, brought unprecedented levels of security from 2003. Congress consists of 435-member House of Representatives, and a 100-member Senate; President elected every 4 years by a college of state representatives, appoints an executive Cabinet responsible to Congress; divided into 50 federal states and the District of Columbia; each state having its own two-body legislature and governor.

Head of State/Government (President)
Vice President in parentheses
1945–53 Harry S Truman (33rd) *Dem No Vice President 1945–9* (Alben W Barkley, 1949–53)
1953–61 Dwight David Eisenhower (34th) *Rep* (Richard Milhous Nixon)
1961–3 John Fitzgerald Kennedy (35th) *Dem* (Lyndon Baines Johnson)
1963–9 Lyndon Baines Johnson (36th) *Dem No Vice President 1963–5* (Hubert Horatio Humphrey, 1965–9)
1969–74 Richard Milhous Nixon (37th) *Rep* (Spiro Theodore Agnew, 1969–73) *No Vice President Oct–Dec 1973* (Gerald Rudolph Ford, 1973–4)

1974–7 Gerald Rudolph Ford (38th) *Rep No Vice President Aug–Dec 1974* (Nelson Aldrich Rockefeller, 1974–7)
1977–81 James Earl (Jimmy) Carter (39th) *Dem* (Walter Frederick Mondale)
1981–9 Ronald Wilson Reagan (40th) *Rep* (George Herbert Walker Bush)
1989–92 George Herbert Walker Bush (41st) *Rep* (J Danforth Quayle)
1992–2001 William Jefferson Clinton (42nd) *Dem* (Alfred Gore)
2001– George (W) Bush (43rd) *Rep* (Dick Cheney)
Dem Democrat *Rep* Republican

American States

Timezones

Two sets of figures indicate that different zones operate in a state; the second figure refers to Summer Time (Apr–Oct, approximately):

2 Aleutian/Hawaii Standard Time : 3 Alaska Standard Time : 4 Pacific Standard Time : 5 Mountain Standard Time : 6 Central Standard Time : 7 Eastern Standard Time

Name / Area (km² / sq mi) / Capital / Time Zone / Population Figures (2000e) / Nickname(s)

Alabama (AL)/ 133 911 / 51 705 / Montgomery / 7/8 / 4 387 000 / Camellia State, Heart of Dixie, Yellowhammer
Alaska (AK) / 1 518 748 / 586 412 / Juneau / 3/4 / 624 000 / Mainland State, The Last Frontier, The Great Land
Arizona (AZ) / 295 249 / 114 000 / Phoenix / 5 / 4 893 000 / Apache State, Grand Canyon State
Arkansas (AR) / 137 403 / 53 187 / Little Rock / 6/7 / 2 564 000 / Bear State, Land of Opportunity
California (CA) / 411 033 / 158 706 / Sacramento / 4/5 / 33 609 000 / Golden State
Colorado (CO) / 269 585 / 104 091 / Denver / 5/6 / 4 145 000 / Centennial State
Connecticut (CT) / 12 996 / 5 018 / Hartford / 7/8 / 3 292 000 / Nutmeg State, Constitution State, The Insurance State
Delaware (DE) / 5 296 / 2 045 / Dover / 7/8 / 763 000 / Diamond State, First State, Blue Hen State
District of Columbia (DC) / 173·5 / 67·0 / Washington / 7/8 / 516 000
Florida (FL) / 151 934 / 58 664 / Tallahassee / 6/7, 7/8 / 15 323 000 / Everglade State, Sunshine State, Peninsular State
Georgia (GA) / 152 571 / 58 910 / Atlanta / 7/8 / 7 944 000 / Empire State of the South, Peach State
Hawaii (HI) / 16 759 / 6 471 / Honolulu / 2 / 1 181 000 / Aloha State
Idaho (ID) / 216 422 / 83 564 / Boise / 4/5, 5/6 / 1 273 000 / Gem State
Illinois (IL) / 145 928 / 56 345 / Springfield / 6/7 / 12 189 000 / Prairie State, Land of Lincoln
Indiana (IN) / 93 716 / 36 185 / Indianapolis / 6/7, 7/8 / 5 979 000 / Hoosier State
Iowa (IA) / 145 747 / 56 275 / Des Moines / 6/7 / 2 878 000 / Hawkeye State, Corn State
Kansas (KS) / 213 089 / 82 277 / Topeka / 5/6, 6/7 / 2 670 000 / Sunflower State, Jayhawker State
Kentucky (KY) / 104 658 / 40 410 / Frankfort / 6/7, 7/8 / 3 989 000 / Bluegrass State
Louisiana (LA) / 123 673 / 47 752 / Baton Rouge / 6/7 / 4 381 000 / Pelican State, Sugar State, Creole State
Maine (ME) / 86 153 / 33 265 / Augusta / 7/8 / 1 258 000 / Pine Tree State, Lumber State
Maryland (MD) / 27 090 / 10 460 / Annapolis / 7/8 / 5 213 000 / Old Line State, Free State

Massachusetts (MA) / 21 455 / 8 284 / Boston / 7/8 / 6 206 000 / Bay State, Old Colony
Michigan (MI) / 151 579 / 58 527 / Lansing / 6/7, 7/8 / 9 903 000 / Wolverine State, Great Lake State
Minnesota (MN) / 218 593 / 84 402 / St Paul / 6/7 / 4 823 000 / Gopher State, North Star State
Mississippi (MS) / 123 510 / 47 689 / Jackson / 6/7 / 2 785 000 / Magnolia State
Missouri (MO) / 180 508 / 69 697 / Jefferson City / 6/7 / 5 501 000 / Bullion State, Show Me State
Montana (MT) / 380 834 / 147 046 / Helena / 5/6 / 886 000 / Treasure State, Big Sky Country
Nebraska (NE) / 200 342 / 77 352 / Lincoln / 5/6, 6/7 / 1 671 000 / Cornhusker State, Beef State
Nevada (NV) / 286 341 / 110 561 / Carson City / 4/5 / 1 878 000 / Silver State, Sagebrush State
New Hampshire (NH) / 24 032 / 9 279 / Concord / 7/8 / 1 217 000 / Granite State
New Jersey (NJ) / 20 167 / 7 787 / Trenton / 7/8 / 8 192 000 / Garden State
New Mexico (NM) / 314 914 / 121 593 / Santa Fe / 5/6 / 1 747 000 / Sunshine State, Land of Enchantment
New York (NY) / 127 185 / 49 108 / Albany / 7/8 / 18 233 000 / Empire State
North Carolina (NC) / 136 407 / 52 699 / Raleigh / 7/8 7 758 000 / Old North State, Tar Heel State
North Dakota (ND) / 180 180 / 69 567 / Bismarck / 5/6, 6/7 / 630 000 / Flickertail State, Sioux State
Ohio (OH) / 107 040 / 41 330 / Columbus / 7/8 / 11 279 000 / Buckeye State
Oklahoma (OK) / 181 083 / 69 919 / Oklahoma City / 6/7 / 3 378 000 / Sooner State
Oregon (OR) / 251 409 / 97 073 / Salem / 4/5 / 3 349 000 / Sunset State, Beaver State
Pennsylvania (PA) / 117 343 / 45 308 / Harrisburg / 7/8 / 11 982 000 / Keystone State
Rhode Island (RI) / 3 139 / 1 212 / Providence / 7/8 / 994 000 / Little Rhody, Plantation State, Ocean State
South Carolina (SC) / 80 579 / 31 113 / Columbia / 7/8 / 3 932 000 / Palmetto State
South Dakota (SD) / 199 723 / 77 116 / Pierre / 5/6, 6/7 / 735 000 / Sunshine State, Coyote State
Tennessee (TN) / 109 149 / 42 144 / Nashville / 6/7, 7/8 / 5 533 000 / Volunteer State
Texas (TX) / 691 003 / 266 807 / Austin / 5/6, 6/7 / 20 385 000 / Lone Star State
Utah (UT) / 219 880 / 84 899 / Salt Lake City / 5/6 / 2 169 000 / Mormon State, Beehive State
Vermont (VT) / 24 899 / 9 614 / Montpelier / 7/8 / 597 000 / Green Mountain State
Virginia (VA) / 105 582 / 40 767 / Richmond / 7/8 / 6 955 000 / Old Dominion State, Mother of Presidents
Washington (WA) / 176 473 / 68 139 / Olympia / 4/5 / 5 825 000 / Evergreen State, Chinook State
West Virginia (WV) / 62 758 / 24 232 / Charleston / 7/8 / 1 802 000 / Panhandle State, Mountain State
Wisconsin (WI) / 145 431 / 56 153 / Madison / 6/7 / 5 227 000 / Badger State, America's Dairyland
Wyoming (WY) / 253 315 / 97 809 / Cheyenne / 5/6 / 479 000 / Equality State

in Westminster Abbey; in the USA in Arlington National Cemetery.

Unleavened Bread, Feast of *Passover*

Unrepresented Nations and Peoples' Organization A body established in 1991 to represent ethnic and minority groups unrecognized by the United Nations, with the aim of defending the right of self-determination of oppressed peoples. The body had 69 members in 2007.

Unsworth, Barry (Forster) (1930–) Novelist, born in Wingate, Co Durham. His works include *The Greeks Have a Word for It* (1967), *Mooncranker's Gift* (1973), *Pascali's Island* (1980, filmed 1988), *Sacred Hunger* (1992, co-winner Booker), *The Songs of the Kings* (2003), and *The Ruby in Her Navel* (2006).

Unter den Linden [unter den lindn] A boulevard running between Marx–Engels Platz and the Brandenburg Gate, in the heart of Berlin, Germany. Formerly a stately avenue lined with lime trees and historic buildings, much of its character was destroyed during World War 2.

untouchables *caste*

Upanishads [oopanishadz] The last section of the Hindu scriptures (the Veda), composed in Sanskrit between 800 and 400 BC. The name, meaning 'to sit near', refers to the secret transmission of these teachings by gurus.

upas tree [yoopas] An evergreen tree (*Antiaris toxicaria*) native to Malaysia; flowers tiny, green; milky latex makes a powerful arrow-poison. In the 18th-c, misunderstanding led to the belief that poisonous emanations from the tree killed all life for miles around. (Family: Moraceae.)

Updike, John (Hoyer) (1932–) Writer, born in Shillington, PA. His novels, exploring human relationships in contemporary US society, include *Rabbit, Run* (1960), *Rabbit is Rich* (1981, Pulitzer), *Rabbit at Rest* (1990, Pulitzer), *The Witches of Eastwick* (1984, filmed 1987), and *Terrorist* (2006). His several collections of short stories include *Licks of Love* (2001).

Up-Helly-Aa [uhp heli ah] A festival held annually in Lerwick in the Shetland Islands, UK, on the last Tuesday in January, ending in the burning of a replica Viking longship.

Upper Volta *Burkina Faso*

Uppsala [upsala] 59°55N 17°38E, pop (2000e) 179 000. City in E Sweden; archbishopric; railway; educational centre, with university (1477) and many other academic institutions; cathedral (13th–15th-c), with tombs of Gustavus Vasa and other kings; castle (16th-c).

Upsilon Andromedae The first star other than the Sun known to have a multiple-planet system. The existence of three planets around the star was confirmed in 1999. All the planets are much larger and heavier than the Earth, with masses up to about five times that of Jupiter. Upsilon Andromedae lies 44 light years away and is faintly visible to the naked eye at 4th magnitude.

Ur [oor] The early home of the Jewish patriarch Abraham, an ancient Sumerian city-state lying to the SE of Babylon. At its zenith in the third millennium BC, it was destroyed by Elam c.2000 BC, and finally abandoned in the 4th-c BC.

uraemia / uremia [yooreemia] A rise in the concentration of urea in the blood, one of the first chemical abnormalities to be detected in kidney failure.

Uralic languages A family of languages descended from an ancestor spoken in the region of the N Ural Mts over 7000 years ago. The major languages are Finnish, Estonian, and Lapp, with an isolated member, Magyar, in Hungary. Numerous other languages are scattered through N Russia.

Ural Mountains [yooral(z)] or **The Urals**, Russ **Uralskiy Khrebet** Mountain range in Russia, forming the traditional boundary between Europe and Asia, and separating the E European Plain (W) from the W Siberian Lowlands (E); extends 1750 km/1100 mi S; generally 200–1000 m/700–3300 ft high; N Urals contain

the highest peak, Mt Narodnaya (1894 m/6214 ft); heavily forested; rich mineral deposits.

Urania [yooraynia] In Greek mythology, the Muse of astronomy.

uraninite *pitchblende*

uranium U, element 92, density 19 g/cm^3, melting point 1132°C. The heaviest of the naturally occurring elements. It has no stable isotopes, but the commonest (^{238}U) has a half-life of more than 10^9 years. Uranium compounds are now used almost exclusively for conversion to plutonium in nuclear fuel applications.

uranium–lead dating A method of radiometric dating for old rocks, using the fact that the radioactive isotope uranium-238 decays with a known half-life to give lead-206 and another isotope of uranium, uranium-235, decays to give lead-207. The amount of each isotope in a rock can be used to determine its absolute age.

Uranus (astronomy) [yooranuhs, yuraynuhs] The seventh major planet from the Sun, discovered by William Herschel in 1781; a smaller 'gas giant' than Jupiter or Saturn, and a near-twin to Neptune. It has the following characteristics: mass 8·7 × 10^{25} kg; radius 25 559 km/15 882 mi; mean density 1·3 g/cm^3; rotational period 84·01 years; orbital period 17·2 h (retrograde); eccentricity of orbit 0·047; inclination of equator 98°; mean distance from the Sun 2·87 × 10^9 km/1·78 × 10^9 mi. Composed mainly of hydrogen and helium, like Jupiter and Saturn, Uranus has a larger percentage of ammonia and methane. Methane gas in the upper atmosphere accounts for the planet's greenish hue. It is highly unusual in having a rotation axis tilted so that the poles lie almost in the ecliptic, and its equatorial plane with rings and moons lies almost perpendicular to the ecliptic.

It was observed at close range for the first time by Voyager 2 in 1986, which discovered two new rings to add to the nine already observed telescopically, and in 2005 two further rings were observed by the Hubble Space Telescope. The rings are very dark, narrow, widely separated, and slightly eccentric. It was discovered in 2006 that the planet has a blue ring – only the second found in the Solar System. There are five major moons (Miranda, Ariel, Umbriel, Titania, Oberon) in synchronous rotation; 10 additional small moons were discovered by Voyager, and others have since been observed, making 27 in all (as of 2007).

Uranus (mythology) [yooranuhs, yuraynuhs] or **Ouranus** In Greek mythology, the earliest sky-god, who was the father of the Titans. He is equivalent to Roman **Caelus**, 'the heavens'.

Urdu *Indo-Aryan languages*

urea [yureea] $H_2N–CO–NH_2$, melting point 135°C. A colourless solid, manufactured by heating ammonia and carbon dioxide under pressure: also called **carbamide**. It is used as an animal feed additive as well as a fertilizer, and is the starting material for urea resins.

urethritis [yoorethriytis] Inflammation of the urethra, caused by one of several organisms such as *Neisseria gonorrhoeae* and *Chlamydia*. The symptoms include a burning sensation on passing urine, and frequency of urination.

Urey, Harold (Clayton) [yooree] (1893–1981) Chemist and pioneer in the study of the Solar System, born in Walkerton, IN. In 1932 he isolated heavy water and discovered deuterium, for which he received the Nobel Prize for Chemistry in 1934. His work on lunar and planetary formation laid the scientific foundation for the space age exploration of the Solar System.

Urfé, Honoré d' [ürfay] (1568–1625) Writer, born in Marseille, France. He was the author of the pastoral romance, *Astrée* (1610–27), regarded as the first French novel.

uric acid [yoorik] An acid derived from purine, $C_5H_4N_4O_3$; like urea, used by animals as a means of excreting nitrogen.

Deposits of crystals of uric acid and its salts cause pain in gout and rheumatism.

Urim and Thummim [oorim, thuhmim] Objects of uncertain description, kept in the breastplate and vestments of the Israelite high priest. They were apparently used to discern God's answer to 'yes'-or-'no' questions put to him.

urinary stones The formation of calculi within the kidneys, ureters, and bladder. They commonly consist of salts of calcium, magnesium, ammonium phosphate, carbonate, and oxalate. They tend to form when the urine becomes too concentrated. Other factors associated with their formation include high dietary calcium and oxalate intake, and familial factors.

urinary system The physiological system involved in the production, storage, and excretion of urine. In mammals it consists of a pair of kidneys each connected to a muscular sac (the *bladder*) by a narrow fibromuscular tube (the *ureter*); a single *urethra* links the bladder to the exterior.

urine A liquid or semi-solid solution produced by the kidneys in vertebrates (eg humans), Malpighian tubules in some invertebrates (eg insects), and nephridia in most invertebrates (eg annelids, molluscs). It consists of water, the end-products of metabolism (eg urea, uric acid, hydrogen ions), dietary constituents taken in excess (eg salts, vitamins), and foreign substances (eg drugs), or their derivatives. The expulsion of urine from the bladder is often referred to as *micturition*.

URL *World Wide Web*

Ursa Major [ersa mayjer] (Lat 'great bear') A huge and conspicuous constellation, containing the Plough. It is mentioned extensively in literature from the earliest times, and is one of the two constellations (the other being Orion) that most people in the N hemisphere can locate without difficulty.

Ursa Minor [ersa miyner] (Lat 'little bear') The constellation around the N celestial pole. Its brightest star is Polaris.

Ursulines Worldwide congregations of sisters engaged in the education of girls. The principal and oldest congregation was founded in 1535 by St Angela Merici as the Company of St Ursula, after the 4th-c legendary saint and martyr.

urticaria [ertikairia] An allergic reaction affecting the skin, resulting in the formation of red, itching weals and blisters; also known as **nettle rash** or **hives**; it can occur as part of a generalized response to an allergen.

Uruguay, River (Span *Río*), Port **Rio Uruguai** South American river; rises in S Brazil, joins the R Paraná to form the R Plate; length c.1600 km/1000 mi.

Uruguay *p.972*

Uruk [ooruk] One of the greatest city-states of Sumer, lying to the NW of Ur. The home of the legendary Gilgamesh, it is also the site of the earliest writing ever found. It survived well into the Parthian period (3rd-c AD).

Ürümqi [urumchee], **Urumchi**, or **Wulumuqi**, also spelled **Wulu-mu-ch'i** 43°43N 87°38E, pop (2000e) 1 357 000. City in NW China; airfield; railway; eight universities; two medical schools; agricultural college (1952); communist base in 1930s and 1940s.

urus [yoorus] *aurochs*

USA *United States of America*

Usama bin Laden *Osama bin Laden*

Usborne, Mount 51°35S 58°57W. Mountain on the island of East Falkland; highest point in the Falkland Is, rising to 705 m/2313 ft.

USENET Originally, a term referring to a network of computers all running the Unix operating system and each communicating with the others. Since the advent of the Internet it has come to mean the world wide set of all newsgroups.

Usher *Ussher*

Uspallata [uspayahta] 32°50S 70°04W. Pass in the Andes between Mendoza (Argentina) and Santiago (Chile); rises to 3900 m/12 795 ft; statue of Christ of the Andes (1904).

Ussher or **Usher, James** (1581–1656) Clergyman, born in Dublin. His major work was the *Annales veteris et novi testamenti* (1650–4, Annals of the Old and New Testament), which gave a long-accepted chronology of Scripture, and fixed the Creation at 4004 BC.

USSR *Soviet Union*

Ustinov *Izhevsk*

Ustinov, Sir Peter (Alexander) [yustinof] (1921–2004) Actor and playwright, born in London, the son of White Russian parents. A prolific playwright, his works include *The Love of Four Colonels* (1951), *Romanoff and Juliet* (1956), and *Overheard* (1981). His many films include *Spartacus* (1961), *Topkapi* (1965), *Death on the Nile* (1978), *Appointment with Death* (1988), and *The Bachelor* (1999), and in his later years he established a reputation as a raconteur and as an ambassador for UNICEF.

Usumacinta, River [oosumaseenta] River in Guatemala and Mexico, enters the Gulf of Mexico; length (with the Chixoy, which rises in Guatemala) c.965 km/600 mi.

US War of Independence *American Revolution*

Utah [yootaw] pop (2000e) 2 223 200; area 219 880 km²/84 899 sq mi. State in W USA, the 'Beehive State'; first white exploration by the Spanish, 1540; acquired by the USA through the Treaty of Guadalupe Hidalgo, 1848; arrival of the Mormons, 1847; Utah Territory organized, 1850; antagonism between Mormon Church and Federal law led to the 'Utah War', 1857–8; joined the Union as the 45th state, 1896; capital, Salt Lake City; contains the Great Salt Lake in the NW; the Wasatch Range runs N–S; highest point, Kings Peak (4123 m/13 527 ft); mountainous and sparsely inhabited E region (containing four-fifths of the population) lie along W foothills of the Wasatch Range; Great Basin further W; arid Great Salt Lake Desert in the NW.

Utamaro, (Kitagawa) [ootamahroh], originally **Kitagawa Nebsuyoshi** (1753–1806) Painter and master of the colour print, born in Edo (modern Tokyo). He came to specialize in portraits of court ladies, painted flowers, birds and fish, and carried the technique of the *ukiyo-e* to its highest artistic level.

uterine tubes A pair of long ducts passing outwards from the upper part of the uterus towards the ovary, also known as the **Fallopian tubes**, after Italian anatomist Gabriele Fallopius (1523–62).

uterus [yooteruhs] A pear-shaped, thick-walled muscular organ of females which projects upwards and forwards above the bladder from the upper part of the vagina; also known as the **womb**. It consists of a *fundus* (the region of the body above the level of entrance of the uterine tubes), a *body*, and the *cervix* (separated from the body by a slight narrowing). In the human female the non-pregnant uterus is c.7·5 cm/3 in in length and weighs 40 g/1·4 oz. During pregnancy it increases in size to become c.30 cm/12 in in length and can weigh as much as 1 kg/2·2 lb by the eighth month.

Uther Pendragon [yoother pendragn] In the Arthurian legends, a king of Britain, who was the father of King Arthur by Ygraine, the wife of Duke Gorlois of Cornwall.

utilitarianism In ethics, the theory that all actions are to be judged by their consequences for the general welfare; 'the greatest happiness of the greatest number' is the sole criterion of moral choice. It flourished particularly in the 19th-c.

utility In computing, a term used for a computer program which carries out a specific function needed by a computer centre, but which is not sufficiently extensive to justify the development of a computer package. Normally a function such as sort and merge is provided as a utility.

Utopia (Gr 'nowhere') A name for a fictional republic, invented

Uruguay

☐ International Airport

[**yoo**ruhgwiy], official name **Oriental Republic of Uruguay**, Span **República Oriental del Uruguay**

Local name Uruguay
Timezone GMT -3
Area 176 215 km²/68 018 sq mi
Population total (2002e) 3 383 000
Status Republic
Date of independence 1828
Capital Montevideo

Language Spanish (official)
Ethnic groups European (mainly Spanish, Italian) (90%), mestizo (8%)
Religions Roman Catholic (60%), Protestant (2%), Jewish (2%), unaffiliated (30%)
Physical features Located in E South America; grass covered plains (S) rise to a high, sandy plateau, traversed SE and NW by the Cuchilla Grande and Cuchilla de Haedo, rising to 501 m/1644 ft at Cerro Mirados; R Negro flows SW to meet the R Uruguay on the Argentine frontier.
Climate Temperate, with warm summers, mild winters; average annual temperature 10°C (Jul), 22°C (Jan) in Montevideo; average annual rainfall 978 mm/38 in; rainy season (Apr–May), occasional droughts.
Currency 1 New Uruguayan Peso (UYU) = 100 centésimos
Economy Traditionally based on livestock and agriculture; meat, wool, fish, wheat, barley, maize, rice; naturally-occurring minerals include granite and marble; hydroelectric power, food processing and packing, light engineering, cement, textiles, leather, steel.
GDP (2002e) $26·82 bn, per capita $7900
Human Development Index (2002) 0·831
History Originally occupied by Charrúas Indians; visited by the Spanish, 1516; part of the Spanish Viceroyalty of Río de la Plata, 1726; province of Brazil, 1814–25; independence as the Eastern Republic of Uruguay, 1828; unrest caused by Tupamaro guerrillas in late 1960s and early 1970s; military rule until 1985; a President is advised by a Council of Ministers; bicameral legislature consists of a Senate and Chamber of Deputies.

Head of State/Government
1966–7 Alberto Heber Usher
1967 Oscar Daniel Gestido
1967–72 Jorge Pacheco Areco
1972–6 Juan María Bordaberry Arocena
1976–81 Aparicio Méndez
1981–5 Gregorio Conrado Alvarez Armelino
1985–90 Julio María Sanguinetti Cairolo
1990–4 Luis Alberto Lacalle Herrera
1995–2000 Julio María Sanguinetti Cairolo
2000–5 Jorge Luis Batlle Ibáñez
2005– Tabare Vazquez

by Sir Thomas More in *Utopia* (1516); hence, any imaginary (and by implication, unattainable) ideal state. The term **dystopia** refers to the reverse, a nightmare state such as in Orwell's *Nineteen Eighty Four* (1949).

utopianism A general term to describe a political philosophy distinguished by its belief in an ideal future state of global social harmony. Its supporters work to establish the basis for the **utopia** of the future.

Utrecht [**yoo**trekt], Dutch [**oo**trekht], Lat **Trajectum ad Rhenum** 52°06N 5°07E, pop (2000e) 244 000. City in W Netherlands; political and cultural centre; Union of Utrecht, 1579; Treaties of Utrecht, 1713–14; archbishopric; railway; university (1634); cathedral (1254).

Utrecht, Treaties of (1713–14) The peace settlement ending the War of the Spanish Succession, a series of agreements between France, Spain, Britain, Holland, and the League of Augsburg. The Bourbons made considerable concessions, but Louis XIV's grandson, Philip V, retained the throne of Spain.

Utrecht School A group of Dutch painters who went to Rome early in the 17th-c and were deeply influenced by Caravaggio.

Utrillo, Maurice [**oo**treeloh] (1883–1955) Painter, born in Paris. He

was a prolific artist, producing picture-postcard views of the streets of Paris, particularly old Montmartre.

Uttar Pradesh [**oo**tar pra**daysh**] pop (2001e) 163 283 000; area 294 413 km²/113 643 sq mi. State in NC India; known as the Bengal Presidency until 1833, then divided into provinces of Agra and Oudh; under one administration, 1877; called United Provinces of Agra and Oudh, 1902; renamed as United Provinces, 1935; adopted present name in 1950; capital, Lucknow; governed by a Legislative Council and Legislative Assembly; official language, Hindi; largest producer of foodgrains in India.

Uttley, Alison, *née* **Alice Jane Taylor** (1884–1976) Writer of children's stories, born on a farm in Derbyshire. *The Country Child* (1931) was followed by a series of books, mainly for children, which revealed her knowledge of the countryside.

U2 [yoo **too**] Irish rock band made up of **Bono** (real name Paul Hewson, 1960– , vocals), **the Edge** (real name David Evans, 1961– , guitar), **Adam Clayton** (1960– , bass), and **Larry Mullen** (1961– , drums). Formed in Dublin in 1976, the group found huge international success in the 1980s and 1990s. Bono in particular has campaigned actively on human-rights issues and in 2007 received an honorary knighthood for his humani-

Uzbekistan

□ International Airport

[uzbekistahn], official name **Republic of Uzbekistan**, Uzbek **Ozbekistan Jumhuriyäti**

Local name Ozbekiston Republikasy

Timezone GMT +5

Area 447 400 km²/172 696 sq mi

Population total (2002e) 25 484 000

Status Republic

Date of independence 1991

Capital Tashkent

Language Uzbek

Ethnic groups Uzbek (71%), Russian (8%), Tajik (5%), Kazakh (4%)

Religion Sunni Muslim

Physical features Located in C and N Middle Asia; four-fifths of area is flat, sandy plain/desert (W); Turan Plain (NW) rises near the Aral Sea to 90 m/300 ft above sea level; delta of major river R Amu Darya forms alluvial plain over C Kara-Kalpak; Sultan-Uizdag Mts rise to 500 m/1600 ft; Kyzyl Kum broken by hills in SE; lowest point, Mynbulak, -12 m/-39 ft; Pskem Mts in E rise to 4299 m/14 104 ft at Beshtor Peak.

Climate Dry and continental; average annual temperatures in S, -12°C (Jan), 32–40°C (Jul); low rainfall.

Currency 1 Som (UZS) = 100 tiyin

Economy Deposits of coal, natural gas, oil, gold, lead, copper, and zinc; third largest cotton-growing area in the world; silk, wool; agriculture dependent on irrigated land; abundant orchards and vineyards; industry powered hydroelectrically.

GDP (2002e) $66·06 bn, per capita $2600

Human Development Index (2002) 0·727

History Conquered by Alexander the Great, 4th-c BC; invaded by Mongols under Genghis Khan, 13th-c; Genghis Khan's grandson, Shibaqan, inherited the area; converted to Islam in 14th-c, under the ruler of Kipchak, Uzbek; became part of Tamerlane the Great's empire, 16th-c; conquered by Russia, mid-19th-c; became the Uzbek Republic in 1924, and Uzbekistan Soviet Socialist Republic in 1925; declared independence, 1991, joined CIS in 1991; governed by a President, Prime Minister, and 250-member Supreme Assembly; new constitution adopted, 1992; proposal for a bicameral legislature approved, 2002.

Head of State
1991– Islam A Karimov

Head of Government
1991–5 Abdulhashim Mutalov
1995–2003 Otkir Sultonov
2003– Shavkat Mirziyoev

---

tarian work. Their albums include *The Joshua Tree* (1987), *Achtung Baby* (1991), and *All That You Can't Leave Behind* (2002). The group won five prizes at the 48th Grammy Awards, including best album for *How To Dismantle An Atomic Bomb* (2004), bringing their total Grammys to 24. In 2005 the band was inducted into the Rock and Roll Hall of Fame.

uvula [yoovyula] The conical, midline muscular extension of the soft palate, of variable length in humans (5–20 mm/0·2–0·8 in). It is elevated in swallowing, and is occasionally used in the production of speech sounds (eg the French 'uvular r').

Uxmal [ooshmahl] An ancient Mayan city in the Yucatan peninsula, Mexico. It flourished AD c.600–1000, and was finally abandoned c.1450.

Uzbekistan *see panel*

Vaal River [vahl] River in South Africa; length 1200 km/750 mi; a major tributary of the Orange R.

Vaasa [vahsa], Swed **Vasa**, formerly **Nikolainkaupunki** 63°06N 21°38E, pop (2000e) 55 000. Seaport in SW Finland; established, 1606; destroyed by fire, 1852; rebuilt on present site, c.1860; airfield; railway; shortest ferry route between Finland and Sweden.

Vac [vats] 47°49N 19°10E, pop (2000e) 34 300. River port and summer resort town in NC Hungary; on R Danube; bishopric; railway; cathedral.

vaccination The induction of immunity against infectious agents. The name is derived from *vaccinia* or cowpox – the virus that was administered by Edward Jenner in 1792 to protect against smallpox. It involves the introduction into the body of a small quantity of living or dead micro-organisms, or proteins (antigens) derived from them. This sensitizes the body to recognize the micro-organism as foreign and to mount an effective immune response against it in the event of a future infection, thereby preventing the development of the disease. Vaccines have been used successfully to protect against a variety of infectious diseases, and smallpox has been eradicated by a worldwide vaccination programme. Recently, there have been concerns about possible harmful side-effects, but there is no clear evidence to link vaccinations with the adverse reactions reported.

vacuum Any space in which no matter is present. In the laboratory, near vacuum is achieved by pumping out air from an enclosed chamber. A perfect vacuum can never be attained; the closest is interstellar space.

vacuum technology A technology which produces and uses pressures from a thousand to one million million times less than the atmosphere. Thin coatings (metal or non-metal) are made by evaporation in a vacuum, and used in optical instruments or the electronics industry. The technology is used to provide vacuums inside television tubes, X-ray tubes, particle accelerators, and for dehydration at low temperatures ('freeze drying').

Vadim, Roger [vadim], originally **Roger Vadim Plemiannikov** (1928–2000) Film director, born in Paris. His *Et Dieu créa la femme* (1956, And God Created Woman), starring his wife Brigitte Bardot as a sex-kitten, was a massive box-office success, and paved the way for further sex-symbol presentations of his later wives, Annette Stroyberg in *Les Liaisons dangereuses* (1959, Dangerous Liaisons), Jane Fonda in *Barbarella* (1968), and his lover, Catherine Deneuve, in *La Vice et la vertue* (1962, Vice and Virtue).

Vaduz [vahdoots] 47°08N 9°32E, pop (2000e) 5500. Capital of Liechtenstein, in the R Rhine valley; 12th-c castle (rebuilt, 20th-c).

vagina A variable-sized fibro-muscular tube, open at its lower end, which communicates at its upper end with the cavity of the uterus. In virgins the lower opening is partly closed by a thin crescent-fold (the *hymen*).

vagus [vayguhs] The 10th cranial nerve. It descends in the neck, supplying the muscles of the larynx and pharynx; in the thorax it supplies the oesophagus, trachea, lungs, heart, and great vessels; in the abdomen it supplies the stomach, the small and part of the large intestine, the pancreas, and the liver.

valence or **valency** [vaylens, vaylensee] The combining power of an atom expressed either as (1) the **covalence**, or net number of bonds an atom makes, weighting double bonds as two, etc, or (2) the **electrovalence**, essentially equivalent to the oxidation state.

Valencia (Spain) [valensia], Span [valenthia] pop (2000e) 3 881 000; area 23 260 km²/8978 sq mi. Autonomous region of E Spain, occupying a narrow coastal area from the Ebro delta to R Segura; a former Moorish kingdom, under Spanish rule from 1238; includes tourist resorts on the Costa Blanca and Costa del Azahar; chief town, Valencia, pop (2000e) 763 000, on R Turia; third largest city in Spain; archbishopric; airport; railway; car ferries to Balearics and Canary Is; university (1500); cathedral (13th–15th-c).

Valencia (Venezuela) [valensia] 10°11N 67°59W, pop (2000e) 1 093 000. Third largest city in Venezuela; on R Cabriales; railway; university (1852); cathedral (18th-c); noted for its oranges.

valentine (card) *St Valentine's Day*

Valentino [valenteenoh], popular name of **Valentino Garavani** (1933–) Fashion designer, born in Rome. He opened his own house in Rome in 1959, but achieved worldwide recognition with his 1962 show in Florence.

Valentino, Rudolph [valenteenoh] (1895–1926) Film actor, born in Castellaneta, Italy. His performances in *The Sheikh* (1921), *Blood and Sand* (1922), and other silent film dramas made him the leading 'screen lover' of the 1920s.

Vale of Glamorgan, Welsh **Bro Morgannwg** pop (2001e) 119 300; area 337 km²/130 sq mi. County (unitary authority from 1996) in S Wales, UK; administrative centre, Barry; tourism at Barry I.

Valera, Eamon de *de Valera, Eamon*

valerian A perennial herb native to Europe and Asia; flowers pink, in dense terminal heads; fruits with a parachute of feathery hairs. (Family: Valerianaceae.)

Valéry, (Ambroise) Paul (Toussaint Jules) [valayree] (1871–1945) Poet and critic, born in Sète, France. After writing a great deal of poetry he relapsed into a 20 years' silence, taken up with mathematics and philosophical speculations, later published as *Cahiers* (29 vols, 1957–60). He emerged in 1917 with a new Symbolist poetic outlook and technique.

Valetta *Valletta*

Valhalla [valhala] In Norse mythology, a great hall built by Odin to house warriors who die bravely in battle.

Valium *benzodiazepines*

Valkyries [valkeereez, valkireez] (Old Norse 'choosers of the slain') In Norse and German mythology, the Maidens of Odin. They rode out to collect warriors killed in battle for Valhalla.

Valladolid [valyadoleeth] 41°38N 4°43W, pop (2000e) 333 000. City in NWC Spain; on R Pisuerga; archbishopric; airport; railway; Columbus died here; university (1346); cathedral (16th-c).

Valle d'Aosta [valay daosta], Fr **Val d'Aoste** pop (2000e) 117 000; area 3263 km²/1259 sq mi. Autonomous region of Italy (1948), bounded W by France and N by Switzerland; population mostly French-speaking; access route to the Great and Little St Bernard Passes.

Valles Marineris [valez marinairis] A vast, complex system of interconnected canyons stretching for c.4000 km/2500 mi around Mars. Generally the canyons are over 3 km/1½ mi deep and over 100 km/60 mi wide. They were discovered by Mariner 9 orbiter in 1972, and studied in detail by Viking orbiters.

Valletta or **Valetta** [valeta] 35°54N 14°32E, pop (2000e) 107 000. Capital of Malta; a world heritage site; founded by the Knights of St John, 1566; airport; university (1769); cathedral (16th-c).

valley An elongated trough in the Earth's surface, most commonly formed by the erosional action of rivers over a long period of time. It may also be carved out by a glacier, in which case it is U-shaped rather than (as in a river valley) V-shaped.

Valley Forge National historical park in Pennsylvania, USA, 7 km/4 mi SE of Phoenixville; winter headquarters of George Washington, 1777–8; renowned for the endurance and loyalty shown by the troops during the severe winter.

Valley of the Kings A remote limestone wadi on the W bank of the R Nile at Luxor, 650 km/400 mi S of Cairo. Cut into its walls are the tombs of the Egyptian kings of the New Kingdom (XVIII–XX Dynasties, 1550–1070 BC), such as Rameses VI and Tutankhamun.

Valois, Dame Ninette de [valwah], originally **Edris Stannus** (1898–2001) Dancer, born in Blessington, Co Wicklow, Ireland. In 1931 she founded the Sadler's Wells Ballet, continuing as its artistic director until 1963. She is regarded as the pioneer of British ballet, both in her own choreography and in the development of a school and two major companies.

Valois [valwah] A ruling dynasty of France from the accession of Philip VI, Count of Valois (1328), to the death of Henry III (1589).

Valparaíso [valparaeesoh] 33°03S 71°07W, pop (2000e) 333 900. Chile's main port and a major commercial centre; founded, 1536; most old buildings destroyed by earthquakes; railway; cathedral; Naval Academy; two universities (1926, 1928).

valve *thermionic valve*

vampire In Slavic and Greek folklore a dead person of either sex whose body does not decompose after burial as expected. Vampires, like other ghosts, seek to take living people with them into the after-life. Typically, they rise at night to prey on and suck the blood of the living. Like other ghosts too, vampires are repelled by crucifixes, garlic, and daylight, and can be destroyed by being beheaded or pierced through the heart with a wooden stake. Bram Stoker's *Dracula* (1897) popularized and distorted the myth.

vampire bat A bat of family Desmodontidae, native to the New World tropics; makes shallow incision with incisors (prey usually not disturbed) and laps blood; bat's saliva prevents blood clotting; three species.

Van, Lake, Turkish **Van Gölü** area 3173 km²/1225 sq mi. Salt lake in mountainous E Anatolia, Turkey; length, 120 km/75 mi; width, 80 km/50 mi; home of the ancient Armenian civilization.

vanadium [vanaydium] V, element 23, density 6·1 g/cm³, melting point 1890°C. A transition metal, not occurring free in nature, and often replacing phosphorus as an impurity in phosphate rocks. Its main uses are in steel production, usually in combination with chromium.

Van Allen radiation belts Two rings of high-energy-charged particles surrounding the Earth, probably originating in the Sun and trapped by the Earth's magnetic field. The lower, more energetic belt is at c.300 km/185 mi from the Earth's surface; the outer belt at c.16 000 km/10 000 mi. They were discovered in 1958 by US physicist James Van Allen (1914–2006) from satellite data.

Vanbrugh, Sir John [vanbruh] (1664–1726) Playwright and Baroque architect, born in London. He scored a success with his comedies *The Relapse* (1696) and *The Provok'd Wife* (1697), and became a theatre manager with Congreve. As architect, he designed Castle Howard, Yorkshire (1699–1726).

Van Buren, Martin (1782–1862) US statesman and eighth president (1837–41), born in Kinderhook, NY. In 1824 he was a member of the group which founded the Democratic Party. Arriving in office during the financial panic of 1837, his measure introducing a treasury independent of private banks created opposition, and he was overwhelmingly defeated in 1840.

Vance, Cyrus (Roberts) (1917–2002) Lawyer and statesman, born in Clarksburg, WV. He served as secretary of state under President Carter, resigning in 1980 over the handling of the crisis when US diplomats were being held hostage in Iran. He worked with Lord Owen for the UN Security Council as the secretary-general's representative during the Yugoslavian conflict, and was instrumental in drawing up the unsuccessful Vance–Owen peace initiative (1992–3).

Vancouver 49°13N 123°06W, pop (2000e) 528 600; (Greater Vancouver) 1 468 000. Seaport in SW British Columbia, Canada; third largest city in Canada; settled c.1875, named Granville; reached by railway, 1886; city and modern name, 1886; airport; two universities (1908, 1963); professional teams, Vancouver Canucks (ice hockey), BC Lions (football); Chinatowns, second largest Chinese community in North America.

Vandals A Germanic people, originally perhaps from the Baltic area, who settled in the Danube valley in the 4th-c. They invaded Gaul (406), crossed into Spain, conquered Roman Africa (429–39), and sacked Rome (455).

Van de Graaff, Robert J(emison) (1901–67) Physicist, born in Tuscaloosa, AL. He constructed an improved type of electrostatic generator (later called the **Van de Graaff generator**), and developed this into the **Van de Graaff accelerator**, which became a major tool of atomic and nuclear physicists.

Vanderbilt, Cornelius, known as **Commodore** (1794–1877) Financier, born on Staten I, NY. By age 40 he had become the owner of steamers running to Boston and up the Hudson; and in 1849, during the gold rush, he established a route to California. At 70 he became a railroad financier. He endowed Vanderbilt University in Nashville, TN.

van der Post, Sir Laurens (Jan) [post] (1906–96) Writer, born in Philippolis, South Africa. He was best known for his books in the mixed genres of travel, anthropology, and metaphysical speculation, such as *Venture to the Interior* (1951) and *The Lost World of the Kalahari* (1958).

van der Waals, Johannes Diderik [wahlz] (1837–1923) Physicist, born in Leyden, The Netherlands. He extended the classical 'ideal' gas laws (of Boyle and Charles) to describe the behaviour of real gases, deriving the **van der Waals equation of state** in 1873. He was awarded the Nobel Prize for Physics in 1910.

Van Diemen's Land *Tasmania*

van Dyck, Sir Anthony [diyk] (1599–1641) Painter, born in Antwerp, Belgium. He travelled widely in Italy, where he painted portraits and religious subjects, and in 1632 went to London, where he was knighted by Charles I and made painter-in-ordinary. His work greatly influenced the British school of portraiture in the 18th-c, and left a thoroughly romantic glimpse of the Stuart monarchy.

Van Dyke, Dick (1925–) Popular entertainer, born in West Plains, MO. His television series, *The Dick Van Dyke Show* (1961–6), was highly popular, and won him Emmys in 1962, 1964, and 1965.

His film career includes *Mary Poppins* (1964) and *Chitty, Chitty, Bang, Bang* (1968), and he returned to the screen as Fletcher in *Dick Tracy* (1990).

Vane, Sir Henry (1613–62) English statesman, born in Hadlow, Kent. He helped to impeach Strafford, promoted the Solemn League and Covenant, supported the parliamentary cause in the Civil War, and during the Commonwealth became one of the Council of State (1649–53). At the Restoration, he was imprisoned and executed.

Vänern, Lake [venern] area 5585 km²/2156 sq mi. Lake in SW Sweden; length, 146 km/91 mi; maximum depth, 98 m/321 ft.

van Gogh, Vincent (Willem) [hokh], Br Eng [gof], US Eng [goh] (1853–90) Painter, born in Groot-Zundert, The Netherlands. At Nuenen he painted his first masterpiece, a domestic scene of peasant poverty, 'The Potato Eaters' (1885, Amsterdam). At Arles, the Provençal landscape gave him many of his best subjects, such as 'Sunflowers' (1888, Tate, London) and 'The Bridge' (1888, Cologne). He showed increasing signs of mental disturbance and, after some time in an asylum, he committed suicide. One of the pioneers of Expressionism, he used colour primarily for its emotive appeal, and profoundly influenced the Fauves and other experimenters of 20th-c art.

vanilla An evergreen climbing orchid (*Vanilla planifolia*), native to Central America. The large green flowers are followed by slender pods up to 15 cm/6 in long, which turn black when dried and contain the essence *vanillin*, used as flavouring. (Family: Orchidaceae.)

van Meegeren, Han or **Henricus** [maygeren] (1889–1947) Artist and forger, born in Deventer, The Netherlands. In 1945 he was accused of selling art treasures to the Germans. To clear himself, he confessed to having forged the pictures, and also the famous 'Supper at Emmaus', which had been 'discovered' in 1937 and was widely accepted to be by Vermeer. In 1947 he was imprisoned, and died a few weeks later.

Vannes [van], ancient **Dariorigum** 47°40N 2°47W, pop (2000e) 50 600. Port in NW France; railway; picturesque Old Town, cathedral (13th–19th-c).

van Nistelrooy, Ruud [nistelroy], properly **Rutgerus van Nistelrooy** (1976–) Footballer, born in Oss, SE Netherlands. After playing for several Dutch clubs (from 1993) he moved to Manchester United Football Club for a British record transfer fee of £19 million in 2001. He transferred to Real Madrid in July 2006, when he had gained 54 international caps.

Vanua Levu [vanooa layvoo] area 5556 km²/2145 sq mi. Mountainous volcanic island in SW Pacific Ocean; second largest of the Fiji Is; length 176 km/109 mi; chief town, Labasa; severely damaged by Cyclone Ami (Jan 2003).

Vanuatu *p.977*

Van Vleck, John H(asbrouck) (1899–1980) Physicist, born in Middletown, CT. He founded the modern theory of magnetism based on quantum theory, and also devised theories of magnetic behaviour in crystals. His classic treatise, *The Theory of Electric and Magnetic Susceptibilities* (1932), earned him the title 'the father of modern magnetism'. He shared the Nobel Prize for Physics in 1977.

Varanasi *Benares*

variable star Any star with a luminosity that is not constant. The variation can be regular or irregular. The principal types are Cepheid variables, RR Lyrae stars, and the long-period Mira variables.

variations (music) A type of musical composition in which a theme is presented a number of times in different guises or with fresh embellishments. The theme itself may be the composer's own (eg Haydn's *Variations in F minor* for piano), or someone else's (eg Brahm's *Variations on a Theme of Paganini*), or a folksong (eg Delius's *Brigg Fair*).

varicose veins Distended veins which result from obstruction to the flow of blood within them or incompetence of their valves. They may occur anywhere in the body, but the veins in the legs are most often affected. When severe, they lead to pain and swelling.

Varna, formerly **Stalin** (1949–56), Lat **Odessus** 43°13N 27°56E, pop (2000e) 298 400. Resort in E Bulgaria; site of defeat by the Turks (1444); third largest town and largest harbour in Bulgaria; airport; railway; Roman thermae and baths.

varnish A liquid which dries to a hard protective transparent or decorative film, consisting of a solution of gums in oil with a thinner such as turpentine. **Spirit varnishes** have resins (such as, notably, shellac) dissolved in alcohol (industrial or methylated spirit). Modern varieties have polymers such as polyurethane in solvents.

varnish tree *lacquer tree*

Varro, Marcus Terentius (116–27 BC) Roman scholar and author, born in Reate, Italy. He wrote over 600 books, covering a wide range of subject matter; only his work on agriculture and part of his book on Latin survive.

varve dating A method of dating the ages of Pleistocene shales, by counting the layers (**varves**) found in the fine lake sediments deposited by the water flowing from glaciers. The layered arrangement arises from the alternation of fine and coarser material from winter to summer.

Vasa (Finland) *Vaasa*

Vasa (Sweden) A royal dynasty that provided all Swedish monarchs from 1523 to 1818, with only two exceptions. It was founded by Gustavus I (r.1523–60), who led the country's conversion to the Lutheran Reformation and ousted foreign powers.

Vasarely, Viktor [voshoraylee] (1908–97) Painter, born in Pecs, Hungary. His particular kind of geometrical–abstract painting, which he began to practise c.1947, pioneered the visually disturbing effects that were later called Op Art.

Vasari, Giorgio [vazahree] (1511–74) Art historian, born in Arezzo, Italy. He was an architect and painter, best known for his design of the Uffizi in Florence, but today his fame rests on his *Lives of the Most Eminent Italian Architects, Painters, and Sculptors* (1550), which remains the major source of information on its subject.

vascular plant Any plant possessing xylem and phloem, distinct conducting tissues which together make up the vascular system; they include flowering plants, gymnosperms, ferns, clubmosses, and horsetails, and in some classifications form the division Tracheophyta. Additional differences between vascular plants and the non-vascular bryophytes and algae are the presence of stomata, and the sporophyte as the dominant generation.

vasectomy *sterilization* 1

vassal A freeman who had acknowledged the lordship of a superior by giving homage and swearing fealty, normally in return for a fief. The lord's default, especially in giving protection, rendered the relationship void, as did the disobedient vassal's withholding of military assistance and general support.

VAT Acronym for **value-added tax**, an indirect tax levied on products or services as a percentage of their value. The customer pays VAT in addition to the normal price. The seller pays VAT on the value of sales, less VAT on purchased inputs. VAT is used in many countries; in the UK it was introduced in 1973, replacing purchase tax. Some goods, such as food in the UK, or businesses below a minimum turnover, are exempt.

Vatican City, Ital **Stato della Città del Vaticano** pop c.1000; area 44 ha/109 acres. Papal sovereign state in Rome, on the W bank of the R Tiber; created in 1929 by the Lateran Treaty; timezone GMT +1; includes St Peter's, the Vatican Palace and Museum,

Vanuatu

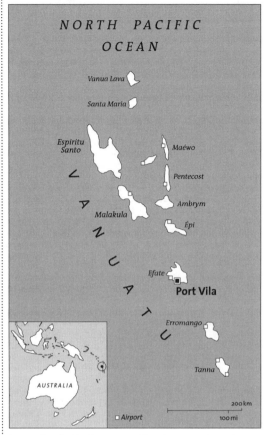

NORTH PACIFIC
OCEAN

Vanua Lava

Santa Maria

Espiritu
Santo

Maéwo

Pentecost

Ambrym

Malakula

Épi

Efate

Port Vila

Erromango

Tanna

AUSTRALIA

200 km
100 mi

☐ Airport

Status Independent republic within the Commonwealth
Date of independence 1980
Capital Port Vila (on Efate Island)
Languages Bislama, English, and French (official)
Ethnic groups Melanesian (95%), Micronesian, Polynesian, and European minorities
Religions Christian (70%) (Presbyterian 40%, Roman Catholic 15%, Anglican 15%), indigenous beliefs (8%), other (15%)
Physical features Mountainous, volcanic Y-shaped island chain in SW Pacific Ocean, 400 km/250 mi NE of New Caledonia; consisting of 12 islands and 60 islets; two-thirds of population occupy the 4 main islands of Efate, Espiritu Santo, Malekula, and Tanna; highest peak, rises to 1888 m/6194 ft, on Espiritu Santo; islands comprise raised coral beaches fringed by reefs; several active volcanoes.
Climate Tropical, high temperatures; hot and rainy season (Nov–Apr) when cyclones may occur; average annual temperatures, 27°C (Jan), 22°C (Jul) in Vila; average annual rainfall 2310 mm/91 in.
Currency 1 Vatu (VUV) = 100 centimes
Economy Agriculture; subsistence farming and plantations; yams, breadfruit, taro, copra, beef, cocoa, coffee, timber; manganese, fish processing, foodstuffs, crafts; tourism rapidly increasing, especially from cruise ships.
GDP (2002e) $563 mn, per capita $2900
Human Development Index (2002) 0·542
History Visited by the Spanish, 1606; charted and named the New Hebrides by British explorer James Cook, 1774; under Anglo-French administration as the condominium of the New Hebrides, 1906; escaped Japanese occupation during World War 2; independence as the Republic of Vanuatu, 1980; inter-tribal violence led to a state of emergency (Mar 2007); governed by a President, Prime Minister, Cabinet, and representative Assembly.

Head of State
1999–2004 John Bennett Bani
2004 Alfred Maseng Nalo
2004 Roger Abiut *Acting*
2004– Kalkot Mataskelekele
Head of Government
1999–2001 Barak Sope
2001–4 Edward Natapei
2004 Serge Vohor
2004– Ham Lini

[vanooahtoo], official name **Republic of Vanuatu**, formerly **New Hebrides**
Local name Ripablik Blong Vanuatu
Timezone GMT +11
Area 14 763 km²/5698 sq mi
Population total (2002e) 207 000

---

several buildings in Rome, and the pope's summer villa at Castel Gandolfo; issues its own stamps, and formerly its own coinage; it adopted the euro in 2002.

Vatican Councils Two councils of the Roman Catholic Church. The **First Vatican Council** (1869–70) was called by Pope Pius IX to deal with doctrine, discipline and canon law, foreign missions, and the relationship between Church and state. It is best remembered for the decree on papal infallibility (1870). The **Second Vatican Council** (1962–5) was called by Pope John XXIII, with the task of renewing religious life and bringing up-to-date the belief, structure, and discipline of the Church (*aggiornamento*).

Vättern, Lake [vetern], also **Vetter** or **Wetter** area 1912 km²/738 sq mi. Lake in S Sweden; extends 130 km/81 mi; maximum width 30 km/19 mi.

Vauban, Sebastien le Prestre de [vohbã] (1633–1707) French soldier and military engineer, born in Saint Léger. He brought about a revolution in siege warfare and fortification, directing siege operations throughout Louis XIV's campaigns, and surrounding the kingdom with a cordon of fortresses (1667–88).

vaudeville In the USA, a variety show tradition stemming from the family entertainments created by Tony Pastor from 1881 onwards. In France, the term was originally used for the dumb shows with songs of the Paris fairs, and later for the light satirical songs popular in 18th-c theatres.

Vaughan, Henry [vawn] (1622–95) Religious poet, born in Newton-by-Usk, S Wales. His best-known works are the pious meditations, *Silex scintillans* (1650, enlarged 1655) and the prose devotions *The Mount of Olives* (1652).

Vaughan, Michael (1974–) Cricketer, born in Eccles, Manchester. A batsman and bowler, he played county cricket for Yorkshire and made his Test debut for England against South Africa at Johannesburg in 1999. In 2003 he was named captain of England's one-day team, and then appointed Test captain. He led

England to a Test series win over Bangladesh (Nov 2003), and a successful season in 2004 included a 4–0 victory over the West Indies. At the end of the year he led England's controversial tour of Zimbabwe, winning the series of one-day matches. In the following Test series against South Africa, England achieved a record-breaking eighth successive Test victory with a win in the opening match, and went on to win the series 2–1. In 2005 he captained England at home in their successful bid to regain the Ashes for the first time since 1987 in a closely fought Test series hailed as the best ever. He missed most of the 2006 season because of injury but returned as captain in January 2007 for a one-day series against Australia and New Zealand.

Vaughan Williams, Ralph [vawn] (1872–1958) Composer, born in Down Ampney, Gloucestershire. He developed a national style of music which derived from English choral tradition, especially of the Tudor period, and folksong. His works include nine symphonies, the opera *The Pilgrim's Progress* (1948–9), and scores for the stage and cinema, such as *The Wasps* (1909) and *Scott of the Antarctic* (1948).

vault An arched covering over any building; usually built of stone or brick, and sometimes imitated in wood or plaster. Various configurations exist, including the barrel, cross, domical, fan, and rib vaults.

Vavilov, Nikolay Ivanovich [vavilof] (1887–1943) Plant geneticist, born in Moscow. In 1930 he was appointed by Lenin to direct Soviet agricultural research, and established 400 institutes, and a collection of 26 000 varieties of wheat. His reputation was challenged by Lysenko, who denounced him at a genetics conference in 1937. Vavilov was arrested in 1940, and is thought to have died in a Siberian concentration camp.

VDU *visual display unit*

Veblen, Thorstein (Bunde) [veblen] (1857–1929) Economist and social scientist, born in Cato, WI. His best-known work is *The Theory of the Leisure Class* (1899), in which he attempted to apply an evolutionary approach to the study of economics.

vector (mathematics) In mathematics, a quantity having magnitude and direction. Vector quantities include position (showing the position of one point relative to another), displacement (the distance in a certain direction), velocity, acceleration, force, and momentum. They contrast with the *scalar* quantities of distance, time, mass, energy, etc, which have magnitude only.

vector (medicine) An organism, commonly an arthropod, which acts as an intermediary agent in transferring a pathogenic micro-organism from one host to another. Examples are ticks in typhus, and mosquitoes in malaria.

Veda [vayda] The 'sacred knowledge' of the Hindus, dating from c.1500 BC, contained in the four collections called the *Vedas*, the *Brahmanas* appended to them, and the *Aranyakas* and *Upanishads* which serve as an epilogue or conclusion. Originally the Veda consisted of the **Rig-veda** (sacred songs or hymns of praise), **Sama-veda** (melodies and chants used by priests during sacrifices), and **Yajur-veda** (sacrificial formulae); to which was later added the **Athara-veda** (spells, charms, and exorcistic chants).

Vedanta (Sanskrit 'conclusion of the Veda') Originally the teachings of the Upanishads; later, a trend in Indian philosophy advocating the identity of the individual self, *atman*, with a transindividual super-self, *brahman*, an undifferentiated being-and-consciousness considered the single source of cognition and action.

Vega [vayga] *Lyra*

Vega (Carpio), Lope (Félix) de [vayga] (1562–1635) Playwright and poet, born in Madrid. He first made his mark as a ballad writer, and after 1588 produced a wide range of historical and contemporary dramas – about 2000 plays and dramatic pieces, of which over 400 still survive.

vegan *vegetarianism*

VEGA project [vayga] A highly successful Soviet mission to Venus and Halley's Comet undertaken 1984–6; the name is an acronym based on the Russian equivalents for 'Venus' and 'Halley'. Two spacecraft each deployed a lander and a balloon at Venus (Jun 1985), then used a Venus gravity assist to fly on to intercept Halley's Comet (6 and 9 Mar 1986), Vega 2 passing within 8900 km/5530 mi of its nucleus. The balloons were deployed at 54 km/34 mi altitude and tracked for two days by an international network of antennas. The mission also provided the first close-up view of the comet's nucleus, and the first measurements of gas and dust properties, before being severely battered by Halley dust, becoming non-operational.

vegetable In a broad sense, anything of or concerning plants; but commonly referring to a plant or its parts, other than fruits and sometimes seeds, used for food. The term is often qualified by reference to the particular parts eaten (eg leaf vegetable, root vegetable). A number of foods often called vegetables are actually fruits, such as the tomato.

vegetarianism The practice of eating a diet devoid of meat. People who follow a diet containing dairy products and eggs are known as **ovo-lacto-vegetarians**. Those who shun all animal foods are known as **vegans**. The vegetarian diet may be healthier than that of the omnivore, since it is likely to contain less fat and more fibre. There are few nutritional disadvantages, the only possible problem being in the low availability of iron in vegetable foods. Veganism, however, does pose problems, with low dietary intakes of available calcium, iron, and zinc, and little or no dietary intake of vitamin B_{12}, which is not found in plants.

vein A vessel usually conveying deoxygenated blood from tissues back to the heart. **Deep veins** accompany arteries; **superficial veins** lie in the subcutaneous tissue, and often appear as blue channels just below the skin (eg at the wrist and on the forearm). Blood flow in veins is slower and at a lower pressure than in arteries; consequently veins are often larger and their walls are thinner.

Vejle [viyluh] 55°43N 9°30E, pop (2000e) 52 900. Seaport and manufacturing town in E Jutland, Denmark; railway; church (13th-c); 28 km/17 mi W is Billund, with Legoland®, a miniature town built of Lego® plastic bricks.

Vela [veela] (Lat 'sails') A S constellation in the Milky Way whose four brightest stars form a near quadrilateral. It includes the Vela pulsar.

Velázquez, Diego (Rodriguez de Silva) [velathketh] (1599–1660) Painter, born in Seville, Spain. He produced several domestic genre pieces and court portraits, but is best known for his three late masterpieces, 'Las Meninas' (1655, The Maids of Honour; Madrid), 'Las Hilanderas' (c.1657, The Tapestry Weavers; Madrid), and 'Venus and Cupid', known as 'The Rokeby Venus' (c.1658, National Gallery, London).

Velde, Henry (Clemens) van de [velduh] (1863–1957) Architect, born in Antwerp, Belgium. He established the famous Weimar School of Arts and Crafts (1906) from which developed the Bauhaus.

Velde, Willem van de [velduh], known as **the Elder** (c.1611–93) Marine painter, born in Leyden, The Netherlands. He came to England in 1657, and painted large pictures of sea battles for Charles II and James II. His son, **Willem van de Velde, the Younger** (1633–1707) became court painter to Charles II (of England) in 1674. A second son, **Adriaen van de Velde** (1636–72), was a landscape painter.

veld(t) [velt] The undulating plateau grassland of S Africa, primarily in Zimbabwe and the Republic of South Africa. It can be divided into the **high veld** (over 1500 m/c.5000 ft), **middle veld** (900–1500 m/c.3000–5000 ft) and **low veld** (under 900 m/c.3000 ft).

Veliko Turnovo [velikuh toornovuh] 43°04N 25°39E, pop (2000e)

60 400. City in NEC Bulgaria; on the R Yantra; capital of the second Bulgarian kingdom (1187–1393); airport; railway; Tsarevets Hill.

Velingrad 42°01N 23°59E, pop (2000e) 23 200. Spa town in S Bulgaria; a therapeutic centre, with 70 thermal springs; railway.

vellum parchment

velocity For *linear motion*, the rate of change of distance with time in a given direction; velocity *v*, units m/s. For *rotational motion*, it is the rate of change of angle with time; **angular velocity** ω, units radian/s. Both are vector quantities.

velocity of light A universal constant, the same value for all observers and all types of electromagnetic radiation; symbol *c*, approximate value 2.998×10^8 m/s (roughly 186 000 mi/s).

Veltman, Martinus (J G) (1931–) Physicist, born in The Netherlands. He became professor of physics at Utrecht (1966) and at the University of Michigan (1981). He shared the 1999 Nobel Prize for Physics for his role in elucidating the quantum structure of electroweak interactions.

Velvet Underground US rock band, formed in 1966, originally with **Lou Reed** (1944– , vocals, songwriter), **John Cale** (1940– , vocals, various instruments, songwriter), **Sterling Morrison** (1942–95, bass guitar), **Maureen Tucker** (1944– , drums), and (slightly later) **Nico** (pseudonym of **Christa Päffgen**, 1940–88, vocals). Their albums *The Velvet Underground and Nico* (1967) and *White Heat/White Light* (1968) have since become rock classics. The band broke up in 1970.

velvet worm A primitive terrestrial arthropod; body cylindrical, segmented, length up to 150 mm/6 in; head with a pair of antennae and a pair of jaws; c.70 species, mostly nocturnal. (Phylum: Arthropoda. Subphylum: Onychophora.)

Venables, Terry, popular name of **Terence Frederick Venables** (1943–) Football player and manager, born in London. He played with Chelsea (1958–66), Tottenham Hotspur (1966–8) and Queens Park Rangers (1968–73), then managed Crystal Palace (1976–80), Queens Park Rangers (1980–4), Barcelona (1984–7), and Tottenham Hotspur (1987–93). He was the English national team coach (1994–6), then coach to the Australian national side. He returned to English football as coach with Middlesbrough (2000) and Leeds United (2002–3), and was appointed assistant coach to the England team in 2006.

Venda [venda] Former independent black homeland in NE South Africa; self-government, 1973; granted independence by South Africa (not recognized internationally), 1979; military coup, 1990; incorporated into Northern Province in the South African constitution of 1994.

Vendée, Wars of the [vãday] French counter-revolutionary insurrections in the W provinces against the central government in Paris. The brutal rising in La Vendée (1793), when priests and nobles encouraged the conservative peasantry to rebel against the Convention's conscription and anticlerical policies, was a precedent for other provincial revolts in 1795, 1799, 1815, and 1832.

Vendôme, Louis Joseph, duc de (Duke of) [vãdohm] (1654–1712) French general, born in Paris, the great-grandson of Henry IV. He commanded in Italy and Flanders during the War of the Spanish Succession (1701–13), was victorious at Cassano (1705) and Calcinato (1706), but defeated at Oudenaarde by Marlborough (1708).

Venera Programme [venaira] A highly successful evolutionary series of Soviet space missions to Venus, 1961–83. Its highlights include: the first complete descent to the surface (Venera 5, 1969); the first TV pictures from the surface (Venera 9, 1975); and the first balloons deployed and tracked in the atmosphere (VEGA, 1985).

venereal disease (VD) A range of infectious diseases usually transmitted by sexual contact and occasionally in other ways. Examples include AIDS, hepatitis B and C virus infection, syphilis, gonorrhoea, herpes, and chancroid.

Venetian School The art associated with Venice, beginning with the building of the Basilica of St Mark in the 11th-c. Painting developed from the 14th-c onwards, leading masters including Bellini, Giorgione, Titian, Veronese, and Tintoretto. The Baroque period saw the building of magnificent churches such as Sta Maria della Salute, and the 18th-c saw a final flowering in painting, with Tiepolo, Canaletto, and Guardi.

Venezuela *p.980*

Venice, Ital **Venezia**, Lat **Venetia** 45°26N 12°20E, pop (2000e) 317 000. Seaport in NE Italy, at the head of the Adriatic Sea; 4 km/2 mi from the Italian mainland in a salt-water lagoon; built on 118 small islands, and crossed by numerous canals, notably the Grand Canal, the main traffic artery; the houses and palaces are built on piles; connects with the mainland by a road and rail causeway, and by ferries; patriarch-archbishopric; airport; railway; a major tourist area; St Mark's Cathedral (remodelled 11th-c) and Campanile (97 m/319 ft-high bell-tower, rebuilt 1905–12), Doge's Palace (14th–15th-c), Bridge of Sighs (c.1595), Church of Saints John and Paul (13th-c); city has sunk 23 cm/9 in during the last century; fresh anxiety since the 1980s over the risk to the city from flooding and pollution; Moses Project with underwater barriers to prevent tidal flooding launched, 2003 (planned completion 2011); Venice and the lagoon are world heritage sites.

Venn diagram In mathematics, a diagram illustrating the relations between sets, devised by the English logician, John Venn (1834–1923). For example, the diagram shows that Set *A* is a subset of *B*, and *B* does not contain any elements of *C*, ie *B* and *C* are disjoint.

ventricles 1 The chambers of the heart which eject blood into the pulmonary trunk (right ventricle) or the aorta (left ventricle). **2** The spaces within the brain where cerebrospinal fluid (CSF) is produced. There are four ventricles, below which a central canal extends into the spinal cord.

Ventris, Michael (George Francis) (1922–56) Linguist, born in Wheathampstead, Hertfordshire. He investigated Minoan scripts found on tablets excavated at palace sites in Crete (Linear B), and in 1952 announced that the language was early Greek, a conclusion later confirmed by other scholars.

Ventura Publisher® [ventyoora] A desk-top publishing package developed by Xerox for the preparation of large textual documents such as scientific papers and books.

Venturi tube [ventooree] A device for measuring the amount of fluid flowing in a tube; named after the Italian physicist Giovanni Battista Venturi (1746–1822). The tube is constricted to form a throat, and pressure is measured on either side, the pressure difference indicating the rate of flow.

Venus (astronomy) The second major planet from the Sun, attaining the greatest brilliancy in the night sky, outshining all the stars, hence its poetic names 'morning/evening star'. There are no natural satellites. It has the following characteristics: mass 4.87×10^{24} kg; radius 6052 km/3760 mi; mean density 5.2 g/cm³; equatorial gravity 887 cm/s²; rotational period 243 days (retrograde); orbital period 224.7 days; obliquity 0°; orbital eccentricity 0.007; mean distance from the Sun 108.2×10^6 km/67.2×10^6 mi. It is a near twin to Earth in size and density, but with a radically different atmosphere of mainly carbon dioxide, 90 times denser than our own, and with surface temperatures near 460°C. The thick atmosphere and cloud cover create a greenhouse effect that maintains high temperatures. There is no observable magnetic field. About 85% consists of volcanic plains marked by thousands of individual volcanic constructs and relatively few impact craters.

Venus (mythology) Originally an obscure Italian deity of the

Venezuela

□ International Airport - - - Disputed border

[venezwayla], official name **Bolivarian Republic of Venezuela**, Span **República Bolivariana de Venezuela**

Local name República Bolivariana de Venezuela

Timezone GMT -4

Area 912 050 km²/352 051 sq mi

Population total (2002e) 25 093 000

Status Republic

Date of independence 1830

Capital Caracas

Languages Spanish (official), Italian, c.25 Indian languages also spoken in the interior

Ethnic groups Mestizo (69%), European (20%), African origin (9%), Indian (2%)

Religions Roman Catholic (92%), Protestant (2%)

Physical features Occupies most of the N coast of South America; Guiana Highlands (SE) cover almost half the country; Venezuelan Highlands in the W and along the coast, highest point, Pico Bolívar 5007 m/16 411 ft; vast grasslands (Llanos) in the Orinoco basin; chief river, Orinoco; largest lake in South America, L Maracaibo, 21 486 km²/8296 sq mi; highest waterfall in the world, Angel Falls 979 m/3212 ft.

Climate Tropical, generally hot and humid; average annual temperatures 18°C (Jan), 21°C (Jul) in Caracas; one rainy season (Apr–Oct); average annual rainfall 833 mm/33 in.

Currency 1 Bolívar (VEB) = 100 céntimos

Economy Since 1920s, based on oil from Maracaibo (now provides over 90% of export revenue); aluminium (second-highest source of revenue); iron ore, gold, diamonds; only 4% of the land is under permanent cultivation; beef and dairy farming; coffee, cocoa, cotton, rice, tobacco, sugar.

GDP (2002e) $131·7 bn, per capita $5400

Human Development Index (2002) 0·770

History Originally inhabited by Caribs and Arawaks; seen by Columbus, 1498; Spanish settlers, 1520; frequent revolts against Spanish colonial rule; independence movement under Simón Bolívar, led to establishment of State of Gran Colombia (Colombia, Ecuador, Venezuela), 1821; independent republic, 1830; short-lived military coup, April 2002; President Chavez' position confirmed by referendum amid opposition claims of ballot-rigging, 2004; Chávez (re-elected Dec 2006) granted power to rule by decree, Jan 2007; governed by an elected unicameral National Assembly (new constitution 1999).

Head of State/Government

1959–64 Romulo Betancourt
1964–9 Raul Leoni
1969–74 Rafael Caldera Rodriguez
1974–9 Carlos Andrés Pérez
1979–84 Luis Herrera Campins
1984–9 Jaime Lusinchi
1989–93 Carlos Andrés Pérez
1993 Ramon José Velásquez *Interim*
1994–8 Rafael Caldera Rodríguez
1998–2002 Hugo Chavez Fríaz
2002 Pedro Carmona *Transitional*
2002– Hugo Chavez Fríaz

vegetable garden, she was identified with Aphrodite, and, as a Roman goddess, took over the latter's mythology and attributes.

Venus Express The European Space Agency's first mission to Venus. The spacecraft lifted off on a Soyuz-Fregat rocket from the Baikonur Cosmodrome in Kazakhstan in November 2005, beginning its five-month long journey to the planet. A probe successfully entered an elliptical orbit around Venus (Apr 2006) to begin studying its atmosphere, which has experienced rapid greenhouse warming. Scientists hope the mission (extended from two years until 2009) will enhance their knowledge of the mechanisms of climate change on our own world.

Venus's fly trap A small carnivorous perennial (*Dionaea muscipula*), native only to the pine barrens of SE USA. Each leaf is divided into a lower, winged portion and an upper portion (the trap) formed by two lobes each bearing three trigger hairs and fringed with teeth. Stimulation of these hairs by an insect causes the lobes to snap shut, the teeth crossing to trap the prey. (Family: Droseraceae.)

Veracruz [vayrakroos] 19°11N 96°10W, pop (2000e) 394 000. Seaport in E Mexico; site of Cortés landing, 1519; airport; railway; principal port of entry for Mexico; Castle of San Juan de Ulúa (1565).

verbena *lemon verbena*; *vervain*

Verdi, Giuseppe (Fortunino Francesco) [vairdee] (1813–1901) Composer, born in Le Roncole, Italy. His first major success was *Nabucco* (1842). *Rigoletto* (1851), *Il Trovatore* (1853), and *La Traviata* (1853) established him as the leading Italian operatic composer of the day. His spectacular *Aïda* was commissioned for the new opera house in Cairo, built in celebration of the Suez Canal (1871). Apart from the *Requiem* (1874), there was then a lull in output until, in his old age, he produced *Otello* (1887) and *Falstaff* (1893).

verdigris [verdigree] Basic copper carbonate, approximately

$Cu_3(CO_3)_2(OH)_2$, formed in the atmospheric corrosion of copper surfaces. It is green in colour.

Verdun *World War 1*

Vereeniging, Peace of [veray**ni**ging] (1902) The peace treaty which ended the Boer War, signed at Pretoria. The Boers won three important concessions: an amnesty for those who had risen in revolt within the Cape Colony; a promise that the British would deny the franchise to Africans until after the Boer republics were returned to representative government; and additional financial support for reconstruction.

Vergil *Virgil*

verificationism In philosophy, the criterion of significance applied by logical positivists. A statement or principle was said to be meaningful only if it was analytical or if it could in principle be verified by empirical observation. The effect, and the intention, was to discriminate in favour of science, logic, and mathematics and against metaphysics, theology, and normative ethics.

Verlaine, Paul (Marie) [ver**len**] (1844–96) Poet, born in Metz, France. He mixed with the leading Parnassian writers, and achieved success with his second book of poetry, *Fêtes galantes* (1869). He travelled in Europe with the young poet Rimbaud, but their friendship ended in Brussels (1873) when Verlaine, drunk and desolate at Rimbaud's intention to leave, shot him in the wrist. While in prison he wrote *Romances sans paroles* (1874, Songs Without Words). Later works include critical studies, notably *Les Poètes maudits* (1884), short stories, and sacred and profane verse.

Vermeer, Jan [ver**mayr**] (1632–75) Painter, born in Delft, The Netherlands. He painted small, detailed domestic interiors, notable for their use of perspective and treatment of the various tones of daylight. Forty of his paintings are known, among them the 'Allegory of Painting' (c.1665, Vienna) and 'Woman Reading a Letter' (c.1662, Amsterdam).

vermiculite [ver**mik**yuliyt] A group of clay minerals formed by the alteration of micas. They consist of porous and flaky particles which expand to about 20 times their volume when heated, producing low-density, thermally insulating, and inert material. This is used in plaster, insulation, and packing material, and as a medium for raising plants from seed.

vermilion *mercury* (chemistry)

Vermont [ver**mont**] pop (2000e) 608 800; area 24 899 km²/9614 sq mi. New England state in NE USA; the 'Green Mountain State'; explored by Champlain, 1609; first settlement established at Fort Dummer, 1724; 14th state admitted to the Union, 1791; capital, Montpelier; the Green Mts run N–S through the C; highest point, Mt Mansfield (1339 m/4393 ft); forestry and timber products, arable farming, dairy products, maple syrup, marble and granite.

vermouth A fortified red or white wine. Pure alcohol is used for the fortification, up to the same alcohol level as sherry, and various herbs and spices are added for flavour.

vernal equinox *equinox*

Verne, Jules (1828–1905) Writer, born in Nantes, France. He developed a new vein in fiction, exaggerating and anticipating the possibilities of science. His best-known books are *Voyage au centre de la terre* (1864, Journey to the Centre of the Earth), *Vingt mille lieues sous les mers* (1870, Twenty Thousand Leagues under the Sea), and *Voyage autour du monde en quatre-vingts jours* (1873, Around the World in Eighty Days). Several successful films have been made from his novels.

Vernon, Edward, nickname **Old Grog** (1684–1757) British admiral, born in London. In 1739, during the War of Jenkins' Ear, his capture of Portobello made him a national hero. He was nicknamed 'Old Grog', from his grogram coat, and in 1740 ordered the dilution of navy rum with water, the mixture being thereafter known as 'grog'.

Verona [ve**rohna**] 45°26N 11°00E, pop (2000e) 264 000. City in N Italy, on the R Adige; important communications centre; railway; agricultural market centre; many Roman and mediaeval remains; cathedral (12th–15th-c); a world heritage site.

Veronese, Paolo [vayro**nayzay**], originally **Paolo Caliari** (c.1528–88) Venetian decorative painter, born in Verona, Italy. His major paintings include 'The Marriage Feast at Cana' (1562–3, Louvre), 'The Adoration of the Magi' (1573, National Gallery, London), and 'Feast in the House of the Levi' (1573, Venice), which brought him before the Inquisition for trivializing religious subjects.

Verrazano-Narrows Bridge A major steel suspension bridge across the entrance to New York harbour; constructed in 1959–64; length of main span 1298 m/4260 ft; Narrows named after the Italian explorer, Giovanni da Verrazano (1485–1528).

Verrocchio, Andrea del [ve**rohkioh**], originally **Andrea del Cione** (c.1435–88) Sculptor, painter, and goldsmith, born in Florence, Italy. He is best known for his magnificent equestrian statue of Colleoni at Venice.

verruca [vuh**rooka**] *wart*

Versace, Gianni [ver**sachee**] (1946–97) Fashion designer, born in Reggio di Calabria, Italy. He launched his own ready-to-wear collection in 1978, and became known for his glamorous styles, producing a range of siren dresses that became his trademark, and often using innovative materials and techniques. He was shot dead by an assassin outside his home in Miami Beach, Florida.

Versailles [vair**siy**] A chateau built for Louis XIII at the village of Versailles, 23 km/14 mi SW of Paris in the 17th-c, and transformed under Louis XIV to create a palace, unequalled in its display of wealth, in which to house the entire court. Later extensions were the Grand Trianon (a smaller residence in the palace grounds) and the Petit Trianon (added by Louis XV). The palace was ransacked during the French Revolution, but has been restored to its original state, and is now a world heritage site.

Versailles, Treaty of [vair**siy**] A peace treaty drawn up in 1919 between Germany and the Allied powers at Paris. Germany and her allies were made responsible for reparation payments. Germany lost all overseas colonies, and considerable territory to Poland in the E. The Rhineland was demilitarized and occupied by Allied troops, and German armed forces were strictly limited.

verse A single line of poetry, a stanza, or poetry in general ('English verse'). *Versification* refers to the technical characteristics of a given poetic form, and also to the exploitation of these by a given poet. *Verse* also has a special use in biblical contexts, where it refers to a traditional division of the text of a chapter.

vertebra *vertebral column*

vertebral column The backbone of all vertebrates: a series of bony elements (**vertebrae**) separated by **intervertebral discs**, and held together by ligaments and muscles. In the majority of vertebrates the column lies horizontally, being supported by hindlimbs and forelimbs. In humans it is held erect and supported by the hindlimbs only. It carries and supports the thorax, and gives attachment to many muscles; it surrounds and protects the spinal cord from mechanical trauma; it acts as a shock-absorber (by virtue of its curvatures and the presence of the intervertebral discs); and it can transmit forces from one part of the body to another. In humans it is 72–75 cm/28–30 in long (c.40% of an individual's height) and consists of 7 cervical, 12 thoracic, 5 lumbar, 5 fused sacral, and 4 fused coccygeal vertebrae. Each intervertebral disc consists of a central gelatinous core surrounded by rings of fibrous tissue. During the course of the day the discs gradually lose water and become thinner; consequently at the end of the day an individual is not as tall as first thing in the morning (the difference may be as large as 2 cm/0·8 in. Similarly, with increasing age the discs also lose water, so that an individual's height may decrease in later life.

Vertebrata *Chordata*

Vertical Take-Off and Landing *VTOL*

vertigo An abnormal sensation of movement, either of the body in space, or of other objects around it; affected individuals complain of feeling dizzy or giddy. It is usually a symptom of disorders such as infections that affect the balance apparatus located in the inner ear.

Verulamium [veryulaymium] A Belgic town in Roman Britain which stood on the site of present-day St Albans. Completely destroyed in the Revolt of Boadicea (Boudicca) in AD 60, it was later rebuilt and became a focal point for the Romanization of the province.

vervain A tough-stemmed perennial (*Verbena officinalis*), growing to 60 cm/2 ft, native to Europe, Asia, and N Africa; flowers lilac, in slender spikes. (Family: Verbenaceae.)

vervet monkey A guenon (*Cercopithecus aethiops*) native to Africa S of the Sahara; yellow-brown with a black face surrounded by white whiskers.

Verwoerd, Hendrik (Frensch) [fervoort] (1901–66) South African statesman and prime minister (1958–66), born in Amsterdam. His administration was marked by the highly controversial policy of apartheid, and the establishment of South Africa as a Republic (1962). He was assassinated in Cape Town.

Very, Edward Wilson [veeree] (1847–1910) US ordnance expert and inventor. In 1877 he invented chemical flares (**Very lights**) for signalling at night.

Very Large Array The world's most elaborate full synthesis radio telescope at Socorro, NM, consisting of 27 antennae arranged on rail tracks forming a Y. It is used to investigate the structure of gaseous nebulae in our Galaxy, and of remote radio galaxies and quasars.

very large scale integration (VLSI) A technique of manufacturing integrated circuits with a very high number of individual components. It is usually defined to refer to integrated circuits containing more than 100 000 components in one chip.

Vesalius, Andreas [vezaylius], Lat name of **Andries van Wesel** (1514–64) Anatomist, born in Brussels. His major work was *De humani corporis fabrica libri septem* (1543, The Seven Books on the Structure of the Human Body), which greatly advanced the science of anatomy with its detailed descriptions and drawings.

Vespasian [vespayzhn], in full **Titus Flavius Vespasianus** (9–79) Roman emperor (69–79), born near Reate, Latium, the founder of the Flavian dynasty (69–96). He ended the civil wars that had been raging since Nero's overthrow, and put the state on a sound financial footing. Among his many lavish building projects was the Colosseum.

Vespers The evening hour of the divine office of the Western Church. In monastic, cathedral, and collegiate churches the Roman Catholic Church it is sung daily between 3 and 6 pm.

Vespucci, Amerigo [vespoochee] (1454–1512) Explorer, born in Florence, Italy. He promoted a voyage to the New World in the track of Columbus, and explored the coast of Venezuela. His name was given to America through an inaccurate account of his travels, in which he is represented as having discovered the mainland in 1497.

Vesta (astronomy) The fourth asteroid discovered (1807). It is the only asteroid that can ever be seen with the unaided eye, mainly on account of its high reflectivity.

Vesta (mythology) Roman goddess of the hearth. Her sacred fire, and a shrine containing sacred objects, were kept in a round building, and tended by the **Vestal Virgins**.

vestibular apparatus [vestibyuler] The part of the internal ear concerned with balance, consisting of a series of spaces and tubes within the temporal bone of the skull. It contains the *saccule* and *utricle*, which convey information regarding head position by responding to linear and tilting movements, and three *semicircular canals*, which convey information about rotatory and angular movements of the head.

vestments Special and distinctive garments worn by clergy in religious worship and liturgy of the Christian Church.

Vestris, Madame, popular name of **Lucia Elizabeth Vestris** or **Mathews**, *née* **Bartolozzi** (1797–1856) Actress, born in London. She appeared at Drury Lane in 1820, becoming famous in a wide range of roles, was lessee of the Olympic Theatre for nine years, and later managed Covent Garden and the Lyceum.

Vesuvius [vesoovius], Ital **Vesuvio** 40°49N 14°26E. Active volcano in SW Italy, 15 km/9 mi SE of Naples; height 1277 m/4190 ft; crater circumference, 1400 m/4593 ft, depth 216 m/709 ft; first recorded eruption AD 79, overwhelming Pompeii, Herculaneum, and Stabiae; last eruption, 1944.

vetch A member of a large group of annuals or perennials, often climbing or scrambling, native to N temperate regions and South America; also called **tare**; generally of little economic importance, and sometimes an agricultural pest. (Genus: *Vicia*, 140 species. Family: Leguminosae.)

Veterans' Day A public holiday in the USA (Nov 11), held to honour veterans of all wars; originally instituted as **Armistice Day** after World War 1, by which name it was known until 1954.

veterinary science The science concerned with the diseases of animals, especially their treatment or their avoidance. It is applied primarily to domesticated animals, or to captive animals in zoos. Most countries have a national veterinary association, such as the **British Veterinary Association (BVA)** and the **American Veterinary Medical Association (AVMA)**. Internationally veterinary matters are dealt with by the **World Veterinary Association (WVA)**, founded in 1863. The international aspects of companion animal veterinary medicine come under the **World Small Animal Veterinary Association (WSAVA)**, founded in 1958.

Vézelay church [vayzelay] The 12th-c abbey church of St Madeleine, a world heritage monument at Vézelay, France.

VHS (Video Home System) The trade name for a videotape cassette recorder introduced in 1975 by JVC/Matsushita for the domestic market, and widely adopted by other manufacturers. It uses $\frac{1}{2}$ in (12·7 mm) tape at a speed of 2·34 cm/in per second in a cassette 189 × 104 × 25 mm/$7\frac{1}{2}$ × 4 × 1 in. It has a playing time of up to 4 hours, and has proved to be the most internationally popular home VTR system. **Super-VHS** is an improved version with separate luminance and chrominance signals, using metal particle tape to give higher picture definition and colour quality.

Viagra® Trade-name of an anti-impotence drug developed by the Pfizer Corporation in the USA, made available in 1998. Its action, increasing blood flow to the male genitals, was first noted as part of research into treatment for heart disease.

Vian, Boris [veeã] (1920–59) Playwright, novelist and poet, born in Ville d'avray, France. He won a cult following for such tragicomic novels such as *L'ecume des jours* (1947, trans Froth on the Daydream) and *L'arrache-coeur* (1953, trans Heartsnatcher).

Viborg [veebaw(r)] 56°28N 9°25E, pop (2000e) 30 000. Ancient city in NC Jutland, Denmark; railway; Gothic cathedral (12th-c, restored 1864–76).

vibraphone A musical instrument resembling a xylophone, but with metal bars and resonators fitted with electrically operated vanes, producing a vibrating, tremolo effect. It is usually played with soft beaters.

vibration *oscillation*

Vibrio A genus of straight or curved rod-shaped bacteria, typically with flagella at one end. They are found in aquatic environments and animal intestines, and include the causative agent of cholera. (Kingdom: Monera. Family: Vibrionaceae.)

viburnum *guelder rose*

vicar (Lat *vicarius*, 'substitute') Literally, one who takes the place of another; for example, the pope is said to be the Vicar of Christ. In Anglican Churches, the term applies technically to the priest acting for the rector, but is widely used for any parish priest or minister.

Vicente, Gil [veesentay] (c.1470–c.1537) Portuguese playwright and poet. He wrote on religious, national, and social themes, as well as farces, and pastoral and romantic plays, all with great lyricism and a predominantly comical spirit.

Vicenza [vichentsa], ancient **Vicetia** 45°33N 11°33E, pop (2000e) 113 000. City in NE Italy; railway junction; cathedral (15th-c).

viceroy The governor of a colony or province, acting in the name and by the authority of the supreme ruler, the monarch. Following the Indian Mutiny in 1857, India was brought directly under the British government (1858), who sent a viceroy to act as governor under a London-based secretary of state within the Cabinet.

Vichy [veeshee] The informal name of the French political regime between 1940 and 1945, a client regime of Germany; officially **l'etat Français** ('the French State'). Established at the spa town of Vichy following Germany's defeat of France (1940), its head of state was Marshal Philippe Pétain.

Vickers test *hardness*

Vickrey, William (1914–96) Economist, born in Victoria, British Columbia, Canada. He shared the Nobel Prize for Economics in 1996 for his work in analyzing the consequences of incomplete financial information.

Vicksburg 32°21N 90°53W, pop (2000e) 26 400. Port in W Mississippi, USA; on the Mississippi R; settled, 1791; captured by Union forces during the Civil War (1863) after a long siege (the 'Vicksburg Campaign'); national cemetery nearby; railway; important processing and shipping centre for cotton, timber, and livestock area.

Vicky, pseudonym of **Victor Weisz** (1913–66) Political cartoonist, born in Berlin. He emigrated to Britain in 1935, and established himself as the leading left-wing political cartoonist of the period.

Vico, Giambattista [veekoh] (1668–1744) Historical philosopher, born in Naples, Italy. In his *Scienza nuova* (1725, New Science), he attempted to systematize the humanities into a single human science in a cyclical theory of the growth and decline of societies.

Victor Emmanuel III (1869–1947) King of Italy (1900–46), born in Naples, Italy. He initially ruled as a constitutional monarch, but defied parliamentary majorities by bringing Italy into World War 1 on the side of the Allies in 1915, and in 1922 when he offered Mussolini the premiership. The fascist government then reduced him to a figurehead. He abdicated in 1946.

Victoria (Australia) pop (2000e) 4 689 000; area 227 600 km²/87 900 sq mi. State in SE Australia; named by Captain Cook, 1770; Melbourne settled, 1835; separated from New South Wales, 1851; gold discovered at Ballarat, 1851; E is the Great Dividing Range, known in this region as the Australian Alps; highest point Mt Bogong (1986 m/6516 ft); about 36% of the land occupied by forest; SW region known as Gippsland; several inland lakes, mostly very saline; contains 25% of the Australian population concentrated into 3% of the land; capital, Melbourne; major contribution to Australia's agricultural output; coal mining (Latrobe Valley one of the world's largest deposits of brown coal); oil and natural gas fields in the Gippsland Basin and Bass Strait.

Victoria (Canada) 48°25N 123°22W, pop (2000e) 79 800. Capital of British Columbia, Canada, at SE end of Vancouver I; founded as fur-trading post, 1843; colonial capital, 1866; airfield; railway; university (1963); Commonwealth Games (1994).

Victoria (Seychelles) 4°37S 55°28E, pop (2000e) 25 400. Seaport capital of the Seychelles, Indian Ocean; on the NE coast of Mahé I.

Victoria, in full **Alexandrina Victoria** (1819–1901) Queen of Great Britain (1837–1901) and (from 1876) Empress of India, born in London, the only child of George III's fourth son, Edward, and Victoria Maria Louisa of Saxe-Coburg. Taught by Lord Melbourne, her first prime minister, she had a clear grasp of constitutional principles and the scope of her own prerogative, which she resolutely exercised in 1839 by setting aside the precedent which decreed dismissal of the current ladies of the bedchamber, thus causing Peel not to take up office as prime minister. In 1840 she married Prince Albert of Saxe-Coburg and Gotha, and had four sons and five daughters. Strongly influenced by her husband, after his death (1861) she went into lengthy seclusion, which brought her unpopularity; but with her recognition as Empress of India, and the celebratory golden (1887) and diamond (1897) jubilees, she increased the prestige of the monarchy.

Victoria, Tomás Luis de, Ital **Vittoria, Tommaso Ludovico da** (c.1548–1611) Composer, born in Ávila, Spain. He wrote only religious music, his 180 works including several books of motets and over 20 Masses.

Victoria, Lake area 69 500 km²/26 827 sq mi. Lake in E Africa; largest lake on the African continent; altitude 1300 m/4265 ft; 400 km/250 mi long; 240 km/150 mi wide; contains several islands, notably the Sese archipelago; European discovery by John Speke, 1858; extensively explored by Stanley, 1875; originally called Ukewere, renamed in honour of Queen Victoria.

Victoria and Albert Museum A museum of fine and applied arts, opened in London in 1852 as the Museum of Manufactures. In 1899, when Queen Victoria laid the foundation stone of the present building, she requested that it be renamed the Victoria and Albert. In 2002 the museum celebrated its 150th anniversary and is currently undergoing major redevelopment.

Victoria Cross (VC) In the UK, the highest military decoration, instituted by Queen Victoria in 1856 and awarded 'for conspicuous bravery in the face of the enemy'. The medal is inscribed 'For valour'; the ribbon is crimson.

Victoria Desert *Great Victoria Desert*

Victoria Falls, indigenous name **Mosi oa Tunya** ('the smoke that thunders') Waterfalls on the Zambezi R; height, 61–108 m/200–354 ft; width, 1688 m/5538 ft; European discovery by Livingstone, 1855; named after Queen Victoria; major tourist attraction.

Victoria Island Island in Northwest Territories, Canada, in the Arctic Ocean; area 217 290 km²/83 874 sq mi; 515 km/320 mi long; 274–595 km/170–370 mi wide; named for Queen Victoria; sparse population.

Victoria Nile Upper reach of River Nile in NW Uganda; flows from the N end of L Victoria; ends in a swampy delta at the NE end of L Albert; length 420 km/260 mi.

Victoria Peak 22°18N 114°08E. Principal peak on Hong Kong Island, SE Asia; height, 554 m/1818 ft; named after Queen Victoria; Peak Tramway (opened 1888).

Victory, HMS Nelson's flagship at the battle of Trafalgar (1805). She is now in permanent dry dock, but still flies the white ensign as flagship to the commander-in-chief, Portsmouth.

vicuña [vikunya] A wild member of the camel family (*Vicugna vicugna*), native to high grassland in the C Andes; resembles a llama, but smaller; produces the finest wool in the world.

Vidal, (Eugene Luther) Gore [vidal], pseudonym **Edgar Box** (1925–) Writer, born in West Point, NY. His many novels include several satirical comedies, such as *Myra Breckinridge* (1968) and *Duluth* (1983), the historical trilogy, *Burr* (1973), *1876* (1976), and *Lincoln* (1984), and a fictional history of America. Later works include a volume of memoirs, *Screening History* (1992), and the novels, *The Smithsonian Institution* (1999) and *Against the Day* (2006).

video Strictly, that part of the television signal which carries the picture information, as distinct from the audio signal carrying the sound; but by extension the term has become generally accepted to cover the electronic recording and reproduction of combined picture and sound, especially in its non-broadcast application.

videoconferencing The use of computer networks and virtual reality to enable groups in separate locations to conduct a conference with the impression that they are all in the same room. The use of computer networks allows the participants to have shared access to computer files and programs.

video disk A reproduction medium in which both picture and sound are recorded as an extremely fine spiral track on a flat circular disk. A series of pits in a reflective surface is optically scanned with a helium-neon laser, and the reflected beam read by a photo-diode to produce the signal. A 30 cm/12 in diameter disk can contain an hour's programme, and access from one part of the programme to another can be very rapid.

video games *electronic games*

videogram A complete programme recorded as a videotape cassette or video disk for distribution by sale or hire.

videotape A high-quality magnetic coating on a flexible polyester base for recording and reproducing video signals. It has been made in widths of 2 in (50·8 mm, now obsolete), 1 in (25·4 mm), $\frac{3}{4}$ in (19 mm), $\frac{1}{2}$ in (12·7 mm), $\frac{1}{3}$ in (8 mm), and $\frac{1}{4}$ in (6·3 mm); the latter two widths are used for domestic applications.

videotape recorder (VTR) A device for recording the picture and sound signals from a television camera on magnetic tape. To obtain a writing speed sufficient for the very high frequencies of a television signal, the recording head must travel rapidly across the moving magnetic tape. Modern VTRs use a narrow tape with helical scanning, each diagonal track recording a single TV field, with audio and control on the edges. Several systems were devised, including U-matic, Betamax, and VHS, all incompatible; U-matic was preferred for professional production and VHS for domestic use. In the 1980s two more helical systems for high-quality production and broadcast were introduced, Betacam in 1981 and M-II in 1986. In 1987–8, digital recording on videotape (DVTR) became available in the D1 and D2 formats, and soon after, the first digital recorders using solid-state storage chips.

videotex An interactive information service using a telephone link between the user and a central computer, such as Prestel, run by British Telecom in the UK in the 1990s. It can be used for home banking, armchair shopping, ticket ordering, and other such functions.

videowall A rectangular grouping of a number of separate video monitor screens, from 3 × 3 units upwards. They can be programmed for the display of individual single, multiple, or combination images with a sound track from videotape or disk recordings.

Vidor, King (Wallis) [veedaw(r)] (1894–1982) Film director, born in Galveston, TX. He made the silent classics *The Big Parade* (1925) and *The Crowd* (1928); later films included *Northwest Passage* (1940) and the big screen epic *Solomon and Sheba* (1959). He received an honorary Oscar in 1979.

Vienna, Ger *Wien* 48°13N 16°22E, pop (2000e) 1 597 000. Capital city of Austria; on the R Danube; C area surrounded by the monumental buildings and gardens of the Ringstrasse, developed 1859–88; badly damaged in World War 2, and occupied by the Allies, 1945–55; UNO-City, conference and office complex (opened 1979); archbishopric; university of technology (1815); university (1873–84); Spanish Riding School; associations with many composers in 18th–19th-c; cathedral,

Schottenkirche (12th-c, rebuilt 1638–48); Ruprechtskirche (12th–13th-c); Palace of Schönbrunn; Opera House; Burgtheater, Mozart museum (2006).

Vienna, Congress of (1814–15) A European assembly convened at the instigation of the four victorious powers (Austria, Britain, Prussia, and Russia) to redefine the territorial map of Europe after the defeat of Napoleon.

Vienna Circle A group of philosophers, scientists, and mathematicians centred on Vienna University in the 1920s and 1930s. It was founded by Schlick, and had among its associates Gödel, Neurath, and Carnap. It became an international focus for logical positivism.

Vientiane [vyentyan], Lao **Viangchan** 17°59N 102°38E, pop (2000e) 560 000. Capital city of Laos, SE Asia; port on R Mekong; airport; university (1958).

Viet Cong or **Vietcong** ('Vietnamese Communists') The name given by the South Vietnamese government in 1959 to all the guerrilla forces that fought them during the Vietnam War. In 1960 they formed the National Liberation Front.

Viet Minh or **Vietminh** The abbreviation of **Viet Nam Doc Lap Dong Minh** ('League for the Independence of Vietnam'), a politico-military organization formed by Ho Chi-minh in 1941. In 1945 it formed a government in Hanoi, and its army defeated the French at Dien Bien Phu in 1954.

Vietnam *p.985*

Vietnamese An Austro-Asiatic language, spoken in Vietnam, Laos, and Cambodia by over 50 million people. A Latin-based alphabet, called *Quoc-ngu* (national language) was introduced in the 17th-c.

Vietnam War (1946–75) Hostilities between communist North Vietnam and non-communist South Vietnam, and others, also known as the **First** and **Second Indo-Chinese Wars**. The first began in 1946 after the breakdown of negotiations between France and the Viet Minh under Ho Chi-minh, and ended with the defeat of the French at Dien Bien Phu in 1954. The subsequent Geneva settlement left North Vietnam under communist rule. From 1961, US aid to the South increased considerably. From 1965, US aircraft bombarded the North, and by 1968 over 500 000 US troops were involved. These troops were withdrawn in 1973, and hostilities ceased in 1975, when the North's victory was completed with the capture of Saigon (renamed Ho Chi Minh City).

viewdata *videotex*

Vignola, Giacomo (Barozzi) da [veenyohla] (1507–73) Architect, born in Vignola, Italy. In Rome he designed the Villa di Papa Giulio and the Church of the Gesú, which had a great influence on French and Italian church architecture.

Vigny, Alfred Victor, comte de (Count of) [veenyee] (1797–1863) Romantic writer, born in Loches, France. His best-known works include the historical novel, *Cinq-Mars* (1826), a volume of exhortatory tales, *Stello* (1832), and the Romantic drama, *Chatterton* (1835).

Vigo [veegoh] 42°12N 8°41W, pop (2000e) 278 000. Naval and commercial port in Galicia, NW Spain; airport; boat services to the Canary Is; watersports; castle.

Viking project The first successful landing mission to Mars, consisting of two highly instrumented orbiter-lander spacecraft. Launched in 1975 by NASA, the first landing (20 Jul 1976) was on Chryse Planitia and the second (3 Sep 1976) on Utopia Planitia. Although evidence for life was not found, data from other lander and orbiter experiments have provided the basis for continuing intensive research on Martian evolution and climate.

Vikings Raiders, traders, and settlers from Norway, Sweden, and Denmark, who between the late 8th-c and the mid-11th-c conquered and colonized large parts of Britain (from 787), Normandy, and Russia; attacked Spain, Morocco, and Italy;

Vietnam

☐ International Airport

annual temperatures 17°C (Jan), 29°C (Jul) in Hanoi; average annual rainfall 1830 mm/72 in; typhoons and flooding frequent in N and SW.

Currency 1 Dông (VND) = 10 hao = 100 xu

Economy Agriculture (employs over 70% of the workforce); however, natural disasters, war, and political unrest have adversely affected economy; Vietnam War brought depopulation of the countryside and considerable destruction of forest and farmland; exports include coal, minerals, rice, rubber, sugar cane.

GDP (2002e) $183·8 bn, per capita $2300

Human Development Index (2002) 0·688

History Under the influence of China for many centuries; regions of Tongking (N), Annam (C), and Cochin-China (S) united as Vietnamese Empire, 1802; French protectorates established in Cochin-China, 1867, and in Annam and Tongking, 1884; formed the French Indo-Chinese Union with Cambodia and Laos, 1887; occupied by the Japanese in World War 2; communist Viet-Minh League under Ho Chi-minh formed after the War, not recognized by France; Indo-Chinese war, resulting in French withdrawal, 1946–54; 1954 armistice divided the country between the communist 'Democratic Republic' in the N, and the 'state' of Vietnam in the S; civil war led to US intervention on the side of S Vietnam, 1965; fall of Saigon, 1975; reunification as the Socialist Republic of Vietnam, 1976; large numbers of refugees tried to find homes in the W in the late 1970s; Hanoi invaded neighbouring Cambodia, overthrowing hostile Khmer Rouge government, 1978; Chinese responded with invasion of Vietnam in 1979 – greatly increased the number trying to leave the country by sea (Vietnamese boat people); in 1984, Hanoi agreed to talks with US about whereabouts of missing US servicemen; limited troop withdrawals from Laos and Cambodia, 1989; Vietnam supported Cambodian peace agreement, 1991; new constitution, 1992, replaced Council of Ministers with a Prime Minister and a Cabinet.

Head of State
1976–80 Ton Duc Thang
1980–1 Nguyen Hun Tho *Acting*
1981–7 Truongh Chinh
1987–92 Vo Chi Cong
1992–7 Le Duc Anh
1997– Tran Duc Luong

Head of Government
1976–87 Pham Van Dong
1987–8 Pham Hung
1988 Vo Van Kiet *Acting*
1988–91 Do Muoi
1991–7 Vo Van Kiet
1997–2006 Phan Van Khai
2006– Nguyen Tan Dung

General Secretary
1960–80 Le Duan
1986 Truong Chinh
1986–91 Nguyen Van Linh
1991–7 Do Muoi
1997–2001 Le Kha Phieu
2001– Nong Duc Manh

official name Socialist Republic of Vietnam, Vietnamese **Cong Hoa Xa Hoi Chu Nghia Viet Nam**

Local name Công Hòa Xã Hôi Chu Nghĩa Viêt Nam (Vietnamese)

Timezone GMT +7

Area 329 566 km²/127 212 sq mi

Population total (2002e) 79 939 000

Status Socialist republic

Date of independence 1976

Capital Hanoi

Languages Vietnamese (official), French, Chinese, English, Khmer

Ethnic groups Vietnamese (85–90%), Chinese (3%), various minorities include Khmer, Cham, Hmong, Nung, and Tay

Religions Buddhist (principal), Taoist, Confucian, Muslim, Roman Catholic, Hoa Hoa, Cao Dai, Protestant, and animist beliefs

Physical features Occupies a narrow strip along the coast of the Gulf of Tongking and the S China Sea on Indochinese peninsula in SE Asia; highest peak Fan si Pan, 3143 m/10 312 ft; Mekong R delta (S) and Red R delta (N) linked by narrow coastal plain; heavily forested mountains and plateaux.

Climate Tropical, monsoon climate; sub-tropical in N; average

traded with Byzantium, Persia, and India; discovered and occupied Iceland and Greenland; and reached the coast of North America (c.1000). As sea-borne raiders they gained a deserved reputation for destructiveness, but as merchants and settlers they played an influential role in the development of mediaeval Europe.

Vila [veela], also **Port-Vila** 17°45S 168°18E, pop (2000e) 24 600. Port and capital town of Vanuatu, on the SW coast of Efate I; airport.

Vila Real [veela rayal] 41°17N 7°48W, pop (2000e) 15 300. Town in N Portugal; on R Corgo, 77 km/48 mi NE of Oporto; airfield; Mateus wine produced nearby; cathedral.

Villa, Pancho [veeyah], also known as **Francisco Villa**, originally **Doroteo Arango** (1878–1923) Mexican revolutionary, born in Hacienda de Río Grande, Mexico. In a fierce struggle for control of the Mexican Revolution, he was defeated by Venustiano Carranza, and eventually made peace with the government (1920).

Villahermosa [veelya-airmohsa] 18°00N 92°53W, pop (2000e) 470 000. River port in SE Mexico, on the R Grijalva; university (1958).

Villa-Lobos, Heitor [veela lohbush] (1887–1959) Composer and conductor, born in Rio de Janeiro, Brazil. His many compositions include 12 symphonies, as well as operas, large-scale symphonic poems, concertos, ballets, and the nine suites *Bachianas Brasileiras* (1930–45), in which he treats Brazilian-style melodies in the manner of Bach.

Villars, Claude Louis Hector, duc de (Duke of) [veelah(r)] (1653–1734) Marshal under Louis XIV, born in Moulins, France. In the War of the Spanish Succession (1701–13) he inflicted heavy losses on Marlborough at Malplaquet (1709), and defeated the British and Dutch at Denain (1712).

Villas-Boas Brothers A family of brothers – **Orlando Villas-Boas** (1916–2002), **Claudio Villas-Boas** (1918–98), and **Leonardo Villas-Boas** (1920–61) – who devoted their lives to the care and welfare of the Indians living around the Xingu R, Matto Grosso, Brazil, previously unknown tribes whom they met during a military expedition to the interior in 1943. They were twice nominated for the Nobel Peace Prize.

Villehardouin, Geoffroi de [veelah(r)dwĩ] (c.1160–c.1213) Mediaeval chronicler, born near Bar-sur-Aube, France. He took part in the Fourth Crusade, and described the events from 1198 to 1207, including the capture of Constantinople in 1204.

villein [vilayn] (Old Fr 'village dweller') In mediaeval England, a legally unfree peasant or serf who was tied to the manor, liable to arbitrary obligations (including labour services on the lord's estate), denied control over goods and property, and wholly bound to the lord's jurisdiction.

Villeneuve, Jacques [veelnoev] (1971–) Motor-racing driver, born in Quebec, Canada. In 1995 he became the youngest driver to win the PPG Indy Car World Series title. He joined Formula One in 1996, driving for the Williams-Renault team, finished second in the World Driver's Championship, and won the Championship in 1997.

Villeneuve, Pierre (Charles Jean Baptiste Sylvestre) de [veelnoev] (1763–1806) French admiral, born in Valensole, France. In 1805 he was in charge of the French fleet at Trafalgar, where he was taken prisoner.

Villiers de L'Isle Adam, comte (Count) **(Philippe) Auguste (Mathias)** [veelyay duh leel adã] (1838–89) Writer, born in St-Brieuc, France. A pioneer of the Symbolist movement, he wrote many poems, short stories (eg *Contes cruels*, 1883, Cruel Tales), novels (eg *Isis*, 1862), and plays (eg *La Révolte*, 1870, The Revolt).

Villon, François [veeyõ], pseudonym of **François de Montcorbier** or **François des Loges** (1431–c.1465) Poet, born in Paris. His works include *Le Lais* (The Legacy, also known as *Le Petit Testament*), and his long poetic sequence, *Le Grand Testament* (1461). He is known to have taken part in several crimes, and in 1463 received a death sentence, commuted to banishment.

Vilnius [veelnius], formerly **Wilno** (1920–39), also **Vilna** 54°40N 25°19E, pop (2000e) 585 000. Capital city of Lithuania, on R Vilnya; one of the largest industrial centres of the Soviet Baltic region; formerly part of Poland; ceded to Russia, 1795; occupied by Germany in World War 2; airport; railway junction; university (1579); cathedral (1777–1801); castle.

Vimy Ridge [veemee] An escarpment 8 km/5 mi NE of Arras, a strongly held part of the German defence line on the Western Front in World War 1. It was successfully stormed by the Canadian Corps of the British 1st Army (1917).

Viña del Mar [veenya thel mah(r)] 33°02S 71°35W, pop (2000e) 351 900. Seaside town in Valparaíso province, C Chile; residential suburb and popular South American resort.

Vincent de Beauvais [vĩsã duh bohvay], Lat **Vincentius Bellovacensis** (c.1190–c.1264) French Dominican priest and encyclope-

dist. He compiled his *Speculum majus* (Great Mirror) on a wide range of natural, doctrinal, and historical subjects.

Vincent de Paul, St (c.1580–1660) Priest and philanthropist, born in Pouy, France. He formed associations for helping the sick, and in 1625 founded the Congregation of Priests of the Missions (or 'Lazarists', from their priory of St Lazare) and (1634) the Sisterhood of Charity. He was canonized in 1737. Feast day 27 September.

Vincentians *Lazarists*

Vinci, Leonardo da *Leonardo da Vinci*

vine *climbing plant; grapevine*

vinegar A sour liquid used as a food preservative or domestic flavour enhancer. It derives from the oxidization of alcohol by bacteria, the ethanol being converted to acetic acid.

Vingt, les [lay vĩ] A group of 20 modern painters, including Ensor, founded in Brussels in 1884. For 10 years they held exhibitions showing pictures by leading Postimpressionists.

vingt-et-un *pontoon*

Vinland [veenland] A generalized Norse name meaning 'Berry Land' or 'Vine Land', applied to the E coast of North America from the time of its first sighting by the Viking Leif Eriksson AD c.985. Accounts of the Norse discovery of America in Icelandic sagas are confirmed by archaeological evidence.

Vinson Massif Highest peak in Antarctica, rising to 4897 m/ 16 066 ft in the Ellsworth Mts.

vinyl An important organic chemical grouping (CH_2=CH–). Many types of polymer are based on it.

viola A bowed string instrument, in all essential respects like a violin but slightly larger and tuned a fifth lower.

viola da gamba Strictly speaking, any member of the viol family – bowed string instruments held upright on the knees, or between the legs, of the player; more generally, the bass instrument of that family, loosely resembling a cello but with sloping shoulders, a flat back, six strings, and a fretted fingerboard like a guitar's.

violet An annual or perennial native to most temperate regions, many being alpine species; flowers 5-petalled, blue, yellow, white, or these colours combined, sometimes fragrant. It includes the species and varieties commonly known as **pansies**. (*Viola*, 500 species. Family: Violaceae.)

violin The most widespread of all bowed string instruments. The four-string violin was developed in the 16th-c from earlier three-string types, and reached its highest point of perfection between 1650 and 1730 in the hands of Stradivari and the Amati and Guarneri families. The other regular members of the violin family are the viola, cello, and double bass.

Viollet-le-Duc, Eugène (Emmanuel) [vyohlay luh dük] (1814–79) Architect and archaeologist, born in Paris. His restorations included the cathedrals of Notre Dame, Amiens, and Laon, and the Château de Pierrefonds.

violoncello *cello*

viper A venomous snake of family Viperidae (187 species), worldwide except Australia; thick body; head usually triangular, broad; fangs attached to front of upper jaw.

Virgil or **Vergil**, in full **Publius Vergilius Maro** (70–19 BC) Latin poet, born in Andes, Italy. His works include *Eclogues* (37 BC), the *Georgics*, or *Art of Husbandry* (36–29 BC), and for the rest of his life he worked at the request of the emperor on the *Aeneid*.

virginals A keyboard instrument with a mechanism similar to that of the harpsichord, but with strings set at right angles to the keys (as in the clavichord). It was widely used from the 15th-c to the 17th-c.

Virgin Birth The Christian belief that Jesus Christ had no human father, but was conceived through the power of the Holy Spirit without his mother, Mary, losing her virginity.

Virginia pop (2000e) 7 078 500; area 105 582 km²/40 767 sq mi. State in E USA; 'Old Dominion'; first permanent British settle-

Virgin Islands, British

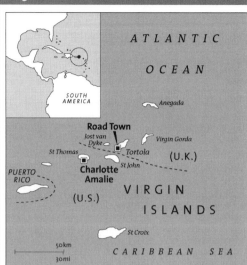

☐ International Airport

(UK British Overseas Territory)

Timezone GMT -4

Area 153 km²/59 sq mi

Population total (2002e) 21 000

Capital Road Town (on Tortola Island)

Physical features Island group at the NW end of the Lesser Antilles chain, E Caribbean, NE of Puerto Rico; comprises 4 large islands (Tortola, Virgin Gorda, Anegada, Jost Van Dyke) and over 30 islets and cays; only 16 inhabited; hilly terrain, except for flat coral island of Anegada; highest point, Sage Mt, 540 m/1772 ft, on Tortola I.

Climate Subtropical climate; average annual temperatures 17–28°C (Jan), 26–31°C (Jul); average annual rainfall 1 270 mm/50 in.

Currency 1 US Dollar (USD) = 100 cents

Economy Tourism (accounts for 50% of national income); construction and stone extraction; rum, paint, gravel, livestock, coconuts, sugar cane, fruit and vegetables, fish.

History Tortola colonized by British planters, 1666; constitutional government, 1774; part of the Leeward Is, 1872; separate Crown Colony, 1956; governor represents the British sovereign; Executive Council and Legislative Council.

Virgin Islands, United States

official name **Virgin Islands of the United States**, formerly **Danish West Indies** (to 1917)

Local name US Virgin Islands

Timezone GMT -4

Area 342 km²/132 sq mi

Population total (2000e) 121 000 (St Croix 53 900, St Thomas 51 400, St John 2900)

Status Territory

Capital Charlotte Amalie (on St Thomas Island)

Languages English (official), with Spanish and Creole widely spoken

Ethnic groups West Indian, French, Hispanic

Religion Protestant

Physical features Nine islands and 75 islets in the Lesser Antilles, Caribbean Sea; three main inhabited islands, St Croix, St Thomas, and St John; volcanic origin, mostly hilly or rugged and mountainous; highest peak, Crown Mt, 474 m/1555 ft on St Thomas.

Climate Subtropical climate; average annual temperatures 21–9°C (Dec–Mar), 24–31°C (Jun–Sep); low humidity; rainy season (May–Nov); subject to severe droughts, floods and earthquakes.

Currency 1 US Dollar (USD) = 100 cents

Economy Tourism (chief industry); St Croix industries include oil and alumina products, clocks and watches, textiles, rum, fragrances, petrochemicals; vegetables, fruit, sorghum.

GDP (2002e) $2·4 bn, per capita $19 000

History Originally inhabited by Ciboney Indians, followed by Arawak Indians, then Caribs; discovered by Columbus in 1493; Denmark colonized St Thomas and St John, 1665 and 1718, and bought St Croix from France, 1733; purchased by US, 1917; now an unincorporated territory of the US; a Governor heads a unicameral legislature.

Head of State/Government
1991–97 Bailey Olter
1997–9 Jacob Nena
1999– Charles Wesley Turnbull

Virgin Islands, British *see panel*
Virgin Islands, United States *see panel*
Virgo (Lat 'virgin') A constellation of the zodiac, which contains the first quasar to be recognized as such, 3C 273, and one of the largest galaxies known, M87. Its brightest star is Spica. Virgo lies on the celestial equator, between Leo and Libra.
viroid A fragment of infectious nucleic acid that resembles a virus. It typically consists of a small loop of ribonucleic acid not enclosed within a protein shell.
virtual reality A computing technique in which the computer user sees only a computer output screen, and all the movements and sounds from the user are recorded by the computer. This allows the computer to simulate another environment in which users might well believe they are wholly involved. Virtual reality is used in a wide range of contexts, such as flight simulators for training pilots, videoconferencing suites, and computer games.
virus The smallest infectious particle, 10–300 nm in diameter. Viruses infect other micro-organisms such as bacteria, fungi, and algae, as well as higher plants and animals. The genetic material of each virus is present as a molecule of either ribonucleic acid or deoxyribonucleic acid, encased inside a protein shell. Viruses replicate only in living cells, their nucleic acid directing the host cell to synthesize material required for producing more virus. The study of viruses is known as **virology**.

ment in America (at Jamestown, 1607); named after Elizabeth I (the 'Virgin Queen'); one of the first colonies to move for independence; scene of the British surrender at Yorktown, 1781; 10th of the original 13 states to ratify the Constitution, 1788; scene of several major battles in the Civil War (Richmond was the Confederacy capital); re-admitted to the Union, 1870; highest point, Mt Rogers (1743 m/5718 ft); flat and swampy coastal area (the Tidewater region); to the W, land rises into the rolling, fertile Piedmont, interrupted further W by the Blue Ridge Mts; W of these lies a series of beautiful valleys (the Valley of Virginia), notably the Shenandoah; capital, Richmond; tobacco (chief agricultural crop); the area's scenery and history make tourism a major state industry.

Virginia Resolutions *Kentucky and Virginia Resolutions*

The Main Types Of Vitamin

Fat soluble vitamins

Vitamin	Chemical name	Precursor	Main symptom of deficiency	Dietary source
A	retinol	β-carotene	xerophthalmia (eye disease)	retinol: milk, butter, cheese, egg yolk, liver, and fatty fish carotene: green vegetables, yellow and red fruits and vegetables, especially carrots
D	cholecalciferol	UV-activated 7-dehydro-cholesterol	rickets, osteomalacia	liver oils of fatty fish, margarine, some fortified milks, and breakfast cereals
K	phytomenadione		haemorrhagic problems	green leafy vegetables and liver
E	α tocopherol		extremely rare in humans	vegetable oils

Water soluble vitamins

Vitamin	Chemical name	Main symptom of deficiency	Dietary source
C	ascorbic acid	scurvy	citrus fruits, potatoes, green leafy vegetables
B–vitamins			
B_1	thiamine	beriberi	seeds and grains; widely distributed
B_2	riboflavin	failure to thrive	liver, milk, cheese, yeast, leafy vegetables
–	nicotinic acid	pellagra	meat, fish, wholemeal cereals, pulses
B_6	pyridoxine	dermatitis; neurological disorders	cereals, liver, meat, fruits, leafy vegetables
B_{12}	cyanocobalamin	anaemia	meat, milk, liver, egg yolk
–	folic acid	anaemia	liver, green vegetables, nuts
–	pantothenic acid	dermatitis	widespread
–	biotin	dermatitis	liver, kidney, yeast extracts

Visayan Islands [visiyan] area 61 991 km²/23 928 sq mi. Island group in the C Philippines; chief islands include Cebu, Bohol, Panay, Leyte, Samar, Negros, Masbate.

viscacha [viskacha] A cavy-like rodent from South America; resembles a large chinchilla; four species in genera *Lagostomus* and *Lagidium*. (Family: Chinchillidae.)

Visconti, Luchino [viskontee] (1906–76) Stage and film director, born in Milan, Italy. His first film, *Ossessione* (1942, Obsession), took Italy by storm, with its strict realism and concern with social problems. Later films included *Il gattopardo* (1963, The Leopard) and *Morte a Venezia* (1971, Death in Venice).

viscose The solution of cellulose from which regenerated cellulose fibre (rayon) is produced. Discovered in 1892, the viscose process is still the basis of most rayon manufacturing.

viscosity [viskositee] A measure of a fluid's reluctance to flow, corresponding to internal friction in the fluid as one portion of the fluid seeks to slide over another; symbol η, units Pa.s (pascal.second); formerly referred to as *poise*. It is defined as the ratio of shear stress to the rate of change of shear strain.

viscount (Lat *vice-comes* 'deputy of a count') In the UK, the second and lowest rank of the peerage, often the second title of an earl or marquess bestowed as a courtesy title on his eldest son.

Vishinsky *Vyshinsky, Andrei*

Vishnu [vishnoo] A major Hindu deity, second in the triad (*Trimurti*) of gods manifesting the cosmic functions of the Supreme Being. The preserver of the universe and the embodiment of goodness and mercy, he is believed to have assumed visible form in nine descents (*avataras*), of which his appearances as Rama and Krishna are the most important.

visibles *invisibles*

Visigoths A Germanic people who fled from the Huns in 376 into the Roman Empire, and eventually founded the Visigothic kingdom, embracing at its height in the 7th-c Portugal, virtually all Spain, and part of S Gaul. It was extinguished by the Arab conquest of 711.

Vistula, River [vistyula], Pol **Wisa** Longest river in Poland; rises in the Carpathians and flows for 1047 km/651 mi to meet the Baltic Sea at Gdańsk.

Visual Basic A high-level computer programming language, and the development software to suppport it, enabling programmers to create user-interactive programs very quickly. Developed by Microsoft, it provides visual programming facilities (the ability to create code by manipulating icons) as well as more traditional text-based programming methods.

visual display unit (VDU) The screen attached to a computer. Most VDUs are based on cathode-ray-tube technology similar to that used in television sets, and both single colour and full colour versions are used. An increasing number of VDUs are being based on liquid crystal displays, particularly in portable computer applications.

vitamins Organic substance present in minute quantities in natural foods that are essential for health, classified as either **water-soluble** or **fat-soluble**. Specific abnormalities result if they are absent from the diet or present in insufficient amounts. *see panel*

Viti Levu [veetee layvoo] area 10 429 km²/4026 sq mi. Largest and most important island of Fiji; length 144 km/89 mi; width 104 km/65 mi; mountainous interior, rising to 1324 m/4344 ft at Tomaniivi (Mt Victoria); capital, Suva; airport.

vitriol *sulphuric acid*

Vitruvius [vitroovius], in full **Marcus Vitruvius Pollio** (1st-c) Roman architect and military engineer. He wrote the 10-volume *De architectura* (On Architecture), the only extant Roman treatise on this subject.

Vittoria, Tommasso Ludovica da *Victoria, Tomás Luis de*

Vittoria [veetohria], Span **Vitoria** 42°51N 2°40W, pop (2000e) 208 000. Basque city in N Spain; scene of French defeat in the Peninsular War, 1813; bishopric; airport; railway; old and new cathedrals.

Vittorino da Feltre [vitoreenoh da feltray], originally **Vittorino dei Ramboldini** (c.1378–1446) Educationist, born in Feltre, Italy. In Mantua he founded a school for both rich and poor children (1425), in which he devised new methods of instruction, integrating the development of mind and body through the study of the Classics and Christianity.

Vivaldi, Antonio (Lucio) [vivaldee] (1678–1741) Violinist and composer, born in Venice, Italy. *L'estro armonico* (1712) gave him a European reputation and *The Four Seasons* (1725), an early example of programme music, proved highly popular; he also wrote operas, sacred music, and over 450 concertos.

Vivekananda [vivaykananda], also known as **Swami Vivekananda**, originally **Narendranath Datta** or **Dutt** (1863–1902) Hindu philosopher, born in Calcutta, India. After meeting Ramakrishna, he became his leading disciple, establishing the headquarters of the Ramakrishna Order at Belur Math on the Ganges, near Calcutta. He attempted to combine Indian spirituality with Western materialism, and became the main force behind the Vedanta movement in the West.

Viverridae [viveridee] A family of small to medium-sized carnivores native to the S Old World; 72 species; long thin body, long tail, pointed muzzle, short legs; coat often spotted or banded.

Vivés, Juan Luis [veevays], Lat **Ludovicus Vives** (1492–1540) Philosopher and humanist, born in Valencia, Spain. His writings include *Adversus Pseudodialecticos* (1570, Against the Pseudo-Dialecticians), and several other works on educational theory and practice.

viviparity [viviparitee] In animals, the production of live young rather than eggs. The embryos grow within the mother's body, which provides nourishment via a placenta or similar structure. In plants, it refers to the production of seeds that germinate within the fruit while still attached to the parent plant.

vivisection The practice of dissecting live animals for experimental purposes. Research includes experiments which look for the effects of new drugs, food additives, cosmetics, and a wide range of chemicals on the body tissue and behaviour of such animals as guinea pigs, rabbits, rats, and monkeys, as an alternative to using human subjects. Such research is now strictly controlled by legislation in most Western nations, but nonetheless can provoke considerable public opposition, including the use of violence against scientists by animal rights extremists.

Vlaanderen [vlanderen] *Flanders*

Vladimir I, St, in full **Vladimis Svyatoslavich**, known as **the Great** (956–1015) Grand Prince of Kiev (c.978–1015). One of ancient Russia's most illustrious rulers, in 988 he was converted to Christianity, and adopted the Greek Orthodox rite as the official religion of Russia. He was later canonized. Feast day 27 September.

Vladivostok [vladivostok] 43°10N 131°53E, pop (2000e) 645 000. Seaport in Russia, on the East Sea (Sea of Japan); chief Soviet port on the Pacific Ocean (kept open in winter by ice-breakers); base for fishing and whaling fleets; founded, 1860; terminus of the Trans-Siberian Railway; university (1920); naval base.

Vlaminck, Maurice de [vlamïk] (1876–1958) Artist, born in Paris. By 1905 he was one of the leaders of the *Fauves*, using typically brilliant colour, then painted more realist landscapes (1908–14), and later developed a more sombre Expressionism.

Vlissingen *Flushing*

Vlorë or **Vlora** [vloruh], Ital **Valona**, ancient **Aulon** 40°27N 19°30E, pop (2000e) 84 300. Seaport in SW Albania; a 5th-c bishopric; independence proclaimed here in 1912; railway.

VLSI *very large scale integration*

Vltava, River [vuhltava], Ger **Moldau** River in the Czech Republic, formed in the Bohemian Forest; meets the R Elbe; length 427 km/265 mi.

VOA *Voice of America*

vocal cords Two muscular folds in the larynx, behind the Adam's apple. They are brought together to impede the airflow during speech, when they vibrate and produce voice, used in the articulation of vowels and many consonants. They are also used to vary the pitch of the voice and in the production of several distinctive tones of voice.

vocational education Education which is aimed at the preparation of students for employment. Often undertaken in colleges of further education, it can also take place on the job in the workplace itself. A wide range of vocational qualifications is usually available, some from chartered award-giving institutions, others from professional organizations.

vodka A colourless spirit produced from potatoes, the national drink of Poland and Russia. It is almost tasteless, and is thus used in many mixed drinks, such as the 'Bloody Mary' (vodka and tomato juice).

Voice of America (VOA) The external broadcasting service of the US government, founded in 1942. By 2000, the VOA was broadcasting worldwide in English and 52 other languages.

Voight, Jon(athan) [voyt] (1938–) Film actor, born in Yonkers, NY. He gained recognition for his role in *Midnight Cowboy* (1969, Oscar nomination). Among his many films are *Deliverance* (1972), *Coming Home* (1978, Best Actor Oscar), *Runaway Train* (1985, Oscar nomination), and *September Dawn* (2006). In 2001 he appeared with his daughter, actress Angelina Jolie, in *Lara Croft: Tomb Raider*.

Volans [vohlanz] (Lat 'flying fish') A tiny and inconspicuous S constellation near the Large Magellanic Cloud.

volcano A vent or fissure in the Earth's crust where molten lava is erupted onto the surface. Most volcanoes are confined to the zones along boundaries between crustal plates, and are closely associated with earthquakes, as in the circum-Pacific 'ring of fire'; but there are notable exceptions, such as the Hawaiian Is, which have formed on a 'hot spot' in the Earth's crust. The scientific study of volcanoes is known as **vulcanology**.

Volcanus *Vulcan*

vole A mouse-like rodent native to Asia, Europe, and North America; most species with large head, blunt snout, and short tail; closely related to lemmings. (Tribe: Microtini, 96 species.)

Volga, River, ancient **Rha** Longest river of Europe, in C European Russia; rises in the Valdai Hills; enters the Caspian Sea in a broad delta, length, 3531 km/2194 mi.

Volgograd [volgograd], formerly **Tsaritsyn** (to 1925), **Stalingrad** (1925–61) 48°45N 44°30E, pop (2000e) 1 200 000. City in SE European Russia, on R Volga; founded, 16th-c; largely destroyed in World War 2; airport; railway.

volleyball An indoor court game, played by two teams of six-a-side. Players hit a large ball with their hands or arms over a raised net in the hope of forcing an error, and thus score points. It was invented in 1895 by William G Morgan at the YMCA, Holyoke, MA, USA.

Volsungasaga [volsungasahga] A 13th-c German epic deriving in part from the Norse *Edda*. It tells the story of the dynasty of the Volsungs, which is linked to that of the Nibelungs.

volt SI unit of electrical potential difference; symbol V; named after Alessandro Volta; if the power dissipated between two points along a wire carrying a current of 1 amp is 1 watt, then the potential difference between the two points equals 1 volt.

Volta, Alessandro (Giuseppe Antonio Anastasio) [volta] (1745–1827) Physicist, born in Como, Italy. He experimented on current electricity, and invented an electric battery which gave the first reliable supply.

voltage *potential difference*

Voltaire [voltair], pseudonym of **François Marie Arouet** (1694–1778) Writer, the embodiment of the 18th-c Enlightenment, born in Paris. His tragedy *Oedipe* brought him fame, but he gained enemies at court, and was forced to go into exile for a time. He later wrote plays, poetry, historical and scientific treatises, and his *Lettres Philosophiques* (1733, Philosophical Letters). From 1762 he produced a range of anti-religious writings and the *Dictionnaire philosophique* (1764, Philosophical Dictionary).

voltmeter An instrument used for measuring potential difference or electromotive force between points in a circuit. Most voltmeters consist of an ammeter connected in line with a high resistance, and calibrated in volts.

Voluntary Reserve *Territorial Army*

Voluntary Service Overseas (VSO) A British charity founded in 1958 to send skilled volunteers to work for two-year periods in developing countries. The host government provides a living allowance and accommodation; VSO provides briefing, air fare, and a grant.

von Braun, Wernher *Braun, Wernher von*

V-1 The abbreviation of *Vergeltungswaffe-1* (Ger 'revenge weapon 1'); small, winged, pilotless aircraft powered by a pulse jet motor, developed by the Luftwaffe. They carried a tonne of high explosive at a speed of c.800 kph/500 mph. Between 1944 and 1945, 5823 were launched against Britain. From the noise of their motors, they were also known as **buzz-bombs**.

von Klitzing constant A constant which forms the international standard of resistance measurement; symbol R_K, defined as h/e^2, where h is Planck's constant and e is the electron charge; named after Klaus von Klitzing (1943–).

Vonnegut, Kurt (Jr) [voneguht] (1922–2007) Novelist, born in Indianapolis, IN. His novels are satirical fantasies, usually cast in the form of science fiction, as in *Player Piano* (1952), *Breakfast of Champions* (1973; filmed 1999), *Galapagos* (1985), and *Timequake* (1997). He is best known for *Slaughterhouse-Five* (1969).

Von Neumann, John [noyman], originally **Johann von Neumann** (1903–57) Mathematician, born in Budapest. He wrote a major work on quantum mechanics (1932), which led him to a new axiomatic foundation for set theory. His work on high-speed calculations for H-bomb development contributed to the development of computers, and he also introduced game theory (1944), which was a major influence on economics.

voodoo The popular religion of Haiti, also found in the West Indies and parts of South America. A blending of Roman Catholicism with W African religion, its followers attend both the church and the voodoo temple, where a voodoo priest or priestess leads a ritual invoking of the spirits of the voodoo world through magical diagrams, songs, and prayer.

Voortrekkers *Afrikaners; Great Trek*

Voronezh [voronyesh] 51°40N 39°10E, pop (2000e) 888 000. River port in EC European Russia, on R Voronezh; founded as a fortress, 1586; airport; railway; university (1918).

Voroshilov, Kliment Yefremovich [vorosheelof] (1881–1969) Soviet marshal, statesman, and president (1953–60), born near Dniepropetrovsk, Ukraine. He played a military rather than a political role in the 1917 Revolution, and as commissar for defence (1925–40) was responsible for the modernization of the Red Army. He became head of state after Stalin's death.

Voroshilovgrad *Lugansk*

Vorster, John [faw(r)ster], originally **Balthazar Johannes Vorster** (1915–83) South African statesman, prime minister (1966–78), and president (1978–9), born in Jamestown, South Africa. He was minister of justice under Verwoerd (1961), whom he succeeded, maintaining the policy of apartheid.

vortex A rotational form of fluid flow. Lines of flow are curved, and may even form closed loops. Examples of vortices are whirlpools, tornadoes, and the circulating eddies caused by obstructions in rivers.

Vorticism A modern art movement started in England in 1913, partly inspired by the Futurists. Leading members included Wyndham Lewis, C R W Nevinson (1889–1946), and Henri Gaudier-Brzeska.

Vortigern [vaw(r)tijern] (fl.425–50) Semi-legendary British king. According to Bede, he recruited Germanic mercenaries led by Hengist and Horsa to help fight off the Picts after the final withdrawal of the Roman administration from Britain (409).

Vosges Mountains [vohzh], ancient **Vosegus** area 7425 km²/ 2866 sq mi. Range of hills in NE France; highest point, Ballon de Guebwiller (1423 m/4669 ft), length, 250 km/155 mi.

Vostok [vostok] ('East') The first generation of Soviet crewed spacecraft, carrying a single person. Vostok 1 carried the first human into space (12 Apr 1961) – Yuri Gagarin, who orbited Earth once on a flight of 118 min. The last Vostok flight carried Valentina Tereshkova, the first woman to fly in space (Vostok 6, 16 Jun 1963). **Voskhod** ('Sunrise') was an intermediate-generation Soviet-crewed spacecraft following Vostok and preceding Soyuz; it made only two flights, in 1964 and 1965.

vowel One of the two main categories of speech sound (the other being **consonant**). It is produced when the air flows freely through the mouth without constriction from the pharynx, tongue, or lips; it also forms the nucleus of the syllable, and (unlike a consonant) can stand alone (as in such words as *I* and *a* in English).

Voyager project A multiple outer-planet flyby mission undertaken by NASA to make the first detailed exploration beyond Mars, and designed to take advantage of a rare (every 175 years) celestial alignment of Jupiter, Saturn, Uranus, and Neptune. Twin spacecraft in the Mariner series were launched in 1977. They flew through the Jovian system (Mar, Jul 1979) and, with a boost from Jupiter's gravity, flew on to Saturn (encounters Nov 1980, Aug 1981). Voyager 1's trajectory is taking it upward out of the ecliptic and in November 2003, at 8 bn mi/13·5 bn km from Earth, it was about to leave the Solar System and begin its transition into interstellar space; Voyager 2 used Saturn's gravity to fly on to the historic encounters with Uranus (Jan 1986) and Neptune (Aug 1989).

voyeurism A repeated tendency to observe others engaging in intimate, including sexual, behaviour. Sexual excitement often occurs in anticipation of the voyeuristic act, which may be accompanied by masturbation.

Voznesensky, Andrey Andreyevich [vozhneshenskee] (1933–) Poet, born in Moscow. His best-known volume *Antimiry* (Antiworlds) appeared in 1964, and the more difficult poems of *Soblazn* (Temptation) in 1979. Later works include *Epitaph for Vysotsky* (1990).

VRSA (vancomycin resistant *Staphylococcus aureus*) *Methicillin Resistant Staphylococcus aureus (MRSA)*

VSO *Voluntary Service Overseas*

VTOL [veetol] Acronym used for a fixed-wing aircraft specially designed for **Vertical Take-Off and Landing**. The most successful aircraft of this type is the Hawker Siddeley Harrier, which can deflect the thrust from its jet engine from the vertical to the horizontal while in flight.

V-2 The abbreviation of *Vergeltungswaffe-2* (Ger 'revenge weapon 2'); a guided ballistic missile developed by the German army, which began rocket experiments under the direction of Wernher von Braun in 1937. It was unstoppable, but wildly inaccurate. Between September 1944 and March 1945, 1054 fell on Britain.

Vuillard, (Jean) Edouard [vweeyah(r)] (1868–1940) Painter and printmaker, born in Cuiseaux, France. One of the later Impressionists, a member of *Les Nabis*, he executed mainly flower pieces and simple interiors, painted with a great sense of light and colour.

Vulcan, also **Vulcanus** or **Volcanus** The Roman god of fire, sometimes called **Mulciber**. He was identified with the Greek Hephaestus.

vulcanite or **ebonite** A hard black material made by the vulcanization of rubber with a high proportion of sulphur (2:1). It was important as an insulator before the coming of modern synthetics.

vulcanization The modification of the properties of rubber by chemical treatment, mainly with sulphur. The technique, which originated in 1839, improves tensile strength, elasticity, and abrasion resistance.

vulcanology *volcano*

Vulgate [vuhlgayt] The Latin translation of the Christian Bible, originating with Jerome (c.405). It emerged in Western Christianity as the favourite Latin version (*vulgate* meaning the 'common' edition), and in 1546 the Council of Trent recognized it as the official Latin text of the Roman Catholic Church.

Vulpecula [vulpekyula] (Lat 'little fox') A small N constellation in the Milky Way.

vulture A bird of prey specialized to feed on carrion; head often lacking long feathers. There are two groups. **Old World vultures** (Family: Accipitridae, 14 species) were formerly worldwide but now absent from the Americas; no sense of smell. **New World** or **cathartid vultures** (Family: Cathartidae, 7 species) are now restricted to the Americas.

Vygotsky, Lev Semenovich [vigotskee] (1896–1934) Psychologist, born in Orsha, Belarus. His writings, such as *Thought and Language* (1934–62) and *Mind in Society* (1978), have had a major influence on Russian and (since the 1960s) Western psychology.

Vyshinsky, Andrey Yanuaryevich [vishinskee] (1883–1954) Jurist and politician, born in Odessa, Ukraine. He was the public prosecutor at the state trials (1936–8) which removed Stalin's rivals, and later became the Soviet delegate to the United Nations (1945–9, 1953–4), and foreign minister (1949–53).

Waddington, C(onrad) H(al) (1905–75) Embryologist and geneticist, born in Evesham, Worcestershire. He introduced important concepts into evolutionary theory, and also helped to popularize science in such general books as *The Ethical Animal* (1960).

wadi [wodee] A desert ravine or steep-sided gorge formed during flash floods, but generally containing water only during rainy seasons.

Wagga Wagga 35°07S 147°24E, pop (2000e) 59 000. Town in New South Wales, Australia; centre of a rich agricultural area; railway; airfield; university, 1989.

Wagner, Otto [vahgner] (1841–1918) Architect and teacher, born in Penzing, Austria. The founder of the Vienna School, he became an important advocate of purely functional architecture, notably through his book *Modern Architecture* (1895).

Wagner, (Wilhelm) Richard [vahgner] (1813–83) Composer, born in Leipzig, Germany. His *Rienzi* (1842) was a great success at Dresden, but his next operas, including *Tannhäuser* (1845), were failures. In 1853 he began to write *Das Rheingold* (The Rhinegold), followed by *Die Walküre* (1856, The Valkyries) and the first two acts of *Siegfried* (1857). In 1864 he was saved from ruin by the eccentric young King of Bavaria, Ludwig II, who became a fanatical admirer of his work. His first wife, Minna, having died in 1866, Wagner then married Cosima von Bülow, the wife of his musical director, after her divorce. *Die Meistersinger* was completed in 1867, and *Götterdämmerung* in 1874. He opened the now famous theatre at Bayreuth in 1876 with a performance of the whole *Ring* cycle. *Parsifal*, his last opera, was staged in 1882. His son **Siegfried Wagner** (1869–1930) was director of the Bayreuth theatre from 1909. His grandson **Wieland Wagner** (1917–66) took over the directorship in 1951, followed by Wieland's brother, **Wolfgang Wagner** (1919–).

wagtail A small, ground-dwelling songbird, found worldwide; plumage usually bold, black-and-white, yellow, or green (dull species are called **pipits**); long tail which wags vertically. (Family: Motacillidae, 48 species.)

Wahhabis [wahabeez] An 18th-c Islamic movement which derives from Mohammed ibn Abd al-Wahhab, a religious reformer, and Mohammed ibn Saud, the ancestor of the present rulers of Saudi Arabia. It maintains that legal decisions must be based exclusively on the Qur'an and the *Sunna*. The original Wahhabis banned music, dancing, poetry, silk, gold, and jewellery, and in the 20th-c attacked telecommunications as innovations not sanctioned by God.

Waikato, River [wiykatoh] River in North Island, New Zealand; length 425 km/264 mi; rises in L Taupo; enters the Tasman Sea.

Waikiki Beach [wiykeekee] Resort beach in SE Honolulu on the Pacific island of Oahu, Hawaii state, USA; surfing popular on the reef.

Wain, John (Barrington) [wayn] (1925–94) Writer and critic, born in Stoke-on-Trent, Staffordshire. His novels include *Hurry on Down* (1953) and *The Contenders* (1958), and his poetry includes

Weep Before God (1961). Among his later books are *Young Shoulders* (1982, Whitbread) and *Comedies* (1990).

Waitangi, Treaty of [wiytangee] A compact signed by Maori representatives and Governor William Hobson at Waitangi (6 Feb 1840) on the occasion of the British annexation of New Zealand. Waitangi Day is the national day of New Zealand.

Waite, Terry [wayt], popular name of **Terence (Hardy) Waite** (1939–) Adviser to the Archbishop of Canterbury on Anglican Communion Affairs (1980–92), born in Bollington, Cheshire. As the Archbishop's special envoy, he was particularly involved in negotiations to secure the release of hostages held in the Middle East. He was himself kidnapped in Beirut in January 1987, and not released until November 1991. A volume of memoirs, *Taken on Trust* was published in 1993. He is founder-president of Y-Care International (1984) and also founded Hostage UK, providing support for hostage families.

Waitz, Grete [viyts], *née* **Andersen** (1953–) Athlete, born in Oslo. She was the world's leading female road athlete, the world marathon champion in 1983, the Olympic silver medallist in 1984, and on four occasions set world best times for the marathon.

Wajda, Andrzej [viyda] (1926–) Film director, born in Suwałki, Poland. He is best known outside Poland for *Czlowiek z marmary* (1977, Man of Marble), dealing with the Stalinist era, and *Czlowiek z zelaza* (1981, Man of Iron). Later works include *Korczak* (1990), *Wielki tydzien* (1995, Holy Week), and *Zemsta* (2002, The Revenge). He received an honorary Oscar in 2000.

Wakefield 53°42N 1°29W, pop (2001e) 315 200. Administrative centre of West Yorkshire, N England; on the R Calder; a woollen centre since the 16th-c; railway; site of Battle of Wakefield (1460) in Wars of the Roses.

Wakefield settlements Settlements of British migrants organized according to Edward Gibbon Wakefield's (1796–1862) ideas of 'systematic colonization'. The aim was to maintain traditional standards of order and refinement by transplanting a cross-section of English society, and restricting land ownership to the wealthy. The settlements were Adelaide, in Australia; and Wellington, Wanganui, New Plymouth, Nelson, Otago, and Canterbury in New Zealand.

Wake Islands 19°18N 166°36E; pop (2000e) 200; area 10 km²/ 4 sq mi. Horseshoe-shaped coral atoll enclosing three islands in C Pacific Ocean; annexed by USA, 1898; seaplane base opened, 1935; under control of US Air Force since 1972.

Walachia *Moldavia and Wallachia*

Walburga, Walpurga, or **Walpurgis, St** *Walpurga*

Walcott, Derek (Alton) [wolkot] (1930–) Poet and playwright, born in Castries, St Lucia. He founded the Trinidad Theatre Workshop in 1959, and his poetry includes *Collected Poems* (1986), *The Bounty* (1997), *Tiepelo's Hound* (2000), and *The Prodigal* (2005). He was awarded the Nobel Prize for Literature in 1992.

Waldenses or **Waldensians** A small Christian community originating in a reform movement initiated by Peter Waldo at Lyon,

France, in the 12th-c. They rejected the authority of the pope, prayers for the dead, and veneration of the saints. After the Reformation, as Protestants, they continued mainly in N Italy.

Waldheim, Kurt [valthiym] (1918–) Austrian statesman and president (1986–92), born near Vienna. He was Austrian representative at the United Nations (1964–8, 1970–1), foreign minister (1968–70), and UN secretary-general (1972–81). His presidential candidature was controversial, because of claims that he had lied about his wartime activities, and been involved in anti-Jewish and other atrocities, but he denied the allegations.

Wales *p.994*

Wales, Princess of *Diana, Princess of Wales*

Wałęsa, Lech [vawensa] (1943–) Polish trade unionist and president (1990–5), born in Popowo, Poland. A former Gdańsk shipyard worker, he became leader of the independent trade union, Solidarity, which challenged the Polish government's policies. He was detained by the authorities in 1981, but released in 1982, and awarded the Nobel Peace Prize in 1983. He continued to be a prominent figure in Polish politics, was much involved in the negotiations which led to Solidarity being involved in government in 1989, and was elected president the following year but defeated by Alexander Kwasniewski in 1995. He quit Solidarity in 2006.

Walker, Alice (Malsenior) (1944–) Novelist and poet, born in Eatonton, GA. She is best known for her novels, notably *The Color Purple* (1982, Pulitzer), later made into a successful film. Later novels include *By the Light of My Father's Smile* (1998) and *Now is the Time to Open Your Heart* (2004), and she has also written volumes of short stories and essays.

Walker, John E (1941–) Chemist, born in Halifax, West Yorkshire. He studied at Oxford, then worked at the Molecular Biology Laboratory in Cambridge. He shared the 1997 Nobel Prize for Chemistry for his contribution towards the elucidation of the enzymatic mechanism underlying the synthesis of adenosine triphosphate.

walking Either a leisurely pursuit or a competitive sport. As a sport, both road and track walking are popular. The rules governing the use of the feet are strict: one foot must be touching the ground at all times, and the lead leg must be straight as it passes under the torso. It has been an Olympic event since 1956, over distances of 20 km (12·4 mi) and 50 km (31 mi).

Walkley Award Annual awards in recognition of excellence in Australian journalism, established in 1956 by Sir William Gaston Walkley, founder of Ampol Petroleum in Australia. The prestigious awards now cover more than 30 categories. In 2000 the federal council of the Media, Entertainment and Arts Alliance formally established the Walkley Foundation for Journalism.

wallaby *kangaroo*

Wallace, Alfred Russel (1823–1913) Naturalist, born in Usk, Monmouthshire. He contributed greatly to the scientific foundations of zoogeography, including his proposal for the evolutionary distinction between the fauna of Australia and Asia ('Wallace's line').

Wallace, (Richard Horatio) Edgar (1875–1932) Writer, born in London. He wrote over 170 novels and plays, and is best remembered for his crime novels, such as *The Clue of the Twisted Candle*.

Wallace, Lew(is) (1827–1905) Writer and soldier, born in Brookville, IN. He was author of the successful religious novel *Ben Hur* (1880), which has twice formed the subject of a spectacular film (1927, 1959).

Wallace, Sir William (c.1270–1305) Scottish knight and champion of the independence of Scotland, probably born in Elderslie, Renfrewshire. He routed the English army at Stirling (1297), and took control of the government of Scotland as 'Guardian', but

was defeated by Edward I at Falkirk (1298), and executed in London.

Wallachia [wolaykia] *Moldavia and Wallachia*

Wallenstein or **Waldstein, Albrecht (Wenzel Eusebius), Herzog von** (Duke of) [wolenstiyn], Ger [valenshtiyn] (1583–1634) Bohemian general, born in Heřmanice, Czech Republic. During the Thirty Years' War he became commander of the Imperial armies and won a series of victories (1625–9), but was defeated by Gustavus Adolphus at Lützen (1632). His intrigues led to an Imperial proclamation of treason, resulting in his assassination.

Waller, Edmund (1606–87) Poet and politician, born in Coleshill, Buckinghamshire. In 1643 he plunged into a conspiracy (**Waller's plot**) against parliament, was arrested, and banished, but returned to England in 1651. His collected poems were published in 1645.

Waller, Fats, popular name of **Thomas Wright Waller** (1904–43) Jazz pianist, organist, singer, and songwriter, born in New York City. Among his many hits are 'Ain't Misbehavin'' (1929) and 'Keeping Out of Mischief Now' (1932).

walleye Large freshwater fish (*Stizostedion vitreum*) related to the zander, found in rivers and lakes of E North America; length up to 90 cm/3 ft. (Family: Percidae.)

wallflower A perennial reaching 20–60 cm/8–24 in (*Cheiranthus cheiri*), native to the E Mediterranean; flowers yellow to orange-red, fragrant. (Family: Cruciferae.)

Walliams, David, originally **Williams** (1971–) Actor and comedian, born in Surrey. He studied drama at Bristol University, and appeared in many stage productions with the National Youth Theatre, where he met **Matt Lucas** (1974–) in 1990. In 1995 they teamed up to take their 'Sir Bernard Chumley and Friends' show to the Edinburgh Festival. Together they wrote and performed a character comedy sketch show, *Little Britain*, for BBC Radio 4, which successfully transferred to television in 2003. The show won the best comedy category at the Comedy Awards (2004, 2005), and an International Emmy for best comedy (2006).

Wallis, Sir Barnes (Neville) (1887–1979) Aeronautical engineer and inventor, born in Ripley, Derbyshire. His many successes include the design of the Wellington bomber, and the 'bouncing bombs' which destroyed the Mohne and Eder dams. In the 1950s he designed the first swing-wing aircraft.

Wallis, John (1616–1703) Mathematician, born in Ashford, Kent. His *Arithmetica infinitorum* (1655, The Arithmetic of Infinitesimals) anticipated calculus, and he also wrote on proportion, mechanics, grammar, logic, theology, and the teaching of the deaf.

Wallis and Futuna Islands, official name **Territory of the Wallis and Futuna Islands** pop (2000e) 15 300; area 274 km²/ 106 sq mi. Island group in the SC Pacific Ocean, NE of Fiji; a French overseas territory comprising the Wallis Is and the Hooru Is, 230 km/140 mi apart; capital, Matu Utu on Uvéa; chief ethnic group, Polynesian; chief religion, Roman Catholicism; unit of currency, the euro; Wallis Is (area 159 km²/61 sq mi) include Uvéa, rising to 145 m/476 ft at Mt Lulu; Hooru Is (115 km²/ 44 sq mi) include Futuna and Alofi, mountainous and volcanic; warm and damp climate; French protectorate, 1842; overseas territory of France, 1961; governed by an administrator, assisted by a Territorial Assembly; France confirmed its recognition of King Tomasi Kulimoetoke as monarch of the territory, 2005.

Wallonia French-speaking region of S Belgium; pop (2000e) 3 246 000. Walloons (36% of Belgian population); many towns renowned for their art treasures.

Walloon *Fleming and Walloon*

Wall Street A street in Manhattan, New York City, where the New York Stock Exchange is located. The road follows what once was the walled N boundary of the original Dutch colony.

walnut A deciduous, spreading tree (*Juglans regia*), growing to

Wales

1	Anglesey	12	Vale of Glamorgan
2	Gwynedd	13	Merthyr Tydfil
3	Aberconwy & Colwyn	14	Blaenau Gwent
4	Powys	15	Torfaen
5	Cardiganshire	16	Caerphilly
6	Carmarthenshire	17	Newport
7	Pembrokeshire	18	Cardiff
8	Swansea	19	Monmouthshire
9	Neath & Port Talbot	20	Denbighshire
10	Bridgend	21	Flintshire
11	Rhondda Cynon Taff	22	Wrexham

□ International Airport

Welsh **Cymru** [kuhm**ree**] (UK)
Local name Cymru (Welsh)

Area 20 761 km²/8014 sq mi

Population total (2001e) 2 903 100

Status Principality (Constituent part of the United Kingdom)

Capital Cardiff

Languages English, Welsh

Physical features Situated on the W coast of the UK, divided into 8 counties since 1974; includes the island of Anglesey off the NW coast; land rises to 1085 m/3560 ft at Snowdon (NW), also Cambrian Mts (C); Brecon Beacons (S); drained by the Severn, Clwyd, Dee, Conwy, Dovey, Taff, Towy, and Wye rivers.

Economy Coal; slate, lead, steel; industrialized S valleys and coastal plain; tourism in N and NW; ferries to Ireland at Holyhead, Fishguard; important source of water for England.

History Rhodri Mawr united Wales against Saxons, Norse, and Danes, 9th-c; Edward I of England established authority over Wales, building several castles, 12th–13th-c; Edward I's son created first Prince of Wales, 1301; 14th-c revolt under Owen Glendower; politically united with England by Act of Union, 1535; centre of Non-conformist religion since 18th-c; University of Wales, 1893, with constituent colleges; political nationalist movement (Plaid Cymru) returned first MP, 1966; Welsh television channel; 1979 referendum opposed devolution; successful referendum for devolved Welsh Assembly, 1997; Welsh Assembly, 1999.

Name / Area (km² / sq mi) / Population total (2000e) / Admin centre

Anglesey / 719 / 277 / 67 900 / Llangefni
Blaenau Gwent / 109 / 42 / 74 000 / Ebbw Vale
Bridgend / 246 / 95 / 132 200 / Bridgend
Caerphilly / 729 / 108 / 172 700 / Hengoed
Cardiff / 139 / 54 / 312 100 / Cardiff
Cardiganshire / 1797 / 694 / 70 400 / Aberystwyth
Carmarthenshire / 2398 / 926 / 170 700 / Carmarthen
Conwy / 1130 / 436 / 111 800 / Colwyn Bay
Denbighshire / 844 / 326 / 92 200 / Ruthin
Flintshire / 437 / 169 / 146 800 / Mold
Gwynedd / 3869 / 1494 / 119 200 / Caernarfon
Merthyr Tydfil / 111 / 43 / 60 100 Merthyr Tydfil
Monmouthshire / 851/ 328 / 85 000 / Cwmbran
Neath and Port Talbot / 442 / 171 / 141 500 / Port Talbot
Newport / 191 / 74 / 138 800 / Newport
Pembrokeshire / 1590 / 614 / 114 700 / Haverfordwest
Powys / 5204 / 2009 / 123 200 / Llandrindod Wells
Rhondda, Cynon Taff / 424 / 164 / 241 400 / Clydach Vale
Swansea / 378 / 164 / 233 000 / Swansea
Torfaen / 12649 / 91 500 / Pontypool
Vale of Glamorgan / 337 / 130 / 120 300 / Barry
Wrexham / 499 / 130 / 124 600 / Wrexham

30 m/100 ft, native to the Balkans; fruit 4–5 cm/1½–2 in, smooth, green. The wrinkled woody seed is the familiar walnut. The timber is used commercially, especially for furniture. (Family: Juglandaceae.)

Walpole, Horace (or **Horatio**), **4th Earl of Orford** (1717–97) Writer, born in London, the fourth son of Sir Robert Walpole. He produced a number of literary collections and a Gothic novel, *The Castle of Otranto* (1764).

Walpole, Sir Hugh (Seymour) (1884–1941) Writer, born in Auckland, New Zealand. His many novels were very popular during his lifetime, and include *The Secret City* (1919), *The Cathedral* (1922), and the four-volume family saga, *The Herries Chronicle* (1930–3).

Walpole, Sir Robert, 1st Earl of Orford (1676–1745) English statesman and leading minister (1721–42) of George I and George II, born in Houghton, Norfolk. Sent to the Tower for alleged corruption during the Tory government (1712), he was recalled by George I, and made a privy councillor and (1715) Chancellor of the Exchequer. He was Chancellor again in 1721 and widely recognized as 'prime minister'. Regarded as indispensable by both George I and George II, his period in office is widely held to have increased the influence of the House of Commons in the Constitution.

walrus A marine mammal (*Odobenus rosmarus*) of family Odobenidae; resembles a large sea-lion with a broad bristly snout; canine teeth enormous, forming tusks; skin with little hair; inhabits coastal Arctic waters.

Walsingham, Sir Francis [wolsingam] (c.1530–90) English statesman, secretary of state to Elizabeth I (1573–90), born in Chislehurst, Kent. A strong opponent of the Catholics, he developed a complex system of espionage at home and abroad, enabling him to reveal the plots of Throckmorton and Babington against the Queen.

Walter, Bruno [valter], originally **Bruno Walter Schlesinger** (1876–1962) Conductor, born in Berlin. He directed the Munich Opera (1913–22), and from 1919 was chief conductor of the Berlin Philharmonic. He also conducted the Berlin Opera (1925–9) and at Leipzig (1929–33), then settled in the USA, where he became chief conductor of the New York Philharmonic in 1951.

Walter, Harriet (Mary) (1956–) British actress. She has frequently worked with the Royal Shakespeare Company, her roles including Lady Macbeth (1999) and Beatrice (2002). Her films include *Sense and Sensibility* (1996), *Onegin* (1999), *Villa des Roses* (2002), and *Babel* (2006). She is an associate artist with Peter Hall's Cannon's Mouth theatre company.

Walter, Hubert (c.1140–1205) English clergyman and statesman, who accompanied Richard I on the Third Crusade (1190–3). He was appointed Archbishop of Canterbury in 1193, and justiciar of England, responsible for all the business of government until his resignation in 1198. On John's accession (1199), he became chancellor.

Walter, John (1739–1812) Printer and newspaper publisher, born in London. In 1785 he founded *The Daily Universal Register* newspaper, which in 1788 was renamed *The Times*.

Walters, Julie (1950–) Actress, born in Birmingham, West Midlands. She made her stage debut in *Educating Rita* (1980), for which she won a BAFTA award in the film version (1983). Later films include *Billy Elliot* (2000, BAFTA) and *Calendar Girls* (2003). On television she partnered Victoria Wood in the comedy series *Wood and Walters* (from 1981), *Victoria Wood As Seen On TV* (1984–7), and *Dinner Ladies* (1998–2000). Later television work includes *Canterbury Tales: The Wife of Bath* (2003, BAFTA) and *The Ruby in the Smoke* (2006).

Walther von der Vogelweide [valter fon der fohglviyduh] (c.1170–1230) German lyric poet. In 1204 he outshone his rivals in the great contest at the Wartburg.

Walton, Izaak (1593–1683) Writer, born in Stafford, Staffordshire. Best known for his treatise on fishing and country life, *The Compleat Angler* (1653), he also wrote several biographies.

Walton, Sir William (Turner) (1902–83) Composer, born in Oldham, Lancashire. He became known through his instrumental setting of poems by Edith Sitwell, *Façade* (1923). His works include two symphonies, concertos for violin, viola, and cello, the biblical cantata *Belshazzar's Feast* (1931), and the opera *Troilus and Cressida* (1954).

waltz A dance in triple time which became the most popular ballroom dance in 19th-c Europe – despite the initial shock caused by the requirement that the man should grasp his female partner at the waist. Austrian composer Joseph Lanner (1801–43) and the Strauss family established the style in Vienna.

Walvis Bay [wolvis], Afrikaans **Walvisbaai** 22°59S 14°31E, pop (2000e) 35 000. Seaport in WC Namibia; Walvis Bay enclave (area 1124 km²/434 sq mi) formerly administered by South Africa as part of Cape Province; annexed by the Dutch, 1792; taken by Britain, 1878; incorporated into Cape Colony, 1884; a South African enclave after Namibian independence, transferred to Namibia, 1994; airfield; railway terminus; handles most of Namibia's trade.

wampum [wompuhm] Beads used as a form of exchange, mnemonic devices, and guarantees of promises by certain Iroquois-speaking North American Indian groups. They were made of bits of seashells cut, drilled, and strung into belts or strands.

wandering Jew A species of tradescantia (*Tradescantia fluminensis*) with variegated leaves. (Family: Commelinaceae.)

Wandering Jew A character in Christian legend who taunted Christ as he carried his cross, and was condemned to wander the Earth until the end of the world or until Christ's second coming.

wandering sailor A species of tradescantia (*Tradescantia blossfeldiana*), with leaves maroon on undersides. (Family: Commelinaceae.)

Wanganui, River [wanganooee] River in W North Island, New Zealand; rises NW of L Taupo; enters the Tasman Sea; length 290 km/180 mi; town of Wanganui near the mouth, pop (2000e) 46 000.

Wankel engine [vangkl] A particular form of internal combustion engine whose piston rotates about a horizontal axis in a specially shaped combustion chamber, rather than oscillating within a cylinder, as in a conventional internal combustion engine. It is named after its designer, German engineer Felix Wankel (1902–88).

wapiti [wopitee] *red deer*

Warbeck, Perkin (c.1474–99) Pretender to the English throne, born in Tournai, Belgium. In 1492 he professed to be Richard, Duke of York, the younger of Edward's two sons who were murdered in the Tower. He made an ineffectual landing in Kent (1495), then landed in Cornwall (1497), but was captured and executed.

warble fly A small, robust fly; larvae live as parasites under the skin of mammals, causing swellings (*warbles*). (Order: Diptera. Family: Oestridae, c.60 species.)

warbler A songbird of the families Sylviidae (**Old World warblers**, 350 species), Parulidae (**American warblers** or **wood warblers**, 114 species), Acanthizidae (**Australian warblers**, 65 species), or Maluridae (**Australian wren-warblers**, 26 species).

Ward, Artemus Browne, Charles Farrar

Ward, Dame Barbara (Mary), Baroness Jackson of Lodsworth (1914–81) Journalist, economist, and conservationist, born in York, North Yorkshire. A prolific and popular writer on politics, economics, and ecology, her books included *Spaceship Earth* (1966) and *Only One Earth* (1972).

wardship proceedings Proceedings whereby the custody of a person under the age of 18 living in England and Wales, or an English subject living outside the jurisdiction of the English courts, is transferred to the Family Division of the High Court. Being made a **ward of court** results in all major decisions in a child's life being subject to the approval of the court. The wardship may be ended by a court order or on the child becoming 18. Wardship proceedings do not exist in all jurisdictions.

warez [wairz] Illegally copied or pirated software. This is usually computer application software, but may be any pirated digital media. There is a tendency among the distributors of warez to append a 'z' to any word to denote its illegal provenance. Thus there are websites containing 'tunez', 'filez', or 'crackz'.

Warhol, Andy [waw(r)hohl], originally **Andrew Warhola** (1927–87) Artist and film-maker, born in Pittsburgh, PA. He was a pioneer in 1961 of Pop Art, with his brightly-coloured exact reproductions of familiar everyday objects such as the famous soup-can label. His films include the 3-hour silent observation of a sleeping man, *Sleep* (1963). In the 1960s he also turned to music, founding a rock revue called The Exploding Plastic Inevitable (1966–7). The Andy Warhol Museum opened in Pittsburgh in 1994.

warlords Chinese provincial military rulers who engaged in a bitter power struggle and civil war after the death of Yuan Shikai in 1916. They were eventually subdued by Jiang Jieshi in 1927.

Warlpiri The dominant language of the central desert of Australia. Warlpiri country was colonized by cattle stations (ranches) during the early 20th-c, and some cattle stations are now Aboriginal-owned.

Warne, Shane (Keith) (1969–) Cricketer, born in Melbourne, Victoria, Australia. A hugely charismatic leg-spinner, his mix of acute spin and control has made him highly effective, particularly against England. He is the first spin bowler to take 500 Test wickets, reaching the milestone in March 2004. In 2000 he was named as one of Wisden's Five Cricketers of the Century. In 2003 he received a one-year ban for drug-related offences. He was part of Australia's losing side in the 2005 Ashes series but gained praise for his all-round performance, receiving the Australia Man of the Series award, and becoming the first bowler to take 600 Test wickets. He was an integral part of Australia's victory in the 2006–7 Ashes series in Australia during which he took a record 700th wicket, making him the most successful bowler in Test cricket history. He retired from international cricket at the end of the series.

Warner, Jack, originally **Jack Leonard Eichelbaum** (1892–1978) Film producer, born in London, Ontario, Canada. He was the youngest of the four **Warner Brothers** (the others being **Harry**, **Albert**, and **Sam**) who set up studios in 1923. Warners were the first to introduce sound into their films, and had a major success with *The Jazz Singer* (1927). Jack's later productions included *My Fair Lady* (1964) and *Camelot* (1967).

Warnock (of Weeke), (Helen) Mary Warnock, Baroness, *née* **Wilson** (1924–) British philosopher and educationist. A fellow and tutor in philosophy at St Hugh's College, Oxford (1949–66, 1976–84), she has chaired several important committees of inquiry into such topics as special education (1974–8), animal experiments (1979–85), higher education (1984), teaching quality (1990), and bioethics (1992–4).

War of 1812 (1812–14) A war between Britain and the USA, declared by the latter on the basis of British conduct towards neutral US shipping during the Napoleonic Wars. It brought the British capture of Washington, DC, and the bombardment of Baltimore. US victories in several sea duels and at New Orleans (fought after the Treaty of Ghent had restored peace) became central elements in the US military self-image.

War of Independence, US *American Revolution*

War of the Pacific A war fought by Chile with Peru and Bolivia (in alliance since 1873) and arising out of Chilean grievances in the Atacama desert, then Bolivian-held. Chile made large territorial gains.

warranty *condition*

Warren, Earl (1891–1974) US Republican politician and judge, born in Los Angeles, CA. He became chief justice in 1954, and was responsible for the epochal decision in *Brown* v. *Board of Education of Topeka, KS* (1954), outlawing school segregation. He was chairman of the federal commission that investigated the assassination of President Kennedy.

Warren, J Robin (1937–) Pathologist, born in Adelaide, South Australia. He studied at the University of Adelaide (1961) and joined the Royal Melbourne Hospital as registrar in clinical pathology (1964–6) and registrar in pathology (1966–8). In 1968–99 he was pathologist at the Royal Perth Hospital. In 2005 he shared the Nobel Prize for Physiology or Medicine with Barry Marshall for their discovery of the bacterium *Helicobacter pylori* and its role in gastritis and peptic ulcer disease.

Warren, Robert Penn (1905–89) Writer, born in Guthrie, KY. Recipient of two Pulitzer Prizes (for fiction in 1947, for poetry in 1958), he established an international reputation with his political novel, *All the King's Men* (1943, Pulitzer; filmed 1949).

Warrington 53°24N 2°37W, pop (2001e) 191100. Town in Cheshire, NWC England; on the R Mersey; designated a 'new town' in 1968; unitary authority from 1998; railway.

Warsaw, Polish **Warszawa** 52°15N 21°00E, pop (2000e) 1 665 000. River-port capital of Poland, on R Vistula; city centre is a world heritage site; established, 13th-c; capital of the Duchy of Mazovia, 1413; capital of Poland, 1596; occupied by Germany in both World Wars; Jewish ghetto established in 1940, with uprising and death of most residents in 1943; largely destroyed in World War 2; post-war reconstruction of the mediaeval old town followed the pre-war street pattern; airport; railway; Polish Academy of Sciences; two universities (1818, 1945); cathedral (14th-c, restored), royal castle.

Warsaw Ghetto The Nazi-enforced Jewish quarter of Warsaw, established in 1940 following the German occupation of Poland in World War 2. Some 500 000 Jews were isolated in a ghetto of less than 2·6 km² (1 sq mi), through which Poles were allowed to pass. Between July and October 1942 more than 300 000 were sent to concentration camps, where they died in the gas chambers. In reprisal for a Jewish uprising (Feb 1943) in the ghetto, an estimated 50 000 were killed. When Warsaw was liberated (Jan 1945) by Soviet troops, only about 200 Jews remained.

Warsaw Pact The countries which signed the East European Mutual Assistance Treaty in Warsaw in 1955: Albania, Bulgaria, Czechoslovakia, East Germany, Hungary, Poland, Romania, and the USSR. Albania withdrew in 1968. The pact established a unified military command for the armed forces of all the signatories. It was a communist response, in part, to the formation of NATO by the West, and was formally dissolved in 1991.

Warsaw uprising The name given to two uprisings during the German occupation of Poland during World War 2. **1** The 1943 Warsaw Ghetto uprising (19 Apr–16 May) was a reaction to the massive daily transportation of Jews from July 1942 onwards from the Ghetto to the extermination camp at Treblinka. It was brutally suppressed by the Waffen-SS and the police, leading to the deaths of a further 50 000 Jews. **2** The 1944 uprising (Aug–Oct) by the home army of the Polish government-in-exile in London was led by General Tadeusz Bòr-Komorowski in an attempt to oust the German army and seize control of the city before it was occupied by the advancing Soviet army. Polish resistance troops gained control of the city against a weak German garrison. Heavy German air raids lasting 63 days preceded a strong German counter-attack. The Soviet army failed to help the insurgents or allow Western allies to airlift supplies to the Poles. Supplies ran out and the Poles surrendered. German forces then systematically deported the population of Warsaw, including the main body of Poles that supported the Polish government in exile, and razed the city. Up to 180 000 people died. The Red Army resumed its advance and occupied Warsaw, establishing a communist provisional government (1 Jan 1945) and assuring Soviet control over Poland.

warships Vessels designed for use in wartime. Navies of the world still employ a vast range of warships, but the use of highly sophisticated guided-missile weaponry has made their roles less easily defined than those of the World War 2 period.

wart A small benign overgrowth in the outer layer of the skin, arising from a virus infection; also known as a **verruca**. Warts are common in children, and unpredictable in occurrence.

wart disease A disease (*Synchytrium endobioticum*) causing excessive cell division in the tubers of potatoes, resulting in the growth of soft warty tissues which destroy their economic value. All new European varieties are now officially tested, and only those showing immunity are released for cultivation. (Order: Chytridiales.)

warthog A wild pig native to Africa S of the Sahara (*Phacochoerus aethiopicus*); sparse covering of shaggy hair; face broad, flattened, with four wart-like knobs of thickened skin; large curved tusks.

Warwick [worik] 52°17N 1°34W, pop (2001e) 126 000. County town of Warwickshire, C England; on the R Avon; founded in 914; railway; university (1965); 14th-c castle; annual Mop Fair.

Warwick, Richard Neville, Earl [worik], also known as **Warwick the Kingmaker** (1428–71) English soldier and politician, who exercised great power during the first phase of the Wars of the Roses. He championed the Yorkist cause, captured Henry VI at Northampton, and had his cousin, Edward of York, proclaimed king as Edward IV (1461). When Edward tried to assert his independence, Warwick joined the Lancastrians, and restored Henry VI to the throne (1470). He was killed by Edward IV at the Battle of Barnet.

Warwickshire [woriksheer] pop (2001e) 505 900; area 1981 km²/ 765 sq mi. County of C England; county town, Warwick; castles at Kenilworth and Warwick; Shakespeare industry at Stratford; annual Mop Fairs.

Wasa [vahsa] A four-masted Swedish warship of 1628 which foundered on her maiden voyage. She was salvaged in 1961 and preserved in dry dock in Stockholm.

Wash, The Shallow inlet of the North Sea on E coast of England; between Norfolk (S) and Lincolnshire (W and N).

Washington (DC) 38°54N 77°02W, pop (2000e) 572 000. Capital of the USA, co-extensive with the District of Columbia; on the E bank of the Potomac R; the US legislative, administrative, and judicial centre: the Federal Government provides most of the city's employment; occupied by the Federal Government, 1800; sacked and burned by the British, 1814; two airports; railway; five universities; professional teams, Bullets (basketball), Capitals (ice hockey), Redskins (football); the International Spy Museum opened in 2002.

Washington (state) pop (2000e) 5 894 100; area 176 473 km²/ 68 139 sq mi. State in NW USA; the 'Evergreen State'; first settled in the late 18th-c, part of Oregon Territory; Britain and the USA quarrelled over the region until the international boundary was fixed by treaty to lie along the 49th parallel, 1846; became a territory, 1853; joined the Union as the 42nd state, 1889; Seattle an important outfitting point during the Alaskan gold rush, 1897–9; Olympic Mts in the NW; Puget Sound to the E, extending c.160 km/100 mi inland, with numerous bays and islands; Cascade Range runs N–S through the middle of the state; mountainous and forested in the W; dry and arid in the E; highest point, Mt Rainier (4395 m/14 419 ft); Mt St Helens volcano in the S (erupted May 1980); North Cascades National Park; capital, Olympia; apples (nation's largest crop); wide range of minerals; major tourist area; substantial Indian population and several reservations.

Washington, Booker T(aliaferro) (1856–1915) Black leader and educationist, born a slave in Franklin Co, VA. In 1881 he was appointed principal of the newly-opened Tuskegee Institute, Alabama, and built it up into a major centre of black education. He was the foremost black leader in late 19th-c USA, but his policies were repudiated by the 20th-c civil rights movement.

Washington, George (1732–99) Commander of American forces and first president of the USA, born in Bridges Creek, VA. He represented Virginia in the first (1774) and second (1775) Continental Congresses, and was given command of the American forces, where he displayed great powers as a strategist and leader. He inflicted notable defeats on the enemy at Trenton and Princeton (1777), then suffered defeats at the Brandywine and Germantown, but held his army together through the winter of 1777–8 at Valley Forge, and forced the surrender of Cornwallis at Yorktown in 1781. In 1787 he became president, remaining neutral while political parties were formed, but eventually joining the Federalist Party.

Washington Monument A marble column in honour of George Washington, designed by Robert Mills (1781–1855) and erected (1848–84) in Washington, DC. The tower is 169 m/555 ft high.

wasp The common name of several different types of solitary and social insects of the order Hymenoptera. Social wasps (mainly in the family Vespidae) are usually banded black and yellow; females inflict painful stings.

Wasserman, August Paul von [vaserman] (1866–1925) Bacteriologist, born in Bamberg, Germany. He discovered a blood-serum test for syphilis in 1906 (the **Wasserman reaction**).

waste disposal The disposal of waste from domestic, industrial, and agricultural sources; a major environmental concern. Methods commonly used include burial in landfill sites and at sea, incineration (sometimes for power generation), and the production of refuse-derived fuel pellets which can be used as an energy source.

watch A small timepiece for wear or in the pocket. Watches have been made ever since the invention of the mainspring (c.1500) made portable clocks possible. In recent times electrical movements have been much used, a small battery replacing the mainspring as a source of energy. The traditional analogue display (by rotation of hands) is often replaced by a digital display using a liquid crystal display (LCD) face.

water H_2O. The commonest molecular compound on Earth; a liquid, freezing to ice at 0°C and boiling to steam at 100°C. It covers about 70% of the Earth's surface, and dissolves almost everything to some extent. However, it is a poor solvent for substances which are found in solution as molecules (eg oxygen, methane). It is essential to life, and occurs in all living organisms. Unusually, the solid is less dense than the liquid; this results in ice floating, and accounts for the destructiveness of continued freezing and thawing. Water containing substantial concentrations of calcium and magnesium ions is called 'hard', and is 'softened' by replacing these ions with sodium or potassium, which do not form insoluble products with soaps.

water avens *avens*

water bear A microscopic animal possibly related to the arthropods; body short, bearing four pairs of stumpy legs usually armed with claws; c.400 species, found in surface water-films on mosses, lichens, algae, plant litter, and soil. (Phylum: Tardigrada.)

water beetle A dark, shiny beetle up to 40 mm/1½ in long; silvery in appearance underwater; abundant in the tropics. (Order: Coleoptera. Family: Hydrophilidae, c.2000 species.)

water birth A technique in which a mother gives birth to her baby while seated in a pool of warm water. There are well documented reductions in the requirement for analgesia, duration of labour, incidence of tears in the vagina, need for episiotomy, and incidence of fetal distress. Some psychotherapists also believe that the birth of a baby into a warm and quiet environment avoids the trauma of delivery, and thus reduces the incidence of psychological problems in later life.

water boatman A predatory aquatic bug that swims upside-down in water, using its paddle-like hindlegs; distributed worldwide. (Order: Heteroptera. Family: Notonectidae, c.200 species.)

water buffalo A SE Asian member of the cattle family; lives near

Highest Waterfalls

Name	Height		Location
	m	ft	
Angel (upper fall)	807	2 648	Venezuela
Itatinga	628	2 060	Brazil
Cuquenan	610	2 000	Guyana/Venezuela
Ormeli	563	1 847	Norway
Tysse	533	1 749	Norway
Pilao	524	1 719	Brazil
Ribbon	491	1 612	USA
Vestre Mardola	468	1 535	Norway
Roraima	457	1 500	Guyana
Cleve-Garth	450	1 476	New Zealand

Distances are given for individual leaps.

water; closely related to the anoa; two species: *Bubalis bubalis* (**Asian water buffalo**, **carabao**, or **arni** – widely domesticated), and *Bubalis mindorensis* (**tamaraw** or **tamarau**).

water chestnut A free-floating aquatic annual (*Trapa natans*), native to warm parts of Europe, Asia, and Africa; flowers white, 4-petalled; fruits woody, triangular with 2–4 spiny horns. Fast-growing, it forms thick, floating mats which can block waterways. The fruit, rich in starch and fat, forms a staple food in much of Asia. (Family: Trapaceae.)

watercolour Any form of painting in which the pigment is mixed with a water-soluble medium such as gum arabic. Watercolour was used in ancient Egypt and China, and mediaeval manuscripts were illuminated with water-based paint. The great masters of watercolour were all English.

watercress A semi-aquatic perennial (*Nasturtium officinale*), native to Europe and Asia; flowers small, white, cross-shaped. It has been cultivated since the 19th-c as a salad plant rich in vitamin C. Its peppery tasting leaves stay green in the autumn. (Family: Cruciferae.)

water-crowfoot An aquatic species of buttercup, growing in still or slow-moving water. The predominantly white flowers project above the water. (Genus: *Ranunculus* subgenus *Batrachium*, c.30 species. Family: Ranunculaceae.)

water deer A deer native to China and Korea (*Hydropotes inermis*), and introduced in UK and France; the only true deer without antlers; also known as **Chinese water deer**.

waterfall A sudden interruption in the course of a river or stream where water falls more or less vertically, in some cases for a considerable distance, such as over the edge of a plateau or where overhanging softer rock has been eroded away. The spectacular Niagara Falls and Victoria Falls are probably the best-known, but are not among the world's highest waterfalls. *see panel*

water flea A small aquatic crustacean; characterized by a jerky swimming motion using large antennae for propulsion; body short; c.450 species, most in fresh water. (Class: Branchiopoda. Order: Cladocera.)

Waterford, Ir **Phort Láirge** pop (2000e) 92 000; area 1839 km²/ 710 sq mi. County in Munster province, S Ireland; Knockmealdown Mts in the W; popular resorts on S coast; capital, Waterford, pop (2000e) 42 000; on R Suir; cathedral (1793), priory (1226); known for its glassware.

waterfowl Aquatic birds, especially ducks, geese, and swans; also known as **wildfowl**. The name *waterfowl* is often used for populations kept in captivity; *wildfowl* for wild birds, especially those hunted.

water gas A gas produced by passing steam over hot coke to give hydrogen and carbon monoxide. This process yields a gas of high energy content.

Watergate (1972–4) A political scandal that led to the first resignation of a president in US history (Richard Nixon, in office 1968–74). The actual 'Watergate' is a hotel and office complex in Washington, DC, where the Democratic Party had its headquarters. During the presidential campaign of 1972, a team of burglars was caught inside Democratic headquarters, and their connections were traced to the White House. Investigations revealed that high officials very close to President Nixon were implicated, and that Nixon himself was aware of illegal measures to cover up that implication. A number of officials were eventually imprisoned. Nixon himself left office when it became clear that he was likely to be impeached.

water glass A concentrated aqueous solution of sodium silicate (Na_2SiO_3), which sets to a hard, transparent layer, and is used as a waterproofing agent and a preservative.

Waterhouse, Alfred (1830–1905) Architect, born in Liverpool, Merseyside. He built the romanesque Natural History Museum in London (1873–81), and from his great use of red brick came the name 'red-brick university'.

water hyacinth A free-floating perennial aquatic plant (*Eichhornia speciosa*), native to South America; flowers funnel-shaped, violet. It grows and spreads rapidly, and is probably the world's most troublesome aquatic weed. (Family: Pontederiaceae.)

waterlily An aquatic perennial found in still or very slow-moving water; large, floating, or slightly emergent leaves and flowers; flowers bowl-shaped with numerous petals and stamens. (Family: Nymphaeaceae.)

Waterloo, Battle of (18 Jun 1815) The final defeat of Napoleon, ending the French Wars and the emperor's last bid for power in the Hundred Days. It was a hard-fought battle, in which Blücher's Prussian force arrived at the climax to support Wellington's mixed Allied force.

Waterloo Cup *bowls; coursing*

water-melon A trailing vine (*Citrullus lanatus*) with tendrils, native to the Mediterranean, Africa, and tropical Asia; flowers yellow, funnel-shaped; fruit up to 60 cm/2 ft long, ovoid, rind dark green, leathery; black seeds embedded in red flesh. It is cultivated for fruit, especially in the USA. (Family: Cucurbitaceae.)

water milfoil A submerged aquatic perennial, found almost everywhere; leaves feathery; flowers small, in slender spikes above water, reddish or yellowish. (Genus: *Myriophyllum*, 45 species. Family: Halagoraceae.)

water polo Developed in Britain in 1869, and played by teams of seven-a-side in a swimming pool. The object is to score goals by propelling the ball into the opposing team's goal at the end of the pool.

water rat A term used generally for many unrelated rats which inhabit the edge of bodies of water. Some species have webbed hind feet and waterproof fur.

water scorpion An aquatic bug that lives submerged, breathing through a tubular tail that reaches the surface; c.200 species, found in still or slow-moving waters. (Order: Heteroptera. Family: Nepidae.)

water spider The only spider that lives permanently submerged; breathes by means of air film over body surface; bite venomous, causing vomiting and fever. (Order: Araneae. Family: Agelenidae.)

water-spout The marine equivalent of a tornado; a rapidly rotating funnel of air which extends from the cloud base to the water surface, picking up water.

water table The surface below which the ground is saturated with water. The position of the water table varies with the topography and amount of rainfall; where it intersects the surface, springs are formed.

water vole A vole of genus *Arvicola*; three species, from NW North America, from Europe, and Asia; also known as **bank vole**.

Watling Street *Roman roads*

Watson, James D(ewey) (1928–) Geneticist, born in Chicago, IL. With Crick and Wilkins he helped to discover the molecular structure of DNA, sharing with them the Nobel Prize for Physiology or Medicine in 1962. He was awarded an honorary knighthood in 2001.

Watson, Russell (1974–) Tenor, born in Salford, Greater Manchester. His debut album, *The Voice* (2000), topped the UK classical chart for many months. Later albums include *Encore* (2001) and *Amore Musica* (2004).

Watson, Tom, popular name of **Thomas (Sturges) Watson** (1949–) Golfer, born in Kansas City, MO. He has won the (British) Open five times (1975, 1977, 1980, 1982–3), the US Open (1982), and the Masters (1977, 1981).

Watt, James (1736–1819) Inventor, born in Greenock, Inverclyde. He studied steam as a motive force, went into partnership with Matthew Boulton (1728–1809), and manufactured a new engine at Birmingham in 1774. Several other inventions followed, including the design of a steam locomotive (1784). The SI unit of power is named after him.

watt SI unit of power; symbol W; named after James Watt; the production of 1 joule of energy per second corresponds to a power of 1 watt; commonly used as **kilowatts** (kW, 10^3 W) or **megawatts** (MW, 10^6 W).

Watteau, (Jean) Antoine [vatoh] (1684–1721) Rococo painter, born in Valenciennes, France. The mythological 'L'embarquement pour l'île de Cythère' (Embarkation for the island of Cythera, 1717, Louvre) won him membership of the Academy. He is also known for his 'Fêtes galantes' (Scenes of Gallantry), quasi-pastoral idylls in court dress which became fashionable in high society.

wattle Any of a large group of mainly trees or shrubs, native to many tropical and subtropical areas, but notably Australia where (together with the eucalypts) they form the dominant tree vegetation; flowers mostly yellow, very small but numerous, in clusters. Many are useful timber trees, producing very hard tough wood. The bark and pods are employed for tanning. Some yield gum arabic. Commonly cultivated species include the **blue-leaved wattle** (*Acacia cyanophylla*) from W Australia, a small tree growing to 10 m/30 ft, and the **silver wattle** (*Acacia dealbata*) from SE Australia and Tasmania, a tree growing to 30 m/100 ft.

wattle and daub A framework of interlaced twigs and rods plastered with mud or clay. The walls of timber-framed houses were often made in this way, and when protected from the weather by good overhanging eaves, could last for hundreds of years.

wattmeter An instrument for measuring electric power. Many types are used, the most common being the **electrodynamic wattmeter** which depends on the interaction of fields in two sets of coils.

Watts, George Frederick (1817–1904) Painter, born in London. He became known for his penetrating portraits of notabilities, 150 of which he presented to the National Portrait Gallery in 1904.

Watts Towers A group of sculptures incorporating metal, stone, cement, tiles, glass, and waste materials, in the Watts district of Los Angeles, CA. The towers were completed in 1954, having been constructed over a period of 35 years by Simon Rodin (1879–1965).

Waugh, Evelyn (Arthur St John) [waw] (1903–66) Writer, born in London. His social satirical novels include *Decline and Fall* (1928), *Vile Bodies* (1930), and *Scoop* (1938). He became a Catholic in 1930, and his later books display a more serious attitude, as seen in the religious theme of *Brideshead Revisited* (1945), and his war trilogy, beginning with *Men at Arms* (1952). His son

(Alexander) Auberon Waugh (1939–2001) became a novelist and journalist, known for his critical reviews and essays.

WAV [wav] *digital media*

wave (oceanography) In oceanography, a disturbance moving under or along the surface of the water. Most ocean surface waves are generated by the wind blowing over the surface of the sea, imparting energy to the water. They can be transmitted over thousands of miles of ocean, often losing little energy until they break upon a shore.

wave (physics) *wave motion*

wavelength The distance between two successive crests of a wave along the direction of propagation; symbol λ, units m (metres). The wavelength of light is 390–780 nm; the wavelength of sound, 16 mm–16 m.

Wavell, Archibald Percival Wavell, 1st Earl [wayvl] (1883–1950) British field marshal, born in Colchester, Essex. In 1939 he was given the Middle East Command, defeated the Italians in N Africa, but failed against Rommel, and in 1941 was transferred to India, where he became viceroy (1943).

wave motion *p.1000*

wax A substance of a firm but plastic solid consistency, with a low coefficient of friction, and water-repellant. **Mineral waxes**, notably **paraffin wax**, are hydrocarbons of high molecular weight with a microcrystalline structure. **Plant** and **animal waxes** are esters of fatty acids, which fulfil a mainly protective function (as **beeswax** in the honeycomb). Beeswax has a long history as a preferred material for candles and polishes, and as a medium for modelling.

waxbill A songbird of the weaver-finch family Estrildidae (17 species); native to Africa, Arabia, and S Asia to N Australia.

wax flower *wax plant*

wax plant An evergreen climbing perennial (*Hoya carnosa*), reaching 6 m/20 ft or more, native to Australia; leaves elliptical, glossy and rather fleshy; flowers in drooping heads, fragrant, 5-petalled, waxy-white with red centre; also called **wax flower**. (Family: Asclepiadaceae.)

waxwing A songbird of the N hemisphere; grey-brown with black tail; head with crest; some individuals with red, wax-like tips to some wing feathers. (Family: Bombicillidae, 3 species.)

Wayland In Norse, German, and Old English legends, a clever inventor, also known as **Wayland the Smith**. Many heroes carry swords made by him; his 'Smithy' is a dolmen on the Berkshire Downs, UK.

Wayne, Anthony, known as **Mad Anthony** (1745–96) Revolutionary soldier, born in Easttown, PA. He commanded at Ticonderoga until 1777, when he joined Washington in New Jersey. He fought at the Brandywine (1777), led the attack at Germantown, captured supplies for the army at Valley Forge, carried Stony Point, and saved Lafayette in Virginia (1781).

Wayne, John, originally **Marion Michael Morrison**, nickname **the Duke** (1907–79) Film actor, born in Winterset, IA. He achieved stardom as the Ringo Kid in *Stagecoach* (1939), and went on to make over 80 films, many in the Western genre typically starring as a tough but warm-hearted gunfighter or lawman, such as *She Wore a Yellow Ribbon* (1949), *The Man who Shot Liberty Vallance* (1962), and *True Grit* (1969, Oscar).

weak interaction The feeble short-range force responsible for radioactive beta decay, characterized by the presence of a particle called the neutrino; also known as **weak nuclear force**. It is mediated by W and Z particles.

weak nuclear force *weak interaction*

Weald, The [weeld] Area in Kent, Surrey, and Sussex, SE England, between North and South Downs; fertile agricultural area.

weapons of mass destruction (WMD) Weapons which are capable of a high level of physical destruction or which can be used to kill large numbers of people. They include nuclear, biological,

wave motion

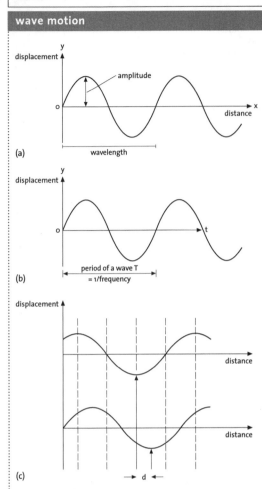

(a) wavelength

(b) period of a wave T = 1/frequency

(c)

A disturbance from equilibrium which propagates in time from one place to another. Many phenomena are governed by waves, such as electromagnetic waves, quantum matter waves for electrons, seismic waves, and vibration. **Longitudinal waves** occur when the displacement is in the same direction as the wave propagation (eg sound waves). **Transverse waves** correspond to a displacement perpendicular to the direction of wave propagation (eg ripples on water). **Standing waves** (also called **stationary waves**) result from interference between waves travelling in opposite directions (eg on a guitar string, where waves run along the string, reflected from end to end). For standing waves, the ratio of the instantaneous value of displacement at one point to that at another does not change. **Periodic waves** (ie waves produced by some regular repeating motion) are described by amplitude A, frequency f or period T, and wavelength λ; wave velocity $v = f\lambda$ m/s. **Sine waves** may be expressed as $y = A\sin 2\pi(ft - x/\lambda)$. Complicated periodic waves can be expressed as sums of sine waves using Fourier analysis.
(a) Sine wave at a fixed time, showing amplitude and wavelength.
(b) Sine wave at a fixed position, showing period T.
(c) Two sine waves *out-of-phase*, with a phrase difference ϕ given by $\phi = 2\pi d/\lambda$.

chemical (NBC), and radiological weapons. Nuclear weapons include atomic and hydrogen bombs. Biological weapons include the use of such diseases as anthrax, botulinum toxin, ricin, plague, and smallpox. Chemical weapons include the use of mustard gas, sarin, VX, soman, and tabun. Radiological weapons are so-called 'dirty' bombs containing radioactive material. In arms control usage, the term excludes devices which transport or propel such weapons, as long as they are clearly separate from the weapons. The notion achieved worldwide prominence in 2003–4 in relation to the international campaign to find and eliminate weapons of mass destruction in Iraq.

weasel A small carnivorous mammal with a long thin body, short legs, and small head; tail usually half length of body; brown with pale underparts (may be all white in winter). (Genus: *Mustela*, 9 species. Family: Mustelidae.)

weather The atmospheric processes operating at a location at a particular time: for example, day-to-day conditions of temperature, precipitation, atmospheric pressure, and wind; the scientific study of weather is *meteorology*. Weather differs from climate in that it is concerned with short-term meteorological events, whereas climate encompasses all the weather characteristics of a place, and is concerned with the long-term behaviour of atmospheric processes.

weather balloon *radiosonde balloon*

weather satellite A satellite used to record global weather patterns. It contains several remote sensing instruments, and measurements are made of atmospheric energy fluxes, atmospheric and surface temperatures, cloud cover, and amounts of water vapour.

Weaver, Sigourney, originally **Susan Alexandra Weaver** (1949–) Film actress, born in New York City. She became well known through her role as astronaut Ripley in the film *Alien* (1979). Later films include *Ghostbusters* (1984), the three *Aliens* sequels, *The Ice Storm* (1997), and *Snow Cake* (2006).

weaver *weaverbird*

weaverbird A finch-like songbird, also known as **weaver**. Many (not all) species weave nests suspended from branches. The group sometimes includes **weaver-finches**.

weaver-finch A finch-like bird, also known as the **estrildid finch** or (sometimes) the **waxbill**; native to the Old World tropics. (Family: Estrildidae, c.130 species.)

weaving An ancient craft in which fabric is produced by interlacing *warp* (lengthwise) and *weft* (crosswise) threads on machines called *looms*. Hand looms are known from very early times. They developed little until the Industrial Revolution, when the flying shuttle was invented by John Kay, in association with Richard Arkwright, in 1733, followed later in the century by Cartwright's power loom (1785).

Webb Social reformers, historians, and economists: **Sidney James Webb** (1859–1947) and **(Martha) Beatrice Webb**, *née* **Potter** (1858–1943), born in London and Standish, Gloucestershire, respectively, and married in 1892. They began a joint life of service to Socialism and trade unionism, publishing their classic *History of Trade Unionism* (1894), *English Local Government* (9 vols, 1906–29), and other works. They also started the New Statesman (1913).

Webb, Karrie (1974–) Golfer, born in Ayr, Queensland, Australia. She won the Women's British Open title in 1995, the youngest ever winner, and won it again in 1997 and 2002. Further achievements include the Australian Ladies' Masters (1998, 1999, 2000), Du Maurier Classic (1999), US Women's Open (2000, 2001), the LPGA title (2001), and the Evian Masters (2006).

Webb, Sidney James *Webb*

Webber, Andrew Lloyd *Lloyd Webber, Andrew*

Weber, Carl (Maria Friedrich) von [vayber] (1786–1826) Composer and pianist, born in Eutin, Germany. He is known as the founder of German romantic opera, notably in *Der Freischütz* (1821, The Freeshooter), *Euryanthe* (1823), and *Oberon* (1826), and he also wrote several orchestral works, piano, chamber, and church music, and many songs.

Weber, Max [vayber] (1864–1920) Economist, born in Erfurt, Germany. His best-known work is *Die protestantische Ethik und der Geist des Kapitalismus* (1904, The Protestant Ethic and the Spirit of Capitalism), which was a major influence on sociological theory.

weber [vayber] SI unit of magnetic flux; symbol *Wb*; named after German scientist Wilhelm Weber (1804–91); defined as the amount of flux which, when allowed to decrease steadily to zero in 1 second, will produce 1 volt of electromotive force in the loop of wire through which the flux passes.

Webern, Anton (Friedrich Ernst von) [vaybern] (1883–1945) Composer, born in Vienna. He studied under Schoenberg, and became one of his first musical disciples, making wide use of 12-tone techniques. His works include a symphony, cantatas, chamber music, a concerto for nine instruments, and songs.

Webster, Daniel (1782–1852) US orator, lawyer, and statesman, born in Salisbury, NH. He helped found the Whig Party, was twice secretary of state (1841–3, 1850–2), and was instrumental in arranging a political compromise over slavery between North and South in 1850. The *Webster–Ashburton Treaty* (1842) between Britain and the USA established the present-day boundaries between NE USA and Canada.

Webster, John (c.1580–c.1625) English playwright. He collaborated with several other writers, especially Dekker, but is best known for his two tragedies, *The White Devil* (1612) and *The Duchess of Malfi* (1623).

Webster, Noah (1758–1843) Lexicographer, born in Hartford, CT. He achieved fame with the first part (later known as 'Webster's Spelling Book') of *A Grammatical Institute of the English Language* (1783). He is best known for his *American Dictionary of the English Language* (2 vols, 1828), which was a major influence on US dictionary practice.

Webster–Ashburton Treaty (1842) An agreement between Britain and the USA which established the present-day boundary between NE USA and Canada. The parties involved were US secretary of state Daniel Webster and Alexander Baring, Baron Ashburton (1774–1848).

Weddell Sea Arm of the Atlantic Ocean, SE of Argentina; named after James Weddell (1787–1834), who claimed to have discovered the sea in 1823.

Wedekind, Frank [vaydekint] (1864–1918) Playwright, born in Hanover, Germany. He is best known for his unconventional tragedies, in which he anticipated the Theatre of the Absurd, such as *Die Büchse der Pandora* (1903, Pandora's Box).

Wedgwood, Dame Cicely (Veronica) (1910–97) Historian, born in Stocksfield, Northumberland. Her books include *Oliver Cromwell* (1939), *William the Silent* (1944), and *The Thirty Years' War* (1938).

Wedgwood, Josiah (1730–95) Potter, born in Burslem, Staffordshire. Inspired by antique models, he invented unglazed black basalt ware and blue jasper ware with raised designs in white. His concern over social welfare led him to build a village for his workmen at Etruria, Staffordshire.

Weeks, Feast of *Shabuoth*

Weelkes, Thomas (c.1575–1623) Madrigal composer, probably born in Elsted, Surrey. Nearly 100 of his madrigals have survived, as well as some instrumental music, and fragments of his sacred music.

weeping willow Any of several species of willow, all making quite large trees, with the smaller branches pendulous, often reaching the ground. Many are ornamentals, and arose in cultivation. (Family: Salicaceae.)

weever Bottom-dwelling fish with powerful poison spines on first dorsal fin and gill covers; eyes large and placed on top of head, mouth oblique. (Genus: *Trachinus*. Family: Trachinidae.)

weevil A robust beetle with a characteristic snout on the front of the head; wing cases often sculptured and toughened; antennae club-like, with elbow joint; species include many important pests such as the grain weevil and cotton boll weevil. (Order: Coleoptera. Family: Curculionidae, c.60 000 species.)

Wegener, Alfred (Lothar) [vaygener] (1880–1930) Explorer and geophysicist, born in Berlin. His theory of continental drift is named after him (**Wegener's hypothesis**), and is the subject of his main publications.

Weigel, Helene [viygl] (1900–71) Actress-manager, born in Vienna. She married Bertolt Brecht in 1929, and became a leading exponent of his work. She took control of the Berliner Ensemble after Brecht's death in 1956.

weigela [wiyjeela] A small deciduous shrub native to E Asia; flowers trumpet-shaped, 5-lobed, pink or crimson, in clusters. (Genus: *Weigela*, 12 species. Family: Caprifoliaceae.)

weight The downwards force on an object due to the gravitational attraction of the Earth; symbol *G*, units N (newton); distinct from mass. Weight decreases with altitude.

weightlifting A test of strength by lifting weights attached to both ends of a metal pole (*barbell*). Weightlifting formed part of the Ancient Olympic Games. It was introduced as a sport c.1850, and held its first world championship in 1891. Competitors have to make two successful lifts: the *snatch*, taking the bar directly above the head, and the *clean and jerk*, taking the bar onto the chest then above the head with outstretched arms. Another form of weightlifting is **powerlifting**, which calls for sheer strength as opposed to technique. This takes three forms: the *squat*, *dead lift*, and *bench press*.

Weil, Simone [vayl] (1909–43) Philosophical writer and mystic, born in Paris. Her posthumously published works include *La Pesanteur et la grâce* (1946, Gravity and Grace) and *Attente de Dieu* (1950, Waiting for God).

Weill, Kurt [viyl] (1900–50) Composer, born in Dessau, Germany. He is best known for his collaboration with Brecht in *Die Dreigroschenoper* (1928, The Threepenny Opera), its best-known song, 'Mack the Knife', becoming an international classic.

Weil's disease [viyl] An infectious disease caused by *Leptospira icterohaemorrhagiae*, also known as **leptospirosis**, commonly carried by rodents. The disease causes a flu-like illness, followed by kidney and liver damage, and there is a mortality of c.20%. It is named after German physician Adolf Weil (1848–1916).

Weimar [viymah(r)] 50°59N 11°20E, pop (2000e) 67 100. City in S Germany, on R Ilm; railway; colleges of technology, music, and architecture; associations with Schiller, Goethe, Liszt; castle; fire in 2004 at the Anna-Amalia Library destroyed over 30 000 priceless books and damaged 40 000.

Weimar Republic [viymah(r)] The name by which the German federal republic of 1919–33 is known. In 1919 a National Constituent Assembly met at Weimar, and drew up a constitution for the new republic. It was suspended by Hitler in 1933.

Weinberger, Caspar (Willard) [wiynberger] (1917–2006) US statesman, born in San Francisco, CA. He served in the Nixon and Ford administrations, then became secretary of defense after Reagan's election victory in 1980.

Weissmuller, Johnny [wiyzmuhler], popular name of **(Peter) John** (originally **Jonas**) **Weissmuller** (1904–84) Swimmer, born in Freidorf, Romania. In 1922 he made history by becoming the first person to swim 100 m (109 yd) in under one minute. He starred in 12 Tarzan films between 1932 and 1948.

Weizmann, Chaim (Azriel) [viytsman, khiym] (1874–1952) Jewish statesman and president of Israel (1949–52), born near Pinsk, Russia. President of the Zionist Organization (1920–30, 1935–46), and of the Jewish Agency (from 1929), he played a major role in the establishment of the state of Israel (1948), and was its first president.

Welch, Raquel, originally **Raquel Tejada** (1940–) Actress, born in Chicago, IL. She made her film debut in 1964, and was launched as a sex symbol after her scantily-clad appearance in *One Million Years* BC (1966). She received a Best Actress Golden Globe Award for *The Three Musketeers* (1973). During the 1980s she appeared in a number of TV series, and her later feature films include *Legally Blonde* (2001) and *Forget About It* (2005).

weld A biennial, native to Europe, W Asia, and N Africa (*Reseda luteola*); stem in second year growing to 1·5 m/5 ft; flowers small, yellowish, 4-petalled in long spike; fruit a 3-lobed capsule; also called **dyer's rocket**. It was once cultivated as a source of bright yellow dye. (Family: Resedaceae.)

Weldon, Fay, originally **Franklin**, *née* **Birkinshaw** (1931–) Writer, born in Alvechurch, Worcestershire. Her work deals with contemporary feminist themes, as in *Female Friends* (1975), and caustic satires of male-dominated society, as in *Darcy's Utopia* (1989). Later books include *Wicked Women* (1995), *Big Girls Don't Cry* (1998), *Mantrapped* (2004), and *She May Not Leave* (2005).

Welensky, Sir Roy [welenskee] (1907–91) Rhodesian statesman, born in Salisbury, Zimbabwe (formerly Southern Rhodesia). From 1956 to its break-up in 1963 he was prime minister of the Federation of Rhodesia and Nyasaland. His handling of the constitutional crisis in 1959 aroused much controversy.

welfare state A system of government whereby the state assumes responsibility for protecting and promoting the welfare of its citizens in such areas as health, income maintenance, unemployment, and pensions. A comprehensive system was established in the UK following World War 2, funded out of national insurance contributions and taxation. In recent years concern has been expressed about the proportion of the budget consumed by welfare services.

Welland, Colin (Williams) (1934–) Actor and playwright, born in Liverpool, Merseyside. In 1970, 1973, and 1974 he was voted best television playwright in Britain, his work including *Roll on Four O'clock* (1970) and *Bambino Mio* (1994). His screenplays include *Chariots of Fire* (1981) and *Twice in a Lifetime* (1987).

Welland Ship Canal Canal in Ontario, E Canada, linking L Erie and L Ontario, bypassing Niagara Falls; first canal opened, 1829; modern canal, 1932; length 61 km/38 mi.

Welles, (George) Orson (1915–85) Film director, producer, writer, and actor, born in Kenosha, WI. In 1938 his radio production of Wells's *War of the Worlds* was so realistic that it caused panic in the USA. In 1941, he wrote, produced, directed, and acted in the film *Citizen Kane*, a revolutionary landmark in cinema technique, and this was followed by *The Magnificent Ambersons* (1942). He played a variety of memorable stage and film roles, the most celebrated being that of Harry Lime in *The Third Man* (1949).

Wellesley, Arthur *Wellington, 1st Duke of*

Wellesley (of Norragh), Richard (Colley) Wellesley, 1st Marquess (1760–1842) Colonial administrator, born in Dangan, Co Meath, Ireland, the brother of Arthur Wellesley. While he was Governor-General of India (1797–1805), British rule in India became supreme: the influence of France was extinguished, and the power of the princes reduced by the crushing of Tippoo Sahib (1799) and the Marathas (1803).

Wellington 41°17S 174°47E, pop (2000e) 355 000. Capital city of New Zealand, on S coast of North Island; founded, 1840; capital, 1865; airport; railway; ferry to South Island; university (1899); Government Building, Parliament Buildings (1922, 1980), cathedral (1866).

Wellington, Arthur Wellesley, 1st Duke of (1769–1852) British general, statesman, and prime minister (1828–30), born in Dublin, Ireland, the brother of Richard Wellesley. He defeated the Danes during the Copenhagen expedition (1807), and in the Peninsu-

lar War drove the French out of Portugal and Spain, gaining victories at Talavera (1809), Salamanca (1812), and Toulouse (1814). After Napoleon's escape from Elba, he routed the French at Waterloo (1815). His period as prime minister significantly weakened the Tory Party, which split over the question of Catholic emancipation, and was further weakened by disagreements over trade and reform.

wellingtonia *mammoth tree*

Wells, H(erbert) G(eorge) (1866–1946) Writer, born in Bromley, Greater London. He achieved fame with scientific fantasies such as *The Time Machine* (1895) and *War of the Worlds* (1898), and wrote a range of comic social novels which proved highly popular, notably *Kipps* (1905) and *The History of Mr Polly* (1910). A member of the Fabian Society, he also wrote several socio-political works dealing with the role of science and the need for world peace.

wels Large nocturnal freshwater catfish (*Silurus glanis*) found in large rivers and lakes of E Europe; length up to 3 m/10 ft; body devoid of scales, mouth with long barbels, anal fin long. (Family: Siluridae.)

Welsh The Celtic language spoken in Wales, assigned equal status with English in all legal and administrative affairs. Of all the extant Celtic languages, Welsh enjoys the most vibrant literary scene, which continues a tradition dating from the epic poem *Taliesin* (c.6th-c), and the prose tales of the *Mabinogi*, preserved in mediaeval manuscripts. Its high point is the annual, weeklong, high-culture festival, the National Eisteddfod, which has become the focal point of Welsh identity for many. A Welsh-language television channel has broadened the range of information and entertainment sources in the media. There are c.580 000 speakers of Welsh (2001 census).

Welsh, Irvine (1957–) Writer, born in Edinburgh. He became known with his controversial first novel, *Trainspotting* (1993; filmed 1996), and later books include *Filth* (1998), *Porno* (2002), and *The Bedroom Secrets of the Master Chefs* (2006).

Welsh Assembly, properly **National Assembly for Wales** A legislative body established under the 1998 Government of Wales Act, following a 1997 referendum. It was formally opened in 1999, taking over the powers and authority previously exercised by the secretary-of-state for Wales. Broadly these include responsibility for secondary legislation in all policy areas except foreign affairs, defence, broadcasting, the emergency services and the justice system, and the exchequer function. The Assembly receives its revenue through a block grant from the Westminster parliament, which retains responsibility for primary legislation. A presiding officer elected by the 60 members oversees the Assembly (a post first held by Lord Dafydd Elis Thomas). The political leader of the Assembly is the first secretary, and Labour's Alun Michael was the first to hold the position, until forced to resign in 2000 (to be followed by Rhodri Morgan). The first election resulted in the formation of a minority Labour administration.

Welsh corgi *corgi*

Welsh Nationalist Party *Plaid Cymru*

welwitschia [welwichia] A peculiar gymnosperm (*Welwitschia mirabilis*) found only in the deserts of SW Africa. Its turnip-like stem produces just two strap-shaped leaves several metres long, which grow throughout the plant's life of over a century. (Family: Gnetaceae.)

Welwyn Garden City [welin] 51°48N 0°13W, pop (2000e) 41 900. Town in Hertfordshire, SE England; founded in 1919 by Ebenezer Howard; designated a 'new town' in 1948; railway.

Wembley Stadium One of the most famous football stadiums in the world, built at Wembley in NE London in 1923, with a capacity of 92 000. It was used for a wide range of sports and other occasions, such as pop concerts and religious meetings. It was demolished in 2003 to make way for a new national stadium on the same site, completed in 2007.

Wenceslaus or **Wenceslas, St** [wenseslas], known as **Good King Wenceslas** (c.903–35) Duke and patron of Bohemia, born in Stochov, Czech Republic. He encouraged Christianity in Bohemia, against the wishes of his mother, and was murdered by his brother Boleslaw. He became the patron saint of Bohemia and Czechoslovakia. Feast day 28 September.

Wentworth, Thomas *Strafford, Earl of*

Wentworth, W(illiam) C(harles) (1790–1872) Australian landowner and politician, born on Norfolk I. He was a staunch champion of self-government for Australia, which he made the policy of his newspaper *The Australian* (established 1824).

werewolf In traditional belief, a person assuming the form of a wolf, usually involuntarily and temporarily. There are traces of the belief in Ancient Greek religion, and it existed in much of Europe, but especially in the Balkans. It seems to be related to some kind of initiation rite, in which youths wore animal skins.

Wergeland, Henrik Arnold [vergeland] (1808–45) Poet, playwright, and patriot, born in Kristiansand, Norway. He is best known for his poetry, notably his Creation epic, *Skabelsen, Mennesket, og Messias* (1830, Creation, Humanity, and Messiah). He became Norway's national poet.

Wesak [wesahk] A Buddhist festival held in May to celebrate the birth, enlightenment, and death of the Buddha.

Weser, River [vayzer], ancient **Visurgis** Major river in Germany, formed by the confluence of the Werra and Fulda Rivers; enters the North Sea; length 440 km/273 mi.

Wesker, Sir Arnold (1932–) Playwright, born in London. The Kahn family trilogy, *Chicken Soup with Barley*, *Roots*, and *I'm Talking about Jerusalem* (1958–60), echo the march of events, pre- and post-World War 2, in a left-wing family. Later plays include *Chips with Everything* (1962), *Caritas* (1981), *Tokyo* (1994), and *Longitude* (2002). Further works include a collection of stories, *The King's Daughters* (1996), and a novel, *Honey* (2005). He was knighted in 2006.

Wesley, John (1703–91) Evangelist and founder of Methodism, born in Epworth, Lincolnshire. He became leader of a small group which had gathered round his brother **Charles Wesley** (1707–88), nicknamed the Methodists. In 1738, at a meeting in London, he experienced an assurance of salvation which led him to preach, but his zeal alarmed most of the parish clergy, who closed their pulpits against him. This drove him into the open air at Bristol (1739), where he founded the first Methodist chapel, and then the Foundry at Moorfields, London, which became their headquarters. His many writings included collections of hymns, sermons and journals, and a magazine.

Wessex A kingdom of the Anglo-Saxon heptarchy, with its main centres at Winchester and Hamwic (Southampton). Under Alfred (871–99), Wessex – by then incorporating Kent and Sussex – was the only English kingdom to withstand the onslaughts of the Danes.

West, Benjamin (1738–1820) Painter, born in Springfield, PA. He settled in London in 1763. The representation of modern instead of classical costume in his best-known picture, 'The Death of General Wolfe' (c.1771), was an innovation in British historical painting.

West, Frederick (1941–95) and **Rosemary West** (1953–) Serial murderers: Frederick, a builder born in Much Marcle, Herefordshire, and his wife Rosemary, born in Devon, SW England. In 1994 they were accused of killing 10 women, among them the former wife and a daughter of Frederick West, following the discovery of numerous bodies buried in their garden and house at 25 Cromwell Street, Gloucester. In 1995 Frederick was found hanged in his Birmingham prison cell while awaiting trial. Rosemary was convicted of 10 murders and sentenced to life imprisonment.

West, Mae (1893–1980) Actress, born in New York City. Throughout the 1930s she appeared in a series of racy comedies, all celebrating the sexually emancipated woman, although under much pressure from censorship. Her name was given to an airman's pneumatic life-jacket which, when inflated, was considered to give the wearer the generous bosom for which she was noted.

West, Nathanael, pseudonym of **Nathan Wallenstein Weinstein** (1903–40) Novelist, born in New York City. He wrote four short fantasy novels, of which the best known are *Miss Lonelyhearts* (1933) and his satire on Hollywood, *The Day of the Locust* (1939).

West, Dame Rebecca, pseudonym of **Cicily Isabel Andrews**, *née* **Fairfield** (1892–1983) Novelist and critic, born in London. She is best known for her studies arising out of the Nuremberg war trials: *The Meaning of Treason* (1949) and *A Train of Powder* (1955). Her novels include *The Thinking Reed* (1936) and *The Birds Fall Down* (1966).

West Bank pop (2000e) 1 662 000; region of the Middle East W of the R Jordan and the Dead Sea; part of the former mandate of Palestine, administered by Jordan, 1949–67; seized by Israel in the 1967 War, and remained under Israeli occupation; area includes Old (East) Jerusalem, as well as Bethlehem, Jericho, Hebron, and Nablus; a focus of territorial aspirations by the Palestine Liberation Organization; scene of an uprising (*Intifada*) against the Israelis (1987–91); parts of the West Bank have been returned to the Palestine National Authority (Jericho and Hebron). In 2004, work was still in progress on the West Bank Barrier, a 690 km/430 mi construction to prevent the incursion of terrorists into Israel, in spite of it being declared illegal by the International Court of Justice in The Hague.

West Bengal [benggawl] pop (2001e) 80 221 200; area 87 853 km²/33 911 sq mi. State in NE India; created in 1947; capital, Kolkata (Calcutta); governed by a Legislative Assembly.

westerlies The prevailing winds found at mid-latitudes, between 30° and 60°N and S of the Equator. Westerlies in the S hemisphere are stronger because there is a smaller land mass, and are known as the **Roaring Forties**, from the latitudes at which they occur.

Western Australia pop (2000e) 1 754 000; area 2 525 500 km²/975 000 sq mi. State in W Australia; Dutchman Dirk Hartog landed here in 1616, and Englishman William Dampier in 1688; Britain's first non-convict settlement on the Swan R, 1829; governed at first by New South Wales; separate colony, 1890; a third of the total area of Australia; over 90% occupied by the Great Plateau (mean altitude 600 m/2000 ft); highest point, Mt Meharry (1245 m/4085 ft); Great Sandy Desert, Gibson Desert, Great Victoria Desert, Nullarbor Plain in the E; capital, Perth.

Western Cape One of the nine new provinces established by the South African constitution of 1994, in SW South Africa; capital, Cape Town (also legislative capital of South Africa); pop (2000e) 4 332 000; area 129 386 km²/49 943 sq mi; chief languages, Afrikaans (63%), English (20%), Xhosa; tourism (Table Mountain, Robben I, Cape of Good Hope, Cape Agulhas); South Africa's richest province.

Western European Union An organization of 10 W European nations, founded in 1954 to co-ordinate defence and other policies, replacing the defunct European Defence Community, and reactivated in the 1980s; its members are Belgium, France, Germany, Greece, Italy, Luxembourg, The Netherlands, Portugal, Spain, and the UK. Several E European countries are linked to it under the heading of Associate Partners.

Western Isles pop (2000e) 29 500; area 2898 km²/1119 sq mi. Administrative region in Scotland; group of islands off the W coast (Outer Hebrides); main islands, Lewis, North Uist, Benbecula, South Uist, Barra; c.210 km/130 mi N–S; capital, Storno-

Western Sahara

□ International Airport — — Boundary status disputed

Timezone GMT
Area 252 126 km²/97 321 sq mi
Population total (2002e) 308 000
Status Under dispute, still officially part of Morocco

Capital al-Aioun
Languages Arabic (Hassaniya and Moroccan), French, Berber dialects, Spanish
Ethnic groups Mainly of Arab and Berber descent
Religion Sunni Muslim
Physical features Located in NW Africa, between Morocco (N), Mauritania (S), and Atlantic Ocean (E); low, flat terrain rising to small mountains in S and NE.
Climate Hot, dry desert; limited rainfall; fog and heavy dew produced by cold offshore currents.
Currency 1 Moroccan Dirham (MAD) = 100 Moroccan francs
Economy Limited by low rainfall and few natural resources; fishing and phosphate mining are main sources of income.
History Spanish province known as Spanish Sahara (Western Sahara) since 1884; partitioned by Morocco and Mauritania after its Spanish status ended in 1975; independence proclaimed in 1976, as Saharan Arab Democratic Republic (SADR); Morocco refused to withdraw its claim to the region, resulting in fighting between Morocco and Polisario guerrillas; Mauritania withdrew its claim after signing a peace treaty with the Polisario Front, 1979; SADR admitted to the Organization of African Unity, 1982; UN-supervised talks to decide the region's future, 1990; Polisario guerrilla warfare stopped under UN ceasefire, 1991; renewed fighting, 1993; agreement to UN proposal for a referendum, 1994, but implementation postponed in 1996.

Main SADR government leaders
Head of State
1982– Mohammed Abdelazziz
Head of Government
1999– Bouchraya Hamoudi Bayoune
Officially administered by the Moroccan government.

way, on Lewis; Harris tweed; name often used to refer to both Inner and Outer Hebrides.

Western Reserve Territory in NW Ohio successfully claimed by the state of Connecticut in 1786, during the final settlement of interstate boundary disputes that dated from the colonial era.

Western Sahara see panel

Western Samoa Samoa

Western Wall The only surviving part of the Second Temple of Jerusalem and, as such, the most sacred of Jewish sites. Traditionally a place of prayer and lamentation during the dispersion of the Jews, it was formerly often referred to as the **Wailing Wall**.

West Germany Germany

West Indies Federation (1958–1962) An unsuccessful attempt to establish a single government for the English-speaking West Indies.

Westinghouse, George (1846–1914) Engineer, born in Central Bridge, NY. In 1863 he invented an air-brake for railways, and also the gas meter and a system of conducting natural gas through pipes safely into homes. A pioneer in the use of alternating current for distributing electric power, he founded the Westinghouse Electrical Co in 1886.

West Irian Irian Jaya

Westman Islands, Icelandic **Vestmannaeyjar** pop (2000e) 5560; area 21 km²/8 sq mi. Group of 15 islands and 30 reefs off the S coast of Iceland; island of Surtsey was formed during eruptions in 1963–6.

Westmeath [westmeeth], Ir **na h-Iarmhidhe** pop (2000e) 63 000; area 1764 km²/681 sq mi. County in Leinster province, C Ireland; capital, Mullingar.

West Midlands pop (2001e) 5 267 300; area 899 km²/347 sq mi. County of C England; adminstrative centre, Birmingham; metropolitan council abolished in 1986.

Westminster, City of 51°30N 0°09W, pop (2001e) 181 300. Borough of C Greater London, England; N of the R Thames; administrative centre of the UK; includes the major tourist area from Westminster Bridge through Trafalgar Square to the West End.

Westminster, Palace of Houses of Parliament

Westminster, Statutes of Part of a comprehensive legislative programme undertaken by Edward I to reform English law and administration. Three Statutes were passed, in 1275, 1285, and 1290.

Westminster Abbey The church of St Peter in Westminster, London. The first recorded abbey church, consecrated in 1065, was replaced from 1245 by the present building in early English Gothic style. It serves as a coronation church and national shrine, with many memorials to those who have shaped the country's history and culture.

Westminster Assembly A body of clerics and laymen convened by the English Long Parliament in 1643 to arrange a religious settlement to replace the Church of England. Dominated by Presbyterians, it produced a directory of public worship to replace the Prayer Book, and the Westminster Confession of Faith.

Westminster Confession of Faith The main Presbyterian Confession of Faith, adopted by the Westminster Assembly, England, in 1643. It became the major confessional influence among Reformed Churches of the English-speaking world.

Westmorland Former county of NW England; part of Cumbria since 1974.

Westphalia NW German principality, first settled by Saxons c.700, later forming part of the Lower Rhine–Westphalian Circle of the Empire (1512).

West Point A US military academy founded by Act of Congress in 1802 at the West Point military station on the Hudson R in the state of New York.

West Sussex *Sussex, West*

West Virginia pop (2000e) 1 808 300; area 62 758 km²/24 232 sq mi. State in E USA; the 'Mountain State'; part of Virginia until the Civil War, when the area remained loyal to the Union, and split from Confederate East Virginia, 1861; 35th state admitted to the Union as West Virginia, 1863; capital, Charleston; Allegheny Mts dominate the E; highest point Mt Spruce Knob (1481 m/4859 ft); a rugged, hilly state, most of which is in the Allegheny Plateau; 65% forested; nation's leading producer of bituminous coal; major producer of natural gas; both summer and winter tourism.

wet rot A type of timber decay caused by the cellar fungus, *Coniophora puteana*; found only in wood with a high moisture content.

Wexford (county), Ir **Loch Garman** pop (2000e) 103 000; area 2352 km²/908 sq mi. County in Leinster province, SE Ireland; Wicklow Mts (N), Blackstairs Mts (W); capital, Wexford, pop (2000e) 16 000; main seaport, Rosslare; rich farmland (cattle) and resort area.

Weyden, Rogier van der [viydn] (c.1400–64) Religious painter, born in Tournai, Belgium. He executed many portraits and altarpieces, and among his best-known works are 'The Descent from the Cross' (c.1435–40, Madrid) and the 'Last Judgment' altarpiece (c.1450, Beaune).

whale An aquatic mammal of worldwide order Cetacea (79 species); resembles fish in shape (although tail blades – *flukes* – are horizontal, not vertical); breathes air through opening(s) on top of head; has insulating layer of oily blubber under skin; two major groups: **toothed whales** (5 families with 69 species, including the sperm whale, killer whale, dolphin, and porpoise); larger **baleen whales** (3 families with 10 species, including rorquals, grey whales, and right whales).

whalebone *baleen*

whale shark The largest of all fishes (*Rhincodon typus*), widely distributed in surface waters of tropical seas; length up to 18 m/ 60 ft; weight up to 20 tonnes. (Family: Rhincodontidae.)

whaling The hunting of whales for oil, meat, and blubber, which has resulted in a serious decline in whale populations and the near-extinction of several species. The International Whaling Commission, established in 1946, exists to regulate the industry, but overfishing continues. A moratorium on commercial whaling was set up in 1986, but not all countries have agreed to it, and several have used loopholes, which allow the killing of whales for scientific research, in order to continue whaling.

Wharton, Edith (Newbold), *née* Jones (1862–1937) Novelist, born in New York City. She wrote mainly about upper-class New York society, and is best known for her novels, *The House of Mirth* (1905), *Ethan Frome* (1911), and *The Age of Innocence* (1920, Pulitzer).

wheat A cereal second only to rice in importance, originating in the Middle East but cultivated throughout temperate regions of the world. The various species yield different qualities of flour, such as **bread wheat** (*Triticum aestivum*) and **durum wheat** (*Triticum durum*) from which pasta is made. Wheat is the most suitable for making bread, because of the presence of the elastic protein gluten. (Genus: *Triticum*, 20 species. Family: Gramineae.)

wheatear A thrush native to the N hemisphere and S Africa; the name is a corruption of 'white arse' (after white rump). (Genus: *Oenanthe*, 20 species.)

Wheatley, Dennis (Yates) (1897–1977) Novelist, born in London.

He produced an enormously popular mix of satanism and historical fiction. Indicative titles in a lurid oeuvre are *The Devil Rides Out* (1935), *The Scarlet Impostor* (1942), and *The Sultan's Daughter* (1963).

Wheatstone, Sir Charles (1802–75) Physicist, born in Gloucester, Gloucestershire. He invented the concertina (1829), took out a patent for an electric telegraph (1837), and invented a sound magnifier for which he introduced the term *microphone*. **Wheatstone's bridge**, a device for the comparison of electrical resistances, was brought to notice (though not invented) by him.

wheel One of the most important innovations in human material culture, allowing continuous rotary motion, and the continuous conversion of rotary motion into linear motion, and vice versa. The earliest wheels are found c.3500 BC; the earliest with spokes c.2000 BC. Other improvements were the separate axle, the reinforced hub, which could be lubricated, and the metal tyre, which strengthened the rim.

Wheeler, Sir (Robert Eric) Mortimer (1890–1976) Archaeologist, born in Glasgow. He carried out notable excavations in Britain at Verulamium (St Albans) and Maiden Castle, and from 1944–7 was director-general of archaeology in India. He was well known for spirited popular accounts of his subject, in books and on television.

wheel window *rose window*

whelk A marine snail with a spirally coiled external shell; aperture closed off by a chitinous covering once head and body are drawn inside. (Class: Gastropoda. Order: Neogastropoda.)

Whichcote, Benjamin (1609–83) Philosopher and theologian, born in Stoke, Shropshire. He became provost of King's College, Cambridge (1644–60), and is regarded as the spiritual founder of the Cambridge Platonists.

Whicker, Alan (Donald) [wiker] (1925–) British broadcaster and journalist, born in Cairo. He served with the Army Film Unit in World War 2, and was a war correspondent in Korea before joining the BBC (1957–68). He began his *Whicker's World* documentary series in 1958, and became British television's most travelled man. His publications include books about his travels and two volumes of autobiography, *Within Whicker's World* (1982) and *Whicker's World: Take 2* (2001). He returned to the battlefields of his youth to film *Whicker's War* (2004) for Channel 4.

whidah *whydah*

Whig Party (USA) One of two major US political parties during the decades prior to the Civil War. The name was adopted in 1834 to signify opposition to 'King' Andrew Jackson (president, 1829–37). The Whigs stood for greater governmental intervention in the economy than did the Democrats, who followed Jackson, but both parties agreed on the necessity of keeping the slavery issue out of politics. The Whigs collapsed in 1854, precisely because the slavery issue could no longer be contained.

Whigs (UK) A British political party which emerged in 1679–80 as the group agitating for the exclusion of James, Duke of York, on the grounds of his Catholicism. The name was probably a contraction of 'Whiggamores' – militant Scottish Presbyterians. During its long period of dominance in British politics after 1714, it drew much strength from defending 'the principles of 1688', which included limited monarchy and the importance of parliament. Most of its leaders were great landowners who used political patronage to create family-based groupings in parliament. Whig fortunes waned in the late 18th-c, and Whigs became leading members of the new Liberal party from the mid-19th-c.

whimbrel A curlew (*Numenius phaeopus*) which breeds in the N hemisphere on tundra and moors; migrates to shores in the S hemisphere; striped head; also known as the **seven whistler**.

whinchat A bird of the thrush family Murcicapidae, native to Europe, N Africa, and W Asia (*Saxicola rubetra*); mottled above, pale beneath, with light 'eyebrow' line.

whip A party official in a legislative chamber responsible for ensuring that members attend and vote in accordance with party policy; the name derives from the jargon of hunting, a 'whipper in'.

whippet A small slender breed of dog developed in Britain by cross-breeding small greyhounds with terriers.

Whipple, Fred (Lawrence) (1906–2004) Astronomer, born in Red Oak, IA. He studied at California University, and became professor of astronomy at Harvard in 1950. An expert on the Solar System, he became known especially for his work on comets, and the six he discovered were all named after him. He was director of the Smithsonian Astrophysical Observatory in Cambridge, MA (1955–1973) and oversaw its merger with the Harvard Observatory to form the Harvard–Smithsonian Centre for Astrophysics. A paper he published in the Astrophysical Journal in 1950 suggested that comets are composed of ice and dust, and later work has confirmed this 'dirty snowball' model. The Fred Lawrence Whipple Observatory in Amado, AZ, contains the largest mirror telescope in the US.

Whipple, George H(oyt) (1878–1976) Pathologist, born in Ashland, NH. He shared the Nobel Prize for Physiology or Medicine in 1934 for the discovery of the lifesaving liver therapy against pernicious anaemia.

whip-poor-will A North American bird (a goatsucker, *Caprimulgus vociferus*); inhabits open woodland.

whip scorpion A nocturnal, predatory arthropod; body scorpion-like, up to 75 mm/3 in long, ending in a long whip-like tail; found in the tropics and subtropics. (Class: Arachnida. Order: Uropygi, c.85 species.)

whirligig A dark, shiny beetle that lives in groups on the surface of ponds; fast-moving, typically swimming in small circles; eyes divided for vision above and below water surface. (Order: Coleoptera. Family: Gyrinidae.)

whirlwind A column of air rotating rapidly around a localized centre of low pressure. It is caused by local surface heating, which results in instability and convectional uprising.

whiskey *whisky*

Whiskey Rebellion (1794) An insurrection of farmers in W Pennsylvania, USA, against the excise tax imposed by the federal government on whiskey, which they made in large quantities from their crops of grain. It was suppressed by government forces.

whisk fern A member of a group of only 10 living species plus various fossil forms, considered the most primitive of vascular plants and possible ancestors of the ferns. Fossil forms date mainly from the Devonian period, the most famous being *Rhynia*. (Class: Psilophyta.)

whisky (Ireland/US **whiskey**) A spirit distilled from fermented grain, such as barley, rye, or wheat; the main spirit produced and consumed in Ireland and Scotland. Whiskies can be single malt, a product of a single distillate, or a blend of several batches.

whist A non-gambling card game, normally played with four people in pairs. Each player receives 13 cards, and the object is to win more tricks than the opposing pair. Trumps are decided before each game, and at **whist drives** trumps are normally played in the following order; hearts, clubs, diamonds, spades. A round of 'no trumps' is also common.

Whistler, James (Abbott) McNeill (1834–1903) Artist, born in Lowell, MA. He is best known for his evening scenes ('nocturnes'), such as 'Old Battersea Bridge' (c.1872–5, Tate, London), and for the famous portrait of his mother (1871–2, Musée d'Orsay, Paris).

Whistler, Rex (John) (1905–44) Artist, born in Eltham, Kent. He studied at the Slade School of Art in London, and excelled in the rendering of 18th-c life, ornament, and architecture, particularly in book illustration, murals, and designs for the theatre and ballet. In 1936 he painted a series of murals for the 6th Marquess of Anglesey at Plas Newydd, Anglesey, now considered to be his masterpiece. In 2005, a major exhibition of his works was held there to celebrate the centenary of his birth.

Whitbread Book Awards *Costa Book Awards*

Whitby, Synod of A meeting in Britain in 663/4 when the differences in organization between Roman and Celtic Christianity were debated. Roman concepts of church order prevailed.

White, Gilbert (1720–93) Clergyman and naturalist, born in Selborne, Hampshire. His *Natural History and Antiquities of Selborne* (1789) has become an English classic.

White, Patrick (Victor Martindale) (1912–90) Writer, born in London. His first novel, *Happy Valley*, appeared in 1939, and he has since written several novels, short stories, and plays, achieving international success with *The Tree of Man* (1954). He received the Nobel Prize for Literature in 1973.

White, T(erence) H(anbury) (1906–64) Novelist, born in Mumbai (Bombay), India. With the exception of the largely autobiographical *The Goshawk* (1951), his best work was in the form of legend and fantasy, especially his sequence of novels about King Arthur, beginning with *The Sword in the Stone* (1937).

white ant *termite*

White Australia Policy The unofficial national policy of Australia from 1901 to the 1960s, designed to exclude non-European migrants; it was particularly aimed at Asians, Pacific Islanders, and Africans who, it was feared, might come to dominate Europeans. In the late 1960s, the policy was progressively dismantled.

whitebait Small silvery fish found abundantly in shallow coastal waters and estuaries; includes the N Atlantic first-year herrings, *Clupea harengus*, and young sprats, *Sprattus sprattus*.

whitebeam A spreading, deciduous tree or shrub (*Sorbus aria*), native to Europe; flowers white, in clusters; berries red. (Family: Rosaceae.)

white bryony A perennial with a large, white, tuber-like base (*Bryonia dioica*), native to Europe, W Asia, and N Africa; flowers greenish-white, 5-petalled; berry changing from green through white and orange to red. (Family: Cucurbitaceae.)

White Canons *Premonstratensians*

white cedar A species of *arbor vitae* (*Thuja occidentalis*), native to E North America, which provides white or yellowish timber. (Family: Cupressaceae.)

white currant *red currant*

white dwarf A small, dim star in the final stages of its evolution. White dwarfs are defunct stars, collapsed to about the diameter of the Earth, at which stage they stabilize, with their electrons forming a degenerate gas, the pressure of which is sufficient to balance gravitational force.

white-eye A small songbird, native to Old World tropical regions; white ring around eye. (Family: Zosteropidae, c.85 species.)

Whitefield, George [whitfeeld] (1714–70) Methodist evangelist, born in Gloucester, Gloucestershire. Associated with the Wesleys at Oxford, he founded no distinct sect, but many of his adherents followed the Countess of Huntingdon in Wales, and formed the Calvinistic Methodists. He made several visits to America, where he played an important role in the Great Awakening.

whitefish Any of a small group of freshwater and brackish-water fishes widespread in lakes and large rivers of the N hemisphere; species include the vendace, cisco, and houting. (Genus: *Coregonus*. Family: Salmonidae.)

whitefly A small, sap-sucking bug; adults active fliers; bodies and wings covered with a waxy, white powder; commonly produces honeydew, and attended by ants. (Order: Homoptera. Family: Aleyrodidae, c.1200 species.)

White Friars *Carmelites*

Whitehall A wide thoroughfare lying between Parliament and Trafalgar Squares in London, and by association the offices of central government which line it.

Whitehead, A(lfred) N(orth) (1861–1947) Mathematician and philosopher, born in Ramsgate, Kent. He collaborated with his former pupil, Bertrand Russell, in writing the *Principia Mathematica* (1910–13). Other more popular works include *Adventures of Ideas* (1933) and *Modes of Thought* (1938).

Whitehorse 60°41N 135°08W, pop (2000e) 20 000. Capital of Yukon territory, NW Canada; on the R Lewes; founded during Klondike gold rush, 1900.

White Horse, Vale of the Site in Oxfordshire, England, of a stylized representation of a horse, carved on the chalk hillside about 3000 years ago. Perhaps originally a cult object for the local Celtic tribe, the Belgae, it has inspired many imitations.

White House The official residence of the US president, situated on Pennsylvania Avenue in Washington, DC. The 132-room Neoclassical mansion was built (1793–1801) from the designs of James Hoban (1762–1831), who also supervised its reconstruction (1814–29) after it was burnt down by the British in 1814.

Whitelaw, William (Stephen Ian) Whitelaw, 1st Viscount, popularly known as **Willie Whitelaw** (1918–99) British Conservative statesman, born in Nairn, Highland. His posts included secretary of state for Northern Ireland (1972–3) and for employment (1973–4), and home secretary (1979–83). He was Leader of the House of Lords until 1988.

Whiteman, Paul (1890–1967) Jazz bandleader, composer, and arranger, born in Denver, CO. Known in his early days as 'the King of Jazz', he was the most popular bandleader of the 1920s and early 1930s, before the swing era.

White Nile or **Bahr El Ablad** Upper reach of R Nile in S and E Sudan; a continuation of the Albert Nile; joined at Khartoum by the Blue Nile, forming the R Nile proper; length 1900 km/ 1180 mi.

whiteout A condition which occurs when there is a scattering of light between the base of low cloud and a bright snow surface, making it difficult to locate the horizon. The term is also used for blizzard conditions in which it is difficult to determine direction.

white paper In the UK, a government publication setting out its policy and legislative intentions in a specific area. Different degrees of scope exist for consultation before the proposals are put into effect.

Whiteread, Rachel (1963–) Artist and sculptor, born in London. She became known for her casts of ordinary domestic objects, such as wardrobes and baths. In 1993 she captured the public imagination with her life-sized cement cast of a three-storey terraced house in East London. The project gained her the Turner Prize and was demolished soon afterwards. Later work includes a plastercast *Untitled (Room 101)* (2003).

White Russia *Belarus*

White Russians The name collectively given to counter-revolutionary forces led by ex-tsarist officers, which fought unsuccessfully against the Bolshevik Red Army during the Russian Civil War (1918–22).

White Sands An area of white gypsum sand dunes in S New Mexico, USA, designated a national monument in 1933. The first nuclear explosion took place here in July 1945.

White Sea, Russian **Beloye More** area c.95 000 km²/36 670 sq mi. Arm of the Arctic Ocean and inlet of the Barents Sea, NW European Russia; ice-breakers keep some sea channels open in winter.

white shark Large and extremely aggressive shark (*Carcharodon carcharias*), considered the most dangerous of all sharks; widespread in tropical to temperate seas; length up to 6 m/20 ft; grey to brown above, underside white; teeth large and finely serrated; many attacks on humans. (Family: Lamnidae.)

Whitewater scandal A series of allegations of financial misconduct levelled against Bill and Hillary Clinton, relating to a commercial land development in the 1980s. Whitewater was the name of an Arkansas property development corporation in which (at the time) Governor Clinton and his wife (a member of a local law firm) were partners. The allegations surfaced in the media following Clinton's inauguration as president in 1993, but despite probes by the Senate and a special prosecutor, the Clintons were never charged with wrongdoing.

white whale *beluga* (mammal)

Whitgift, John (c.1530–1604) Clergyman, born in Grimsby, North East Lincolnshire. He became Archbishop of Canterbury (1583) and a Privy Councillor (1586). A champion of conformity, he vindicated the Anglican position against the Puritans.

whiting European codfish (*Merlangius merlangus*) widely distributed in shallow shelf waters from N Norway to the Black Sea; length up to 70 cm/28 in. (Family: Gadidae.)

Whiting, John (Robert) (1917–63) Playwright, born in Salisbury, Wiltshire. His best-known work was *The Devils* (1961), a dramatization of Huxley's *The Devils of Loudon*.

Whitlam, (Edward) Gough [gof] (1916–) Australian statesman and Labor prime minister (1972–5). He ended conscription and relaxed the policy on non-white immigrants. He was dismissed by the governor-general after the opposition blocked his money bills in the upper house of the Senate – the first time that the crown had so acted against an elected prime minister.

Whitman, Walt(er) (1819–92) Poet, born in Long Island, NY. An outstanding proponent of free verse, his major poetic work was *Leaves of Grass* (1855), which grew in successive editions to over 400 pages. His later prose works include *Democratic Vistas* (1871) and *Specimen Days and Collect* (1882–3).

Whitney, Eli (1765–1825) Inventor, born in Westborough, MA. He invented a cotton-gin (patented 1793) for separating cotton fibre from the seeds, and in 1798 developed a new system for the mass-production of firearms.

Whitsunday or **Whit Sunday** In the Christian Church, the seventh Sunday after Easter, commemorating the day of Pentecost. The name Whit ('white') Sunday derives from the white robes traditionally worn by those baptized on this day.

Whittier, John Greenleaf (1807–92) Quaker poet and abolitionist, born near Haverhill, MA. He is best known for a collection of poems and stories, *Legends of New England* (1831). Later works include *In War Time* (1864) and *At Sundown* (1892).

Whittington, Dick, popular name of **Richard Whittington** (c.1358–1423) English merchant, who set out at 13 for London, where he found work as an apprentice, and in 1397 became Lord Mayor of London. The legend of his cat is an accepted part of English folklore.

Whittle, Sir Frank (1907–96) Inventor and aviator, born in Coventry, Warwickshire. He successfully developed the jet engine for aircraft (1941), and became government technical adviser on engine design (1946–8).

Whitworth, Kathy, popular name of **Kathrynne Ann Whitworth** (1939–) Golfer, born in Monahans, TX. The most successful woman golfer of all time, she has won all the women's 'Majors' except the US Open. She turned professional in 1958.

WHO *United Nations*

whooping cough An acute severe bronchitis caused by *Bordetella pertussis*, mainly affecting children; also known as **pertussis**. It is characterized by a series of violent coughs followed by a deep inspiration (the 'whoop'). The condition carries a high mortality in infants, and active immunization is highly desirable.

whortleberry *bilberry; cowberry*

Whovian *Doctor Who*

whydah [widuh] A songbird of the genus *Vidua* (8 species), treated variously as a weaver-finch or weaverbird, and sometimes put in a separate family (Viduidae); finch-like; male with very long tail; also known as **whidah** or **widow finch**.

Whymper, Edward (1840–1911) Wood-engraver and mountaineer, born in London. During 1860–9 he conquered several hitherto unscaled peaks of the Alps, including the Matterhorn (1865).

Wichita [wichitaw] 37°42N 97°20W, pop (2000e) 344300. City in S Kansas, USA, on the Arkansas R; settled, 1866; city status, 1870; airport; railway; two universities (1892, 1898); chief commercial and industrial centre in S Kansas; Cow Town (1870s replica).

Wicklow, Ir **Cill Mhantáin**, nickname **the Garden of Ireland** pop (2000e) 98 000; area 2025 km²/782 sq mi. County in Leinster province, E Ireland; Wicklow Mts (W); capital, Wicklow (pop (2000e) 5300); agriculture; resort towns (eg Bray).

Widdecombe, Ann (Noreen) [widikum] (1947–) British stateswoman, born in Bath, S England. She was elected as Conservative MP for Maidstone in 1987. She became minister-of-state for employment (1994–5) and at the Home Office (1995–7), then shadow secretary for health (1998–9) and shadow home secretary (1999–2001). She attracted publicity when she converted from Anglicanism to Roman Catholicism over the issue of women priests. In 2005 she took on the role of real-life agony aunt in the BBC 2 TV series *Ann Widdecombe to the Rescue*.

wide area network (WAN) *local area network*

widgeon *wigeon*

Widor, Charles Marie (Jean Albert) [weedaw(r)] (1844–1937) Composer, born in Lyon, France. He composed 10 symphonies for the organ, as well as a ballet, chamber music, and other orchestral works.

widow bird / finch *whydah*

Wieland, Christoph Martin [veelant] (1733–1813) Writer, born near Biberach, Germany. He made the first German translation of Shakespeare (1762–6), and wrote a number of popular romances, notably *Agathon* (1766–7). His best-known work is the heroic poem *Oberon* (1780).

Wieman, Carl E (1951–) Physicist, born in Corvallis, OR. A researcher at the National Institute of Standards and Technology at the University of Colorado, he shared the 2001 Nobel Prize for Physics for the achievement of Bose–Einstein condensation in dilute gases of alkali atoms, and for early fundamental studies of the properties of the condensates.

Wien [veen] *Vienna*

Wiener, Norbert [weener] (1894–1964) Mathematical logician, the founder of cybernetics, born in Columbia, MO. His study of the handling of information by electronic devices, based on the feedback principle, encouraged comparison between these and human mental processes in *Cybernetics* (1948) and other works.

Wiesbaden [veezbahdn] 50°05N 8°15E, pop (2000e) 267000. City in Germany; on the R Rhine; railway; popular health resort; traditional wine centre.

Wieschaus, Eric F(rancis) [veeshows] (1947–) Developmental biologist, born in South Bend, IA. He shared the Nobel Prize for Physiology or Medicine in 1995 for his research into how genes control early development of the human embryo.

Wigan 53°33N 2°38W, pop (2001e) 301400. Town in Greater Manchester, NW England; a borough since 1246; railway; Wigan Pier, now a museum, made famous by George Orwell, in *The Road to Wigan Pier* (1932); football league team, Wigan Athletic (Latics).

wigeon or **widgeon** A dabbling duck of the genus *Anas*; includes the **European wigeon** (*Anas penelope*), from Eurasia and N Africa, and the **North American wigeon** or **baldpate** (*Anas americana*).

Wiggin, Kate Douglas, *née* **Smith** (1856–1923) Novelist and kindergarten educator, born in Philadelphia, PA. She led the kindergarten movement in the USA, but is best remembered for her children's novels, notably *Rebecca of Sunnybrook Farm* (1903).

Wight, Isle of, Lat **Vectis** pop (2001e) 132700; area 381 km²/147 sq mi. Island county off the S coast of England, a unitary authority from 1995; in the mouth of Southampton Water, separated from Hampshire by the Solent and Spithead; imposing cliffs of the vertical sandstone Needles near Alum Bay; county town, Newport; ferry services from Portsmouth, Southampton, Lymington; tourism; yachting (especially Cowes Regatta Week).

Wightman Cup An annual lawn tennis competition involving professional women's teams from the USA and UK. It was first held in 1923, and named after the former US player Hazel Wightman (*née* Hotchkiss) (1886–1974). It was scrapped in 1992.

Wigman, Mary, originally **Marie Wiegmann** (1886–1973) Dancer, choreographer, and teacher, born in Hanover, Germany. She opened a school in Dresden in 1920, and created numerous solo and group dances which typified German expressionist dancing.

Wilberforce, William (1759–1833) British politician, evangelist, and philanthropist, born in Hull, NE England. In 1788 he began the movement which resulted in the abolition of the slave trade in the British West Indies in 1807. He died one month before the Slavery Abolition Act was passed in parliament.

Wilbur, Richard (Purdy) (1921–) Poet, born in New York City. Based in Cummington, MA, he has won acclaim for his translations as well as for his own lyrical poetry, as in *New and Collected Poems* (1988). *The Pig in the Spigot* appeared in 2000. He was named poet laureate of the USA in 1987.

Wilbye, John (1574–1638) Madrigal composer, born in Diss, Norfolk. He is known for only 66 madrigals, but these are renowned for his careful setting of literary texts, and for several translations of Italian poems.

Wilczek, Frank (1951–) Theoretical physicist, born in New York City. Professor of physics at the University of California in Santa Barbara (1981–8), in 2000 he moved from the Institute of Advanced Study to be professor of physics at the Massachusetts Institute of Technology. In 2004 he shared the Nobel Prize for Physics for work contributing to the discovery and exploration of the force that binds particles inside an atomic nucleus.

wild boar A wild ancestor (*Sus scrofa*) of the domestic pig, native to Europe, NW Africa, and S Asia; thick dark hair; male with tusks; domesticated in SE Asia 5–10 000 years ago.

wild cat A member of the cat family (*Felis silvestris*), found from N Europe to Africa and India; ancestor of the domestic cat, but larger, with a shorter, thicker tail.

Wilde, Oscar (Fingal O'Flahertie Wills) (1854–1900) Writer, born in Dublin. Celebrated for his wit and flamboyant manner, he became a leading member of the 'art for art's sake' movement. His early work included his *Poems* (1881), the novel *The Picture of Dorian Gray* (1891), and several comic plays, notably *Lady Windermere's Fan* (1892) and *The Importance of being Earnest* (1895). *The Ballad of Reading Gaol* (1898) and *De profundis* (1905) reveal the effect of two years' hard labour for homosexual practices.

wildebeest [wilduhbeest, vilduhbeest] An African grazing antelope; sturdy, with a large convex face; short horns spread sideways with upturned tips; long mane; long fringe of hairs along throat; also known as **gnu**. (Genus: *Connochaetes*, 2 species.)

Wilder, Billy, originally **Samuel Wilder** (1906–2002) Film director and scriptwriter, born in Sucha Poland (formerly Austria), Austria. His films include *The Lost Weekend* (1945, Oscar),

Sunset Boulevard (1950), and *The Apartment* (1960, Oscar). He received the American Film Institute Life Achievement Award in 1986.

Wilder, Gene, originally **Jerome Silberman** (1935–) Film actor, writer, and director, born in Milwaukee, WI. He received a Best Supporting Actor Oscar nomination for *The Producers* (1968), later films including *Blazing Saddles* (1974) and *Young Frankenstein* (1974). Known also as a screenwriter and director, he returned to the stage in 1996, starring in the London production of *Laughter on the 23rd Floor*.

Wilder, Thornton (Niven) (1897–1975) Writer, born in Madison, WI. His first novel, *The Cabala* (1926), was followed by the very successful *The Bridge of San Luis Rey* (1927), and the plays *Our Town* (1938) and *The Skin of Our Teeth* (1942), which all won Pulitzer Prizes.

Wilderness Campaign 1 (1864) An indecisive conflict in the American Civil War between the Union army under General Grant and the Confederate army under General Lee, fought in the Wilderness area of Virginia. **2** (1755) The term **Battle of the Wilderness** is also used for a conflict in Western Pennsylvania, in which Indians and French troops decimated a larger British army under General Edward Braddock.

Wilderness Road The early route across the S Appalachian Mts, from the Holston R through Cumberland Gap to Boonesborough on the Kentucky R. It was constructed in 1775 by a party led by Daniel Boone.

wildlife refuge An area set aside for the protection and conservation of wildlife (eg Serengeti National Park, Tanzania, and Australia's Great Barrier Reef). Ideally, it should be a wilderness area large enough to sustain its plant and animal population.

Wildlife Trusts *Royal Society for Nature Conservation*

Wiles, Andrew (John) (1953–) Mathematician, born in Cambridge, Cambridgeshire. In 1993 he announced that he had solved one of mathematics' oldest mysteries, Fermat's last theorem, and acceptance of his proposal followed in 1994.

Wilfrid or **Wilfrith, St** (634–709) Monk and bishop, born in Northumbria, England. As Bishop of York (c.665), he was involved in controversy over the organization of the Church in Britain, and was the first churchman to appeal to Rome to settle the issue. Feast day 12 October.

Wilhelmina (Helena Pauline Maria) [wiluhmeena] (1880–1962) Queen of The Netherlands (1890–1948), born in The Hague. During World War 2, though compelled to seek refuge in Britain, she steadfastly encouraged Dutch resistance to the German occupation. In 1948, she abdicated in favour of her daughter **Juliana**.

Wilkes, John (1727–97) British politician and journalist, born in London. He became an MP (1757), and attacked the ministry in his weekly journal, *North Briton* (1762–3), for which he was expelled from the house. Re-elected on several occasions, and repeatedly expelled, he came to be seen as a champion of liberty, and an upholder of press freedom. He finally gained admission to parliament in 1774.

Wilkes Land Area of Antarctica between Queen Mary Land (W) and Terre Adélie, lying mostly between 105° and 135° E.

Wilkie, Sir David (1785–1841) Painter, born in Cults, Fife. His fame mainly rests on his genre painting, but he also painted portraits, and in his later years sought to emulate the richness of colouring of the old masters, choosing more elevated subjects.

Wilkins, Sir George (Hubert) (1888–1958) Polar explorer, born in Mt Bryan East, Australia. He flew from England to Australia (1919), explored the Antarctic with Shackleton (1920–2), and made a pioneer flight from Alaska to Spitsbergen over polar ice (1928).

Wilkins, Maurice (Hugh Frederick) (1916–2004) Biophysicist, born in Pongaroa, New Zealand. With Crick and Watson he shared the

Nobel Prize for Physiology or Medicine in 1962 for work on the structure of DNA.

Wilkins, Roy (1910–81) Journalist and civil rights leader, born in St Louis, MO. He edited the newspapers of the National Association for the Advancement of Colored People (1934–49), and was then appointed the organization's executive secretary, retiring in 1977.

Wilkinson, Jonny (1979–) Rugby Union player, born in Surrey, England. He signed as a fly-half for Newcastle Falcons, and made his debut for England against Ireland in 1998. In the 1999 Five Nations competition he scored all of England's points against Ireland with seven penalties, a record-equalling achievement, and in the inaugural 2000 Six Nations campaign he established a new championship points tally. In the 2003 World Cup, he scored all England's points in the 24–7 semi-final win over France, and in the final against Australia secured his country's victory with a drop-goal in the last minutes of extra time. He was voted the International Rugby Players' Association player of the year in 2003, and also won the BBC Sports Personality of the Year Award. Appointed England captain in 2004, he was dogged by injury and frequently out of the game. At the start of 2007 he was recalled to the England team for the Six Nations championship.

will (law) A document in which a person (the *testator* or *testatrix*) sets out the way in which his or her property (the *estate*) is to be distributed to beneficiaries after death. In order to be valid, a will must comply with certain requirements (which vary between jurisdictions): for example, in the UK it must be signed in the presence of two witnesses, both of whom are present at the same time. If a person dies without making a will (dies *intestate*), statutory rules in some jurisdictions govern the distribution of property.

Willandra Lakes A world heritage site covering c.6000 km²/ 2300 sq mi in the Murray R Basin in New South Wales, Australia. The region provides a remarkable 'fossil landscape', generally unmodified since the end of the Pleistocene ice age.

Willard, Emma, *née* **Hart** (1787–1870) Educator, born in Berlin, CT. As founder of the Troy (NY) Female Seminary in 1821 (now the Emma Willard School), she was instrumental in the emergence of intellectually demanding secondary education for American women. Her campaigns paved the way for co-education.

Willemstad [vilemstaht] 12°12N 68°56W, pop (2000e) 53 000. Capital town of the Netherlands Antilles, on SW coast of Curaçao I; established by the Dutch as a trading centre, mid-17th-c; airport; free port; inner city and harbour, a world heritage site.

Willendorf [vilendaw(r)f] A prehistoric site near Krems, lower Austria, with Gravettian occupation dated c.32–28 000 BC. It is celebrated for the 'Willendorf Venus', a limestone statuette, 11 cm/4⅜ in high, painted with red ochre, which presumably served as a fertility or house goddess.

William I (of England), known as **the Conquerer** (c.1028–87) Duke of Normandy (1035–87) and the first Norman king of England (1066–87), the illegitimate son of Duke Robert of Normandy. Edward the Confessor most probably designated him as future King of England in 1051. When Harold Godwinson took the throne as Harold II, William invaded with the support of the papacy, defeated and killed Harold at the Battle of Hastings, and was crowned king on Christmas Day 1066. By the time of the Domesday Book (1086), the leaders of Anglo-Saxon society S of the Tees had been almost entirely replaced by a new ruling class of Normans, Bretons, and Flemings, who were closely tied to William by feudal bonds.

William I (of Germany), Ger **Wilhelm** (1797–1888) King of Prussia (1861–88) and first German emperor (1871–88), born in Berlin, the second son of Frederick William III. He placed Bismarck at the head of the ministry, and was victorious against Denmark (1864), Austria (1866), and France (1871). The rapid rise of socialism in Germany led to severe repressive measures, and he survived several attempts at assassination.

William I (of the Netherlands), **Prince of Orange**, known as **William the Silent** (1533–84) First of the hereditary stadtholders of the United Provinces of the Netherlands (1572–84), born in Dillenburg, Germany. In 1568 he took up arms against the Spanish crown, and became stadtholder of the Northern provinces, united in the Union of Utrecht (1579). He was assassinated by a Spanish agent. His byname comes from his ability to keep secret Henry II's scheme to massacre all the Protestants of France and the Netherlands, confided to him when he was a French hostage in 1559.

William I (of Scotland), known as **William the Lion** (c.1142–1214) King of Scots (1165–1214), the brother and successor of Malcolm IV. In 1173–4 he invaded Northumberland during the rebellion against Henry II, but was defeated at Alnwick. He was nevertheless able to make Scotland a much stronger kingdom.

William II (of England), known as **William Rufus** (c.1056–1100) King of England (1087–1100), the second surviving son of William the Conqueror. His main goal was the recovery of Normandy from his elder brother Robert Curthose, and from 1096, when Robert departed on the First Crusade, William ruled the duchy as *de facto* duke. He also led expeditions to Wales (1095, 1097), and came to exercise a controlling influence over Scottish affairs. He exploited his rights over the Church and the nobility, and quarrelled with Anselm, Archbishop of Canterbury. He was killed by an arrow while hunting in the New Forest.

William II (of Germany), Ger **Wilhelm**, known as **Kaiser Wilhelm** (1859–1941) German Emperor and King of Prussia (1888–1918), born in Potsdam, Germany, the eldest son of Frederick III and Victoria, daughter of Britain's Queen Victoria. He dismissed Bismarck (1890), and began a long period of personal rule, displaying a bellicose attitude in international affairs. During World War 1 he became a mere figurehead, and when the German armies collapsed, he abdicated.

William III (of Great Britain), known as **William of Orange** (1650–1702) Stadtholder of the United Provinces (1672–1702) and King of Great Britain (1689–1702), born in The Hague, the son of William II of Orange by Mary, the eldest daughter of Charles I of England. In 1677 he married his cousin, **Mary** (1662–94), the daughter of James II by Anne Hyde. Invited to redress the grievances of the country, he landed at Torbay in 1688 with an English and Dutch army, and forced James II to flee. He defeated James's supporters at Dunkeld (1689) and at the Boyne (1690), then concentrated on the War of the League of Augsburg against France (1689–97), in which he was finally successful.

William IV, known as **the Sailor King** (1765–1837) King of Great Britain and Ireland, and King of Hanover (1830–7), born in London, the third son of George III. He was the last monarch to use prerogative powers to dismiss a ministry with a parliamentary majority when he sacked Melbourne in 1834.

William, Prince *Charles, Prince of Wales*

William of Malmesbury [mahmzbree] (c.1090–c.1143) English chronicler and Benedictine monk, the librarian of Malmesbury Abbey, Wiltshire. His main works include *Gesta regum anglorum*, a general history of England from the coming of the Anglo-Saxons.

William of Ockham or **Occam** [okam], known as **the Venerable Inceptor** (c.1285–c.1349) Philosopher and theologian, born in the village of Ockham, Surrey. He became involved in a dispute between the Franciscans and Pope John XXII over apostolic poverty. He is especially known for his use of the principle of parsimony (**Ockham's razor**): 'Do not multiply entities beyond necessity' – a theory should not propose the existence of anything more than is needed for its explanations.

William of Tyre (c.1130–86) Chronicler and churchman, born in Palestine of French parents. He was appointed Archbishop of Tyre in 1175. His main work, *Historia rerum in partibus transmarinis gestarum* (History of Deeds in Foreign Parts), deals with the history of Palestine from 614 to 1184.

William of Wykeham or **Wickham** [wikam] (1324–1404) English statesman and clergyman, born in Wickham, Hampshire. He was appointed Bishop of Winchester (1367), and was twice Chancellor of England (1367–71, 1389–91).

Williams, (George) Emlyn (1905–87) Playwright and actor, born in Pen-y-ffordd, Flintshire. He achieved success as a dramatist with *A Murder has been Arranged* (1930) and the psychological thriller, *Night Must Fall* (1935). He featured in several films, and gave widely acclaimed readings from the works of Dickens, Dylan Thomas, and Saki.

Williams, Hank, popular name of **Hiram King Williams** (1923–53) Country singer, composer, and guitarist, born in Mount Olive West, AL. His many hit records include 'Lovesick Blues' (1949) and 'Hey, Good Lookin''. His son, **Hank Williams Jr** (1949–), continues as a successful country singer and songwriter.

Williams, Jody (1950–) US activist, born in Putney, VT, the campaign coordinator for the International Campaign to Ban Landmines. She shared the 1997 Nobel Peace Prize along with the organization for their work towards the banning and clearing of anti-personnel mines.

Williams, John (Christopher) (1942–) Guitarist, born in Melbourne, Victoria, Australia. Resident in England since 1952, several classical composers have written works for him. He founded a rock group known as Sky (1979–84) and later formed the contemporary music group Attacca.

Williams, John (Towner) (1932–) Film composer and conductor, born in New York City. He is the leading screen composer of his generation, his early films including *Superman* (1978) and the *Star Wars* and *Indiana Jones* series. In 1980 he became conductor of the Boston Pops, retiring from that post in 1992 to devote his time to composing. Later scores include *A.I. Artificial Intelligence* (2001), *Harry Potter and the Philosopher's Stone* (2001), *Star Wars Episode II* (2002), and *The Terminal* (2004).

Williams, J(ohn) P(eter) R(hys) (1949–) Rugby union player, born in Bridgend, S Wales. When he retired he was the most capped Welshman, with 55 appearances, and the game's most capped fullback (54).

Williams, Mark (1975–) Snooker player, born in Cwm, S Wales. He turned professional in 1992. His first major tournament win was the Regal Welsh Open in 1996, and further titles include the Benson and Hedges Masters (1998, 2003), UK Championship (1999, 2002), World Professional Championship (2000, 2003), and the LG Cup (2003). He was ranked world number 1 in 2000–1 and 2003.

Williams, Robbie (1974–) Pop singer, born in Stoke-on-Trent, Staffordshire. At age 16 he joined British boy band Take That (1991), leaving four years later to pursue a solo career. He has enjoyed regular success in the singles charts and his albums include *Life Thru a Lens* (1997), *Sing When You're Winning* (2000), *Escapology* (2002), and *Rudebox* (2006).

Williams, Robin (1952–) Film actor and entertainer, born in Chicago, IL. He starred in the television series *Mork and Mindy* (1978–82), and made his film debut in *Popeye* (1981). He earned Oscar nominations for *Good Morning Vietnam* (1987) and *Dead Poets Society* (1989), and a Best Supporting Actor Oscar for *Good Will Hunting* (1997). Later films include *Bicentennial Man* (1999), *Insomnia* (2002), and *Man of the Year* (2006).

Williams, Roger (c.1604–83) Colonist who founded Rhode Island, born in London. He became an extreme Puritan, and emigrated to New England in 1630. He purchased lands from the Indians, and founded the city of Providence (1636), allowing full religious toleration, becoming its first president (1654–8).

Williams, Rowan (1950–) Anglican clergyman, born in Swansea, S Wales. Professor of divinity at Oxford (1986–92), he was consecrated Bishop of Monmouth in 1992, becoming Archbishop of Wales in 2000. In 2002 he succeeded George Carey as Archbishop of Canterbury. He has written a number of books on the history of theology and spirituality.

Williams, Serena (1981–) Tennis player, born in Saginaw, MI, the sister of Venus Williams. Coached by her father, her singles titles include the US Open (1999, 2002), the French Open (2002), Wimbledon (2002, 2003), and the Australian Open (2003, 2005). She also partnered her sister to gain doubles titles in the US Open (1999), French Open (1999), Wimbledon (2000, 2002), and Australian Open (2001, 2003). At the start of 2007 her world ranking had slipped from 15 to 95, having been out of the game for six months through injury, but rose to 14 after winning the Australian Open singles title.

Williams (of Crosby), Shirley (Vivien Teresa Brittain) Williams, Baroness, *née* **Catlin** (1930–) British stateswoman, born in London. She became a Labour MP in 1964, and was secretary of state for prices and consumer protection (1974–6), and for education and science (1976–9). She became a co-founder of the Social Democratic Party in 1981, and the party's first elected MP later that year. She lost her seat in the 1983 general election, but remained as the SDP's president (1982–7). She later moved to the USA, but remains involved in British politics, and was made a life peer in 1993. From 2000–4 she was leader of the Liberal Democrats in the House of Lords.

Williams, Tennessee, pseudonym of **Thomas Lanier Williams** (1911–83) Playwright, born in Columbus, MS. He achieved success with *The Glass Menagerie* (1944). His later plays, almost all set in the Deep South against a background of decadence and degradation, include *A Streetcar Named Desire* (1947, Pulitzer), *Cat on a Hot Tin Roof* (1955, Pulitzer), *Suddenly Last Summer* (1958), and *Night of the Iguana* (1961). He also wrote short stories, essays, poetry, memoirs, and two novels.

Williams, Venus (1980–) Tennis player, born in Lynwood, CA. Coached by her father, she became the dominant female player of 2000, that year winning the Wimbledon singles title, the US Open, and Olympic gold in Sydney. She also won the Wimbledon doubles title, partnered by her younger sister, Serena Williams. She retained the Wimbledon and the US Open singles titles in 2001, but in 2003 she was defeated by her sister in the Wimbledon singles final. After a loss of form in 2004, she came back to win the Wimbledon singles title for a third time in 2005. She suffered injury problems during 2006 and by the start of 2007 her ranking had fallen to 48.

Williams, William Carlos (1883–1963) Writer and physician, born in Rutherford, NJ. He developed a distinctly American style for his shorter lyrics, which commanded attention from *Spring and All* (1923), and he adapted this for his 'personal epic', *Paterson* (1946–51). He also wrote plays, essays, a trilogy of novels, and criticism, including *In The American Grain* (1925).

Williamsburg 37°17N 76°43W, pop (2000e) 12 000. City in SE Virginia, USA; settled, 1633 (as Middle Plantation, renamed 1699); state capital, 1699–1780; Colonial Williamsburg is a major building restoration scheme; College of William and Mary (1693).

Williamson, Malcolm (Benjamin Graham Christopher) (1931–2003) Composer, born in Sydney, New South Wales, Australia. His compositions include the operas *Our Man in Havana* (1963) and *The Red Sea* (1972), as well as a wide variety of orchestral, vocal, choral, and other works. He was made Master of the Queen's Musick in 1975.

Willis, Bruce (1955–) Film actor, born in West Germany, but moved to the USA as a young child. He became widely known in the television series *Moonlighting* (1985–9), and achieved star status for his role in the *Die Hard* series (1988,

1990, 1995). Later films include *Pulp Fiction* (1994), *Armageddon* (1998), *The Sixth Sense* (1999), and *Sin City* (2005).

will o' the wisp *ignis fatuus*

willow A member of a large genus of mostly N temperate deciduous trees and shrubs; flowers in separate male and female catkins; seeds plumed with silky hairs for wind dispersal. Willows show a wide range of form, from low, creeping arctic species to large trees, many growing in or near water. They are a source of withies for basketwork, and cricket bats. (Genus: *Salix*, 500 species. Family: Salicaceae.)

willow-herb A member of a somewhat variable genus of mostly perennials, native throughout temperate and arctic regions; flowers with four rose, purple, sometimes white petals on top of a long, purplish ovary; fruit a capsule containing numerous white-plumed seeds. (Genus: *Epilobium*, 215 species. Family: Onagraceae.)

willow pattern A decorative scene used on pottery table-wares, showing a Chinese landscape, with figures, buildings, and a bridge, carried out in blue transfer-printing on white. It was first engraved by Thomas Minton c.1780, and widely copied by many factories.

Wills, Helen (Newington) *Moody, Helen (Newington) Wills*

Wilmington 39°45N 75°33W, pop (2000e) 72 700. Port in N Delaware, USA; founded by the Swedes as Fort Christina, 1638; taken by the British and renamed Willington, 1731; renamed Wilmington, 1739; city status, 1832; largest city in the state; airfield; railway; chemicals ('the chemical capital of the world'); home of several large corporations.

Wilmot Proviso (1846) A motion introduced in the US Congress by David Wilmot (Democrat, Pennsylvania) to forbid the expansion of slavery into territory acquired during the Mexican War. It passed the House of Representatives but not the Senate.

Wilson, Sir Angus (Frank Johnstone) (1913–91) Writer, born in Bexhill, East Sussex. His works include the novels *Anglo-Saxon Attitudes* (1956) and *The Old Men at the Zoo* (1961), the play *The Mulberry Bush* (1955), and two volumes of short stories.

Wilson, Brian *Beach Boys, The*

Wilson, Carl *Beach Boys, The*

Wilson, C(harles) T(homson) R(ees) (1869–1959) Pioneer of atomic and nuclear physics, born in Glencorse, Midlothian. His major achievement was to devise the cloud chamber method for observing the track of alpha particles and electrons. In 1927 he shared the Nobel Prize for Physics.

Wilson, Colin (Henry) (1931–) Novelist and writer on philosophy, sociology, and the occult, born in Leicester, Leicestershire. His books include *The Mind Parasites* (1966), *Poltergeist!* (1981), *Written in Blood* (1989), *From Atlantis to the Sphinx* (1996), and *Alien Dawn* (1999). His psychic interests brought him status as a cult figure in the 1980s.

Wilson, Colin St John (1922–) Architect, born in Cheltenham, Gloucestershire. He became professor of architecture at Cambridge (1975–89, now emeritus), and was made a fellow of Pembroke College in 1977. His many design projects include the extension to the British Museum (1973–9) and the new British Library (1962–97) in Euston Road, London.

Wilson, Dennis *Beach Boys, The*

Wilson, Edmund (1895–1972) Literary and social critic, born in Red Bank, NJ. He was a prolific and wide-ranging author, producing several studies on aesthetic, social, and political themes, as well as verse, plays, travel books, and historical works.

Wilson, Edward O(sborne) (1929–) Biologist, born in Birmingham, AL. His book *Sociobiology: the New Synthesis* (1975) virtually founded the subject of sociobiology. Other works include *On Human Nature* (1978, Pulitzer), and in 1990 he received Sweden's Crafoord Prize.

Wilson (of Rievaulx), (James) Harold Wilson, Baron (1916–95) British statesman and prime minister (1964–70, 1974–6), born in Huddersfield, West Yorkshire. He was President of the Board of Trade (1947–51), and in 1963 succeeded Gaitskell as Leader of the Labour Party. His economic plans were badly affected by a balance of payments crisis, leading to severe restrictive measures. He was also faced with the problem of Rhodesian independence, and opposition to Britain's proposed entry into the European Economic Community. Following his third general election victory, he resigned as Labour leader in 1976.

Wilson (of Libya and of Stowlangtoft), Henry Maitland Wilson, Baron (1881–1964) British field marshal, born in London. He led the initial British advance in Libya (1940–1) and the unsuccessful Greek campaign (1941), and became commander-in-chief Middle East (1943) and supreme allied commander in the Mediterranean theatre (1944).

Wilson, Jacqueline (1945–) Writer, born in Bath, SW England. She began work as a journalist, working on the popular teenage magazine *Jackie* which was named after her. She went on to become a full-time writer and her many books for children include *The Suitcase Kid* (1993), *The Lottie Project* (1998), *Girls in Tears* (2002), and *Candy Floss* (2006). *The Story of Tracy Beaker* (1992) and *Double Act* (1996) were successfully filmed for television. She was named the most borrowed author in the UK library lending chart for three successive years (2004–6), and in 2005 was made Children's Laureate.

Wilson, Richard (1714–82) Landscape painter, born in Penygroes, Powys. He began as a portrait painter, but after a visit to Italy (1752–6) turned to landscapes and became one of the leading painters of his time.

Wilson, Richard (1936–) Actor and director, born in Greenock, Scotland. His film work includes roles in *A Passage to India* (1984) and *The Man Who Knew Too Little* (1997), but it was his characterization of Victor Meldrew in several series of *One Foot in the Grave* (1990–2000, BAFTAs in 1991 and 1993) that made him a national figure. He was elected Rector of Glasgow University in 1996.

Wilson, Robert (1941–) Epic theatre-maker, director, and designer, born in Waco, TX. America's most flamboyant postmodern creator of theatrical spectacle, he mixes a combination of movement, music, and imagery, often in very long performances. *The CIVIL WarS* (begun in 1984) was one of the most ambitious theatrical events ever proposed. Later productions include *Wings on a Rock* and *Scourge of Hyacinth* (both 1999).

Wilson, (Thomas) Woodrow (1856–1924) US statesman and 28th president (1913–21), born in Staunton, VA. Elected Democratic president in 1912 and 1916, his administration saw the prohibition and women's suffrage amendments to the constitution, America's participation in World War 1, his peace plan proposals (the *Fourteen Points*), and his championship of the League of Nations. He received the Nobel Peace Prize in 1919.

Wiltshire pop (2001e) 433 000; area 3481 km²/1344 sq mi. County of S England; chalk downland of Salisbury Plain at the centre; county town, Trowbridge; Thamesdown a unitary authority from 1997; many ancient prehistoric remains, such as Stonehenge; Marlborough Downs, Savernake Forest, Longleat House.

Wimbledon Residential district in Merton borough, S Greater London, UK; headquarters of the All England Tennis Club; annual lawn tennis championships (Jun–Jul).

WIMP interface *graphic user interface*

Winchester, Lat **Venta Belgarum**, Anglo-Saxon **Wintanceaster** 51°04N 1°19W, pop (2001e) 107 200. City and county town in Hampshire, S England; on the R Itchen; Roman settlement the fifth largest in Britain; capital of Wessex in 519, and capital of England in 827; Domesday Book compiled here; railway; longest Gothic cathedral N of the Alps (11th–16th-c); Winchester College (1382), oldest public school in England; 12th-c St Cross Hospital; 13th-c castle hall, containing a mediaeval 'replica' of Arthur's Round Table.

Winckelmann, Johann (Joachim) [vingkelman] (1717–68) Archaeologist and art historian, born in Stendal, Germany. His works include the pioneering study, *Geschichte der Kunst des Alterthums* (1764, History of the Art of Antiquity).

wind The movement of air along the pressure gradient from areas of high to lower pressure; one of the basic elements of weather. Pressure gradients develop through the unequal cooling or heating of a layer of atmosphere. The steeper the gradient, the stronger the wind. In the N hemisphere the Coriolis force deflects wind to the right, and in the S hemisphere to the left. At low altitudes, the frictional force of the Earth's surface reduces the influence of the Coriolis force, diverting the wind towards the centre of the low pressure area.

wind chill An effect of wind decreasing the apparent temperature felt by a human body. Strong winds increase the heat loss from exposed flesh, and so at low temperatures may induce hypothermia at a higher air temperature than would occur in calm conditions. For example, an air temperature of −18°C with no wind would be equivalent to −38°C at 7 m/23 ft/s.

Windermere (lake) Largest lake in England, in the Lake District; extending 18 km/11 mi S from Ambleside; largest island, Belle Isle.

Windermere (town) 54°23N 2°54W, pop (2000e) 8380. Lakeside resort town in Cumbria, NW England; on L Windermere; railway; major tourist centre; Rydal Mount (10 km/6 mi NW), Wordsworth's home from 1813 to 1850; Brantwood, home of Ruskin.

Windhoek [vinthuk] 22°34S 17°06E, pop (2000e) 200 000. Capital of Namibia; altitude, 1650 m/5413 ft; occupied by South African forces, 1915; capital of German South-West Africa, 1922; airport; railway; cathedral.

wind instrument *aerophone*

windmill A mill worked by the action of wind on sails. Windmills have been used principally for grinding corn, cleansing (*fulling*) cloth, and for drainage. There are three types: **post mills**, where the mill itself revolves on a central post to face the wind, and **tower mills** (built of brick) and **smock mills** (built of timber), where only the cap revolves. Windmills were in common use until the end of the 19th-c, when they were largely superseded by the advent of steam power.

windows A form of graphic user interface in which the computer presents on a screen a set of sub-screens (windows), each sub-screen corresponding to a different program running in the computer. The sub-screens can be moved about, placed one on top of another, or temporarily shrunk in order to minimize the amount of information presented on the screen at any time, and to allow different programs to pass files between them. *Windows* is also the name of a registered trade mark of a multitasking operating environment for the IBM PC marketed by Microsoft.

windpipe *trachea*

Windscale *Sellafield*

Windsor (Canada) 42°18N 83°00W, pop (2000e) 214 200. Town in S Ontario, Canada, on Detroit R, opposite Detroit, MI; founded 1835; rapid industrial growth in 19th-c; railway; university (1857).

Windsor (UK) 51°30N 0°38W, pop (2000e) 33 800. Town linked with Eton in Windsor and Maidenhead unitary authority, S England; on R Thames; railway; Windsor Castle, Eton College (1440); Legoland theme park nearby; Royal Windsor Horse Show (May).

Windsor, Duke and Duchess of *Edward VIII*

Windsor, Lady Louise *Edward, Prince*

Windsor, House of The name of the British royal family since 1917. This unequivocally English name resulted from a Declaration by George V, a member of the House of Saxe-Coburg-Gotha. It was felt that a Germanic surname for the British monarchy was inappropriate, especially during a war against Germany.

Windsor Castle The largest of England's castles, situated on the R Thames at Windsor, S England. It was founded by William I and first used as a royal residence by Henry I. It was severely damaged by fire in 1992. Restoration work was completed in 1997.

wind tunnel *aerodynamics*

wind-up power Self-contained energy which stores human energy in a mechanical device and releases it in a controlled fashion over a period of time. Pioneered by British inventor Trevor Baylis to power his wind-up radio (1993) and Freeplay's torch (launched in 1998), it works on the principle that a spring inside the device is wound up by hand, releasing power as it unwinds (a wind-up time of 25 seconds allows a play-back time of 30 minutes). Clockwork generators are fitted with a special spring called a *tensator*, or *constant force spring*, which delivers its stored mechanical energy more evenly than the coiled springs used in ordinary clockwork.

Windward Islands (Caribbean) Island group of the Lesser Antilles in the Caribbean Sea; S of the Leeward Is, from Martinique (N) to Grenada (S), excluding Trinidad and Tobago; so called because of their exposure to the prevailing NE trade winds; formerly the name of a British colony comprising Dominica, St Lucia, St Vincent, and Grenada.

Windward Islands (French Polynesia), Fr **Iles du Vent** pop (2000e) 164 000. Island group of the Society Is, French Polynesia; comprises Tahiti, Moorea, and the smaller Mehetia, Tetiaroa, and Tubuai Manu Is; capital, Papeete.

wine The alcoholic beverage produced from the fermentation of grapes or other fruits. The alcohol content varies, but is usually 12%, the point at which fermentation stops. A wine's taste is determined by the type of grape used, the soil in which it is grown, and the local climate. It may be white, red, or rosé, dry or sweet, still or sparkling. White wine can be made from red (or black) grapes as well as white (or green): the final colour depends on whether the skins are left to ferment with the juice. Sweet wine is taken from the vat before fermentation has finished, while some sugar remains; dry wine is left to ferment until all the sugar has been converted to alcohol. Sparkling wine is produced by bottling it before the fermentation process is completed, so that fermentation continues in the bottle. Fermentation is stopped by the addition of alcohol (eg brandy) to produce fortified wines (eg sherry and port). Known since ancient times, viniculture was taken to Italy by the Greeks, and by the Romans to Gaul. France has long been regarded as the producer of the greatest wines, in Bordeaux (claret) and Burgundy. France and Italy are the leading producers, with Spain and Germany also traditional centres. The 20th-c saw the development of vineyards all over the world.

Winfrey, Oprah (Gail) [winfree] (1954–) Television talk-show host, actor, and producer, born in Kosciusko, MS. She launched the highly successful *Oprah Winfrey Show* (1986–), winner of 38 Emmy awards by 2004. She established Harpo Productions in Chicago, her films including *The Color Purple* (1985, Oscar nomination), and her work as producer includes a Broadway musical version of *The Color Purple* (2005). She is also known for her exercise and dieting programmes, and as an activist in support of children's rights. She received the inaugural Bob Hope Humanitarian Award in 2002.

Wingate, Orde (Charles) (1903–44) British general, born in Naini Tal, India. He served in the Sudan (1928–33) and Palestine (1936–9), where he helped create a Jewish defence force, and in the Burma theatre (1942) organized the Chindits.

winkle *periwinkle* (zoology)

Winkler, Hans-Günther [vingkler] (1926–) Show jumper, born in

Wuppertal-Barmen, Germany. He is the only man to have won five Olympic gold medals (for West Germany) at show jumping: the team golds in 1956, 1960, 1964, and 1972, and the individual title on *Halla* in 1956.

Winnipeg 49°53N 97°10W, pop (2000e) 691 000. Capital of Manitoba province, C Canada, on the Red R; established 1738 as Fort Rouge; fur-trading post, 1806; modern name, 1873; expansion after arrival of railway, 1881; airport; universities (1877, 1967); professional teams, Winnipeg Jets (ice hockey), Winnipeg Blue Bombers (football); Centennial Arts Centre, Civic Auditorium (home of Winnipeg Symphony Orchestra), Royal Winnipeg Ballet.

Winnipeg, Lake Lake in SC Manitoba province, S Canada; length 386 km/240 mi; breadth 88 km/55 mi; area 24 390 km^2/9414 sq mi.

Winslet, Kate (1975–) Actress, born in Reading, Berkshire. Her breakthrough into films came with *Heavenly Creatures* (1994), and later successes include *Sense and Sensibility* (1995), *Titanic* (1997), *Iris* (2001), *Finding Neverland* (2004), and *Little Children* (2006, Best Actress Oscar nomination). She married director Sam Mendes in 2003.

Winston, Robert (Maurice Lipson), Baron (1940–) Obstetrician, gynaecologist, and broadcaster, born in London. He became professor of fertility studies at the Imperial College School of Medicine in 1987. In the 1970s he developed gynaecological microsurgery and undertook the first human tubal transplant, and in 1981 founded the National Health Service's in vitro fertilization (IVF) programme. He is well known as a television presenter of series such as *Child of Our Time* (BBC, 2001–5) and *Walking With Cavemen* (2003). He was created a life peer in 1995.

Winston-Salem 36°06N 80°15W, pop (2000e) 185 800. City in NC North Carolina, USA; Winston founded in 1849, Salem in 1766; towns united, 1913; Wake Forest University (1834); railway; the nation's chief tobacco manufacturer.

wintergreen A member of a family of small evergreen perennials, native to N temperate and arctic regions; flowers drooping, bell-shaped, 5-petalled, pink or white. (Family: Pyrolaceae.)

Winterhalter, Franz Xaver [vinterhalter] (1806–73) Painter, born in Menzenschwand, Germany. In 1834 he went to Paris, where he became the fashionable artist of his day, painting many royal figures.

Winter Palace *Hermitage*

Winterthur [vintertoor] 47°30N 8°45E, pop (2000e) 90 000. Town in Switzerland; near the R Töss, NE of Zürich; railway junction.

Winter War *Russo-Finnish War*

Winthrop, John (1588–1649) Colonist, born in Edwardstone, Suffolk. He was appointed governor of Massachusetts colony in 1629, and was a major influence in forming the political institutions of the Northern states of America.

Winton, Tim(othy John) (1960–) Writer, born in Perth, Western Australia. He jointly won the Australian–Vogel award in 1981 with his first novel *An Open Swimmer*. He has won the Miles Franklin Award three times – for *Shallows* (1984), *Cloudstreet* (1991, also winner of the British Deo Gloria award), and *Dirt Music* (2001). Other novels include *The Riders* (1994) and *Small Mercies* (2006).

wire service *news agency*

wireworm *click beetle*

Wisconsin [wiskonsin] pop (2000e) 5 363 700; area 145 431 km^2/56 153 sq mi. State in N USA; the 'Badger State'; first settled by French traders, 1670; surrendered to the British, 1763; ceded to the USA, 1783 (part of the Northwest Territory); Territory of Wisconsin formed, 1836; 30th state to join the Union, 1848; c.26 000 km^2/10 000 sq mi of L Michigan lie within the state boundary; capital, Madison; highest point, Timms Hill (595 m/

1952 ft); glaciated terrain in the N and W, largely forested; over 8500 lakes; produces more milk, butter, and cheese than any other state; over a third of the nation's cheese production; heavy industry in the Milwaukee area.

Wisdom, Book of *Wisdom of Solomon*

wisdom literature In the Hebrew Bible/Old Testament, a group of writings, usually including Proverbs, Ecclesiastes, the Song of Songs, and Job. Among the Apocrypha, it also includes Ecclesiasticus and the Wisdom of Solomon. The literature is usually traced to a special class of sages in Israel who sought to draw lessons for life from general human experience rather than from revealed religious truths.

Wisdom of Solomon or **Book of Wisdom** A book of the Old Testament Apocrypha, purportedly from Solomon, but usually attributed to an unknown Alexandrian Jew c.1st-c BC.

Wise, Ernie *Morecambe, Eric*

Wiseman, Nicholas (Patrick Stephen), Cardinal (1802–65) Roman Catholic churchman, born in Seville, Spain. His appointment as the first Archbishop of Westminster and a cardinal (1850) called forth a storm of religious excitement, which led to the passing of the Ecclesiastical Titles Assumption Act.

Wise Men *Magi* 2

wisent [veezent] *bison*

Wishart, George [wishert] (c.1513–46) Reformer and martyr, born in Pitarrow, Aberdeenshire. He preached the Lutheran doctrine in several towns, and was arrested and burned at St Andrews. One of his converts was John Knox.

wisteria A deciduous climbing shrub from E Asia and North America; pea-flowers fragrant, lilac, violet, or white, in long pendulous clusters. It is often grown for ornament. (Genus: *Wisteria*, 6 species. Family: Leguminosae.)

witan or **witenagemot** (Old English 'meeting of wise men') The council of the Anglo-Saxon kings, once regarded as the first English 'parliament'.

witchcraft The alleged possession and exercise of magical or psychic powers, especially involving the manipulation of natural objects or events; often called *black magic* if harmful to people, *white magic* if helpful. In Europe the Christian Church began persecuting witches in the 14th-c, alleging that witches consciously made a pact with Satan. Contemporary witchcraft in the West sees itself as an alternative religion, celebrating gods drawn from various European pre-Christian religions, and exercising its magical powers in beneficial ways.

witch hazel A deciduous shrub or small tree, native to E Asia and eastern North America; flowers in short-stalked clusters, each with four long strap-shaped yellow petals. The bark yields an astringent lotion. (Genus: *Hamamelis*, 6 species. Family: Hamamelidaceae.)

witchweed A higher plant parasite (*Striga hermonthica*) causing severe damage to the roots of sorghum, millet, sugar cane, and other tropical grain crops, and also occasionally attacking pigeon pea and other legumes. It is most serious in Africa and the drier parts of India, but has also been reported from North America. (Family: Scrophulariaceae.)

withdrawal syndrome Symptoms which occur when an addictive substance is no longer available to someone who has become addicted to it; they include nausea, vomiting, stomach cramps, anxiety, panic attacks, palpitations, headaches, hallucinations, sweating, shaking, and possibly convulsions. The treatment of drug dependency involves replacing the body's biochemical requirement for the drug with a similar but less addictive substance. Diminishing doses of the substance are given until eventually all medication can be withdrawn.

Witherspoon, (Laura Jean) Reese (1976–) Film actress, born in Baton Rouge, LA. She made her film debut with *The Man in the Moon* (1991), and later films include *A Far Off Place* (1993), *Freeway* (1996), and *Cruel Intentions* (1999), but it was with *Legally*

Blonde (2001) that she established her reputation. In 2005, her performance as singer June Carter in the biopic of Johnny Cash, *Walk the Line*, won her a Best Actress Oscar and BAFTA.

Witt, Katerina [vit] (1965–) Figure skater, born in Karl-Marx-Stadt, Germany. She was world champion in 1984–5 and 1987–8, and Olympic champion in 1984 and 1988.

Wittenberg [vitnberg] 51°53N 12°39E, pop (2000e) 55 700. Town in EC Germany; on R Elbe; associated with the beginning of the Reformation, 1517; part of Prussia, 1814; railway; university (1817); Schlosskirche, to the doors of which Luther nailed his 95 theses.

Wittgenstein, Ludwig (Josef Johann) [witgenstiyn], Ger [vitgenshtiyn] (1889–1951) Philosopher, born in Vienna. He produced major works on the philosophy of language, notably *Tractatus logico-philosophicus* (1921) and the posthumously-published *Philosophische Untersuchungen* (1953, Philosophical Investigations), in which he studies the 'language games' whereby language is given its meaning in actual *use*.

Witwatersrand [witwawterzrand], Afrikaans [vuhtvahtersrant] or **The Rand** ('white water's reef') Region centred on a ridge of gold-bearing rock in South Africa; length 100 km/60 mi; width 40 km/25 mi; Johannesburg located near its centre; the power house of the South African economy; gold discovered in 1886 (produces over half the world's supply).

woad A biennial or perennial (*Isatis tinctoria*) with numerous yellow, cross-shaped flowers and pendulous, purplish capsules. The blue dye used by Ancient Britons (and still produced until the 19th-c) is made by exposing part-dried, crushed leaves to the air. (Family: Cruciferae.)

Wodehouse, Sir P(elham) G(renville) [wudhows] (1881–1975) Novelist, born in Guildford, Surrey. He established his reputation with the creation of Bertie Wooster and his 'gentleman's gentleman' Jeeves. A prolific writer, he produced a succession of novels, short stories, sketches, and librettos.

Woden *Odin*

Wogan, Terry [wohgn], popular name of **Michael Terence Wogan** (1938–) Broadcaster and writer, born in Limerick, Ireland. He began as a radio announcer in Ireland, and joined the BBC in 1965. His television shows include *Blankety Blank* (1977–81), the annual Eurovision Song Contests, and an early evening chat-show (1982–92). The recipient of many broadcasting 'personality of the year' awards, he returned to radio work in 1993 presenting *Wake Up to Wogan*. An autobiography, *Mustn't Grumble*, appeared in 2006. He was awarded an honorary knighthood in 2005.

Wöhler, Friedrich [voeler] (1800–82) Chemist, born near Frankfurt, Germany. He isolated aluminium (1827) and beryllium (1828). His synthesis of urea from ammonium cyanate in 1828 was a turning point for organic chemistry.

Wojtyła, Karol Jozef *John Paul II*

Wolf, Hugo (Philipp Jakob) [volf] (1860–1903) Composer, born in Windischgraz, Slovenia (formerly Austria). From 1888 he composed c.300 songs, settings of poems by Goethe and others, and wrote an opera, *Der Corregidor* (1895), and other works.

wolf A member of the dog family; two species: the **grey** (or **timber**) **wolf** (*Canis lupus*), the largest wild dog and ancestor of the domestic dog, native to forests throughout the temperate N hemisphere (distribution now patchy); and the rare **red wolf** (*Canis rufus*) of E USA.

Wolfe, Charles (1791–1823) Poet, born in Dublin. He is remembered for his poem 'The Burial of Sir John Moore' (1817), which caught the admiration of the people.

Wolfe, James (1727–59) British soldier, born in Westerham, Kent. In 1758 he was prominent in the capture of Louisburg, and commanded in the famous capture of Quebec (1759), where he was killed.

Wolfe, Thomas (Clayton) (1900–38) Novelist, born in Asheville,

NC. He wrote several plays, but found success with novels, notably *Look Homeward, Angel* (1929) and *Of Time and the River* (1935). Some of his best work is to be found in the stories in *From Death to Morning* (1935).

Wolfe, Tom, popular name of **Thomas Kennerly Wolfe** (1931–) Journalist, pop-critic, and novelist, born in Richmond, VA. A proponent of New Journalism, his books include *The Electric Kool-Aid Acid Test* (1968). Among his novels are the best seller *The Bonfire of the Vanities* (1988) and *I Am Charlotte Simmons* (2004). The non-fiction *Hooking Up* appeared in 2000.

Wolfenden, John (Frederick) Wolfenden, Baron [wulfenden] (1906–85) Educationist, born in Halifax, West Yorkshire. He was best known for his government investigation of homosexuality and prostitution (the **Wolfenden Report**, 1957).

Wolfensohn, Jim, popular name of **James D Wolfensohn** (1933–) President of the World Bank, (1995–2005), born in Sydney, Australia. He worked in Australia, London, and New York, eventually establishing an investment bank in his own name. Under his tutelage, the World Bank sought to find ways of reducing the burden of debt on the world's poorest countries. He was awarded an honorary knighthood in 1995.

Wolf-Ferrari, Ermanno [volf ferahree] (1876–1948) Composer, born in Venice, Italy. His best-known works are *I quattro rusteghi* (1906, trans The School for Fathers) and *Il segreto di Susanna* (1909, Susanna's Secret). He also composed choral and chamber works, and music for organ and piano.

wolffia A tiny floating freshwater herb (*Wolffia arhiza*) consisting only of a minute green body 0·5–1 mm/0·02–0·04 in across, with a budding pouch from which new plants are produced. It is the smallest flowering plant in the world. (Family: Lemnaceae.)

Wölfflin, Heinrich [voelflin] (1864–1945) Art historian, born in Winterthur, Switzerland. He was one of the founders of modern art history, as seen in such works as *Principles of Art History* (1915).

wolfhound *borzoi; Irish wolfhound*

Wolfit, Sir Donald [wulfit] (1902–68) Actor-manager, born in Newark, Nottinghamshire. He formed his own company in 1937, and became known for his Shakespeare performances. He also appeared in several films.

Wolfowitz, Paul (Dundes) [wulfovits] (1943–) President of the World Bank (2005–7), born in Brooklyn, NY. In 1981 he was appointed head of the US state department policy planning staff, and further posts include US ambassador to Indonesia (1986–9), under-secretary for defence policy (1989–93), and deputy defence secretary (from 2001). In 2005 he took up the role of head of the World Bank, resigning in 2007.

wolfram [wulfram] *tungsten*

wolframite [wulframiyt] An iron manganese tungstate mineral ((Fe,Mn)WO$_4$), found in pegmatites and hydrothermal veins as tabular crystals or brown masses. It is the principal ore of tungsten.

Wolfram von Eschenbach [volfram fon eshenbakh] (c.1170–c.1220) Poet, born near Ansbach, Germany. He is best known for his epic *Parzival* (c.1200–10), which introduced the theme of the Holy Grail into German literature.

Wolfsburg [volfsboork] 52°27N 10°49E, pop (2000e) 131 000. City in Germany; founded, 1938; railway; known as the 'Volkswagen town' (site of car factory).

Wolfson, Sir Isaac (1897–1991) Businessman, born in Glasgow, W Scotland. In 1955 he set up the **Wolfson Foundation** for the advancement of health, education, and youth activities in the UK and the Commonwealth.

Wollongong [wolongong] 34°25S 150°52E, pop (2000e) 192 300. Urban centre in SE New South Wales, Australia; railway; university (1975).

Wollstonecraft, Mary [wulstonkraft], married name **Godwin** (1759–97) Feminist and educationist, born in London. In 1792 she wrote *Vindication of the Rights of Woman*, advocating equality of the sexes. She married William Godwin in 1797.

Wolof [wolof] A West Atlantic-speaking agricultural people of Senegal and Gambia. They are traditionally grouped into a state with elaborate hierarchical distinctions.

Wolpe, Joseph [volpay] (1915–97) Psychiatrist, born in Johannesburg, South Africa. He was co-author of *Behavioural Therapy Techniques* (1966), with which he founded the field of behavioural therapy, widely used in the treatment of neurotic disorders.

Wolseley, Garnet (Joseph) Wolseley, 1st Viscount [wulzlee] (1833–1913) British field marshal, born in Golden Bridge, Co Dublin, Ireland. He served in campaigns in many parts of the world, including the Crimea, India, China, and Canada, and led the attempted rescue of General Gordon at Khartoum. As army commander-in-chief (1895–1901), he carried out several reforms, and mobilized forces for the Boer War (1899–1902).

Wolsey, Thomas, Cardinal [wulzee] (c.1475–1530) English cardinal and statesman, born in Ipswich, Suffolk. Under Henry VIII, he became Archbishop of York (1514) and a cardinal (1515). Made Lord Chancellor (1515–29), he was Henry VIII's leading adviser. When he failed to persuade the pope to grant Henry's divorce, he was arrested, and died while travelling to London.

Wolverhampton [wulverhamptn] 52°36N 2°08W, pop (2001e) 236 600. Industrial town in West Midlands, C England; collegiate church founded here in 994; city status, 2000; railway; university, 1992; football league team, Wolverhampton Wanderers (Wolves).

wolverine A mammal of family Mustelidae, native to the N forests and tundra of Scandinavia, Asia, and North America; stocky (length, 1 m/3$^1\!/_4$ ft), pointed muzzle, bushy tail; dark brown, often pale on face and sides; also known as **glutton**. (*Gulo gulo*.)

womb *uterus*

wombat A nocturnal Australian marsupial; length, up to 1·3 m/ 4 ft; bear-like, with a stout body, very small tail; round head, blunt muzzle with a large nose pad; digs burrows. (Family: Vombatidae, 3 species.)

Women's Institutes, National Federation of (WI) A women's voluntary organization, started in Canada in 1897 by Adelaide Hoodless to provide classes in domestic science and home-making. The WI spread to Britain in 1915, and to other Commonwealth countries later.

women's liberation movement A broad cultural and political movement initiated by women to improve their social position by freeing themselves from the constraints and disadvantages of a society said to be dominated by men. 'Women's lib' has very strong roots in the USA and Europe, and has been politicized, especially by radical feminists who claim the continued existence of male dominance in capitalist societies.

Women's Royal Voluntary Service (WRVS) In the UK, an organization founded in 1938 (designated Royal in 1966), made up of unpaid helpers who do community work. They pioneered the first home help scheme (1944), and run the 'meals on wheels' service for the housebound elderly, as well as providing voluntary workers for day centres, hospitals, playgroups, prison visiting, and rural transport.

women's services Military organizations in which women enlist for non-combatant duty. In Britain, there are separate corps for army, navy, and air force. The **Women's Royal Army Corps** (**WRAC**) was founded in 1949, directly succeeding the Auxiliary Territorial Service (ATS) within which large numbers of women had served during World War 2. British women had served during World War 1 in the **Women's Auxiliary Army Corps** (**WAAC**) formed in 1917. The **Women's Royal Naval Service** (**WRNS**), popularly known as 'the Wrens', was first formed in 1917. The **Women's Royal Air Force** (**WRAF**) was formed in 1918, and later became known as the **Women's Auxiliary Air Force (WAAF)**. In the USA, the **Women's Army Corps (WAC)** was established in 1948, and dissolved in 1978.

women's studies The study of the history and contemporary role of girls and women. More available in further and higher education than in schools, it is favoured by feminist groups, who feel that girls and women are disadvantaged and that the nature of this disadvantage is often not mentioned in education.

Wonder, Stevie, originally **Steveland Judkins** or **Steveland Morris** (1950–) Soul singer, songwriter, and instrumentalist, born in Saginaw, MI. He was blind from birth, played the harmonica, drums, keyboards, and guitar from an early age, and was signed to Motown Records in 1961. His first album *Little Stevie Wonder: the 12-Year-Old Genius* (1963) was an immediate success. Later albums include *Songs In The Key Of Life* (1976), *Hotter Than July* (1980), *Natural Wonder* (1995), and *A Time to Love* (2005).

Wood, Elijah (Jordan) (1981–) Actor, born in Cedar Rapids, IA. He moved with his family to Los Angeles in 1988 where he gained a number of small film parts before playing a starring role in *Paradise* (1991). He became well known following his role as Frodo Baggins in *The Lord of the Rings* trilogy (2001–3). Later films include *Green Street* (2005) and *Bobby* (2006).

Wood, Sir Henry (Joseph) (1869–1944) Conductor, born in London. In 1895 he helped to found the Promenade Concerts which he conducted annually until his death. He composed operettas and an oratorio, but his international reputation was gained as a conductor.

Wood, Victoria (1953–) Comedy performer and writer, born in Prestwich, Lancashire. She studied drama at Birmingham University, and began singing her own comic songs on local radio and television while still a student. Her television work includes *Wood and Walters* (1981–2), *Victoria Wood As Seen on TV* (1984–7), *An Audience With Victoria Wood* (1988, BAFTA), and *Dinner Ladies* (1998–2000). She went on to write and star in the stage musical *Acorn Antiques* (2005), and the wartime drama *Housewife, 49* for ITV (2006).

wood The bulk of the tissue making up the trunk and branches of trees and shrubs. For commercial purposes, it is divided into two types: **softwoods**, derived from gymnosperms, and **hardwoods**, which have a less regular grain and are derived from flowering plants. The terms are misleading, as some softwoods are very hard and durable.

wood alcohol *methanol*

wood avens *avens*

woodbine *honeysuckle*

wood block A percussion instrument (also known as a **Chinese block**) in the form of a hollowed rectangular or spherical block of wood, with one or more slits in the surface, which is struck with a wooden stick.

woodchat A shrike native to Europe, Africa, and W Asia (*Lanius senator*); top of head and neck chestnut-brown; breast white; also known as **woodchat shrike**.

woodchuck A marmot native to North America (*Marmota monax*); large (length, 80 cm/30 in), aggressive; may dig a den in woodland for the winter months; also known as **groundhog**.

woodcock A short-legged sandpiper, native to the Old World and E North America; mottled brown; bill long, straight. (Genus: *Scolopax*, 6 species.)

woodcreeper A bird native to the New World tropics; tail stiffened as in woodpeckers; many shapes of bill; also known as a **woodhewer**. (Family: Dendrocolaptidae, 47 species; sometimes placed in family Furnariidae.)

woodcut One of the simplest and oldest methods of relief-printing. The design is gouged into the smooth surface of a block of wood, and sticky ink rolled over the top. The cut-away areas print as white patches, the rest as solid black.

Woodhead, Chris(topher Anthony) (1946–) British teacher and educational administrator. He was an English teacher and local government education officer before becoming chief executive for the National Curriculum Council (1991–3) and School Curriculum and Assessment Authority (1993–4). He was appointed chief inspector for schools at the Office for Standards in Education (OFSTED) (1994–2001).

Woodhenge Prehistoric site in Wiltshire, S England; 3 km/1¾ mi NE of Stonehenge; discovered by aerial reconnaissance in 1926. It apparently consisted of a number of concentric ovals of wooden pillars oriented for the same ritualistic forms as were in use at Stonehenge.

woodhewer *woodcreeper*

Woodland culture A generic term for the Indian culture of the E USA as far W as the Great Plains, c.700 BC–AD 1500. It is characterized archaeologically by burial mounds, cord-impressed pottery, and tobacco smoking.

woodlouse A terrestrial crustacean found under stones, in litter and soil; abdominal limbs modified for aerial breathing and for reproduction; thoracic legs adapted for walking. (Order: Isopoda, c.3500 species.)

woodpecker A bird of the family Picidae (198 species); clings to tree trunks; tail stiff and presses against tree for support except in small **piculets** (Subfamily: Picumninae, 27 species) and **wrynecks**.

wood pigeon A pigeon native to Europe, N Africa, and W Asia (*Columba palumbus*); plumage dark grey with white patch on neck; also known as **ringdove**.

woodrush A tufted perennial, found almost everywhere; leaves grass-like, fringed with long, colourless hairs. (Genus: *Luzula*, 80 species. Family: Juncaceae.)

Woods, Tiger, popular name of **Eldrick Woods** (1976–) Golfer, born in Cypress, CA. He turned professional in 1996, and shot to fame after winning the US Masters at Augusta in 1997 at the age of 21. Later successes include the US PGA title (1999, 2000, 2006), the US Open (2000, 2002), the Open Championhip (2000, 2005, 2006), and the US Masters (2001, 2002, 2005). In 2005 he was voted the US PGA Tour Player of Year for the seventh time in nine years.

Woodstock Small town in Ulster Co, SE New York; tourist centre; in the foothill of the Catskill Mts; noted for its artists' colony; became world famous for the 3-day rock festival held nearby as part of the Woodstock Music and Art Fair in 1969, the largest rock festival of the 1960s, recorded in the film *Woodstock* (1970).

woodwind instrument A musical instrument made principally from wood (or, in the case of the saxophone and some flutes, from metal), in which a column of air is activated by the player blowing across a mouth-hole (as in the flute or piccolo), through a duct (as in the recorder), or against a single or double reed (as in the bassoon, cor anglais, oboe, and clarinet).

woodworm *furniture beetle*

woody nightshade A scrambling woody perennial (*Solanum dulcamara*), native to Europe, Asia, and N Africa; flowers with five purple petals, and a cone of yellow stamens; berries oval, green turning yellow and finally red when ripe, mildly poisonous; also called **bittersweet**. (Family: Solanaceae.)

Wookey Hole Limestone caves near the village of Wookey in Somerset, SW England; on the SW slopes of the Mendip Hills.

wool The fibre obtained from the fleeces of sheep. There are many qualities of wool, from fine soft wools obtained from the merino sheep of Australia, South Africa, and Argentina to coarse fibres which come from sheep in the cooler climates of New Zealand, Europe, and North America. Medium quality wools are used in clothing, including knitwear of the Shetland type; coarse wools are used mainly for carpets and other furnishings.

Woolf, (Adeline) Virginia, *née* **Stephen** (1882–1941) Novelist, born in London. A leading member of the Bloomsbury Group, she made a major contribution to the development of the novel, in such works as *Mrs Dalloway* (1925), *To the Lighthouse* (1927), and *The Waves* (1931), noted for their impressionistic style. Publication of her *Diary* (5 vols, 1977–84) and *Letters* (6 vols, 1975–80) has further enhanced her reputation.

Woolley, Sir (Charles) Leonard (1880–1960) Archaeologist, born in London. He directed the important excavations (1922–34) at Ur in Mesopotamia, and wrote several popular accounts of his work, notably *Digging up the Past* (1930).

woolly monkey A New World monkey; large round head, long grasping tail; short dense woolly coat; plain dark colour; also known as **barrigudo**. (Genus: *Lagothrix*, 2 species.)

woolly rhinoceros An extinct rhinoceros (*Coelodonta antiquitatis*), once native to Europe and N Asia; length, 3·5 m/11 ft; thick coat of long hair; snout with two horns.

woolsack A large red cushion filled with wool that the Lord Chancellor sits on in the UK House of Lords. It is said to represent the authority of the Lord Chancellor who presides over the proceedings of the House.

Woolworth, Frank W(infield) (1852–1919) Merchant, born in Rodman, NY. In 1879 he opened a store in Utica, NY, for 5-cent goods only; this failed, but a second store, in Lancaster, PA, selling also 10-cent goods, was successful. He then built a chain of similar stores, setting up the F W Woolworth Company in 1905.

Woosnam, Ian (1958–) Golfer, born in Oswestry, Shropshire. He turned professional in 1976, won the Swiss Open in 1982, and in 1991 was ranked world number 1, a position he held for almost a year. Further titles include the US Masters (1991), the Volvo PGA Championship (1997), and the Cisco World Match Play Championship at Wentworth (2001). A member of successive European Ryder Cup teams between 1983 and 1997, he was chosen team vice-captain in 2002, and in 2006 captained Europe to a decisive win over the USA.

Wootton (of Abinger), Barbara Frances Wootton, Baroness (1897–1988) Social scientist, born in Cambridge, Cambridgeshire. She is best known for her work, *Testament for Social Science* (1950), in which she attempted to assimilate the social to the natural sciences.

Worcester (UK) [wuster], Anglo-Saxon **Wigorna Ceaster** 52°11N 2°13W, pop (2000e) 91 600. City and administrative centre of Worcestershire (from 1998), WC England; on the R Severn; founded AD c.680; site of Cromwell's victory in Civil War; railway, university; cathedral (14th-c); Worcester porcelain, from 1751; Three Choirs Festival in rotation with Hereford and Gloucester (Sep).

Worcestershire [wustersheer] pop (2004e) 552 000; area 1813 km²/700 sq mi. County in WC England, UK (formerly Hereford and Worcester, 1974–98); drained by Severn and Avon Rivers; county town Worcester.

word class A group of words which share several grammatical properties, such as the same kind of inflection or position in sentence structure; also known as **part of speech**. The grouping of words into classes was first carried out by the Greeks, and the main classes (noun, verb, etc) have since been universally used in language description.

Worde, Wynkyn de [werd] (?–?1535) London printer, born in Holland or in Alsace. He was a pupil of Caxton, and in 1491 succeeded to his stock-in-trade. He made great improvements in printing and typecutting.

word processor A computer program, normally running on a personal computer, which allows the computer to be used as a sophisticated typewriter. Documents can be held as whole documents; they can be fully edited before they are printed; and they can be repeatedly updated. The term is now little used.

Wordsworth, Dorothy (1771–1855) Writer born in Cockermouth, Cumbria, the sister of William Wordsworth. Her *Journals* show a keen sensibility and acute observation of nature.

Wordsworth, William (1770–1850) Poet, born in Cockermouth, Cumbria. Following travels in Europe, he set up house at Racedown, Dorset, with his sister, Dorothy, where he began to write poetry exploring the lives of humble folk living in close contact with nature. *Lyrical Ballads* (1798), written with Coleridge, was the first manifesto of the new Romantic poetry. He later moved to Dove Cottage, Grasmere with Dorothy, married Mary Hutchinson in 1802, and wrote much of his best work, including his poetic autobiography, *The Prelude* (1805, published posthumously in 1850). He succeeded Southey as poet laureate in 1843.

work The product of force and distance; symbol W, units J (joule). Applying a force F to an object over a distance d means work $W = Fd$ is done, equal to the object's increase in kinetic energy. The rate of doing work is *power*.

workfunction The minimum energy which must be supplied to extract an electron from a solid; symbol Φ, units J (joule), or more often eV (electronvolt). It is a measure of how tightly electrons are bound to a material.

work-hardening An alteration in the properties of a metal by repeated hammering, rolling, or other forming processes. The process may be deleterious, in producing brittleness, or advantageous, in increasing strength.

workhouse A building used for the accommodation, and often employment, of the unemployed poor in Britain. Workhouses gained special notoriety after the Poor Law Amendment Act (1834), when the policy was to increase their number and place as many able-bodied paupers as possible in them. This policy was much criticized by reformers, who unearthed many 'workhouse scandals'. Workhouses survived until the later 1920s.

Working Men's Clubs and Institutes Union In the UK, clubs that provide education and recreation for working men; originally founded as an alternative to the public house. The Union was created in 1862, the inspiration of the Rev Henry Solly; initially the clubs did not serve alcohol, but now provide it at a lower price than in public houses, which helps to contribute to their popularity.

Works Projects Administration (WPA) (1935–43) A US federal agency established under President Roosevelt to combat unemployment during the Great Depression. Originally called the **Works Progress Administration**, it built transportation facilities, parks, and buildings.

work study *time and motion study*

work-to-rule *industrial action*

world (maps) *pp.1018–21*

World Bank *IBRD*

World Commission on Environment and Development, also known as the **Brundtland Commission** An independent body established by the UN in 1983 to formulate 'a global agenda for change'. Its purpose was to propose strategies for sustainable development by the year 2000, to promote co-operation between nations at different stages of economic development, and to consider ways by which the international community can deal with environmental concerns. It published the Brundtland Report, *Our Common Future*, in 1987, and convened the Earth Summits in 1992 and 1997.

World Council of Churches An interdenominational council of Churches, formed in Amsterdam in 1948. Originating in the ecumenical movement of the early 20th-c, its main task is to seek the unity of the Church. It comprises most of the mainline Christian denominations with the exception of the Roman Catholic Church, with which it keeps close contact. Its headquarters is in Geneva.

World (physical)

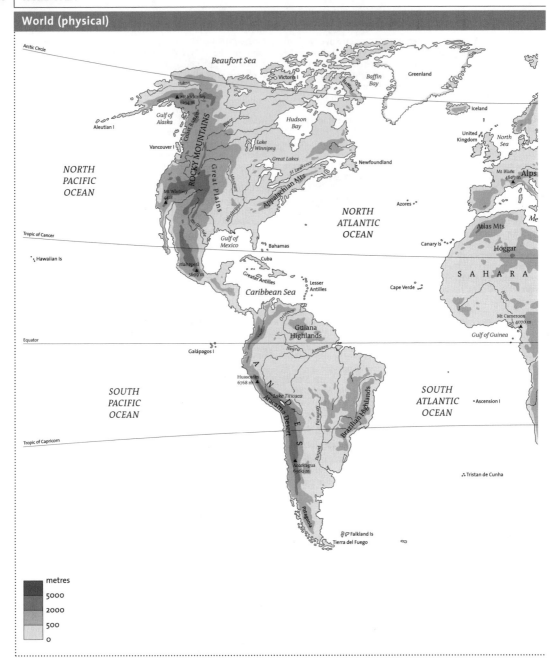

World Court *International Court of Justice*

World Cup (Association Football) The world's largest single-sport event, organized by the Fédération Internationale de Football Association. The first World Cup was held in Uruguay in 1930, when 16 teams entered. In 1998 and 2002, 32 nations competed. The trophy is named after Jules Rimet (1873–1956), the Associations's former president (1921–56).

World Cup (cricket) A world championship which has been played on roughly a four-yearly cycle since 1975, using a limited-over one-day format: initially 60 overs, 50 overs since 1987. It expanded from 8 competitors to 12 in 1996. The winners have been the West Indies (1975, 1979), India (1983), Australia (1987, 1999, 2003, 2007), Pakistan (1992), and Sri Lanka (1996).

World Cup (Rugby League) A world championship played at irregular intervals under a variety of formats from 1954, limited

ARCTIC OCEAN

Svalbard

Severnaya
Zemlya

New Siberian Is

Novaya
Zemlya

Bering Sea

URAL MTS

Ob

Yenisei

Lena

Central
Siberian
Plateau

West
Siberian
Plateau

Sea of
Okhotsk

Kamchatka
Peninsula

NORTH
PACIFIC
OCEAN

Volga

Caspian
Sea

Aral Sea

Lake Balkhash

Syr Darya

Lake Baikal

Amur

Sakhalin

Kuril Is

Black Sea

Caucasus Mts

Amu Darya

Gobi

Sea of
Japan

Honshu

diterannean Sea

Euphrates

Tigris

Tien Shan

Kunlan Shan

Huang

Chang

East China
Sea

Libyan
Desert

Nile

Persian Gulf

HIMALAYAS

Indus

Mt Everest 8848 m

Ganges

Taiwan

Tibesti

Red Sea

Arabian
Peninsula

Hainan

Arabian
Sea

Andaman Is

South
China
Sea

Philippine Is

Ethiopian
Highlands

Lake Turkana

Maldives

Nicobar Is

Sri Lanka

Congo

Lake
Victoria

Killmanjaro 5895 m

Lake Tanganyika

Seychelles

Sumatra

Borneo

Celebes

New
Guinea

Bismarck
Archipelago

Solomon Is

Lake
Malawi

Comoros

Java

Timor

INDIAN
OCEAN

Coral Sea

Vanuatu

Fiji Is

Zambezi

Madagascar

Mauritius

Réunion

Great Sandy
Desert

New
Caledonia

Kalahari
Desert

Mozambique Channel

Limpopo

MacDonnell
Ranges

Lake Eyre

Darling

Great Dividing Range

Mt Kosciusko
2230 m

SOUTHERN OCEAN

Tasmania

Tasman
Sea

New Zealand

Mt Cook 3764 m

0   5000 km

0   3000 miles

in scope and impact by having no more than five teams before 1995. Great Britain beat France in the first final, but Australia have been either champions or runners-up in every competition since. The 2000 competition had 16 teams. The next competition is in 2008.

World Cup (Rugby Union) A world championship which has been played on a four-yearly cycle since 1987. The tournament had expanded to 20 teams by 1999, with 69 entrants. It was won by

New Zealand in 1987, Australia in 1991 and 1999, South Africa in 1995, and England in 2003. The Women's World Cup has been played since 1991, won by the USA (1991), England (1994), and New Zealand (1998, 2002).

World Federation of Trade Unions (WFTU) A leftist-oriented organization of world trade union federations, set up in 1945 by the World Trade Union Congress. The democratic unions of W Europe and North America broke away in 1949, and subse-

World (political)

Arctic Circle

Greenland
(Denmark)

Alaska
(USA)

ICELAND

NORWAY

SWE

CANADA

UNITED
KINGDOM

IRELAND

NETH.
GER.
BEL.
LUX.
CZ.
AU.
SW.

FRANCE

ITALY

UNITED STATES
OF AMERICA

PORTUGAL

SPAIN

MALTA
TUNISIA

Tropic of Cancer

MEXICO

Bermuda
(UK)

Canary Is
(Spain)

MOROCCO

WESTERN
SAHARA

ALGERIA

Hawaiian Is.
(USA)

BAHAMAS

CUBA

Puerto Rico
(USA)

DOM.

MAURITANIA

MALI

NIGER

BELIZE
HONDURAS

JAMAICA

HAITI

ANTIGUA AND BARBUDA

ST. KITTS-
NEVIS

DOMINICA
ST. LUCIA

CAPE
VERDE

SENEGAL

GAMBIA

BURKINA
FASO

GUATEMALA

EL SALVADOR

NICARAGUA

ST. VINCENT

BARBADOS
GRENADA

TRINIDAD AND TOBAGO

GUINEA BISSAU

GUINEA

BE.

NIGERIA

SIERRA LEONE

C. TE
D'IVOIRE

G.

COSTA RICA

PANAMA

VENEZUELA

GUYANA

LIBERIA

CAMEROON

SURINAME

French Guiana

COLOMBIA

S O TOME &
PRINCIPE

EQ.

GABON

Equator

Galapagos Is
(Ecuador)

ECUADOR

CONGO

Cabinda (ANGOLA)

PERU

BRAZIL

BOLIVIA

PARAGUAY

NAMIBIA

Tropic of Capricorn

URUGUAY

CHILE

ARGENTINA

Falkland Is
(UK)

A.	ANDORRA	G.	GHANA
AL.	ALBANIA	GER.	GERMANY
AR.	ARMENIA	HUN.	HUNGARY
AU.	AUSTRIA	L.	LEBANON
AZ.	AZERBAIJAN	LITH.	LITHUANIA
BANG.	BANGLADESH	LUX.	LUXEMBOURG
B.	BOSNIA-HERZEGOVINA	M.	FORMER YUGOSLAV REPUBLIC OF MACEDONIA
BE.	BENIN	Mo	MONTENEGRO
BEL.	BELGIUM	NETH.	NETHERLANDS
BU.	BURUNDI	R.	RUSSIA
C.A.R.	CENTRAL AFRICAN REPUBLIC	RW.	RWANDA
CR.	CROATIA	S.	SLOVENIA
CYP.	CYPRUS	Se	SERBIA
CZ.	CZECH REPUBLIC	SL.	SLOVAKIA
DEN.	DENMARK	SW.	SWITZERLAND
DOM.	DOMINICAN REPUBLIC	T.	TOGO
EQ.	EQUATORIAL GUINEA	U.A.E.	UNITED ARAB EMIRATES

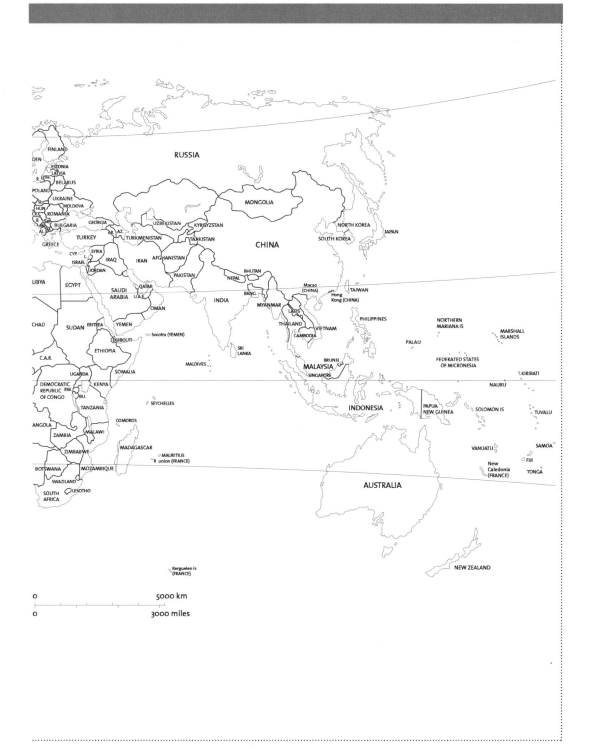

FINLAND
DEN
ESTONIA
R. LATVIA
LITH. BELARUS
POLAND
SL. UKRAINE
HUN.
CZ. ROMANIA
B. MOLDOVA
SE. BULGARIA
AL.
GREECE
TURKEY
CYP. SYRIA
L.
ISRAEL
JORDAN
LIBYA
EGYPT
SAUDI
ARABIA
OMAN
CHAD
SUDAN ERITREA
YEMEN
DJIBOUTI
ETHIOPIA
C.A.R.
UGANDA
SOMALIA
DEMOCRATIC KENYA
REPUBLIC RW.
OF CONGO BU.
TANZANIA
ANGOLA
COMOROS
ZAMBIA
MALAWI
ZIMBABWE
MADAGASCAR
BOTSWANA
MOZAMBIQUE
SWAZILAND
SOUTH LESOTHO
AFRICA

RUSSIA

GEORGIA
AR. AZ.
TURKMENISTAN
UZBEKISTAN KYRGYZSTAN
TAJIKISTAN
AFGHANISTAN
IRAN
PAKISTAN
QATAR
U.A.E.

MONGOLIA

NORTH KOREA
SOUTH KOREA
JAPAN

CHINA

IRAQ

BHUTAN
NEPAL
INDIA
BANG.
MYANMAR

Macao
(CHINA)
Hong
Kong (CHINA)
TAIWAN

SRI
LANKA
MALDIVES

LAOS
THAILAND
VIETNAM
CAMBODIA

PHILIPPINES

NORTHERN
MARIANA IS

MARSHALL
ISLANDS

PALAU

FEDERATED STATES
OF MICRONESIA

BRUNEI
MALAYSIA
SINGAPORE

Socotra (YEMEN)

SEYCHELLES

INDONESIA

KIRIBATI

NAURU

PAPUA
NEW GUINEA
SOLOMON IS

TUVALU

VANUATU

SAMOA

New
Caledonia
(FRANCE)

FIJI

TONGA

MAURITIUS
R union (FRANCE)

AUSTRALIA

Kerguelen Is
(FRANCE)

NEW ZEALAND

0   5000 km

0   3000 miles

quently formed the International Confederation of Free Trade Unions. The largest WFTU affiliates are now in the developing nations of Asia, Latin America, and Africa.

World Health Organization (WHO) A specialized agency formed in 1948 within the United Nations to advance international co-operation for the improvement in health of peoples in all countries. It is primarily concerned with the control of epidemic diseases, vaccination and other programmes, worldwide sanitation, and water supplies. There were 193 member countries in 2007.

world heritage site A site (natural or cultural) recognized by the international community (in the shape of the World Heritage Convention founded by the General Conference of UNESCO in 1972) as possessing universal value, and thus coming under a collective responsibility. A country nominates a site to the Convention, and a decision on whether to include it in the world heritage list is made by an international 21-member committee. In 2007 there were 830 sites in 138 states.

World Series America's annual baseball championship, first played in 1903. Despite its title, only America's Major League baseball teams compete, with the winner of the American League meeting the winner of the National League over the best of seven games.

World Trade Center A complex of buildings occupying 6·5 ha/16 acres in lower Manhattan, New York City, USA. Its two 110-storey skyscrapers were the world's tallest buildings from their completion in 1973 until topped by the Sears Tower a year later. The New York landmark collapsed after two aircraft were flown deliberately at the 414 m/1360 ft towers in a terrorist attack on 11 September 2001, with a loss of life estimated (Jul 2004) to be 2749. The '9/11 Commission Report' (2004) into the incident delivered a scathing attack on US authorities. In 2003 plans were announced for a replacement building, the Freedom Tower (architects David Childs and Daniel Libeskind), which would be the world's tallest building at 541 m/1776 ft. The cornerstone was laid on 4 July 2004 and the tower is due for completion in 2009. Work to redevelop the rest of the site began in 2006.

World Trade Organization (WTO) A permanent body created in 1994 at the conclusion of the GATT Uruguay Round of talks to succeed GATT in monitoring international trade and resolve disputes. It began work in 1995, with headquarters in Geneva. It meets every two years, and is overseen by a General Council. It had 150 members at the start of 2007.

World War 1 (1914–18) A war whose origins lay in the reaction of other great powers to the ambitions of the German Empire after 1871. The assassination of the heir to the Habsburg throne, Franz Ferdinand, at Sarajevo in Bosnia (28 Jun 1914), triggered the war. Austria declared war on Serbia (28 Jul); Russia mobilized in support of Serbia (29–30 Jul); and Germany declared war on Russia (1 Aug), and on France (3 Aug). The German invasion of neutral Belgium (4 Aug) brought the British into the war on the French side. Japan joined Britain, France, and Russia under the terms of an agreement with Britain (1902, 1911), and Italy joined the Allies in May 1915. Turkey allied with Germany (Nov 1914), and they were joined by Bulgaria (Oct 1915).

Military campaigning centred on France and Belgium in W Europe, and on Poland and W Russia in E Europe. The British Expeditionary Force and French army prevented the Germans, at the first battle of Ypres, from reaching the Channel ports. By the end of 1914, a static defence line had been established from the Belgian coast to Switzerland. The Allies attempted to break the stalemate by a campaign in Gallipoli (Apr 1915–Jan 1916), but failed. For 3 years, an Allied army was involved in a Macedonian campaign, and there was also fighting in Mesopotamia against Turkey. The Allies organized a large offensive for the W

front in 1916, but were forestalled by the Germans, who attacked France at Verdun (Feb–Jul). To relieve the situation, the Battle of the Somme was launched, but proved indecisive. The Germans then unleashed unrestricted submarine warfare (Jan 1917) to cripple Britain economically. The USA declared war (2 Apr 1917) when British food stocks were perilously low, and the German submarine menace was finally overcome by the use of convoys. In the spring of 1918, the Germans launched a major attack in the W, but were driven back, with the USA providing an increasing number of much-needed troops. By November, when the armistice was signed, the Allies had recaptured E Belgium and nearly all French territory.

World War 2 (1939–45) The most destructive war in history. Its origins lay in three different conflicts which merged after 1941: Germany's desire for European expansion; Japan's struggle against China; and a resulting conflict between Japanese ambitions and US interests in the Pacific. After the German invasion of Czechoslovakia (Mar 1939), Britain and France pledged support to Poland. Germany concluded an alliance with Russia (Aug 1939), and then invaded Poland (1 Sep). Britain and France declared war on Germany (3 Sep), but could not prevent Poland from being overrun in four weeks. For six months there was a period of 'phoney war', when little fighting took place, but the Germans then occupied Norway and Denmark (Apr 1940), and Belgium and Holland were invaded (10 May). There followed the Battle of Britain, in which Germany tried to win air supremacy over Britain, but failed. Germany launched submarine attacks against British supply routes, but then moved E and invaded Greece and Yugoslavia (Apr 1941). British military efforts were concentrated against Italy in the Mediterranean and N Africa. Rommel was sent to N Africa with the Afrika Corps, and campaigning continued here for three years until Allied troops finally ejected German and Italian forces in mid-1943, invaded Sicily and then Italy itself, and forced Italy to make a separate peace (3 Sep 1943).

In June 1941, Germany invaded her ally Russia along a 2000 mi front. After spectacular early successes, from November 1942 they were gradually driven back, and were finally driven out of Russia in August 1944. Leningrad (now St Petersburg) was under siege for nearly 2½ years (until Jan 1944). A second front was launched against Germany by the Allies (Jun 1944), through the invasion of Normandy, and Paris was liberated (25 Aug). The Allies advanced into Germany (Feb 1945) and linked with the Russians on the R Elbe (28 Apr). The Germans surrendered unconditionally at Reims (7 May 1945).

In the Far East, Japan's desire for expansion led to her attack on Pearl Harbor and other British and US bases (7 Dec 1941), galvanizing the USA to declare war against Japan the next day. In reply Japan's allies, Germany and Italy, declared war on the USA (11 Dec). Within four months, Japan controlled SE Asia and Burma. Not until June 1942 did naval victories in the Pacific stem the advance. Bitter fighting continued until 1945, when, with Japan on the retreat, the USA dropped two atomic bombs on Hiroshima and Nagasaki (6 and 9 Aug). Japan then surrendered (14 Aug).

World Wide Fund for Nature (WWF) An international voluntary organization, founded in 1961 as the **World Wildlife Fund**, with its headquarters in Switzerland; international president, the Duke of Edinburgh. It aims to create awareness of the need for conservation of endangered wild animals, plants, and places, and promote the wise use of the world's natural resources. In 2007 its global network was active in more than 90 countries.

World Wide Web The full collection of all the computers linked to the Internet which hold documents that are mutually accessible through use of a standard protocol (the HyperText

Transfer Protocol, HTTP); usually abbreviated to **Web** or **W3** and in site addresses presented as the acronym **www**. The creator of the Web, computer scientist Tim Berners-Lee, has defined it as 'the universe of network-accessible information, an embodiment of human knowledge'. It was devised in 1990 as a means of enabling high-energy physicists in different institutions to share information within their field, but it rapidly spread to other fields, and is now all-inclusive. A **Web site** is an individual computer holding documents capable of being transferred to and presented by browsers, using one of the standard formats (usually HTML or XML). Web sites are identified by a unique address, or **URL** (**Uniform Resource Locator**), with different 'pages' of data at the site distinguished by means of labels separated by forward slashes. A further necessary element of the Web is the search engine, a means of locating documents by content rather than by location. The **World Wide Web Consortium** (**W3C**) is an international industry organization, founded in 1994 to develop common protocols for the Web.

World Wildlife Fund *World Wide Fund for Nature*

worm The common name for a wide range of long-bodied, legless invertebrate animals.

Worms [vorms], Eng [wermz], Lat **Borbetomagus** 49°38N 8°23E, pop (2000e) 78 500. River port in Germany; on R Rhine; one of the oldest towns in Germany; capital of kingdom of Burgundy, 5th-c; scene of many Imperial Diets; badly bombed in World War 2; railway; centre of the wine trade (notably for Liebfraumilch); cathedral (11th–12th-c).

Worms, Diet of Meetings of the estates of the German empire in 1521 and 1545, which sealed the religious fate of 16th-c Germany. At the first, Luther was condemned, following papal declarations of heresy; at the second, an attempt to heal the religious divisions between Catholics and Lutherans failed.

wormwood An aromatic perennial (*Artemisia absinthium*) growing to 90 cm/3 ft, native to Europe and Asia; flower-heads numerous, yellow, drooping. It is cultivated as a flavouring, and also used in the preparation of absinthe liqueur. (Family: Compositae.)

Worrall, Denis John (1935–) South African politician, born in Benoni, South Africa. He established the Independent Party, which in 1989 merged with other white Opposition parties to form the reformist Democratic Party. A co-leader of this party, he was elected to parliament in 1989.

Worthing 50°48N 0°23W, pop (2001e) 97 500. Resort town in West Sussex, S England; railway.

Wotan *Odin*

wound A breach in the skin, which may also involve underlying tissues and deeper structures, usually caused by physical injury, but also by heat or chemicals. Damage to the body results from the direct effect of the injury, particularly if vital organs are involved, and also from infection of the wound with disease-causing micro-organisms.

Wounded Knee The site in S Dakota of the final defeat of Sioux Indians (29 Dec 1890). The 'battle' was in fact a massacre by US troops.

woundwort An annual or perennial, found almost everywhere; flowers 2-lipped, usually white to pink or purple with darker spots, in whorls. It had an old herbal use in salves for treating cuts. (Genus: *Stachys*, 300 species. Family: Labiatae.)

Wouwerman, Philips [vowverman], also found as **Wouwermans** (c.1619–68) Painter of battle and hunting scenes, born in Haarlem, The Netherlands. His pictures are mostly small landscapes, with several figures in energetic action. He had two brothers, also painters, **Peter Wouwerman** (1623–82) and **Jan Wouwerman** (1629–66), who chose similar subjects.

W particle A particle that carries weak nuclear force; symbol *W*; mass 80·4 GeV; charge +1 (*W*⁺) or −1 (*W*⁻); spin 1; decays to an

electron or muon or tau plus corresponding neutrino; discovered in 1983.

WRAC *women's services*

Wrangel, Ferdinand Petrovich, Baron von [vranggl] (1794–1870) Explorer, born in Pskov, Russia. He travelled in Arctic waters and on Siberian coasts, and made valuable surveys and observations.

Wrangel Island [vrangl], Russ **Ostrov Vrangelya** area 5180 km²/2000 sq mi. Tundra-covered island in the W Chukchi Sea; length, 120 km/75 mi; width, 72 km/45 mi; rises to 1097 m/3599 ft; ceded to Russia, 1924; small settlements of Chukchi and Eskimo.

wrasse [ras] Any of a large group of mostly small colourful fishes widespread in tropical to temperate seas; length typically 10–30 cm/4–12 in. (Family: Labridae, 15 genera.)

wreckfish Large heavy-bodied fish (*Polyprion americanus*) found mainly in the tropical Atlantic; length up to 2 m/6½ ft; also called **stonebass**. (Family: Serranidae.)

Wren, Sir Christopher (1632–1723) Architect, born in East Knoyle, Wiltshire. After the Great Fire of London (1666), he drew designs for rebuilding the whole city, but his scheme was never implemented. In 1669 he designed the new St Paul's (building begun 1675) and many other public buildings in London, such as the Greenwich Observatory.

Wren, P(ercival) C(hristopher) (1875–1941) Writer, born in Deptford, Devon. He joined the Indian Educational Service in 1903, published textbooks and a guide to the theory and practice of education, and over 30 novels, notably *Beau Geste* (1924) and *Beau Sabreur* (1926).

wren A small songbird of the New World family Troglodytidae (**wrens**, c.65 species, one extending to the N Old World); name also used for Maluridae (**Australian wrens/wren-warblers**, 26 species, including the **fairy** or **blue wrens**, **grasswrens**, and **emu-wrens**); Xenicidae, sometimes called Acanthisittidae (**New Zealand wrens**, 3 species); and for many small birds of other families.

wren babbler A small babbler, found from India to SE Asia; inhabits woodland; eats mainly insects, some snails, possibly seeds. (Tribe: Pomatorhinini, 22 species.)

wren-warbler *emu wren; warbler*

wrestling The sport of one person fighting against another, but without the use of fists. In most cases the object is to fell your opponent to the ground. Many forms exist, the most popular amateur forms being **freestyle** and **Graeco-Roman**. In the latter, holds below the waist and the use of the legs are prohibited. Other forms include **Sambo**, which originated in Russia; **Sumo**, the national sport of Japan; British variations **Cumberland and Westmoreland** and **Devon and Cornwall**; and **Yagli**, the national sport of Turkey. Women's wrestling has also developed in recent years.

Wrexham [reksm], Welsh **Wrecsam** pop (2001e) 128 500; area 499 km²/193 sq mi. County (unitary authority from 1996) in NE Wales, UK; administrative centre, Wrexham; Wrexham cathedral, Church of St Giles (15th-c); football league team, Wrexham (Robins).

Wright, Frank Lloyd (1867–1959) Architect, born in Richland Center, WI. He became known for his low-built, prairie-style residences, but soon launched out into more controversial designs, and is regarded as the leading designer of modern private dwellings, planned in conformity with the natural features of the land. Among his larger works is the Guggenheim Museum of Art in New York City.

Wright, Judith (Arundell) (1915–2000) Poet, born near Armidale, New South Wales. She was one of the first white writers to recognize Aboriginal claims, in *The Moving Image (1946)*. Her *Collected Poems: 1942–1985* appeared in 1994, and the first volume of her autobiography, *Half a Lifetime*, was published in 1999.

Wright, Richard (Nathaniel) (1908–60) Novelist, short-story writer, and critic, born on a plantation in Natchez, MS. Among the first African-Americans to write about their ill-treatment by whites, he is best known for his *Native Son* (1940), the first substantial novel of US black revolt, and for his autobiography *Black Boy* (1945).

Wright, Sewall (1889–1988) Geneticist and statistician, born in Melrose, MA. He drew attention to random fluctuations in gene frequencies in small populations, and the possibility that alleles could be lost or fixed by chance rather than by natural selection. This concept of genetic drift (the **Sewall Wright effect**) was strongly criticized at the time, but is now widely accepted.

Wright brothers Aviation pioneers: **Orville Wright** (1871–1948), born in Dayton, OH, and **Wilbur Wright** (1867–1912), born near Millville, IN. They were the first to fly in a powered heavier-than-air machine (17 Dec 1903), at Kitty Hawk, NC. They formed an aircraft production company in 1909.

wrist A region of the upper limb between the forearm and the hand, consisting of eight *carpal* bones arranged in two rows. The rows make an arch forming part of a tunnel (the *carpal tunnel*), which transmits nearly all the structures entering the hand.

writing systems *alphabet; cuneiform; epigraphy; graphology* **2**; *hieroglyphics; ideography; logography; pictography; syllabary*

Wrocław [vrotswaf], Ger Breslau 51°05N 17°00E, pop (2000e) 651 000. River port in W Poland, on R Oder; capital of lower Silesia; founded, 10th-c; badly damaged in World War 2; airport; railway junction; technical university (1945); cathedral (13th-c).

wrought iron A form of iron, of very low carbon content, once much used by blacksmiths, but now mostly replaced by steel. It is less brittle than cast iron. Famous wrought iron structures were the SS *Great Britain* (1856) and the Eiffel Tower (1889). It is not much used now, except for decorative purposes.

WRVS *Women's Royal Voluntary Service*

wrybill A small plover, native to New Zealand (*Anarhynchus frontalis*); bill straight when seen from side, but tip bends to right; inhabits river beds and sand flats.

wryneck A short-billed, uncharacteristic woodpecker, native to Europe, Asia, and Africa; mottled brown. (Genus: *Jynx*, 2 species. Subfamily: Jynginae.)

Wu, Empress, in full **Wu Zhao** (?625–?706) Empress of China, the only woman ever to rule China in her own name. A concubine of Emperor Taizong, she married his son, Emperor Gaozong. After his death (683) she first ruled through her own sons, then after a reign of terror she seized the title *emperor* in 690 with the dynastic name Zhou (Chou). She was forced to abdicate in 705.

Wuhan or **Wu-han** [woohan], **Han-kow**, or **Han-kou** 30°35N 114°19E, pop (2000e) 4 504 000. Inland port in EC China; at confluence of Han Shui and Yangtze Rivers; commercial centre of C China; airfield; railway; university (1913); Central China Engineering Institute; Guiyuan Buddhist Temple (c.1600), now a museum.

Wulfila *Ulfilas*

Wuppertal [vupertahl] 51°15N 7°10E, pop (2000e) 392 000. Industrial city in Germany; on R Wupper in the Ruhr valley; includes the former towns of Barmen, Elberfeld, and Vohwinkel; university (1972).

Würzburg [vürtsboork] 49°48N 9°57E, pop (2000e) 135 000. Industrial city in Germany; on R Main; railway; centre of wine production and trade in Franconia; university (1582); cathedral (11th–13th-c), Marienberg (fortress, 13th-c); Würzburg Residence (episcopal palace built by Balthasar Neumann, 1719–44), a world heritage site.

Wüthrich, Kurt [vütrikh] (1938–) Chemist, born in Aarberg, Swit-

zerland. A researcher at the Swiss Federal Institute of Technology in Zürich and The Scripps Research Institute in La Jolla, CA, he shared the 2002 Nobel Prize for Chemistry for his development of nuclear magnetic resonance spectroscopy for determining the three-dimensional structure of biological macromolecules in solution.

www *World Wide Web*

Wyatt, James (1746–1813) Architect, born in Burton Constable, Staffordshire. He achieved fame with his Neoclassical design for the London Pantheon (1772). His best-known work is the Gothic Revival Fonthill Abbey (1796–1807), which largely collapsed in the 1820s.

Wyatt, Sir Thomas, known as **the Elder** (1503–42) Courtier and poet, born in Allington, Kent. In 1557 his poems, published in *Tottel's Miscellany*, helped to introduce the Italian sonnet and other forms into English literature.

Wycherley, William [wicherlee] (c.1640–1716) Playwright, born in Clive, Shropshire. He wrote several satirical comedies, notably *The Country Wife* (1675) and *The Plain Dealer* (1677), both based on plays by Molière.

Wycliffe or **Wicliffe, John** [wiklif], also spelled **Wyclif, Wycliff** (c.1330–84) Religious reformer, born near Richmond, Yorkshire. He attacked the Church hierarchy, priestly powers, and the doctrine of transubstantiation, wrote many popular tracts in English (as opposed to Latin), and issued the first English translation of the Bible (1380). His followers were known as Lollards, and the influence of his teaching was widespread in England, in many respects anticipating the Reformation.

Wye, River 1 River rising on Plynlimon, C Wales; flows 208 km/ 129 mi to meet the R Severn estuary; notable for its valley scenery. **2** River rising in Buckinghamshire, SC England; flows 15 km/ 9 mi to meet the R Thames. **3** River rising near Buxton in Derbyshire, C England; flows 32 km/20 mi SE to meet the R Derwent.

Wyler, William [wiyler] (1902–81) Film director, born in Mulhouse, France (formerly Germany). In 1935 his association with the producer Sam Goldwyn resulted in several successes, including *Mrs Miniver* (1942, Oscar), *The Best Years of Our Lives* (1946), *Ben Hur* (1959, Oscar), and *Funny Girl* (1968).

Wyndham, John [windam], pseudonym of **John Wyndham Parkes Lucas Beynon Harris** (1903–69) Science-fiction writer, born in Knowle, West Midlands. His novels included *The Day of the Triffids* (1951), *The Kraken Wakes* (1953), and *The Midwich Cuckoos* (1957). He also published collections of short stories, such as *The Seeds of Time* (1969).

Wynkyn de Worde *Worde, Wynkyn de*

Wyoming [wiyohming] pop (2000e) 493 800; area 253 315 km²/ 97 809 sq mi. State in W USA; the 'Equality State'; most of the region acquired by the USA from France in the Louisiana Purchase, 1803; total American jurisdiction, 1848; Wyoming Territory established, 1868; first territory or state to adopt women's suffrage, 1869; admitted to the Union as the 44th state, 1890; conflicts between cattle and sheep ranchers in the 1890s; contains the Wind River Indian reservation; a sparsely populated state; several ranges of the Rocky Mts (largely forested); highest point, Gannett Peak (4201 m/13 782 ft); eroded 'badlands' in the extreme NE; capital, Cheyenne; ranching and farming on the fertile Great Plains (E); an important mining state; very little manufacturing; major tourist area; national parks at Grand Teton and Yellowstone.

WYSIWYG [wizeewig] Acronym for **what you see is what you get**, used to refer to those computer systems, usually word processors or desktop publishing systems, where the display on the screen exactly mimics the final result produced by the printer.

Wyss, Johann Rudolf [vees] (1781–1830) Writer, born in Bern, Switzerland. He is best known for his completion and editing of *Der Schweizerische Robinson* (1812–13, trans The Swiss Family Robinson), written by his father, **Johann David** (1743–1818).

Wyszyński, Stefan, Cardinal [vishinskee] (1901–81) Polish cardinal, born in Zuzela, Poland. Following his indictment of the Com-munist campaign against the Church, he was imprisoned (1953). Freed in 1956, he agreed to a reconciliation between Church and state under the Gomułka regime, but relations remained uneasy.

wytch elm *elm*

Xanthophyceae [zanthuhfiysee-ee] *yellow-green algae*

Xavier, Francis, St *Francis Xavier, St*

Xena (2003 UB313) *Eris*

Xenakis, Iannis [zenahkees] (1922–2001) Composer, born in Braila, Romania. He developed a highly complex style which incorporated mathematical concepts of chance and probability (so-called *stochastic music*), as well as electronic techniques.

Xenocrates [zenokratees] (c.395–314 BC) Greek philosopher and scientist, born in Chalcedon on the Bosphorus. He was a pupil of Plato, and in 339 BC succeeded Speusippus as head of the Academy which Plato had founded.

xenoglossia [zenoglosia] *glossolalia*

xenon [zenon] Xe, element 54, boiling point −107°C. The fifth of the noble gases recovered from the atmosphere, of which it makes up only 0·000009%. Like the other noble gases, it is used in gas discharge tubes.

Xenophanes [zenofaneez] (c.570–c.480 BC) Greek philosopher, born in Colophon, Ionia. He attacked traditional Greek conceptions of the gods, arguing against anthropomorphism and polytheism.

Xenophon [zenofon] (c.435–354 BC) Athenian historian, essayist, and soldier, born in Attica. In 401 BC he served with a group of 10 000 Greek mercenaries under Persian Prince Cyrus. After Cyrus was killed, the Greeks were isolated over 1500 km/ 900 mi from home, but under Xenophon the group successfully fought their way back to the Black Sea. This heroic feat formed the basis of his major work, *Anabasis Kyrou* (The Expedition of Cyrus).

xerographic printer In computing, a printer which uses electrostatic techniques to provide text and/or graphics. Most photocopiers are of this type. Laser printers generally use this basic technology, which has the advantage of being silent, and capable of very high quality reproduction.

xerography [zerografee] The most widely used method of photocopying, first devised in the late 1930s by US physicist Chester F Carlson, but not developed commercially until the 1950s. A photoconductive surface is charged and exposed to the image to be copied; the charge is lost except in the image areas. The secondary image so produced is developed with a charged pigment which is transferred to copy paper and fixed by heat.

Xerxes I [zerkseez] (c.519–465 BC) Achaemenid king of Persia (485–465 BC), the son of Darius I. He is remembered in the West mainly for the failure of his forces against the Greeks in the Second Persian War.

Xhosa [khohsa] A cluster of Bantu-speaking peoples of the Transkei and Ciskei, South Africa. Xhosa is the most widely spoken African language in South Africa.

Xiamen, Hsia-men, or **Amoy** [shyahmuhn] 24°26N 118°07E, pop (2000e) 738 400. Subtropical port city in SE China; on island in Taiwan Strait; connected to mainland by 5 km/3 mi-long causeway (1949); first settled during S Song dynasty (1127–1279); made an open port, 1842; designated a special economic zone, 1981; new harbour; airfield; railway; university (1921); centre of growing unofficial trade between China and Taiwan.

Xian [shyahn], also spelled **Xi'an** or **Sian** 34°16N 108°54E, pop (2000e) 3 202 000. City in C China; first capital of feudal China; airport; railway; university (1937); Mausoleum of Emperor Qin Shihuangdi (30 km/18 mi E); terracotta warriors of Emperor Qin, discovered 1974; Big Wild Goose pagoda (652); Great Mosque (742); scene of the Xian incident (1936).

Xian incident [shyahn], also spelled **Xi'an** or **Sian** (Dec 1936) an incident in which Jiang Jieshi (Chiang Kai-shek) was held hostage in Xian by one of his own commanders, the 'young marshal' Zhang Xueliang (1901–2001), who demanded an anti-Japanese united front. He was released only on the intervention of Zhou Enlai. A united front of Communist and Nationalist forces resulted.

Xingu [sheenggoo] National park in WC Brazil; crossed by branches of the Xingu R (length c.1980 km/1230 mi), a S tributary of the Amazon; created in 1961 by the Villas-Boas brothers to protect the Indian tribes, but in recent years it has suffered from property developers.

Xinhua [shinwah] The national news agency of the People's Republic of China, with headquarters in Beijing. Founded as the communist Red China News Agency in 1931, and renamed *Hsin Hua* in 1937 (*Xinhua* since 1979), it is sometimes known nowadays as the New China News Agency.

Xining [sheening], **Hsi-ning**, or **Sining** 36°35N 101°55E, pop (2000e) 777 900. City in WC China; airfield; railway.

Xizang *Tibet*

XML *document description language*

X-ray astronomy A general term for the study of the X-rays from cosmic sources. It needs satellite-borne instruments, because X-rays do not penetrate our atmosphere.

X-ray diffraction An interference effect in which atoms in a material scatter X-rays to give a pattern of spots or concentric rings. These may be recorded, and their position and intensity used to determine the material's structure. The technique was discovered in 1912 by German physicist Max von Laue (1879–1960).

X-rays Invisible electromagnetic radiation having a much shorter wavelength than light, between 10^{-8} and 3×10^{-11} metres; discovered by Wilhelm Röntgen in 1895, and originally called **Röntgen rays**. They are produced by the transitions of electrons in the inner levels of excited atoms, or by the rapid deceleration of charged particles. X-rays are useful in medicine, since different components of the body absorb X-rays to a different extent, but enough radiation passes through the body to register on a photograhic plate beyond.

xylem [ziylem] A tissue composed of several types of conducting cells and supporting fibres which transports water and minerals up from the roots to all other parts of a plant. It forms the 'wood' of woody plants.

xylophone A percussion instrument known in various forms since the 14th-c. The modern orchestral instrument has two rows of wooden bars arranged like a piano keyboard, with a compass of $3\frac{1}{2}$–4 octaves. These are mounted over tubular resonators and played with hard wooden sticks.

X–Y plotter A form of pen recorder where one or more pens can be placed anywhere on the drawing surface. This allows complicated drawings and text to be produced.

yacht A sailing or power-driven vessel used for the pleasure of the owner. The first known yacht race was between Charles II and his brother James in 1661 from Greenwich to Gravesend and back. Yachting increased steadily in popularity throughout the 19th-c, and received a great boost from the continuing interest of Edward, Prince of Wales and other royals.

Yahweh [yahway] or **YHWH** The name of the God of Israel, usually taken to mean 'He is/will be', 'He comes to be/creates', or 'He causes to fall'. The unvocalized YHWH (known as the **Tetragrammaton**) is considered by Jews too sacred to pronounce aloud, and is usually replaced orally by *Adonai* ('Lord') when it is read from the Bible. Christians erroneously vocalized it as 'Jehovah'.

yak A member of the cattle family, native to the high Tibetan Plateau; thick shaggy brown coat; white muzzle; widely spread upturned horns; females crossbred with male domestic cattle or zebu; hybrid offspring (a *dzo*) economically important as draught animals. (*Bos mutus.*)

Yakut A Turkic-speaking Mongoloid people of NE Siberia, and the main group in the area. They are sedentary cattle and reindeer herders, and fishermen.

yakuza [yakuza] A Japanese gangster. The yakuza belong to recognized groups, cultivate a pseudo-samurai loyalty, and are proud of their traditions. Like the Mafia, they are widely involved in such activities as gambling, extortion, and racketeering.

Yale University *Ivy League*

Yalow, Rosalyn S(ussman) [yaloh] (1921–) Medical physicist, born in New York City. In the 1950s she devised the technique of radio-immunoassay, and shared the Nobel Prize for Physiology or Medicine in 1977.

Yalta Conference A meeting at Yalta, in the Crimea, during World War 2 (4–11 Feb 1945), between Churchill, Stalin, and Roosevelt. Among matters agreed were the disarmament and partition of Germany, the Russo–Polish frontier, and the establishment of the United Nations.

Yalu, River River forming the N border between North Korea and NE China; rises in the Changbai Shan range; flows into Korea Bay; length 790 km/490 mi.

yam A tuberous perennial, native to tropical and subtropical regions. Some 60 species are important food plants, especially in SE Asia, W Africa, and South America, where they are cultivated for the starchy tubers. In recent years some species have become important as a source of a steroid-type chemical used in oral contraceptives. (Genus: *Dioscorea*. Family: Dioscoreaceae.)

Yamoussoukro [yamoosookroh] 6°49N 5°17W, pop (2000e) 194 900. Capital of Côte d'Ivoire; weekend resort town; presidential residence.

Yamuna or **Jumna, River** [yahmuna] River of NW India; rises in the Himalayas; joins the R Ganges; length 1370 km/850 mi; confluence with the Ganges is one of the most sacred Hindu places.

yang *yin and yang*

Yangchow *Yangzhou*

Yangon, formerly (to 1989) **Rangoon** 16°47N 96°10E, pop (2000e) 3 445 000. Chief port and former capital (until 2005) of Myanmar; on R Yangon; settlement in 6th-c; capital, 1886; large Indian and Chinese population; airport (Mingaladon); railway; university (1920); Sule and Botataung Pagodas (both over 2000 years old), Shwedagon Pagoda (height 99.4 m/ 326 ft).

Yangtze River [yangksee] or **Yangtse-kiang**, in Chinese now normally **Chang Jiang** Longest river in China and third longest in the world; length c.6300 km/3900 mi; rises in the Tanggula Shan range; enters the E China Sea; provides c.40% of China's electricity; Three Gorges Dam project, begun in 1994 (completion scheduled, 2009); major transportation artery between E and W China; densely populated river basin contains about a quarter of China's cultivated land; increasing concern over conservation of aquatic resources (2007).

Yangzhou or **Yangchow** [yahngjoh] 32°25N 119°26E, pop (2000e) 508 600. City in E China, on Yangtze and Hua Rivers; first settled during Spring and Autumn Period, 770–476 BC; largest multiple-purpose water control project in China (1961–75); artistic centre for crafts, lacquerware screens, jade carving and printing.

Yao (Africa) [yow] A cluster of agricultural Bantu-speaking peoples of Tanzania, Malawi, and Mozambique. The majority are Muslims.

Yao (Asia) A mountain village people of SE Asia, dispersed and culturally diverse. They live chiefly in China, with some also in Thailand, Vietnam, and Laos.

Yaoundé or **Yaundé** [yaoonday] 3°51N 11°31E, pop (2000e) 1 109 000. Capital of Cameroon, W Africa; established as military post by Germans in 1899; occupied by Belgian colonial troops, 1915; capital of French Cameroon, 1921; airport; railway to the coast (Douala); university (1962).

Yap pop (2000e) 17 200; area 119 km²/46 sq mi. One of the Federated States of Micronesia, W Pacific; comprises four large islands with some 130 outer islands; airport; capital, Colonia.

yapok [yapok] A marsupial native to Central and South America (*Chironectes minimus*); slender with long legs, pointed head, long naked tail; the only truly semiaquatic marsupial; hind feet webbed; also known as **water opossum**. (Family: Didelphidae.)

yarn The spun thread from which woven, knitted, and other fabrics are manufactured. Yarns vary widely in their properties, depending upon fibre content, count, and the spinning process used.

Yaroslavl [yaroslafl] 57°34N 39°52E, pop (2000e) 633 000. River port in E European Russia; founded c.1024; railway; university (1971); monastery (12th-c).

yarrow A perennial (*Achillea millefolium*) growing to 60 cm/2 ft, native to Europe and W Asia; flower-heads numerous, in dense, flat-topped clusters; also called **milfoil**. It was formerly employed extensively in herbal medicine. (Family: Compositae.)

Yassin or **Yasin, Sheikh Ahmad** (1936–2004) Founder of the Islamic Resistance Movement, Hamas, born in Majdal, Palestine. Paralysed since childhood, he grew up in Palestinian refugee camps in the Gaza Strip. In 1970, he organised the *al-Mujama al-Islami* 'The Islamic Compound' which opened mosques, hospitals, and libraries. In 1979, he founded the radical group *Majd al-Mujahedin* 'The Pride of the Faithful Warriors'. He was imprisoned by the Israelis in 1984 for organising violence but released in 1985. In 1987 he founded Hamas with the goal of replacing Israel with an Islamic state and played a leading role in the 1987 Palestinian intifada. With the banning of Hamas in 1989, Yassin received two life sentences but was released in 1997, following Israel's assassination attempt on Khalid Mishaal, the Hamas spokesman in Jordan. He was assassinated in an Israeli missile attack in March 2004.

Yates, Dornford, pseudonym of **Cecil William Mercer** (1885–1960) Novelist, born in London. He achieved great popularity with an entertaining series of fanciful escapist adventure fiction, such as *Berry and Co* (1921).

Yavneh [yavne] *Jabneh*

yawl *ketch*

yaws An infectious disease of tropical regions caused by the bacterium *Treponema pertenue*. It is largely confined to eruptions in the skin.

yeast A fungus that can occur as single cells; typically reproduces by budding or by fission; used in fermentation processes in the brewing and baking industries. (Subdivision: Ascomycetes. Order: Endomycetales.)

Yeats, W(illiam) B(utler) [yayts] (1865–1939) Poet and playwright, born near Dublin. In 1888 he published *The Wanderings of Oisin*, a long narrative poem that established his reputation. With his patron, Lady Gregory, he founded the Irish Literary Theatre in 1899, and was a director of the Abbey Theatre, Dublin, from 1904. He wrote nearly 30 plays, including *The Countess Cathleen* (1892), *The Land of Heart's Desire* (1894), and *Cathleen ni Houlihan* (1903). Many of his best-known poems appeared in *The Tower* (1928), *The Winding Stair* (1929), and *A Full Moon in March* (1935). He received the Nobel Prize for Literature in 1923.

Yekaterinburg or **Ekaterinburg** [yekatuhrinberg], formerly **Sverdlovsk** (1924–91) 56°52N 60°35E, pop (2000e) 1 365 000. Industrial city in E European Russia; on R Iset; founded as a military stronghold and trading centre, 1723; tsar and his family shot here, 1918; airport; on the Trans-Siberian Railway; university (1920).

yellow fever A disease occurring in Africa and South America caused by a virus which infests monkeys and is transmitted to humans by mosquitoes. It is often a mild short-lived feverish illness, but may become severe, with jaundice, kidney failure, and even death.

yellowfin tuna Species of tuna fish (*Thunnus albacares*) widespread in surface waters of tropical and warm temperate seas; length up to 2 m/6½ ft; golden band along side of body, dorsal and anal fins yellow; heavily exploited commercially. (Family: Scombridae.)

yellow-green algae Aquatic algae containing the photosynthetic pigments chlorophyll *a* and *c*, and various carotenoids which produce the yellow-green colour of the chloroplasts; they vary in form from single cells to filaments. (Class: Xanthophyceae.)

yellowhammer (Ger *ammer*, 'bunting') A bird, a species of bunting (*Emberiza citronella*), native to NW regions of the Old World; black and yellow streaked plumage with chestnut rump; also known as the **yellow bunting**. The name is used in the USA for the woodpecker, *Colaptes auratus*.

Yellowknife 62°30N 114°29W, pop (2000e) 17 000. Capital of North West Territories, Canada, on NW shore of Great Slave Lake at mouth of Yellowknife R; founded, 1935; capital, 1967.

Yellow River, Chin **Huang Ho** or **Huang He** Second longest river in China; length 5464 km/3395 mi; rises in Bayan Har Shan Range; enters the Bo Hai Gulf; flooding now increasingly controlled by dykes; several conservancy projects on upper and middle reaches; in 2004 it was revealed that it now fails to reach the sea for over 200 days each year due to huge drawings for cotton irrigation, and that tens of millions of people may be forced to migrate to the cities; one third of fish species reported extinct in 2007.

Yellow Sea, Chin **Hwang Hai** Inlet of the Pacific Ocean, bounded by China (N, W) and by N and S Korea (E); maximum width c.650 km/400 mi; maximum depth c.150 m/500 ft; named for its colour, because of the silt brought down by its rivers.

Yellowstone Largest US national park, and the world's first, mainly in NW Wyoming; contains over 3000 hot springs and geysers, including Old Faithful, a geyser that spurts water at regular intervals; area 8992 km²/3472 sq mi.

yellow wood A member of a large genus of evergreen conifers found in the mountains of warm temperate and tropical regions of the S hemisphere. They are important forest trees, especially in Australasia, yielding valuable timber. (Genus: *Podocarpus*, 100 species. Family: Pinaceae.)

Yeltsin, Boris (Nikolayevich) (1931–2007) Russian president (1991–9), born in Butka, Russia. Inducted into the Central Committee in 1981 by Gorbachev, he was appointed Moscow party chief, and set about renovating the corrupt 'Moscow machine'. In 1987, after he had bluntly criticized party conservatives for sabotaging *perestroika*, he was downgraded to a lowly administrative post. He returned to public attention in 1989 as a member of the new Congress of USSR People's Deputies, and in 1990 was elected president of the Russian Federation. Following the attempted coup to oust Gorbachev in 1991, his political standing greatly increased when he led the protestors who defeated the coup, and following the break-up of the Soviet Union he remained in power as president. He continued to press for reform, but met increasing resistance from more conservative elements in the parliament. Although successful in the 1996 elections, continuing ill health caused him major difficulties. He resigned on New Year's Eve, 1999.

Yemen *p.1030*

Yenisey or **Yenisei, River** [yenisay] River in C Siberian Russia; rises in the E Sayanskiy Khrebet; enters the Kara Sea; length, 3487 km/2167 mi.

yeoman A person in late mediaeval England qualified, by holding freehold land and property worth 40 shillings or more, to serve on juries and vote for knights of the shire. In the early modern period, the name is used for the better-off freeholders or tenant-farmers who were often dominant in village life and administration.

Yeomen of the Guard The oldest of the four corps of the British sovereign's personal bodyguard, known also as **Beefeaters**, supposedly in tribute to their healthy appearance. They are called out for special duties only, when they wear their basically Tudor uniforms. The same uniforms are worn by the **Yeomen Warders** of the Tower of London.

Yerevan or **Erivan** [yerevan] 40°10N 44°31E, pop (2000e) 1 337 000. Capital city of Armenia; on R Razdan; altitude of highest part, 1042 m/3419 ft; one of the world's most ancient cities; ceded to Russia, 1828; airfield; railway; university.

Yesenin, Sergey Alexandrovich [yesaynin] (1895–1925) Poet, born in Konstantino (later renamed Yesenino), Russia to a peasant family. He gained literary success with his first volume *Radunitsa* (1916, Mourning for the Dead). His suicide in St Petersburg prompted a wave of imitative suicides in Russia.

yeti A supposed ape-like creature said to live at the edge of the snow-line in high valleys of the Himalayan Mts; generally described as large, covered in brown hair, and walking upright like a human; first reported in 1889; footprints of length 15–

Yemen

☐ International Airport   - - - - No defined boundary

official name **Republic of Yemen**, Arabic **al-Jumhurijah al-Yemenijah**

Local name al-Yaman (Arabic)

Timezone GMT +3

Area 531 570 km²/205 186 sq mi

Population total (2002e) 19 495 000

Status Republic

Date of independence 1967

Capitals Sana (political), Aden (commercial)

Languages Arabic (official), English

Ethnic groups Arab (96%), with Indo-Pakistani, Somali, Amhara and Swahili, Persian, Jewish, and European minorities

Religions Muslim (Sunni 53%, Shiite 47%), small Christian, Hindu, and Yemeni Jew minorities

Physical features Occupies the SW corner of the Arabian peninsula; narrow coastal plain, backed by mountains rising to 3000–3500 m/10 000–11 500 ft; highlands, central plateau and mari-

time range of former South Yemen form the most fertile part of the country; former North Yemen is largely desert and mountainous.

Climate Hot and humid climate; lowland and desert regions in NE receive an average annual rainfall of 100 mm/4 in; hot and humid on Tihamat coastal strip with mean temperature of 29°C; mild and temperate in interior highlands, with cool winters; average annual temperatures 25°C (Jan), 32°C (Jul) in Aden; average annual rainfall, 46 mm/1·8 in.

Currency 1 Yemeni Riyal (YER) = 100 fils (former N Yemen)

Economy Based on agriculture (largely subsistence) and light industry; cotton has overtaken coffee as chief cash crop; irrigation schemes likely to increase area under cultivation; qat, a narcotic leaf, now a major enterprise; hides, vegetables, dried fish; crude- and refined-oil industry; textiles, cement, aluminium, salt.

GDP (2002e) $15·07 bn, per capita $800

Human Development Index (2002) 0·479

History Part of the Minaean kingdom, 1200–650 BC; converted to Islam in 7th-c; Turkish occupation, 1538–1630 and 1872–1918; between and after Turkish rule, Yemen under the rule of the Hamid al-Din dynasty; sovereignty of Yemen acknowledged by Saudi Arabia and Britain, 1934; joined Arab League, 1945; Egypt-backed revolution in 1962, resulting in civil war; Yemen Arab Republic (North Yemen) declared, 1962; royalists defeated, 1969; neighbouring People's Republic of South Yemen established, 1967, when Britain ended 129 years of rule in Aden and the Marxist National Liberation Front took over; the People's Republic comprised Aden and 16 of the 20 protectorate states once under British control; renamed People's Democratic Republic of Yemen, 1970; negotiations to merge the two Yemens, 1979; unification proclaimed and ratified, 1990; new state called Republic of Yemen; former President of North Yemen declared President of the unified state, and former President of South Yemen became Prime Minister, supported Iraq during Gulf War, 1991; coalition government formed, 1993; governed by a President, Prime Minister, House of Representatives and Advisory Council; South Yemen declared independence as Democratic Republic of Yemen, 1994; subsequent civil war won by North Yemen.

Head of State

1990– Ali Abdullah Saleh

Head of Government

1990–4 Haider Abu Bakr al-Attas

1994–7 Abdel Aziz Abdel-Ghani

1997–8 Farag Said Ben Ghanem

1998–2001 Abdul Karim al-Iriani

2001– Abd al-Qadir Abd al-Rahman Ba Jammal

30 cm/6–12 in have been photographed, but various expeditions have failed to find it; also known as **abominable snowman**.

Yevtushenko, Yevgeny (Alexandrovich) [yevtushengkoh] (1933–) Poet, born in Zima, Russia. His early poetry, such as *The Third Snow* (1955), made him a spokesman for the young post-Stalin generation. Major poems include *Stantsiya Zima* (1956, Zima Junction), considering issues raised by the death of Stalin, and *Babi Yar* (1962) which attacked anti-Semitism. In 1960 he began to travel abroad to give readings of his poetry. Among later works are *Pre-morning* (1995). His first major stage piece, *Under the Skin of the Statue of Liberty*, was a huge success in 1972.

yew A small evergreen tree or shrub, native to the western N hemisphere; leaves narrow, flattened, spreading in two hori-

zontal rows. The foliage and seeds are highly poisonous. Popular for cemeteries, topiary, and mazes, yews were once the source of the finest longbows. (Genus: *Taxus*, 10 species. Family: Taxaceae.)

Yiddish A language used by E European Jews, developed from Old High German in the 9th-c, and written using the Hebrew alphabet. It flourished as a medium of literature in the 19th-c, but its literary use has diminished following the establishment of Hebrew as the official language of Israel.

yield The interest paid on a stock, share, or bond in relation to its current market value, in percentage terms. If a company pays a dividend of 20p a share, before tax is deducted, and the share price is 400p, then the dividend yield is 5%.

yield stress The lowest stretching stress at which a material undergoes an irreversible plastic deformation, producing what is called a 'permanent set' in the material; symbol σ_y, units Pa (pascal).

yin and yang The Chinese concept that everything is explicable in terms of two complementary but opposing principles. Yang represents heaven, and is the positive, male force which is characteristically aggressive, stimulating, light, hot, and dry. Yin is seen as the negative, female force, which is characteristically cold, dark, heavy, and damp. Yang people are active, alert, energetic, and precise, but suffer with problems of anxiety, stress, tension, irritability, and inability to relax. Yin people are calm, relaxed, peaceful, and creative, but are prone to laziness, depression, and lethargy. Representing all experience in a dynamic framework, the yin–yang concept has underpinned Chinese cyclical views of history, and was developed in a sophisticated form by Han times (3rd-c BC–AD 3rd-c).

Yinchuan or **Yinch'uan** [yinchwahn] 38°30N 106°19E, pop (2000e) 559 500. Capital of Ningxia autonomous region, N China; airfield; commercial centre; centre of agricultural trade; Muslims are a third of the population.

ylang-ylang [eelang eelang] An evergreen tree (*Cananga odorata*) growing to 25 m/80 ft, native to Malaysia and the Philippines; flowers 6-petalled, dull yellow, fragrant. Ylang-ylang or macassar oil from the flowers is used in perfumes. (Family: Annonaceae.)

YMCA Abbreviation of **Young Men's Christian Association**, a charity founded in London in 1844 to promote the spiritual, social, and physical welfare of boys and young men. It is a global network of over 120 autonomous national movements and currently serves over 45 million youths and families worldwide.

yoga In Indian religious tradition, any of various physical and contemplative techniques designed to free the superior, conscious element in a person from involvement with the inferior material world. More narrowly, Yoga is a school of Hindu philosophy.

yogurt or **yoghurt** A product, originating in the Balkans, obtained by fermenting milk with the bacteria *Lactobacillus bulgaricus* and *Streptococcus acidophilus*. Various sweetenings and flavourings may be added.

Yogyakarta [yagyakah(r)ta] or **Yogya** 7°48S 110°24E, pop (2000e) 547 000. City in SC Java, Indonesia; cultural centre of Java; airfield; railway; two universities (1945, 1949); ancient temples of Borobudur and Prambanan.

Yokohama [yohkohhahma] 35°28N 139°28E, pop (2000e) 3 325 000. Port in C Honshu, Japan; second largest city in Japan, handling 15% of foreign trade; first port to be opened to foreign trade, 1859; linked to Tokyo by first Japanese railway, 1872; largely destroyed by earthquake in 1923, and by bombing in 1945; railway; two universities (1949); Yokohama International Stadium (1997).

Yolngu The Aboriginal people and language of NE Arnhem Land; sometimes called **Murngin**. Three Yolngu clans were the plaintiffs in a land rights case in 1968, and their failure to secure legal recognition led directly to the introduction of the first Australian land rights legislation in 1976.

Yom Kippur [yohm kipoor, yom kipur] The Day of Atonement, a Jewish holy day (10 Tishri) coming at the end of 10 days of penitence which begin at Rosh Hashanah; a day devoted to fasting, prayer, and repentance for past sins.

Yom Kippur War *Arab–Israeli Wars*

yoni [yohnee] *lingam*

Yonkers 40°56N 73°54W, pop (2000e) 196 100. Town in SE New York, USA; a residential suburb on the Hudson R; railway; St Andrews golf course (first course in the USA).

York (UK), Lat **Eboracum** 53°58N 1°05W, pop (2000e) 103 000.

City in North Yorkshire, N England; unitary authority from 1996 (pop (2000e) 176 000); Roman settlement founded in AD 71 as capital of the Roman province of Britannia; thereafter a royal and religious centre, capital of Anglo-Saxon Northumbria; captured by the Danes, 867, known as **Jorvik**; Archbishop of York bears the title Primate of England; expanded rapidly in the 19th-c as a railway centre; university (1963); 14th-c city walls; York Minster (12th–15th-c), south transept badly damaged by fire in 1984, since restored; National Railway Museum; Jorvik Viking Centre (1984); football league team, York City.

York, Duke of In the UK, a title often given to the second son of the sovereign. It is currently held by Andrew, the second son of Queen Elizabeth II.

York, House of The younger branch of the English Plantagenet dynasty, founded by Edmund of Langley, the fourth son of Edward III and first Duke of York (1385–1402), whence came three kings of England: Edward IV (1461–83), who usurped the Lancastrian king Henry VI; Edward V (1483); and Richard III (1483–5) killed at Bosworth Field.

York, Alvin (Cullum) (1887–1964) US soldier and popular hero, born in Pall Mall, TN. While in France during World War 1, he led a small detachment against a German machine-gun emplacement, in which he killed 25 of the enemy, inducing 132 Germans to surrender. Gary Cooper portrayed him in the movie *Sergeant York* (1941).

Yorkshire, North pop (2000e) 738 300; excluding York, 605 300; area 8309 km²/3207 sq mi. County in N England, created in 1974; largest county in England; York and Middlesbrough given status as unitary authorities from 1996; Pennines in the W; Vale of York, North Yorkshire Moors, Cleveland Hills in the E; county town, Northallerton; Rievaulx Abbey, Yorkshire Dales national park, Castle Howard, York Minster, Fountains Abbey.

Yorkshire, South pop (2001e) 1 266 300; area 1560 km²/602 sq mi. Area of N England, created in 1974, divided into four metropolitan borough councils: Sheffield, Rotherham, Doncaster, Barnsley (administrative centre).

Yorkshire, West pop (2001e) 2 079 200; area 2039 km²/787 sq mi. County of N England; administrative centre, Wakefield; metropolitan council abolished in 1986; Ilkley Moor, Haworth Parsonage (home of the Brontës), Peak District National Park.

Yorkshire Dales National park in North Yorkshire and Cumbria, England; area 1761 km²/680 sq mi; established in 1954; limestone scenery, popular with potholers and fell walkers.

Yorkshire terrier A British toy terrier; very small, with long fine brown and blue-grey hair; coat reaches ground; head with large erect ears and very long hair.

Yorktown 37°14N 76°30W. Town in SE Virginia, USA, at the mouth of the York R; settled, 1631; now in Colonial National Historical Park; besieged during the Revolution, 1781, and the Civil War, 1862.

Yorktown Campaign (30 Aug–19 Oct 1781) The final campaign of the US War of Independence, ending with the entrapment at Yorktown, VA, of the British army under Lord Cornwallis by troops under Washington and a French fleet under Admiral de Grasse (1722–88).

Yoruba [yoruhba] A cluster of Kwa-speaking peoples of SW Nigeria and Benin. Their dominant state in the 17th–18th-c was the kingdom of Oyo.

Yosemite [yohsemitee] ('grizzly bear') National park in E California, USA, in the Sierra Nevada; rises to 3990 m/13 090 ft in Mt Lyell; Yosemite Falls (highest in North America); area 3083 km²/1189 sq mi.

Young, Andrew (Jackson), Jr (1932–) Civil rights activist, Protestant minister, and public official, born in New Orleans, LA. As a minister, he joined the Southern Christian Leadership Conference in 1960, and came to be one of the closest associates of

Martin Luther King, Jr. He later became US representative to the UN, but was forced to resign after it was revealed that he had met secretly with members of the PLO.

Young, Brigham (1801–77) Mormon leader, born in Whitingham, VT. Converted in 1832, he became president of the Church upon the death of Joseph Smith in 1844. He led the Mormons to Utah (1847), where they founded Salt Lake City. He established over 300 towns and settlements, had over 20 wives (estimates vary), and was the father of more than 40 children.

Young, Cy, popular name of **Denton True Young** (1867–1955) Baseball pitcher, born in Gilmore, OH. One of the first of baseball's greats, during his career he threw 749 and won 511 games, both records. National and American League's leading pitchers win the **Cy Young Award** every year.

Young, John (1930–) Astronaut, born in San Francisco, CA. He has flown in space a record six times: twice in the Gemini programme, twice in the Apollo programme (Apollos 10 and 16), and twice as commander of the space shuttle, including its first flight, STS-1, in 1981.

Young, Lester (Willis), nickname **Prez** (1909–59) Influential and much-imitated jazz musician, born in Woodville, MS. Originally a drummer, he became a master of the tenor and alto saxophones, becoming known in the 1930s and 1940s. Billie Holiday gave him his nickname, short for 'President'.

Young, Simone (1961–) Conductor, born in Sydney, New South Wales, Australia. She became the first woman to conduct the Vienna Volksoper, the Vienna Staatsoper, and the Paris Opera, and was chief conductor and musical director for Opera Australia (2001–3). In 2005 she was appointed general manager and music director of Hamburg State Opera, and music director of the Philharmonic State Orchestra, Hamburg.

Young, Thomas (1773–1829) Physicist, physician, and Egyptologist, born in Milverton, Somerset. He established the wave theory of light, and made a fundamental contribution to the deciphering of the inscriptions on the Rosetta Stone.

Young Ireland An Irish protest movement, founded in 1840, arguing for repeal of the Act of Union. It set up an Irish Confederation in 1847, which returned several nationalists to parliament.

Young Italy (Ital **Giovine Italia**) An Italian patriotic organization which played an important role in the early stages of the Risorgimento, founded in Marseille (1833) by Mazzini. It played a significant part in the revolutions of 1848.

Young Men's Christian Association *YMCA*

Young Men's / Women's Hebrew Association (YMHA/YWHA) In the USA, an organization to promote health, social activities, and Jewish culture. The first YMHA was founded in 1854, and the first independent YWHA in 1902.

young offender institution An institution in the UK where adolescent and young adult offenders between 15 and 21 may be detained either on remand or following a sentence of the court. In the USA, detention centres for both male and female offenders are often known as *juvenile halls*, *youth camps*, or *youth authorities*.

Young's modulus Linear stress divided by linear strain, a constant for a given material; symbol *E*, units Pa (pascal); also called the **modulus of elasticity** or the **elastic modulus**; named after British physicist Thomas Young. A high Young's modulus means that material is stiffer.

Young Turks The modernizing and westernizing reformers in the early 20th-c Ottoman Empire. With the support of disaffected army elements under Enver Pasha, they rebelled against Sultan Abd-ul-Hamid II in 1908, and deposed him in 1909.

Young Vic *Old Vic Theatre*

Young Women's Christian Association *YWCA*

Yourcenar, Marguerite [yersenah(r)], pseudonym of **Marguerite de Crayencour** (1903–87) Novelist, born in Brussels. She is best known for her historical novel *Mémoires d'hadrien* (1951, Memoirs of Hadrian), and for being the first woman to be elected to the Académie Française.

youth court A court introduced in England and Wales in 1991 to replace the existing juvenile courts. Youth courts deal with most young offenders from the age of criminal responsibility (10 in England and Wales) up to the age of 18. In England and Wales, the Crime and Disorder Act (1998) contains radical measures designed to prevent crime and anti-social behaviour by young offenders.

Youth Hostels Association (YHA) *International Youth Hostel Association*

Ypres [eepr], Flemish **Ieper** 50°51N 2°53E, pop (2000e) 35 800. Town in W Belgium, close to the French border; long associated with the cloth trade; devastated in World War 1; Menin Gate (Menenpoort) memorial, graveyards, and Garden of Peace provide a place of pilgrimage; railway; cloth hall (13th-c); cathedral.

Ypres, Battles of (1914–17) [eepr] Major battles in World War 1, taking place in three stages. The first (30 Oct–24 Nov 1914) ended in stalement, beginning a protracted period of trench warfare on the Western Front. In the second (22 Apr–27 May 1915), the Germans used chemical warfare – chlorine gas. In the third stage (July–Nov 1917), after constant Allied bombardment, the Germans won the advantage, deploying mustard gas and machine-gunfire. Canadian infantrymen eventually took Passchendaele after months of bitter fighting in battlefield swamps. By the end of the battle, Allied troops had gained a mere 8 km/5 mi. More than half a million men perished.

Ysselmeer *Ijsselmeer*

yttrium [yitrium] Y, element 39, density 4·5 g/cm³, melting point 1522°C. A relatively rare element occurring in ores of the lanthanide elements, many of whose properties it shares. It is a constituent of many superconducting ceramics.

Yuan dynasty [yooan] or **Mongol dynasty** (1279–1368) A Chinese dynasty founded by Kublai Khan (1264), who took the name Yuan in 1271 and conquered the Song dynasty in 1279. There were significant developments in astronomy, medicine, shipbuilding, and technology; and a vernacular literary genre evolved, with new dramatic forms. The dynasty was eventually overthrown by a Chinese uprising led by Zhu Yuanzhang, the first Ming emperor.

Yuan Shikai [yüan sheekiy], also spelled **Yuan Shih-k'ai** (1859–1916) Chinese statesman and soldier, born in Xiancheng, Henan, China, the first president of the Republic established in 1912. He lost support by procuring the murder of the parliamentary leader of the Nationalists, making war on them, and proclaiming himself emperor (1915), and he was forced to abdicate.

Yucatán [yukatahn] pop (2000e) 1 640 000; area 38 402 km²/14 823 sq mi. State in SE Mexico, on the N Yucatán peninsula; capital, Mérida; numerous Mayan ruins, including Chichén Itzá and Uxmal; the name also often given to the whole peninsula.

yucca An evergreen perennial native to the USA, Mexico, and the Caribbean; somewhat palm-like in appearance, trunk short, thick; leaves sword-shaped; flowers night-scented, white, bell-shaped and hanging, in spikes. (Genus: *Yucca*, 40 species. Family: Agavaceae.)

Yugoslavia *Montenegro*; *Serbia*

Yugoslavian Civil War (1991–5) A conflict resulting from the declaration of independence by Slovenia, Macedonia, and Croatia, considered illegal by the central Yugoslav government. The first major European conflict since World War 2, it began as a confrontation between Croatia and the Serb-dominated national army, and developed into civil war. Croatian independence was internationally recognized in 1991, but fighting continued between Croats and Muslims in Bosnia, and between Croats and Serb guerrillas in Krajina (a Serb-dominated enclave in Croatia), who wished to see the area as part of a 'Greater Serbia'.

UN recognition of Bosnia-Herzegovina independence in 1992 was opposed by Serbs. UN sanctions were imposed on Yugoslavia (and suspension from the UN) following its support of Serb guerrillas in Bosnia and the Serbian policy of 'ethnic cleansing' (driving Muslims from areas shared with ethnic Serbs). Croatian-dominated Western Herzegovina proclaimed itself autonomous, raising the possibility of a 'Greater Croatia'.

There was continued fighting throughout 1993, despite several rounds of negotiations. An internationally sponsored plan introduced 'safe areas' for Muslims in Bosnia, to be monitored by a UN Protection Force. Serb attacks on Sarajevo, 1994, led to a NATO ultimatum, the imposition of a 'no-fly' zone, and NATO bombing of Serb forces in response to attacks on safe areas, but with little military effect. Serb reprisals against the UN included hostage-taking. A Muslim-Croat accord to set up a federation in Bosnia-Herzegovina was also rejected by the Serbs. In 1995, further Serb bombardment of Sarajevo resulted in NATO air strikes and more hostage-taking. Serbs captured the Muslim safe-area enclave of Srebrenica, which brought reports of major atrocities. A successful Croatian offensive in Krajina and NW Bosnia restored territorial balance in the area. A Serb attack on Sarajevo led to NATO/UN attacks on Bosnian Serb targets, and Serb withdrawal. A ceasefire was arranged (Oct) and a peace treaty was signed in Dayton, Ohio (Nov). Bosnia was to stay a single state, made up of the Bosnian–Croat Federation and the Bosnian Serb Republic, with a united Sarajevo, and the establishment of a NATO peace implementation force.

An International Criminal Tribunal was set up by the UN Security Council in 1993 in The Hague, following the discovery of evidence pointing to civilian massacres in war-torn areas. Several people have since been tried for crimes against humanity. In 2006 Bosnia and Herzogovina accused Serbia, as a state, of genocide. In the first ruling of this kind (Feb 2007), the UN International Court of Justice found this charge unproven, but agreed that the Srebrenica incident was a case of genocide.

Yukon [yookon] pop (2000e) 31100; area 483 450 km²/ 186 660 sq mi. Territory in NW Canada; capital, Whitehorse; area of plateaux and mountain ranges, rising to 5950 m/ 19 521 ft at Mt Logan; tundra in N; several lakes; Hudson's Bay Company fur-trading post, 1842; gold prospectors from 1873; district of Northwest Territories, 1895; separate territory when Klondike gold rush at its height, 1898; governed by an Executive Council appointed from a Legislative Assembly.

Yukon River Major river in North America, in Yukon territory and Alaska; rises in the Rocky Mts, enters the Bering Sea; length to the head of the longest headstream (the Nisutlin) 3185 km/ 1979 mi; ice-bound most of the year (Oct–Jun).

Yunupingu, Mandawuy [yunupinggoo, mandawoy] (1956–) Singer, born in Yirrkala, a former Methodist mission in NE Arnhem Land, Australia. A member of one of the leading families in the Gumatj clans, in 1986 he established the group *Yothu Yindi* ('mother–child' in Yolngu-matha). In 1993 he was made Australian of the Year, an honour also bestowed on his brother **Galarrwuy** in 1978.

Yunus, Muhammad (1940–) Banker and economist, born in Bathua, Chittagong, Bangladesh. He studied at Dhaka University (1957–61) and later gained a Fulbright scholarship to study at Vanderbilt University, USA, where he gained his doctorate (1969). Returning to Bangladesh, he joined Chittagong University as an economics professor. He took up the cause of fighting poverty in his country following a famine there in 1974, and developed the concept of microfinance, the extension of small loans to those too poor to qualify for traditional bank loans. To this end he founded the Grameen Bank and Foundation to fight poverty. He was awarded the 2006 Nobel Peace Prize jointly with the Grameen Bank for 'their efforts to create economic and social development from below'.

Yurak *Nenets*

Yushchenko, Viktor (1954–) Ukrainian prime minister (1999–2001) and president (2004–), born in NE Ukraine. He studied accountancy and joined the Soviet State Bank, rising to become governor of the National Bank of Ukraine (1995). President Kuchma appointed him prime minister in 1999 but he was dismissed in 2001 and went on to form the opposition Our Ukraine bloc. During the 2004 presidential campaign there were many attempts by the opposition, led by Viktor Yanukovych, to discredit him. The result awarded victory to Yanukovych but mass public protest in Kiev forced the poll to be declared invalid by Ukraine's Supreme Court. The poll was re-run with Yushchenko declared the winner, gaining 52% of the vote. In 2005 Queen Elizabeth II presented him with the first Chatham House Prize.

YWCA Abbreviation of **Young Women's Christian Association**, a charity formed in London in 1877 by the joining of a prayer union and a home for nurses travelling to and from the Crimean War. It is now active in 125 countries.

Z

Zabrze [zabuhrzhe], Ger **Hindenburg** 50°18N 18°47E, pop (2000e) 202 000. Mining and industrial city in S Poland; second largest city in upper Silesian industrial region; railway.

Zacharias *Zechariah, Book of*

Zacynthus [zakinthus], Gr **Zákinthos** pop (2000e) 34 200; area 406 km²/157 sq mi. Third largest of the Ionian Is, W Greece; length 40 km/25 mi; capital, Zacynthus; devastated by earthquakes in 1953.

Zadar [zadah(r)], Ital **Zara** 44°07N 15°14E, pop (2000e) 124 600. Seaport and resort town in Croatia, on the Adriatic; conquered by Venice, 1000; passed to Austria, 1797; enclave of Italy, 1920–47; airfield; railway; car ferries to Ancona (Italy); cathedral.

Zadkine, Ossip [zadkeen] (1890–1967) Sculptor, born in Smolensk, Russia. He developed an individual Cubist style, making effective use of the play of light on concave surfaces, as in 'The Three Musicians' (1926) and 'Destroyed City' (1952, Rotterdam).

Zadokites [zaydokiyts] Descendants of Zadok, a priest apparently of Aaronic lineage who was appointed high priest, serving in Solomon's temple. His family continued to hold this office until Jerusalem fell in 587 BC, and again later in the Second Temple period. The Qumran community continued to look for a renewal of the Zadokite priesthood.

Zagreb [zagreb], Ger **Agram**, Hung **Zágráb**, ancient **Andautonia** 45°48N 15°58E, pop (2000e) 724 600. Capital city of Croatia; on R Sava; Croat cultural centre; airport; railway; university (1669); cathedral.

Zaharias, Babe *Didrikson, Babe*

Zaire *Congo, Democratic Republic of*

Zaire, River *Congo, River*

zakat [zakat] The alms tax obligatory on all Muslims, and the third of the five 'pillars' of Islam. Traditionally, it consisted of a 2·5% annual levy on income and capital.

Zambezi [zambeezee] or **Zambesi, River**, Port **Zambeze** River in SE Africa, flowing through Angola, Zimbabwe, Zambia, Namibia, and Mozambique; length c.2700 km/1700 mi; rises in NW Zambia; Victoria Falls, L Kariba, and Kariba Dam; enters the Mozambique Channel as a marshy delta; middle course explored by Livingstone in the early 1850s.

Zambia *p.1035*

Zamboanga or **Zamboanga City** [sambohangga] 6°55N 122°05E, pop (2000e) 542 000. Seaport in W Mindanao, Philippines; founded, 1635; airfield.

Zamenhof, L(azarus) L(udwig) [zamenof], pseudonym **Doktoro Esperanto** (1859–1917) Physician and oculist, the inventor of Esperanto, born in Białystok, Poland. His aims were to promote international tolerance and world peace, which he hoped to achieve through the use of an artificial language.

Zamyatin, Yevgeny Ivanovich [zamyatin], also spelled **Zamiatin** (1884–1937) Writer, born in Lebedyan, Russia. In 1921 he was a founder member of the Modernist group, the Serapion Brothers. He is best known for the novel *My* (1920, We).

zander Freshwater fish (*Stizostedion lucioperca*) found in large rivers and lakes of E Europe; length up to c.1 m/3¼ ft; greenish-grey on back, underside white; a voracious predator; also called **pikeperch**. (Family: Percidae.)

Zante [zantay] *Zacynthus*

Zanuck, Darryl F(rancis) [zanuhk] (1902–79) US film producer, born in Wahoo, NE. He became a co-founder of Twentieth-Century Pictures (later Twentieth-Century Fox) in 1933. Among his many successful films are *The Jazz Singer* (1927), *The Longest Day* (1962), and *The Sound of Music* (1965).

Zanzibar (island) [zanzibah(r)] pop (2000e) 494 000; area 1554 km²/971 sq mi. Island region of Tanzania; separated from the mainland by the 40 km/25 mi-wide Zanzibar Channel; length, 85 km/53 mi; width, 39 km/24 mi; highest point, 118 m/387 ft; capital, Zanzibar; largely Islamic since the 10th-c; developed under Omani Arab rule into the commercial centre of the W Indian Ocean, 17th-c; now a world centre of clove production; annexed by Germany, 1885; British protectorate, 1891; independence, 1963; ruling Sultanate overthrown in 1964, and the People's Republic of Zanzibar created; joined with Tanganyika, Zanzibar, and Pemba, now forming Tanzania; later the United Republic of Tanzania.

Zapata, Emiliano [sapahta] (1879–1919) Mexican revolutionary, born in Anencuilio, Mexico. After the onset of the Mexican Revolution, he mounted a land distribution programme in areas under his control.

Zaporozhye [zapuhrozhye], formerly **Aleksandrovsk** (to 1921) 47°50N 35°10E, pop (2000e) 881 000. River port in Ukraine, on R Dnepr; founded as a fortress, 1770; airfield; railway; major industrial and energy-producing centre.

Zapotecs A pre-Columbian Middle American Indian civilization of S Mexico (300 BC–AD 300), influenced by Olmec culture. It was centred on Monte Alban.

Zappa, Frank, popular name of **Francis Vincent Zappa** (1940–93) Avant-garde rock musician and composer, born in Baltimore, MD. He led the satirical 'underground' band The Mothers of Invention in the 1960s and 1970s, making inventive and often scabrous albums such as *Freak-Out!* (1966) and *We're Only in it for the Money* (1967).

Zarathustra *Zoroaster*

Zaria [zaria] 11°01N 7°44E, pop (2000e) 420 000. Town in SW Nigeria; founded, 16th-c; airfield; railway junction; university (1962).

Zarqa [zah(r)ka] 32°04N 36°05E, pop (2000e) 700 000. Industrial town in N Jordan; large phosphate reserves nearby; airfield; railway.

zarzuela [thah(r)thwayla] A type of popular Spanish opera with spoken dialogue. The name derives from the palace near Madrid (now the king's residence) where the genre was first staged in the 17th-c.

Zatopek, Emil [zatopek] (1922–2000) Athlete, born in Kopřivnice, Czech Republic. He won the 10 000 m title at the London Olympics in 1948, subsequently breaking 13 world records, and winning the 5000 m, 10 000 m, and the marathon at the 1952 Olympics.

Zambia

600 km
300 mi

AFRICA

Lake Tanganyika

TANZANIA

D.R. CONGO

Kalambo Falls

Lake
Mweru

Mbala
2067m

Mansa

Kasama

Solwezi

Mufulira

Kitwe

Zambezi

Ndola

Luangwa
Nat. Parks

Kafue
National
Park

Z A M B I A

Kabwe

Chipata

Lusaka

Victoria
Falls

Kalomo

Kariba Dam

Maramba
(Livingstone)

Lake Kariba

ZIMBABWE

MOZAMBIQUE

NAM.

BOTSWANA

ANGOLA

MAL.

☐ International Airport   ∴ World heritage site

[zambia], official name **Republic of Zambia**, formerly **Northern Rhodesia** (to 1964)

Local name Zambia

Timezone GMT +2

Area 752 613 km²/290 586 sq mi

Population total (2002e) 9 959 000

Status Independent republic within the Commonwealth

Date of independence 1964

Capital Lusaka

Languages English (official), with c.70 local languages (including Tonga, Kaonde, Lunda, and Luvale) also spoken

Ethnic groups Bantu (99%), including Bemba Nyanja, Barotse, Mambwe, and Swahili peoples

Religions Christian (75%), local beliefs (23%), Muslim and Hindu (1%)

Physical features High plateau in SC Africa, altitude 1000–1400 m/3300–4600 ft; highest point, 2067 m/6781 ft, SE of Mbala; a number of rivers drain southwards to join Zambezi R in N, including R Luangwa; highest waterfall, Kalambo Falls, 221 m/726 ft; artificial L Kariba in S, 440 km²/170 sq mi.

Climate Warm temperate climate on plateau; tropical in lower valleys; although in C Africa and subequatorial, protected from very high temperatures by altitude; three distinct seasons, hot, dry (Aug–Oct), warm, wet (Nov–Apr), dry, cool (May–Jul); average annual temperatures, 21°C (Jan), 16°C (Jul) in Lusaka; average annual rainfall 840 mm/33 in.

Currency 1 Kwacha (ZMK) = 100 ngwee

Economy Based on copper and cobalt, (provide over 50% of national income); lead, zinc, tobacco, coal; corn, tobacco, rice, sugar cane, groundnuts, cotton; sugar refining, glassware, tyres, brewing, oil refining.

GDP (2002e) $8·24 bn, per capita $800

Human Development Index (2002) 0·433

History European influence followed Livingstone's discovery of the Victoria Falls, 1855; administered by the British South Africa Company under Rhodes; Northern and Southern Rhodesia declared a British sphere of influence, 1889–90; became Northern Rhodesia, 1911; British Crown Colony, 1924; joined with Southern Rhodesia and Nyasaland as the Federation of Rhodesia and Nyasaland, 1953; Federation dissolved, 1963; independence as the Republic of Zambia, 1964; governed by a President and National Assembly; new multi-party constitution adopted in 1991.

Head of State/Government (President)
1964–91 Kenneth Kaunda
1991–2002 Frederick Chiluba
2002– Levy Mwanawasa
(Vice-President)
1989–91 Malimba Masheke
1991–4 Levy Mwanawasa
1994–7 Godfrey Miyanda
1997–2001 Christon Tembo
2001–3 Enoch Kavindele
2003–4 Nevers Mumba
2004–6 Lupando Mwape
2006– Rupiah Banda

Zealand, Dan **Sjælland**, Ger **Seeland** area 7000 km²/2700 sq mi. Largest of the islands of Denmark; separated from Sweden by The Sound, but now linked (2000) by the Øresund bridge; length 128 km/80 mi; rises to 126 m/413 ft; chief towns include Copenhagen.

Zealots [zelots] A militant Jewish sect which came into prominence in Palestine in the 1st-c AD. Its aim was to cast off the Roman yoke, using violence if necessary.

zebra An African wild horse; stocky with bold black and white stripes; three species: *Equus grevyi* (**Grevy's zebra**, **imperial zebra**, or **hippotigris**) with narrow stripes; *Equus zebra* (**mountain zebra**) with short crosswise stripes on top of hindquarters; and *Equus burchelli* (**common zebra**, **plains zebra**, or **Burchell's zebra**) with variable markings.

zebra fish Small, colourful fish (*Therapon jarbua*) common in shallow inshore waters of the Indian Ocean and W Pacific; length up to 30 cm/1 ft; grey to silver with dark horizontal banding. (Family: Theraponidae.)

zebrass An animal resulting from the mating of a male zebra and a female ass.

zebu [zeeboo] S Asian domestic cattle; usually pale with upturned horns; fatty hump on shoulders; heavy hanging skin along throat; traditionally considered sacred in India; also known as **Brahman cattle** or **humped cattle**. (*Bos taurus*, sometimes called *Bos indicus*.)

Zechariah or **Zacharias, Book of** [zekariya] One of 12 so-called 'minor' prophetic writings of the Hebrew Bible/Old Testament, attributed to Zechariah, writing c.520–518 BC after returning to Jerusalem from exile.

Zeebrugge [zaybruguh] 51°20N 3°12E. Belgian ferry port, the scene of a major shipping disaster in March 1987, when the Townsend Thoresen ferry, *Herald of Free Enterprise*, foundered just outside the harbour, with the loss of 193 lives. The accident resulted from the main car deck doors having been left open to the sea.

Zeeland [zaylant] pop (2000e) 376 000; land area 1786 km²/689 sq mi. Province in West Netherlands; capital, Middelburg; entire area reclaimed from the sea by artificial dykes, and mostly below sea-level; scene of major flooding in 1953.

Zeffirelli, Franco [zefirelee] (1923–) Stage, opera, and film director, born in Florence, Italy. His films include *The Taming of the Shrew* (1966), *Romeo and Juliet* (1968), *Jane Eyre* (1996), *Tea with Mussolini* (1998), and *Callas Forever* (2002). Other works are film versions of the operas *La traviata* (1983) and *Otello* (1986), and *Jesus of Nazareth* (1977) for television.

Zeiss, Carl [tsiys] (1816–88) Optician, born in Weimar, Germany. In 1846 he established a factory at Jena which became noted for the production of lenses, microscopes, and other optical instruments.

Zellweger, Renée (Kathleen) [zelweger] (1969–) Actress, born in Katy, TX. She made her film debut in *My Boyfriend's Back* (1993). Later films include *Jerry Maguire* (1996), *Nurse Betty* (2000), *Bridget Jones's Diary* (2001, sequel 2004), *Chicago* (2002), *Cold Mountain* (2003, Best Supporting Actress Oscar; BAFTA), and *Miss Potter* (2006).

Zen Buddhism [zen budizm] A meditation school of Buddhism introduced into Japan by monks returning from China in the 12th-c. Zen stresses the personal experience of enlightenment based on a simple life lived close to nature, and upon methods of meditation which avoid complicated rituals and abstruse thought.

zener diode [zeener diyohd] A semiconductor junction diode which produces a sharply increased reverse current when the reverse bias voltage reaches a certain value; named after US physicist Clarence Zener (1905–93).

zenith *nadir*

Zeno of Citium [zeenoh, sishium] (c.336–c.265 BC) Greek philosopher, the founder of Stoicism, born in Citium, Cyprus. He opened a school at the *Stoa poikile* ('painted colonnade'), from which the name of his philosophy derives.

Zeno of Elea [zeenoh, eelia] (c.490–c.420 BC) Greek philosopher and mathematician, a native of Elea, Italy. He became known for a series of paradoxes, many of which denied the possibility of spatial division or motion. The best known is 'Achilles and the Tortoise', whose conclusion is that no matter how fast Achilles runs, he cannot overtake a tortoise, if the tortoise has a head start.

zeolites [zeeoliyts] A group of hydrous aluminosilicate minerals containing sodium, potassium, calcium, and barium, and formed by the alteration of feldspars. They are characterized by structures into which gases, ions, and molecules can easily diffuse, and hence they are used as molecular sieves and ion exchangers for water softening.

Zephaniah, Benjamin [zefaniya] (1958–) Poet, born in Birmingham, West Midlands, who spent much of his childhood in Jamaica. His first book, *Pen Rhythms* (1981), was followed by *The Dread Affair* (1985), a passionate condemnation of aggression. Later works include *Too Black, Too Strong* (2001) and *J is for Jamaica* (2006). He has also worked with several Jamaican reggae bands, including the Wailers.

Zephaniah, Book of [zefaniya] One of 12 so-called 'minor' prophetic writings of the Hebrew Bible/Old Testament, attributed to Zephaniah, son of Cushi and descendant of Hezekiah, active in Josiah's reign (7th-c BC), but unknown apart from this work.

Zeppelin, Ferdinand (Adolf August Heinrich), Graf von (Count of) (1838–1917) German army officer, born in Konstanz, Germany. In 1897–1900 he constructed his first airship, setting up a factory for their construction at Freidrichshafen.

Zermatt [zermat] 46°01N 7°45E, pop (2000e) 4800. Fashionable skiing resort and popular mountaineering centre in the Pennine Alps, S Switzerland.

zero-emission vehicle (ZEV) A type of motor vehicle with no tailpipe pollutants. During the 1980s, approaches using alternative fuels made progress towards this goal, but only specially designed vehicles powered by electricity seem likely to achieve it.

Zeta-Jones, Catherine [zeeta] (1969–) Actress and singer, born in Swansea, S Wales. She became known through her role in the BBC television series *The Darling Buds of May* (1991), and went on to feature film-success with *The Mask of Zorro* (1998). Later films include *Traffic* (2000), in which she co-starred with husband Michael Douglas (married 2000), *Chicago* (2002, BAFTA; Oscar Best Supporting Actress), and *The Legend of Zorro* (2005).

Zeus [zyoos] In Greek mythology, the supreme god, equivalent to Jupiter. He is usually depicted with thunderbolt and eagle, and associated with the oak-tree.

Zeus, statue of [zyoos] A colossal statue, wrought in ivory and gold over a core of wood, formerly located in the Temple of Zeus at Olympia. It was one of the foremost works of the great Athenian sculptor, Phidias.

Zeuxis [zyooksis] (5th-c BC) Greek painter, born in Heraclea. He excelled in the representation of natural objects.

ZEV *zero-emission vehicle*

Zewail, Ahmed H(assan) [zuhwayl] (1946–) Chemist and physicist, born in Egypt. He joined the California Institute of Technology in 1976. He received the 1999 Nobel Prize for Chemistry for his studies of the transition states of chemical reactions using femtosecond spectroscopy.

Zhang Yimou, sometimes credited as **Yi-Mou Zhang** (1951–) Film director and actor, born in Xian, China. He struggled to be admitted to the Beijing Film Academy, and became one of the first group of students to be accepted after it re-opened in 1978. In 1986 he started work at the Xian Film Studios, where he played the lead in Wu Tianming's *Lao jing* (1986, Old Well), for which he won the Best Actor Award at the 1987 Tokyo International Film Festival. His debut as a director came in 1987 with *Hong gao liang* (Red Sorghum), which won him critical acclaim. Later films include *Yi Ge Dou Bu Neng Shao* (1999, Not One Less), *Wo De Fu Qin Mu Qin* (2000, The Road Home), and *Shi mian mai fu* (2004, House of Flying Daggers). Several of his films have won prestigious international awards.

Zhdanov *Mariupol*

Zhengzhou [juhngjoh], **Chengchow**, or **Cheng-chou** 34°35N 113°38E, pop (2000e) 2 003 000. Capital of Henan province, NC China; major market and transportation centre first settled before 1000 BC; airfield; railway junction.

Zhenjiang, Chen-chiang, or **Chinkiang** [juhnjiahng] 32°08N 119°30E, pop (2000e) 552 200. River port in E China, at confluence of Yangtze R and Grand Canal; founded, 545 BC; railway; scenic area; Jinshan Temple (4th-c).

Zhitomir or **Jitomir** [zhitomyir] 50°18N 28°40E, pop (2000e) 293 000. City in WC Ukraine; on R Teterev; founded, 9th-c; railway junction.

Zhou or **Chou dynasty** [joh] (1027–256 BC) The second historical Chinese dynasty. Accounts of its origins are a mixture of history and legend. Its capital was at Hao (near Xi'an) until 771 BC, and at Luoyi (near Luoyang) until its occupation by the Qin in 256 BC. A form of feudal monarchy, the Zhou saw the first flowering of Chinese historical, philosophical, and literary writing.

Zhou Enlai [joh enliy], also spelled **Chou En-lai** (1898–1975) One of the leaders of the Communist Party of China, and prime minister of the Chinese People's Republic from its inception in 1949 until his death. As minister of foreign affairs (and concurrently prime minister) he vastly increased China's international influence. Perhaps his greatest triumph of mediation was during the Cultural Revolution, when he worked to preserve national unity against the forces of anarchy.

Zhu De [joo de], also spelled **Chu-teh** (1886–1976) Chinese communist general, born in Yilong, Sichuan, China. He joined Mao Zedong to found the Jiangxi Soviet and together they built the Red Army. With Mao he led the Long March in 1934, and from 1949 he was commander-in-chief of the Chinese armed forces.

Zhu Jiang, Chu-chiang or **Chu-kiang** [joo jiahng], Eng **Pearl River**

River in S China; forms wide estuary between Hong Kong and Macao; length 2197 km/1365 mi; densely populated, fertile river valley.

Zhukov, Giorgiy Konstantinovich [zhookof] (1896–1974) Soviet marshal, born in Strelkovka, Russia. He became army chief-of-staff (1941), lifted the siege of Moscow, and in 1943 his counter-offensive was successful at Stalingrad. In 1944–5 he captured Warsaw, conquered Berlin, and accepted the German surrender.

Zhu Rongji [joo rongjee] (1928–) Chinese politician and prime minister (1998–2003), born in Changsha, Hunan. Exiled twice under Mao Zedong, he became Mayor of Shanghai (1988–91), known for his peaceful resolution of student protests there in 1989. He was appointed vice premier in 1991, and in his role as the government's chief economic policy maker (1993–8) introduced a successful austerity programme.

Zia ul-Haq, Muhammad [zeea ul hak] (1924–88) Pakistani general and president (1978–88), born near Jullundhur, Punjab, India. He led a bloodless coup in 1977, imposed martial law, banned political activity, and introduced an Islamic code of law. Despite international protest, he sanctioned the hanging of former President Bhutto in 1979.

Ziaur Rahman [zeeaoor ramahn] (1935–81) Bangladeshi soldier and president (1977–81). Appointed chief of army staff after the assassination of Mujibur Rahman (1975), he became the dominant figure within the military. He survived many attempted coups, but was finally assassinated in Dhaka.

Zibo [tsoeboh] or **Tzu-po** 36°51N 118°01E, pop (2000e) 2 770 000. Industrial city in Shandong province, E China; railway.

Zidane, Zinédine [zeedan], nickname **Zizou** (1972–) Footballer, born in Castellane, near Marseille, France, the son of Algerian immigrant parents. He signed as a schoolboy for Cannes FC, and later joined Juventus. He was a key player for his country in the 1998 FIFA World Cup Final, scoring two goals in France's 3–0 victory over Brazil, and was hailed as a national hero. He was European Footballer of the Year (1998) and FIFA World Footballer of the Year (1998, 2000, 2003). In 2001 he signed for Real Madrid for a world record transfer fee of £47·2 million. His last appearance before retiring from football was in the 2006 World Cup final against Italy – an event marred by a head-butting incident for which he received a red card. Following France's defeat in the 2006 World Cup final, he received the Golden Ball award as best player, and retired from football with 108 caps.

zidovudine *AZT*

Ziegfeld, Florenz [zeegfeld] (1869–1932) Theatre manager, born in Chicago, IL. His *Follies of 1907* ran for 24 editions to 1943, and made his name synonymous with extravagant theatrical production.

Ziegler, Karl [zeegler] (1898–1973) Chemist, born in Helsa, Germany. With Italian chemist Giulio Natta (1903–79) he was awarded the 1963 Nobel Prize for Chemistry for his research into long-chain polymers leading to new developments in industrial materials, such as polypropylene.

ziggurat [zigurat] A temple tower, in the shape of a mountain, found throughout ancient Sumeria and the adjacent region of Elam. It consisted of a high, pyramidal mound, constructed in stages and surmounted by a shrine. Access to the shrine was by a series of external stairways or ramps.

Zimbabwe *p.1038*

Zimmer walking frame A self-standing metal frame consisting of two double legs at the sides, joined together by a bar in front; the name derives from the US orthopaedic company which manufactures it. It is used to assist walking by elderly persons, or those with pain or weakness in the legs.

zinc Zn, element 30, density 7 g/cm^3, melting point 420°C. An active, silvery-blue metal, never occurring uncombined, but found in many minerals, especially as a sulphide. It has been used from earliest times as an alloy with copper (*brass*). It owes its corrosion resistance to an adherent oxide coating, and is used as a plating to protect iron (*galvanizing*). It is also used in primary batteries as an anode. **Zinc oxide** (ZnO) is used as a pigment, filler, and mild antiseptic in cosmetics, pharmaceuticals, paints, and plastics. **Zinc sulphide** (ZnS) is used in luminous screens.

zinc blende *sphalerite*

Zinjanthropus [zinjanthropus] The former name of *Australopithecus boisei*, based on a cranium found by Louis and Mary Leakey at Olduvai Gorge in 1959.

Zinkernagel, Rolf M [zingkernahgel] (1944–) Immunologist, born in Basel, Switzerland. He shared the Nobel Prize for Physiology or Medicine in 1996 for his contribution to the discovery of how the immune system recognizes virus-infected cells – research which was first reported in 1974.

zinnia An annual, perennial, or small shrub, distributed throughout the USA and S into South America, but predominantly Mexican; chrysanthemum-like flower-heads, showy. (Genus: *Zinnia*, 22 species. Family: Compositae.)

Zinoviev, Grigoriy Yevseyevich [zinovyef], originally **Grigoriy Yevseyevich Radomyslskiy** (1883–1936) Russian Jewish revolutionary and politician, born in the Ukraine. Charged with organizing terrorist activities, he was executed following the first of Stalin's Great Purge trials in Moscow. The so-called **Zinoviev letter** urging British Communists to incite revolution in Britain contributed to the downfall of the Labour government in the 1924 general elections; fresh research reported in 1999 confirmed the view that this letter was a forgery.

Zinzendorf, Nicolaus Ludwig, Graf von (Count of) [tsintsendaw(r)f] (1700–60) Religious leader, born in Dresden, Germany. He invited the persecuted Moravians to his estates, and there founded for them the colony of *Herrnhut* ('the Lord's keeping'). He later became Bishop of the Moravian Brethren.

Zion or **Sion** [ziyon] (Heb probably 'fortress' or 'rock') Term used in the Hebrew Bible and Jewish literature in various ways: for one of the hills in Jerusalem; for the mount on which the Temple was built; for the Temple itself; and symbolically for Jerusalem or even Israel as a whole. Today 'Mount Zion' usually denotes the SW hill in Jerusalem just S of the city wall.

Zionism The movement which sought to recover for the Jewish people their historic Palestinian homeland (the *Eretz Israel*) after centuries of dispersion. The modern movement arose in the late 19th-c with plans for Jewish colonization of Palestine, and under Theodor Herzl also developed a political programme. Its objectives were supported by the British Balfour Declaration in 1917, as long as rights for non-Jews in Palestine were not impaired. Zionism is still active, as a movement encouraging diaspora Jews to immigrate to and take an interest in the Jewish state.

zircon [zerkn] A zirconium silicate (ZrSiO$_4$) mineral commonly occurring in very small amounts in a wide variety of rocks. It is very hard, and is used as a gemstone. It is the principal source of zirconium.

zither A musical instrument consisting of a box strung with five fretted and about 30 open (unfretted) strings. The fretted strings are stopped by the fingers of the left hand and plucked with a plectrum worn on the right thumb; the right-hand fingers pluck the open strings.

Žižka, Jan [zhishka] or **Ziska, John** (c.1370–1424) Bohemian Hussite leader, born in Trocznov, Czech Republic. During the Civil War he was chosen leader of the popular party, captured Prague (1421), and erected the fortress of Tabor, his party coming to be called Taborites. He continued to lead his troops in a series of victories, compelling Emperor Sigismund to offer the Hussites religious liberty.

zodiac A zone of fixed stars, approximately 16° in width, which

Zimbabwe

□ International Airport   ∴ World heritage site

[zimbabway], official name **Republic of Zimbabwe**, formerly **Southern Rhodesia** (to 1979)

Local name Zimbabwe

Timezone GMT +2

Area 390 759 km²/150 873 sq mi

Population total (2002e) 11 377 000

Status Independent republic within the Commonwealth

Date of independence 1980

Capital Harare

Languages English (official), Ndebele and Shona widely spoken

Ethnic groups Bantu (97%) (including Shona 71%, Ndebele 16%), European (2%)

Religions Syncretic Christian/local beliefs (50%), Christian (25%), traditional animist beliefs (24%), small Muslim minority

Physical features Landlocked country in SC Africa; mostly savan-

nah (tropical grassland); Highveld ridge crosses SW to NE to join the Inyanga Mts on Mozambique border, highest point, Mt Inyangani, 2592 m/8504 ft; Highveld flanked by lower plateau, Middleveld; Lowveld, altitude, 300 m/1000 ft, lies NE; tropical hardwood forests (SE); chief rivers, Zambezi, Limpopo, and Sabi.

Climate Subtropical climate, strongly influenced by altitude; average annual temperature 21°C (Jan), 14°C (Jul) in Harare; average annual rainfall 828 mm/33 in; rainfall increases from SW to NE; wet season (Nov–Mar).

Currency 1 Zimbabwe Dollar (ZWD) = 100 cents

Economy Agriculture (involves 70% of population), manufacturing and mining; sugar, cotton, livestock; natural resources, gold, copper, chrome, nickel, tin, asbestos; tourism to national parks; major industries in steel, textiles, vehicles, and chemicals.

GDP (2002e) $26·07 bn, per capita $2100

Human Development Index (2002) 0·551

History Mediaeval Bantu kingdom during 12–16th-c, with capital at Great Zimbabwe; visited by Livingstone in the 1850s; Southern Rhodesia under British influence in the 1880s as the British South Africa Company under Cecil Rhodes; divided into Northern and Southern Rhodesia, 1911; Southern Rhodesia became a self-governing British colony, 1923; Northern and Southern Rhodesia and Nyasaland formed a multi-racial federation, 1953; independence of Nyasaland and Northern Rhodesia, 1963; opposition to the independence of Southern Rhodesia under African rule resulted in a Unilateral Declaration of Independence (UDI) by the White-dominated government, 1965; economic sanctions and internal guerrilla activity forced the government to negotiate with the main African groups: the Zimbabwe African People's Union (ZAPU), led by Joshua Nkomo, the Zimbabwe African National Union (ZANU), led by Robert Mugabe, and the United African National Council (UANC), led by Bishop Abel Muzorewa; independence as the Republic of Zimbabwe, 1980; since 1987, the post of executive President has combined the posts of Head of State and Head of Government; bicameral legislature replaced, 1990, by new single-chamber Parliament, the House of Assembly; political crisis over land redistribution, focused on white farmers, 2000 and ongoing; increasing international concern over democracy within the country, especially in relation to the election process in 2002, sanctions imposed by EU; suspended from the Commonwealth for one year in March 2002, reaffirmed in 2003, after which Mugabe announced his country's withdrawal from the organization; sanctions extended, 2004; Mugabe re-elected, Mar 2005; civil unrest arising from domestic policy and annual inflation rate of c.1600%, Feb 2007.

Head of State/Government

1980–7 Canaan Sodindo Banana

1987– Robert Gabriel Mugabe

---

marks the apparent courses of the Sun, Moon, and planets (apart from Pluto) about the Earth. Early astronomers projected patterns on to this area of sky, creating 12 groupings or constellations. The **tropical zodiac** takes the equinoxial position as a starting point, irrespective of the underlying constellation. On the 21st of each month (approximately) the Sun appears to change sign in the tropical zodiac, from Aries through Taurus, Gemini, Cancer, Leo, Virgo, Libra, Scorpius (Scorpio), Sagittarius, Capricorn, Aquarius and Pisces. The disposition of the planets within the signs of the zodiac furnishes important information to the astrologer.

zodiacal light A permanent glow of light, readily visible in the tropics after sunset as a cone of light extending from the horizon. It is sunlight reflected from dust in interplanetary space.

Zoffany, John or **Johann** [tsofanee] (1734–1810) Portrait painter, born in Frankfurt (am Main), Germany. His speciality was the conversation piece.

Zog I [zohg], originally **Ahmed Bey Zogu** (1895–1961) Albanian prime minister (1922–4), president (1925–8), and king (1928–39), born in Burgajet, Albania. He formed a republican government in 1922, and after a period in exile became president, later proclaiming himself king. When Albania was overrun by the Italians (1939), he fled to Britain, and formally abdicated in 1946.

Zohar [zohhah(r)] The main text of the Jewish Kabbalah. Discovered in Spain in the late 13th-c, it was said to be the mystical teachings of Rabbi Simeon bar Yochai and his followers, who lived in Palestine in the 2nd–3rd-c. There have always been doubts about its authenticity.

zokor *mole rat*

Zola, Emile (Edouard Charles Antoine) [zohla] (1840–1902) Novelist, born in Paris. After his first major novel, *Thérèse Raquin* (1867), he began the long series called *Les Rougon-Macquart*, a sequence of 20 books described in the subtitle as 'the natural and social history of a family under the Second Empire', including such acclaimed studies as *Nana* (1880), *Germinal* (1885), and *La Bête humaine* (1890, trans The Beast in Man). In 1898 he espoused the cause of Dreyfus in his open letter *J'accuse*.

Zollverein [tsolferiyn] A German customs union, based on the enlarged Prussia of 1814, and officially constituted in 1834. It represented an important stage in the German unification process.

zoogeography [zohuhjiografee] The study of the past and present geographical distribution of animals and animal communities.

zoology The branch of biology dealing with the study of animals. It includes their anatomy, behaviour, ecology, evolution, genetics, and physiology.

zoom A visual effect in motion pictures or video, enlarging or diminishing the image as though rapidly approaching or receding. Originally made by actual camera movement, it is now provided by a **zoom lens** whose focal length, and hence its magnification, can be continuously varied.

zooplankton *plankton*

zoosemiotics [zohohsemiotiks] The science of animal communication. Combining semiotics and ethology, this interdisciplinary field seeks to understand the many complex systems of meaning employed by animals, such as bird calls, bee-dancing, and grasshopper signals.

zorilla [thoreelya] An African mammal (*Ictonyx striatus*) of family Mustelidae; long coat and long brush-like tail; black with white markings on face, long white stripes along body; superficially resembles the skunk; also known as **striped polecat**.

Zorn, Anders (Leonhard) (1860–1920) Etcher, sculptor, and painter, born in Mora. His paintings deal mainly with Swedish peasant life. He achieved European fame as an etcher, known for his series of nudes, and for his portraits.

Zoroaster [zorohaster], Greek form of **Zarathustra** (6th-c BC) Iranian prophet and founder of the ancient Parsee religion which bears his name. He appears as a historical person only in the earliest portion of the Avesta.

Zoroastrianism [zorohastrianizm] The worship of a supreme God, Ahura Mazda, in Iran during the first millennium BC. Rites of worship were performed by priests (*Magi*), and there was a body of scriptures called *Avesta*, the earliest part of which was made up of hymns attributed to a religious teacher, Zoroaster. Today it is practised by Parsees.

Z particle A particle that carries weak nuclear force; symbol *Z*; mass 91·2 GeV; charge zero; spin 1; decays for example to an electron plus positron, or a muon plus antimuon, or a neutrino plus antineutrino; it was discovered in 1983.

Zuccarelli, Francesco [tsukaraylee] (1702–88) Painter, born in Pitigliano, Italy. His pastoral landscapes, populated by shepherds and maidens and painted in a soft Rococo style, were very popular, especially in England.

Zuccari or **Zuccaro, Taddeo** [tsukahree] (1529–66) Painter, born in Vado, Italy, who executed several frescoes and easel pieces. His brother **Federigo Zuccari** (c.1543–1609) painted portraits and frescoes, and became an influential art theorist. The two brothers were leaders of the Roman late Mannerist school.

zucchini [zukeenee] *courgette*

Zuckerman (of Burnham Thorpe), Solly Zuckerman, Baron (1904–93) Zoologist, born in Cape Town, South Africa, and chief scientific adviser to the British government (1964–71). He carried

out extensive research into primates, publishing such classic works as *The Social Life of Monkeys and Apes* (1932).

Zug [tsug] 47°10N 8°31E, pop (2000e) 22 500. Town in C Switzerland; railway junction; noted for its local kirsch; Gothic church (15th–16th-c).

Zugspitze [tsukshpitsuh] 47°25N 11°00E. Mountain in S Germany, rising to 2962 m/9718 ft on the Wettersteingebirge of the Bavarian Alps.

Zuider Zee *Ijsselmeer*

Zukofsky, Louis [zukofskee] (1904–78) Poet, born in New York City. A leading experimentalist after Pound, his works appear in *An Objectivist Anthology* (1932) and *All: The Collected Short Poems* (1965, 1967).

Zulu A Bantu-speaking agricultural and cattle people of Natal, South Africa; one of the Nguni group. Formed into a kingdom in the early 19th-c, they became a formidable fighting force; but were conquered by the Boers and British, and much of their territory annexed. They have retained a strong self-identity, and are organized politically into the modern Inkatha movement under their leader Chief Mangosuthu Buthelezi. Their territory, greatly contracted, became one of the 'Homelands' of South Africa during the apartheid period: KwaZulu.

Zuni [zoonyee] A North American Indian group of the American SW, living in New Mexico and Arizona; one of the Pueblo peoples. Many are now assimilated to US culture.

Zurbarán, Francisco de [thoorbaran] (1598–1664) Religious painter, born in Fuente de Cantos, Spain. Apart from a few portraits and still-life studies, his main subjects were monastic and historical, and he came to be called 'the Spanish Caravaggio'.

Zürich [zoorikh], Ger [tsüreekh] 47°22N 8°32E, pop (2000e) 357 000. Financial centre in N Switzerland; on R Limmat, at NW end of L Zurich; largest city in Switzerland; Swiss Federal Institute of Technology (1855); joined Swiss Confederation, 1351; airport; railway; university (1833); Swiss Federal Institute of Technology (1855); Grossmünster (11th–14th-c), Fraumünster (13th-c, restored).

Zweig, Arnold [tsviyk] (1887–1968) Writer, born in Glogau, Germany. He is best known for his pacifist novel, *Der Streit um den Sergeanten Grischa* (1928, The Case of Sergeant Grischa).

Zweig, Stefan [tsviyk] (1881–1942) Writer, born in Vienna. His best-known work was his set of historical portraits, *Sternstunden der Menschheit* (1928, trans The Tide of Fortune).

Zwickau [tsvikow] 50°43N 12°30E, pop (2000e) 124 000. Mining and industrial city in S Germany; on R Mulde; a free imperial city, 1290–1323; railway; birthplace of Schumann.

Zwingli, Huldrych or **Ulrich** [tsvinglee], Lat **Ulricus Zuinglius** (1484–1531) Protestant reformer, born in Wildhaus, Switzerland. In 1518, he opposed the selling of indulgences, and espoused the Reformed doctrines, but in 1524 split with Luther over the question of the Eucharist.

zwitterion [tsviteriyon] A molecule containing both a positive and a negative charge simultaneously. It is the predominant form of an amino acid in solution.

Zwolle [zvoluh] 52°31N 6°06E, pop (2000e) 102 000. City in E Netherlands; railway; canal junction; major cattle market; St Michaelskerk (15th-c).

Zworykin, Vladimir (Kosma) [tsvorikin] (1889–1982) Physicist, born in Murom, Russia. In 1923–4 he patented an all-electronic television system using a scanned camera-tube (the *iconoscope*), in 1929 demonstrated a cathode-ray display (the *kinescope*), and in later years contributed to the development of colour television and the electron microscope. He is regarded as 'the father of modern television'.

zydeco [ziydekoh] US dance music from SW Louisiana and W Texas, the black counterpart to white 'Cajun' music. The instrumentation usually includes piano accordion, saxophone, guitar, and washboard; there are influences from blues and, perhaps, the Carribean; and the music is fast, swinging, and syncopated.

zygomorphic flower A flower which is bilaterally symmetrical, so that it can be divided into equal halves in one plane only. It is often found in the more advanced plant families.

zygote [ziygoht] The fertilized egg of a plant or animal, formed by the fusion of male (*sperm*) and female (*ovum*) gametes. It is usually diploid (possessing a double chromosome set), having received a haploid chromosome set from each gamete.